PHILIP'S

STREET ATLAS
London

First published 2000 by

Philip's, a division of
Octopus Publishing Group Ltd
2–4 Heron Quays
London E14 4JP

Third edition 2007
Second impression 2007
LONCB

© Philip's 2007

Ordnance Survey®

This product includes mapping data licensed from Ordnance Survey®, with the permission of the Controller of Her Majesty's Stationery Office.© Crown copyright 2007. All rights reserved. Licence number 100011710

This product contains driver restriction information derived from Teleatlas © TeleatlasDRI

The information for the speed camera locations is used with permission of the London Safety Camera Partnership and is correct at the time of publishing. New sites will be installed by the LSCP, for the latest list visit www.lscp.org.uk

Printed and bound in Spain by Cayfosa-Quebecor.

Contents

II	Our Top 10 Tips to avoid parking penalties	
V	Mobile speed camera sites	
VI	**Key to map pages**	
VIII	Administrative and Postcode boundaries	
X	**Route planning**	
XXVIII	**Key to map symbols**	
1	**Street maps**	
228	**Keys to enlarged map pages and symbols**	
229	**Enlarged street maps**	
271	**Index**	
398	**List of numbered locations**	
412	Hospitals	
413	Places of interest	
414	Shopping, theatres, cinemas	
416	Central London buses	
418	Local rail and London Underground	

Digital Data

The exceptionally high-quality mapping found in this atlas is available as digital data in TIFF format, which is easily convertible to other bitmapped (raster) image formats.

The index is also available in digital form as a standard database table. It contains all the details found in the printed index together with the National Grid reference for the map square in which each entry is named.

For further information and to discuss your requirements, please contact james.mann@philips-maps.co.uk

Our Top 10 Tips
to avoid parking penalties

David Willis / Alamy

Parking fines 2005/6	
Borough	fines
1 Westminster	715085
2 Camden	448085
3 Kensington and Chelsea	294932
4 Lambeth	255066
5 Wandsworth	245475
6 Ealing	212656
7 Islington	210685
8 Newham	188465
9 Barnet	168681
10 Hammersmith and Fulham	165196
11 Hackney	140966
12 Waltham Forest	140216
13 Southwark	135045
14 Haringey	134551
15 Brent	133561
16 Enfield	100087
17 Redbridge	95966
18 Hounslow	92764
19 Croydon	86534
20 Harrow	83303
21 Tower Hamlets	72858
22 Richmond upon Thames	72526
23 Bromley	69538
24 Bexley	65739
25 Kingston upon Thames	63980
26 Lewisham	63250
27 Hillingdon	61211
28 Merton	56860
29 Sutton	48965
30 Greenwich	48892
31 Barking and Dagenham	42416
32 Havering	40141
33 City of London	37478
34 Transport for London	304305
	5,095,478

When it comes to parking, London's streets are mean and its traffic regulators keen. Lucky motorists might find a marked bay, or at night a patch of single line, but that could just be the start of the problem. It's all too easy to pick the wrong space or the wrong time of day.

Getting a ticket for over-staying, or using a suspended bay or a resident's only space, is invariably expensive and sometimes the pain doesn't end there. What's the worst that can happen? Well, the car could be clamped or towed away. But in either case it's excruciatingly costly and time-consuming to retrieve the vehicle, especially after 10pm, when London black cab prices go through the roof.

Why has parking become so hazardous? The whole process used to be much less complex, and far easier to understand. The hours of parking control were fairly standard right across the capital, and enforcement was also uniform, with traffic wardens attached to the police service. Then came the Road Traffic Act 1991, which took responsibility away from the police and into the hands of local authorities.

The post-code lottery

Since 1994 parking in London has been run by the borough councils. Most choose to employ private contractors to operate the parking penalty service. In common with all other companies,

these outfits are in pursuit of profit – and they haven't been disappointed. Parking fines are big business in London these days.

Latest figures show that more than five million parking penalties were levied on motorists in 2005/6 (see table). In bald terms, that's nearly one for every person living in Greater London. These penalties produced an income for the boroughs of some £279 million in a year. Once the operators have taken their slice, the money goes into the coffers of London's 33 boroughs as well as Transport for London, which has recently stepped up its enforcement activities, especially on red routes.

There is huge variation among the 32 boroughs, with central London by far the riskiest place to park. Westminster held the 2005 record for issuing the greatest number of fines, even though its total of 715,085 was about 100,000 less than the previous year. The fewest parking fines were given in the City of London.

There is one piece of good news. A third fewer cars were clamped than in 2004/5 – nearly 50,000 fewer. But there was a sharp 18% increase in cars removed to pounds. To acknowledge this grim statistic, Philip's London street atlases are now the first to locate Car Pounds on the maps using this symbol: 🚗

The figures also reveal the trend-setters among the boroughs:

Camden for the most cars clamped.

Westminster for the most cars removed to pounds.

The boroughs where the number of tickets issued grew the fastest were: Ealing (+55%), Enfield (+47%) and Hackney (+46%)

The boroughs who saw the biggest falls were: Greenwich (-21%), Richmond (-25%) and Islington (-26%)

The sheer number of different authorities shelling out penalties can make the London street parking issue seem baffling. Arrangements in Richmond

Top 10 Tips

1 Check borough boundaries. One common pitfall for London's drivers is to pump cash into a meter belonging to one borough while being parked in another. This is especially problematic around the London museums. Numerous visitors perfectly willing to pay the charge have fed money into a meter belonging to the Royal Borough of Kensington and Chelsea when they have inadvertently parked in a bay operated by Westminster council. The signage, campaigners claim, is inadequate – so beware.

2 Keep plenty of loose change if you intend to use parking meters. If a parking attendant happens along while you have toddled off to find the correct coinage you have no defence against a ticket.

3 If you've been caught fair and square, pay the ticket within 14 days to take advantage of the cash discount scheme. Prompt settlement usually means coughing up just half the full amount.

4 Assume nothing. Just because you are often permitted to park on single yellow lines after 6.30 doesn't mean it is always so. There are an increasing number of parking places reserved for 'residents only' and these are frequently governed by a 10pm rule. Moreover some zones are 24 hour no parking areas. Look for signs to indicate what

rules apply to the parking space before moving into it. Don't forget that some parking areas are watched by cameras that can capture your licence plate, so don't imagine you are safe to contravene regulations on the basis that parking attendants will have ended their shift. If you have received a penalty charge notice in an area where the signs outlining the regulations on parking are obscured by trees or even missing then you may have grounds for appeal. Take photographs as evidence before embarking on the appeals process.

5 If you return to your vehicle while a parking attendant is in the process of writing the ticket don't hesitate to drive off if you can do so without endangering anyone. Parking offences are not criminal offences, so you are not leaving the scene of a crime. The relevant legislation makes it clear that the completed ticket must be either given to the driver or attached to the vehicle. If not, the ticket is invalid.

6 There are loopholes in parking regulations to capitalise upon. A ticket is invalid if the parking attendant is not wearing full uniform, including a hat, or if his identification number is not clearly visible. There might be discrepancies in the ticket regarding the timings or your vehicle. Sometimes the markings on the road are awry or the position of the meter is misleading. If the parking attendant is present request that he makes a note of your

objections as this may assist in any pending appeals process.

7 Don't be afraid to appeal against a penalty that in your view has been wrongly issued. The number of appeals is surprisingly small (fewer than 1%) and yet more than 60% are successful. It generally costs nothing to appeal so what have you got to lose? At first glance the process is daunting but stick with it if you feel you have been unfairly targeted with a ticket. Whatever you do, don't ignore it! See 'How to appeal' on the following page.

8 When cars are clamped or towed retrieve the vehicle fast – within 24 hours if possible. This is an expensive business because drivers must pay the penalty charge notice as well as a fee to release the vehicle. If it's not recovered promptly expect a daily charge for 'storage' on top. Afterwards, study the timings on the ticket. Most councils permit a 15 or 20 minute grace period after a parking ticket has run out before clamping or towing. Anything less than that is grounds for appeal. Remember, if you return to your vehicle before the clamp is locked or before the wheels are raised from the ground if it is being towed then the penalty charge notice is invalid.

9 Look out for cashless parking zones. Some are already on trial in central London. Drivers can ring a database to establish an arrival time. Then the clock

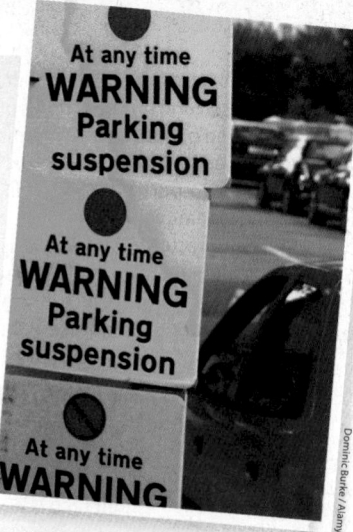

Parking on a suspended bay will almost certainly result in your car being towed to the borough pound.

starts running until the driver calls again to signal departure. The amount due is automatically debited from the driver's account. There's no doubt that new technology will play its part on the parking scene in the over-crowded capital. And it's sensible recognition at last that drivers may have many talents but are not as yet blessed with the foresight to know the precise moment that they will return to their vehicles.

10 Don't forget the other offences. London drivers not only have to be careful about parking. There's the congestion charge to consider as well as fines for using bus lanes illegally and other moving traffic fines orchestrated by local authorities. Congestion charge boundaries, bus lanes, red lights and yellow box junctions are generally monitored by enforcement cameras and evidence is extremely difficult to dispute.

may be substantially different to those in Redbridge. Charges and hours of operation for meters and ticket machines vary hugely, sometimes even on opposite sides of the same street. So there's

'stranger danger' not only for those from outside London, or suburbanites driving into central London, but even for Inner Londoners crossing borough borders.

But that isn't what most alarms the average motorist. There's a widely held belief that wardens have quotas to fill, and can get bonuses for over-achieving. Examples of predatory behaviour are

legendary. Favourite times for ticketing are the first and last 10 minutes of the controlled period, when wardens are often seen out in large numbers. There have been reports of tickets being issued to removal vans during house moves, to security company vans when rogue burglar alarms are clanging, and to numerous traders unloading goods for their shops – sometimes in the middle of the night.

In short, it is not only motorists who have broken parking regulations that are being fined, but also the unwary and the downright unlucky - in the right place, at the right time but with a wrong-minded attendant in the vicinity.

Some of the villains have been weeded out. Certain boroughs are ensuring those patrolling the streets have undergone a re-education process that will cast them as a friend to the motorist rather than a foe. It's not in your best interest to assume the whole system is unfair and take out your frustrations upon the parking attendant who just might have ticketed you legitimately.

However, the activities of a few parking regulators deserve close scrutiny. Clampers in particular have earned themselves a cowboy image that is finally arousing the interest of the legislators. A House of Commons Transport Committee Report has urged that operators should 'consider restricting clamping to persistent offenders and unregistered vehicles'. There's even talk in the document that towing a car may be incompatible with our human rights. That's perhaps why the number of cars being clamped in the capital has gone down by some 50,000.

Of course, there are always reasons to justify a harsh parking regime. It keeps London traffic on the move, making

Clamping rates are falling but you are still at risk – especially in Camden and Westminster.

How to appeal

■ **Begin with a letter sent by recorded delivery within 14 days.** That generally means the clock will stop on the prompt payment discount scheme and it will still be available if the initial appeal is unsuccessful – although some councils claim the reduced amount isn't open to those who embark on this route. Keep copies of the correspondence and any supporting evidence you send with it. Always quote the Penalty Charge Notice number. If you hear nothing for more than 56 days then the council is deemed out of time and the ticket should be cancelled.

■ **Do not pay any part of the fine if you are intending to appeal. Once payment is received by the authority the case is closed.**

■ **If your appeal is turned down don't accept a letter couched in general terms.** Write back to ask about the specifics of your case. The council will either stand by the notice and issue a Notice of Rejection or allow the appeal.

■ **If the authority endorses the ticket its next step is to issue a Notice to Owner and that should happen within six months.** According to the Road Traffic Act of 1991 the owner is liable for violations linked to his vehicle. Disturbingly, it is only at this stage that many motorists discover they are being pursued for a parking offence. If you are the sole driver of a vehicle that hasn't been stolen the ticket has clearly not been either attached to the vehicle or handed to you, the driver, as the law demands. Respond within 28 days filing the relevant information. This is known as Formal Representation. (If you do not answer in the specified time the council may well up the fine and send in the bailiffs to recover the amount.)

■ **If this petition is rejected by the local authority then it's time to take the case to the Parking and Traffic Appeals Service.** You can select a postal or personal adjudication. Internet advice favours face time with the adjudicator as local councils are known to frequently cave in at the prospect of putting evidence before an official tribunal on the grounds of cost, although there's no guarantee of this happening. The adjudicator's decision is final as there is no recourse to law.

journey times more predictable and curtailing traffic mayhem. That's the official line – which never mentions just how valuable the income generated by parking penalties is to the enforcers. Further, authorities don't talk about targets in relation to parking fines, rather 'baseline performance indicators'.

So if you are going to park in London, especially in the centre, beware, be aware – and know your rights. If you do get fined and you think you have a case, be prepared to appeal. Fewer than 1% of motorists did appeal in 2004/5 (do we detect money-raising by inertia?),

but over 60% of those appeals were allowed. Remember, if you do not get a response to your appeal within 56 days, your appeal is automatically allowed.

Helpful information

The Knowledge A telephone advisory service run by off-duty London taxi drivers. They will help with problems including parking and directions. The number is 0906 265 6565 (premium rate) or try *www.theknowledge.com*

Transport for London (TfL) Responsible for 360 miles of roads, 4,600 traffic lights and London's red routes. It is also a fine-issuing authority. Contact Tfl on 0207 2221234 or *www.tfl.gov.uk.*

www.ticketbusters.co.uk is a website devoted to assisting London motorists, offering tailored advice on parking ticket appeals.

www.parkingticket.co.uk also offers support for London drivers.

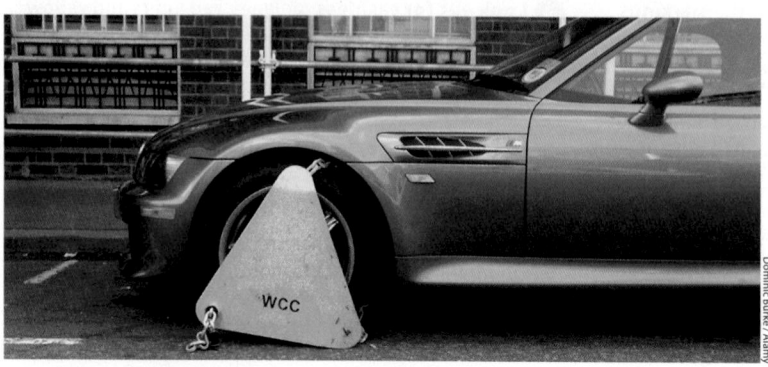

Dominic Burke / Alamy

Mobile speed camera sites

This table lists the sites where the local safety camera partnership may enforce speed limits through the use of mobile cameras or detectors. These are usually set up on the roadside or a bridge spanning the road and operated by a police or civilian enforcement officer.

Barking & Dagenham

A13
Alfreds Way IG11
Alfreds Way IG12
Ripple Rd IG11
Ripple Rd RM9

A406
Barking Relief Rd IG11

A1153
Porters Avenue RM8

B178
Ballards Rd RM10

Barnet

A5
Hendon Broadway NW9

A406
North Circular Rd N3

Unclassified
Oakleigh Rd South N11

Bexley

A20
Sidcup Rd SE9

Unclassified
Abbey Rd DA17
Bellegrove Rd DA16
Erith Rd DA17
Farady Avenue DA14
King Harolds Way DA17
Lower Rd DA17
Penhill Rd DA5
Pickford Lane DA7
Well Hall Rd SE9
Woolwich Rd DA17

Brent

A5
Edgware Rd NW2

A406
North Circular Rd NW2
North Circular Rd NW10

A4006
Kenton Rd HA3

Unclassified
Crest Rd NW2
Fryent Way, Kingsbury NW9
Hillside NW10
Kingsbury Rd NW9
Watford Rd, Wembley HA0
Watford Rd, Sudbury HA0
Woodcock Hill HA3

Bromley

A20
Sidcup By-Pass DA14

A213
Croydon Rd SE20

A222
Bromley Rd BR2
Bromley Rd BR3

Unclassified
Beckenham Rd BR3
Burnt Ash Lane BR1
Crystal Palace Park Rd SE26
Elmers End Rd BR3
Main Rd TN16
Sevenoaks Way BR5
Wickham Way BR3

Camden

A501
Euston Rd NW1

Chadwell

M11
Chadwell IG8

City of Westminster

A40
Westway W2

Unclassified
Great Western Rd W11
Millbank SW1
Vauxhall Bridge Rd SW1

Croydon

A22
Godstone Rd CR8

A215
Beulah Hill SE19

A217
Garratt Lane SW18

Unclassified
Brigstock Rd CR7
Coulsdon Rd, Coulsdon CR5
Long Lane, Addiscombe CR0
Portnalls Rd, Coulsdon CR5
Thornton Rd CR0

Ealing

A40
Perivale UB6
Western Avenue UB5
Western Avenue UB6

Unclassified
Greenford Rd, Greenford UB6
Greenford Rd, Southall UB1
Horn Lane W3
Lady Margaret Rd UB1
Ruislip Rd UB5
Uxbridge Rd UB2

Egham

M25
Egham TW20

Elmbridge

M25
Byfleet KT14

Enfield

A10
Great Cambridge Rd N18

A110
Enfield Rd EN2

Unclassified
Fore Street N9

Forest Hill

Unclassified
Stanstead Rd SE23

Greenwich

A20
Sidcup Rd SE9

Unclassified
Beresford Street SE18
Court Rd SE9
Creek Rd SE10
Glenesk Rd SE9
Rochester Way SE3
Rochester Way SE9
Woolwich Church Street SE18

Hackney

A10
Stamford Hill N16

Unclassified
Clapton Common E5
Seven Sisters Rd N4
Upper Clapton Rd E5

Hammersmith & Fulham

A40
Westway W2
Westway W12

A219
Scrubs Lane W12

Unclassified
Fulham Palace Rd SW6
Uxbridge Rd W12

Haringey

A503
Seven Sisters Rd N15

Unclassified
Belmont Rd N15
Bounds Green Rd N11
Seven Sisters Rd N4
White Hart Lane N22

Harrow

Unclassified
Alexandra Avenue HA2
Harrow View HA3
Honeypot Lane NW9
Porlock Avenue HA2
Uxbridge Rd, Harrow Weald HA3
Watford Rd HA1

Havering

Unclassified
Brentwood Rd, Romford RM1
Chase Cross Rd RM5
Eastern Avenue RM14
Eastern Avenue East RM14
Hall Lane RM14
Ingrebourne Gardens, Upminster RM14
Ockenden Rd RM14

Parkstone Avenue, Hornchurch RM11
Wingletye Lane RM11

Hillingdon

M25
Colnbrook SL3
West Drayton UB7

A40
Western Avenue, Ruislip UB10

A312
Hayes UB3

Unclassified
Church Hill, Harefield UB9
Cowley Rd, Uxbridge UB8
Cowley High Rd UB8
Joel Street, Northwood Hills HA6
Kingshill Avenue, Hayes UB4
Park Rd UB8
Stockley Rd UB7
Uxbridge Rd, Hayes UB4

Hounslow

A4
Great West Rd, Brentford TW8
Great West Rd, Hounslow TW7
Great West Rd, Hounslow W4

A315
High Street TW8

Unclassified
Castle Way, Hanworth TW13
Great West Rd TW5
Harlington Rd West TW14
Hatton Rd, Bedfont TW14

Islington

Unclassified
Holloway Rd N19
Seven Sisters Rd N4
Upper Street N1

Kensington & Chelsea

Unclassified
Barlby Rd W10
Chelsea Embankment SW3
Chesterton Rd W10
Holland Park Avenue W11
Holland Villas Rd W14
Kensington Park Rd W11
Kensington Rd SW7
Ladbroke Grove W11
Latimer Rd W10
Royal Hospital Rd SW3
Sloane Street SW1
St Helens Gardens W10

Kingston upon Thames

A3
Kingston By-Pass SW20

A240
Kingston Rd KT4

Unclassified
Manor Drive North KT3
Richmond Rd KT2

Lambeth

Unclassified
Atkins Rd SW12
Brixton Hill SW2
Brixton Rd SW9
Clapham Rd SW9
Herne Hill Rd SE24
Kennington Park Rd SE11
Kings Avenue SW4
Streatham High Rd SW16

Lewisham

A21
Bromley Rd BR1

Unclassified
Brockley Rd SE4
Brockley Rd SE23
Bromley Rd SE6
Brownhill Rd SE6
Burnt Ash Hill SE12
Lee High Rd SE12
Lewisham Way SE4
Westwood Hill SE26

Merton

A298
Bushey Rd SW20

Unclassified
Central Rd SM4
High Street, Colliers Wood SW19
Hillcross Avenue SM4
London Rd CR4
Martin Way SM4
Martin Way SW20
Ridgway Place SW19
West Barnes Lane SW20

Newham

A13
Alfreds Way IG11

A124
Barking Rd E6

A1020
Royal Albert Dock Way E6
Royal Docks Rd E6

Unclassified
Barking Rd E13
Romford Rd E7

Redbridge

A406
Southend Rd IG8

Unclassified
Manford Way, Hainault IG7
Woodford Avenue IG8
Woodford Rd E18

Richmond upon Thames

A205
Upper Richmond Rd West SW14

Unclassified
Kew Rd TW9
Sixth Cross Rd TW2
Uxbridge Rd TW12

Ruislip

Unclassified
Field End Rd HA4

Runnymeade

M25
Runnymede TW20

Southwark

Unclassified
Albany Rd SE5
Alleyn Park SE21
Brenchley Gardens SE15
Camberwell New Rd SE5
Denmark Hill SE5
Kennington Park Rd SE11
Linden Grove SE15
Old Kent Rd SE1
Old Kent Rd SE14
Old Kent Rd SE17
Peckham Rye SE15
Salter Rd SE16
Southwark Pk Rd SE16
Sunray Avenue SE24

Spelthorne

M25
Staines TW18

Sutton

A232
Cheam Rd SM1

B272
Foresters Drive SM6

B278
Green Lane SM4

B279
Tudor Drive SM4

Unclassified
Malden Rd SM3
Middleton Rd SM5
Beddington Lane CR0
Cheam Common Rd KT4

Tower Hamlets

A102
Homerton High Street E9

Unclassified
Bow Rd E3
Cambridge Heath Rd E2
Manchester Rd E14
Mile End Rd E1
Upper Clapton Rd E5
Westferry Rd E14

Waltham Forest

Unclassified
Chingford Rd E4
Chingford Rd E17
Hoe Street E17
Larkshall Rd E4

Wandsworth

A3
Kingston Rd SW15

A214
Trinity Rd SW18

A3220
Latchmere Rd SW11

Unclassified
Battersea Park Rd SW11
Garratt Lane SW18
Upper Richmond Rd SW15

Windsor & Maidenhead

M25
Wraysbury TW19

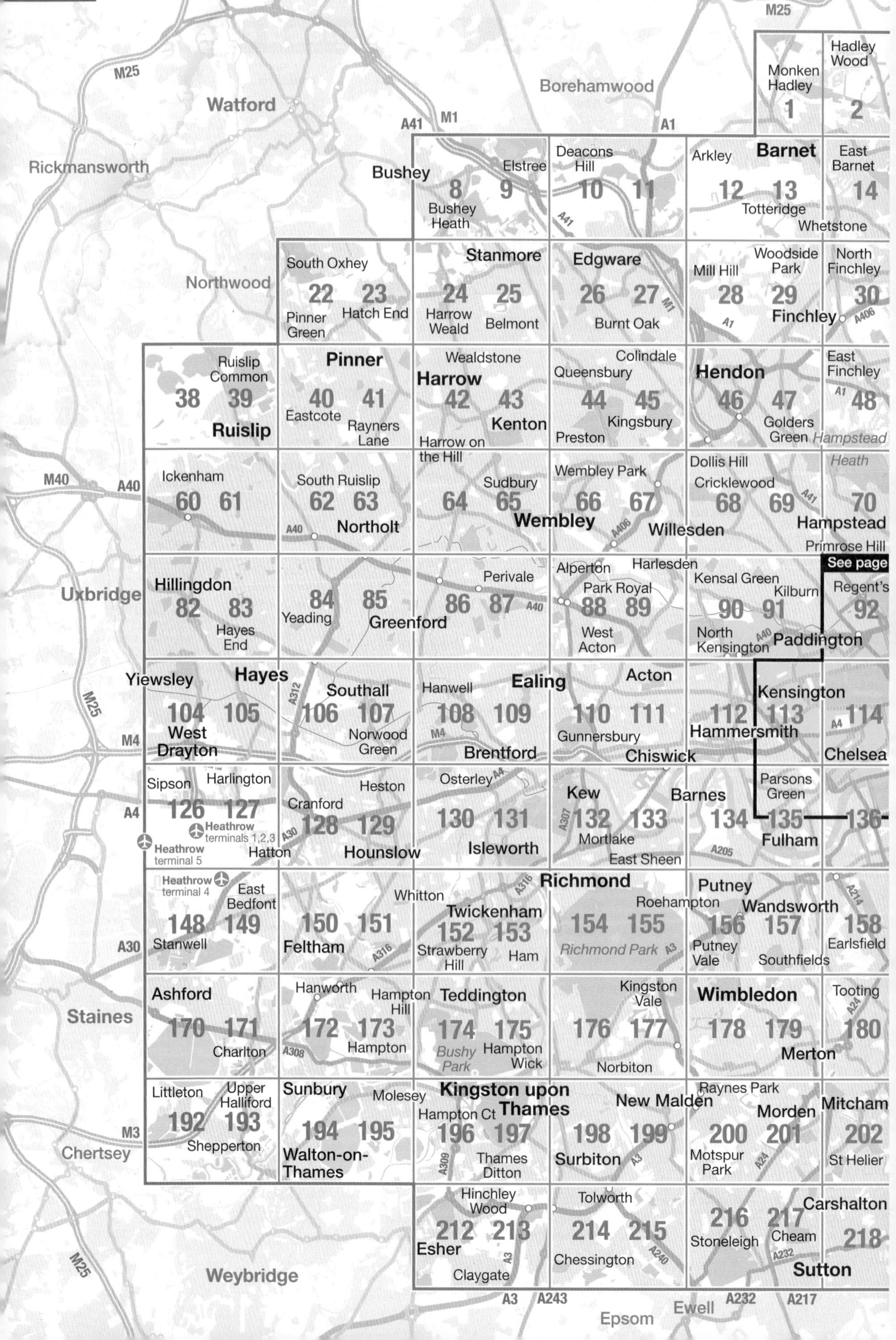

Potters Bar

M25

M25

Watford

Rickmansworth

Borehamwood

Monken Hadley **1**

Hadley Wood **2**

M1

A41

A1

Bushey

Elstree

8

9

Bushey Heath

Deacons Hill

10

11

A41

Arkley

12

Barnet

13

Totteridge

Whetstone

East Barnet **14**

Northwood

South Oxhey

22

23

Hatch End

Pinner Green

Stanmore

24

25

Harrow Weald

Belmont

Edgware

26

27

Burnt Oak

M1

Mill Hill

28

Woodside Park **29**

Finchley

North Finchley **30**

A406

A1

Ruislip Common **38**

39

Ruislip

Pinner

40

41

Eastcote

Rayners Lane

Harrow on the Hill

Wealdstone

Harrow

42

43

Kenton

Colindale

Queensbury

44

45

Kingsbury

Preston

Hendon

46

47

Golders Green

East Finchley **48**

A1

Hampstead

M40

A40

Ickenham

60

61

South Ruislip

62

63

Northolt

A40

Wembley Park

Sudbury

64

65

Wembley

Dollis Hill

Cricklewood

68

69

Willesden

Heath

A41

70

Hampstead

Primrose Hill

Uxbridge

Hillingdon

82

83

Hayes End

Yeading

84

85

Greenford

Perivale

86

87

A40

Alperton

Park Royal **88**

89

West Acton

Harlesden

Kensal Green

90

91

North Kensington

Kilburn

A40

Paddington

See page

Regent's **92**

Yiewsley

Hayes

104

105

West Drayton

A312

Southall

106

107

Norwood Green

Hanwell

108

109

Brentford

M4

Ealing

110

111

Gunnersbury

Chiswick

Acton

Acton

North Kensington

112

Kensington

113

Hammersmith

A4

114

Chelsea

M4

A4

Sipson

Harlington

126

127

Heathrow terminals 1,2,3

Heathrow terminal 5

Cranford

128

129

Hounslow

Hatton

Heston

Osterley

A4

130

131

Isleworth

A307

Kew

132

133

Mortlake

East Sheen

Barnes

134

Parsons Green

135

Fulham

A205

136

Heathrow terminal 4

Stanwell

148

East Bedfont **149**

A30

Feltham

150

151

A316

Whitton

Twickenham

152

153

Strawberry Hill

Ham

Richmond

Roehampton

154

155

Richmond Park

A3

Putney

156

Putney Vale

Wandsworth

157

Southfields

A214

158

Earlsfield

Ashford

170

171

Charlton

Hanworth

172

173

Hampton

A308

Hampton Hill

Teddington

174

175

Bushy Park

Hampton Wick

Kingston Vale

176

177

Norbiton

Wimbledon

178

179

Merton

Tooting

A24

180

Littleton

Upper Halliford **193**

192

Shepperton

M3

Chertsey

Sunbury

194

195

Walton-on-Thames

Molesey

Hampton Ct

Kingston upon Thames

196

197

Thames Ditton

A309

New Malden

198

199

Surbiton

A3

Raynes Park

200

201

Motspur Park

A24

Morden

Mitcham

202

St Helier

Weybridge

Hinchley Wood

212

213

Esher

Claygate

A3

Tolworth

214

215

Chessington

A243

A240

Stoneleigh

216

217

Cheam

A232

Carshalton

218

Sutton

A3

A243

Ewell

Epsom

A232

A217

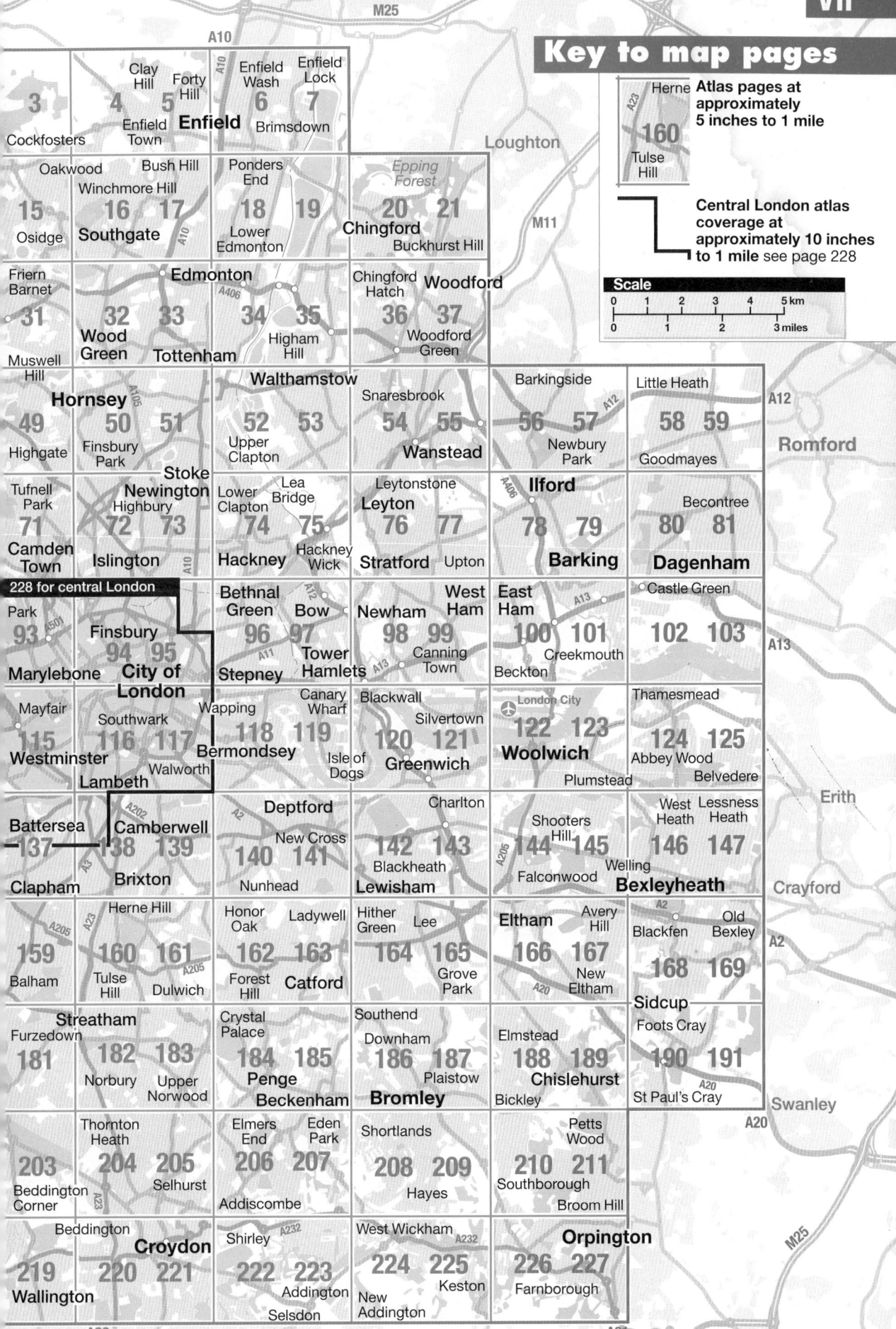

Key to map pages

Herne
Atlas pages at approximately 5 inches to 1 mile
A23
160
Tulse Hill

Central London atlas coverage at approximately 10 inches to 1 mile see page 228

Scale
0 1 2 3 4 5 km
0 1 2 3 miles

M25
A10
A10
M11
M25
A20
A21
A23

3 Cockfosters

Clay Hill **4** Forty Hill **5**
Enfield Town **Enfield**

Enfield Wash **6** Enfield Lock **7**
Brimsdown

Loughton

Oakwood **15** Osidge

Bush Hill **16 17**
Winchmore Hill **Southgate**

Ponders End **18 19**
Lower Edmonton

Epping Forest **20 21**
Chingford Buckhurst Hill

Friern Barnet **31**
Muswell Hill

Edmonton
A406 **32 33**
Wood Green **Tottenham**

34 35
Higham Hill

Chingford Hatch **36 37** **Woodford**
Woodford Green

Hornsey **49**
Highgate

50 51
Finsbury Park

Walthamstow **52 53**
Upper Clapton

Snaresbrook **54 55**
Wanstead

Barkingside **56 57**
Newbury Park

Little Heath **58 59**
Goodmayes

A12
Romford

Tufnell Park **71**
Camden Town

72 73
Highbury **Stoke Newington**
Islington

Lower Clapton **74 75**
Hackney Hackney Wick

Leytonstone **76 77**
Leyton **Stratford** Upton

Ilford **78 79**
Barking

Becontree **80 81**
Dagenham

228 for central London
Park **93**
Marylebone

Finsbury **94 95**
City of London
Stepney

Bethnal Green Bow **96 97**
Tower Hamlets

West Ham **98 99**
Newham Canning Town

East Ham **100 101**
A13 Creekmouth
Beckton

Castle Green **102 103**
A13

Mayfair **115**
Westminster
Lambeth

Southwark **116 117**
Walworth **Bermondsey**

Wapping **118 119**
Canary Wharf Isle of Dogs

Blackwall **120 121**
Silvertown **Greenwich**

London City **122 123**
Woolwich Plumstead

Thamesmead **124 125**
Abbey Wood Belvedere

Erith

Battersea **137**
Clapham

138 139
Camberwell **Brixton**

Deptford **140 141**
New Cross Nunhead

Charlton **142 143**
Blackheath **Lewisham**

Shooters Hill **144 145**
Falconwood Welling

West Heath Lessness Heath **146 147**
Bexleyheath

Crayford
A2

Herne Hill **159**
Balham **160 161**
Tulse Hill Dulwich

Honor Oak **162 163**
Forest Hill **Catford**
Ladywell

Hither Green **164 165**
Lee Grove Park

Eltham **166 167**
New Eltham
Avery Hill

Blackfen **168 169**
Old Bexley
Sidcup
A2

Streatham **181**
Furzedown
182 183
Norbury Upper Norwood

Crystal Palace **184 185**
Penge **Beckenham**

Southend **186 187**
Downham Plaistow **Bromley**

Elmstead **188 189**
Chislehurst
Bickley

Foots Cray **190 191**
St Paul's Cray
A20

Swanley
A20

Thornton Heath **203**
Beddington Corner
204 205
Selhurst

Elmers End **206 207**
Eden Park
Addiscombe

Shortlands **208 209**
Hayes

Petts Wood **210 211**
Southborough
Broom Hill

M25

Beddington **219**
Wallington
Croydon **220 221**
Shirley **222 223**
Addington Selsdon

West Wickham **224 225**
Keston
New Addington

Orpington **226 227**
Farnborough

A23
A21

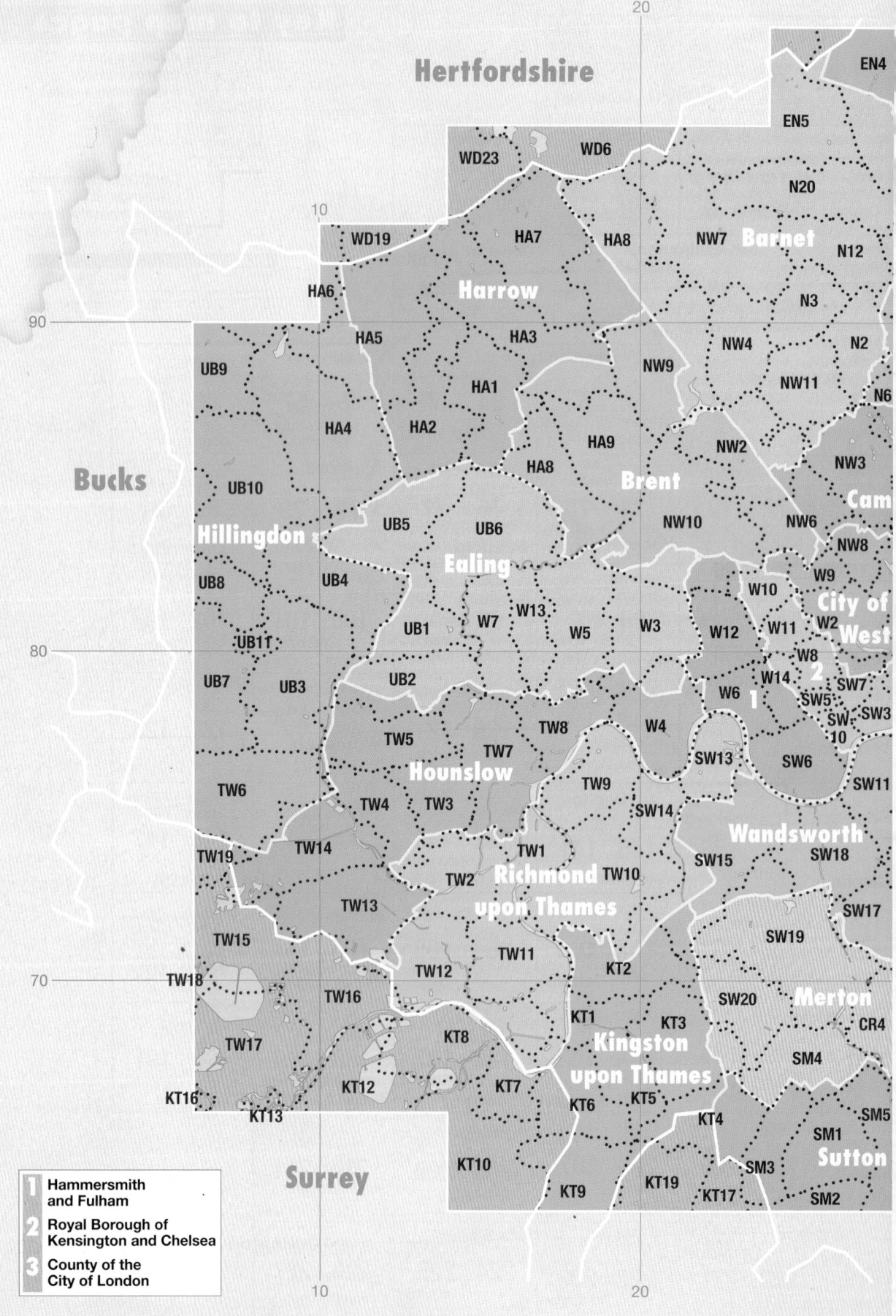

Hertfordshire

WD23 WD6

EN4

EN5

N20

WD19 HA7 HA8 NW7 **Barnet** N12

HA6 **Harrow** N3

HA5 HA3 NW9 N2

HA1 NW4 NW11 N6

Bucks HA4 HA2 HA9 NW2 NW3

UB9 HA8 **Brent** NW8

UB10 UB5 UB6 NW10 NW6 **Cam**

Hillingdon **Ealing** NW8

UB8 UB4 W10 W9 **City of**

UB1 W7 W13 W5 W3 W12 W11 W2 **West**

UB11 W8

UB7 UB3 UB2 W6 W14 **2** SW7

W4 **1** SW5 SW3

TW5 TW7 SW13 SW6 SW 10

TW6 **Hounslow** TW9 SW14 SW11

TW4 TW3 **Wandsworth**

TW14 TW1 SW15 SW18

TW19 TW2 **Richmond** TW10 SW17

TW13 **upon Thames** SW19

TW15 TW11 SW20 **Merton**

TW18 TW12 KT2 CR4

TW16 KT1 KT3 SW20 SM4

TW17 KT8 **Kingston** SM5

KT16 KT12 KT7 **upon Thames** KT5 SM1

KT13 KT6 KT4 SM3 **Sutton**

KT10 KT19 SM2

Surrey KT9 KT17

---

1 Hammersmith
and Fulham

2 Royal Borough of
Kensington and Chelsea

3 County of the
City of London

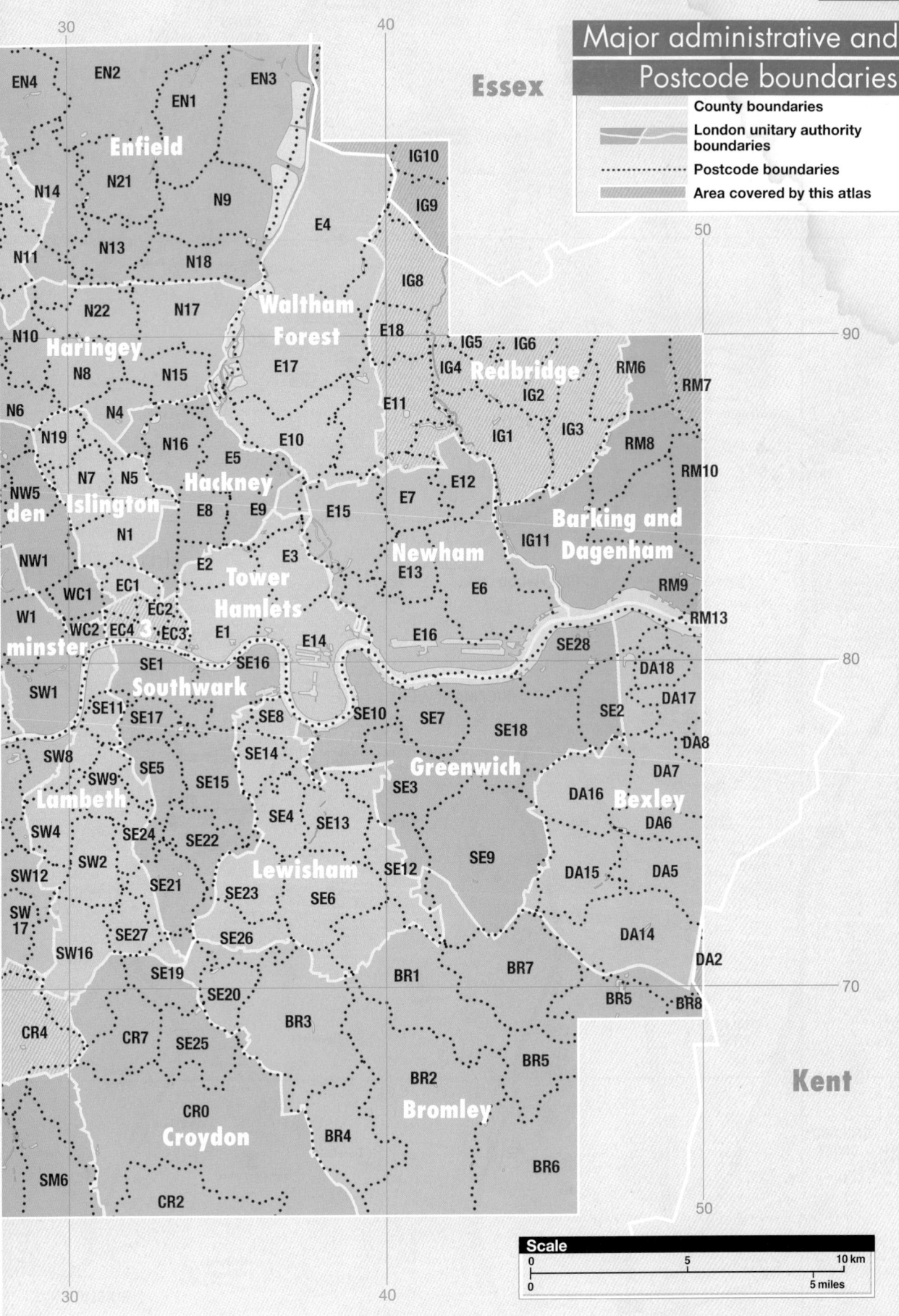

Major administrative and Postcode boundaries

County boundaries
London unitary authority boundaries
Postcode boundaries
Area covered by this atlas

Essex

Kent

EN4 · EN2 · EN1 · EN3
Enfield
N14 · N21 · N9
N11 · N13 · N18 · E4 · IG10
N10 · N22 · N17 · IG9
Haringey · N8 · N15 · Waltham Forest · E18 · IG8
N6 · N4 · N16 · E17 · E11 · IG5 · IG6 · RM6 · RM7
N19 · E10 · IG4 · Redbridge · RM8
N7 · N5 · E5 · IG2 · IG3 · RM10
NW5 · Hackney · E8 · E9 · E15 · E12 · IG1
den · Islington · E7 · RM8
N1 · E2 · E3 · Newham · Barking and Dagenham
NW1 · Tower · E13 · IG11 · RM9
W1 · WC1 · EC1 · Hamlets · E6 · RM13
minster · WC2 · EC2 · EC4 · EC3 · E1 · E14 · E16 · SE28 · DA18
SW1 · SE1 · SE16 · SE2 · DA17
SE11 · Southwark · SE8 · SE10 · SE7 · SE18 · DA8
SW8 · SE17 · SE14 · DA7
SW9 · SE5 · SE15 · SE3 · Greenwich · DA16 · Bexley · DA6
Lambeth · SE4 · SE13 · DA15 · DA5
SW4 · SE24 · SE22 · SE12 · SE9
SW2 · SE21 · Lewisham · SE6 · DA14
SW12 · SE23
SW17 · SE27 · SE26 · DA2
SW16 · SE19 · BR1 · BR7 · BR5 · BR8
CR4 · SE20
CR7 · SE25 · BR3 · BR5
CR0 · BR2
Croydon · BR4 · Bromley
SM6 · BR6
CR2

Route planning

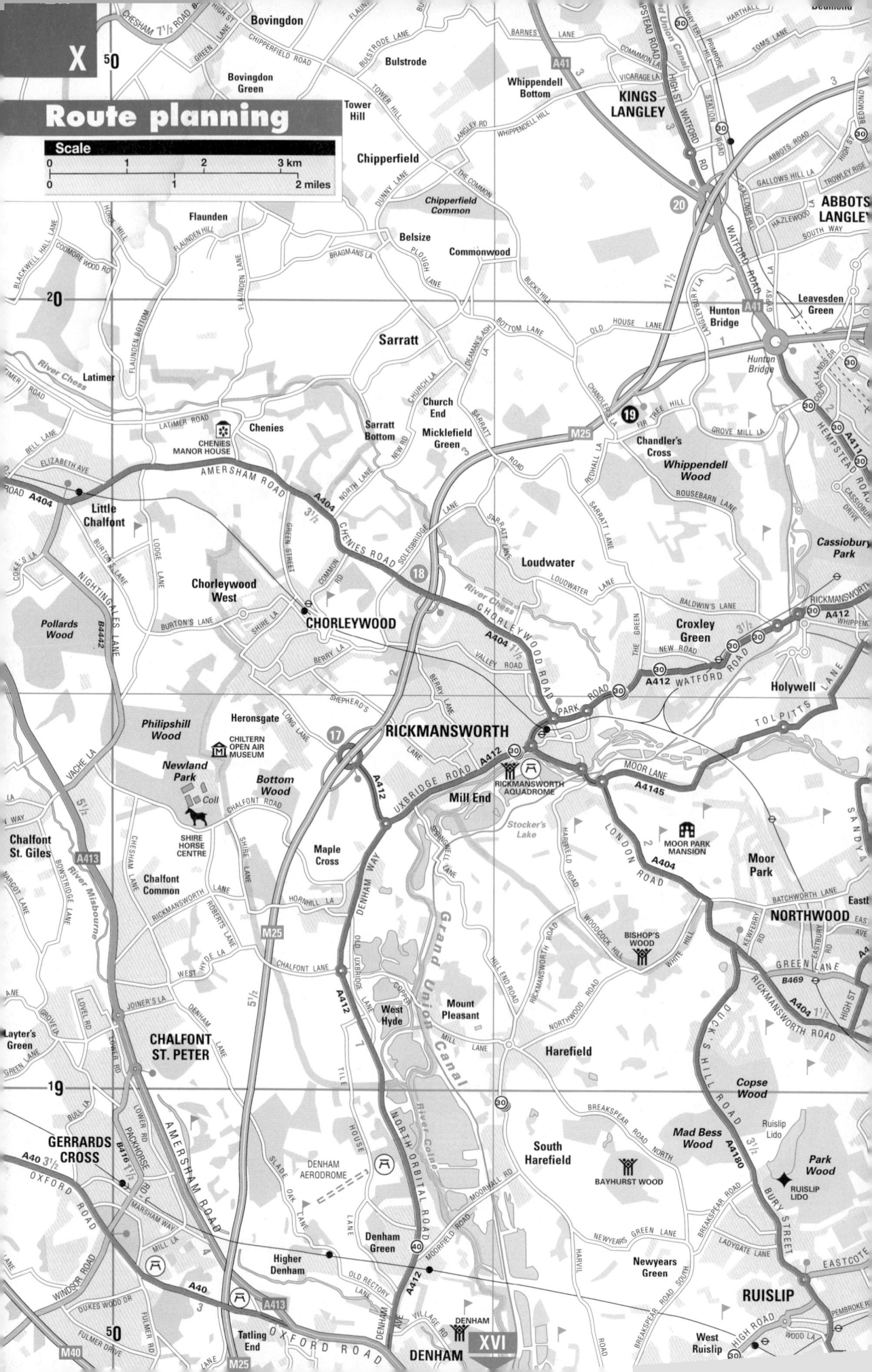

Scale
0 1 2 3 km
0 1 2 miles
Bovingdon
Bovingdon Green
Bulstrode
Tower Hill
Chipperfield
Chipperfield Common
Whippendell Bottom
KINGS LANGLEY
ABBOTS LANGLEY
Flaunden
Belsize
Commonwood
Leavesden Green
Hunton Bridge
Sarratt
Latimer
River Chess
Chenies
CHENIES MANOR HOUSE
Church End
Sarratt Bottom
Micklefield Green
Chandler's Cross
Whippendell Wood
Little Chalfont
Chorleywood West
CHORLEYWOOD
Loudwater
Cassiobury Park
Pollards Wood
Croxley Green
Holywell
Philipshill Wood
Heronsgate
CHILTERN OPEN AIR MUSEUM
RICKMANSWORTH
Newland Park
Bottom Wood
Mill End
RICKMANSWORTH AQUADROME
Stocker's Lake
SHIRE HORSE CENTRE
Chalfont St. Giles
Maple Cross
MOOR PARK MANSION
Moor Park
Chalfont Common
NORTHWOOD
Grand Union Canal
BISHOP'S WOOD
West Hyde
Mount Pleasant
Layter's Green
CHALFONT ST. PETER
Harefield
Copse Wood
GERRARDS CROSS
South Harefield
Mad Bess Wood
Ruislip Lido
Park Wood
RUISLIP LIDO
DENHAM AERODROME
BAYHURST WOOD
Higher Denham
Denham Green
Newyears Green
RUISLIP
Tatling End
DENHAM
West Ruislip
XVI

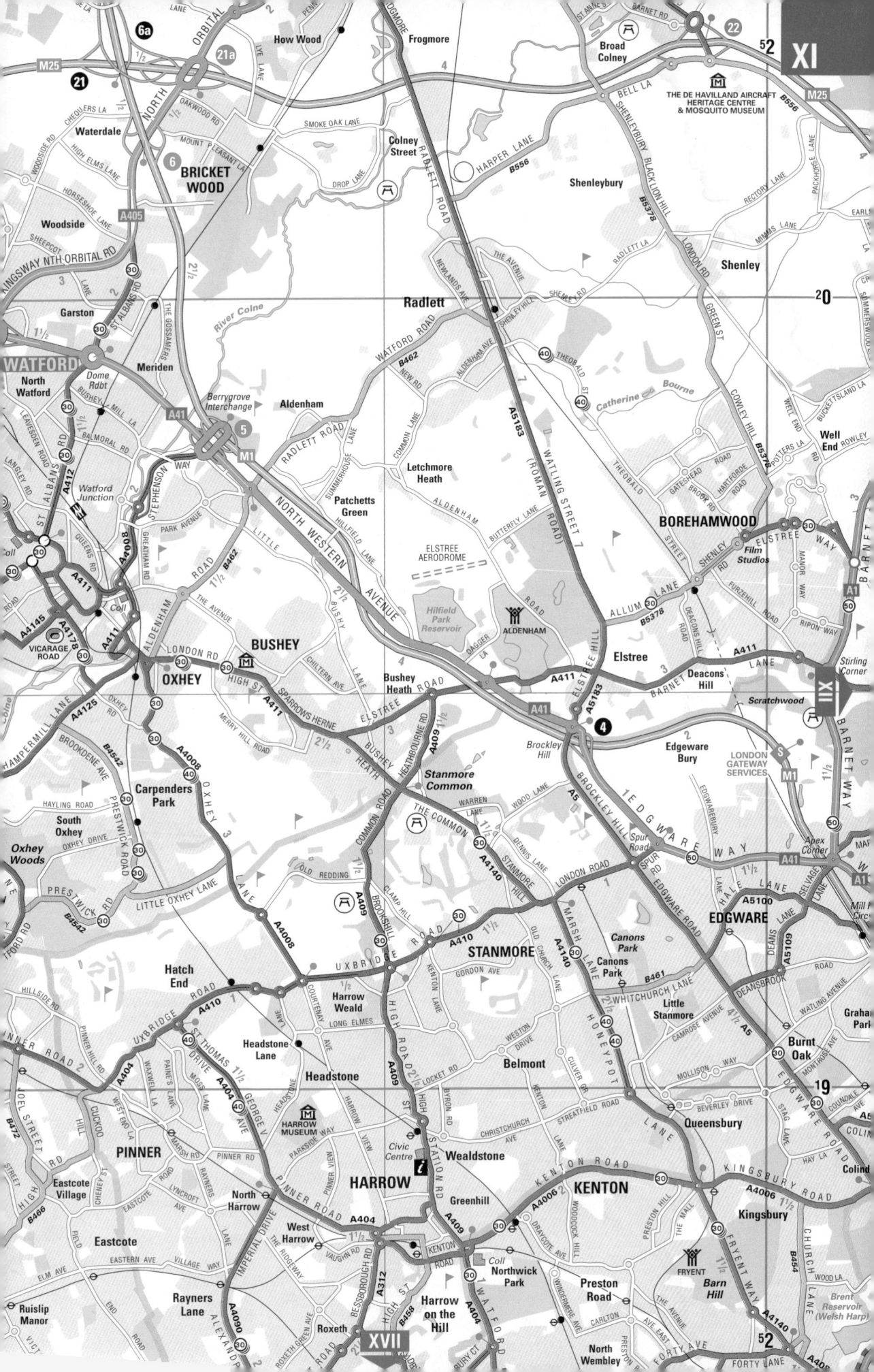

XI
How Wood
Frogmore
Broad Colney
THE DE HAVILLAND AIRCRAFT HERITAGE CENTRE & MOSQUITO MUSEUM
M25
Waterdale
BRICKET WOOD
Colney Street
Shenleybury
Woodside
Shenley
Radlett
Garston
WATFORD
North Watford
Dome Rdbt
Meriden
Berrygrove Interchange
Aldenham
Letchmore Heath
Patchetts Green
Watford Junction
ELSTREE AERODROME
BOREHAMWOOD
Film Studios
Well End
Hilfield Park Reservoir
ALDENHAM
BUSHEY
OXHEY
Bushey Heath
Elstree
Deacons Hill
Scratchwood
Stirling Corner
Brockley Hill
Edgeware Bury
LONDON GATEWAY SERVICES
Carpenders Park
South Oxhey
Oxhey Woods
Stanmore Common
Apex Corner
Spur Road
EDGWARE
Mill Hill Circus
Hatch End
STANMORE
Canons Park
Harrow Weald
Little Stanmore
Headstone Lane
Headstone
Belmont
Burnt Oak
HARROW MUSEUM
Queensbury
PINNER
Civic Centre
Wealdstone
HARROW
KENTON
Eastcote Village
North Harrow
Greenhill
Kingsbury
West Harrow
Eastcote
Northwick Park
Preston Road
FRYENT
Barn Hill
Rayners Lane
Harrow on the Hill
Brent Reservoir (Welsh Harp)
Ruislip Manor
Roxeth
XVII
North Wembley
M1
A41
A411
A5183
A5
A409
A4008
A4140
A410
A404
A4006
A312
A4090
A5109
A5100
A1
B556
B5378
B462
B461
B4542
B466
B472
B454
B458
River Colne
Catherine Bourne
North Orbital
Watling Street (Roman Road)
North Western Avenue
Uxbridge Road
Kenton Road
Kingsbury Road
Edgware Road
Barnet Way
Elstree Way
Edgware Way

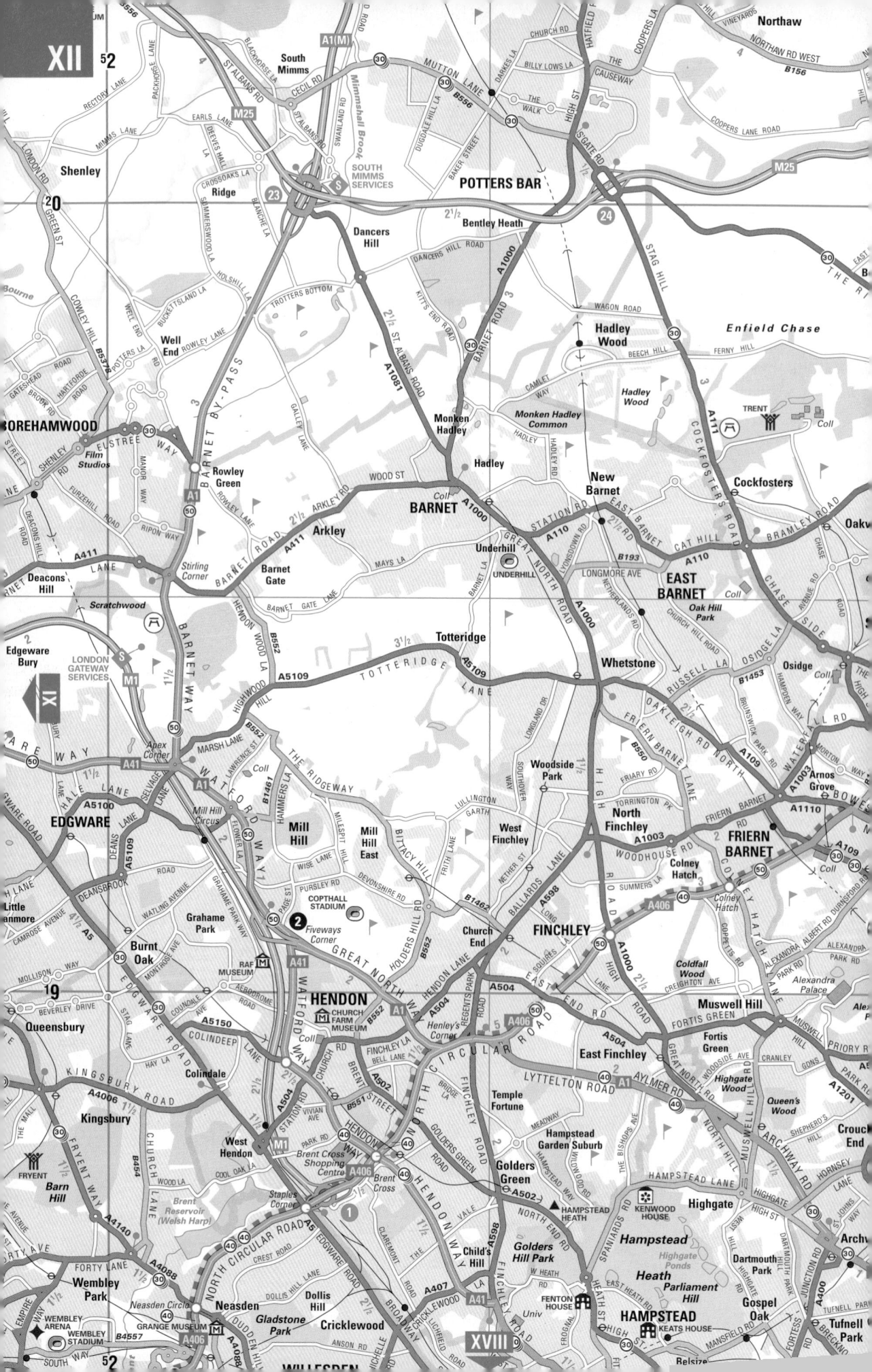

52
20
19
Northaw
NORTHAW RD WEST
B156
COOPERS LANE ROAD
THE CAUSEWAY
South Mimms
Mimmshall Brook
SOUTH MIMMS SERVICES
A1(M)
M25
MUTTON LANE
B556
CHURCH RD
BILLY LOWS LA
DARKES LA
DUGDALE HILL LA
BAKER STREET
HATFIELD RD
HIGH ST
THE WALK
POTTERS BAR
ST ALBANS RD
BLACKHORSE LA
CECIL RD
SWANLAND RD
RECTORY LANE
PACKHORSE LANE
EARLS LANE
MIMMS LANE
DEEVES HALL LA
LONDON RD
Shenley
CROSSOAKS LA
Ridge
SUMMERSWOOD LA
BLANCHE LA
23
24
Bentley Heath
Dancers Hill
DANCERS HILL ROAD
STAG HILL
THE RIDGEWAY
Enfield Chase
GREEN ST
COWLEY HILL
B5378
HOLSHILL LA
BUCKETTSLAND LA
WELL END RD
TROTTERS BOTTOM
KITTS END ROAD
BARNET ROAD
A1000
WAGON ROAD
Hadley Wood
BEECH HILL
FERNY HILL
Well End
ROWLEY LANE
POTTERS LA
GATESHEAD ROAD
HARTFORDE ROAD
BROOK RD
BARNET BY-PASS
GALLEY LANE
ST. ALBANS ROAD
A1081
CAMLET WAY
Monken Hadley Common
Hadley Wood
TRENT
Coll
COCKFOSTERS ROAD
A111
BOREHAMWOOD
ELSTREE WAY
SHENLEY RD
Film Studios
MANOR WAY
Monken Hadley
Hadley
HADLEY RD
Rowley Green
A1
FURZEHILL ROAD
RIPON WAY
DEACONS HILL ROAD
WOOD ST
ARKLEY RD
Arkley
BARNET
New Barnet
EAST BARNET RD
STATION RD
A110
Cockfosters
BRAMLEY ROAD
CAT HILL
Oakwood
A411
LANE
Deacons Hill
Stirling Corner
BARNET ROAD
Barnet Gate
MAYS LA
Underhill
UNDERHILL
BARNET LA
GREAT NORTH ROAD
LYONSDOWN RD
B193
LONGMORE AVE
EAST BARNET
Oak Hill Park
CHURCH HILL ROAD
CHASE SIDE
Scratchwood
BARNET GATE LANE
HENDON WOOD LA
B552
NETHERLANDS RD
Edgeware Bury
LONDON GATEWAY SERVICES
M1
BARNET WAY
Totteridge
TOTTERIDGE LANE
A5109
Whetstone
RUSSELL LA
OSIDGE LA
Osidge
B1453
HAMPDEN WAY
HIGHWOOD HILL
OAKLEIGH RD NORTH
BRUNSWICK PARK RD
WATERFALL RD
FRIERN BARNET LANE
B550
A109
CARE WAY
A41
Apex Corner
MARSH LANE
LAWRENCE ST
HAMMERS LA
B1461
THE RIDGEWAY
LONGLAND DR
SOUTHOVER
Woodside Park
FRIARY RD
TORRINGTON PK
Arnos Grove
A1003
BOWES
HALE LANE
A5100
EDGWARE
SELVAGE LANE
Mill Hill Circus
WATFORD WAY
FLOWER LA
Mill Hill
Mill Hill East
MILESPIT HILL
BITTACY HILL
LULLINGTON GARTH
FRITH LANE
West Finchley
North Finchley
FRIERN BARNET
A1110
EDGWARE ROAD
DEANS LANE
DEANSBROOK ROAD
WATLING AVENUE
GRAHAME PARK WAY
WISE LANE
PURSLEY RD
DEVONSHIRE RD
PAGE ST
COPTHALL STADIUM
HOLDERS HILL RD
B1462
NETHER ST
BALLARDS LANE
A598
WOODHOUSE RD
Colney Hatch
SUMMERS LA
A406
COLNEY HATCH LANE
Little Stanmore
CAMROSE AVENUE
A5
Grahame Park
Fiveways Corner
GREAT NORTH WAY
Church End
FINCHLEY
Colney Hatch
COPPETTS RD
ALBERT RD
DURNSFORD RD
ALEXANDRA PARK RD
Burnt Oak
MONTROSE AVE
RAF MUSEUM
Coldfall Wood
CREIGHTON AVE
Alexandra Palace
MOLLISON WAY
BEVERLEY DRIVE
Queensbury
STAG LANE
AERODROME ROAD
HENDON
CHURCH FARM MUSEUM
HENDON LANE
REGENTS PARK ROAD
A504
SQUIRES LA
EAST END RD
HIGH ROAD
Muswell Hill
FORTIS GREEN
MUSWELL HILL
PRIORY RD
A5150
COLINDEEP LANE
Henley's Corner
NORTH CIRCULAR ROAD
East Finchley
Fortis Green
CRANLEY GDNS
PARK RD
Colindale
HAY LA
FINCHLEY LA
BELL LANE
BRENT STREET
A502
LYTTELTON ROAD
AYLMER RD
GREAT NORTH RD
WOODSIDE AVE
Highgate Wood
Queen's Wood
A1201
KINGSBURY ROAD
A4006
Kingsbury
STATION RD
VIVIAN AVE
B551
BRIDGE LA
Temple Fortune
MEADWAY
THE BISHOPS AVE
NORTH HILL
MUSWELL HILL RD
SHEPHERD'S HILL
ARCHWAY RD
Crouch End
THE MALL
FRYENT WAY
B454
CHURCH LANE
West Hendon
PARK RD
Brent Cross Shopping Centre
HENDON WAY
GOLDERS GREEN ROAD
FINCHLEY ROAD
Hampstead Garden Suburb
HAMPSTEAD WAY
WILDWOOD RD
HAMPSTEAD LANE
HORNSEY LANE
FRYENT
Barn Hill
WOOD LA
COOL OAK LA
Brent Cross
Golders Green
Highgate
HIGHGATE HILL
Brent Reservoir (Welsh Harp)
Staples Corner
A4140
CLAREMONT ROAD
VALE
HAMPSTEAD HEATH
KENWOOD HOUSE
NORTH END RD
Hampstead
Highgate Ponds
HIGH ST
ST JOHNS WAY
Archway
FORTY AVE
FORTY LANE
A4088
CREST ROAD
DOLLIS HILL LANE
EDGWARE ROAD
Child's Hill
Golders Hill Park
W HEATH RD
SPANIARDS RD
Heath
Parliament Hill
Dartmouth Park
DARTMOUTH PARK HILL
JUNCTION RD
A400
Wembley Park
Neasden Circle
Neasden
Dollis Hill
Gladstone Park
Cricklewood
BROADWAY
A407
CRICKLEWOOD LA
A41
FENTON HOUSE
Univ
FROGNAL
HEATH ST
EAST HEATH RD
Gospel Oak
TUFNELL PARK RD
Tufnell Park
EMPIRE WAY
WEMBLEY ARENA
WEMBLEY STADIUM
GRANGE MUSEUM
B4557
DUDDEN HILL
ANSON RD
LICHFIELD ROAD
HAMPSTEAD
KEATS HOUSE
MANSFIELD RD
FORTESS RD
Belsize
SOUTH WAY
WILLESDEN
XVIII
IX

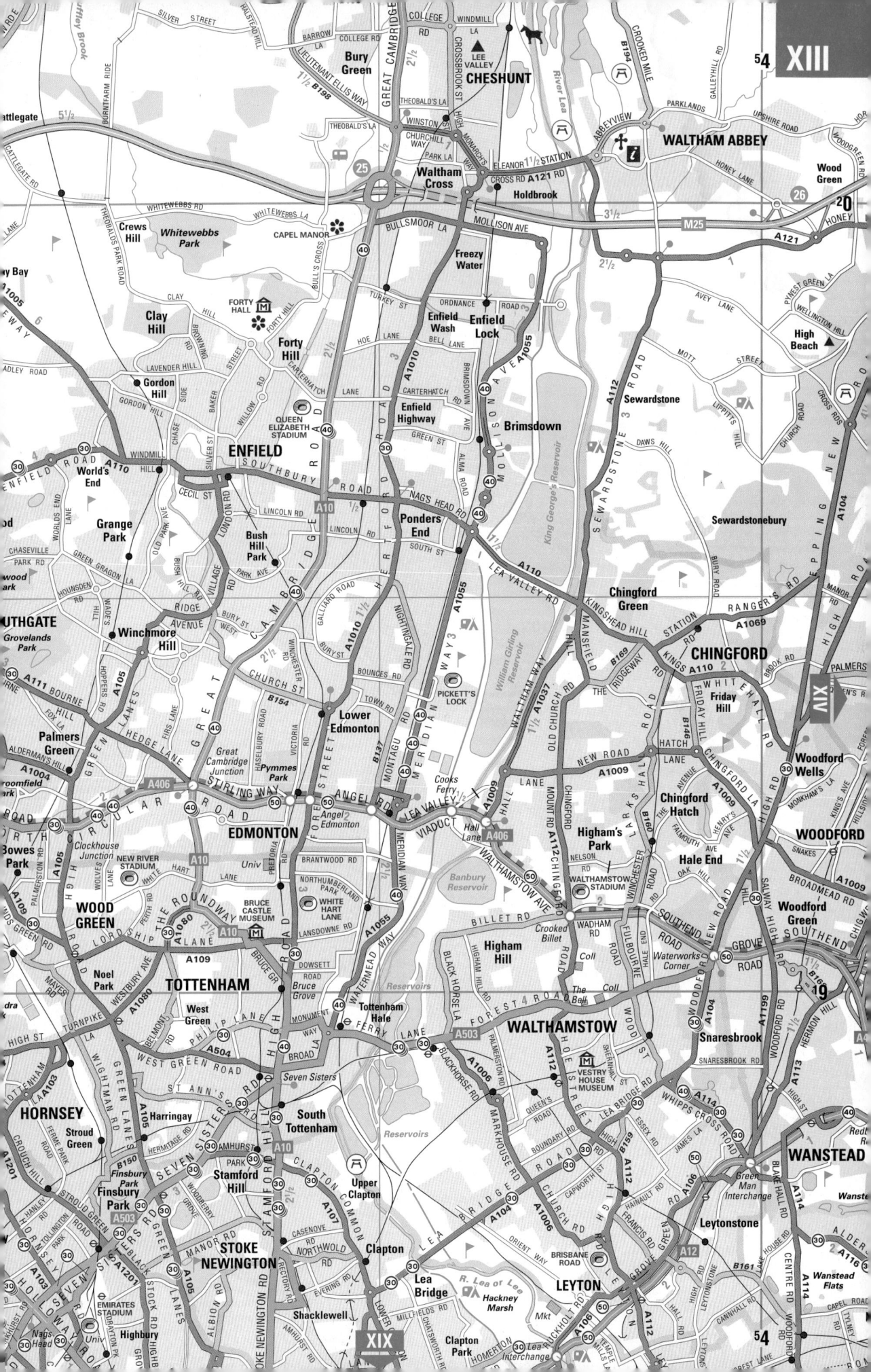
CHESHUNT
Bury Green
LEE VALLEY
River Lea
WALTHAM ABBEY
Waltham Cross
Holdbrook
Wood Green
Crews Hill
Whitewebbs Park
CAPEL MANOR
FORTY HALL
Clay Hill
Forty Hill
Freezy Water
Enfield Wash
Enfield Lock
Gordon Hill
QUEEN ELIZABETH STADIUM
Enfield Highway
Brimsdown
Sewardstone
High Beach
ENFIELD
World's End
Grange Park
Bush Hill Park
Ponders End
King George's Reservoir
Sewardstonebury
Chingford Green
SOUTHGATE
Grovelands Park
Winchmore Hill
William Girling Reservoir
CHINGFORD
Friday Hill
Palmers Green
Great Cambridge Junction
Pymmes Park
Lower Edmonton
PICKETT'S LOCK
Cooks Ferry
Woodford Wells
Chingford Hatch
EDMONTON
Angel Edmonton
Clockhouse Junction
NEW RIVER STADIUM
Banbury Reservoir
Higham's Park
Hale End
WOODFORD
Bowes Park
WOOD GREEN
BRUCE CASTLE MUSEUM
WHITE HART LANE
WALTHAMSTOW STADIUM
Crooked Billet
Woodford Green
Higham Hill
Waterworks Corner
Noel Park
TOTTENHAM
Bruce Grove
Reservoirs
West Green
Tottenham Hale
WALTHAMSTOW
Snaresbrook
Seven Sisters
VESTRY HOUSE MUSEUM
HORNSEY
Harringay
South Tottenham
Stroud Green
Stamford Hill
Upper Clapton
WANSTEAD
Finsbury Park
Green Man Interchange
Leytonstone
STOKE NEWINGTON
Clapton
Lea Bridge
LEYTON
Wanstead Flats
EMIRATES STADIUM
Shacklewell
Hackney Marsh
Highbury
Clapton Park
Lea Interchange
XIV
XIX
M25
A10
A406
A503
A12

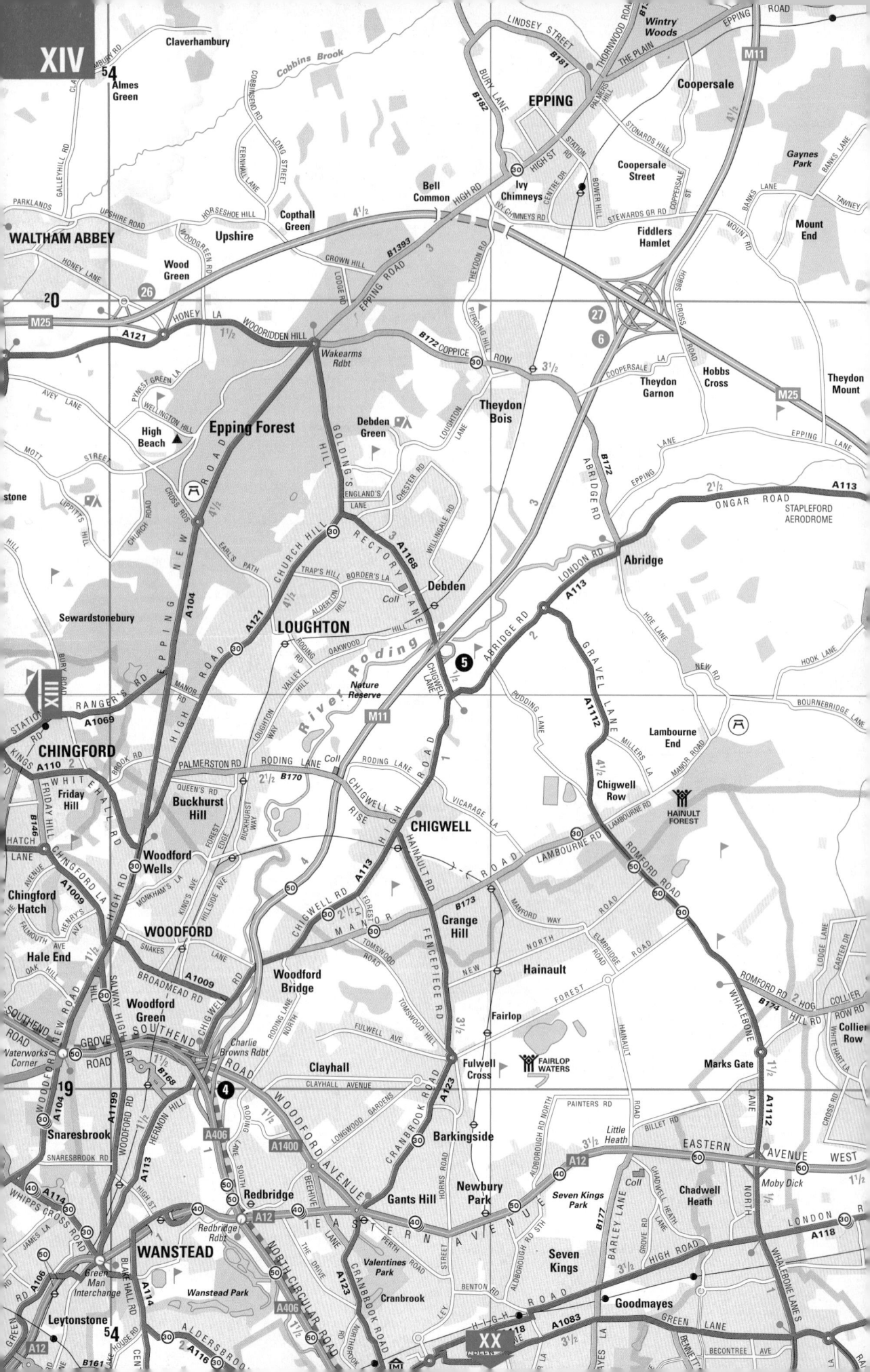
Claverhambury
Almes Green
Cobbins Brook
Wintry Woods
Coopersale
EPPING
Ivy Chimneys
Bell Common
Coopersale Street
Gaynes Park
Copthall Green
Fiddlers Hamlet
Mount End
WALTHAM ABBEY
Upshire
Wood Green
Theydon Garnon
Hobbs Cross
Theydon Mount
Wakearms Rdbt
Theydon Bois
High Beach
Epping Forest
Debden Green
STAPLEFORD AERODROME
Abridge
Debden
Sewardstonebury
LOUGHTON
River Roding
Nature Reserve
Lambourne End
CHINGFORD
Friday Hill
Buckhurst Hill
Chigwell Row
HAINULT FOREST
CHIGWELL
Woodford Wells
Chingford Hatch
Grange Hill
WOODFORD
Hale End
Hainault
Woodford Bridge
Woodford Green
Fairlop
Charlie Browns Rdbt
Waterworks Corner
Clayhall
Fulwell Cross
FAIRLOP WATERS
Marks Gate
Collier Row
Snaresbrook
Barkingside
Little Heath
Moby Dick
Redbridge
Gants Hill
Newbury Park
Seven Kings Park
Chadwell Heath
Redbridge Rdbt
WANSTEAD
Valentines Park
Seven Kings
Green Man Interchange
Wanstead Park
Cranbrook
Goodmayes
Leytonstone
M25
M11
A121
A104
A1069
A110
A113
A1168
A1112
A1009
A12
A406
A1400
A123
A1199
A114
A106
A116
A118
A1083
B1393
B172
B181
B182
B170
B173
B174
B177
B146
B168
B161
EPPING ROAD
HIGH ROAD
EPPING NEW ROAD
LONDON RD
ONGAR ROAD
ABRIDGE RD
GRAVEL LANE
ROMFORD ROAD
LAMBOURNE RD
MANOR ROAD
EASTERN AVENUE
WOODFORD AVENUE
NORTH CIRCULAR ROAD
SOUTHEND ROAD
HIGH ROAD
GREEN LANE
XIII
XX

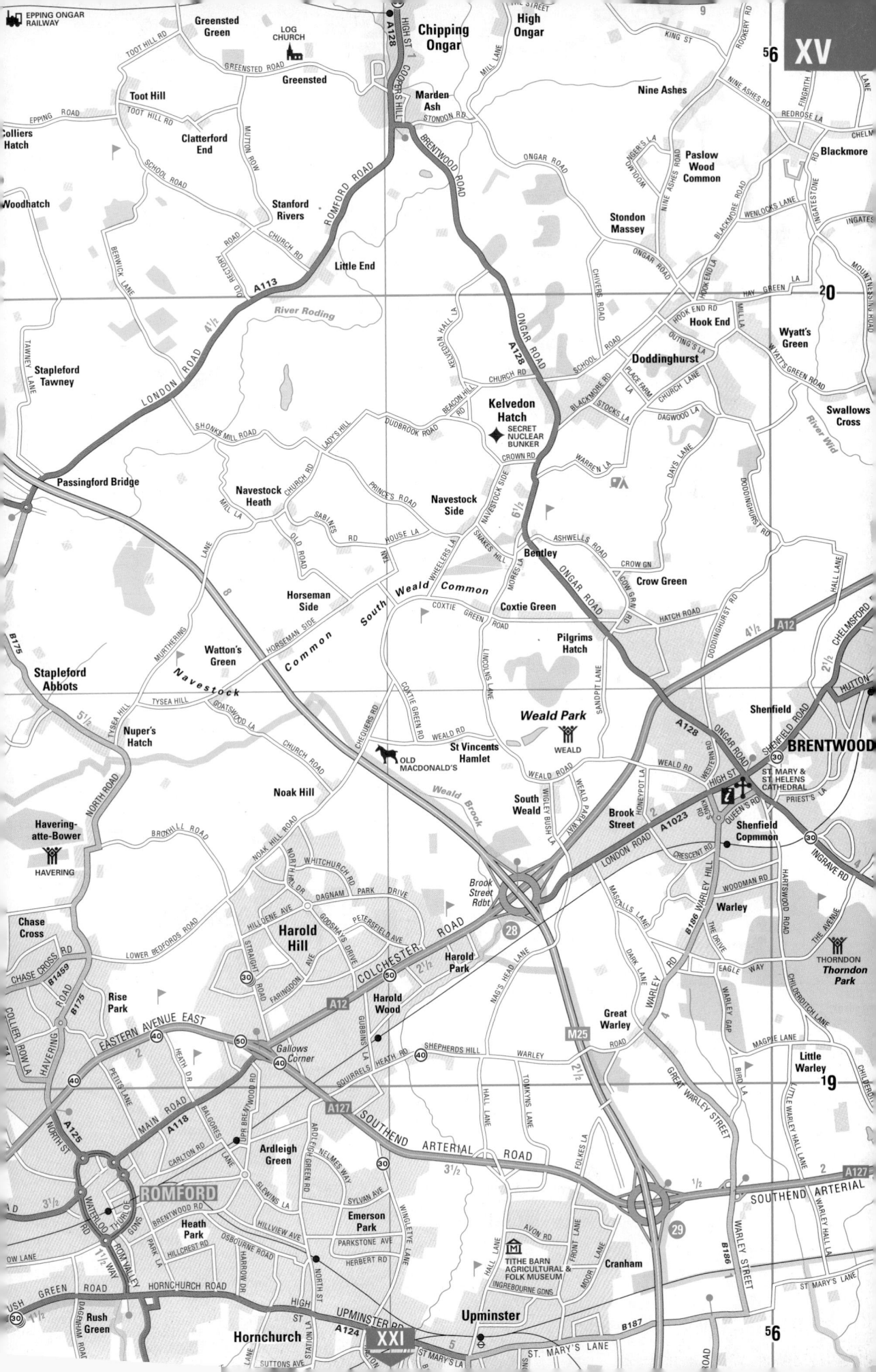
Chipping Ongar
High Ongar
Greensted Green
Greensted
Toot Hill
Clatterford End
Marden Ash
Nine Ashes
Blackmore
Paslow Wood Common
Stanford Rivers
Stondon Massey
Little End
Hook End
Wyatt's Green
Doddinghurst
Stapleford Tawney
Kelvedon Hatch
Swallows Cross
Passingford Bridge
Navestock Heath
Navestock Side
Bentley
Crow Green
Horseman Side
Coxtie Green
Pilgrims Hatch
Watton's Green
Stapleford Abbots
Weald Park
Shenfield
Nuper's Hatch
St Vincents Hamlet
BRENTWOOD
Noak Hill
South Weald
Brook Street
Shenfield Common
Havering-atte-Bower
Warley
Chase Cross
Harold Hill
Harold Park
Thorndon Park
Rise Park
Harold Wood
Great Warley
Little Warley
Gallows Corner
Ardleigh Green
ROMFORD
Emerson Park
Heath Park
Cranham
Rush Green
Upminster
Hornchurch

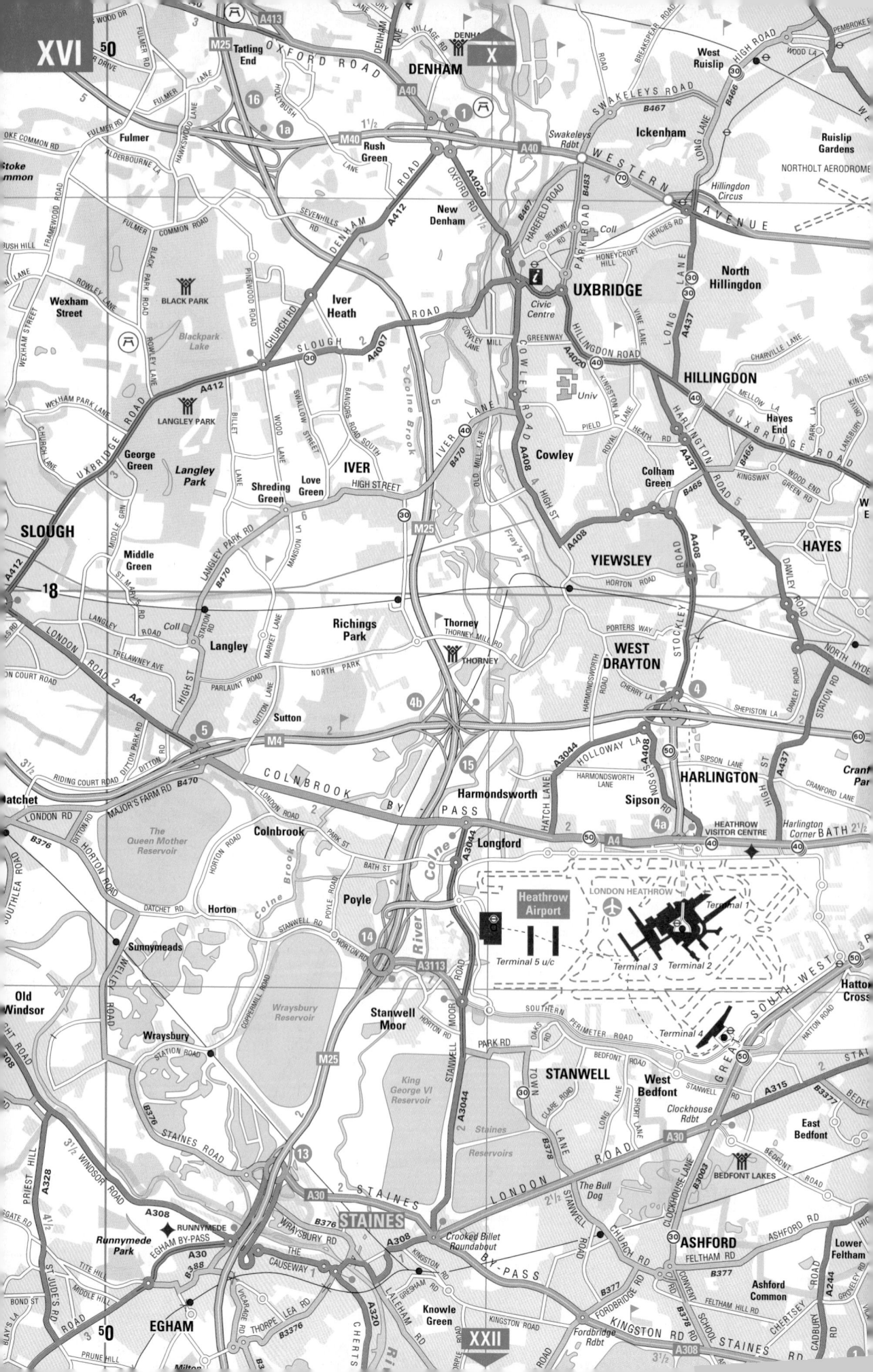
XVI
50
X
XXII
Tatling End
OXFORD ROAD
DENHAM
Fulmer
Rush Green
M40
M25
A40
A413
Swakeleys Rdbt
WESTERN AVENUE
SWAKELEYS ROAD
B467
Ickenham
West Ruislip
HIGH ROAD
B466
Ruislip Gardens
NORTHOLT AERODROME
Hillingdon Circus
LONG LANE
North Hillingdon
New Denham
A4020
A412
DENHAM ROAD
SEVENHILLS RD
FULMER COMMON ROAD
BLACK PARK
Blackpark Lake
Wexham Street
Iver Heath
UXBRIDGE
Civic Centre
Coll
HAREFIELD ROAD
PARK ROAD
B483
HONEYCROFT HILL
VINE LANE
A437
HILLINGDON ROAD
HILLINGDON
CHARVILLE LANE
Hayes End
UXBRIDGE ROAD
SLOUGH ROAD
A4007
CHURCH RD
PINEWOOD ROAD
ROWLEY LANE
WEXHAM PARK LANE
LANGLEY PARK
Langley Park
George Green
UXBRIDGE ROAD
SLOUGH
Middle Green
Shreding Green
Love Green
IVER
HIGH STREET
IVER LANE
B470
COWLEY ROAD
A408
Univ
Cowley
Colham Green
HARLINGTON ROAD
Colne Brook
Fray's R
YIEWSLEY
HORTON ROAD
STOCKLEY ROAD
HAYES
DAWLEY ROAD
LANGLEY PARK RD
MANSION LA
18
Richings Park
Thorney
THORNEY MILL RD
THORNEY
Langley
LONDON ROAD
A4
WEST DRAYTON
PORTERS WAY
NORTH HYDE
Sutton
NORTH PARK
PARLAUNT ROAD
M4
SHEPISTON LA
COLNBROOK BY-PASS
Harmondsworth
HOLLOWAY LA
A3044
HATCH LANE
HARMONDSWORTH LANE
SIPSON LANE
Sipson
HARLINGTON
Cranford Park
CRANFORD LANE
Datchet
RIDING COURT ROAD
MAJOR'S FARM RD
LONDON RD
B376
HORTON ROAD
The Queen Mother Reservoir
Colnbrook
Longford
HEATHROW VISITOR CENTRE
Harlington Corner
BATH ROAD
SOUTHLEA ROAD
Horton
DATCHET RD
Poyle
POYLE ROAD
River Colne
Heathrow Airport
LONDON HEATHROW
Terminal 1
Terminal 2
Terminal 3
Terminal 5 u/c
Terminal 4
Sunnymeads
STANWELL RD
A3113
Wraysbury Reservoir
Stanwell Moor
SOUTHERN PERIMETER ROAD
GREAT SOUTH-WEST ROAD
Hatton Cross
Old Windsor
WELLEY ROAD
Wraysbury
STATION ROAD
COPPERMILL ROAD
King George VI Reservoir
PARK RD
STANWELL
West Bedfont
Clockhouse Rdbt
A315
East Bedfont
Staines Reservoirs
A30
LONDON ROAD
B378
TOWN LANE
BEDFONT LAKES
STAINES ROAD
WINDSOR ROAD
PRIEST HILL
A328
STAINES
A308
The Bull Dog
CLOCKHOUSE LANE
B3003
ASHFORD
ASHFORD RD
Lower Feltham
RUNNYMEDE
Runnymede Park
EGHAM BY-PASS
WRAYSBURY RD
THE CAUSEWAY
Crooked Billet Roundabout
BY-PASS
CHURCH RD
FELTHAM RD
B377
Ashford Common
A244
EGHAM
A320
LALEHAM RD
Knowle Green
KINGSTON ROAD
FORDBRIDGE RD
Fordbridge Rdbt
KINGSTON RD
STAINES RD
CHERTSEY ROAD
THORPE LEA RD
B3376
B388
ST JUDE'S RD
PRUNE HILL

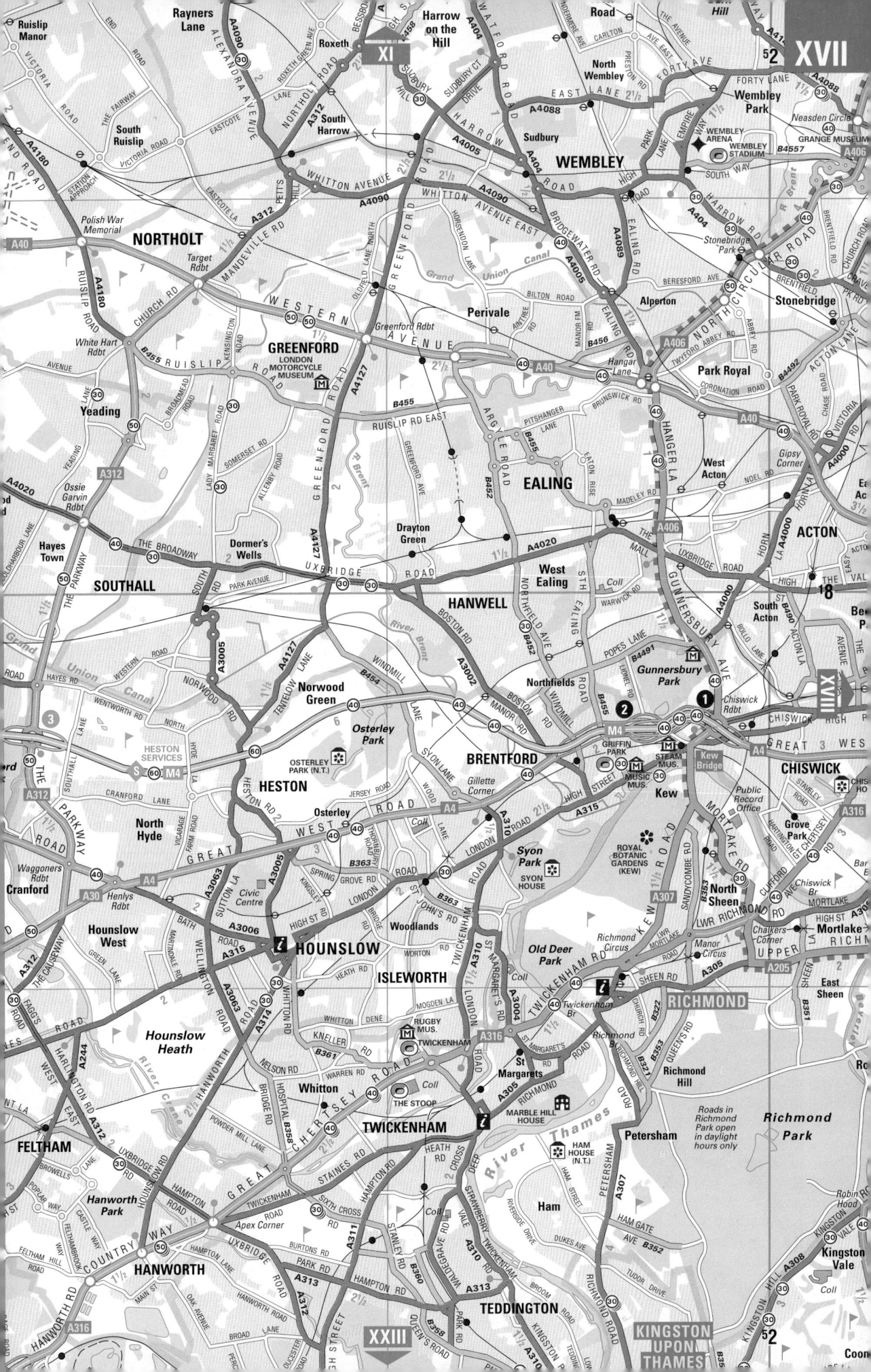

XVII
XI
XXIII
XVIII
Rayners Lane
Harrow on the Hill
Ruislip Manor
Roxeth
South Harrow
South Ruislip
North Wembley
Wembley Park
Sudbury
WEMBLEY
WEMBLEY ARENA
WEMBLEY STADIUM
GRANGE MUSEUM
Neasden Circle
NORTHOLT
Polish War Memorial
Target Rdbt
Stonebridge Park
Stonebridge
Alperton
Perivale
Greenford Rdbt
GREENFORD
LONDON MOTORCYCLE MUSEUM
White Hart Rdbt
Yeading
Hangar Lane
Park Royal
West Acton
Gipsy Corner
EALING
Ossie Garvin Rdbt
Hayes Town
Dormer's Wells
Drayton Green
West Ealing
ACTON
SOUTHALL
HANWELL
South Acton
Gunnersbury Park
Norwood Green
Northfields
Chiswick Rdbt
Osterley Park
HESTON SERVICES
OSTERLEY PARK (N.T.)
BRENTFORD
GRIFFIN PARK
STEAM MUS.
MUSIC MUS.
Kew Bridge
CHISWICK
HESTON
Gillette Corner
Kew
North Hyde
Osterley
Public Record Office
Grove Park
ROYAL BOTANIC GARDENS (KEW)
Syon Park
SYON HOUSE
Waggoners Rdbt
Cranford
Henlys Rdbt
Civic Centre
North Sheen
Chiswick Br
Mortlake
Chalkers Corner
Woodlands
Hounslow West
HOUNSLOW
Richmond Circus
Manor Circus
Old Deer Park
ISLEWORTH
Twickenham Br
RICHMOND
East Sheen
Hounslow Heath
RUGBY MUS.
TWICKENHAM
Richmond Br
St Margarets
Richmond Hill
Whitton
THE STOOP
MARBLE HILL HOUSE
FELTHAM
TWICKENHAM
Petersham
Roads in Richmond Park open in daylight hours only
Richmond Park
HAM HOUSE (N.T.)
Hanworth Park
Ham
Apex Corner
Robin Hood
Kingston Vale
HANWORTH
TEDDINGTON
KINGSTON UPON THAMES
River Thames

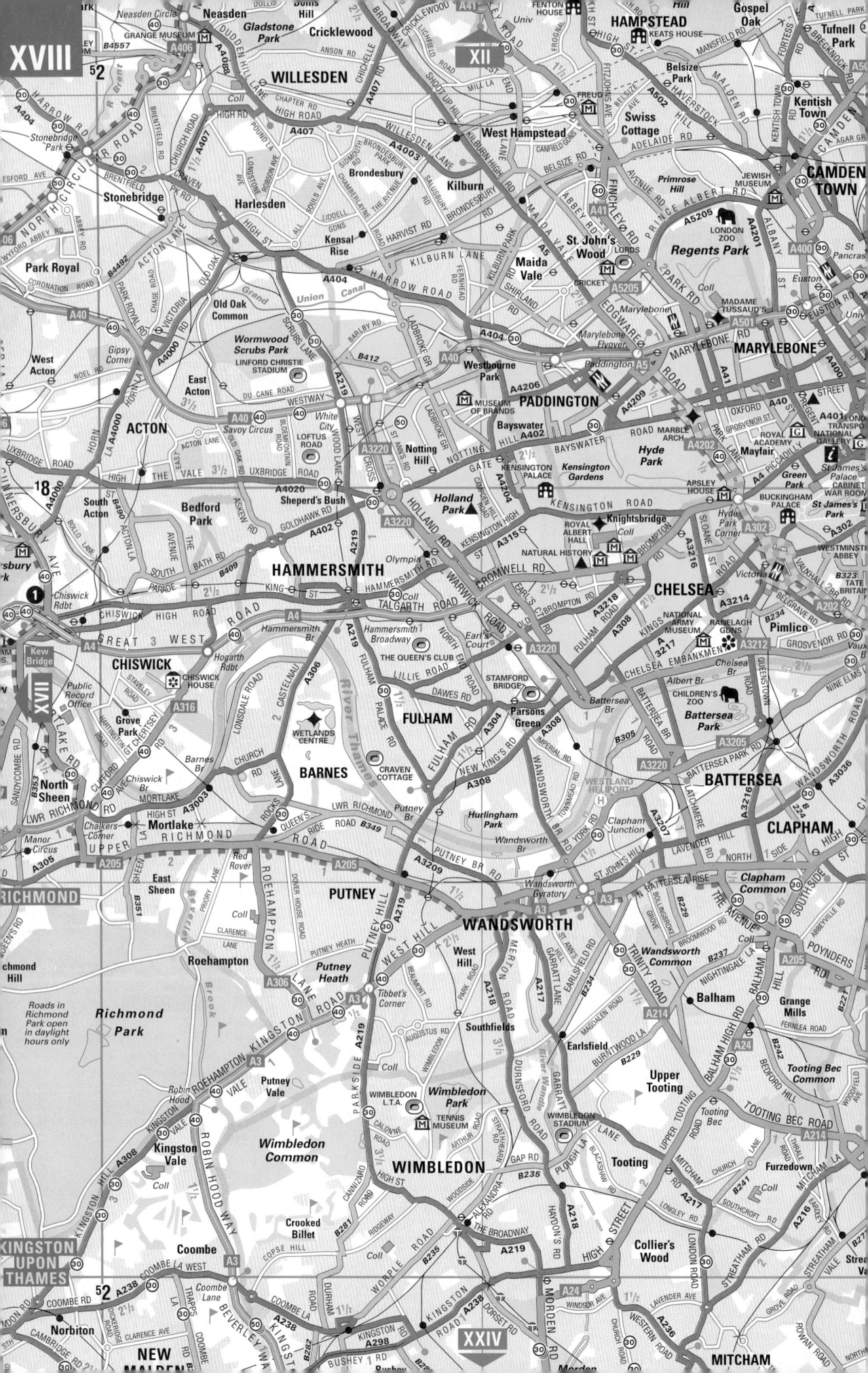

XVIII
XII
XXIV
XVII
Neasden
Neasden Circle
GRANGE MUSEUM
Gladstone Park
Cricklewood
WILLESDEN
HAMPSTEAD
KEATS HOUSE
FENTON HOUSE
Gospel Oak
Tufnell Park
Kentish Town
Belsize Park
Swiss Cottage
FREUD
West Hampstead
Brondesbury
Kilburn
Primrose Hill
JEWISH MUSEUM
CAMDEN TOWN
Stonebridge Park
Stonebridge
Harlesden
Kensal Rise
St. John's Wood
LORDS
CRICKET
LONDON ZOO
Regents Park
Maida Vale
Park Royal
Old Oak Common
Grand Union Canal
MADAME TUSSAUD'S
Euston
St Pancras
Marylebone
MARYLEBONE
Wormwood Scrubs Park
LINFORD CHRISTIE STADIUM
Gipsy Corner
West Acton
East Acton
Westbourne Park
Paddington
PADDINGTON
MUSEUM OF BRANDS
ACTON
Savoy Circus
White City
LOFTUS ROAD
Notting Hill
Bayswater
KENSINGTON PALACE
Kensington Gardens
Hyde Park
MARBLE ARCH
ROYAL ACADEMY
Mayfair
NATIONAL GALLERY
Green Park
APSLEY HOUSE
BUCKINGHAM PALACE
St James's Park
South Acton
Bedford Park
Sheperd's Bush
Holland Park
Knightsbridge
ROYAL ALBERT HALL
NATURAL HISTORY
Hyde Park Corner
Victoria
WESTMINSTER ABBEY
HAMMERSMITH
Olympia
Chiswick Rdbt
CHELSEA
Pimlico
Hammersmith Br
Hammersmith Broadway
THE QUEEN'S CLUB
Earl's Court
NATIONAL ARMY MUSEUM
RANELAGH GDNS
Kew Bridge
CHISWICK
Hogarth Rdbt
CHISWICK HOUSE
Public Record Office
STAMFORD BRIDGE
Chelsea Br
Albert Br
CHILDREN'S ZOO
Battersea Park
Grove Park
WETLANDS CENTRE
River Thames
FULHAM
Parsons Green
Battersea Br
North Sheen
Barnes Br
Chiswick Br
BARNES
CRAVEN COTTAGE
WESTLAND HELIPORT
BATTERSEA
Mortlake
Chalkers Corner
Manor Circus
Putney Br
Hurlingham Park
Clapham Junction
CLAPHAM
Wandsworth Br
RICHMOND
East Sheen
Red Rover
PUTNEY
Wandsworth Gyratory
Clapham Common
WANDSWORTH
Roehampton
West Hill
Wandsworth Common
Richmond Hill
Putney Heath
Tibbet's Corner
Balham
Grange Mills
Roads in Richmond Park open in daylight hours only
Richmond Park
Southfields
Earlsfield
River Wandle
Upper Tooting
Tooting Bec Common
Robin Hood
Putney Vale
WIMBLEDON L.T.A.
Wimbledon Park
TENNIS MUSEUM
WIMBLEDON STADIUM
Tooting Bec
Kingston Vale
Wimbledon Common
WIMBLEDON
Tooting
Furzedown
Crooked Billet
KINGSTON UPON THAMES
Coombe
Collier's Wood
Coombe Lane
Norbiton
NEW MALDEN
MITCHAM

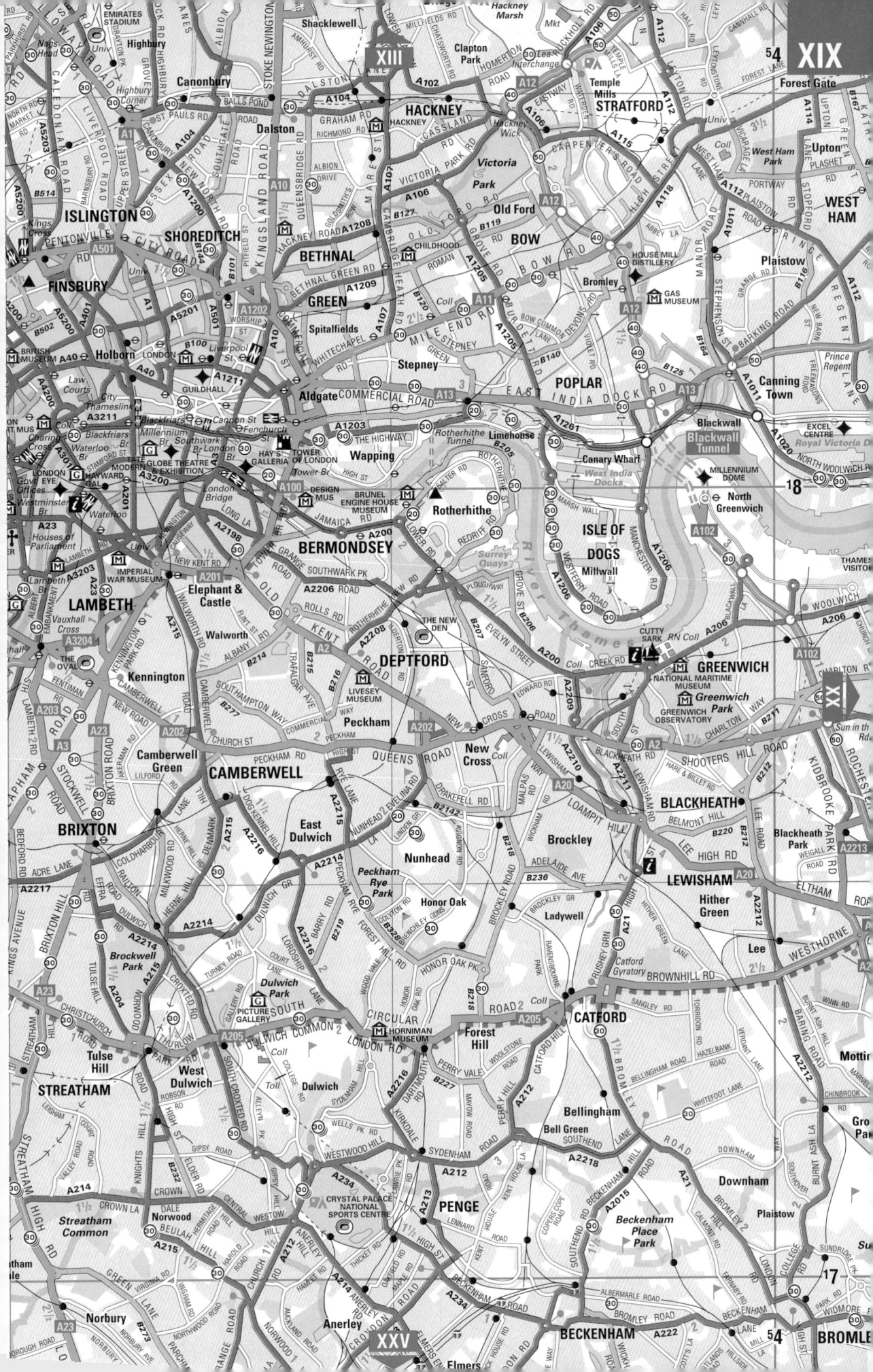

EMIRATES STADIUM
Highbury
Shacklewell
Hackney Marsh
Clapton Park
Lea Interchange
Temple Mills
Forest Gate
Canonbury
Highbury Corner
HACKNEY
STRATFORD
Dalston
Hackney Wick
Victoria Park
Upton
West Ham Park
ISLINGTON
SHOREDITCH
Old Ford
WEST HAM
BETHNAL GREEN
BOW
CHILDHOOD
HOUSE MILL DISTILLERY
Plaistow
FINSBURY
Bromley
GAS MUSEUM
Spitalfields
Holborn
Liverpool St
Stepney
BRITISH MUSEUM
LONDON
GUILDHALL
POPLAR
Prince Regent
Canning Town
Law Courts
City Thameslink
Aldgate
Blackwall
EXCEL CENTRE
Royal Victoria Dock
Blackfriars
Cannon St
Fenchurch St
Limehouse
Blackwall Tunnel
Charing Cross
Waterloo
Millennium Br
Southwark Br
London Br
HAY'S GALLERIA
TOWER OF LONDON
Wapping
Rotherhithe Tunnel
Canary Wharf
West India Docks
MILLENNIUM DOME
TATE MODERN
GLOBE THEATRE & EXHIBITION
Tower Br
LONDON EYE
HAYWARD GAL
London Bridge
DESIGN MUS
BRUNEL ENGINE HOUSE MUSEUM
Rotherhithe
North Greenwich
Govt Offices
Westminster
Waterloo
ISLE OF DOGS
Houses of Parliament
BERMONDSEY
Surrey Quays
Millwall
IMPERIAL WAR MUSEUM
Elephant & Castle
Lambeth Br
LAMBETH
Walworth
THE NEW DEN
River Thames
Vauxhall Cross
CUTTY SARK
RN Coll
GREENWICH
THE OVAL
Kennington
DEPTFORD
LIVESEY MUSEUM
NATIONAL MARITIME MUSEUM
Greenwich Park
GREENWICH OBSERVATORY
Peckham
New Cross
Camberwell Green
CAMBERWELL
BLACKHEATH
Blackheath Park
BRIXTON
East Dulwich
Brockley
Nunhead
LEWISHAM
Peckham Rye Park
Honor Oak
Hither Green
Ladywell
Lee
Brockwell Park
Catford Gyratory
Dulwich Park
PICTURE GALLERY
HORNIMAN MUSEUM
CATFORD
Forest Hill
Tulse Hill
West Dulwich
Dulwich
STREATHAM
Bellingham
Bell Green
Downham
CRYSTAL PALACE NATIONAL SPORTS CENTRE
PENGE
Streatham Common
Norwood
Beckenham Place Park
Plaistow
Norbury
Anerley
BECKENHAM
BROMLEY
Elmers End
XIII
XX
XXV
54
18
17

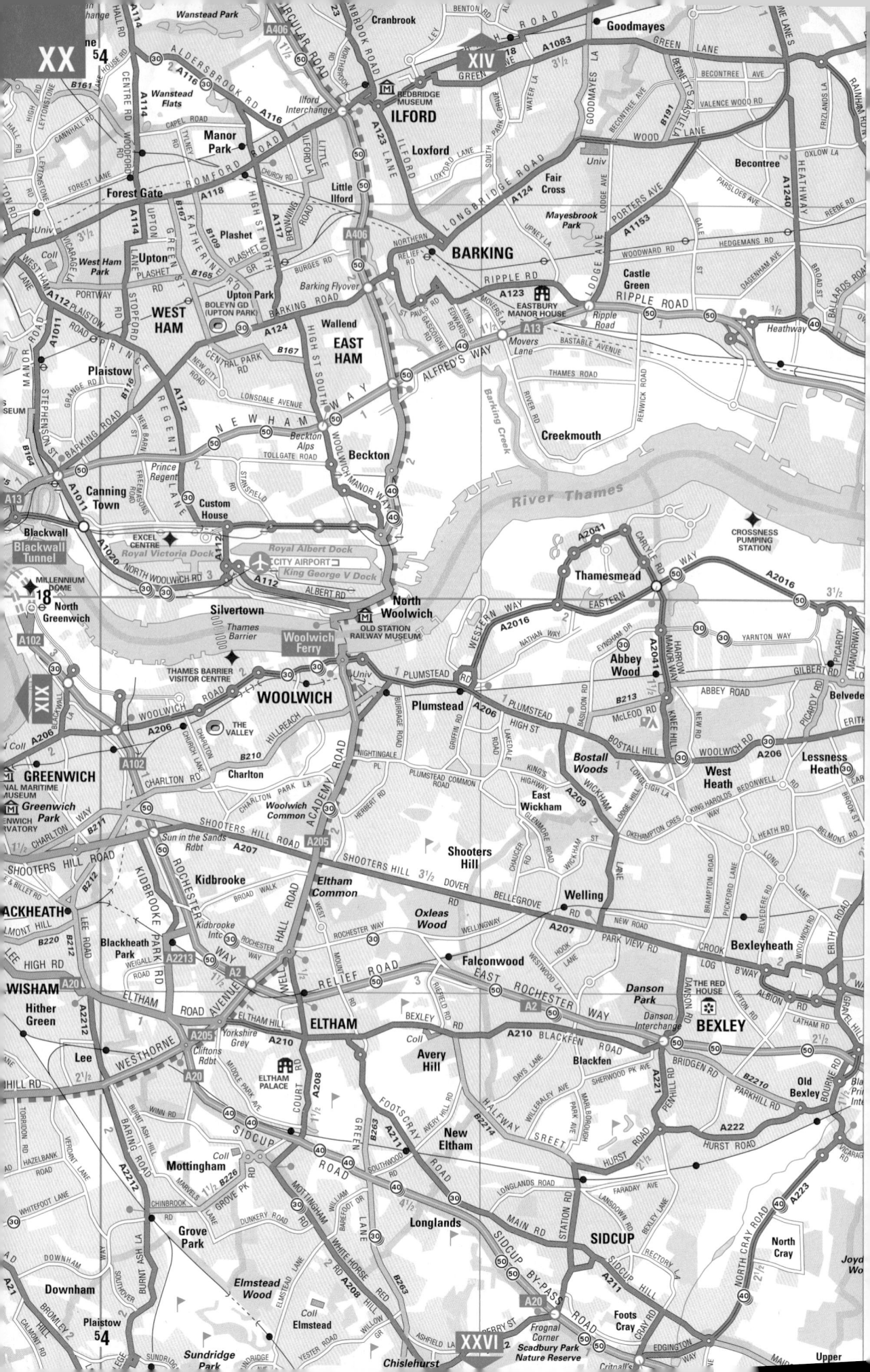
XX
XIV
XIX
XXVI
Wanstead Park
Cranbrook
Goodmayes
Wanstead Flats
Ilford Interchange
REDBRIDGE MUSEUM
ILFORD
Manor Park
Loxford
Forest Gate
Little Ilford
Becontree
Fair Cross
Mayesbrook Park
Plashet
West Ham Park
Upton
BARKING
Castle Green
Upton Park
BOLEYN GD (UPTON PARK)
Barking Flyover
EASTBURY MANOR HOUSE
Ripple Road
Heathway
WEST HAM
Wallend
EAST HAM
Movers Lane
Plaistow
Creekmouth
Beckton Alps
Beckton
Barking Creek
River Thames
Prince Regent
Canning Town
Custom House
CROSSNESS PUMPING STATION
Blackwall
Blackwall Tunnel
EXCEL CENTRE
Royal Victoria Dock
Royal Albert Dock
CITY AIRPORT
King George V Dock
Thamesmead
MILLENNIUM DOME
North Greenwich
Silvertown
Thames Barrier
North Woolwich
OLD STATION RAILWAY MUSEUM
Woolwich Ferry
THAMES BARRIER VISITOR CENTRE
Abbey Wood
WOOLWICH
Plumstead
Belvedere
THE VALLEY
Bostall Woods
West Heath
Lessness Heath
GREENWICH
NATIONAL MARITIME MUSEUM
Charlton
Greenwich Park
Woolwich Common
East Wickham
Sun in the Sands Rdbt
Shooters Hill
Kidbrooke
Eltham Common
Welling
BLACKHEATH
Oxleas Wood
Kidbrooke Intc
Blackheath Park
Falconwood
Bexleyheath
LEWISHAM
Danson Park
THE RED HOUSE
Hither Green
Danson Interchange
BEXLEY
Yorkshire Grey
ELTHAM
Lee
Cliftons Rdbt
Avery Hill
Blackfen
ELTHAM PALACE
Old Bexley
New Eltham
Mottingham
Longlands
Grove Park
SIDCUP
North Cray
Downham
Elmstead Wood
Elmstead
Foots Cray
Plaistow
Frognal Corner
Scadbury Park Nature Reserve
Sundridge Park
Chislehurst
Upper

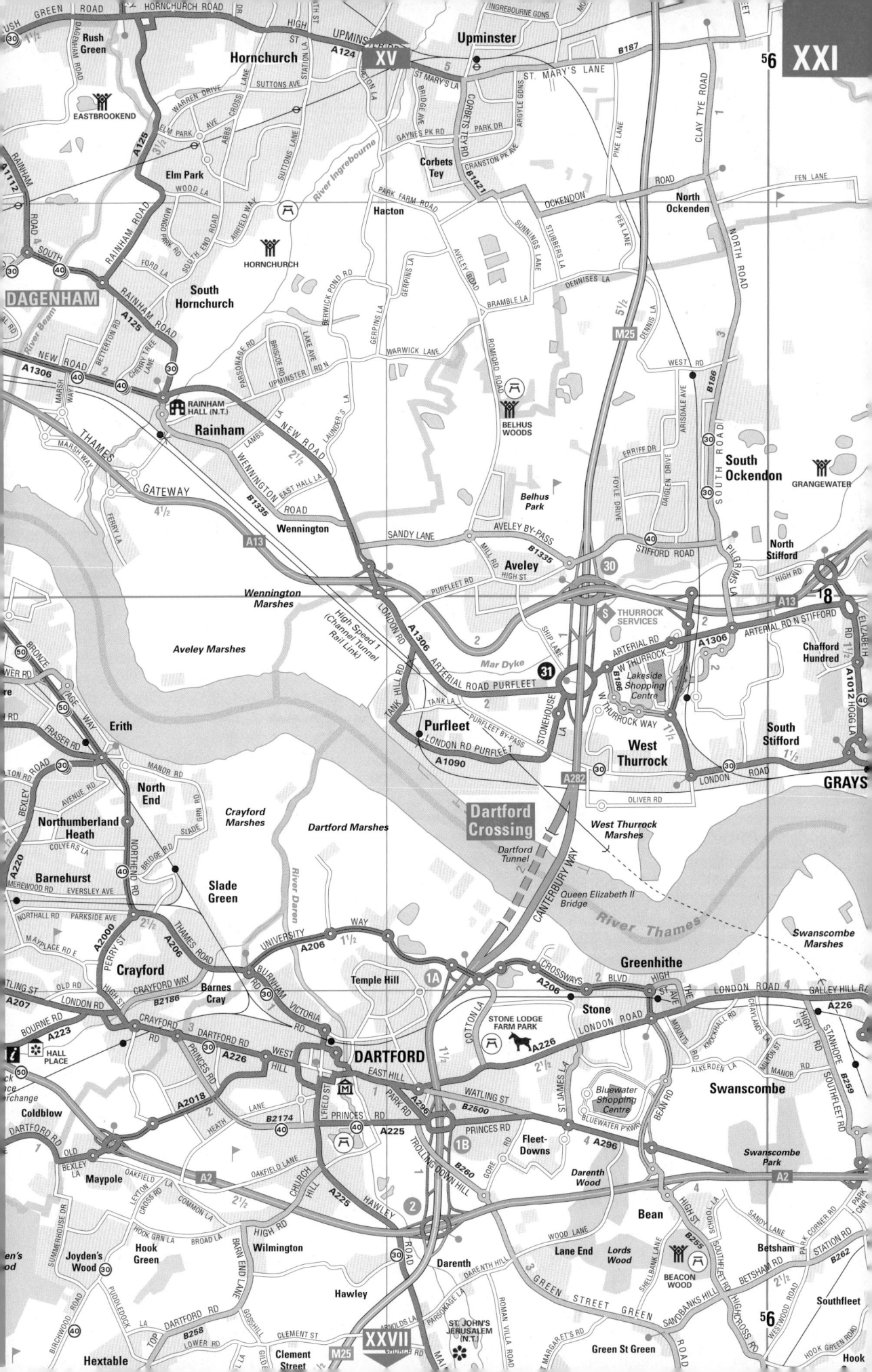

Rush Green
Hornchurch
XV
Upminster
EASTBROOKEND
Elm Park
Corbets Tey
Hacton
North Ockenden
HORNCHURCH
South Hornchurch
DAGENHAM
River Ingrebourne
River Beam
RAINHAM HALL (N.T.)
Rainham
BELHUS WOODS
South Ockendon
GRANGEWATER
Belhus Park
Wennington
North Stifford
Aveley
Wennington Marshes
THURROCK SERVICES
High Speed 1 (Channel Tunnel Rail Link)
Aveley Marshes
Mar Dyke
Lakeside Shopping Centre
Chafford Hundred
Erith
Purfleet
West Thurrock
South Stifford
GRAYS
North End
Crayford Marshes
Dartford Marshes
Dartford Crossing
Northumberland Heath
Dartford Tunnel
West Thurrock Marshes
Barnehurst
River Darent
Queen Elizabeth II Bridge
Slade Green
River Thames
Swanscombe Marshes
Crayford
Temple Hill
Greenhithe
Barnes Cray
Stone
STONE LODGE FARM PARK
HALL PLACE
DARTFORD
Coldblow
Bluewater Shopping Centre
Swanscombe
Fleet-Downs
Swanscombe Park
Maypole
Darenth Wood
Bean
Hook Green
Wilmington
Lane End
Lords Wood
Betsham
Joyden's Wood
Darenth
BEACON WOOD
Hawley
Southfleet
ST. JOHN'S JERUSALEM (N.T.)
Green St Green
Hextable
Clement Street
XXVII
Hook
GREEN ROAD
HORNCHURCH ROAD
UPMINSTER RD
HIGH ST
A124
B187
ST. MARY'S LANE
CLAY TYE ROAD
DAGENHAM ROAD
SUTTONS AVE
STATION LA
WARREN DRIVE
CORBETS TEY RD
ARGYLE GDNS
BRIDGE AVE
PARK DR
GAYNES PK RD
ELM PARK AVE
ABBS CROSS LANE
SUTTONS LANE
A125
PIKE LANE
CRANSTON PK AVE
B1421
OCKENDON ROAD
FEN LANE
A1112
RAINHAM ROAD
WOOD LA
PARK FARM ROAD
MUNGO PARK RD
AIRFIELD WAY
SOUTH END ROAD
PEA LANE
STUBBERS LA
SUNNINGS LANE
AVELEY ROAD
NORTH ROAD
SOUTH RD
FORD LA
BERWICK POND RD
GERPINS LA
DENNISES LA
BRAMBLE LA
M25
DENNIS LA
A125
NEW ROAD
BETTERTON RD
CHERRY TREE LANE
PARSONAGE RD
BRISCOE RD
LAKE AVE
WARWICK LANE
ROMFORD ROAD
WEST RD
B186
A1306
MARSH WAY
UPMINSTER RD N
LAUNDER'S LA
ARISDALE AVE
THAMES GATEWAY
LAMBS LA
NEW ROAD
WENNINGTON ROAD
ERRIFF DR
DAIGLEN DRIVE
FOYLE DRIVE
SOUTH ROAD
EAST HALL LA
B1335
FERRY LA
A13
SANDY LANE
AVELEY BY-PASS
STIFFORD ROAD
PILGRIMS LA
MILL RD
HIGH ST
HIGH RD
PURFLEET RD
LONDON RD
SHIP LANE
ARTERIAL RD
W THURROCK
A1306
ARTERIAL RD N STIFFORD
ELIZABETH RD
BRONZE AGE WAY
TANK HILL RD
ARTERIAL ROAD PURFLEET
TANK LA
W THURROCK WAY
A1012 HOGG LA
STONEHOUSE LA
PURFLEET BY-PASS
FRASER RD
LONDON RD PURFLEET
A1090
LONDON ROAD
A282
OLIVER RD
MANOR RD
BEXLEY RD
AVENUE RD
SLADE GRN RD
NORTHEND RD
COLYERS LA
BRIDGE RD
A220
CANTERBURY WAY
EVERSLEY AVE
NORTHALL RD
PARKSIDE AVE
THAMES ROAD
MAYPLACE RD E
A2000
PERRY ST
A206
UNIVERSITY WAY
CROSSWAYS BLVD
HIGH ST
THE AVE
LONDON ROAD
GALLEY HILL RD
A226
OLD RD
CRAYFORD WAY
BURNHAM RD
VICTORIA RD
A207
LONDON RD
B2186
COTTON LA
MOUNTS RD
KNOCKHALL RD
CRAYLANDS LA
HIGH ST
STANHOPE RD
BOURNE RD
A223
CRAYFORD RD
DARTFORD RD
A226
PRINCES RD
WEST HILL
MILTON ST
MANOR RD
ALKERDEN LA
SOUTHFLEET RD
B259
EAST HILL
PARK RD
A296
WATLING ST
ST JAMES LA
BEAN RD
A2018
HEATH LANE
B2174
L'FIELD ST
PRINCES RD
A225
B2500
PRINCES RD
BLUEWATER P'KWAY
DARTFORD RD
OLD BEXLEY LA
OAKFIELD LA
LEYTON CROSS RD
OAKFIELD LANE
CHURCH HILL
TROLLING DOWN HILL
B260
GORE RD
A296
A2
COMMON LA
HAWLEY ROAD
SUMMERHOUSE DR
HOOK GRN LA
BROAD LA
HIGH RD
WOOD LANE
HIGH ST
SCHOOL LA
SANDY LANE
PARK CORNER RD
STATION RD
B255
BARN END LANE
DARENTH HILL
SHELLBANK LANE
SOUTHFLEET RD
BETSHAM RD
B262
PUDDLEDOCK LA
BIRCHWOOD ROAD
TOP DARTFORD RD
B258
LOWER RD
GOSSHILL
CLEMENT ST
ARNOLDS LA
PARSONAGE LA
ROMAN VILLA ROAD
GREEN STREET GREEN
ST MARGARET'S RD
SANDBANKS HILL
HIGHCROSS RD
WESTWOOD ROAD
HOOK GREEN ROAD
M25
CHURCH RD
56

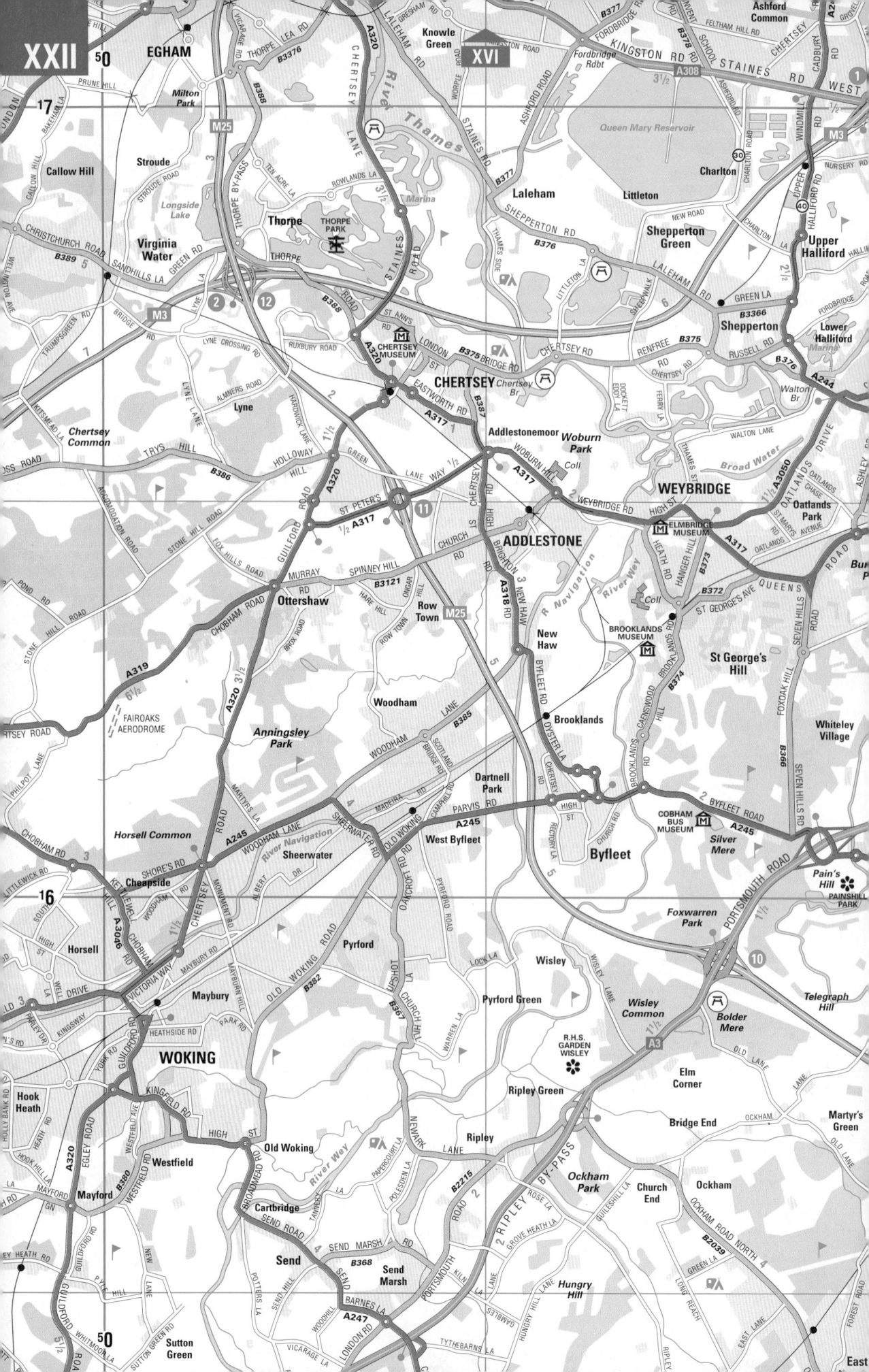

XXII
XVI
EGHAM
Milton Park
Stroude
Callow Hill
Longside Lake
Virginia Water
Thorpe
THORPE PARK
Knowle Green
River Thames
Marina
Laleham
Littleton
Queen Mary Reservoir
Ashford Common
Fordbridge Rdbt
Charlton
Shepperton Green
Upper Halliford
Shepperton
Lower Halliford
Walton Br
Chertsey Br
CHERTSEY
CHERTSEY MUSEUM
Lyne
Chertsey Common
Addlestonemoor
Woburn Park
Coll
WEYBRIDGE
ELMBRIDGE MUSEUM
Broad Water
Oatlands Park
ADDLESTONE
Ottershaw
Row Town
R Navigation
River Wey
BROOKLANDS MUSEUM
New Haw
St George's Hill
Woodham
FAIROAKS AERODROME
Anningsley Park
Brooklands
Whiteley Village
Dartnell Park
West Byfleet
Byfleet
COBHAM BUS MUSEUM
Silver Mere
Horsell Common
Sheerwater
Cheapside
River Navigation
Pain's Hill
PAINSHILL PARK
Foxwarren Park
Horsell
Pyrford
Wisley
Maybury
Pyrford Green
Wisley Common
Bolder Mere
Telegraph Hill
WOKING
R.H.S. GARDEN WISLEY
Elm Corner
Hook Heath
Ripley Green
Bridge End
Martyr's Green
Westfield
Old Woking
Ripley
Ockham Park
Church End
Ockham
Mayford
Cartbridge
Send
Send Marsh
Hungry Hill
Sutton Green
East
M25
M3
A3
A308
A320
A317
A318
A319
A245
A3046
A3050
A244
A247
B377
B378
B376
B375
B3366
B3376
B388
B389
B386
B387
B3121
B385
B372
B373
B374
B366
B382
B367
B380
B2215
B2039
B368

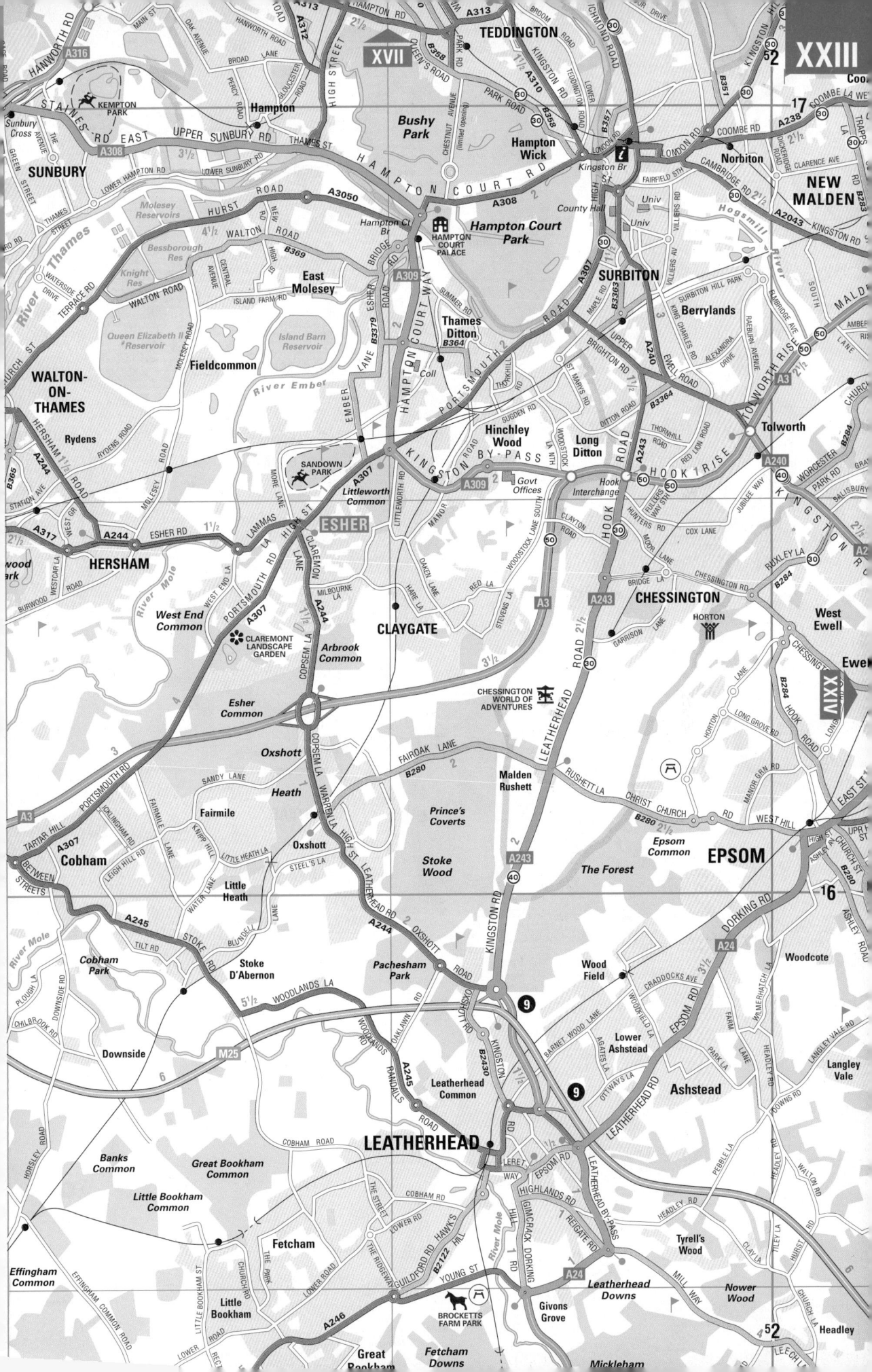

XXIII
XVII
XXIV
TEDDINGTON
Hampton
KEMPTON PARK
Sunbury Cross
SUNBURY
Bushy Park
Hampton Wick
Kingston Br
Norbiton
NEW MALDEN
Molesey Reservoirs
Bessborough Res
Knight Res
River Thames
Hampton Ct Br
HAMPTON COURT PALACE
Hampton Court Park
County Hall
Univ
Hogsmill River
SURBITON
East Molesey
Queen Elizabeth II Reservoir
Island Barn Reservoir
Fieldcommon
Thames Ditton
Coll
Berrylands
WALTON-ON-THAMES
River Ember
Rydens
SANDOWN PARK
Hinchley Wood
Long Ditton
Tolworth
Littleworth Common
ESHER
Govt Offices
Hook Interchange
HERSHAM
River Mole
West End Common
CLAREMONT LANDSCAPE GARDEN
CLAYGATE
Arbrook Common
CHESSINGTON
HORTON
West Ewell
Esher Common
CHESSINGTON WORLD OF ADVENTURES
Oxshott
Heath
Malden Rushett
Fairmile
Prince's Coverts
Stoke Wood
Epsom Common
EPSOM
The Forest
Cobham
Little Heath
Cobham Park
Stoke D'Abernon
Pachesham Park
Wood Field
Woodcote
Lower Ashstead
Downside
Leatherhead Common
Ashstead
Langley Vale
LEATHERHEAD
Banks Common
Great Bookham Common
Little Bookham Common
Fetcham
Tyrell's Wood
Effingham Common
Leatherhead Downs
Nower Wood
Little Bookham
BROCKETTS FARM PARK
Givons Grove
Headley
Great Bookham
Fetcham Downs
Mickleham
HAMPTON COURT RD
KINGSTON BY-PASS
HOOK RISE
PORTSMOUTH RD
LEATHERHEAD ROAD
KINGSTON RD
DORKING RD
EPSOM RD
WOODLANDS LA
COBHAM ROAD
LEATHERHEAD BY-PASS
A3
A307
A308
A309
A3050
A243
A244
A245
A24
A240
A246
B280
B2122
B2430
M25
17
16
52

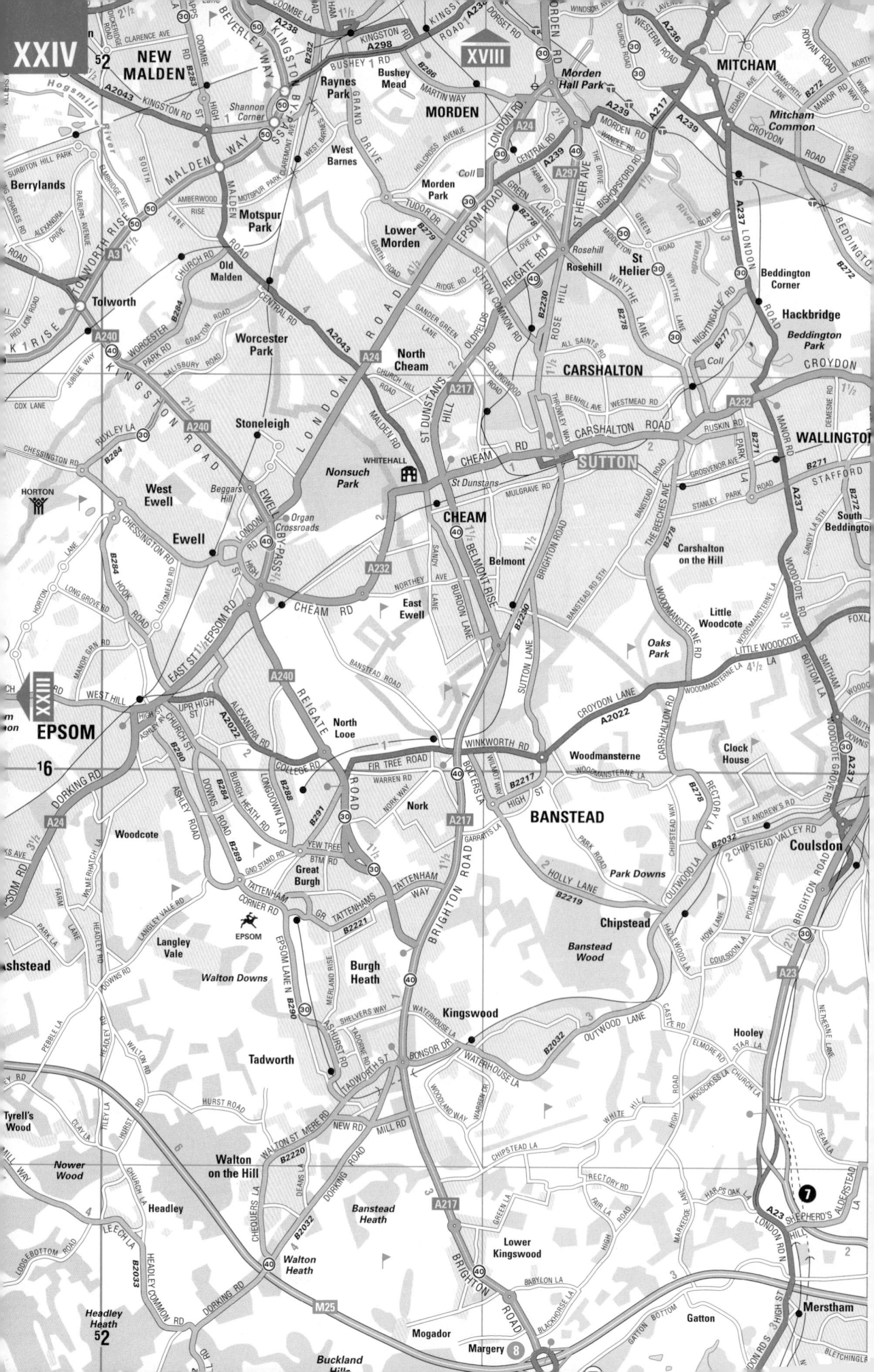

XXIV
XVIII
XXIII
NEW MALDEN
Raynes Park
Bushey Mead
MORDEN
Morden Hall Park
MITCHAM
Mitcham Common
Hogsmill River
Shannon Corner
West Barnes
Berrylands
Motspur Park
Morden Park
Lower Morden
Old Malden
Tolworth
Rosehill
St Helier
Beddington Corner
Hackbridge
Beddington Park
Worcester Park
North Cheam
CARSHALTON
Stoneleigh
WALLINGTON
SUTTON
HORTON
West Ewell
Beggars Hill
Nonsuch Park
WHITEHALL
St Dunstans
CHEAM
South Beddington
Ewell
Organ Crossroads
Belmont
Carshalton on the Hill
East Ewell
Little Woodcote
Oaks Park
EPSOM
North Looe
Clock House
Woodmansterne
Nork
BANSTEAD
Woodcote
Great Burgh
Coulsdon
Park Downs
Chipstead
Langley Vale
Banstead Wood
Burgh Heath
Walton Downs
Kingswood
Hooley
Tadworth
Tyrell's Wood
Walton on the Hill
Nowev Wood
Headley
Banstead Heath
Lower Kingswood
Walton Heath
Headley Heath
Merstham
Gatton
Mogador
Margery
Buckland Hills
River Wandle
Coll
ashstead
A3
A24
A217
A232
A237
A240
A2043
A2022
A23
A236
A238
A239
A297
A298
M25
B2230
B278
B284
B2032
B2219
B2217
B2221
B280
B288
B289
B290
B291
B2220
B2033
B271
B272
B277
B279
B282
B283
B286
KINGSTON BY-PASS
KINGSTON ROAD
MALDEN WAY
LONDON ROAD
EPSOM ROAD
REIGATE ROAD
BRIGHTON ROAD
CARSHALTON ROAD
CHEAM ROAD
CROYDON LANE
WINKWORTH RD
FIR TREE ROAD
HOLLY LANE
OUTWOOD LANE
DORKING ROAD
TATTENHAM WAY
EWELL BY-PASS
HIGH ST
WEST HILL
16
52

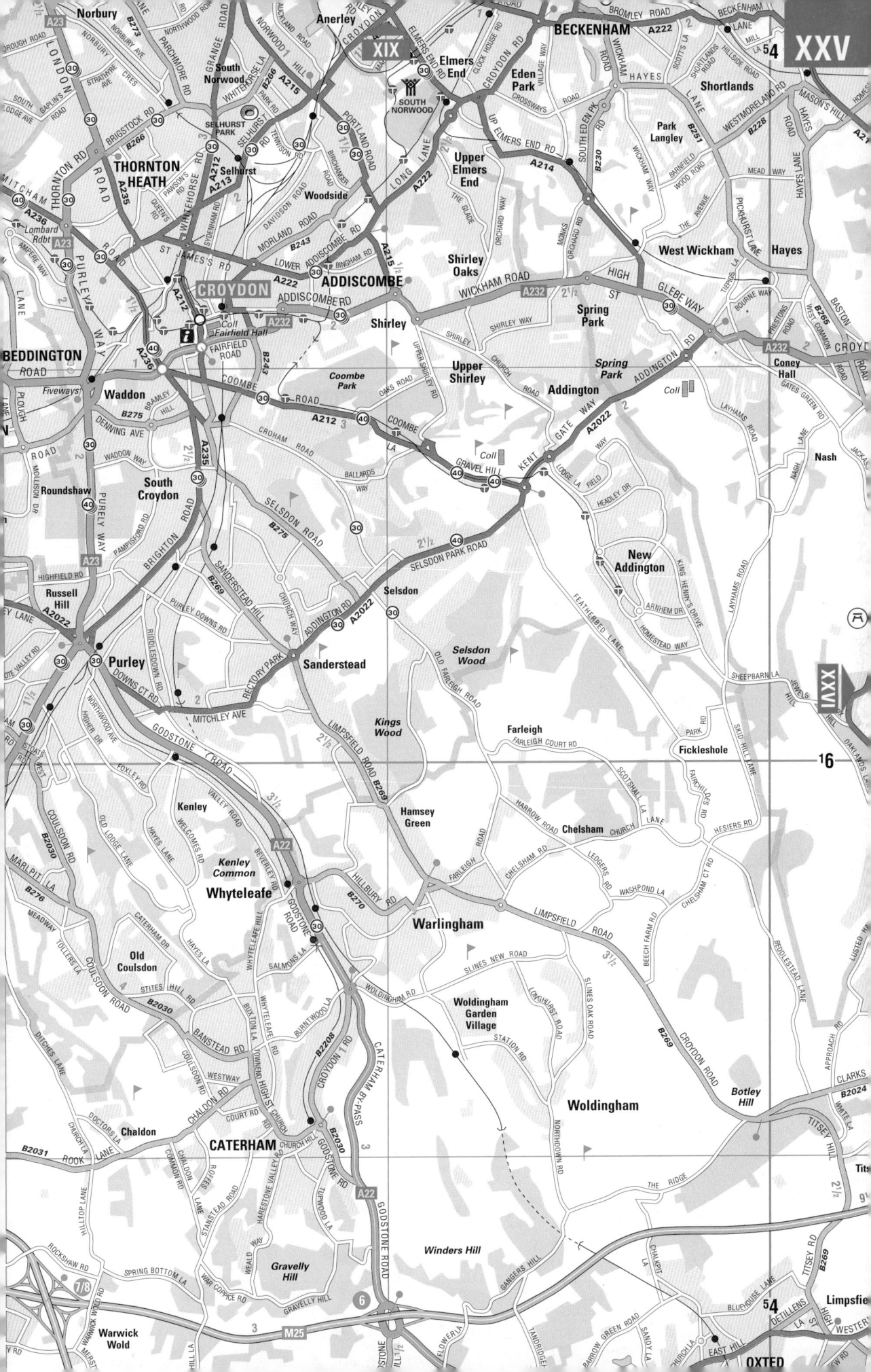
XXV
XIX
XXVI
54
16
Norbury
Anerley
BECKENHAM
Elmers End
Eden Park
South Norwood
SOUTH NORWOOD
Shortlands
Park Langley
SELHURST PARK
THORNTON HEATH
Selhurst
Upper Elmers End
Woodside
Lombard Rdbt
West Wickham
Hayes
Shirley Oaks
CROYDON
ADDISCOMBE
Coll
Fairfield Hall
Spring Park
BEDDINGTON
Shirley
Coney Hall
Coombe Park
Upper Shirley
Addington
Fiveways
Waddon
Nash
South Croydon
Roundshaw
New Addington
Russell Hill
Selsdon
Purley
Sanderstead
Selsdon Wood
Kings Wood
Farleigh
Fickleshole
Kenley
Hamsey Green
Chelsham
Kenley Common
Whyteleafe
Warlingham
Old Coulsdon
Woldingham Garden Village
Woldingham
Botley Hill
Chaldon
CATERHAM
Winders Hill
Gravelly Hill
Warwick Wold
OXTED
Limpsfield
Tits
7/8
6
M25
A23
A22
A212
A213
A215
A222
A232
A235
A236
A2022
A214
B2030
B2031
B2024
B2208
B269
B270
B275
B276
B243
B266
B273
B228
B230
B251
B265
BROMLEY ROAD
CROYDON RD
WICKHAM ROAD
GLEBE WAY
ADDINGTON RD
SELSDON PARK ROAD
LIMPSFIELD ROAD
GODSTONE ROAD
CATERHAM BY-PASS
CROYDON ROAD
PURLEY WAY
BRIGHTON ROAD
COULSDON ROAD
CHALDON RD
TITSEY HILL

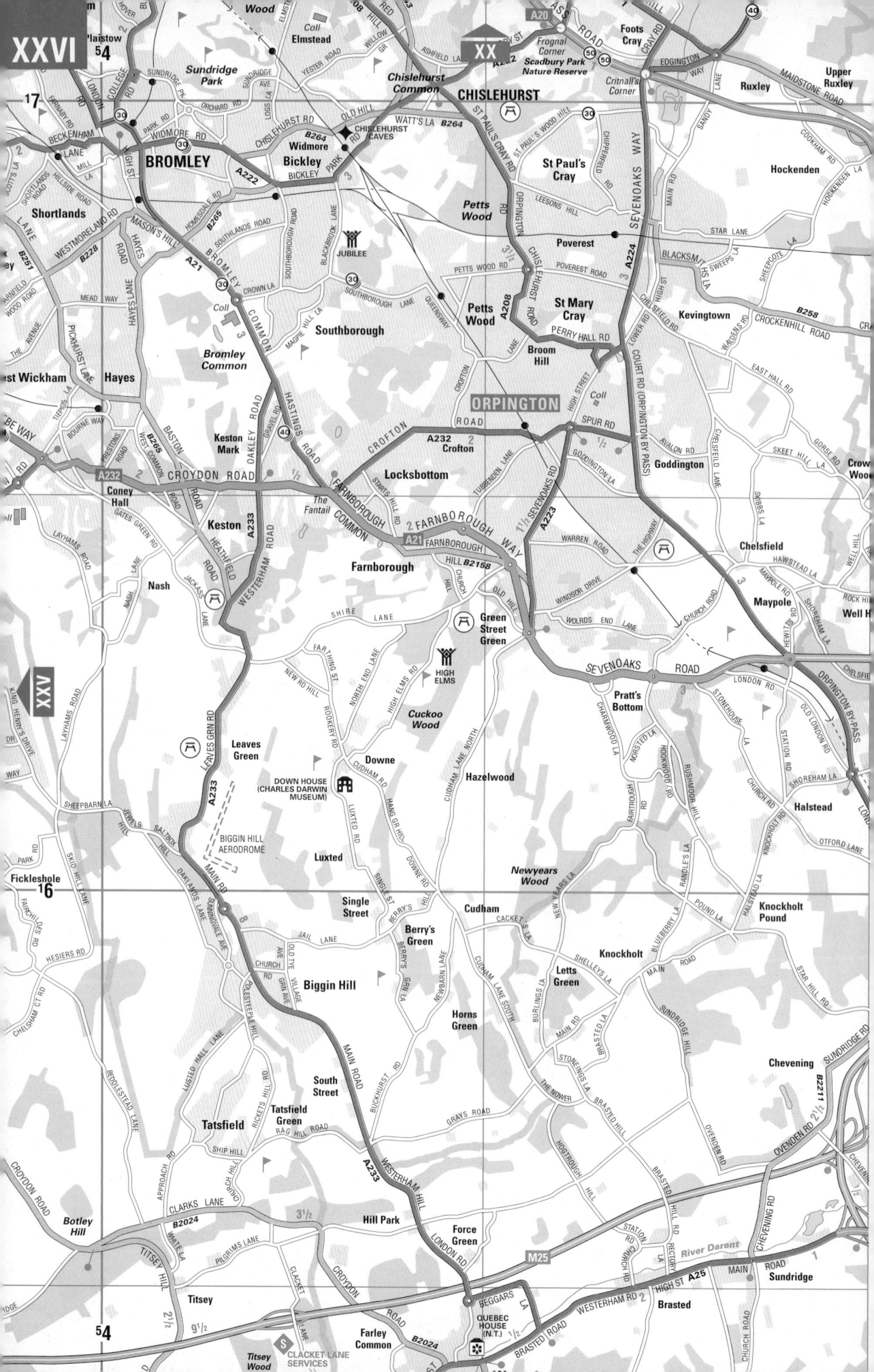
XXVI
XX
XXV
Plaistow
Sundridge Park
Elmstead
Chislehurst Common
CHISLEHURST
Frognal Corner
Scadbury Park Nature Reserve
Foots Cray
Critnall's Corner
Ruxley
Upper Ruxley
BROMLEY
Widmore
Bickley
CHISLEHURST CAVES
St Paul's Cray
Hockenden
Shortlands
Petts Wood
Poverest
St Mary Cray
Kevingtown
JUBILEE
Southborough
Bromley Common
Broom Hill
ORPINGTON
Hayes
Keston Mark
Crofton
Goddington
Locksbottom
Coney Hall
The Fantail
Keston
Farnborough
Chelsfield
Nash
Maypole
Green Street Green
HIGH ELMS
Pratt's Bottom
Cuckoo Wood
Leaves Green
Downe
DOWN HOUSE (CHARLES DARWIN MUSEUM)
Hazelwood
Halstead
BIGGIN HILL AERODROME
Luxted
Newyears Wood
Fickleshole
Single Street
Cudham
Knockholt Pound
Berry's Green
Knockholt
Letts Green
Biggin Hill
Horns Green
Chevening
South Street
Tatsfield Green
Tatsfield
Botley Hill
Hill Park
Force Green
River Darent
Sundridge
Titsey
Brasted
QUEBEC HOUSE (N.T.)
Farley Common
CLACKET LANE SERVICES
Titsey Wood
A20
A21
A222
A224
A232
A208
A223
A233
A25
M25
B264
B265
B228
B251
B258
B2158
B2024
B2211
SEVENOAKS WAY
SEVENOAKS ROAD
CROYDON ROAD
FARNBOROUGH WAY
WESTERHAM ROAD
MAIN ROAD
WESTERHAM HILL
ORPINGTON BY-PASS
17
16
54

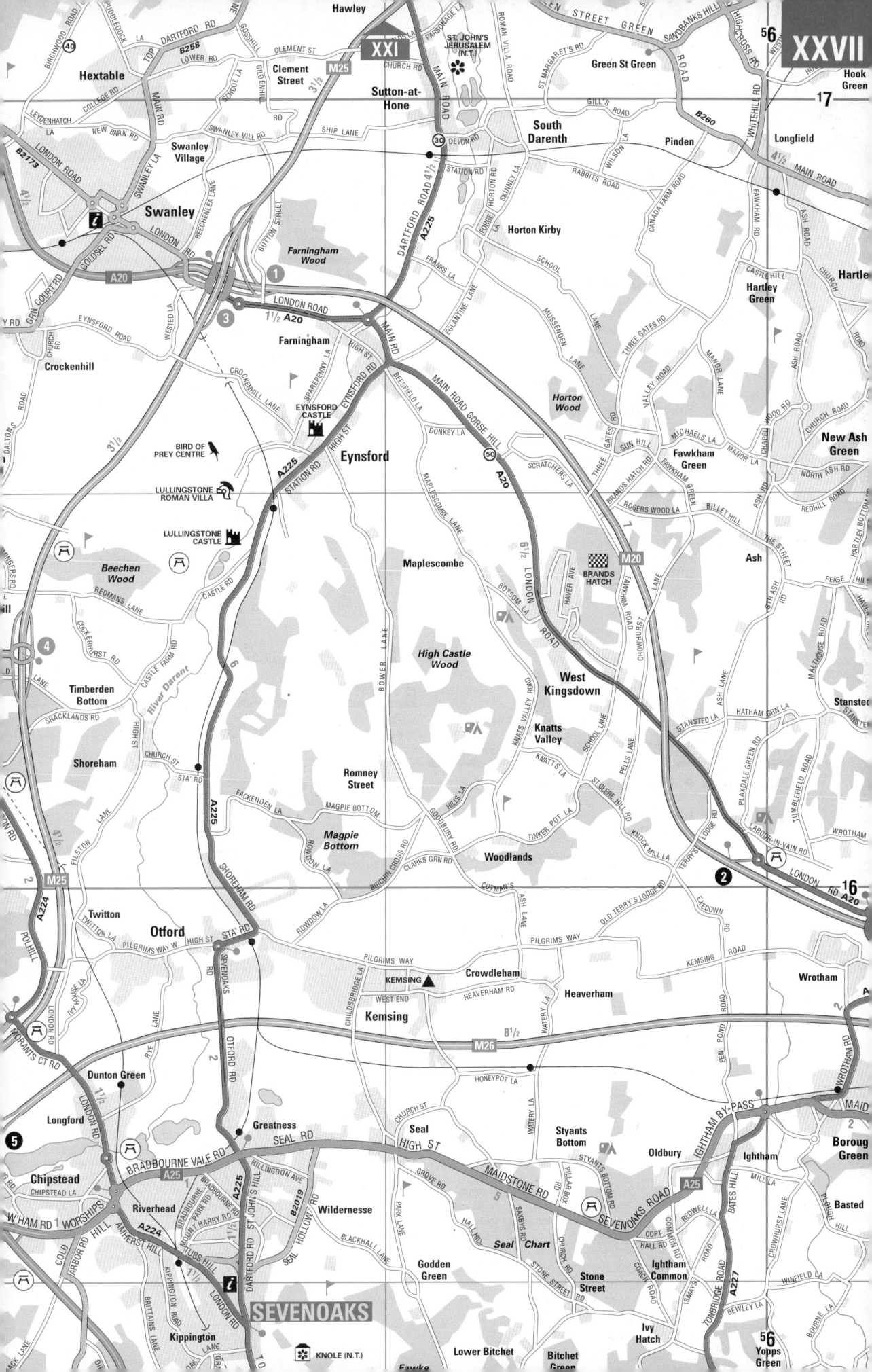
XXVII
XXI
56
17
16
Hawley
Hextable
Clement Street
Sutton-at-Hone
ST. JOHN'S JERUSALEM (N.T.)
Green St Green
Hook Green
South Darenth
Pinden
Longfield
Swanley Village
Swanley
Farningham Wood
Horton Kirby
Hartley Green
Farningham
Crockenhill
EYNSFORD CASTLE
Eynsford
BIRD OF PREY CENTRE
LULLINGSTONE ROMAN VILLA
LULLINGSTONE CASTLE
Horton Wood
Fawkham Green
New Ash Green
Beechen Wood
Maplescombe
BRANDS HATCH
Ash
High Castle Wood
West Kingsdown
Timberden Bottom
River Darent
Knatts Valley
Shoreham
Romney Street
Magpie Bottom
Woodlands
Twitton
Otford
KEMSING
Crowdleham
Heaverham
Kemsing
Wrotham
Dunton Green
Longford
Greatness
Seal
Styants Bottom
Oldbury
Ightham
Borough Green
Chipstead
Riverhead
Wildernesse
Seal Chart
Basted
Godden Green
Stone Street
Ightham Common
SEVENOAKS
Kippington
KNOLE (N.T.)
Lower Bitchet
Bitchet Green
Ivy Hatch
Yopps Green
M25
M20
M26
A20
A225
A224
A25
A227
B2019
B258
B260
B2173

Key to map symbols

Roads

- **Motorway with junction number** (22a)
- **Primary route** – single, dual carriageway
- **A road** – single, dual carriageway
- **B road** – single, dual carriageway
- **Through-route** – single, dual carriageway
- **Minor road** – single, dual carriageway
- **Road under construction**
- **Rural track, private road or narrow road in urban area**
- **Path, bridleway, byway open to all traffic, road used as public path**
- **Tunnel, covered road**
- **Speed camera** – single, multiple
- **Congestion Charge Zone boundary** Roads within the zone are outlined in green
- **Gate or obstruction, car pound**
- P P&R **Parking, park and ride**
- Crooked Billet **Road junction name**
- **Pedestrianised, restricted access area**

Public transport

-  **Railway station, private rail station**
- **London Underground station, Docklands Light Railway station**
- **Tramway or miniature railway**
- **Bus or coach station, tram stop**

Scale

4.83 inches to 1 mile   1:13 118

0	220yds	440yds	660yds	½ mile

0	250m	500m	750m	1km

Emergency services

-   **Ambulance, police, fire station**
- H ✚ **Hospital, accident and emergency entrance**

General features

- **Market, public amenity site**
- **Sports stadium**
- *i* PO **Information centre, post office**
- VILLA   House **Roman, non-Roman antiquity**
- 100   .304 **House number, spot height** – metres
- ✝ **Christian place of worship**
- **Mosque, synagogue**
- ◻ **Other place of worship**
- **Houses, important buildings**
- **Woods, parkland / common**
- 123 **Adjoining page number**

Leisure facilities

- **Camp site, caravan site**
- **Golf course, picnic site, view point**

Boundaries

- **NW6**  **Postcode boundaries**
- Westminster **County and unitary authority boundaries**

Water features

- Barking Creek **Water name**
- **Tidal water**
- **River or canal** – minor, major
- **Stream**
- **Water**

Abbreviations

Acad	Academy	Coll	College	Glf Crs	Golf Course	Ct	Law Court	Obsy	Observatory	Sh Ctr	Shopping Centre

Acad	Academy	Coll	College	Glf Crs	Golf Course
Allot Gdns	Allotments	Ct	Court	Drv Rng	Golf Driving Range
Bndstd	Bandstand	Crem	Crematorium		
Btcl	Botanical	Crkt	Cricket	Gn	Green
Bwg Gn	Bowling	Ent	Enterprise	Gd	Ground
Cemy	Cemetery	Ex H	Exhibition Hall	Hort	Horticultural
Ctr	Centre			Ind Est	Industrial Estate
C Ctr	Civic Centre	Fball	Football		
CH	Club House	Gdns	Gardens	Inst	Institute
Ctry Pk	Country Park	Glf C	Golf Course	Int	Interchange

Ct	Law Court	Obsy	Observatory	Sh Ctr	Shopping Centre
L Ctr	Leisure Centre	Pav	Pavilion		
		Pk	Park	Sp	Sports
LC	Level Crossing	Pl Fld	Playing Field	Stad	Stadium
Liby	Library	Pal	Royal Palace	Sw Pool	Swimming Pool
Mkt	Market	PH	Public House		
Meml	Memorial	Recn Gd	Recreation Ground	Tenn Cts	Tennis
Mon	Monument			TH	Town Hall
Mus	Museum	Resr	Reservoir	Trad Est	Trading Estate
Nat Res	Nature Reserve	Ret Pk	Retail Park		
		Sch	School	Univ	University
				YH	Youth Hostel

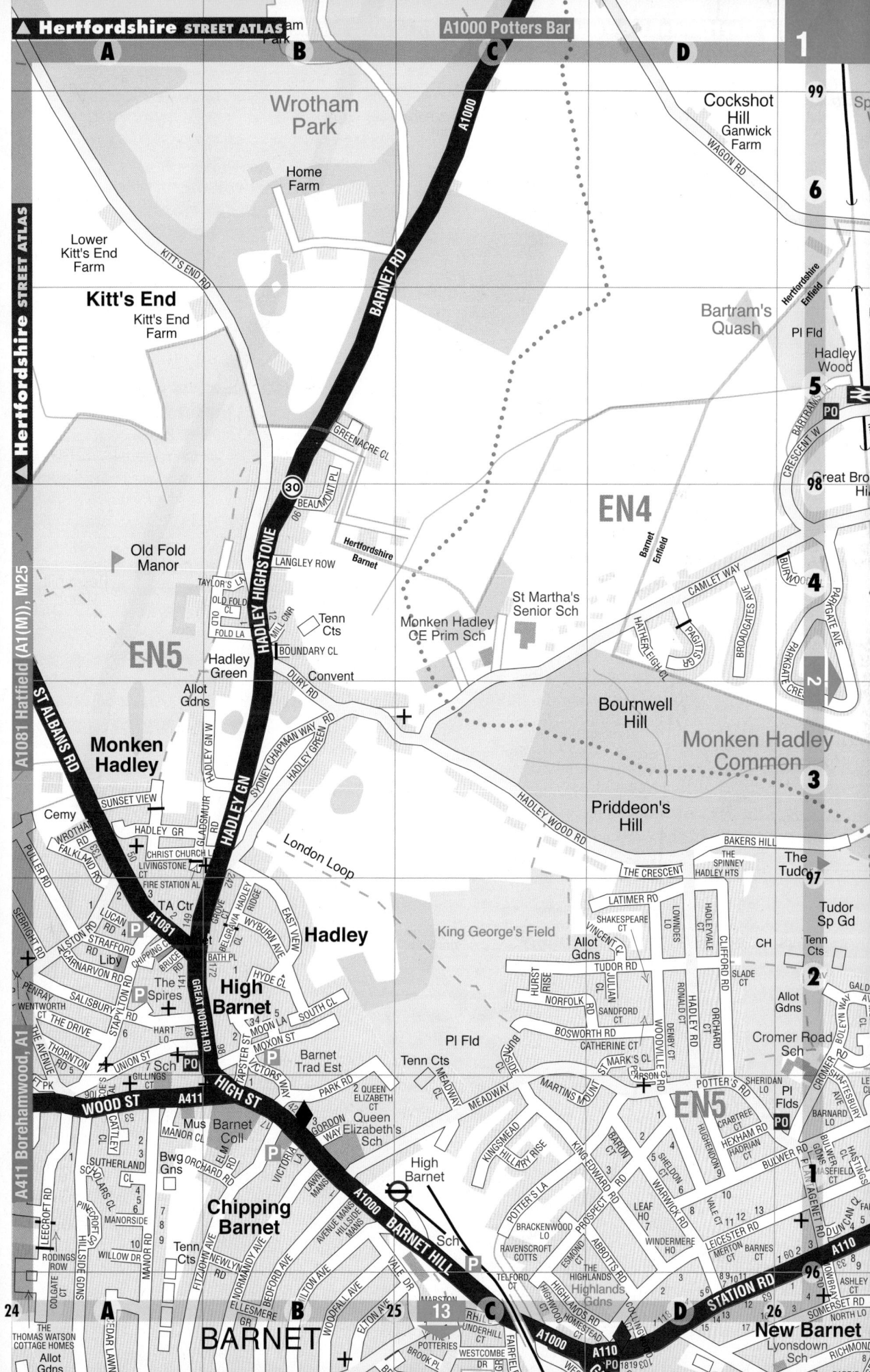
A1000 Potters Bar
A
B
C
D
1
99
6
5
98
4
3
2
97
96
1
24
25
26
13
Wrotham Park
Home Farm
Lower Kitt's End Farm
Kitt's End
Kitt's End Farm
Cockshot Hill
Ganwick Farm
WAGON RD
A1000
BARNET RD
KITT'S END RD
Bartram's Quash
Hertfordshire Enfield
Pl Fld
Hadley Wood
PO
BARTRAMS LA
CRESCENT W
Great Bro
GREENACRE CL
BEAUMONT PL
30
Hertfordshire Barnet
EN4
Barnet Enfield
Old Fold Manor
HADLEY HIGHSTONE
LANGLEY ROW
TAYLOR'S LA
OLD FOLD CL
OLD FOLD LA
MILL CNR
Tenn Cts
Monken Hadley CE Prim Sch
St Martha's Senior Sch
CAMLET WAY
BROADGATES AVE
BURWOOD
PARKGATE AVE
PARKGATE CRES
PAGITTS GR
HATHERLEIGH CL
BOUNDARY CL
EN5
Hadley Green
Convent
DURY RD
Allot Gdns
Bournwell Hill
Monken Hadley Common
Priddeon's Hill
ST ALBANS RD
Monken Hadley
HADLEY GN W
SYDNEY CHAPMAN WAY
HADLEY GREEN RD
HADLEY GN
SUNSET VIEW
Cemy
WROTHAM RD
FALKLAND RD
HADLEY GR
GLADSMUIR RD
CHRIST CHURCH LA
LIVINGSTONE CT
FIRE STATION AL
London Loop
HADLEY WOOD RD
BAKERS HILL
THE CRESCENT
THE SPINNEY
HADLEY HTS
The Tudor
Tudor Sp Gd
PULLER RD
SEBRIGHT RD
TA Ctr
A1081
LUCAN RD
ALSTON RD
STRAFFORD RD
CARNARVON RD
Liby
CHIPPING CL
BRUCE RD
GROVE CT
BELGRAVIA CL
HADLEY RIDGE
WYBURN AVE
EAST VIEW
Hadley
King George's Field
LATIMER RD
SHAKESPEARE CT
VINCENT CL
LOWNDES LO
HADLEYVALE CT
CLIFFORD RD
CH
Tenn Cts
SLADE CT
GALDANA AV
BATH PL
HYDE CL
The Spires
High Barnet
SOUTH CL
PENRAY
WENTWORTH
SALISBURY RD
STAPYLTON RD
GREAT NORTH RD
HART LO
MOON LA
MOXON ST
TAPSTER ST
THE DRIVE
THE AVENUE
THORNTON RD
UNION ST
Sch
PO
Barnet Trad Est
Pl Fld
Tenn Cts
TUDOR RD
HURST RISE
JULIAN CL
NORFOLK RD
SANDFORD CT
BOSWORTH RD
CATHERINE CT
ST MARK'S CL
RONALD CT
DENBY CT
HADLEY RD
ORCHARD CT
WOODVILLE RD
Allot Gdns
Cromer Road Sch
BOLEYN WAY
CROMER RD
SHAFTESBURY AVE
VICTORS WAY
PARK RD
QUEEN ELIZABETH CT
MEADWAY CL
MEADWAY
BURNSIDE CL
MARTINS MOUNT
POTTER'S RD
SHERIDAN LO
Pl Flds
PO
BARNARD LO
GILLINGS CT
WOOD ST
A411
HIGH ST
Mus
MANOR CL
Barnet Coll
ELM DR
GORDON WAY
Queen Elizabeth's Sch
KINGSMEAD
HILLARY RISE
BARON CT
KING EDWARD RD
EN5
CRABTREE CT
HEXHAM RD
HADRIAN CT
HUGHENDON
SHELDON CT
BULWER RD
BULWER GDNS
MASEFIELD CT
HASTINGS
CATLEY CL
SUTHERLAND CL
SCHOLARS CL
Bwg Gns
ORCHARD RD
VICTORIA LA
LAWN MANS
High Barnet
POTTER'S LA
PROSPECT RD
WARWICK RD
LEAF HO
VALE CT
PLANTAGENET RD
DUNCAN CL
Chipping Barnet
LEECROFT RD
PINECROFT CR
MANORSIDE
HILLSIDE GDNS
A1000
BARNET HILL
AVENUE MANS
HILLSIDE MANS
Sch
BRACKENWOOD LO
RAVENSCROFT COTTS
ESMOND CT
ABBOTTS RD
WINDERMERE HO
LEICESTER RD
MERTON CT
BARNES CT
A110
RODINGS ROW
WILLOW DR
MANOR RD
Tenn Cts
FITZJOHN AVE
NEWLYN RD
NORMANDY AVE
BEDFORD AVE
HILTON AVE
WOODFALL AVE
VALE DR
TELFORD CT
THE HIGHLANDS
Highlands Gdns
HIGHLANDS RD
HIGHWOOD CT
HOMESTEAD CT
STATION RD
ASHLEY CT
SOMERSET RD
NORTH LO
COLGATE CT
THE THOMAS WATSON COTTAGE HOMES
Allot Gdns
CEDAR LAWN
ELLESMERE GR
BARNET
ELTON AVE
MARSTON
THE POTTERIES
BROOK PL
UNDERHILL CT
WESTCOMBE DR
FAIRFIELD
A1000
A110
New Barnet
Lyonsdown Sch
RICHMOND
A411 Borehamwood, A1
A1081 Hatfield (A1(M)), M25

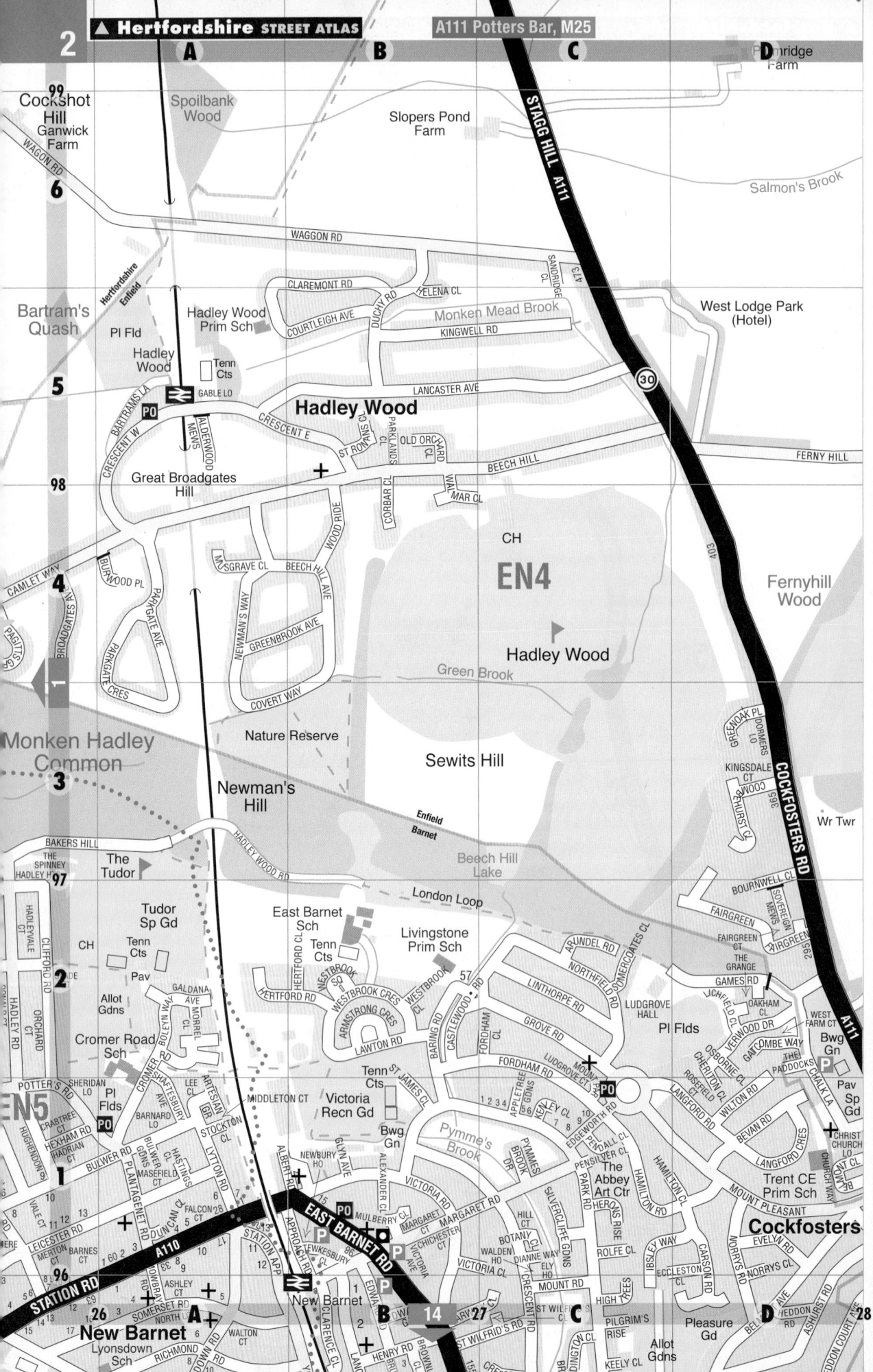

Cockshot Hill
99
Ganwick Farm
WAGGON RD
6

Spoilbank Wood

Slopers Pond Farm

STAGG HILL A111

Bromridge Farm

Salmon's Brook

WAGGON RD

CLAREMONT RD
DUCHY RD
HELENA CL
Monken Mead Brook
KINGWELL RD

SANDRIDGE CL

West Lodge Park (Hotel)

Bartram's Quash
Pl Fld
Hadley Wood Prim Sch
Hadley Wood
Tenn Cts
GABLE LO
ALDERWOOD MEWS
Hertfordshire / Enfield
BARTRAMS LA
CRESCENT W
PO
5

COURTLEIGH AVE
LANCASTER AVE

Hadley Wood

30

FERNY HILL

98
Great Broadgates Hill
CRESCENT E
ST RONANS
PARKLANDS
OLD ORCHARD CL
CORBAR CL
WAL MAR CL
BEECH HILL

CAMLET WAY
BURWOOD PL
BROADGATES AV
PARKGATE AVE
PARKGATE CRES
MUSGRAVE CL
NEWMAN'S WAY
BEECH HILL AVE
GREENBROOK AVE
WOOD RIDE
4

CH

EN4

Fernyhill Wood

403

PAGITTS ?
1
COVERT WAY
Green Brook
Hadley Wood

Monken Hadley Common
3
Nature Reserve
Sewits Hill

Newman's Hill

Enfield / Barnet

GRESOAK PL
DORMERS LO
KINGSDALE CT
COOMHURST CT
COCKFOSTERS RD
Wr Twr
998

BAKERS HILL
THE SPINNEY
Hadley H
97
The Tudor
HADLEY WOOD RD
Beech Hill Lake
London Loop
BOURNWELL CT
FAIRGREEN
SOVEREIGN MEWS
FAIRGREEN CT
THE GRANGE
GAMES RD

Tudor Sp Gd
CH
Tenn Cts
Pav
East Barnet Sch
Tenn Cts
Livingstone Prim Sch
57
ARUNDEL RD
NORTHFIELD RD
SOMERCOATES CL
Ludgrove Hall
Pl Flds
OAKHAM CL
VERWOOD DR
WEST FARM CT
Bwg Gn
P
2
HADLEYVALE CT
CLIFFORD RD
Allot Gdns
GALDANA AVE
BOLEYN WAY
MORREL CT
HERTFORD CL
HERTFORD RD
WESTBROOK SQ
WESTBROOK CRES
WESTBROOK CL
BARING RD
CASTLEWOOD RD
LINTHORPE RD
GROVE RD
FORDHAM CL
LUDGROVE MCT
LICHFIELD CT
OSBORNE CL
CHERITON CL
ROSEFIELD CL
WILTON RD
GATCOMBE WAY
THE PADDOCKS
Pav Sp Gd
P
CHALK LA

ORCHARD CT
HADLEY RD
Cromer Road Sch
LAWTON RD
FORDHAM RD
Pav Sp Gd
BEVAN RD
LANGFORD RD
HAMILTON CL
LANGFORD CRES
MOUNT PLEASANT
CHRIST CHURCH LO
CHURCH WAY
Trent CE Prim Sch

POTTER'S RD
SHERIDAN LO
Pl Flds
SHAFTESBURY AVE
BARNARD LO
STOCKTON CL
LEE RD
ARTESIAN GR
MIDDLETON CT
Victoria Recn Gd
ST JAMES CL
Tenn Cts
1 2 3 4 5 6
APPLETREE GDNS
KEMPLEY CL
7 8 9 10
EDGEWORTH CL
Pl Flds
PENSILVER CL
PALL CL
The Abbey Art Ctr
HERONS RISE
PARK RD
HAMILTON RD
IBSLEY WAY
EVELYN RD
CHRIST CHURCH LO
Cockfosters

EN5
1
CRABTREE CT
HIGHENDON CT
HEXHAM RD
HADRIAN CL
BULWER RD
HASTINGS RD
PLANTAGENET RD
MASEFIELD GDNS
LYTTON RD
ALBERT RD
FALCON CT
DUNCAN RD
STATION APP
Bwg Gn
NEWBURY HO
GLYN AVE
ALEXANDER RD
MULBERRY CL
Victoria Recn Gd
PYMMES BROOK DR
PYMME'S Brook
Pymme's Brook
SILVERCLIFFE GDNS
HILL CT
BOTANY CL
WALDEN HO
DIANNE WAY
ELY HO
ROLFE CL
NORRYS RD
NORRYS RD
PLEASURE Gd
CARSON RD
ECCLESTON CL
BELL AVE
EDDON CL
WEDDON CL
ASHURST RD

96
STATION RD
26
A110
60
LEICESTER RD
MERTON RD
BARNES CT
VALE RD
SOMERSET RD
NORTH LO
COWBRAY CT
ASHLEY CT
SDOWN RD
RICHMOND RD
WALTON CT
STATION APP
New Barnet
EAST BARNET RD
PO
P
TEWKESBURY
CLARENCE CL
EDNA RD
APPROACH RD
MARGARET RD
MARGARET RD
CHICHESTER RD
VICTORIA RD
VICTORIA AVE
VICTORIA CL
MOUNT RD
CRESCENT RD
ST WILFRID'S RD
ST WILFRID'S RD
HIGH TREES
PILGRIM'S RISE
Allot Gdns
KEELY CL
EDDON COURT RD

New Barnet
Lyonsdown Sch
17
HENRY RD
LANC
BROWNLOW
CRESCENT

A　　　　B　　14　27　　　　C　　　　D　　28

Vault Hill Wood

Wood

Roundhedge Hill

Salmon's Brook

Botany Bay Farm

Botany Bay

EN2

THE RIDGEWAY

A1005

99

6

Duncan's Wood

Ash Wood

Cu

Park Farm

5

FERNY HILL

Ferny Hill Farm

Obelisk

Moat Wood

P

Ride Wood

Parkside Farm

HADLEY RD

98

Leeging Beech

EN4

Rough Lot

Enfield Chase

London Loop

4

4

Seedfield Spinney

Icehouse Wood

Williams Wood

3

Oak Wood

Trent Country Park

Middlesex Univ Trent Park

SHAWS WOOD COTTS

Shaws Wood

97

ROOKERY COTTS

Pav

Sp Gd

2

Church Wood

Merryhills Brook

South Lodge Farm

A110

Triangular Wood

SNAKES LA

Trent Park

Trent Park Equestrian Ctr

EASTPOLE COTTS

EASTPOLE COTTS

SOUTH LODGE CRES

LAKESIDE

SOUTH LODGE CRES

GREYSTOKE GDNS

SOUTH GDNS

LOWTHE

Cemy

P

Cockfosters

LONSDALE DR

NETHER

CULGAITH GDNS

1

COCKFOSTERS RD

COCKFOSTERS PAR

NORFOLK CL

WEST CL

EAST CL

CHADDLEWOOD

GALVA CL

MOUNT CL

BRAEMORE

HEDDON

STATION PAR

N14 CH

WESTPOLE AVE

BRAMLEY RD

PO

BRAYTON GDNS

GROSVENOR GDNS

BELGRAVE GDNS

CURTHWAITE GDNS

MERRYHILLS DR

BRAMTWOOD GDNS

CLIFTON GDNS

WEOENDD GDNS

ASBURY CT

96

A11

Betjeman CT 1
TAVERNERS LO 2

28

A

FRESTON GDNS

LEYS GDNS

GLOUCESTER GDNS

KENT DR

Southgate Sch Pl Fld

B

SUSSEX WAY

29

15

RIDGEVIEW CT

MERRYHILLS

STAFFORD CL

WOODVILLE CT

HARPER CL

Oakwood

C

GERRARD'S CL

BELGRAVE CT

CARLTON AVE

SOUTH LODGE DR

D

BEVERIDGE CT
JENNER CT
30

LOWER

WOODEND AVE

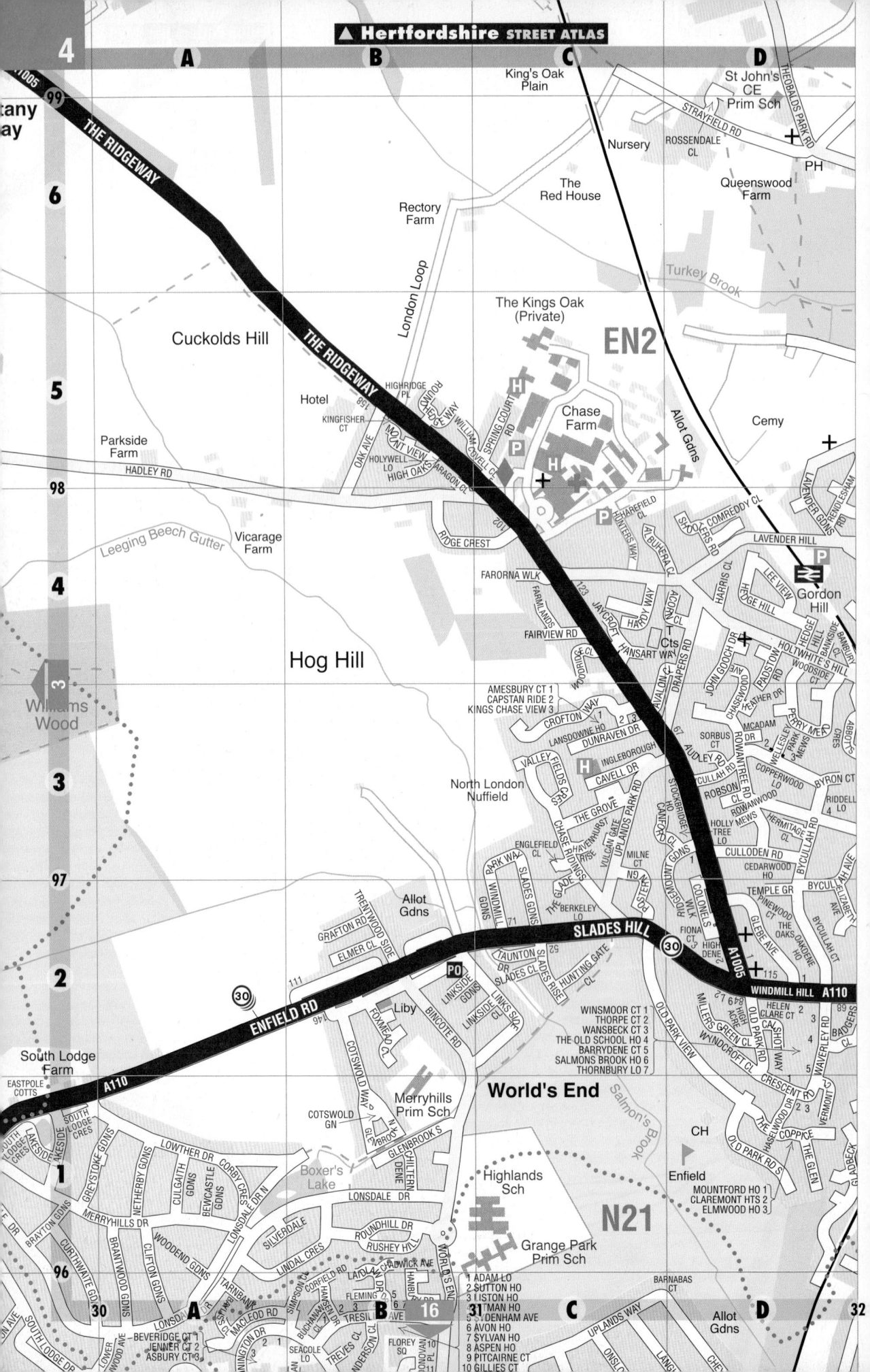
THE RIDGEWAY
A1005
Cuckolds Hill
Hog Hill
King's Oak Plain
Rectory Farm
The Red House
Nursery
St John's CE Prim Sch
STRAYFIELD RD
ROSSENDALE CL
THEOBALDS PARK RD
PH
Queenswood Farm
Turkey Brook
London Loop
The Kings Oak (Private)
EN2
Chase Farm
Allot Gdns
Cemy
Hotel
Parkside Farm
HADLEY RD
HIGHRIDGE PL
KINGFISHER CT
OAK AVE
ROUNDHEDGE WAY
WILLIAM COVELL CL
SPRING COURT RD
MOUNT VIEW
HOLYWELL LO
HIGH OAKS
ARAGON CL
Leeging Beech Gutter
Vicarage Farm
RIDGE CREST
HAREFIELD CL
HUNTERS WAY
ALBUHERA CL
SHOOTERS RD
COMREDDY CL
LAVENDER HILL
LAVENDER GDNS
RENDLESHAM RD
Gordon Hill
FARORNA WLK
FARMLANDS
JAYCROFT
HARDY WAY
ACORN CL
HARRIS CL
LEE VIEW
HEDGE HILL
FAIRVIEW RD
WOODRIDGE CL
HANSART WAY
Cts
DRAPERS RD
JOHN GOOCH DR
PADSTOW RD
HOLTWHITE'S HILL
BANKSIDE CL
BANBURY
WOODSIDE CT
AMESBURY CT 1
CAPSTAN RIDE 2
KINGS CHASE VIEW 3
CROFTON WAY
LANSDOWNE HO
DUNRAVEN DR
AVALON CL
CHASEWOOD AVE
HEATHER DR
PERRY MEAD
ABBOTS CRES
SORBUS CT
MCADAM DR
WELLESLEY PARK MEWS
AUDLEY RD
VALLEY FIELDS CRES
INGLEBOROUGH
CAVELL DR
North London Nuffield
BYCULLAH RD
ROWANTREE RD
COPPERWOOD LO
BYRON CT
ROBSON CL
ROWANWOOD
RIDDELL LO
THE GROVE
UPLANDS PARK RD
STOCKBRIDGE HO
CANFORD CL
HOLLY TREE LO
HERMITAGE CL
ENGLEFIELD CL
CHASE RIDINGS
HAVENHURST RISE
VULCAN GATE
MILNE CT
CULLODEN RD
CEDARWOOD HO
PARK WAY
WINDMILL GDNS
SLADES GDNS
THE GLADE
POSTERN GN
RIDGEMONT GDNS
COLONELS WLK
TEMPLE GR
PINEWOOD CT
BYCULLAH AVE
ELIZABETH CT
Allot Gdns
TRENTWOOD SIDE
GRAFTON RD
ELMER CL
BERKELEY LO
SLADES HILL
FIONA CT
HIGH DENE
GLEBE AVE
THE OAKS
OAKDENE HO
BYCULLAH CT
TAUNTON DR
SLADES CL
SLADES RISE
HUNTING GATE CL
WINDMILL HILL A110
PO
LINKSIDE GDNS
LINKSIDE
LINKS SIDE CL
ENFIELD RD
Liby
FOXMEAD CL
BINCOTE RD
WINSMOOR CT 1
THORPE CT 2
WANSBECK CT 3
THE OLD SCHOOL HO 4
BARRYDENE CT 5
SALMONS BROOK HO 6
THORNBURY LO 7
OLD PARK VIEW
MILLERS GREEN CL
HIGH ACRE
OLD PARK RD
HELEN CLARE CT
CALSHOT WAY
WAVERLEY RD
BADGERS CL
WYNDCROFT CL
CRESCENT RD
VERMONT CL
South Lodge Farm
EASTPOLE COTTS
A110
COTSWOLD WAY
Merryhills Prim Sch
World's End
Salmon's Brook
CH
Enfield
THE HASELWOOD DR
THE COPPICE
THE GLEN
OLD PARK RD S
GLADBECK
COTSWOLD GN
GLENBROOK N
GLENBROOK S
SOUTH LODGE CRES
LAKESIDE
LOWTHER DR
CORBY CRES
GREYSTOKE GDNS
NETHERBY GDNS
CULGAITH GDNS
BEWCASTLE GDNS
LONSDALE DR N
CHILTERN DENE
Boxer's Lake
Highlands Sch
MOUNTFORD HO 1
CLAREMONT HTS 2
ELMWOOD HO 3
LONSDALE DR
MERRYHILLS DR
BRAYTON GDNS
CURTHWAITE GDNS
BRANTWOOD GDNS
CLIFTON GDNS
WOODEND GDNS
SILVERDALE
ROUNDHILL DR
RUSHEY HILL
LINDAL CRES
N21
Grange Park Prim Sch
WORLD'S END LA
CHADWICK AVE
LAIDLAW DR
FLEMING
HANBURY DR
CORFIELD RD
SIMPSON CL
HANSEN DR
BUCHANAN CL
TARNBANK
TRESILIAN AVE
MACLEOD RD
1 ADAM LO
2 SUTTON HO
3 LISTON HO
4 ATMAN HO
5 SYDENHAM AVE
6 AVON HO
7 SYLVAN HO
8 ASPEN HO
9 PITCAIRNE CT
10 GILLIES CT
BARNABAS CT
UPLANDS WAY
Allot Gdns
BEVERIDGE CT 1
JENNER CT 2
ASBURY CT 3
SEACOLE LO
TREVES CL
FLOREY SQ
DONOVAN PL
16
A B C D
30 31 32
99 98 97 96
6 5 4 3 2 1
Williams Wood
3

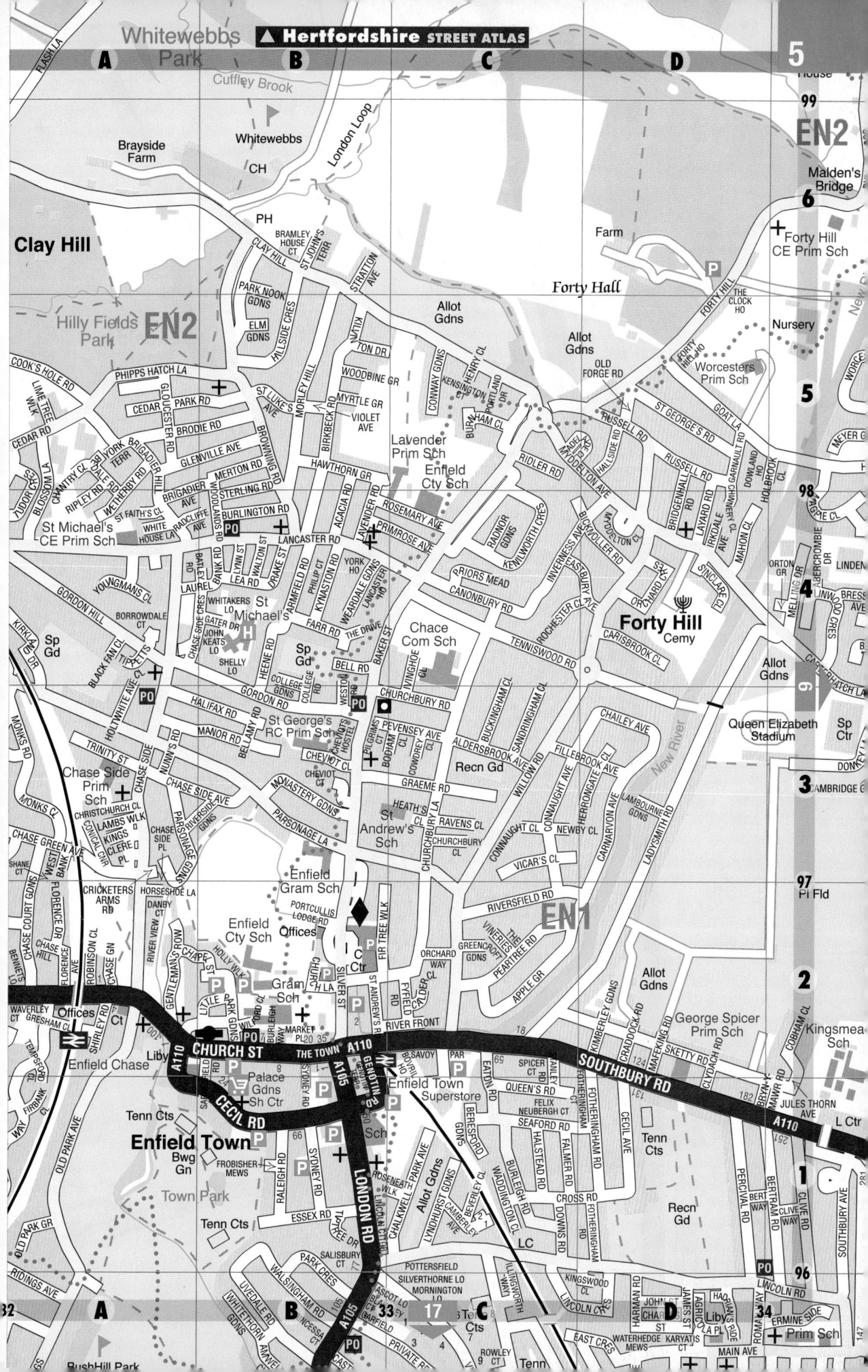

Hertfordshire STREET ATLAS
A
B
C
D
5
Whitewebbs Park
Cuffley Brook
FLASH LA
Whitewebbs
Brayside Farm
CH
London Loop
EN2
99
Malden's Bridge
6
PH
Clay Hill
BRAMLEY HOUSE CT
ST JOHN'S TERR
CLAY HILL
STRATTON AVE
Farm
Forty Hill CE Prim Sch
Forty Hall
FORTY HILL
THE CLOCK HO
Nursery
PARK NOOK GDNS
ELM GDNS
HILLSIDE CRES
Allot Gdns
Hilly Fields Park
EN2
KILN
TON DR
HENRY CL
CONWAY GDNS
KENSINGTON CT
PORTLAND DR
OLD FORGE RD
FORTY HILL HO
Worcesters Prim Sch
COOK'S HOLE RD
PHIPPS HATCH LA
LIME TREE WLK
GLOUCESTER RD
CEDAR
PARK RD
ST LUKE'S AVE
MORLEY HILL
WOODBINE GR
MYRTLE GR
BIRKBECK RD
VIOLET AVE
BURNHAM CL
ADELA AVE
MYDDELTON AVE
HALLSIDE RD
RUSSELL RD
ST GEORGE'S RD
GOAT LA
5
CEDAR RD
BRODIE RD
GLENVILLE AVE
BROWNING RD
Lavender Prim Sch
Enfield Cty Sch
RIDLER RD
RUSSELL RD
GARNAULT RD
DOWNLAND HO
HOLBROOK CL
MEYER GR
BLOSSOM LA
TUDOR CRES
CHANTRY CL
YORK TERR
DALE RD
RIPLEY RD
WETHERBY RD
BRIGADIER HILL
MERTON RD
BRIGADIER AVE
STERLING RD
WOODLANDS RD
HAWTHORN GR
ACACIA RD
LAVENDER RD
ROSEMARY AVE
PRIMROSE AVE
BRIDGENHALL RD
LAYARD RD
IRKDALE AVE
CHIMNEY CL
MAHON CL
98
AGPIE CL
St Michael's CE Prim Sch
ST FAITH'S CL
WHITE HOUSE LA
RADCLIFFE AVE
BURLINGTON RD
PO
LANCASTER RD
RADNOR GDNS
KENILWORTH CRES
INVERNESS AVE
BICKMOLLER RD
MYDDELTON CL
EASTBURY AVE
ABERCROMBIE DR
LINDEN
BATLEY RD
BANK RD
LYNN ST
WALTON ST
DRAKE ST
ARMFIELD RD
PHILIP CT
KYNASTON RD
YORK HO
WEARDALE GDNS
LANCASTER HO
PRIORS MEAD
ORTON GR
MELLING DR
YOUNGMANS CL
LAUREL
LEA RD
CANONBURY RD
ORCHARD CL
SINCLARE CL
4
LINWOOD CRES
BRESS AVE
GORDON HILL
BORROWDALE CT
CHASE SIDE CRES
WHITAKERS LO
St Michael's
GATER DR
JOHN KEATS LO
H
FARR RD
THE DRIVE
Chace Com Sch
ROCHESTER CL
Forty Hill Cemy
KIRKLAND DR
Sp Gd
TIPPETTS CL
SHELLY LO
HEENE RD
Sp Gd
BELL RD
BAKER ST
VINGHOE CL
TENNISWOOD RD
CARISBROOK CL
Allot Gdns
BLACK FAN CL
HOLTWHITE AVE
PO
COLLEGE GDNS
COLLEGE RD
WESTON RD
GORDON RD
PO
CHURCHBURY RD
BUCKINGHAM CL
SANDRINGHAM CL
CHAILEY AVE
CARTERHATCH LA
9
MONKS RD
HALIFAX RD
BELLAMY RD
St George's RC Prim Sch
CHEVIOTS HOSTEL
PILGRIMS CT
PEVENSEY AVE
BODIAM CL
COWDREY CL
ALDERSBROOK AVE
WILLOW RD
FILLEBROOK AVE
New River
Queen Elizabeth Stadium
Sp Ctr
TRINITY ST
MANOR RD
NUNN'S RD
CHEVIOT CL
Recn Gd
HERRONGATE CL
DONKEY
Chase Side Prim Sch
CHASE SIDE
CHASE SIDE AVE
MONASTERY GDNS
CHEVIOT CT
GRAEME RD
CONNAUGHT AVE
3
CAMBRIDGE
MONKS CL
CHRISTCHURCH CL
RIVERSIDE GDNS
HEATH'S CL
RAVENS CL
CARNARVON AVE
LAMBOURNE GDNS
LADYSMITH RD
LAMBS WLK
KINGS CLERE PL
CHASE SIDE PL
PARSONAGE GDNS
PARSONAGE LA
St Andrew's Sch
CHURCHBURY LA
CHURCHBURY CL
CONNAUGHT CL
NEWBY CL
CHASE GREEN AVE
SHANE CT
WEST BANK
FLORENCE DR
CONICAL CNR
VICAR'S CL
Enfield Gram Sch
97
Pi Fld
CHASE COURT GDNS
CRICKETERS ARMS RD
HORSESHOE LA
DANBY CT
RIVERSFIELD RD
PORTCULLIS LODGE RD
FIR TREE WLK
EN1
CHASE HILL
ROBINSON CL
CHASE GN
RIVER VIEW
GENTLEMAN'S ROW
Enfield Cty Sch
Offices
THE VINERIES
BENNETS
CHAPEL ST
HOLLY WLK
C Ctr
ORCHARD WAY
GREENCROFT GDNS
PEARTREE RD
Allot Gdns
2
CHURCH LA
ST ANDREW'S RD
CALDER CL
APPLE GR
KIMBERLEY GDNS
CRADDOCK RD
MAFEKING RD
COBHAM CL
Kingsmead Sch
Gram Sch
SILVER ST
FYFIELD RD
George Spicer Prim Sch
WAVERLEY CT
GRESHAM CL
Offices
SHIRLEY RD
Ct
LITTLE PARK GDNS
WILFORD CL
BURLEIGH WAY
MARKET PL
RIVER FRONT
CHURCH ST
THE TOWN
A110
A110
SAVOY
PAR
SOUTHBURY RD
SKETTY RD
CLYDACH RD
BRYN-Y-MAWR RD
TEMPSFORD
Enfield Chase
Liby
A105
GENOTIN TERR
GENOTIN RD
BOVRIL HO
EATON RD
SPICER CT
STANLEY RD
QUEEN'S RD
FOTHERINGHAM RD
JULES THORN AVE
FIRBANK CL
Palace Gdns Sh Ctr
SYDNEY RD
Enfield Town Superstore
FELIX NEUBERGH CT
SEAFORD RD
CECIL AVE
A110
L Ctr
Tenn Cts
CECIL RD
BERESFORD GDNS
HALSTEAD RD
FALMER RD
Tenn Cts
OLD PARK AVE
Enfield Town
Sch
Bwg Gn
FROBISHER MEWS
RALEIGH RD
SYDNEY RD
LONDON RD
ROSENEATH WLK
CHALKWELL PARK AVE
Allot Gdns
LYNDHURST GDNS
CAMBERLEY AVE
BEVERLEY CL
WADDINGTON CL
BURLEIGH RD
CROSS RD
DOWNS RD
PERCIVAL RD
BERTRAM RD
BERT WAY
CLIVE WAY
CLIVE RD
1
SOUTHBURY AVE
Town Park
Tenn Cts
ESSEX RD
TREE DR
LINCOLN CT
LC
Recn Gd
OLD PARK GR
SALISBURY CT
PARK CRES
POTTERSFIELD
SILVERTHORNE LO
MORNINGTON LO
ILLINGWORTH WAY
KINGSWOOD CL
PO
96
LINCOLN RD
RIDINGS AVE
WALSINGHAM RD
UVEDALE RD
WHITETHORN GDNS
ASCOT LO
BEVERLEY CT
GARFIELD
LINCOLN CRES
HARMAN RD
JOHN CT
CHARLES ST
JAMES ST
AGRICOLA PL
HADRIAN'S RIDE
Liby
ROMAN WAY
ERMINE SIDE
Prim Sch
32
A
B
33
17
C
D
34
A105
PRINCESS CT
PO
PRIVATE RD
EAST CRES
WATERHEDGE MEWS
KARYATIS CT
MAIN AVE
ROWLEY CT
Tenn
BushHill Park

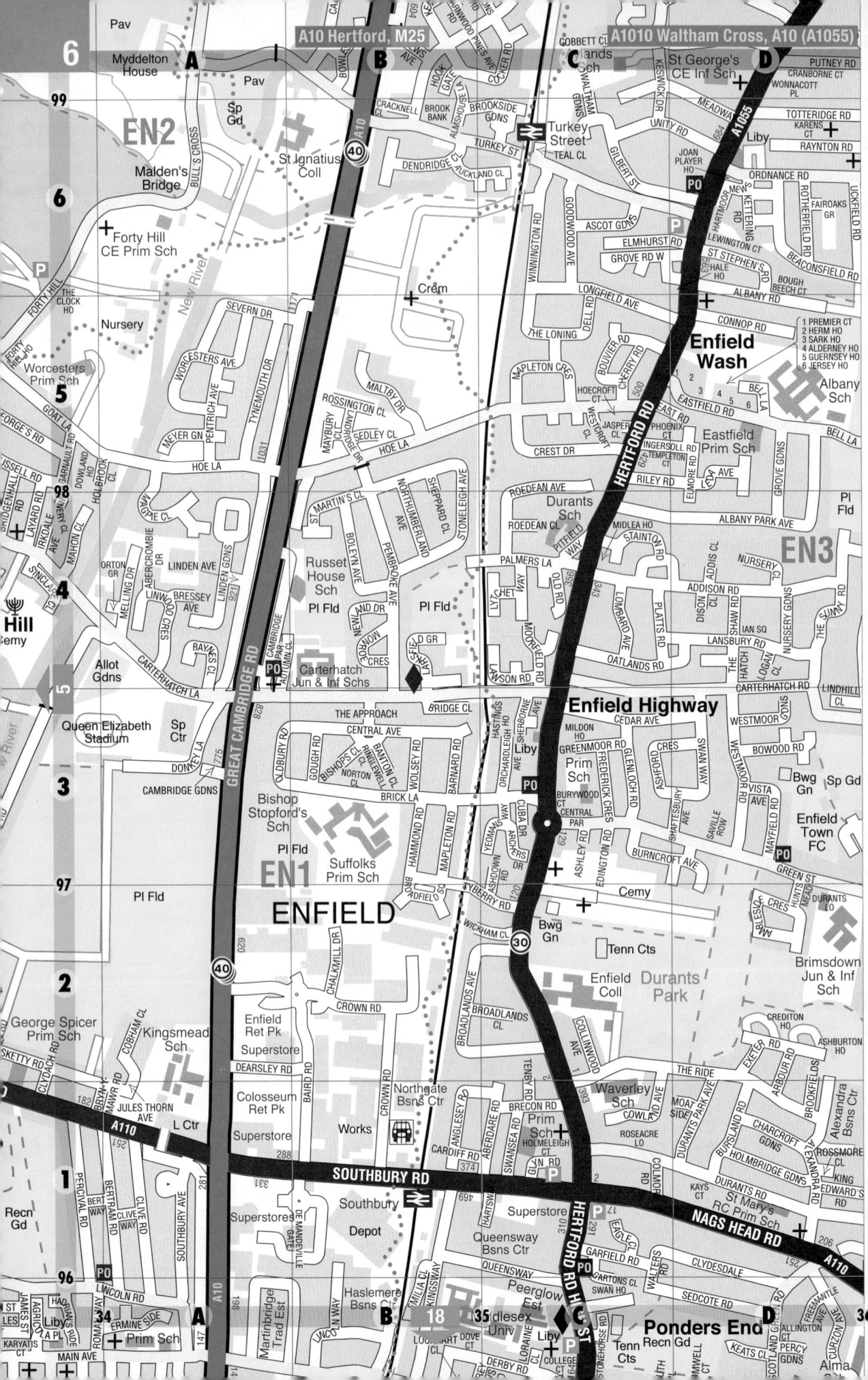

A10 Hertford, M25
A1010 Waltham Cross, A10 (A1055)
6
A
B
C
D
Pav
Myddelton House
Sp Gd
EN2
Malden's Bridge
BULL'S CROSS
St Ignatius Coll
CRACKNELL CL
BROOK BANK
BROOKSIDE GDNS
ALMSHOUSE LA
HOOK GATE
DENDRIDGE CL
AUCKLAND CL
TURKEY ST
Turkey Street
TEAL CL
COBBETT CL
WALTHAM GDNS
KESWICK DR
St George's CE Inf Sch
PUTNEY RD
CRANBORNE CT
WONNACOTT PL
MEADWAY
UNITY RD
TOTTERIDGE RD
KARENS CT
Liby
RAYNTON RD
A1055
GILBERT ST
JOAN PLAYER HO
ORDNANCE RD
PO
FAIRDAKS GR
UCKFIELD RD
ROTHERFIELD RD
KETTERING RD
HARTMOOR MEWS
ASCOT GDNS
ELMHURST RD
GROVE RD W
LEWINGTON CT
ST STEPHEN'S RD
HALE HO
BEACONSFIELD RD
BOUGH BEECH CT
ALBANY RD
GOODWOOD AVE
WINNINGTON RD
Forty Hill CE Prim Sch
FORTY HILL
THE CLOCK HO
New River
Crem
LONGFIELD AVE
CONNOP RD
Enfield Wash
1 PREMIER CT
2 HERM HO
3 SARK HO
4 ALDERNEY HO
5 GUERNSEY HO
6 JERSEY HO
THE LONING
DELL RD
BOUVIER RD
CHERRY RD
SEVERN DR
Nursery
FORTY HILL HO
Worcesters Prim Sch
WORCESTERS AVE
TYNEMOUTH DR
PENTRICH AVE
MEYER GN
MALTBY DR
ROSSINGTON CL
MAPLETON CRES
HOECROFT CT
Albany Sch
BELL LA
EASTFIELD RD
EAST RD
5
GOAT LA
FORGE'S RD
GARNAULT RD
DOWLAND RD
HOLBROOK CL
HOE LA
MAYBURY CL
LANDRIDGE DR
SEDLEY CL
WESTCROFT CL
JASPER CL
PHOENIX CT
INGERSOLL RD
TEMPLETON CT
Eastfield Prim Sch
HERTFORD RD
CREST DR
ELMORE RD
LEDA AVE
RILEY RD
GROVE GDNS
Pl Fld
ISSELL RD
98
LAYARD RD
IRKDALE AVE
MAHON CL
MAGPIE CL
ST MARTIN'S CL
NORTHUMBERLAND AVE
SHEPPARD CL
STONELEIGH AVE
ROEDEAN AVE
Durants Sch
ROEDEAN CL
PITFIELD WAY
MIDLEA HO
STAINTON RD
ALBANY PARK AVE
EN3
ADDIS CL
NURSERY CL
ABERCROMBIE DR
ORTON GR
LINDEN AVE
LINDEN GDNS
BOLEYN AVE
PEMBROKE AVE
Russet House Sch
PALMERS LA
LYTCHET WAY
OLD RD
ADDISON RD
MELLING DR
SINCLARE CL
4
LINWOOD CRES
BRESSEY AVE
Pl Fld
NEWLAND DR
MONROE CRES
LOMBARD AVE
PLATTS RD
DISON CL
SHAW RD
IAN SQ
NURSERY GDNS
THE SUNNY RD
LANSBURY RD
MOORFIELD RD
Hill Cemy
BAYNES CL
CAMBRIDGE PAR
AUTUMN CL
Allot Gdns
CARTERHATCH LA
Carterhatch Jun & Inf Schs
LAKESFIELD GR
LAWSON RD
OATLANDS RD
THE HATCH
LOGAN CL
CARTERHATCH RD
LINDHILL CL
GREAT CAMBRIDGE RD
Queen Elizabeth Stadium
Sp Ctr
THE APPROACH
BRIDGE CL
HASTINGS AVE
SHERBORNE AVE
Enfield Highway
CEDAR AVE
WESTMOOR GDNS
CENTRAL AVE
OLDBURY RD
GOUGH RD
BISHOPS CL
RINGLEWELL CL
BANTON CL
WOLSEY RD
BARNARD RD
ORCHARDLEIGH AVE
MILDON HO
GREENMOOR RD
FREDERICK CRES
GLENLOCH RD
ASHFORD CRES
SWAN WAY
WESTMOOR RD
BOWOOD RD
DONKEY LA
CAMBRIDGE GDNS
NORTON CL
Liby
Prim Sch
BRICK LA
BURYWOOD CT
CENTRAL PAR
SHAFTESBURY AVE
VISTA AVE
Bwg Gn
Sp Gd
3
Bishop Stopford's Sch
HAMMOND RD
MAPLETON RD
YEOMANS WAY
CUBA DR
ARCHERS DR
ASHLEY RD
EDINGTON RD
SAVILLE ROW
MAYFIELD RD
Enfield Town FC
Pl Fld
Suffolks Prim Sch
EN1
ASHDOWN RD
BURNCROFT AVE
GREEN ST
97
BROADFIELD SQ
TYBERRY RD
Cemy
DURANTS LO
HUNTS MEAD
AMBLESIDE CRES
ENFIELD
WICKHAM CL
Bwg Gn
Tenn Cts
CHALKMILL DR
Enfield Coll
Durants Park
Brimsdown Jun & Inf Sch
2
CROWN RD
BROADLANDS AVE
BROADLANDS CL
George Spicer Prim Sch
COBHAM CL
Kingsmead Sch
Enfield Ret Pk
Superstore
COLLINWOOD AVE
CREDITON HO
EXETER RD
ARBOUR RD
ASHBURTON HO
DEARSLEY RD
BAIRD RD
SKETTY RD
CLYDACH RD
BRYN-Y-MAWR RD
JULES THORN AVE
Colosseum Ret Pk
Northgate Bsns Ctr
TENBY RD
Waverley Sch
THE RIDE
BROOKFIELDS
Alexandra Bsns Ctr
A110
L Ctr
Superstore
Works
ANGLESEY RD
ABERDARE RD
BRECON RD
Prim Sch
HOLMELEIGH CT
COWLAND AVE
MOAT SIDE
ROSEACRE LO
DURANTS PARK AVE
BURSLAND RD
CHARCROFT GDNS
HOLMBRIDGE GDNS
ROSSMORE CL
KING EDWARD'S RD
CARDIFF RD
SWANSEA RD
GLYN RD
SOUTHBURY RD
COLMORE RD
1
PERCIVAL RD
BERT WAY
BERTRAM RD
CLIVE WAY
CLIVE RD
SOUTHBURY AVE
Recn Gd
Superstores
DE MANDEVILLE GATE
Southbury
Depot
HARTSWAY
Superstore
Queensway Bsns Ctr
HERTFORD RD
KAYS CT
DURANTS RD
St Mary's RC Prim Sch
NAGS HEAD RD
ALEXANDRA RD
EAGLE CL
GARFIELD RD
WALTERS RD
CLYDESDALE
96
LINCOLN RD
QUEENSWAY
GARTONS CL
SWAN HO
SEDCOTE RD
Haslemere Bsns Ctr
Peerglow Est
Martinbridge Trad Est
ROMAN WAY
HADRIAN'S RIDE
ERMINE SIDE
Prim Sch
AGRICOLA PL
Liby
JAMES ST
KARYATIS CT
MAIN AVE
34
18
35
Middlesex Univ
LINCOLN WAY
KINGSWAY
LOCKHART CL
DOVE CT
DERBY RD
LORAINE CL
Liby
COLLEGE CT
STONEHORSE RD
HIGH ST
Tenn Cts
Ponders End
Recn Gd
SCOTLAND GREEN RD
ALLINGTON CT
PERCY GDNS
KEATS CL
FREEMANTLE AVE
CURZON AVE
Alma

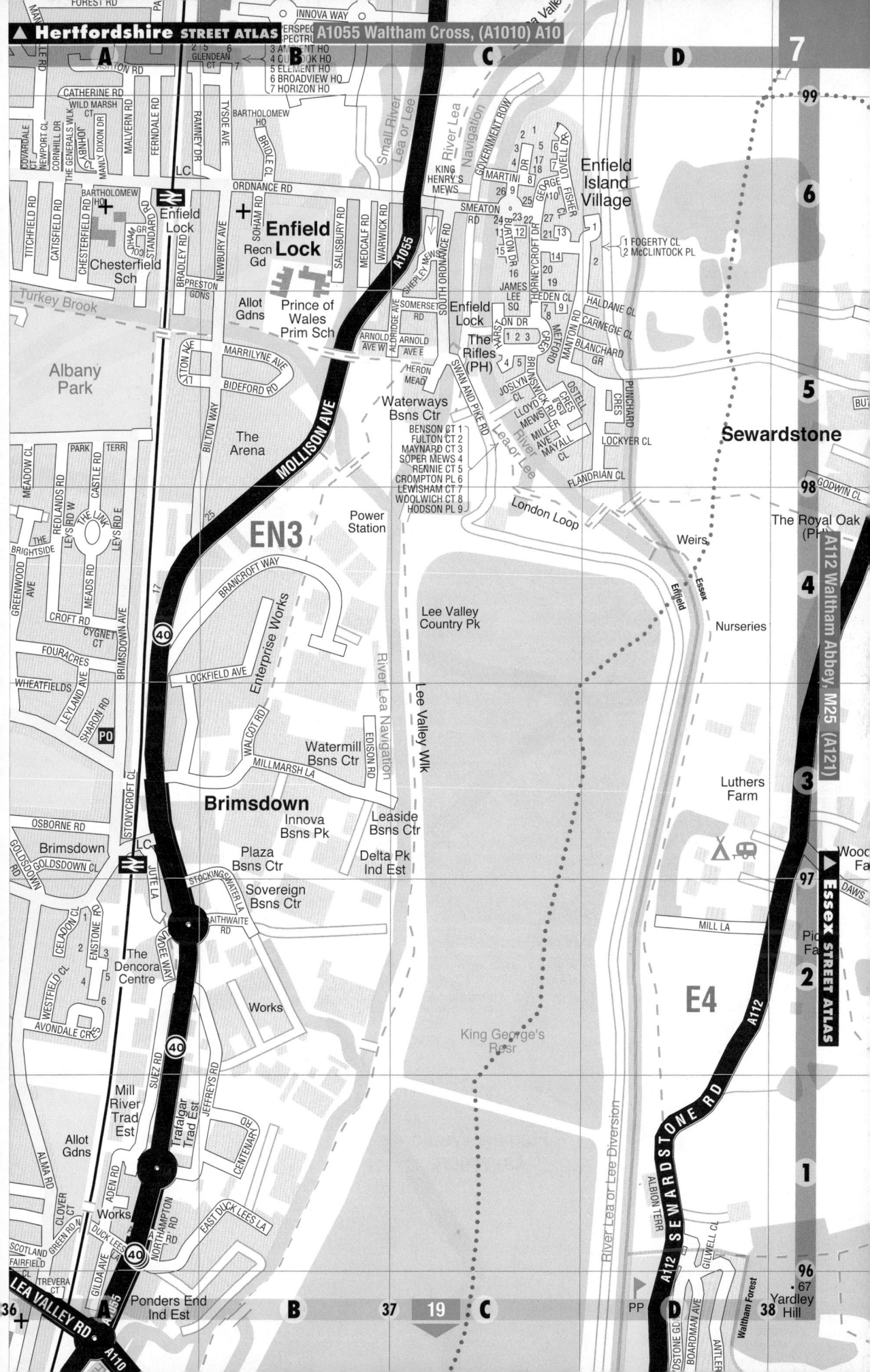

A

FOREST RD

INNOVA WAY

ASTON RD

CATHERINE RD
WILD MARSH CT
MALVERN RD
FERNDALE RD
RAMNEY DR
TYSOE AVE
BARTHOLOMEW HO
BRIDLE PATH

COVERDALE CT
NEWPORT CL
THE GENERALS WLK
CORNHILL DR
MANLY DIXON DR

GLENDEAN CT

1 AMBIENT HO
2 SPECTRUM HO
3 CURRENT HO
4 CUBROOK HO
5 ELEMENT HO
6 BROADVIEW HO
7 HORIZON HO

ORDNANCE RD

TITCHFIELD RD
CATISFIELD RD
CHESTERFIELD RD
BARTHOLOMEW HO

SOHAM RD
NEWBURY AVE
SALISBURY RD
MEDCALF RD
WARWICK RD

BARTHOLOMEW HO

Enfield Lock

Enfield Lock

Chesterfield Sch

Recn Gd

Prince of Wales Prim Sch

BRADLEY RD
PRESTON GDNS

Turkey Brook

Allot Gdns

KING HENRY'S MEWS

SMEATON RD

Enfield Island Village

GOVERNMENT ROW

MARTINI

GEORGE

FISHER
LOVELL DR

1 FOGERTY CL
2 McCLINTOCK PL

Albany Park

STON AVE
MARRILYNE AVE
BIDEFORD RD

The Arena

SOMERSET RD
ARNOLD AVE W
ARNOLD AVE E
ALDRIDGE AVE

HERON MEAD

Waterways Bsns Ctr

BENSON CT 1
FULTON CT 2
MAYNARD CT 3
SOPER MEWS 4
RENNIE CT 5
CROMPTON PL 6
LEWISHAM CT 7
WOOLWICH CT 8
HODSON PL 9

Enfield Lock

The Rifles (PH)

SWAN AND PIKE RD

JOSLYN CL

BRUNSWICK CL

JAMES LEE SQ

THEDEN CL

HARSTON DR
1 2 3

LLOYD MEWS

OSTELL CRES
CRES

MILLER AVE
MAYALL CL

BURTON DR
THORNEYCROFT DR

METFORD
MANTON RD
HALDANE CL
CARNEGIE CL
BLANCHARD GR
PUNCHARD CRES
LOCKYER CL
FLANDRIAN CL

Sewardstone

GODWIN CL

The Royal Oak (PH)

Weirs

Nurseries

Enfield

Essex

EN3

MOLLISON AVE

Power Station

Lee Valley Country Pk

Lee Valley Wlk

River Lea Navigation

London Loop

A112 Waltham Abbey, M25 (A121)

ESSEX STREET ATLAS

MEADOW CL
REDLANDS RD
LEYS RD W
LEYS RD E
CASTLE RD
PARK TERR
THE LINK

THE BRIGHTSIDE
GREENWOOD AVE
CROFT RD
MEADS RD
CYGNET CT

BRANCROFT WAY

Enterprise Works

LOCKFIELD AVE

Luthers Farm

FOURACRES
WHEATFIELDS
LEYLAND AVE
SHARON RD

PO

WALCOT RD
EDISON RD
MILLMARSH LA

Watermill Bsns Ctr

BRIMSDOWN AVE

STONYCROFT CL

Leaside Bsns Ctr

Brimsdown

Innova Bsns Pk

Plaza Bsns Ctr

Sovereign Bsns Ctr

Delta Pk Ind Est

MILL LA

Luthers Farm

OSBORNE RD

GOLDSDOWN CL

Brimsdown

GOLDSDOWN RD

JUTE LA
STOCKINGSWATER LA
AITHWAITE RD

The Dencora Centre

CELADON CL
ENSTONE RD

WESTFIELD CL

AVONDALE CRES

Works

E4

King George's Resr

MILL RIVER TRAD EST

SUEZ RD
TRAFALGAR TRAD EST
JEFFREYS RD
CENTENARY RD

Allot Gdns

ALMA RD
CLOVER CT
TREVERA CT

SCOTLAND GREEN RD N
FAIRFIELD CL

GILDA AVE
ADEN RD
NORTHAMPTON RD
EAST DUCK LEES LA
DUCK LEES LA

Works

River Lea or Lee Diversion

SEWARDSTONE RD

ALBION TERR

GILWELL CL

Waltham Forest

Yardley Hill

Wood Fa

Pic Fa

67

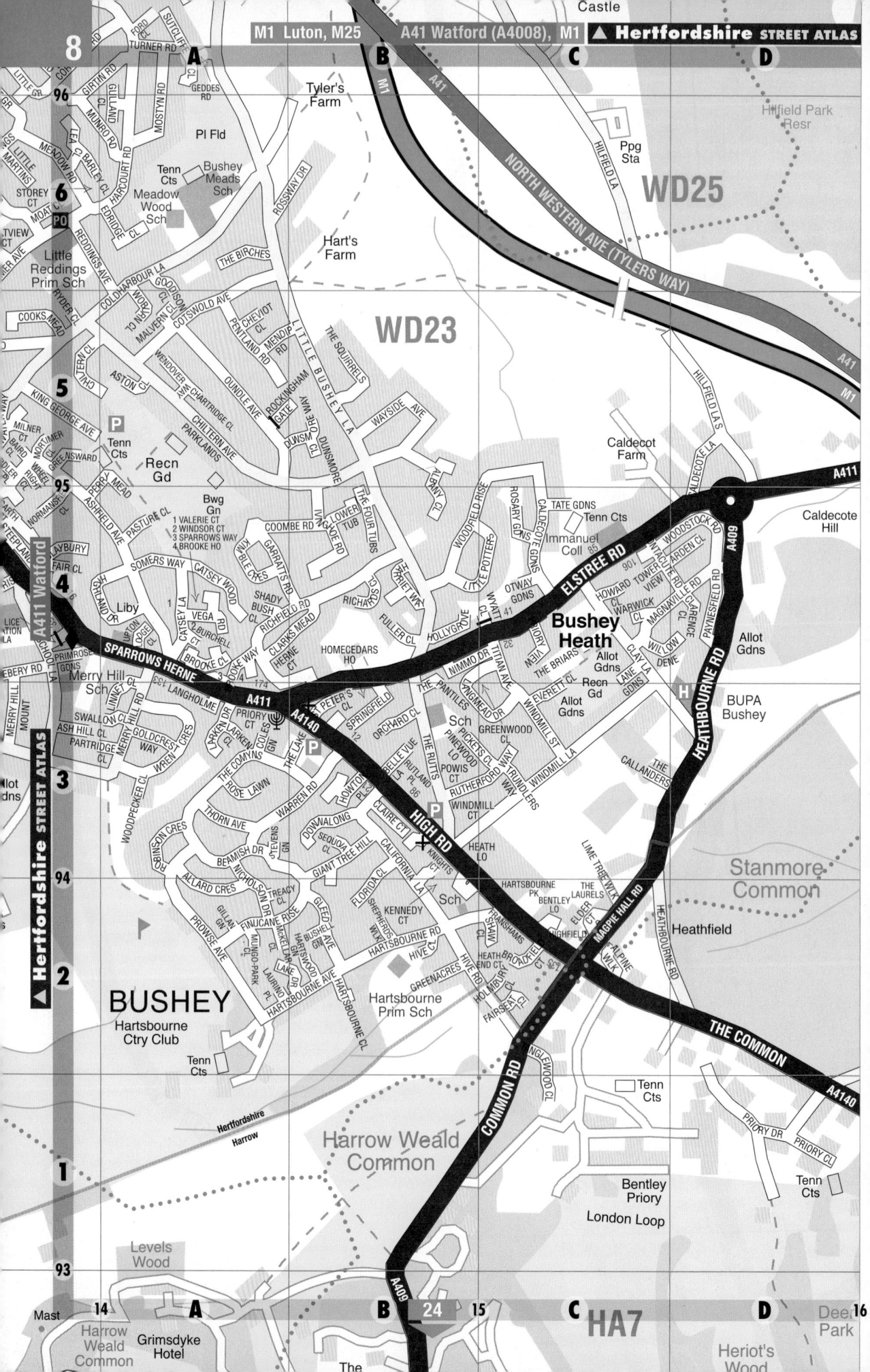
8
M1 Luton, M25
A41 Watford (A4008), M1
▲ Hertfordshire STREET ATLAS
A
B
C
D
Castle
Tyler's Farm
Hilfield Park Resr
Ppg Sta
WD25
NORTH WESTERN AVE (TYLERS WAY)
A41
M1
HILFIELD LA
TURNER RD
SUTCLIFFE CL
GEDDES RD
GIRTIN RD
GULLAND CL
MOSTYN RD
MUNRO RD
LEA CL
BARLEY CL
MEADOW RD
HARCOURT RD
LITTLE MARTINS
STOREY CT
MOAT CL
EDRIDGE CL
Pl Fld
Tenn Cts
Bushey Meads Sch
Meadow Wood Sch
ROSSWAY DR
Hart's Farm
Little Reddings Prim Sch
REDDINGS AVE
THE BIRCHES
COLDHARBOUR LA
GOODISON CL
WORLD CL
MALVERN CL
COTSWOLD AVE
CHEVIOT CL
PENTLAND RD
MENDIP RD
COOKS MEAD
RYDER CL
WD23
THE SQUIRRELS
LITTLE BUSHEY LA
CHILTERN CL
ASTON CL
WENDOVER WAY
CHARTRIDGE CL
OUNDLE AVE
ROCKINGHAM GATE
CHILTERN AVE
PARKLANDS
KING GEORGE AVE
MILNER CT
MORTIMER CL
BAIRD CL
WHEELWRIGHT CL
GREENSWARD
Tenn Cts
Recn Gd
DUWSM CL
DUNSMORE WAY
DUNSMORE
WAYSIDE AVE
ALBANY CL
Caldecot Farm
CALDECOTE LA
HILLFIELD LA S
A411
Caldecote Hill
95
NORMANSFIELD CL
PERRY MEAD
ASHFIELD AVE
PASTURE CL
Bwg Gn
1 VALERIE CT
2 WINDSOR CT
3 SPARROWS WAY
4 BROOKE HO
COOMBE RD
LOWER TUB
THE FOUR TUBS
IVINGHOE RD
WOODFIELD RISE
ROSARY GDNS
CALDECOTE GDNS
TATE GDNS
Tenn Cts
Immanuel Coll
ELSTREE RD
WOODSTOCK RD
ARDEN CL
A409
LAYBURY
FAIR CL
A411 Watford
SOMERS WAY
CATSEY WOOD
KIMBLE CRES
GARRATTS RD
SHADY BUSH CL
RICHFIELD RD
RICHARDS CL
HARRIET WAY
LITTLE POTTERS
OTWAY GDNS
WYATT CL
HOWARD CL
TOWER VIEW
MONTACUTE RD
MAGNAVILLE RD
CLARENCE CL
PAYNESFIELD RD
Allot Gdns
Liby
CATSEY LA
VEGA RD
BURCHELL CT
CLARKS MEAD
HERNE CT
FULLER CL
HOLLYGROVE
Bushey Heath
WARWICK CL
WILLOW DENE
PRIORY VIEW
TITIAN AVE
NIMMO DR
THE BRIARS
Allot Gdns
CLAY LA
LANE GDNS
SPARROWS HERNE
PRIMROSE GDNS
BROOKE CL
BROOKE WAY
HOMECEDARS HO
Merry Hill Sch
LANGHOLME
A411
A4140
PRIORY CT
COLES GN
ST PETER'S CL
SPRINGFIELD
ORCHARD CL
THE PANTILES
Sch
LONGMEAD DR
GREENWOOD CL
EVERETT CL
Recn Gd
Allot Gdns
WINDMILL ST
HEATHBOURNE RD
BUPA Bushey
LINNET CL
SWALLOW CL
ASH HILL CL
PARTRIDGE CL
MERRY HILL RD
GOLDCREST WAY
WREN CRES
LARKEN DR
LARKEN CL
THE LAKE
THE COMYNS
ROSE LAWN
BELLE VUE LA
RUTLAND PL
THE RUTTS
PINEWOOD LO
POWIS CT
PICKETS CL
RUTHERFORD WAY
TRUNDLERS WAY
WINDMILL LA
THE CALLANDERS
3
WOODPECKER CL
THORN AVE
WARREN RD
HOWTON PL
CLAIRE CT
HIGH RD
WINDMILL CT
ROBINSON CRES
DOWNALONG
SEQUOIA CL
STEVENS GN
BEAMISH DR
GIANT TREE HILL
CALIFORNIA LA
KNIGHTS CT
HEATH LO
LIME TREE WLK
Stanmore Common
94
ALLARD CRES
NICHOLSON DR
TREACY CL
FLORIDA CL
Sch
HARTSBOURNE PK
THE LAURELS
BENTLEY LO
ELDER CT
MAGPIE HALL RD
Heathfield
GILLAN GN
FINUCANE RISE
MUNGO-PARK CL
MCKELLAR CL
HARTSWOOD GN
BUSHELL GN
GLEED AVE
SHEPHERDS WLK
KENNEDY CT
HARTSBOURNE RD
SHAW CL
FRANSHAMS
HIGHFIELD
ALPINE WLK
PROWSE AVE
HIVE CL
HEATH END CT
BROADFIELD CT
2
LAURINO PL
LAKE DR
HARTSBOURNE AVE
HARTSBOURNE CL
GREENACRES
HIVE RD
HOLMBURY CT
FAIRSEAT CL
BUSHEY
Hartsbourne Ctry Club
Hartsbourne Prim Sch
THE COMMON
Tenn Cts
COMMON RD
INGLEWOOD CL
Tenn Cts
A4140
Hertfordshire
Harrow
Harrow Weald Common
PRIORY DR
PRIORY CL
1
Bentley Priory
London Loop
Tenn Cts
Levels Wood
93
A409
Mast
14
24
15
16
HA7
Deer Park
Harrow Weald Common
Grimsdyke Hotel
The
Heriot's Wood
Hertfordshire STREET ATLAS

A · B · C · D

Allot Gdns

96

ALLUM LA

Home Farm

Aldenham Ctry Pk

Laboratory

LISTER COTTS

DAGGER LA

Aldenham Resr

Sailing Club

Pav

ALDENHAM RD

Cemy

6

ROMELAND CT

ELSTREE HILL N

B5378

A5183

THE BARTONS

St Nicholas CE Prim Sch

ROMELAND

St Nicholas CL

Elstree

Sp Gd

Tenn Cts

LANDS' END

NEW RD

TREE CT

OAK TREE CT

GEORGES MEAD

5

WD6

WATFORD RD

PH

SCHUBERT RD

BRITTEN CL

FOX CL

RODGERS CL

WEBBER CL

DELIUS CL

BEETHOVEN RD

SULLIVAN WAY

BEEHIVE

HIGH ST

PO

A411

VALENTINE CT

MAY GDNS

FORTUNE LA

SUMMER GR

WEST VIEW GDNS

Tenn Cts

The L

ELSTREE RD

Lismirrane Ind Pk

DYLAN CL

ELGAR CL

COATES RD

ELSTREE HILL S

A5183

Edgwarebury House Farm

95

Te C

WD23

Hertfordshire

Harrow

NORTH WESTERN AVE (WATFORD BY-PASS)

CENTENNIAL AVE

Centennial Pk

Centennial Ct

4

London Loop

Brockleyhill Farm

A5

4

Hertfordshire

Barnet

M1

10

Sp Gd

Brockley Grange

Tenn Cts

BROCKLEY HILL HO

3

HA8

Annandale

NUTT GR

A41 EDGWARE WAY (WATFORD BY-PASS)

94

Works

HA7

SIR HENRY FLOYD CT

Grove Farm

Royal National Orthopaedic

H

Pear Wood Cottages

BROCKLEY HILL

Brockley Hill

CH

Barnet

Harrow

2

THE LIMES

Limes House

WARREN LA

WOOD LA

Wood Farm

Pear Wood

Crkt Gd

LANCASTER HO

Pav

SPRINGFIELD CL

HILLTOP WY

Tenn Cts

Springbok House

Cloisters Wood

Tenn Cts

JULIUS CAESAR WAY

AUGUSTUS CL

CLAUDIUS CL

1

BROOMFIELD HO 1
FALLOWFIELD CT 2
HILL HO 3
WELLINGTON HO 4

LITTLE COMMON

DENNIS LA

A5

A5

Brockley Hill

FAUNA CL

CHEVALIER CL

BERRY HILL

BROCKLEY AVE

PARTRIDGE

REFS

93

FALLOWFIELD

AYLMER RISE

AYLMER DR

STANMORE HILL

30

AYLMER CL

PINE CL

HERIOTS CL

OLD FORGE CL

SPRING LAKE

Stanmore Hall

HALL LA

DENNIS LA

KN

GLANLEAM RD

NEWLANDS CL

GRANTHAM CL

HAMLYN CL

PIPERS

GREEN LA

REENGLASS RD

KER

OCKLEYSIDE

PO

Elstree

Deacons Hill

WD6

NW7

Edgware Bury

HA8

HA7

DUNBLANE CL 1
KINROSS CL 2
MOIDART CT 3
MALLAIG CT 4
OBAN CT 5
ARRAN CT 6
TORRIDON CT 7
ROSS CT 8

PARKLANDS PL 6
COMPASS CL 7

1 WARE CT
2 WAKEMAN HO
3 ABINGDON CT
4 CHICHELE HO
5 HAVILLAND CT

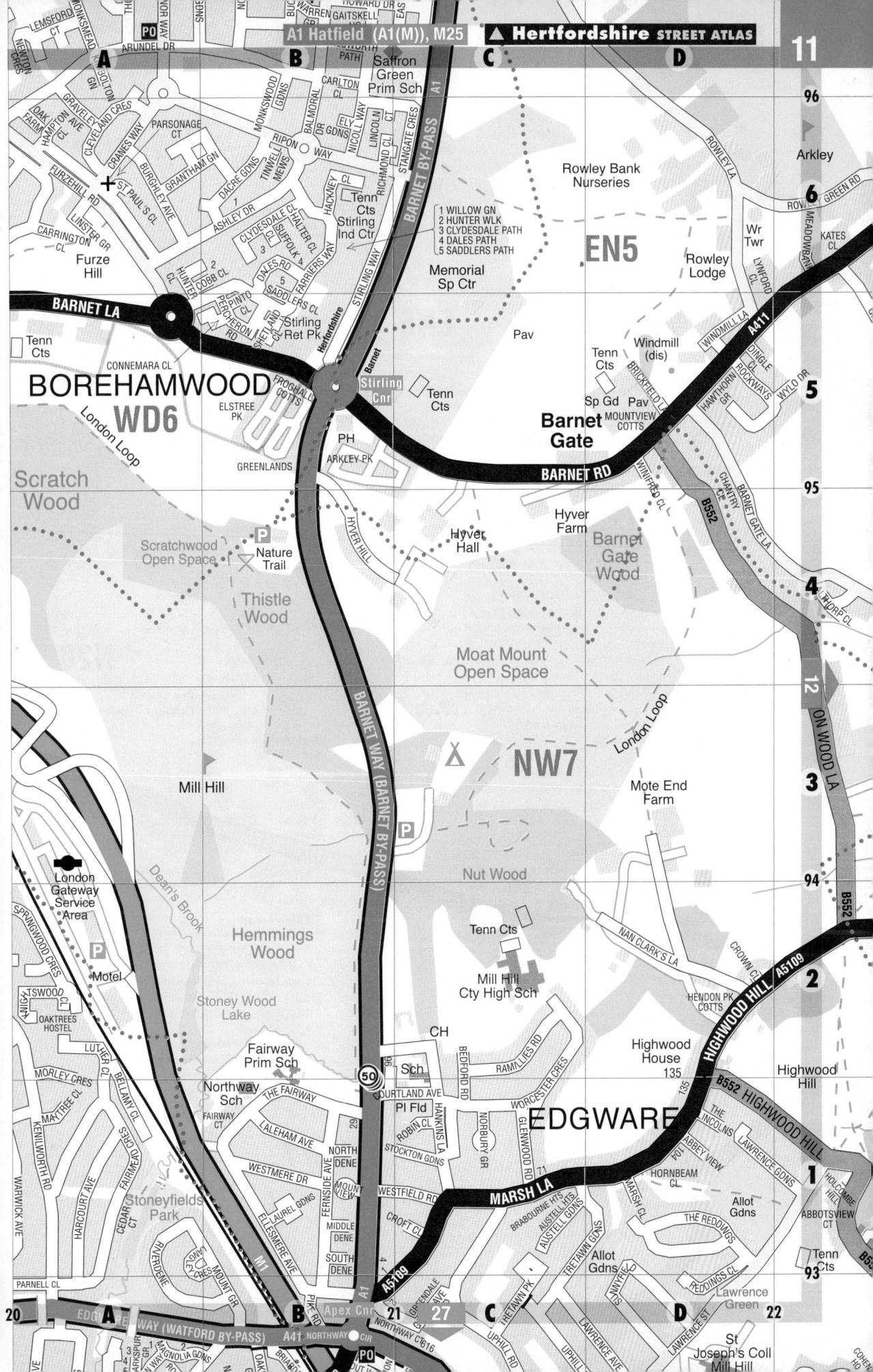
BOREHAMWOOD
WD6
EN5
NW7
EDGWARE
Barnet Gate
Arkley
Furze Hill
Scratch Wood
Scratchwood Open Space
Nature Trail
Thistle Wood
Moat Mount Open Space
Mill Hill
London Gateway Service Area
Hemmings Wood
Stoney Wood Lake
Nut Wood
Mill Hill Cty High Sch
Fairway Prim Sch
Northway Sch
Stoneyfields Park
Highwood House
Highwood Hill
Mote End Farm
Hyver Farm
Hyver Hall
Barnet Gate Wood
Rowley Bank Nurseries
Rowley Lodge
Memorial Sp Ctr
Saffron Green Prim Sch
Stirling Cnr
BARNET LA
BARNET RD
BARNET BY-PASS
BARNET WAY (BARNET BY-PASS)
HIGHWOOD HILL
MARSH LA
EDGWARE WAY (WATFORD BY-PASS)
London Loop
1 WILLOW GN
2 HUNTER WLK
3 CLYDESDALE PATH
4 DALES PATH
5 SADDLERS PATH
Lawrence Green
St Joseph's Coll Mill Hill
Apex Cnr

12
27

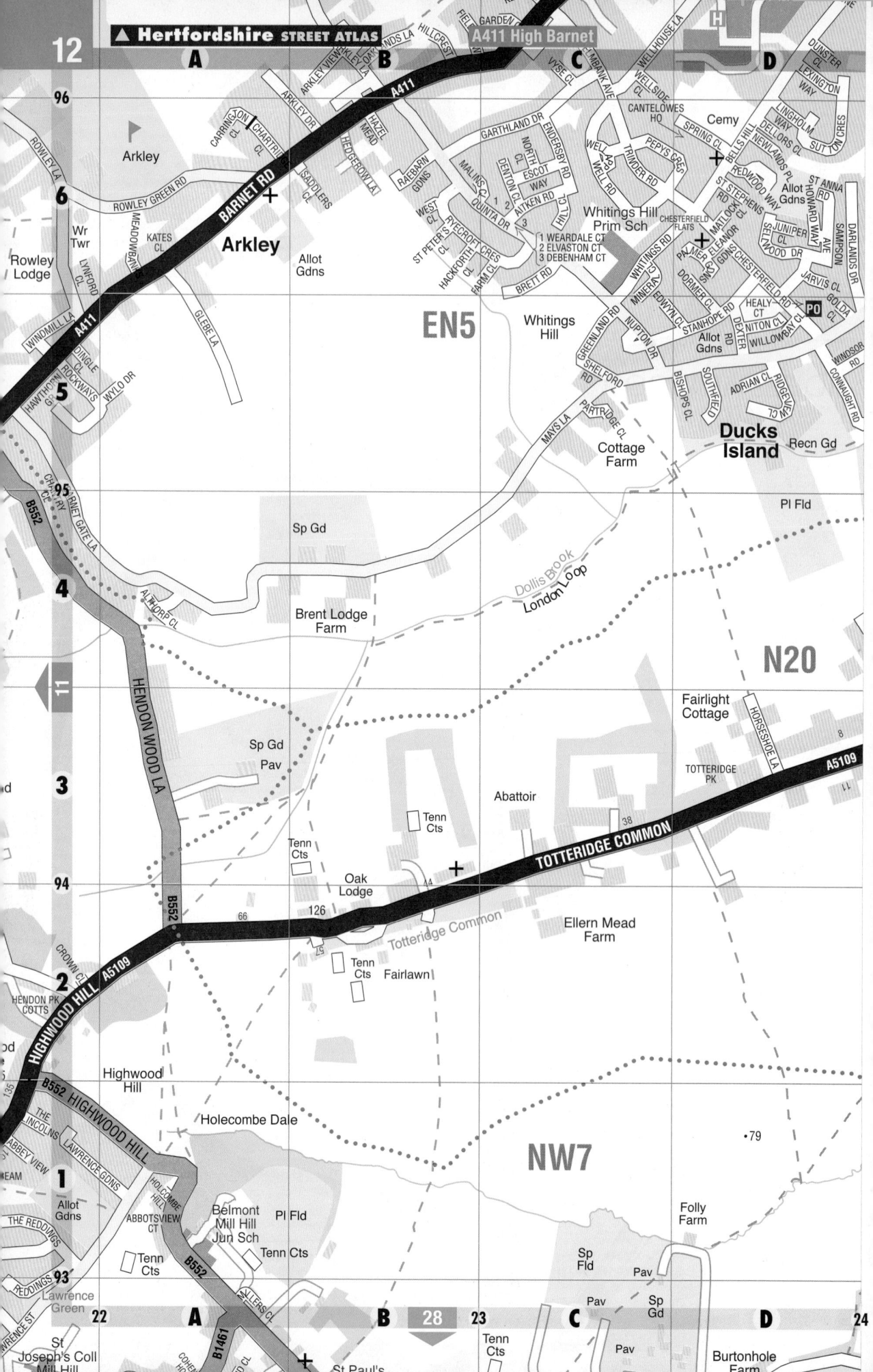
A411 High Barnet
A
B
C
D
96
6
5
95
4
11
3
94
2
1
93
22
28
23
24
Arkley
Rowley Lodge
Wr Twr
Arkley
Allot Gdns
EN5
Whitings Hill
Whitings Hill Prim Sch
Cantelowes Ho
Cemy
Allot Gdns
Ducks Island
Recn Gd
Cottage Farm
Pl Fld
Sp Gd
Brent Lodge Farm
Dollis Brook
London Loop
N20
Fairlight Cottage
Totteridge Pk
Sp Gd
Pav
Abattoir
Tenn Cts
Tenn Cts
Oak Lodge
Totteridge Common
Ellern Mead Farm
Tenn Cts
Fairlawn
Highwood Hill
Holecombe Dale
NW7
Folly Farm
Belmont Mill Hill Jun Sch
Pl Fld
Tenn Cts
Tenn Cts
Sp Fld
Pav
Pav
Sp Gd
Pav
Tenn Cts
Burtonhole Farm
St Joseph's Coll Mill Hill
St Paul's
Lawrence Green
A411
BARNET RD
B552
A5109
HENDON WOOD LA
TOTTERIDGE COMMON
HIGHWOOD HILL
B552 HIGHWOOD HILL
B1461
ROWLEY LA
ROWLEY GREEN RD
MEADOWBANKS
KATES CL
LYNFORD CL
WINDMILL LA
DINGLE CL
ROCKWAYS
WYLO DR
HAWTHORN GR
CARRINGTON CL
CHARTRIDGE CL
ARKLEY DR
ARKLEY VIEW
SADDLERS CL
HEDGEROW LA
HAZEL MEAD
HILLCREST
RAEBARN GDNS
WEST CL
ST PETER'S CL
RYECROFT CRES
HACKFORTH CL
FARM CL
MALINS CL
QUINTA DR
DENTON CL
NORTH CL
ESCOT WAY
AITKEN RD
HILL CL
ENDERSBY RD
GARTHLAND DR
VYSE CL
ELMBANK AVE
WELLHOUSE LA
WELLSIDE CL
WELL APP
WELL RD
TRIMDER RD
PEPYS CRES
SPRING CL
BELLS HILL
1 WEARDALE CT
2 ELVASTON CT
3 DEBENHAM CT
BRETT RD
CHESTERFIELD FLATS
WHITINGS RD
MINERVA CL
EDWYN CL
PALMER GDNS
ELEANOR CL
MATLOCK CL
ST STEPHENS RD
REDWOOD WAY
NEWLANDS PL
DELLORS CL
LINGHOLM WAY
SUTTON CRES
LEXINGTON WAY
DUNSTER CL
ST ANNA RD
HOWARD WAY
JUNIPER CL
SELLWOOD DR
SAMPSON AVE
DARLANDS DR
JARVIS CL
GOLDA CL
CHESTERFIELD RD
HEALY CT
DORMER CL
STANHOPE RD
DEXTER RD
NITON CL
WILLOWBAY CL
WINDSOR RD
CONNAUGHT RD
GREENLAND RD
NUPTON DR
SHELFORD RD
BISHOPS CL
SOUTHFIELD
ADRIAN CL
RIDGEVIEW CL
MAYS LA
PARTRIDGE CL
GLEBE LA
CHANTRY CL
BARNET GATE LA
ALTHORP CL
HORSESHOE LA
CROWN CL
HENDON PK COTTS
THE LINCOLNS
LAWRENCE GDNS
ABBEY VIEW
THE REDDINGS
REDDINGS
HOLCOMBE HILL
ABBOTSVIEW CT
PO

A411 High Barnet
11
28

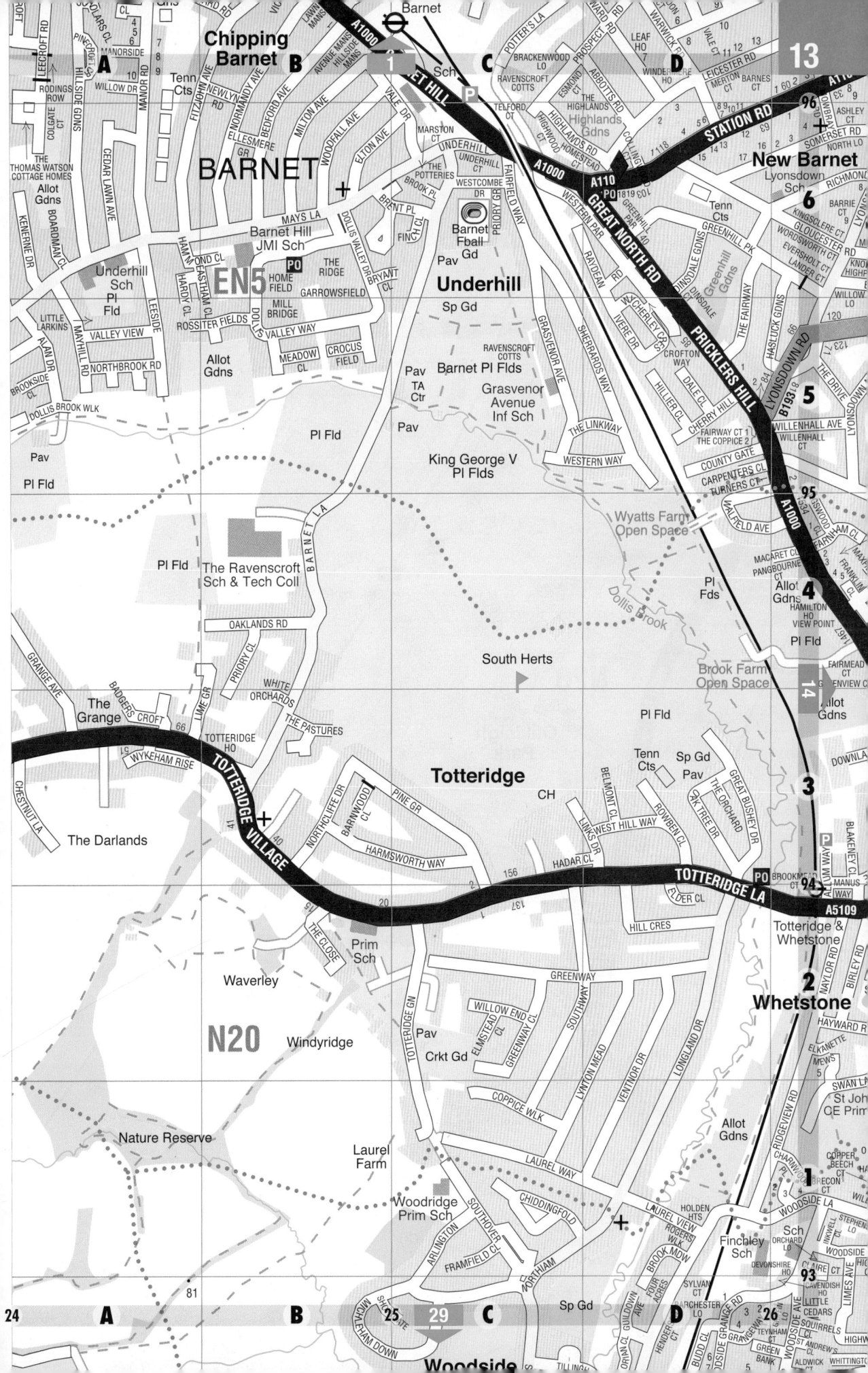
Barnet
Chipping Barnet
BARNET
EN5
Underhill
Underhill Sch
Barnet Hill JMI Sch
Barnet Fball Gd
Highlands Gdns
New Barnet
Lyonsdown Sch
Greenhill Gdns
STATION RD
GREAT NORTH RD
PRICKLERS HILL
A1000
A110
B193
LYONSDOWN RD
MAYS LA
UNDERHILL
FAIRFIELD WAY
WESTERN PAR
DOLLIS VALLEY DR
GARROWSFIELD
ROSSITER FIELDS
VALLEY WAY
VALLEY VIEW
NORTHBROOK RD
DOLLIS BROOK WLK
Barnet Pl Flds
Grasvenor Avenue Inf Sch
GRASVENOR AVE
SHERRARDS WAY
THE LINKWAY
WESTERN WAY
King George V Pl Flds
Wyatts Farm Open Space
Dollis Brook
Brook Farm Open Space
The Ravenscroft Sch & Tech Coll
BARNET LA
OAKLANDS RD
South Herts
Totteridge
The Grange
GRANGE AVE
WYKEHAM RISE
TOTTERIDGE VILLAGE
TOTTERIDGE LA
A5109
The Darlands
CHESTNUT LA
NORTHCLIFFE DR
HARMSWORTH WAY
BELMONT CL
WEST HILL WAY
GREAT BUSHEY DR
Totteridge & Whetstone
Whetstone
Prim Sch
Waverley
Windyridge
N20
Nature Reserve
TOTTERIDGE GN
Crkt Gd
GREENWAY
SOUTHWAY
LYNTON MEAD
VENTNOR DR
LONGLAND DR
COPPICE WLK
LAUREL WAY
Laurel Farm
Woodridge Prim Sch
Allot Gdns
Finchley Sch
WOODSIDE LA
RIDGEVIEW RD
St John's CE Prim
Woodside
24
A
B
25
29
C
D
26
14

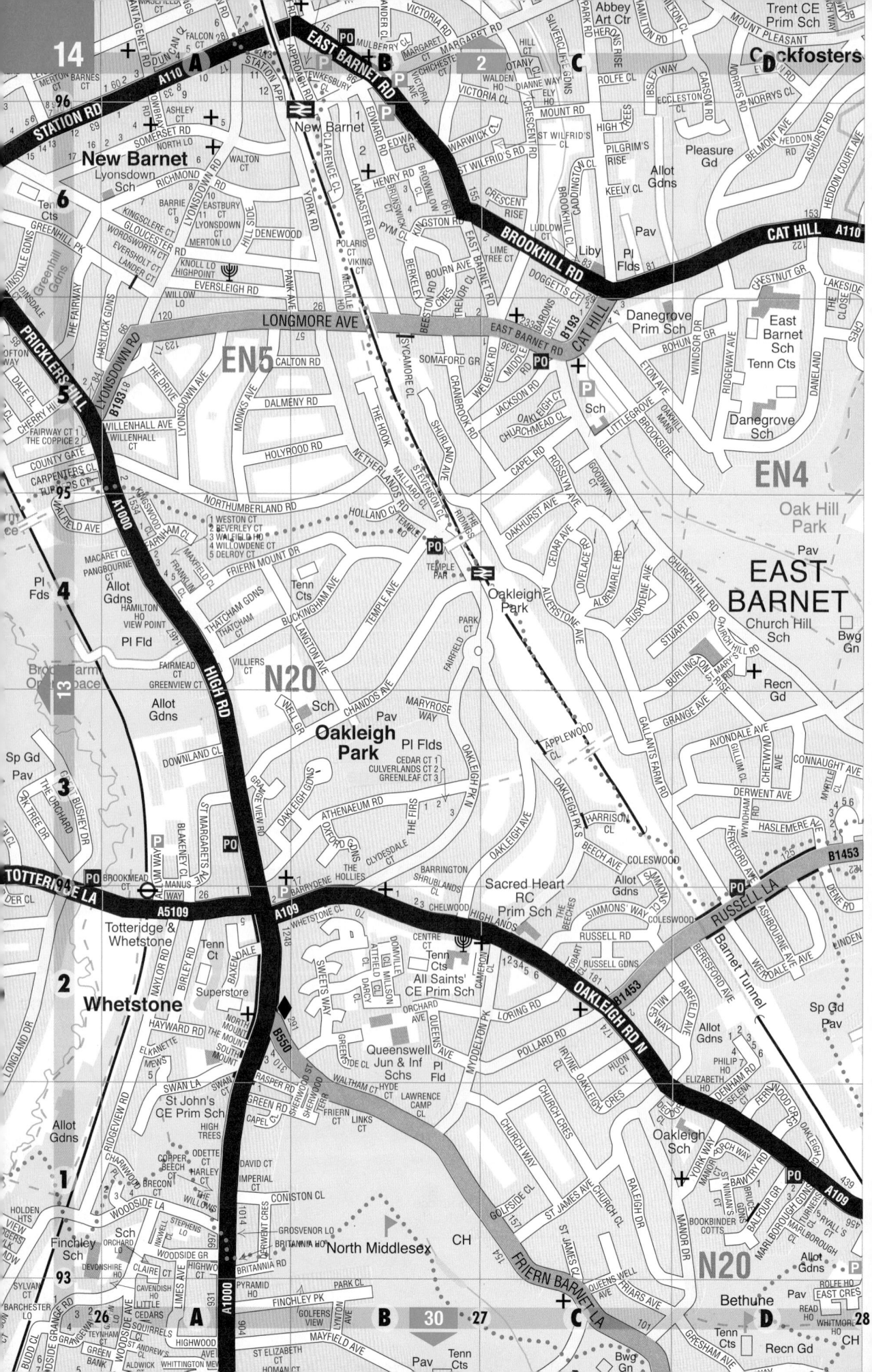
New Barnet
Cockfosters
Trent CE Prim Sch
Abbey Art Ctr
EAST BARNET RD
STATION RD
A110
CAT HILL
BROOKHILL RD
LONGMORE AVE
EN5
EN4
N20
Lyonsdown Sch
Pleasure Gd
Allot Gdns
Danegrove Prim Sch
East Barnet Sch
Danegrove Sch
Oak Hill Park
EAST BARNET
Church Hill Sch
Oakleigh Park
PRICKLERS HILL
A1000
HIGH RD
Totteridge & Whetstone
Whetstone
TOTTERIDGE LA
A5109
A109
OAKLEIGH RD N
RUSSELL LA
B1453
Barnet Tunnel
Sacred Heart RC Prim Sch
All Saints' CE Prim Sch
Queenswell Jun & Inf Schs
St John's CE Prim Sch
Oakleigh Sch
Finchley Sch
North Middlesex
FRIERN BARNET LA
B550
Bethune Recn Gd
Superstore
30
2
13
28
Greenhill Gdns
Brook Farm Open Space
Sp Gd
Pl Fld
Tenn Cts
Liby
Pav
CH

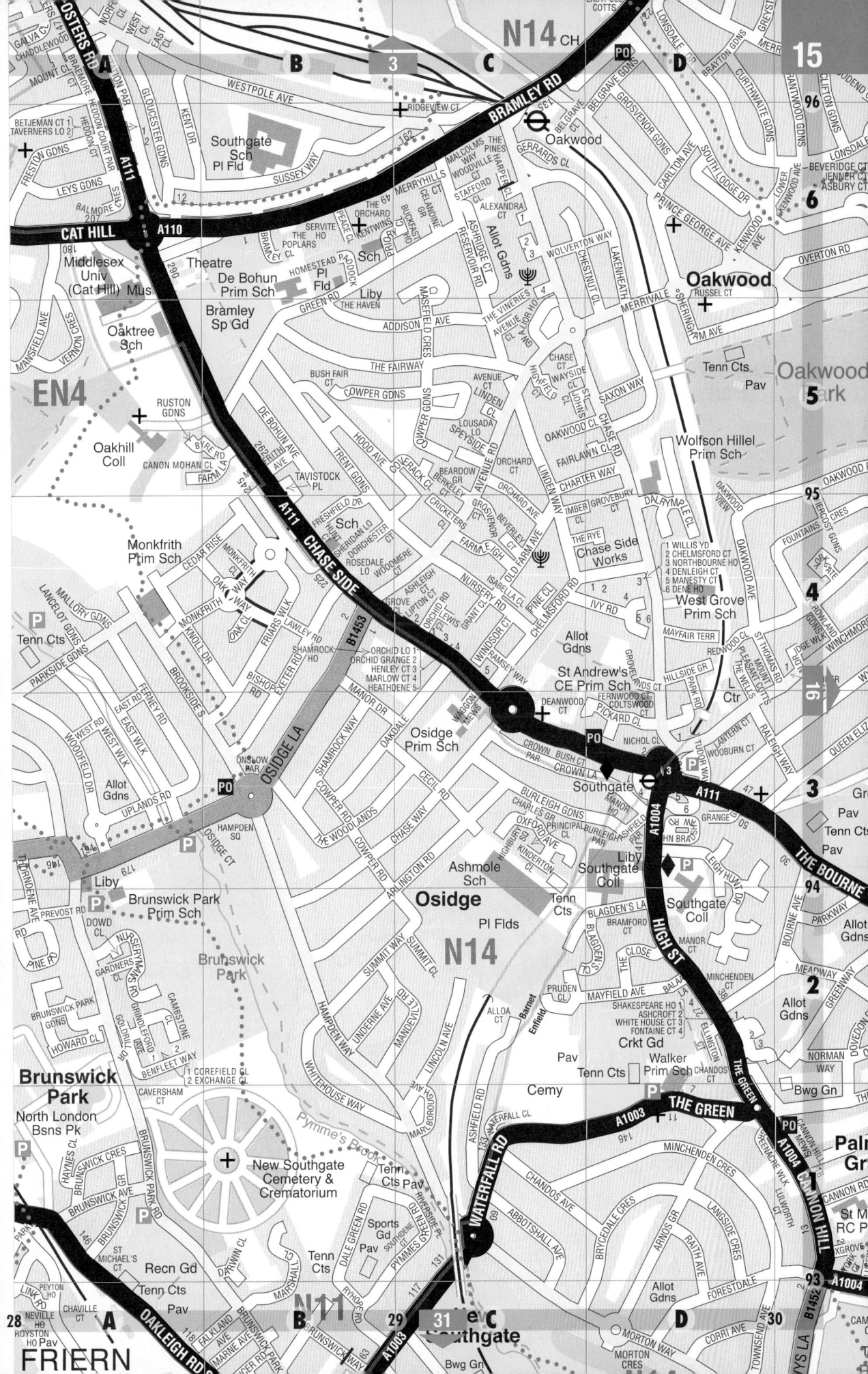
15
N14
A
B
3
C
D
BRAMLEY RD
WESTPOLE AVE
RIDGEVIEW CT
Southgate Sch Pl Fld
SUSSEX WAY
GLOUCESTER GDNS
KENT DR
Oakwood
BELGRAVE GDNS
GROSVENOR GDNS
CARLTON AVE
SOUTH LODGE DR
CURTHWAITE GDNS
BRAYTON GDNS
LONSDALE DR
96
CLIFTON GDNS
BEVERIDGE CT
JENNER CT
ASBURY CT
6
PRINCE GEORGE AVE
KENWOOD AVE
OVERTON RD
Oakwood
RUSSEL CT
SHERINGHAM AVE
MERRIVALE
CAT HILL
A110
A111
FRESTON GDNS
LEYS GDNS
BETJEMAN CT 1
TAVERNERS LO 2
CHADDLEWOOD
MOUNT CL
Middlesex Univ (Cat Hill)
Mus
Theatre
De Bohun Prim Sch
Bramley Sp Gd
Oaktree Sch
MANSFIELD AVE
VERNON CRES
EN4
RUSTON GDNS
Oakhill Coll
CANON MOHAN CL
FARM LA
BYRE RD
MERRYHILLS
THE ORCHARD
KENTWINS
SERVITE HO
THE POPLARS
HOMESTEAD PL
Pl Fld
Sch
Liby
THE HAVEN
GREEN RD
ADDISON AVE
THE FAIRWAY
BUSH FAIR CT
COWPER GDNS
MASEFIELD CRES
STAFFORD CL
ALEXANDRA CT
Allot Gdns
RESERVOIR RD
ASHRIDGE CT
GERRARDS CL
WOLVERTON WAY
CHESTNUT CL
LAKENHEATH
THE VINERIES
AVENUE CL
HIGHFIELD CT
CHASE CT
WAYSIDE CL
SAXON WAY
Tenn Cts
Pav
Oakwood Park
5
Wolfson Hillel Prim Sch
OAKWOOD CL
FAIRLAWN CL
CHARTER WAY
CHASE RD
LINDEN WAY
AVENUE RD
HOOD AVE
TRENT GDNS
DE BOHUN AVE
TAVISTOCK PL
SPEYSIDE
LOUSADA LO
ORCHARD CT
ORCHARD AVE
BEARDOW GR
CRICKETERS CL
GROSVENOR CL
BEVERLEY CT
FARM LEIGH
OLD FARM AVE
IMBER CL
GROVEBURY CT
DALRYMPLE CL
THE RYE
Chase Side Works
1 WILLIS YD
2 CHELMSFORD CT
3 NORTHBOURNE HO
4 DENLEIGH CT
5 MANESTY CT
6 DENE HO
West Grove Prim Sch
OAKWOOD VIEW
OAKWOOD AVE
95
FOUNTAINS CRES
4
Monkfrith Prim Sch
CEDAR RISE
MONKFRITH WAY
OAK CL
FRIARS WLK
CHASE SIDE
Sch
FRESHFIELD DR
SHERIDAN LO
DORCHESTER CT
ROSEDALE LO
WOODMERE CT
ASHLEIGH CT
LIPTON CT
ORCHID RD
NURSERY RD
ISABELLA CL
PINE CL
CHELMSFORD RD
IVY RD
MALLORY GDNS
LANCELOT GDNS
Tenn Cts
PARKSIDE GDNS
KNOLL DR
BROOKSIDE S
LAWLEY RD
EXETER RD
BISHOP RD
SHAMROCK HO
B1453
ORCHID LO 1
ORCHID GRANGE 2
HENLEY CT 3
MARLOW CT 4
HEATHDENE 5
WINDSOR CT
RAMSEY WAY
Allot Gdns
St Andrew's CE Prim Sch
GROVELANDS CT
HILLSIDE GR
MAYFAIR TERR
REDWOOD CL
ST THOMAS RD
L Ctr
16
WINCHMORE
DEANWOOD CT
FERNWOOD CT
COLTSWOOD CT
PICKARD CL
NICHOL CL
TUDOR WAY
LANTERN CL
WOOBURN CT
RALEIGH WAY
QUEEN ELIZ
3
EAST RD
FERNEY RD
WEST RD
WEST WLK
EAST WLK
WOODFIELD DR
Allot Gdns
UPLANDS RD
ONSLOW PAR
OSIDGE LA
PO
HAMPDEN SQ
OSIDGE CT
MANOR DR
OAKDALE
SHAMROCK WAY
Osidge Prim Sch
WAGGON MEWS
CROWN BUSH CT
CROWN LA
Southgate
A1004
GRANGE
THE BOURNE
Tenn Cts
Pav
COWPER RD
THE WOODLANDS
CECIL RD
CHASE WAY
BURLEIGH GDNS
CHARLES GR
OXFORD AVE
PRINCIPAL CL
BURLEIGH PAR
ASHFIELD PAR
KINDERTON CL
HIGHBURY GR
Liby
Southgate Coll
Southgate Coll
LEIGH HUNT DR
94
BOURNE AVE
PARKWAY
Allot Gdns
Liby
Brunswick Park Prim Sch
PREVOST RD
DOWD CL
NURSERYMANS RD
THORNDENE AVE
PINE RD
ARLINGTON RD
Ashmole Sch
Osidge
Pl Flds
N14
Tenn Cts
BLAGDEN'S LA
BRAMFORD CT
HIGH ST
THE CLOSE
MANOR CT
MINCHENDEN CT
SUMMIT WAY
SUMMIT CL
Brunswick Park
GARDNERS CL
CAMBSTONE CL
GRINDLEFORD AVE
BRUNSWICK PARK GDNS
HOWARD CL
BENFLEET WAY
1 COREFIELD CL
2 EXCHANGE CL
HAMPDEN WAY
UNDERNE AVE
MANDEVILLE RD
LINCOLN AVE
ALLOA CT
PRUDEN CL
MAYFIELD AVE
SHAKESPEARE HO 1
ASHCROFT 2
WHITE HOUSE CT 3
FONTAINE CT 4
Crkt Gd
ELLINGTON CT
MEADWAY
GREENWAY
2
Allot Gdns
NORMAN WAY
Bwg Gn
Brunswick Park
North London Bsns Pk
CAVERSHAM CT
WHITEHOUSE WAY
MARLBOROUGH AVE
Pav
Tenn Cts
Walker Prim Sch
CHANDOS CT
Cemy
ASHFIELD RD
WATERFALL CL
A1003
THE GREEN
THE GREEN
CANNON MEWS
A1004
Palm Gr
HAYNES CL
BRUNSWICK CRES
BRUNSWICK AVE
BRUNSWICK GR
BRUNSWICK PARK RD
New Southgate Cemetery & Crematorium
Pymme's Brook
Tenn Cts Pav
MINCHENDEN CRES
GREENACRE WLK
LULWORTH CT
CANNON HILL
CANNON RD
1
St M RC P
WATERFALL RD
CHANDOS AVE
ABBOTSHALL AVE
BRYCEDALE CRES
ARNOS GR
RAITH AVE
LANGSIDE CRES
ST MICHAEL'S CT
Recn Gd
DARWIN CL
MARSHALL CL
Tenn Cts
Sports Gd
Pav
DALE GREEN RD
SOUTHDENE CT
PYMMES GREEN RD
RIVERSIDE PL
Allot Gdns
FORESTDALE
93
A1004
B1452
Tenn Cts
Pav
PEYTON HO
LINK RD
CHAVILLE CT
NEVILLE HO
ROYSTON HO
28
Pav
FRIERN
OAKLEIGH RD
FALKLAND AVE
MARNE AVE
BRUNSWICK PARK
N11
RYHOPE RD
29
31
C
New Southgate
D
MORTON WAY
MORTON CRES
CORRI AVE
TOWNSEND AVE
30
Bwg Gn

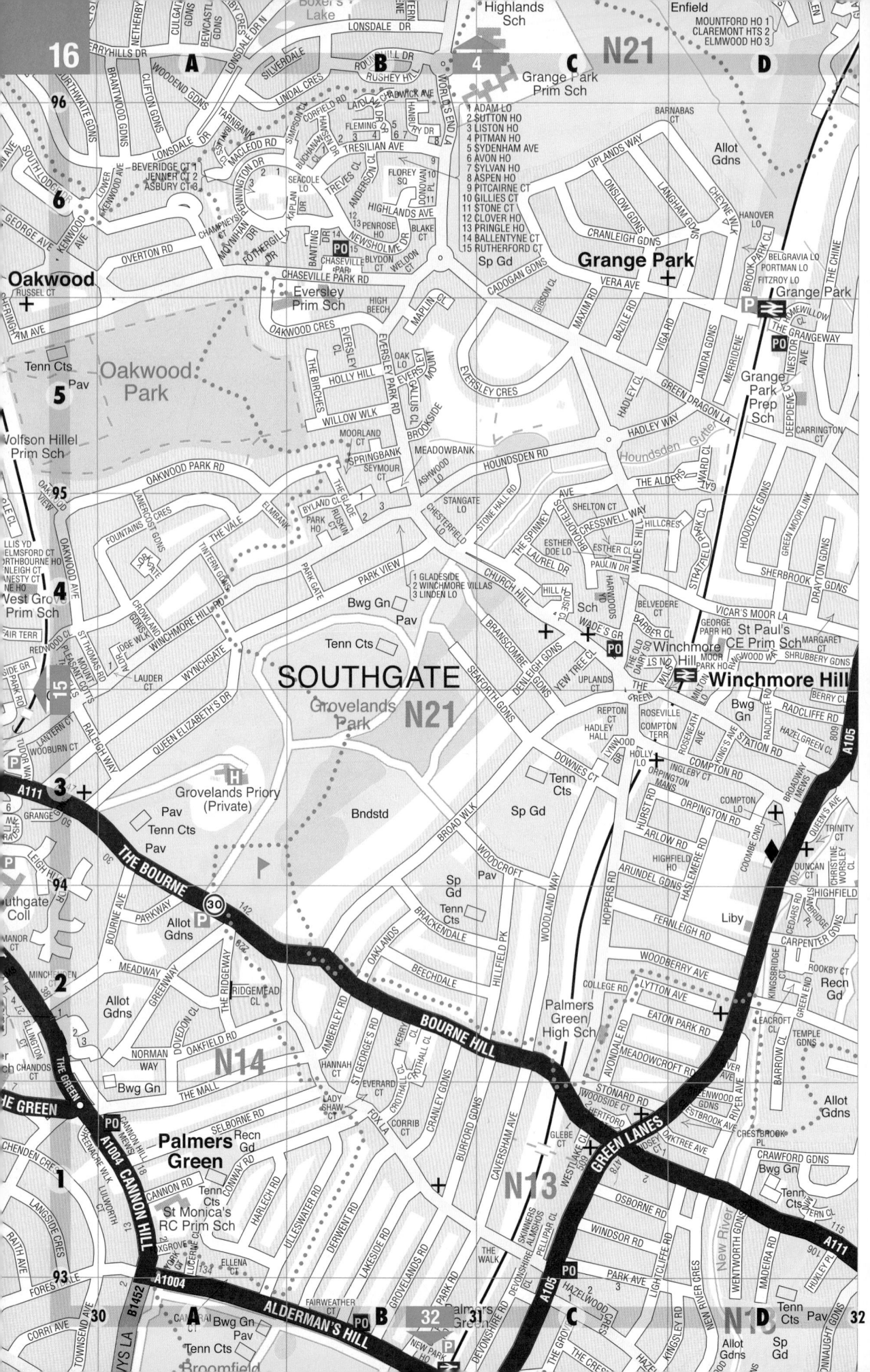
16
A
B
C
D
4
N21
Highlands Sch
Enfield
Grange Park Prim Sch
1 ADAM LO
2 SUTTON HO
3 LISTON HO
4 PITMAN HO
5 SYDENHAM AVE
6 AVON HO
7 SYLVAN HO
8 ASPEN HO
9 PITCAIRNE CT
10 GILLIES CT
11 STONE CT
12 CLOVER HO
13 PRINGLE HO
14 BALLENTYNE CT
15 RUTHERFORD CT
MOUNTFORD HO 1
CLAREMONT HTS 2
ELMWOOD HO 3
BEVERIDGE CT 1
JENNER CT 2
ASBURY CT 3
Oakwood
Eversley Prim Sch
Grange Park
Oakwood Park
Tenn Cts
Pav
Wolfson Hillel Prim Sch
West Grove Prim Sch
1 GLADESIDE
2 WINCHMORE VILLAS
3 LINDEN LO
SOUTHGATE
Grovelands Park
N21
Winchmore Hill
St Paul's CE Prim Sch
Grange Park Prep Sch
Grovelands Priory (Private)
Bndstd
Sp Gd
Allot Gdns
Palmers Green High Sch
THE BOURNE
BOURNE HILL
GREEN LANES
CANNON HILL
ALDERMAN'S HILL
A111
A105
A1004
B1452
N14
N13
Palmers Green
St Monica's RC Prim Sch
Southgate Coll
15
32
96
95
94
93
30
31
32
6
5
4
3
2
1

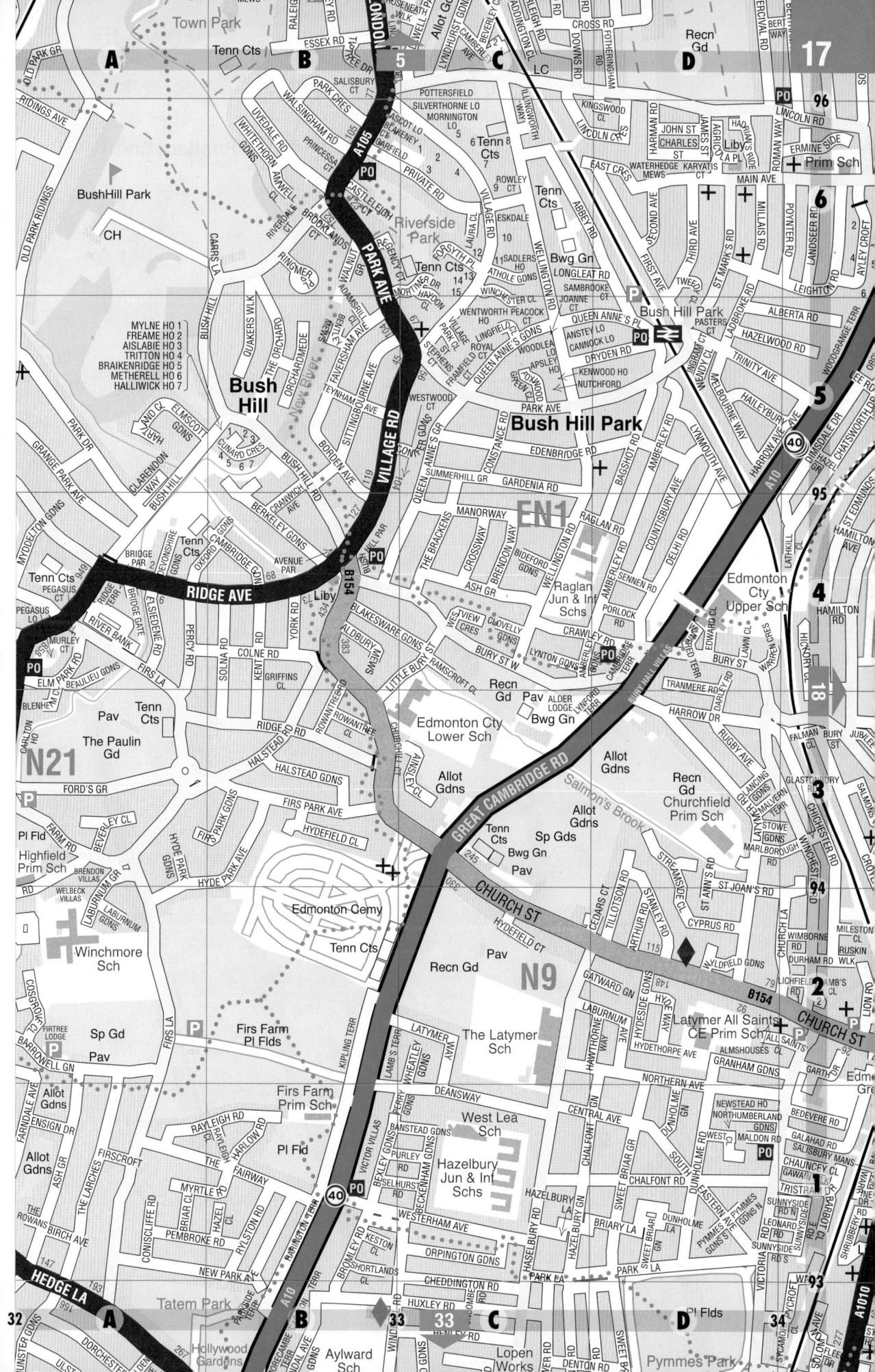
17
A
B
C
D
5
6
4
3
2
1
32
33
34
18
Town Park
Tenn Cts
ESSEX RD
OLD PARK GR
RIDINGS AVE
BushHill Park
CH
OLD PARK RIDINGS
SALISBURY CT
PARK CRES
WALSINGHAM RD
UVEDALE RD
WHITETHORN GDNS
PRINCESSA CT
ANNWELL CL
RIVERDALE CT
BROOKLANDS CT
CASTLELEIGH CT
A105
PARK AVE
Riverside Park
POTTERSFIELD
SILVERTHORNE LO
MORNINGTON LO
ASCOT LO
BLAKENEY
GARFIELD
PRIVATE RD
VILLAGE RD
LAURA CL
ROWLEY CT
ESKDALE
ILLINGWORTH WAY
LYNDHURST GDNS
CROSS RD
FOTHERINGHAM RD
DOWNS RD
Recn Gd
KINGSWOOD CL
LINCOLN CRES
HARMAN RD
JOHN ST
CHARLES ST
JAMES ST
AGRICOLA PL
Liby
HADRIANS RIDE
ROMAN WAY
LINCOLN RD
ERMINE SIDE
Prim Sch
EAST CRES
WATERHEDGE MEWS
KARYATIS CT
MAIN AVE
SECOND AVE
FIRST AVE
THIRD AVE
ST MARK'S RD
MILLAIS RD
POYNTER RD
LANDSEER RD
AYLEY CROFT
LEIGHTON RD
ABBEY RD
WELLINGTON RD
Tenn Cts
Bwg Gn
LONGLEAT RD
SAMBROOKE CT
JOANNE CT
QUEEN ANNE'S PL
Bush Hill Park
PASTERS CT
ALBERTA RD
HAZELWOOD RD
TRINITY AVE
HAILEYBURY AVE
MELBOURNE WAY
WENDY CL
INGRAM CT
LADBROKE RD
WOODGRANGE TERR
HARROW AVE
DIMSDALE DR
CHATSWORTH DR
ST EDMUNDS
HAMILTON AVE
HAMILTON RD
A10
40
95
96
94
93
RINGMER PL
WALNUT GR
REGENCY CT
FORSYTH PL
MORTIMER DR
HAYDON CL
SADLERS HO
ATHOLE GDNS
WINCHESTER CL
WENTWORTH HO
PEACOCK CT
LINGFIELD CL
ROYAL CT
QUEEN ANNE'S GDNS
WOODLEA LO
APSLEY HO
ANSTEY LO
CANNOCK LO
DRYDEN RD
KENWOOD HO
NUTCHFORD
FOXWOOD GREEN CL
STEPHENS
FRAMFIELD CT
VILLAGE PARK CL
ADAMSRILL CL
BENTLEY MEWS
FAVERSHAM AVE
TEYNHAM AVE
SITTINGBOURNE AVE
BORDEN AVE
VILLAGE RD
WESTWOOD CT
COWPER GDNS
QUEEN ANNE'S GR
CONSTANCE RD
PARK AVE
EDENBRIDGE RD
BAGSHOT RD
AMBERLEY RD
LYNMOUTH AVE
SUMMERHILL GR
GARDENIA RD
COUNTISBURY AVE
DELHI RD
EN1
MANORWAY
THE BRACKENS
CROSSWAY
BRENDON WAY
BIDEFORD GDNS
RAGLAN RD
SENNEN RD
Raglan Jun & Inf Schs
ASH GR
WESTVIEW CRES
CLOVELLY GDNS
PORLOCK RD
CRAWLEY RD
LYNTON GDNS
CAMBRIDGE TERR
BURY ST W
Edmonton Cty Upper Sch
EDWARD CL
LAWN CL
WARREN CRES
HICKORY CL
BURY ST
TRANMERE RD
DARLEY RD
HARROW DR
RUGBY AVE
FALMAN CL
BURY ST
JUBILEE
MYLNE HO 1
FREAME HO 2
AISLABIE HO 3
TRITTON HO 4
BRAIKENRIDGE HO 5
METHERELL HO 6
HALLIWICK HO 7
CARRS LA
BUSH HILL
QUAKERS WLK
THE ORCHARD
ORCHARDMEDE
New River
Bush Hill
HARTLAND CL
ELMSCOTT GDNS
CUNARD CRES
CLARENDON WAY
BUSH HILL
PARK DR
GRANGE PARK AVE
BUSH HILL RD
CRANWICH AVE
BERKELEY GDNS
MYDDELTON GDNS
Tenn Cts
PEGASUS CT
BRIDGE PAR
DEVONSHIRE GDNS
Tenn Cts
OXFORD GDNS
CAMBRIDGE GDNS
AVENUE PAR
BUSH HILL PAR
B154
RIDGE AVE
PEGASUS LO
RIDGE TERR
BRIDGE GATE
ELSIEDENE RD
PERCY RD
SOLNA RD
KENT RD
YORK RD
Liby
RIVER BANK
MURLEY CT
COLNE RD
GRIFFINS CL
ELM PARK RD
BEAULIEU GDNS
FIRS LA
BLENHEIM CL
CARLTON HO
Pav
Tenn Cts
The Paulin Gd
N21
RIDGE RD
HALSTEAD RD
HALSTEAD GDNS
BLAKESWARE GDNS
ALDBURY MEWS
LITTLE BURY ST
RAMSCROFT CL
ROWANTREE RD
ROWANTREE CL
CHURCHILL CT
AINSLEY CL
Edmonton Cty Lower Sch
Recn Gd
Pav
ALDER LODGE
Bwg Gn
LYNFORD TERR
BURY HALL VILLAS
GREAT CAMBRIDGE RD
Allot Gdns
Allot Gdns
Allot Gdns
Salmon's Brook
Recn Gd
Churchfield Prim Sch
LANCING GDNS
MALVERN TERR
GLASTONBURY
CHICHESTER RD
SALMONS
STOWE GDNS
MARLBOROUGH RD
WINCHESTER RD
FORD'S GR
FIRS PARK AVE
FIRS PARK GDNS
HYDEFIELD CL
BEVERLEY CL
Pl Fld
FARM RD
Highfield Prim Sch
BRENDON VILLAS
LABURNUM GR
WELBECK VILLAS
LABURNUM GDNS
HYDE PARK GDNS
HYDE PARK AVE
Edmonton Cemy
Tenn Cts
Sp Gds
Bwg Gn
Pav
CHURCH ST
HYDEFIELD CT
CEDARS CT
TILLOTSON RD
ARTHUR RD
STANLEY RD
STREAMSIDE CL
ST ANN'S RD
ST JOAN'S RD
CYPRUS RD
CHURCH LA
WIMBORNE RD
DURHAM RD
MILESTONE CL
RUSKIN WLK
WYLDFIELD GDNS
Winchmore Sch
Recn Gd
Pav
N9
COSGROVE CL
FIRTREE LODGE
Sp Gd
Pav
BARROWELL GN
FIRS LA
Firs Farm Pl Flds
KIPLING TERR
LATYMER WAY
LAMB'S TERR
WHEATLEY GDNS
The Latymer Sch
GATWARD GN
LABURNUM AVE
HAWTHORNE WAY
HYDESIDE GDNS
HYDE WAY
Latymer All Saints CE Prim Sch
HYDETHORPE AVE
ALL SAINTS CL
ALMSHOUSES
LICHFIELD RD
LAMB'S CL
CHURCH ST
LION RD
GRANHAM GDNS
GARTH DR
Allot Gdns
FARNDALE AVE
ENSIGN DR
Firs Farm Prim Sch
DEANSWAY
PERRY GDNS
NORTHERN AVE
CENTRAL AVE
DUNHOLME GN
NEWSTEAD HO
NORTHUMBERLAND GDNS
BEDEVERE RD
Allot Gdns
ASH GR
RAYLEIGH RD
RAYLEIGH CL
HARLOW RD
Pl Fld
FIRSCROFT
THE LARCHES
THE FAIRWAY
West Lea Sch
BANSTEAD GDNS
PURLEY RD
SELHURST RD
BEXLEY GDNS
VICTOR VILLAS
BECKENHAM GDNS
Hazelbury Jun & Inf Schs
CHALFONT GN
SWEET BRIAR GR
CHALFONT RD
DUNHOLME RD
SOUTH EASTERN AVE
WEST CL
MALDON RD
GALAHAD RD
SALISBURY MANS
CHAUNCEY CL
GAWAIN WLK
TRISTRAM DR
MYRTLE RD
BRIAR CL
HAZEL CL
RYLSTON RD
CONISCLIFFE RD
PEMBROKE RD
THE ROWANS
BIRCH AVE
WESTERHAM AVE
HAZELBURY LA
HASELBURY RD
HAZELBURY GN
BRIARY LA
DUNHOLME LA
PYMMES GDNS N
PYMMES GDNS S
SUNNYSIDE RD N
SUNNYSIDE RD E
SUNNYSIDE RD S
LEONARD RD
BARBOT CL
SHRUBBERY RD
VICTORIA RD
KESTON CL
BROMLEY RD
ORPINGTON GDNS
NEW PARK AVE
SHORTLANDS CL
CHEDDINGTON RD
HUXLEY RD
PARK LA
PARK LA
PYCROFT WAY
HEDGE LA
Tatem Park
PARKSIDE TERR
HARINGTON TERR
Pl Flds
A1010
Hollywood Gardens
DORCHESTER
Aylward Sch
WINDMILL RD
HENLEY RD
Lopen Works
DENTON RD
Pymmes Park
MUNSTER GDNS

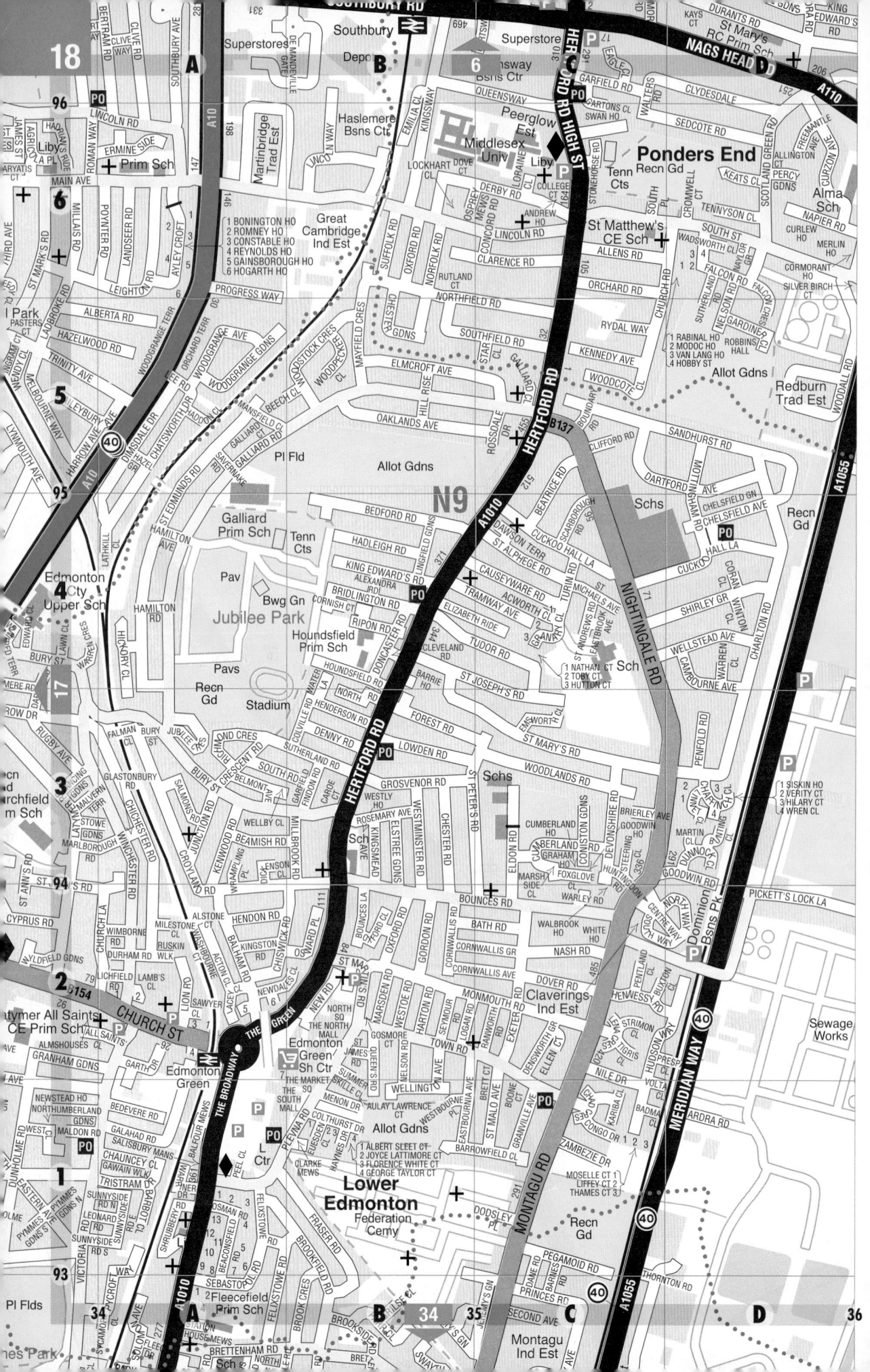

Southbury Rd
Southbury
Superstores
De Mandeville Gate
Depot
Superstore
Queensway Bsns Ctr
Queensway
Hertford Rd
High St
Nags Head Rd
A110
Durants Rd
Kays Ct
St Mary's RC Prim Sch
King Edward's Rd
Garfield Rd
Eagle Ct
Clydesdale
Cartons Cl
Swan Ho
Walters Rd
Sedcote Rd
Peerglow Est
Middlesex Univ
Liby
Haslemere Bsns Ctr
Martinbridge Trad Est
Lincoln Way
Emilia Cl
Kingsway
Ponders End
Recn Gd
Tenn Cts
Scotland Green Rd
Freemantle St
Allington Ct
Percy Gdns
Keats Cl
Curzon Ave
Alma Sch
Napier Rd
Curlew Ho
Merlin Ho
Cormorant Ho
Silver Birch Ct
Lockhart Cl
Dove Ct
Loraine Cl
College Ct
Stonehorse Rd
Derby Rd
Osprey Mews
Concord Rd
Andrew Ho
Lincoln Rd
St Matthew's CE Sch
Cromwell Ct
Tennyson Cl
South St
South Pl
Wadsworth Cl
Naylor Gr
Falcon Rd
Falcon Cres
Allens Rd
Clarence Rd
Orchard Rd
Church Rd
Sutherland Rd
Nelson Rd
Gardiner Cl
Robbins Hall
Great Cambridge Ind Est
Suffolk Rd
Oxford Rd
Norfolk Rd
Rutland Ct
Northfield Rd
Southfield Rd
Rydal Way
Kennedy Ave
Woodcote Cl
1 Rabinal Ho
2 Modoc Ho
3 Van Lang Ho
4 Hobby St
Allot Gdns
Redburn Trad Est
Woodall Rd
Chester Gdns
Star Cl
Galliard Cl
Mayfield Cres
Woodpecker Cl
Woodstock Cres
Elmcroft Ave
Hill Rise
Oaklands Ave
Rossdale Dr
Boundary Rd
B137
Clifford Rd
Sandhurst Rd
Dartford Ave
Nottingham Rd
Chelsfield Gn
Chelsfield Ave
Schs
Recn Gd
A1055
Bertram Rd
Clive Way
Clive Rd
Southbury Ave
A10
Lincoln Rd
Hadrian's Ride
Agricola Pl
Roman Way
Ermine Side
Prim Sch
James St
Caryatis Ct
Main Ave
Millais Rd
Poynter Rd
Landseer Rd
Ayley Croft
St Mark's Rd
Third Ave
Leighton Rd
1 Bonington Ho
2 Romney Ho
3 Constable Ho
4 Reynolds Ho
5 Gainsborough Ho
6 Hogarth Ho
Progress Way
Ladbroke Rd
Alberta Rd
Pasters Ct
Hazelwood Rd
Woodgrange Terr
Orchard Terr
Woodgrange Ave
Woodgrange Gdns
Trinity Ave
Wendy Cl
Melbourne Way
Leybury Way
Harrow Ave
Dimsdale Dr
Chatsworth Dr
Haddon Cl
Mansfield Cl
Beech Cl
Galliard Ct
Galliard Rd
Savernake Rd
Lynmouth Ave
Hazel Gr
St Edmunds Rd
Pl Fld
Allot Gdns
N9
A1010
Beatrice Rd
Scarborough Rd
Bedford Rd
Galliard Prim Sch
Tenn Cts
Hamilton Ave
Lathkill Cl
Hadleigh Rd
Lingfield Gdns
Dawson Terr
Cuckoo Hall La
St Alphege Rd
Edmonton Cty Upper Sch
Pav
Bwg Gn
Jubilee Park
King Edward's Rd
Alexandra Rd
Bridlington Rd
Cornish Ct
Causeyware Rd
Tramway Ave
Acworth Cl
Turin Rd
St Michaels Ave
Nightingale Rd
Shirley Gr
Coran Cl
Winton Cl
Hamilton Rd
Hickory Cl
Edward Cl
Lawn Cl
Warren Cres
Ripon Rd
Houndsfield Prim Sch
Elizabeth Ride
Granary Cl
St Andrews Rd
Eastbrook Ave
Wellstead Ave
Warren Cl
Charlton Rd
Bury St
Doncaster Rd
Cleveland Rd
Tudor Rd
1 Nathan Ct
2 Toby Ct
3 Hutton Ct
Sch
Camborne Ave
Pavs
Recn Gd
Stadium
Houndsfield Rd
Water La
Barrie Ho
St Joseph's Rd
North Rd
Henderson Rd
Colville Rd
Forest Rd
Emsworth Cl
Penfold Rd
Denny Rd
Falman Cl
Bury St
Jubilee Cres
Richmond Cres
Crescent Rd
Sutherland Rd
Lowden Rd
St Mary's Rd
Woodlands Rd
Rugby Ave
Glastonbury Rd
Belmont Ave
South Rd
Garfield Rd
Findon Rd
Carde Cl
Grosvenor Rd
Westly Ho
St Peter's Rd
Schs
Brierley Ave
Goodwin Ho
Chaffinch Cl
Linnet Cl
Bunting Cl
1 Siskin Ho
2 Verity Ct
3 Hilary Ct
4 Wren Cl
Latymer Gdns
Malvern Terr
Stowe Gdns
Marlborough Rd
Chichester Rd
Winchester Rd
Salmons Rd
Junction Rd
Wellby Cl
Beamish Rd
Millbrook Rd
Rosemary Ave
Kingsmead Ave
Elstree Gdns
Westminster Rd
Chester Rd
Eldon Rd
Cumberland Ho
Cumberland Ct
Graham Ho
Coniston Gdns
Devonshire Rd
Steering Cl
Huntingdon Rd
Martin Cl
Dunnock Cl
Goodwin Rd
Archfield Sch
Croyland Rd
Kenwood Rd
Wrampling Pl
Dickenson Cl
Marsh Side Cl
Foxglove Cl
Warley Rd
Bounces Rd
Pickett's Lock La
St Ann's Rd
Cyprus Rd
Church La
Wimborne Cl
Alstone Ct
Milestone Ct
Ruskin Wlk
Durham Rd
Washbourne Ct
Hendon Rd
Kingston Rd
Chiswick Rd
Ward Pl
Bounces La
Pitford Cl
Oxford Rd
Gordon Rd
Cornwallis Rd
Bath Rd
Cornwallis Gr
Cornwallis Ave
Walbrook Ho
White Ho
Nash Rd
North Way
Centre Way
South Way
Dominion Bsns Pk
Wyldfield Gdns
Lichfield Rd
Lamb's Cl
Lion Rd
Balham Rd
Acton Cl
Lacey Cl
Newdales Cl
St Martin's Rd
Marsden Rd
Westoe Rd
Harton Rd
Seymour Rd
Logan Rd
Monmouth Rd
Dover Rd
Claverings Ind Est
Pentland Cl
Buxton Rd
Hennessy Rd
B154
Church St
Latymer All Saints CE Prim Sch
All Saints' Cl
Almshouses
Sawyer Cl
The Green
New Rd
North Sq
The North Mall
Gosmore Ct
St James Rd
Queen's Rd
Ranworth Rd
Exeter Rd
Town Rd
Densworth Gr
Ellen Ct
Strimon Cl
Tigris Cl
Lena Cres
Hudson Way
Graham Gdns
Garth Rd
Edmonton Green
The Broadway
Edmonton Green Sh Ctr
The Market Sq
The South Mall
Skille Cl
Summer Rd
Nelson Rd
Wellington Ave
Brett Ct
Boone Ct
Nile Dr
Volta Cl
Menon Dr
Aulay Lawrence Ct
Westbourne Pl
Newstead Ho
Northumberland Gdns
West Cl
Maldon Rd
Bedevere Rd
Galahad Rd
Salisbury Mans
Chauncey Cl
Gawain Wlk
Tristram Dr
Balfour Mews
Colthurst Dr
Euesden Cl
Haynes Dr
Allot Gdns
Eastbournia Ave
St Malo Ave
Granville Ave
Chad Cres
Kariba Cl
Congo Dr
Badma Cl
Ardra Rd
Meridian Way
Sewage Works
Dunholme Rd
Eastern Ave
Pymmes Gdns N
Pymmes Gdns S
Sunnyside Rd N
Sunnyside Rd E
Sunnyside Rd S
Leonard Rd
Barbot Cl
Peel Cl
L Ctr
Plevna Rd
Clarke Mews
1 Albert Sleet Ct
2 Joyce Lattimore Ct
3 Florence White Ct
4 George Taylor Ct
Barrowfield Cl
Zambezie Dr
Moselle Ct
Liffey Ct
Thames Ct
Lower Edmonton
Federation Cemy
Dodsley Pl
Montagu Rd
Recn Gd
Victoria Rd
Shrubbery Rd
Cosman Rd
Beaconsfield Rd
Felixstowe Rd
Fraser Rd
Brookfield Rd
Brook Cres
Pegamoid Rd
Dane Rd
Barnes Rd
Thornton Rd
Princes Rd
Pl Flds
Sebastopol Rd
Fleecefield Prim Sch
Station House Mews
Brettenham Rd
Brookside Rd
Second Ave
Montagu Ind Est
Jeremy's Gn
Sch
Pymmes Park
Sycamore Cl
Solomon Ave
A1010
A
B
C
D
1
2
3
4
5
6
17
93
94
95
96
34
35
36

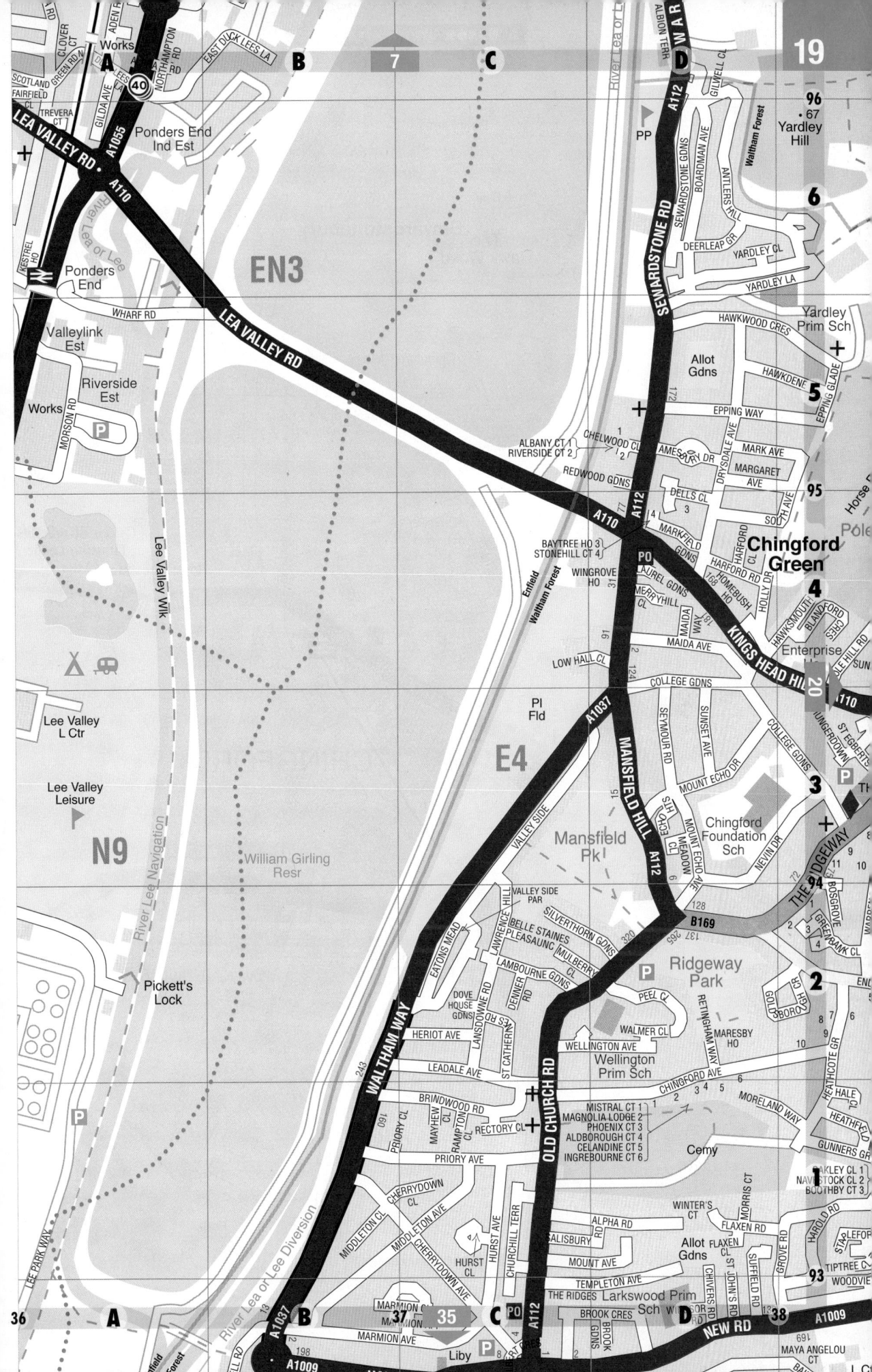
EN3
E4
N9
Ponders End Ind Est
Ponders End
Valleylink Est
Riverside Est
Works
Lee Valley Wlk
Lee Valley L Ctr
Lee Valley Leisure
River Lee Navigation
William Girling Resr
Pickett's Lock
LEA VALLEY RD
WHARF RD
MORSON RD
EAST DUCK LEES LA
NORTHAMPTON RD
GILDA AVE
SCOTLAND GREEN RD
FAIRFIELD CL
TREVERA CT
KESTREL HO
Yardley Hill
Waltham Forest
SEWARDSTONE RD
SEWARDSTONE GDNS
BOARDMAN AVE
ANTLERS HILL
DEERLEAP GR
YARDLEY CL
YARDLEY LA
GILWELL CL
ALBION TERR
PP
Yardley Prim Sch
HAWKWOOD CRES
HAWKDENE
EPPING GLADE
EPPING WAY
Allot Gdns
ALBANY CT 1
RIVERSIDE CT 2
CHELWOOD CL
AMESBURY DR
MARK AVE
MARGARET AVE
DRYSDALE AVE
REDWOOD GDNS
DELLS CL
SOUTH AVE
MARKFIELD GDNS
HARFORD CL
HARFORD RD
HOMEBUSH HO
HOLLY DR
BAYTREE HO 3
STONEHILL CT 4
WINGROVE HO
LAUREL GDNS
MERRYHILL CL
MAIDA WAY
MAIDA AVE
Chingford Green
Pole
Horse
KINGS HEAD HILL
HAWKSMOUTH
BLANDFORD CRES
Enterprise
LOW HALL CL
COLLEGE GDNS
SEYMOUR RD
SUNSET AVE
MOUNT ECHO DR
MANSFIELD HILL
Pl Fld
Enfield
Chingford Foundation Sch
ST EGBERTS
HUNGERDOWN
Mansfield Pk
VALLEY SIDE
ECHO HTS
MEADOW CL
MOUNT ECHO AVE
NEVIN DR
THE RIDGEWAY
BOSGROVE
GREENBANK CL
VALLEY SIDE PAR
EATONS MEAD
LAWRENCE HILL
BELLE STAINES PLEASAUNCE
SILVERTHORN GDNS
MULBERRY CL
LAMBOURNE GDNS
B169
Ridgeway Park
GOLDSBOROUGH CR
DOVE HOUSE GDNS
LANSDOWNE RD
DENNER RD
PEEL CL
WALMER CL
RETINGHAM WAY
MARESBY HO
HEATHCOTE GR
HERIOT AVE
ST CATHERINES RD
WELLINGTON AVE
Wellington Prim Sch
LEADALE AVE
CHINGFORD AVE
HALE
MORELAND WAY
HEATHFIELD
WALTHAM WAY
BRINDWOOD RD
MAYHEW CL
RAMPTON CL
RECTORY CL
PRIORY CL
OLD CHURCH RD
MISTRAL CT 1
MAGNOLIA LODGE 2
PHOENIX CT 3
ALDBOROUGH CT 4
CELANDINE CT 5
INGREBOURNE CT 6
Cemy
GUNNERS GR
OAKLEY CL 1
NAVESTOCK CL 2
BOOTHBY CT 3
PRIORY AVE
CHERRYDOWN CL
MIDDLETON CL
MIDDLETON AVE
CHERRYDOWN AVE
WINTER'S CT
MORRIS CT
FLAXEN RD
FLAXEN CL
HAROLD RD
STAPLEFORD
ALPHA RD
SALISBURY RD
HURST AVE
HURST CL
CHURCHILL TERR
MOUNT AVE
Allot Gdns
ST JOHN'S RD
SUFFIELD RD
GROVE RD
TIPTREE
WOODVIEW
TEMPLETON AVE
THE RIDGES
Larkswood Prim Sch
CHIVERS RD
WINDSOR RD
LEE PARK WAY
River Lea or Lee Diversion
River Lea or Lee
MARMION CL
MARMION AVE
BROOK CRES
BROOK GDNS
NEW RD
MAYA ANGELOU CT
Liby
A1009
A1037
A112
A110
A1055
PO
20
35
36
37
38
93
94
95
96
7
A
B
C
D
1
2
3
4
5
6

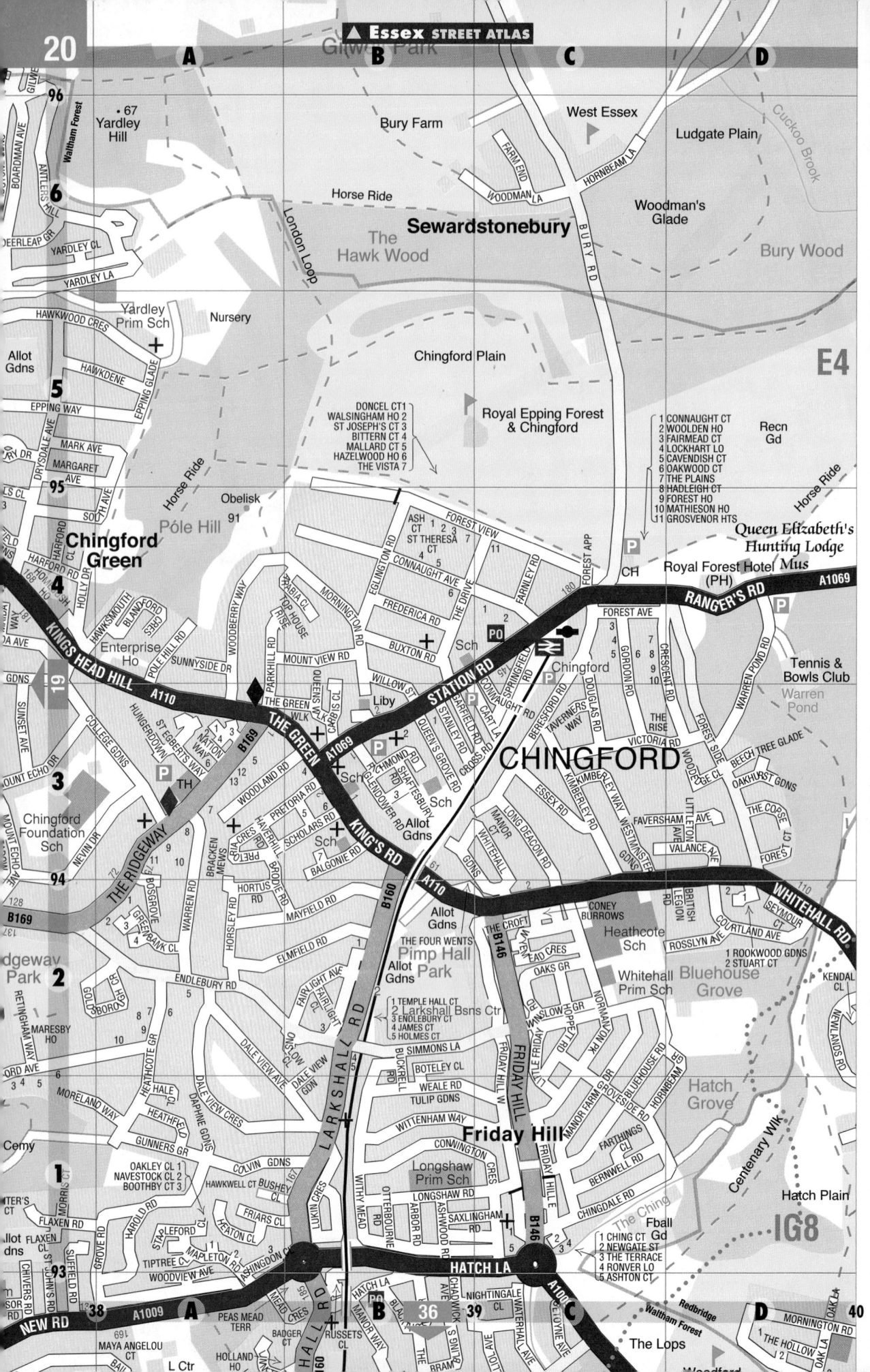
20
Essex STREET ATLAS
A
B
C
D
Gilwell Park
Bury Farm
West Essex
Ludgate Plain
Cuckoo Brook
67
Yardley Hill
Waltham Forest
96
BOARDMAN AVE
ANTLERS HILL
FARM END
HORNBEAM LA
WOODMAN LA
Horse Ride
6
London Loop
Sewardstonebury
Woodman's Glade
DEERLEAP GR
YARDLEY CL
The Hawk Wood
BURY RD
Bury Wood
YARDLEY LA
HAWKWOOD CRES
Yardley Prim Sch
Nursery
Allot Gdns
Chingford Plain
E4
HAWKDENE
EPPING GLADE
5
EPPING WAY
Royal Epping Forest & Chingford
DONCEL CT 1
WALSINGHAM HO 2
ST JOSEPH'S CT 3
BITTERN CT 4
MALLARD CT 5
HAZELWOOD HO 6
THE VISTA 7
1 CONNAUGHT CT
2 WOOLDEN HO
3 FAIRMEAD CT
4 LOCKHART LO
5 CAVENDISH CT
6 OAKWOOD CT
7 THE PLAINS
8 HADLEIGH CT
9 FOREST HO
10 MATHIESON HO
11 GROSVENOR HTS
Recn Gd
DRYSDALE AVE
MARK AVE
MARGARET AVE
95
Horse Ride
Obelisk
91
Pole Hill
SOUTH AVE
HARFORD CL
Chingford Green
HARFORD RD
HOLLY DR
4
FOREST VIEW
ASH CT
ST THERESA CT
EGLINTON RD
CONNAUGHT AVE
FOREST APP
Queen Elizabeth's Hunting Lodge Mus
Royal Forest Hotel (PH)
CH
RANGER'S RD
A1069
HAWKSMOUTH
BLANDFORD CRES
Enterprise Ho
POLE HILL RD
SUNNYSIDE DR
WOODBERRY WAY
ARABIA CL
TOP HOUSE RISE
MORNINGTON RD
FREDERICA RD
THE DRIVE
FARNLEY RD
FOREST AVE
GORDON RD
CRESCENT RD
WARREN POND RD
PO
BUXTON RD
Sch
Chingford
Tennis & Bowls Club
Warren Pond
KINGS HEAD HILL
A110
PARKHILL RD
MOUNT VIEW RD
QUEENS WALK
CARBIS CL
WILLOW ST
STATION RD
GARFIELD RD
CONNAUGHT RD
SPRINGFIELD RD
Liby
THE GREEN WLK
19
SUNSET AVE
COLLEGE GDNS
HUNGERDOWN
ST EGBERTS WAY
NATION WAY
B169
THE GREEN
A1069
STANLEY RD
CART LA
BERESFORD RD
TAVERNERS WAY
DOUGLAS RD
THE RISE
VICTORIA RD
FOREST SIDE
BEECH TREE GLADE
WOODEND GE CL
OAKHURST GDNS
MOUNT ECHO DR
3
RICHMOND RD
QUEEN'S GROVE RD
CROSS RD
CHINGFORD
KIMBERLEY WAY
KIMBERLEY RD
TH
WOODLAND RD
PRETORIA RD
GLENDOWER RD
SHAFTESBURY
Sch
ESSEX RD
LONG DEACON RD
MANOR CT
WHITEHALL GDNS
WESTMINSTER GDNS
FAVERSHAM AVE
LITTLETON AVE
VALANCE AVE
THE COPSE
FOREST CT
Chingford Foundation Sch
NEVIN DR
THE RIDGEWAY
HAVERHILL RD
SCHOLARS RD
BALGONIE RD
BRACKEN MEWS
KING'S RD
Allot Gdns
MOUNT ECHO AVE
94
BOSGROVE
HORTUS RD
BRODIE RD
WARREN RD
A110
BRITISH LEGION RD
WHITEHALL RD
B169
HORSLEY RD
MAYFIELD RD
B160
Allot Gdns
CONEY BURROWS
THE CROFT
Heathcote Sch
SEYMOUR CT
COURTLAND AVE
ROSSLYN AVE
1 ROOKWOOD GDNS
2 STUART CT
Ridgeway Park
2
GREENBANK CL
ELMFIELD RD
THE FOUR WENTS
Pimp Hall Park
HEAD CRES
OAKS GR
Whitehall Prim Sch
Bluehouse Grove
KENDAL CL
ENDLEBURY RD
FAIRLIGHT AVE
FAIRLIGHT CL
Allot Gdns
1 TEMPLE HALL CT
2 Larkshall Bsns Ctr
3 ENDLEBURY CT
4 JAMES CT
5 HOLMES CT
WINSLOW GR
HOPPETT RD
NORMANTON PK
GOLDSBOROUGH CR
RETINGHAM WAY
MARESBY HO
ONSLOW CL
DALE VIEW AVE
LARKSHALL RD
SIMMONS LA
FRIDAY HILL W
FRIDAY HILL
NEWLANDS RD
ORD AVE
HEATHCOTE GR
DALE VIEW GDNS
BUCKRELL RD
BOTELEY CL
WEALE RD
LITTLE FRIDAY RD
BLUEHOUSE RD
HORNBEAM GR
MORELAND WAY
HALE CL
HEATHFIELD
DALE VIEW CRES
DAPHNE GDNS
TULIP GDNS
WITTENHAM WAY
MANOR FARM DR
GROVESIDE RD
Hatch Grove
Cemy
GUNNERS GR
Friday Hill
FARTHINGS CL
Centenary Wlk
1
MORRIS CT
OAKLEY CL 1
NAVESTOCK CL 2
BOOTHBY CT 3
COLVIN GDNS
HAWKWELL CT
BUSHEY CL
CONNINGTON CRES
Longshaw Prim Sch
BERNWELL RD
HUNTER'S CT
FLAXEN RD
HAROLD RD
STAPLEFORD CL
FRIARS CL
HEATON CL
LUKIN CRES
WITHY MEAD
OTTERBOURNE RD
LONGSHAW RD
ARBOR RD
ASHWOOD RD
SAXLINGHAM RD
FRIDAY HILL E
CHINGDALE RD
The Ching
Hatch Plain
Allot Gdns
FLAXEN CL
GROVE RD
TIPTREE CL
MAPLETON RD
ASHINGDON CL
Fball Gd
1 CHING CT
2 NEWGATE ST
3 THE TERRACE
4 RONVER LO
5 ASHTON CT
IG8
93
ST JOHN'S RD
SUFFIELD RD
CHIVERS RD
WOODVIEW AVE
HATCH LA
B146
A1009
NEW RD
38
A1009
PEAS MEAD TERR
MEAD CRES
HATCH LA
PO
36
39
NIGHTINGALE CL
WATERHALL AVE
A1009
STONE AVE
Redbridge
Waltham Forest
The Lops
MORNINGTON RD
THE HOLLOW
OAK LA
40
MAYA ANGELOU CT
BADGER CT
RUSSETS CL
MANOR WAY
HOLLAND HO
L Ctr
HALL RD

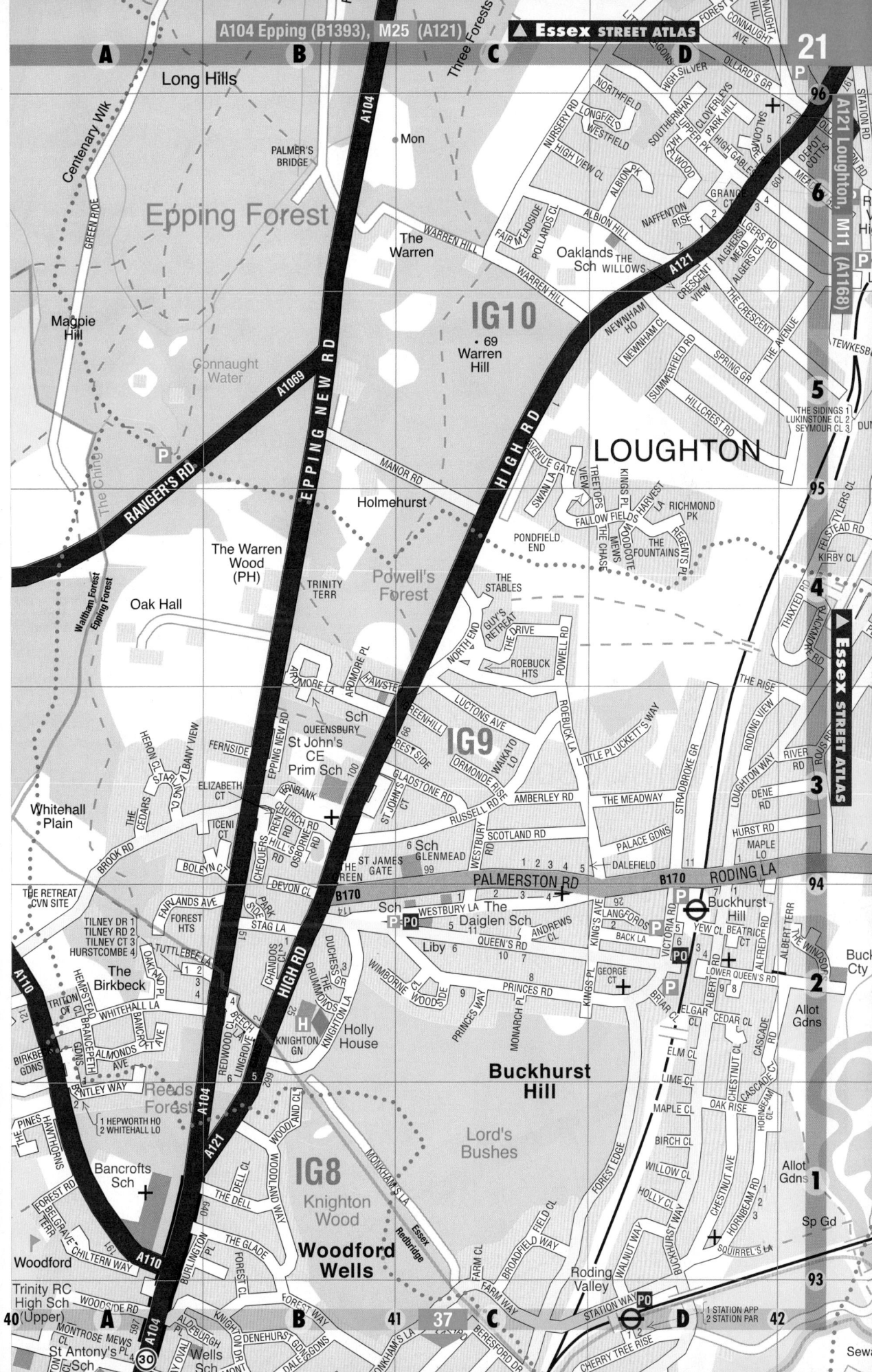
A104 Epping (B1393), M25 (A121)
Essex STREET ATLAS
A121 Loughton, M11 (A1168)
Long Hills
Centenary Wlk
Epping Forest
Magpie Hill
Connaught Water
PALMER'S BRIDGE
Mon
The Warren
IG10
69 Warren Hill
Oaklands Sch
LOUGHTON
Holmehurst
The Warren Wood (PH)
Oak Hall
Powell's Forest
TRINITY TERR
Whitehall Plain
IG9
St John's CE Prim Sch
THE RETREAT CVN SITE
The Birkbeck
The Daiglen Sch
Buckhurst Hill
Holly House
Reeds Forest
Lord's Bushes
IG8
Knighton Wood
Woodford Wells
Bancrofts Sch
Woodford
Trinity RC High Sch (Upper)
St Antony's Sch
Wells Sch
Roding Valley
Allot Gdns
Sp Gd
Buck Cty
RANGER'S RD
EPPING NEW RD
HIGH RD
PALMERSTON RD
RODING LA
B170
A1069
A104
A121
A110
Essex Redbridge
Waltham Forest Epping Forest
1 HEPWORTH HO
2 WHITEHALL LO
TILNEY DR 1
TILNEY RD 2
TILNEY CT 3
HURSTCOMBE 4
THE SIDINGS 1
LUKINSTONE CL 2
SEYMOUR CL 3
1 STATION APP
2 STATION PAR
A B C D
40 41 37 42
93 94 95 96
1 2 3 4 5 6
30

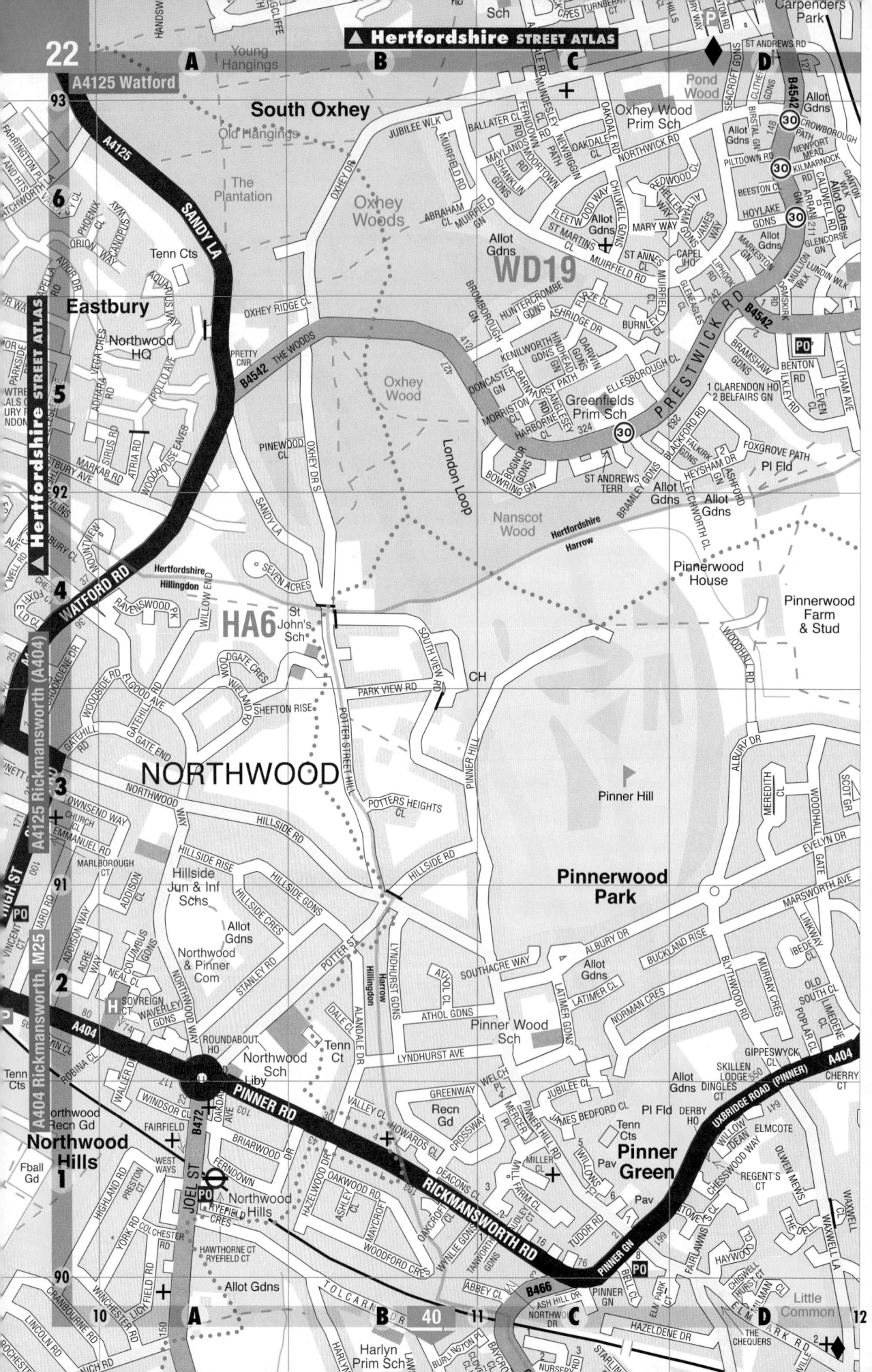
A
B
C
D
A4125 Watford
Young Hangings
South Oxhey
Old Hangings
The Plantation
Oxhey Woods
Oxhey Wood
Pond Wood
Oxhey Wood Prim Sch
Carpenders Park
WD19
Eastbury
Northwood HQ
Tenn Cts
SANDY LA
A4125
WATFORD RD
THE WOODS
B4542
PRESTWICK RD
Greenfields Prim Sch
London Loop
Nanscot Wood
Hertfordshire
Harrow
Hillingdon
Pinnerwood House
Pinnerwood Farm & Stud
HA6
St John's Sch
NORTHWOOD
Pinner Hill
Pinnerwood Park
Hillside Jun & Inf Schs
Allot Gdns
Northwood & Pinner Com
Northwood Sch
Tenn Ct
Pinner Wood Sch
Recn Gd
Pinner Green
Northwood Hills
Northwood Recn Gd
Fball Gd
PINNER RD
RICKMANSWORTH RD
UXBRIDGE ROAD (PINNER)
A404
B466
B472
JOEL ST
A4125 Rickmansworth (A404)
A404 Rickmansworth, M25
Hertfordshire STREET ATLAS
Harlyn Prim Sch
Little Common
93
6
5
92
4
3
91
2
1
90
10
11
12
40

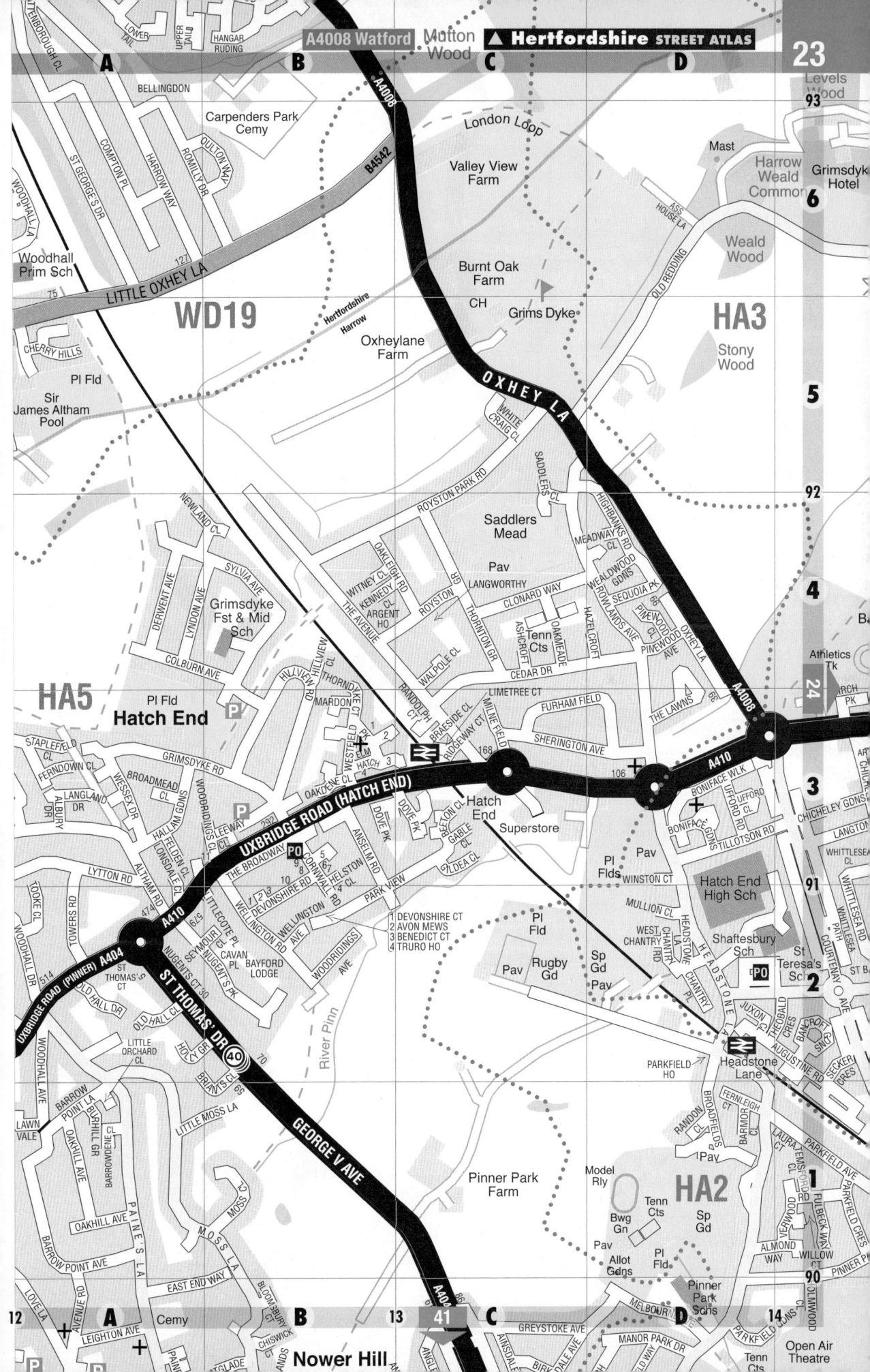
A4008 Watford
Mutton Wood
A B C D
Levels Wood
93
Bellingdon
Carpenders Park Cemy
London Loop
Valley View Farm
Mast
Harrow Weald Common
Grimsdyke Hotel
6
Ass House La
Weald Wood
Compton Pl
St George's Dr
Harrow Way
Romilly Dr
Oulton Way
B4542
A4008
Woodhall Prim Sch
Little Oxhey La
127
75
Burnt Oak Farm
CH
Grims Dyke
Old Redding
WD19
HA3
Hertfordshire
Harrow
Oxheylane Farm
Stony Wood
Cherry Hills
Pl Fld
Sir James Altham Pool
5
Oxhey La
White Craig Cl
Saddlers Cl
92
Royston Park Rd
Saddlers Mead
Highbanks Rd
Newland Cl
Meadway Cl
Pav
Sylvia Ave
Oakleigh Rd
Witney Cl
Kennedy Cl
Argent Ho
Langworthy
Clonard Way
Wealdwood Gdns
Sequoia Pk
4
Derwent Ave
Lyndon Ave
Grimsdyke Fst & Mid Sch
The Avenue
Royston Gr
Thornton Gr
Ashcroft
Tenn Cts
Oakmeade
Hazelcroft
Rowlands Ave
Pinewood Cl
Pinewood Ave
Oxhey La
Athletics Tk
Colburn Ave
Hillview Rd
Hillview Cl
Thorndyke Ct
Walpole Cl
Cedar Dr
HA5
Pl Fld
Hatch End
Mardon
Randolph Ct
Braeside Cl
Limetree Ct
Milne Field
Furham Field
The Lawns
A4008
24
Stapleford Cl
Ferndown Cl
Grimsdyke Rd
Westfield Pk
Elm Hatch
Ridgeway Ct
168
Sherington Ave
106
A410
Langland Dr
Albury Dr
Wessex Dr
Broadmead Cl
Hallam Gdns
Woodridings Cl
Oakdene Cl
Uxbridge Road (Hatch End)
Hatch End
Superstore
Boniface Wlk
Ufford Rd
Ufford Cl
3
Chicheley Gdns
Boniface Gdns
Tillotson Rd
Langton
Sleeway
Felden Cl
Lonsdale Cl
292
The Broadway
PO
Cornwall Rd
Dove Pk
Anselm Rd
Beeton Cl
Gable Cl
Oldea Cl
Pl Flds
Pav
Whittlesea Cl
Lytton Rd
Altham Rd
Helston Cl
Devonshire Rd
Wellington Rd
Wellington Ave
Park View
Winston Ct
Hatch End High Sch
91
Tooke Cl
Towers Rd
Woodhall Dr
474
A410
Littlecote Pl
Seymour Cl
Cavan Pl
Bayford Lodge
Woodridings Ave
1 Devonshire Ct
2 Avon Mews
3 Benedict Ct
4 Truro Ho
Pl Fld
Mullion Cl
West Chantry
Chantry Rd
Headstone La
Shaftesbury Sch
St Teresa's Sch
Whittlesea Path
Courtenay Ave
Rugby Gd
Sp Gd
Pav
2
Uxbridge Road (Pinner) A404
514
St Thomas' Ct
Nugents Ct
Nugent's Pk
St Thomas' Dr
Old Hall Dr
Old Hall Cl
River Pinn
Chantry Pl
Juxon Cl
Theobald Cres
Bancroft Gdns
Augustine Rd
Secker Cres
Woodhall Ave
Little Orchard Cl
Holly Gr
40
70
Briants Cl
Parkfield Ho
Headstone Lane
Barrow Point La
Burhill Gr
Little Moss La
George V Ave
Randon Cl
Broadfields
Fernleigh Ct
Barmor Cl
Laura Cl
Parkfield Ave
Lawn Vale
Oakhill Ave
Barrowdene Cl
Moss Cl
Pinner Park Farm
Model Rly
HA2
Tensford
Fulbeck Way
Parkfield Cres
1
Oakhill Ave
Paine's La
Moss La
Bwg Gn
Tenn Cts
Sp Gd
Verwood Rd
Almond Way
Willow Ct
Barrow Point Ave
Pav
Allot Gdns
Pl Fld
Pinner Park Sch
90
Pinner Pk
East End Way
Love La
Avenue Rd
Bloomsbury Ct
Melbourne
Olmwood
12
Cemy
13
41
14
Parkfield Gdns
Leighton Ave
Chiswick Ct
Nower Hill
Greystoke Ave
Manor Park Dr
Open Air Theatre
Tenn Cts

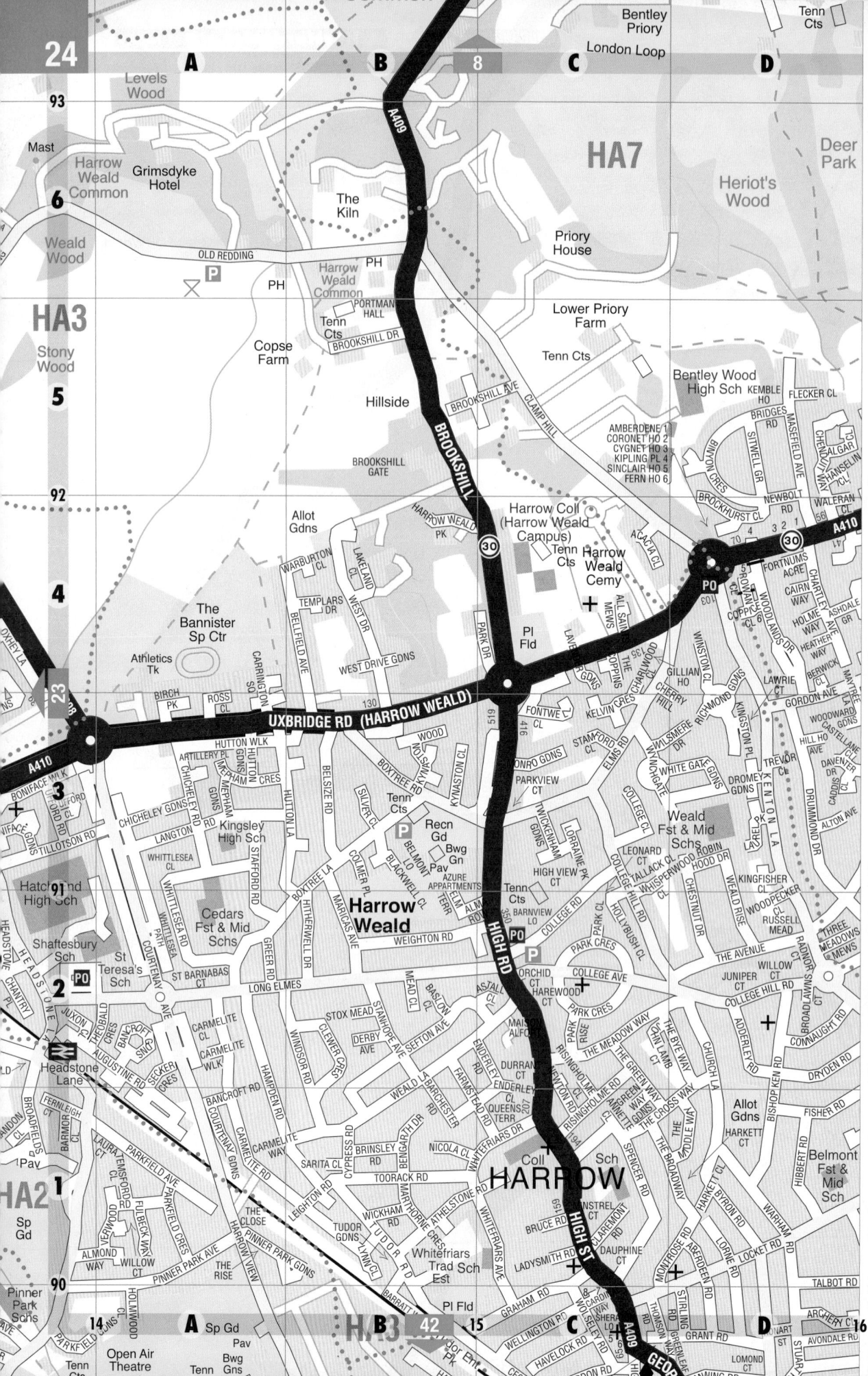
A
B
8
C
D
Bentley Priory
London Loop
Tenn Cts
Levels Wood
93
Mast
Harrow Weald Common
Grimsdyke Hotel
6
The Kiln
HA7
Deer Park
Heriot's Wood
A409
Weald Wood
OLD REDDING
PH
Priory House
Harrow Weald Common
PORTMAN HALL
HA3
Stony Wood
Tenn Cts
BROOKSHILL DR
Copse Farm
Lower Priory Farm
Tenn Cts
5
Hillside
BROOKSHILL AVE
CLAMP HILL
Bentley Wood High Sch
KEMBLE HO
FLECKER CL
BRIDGES RD
BROOKSHILL
BROOKSHILL GATE
AMBERDENE 1
CORONET HO 2
CYGNET HO 3
KIPLING PL 4
SINCLAIR HO 5
FERN HO 6
BINYON CRES
SITWELL GR
MASEFIELD AVE
CHESTERTON
ALGAR CL
HANSELIN CL
92
BROCKHURST CL
NEWBOLT RD
WALERAN CL
A410
Allot Gdns
HARROW WEALD PK
Harrow Coll (Harrow Weald Campus)
Tenn Cts
Harrow Weald Cemy
ACACIA CL
30
WARBURTON CL
LAKELAND CL
FORTNUMS ACRE
PO
4
TEMPLARS DR
WEST DR
ALL SAINTS MEWS
ROWAN CL
CAIRN WAY
CHARTLEY AVE
ASHDALE GR
The Bannister Sp Ctr
BELLFIELD AVE
PARK DR
Pl Fld
COPPICE CL
WOODLANDS DR
HOLME WAY
HEATHER WAY
Athletics Tk
CARRINGTON SQ
WEST DRIVE GDNS
THE COPPINS
CHARLWOOD CL
GILLIAN HO
WINSTON CL
BERWICK CL
LAWRIE CT
OXHEY LA
23
BIRCH PK
ROSS CL
130
UXBRIDGE RD (HARROW WEALD)
FONTWELL CL
KELVIN CRES
CHERRY HILL
RICHMOND GDNS
KINGSTON PL
GORDON AVE
WOODWARD GDNS
MAYTREE LA
CASTELLANE CL
HUTTON WLK
HUTTON GDNS
WOOD
519
416
STAMFORD CL
ELMS RD
WILSMERE DR
HILL HO AVE
ARTILLERY PL
CHICHELEY RD
MEPHAM CRES
BOXTREE RD
KYNASTON CL
MONRO GDNS
WYNCHGATE
WHITE GATE GDNS
TREVOR CL
DAVENTER DR
BONIFACE WLK
UFFORD CL
MEPHAM GDNS
BELSIZE RD
HUTTON LA
SILVER CL
Tenn Cts
PARKVIEW CT
TWICKENHAM GDNS
COLLEGE CL
DROMEY GDNS
KENTON LA
DRUMMOND DR
CADDIS CL
3
UFFORD RD
CHICHELEY GDNS
LANGTON RD
Kingsley High Sch
Recn Gd
Bwg Gn
LORRAINE PK
Weald Fst & Mid Schs
ALTON AVE
TILLOTSON RD
WHITTLESEA CL
BELMONT LO
Pav
AZURE APARTMENTS
HIGH VIEW CT
LEONARD CT
TALLACK CL
WHISPERWOOD CL
ROBIN HOOD DR
LAUREL PK
Hatch End High Sch
91
STAFFORD RD
BOXTREE LA
COLMER PL
BLACKWELL CL
ELM TERR
ALMA ROW
Tenn Cts
COLLEGE HILL RD
CHESTNUT DR
WEALD RISE
KINGFISHER CL
WOODPECKER CL
Cedars Fst & Mid Schs
WHITTLESEA PATH
WHITTLESEA RD
HITHERWELL DR
MARICAS AVE
Harrow Weald
350
HIGH RD
BARNVIEW LO
COLLEGE RD
PARK CL
HOLLYBUSH CL
RUSSELL MEAD
THREE MEADOWS MEWS
HEADSTONE LA
Shaftesbury Sch
COURTENAY AVE
WEIGHTON RD
PO
PARK CRES
THE AVENUE
RADNOR CT
St Teresa's Sch
ST BARNABAS CT
GREER RD
WILLOW CT
JUNIPER CT
CHANTRY PL
2
PO
LONG ELMES
MEAD CL
ORCHID CT
COLLEGE AVE
HAREWOOD CT
COLLEGE HILL RD
BROADLAWNS CT
THEOBALD CRES
JUXON CL
BANCROFT GDNS
CARMELITE CL
STOX MEAD
STANHOPE AVE
BASLOW CL
ASTALL CL
PARK CRES
CONNAUGHT RD
AUGUSTINE RD
CARMELITE WLK
DERBY AVE
SEFTON AVE
CLEWER CRES
MAISON ALFORT
PARK RISE
THE MEADOW WAY
CHILLAMB CT
THE BYE WAY
CHURCH LA
ADDERLEY RD
Headstone Lane
SECKER CRES
HAMPDEN RD
WINDSOR RD
ENDERLEY RD
DURRANT CT
ENDERLEY CL
RISINGHOLME CL
THE GREEN WAY
DRYDEN RD
BROADFIELDS
FERNLEIGH CT
BARMOR CL
BANCROFT RD
COURTENAY GDNS
FARMSTEAD RD
WEALD LA
BARCHESTER RD
QUEENS TERR
207
NEWTON RD
RISINGHOLME RD
GREEN WAY GDNS
ANNETTE CL
THE CROSS WAY
THE MIDDLE WAY
Allot Gdns
BISHOP KEN RD
FISHER RD
Pav
LAURA CT
TEMSFORD CL
PARKFIELD AVE
CARMELITE RD
CARMELITE WAY
CYPRESS RD
BRINSLEY RD
BENGARTH DR
NICOLA CL
WHITEFRIARS DR
194
HARKETT CT
HIBBERT RD
Belmont Fst & Mid Sch
HA2
1
FULBECK WAY
PARKFIELD CRES
SARITA CL
TOORACK RD
Coll
HARROW
Sch
SPENCER RD
THE BROADWAY
HARKETT CL
BYRON RD
Sp Gd
VERWOOD RD
THE CLOSE
LEIGHTON RD
WICKHAM RD
MARTHORNE CRES
ATHELSTONE RD
WHITEFRIARS AVE
MINSTREL CT
CLAREMONT RD
WARHAM RD
ALMOND WAY
WILLOW CT
HARROW VIEW
PINNER PARK GDNS
TUDOR GDNS
TUDOR RD
LYNN CL
BRUCE RD
HIGH ST
159
DAUPHINE CT
MONTROSE RD
ABERDEEN RD
LORNE RD
LOCKET RD
PINNER PARK AVE
THE RISE
Whitefriars Trad Sch Est
LADYSMITH RD
90
TALBOT RD
Pinner Park Schs
HOLMWOOD CL
BARRATT WAY
Pl Fld
GRAHAM RD
8
CARDINAL WAY
STIRLING RD
THOMSON RD
ARCHERY CL
14
A
Sp Gd
HA3
B
42
15
WELLINGTON RD
C
SHERATON LO
A409
GREENLEAF RD
GRANT RD
D
16
ST
AVONDALE RD
PARKFIELD GDNS
Pav
HAVELOCK RD
WOLSELEY RD
LOMOND CT
STUART RD
Open Air Theatre
Tenn Cts
Bwg Gns
Tenn
GEORGE

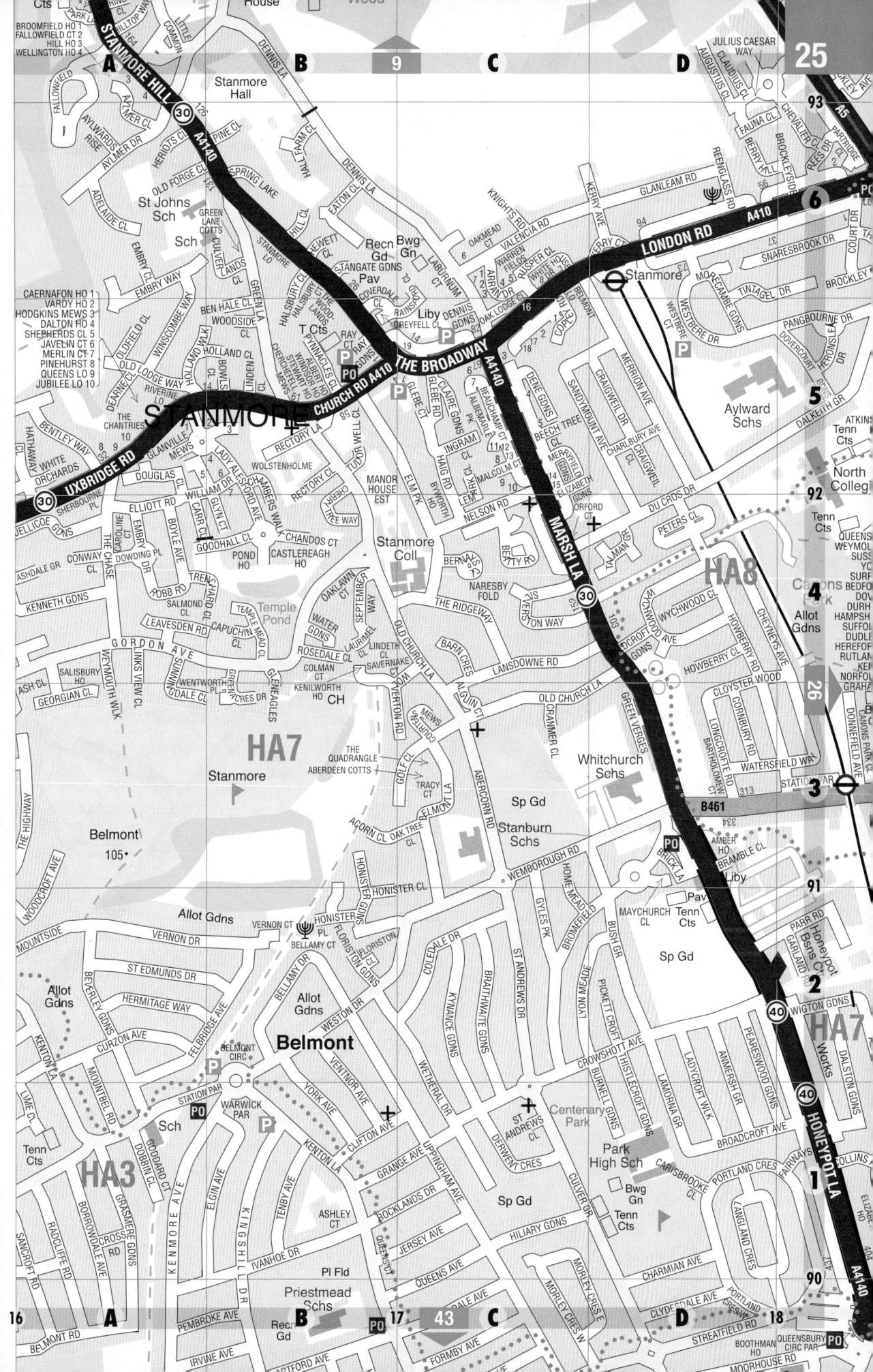

A
B
9
C
D
STANMORE
HA7
HA8
HA3
Stanmore Hall
St Johns Sch
Stanmore Coll
Temple Pond
Aylward Schs
Whitchurch Schs
Stanburn Schs
Park High Sch
Priestmead Schs
Belmont
Centenary Park
Allot Gdns
Stanmore
UXBRIDGE RD
CHURCH RD A410
THE BROADWAY
LONDON RD
A410
STANMORE HILL
A4140
MARSH LA
HONEYPOT LA
A5
B461
KENTON LA
GORDON AVE
OLD CHURCH LA
WEMBOROUGH RD
DU CROS DR
LANSDOWNE RD
CLIFTON AVE
STATION PAR
WARWICK PAR
6
5
4
3
2
1
26
A
B
17
43
C
D
18
16

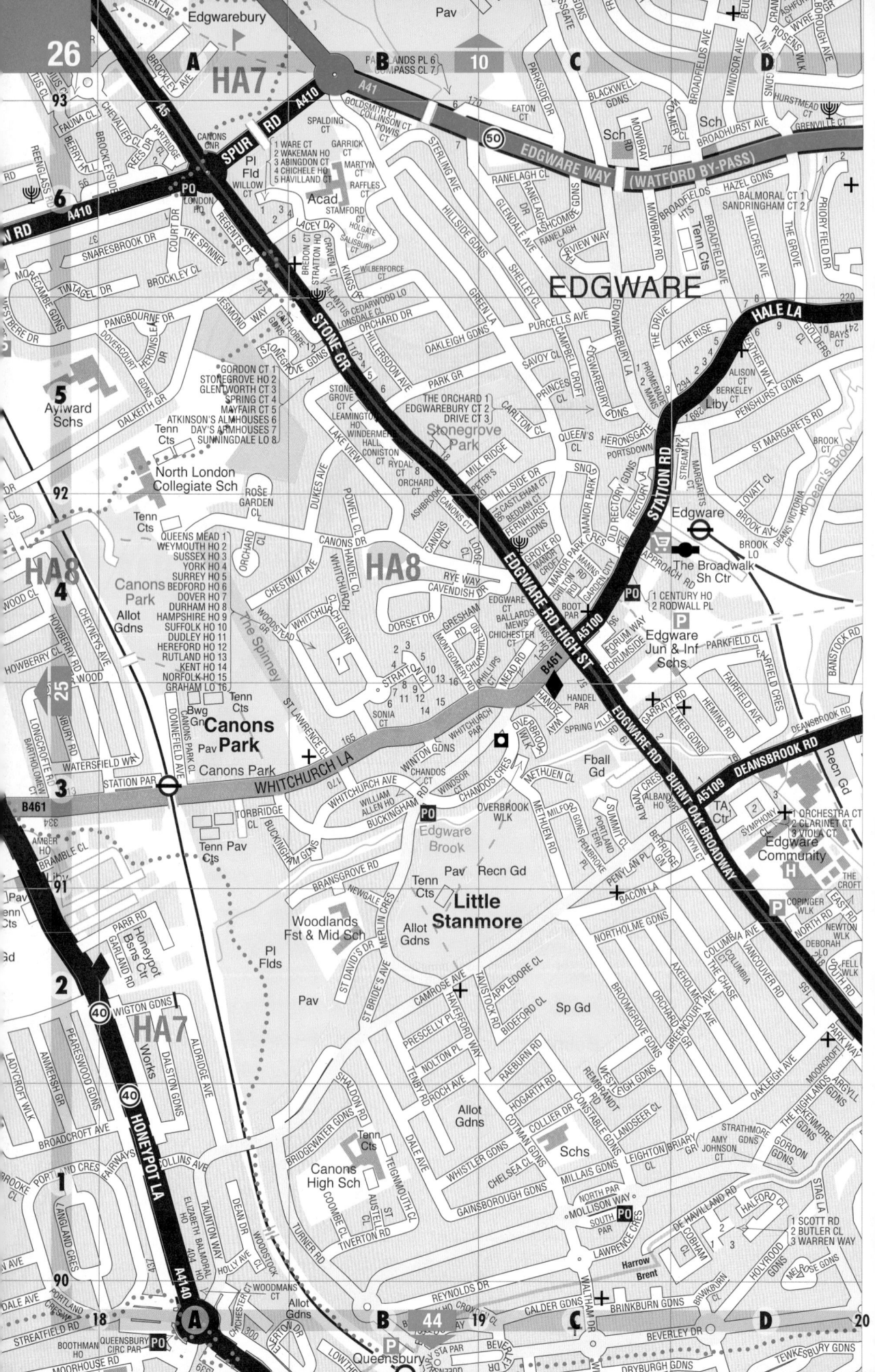
26
Edgwarebury
Pav
A
B
C
D
10
HA7
PARKLANDS PL 6
COMPASS CL 7
A41
A410
A5
SPUR RD
CANONS CNR
Pl Fld
WILLOW CT
LONDON HO
PO
93
6
FAUNA CL
CHEVALIER CL
BERRY HILL
BROCKLEYSIDE
REES DR
PARTRIDGE
BROCKLEY AVE
REENGLASS RD
SNARESBROOK DR
COURT DR
THE SPINNEY
REGENTS CT
BROCKLEY CL
MORECAMBE GDNS
TINTAGEL DR
GOLDSMITH CT
COLLINSON CT
POWIS CT
SPALDING CT
1 WARE CT
2 WAKEMAN HO
3 ABINGDON CT
4 CHICHELE HO
5 HAVILLAND CT
GARRICK CT
MARTYN CT
RAFFLES CT
Acad
STAMFORD CT
HOLGATE CT
SALISBURY CT
LACEY DR
BREDON CT
CRAVEN CT
STRATTON HO
KINGS DR
WILBERFORCE CT
AILANTUS CT
CEDARWOOD LO
LONSDALE CL
ORCHARD DR
STERLING AVE
HILLSIDE GDNS
GREEN LA
GLENDALE AVE
SHELLEY CL
EATON CT
PARKSIDE DR
BLACKWELL GDNS
MOWBRAY RD
Sch
DELMER CL
BROADFIELDS AVE
WINDSOR AVE
Sch
BROADHURST AVE
HURSTMEAD CT
GRENVILLE CT
50
EDGWARE WAY
(WATFORD BY-PASS)
RANELAGH CL
RANELAGH DR
ASHCOMBE GDNS
RANELAGH CL
FAIRVIEW WAY
BROADFIELDS HTS
Tenn Cts
BROADFIELD AVE
HAZEL GDNS
BALMORAL CT 1
SANDRINGHAM CT 2
HILLCREST AVE
THE GROVE
PRIORY FIELD DR
EDGWARE
HALE LA
GOLDERS CL
BAYS CT
THE DRIVE
THE RISE
FEATHER WLK
ALISON CT
BERKELEY CT
Liby
PENSHURST GDNS
ST MARGARETS RD
BROOK CT
Dean's Brook
PURCELLS AVE
CAMPBELL CROFT
EDGWAREBURY LA
EDGWAREBURY GDNS
PROMENADE MANS
SAVOY CL
PRINCES CL
OAKLEIGH GDNS
PARK GR
THE ORCHARD 1
EDGWAREBURY CT 2
DRIVE CT 3
CARLTON CL
QUEEN'S CL
HERONSGATE
PORTSDOWN
STATION RD
STREAM LA
MARGARETS CT
LOVATT CL
BROOK AVE
DEANS VICTORIA HO
Edgware
BROOK LO
The Broadwalk Sh Ctr
APPROACH RD
1 CENTURY HO
2 RODWALL PL
Edgware Jun & Inf Schs
PARKFIELD CL
FAIRFIELD CL
BANSTOCK RD
FAIRFIELD AVE
FAIRFIELD CRES
HEMING RD
GARRATT RD
ELMER GDNS
DEANSBROOK RD
A5109
Recn Gd
STONE GR
HILLERSDON AVE
STONEGROVE GDNS
CALTHORPE GDNS
JESMOND WAY
PANGBOURNE DR
DOVERCOURT GDNS
HERONSLEA DR
DALKEITH GR
WESTBERE DR
5
Aylward Schs
GORDON CT 1
STONEGROVE HO 2
GLENTWORTH CT 3
SPRING CT 4
MAYFAIR CT 5
ATKINSON'S ALMSHOUSES 6
DAY'S ARMHOUSES 7
SUNNINGDALE LO 8
Tenn Cts
North London Collegiate Sch
ROSE GARDEN CL
STONE GROVE CT
LEAMINGTON HO
WINDERMERE HALL
CONISTON CT
RYDAL CT
ORCHARD CT
LAKE VIEW
Stonegrove Park
MILL RIDGE
PETER'S CL
HILLSIDE DR
CASTLEHAM CT
BEDDAN CT
FERNHURST GDNS
MANOR PARK GDNS
OLD RECTORY GDNS
RECTORY LA
GROVE RD
MANOR CROFT
MANOR PARK CRES
CHILTON RD
MANNS RD
GARDEN CITY
92
DUKES AVE
POWELL CL
ASHBROOK
CANONS CT
CANONS CL
LODGE CL
CANONS DR
Tenn Cts
QUEENS MEAD 1
WEYMOUTH HO 2
SUSSEX HO 3
YORK HO 4
SURREY HO 5
BEDFORD HO 6
DOVER HO 7
DURHAM HO 8
HAMPSHIRE HO 9
SUFFOLK HO 10
DUDLEY HO 11
HEREFORD HO 12
RUTLAND HO 13
KENT HO 14
NORFOLK HO 15
GRAHAM LO 16
HA8
4
Canons Park
Allot Gdns
ORCHARD CL
CHESTNUT AVE
WHITCHURCH CL
HANDEL CL
HA8
RYE WAY
CAVENDISH DR
EDGWARE RD HIGH ST
A5100
BOOT PAR
EDGWARE CT
BALLARDS MEWS
CHICHESTER CT
DORSET DR
GRESHAM RD
MONTGOMERY RD
CHURCHILL RD
PHILLIPS CT
MEAD RD
LANSON HO
FORUM WAY
FORUMSIDE
WOODSTEAD GR
WHITCHURCH GDNS
The Spinney
CHEYNEYS AVE
HOWBERRY RD
HOWBERRY CL
WOOD CL
LONGCROFT RD
STRATTON CL
SONIA CT
B461
HANDEL WAY
HANDEL PAR
SPRING VILLA RD
EDGWARE RD
BURNT OAK BROADWAY
25
Bwg Gn
Tenn Cts
Canons Park
Pav
CANONS PARK CL
DONNEFIELD AVE
ST LAWRENCE CL
WHITCHURCH PAR
OVERBROOK WLK
WATERSFIELD WAY
BARTHOLOMEW CT
3
STATION PAR
Canons Park
WHITCHURCH LA
WINTON GDNS
CHANDOS CT
WINDSOR CT
CHANDOS CRES
METHUEN CL
Fball Gd
ALBANY CRES
ALBANY HO
TA Ctr
1 ORCHESTRA CT
2 CLARINET CT
3 VIOLA CT
SYMPHONY CL
Edgware Community
THE CROFT
TORBRIDGE CL
WHITCHURCH AVE
WILLIAM ALLEN HO
BUCKINGHAM RD
PO
OVERBROOK WLK
METHUEN RD
MILFORD GDNS
PORTLAND TERR
SUMMIT CL
PEMBROKE PL
BERRIDGE GN
SELWYN CT
AMBER HO
BRAMBLE CL
Tenn Pav Cts
Edgware Brook
BUCKINGHAM GDNS
BRANSGROVE RD
NEWGALE GDNS
Pav
Recn Gd
PENYLAN PL
BACON LA
COPINGER WLK
EAST RD
NORTH RD
NEWTON WLK
DEBORAH LO
FELL WLK
SOUTH RD
91
Liby
Tenn Cts
Little Stanmore
Woodlands Fst & Mid Sch
Allot Gdns
MERLIN CRES
PARR RD
Honeypot Bsns Ctr
GARLAND RD
NORTHOLME GDNS
COLUMBIA AVE
COLUMBIA CT
THE CHASE
VANCOUVER RD
Pl Flds
ST DAVID'S DR
ST BRIDE'S AVE
CAMROSE AVE
APPLEDORE CL
BIDEFORD CL
TAVISTOCK RD
HAVERFORD WAY
PRESCELLY PL
Sp Gd
BROOMGROVE GDNS
ORCHARD GR
AXEHOLME AVE
GREENCOURT AVE
2
40
WIGTON GDNS
HA7
Works
Pav
PEARESWOOD GDNS
AMMERSH GR
LADYCROFT WLK
DALSTON GDNS
ALDRIDGE AVE
NOLTON PL
TENBY RD
ROCH AVE
RAEBURN RD
HOGARTH RD
REMBRANDT RD
WESTLEIGH GDNS
PARK WAY
MOORCROFT
OAKLEIGH AVE
THE HIGHLANDS
ARGYLL GDNS
KENMORE GDNS
40
HONEYPOT LA
BROADCROFT AVE
FAIRWAYS
COLLINS AVE
SHALDON RD
BRIDGEWATER GDNS
Tenn Cts
DALE AVE
Allot Gdns
COLLIER DR
CONSTABLE GDNS
LANDSEER CL
COTMAN GDNS
WHISTLER GDNS
CHELSEA CL
Schs
LEIGHTON CL
BRIARY GR
AMY JOHNSON CT
STRATHMORE GDNS
GORDON GDNS
Canons High Sch
TEIGNMOUTH CL
1
PORTLAND CRES
LANGLAND CRES
ELIZABETH HO
BALMORAL HO
TAUNTON WAY
DEAN DR
COOMBE CL
AUSTELL GDNS
GAINSBOROUGH GDNS
MILLAIS GDNS
NORTH PAR
MOLLISON WAY
SOUTH PAR
PO
LAWRENCE CRES
DE HAVILLAND RD
COBHAM CL
HALFORD CL
1 SCOTT RD
2 BUTLER CL
3 WARREN WAY
STAG LA
HOLYROOD GDNS
MELROSE GDNS
TURNER RD
TIVERTON RD
HOLLY AVE
WOODSTOCK
Harrow
Brent
90
A4140
REYNOLDS DR
WALTHAM DR
BRINKBURN GDNS
BRINKBURN CL
WOODMANS CT
CHICHESTER CT
Allot Gdns
CALDER GDNS
CROXDEN CL
18
A
B
44
19
C
D
20
STREATFIELD RD
BOOTHMAN HO
QUEENSBURY CIRC PAR
PO
MOORHOUSE RD
ELLERTON RD
Queensbury
STATION PAR
BEVERLEY DR
DRYBURGH GDNS
TEWKESBURY GDNS

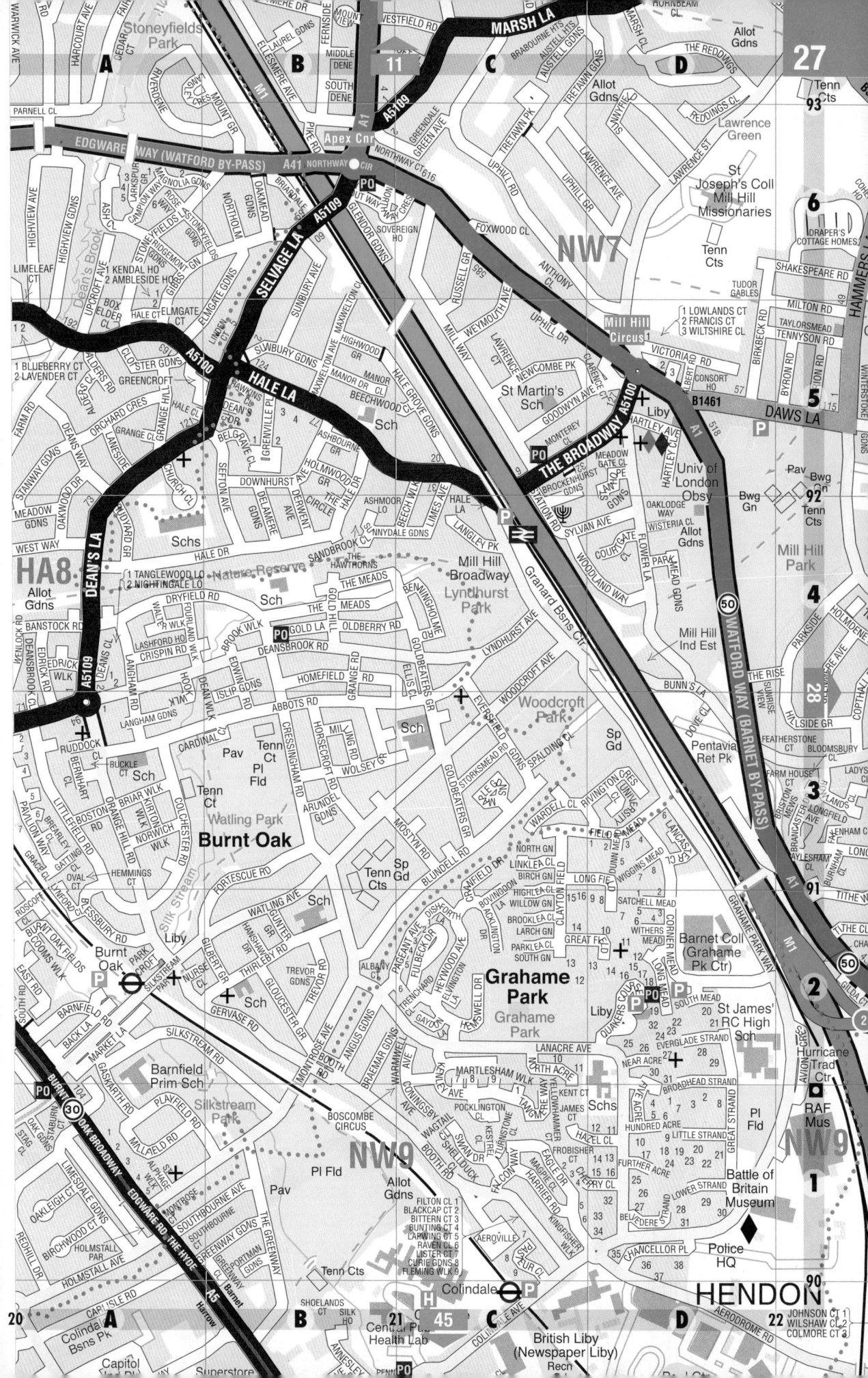
11
MARSH LA
Stoneyfields Park
WARWICK AVE
HARCOURT AVE
ELLESMERE AVE
LAUREL GDNS
FERNSIDE
MOUNT VIEW
WESTFIELD RD
MIDDLE DENE
SOUTH DENE
BRABOURNE HTS
AUSTELL HTS
AUSTELL GDNS
TRETAWN GDNS
MARSH CL
THE REDDINGS
REDDINGS CL
Allot Gdns
Tenn Cts
93
PARNELL CL
EDGWARE WAY (WATFORD BY-PASS)
A41
NORTHWAY CIR
Apex Cnr
A1
A5109
M1
NORTHWAY CT
GREEN AVE
GREENDALE
TRETAWN PK
UPHILL RD
UPHILL GR
LAWRENCE AVE
LAWRENCE ST
SUNNYFIELD
Lawrence Green
St Joseph's Coll Mill Hill Missionaries
6
DRAPER'S COTTAGE HOMES
SHAKESPEARE RD
MILTON RD
TAYLORSMEAD
TENNYSON RD
HAMMERS LA
TUDOR GABLES
1 LOWLANDS CT
2 FRANCIS CT
3 WILTSHIRE CL
NW7
FOXWOOD CL
ANTHONY CL
RUSSELL GR
WEYMOUTH AVE
MILL WAY
UPHILL DR
LAWRENCE CT
NEWCOMBE PK
CLARENCE CT
Mill Hill Circus
VICTORIA RD
ALBERT RD
CONSORT HO
BIRKBECK RD
BYRON RD
B1461
DAWS LA
5
WINTERSTOKE GDNS
HIGHVIEW AVE
HIGHVIEW GDNS
LIMELEAF CT
UPCROFT AVE
1 KENDAL HO
2 AMBLESIDE HO
BOX ELDER CL
HALE CT
ELMGATE CT
ELMGATE GDNS
SELVAGE LA
SUNBURY AVE
MAXWELTON CL
MAXWELTON AVE
SUNBURY GDNS
HIGHWOOD GR
MANOR DR
MANOR CL
GLENDOR GDNS
SOVEREIGN HO
OAKMEAD GDNS
NORTHOLM
STONEYFIELDS GDNS
RIDGEMONT GDNS
GIBBS GN
MAGNOLIA GDNS
CAMPION WAY
LARKSPUR GR
ASH CL
Dean's Brook
1 BLUEBERRY CT
2 LAVENDER CT
ALDERS RD
GLOSTER GDNS
GREENCROFT
A5100
HALE LA
HALE CL
GRANGE HILL
GRANGE CL
DEAN'S DR
BELGRAVE CL
GRENVILLE PL
BEECHWOOD CL
HALE GROVE GDNS
Sch
St Martin's Sch
GOODWYN AVE
MONTEREY CL
THE BROADWAY
Liby
HARTLEY AVE
HARTLEY CL
Univ of London Obsy
Pav
Bwg Gn
92
Tenn Cts
FARM RD
DEANS WAY
ORCHARD CRES
LANESIDE
STANWAY GDNS
OAKWOOD DR
MEADOW GDNS
WEST WAY
CHURCH CL
SEFTON AVE
DOWNHURST AVE
DELAMERE GDNS
DERWENT AVE
HOLMWOOD GR
THE CIRCLE
THE HALE DR
ASHBOURNE GR
ASHMOOR LO
BEECH WLK
LIMES AVE
HALE LA
LANGLEY PK
MEADOW GATE CL
BROCKENHURST GDNS
STATION RD
SYLVAN AVE
OAKLODGE WAY
WISTERIA CL
COURTGATE CL
FLOWER LA
PARK MEAD GDNS
Allot Gdns
Mill Hill Park
HA8
DEAN'S LA
Schs
HALE DR
SANDBROOK CL
SUNNYDALE GDNS
THE HAWTHORNS
1 TANGLEWOOD LO
2 NIGHTINGALE LO
Nature Reserve
Mill Hill Broadway
Lyndhurst Park
Granard Bsns Ctr
WOODLAND WAY
4
Mill Hill Ind Est
WATFORD WAY (BARNET BY-PASS)
50
Allot Gdns
BANSTOCK RD
DRYFIELD RD
WALTER WLK
FOURLAND WLK
LASHFORD HO
CRISPIN RD
BROOK WLK
GOLD LA
THE MEADS
BENNINGHOLME RD
OLDBERRY RD
DEANSBROOK RD
GOLDBEATERS GR
ELLIS CL
LYNDHURST AVE
WOODCROFT AVE
PARKSIDE
HOLMDENE AVE
THE RISE
SUNRISE VIEW
BUNN'S LA
28
HILLSIDE GR
COPTHALL
WENLOCK RD
DEANSBROOK CL
EDRICK RD
EDRICK WLK
A5109
DEANS CL
LANGHAM RD
HOOK WLK
EDWIN RD
ISLIP GDNS
DEAN WLK
HOMEFIELD RD
GRANGE RD
ABBOTS RD
LANGHAM GDNS
EVERSFIELD GDNS
Woodcroft Park
Sp Gd
DOVE CL
Pentavia Ret Pk
FEATHERSTONE CT
BLOOMSBURY CL
FARM HOUSE CT
RUDDOCK CL
BERNHART CL
BUCKLE CT
Sch
CARDINAL RD
Pav
Tenn Ct
Pl Fld
CRESSINGHAM RD
HORSECROFT RD
MILLING RD
WOLSEY GR
STORKSMEAD RD
SPALDING CL
GOLDBEATERS GR
RIVINGTON CRES
UNIVERSITY CL
3
ROWLANDS CL
LONGFIELD AVE
BRISTON MEWS
BRANCASTER DR
FAKENHAM CL
AYLESHAM CL
BURNHAM CL
PAVILION WAY
LITTLEFIELD RD
BREARLEY CL
BOSTON RD
ORANGE HILL RD
BRIAR WLK
KIRTON WLK
NORWICH WLK
COLCHESTER RD
Tenn Ct
Watling Park
Burnt Oak
ARUNDEL GDNS
MOSTYN RD
WARDELL CL
FIELD MEAD
DUNN MEAD
LANCASTER CL
NORTH GN
LINKLEA CL
BIRCH GN
LONG FIELD
WIGGINS MEAD
GATTING CL
OVAL CT
GRACE CL
HEMMINGS CT
FORTESCUE RD
Silk Stream
Tenn Cts
Sp Gd
BLUNDELL RD
CRANFIELD DR
HIGHLEA CL
WILLOW GN
BROOKLEA CL
LARCH GN
PARKLEA CL
SOUTH GN
CLAYTON FIELD
SATCHELL MEAD
WITHERS MEAD
CORNER MEAD
GREAT FIELD
91
TITHE WLK
THE CL
ROSCOFF CL
LYNFORD CL
BLESSBURY RD
BURNT OAK FIELDS
COOMS WLK
WATLING AVE
GUNTER GR
HANSHAW DR
Sch
Liby
Burnt Oak
PARK CROFT
SILKSTREAM PAR
NURSE CL
GILBERT GR
THIRLEBY RD
GLOUCESTER GR
TREVOR GDNS
TREVOR RD
ALBANY CT
PAGEANT AVE
FULBECK DR
DISHFORTH LA
HEYWOOD AVE
ACKLINGTON DR
BOVINGDON LA
TRENCHARD CL
ELVINGTON LA
GAYDON LA
HEMSWELL DR
Grahame Park
Grahame Park
Barnet Coll (Grahame Pk Ctr)
GRAHAME PARK WAY
LONG MEAD
QUAKERS COURSE
SOUTH MEAD
St James' RC High Sch
2
GILDA CR
EAST RD
SOUTH RD
BARNFIELD RD
BACK LA
MARKET LA
GERVASE RD
Sch
MONTROSE AVE
BOOTH RD
ANGUS GDNS
BRAEMAR GDNS
WARMWELL AVE
LANACRE AVE
NORTH ACRE
NEAR ACRE
EVERGLADE STRAND
AVION CRES
Hurricane Trad Ctr
SILKSTREAM RD
GASKARTH RD
Barnfield Prim Sch
PLAYFIELD RD
Silkstream Park
MARTLESHAM WLK
KENLEY AVE
CONINGSBY AVE
POCKLINGTON CL
TANGMERE WAY
YELLOWHAMMER CT
KENT CT
JAMES CT
Schs
BROADHEAD STRAND
FIVE ACRE
HUNDRED ACRE
LITTLE STRAND
GREAT STRAND
Pl Fld
RAF Mus
NW9
BURNT OAK BROADWAY
30
STABURN
OAK GDNS
STAG CL
MILLFIELD RD
ALPHAGE WLK
BOSCOMBE CIRCUS
NW9
WAGTAIL CL
SHELDUCK CL
SWAN DR
KESTREL CL
TURNSTONE CL
HAZEL CL
FROBISHER RD
CHERRY CL
FURTHER ACRE
Battle of Britain Museum
1
LIMESDALE GDNS
OAKLEIGH CT
EDGWARE RD THE HYDE
A5
SOUTHBOURNE AVE
SOUTHBOURNE CT
MONTROSE CT
Pav
Pl Fld
Allot Gdns
BOOTH RD
FALCON WAY
HARRIER RD
EAGLE DR
MAGPIE CL
KINGFISHER WLK
LOWER STRAND
BELVEDERE STRAND
FILTON CL 1
BLACKCAP CT 2
BITTERN CT 3
BUNTING CT 4
LAPWING CT 5
RAVEN CL 6
LISTER CT 7
CURIE GDNS 8
FLEMING WLK 9
AEROVILLE
PASTEUR CL
CHANCELLOR PL
Police HQ
BIRCHWOOD CT
HOLMSTALL PAR
HOLMSTALL AVE
REDHILL DR
GREENWAY GDNS
GREENWAY CL
PORTMAN GDNS
THE GREENWAY
Tenn Cts
Colindale
90
HENDON
CARLISLE RD
Barnet
Harrow
Colindale Bsns Pk
SHOELANDS CT
SILK HO
Central Public Health Lab
45
COLINDALE AVE
British Liby (Newspaper Liby)
AERODROME RD
JOHNSON CT 1
WILSHAW CL 2
COLMORE CT 3
Capitol
Superstore
ANNESLEY
Recn
20
A
B
21
C
D
22

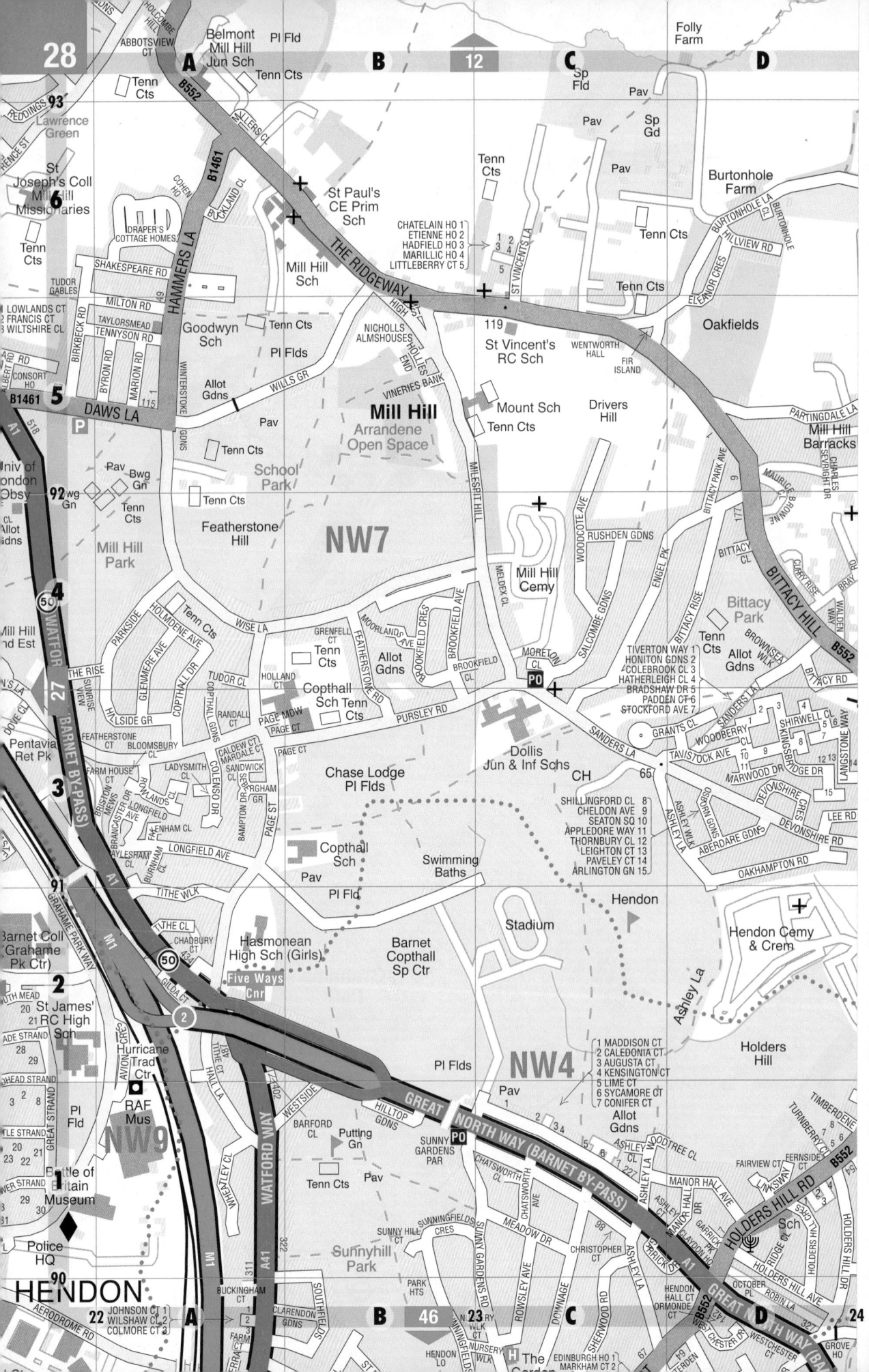
12
46
Mill Hill
NW7
NW4
NW9
HENDON
Arrandene Open Space
Mill Hill Park
Bittacy Park
Sunnyhill Park
THE RIDGEWAY
GREAT NORTH WAY (BARNET BY-PASS)
WATFORD WAY
BITTACY HILL
HOLDERS HILL RD
CHATELAIN HO 1
ETIENNE HO 2
HADFIELD HO 3
MARILLIC HO 4
LITTLEBERRY CT 5
TIVERTON WAY 1
HONITON GDNS 2
COLEBROOK CL 3
HATHERLEIGH CL 4
BRADSHAW DR 5
PADDEN CT 6
STOCKFORD AVE 7
SHILLINGFORD CL 8
CHELDON AVE 9
SEATON SQ 10
APPLEDORE WAY 11
THORNBURY CL 12
LEIGHTON CT 13
PAVELEY CT 14
ARLINGTON GN 15
1 MADDISON CT
2 CALEDONIA CT
3 AUGUSTA CT
4 KENSINGTON CT
5 LIME CT
6 SYCAMORE CT
7 CONIFER CT
JOHNSON CT 1
WILSHAW CL 2
COLMORE CT 3
EDINBURGH HO 1
MARKHAM CT 2
LOWLANDS CT
FRANCIS CT
WILTSHIRE CL

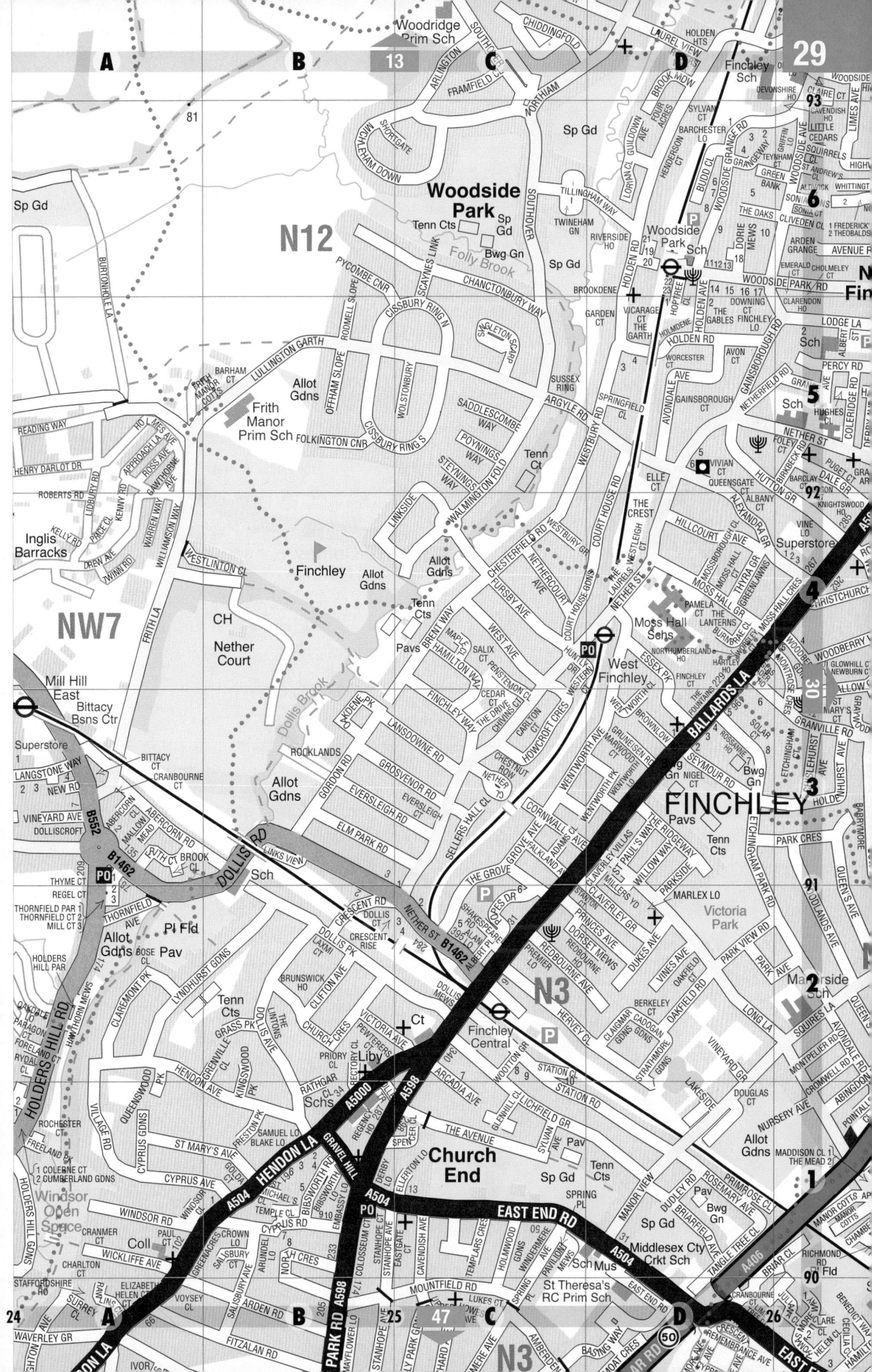
29
A
B
13
C
D
Woodridge Prim Sch
CHIDDINGFOLD
LAUREL VIEW
HOLDEN HTS
Finchley Sch
WOODSIDE
DEVONSHIRE HO
CLAIRE CT
93
CAVENDISH HO
LITTLE CEDARS
SQUIRRELS
LIMES AVE
HIGHW
ARLINGTON
SOUTHOVER
FRAMFIELD CL
NORTHAM
BROOK MDW
FOUR ACRES
SYLVAN CT
BARCHESTER LO
WOODSIDE GRANGE RD
81
SHORTGATE
MICHLEHAM DOWN
Sp Gd
GUILDOWN AVE
LORIAN CL
HENDERSON CT
BUDD CL
GRANGEWAY
TEYNHAM CT
GREEN BANK
ST ANDREW'S CL
ALDWICK
WHITTINGT
Sp Gd
Woodside Park
Sp Gd
Tenn Cts
Bwg Gn
Folly Brook
N12
TILLINGHAM WAY
TWINEHAM GN
RIVERSIDE HO
Woodside Park Sch
SONIA GDNS
SONIA CT
6
THE OAKS
DORIE MEWS
CLIVEDEN CL
1 FREDERICK CT
2 THEOBALDS
ARDEN GRANGE
AVENUE R
EMERALD CT
CHOLMELEY CT
WOODSIDE PARK RD
Fin
BURTONHOLE LA
PYCOMBE CNR
SCAYNES LINK
CHANCTONBURY WAY
BROOKDENE
VICARAGE CT
THE GARTH
HOPTREE CL
HOLDEN AVE
THE GABLES
DOWNING CT
FINCHLEY LO
CLARENDON HO
LODGE LA
CISSBURY RING N
RODMELL SLOPE
SINGLETON SCARP
GARDEN CT
HOLMDENE
HOLDEN RD
WORCESTER CT
AVON CT
GAINSBOROUGH RD
Sch
ALBERT ST
PERCY RD
LULLINGTON GARTH
BARHAM CT
FRITH MANOR COTTS
OFFHAM SLOPE
WOLSTONBURY
Allot Gdns
SUSSEX RING
AVONDALE RD
AVE
GAINSBOROUGH CT
NETHERFIELD RD
5
HUGHES CL
COLERIDGE RD
Frith Manor Prim Sch
ARGYLE RD
SPRINGFIELD CL
SADDLESCOMBE WAY
READING WAY
HOLMES AVE
APPROACH LA
ROSS AVE
GAWTHORNE AVE
HENRY DARLOT DR
FOLKINGTON CNR
CISSBURY RING S
POYNINGS WAY
Tenn Ct
WESTBURY RD
NETHER ST
FOLEY CT
BIRKBECK RD
PUGET CT
DALE GR
STEYNINGS WAY
WALMINGTON FOLD
VIVIAN CT
QUEENSGATE CT
ELLE CT
BARCLAY CT
92
KNIGHTSWOOD HO
ROBERTS RD
LIDBURY RD
KENNY RD
PRICE CL
WARREN WAY
WILLIAMSON WAY
LINKSIDE
COURT HOUSE RD
THE CREST
HUTTON GR
ALBANY CT
ALEXANDRA GR
VINE LO
Inglis Barracks
KELLY RD
DREW AVE
WINN RD
WESTLINTON CL
Allot Gdns
Finchley
Allot Gdns
CHESTERFIELD RD
WESTBURY GR
WESTLEIGH CT
HILLCOURT AVE
MOSSBOROUGH CL
MOSS HALL CT
THYRA GR
GREENLAWNS
Superstore
NW7
FRITH LA
CH
Nether Court
Tenn Cts
Pavs
FURSBY AVE
NETHERCOURT AVE
COURT HOUSE GDNS
THE LAURELS
MOSS HALL GR
MOSS HALL CRES
4
CHRISTCHURCH
PAMELA CT
THE LANTERNS
Moss Hall Schs
BURMBRAE CL
BRENT WAY
MAPLE CL
HAMILTON WAY
SALIX CT
WEST AVE
PENSTEMON CL
HUNT DR
PO
West Finchley
NORTHUMBERLAND HO
WOODBERRY W
GLOWHILL CT
NEWBURN CT
Mill Hill East
Bittacy Bsns Ctr
Dollis Brook
OAKDENE PK
LANSDOWNE RD
FINCHLEY WAY
CEDAR CT
THE DRIVE
CHIVINS CT
CARLTON CT
HOWCROFT CRES
WESTERN CT
ESSEX PK
FINCHLEY CT
HARTLEY HO
THE FOUNTAINS
BALLARDS LA
MONTROSE CRES
30
ST MARY'S CT
GRANVILLE RD
Superstore
BITTACY CT
CRANBOURNE CT
ROCKLANDS
GORDON RD
GROSVENOR RD
CHESTNUT ROW
NETHER CL
WENTWORTH AVE
MARWOOD CT
GRUNEISEN RD
BROWNLOW RD
SEYMOUR RD
ROSSANNE HO
SOLAR CT
ETCHINGHAM CT
CASTLEHURST AVE
NETHERHURST AVE
BABRYMORE
LANGSTONE WAY
NEW RD
VINEYARD AVE
DOLLISCROFT
Allot Gdns
EVERSLEIGH RD
EVERSLEIGH CT
WENTWORTH PK
WENTWORTH LO
Bwg Gn
NIGEL CT
FINCHLEY
3
HOLDE
ABERCORN CL
MALLOW MEAD
ABERCORN RD
B552
B1462
ELM PARK RD
SELLERS HALL CL
CORNWALL AVE
ADAMS CL
FALKLAND AVE
CLAVERLEY VILLAS
ST PAUL'S WAY
WILLOW WAY
THE RIDGEWAY
Pavs
Tenn Cts
ETCHINGHAM PARK RD
PARK CRES
QUEEN'S AVE
FRITH CT
BROOK CL
DOLLIS RD
LINKS VIEW
THYME CT
REGEL CT
PO
THORNFIELD PAR
THORNFIELD CT
MILL CT
Sch
THE GROVE
GROVE AVE
MILLERS YD
PARKSIDE
MARLEX LO
91
WOODLANDS AVE
THORNFIELD AVE
Allot Gdns
BOSE CL
Pav
Pl Fld
HOLDERS HILL PAR
CRESCENT RD
DOLLIS CT
CRESCENT RISE
NETHER ST
B1462
SHAKESPEARE RD
ALAN LO
ALBERT PL
POPES DR
STANTON CT
CLAVERLEY GR
PRINCES AVE
DORSET MEWS
REDBOURNE HO
REDBOURNE AVE
PREMIER LO
DUKES AVE
VINES AVE
OAKFIELD CT
Victoria Park
PARK VIEW RD
PARK AVE
Manorside Sch
2
LYNDHURST GDNS
LAXMI CT
DOLLIS PK
CLIFTON AVE
BRUNSWICK HO
N3
HERVEY CL
BERKELEY CT
OAKFIELD RD
LONG LA
SQUIRES LA
QUEEN'S
CLAREMONT PK
Tenn Cts
GRASS PK
DOLLIS AVE
THE LINTONS
CHURCH CRES
VICTORIA AVE
PEWTERERS CT
DOLLIS MEWS
Finchley Central
CLAIGMAR GDNS
CADOGAN GDNS
STRATHMORE GDNS
VINEYARD GR
AVONDALE RD
MONTPELIER RD
OAKDALE
PARAGON CT
FORELAND CT
RYDAL CL
HOLDERS HILL RD
HAWTHORN MEWS
PRIORY CL
Liby
Ct
GRENVILLE CL
KINGSWOOD PK
HENDON AVE
RATHGAR CL
RECTORY CL
ARCADIA AVE
WOOTTON GR
STATION CL
STATION RD
LAKESIDE
DOUGLAS CT
CROMWELL RD
ABINGDON
QUEENSWOOD PK
VILLAGE RD
CYPRUS GDNS
FRESTON PK
SAMUEL LO
BLAKE LO
Schs
A5000
A598
GLENHILL CL
LICHFIELD GR
THE AVENUE
SYLVAN AVE
Pav
NURSERY AVE
POINTALL
ROCHESTER CT
FREELAND PK
1 COLERNE CT
2 CUMBERLAND GDNS
ST MARY'S AVE
GOLDA CT
CYPRUS AVE
HENDON LA
GRAVEL HILL
REGENCY HO
SPENCER CL
DERBY LO
Church End
Tenn Cts
Sp Gd
MANOR VIEW
DUDLEY RD
ROSEMARY AVE
PRIMROSE CL
Allot Gdns
MADDISON CL
THE MEAD
1
Windsor Open Space
WINDSOR CL
WINDSOR RD
ST MICHAEL'S CL
TEMPLE CL
BIBSWORTH RD
BIBSWORTH LO
EMBASSY LO
ELLERTON LO
A504
EAST END RD
SPRING PL
Pav
Bwg Gn
MANOR COTTS
HOLDERS HILL GDNS
CRANMER CT
Coll
PAUL CT
CROWN LO
CYPRUS RD
NORTH CRES
PO
COLOSSEUM CT
STANHOPE CT
EASTGATE CT
CAVENDISH AVE
TEMPLARS CRES
HOLMWOOD GDNS
WINDERMERE AVE
PAVILION MEWS
Sp Gd
Middlesex Cty Crkt Sch
BRIARFIELD AVE
TANGLE TREE CL
A406
RICHMOND RD
CHAMBE
WICKLIFFE AVE
CHARLTON CT
SALISBURY CT
ARUNDEL LO
GREENACRES
STAFFORDSHIRE HO
ELIZABETH CT
HELEN CT
VOYSEY CL
SALISBURY AVE
ARDEN RD
MOUNTFIELD RD
LUKES CT
Sch
Mus
St Theresa's RC Prim Sch
EAST END RD
BRIAR CL
90
Fld
CRANBOURNE CT
BENEDICT WAY
24
SURREY CL
A
B
25
47
C
D
26
WAVERLEY GR
FITZALAN RD
PARK RD
A598
MAYFLOWER LO
STANHOPE AVE
N3
AMBERDEN
BASING WAY
50
CRESCENT
REMEMBRANCE AVE
HELEN CL
CECILIA CL
EAST
IVOR

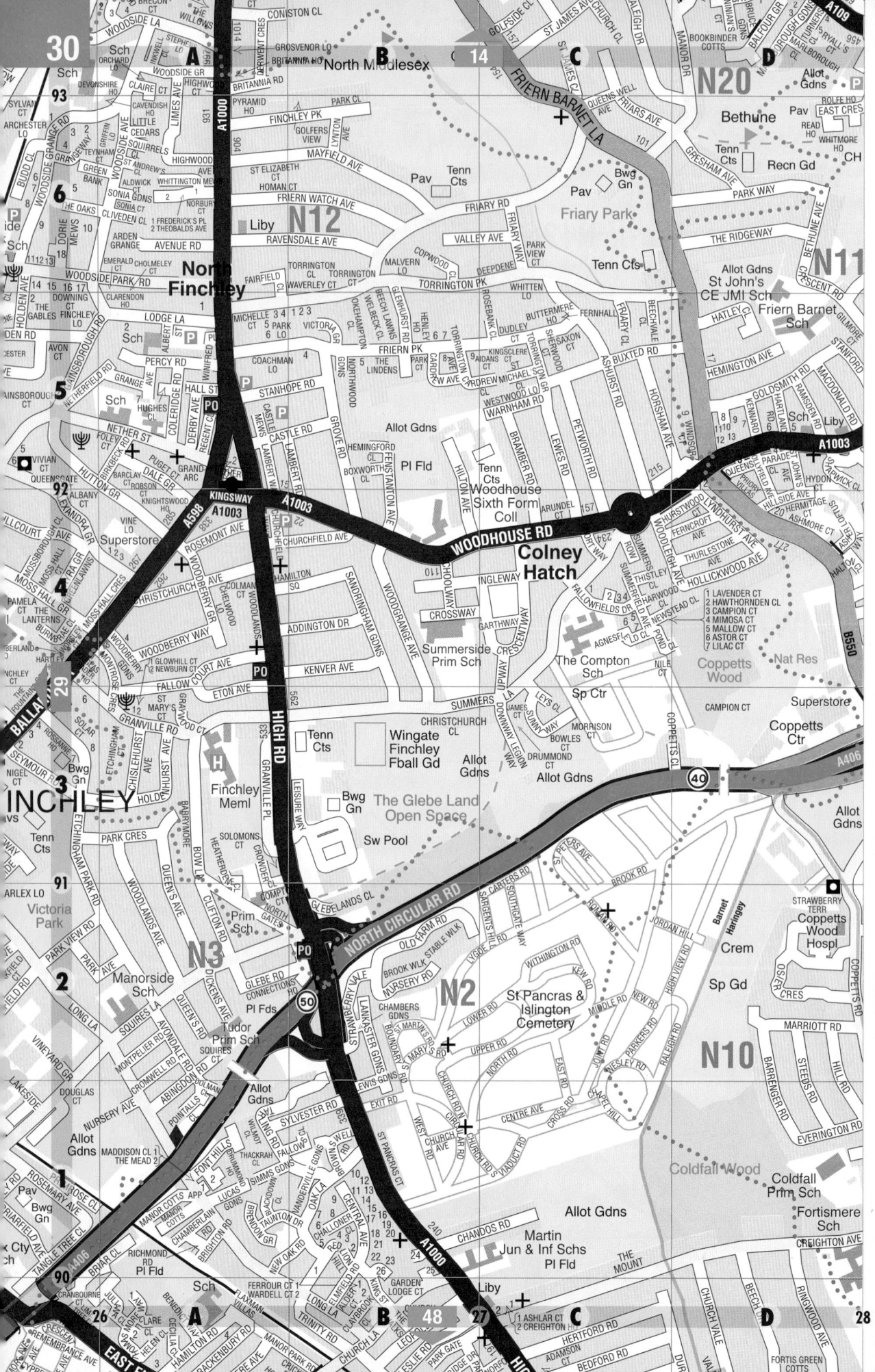

30
14
48
29
26
27
28
A
B
C
D
1
2
3
4
5
6
90
91
92
93
N12
N20
N11
N3
N2
N10
North Middlesex
North Finchley
Colney Hatch
INCHLEY
Friary Park
Bethune
Recn Gd
Allot Gdns
St John's CE JMI Sch
Friern Barnet Sch
Woodhouse Sixth Form Coll
Summerside Prim Sch
The Compton Sch
Sp Ctr
Coppetts Wood
Nat Res
Superstore
Coppetts Ctr
Wingate Finchley Fball Gd
Finchley Meml
The Glebe Land Open Space
Sw Pool
Manorside Sch
Tudor Prim Sch
Victoria Park
St Pancras & Islington Cemetery
Crem
Sp Gd
Coppetts Wood Hospl
Coldfall Wood
Coldfall Prim Sch
Fortismere Sch
Martin Jun & Inf Schs
Pl Fld
Pl Fds
Liby
Tenn Cts
Bwg Gn
Pav
Barnet
Haringey
A1000
A1003
A598
A406
A109
B550
HIGH RD
NORTH CIRCULAR RD
WOODHOUSE RD
KINGSWAY
FRIERN BARNET LA
WOODSIDE PARK RD
WOODSIDE LA
BALLARDS LA
EAST END RD
LODGE LA
FRIERN PK
TORRINGTON PK
FRIARY RD
FRIERN WATCH AVE
RAVENSDALE AVE
MAYFIELD AVE
FINCHLEY PK
NETHER ST
CHRISTCHURCH AVE
FALLOW COURT AVE
GRANVILLE RD
LONG LA
CHANDOS RD
CREIGHTON AVE
HEMINGTON AVE
BUXTED RD
SUMMERS LA
PARK WAY
THE RIDGEWAY
GRESHAM AVE
EVERINGTON RD
MARRIOTT RD
HERTFORD RD
BEDFORD RD
CHURCH LA

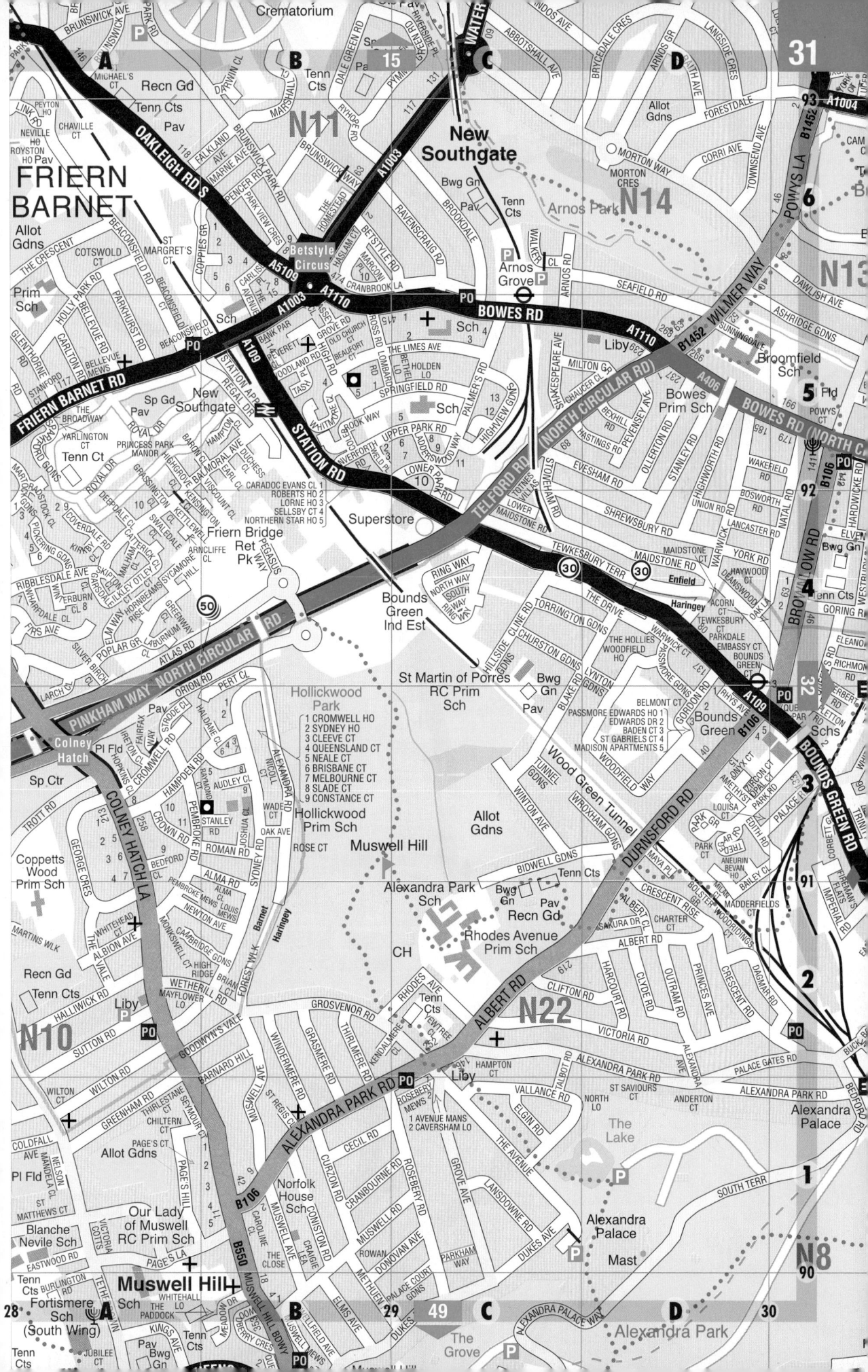

31
Crematorium
A
B
15
C
D
FRIERN BARNET
New Southgate
N11
N14
N13
N22
N10
N8
Arnos Park
Arnos Grove
Betstyle Circus
Friern Bridge Ret Pk
Bounds Green Ind Est
Bounds Green
Hollickwood Park
Hollickwood Prim Sch
Muswell Hill
Alexandra Park Sch
Rhodes Avenue Prim Sch
Alexandra Palace
The Lake
Mast
Alexandra Park
Colney Hatch
Coppetts Wood Prim Sch
Blanche Nevile Sch
Our Lady of Muswell RC Prim Sch
Fortismere Sch (South Wing)
Norfolk House Sch
St Martin of Porres RC Prim Sch
Bowes Prim Sch
Broomfield Sch
Superstore
Wood Green Tunnel
OAKLEIGH RD S
FRIERN BARNET RD
BOWES RD
STATION RD
TELFORD RD (NORTH CIRCULAR RD)
PINKHAM WAY NORTH CIRCULAR RD
COLNEY HATCH LA
ALEXANDRA PARK RD
ALBERT RD
DURNSFORD RD
BOUNDS GREEN RD
WILMER WAY
POWYS LA
BROWNLOW RD
MUSWELL HILL BDWY
ALEXANDRA PALACE WAY
A1003
A1110
A5109
A109
A406
B1452
A1004
B106
B550
28
A
B
29
49
C
D
30
The Grove

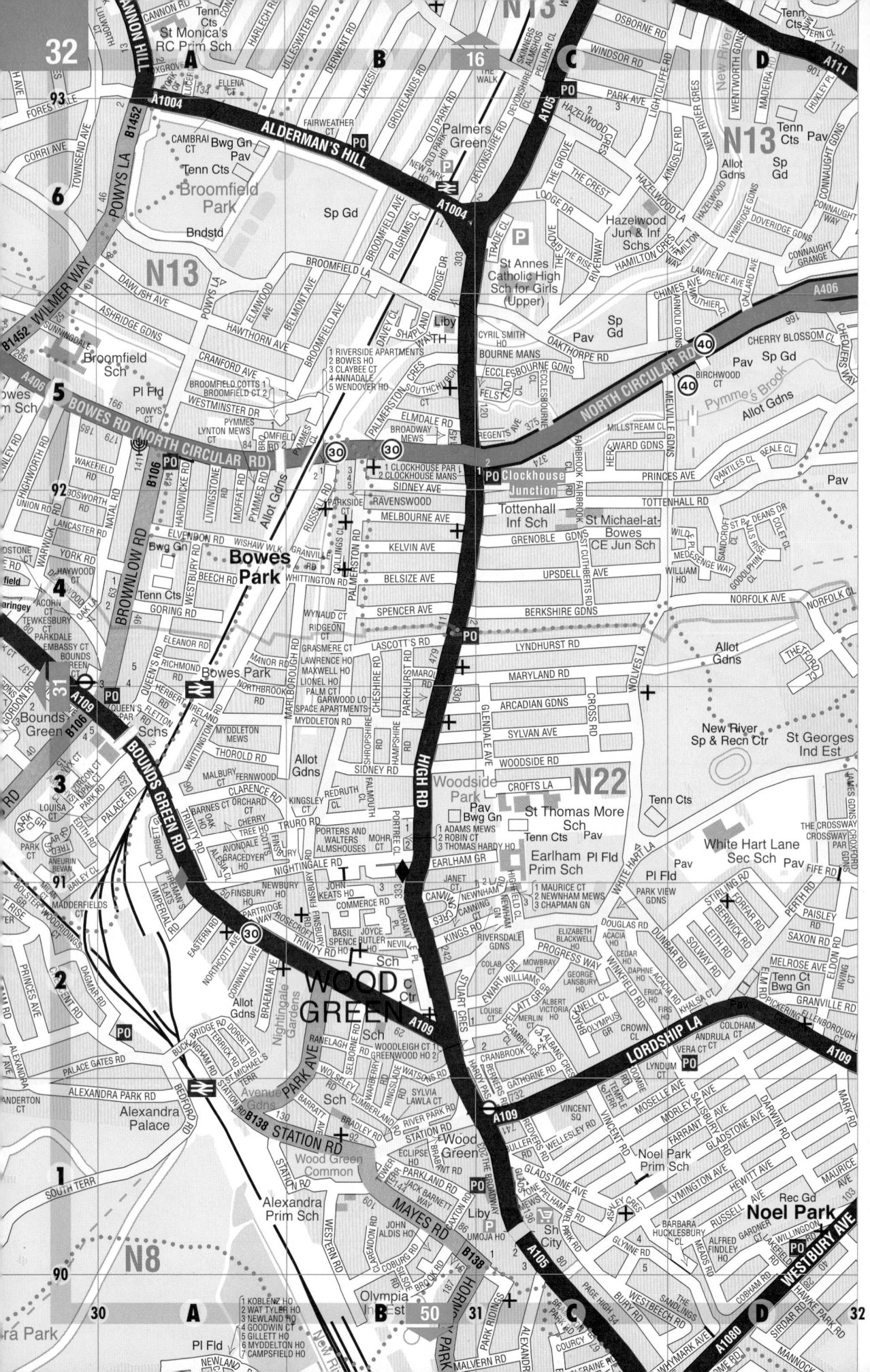

32
A
B
C
D
16
N13
St Monica's RC Prim Sch
ALDERMAN'S HILL
A1004
Palmers Green
Broomfield Park
Bwg Gn Pav
Tenn Cts
Bndstd
Sp Gd
WILMER WAY
POWYS LA
B1452
A105
Hazelwood Jun & Inf Schs
St Annes Catholic High Sch for Girls (Upper)
NORTH CIRCULAR RD
A406
BOWES RD (NORTH CIRCULAR RD)
Broomfield Sch
Pl Fld
Pymme's Brook
Allot Gdns
Clockhouse Junction
Tottenhall Inf Sch
St Michael-at-Bowes CE Jun Sch
Bowes Park
BROWNLOW RD
B106
HIGH RD
Woodside Park
St Thomas More Sch
Earlham Prim Sch
N22
White Hart Lane Sec Sch
New River Sp & Recn Ctr
St Georges Ind Est
Bounds Green
BOUNDS GREEN RD
A109
WOOD GREEN
LORDSHIP LA
Alexandra Palace
STATION RD
B138
Wood Green Common
Alexandra Prim Sch
MAYES RD
Noel Park
Noel Park Prim Sch
WESTBURY AVE
A1080
Wood Green
Sh City
N8
Olympia Ind Est
50
30
31
1
2
3
4
5
6
90
91
92
93

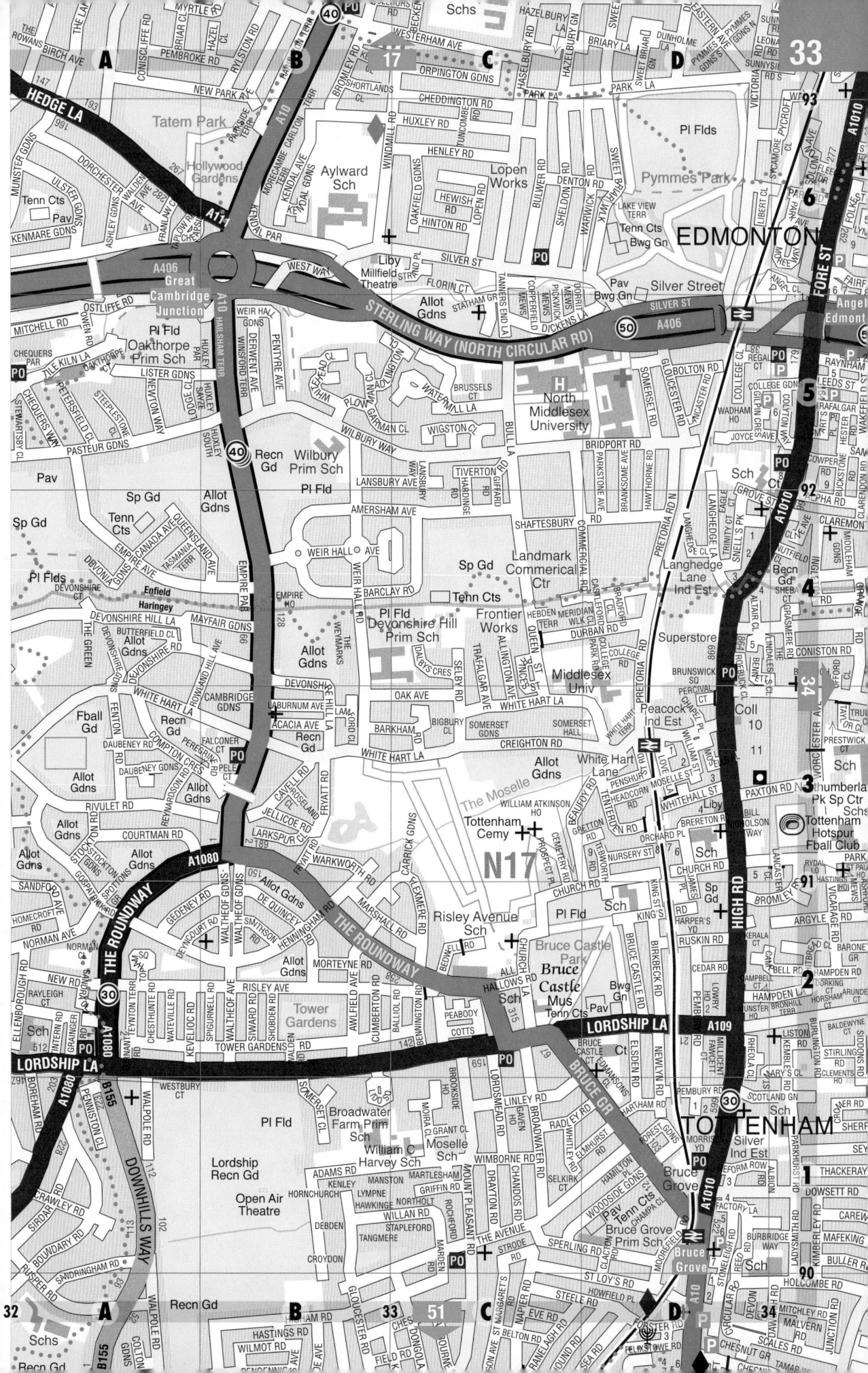
EDMONTON
TOTTENHAM
N17
Great Cambridge Junction
STERLING WAY (NORTH CIRCULAR RD)
A406
A10
A1010
A1080
A111
A109
B155
HIGH RD
FORE ST
LORDSHIP LA
THE ROUNDWAY
BRUCE GR
DOWNHILLS WAY
HEDGE LA
Tatem Park
Hollywood Gardens
Aylward Sch
Lopen Works
Pymmes Park
Pl Flds
Silver Street
North Middlesex University
Wilbury Prim Sch
Oakthorpe Prim Sch
Landmark Commerical Ctr
Frontier Works
Devonshire Hill Prim Sch
Langhedge Lane Ind Est
Superstore
Middlesex Univ
Peacock Ind Est
White Hart Lane
Tottenham Cemy
The Moselle
Tottenham Hotspur Fball Club
Northumberland Pk Sp Ctr
Risley Avenue Sch
Bruce Castle Park
Bruce Castle Mus
Tower Gardens
Broadwater Farm Prim Sch
William C Harvey Sch
Moselle Sch
Lordship Recn Gd
Open Air Theatre
Bruce Grove Prim Sch
Bruce Grove
Silver Ind Est
Liby
Millfield Theatre
Enfield
Haringey
Angel Edmonton
17
34
51
32
A B C D
1 2 3 4 5 6

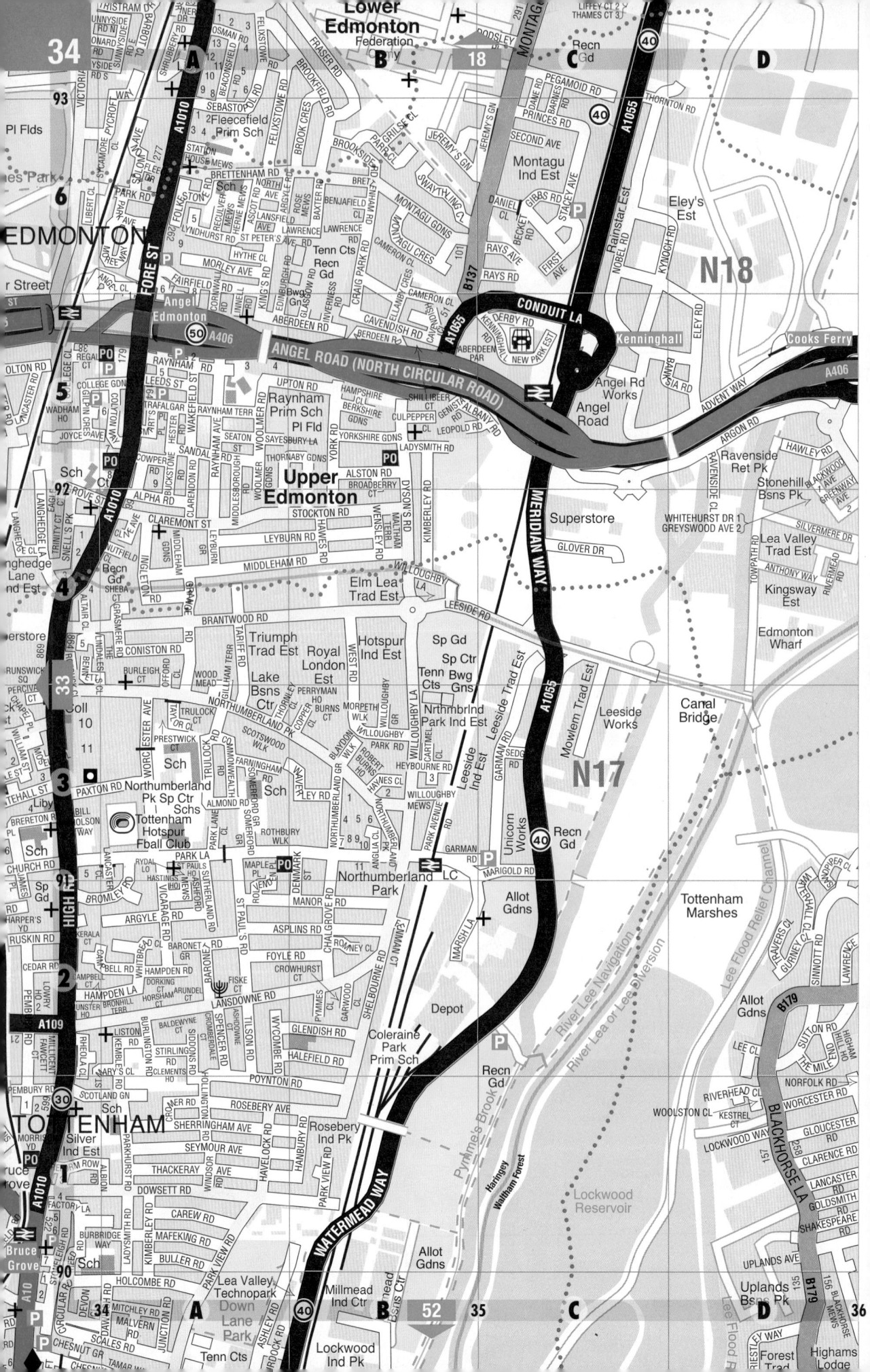
34
Lower Edmonton
Federation
18
EDMONTON
N18
Upper Edmonton
N17
Angel Edmonton
ANGEL ROAD (NORTH CIRCULAR ROAD)
A406
A1010
A1055
B137
CONDUIT LA
MERIDIAN WAY
WATERMEAD WAY
FORE ST
HIGH RD
Montagu Ind Est
Eley's Est
Angel Road
Angel Rd Works
Kenninghall
Cooks Ferry
Ravenside Ret Pk
Stonehill Bsns Pk
Superstore
Lea Valley Trad Est
Kingsway Est
Edmonton Wharf
Elm Lea Trad Est
Triumph Trad Est
Royal London Est
Hotspur Ind Est
Lake Bsns Ctr
Nrthmbrlnd Park Ind Est
Leeside Ind Est
Leeside Trad Est
Mowlem Trad Est
Leeside Works
Canal Bridge
Unicorn Works
Northumberland Park
Tottenham Hotspur Fball Club
Northumberland Pk Sp Ctr
Tottenham Marshes
River Lee Navigation
River Lea or Lee Diversion
Lee Flood Relief Channel
Pymme's Brook
Lockwood Reservoir
Depot
Coleraine Park Prim Sch
Rosebery Ind Pk
Lea Valley Technopark
Millmead Ind Ctr
Lockwood Ind Pk
Down Lane Park
Uplands Bsns Pk
BLACKHORSE LA
B179
TOTTENHAM
Bruce Grove
Silver Ind Est
Raynham Prim Sch
Fleecefield Prim Sch
33
52
35
36
A
B
C
D

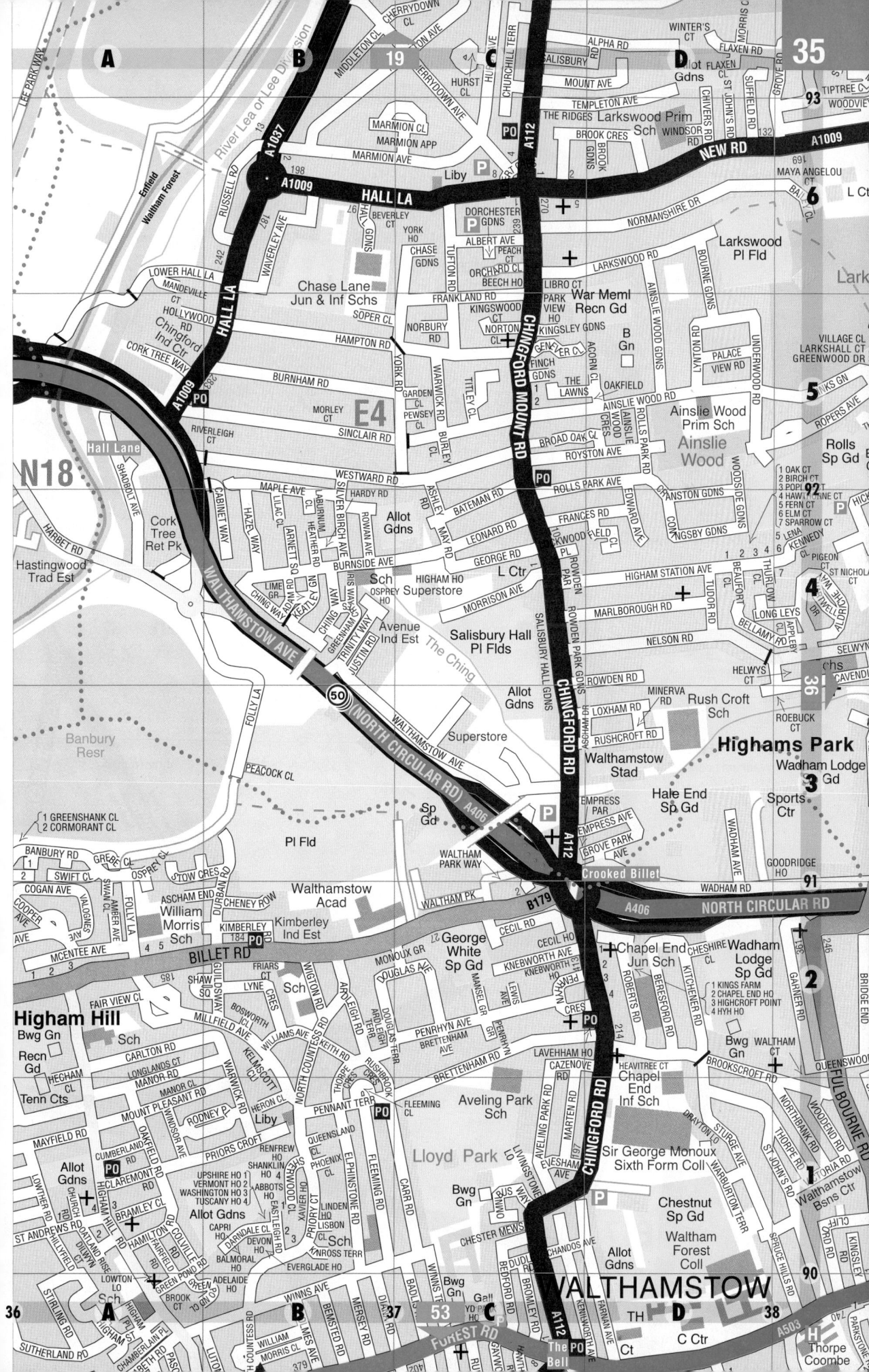
A
B
C
D
19
N18
E4
Higham Hill
Highams Park
WALTHAMSTOW
Chingford Mount Rd
Chingford Rd
Hall La
Hall Lane
New Rd
Walthamstow Ave
North Circular Rd
Billet Rd
Forest Rd
Fulbourne Rd
Crooked Billet
Larkswood Prim Sch
Chase Lane Jun & Inf Schs
War Meml Recn Gd
Ainslie Wood Prim Sch
Ainslie Wood
Larkswood Pl Fld
Salisbury Hall Pl Flds
Walthamstow Stad
Rush Croft Sch
Hale End Sp Gd
Banbury Resr
Walthamstow Acad
William Morris Sch
Kimberley Ind Est
George White Sp Gd
Chapel End Jun Sch
Wadham Lodge Sp Gd
Aveling Park Sch
Lloyd Park
Sir George Monoux Sixth Form Coll
Chestnut Sp Gd
Waltham Forest Coll
Cork Tree Ret Pk
Hastingwood Trad Est
Avenue Ind Est
Superstore
The Ching
Walthamstow Bsns Ctr
Thorpe Combe
The Bell
36
37
38
53
90
91
92
93

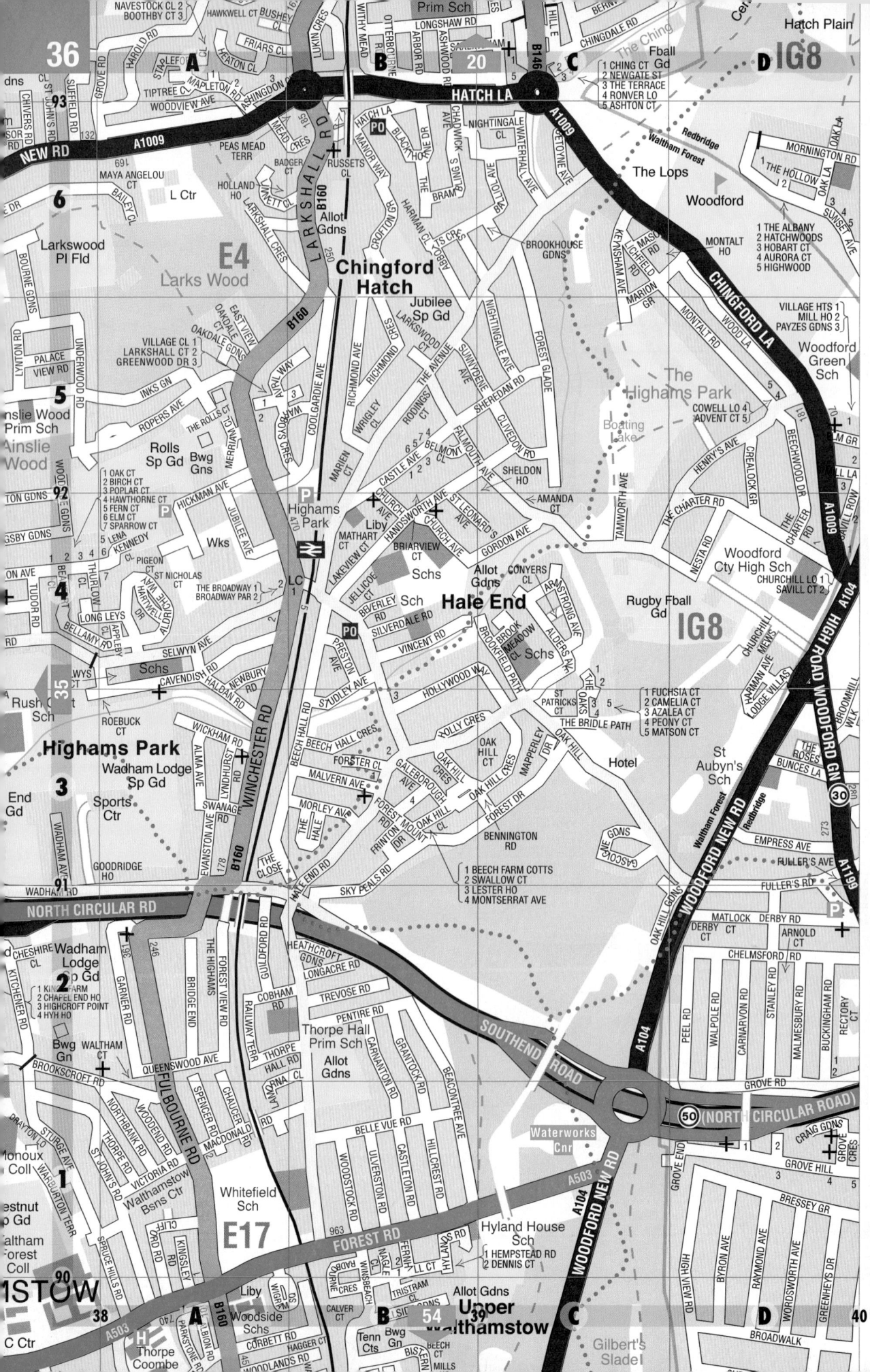
36
A
B
C
D
20
IG8
Hatch Plain
Fball Gd
The Ching
NAVESTOCK CL 2
BOOTHBY CT 3
HAWKWELL CT
BUSHEY CL
HAROLD RD
FRIARS CL
HEATON CL
STAPLEFORD
MAPLETON RD
TIPTREE CL
ASHINGDON
WOODVIEW AVE
GROVE RD
SUFFIELD RD
ST JOHN'S RD
CHIVERS RD
93
132
NEW RD
A1009
LUKIN CRES
WITHY MEAD
OTTERBOURNE
Prim Sch
LONGSHAW RD
ARBOR RD
ASHWOOD RD
HATCH LA
CHINGDALE RD
1 CHING CT
2 NEWGATE ST
3 THE TERRACE
4 RONVER LO
5 ASHTON CT
B146
HILL E
PO
HATCH LA
MANOR WAY
BLACKTHORNE DR
CHADWICK AVE
NIGHTINGALE CL
WATERHALL AVE
CETOYNE AVE
Redbridge
Waltham Forest
The Lops
MORNINGTON RD
OAK LA
THE HOLLOW
SUNSET AVE
Woodford
PEAS MEAD TERR
MEAD CRES
BADGER CT
RUSSETS CL
MAYA ANGELOU CT
HOLLAND HO
LARKSHALL RD
LARKSHALL CRES
BAILEY CL
L Ctr
Allot Gdns
B160
CROFTON GR
HARMAN CL
THE BRAM
BALLIOL AVE
BROOKHOUSE GDNS
KEYNSHAM AVE
LICHFIELD RD
MASON RD
MONTALT HO
1 THE ALBANY
2 HATCHWOODS
3 HOBART CT
4 AURORA CT
5 HIGHWOOD
6
Larkswood Pl Fld
E4
Larks Wood
Chingford Hatch
Jubilee Sp Gd
BOURNE GDNS
CHINGFORD LA
MARION GR
MONTALT RD
WOOD LA
VILLAGE HTS 1
MILL HO 2
PAYZES GDNS 3
Woodford Green Sch
LYNTON RD
PALACE VIEW RD
UNDERWOOD RD
OAKDALE CT
OAKDALE GDNS
EAST VIEW
VILLAGE CL 1
LARKSHALL CT 2
GREENWOOD DR 3
AVRIL WAY
COOLGARDIE AVE
RICHMOND AVE
RICHMOND CRES
LARKSWOOD CT
THE AVENUE
SUNNYDENE AVE
NIGHTINGALE AVE
FOREST GLADE
The Highams Park
Boating Lake
COWELL LO 4
ADVENT CT 5
5
INKS GN
ROPERS AVE
THE ROLLS CT
MERRIAM CL
WARBOYS CRES
WRIGLEY CL
RODINGS CT
SHERIDAN RD
CLIVEDON RD
BELMONT CL
FALMOUTH AVE
CASTLE AVE
MARIEN CT
Ainslie Wood Prim Sch
Ainslie Wood
Rolls Sp Gd
Bwg Gns
1 OAK CT
2 BIRCH CT
3 POPLAR CT
4 HAWTHORNE CT
5 FERN CT
6 ELM CT
7 SPARROW CT
HICKMAN AVE
JUBILEE AVE
Wks
Highams Park
CHURCH AVE
HANDSWORTH AVE
ST LEONARD'S AVE
SHELDON HO
AMANDA CT
TAMWORTH AVE
HENRY'S AVE
CREALOCK GR
BEECHWOOD DR
THE CHARTER RD
THE CHARTER RD
NESTA RD
A1009
92
TON GDNS
WOODSIDE GDNS
GSBY GDNS
LENA KENNEDY CL
PIGEON CT
ST NICHOLAS CT
THE BROADWAY 1
BROADWAY PAR 2
LC
MATHART CT
Liby
BRIARVIEW CT
LAKEVIEW CT
GORDON AVE
Schs
Allot Gdns
CONYERS CL
ARMSTRONG AVE
Hale End
Woodford Cty High Sch
CHURCHILL LO 1
SAVILL CT 2
A104
4
ON AVE
TUDOR RD
BEAUFORT CL
THURLOW
HARTWELL DR
ALDRIDGE WAY
LONG LEYS
APPLEBY
BELLAMY RD
JELLICOE CT
BEVERLEY RD
Sch
SILVERDALE RD
VINCENT RD
PO
BROOK MEADOW
BROOKFIELD PATH
ALDERS AVE
Schs
Rugby Fball Gd
IG8
CHURCHILL MEWS
HARMAN AVE
LODGE VILLAS
HIGH ROAD WOODFORD GN
SELWYN AVE
CAVENDISH RD
HALDAN RD
NEWBURY RD
Schs
35
Rush Croft Sch
ROEBUCK CT
PRESTON AVE
STUDLEY AVE
HOLLYWOOD WAY
THE OAKS
ST PATRICKS CT
1 FUCHSIA CT
2 CAMELIA CT
3 AZALEA CT
4 PEONY CT
5 MATSON CT
THE BRIDLE PATH
BROOMHILL WLK
Highams Park
WICKHAM RD
ALMA AVE
LYNDHURST RD
WINCHESTER RD
BEECH HALL RD
BEECH HALL CRES
HOLLY CRES
OAK HILL CT
MAPPERLEY DR
OAK HILL
Hotel
St Aubyn's Sch
THE ROSES
BUNCES LA
Wadham Lodge Sp Gd
3
End Gd
Sports Ctr
SWANAGE RD
FORSTER CL
MALVERN AVE
GALEBOROUGH AVE
OAK HILL CRES
FOREST DR
WOODFORD NEW RD
30
MORLEY AVE
THE HALE
FOREST MOUNT RD
FRINTON DR
OAK HILL CL
BENNINGTON RD
GASCOIGNE GDNS
EMPRESS AVE
WADHAM AVE
EVANSTON AVE
GOODRIDGE HO
THE CLOSE
HALE END RD
SKY PEALS RD
1 BEECH FARM COTTS
2 SWALLOW CT
3 LESTER HO
4 MONTSERRAT AVE
FULLER'S AVE
FULLER'S RD
A1199
91
WADHAM RD
NORTH CIRCULAR RD
OAK HILL GDNS
MATLOCK CT
DERBY RD
DERBY CT
ARNOLD CT
CHELMSFORD RD
CHESHIRE CL
Wadham Lodge Sp Gd
2
KITCHENER RD
1 KINGS FARM
2 CHAPEL END HO
3 HIGHCROFT POINT
4 HYH HO
GARNER RD
BRIDGE END
THE HIGHAMS
FOREST VIEW RD
GUILDFORD RD
HEATHCROFT GDNS
LONGACRE RD
TREVOSE RD
COBHAM RD
RAILWAY TERR
PENTIRE RD
Thorpe Hall Prim Sch
SOUTHEND ROAD
A104
PEEL RD
WALPOLE RD
CARNARVON RD
STANLEY RD
MALMESBURY RD
BUCKINGHAM RD
RECTORY CT
Bwg Gn
WALTHAM CT
QUEENSWOOD AVE
THORPE HALL RD
CARNANTON RD
GRANTOCK RD
BEACONTREE AVE
Allot Gdns
BROOKSCROFT RD
NORTHBANK RD
WOODEND RD
FULBOURNE RD
SPENCER RD
CHAUCER RD
LAVERNA CL
GROVE RD
50
(NORTH CIRCULAR ROAD)
Waterworks Cnr
DRAYTON
STURGE AVE
THORPE RD
ST JOHN'S RD
VICTORIA RD
MACDONALD RD
BELLE VUE RD
CRAIG GDNS
GROVE CRES
GROVE HILL
GROVE END
Monoux Coll
1
WARBURTON TERR
Walthamstow Bsns Ctr
Whitefield Sch
A503
WOODSTOCK RD
ULVERSTON RD
CASTLETON RD
HILLCREST RD
BRESSEY GR
Chestnut Sp Gd
Waltham Forest Coll
SPRUCE HILLS RD
CLIFFORD RD
KINGSLEY RD
E17
FOREST RD
963
Hyland House Sch
1 HEMPSTEAD RD
2 DENNIS CT
WOODFORD NEW RD
HIGH VIEW RD
BYRON AVE
RAYMOND AVE
WORDSWORTH AVE
GREENHEYS DR
90
STOW
Liby
Woodside Schs
WIGRAM
TRISTRAM
CALVER CT
Allot Gdns
Upper Walthamstow
38
A
B160
B
54
39
C
D
40
BROADWALK
C Ctr
Thorpe Coombe
PARKSTONE RD
ALBION RD
CORBETT RD
HAGGER CT
WOODLANDS RD
Tenn Cts
Bwg Gn
BEECH CT
BISTERNE
Gilbert's Slade

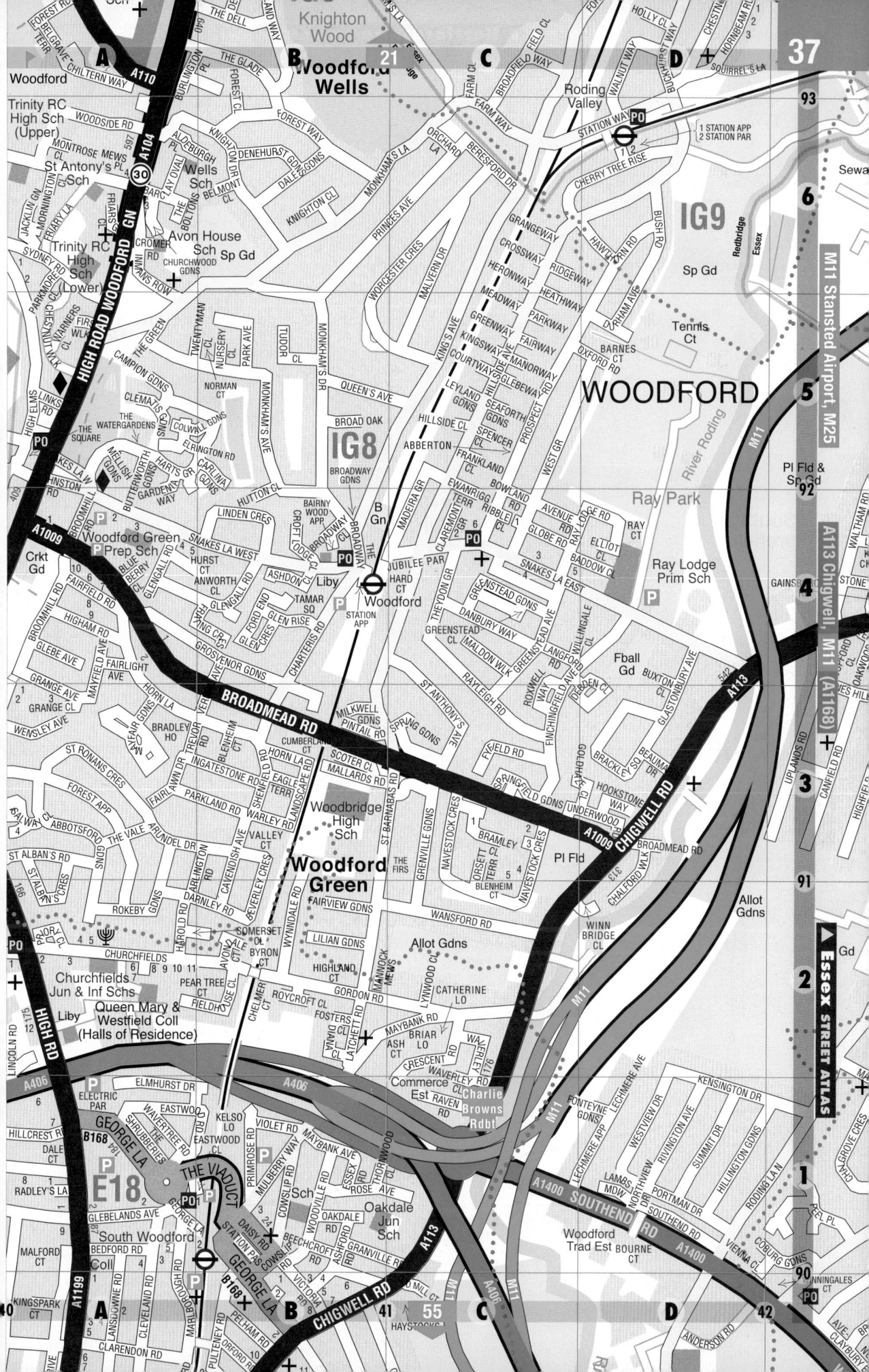

Knighton Wood
21
Woodford Wells
Woodford
Trinity RC High Sch (Upper)
St Antony's Sch
Wells Sch
Avon House Sch
Sp Gd
Trinity RC High Sch (Lower)
HIGH ROAD WOODFORD GN
A104
A110
Roding Valley
STATION WAY
1 STATION APP
2 STATION PAR
CHERRY TREE RISE
IG9
Redbridge
Essex
Sp Gd
Tennis Ct
WOODFORD
River Roding
Ray Park
M11
M11 Stansted Airport, M25
A113 Chigwell, M11 (A1168)
Pl Fld & Sp Gd
IG8
BROAD OAK
BROADWAY GDNS
ABBERTON
Woodford Green Prep Sch
Crkt Gd
A1009
Liby
Woodford
STATION APP
Ray Lodge Prim Sch
SNAKES LA EAST
SNAKES LA WEST
Fball Gd
BROADMEAD RD
CHIGWELL RD
A113
Woodbridge High Sch
Woodford Green
Pl Fld
Allot Gdns
WINN BRIDGE CL
Churchfields Jun & Inf Schs
Queen Mary & Westfield Coll (Halls of Residence)
Liby
HIGH RD
A406
Charlie Browns Rdbt
Commerce Est
E18
THE VIADUCT
GEORGE LA
B168
South Woodford
Coll
Oakdale Jun Sch
A1400 SOUTHEND RD
Woodford Trad Est
CHIGWELL RD
A1199
Essex STREET ATLAS
55
41
42
HAYSTOCKS
A B C D
93 6 5 92 4 3 91 2 1 90

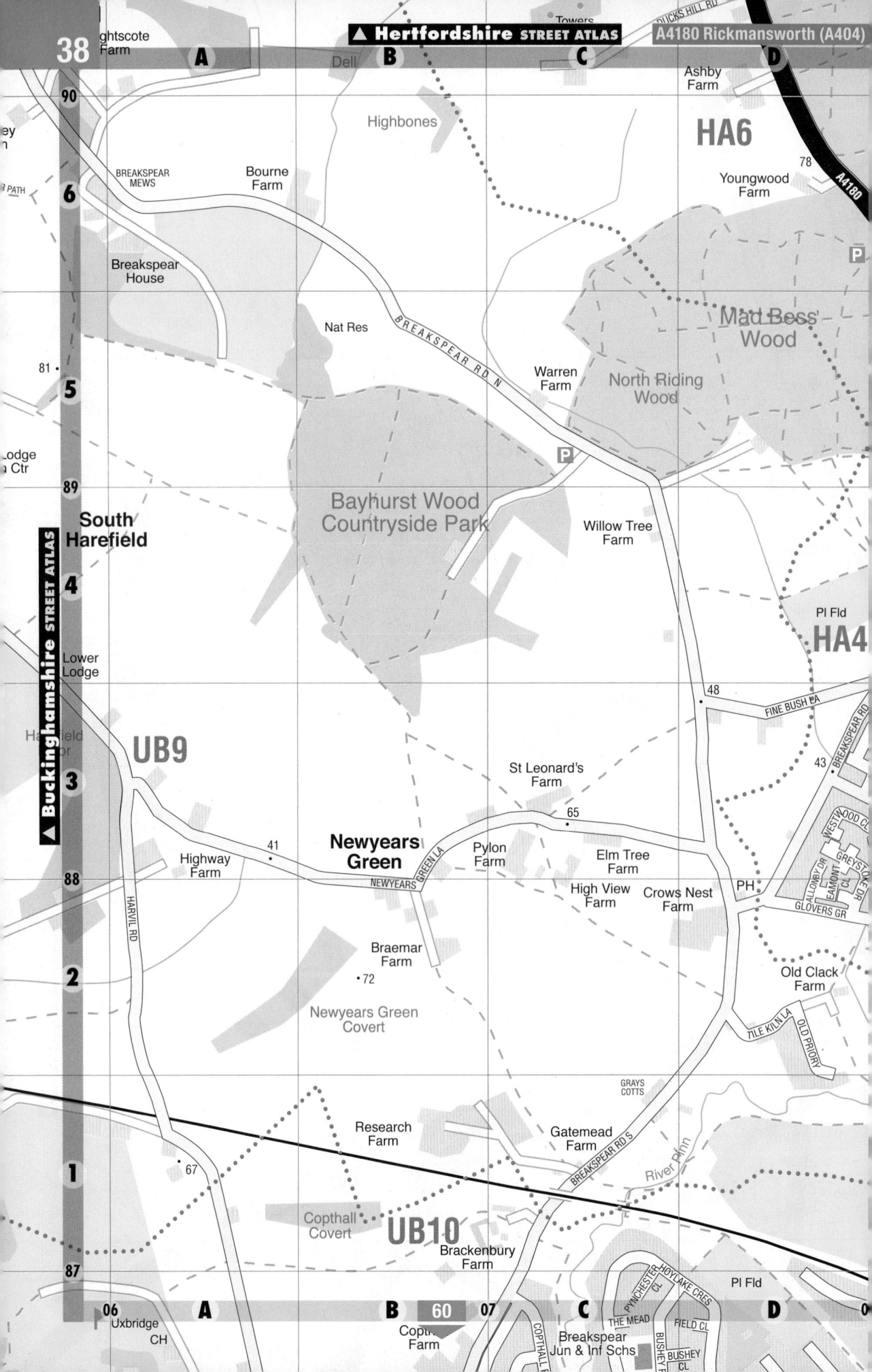
Knightscote Farm
Dell
Towers
DUCKS HILL RD
Ashby Farm
Highbones
HA6
78
Youngwood Farm
A4180
BREAKSPEAR MEWS
Bourne Farm
Breakspear House
Nat Res
BREAKSPEAR RD N
Warren Farm
North Riding Wood
Mad Bess Wood
81
Lodge
Ctr
Bayhurst Wood Countryside Park
South Harefield
Willow Tree Farm
Lower Lodge
Pl Fld
HA4
48
FINE BUSH LA
BREAKSPEAR RD
43
UB9
St Leonard's Farm
65
Newyears Green
41
Highway Farm
GREEN LA
NEWYEARS
Pylon Farm
Elm Tree Farm
High View Farm
Crows Nest Farm
PH
WESTWOOD CL
ALLONBY DR
EAMONT CL
GREYSTOKE DR
GLOVERS GR
HARVIL RD
Braemar Farm
72
Newyears Green Covert
Old Clack Farm
TILE KILN LA
OLD PRIORY
GRAYS COTTS
Research Farm
Gatemead Farm
BREAKSPEAR RD S
River Pinn
67
Copthall Covert
UB10
Brackenbury Farm
PYNCHESTER CL
HOYLAKE CRES
Pl Fld
THE MEAD
FIELD CL
COPTHALL
BUSHEY CL
BUSHEY RD
Breakspear Jun & Inf Schs
Uxbridge CH
Copthall Farm
90
6
5
89
4
3
88
2
1
87
06
07
A
B
C
D

▲ Buckinghamshire STREET ATLAS

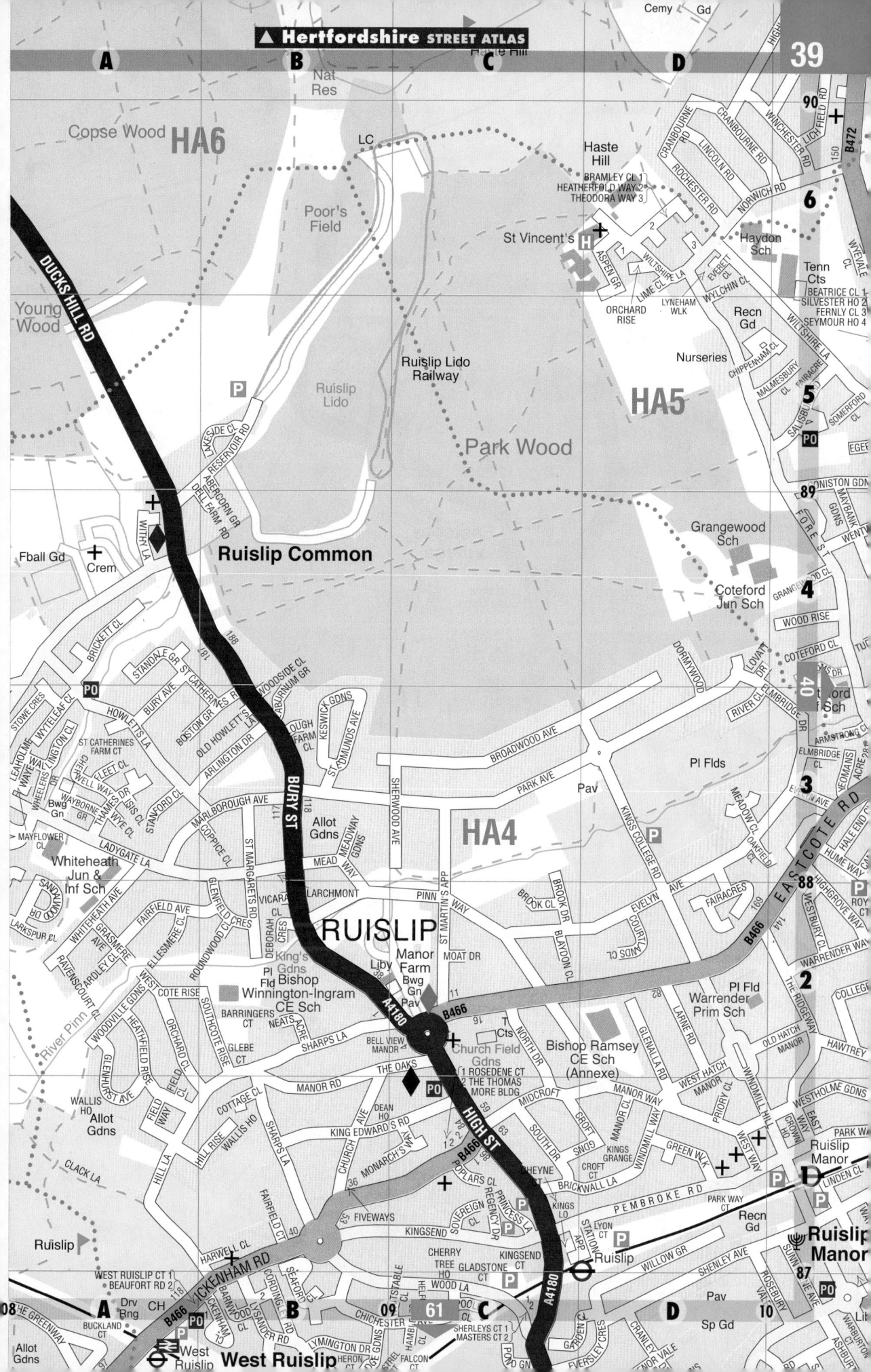
A
B
C
D
Cemy
Gd
Haste Hill
Nat Res
Copse Wood
HA6
LC
Poor's Field
Young Wood
DUCKS HILL RD
Haste Hill
BRAMLEY CL 1
HEATHERFOLD WAY 2
THEODORA WAY 3
St Vincent's
ASPEN GR
LIME CL
WILTSHIRE LA
ORCHARD RISE
LYNEHAM WLK
WYLCHIN CL
EVERETT CL
CRANBOURNE RD
LINCOLN RD
ROCHESTER RD
NORWICH RD
WINCHESTER RD
LICHFIELD RD
B472
90
150
6
Haydon Sch
Tenn Cts
BEATRICE CL 1
SILVESTER HO 2
FERNLY CL 3
SEYMOUR HO 4
WYEVALE CL
Recn Gd
Nurseries
CHIPPENHAM CL
MALMESBURY CL
FAIRACRE
SALISBURY RD
SOMERFORD CL
EGERTON
5
PO
Ruislip Lido Railway
Ruislip Lido
P
HA5
Park Wood
LAKESIDE CL
RESERVOIR RD
ABERCORN GR
DELL FARM RD
WITHY LA
Ruislip Common
Fball Gd
Crem
Grangewood Sch
CONISTON GDNS
89
FORE ST
MAYBANK GDNS
WENTWORTH
GRANGEWOOD CL
4
Coteford Jun Sch
WOOD RISE
COTEFORD CL
DORMYWOOD
LOVATT DR
RIVER CL
ELMBRIDGE DR
40
ARMSTRONG CL
ELMBRIDGE CL
BRICKETT CL
188
187
STANDALE GR
ST CATHERINES RD
WOODSIDE CL
LABURNUM GR
PO
STOWE CRES
WYTELEAF CL
HOWLETTS LA
BURY AVE
BOSTON GR
OLD HOWLETT'S LA
ARLINGTON DR
LOUGH FARM CL
KESWICK GDNS
ST EDMUNDS AVE
BROADWOOD AVE
Pl Flds
ST CATHERINES FARM CT
LEAHOLME WAYE
FLEET CL
WHEELERS DR
WAYBORNE GR
THAMES DR
ISIS CL
WYE CL
STANFORD CL
MARLBOROUGH AVE
COPPICE CL
BURY ST
118
117
Allot Gdns
MEADWAY GDNS
SHERWOOD AVE
PARK AVE
Pav
3
EVELYN AVE
YEOMANS ACRE
EASTCOTE RD
HALE END CL
HUME WAY
MEADOW CL
OAKFIELD CL
Bwg Gn
MAYFLOWER CL
LADYGATE LA
Whiteheath Jun & Inf Sch
MEAD WAY
HA4
KINGS COLLEGE RD
P
88
HIGHGROVE WAY
WESTBURY CL
SANDWOOD DR
LARKSPUR CL
WHITEHEATH AVE
GRASMERE AVE
FAIRFIELD AVE
ELLESMERE CL
GLENFIELD CRES
ST MARGARETS RD
VICARAGE CL
LARCHMONT
PINN WAY
ST MARTIN'S APP
BROOK CL
BROOK DR
BLAYDON CL
COURTLANDS CL
FAIRACRES
169
144
B466
WARRENDER WAY
RAVENSCOURT CL
ARDLEY CL
ROUNDWOOD CL
DEBORAH CRES
RUISLIP
King's Gdns
Pl Fld
Bishop Winnington-Ingram CE Sch
Liby
Manor Farm
Bwg Gn
Pav
MOAT DR
2
THE RIDGEWAY
COLLEGE
WOODVILLE GDNS
COTE RISE
HEATHFIELD RISE
ORCHARD CL
SOUTHCOTE RISE
BARRINGERS CT
NEATS ACRE
A4180
B466
11
16
82
Pl Fld
Warrender Prim Sch
River Pinn
SHARPS LA
BELL VIEW MANOR
T Cts
Church Field Gdns
NORTH DR
Bishop Ramsey CE Sch (Annexe)
GLENALLA RD
LARNE RD
OLD HATCH MANOR
HAWTREY
GLENHURST AVE
FIELD CL
GLEBE CT
THE OAKS
1 ROSEDENE CT
2 THE THOMAS MORE BLDG
WEST HATCH MANOR
WINDMILL HILL
WALLIS HO
Allot Gdns
COTTAGE CL
MANOR RD
PO
MIDCROFT
MANOR WAY
PRIORY CL
WESTHOLME GDNS
FIELD WAY
WALLIS HO
DEAN HO
KING EDWARD'S RD
HIGH ST
SOUTH DR
CROFT GDNS
MANOR CL
WINDMILL WAY
CROWN HO
EAST WAY
PARK WAY
HILL RISE
SHARPS LA
CHURCH AVE
MONARCH'S WAY
KINGS GRANGE
GREEN WLK
WEST WAY
Ruislip Manor
CLACK LA
HILL LA
36
POPLARS CL
CROFT CT
CHEYNE CT
BRICKWALL LA
PEMBROKE RD
P
LINDEN CL
FIVEWAYS
SOVEREIGN CL
REGENCY DR
PRINCESS LA
KINGS LO
PARK WAY CT
FAIRFIELD CT
KINGSEND
STATION APP
LYON CT
Recn Gd
Ruislip
HARWELL CL
40
CHERRY TREE HO
KINGSEND CT
GLADSTONE CT
Ruislip
WILLOW GR
SHENLEY AVE
Ruislip Manor
WEST RUISLIP CT 1
BEAUFORT RD 2
ICKENHAM RD
CORDINGLEY RD
SEAFORTH
WOOD LA
87
PO
Drv Rng
CH
118
WHITSTABLE CL
ROSEBURY VALE
SUNNINGDALE AVE
Pav
THE GREENWAY
B466
PO
BUCKLAND CT
LYSANDER RD
09
61
POOL CL
10
Sp Gd
CHICHESTER
HAMBLE CL
SHERLEYS CT 1
MASTERS CT 2
GARDEN CL
EVERSLEY CRES
CRANLEY DR
WARBURTON CT
Allot Gdns
West Ruislip
LYMINGTON DR
HERON CT
FALCON CT
POND GN
West Ruislip
ASHBURNHAM
08

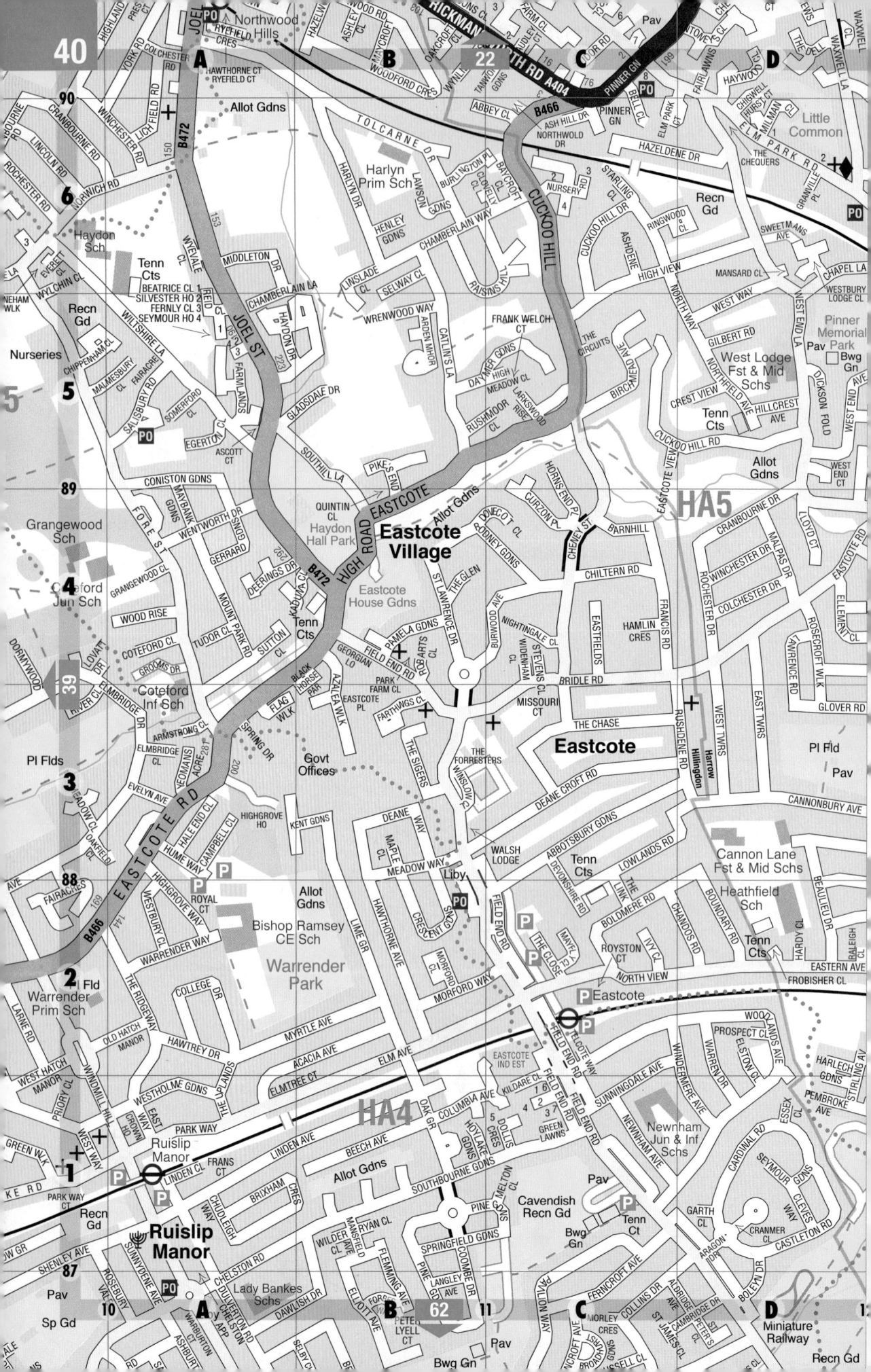
Northwood Hills
Allot Gdns
Harlyn Prim Sch
Haydon Sch
Tenn Cts
Recn Gd
Nurseries
Little Common
Recn Gd
Pinner Memorial Park
West Lodge Fst & Mid Schs
Tenn Cts
Allot Gdns
HA5
Grangewood Sch
Coteford Jun Sch
Haydon Hall Park
Eastcote Village
Eastcote House Gdns
Tenn Cts
Coteford Inf Sch
Pl Flds
Govt Offices
Eastcote
Pl Fld
Pav
Cannon Lane Fst & Mid Schs
Heathfield Sch
Tenn Cts
Allot Gdns
Bishop Ramsey CE Sch
Warrender Park
Warrender Prim Sch
Liby
Eastcote Ind Est
HA4
Newnham Jun & Inf Schs
Ruislip Manor
Allot Gdns
Cavendish Recn Gd
Bwg Gn
Tenn Ct
Recn Gd
Lady Bankes Schs
Sp Gd
Miniature Railway
Recn Gd
Bwg Gn
EASTCOTE RD
HIGH ROAD EASTCOTE
JOEL ST
CUCKOO HILL
RICKMANSWORTH RD A404
PINNER GN
FIELD END RD
22
39
62

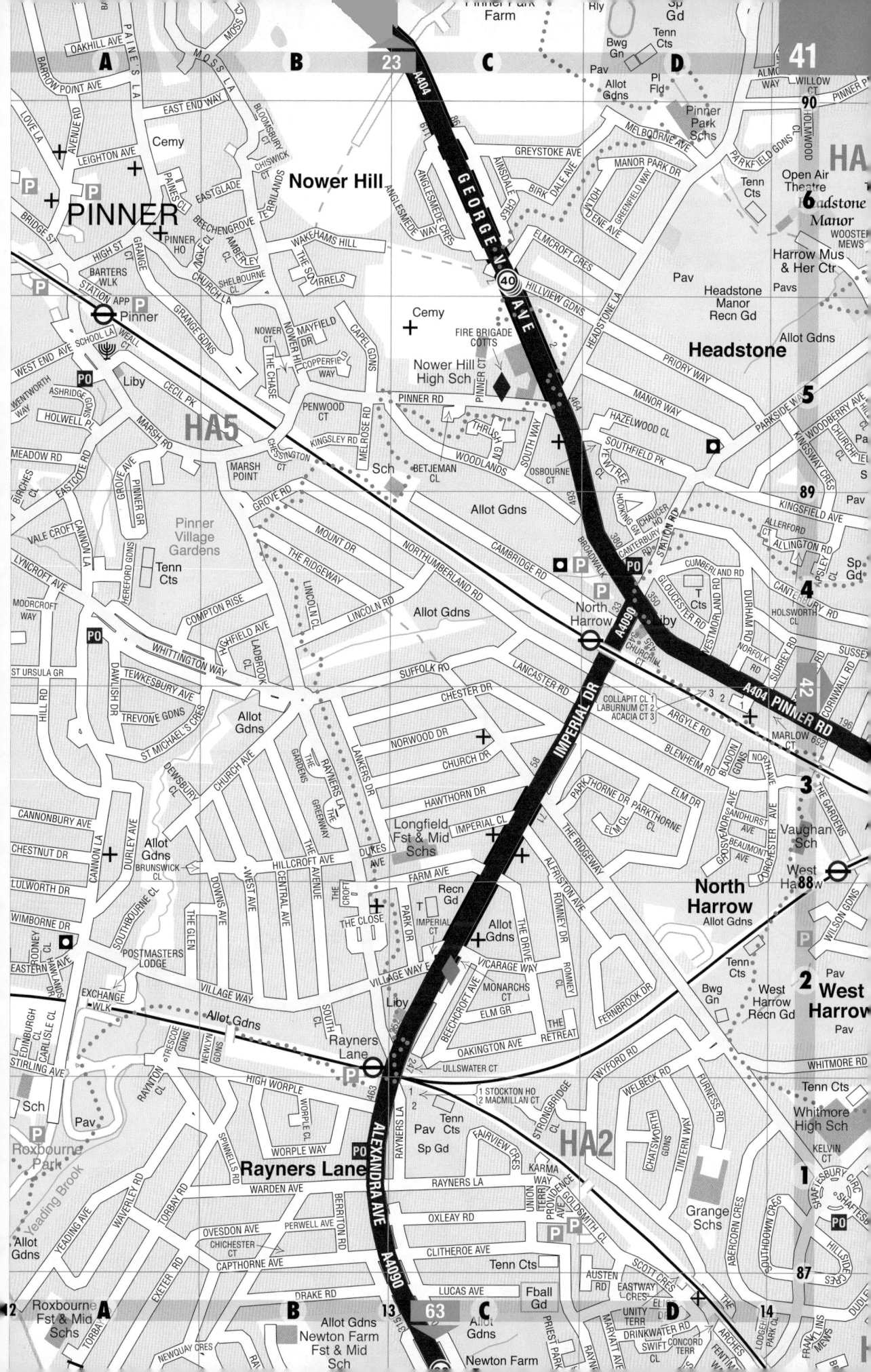
23
A
B
C
D
PINNER
Nowher Hill
Headstone
HA5
HA2
North Harrow
West Harrow
Rayners Lane
Pinner
Pinner Village Gardens
Pinner Park Farm
Headstone Manor
Harrow Mus & Her Ctr
Headstone Manor Recn Gd
Nower Hill High Sch
Longfield Fst & Mid Schs
Vaughan Sch
Whitmore High Sch
Grange Schs
Roxbourne Park
Roxbourne Fst & Mid Schs
Newton Farm Fst & Mid Sch
Yeading Brook
GEORGE V AVE
A404
PINNER RD
IMPERIAL DR
A4090
ALEXANDRA AVE
42
63
90
89
88
87
6
5
4
3
2
1
12
13
14

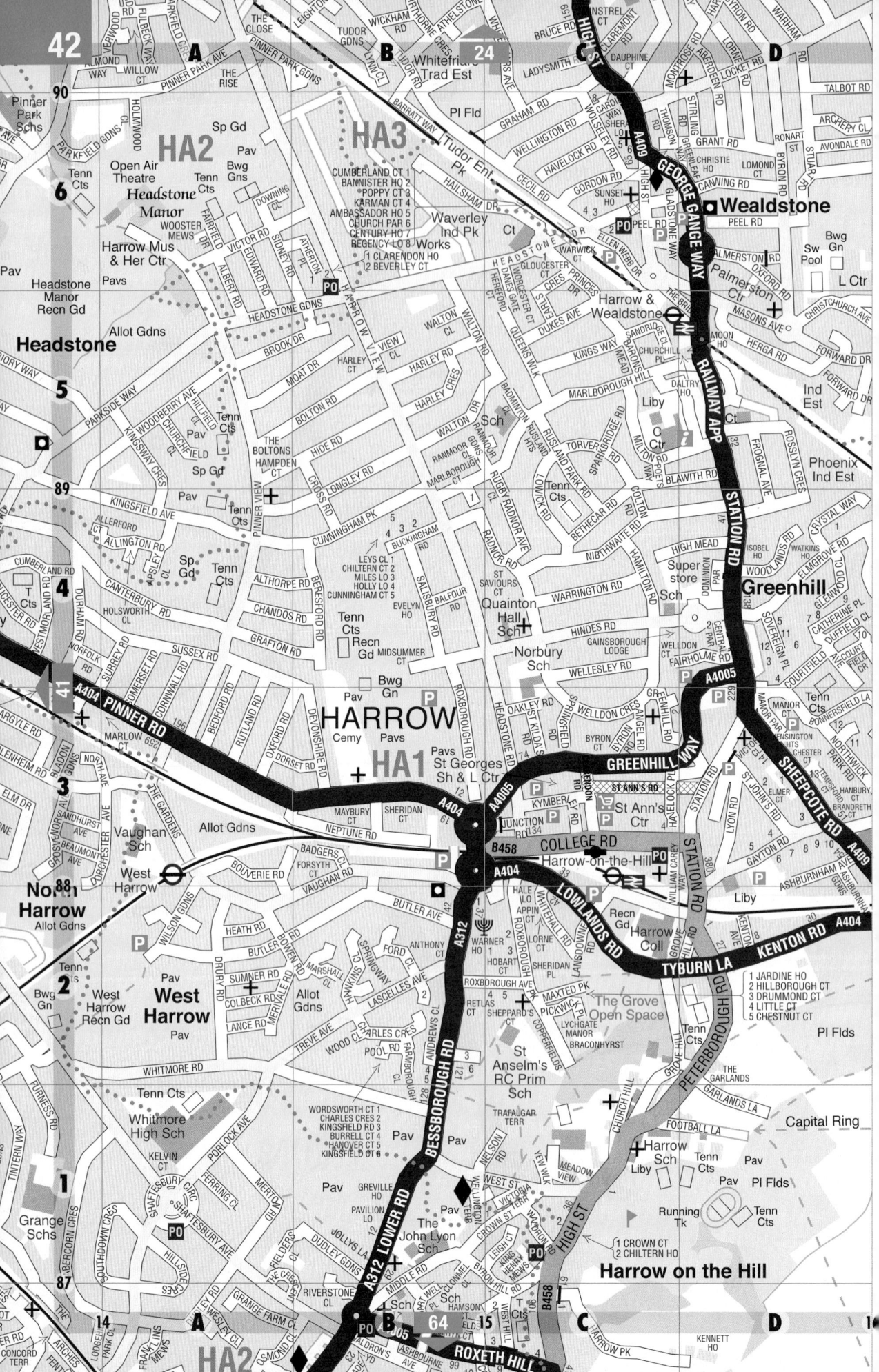

HA2
HA3
HA1
Headstone
Headstone Manor
Harrow Mus & Her Ctr
Headstone Manor Recn Gd
Wealdstone
Harrow & Wealdstone
Greenhill
HARROW
St Georges Sh & L Ctr
St Ann's Ctr
Harrow-on-the-Hill
North Harrow
West Harrow
West Harrow Recn Gd
Whitmore High Sch
Vaughan Sch
The Grove Open Space
St Anselm's RC Prim Sch
Harrow Sch
The John Lyon Sch
Harrow on the Hill
Capital Ring
Waverley Ind Pk
Whitefriars Trad Est
Phoenix Ind Est
Tudor Ent Pk
Harrow Coll
Pinner Park Schs
Grange Schs
Quainton Hall Sch
Norbury Sch
A404 PINNER RD
A409 GEORGE GANGE WAY
STATION RD
SHEEPCOTE RD
GREENHILL WAY
A404 KENTON RD
TYBURN LA
LOWLANDS RD
A312 LOWER RD
BESSBOROUGH RD
ROXETH HILL
HIGH ST
PETERBOROUGH RD
COLLEGE RD
24
41
64

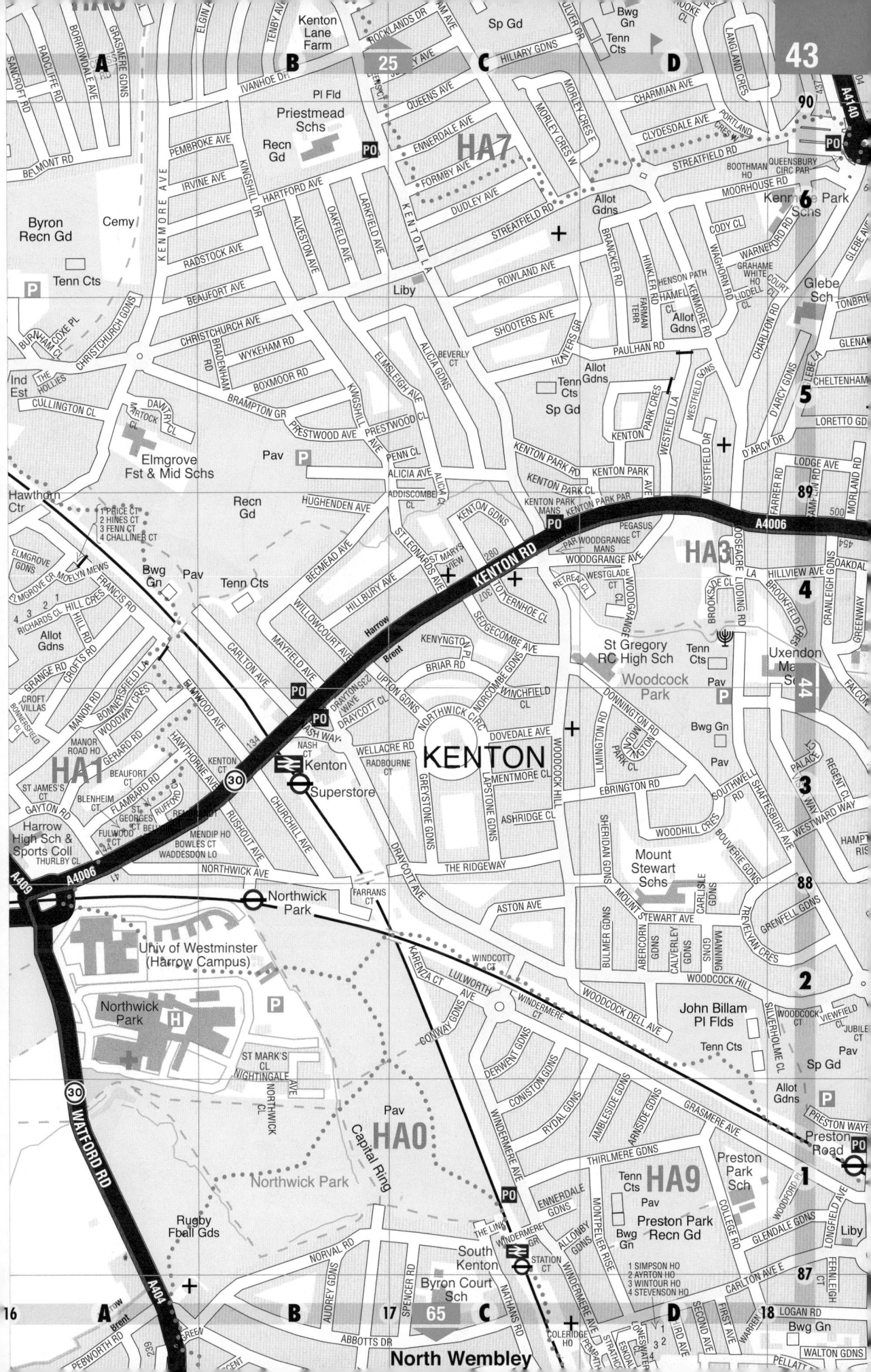
A
B
C
D
25
Kenton Lane Farm
Sp Gd
Bwg Gn
Tenn Cts
RADCLIFFE RD
BORROWDALE AVE
GRASMERE GDNS
SANCROFT RD
ROCKLANDS DR
TENBY AVE
ELGIN AVE
HILIARY GDNS
IVANHOE DR
LANGLAND CRES
Pl Fld
Priestmead Schs
Recn Gd
PO
QUEENS AVE
ENNERDALE AVE
HA7
MORLEY CRES E
MORLEY CRES W
CHARMIAN AVE
CLYDESDALE AVE
PORTLAND CRES W
STREATFIELD RD
BOOTHMAN HO
QUEENSBURY CIRC PAR
MOORHOUSE RD
A4140
90
BELMONT RD
PEMBROKE AVE
IRVINE AVE
KINGSHILL DR
HARTFORD AVE
FORMBY AVE
DUDLEY AVE
KENTON LA
Allot Gdns
Kenmore Park Schs
6
Byron Recn Gd
Cemy
KENMORE AVE
RADSTOCK AVE
ALVESTON AVE
OAKFIELD AVE
LARKFIELD AVE
CODY CL
WARNEFORD RD
GLEBE AVE
Tenn Cts
P
BEAUFORT AVE
Liby
ROWLAND AVE
BRANCKER RD
HINKLER RD
HENSON PATH
HAMEL CL
FARMAN TERR
KENMORE RD
WAGHORN RD
GRAHAME WHITE HO
LIDDELL CL
COURT CL
Glebe Sch
TONBRIDGE
CHRISTCHURCH GDNS
COXE PL
BURNHAM CL
CHRISTCHURCH AVE
BRADENHAM RD
WYKEHAM RD
SHOOTERS AVE
Allot Gdns
CHARLTON RD
GLENALMOND
BEVERLY CT
HUNTERS GR
PAULHAN RD
Ind Est
THE HOLLIES
BOXMOOR RD
ELMSLEIGH AVE
ALICIA GDNS
Allot Gdns
Tenn Cts
WESTFIELD GDNS
D'ARCY GDNS
GLEBE LA
CHELTENHAM
CULLINGTON CL
DAWTRY CL
MARTOCK CL
BRAMPTON GR
KINGSHILL AVE
Sp Gd
KENTON PARK CRES
WESTFIELD LA
5
LORETTO GDNS
PRESTWOOD AVE
PRESTWOOD CL
WESTFIELD DR
D'ARCY DR
Elmgrove Fst & Mid Schs
Pav
PENN CL
KENTON PARK RD
KENTON PARK
LODGE AVE
FARRER RD
MORLAND RD
ALICIA AVE
ALICIA CL
KENTON PARK CL
Hawthorn Ctr
1 PRICE CT
2 HINES CT
3 FENN CT
4 CHALLINER CT
Recn Gd
HUGHENDEN AVE
ADDISCOMBE CL
KENTON GDNS
KENTON PARK MANS
KENTON PARK PAR
89
500
A4006
PEGASUS CT
ELMGROVE GDNS
ELMGROVE CR
MOELYN MEWS
FRANCIS RD
Bwg Gn
Pav
Tenn Cts
BECMEAD AVE
ST LEONARDS AVE
ST MARYS VIEW
280
KENTON RD
WOODGRANGE MANS
WOODGRANGE AVE
HA3
GOOSEACRE LA
HILLVIEW AVE
OAKDALE
RICHARDS CL
HILL CRES
HILL RD
HILLBURY AVE
WESTGLADE CT
RETREAT CL
TOTTERNHOE CL
WOODGRANGE CL
BROOKSIDE CL
LIDDING RD
BROOKFIELD CRES
CRANLEIGH GDNS
GREENWAY
4
Allot Gdns
GRANGE RD
CROFTS RD
CARLTON AVE
WILLOWCOURT AVE
Harrow
Brent
KENYNGTON PL
SEDGECOMBE AVE
St Gregory RC High Sch
Tenn Cts
Uxendon Manor Sch
44
FALCON
CROFT VILLAS
BONNERSFIELD CL
BONNERSFIELD LA
MANOR RD
WOODWAY CRES
ELMWOOD AVE
MAYFIELD AVE
PO
BRIAR RD
UPTON GDNS
NORCOMBE GDNS
WINCHFIELD CL
Woodcock Park
Pav
DONNINGTON RD
MANOR ROAD HO
GERARD RD
DRAYTON WAYE
DRAYCOTT CL
NORTHWICK CIRC
DOVEDALE AVE
ILMINGTON RD
MOUNT PARK CL
Bwg Gn
NASH WAY
NASH CT
KENTON
WELLACRE RD
HA1
BEAUFORT CT
HAWTHORNE AVE
KENTON CT
Kenton
RADBOURNE CT
Pav
PALACE CT
REGENT CL
ST JAMES'S CT
BLENHEIM CT
FLAMBARD RD
RUFFORD CL
30
Superstore
GREYSTONE GDNS
LAPSTONE GDNS
MENTMORE CL
WOODCOCK HILL
EBRINGTON RD
SOUTHWELL RD
SHAFTESBURY AVE
3
GAYTON RD
ST GEORGES CT
MENDIP HO
BOWLES CT
WADDESDON LO
RUSHOUT AVE
ASHRIDGE CL
SHERIDAN GDNS
WOODHILL CRES
WESTWARD WAY
Harrow High Sch & Sports Coll
FULWOOD CT
THURLBY CL
CHURCHILL AVE
DRAYCOTT AVE
THE RIDGEWAY
Mount Stewart Schs
BOUVERIE GDNS
A409
A4006
NORTHWICK AVE
FARRANS CT
CARLISLE GDNS
88
Northwick Park
ASTON AVE
MOUNT STEWART AVE
GRENFELL GDNS
Univ of Westminster (Harrow Campus)
BULMER GDNS
ABERCORN GDNS
CALVERLEY GDNS
MANNING GDNS
TREVELYAN CRES
KARENZA CT
WINDCOTT CT
LULWORTH AVE
WOODCOCK HILL
2
Northwick Park
H
P
WINDERMERE CT
WOODCOCK DELL AVE
John Billam Pl Flds
WOODCOCK CT
VIEWFIELD CL
JUBILEE
CONWAY GDNS
DERWENT GDNS
Tenn Cts
Pav
ST MARK'S CL
NIGHTINGALE AVE
NORTHWICK CL
SILVERHOLME CL
Sp Gd
CONISTON GDNS
Allot Gdns
30
Pav
RYDAL GDNS
AMBLESIDE GDNS
ARNSIDE GDNS
GRASMERE AVE
PRESTON WAYE
WATFORD RD
Capital Ring
HA0
Preston Road
PO
WINDERMERE AVE
THIRLMERE GDNS
Preston Park Sch
Northwick Park
Tenn Cts
HA9
1
Pav
ENNERDALE GDNS
WOODFORD PL
LONGFIELD AVE
Rugby Fball Gds
PO
ALLONBY GDNS
MONTPELIER RISE
COLLEGE RD
Preston Park Recn Gd
GLENDALE GDNS
Liby
THE LINK
WINDERMERE GR
Bwg Gn
NORVAL RD
South Kenton
STATION CT
1 SIMPSON HO
2 AYRTON HO
3 WINTOUR HO
4 STEVENSON HO
FERNLEIGH CT
AUDREY GDNS
SPENCER RD
Byron Court Sch
CARLTON AVE E
87
A404
Brent
16
A
B
17
65
C
NATHANS RD
D
18
LOGAN RD
PEBWORTH RD
239
ABBOTTS DR
COLERIDGE HO
SECOND AVE
FIRST AVE
Bwg Gn
North Wembley
WALTON GDNS

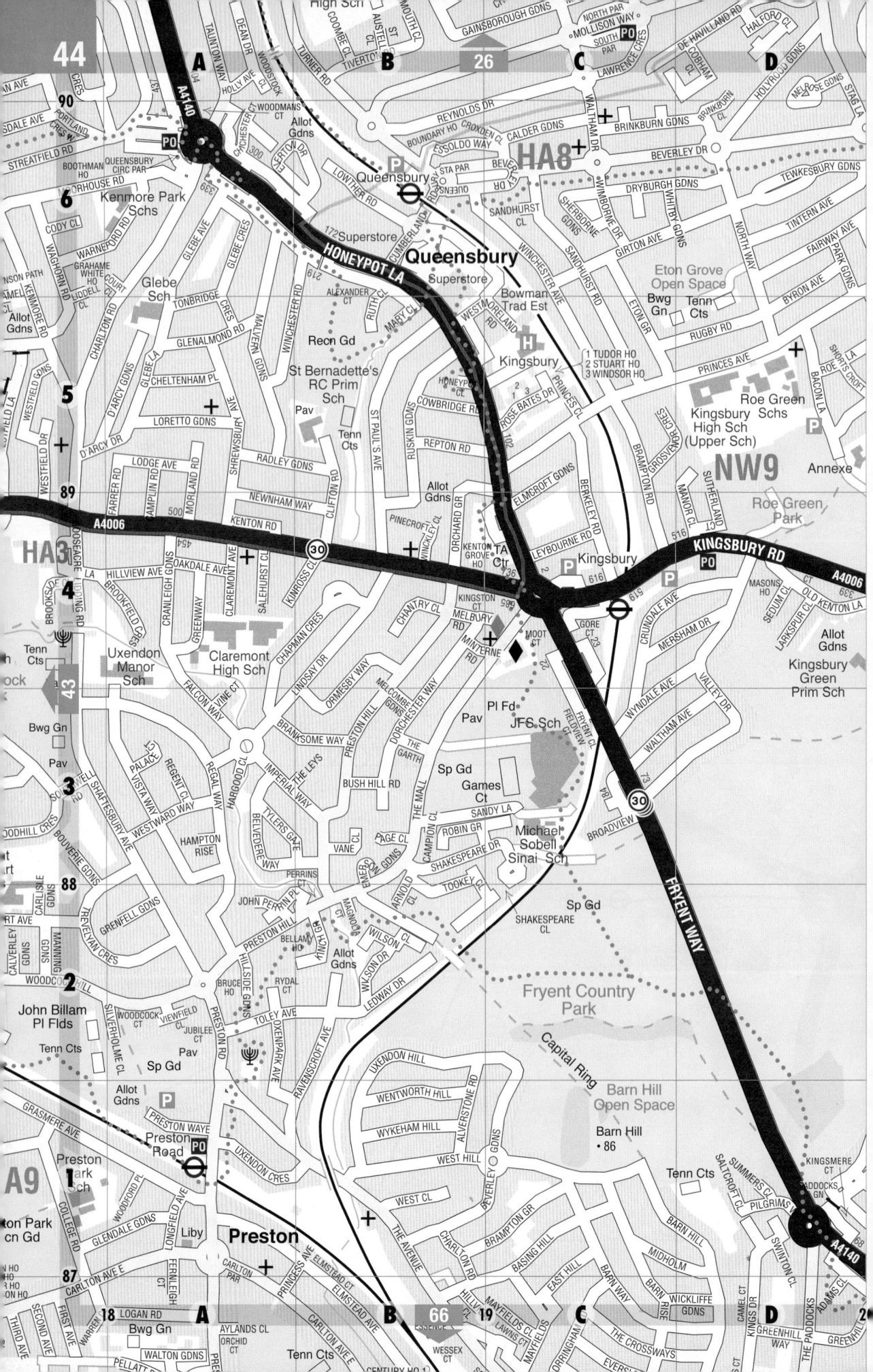
A
B
C
D
26
66
43
90
89
88
87
6
5
4
3
2
1
18
19
HA8
HA3
NW9
A9
A4140
A4006
HONEYPOT LA
KINGSBURY RD
FRYENT WAY
30
Queensbury
Kingsbury
Preston
Preston Road
Kenmore Park Schs
Glebe Sch
Allot Gdns
Recn Gd
St Bernadette's RC Prim Sch
Pav
Tenn Cts
Superstore
Bowman Trad Est
Kingsbury
1 TUDOR HO
2 STUART HO
3 WINDSOR HO
Eton Grove Open Space
Bwg Gn
Roe Green Schs
Kingsbury High Sch (Upper Sch)
Annexe
Roe Green Park
TA Ctr
Claremont High Sch
Uxendon Manor Sch
Kingsbury Green Prim Sch
JFS Sch
Pl Fd
Sp Gd
Games Ct
Michael Sobell Sinai Sch
Fryent Country Park
Capital Ring
Barn Hill Open Space
Barn Hill
• 86
John Billam Pl Flds
Preston Park Sch
Liby
STREATFIELD RD
MOORHOUSE RD
REYNOLDS DR
BEVERLEY DR
CALDER GDNS
BRINKBURN GDNS
TEWKESBURY GDNS
DRYBURGH GDNS
GIRTON AVE
WINCHESTER AVE
GLENALMOND RD
CHELTENHAM PL
LORETTO GDNS
RADLEY GDNS
NEWNHAM WAY
KENTON RD
HILLVIEW AVE
OAKDALE AVE
PRINCES AVE
RUGBY RD
BYRON AVE
CHARLTON RD
WESTFIELD DR
GLEBE AVE
MALVERN GDNS
SHREWSBURY AVE
CLIFTON RD
ST PAUL'S AVE
RUSKIN GDNS
COWBRIDGE RD
REPTON RD
ELMCROFT GDNS
LEYBOURNE RD
BERKELEY RD
BRAMPTON RD
CRUNDALE AVE
MERSHAM DR
WYNDALE AVE
VALLEY DR
WALTHAM AVE
BROADVIEW
OLD KENTON LA
LARKSPUR CL
CHAPMAN CRES
LINDSAY DR
ORMESBY WAY
BRANKSOME WAY
PRESTON HILL
DORCHESTER WAY
BUSH HILL RD
THE MALL
SANDY LA
ROBIN GR
SHAKESPEARE DR
TOOKEY CL
WESTWARD WAY
SHAFTESBURY AVE
REGAL WAY
IMPERIAL WAY
THE LEYS
BELVEDERE WAY
TYLERS GATE
HAMPTON RISE
PRESTON RD
TOLEY AVE
OXENPARK AVE
RAVENSCROFT AVE
LEDWAY DR
WILSON DR
UXENDON HILL
WENTWORTH HILL
WYKEHAM HILL
WEST HILL
WEST CL
ALVERSTONE RD
BEVERLEY GDNS
THE AVENUE
BRAMPTON GR
BASING HILL
EAST HILL
BARN WAY
MIDHOLM
BARN HILL
BARN RISE
WICKLIFFE GDNS
THE CROSSWAYS
SUMMERS CL
SALTCROFT CL
PILGRIMS WAY
SWINTON CL
KINGS DR
THE PADDOCKS
GREENHILL WAY
GRASMERE AVE
PRESTON WAYE
UXENDON CRES
GLENDALE GDNS
WOODFORD PL
LONGFIELD AVE
COLLEGE RD
CARLTON AVE E
FERNLEIGH CT
LOGAN RD
WALTON GDNS
AYLANDS CL
ELMSTEAD AVE
PRINCESS AVE
WOODCOCK HILL
SILVERHOLME CL
GRENFELL GDNS
TREVELYAN CRES
BOUVERIE GDNS
D'ARCY DR
D'ARCY GDNS
LODGE AVE
FARRER RD
MORLAND RD
CRANLEIGH GDNS
GREENWAY
CLAREMONT AVE
KINROSS CL
CHANTRY CL
MELBURY RD
MINTERNE RD
ORCHARD GR
WINCHESTER RD
LOWTHER RD
CUMBERLAND RD
MARY CL
ESSOLDO WAY
SANDHURST RD
SHERBORNE GDNS
WIMBORNE DR
WHITBY GDNS
ETON GR
NORTH WAY
TINTERN AVE
FAIRWAY AVE
HOLYROOD GDNS
GAINSBOROUGH GDNS
LAWRENCE CRES
TURNER RD
TAUNTON WAY
DEAN DR
HOLLY AVE
WARNEFORD RD
CODY CL
WAGHORN RD
KENMORE RD
TONBRIDGE CRES
GLEBE LA
GLEBE CRES

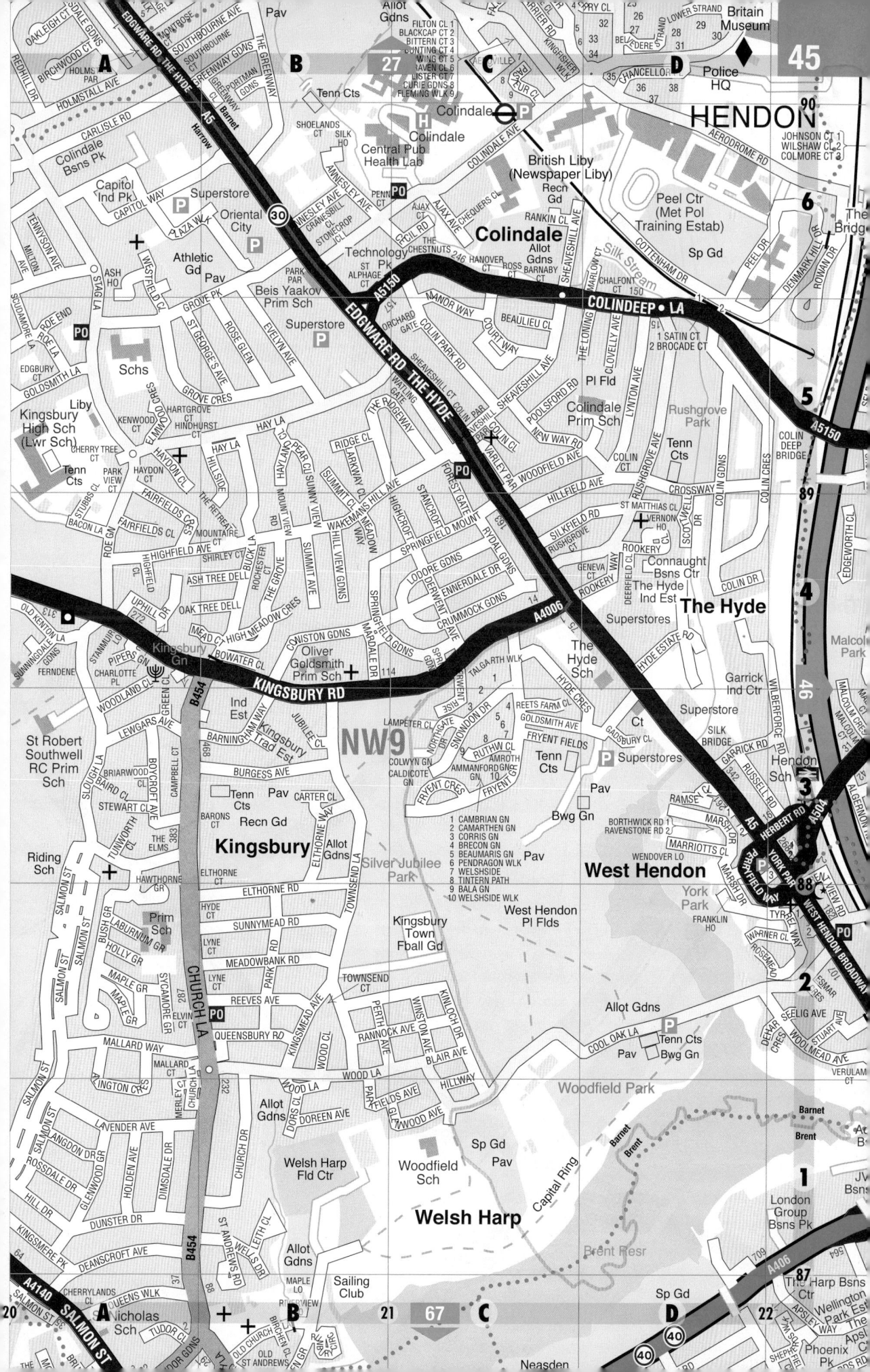
45
HENDON
Britain Museum
Police HQ
Colindale
Central Pub Health Lab
British Liby (Newspaper Liby)
Peel Ctr (Met Pol Training Estab)
Sp Gd
Colindale Bsns Pk
Capitol Ind Pk
Superstore
Oriental City
Athletic Gd
Pav
Technology Pk
Beis Yaakov Prim Sch
Schs
Kingsbury High Sch (Lwr Sch)
Liby
Tenn Cts
Colindale Prim Sch
Pl Fld
Rushgrove Park
Colin Deep Bridge
Connaught Bsns Ctr
The Hyde Ind Est
The Hyde
Superstores
The Hyde Sch
Garrick Ind Ctr
Silk Bridge
Hendon Sch
Kingsbury Gn
Oliver Goldsmith Prim Sch
Ind Est
Kingsbury Trad Est
NW9
St Robert Southwell RC Prim Sch
Riding Sch
Recn Gd
Kingsbury
Allot Gdns
Silver Jubilee Park
Kingsbury Town Fball Gd
West Hendon Pl Flds
Bwg Gn
West Hendon
York Park
Prim Sch
Woodfield Park
Welsh Harp Fld Ctr
Woodfield Sch
Welsh Harp
Capital Ring
Brent Resr
Sailing Club
St Nicholas Sch
London Group Bsns Pk
The Harp Bsns Ctr
Wellington Park Est
Neasden
EDGWARE RD THE HYDE
A5
COLINDEEP LA
A5150
KINGSBURY RD
A4006
CHURCH LA
B454
A4140 SALMON ST
A406
WEST HENDON BROADWAY
1 CAMBRIAN GN
2 CAMARTHEN GN
3 CORRIS GN
4 BRECON GN
5 BEAUMARIS GN
6 PENDRAGON WLK
7 WELSHSIDE
8 TINTERN PATH
9 BALA GN
10 WELSHSIDE WLK
1 FILTON CL
2 BLACKCAP CT
3 BITTERN CT
4 BUNTING CT
5 WING CT
6 RAVEN CL
7 LISTER CT
8 CURIE GDNS
9 FLEMING WLK
1 JOHNSON CT
2 WILSHAW CL
3 COLMORE CT
1 SATIN CT
2 BROCADE CT
27
67
A B C D
20 21 22
90 89 88 87
46

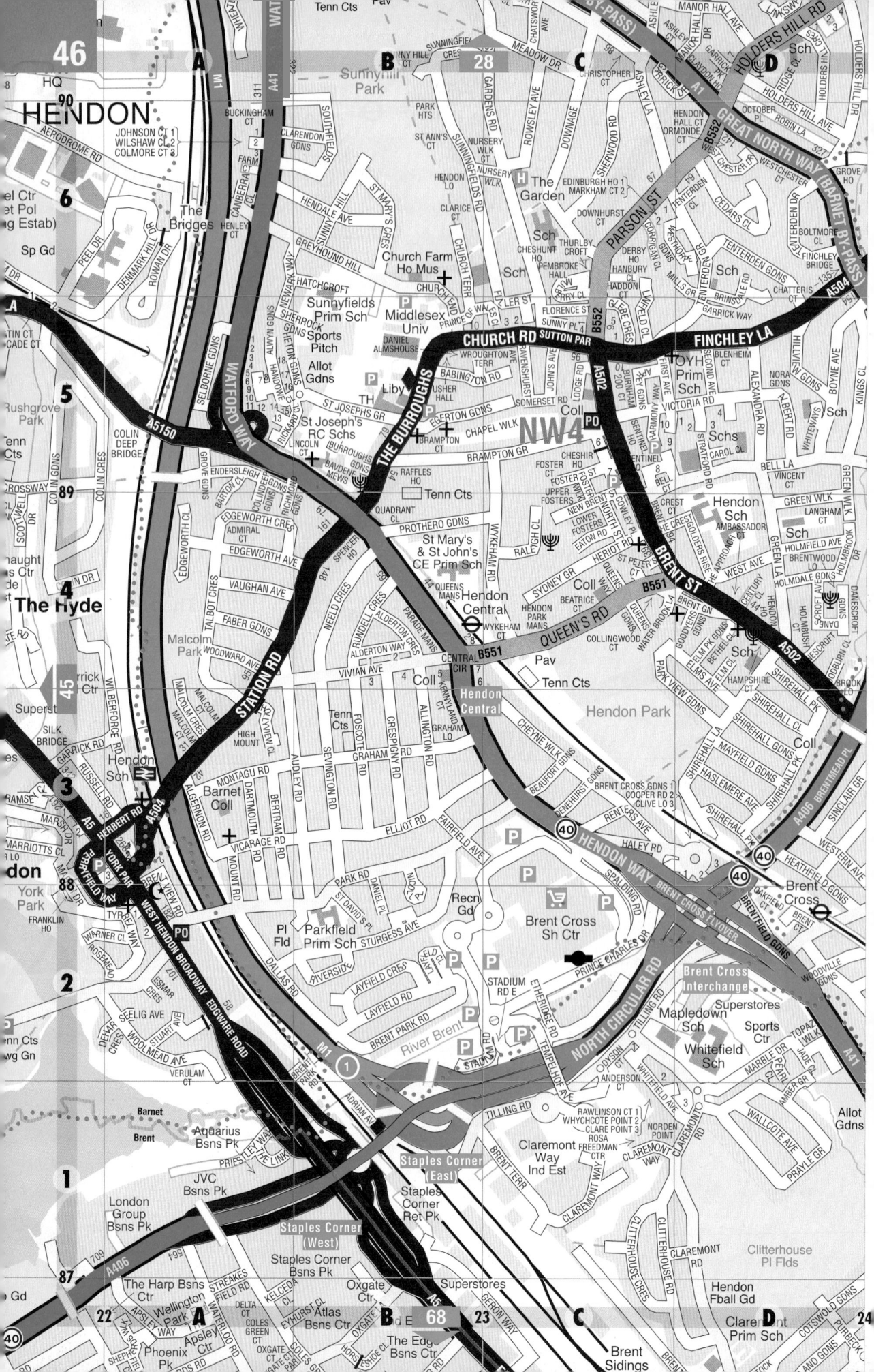
46
28
45
68
A
B
C
D
6
5
4
3
2
1
90
89
88
87
22
23
24
HENDON
The Hyde
NW4
Tenn Cts
Pav
HQ
AERODROME RD
el Ctr
et Pol
g Estab)
Sp Gd
Rushgrove Park
Tenn Cts
Silk Bridge
Superst
Hendon Sch
York Park
FRANKLIN HO
ldon
Barnet
Brent
Sunnyhill Park
PARK HTS
ST ANN'S CT
SUNNINGFIELDS RD
GARDENS RD
ROWSLEY AVE
DOWNAGE
SHERWOOD RD
ASHLEY LA
MEADOW DR
CHRISTOPHER CT
CHATSWORTH AVE
MANOR HALL AVE
MANOR HALL DR
HOLDERS HILL RD
HOLDERS HILL AVE
HOLDERS HILL DR
HOLDERS HILL CRES
RIDGE CL
OCTOBER PL
ROBIN LA
GREAT NORTH WAY (BARNET BY-PASS)
A1
B552
HENDON HALL CT
ORMONDE CT
WESTCHESTER DR
GROVE HO
TENTERDEN DR
BOLTMORE CL
FINCHLEY BRIDGE
CEDARS CL
TENTERDEN GDNS
TENTERDEN GR
TENTERDEN CL
CHATTERIS CT
BRINSDALE RD
GARRICK WAY
PARSON ST
EDINBURGH HO 1
MARKHAM CT 2
DOWNHURST CT
THURLBY CROFT
DERBY HO
HANBURY CT
HADDON CT
GLEBE CRES
LAWFIELD CL
CHESHUNT HO
PEMBROKE HALL
FLORENCE ST
SUNNY PL
The Garden
Sch
NURSERY WLK CT
NURSERY WLK
HENDON LO
CLARICE CT
CHURCH TERR
Church Farm Ho Mus
CHURCH END
PRINCE OF WALES CL
FULLER ST
CHURCH RD
SUTTON PAR
FINCHLEY LA
A504
A502
BLENHEIM CT
OYH Prim Sch
SECOND AVE
FIRST AVE
ALEXANDRA RD
NORA GDNS
ALBERT RD
HILLVIEW GDNS
BOYNE AVE
KINGS CL
WHITEWAYS
BURNHAM CT
VICTORIA RD
HARMONY WAY
SENTINEL HO
Schs
CAROL CL
BELL LA
VINCENT CT
GREEN WLK
LANGHAM CT
Hendon Sch
AMBASSADOR CT
HOLMFIELD AVE
BRENTWOOD LO
HOLMDALE GDNS
HOLMBROOK DR
DANESCROFT
BELL CT
CREST CT
THE CREST
GOLDERS RISE
THE APPROACH
WEST AVE
GREEN LA
CENTURY HO
HOLMBUSH CT
DANESCROFT AVE
BRENT ST
BRENT GN
GOODYERS GDNS
ELM PK GDNS
BETHEL CL
ELMS AVE
ELM CL
PARK VIEW GDNS
HAMPSHIRE CT
SHIREHALL PK
SHIREHALL CL
SHIREHALL GDNS
SHIREHALL LA
MAYFIELD GDNS
HASLEMERE AVE
SHIREHALL PK
Coll
SINCLAIR GR
A406 BRENTMEAD PL
WESTERN AVE
HEATHFIELD GDNS
Brent Cross
BRENTFIELD GDNS
WOODVILLE GDNS
OAKFIELD CT
BRENT CT
HENDON WAY
BRENT CROSS FLYOVER
HALEY RD
RENTERS AVE
BRENT CROSS GDNS 1
COOPER RD 2
CLIVE LO 3
DENEHURST GDNS
BEAUFORT GDNS
CHEYNE WLK
SPALDING RD
Hendon Park
Tenn Cts
Pav
QUEEN'S RD
B551
COLLINGWOOD CT
WATER BROOK LA
QUEENS GDNS
BEATRICE CT
HENDON PARK MANS
SYDNEY GR
QUEENS WAY
Coll
HERIOT RD
ST PETER'S CT
EATON RD
LOWER FOSTERS
UPPER FOSTERS
NORTH ST
COWLEY PL
NEW BRENT ST
FOSTER CT
FOSTER ST
CHESHIR HO
RALEIGH CL
WYKEHAM RD
WYKEHAM CT
Hendon Central
Hendon Central
CENTRAL CIR
QUEENS MANS
St Mary's & St John's CE Prim Sch
PROTHERO GDNS
QUADRANT CL
RAFFLES HO
Tenn Cts
BRAMPTON GR
BRAMPTON CT
CHAPEL WLK
EGERTON GDNS
SOMERSET RD
LODGE RD
JOHN'S AVE
RAVENSHURST AVE
WROUGHTON TERR
BABINGTON RD
USHER HALL
Liby
TH
DANIEL ALMSHOUSE
Middlesex Univ
THE BURROUGHS
BURROUGHS GDNS
BAYDENE MEWS
LINCOLN CT
St Joseph's RC Schs
ST JOSEPHS GR
Allot Gdns
Sports Pitch
Sunnyfields Prim Sch
SHERROCK GDNS
HATCHCROFT
NEWARK WAY
GREYHOUND HILL
HENDALE AVE
SUNNY HILL
ST MARY'S CRES
SOUTHFIELDS
CLARENDON GDNS
BUCKINGHAM CT
JOHNSON CT 1
WILSHAW CL 2
COLMORE CT 3
FARM CT
CANBERRA CT
HENLEY CT
The Bridges
PEEL DR
DENMARK HILL DR
ROWAN DR
A41
M1
WATFORD WAY
SELBORNE GDNS
ALWYN GDNS
HETON GDNS
HANDOWE CL
RICKARD CL
A5150
COLIN DEEP BRIDGE
COLIN GDNS
COLIN CRES
CROSSWAY
SCOTSWELL DR
COLIN DR
GROVE GDNS
ENDERSLEIGH GDNS
BARTON CL
COLINDEEP GDNS
RICHMOND GDNS
EDGEWORTH CRES
ADMIRAL CT
EDGEWORTH AVE
EDGEWORTH CL
TALBOT CRES
VAUGHAN AVE
FABER GDNS
WOODWARD AVE
Malcolm Park
MALCOLM CRES
MALCOLM CT
STATION RD
SPENCER HO
NEELD CRES
RUNDELL CRES
ALDERTON CRES
ALDERTON WAY
PARADE MANS
VIVIAN AVE
Coll
KENNYLAND CT
ALLINGTON RD
GRAHAM LO
CRESPIGNY RD
FOSCOTE RD
SEVINGTON RD
AUDLEY RD
GRAHAM RD
Tenn Cts
HIGH MOUNT
HILLVIEW CL
MONTAGU RD
Barnet Coll
DARTMOUTH RD
BERTRAM RD
ALGERNON RD
VICARAGE RD
MOUNT RD
ELLIOT RD
FAIRFIELD AVE
PARK RD
DANIEL PL
NICOLL PL
ST DAVID'S PL
Pl Fld
Parkfield Prim Sch
STURGESS AVE
RIVERSIDE
LAYFIELD CRES
LAYFIELD RD
LAYFIELD CL
BRENT PARK RD
DALLAS RD
Recn Gd
Brent Cross Sh Ctr
PRINCE CHARLES DR
STADIUM RD E
STADIUM RD
ETHERIDGE RD
TEMPELHOF AVE
River Brent
NORTH CIRCULAR RD
Brent Cross Interchange
Superstores
Mapledown Sch
Whitefield Sch
Sports Ctr
MARBLE DR
PEARL CL
JADE CL
TOPAZ WLK
AMBER GR
WALLCOTE AVE
PRAYLE GR
Allot Gdns
TILLING RD
ODYSON CT
ANDERSON CT
WHITEFIELD AVE
CLAREMONT RD
RAWLINSON CT 1
WHYCHCOTE POINT 2
CLARE POINT 3
ROSA FREEDMAN CTR
NORDEN POINT
CLAREMONT WAY
Claremont Way Ind Est
BRENT TERR
CLITTERHOUSE CRES
CLITTERHOUSE RD
CLAREMONT RD
Clitterhouse Pl Flds
Hendon Fball Gd
Claremont Prim Sch
COTSWOLD GDNS
PURBECK
Brent Sidings
GERON WAY
Superstores
Staples Corner (East)
Staples Corner Ret Pk
Staples Corner (West)
Staples Corner Bsns Pk
Oxgate Ctr
Atlas Bsns Ctr
The Edge Bsns Ctr
OXGATE
EYHURST CL
KELCEDA CL
COLES GREEN CT
OXGATE CT
DELTA CT
WATERLOO RD
STREAKES FIELD RD
The Harp Bsns Ctr
Wellington Park
APSLEY WAY
Apsley Ctr
Phoenix Pk
A406
A5
London Group Bsns Pk
JVC Bsns Pk
PRIESTLEY WAY
THE LINK
Aquarius Bsns Pk
BRENT PARK RD
ADRIAN AV
EDGWARE ROAD
WEST HENDON BROADWAY
VERULAM CT
WOOLMEAD AVE
STUART AVE
SEELIG AVE
ESMAR CRES
ROSEMEAD
DEHAR CRES
WARNER CL
TYREL WAY
BRENT VIEW RD
PARFIELD WAY
YORK PAR
HERBERT RD
MARSH DR
MARRIOTTS CL
RAMSEY CL
RUSSELL RD
GARRICK RD
WILBERFORCE RD
PO
40
1

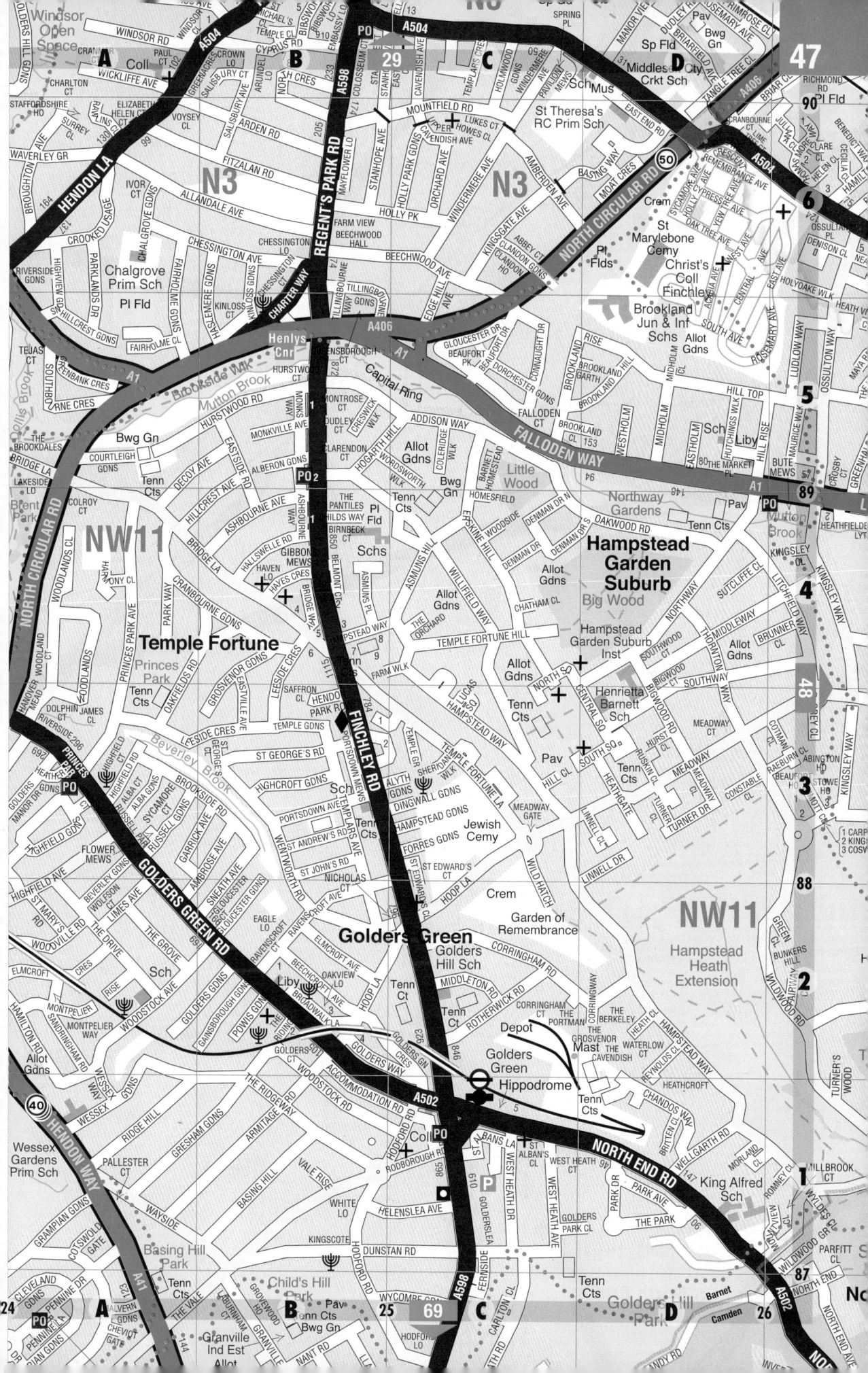
29
69
48
A
B
C
D
1
2
3
4
5
6
N3
N3
NW11
NW11
Windsor Open Space
Coll
Temple Fortune
Hampstead Garden Suburb
Golders Green
Hampstead Heath Extension
Big Wood
Little Wood
Northway Gardens
Henlys Cnr
Capital Ring
Mutton Brook
Brookside Wlk
Beverley Brook
Dollis Brook
Chalgrove Prim Sch
Pl Fld
St Theresa's RC Prim Sch
Middlesex Cty Crkt Sch
Sp Fld
Bwg Gn
St Marylebone Cemy
Crem
Christ's Coll Finchley
Brookland Jun & Inf Schs
Allot Gdns
Tenn Cts
Schs
Jewish Cemy
Garden of Remembrance
Golders Hill Sch
Hampstead Garden Suburb Inst
Henrietta Barnett Sch
Golders Green Hippodrome
Depot
Mast
King Alfred Sch
Wessex Gardens Prim Sch
Basing Hill Park
Child's Hill Park
Golders Hill Park
Granville Ind Est
Liby
Pav
Barnet
Camden
REGENT'S PARK RD
FINCHLEY RD
NORTH CIRCULAR RD
HENDON LA
HENDON WAY
GOLDERS GREEN RD
NORTH END RD
FALLODEN WAY
A1
A41
A406
A502
A504
A598
WINDSOR RD
WICKLIFFE AVE
ARDEN RD
FITZALAN RD
ALLANDALE AVE
CHESSINGTON AVE
CHARTER WAY
MOUNTFIELD RD
HOLLY PK
BEECHWOOD AVE
KINGSGATE AVE
AMBERDEN AVE
WINDERMERE AVE
STANHOPE AVE
ORCHARD AVE
EAST END RD
ADDISON WAY
HOGARTH HILL
WILLIFIELD WAY
TEMPLE FORTUNE HILL
TEMPLE FORTUNE LA
HAMPSTEAD WAY
CENTRAL SQ
NORTH SQ
SOUTH SQ
MEADWAY
SOUTHWAY
NORTHWAY
OAKWOOD RD
BRIDGE LA
HURSTWOOD RD
PRINCES PARK AVE
WOODLANDS
CRANBOURNE GDNS
ST GEORGE'S RD
HIGHCROFT GDNS
WENTWORTH RD
CORRINGHAM RD
HOOP LA
WILD HATCH
WOODSTOCK AVE
ACCOMMODATION RD
THE RIDGEWAY
HODFORD RD
WEST HEATH DR
WEST HEATH AVE
DUNSTAN RD
HELENSLEA AVE
WELLGARTH RD
PARK AVE
THE PARK
WILDWOOD RD
KINGSLEY WAY
LITCHFIELD WAY
HILL TOP
WESTHOLM
MIDHOLM
EASTHOLM
SOUTH AVE
ROSEMARY AVE
LUDLOW WAY
ASMUNS HILL
ERSKINE HILL
HEATHGATE
BIGWOOD RD
TURNER DR
LINNELL DR
CHANDOS WAY
HEATH CL
WAYSIDE
RIDGE HILL
GRESHAM GDNS
BASING HILL
VALE RISE
THE VALE
WYCOMBE GDNS
NANT RD
HIGHFIELD AVE
THE DRIVE
LIMES AVE
THE GROVE
SNEATH AVE
GARRICK AVE
BROOKSIDE RD
RIVERSIDE DR
WAVERLEY GR
BROUGHTON AVE
PARKLANDS DR
FAIRHOLME GDNS
HASLEMERE GDNS
DECOY AVE
EASTSIDE RD
HILLCREST AVE
ASHBOURNE AVE
MONKVILLE AVE
HOMESFIELD
DENMAN DR

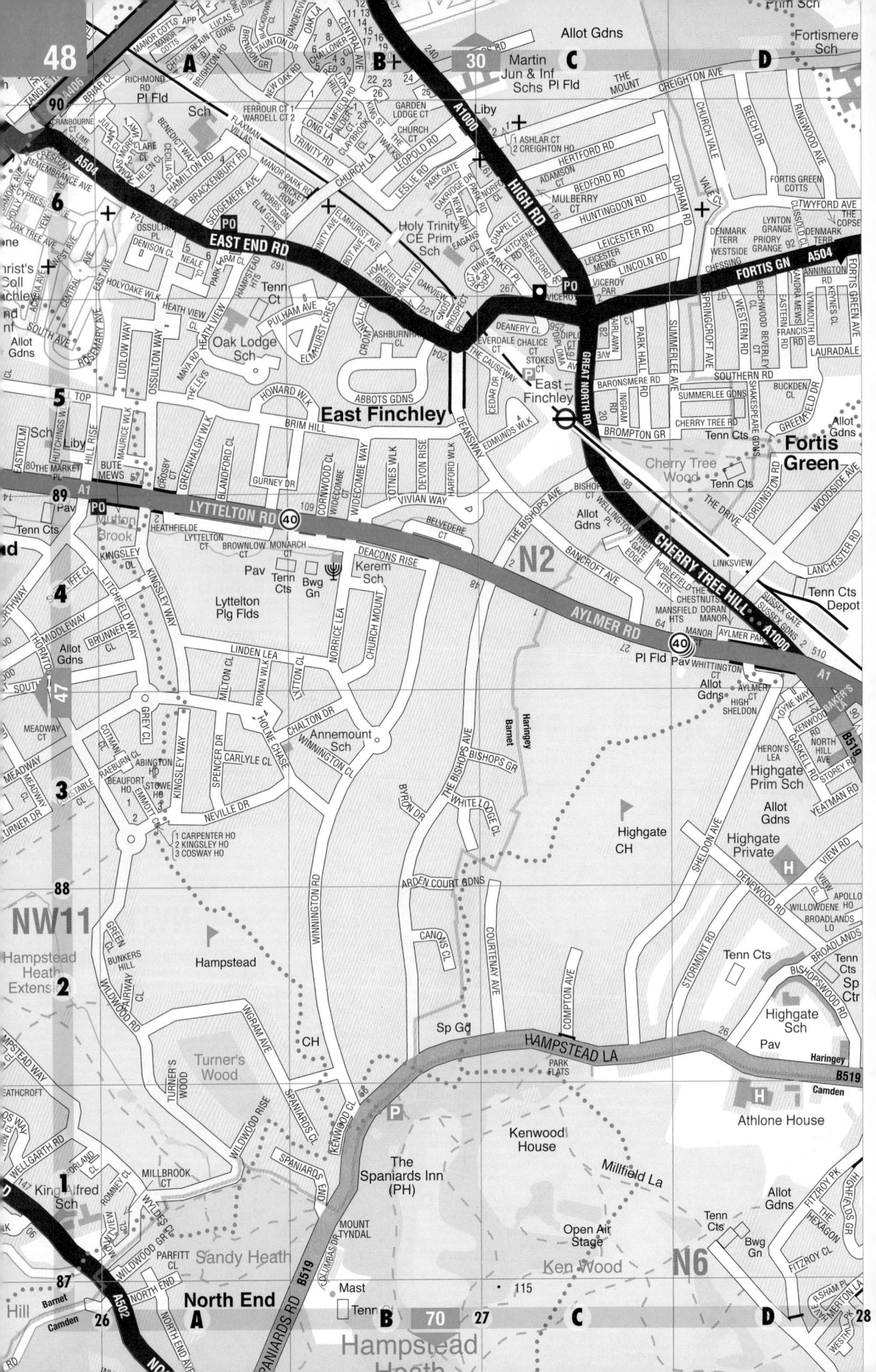

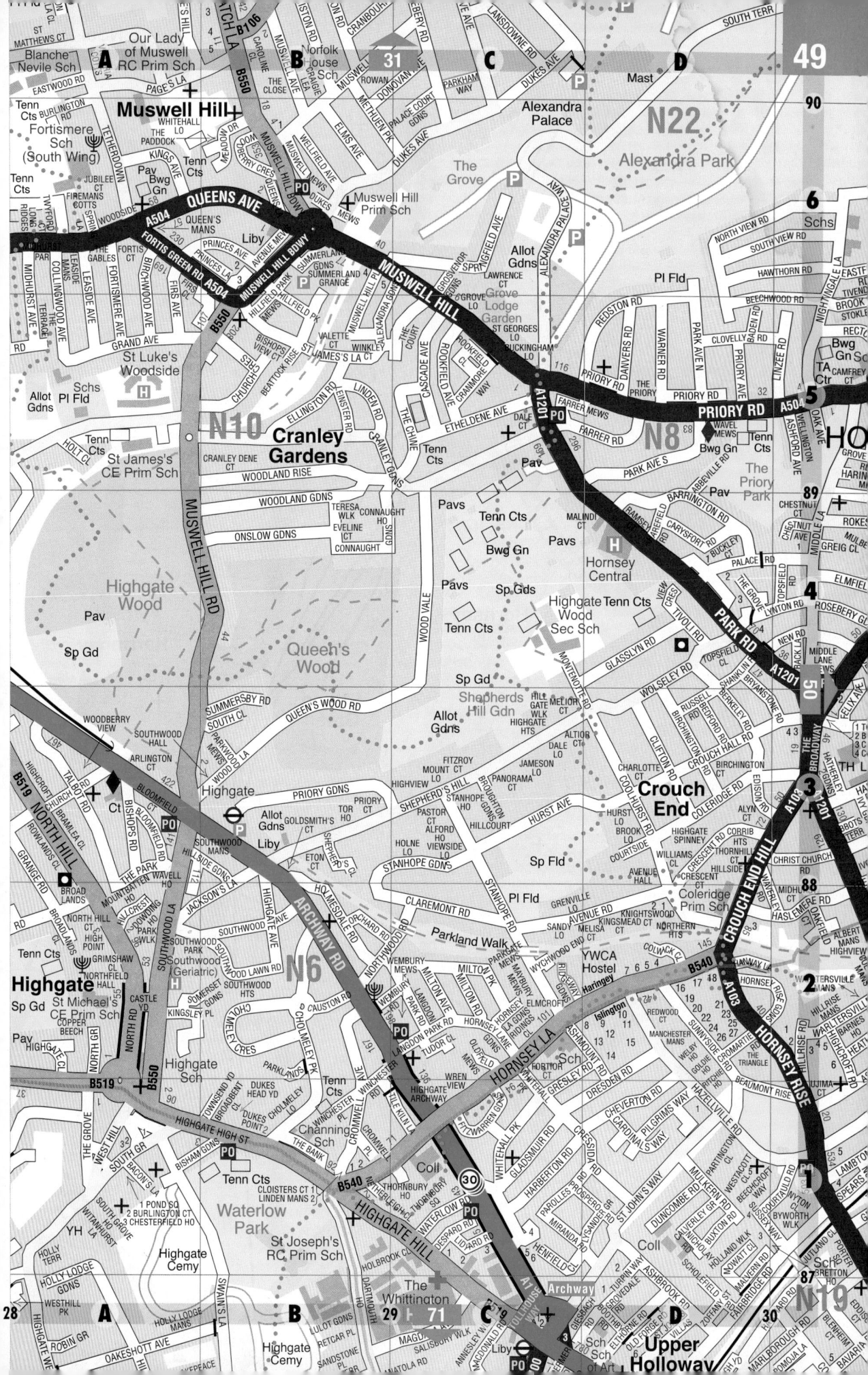

Muswell Hill
Alexandra Palace
Alexandra Park
N22
The Grove
N10
Cranley Gardens
N8
Hornsey Central
Highgate Wood
Queen's Wood
Crouch End
Highgate
N6
Waterlow Park
Highgate Cemy
The Whittington
Upper Holloway
N19
Archway
Queens Ave
Muswell Hill
Priory Rd
Muswell Hill Rd
Archway Rd
Hornsey La
Park Rd
Crouch End Hill
Hornsey Rise
Highgate Hill
North Hill
Parkland Walk
Shepherds Hill Gdn
The Priory Park
Fortismere Sch (South Wing)
Our Lady of Muswell RC Prim Sch
Blanche Nevile Sch
Norfolk House Sch
St Luke's Woodside
St James's CE Prim Sch
Highgate Wood Sec Sch
Coleridge Prim Sch
YWCA Hostel
St Michael's CE Prim Sch
Channing Sch
St Joseph's RC Prim Sch
Highgate Sch

31
50
71

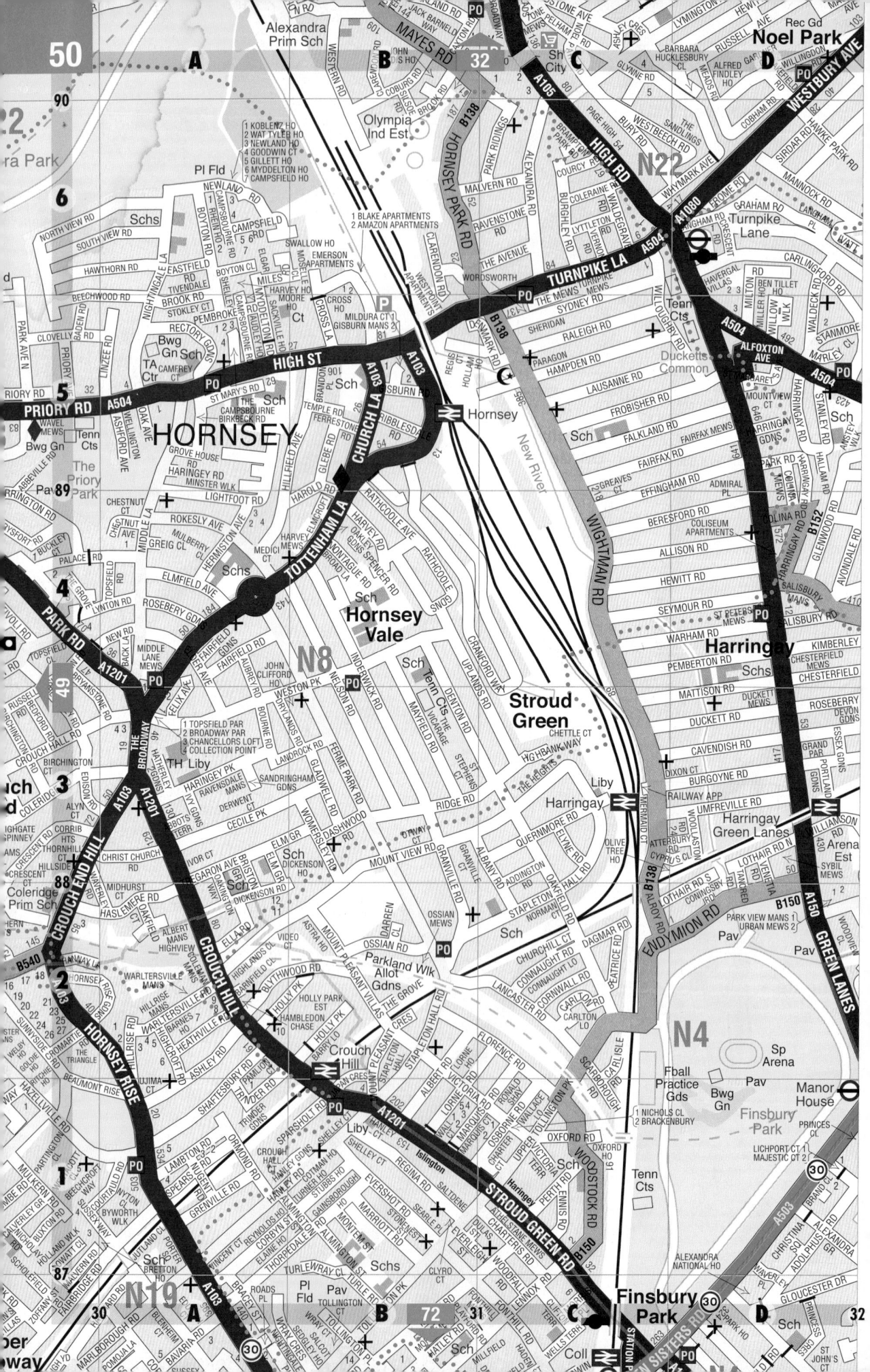

A
B
C
D
32
90
6
5
89
4
49
3
88
2
1
87
30
31
72
N19
N22
N8
N4
Noel Park
HORNSEY
Hornsey Vale
Stroud Green
Harringay
Harringay Green Lanes
Turnpike Lane
Finsbury Park
Manor House
Crouch Hill
Hornsey
Alexandra Prim Sch
Olympia Ind Est
Sh City
Rec Gd
The Priory Park
Ducketts Common
New River
Parkland Wlk
Allot Gdns
Coleridge Prim Sch
Sp Arena
Fball Practice Gds
Finsbury Park
Arena Est
TURNPIKE LA
HIGH ST
PRIORY RD
HIGH RD
WESTBURY AVE
GREEN LANES
WIGHTMAN RD
HORNSEY PARK RD
TOTTENHAM LA
CHURCH LA
PARK RD
THE BROADWAY
CROUCH END HILL
CROUCH HILL
HORNSEY RISE
STROUD GREEN RD
ENDYMION RD
SEVEN SISTERS RD
STATION PL
WOODSTOCK RD
MAYES RD
A504
A105
A1080
A103
A1201
A150
A503
B138
B150
B152
B540

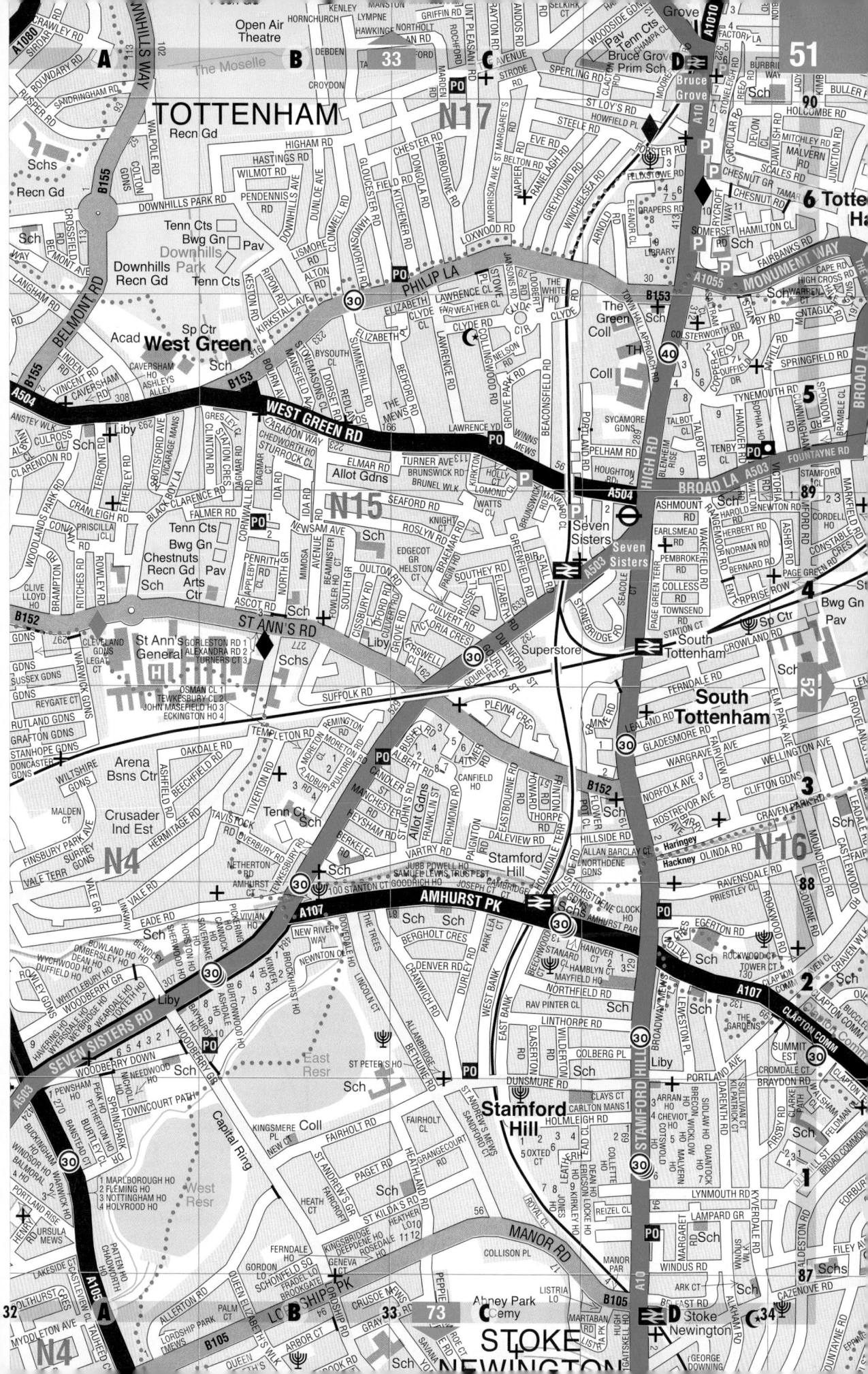
TOTTENHAM
N17
N15
N4
N16
West Green
South Tottenham
Stamford Hill
STOKE NEWINGTON
Open Air Theatre
The Moselle
Bruce Grove
Bruce Grove Prim Sch
Seven Sisters
Downhills Park
Downhills Recn Gd
Chestnuts Recn Gd
St Ann's General
Arena Bsns Ctr
Crusader Ind Est
East Resr
West Resr
Capital Ring
Abney Park Cemy
The Green Coll
Superstore
WEST GREEN RD
ST ANN'S RD
AMHURST PK
SEVEN SISTERS RD
HIGH RD
STAMFORD HILL
BROAD LA
PHILIP LA
MONUMENT WAY
LORDSHIP PK
MANOR RD
DOWNHILLS PARK RD
BELMONT RD
DOWNHILLS WAY
CLAPTON COMM
A10
A1010
A504
A503
A107
A105
A1055
B155
B153
B152
B105
33
73
52
32
34
87
88
89
90
A
B
C
D
1
2
3
4
5
6

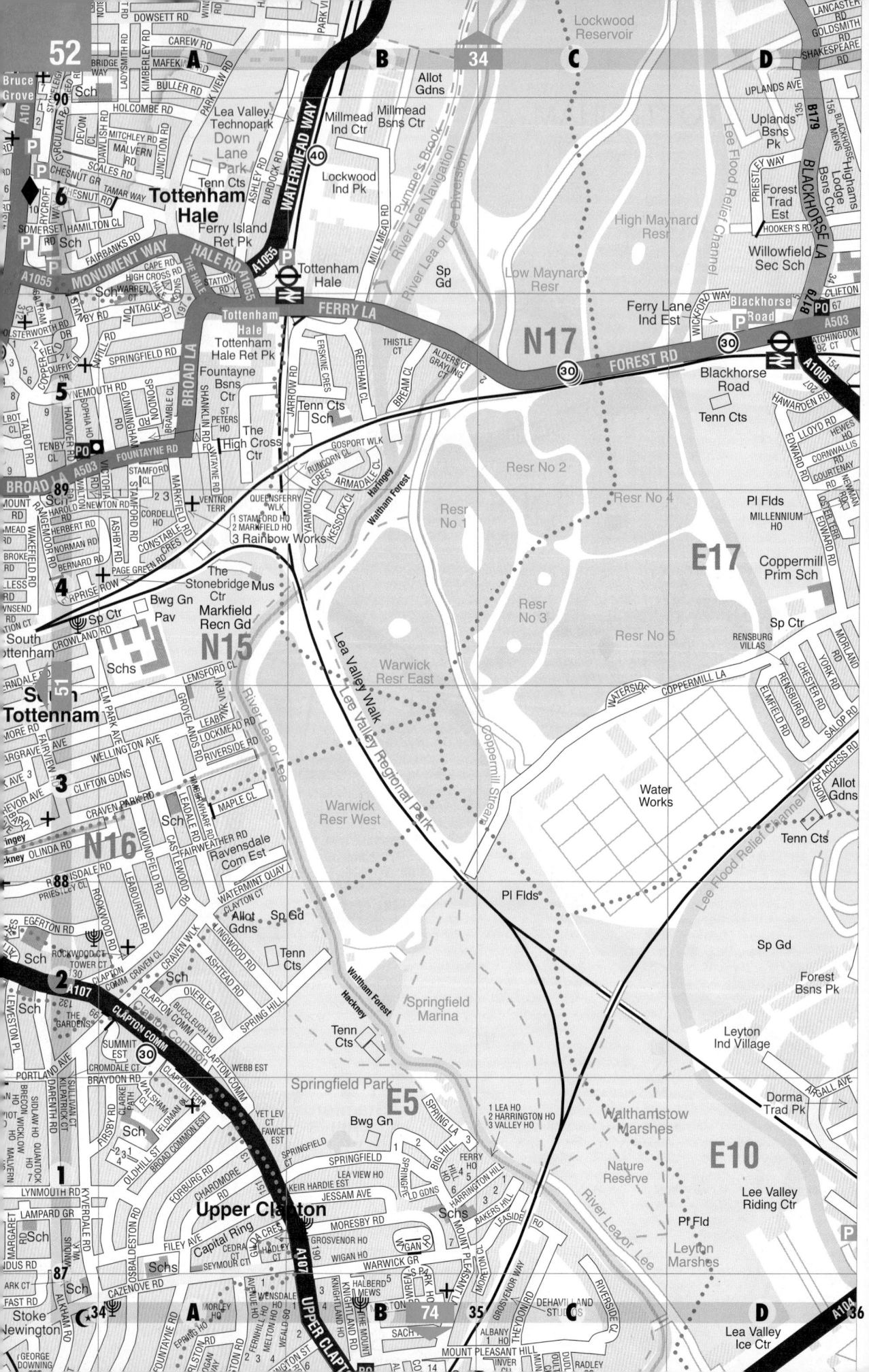
A
B
34
C
D
Tottenham Hale
Lea Valley Technopark
Down Lane Park
Millmead Ind Ctr
Millmead Bsns Ctr
Allot Gdns
Lockwood Reservoir
Lockwood Ind Pk
Uplands Bsns Pk
Forest Trad Est
Highams Lodge Bsns Ctr
Willowfield Sec Sch
High Maynard Resr
Low Maynard Resr
Ferry Island Ret Pk
Tottenham Hale Ret Pk
Fountayne Bsns Ctr
High Cross Ctr
Ferry Lane Ind Est
Blackhorse Road
N17
FOREST RD
FERRY LA
MONUMENT WAY
HALE RD
BROAD LA
WATERMEAD WAY
BLACKHORSE LA
Resr No 1
Resr No 2
Resr No 3
Resr No 4
Resr No 5
E17
Coppermill Prim Sch
3 Rainbow Works
The Stonebridge Ctr
Mus
Markfield Recn Gd
N15
South Tottenham
Warwick Resr East
Warwick Resr West
Lea Valley Walk
Lee Valley Regional Park
Coppermill Stream
Water Works
COPPERMILL LA
N16
Ravensdale Com Est
Pl Flds
Lee Flood Relief Channel
Springfield Marina
Springfield Park
E5
Walthamstow Marshes
Nature Reserve
Leyton Marshes
E10
Leyton Ind Village
Dorma Trad Pk
Forest Bsns Pk
Lee Valley Riding Ctr
Lea Valley Ice Ctr
Upper Clapton
Capital Ring
CLAPTON COMMON
UPPER CLAPTON RD
Stoke Newington
River Lea or Lee
74
35
36
51

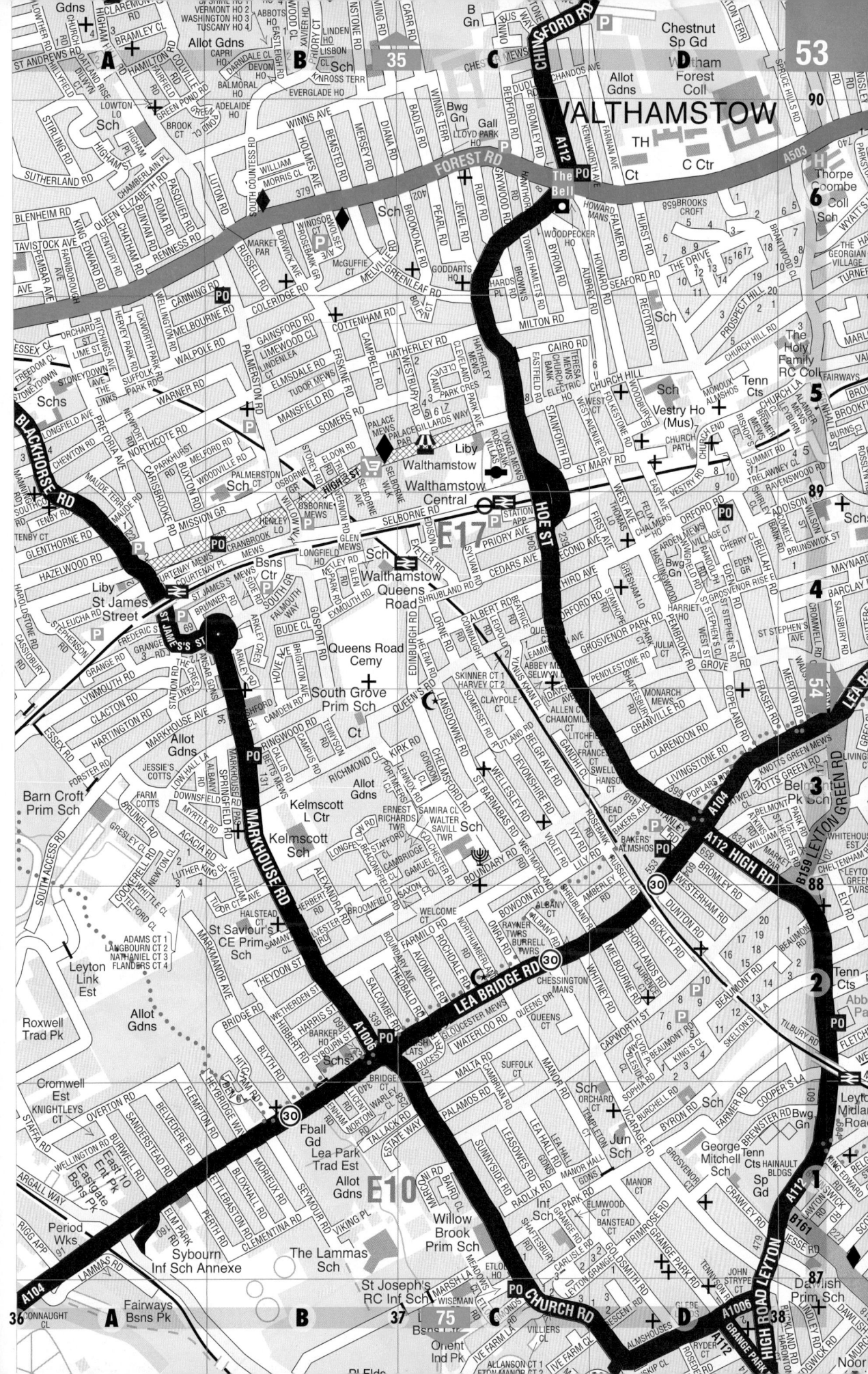
35
75
54
A
B
C
D
90
89
88
87
36
37
38
6
5
4
3
2
1
WALTHAMSTOW
E17
E10
FOREST RD
CHINGFORD RD
HOE ST
BLACKHORSE RD
MARKHOUSE RD
LEA BRIDGE RD
HIGH RD
HIGH ROAD LEYTON
CHURCH RD
LEYTON GREEN RD
A112
A503
A104
A1006
B159
B161
The Bell
Walthamstow Central
Walthamstow Queens Road
St James Street
Queens Road Cemy
South Grove Prim Sch
Kelmscott L Ctr
Kelmscott Sch
Barn Croft Prim Sch
St Saviour's CE Prim Sch
Leyton Link Est
Roxwell Trad Pk
Cromwell Est
East 10 Ent Pk
Eastgate Bsns Pk
Period Wks
Sybourn Inf Sch Annexe
Fball Gd
Lea Park Trad Est
Willow Brook Prim Sch
The Lammas Sch
St Joseph's RC Inf Sch
Fairways Bsns Pk
Orient Ind Pk
George Mitchell Sch
Chestnut Sp Gd
Waltham Forest Coll
Thorpe Coombe Coll
The Holy Family RC Coll
Vestry Ho (Mus)
Walthamstow Liby
Dawlish Prim Sch
Leyton Midland Road
Allot Gdns
HIGH ST
ST JAMES'S ST
SELBORNE RD
GROSVENOR PARK RD
MARKHOUSE AVE
CHURCH HILL
ST MARY RD
ORFORD RD
MILTON RD
WINNS AVE
QUEEN ELIZABETH RD

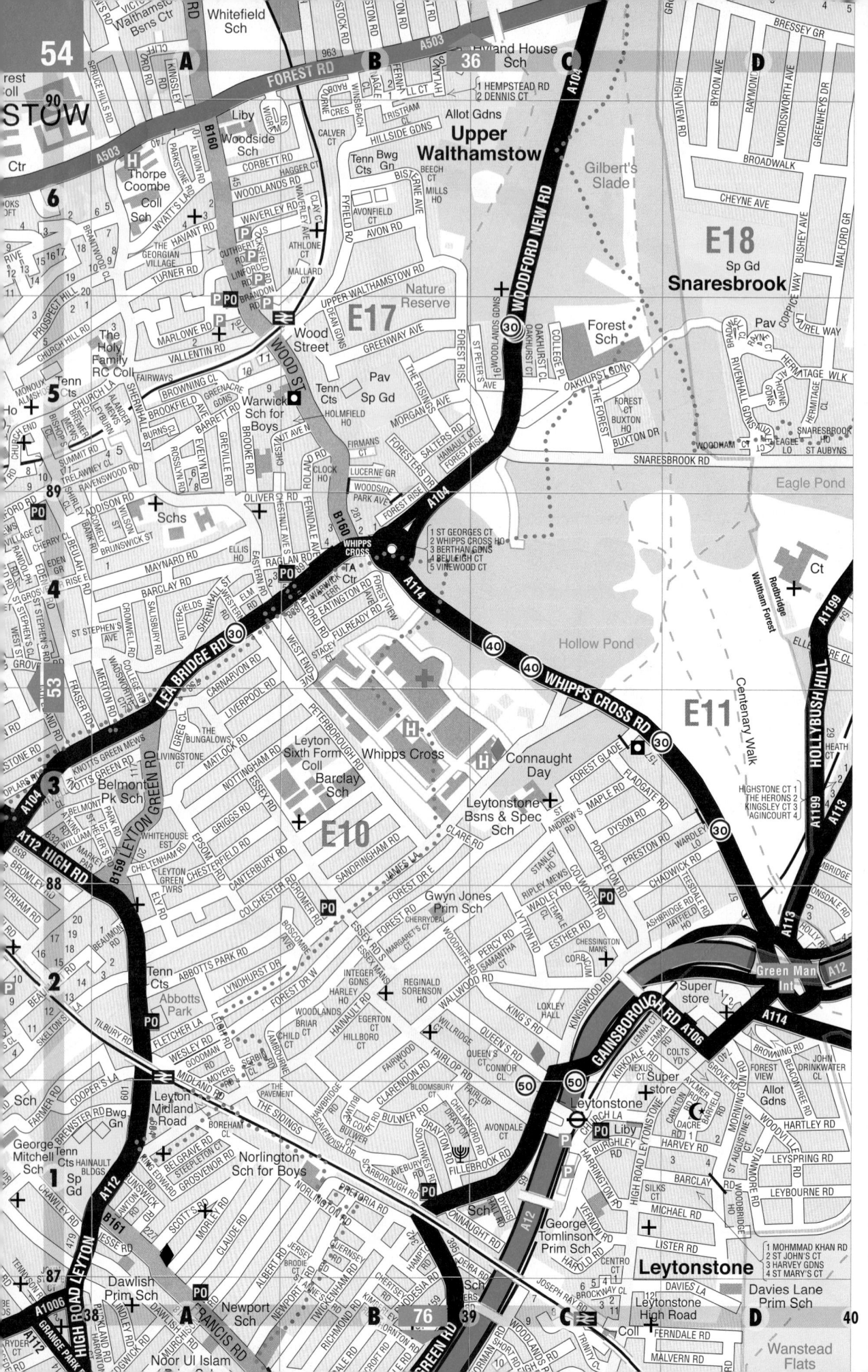
Upper Walthamstow
E17
E18
Snaresbrook
E10
E11
Leytonstone
Whipps Cross
Wood Street
Hollow Pond
Eagle Pond
Gilbert's Slade
Centenary Walk
FOREST RD
WOODFORD NEW RD
LEA BRIDGE RD
WHIPPS CROSS RD
HOLLYBUSH HILL
GAINSBOROUGH RD
HIGH ROAD LEYTON
LEYTON GREEN RD
SNARESBROOK RD
WOOD ST
Leyton Midland Road
Leytonstone High Road
Green Man Int
Whipps Cross
Leyton Sixth Form Coll
Barclay Sch
Connaught Day
Leytonstone Bsns & Spec Sch
Gwyn Jones Prim Sch
Norlington Sch for Boys
Dawlish Prim Sch
Newport Sch
Noor Ul Islam
George Tomlinson Prim Sch
Davies Lane Prim Sch
Forest Sch
Warwick Sch for Boys
The Holy Family RC Coll
Thorpe Coombe
Woodside Sch
Whitefield Sch
Ryland House Sch
Belmont Pk Sch
George Mitchell Sch
Abbotts Park
Nature Reserve
Wanstead Flats
Redbridge
Waltham Forest

36
53
76

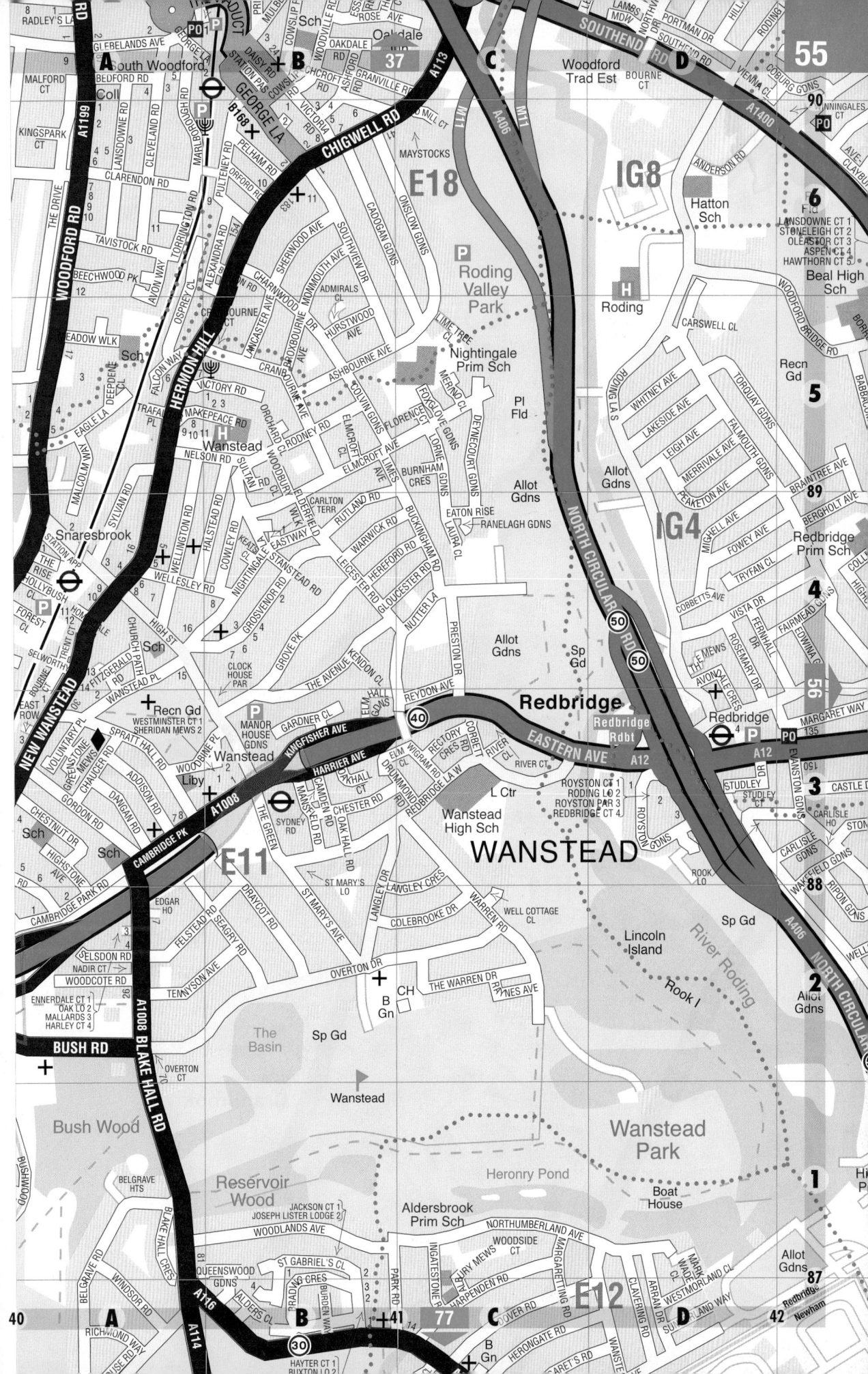

RADLEY'S LA
GLEBELANDS AVE
South Woodford
BEDFORD RD
MALFORD CT
Coll
KINGSPARK CT
WOODFORD RD
A1199
LANSDOWNE RD
CLEVELAND RD
MARLBOROUGH RD
CLARENDON RD
THE DRIVE
TAVISTOCK RD
TORRINGTON RD
BEECHWOOD PK
AVON WAY
OSPREY CL
ALEXANDRA RD
MEADOW WLK
Sch
FALCON WAY
HERMON HILL
DEEPDENE CL
EAGLE LA
MALCOLM WAY
VICTORY RD
TRAFALGAR PL
MAKEPEACE RD
Wanstead
NELSON RD
SYLVAN RD
Snaresbrook
STATION APP
THE RISE
HOLLYBUSH
FOREST CL
SELWORTHY
TRENT CT
NEW WANSTEAD
CHURCH PATH
FITZGERALD RD
WANSTEAD PL
HIGH ST
Recn Gd
WESTMINSTER CT 1
SHERIDAN MEWS 2
VOLUNTARY PL
GREENSTONE MEWS
CHAUCER RD
SPRATT HALL RD
ADDISON RD
DANGAN RD
GORDON RD
CHESTNUT DR
HIGHSTONE AVE
CAMBRIDGE PARK RD
CAMBRIDGE PK
A1008
EDGAR HO
ELSDON RD
NADIR CT
WOODCOTE RD
ENNERDALE CT 1
OAK LO 2
MALLARDS 3
HARLEY CT 4
BUSH RD
A1008 BLAKE HALL RD
OVERTON CT
Bush Wood
BUSHWOOD
BELGRAVE HTS
BELGRAVE RD
WINDSOR RD
RICHMOND WAY
BLAKE HALL CRES
A116
A114
Reservoir Wood
QUEENSWOOD GDNS
ALDERS CL
ST GABRIEL'S CL
BRADING CRES
BURDEN WAY
JACKSON CT 1
JOSEPH LISTER LODGE 2
WOODLANDS AVE
PARK RD
HAYTER CT 1
BUXTON LO 2
Sch
COWSLIP RD
WOODVILLE RD
OAKDALE RD
Oakdale
DAISY RD
STATION PAS
GEORGE LA
B168
PELHAM RD
PULTENEY RD
ORFORD RD
VICTORIA RD
CHURCHFIELDS
ASHFORD RD
GRANVILLE RD
MILL CT
CHIGWELL RD
A113
MAYSTOCKS
E18
CADOGAN GDNS
ONSLOW GDNS
SOUTHVIEW DR
SHERWOOD AVE
MONMOUTH AVE
CHARNWOOD DR
ADMIRALS CL
HURSTWOOD AVE
CRANBOURNE CT
LANCASTER AVE
BROXBOURNE AVE
ASHBOURNE AVE
CRANBOURNE AVE
COLVIN GDNS
ORCHARD CL
RODNEY RD
ELMCROFT CL
ELMCROFT AVE
FLORENCE CT
LIMES AVE
FOXGLOVE GDNS
MERINO CL
LORNE GDNS
DEYNECOURT GDNS
BURNHAM CRES
WOODBURY CL
SULTAN RD
ELDERFIELD WLK
CARLTON TERR
RUTLAND RD
EASTWAY
KEATS CL
NIGHTINGALE LA
STANSTEAD RD
WARWICK RD
HEREFORD RD
BUCKINGHAM RD
WELLINGTON RD
HALSTEAD RD
COWLEY RD
WELLESLEY RD
GROSVENOR RD
LEICESTER RD
GLOUCESTER RD
NUTTER LA
PRESTON DR
EATON RISE
LAURA CL
RANELAGH GDNS
GROVE PK
CLOCK HOUSE PAR
THE AVENUE
KENDON CL
ELM HALL GDNS
REYDON AVE
MANOR HOUSE GDNS
GARDNER CL
WOODBINE PL
Liby
KINGFISHER AVE
HARRIER AVE
THE GREEN
SYDNEY RD
CAMDEN RD
MANSFIELD RD
OAKHALL CT
CHESTER RD
OAK HALL RD
ELM CL
WIGRAM RD
DRUMMOND RD
RECTORY CRES
CORBETT RD
REDBRIDGE LA W
RIVER CL
RIVER CT
L Ctr
Wanstead High Sch
WANSTEAD
E11
ST MARY'S LO
ST MARY'S AVE
LANGLEY DR
LANGLEY CRES
COLEBROOKE DR
WARREN RD
WELL COTTAGE CL
DRAYCOT RD
FELSTEAD RD
SEAGRY RD
TENNYSON AVE
OVERTON DR
THE WARREN DR
RAYNES AVE
B Gn
CH
The Basin
Sp Gd
Wanstead
Heronry Pond
Aldersbrook Prim Sch
NORTHUMBERLAND AVE
INGATESTONE RD
WOODSIDE CT
BURY MEWS
HARPENDEN RD
MARGARETTING RD
DOVER RD
HERONGATE RD
E12
CLAVERING RD
ARRAN DR
MARK WADE CL
WESTMORLAND CL
SUNLAND WAY
Redbridge
Newham
Roding Valley Park
Nightingale Prim Sch
LIME TREE CL
Pl Fld
Allot Gdns
Woodford Trad Est
BOURNE CT
M11
A406
SOUTHEND RD
LAMBS MDW
NORTHVIEW DR
PORTMAN DR
SOUTHEND DR
RODING LA
VIENNA CL
COBURG GDNS
A1400
ANDERSON RD
IG8
Hatton Sch
LANSDOWNE CT 1
STONELEIGH CT 2
OLEASTOR CT 3
ASPEN CT 4
HAWTHORN CT 5
Beal High Sch
H
Roding
CARSWELL CL
WOODFORD BRIDGE RD
Recn Gd
RODING LA S
WHITNEY AVE
LAKESIDE AVE
TORQUAY GDNS
LEIGH AVE
MERRIVALE AVE
FALMOUTH GDNS
PEAKETON AVE
BRAINTREE AVE
BERGHOLT AVE
IG4
MICHELL AVE
FOWEY AVE
Redbridge Prim Sch
TRYFAN CL
COBBETTS AVE
VISTA DR
FERNHALL DR
FAIRMEAD GDNS
EDWINA GDNS
THE MEWS
ROSEMARY DR
AVONDALE CRES
NORTH CIRCULAR RD
Sp Gd
Redbridge
Redbridge Rdbt
EASTERN AVE
A12
MARGARET WAY
STUDLEY DR
STUDLEY CT
EVANSTON GDNS
CASTLE
CARLISLE HO
CARLISLE GDNS
WAKEFIELD GDNS
RIPON GDNS
ROYSTON CT 1
RODING LO 2
ROYSTON PAR 3
REDBRIDGE CT 4
ROYSTON GDNS
ROOK LO
Lincoln Island
River Roding
Rook I
Wanstead Park
Boat House
Allot Gdns
A406 NORTH CIRCULAR
A
B
C
D
37
56
77
40
41
42
87
88
89
90
1
2
3
4
5
6

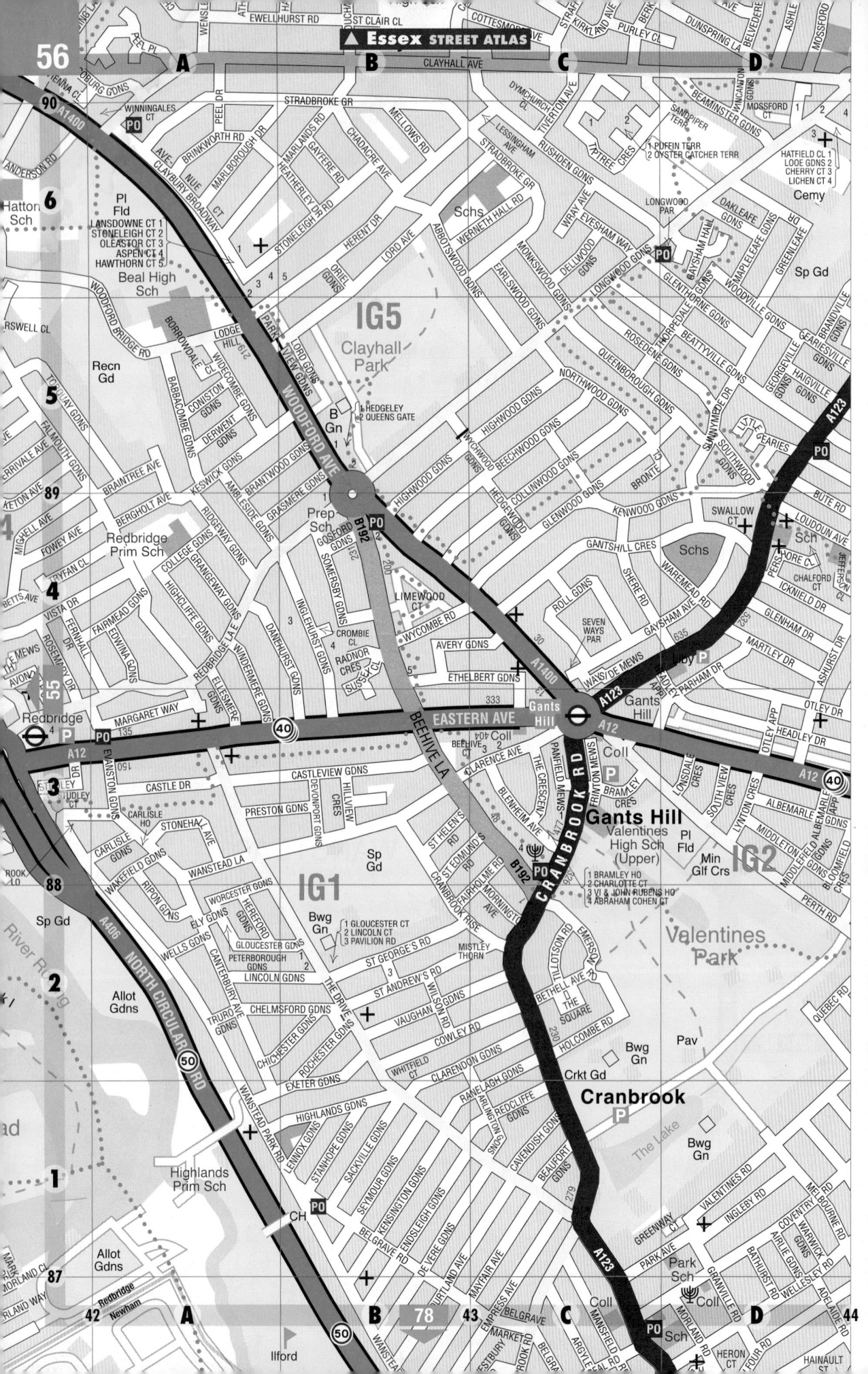
Essex STREET ATLAS
A
B
C
D
CLAYHALL AVE
STRADBROKE GR
IG5
Clayhall Park
WOODFORD AVE
Beal High Sch
Redbridge Prim Sch
EASTERN AVE
Gants Hill
CRANBROOK RD
BEEHIVE LA
IG1
IG2
Valentines High Sch (Upper)
Valentines Park
Cranbrook
The Lake
NORTH CIRCULAR RD
Highlands Prim Sch
Allot Gdns
Redbridge
Newham
Ilford
78
55
42
43
44
87
88
89
90
1
2
3
4
5
6

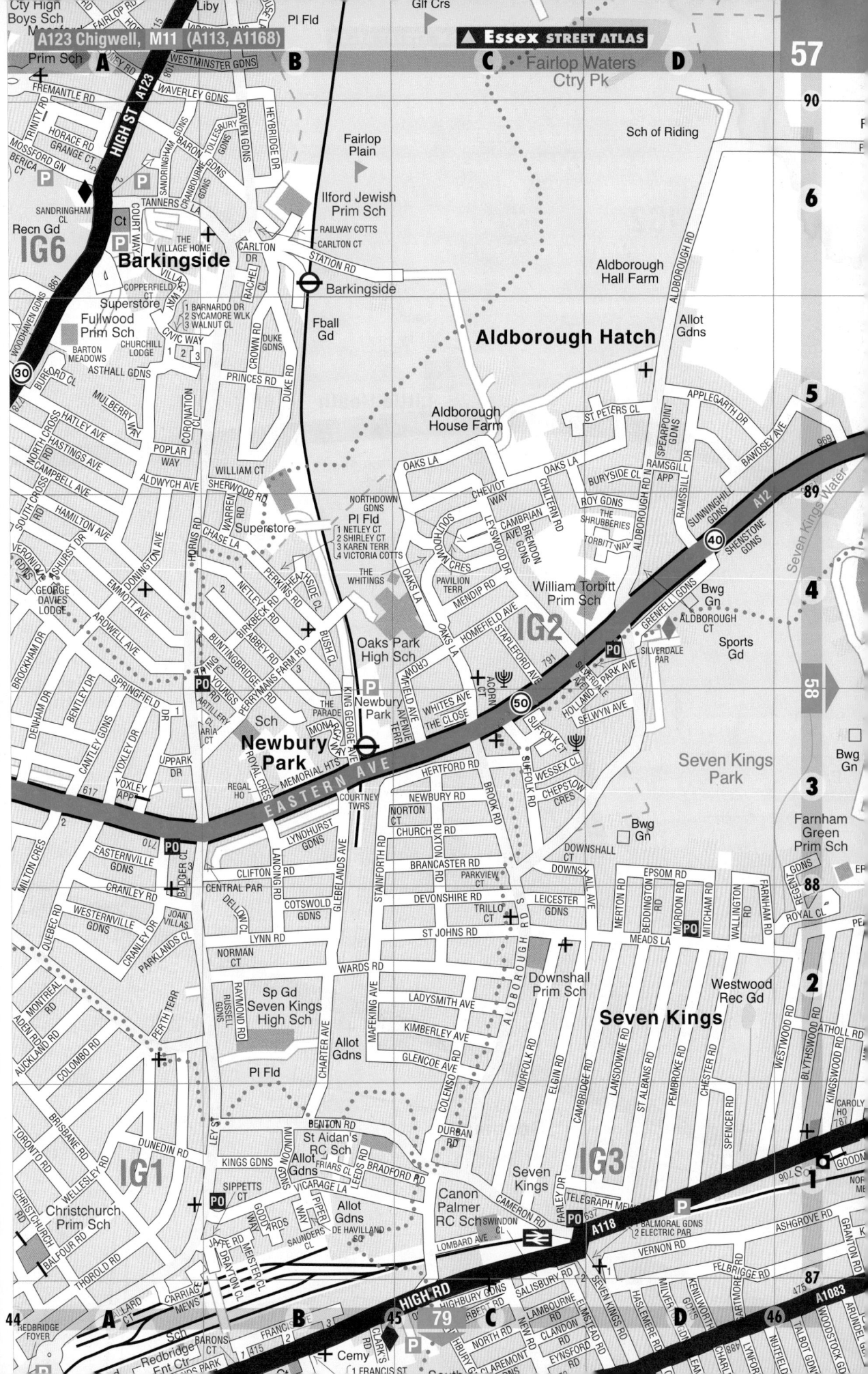
Barkingside
Aldborough Hatch
Newbury Park
Seven Kings
IG6
IG2
IG1
IG3
Fairlop Waters Ctry Pk
Fairlop Plain
Sch of Riding
Ilford Jewish Prim Sch
Aldborough Hall Farm
Aldborough House Farm
Fullwood Prim Sch
William Torbitt Prim Sch
Oaks Park High Sch
Seven Kings Park
Farnham Green Prim Sch
Downshall Prim Sch
Westwood Rec Gd
Sp Gd Seven Kings High Sch
St Aidan's RC Sch
Canon Palmer RC Sch
Christchurch Prim Sch
EASTERN AVE
HIGH ST
HIGH RD
A123
A12
A118
A1083
Seven Kings Water

58
79
44
45
46
30
40
50

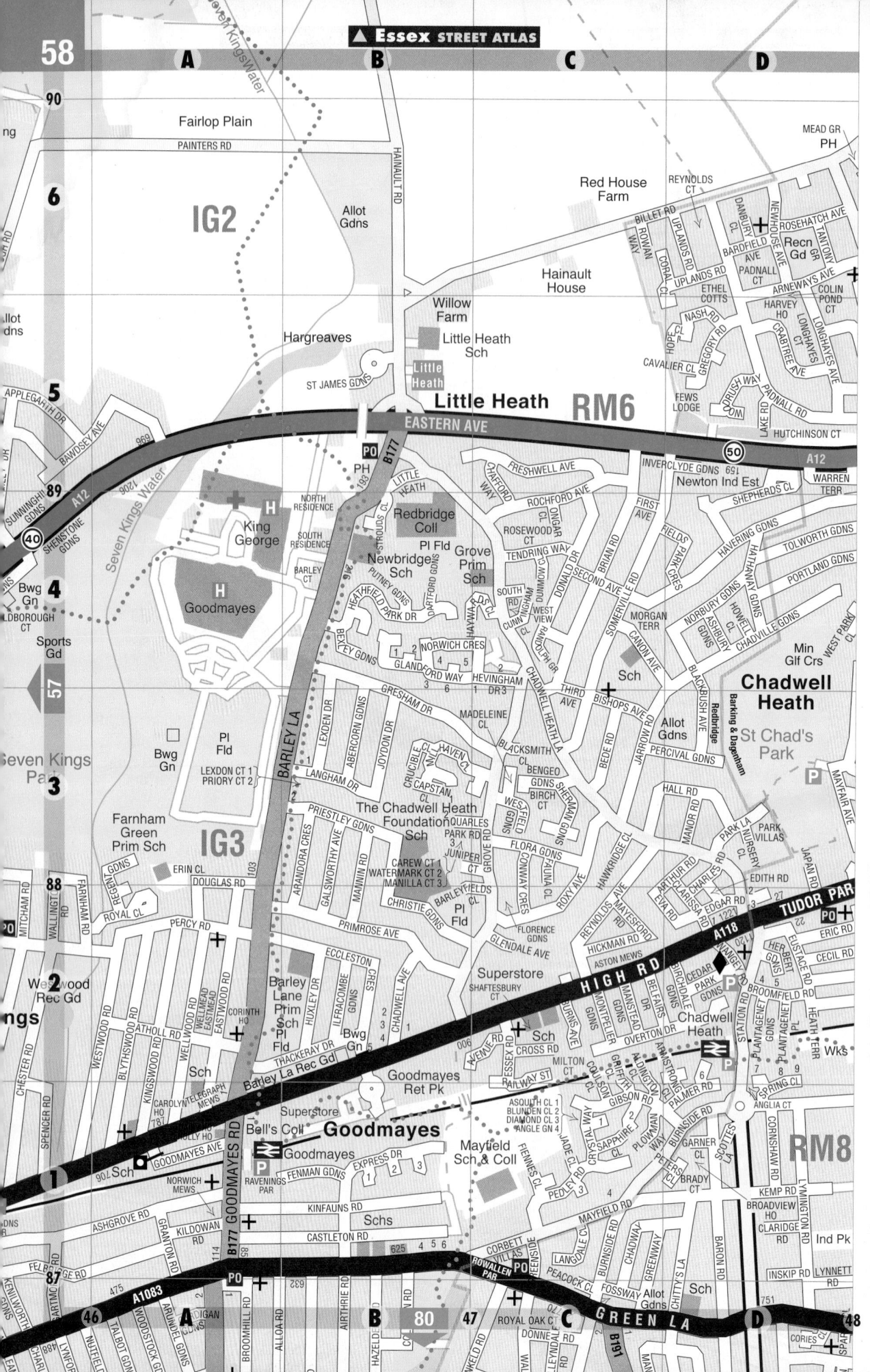

Fairlop Plain
PAINTERS RD
HAINAULT RD
IG2
Allot Gdns
Red House Farm
Hainault House
Willow Farm
Little Heath Sch
Hargreaves
Little Heath
RM6
EASTERN AVE
A12
Newton Ind Est
King George
Goodmayes
Redbridge Coll
Newbridge Sch
Grove Prim Sch
Chadwell Heath
St Chad's Park
Seven Kings Park
IG3
Farnham Green Prim Sch
The Chadwell Heath Foundation Sch
BARLEY LA
HIGH RD
A118
TUDOR PAR
Superstore
Chadwell Heath
Goodmayes Ret Pk
Goodmayes
Bell's Coll
Mayfield Sch & Coll
Barley Lane Prim Sch
Westwood Rec Gd
GOODMAYES RD
B177
A1083
GREEN LA
RM8
Ind Pk
Wks
Min Glf Crs
Barking & Dagenham
Redbridge

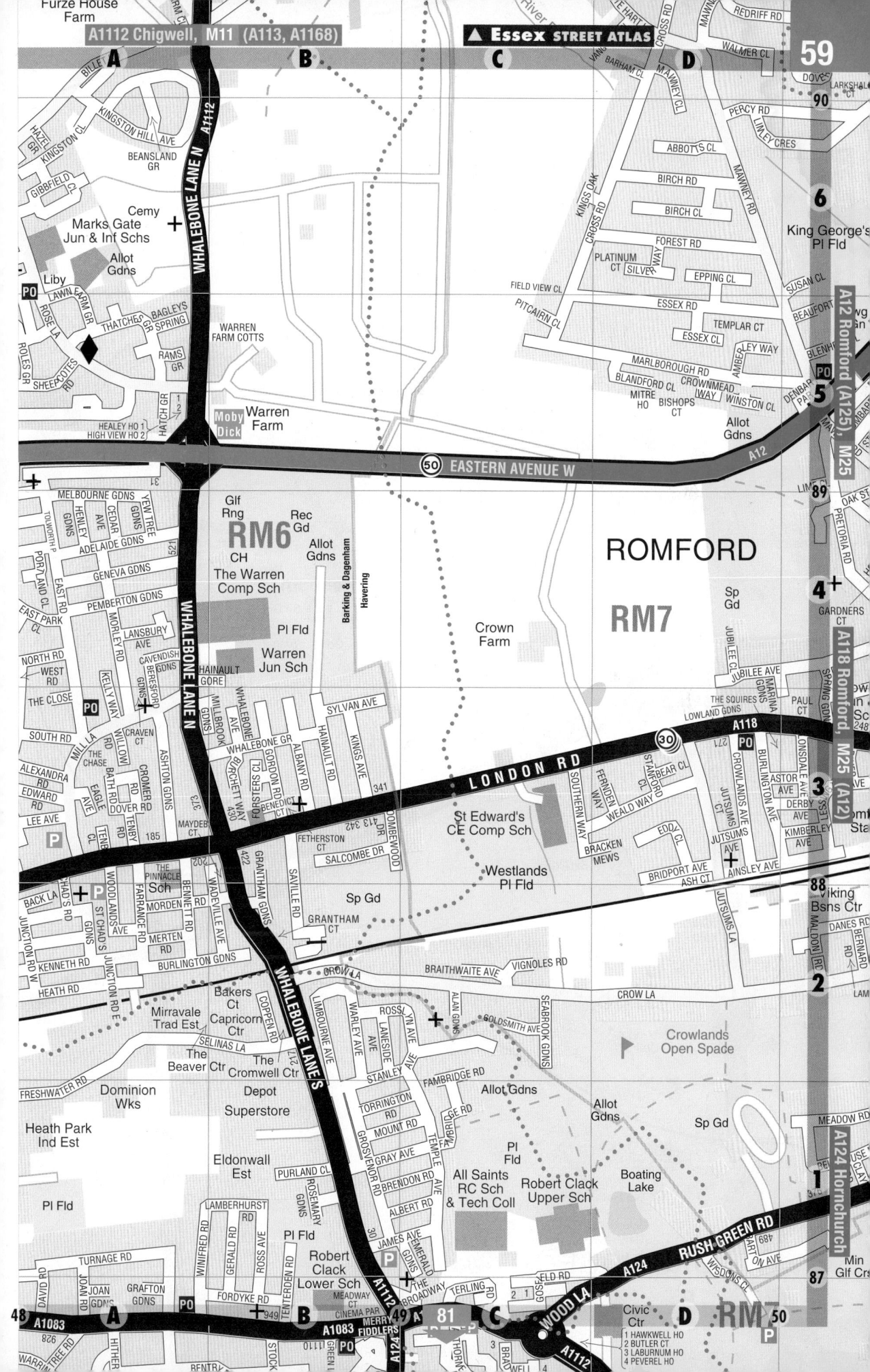
Furze House Farm
A
B
C
D
WHALEBONE LANE N
A1112
KINGSTON HILL AVE
KINGSTON CL
BEANSLAND GR
GIBBFIELD CL
Cemy
Marks Gate Jun & Inf Schs
Allot Gdns
Liby
LAWN FARM GR
ROSE LA
THATCHES GR
BAGLEYS SPRING
RAMS GR
SHEEPCOTES RD
ROLES GR
HATCH GR
HEALEY HO
HIGH VIEW HO
WARREN FARM COTTS
Moby Dick
Warren Farm
EASTERN AVENUE W
A12
RM6
ROMFORD
RM7
Glf Rng
Rec Gd
Allot Gdns
CH
The Warren Comp Sch
Pl Fld
Warren Jun Sch
Barking & Dagenham
Havering
Crown Farm
MELBOURNE GDNS
HENLEY GDNS
CEDAR AVE
YEW TREE GDNS
ADELAIDE GDNS
GENEVA GDNS
PEMBERTON GDNS
PORTLAND CL
EAST RD
EAST PARK CL
LANSBURY AVE
MORLEY RD
CAVENDISH GDNS
BERESFORD GDNS
NORTH RD
WEST RD
THE CLOSE
KELLY WAY
SOUTH RD
MILL LA
WILLOW
CRAVEN CT
THE CHASE
ALEXANDRA RD
EDWARD RD
EAGLE AVE
BATH RD
DOVER RD
CROMER RD
TENBY RD
ASHTON GDNS
LEE AVE
HAINAULT GORE
MILLBROOK GDNS
WHALEBONE AVE
WHALEBONE GR
BURCHETT WAY
FORSTERS CL
GORDON RD
ALBANY RD
BENEDICT CT
HAINAULT RD
KINGS AVE
SYLVAN AVE
MAYDEB CT
LONDON RD
A118
FETHERSTON CT
SALCOMBE DR
COOMBEWOOD DR
St Edward's CE Comp Sch
Westlands Pl Fld
SOUTHERN WAY
FERNDEN WAY
STAMFORD CL
BEAR CL
WEALD WAY
BRACKEN MEWS
EDDY CL
BRIDPORT AVE
ASH CT
JUTSUMS CT
JUTSUMS AVE
AINSLEY AVE
CROWLANDS AVE
BURLINGTON AVE
ASTOR AVE
DERBY AVE
KIMBERLEY AVE
LONSDALE AVE
JUBILEE CL
JUBILEE AVE
MARINA GDNS
THE SQUIRES
LOWLAND GDNS
PAUL CT
SPRING GDNS
Sp Gd
GARDNERS CT
PRETORIA RD
OAK ST
BACK LA
CHAD'S RD
THE PINNACLE
Sch
WOODLANDS AVE
FARRANCE RD
MORDEN RD
BENNETT RD
MERTEN RD
WADEVILLE AVE
GRANTHAM GDNS
SAVILLE RD
GRANTHAM CT
Sp Gd
JUNCTION RD W
KENNETH RD
ST CHAD'S GDNS
JUNCTION RD E
HEATH RD
BURLINGTON GDNS
Bakers Ct
Capricorn Ctr
COPPEN RD
Mirravale Trad Est
SELINAS LA
The Beaver Ctr
The Cromwell Ctr
WHALEBONE LANE S
CROW LA
BRAITHWAITE AVE
VIGNOLES RD
JUTSUMS LA
Viking Bsns Ctr
MALDON RD
DANES RD
BERNARD RD
LIMBOURNE AVE
WARLEY AVE
ROSSLYN AVE
LANESIDE AVE
ALAN GDNS
GOLDSMITH AVE
SEABROOK GDNS
Crowlands Open Space
FRESHWATER RD
Dominion Wks
Depot
Superstore
Heath Park Ind Est
STANLEY AVE
TORRINGTON RD
MOUNT RD
FAMBRIDGE RD
Allot Gdns
Allot Gdns
Sp Gd
MEADOW RD
Eldonwall Est
GROSVENOR RD
GRAY AVE
TEMPLE AVE
BRENDON RD
ALBERT RD
Pl Fld
All Saints RC Sch & Tech Coll
Robert Clack Upper Sch
Boating Lake
PURLAND CL
ROSEMARY GDNS
LAMBERHURST RD
WINIFRED RD
GERALD RD
ROSS AVE
Pl Fld
Pl Fld
TENTERDEN RD
Robert Clack Lower Sch
JAMES AVE
EMERALD GDNS
THE BROADWAY
TERLING RD
RUSH GREEN RD
A124
WISDONS CL
NORTON AVE
TURNAGE RD
DAVID RD
JOAN RD
JOAN GDNS
GRAFTON GDNS
FORDYKE RD
MEADWAY CT
CINEMA PAR
MERRY FIDDLERS
WOOD LA
Civic Ctr
1 HAWKWELL HO
2 BUTLER CT
3 LABURNUM HO
4 PEVEREL HO
A1083
A1112
A124
HITHER
WARRINGTREE RD
STOCK
81
Min
Gfl Cr
48
49
50
87
88
89
90
1
2
3
4
5
6
REDRIFF RD
WALMER CL
CROSS RD
MAWNEY CL
BARHAM CL
PERCY RD
LIMLEY CRES
ABBOTTS CL
BIRCH RD
BIRCH CL
MAWNEY RD
KINGS OAK
CROSS RD
FOREST RD
PLATINUM CT
SILVER WAY
EPPING CL
FIELD VIEW CL
ESSEX RD
PITCAIRN CL
TEMPLAR CT
ESSEX CL
LEY WAY
AMBER
MARLBOROUGH RD
BLANDFORD CL
CROWNMEAD WAY
MITRE HO
BISHOPS CT
WINSTON CL
Allot Gdns
DENBAR PAR
King George's Pl Fld
SUSAN CL
BEAUFORT
A12 Romford (A125), M25
A118 Romford, M25 (A12)
A124 Hornchurch

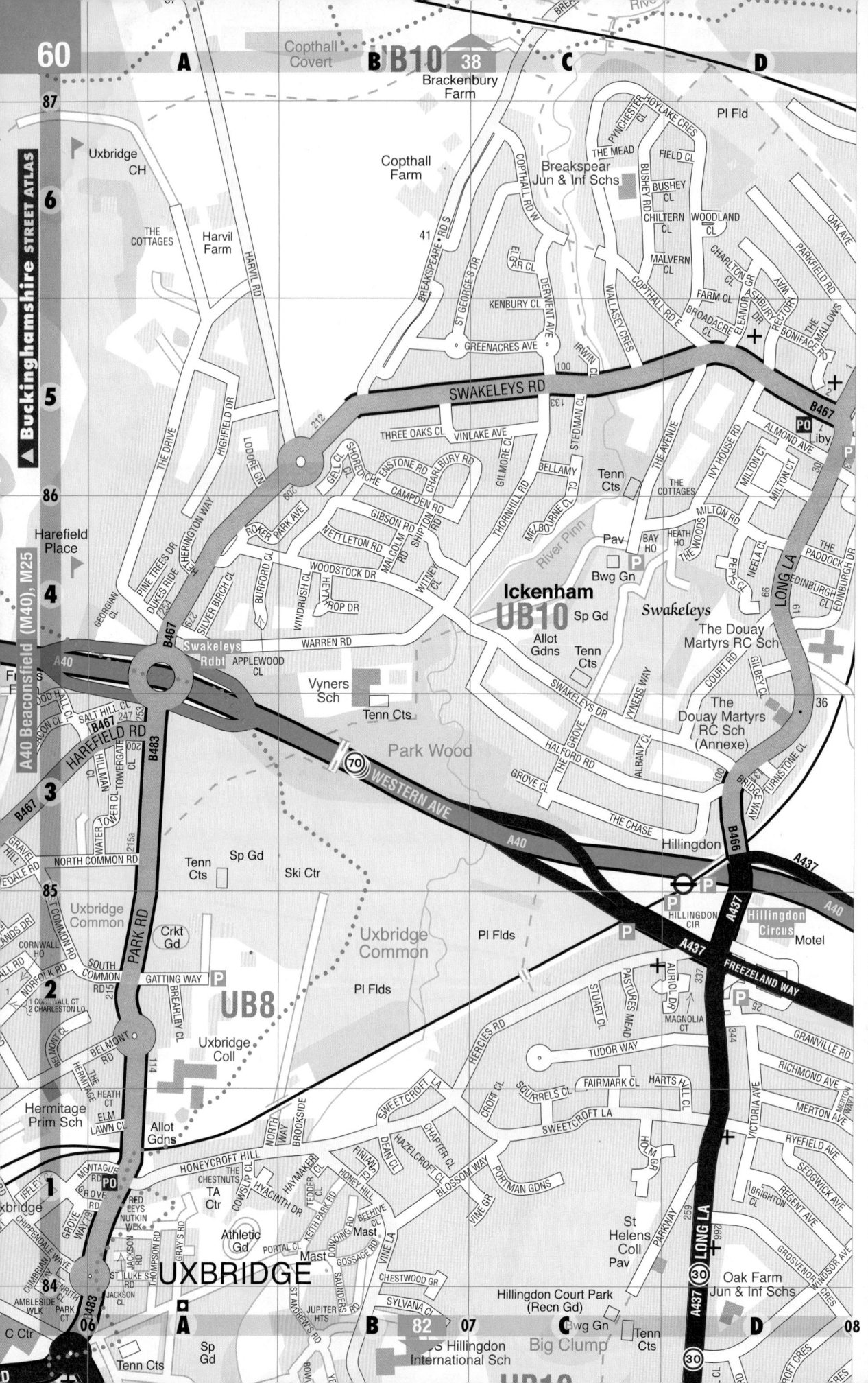

A
B
C
D
UB10
38
Copthall Covert
Brackenbury Farm
Uxbridge CH
Copthall Farm
Breakspear Jun & Inf Schs
Pl Fld
THE COTTAGES
Harvil Farm
HARVIL RD
BREAKSPEARE RD S
ST GEORGE'S DR
COPTHALL RD W
DERWENT AVE
KENBURY CL
GREENACRES AVE
ELGAR CL
THE MEAD
PYNCHESTER CL
HOYLAKE CRES
FIELD CL
BUSHEY RD
BUSHEY CL
CHILTERN CL
WOODLAND CL
MALVERN CL
WALLASEY CRES
COPTHALL RD E
CHARLTON CL
FARM CL
BROADACRE CL
ELEANOR GR
ASHBURY DR
RECTORY WAY
BONIFACE RD
THE MALLOWS
PARKFIELD RD
OAK AVE
IRWIN CL
SWAKELEYS RD
B467
THE DRIVE
HIGHFIELD DR
LODORE GN
HETHERINGTON WAY
PINE TREES DR
DUKES RIDE
GEORGIAN CL
SILVER BIRCH CL
ROKER PARK AVE
BURFORD CL
WINDRUSH CL
HEYTHROP DR
WOODSTOCK DR
NETTLETON RD
GIBSON RD
MALCOLM RD
SHIPTON RD
CAMPDEN RD
ENSTONE RD
CHARLBURY RD
SHOREDITCH CL
GELL CL
THREE OAKS CL
VINLAKE AVE
GILMORE CL
THORNHILL RD
BELLAMY CL
MELBOURNE CL
STEDMAN CL
WITNEY CL
Tenn Cts
THE AVENUE
THE COTTAGES
IVY HOUSE RD
ALMOND AVE
MILTON CT
MILTON RD
THE WOODS
BAY HO
HEATH HO
Pav
Bwg Gn
River Pinn
Ickenham
UB10
Sp Gd
Swakeleys
PEPYS CL
NEELA CL
LONG LA
THE PADDOCK
EDINBURGH DR
EDINBURGH CL
Liby
The Douay Martyrs RC Sch
Allot Gdns
Swakeleys Rdbt
APPLEWOOD CL
WARREN RD
Vyners Sch
Tenn Cts
SWAKELEYS DR
VYNERS WAY
COURT RD
GILBEY CL
The Douay Martyrs RC Sch (Annexe)
Park Wood
WESTERN AVE
A40
HALFORD RD
THE GROVE
ALBANY CL
GROVE CL
THE CHASE
TURNSTONE CL
BRIDGE WAY
B466
Hillingdon
A437
A40 Beaconsfield (M40), M25
HAREFIELD RD
SALT HILL CL
HILLMAN CL
TOWERGATE CL
WATER TOWER CL
B483
NORTH COMMON RD
GRAVEL HILL
Tenn Cts
Sp Gd
Ski Ctr
HILLINGDON CIR
Hillingdon Circus
Motel
Uxbridge Common
Pl Flds
FREEZELAND WAY
PARK RD
Crkt Gd
CORNWALL HO
SOUTH COMMON RD
NORFOLK RD
GATTING WAY
BREARLEY CL
UB8
Uxbridge Coll
PASTURES MEAD
STUART CL
AURIOL DR
MAGNOLIA CT
HERCIES RD
TUDOR WAY
GRANVILLE RD
RICHMOND AVE
MERTON AVE
BELMONT CL
BELMONT RD
THE HERMITAGE
HEATH CT
ELM LAWN CL
Hermitage Prim Sch
Allot Gdns
NORTH WAY
BROOKSIDE
SWEETCROFT LA
CROFT CL
SQUIRRELS CL
FAIRMARK CL
HARTS HALL CL
VICTORIA AVE
RYEFIELD AVE
SEDGWICK AVE
HOLM GR
HONEYCROFT HILL
THE CHESTNUTS
COWSLIP CL
HYACINTH DR
HAYMAKER CL
TEDDER CL
KEITH PARK RD
HONEY HILL
FINIAN CL
DEAN CL
HAZELCROFT CL
CHAPTER CL
BLOSSOM WAY
PORTMAN GDNS
VINE GR
BEEHIVE CL
VINE LA
MONTAGUE RD
GROVE RD
GROVE WAY
RED LEYS
NUTKIN WLK
TA Ctr
Athletic Gd
PORTAL CL
DOWDING RD
GOSSAGE RD
Mast
PARKWAY
St Helens Coll
Pav
BRIGHTON CL
REGENT AVE
GROSVENOR CRES
WINDSOR AVE
CHIPPENDALE WAYE
CUMBRIAN WAY
PENRITH CL
AMBLESIDE WLK
PARK CT
JACKSON RD
THOMPSON RD
GRAY'S RD
ST LUKE'S RD
JACKSON CL
UXBRIDGE
SAUNDERS RD
ST ANDREW'S RD
JUPITER HTS
CHESTWOOD GR
SYLVANA CL
Hillingdon Court Park (Recn Gd)
Oak Farm Jun & Inf Schs
Sp Gd
Tenn Cts
Hillingdon International Sch
Big Clump
Bwg Gn
82
07
08
06
87
86
85
84
6
5
4
3
2
1
Buckinghamshire STREET ATLAS

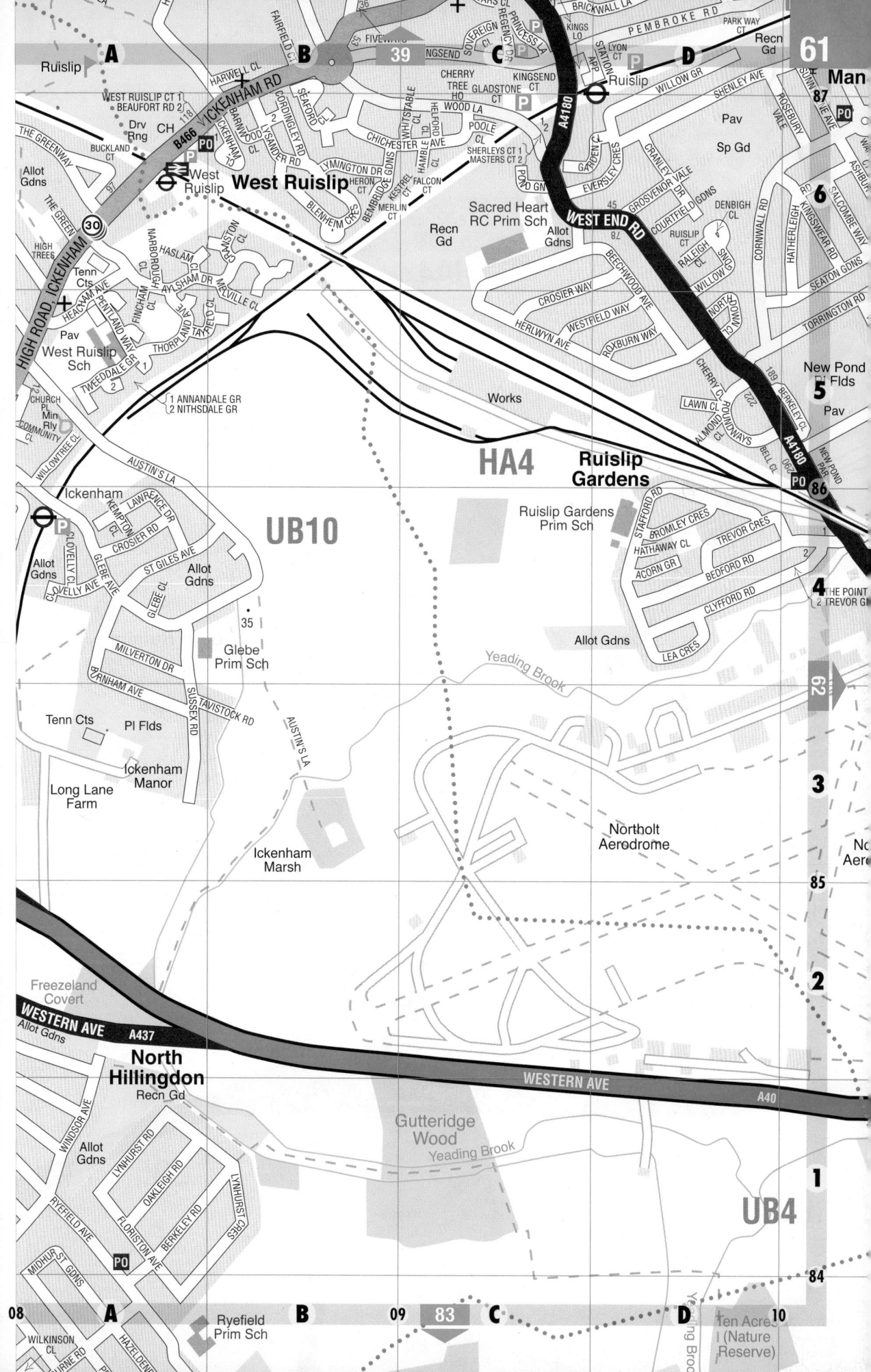
61
39
83
62
A
B
C
D
08
09
10
6
5
4
3
2
1
87
86
85
84
Ruislip
West Ruislip
Ruislip Gardens
Ickenham
North Hillingdon
HA4
UB10
UB4
ICKENHAM RD
B466
HIGH ROAD, ICKENHAM
WEST END RD
A4180
WESTERN AVE
A437
A40
Sacred Heart RC Prim Sch
West Ruislip Sch
Ruislip Gardens Prim Sch
Glebe Prim Sch
Ryefield Prim Sch
Ickenham Manor
Long Lane Farm
Ickenham Marsh
Northolt Aerodrome
Gutteridge Wood
Yeading Brook
Freezeland Covert
Ten Acres (Nature Reserve)
New Pond Pl Flds
Works
Allot Gdns
Recn Gd
Tenn Cts
Pl Flds
Pav
Sp Gd
Drv Rng
CH
1 ANNANDALE GR
2 NITHSDALE GR
WEST RUISLIP CT 1
BEAUFORT RD 2
SHERLEYS CT 1
MASTERS CT 2
1 THE POINT
2 TREVOR GR
AUSTIN'S LA
MILVERTON DR
BURNHAM AVE
TAVISTOCK RD
SUSSEX RD
ST GILES AVE
GLEBE AVE
CLOVELLY AVE
CROSIER RD
LAWRENCE DR
KEMPTON CL
WILLOWTREE CL
THORPLAND AVE
AYLSHAM DR
MELVILLE CL
PENTLAND WAY
TWEEDDALE GR
FINCHAM CL
NARBOROUGH CL
HASLAM CL
CRANSTON CL
CROSIER WAY
WESTFIELD WAY
HERLWYN AVE
ROXBURN WAY
BEECHWOOD AVE
GROSVENOR VALE
EVERSLEY CRES
CRANLEY DR
COURTFIELD GDNS
DENBIGH CL
RALEIGH CL
WILLOW GDNS
CORNWALL RD
HATHERLEIGH RD
KINGSWEAR RD
SALCOMBE WAY
SEATON GDNS
TORRINGTON RD
ROSEBURY VALE
SHENLEY AVE
WILLOW GR
PEMBROKE RD
BRICKWALL LA
STATION APP
KINGSEND CT
GLADSTONE CT
WOOD LA
POOLE CL
HELFORD CL
HAMBLE CL
WHITSTABLE CL
CHICHESTER AVE
LYMINGTON DR
BLENHEIM CRES
BEMBRIDGE GDNS
KESTREL CT
FALCON CT
MERLIN CT
HERON CT
LYSANDER RD
CORDINGLEY RD
SEAFORD CL
HARWELL CL
BUCKLAND CT
THE GREENWAY
STAFFORD RD
BROMLEY CRES
HATHAWAY CL
ACORN GR
TREVOR CRES
BEDFORD RD
CLYFFORD RD
LEA CRES
CHERRY CL
LAWN CL
ALMOND CL
ROUNDWAYS
BERKELEY CL
BELL CL
NEW POND PAR
WINDSOR AVE
LYNHURST RD
OAKLEIGH RD
BERKELEY RD
LYNHURST CRES
FLORISTON AVE
RYEFIELD AVE
MIDHURST GDNS
WILKINSON CL
HAZELDENE

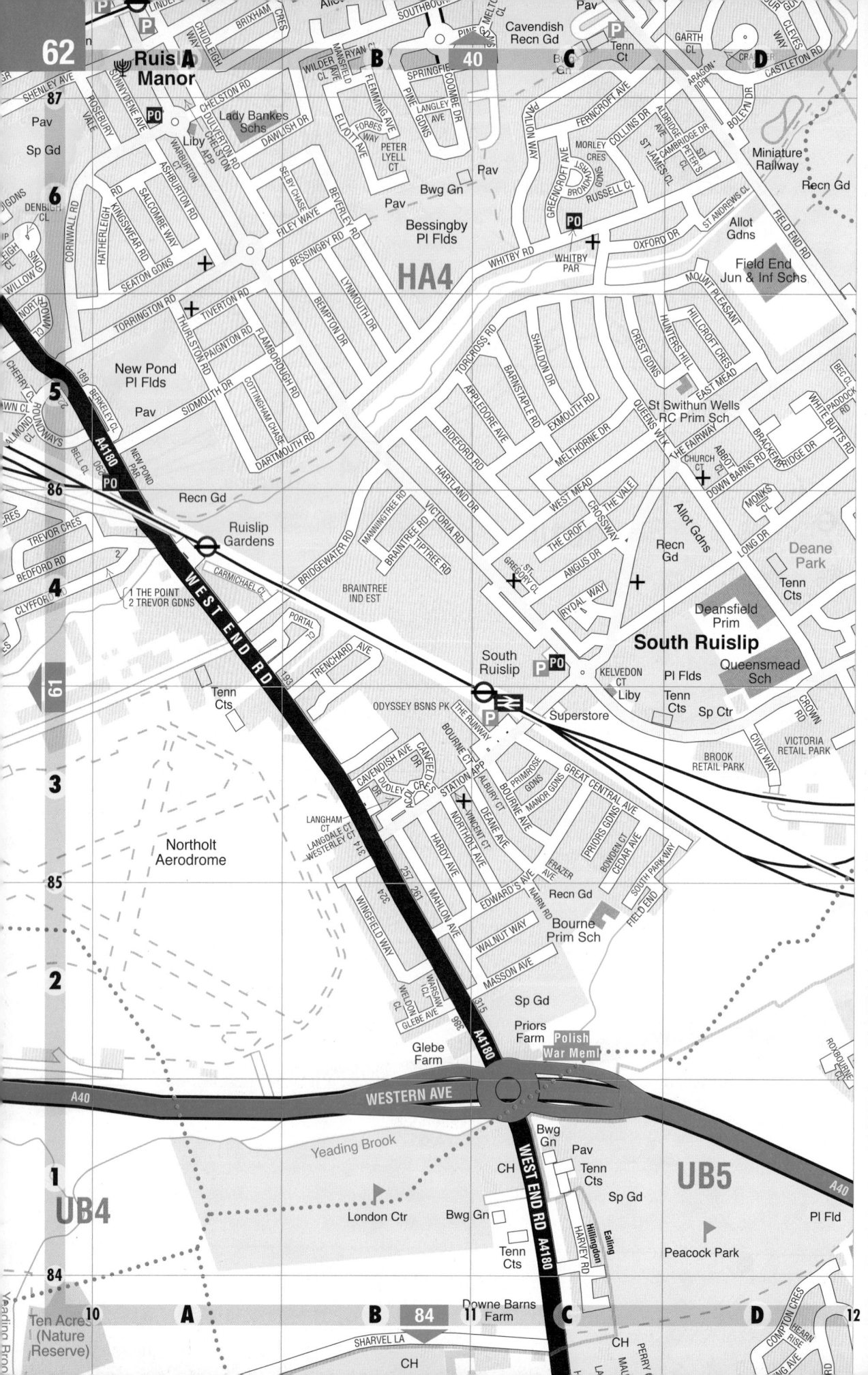

Ruislip Manor
A
B
40
C
D
SHENLEY AVE
SUNNYDENE AVE
ROSEBURY VALE
CHUDLEIGH WAY
BRIXHAM CRES
SOUTHBOURNE
PINE GDNS
MELTON CL
Cavendish Recn Gd
Pav
Tenn Ct
GARTH CL
CLEVES WAY
CASTLETON RD
ARAGON DR
CRAY
87
Pav
Sp Gd
PO
Liby
CHELSTON RD
DULVERTON RD
CHELSTON APP
Lady Bankes Schs
DAWLISH DR
WILDER CL
RYAN CL
MANSFIELD AVE
FLEMMING AVE
SPRINGFIELD
COOMBE DR
LANGLEY AVE
FORBES WAY
ELLIOTT AVE
PETER LYELL CT
PINE GDNS
PAVILION WAY
FERNCROFT AVE
COLLINS DR
ALDRIDGE AVE
CAMBRIDGE DR
ST PETER'S CL
ST JAMES CL
MORLEY CRES
GREENCROFT AVE
BROADHURST GDNS
RUSSELL CL
BOLEYN DR
Miniature Railway
Recn Gd
6
DENBIGH CL
WILLOW
CORNWALL RD
HATHERLEIGH RD
KINGSWEAR RD
SALCOMBE WAY
ASHBURTON RD
WARBURTON CT
SELBY CHASE
FILEY WAYE
BEVERLEY RD
Pav
Bwg Gn
Pav
Bessingby Pl Flds
ST ANDREWS CL
Allot Gdns
FIELD END RD
OXFORD DR
WHITBY RD
WHITBY PAR
SEATON GDNS
BESSINGBY RD
LYNMOUTH DR
HA4
Field End Jun & Inf Schs
MOUNT PLEASANT
TORRINGTON RD
TIVERTON RD
THURLSTON RD
PAIGNTON RD
FLAMBOROUGH RD
BEMPTON DR
NORTHDOWN CL
TORCROSS RD
SHALDON DR
CREST GDNS
HUNTERS HILL
HILLCROFT CRES
New Pond Pl Flds
BARNSTAPLE RD
5
CHERRY CL
BERKELEY CL
Pav
SIDMOUTH DR
COTTINGHAM CHASE
APPLEDORE AVE
EXMOUTH RD
EAST MEAD
BEC CL
PADDOCK RD
WHITE BUTTS RD
ALMOND CL
ROUNDWAYS
St Swithun Wells RC Prim Sch
QUEENS WALK
THE FAIRWAY
BIDEFORD RD
MELTHORNE DR
DARTMOUTH RD
A4180
BELL CL
NEW POND PAR
ABBOT CL
BRACKENBRIDGE DR
CHURCH CT
DOWN BARNS RD
HARTLAND DR
86
PO
Recn Gd
WEST MEAD
THE VALE
CROSSWAY
MONKS CL
MANNINGTREE RD
VICTORIA RD
THE CROFT
Allot Gdns
TREVOR CRES
Ruislip Gardens
BRAINTREE RD
TIPTREE RD
Recn Gd
LONG DR
Deane Park
BEDFORD RD
BRIDGEWATER RD
ANGUS DR
ST GREGORY CL
Tenn Cts
4
CLYFFORD RD
CARMICHAEL CL
1 THE POINT
2 TREVOR GDNS
BRAINTREE IND EST
RYDAL WAY
Deansfield Prim
WEST END RD
PORTAL CL
TRENCHARD AVE
South Ruislip
South Ruislip
61
KELVEDON CT
Queensmead Sch
Pl Flds
Tenn Cts
Liby
Tenn Cts
Sp Ctr
ODYSSEY BSNS PK
THE RUNWAY
Superstore
CROWN RD
BOURNE CT
BROOK RETAIL PARK
CIVIC WAY
VICTORIA RETAIL PARK
CAVENDISH AVE
CANFIELD DR
STATION APP
PRIMROSE GDNS
GREAT CENTRAL AVE
DUDLEY DR
ACOL CRES
ALBURY CT
BOURNE AVE
MANOR GDNS
3
LANGHAM CT
LANGDALE CT
WESTERLEY CT
VINCENT CT
DEANE AVE
PRIORS GDNS
BOWDEN CT
CEDAR AVE
SOUTH PARK WAY
Northolt Aerodrome
HARDY AVE
NORTHOLT AVE
85
FRAZER AVE
EDWARD'S AVE
NAIRN RD
Recn Gd
FIELD END
WINGFIELD WAY
MAHLON AVE
WALNUT WAY
Bourne Prim Sch
2
MASSON AVE
WELDON CL
WARSAW CL
GLEBE AVE
Sp Gd
Priors Farm
Polish War Meml
Glebe Farm
ROXBOURNE CL
A40
WESTERN AVE
Yeading Brook
Bwg Gn
Pav
CH
Tenn Cts
1
UB5
Sp Gd
A40
UB4
London Ctr
Bwg Gn
Pl Fld
Hillingdon
Ealing
HARVEY RD
Tenn Cts
Peacock Park
84
COMPTON CRES
HEARN RISE
Ten Acres (Nature Reserve)
10
A
B
84
11
Downe Barns Farm
C
D
12
SHARVEL LA
CH
CH

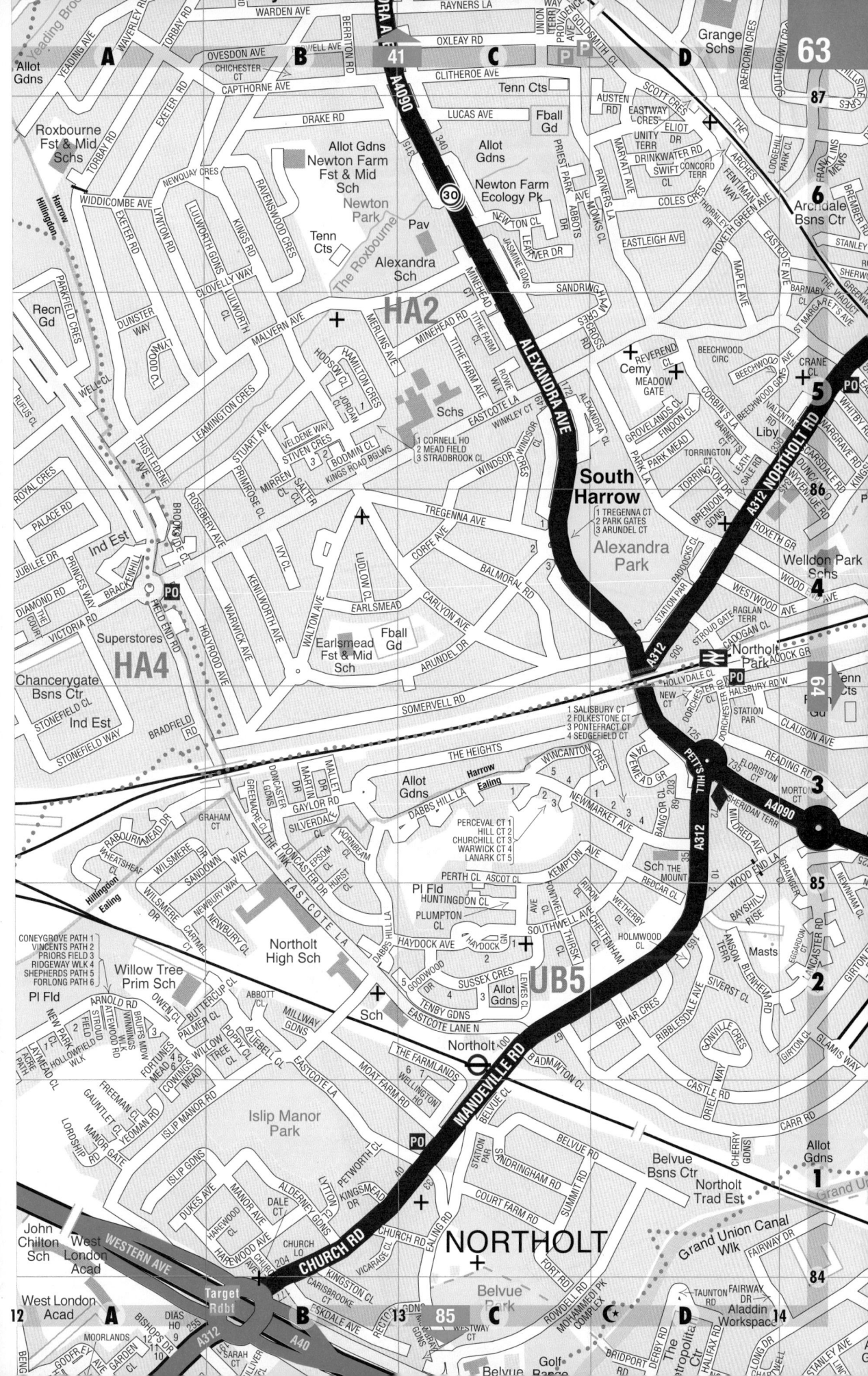

South Harrow
NORTHOLT
HA2
HA4
UB5
Northolt
Northolt Park
Alexandra Park
Islip Manor Park
Newton Park
Roxbourne Fst & Mid Schs
Newton Farm Fst & Mid Sch
Newton Farm Ecology Pk
Alexandra Sch
Earlsmead Fst & Mid Sch
Northolt High Sch
Willow Tree Prim Sch
John Chilton Sch
West London Acad
Belvue Bsns Ctr
Northolt Trad Est
Chancerygate Bsns Ctr
Welldon Park Schs
Archdale Bsns Ctr
Grange Schs
Aladdin Workspace
Grand Union Canal Wlk
ALEXANDRA AVE
NORTHOLT RD
MANDEVILLE RD
CHURCH RD
WESTERN AVE
PETTS HILL
A4090
A312
A40
Target Rdbt

41
64
85

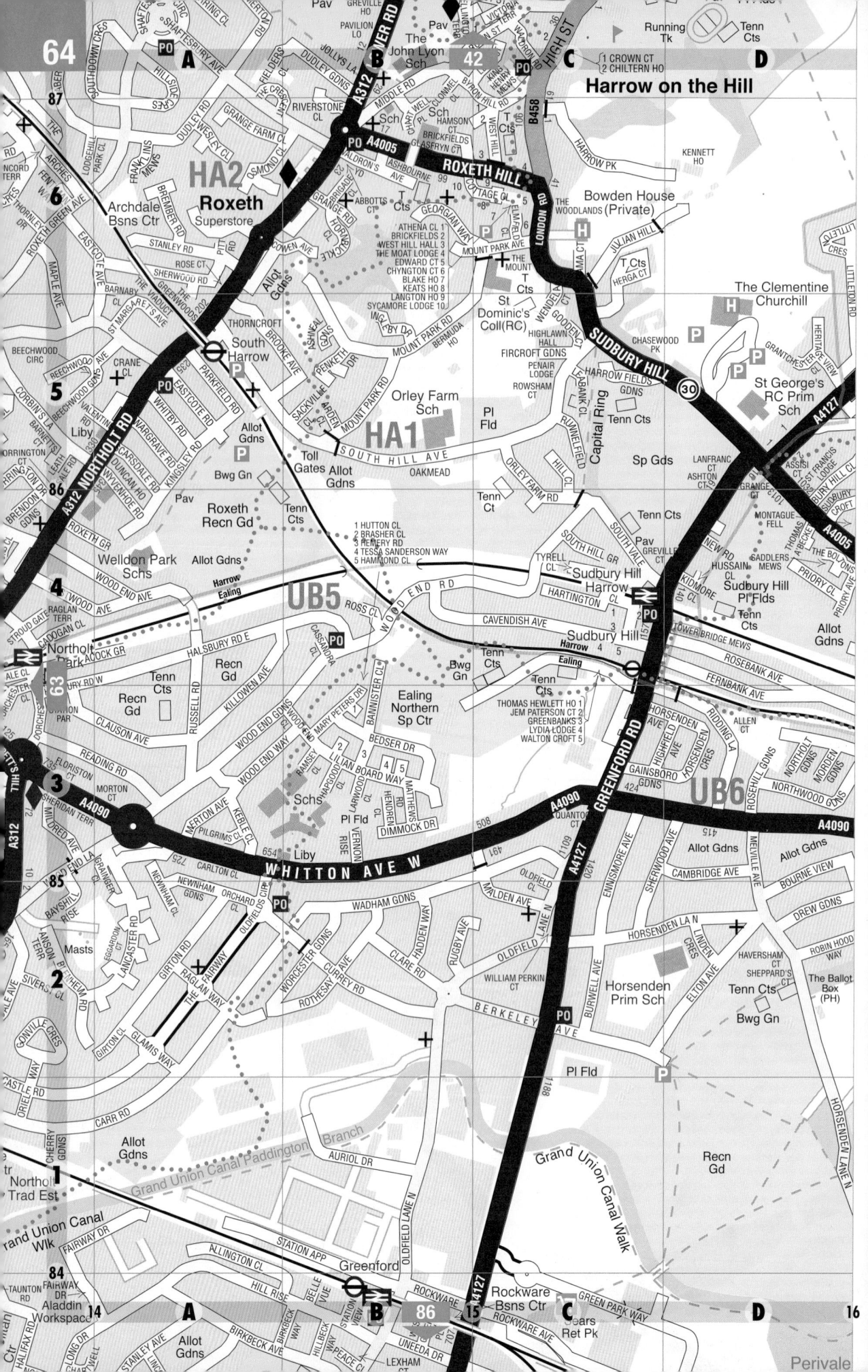
Harrow on the Hill
HA2
Roxeth
HA1
UB5
UB6
A312 NORTHOLT RD
ROXETH HILL
SUDBURY HILL
WHITTON AVE W
GREENFORD RD
A4090
A4127
A4005
B458
LONDON RD
HIGH ST
South Harrow
Sudbury Hill Harrow
Sudbury Hill
Northolt Park
Greenford
The John Lyon Sch
Bowden House (Private)
The Clementine Churchill
St George's RC Prim Sch
St Dominic's Coll(RC)
Orley Farm Sch
Archdale Bsns Ctr
Superstore
Roxeth Recn Gd
Welldon Park Schs
Ealing Northern Sp Ctr
Horsenden Prim Sch
Capital Ring
Grand Union Canal Paddington Branch
Grand Union Canal Walk
Rockware Bsns Ctr
Aladdin Workspace
Northolt Trad Est
Sears Ret Pk
Perivale
The Ballot Box (PH)
SOUTH HILL AVE
WOOD END RD
CAVENDISH AVE
HORSENDEN LANE N
OLDFIELD LANE N
BERKELEY AVE
1 CROWN CT
2 CHILTERN HO
ATHENA CL 1
BRICKFIELDS 2
WEST HILL HALL 3
THE MOAT LODGE 4
EDWARD CT 5
CHYNGTON CT 6
BLAKE HO 7
KEATS HO 8
LANGTON HO 9
SYCAMORE LODGE 10
1 HUTTON CL
2 BRASHER CL
3 HEMERY RD
4 TESSA SANDERSON WAY
5 HAMMOND CL
THOMAS HEWLETT HO 1
JEM PATERSON CT 2
GREENBANKS 3
LYDIA LODGE 4
WALTON CROFT 5
42
63
86
A
B
C
D
87
86
85
84
14
15
16
1
2
3
4
5
6

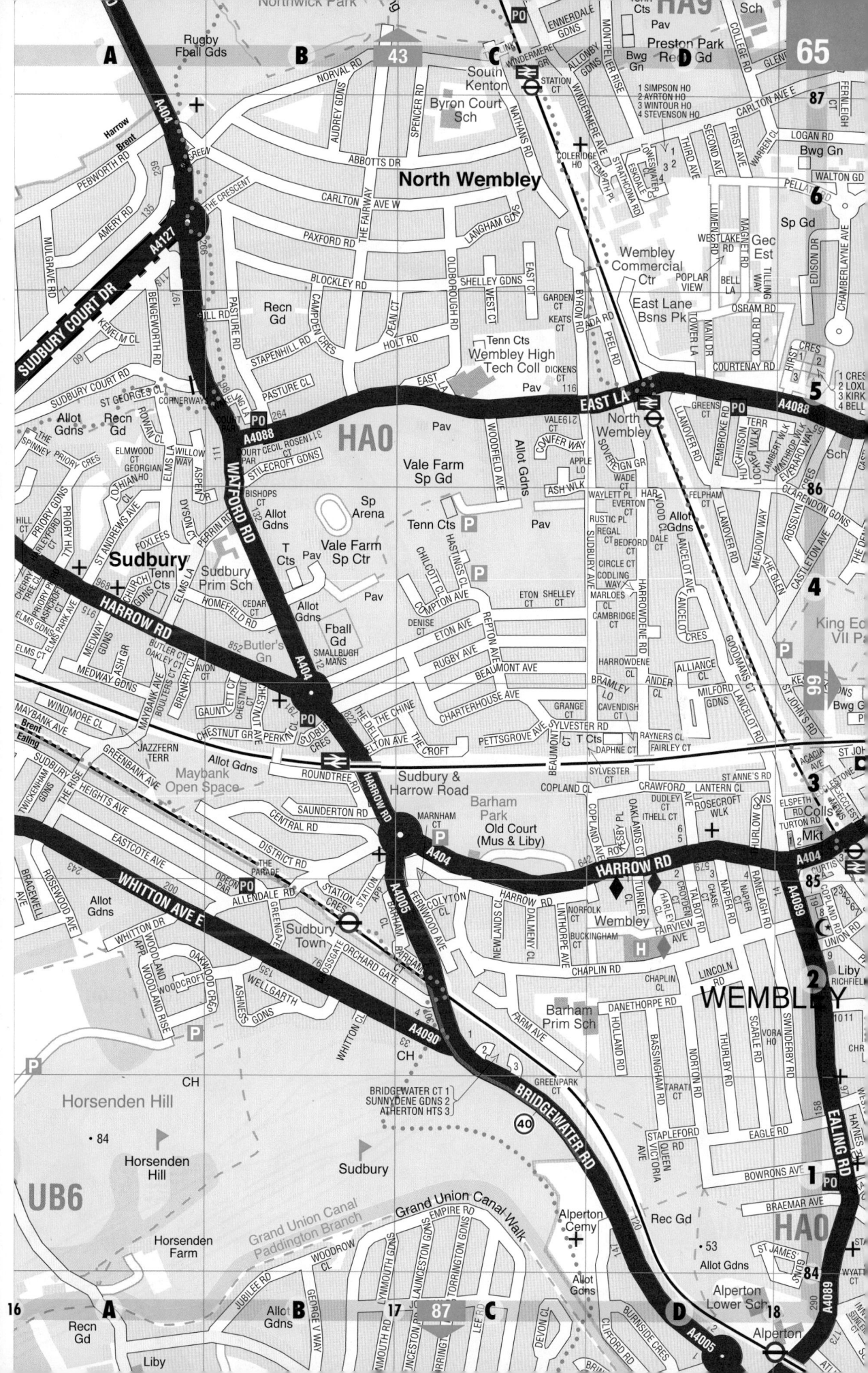
65
43
87
69
A
B
C
D
16
17
18
Northwick Park
Rugby Fball Gds
South Kenton
Byron Court Sch
Preston Park Rec Gd
HA9
North Wembley
NORVAL RD
AUDREY GDNS
SPENCER RD
NATHANS RD
ABBOTTS DR
CARLTON AVE W
PAXFORD RD
LANGHAM GDNS
BLOCKLEY RD
SHELLEY GDNS
EAST CT
WEST CT
OLDBOROUGH RD
DEAN CT
CAMPDEN CRES
STAPENHILL RD
HOLT RD
PASTURE RD
PASTURE CL
Recn Gd
Tenn Cts
Wembley High Tech Coll
DICKENS CT
GARDEN CT
KEATS CT
BYRON RD
ADA RD
PEEL RD
EAST LA
A4088
HA0
Pav
Vale Farm Sp Gd
Sp Arena
Vale Farm Sp Ctr
Allot Gdns
Fball Gd
Butler's Gn
SMALLBUGH MANS
WOODFIELD AVE
CONIFER WAY
ASH WLK
SOVEREIGN GR
HARROWDENE RD
SUDBURY AVE
CHILCOTT CL
HASTINGS CL
COMPTON AVE
ETON AVE
RUGBY AVE
BEAUMONT AVE
CHARTERHOUSE AVE
REPTON AVE
PETTSGROVE AVE
SYLVESTER RD
THE CHINE
THE DELL
ELTON AVE
THE CROFT
Wembley Commercial Ctr
East Lane Bsns Pk
Gec Est
WESTLAKE RD
POPLAR VIEW
BELL LA
OSRAM RD
TOWER LA
MAIN DR
QUAD RD
COURTENAY RD
LUMEN RD
MAGNET RD
TILLING WAY
EDISON DR
CHAMBERLAYNE AVE
SECOND AVE
FIRST AVE
THIRD AVE
LOGAN RD
WALTON GD
PELLATT RD
CARLTON AVE E
WINDERMERE AVE
MONTPELIER RISE
ALLONBY GDNS
ENNERDALE GDNS
COLLEGE RD
1 SIMPSON HO
2 AYRTON HO
3 WINTOUR HO
4 STEVENSON HO
North Wembley
LLANOVER RD
PEMBROKE RD
HUTCHINSON TERR
CLARENDON GDNS
ROSSLYN CRES
CASTLETON AVE
MEADOW WAY
THE GLEN
LANCELOT AVE
LANCELOT CRES
GOODMANS CT
LANCELOT RD
ST JOHN'S RD
ALLIANCE CL
MILFORD GDNS
King Edward VII Pk
Sudbury
SUDBURY COURT DR
SUDBURY COURT RD
A4127
A404
WATFORD RD
HARROW RD
PEBWORTH RD
AMERY RD
MULGRAVE RD
BENGEWORTH RD
KENELM CL
THE CRESCENT
ST GEORGES CL
CORNERWAYS
ROWAN CL
ELMS LA
WILLOW WAY
ASPEN DR
DYSON CT
PERRIN RD
STILECROFT GDNS
BISHOPS CT
PRIORY CRES
PRIORY GDNS
PRIORY HILL
ST ANDREWS AVE
FOXLEES
Sudbury Prim Sch
HOMEFIELD RD
CHURCH GDNS
MEDWAY GDNS
ASH GR
MAYBANK AVE
BOULTERS CT
BRENERY CL
GAUNT CT
CHESTNUT GR
PERKIN CL
SUDBURY CRES
WINDMORE CL
GREENBANK AVE
JAZZFERN TERR
Maybank Open Space
SUDBURY HEIGHTS AVE
THE RISE
TWICKENHAM GDNS
EASTCOTE AVE
ROSEWOOD AVE
BRACEWELL AVE
WHITTON AVE E
WHITTON DR
WOODLAND APP
WOODLAND RISE
WOODCROFT
OAKWOOD CRES
ASHNESS GDNS
WELLGARTH
ROUNDTREE RD
SAUNDERTON RD
CENTRAL RD
DISTRICT RD
THE PARADE
ODEON PAR
ALLENDALE RD
GREENGATE
STATION CRES
STATION APP
Sudbury Town
ORCHARD GATE
WHITTON CL
A4090
Sudbury & Harrow Road
Barham Park
Old Court (Mus & Liby)
MARNHAM CT
A4005
BARHAM CL
FERNWOOD AVE
COLYTON CL
NEWLANDS CL
DALMENY CL
LINTHORPE AVE
COPLAND AVE
COPLAND CL
OAKLANDS CT
TURNER CL
HARLEY CL
CROYDEN CT
CHASE CT
TALBOT RD
NAPIER RD
RANELAGH RD
Wembley
FAIRVIEW AVE
CHAPLIN RD
LINCOLN RD
Barham Prim Sch
FARM AVE
DANETHORPE RD
HOLLAND RD
BASSINGHAM RD
NORTON RD
THURLBY RD
SCARLE RD
SWINDERBY RD
WEMBLEY
EALING RD
A4089
EAGLE RD
BOWRONS AVE
BRAEMAR AVE
STAPLEFORD RD
QUEEN VICTORIA AVE
Rec Gd
ST JAMES' GDNS
Alperton Lower Sch
Alperton
BRIDGEWATER RD
BRIDGEWATER CT 1
SUNNYDENE GDNS 2
ATHERTON HTS 3
GREENPARK CT
Horsenden Hill
Horsenden Farm
UB6
Grand Union Canal Paddington Branch
Grand Union Canal Walk
EMPIRE RD
SUNNYMEDE GDNS
TORRINGTON GDNS
LAUNCESTON GDNS
LYNMOUTH GDNS
WOODROW CL
JUBILEE RD
GEORGE V WAY
Alperton Cemy
DEVON CL
CLIFFORD RD
BURNSIDE CRES
Recn Gd
Liby
Harrow
Brent
Ealing

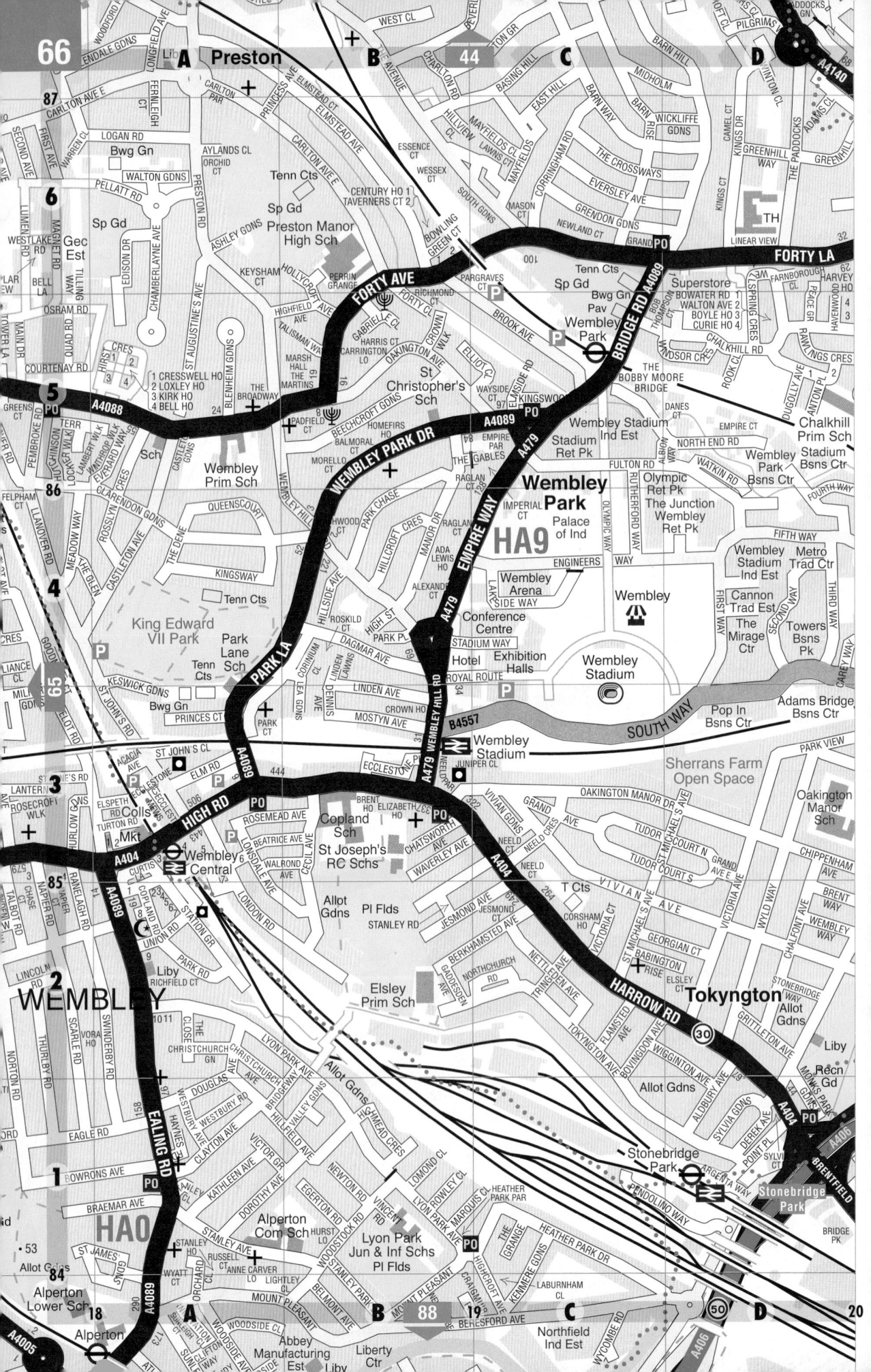
A
B
C
D
44
88
Preston
Wembley Park
Wembley
WEMBLEY
Tokyngton
HA9
HA0
FORTY AVE
FORTY LA
A4088
A4089
A479
A404
A4140
B4557
A406
A4005
BRIDGE RD
EMPIRE WAY
WEMBLEY PARK DR
PARK LA
HIGH RD
EALING RD
HARROW RD
WEMBLEY HILL RD
SOUTH WAY
PRESTON RD
CARLTON AVE E
LOGAN RD
PELLATT RD
EDISON DR
CHAMBERLAYNE AVE
ST AUGUSTINE'S AVE
BLENHEIM GDNS
ASHLEY GDNS
KEYSHAM CT
HOLLYCROFT AVE
HIGHFIELD AVE
TALISMAN WAY
MARSH HALL
THE MARTINS
THE BROADWAY
1 CRESSWELL HO
2 LOXLEY HO
3 KIRK HO
4 BELL HO
OSRAM RD
COURTENAY RD
QUAD RD
MAIN DR
TILLING WAY
MAGNET RD
LUMEN RD
WESTLAKE RD
BELL LA
Gec Est
Sp Gd
Tenn Cts
Preston Manor High Sch
Bwg Gn
WALTON GDNS
AYLANDS CL
ORCHID CT
ELMSTEAD AVE
ELMSTEAD CT
PRINCESS AVE
THE AVENUE
WEST CL
CHARLTON RD
BASING HILL
EAST HILL
HILLVIEW CL
MAYFIELDS CL
LAWNS CT
MAYFIELDS
CORRINGHAM RD
BARN WAY
BARN HILL
MIDHOLM
BARN RISE
WICKLIFFE GDNS
THE CROSSWAYS
EVERSLEY AVE
GRENDON GDNS
NEWLAND CT
MASON CT
SOUTH GDNS
ESSENCE CT
WESSEX CT
CENTURY HO 1
TAVERNERS CT 2
BOWLING GREEN CT
PERRIN GRANGE
RICHMOND CT
PARGRAVES CT
BROOK AVE
FORTY CL
GABRIELLE CL
HARRIS CT
CARRINGTON LO
OAKINGTON AVE
CROWN WLK
ELLIOT CL
St Christopher's Sch
BEECHCROFT GDNS
PADFIELD CT
HOMEFIRS HO
BALMORAL CT
MORELLO CT
WAYSIDE CT
ELMSIDE RD
KINGSWOOD
EMPIRE PAR
THE GABLES
RAGLAN CT
PARK CHASE
HILLCROFT CRES
MANOR DR
ADA LEWIS HO
ALEXANDRA CT
IMPERIAL CT
Palace of Ind
ENGINEERS WAY
Wembley Arena
LAKESIDE WAY
Conference Centre
STADIUM WAY
Hotel
Exhibition Halls
ROYAL ROUTE
Wembley Stadium
Wembley Stadium Ind Est
Stadium Ret Pk
FULTON RD
RUTHERFORD WAY
OLYMPIC WAY
Olympic Ret Pk
The Junction Wembley Ret Pk
NORTH END RD
ALBION WAY
WATKIN RD
EMPIRE CT
DANES CT
THE BOBBY MOORE BRIDGE
Tenn Cts
Sp Gd
Bwg Gn
Pav
Superstore
BOWATER RD 1
WALTON AVE 2
BOYLE HO 3
CURIE HO 4
BOB THOMPSON CT
WINDSOR CRES
CHALKHILL RD
ROOK CL
RAWLINGS CRES
DUGOLLY AVE
ANTON PL
Chalkhill Prim Sch
Wembley Park Bsns Ctr
Stadium Bsns Ctr
FOURTH WAY
FIFTH WAY
Wembley Stadium Ind Est
Metro Trad Ctr
Cannon Trad Est
The Mirage Ctr
Towers Bsns Pk
FIRST WAY
SECOND WAY
THIRD WAY
CAREY WAY
Adams Bridge Bsns Ctr
Pop In Bsns Ctr
LINEAR VIEW
KINGS DR
KINGS CT
CAMEL CT
GREENHILL WAY
THE PADDOCKS
ADAMS CL
GREENHILL
PILGRIMS WAY
PADDOCKS GN
WINTON CL
FARNBOROUGH CL
HARVEY HO
PEACE GR
HAVENWOOD
WELLSPRING CRES
TH
GRAND PO
Wembley Prim Sch
QUEENSCOURT
CLARENDON GDNS
ROSSLYN CRES
CASTLETON AVE
THE DENE
KINGSWAY
THE GLEN
MEADOW WAY
LLANOVER RD
FELPHAM CT
King Edward VII Park
Park Lane Sch
KESWICK GDNS
ST JOHN'S RD
PRINCES CT
ST JOHN'S CL
ACACIA AVE
ELM RD
ECCLESTONE CT
ECCLESTONE PL
CORINIUM CL
LEA GDNS
DENNIS AVE
LINDEN LAWNS
LINDEN AVE
DAGMAR AVE
CROWN HO
MOSTYN AVE
PARK CT
HILLSIDE AVE
ROSKILD CT
HIGH ST
PARK PL
JUNIPER CL
NEELD PAR
Sherrans Farm Open Space
PARK VIEW
OAKINGTON MANOR DR
Oakington Manor Sch
GRAND AVE
TUDOR COURT N
TUDOR COURT S
GRAND AVE E
ST MICHAEL'S AVE
VIVIAN AVE
VIVIAN GDNS
NEELD CRES
NEELD CT
CHIPPENHAM AVE
BRENT WAY
WEMBLEY WAY
WYLD WAY
CHALFONT AVE
VICTORIA AVE
VICTORIA CT
CORSHAM HO
T Cts
GEORGIAN CT
BABINGTON RISE
ELSLEY CT
STONEBRIDGE WAY
Allot Gdns
GRITTLETON AVE
Liby
Recn Gd
MONKS PARK GDNS
Copland Sch
BRENT HO
ELIZABETH HO
St Joseph's RC Schs
CHATSWORTH AVE
WAVERLEY AVE
ROSEMEAD AVE
BEATRICE AVE
WALROND AVE
CECIL AVE
LONSDALE AVE
LONDON RD
Allot Gdns
Pl Flds
STANLEY RD
JESMOND AVE
JESMOND CT
BERKHAMSTED AVE
NORTHCHURCH RD
GADDESDEN AVE
NETTLEDEN AVE
TRING AVE
Elsley Prim Sch
Wembley Central
Colls
Mkt
LANTERN CL
ROSECROFT WLK
ELSPETH RD
TURTON RD
CURTIS LA
COPLAND RD
UNION RD
STATION GR
PARK RD
Liby
RICHFIELD CT
CHASE CT
NAPIER RD
RANELAGH RD
TALBOT RD
LINCOLN RD
HURLOW GDNS
GREENS CT
PEMBROKE RD
HUTCHINSON TERR
LOCKER WLK
LAMBERT WLK
WINTHROP WLK
EVERARD WAY
CASTLETON GDNS
THE CLOSE
CHRISTCHURCH GN
CHRISTCHURCH AVE
LYON PARK AVE
BRIDGEWAY
VALLEY GDNS
HILLFIELD AVE
HIGHMEAD CRES
Allot Gdns
DOUGLAS AVE
WESTBURY AVE
WESTBURY RD
HAYNES CL
CLAYTON AVE
VICTOR GR
DOROTHY AVE
KATHLEEN AVE
NEWTON RD
EGERTON RD
VINCENT RD
LOMOND CL
LYON PARK AVE
ROWLEY CL
MARQUIS CL
HEATHER PARK PAR
HEATHER PARK DR
THE GRANGE
KENMERE GDNS
LABURNHAM CL
HIGHCROFT AVE
CRAIGMUIR
MOUNT PLEASANT
BELMONT AVE
STANLEY PARK
WOODSTOCK RD
Alperton Com Sch
HURST LO
Lyon Park Jun & Inf Schs
Pl Flds
STANLEY AVE
STANLEY HO
RUSSELL CT
ANNE CARVER LO
LIGHTLEY CL
WYATT CT
ORCHARD CL
WOODSIDE CL
WOODSIDE AVE
Abbey Manufacturing Est
Liby
Liberty Ctr
Northfield Ind Est
WYCOMBE RD
BERESFORD AVE
NORTON RD
THURLBY RD
SCARLE RD
SWINDERBY RD
VORA HO
EAGLE RD
BOWRONS AVE
BRAEMAR AVE
ST JAMES' GDNS
Allot Gdns
Alperton Lower Sch
Alperton
Stonebridge Park
ARGENTA WAY
PENDOLINO WAY
ALDBURY AVE
SYLVIA GDNS
DEREK AVE
POINT PL
WIGGINTON AVE
BOVINGDON AVE
FLAMSTED AVE
TOKYNGTON AVE
BRENTFIELD
BRIDGE PK
87
86
85
84
18
19
20
6
5
4
3
2
1
65

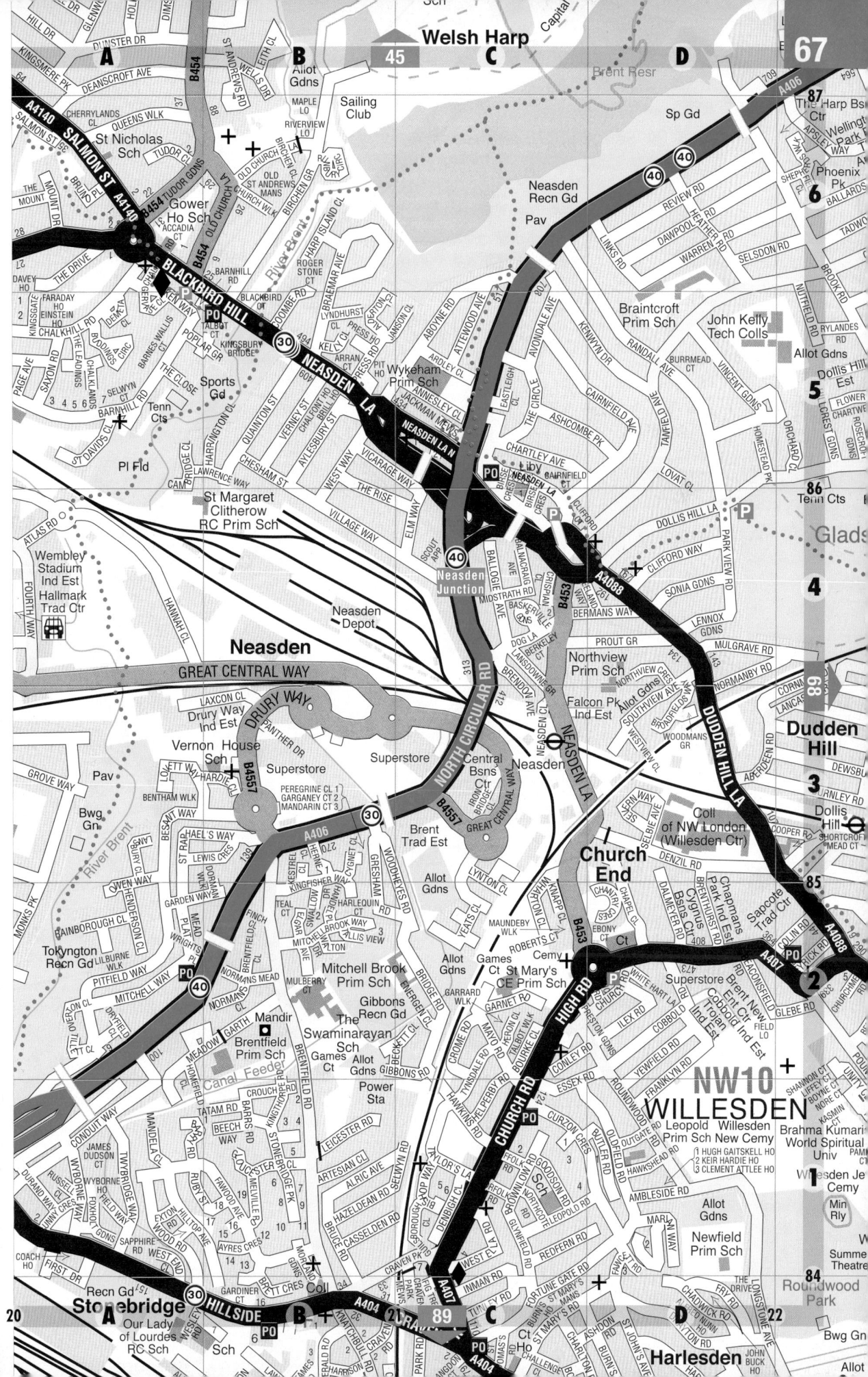

67
Welsh Harp
45
A
B
C
D
Brent Resr
Allot Gdns
Sailing Club
Sp Gd
Neasden Recn Gd
Pav
St Nicholas Sch
Gower Ho Sch
SALMON ST
A4140
B454
BLACKBIRD HILL
NEASDEN LA
NEASDEN LA N
Wykeham Prim Sch
Braintcroft Prim Sch
John Kelly Tech Colls
Allot Gdns
Dollis Hill Est
Sports Gd
Tenn Cts
Pl Fld
St Margaret Clitherow RC Prim Sch
Wembley Stadium Ind Est
Hallmark Trad Ctr
Neasden Depot
Neasden
Neasden Junction
GREAT CENTRAL WAY
Drury Way Ind Est
Vernon House Sch
Superstore
Central Bsns Ctr
Northview Prim Sch
Falcon Pk Ind Est
DUDDEN HILL LA
Dudden Hill
Dollis Hill
NORTH CIRCULAR RD
A406
A4088
B453
B4557
Brent Trad Est
Coll of NW London (Willesden Ctr)
Church End
Tokyngton Recn Gd
Mitchell Brook Prim Sch
Gibbons Recn Gd
Mandir
The Swaminarayan Sch
Brentfield Prim Sch
Canal Feeder
Power Sta
Games Ct
St Mary's CE Prim Sch
Cemy
Superstore
Chapmans Park Ind Est
Cygnus Bsns Ctr
Sapcote Trad Ctr
Brent New Ent Ctr
Cobbold Ind Est
Trojan Ind Est
HIGH RD
CHURCH RD
A407
NW10
WILLESDEN
Leopold Prim Sch
Willesden New Cemy
Brahma Kumaris World Spiritual Univ
Willesden Jewish Cemy
Allot Gdns
Newfield Prim Sch
Roundwood Park
Stonebridge
HILLSIDE
A404
Our Lady of Lourdes RC Sch
Harlesden
89
20
21
22
84
85
86
87
68

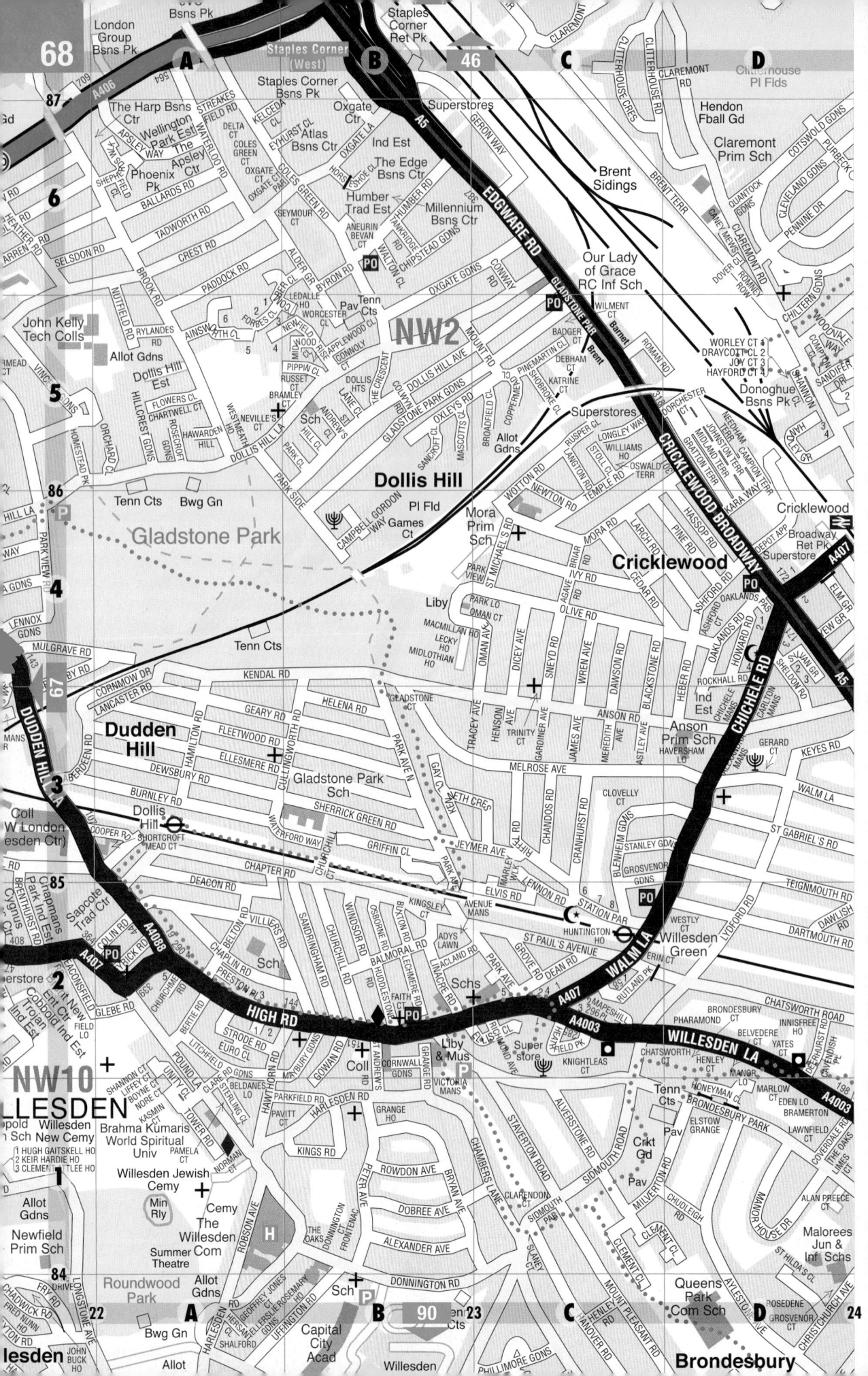

A
B
C
D
46
Staples Corner (West)
Staples Corner Bsns Pk
London Group Bsns Pk
Staples Corner Ret Pk
The Harp Bsns Ctr
Wellington Park Est
Atlas Bsns Ctr
Oxgate Ctr
Ind Est
The Edge Bsns Ctr
Humber Trad Est
Millennium Bsns Ctr
Superstores
Brent Sidings
Hendon Fball Gd
Claremont Prim Sch
Clitterhouse Pl Flds
Our Lady of Grace RC Inf Sch
NW2
EDGWARE RD
John Kelly Tech Colls
Allot Gdns
Dollis Hill Est
Donoghue Bsns Pk
Dollis Hill
Pl Fld
Games Ct
Tenn Cts
Bwg Gn
Gladstone Park
Mora Prim Sch
Cricklewood
CRICKLEWOOD BROADWAY
Cricklewood
Broadway Ret Pk
Superstore
Liby
Dudden Hill
DUDDEN HILL LA
Gladstone Park Sch
Anson Prim Sch
CHICHELE RD
Dollis Hill
Coll of NW London (Willesden Ctr)
Sapcote Trad Ctr
Chapmans Park Ind Est
HIGH RD
Willesden Green
WALM LA
WILLESDEN LA
Coll
Liby & Mus
Super store
NW10
WILLESDEN
Willesden New Cemy
Brahma Kumaris World Spiritual Univ
Willesden Jewish Cemy
The Willesden Com
Summer Theatre
Newfield Prim Sch
Roundwood Park
Capital City Acad
Queens Park Com Sch
Malorees Jun & Inf Schs
Brondesbury
90
6
5
4
3
2
1
87
86
85
84
22
23
24

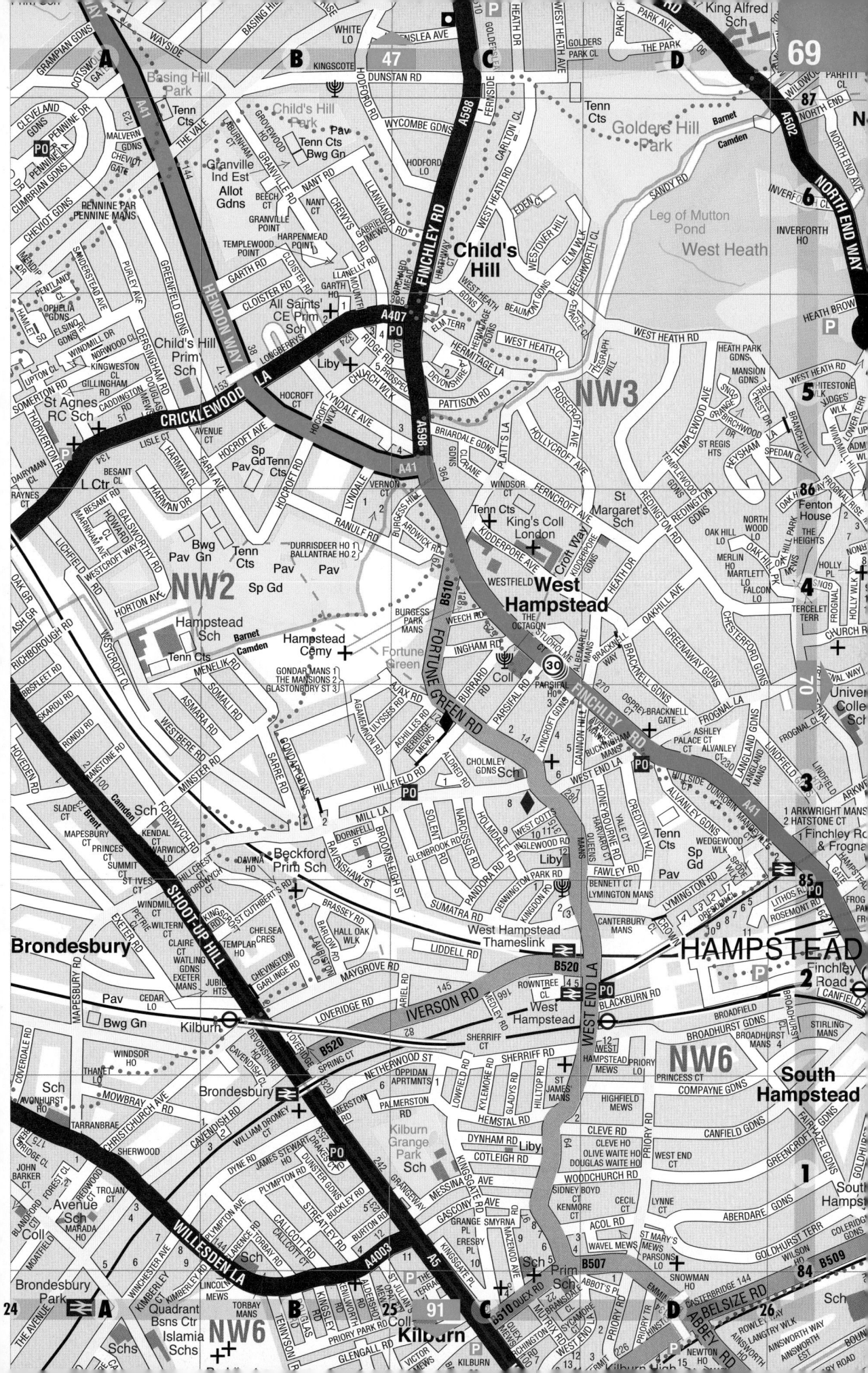
69
A
B
C
D
47
70
91
24
25
26
1
2
3
4
5
6
Basing Hill Park
Child's Hill Park
Golders Hill Park
Leg of Mutton Pond
West Heath
Child's Hill
NW3
NW2
NW6
West Hampstead
HAMPSTEAD
South Hampstead
Brondesbury
Brondesbury Park
Kilburn
Kilburn Grange Park
Fortune Green
Hampstead Cemy
Hampstead Sch
King's Coll London
St Margaret's Sch
Child's Hill Prim Sch
All Saints' CE Prim Sch
St Agnes RC Sch
Beckford Prim Sch
Granville Ind Est
Allot Gdns
King Alfred Sch
Fenton House
Quadrant Bsns Ctr
Islamia Schs
Avenue Sch
Finchley Road
West Hampstead Thameslink
Inverforth Ho
Barnet
Camden
Brent
HENDON WAY
FINCHLEY RD
CRICKLEWOOD LA
NORTH END WAY
FORTUNE GREEN RD
WEST END LA
SHOOT-UP HILL
WILLESDEN LA
IVERSON RD
ABBEY RD
BELSIZE RD
A41
A598
A407
A502
A5
A4003
B510
B520
B507
B509
WEST HEATH RD
REDINGTON RD
FROGNAL LA
MILL LA
HOCROFT AVE
PLATT'S LA
KIDDERPORE AVE
BROADHURST GDNS
ABERDARE GDNS
GOLDHURST TERR
PRIORY RD
QUEX RD
KINGSGATE RD
MAYGROVE RD
LOVERIDGE RD
MENELIK RD
MINSTER RD
FORDWYCH RD
MAPESBURY RD
RICHBOROUGH RD
DUNSTAN RD
HODFORD RD
GRANVILLE RD
NANT RD
LLANVANOR RD
PATTISON RD
FERNCROFT AVE
HOLLYCROFT AVE
ROSECROFT AVE
WEST HEATH AVE
SANDY RD
CHURCH RD
LYNDALE AVE
RANULF RD
BURRARD RD
INGHAM RD
SUMATRA RD
HILLFIELD RD
NARCISSUS RD
SOLENT RD
AGAMEMNON RD
ACHILLES RD
CHRISTCHURCH AVE
CAVENDISH RD
DYNE RD
PLYMPTON RD
CANFIELD GDNS
COMPAYNE GDNS
CLEVE RD
WOODCHURCH RD
MESSINA AVE
GREENCROFT GDNS
FAIRHAZEL GDNS

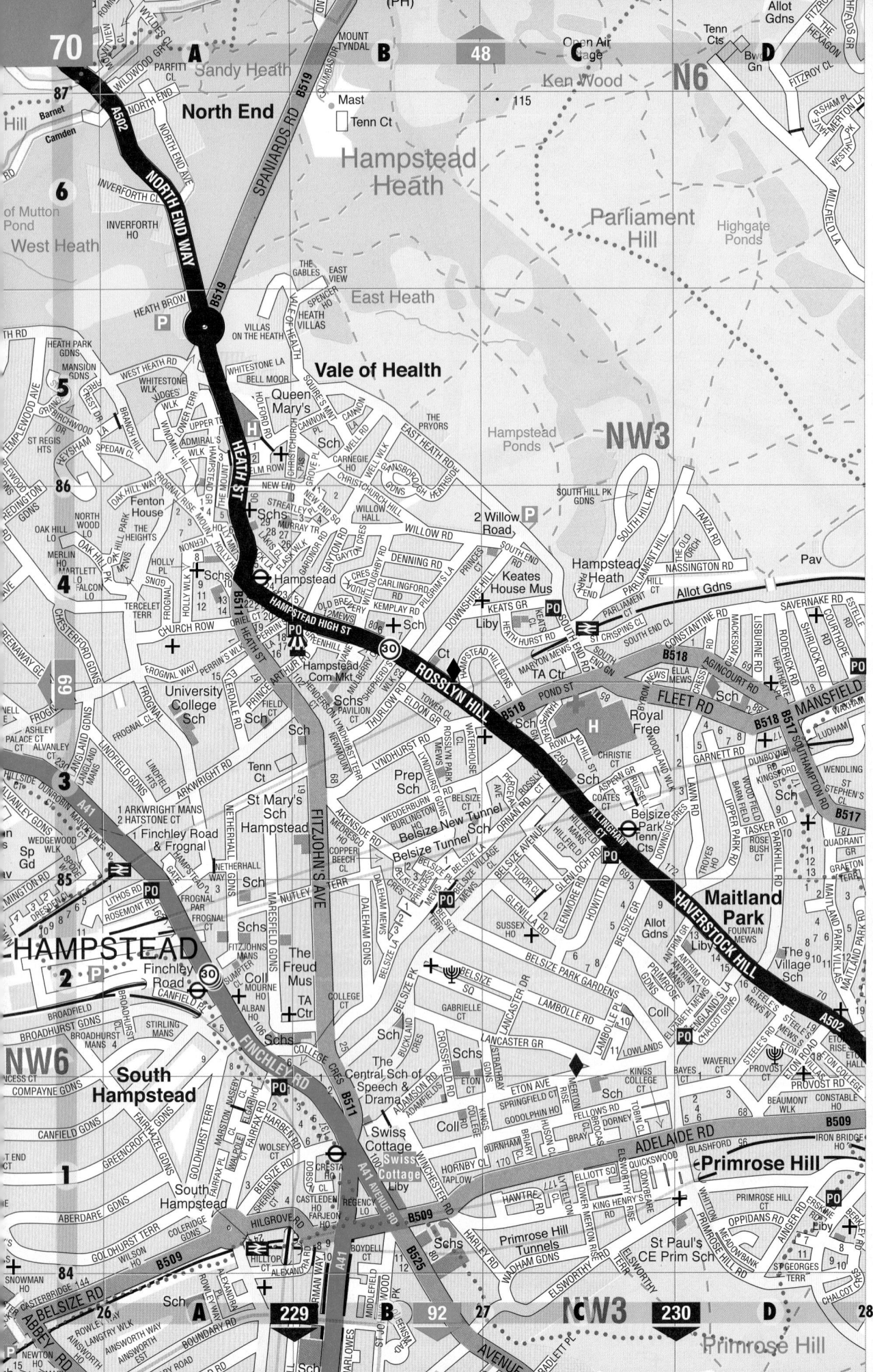

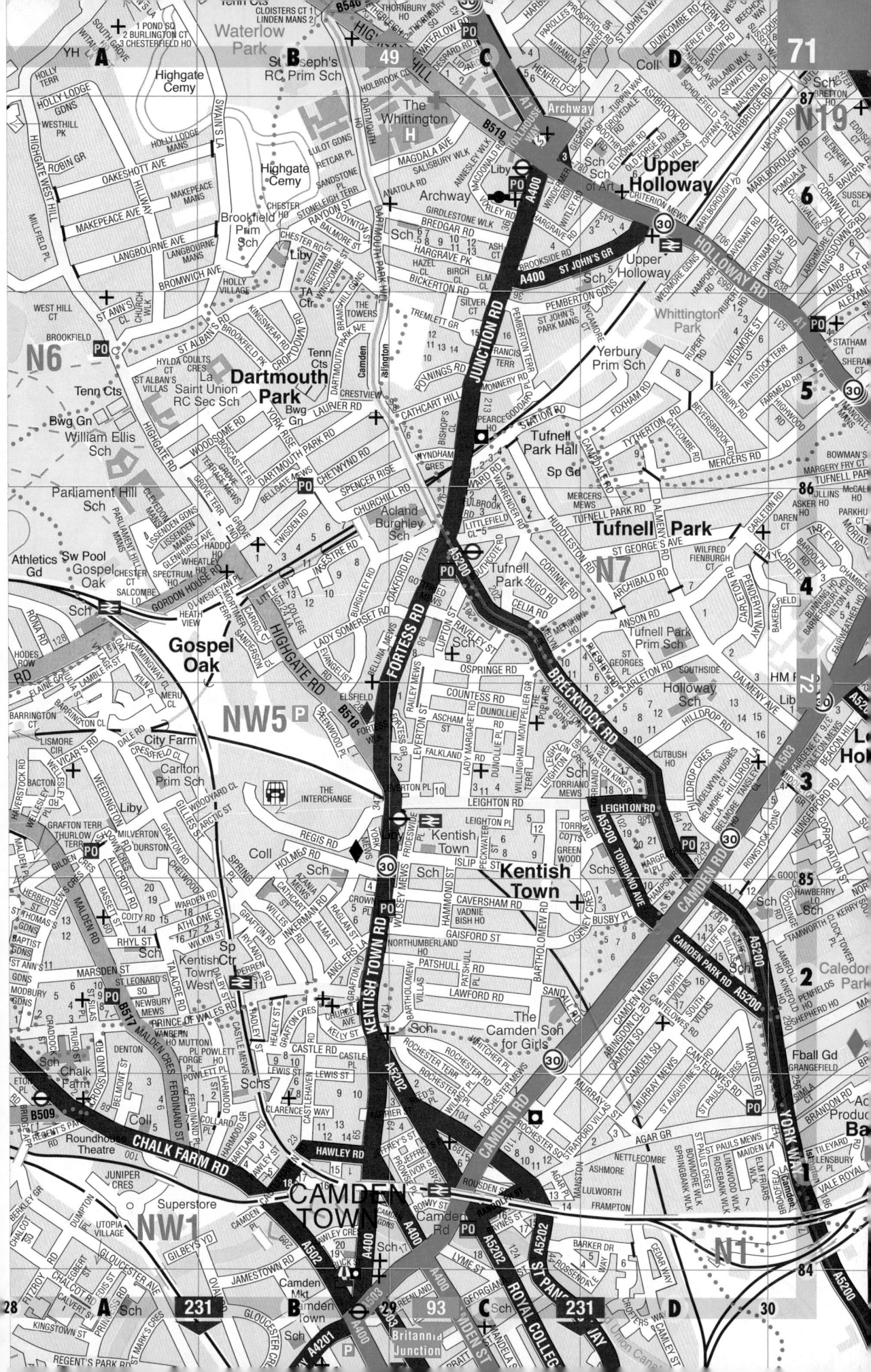

Waterlow Park
Highgate Cemy
St Joseph's RC Prim Sch
The Whittington
Archway
Upper Holloway
N19
Whittington Park
Yerbury Prim Sch
Highgate Cemy
Brookfield Prim Sch
N6
Dartmouth Park
Saint Union RC Sec Sch
William Ellis Sch
Parliament Hill Sch
Tufnell Park Hall
Tufnell Park
N7
Acland Burghley Sch
Athletics Gd
Sw Pool
Gospel Oak
Tufnell Park Prim Sch
Holloway Sch
NW5
City Farm
Carlton Prim Sch
THE INTERCHANGE
Kentish Town
Kentish Town West
The Camden Sch for Girls
Roundhouse Theatre
CHALK FARM RD
CAMDEN TOWN
NW1
Camden Mkt
Camden Rd
N1
Britannia Junction
Caledonian Park
Fball Gd
HOLLOWAY RD
JUNCTION RD
FORTESS RD
KENTISH TOWN RD
BRECKNOCK RD
CAMDEN RD
YORK WAY
HIGHGATE RD
ROYAL COLLEGE ST
ST PANCRAS WAY

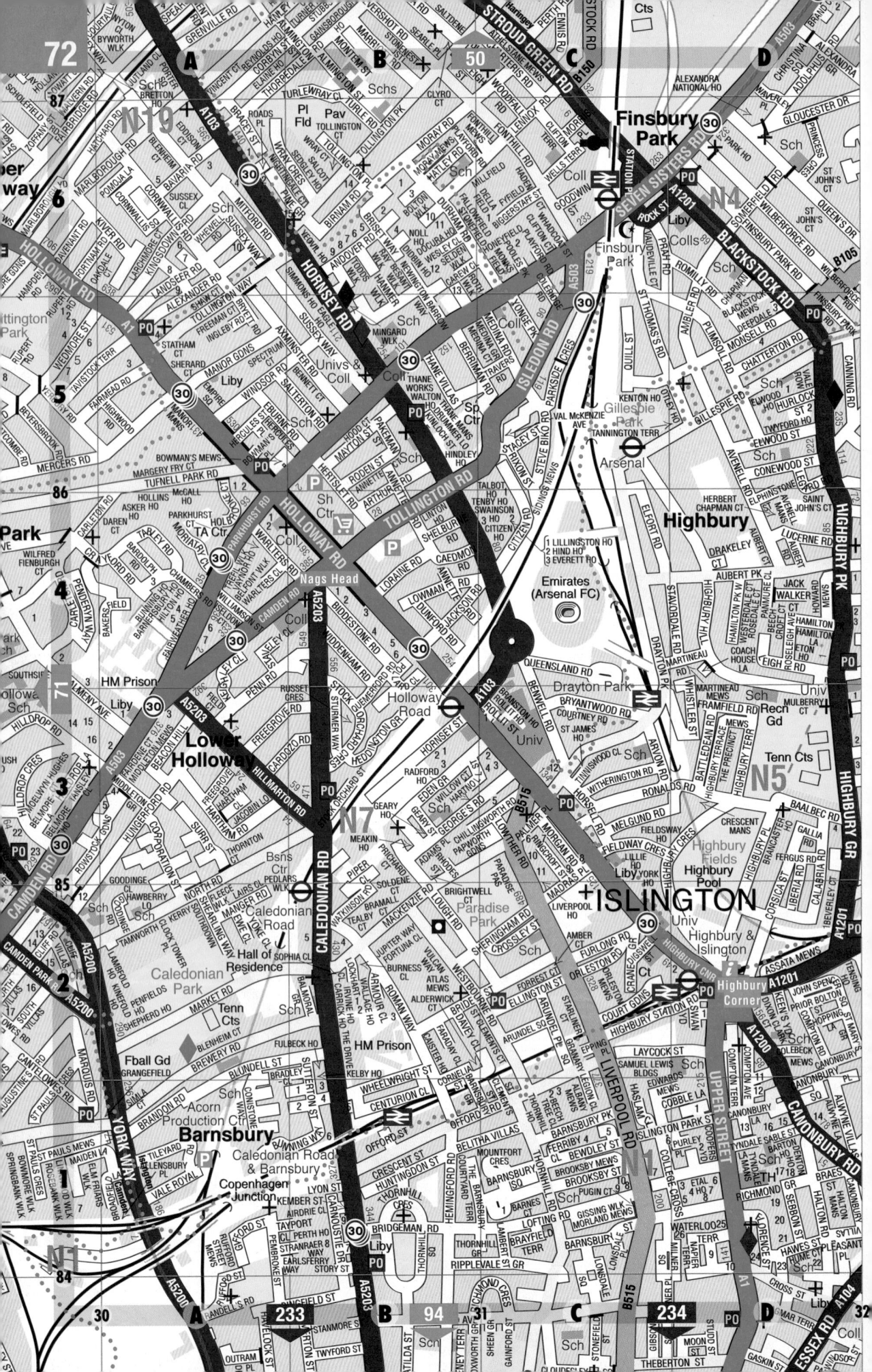
A
B
C
D
50
N19
Finsbury Park
N4
Highbury
N5
N7
ISLINGTON
Lower Holloway
Barnsbury
Nags Head
Holloway Road
Caledonian Road
Caledonian Road & Barnsbury
Copenhagen Junction
Drayton Park
Arsenal
Emirates (Arsenal FC)
Gillespie Park
Highbury Fields
Highbury Pool
Highbury & Islington
Highbury Corner
Caledonian Park
Paradise Park
HM Prison
Acorn Production Ctr
Hall of Residence
Alexandra National Ho
HOLLOWAY RD
HORNSEY RD
SEVEN SISTERS RD
BLACKSTOCK RD
STROUD GREEN RD
TOLLINGTON RD
CAMDEN RD
CALEDONIAN RD
YORK WAY
LIVERPOOL RD
UPPER STREET
HIGHBURY PK
HIGHBURY GR
CANONBURY RD
ESSEX RD
ISLEDON RD
PARKHURST RD
HILLMARTON RD
A1
A103
A503
A5203
A5200
A1201
A1200
A104
B150
B515
B105
N1
6
5
4
3
2
1
87
86
85
84
30
31
32
71
233
94
234

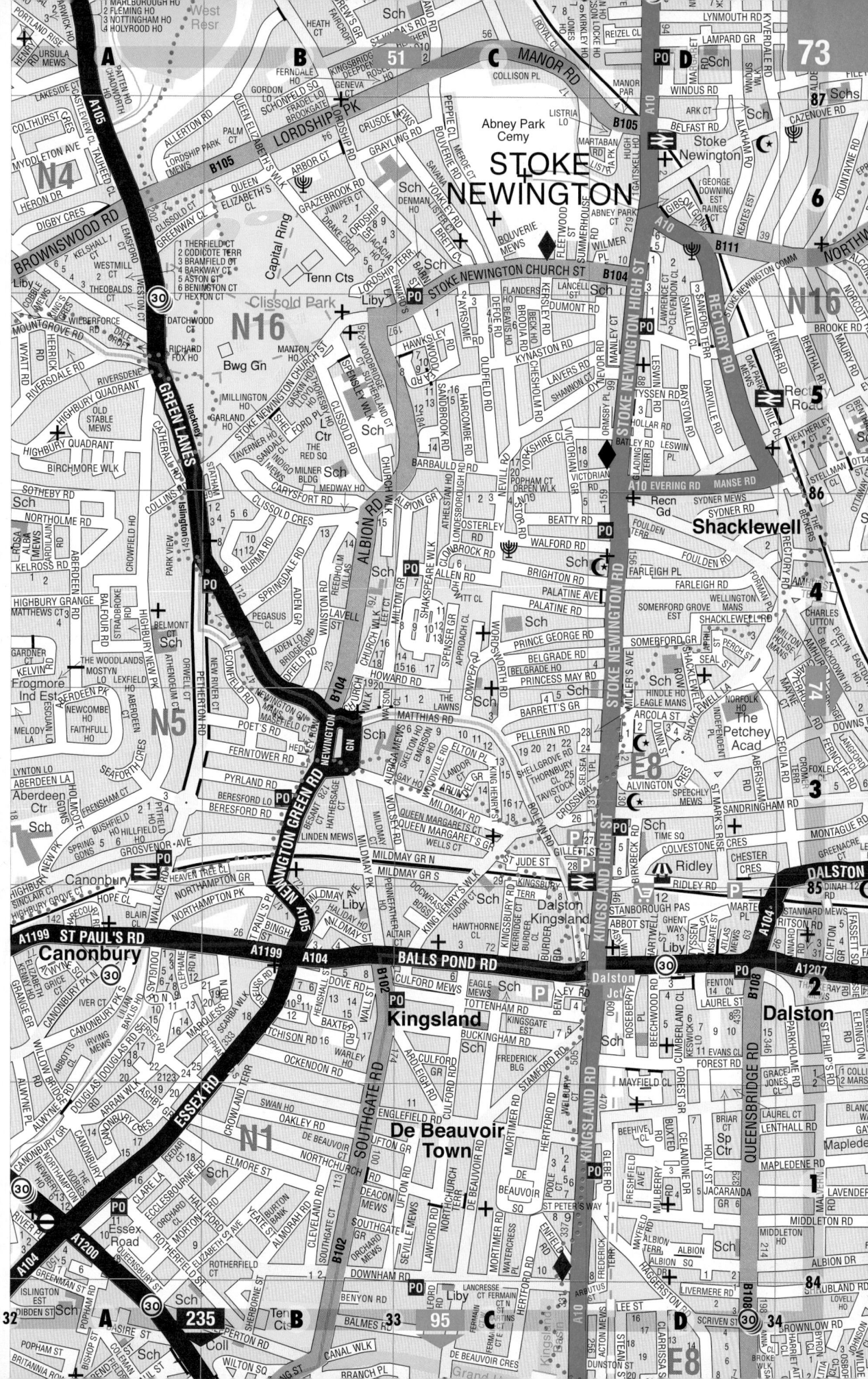

73
A
B
C
D
51
235
95
32
33
34
74
85
84
86
87
1
2
3
4
5
6
N4
N16
N5
N1
E8
STOKE NEWINGTON
Stoke Newington
Abney Park Cemy
Clissold Park
Capital Ring
Tenn Cts
Bwg Gn
West Resr
Shacklewell
Rectory Road
Canonbury
Kingsland
Dalston Kingsland
Dalston Jct
Dalston
De Beauvoir Town
Essex Road
Frogmore Ind Est
Aberdeen Ctr
The Petchey Acad
Ridley
Recn Gd
Sp Ctr
Kingsland Basin
GREEN LANES
LORDSHIP PK
MANOR RD
BROWNSWOOD RD
STOKE NEWINGTON CHURCH ST
STOKE NEWINGTON HIGH ST
KINGSLAND HIGH ST
KINGSLAND RD
RECTORY RD
NEWINGTON GREEN RD
ESSEX RD
ST PAUL'S RD
BALLS POND RD
SOUTHGATE RD
QUEENSBRIDGE RD
ALBION RD
EVERING RD
MANSE RD
CLISSOLD CRES
GROSVENOR AVE
MILDMAY GR N
MILDMAY GR S
A105
A10
A104
A1199
A1207
A1200
B105
B104
B111
B102
B108
DALSTON LA

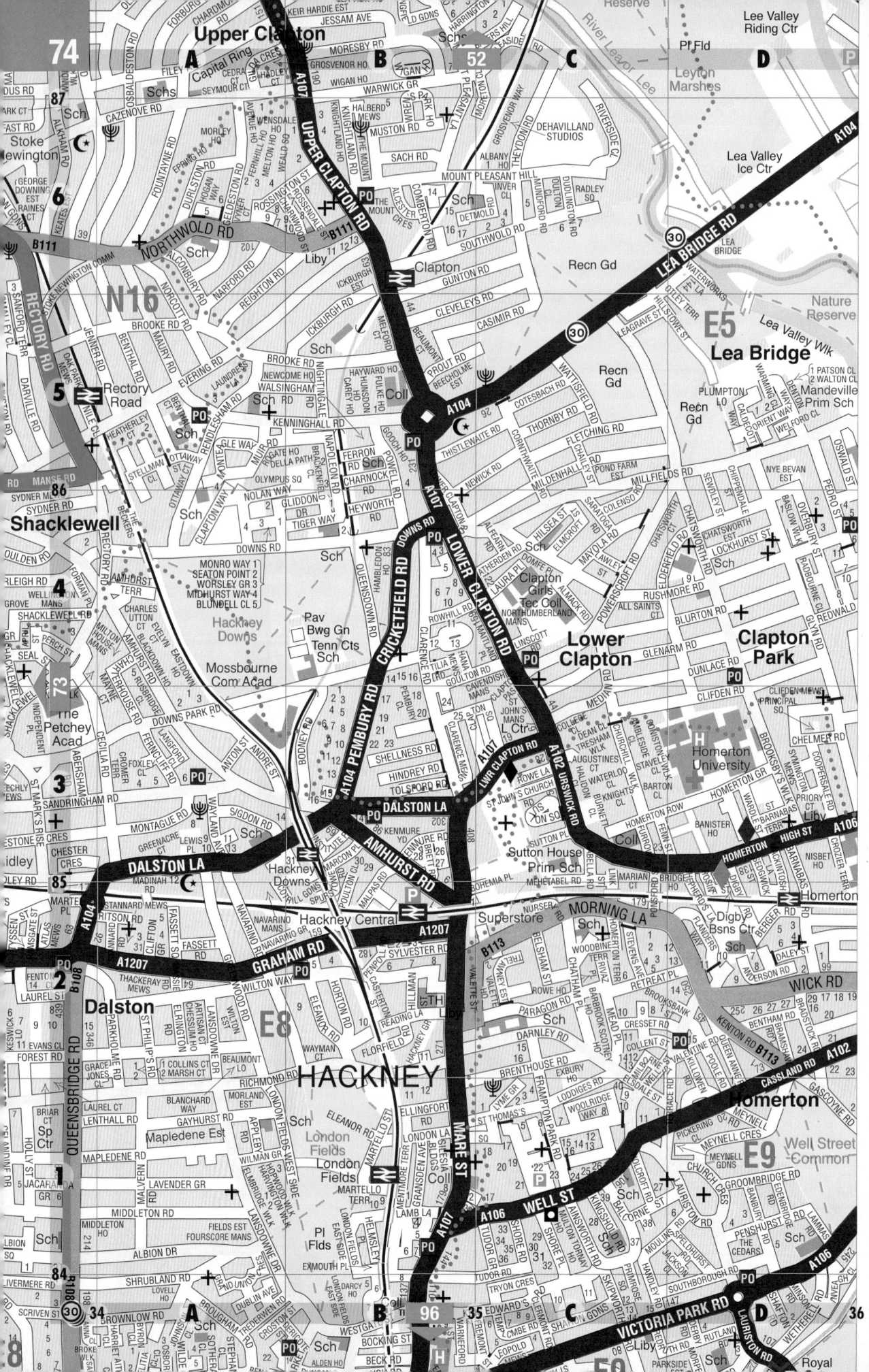

74
Upper Clapton
A
B
C
D
52
Lee Valley Riding Ctr
Leyton Marshes
River Lea or Lee
Dehavilland Studios
Lea Valley Ice Ctr
Stoke Newington
Capital Ring
Upper Clapton Rd
Northwold Rd
Clapton
Lea Bridge Rd
Recn Gd
Nature Reserve
Lea Valley Wlk
E5
Lea Bridge
N16
Rectory Rd
Rectory Road
Mandeville Prim Sch
Shacklewell
Hackney Downs
Mossbourne Com Acad
Cricketfield Rd
Lower Clapton Rd
Lower Clapton
Clapton Park
Clapton Girls Tec Coll
Homerton University
The Petchey Acad
Pembury Rd
Dalston La
Amhurst Rd
Sutton House Prim Sch
Homerton High St
Homerton
Hackney Central
Morning La
Superstore
Digby Bsns Ctr
Graham Rd
Wick Rd
Dalston
E8
HACKNEY
Mare St
Queensbridge Rd
London Fields
Mapledene Est
Well St
Homerton
Well Street Common
E9
Victoria Park Rd
Cassland Rd
96
34
35
36
1
2
3
4
5
6
73
84
85
86
87

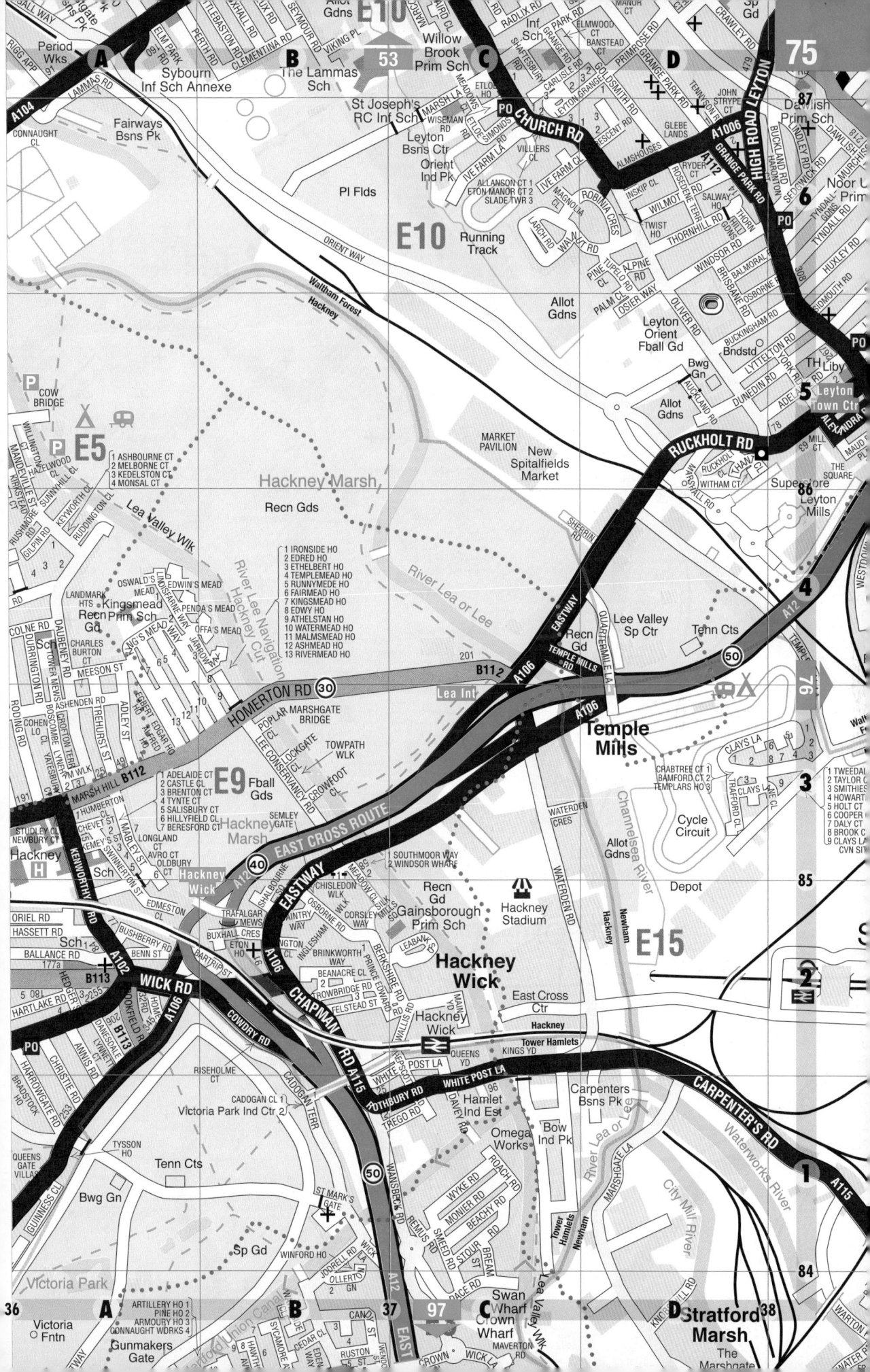

75
53
97
76
36
37
38
84
85
86
87
A
B
C
D
1
2
3
4
5
6
E10
E5
E9
E15
Period Wks
Sybourn Inf Sch Annexe
The Lammas Sch
Willow Brook Prim Sch
Inf Sch
Fairways Bsns Pk
St Joseph's RC Inf Sch
Leyton Bsns Ctr
Orient Ind Pk
Pl Flds
Running Track
Dawlish Prim Sch
Noor Ul Prim
Allot Gdns
Leyton Orient Fball Gd
Bndstd
TH
Liby
Leyton Town Ctr
Bwg Gn
MARKET PAVILION
New Spitalfields Market
Superstore
Leyton Mills
COW BRIDGE
Hackney Marsh
Recn Gds
Lea Valley Wlk
River Lee Navigation Hackney Cut
River Lea or Lee
Lee Valley Sp Ctr
Tenn Cts
Temple Mills
Kingsmead Prim Sch
Recn Gd
Lea Int
Fball Gds
Cycle Circuit
Depot
Hackney
Hackney Wick
Hackney Stadium
Recn Gd
Gainsborough Prim Sch
East Cross Ctr
Carpenters Bsns Pk
Hamlet Ind Est
Omega Works
Bow Ind Pk
Victoria Park Ind Ctr
Tenn Cts
Bwg Gn
Sp Gd
Victoria Park
Victoria Fntn
Gunmakers Gate
Swan Wharf
Crown Wharf
Stratford Marsh
The Marshgate
Channelsea River
Waterworks River
City Mill River
Hertford Union Canal
Waltham Forest
Hackney
Newham
Tower Hamlets
CHURCH RD
HIGH ROAD LEYTON
RUCKHOLT RD
EASTWAY
EAST CROSS ROUTE
HOMERTON RD
MARSH HILL
WICK RD
CHAPMAN RD
WHITE POST LA
CARPENTER'S RD
ORIENT WAY
TEMPLE MILLS LA
QUARTERMILE LA
WATERDEN RD
KENWORTHY RD
WANSBECK RD
MARSHGATE LA
A104
A106
A12
A102
A112
A1006
A115
B112
B113
1 ASHBOURNE CT
2 MELBORNE CT
3 KEDELSTON CT
4 MONSAL CT
1 IRONSIDE HO
2 EDRED HO
3 ETHELBERT HO
4 TEMPLEMEAD HO
5 RUNNYMEDE HO
6 FAIRMEAD HO
7 KINGSMEAD HO
8 EDWY HO
9 ATHELSTAN HO
10 WATERMEAD HO
11 MALMSMEAD HO
12 ASHMEAD HO
13 RIVERMEAD HO
1 ADELAIDE CT
2 CASTLE CT
3 BRENTON CT
4 TYNTE CT
5 SALISBURY CT
6 HILLYFIELD CL
7 BERESFORD CT
1 SOUTHMOOR WAY
2 WINDSOR WHARF
CRABTREE CT 1
BAMFORD CT 2
TEMPLARS HO 3
1 TWEEDAL
2 TAYLOR C
3 SMITHIES
4 HOWART
5 HOLT CT
6 COOPER
7 DALY CT
8 BROOK C
9 CLAYS LA
ALLANSON CT 1
ETON MANOR CT 2
SLADE TWR 3
ARTILLERY HO 1
PINE HO 2
ARMOURY HO 3
CONNAUGHT WORKS 4
CADOGAN CL 1

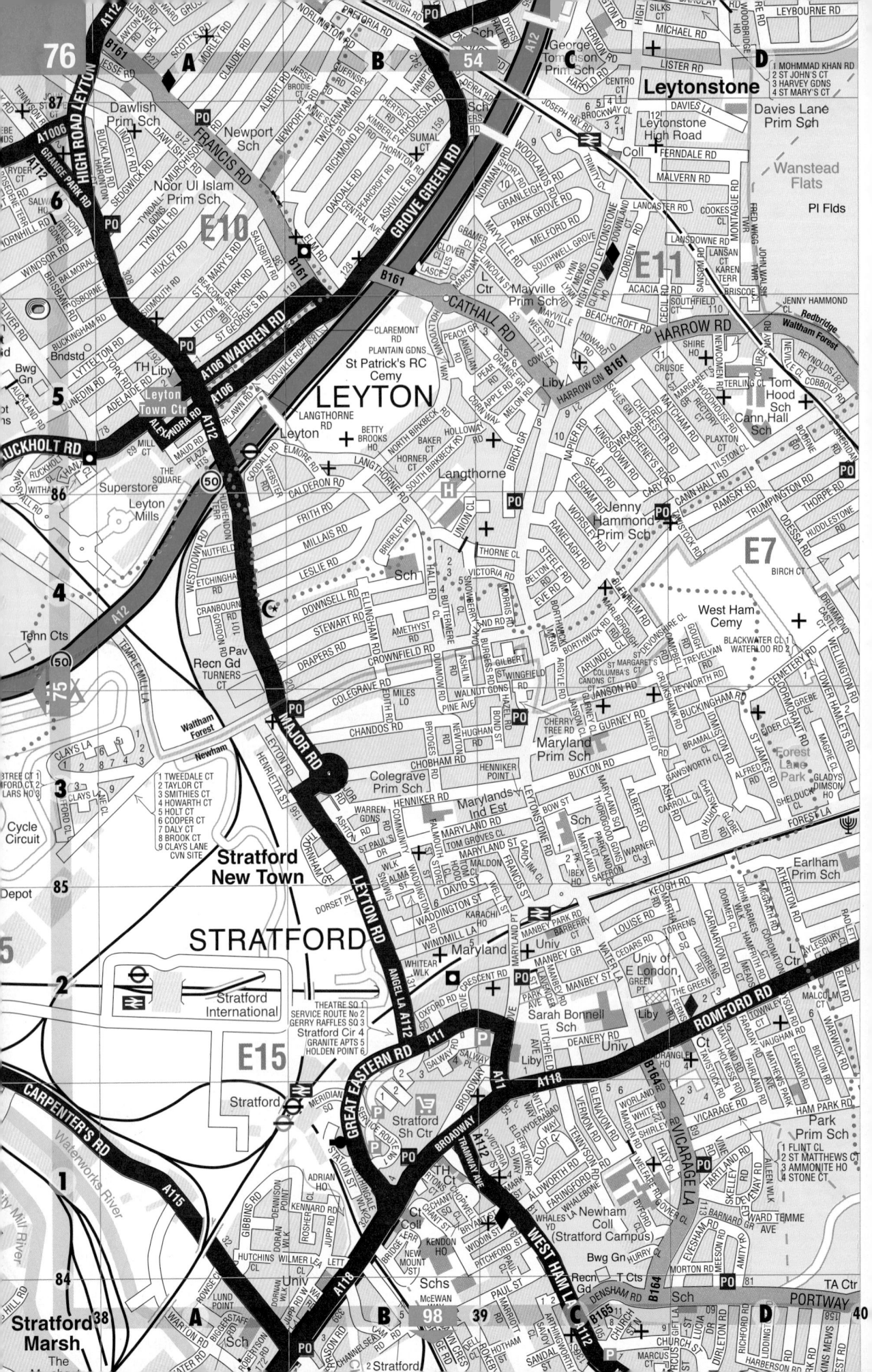
Leytonstone
Davies Lane Prim Sch
Wanstead Flats
Pl Flds
Dawlish Prim Sch
Newport Sch
Noor Ul Islam Prim Sch
E10
E11
E7
E15
LEYTON
St Patrick's RC Cemy
Mayville Prim Sch
Leyton Town Ctr
Leyton Mills
Superstore
Langthorne
Jenny Hammond Prim Sch
Tom Hood Sch
Cann Hall Sch
West Ham Cemy
Maryland Prim Sch
Colegrave Prim Sch
Marylands Ind Est
Forest Lane Park
Earlham Prim Sch
Stratford New Town
STRATFORD
Stratford International
Stratford Sh Ctr
Sarah Bonnell Sch
Newham Coll (Stratford Campus)
Park Prim Sch
Univ of E London
Cycle Circuit
Tenn Cts
Recn Gd
Stratford Marsh
Waterworks River
Waltham Forest
Newham
Redbridge
HIGH ROAD LEYTON
GROVE GREEN RD
FRANCIS RD
A106 WARREN RD
CATHALL RD
HARROW RD
LEYTON RD
MAJOR RD
ROMFORD RD
GREAT EASTERN RD
BROADWAY
WEST HAM LA
VICARAGE LA
CARPENTER'S RD
PORTWAY
ANGEL LA A112
A12
A11
A118
A115
B161
B164
54
98
75
40

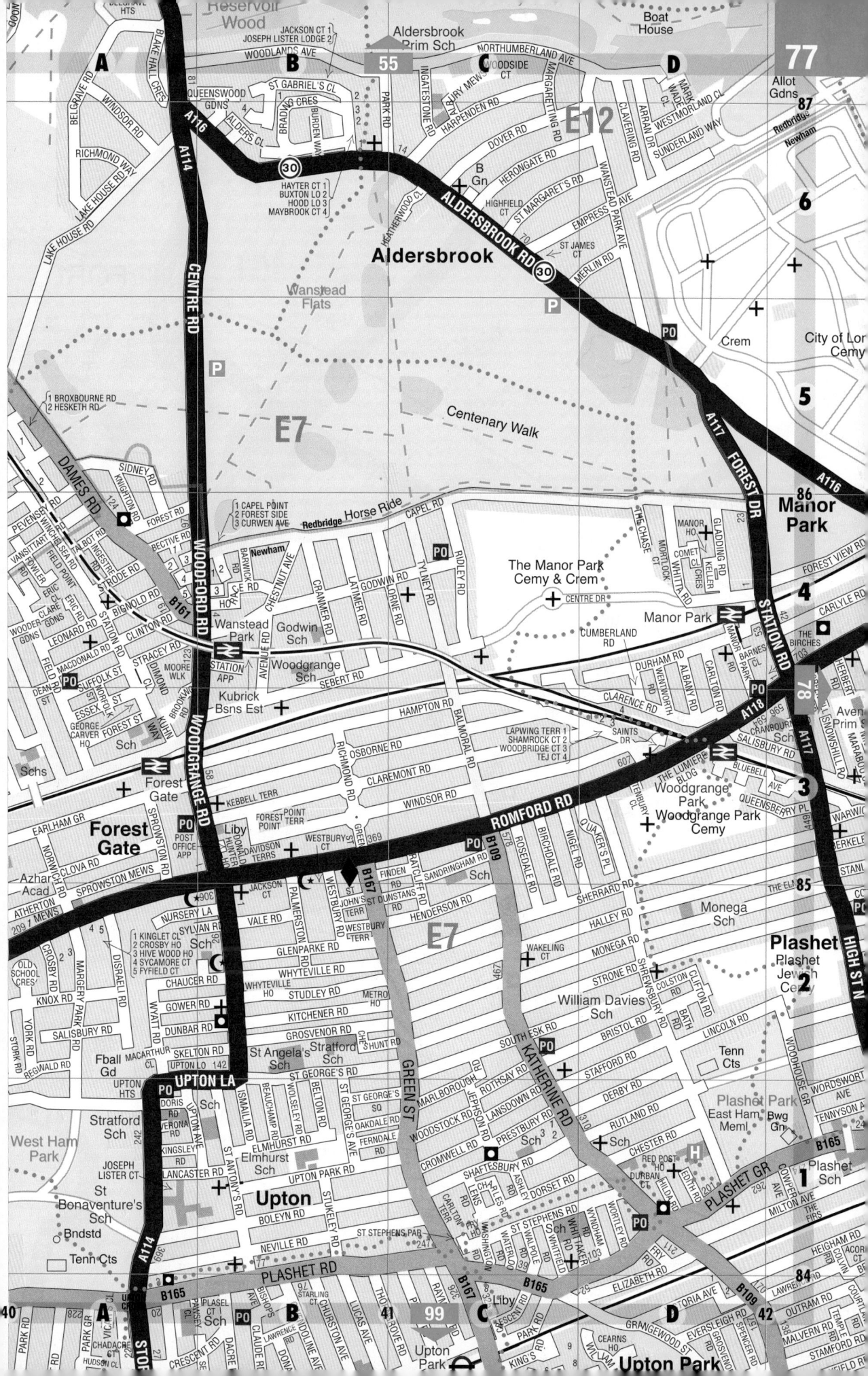

77
55
78
99
A
B
C
D
Reservoir Wood
Aldersbrook Prim Sch
Boat House
E12
Aldersbrook
Wanstead Flats
Centenary Walk
E7
Crem
City of London Cemy
Manor Park
The Manor Park Cemy & Crem
Allot Gdns
Redbridge
Newham
Redbridge Horse Ride
Forest Gate
Wanstead Park
Godwin Sch
Woodgrange Sch
Kubrick Bsns Est
Woodgrange Park
Woodgrange Park Cemy
Monega Sch
Plashet
Plashet Jewish Cemy
William Davies Sch
Tenn Cts
Plashet Park
East Ham Meml
Plashet Sch
St Angela's Sch
Stratford Sch
Elmhurst Sch
Upton
West Ham Park
St Bonaventure's Sch
Bndstd
Fball Gd
Upton Park
Azhar Acad
A114
A116
A117
A118
B161
B165
B167
B109
CENTRE RD
WOODFORD RD
WOODGRANGE RD
ALDERSBROOK RD
ROMFORD RD
FOREST DR
STATION RD
HIGH ST N
GREEN ST
KATHERINE RD
PLASHET RD
PLASHET GR
UPTON LA
DAMES RD
LAKE HOUSE RD
WOODLANDS AVE
NORTHUMBERLAND AVE
WANSTEAD PARK AVE
CAPEL RD
87
86
85
84
6
5
4
3
2
1
40
41
42

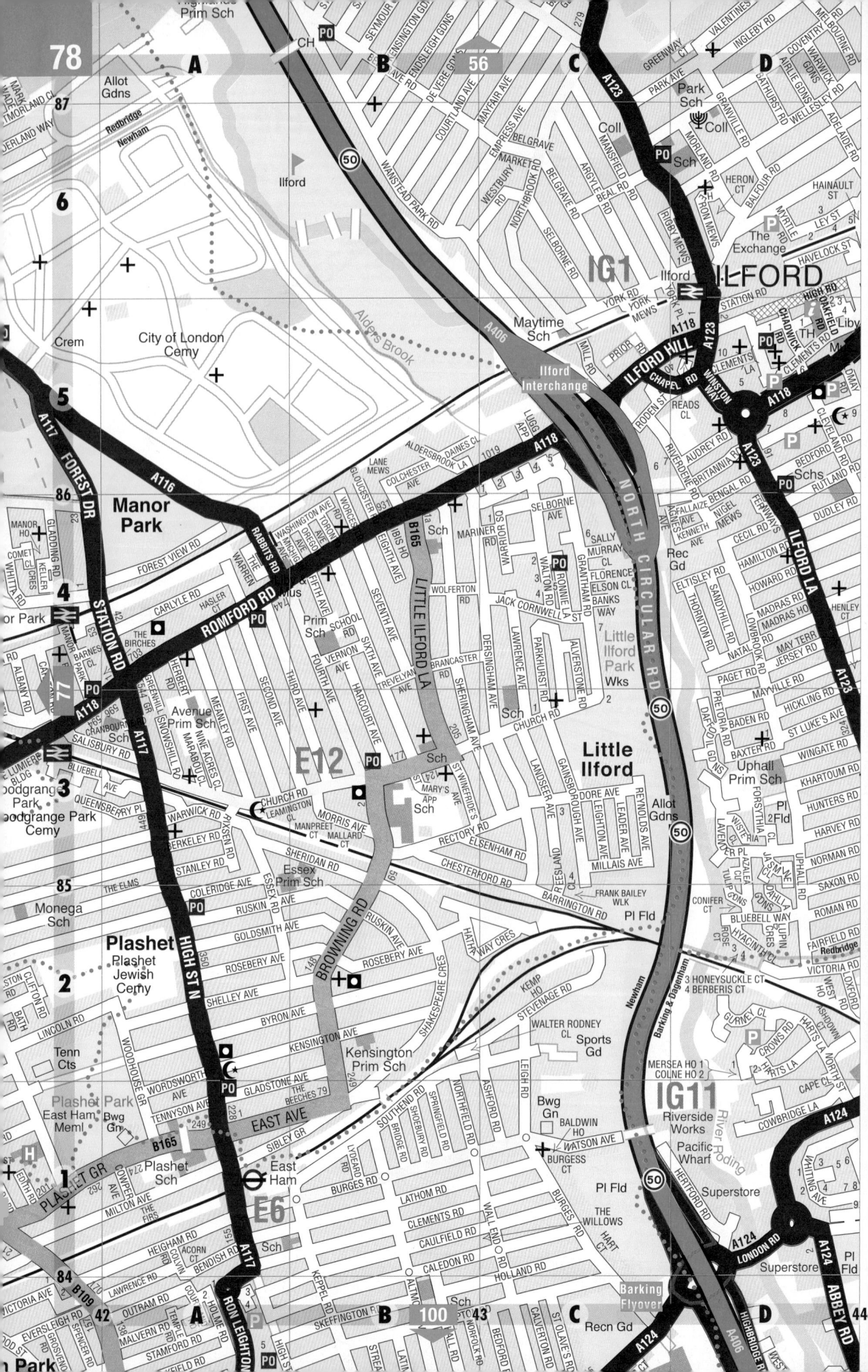
56
100
77
A
B
C
D
87
6
5
86
4
3
85
2
1
84
42
43
44
Allot Gdns
Redbridge
Newham
Ilford
City of London Cemy
Crem
Manor Park
FOREST DR
A117
A116
A118
A123
A124
A406
B165
B109
FOREST VIEW RD
RABBITS RD
ROMFORD RD
STATION RD
HIGH ST N
ILFORD HILL
ILFORD LA
NORTH CIRCULAR RD
LITTLE ILFORD LA
Ilford Interchange
Aldersbrook
IG1
ILFORD
The Exchange
Park Sch
Coll
Sch
Maytime Sch
WANSTEAD PARK RD
BELGRAVE RD
SELBORNE RD
YORK RD
CHAPEL RD
WINSTON WAY
CLEMENTS RD
HAVELOCK ST
Little Ilford Park
Wks
Rec Gd
Little Ilford
Allot Gdns
Uphall Prim Sch
Pl Fld
E12
Prim Sch
Avenue Prim Sch
Essex Prim Sch
Monega Sch
Plashet
Plashet Jewish Cemy
Tenn Cts
Plashet Park
East Ham Meml
Bwg Gn
Plashet Sch
PLASHET GR
East Ham
E6
Kensington Prim Sch
BROWNING RD
EAST AVE
BARKING RD
Sports Gd
Riverside Works
Pacific Wharf
River Roding
IG11
Superstore
Barking Flyover
Barking & Dagenham
LONDON RD
ABBEY RD
Recn Gd
RON LEIGHTON WAY
Pl Fld
THE WILLOWS
HIGHBRIDGE RD

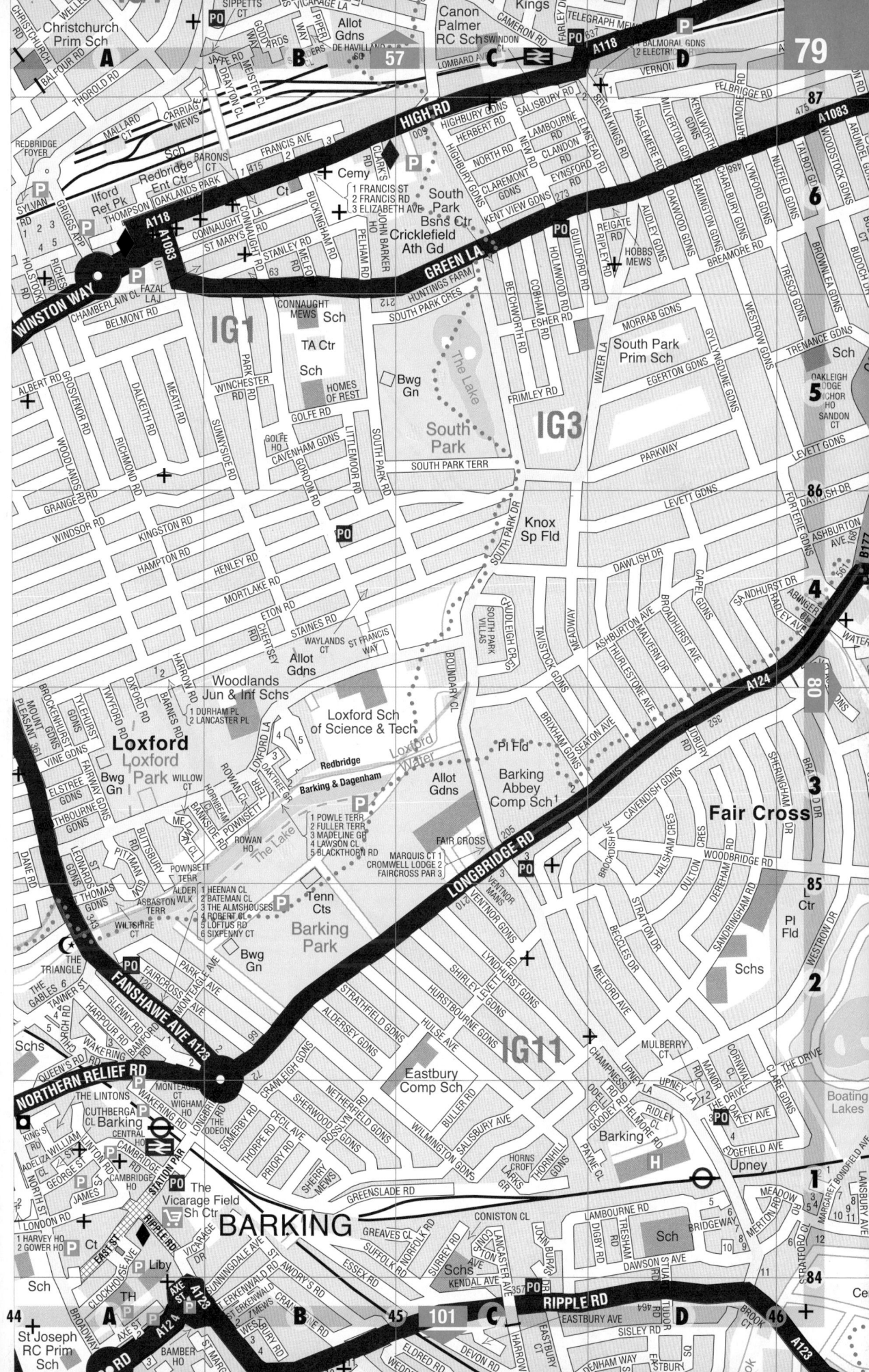
79
57
80
101
A
B
C
D
87
86
85
84
44
45
46
6
5
4
3
2
1
IG1
IG3
IG11
HIGH RD
GREEN LA
WINSTON WAY
LONGBRIDGE RD
FANSHAWE AVE A123
NORTHERN RELIEF RD
RIPPLE RD
A118
A1083
A124
A123
B177
Christchurch Prim Sch
Canon Palmer RC Sch
Kings
Allot Gdns
Redbridge Ent Ctr
Ilford Ret Pk
Cemy
South Park Bsns Ctr
Cricklefield Ath Gd
TA Ctr
Homes of Rest
Bwg Gn
The Lake
South Park
South Park Prim Sch
Knox Sp Fld
Woodlands Jun & Inf Schs
Loxford Sch of Science & Tech
Loxford
Loxford Park
Loxford Water
Redbridge
Barking & Dagenham
Pl Fld
Barking Abbey Comp Sch
Fair Cross
Tenn Cts
Barking Park
Eastbury Comp Sch
Barking
BARKING
The Vicarage Field Sh Ctr
Liby
Upney
Boating Lakes
St Joseph RC Prim Sch
Schs
L Ctr
The Triangle
The Gables
Oakleigh Lodge
Anchor Ho
Sandon Ct
Redbridge Foyer
Fazal Laj

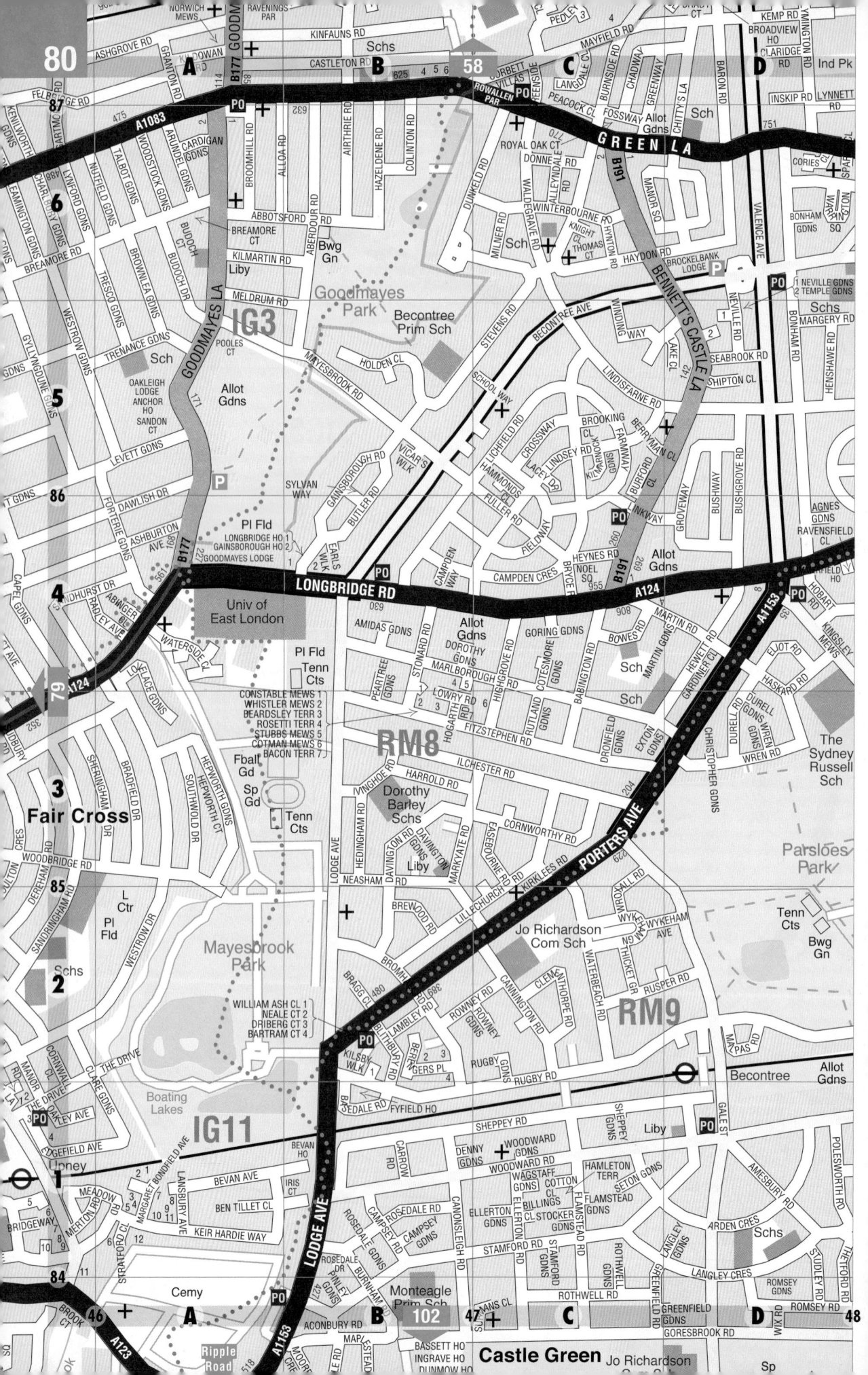

58
79
102
A
B
C
D
87
6
5
86
4
3
85
2
1
84
46
47
48
NORWICH MEWS
RAVENINGS PAR
KINFAUNS RD
Schs
ASHGROVE RD
KILDOWAN RD
CASTLETON RD
GOODMAYES LA
B177
PEDLEY
MAYFIELD RD
KEMP RD
BROADVIEW HO
CLARIDGE RD
Ind Pk
CORBETT VILLAS
ROWALLEN PAR
LANGDALE CL
BURNSIDE RD
CHADWAY
GREENWAY
CHITTY'S LA
BARON RD
LYMINGTON RD
INSKIP RD
LYNNETT RD
FELBRIGGE RD
A1083
KENILWORTH GDNS
GARTMORE RD
TALBOT GDNS
WOODSTOCK GDNS
ARUNDEL GDNS
CARDIGAN GDNS
BROOMHILL RD
ALLOA RD
AIRTHRIE RD
HAZELDENE RD
COLINTON RD
PEACOCK CL
FOSSWAY
Allot Gdns
Sch
GREEN LA
ROYAL OAK CT
DONNE PL
ALLEYNDALE RD
B191
MANOR SQ
VALENCE AVE
CORIES CL
LEAMINGTON RD
CHARLBURY GDNS
LYNFORD GDNS
NUTFIELD GDNS
ABBOTSFORD RD
ABERDOUR RD
DUNKELD RD
MILNER RD
WALDEGRAVE RD
WINTERBOURNE RD
KNIGHT CL
THOMAS CT
HYNTON RD
BONHAM GDNS
WARRINGTON SQ
BREAMORE RD
BREAMORE CT
BUDOCH CT
BUDOCH DR
KILMARTIN RD
Liby
Bwg Gn
HAYDON RD
BROCKELBANK LODGE
BENNETT'S CASTLE LA
1 NEVILLE GDNS
2 TEMPLE GDNS
TRESCO GDNS
BROWNLEA GDNS
MELDRUM RD
Goodmayes Park
Becontree Prim Sch
IG3
STEVENS RD
BECONTREE AVE
WINDING WAY
NEVILLE RD
BONHAM RD
MARGERY RD
WESTROW GDNS
GYLLYNGDUNE GDNS
TRENANCE GDNS
POOLES CT
HOLDEN CL
MAYESBROOK RD
SCHOOL WAY
LINDISFARNE RD
LAKE CL
SEABROOK RD
SHIPTON CL
HENSHAWE RD
OAKLEIGH LODGE
ANCHOR HO
SANDON CT
LEVETT GDNS
CROSSWAY
LICHFIELD RD
BROOKING CL
BERRYMAN CL
FARMWAY
LINDSEY RD
KILMARNOCK GDNS
LACEY DR
VICAR'S WLK
GAINSBOROUGH RD
SYLVAN WAY
BUTLER RD
HAMMONDS CL
FULLER RD
BURFORD CL
BUSHWAY
BUSHGROVE RD
GROVEWAY
LINKWAY
AGNES GDNS
RAVENSFIELD CL
DAWLISH DR
FORTERIE GDNS
ASHBURTON AVE
Pl Fld
LONGBRIDGE HO 1
GAINSBOROUGH HO 2
GOODMAYES LODGE
EARLS WLK
CAMPDEN WAY
FIELDWAY
HEYNES RD
NOEL SQ
BRYCE RD
CAMPDEN CRES
SOMMERFIELD HO
CAPEL GDNS
SANDHURST DR
ABINGER CL
RADLEY AVE
LONGBRIDGE RD
A124
Univ of East London
AMIDAS GDNS
Allot Gdns
GORING GDNS
BOWES RD
MARTIN RD
HOBART RD
KINGSLEY MEWS
WATERSIDE CL
Pl Fld
Tenn Cts
STONARD RD
DOROTHY GDNS
COTESMORE GDNS
HIGHGROVE RD
BABINGTON RD
MARTIN GDNS
HEWETT RD
GARDINER CL
ELIOT RD
HASKARD RD
LOCKSLEY PLACE GDNS
CONSTABLE MEWS 1
WHISTLER MEWS 2
BEARDSLEY TERR 3
ROSETTI TERR 4
STUBBS MEWS 5
COTMAN MEWS 6
BACON TERR 7
PEARTREE GDNS
MARLBOROUGH RD
LOWRY RD
HOGARTH RD
RUTLAND GDNS
FITZSTEPHEN RD
DRONFIELD GDNS
EXTON GDNS
CHRISTOPHER GDNS
DURELL RD
DURELL GDNS
WREN GDNS
WREN RD
The Sydney Russell Sch
SUDBURY CT
SHERINGHAM DR
BRADFIELD DR
HEPWORTH GDNS
HEPWORTH CT
SOUTHWOLD DR
Fball Gd
Sp Gd
RM8
ILCHESTER RD
IVINGHOE RD
HARROLD RD
Dorothy Barley Schs
A1153
PORTERS AVE
Fair Cross
HEDINGHAM RD
DAVINGTON RD
DAVINGTON GDNS
MARKYATE RD
EASEBOURNE RD
CORNWORTHY RD
Parsloes Park
WOODBRIDGE RD
DEREHAM RD
SANDRINGHAM RD
LODGE AVE
NEASHAM RD
LILLECHURCH RD
KIRKLEES RD
WROXHAM RD
L Ctr
Pl Fld
WESTROW DR
BREWOOD RD
Jo Richardson Com Sch
WYKEHAM AVE
Tenn Cts
Bwg Gn
Mayesbrook Park
BROMHALL RD
WATERBEACH RD
THICKET GR
RUSPER RD
Schs
BRAGG CL
CANNINGTON RD
CLEMENTHORPE RD
ROWNEY RD
ROWNEY GDNS
RM9
WILLIAM ASH CL 1
NEALE CT 2
DRIBERG CT 3
BARTRAM CT 4
LAMBLEY RD
MALPAS RD
CORNWALL CL
CLARE GDNS
THE DRIVE
KILSBY WLK
BLITHBURY RD
BERENGERS PL
RUGBY GDNS
RUGBY RD
Becontree
Allot Gdns
Boating Lakes
MANOR RD
OAKLEY AVE
IG11
BASEDALE RD
FYFIELD HO
SHEPPEY RD
SHEPPEY GDNS
Liby
GALE ST
EDGEFIELD AVE
Upney
BEVAN HO
CARROW RD
DENNY GDNS
WOODWARD GDNS
WOODWARD RD
HAMLETON TERR
SETON GDNS
POLESWORTH RD
MARGARET BONDFIELD AVE
BEVAN AVE
IRIS CT
MEADOW RD
MERTON RD
BRIDGEWAY
BEN TILLET CL
LANSBURY AVE
KEIR HARDIE WAY
ROSEDALE RD
CAMPSEY RD
CAMPSEY GDNS
CANONSLEIGH RD
WAGSTAFF GDNS
COTTON CL
BILLINGS CL
STOCKER GDNS
FLAMSTEAD GDNS
FLAMSTEAD RD
ELLERTON GDNS
ELLERTON RD
AMESBURY RD
ARDEN CRES
LANGLEY GDNS
STRATFORD CL
STAMFORD RD
STAMFORD GDNS
ROTHWELL GDNS
ROSEDALE DR
ROSEDALE GDNS
PINLEY GDNS
BURNHAM RD
Monteagle Prim Sch
ROTHWELL RD
GREENFIELD RD
LANGLEY CRES
ROMSEY GDNS
STUDLEY RD
THETFORD RD
Cemy
BROOK CT
A123
SUMMONS CL
GREENFIELD GDNS
ROMSEY RD
WIX RD
ACONBURY RD
MAPLESTEAD RD
GORESBROOK RD
BASSETT HO
INGRAVE HO
DUNMOW HO
Ripple Road
Castle Green
Jo Richardson
Sp

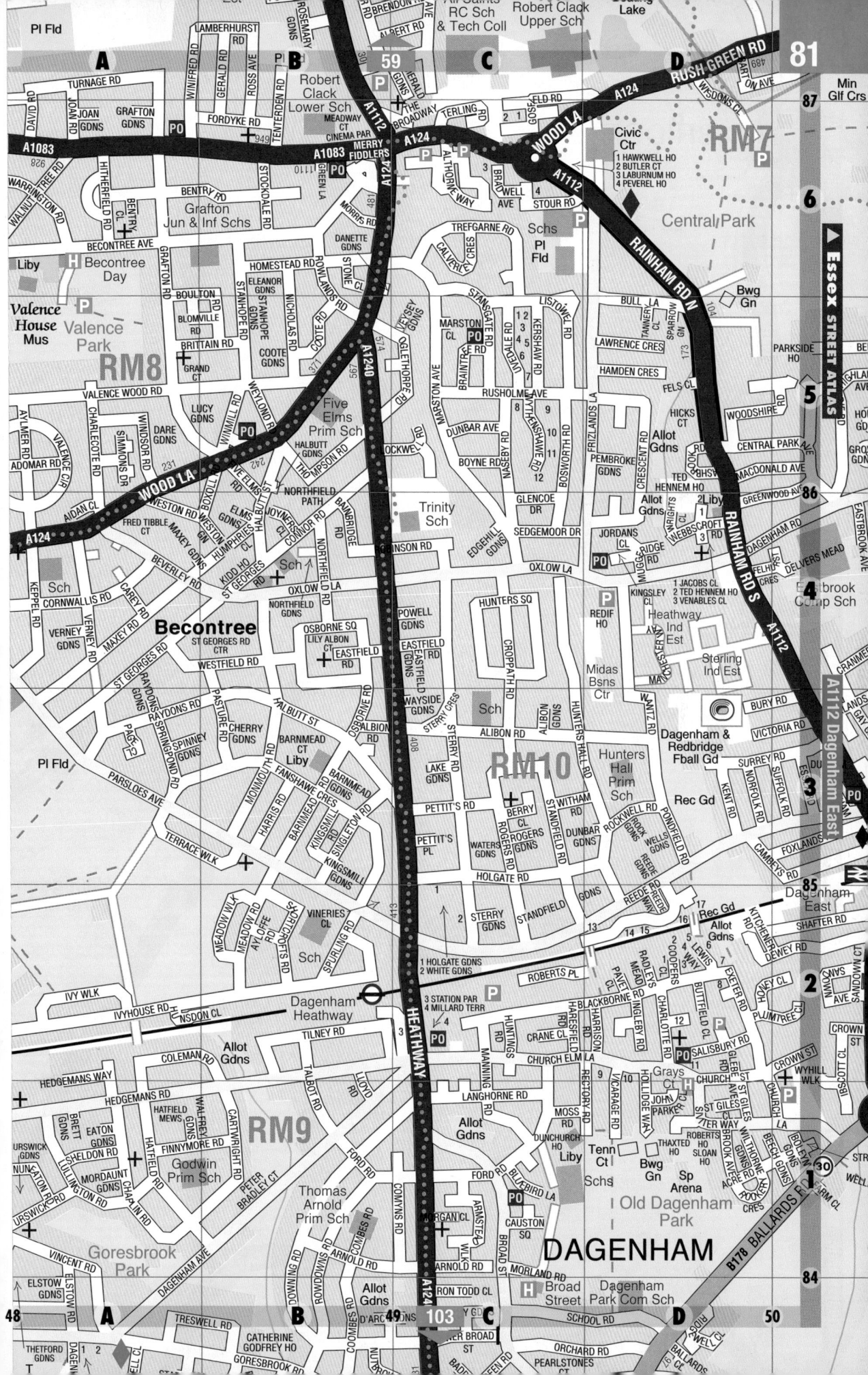
A
B
C
D
59
103
87
86
85
84
6
5
4
3
2
1
48
49
50
Essex STREET ATLAS
A1112 Dagenham East
RM7
RM8
RM9
RM10
Becontree
DAGENHAM
Valence House Mus
Valence Park
Central Park
Old Dagenham Park
Goresbrook Park
Dagenham Heathway
Dagenham East
Dagenham & Redbridge Fball Gd
Robert Clack Lower Sch
Grafton Jun & Inf Schs
Five Elms Prim Sch
Trinity Sch
Hunters Hall Prim Sch
Godwin Prim Sch
Thomas Arnold Prim Sch
Eastbrook Comp Sch
Dagenham Park Com Sch
Heathway Ind Est
Sterling Ind Est
Midas Bsns Ctr
Civic Ctr
WOOD LA
RAINHAM RD N
RAINHAM RD S
HEATHWAY
RUSH GREEN RD
BALLARDS RD

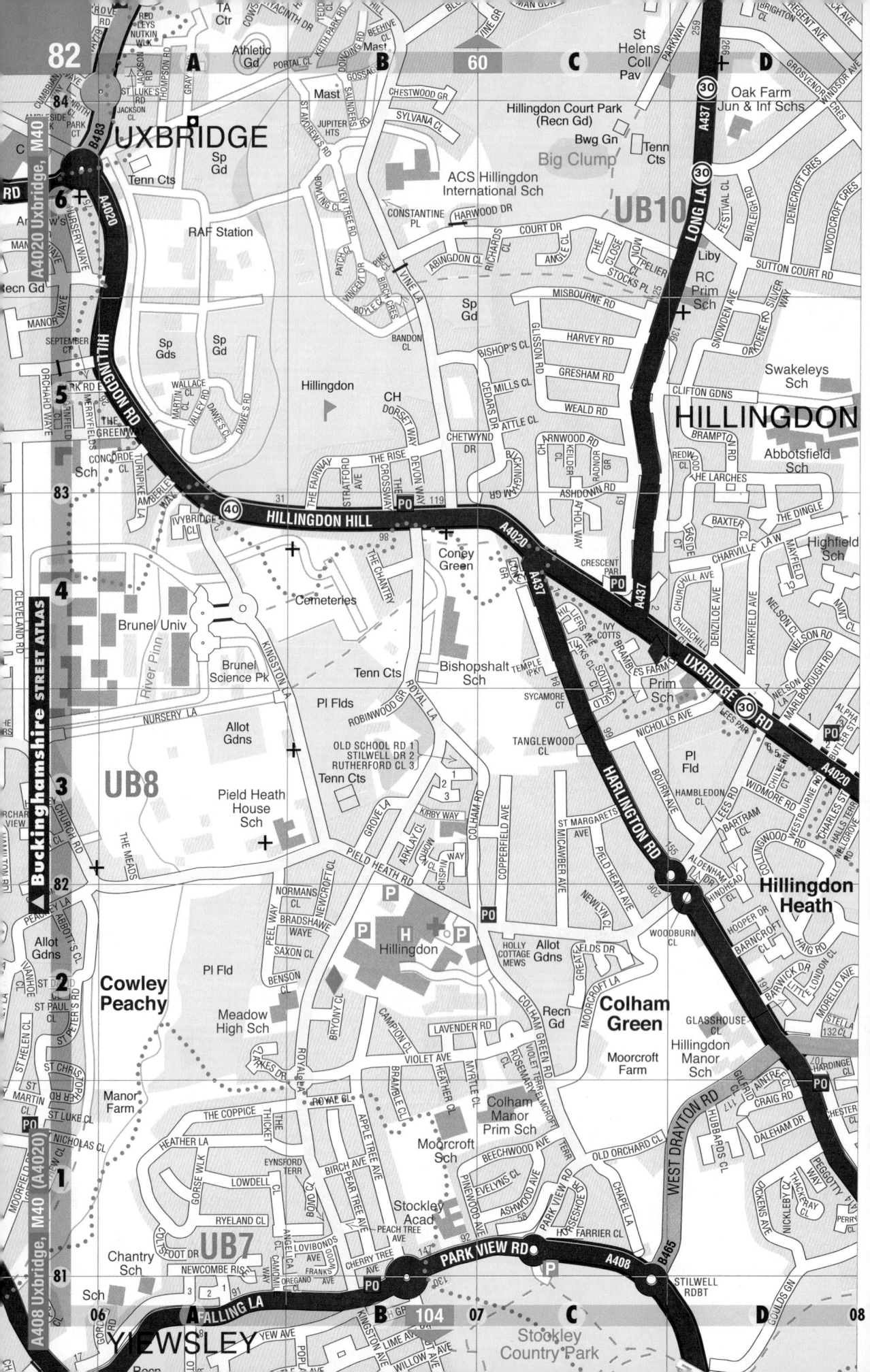
UXBRIDGE
HILLINGDON
UB10
UB8
UB7
YIEWSLEY
Hillingdon Heath
Colham Green
Cowley Peachy
HILLINGDON HILL
HILLINGDON RD
HARLINGTON RD
UXBRIDGE RD
LONG LA
PARK VIEW RD
FALLING LA
WEST DRAYTON RD
Brunel Univ
Brunel Science Pk
RAF Station
Cemeteries
ACS Hillingdon International Sch
Hillingdon Court Park (Recn Gd)
Big Clump
Oak Farm Jun & Inf Schs
Swakeleys Sch
Abbotsfield Sch
Highfield Sch
Bishopshalt Sch
Pield Heath House Sch
Meadow High Sch
Moorcroft Sch
Colham Manor Prim Sch
Stockley Acad
Chantry Sch
Hillingdon Manor Sch
Stockley Country Park
Athletic Gd
St Helens Coll Pav
Coney Green
Moorcroft Farm
Manor Farm
Hillingdon
STILWELL RDBT
Buckinghamshire STREET ATLAS
A4020 Uxbridge, M40
A408 Uxbridge, M40 (A4020)
60
104
06
07
08
A
B
C
D
1
2
3
4
5
6
81
82
83
84

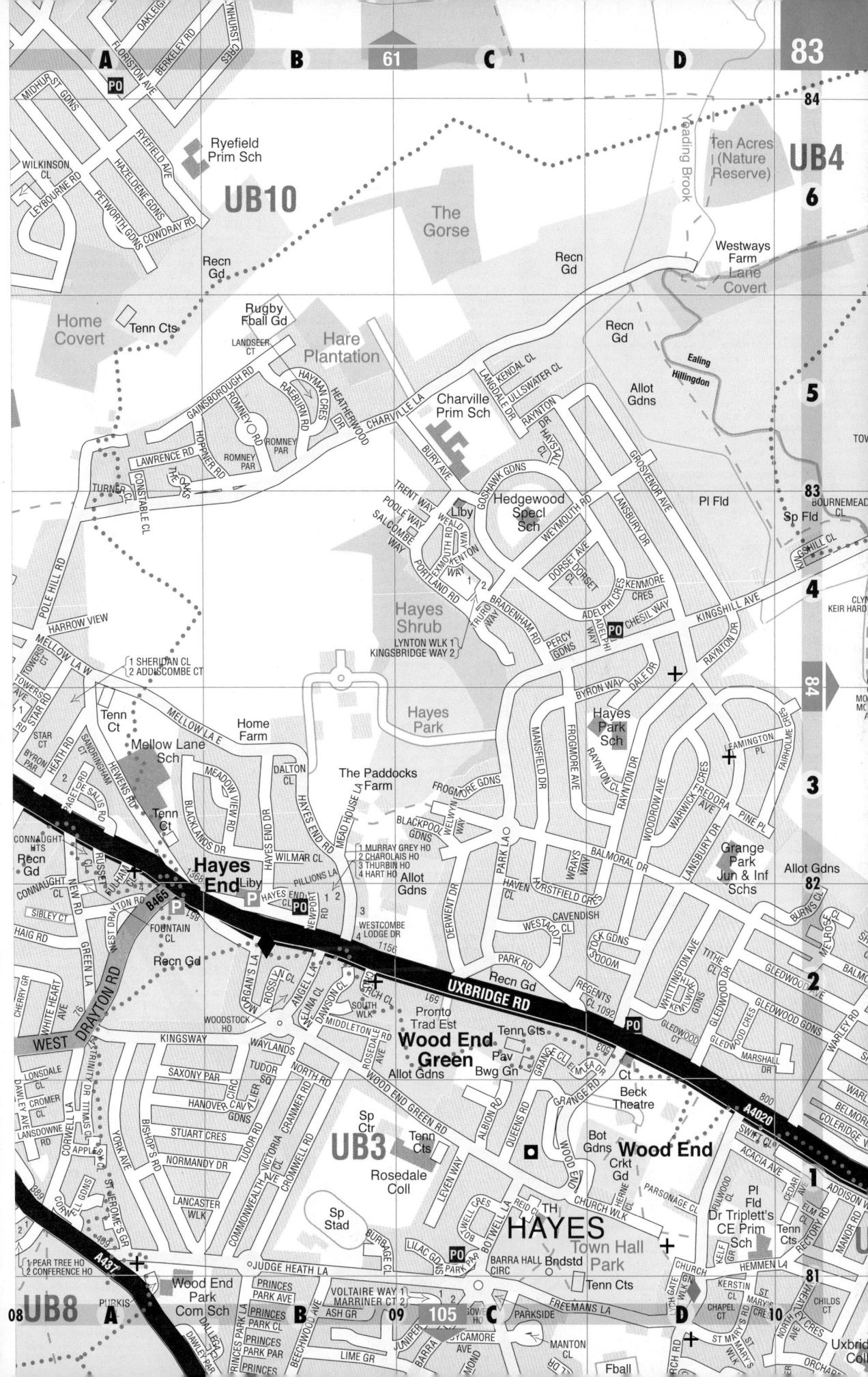

84

OAKLEIGH
FLORISTON AVE
MIDHURST GDNS
BERKELEY RD
YNEHURST CRES
PO
Ryefield Prim Sch
UB10
The Gorse
Recn Gd
Westways Farm Lane Covert
Ten Acres (Nature Reserve)
UB4
6

WILKINSON CL
LEYBOURNE RD
HAZELDENE GDNS
RYEFIELD AVE
PETWORTH GDNS
COWDRAY RD
Recn Gd
Recn Gd
Ealing Hillingdon
5

Home Covert
Tenn Cts
Rugby Fball Gd
LANDSEER CT
Hare Plantation
Charville Prim Sch
KENDAL CL
LANGDALE DR
ULLSWATER CL
RAYNTON DR
HAYSALL
Allot Gdns
Recn Gd
Pl Fld
Sp Fld
BOURNEMEAD
83

GAINSBOROUGH RD
HAYMAN CRES
HEATHERWOOD DR
CHARVILLE LA
BURY AVE
GOSHAWK GDNS
WEYMOUTH RD
GROSVENOR AVE
LANSBURY DR
KINGSHILL CL
4

LAWRENCE RD
HOPPNER RD
ROMNEY RD
RALBURN RD
ROMNEY PAR
THE OAKS
TRENT WAY
POOLE WAY
SALCOMBE WAY
WEALD
Liby
KYMOCKTON RD
KENTON
Hedgewood Specl Sch
DORSET AVE
DORSET CL
ADELPHI CRES
KENMORE CRES
CHESIL WAY
KINGSHILL AVE
CLYN KEIR HARD
TURNER CL
CONSTABLE CL
PORTLAND RD
TRURO WAY
PERCY GDNS
ADELPHI WAY
PO
RAYNTON DR
84

HARROW VIEW
Hayes Shrub
BRADENHAM RD
LYNTON WLK 1
KINGSBRIDGE WAY 2
BYRON WAY
DALE DR
MO MO

MELLOW LA W
TOWERS RD
TOWERS AVE
STAR RD
1 SHERIDAN CL
2 ADDISCOMBE CT
Hayes Park
Hayes Park Sch
LEAMINGTON PL
FAIRHOLME CRES
PINE PL
3

STAR CT
BYRON PAR
HEATH RD
SANDRINGHAM RD
Tenn Ct
MELLOW LA E
Home Farm
MANSFIELD DR
FROGMORE AVE
RAYNTON DR
WARWICK CRES
FREDORA AVE
LANSBURY DR
CONNAUGHT HTS
Recn Gd
DE SALIS RD
HEWENS RD
Mellow Lane Sch
MEADOW VIEW RD
BLACKLANDS DR
DALTON CL
The Paddocks Farm
FROGMORE GDNS
WOODROW AVE
Grange Park Jun & Inf Schs
Allot Gdns
82

CONNAUGHT CL
NEW RD
PAGET RD
RUSSET CL
FULHAM
Tenn Ct
HAYES END DR
WILMAR RD
MEAD HOUSE LA
1 MURRAY GREY HO
2 CHAROLAIS HO
3 THURBIN HO
4 HART HO
Allot Gdns
BLACKPOOL GDNS
WELWYN
PARK LA
WRAYS WAY
BALMORAL DR
BURNS RD
MELROSE
SIBLEY CT
HAIG RD
GREEN LA
DRAYTON RD
B465
Hayes End
Liby
PO
PILLIONS LA
NEWPORT RD
WESTCOMBE LODGE DR
DERWENT DR
HURSTFIELD CRES
HAVEN CL
CAVENDISH
WESTACOTT CL
STOCK GDNS
SDOOM
TITHE CL
WHITTINGTON AVE
GLEDWOOD DR
GLEDWOOD AVE
GLEDWOOD GDNS
WARLEY AVE

CHERRY GR
WHITE HEART AVE
FOUNTAIN CL
Recn Gd
MORGAN'S LA
ROSSLYN CL
ANGEL LA
MELINA CL
DAWSON CL
MIDDLETON CL
BIRCH CL
SOUTH WLK
Pronto Trad Est
Park RD
Recn Gd
REGENTS CL 1092
UXBRIDGE RD
A4020
PO
GLEDWOOD CRES
MARSHALL DR
GLEDWOOD CT
BALM

LONSDALE CL
CROMER CL
LANSDOWNE CL
DAWLEY AVE
APPLE
CORWELL LA
ST JEROME'S GR
TRINITY DR
TITMUSS CT
WOODSTOCK HO
WEST
KINGSWAY
WAYLANDS
TUDOR SQ
NORTH RD
ROSEDALE RD
WOOD END GREEN RD
ANGEL LA
Wood End Green
Allot Gdns
Tenn Cts
Pav
Bwg Gn
GRANGE CL
ELMA RD
GRANGE RD
Beck Theatre
Ct
WARL BELMOR COLERIDGE
SWIFT CL
ACACIA AVE

YORK AVE
BISHOPS RD
HANOVER CAV GDNS
STUART CRES
NORMANDY DR
VICTORIA CT
CAVALIER CRES
CROMWELL RD
CRAMMER RD
Sp Ctr
UB3
Tenn Cts
WOOD END GREEN RD
ALBION RD
QUEENS RD
WOOD END
Bot Gdns
Wood End
Crkt Gd
PARSONAGE RD
FULWOOD CL
Pl Fld
Dr Triplett's CE Prim Sch
Tenn Cts
CEDAR ELM RECTORY RD
1

DAWLEY AVE
CORW
LANCASTER WLK
Sp Stad
Rosedale Coll
LEVEN WAY
LILAC AVE
BURBAGE RD
WELL CRES
BOTWELL LA
REID CL
HAYES
CHURCH WLK
HERNE
Town Hall Park
CHURCH
KELF RD
ST MARY'S
MANOR RD
81

1 PEAR TREE HO
2 CONFERENCE HO
UB8
A437
A
PURKIS
Wood End Park Com Sch
PRINCES PARK AVE
PRINCES PARK CL
PRINCES PARK PAR
JUDGE HEATH LA
ASH GR
VOLTAIRE WAY 1
MARRINER CT 2
PO
BARRA HALL CIRC
BARRA HALL PARK
Bndstd
Tenn Cts
KINGATE
KERSTIN CL
CHAPEL CT
ST MARY'S CRES
CHILDS CT

DAWLEY RD
BEECHWOOD AVE
LIME GR
SYCAMORE AVE
BARRA
JUNIPER
PARKSIDE
FREEMANS LA
MANTON CL
ST MARY'S WLK
ORCH
Uxbridge Coll

Fball

83

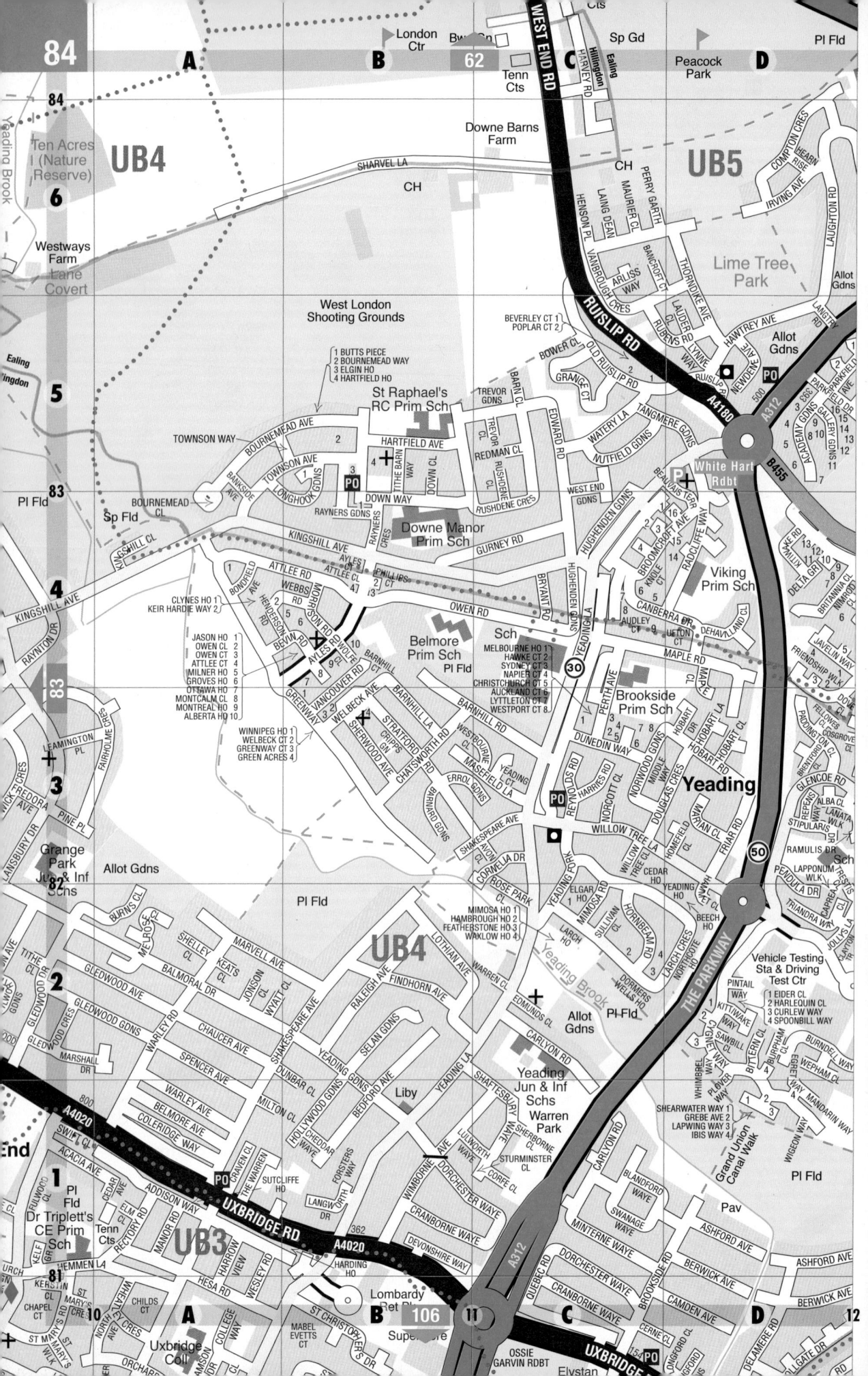

A
B
62
C
D
London Ctr
Tenn Cts
Sp Gd
Peacock Park
Pl Fld
Hillingdon
Ealing
HARVEY RD
WEST END RD
Downe Barns Farm
UB4
UB5
Ten Acres (Nature Reserve)
Yeading Brook
SHARVEL LA
CH
Westways Farm
Lane Covert
West London Shooting Grounds
HENSON PL
LAING DEAN
MAURIER CL
PERRY GARTH
COMPTON CRES
HEARN RISE
IRVING AVE
LAUGHTON RD
Lime Tree Park
Allot Gdns
VANBROUGH CRES
ARLISS WAY
BANCROFT CT
THORNDIKE AVE
LAUDER CL
RUBENS RD
LYNNE WAY
HAWTREY AVE
LANGTRY RD
NEWDENE AVE
RUISLIP RD
A4180
A312
B455
White Hart Rdbt
BEVERLEY CT 1
POPLAR CT 2
BOWER CL
OLD RUISLIP RD
GRANGE CT
1 BUTTS PIECE
2 BOURNEMEAD WAY
3 ELGIN HO
4 HARTFIELD HO
St Raphael's RC Prim Sch
TREVOR GDNS
BARN CL
EDWARD RD
WATERY LA
TANGMERE GDNS
NUTFIELD GDNS
TOWNSON WAY
BOURNEMEAD AVE
HARTFIELD AVE
TITHE BARN WAY
DOWN CL
TREVOR CL
REDMAN CL
RUSHDENE CL
RUSHDENE CRES
BANKSIDE AVE
TOWNSON AVE
LONGHOOK GDNS
DOWN WAY
RAYNERS GDNS
WEST END GDNS
BEAUVAIS TERR
PARKFIELD AVE
PARKFIELD DR
ACADEMY GDNS
GALLERY GDNS
Pl Fld
Sp Fld
BOURNEMEAD CL
KINGSHILL CL
KINGSHILL AVE
Downe Manor Prim Sch
RAYNERS CRES
GURNEY RD
HUGHENDEN GDNS
BROOMCROFT AVE
RADCLIFFE WAY
KNOLE CT
Viking Prim Sch
KILLOWEN GDNS
DELTA GR
BRITANNIA CL
NIMROD
AYLES CT
ATTLEE CL
PHILLIPS CT
ATTLEE RD
BONDFIELD AVE
WEBBS RD
MORRISON RD
CLYNES HO 1
KEIR HARDIE WAY 2
OWEN RD
BRYANT RD
YEADING LA
CANBERRA DR
AUDLEY CT
UFTON CT
DEHAVILLAND CL
JAVELIN WAY
FRIENDSHIP WLK
RAYNTON DR
HENDERSON RD
BEVIN RD
AYLES RD
WOLFE CL
Belmore Prim Sch
Sch
MAPLE RD
MAPLE CL
JASON HO 1
OWEN CL 2
OWEN CT 3
ATTLEE CT 4
MILNER HO 5
GROVES HO 6
OTTAWA HO 7
MONTCALM CL 8
MONTREAL HO 9
ALBERTA HO 10
MELBOURNE HO 1
HAWKE CT 2
SYDNEY CT 3
NAPIER CT 4
CHRISTCHURCH CT 5
AUCKLAND CT 6
LYTTLETON CT 7
WESTPORT CT 8
BARNHILL CT
BARNHILL RD
BARNHILL LA
VANCOUVER RD
GREENWAY
WELBECK AVE
STRATFORD RD
CRIPPS GN
SHERWOOD AVE
CHATSWORTH RD
WESTBOURNE CL
MASEFIELD LA
YEADING CT
PERTH AVE
Brookside Prim Sch
HOBART DR
HOBART LA
HOBART CL
HOBART RD
DUNEDIN WAY
FELLOWES CL
COSGROVE CL
PADDINGTON CL
BRENTFORD CL
LEAMINGTON PL
FAIRHOLME CRES
WINNIPEG HO 1
WELBECK CT 2
GREENWAY CT 3
GREEN ACRES 4
REYNOLDS RD
HARRIES RD
NORCOTT CL
NORWOOD GDNS
MIDDLE WAY
DOUGLAS CRES
Yeading
GLENCOE RD
ALBA CL
LANATA WLK
STIPULARIS DR
REPENS WAY
FREDORA AVE
PINE PL
LANSBURY DR
ERROL GDNS
BARNARD GDNS
SHAKESPEARE AVE
AVON CL
WILLOW TREE LA
WILLOW TREE CL
HOMEFIELD CL
MARIAN CL
FRIAR RD
RAMULIS DR
LAPPONUM WLK
PENDULA DR
Grange Park Jun & Inf Schs
Allot Gdns
CORNELIA DR
ROSE PARK CL
YEADING FORK
ELGAR HO
MIMOSA RD
CEDAR HO
YEADING HO
HAMLET CL
TRIANDRA WAY
CAPREA CL
JOLLYS LA
Pl Fld
BURNS CL
MELROSE CL
MIMOSA HO 1
HAMBROUGH HO 2
FEATHERSTONE HO 3
WAXLOW HO 4
SULLIVAN CL
HORNBEAM RD
LARCH HO
BEECH HO
Vehicle Testing Sta & Driving Test Ctr
SHELLEY CL
MARVELL AVE
KEATS CL
JONSON CL
WYATT CL
LOTHIAN AVE
WARREN CL
LARCH CRES
NORTHCOTE AVE
DORMERS WELLS HO
TITHE CL
GLEDWOOD AVE
BALMORAL DR
FINDHORN AVE
RALEIGH AVE
PINTAIL WAY
1 EIDER CL
2 HARLEQUIN CL
3 CURLEW WAY
4 SPOONBILL WAY
GLEDWOOD DR
GLEDWOOD GDNS
GLEDWOOD CRES
WARLEY RD
CHAUCER AVE
SHAKESPEARE AVE
SELAN GDNS
EDMUNDS CL
Allot Gdns
Pl Fld
THE PARKWAY
KITTIWAKE WAY
SAWBILL CL
BITTERN CL
BURPHAM CL
BURNDELL WAY
WEPHAM CL
EGRET WAY
MANDARIN WAY
MARSHALL DR
SPENCER AVE
DUNBAR CL
YEADING GDNS
CARLYON RD
WARLEY AVE
MILTON CL
HOLLYWOOD GDNS
BEDFORD AVE
Liby
YEADING LA
SHAFTESBURY WAYE
Yeading Jun & Inf Schs
Warren Park
CYGNET WAY
PLOVER WAY
WHIMBREL WAY
SHEARWATER WAY 1
GREBE AVE 2
LAPWING WAY 3
IBIS WAY 4
WIGEON WAY
Grand Union Canal Walk
BELMORE AVE
COLERIDGE WAY
A4020
SWIFT CL
ACACIA AVE
CHEDDAR WAYE
FORSTERS WAY
SHERBORNE CL
LULWORTH WAYE
STURMINSTER CL
CORFE CL
CARLYON RD
BLANDFORD WAYE
SWANAGE WAYE
Pl Fld
CEDAR AVE
ELM CL
CRAVEN CL
THE WARREN
SUTCLIFFE HO
LANGWORTH DR
WIMBORNE AVE
DORCHESTER WAYE
Pav
FULWOOD CL
Pl Fld
Dr Triplett's CE Prim Sch
Tenn Cts
RECTORY RD
ADDISON WAY
UXBRIDGE RD
CRANBORNE WAYE
MINTERNE WAYE
ASHFORD AVE
UB3
MANOR RD
HARROW VIEW
WESLEY RD
A4020
DEVONSHIRE WAY
A312
QUEBEC RD
DORCHESTER WAYE
BROOKSIDE RD
BERWICK AVE
HEMMEN LA
HARDING HO
KERSTIN CL
CHAPEL CT
ST MARY'S CRES
HESA RD
CHILDS CT
Lombardy Ret Pk
CRANBORNE WAYE
CAMDEN AVE
ST MARY'S RD
WHEATLEY CRES
NORTH AVE
COLLEGE WAY
MABEL EVETTS CT
ST CHRISTOPHER'S DR
106
CERNE CL
LONGFORD CL
DELAMERE RD
Uxbridge Coll
OSSIE GARVIN RDBT
Elystan
UXBRIDGE RD
10
11
12
84
83
82
81
6
5
4
3
2
1
30
50

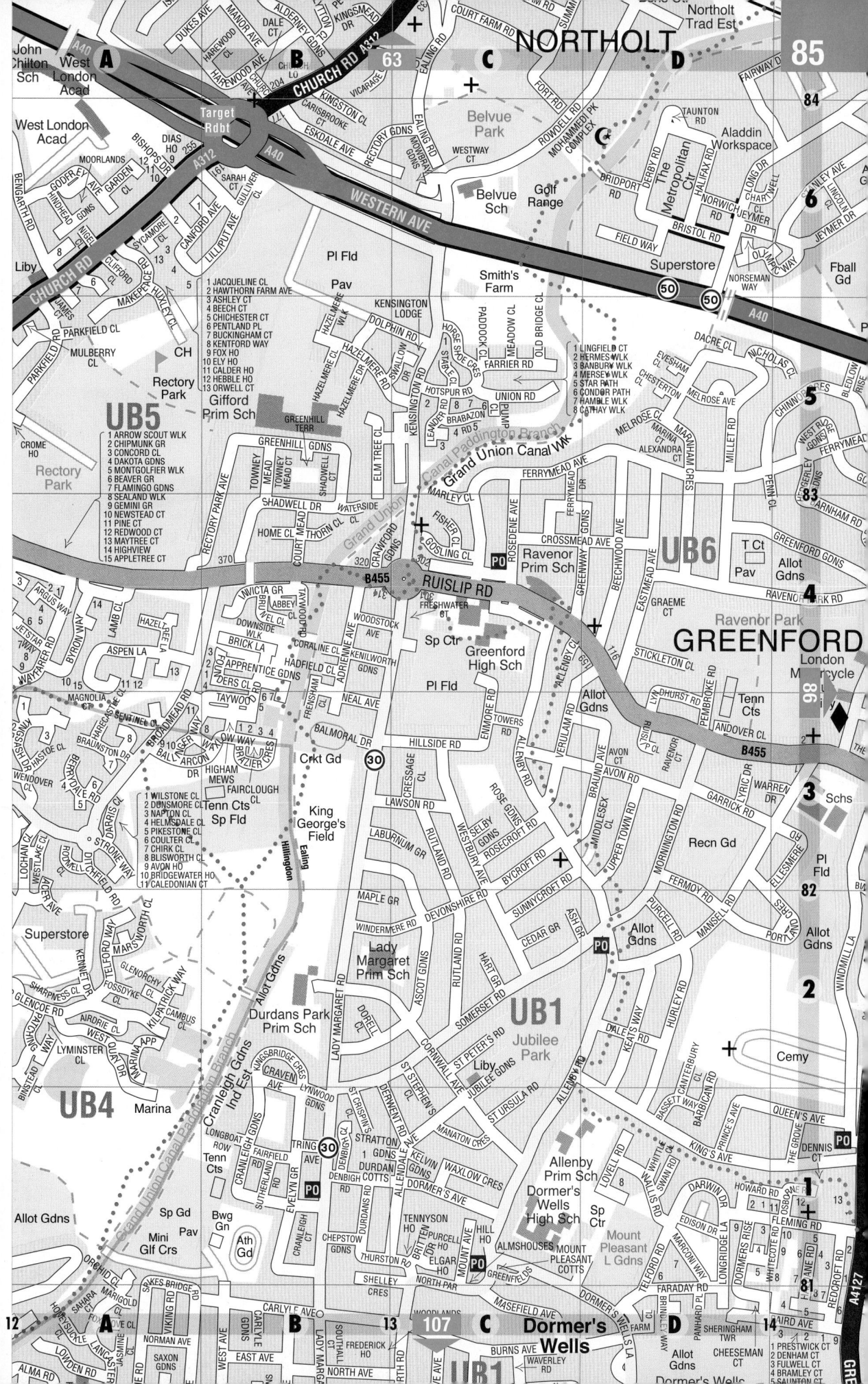

85
NORTHOLT
Northolt Trad Est
GREENFORD
UB5
UB6
UB1
UB4
Dormer's Wells
63
84
6
5
83
4
98
3
82
2
1
81
107
12
13
14
A
B
C
D
John Chilton Sch
West London Acad
Target Rdbt
CHURCH RD A312
CHURCH RD
WESTERN AVE
A40
A312
Belvue Park
Belvue Sch
Golf Range
Mohammedi Pk Complex
The Metropolitan Ctr
Aladdin Workspace
Superstore
Smith's Farm
Fball Gd
Pl Fld
Pav
Kensington Lodge
Rectory Park
Gifford Prim Sch
Grand Union Canal Paddington Branch
Grand Union Canal Wk
RUISLIP RD
B455
Ravenor Prim Sch
Greenford High Sch
Sp Ctr
Ravenor Park
Allot Gdns
Tenn Cts
Crkt Gd
King George's Field
Recn Gd
Lady Margaret Prim Sch
Durdans Park Prim Sch
Jubilee Park
Cranleigh Gdns Ind Est
Marina
Superstore
Cemy
Allenby Prim Sch
Dormer's Wells High Sch
Mount Pleasant L Gdns
Sp Gd
Mini Glf Crs
Ath Gd
Bwg Gn
Schs
Hillingdon
Ealing
1 JACQUELINE CL
2 HAWTHORN FARM AVE
3 ASHLEY CT
4 BEECH CT
5 CHICHESTER CT
6 PENTLAND PL
7 BUCKINGHAM CT
8 KENTFORD WAY
9 FOX HO
10 ELY HO
11 CALDER HO
12 HEBBLE HO
13 ORWELL CT
1 LINGFIELD CT
2 HERMES WLK
3 BANBURY WLK
4 MERSEY WLK
5 STAR PATH
6 CONDOR PATH
7 HAMBLE WLK
8 CATHAY WLK
1 ARROW SCOUT WLK
2 CHIPMUNK GR
3 CONCORD CL
4 DAKOTA GDNS
5 MONTGOLFIER WLK
6 BEAVER GR
7 FLAMINGO GDNS
8 SEALAND WLK
9 GEMINI GR
10 NEWSTEAD CT
11 PINE CT
12 REDWOOD CT
13 MAYTREE CT
14 HIGHVIEW
15 APPLETREE CT
1 WILSTONE CL
2 DUNSMORE CL
3 NAPTON CL
4 HELMSDALE CL
5 PIKESTONE CL
6 COULTER CL
7 CHIRK CL
8 BLISWORTH CL
9 AVON HO
10 BRIDGEWATER HO
11 CALEDONIAN CT
1 PRESTWICK CT
2 DENHAM CT
3 FULWELL CT
4 BRAMLEY CT

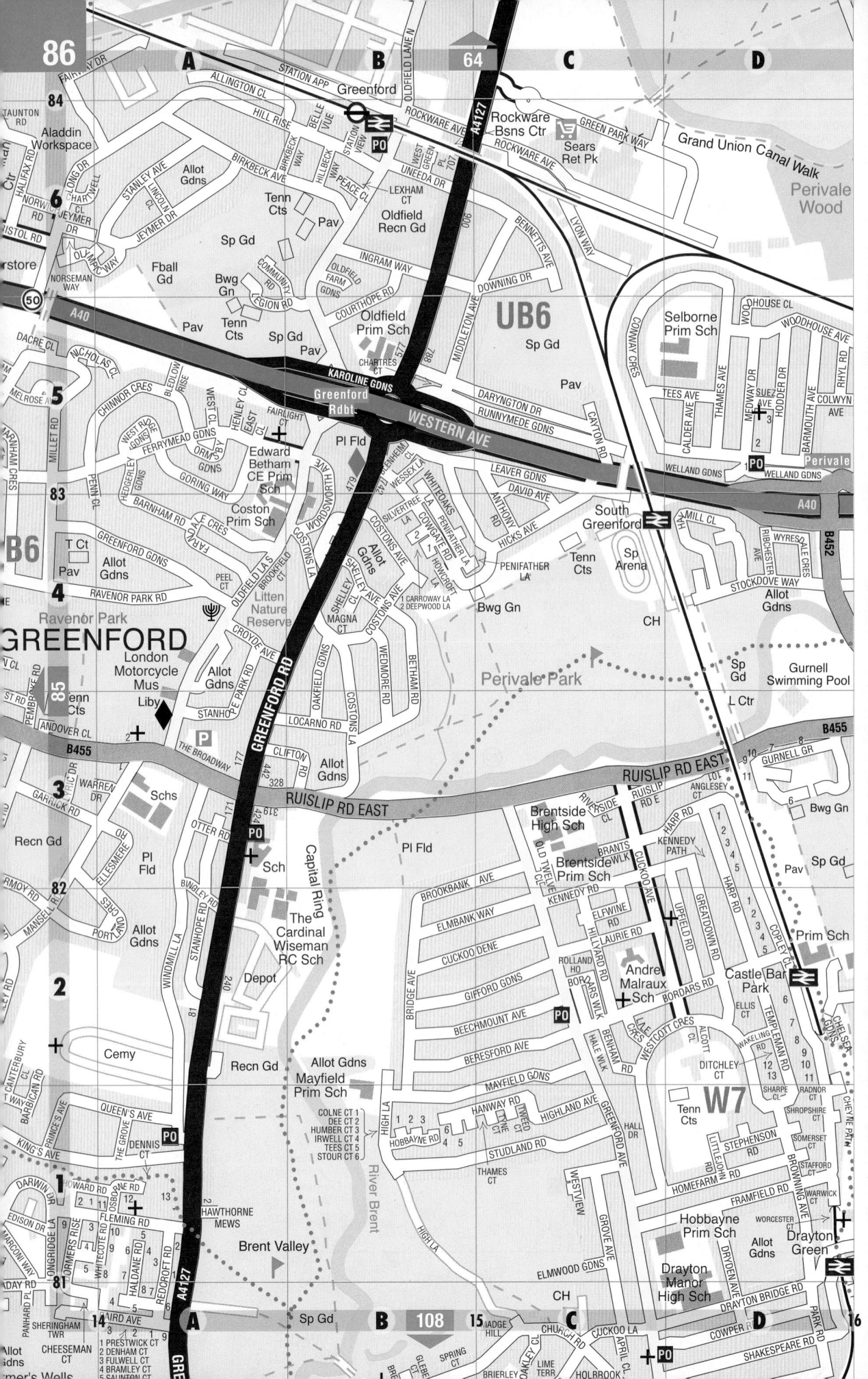
A
B
C
D
64
Greenford
Rockware Bsns Ctr
Sears Ret Pk
Grand Union Canal Walk
Perivale Wood
Aladdin Workspace
Allot Gdns
Tenn Cts
Pav
Oldfield Recn Gd
Sp Gd
Fball Gd
Bwg Gn
UB6
Selborne Prim Sch
Oldfield Prim Sch
Greenford Rdbt
WESTERN AVE
A40
Edward Betham CE Prim Sch
Coston Prim Sch
South Greenford
Sp Arena
Perivale
Litten Nature Reserve
Ravenor Park
GREENFORD
London Motorcycle Mus
Liby
Perivale Park
Gurnell Swimming Pool
L Ctr
RUISLIP RD EAST
GREENFORD RD
B455
Schs
Recn Gd
Pl Fld
Capital Ring
The Cardinal Wiseman RC Sch
Brentside High Sch
Brentside Prim Sch
Andre Malraux Sch
Castle Bar Park
Prim Sch
Depot
Cemy
Mayfield Prim Sch
Allot Gdns
River Brent
Brent Valley
W7
Hobbayne Prim Sch
Drayton Green
Drayton Manor High Sch
CH
Sp Gd
108
A4127

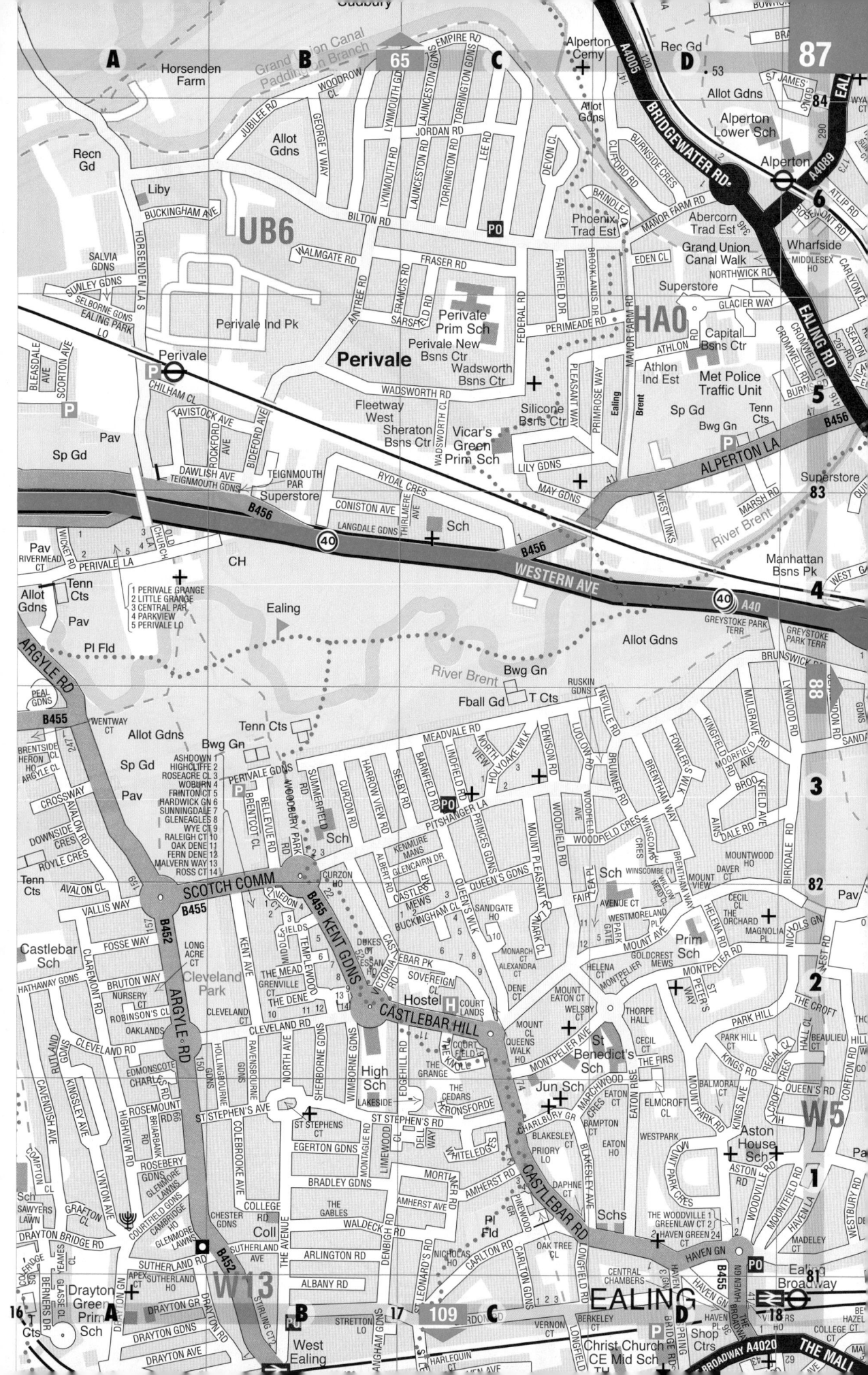
A
B
C
D
65
Horsenden Farm
Grand Union Canal Paddington Branch
Alperton Cemy
Rec Gd
Allot Gdns
Alperton Lower Sch
Alperton
Recn Gd
Liby
UB6
Phoenix Trad Est
Abercorn Trad Est
Grand Union Canal Walk
Wharfside
Superstore
HA0
Perivale Ind Pk
Perivale
Perivale Prim Sch
Perivale New Bsns Ctr
Wadsworth Bsns Ctr
Capital Bsns Ctr
Athlon Ind Est
Met Police Traffic Unit
Fleetway West
Sheraton Bsns Ctr
Vicar's Green Prim Sch
Silicone Bsns Ctr
Sp Gd
Pav
Superstore
Sch
WESTERN AVE
A40
B456
ALPERTON LA
River Brent
Manhattan Bsns Pk
CH
Ealing
Allot Gdns
Pl Fld
Bwg Gn
Fball Gd
T Cts
Tenn Cts
ARGYLE RD
B455
SCOTCH COMM
KENT GDNS
CASTLEBAR HILL
Hostel
High Sch
Castlebar Sch
Cleveland Park
St Benedict's Sch
Prim Sch
Aston House Sch
Jun Sch
Schs
CASTLEBAR RD
W5
W13
Coll
Drayton Green Prim Sch
West Ealing
EALING
Ealing Broadway
Christ Church CE Mid Sch
Shop Ctrs
THE MALL
A4020
BROADWAY
109
16
17
18
81
82
83
84
88
1
2
3
4
5
6

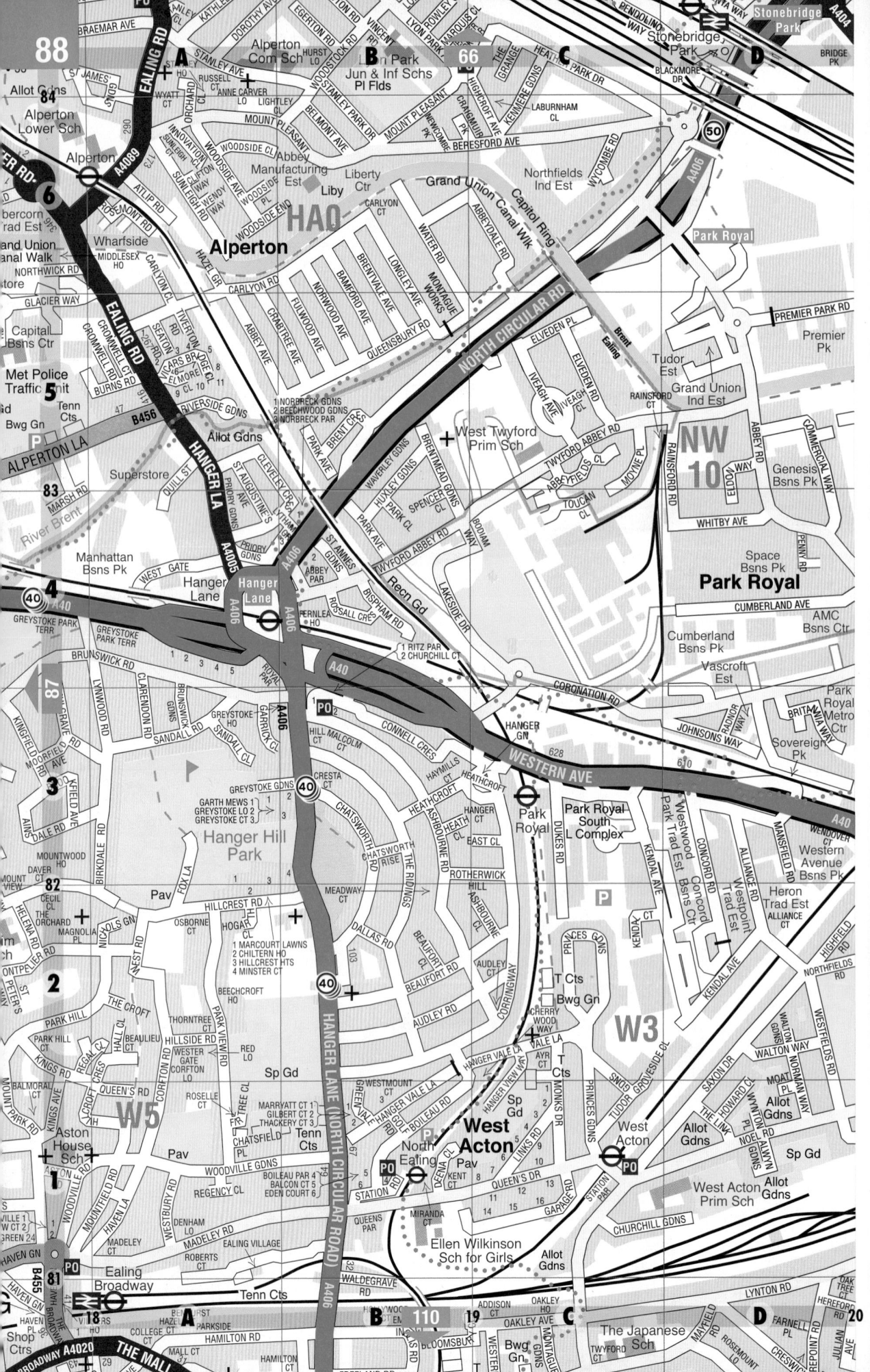
Alperton
Park Royal
West Acton
Hanger Hill Park
North Circular Rd
Western Ave
Hanger Lane
Ealing Rd
HA0
NW10
W3
W5
66
87
110

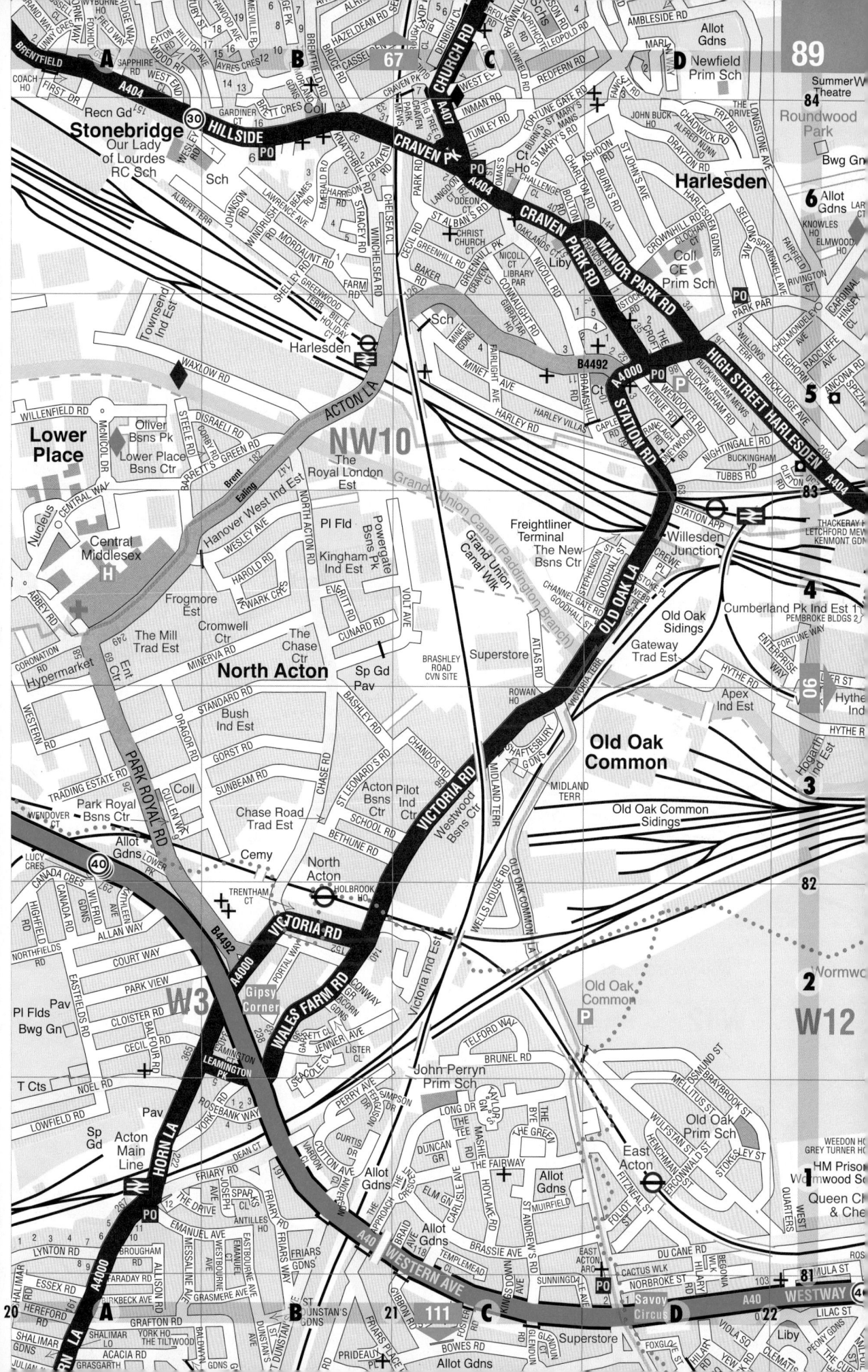

Stonebridge
Harlesden
NW10
Lower Place
North Acton
Old Oak Common
W3
W12
HILLSIDE
CRAVEN PK
CHURCH RD
CRAVEN PARK RD
MANOR PARK RD
HIGH STREET HARLESDEN
STATION RD
OLD OAK LA
VICTORIA RD
ACTON LA
PARK ROYAL RD
WALES FARM RD
HORN LA
WESTERN AVE
WESTWAY
Grand Union Canal (Paddington Branch)
Willesden Junction
Freightliner Terminal
Old Oak Common Sidings
Old Oak Sidings
Central Middlesex
Hypermarket
Superstore
Gipsy Corner
Savoy Circus
East Acton
North Acton
Acton Main Line
Roundwood Park
Harlesden
Old Oak Prim Sch
John Perryn Prim Sch
HM Prison Wormwood Scrubs
Newfield Prim Sch
Coll CE Prim Sch
Our Lady of Lourdes RC Sch
Townsend Ind Est
Oliver Bsns Pk
Lower Place Bsns Ctr
The Royal London Est
Hanover West Ind Est
Powergate Bsns Pk
Kingham Ind Est
Frogmore Est
Cromwell Ctr
The Mill Trad Est
The Chase Ctr
Bush Ind Est
Park Royal Bsns Ctr
Chase Road Trad Est
Acton Bsns Ctr
Pilot Ind Ctr
Westwood Bsns Ctr
Victoria Ind Est
Cumberland Pk Ind Est
Gateway Trad Est
Apex Ind Est
Hogarth Ind Est
The New Bsns Ctr
A404
A407
A4000
B4492
A40
67
111
90
A
B
C
D
1
2
3
4
5
6
20
21
22
81
82
83
84

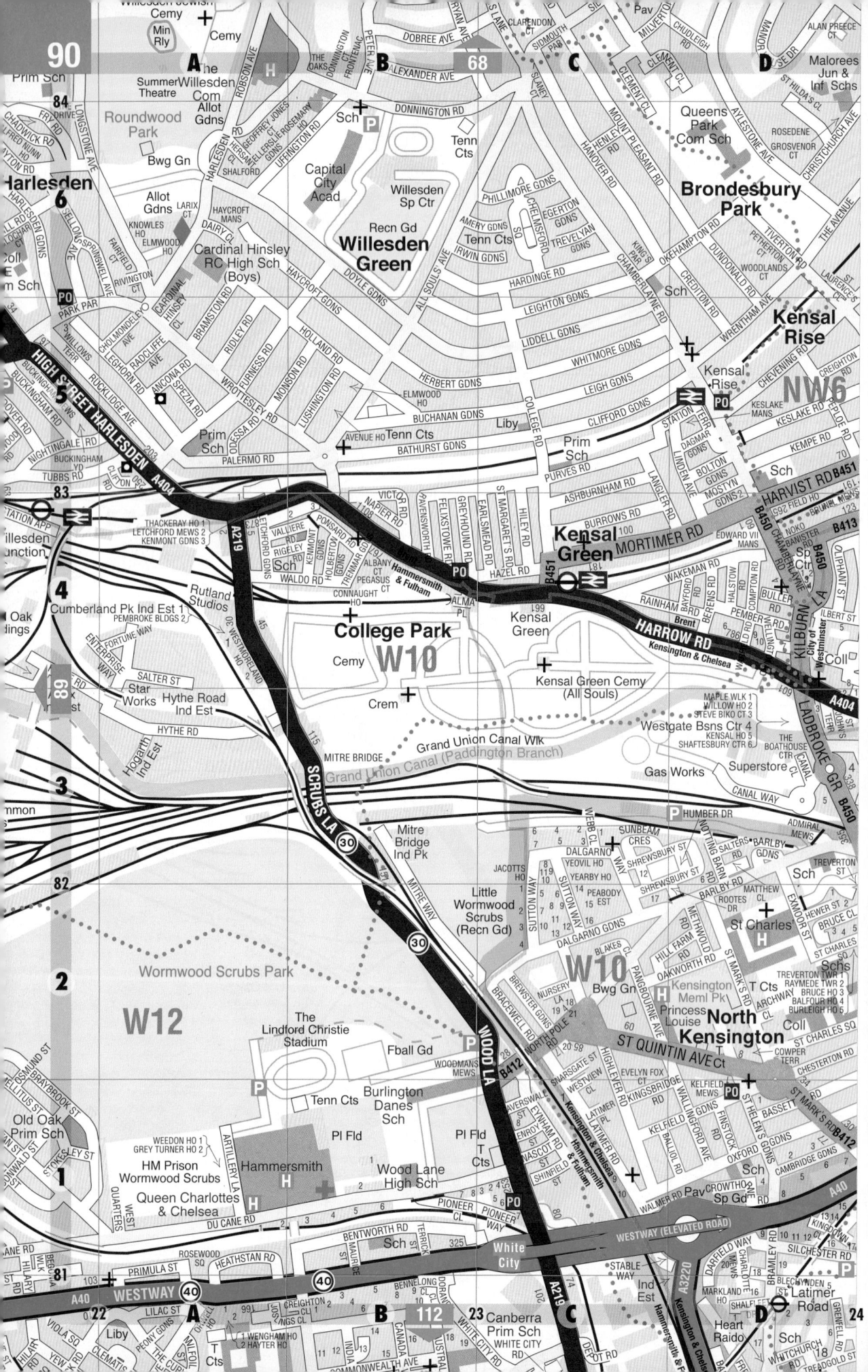
A
B
C
D
68
Harlesden
Willesden Green
Brondesbury Park
Kensal Rise
NW6
Kensal Green
College Park
W10
W12
North Kensington
Cemy
Min Rly
The Willesden Com Allot Gdns
Summer Theatre
Prim Sch
Roundwood Park
Bwg Gn
Allot Gdns
Capital City Acad
Willesden Sp Ctr
Recn Gd
Tenn Cts
Cardinal Hinsley RC High Sch (Boys)
Queens Park Com Sch
Malorees Jun & Inf Schs
Sch
Liby
Prim Sch
HIGH STREET HARLESDEN
A404
A219
HARROW RD
MORTIMER RD
HARVIST RD
B451
B450
B413
KILBURN LA
Kensington & Chelsea
Hammersmith & Fulham
Brent
City of Westminster
Rutland Studios
Cumberland Pk Ind Est
Star Works
Hythe Road Ind Est
HYTHE RD
Hogarth Ind Est
Kensal Green Cemy (All Souls)
Crem
Grand Union Canal Wlk
Grand Union Canal (Paddington Branch)
MITRE BRIDGE
SCRUBS LA
Mitre Bridge Ind Pk
MITRE WAY
Westgate Bsns Ctr
Gas Works
Superstore
CANAL WAY
LADBROKE GR
Little Wormwood Scrubs (Recn Gd)
Wormwood Scrubs Park
The Lindford Christie Stadium
Fball Gd
Burlington Danes Sch
HM Prison Wormwood Scrubs
Queen Charlottes & Chelsea
Hammersmith
Wood Lane High Sch
WOOD LA
DU CANE RD
ST QUINTIN AVE
St Charles
Kensington Meml Pk
Princess Louise
Old Oak Prim Sch
WESTWAY
WESTWAY (ELEVATED ROAD)
White City
A40
A3220
Latimer Road
Canberra Prim Sch
Ind Est
Heart Raido
84
83
82
81
6
5
4
3
2
1
22
23
24
112

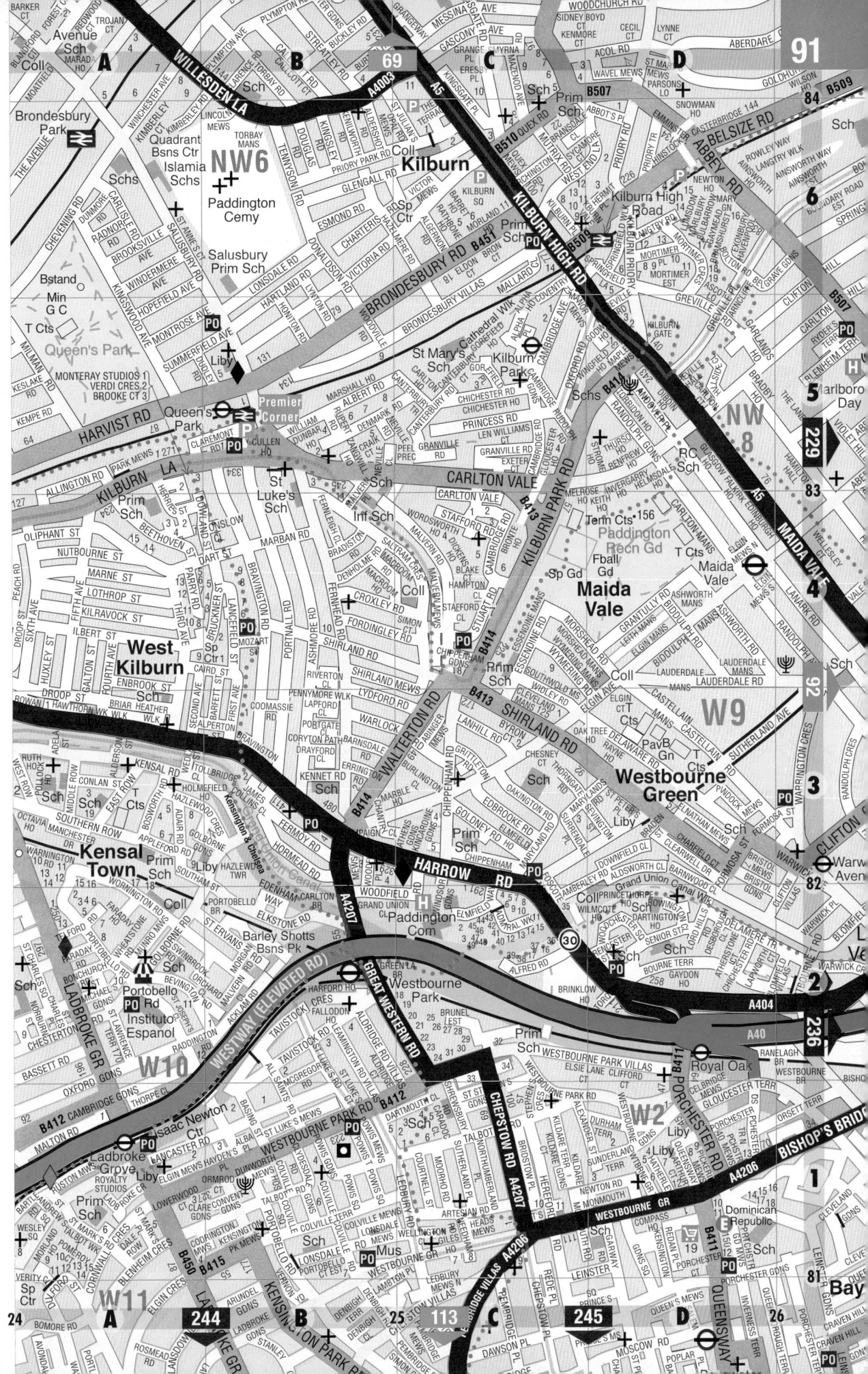

91
A
B
C
D
69
84
229
92
83
82
236
81
24
25
26
244
113
245
1
2
3
4
5
6
NW6
NW8
W9
W10
W2
W11
Kilburn
Maida Vale
West Kilburn
Kensal Town
Westbourne Green
Westbourne Park
Royal Oak
Ladbroke Grove
Queen's Park
Kilburn High Road
Kilburn Park
Brondesbury Park
Paddington Cemy
Salusbury Prim Sch
Quadrant Bsns Ctr
Islamia Schs
Paddington Recn Gd
Paddington Com
Barley Shotts Bsns Pk
Portobello Rd Instituto Espanol
Isaac Newton Ctr
Dominican Republic
Premier Corner
Grand Union Canal
Kensington & Chelsea
WILLESDEN LA
KILBURN HIGH RD
BRONDESBURY RD
BRONDESBURY VILLAS
HARVIST RD
KILBURN LA
CARLTON VALE
KILBURN PARK RD
MAIDA VALE
SHIRLAND RD
WALTERTON RD
HARROW RD
GREAT WESTERN RD
WESTWAY (ELEVATED RD)
WESTBOURNE PARK RD
WESTBOURNE PARK VILLAS
WESTBOURNE GR
CHEPSTOW RD
PORCHESTER RD
QUEENSWAY
BISHOP'S BRIDGE RD
LADBROKE GR
KENSINGTON PARK RD
ELGIN CRES
PEMBRIDGE VILLAS
BELSIZE RD
ABBEY RD
A5
A4003
A404
A40
A4207
A4206
B507
B509
B510
B451
B413
B414
B411
B412
B415
B450

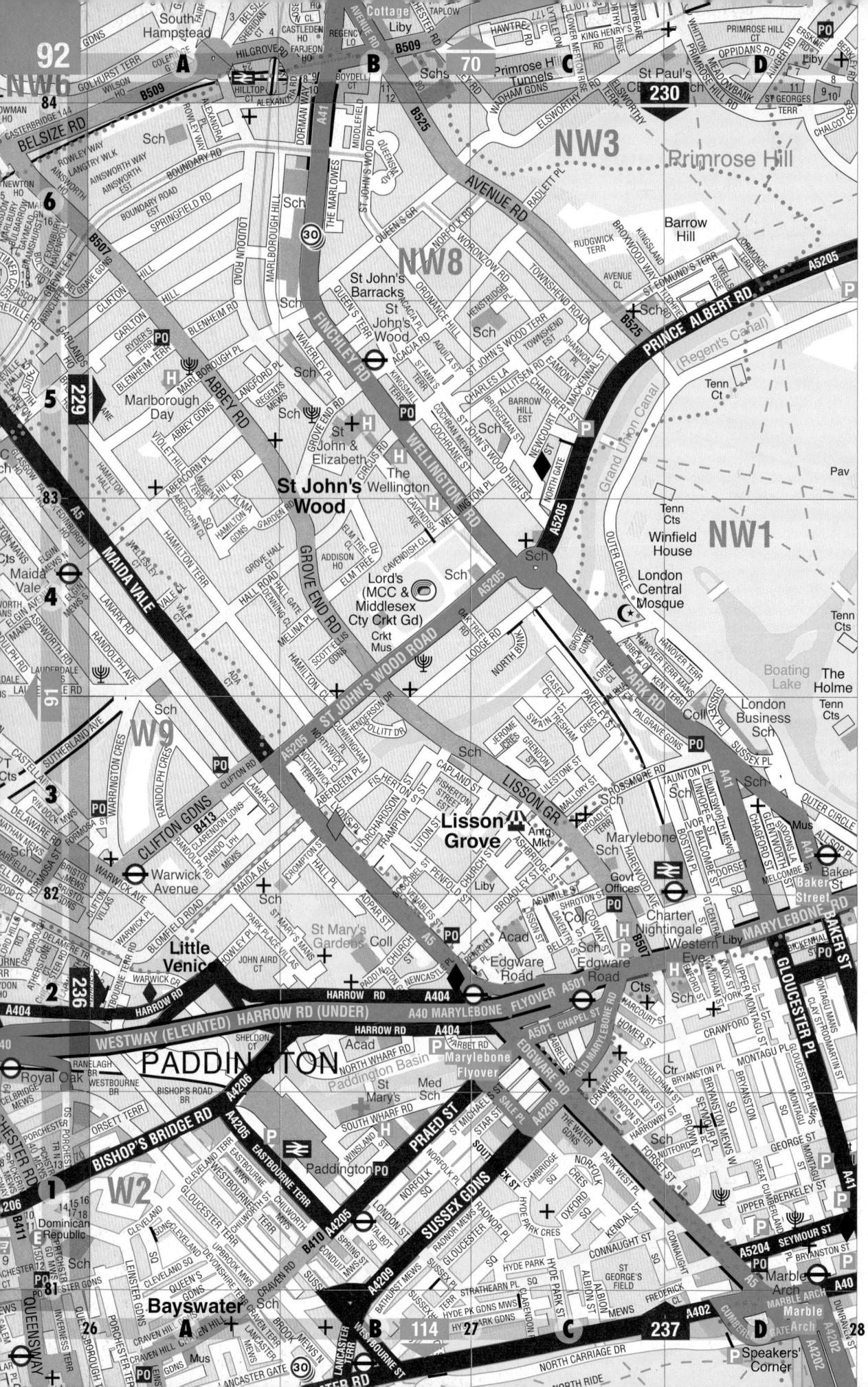
South Hampstead
NW6
NW3
NW8
NW1
W9
W2
Primrose Hill
Primrose Hill Tunnels
St Paul's
230
70
229
236
91
114
237
Barrow Hill
St John's Barracks
St John's Wood
The Wellington
Lord's (MCC & Middlesex Cty Crkt Gd)
Crkt Mus
Marlborough Day
Maida Vale
Warwick Avenue
Little Venice
PADDINGTON
Paddington Basin
Paddington
Royal Oak
Bayswater
Dominican Republic
Lisson Grove
Antq Mkt
Marylebone
Govt Offices
Charter Nightingale
Western Eye
Edgware Road
Marylebone Flyover
St Mary's Gardens
London Central Mosque
Winfield House
London Business Sch
Boating Lake
The Holme
Baker Street
Marble Arch
Speakers' Corner
Grand Union Canal
(Regent's Canal)
PRINCE ALBERT RD
AVENUE RD
FINCHLEY RD
WELLINGTON RD
ABBEY RD
MAIDA VALE
GROVE END RD
ST JOHN'S WOOD ROAD
PARK RD
LISSON GR
OUTER CIRCLE
HARROW RD
WESTWAY (ELEVATED) HARROW RD (UNDER)
A40 MARYLEBONE FLYOVER
EDGWARE RD
PRAED ST
SUSSEX GDNS
BISHOP'S BRIDGE RD
EASTBOURNE TERR
MARYLEBONE RD
GLOUCESTER PL
BAKER ST
SEYMOUR ST
BELSIZE RD
BOUNDARY RD
CLIFTON GDNS
WARWICK AVE
QUEENSWAY
NORTH CARRIAGE DR
A B C D

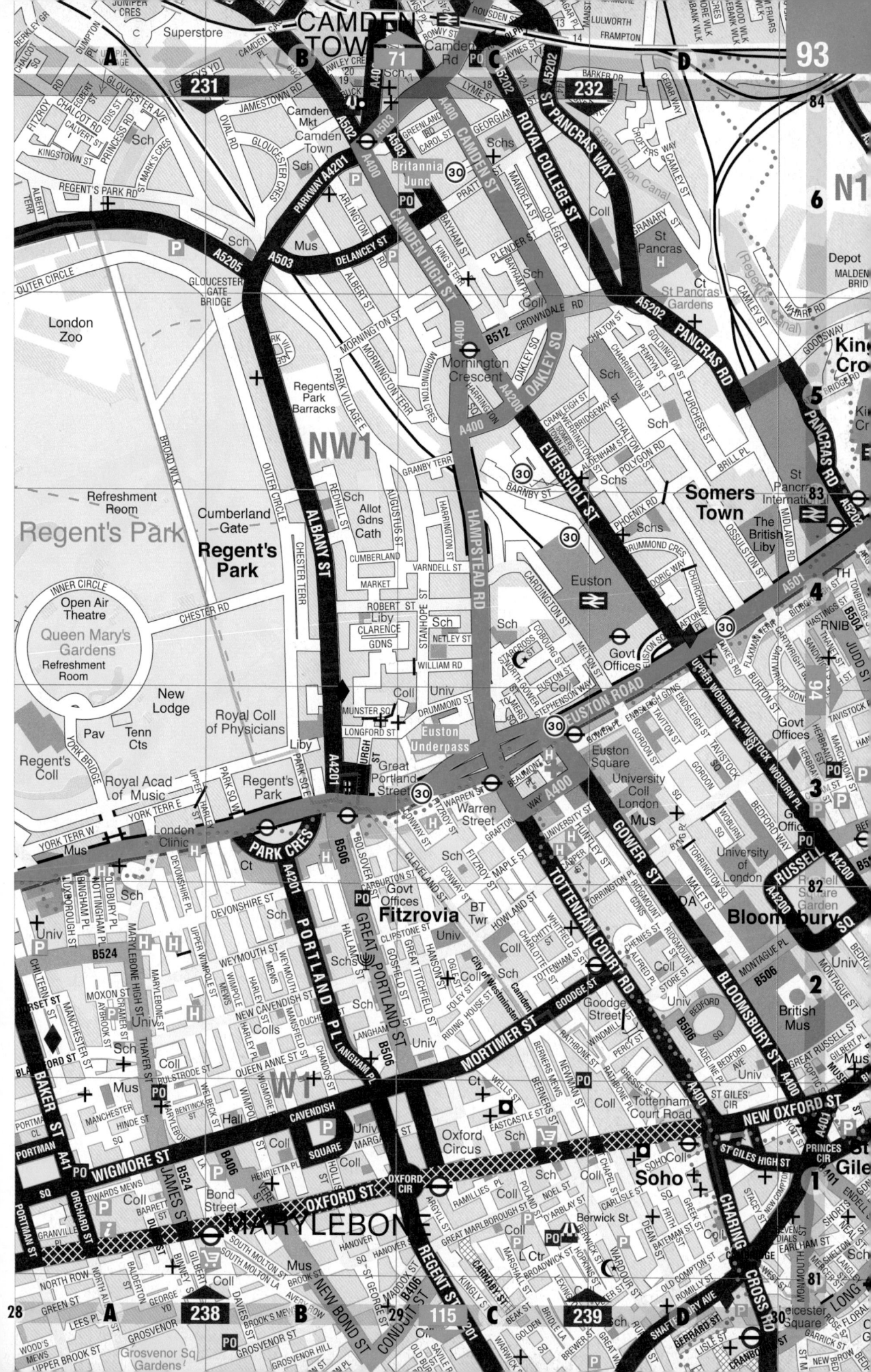

CAMDEN TOWN
Camden Rd
Camden Mkt
Camden Town
Britannia Junc
Superstore
A
B
C
D
71
231
232
84
6
N1
5
4
3
2
1
83
94
82
81
28
29
30
238
115
239
JAMESTOWN RD
GLOUCESTER AVE
GLOUCESTER CRES
OVAL RD
PRINCESS RD
KINGSTOWN ST
CHALCOT RD
REGENT'S PARK RD
ST MARK'S CRES
PARKWAY A4201
ARLINGTON RD
CAMDEN HIGH ST
CAMDEN ST
ROYAL COLLEGE ST
ST PANCRAS WAY
Grand Union Canal
Regent's Canal
DELANCEY ST
PRATT ST
BAYHAM ST
KING'S TERR
PLENDER ST
MANDELA ST
COLLEGE PL
CROWNDALE RD
OAKLEY SQ
A5202
PANCRAS RD
St Pancras
St Pancras Gardens
CAMLEY ST
Depot
GOODSWAY
OUTER CIRCLE
GLOUCESTER GATE BRIDGE
London Zoo
MORNINGTON ST
MORNINGTON TERR
MORNINGTON CRES
Mornington Crescent
PARK VILLAGE E
Regents Park Barracks
NW1
HAMPSTEAD RD
EVERSHOLT ST
Somers Town
CHALTON ST
PURCHESE ST
BRILL PL
OSSULSTON ST
MIDLAND RD
St Pancras International
The British Liby
PHOENIX RD
POLYGON RD
DRUMMOND CRES
CHURCHWAY
Euston
Govt Offices
CARDINGTON ST
MELTON ST
EUSTON ROAD
Euston Square
BROAD WLK
Refreshment Room
Regent's Park
Cumberland Gate
OUTER CIRCLE
CHESTER TERR
ALBANY ST
REDHILL ST
AUGUSTUS ST
Allot Gdns
Cath
CUMBERLAND MARKET
VARNDELL ST
ROBERT ST
Liby
CLARENCE GDNS
STANHOPE ST
NETLEY ST
WILLIAM RD
DRUMMOND ST
INNER CIRCLE
Open Air Theatre
Queen Mary's Gardens
CHESTER RD
New Lodge
Royal Coll of Physicians
Pav
Tenn Cts
Regent's Coll
YORK BRIDGE
Royal Acad of Music
YORK TERR E
YORK TERR W
London Clinic
PARK SQ E
PARK SQ W
Great Portland Street
Euston Underpass
Warren Street
PARK CRES
WARREN ST
GRAFTON WAY
University Coll London
GOWER ST
TOTTENHAM COURT RD
TORRINGTON PL
MALET ST
University of London
RUSSELL SQ
Russell Square Garden
Bloomsbury
WOBURN PL
TAVISTOCK SQ
TAVISTOCK PL
UPPER WOBURN PL
BEDFORD WAY
GORDON SQ
ENDSLEIGH GDNS
BURTON ST
CARTWRIGHT GDNS
HASTINGS ST
JUDD ST
RNIB
TH
BOLSOVER ST
CLEVELAND ST
Fitzrovia
BT Twr
GREAT PORTLAND ST
PORTLAND PL
A4201
DEVONSHIRE PL
DEVONSHIRE ST
WEYMOUTH ST
NEW CAVENDISH ST
HARLEY ST
WIMPOLE ST
MARYLEBONE HIGH ST
UPPER WIMPOLE ST
QUEEN ANNE ST
CHANDOS ST
LANGHAM PL
MORTIMER ST
GOODGE ST
Goodge Street
CHARLOTTE ST
WHITFIELD ST
BEDFORD SQ
BLOOMSBURY ST
MONTAGUE PL
British Mus
GREAT RUSSELL ST
NEW OXFORD ST
ST GILES HIGH ST
ST GILES' CIR
Tottenham Court Road
W1
CHILTERN ST
MANCHESTER ST
BAKER ST
THAYER ST
CAVENDISH SQUARE
WIGMORE ST
OXFORD ST
OXFORD CIR
Oxford Circus
Bond Street
JAMES ST
ORCHARD ST
PORTMAN SQ
PORTMAN ST
MARYLEBONE
REGENT ST
ARGYLL ST
GREAT MARLBOROUGH ST
CARNABY ST
BROADWICK ST
Soho
SOHO SQ
CHARING CROSS RD
Berwick St
WARDOUR ST
DEAN ST
FRITH ST
GREEK ST
OLD COMPTON ST
SHAFTESBURY AVE
GERRARD ST
Leicester Square
PRINCES CIR
St Giles
NEW BOND ST
SOUTH MOLTON ST
HANOVER SQ
ST GEORGE ST
CONDUIT ST
MADDOX ST
BROOK'S MEWS
GROSVENOR ST
Grosvenor Sq Gardens
UPPER BROOK ST
NORTH ROW
GREEN ST
LEES PL

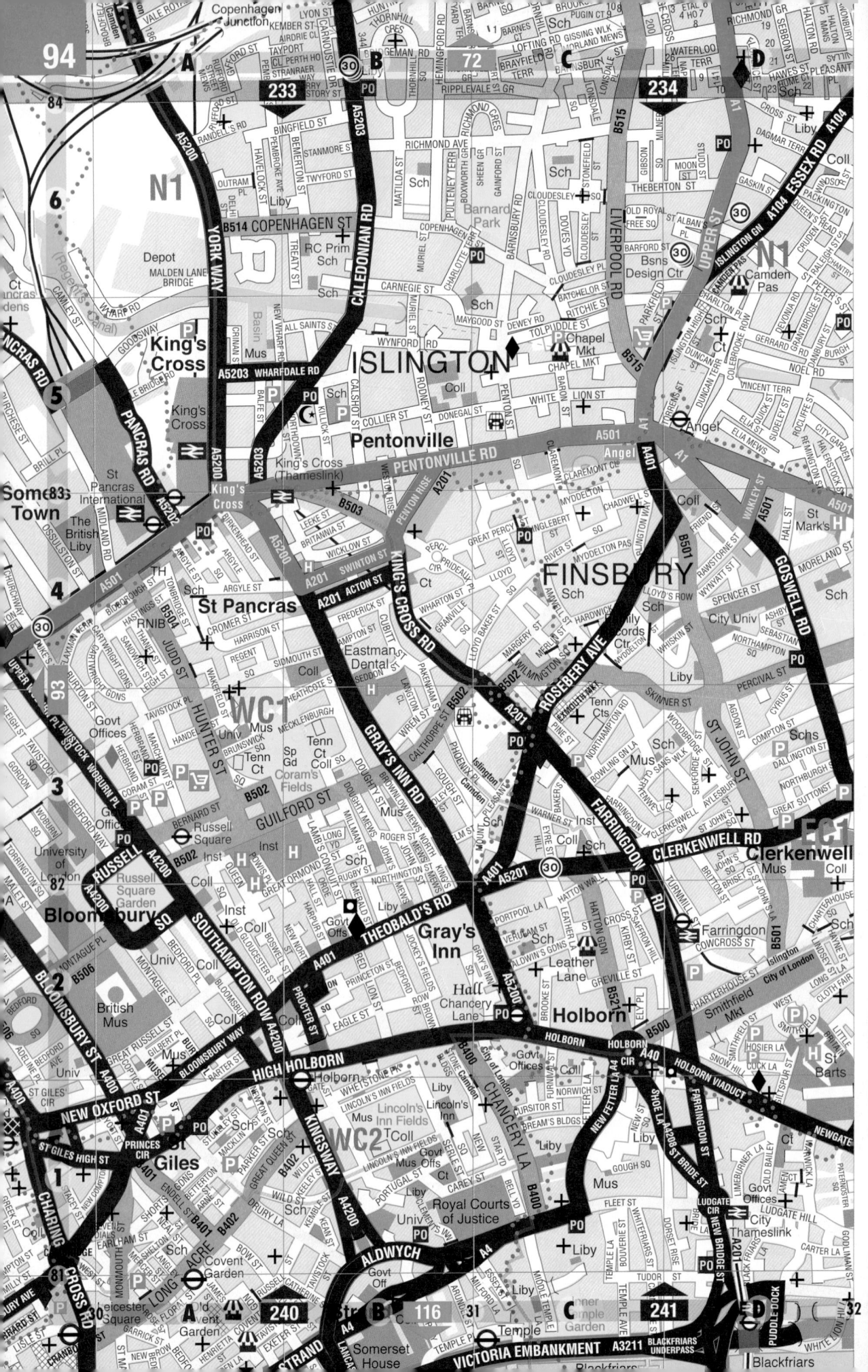
Copenhagen Junction
A
B
C
D
72
233
234
N1
6
5
4
3
2
1
84
83
82
81
93
YORK WAY
CALEDONIAN RD
B514 COPENHAGEN ST
RICHMOND AVE
RIPPLEVALE GR
LIVERPOOL RD
UPPER ST
ESSEX RD
ISLINGTON GN
Barnard Park
Depot
MALDEN LANE BRIDGE
RC Prim Sch
Regent's Canal
King's Cross
Basin
ISLINGTON
Chapel Mkt
CHAPEL MKT
Camden Pas
Bsns Design Ctr
Angel
A5203 WHARFDALE RD
Pentonville
PENTONVILLE RD
King's Cross (Thameslink)
St Pancras International
PANCRAS RD
Somers Town
The British Liby
MIDLAND RD
OSSULSTON ST
St Pancras
FINSBURY
KING'S CROSS RD
ROSEBERY AVE
GOSWELL RD
ST JOHN ST
City Univ
Family Records Ctr
Eastman Dental
WC1
HUNTER ST
JUDD ST
Coram's Fields
GUILFORD ST
GRAY'S INN RD
THEOBALD'S RD
Gray's Inn
Russell Square
Russell Square Garden
RUSSELL SQ
University of London
Bloomsbury
SOUTHAMPTON ROW
FARRINGDON RD
CLERKENWELL RD
Clerkenwell
EC1
Farringdon
COWCROSS ST
Smithfield Mkt
St Barts
HOLBORN VIADUCT
HOLBORN CIR
Holborn
Leather Lane
Chancery Lane
HIGH HOLBORN
Holborn
BLOOMSBURY WAY
BLOOMSBURY ST
British Mus
NEW OXFORD ST
ST GILES HIGH ST
St Giles
CHARING CROSS RD
KINGSWAY
Lincoln's Inn Fields
WC2
Lincoln's Inn
CHANCERY LA
Royal Courts of Justice
FLEET ST
NEW FETTER LA
City Thameslink
LUDGATE HILL
NEW BRIDGE ST
NEWGATE
ALDWYCH
STRAND
LONG ACRE
Covent Garden
Leicester Square
Somerset House
Temple
Inner Temple Garden
VICTORIA EMBANKMENT
BLACKFRIARS UNDERPASS
Blackfriars
240
116
241
31
32

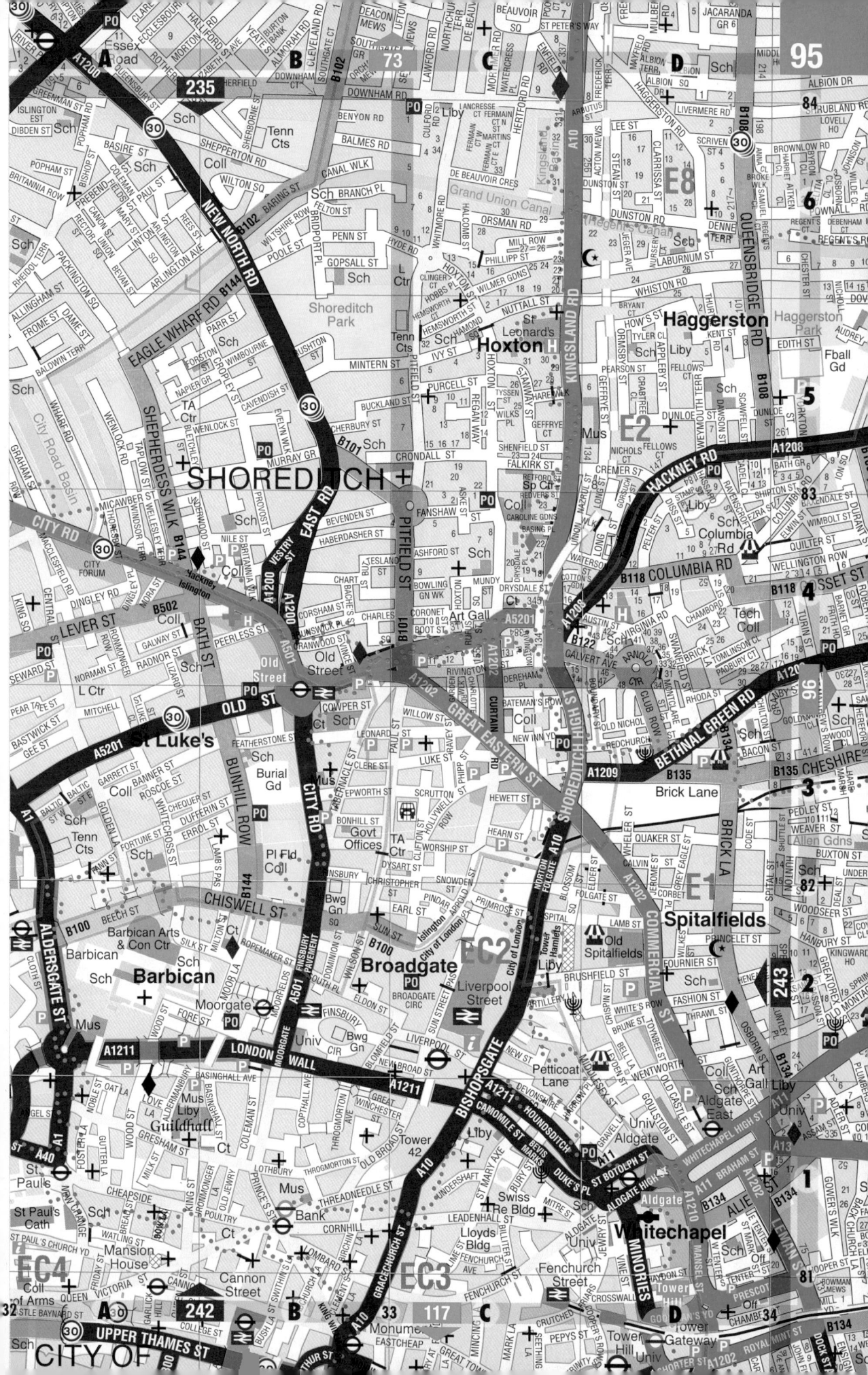

95
A
B
C
D
73
235
242
117
243
96
SHOREDITCH
Hoxton
Haggerston
Haggerston Park
Shoreditch Park
St Luke's
Barbican
Broadgate
Spitalfields
Whitechapel
Brick Lane
E8
E2
E1
EC2
EC3
EC4
Grand Union Canal
Regent's Canal
City Road Basin
Kingsland Basin
Essex Road
Old Street
Moorgate
Liverpool Street
Bank
Mansion House
Cannon Street
Fenchurch Street
Tower Hill
Tower Gateway
Aldgate
Aldgate East
St. Paul's
Monument
Barbican Arts & Con Ctr
Guildhall
St Paul's Cath
Tower 42
Swiss Re Bldg
Lloyds Bldg
Petticoat Lane
Old Spitalfields
Columbia Rd
Bunhill Fields Burial Gd
NEW NORTH RD
KINGSLAND RD
QUEENSBRIDGE RD
HACKNEY RD
CITY RD
OLD ST
EAST RD
PITFIELD ST
GREAT EASTERN ST
SHOREDITCH HIGH ST
COMMERCIAL ST
BISHOPSGATE
LONDON WALL
ALDERSGATE ST
BETHNAL GREEN RD
WHITECHAPEL HIGH ST
MINORIES
UPPER THAMES ST
CITY OF

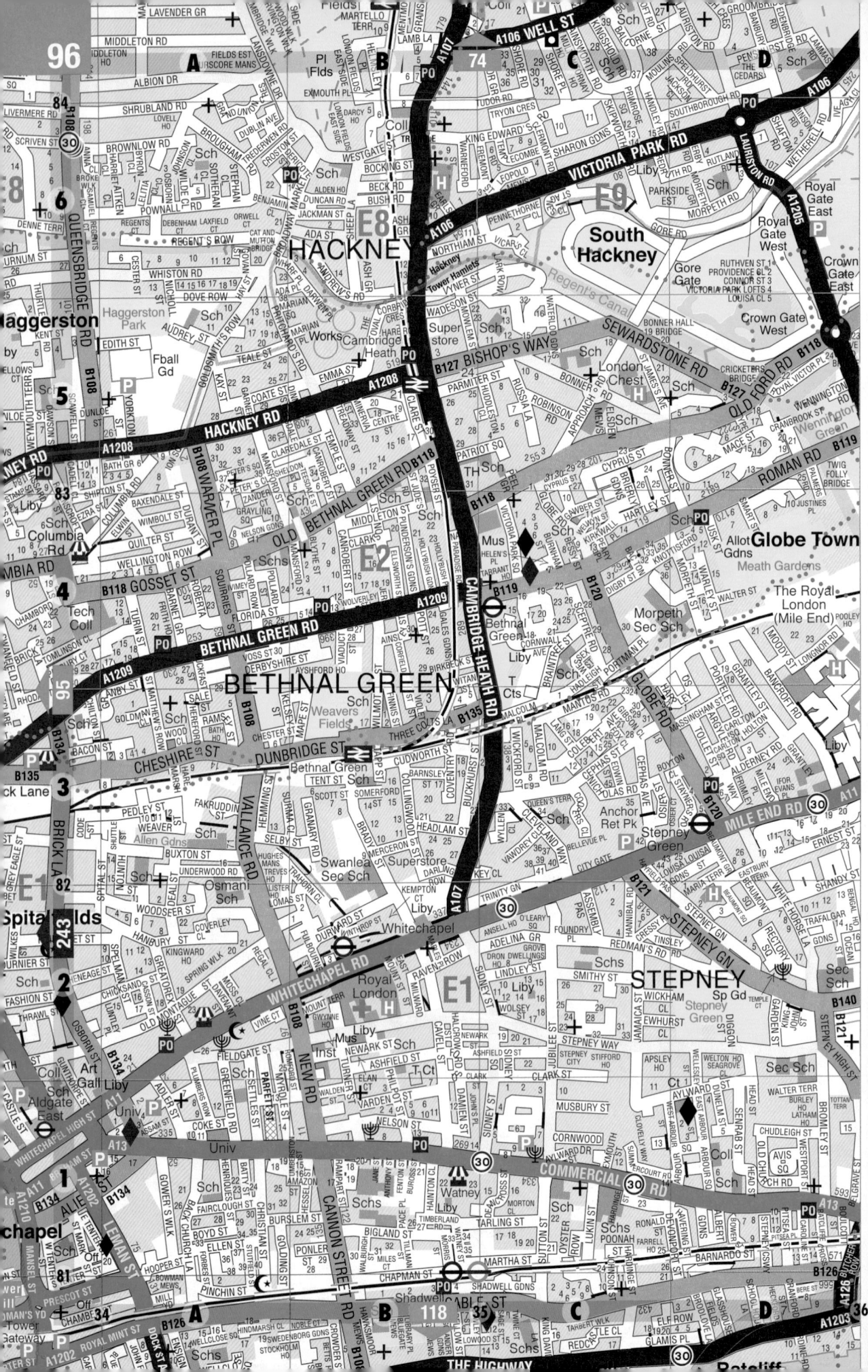
HACKNEY
E8
E9
South Hackney
Haggerston
Haggerston Park
BETHNAL GREEN
E2
Globe Town
Meath Gardens
STEPNEY
E1
Spitalfields
Whitechapel
Shadwell
Ratcliff
QUEENSBRIDGE RD
HACKNEY RD
VICTORIA PARK RD
BISHOP'S WAY
SEWARDSTONE RD
OLD FORD RD
ROMAN RD
OLD BETHNAL GREEN RD
GOSSET ST
BETHNAL GREEN RD
CAMBRIDGE HEATH RD
WARNER PL
CHESHIRE ST
DUNBRIDGE ST
VALLANCE RD
BRICK LA
WHITECHAPEL RD
MILE END RD
STEPNEY GN
COMMERCIAL RD
CANNON STREET RD
NEW RD
LEMAN ST
THE HIGHWAY
GLOBE RD
WELL ST
MARE ST
Regent's Canal
Cambridge Heath
Bethnal Green
Stepney Green
Aldgate East
Royal London
Weavers Fields
Allen Gdns
Osmani Sch
Swanlea Sec Sch
Morpeth Sec Sch
The Royal London (Mile End)
London Chest
Royal Gate East
Royal Gate West
Crown Gate East
Crown Gate West
Gore Gate
Columbia Rd
Anchor Ret Pk
Stepney Green
A B C D
1 2 3 4 5 6
74
95
118
36

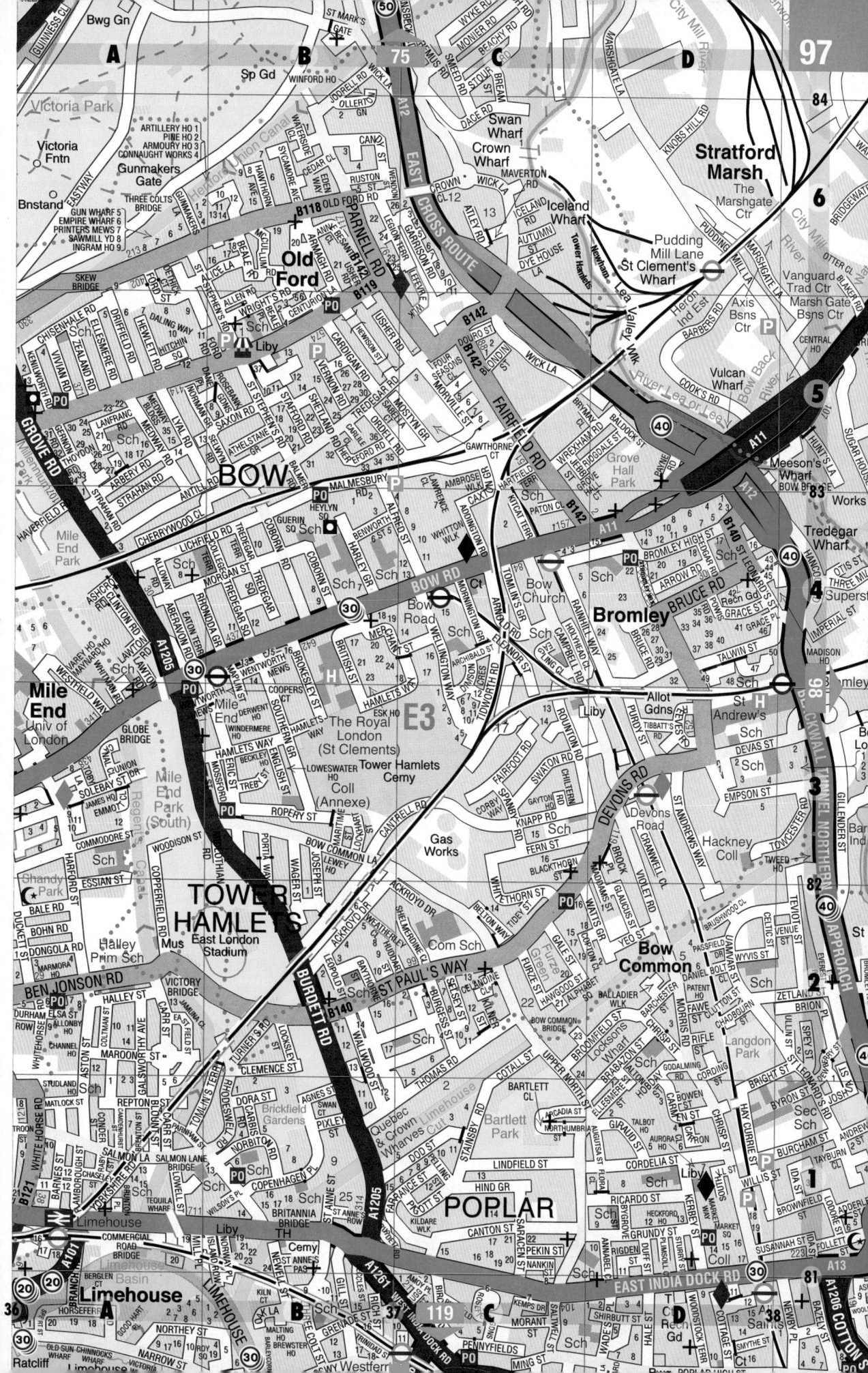

BOW
Old Ford
Bromley
TOWER HAMLETS
POPLAR
Limehouse
Mile End
Stratford Marsh
Bow Common
E3
Victoria Park
Mile End Park
The Royal London (St Clements)
Tower Hamlets Cemy
Gas Works
East London Stadium
Langdon Park
Bartlett Park
Hackney Coll
Mile End Park (South)
Univ of London

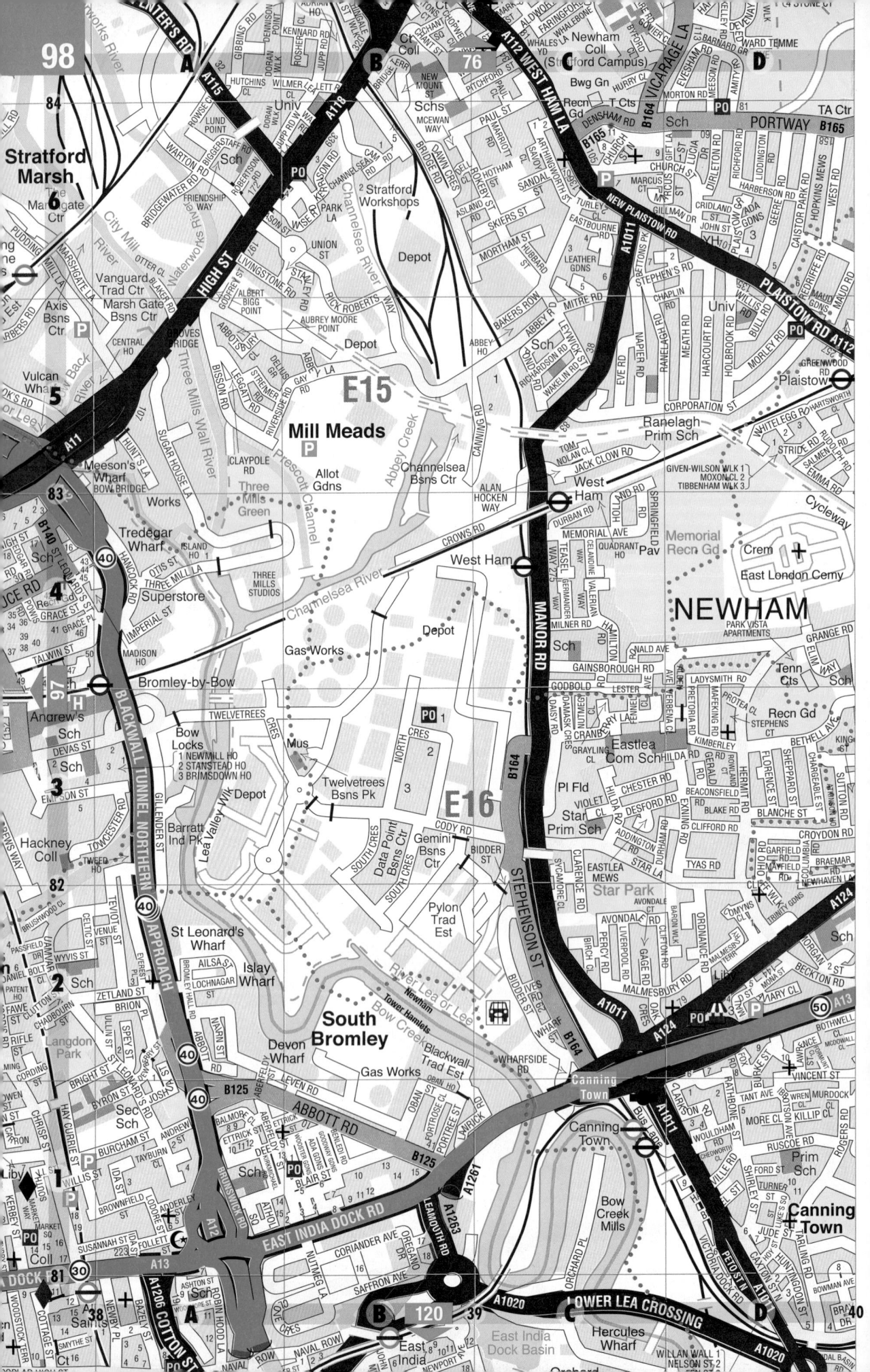
Stratford Marsh
Stratford Workshops
Depot
Newham Coll (Stratford Campus)
Univ
Schs
HIGH ST
A11
A112 WEST HAM LA
NEW PLAISTOW RD
PLAISTOW RD A112
PORTWAY B165
VICARAGE LA B164
Vanguard Trad Ctr
Marsh Gate Bsns Ctr
Axis Bsns Ctr
Vulcan Wharf
City Mill River
Waterworks River
Channelsea River
Three Mills Wall River
Prescott Channel
Abbey Creek
E15
Mill Meads
Allot Gdns
Channelsea Bsns Ctr
Meeson's Wharf
Tredegar Wharf
Three Mills Green
Three Mills Studios
Superstore
Gas Works
Bromley-by-Bow
BLACKWALL TUNNEL NORTHERN APPROACH
Bow Locks
1 NEWMILL HO
2 STANSTEAD HO
3 BRIMSDOWN HO
Mus
Twelvetrees Bsns Pk
Barratt Ind Pk
Lea Valley Wlk
E16
Data Point Bsns Ctr
Gemini Bsns Ctr
Pylon Trad Est
St Leonard's Wharf
Islay Wharf
South Bromley
Devon Wharf
Bow Creek
River Lea or Lee
Blackwall Trad Est
Hackney Coll
Langdon Park
Sec Sch
ABBOTT RD
EAST INDIA DOCK RD
A13
A1206 COTTON ST
Canning Town
Bow Creek Mills
LOWER LEA CROSSING
A1020
East India Dock Basin
Hercules Wharf
West Ham
MANOR RD
Ranelagh Prim Sch
Memorial Recn Gd
Crem
East London Cemy
NEWHAM
Plaistow
Cycleway
Eastlea Com Sch
Star Prim Sch
Star Park
STEPHENSON ST
A1011
A124
76
120
97

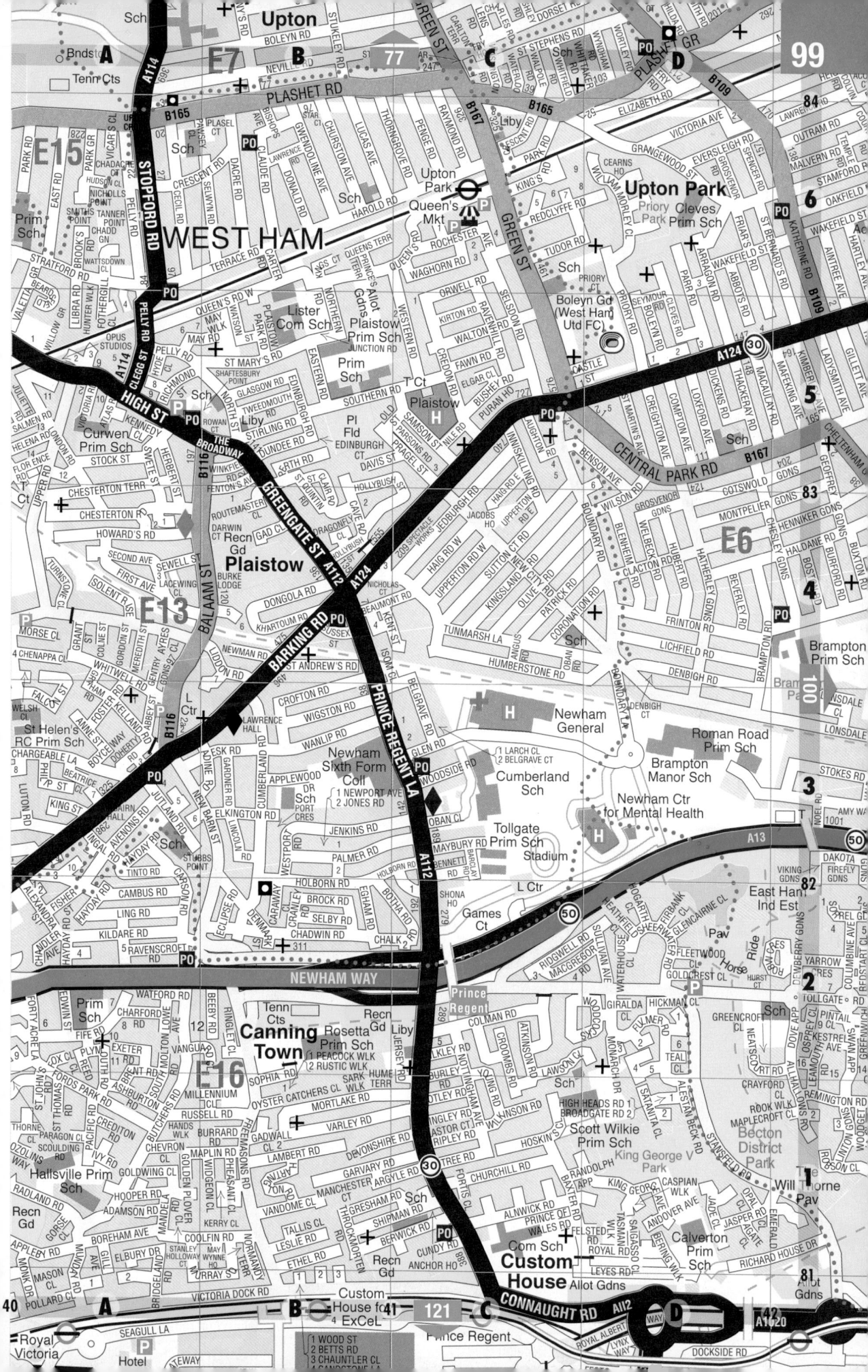
Upton
Upton Park
WEST HAM
Plaistow
Canning Town
Custom House
E7
E15
E13
E6
E16
STOPFORD RD
HIGH ST
THE BROADWAY
GREENGATE ST
BARKING RD
PRINCE REGENT LA
NEWHAM WAY
CONNAUGHT RD
CENTRAL PARK RD
GREEN ST
PLASHET RD
PLASHET GR
BOLEYN RD
BALAAM ST
A114
A124
A112
A13
A1020
B165
B167
B109
B116
Upton Park
Queen's Mkt
Boleyn Gd (West Ham Utd FC)
Plaistow
Newham General
Cumberland Sch
Brampton Manor Sch
Roman Road Prim Sch
Newham Ctr for Mental Health
Tollgate Prim Sch
Stadium
East Ham Ind Est
Becton District Park
King George V Park
Scott Wilkie Prim Sch
Calverton Prim Sch
Newham Sixth Form Coll
Lister Com Sch
Plaistow Prim Sch
Curwen Prim Sch
St Helen's RC Prim Sch
Hallsville Prim Sch
Rosetta Prim Sch
Priory Park
Cleves Prim Sch
Brampton Prim Sch
Prince Regent
Custom House for ExCeL
Royal Victoria
77
100
121
A
B
C
D
1
2
3
4
5
6

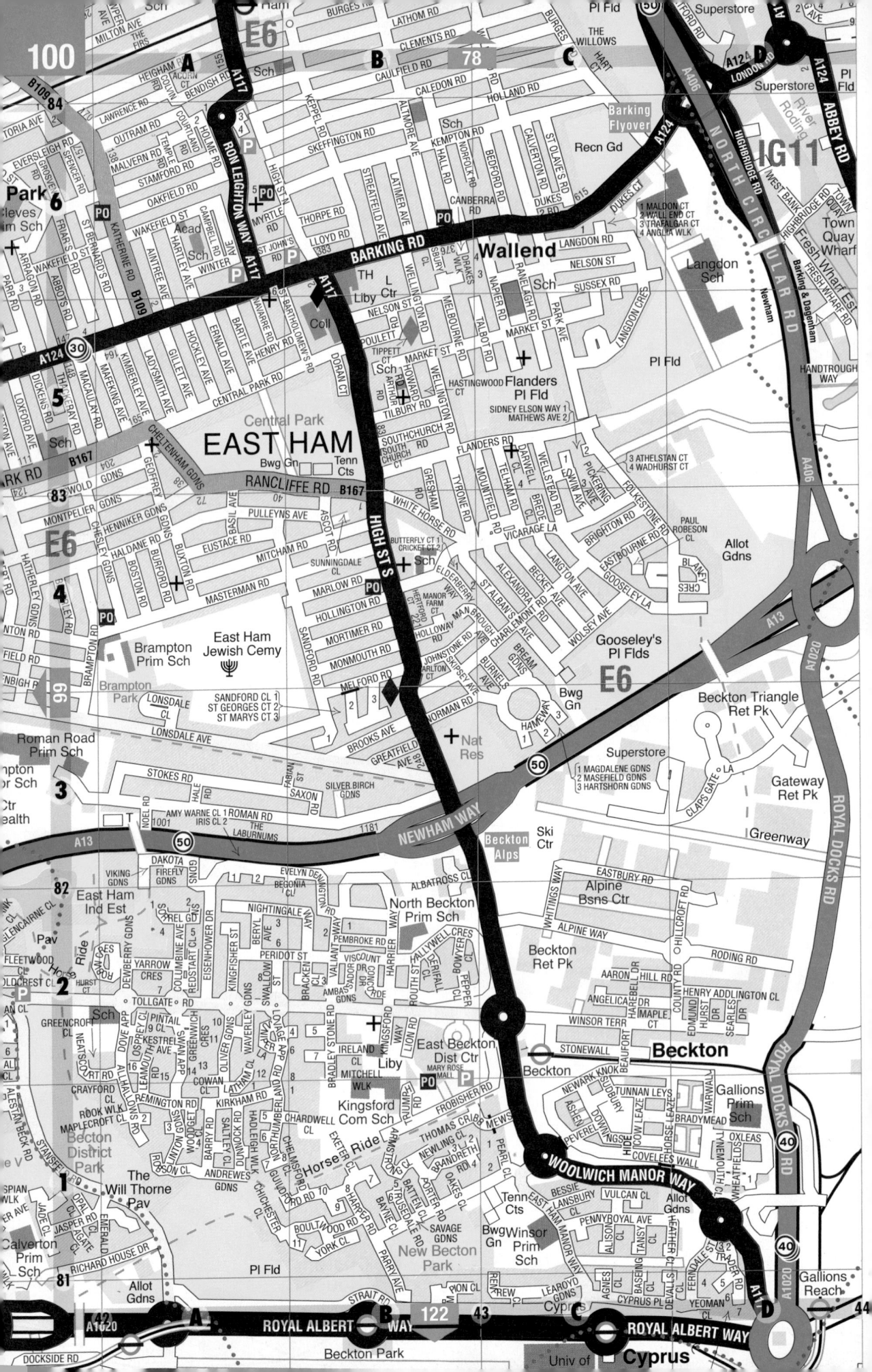
78
A
B
C
D
E6
IG11
BURGES RD
LATHOM RD
CLEMENTS RD
CAULFIELD RD
CALEDON RD
HOLLAND RD
THE WILLOWS
Superstore
Pl Fld
A124
LONDON RD
A406
ABBEY RD
River Roding
Barking Flyover
Recn Gd
NORTH CIRCULAR RD
HIGHBRIDGE RD
WEST BANK
TOWN QUAY
Town Quay Wharf
Fresh Wharf Est
FRESH WHARF RD
Barking & Dagenham
Newham
MILTON AVE
THE FIRS
HEIGHAM RD
ACORN CT
BENDISH RD
COLVIN RD
B109
LAWRENCE RD
OUTRAM RD
MALVERN RD
STAMFORD RD
OAKFIELD RD
EVERSLEIGH RD
GROSVENOR RD
SPENCER RD
TORIA AVE
RON LEIGHTON WAY
A117
HOLME RD
COURTLAND RD
TEMPLE RD
KEPPEL RD
SKEFFINGTON RD
ALTMORE AVE
KEMPTON RD
HALL RD
NORFOLK RD
BEDFORD RD
CALVERTON RD
ST OLAVE'S RD
DUKES RD
DUKES CT
CANBERRA RD
1 MALDON CT
2 WALL END CT
3 TRAFALGAR CT
4 ANGLIA WLK
Park
Cleves Prim Sch
WAKEFIELD ST
ARRAGON RD
FRIARS RD
ST BERNARD'S RD
KATHERINE RD
CAMPBELL RD
HARTLEY AVE
AINTREE AVE
WINTER AVE
Acad
Sch
MYRTLE RD
ST JOHN'S RD
HIGH ST N
STREATFEILD AVE
LATIMER AVE
THORPE RD
LLOYD RD
BARKING RD
Wallend
LANGDON RD
NELSON ST
SUSSEX RD
Langdon Sch
PARR RD
ABBOTS RD
B109
TH
L Ctr
Liby
Coll
NELSON ST
WELLINGTON RD
MELBOURNE RD
NAPIER RD
RANELAGH RD
PARK AVE
LANGDON CRES
MARKET ST
TALBOT RD
A124
DICKENS RD
THACKERAY RD
MACAULAY RD
MAFEKING AVE
KIMBERLEY AVE
LADYSMITH AVE
GILLETT AVE
HOCKLEY AVE
ERNALD AVE
BARTLE AVE
NAVARRE RD
HENRY RD
ST BARTHOLOMEW'S RD
CENTRAL PARK RD
DORAN CT
POULETT RD
TIPPETT CT
ARTHUR RD
HOWARD RD
TILBURY RD
HASTINGWOOD CT
Flanders Pl Fld
SIDNEY ELSON WAY 1
MATHEWS AVE 2
Pl Fld
HANDTROUGH WAY
LOXFORD AVE
Central Park
EAST HAM
Bwg Gn
Tenn Cts
SOUTHCHURCH RD
SOUTH CHURCH CT
FLANDERS RD
CHELTENHAM GDNS
RANCLIFFE RD
B167
GEOFFREY GDNS
GDNS
WOLD
MONTPELIER GDNS
HENNIKER GDNS
HALDANE RD
BOSTON RD
BURFORD RD
BUXTON RD
BASIL AVE
EUSTACE RD
PULLEYNS AVE
MITCHAM RD
MASTERMAN RD
ASCOT RD
SUNNINGDALE CL
HIGH ST S
WHITE HORSE RD
GRESHAM RD
TYRONE RD
MOUNTFIELD RD
TELHAM RD
DARWELL CL
WELLSTEAD RD
BREDE CL
EDWIN AVE
PICKERING AVE
VICARAGE LA
3 ATHELSTAN CT
4 WADHURST CT
FOLKESTONE RD
BRIGHTON RD
EASTBOURNE RD
GOOSELEY LA
PAUL ROBESON CL
BLANEY CRES
Allot Gdns
A406
E6
HATHERLEY GDNS
CHESLEY GDNS
BUTTERFLY CT 1
CRICKET CT 2
Sch
ELDERBERRY WAY
MANOR FARM CT
HERTFORD CT
MARLOW RD
HOLLINGTON RD
MORTIMER RD
MONMOUTH RD
SANDFORD RD
HOLLOWAY RD
MANBROUGH AVE
ST ALBAN'S AVE
ALEXANDRA RD
CHARLEMONT RD
BECKET AVE
LANGTON AVE
WOLSEY AVE
JOHNSTONE RD
CARLTON CT
SKIPSEY AVE
BURNELS AVE
BREAM GDNS
Gooseley's Pl Flds
A13
A1020
BRAMPTON RD
Brampton Prim Sch
East Ham Jewish Cemy
Brampton Park
LONSDALE CL
LONSDALE AVE
SANDFORD CL 1
ST GEORGES CT 2
ST MARYS CT 3
MELFORD RD
BROOKS AVE
NORMAN RD
GREATFIELD AVE
Nat Res
HAMEWAY
Bwg Gn
E6
Beckton Triangle Ret Pk
Superstore
1 MAGDALENE GDNS
2 MASEFIELD GDNS
3 HARTSHORN GDNS
CLAPS GATE LA
Gateway Ret Pk
ROYAL DOCKS RD
Roman Road Prim Sch
STOKES RD
HALE RD
FABIAN ST
SAXON RD
SILVER BIRCH GDNS
NOEL RD
AMY WARNE CL 1
IRIS CL 2
ROMAN RD
THE LABURNUMS
NEWHAM WAY
Beckton Alps
Ski Ctr
Greenway
A13
DAKOTA GDNS
FIREFLY GDNS
VIKING GDNS
EVELYN DENINGTON RD
BEGONIA CL
ALBATROSS CL
EASTBURY RD
WHITINGS WAY
Alpine Bsns Ctr
HILLCROFT RD
ALPINE WAY
East Ham Ind Est
SORREL GDNS
NIGHTINGALE WAY
BERYL AVE
North Beckton Prim Sch
PEMBROKE RD
HARRIER WAY
VALIANT WAY
HALLYWELL CRES
BOWYER CL
Beckton Ret Pk
RODING RD
GLENCAIRNE CL
Pav
FLEETWOOD CL
Horse Ride
ROBINA CL
DEWBERRY GDNS
COLUMBINE AVE
REDSTART CL
EISENHOWER DR
KINGFISHER ST
PERIDOT ST
VISCOUNT DR
CONCORDE DR
AMBASSADOR GDNS
SWALLOW ST
BRACKEN CL
ROUTH ST
DERIFALL CL
PEPPER CL
AARON HILL RD
HAREBELL DR
ANGELICA DR
MAPLE CT
COUNTY RD
EDMUND HURST DR
SEARLES DR
HENRY ADDLINGTON CL
OLDCREST CL
HURST CT
YARROW CRES
TOLLGATE RD
Sch
GREENCROFT CL
DOVE APP
OSPREY CL
PINTAIL CL
KESTREL AVE
SWAN APP
GREENWICH CRES
OLIVER GDNS
WAVERLEY GDNS
LATHAM CL
BRADLEY STONE RD
KINGSFORD WAY
LION RD
IRELAND CL
Liby
East Beckton Dist Ctr
MARY ROSE MALL
WINSOR TERR
STONEWALL
Beckton
Beckton
NEATSCOURT RD
LEAMOUTH RD
ALLHALLOWS RD
COWAN CL
KIRKHAM RD
NORTHUMBERLAND RD
MITCHELL WLK
CRAYFORD CL
ROOK WLK
MAPLECROFT CL
REMINGTON RD
LINTON GDNS
WOODGET CL
BARRY RD
SALTLEY CL
DUNNOCK RD
HADLEIGH WLK
CHARDWELL CL
Kingsford Com Sch
TRIUMPH RD
FROBISHER RD
THOMAS CRIBB MEWS
NEWARK KNOK
SUDBURY
TUNNAN LEYS
ASHEN
DOWNINGS
PEVEREL
HIDE
COW LEAZE
HORSE LEAZE
COVELEES WALL
BRADYMEAD
WARWALL
Gallions Prim Sch
OXLEAS
TYNEMOUTH CL
WHEATFIELDS
Becton District Park
STANSFELD RD
ROBSON CL
ANDREWES GDNS
CHELMSFORD CL
CHICHESTER CL
GUILDFORD RD
EXETER RD
Horse Ride
ARMSTRONG CL
NEWLING CL
BRANDRETH RD
PEARL CL
WOOLWICH MANOR WAY
BESSIE LANSBURY CL
VULCAN CL
Allot Gdns
The Will Thorne Pav
JADE CL
OPAL CL
JASPER RD
AGATE CL
EMERALD
Calverton Prim Sch
RICHARD HOUSE DR
Pl Fld
HARPER RD
BAYNE CL
TRUSEDALE RD
BATTEN CL
PORTER RD
OAKES CL
SAVAGE GDNS
New Becton Park
PARRY AVE
BOULTWOOD RD
YORK CL
Tenn Cts
Bwg Gn
Winsor Prim Sch
EAST HAM MANOR WAY
PENNYROYAL AVE
ALISON CL
TANSY CL
HEATHER CL
FERNDALE ST
TRADER RD
AGNES CL
BASEING CL
DEVALLS CL
CYPRUS PL
YEOMAN CL
LEAROYD GDNS
Gallions Reach
Allot Gdns
STRAIT RD
ROYAL ALBERT WAY
Cyprus
122
42
43
44
A1020
DOCKSIDE RD
Beckton Park
Univ of
Cyprus
81
82
83
84
1
2
3
4
5
6

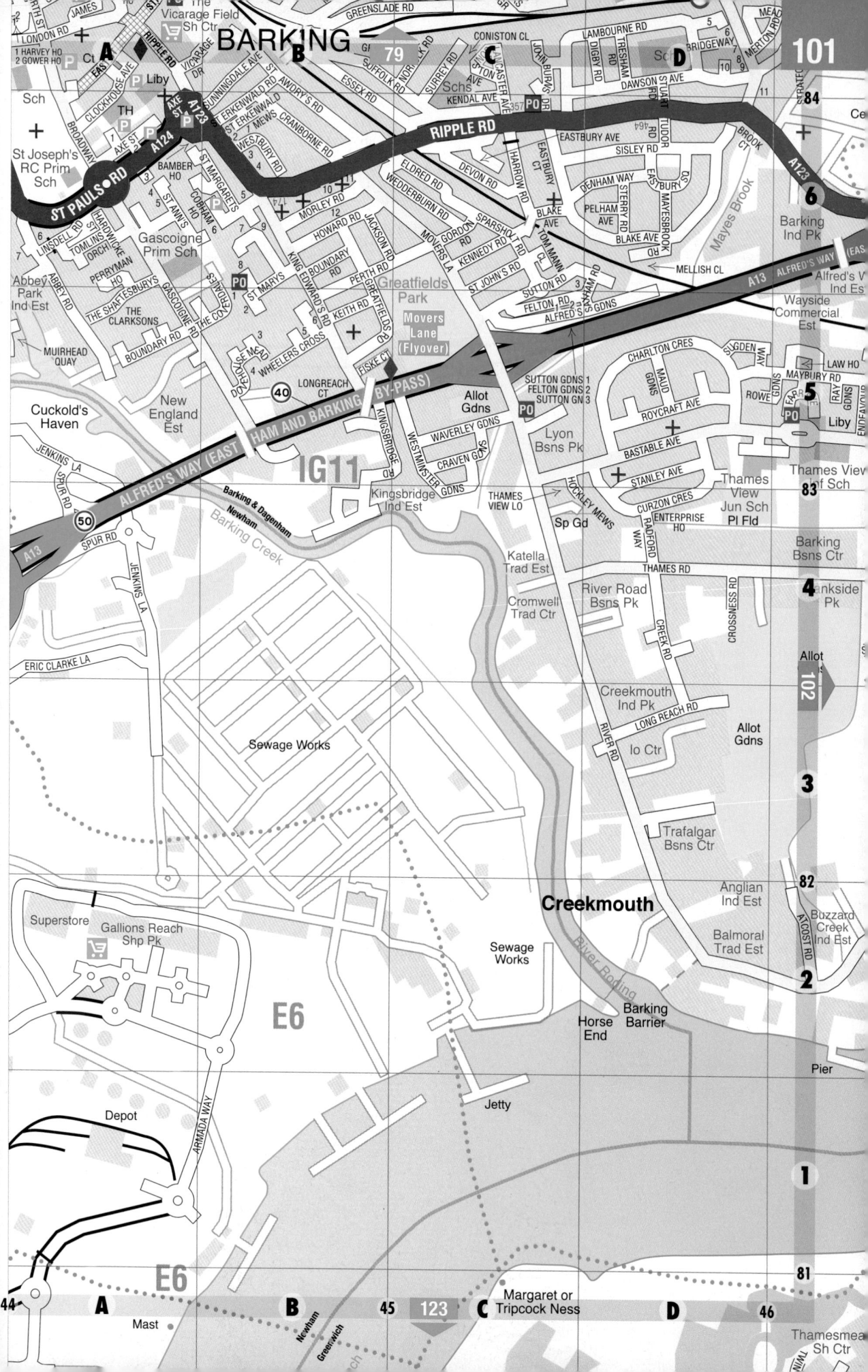
BARKING
Vicarage Field Sh Ctr
St Joseph's RC Prim Sch
Gascoigne Prim Sch
Abbey Park Ind Est
Muirhead Quay
Cuckold's Haven
New England Est
Greatfields Park
Movers Lane (Flyover)
Longreach Ct
Kingsbridge Ind Est
IG11
Alfred's Way (East Ham and Barking By-Pass)
Ripple Rd
St Pauls Rd
Barking Ind Pk
Alfred's Way Ind Est
Wayside Commercial Est
Lyon Bsns Pk
Thames View Inf Sch
Thames View Jun Sch
Barking Bsns Ctr
Katella Trad Est
Cromwell Trad Ctr
River Road Bsns Pk
Creekmouth Ind Pk
Trafalgar Bsns Ctr
Anglian Ind Est
Balmoral Trad Est
Buzzard Creek Ind Est
Barking Creek
Barking & Dagenham
Newham
Sewage Works
Creekmouth
River Roding
Barking Barrier
Horse End
Superstore
Gallions Reach Shp Pk
E6
Depot
Jetty
Pier
Margaret or Tripcock Ness
Thamesmead Sh Ctr
Mast
Newham
Greenwich
Mayes Brook
79
102
123

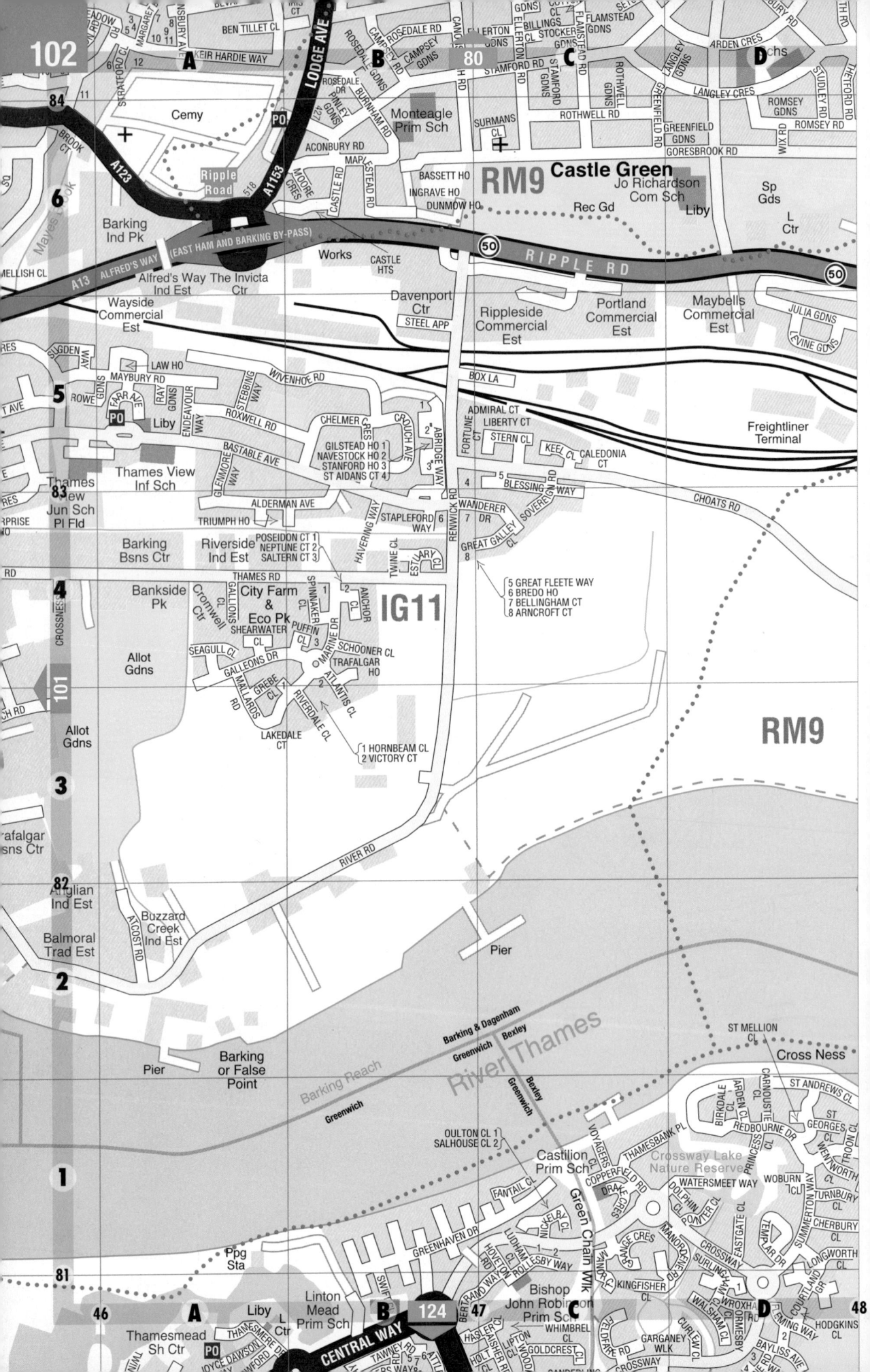
Castle Green
RM9
IG11
Cemy
Ripple Road
LODGE AVE
A1153
A123
A13 ALFRED'S WAY (EAST HAM AND BARKING BY-PASS)
RIPPLE RD
Monteagle Prim Sch
Jo Richardson Com Sch
Liby
Rec Gd
Sp Gds
L Ctr
Barking Ind Pk
Works
Alfred's Way Ind Est
The Invicta Ctr
Wayside Commercial Est
Davenport Ctr
Rippleside Commercial Est
Portland Commercial Est
Maybells Commercial Est
Freightliner Terminal
Thames View Inf Sch
Thames View Jun Sch Pl Fld
Barking Bsns Ctr
Riverside Ind Est
Bankside Pk
City Farm & Eco Pk
Cromwell Ctr
Allot Gdns
Anglian Ind Est
Buzzard Creek Ind Est
Balmoral Trad Est
Pier
Barking or False Point
River Thames
Barking Reach
Cross Ness
Crossway Lake Nature Reserve
Castilion Prim Sch
Green Chain Wlk
Bishop John Robinson Prim Sch
Linton Mead Prim Sch
Thamesmead Sh Ctr
Ppg Sta
CENTRAL WAY
RIVER RD
RENWICK RD
CHOATS RD
THAMES RD
5 GREAT FLEETE WAY
6 BREDO HO
7 BELLINGHAM CT
8 ARNCROFT CT
1 HORNBEAM CL
2 VICTORY CT
1 OULTON CL
2 SALHOUSE CL
80
101
124
A B C D
1 2 3 4 5 6
46 47 48
81 82 83 84

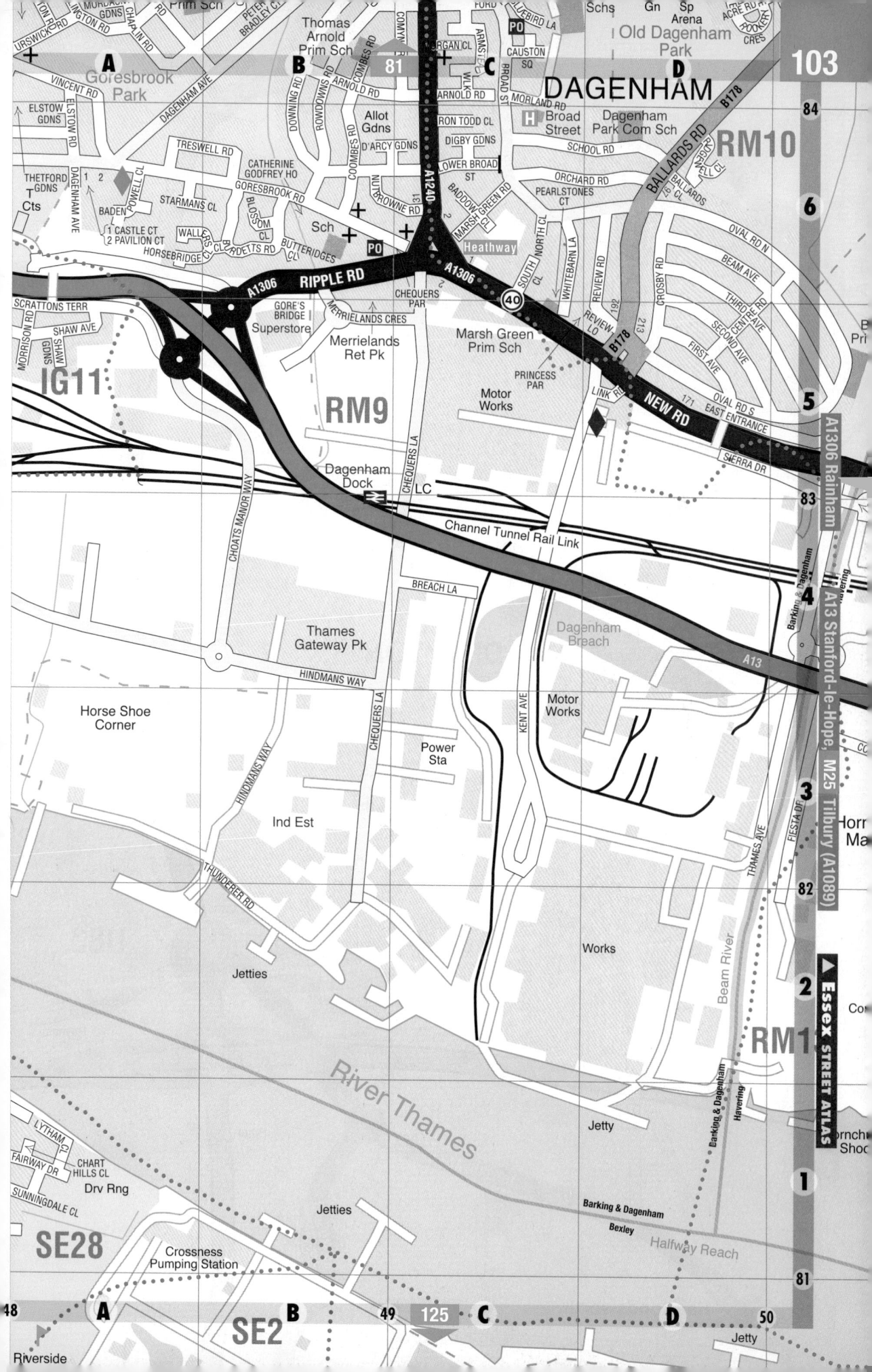
103
DAGENHAM
Old Dagenham Park
Goresbrook Park
Thomas Arnold Prim Sch
Allot Gdns
Broad Street
Dagenham Park Com Sch
RM10
RIPPLE RD
A1306
A1240
NEW RD
BALLARDS RD
B178
Heathway
Merrielands Ret Pk
Superstore
Marsh Green Prim Sch
Motor Works
IG11
RM9
Dagenham Dock
LC
Channel Tunnel Rail Link
CHOATS MANOR WAY
CHEQUERS LA
BREACH LA
Thames Gateway Pk
HINDMANS WAY
Dagenham Breach
A13
KENT AVE
Horse Shoe Corner
Power Sta
Ind Est
THUNDERER RD
Jetties
Works
Beam River
THAMES AVE
FIESTA DR
River Thames
Jetty
Barking & Dagenham
Bexley
Havering
Halfway Reach
SE28
SE2
Crossness Pumping Station
Drv Rng
CHART HILLS CL
FAIRWAY DR
SUNNINGDALE CL
LYTHAM CL
Riverside
A1306 Rainham
A13 Stanford-le-Hope, M25 Tilbury (A1089)
Essex STREET ATLAS
81
125
48
49
50
84
83
82
81

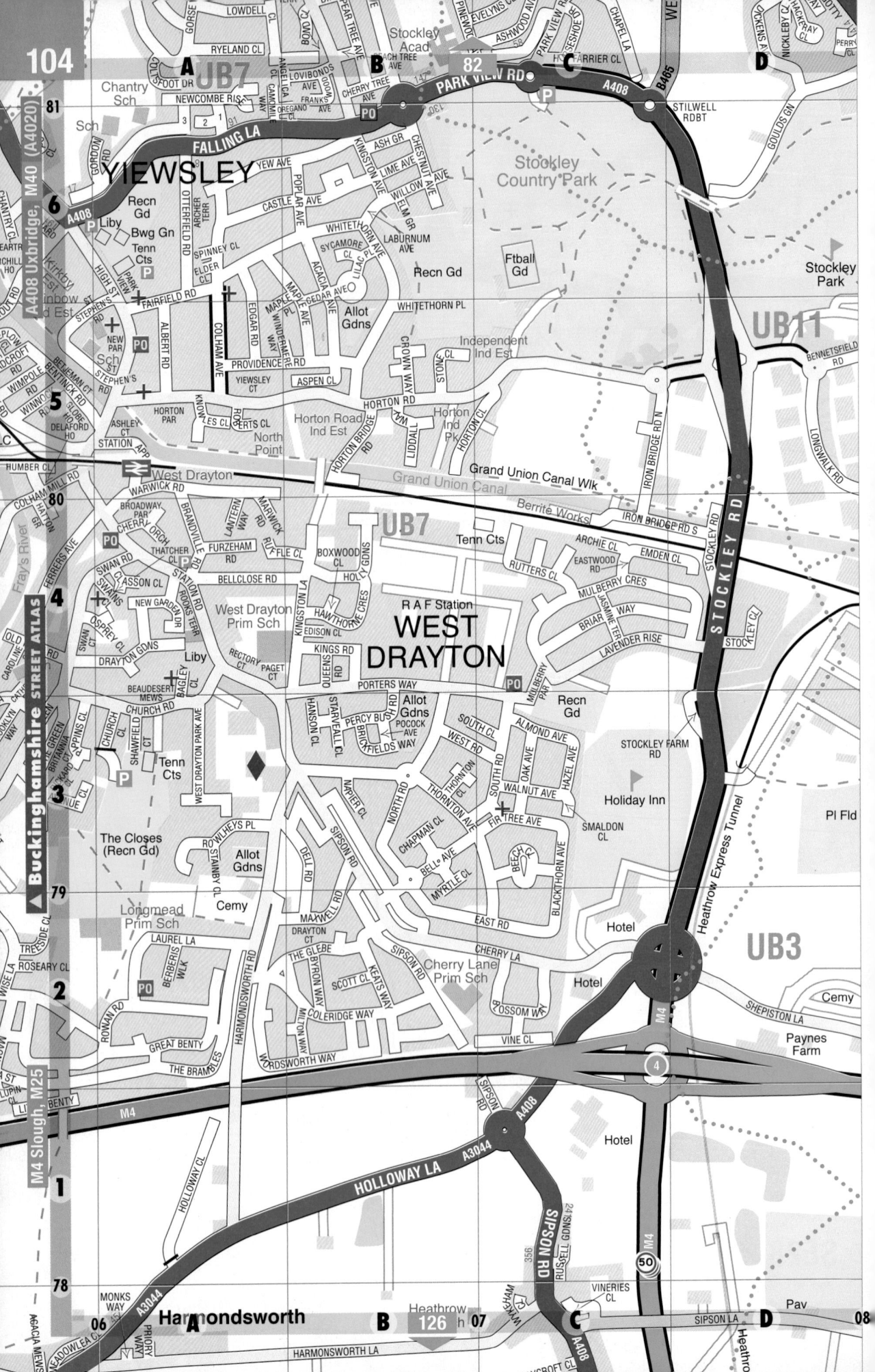

104
A408 Uxbridge, M40 (A4020)
Buckinghamshire STREET ATLAS
M4 Slough, M25
A
B
C
D
82
126
81
80
79
78
6
5
4
3
2
1
06
07
08
UB7
UB11
UB3
YIEWSLEY
WEST DRAYTON
R A F Station
Harmondsworth
Stockley Country Park
Stockley Park
Stockley Acad
Chantry Sch
FALLING LA
PARK VIEW RD
A408
B465
STILWELL RDBT
STOCKLEY RD
Grand Union Canal
Grand Union Canal Wlk
Berrite Works
IRON BRIDGE RD N
IRON BRIDGE RD S
Independent Ind Est
Horton Road Ind Est
Horton Ind Pk
HORTON RD
HORTON BRIDGE RD
North Point
West Drayton
West Drayton Prim Sch
Longmead Prim Sch
Cherry Lane Prim Sch
The Closes (Recn Gd)
Holiday Inn
Heathrow Express Tunnel
HOLLOWAY LA
A3044
SIPSON RD
SIPSON LA
HARMONDSWORTH LA
HARMONDSWORTH RD
CHERRY LA
SHEPISTON LA
Paynes Farm
STOCKLEY FARM RD
PORTERS WAY
STATION RD
KINGSTON LA
COLHAM AVE
FAIRFIELD RD
PROVIDENCE RD
WHITETHORN PL
CASTLE AVE
YEW AVE
HIGH ST
WARWICK RD
BELLCLOSE RD
DRAYTON GDNS
CHURCH RD
WEST DRAYTON PARK AVE
EAST RD
WEST RD
SOUTH RD
NORTH RD
WORDSWORTH WAY
COLERIDGE WAY
GREAT BENTY
THE BRAMBLES
LAUREL LA
MULBERRY CRES
LAVENDER RISE
ARCHIE CL
EMDEN CL
RUTTERS CL
Fray's River
M4
4
50
Hotel
Cemy
Pl Fld
Pav

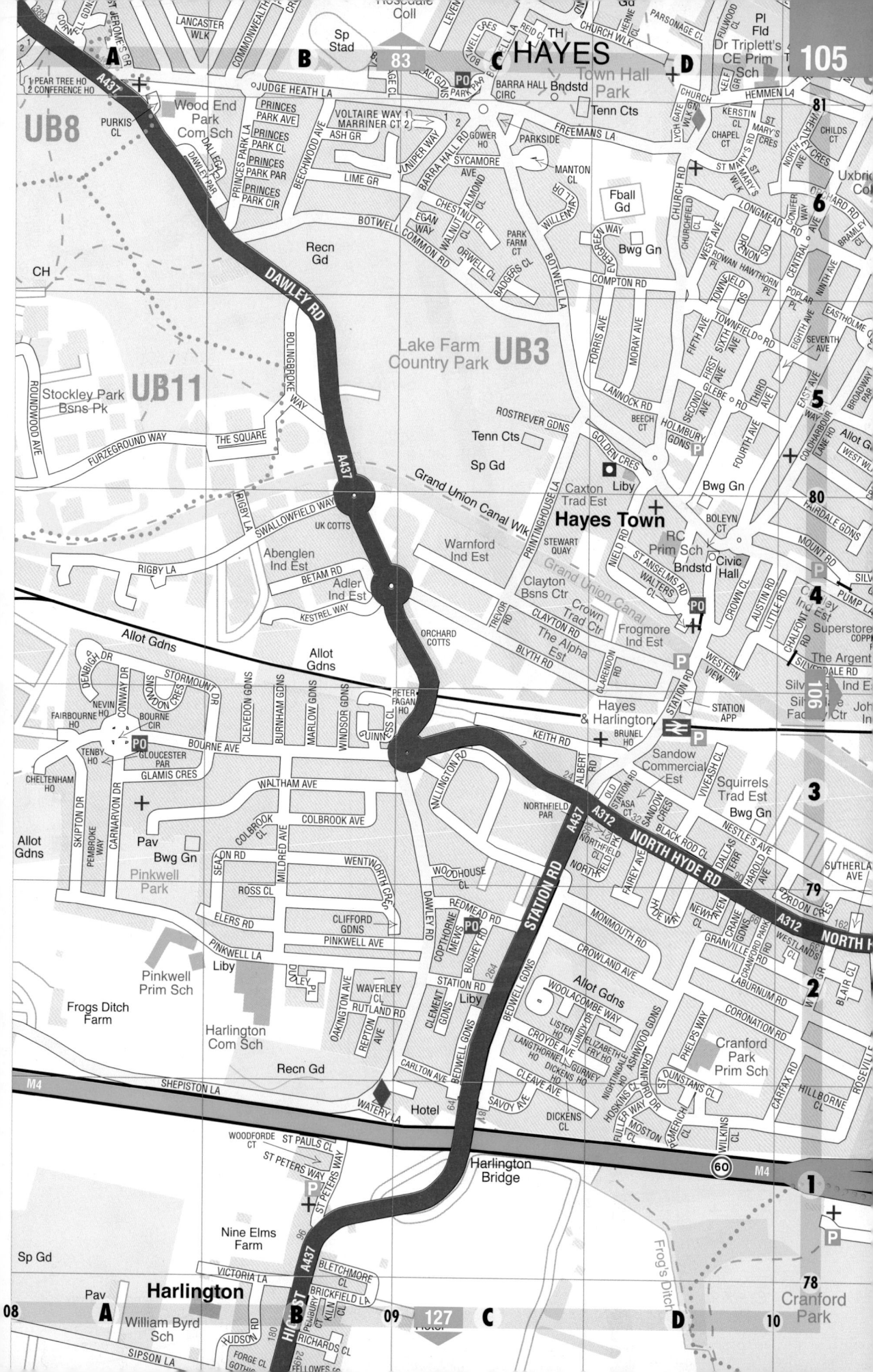
HAYES
UB8
UB3
UB11
Hayes Town
Harlington
Lake Farm Country Park
Stockley Park Bsns Pk
Grand Union Canal
Grand Union Canal Wlk
DAWLEY RD
STATION RD
NORTH HYDE RD
Hayes & Harlington
Harlington Bridge
Pinkwell Park
Cranford Park
M4

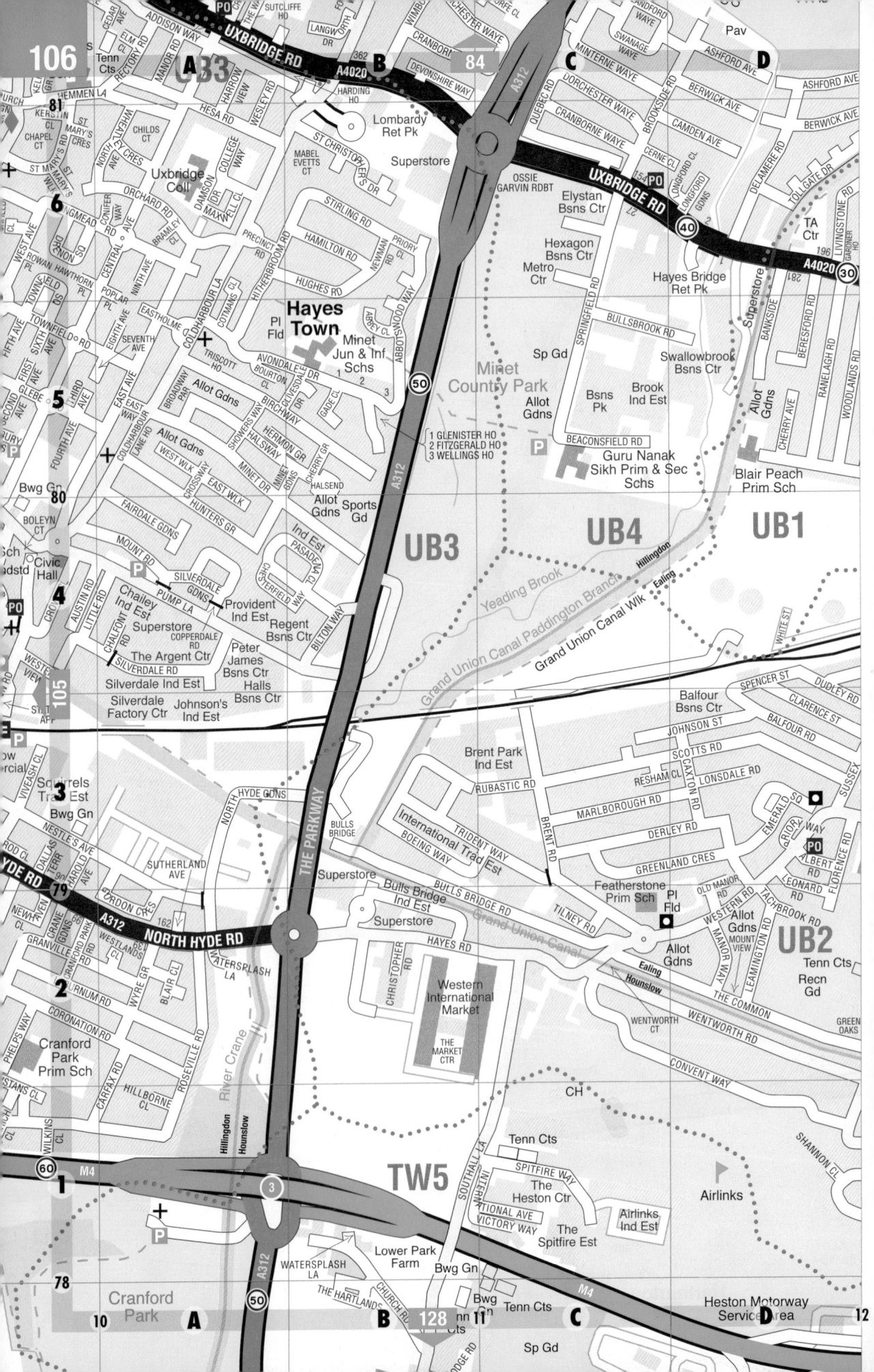
UXBRIDGE RD
A4020
ADDISON WAY
SUTCLIFFE HO
LANGWORTH DR
CRANBORNE RD
DEVONSHIRE WAY
84
A312
MINTERNE WAYE
SWANAGE WAYE
ASHFORD AVE
Pav
HEMMEN LA
Tenn Cts
MANOR RD
HARROW VIEW
WESLEY RD
HARDING HO
HESA RD
CHILDS CT
Lombardy Ret Pk
ST CHRISTOPHER'S DR
MABEL EVETTS CT
Superstore
QUEBEC RD
DORCHESTER WAYE
CRANBORNE WAYE
BROOKSIDE RD
BERWICK AVE
CAMDEN AVE
CERNE CL
LONGFORD CL
DELAMERE RD
TOLLGATE DR
CHAPEL CT
ST MARY'S CRES
WHEATLEY CRES
Uxbridge Coll
COLLEGE WAY
DAMSON DR
MAXWELL CL
OSSIE GARVIN RDBT
Elystan Bsns Ctr
LIVINGSTONE RD
TA Ctr
ORCHARD RD
BRAMLEY CL
STIRLING RD
HAMILTON RD
PRIORY CL
NEWMAN RD
Hexagon Bsns Ctr
Metro Ctr
Hayes Bridge Ret Pk
HUGHES RD
PRECINCT RD
HITHERBROOM RD
COLDHARBOUR LA
COTMANS CL
NINTH AVE
CENTRAL AVE
POPLAR AVE
EIGHTH AVE
SEVENTH AVE
EASTHOLME
TOWNFIELD RD
FIFTH AVE
SIXTH AVE
FIRST AVE
Hayes Town
Pl Fld
Minet Jun & Inf Schs
ABBOTSWOOD WAY
ABBEY CL
AVONDALE DR
BOURTON CL
TRISCOTT HO
CLIVESDALE DR
GADE CL
SPRINGFIELD RD
BULLSBROOK RD
Sp Gd
Swallowbrook Bsns Ctr
BANKSIDE
BERESFORD RD
RANELAGH RD
WOODLANDS RD
Minet Country Park
Allot Gdns
Bsns Pk
Brook Ind Est
BEACONSFIELD RD
1 GLENISTER HO
2 FITZGERALD HO
3 WELLINGS HO
Guru Nanak Sikh Prim & Sec Schs
CHERRY AVE
Blair Peach Prim Sch
EAST AVE
EAST WAY
BROADWAY PAR
SHOWERS WAY
BIRCHWAY
HALSWAY
HERMON GR
CHERRY GR
MINET DR
MINET GDNS
HALSEND
WEST WLK
EAST WLK
CROSSWAY
HUNTERS GR
FAIRDALE GDNS
FOURTH AVE
THIRD AVE
GLEBE AVE
SECOND AVE
Bwg Gn
80
BOLEYN CT
Civic Hall
Sports Gd
Ind Est
PASADENA CL
UB3
UB4
UB1
Yeading Brook
Grand Union Canal Paddington Branch
Grand Union Canal Wlk
Hillingdon
Ealing
MOUNT RD
SILVERDALE GDNS
PUMP LA
AUSTIN RD
LITTLE RD
Chailey Ind Est
Superstore
COPPERDALE RD
Provident Ind Est
Regent Bsns Ctr
CHESTERFIELD WAY
BILTON WAY
WHITE ST
CHALFONT RD
The Argent Ctr
SILVERDALE RD
Silverdale Ind Est
Silverdale Factory Ctr
Peter James Bsns Ctr
Halls Bsns Ctr
Johnson's Ind Est
105
SPENCER ST
DUDLEY RD
CLARENCE ST
BALFOUR RD
Balfour Bsns Ctr
JOHNSON ST
SCOTTS RD
Brent Park Ind Est
RESHAM CL
LONSDALE RD
CAXTON RD
SUSSEX
VIVEASH CL
Squirrels Trad Est
Bwg Gn
HYDE GDNS
NORTH
RUBASTIC RD
BRENT RD
MARLBOROUGH RD
EMERALD SQ
PRIORY WAY
DERLEY RD
NESTLE'S AVE
DALLAS TERR
HAROLD AVE
SUTHERLAND AVE
BULLS BRIDGE
International Trad Est
TRIDENT WAY
BOEING WAY
GREENLAND CRES
ALBERT RD
FLORENCE RD
LEONARD RD
THE PARKWAY
Superstore
Bulls Bridge Ind Est
BULLS BRIDGE RD
Featherstone Prim Sch
Pl Fld
OLD MANOR RD
WESTERN RD
TACHBROOK RD
TILNEY RD
NORTH HYDE RD
79
GORDON CRES
CRANE GDNS
CRANFORD PARK RD
WESTLANDS CL
GRANVILLE RD
162
Superstore
HAYES RD
Grand Union Canal
Allot Gdns
MANOR WAY
MOUNT VIEW
LEAMINGTON RD
UB2
Tenn Cts
Recn Gd
WATERSPLASH LA
WYRE GR
BLAIR CL
LABURNUM RD
CHRISTOPHER RD
Western International Market
Ealing
Hounslow
THE COMMON
CORONATION RD
WENTWORTH CT
WENTWORTH RD
GREEN OAKS
Cranford Park Prim Sch
CARFAX RD
ROSEVILLE RD
HILLBORNE CL
River Crane
THE MARKET CTR
CONVENT WAY
CH
PHELPS WAY
WILKINS CL
Hillingdon
Hounslow
Tenn Cts
SHANNON CL
M4
60
1
TW5
SOUTHALL LA
SPITFIRE WAY
The Heston Ctr
INTERNATIONAL AVE
VICTORY WAY
Airlinks Ind Est
The Spitfire Est
Airlinks
3
WATERSPLASH LA
Lower Park Farm
Bwg Gn
THE HARTLANDS
CHURCH RD
78
50
Cranford Park
10
A
B
128
11
C
Tenn Cts
Heston Motorway Service Area
D
12
Sp Gd

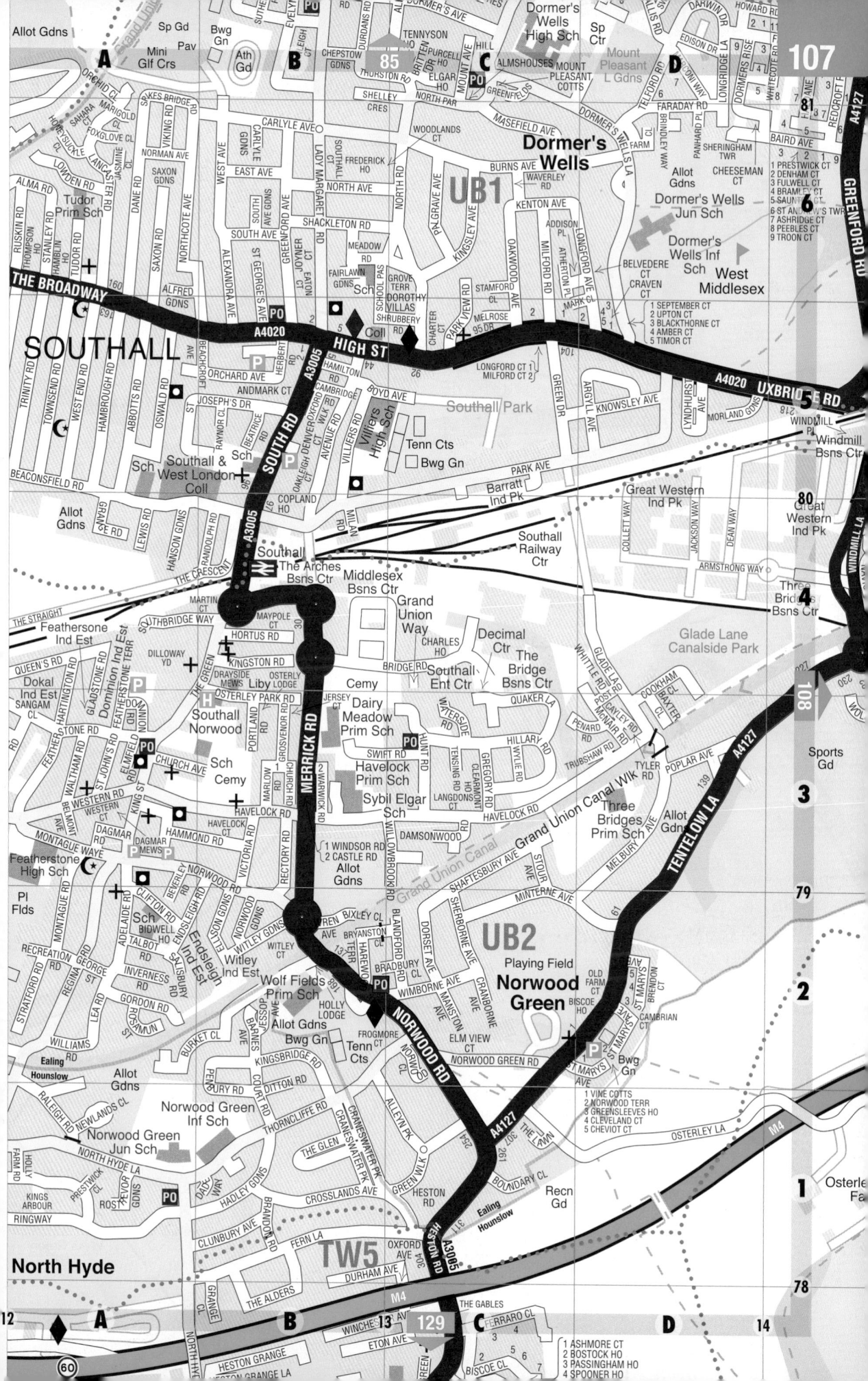
Allot Gdns
Sp Gd
Pav
Bwg Gn
Mini Glf Crs
Ath Gd
Grand Union
A
B
C
D
85
Dormer's Wells High Sch
Sp Ctr
Mount Pleasant L Gdns
DORMER'S AVE
TENNYSON HO
PURCELL HO
ELGAR HO
BRITTEN DR
MOUNT AVE
HILL
ALMSHOUSES
MOUNT PLEASANT COTTS
GREENFIELDS
CHEPSTOW GDNS
THURSTON RD
SHELLEY CRES
NORTH PAR
DURDANS RD
EVELYN
LEIGH CT
DARWIN DR
EDISON DR
HOWARD RD
LONGRIDGE LA
DORMERS RISE
WHITECOTE RD
REDCROFT
TELFORD RD
MARCONI WAY
FARADAY RD
BRINDLEY WAY
PANHARD PL
DORMER'S WELLS LA
FARM
MASEFIELD AVE
WOODLANDS CT
CARLYLE AVE
FREDERICK HO
Dormer's Wells
BURNS AVE
WAVERLEY RD
UB1
KENTON AVE
ADDISON PL
ATHERTON PL
LONGFORD AVE
MILFORD RD
OAKWOOD AVE
KINGSLEY AVE
PALGRAVE AVE
NORTH RD
SHERINGHAM TWR
CHEESEMAN CT
Allot Gdns
BAIRD AVE
1 PRESTWICK CT
2 DENHAM CT
3 FULWELL CT
4 BRAMLEY CT
5 SAUNTON CT
6 ST ANDREW'S TWR
7 ASHRIDGE CT
8 PEEBLES CT
9 TROON CT
81
A4127
GREENFORD RD
Dormer's Wells Jun Sch
Dormer's Wells Inf Sch
West Middlesex
BELVEDERE CT
CRAVEN CT
1 SEPTEMBER CT
2 UPTON CT
3 BLACKTHORNE CT
4 AMBER CT
5 TIMOR CT
MARK CL
ORCHID CL
HONEYSUCKLE CL
SAHARA CT
MARIGOLD CL
FOXGLOVE CL
JASMINE CL
LANCASTER RD
LOWDEN RD
SYKES BRIDGE RD
VIKING RD
NORMAN AVE
SAXON GDNS
DANE RD
ALMA RD
Tudor Prim Sch
RUSKIN RD
THOMPSON HO
STANLEY RD
HAMBLIN HO
TUDOR RD
SAXON RD
NORTHCOTE AVE
WEST AVE
CARLYLE GDNS
EAST AVE
SOUTH AVE
SOUTH AVE GDNS
NORTH AVE
GREENFORD AVE
LADY MARGARET RD
SOUTHALL CT
SHACKLETON RD
MEADOW RD
JOYNER CT
EATON CT
FAIRLAWN GDNS
Sch
SCHOOL PAS
GROVE TERR
DOROTHY VILLAS
SHRUBBERY RD
CHARTER CT
PARK VIEW RD
STAMFORD CL
MELROSE DR
THE BROADWAY
160
163
ALFRED GDNS
ALEXANDRA AVE
ST GEORGE'S AVE
PO
Coll
A4020
HIGH ST
SOUTHALL
BEACHCROFT AVE
HERBERT RD
ORCHARD AVE
ANDMARK CT
HAMILTON RD
CAMBRIDGE RD
BOYD AVE
A3005
LONGFORD CT 1
MILFORD CT 2
GREEN DR
ARGYLL AVE
KNOWSLEY AVE
LYNDHURST AVE
MORLAND GDNS
UXBRIDGE RD
218
WINDMILL PL
Windmill Bsns Ctr
Southall Park
TRINITY RD
TOWNSEND RD
WEST END RD
HAMBROUGH RD
ABBOTTS RD
OSWALD RD
ST JOSEPH'S DR
RAYNOR CL
BEATRICE RD
SOUTH RD
OAKLEIGH CT
DENVER CT
OXFORD WLK
AVENUE RD
VILLIERS RD
Villiers High Sch
Tenn Cts
Bwg Gn
Sch
Southall & West London Coll
BEACONSFIELD RD
PARK AVE
Barratt Ind Pk
Great Western Ind Pk
COLLETT WAY
JACKSON WAY
DEAN WAY
80
Great Western Ind Pk
WINDMILL LA
Allot Gdns
GRANGE RD
LEWIS RD
HANSON GDNS
RANDOLPH RD
COPLAND HO
MILAN RD
Southall Railway Ctr
ARMSTRONG WAY
THE CRESCENT
Southall
The Arches Bsns Ctr
Middlesex Bsns Ctr
Grand Union Way
Three Bridges Bsns Ctr
4
THE STRAIGHT
MARTIN CT
SOUTHBRIDGE WAY
MAYPOLE CT
HORTUS RD
Feathersone Ind Est
Dominion Ind Est
DILLOWAY YD
CHARLES HO
Decimal Ctr
The Bridge Bsns Ctr
Glade Lane Canalside Park
QUEEN'S RD
GLADSTONE RD
FEATHERSTONE TERR
Dokal Ind Est
SANGAM CL
HARTINGTON RD
KINGSTON RD
DRAYSIDE MEWS
Liby
OSTERLY LODGE
OSTERLEY PARK RD
BRIDGE RD
Southall Ent Ctr
Cemy
GLADE LA
WHITTLE RD
POST RD
CAYLEY RD
MCNAIR RD
COOKHAM CL
BAXTER CL
108
Southall Norwood
DOMINION RD
JERSEY CT
Dairy Meadow Prim Sch
WYTERSIDE RD
QUAKER LA
PENARD RD
TRUBSHAW RD
FEATHERSTONE RD
WALTHAM RD
ST JOHN'S RD
ELMFIELD RD
PORTLAND RD
GROSVENOR RD
MERRICK RD
HUNT RD
HILLARY RD
WYLIE RD
TYLER RD
POPLAR AVE
Sports Gd
CHURCH AVE
Sch
Cemy
MARLOW CT
CHURCH RD
WARWICK RD
SWIFT RD
Havelock Prim Sch
TENSING RD
CLEARMONT HO
GREGORY RD
139
A4127
TENTELOW LA
WESTERN RD
BELMONT AVE
WESTERN CT
KING ST
HAVELOCK RD
Sybil Elgar Sch
LANGDONS CT
HAVELOCK RD
Grand Union Canal Wlk
Three Bridges Prim Sch
Allot Gdns
3
DAGMAR RD
HAVELOCK CT
DAGMAR MEWS
HAMMOND RD
VICTORIA RD
RECTORY RD
DAMSONWOOD RD
MELBURY AVE
MONTAGUE WAYE
Featherstone High Sch
NORWOOD RD
BEVERLEY RD
1 WINDSOR RD
2 CASTLE RD
Allot Gdns
Grand Union Canal
SHAFTESBURY AVE
STOUR AVE
Pl Flds
MONTAGUE RD
ADELAIDE RD
CLIFTON RD
ENDSLEIGH RD
ELLISON GDNS
NORWOOD GDNS
WILLOWBROOK RD
MINTERNE AVE
79
Sch
BIDWELL HO
TALBOT RD
Endsleigh Ind Est
WITLEY GDNS
WREN AVE
BIXLEY CL
BRYANSTON CT
BLANDFORD RD
DORSET AVE
SHERBORNE AVE
61
UB2
WITLEY CT
Witley Ind Est
HAREWOOD TERR
BRADBURY CL
RECREATION RD
GEORGE ST
STRATFORD RD
REGINA RD
INVERNESS RD
SALISBURY RD
Wolf Fields Prim Sch
WIMBORNE AVE
Playing Field
Norwood Green
OLD FARM CT
BISCOE HO
ST MARYS AVE
BRENDON CT
CAMBRIAN CL
2
GORDON RD
LEA RD
ROSAMUN ST
JESSOP AVE
HOLLY LODGE
NORWOOD RD
MANSTON AVE
CRANBORNE AVE
Allot Gdns
Bwg Gn
Tenn Cts
FROGMORE CT
ELM VIEW CT
WILLIAMS RD
BURKET CL
BARNES AVE
KINGSBRIDGE RD
NORWOOD CL
NORWOOD GREEN RD
ST MARYS AVE
Bwg Gn
Ealing
Hounslow
Allot Gdns
PENBURY RD
COURT RD
DITTON RD
1 VINE COTTS
2 NORWOOD TERR
3 GREENSLEEVES HO
4 CLEVELAND CT
5 CHEVIOT CT
RALEIGH RD
NEWLANDS CL
Norwood Green Inf Sch
THORNCLIFFE RD
CRANESWATER
CRANESWATER PK
A4127
THE LAWN
OSTERLEY LA
M4
Norwood Green Jun Sch
NORTH HYDE LA
THE GLEN
ALLEYN PK
254
307
261
HOLLY FARM RD
PRESTWICK CL
ROSTREVOR GDNS
DADE WAY
HADLEY GDNS
GREEN WLK
BOUNDARY CL
Recn Gd
1
Osterley Fa
KINGS ARBOUR
RINGWAY
CLUNBURY AVE
BRANDON RD
CROSSLANDS AVE
HESTON RD
Ealing
Hounslow
311
HESTON RD
A3005
FERN LA
TW5
OXFORD AVE
304
North Hyde
DURHAM AVE
GRANGE CL
THE ALDERS
M4
78
THE GABLES
12
A
B
C
D
13
14
129
WINCHESTER AV
ETON AVE
FERRARO CL
1 ASHMORE CT
2 BOSTOCK HO
3 PASSINGHAM HO
4 SPOONER HO
HESTON GRANGE
HESTON GRANGE LA
NORTH HYDE
BISCOE CL
60

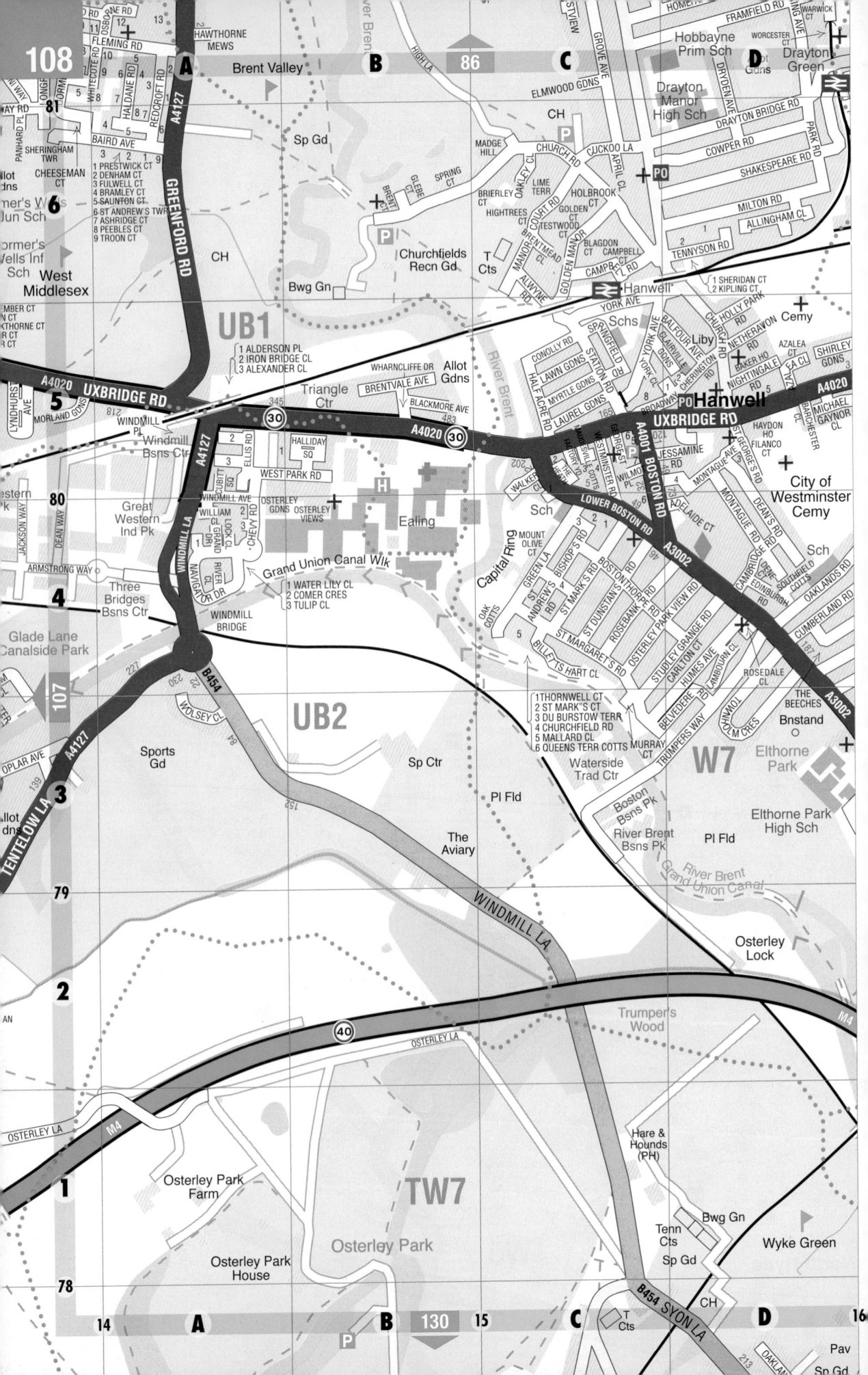

HAWTHORNE MEWS
Brent Valley
86
HIGH LA
GROVE AVE
FRAMFIELD RD
Hobbayne Prim Sch
Drayton Green
ELMWOOD GDNS
Drayton Manor High Sch
DRAYTON BRIDGE RD
COWPER RD
SHAKESPEARE RD
MILTON RD
ALLINGHAM CL
TENNYSON RD
FLEMING RD
WHITECOTE RD
HALDANE RD
REDCROFT RD
BAIRD AVE
SHERINGHAM TWR
CHEESEMAN CT
1 PRESTWICK CT
2 DENHAM CT
3 FULWELL CT
4 BRAMLEY CT
5 SAUNTON CT
6 ST ANDREW'S TWR
7 ASHRIDGE CT
8 PEEBLES CT
9 TROON CT
GREENFORD RD
A4127
Sp Gd
CH
MADGE HILL
CHURCH RD
CUCKOO LA
APRIL CL
SPRING CT
GLEBE CT
BRENT CT
OAKLEY CL
LIME TERR
BRIERLEY CT
HIGHTREES CT
HOLBROOK CT
GOLDEN CT
TESTWOOD CT
BLAGDON CT
CAMPBELL CT
MANOR COURT RD
BRENTMEAD CL
GOLDEN MANOR
ALWYNE RD
Churchfields Recn Gd
T Cts
Bwg Gn
Hanwell
1 SHERIDAN CT
2 KIPLING CT
West Middlesex
UB1
1 ALDERSON PL
2 IRON BRIDGE CL
3 ALEXANDER CL
WHARNCLIFFE DR
BRENTVALE AVE
BLACKMORE AVE
Allot Gdns
Triangle Ctr
River Brent
YORK AVE
Schs
CONOLLY RD
LAWN GDNS
MYRTLE GDNS
LAUREL GDNS
HALF ACRE RD
SPRINGFIELD RD
STATION RD
BALFOUR AVE
CLAIRVILLE GDNS
Liby
HOLLY PARK
NETHERAVON RD
BAKER HO
NIGHTINGALE RD
AZALEA CT
SHIRLEY GDNS
Cemy
A4020
UXBRIDGE RD
MORLAND GDNS
LYNDHURST AVE
WINDMILL PL
Windmill Bsns Ctr
HALLIDAY SQ
WEST PARK RD
ELLIS RD
CUBITT SQ
WINDMILL AVE
OSTERLEY GDNS
OSTERLEY VIEWS
Ealing
WILLIAM CL
LOCK CL
GRAND DRI
CHEVY RD
RIVER CL
NAVIGATOR DR
Great Western Ind Pk
JACKSON WAY
DEAN WAY
ARMSTRONG WAY
Three Bridges Bsns Ctr
Grand Union Canal Wlk
1 WATER LILY CL
2 COMER CRES
3 TULIP CL
WINDMILL BRIDGE
WINDMILL LA
Hanwell
BROADWAY
A4001 BOSTON RD
JESSAMINE
HAYDON HO
FILANCO CT
MICHAEL GAYNOR CL
BARCHESTER CL
ST GEORGE'S RD
MONTAGUE AVE
City of Westminster Cemy
WALKER CL
WESTMINSTER RD
GEORGE ST
WILMOT PL
LOWER BOSTON RD
ADELAIDE CT
Sch
MOUNT OLIVE CT
Capital Ring
GREEN LA
BISHOP'S RD
ST MARK'S RD
BOSTON GDNS
BOSTONTHORPE RD
ROSEBANK RD
OSTERLEY PARK VIEW RD
ST ANDREW'S RD
ST DUNSTAN'S RD
OAK COTTS
ST MARGARET'S RD
BILLETS HART CL
STUBLEY GRANGE RD
CARLTON CT
HUMES AVE
LAMBOURN CL
A3002
MONTAGUE RD
DEAN'S RD
CAMBRIDGE RD
DENE CT
EDINBURGH RD
SOUTHFIELD COTTS
OAKLANDS RD
CUMBERLAND RD
ROSEDALE CL
THE BEECHES
Bnstand
Glade Lane Canalside Park
107
B454
WOLSEY CL
UB2
1 THORNWELL CT
2 ST MARK'S CT
3 DU BURSTOW TERR
4 CHURCHFIELD RD
5 MALLARD CL
6 QUEENS TERR COTTS
MURRAY CT
TRUMPERS WAY
BELVEDERE RD
TOWNHOLM CRES
W7
Elthorne Park
Waterside Trad Ctr
Sports Gd
POPLAR AVE
TENTELOW LA
Sp Ctr
Pl Fld
The Aviary
Boston Bsns Pk
River Brent Bsns Pk
Elthorne Park High Sch
Grand Union Canal
WINDMILL LA
Osterley Lock
Trumper's Wood
M4
OSTERLEY LA
Hare & Hounds (PH)
Osterley Park Farm
TW7
Bwg Gn
Tenn Cts
Sp Gd
Wyke Green
Osterley Park
Osterley Park House
CH
B454 SYON LA
T Cts
130
Pav
Sp Gd
A B C D
14 15 16
1 2 3 4 5 6
78 79 80 81

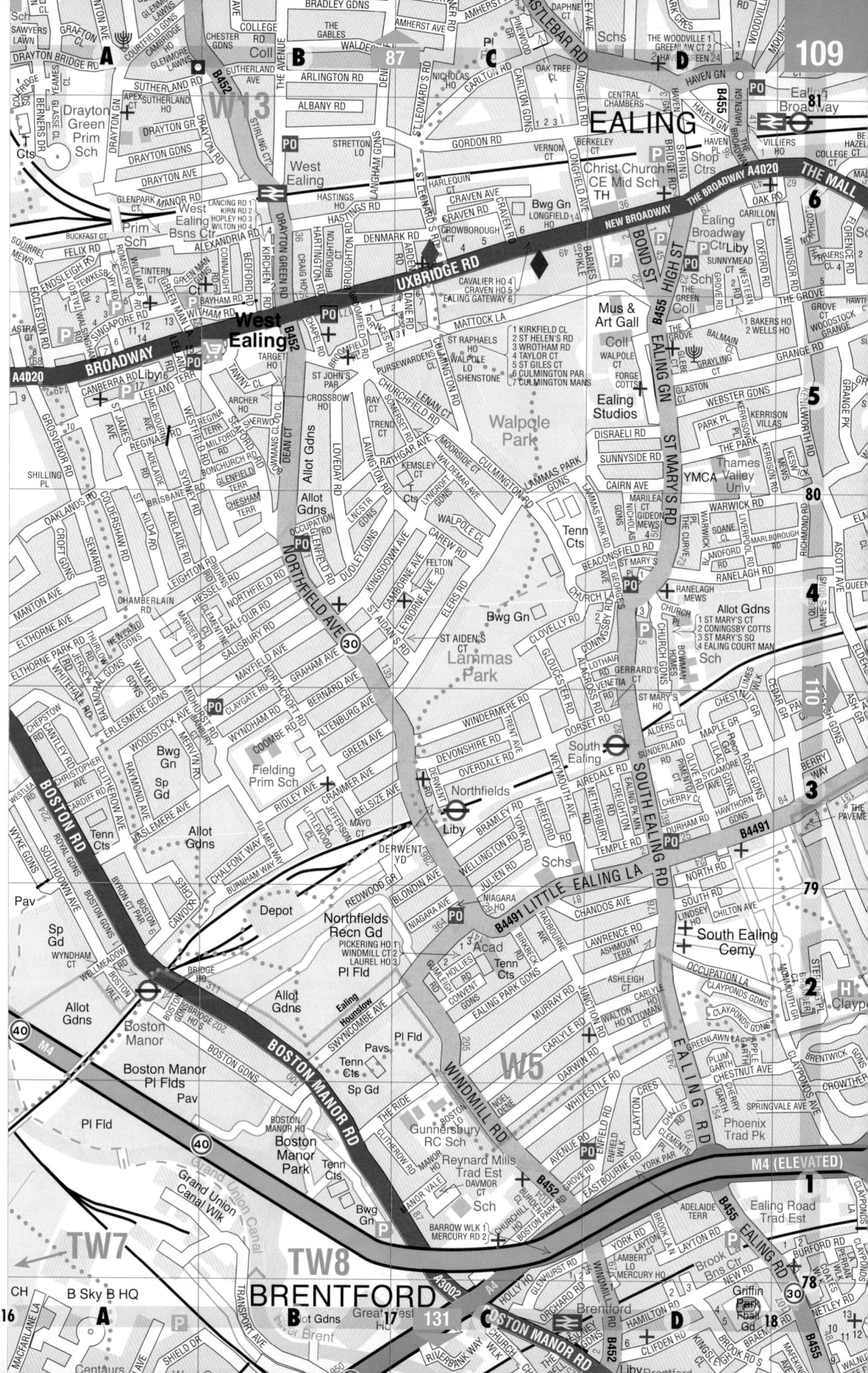

109
87
110
131
EALING
W13
W5
TW7
TW8
BRENTFORD
West Ealing
Ealing Broadway
South Ealing
Northfields
Boston Manor
Brentford
UXBRIDGE RD
BROADWAY
A4020
NEW BROADWAY
THE BROADWAY
THE MALL
HIGH ST
BOND ST
EALING GN
ST MARY'S RD
SOUTH EALING RD
EALING RD
NORTHFIELD AVE
BOSTON RD
BOSTON MANOR RD
WINDMILL RD
LITTLE EALING LA
B4491
B455
B452
A3002
A4
M4
M4 (ELEVATED)
Walpole Park
Lammas Park
Mus & Art Gall
Ealing Studios
Thames Valley Univ
YMCA
Christ Church CE Mid Sch
Drayton Green Prim Sch
Fielding Prim Sch
Northfields Recn Gd
Depot
South Ealing Cemy
Phoenix Trad Pk
Ealing Road Trad Est
Gunnersbury RC Sch
Reynard Mills Trad Est
Boston Manor Park
Boston Manor Pl Flds
Grand Union Canal
Grand Union Canal Wlk
Griffin Park Fball Gd
B Sky B HQ
Brook La Bns Ctr
DRAYTON BRIDGE RD
DRAYTON GN
DRAYTON GR
DRAYTON GDNS
DRAYTON AVE
SUTHERLAND RD
ARLINGTON RD
ALBANY RD
BRADLEY GDNS
GORDON RD
MATTOCK LA
CULMINGTON RD
LAMMAS PARK RD
LAMMAS PARK GDNS
WALPOLE CL
CLOVELLY RD
GLOUCESTER RD
WINDERMERE RD
DEVONSHIRE RD
OVERDALE RD
DORSET RD
WEYMOUTH AVE
WARWICK RD
RANELAGH RD
RICHMOND RD
ASCOTT AVE
KENILWORTH RD
WEBSTER GDNS
DISRAELI RD
SUNNYSIDE RD
CAIRN AVE
BEACONSFIELD RD
CHURCH LA
OCCUPATION LA
CLAYPONDS GDNS
CLAYPONDS AVE
GREENLAWN LA
CHESTNUT AVE
SPRINGVALE AVE
MURRAY RD
CARLYLE RD
DARWIN RD
WHITESTILE RD
JUNCTION RD
CHANDOS AVE
LAWRENCE RD
EALING PARK GDNS
NIAGARA AVE
JULIEN RD
WELLINGTON RD
BRAMLEY RD
BLONDIN AVE
REDWOOD GR
SWYNCOMBE AVE
MAYFIELD AVE
SALISBURY RD
BALFOUR RD
NORTHFIELD RD
LEIGHTON RD
ADELAIDE RD
ST KILDA RD
BRISBANE RD
SYDNEY RD
OAKLANDS RD
COLDERSHAW RD
SEWARD RD
CROFT GDNS
MANTON AVE
ELTHORNE AVE
ELTHORNE PARK RD
WALMER GDNS
ERLESMERE GDNS
WOODSTOCK AVE
MIDHURST RD
WYNDHAM RD
COOMBE RD
RIDLEY AVE
CRANMER AVE
BELSIZE AVE
GREEN AVE
ALTENBURG AVE
BERNARD AVE
GRAHAM AVE
DUDLEY GDNS
KINGSDOWN AVE
CAMBORNE AVE
LEYBORNE AVE
ELERS RD
CAREW RD
HASLEMERE AVE
RAYMOND AVE
CLITHEROW AVE
CHALFONT WAY
BURNHAM WAY
SOUTHDOWN AVE
WYKE GDNS
BOSTON GDNS
BOSTON RD
CLAYTON CRES
ENFIELD RD
EASTBOURNE RD
GROVE RD
AVENUE RD
BURFORD RD
CLIFDEN RD
HAMILTON RD
LAYTON RD
YORK RD
TRANSPORT AVE
SHIELD DR
MACFARLANE LA

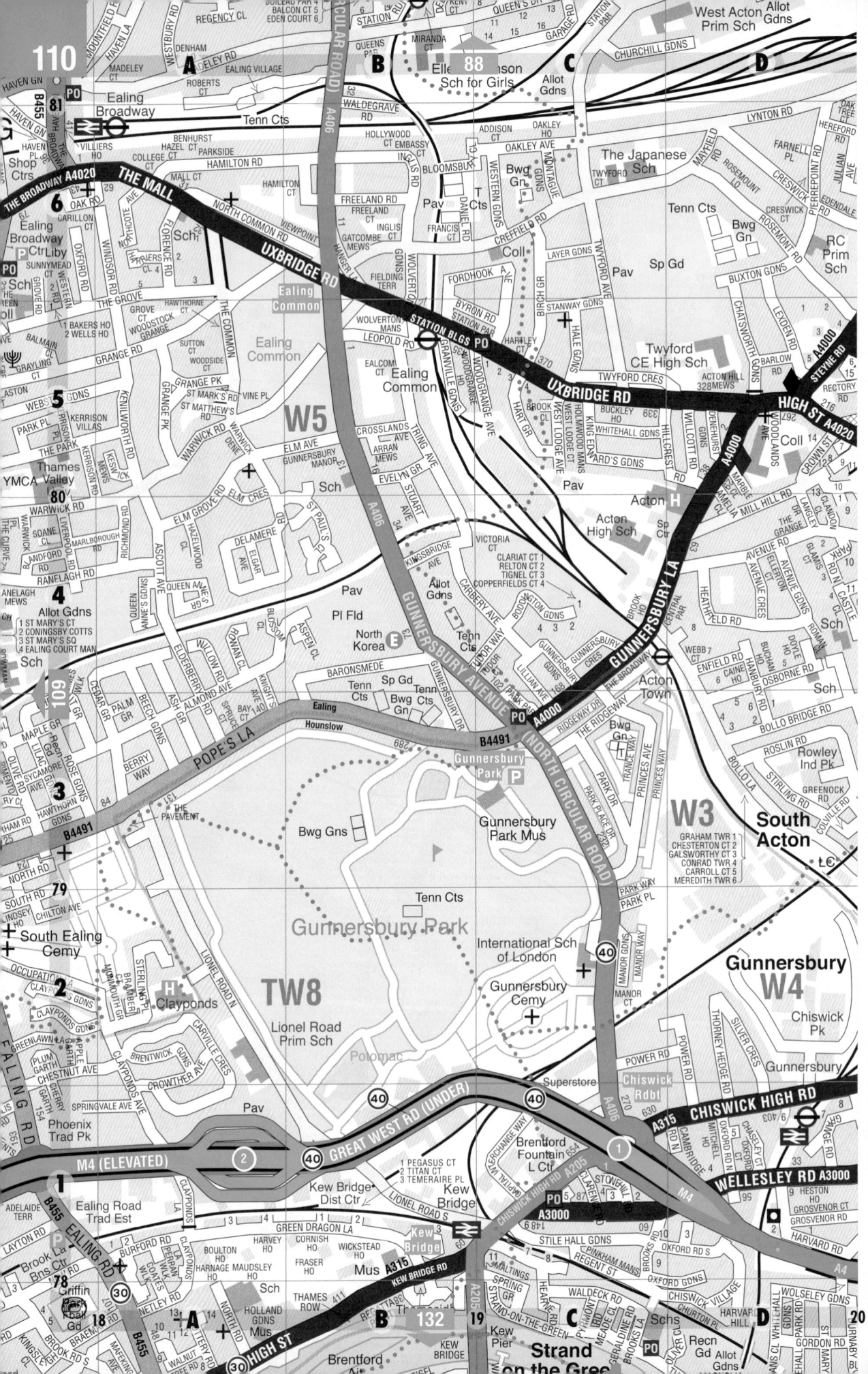

88
West Acton Prim Sch
Allot Gdns
Ellen Wilkinson Sch for Girls
Ealing Broadway
Tenn Cts
The Japanese Sch
THE BROADWAY A4020
THE MALL
UXBRIDGE RD
NORTH COMMON RD
Ealing Broadway Ctr
Ealing Common
W5
Twyford CE High Sch
UXBRIDGE RD
HIGH ST A4020
Acton High Sch
Acton
GUNNERSBURY LA
GUNNERSBURY AVENUE
NORTH CIRCULAR ROAD
A406
Thames Valley Univ
North Korea
Acton Town
POPE'S LA
B4491
Gunnersbury Park
Gunnersbury Park Mus
W3
South Acton
Rowley Ind Pk
Gunnersbury Park
South Ealing Cemy
International Sch of London
Gunnersbury Cemy
Gunnersbury
W4
Chiswick Pk
TW8
Lionel Road Prim Sch
Claypond
Potomac
Chiswick Rdbt
CHISWICK HIGH RD
GREAT WEST RD (UNDER)
M4 (ELEVATED)
Phoenix Trad Pk
Brentford Fountain L Ctr
Kew Bridge Dist Ctr
Kew Bridge
WELLESLEY RD A3000
Ealing Road Trad Est
EALING RD
KEW BRIDGE RD
Mus
HIGH ST
132
Strand on the Green
109

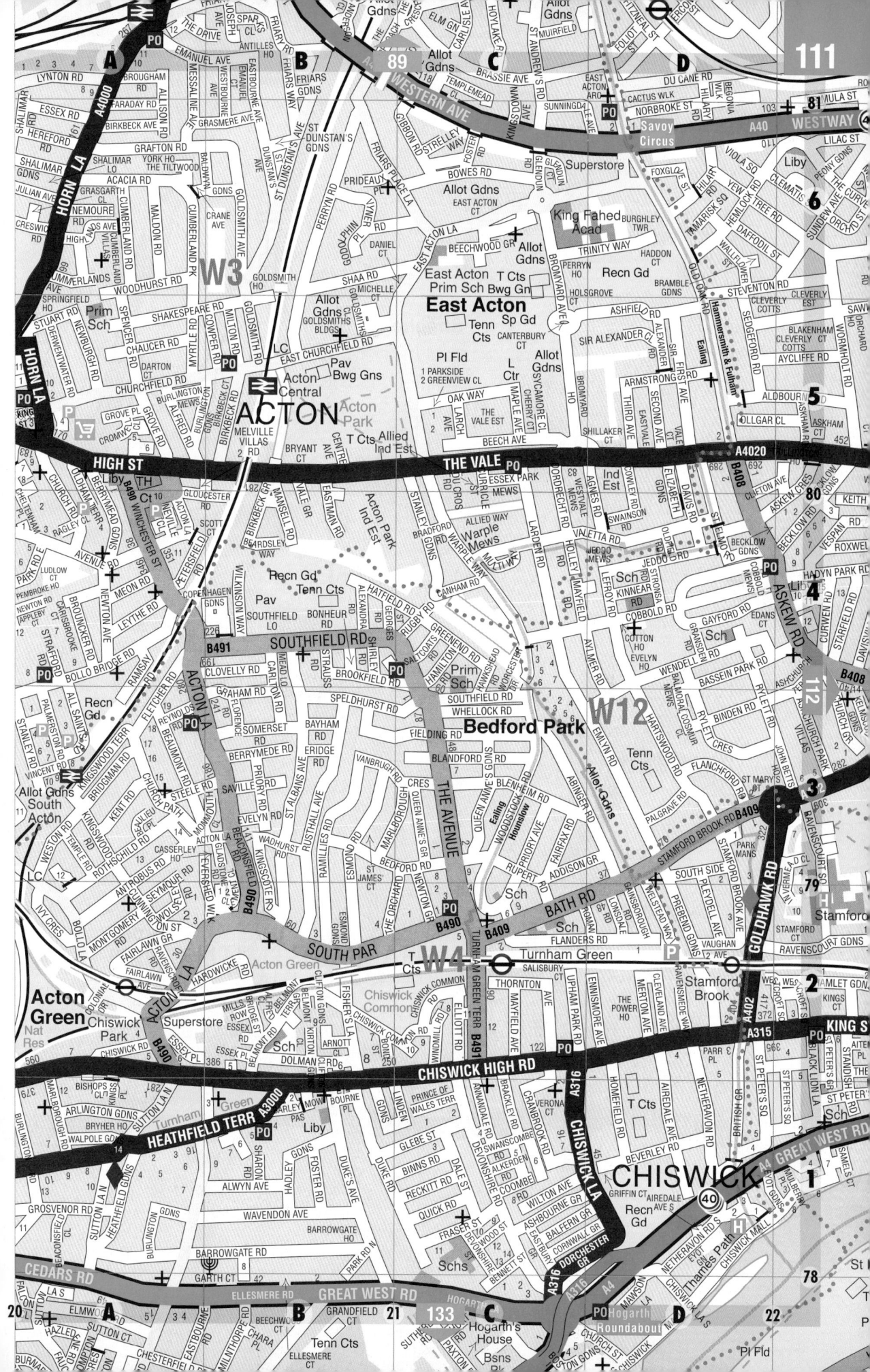
A
B
C
D
89
WESTERN AVE
A40
WESTWAY
Savoy Circus
DU CANE RD
EAST ACTON ARC
CACTUS WLK
NORBROKE ST
SUNNINGDALE AVE
BRASSIE AVE
TEMPLEMEAD CL
ELM GN
CARLISLE AVE
HOYLAKE RD
ST ANDREW'S RD
FITZNEAL ST
FOLIOT ST
LILAC ST
MULA ST
VIOLA SQ
PEONY GDNS
CLEMATIS ST
THE CURVE
SUNDEW AVE
ORCHID ST
YEW TREE RD
HEMLOCK RD
TAMARISK SQ
DAFFODIL ST
WALLFLOWER ST
FOXGLOVE ST
HILARY RD
Liby
Superstore
BOWES RD
GLENDUN RD
King Fahed Acad
BURGHLEY TWR
TRINITY WAY
HADDON CT
Recn Gd
BRAMBLE GDNS
PERRYN HO
HOLSGROVE CT
STEVENTON RD
CLEVERLY COTTS
CLEVERLY EST
BLAKENHAM CT
AYCLIFFE RD
ASHFIELD RD
SIR ALEXANDER CL
ALEXANDER CL
SIR FIRST AVE
ARMSTRONG RD
ALDBOURNE RD
OLLGAR CL
ASKHAM CT
OLD OAK RD
Hammersmith & Fulham
Ealing
SEDGEFORD RD
WORMHOLT RD
East Acton
East Acton Prim Sch
T Cts
Bwg Gn
Sp Gd
Tenn Cts
CANTERBURY CT
Allot Gdns
Pl Fld
L Ctr
OAK WAY
THE VALE EST
BEECH AVE
MAPLE AVE
SYCAMORE CL
CHERRY CT
BROMYARD AVE
SHILLAKER CT
THIRD AVE
SECOND AVE
EASTVALE
EAST ACTON LA
BEECHWOOD GR
DANIEL CT
SHAA RD
MICHELLE CT
GOLDSMITHS BLDGS
EAST CHURCHFIELD RD
PRIDEAUX PL
FRIARS PLACE LA
PERRYN RD
VYNER RD
Allot Gdns
EAST ACTON CT
FRIARS GDNS
ST DUNSTAN'S GDNS
ST DUNSTAN'S RD
W3
GOLDSMITH HO
GOLDSMITH AVE
CRANE AVE
CUMBERLAND PK
MALDON RD
ALLISON RD
BROUGHAM RD
EMANUEL AVE
ANTILLES HO
FRIARY RD
FRIARS WAY
THE DRIVE
LYNTON RD
FARADAY RD
BIRKBECK AVE
ESSEX RD
HEREFORD RD
SHALIMAR RD
SHALIMAR GDNS
GRAFTON RD
YORK HO
THE TILTWOOD
ACACIA RD
JULIAN AVE
GRASGARTH CL
NEMOURE RD
HORN LA
A4000
SUMMERLANDS AVE
SPRINGFIELD HO
WOODHURST RD
STUART RD
Prim Sch
SHAKESPEARE RD
CHAUCER RD
DARTON CT
CHURCHFIELD RD
MILTON RD
COWPER RD
GOLDSMITH RD
MYRTLE RD
Acton Central
Pav
Bwg Gns
ACTON
Acton Park
MELVILLE VILLAS RD
BRYANT CT
T Cts
Allied Ind Est
GROVE PL
CROMWELL
BURLINGTON MEWS
HIGH ST
Liby
THE VALE
A4020
B408
ESSEX PARK MEWS
DU CROS RD
Ind Est
SWAINSON RD
VALETTA RD
JEDDO MEWS
JEDDO RD
BECKLOW GDNS
ASKEW CRES
ASKEW RD
80
KEITH
VESPAN RD
ROXWELL
HADYN PARK RD
4
B490
WINCHESTER ST
GLOUCESTER RD
SCOTT CT
PETERSFIELD RD
ACTON LA
BIRKBECK RD
MANSELL RD
VALE GR
EASTMAN RD
Acton Park Ind Est
BEARDSLEY WAY
Recn Gd
Tenn Cts
Pav
COPENHAGEN GDNS
WILKINSON WAY
SOUTHFIELD LO
BONHEUR RD
HATFIELD RD
ALEXANDRA RD
GEORGES RD
RUGBY RD
BRADFORD RD
ALLIED WAY
Warple Mews
WARPLE WAY
CANHAM RD
LARDEN RD
HOLLEY RD
MAYFIELD RD
LEFROY RD
Sch
KINNEAR RD
COBBOLD RD
STRONSA RD
GAYFORD RD
EDANS CT
CURWEN RD
STARFIELD RD
COTTON HO
EVELYN HO
WENDELL RD
BASSEIN PARK RD
BINDEN RD
RYLETT RD
RYLETT CRES
FLANCHFORD RD
W12
Bedford Park
Tenn Cts
HARTSWOOD RD
EMLYN RD
AYLMER RD
112
B408
3
B491
SOUTHFIELD RD
STRAUSS RD
SHIRLEY RD
BROOKFIELD RD
SALTCOATS RD
GREENEND RD
HAMILTON RD
Prim Sch
HAWKSHEAD RD
WORCESTER RD
SOUTHFIELD RD
WHELLOCK RD
CLOVELLY RD
GRAHAM RD
FLORENCE RD
SOMERSET RD
BERRYMEDE RD
PRIORY RD
SAVILLE RD
EVELYN RD
SPELDHURST RD
BAYHAM RD
ERIDGE RD
FIELDING RD
BLANDFORD RD
VANBRUGH RD
ST ALBANS AVE
RUSTHALL AVE
RAMILLIES RD
ESMOND RD
MARLBOROUGH CRES
QUEEN ANNE'S GR
THE AVENUE
BLENHEIM RD
WOODSTOCK RD
Ealing
Hounslow
PRIORY AVE
FAIRFAX RD
ABINGER RD
Allot Gdns
PALGRAVE RD
STAMFORD BROOK RD
B409
ST MARY'S CT
RAVENSCOURT SQ
ACTON LA
NEWTON AVE
MEON RD
LEYTHE RD
BOLLO BRIDGE RD
RAMSAY RD
FLETCHER RD
REYNOLDS RD
BEAUMONT RD
CHURCH PATH
STEELE RD
KINGSWOOD TERR
BRIDGMAN RD
KENT RD
BEAULIEU PL
ROTHSCHILD RD
ANTROBUS RD
SEYMOUR RD
CUNNINGTON ST
MONTGOMERY RD
WOLSELEY RD
CASSERLEY HO
MONMOUTH RD
GLADSTONE RD
EVERSHED WLK
BEACONSFIELD RD
KINGSCOTE RD
WADHURST RD
BEDFORD RD
NEWTON GR
ST JAMES' CT
THE ORCHARD
RUPERT RD
ADDISON GR
Sch
BATH RD
ROMAN RD
LONSDALE RD
GAINSBOROUGH RD
WELSTEAD WAY
PREBEND GDNS
PLEYDELL AVE
STAMFORD BROOK AVE
SOUTH SIDE
PARK MANS
GOLDHAWK RD
VERMEAD CL
79
Stamford
STAMFORD CT
RAVENSCOURT GDNS
Recn Gd
Allot Gdns
South Acton
LUDLOW CT
PEMBROKE HO
NEWTON RD
APPLEBY CT
CARISBROOKE
BROUNCKER RD
STRAFFORD RD
ALL SAINTS RD
PALMERSTON RD
STANLEY RD
VINCENT RD
WESTON RD
TEMPLE RD
BOLLO LA
IVY CRES
LC
FAIRLAWN GR
FAIRLAWN AVE
RAVENSCROFT RD
HARDWICKE RD
SOUTH PAR
Acton Green
W4
T Cts
Turnham Green
TURNHAM GREEN TERR
B491
SALISBURY CT
FLANDERS RD
VAUGHAN AVE
Stamford Brook
THORNTON AVE
UPHAM PARK RD
ENNISMORE AVE
THE POWER HO
MERTON AVE
CLEVELAND AVE
RAVENSMEDE WAY
A402
2
HAMLET GDNS
KINGS CT
Acton Green
Chiswick Park
Nat Res
Superstore
MILLS ROW
ESSEX PL
BELMONT RD
BELMONT TERR
CLIFTON GDNS
FISHER'S LA
Chiswick Common
CHISWICK COMMON RD
ELLIOTT RD
WINDMILL RD
MAYFIELD AVE
Sch
ARNOTT CL
DOLMAN RD
BOURNE PL
CHISWICK HIGH RD
A315
KING ST
A316
CHISWICK LA
BISHOPS CL
ARLINGTON GDNS
BRYHER HO
WALPOLE GDNS
HEATHFIELD TERR
A3000
Turnham Green
SUTTON LA N
MARLBOROUGH RD
Liby
LINDEN GDNS
PRINCE OF WALES TERR
ANNANDALE RD
BRACKLEY RD
CRANBROOK RD
VERONA CT
HOMEFIELD RD
T Cts
AIREDALE AVE
NETHERAVON RD
BRITISH GR
ST PETER'S SQ
BLACK LION LA
STANDISH
Sch
GREAT WEST RD
A4
GLEBE ST
BINNS RD
RECKITT RD
QUICK RD
DALE ST
DEVONSHIRE RD
SWANSCOMBE RD
ALKERDEN RD
COOMBE RD
WILTON AVE
ASHBOURNE GR
BALFERN GR
CORNWALL GR
BEVERLEY RD
CHISWICK
GRIFFIN CT
AIREDALE AVE S
Recn Gd
40
H
NETHERAVON RD S
EYOT GDNS
Thames Path
CHISWICK MALL
MULBERRY PL
1
78
ARLINGTON GDNS
GROSVENOR RD
HEATHFIELD GDNS
BURLINGTON GDNS
ALWYN AVE
WAVENDON AVE
HADLEY GDNS
FOSTER RD
DUKE'S AVE
DUKE RD
BARROWGATE HO
BARROWGATE RD
GARTH CT
FRASER ST
WOOD ST
Schs
BENNETT ST
DORCHESTER GR
CEDARS RD
GREAT WEST RD
ELLESMERE RD
HOGARTH
Hogarth Roundabout
MAWSON LA
CHISWICK LA S
20
A
B
21
133
C
D
22
ELMWOOD RD
SUTTON CT
HAZLEDENE RD
CHESTERFIELD RD
EASTBOURNE RD
MILNTHORPE RD
BEECHWOOD CT
GRANDFIELD CT
Tenn Cts
ELLESMERE CT
Hogarth's House
Bsns
CHURCH ST
Pl Fld

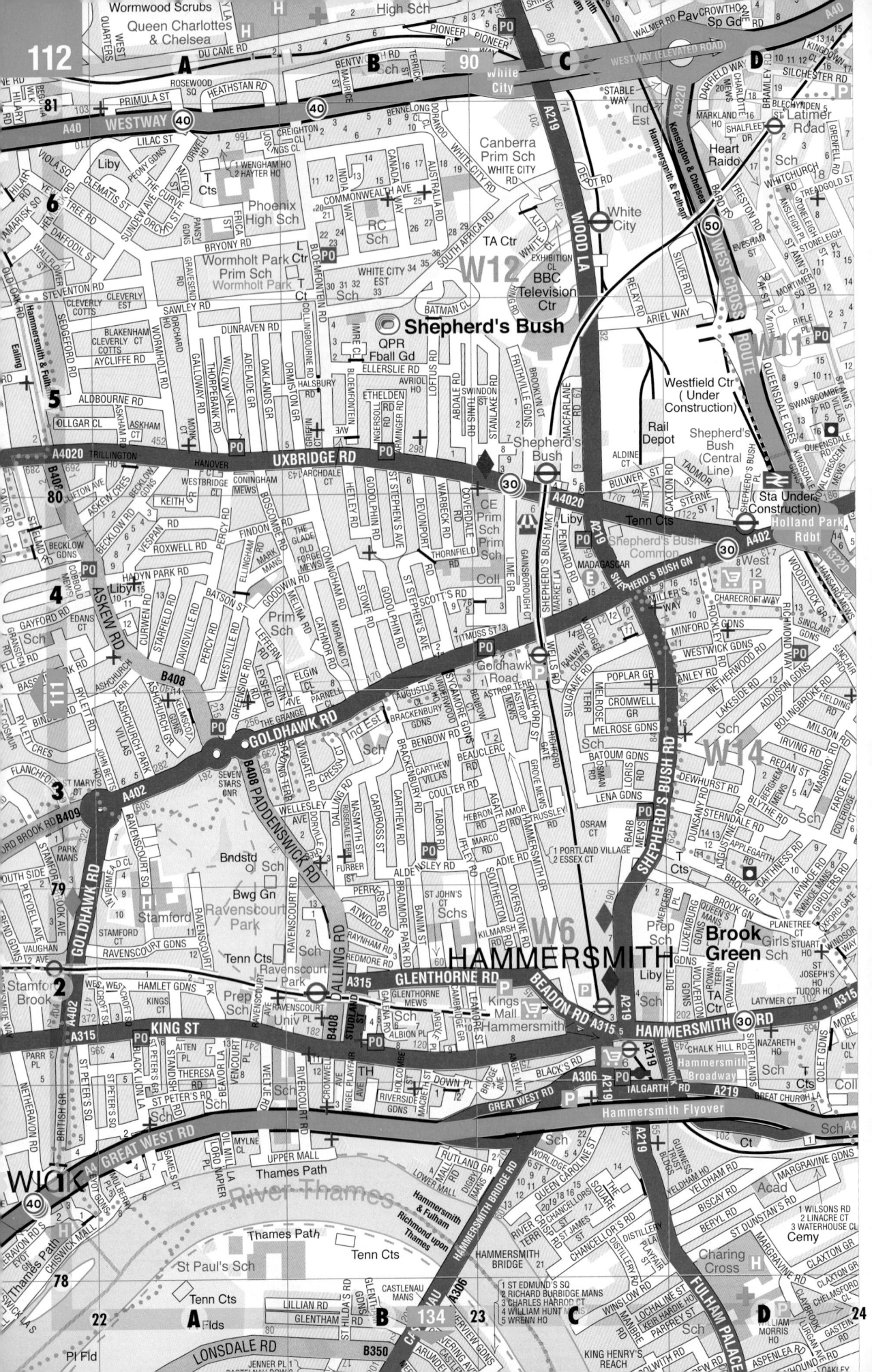

Wormwood Scrubs
Queen Charlottes & Chelsea
High Sch
DU CANE RD
PIONEER CL
PIONEER WAY
90
White City
WESTWAY (ELEVATED ROAD)
WALMER RD
Pav
CROWTHORNE RD
Sp Gd
KINGSDOWN CL
SILCHESTER RD
A
B
C
D
ROSEWOOD SQ
HEATHSTAN RD
BENTWORTH RD
Sch
PRIMULA ST
81
A40
WESTWAY
40
BENNELONG CL
DORANDO CL
STABLE WAY
Ind Est
A219
A3220
Kensington & Chelsea
Hammersmith & Fulham
DARFIELD WAY
CHARLOTTE MEWS
BRAMLEY RD
BLECHYNDEN ST
Latimer Road
SHALFLEET DR
MARKLAND HO
Heart Raido
GRENFELL RD
LILAC ST
VIOLA SQ
Liby
PEONY GDNS
CLEMATIS ST
THE CURVE
SUNDEW AVE
ORCHID ST
1 WENGHAM HO
2 HAYTER HO
T Cts
Phoenix High Sch
CREIGHTON CL
Canberra Prim Sch
WHITE CITY RD
WHITE CITY RD
COMMONWEALTH AVE
CANADA WAY
AUSTRALIA RD
INDIA WAY
RC Sch
DEPOT RD
White City
WOOD LA
50
WEST CROSS ROUTE
FRESTON RD
WHITCHURCH RD
TREADGOLD ST
STONELEIGH PL
STONELEIGH ST
ANSLEIGH PL
6
TREE RD
DAFFODIL ST
WALLFLOWER ST
TAMARISK SQ
BRYONY RD
Wormholt Park Prim Sch
Wormholt Park
L Ctr
PO
WHITE CITY EST
SOUTH AFRICA RD
TA Ctr
W12
EXHIBITION CL
BBC Television Ctr
SILVER RD
EVESHAM ST
ST ANN'S RD
MORTIMER SQ
RIFLE PL
W11
STEVENTON RD
CLEVERLY COTTS
CLEVERLY EST
SAWLEY RD
DUNRAVEN RD
BATMAN CL
Shepherd's Bush
RELAY RD
ARIEL WAY
QUEENSDALE CRES
OLD OAK RD
Hammersmith & Fulham
Ealing
SEDGEFORD RD
BLAKENHAM CT
CLEVERLY COTTS
AYCLIFFE RD
WORMHOLT RD
ORCHARD HO
GALLOWAY RD
THORPEBANK RD
WILLOW VALE
ADELAIDE GR
OAKLANDS GR
ORMISTON GR
COLLINGBOURNE RD
HALSBURY RD
IMRE CL
QPR Fball Gd
ELLERSLIE RD
AVRIOL HO
LOFTUS RD
BLOEMFONTEIN RD
BLOEMFONTEIN AVE
ETHELDEN RD
ABDALE RD
SWINDON ST
STANLAKE RD
FRITHVILLE GDNS
BROOKLYN CT
MACFARLANE RD
Westfield Ctr (Under Construction)
Rail Depot
Shepherd's Bush (Central Line)
SWANSCOMBE RD
ST ANN'S VILLAS
QUEENSDALE RD
5
ALDBOURNE RD
OLLGAR CL
ASKHAM CT
ASKHAM RD
MONK CT
INGERSOLL RD
ARMINGER RD
A4020
TRILLINGTON HO
HANOVER CL
UXBRIDGE RD
ARCHDALE CT
Shepherd's Bush
ALDINE CT
BULWER ST
CAXTON RD
TADMOR ST
STERNE ST
SHEPHERD'S BUSH PL
Sta Under Construction
Holland Park Rdbt
ROYAL CRESCENT MEWS
KINGSDALE GDNS
B408
80
CLIFTON AVE
ASKEW CRES
BECKLOW GDNS
WESTBRIDGE CL
CONINGHAM MEWS
KEITH GR
HETLEY RD
GODOLPHIN RD
ST STEPHEN'S AVE
DEVONPORT RD
WARBECK RD
COVERDALE RD
30
CE Prim Sch
Prim Sch
Liby
Tenn Cts
A402
A3220
ST ELMO RD
BECKLOW GDNS
BECKLOW RD
VESPAN RD
ROXWELL RD
FINDON RD
BOSCOMBE RD
THE GLADE
OLD FORGE MEWS
CONINGHAM RD
THORNFIELD RD
LIME GR
GAINSBOROUGH CT
SHEPHERD'S BUSH MKT
PENNARD RD
Shepherd's Bush Common
MADAGASCAR
SHEPHERD'S BUSH GN
West 12
WOODSTOCK GR
HANSARD MEWS
COBBOLD MEWS
HADYN PARK RD
Liby
4
PERCY RD
ELLINGHAM RD
MARK MANS
GOODWIN RD
STOWE RD
SCOTT'S RD
Coll
MARKET LA
E
MILLER'S WAY
CHARECROFT WAY
RICHMOND WAY
SINCLAIR GDNS
BATSON ST
MELINA RD
CATHNOR RD
MORLAND CT
TITMUSS ST
MINFORD GDNS
WESTWICK GDNS
NETHERWOOD RD
ROCKLEY RD
GAYFORD RD
EDANS CT
Sch
ASKEW RD
CURWEN RD
STARFIELD RD
DAVISVILLE RD
PERCY RD
WESTVILLE RD
Prim Sch
LEFFERN RD
ELGIN AVE
ELGIN CL
PARNELL CL
Goldhawk Road
ASTROP TERR
ASTROP MEWS
RICHFORD ST
RICHFORD GATE
WELLS RD
SULGRAVE RD
RAILWAY COTTS
WOODGER RD
POPLAR GR
CROMWELL GR
MELROSE GDNS
MELROSE TERR
STANLEY RD
LAKESIDE RD
ADDISON GDNS
BOLINGBROKE RD
FIELDING RD
MILSON RD
GRANSDEN RD
111
RYLETT RD
ASHCHURCH TERR
ASHCHURCH PARK VILLAS
ASHCHURCH GR
KELMSCOTT GDNS
B408
GREENSIDE RD
LEYSFIELD RD
THE GRANGE
GOLDHAWK RD
AUGUSTUS CL
BRACKENBURY GDNS
SYCAMORE GDNS
BENBOW CT
Ind Est
Sch
BENBOW RD
BEAUCLERC RD
W14
IRVING RD
REDAN ST
MASBRO RD
FAROE RD
RYLETT CRES
FLANCHFORD RD
3
ST MARY'S CT
JOHN BETTS HO
SEVEN STARS CNR
B408 PADDENSWICK RD
BRAGANZA TERR
WINGATE RD
CRESSY CT
BRACKENBURY RD
CARTHEW VILLAS
COULTER RD
GROVE MEWS
Sch
BATOUM GDNS
LORIS RD
OSMAN RD
LENA GDNS
SHEPHERD'S BUSH RD
DEWHURST RD
STERNDALE RD
BLYTHE RD
BERGHEM MEWS
Sch
COLERIDGE CL
B409
A402
BROOK RD
PARK MANS
STAMFORD BROOK AVE
RAVENSCOURT SQ
Bndstd
Sch
Bwg Gn
WELLESLEY AVE
DORVILLE CRES
DALLING RD
NASMYTH ST
ROSEDALE TERR
CARDROSS ST
CARTHEW RD
TABOR RD
HEBRON RD
AGATE RD
AMOR RD
TRUSSLEY RD
OSRAM CT
BARB MEWS
DUNSANY RD
AUGUSTINE RD
APPLEGARTH RD
CAITHNESS RD
AYNHOE RD
GIRDLERS RD
SOUTH SIDE
79
GOLDHAWK RD
PLEYDELL AVE
Stamford
Ravenscourt Park
FURBER ST
PERRERS RD
BRADMORE PARK RD
BANIM ST
ALDENSLEY RD
MARCO RD
ADIE RD
IFFLEY RD
SOUTHERTON RD
OVERSTONE RD
HAMMERSMITH GR
1 PORTLAND VILLAGE
2 ESSEX CT
T Cts
BROOK GN
OXFORD GATE
PLANETREE CT
VAUGHAN AVE
STAMFORD CT
RAVENSCOURT GDNS
RAVENSCOURT RD
Sch
ATWOOD RD
RAYNHAM RD
REDMORE RD
ST JOHN'S CT
Schs
KILMARSH RD
W6
Prep Sch
LUXEMBURG GDNS
QUEEN'S MANS
Brook Green
Girls' Sch
STUART HO
WINDSOR WAY
Stamford Brook
2
HAMLET GDNS
KINGS CT
Tenn Cts
Ravenscourt Park
Prep Sch
Ravenscourt
Univ
A315
GLENTHORNE RD
GLENTHORNE MEWS
HAMMERSMITH
Kings Mall
BEADON RD
Liby
ROWAN RD
TA Ctr
ST JOSEPH'S HO
TUDOR HO
LATYMER CT
A402
A315
KING ST
BLACK LION LA
ST PETER'S GR
AITEN PL
STANDISH RD
THERESA RD
VENCOURT PL
WELTJE RD
RIVERCOURT RD
CROMWELL AVE
NIGEL PLAYFAIR AVE
HOLCOMBE ST
ALBION PL
GALENA RD
STUDLAND ST
DALLING RD
TH
DOWN PL
RIVERSIDE GDNS
MACBETH ST
Hammersmith
ANGEL WLK
BLACK'S RD
A306
BUTTERWICK
HAMMERSMITH RD
CHALK HILL RD
Hammersmith Broadway
SHORTLANDS
NAZARETH HO
Sch
T Cts
COLET GDNS
LILY CL
Coll
PARR PL
NETHERAVON RD
ST PETER'S SQ
ST PETER'S RD
Sch
BRITISH GR
TALGARTH RD
A219
GREAT WEST RD
Hammersmith Flyover
GREAT CHURCH LA
Sch
A4 GREAT WEST RD
SAMUELS CT
LORD NAPIER
OIL MILL LA
MYLNE CL
UPPER MALL
Thames Path
River Thames
RUTLAND GR
LOWER MALL
DIGBY MANS
HAMMERSMITH BRIDGE RD
WORLIDGE ST
QUEEN CAROLINE ST
THE SQUARE
GUINNESS TRUST BLDGS
YELDHAM HO
YELDHAM RD
BISCAY RD
MARGRAVINE GDNS
Acad
ST DUNSTAN'S RD
1 WILSONS RD
2 LINACRE CT
3 WATERHOUSE CL
Cemy
CHISWICK
40
CHISWICK MALL
Hammersmith & Fulham
Richmond upon Thames
RIVER TERR
CHANCELLORS ST
ST JAMES ST
CHANCELLOR'S RD
DISTILLERY LA
DISTILLERY RD
PLAYFAIR ST
BERYL RD
Charing Cross
MARGRAVINE RD
CLAXTON GR
EYOT GDNS
Thames Path
78
St Paul's Sch
Tenn Cts
HAMMERSMITH BRIDGE
21
1 ST EDMUND'S SQ
2 RICHARD BURBIDGE MANS
3 CHARLES HARROD CT
4 WILLIAM HUNT MANS
5 WRENN HO
WINSLOW RD
LOCHALINE ST
KEIR HARDIE HO
PARFREY ST
FULHAM PALACE RD
WILLIAM MORRIS HO
CHELMSFORD CL
GASTEIN RD
24
Tenn Cts
CASTLENAU MANS
ST HILDA'S RD
GLENTHAM GDNS
LILLIAN RD
GLENTHAM RD
134
22
A
Flds
B
23
C
D
Pl Fld
LONSDALE RD
B350
CASTELNAU
RIVERVIEW GDNS
KING HENRY'S REACH
ASPENLEA RD

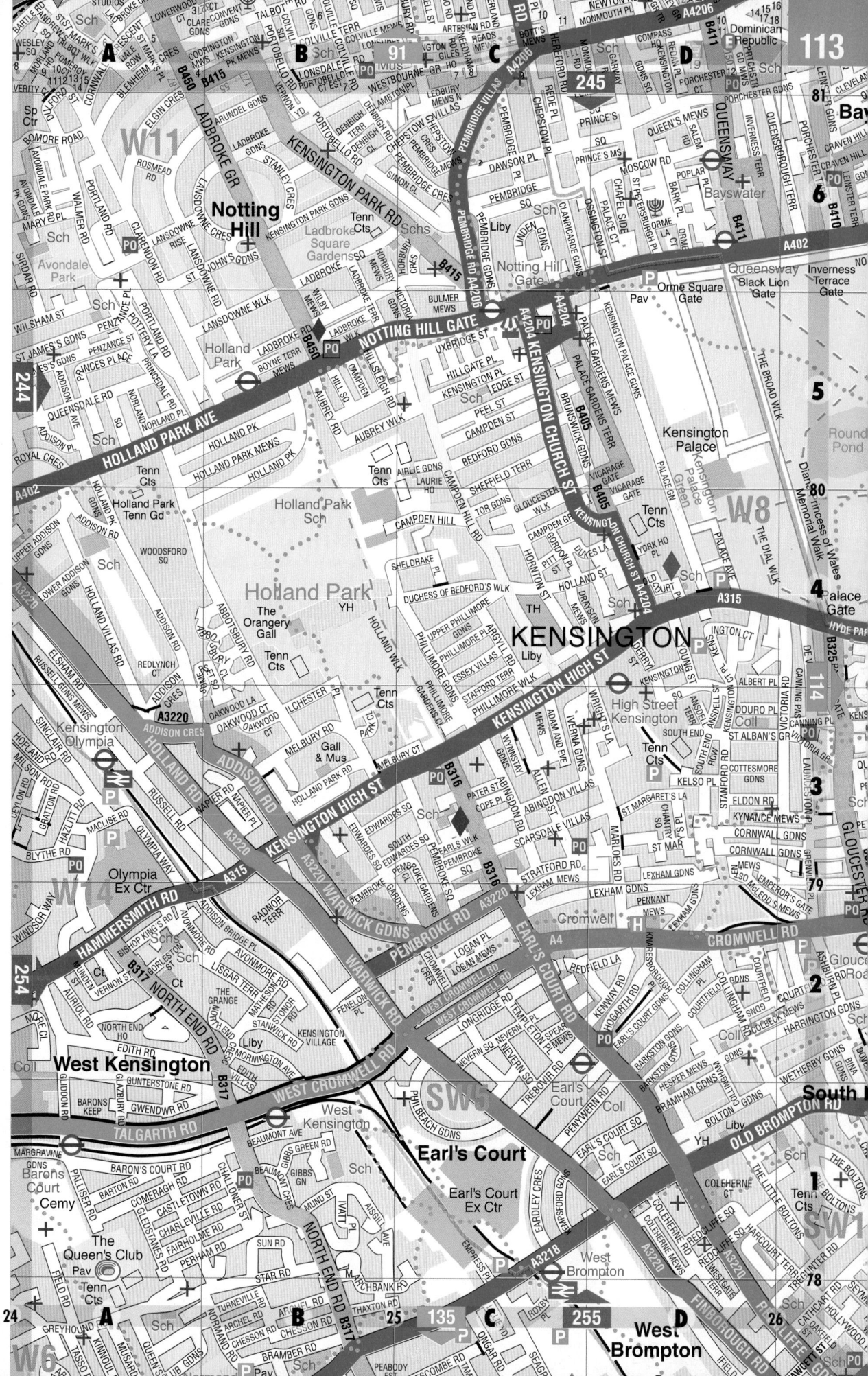

113
W11
Notting Hill
Ladbroke Square Gardens
Notting Hill Gate
NOTTING HILL GATE
HOLLAND PARK AVE
Holland Park
KENSINGTON PARK RD
LADBROKE GR
PEMBRIDGE VILLAS
QUEENSWAY
Bayswater
Queensway
Black Lion Gate
Orme Square Gate
Inverness Terrace Gate
A402
Kensington Palace
Kensington Palace Green
THE BROAD WLK
Round Pond
Diana Princess of Wales Memorial Walk
W8
KENSINGTON CHURCH ST
Palace Gate
A315
HYDE PARK
KENSINGTON
Liby
High Street Kensington
KENSINGTON HIGH ST
Holland Park Sch
Holland Park Tenn Gd
The Orangery Gall
YH
Kensington Olympia
Olympia Ex Ctr
W14
HAMMERSMITH RD
A3220
HOLLAND RD
ADDISON RD
WARWICK GDNS
WARWICK RD
PEMBROKE RD
EARL'S COURT RD
CROMWELL RD
A4
Cromwell
SW5
Earl's Court
Earl's Court Ex Ctr
WEST CROMWELL RD
West Kensington
TALGARTH RD
NORTH END RD
Barons Court
Cemy
The Queen's Club
West Brompton
OLD BROMPTON RD
South
GLOUCESTER RD
SW10
W6
244
254
91
245
114
135
255
24
25
26
A
B
C
D
1
2
3
4
5
6
78
79
80
81

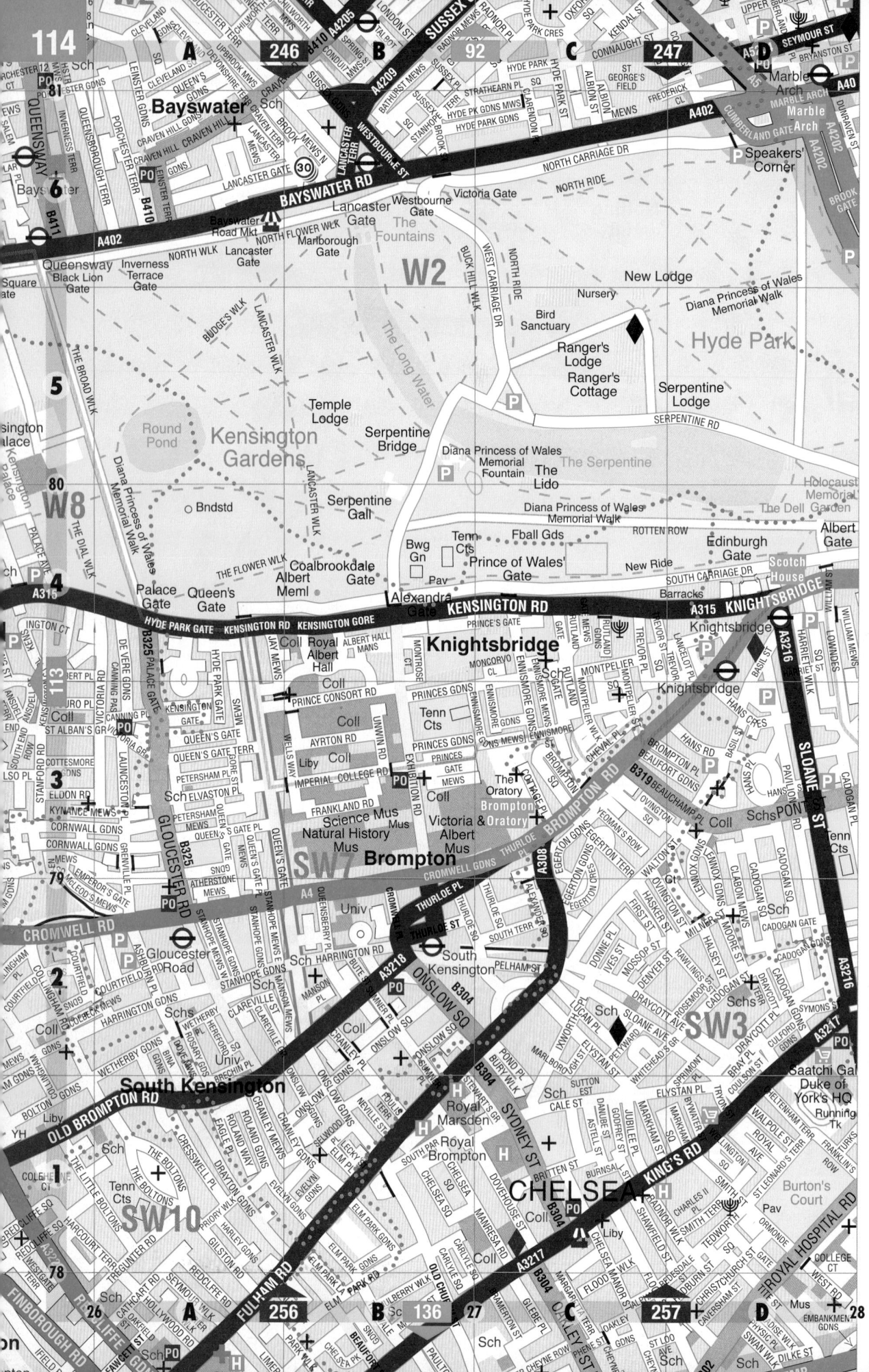
A
B
C
D
246
92
247
256
136
257
Bayswater
Queensway
Bayswater Rd
A402
Lancaster Gate
Westbourne Gate
Victoria Gate
Marlborough Gate
Queensway Black Lion Gate
Inverness Terrace Gate
Bayswater Road Mkt
The Fountains
W2
North Carriage Dr
North Ride
North Wlk
Speakers' Corner
Marble Arch
Cumberland Gate
New Lodge
Nursery
Bird Sanctuary
Ranger's Lodge
Ranger's Cottage
Serpentine Lodge
Hyde Park
Diana Princess of Wales Memorial Walk
The Long Water
Buck Hill Wlk
West Carriage Dr
Serpentine Rd
Kensington Gardens
Round Pond
Temple Lodge
Serpentine Bridge
Diana Princess of Wales Memorial Fountain
The Lido
The Serpentine
Serpentine Gall
Bndstd
Holocaust Memorial
The Dell
Rotten Row
Fball Gds
Tenn Cts
Bwg Gn
Pav
Prince of Wales' Gate
Coalbrookdale Gate
Albert Meml
Edinburgh Gate
Albert Gate
New Ride
South Carriage Dr
Scotch House
Barracks
The Broad Wlk
The Flower Wlk
Lancaster Wlk
Budge's Wlk
The Dial Wlk
Palace Ave
W8
Kensington Palace
Palace Gate
Queen's Gate
Alexandra Gate
Kensington Rd
A315
Kensington Gore
Hyde Park Gate
Knightsbridge
Royal Albert Hall
Prince Consort Rd
Exhibition Rd
Imperial College Rd
Science Mus
Natural History Mus
Victoria & Albert Mus
Brompton Oratory
The Oratory
Brompton
SW7
Brompton Rd
Cromwell Gdns
Cromwell Rd
A4
Gloucester Rd
Gloucester Road
Queen's Gate
Thurloe Pl
Thurloe St
South Kensington
Onslow Sq
Pelham St
Sloane St
A3216
Cadogan Sq
Pont St
Sloane Ave
SW3
King's Rd
A3217
Chelsea
Royal Marsden
Royal Brompton
Sydney St
Fulham Rd
Old Brompton Rd
South Kensington
The Boltons
SW10
Finborough Rd
Redcliffe Gdns
Saatchi Gal
Duke of York's HQ
Running Tk
Burton's Court
Royal Hospital Rd
Sloane Ave
Draycott Ave
Walton St
Ovington Sq
Beauchamp Pl
Hans Cres
Montpelier Sq
Ennismore Gdns
Princes Gdns
Seymour St
Sussex Gdns
Westbourne St
Connaught St

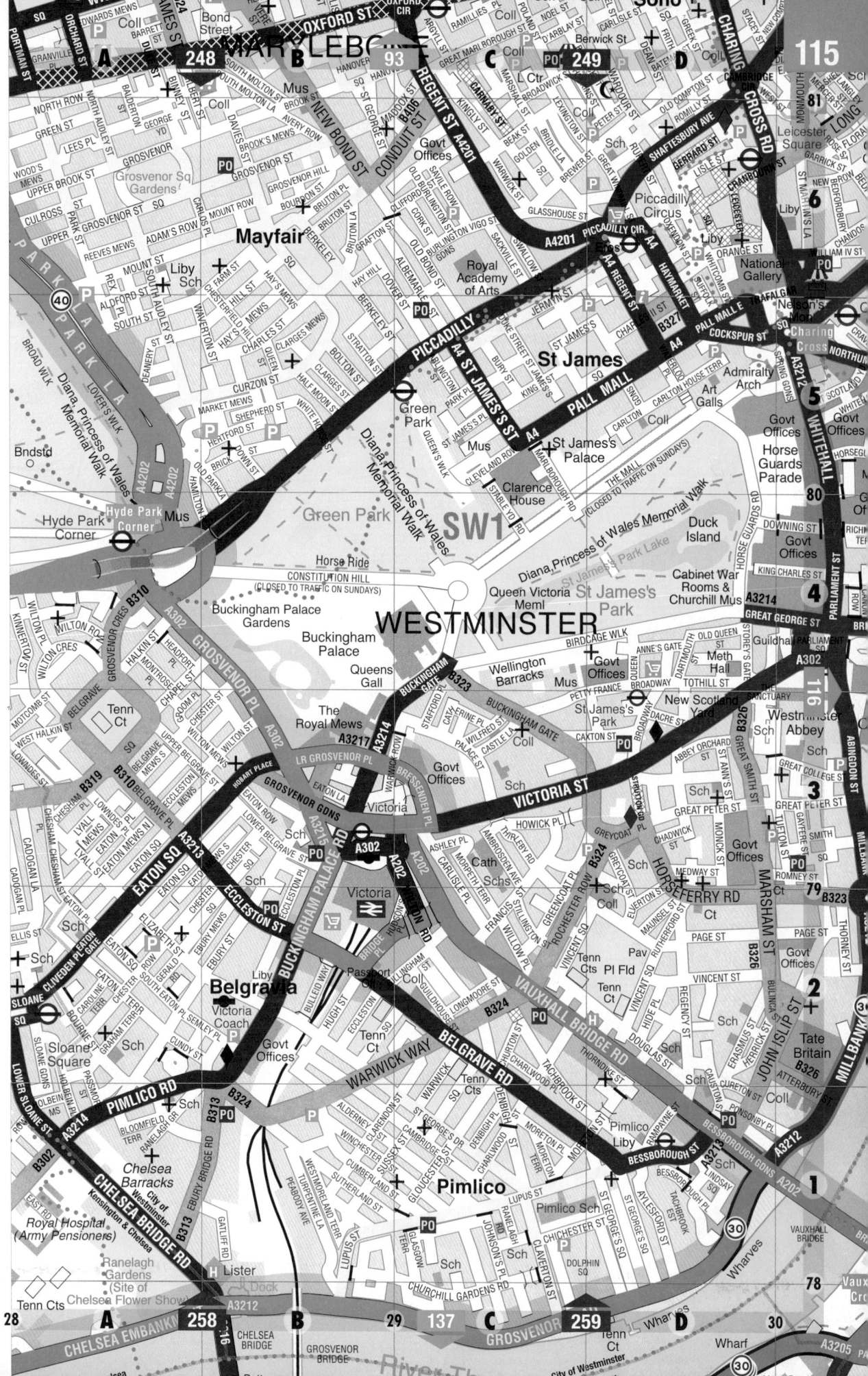
248
93
249
A
B
C
D
MARYLEBONE
Soho
OXFORD ST
OXFORD CIR
Bond Street
REGENT ST A4201
NEW BOND ST
CONDUIT ST
CHARING CROSS RD
CAMBRIDGE CIR
SHAFTESBURY AVE
Leicester Square
Mayfair
Grosvenor Sq Gardens
GROSVENOR ST
PARK LA
Piccadilly Circus
PICCADILLY CIR
Eros
HAYMARKET
National Gallery
TRAFALGAR
Nelson's Mon
Charing Cross
Royal Academy of Arts
PICCADILLY
St James
PALL MALL
Admiralty Arch
Art Galls
Green Park
Diana, Princess of Wales Memorial Walk
Hyde Park Corner
ST JAMES'S ST
St James's Palace
Clarence House
THE MALL
(CLOSED TO TRAFFIC ON SUNDAYS)
SW1
Horse Ride
CONSTITUTION HILL
(CLOSED TO TRAFFIC ON SUNDAYS)
Duck Island
St James's Park Lake
St James's Park
Queen Victoria Meml
Horse Guards Parade
WHITEHALL
DOWNING ST
KING CHARLES ST
Cabinet War Rooms & Churchill Mus
WESTMINSTER
Buckingham Palace Gardens
Buckingham Palace
Queens Gall
The Royal Mews
BIRDCAGE WLK
Wellington Barracks
BUCKINGHAM GATE
GREAT GEORGE ST
PARLIAMENT ST
New Scotland Yard
Westminster Abbey
116
VICTORIA ST
GROSVENOR PL
LR GROSVENOR PL
GROSVENOR GDNS
Victoria
BELGRAVE SQ
EATON SQ
ECCLESTON ST
BUCKINGHAM PALACE RD
VAUXHALL BRIDGE RD
HORSEFERRY RD
MARSHAM ST
Belgravia
Victoria Coach
Sloane Square
PIMLICO RD
WARWICK WAY
BELGRAVE RD
Tate Britain
MILLBANK
JOHN ISLIP ST
Pimlico
BESSBOROUGH ST
BESSBOROUGH GDNS
Chelsea Barracks
CHELSEA BRIDGE RD
City of Westminster
Kensington & Chelsea
Royal Hospital (Army Pensioners)
Ranelagh Gardens (Site of Chelsea Flower Show)
Lister
CHURCHILL GARDENS RD
Wharves
VAUXHALL BRIDGE
GROSVENOR RD
CHELSEA EMBANKMENT
CHELSEA BRIDGE
GROSVENOR BRIDGE
258
137
259
28
29
30
81
6
5
80
4
3
79
2
1
78

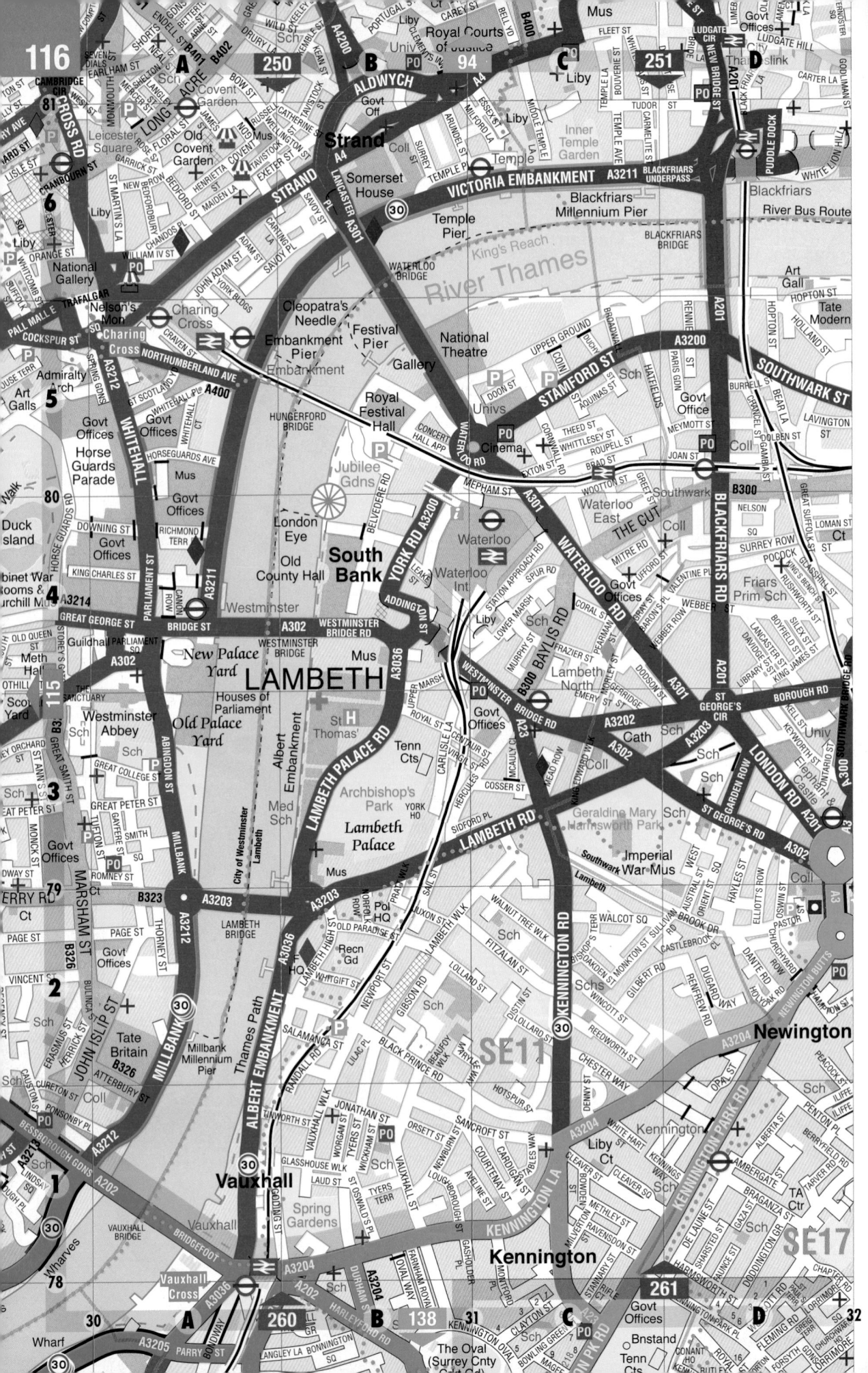
250
94
251
A
B
C
D
Royal Courts of Justice
Mus
Liby
Univ
PO
Govt Offices
LUDGATE CIR
LUDGATE HILL
FLEET ST
NEW BRIDGE ST
Thameslink
CARTER LA
ALDWYCH
Strand
STRAND
Covent Garden
Old Covent Garden
LONG ACRE
Leicester Square
CAMBRIDGE CIR
CHARING CROSS RD
CRANBOURN ST
SEVEN DIALS
EARLHAM ST
SHORTS GDNS
ENDELL ST
MONMOUTH ST
NEAL ST
BOW ST
DRURY LA
KINGSWAY
Govt Off
Coll
Inner Temple Garden
Temple
TEMPLE AVE
TUDOR ST
CARMELITE ST
BOUVERIE ST
WHITEFRIARS ST
MIDDLE TEMPLE LA
ESSEX ST
MILFORD LA
ARUNDEL ST
SURREY ST
TEMPLE PL
PUDDLE DOCK
WHITE LION HILL
BLACKFRIARS UNDERPASS
VICTORIA EMBANKMENT
A3211
Blackfriars
Blackfriars Millennium Pier
River Bus Route
BLACKFRIARS BRIDGE
Somerset House
LANCASTER PL
A301
SAVOY ST
SAVOY PL
CARTING LA
ADAM ST
JOHN ADAM ST
YORK BLDGS
Temple Pier
King's Reach
River Thames
WATERLOO BRIDGE
Art Gall
HOPTON ST
Tate Modern
HOLLAND ST
National Gallery
Nelson's Mon
TRAFALGAR SQ
PALL MALL E
COCKSPUR ST
Charing Cross
CRAVEN ST
NORTHUMBERLAND AVE
Embankment
Embankment Pier
Cleopatra's Needle
Festival Pier
National Theatre
Gallery
Royal Festival Hall
HUNGERFORD BRIDGE
Jubilee Gdns
London Eye
Old County Hall
South Bank
BELVEDERE RD
YORK RD A3200
Waterloo
Waterloo Int
Cinema
Univs
UPPER GROUND
STAMFORD ST
A3200
SOUTHWARK ST
Sch
HATFIELDS
Govt Office
MEYMOTT ST
JOAN ST
Southwark
B300
BLACKFRIARS RD
NELSON SQ
SURREY ROW
LOMAN ST
THE CUT
Waterloo East
WOOTTON ST
THEED ST
WHITTLESEY ST
ROUPELL ST
CORNWALL RD
WATERLOO RD
MEPHAM ST
Admiralty Arch
Art Galls
WHITEHALL
A3212
Govt Offices
Horse Guards Parade
HORSEGUARDS AVE
Mus
Duck Island
HORSE GUARDS RD
DOWNING ST
RICHMOND TERR
KING CHARLES ST
Cabinet War Rooms & Churchill Mus
PARLIAMENT ST
A3211
Westminster
GREAT GEORGE ST
BRIDGE ST
A302
WESTMINSTER BRIDGE RD
WESTMINSTER BRIDGE
ADDINGTON ST
STATION APPROACH RD
LOWER MARSH
BAYLIS RD
Lambeth North
Govt Offices
Friars Prim Sch
WEBBER ST
ST GEORGE'S CIR
BOROUGH RD
Cath
LONDON RD
Elephant & Castle
A300 SOUTHWARK BRIDGE RD
Guildhall
PARLIAMENT SQ
Meth Hall
Scot Yard
New Palace Yard
LAMBETH
Houses of Parliament
Old Palace Yard
Westminster Abbey
ABINGDON ST
MILLBANK
Albert Embankment
St Thomas'
LAMBETH PALACE RD
Tenn Cts
Archbishop's Park
Lambeth Palace
Med Sch
LAMBETH RD
Geraldine Mary Harmsworth Park
Imperial War Mus
ST GEORGE'S RD
KENNINGTON RD
GREAT PETER ST
GREAT SMITH ST
MARSHAM ST
HORSEFERRY RD
B323
A3203
LAMBETH BRIDGE
THORNEY ST
PAGE ST
Govt Offices
VINCENT ST
JOHN ISLIP ST
Tate Britain
B326
ATTERBURY ST
Pol HQ
Recn Gd
LAMBETH HIGH ST
LAMBETH WLK
KENNINGTON RD
Sch
SE11
Schs
WALCOT SQ
BROOK DR
Newington
NEWINGTON BUTTS
A3204
Kennington
KENNINGTON PARK RD
SE17
TA Ctr
Millbank Millennium Pier
Thames Path
ALBERT EMBANKMENT
Vauxhall
Spring Gardens
VAUXHALL BRIDGE
BRIDGEFOOT
Vauxhall Cross
Wharves
KENNINGTON LA
Liby Ct
Kennington
HARLEYFORD RD
A202
260
138
261
The Oval (Surrey Cnty Crkt Gd)
Bnstand
Tenn Cts
Govt Offices
KENNINGTON OVAL
PARRY ST
BONDWAY
A3205
Wharf
1
2
3
4
5
6
78
79
80
81
115
30
31
32

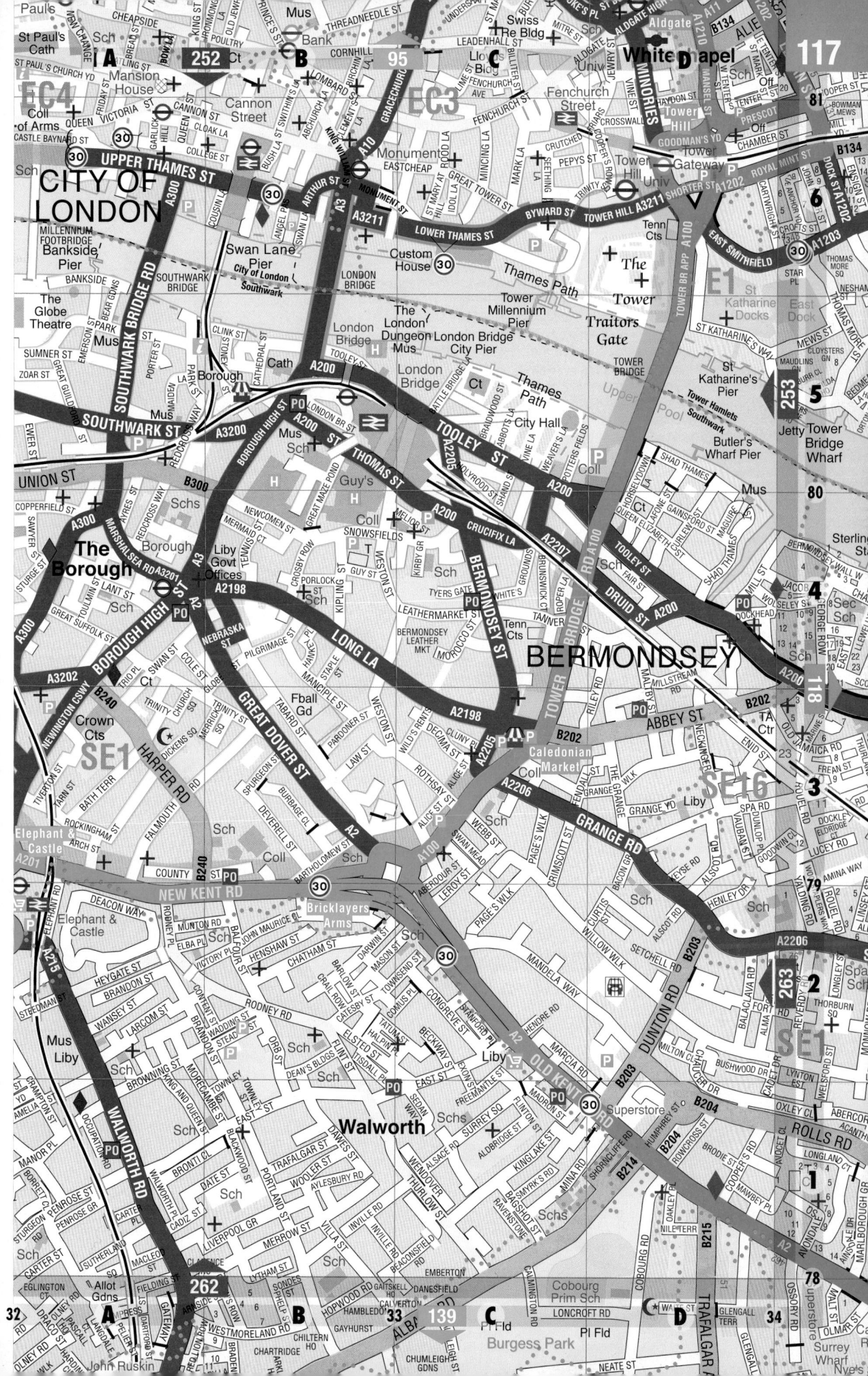

A
B
C
D
117
252
95
118
253
262
263
139
6
5
4
3
2
1
81
80
79
78
32
33
34
CITY OF LONDON
EC4
EC3
E1
SE1
SE16
BERMONDSEY
The Borough
Walworth
Whitechapel
St Paul's Cath
Mansion House
Cannon Street
Bank
Monument
Fenchurch Street
Aldgate
Tower Hill
Tower Gateway
The Tower
Traitors Gate
Tower Millennium Pier
London Bridge City Pier
London Bridge
The London Dungeon Mus
Custom House
Swan Lane Pier
City of London
Southwark
Tower Hamlets
Millennium Footbridge
Bankside Pier
The Globe Theatre
Borough
Guy's
City Hall
Thames Path
St Katharine Docks
St Katharine's Pier
East Dock
Butler's Wharf Pier
Tower Bridge Wharf
Jetty
Upper Pool
Swiss Re Bldg
Lloyds Bldg
Liby Govt Offices
Bermondsey Leather Mkt
Fball Gd
Crown Cts
Caledonian Market
Elephant & Castle
Bricklayers Arms
Superstore
Cobourg Prim Sch
Burgess Park
Pl Fld
Allot Gdns
John Ruskin
Surrey Wharf
UPPER THAMES ST
LOWER THAMES ST
QUEEN VICTORIA ST
CANNON ST
CHEAPSIDE
CORNHILL
LEADENHALL ST
THREADNEEDLE ST
FENCHURCH ST
EASTCHEAP
GREAT TOWER ST
BYWARD ST
TOWER HILL
MINORIES
ROYAL MINT ST
EAST SMITHFIELD
ST KATHARINE'S WAY
SOUTHWARK BRIDGE RD
SOUTHWARK ST
BOROUGH HIGH ST
TOOLEY ST
THOMAS ST
CRUCIFIX LA
BERMONDSEY ST
LONG LA
GREAT DOVER ST
TOWER BRIDGE RD
DRUID ST
ABBEY ST
GRANGE RD
OLD KENT RD
NEW KENT RD
WALWORTH RD
DUNTON RD
ROLLS RD
UNION ST
MARSHALSEA RD
HARPER RD
NEWINGTON CSWY
TOWER BR APP
SHAD THAMES
JAMAICA RD
MANDELA WAY
RODNEY RD
EAST ST
WESTMORELAND RD
TRAFALGAR AV
A3211
A200
A2
A3
A100
A2198
A2206
A3200
A3202
A300
A10
A11
A1202
A1203
A1210
A215
A201
A2205
A2207
B202
B203
B204
B214
B215
B240
B300
B134

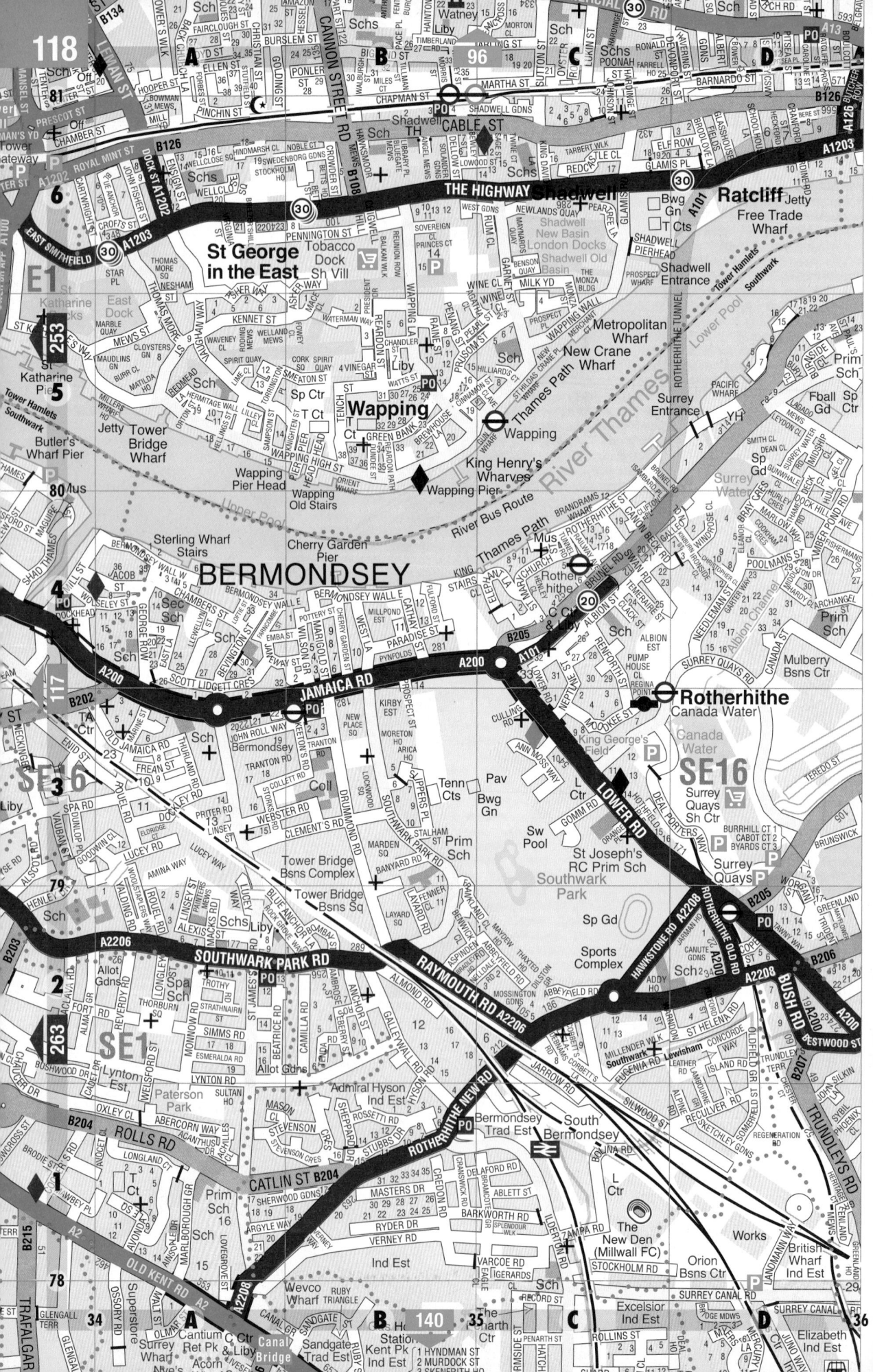
St George in the East
Wapping
Shadwell
Ratcliff
Free Trade Wharf
Tobacco Dock Sh Vill
Shadwell New Basin
London Docks
Shadwell Old Basin
St Katharine Docks
St Katharine Pier
Butler's Wharf Pier
Tower Bridge Wharf
Wapping Pier Head
Wapping Old Stairs
Wapping Pier
King Henry's Wharves
Metropolitan Wharf
New Crane Wharf
Thames Path
River Thames
Upper Pool
Lower Pool
River Bus Route
Sterling Wharf Stairs
Cherry Garden Pier
BERMONDSEY
Rotherhithe
Canada Water
Surrey Quays Sh Ctr
Surrey Quays
Southwark Park
St Joseph's RC Prim Sch
Sports Complex
Tower Bridge Bsns Complex
Tower Bridge Bsns Sq
Mulberry Bsns Ctr
King George's Field
Bermondsey Trad Est
South Bermondsey
The New Den (Millwall FC)
Orion Bsns Ctr
British Wharf Ind Est
Excelsior Ind Est
Admiral Hyson Ind Est
Paterson Park
Lynton Est
Surrey Wharf
Cantium Ret Pk
Canal Bridge
Sandgate Trad Est
Elizabeth Ind Est
Wevco Wharf
SE16
SE1
E1
THE HIGHWAY
CABLE ST
JAMAICA RD
LOWER RD
SOUTHWARK PARK RD
RAYMOUTH RD
ROTHERHITHE NEW RD
ROLLS RD
CATLIN ST
OLD KENT RD
EAST SMITHFIELD
ROYAL MINT ST
CANNON STREET RD
COMMERCIAL RD
TRUNDLEYS RD
BUSH RD
ROTHERHITHE TUNNEL
WAPPING HIGH ST
WAPPING LA
Tower Hamlets
Southwark
Lewisham
1 HYNDMAN ST
2 MURDOCK ST
3 SKENFRITH HO

96
253
117
263
140

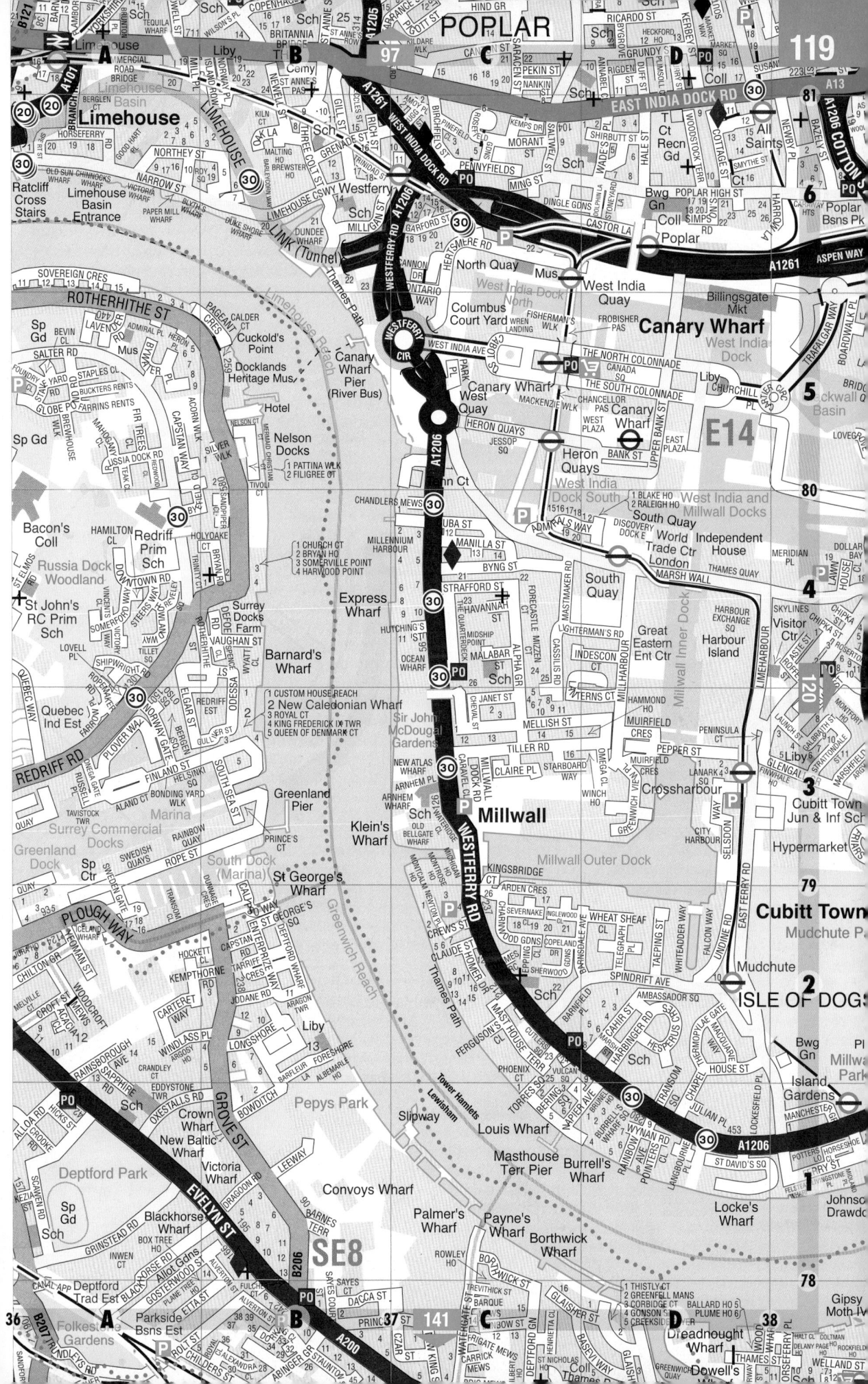
POPLAR
97
A
B
C
D
Limehouse
Limehouse Basin
Ratcliff Cross Stairs
Limehouse Basin Entrance
LIMEHOUSE LINK (Tunnel)
Westferry
WEST INDIA DOCK RD
EAST INDIA DOCK RD
A13
A1261
ASPEN WAY
Poplar
All Saints
Poplar Bsns Pk
North Quay
West India Quay
West India Dock North
Columbus Court Yard
Billingsgate Mkt
Canary Wharf
West India Dock
WESTFERRY CIR
Canary Wharf Pier (River Bus)
Cuckold's Point
Docklands Heritage Mus
THE NORTH COLONNADE
THE SOUTH COLONNADE
CHURCHILL PL
Heron Quays
West India Dock South
E14
South Quay
West India and Millwall Docks
World Trade Ctr London
Independent House
MARSH WALL
Harbour Island
Great Eastern Ent Ctr
Millwall Inner Dock
Crossharbour
Millwall
Millwall Outer Dock
Mudchute
ISLE OF DOGS
Cubitt Town
Mudchute Pk
Island Gardens
Locke's Wharf
Rotherhithe
ROTHERHITHE ST
Nelson Docks
Surrey Docks Farm
Barnard's Wharf
Russia Dock Woodland
Redriff Prim Sch
Bacon's Coll
St John's RC Prim Sch
Quebec Ind Est
REDRIFF RD
Surrey Commercial Docks
Greenland Dock
South Dock (Marina)
Greenland Pier
Klein's Wharf
St George's Wharf
Sir John McDougal Gardens
Express Wharf
Limehouse Reach
Greenwich Reach
Thames Path
WESTFERRY RD
A1206
PLOUGH WAY
EVELYN ST
GROVE ST
Pepys Park
Deptford Park
Crown Wharf
New Baltic Wharf
Victoria Wharf
Convoys Wharf
Blackhorse Wharf
Palmer's Wharf
Payne's Wharf
Borthwick Wharf
Louis Wharf
Masthouse Terr Pier
Burrell's Wharf
Slipway
Tower Hamlets
Lewisham
SE8
Deptford Trad Est
Parkside Bsns Est
Folkestone Gardens
Dreadnought Wharf
Dowell's Wharf
A200
141
36
37
38
120
81
80
79
78
6
5
4
3
2
1

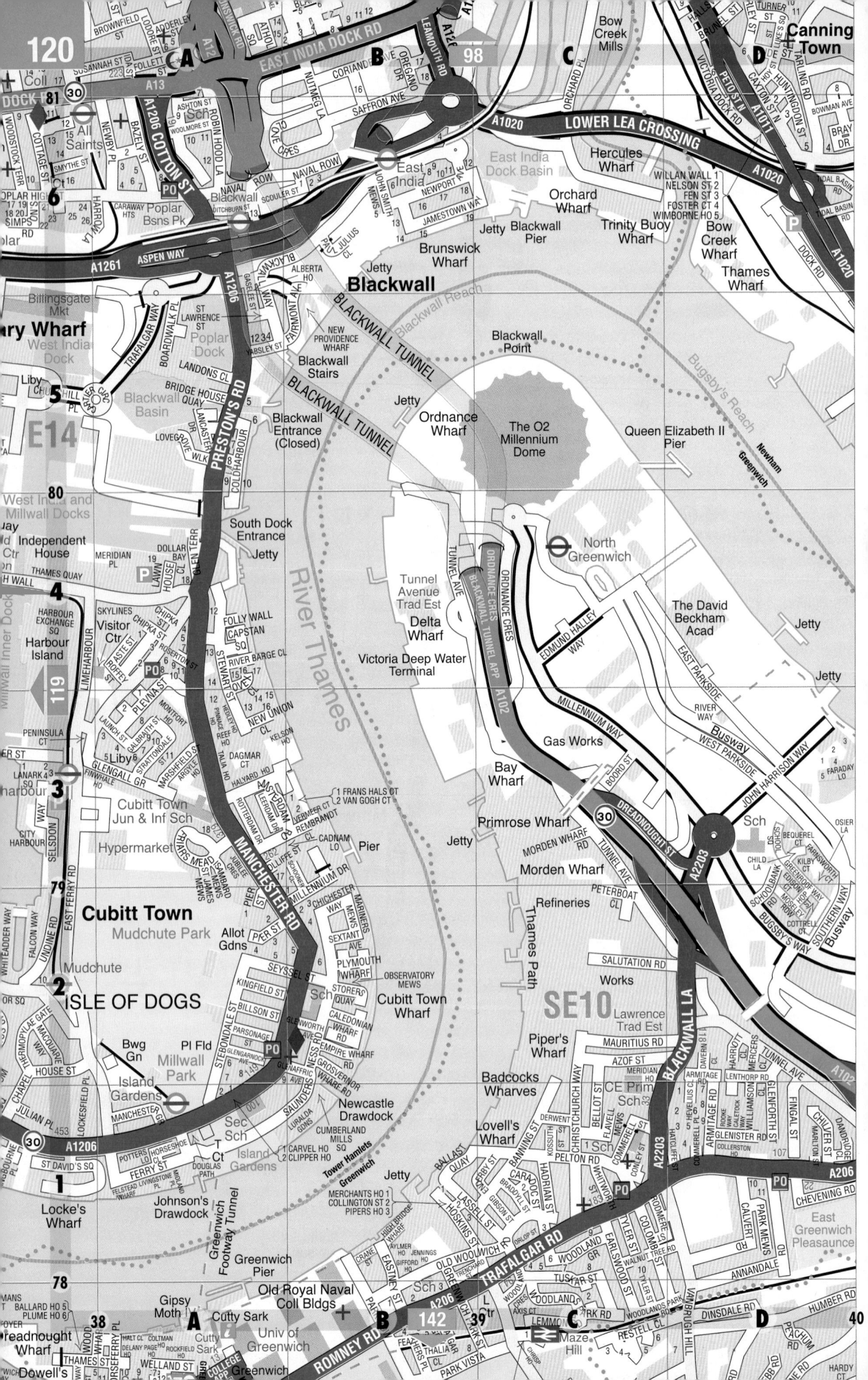
A
B
C
D
98
Canning Town
Bow Creek Mills
BROWNFIELD ST
LODORE ST
ADDERLEY ST
EAST INDIA DOCK RD
LEAMOUTH RD
ATHOL SQ
SUSANNAH ST
IDA ST
FOLLETT ST
A13
A12
CORIANDER AVE
OREGANO DR
NUTMEG LA
SAFFRON AVE
CLOVE CRES
ORCHARD PL
BRUNEL ST
VICTORIA DOCK RD
PETO ST N
CAXTON ST N
HOY ST
TARLING RD
HUNTINGDON ST
BOWMAN AVE
BRAY DR
A1011
A1020
LOWER LEA CROSSING
DOCK RD
Coll
81
30
All Saints
WOODSTOCK TERR
COTTAGE ST
SMYTHE ST
NEWBY PL
BAZELY ST
A1206 COTTON ST
ASHTON ST
WOOLMORE ST
ROBIN HOOD LA
Sch
PO
Hercules Wharf
East India Dock Basin
East India
NAVAL ROW
JOHN SMITH MEWS
NEWPORT AVE
JAMESTOWN WAY
WILLAN WALL
NELSON ST
FEN ST
FOSTER CT
WIMBORNE HO
TIDAL BASIN RD
6
POPLAR HIGH ST
SIMPSON'S RD
HARROW LA
CARAWAY HTS
Poplar Bsns Pk
Blackwall
DITCHBURN ST
SCOULER ST
Orchard Wharf
Trinity Buoy Wharf
Bow Creek Wharf
Thames Wharf
Jetty
Blackwall Pier
Brunswick Wharf
JULIUS CL
A1261
ASPEN WAY
A1206
BLACKWALL WAY
ALBERTA HO
GASLEE ST
FAIRMONT AVE
Blackwall
Billingsgate Mkt
ary Wharf
West India Dock
TRAFALGAR WAY
BOARDWALK PL
ST LAWRENCE ST
Poplar Dock
YABSLEY ST
NEW PROVIDENCE WHARF
Blackwall Stairs
BLACKWALL TUNNEL
Blackwall Reach
Blackwall Point
Bugsby's Reach
Liby
CHURCHILL PL
5
CARTIER CIRC
Blackwall Basin
BRIDGE HOUSE QUAY
LANDONS CL
PRESTON'S RD
LANCASTER DR
COLDHARBOUR
LOVEGROVE WLK
Blackwall Entrance (Closed)
Jetty
Ordnance Wharf
The O2 Millennium Dome
Queen Elizabeth II Pier
Newham
Greenwich
E14
80
West India and Millwall Docks
Independent House
MERIDIAN PL
THAMES QUAY
DOLLAR BAY CL
LAWN HOUSE CL
GLEN TERR
South Dock Entrance
Jetty
River Thames
Tunnel Avenue Trad Est
TUNNEL AVE
ORDNANCE CRES
BLACKWALL TUNNEL APP
North Greenwich
4
HARBOUR EXCHANGE SQ
Harbour Island
SKYLINES
Visitor Ctr
LIMEHARBOUR
CHIPKA ST
FOLLY WALL
CAPSTAN SQ
RIVER BARGE CL
STEWART ST
ROSERTON ST
ASTE ST
ROFFEY ST
Delta Wharf
Victoria Deep Water Terminal
EDMUND HALLEY WAY
The David Beckham Acad
Jetty
EAST PARKSIDE
Jetty
119
Millwall Inner Dock
PLEVNA ST
MONTCALM HO
LAUNCH ST
GALBRAITH ST
STRATTONDALE ST
MARSHFIELD ST
ARGYLE HO
PINNACE HO
REEF HO
TALIA HO
NEW UNION CL
KELSON HO
A102
MILLENNIUM WAY
RIVER WAY
Busway
WEST PARKSIDE
JOHN HARRISON WAY
FARADAY LO
PENINSULA CT
ER ST
LANARK SQ
3
Liby
GLENGALL GR
DAGMAR CT
HALYARD HO
Gas Works
BOORD ST
Bay Wharf
Cubitt Town Jun & Inf Sch
AMSTERDAM RD
LEERDAM DR
ROTTERDAM DR
1 FRANS HALS CT
2 VAN GOGH CT
VERMEER CT
REMBRANDT CL
CITY HARBOUR
SELSDON WAY
Hypermarket
FRIARS MEAD
ISAMBARD MEWS
ST JAMES MEWS
JUBILEE CRES
MANCHESTER RD
CADNAM LO
Pier
Primrose Wharf
Jetty
DREADNOUGHT ST
MORDEN WHARF RD
TUNNEL AVE
Morden Wharf
A2203
Sch
SCHOOL SQ
BEQUEREL CT
CHILD LA
KILBY CT
FARNSWORTH CT
OSIER LA
79
EAST FERRY RD
Cubitt Town
Mudchute Park
Allot Gdns
PIER ST
PAR ST
MILLENNIUM DR
CHICHESTER WAY
MARINERS MEWS
SEXTANT AVE
PLYMOUTH WHARF
Refineries
PETERBOAT CL
SCHOOLBANK RD
GREENROOF WAY
EDISON DR
MOSELEY ROW
COTTRELL CT
BUGSBY'S WAY
SOUTHERN WAY
Busway
WHITEADDER WAY
FALCON WAY
UNDINE RD
Mudchute
2
ISLE OF DOGS
SEYSSEL ST
KINGFIELD ST
BILLSON ST
STEBONDALE ST
PARSONAGE ST
GLENGARNOCK AVE
OBSERVATORY MEWS
STOREHOUSE QUAY
Cubitt Town Wharf
CALEDONIAN WHARF RD
Thames Path
SALUTATION RD
Works
SE10
Lawrence Trad Est
OR SQ
THERMOPYLAE GATE
MACQUARIE WAY
Bwg Gn
Pl Fld
Millwall Park
GLENWORTH AVE
EMPIRE WHARF RD
PO
Piper's Wharf
MAURITIUS RD
BLACKWALL LA
AZOF ST
MERIDIAN HO
DAVERN CL
HARVOTT CT
MERCERS CT
TUNNEL AVE
A102
HOUSE ST
CHAPEL HO
Island Gardens
GLENAFFRIC AVE
GROSVENOR WHARF RD
NESS ST
SAUNDERS NESS RD
Newcastle Drawdock
Badcocks Wharves
CHRISTCHURCH WAY
BELLOT ST
FLAVELL MEWS
CE Prim Sch
COMMERELL ST
ARMITAGE HO
ARMITAGE RD
LENTHORP RD
WILLIAMSON CL
GLENFORTH ST
FINGAL ST
CHILVER ST
DANDRIDGE CL
JULIAN PL
453
LOCKESFIELD PL
MANCHESTER GR
Sec Sch
LURALDA GDNS
CUMBERLAND MILLS SQ
DERWENT
Lovell's Wharf
BANNING ST
KOSSUTH ST
GLENISTER RD
COLLERSTON HO
MARLTON ST
30
A1206
POTTERS HO
HORSESHOE CL
Ct
Island Gardens
1 CARVEL HO
2 CLIPPER HO
Tower Hamlets
Greenwich
PELTON RD
Sch
HATCLIFFE ST
A2203
107
A206
ST DAVID'S SQ
FERRY ST
DOUGLAS PATH
1
FELSTEAD WHARF
LIVINGSTONE PL
MIDLAND PL
Jetty
BALLAST QUAY
ENDERBY ST
CARADOC ST
HADRIAN ST
LEMMON
WHITWORTH ST
CONLEY ST
PO
PO
CHEVENING RD
Locke's Wharf
Johnson's Drawdock
Greenwich Footway Tunnel
MERCHANTS HO
COLLINGTON ST
PIPERS HO
HOSKINS ST
LASSELL ST
GIBSON ST
BRADDYLL ST
TRAFALGAR RD
TYLER ST
COLOMB ST
RODMERE ST
CALVERT RD
PARK MEWS
East Greenwich Pleasaunce
Greenwich Pier
HIGH BRIDGE WHARF
CRANE ST
AYLMER HO
JENNINGS HO
GIFFORD HO
OLD WOOLWICH RD
TRENCHARD ST
ORLOP ST
WOODLAND GR
EARLSWOOD ST
WALNUT TREE RD
ANNANDALE RD
78
Old Royal Naval Coll Bldgs
Sch
EASTNEY ST
GREENWICH CHURCH ST
TUSKAR ST
WOODLAND CRES
WOODLANDS PARK RD
VANBRUGH HILL
DINSDALE RD
HUMBER RD
BALLARD HO
PLUME HO
Gipsy Moth
A
Cutty Sark
B
142
39
Ctr
AXIS CT
C
PARK RD
D
40
38
Dreadnought Wharf
HALT CL
COLTMAN HO
DELANY PAGE HO
ROCKFIELD HO
Cutty Sark
Univ of Greenwich
ROMNEY RD
FEATHERS PL
THALIA CL
PARK VISTA
CHRISP ST
Maze Hill
RESTELL CL
PEACHUM RD
HARDY CT
THAMES ST
WELLAND ST
COLLEGE APP
Greenwich
Dowell's

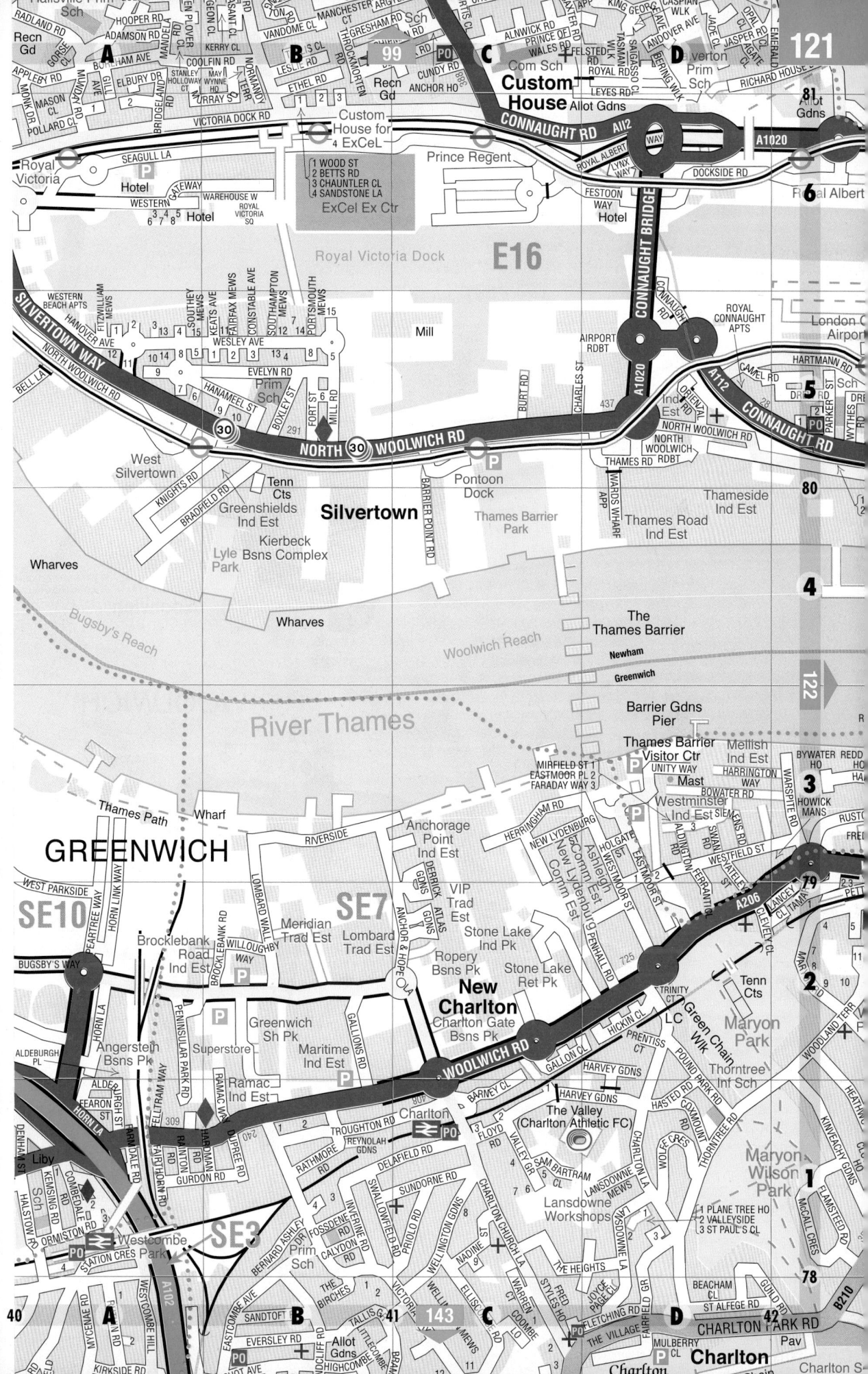

121
99
Custom House
Custom House for ExCeL
Prince Regent
Royal Victoria
CONNAUGHT RD
A112
A1020
ROYAL ALBERT WAY
DOCKSIDE RD
Royal Albert
Allot Gdns
81
Hotel
WESTERN GATEWAY
WAREHOUSE W
ROYAL VICTORIA SQ
SEAGULL LA
1 WOOD ST
2 BETTS RD
3 CHAUNTLER CL
4 SANDSTONE LA
ExCel Ex Ctr
FESTOON WAY
CONNAUGHT BRIDGE
Royal Victoria Dock
E16
VICTORIA DOCK RD
Recn Gd
Com Sch
Mill
AIRPORT RDBT
ROYAL CONNAUGHT APTS
London City Airport
HARTMANN RD
SILVERTOWN WAY
NORTH WOOLWICH RD
WESLEY AVE
EVELYN RD
HANAMEEL ST
Prim Sch
BOXLEY ST
FORT ST
MILL RD
BURT RD
CHARLES ST
NORTH WOOLWICH RDBT
THAMES RD
Ind Est
West Silvertown
Pontoon Dock
Tenn Cts
Greenshields Ind Est
Silvertown
Thames Barrier Park
Thames Road Ind Est
Thameside Ind Est
Kierbeck Bsns Complex
Lyle Park
Wharves
BARRIER POINT RD
KNIGHTS RD
BRADFIELD RD
WARDS WHARF APP
80
4
Bugsby's Reach
Woolwich Reach
The Thames Barrier
Newham
Greenwich
122
River Thames
Barrier Gdns Pier
Thames Barrier Visitor Ctr
Mellish Ind Est
Mast
Westminster Ind Est
MIRFIELD ST 1
EASTMOOR PL 2
FARADAY WAY 3
UNITY WAY
HARRINGTON WAY
BOWATER RD
3
Thames Path
Wharf
GREENWICH
RIVERSIDE
Anchorage Point Ind Est
HERRINGHAM RD
NEW LYDENBURG ST
New Lydenburg Comm Est
Ashleigh Comm Est
WESTMOOR ST
EASTMOOR ST
WESTFIELD ST
A206
79
SE10
SE7
WEST PARKSIDE
PEARTREE WAY
HORN LINK WAY
LOMBARD WALL
Meridian Trad Est
Lombard Trad Est
VIP Trad Est
Stone Lake Ind Pk
Ropery Bsns Pk
Stone Lake Ret Pk
ANCHOR & HOPE LA
New Charlton
Charlton Gate Bsns Pk
Brocklebank Road Ind Est
WILLOUGHBY WAY
BUGSBY'S WAY
Greenwich Sh Pk
Superstore
Maritime Ind Est
GALLIONS RD
Angerstein Bsns Pk
Ramac Ind Est
WOOLWICH RD
Tenn Cts
2
Maryon Park
Green Chain Wlk
Thorntree Inf Sch
The Valley (Charlton Athletic FC)
Charlton
HARVEY GDNS
FLOYD RD
VALLEY GR
SAM BARTRAM CL
Lansdowne Workshops
CHARLTON LA
CHARLTON CHURCH LA
Maryon Wilson Park
1
1 PLANE TREE HO
2 VALLEYSIDE
3 ST PAUL'S CL
78
Westcombe Park
SE3
A102
Liby
Prim Sch
THE HEIGHTS
BEACHAM CL
ST ALFEGE RD
CHARLTON PARK RD
B210
THE VILLAGE
Charlton
Pav
40
41
143
42
A
B
C
D

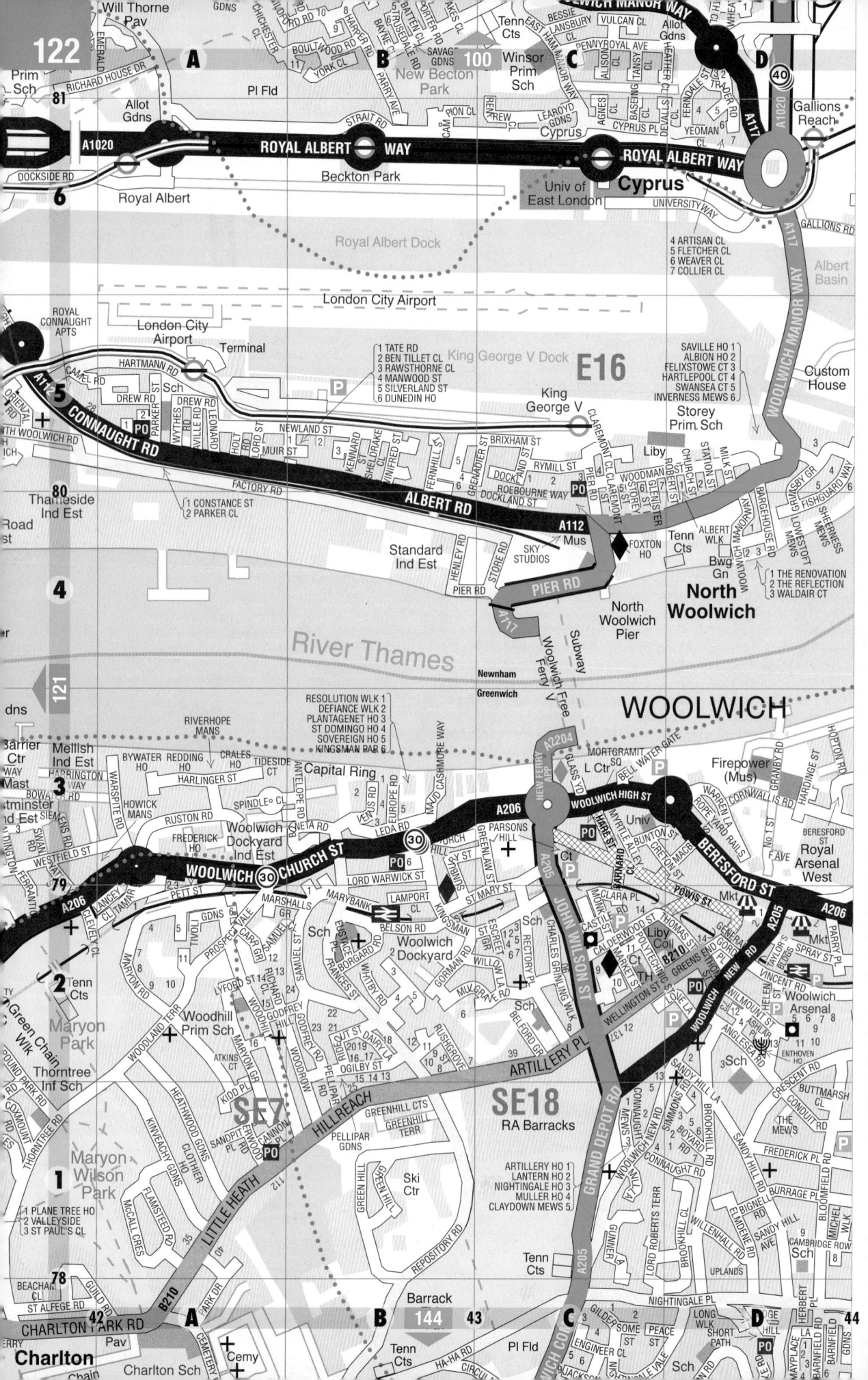

ROYAL ALBERT WAY
Beckton Park
Cyprus
Univ of East London
Royal Albert Dock
London City Airport
King George V Dock
E16
CONNAUGHT RD
ALBERT RD
PIER RD
North Woolwich
River Thames
WOOLWICH
WOOLWICH CHURCH ST
WOOLWICH HIGH ST
BERESFORD ST
JOHN WILSON ST
Woolwich Dockyard
SE18
SE7
RA Barracks
Maryon Park
Maryon Wilson Park
GRAND DEPOT RD
Royal Arsenal West
Charlton

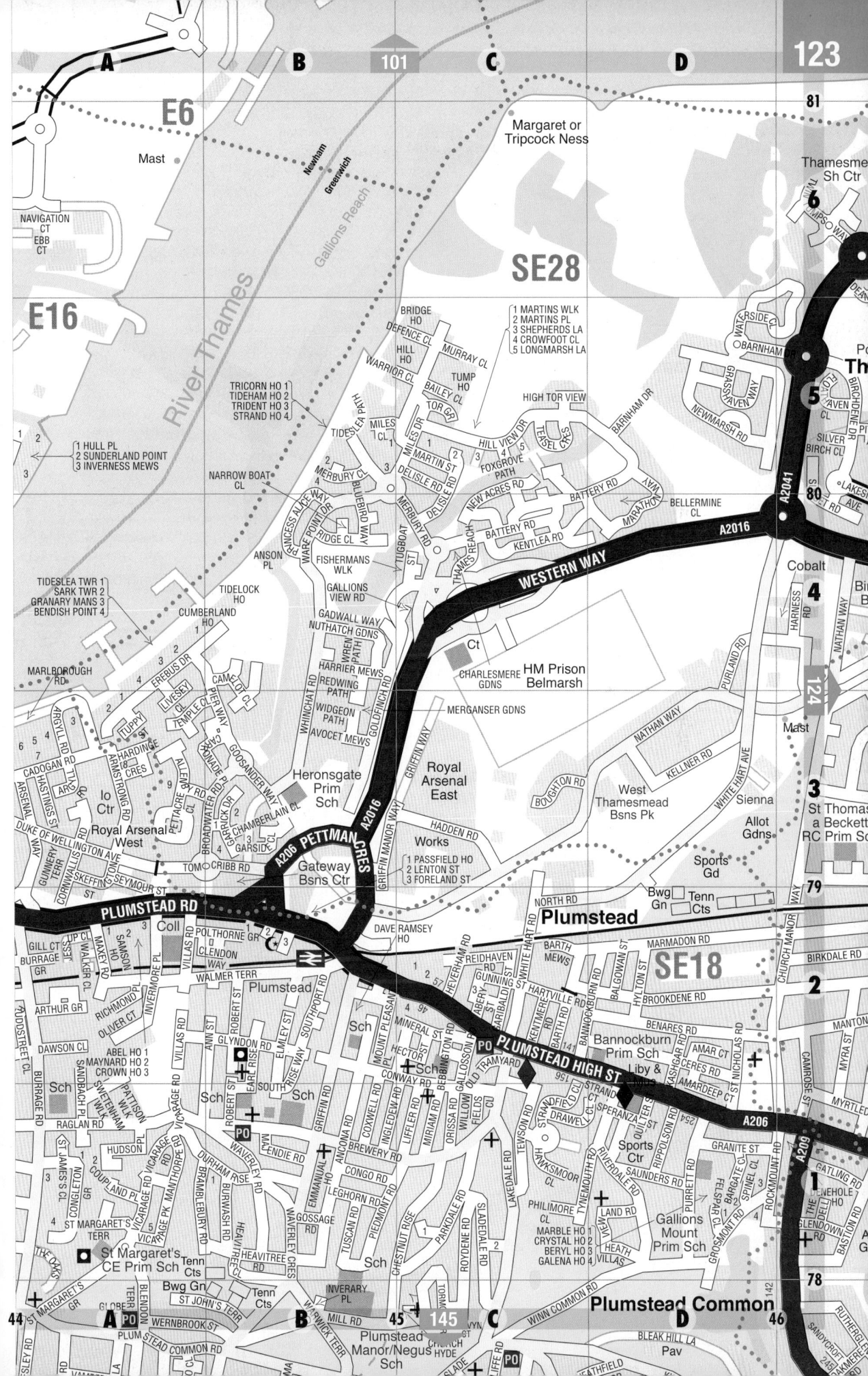

E6

Mast

NAVIGATION
CT
EBB
CT

E16

River Thames

Gallions Reach

Newham

Greenwich

Margaret or
Tripcock Ness

SE28

Thamesme
Sh Ctr

1 HULL PL
2 SUNDERLAND POINT
3 INVERNESS MEWS

TRICORN HO 1
TIDEHAM HO 2
TRIDENT HO 3
STRAND HO 4

NARROW BOAT
CL

TIDESLEA TWR 1
SARK TWR 2
GRANARY MANS 3
BENDISH POINT 4

MARLBOROUGH
RD

CUMBERLAND
HO

TIDELOCK

ANSON
PL

BRIDGE
HO
DEFENCE CL
HILL
HO
WARRIOR CL
TIDESLEA PATH

MILES
CL

MURRAY CL

TUMP
HO
BAILEY CL
TOR GR

MILES DR

MERBURY CL

BLUEBIRD WAY
RIDGE CL

TUGBOAT
ST

THAMES REACH

MERBURY RD
DELISLE RD
DELISLE ED

MARTIN ST

NEW ACRES RD

HIGH TOR VIEW

1 MARTINS WLK
2 MARTINS PL
3 SHEPHERDS LA
4 CROWFOOT CL
5 LONGMARSH LA

HILL VIEW DR

TEASEL CRES

FOXGROVE
PATH

HILL VIEW DR

BATTERY RD

BATTERY RD
KENTLEA RD

BARNHAM DR

MARATHON

BARNHAM
WAY

BELLERMINE
CL

A2016

WESTERN WAY

Cobalt

WATERSIDE
BARNHAM

GRASSHAVEN WAY

NEWMARSH RD

A2041

BIRCHDENE DR
FLOTHAVEN CL

SILVER
BIRCH CL

LAKES
AVE

RD

Th

6

5

80

124

PRINCESS ALICE WAY
WARE POINT DR

FISHERMANS
WLK
GALLIONS
VIEW RD

GADWALL WAY
NUTHATCH GDNS
WREN
PATH
HARRIER MEWS
REDWING
PATH
WIDGEON
PATH
AVOCET MEWS

WHINCHAT RD
GOLDFINCH RD

Ct

CHARLESMERE
GDNS

MERGANSER GDNS

HM PRISON
Belmarsh

PURLAND RD

NATHAN WAY

KELLNER RD

BOUGHTON RD

West
Thamesmead
Bsns Pk

HARNESS
RD

NATHAN WAY

WHITE HART AVE

Sienna

Allot
Gdns

Sienna

Sports
Gd

Mast

4

3

79

St Thomas
a Beckett
RC Prim Sch

ARGYLL RD
CADOGAN RD
HASTINGS ST

ARSENAL
RD

DUKE OF WELLINGTON AVE

GUNNERY
TERR

CORNWALLIS
ST

SKEFFINGTON
ST

MARLBOROUGH
RD

EREBUS DR
LIVESEY

TUPPY

HARDINGE
CRES

TEMPLE CL

PIER WAY
CAMEL CT

ARMSTRONG RD

Io
Ctr

Royal Arsenal
West

PETTACRE CL
BROADWATER RD
CHAPLIN CL

GARRICK DR

GOOSANDER WAY

CHAMBERLAIN CL
GARSIDE

A206 PETTMAN CRES

A2016

GRIFFIN MANOR WAY

GRIFFIN WAY

Royal
Arsenal
East

HADDEN RD

Works

1 PASSFIELD HO
2 LENTON ST
3 FORELAND ST

Heronsgate
Prim Sch

Gateway
Bsns Ctr

TOM CRIBB RD

SEYMOUR ST

PLUMSTEAD RD

Plumstead

NORTH RD

Bwg
Gn

Tenn
Cts

WAY

2

1

78

Coll

GILL CT
BURRAGE
GR

SAMSON
ST

WALKER CL
MAXEY RD

CLENDON
WAY

POLTHORNE GR

INVERMORE PL

WALMER TERR

Plumstead

DAVE RAMSEY
HO

REIDHAVEN
RD

HEVERHAM RD

WHITE HART RD

GUNNING ST
GARIBALDI ST

BARTH
MEWS

MARMADON RD

BALGOWAN ST

HYLTON ST

BANNOCKBURN ST

BENARES RD

BROOKDENE RD

SE18

BIRKDALE RD

MANTON

RICHMOND
ARTHUR GR
DAWSON CL

ABEL HO 1
MAYNARD HO 2
CROWN HO 3

Sch

BURRAGE RD

PUDDSTREET RD

ST JAMES'S
CL

ST MARGARET'S
TERR

Sch

HUDSON

COUPLAND PL

PATTISON
WALK
SWETENHAM
WILKINSON

VICARAGE RD
VICARAGE

VICARAGE PK

MANTHORPE RD

BRAMBLEBURY RD

DURHAM RISE

BURWASH RD

WAVERLEY RISE

WAVERLEY RD

HEAVITREE
RD

GOSSAGE
RD

St Margaret's
CE Prim Sch

Bwg Gn

Tenn
Cts

ST MARGARET'S
GR

BLENDON TERR
GLOBE
PO

WERNBROOK ST

ST JOHN'S TERR

PLUM
STEAD COMMON RD

WARWICK TERR

INVERARY
PL

MILL RD

Plumstead
Manor/Negus
Sch

GLYNDON RD

ANN ST

ROBERT ST

EARL RISE

ELMLEY ST

RISE WAY

SOUTHPORT RD

SOUTH

GRIFFIN RD

COXWELL RD

INGLEDEW RD

EMMANUEL RD

CONGO RD

LEGHORN RD

PIEDMONT RD

TUSCAN RD

CHESTNUT RISE

Sch

Sch

PO

WAVERLEY RD

MENDIE RD

ANCONA RD

BREWERY RD

Sch

ORISSA RD

MIRIAM RD

LIFFLER RD

WILLOW
FIELDS

MINERAL ST

HECTOR ST

MOUNT PLEASANT

BEBBINGTON RD

SCHENBURG

CONWAY RD

GALLOSSON RD

BARTH RD

LAKEDALE RD

SLADEDALE RD

PARKDALE RD

ROYDENE RD

TOMLIN

Sch

TEWSON RD

HAWKSMOOR
CL

PHILIMORE
CL

MARBLE HO 1
CRYSTAL HO 2
BERYL HO 3
GALENA HO 4

HEATH
VILLAS

PO
Old Tramyard
PLUMSTEAD HIGH ST

STRANDFIELD
DRAWELL

STRAND

QUILTERS

Sports
Ctr

Liby &

PO

Bannockburn
Prim Sch

KENTMERE RD

HARTVILLE RD

AMBER CT

AMAR CT

CERES RD

AMARDEEP ST

ST NICHOLAS RD

KASHGAR RD

RIPPOLSON RD

SAUNDERS RD

RIVERDALE RD

PURRETT RD

TYNEMOUTH RD

FELSPAR CL

BARGATE CL

SPINEL CL

ROCKMOUNT RD

GROSMONT RD

CHURCH MANOR

MYRA ST

CAMROSE ST

A206

MYRTLE

GRANITE ST

GATLING RD

NEWHOLE
HO

THE
DELL
BLENDOWN ST

BASTION RD

A206

Gallions
Mount
Prim Sch

Plumstead Common

BLEAK HILL LA
Pav

SANDYCROFT

RUTHER

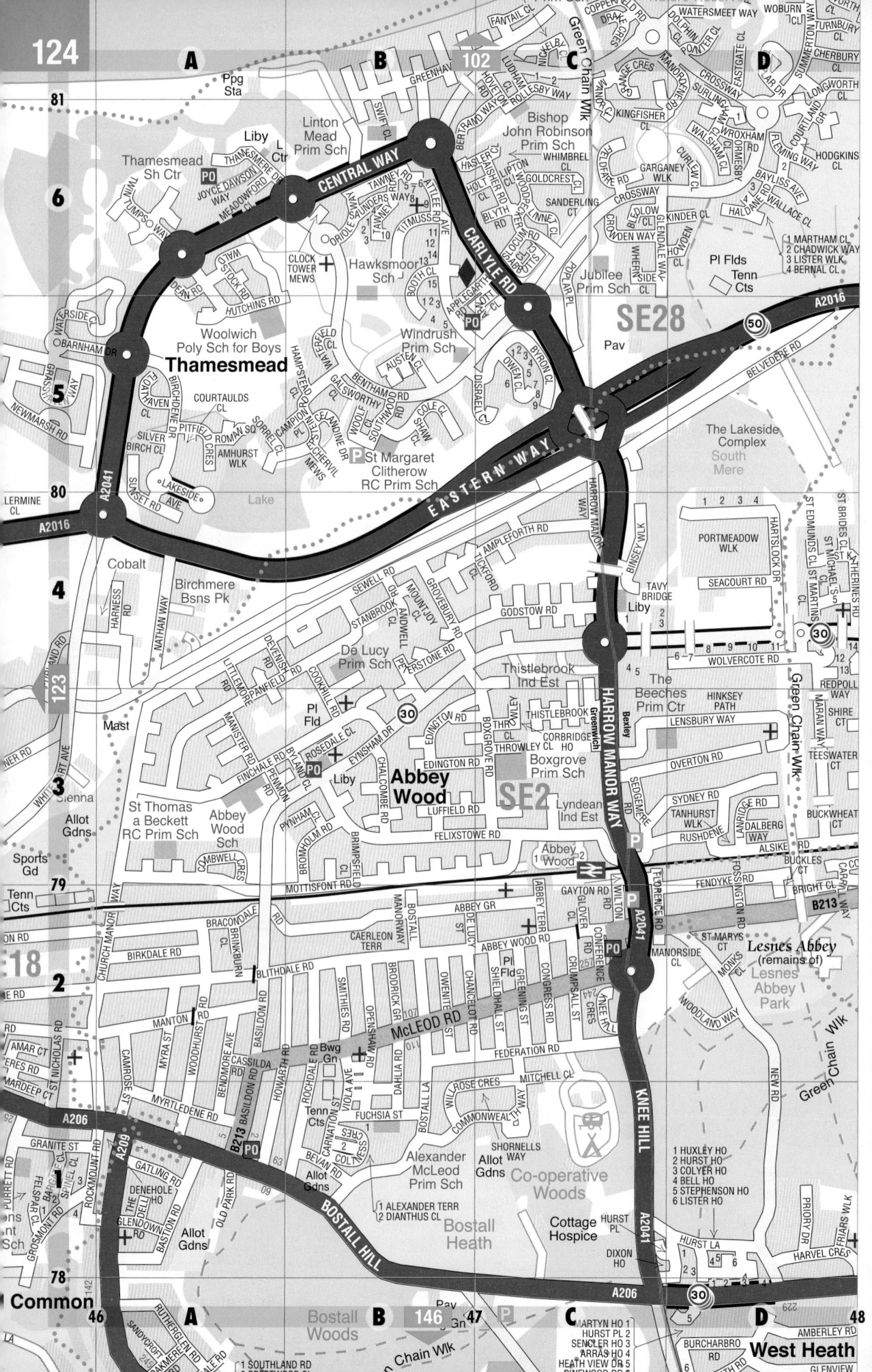

A
B
C
D
102
123
146
81
6
5
80
4
3
79
2
1
78
46
47
48
Thamesmead
Thamesmead Sh Ctr
Linton Mead Prim Sch
Bishop John Robinson Prim Sch
Hawksmoor Sch
Woolwich Poly Sch for Boys
Windrush Prim Sch
St Margaret Clitherow RC Prim Sch
Jubilee Prim Sch
SE28
The Lakeside Complex
South Mere
Lake
Cobalt
Birchmere Bsns Pk
De Lucy Prim Sch
Thistlebrook Ind Est
The Beeches Prim Ctr
Abbey Wood
SE2
Boxgrove Prim Sch
Lyndean Ind Est
St Thomas a Beckett RC Prim Sch
Abbey Wood Sch
Allot Gdns
Sports Gd
Tenn Cts
Lesnes Abbey (remains of)
Lesnes Abbey Park
Alexander McLeod Prim Sch
Co-operative Woods
Bostall Heath
Cottage Hospice
Bostall Woods
West Heath
Common
CENTRAL WAY
CARLYLE RD
EASTERN WAY
HARROW MANOR WAY
KNEE HILL
McLEOD RD
BOSTALL HILL
A2016
A2041
A206
A209
B213
Green Chain Wlk
1 MARTHAM CL
2 CHADWICK WAY
3 LISTER WLK
4 BERNAL CL
1 HUXLEY HO
2 HURST HO
3 COLYER HO
4 BELL HO
5 STEPHENSON HO
6 LISTER HO
1 ALEXANDER TERR
2 DIANTHUS CL
MARTYN HO 1
HURST PL 2
SENCLER HO 3
ARRAS HO 4
HEATH VIEW DR 5

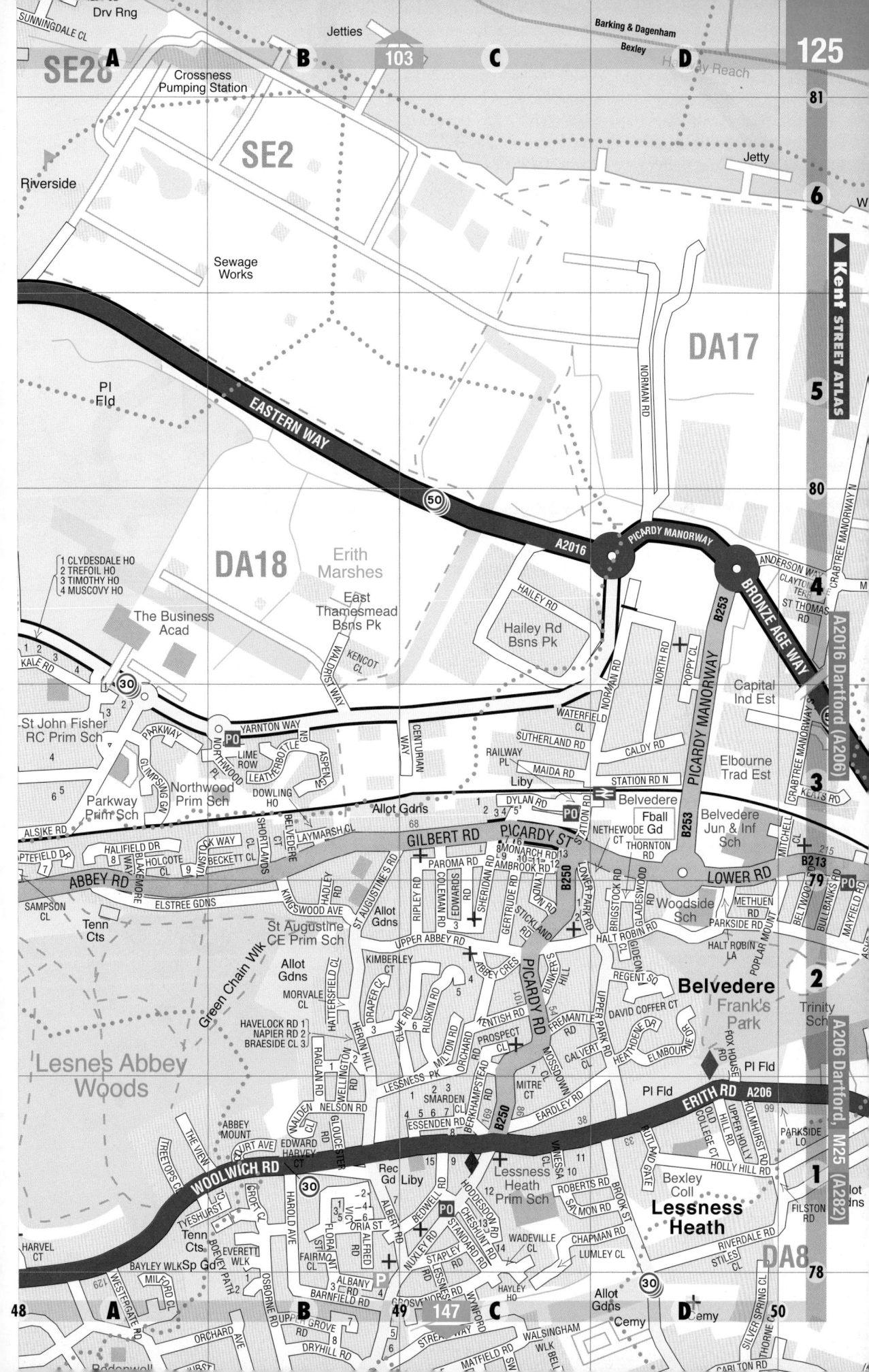
Kent STREET ATLAS
A B C D
103
147
81
80
79
78
6
5
4
3
2
1
48
49
50
Drv Rng
SUNNINGDALE CL
SE28
Jetties
Barking & Dagenham
Bexley
Halfway Reach
Crossness Pumping Station
SE2
Jetty
Riverside
Sewage Works
DA17
NORMAN RD
Pl Fld
EASTERN WAY
50
A2016
PICARDY MANORWAY
ANDERSON WAY
CRABTREE MANORWAY N
CLAYTON TERR
ST THOMAS RD
BRONZE AGE WAY
1 CLYDESDALE HO
2 TREFOIL HO
3 TIMOTHY HO
4 MUSCOVY HO
DA18
Erith Marshes
East Thamesmead Bsns Pk
HAILEY RD
Hailey Rd Bsns Pk
The Business Acad
KALE RD
KENCOT CL
WALDRIST WAY
NORTH RD
POPPY CL
B253
Capital Ind Est
30
St John Fisher RC Prim Sch
PARKWAY
YARNTON WAY
PO
NORTHWOOD PL
LIME ROW
LEATHERBOTTLE GN
ASPEN GN
CENTURIAN WAY
WATERFIELD CL
SUTHERLAND RD
RAILWAY PL
MAIDA RD
CALDY RD
STATION RD N
Elbourne Trad Est
CRABTREE MANORWAY S
KEATS RD
A2016 Dartford (A206)
GLIMPSING GN
Northwood Prim Sch
Parkway Prim Sch
DOWLING HO
Liby
DYLAN RD
Belvedere
Fball Gd
Belvedere Jun & Inf Sch
ALSIKE RD
Allot Gdns
68
SHORTLANDS
BELVEDERE CT
LAYMARSH CL
GILBERT RD
PICARDY ST
STATION RD
NETHEWODE CT
THORNTON RD
MITCHELL CL
B213
215
HALIFIELD DR
TUNSTOCK WAY
BECKETT CL
HOLCOTE CL
BLAKEMORE WAY
MONARCH RD
AMBROOK RD
PAROMA RD
LOWER PARK RD
B250
LOWER RD
METHUEN RD
BELTWOOD RD
BULLBANKS RD
MAYFIELD RD
ABBEY RD
ELSTREE GDNS
KINGSWOOD AVE
HADLEY RD
ST AUGUSTINE'S RD
RIPLEY RD
COLEMAN RD
EDWARDS RD
SHERIDAN RD
GERTRUDE RD
LYNDON RD
STICKLAND RD
BRIGSTOCK RD
GLADESWOOD RD
Woodside Sch
PARKSIDE RD
POPLAR MOUNT
SAMPSON CL
Tenn Cts
St Augustine CE Prim Sch
Allot Gdns
UPPER ABBEY RD
HALT ROBIN RD
HALT ROBIN LA
Green Chain Wlk
KIMBERLEY CT
ABBEY CRES
PICARDY RD
BUNKER'S HILL
GIDEON CL
REGENT SQ
Belvedere
Frank's Park
Trinity Sch
MORVALE CL
HATTERSFIELD CL
DRAPER CL
CLIVE RD
RUSKIN RD
MILTON RD
KENTISH RD
FREMANTLE RD
UPPER PARK RD
DAVID COFFER CT
HEATHDENE DR
ELMBOURNE DR
FOX HOUSE RD
HAVELOCK RD
NAPIER RD
BRAESIDE CL
HERON HILL
ORCHARD
PROSPECT CL
MOSSDOWN CL
CALVERT CL
Pl Fld
Lesnes Abbey Woods
RAGLAN RD
WELLINGTON RD
LESSNESS PK
BERKHAMPSTEAD RD
MITRE CT
EARDLEY RD
Pl Fld
ERITH RD
A206
A206 Dartford, M25 (A282)
SMARDEN CL
ESSENDEN RD
NELSON RD
WALDEN CL
GLOUCESTER RD
OLD COLLEGE CT
HILL RD
UPPER HOLLY HILL RD
HOLMHURST RD
PARKSIDE LO
THE VIEW
ABBEY MOUNT
COURT AVE
EDWARD HARVEY CT
38
99
VANESSA CL
RUTLAND GATE
HOLLY HILL RD
TREETOPS CL
WOOLWICH RD
Rec Gd
Liby
Lessness Heath Prim Sch
Bexley Coll
HARVEL CT
TYESHURST CL
CROFT CL
HAROLD AVE
ALBERT RD
BEDWELL RD
HODDESDON RD
CHESHUNT RD
ROBERTS RD
SALMON RD
BROOK ST
Lessness Heath
FILSTON RD
Tenn Cts
BOEVEY PATH
EVERETT WLK
VICTORIA ST
ALFRED RD
FLORANCE ST
STANDARD RD
NUXLEY RD
WADEVILLE CL
CHAPMAN RD
LUMLEY CL
RIVERDALE RD
STILES CL
DA8
BAYLEY WLK
Sp Gd
MILFORD CL
FAIRMONT CL
ALBANY RD
STAPLEY RD
LESSNESS RD
HAYLEY HO
Allot Gdns
Cemy
SILVER SPRING CL
THORNE CL
WESTERGATE RD
OSBORNE RD
BARNFIELD RD
GROSVENOR RD
WYNFORD
UPPER GROVE RD
ORCHARD AVE
DRYHILL RD
STREAM WAY
WALSINGHAM WLK
MATFIELD RD
CARLTON RD
129
169
98

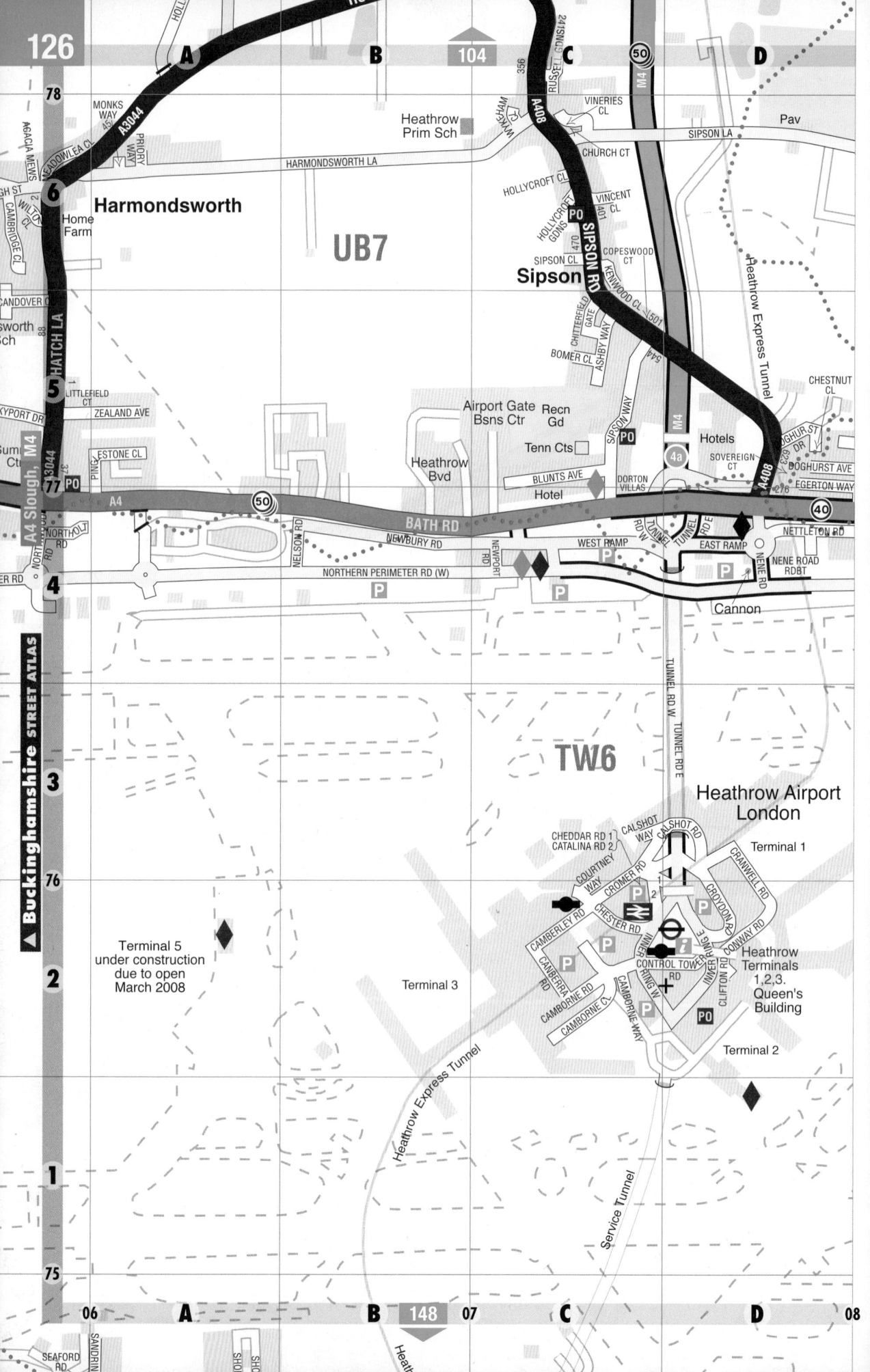

78

MONKS
WAY
MEADOWLEA CL
AGACIA MEWS

HIGH ST
CAMBRIDGE CL
WILTON CL

A3044
PRIORY WAY

HOLLO

VINERIES CL

SIPSON LA
Pav

6
Home Farm

Harmondsworth

Heathrow Prim Sch

A408
WYNHAM

RUSH

356
M4

CHURCH CT

HOLLYCROFT CL

VINCENT CL

UB7

HOLLYCROFT GDNS
PO

SIPSON RD

COPESWOOD CT

Sipson

CANDOVER CT

sworth Sch

HATCH LA

CHITTERFIELD GATE

SIPSON CL
KENWOOD CL

BOMER CL
ASHBY WAY

CHESTNUT CL

5
LITTLEFIELD CT

ZEALAND AVE

Airport Gate Bsns Ctr

Recn Gd

SIPSON WAY

BOGHURST DR

SKYPORT DR

ESTONE CL
PINES

Heathrow Bvd

Tenn Cts
PO

4a

Hotels

SOVEREIGN CT

BOGHURST AVE
EGERTON WAY

M4

77
PO

A3044
M4
A4 Slough, M4

50

A4

BATH RD

BLUNTS AVE
Hotel

DORTON VILLAS

A408

40

NELSON RD

NEWBURY RD

NEWPORT RD

WEST RAMP

TUNNEL RD W
TUNNEL RD E

EAST RAMP

NETTLETON RD

NENE RD
NENE ROAD RDBT

4
NORTHOLT RD

NORTHERN PERIMETER RD (W)

P

P

P

Cannon

P

TW6

Terminal 5 under construction due to open March 2008

TUNNEL RD W
TUNNEL RD E

Heathrow Airport London

CHEDDAR RD 1
CATALINA RD 2

CALSHOT WAY
CALSHOT RD

Terminal 1

76

COURTNEY WAY

CROMER RD

CRANWELL RD

P

CROYDON RD

CONWAY RD

CAMBERLEY RD

CHESTER RD

INNER RING E

Heathrow Terminals 1,2,3. Queen's Building

CAMBERRA RD
CAMBORNE RD

P

P

Terminal 3

CAMBORNE CL

CLIFTON RD

Control Tower
INNER RING W

CAMBORNE WAY

PO

2

Terminal 2

Heathrow Express Tunnel

Service Tunnel

1

75

▲ Buckinghamshire STREET ATLAS

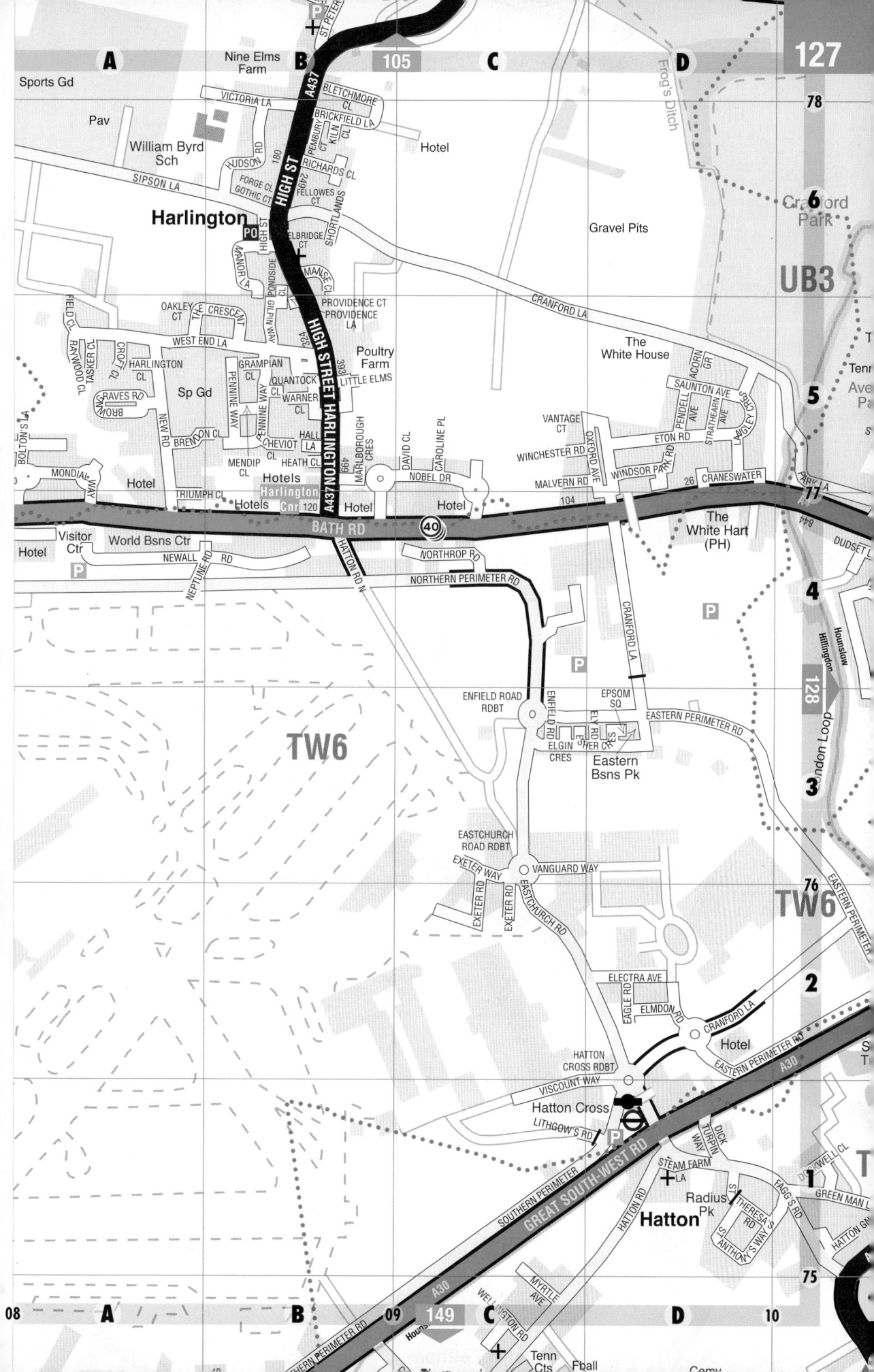

127
105
149
128
A
B
C
D
78
6
5
4
3
2
1
76
77
75
08
09
10
Nine Elms Farm
Sports Gd
Pav
William Byrd Sch
Harlington
Hotel
Gravel Pits
Cranford Park
UB3
Frog's Ditch
SIPSON LA
VICTORIA LA
HIGH ST
BLETCHMORE CL
BRICKFIELD LA
KILN CL
PEMBURY CT
RICHARDS CL
HUDSON RD
FORGE CL
GOTHIC CT
FELLOWES CT
SHORTLANDS
ELBRIDGE CT
MANSE CL
MANOR LA
PONDSIDE CL
GILPIN WAY
PROVIDENCE CT
PROVIDENCE LA
CRANFORD LA
OAKLEY CT
THE CRESCENT
WEST END LA
Poultry Farm
The White House
ACORN GR
SAUNTON AVE
HARLINGTON CL
GRAMPIAN CL
QUANTOCK CL
WARNER CL
LITTLE ELMS
HIGH STREET HARLINGTON
A437
Sp Gd
PENNINE WAY
BRENDON CL
CHEVIOT CL
MENDIP CL
HEATH CL
HALL LA
MARLBOROUGH CRES
DAVID CL
CAROLINE PL
NOBEL DR
VANTAGE CT
WINCHESTER RD
OXFORD AVE
MALVERN RD
WINDSOR PARK RD
ETON RD
PENDELL AVE
STRATHEARN AVE
LANGLEY CRES
CRANESWATER
PARK LA
NEW RD
MONDIAL WAY
TRIUMPH CL
Hotels
Harlington Cnr
BATH RD
A4
The White Hart (PH)
DUDSET
Visitor Ctr
World Bsns Ctr
NEWALL RD
NEPTUNE RD
HATTON RD N
NORTHROP RD
NORTHERN PERIMETER RD
TW6
ENFIELD ROAD RDBT
ENFIELD RD
EPSOM SQ
ELY RD
FISHER CRES
ELGIN CRES
Eastern Bsns Pk
EASTERN PERIMETER RD
London Loop
Hillingdon
Hounslow
EASTCHURCH ROAD RDBT
VANGUARD WAY
EXETER WAY
EXETER RD
EASTCHURCH RD
ELECTRA AVE
EAGLE RD
ELMDON RD
HATTON CROSS RDBT
VISCOUNT WAY
Hatton Cross
LITHGOW'S RD
GREAT SOUTH-WEST RD
A30
SOUTHERN PERIMETER RD
STEAM FARM LA
TURPIN WAY
DICK
Radius Pk
Hatton
HATTON RD
ST THERESA'S RD
ST ANTHONY'S WAY
FAGG'S RD
GREEN MAN LA
MYRTLE AVE
WELLINGTON RD
Tenn Cts
Fball
Cemy

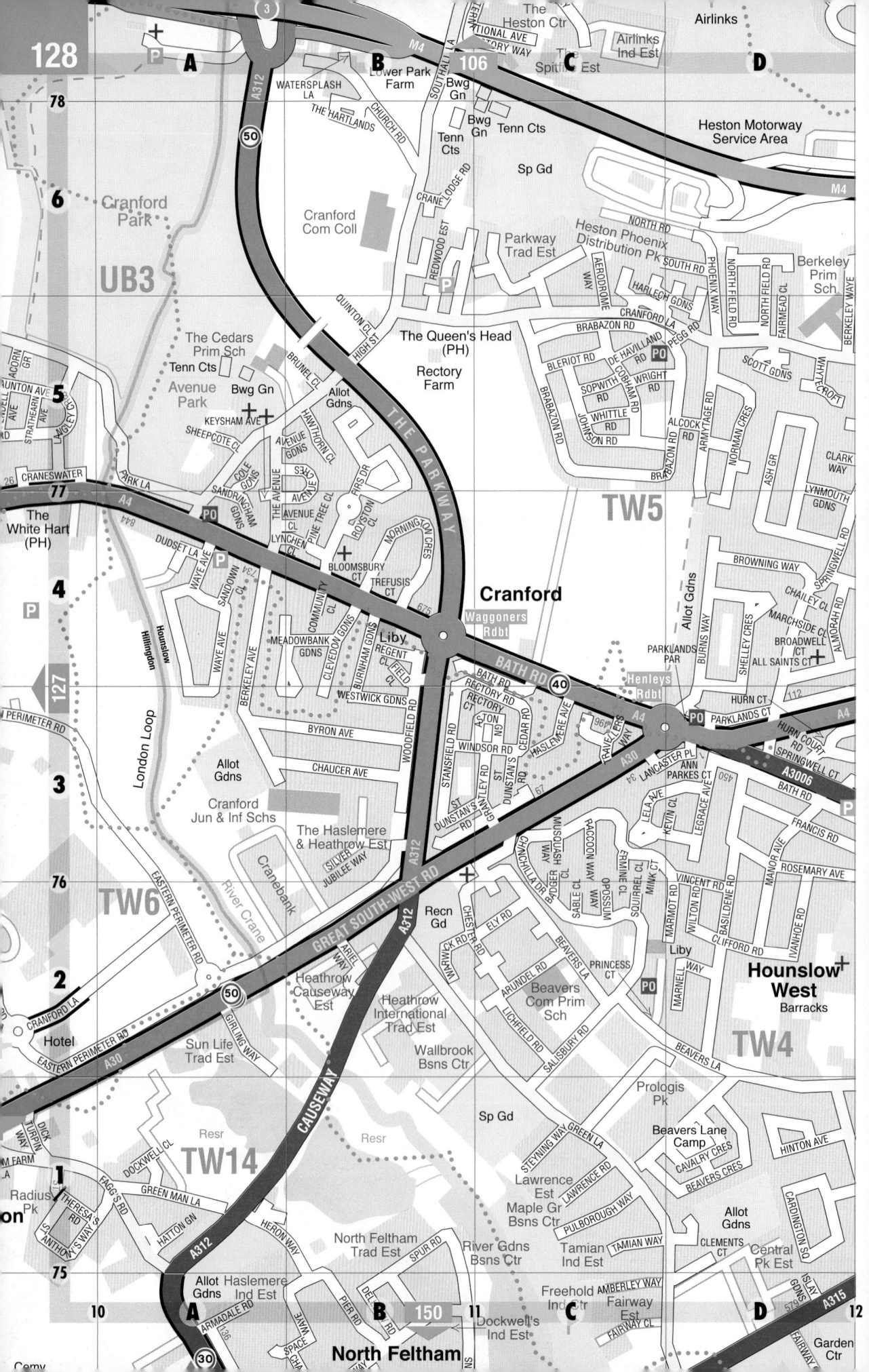

Cranford
Heston Motorway Service Area
Cranford Park
UB3
TW5
TW6
TW14
TW4
Hounslow West
Barracks
North Feltham
Heston Phoenix Distribution Pk
Parkway Trad Est
Cranford Com Coll
The Queen's Head (PH)
Rectory Farm
The Cedars Prim Sch
Avenue Park
The White Hart (PH)
Waggoners Rdbt
Henleys Rdbt
London Loop
Cranford Jun & Inf Schs
The Haslemere & Heathrow Est
Heathrow Causeway Est
Heathrow International Trad Est
Wallbrook Bsns Ctr
Sun Life Trad Est
Beavers Com Prim Sch
Prologis Pk
Beavers Lane Camp
Lawrence Est
Maple Gr Bsns Ctr
Tamian Ind Est
River Gdns Bsns Ctr
North Feltham Trad Est
Haslemere Ind Est
Freehold Ind Ctr
Fairway Est
Dockwell's Ind Est
Central Pk Est
Garden Ctr
Berkeley Prim Sch
Airlinks Ind Est
The Spitfire Est
Lower Park Farm
THE PARKWAY
BATH RD
GREAT SOUTH-WEST RD
CAUSEWAY
M4
A4
A30
A312
A3006
A315
106
127
150

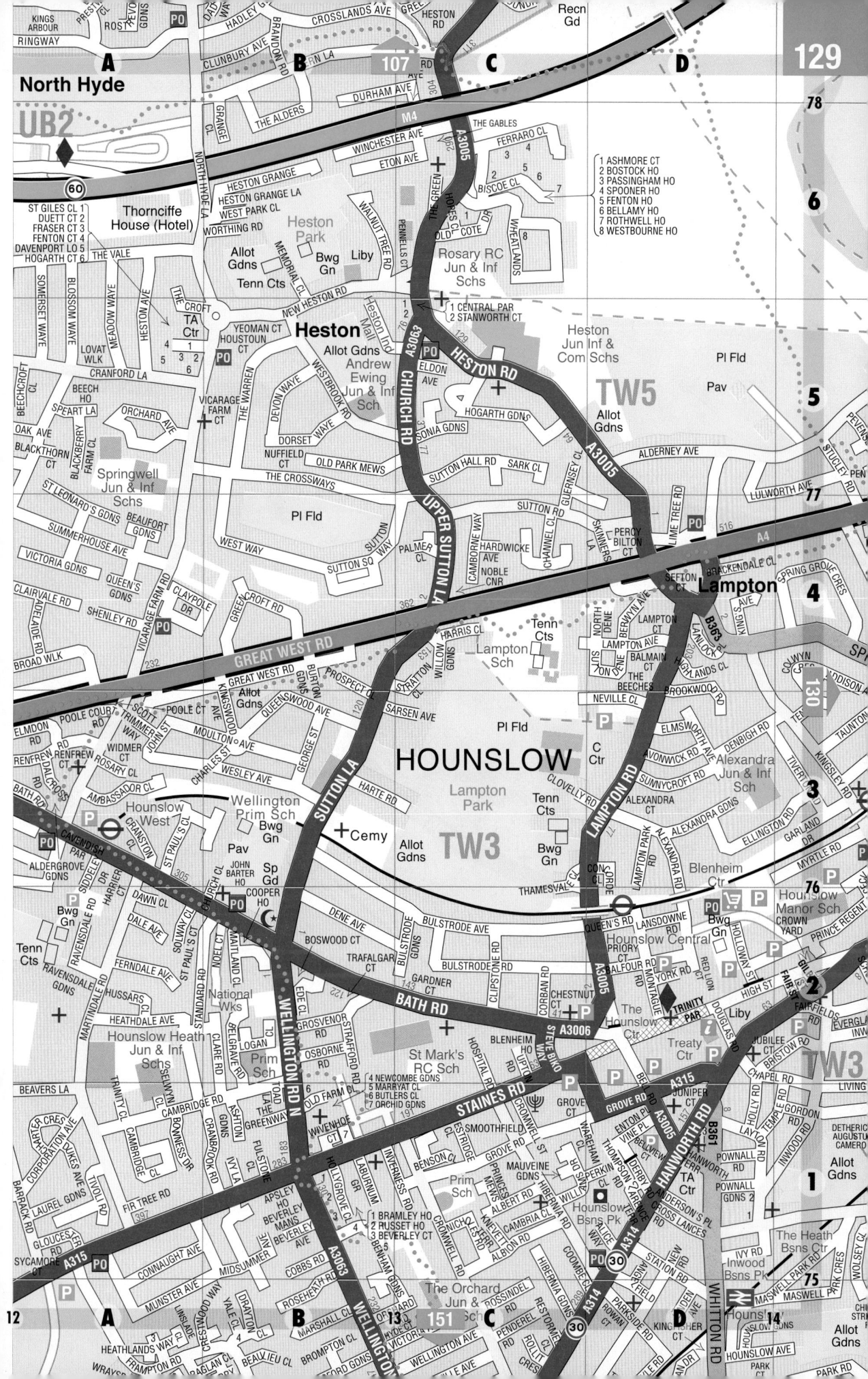

North Hyde
UB2
Heston
HOUNSLOW
Lampton
TW5
TW3
Hounslow West
Hounslow Central
Lampton Park
GREAT WEST RD
BATH RD
STAINES RD
HESTON RD
LAMPTON RD
WELLINGTON RD N
SUTTON LA
UPPER SUTTON LA
CHURCH RD
1 ASHMORE CT
2 BOSTOCK HO
3 PASSINGHAM HO
4 SPOONER HO
5 FENTON HO
6 BELLAMY HO
7 ROTHWELL HO
8 WESTBOURNE HO
ST GILES CL 1
DUETT CT 2
FRASER CT 3
FENTON CT 4
DAVENPORT LO 5
HOGARTH CT 6
1 CENTRAL PAR
2 STANWORTH CT
4 NEWCOMBE GDNS
5 MARRYAT CL
6 BUTLERS CL
7 ORCHID GDNS
1 BRAMLEY HO
2 RUSSET HO
3 BEVERLEY CT

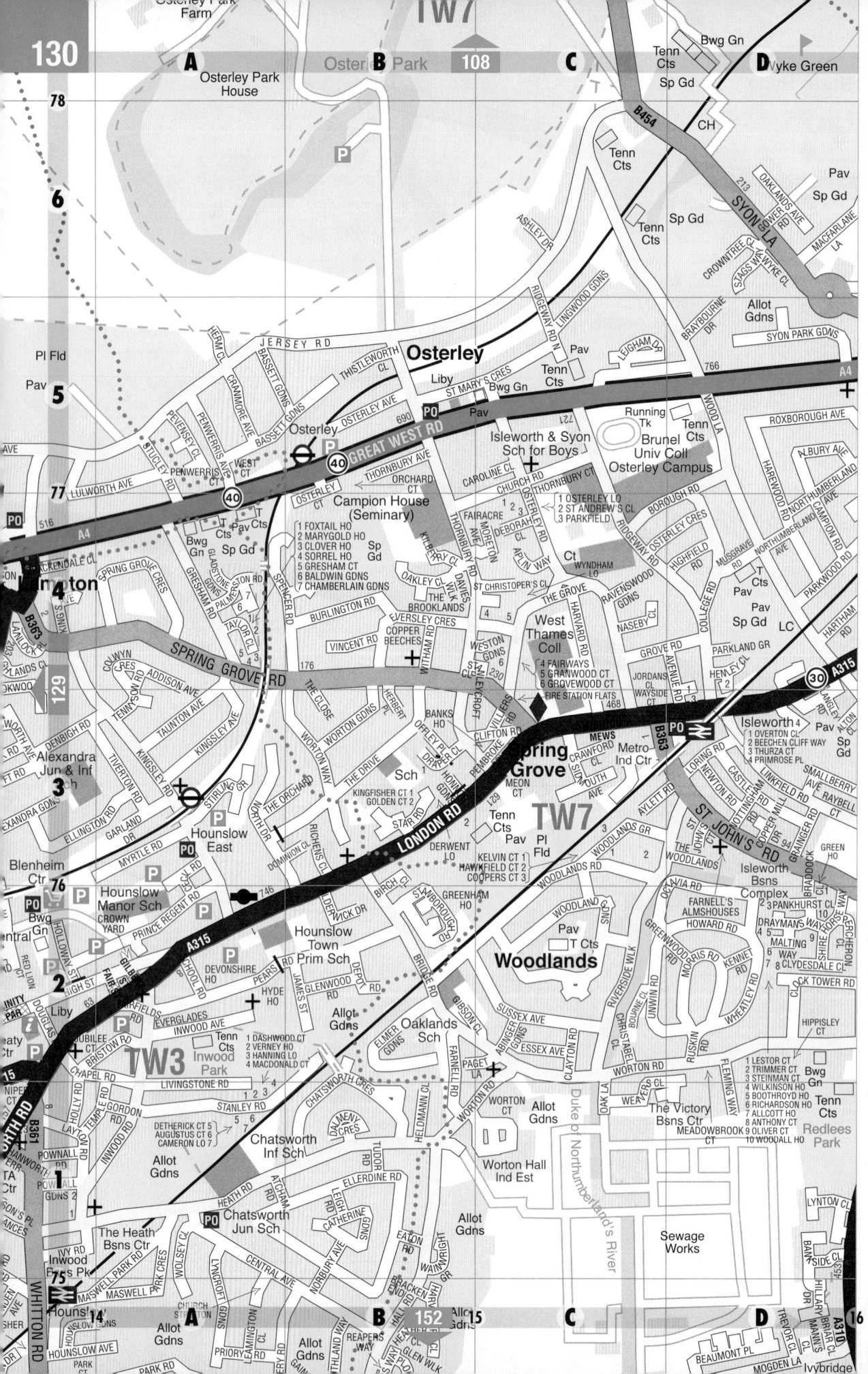
Osterley Park Farm
TW7
Osterley Park
108
Osterley Park House
Wyke Green
Osterley
GREAT WEST RD
A4
Isleworth & Syon Sch for Boys
Brunel Univ Coll Osterley Campus
Campion House (Seminary)
West Thames Coll
SPRING GROVE RD
Spring Grove
LONDON RD
Hounslow East
Hounslow Manor Sch
Hounslow Town Prim Sch
Woodlands
Oaklands Sch
Isleworth
ST JOHN'S RD
Isleworth Bsns Complex
TW3
Inwood Park
Chatsworth Inf Sch
Chatsworth Jun Sch
The Heath Bsns Ctr
Worton Hall Ind Est
Duke of Northumberland's River
Sewage Works
Redlees Park
The Victory Bsns Ctr
Alexandra Jun & Inf Sch
Blenheim Ctr
Hounslow
WHITTON RD
129
152

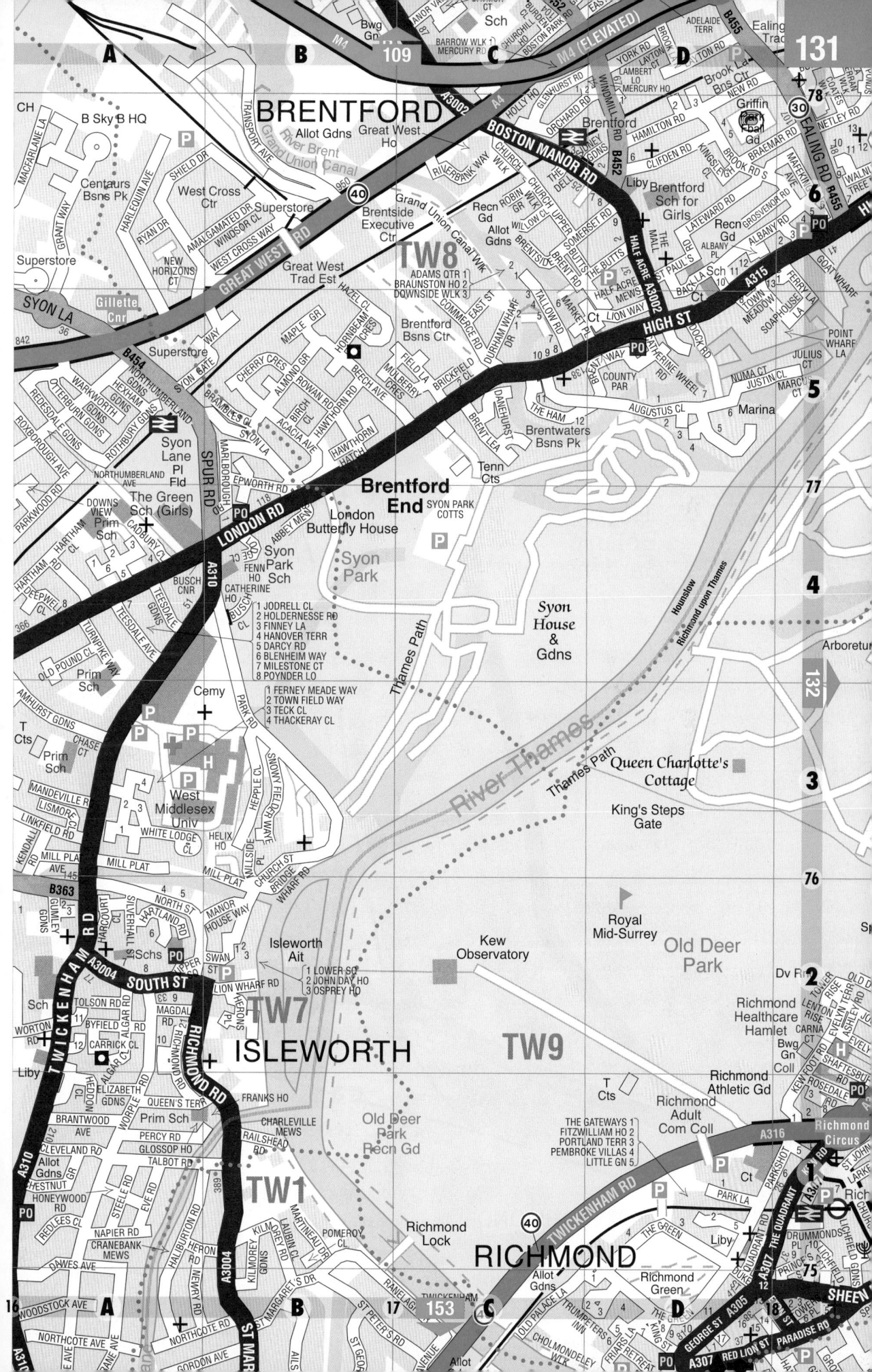

131
BRENTFORD
ISLEWORTH
RICHMOND
TW8
TW7
TW9
TW1
Brentford End
B Sky B HQ
Centaurs Bsns Pk
West Cross Ctr
Superstore
Great West Trad Est
Brentside Executive Ctr
Brentford Bsns Ctr
Brentford Sch for Girls
Griffin Park Fball Gd
Brentwaters Bsns Pk
Marina
London Butterfly House
Syon Park
Syon Park Sch
Syon House & Gdns
Syon Lane
The Green Sch (Girls)
Gillette Cnr
West Middlesex Univ
River Thames
River Brent
Grand Union Canal
Thames Path
Queen Charlotte's Cottage
King's Steps Gate
Isleworth Ait
Kew Observatory
Royal Mid-Surrey
Old Deer Park
Old Deer Park Recn Gd
Richmond Lock
Richmond Healthcare Hamlet
Richmond Athletic Gd
Richmond Adult Com Coll
Richmond Green
Richmond Circus
Arboretum
GREAT WEST RD
LONDON RD
BOSTON MANOR RD
HIGH ST
M4 (ELEVATED)
TWICKENHAM RD
SOUTH ST
RICHMOND RD
SYON LA
HALF ACRE
EALING RD
SPUR RD
Hounslow
Richmond upon Thames
109
132
153

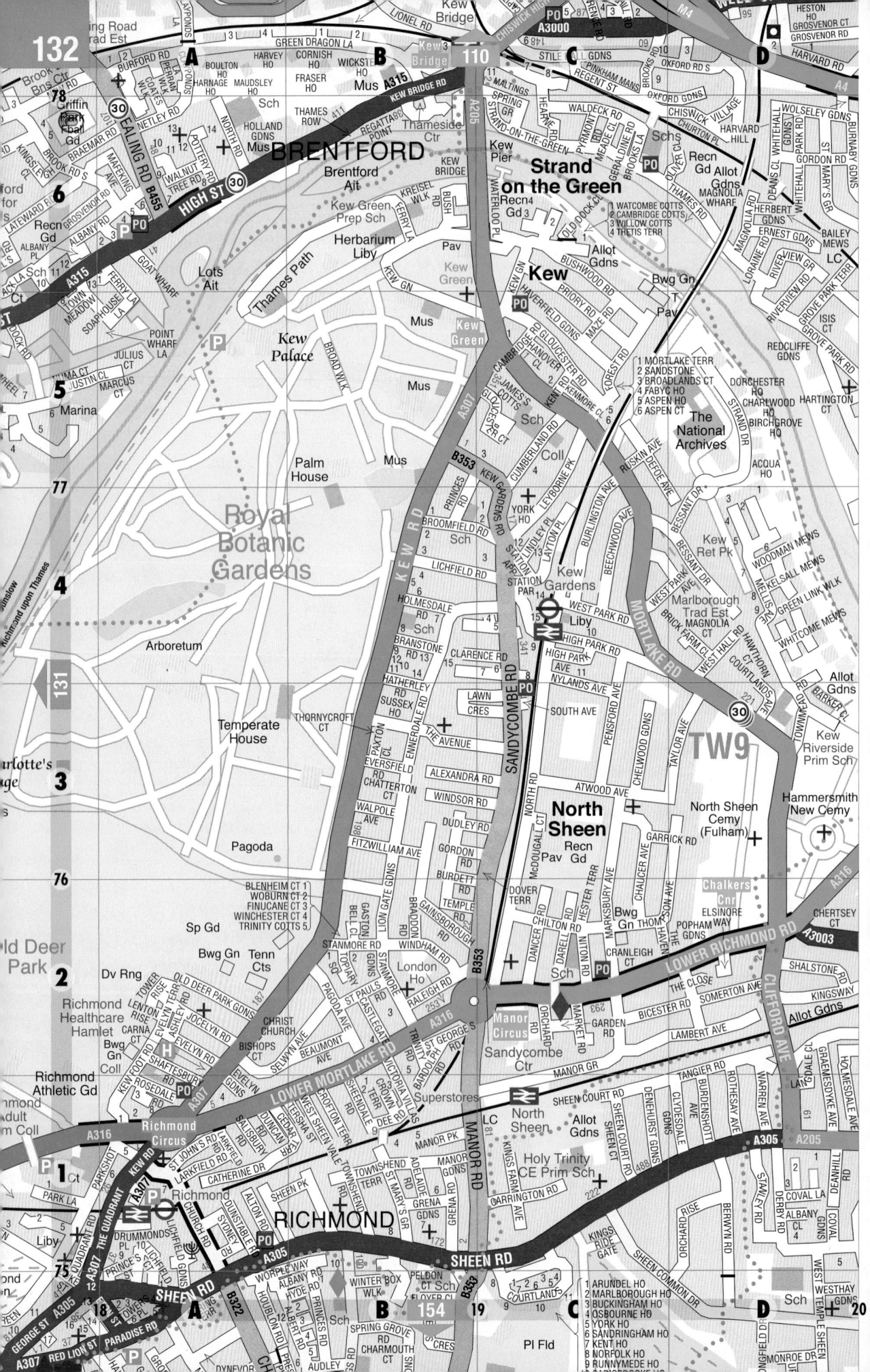

Kew Bridge
110
A B C D
BRENTFORD
Strand on the Green
Kew
Brentford Ait
Lots Ait
Kew Palace
Royal Botanic Gardens
Palm House
Arboretum
Temperate House
Pagoda
Herbarium Liby
Kew Green
Kew Green Prep Sch
Thames Path
Thameside Ctr
Griffin Park Fball Gd
The National Archives
Kew Ret Pk
Marlborough Trad Est
Kew Gardens
TW9
North Sheen
North Sheen Cemy (Fulham)
Hammersmith New Cemy
Chalkers Cnr
Kew Riverside Prim Sch
Manor Circus
Sandycombe Ctr
Superstores
Holy Trinity CE Prim Sch
RICHMOND
Richmond Circus
Richmond Healthcare Hamlet
Richmond Athletic Gd
Old Deer Park
Marina
HIGH ST
KEW RD
KEW BRIDGE RD
MORTLAKE RD
SANDYCOMBE RD
LOWER RICHMOND RD
LOWER MORTLAKE RD
CLIFFORD AVE
MANOR RD
SHEEN RD
EALING RD
A315 A205 A307 A316 A305 A3003 A3000 A4 M4 B353 B455 B322
131
154
1 2 3 4 5 6
75 76 77 78
18 19 20

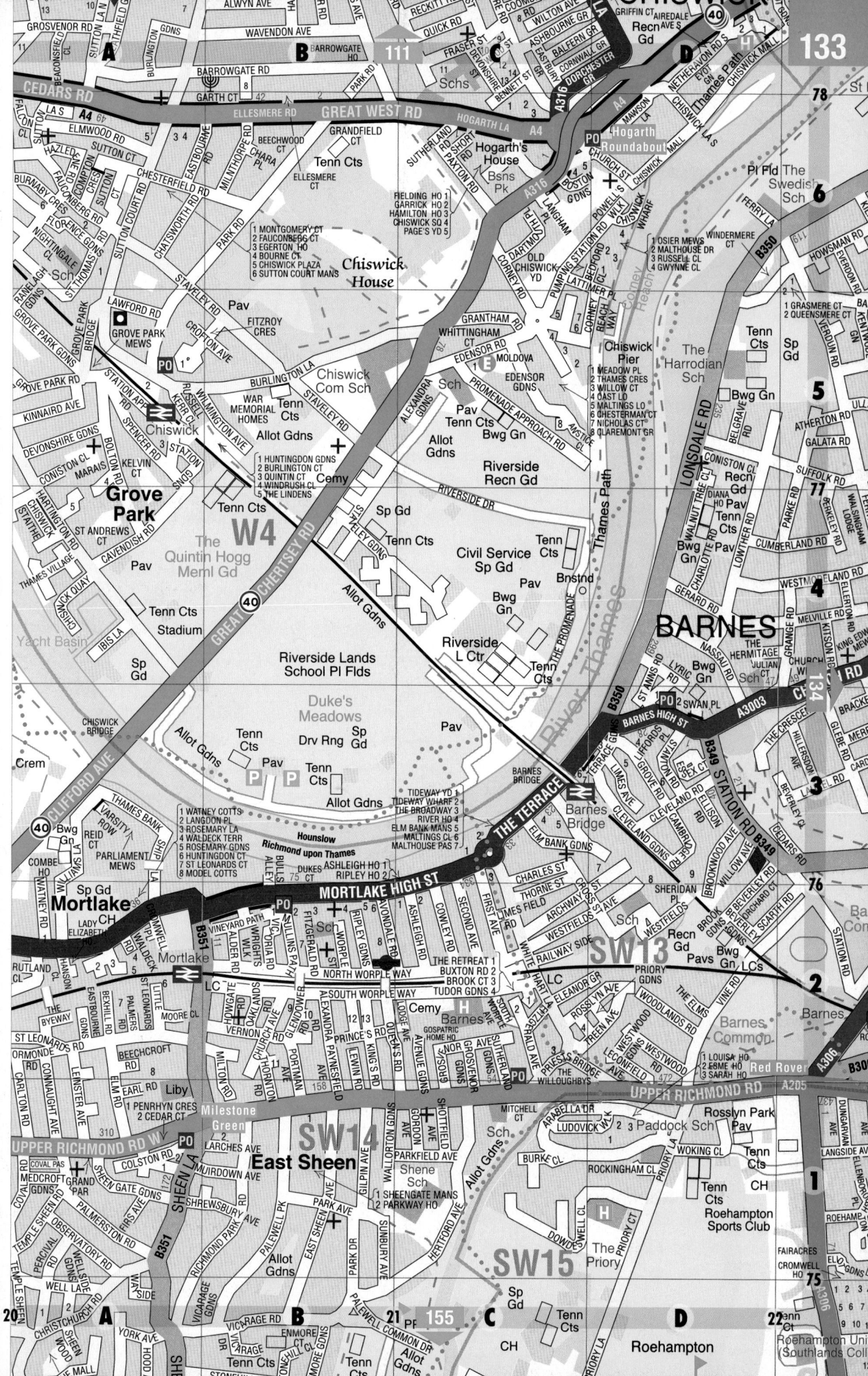
133
111
134
155
78
77
76
75
6
5
4
3
2
1
20
21
22
A
B
C
D
CHISWICK
GREAT WEST RD
CEDARS RD
HOGARTH LA
A4
A316
DORCHESTER GR
Hogarth Roundabout
Hogarth's House
Chiswick House
Chiswick Com Sch
Grove Park
Chiswick
W4
The Quintin Hogg Meml Gd
GREAT CHERTSEY RD
Riverside Recn Gd
Civil Service Sp Gd
Riverside L Ctr
Riverside Lands School Pl Flds
Duke's Meadows
Drv Rng
Chiswick Pier
The Harrodian Sch
The Swedish Sch
River Thames
Thames Path
LONSDALE RD
BARNES
BARNES HIGH ST
STATION RD
CHURCH RD
Barnes Bridge
THE TERRACE
MORTLAKE HIGH ST
Mortlake
CLIFFORD AVE
CHISWICK BRIDGE
BARNES BRIDGE
Yacht Basin
Stadium
Crem
Hounslow
Richmond upon Thames
SW13
SW14
SW15
East Sheen
UPPER RICHMOND RD
UPPER RICHMOND RD W
NORTH WORPLE WAY
SOUTH WORPLE WAY
SHEEN LA
Barnes Common
Rosslyn Park
Roehampton Sports Club
Roehampton
The Priory
Red Rover
A306
A205
A3003
B349
B350
B351
PALEWELL COMMON DR
Milestone Green

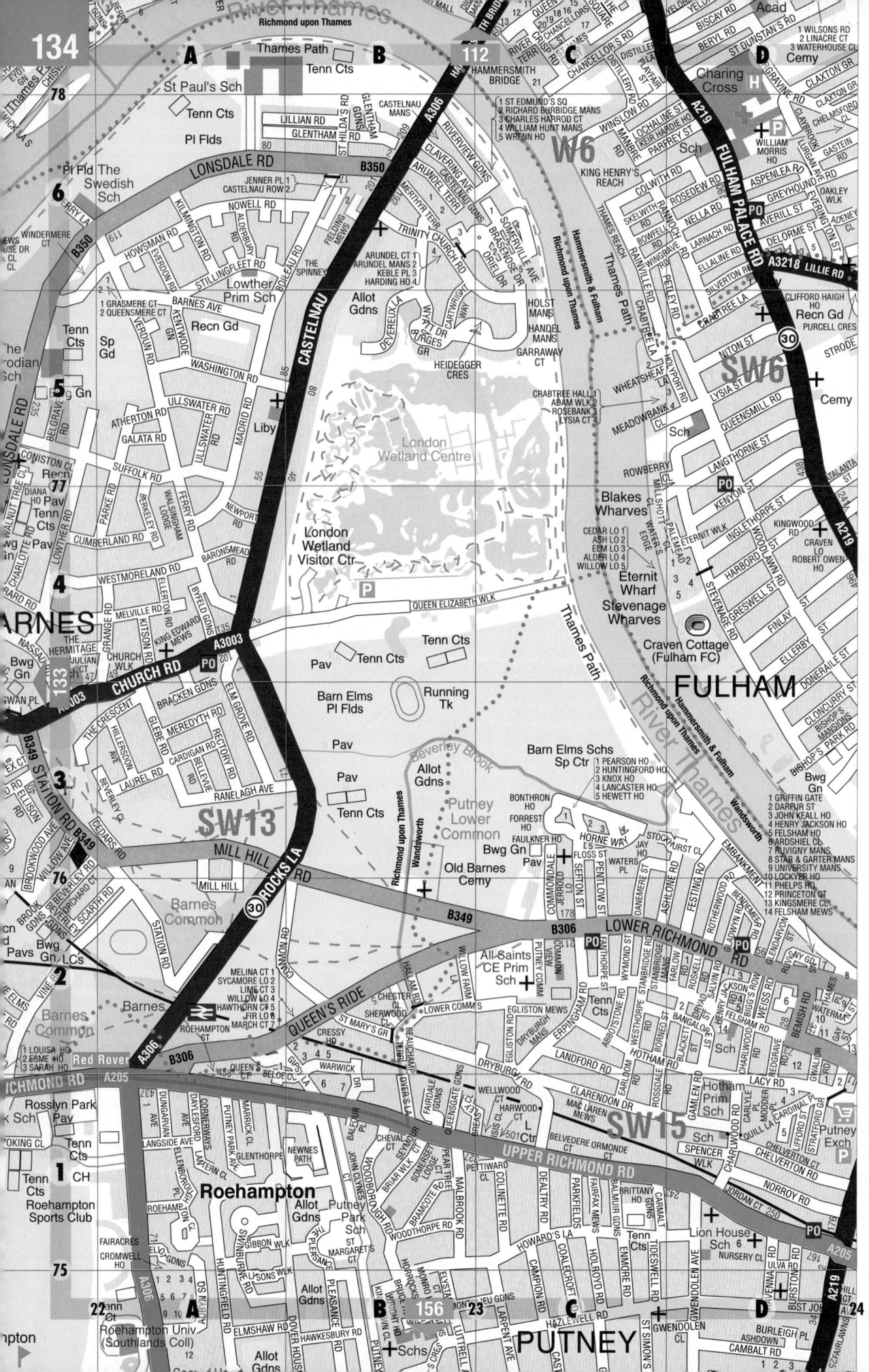

River Thames
Richmond upon Thames
Thames Path
A
B
C
D
112
Tenn Cts
St Paul's Sch
Pl Flds
Hammersmith Bridge
W6
Charing Cross
Fulham Palace Rd
A219
Lonsdale Rd
B350
The Swedish Sch
Castelnau
A306
Lowther Prim Sch
Recn Gd
Sp Gd
Liby
Allot Gdns
London Wetland Centre
London Wetland Visitor Ctr
Queen Elizabeth Wlk
Hammersmith & Fulham
King Henry's Reach
SW6
Lillie Rd
A3218
Cemy
Blakes Wharves
Eternit Wharf
Stevenage Wharves
Craven Cottage (Fulham FC)
FULHAM
Barnes
Church Rd
A3003
Barn Elms Pl Flds
Running Tk
Pav
Beverley Brook
Barn Elms Schs Sp Ctr
Putney Lower Common
Old Barnes Cemy
Wandsworth
SW13
Mill Hill Rd
Rocks La
B349
Barnes Common
Station Rd
Lower Richmond Rd
B306
Queen's Ride
All Saints CE Prim Sch
Roehampton
Upper Richmond Rd
A205
SW15
Putney Exch
Rosslyn Park Sch
Roehampton Sports Club
Roehampton Univ (Southlands Coll)
PUTNEY
Lion House Sch
Hotham Prim Sch
156
133
22
23
24
75
76
77
78
1
2
3
4
5
6

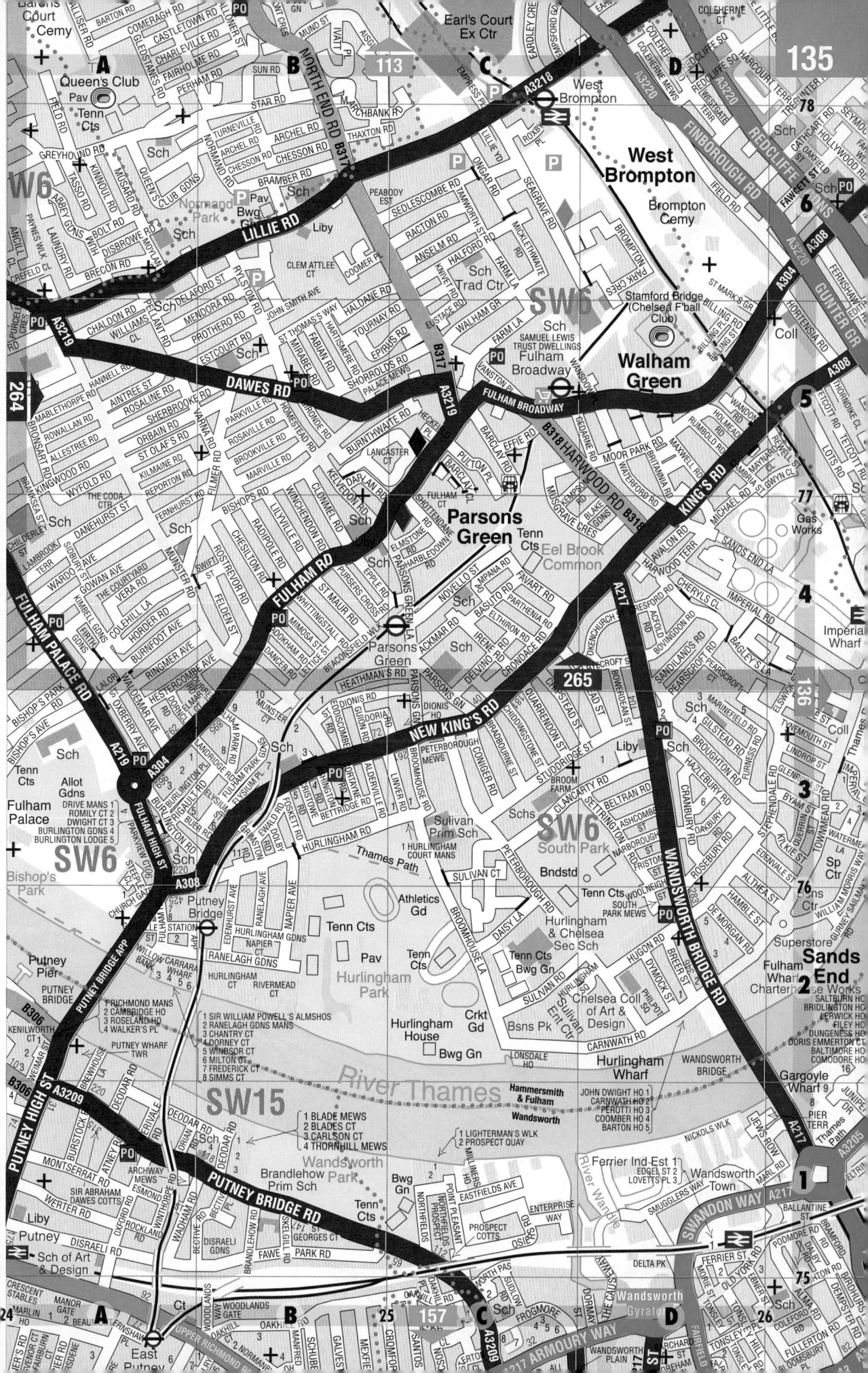

135
113
264
265
136
157
A
B
C
D
E
78
6
5
77
4
3
76
2
1
75
24
25
26
Barons Court Cemy
Queen's Club
Pav
Tenn Cts
W6
Earl's Court Ex Ctr
West Brompton
Brompton Cemy
Stamford Bridge (Chelsea F'ball Club)
Walham Green
Fulham Broadway
SW6
Samuel Lewis Trust Dwellings
Normand Park
Parsons Green
Eel Brook Common
Gas Works
Imperial Wharf
Fulham Palace
Bishop's Park
Allot Gdns
Putney Bridge
Putney Pier
Hurlingham Park
Hurlingham House
Hurlingham Wharf
Hurlingham & Chelsea Sec Sch
Chelsea Coll of Art & Design
South Park
Sulivan Prim Sch
Athletics Gd
Thames Path
River Thames
SW15
Hammersmith & Fulham
Wandsworth
Wandsworth Bridge
Wandsworth Park
Wandsworth Town
Wandsworth Gyratory
Brandlehow Prim Sch
Ferrier Ind Est
River Wandle
Sands End
Fulham Wharf
Gargoyle Wharf
Putney
Sch of Art & Design
East Putney
LILLIE RD
DAWES RD
NORTH END RD
FULHAM RD
FULHAM BROADWAY
FULHAM PALACE RD
FULHAM HIGH ST
NEW KING'S RD
KING'S RD
HARWOOD RD
WANDSWORTH BRIDGE RD
PUTNEY BRIDGE RD
PUTNEY BRIDGE APP
PUTNEY HIGH ST
SWANDON WAY
ARMOURY WAY
FINBOROUGH RD
REDCLIFFE GDNS
GUNTER GR
HURLINGHAM RD
CARNWATH RD
BROOMHOUSE LA
PETERBOROUGH RD
IMPERIAL RD
TOWNMEAD RD
A3218
A3219
A308
A304
A217
A3209
A3220
A219
B317
B318
B306
A3205

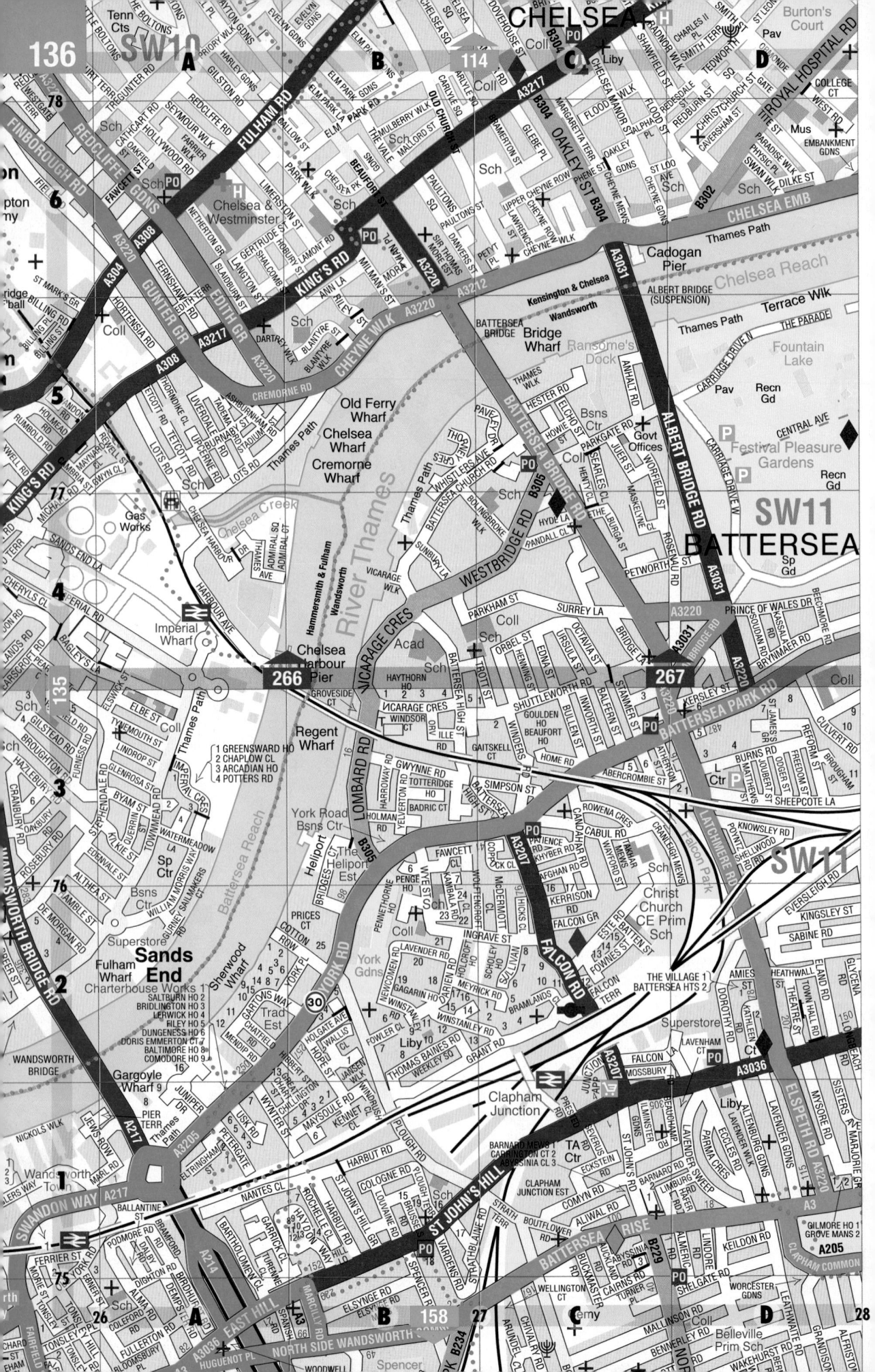
SW10
A
B
C
D
114
CHELSEA
FULHAM RD
KING'S RD
REDCLIFFE GDNS
FINBOROUGH RD
OLD CHURCH ST
BEAUFORT ST
OAKLEY ST
ROYAL HOSPITAL RD
CHELSEA EMB
Chelsea & Westminster
Cadogan Pier
Thames Path
Chelsea Reach
ALBERT BRIDGE (SUSPENSION)
Terrace Wlk
THE PARADE
Fountain Lake
CHEYNE WLK
CREMORNE RD
GUNTER GR
EDITH GR
BATTERSEA BRIDGE
Bridge Wharf
Ransome's Dock
Kensington & Chelsea
Wandsworth
Old Ferry Wharf
Chelsea Wharf
Cremorne Wharf
River Thames
Hammersmith & Fulham
Chelsea Creek
Gas Works
CHELSEA HARBOUR
Imperial Wharf
Chelsea Harbour Pier
266
267
BATTERSEA BRIDGE RD
ALBERT BRIDGE RD
Govt Offices
Festival Pleasure Gardens
Recn Gd
CENTRAL AVE
SW11
BATTERSEA
Sp Gd
PRINCE OF WALES DR
WESTBRIDGE RD
VICARAGE CRES
SURREY LA
BATTERSEA PARK RD
BATTERSEA HIGH ST
135
Regent Wharf
York Road Bsns Ctr
Heliport
LOMBARD RD
YORK RD
LATCHMERE RD
FALCON RD
Christ Church CE Prim Sch
Falcon Park
Sands End
Fulham Wharf
Charterhouse Works
Sherwood Wharf
Battersea Reach
Superstore
WANDSWORTH BRIDGE
WANDSWORTH BRIDGE RD
Gargoyle Wharf
Clapham Junction
CLAPHAM JUNCTION EST
ST JOHN'S HILL
ST JOHN'S RD
BATTERSEA RISE
LAVENDER HILL
ELSPETH RD
Wandsworth Town
SWANDON WAY
EAST HILL
NORTH SIDE WANDSWORTH COMMON
CLAPHAM COMMON
Belleville Prim Sch
158
1
2
3
4
5
6
75
76
77
78
26
27
28

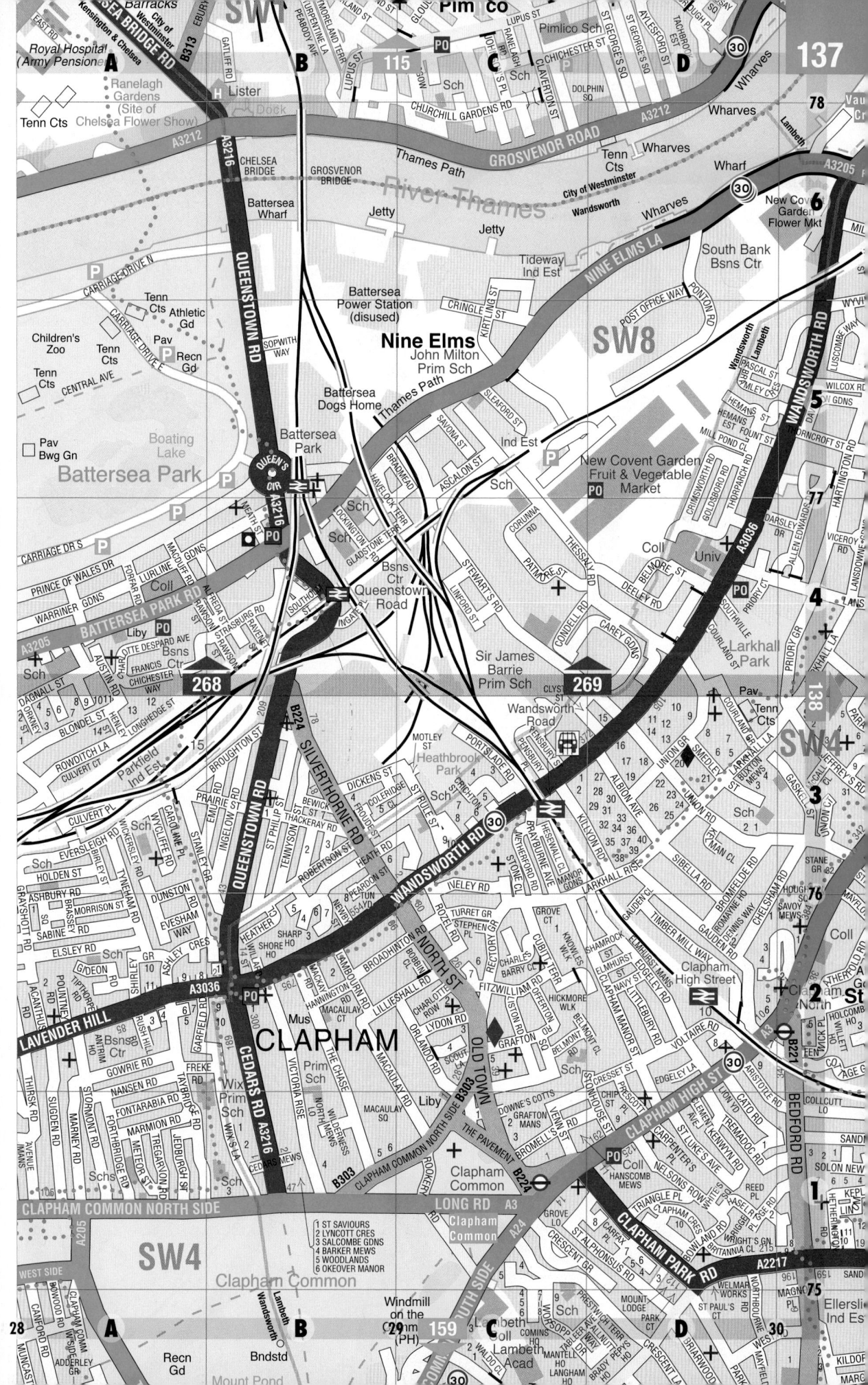
Pimlico
SW1
Royal Hospital (Army Pensioners)
Ranelagh Gardens (Site of Chelsea Flower Show)
CHELSEA BRIDGE RD
GROSVENOR ROAD
A3212
River Thames
Thames Path
CHELSEA BRIDGE
GROSVENOR BRIDGE
Battersea Wharf
Jetty
Wharves
Wharf
City of Westminster
Wandsworth
NINE ELMS LA
A3205
New Covent Garden Flower Mkt
South Bank Bsns Ctr
Tideway Ind Est
Battersea Power Station (disused)
Nine Elms
John Milton Prim Sch
SW8
QUEENSTOWN RD
Battersea Dogs Home
Battersea Park
Boating Lake
Children's Zoo
Athletic Gd
Recn Gd
QUEEN'S CIR
A3216
CARRIAGE DRIVE N
CARRIAGE DRIVE E
CENTRAL AVE
CARRIAGE DR S
PRINCE OF WALES DR
BATTERSEA PARK RD
Queenstown Road
New Covent Garden Fruit & Vegetable Market
WANDSWORTH RD
A3036
Larkhall Park
Sir James Barrie Prim Sch
Wandsworth Road
Heathbrook Park
Parkfield Ind Est
SILVERTHORNE RD
B224
268
269
138
SW4
LAVENDER HILL
CLAPHAM
CEDARS RD
NORTH ST
OLD TOWN
Clapham High Street
CLAPHAM HIGH ST
CLAPHAM PARK RD
A2217
BEDFORD RD
B221
CLAPHAM COMMON NORTH SIDE
LONG RD
A3
Clapham Common
SOUTH SIDE
A24
A205
WEST SIDE
Lambeth Coll
Lambeth Acad
Windmill on the Common (PH)
Bndstd
Recn Gd
Mount Pond
1 ST SAVIOURS
2 LYNCOTT CRES
3 SALCOMBE GDNS
4 BARKER MEWS
5 WOODLANDS
6 OKEOVER MANOR
115
159
A
B
C
D
28
29
30
1
2
3
4
5
6
75
76
77
78

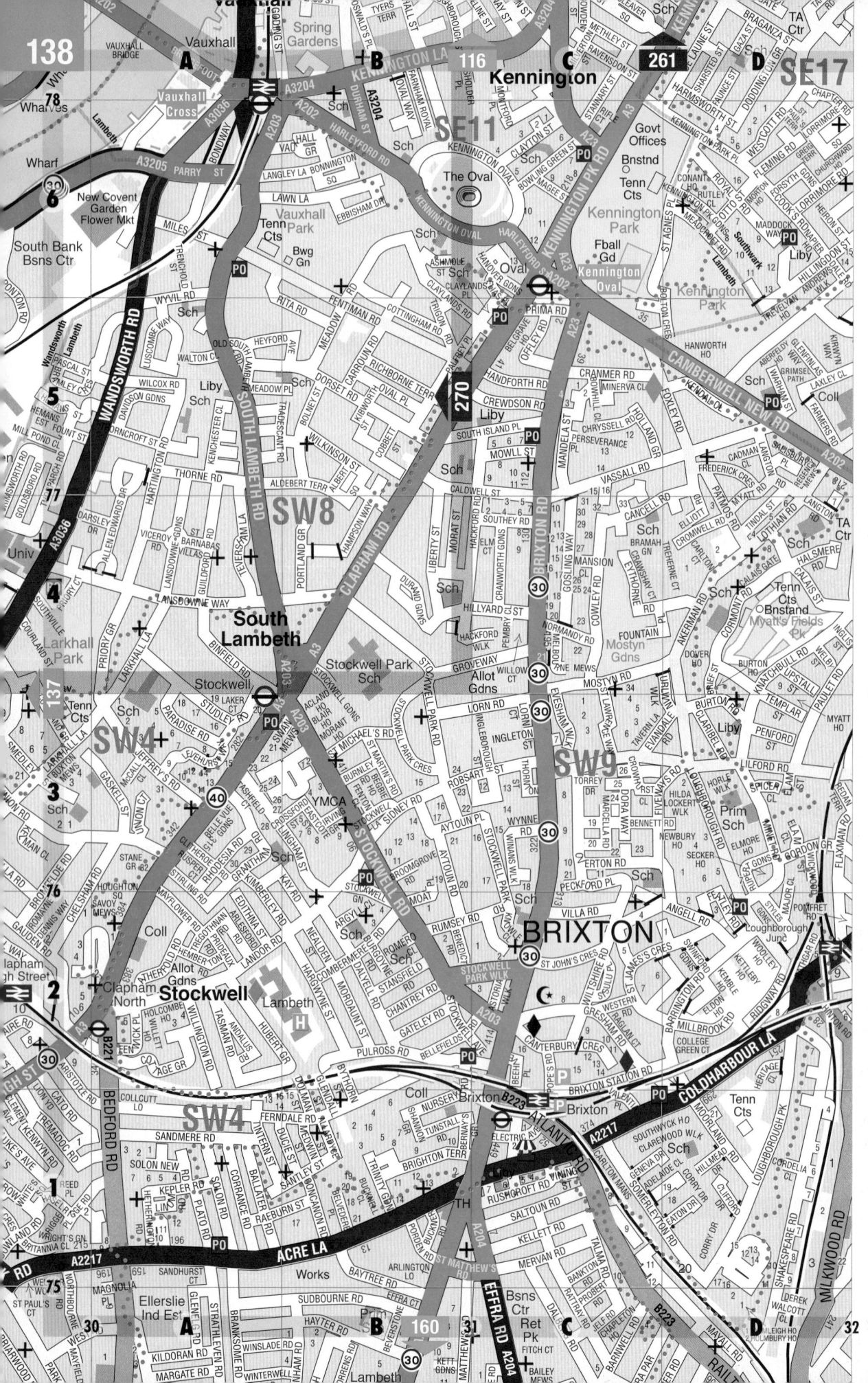
138
A
B
C
D
116
261
270
137
160
Vauxhall
Vauxhall Cross
Spring Gardens
Kennington
SE11
SE17
The Oval
Kennington Oval
Kennington Park
Vauxhall Park
New Covent Garden Flower Mkt
South Bank Bsns Ctr
Wharf
Wharves
Govt Offices
Larkhall Park
South Lambeth
Stockwell
SW8
SW4
SW9
Stockwell Park Sch
Myatt's Fields Pk
Mostyn Gdns
BRIXTON
Brixton
Clapham North
Clapham High Street
Lambeth
Loughborough Junc
Ellerslie Ind Est
Bsns Ctr
Ret Pk
Works
WANDSWORTH RD
SOUTH LAMBETH RD
CLAPHAM RD
BRIXTON RD
KENNINGTON PK RD
KENNINGTON LA
HARLEYFORD RD
KENNINGTON OVAL
CAMBERWELL NEW RD
STOCKWELL RD
COLDHARBOUR LA
ACRE LA
ATLANTIC RD
BEDFORD RD
EFFRA RD
MILKWOOD RD
LANSDOWNE WAY
BINFIELD RD
VASSALL RD
LOUGHBOROUGH RD
A3
A23
A202
A203
A204
A217
A2217
A3036
A3204
A3205
B221
B223
1
2
3
4
5
6
75
76
77
78
30
31
32

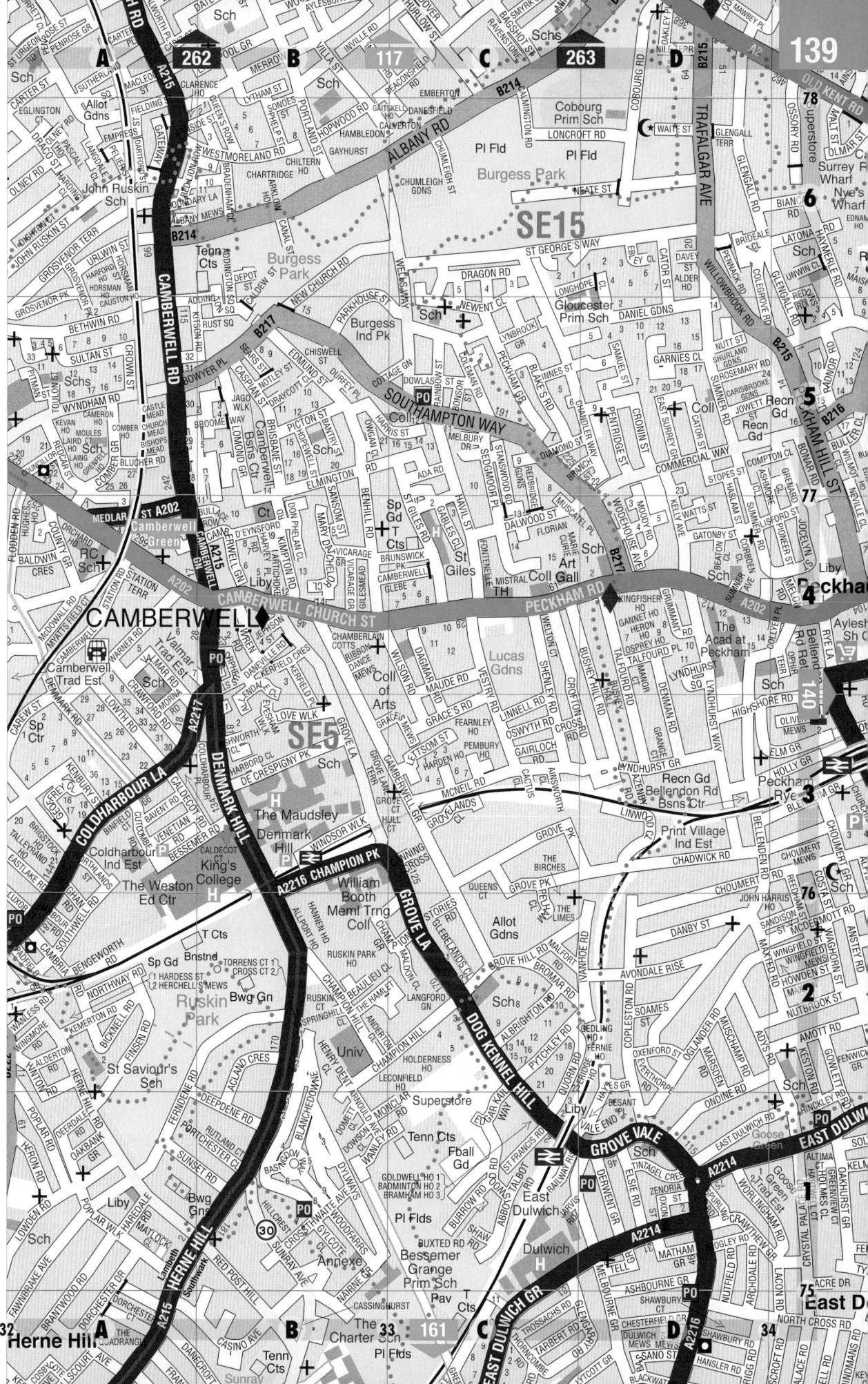
262
117
263
A
B
C
D
SE15
SE5
CAMBERWELL
Camberwell Green
Burgess Park
Burgess Ind Pk
CAMBERWELL RD
CAMBERWELL CHURCH ST
PECKHAM RD
SOUTHAMPTON WAY
ALBANY RD
TRAFALGAR AVE
WILLOWBROOK RD
PECKHAM HILL ST
OLD KENT RD
COLDHARBOUR LA
DENMARK HILL
CHAMPION PK
GROVE LA
DOG KENNEL HILL
GROVE VALE
EAST DULWICH GR
HERNE HILL
EAST DULWICH RD
CRYSTAL PALACE RD
LORDSHIP LA
The Maudsley
Denmark Hill
King's College
The Weston Ed Ctr
William Booth Meml Trng Coll
Ruskin Park
St Saviour's Sch
Coldharbour Ind Est
Camberwell Trad Est
Valmar Trad Est
Lucas Gdns
Coll of Arts
St Giles
The Acad at Peckham
Recn Gd
Bellendon Rd Bsns Ctr
Print Village Ind Est
Peckham Rye
Cobourg Prim Sch
Gloucester Prim Sch
John Ruskin Sch
Allot Gdns
Superstore
Fball Gd
Tenn Cts
Bessemer Grange Prim Sch
Annexe
East Dulwich
Dulwich
Goose Green
Goose Green Trad Est
The Charter Sch
Herne Hill
East D
140
161
32
33
34
75
76
77
78
1
2
3
4
5
6
A215
A202
B214
B217
B215
B216
A2217
A2216
A2214
A2

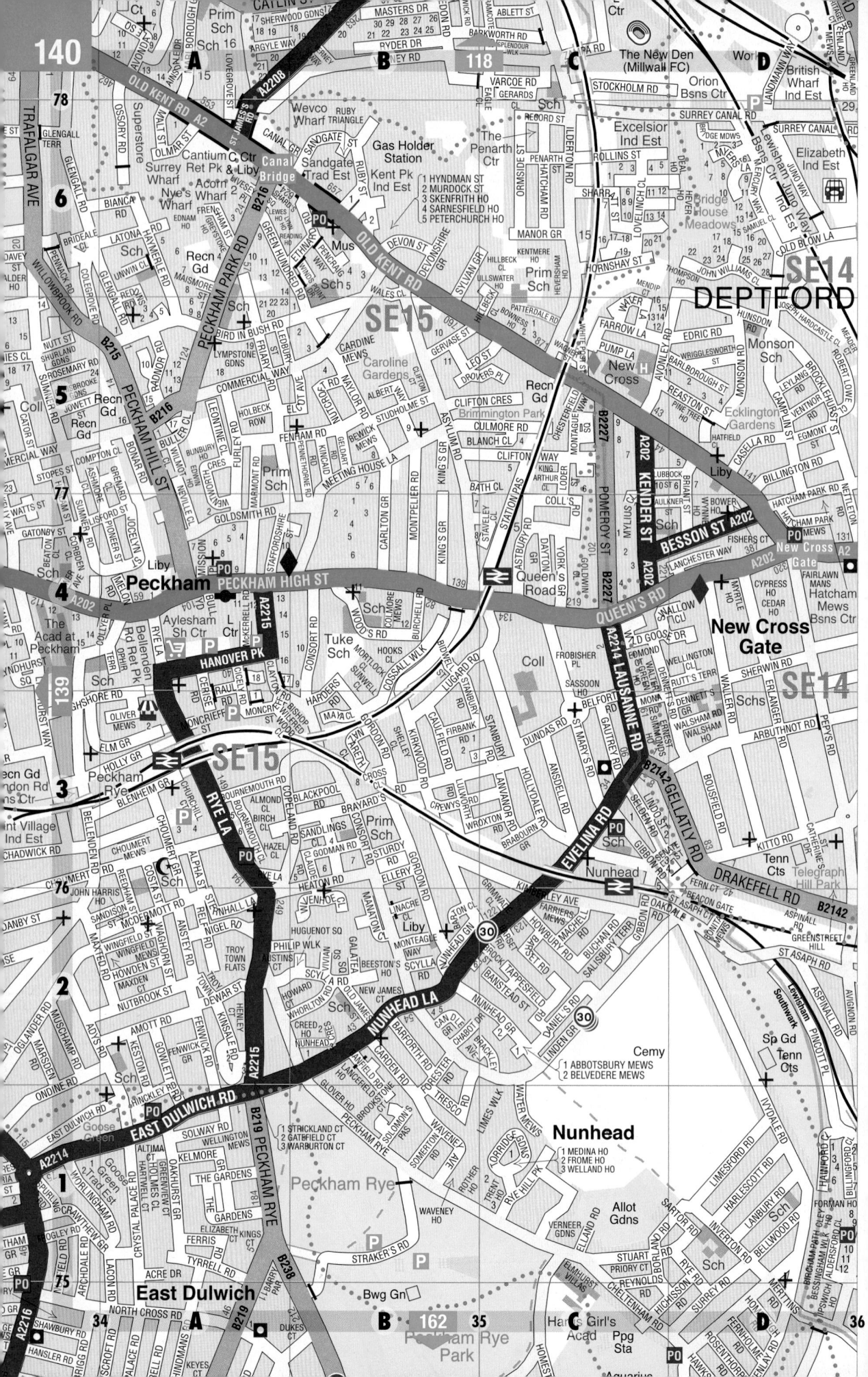
A
B
C
D
118
The New Den
(Millwall FC)
OLD KENT RD A2
TRAFALGAR AVE
Wevco Wharf
RUBY TRIANGLE
Gas Holder Station
Kent Pk Ind Est
Sandgate Trad Est
Canal Bridge
Cantium Ret Pk
Surrey Ret Pk
Superstore
Nye's Wharf
Acorn Wharf
1 HYNDMAN ST
2 MURDOCK ST
3 SKENFRITH HO
4 SARNESFIELD HO
5 PETERCHURCH HO
The Penarth Ctr
Excelsior Ind Est
Orion Bsns Ctr
British Wharf Ind Est
Elizabeth Ind Est
Bridge House Meadows
Lewisham Bsns Ctr
SURREY CANAL RD
STOCKHOLM RD
SE14
DEPTFORD
SE15
PECKHAM PARK RD
PECKHAM HILL ST
WILLOWBROOK RD
Caroline Gardens
Brimmington Park
COMMERCIAL WAY
CLIFTON CRES
ASYLUM RD
New Cross
Monson Sch
Ecklington Gardens
KENDER ST
BESSON ST
New Cross Gate
Peckham
PECKHAM HIGH ST
QUEEN'S RD
Queen's Road
The Acad at Peckham
Aylesham Sh Ctr
Bellenden Rd Ret Pk
HANOVER PK
New Cross Gate
Hatcham Mews Bsns Ctr
Tuke Sch
LAUSANNE RD
Peckham Rye
RYE LA
EVELINA RD
GELLATLY RD
DRAKEFELL RD
Nunhead
Tenn Cts
Telegraph Hill Park
NUNHEAD LA
Troy Town Flats
EAST DULWICH RD
Goose Green
Goose Green Trad Est
PECKHAM RYE
Peckham Rye
1 STRICKLAND CT
2 GATEFIELD CT
3 WARBURTON CT
Nunhead
1 MEDINA HO
2 FROME HO
3 WELLAND HO
1 ABBOTSBURY MEWS
2 BELVEDERE MEWS
Cemy
Allot Gdns
Sp Gd
Lewisham
Southwark
East Dulwich
Bwg Gn
Harris Girl's Acad
Ppg Sta
Peckham Rye Park
162
34
35
36
75
76
77
78
1
2
3
4
5
6
139

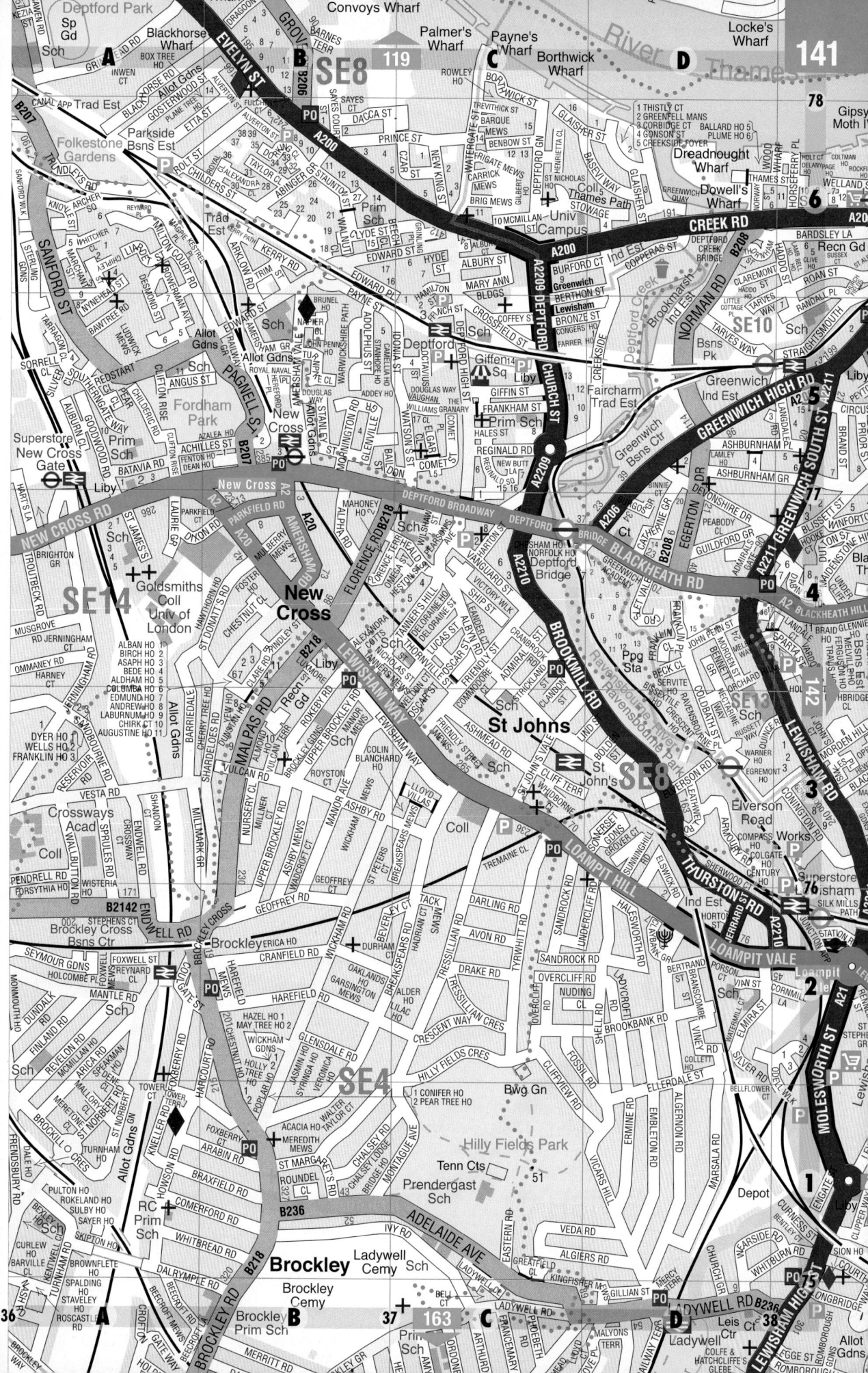

SE8
119
River Thames
Convoys Wharf
Palmer's Wharf
Payne's Wharf
Borthwick Wharf
Locke's Wharf
Blackhorse Wharf
Deptford Park
Dreadnought Wharf
Dowell's Wharf
Gipsy Moth IV
EVELYN ST
A200
CREEK RD
DEPTFORD CHURCH ST
A2209
Deptford
Deptford Creek
NORMAN RD
SE10
GREENWICH HIGH RD
GREENWICH SOUTH ST
A2211
Greenwich
Folkestone Gardens
SANFORD ST
Fordham Park
PAGNELL ST
New Cross
New Cross Gate
NEW CROSS RD
DEPTFORD BROADWAY
Deptford Bridge
BLACKHEATH RD
A2
SE14
Goldsmiths Coll Univ of London
LEWISHAM WAY
BROOKMILL RD
A2210
St Johns
St John's
SE13
LEWISHAM RD
142
Elverson Road
LOAMPIT HILL
LOAMPIT VALE
THURSTON RD
Loampit Vale
MALPAS RD
Brockley
BROCKLEY RD
B218
SE4
Hilly Fields Park
Prendergast Sch
ADELAIDE AVE
B236
Ladywell Cemy
Brockley Cemy
LADYWELL RD
Ladywell
MOLESWORTH ST
A21
LEWISHAM HIGH ST
163
A
B
C
D
1
2
3
4
5
6
7
36
37
38
78
75
76

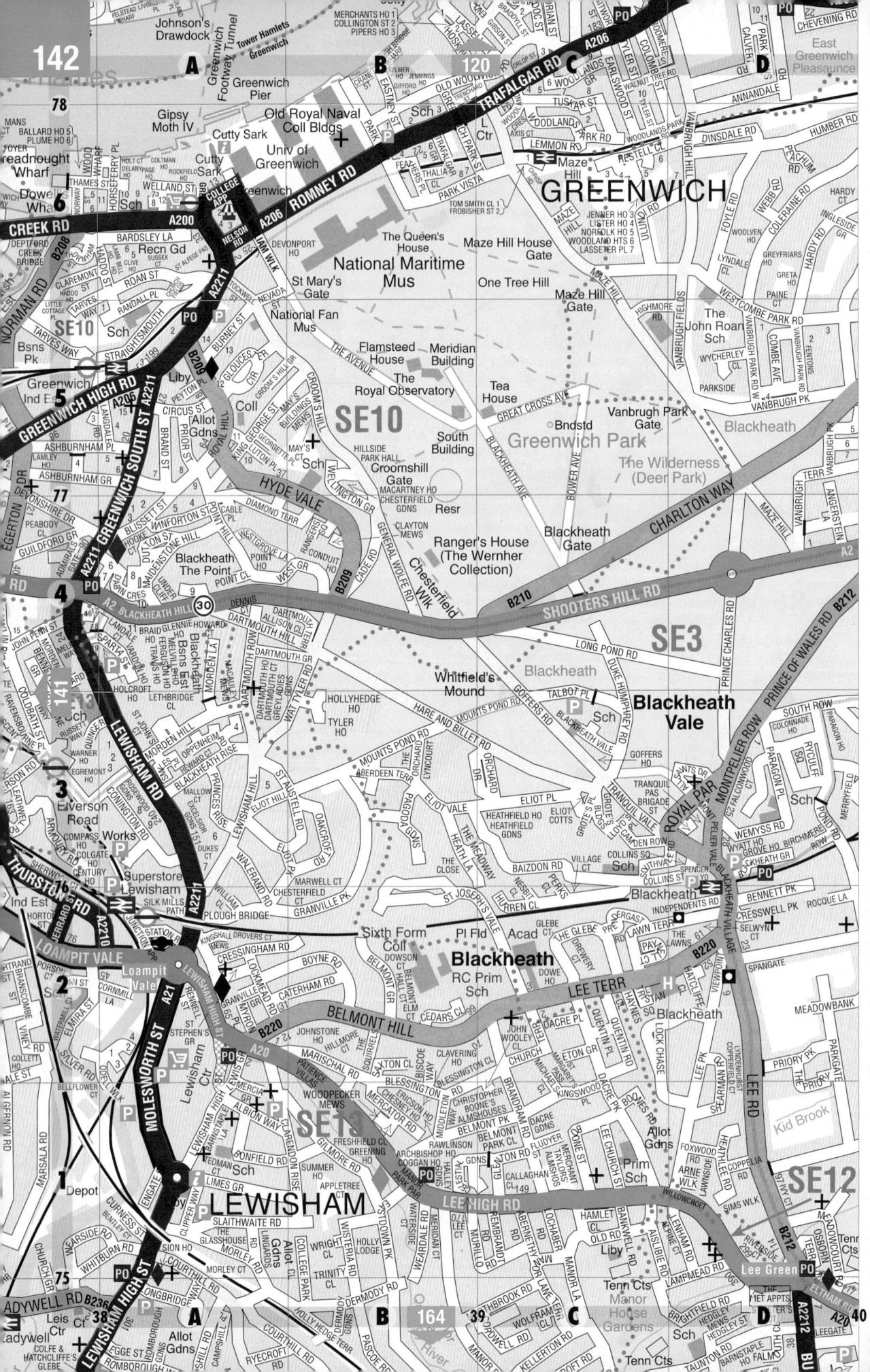
120
A
B
C
D
Johnson's Drawdock
Greenwich Footway Tunnel
Tower Hamlets
Greenwich
Greenwich Pier
Gipsy Moth IV
Old Royal Naval Coll Bldgs
Cutty Sark
Univ of Greenwich
Dreadnought Wharf
Greenwich
TRAFALGAR RD
A206
ROMNEY RD
CREEK RD
A200
GREENWICH
Maze Hill
East Greenwich Pleasaunce
The Queen's House
National Maritime Mus
Maze Hill House Gate
One Tree Hill
Maze Hill Gate
St Mary's Gate
National Fan Mus
Flamsteed House
Meridian Building
The Royal Observatory
Tea House
SE10
Greenwich Park
Bndstd
Vanbrugh Park Gate
Blackheath
The Wilderness (Deer Park)
South Building
Croomshill Gate
Resr
Ranger's House (The Wernher Collection)
Blackheath Gate
Chesterfield Wlk
CHARLTON WAY
SHOOTERS HILL RD
B210
A2
BLACKHEATH HILL
GREENWICH HIGH RD
GREENWICH SOUTH ST
A2211
HYDE VALE
B209
ROYAL HILL
Greenwich Ind Est
Bsns Pk
SE10
Recn Gd
Liby
Coll
Allot Gdns
Blackheath The Point
Blackheath Bsns Est
SE3
Blackheath
Whitfield's Mound
Blackheath Vale
LEWISHAM RD
The John Roan Sch
PRINCE CHARLES RD
PRINCE OF WALES RD
B212
MONTPELIER ROW
ROYAL PAR
Blackheath
BLACKHEATH VILLAGE
LEE TERR
B220
BELMONT HILL
Sixth Form Coll
Pl Fld
Acad
Blackheath RC Prim Sch
Elverson Road
Works
Superstore
Lewisham
LOAMPIT VALE
Loampit Vale
LEWISHAM HIGH ST
A20
A21
MOLESWORTH ST
Lewisham Ctr
SE13
LEWISHAM
LEE HIGH RD
Allot Gdns
Prim Sch
Liby
Tenn Cts
Manor House Gardens
Lee Green
SE12
LEE RD
Kid Brook
MEADOWBANK
Depot
Leis Ctr
Ladywell
Allot Gdns
LADYWELL RD
B236
ELTHAM RD
A2212
A20
164
38
39
40
78
77
76
75
141
6
5
4
3
2
1

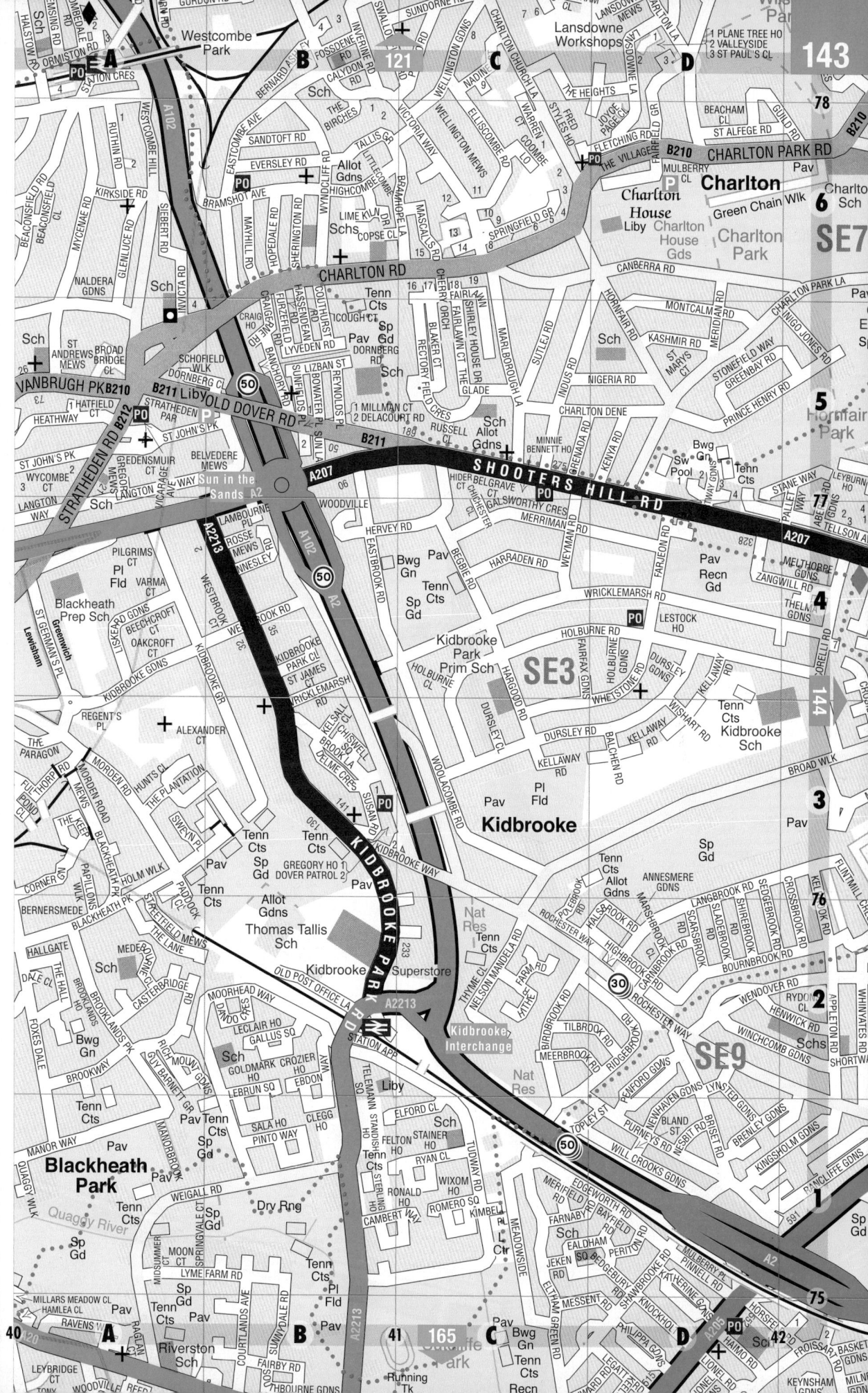

143
121
144
165
A
B
C
D
78
6
5
4
3
2
1
77
76
75
40
41
42
SE7
SE3
SE9
Westcombe Park
Lansdowne Workshops
1 PLANE TREE HO
2 VALLEYSIDE
3 ST PAUL'S CL
Charlton
Charlton House
Charlton House Gds
Charlton Park
Charlton Sch
Hornfair Park
CHARLTON PARK RD
CHARLTON PARK LA
CHARLTON RD
CHARLTON CHURCH LA
CHARLTON DENE
THE VILLAGE
B210
B211
B212
A207
A102
A2
A2213
A205
SHOOTERS HILL RD
OLD DOVER RD
VANBRUGH PK
STRATHEDEN RD
WESTCOMBE HILL
SUNDORNE RD
WELLINGTON GDNS
VICTORIA WAY
CANBERRA RD
MONTCALM RD
KASHMIR RD
NIGERIA RD
STONEFIELD WAY
GREENBAY RD
PRINCE HENRY RD
INDUS RD
SUTLEJ RD
MARLBOROUGH LA
HORNFAIR RD
GRENADA RD
KENYA RD
Green Chain Wlk
Sun in the Sands
WOODVILLE
HERVEY RD
EASTBROOK RD
HARRADEN RD
WRICKLEMARSH RD
HOLBURNE RD
WHETSTONE RD
DURSLEY RD
KELLAWAY RD
BROAD WLK
WOOLACOMBE RD
Kidbrooke Park Prim Sch
Kidbrooke
Kidbrooke Sch
KIDBROOKE PARK RD
KIDBROOKE WAY
KIDBROOKE GDNS
KIDBROOKE GR
Kidbrooke Interchange
Thomas Tallis Sch
Superstore
ROCHESTER WAY
NELSON MANDELA RD
BIRDBROOK RD
WILL CROOKS GDNS
Blackheath Prep Sch
Blackheath Park
BLACKHEATH PK
ST GERMAN'S PL
Lewisham
Greenwich
Quaggy River
Riverston Sch
Running Tk
SUNNYDALE RD
COURTLANDS AVE
WEIGALL RD
ELTHAM GREEN RD
MEADOWSIDE
STATION APP

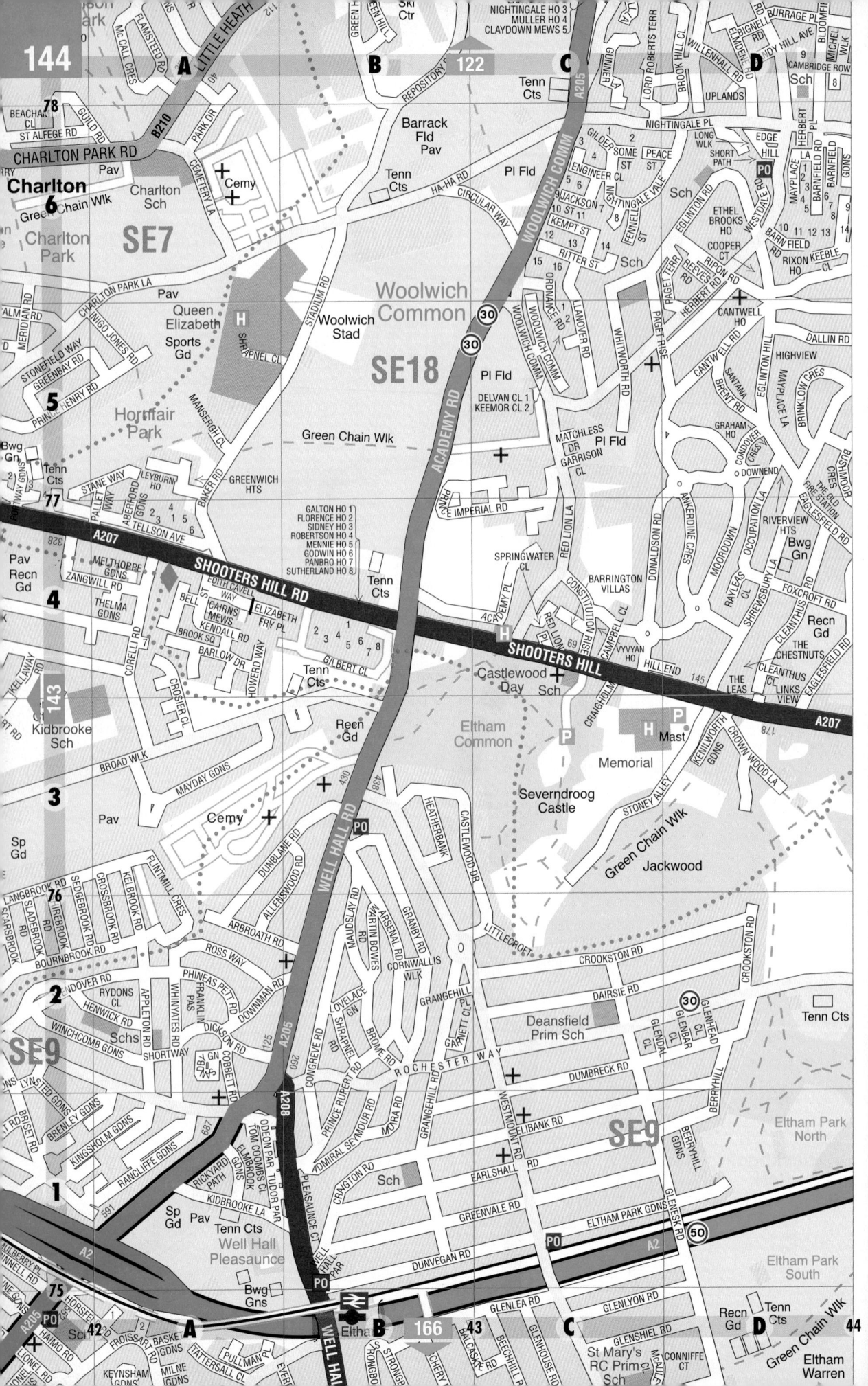

144
A
B
C
D
122
166
143
42
43
44
78
77
76
75
6
5
4
3
2
1
Charlton
SE7
SE18
SE9
Charlton Park
Charlton Sch
Woolwich Common
Woolwich Stad
Queen Elizabeth
Sports Gd
Hornfair Park
Barrack Fld Pav
Kidbrooke Sch
Eltham Common
Severndroog Castle
Memorial
Mast
Jackwood
Castlewood Day Sch
Deansfield Prim Sch
Well Hall Pleasaunce
Eltham Park North
Eltham Park South
Eltham Warren
St Mary's RC Prim Sch
Green Chain Wlk
LITTLE HEATH
CHARLTON PARK RD
B210
ST ALFEGE RD
BEACHAM CL
GUILD RD
FLAMSTEED RD
Mc CALL CRES
PARK DR
CEMETERY LA
REPOSITORY RD
HA-HA RD
CIRCULAR WAY
WOOLWICH COMM
A205
ACADEMY RD
NIGHTINGALE HO 3
MULLER HO 4
CLAYDOWN MEWS 5
GUNNER LA
LORD ROBERTS TERR
BROOK HILL CL
WILLENHALL RD
BIGNELL RD
BURRAGE PL
CAMBRIDGE ROW
MICHEL WLK
UPLANDS
NIGHTINGALE PL
GILDERSOME ST
PEACE ST
ENGINEER CL
JACKSON ST
KEMPT ST
RITTER ST
NIGHTINGALE VALE
FENNELL ST
EGLINTON RD
WESTDALE RD
ETHEL BROOKS HO
COOPER CT
BARNFIELD RD
BARNFIELD GDNS
MAYPLACE LA
HERBERT PL
RIXON HO
KEEBLE CL
REEVES RD
RIPON RD
HERBERT RD
PAGET TERR
PAGET RISE
CANTWELL HO
CANTWELL RD
DALLIN RD
HIGHVIEW
EGLINTON HILL
MAYPLACE LA
BRINKLOW CRES
SANTANA
BRENT RD
GRAHAM HO
CONDOVER CRES
DOWNEND
BUSHMOOR CRES
THE OLD FIRE STATION
EAGLESFIELD RD
RIVERVIEW HTS
OCCUPATION LA
SHREWSBURY LA
FOXCROFT RD
CLEANTHUS RD
CLEANTHUS CL
THE CHESTNUTS
LINKS VIEW
THE LEAS
RAYLEAS CL
MOORDOWN
ANKERDINE CRES
DONALDSON RD
WHITWORTH RD
LLANOVER RD
ORDNANCE RD
DELVAN CL 1
KEEMOR CL 2
MATCHLESS DR
GARRISON CL
PRINCE IMPERIAL RD
RED LION LA
SPRINGWATER CL
BARRINGTON VILLAS
CONSTITUTION RISE
CAMPBELL CL
VYVYAN HO
HILL END
ACADEMY PL
RED LION PL
SHOOTERS HILL
SHOOTERS HILL RD
A207
CRAIGHOLM
KENILWORTH GDNS
CROWN WOOD LA
STONEY ALLEY
CHARLTON PARK LA
INIGO JONES RD
STONEFIELD WAY
GREENBAY RD
PRINCE HENRY RD
MERIDIAN RD
SHRAPNEL CL
STADIUM RD
MANSERGH CL
BAKER RD
GREENWICH HTS
LEYBURN HO
STANE WAY
PALLET WAY
ABERFORD GDNS
TELLSON AVE
PORTWAY GDNS
GALTON HO 1
FLORENCE HO 2
SIDNEY HO 3
ROBERTSON HO 4
MENNIE HO 5
GODWIN HO 6
PANBRO HO 7
SUTHERLAND HO 8
MELTHORPE GDNS
ZANGWILL RD
THELMA GDNS
EDITH CAVELL WAY
BELL ST
CAIRNS MEWS
ELIZABETH FRY PL
KENDALL RD
BROOK SQ
BARLOW DR
HOWERD WAY
GILBERT CL
CORELLI RD
CROSIER CL
KELLAWAY RD
BROAD WLK
MAYDAY GDNS
Cemy
WELL HALL RD
DUNBLANE RD
ALLENSWOOD RD
ARBROATH RD
HEATHERBANK
CASTLEWOOD DR
LITTLECROFT
MAUDSLAY RD
MARTIN BOWES RD
ARSENAL RD
GRANBY RD
CORNWALLIS WLK
GRANGEHILL PL
GRANGEHILL RD
GARNETT CL
CROOKSTON RD
DAIRSIE RD
GLENDAL CL
GLENBAR CL
GLENHEAD CL
DUMBRECK RD
BERRYHILL
BERRYHILL GDNS
ELIBANK RD
WESTMOUNT RD
EARLSHALL RD
GREENVALE RD
ELTHAM PARK GDNS
GLENESK RD
DUNVEGAN RD
GLENLEA RD
GLENLYON RD
GLENSHIEL RD
GLENHOUSE RD
BEECHILL RD
BALCASKIE RD
McAULEY
CONNIFFE CT
ROCHESTER WAY
CONGREVE RD
SHRAPNEL RD
LOVELACE GN
BROME RD
PRINCE RUPERT RD
ADMIRAL SEYMOUR RD
MORA RD
CRAGTON RD
PLEASAUNCE CT
WELL HALL PAR
A208
ODEON PAR
TUDOR PAR
TOM COOMBS CL
ELMBROOK GDNS
RICKYARD PATH
KIDBROOKE LA
LANGBROOK RD
SEDGEBROOK RD
CROSSBROOK RD
KELBROOK RD
FLINTMILL CRES
SLADEBROOK RD
BIREBROOK RD
SCARSBROOK RD
BOURNBROOK RD
ROSS WAY
ENDOVER RD
RYDONS CL
HENWICK RD
APPLETON RD
WHINYATES RD
PHINEAS PETT RD
FRANKLIN PAS
DOWNMAN RD
DICKSON RD
COBBETT RD
WINCHCOMB GDNS
SHORTWAY
LYNSTED GDNS
BRENLEY GDNS
BRISET RD
KINGSHOLM GDNS
RANCLIFFE GDNS
A2
MULBERRY PL
HORSFELD
HAIMO RD
LIONEL RD
FROISSART RD
BASKET GDNS
TATTERSALL CL
MILNE GDNS
KEYNSHAM GDNS
PULLMAN PL
STRONGBOW
Eltham
WELL HALL

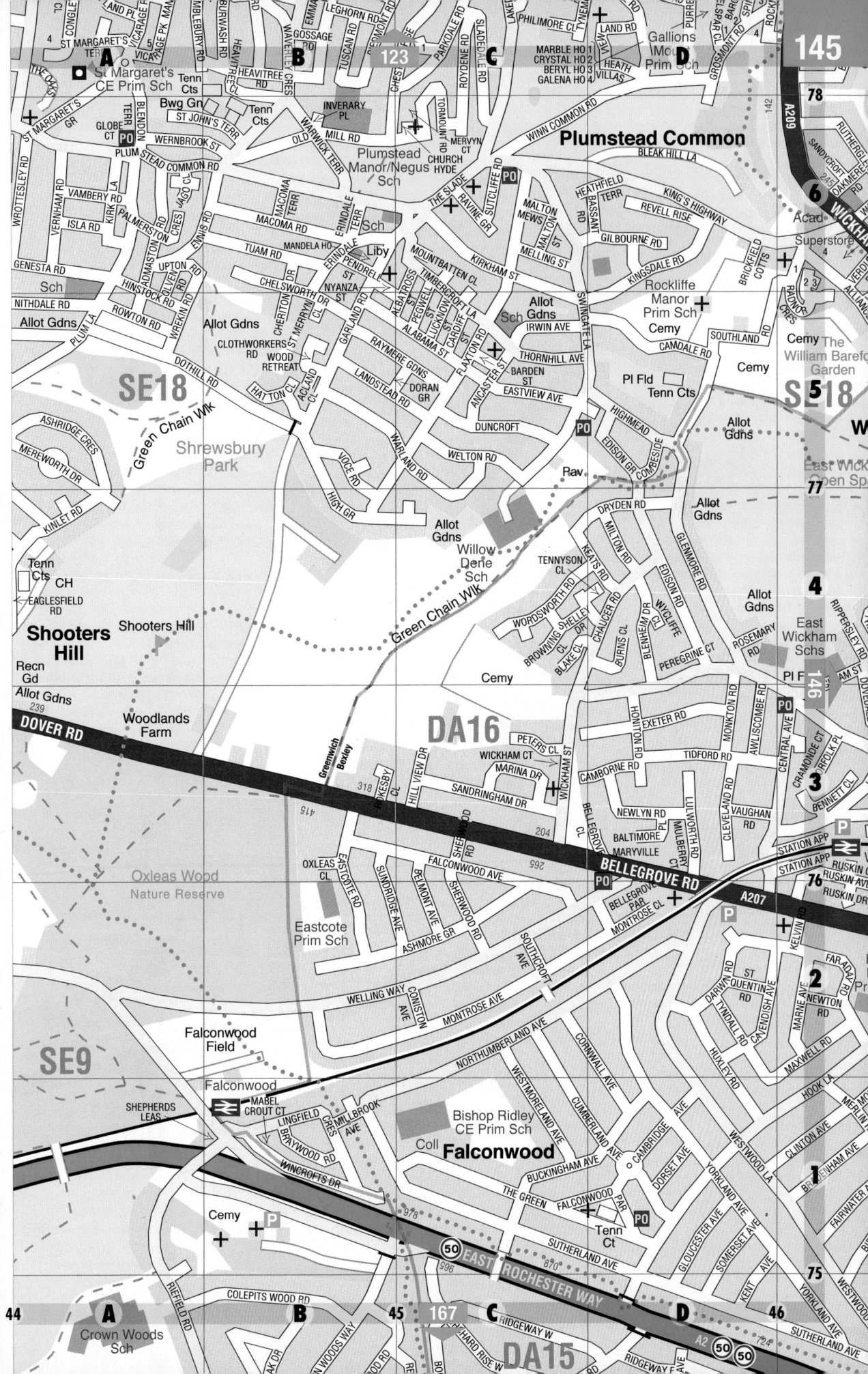
Plumstead Common
Shooters Hill
Falconwood
SE18
DA16
SE9
DA15
Shrewsbury Park
Oxleas Wood
Nature Reserve
Falconwood Field
Green Chain Wlk
DOVER RD
BELLEGROVE RD
EAST ROCHESTER WAY
Willow Dene Sch
Eastcote Prim Sch
Bishop Ridley CE Prim Sch
Crown Woods Sch
St Margaret's CE Prim Sch
Plumstead Manor/Negus Sch
Rockliffe Manor Prim Sch
Gallions Mount Prim Sch
East Wickham Schs
Woodlands Farm
123
146
167
44
45
46
75
76
77
78

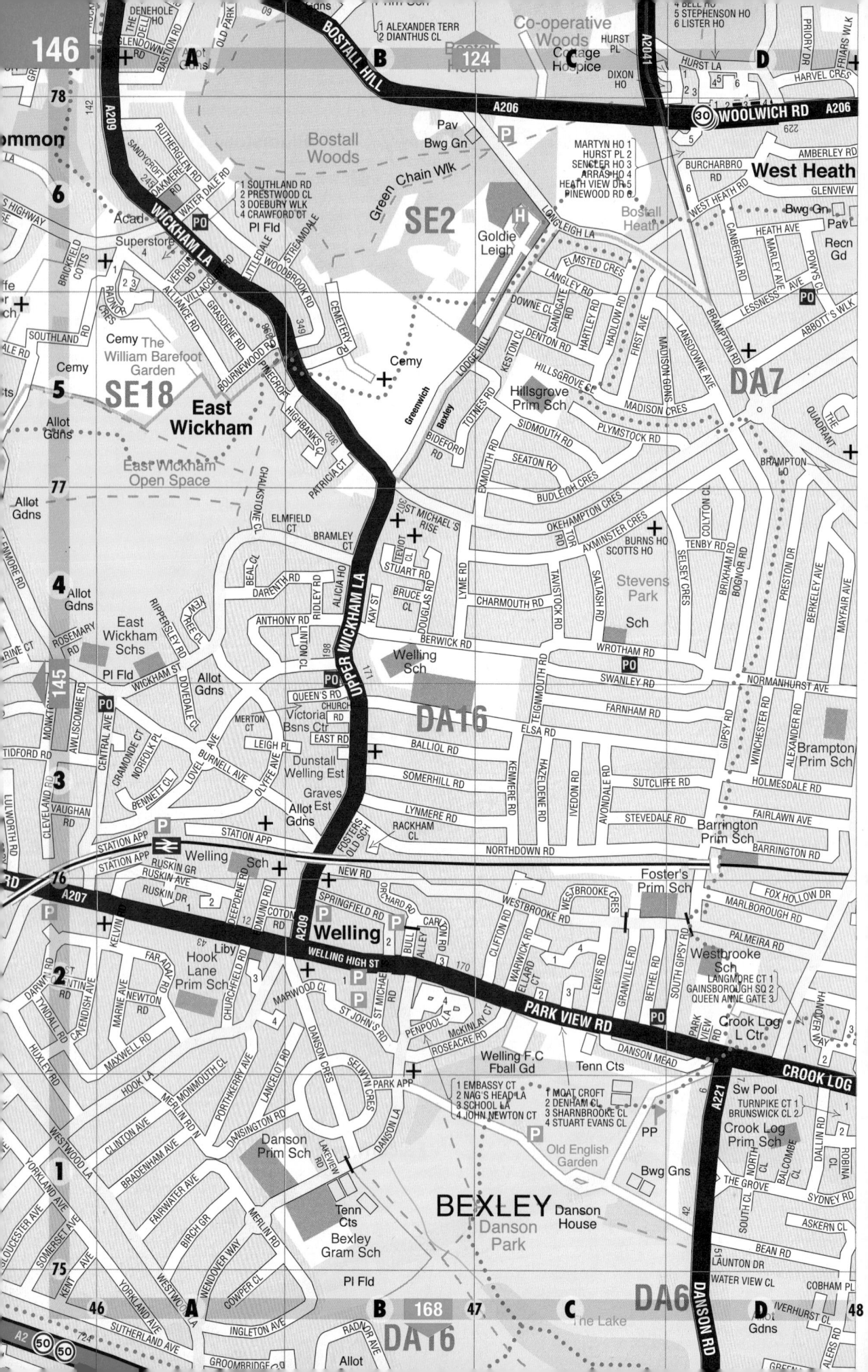
146
124
145
168
A
B
C
D
78
77
76
75
46
47
48
6
5
4
3
2
1
BOSTALL HILL
A206
WOOLWICH RD
A2041
Co-operative Woods
Cottage Hospice
Bostall Heath
Bostall Woods
Green Chain Wlk
SE2
Goldie Leigh
West Heath
DA7
SE18
East Wickham
East Wickham Open Space
The William Barefoot Garden
A209
WICKHAM LA
UPPER WICKHAM LA
DA16
Welling
WELLING HIGH ST
A207
PARK VIEW RD
CROOK LOG
A221
DANSON RD
BEXLEY
Danson Park
Danson House
Old English Garden
The Lake
DA6
Bexley Gram Sch
Danson Prim Sch
Hook Lane Prim Sch
Welling Sch
Welling F.C Fball Gd
Westbrooke Sch
Foster's Prim Sch
Barrington Prim Sch
Brampton Prim Sch
Crook Log Prim Sch
Crook Log L Ctr
Sw Pool
Hillsgrove Prim Sch
Stevens Park
East Wickham Schs
Victoria Bsns Ctr
Dunstall Welling Est
Graves Est
Allot Gdns
Cemy
Superstore
Acad
Pl Fld
Tenn Cts
Bwg Gns
Recn Gd
1 SOUTHLAND RD
2 PRESTWOOD CL
3 DOEBURY WLK
4 CRAWFORD CT
1 ALEXANDER TERR
2 DIANTHUS CL
5 STEPHENSON HO
6 LISTER HO
MARTYN HO 1
HURST PL 2
SENCLER HO 3
ARRAS HO 4
HEATH VIEW DR 5
PINEWOOD RD 6
1 EMBASSY CT
2 NAG'S HEAD LA
3 SCHOOL LA
4 JOHN NEWTON CT
1 MOAT CROFT
2 DENHAM CL
3 SHARNBROOKE CL
4 STUART EVANS CL
LANGMORE CT 1
GAINSBOROUGH SQ 2
QUEEN ANNE GATE 3
TURNPIKE CT 1
BRUNSWICK CL 2
BRAMPTON LO
BURNS HO
SCOTTS HO
NORTHDOWN RD
BERWICK RD
BALLIOL RD
SOMERHILL RD
LYNMERE RD
OKEHAMPTON CRES
BUDLEIGH CRES
PLYMSTOCK RD
HILLSGROVE CL
LODGE HILL
STATION APP
WESTBROOKE RD
DANSON MEAD
BEAN RD
LAUNTON DR
WATER VIEW CL
SYDNEY RD
ASKERN CL
THE GROVE
IVERHURST CL
COBHAM PL

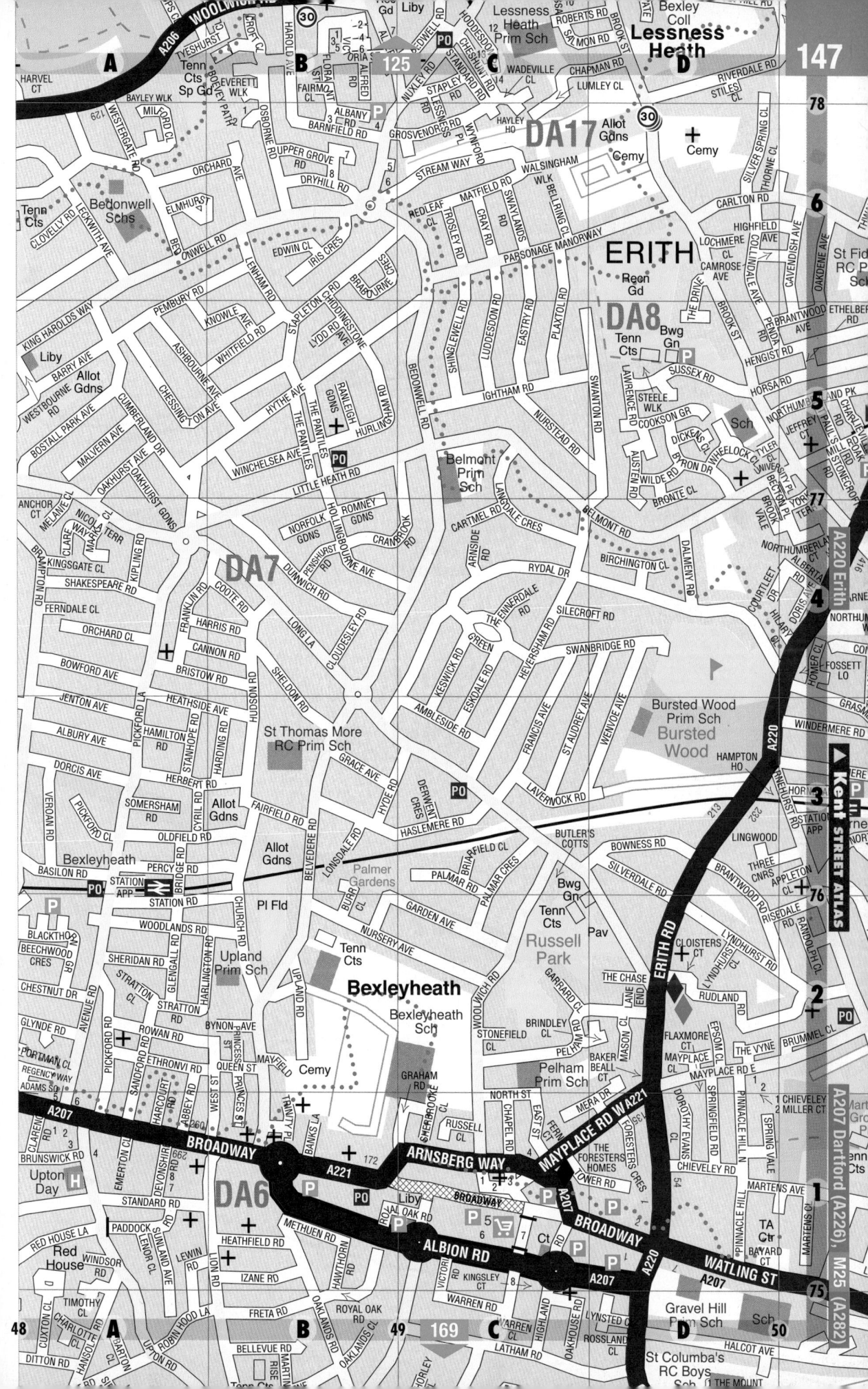

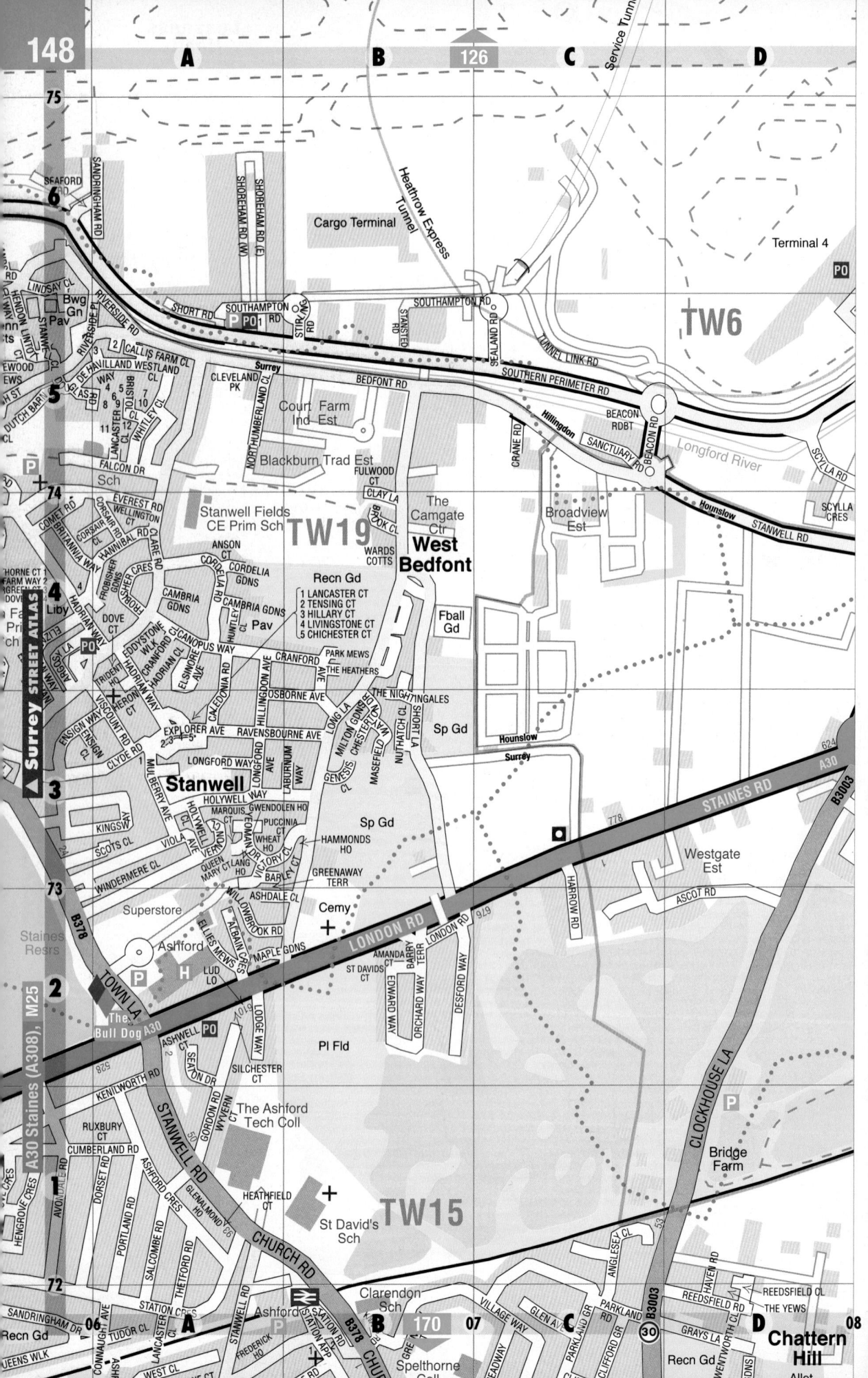

A
B
126
C
D
75
6
5
74
4
3
73
2
1
72
Cargo Terminal
Heathrow Express Tunnel
Service Tunnel
Terminal 4
TW6
SOUTHAMPTON RD
SOUTHERN PERIMETER RD
TUNNEL LINK RD
BEACON RDBT
Longford River
Court Farm Ind Est
Blackburn Trad Est
Stanwell Fields CE Prim Sch
TW19
West Bedfont
The Camgate Ctr
Broadview Est
Recn Gd
Fball Gd
1 LANCASTER CT
2 TENSING CT
3 HILLARY CT
4 LIVINGSTONE CT
5 CHICHESTER CT
Stanwell
Sp Gd
STAINES RD
Westgate Est
LONDON RD
Superstore
Staines Resrs
Ashford
The Bull Dog
Pl Fld
The Ashford Tech Coll
STANWELL RD
CLOCKHOUSE LA
Bridge Farm
TW15
St David's Sch
CHURCH RD
Clarendon Sch
Ashford
Spelthorne Coll
Chattern Hill
Recn Gd
Surrey STREET ATLAS
A30 Staines (A308), M25
06
170
07
08

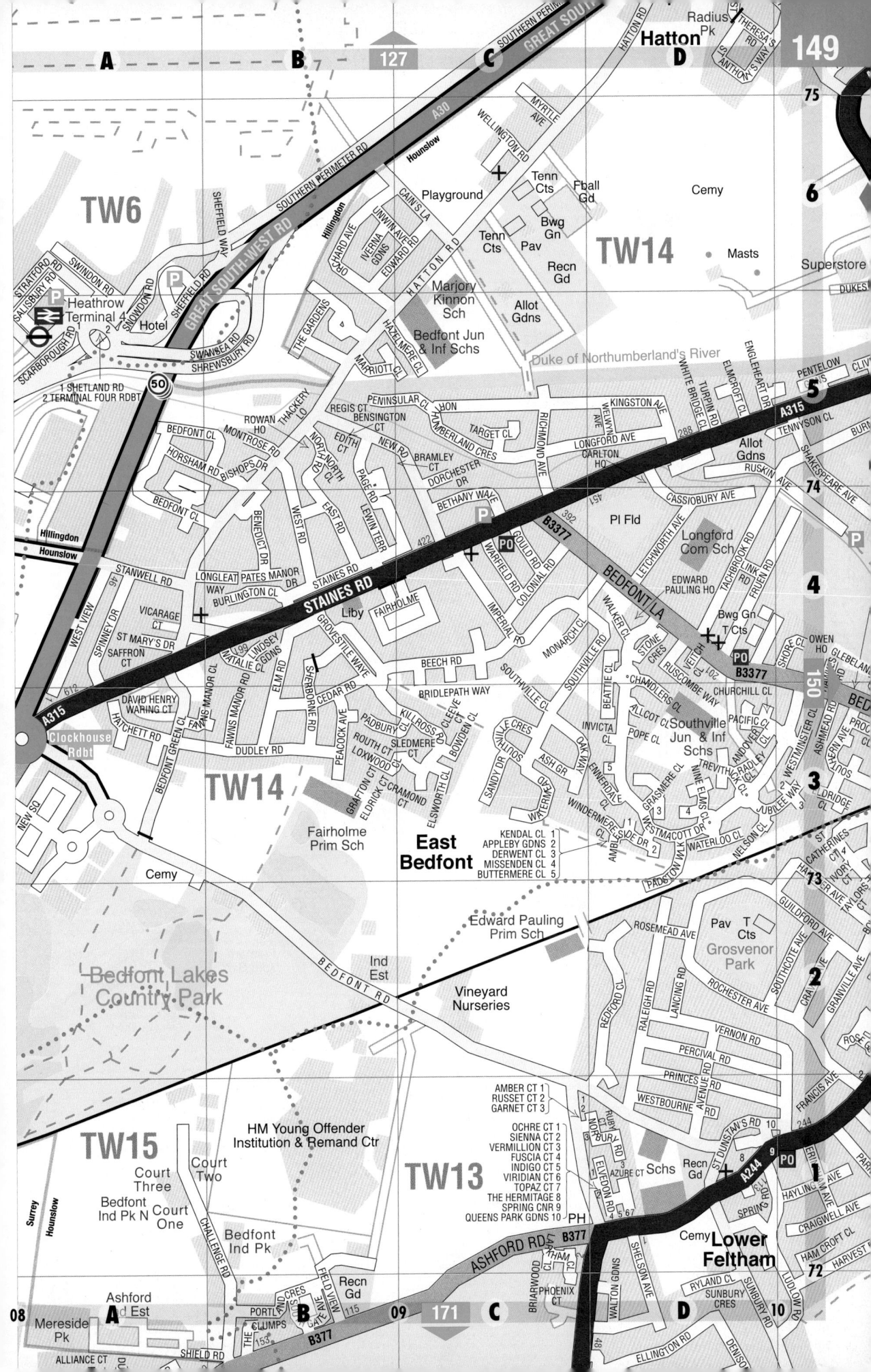
127
171
150
A
B
C
D
75
6
5
74
4
3
73
2
1
72
08
09
10
Hatton
Radius Pk
TW6
TW14
TW15
TW13
Heathrow Terminal 4
Hotel
1 SHETLAND RD
2 TERMINAL FOUR RDBT
GREAT SOUTH-WEST RD
SOUTHERN PERIMETER RD
A30
Hounslow
Hillingdon
Playground
Tenn Cts
Fball Gd
Cemy
Bwg Gn
Pav
Recn Gd
Masts
Superstore
Marjory Kinnon Sch
Bedfont Jun & Inf Schs
Allot Gdns
Duke of Northumberland's River
STAINES RD
A315
B3377
BEDFONT LA
Liby
FAIRHOLME
Pl Fld
Longford Com Sch
EDWARD PAULING HO
Bwg Gn
T Cts
Southville Jun & Inf Schs
Clockhouse Rdbt
Fairholme Prim Sch
East Bedfont
KENDAL CL 1
APPLEBY GDNS 2
DERWENT CL 3
MISSENDEN CL 4
BUTTERMERE CL 5
Edward Pauling Prim Sch
Ind Est
Vineyard Nurseries
Bedfont Lakes Country Park
Grosvenor Park
HM Young Offender Institution & Remand Ctr
Court Two
Court Three
Court One
Bedfont Ind Pk N
Bedfont Ind Pk
Ashford Ind Est
Mereside Pk
Recn Gd
AMBER CT 1
RUSSET CT 2
GARNET CT 3
OCHRE CT 1
SIENNA CT 2
VERMILLION CT 3
FUSCIA CT 4
INDIGO CT 5
VIRIDIAN CT 6
TOPAZ CT 7
THE HERMITAGE 8
SPRING CNR 9
QUEENS PARK GDNS 10
Schs
Recn Gd
Lower Feltham
ASHFORD RD
B377
A244
BEDFONT RD
Surrey
Hounslow

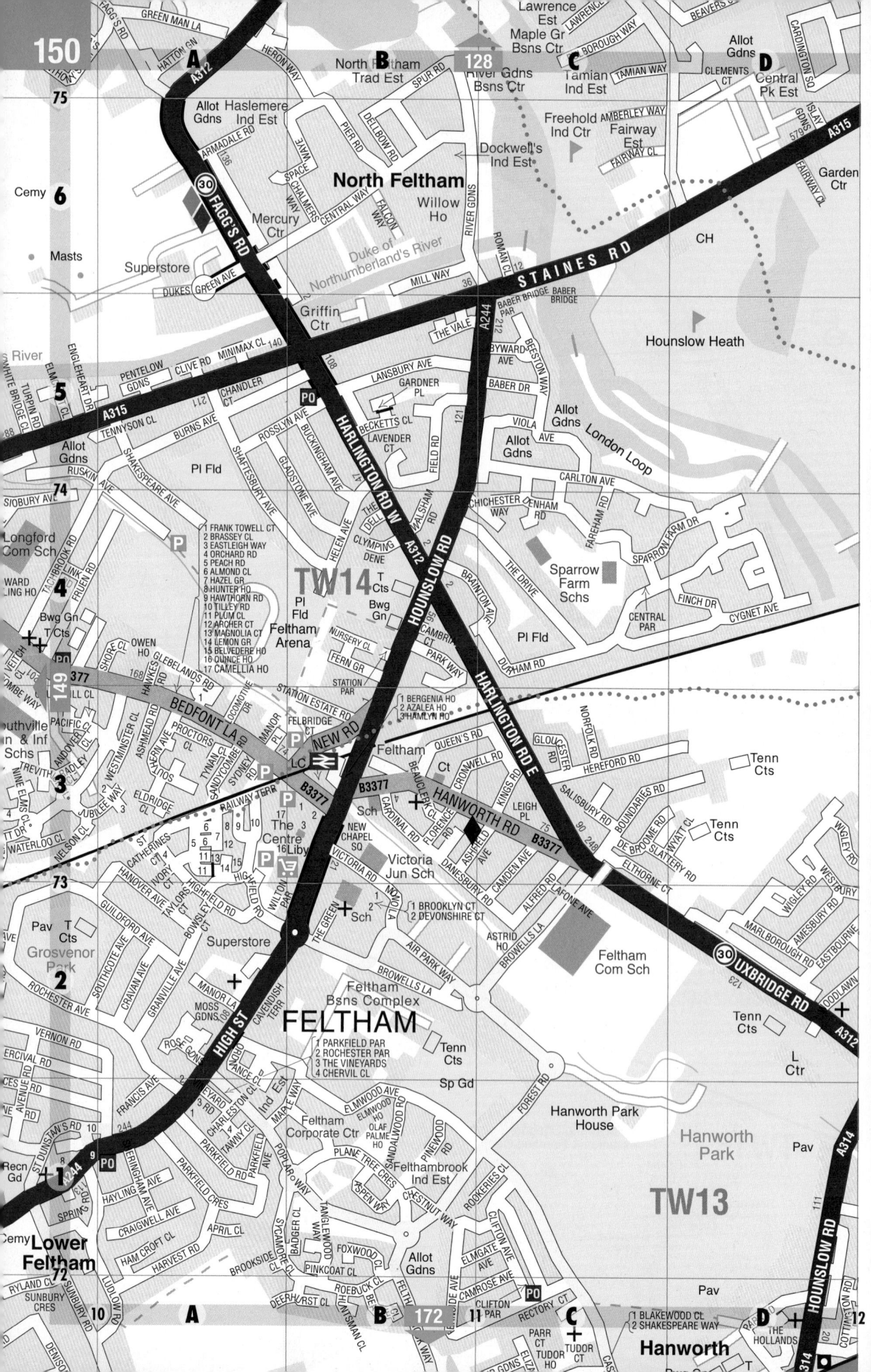
North Feltham
FELTHAM
Lower Feltham
Hanworth
TW14
TW13
Hounslow Heath
Hanworth Park
Hanworth Park House
North Feltham Trad Est
River Gdns Bsns Ctr
Tamian Ind Est
Central Pk Est
Haslemere Ind Est
Freehold Ind Ctr
Fairway Est
Dockwell's Ind Est
Mercury Ctr
Willow Ho
Duke of Northumberland's River
Superstore
Griffin Ctr
Feltham Arena
Sparrow Farm Schs
Longford Com Sch
Victoria Jun Sch
The Centre
Feltham Bsns Complex
Feltham Com Sch
Feltham Corporate Ctr
Felthambrook Ind Est
Grosvenor Park
London Loop
STAINES RD
FAGG'S RD
HARLINGTON RD W
HARLINGTON RD E
HOUNSLOW RD
HANWORTH RD
BEDFONT LA
HIGH ST
UXBRIDGE RD
NEW RD
A312
A315
A244
B3377
A314
1 FRANK TOWELL CT
2 BRASSEY CL
3 EASTLEIGH WAY
4 ORCHARD RD
5 PEACH RD
6 ALMOND CL
7 HAZEL GR
8 HUNTER HO
9 HAWTHORN RD
10 TILLEY RD
11 PLUM CL
12 ARCHER CT
13 MAGNOLIA CT
14 LEMON GR
15 BELVEDERE HO
16 QUINCE HO
17 CAMELLIA HO
1 BERGENIA HO
2 AZALEA HO
3 HAMLYN HO
1 BROOKLYN CT
2 DEVONSHIRE CT
1 PARKFIELD PAR
2 ROCHESTER PAR
3 THE VINEYARDS
4 CHERVIL CL
1 BLAKEWOOD CL
2 SHAKESPEARE WAY
128
172
149

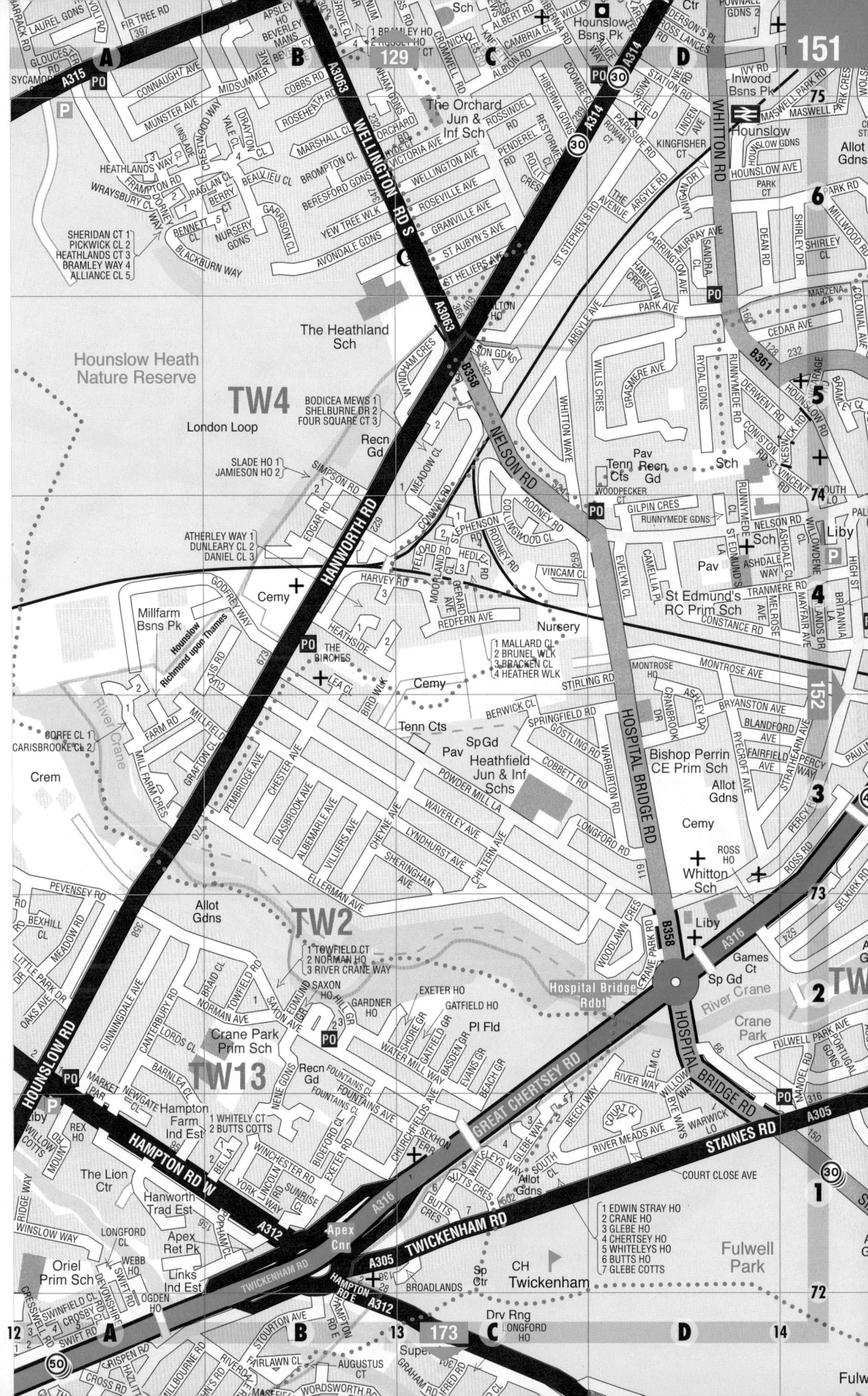

151
129
152
173
A
B
C
D
A
B
C
D
12
13
14
75
6
5
74
4
3
73
2
1
72
TW4
TW2
TW13
Hounslow Heath Nature Reserve
London Loop
The Heathland Sch
The Orchard Jun & Inf Sch
Hounslow Bsns Pk
Inwood Bsns Pk
Hounslow
WELLINGTON RD S
HANWORTH RD
NELSON RD
HOSPITAL BRIDGE RD
WHITTON RD
HOUNSLOW RD
HAMPTON RD W
GREAT CHERTSEY RD
TWICKENHAM RD
STAINES RD
Hospital Bridge Rdbt
Apex Cnr
Millfarm Bsns Pk
Hounslow
Richmond upon Thames
River Crane
Crem
Cemy
Heathfield Jun & Inf Schs
Bishop Perrin CE Prim Sch
St Edmund's RC Prim Sch
Whitton Sch
Crane Park Prim Sch
Crane Park
Hampton Farm Ind Est
The Lion Ctr
Hanworth Trad Est
Apex Ret Pk
Links Ind Est
Oriel Prim Sch
CH Twickenham
Fulwell Park
Drv Rng
Allot Gdns
Nursery
SHERIDAN CT 1
PICKWICK CL 2
HEATHLANDS CT 3
BRAMLEY WAY 4
ALLIANCE CL 5
BODICEA MEWS 1
SHELBURNE DR 2
FOUR SQUARE CT 3
SLADE HO 1
JAMIESON HO 2
ATHERLEY WAY 1
DUNLEARY CL 2
DANIEL CL 3
CORFE CL 1
CARISBROOKE CL 2
1 MALLARD CL
2 BRUNEL WLK
3 BRACKEN CL
4 HEATHER WLK
1 TOWFIELD CT
2 NORMAN HO
3 RIVER CRANE WAY
1 WHITELY CT
2 BUTTS COTTS
1 EDWIN STRAY HO
2 CRANE HO
3 GLEBE HO
4 CHERTSEY HO
5 WHITELEYS HO
6 BUTTS HO
7 GLEBE COTTS
1 BRAMLEY HO
2 RUSSELL HO

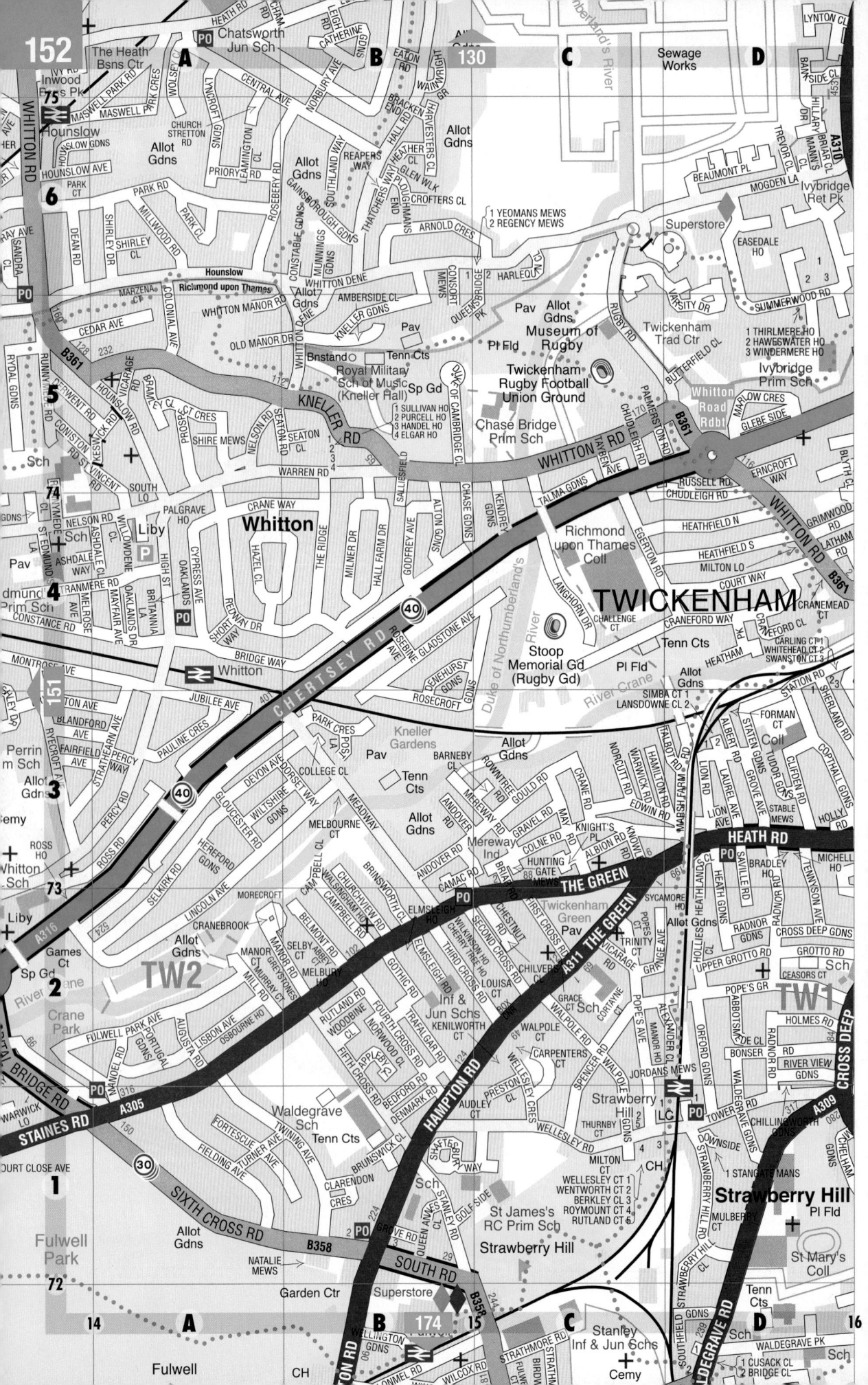

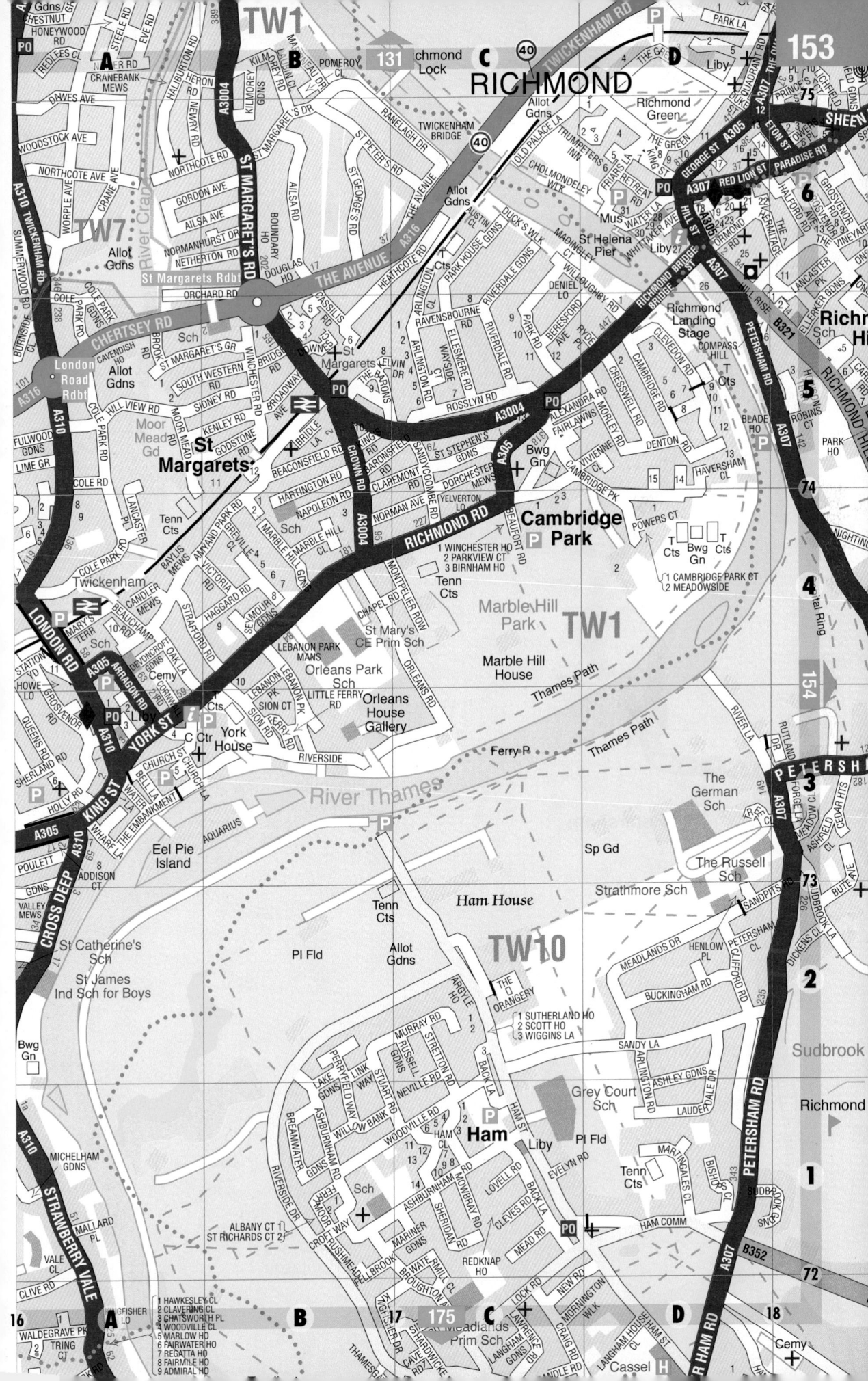
RICHMOND
TW1
TW7
TW10
St Margarets
Cambridge Park
Twickenham
Ham
Richmond Green
River Thames
Marble Hill Park
Marble Hill House
Ham House
Eel Pie Island
Orleans House Gallery
York House
The German Sch
The Russell Sch
Strathmore Sch
Grey Court Sch
St Catherine's Sch
St James Ind Sch for Boys
St Margarets Rdbt
London Road Rdbt
Richmond Landing Stage
St Helena Pier
Twickenham Bridge
Richmond Bridge
Richmond Lock
Thames Path
Sudbrook
Petersham Rd
Richmond Rd
Twickenham Rd
St Margaret's Rd
The Avenue
Chertsey Rd
York St
King St
London Rd
Cross Deep
Strawberry Vale
Ham St
Sandy La
Ham Comm
Crown Rd
Hill St
George St
Red Lion St
Paradise Rd
Sheen Rd
Hill Rise
Richmond Hill
A B C D
131
154
175
16 17 18
72 73 74 75
1 2 3 4 5 6

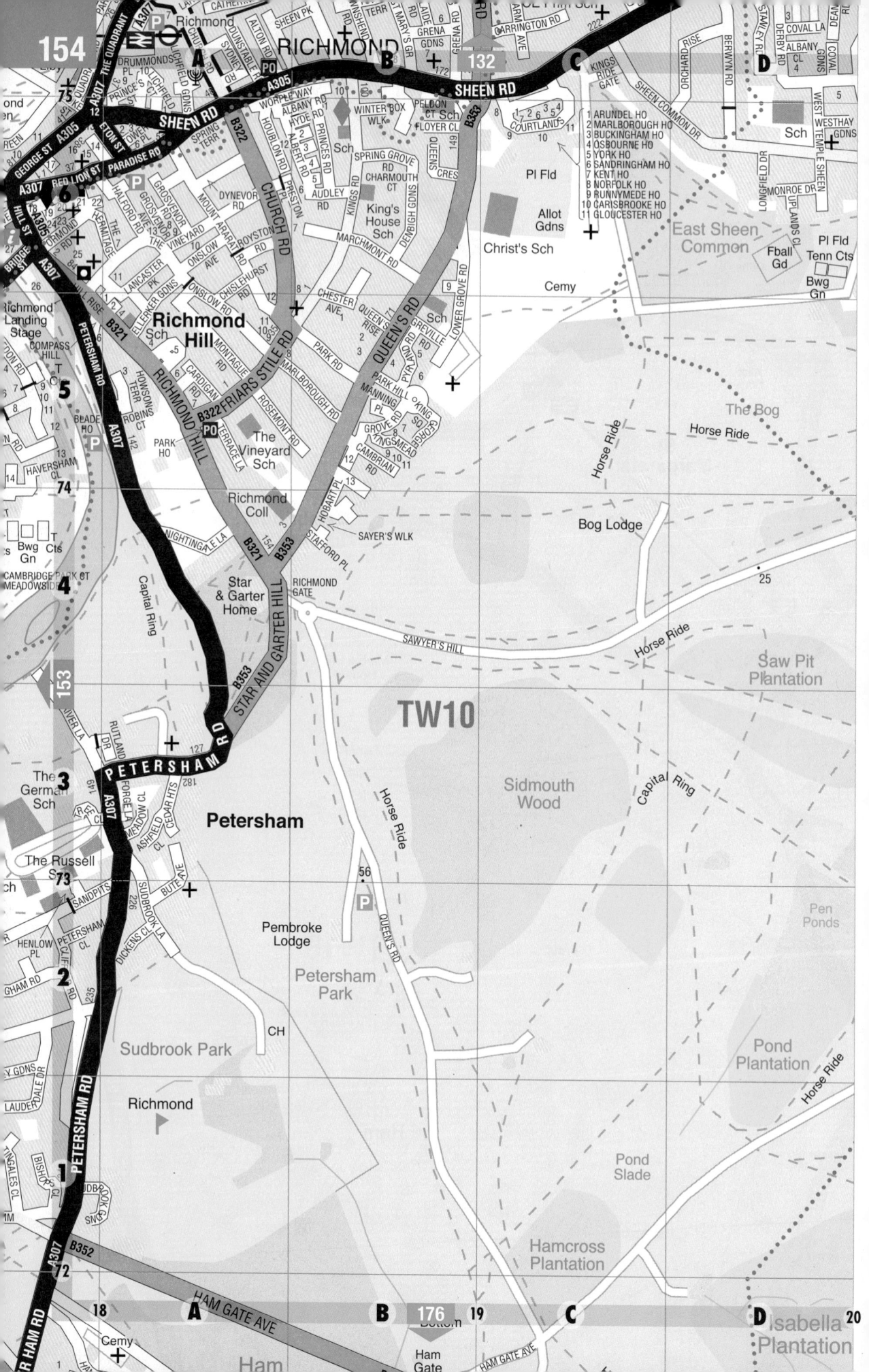
RICHMOND
Richmond Hill
Petersham
TW10
East Sheen Common
SHEEN RD
A305
A307
B321
B322
B353
B352
PETERSHAM RD
RICHMOND HILL
STAR AND GARTER HILL
QUEEN'S RD
CHURCH RD
FRIARS STILE RD
SAWYER'S HILL
HAM GATE AVE
GEORGE ST
HILL ST
THE QUADRANT
PARADISE RD
RED LION ST
ETON ST
BRIDGE ST
KINGS RIDE GATE
SHEEN COMMON DR
ORCHARD RISE
BERWYN RD
COURTLANDS
1 ARUNDEL HO
2 MARLBOROUGH HO
3 BUCKINGHAM HO
4 OSBOURNE HO
5 YORK HO
6 SANDRINGHAM HO
7 KENT HO
8 NORFOLK HO
9 RUNNYMEDE HO
10 CARISBROOKE HO
11 GLOUCESTER HO
Christ's Sch
Allot Gdns
Pl Fld
Cemy
King's House Sch
The Vineyard Sch
Richmond Coll
Star & Garter Home
Richmond Gate
Bog Lodge
The Bog
Horse Ride
Capital Ring
Saw Pit Plantation
Sidmouth Wood
Pen Ponds
Pembroke Lodge
Petersham Park
Sudbrook Park
Pond Plantation
Pond Slade
Hamcross Plantation
Isabella Plantation
The German Sch
The Russell Sch
Richmond Landing Stage
Ham Gate
Ham
Fball Gd
Tenn Cts
Bwg Gn
132
153
176
18
19
20
A
B
C
D
1
2
3
4
5
6

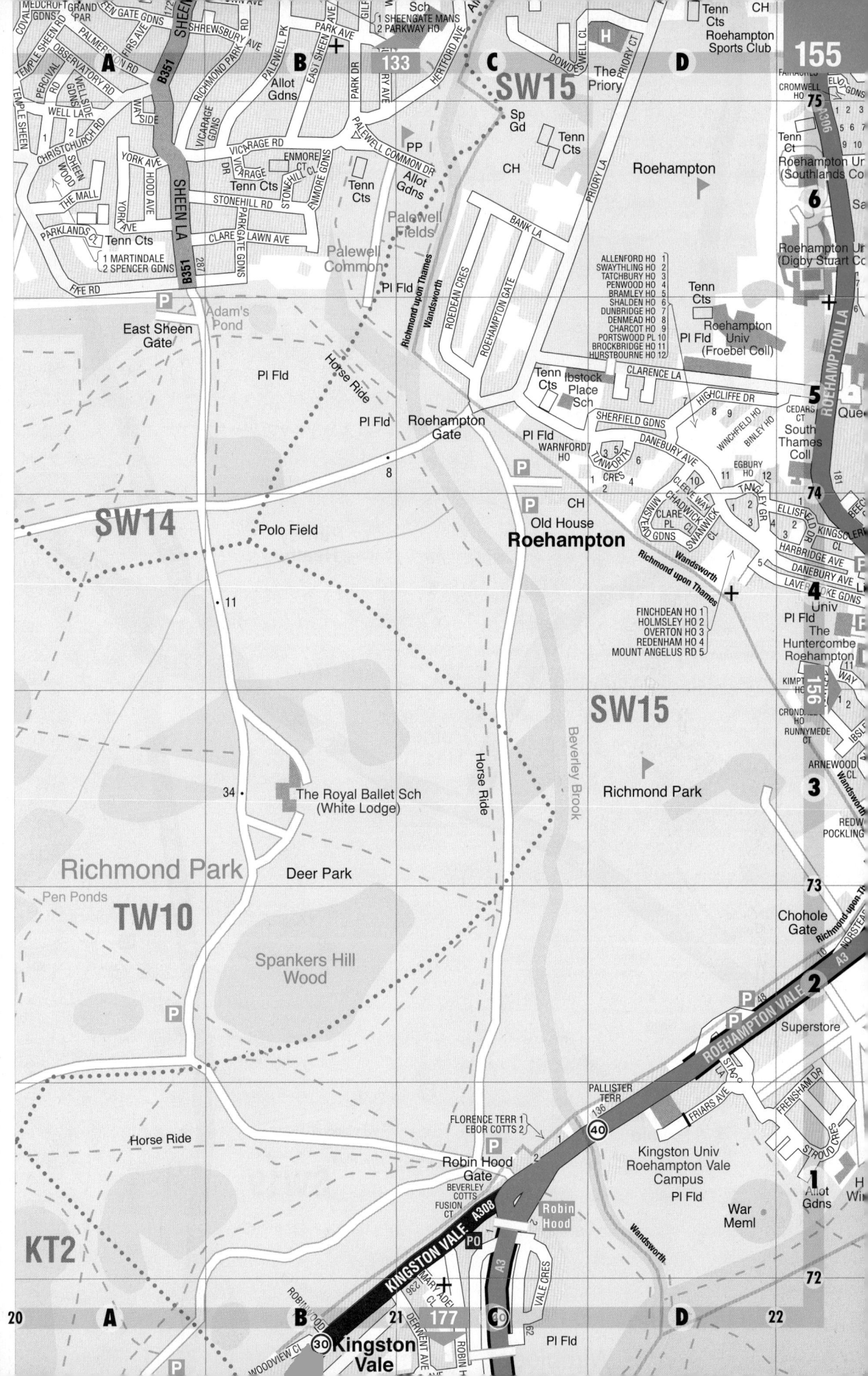
SW15
SW14
SW15
TW10
KT2
Roehampton
Richmond Park
Richmond Park
Polo Field
Deer Park
Spankers Hill Wood
Pen Ponds
The Royal Ballet Sch (White Lodge)
Adam's Pond
East Sheen Gate
Roehampton Gate
Robin Hood Gate
Kingston Vale
Palewell Common
Palewell Fields
Old House
Kingston Univ Roehampton Vale Campus
War Meml
Superstore
Chohole Gate
Beverley Brook
Horse Ride
Horse Ride
Horse Ride
Roehampton Univ (Froebel Coll)
Roehampton Univ (Southlands Coll)
Roehampton Univ (Digby Stuart Coll)
South Thames Coll
Ibstock Place Sch
The Priory
Tenn Cts
Roehampton Sports Club
SHEEN LA
ROEHAMPTON LA
ROEHAMPTON VALE
KINGSTON VALE
CLARENCE LA
DANEBURY AVE
HIGHCLIFFE DR
SHERFIELD GDNS
BANK LA
PRIORY LA
ROEDEAN CRES
ROEHAMPTON GATE
PALEWELL COMMON DR
STONEHILL RD
CLARE LAWN AVE
FIFE RD
THE MALL
CHRISTCHURCH RD
ALLENFORD HO 1
SWAYTHLING HO 2
TATCHBURY HO 3
PENWOOD HO 4
BRAMLEY HO 5
SHALDEN HO 6
DUNBRIDGE HO 7
DENMEAD HO 8
CHARCOT HO 9
PORTSWOOD PL 10
BROCKBRIDGE HO 11
HURSTBOURNE HO 12
FINCHDEAN HO 1
HOLMSLEY HO 2
OVERTON HO 3
REDENHAM HO 4
MOUNT ANGELUS RD 5
1 MARTINDALE
2 SPENCER GDNS
1 SHEENGATE MANS
2 PARKWAY HO
FLORENCE TERR 1
EBOR COTTS 2
Richmond upon Thames
Wandsworth
A
B
C
D
133
177
156
20
21
22
75
74
73
72

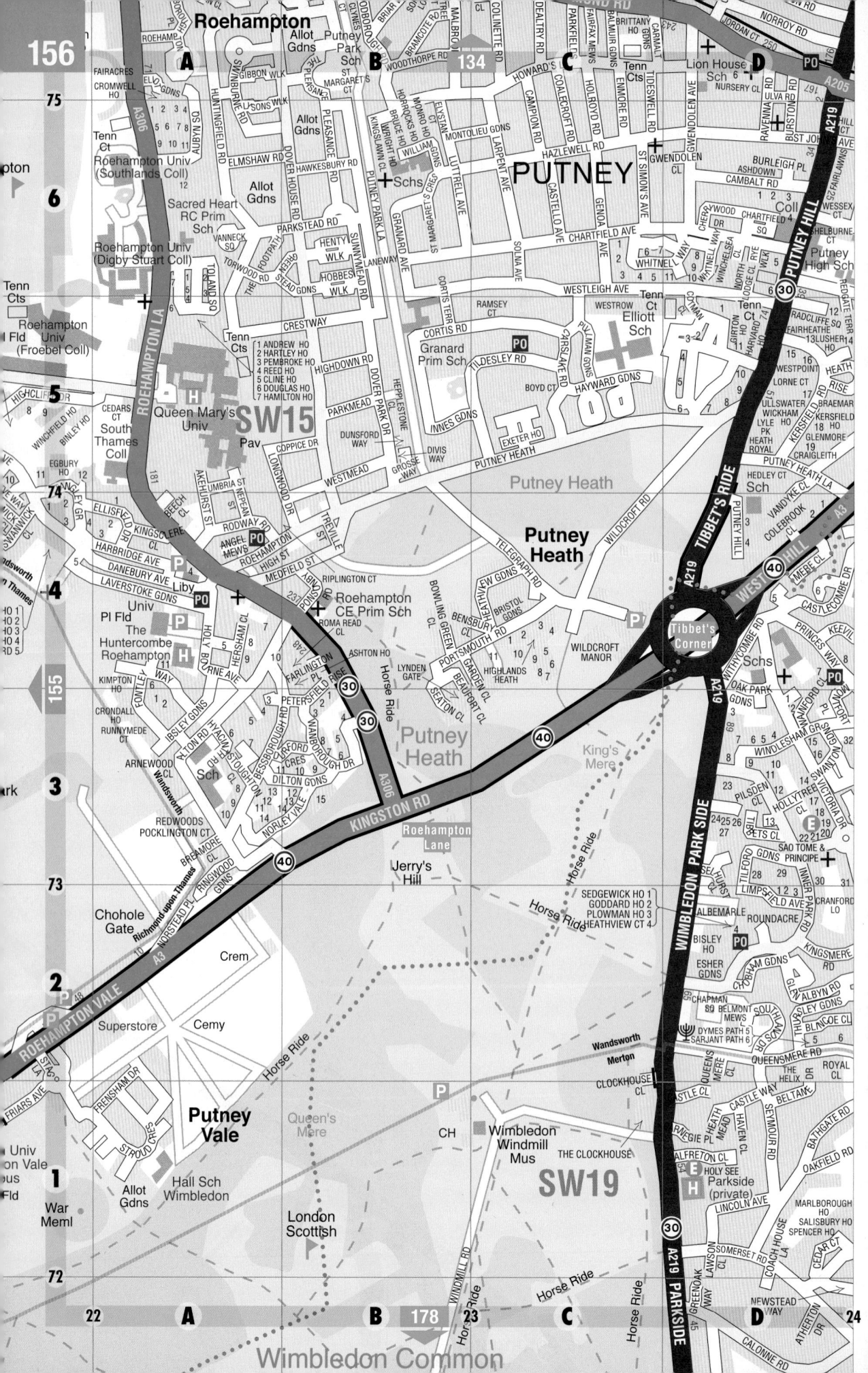
156
134
155
178
Roehampton
PUTNEY
Putney Heath
Putney Vale
Wimbledon Common
SW15
SW19
Tibbet's Corner
Roehampton Lane
Jerry's Hill
King's Mere
Queen's Mere
Horse Ride
Crem
Cemy
Superstore
Wimbledon Windmill Mus
London Scottish
War Meml
Hall Sch Wimbledon
Chohole Gate
Queen Mary's Univ
Roehampton Univ (Southlands Coll)
Roehampton Univ (Digby Stuart Coll)
Roehampton Univ (Froebel Coll)
Sacred Heart RC Prim Sch
Roehampton CE Prim Sch
Granard Prim Sch
Elliott Sch
Putney Park Sch
Putney High Sch
Lion House Sch
South Thames Coll
The Huntercombe Roehampton
Parkside (private)
WILDCROFT MANOR
THE CLOCKHOUSE
KINGSTON RD
ROEHAMPTON LA
ROEHAMPTON VALE
PUTNEY HEATH
PUTNEY HILL
TIBBET'S RIDE
WIMBLEDON PARK SIDE
PARKSIDE
WEST HILL
PUTNEY PARK LA
WESTLEIGH AVE
CHARTFIELD AVE
HAZLEWELL RD
DOVER HOUSE RD
DOVER PARK DR
WILDCROFT RD
TELEGRAPH RD
PORTSMOUTH RD
WINDMILL RD
QUEENSMERE RD
Wandsworth
Merton
Richmond upon Thames
A3
A205
A219
A306

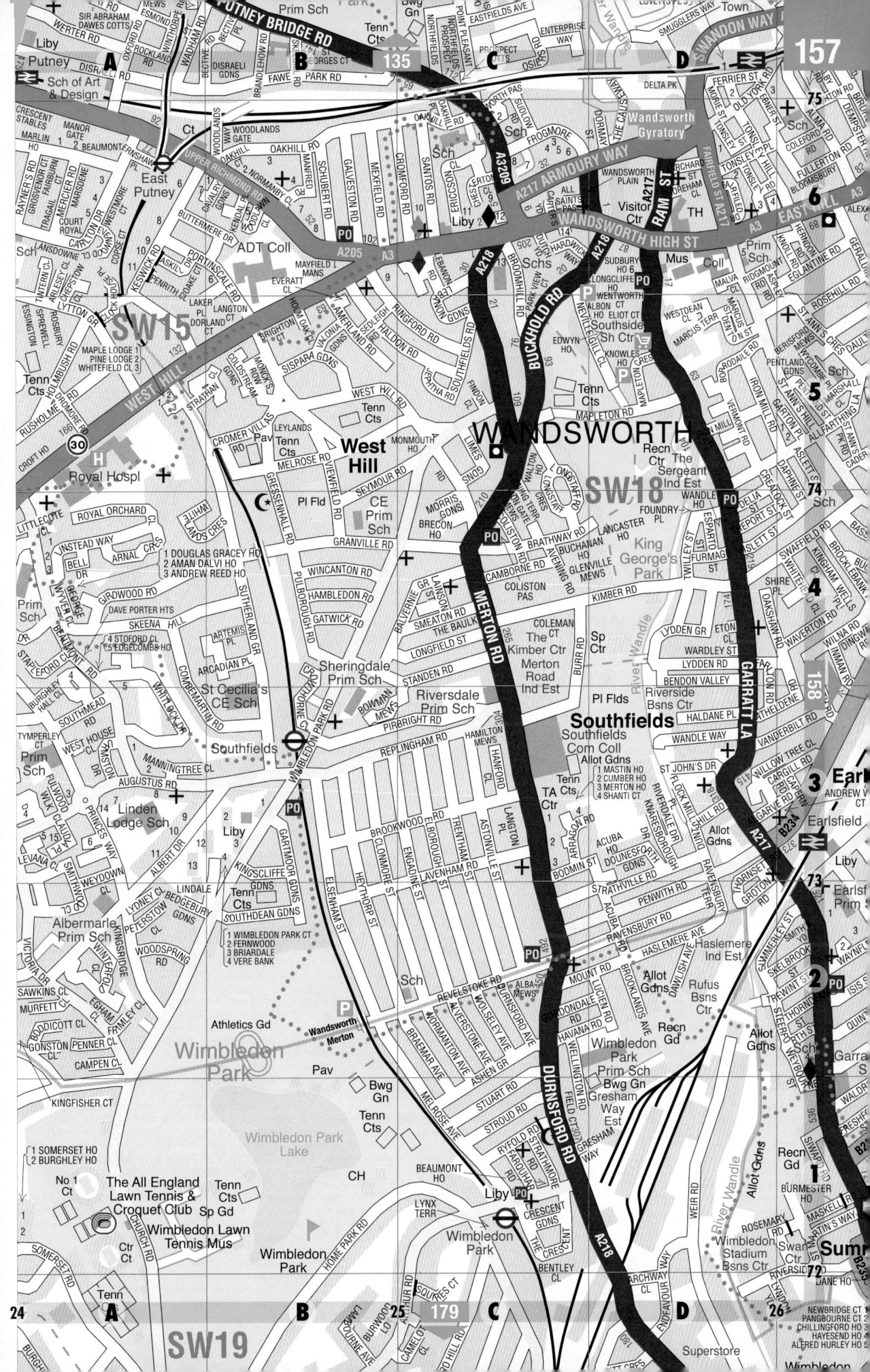
PUTNEY BRIDGE RD
135
Putney
East Putney
UPPER RICHMOND RD
WEST HILL
SW15
Royal Hospl
West Hill
WANDSWORTH
SW18
A217 ARMOURY WAY
Wandsworth Gyratory
WANDSWORTH HIGH ST
EAST HILL
BUCKHOLD RD
MERTON RD
GARRATT LA
King George's Park
Southfields
Southside Sh Ctr
Earlsfield
Wimbledon Park
Wimbledon Park Lake
The All England Lawn Tennis & Croquet Club
Wimbledon Lawn Tennis Mus
DURNSFORD RD
Wimbledon Stadium Bsns Ctr
158
SW19
179

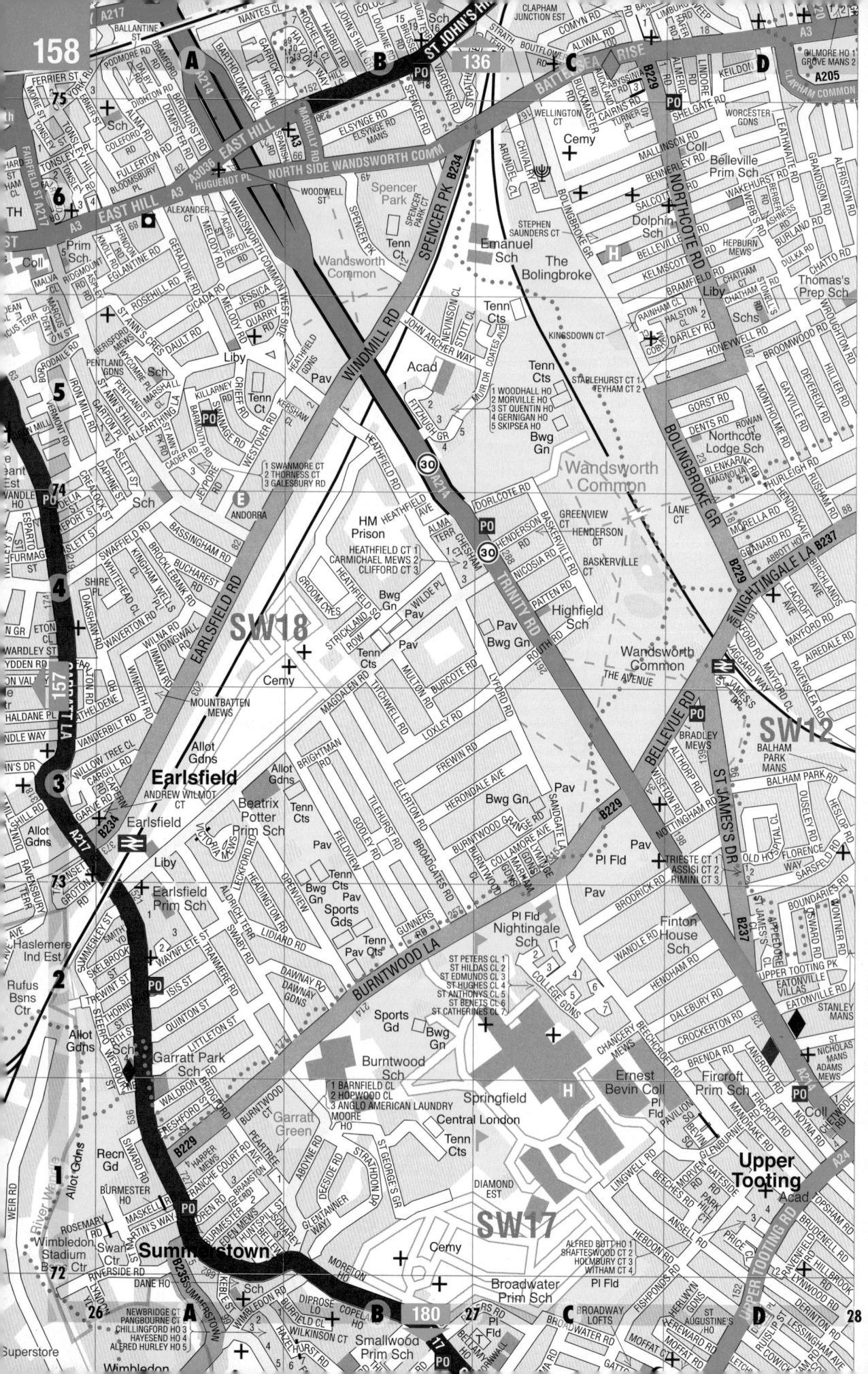

SW18
SW12
SW17
Earlsfield
Summerstown
Upper Tooting
Wandsworth Common
Spencer Park
Emanuel Sch
The Bolingbroke
HM Prison
Springfield
Central London
Burntwood Sch
Garratt Green
Nightingale Sch
Ernest Bevin Coll
Fircroft Prim Sch
Finton House Sch
Beatrix Potter Prim Sch
Earlsfield Prim Sch
Garratt Park Sch
Broadwater Prim Sch
Smallwood Prim Sch
Highfield Sch
Northcote Lodge Sch
Thomas's Prep Sch
Belleville Prim Sch
Dolphin Sch
Wimbledon Stadium Bsns Ctr
Haslemere Ind Est
Rufus Bsns Ctr
River Wandle
EAST HILL
NORTH SIDE WANDSWORTH COMM
WINDMILL RD
TRINITY RD
EARLSFIELD RD
BURNTWOOD LA
NIGHTINGALE LA
BOLINGBROKE GR
NORTHCOTE RD
BELLEVUE RD
ST JAMES'S DR
UPPER TOOTING RD
SPENCER PK
BATTERSEA RISE
GARRATT LA
ST JOHN'S HILL

136
157
180

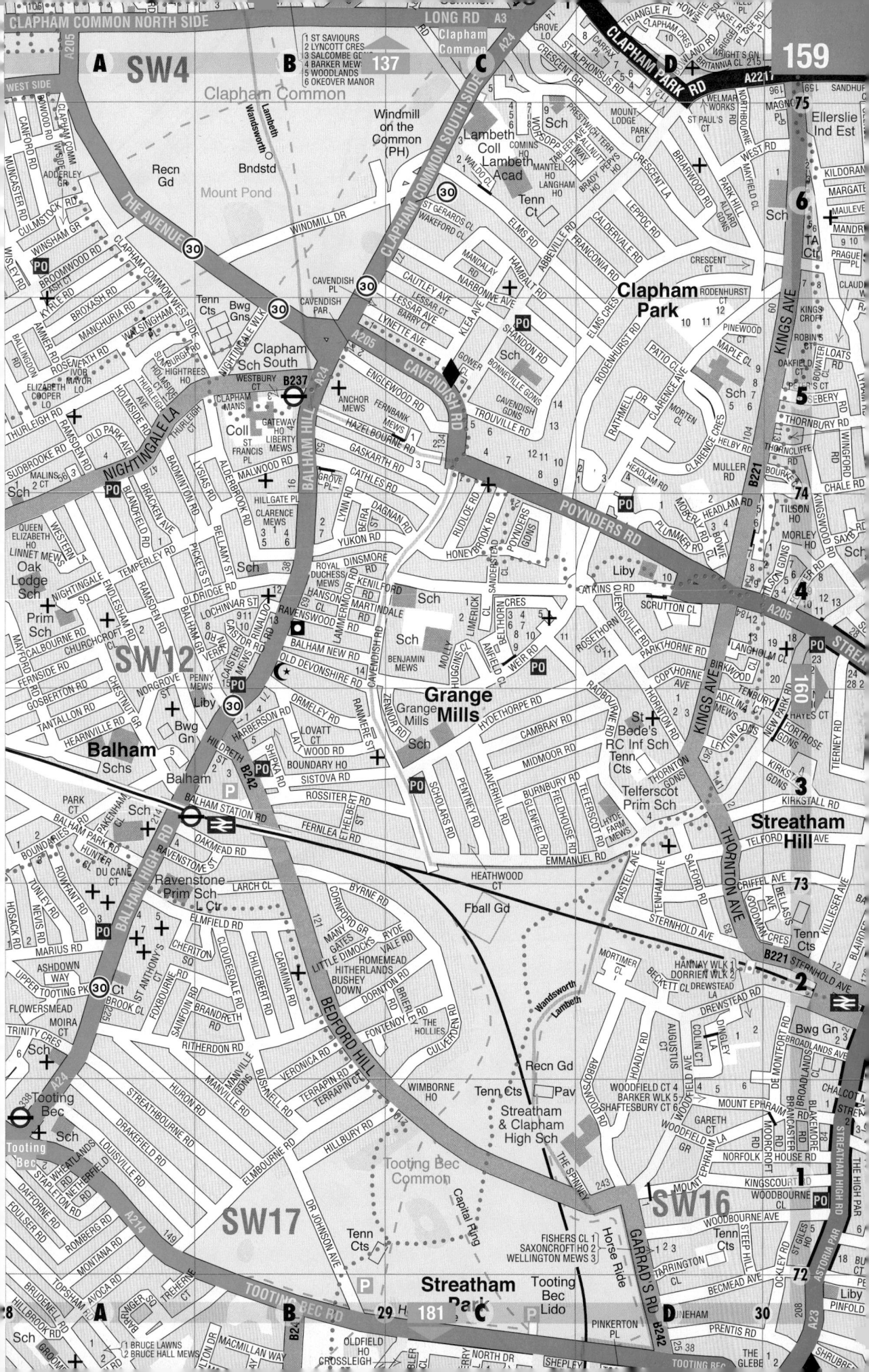
159
CLAPHAM COMMON NORTH SIDE
LONG RD
A3
A205
WEST SIDE
A
B
C
D
SW4
137
1 ST SAVIOURS
2 LYNCOTT CRES
3 SALCOMBE GDNS
4 BARKER MEWS
5 WOODLANDS
6 OKEOVER MANOR
Clapham Common
Clapham Common
Windmill on the Common (PH)
Lambeth
Wandsworth
Recn Gd
Bndstd
Mount Pond
WINDMILL DR
THE AVENUE
CLAPHAM COMMON SOUTH SIDE
CLAPHAM COMMON WEST SIDE
CLAPHAM PARK RD
A2217
TRIANGLE PL
CLAPHAM CRES
CARFAX PL
CRESCENT GR
ST ALPHONSUS RD
GROVE LO
WELMAR WORKS
MOUNT LODGE
PARK CT
ST PAUL'S CT
NORTHBOURNE
MAYFIELD CL
WEST RD
Ellerslie Ind Est
KILDORAN
MARGATE
MAULEVE
MANDRE
PRAGUE PL
Lambeth Coll
Lambeth Acad
PRESTWICH TERR
WORSOPP DR
TABLEER AVE
ALLNUTT WAY
COMINS HO
MANTELL HO
LANGHAM HO
BRADY HO
PEPYS HO
Tenn Ct
Sch
WALDO CL
ST GERARDS CL
WAKEFORD CL
ELMS RD
ABBEVILLE RD
FRANCONIA RD
CALDERVALE RD
LEPPOC RD
CRESCENT LA
BRIARWOOD RD
PARK HILL
ALLARD GDNS
CRESCENT CT
RODENHURST CT
Clapham Park
PINEWOOD CT
MAPLE CL
PATIO CL
CLARENCE AVE
MORTEN CL
CLARENCE CRES
HELBY RD
KINGS AVE
KINGS CROFT
ROBIN'S CT
OAKFIELD CT
LOATS RD
BOWATER CL
PETER'S CT
SEBERY
THORNBURY RD
WINGFORD RD
THORNCLIFFE
BOURKE CL
CHALE RD
TILSON HO
MORLEY HO
TILSON GDNS
KINGSWOOD RD
SAXBY
MANDALAY
HAMBALT RD
NARBONNE AVE
CAUTLEY AVE
LESSAR AVE
BARRY CT
LYNETTE AVE
KLEA AVE
SHANDON RD
BONNEVILLE GDNS
CAVENDISH GDNS
TROUVILLE RD
ELMS CRES
RODENHURST RD
RATHMILL DR
HEADLAM RD
MULLER RD
MOBERLY RD
BOWIE CL
PLUMMER RD
CAVENDISH PL
CAVENDISH PAR
CAVENDISH RD
A205
ENGLEWOOD RD
ANCHOR MEWS
FERNBANK MEWS
HAZELBOURNE RD
GASKARTH RD
CATHLES RD
GROVE PL
LYNN RD
BEIRA ST
DAGNAN RD
YUKON RD
RUDLOE RD
HONEYBROOK RD
POYNDERS GDNS
POYNDERS RD
SANDERSTEAD CL
Liby
CATKINS RD
SCRUTTON CL
QUEENSVILLE RD
PARKTHORNE RD
LANGHOLM CL
STREATHAM
160
BROOMWOOD RD
WINSHAM GR
CULMSTOCK RD
ADDERLEY GR
MUNCASTER RD
CANFORD RD
BOWOOD RD
WISLEY RD
KYRLE RD
ASH CT
BROXASH RD
MANCHURIA RD
WALSINGHAM PL
AMNER RD
BALLINGDON RD
ROSENEATH RD
IVOB MAYOR LO
ELIZABETH COOPER LO
HOLMSIDE RD
THURLEIGH RD
RAMSDEN RD
OLD PARK AVE
SUDBROOKE RD
MALINS CT
Sch
Tenn Cts
Bwg Gns
Clapham South
NIGHTINGALE WLK
WESTBURY CT
B237
HIGHTREES HO
CLAPHAM MANS
GATEWAY HO
LIBERTY MEWS
ST FRANCIS PL
Coll
NIGHTINGALE LA
BADMINTON RD
LYSIAS RD
ALDERBROOK RD
MALWOOD RD
HILLGATE PL
CLARENCE MEWS
BALHAM HILL
A24
QUEEN ELIZABETH HO
WESTERN LA
LINNET MEWS
Oak Lodge Sch
BLANDFIELD RD
BRACKEN AVE
TEMPERLEY RD
BELLAMY ST
PICKETS ST
NIGHTINGALE SQ
ENDLESHAM RD
RAMSDEN RD
OLDRIDGE RD
BALHAM GR
LOCHINVAR ST
Prim Sch
MAYFORD RD
CALBOURNE RD
CHURCHCROFT CL
SW12
FERNSIDE RD
GOSBERTON RD
TANTALLON RD
HEARNVILLE RD
CHESTNUT GR
NORGROVE ST
PENNY MEWS
CAISTOR MEWS
CAISTOR RD
RINALDO RD
RAVENSWOOD RD
BALHAM NEW RD
OLD DEVONSHIRE RD
ROYAL DUCHESS MEWS
DINSMORE RD
HANSON CL
LAMMERMOOR RD
KENILFORD RD
MARTINDALE RD
CAVENDISH RD
Sch
BENJAMIN MEWS
MOLLY HUGGINS CL
LIMERICK CL
ANFIELD CL
BELTHORN CRES
WEIR RD
ROSETHORN CL
COPTHORNE AVE
BIRKWOOD CL
ADELINA MEWS
TENBURY CT
NEW PARK RD
HAYES CT
FORTROSE GDNS
TIERNEY RD
Balham
Schs
Bwg Gn
Liby
HILDRETH ST
HARBERSON RD
ORMELEY RD
LOVATT CT
LAITWOOD RD
BOUNDARY HO
SISTOVA RD
SHIPKA RD
RAMMERE ST
ZENNOR RD
Grange Mills
Grange Mills
HYDETHORPE RD
CAMBRAY RD
MIDMOOR RD
RADBOURNE RD
St Bede's RC Inf Sch
Tenn Cts
THORNTON GDNS
LEYTON GDNS
KIRKSTALL GDNS
KIRKSTALL RD
Streatham Hill
TELFORD AVE
B242
BALHAM STATION RD
ROSSITER RD
ETHELBERT ST
FERNLEA RD
SCHOLARS RD
PENTNEY RD
HAVERHILL RD
BURNBURY RD
GLENFIELD RD
FIELDHOUSE RD
TELFERSCOT RD
HYDE FARM MEWS
Telferscot Prim Sch
THORNTON AVE
PARK CT
BALHAM PARK RD
PAKENHAM CL
BOUNDARIES RD
HUNTER CL
DU CANE CT
BALHAM HIGH RD
OAKMEAD RD
RAVENSTONE ST
Ravenstone Prim Sch
L Ctr
LARCH CL
EMMANUEL RD
HEATHWOOD CT
Fball Gd
RASTELL AVE
TENHAM AVE
SALFORD RD
CRIFFEL AVE
BELLASIS AVE
GOODMAN CRES
KILLIESER AVE
Tenn Cts
BLAIRDERRY
STERNHOLD AVE
B221
ROWFANT RD
TUNLEY RD
NEVIS RD
HOSACK RD
MARIUS RD
ELMFIELD RD
CHERITON SQ
CLOUDESDALE RD
CHILDEBERT RD
CARMINIA RD
BYRNE RD
CORNFORD GR
MANY GATES
LITTLE DIMOCKS
RYDE VALE RD
HOMEMEAD
HITHERLANDS
BUSHEY DOWN
DORNTON RD
BRIERLEY RD
FONTENOY RD
THE HOLLIES
CULVERDEN RD
MORTIMER CL
BECKETT CL
HANNAY WLK 1
DORRIEN WLK 2
DREWSTEAD LA
DREWSTEAD RD
DINGLEY LA
COLIN CT
Bwg Gn
BROADLANDS AVE
CHALCOT
ASHDOWN WAY
UPPER TOOTING PK
Ct
BROOK CL
ST ANTHONY'S CT
FOXBOURNE RD
SAINFOIN RD
BRANDRETH RD
RITHERDON RD
MANVILLE GDNS
MANVILLE RD
FLOWERSMEAD
MOIRA CT
TRINITY CRES
Sch
A24
HURON RD
STREATHBOURNE RD
DRAKEFIELD RD
BUSHNELL RD
VERONICA RD
TERRAPIN RD
TERRAPIN CT
BEDFORD HILL
WIMBORNE HO
Tenn Cts
Pav
Recn Gd
Wandsworth
Lambeth
HOADLY RD
AUGUSTUS CT
WOODFIELD AVE
ABBOTSWOOD RD
WOODFIELD CT 4
BARKER WLK 5
SHAFTESBURY CT 6
MOUNT EPHRAIM LA
GARETH CT
WOODFIELD GR
MOORCROFT RD
BRANCASTER RD
BLAKEMORE RD
DE MONTFORT RD
STREATHAM HIGH RD
Tooting Bec
Tooting Bec
Sch
LOUISVILLE RD
WHEATLANDS RD
STAPLETON RD
NETHERFIELD RD
HILLBURY RD
ELMBOURNE RD
Streatham & Clapham High Sch
THE SPINNEY
NORFOLK HOUSE RD
KINGSCOURT RD
WOODBOURNE CL
SW16
WOODBOURNE AVE
Tooting Bec Common
Capital Ring
DAFFORNE RD
FOULSER RD
ROMBERG RD
MONTANA RD
TOPSHAM RD
AVOCA RD
BRUDENELL RD
HILLBROOK RD
A214
SW17
DR JOHNSON AVE
Tenn Cts
FISHERS CL 1
SAXONCROFT HO 2
WELLINGTON MEWS 3
Horse Ride
GARRAD'S RD
TARRINGTON CL
BECMEAD AVE
Tenn Cts
STEEP HILL
OCKLEY RD
ST GILES HO
THE HIGH PAR
ASTORIA PAR
A23
Liby
PINFOLD
TREHERNE CT
BARRINGER SQ
TOOTING BEC RD
181
Streatham Park
Tooting Bec Lido
PINKERTON PL
B242
D
30
PRENTIS RD
THE GLEBE
SHRUBBERY
Sch
1 BRUCE LAWNS
2 BRUCE HALL MEWS
MACMILLAN WAY
OLDFIELD HO
CROSSLEIGH
NORTH DR
SHEPLEY
TOOTING BEC
B241
6
5
4
3
2
1
75
74
73
72
29
8

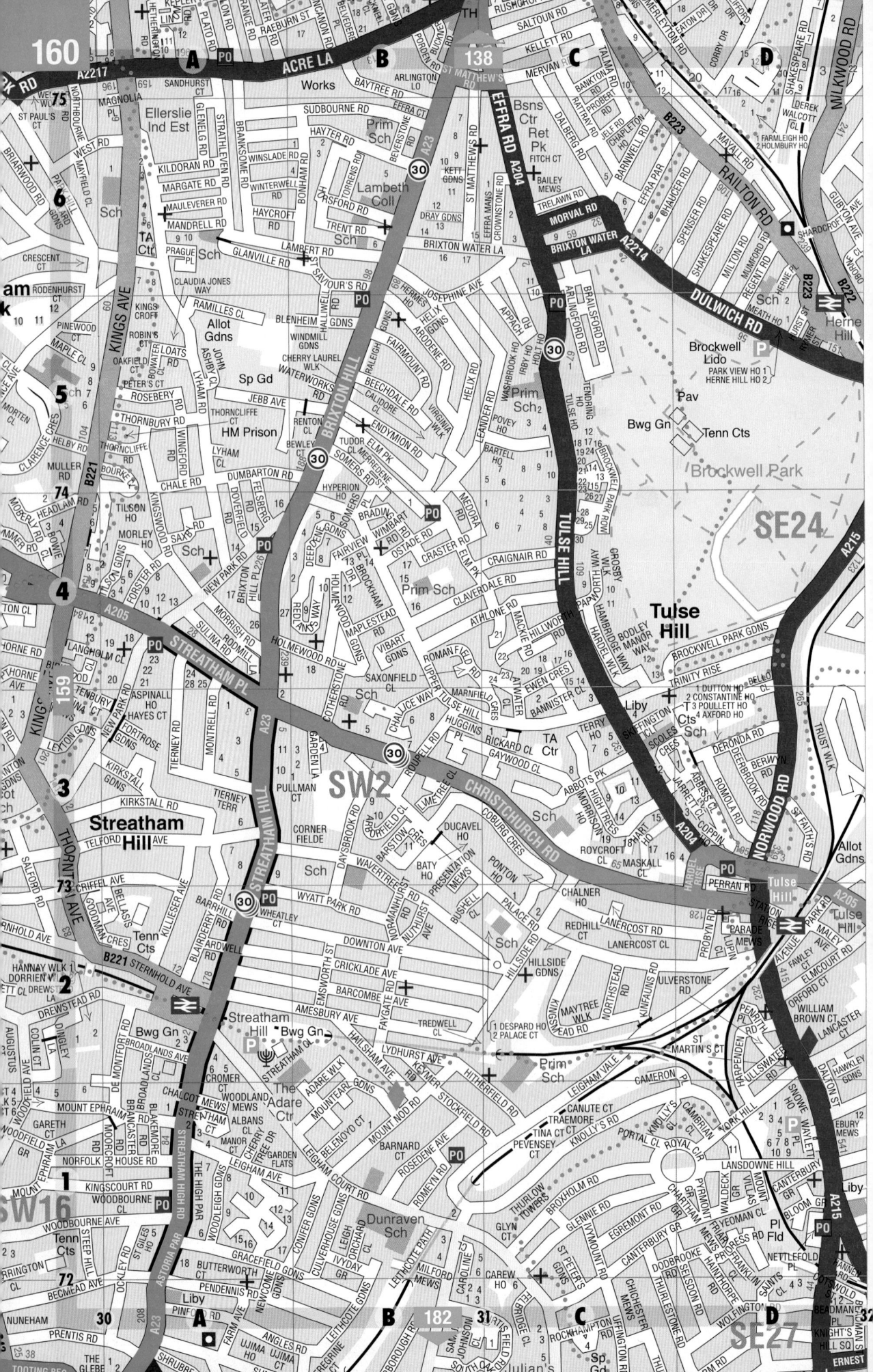
138
182
159
A
B
C
D
ACRE LA
A2217
EFFRA RD
A204
BRIXTON HILL
A23
BRIXTON WATER LA
DULWICH RD
A2214
RAILTON RD
B223
B222
MILKWOOD RD
TULSE HILL
STREATHAM PL
A205
CHRISTCHURCH RD
STREATHAM HILL
STREATHAM HIGH RD
NORWOOD RD
A215
KINGS AVE
B221
THORNTON AVE
STERNHOLD AVE
LEIGHAM COURT RD
LEIGHAM VALE
KNOLLY'S RD
HITHERFIELD RD
ELM PK
CRAIGNAIR RD
CLAVERDALE RD
ATHLONE RD
ROMAN RISE
HOLMEWOOD RD
JEBB AVE
DUMBARTON RD
NEW PARK RD
TELFORD AVE
WYATT PARK RD
DOWNTON AVE
CRICKLADE AVE
BARCOMBE AVE
AMESBURY AVE
MOUNT NOD RD
NORFOLK HOUSE RD
KINGSCOURT RD
WOODBOURNE AVE
BECMEAD AVE
LANSDOWNE HILL
TRINITY RISE
BROCKWELL PARK GDNS
Ellerslie Ind Est
Lambeth Coll
HM Prison
Allot Gdns
Sp Gd
Prim Sch
Bsns Ctr
Ret Pk
Brockwell Lido
Brockwell Park
Bwg Gn
Tenn Cts
Pav
SE24
SW2
SW16
SE27
Tulse Hill
Streatham Hill
Herne Hill
The Adare Ctr
Dunraven Sch
Liby
Works

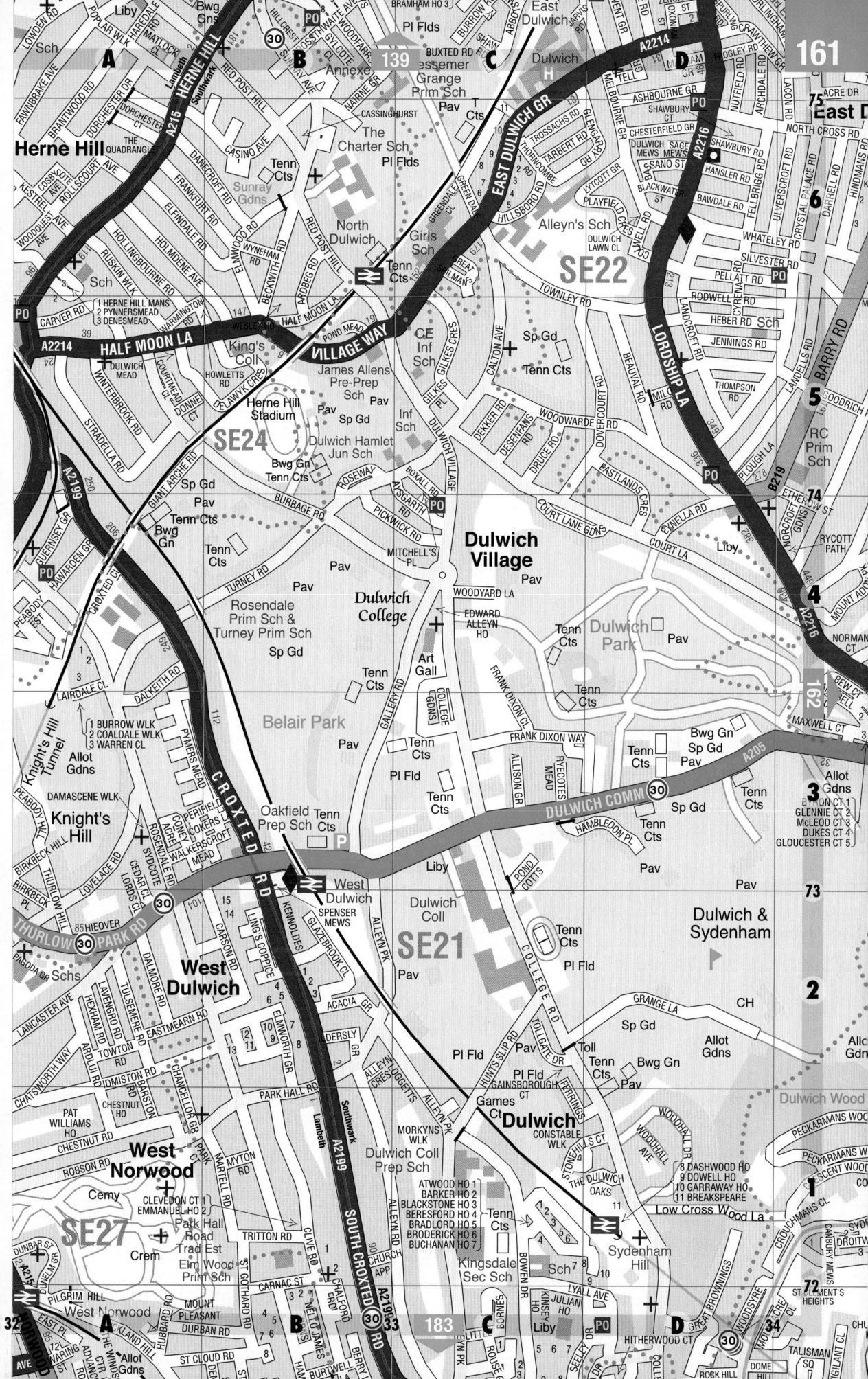
Herne Hill
East Dulwich
Dulwich
Dulwich Village
Dulwich College
Dulwich Park
Belair Park
West Dulwich
West Norwood
Knight's Hill
Dulwich & Sydenham
Sydenham Hill
SE22
SE24
SE21
SE27
HALF MOON LA
VILLAGE WAY
EAST DULWICH GR
LORDSHIP LA
CROXTED RD
SOUTH CROXTED RD
DULWICH COMM
THURLOW PARK RD
HERNE HILL
Low Cross Wood La
Dulwich Wood

139
162
183

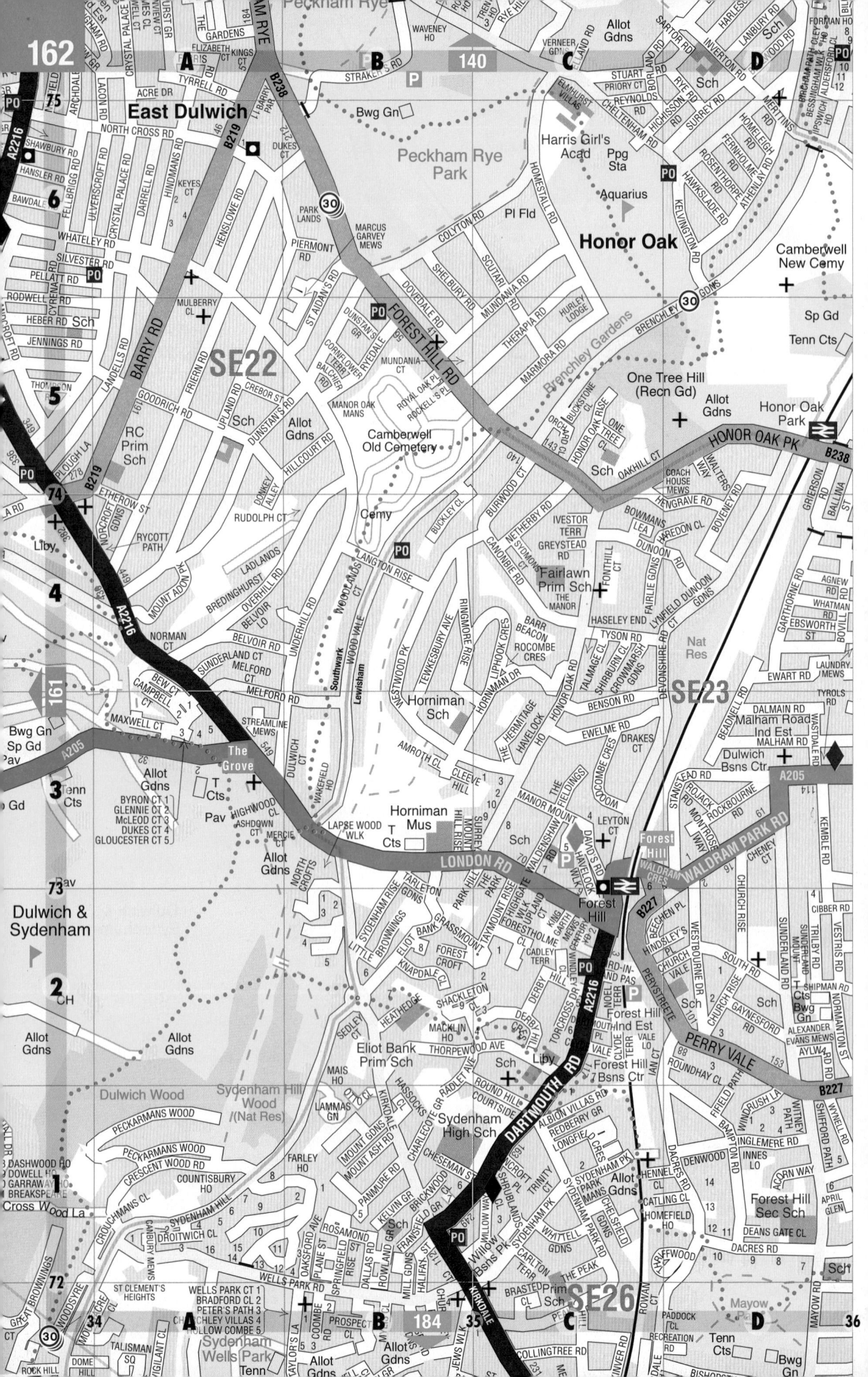
A
B
C
D
140
East Dulwich
Peckham Rye
Peckham Rye Park
Bwg Gn
Allot Gdns
Harris Girl's Acad
Ppg Sta
Aquarius
Sch
Honor Oak
Camberwell New Cemy
Sp Gd
Tenn Cts
One Tree Hill (Recn Gd)
Honor Oak Park
HONOR OAK PK
B238
Brenchley Gardens
SE22
Camberwell Old Cemetery
Cemy
RC Prim Sch
Fairlawn Prim Sch
Nat Res
SE23
Malham Road Ind Est
Dulwich Bsns Ctr
Horniman Sch
Horniman Mus
The Grove
LONDON RD
Forest Hill
WALDRAM PARK RD
A205
A2216
B219
B227
BARRY RD
FOREST HILL RD
DARTMOUTH RD
PERRY VALE
Forest Hill Ind Est
Forest Hill Bsns Ctr
Eliot Bank Prim Sch
Sydenham High Sch
Dulwich & Sydenham
Dulwich Wood
Sydenham Hill Wood (Nat Res)
Cross Wood La
Forest Hill Sec Sch
Willow Bsns Pk
Mayow Park
Sydenham Wells Park
SE26
161
184
34
35
36
72
73
74
75
1
2
3
4
5
6

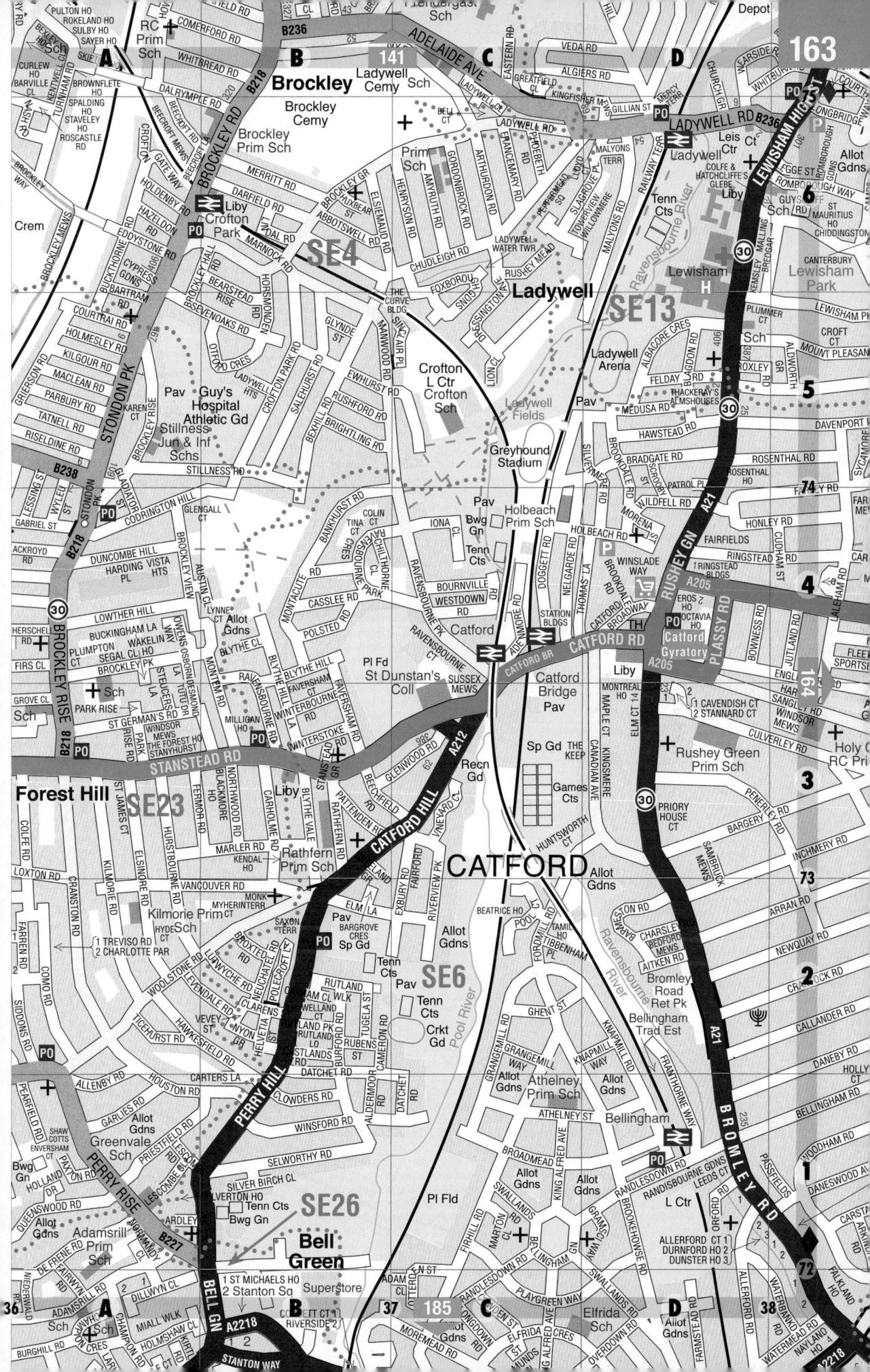
163
A
B
C
D
141
185
164
36
37
38
72
73
74
1
2
3
4
5
6
Brockley
Ladywell
Catford
CATFORD
Forest Hill
Bellingham
Bell Green
SE4
SE13
SE23
SE6
SE26
Brockley Cemy
Ladywell Cemy
Brockley Prim Sch
RC Prim Sch
Crofton Park
Crem
Ladywell Arena
Ladywell Fields
Lewisham Park
Lewisham
Crofton L Ctr
Crofton Sch
Greyhound Stadium
Holbeach Prim Sch
Guy's Hospital Athletic Gd
Stillness Jun & Inf Schs
St Dunstan's Coll
Catford Bridge
Catford Gyratory
Rushey Green Prim Sch
Rathfern Prim Sch
Kilmorie Prim Sch
Athelney Prim Sch
Greenvale Sch
Adamsrill Prim Sch
Elfrida Sch
Bromley Road Ret Pk
Bellingham Trad Est
Superstore
Recn Gd
Sp Gd
Games Cts
Tenn Cts
Crkt Gd
Allot Gdns
Pl Fld
Pl Fd
L Ctr
Pav
Liby
Ravensbourne River
Pool River
BROCKLEY RD
BROCKLEY RISE
STONDON PK
ADELAIDE AVE
LADYWELL RD
LEWISHAM HIGH ST
RUSHEY GN
CATFORD RD
CATFORD BR
CATFORD HILL
STANSTEAD RD
PERRY HILL
PERRY RISE
BROMLEY RD
BELL GN
STANTON WAY
CODRINGTON HILL
DUNCOMBE HILL
LOWTHER HILL
RAVENSBOURNE PK
RAVENSBOURNE PARK
HOLBEACH RD
RINGSTEAD RD
ROSENTHAL RD
HAWSTEAD RD
BRADGATE RD
CULVERLEY RD
BARGERY RD
INCHMERY RD
ARRAN RD
NEWQUAY RD
CALLANDER RD
DANEBY RD
BELLINGHAM RD
WOODHAM RD
BROADMEAD
ATHELNEY ST
RANDLESDOWN RD
PLAYGREEN WAY
SELWORTHY RD
WINSFORD RD
CLOWDERS RD
DATCHET RD
VANCOUVER RD
MARLER RD
HOUSTON RD
ALLENBY RD
QUEENSWOOD RD
A21
A205
A212
A2218
B218
B227
B236
B238

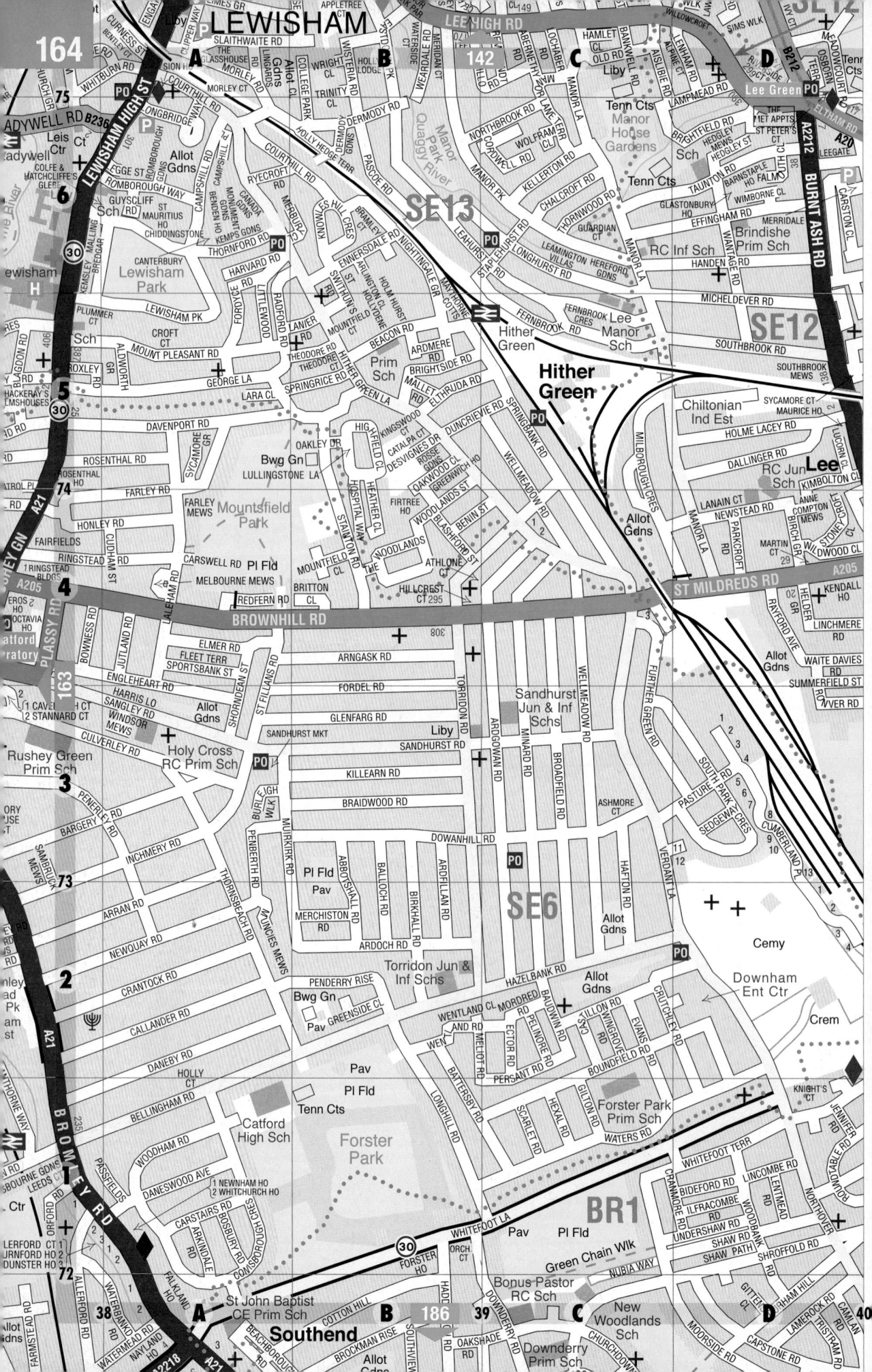
LEWISHAM
LEE HIGH RD
142
A
B
C
D
SE13
SE12
SE6
BR1
Lee Green
Hither Green
Lee
Southend
Lewisham Park
Mountsfield Park
Forster Park
Manor House Gardens
Quaggy River
Manor Park
LEWISHAM HIGH ST
LADYWELL RD
B236
A21
A205
A20
A2212
B212
BURNT ASH RD
BROWNHILL RD
ST MILDREDS RD
BROMLEY RD
WHITEFOOT LA
SLAITHWAITE RD
MORLEY RD
COURTHILL RD
LONGBRIDGE WAY
ROMBOROUGH WAY
CAMPSHILL RD
RYECROFT RD
MERBURY CL
KNOWLES HILL CRES
ENNERSDALE RD
NIGHTINGALE GR
LEAHURST RD
STAPLEHURST RD
LONGHURST RD
MANOR LA
NORTHBROOK RD
KELLERTON RD
CHALCROFT RD
THORNWOOD RD
EFFINGHAM RD
HANDEN RD
MICHELDEVER RD
SOUTHBROOK RD
FERNBROOK RD
HIGHFIELD CL
SPRINGBANK RD
WELLMEADOW RD
HITHER GREEN LA
GEORGE LA
MOUNT PLEASANT RD
DAVENPORT RD
ROSENTHAL RD
FARLEY RD
HONLEY RD
RINGSTEAD RD
CARSWELL RD
MELBOURNE MEWS
REDFERN RD
ARNGASK RD
FORDEL RD
GLENFARG RD
SANDHURST RD
KILLEARN RD
BRAIDWOOD RD
DOWANHILL RD
TORRIDON RD
ARDGOWAN RD
MINARD RD
BROADFIELD RD
FURTHER GREEN RD
VERDANT LA
HAFTON RD
ARDOCH RD
HAZELBANK RD
PENDERRY RISE
GREENSIDE CL
MUIRKIRK RD
CULVERLEY RD
PENERLEY RD
BARGERY RD
INCHMERY RD
ARRAN RD
NEWQUAY RD
CRANTOCK RD
CALLANDER RD
DANEBY RD
BELLINGHAM RD
WOODHAM RD
DANESWOOD AVE
CARSTAIRS RD
BOUNDFIELD RD
PERSANT RD
LONGHILL RD
BATTERSBY RD
SCARLETT RD
HEXAL RD
GILTON RD
WATERS RD
WHITEFOOT TERR
NUBIA WAY
Green Chain Wlk
MOORSIDE RD
CAPSTONE RD
CHURCHDOWN
DOWNDERRY RD
COTTON HILL
BROCKMAN RISE
BEACHBOROUGH
HOLME LACEY RD
DALLINGER RD
NEWSTEAD RD
MILBOROUGH CRES
Chiltonian Ind Est
RAYFORD AVE
SOUTH PARK CRES
SEDGEWAY
CUMBERLAND PL
Cemy
Crem
Downham Ent Ctr
Torridon Jun & Inf Schs
Sandhurst Jun & Inf Schs
Forster Park Prim Sch
Catford High Sch
Holy Cross RC Prim Sch
Rushey Green Prim Sch
St John Baptist CE Prim Sch
Bonus Pastor RC Sch
New Woodlands Sch
Downderry Prim Sch
Lee Manor Sch
Brindishe Prim Sch
Allot Gdns
Pl Fld
Pav
Tenn Cts
Bwg Gn
Liby
163
186
38
39
40
75
74
73
72
1
2
3
4
5
6

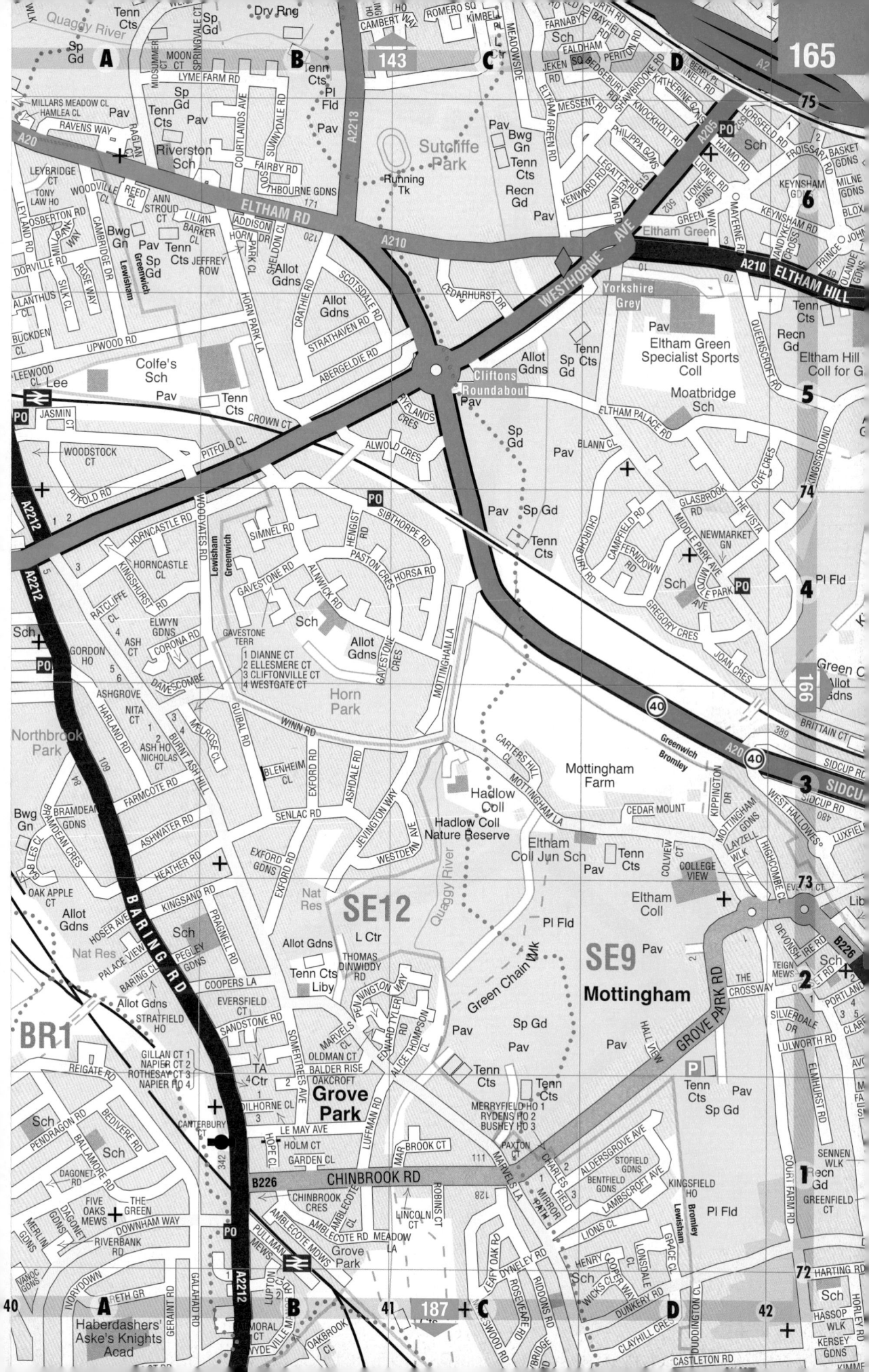

A
B
C
D
143
Quaggy River
Sp Gd
Tenn Cts
Drv Rng
MIDSUMMER CT
MOON CT
SPRINGVALE CT
LYME FARM RD
Pl Fld
Pav
CAMBERT WAY
ROMERO SQ
KIMBELL PL
MEADOWSIDE
FARNABY RD
BAYFIELD RD
Sch
EALDHAM SQ
PERITON RD
JEKEN RD
BEDGEBURY RD
ELTHAM GREEN RD
BERRY PL
KATHERINE GDNS
SHAWBROOKE RD
MESSENT RD
KNOCKHOLT RD
A2
75
MILLARS MEADOW CL
HAMLEA CL
RAVENS WAY
RAGLAN CT
A20
Riverston Sch
COURTLANDS AVE
SUNNYDALE RD
FAIRBY RD
SOUTHBOURNE GDNS
A2213
Sutcliffe Park
Running Tk
Bwg Gn
Recn Gd
PHILIPPA GDNS
LEGATT RD
KEELING RD
KENWARD RD
A205
HORSFELD RD
HAIMO RD
FROISSART RD
BASKET GDNS
KEYNSHAM GDNS
MILNE GDNS
6
LEYBRIDGE CT
TONY LAW HO
WOODVILLE CL
REED CL
ANN STROUD CT
LILIAN BARKER CL
ADDISON CL
ELTHAM RD
A210
LEYLAND RD
OSBERTON RD
MILLBANK WAY
CAMBRIDGE DR
DORVILLE RD
ROSE WAY
SILK CL
ALANTHUS CL
BUCKDEN CL
Lewisham
Greenwich
JEFFREY ROW
HORN PARK CL
SHELDON CL
Allot Gdns
WESTHORNE AVE
LIONEL RD
LIONEL GDNS
MAYERNE RD
ELTHAM GREEN
Eltham Green
VANDYKE CROSS
KEYNSHAM RD
PRINCE JOHN RD
A210 ELTHAM HILL
CRATHIE RD
SCOTSDALE RD
STRATHAVEN RD
ABERGELDIE RD
CEDARHURST DR
Yorkshire Grey
UPWOOD RD
HORN PARK LA
Colfe's Sch
LEEWOOD CL
Lee
PO
JASMIN CT
CROWN CT
Cliftons Roundabout
Allot Gdns
Eltham Green Specialist Sports Coll
Moatbridge Sch
QUEENSCROFT RD
Eltham Hill Coll for G
5
WOODSTOCK CT
PITFOLD CL
PITFOLD RD
RYELANDS CRES
ALWOLD CRES
ELTHAM PALACE RD
BLANN CL
CUFF CRES
KINGSGROUND
74
A2212
HORNCASTLE RD
HORNCASTLE CL
KINGSHURST RD
WOODYATES RD
SIMNEL RD
HENGIST RD
SIBTHORPE RD
PASTON CRES
HORSA RD
GAVESTONE RD
ALNWICK RD
CHURCHBURY RD
CAMPFIELD RD
FERNDOWN RD
GLASBROOK RD
THE VISTA
NEWMARKET GN
MIDDLE PARK AVE
GREGORY CRES
JOAN CRES
Pl Fld
4
RATCLIFFE CL
ELWYN GDNS
ASH CT
CORONA RD
GORDON HO
GAVESTONE TERR
1 DIANNE CT
2 ELLESMERE CT
3 CLIFTONVILLE CT
4 WESTGATE CT
GAVESTONE CRES
MOTTINGHAM LA
Horn Park
Green Chain Allot Gdns
166
DANESCOMBE
ASHGROVE
NITA CT
HARLAND RD
ASH HO
NICHOLAS CT
MELROSE CL
BURNT ASH HILL
GUIBAL RD
WINN RD
40
Greenwich
Bromley
BRITTAIN CT
389
Northbrook Park
BLENHEIM CL
EXFORD RD
ASHDALE RD
CARTERS HILL CL
Mottingham Farm
SIDCUP RD
3
BRAMDEAN GDNS
BRAMDEAN CRES
FARMCOTE RD
ASHWATER RD
SENLAC RD
JEVINGTON WAY
WESTDEAN AVE
Hadlow Coll
Hadlow Coll Nature Reserve
CEDAR MOUNT
KIPPINGTON DR
MOTTINGHAM GDNS
LAYZELL WLK
WEST HALLOWES
LUXFIELD
Bwg Gn
HEATHER RD
EXFORD GDNS
Quaggy River
Eltham Coll Jun Sch
COLVIEW CT
COLLEGE VIEW
HIGHCOMBE CL
OAK APPLE CT
BARING RD
KINGSAND RD
PRAGNELL RD
Nat Res
SE12
L Ctr
Eltham Coll
73
EVELYN CT
Pl Fld
HOSER AVE
PALACE VIEW
PEGLEY GDNS
BARING CL
Allot Gdns
STRATFIELD HO
COOPERS LA
EVERSFIELD CT
SANDSTONE RD
THOMAS DINWIDDY RD
Tenn Cts
Liby
PENNINGTON WAY
SE9
Mottingham
Green Chain Wk
DEVONSHIRE RD
B226
THE CROSSWAY
TEIGN MEWS
2
SILVERDALE DR
PORTLAND
BR1
GILLAN CT 1
NAPIER CT 2
ROTHESAY CT 3
NAPIER HO 4
REIGATE RD
TA Ctr
MARVELS CL
OLDMAN CT
BALDER RISE
OAKCROFT
EDWARD TYLER RD
ALICE THOMPSON CL
HALL VIEW
GROVE PARK RD
LULWORTH RD
ELMHURST RD
SOMERTREES AVE
DILHORNE CL
Grove Park
LUFFMAN RD
MERRYFIELD HO 1
RYDENS HO 2
BUSHEY HO 3
Sp Gd
PENDRAGON RD
BEDIVERE RD
BALLAMORE RD
CANTERBURY CT
LE MAY AVE
HOPE CL
HOLM CT
GARDEN CL
MARBROOK CT
PAXTON CT
CHARLES FIELD
ALDERSGROVE AVE
STOFIELD GDNS
BENTFIELD GDNS
LAMBSCROFT AVE
KINGSFIELD HO
SENNEN WLK
Recn Gd
GREENFIELD CT
COURT FARM RD
1
DAGONET RD
FIVE OAKS MEWS
THE GREEN
DOWNHAM WAY
RIVERBANK RD
MERLIN GDNS
342
B226 CHINBROOK RD
CHINBROOK CRES
AMBLECOTE MDWS
AMBLECOTE CL
AMBLECOTE RD
MEADOW LA
LINCOLN CT
ROBINS CT
MARVELS LA
MIRROR PATH
LIONS CL
GRACE CL
HENRY COOPER WAY
LONSDALE CL
WICKS CL
DUNKERY RD
PULLMAN MEWS
LUPTON CL
LEAFY OAK RD
DYNELEY RD
ROSEVEARE RD
RIDDONS RD
72
HARTING RD
IVORYDOWN
GERAINT RD
GALAHAD RD
40
A
Haberdashers' Aske's Knights Acad
B
41
187
C
D
42
DUDDINGTON CL
CLAYHILL CRES
CASTLETON RD
HASSOP WLK
KERSEY GDNS
HORLEY RD
BALMORAL CT
OAKBROOK CL

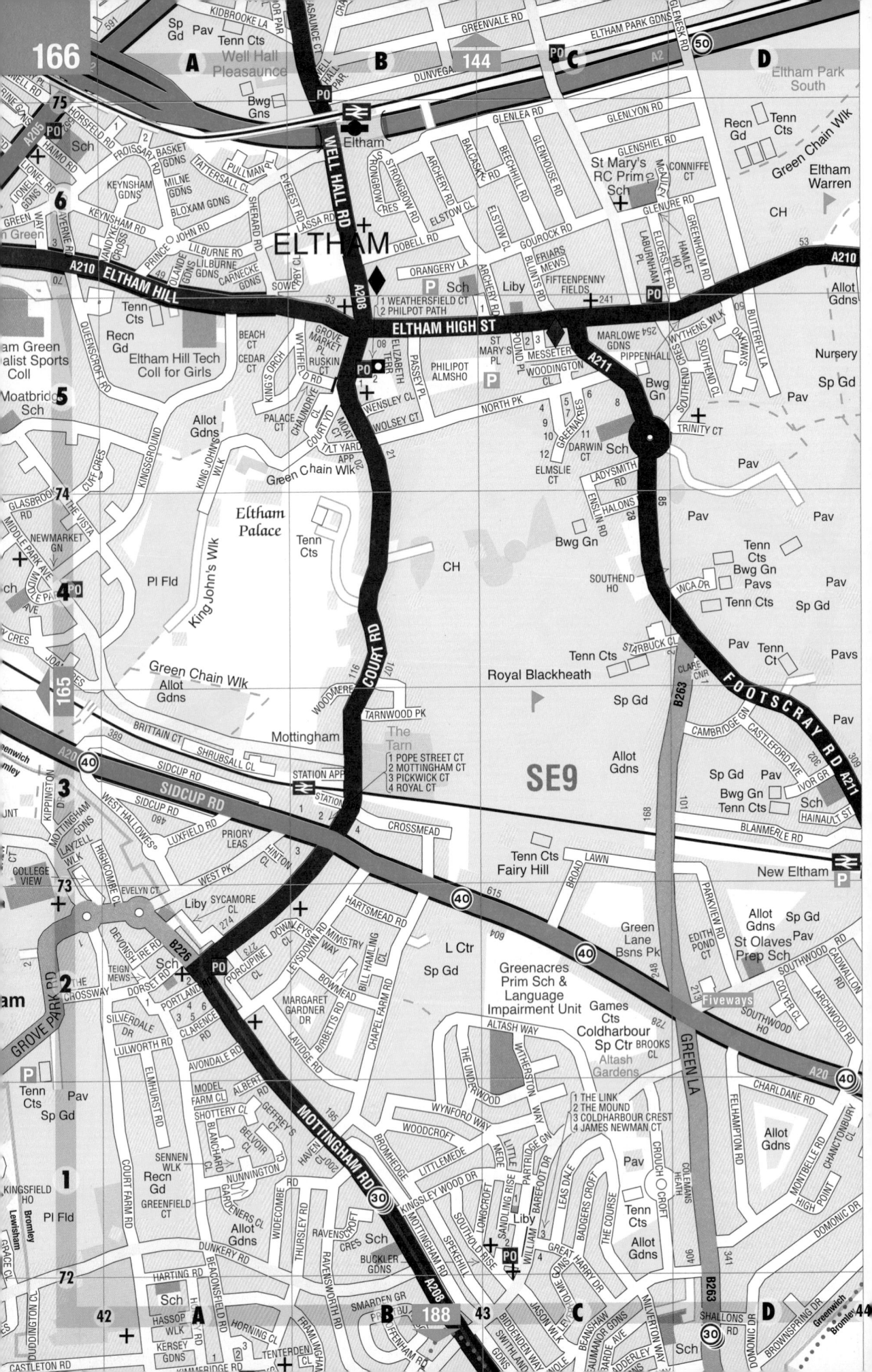

A
B
C
D
144
Well Hall Pleasaunce
Eltham Park South
Eltham
ELTHAM
ELTHAM HILL
ELTHAM HIGH ST
WELL HALL RD
A210
A208
A211
A2
A20
A205
B226
B263
KIDBROOKE LA
GREENVALE RD
ELTHAM PARK GDNS
GLENESK RD
DUNVEGAN
GLENLEA RD
GLENLYON RD
GLENSHIEL RD
GLENURE RD
St Mary's RC Prim Sch
CONIFFE CT
Green Chain Wlk
Eltham Warren
CH
ORANGERY LA
DOBELL RD
GOUROCK RD
FRIARS MEWS
FIFTEENPENNY FIELDS
1 WEATHERSFIELD CT
2 PHILPOT PATH
Liby
Sch
Eltham Hill Tech Coll for Girls
Recn Gd
Tenn Cts
Allot Gdns
Moatbridge Sch
MARLOWE GDNS
PIPPENHALL
Bwg Gn
Nursery
Sp Gd
Pav
TRINITY CT
NORTH PK
PHILIPOT ALMSHO
WOODINGTON CL
MESSETER
DARWIN CT
ELMSLIE CT
LADYSMITH RD
HALONS
ENSLIN RD
Eltham Palace
King John's Wlk
Pl Fld
COURT RD
SOUTHEND HO
INCA DR
Pavs
STARBUCK CL
Royal Blackheath
FOOTSCRAY RD
CLARE CNR
CAMBRIDGE GN
CASTLEFORD AVE
IVOR GR
HAINAULT ST
BLANMERLE RD
SE9
Mottingham
TARNWOOD PK
The Tarn
1 POPE STREET CT
2 MOTTINGHAM CT
3 PICKWICK CT
4 ROYAL CT
STATION APP
CROSSMEAD
SIDCUP RD
BRITTAIN CT
SHRUBSALL CL
165
WEST HALLOWES
LUXFIELD RD
PRIORY LEAS
HINTON CL
WEST PK
EVELYN CT
SYCAMORE CL
New Eltham
Fairy Hill
BROAD LAWN
PARKVIEW RD
Green Lane Bsns Pk
St Olaves Prep Sch
L Ctr
Greenacres Prim Sch & Language Impairment Unit
Games Cts
Coldharbour Sp Ctr
Altash Gardens
BROOKS CL
Fiveways
SOUTHWOOD RD
CADWALLON RD
LARCHWOOD RD
COLYER CL
GREEN LA
HARTSMEAD RD
MINISTRY WAY
BILL HAMLING CL
LEYSDOWN RD
BOWMEAD
MARGARET GARDNER DR
BIRBETTS RD
CHAPEL FARM RD
LAVIDGE RD
ALTASH WAY
THE UNDERWOOD
WITHERSTON WAY
1 THE LINK
2 THE MOUND
3 COLDHARBOUR CREST
4 JAMES NEWMAN CT
WYNFORD WAY
WOODCROFT
LITTLEMEDE
KINGSLEY WOOD DR
CROUCH CROFT
THE COURSE
BADGERS CROFT
LEAS DALE
MOTTINGHAM RD
GROVE PARK RD
THE CROSSWAY
DORSET RD
PORTLAND RD
SILVERDALE DR
LULWORTH RD
AVONDALE RD
ELMHURST RD
COURT FARM RD
SHOTTERY CL
BLANCHARD CL
BELVOIR CL
NUNNINGTON CL
SENNEN WLK
GREENFIELD CT
GARDENERS CL
DUNKERY RD
WIDECOMBE RD
THURSLEY RD
RAVENSWORTH RD
RAVENSCROFT CRES
BUCKLER GDNS
CHARLDANE RD
FELHAMPTON RD
MONTBELLE RD
CHANCTONBURY CL
HIGH POINT
DOMONIC DR
SHALLONS RD
HARTING RD
HASSOP WLK
KERSEY GDNS
HORNING CL
TENTERDEN CL
SMARDEN GR
188
42
43
44
72
73
74
75
KINGSFIELD HO
CASTLETON RD
Lewisham
Bromley
Greenwich

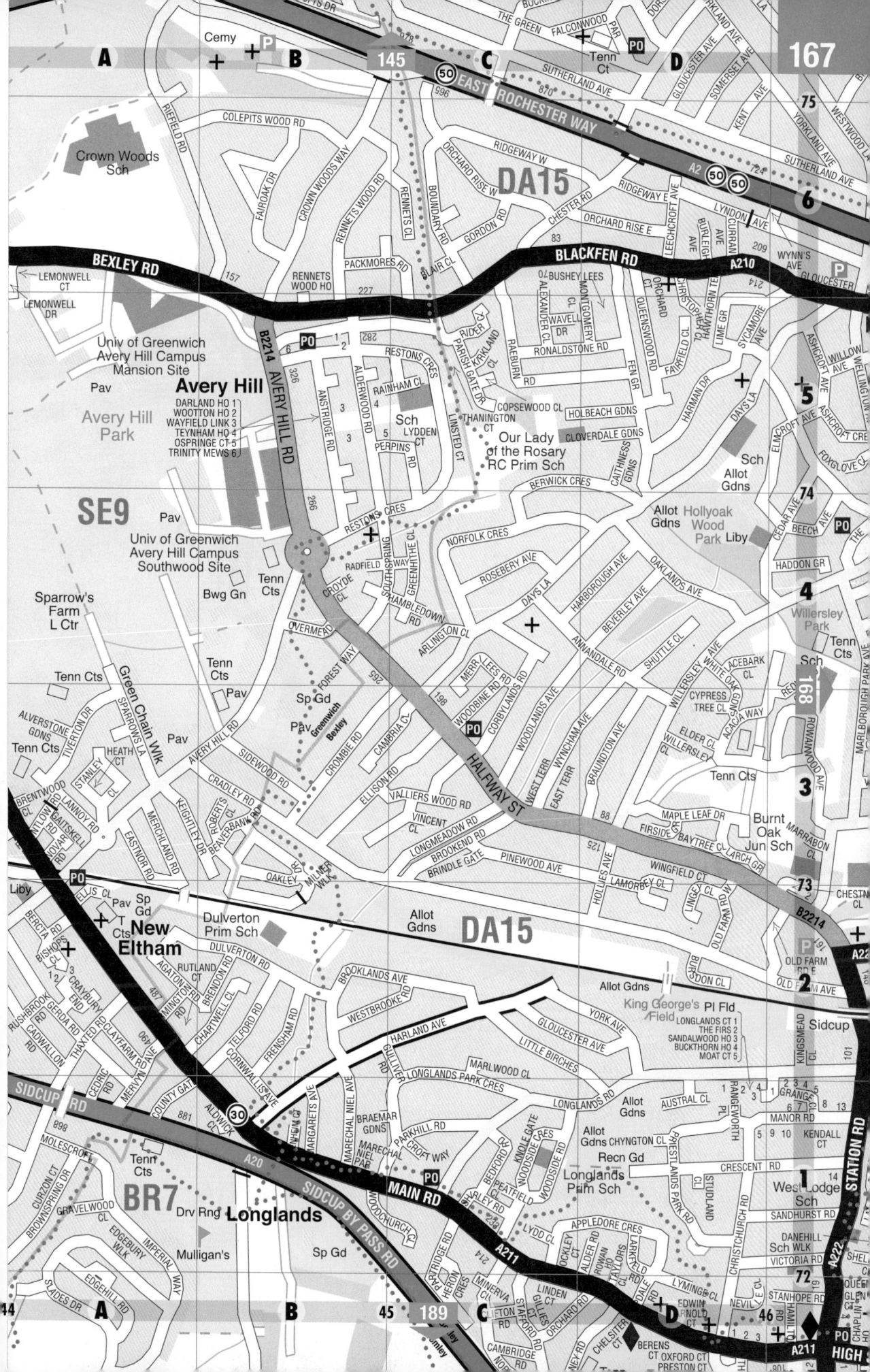
A
B
C
D
145
189
168
44
45
46
6
5
4
3
2
1
75
74
73
72
DA15
SE9
BR7
Cemy
Tenn Ct
THE GREEN
FALCONWOOD PAR
SUTHERLAND AVE
EAST ROCHESTER WAY
GLOUCESTER AVE
SOMERSET AVE
KENT AVE
YORKLAND AVE
WESTWOOD LA
A2
Crown Woods Sch
COLEPITS WOOD RD
RIEFIELD RD
FAIROAK DR
CROWN WOODS WAY
RENNETS WOOD RD
RENNETS CL
BOUNDARY RD
ORCHARD RISE W
RIDGEWAY W
GORDON RD
CHESTER RD
RIDGEWAY E
ORCHARD RISE E
LEECHCROFT AVE
BURLEIGH AVE
CURRAN AVE
LYNDON AVE
WYNN'S AVE
BEXLEY RD
BLACKFEN RD
A210
GLOUCESTER RD
LEMONWELL CT
LEMONWELL DR
RENNETS WOOD HO
PACKMORES RD
BLAIR CL
BUSHEY LEES
ALEXANDER CL
MONTGOMERY CL
WAVELL DR
ORCHARD CT
CHRISTOPHER CL
HAWTHORN TER
LIME GR
SYCAMORE AVE
QUEENSWOOD RD
FAIRFIELD CL
RONALDSTONE RD
RAEBURN RD
FEN GR
HARMAN DR
DAYS LA
ASHCROFT AVE
WILLOW AVE
WELLING
Univ of Greenwich Avery Hill Campus Mansion Site
Avery Hill
Avery Hill Park
Pav
DARLAND HO 1
WOOTTON HO 2
WAYFIELD LINK 3
TEYNHAM HO 4
OSPRINGE CT 5
TRINITY MEWS 6
B2214
AVERY HILL RD
ANSTRIDGE RD
ALDERWOOD RD
RESTONS CRES
RAINHAM CL
Sch
LYDDEN CT
PERPINS RD
LINSTED CT
RIDER CL
KIRKLAND CL
PARISH GATE DR
THANINGTON CT
COPSEWOOD CL
HOLBEACH GDNS
Our Lady of the Rosary RC Prim Sch
CLOVERDALE GDNS
CAITHNESS GDNS
BERWICK CRES
ELMCROFT AVE
FOXGLOVE CL
Allot Gdns
Hollyoak Wood Park
Liby
CEDAR AVE
BEECH AVE
HADDON GR
Univ of Greenwich Avery Hill Campus Southwood Site
Tenn Cts
Bwg Gn
Sparrow's Farm L Ctr
NORFOLK CRES
ROSEBERY AVE
RADFIELD WAY
SOUTHSPRING
GREENHITHE CL
CROYDE CL
SHAMBLEDOWN RD
OVERMEAD
ARLINGTON CL
HARBOROUGH AVE
OAKLANDS AVE
BEVERLEY AVE
Willersley Park
Green Chain Wlk
SPARROWS LA
ALVERSTONE GDNS
TIVERTON DR
HEATH CT
STANLEY CL
FOREST WAY
Sp Gd
Greenwich
Bexley
CROMBIE RD
CAMBRIA CL
MERRILEES RD
WOODBINE RD
CORBYLANDS RD
WOODLANDS AVE
ANNANDALE RD
SHUTTLE CL
WILLERSLEY AVE
WHITE OAK GDNS
LACEBARK CL
CYPRESS TREE CL
ACACIA WAY
ELDER CL
WILLERSLEY CL
ROWANWOOD AVE
MARLBOROUGH PARK AVE
BRENTWOOD CL
LANNOY RD
GAITSKELL RD
NOVAR RD
EASTNOR RD
MERCHLAND RD
KEIGHTLEY DR
ROBERTS CL
BEAVERBANK RD
CRADLEY RD
SIDEWOOD RD
ELLISON RD
VALLIERS WOOD RD
VINCENT CL
HALFWAY ST
WEST TERR
EAST TERR
WYNCHAM AVE
BRAUNDTON AVE
MAPLE LEAF DR
FIRSIDE GR
BAYTREE CL
LARCH GR
Burnt Oak Jun Sch
MARRABON CL
LONGMEADOW RD
BROOKEND RD
BRINDLE GATE
PINEWOOD AVE
HOLLIES AVE
LAMORBEY CL
WINGFIELD CT
LINGEY CL
OLD FARM RD W
CHESTNUT CL
OAKLEY DR
MILNER WLK
Liby
ELLIS CL
Pav
Sp Gd
T Cts
New Eltham
Dulverton Prim Sch
DA15
BERCTA RD
BISHOPS CL
CRAYBURY END
DULVERTON RD
AGATON RD
RUTLAND CT
BRENDON RD
WIMMINGTON RD
BROOKLANDS AVE
WESTBROOKE RD
Allot Gdns
King George's Field
Pl Fld
LONGLANDS CT 1
THE FIRS 2
SANDALWOOD HO 3
BUCKTHORN HO 4
MOAT CT 5
BURSDON CL
OLD FARM RD E
OLD FARM AVE
Sidcup
KINGSMEAD CL
RUSHBROOK RD
GERDA RD
CADWALLON RD
THAXTED RD
CLAYFARM RD
MERVYN AVE
CHARTWELL CL
TELFORD RD
FRENSHAM RD
CORNWALLIS AVE
HARLAND AVE
YORK AVE
GLOUCESTER AVE
LITTLE BIRCHES
MARLWOOD CL
GULLIVER RD
LONGLANDS PARK CRES
LONGLANDS RD
AUSTRAL CL
RANGEWORTH PL
GRANGE CL
MANOR RD
KENDALL CT
SIDCUP RD
CEDRIC RD
COUNTY GATE
ALDWICK CL
MARGARETS AVE
MARECHAL NIEL AVE
BRAEMAR GDNS
MARECHAL NIEL PAR
PARKHILL RD
CROFT WAY
BEDFORD RD
KNOLE GATE
WOODSIDE CRES
WOODSIDE RD
CHYNGTON CL
Recn Gd
PRESTLANDS PARK RD
STUDLAND CL
CRESCENT RD
West Lodge Sch
STATION RD
MOLESCROFT
CURZON CT
BROWNSPRING DR
GRAVELWOOD CL
EDGEBURY WLK
IMPERIAL WAY
Tenn Cts
BR7
Drv Rng
Longlands
Mulligan's
Sp Gd
A20
SIDCUP BY PASS RD
MAIN RD
WOODCHURCH CL
PEATFIELD CL
Longlands Prim Sch
CHRISTCHURCH RD
SANDHURST RD
DANEHILL WLK
VICTORIA RD
A211
LYDD CL
APPLEDORE CRES
ALDER RD
ROWAN HO
TAYLORS CL
LARKFIELD
LYMINGE CL
STANHOPE RD
HAMILTON RD
A222
SHELLEY
QUEEN GLEN CT
CHAPLIN
EDGEHILL RD
SLADES DR
PARTRIDGE RD
HERON CRES
MINERVA CL
CLIFTON RD
STAFFORD RD
LINDEN CT
GILLIES CT
ORCHARD RD
CAMBRIDGE
CHELSITER CT
BERENS CT
OXFORD CT
PRESTON CT
EDWIN ARNOLD CT
NEVILLE CL
HIGH

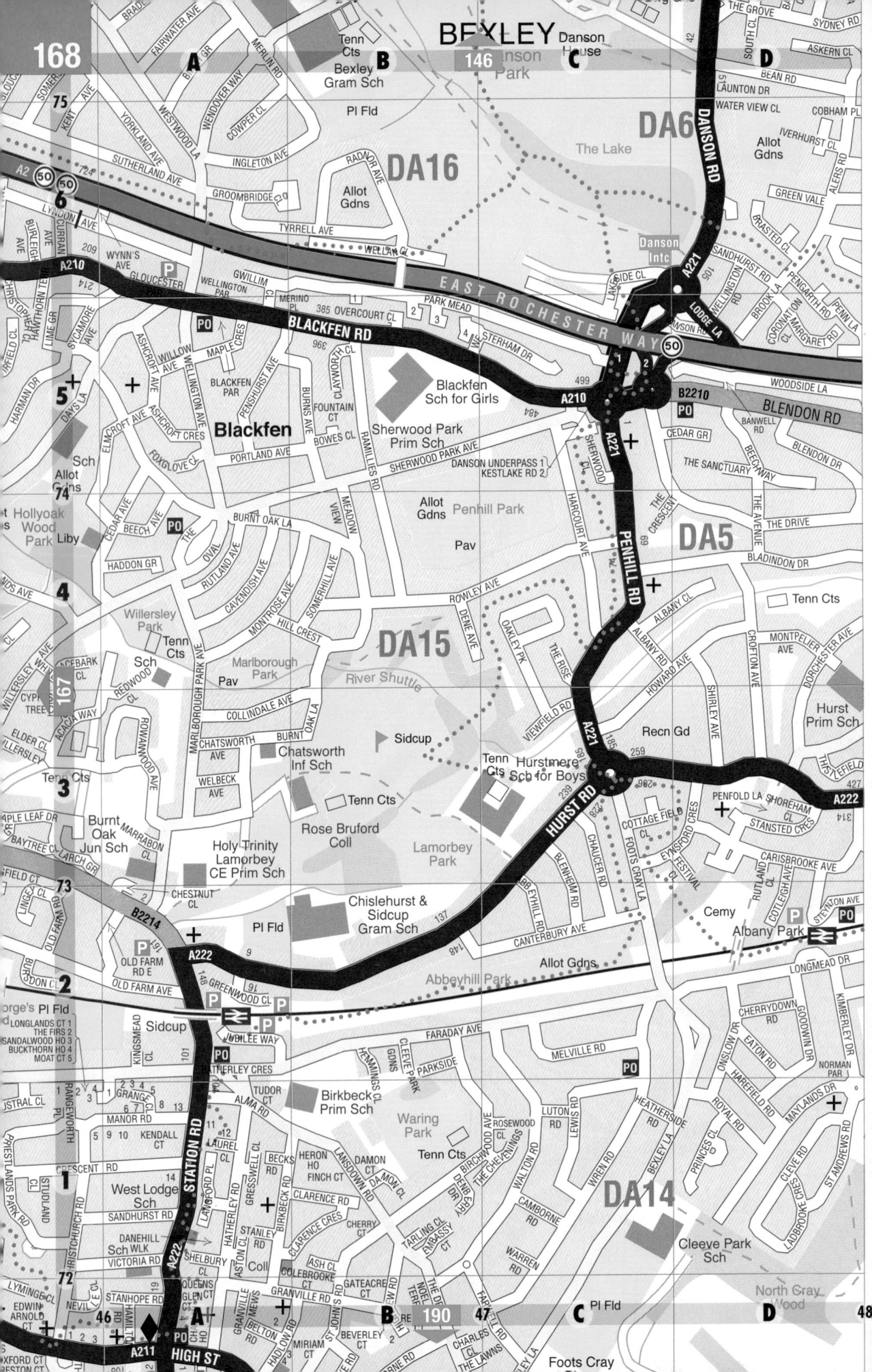
BEXLEY
146
DA16
DA6
DA5
DA15
DA14
Blackfen
Danson Park
The Lake
Danson House
Bexley Gram Sch
Blackfen Sch for Girls
Sherwood Park Prim Sch
Penhill Park
Marlborough Park
Willersley Park
Hollyoak Wood Park
River Shuttle
Sidcup
Chatsworth Inf Sch
Rose Bruford Coll
Lamorbey Park
Hurstmere Sch for Boys
Holy Trinity Lamorbey CE Prim Sch
Chislehurst & Sidcup Gram Sch
Burnt Oak Jun Sch
Hurst Prim Sch
Albany Park
Abbeyhill Park
Birkbeck Prim Sch
Waring Park
West Lodge Sch
Cleeve Park Sch
North Cray Wood
Foots Cray
BLACKFEN RD
EAST ROCHESTER WAY
DANSON RD
PENHILL RD
HURST RD
STATION RD
BLENDON RD
HIGH ST
A2
A210
A221
A222
A211
B2210
B2214
167
190

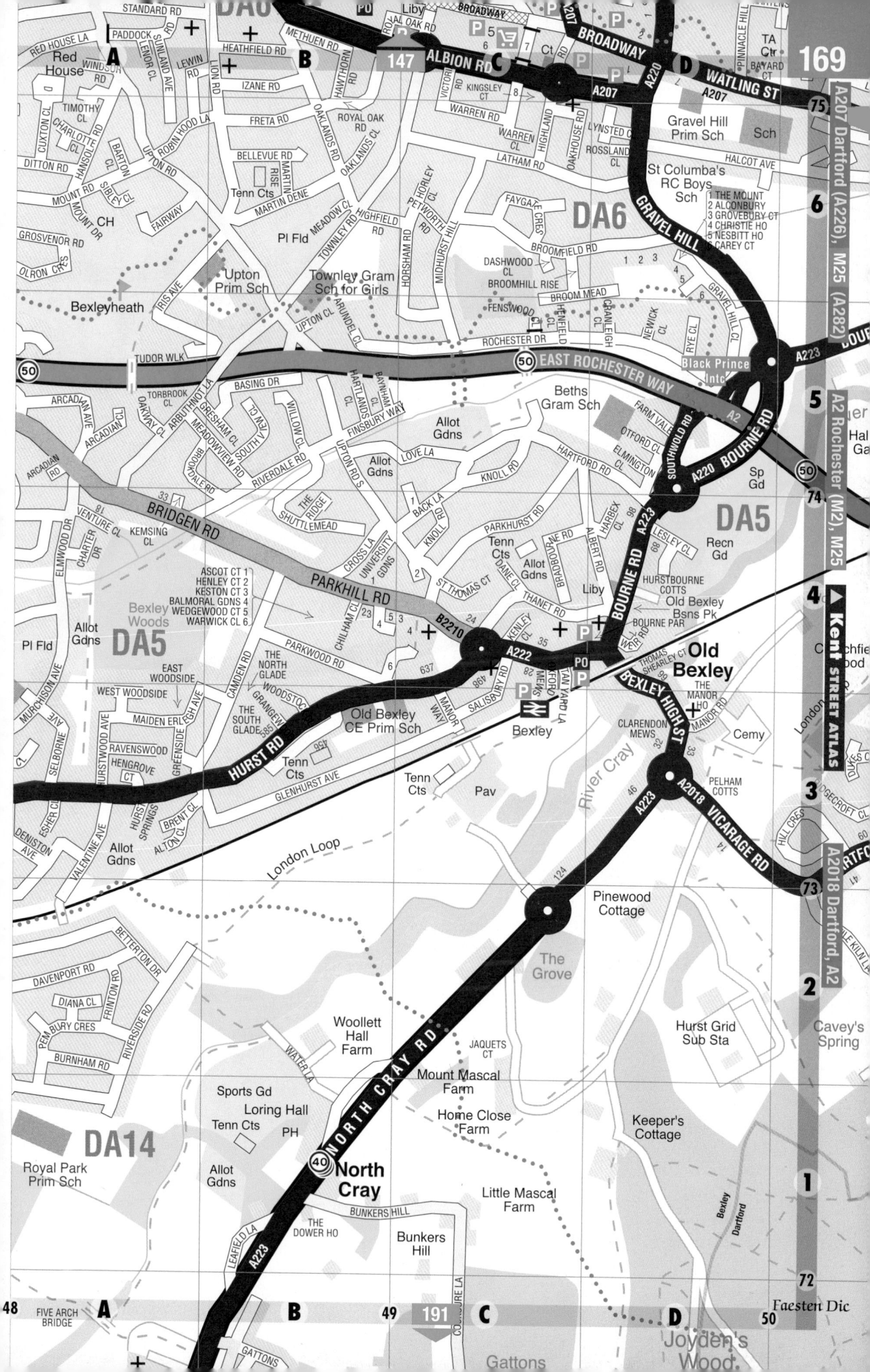
Bexleyheath
Red House
Upton Prim Sch
Townley Gram Sch for Girls
DA6
Gravel Hill Prim Sch
St Columba's RC Boys Sch
Beths Gram Sch
Black Prince Intc
EAST ROCHESTER WAY
BROADWAY
WATLING ST
ALBION RD
GRAVEL HILL
BOURNE RD
BRIDGEN RD
PARKHILL RD
HURST RD
DA5
Bexley Woods
Old Bexley
Old Bexley CE Prim Sch
Bexley
BEXLEY HIGH ST
VICARAGE RD
River Cray
London Loop
Pinewood Cottage
The Grove
Hurst Grid Sub Sta
NORTH CRAY RD
Woollett Hall Farm
Mount Mascal Farm
Home Close Farm
Keeper's Cottage
Loring Hall
DA14
Royal Park Prim Sch
North Cray
Little Mascal Farm
Bunkers Hill
Cavey's Spring
Joyden's Wood
Gattons
FIVE ARCH BRIDGE
A207 Dartford (A226), M25 (A282)
A2 Rochester (M2), M25
A2018 Dartford, A2
Kent STREET ATLAS
147
191

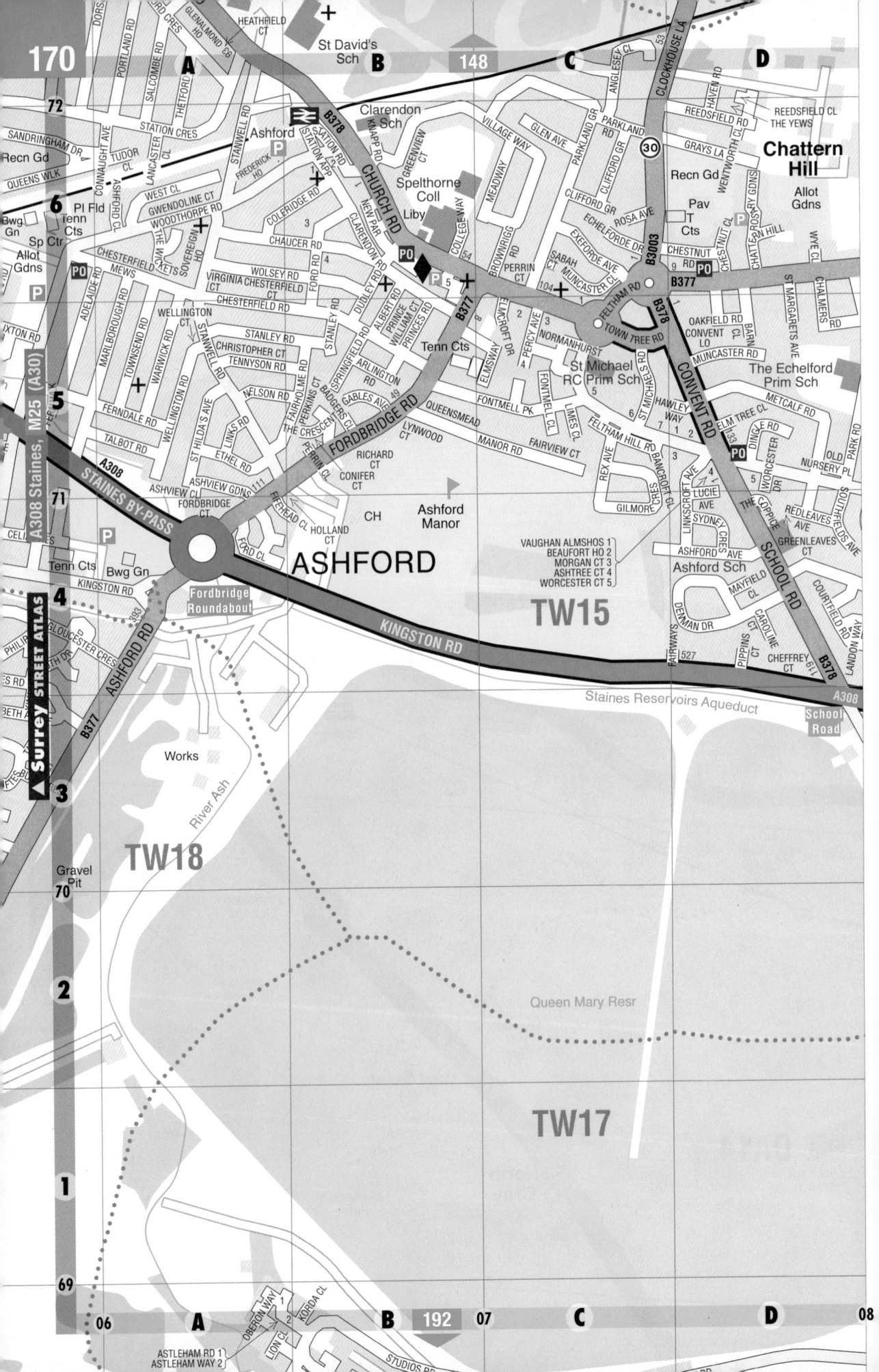
148
A
B
C
D
72
6
5
71
4
3
70
2
1
69
06
07
08
192
St David's Sch
Clarendon Sch
Ashford
Spelthorne Coll
Liby
Tenn Cts
Recn Gd
Chattern Hill
Allot Gdns
Pav
Cts
Pl Fld
Bwg Gn
Sp Ctr
St Michael RC Prim Sch
The Echelford Prim Sch
Ashford Manor
CH
ASHFORD
Ashford Sch
TW15
TW18
TW17
Works
River Ash
Gravel Pit
Queen Mary Resr
Staines Reservoirs Aqueduct
School Road
Fordbridge Roundabout
STAINES BY-PASS
KINGSTON RD
A308
B377
B378
B3003
30
CHURCH RD
FORDBRIDGE RD
CLOCKHOUSE LA
CONVENT RD
SCHOOL RD
ASHFORD RD
FELTHAM RD
TOWN TREE RD
STATION RD
STATION APP
STATION CRES
STANWELL RD
CHESTERFIELD RD
QUEENSMEAD
MANOR RD
FAIRVIEW CT
FONTMELL PK
FELTHAM HILL RD
VILLAGE WAY
GLEN AVE
PARKLAND GR
CLIFFORD GR
ECHELFORDE DR
EXEFORDE AVE
MUNCASTER CL
MUNCASTER RD
OAKFIELD RD
CONVENT LO
METCALF RD
NURSERY PL
KINGSTON RD
GLOUCESTER CRES
DENMAN DR
MAYFIELD CL
FAIRWAYS
VAUGHAN ALMSHOS 1
BEAUFORT HO 2
MORGAN CT 3
ASHTREE CT 4
WORCESTER CT 5
ASTLEHAM RD 1
ASTLEHAM WAY 2
OBERON WAY
KORDA CL
LION CL
STUDIOS RD
A308 Staines, M25 (A30)
Surrey STREET ATLAS

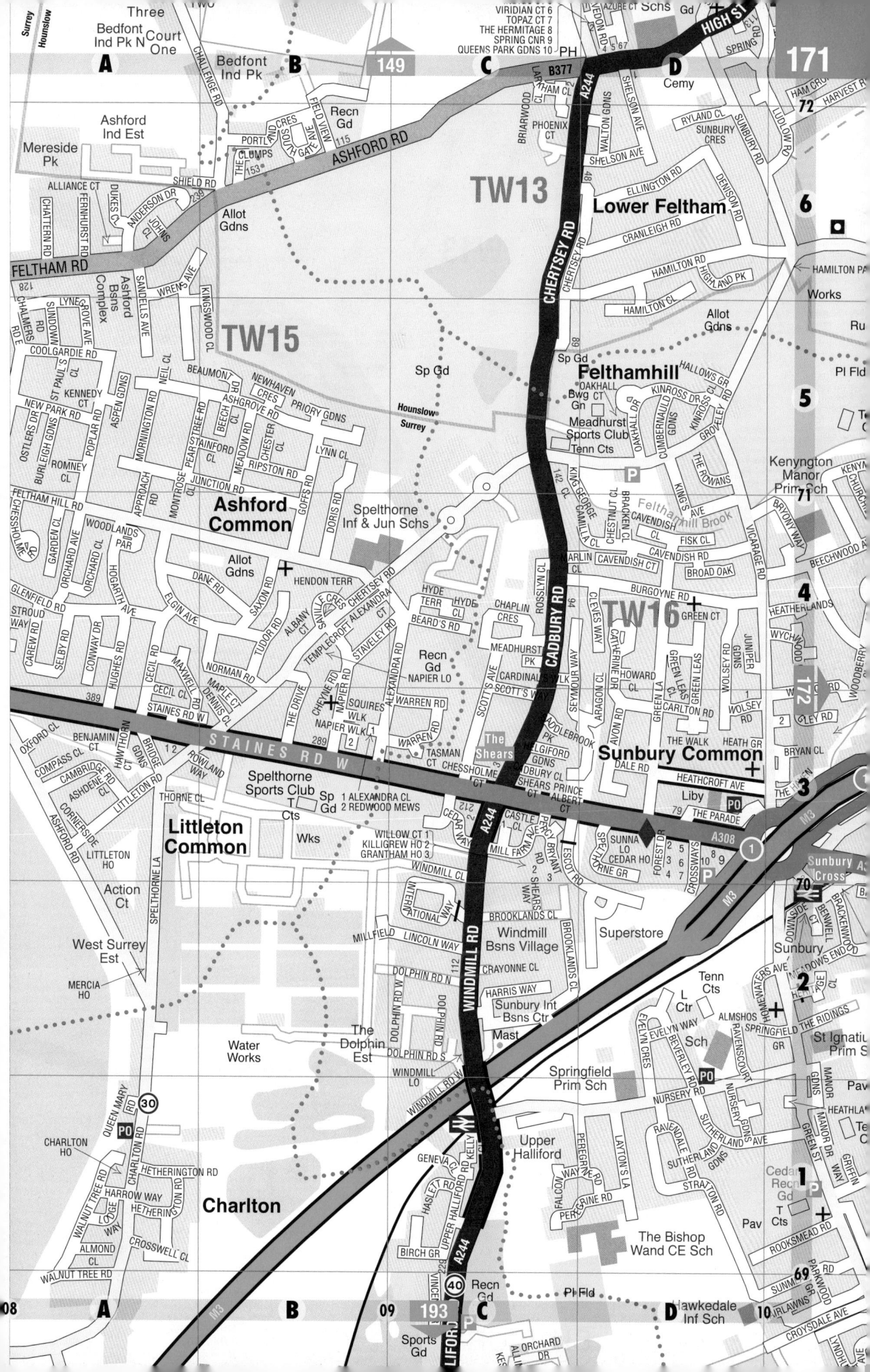
171
149
172
193
A
B
C
D
A
B
C
D
08
09
10
69
70
71
72
1
2
3
4
5
6
Surrey
Hounslow
Three
Bedfont Ind Pk N
Court One
Bedfont Ind Pk
VIRIDIAN CT 6
TOPAZ CT 7
THE HERMITAGE 8
SPRING CNR 9
QUEENS PARK GDNS 10
PH
AZURE CT
Schs
Gd
HIGH ST
SPRING RD
B377
A244
Cemy
HAM CR
HARVEST RD
LARKHAM CL
CHALLENGE RD
FIELD VIEW
Recn Gd
Ashford Ind Est
Mereside Pk
PORTLAND CRES
SOUTH GATE AVE
THE CLUMPS
ASHFORD RD
SHIELD RD
BRIARWOOD
PHOENIX CT
WALTON GDNS
SHELSON AVE
RYLAND CL
SUNBURY CRES
SUNBURY RD
LUDLOW RD
ALLIANCE CT
DUKES CL
ANDERSON DR
JOHNS CL
CHATTERN RD
FERNHURST RD
Allot Gdns
TW13
ELLINGTON RD
Lower Feltham
DENISON RD
CRANLEIGH RD
CHERTSEY RD
HAMILTON RD
HIGHLAND PK
HAMILTON PA
Works
HAMILTON CL
FELTHAM RD
Ashford Bsns Complex
SANDELLS AVE
WRENS AVE
KINGSWOOD CL
CHALMERS RD E
SUNDOWN RD
LYNEGROVE AVE
TW15
Allot Gdns
Ru
COOLGARDIE RD
ST PAUL'S CL
KENNEDY CT
NEW PARK RD
ASPEN GDNS
POPLAR RD
MORNINGTON RD
NEIL CL
BEAUMONT DR
NEWHAVEN CRES
PRIORY GDNS
ASHGROVE RD
Sp Gd
Sp Gd
Felthamhill
HALLOWS GR
OAKHALL CT
Bwg Gn
KINROSS DR
KINROSS CL
GROVELEY RD
Pl Fld
Hounslow
Surrey
Meadhurst Sports Club
Tenn Cts
OAKHALL DR
CUMBERNAULD GDNS
THE ROWANS
OSTLERS DR
BURLEIGH GDNS
ROMNEY CL
BEECH CL
PEARTREE RD
STAINFORD CL
MEADOW RD
CHESTER CL
RIPSTON RD
LYNN CL
JUNCTION RD
MONTROSE RD
APPROACH RD
GOFFS RD
Kenyngton Manor Prim Sch
FELTHAM HILL RD
CHESSHOLME RD
Ashford Common
DORIS RD
Spelthorne Inf & Jun Schs
KING GEORGE CL
CAMILLA CL
CHESTNUT CL
BRACKEN CL
KING'S AVE
CAVENDISH CL
FISK CL
Felthamhill Brook
BRYONY WAY
GARDEN CL
ORCHARD AVE
ORCHARD CL
WOODLANDS PAR
HOGARTH AVE
Allot Gdns
DANE RD
SAXON RD
HENDON TERR
CHERTSEY RD
SAVILLE CRES
ALEXANDRA CT
HYDE TERR
HYDE CL
MARLIN CL
CAVENDISH CT
CAVENDISH RD
BROAD OAK
VICARAGE RD
BEECHWOOD AVE
GLENFIELD RD
STROUD WAY
ELGIN AVE
TUDOR RD
ALBANY CT
TEMPLECROFT
STAVELEY RD
BEARD'S RD
CHAPLIN CRES
ROSSLYN CL
CADBURY RD
CLEVES WAY
TW16
BURGOYNE RD
GREEN CT
HEATHERLANDS
WYCHWOOD
CAREW RD
SELBY RD
CONWAY DR
HUGHES RD
CECIL RD
MAXWELL RD
NORMAN RD
MAPLE CT
DENNIS CL
CECIL CL
Recn Gd
NAPIER LO
MEADHURST PK
CATHERINE DR
HOWARD CL
GREEN LA
GREEN LEAS
GREEN LEAS CL
WOLSEY RD
JUNIPER GDNS
WOLSEY RD
CARDINALS WLK
SCOTT'S WAY
SCOTT'S AVE
SEYMOUR WAY
ARAGON CL
AVON RD
CARLTON RD
THE WALK
HEATH GR
BRYAN CL
389
STAINES RD W
THE DRIVE
CHEYNE RD
NAPIER RD
SQUIRES WLK
ALEXANDRA RD
WARREN RD
WARREN CT
NAPIER WLK
289
TASMAN CT
CHESSHOLME CT
The Shears
WELGIFORD GDNS
CADBURY CL
SHEARS CT
PRINCE ALBERT CT
Sunbury Common
DALE RD
HEATHCROFT AVE
THE HOLLOW
OXFORD CL
BENJAMIN CT
COMPASS CL
CAMBRIDGE RD
ASHDENE CL
HAWTHORN CT
GDNS
BRIDGE RD
ROWLAND WAY
Spelthorne Sports Club
T Cts
Sp Gd
1 ALEXANDRA CL
2 REDWOOD MEWS
Liby
THE PARADE
A308
THORNE CL
LITTLETON RD
CORNERSIDE
ASHFORD RD
Littleton Common
Wks
WILLOW CT 1
KILLIGREW HO 2
GRANTHAM HO 3
CEDAR WAY
CASTLE CL
MILL FARM AVE
PERCY BRYANT RD
ESCOT RD
SPELTHORNE GR
SUNNA LO
CEDAR HO
FOREST DR
CROSSWAYS
M3
Sunbury Cross
LITTLETON HO
Action Ct
WINDMILL CL
INTERNATIONAL WAY
SHEARS WAY
BROOKLANDS CL
BROOKLANDS CL
Superstore
DOWNSIDE CT
BENWELL
BRACKENWOOD
MEADOWS END
Sunbury
West Surrey Est
SPELTHORNE LA
MILLFIELD
LINCOLN WAY
Windmill Bsns Village
CRAYONNE CL
WINDMILL RD
DOLPHIN RD N
HARRIS WAY
Sunbury Int Bsns Ctr
Tenn Cts
L Ctr
HOMEWATERS AVE
HERITAGE CL
MERCIA HO
EVELYN WAY
EVELYN CRES
BEVERLEY RD
RAVENSCOURT
ALMSHOS
SPRINGFIELD GR
THE RIDINGS
St Ignatius Prim S
Water Works
The Dolphin Est
DOLPHIN RD W
DOLPHIN RD
DOLPHIN RD S
Mast
Sch
Springfield Prim Sch
WINDMILL LO
WINDMILL RD W
NURSERY RD
NURSERY GDNS
MANOR GDNS
Pav
QUEEN MARY RD
30
CHARLTON RD
CHARLTON HO
HETHERINGTON RD
KELLY
Upper Halliford
GENEVA CL
PEREGRINE RD
LAYTON'S LA
RAVENDALE RD
SUTHERLAND GDNS
SUTHERLAND AVE
HEATHLANDS
MANOR DR
GREEN ST
GRIFFIN WAY
WALNUT TREE RD
HARROW WAY
LODGE WAY
HETHERINGTON RD
Charlton
HASLETT RD
UPPER HALLIFORD RD
FALCON WAY
PEREGRINE RD
STRATTON RD
Cedar Recn Gd
T Cts
Pav
ALMOND CL
CROSSWELL CL
BIRCH GR
The Bishop Wand CE Sch
ROOKSMEAD RD
PARKWOOD GR
WALNUT TREE RD
40
Recn Gd
Pl Fld
Hawkedale Inf Sch
CURLAWNS
CROYSDALE AVE
Sports Gd
HALLIFORD
ORCHARD DR
LYNDHURST

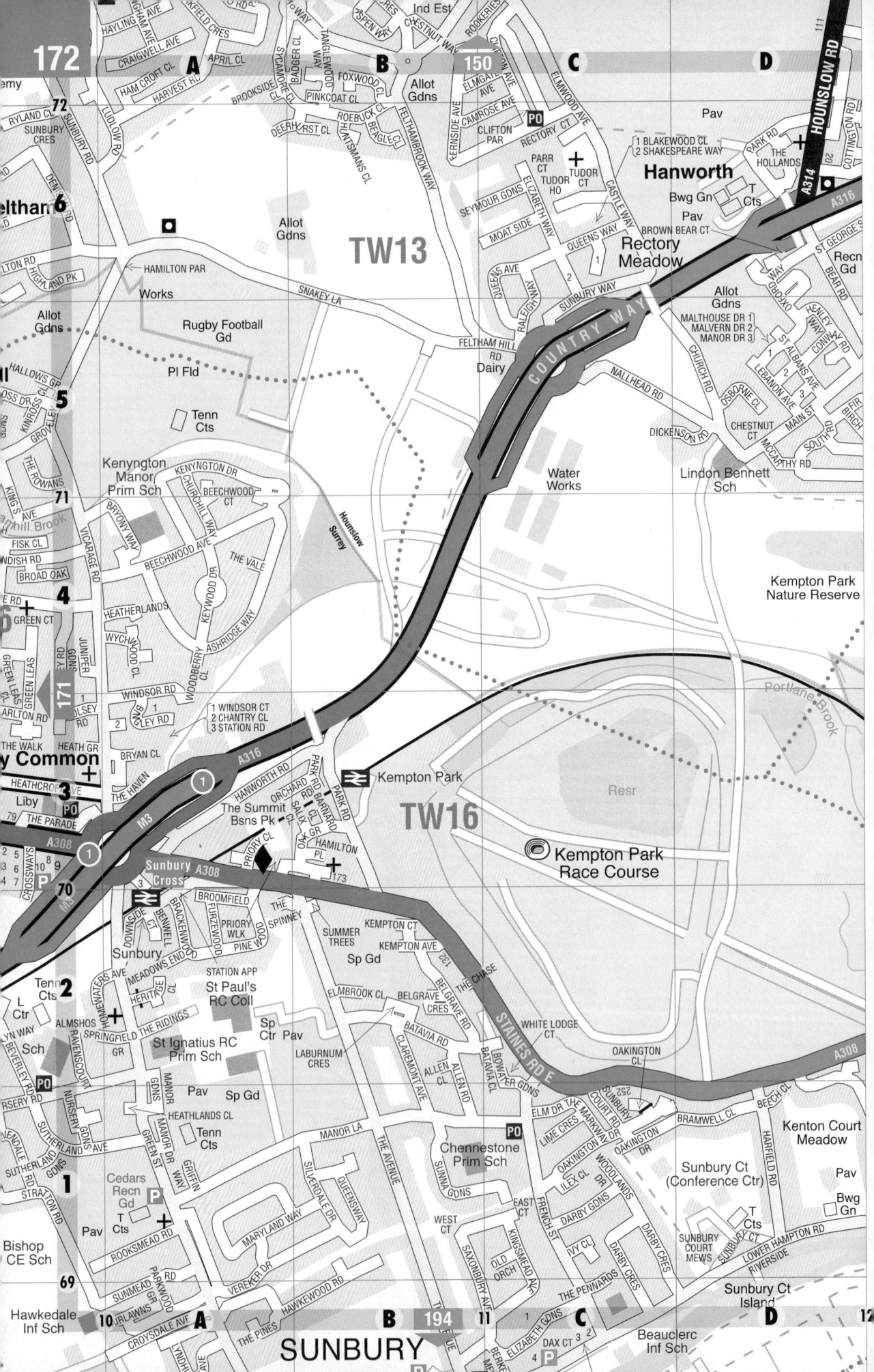
A
B
C
D
150
Hanworth
TW13
Rectory Meadow
Country Way
Kempton Park
TW16
Kempton Park Race Course
Kempton Park Nature Reserve
Lindon Bennett Sch
Water Works
Rugby Football Gd
Kenyngton Manor Prim Sch
The Summit Bsns Pk
Sunbury Cross
St Paul's RC Coll
St Ignatius RC Prim Sch
Chennestone Prim Sch
Sunbury Ct (Conference Ctr)
Kenton Court Meadow
Sunbury Ct Island
Beauclerc Inf Sch
Hawkedale Inf Sch
Bishop CE Sch
Cedars Recn Gd
SUNBURY
194
171
Hounslow Surrey
A316
A308
A314
M3
HOUNSLOW RD
STAINES RD E

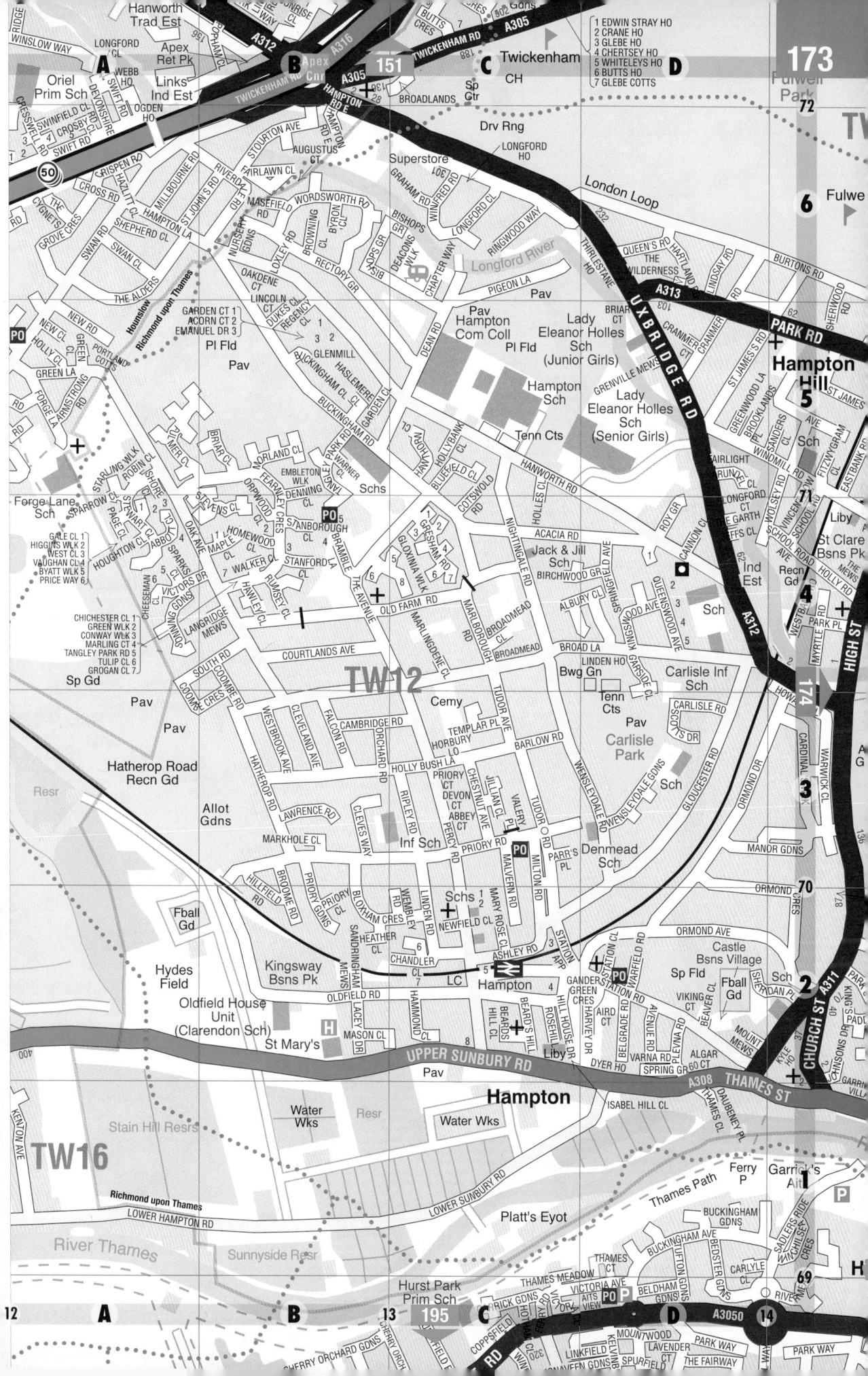

173
151
174
195
A
B
C
D
Hanworth Trad Est
Apex Ret Pk
Links Ind Est
Apex Cnr
Twickenham
CH
Sp Ctr
BROADLANDS
Fulwell Park
1 EDWIN STRAY HO
2 CRANE HO
3 GLEBE HO
4 CHERTSEY HO
5 WHITELEYS HO
6 BUTTS HO
7 GLEBE COTTS
A312
A316
A305
A313
A311
A308
A3050
TWICKENHAM RD
HAMPTON RD E
WINSLOW WAY
LONGFORD CL
WEBB HO
OGDEN HO
Oriel Prim Sch
DEVONSHIRE
SWIFT RD
SWINFIELD CL
CROSBY CL
CRESSWELL RD
STOURTON AVE
AUGUSTUS CT
FAIRLAWN CL
RIVERDALE RD
ST JOHN'S RD
MILLBOURNE RD
HAZLITT CL
CRISPEN RD
CROSS RD
THE CYGNETS
HAMPTON LA
SHEPHERD CL
SWAN RD
SWAN CL
GROVE CRES
THE ALDERS
Drv Rng
Superstore
LONGFORD HO
GRAHAM RD
WINIFRED RD
LONGFORD CL
BISHOPS GR
DEACONS WLK
CHAPTER WAY
RINGWOOD WAY
Longford River
PIGEON LA
London Loop
THIRLESTANE HO
QUEEN'S RD
THE WILDERNESS
HARTLAND RD
LINDSAY RD
BURTONS RD
SHERWOOD RD
PARK RD
Hampton Hill
MASEFIELD RD
WORDSWORTH RD
BROWNING CL
BYRON CL
RECTORY GR
LOXLEY RD
NURSERY GDNS
OAKDENE CT
LINCOLN CT
DUKES CL
REGENCY CL
GARDEN CT 1
ACORN CT 2
EMANUEL DR 3
GLENMILL
HASLEMERE CL
BUCKINGHAM CL
BUCKINGHAM RD
GARDEN CL
Hounslow
Richmond upon Thames
Pl Fld
Pav
NEW RD
NEW CL
HOLLY CL
GREEN CL
PORTLAND COTTS
GREEN LA
FORGE LA
ARMSTRONG RD
DEAN RD
Hampton Com Coll
Lady Eleanor Holles Sch (Junior Girls)
Hampton Sch
Lady Eleanor Holles Sch (Senior Girls)
BRIAR CT
UXBRIDGE RD
GRENVILLE MEWS
CRANMER CT
CRANMER RD
ST JAMES'S RD
GREENWOOD LA
BROOKLANDS PL
SANDERS CL
ST JAMES AVE
FITZWYGRAM CL
EASTBANK RD
Tenn Cts
WINDMILL RD
FAIRLIGHT
ARUNDEL CL
LONGFORD CT
THE GARTH
JEFFS CL
WOLSEY RD
VINCENT ROW
SCHOOL RD
SCHOOL ROAD AVE
HOLLY RD
THE MEWS
Liby
St Clare Bsns Pk
Recn Gd
Ind Est
Sch
Schs
FULMER CL
BRIAR CL
NORLAND CL
EMBLETON WLK
DENNING CL
TANGLEY PARK RD
WARNER CL
HAWTHORN CL
HOLLYBANK CL
BLUEFIELD CL
COTSWOLD RD
HANWORTH RD
HOLLES CL
ROY GR
CANNON CL
Forge Lane Sch
STARLING WLK
ROBIN CL
SPARROW CL
PAGE CL
STEWART CL
SHORE CL
ABBOTT CL
SPARKS CL
HOUGHTON CL
GALE CL 1
HIGGINS WLK 2
WEST CL 3
VAUGHAN CL 4
BYATT WLK 5
PRICE WAY 6
STEVENS CL
OAK AVE
MAPLE CL
HOMEWOOD CL
ORPWOOD CL
FEARNLEY CRES
STANBOROUGH CL
BRAMBLE LA
WALKER CL
STANFORD CL
VICTORS DR
CHEESEMAN CL
HAWLEY CL
RUMSEY CL
GRESHAM RD
GLOXINIA WLK
THE AVENUE
OLD FARM RD
NIGHTINGALE RD
ACACIA RD
Jack & Jill Sch
BIRCHWOOD GR
SPRINGFIELD AVE
ALBURY CL
KINGSWOOD AVE
QUEENSWOOD AVE
CHICHESTER CL 1
GREEN WLK 2
CONWAY WLK 3
MARLING CT 4
TANGLEY PARK RD 5
TULIP CL 6
GROGAN CL 7
LANGRIDGE MEWS
SHIRES CL
COURTLANDS AVE
MARLINGDENE CL
MARLBOROUGH RD
BROADMEAD CL
BROADMEAD
BROAD LA
LINDEN HO
Bwg Gn
GARSIDE CL
Carlisle Inf Sch
CARLISLE RD
SCOTTS DR
TW12
SOUTH RD
COOMBE RD
COOMBE CRES
Sp Gd
Cemy
TUDOR AVE
TEMPLAR PL
HORBURY LO
BARLOW RD
Carlisle Park
WESTBROOK AVE
CLEVELAND AVE
FALCON RD
CAMBRIDGE RD
ORCHARD RD
HOLLY BUSH LA
PRIORY CT
DEVON CT
ABBEY CT
CHESTNUT AVE
JILLIAN CL
VALERY PL
WENSLEYDALE RD
WENSLEYDALE GDNS
GLOUCESTER RD
ORMOND DR
CARDINAL
WARWICK CL
MANOR GDNS
Hatherop Road Recn Gd
Allot Gdns
HATHEROP RD
LAWRENCE RD
CLEVES WAY
RIPLEY RD
PERCY RD
TUDOR RD
MILTON RD
MALVERN RD
PRIORY RD
Inf Sch
MARKHOLE CL
PARR'S PL
Denmead Sch
ORMOND CRES
Resr
Fball Gd
HILLFIELD RD
BROOME RD
PRIORY GDNS
PRIORY CL
BLOXHAM CRES
WEMBLEY RD
LINDEN RD
NEWFIELD CL
MARY ROSE CL
ASHLEY RD
STATION APP
ORMOND AVE
Castle Bsns Village
STATION CL
WARFIELD RD
HEATHER CL
SANDRINGHAM MEWS
CHANDLER CL
LC
Hampton
Hydes Field
Kingsway Bsns Pk
Oldfield House Unit (Clarendon Sch)
OLDFIELD RD
LACEY DR
MASON CL
HAMMOND CL
St Mary's
BEARDS HILL CL
BEARD'S HILL
ROSEHILL
HILL HOUSE DR
GANDER GREEN CRES
STATION RD
HARVEY DR
AIRD CT
BELGRADE RD
AVENUE RD
PLEVNA RD
VIKING CT
BEAVER CL
Sp Fld
SHERIDAN PL
MOUNT MEWS
KYLE HO
CHURCH ST
JOHNSONS DR
KING'S PADD
GARRICK VILLAS
UPPER SUNBURY RD
Liby
DYER HO
VARNA RD
SPRING GR
ALGAR CT
THAMES ST
ISABEL HILL CL
THAMES CL
DAUBENEY PL
KENTON AVE
Stain Hill Resrs
Water Wks
TW16
Ferry P
Garrick's Ait
Thames Path
Richmond upon Thames
LOWER HAMPTON RD
LOWER SUNBURY RD
Platt's Eyot
River Thames
Sunnyside Resr
BUCKINGHAM GDNS
BUCKINGHAM AVE
UFTON GDNS
BEDSTER GDNS
CARLYLE CL
SADLERS RIDE
WINCHILSEY CRES
Hurst Park Prim Sch
THAMES MEADOW
THAMES CT
VICTORIA AVE
AITS VIEW
BELDHAM GDNS
RIVERMEAD
GARRICK GDNS
VICTORIA CL
FERRY RD
HOTHAM CL
COPPSFIELD
MOUNTWOOD
LAVENDER CT
PARK WAY
THE FAIRWAY
LINKFIELD
KELVINBROOK
SPURFIELD
CHERRY ORCHARD GDNS
12
13
14
1
2
3
4
5
6

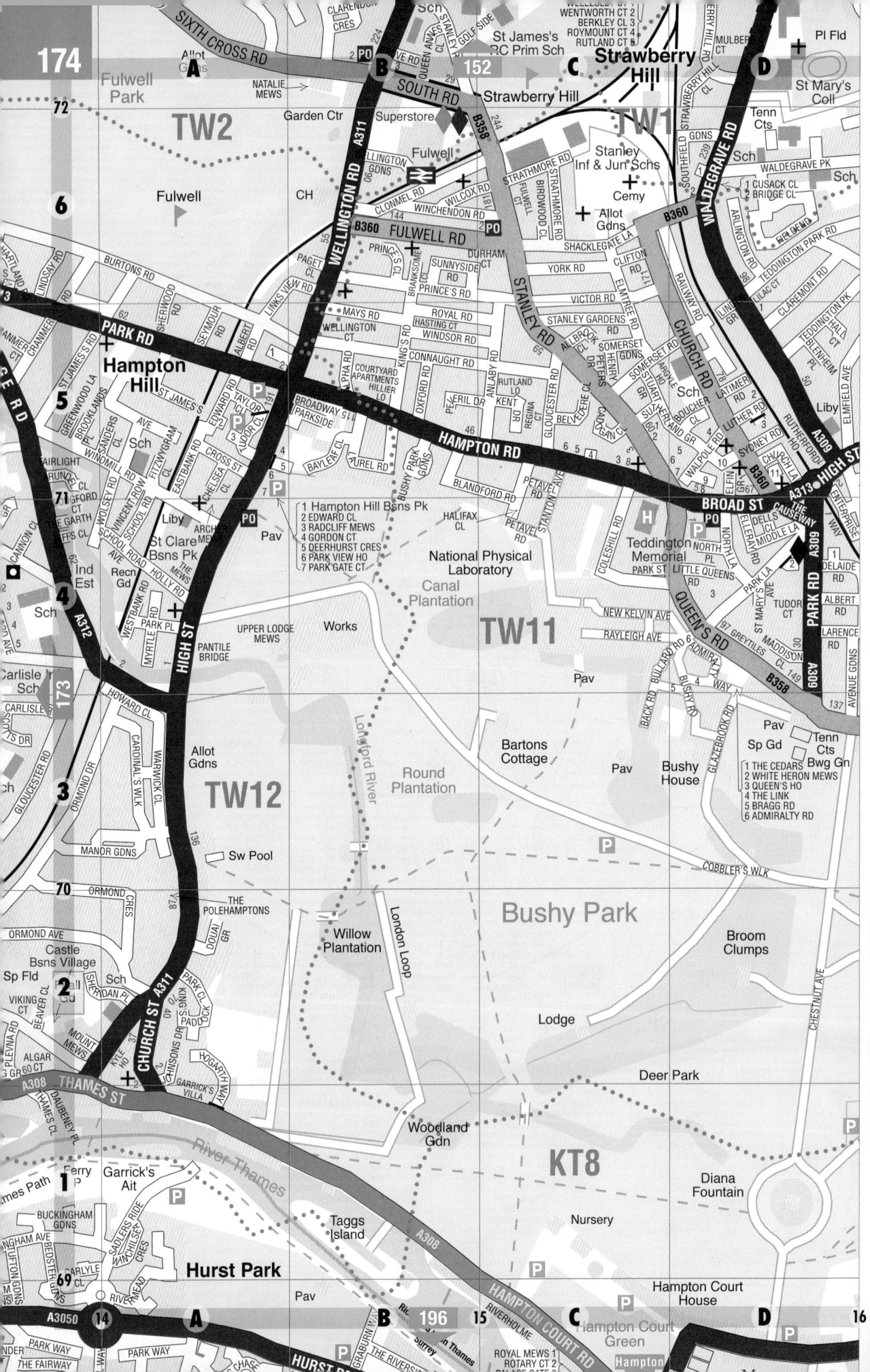

TW2
TW1
TW11
TW12
KT8
Fulwell Park
Fulwell
Strawberry Hill
St James's RC Prim Sch
Hampton Hill
Teddington Memorial
National Physical Laboratory
Canal Plantation
Bushy Park
Bushy House
Round Plantation
Willow Plantation
Broom Clumps
Deer Park
Woodland Gdn
Diana Fountain
Hampton Court House
Hampton Court Green
Hurst Park
Taggs Island
Garrick's Ait
River Thames
Longford River
London Loop
Castle Bsns Village
St Clare Bsns Pk
Bartons Cottage
Stanley Inf & Jun Schs
St Mary's Coll
WELLINGTON RD
HAMPTON RD
PARK RD
HIGH ST
STANLEY RD
CHURCH RD
WALDEGRAVE RD
BROAD ST
QUEEN'S RD
FULWELL RD
SOUTH RD
SIXTH CROSS RD
THAMES ST
HAMPTON COURT RD
CHURCH ST
COBBLER'S WLK
CHESTNUT AVE
1 Hampton Hill Bsns Pk
2 EDWARD CL
3 RADCLIFF MEWS
4 GORDON CT
5 DEERHURST CRES
6 PARK VIEW HO
7 PARK GATE CT
1 THE CEDARS
2 WHITE HERON MEWS
3 QUEEN'S HO
4 THE LINK
5 BRAGG RD
6 ADMIRALTY RD
1 CUSACK CL
2 BRIDGE CL
152
173
196
A
B
C
D

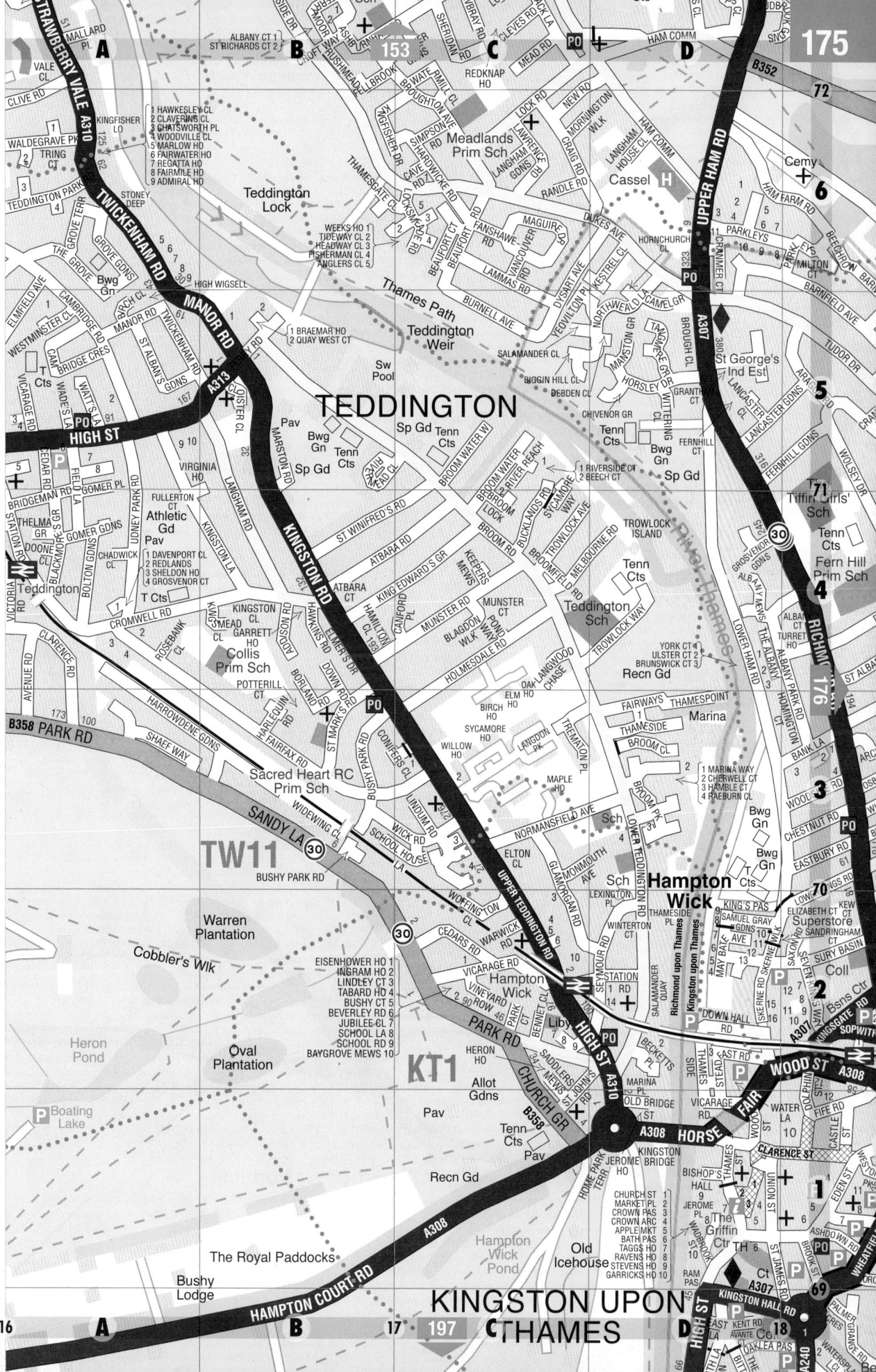

TEDDINGTON
Hampton Wick
KINGSTON UPON THAMES
TW11
KT1
River Thames
Teddington Lock
Teddington Weir
Thames Path
STRAWBERRY VALE A310
TWICKENHAM RD
MANOR RD
A313
HIGH ST
KINGSTON RD
UPPER TEDDINGTON RD
UPPER HAM RD A307
RICHMOND RD
HAM COMM
B352
B358 PARK RD
SANDY LA
PARK RD
CHURCH GR B358
HAMPTON COURT RD A308
HORSE FAIR A308
WOOD ST A308
KINGSTON BRIDGE
KINGSTON HALL RD
HIGH ST A310
Meadlands Prim Sch
Cassel H
St George's Ind Est
Tiffin Girls' Sch
Fern Hill Prim Sch
Teddington Sch
Collis Prim Sch
Sacred Heart RC Prim Sch
Athletic Gd
Teddington
Recn Gd
Marina
Superstore
Warren Plantation
Oval Plantation
Cobbler's Wlk
Heron Pond
Boating Lake
The Royal Paddocks
Bushy Lodge
Hampton Wick Pond
Old Icehouse
Allot Gdns
Bushy Park Rd
The Griffin Ctr
Cemy
Richmond upon Thames
Kingston upon Thames
1 HAWKESLEY CL
2 CLAVERING CL
3 CHATSWORTH PL
4 WOODVILLE CL
5 MARLOW HO
6 FAIRWATER HO
7 REGATTA HO
8 FAIRMILE HO
9 ADMIRAL HO
WEEKS HO 1
TIDEWAY CL 2
HEADWAY CL 3
FISHERMAN CL 4
ANGLERS CL 5
1 BRAEMAR HO
2 QUAY WEST CT
1 DAVENPORT CL
2 REDLANDS
3 SHELDON HO
4 GROSVENOR CT
1 RIVERSIDE CT
2 BEECH CT
YORK CT 1
ULSTER CT 2
BRUNSWICK CT 3
1 MARINA WAY
2 CHERWELL CT
3 HAMBLE CT
4 RAEBURN CL
EISENHOWER HO 1
INGRAM HO 2
LINDLEY CT 3
TABARD HO 4
BUSHY CT 5
BEVERLEY RD 6
JUBILEE CL 7
SCHOOL LA 8
SCHOOL RD 9
BAYGROVE MEWS 10
CHURCH ST 1
MARKET PL 2
CROWN PAS 3
CROWN ARC 4
APPLE MKT 5
BATH PAS 6
TAGGS HO 7
RAVENS HO 8
STEVENS HO 9
GARRICKS HO 10
153
176
197
A B C D
16 17 18
1 2 3 4 5 6

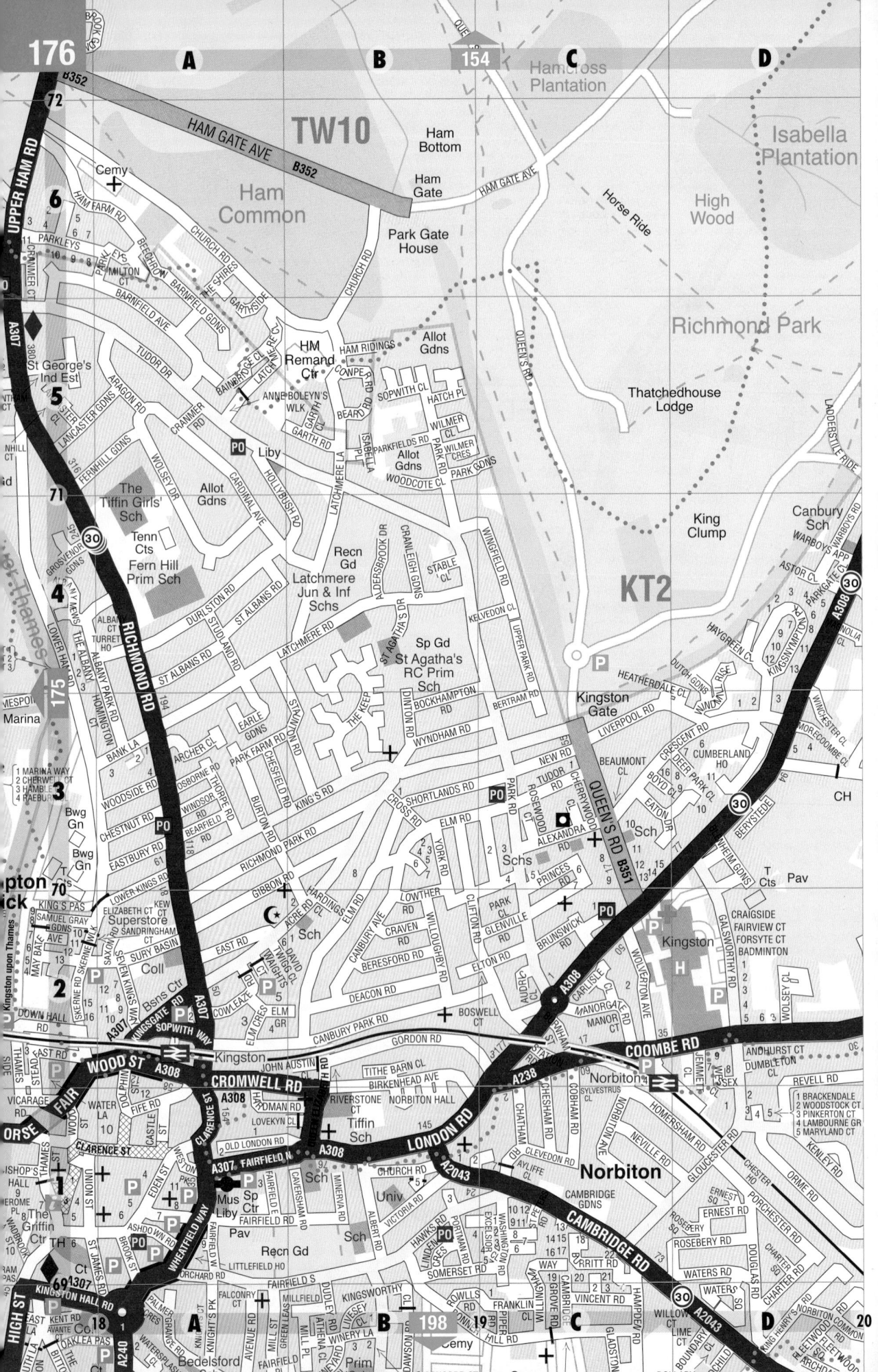
A
B
C
D
154
TW10
Ham Common
Ham Bottom
Ham Gate
Hamcross Plantation
Isabella Plantation
High Wood
Richmond Park
Thatchedhouse Lodge
King Clump
KT2
Kingston Gate
Park Gate House
HM Remand Ctr
The Tiffin Girls' Sch
Fern Hill Prim Sch
Latchmere Jun & Inf Schs
St Agatha's RC Prim Sch
Canbury Sch
Kingston
Norbiton
Tiffin Sch
HAM GATE AVE
UPPER HAM RD
RICHMOND RD
QUEEN'S RD
CROMWELL RD
LONDON RD
COOMBE RD
CAMBRIDGE RD
175
198

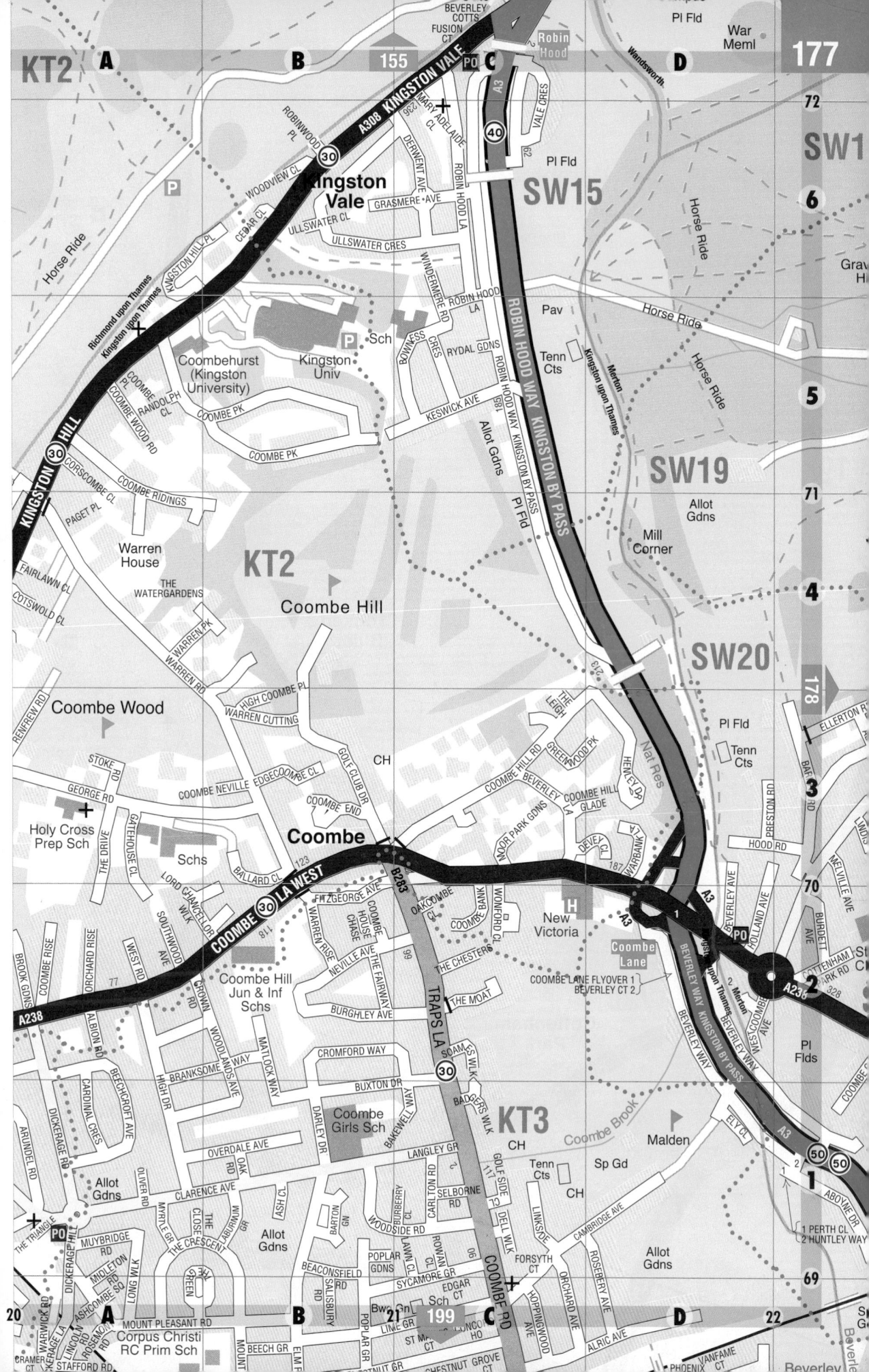
KT2
A
B
155
C
D
Robin Hood
Pl Fld
War Meml
Wandsworth
KINGSTON VALE
A308
BEVERLEY COTTS
FUSION CT
ROBINWOOD PL
MARY ADELAIDE CL
DERWENT AVE
ROBIN HOOD LA
VALE CRES
SW15
SW1
Kingston Vale
WOODVIEW CL
GRASMERE AVE
ULLSWATER CL
ULLSWATER CRES
CEDAR CL
KINGSTON HILL PL
Horse Ride
Richmond upon Thames
Kingston upon Thames
WINDERMERE RD
ROBIN HOOD LA
Pav
Sch
Kingston Univ
Coombehurst (Kingston University)
BOWNESS CRES
RYDAL GDNS
Tenn Cts
Merton
COOMBE PL
RANDOLPH CL
COOMBE WOOD RD
COOMBE PK
KESWICK AVE
ROBIN HOOD WAY KINGSTON BY PASS
Allot Gdns
SW19
KINGSTON HILL
CORSCOMBE CL
COOMBE RIDINGS
PAGET PL
Pl Fld
Allot Gdns
Mill Corner
Warren House
KT2
FAIRLAWN CL
COTSWOLD CL
THE WATERGARDENS
Coombe Hill
WARREN PK
WARREN RD
SW20
178
Coombe Wood
RENFREW RD
HIGH COOMBE PL
WARREN CUTTING
THE LEIGH
GREENWOOD PK
ELLERTON RD
STOKE RD
CH
COOMBE HILL RD
HENLEY DR
Nat Res
GEORGE RD
COOMBE NEVILLE
EDGECOOMBE CL
GOLF CLUB DR
BEVERLEY LA
COOMBE HILL GLADE
PRESTON RD
Holy Cross Prep Sch
COOMBE END
MOOR PARK GDNS
DEVEY CL
WARBANK LA
HOOD RD
Coombe
THE DRIVE
GATEHOUSE CL
Schs
BALLARD CL
LORD CHANCELLOR WLK
COOMBE LA WEST
B283
FITZGEORGE AVE
OAKCOMBE CL
COOMBE BANK
WONFORD CL
New Victoria
A3
BEVERLEY AVE
HOLLAND AVE
MELVILLE AVE
BURDETT AVE
SOUTHWOOD AVE
WARREN RISE
COOMBE HOUSE CHASE
NEVILLE AVE
THE FAIRWAY
THE CHESTERS
Coombe Lane
COTTENHAM PARK RD
BROOK GDNS
COOMBE RISE
ORCHARD RISE
WEST RD
CROWN RD
Coombe Hill Jun & Inf Schs
THE MOAT
COOMBE LANE FLYOVER 1
BEVERLEY CT 2
BEVERLEY WAY KINGSTON BY PASS
WEST COOMBE AVE
A238
ALBION RD
BURGHLEY AVE
TRAPS LA
Pl Flds
BEECHCROFT AVE
CARDINAL CRES
WOODLANDS AVE
MATLOCK WAY
CROMFORD WAY
SOAMES WLK
BRANKSOME WAY
HIGH DR
BUXTON DR
BADGERS WLK
DICKERAGE RD
ARUNDEL RD
Coombe Girls Sch
BAKEWELL WAY
DARLEY DR
KT3
Coombe Brook
Malden
ELY CL
OVERDALE AVE
OAK RD
LANGLEY GR
CH
Tenn Cts
Sp Gd
Allot Gdns
OLIVER RD
CLARENCE AVE
ASH CL
BARTON GN
BURBERRY CL
CARLTON RD
SELBORNE RD
GOLF SIDE CL
ABOYNE DR
1 PERTH CL
2 HUNTLEY WAY
THE TRIANGLE
DICKERAGE HILL
MUYBRIDGE RD
MYRTLE GR
THE CLOSE
THE CRESCENT
LABURNUM GR
Allot Gdns
WOODSIDE RD
LAWN CL
ROWAN CL
DELL WLK
LINKSIDE
CAMBRIDGE AVE
MIDLETON RD
ASHCOMBE SQ
LONG WLK
THE GREEN
BEACONSFIELD RD
POPLAR GDNS
SYCAMORE GR
EDGAR CT
FORSYTH CT
HOPPINGWOOD AVE
ORCHARD AVE
ROSEBERY AVE
Allot Gdns
WARWICK RD
SALISBURY RD
Sch
COOMBE RD
69
20
21
22
199
MOUNT PLEASANT RD
Corpus Christi RC Prim Sch
LINCOLN AVE
ROSEMONT RD
POPLAR GR
LIME GR
ST MARY'S CT
LINCOLN CT
ALRIC AVE
BEECH GR
ELM RD
CRAMER CT
STAFFORD RD
CHESTNUT GR
CHESTNUT GROVE CT
PHOENIX CT
VANFAME CT
72
6
5
71
4
3
70
2
1

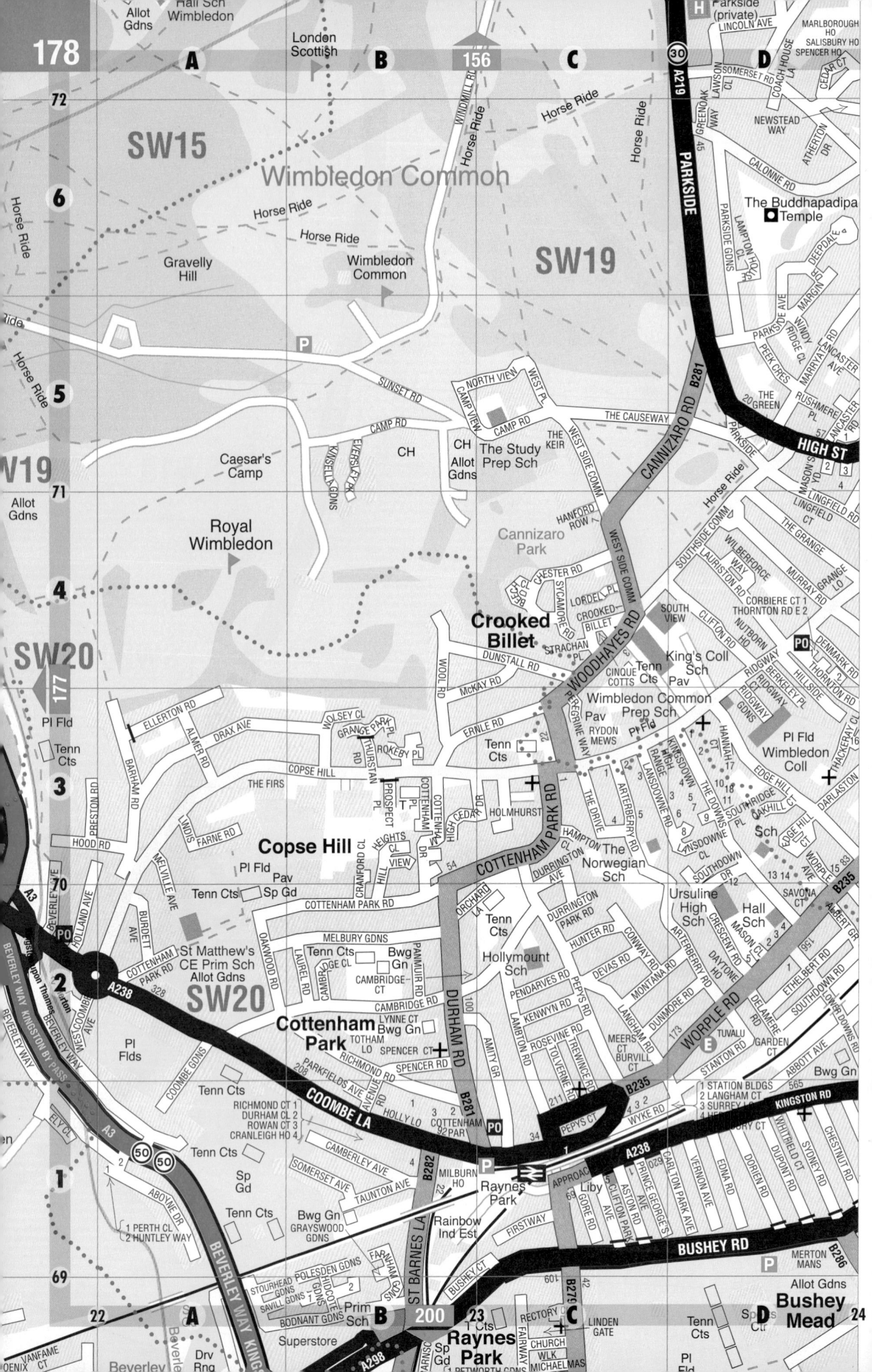

178
A
B
C
D
156
177
200
London Scottish
Hall Sch Wimbledon
Allot Gdns
SW15
SW19
SW20
Wimbledon Common
Horse Ride
Gravelly Hill
Wimbledon Common
Caesar's Camp
Royal Wimbledon
WINDMILL RD
SUNSET RD
CAMP RD
KINSELLA GDNS
EVERSLEY PK
CH
NORTH VIEW
CAMP VIEW
WEST PL
THE CAUSEWAY
THE KEIR
WEST SIDE COMM
CH
Allot Gdns
The Study Prep Sch
HANFORD ROW
Cannizaro Park
CANNIZARO RD
B281
PARKSIDE
A219
30
Parkside (private)
LINCOLN AVE
MARLBOROUGH HO
SALISBURY HO
SPENCER HO
SOMERSET RD
COACH HOUSE LA
CEDAR CT
GREENOAK WAY
LAWSON CL
NEWSTEAD WAY
ATHERTON DR
CALONNE RD
The Buddhapadipa Temple
PARKSIDE GDNS
LAMPTON HOUSE CL
DEEPDALE
MARGIN DR
PARKSIDE AVE
WINDY RIDGE CL
PEEK CRES
MARRYAT RD
LANCASTER AVE
THE GREEN
RUSHMERE PL
HIGH ST
LANCASTER RD
MASON'S YD
LINGFIELD RD
LINGFIELD CT
THE GRANGE
SOUTHSIDE COMM
WILBERFORCE WAY
LAURISTON RD
MURRAY RD
GRANGE LO
CORBIERE CT 1
THORNTON RD E 2
SOUTH VIEW
CLIFTON RD
NUTBORN HO
DENMARK RD
THORNTON RD
HILLSIDE
BERKELEY PL
RIDGWAY
RIDGWAY GDNS
King's Coll Sch
Tenn Cts
Pav
CINQUE COTTS
CHESTER RD
BEECH CL
SYCAMORE RD
LORDELL PL
CROOKED BILLET
Crooked Billet
STRACHAN PL
DUNSTALL RD
WOOL RD
McKAY RD
ERNLE RD
WOODHAYES RD
PEREGRINE WAY
RYDON MEWS
Wimbledon Common Prep Sch
Pav
Pl Fld
KINGSDOWN
HIGH RANGE
HANNAH CT
Pl Fld
Wimbledon Coll
THACKERAY CL
EDGE HILL
DARLASTON
OAKHILL CT
SOUTHRIDGE PL
EDGE HILL CT
Sch
WORPLE AVE
SAVONA CT
ELLERTON RD
DRAX AVE
ALMER RD
WOLSEY CL
GRANGE PARK PL
THURSTAN RD
ROKEBY PL
COPSE HILL
THE FIRS
BARHAM RD
PRESTON RD
HOOD RD
LINDISFARNE RD
PROSPECT PL
COTTENHAM PL
COTTENHAM DR
HIGH CEDAR DR
HOLMHURST
Copse Hill
HEIGHTS CL
HILL VIEW
CRANFORD CL
COTTENHAM PARK RD
THE DRIVE
ARTERBERRY RD
LANSDOWNE RD
THE DOWNS
LANSDOWNE CL
SOUTHDOWN DR
HAMPTON CL
The Norwegian Sch
DURRINGTON AVE
DURRINGTON PARK RD
Ursuline High Sch
Hall Sch
CRESCENT RD
MASON CL
B235
ALBERT GR
Pl Fld
Pav
Tenn Cts
Sp Gd
MELVILLE AVE
BURDETT AVE
HOLLAND AVE
BEVERLEY AVE
A3
PO
MELBURY GDNS
OAKWOOD RD
LAUREL RD
CAMBRIDGE CL
Tenn Cts
Bwg Gn
PANMUIR RD
CAMBRIDGE CT
ORCHARD LA
Tenn Cts
Hollymount Sch
HUNTER RD
CONWAY RD
DEVAS RD
PENDARVES RD
KENWYN RD
PEPYS RD
ROSEVINE RD
MONTANA RD
DUNMORE RD
ARTERBERRY RD
DAYTONE HO
DELAMERE RD
ETHELBERT RD
SOUTHDOWN RD
LOWER DOWNS RD
COTTENHAM PARK RD
St Matthew's CE Prim Sch
Allot Gdns
SW20
A238
WESTCOOMBE AVE
CAMBRIDGE RD
DURHAM RD
AMITY GR
LAMBTON RD
TOLVERNE RD
TREWINCE RD
MEERS CT
BURVILL CT
LANGHAM RD
WORPLE RD
TUVALU
STANTON RD
GARDEN CT
ABBOTT AVE
Bwg Gn
Cottenham Park
LYNNE CT
Bwg Gn
TOTHAM LO
SPENCER CT
RICHMOND RD
SPENCER RD
Pl Flds
COOMBE GDNS
PARKFIELDS AVE
AVENUE RD
HOLLY LO
COTTENHAM PAR
COOMBE LA
B281
PO
PEPYS CT
WYKE RD
1 STATION BLDGS
2 LANGHAM CT
3 SURREY LO
KINGSTON RD
WHITFIELD CT
SYDNEY RD
CHESTNUT RD
DUPONT RD
DORIEN RD
EDNA RD
VERNON AVE
CARLTON PARK AVE
PRINCE GEORGE'S AVE
ASTON RD
CLIFTON PARK AVE
GORE RD
Liby
APPROACH RD
BEVERLEY WAY
KINGSTON BY PASS
Kingston upon Thames
Merton
Tenn Cts
RICHMOND CT 1
DURHAM CL 2
ROWAN CT 3
CRANLEIGH HO 4
CAMBERLEY AVE
SOMERSET AVE
TAUNTON AVE
B282
MILBURN HO
Raynes Park
Tenn Cts
ELY CL
50
ABOYNE DR
1 PERTH CL
2 HUNTLEY WAY
Sp Gd
Tenn Cts
Bwg Gn
GRAYSWOOD GDNS
Rainbow Ind Est
FIRSTWAY
BUSHEY RD
B286
MERTON MANS
Allot Gdns
Bushey Mead
BEVERLEY WAY
ST BARNES LA
BUSHEY CT
POLESDEN GDNS
HIDCOTE GDNS
FARNHAM GDNS
STOURHEAD GDNS
SAVILL GDNS
BODNANT GDNS
Prim Sch
Superstore
A298
B279
RECTORY
LINDEN GATE
CHURCH WLK
Raynes Park
Sp Gd
FAIRWAY
Tenn Cts
Sports Ctr
Pl Fld
Drv Rng
Beverley
VANFAME CT
72
6
5
71
4
3
70
2
1
69
22
23
24

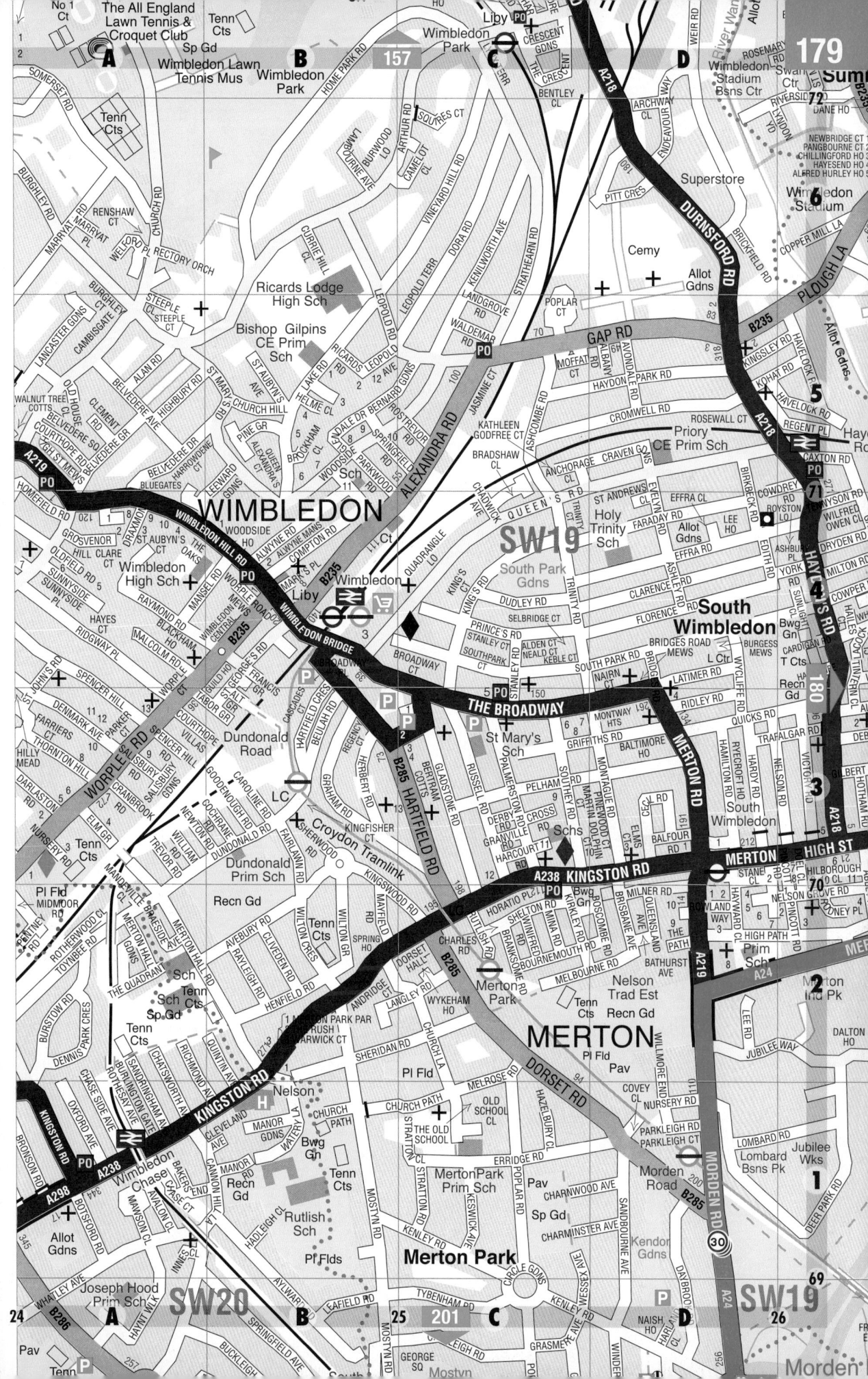

The All England Lawn Tennis & Croquet Club
Wimbledon Lawn Tennis Mus
Wimbledon Park
157
Liby
Wimbledon Park
A
B
C
D
Wimbledon Stadium Bsns Ctr
Wimbledon Stadium
Superstore
Cemy
Allot Gdns
Ricards Lodge High Sch
Bishop Gilpins CE Prim Sch
WIMBLEDON
Wimbledon High Sch
Wimbledon
SW19
South Park Gdns
Holy Trinity Sch
Priory CE Prim Sch
South Wimbledon
St Mary's Sch
Dundonald Road
Dundonald Prim Sch
Croydon Tramlink
Recn Gd
Merton Park
MERTON
Nelson Trad Est
Merton Ind Pk
Lombard Bsns Pk
Jubilee Wks
Morden Road
Merton Park Prim Sch
Rutlish Sch
Merton Park
Joseph Hood Prim Sch
SW20
Wimbledon Chase
Nelson
Kendor Gdns
Morden
180
201
DURNSFORD RD
GAP RD
ALEXANDRA RD
WIMBLEDON HILL RD
WORPLE RD
WIMBLEDON BRIDGE
THE BROADWAY
HARTFIELD RD
MERTON RD
KINGSTON RD
MERTON HIGH ST
HAYDONS RD
MORDEN RD
DORSET RD
PLOUGH LA
A218
A219
A238
A24
A298
B235
B285
B286
1
2
3
4
5
6
24
25
26
69
70
71
72

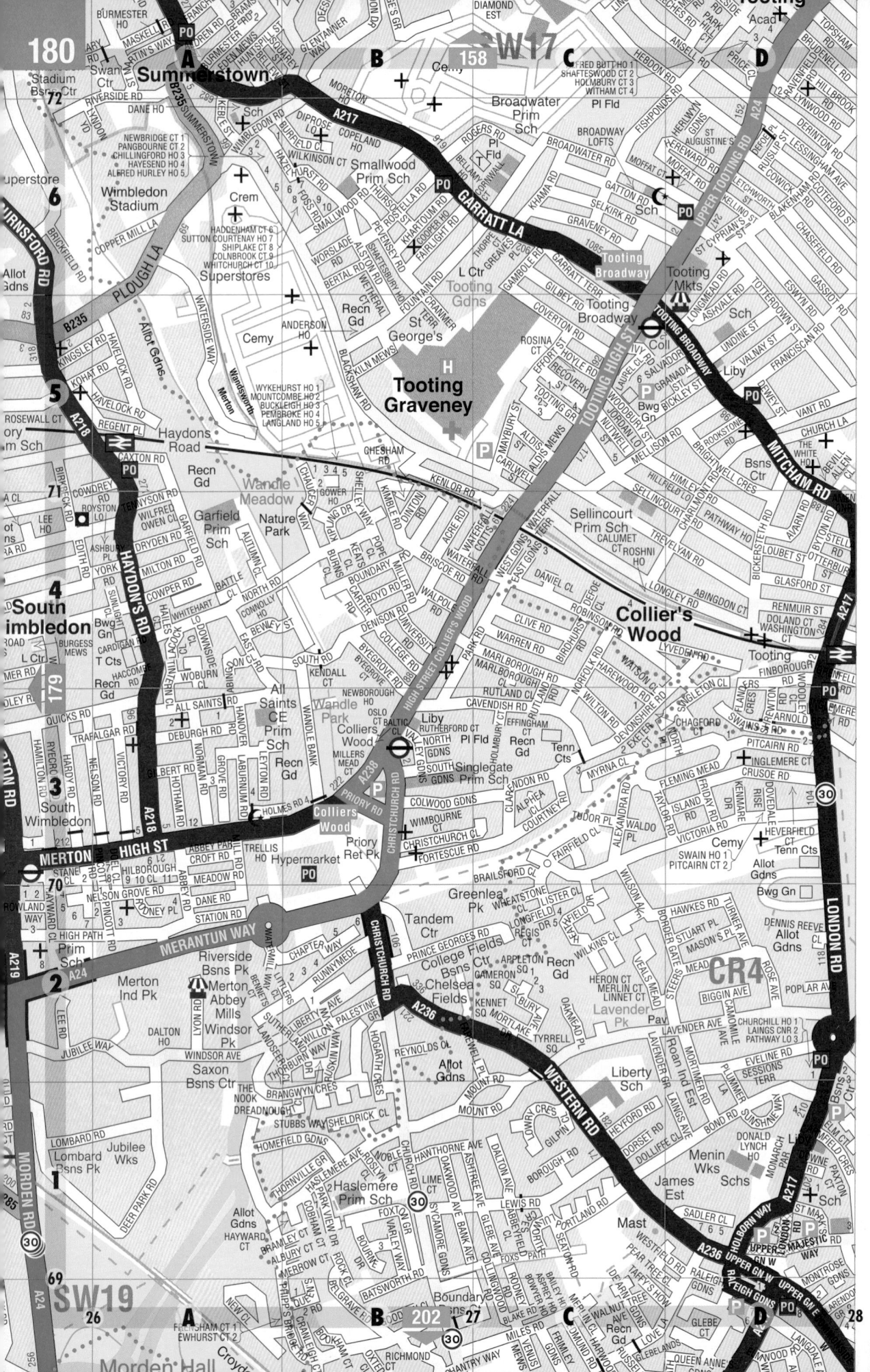
158
SW17
A
B
C
D
Summerstown
Tooting
Wimbledon Stadium
Superstores
Crem
Cemy
Smallwood Prim Sch
Broadwater Prim Sch
GARRATT LA
A217
A218
A219
A24
A236
A238
B235
PLOUGH LA
HAYDON'S RD
DURNSFORD RD
Tooting Broadway
UPPER TOOTING RD
TOOTING HIGH ST
TOOTING BROADWAY
MITCHAM RD
St George's
Tooting Graveney
Haydons Road
Wandle Meadow Nature Park
Garfield Prim Sch
South Wimbledon
All Saints CE Prim Sch
Wandle Park
Colliers Wood
Sellincourt Prim Sch
Collier's Wood
Singlegate Prim Sch
MERTON HIGH ST
MERANTUN WAY
Riverside Bsns Pk
Merton Ind Pk
Merton Abbey Mills
Windsor Pk
Saxon Bsns Ctr
Tandem Ctr
Greenlea Pk
College Fields Bsns Ctr
Chelsea Fields
Lavender Pk
CR4
Liberty Sch
WESTERN RD
LONDON RD
CHRISTCHURCH RD
Menin Wks
James Est
Roan Ind Est
Lombard Bsns Pk
Jubilee Wks
Haslemere Prim Sch
MORDEN RD
SW19
Morden Hall
179
202
26
27
28
1
2
3
4
5
6

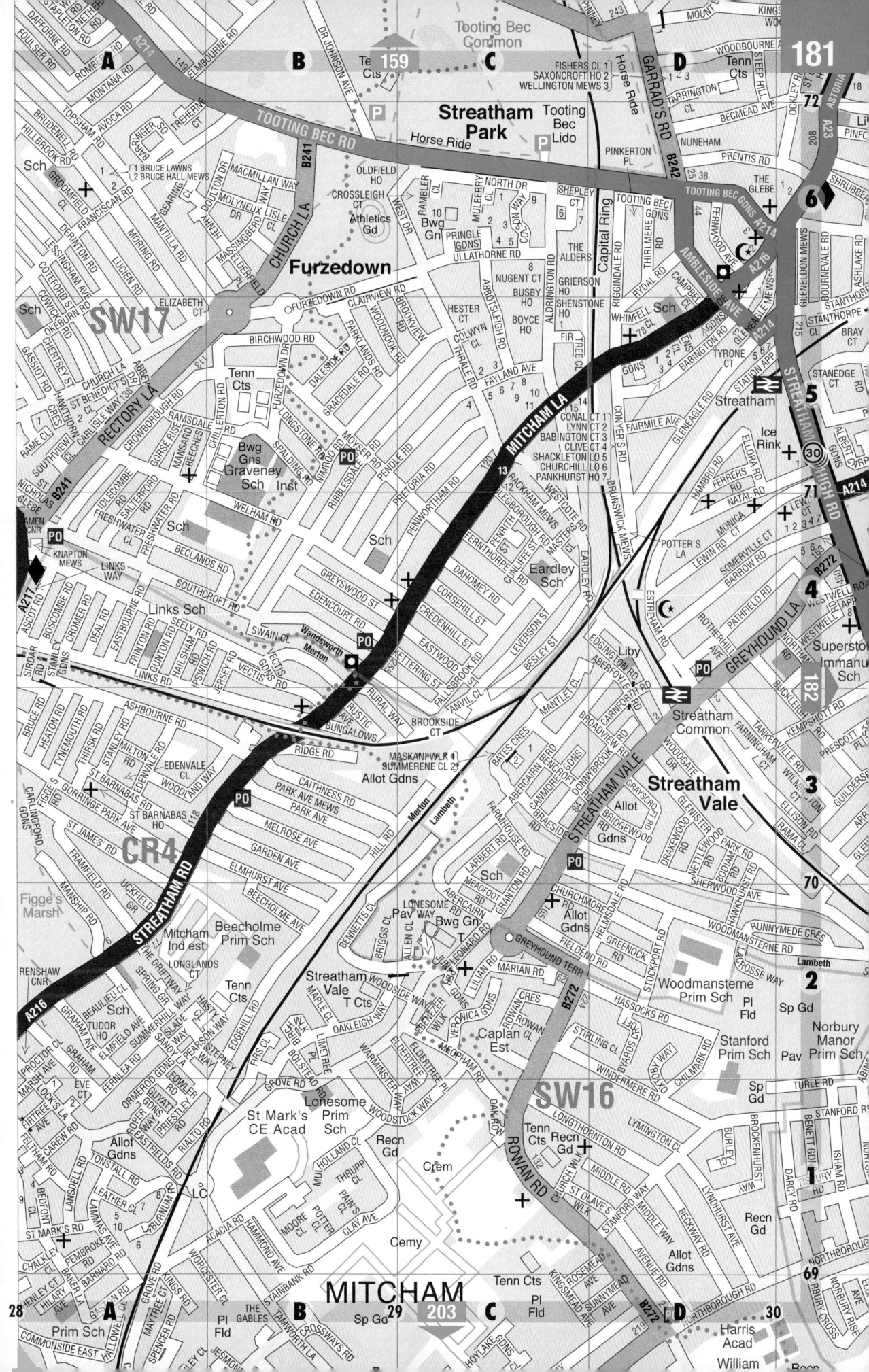

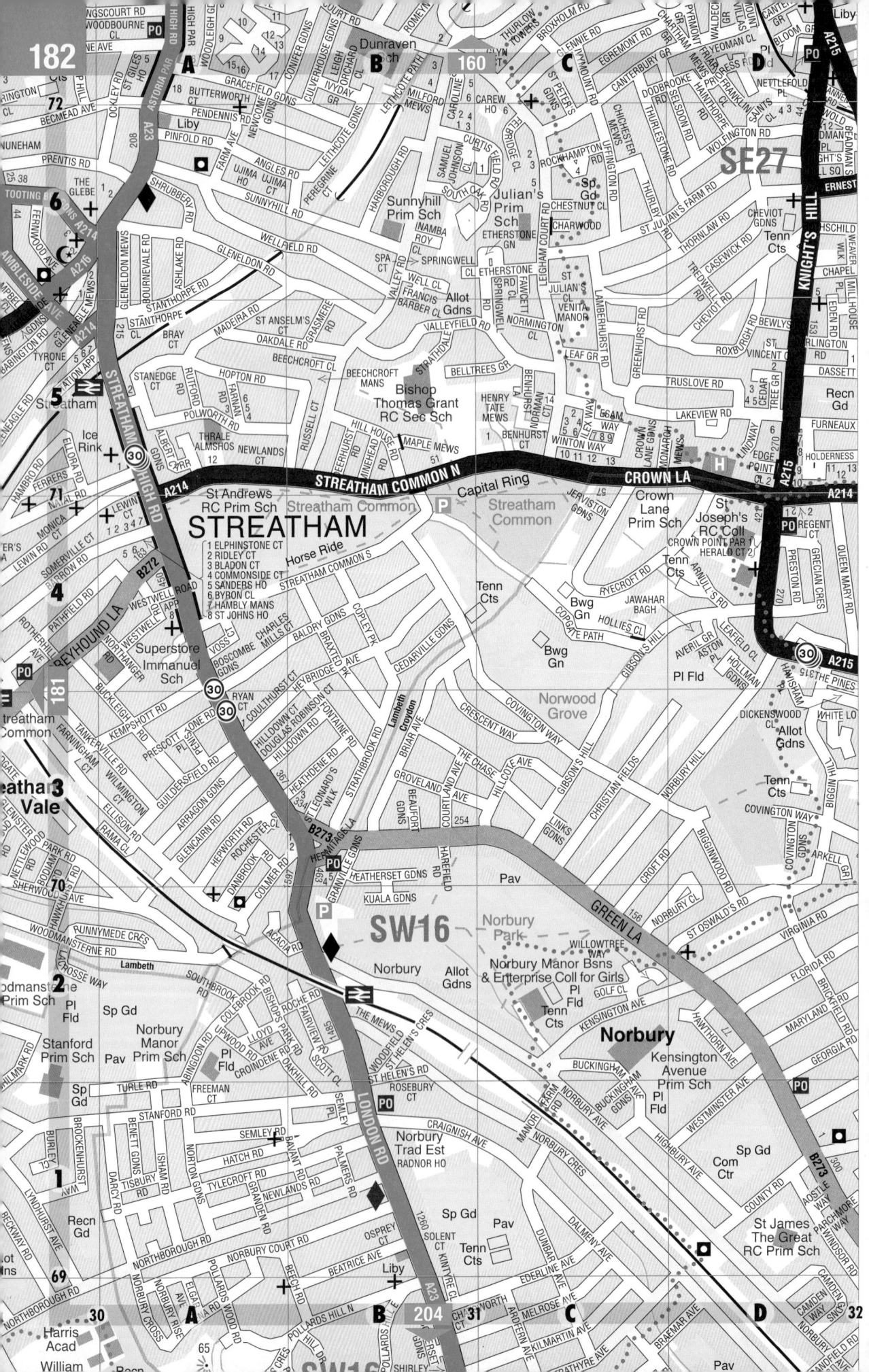
160
A
B
C
D
STREATHAM
SW16
SE27
Norbury
Streatham Common
Capital Ring
Horse Ride
STREATHAM COMMON N
STREATHAM COMMON S
STREATHAM HIGH RD
CROWN LA
GREEN LA
LONDON RD
KNIGHT'S HILL
GREYHOUND LA
ASTORIA PAR
A23
A214
A215
A216
B272
B273
St Andrews RC Prim Sch
1 ELPHINSTONE CT
2 RIDLEY CT
3 BLADON CT
4 COMMONSIDE CT
5 SANDERS HO
6 BYRON CL
7 HAMBLY MANS
8 ST JOHNS HO
Sunnyhill Prim Sch
Julian's Prim Sch
Bishop Thomas Grant RC Sec Sch
Crown Lane Prim Sch
St Joseph's RC Coll
Superstore
Immanuel Sch
Norwood Grove
Norbury Park
Norbury Manor Bsns & Enterprise Coll for Girls
Kensington Avenue Prim Sch
Norbury Manor Prim Sch
Stanford Prim Sch
Norbury Trad Est
St James The Great RC Prim Sch
Harris Acad
Dunraven Sch
Ice Rink
Allot Gdns
Tenn Cts
Bwg Gn
Pl Fld
Sp Gd
Recn Gd
Com Ctr
Pav
Liby
PO
Lambeth
Croydon
Streatham
Streatham Common
Streatham Vale
WELLFIELD RD
GLENELDON RD
VALLEYFIELD RD
HOPTON RD
NEWLANDS CT
COVINGTON WAY
CRESCENT WAY
GIBSON'S HILL
NORBURY HILL
CHRISTIAN FIELDS
BIGGINWOOD RD
KENSINGTON AVE
NORBURY AVE
NORBURY CRES
CRAIGNISH AVE
NORTHBOROUGH RD
NORBURY COURT RD
POLLARDS HILL N
ST OSWALD'S RD
VIRGINIA RD
FLORIDA RD
WESTMINSTER AVE
STANFORD RD
TURLE RD
SEMLEY RD
HATCH RD
TYLECROFT RD
NEWLANDS RD
HEYBRIDGE AVE
GUILDERSFIELD RD
ARRAGON GDNS
GLENCAIRN RD
KEMPSHOTT RD
ST JULIAN'S FARM RD
THORNLAW RD
LEIGHAM COURT RD
LAKEVIEW RD
TRUSLOVE RD
RYECROFT RD
COPGATE PATH
HOLLIES CL
WOODMANSTERNE RD
RUNNYMEDE CRES
LACROSSE WAY
204
30
31
32
181
72
71
70
69
6
5
4
3
2
1

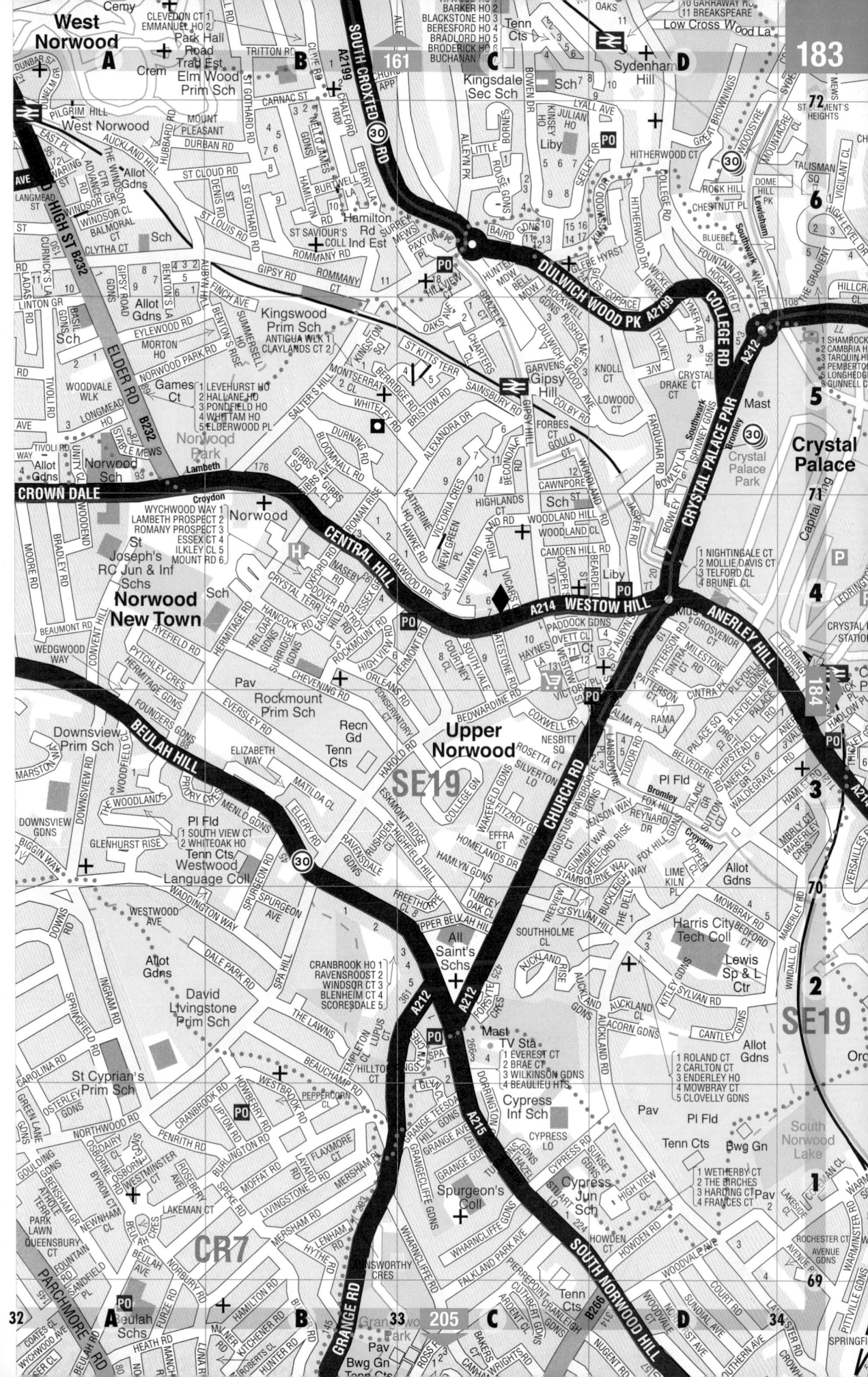
West Norwood
Cemy
Crem
Park Hall Road Trad Est
Elm Wood Prim Sch
Kingsdale Sec Sch
Sydenham Hill
Low Cross Wood La
161
A
B
C
D
SOUTH CROXTED RD
A2199
West Norwood
PILGRIM HILL
AUCKLAND HILL
DURBAN RD
ST CLOUD RD
ST GOTHARD RD
CARNAC ST
CHALFORD RD
HAMILTON RD
BERRY LA
Hamilton Rd
St Saviour's Coll Ind Est
ROMMANY RD
GIPSY RD
HIGH ST B232
ELDER RD
Allot Gdns
Sch
Kingswood Prim Sch
NORWOOD PARK RD
Games Ct
1 LEVEHURST HO
2 HALLANE HO
3 PONDFIELD HO
4 WHITTAM HO
5 ELDERWOOD PL
Norwood Park
Norwood Sch
Lambeth
Croydon
CROWN DALE
WYCHWOOD WAY 1
LAMBETH PROSPECT 2
ROMANY PROSPECT 3
ESSEX CT 4
ILKLEY CL 5
MOUNT RD 6
Norwood
St Joseph's RC Jun & Inf Schs
Norwood New Town
CENTRAL HILL
DULWICH WOOD PK
A2199
COLLEGE RD
HITHERWOOD DR
Gipsy Hill
GIPSY HILL
SAINSBURY RD
ALEXANDRA DR
HIGHLAND RD
WOODLAND RD
CRYSTAL PALACE PAR
A212
Mast
Crystal Palace
Crystal Palace Park
Capital Ring
1 NIGHTINGALE CT
2 MOLLIE DAVIS CT
3 TELFORD CL
4 BRUNEL CL
A214 WESTOW HILL
ANERLEY HILL
184
Mus
Upper Norwood
SE19
CHURCH RD
BEULAH HILL
Downsview Prim Sch
Rockmount Prim Sch
Recn Gd
Tenn Cts
Pl Fld
1 SOUTH VIEW CT
2 WHITEOAK HO
Westwood Language Coll
All Saint's Schs
Harris City Tech Coll
Lewis Sp & L Ctr
David Livingstone Prim Sch
CRANBROOK HO 1
RAVENSROOST 2
WINDSOR CT 3
BLENHEIM CT 4
SCORESDALE 5
Mast
TV Sta
1 EVEREST CT
2 BRAE CT
3 WILKINSON GDNS
4 BEAULIEU HTS
1 ROLAND CT
2 CARLTON CT
3 ENDERLEY HO
4 MOWBRAY CT
5 CLOVELLY GDNS
Cypress Inf Sch
Cypress Jun Sch
St Cyprian's Prim Sch
Spurgeon's Coll
A215
SE19
South Norwood Lake
1 WETHERBY CT
2 THE BIRCHES
3 HARDING CT
4 FRANCES CT
Bwg Gn
CR7
SOUTH NORWOOD HILL
GRANGE RD
PARCHMORE RD
Beulah Schs
Grangewood Park
Pav
32
33
34
205
1
2
3
4
5
6
69
70
71
72

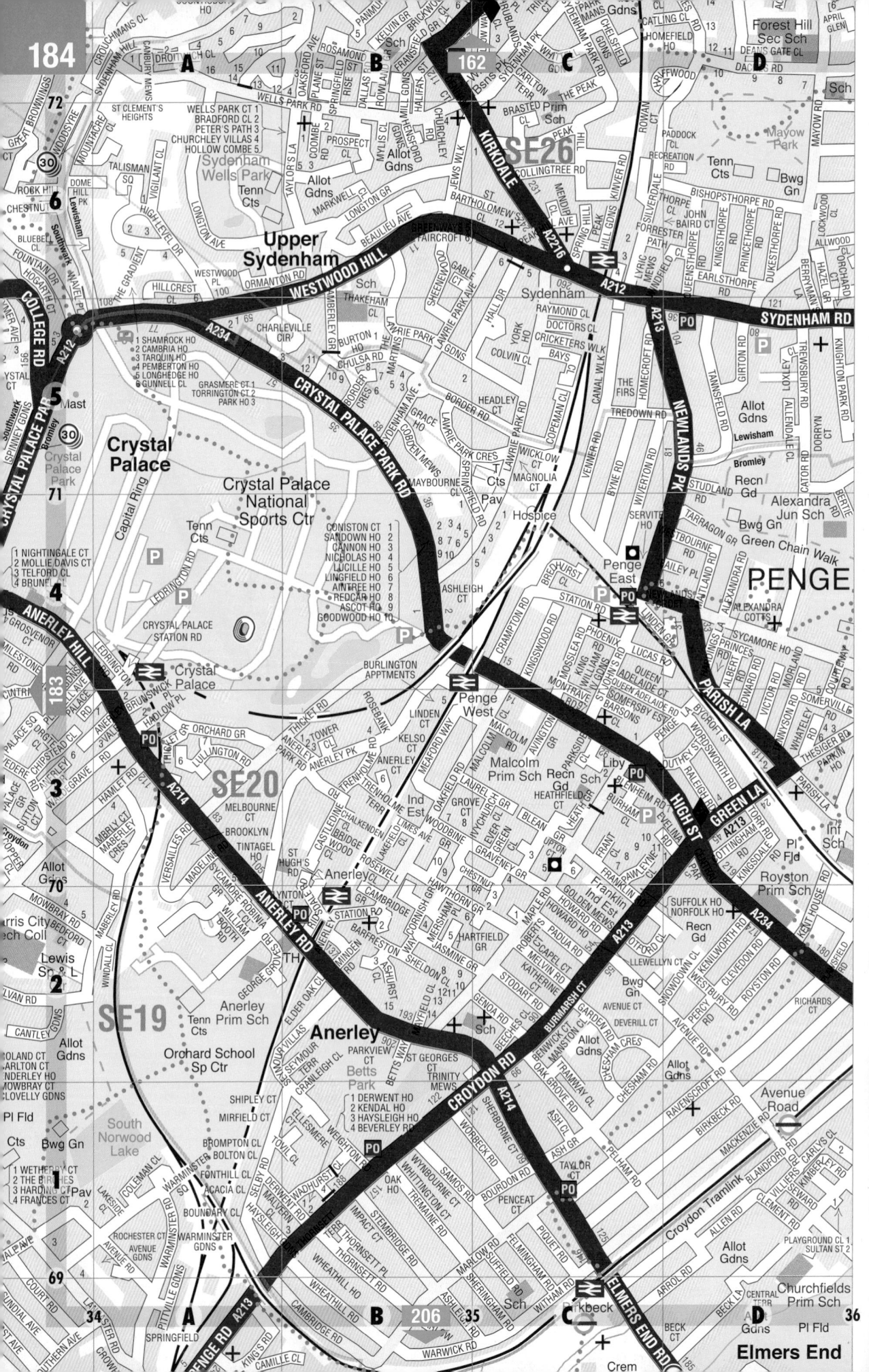
162
SE26
Sydenham Wells Park
Upper Sydenham
WESTWOOD HILL
KIRKDALE
SYDENHAM RD
Sydenham
Forest Hill Sec Sch
Mayow Park
COLLEGE RD
CRYSTAL PALACE PARK RD
Crystal Palace
Crystal Palace National Sports Ctr
Crystal Palace Park
Capital Ring
NEWLANDS PK
Penge East
PENGE
Alexandra Jun Sch
Green Chain Walk
ANERLEY HILL
183
Penge West
SE20
Malcolm Prim Sch
HIGH ST
GREEN LA
PARISH LA
Royston Prim Sch
ANERLEY RD
Anerley
SE19
Anerley Prim Sch
Orchard School Sp Ctr
Betts Park
South Norwood Lake
CROYDON RD
Avenue Road
Croydon Tramlink
Birkbeck
ELMERS END RD
Churchfields Prim Sch
Elmers End
206
Crem
A
B
C
D
34
35
36
72
71
70
69
6
5
4
3
2
1

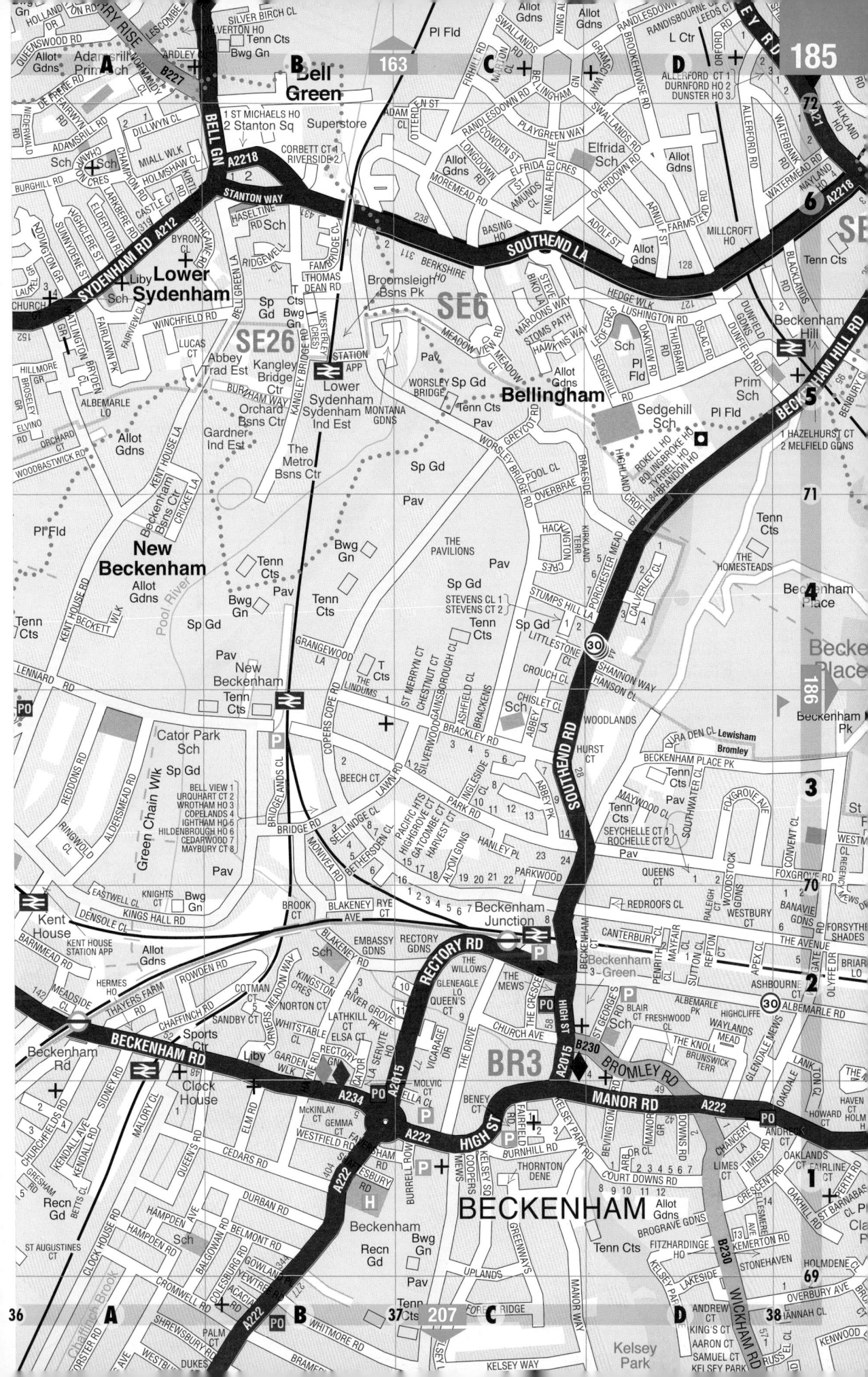

Bell Green
Lower Sydenham
SE26
SE6
Bellingham
New Beckenham
BR3
BECKENHAM
SOUTHEND LA
SYDENHAM RD
SOUTHEND RD
BECKENHAM HILL RD
BECKENHAM RD
MANOR RD
RECTORY RD
HIGH ST
BROMLEY RD
WICKHAM RD
STANTON WAY
Beckenham Junction
Kent House
Clock House
Beckenham Hill
Lower Sydenham
New Beckenham
Beckenham Place
Sedgehill Sch
Cator Park Sch
Elfrida Sch
Kelsey Park
Beckenham Recn Gd
Green Chain Wlk
Pool River
Chaffinch Brook
Lewisham
Bromley

163
186
207

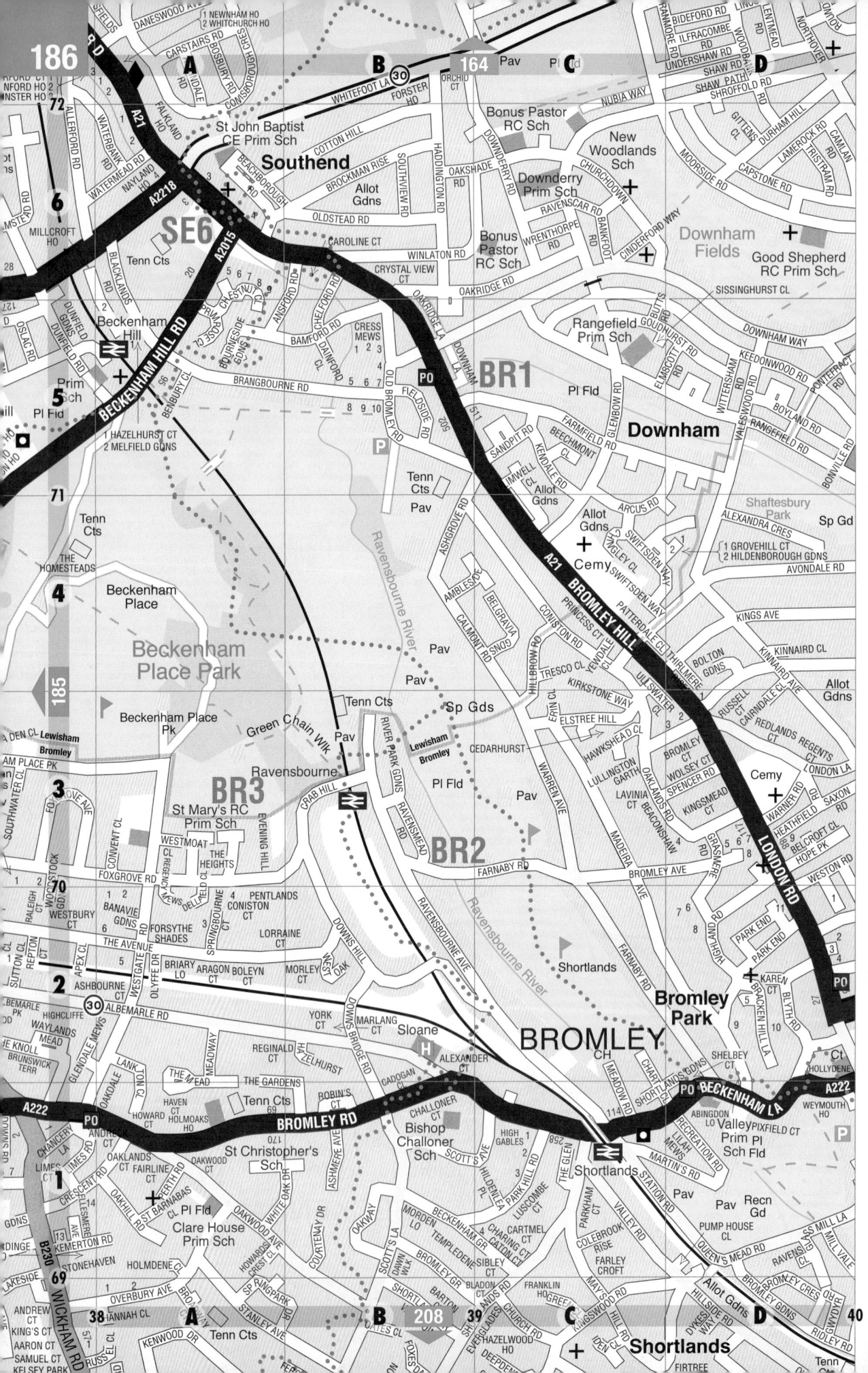

Southend
SE6
Beckenham Hill
BR1
Downham
Downham Fields
Beckenham Place Park
Ravensbourne
BR3
BR2
BROMLEY
Bromley Park
Shortlands
Sloane
St John Baptist CE Prim Sch
Bonus Pastor RC Sch
New Woodlands Sch
Downderry Prim Sch
Good Shepherd RC Prim Sch
Rangefield Prim Sch
St Mary's RC Prim Sch
Bishop Challoner Sch
St Christopher's Sch
Clare House Prim Sch
Valley Prim Sch
BECKENHAM HILL RD
BROMLEY HILL
LONDON RD
BROMLEY RD
BECKENHAM LA
Green Chain Wlk
Ravensbourne River
A21
A2218
A2015
A222
B230
WICKHAM RD
164
185
208

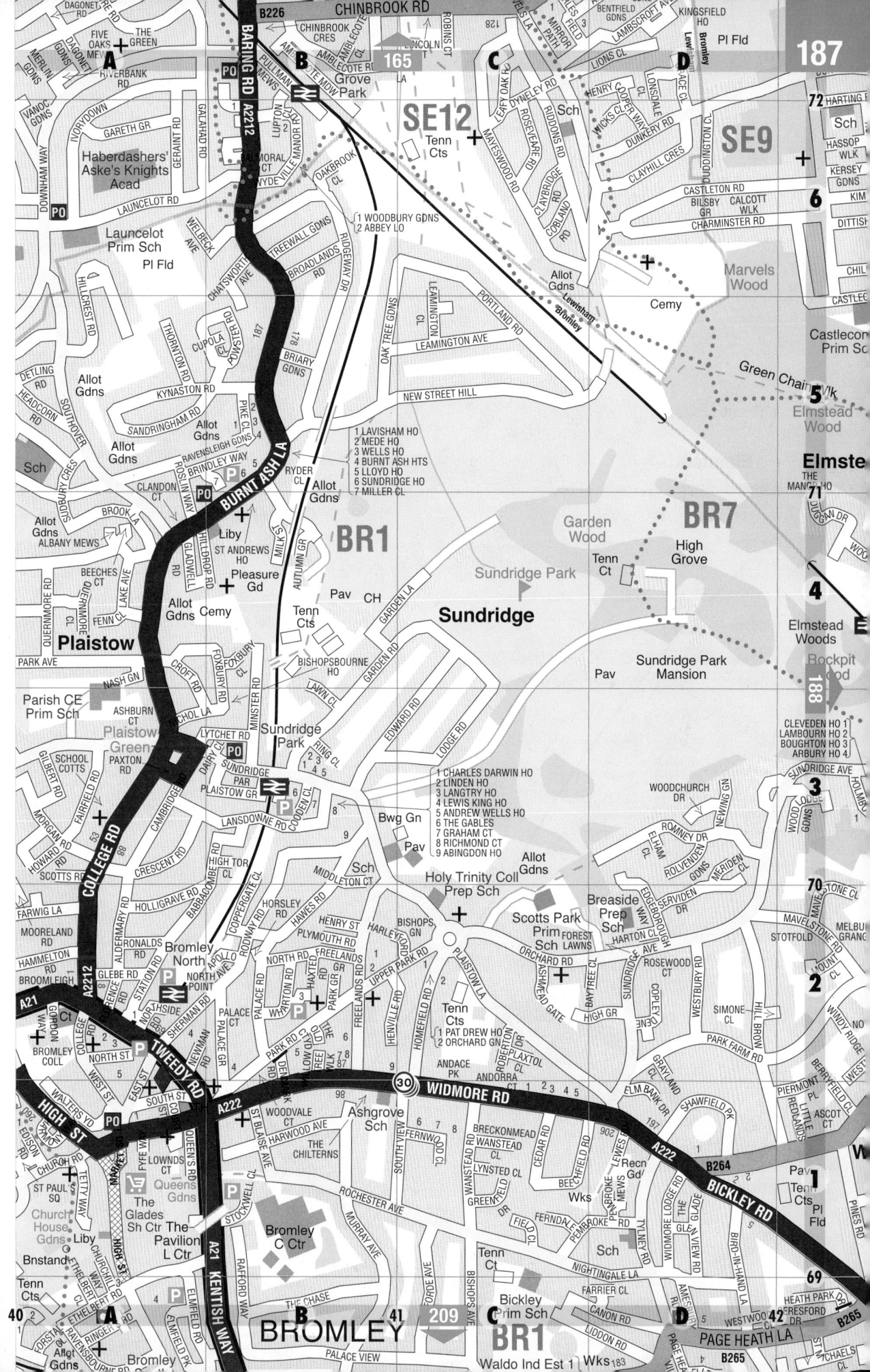
187
A
B
C
D
SE12
SE9
BR1
BR7
165
188
209
CHINBROOK RD
B226
BARING RD
A2212
CHINBROOK CRES
AMBLECOTE CL
AMBLECOTE RD
AMBLECOTE MDW
ROBINS CT
LINCOLN CT
PULLMAN MEWS
Grove Park
DAGONET RD
DAGONET GDNS
FIVE OAKS MEWS
THE GREEN
MERLIN GDNS
RIVERBANK RD
VANOC GDNS
IVORYDOWN
GARETH GR
GERAINT RD
GALAHAD RD
LUPTON CL
VILLE MANOR RD
BALMORAL CT
WYDE
OAKBROOK CL
Haberdashers' Aske's Knights Acad
DOWNHAM WAY
LAUNCELOT RD
Launcelot Prim Sch
Pl Fld
WELBECK AVE
TREEWALL GDNS
BROADLANDS RD
RIDGEWAY DR
1 WOODBURY GDNS
2 ABBEY LO
HILLCREST RD
CHATSWORTH AVE
THORNTON RD
CUPOLA CL
POWSTER RD
BRIARY GDNS
DETLING RD
HEADCORN RD
SOUTHOVER
Allot Gdns
KYNASTON RD
SANDRINGHAM RD
PIKE CL
RAVENSLEIGH GDNS
BRINDLEY WAY
BURNT ASH LA
ROSLIN WAY
CLANDON CT
RYDER CL
1 LAVISHAM HO
2 MEDE HO
3 WELLS HO
4 BURNT ASH HTS
5 LLOYD HO
6 SUNDRIDGE HO
7 MILLER CL
Sch
SUDBURY CRES
BROOK LA
ALBANY MEWS
Liby
ST ANDREWS HO
MILK ST
AUTUMN GR
HILLDROP RD
GLADWELL RD
Pleasure Gd
BEECHES CT
QUERNMORE RD
QUERNMORE CL
LAKE AVE
FENN CL
Cemy
Plaistow
PARK AVE
CROFT RD
FOXBURY RD
FOXBURY CL
MINSTER RD
NASH GN
Parish CE Prim Sch
ASHBURN CT
Plaistow Green
NICHOL LA
LYTCHET RD
DAIRY CL
SCHOOL COTTS
PAXTON RD
GILBERT RD
FAIRFIELD RD
CAMBRIDGE RD
SUNDRIDGE PAR
PLAISTOW GR
MORGAN RD
HOWARD RD
SCOTTS RD
COLLEGE RD
LANSDOWNE RD
CRESCENT RD
HIGH TOR CL
BABBACOMBE RD
COPPERGATE CL
HOLLIGRAVE RD
FARWIG LA
MOORELAND RD
HAMMELTON RD
BROOMLEIGH
ALDERMARY RD
ALDERONALDS RD
GLEBE RD
STATION RD
Bromley North
NORTH POINT
APOLLO AVE
SHERMAN RD
NORTHSIDE
A21
Ct
GORDON CT
COLLEGE RD
BROMLEY COLL
NORTH ST
TWEEDY RD
WEST ST
EAST ST
SOUTH ST
WALTERS YD
HIGH ST
EDISON
CHURCH RD
FYFE WAY
LOWNDS CT
QUEEN'S RD
Queens Gdns
ST PAUL'S SQ
TETTY WAY
MARKET SQ
The Glades Sh Ctr
The Pavilion L Ctr
Church House Gdns
Liby
Bnstand
CHURCHILL WAY
ETHELBERT RD
ETHELBERT CL
RINGERS RD
RAVENSBOURNE RD
FORSTAL CL
Allot Gdns
Bromley
A21 KENTISH WAY
ELMFIELD RD
ELMFIELD PK
RAFFORD WAY
THE CHASE
PALACE VIEW
BROMLEY
BR1
Waldo Ind Est
Wks
SE12
Tenn Cts
LEAFY OAK RD
DYNELEY RD
MAYESWOOD RD
ROSEVEARE RD
RIDDONS RD
CLAYBRIDGE RD
COBLAND RD
MIRROR PATH
BENTFIELD GDNS
LAMBSCROFT AVE
KINGSFIELD HO
LIONS CL
HENRY COOPER WAY
WICKS CL
LONSDALE CL
DUNKERY RD
CLAYHILL CRES
DUDDINGTON CL
CASTLETON RD
BILSBY GR
CALCOTT WLK
CHARMINSTER RD
HARTING RD
HASSOP WLK
KERSEY GDNS
DITTISHAM
Marvels Wood
Cemy
Lewisham
Bromley
LEAMINGTON CL
LEAMINGTON AVE
OAK TREE GDNS
PORTLAND RD
NEW STREET HILL
Castlecombe Prim Sch
Green Chain Wlk
Elmstead Wood
Elmstead
THE MANOR HO
DUGGAN DR
Garden Wood
Tenn Ct
High Grove
Sundridge Park
Sundridge
Pav
CH
Tenn Cts
GARDEN LA
GARDEN RD
BISHOPSBOURNE HO
LAWN CL
EDWARD RD
LODGE RD
RING CL
Sundridge Park
Elmstead Woods
Rockpit Wood
Sundridge Park Mansion
CLEVEDEN HO
LAMBOURN HO
BOUGHTON HO
ARBURY HO
SUNDRIDGE AVE
1 CHARLES DARWIN HO
2 LINDEN HO
3 LANGTRY HO
4 LEWIS KING HO
5 ANDREW WELLS HO
6 THE GABLES
7 GRAHAM CT
8 RICHMOND CT
9 ABINGDON HO
CODDEN CL
Bwg Gn
Pav
Allot Gdns
WOODCHURCH DR
NEWING GN
ROMNEY DR
ELHAM CL
ROLVENDEN GDNS
MERIDEN CL
WOOD LODGE GDNS
Holy Trinity Coll Prep Sch
MIDDLETON CT
Sch
HORSLEY RD
HAWES RD
HENRY ST
PLYMOUTH RD
HARLEYFORD
BISHOPS GN
Scotts Park Prim Sch
FOREST LAWNS
Breaside Prep Sch
EDGEBOROUGH WAY
SERVIDEN DR
HARTON CL
MAVELSTONE CL
MAVELSTONE RD
MELBURY GRANGE
STOTFOLD
MOUNT CL
WINDY RIDGE
ORCHARD RD
ASHMEAD GATE
BAYTREE CL
SUNDRIDGE AVE
ROSEWOOD CT
COPLEY DENE
WESTBURY RD
SIMONE CL
HILL BROW
PARK FARM RD
HIGH GR
NORTH RD
FREELANDS GR
FREELANDS RD
HAXTED RD
WHARTON RD
PARK GR
UPPER PARK RD
PLAISTOW LA
PALACE RD
PALACE CT
PALACE GR
NEWMAN RD
HENVILLE RD
HOMEFIELD RD
Tenn Cts
1 PAT DREW HO
2 ORCHARD GN
ROBERTON DR
PLAXTOL CL
ANDACE PK
ANDORRA CT
PARK RD
WILLOW CT
THE WLK
DENMARK RD
WIDMORE RD
A222
30
ELM BANK DR
GRAYLAND CL
SHAWFIELD PK
BERRYFIELD CL
PIERMONT PL
LITTLE REDLANDS
ASCOT CT
WOODVALE CT
HARWOOD AVE
ST BLAISE AVE
Ashgrove Sch
THE CHILTERNS
SOUTH VIEW
FERNWOOD CL
BRECKONMEAD
WANSTEAD CL
WANSTEAD RD
LYNSTED CL
GREENFIELD DR
CEDAR RD
BEECHFIELD RD
LEWES RD
PEMBROKE MEWS
Recn Gd
Wks
A222
B264
BICKLEY RD
Pav
Tenn Cts
Pl Fld
PINES RD
WIDMORE LODGE RD
THE GLADE
GLEN VIEW RD
BIRD-IN-HAND LA
ROCHESTER AVE
MURRAY AVE
STOCKWELL CL
Bromley C Ctr
FIELD CL
FERNDALE
PEMBROKE RD
TYLNEY RD
Sch
Tenn Ct
NIGHTINGALE LA
FARRIER CL
CANON RD
LIDDON RD
AMESBURY RD
Bickley Prim Sch
BISHOPS AVE
ORDE AVE
HEATH PARK DR
BERESFORD DR
WESTWOOD CL
B265
PAGE HEATH LA
ST MICHAELS CL
PAGE HEATH VILLAS
40
41
42
6
5
4
3
2
1
72
71
70
69

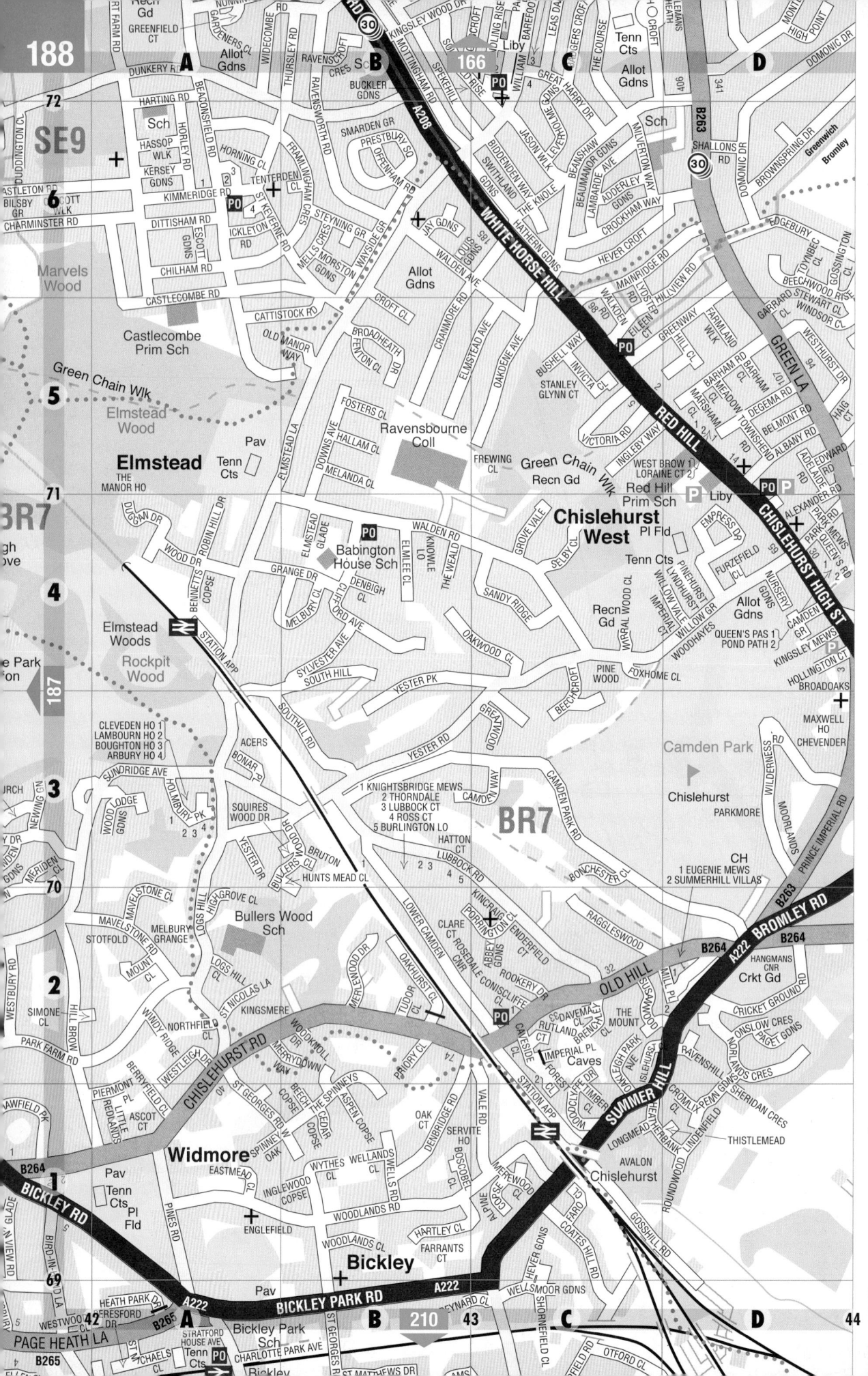

SE9
BR7
Elmstead
Chislehurst West
Widmore
Bickley
Chislehurst
Marvels Wood
Castlecombe Prim Sch
Green Chain Wlk
Elmstead Wood
Elmstead Woods
Rockpit Wood
Ravensbourne Coll
Babington House Sch
Bullers Wood Sch
Red Hill Prim Sch
Camden Park
Bickley Park Sch
WHITE HORSE HILL
RED HILL
CHISLEHURST HIGH ST
GREEN LA
OLD HILL
SUMMER HILL
BROMLEY RD
CHISLEHURST RD
BICKLEY PARK RD
BICKLEY RD
PAGE HEATH LA
A208
A222
B263
B264
B265
166
187
210
44

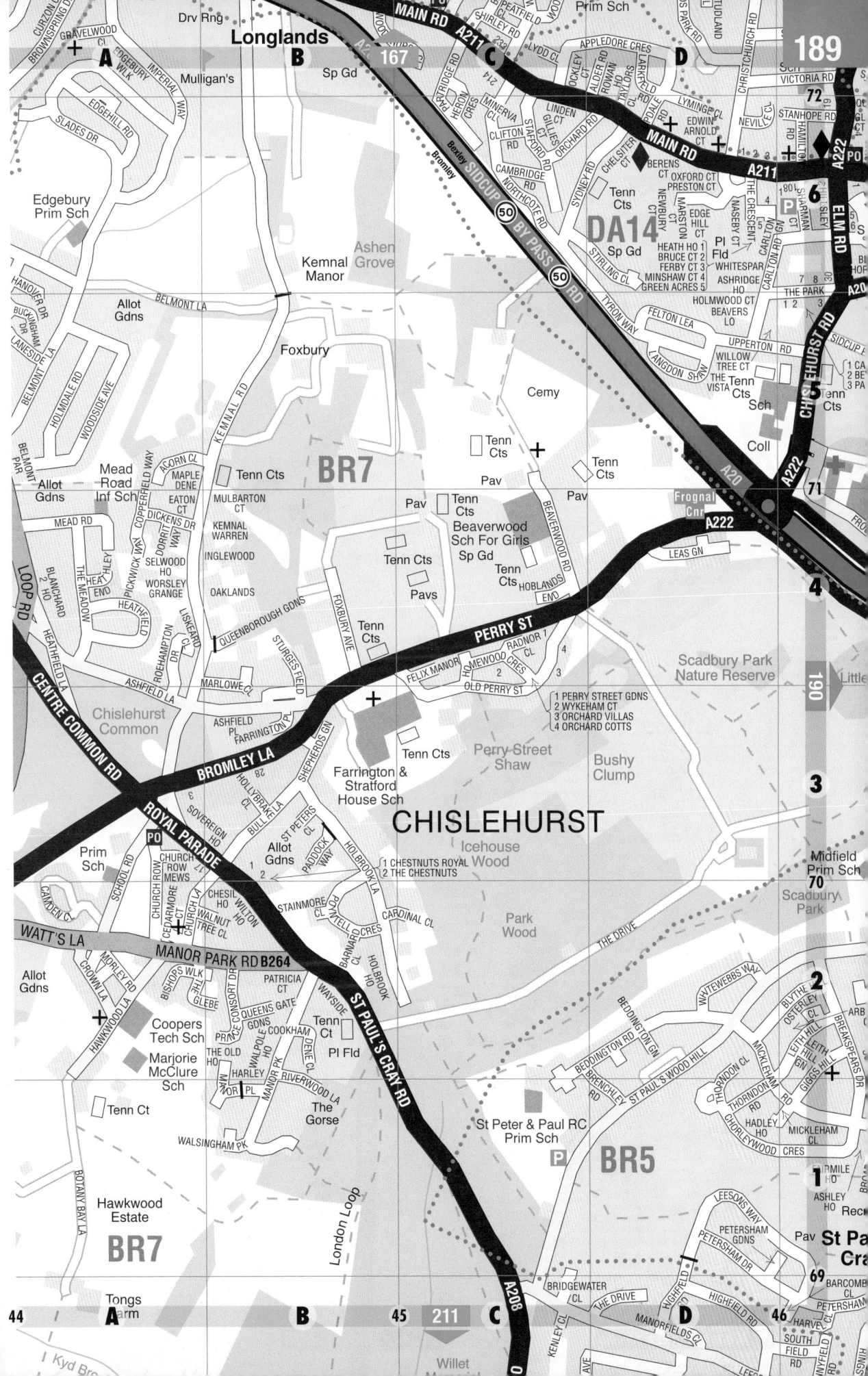

Longlands

MAIN RD A211

SHIRLEY RD
PEATFIELD

Prim Sch

APPLEDORE CRES

D

VICTORIA RD

72

Bexley SIDCUP BY PASS RD

MAIN RD

A211

DA14

A222

PO

6

Edgebury
Prim Sch

Ashen
Grove

Kemnal
Manor

THE PARK

A20

THE
VISTA

Tenn
Cts

A222

71

Belmont La

Foxbury

Cemy

Tenn
Cts

Tenn
Cts

Frognal
Cnr

A222

Allot
Gdns

Tenn Cts

BR7

Pav

Tenn
Cts

Pav

Pav

Tenn
Cts

Mead
Road
Inf Sch

Tenn Cts

Beaverwood
Sch For Girls
Sp Gd

LEAS GN

Tenn
Cts

4

190

Tenn
Cts

Tenn
Cts

PERRY ST

Scadbury Park
Nature Reserve

Little

Chislehurst
Common

Tenn
Cts

OLD PERRY ST

1 PERRY STREET GDNS
2 WYKEHAM CT
3 ORCHARD VILLAS
4 ORCHARD COTTS

3

BROMLEY LA

Tenn Cts

Perry Street
Shaw

Bushy
Clump

ROYAL PARADE

Prim
Sch

CHISLEHURST

Icehouse
Wood

1 CHESTNUTS ROYAL
2 THE CHESTNUTS

Midfield
Prim Sch

70

Park
Wood

Scadbury
Park

WATT'S LA

MANOR PARK RD B264

THE DRIVE

Allot
Gdns

Tenn
Ct

Pl Fld

2

Coopers
Tech Sch

BEDDINGTON RD

ST PAUL'S WOOD HILL

Marjorie
McClure
Sch

Tenn Ct

The
Gorse

St Peter & Paul RC
Prim Sch

BR5

1

WALSINGHAM PK

Hawkwood
Estate

BR7

London Loop

A208

69

Tongs
Farm

44 A

B

45 211 C

D 46

St Pa
Cra

Kyd Bro

Willet

ST PAUL'S CRAY RD

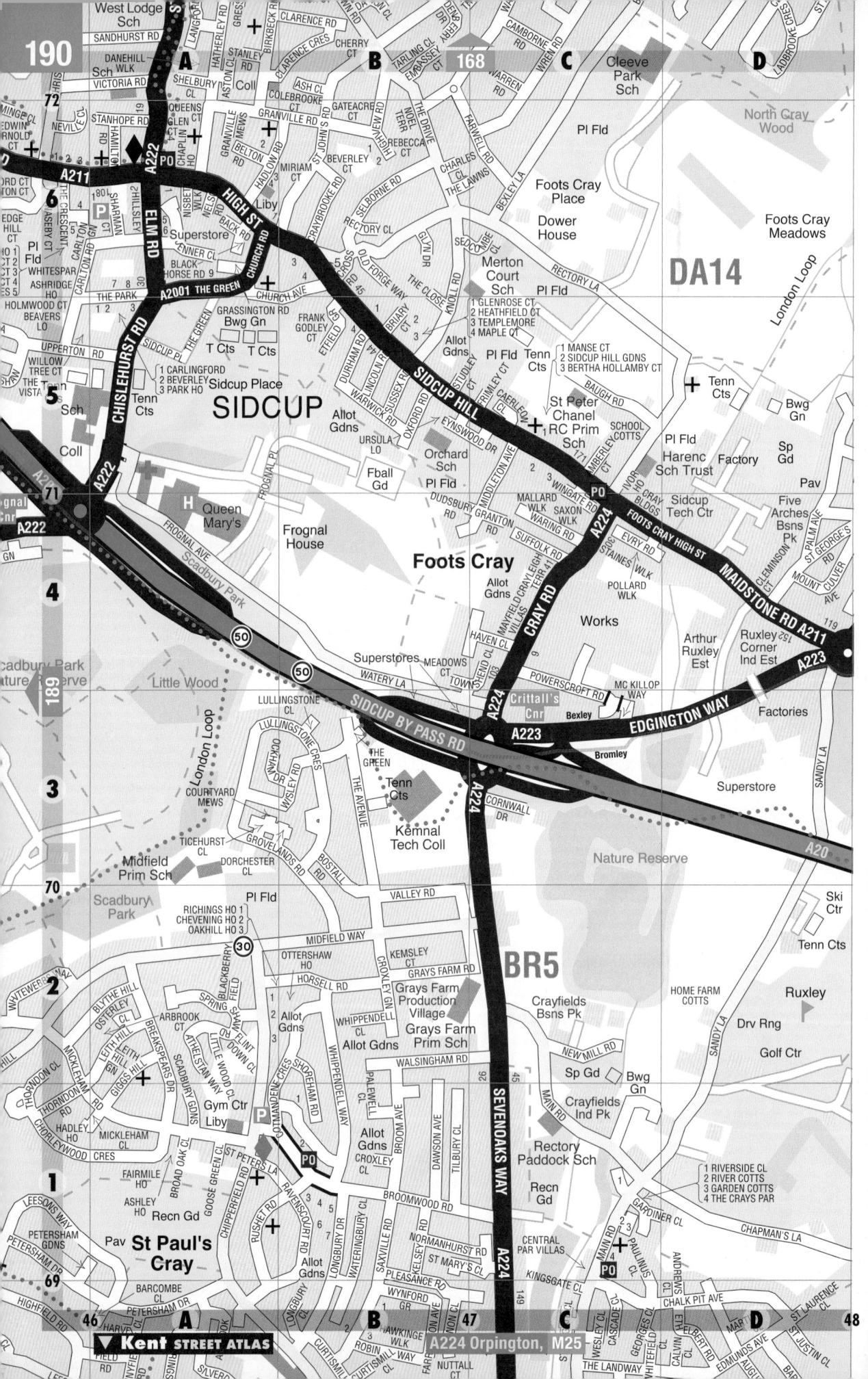
SIDCUP
Foots Cray
St Paul's Cray
DA14
BR5
168
189
A
B
C
D
72
6
5
4
3
70
2
1
69
46
47
48
A211
A222
A2001
A223
A224
A20
HIGH ST
ELM RD
CHISLEHURST RD
SIDCUP HILL
FOOTS CRAY HIGH ST
MAIDSTONE RD A211
CRAY RD
EDGINGTON WAY
SIDCUP BY PASS RD
SEVENOAKS WAY
West Lodge Sch
Cleeve Park Sch
North Cray Wood
Foots Cray Place
Dower House
Foots Cray Meadows
Merton Court Sch
Sidcup Place
Queen Mary's
Frognal House
Scadbury Park
Little Wood
London Loop
St Peter Chanel RC Prim Sch
Orchard Sch
Harenc Sch Trust
Sidcup Tech Ctr
Five Arches Bsns Pk
Arthur Ruxley Est
Ruxley Corner Ind Est
Crittall's Cnr
Kemnal Tech Coll
Nature Reserve
Midfield Prim Sch
Grays Farm Production Village
Grays Farm Prim Sch
Crayfields Bsns Pk
Crayfields Ind Pk
Rectory Paddock Sch
Ruxley
Golf Ctr
Ski Ctr
Superstore
Superstores
Factories
Works
A224 Orpington, M25

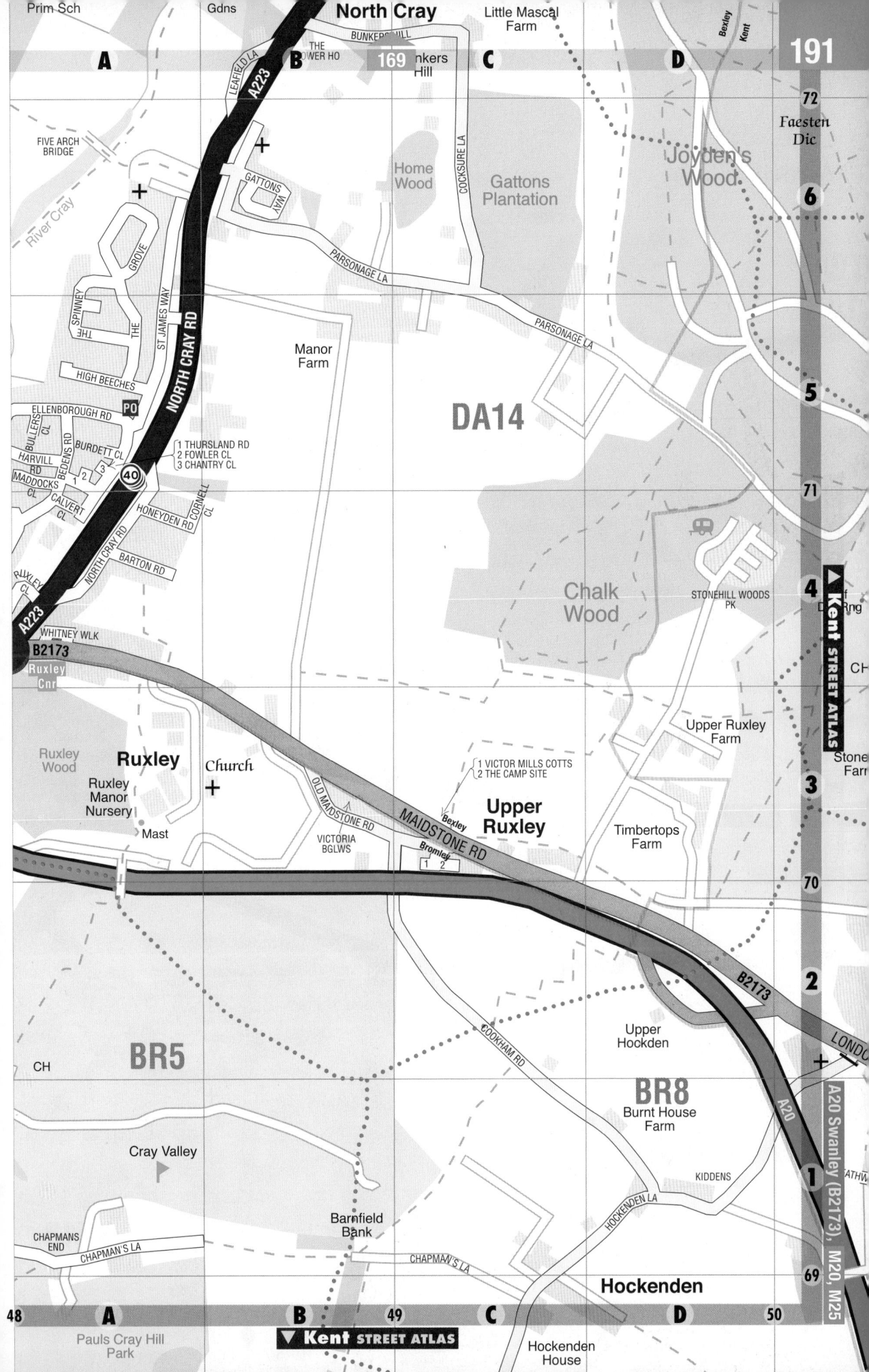

North Cray

Prim Sch

Gdns

Little Mascal Farm

Bexley Kent

72

Faesten Dic

FIVE ARCH BRIDGE

Home Wood

Gattons Plantation

Joyden's Wood

6

River Cray

LEAFIELD LA

A223

THE TOWER HO

Bunkers Hill

COCKSURE LA

THE SPINNEY

THE GROVE

ST JAMES WAY

GATTONS WAY

PARSONAGE LA

PARSONAGE LA

5

HIGH BEECHES

NORTH CRAY RD

Manor Farm

DA14

ELLENBOROUGH RD

PO

BULLERS CL

BEDENS RD

BURDETT CL

1 THURSLAND RD
2 FOWLER CL
3 CHANTRY CL

71

HARVILL RD

MADDOCKS CL

CALVERT CL

40

HONEYDEN RD

CORNELL CL

BARTON RD

RUXLEY CL

A223

Chalk Wood

STONEHILL WOODS PK

4

Stone Rng

CH

WHITNEY WLK

B2173

Ruxley Cnr

Upper Ruxley Farm

Stone Farm

Ruxley Wood

Ruxley

Church

OLD MAIDSTONE RD

MAIDSTONE RD

Bexley

1 VICTOR MILLS COTTS
2 THE CAMP SITE

3

Ruxley Manor Nursery

Mast

VICTORIA BGLWS

Bromley

1 2

Upper Ruxley

Timbertops Farm

70

BR5

COOKHAM RD

Upper Hockden

B2173

2

LONDO

CH

Cray Valley

BR8

Burnt House Farm

A20

A20 Swanley (B2173), M20, M25

1

KIDDENS

CHAPMANS END

CHAPMAN'S LA

Barnfield Bank

CHAPMAN'S LA

HOCKENDEN LA

69

Hockenden

Pauls Cray Hill Park

Hockenden House

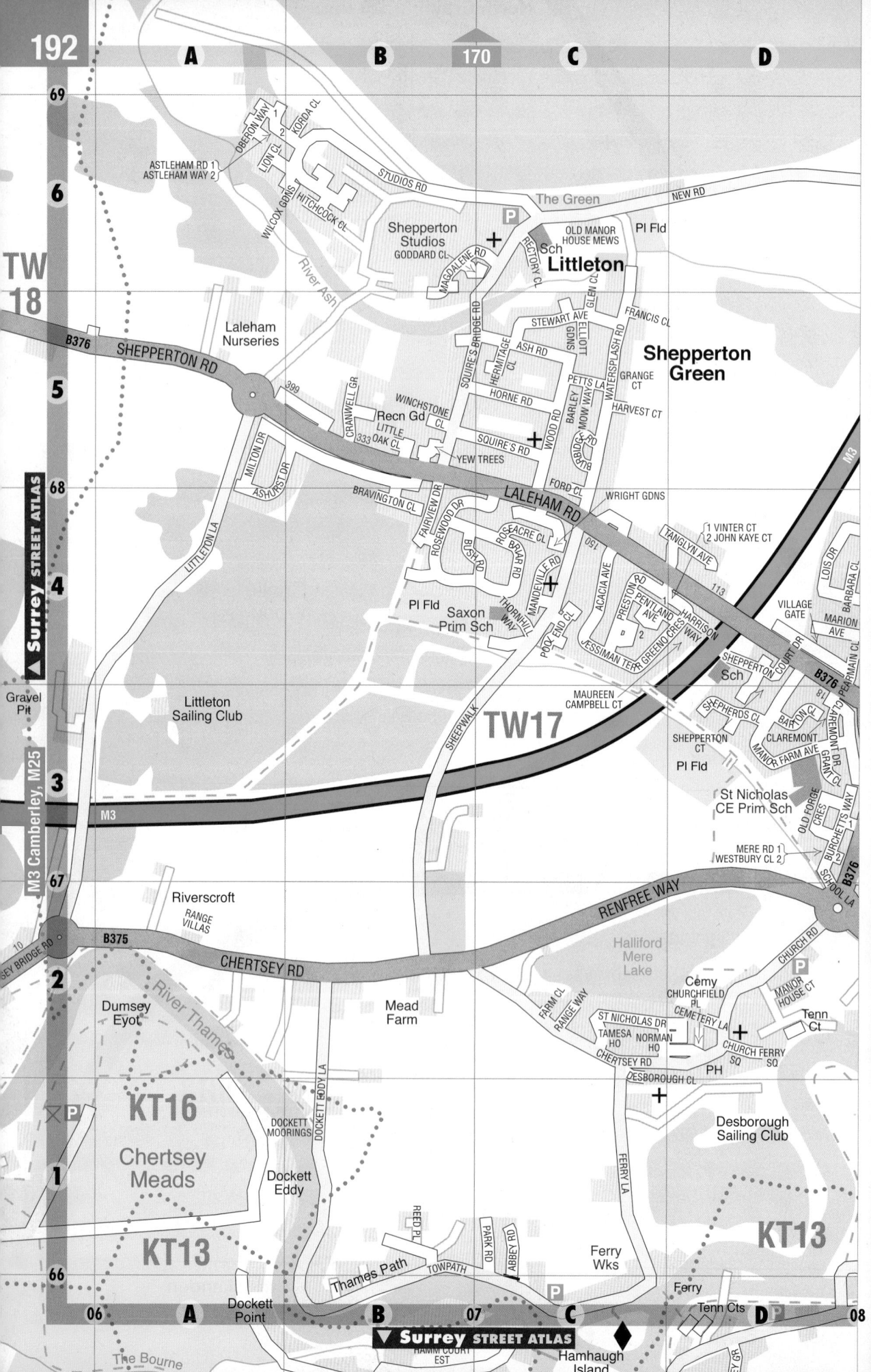

A   B   **170**   C   D

69

6

**TW
18**

▲ **Surrey** STREET ATLAS

M3 Camberley, M25

OBERON WAY
1 KORDA CL
LION CL
2
WILCOX GDNS
HITCHCOCK CL

ASTLEHAM RD 1
ASTLEHAM WAY 2

STUDIOS RD

The Green   NEW RD

P

OLD MANOR
HOUSE MEWS   Pl Fld

Shepperton
Studios   Sch   **Littleton**
GODDARD CL   MAGDALENE RD

River Ash

Laleham
Nurseries

GLEN CL   FRANCIS CL

STEWART AVE   ELLIOTT
GDNS

**Shepperton
Green**

B376   **SHEPPERTON RD**

399

MILTON DR   CRANWELL GR   WINCHSTONE
CL   HERMITAGE
CL   ASH RD   WATERSPLASH RD   GRANGE
CT

Recn Gd   HORNE RD   PETTS LA   HARVEST CT

ASHURST DR   LITTLE
OAK CL   WOOD RD

68   333   SQUIRE'S RD   YEW TREES   BRIDGE
MOW LANE

FAIRVIEW DR   FORD CL
BRAVINGTON CL   **LALEHAM RD**   WRIGHT GDNS

ROSEWOOD DR   1 VINTER CT
2 JOHN KAYE CT

LITTLETON LA   BUSH RD   ROSACRE CL   BRIAR RD   150   TANGLYN AVE

113

4   MANDEVILLE RD   LOIS DR   BARBARA CL

Pl Fld   Saxon
Prim Sch   THORNHILL
WAY   ACACIA AVE   PRESTON
RD   PENTLAND
AVE   HARRISON
WAY   MARION
AVE

POX END CL   JESSIMAN TERR   GREENO CRES   VILLAGE
GATE

Gravel
Pit   Littleton
Sailing Club   D   2   SHEPPERTON
Sch   B376

MAUREEN
CAMPBELL CT   COURT DR   PEPPERMAIN CL
81

TW17   SHEPHERDS CL   CLAREMONT
GRANT CL   BARTON CL   CLAREMONT

SHEPPERTON
CT

M3   St Nicholas
CE Prim Sch

OLD FORGE
CRES   BURCHETTS WAY   SCHOOL LA

67   Pl Fld   MERE RD 1
WESTBURY CL 2   B376

Riverscroft   RENFREE WAY
RANGE
VILLAS

B375   Halliford
Mere Lake   CHURCH RD   P

2   **CHERTSEY RD**   FARM CL   Cemy   CHURCHFIELD
PL   MANOR
HOUSE CT

River Thames   Mead
Farm   RANGE WAY   CEMETERY LA   Tenn
Ct

Dumsey
Eyot   ST NICHOLAS DR   CHURCH FERRY
SQ
TAMESA
HO   NORMAN
HO   PH

Littleton
Sailing Club   CHERTSEY RD

DESBOROUGH CL

KT16   DOCKETT
MOORINGS   DOCKETT EDDY LA   FERRY LA   Desborough
Sailing Club

P   **Chertsey
Meads**   Dockett
Eddy

1

KT13   REED PL   PARK RD   ABBEY RD   Ferry
Wks   **KT13**

66   Thames Path   TOWPATH   P   Ferry   Tenn Cts

06   A   Dockett
Point   B   **07**   C   D   08

HAMM COURT
EST   Hamhaugh
Island

The Bourne

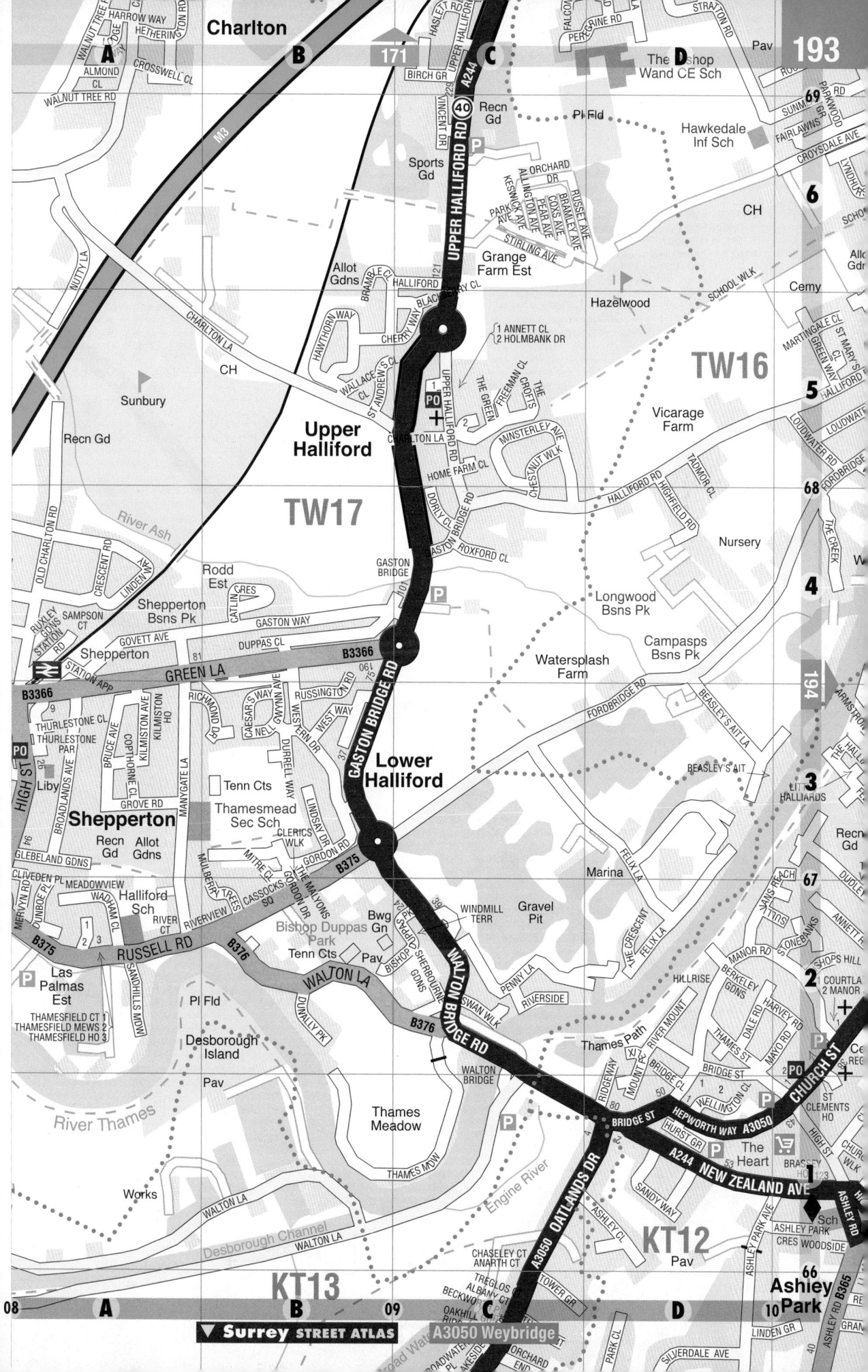
Charlton
A
B
171
C
D
The Bishop Wand CE Sch
Pav
HARROW WAY
HETHERINGTON RD
WALNUT TREE RD
ALMOND CL
CROSSWELL CL
BIRCH GR
UPPER HALLIFORD RD
A244
VINCENT DR
Recn Gd
PERREGRINE RD
STRATTON RD
Pl Fld
Hawkedale Inf Sch
PARKWOOD RD
SUNMEAD
FAIRLAWNS
CROYSDALE AVE
M3
Sports Gd
ORCHARD DR
PARK AVE
ALLINGTON AVE
KESWICK AVE
PEAR AVE
COXS AVE
BRAMLEY AVE
RUSSET AVE
STIRLING AVE
Grange Farm Est
CH
6
NUTTY LA
Allot Gdns
BRAMBLE CL
HALLIFORD CL
BLACKBERRY CL
Hazelwood
SCHOOL WLK
Cemy
HAWTHORN WAY
CHERRY WAY
CHARLTON LA
1 ANNETT CL
2 HOLMBANK DR
MARTINGALE CL
ST MARY'S CL
GREEN WAY
TW16
WALLACE CL
ST ANDREW'S CL
PO
THE GREEN
FREEMAN CL
THE CROFTS
Sunbury
Upper Halliford
Vicarage Farm
HALLIFORD CL
5
LOUDWATER RD
Recn Gd
MINSTERLEY AVE
CHESTNUT WLK
HOME FARM CL
HALLIFORD RD
TADMOR CL
HIGHFIELD RD
68
FORDBRIDGE RD
TW17
OLD CHARLTON RD
River Ash
CRESCENT RD
LINDEN WAY
DORLY CL
GASTON BRIDGE RD
ROXFORD CL
Nursery
THE CREEK
GASTON BRIDGE
Rodd Est
CATLIN CRES
Shepperton Bsns Pk
Longwood Bsns Pk
4
RUXLEY GDNS
SAMPSON CT
STATION RD
GASTON WAY
GOVETT AVE
DUPPAS CL
Campasps Bsns Pk
Shepperton
B3366
Watersplash Farm
GREEN LA
STATION APP
194
B3366
THURLESTONE CL
THURLESTONE PAR
BRUCE AVE
KILMISTON AVE
KILMISTON HO
RICHMOND DR
CAESAR'S WAY
NELL GWYNN AVE
RUSSINGTON RD
WEST WAY
WESTERN DR
FORDBRIDGE RD
BEASLEY'S AIT LA
ARMSTRONG
PO
COPTHORNE CL
MANYGATE LA
DURRELL WAY
Lower Halliford
BEASLEY'S AIT
HIGH ST
BROADLANDS AVE
Liby
Tenn Cts
3
LITTLE HALLIARDS
GROVE RD
Thamesmead Sec Sch
LINDSAY DR
Shepperton
Recn Gd
Allot Gdns
CLERICS WLK
Recn Gd
GLEBELAND GDNS
MITRE CL
GORDON RD
B375
Marina
FELIX LA
67
CLIVEDEN PL
MEADOWVIEW
MERVYN RD
DUNBOE PL
WADHAM CL
Halliford Sch
RIVER CT
MULBERRY TREES
RIVERVIEW
CASSOCKS SQ
GORDON DR
THE MALYONS
Bwg Gn
WINDMILL TERR
Gravel Pit
VANS REACH
DUDLEY
ANNETT
B375
RUSSELL RD
Bishop Duppas Park
Tenn Cts
Pav
UPPER PK
BISHOP DUPPAS PK
SHERBOURNE GDNS
WALTON BRIDGE RD
THE CRESCENT
FELIX LA
MANOR RD
STONEBANKS
SHOPS HILL
B376
Las Palmas Est
SANDHILLS MDW
WALTON LA
PENNY LA
HILLRISE
BERKELEY GDNS
2
1 COURTLA
2 MANOR
THAMESFIELD CT 1
THAMESFIELD MEWS 2
THAMESFIELD HO 3
Pl Fld
DUNALLY PK
SWAN WLK
RIVERSIDE
RIVER MOUNT
DALE RD
HARVEY RD
B376
Thames Path
MOUNT PL
THAMES ST
MAYO RD
Desborough Island
WALTON BRIDGE
RIDGEWAY
BRIDGE CL
BRIDGE ST
PO
CHURCH ST
Pav
WELLINGTON CL
BRIDGE ST
HEPWORTH WAY
A3050
ST CLEMENTS HO
River Thames
Thames Meadow
HURST GR
The Heart
HIGH ST
CHURCH WLK
OATLANDS DR
A244
NEW ZEALAND AVE
BRASSEY HO
THAMES MDW
1
ASHLEY RD
Engine River
SANDY WAY
Works
WALTON LA
ASHLEY CL
ASHLEY PARK AVE
Sch
ASHLEY PARK CRES
WOODSIDE
Desborough Channel
WALTON LA
A3050
KT12
Pav
CHASELEY CT
ANARTH CT
KT13
TREGLOS CT
ALBANY CT
TOWER GR
66
Ashley Park
B365
08
A
B
09
C
D
10
BECKWORTH PL
OAKHILL RD
Surrey STREET ATLAS
A3050 Weybridge
LINDEN GR
PARK CL
SILVERDALE AVE
ORCHARD END

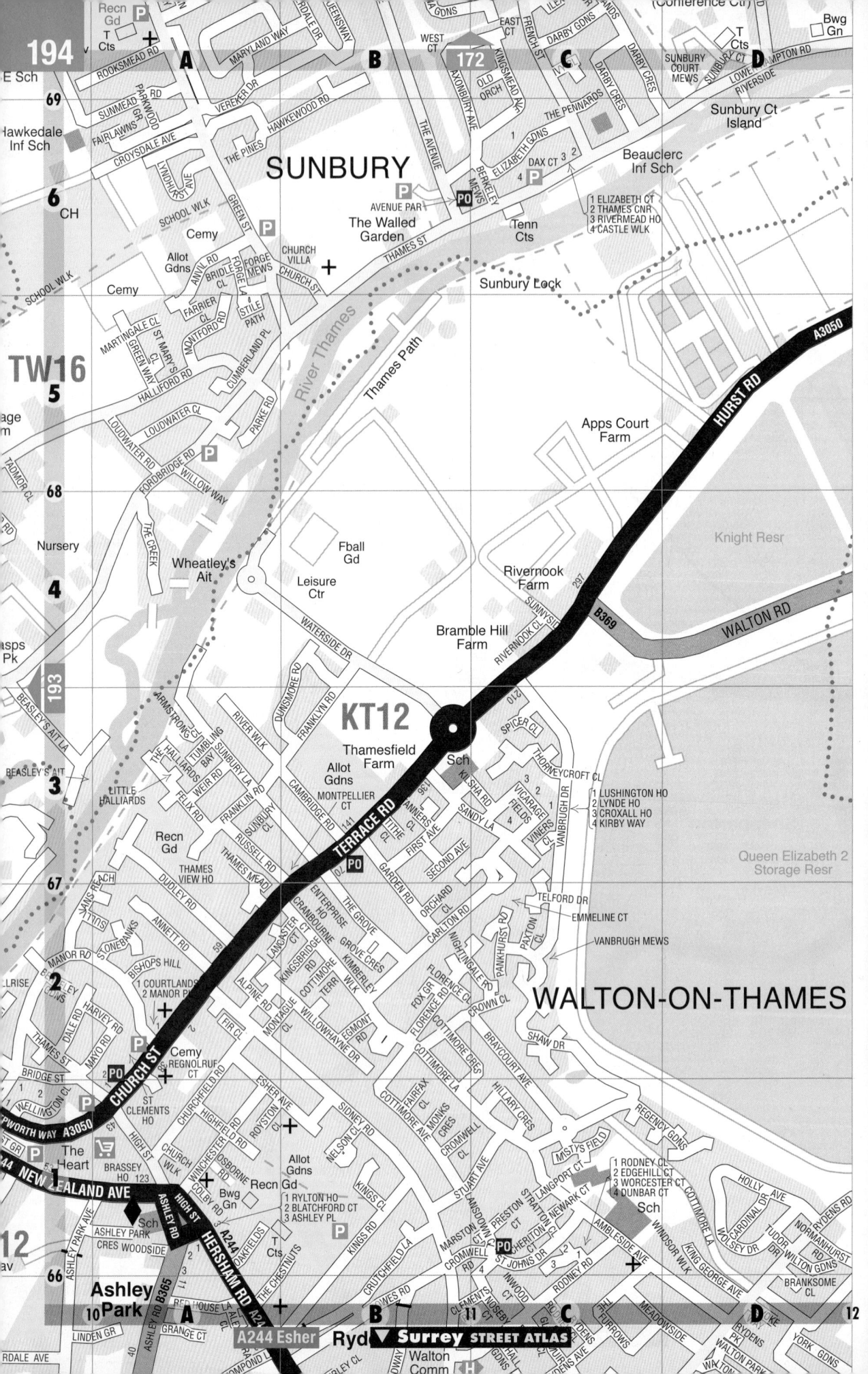

SUNBURY

TW16

KT12

WALTON-ON-THAMES

Ashley Park

River Thames

Thames Path

Knight Resr

Queen Elizabeth 2
Storage Resr

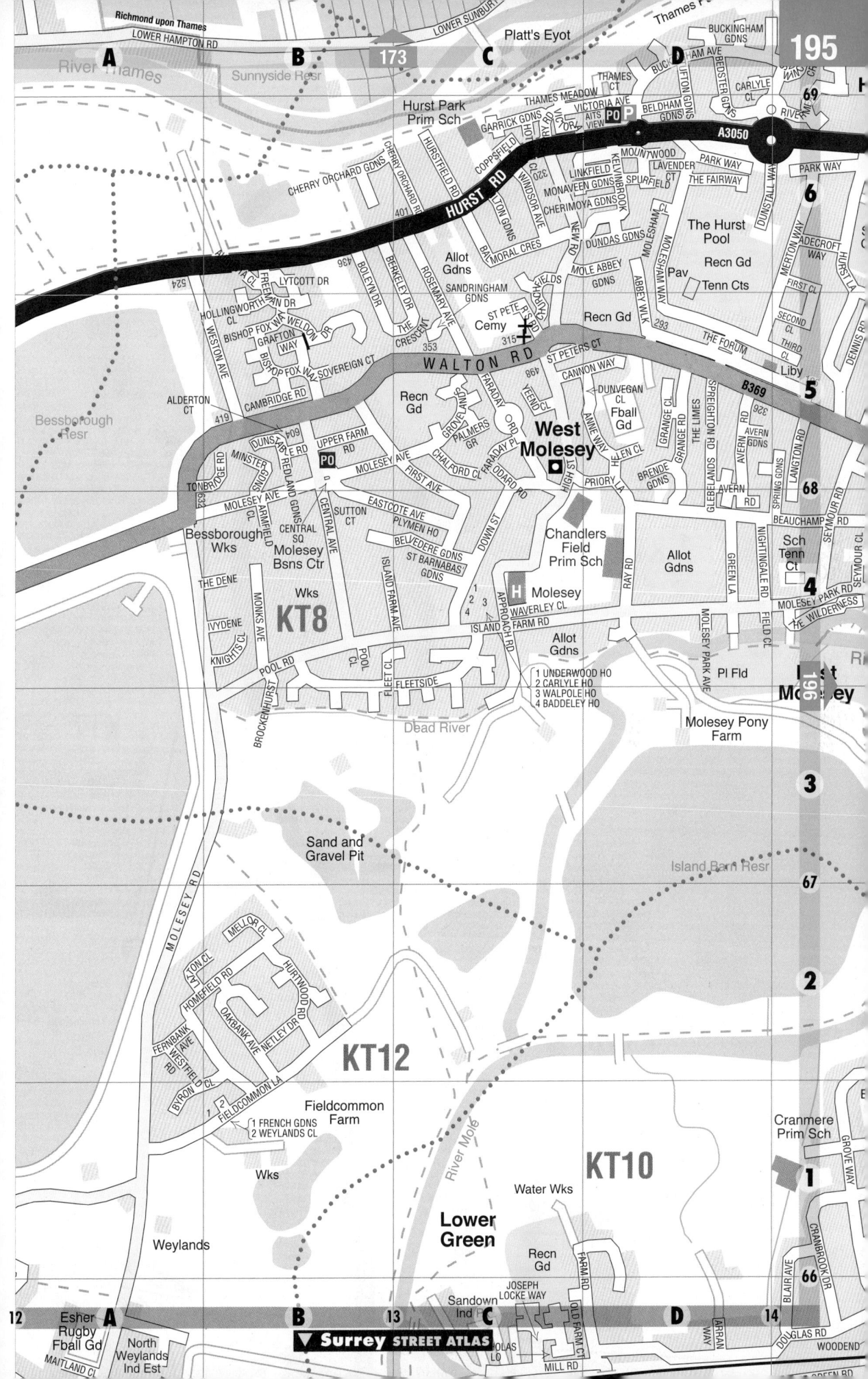

Richmond upon Thames
LOWER HAMPTON RD
LOWER SUNBURY
Platt's Eyot
Thames
BUCKINGHAM GDNS
173
A
B
C
D
River Thames
Sunnyside Resr
BUCKINGHAM AVE
THAMES CT
UFTON GDNS
BEDSTER GDNS
CARLYLE CL
69
THAMES MEADOW
VICTORIA AVE
AITS VIEW
BELDHAM GDNS
RIVER
Hurst Park Prim Sch
GARRICK GDNS
A3050
MOUNTWOOD
PARK WAY
LAVENDER CT
CHERRY ORCHARD GDNS
CHERRY ORCHARD RD
HURSTFIELD RD
COPPSFIELD
WINDSOR AVE
LINKFIELD
KELVINBROOK
SPURFIELD
THE FAIRWAY
DUNSTALL WAY
PARK WAY
MONAVEEN GDNS
CHERIMOYA GDNS
HURST RD
401
6
The Hurst Pool
MERTON WAY
ADECROFT WAY
HURST LA
Recn Gd
Pav
Tenn Cts
DUNDAS GDNS
MOLESHAM CL
MOLESHAM WAY
BALMORAL CRES
NEW RD
Allot Gdns
MOLE ABBEY GDNS
ABBEY WLK
FIRST CL
SECOND CL
THIRD CL
DENNIS RD
436
524
BOLEYN DR
BERKELEY DR
ROSEMARY AVE
LYTCOTT DR
FREEMAN DR
HOLLINGWORTH CL
WESTON AVE
BISHOP FOX WAY
WELDON DR
GRAFTON WAY
SANDRINGHAM GDNS
ST PETERS RD
Cemy
Recn Gd
293
THE FORUM
THE CRESCENT
353
315
ST PETERS CT
Liby
SOVEREIGN CT
WALTON RD
CANNON WAY
B369
5
498
DUNVEGAN CL
CAMBRIDGE RD
Recn Gd
GROVELANDS
FARADAY RD
YEEND CL
Fball Gd
GRANGE CL
GRANGE RD
THE LIMES
SPREIGHTON RD
AVERN RD
326
AVERN GDNS
LANGTON RD
Bessborough Resr
ALDERTON CT
419
604
DUNSTABLE RD
UPPER FARM RD
PALMERS GR
West Molesey
ANNE WAY
HELEN CL
TONBRIDGE RD
MINSTER GDNS
REDLAND GDNS
PO
MOLESEY AVE
CHALFORD CL
FARADAY PL
ODARD RD
HIGH ST
PRIORY LA
BRENDE GDNS
GLEBELANDS RD
AVERN RD
SPRING GDNS
68
632
MOLESEY AVE
ARMFIELD CL
CENTRAL AVE
FIRST AVE
EASTCOTE AVE
SUTTON CT
PLYMEN HO
DOWN ST
Chandlers Field Prim Sch
RAY RD
Allot Gdns
GREEN LA
NIGHTINGALE RD
BEAUCHAMP RD
SEYMOUR RD
SEYMOUR CL
Sch
Tenn Ct
Bessborough Wks
CENTRAL SQ
Molesey Bsns Ctr
BELVEDERE GDNS
ST BARNABAS' GDNS
ISLAND FARM AVE
THE DENE
Wks
MONKS AVE
KT8
Molesey
WAVERLEY CL
APPROACH RD
MOLESEY PARK RD
THE WILDERNESS
4
IVYDENE
KNIGHTS CL
ISLAND FARM RD
MOLESEY PARK AVE
FIELD CL
POOL RD
POOL CL
FLEET CL
FLEETSIDE
Allot Gdns
Pl Fld
1 UNDERWOOD HO
2 CARLYLE HO
3 WALPOLE HO
4 BADDELEY HO
East Molesey
196
BROCKENHURST
Dead River
Molesey Pony Farm
3
Sand and Gravel Pit
Island Barn Resr
67
MOLESEY RD
MELLOR CL
LAYTON CL
HOMEFIELD RD
HURTWOOD RD
OAKBANK AVE
NETLEY DR
2
FERNBANK AVE
WESTFIELD RD
KT12
BYRON CL
FIELDCOMMON LA
Fieldcommon Farm
1 FRENCH GDNS
2 WEYLANDS CL
Wks
River Mole
KT10
Cranmere Prim Sch
GROVE WAY
1
Water Wks
Lower Green
Weylands
Recn Gd
FARM RD
JOSEPH LOCKE WAY
CRANBROOK DR
BLAIR AVE
66
Sandown Ind Pk
OLD FARM CT
ARRAN WAY
12
13
14
Esher Rugby Fball Gd
North Weylands Ind Est
MAITLAND CL
MILL RD
DOUGLAS RD
WOODEND

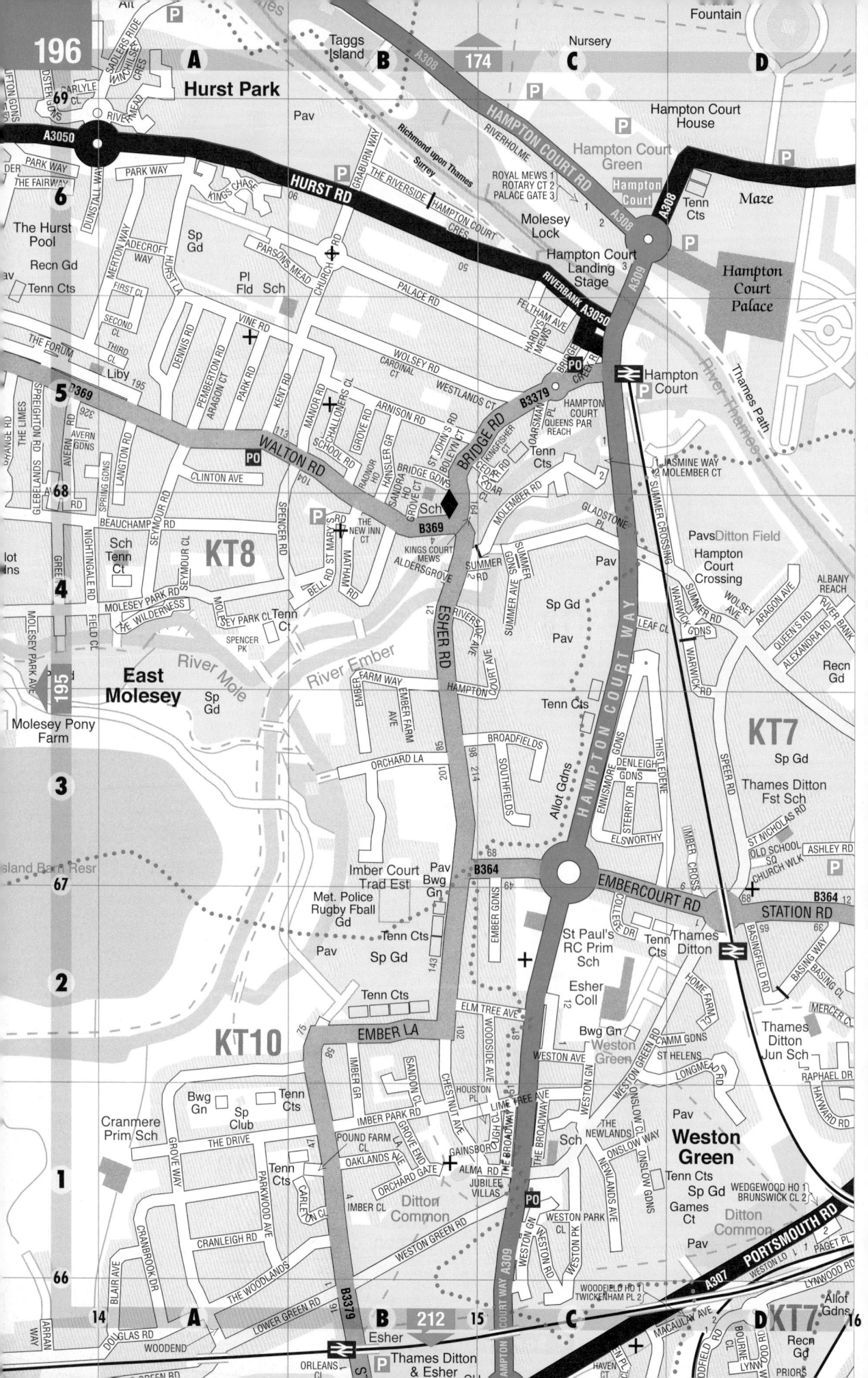
174
212
195
A
B
C
D
Hurst Park
Taggs Island
Nursery
Fountain
Hampton Court House
Hampton Court Green
Hampton Court
Maze
Hampton Court Palace
Molesey Lock
Hampton Court Landing Stage
River Thames
Thames Path
HAMPTON COURT RD
HURST RD
A3050
A308
A309
B369
B3379
B364
A307
WALTON RD
BRIDGE RD
ESHER RD
HAMPTON COURT WAY
EMBERCOURT RD
STATION RD
PORTSMOUTH RD
The Hurst Pool
Recn Gd
Tenn Cts
Richmond upon Thames
Surrey
ROYAL MEWS 1
ROTARY CT 2
PALACE GATE 3
KT8
KT7
KT10
East Molesey
River Mole
River Ember
Molesey Pony Farm
Island Barn Resr
Imber Court Trad Est
Met. Police Rugby Fball Gd
St Paul's RC Prim Sch
Esher Coll
Thames Ditton
Thames Ditton Fst Sch
Thames Ditton Jun Sch
Hampton Court Crossing
Ditton Field
Weston Green
Ditton Common
Cranmere Prim Sch
Esher
Thames Ditton & Esher
Allot Gdns
1 JASMINE WAY
2 MOLEMBER CT
WEDGEWOOD HO 1
BRUNSWICK CL 2
WOODFIELD HO 1
TWICKENHAM PL 2
6
5
4
3
2
1
69
68
67
66
14
15
16

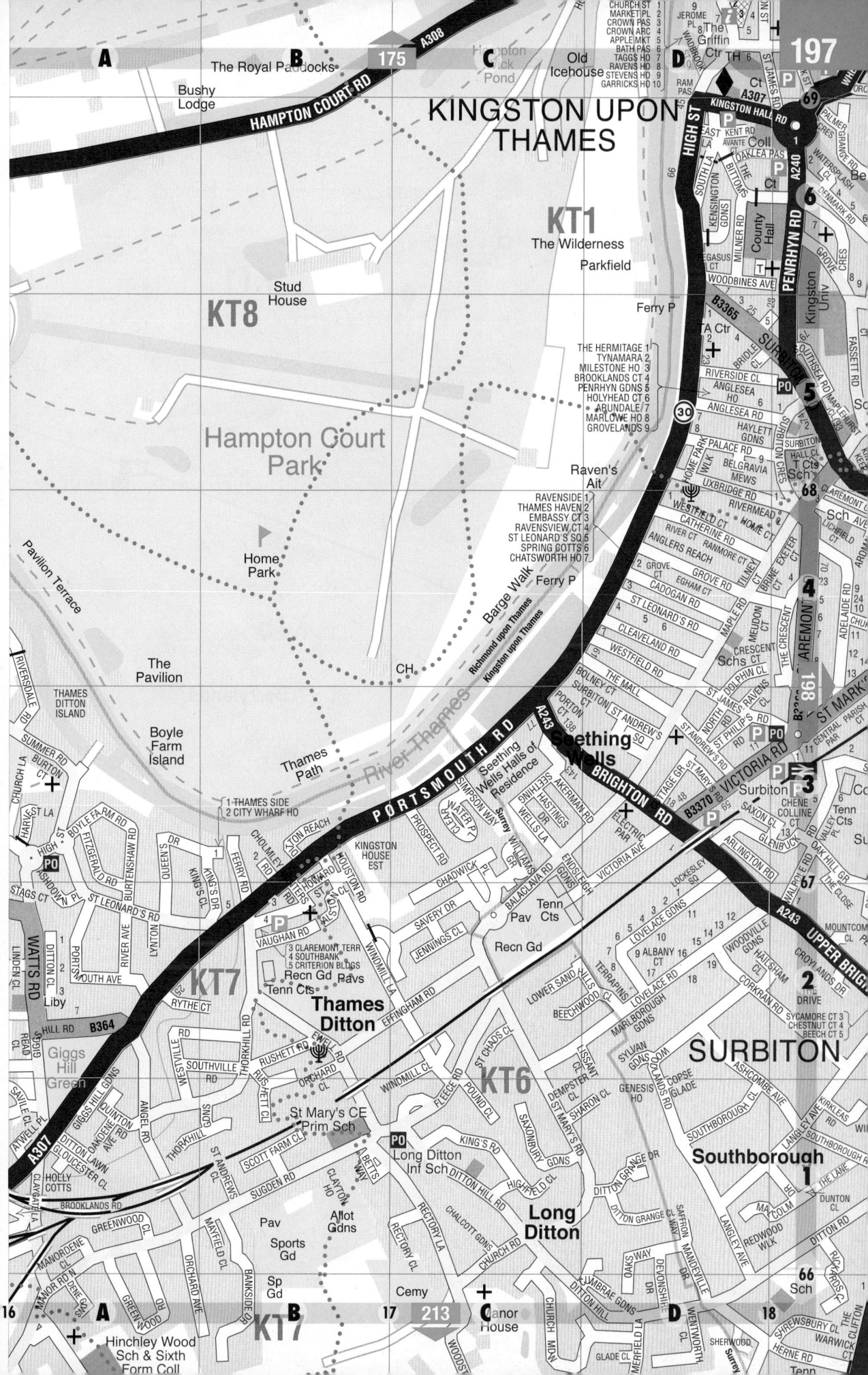

KINGSTON UPON THAMES
KT1
KT8
KT7
KT6
Hampton Court Park
Home Park
The Royal Paddocks
Bushy Lodge
Stud House
HAMPTON COURT RD
A308
175
Old Icehouse
The Wilderness
Parkfield
Ferry P
Raven's Ait
Barge Walk
River Thames
Thames Path
The Pavilion
Pavilion Terrace
THAMES DITTON ISLAND
Boyle Farm Island
PORTSMOUTH RD
A243
Seething Wells
Seething Wells Halls of Residence
BRIGHTON RD
VICTORIA RD
B3370
Surbiton
UPPER BRIGHTON RD
HIGH ST
PENRHYN RD
A240
County Hall
Kingston Univ
B3365
SURBITON RD
A307
KINGSTON HALL RD
Thames Ditton
Giggs Hill Green
WATTS RD
B364
St Mary's CE Prim Sch
Long Ditton Inf Sch
Long Ditton
SURBITON
Southborough
Recn Gd
Tenn Cts
Pav
Sports Gd
Allot Gdns
Cemy
Manor House
Hinchley Wood Sch & Sixth Form Coll
198
213
CHURCH ST 1
MARKET PL 2
CROWN PAS 3
CROWN ARC 4
APPLE MKT 5
BATH PAS 6
TAGGS HO 7
RAVENS HO 8
STEVENS HO 9
GARRICKS HO 10
THE HERMITAGE 1
TYNAMARA 2
MILESTONE HO 3
BROOKLANDS CT 4
PENRHYN GDNS 5
HOLYHEAD CT 6
ARUNDALE 7
MARLOWE HO 8
GROVELANDS 9
RAVENSIDE 1
THAMES HAVEN 2
EMBASSY CT 3
RAVENSVIEW CT 4
ST LEONARD'S SQ 5
SPRING COTTS 6
CHATSWORTH HO 7
1 THAMES SIDE
2 CITY WHARF HO
3 CLAREMONT TERR
4 SOUTHBANK
5 CRITERION BLDGS
SYCAMORE CT 3
CHESTNUT CT 4
BEECH CT 5

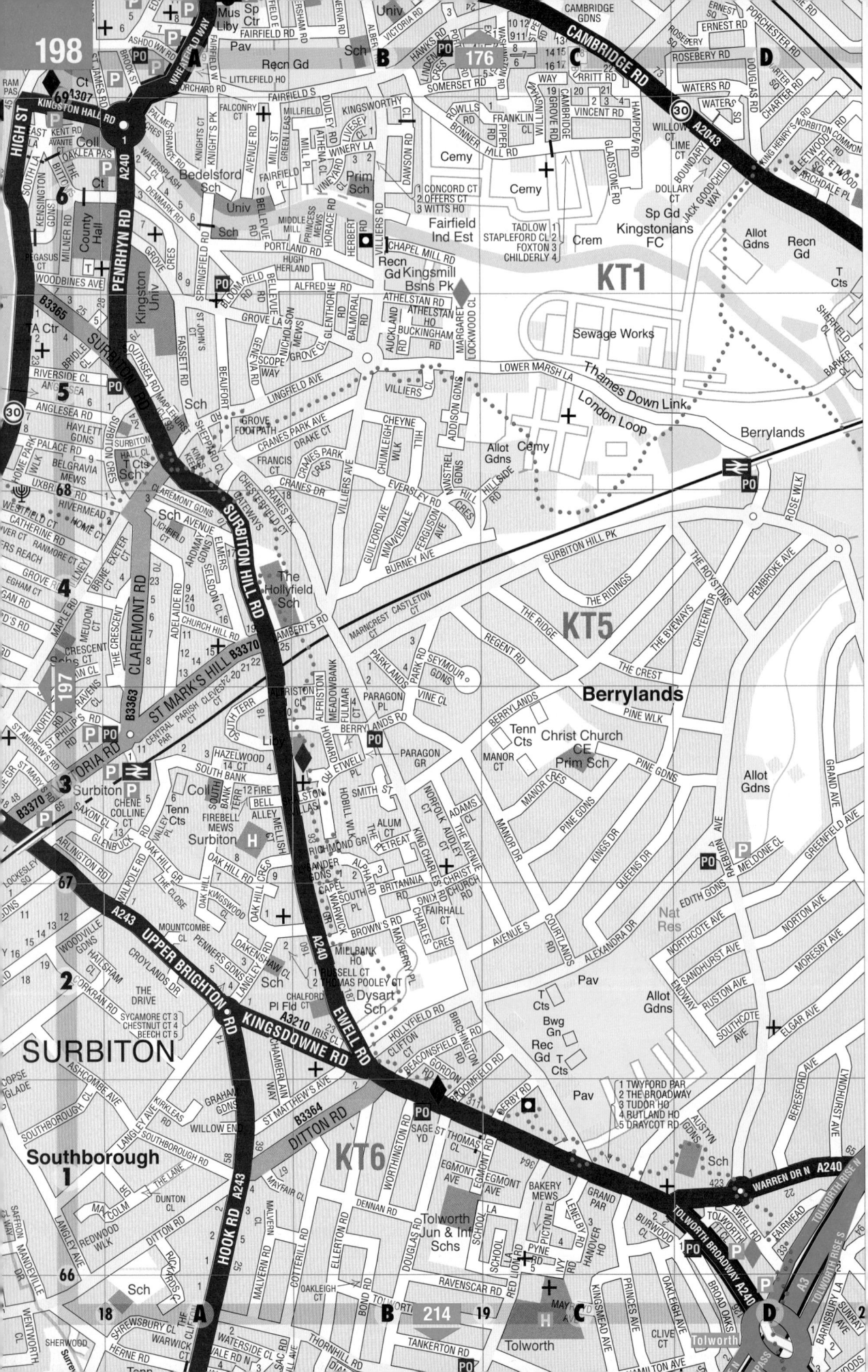
176
KT1
KT5
KT6
Berrylands
SURBITON
Southborough
Surbiton
Tolworth
CAMBRIDGE RD
KINGSTON HALL RD
HIGH ST
PENRHYN RD
SURBITON RD
SURBITON HILL RD
CLAREMONT RD
ST MARK'S HILL
VICTORIA RD
UPPER BRIGHTON RD
KINGSDOWNE RD
EWELL RD
HOOK RD
DITTON RD
TOLWORTH BROADWAY
WARREN DR N
LOWER MARSH LA
Thames Down Link
London Loop
Sewage Works
Kingstonians FC
Fairfield Ind Est
Kingsmill Bsns Pk
County Hall
Kingston Univ
The Hollyfield Sch
Christ Church CE Prim Sch
Tolworth Jun & Inf Schs
Dysart Sch
Bedelsford Sch
Allot Gdns
Recn Gd
Cemy
Crem
Nat Res
197
214
A
B
C
D
1
2
3
4
5
6
18
19

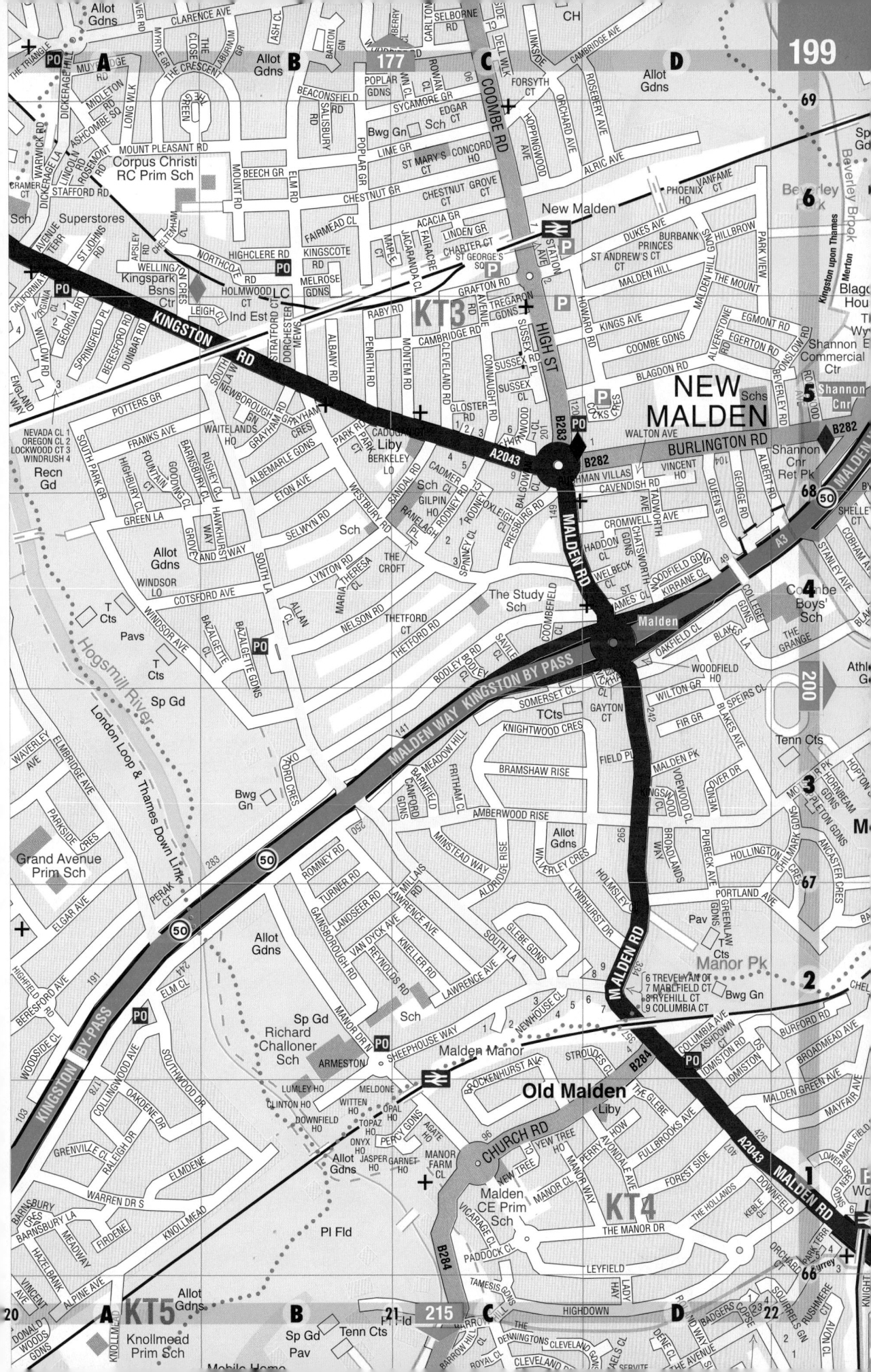
177
A
B
C
D
Allot Gdns
CLARENCE AVE
THE TRIANGLE
DICKERAGE HILL
MUYBRIDGE RD
MIDDLETON RD
ASHCOMBE SQ
LONG WLK
THE CRESCENT
THE CLOSE
THE GREEN
LABURNUM GR
MYRTLE GR
ASH CL
BARTON GN
SELBORNE RD
CARLTON
COOMBE RD
DELL WLK
LINKSIDE
CAMBRIDGE AVE
FORSYTH CT
ROSEBERY AVE
ORCHARD AVE
HOPPINGWOOD AVE
ALRIC AVE
BEACONSFIELD RD
SALISBURY RD
POPLAR GDNS
POPLAR GR
SYCAMORE GR
EDGAR CT
ROWAN CL
Bwg Gn
Sch
LIME GR
ST MARY'S CT
CONCORD HO
MOUNT PLEASANT RD
Corpus Christi RC Prim Sch
MOUNT RD
BEECH GR
ELM RD
CHESTNUT GR
CHESTNUT GROVE CT
WARWICK RD
DICKERAGE LA
LINCOLN RD
ROSEMONT RD
CRAMER CT
STAFFORD RD
Sch
Superstores
AVENUE TERR
ST JOHNS RD
APSLEY RD
CHELTENHAM
NORTHCOTE RD
HIGHCLERE RD
KINGSCOTE RD
MELROSE GDNS
FAIRMEAD CL
MAPLE CT
JACARANDA CL
FAIRACRE
ACACIA GR
LINDEN GR
CHARTER CT
ST GEORGE'S SQ
New Malden
PHOENIX HO
VANFAME CT
DUKES AVE
BURBANK
PRINCES
ST ANDREW'S CT
HILLBROW
PARK VIEW
MALDEN HILL
MALDEN HILL GDNS
THE MOUNT
Beverley Park
Beverley Brook
Kingston upon Thames
Merton
WELLINGTON CRES
Kingspark Bsns Ctr
HOLMWOOD CT
LC
Ind Est
LEIGH CL
CALIFORNIA RD
VIRGINIA CL
GEORGIA RD
SPRINGFIELD PL
BERESFORD RD
DUNBAR RD
WILLOW RD
KINGSTON RD
STRATFORD CT
DORCHESTER MEWS
RABY RD
ALBANY RD
PENRITH RD
MONTEM RD
KT3
GRAFTON RD
TREGARON GDNS
CAMBRIDGE RD
CLEVELAND RD
CONNAUGHT RD
SUSSEX RD
SUSSEX PL
SUSSEX CL
HIGH ST
STATION AVE
HOWARD RD
KINGS AVE
COOMBE GDNS
BLAGDON RD
ALVERSTONE RD
EGMONT RD
EGERTON RD
ONSLOW RD
BEVERLEY RD
Shannon Commercial Ctr
NEW MALDEN
Schs
Shannon Cnr
ENGLAND WAY
NEVADA CL 1
OREGON CL 2
LOCKWOOD CT 3
WINDRUSH 4
POTTERS GR
SOUTH LA
NEWBOROUGH GN
GRAYHAM RD
GRAYHAM CRES
WAITELANDS HO
FRANKS AVE
SOUTH PARK GR
HIGHBURY CL
FOUNTAIN CT
GOODING CL
BARNSBURY CL
RUSHEY CL
HAWKHURST WAY
ALBEMARLE GDNS
PARK RD
PARK CT
CADOGAN CT
Liby
BERKELEY LO
GLOSTER RD
A2043
B283
PO
COX CRES
WALTON AVE
BURLINGTON RD
B282
Shannon Cnr Ret Pk
MALDEN WAY
Recn Gd
ETON AVE
SANDAL RD
CADMER CL
RODNEY RD
Sch
GILPIN HO
WESTBURY RD
RANELAGH PL
SELWYN RD
GREEN LA
GROVE WAY
Sch
Allot Gdns
WINDSOR LO
LYNTON RD
MARIA THERESA CL
THE CROFT
SPINNEY CL
OXLEIGH CL
BALGOWAN CL
PRESBURG RD
MALDEN RD
CAVENDISH RD
VINCENT HO
TADWORTH AVE
QUEEN'S RD
GEORGE RD
ALBERT RD
CROMWELL AVE
HADDON CL
CHATSWORTH GDNS
WELBECK CL
ST JAMES' CL
WOODFIELD GDNS
KIRRANE CL
A3
COLLEGE GDNS
Coombe Boys' Sch
STANLEY AVE
COBHAM AVE
COTSFORD AVE
T Cts
Pavs
WINDSOR AVE
BAZALGETTE CL
BAZALGETTE GDNS
ALLAN CL
NELSON RD
THETFORD CT
THETFORD RD
The Study Sch
COOMBEFIELD CL
Malden
OAKFIELD CL
BLAKES LA
THE GRANGE
T Cts
Hogsmill River
Sp Gd
BODLEY RD
BODLEY CL
SAVILE CL
KINGSTON BY PASS
WOODFIELD HO
WILTON GR
SPEIRS CL
200
SOMERSET CL
TCts
GAYTON CT
FIR GR
BLAKES AVE
Tenn Cts
London Loop & Thames Down Link
WAVERLEY AVE
ELMBRIDGE AVE
OXFORD CRES
MEADOW HILL
FRITHAM CL
KNIGHTWOOD CRES
FIELD PL
MALDEN PK
BRAMSHAW RISE
KINGSWOOD CL
VOEWOOD CL
WENDOVER DR
HORNBEAM GDNS
APPLETON GDNS
Bwg Gn
PARKSIDE CRES
CANFORD GDNS
BARNFIELD
AMBERWOOD RISE
Allot Gdns
Grand Avenue Prim Sch
50
ROMNEY RD
TURNER RD
MINSTEAD WAY
ALDRIDGE RISE
WAVERLEY CRES
BROADLANDS WAY
PURBECK AVE
HOLLINGTON CRES
CHILMARK GDNS
ANCASTER CRES
PERAK CT
ELGAR AVE
GAINSBOROUGH RD
LANDSEER RD
MILLAIS RD
LAWRENCE AVE
HOLMSLEY CL
LYNDHURST DR
PORTLAND AVE
Pav
T Cts
GREENLAW GDNS
Manor Pk
VAN DYCK AVE
REYNOLDS RD
KNELLER RD
SOUTH LA
GLEBE GDNS
6 TREVELYAN CT
7 MARLFIELD CT
8 RYEHILL CT
9 COLUMBIA CT
Bwg Gn
Allot Gdns
HIGHFIELD RD
BERESFORD AVE
ELM CL
MANOR DR N
Sp Gd
Richard Challoner Sch
Sch
SHEEPHOUSE WAY
NEWHOUSE CL
COLUMBIA AVE
ASHDOWN CT
BURFORD RD
BROADMEAD AVE
WOODSIDE CL
KINGSTON BY-PASS
SOUTHWOOD DR
ARMESTON
Malden Manor
STROUDES CL
B284
IDMISTON RD
IDMISTON SQ
MALDEN GREEN AVE
MAYFAIR AVE
COLLINGWOOD AVE
OAKDENE DR
LUMLEY HO
MELDONE
CLINTON HO
WITTEN HO
OPAL HO
DOWNFIELD HO
TOPAZ HO
ONYX HO
PERCY GDNS
AGATE HO
BROCKENHURST AVE
Old Malden
Liby
THE GLEBE
FULLBROOKS AVE
GRENVILLE CL
RALEIGH DR
ELMDENE
JASPER HO
GARNET HO
MANOR FARM CL
Allot Gdns
CHURCH RD
YEW TREE HO
NEW TREE CL
MANOR CL
MANOR WAY
PERRY HOW
AVONDALE AVE
FOREST SIDE
A2043
MALDEN RD
LOWER GN GDNS
WARREN DR S
KNOLLMEAD
Malden CE Prim Sch
KT4
THE HOLLANDS
KEBLE CL
DOWNFIELD
BARNSBURY CRES
BARNSBURY LA
FIRDENE
MEADWAY
Pl Fld
VICARAGE CL
PADDOCK CL
THE MANOR DR
HAZELBANK
ALPINE AVE
LEYFIELD
HAY
LADY
ORCHARD CT
PARK TERR
Surrey
VINCENT AVE
Allot Gdns
TAMESIS GDNS
HIGHDOWN
KT5
A
B
C
D
215
DONALD WOODS GDNS
KNOLLMEAD
Knollmead Prim Sch
Sp Gd
Pav
Tenn Cts
Pl Fld
BARROW HILL
DENNINGTONS
CLEVELAND GDNS
CLEVELAND RD
BADGERS COPSE
SQUIRRELS GN
RUSHMERE CT
DENE CL
THE AVENUE
SERVITE
6
5
4
3
2
1
69
68
67
66
20
21
22

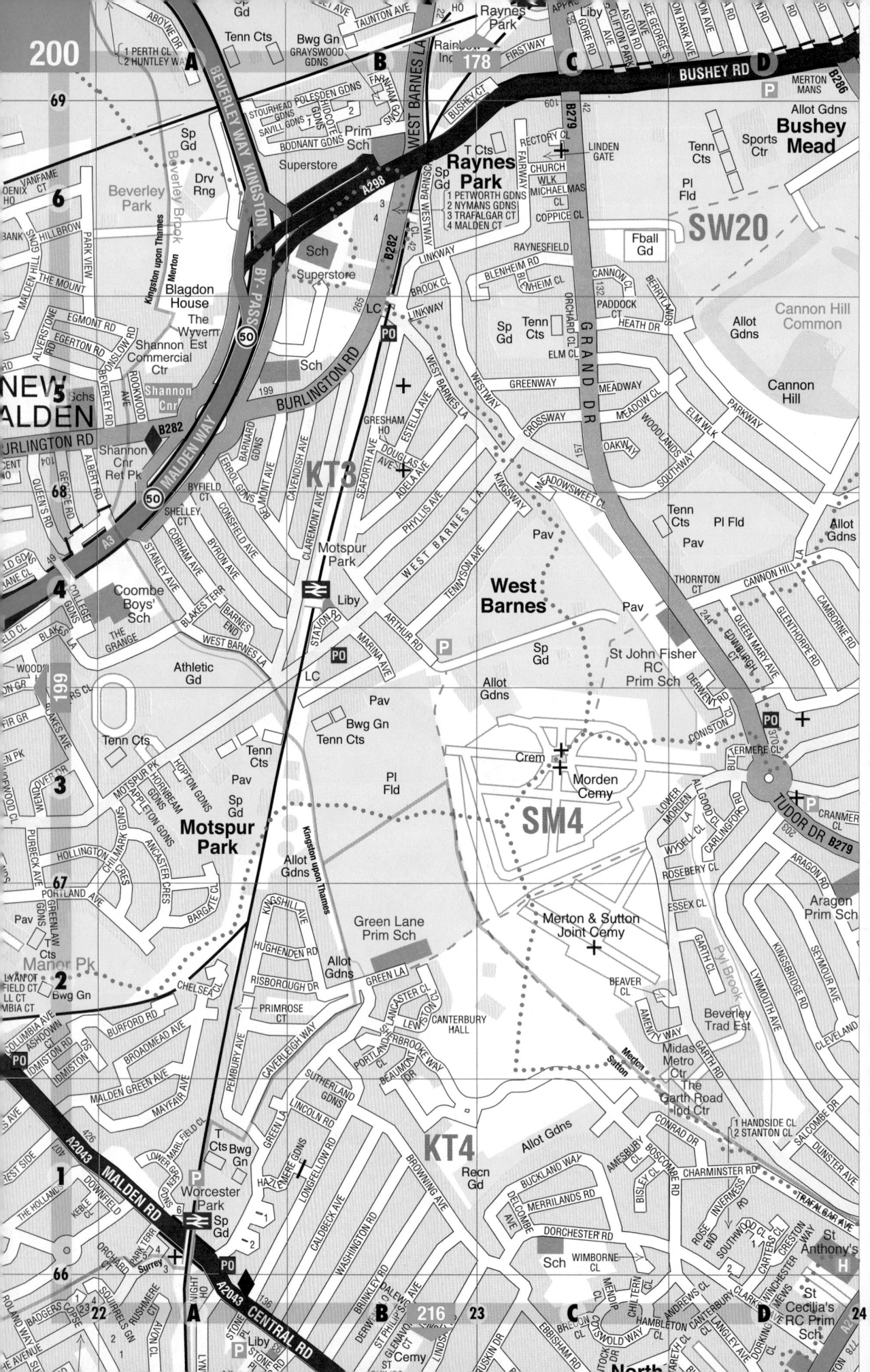

200
178
216
199
Raynes Park
West Barnes
Motspur Park
Bushey Mead
NEW MALDEN
KT3
KT4
SW20
SM4
BUSHEY RD
GRAND DR
BURLINGTON RD
MALDEN WAY
BEVERLEY WAY KINGSTON BY-PASS
WEST BARNES LA
MALDEN RD
CENTRAL RD
TUDOR DR
Worcester Park
Cannon Hill Common
Cannon Hill
Beverley Park
Blagdon House
The Wyvern Est
Shannon Commercial Ctr
Shannon Cnr Ret Pk
Coombe Boys' Sch
Athletic Gd
St John Fisher RC Prim Sch
Crem
Morden Cemy
Merton & Sutton Joint Cemy
Green Lane Prim Sch
Aragon Prim Sch
Beverley Trad Est
Midas Metro Ctr
The Garth Road Ind Ctr
Canterbury Hall
St Anthony's
St Cecilia's RC Prim Sch
Manor Pk
Kingston upon Thames
Merton
Sutton
Surrey

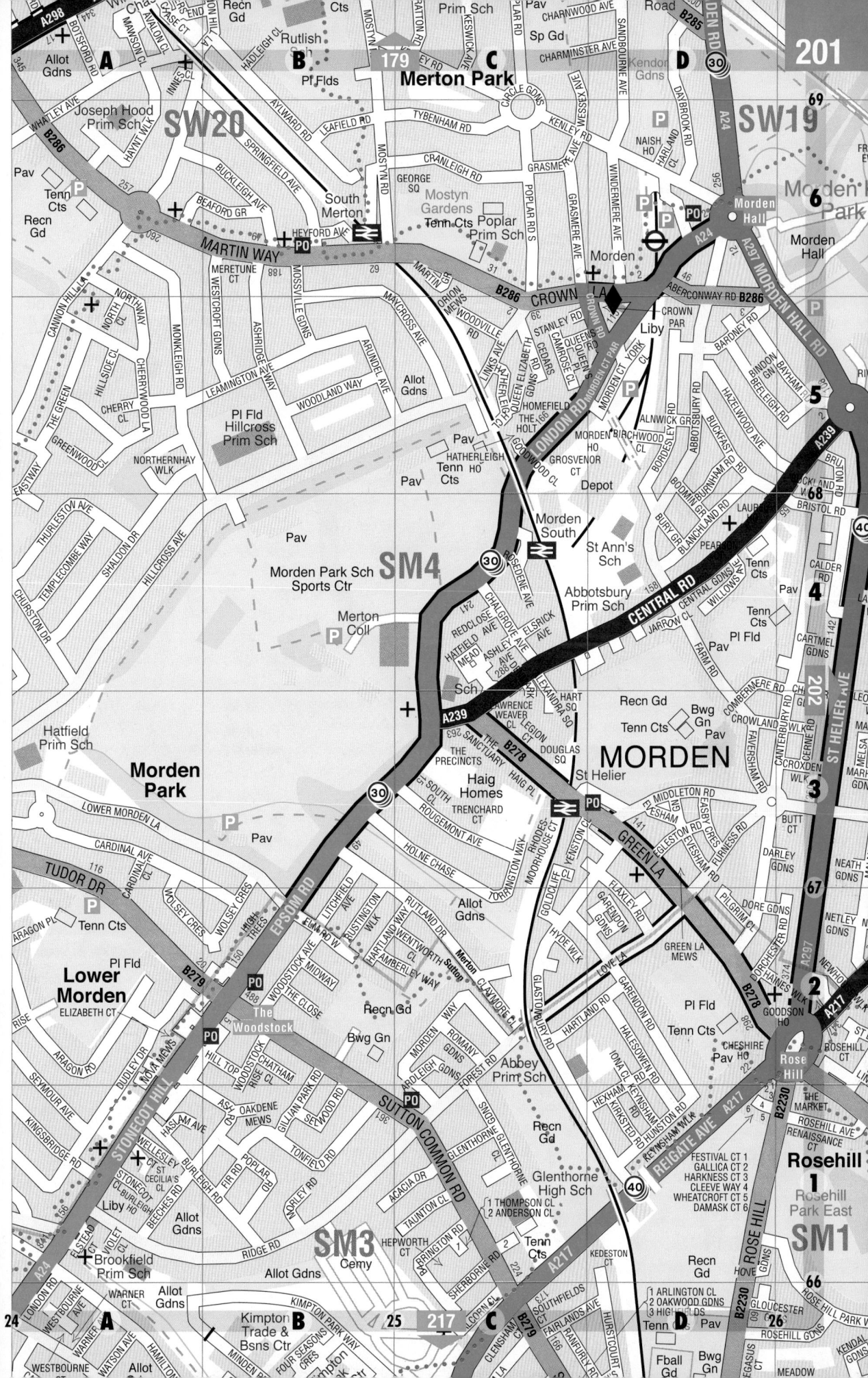

179
A
B
C
D
1
2
3
4
5
6
Merton Park
SW20
SW19
SM4
SM3
SM1
MORDEN
Morden Park
Lower Morden
Rosehill
A298
B286
B285
A24
A297
A239
B278
B279
A217
B2230
Allot Gdns
Joseph Hood Prim Sch
Rutlish Sch
Pl Flds
Prim Sch
Sp Gd
Kendor Gdns
Recn Gd
Tenn Cts
Pav
South Merton
Mostyn Gardens
Poplar Prim Sch
GEORGE SQ
Morden
Morden Hall
Morden Hall Park
Liby
MARTIN WAY
CROWN LA
ABERCONWAY RD
MORDEN HALL RD
LONDON RD
CENTRAL RD
EPSOM RD
STONECOT HILL
SUTTON COMMON RD
REIGATE AVE
ROSE HILL
ST HELIER AVE
GREEN LA
TUDOR DR
Pl Fld Hillcross Prim Sch
Morden Park Sch Sports Ctr
Merton Coll
Morden South
St Ann's Sch
Abbotsbury Prim Sch
Depot
Haig Homes
St Helier
Recn Gd
Bwg Gn
Hatfield Prim Sch
The Woodstock
Abbey Prim Sch
Glenthorne High Sch
Cemy
Brookfield Prim Sch
Kimpton Trade & Bsns Ctr
Rosehill Park East
FESTIVAL CT 1
GALLICA CT 2
HARKNESS CT 3
CLEEVE WAY 4
WHEATCROFT CT 5
DAMASK CT 6
1 THOMPSON CL
2 ANDERSON CL
1 ARLINGTON CL
2 OAKWOOD GDNS
3 HIGHFIELDS
Fball Gd
24
25
26
217
202

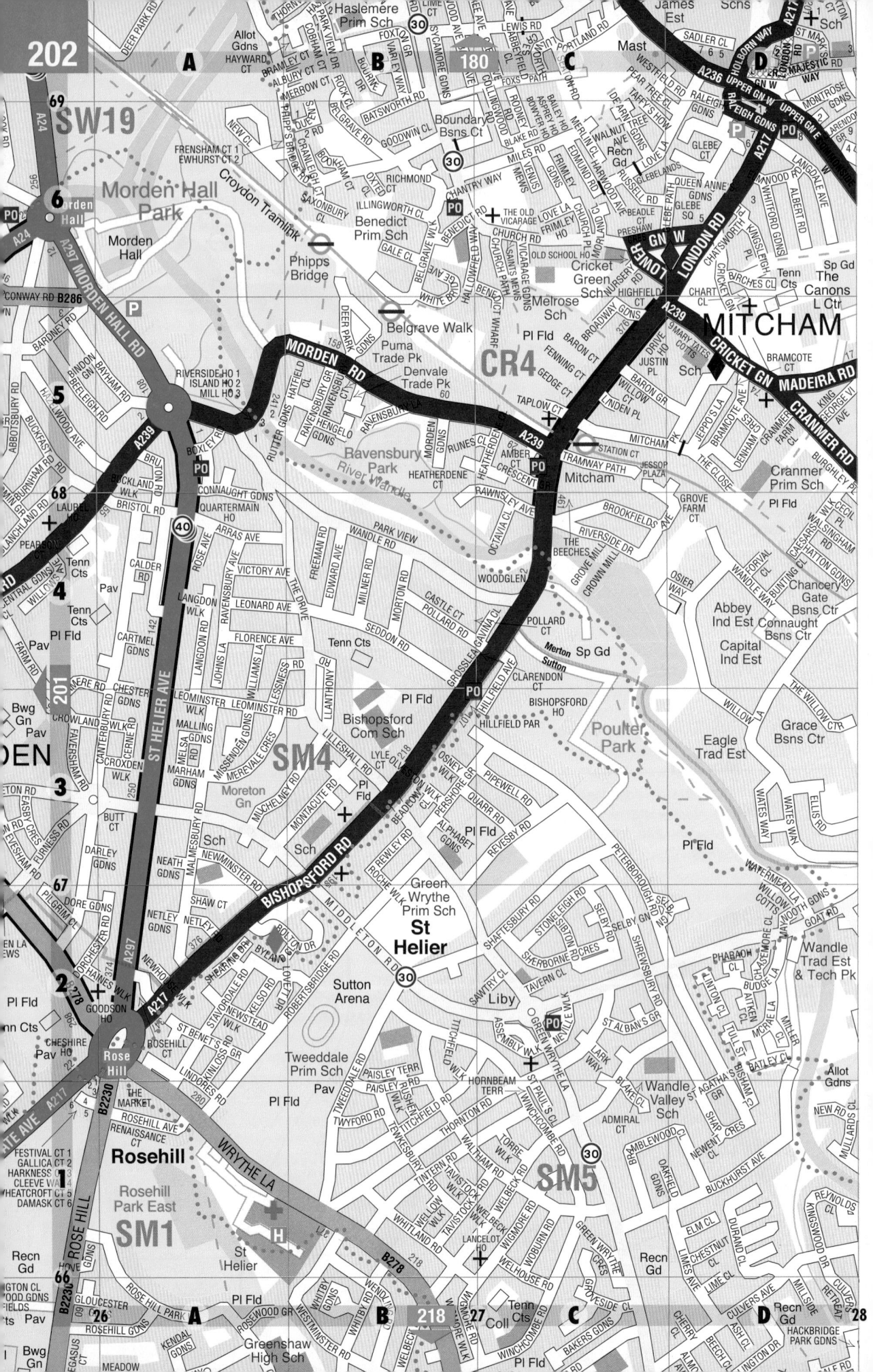

A
B
C
D
180
218
201
SW19
CR4
SM4
SM5
SM1
MITCHAM
St Helier
Rosehill
Morden Hall Park
Morden Hall
Morden Hall
Phipps Bridge
Belgrave Walk
Croydon Tramlink
Haslemere Prim Sch
Benedict Prim Sch
Boundary Bsns Ct
Puma Trade Pk
Denvale Trade Pk
Ravensbury Park
River Wandle
Melrose Sch
Cricket Green Sch
The Canons L Ctr
Cranmer Prim Sch
Mitcham
Abbey Ind Est
Capital Ind Est
Chancery Gate Bsns Ctr
Connaught Bsns Ctr
Eagle Trad Est
Grace Bsns Ctr
Poulter Park
Merton
Sutton
Sp Gd
Bishopsford Com Sch
Moreton Gn
Green Wrythe Prim Sch
Sutton Arena
Tweeddale Prim Sch
Wandle Valley Sch
Wandle Trad Est & Tech Pk
Rosehill Park East
St Helier
Greenshaw High Sch
Liby
Coll
Allot Gdns
Recn Gd
Tenn Cts
Pl Fld
Pav
Sch
Mast
James Est
MORDEN RD
MORDEN HALL RD
BISHOPSFORD RD
ST HELIER AVE
WRYTHE LA
LONDON RD
CRICKET GN
MADEIRA RD
CRANMER RD
UPPER GN W
UPPER GN E
HOLBORN WAY
RALEIGH GDNS
CONWAY RD
ROSE HILL
A24
A297
A239
A217
A236
B286
B278
B2230

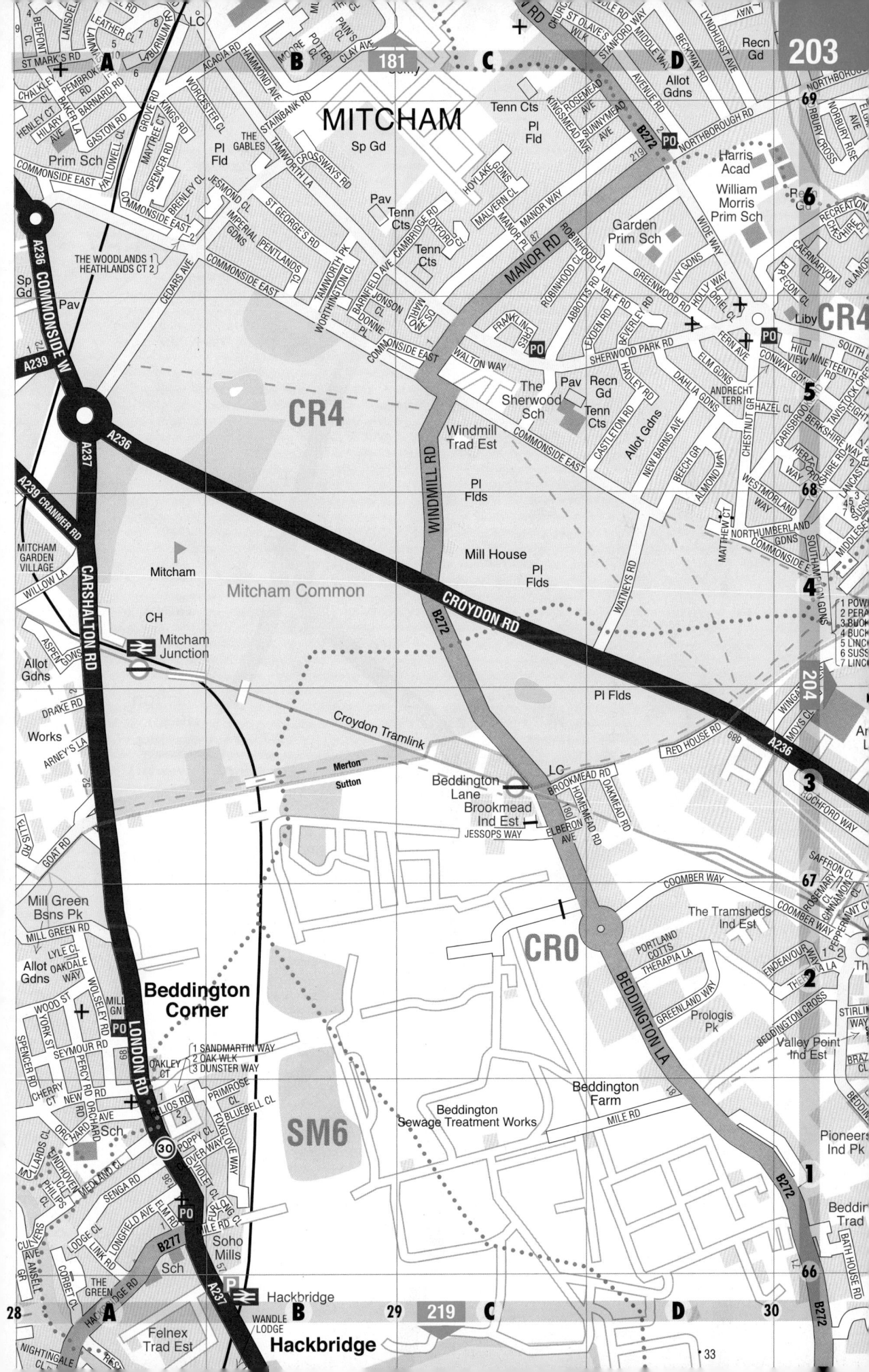
MITCHAM
CR4
CR0
SM6
Mitcham Common
Mitcham Junction
Beddington Corner
Hackbridge
Beddington Sewage Treatment Works
Beddington Farm
Beddington Lane
Brookmead Ind Est
Windmill Trad Est
Mill House
The Sherwood Sch
Garden Prim Sch
William Morris Prim Sch
Harris Acad
Mill Green Bsns Pk
Felnex Trad Est
Soho Mills
The Tramsheds Ind Est
Prologis Pk
Valley Point Ind Est
Pioneers Ind Pk
Croydon Tramlink
CROYDON RD
COMMONSIDE W
COMMONSIDE EAST
CARSHALTON RD
LONDON RD
WINDMILL RD
MANOR RD
BEDDINGTON LA
A236
A237
A239
B272
B277
Merton
Sutton
181
204
219

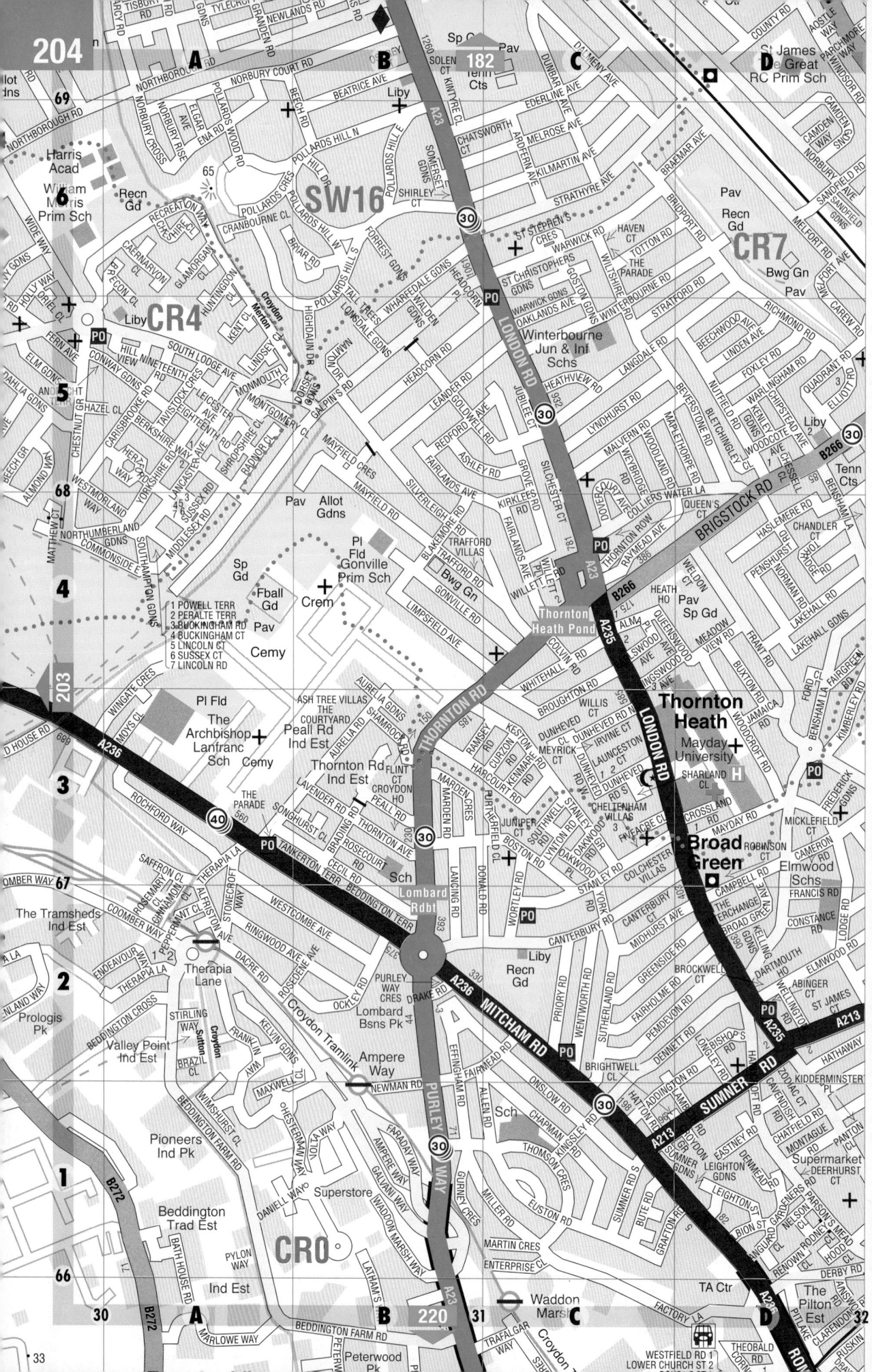
A
B
C
D
182
SW16
CR4
CR7
CR0
Harris Acad
William Morris Prim Sch
St James the Great RC Prim Sch
Winterbourne Jun & Inf Schs
Gonville Prim Sch
Thornton Heath Pond
Thornton Heath
Mayday University
Broad Green
The Archbishop Lanfranc Sch
Peall Rd Ind Est
Thornton Rd Ind Est
Lombard Rdbt
Lombard Bsns Pk
Therapia Lane
The Tramsheds Ind Est
Prologis Pk
Valley Point Ind Est
Pioneers Ind Pk
Beddington Trad Est
Ampere Way
Superstore
Waddon Marsh
Elmwood Schs
The Pilton Est
Peterwood Pk
Croydon Tramlink
LONDON RD
BRIGSTOCK RD
MITCHAM RD
PURLEY WAY
THORNTON RD
SUMNER RD
A23
A235
A236
A213
B266
B272
203
220
1 POWELL TERR
2 PERALTE TERR
3 BUCKINGHAM RD
4 BUCKINGHAM CT
5 LINCOLN CT
6 SUSSEX CT
7 LINCOLN RD
WESTFIELD RD 1
LOWER CHURCH ST 2
30
31
32
33
66
67
68
69
1
2
3
4
5
6

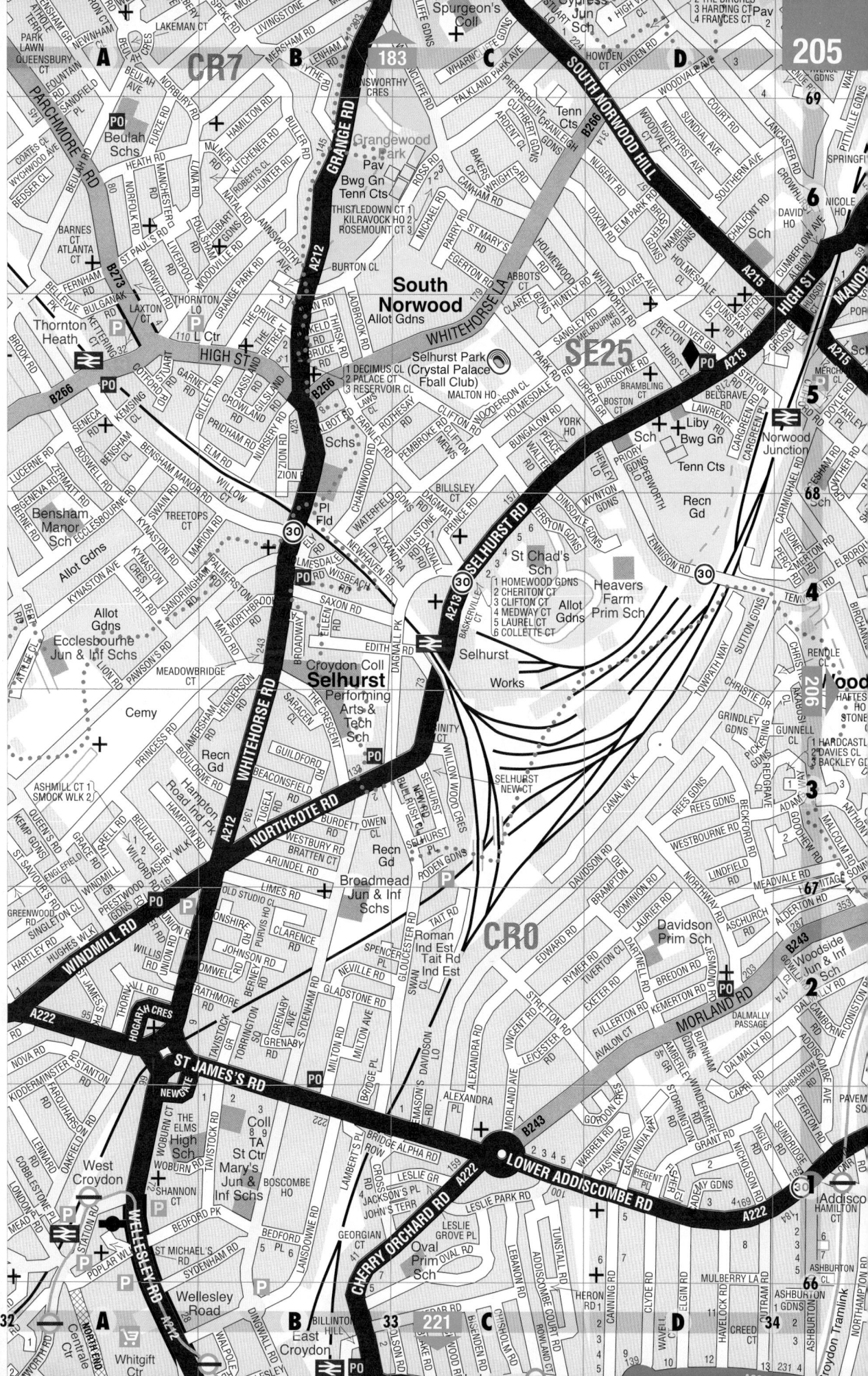

A
B
C
D
CR7
183
South Norwood
SE25
Selhurst Park (Crystal Palace Fball Club)
Thornton Heath
HIGH ST
GRANGE RD
A212
SOUTH NORWOOD HILL
B266
WHITEHORSE LA
Grangewood Park
Allot Gdns
Norwood Junction
Selhurst
Croydon Coll
Performing Arts & Tech Sch
Selhurst Works
Heavers Farm Prim Sch
St Chad's Sch
Bensham Manor Sch
Ecclesbourne Jun & Inf Schs
Cemy
WHITEHORSE RD
NORTHCOTE RD
SELHURST RD
A213
A215
CR0
Davidson Prim Sch
Broadmead Jun & Inf Schs
Roman Ind Est
Tait Rd Ind Est
WINDMILL RD
A222
ST JAMES'S RD
LOWER ADDISCOMBE RD
CHERRY ORCHARD RD
MORLAND RD
B243
Woodside Jun & Inf Sch
WELLESLEY RD
West Croydon
East Croydon
Wellesley Road
Whitgift Ctr
Centrale Ctr
Oval Prim Sch
The Elms High Sch
St Mary's Jun & Inf Schs
Coll
Addiscombe
Croydon Tramlink
206
221
32
33
34
66
67
68
69
1
2
3
4
5
6

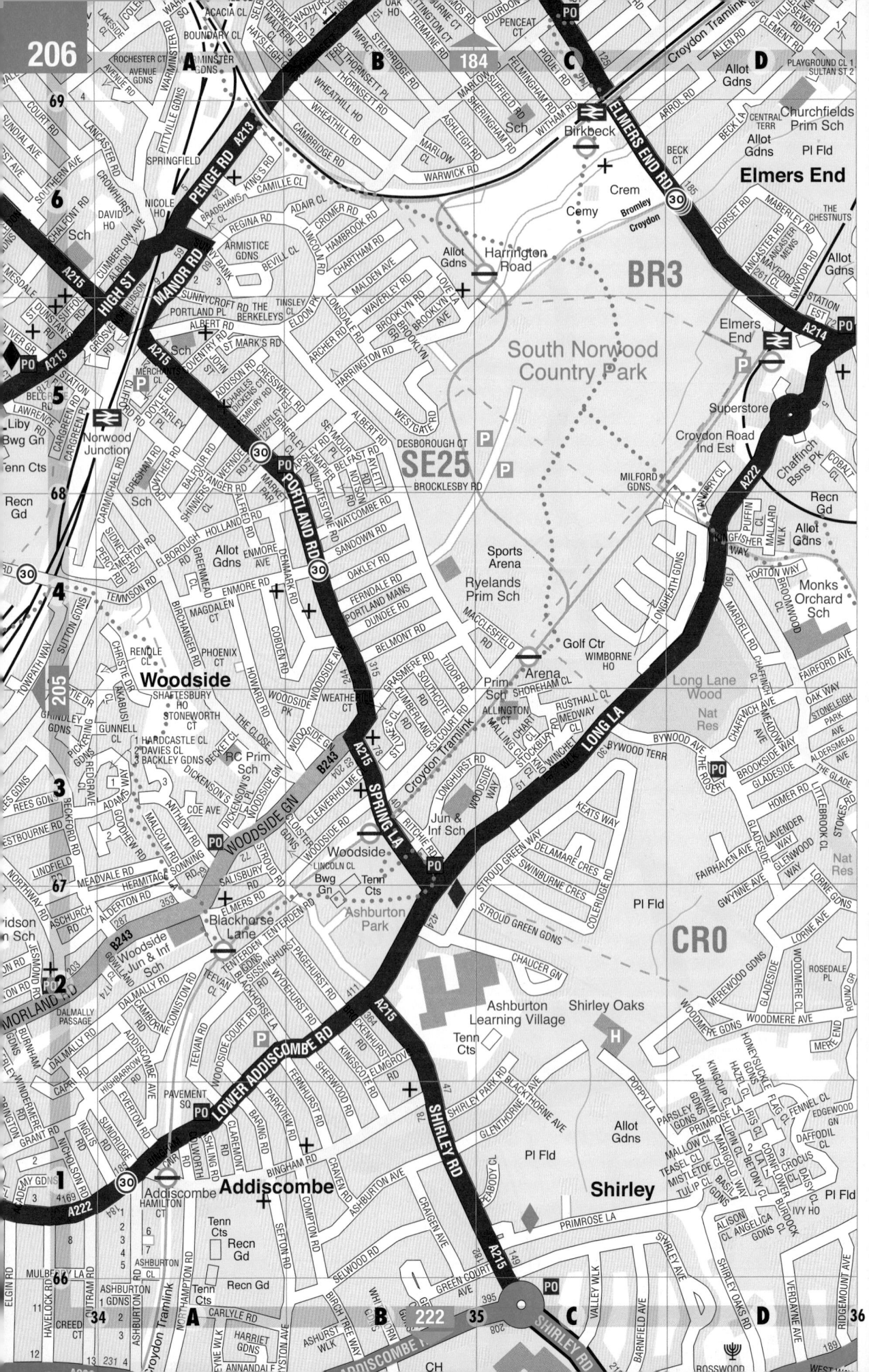
184
A
B
C
D
Birkbeck
Elmers End
BR3
South Norwood Country Park
SE25
Norwood Junction
Woodside
Harrington Road
Arena
Sports Arena
Ryelands Prim Sch
Croydon Road Ind Est
Superstore
Monks Orchard Sch
Long Lane Wood
Woodside
Ashburton Park
Blackhorse Lane
Ashburton Learning Village
Shirley Oaks
CR0
Addiscombe
Shirley
PENGE RD
HIGH ST
MANOR RD
PORTLAND RD
SPRING LA
LONG LA
WOODSIDE GN
LOWER ADDISCOMBE RD
SHIRLEY RD
ELMERS END RD
Croydon Tramlink
Bromley
Croydon
205
222
34
35
36
1
2
3
4
5
6
66
67
68
69

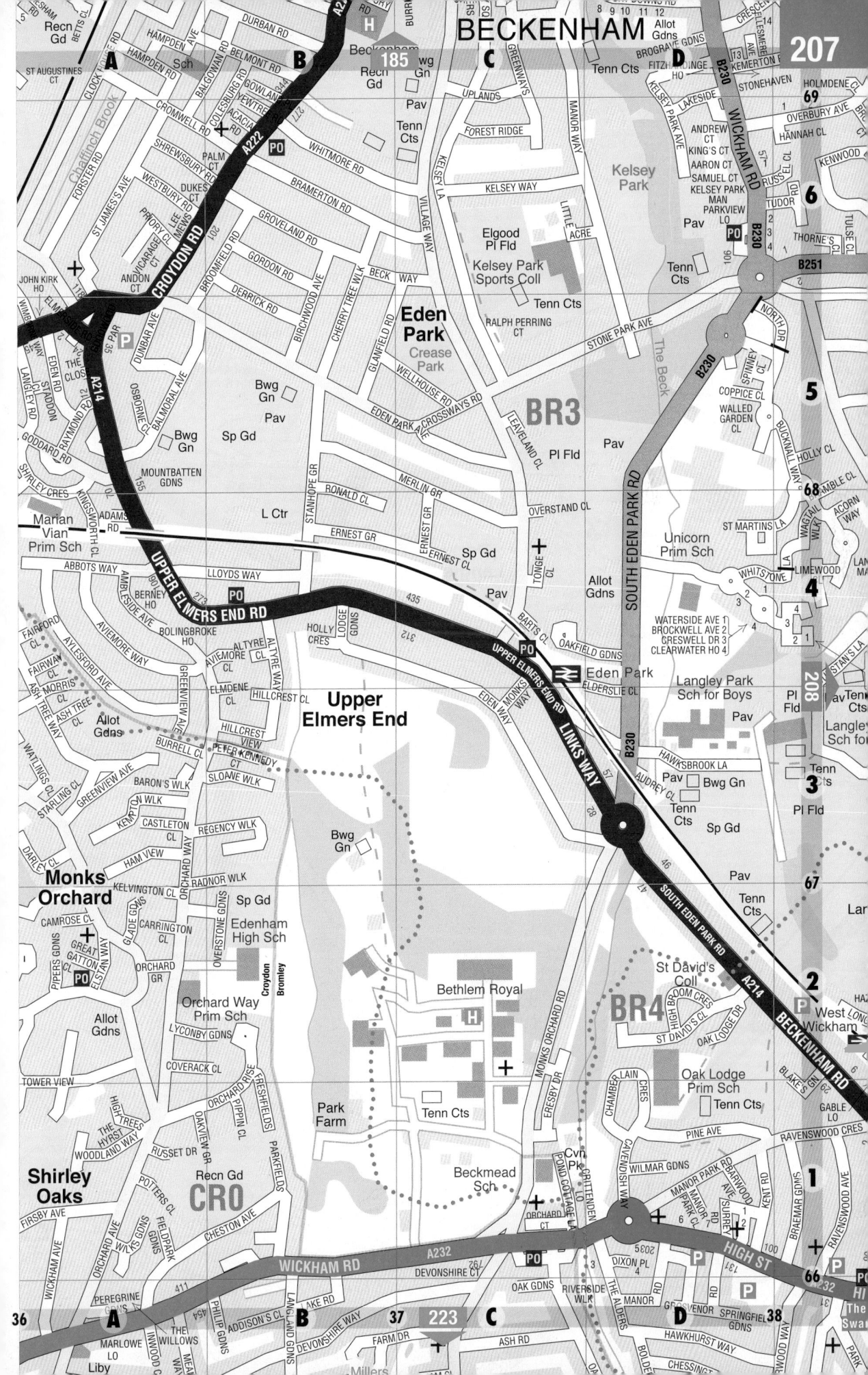

BECKENHAM
207
185
208
223
Beckenham
Recn Gd
Hampden Ave
Hampden Rd
Durban Rd
Belmont Rd
Balgowan Rd
Colesburg Rd
Gowland Pl
Yewtree Rd
Acacia Rd
Cromwell Rd
St Augustines Ct
Clock House Rd
Chaffinch Brook
Forster Rd
Shrewsbury Rd
Westbury Rd
Palm Ct
Dukes Ct
St James's Ave
Priory Cl
Lee Mews
Vicarage Ct
Andon Ct
John Kirk Ho
Croydon Rd
A222
A214
Whitmore Rd
Bramerton Rd
Groveland Rd
Gordon Rd
Derrick Rd
Broomfield Rd
Birchwood Ave
Cherry Tree Wlk
Beck Way
Village Way
Uplands
Greenways
Forest Ridge
Kelsey La
Kelsey Way
Manor Way
Little Acre
Elgood Pl Fld
Kelsey Park Sports Coll
Tenn Cts
Ralph Perring Ct
Stone Park Ave
Kelsey Park
The Beck
Allot Gdns
Brograve Gdns
Fitzhardinge Ho
Kelsey Park Ave
Lakeside
Andrew Ct
King's Ct
Aaron Ct
Samuel Ct
Kelsey Park Man
Parkview Lo
Wickham Rd
B230
B251
Stonehaven
Holmdene Cl
Overbury Ave
Hannah Cl
Kenwood
Russell Cl
Tudor
Thorne's Cl
Tulse Cl
North Dr
Spinney Cl
Coppice Cl
Walled Garden Cl
Bucknall Way
Holly Cl
Bramble Cl
Acorn Way
Wagtail Wlk
St Martins La
Limewood
Whitstone La
Unicorn Prim Sch
Waterside Ave 1
Brockwell Ave 2
Creswell Dr 3
Clearwater Ho 4
Eden Park
Crease Park
Glanfield Rd
Wellhouse Rd
Crossways Rd
Eden Park Ave
BR3
Leaveland Cl
Pl Fld
Pav
South Eden Park Rd
Elmerside Rd
Eden Way
Langley Rd
Raymond Rd
Goddard Rd
The Close
Staddon
Shirley Cres
Kingsworth Cl
Dunbar Ave
Osborne Cl
Balmoral Ave
Bwg Gn
Sp Gd
Mountbatten Gdns
Stanhope Gr
Ronald Cl
Merlin Gr
Ernest Gr
Ernest Cl
Overstand Cl
Tonge Cl
L Ctr
Marian Vian Prim Sch
Adams Rd
Abbots Way
Lloyds Way
Ambleside Ave
Berney Ho
Upper Elmers End Rd
Bolingbroke Ho
Holly Cres
Lodge Gdns
Barts Cl
Oakfield Gdns
Eldersie Cl
Monks Way
Links Way
Langley Park Sch for Boys
Hawksbrook La
Audrey Cl
Fairford Cl
Aylesford Ave
Aviemore Way
Aviemore Cl
Altyre Cl
Altyre Way
Fairway Cl
Morris Cl
Ash Tree Cl
Ash Tree Way
Elmdene Cl
Hillcrest Cl
Hillcrest View
Upper Elmers End
Greenview Ave
Burrell Cl
Peter Kennedy Ct
Sloane Wlk
Watlings Cl
Starling Cl
Baron's Wlk
Kempton Wlk
Castleton Cl
Regency Wlk
Darley Cl
Ham View
Orchard Way
Radnor Wlk
Kelvington Cl
Monks Orchard
Camrose Cl
Great Gatton Cl
Elstan Way
Glade Gdns
Carrington Cl
Overstone Gdns
Edenham High Sch
Pipers Gdns
Orchard Gr
Croydon
Bromley
Orchard Way Prim Sch
Lyconby Gdns
Coverack Cl
Tower View
Allot Gdns
High Trees
The Hyrst
Woodland Way
Orchard Rise
Pippin Cl
Freshfields
Oakview Gr
Russet Dr
Shirley Oaks
Recn Gd
CR0
Potters Cl
Fieldpark Gdns
Wilks Gdns
Orchard Ave
Firsby Ave
Cheston Ave
Parkfields
Bethlem Royal
Park Farm
Beckmead Sch
Monks Orchard Rd
Eresby Dr
Cvn Pk
Pond Cottage La
Crittenden Lo
Orchard Ct
St David's Coll
BR4
High Broom Cres
St David's Cl
Oak Lodge Dr
Chamberlain Cres
Oak Lodge Prim Sch
Pine Ave
Cavendish Way
Wilmar Gdns
Manor Park Rd
Manor Park Cl
Barwood Ave
Surrey Rd
Kent Rd
Braemar Gdns
Ravenswood Ave
Ravenswood Cres
Gable Lo
Blake's Grn
Beckenham Rd
West Wickham
A232
Wickham Rd
Devonshire Ct
High St
Dixon Pl
Oak Gdns
Riverside Wlk
The Alders
Manor Rd
Grosvenor Rd
Springfield Gdns
Hawkhurst Way
Chessington
Wood Way
Peregrine Gdns
Marlowe Lo
The Willows
Inwood Cl
Philip Gdns
Addison's Cl
Langland Gdns
Lake Rd
Devonshire Way
Farm Dr
Ash Rd
Liby
Millers
A
B
C
D
1
2
3
4
5
6
36
37
38
66
67
68
69

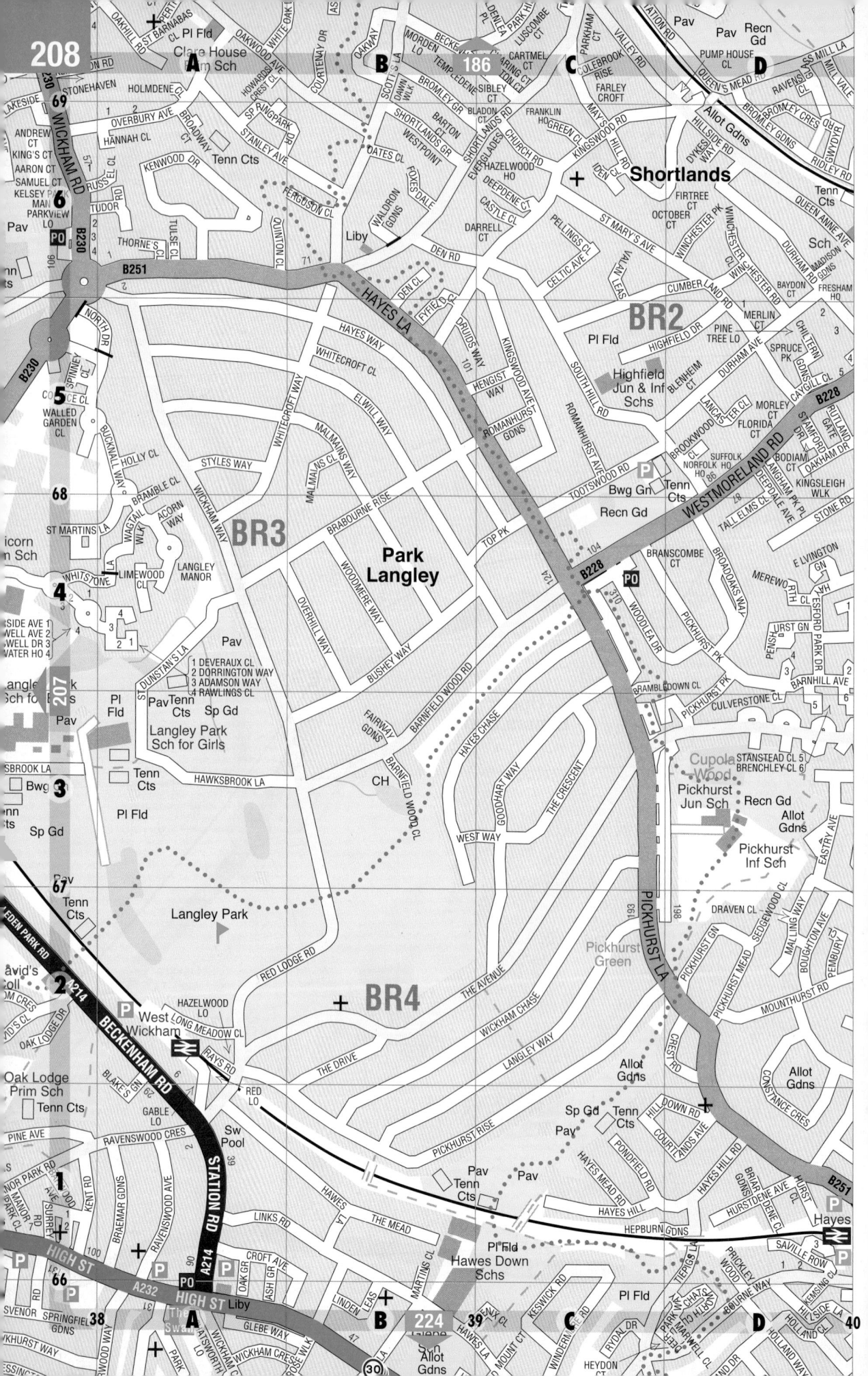

Shortlands
BR2
BR3
Park Langley
BR4
Langley Park
West Wickham
Hayes
Pickhurst Green
Cupola Wood
WICKHAM RD
HAYES LA
WESTMORELAND RD
PICKHURST LA
BECKENHAM RD
STATION RD
HIGH ST
Highfield Jun & Inf Schs
Langley Park Sch for Girls
Pickhurst Jun Sch
Pickhurst Inf Sch
Hawes Down Schs
Oak Lodge Prim Sch
Clare House Prim Sch

186
207
224

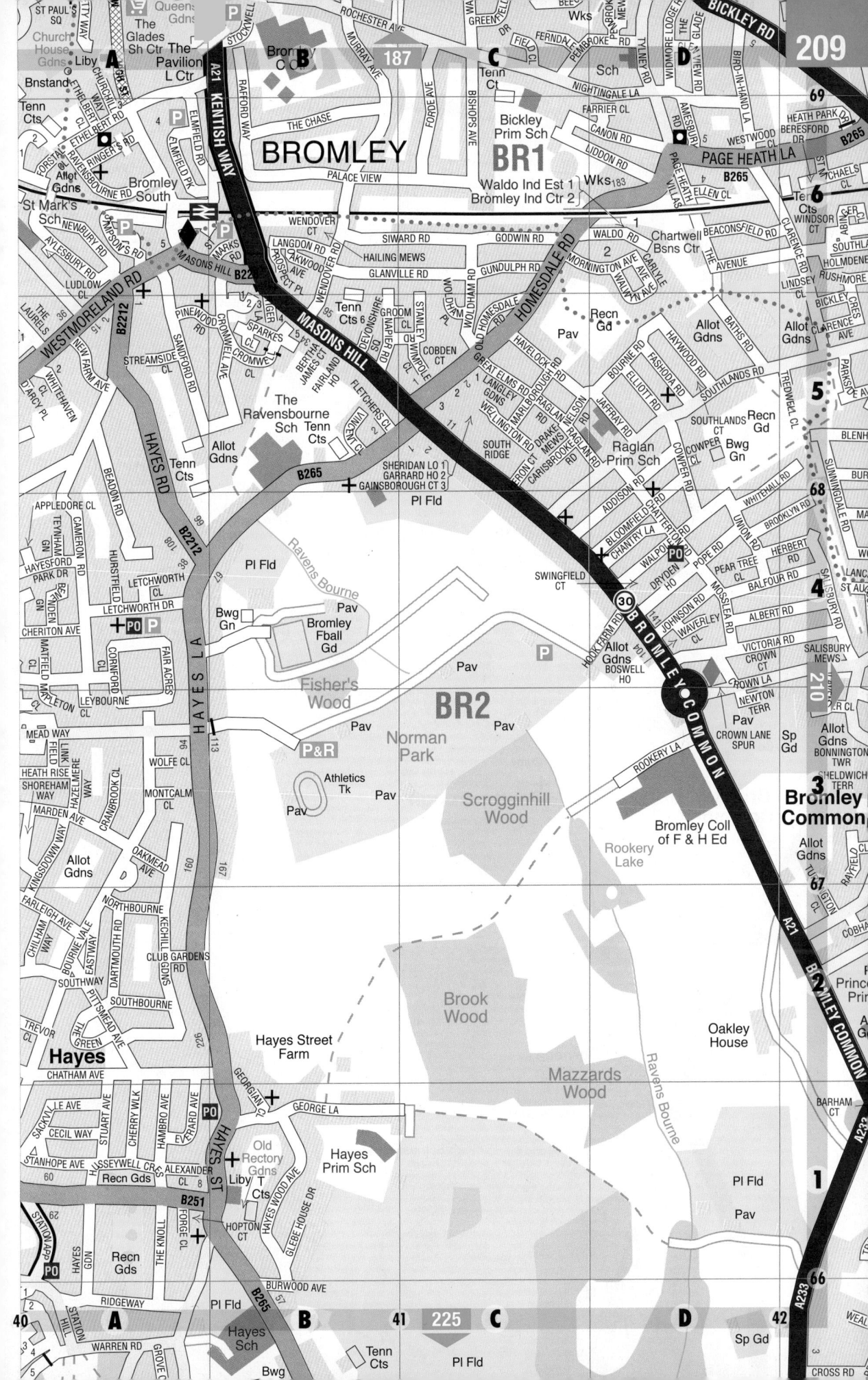
BROMLEY
BR1
BR2
Bromley South
Masons Hill
Kentish Way
Homesdale Rd
Westmoreland Rd
Hayes Rd
Hayes La
Hayes St
Bromley Common
Page Heath La
Bickley Rd
Norman Park
Scrogginhill Wood
Brook Wood
Mazzards Wood
Fisher's Wood
Ravens Bourne
Bromley Fball Gd
Bromley Coll of F & H Ed
Rookery Lake
Oakley House
Hayes Street Farm
Hayes Prim Sch
Hayes
The Ravensbourne Sch
Raglan Prim Sch
Bickley Prim Sch
Waldo Ind Est
Bromley Ind Ctr
Chartwell Bsns Ctr
The Glades Sh Ctr
The Pavilion L Ctr
187
225
210
40
41
42
66
67
68
69

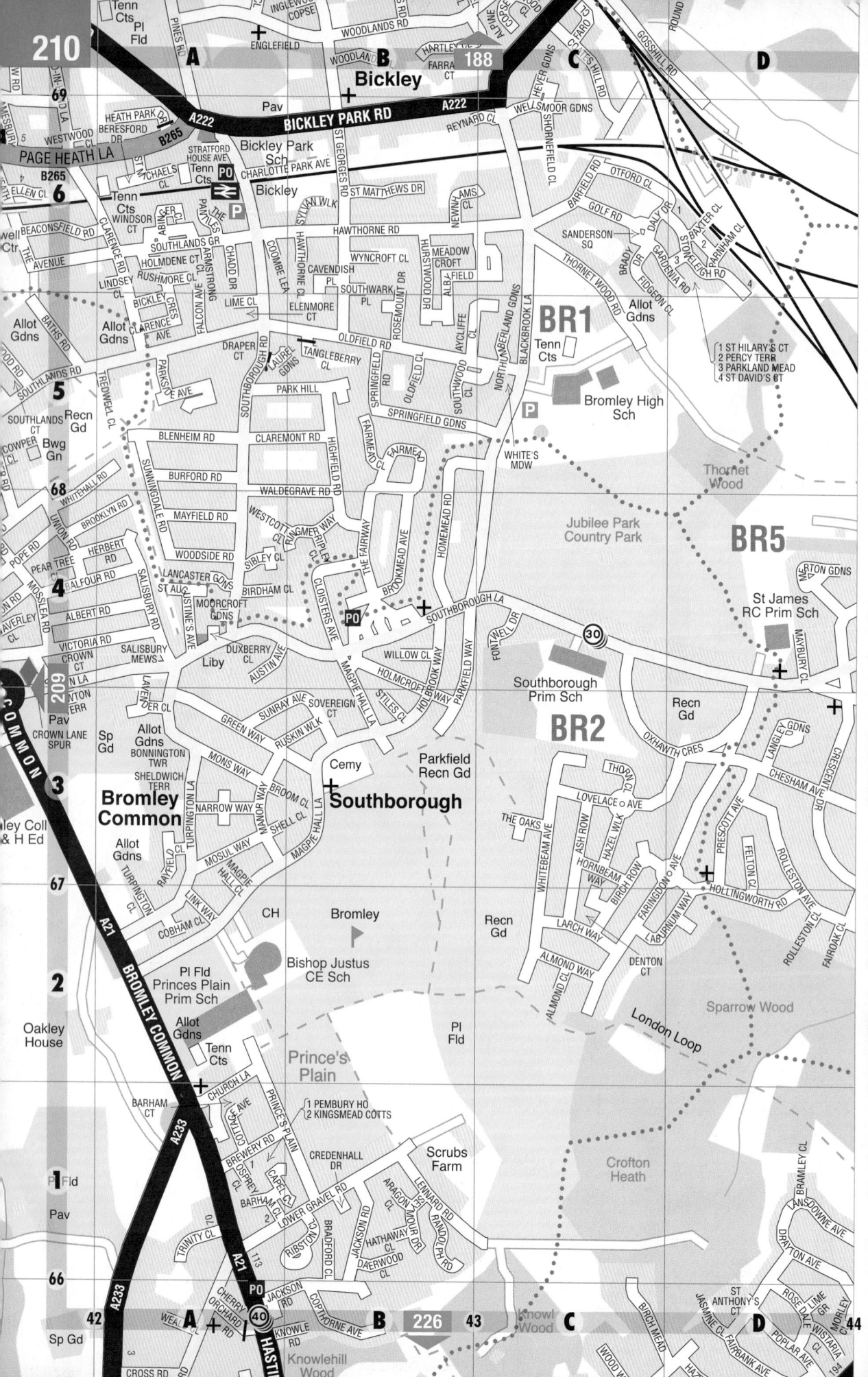

188
226
209
A
B
C
D
1
2
3
4
5
6
66
67
68
69
42
43
44
Bickley
Bickley Park Sch
BICKLEY PARK RD
A222
PAGE HEATH LA
B265
BR1
BR2
BR5
Bromley High Sch
Jubilee Park Country Park
Thornet Wood
St James RC Prim Sch
Southborough Prim Sch
Southborough
Parkfield Recn Gd
Bromley Common
Bishop Justus CE Sch
Princes Plain Prim Sch
Prince's Plain
Scrubs Farm
Crofton Heath
Sparrow Wood
London Loop
Knowl Wood
Knowlehill Wood
Oakley House
BROMLEY COMMON
A21
A233
SOUTHBOROUGH LA
OLDFIELD RD
HAWTHORNE RD
BLACKBROOK LA
LOWER GRAVEL RD
CHURCH LA
1 ST HILARY'S CT
2 PERCY TERR
3 PARKLAND MEAD
4 ST DAVID'S CT
1 PEMBURY HO
2 KINGSMEAD COTTS

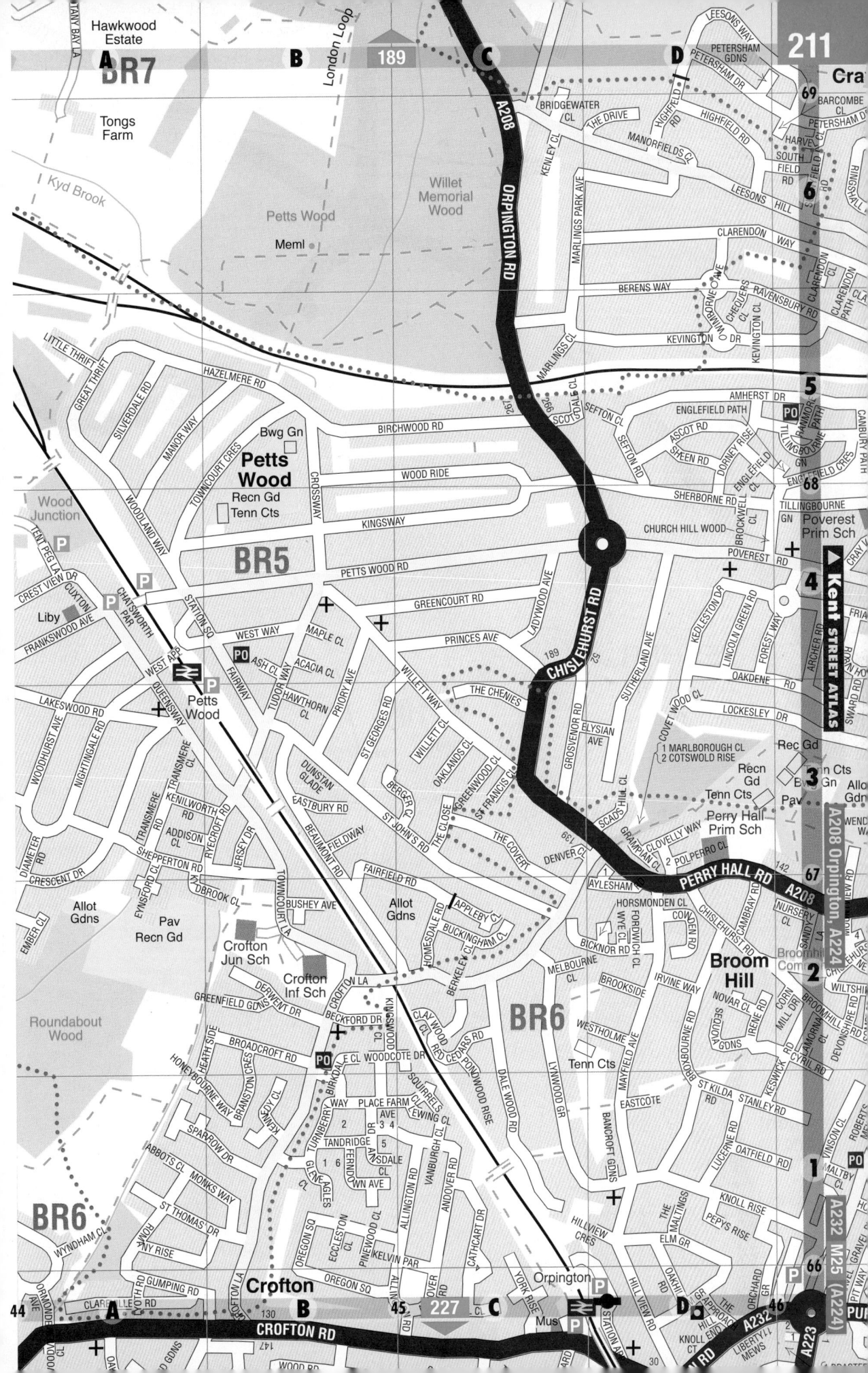
Hawkwood Estate
BR7
Tongs Farm
Kyd Brook
London Loop
189
Petts Wood
Meml
Willet Memorial Wood
A208
ORPINGTON RD
Cray
BRIDGEWATER CL
THE DRIVE
KENLEY CL
HIGHFIELD RD
MANORFIELDS CL
LEESONS WAY
PETERSHAM GDNS
PETERSHAM DR
BARCOMBE CL
PETERSHAM DR
SOUTHFIELD RD
LEESONS HILL
MARLINGS PARK AVE
CLARENDON WAY
BERENS WAY
WIMBORNE AVE
CHEQUERS CL
RAVENSBURY RD
KEVINGTON CL
KEVINGTON DR
CLARENDON PATH
MARLINGS CL
LITTLE THRIFT
GREAT THRIFT
HAZELMERE RD
SILVERDALE RD
MANOR WAY
TOWNCOURT CRES
Bwg Gn
Petts Wood
Recn Gd
Tenn Cts
BIRCHWOOD RD
SCOTSDALE CL
SEFTON CL
SEFTON RD
AMHERST DR
ENGLEFIELD PATH
ASCOT RD
SHEEN RD
DORNEY RISE
ENGLEFIELD CL
TILLINGBOURNE GN
ENGLEFIELD CRES
CANBURY PATH
WOOD RIDE
CROSSWAY
SHERBORNE RD
BROCKWELL CL
TILLINGBOURNE GN
Poverest Prim Sch
Wood Junction
WOODLAND WAY
KINGSWAY
CHURCH HILL WOOD
POVEREST RD
BR5
TENT PEG LA
CREST VIEW DR
CUXTON
Liby
FRANKSWOOD AVE
CHATSWORTH PAR
STATION SQ
PETTS WOOD RD
GREENCOURT RD
LADYWOOD AVE
CHISLEHURST RD
KEDLESTON DR
LINCOLN GREEN RD
FOREST WAY
ARCHER RD
Kent STREET ATLAS
WEST WAY
MAPLE CL
ACACIA CL
ASH CL
PRINCES AVE
SUTHERLAND AVE
OAKDENE RD
WEST APP
Petts Wood
QUEENSWAY
FAIRWAY
TUDOR WAY
HAWTHORN CL
PRIORY AVE
WILLETT WAY
THE CHENIES
COVET WOOD CL
LOCKESLEY DR
LAKESWOOD RD
WOODHURST AVE
NIGHTINGALE RD
TRANSMERE CL
ST GEORGES RD
WILLETT CL
OAKLANDS CL
GREENWOOD CL
ST FRANCIS CL
GROSVENOR RD
ELYSIAN AVE
1 MARLBOROUGH CL
2 COTSWOLD RISE
Rec Gd
Recn Gd
Tenn Cts
Bwg Gn
Pav
Perry Hall Prim Sch
A208 Orpington, A224
TRANSMERE RD
KENILWORTH RD
ADDISON CL
RYECROFT RD
JERSEY DR
DUNSTAN GLADE
EASTBURY RD
BERGER CL
THE CLOSE
ST JOHN'S RD
THE COVERT
SCADS HILL CL
GRAMPIAN CL
CLOVELLY WAY
2 POLPERRO CL
DIAMETER RD
CRESCENT DR
SHEPPERTON RD
KYDBROOK CL
TOWNCOURT LA
BEAUMONT RD
FIELDWAY
FAIRFIELD RD
DENVER CL
AYLESHAM RD
PERRY HALL RD
A208
CAMBRAY RD
NURSERY CL
Allot Gdns
EYNSFORD CL
Pav
Recn Gd
BUSHEY AVE
Allot Gdns
APPLEBY CL
HOMESDALE RD
BUCKINGHAM CL
HORSMONDEN CL
WYE CL
FORDWICH CL
COWDEN RD
CHISLEHURST RD
EMBER CL
Crofton Jun Sch
Crofton Inf Sch
BERKELEY CL
MELBOURNE CL
BICKNOR RD
BROOKSIDE
IRVINE WAY
Broom Hill
Broomhill Comm
CROFTON LA
GREENFIELD GDNS
DERWENT DR
BECKFORD DR
KINGSWOOD CL
CLAYWOOD CL
RED CEDARS RD
BR6
WESTHOLME
NOVAR CL
IRENE RD
CORN MILL DR
BROOMHILL RD
AMORNA CL
WILTSHIRE RD
DEVONSHIRE RD
Roundabout Wood
HEATH SIDE
BROADCROFT RD
HONEYBOURNE WAY
BRANSTON CRES
KENNEDY CL
BIRKDALE CL
WOODCOTE DR
SQUIRRELS CL
PONDWOOD RISE
DALE WOOD RD
LYNWOOD GR
MAYFIELD AVE
Tenn Cts
BROXBOURNE RD
SEQUOIA GDNS
KESWICK RD
CYRIL RD
TURNBERRY WAY
PLACE FARM AVE
EWING CL
EASTCOTE
ST KILDA RD
STANLEY RD
SPARROW DR
TANDRIDGE DR
ARNSDALE CL
FERNDOWN AVE
GLENEAGLES CL
VANBURGH CL
ANDOVER RD
ALLINGTON RD
BANCROFT GDNS
LUCERNE RD
OATFIELD RD
VINSON CL
MALTBY CL
ABBOTS CL
MONKS WAY
ST THOMAS' DR
KNOLL RISE
PEPYS RISE
BR6
WYNDHAM CL
ROWANY RISE
OREGON SQ
ECCLESTON CL
PINEWOOD CL
KELVIN PAR
CATHCART DR
HILLVIEW CRES
THE MALTINGS
ELM GR
A232 M25 (A224)
CLAREVILLE RD
GUMPING RD
CROFTON LA
Crofton
OREGON SQ
YORK RISE
Orpington
HILL VIEW RD
OAKHILL RD
GRASMERE APPROACH
THE APPROACH
ORCHARD GR
CROFTON RD
227
Mus
STATION APP
KNOLL END CT
LIBERTY MEWS
A232
A223
ORMONDE AVE
WOOD RD
44
45
46

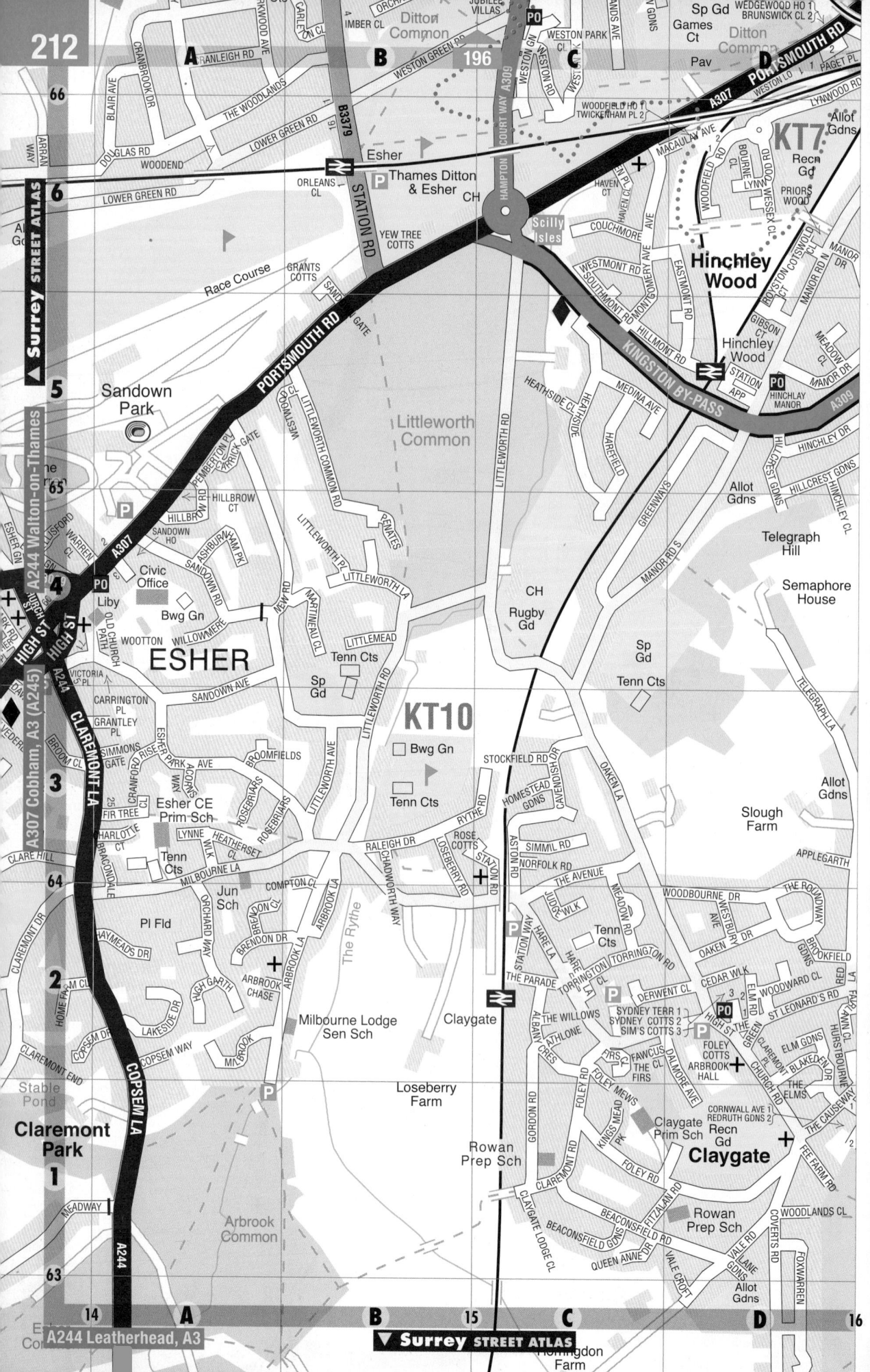
196
A
B
C
D
66
6
5
65
4
3
64
2
1
63
14
15
16
Surrey STREET ATLAS
A244 Walton-on-Thames
A307 Cobham, A3 (A245)
A244 Leatherhead, A3
ESHER
Esher
Thames Ditton & Esher
Sandown Park
Race Course
Littleworth Common
KT10
KT7
Hinchley Wood
Claygate
Claremont Park
Arbrook Common
Ditton Common
Telegraph Hill
Semaphore House
Slough Farm
Loseberry Farm
Milbourne Lodge Sen Sch
Esher CE Prim Sch
Claygate Prim Sch
Rowan Prep Sch
Civic Office
PORTSMOUTH RD
KINGSTON BY-PASS
HAMPTON COURT WAY
STATION RD
LITTLEWORTH RD
CLAREMONT LA
COPSEM LA
HIGH ST
LOWER GREEN RD
WESTON GREEN RD
OAKEN LA
TELEGRAPH LA
MANOR RD S
FOLEY RD
HARE LA
MILBOURNE LA
SANDOWN AVE
RALEIGH DR
CORNWALL AVE 1
REDRUTH GDNS 2
SYDNEY TERR 1
SYDNEY COTTS 2
SIM'S COTTS 3
WOODFIELD HO 1
TWICKENHAM PL 2
WEDGEWOOD HO 1
BRUNSWICK CL 2

Long Ditton

KT7

Hinchley Wood Sch & Sixth Form Coll

Hinchley Wood Prim Sch

Manor House

KT6

Ditton Hill Nurseries

Hill Park Nurseries

KINGSTON BY-PASS

KELVIN GR

KING EDWARD DR

Bwg Gn
Tenn Cts
Recn Gd

Allot Gdns

The Waffrons

Surbiton

CH

Sp Gd
Nursery

Pl Fld

Tenn Cts

Somerset Ave

VALLIS WAY

SELWOOD RD

Pl Fld

Pav

HOLSWORTHY WAY

Lovelace Prim Sch

Kingston upon Thames Surrey

LINDA CT

BRAMHAM GDNS

CHARLES LESSER

RIPON GDNS

BABBACOMBE CL

HATHERLEIGH CL

ROBERTS CT

TIVERTON WAY

WHITEHALL CRES 1
TREWENNA DR 2
CHESSINGTON PAR 3

MANSFIELD RD

POWELL

COURT CRES

CHESHIRE GDNS

SUSSEX GDNS

KT10

Manor Farm

Elm Farm

Lower Wood

DENMAN DR

RED LA

MERLING CL 1
GOLDING CL 2
NICHOLS CL 3
WITHERS CL 4
MITFORD CL 5
VIDLER CL 6
SMEATON CL 7
HUBBARD DR 8

ST CATHERINES CL

SALMONS RD

BOLTON RD

ASHLYNS WAY

St Philip's Sch

LEATHERHEAD RD

ELLINGHAM RD

SIMMONS CL

RAY CL

LOFTHOUSE PL

ORCHID CL

WOODALL

BAILEY CRES

FLEETWOOD CL

BURTON CL

St Philip's Sch

Ellingham Prim Sch

Chessington South Com Coll

KT9

RYTHE CL

GRAPSOME CL

WINEY CL

CHARLES BABBAGE CL

GLADESIDE CL

Barwell

Tenn Cts
Recn Gd

Barwell Bsns Pk

Allot Gdns

Chessington

Barwell Bsns Pk

Glaygate Common

Claygate Common

BARWELL LA

KT9

COXWOLD PATH 1
WETHERBY WAY 2

YORK WAY

CRAKE HILL

HUNTING

VIVIEN CL

Hill

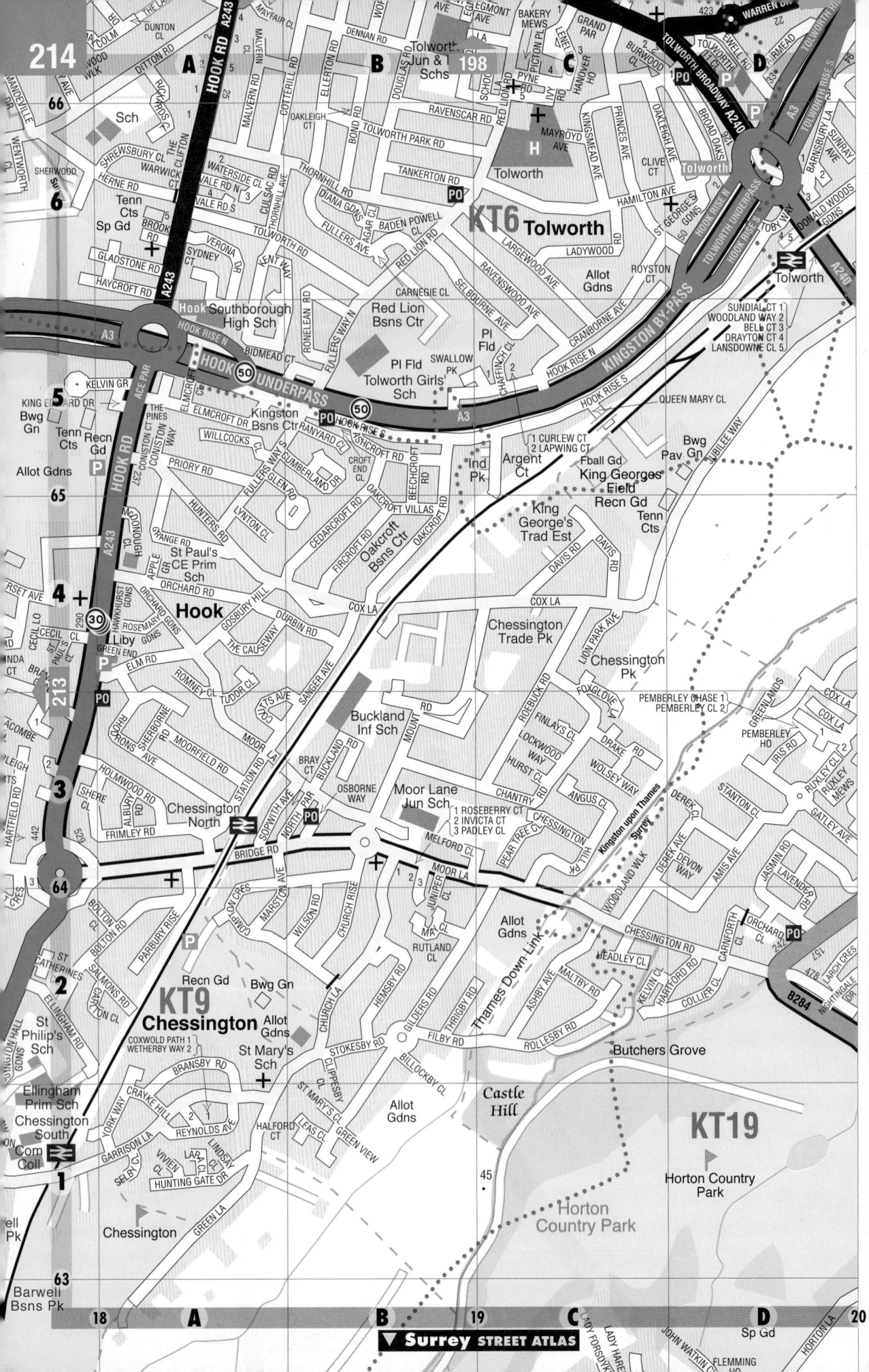
A
B
C
D
198
66
6
5
4
3
2
1
65
64
63
213
18
19
20
A243
HOOK RD
A3
A240
TOLWORTH BROADWAY
TOLWORTH RISE S
TOLWORTH UNDERPASS
HOOK RISE N
HOOK RISE S
HOOK UNDERPASS
KINGSTON BY-PASS
KT6
Tolworth
KT9
Chessington
KT19
Hook
Tolworth Jun & Inf Schs
Tolworth Girls' Sch
Southborough High Sch
Red Lion Bsns Ctr
Kingston Bsns Ctr
Oakcroft Bsns Ctr
St Paul's CE Prim Sch
Chessington Trade Pk
Chessington Pk
King George's Trad Est
King Georges Field
Recn Gd
Tenn Cts
Buckland Inf Sch
Moor Lane Jun Sch
Chessington North
Chessington South
St Philip's Sch
Ellingham Prim Sch
Chessington Com Coll
St Mary's Sch
Castle Hill
Butchers Grove
Horton Country Park
Thames Down Link
Kingston upon Thames
Surrey
Barwell Bsns Pk
Allot Gdns
Bwg Gn
Sp Gd
Argent Ct
Ind Pk
Pl Fld
Liby
DITTON RD
HERNE RD
SHREWSBURY CL
WARWICK CL
GLADSTONE RD
HAYCROFT RD
BROOK RD
SYDNEY CT
VERONA DR
KENT WAY
TOLWORTH RD
THORNHILL RD
THORNHILL RD
DIANA GDNS
AGAR CL
BADEN POWELL CL
FULLERS AVE
RED LION RD
CULSAC RD
COTTERILL RD
MALVERN RD
ELLERTON RD
BOND RD
OAKLEIGH CT
TOLWORTH PARK RD
TANKERTON RD
RAVENSCAR RD
DOUGLAS RD
DENNAN RD
MAYFAIR CL
EGMONT AVE
BAKERY MEWS
PICTON PL
GRAND PAR
PYNE RD
IVY RD
HANOVER HO
BURWOOD CL
MAYROYD AVE
KINGSMEAD AVE
PRINCES AVE
OAKLEIGH AVE
BROAD OAKS
CLIVE CT
HAMILTON AVE
ST GEORGE'S GDNS
LADYWOOD
LARGEWOOD AVE
RAVENSWOOD AVE
SELBOURNE AVE
ROYSTON CT
CRANBORNE AVE
CARNEGIE CL
CHAFFINCH CL
SWALLOW PK
RONELEAN RD
FULLERS WAY N
BIDMEAD CT
ELMCROFT CL
ELMCROFT DR
THE PINES
CONISTON CT
CONISTON WAY
WILLCOCKS CL
RANYARD CL
ASHCROFT RD
CROFT END CL
BEECHCROFT RD
PRIORY RD
CUMBERLAND DR
FULLERS WAY S
GLEN RD
HUNTERS RD
LYNTON CL
CEDARCROFT RD
OAKCROFT VILLAS
OAKCROFT RD
FIRCROFT RD
MCDONOUGH CL
GRANGE RD
APPLE GR
ORCHARD RD
ORCHARD GDNS
HAWKHURST GDNS
ROSEMARY GDNS
GOSBURY HILL
DURBIN RD
THE CAUSEWAY
COX LA
DAVIS RD
LION PARK AVE
ROEBUCK RD
FOXGLOVE LA
FINLAYS CL
LOCKWOOD WAY
HURST CL
CHANTRY RD
DRAKE RD
WOLSEY WAY
ANGUS CL
CHESSINGTON HILL PK
PEAR TREE CL
GREEN END
ELM RD
ROMNEY CL
TUDOR CL
CUTTS AVE
SANGER AVE
MOOR LA
STATION RD
SHERBORNE RD
MOORFIELD RD
RONS AVE
HOLMWOOD RD
SHERE CL
ALBURY RD
FRIMLEY RD
BUCKLAND RD
BRAY CT
SOPWITH AVE
NORTH PAR
OSBORNE WAY
MOUNT RD
BRIDGE RD
MELFORD CL
KELVIN GR
KING EDWARD DR
ACE PAR
CECIL CL
QUEEN MARY CL
JUBILEE WAY
SUNDIAL CT 1
WOODLAND WAY 2
BELL CT 3
DRAYTON CT 4
LANSDOWNE CL 5
TOBY WAY
DONALD WOODS GDNS
1 CURLEW CT
2 LAPWING CT
1 ROSEBERRY CT
2 INVICTA CT
3 PADLEY CL
PEMBERLEY CHASE 1
PEMBERLEY CL 2
PEMBERLEY HO
GREENLANDS
COX LA
IRIS RD
RUXLEY CL
RUXLEY MEWS
STANTON CL
GATLEY AVE
DEREK CL
DEREK AVE
DEVON WAY
AMIS AVE
JASMIN RD
LAVENDER RD
ORCHARD CL
CARNFORTH CL
CHESSINGTON RD
WOODLAND WLK
HEADLEY CL
KELVIN CL
HARTFORD RD
COLLIER CL
MALTBY RD
ASHBY AVE
ROLLESBY RD
LARCH CRES
NIGHTINGALE DR
B284
BOLTON CL
BOLTON RD
PARBURY RISE
COMPTON CRES
MARSTON AVE
WILSON RD
CHURCH RISE
JUNIPER CL
RUTLAND CL
HEMSBY RD
GILDERS RD
THRIGBY RD
FILBY RD
STOKESBY RD
CHURCH LA
CLIPPESBY CL
BILLOCKBY CL
ST MARY'S CL
GREEN VIEW
LEAS CL
HALFORD CT
ST CATHERINES
SALMONS RD
CARLTON CL
ELLINGHAM RD
COXWOLD PATH 1
WETHERBY WAY 2
BRANSBY RD
CRAYKE HILL
YORK WAY
REYNOLDS AVE
LINDSAY CL
GARRISON LA
VIVIEN CL
LARA CL
SELBY CL
HUNTING GATE DR
GREEN LA
HARTFIELD RD
WENTWORTH
SHERWOOD
HORTON LA
JOHN WATKIN CL
LADY HARE
LADY FORSDYKE
FLEMMING HO
WARREN DR
FAIRMEAD
BARNSBURY LA
SUNRAY AVE
Sch
Tenn Cts
Sp Gd
PO
P
H
45
Chessington
Horton Country Park

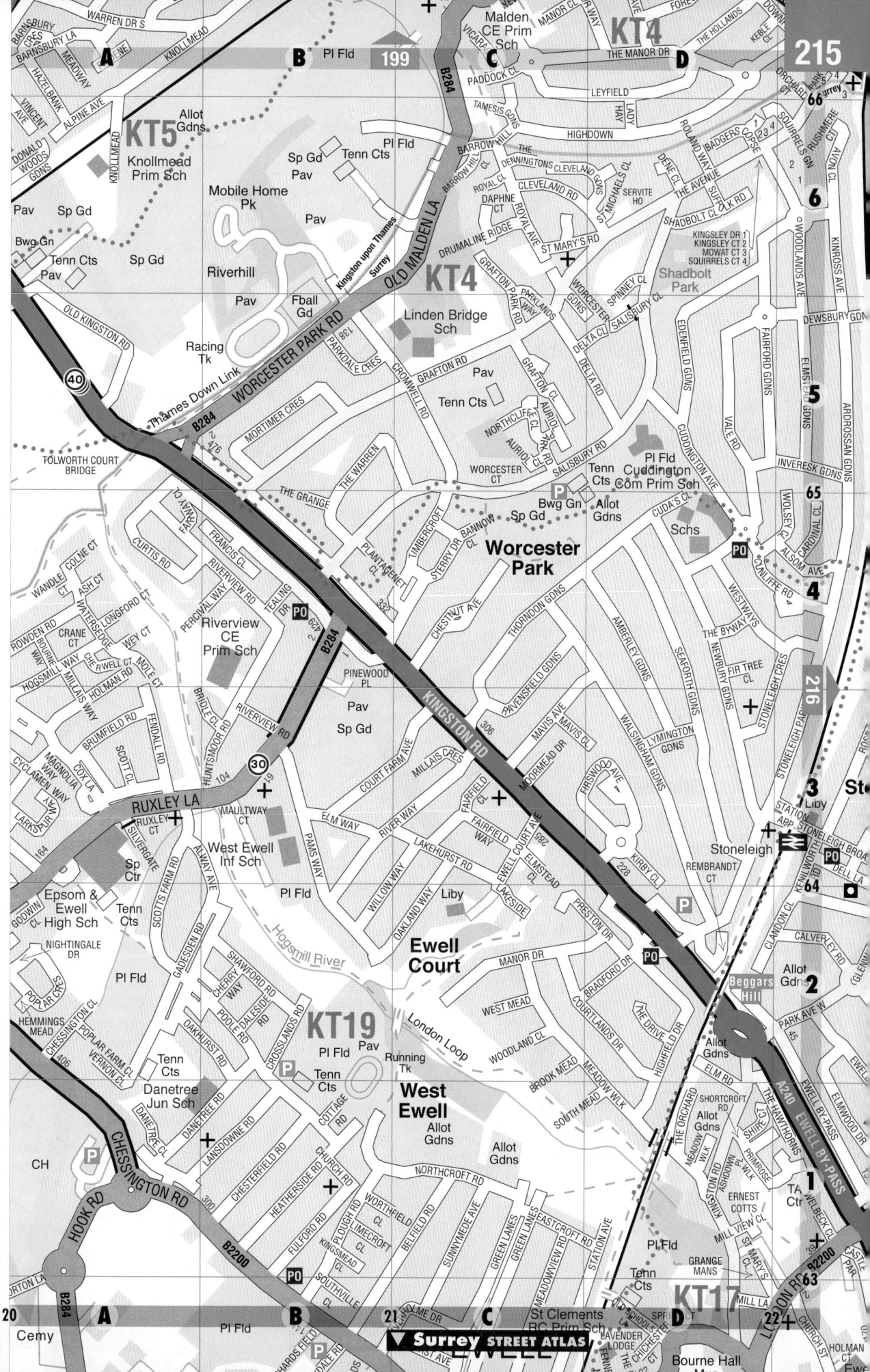
KT4
KT5
KT19
KT17
Malden CE Prim Sch
Knollmead Prim Sch
Mobile Home Pk
Riverhill
Racing Tk
Linden Bridge Sch
Shadbolt Park
Worcester Park
Cuddington Com Prim Sch
Riverview CE Prim Sch
West Ewell Inf Sch
Epsom & Ewell High Sch
Ewell Court
West Ewell
Danetree Jun Sch
Stoneleigh
Beggars Hill
KINGSTON RD
WORCESTER PARK RD
OLD MALDEN LA
RUXLEY LA
CHESSINGTON RD
HOOK RD
EWELL BY-PASS
Hogsmill River
London Loop
Thames Down Link
TOLWORTH COURT BRIDGE
Bourne Hall
St Clements RC Prim Sch
Surrey STREET ATLAS

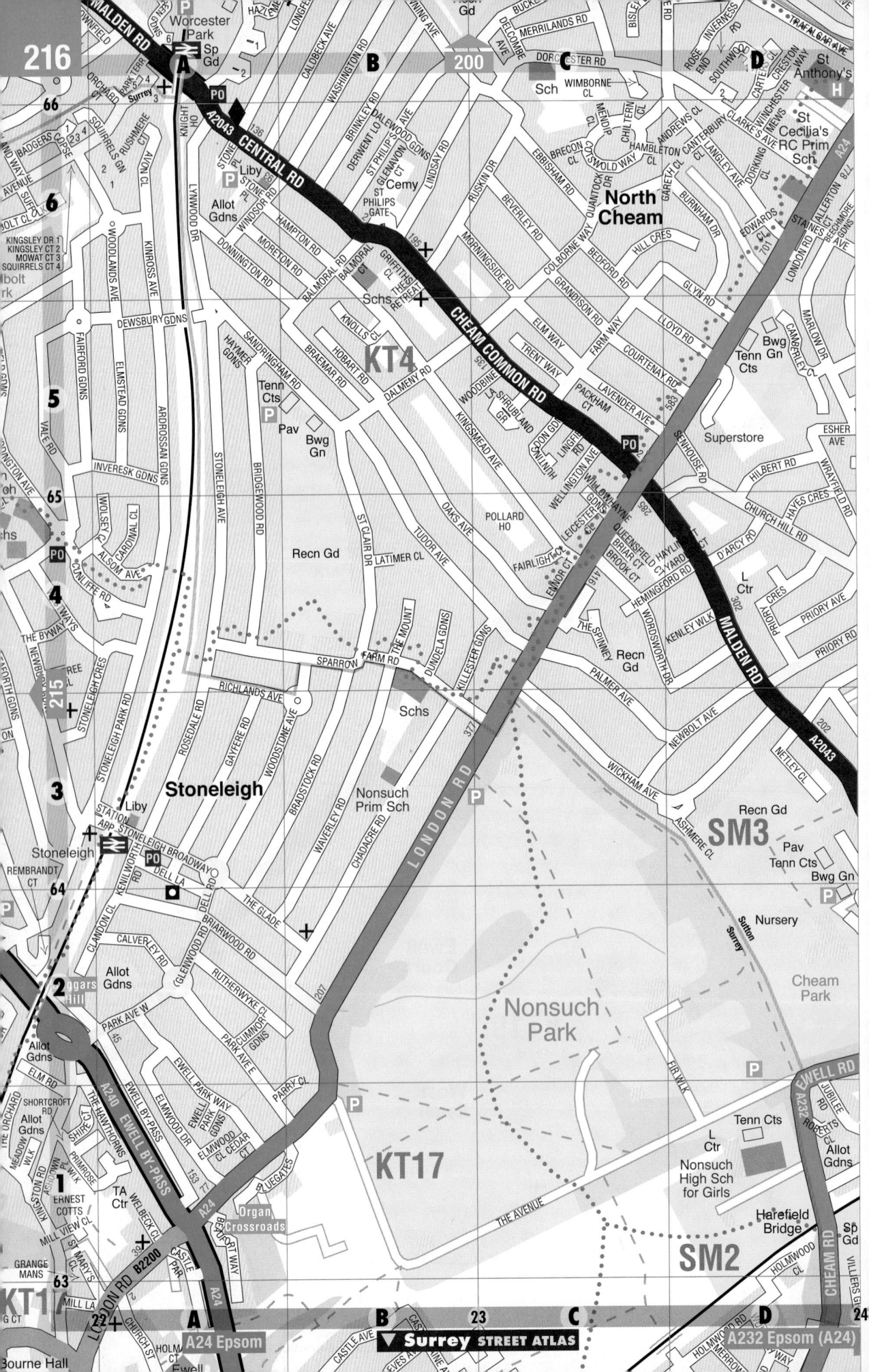

Worcester Park
Sp Gd
200
A
B
C
D
MALDEN RD
CALDBECK AVE
WASHINGTON RD
LONGFELLOW RD
MERRILANDS RD
DELCOMBE AVE
DORCHESTER RD
Sch
WIMBORNE CL
ROSE END
INVERNESS RD
SOUTHWOOD
CARTERS CL
CRESTON WAY
TRAFALGAR AVE
St Anthony's
H
St Cecilia's RC Prim Sch
ORCHARD CT
PARK TERR
Surrey
66
PO
A2043
CENTRAL RD
KNIGHT HO
BADGERS COPSE
SQUIRRELS GN
RUSHMERE CT
AVON CL
BRINKLEY RD
DALEWOOD GDNS
DERWENT LO
ST PHILIP'S AVE
GLENAVON CT
LINDSAY RD
ST PHILIPS GATE
Cemy
Liby
STONE PL
WINDSOR RD
Allot Gdns
LYNWOOD DR
HAMPTON RD
MORETON RD
DONNINGTON RD
BALMORAL RD
BALMORAL CT
GRIFFITHS CL
THE RETREAT
Schs
RUSKIN DR
BEVERLEY RD
MORNINGSIDE RD
EBBISHAM RD
MENDIP
CHILTERN CL
BRECON CL
COTSWOLD WAY
HAMBLETON CL
ANDREWS CL
CANTERBURY CL
CLARKE'S AVE
WINCHESTER MEWS
LANGLEY AVE
DORKING CL
GARETH CL
BURNHAM DR
QUANTOCK DR
North Cheam
COLBORNE WAY
BEDFORD RD
HILL CRES
GLYN RD
GRANDISON RD
EDWARDS CL
STAINES AVE
ALLERTON CT
BEECHMORE GDNS
LONDON RD
A24
6
KINGSLEY DR 1
KINGSLEY CT 2
MOWAT CT 3
SQUIRRELS CT 4
WOODLANDS AVE
KINROSS AVE
DEWSBURY GDNS
FAIRFORD GDNS
ELMSTEAD GDNS
ARDROSSAN GDNS
STONELEIGH AVE
HAYMER GDNS
SANDRINGHAM RD
BRIDGEWOOD RD
KNOLLS CL
HOBART RD
BRAEMAR RD
DALMENY RD
KT4
CHEAM COMMON RD
ELM WAY
TRENT WAY
FARM WAY
LLOYD RD
COURTENAY RD
LAVENDER AVE
PACKHAM CT
WOODBINE
LA SHRUBLAND GR
KINGSMEAD AVE
Tenn Cts
Bwg Gn
Pav
5
VALE RD
INVERESK GDNS
65
WOLSEY CL
CARDINAL CL
ALSOM AVE
CUNLIFFE RD
Recn Gd
ST CLAIR DR
LATIMER CL
TUDOR AVE
OAKS AVE
POLLARD HO
WELLINGTON AVE
WILLOWHAYNE GDNS
LEICESTER CL
FAIRLIGHT CL
ENNOR CT
QUEENSFIELD CT
BRIAR CT
BROOK CT
HAYLING CT
YARD
SENHOUSE RD
Superstore
CAMBERLEY CL
MARLOW DR
ESHER AVE
HILBERT RD
WRAYFIELD RD
HAYES CRES
CHURCH HILL RD
D'ARCY RD
L Ctr
PRIORY CRES
PRIORY AVE
PRIORY RD
HEMINGFORD RD
KENLEY WLK
WORDSWORTH DR
THE SPINNEY
4
THE BYWAY
215
STONELEIGH CRES
STONELEIGH PARK RD
THE MOUNT
DUNDELA GDNS
KILLESTER GDNS
SPARROW FARM RD
RICHLANDS AVE
ROSEDALE RD
GAYFERE RD
WOODSTONE AVE
BRADSTOCK RD
WAVERLEY RD
CHADACRE RD
Nonsuch Prim Sch
PALMER AVE
NEWBOLT AVE
WICKHAM AVE
NETLEY CL
ASHMERE CL
SM3
3
Stoneleigh
STATION APP
STONELEIGH BROADWAY
KENILWORTH RD
DELL LA
DELL RD
THE GLADE
LONDON RD
REMBRANDT CT
64
CLANDON CL
CALVERLEY RD
GLENWOOD RD
BRIARWOOD RD
RUTHERWYKE CL
Nursery
Sutton
Cheam Park
2
PARK AVE W
PARK AVE E
CUMNOR GDNS
Nonsuch Park
Allot Gdns
ELM RD
SHORTCROFT RD
THE ORCHARD
MEADOW WLK
THE HAWTHORNS
SHIRE CT
PRIMROSE WLK
A240
EWELL BY-PASS
EWELL PARK WAY
EWELL PARK GDNS
ELMWOOD DR
ELMWOOD CL
CEDAR CT
PARRY CL
BLUEGATES
FIR WLK
EWELL RD
A232
JUBILEE RD
ROBERTS CL
Tenn Cts
L Ctr
Nonsuch High Sch for Girls
KT17
1
ERNEST COTTS
TA Ctr
WELBECK CL
Organ Crossroads
THE AVENUE
Harefield Bridge
Sp Gd
MILL VIEW CL
ST MARY'S CL
GRANGE MANS
63
B2200
CASTLE PAR
BEAUFORT WAY
SM2
HOLMWOOD CL
CHEAM RD
VILLIERS GR
MILL LA
LONDON RD
CHURCH ST
HOLM CT
22
23
24
A24 Epsom
Surrey STREET ATLAS
A232 Epsom (A24)
Bourne Hall
Ewell
CASTLE AVE
HOLMWOOD RD

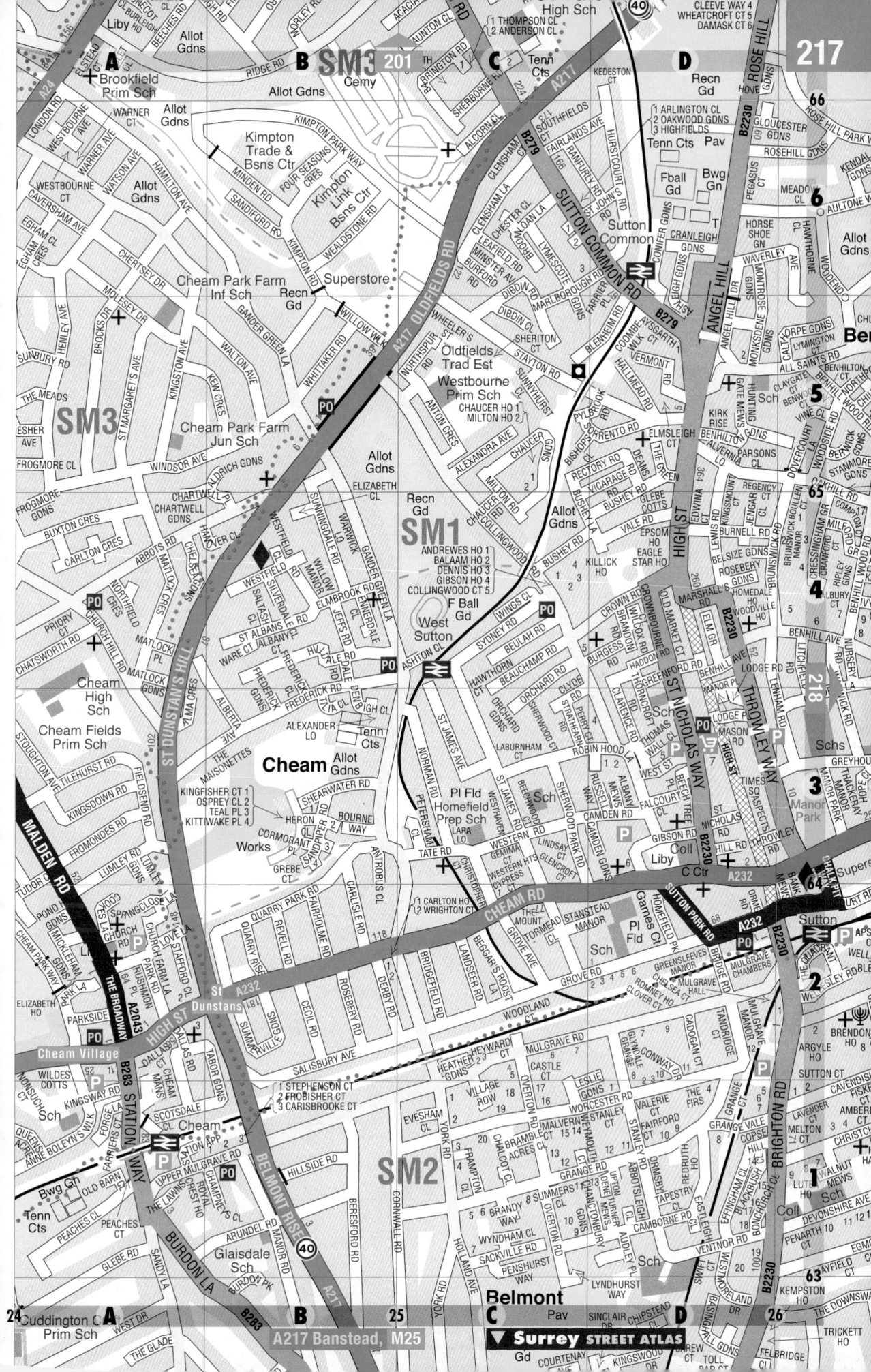
SM3
201
High Sch
Allot Gdns
Liby
Brookfield Prim Sch
Allot Gdns
Cemy
Tenn Cts
Recn Gd
Kimpton Trade & Bsns Ctr
Kimpton Link Bsns Ctr
Four Seasons Cres
Sutton Common
Cheam Park Farm Inf Sch
Superstore
Oldfields Trad Est
Westbourne Prim Sch
Cheam Park Farm Jun Sch
SM3
SM1
Allot Gdns
Recn Gd
F Ball Gd
West Sutton
Cheam High Sch
Cheam Fields Prim Sch
Cheam
Allot Gdns
Tenn Cts
Works
Homefield Prep Sch
Pl Fld
Sch
Games Ct
Coll
Liby
C Ctr
Sutton
Manor Park
Schs
Cheam Village
Cheam
Glaisdale Sch
SM2
Belmont
Cuddington Croft Prim Sch
Bwg Gn
Tenn Cts
A217 Banstead, M25
Surrey STREET ATLAS
A217 OLDFIELDS RD
SUTTON COMMON RD
ST DUNSTAN'S HILL
MALDEN RD
CHEAM RD
HIGH ST
ST NICHOLAS WAY
THROWLEY WAY
ANGEL HILL
ROSE HILL
BRIGHTON RD
BELMONT RISE
STATION WAY
BURDON LA
218
A B C D
24 25 26
63 64 65 66

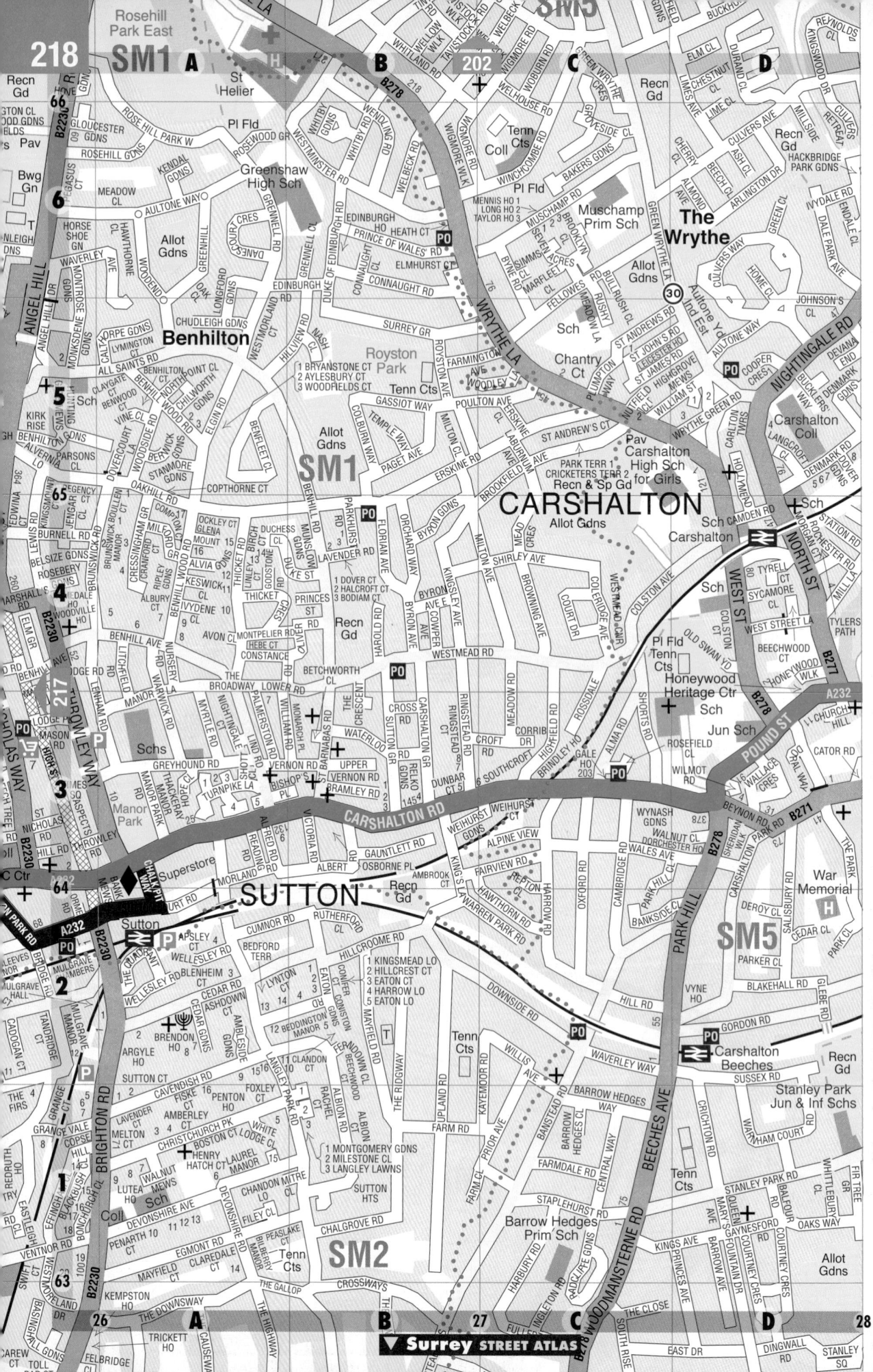

218
SM1
A
B
202
C
D
Rosehill Park East
St Helier
Benhilton
Greenshaw High Sch
Royston Park
The Wrythe
Muschamp Prim Sch
Aultone Yd Ind Est
Carshalton Coll
Pav Carshalton High Sch for Girls
CARSHALTON
Carshalton
Honeywood Heritage Ctr
Jun Sch
War Memorial
SM5
SUTTON
Sutton
Superstore
Manor Park
Carshalton Beeches
Stanley Park Jun & Inf Schs
Barrow Hedges Prim Sch
SM2
WRYTHE LA
CARSHALTON RD
NIGHTINGALE RD
NORTH ST
WEST ST
POUND ST
PARK HILL
BEECHES AVE
WOODMANSTERNE RD
BRIGHTON RD
ANGEL HILL
THROWLEY WAY
WESTMEAD RD
SHIRLEY AVE
DOWNSIDE RD
WAVERLEY WAY
GREYHOUND RD
HILLCROOME RD
CAVENDISH RD
MULGRAVE RD
BENHILL WOOD RD
ERSKINE RD
ST ANDREW'S CT
ROSE HILL PARK W
AULTONE WAY
B278
B2230
B277
B271
A232
217
26
27
28
63
64
65
66
Surrey STREET ATLAS

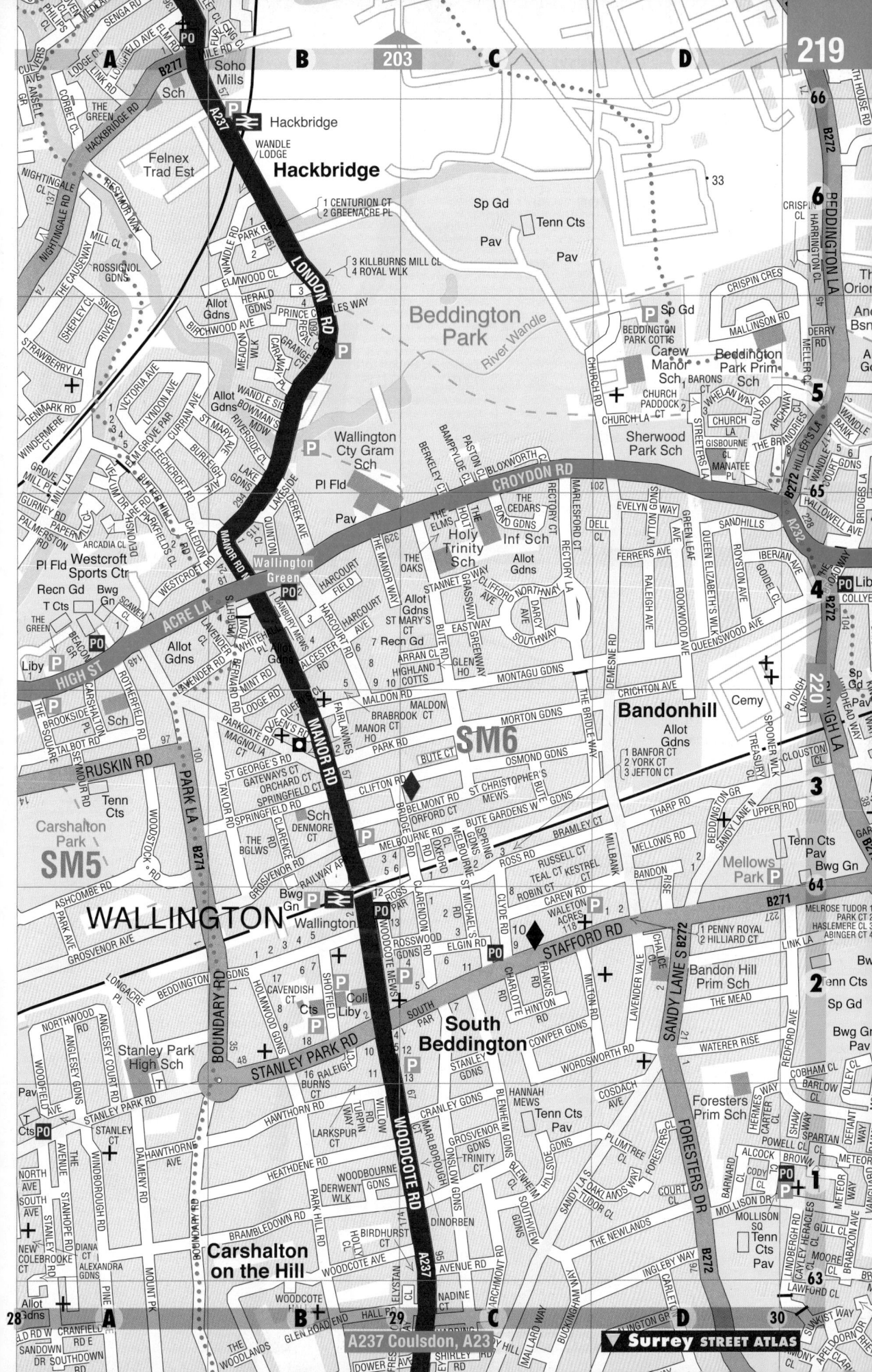
203
A
B
C
D
Hackbridge
Hackbridge
Soho Mills
Felnex Trad Est
WANDLE LODGE
1 CENTURION CT
2 GREENACRE PL
3 KILLBURNS MILL CL
4 ROYAL WLK
LONDON RD
A237
B277
HACKBRIDGE RD
NIGHTINGALE RD
NIGHTINGALE CL
THE CAUSEWAY
ROSSIGNOL GDNS
MILL CL
SHEPLEY CL
STRAWBERRY LA
DENMARK RD
WINDERMERE CT
Sp Gd
Tenn Cts
Pav
Beddington Park
River Wandle
Allot Gdns
ELMWOOD CL
HERALD GDNS
BIRCHWOOD AVE
PRINCE CHARLES WAY
GRANGE CT
MEADOW WLK
VICTORIA AVE
LYNDON AVE
CURRAN AVE
ST MARY AVE
BURLEIGH AVE
LEECHCROFT RD
ELM GROVE PAR
WANDLE SIDE
BOWMAN'S MDW
RIVERSIDE CL
LAKE GDNS
Wallington Cty Gram Sch
Pl Fld
BERKELEY CT
BAMPFYLDE CL
PASTON CL
BLOXWORTH CL
CROYDON RD
RECTORY CL
MARLESFORD CT
BEDDINGTON PARK COTTS
Carew Manor Sch
Beddington Park Prim Sch
CHURCH RD
CHURCH PADDOCK CT
CHURCH LA
BARONS CT
WHELAN WAY
GUY RD
ARCHWAY CL
Sherwood Park Sch
STREETERS LA
GISBOURNE CL
MANATEE PL
THE BRANDRIES
HILLIER'S LA
CRISPIN CRES
CRISPIN CL
MALLINSON RD
DERRY RD
MELLER CL
HARRINGTON CL
BEDDINGTON LA
B272
B272
A232
Westcroft Sports Ctr
Pl Fld
Recn Gd
Bwg Gn
T Cts
Liby
HIGH ST
ACRE LA
Wallington Green
WESTCROFT RD
CALEDON RD
MANOR RD W
QUINTON CL
LAKESIDE
DEREK AVE
THE MANOR WAY
THE ELMS
HOLT CL
Holy Trinity Sch
THE CEDARS
BOND GDNS
Inf Sch
Allot Gdns
STANNET WAY
CLIFFORD AVE
NORTHWAY
DARCY AVE
SOUTHWAY
EASTWAY
GREENWAY
RECTORY LA
DELL CL
EVELYN WAY
LYTTON GDNS
GREEN LEAF AVE
SANDHILLS
FERRERS AVE
RALEIGH AVE
ROOKWOOD AVE
QUEEN ELIZABETH'S WLK
ROYSTON AVE
IBERIAN AVE
GOIDEL CL
QUEENSWOOD AVE
DEMESNE RD
HARCOURT FIELD
HARCOURT AVE
HARCOURT RD
ALCESTER RD
DANBURY MEWS
Recn Gd
ARRAN CL
HIGHLAND COTTS
GLEN HO
MONTAGU GDNS
CRICHTON AVE
Cemy
Bandonhill
Allot Gdns
1 BANFOR CT
2 YORK CT
3 JEFTON CT
MALDON RD
MALDON CT
BRABROOK CT
MANOR CT
MORTON GDNS
THE BRIDLE WAY
SM6
PARK RD
BUTE CT
OSMOND GDNS
CLIFTON RD
BELMONT RD
ST CHRISTOPHER'S MEWS
BUTE GDNS
BUTE GARDENS W
ORFORD CT
BRIDGE RD
MELBOURNE RD
SPRING GDNS
BRAMLEY CT
MILLBANK
THARP RD
MELLOWS RD
BANDON RISE
BEDDINGTON GR
SANDY LANE N
UPPER RD
CLOUSTON CL
SPOONER WLK
TREASURY CL
PLOUGH LA
Tenn Cts
Pav
Mellows Park
Bwg Gn
CARSHALTON PL
BROOKSIDE
THE SQUARE
TALBOT RD
SEYMOUR RD
RUSKIN RD
ROTHERFIELD RD
PARK LA
B274
Tenn Cts
Carshalton Park
SM5
WOODSTOCK RD
ASHCOMBE RD
PARK AVE
GROSVENOR AVE
WALLINGTON
Wallington
MANOR RD
QUEEN'S RD
MAGNOLIA CT
PARKGATE RD
ST GEORGE'S RD
GATEWAYS CT
ORCHARD CT
SPRINGFIELD CT
SPRINGFIELD RD
TAYLOR RD
CLARENCE RD
THE BGLWS
DENMORE CT
GROSVENOR RD
RAILWAY APP
Bwg Gn
ROSS PAR
CLARENDON RD
ST MICHAEL'S RD
ROSS RD
RUSSELL CT
TEAL CT
KESTREL CT
ROBIN CT
CAREW RD
WALETON ACRES
CLYDE RD
STAFFORD RD
B271
1 PENNY ROYAL
2 HILLIARD CT
CHALICE CL
SANDY LANE S
B272
MELROSE TUDOR
PARK CT
HASLEMERE CL
ABINGER CT
LINK LA
Bandon Hill Prim Sch
THE MEAD
LAVENDER VALE
MILTON RD
FRANCIS RD
CHARLOTTE RD
HINTON RD
ELGIN RD
ROSSWOOD GDNS
WOODCOTE MEWS
SOUTH PAR
South Beddington
COWPER GDNS
WORDSWORTH RD
WATERER RISE
REDFORD AVE
Tenn Cts
Sp Gd
LONGACRE PL
BEDDINGTON GDNS
BOUNDARY RD
HOLMWOOD GDNS
CAVENDISH CT
SHOTFIELD
Coll
Liby
Cts
STANLEY PARK RD
Stanley Park High Sch
NORTHWOOD RD
ANGLESEY COURT RD
ANGLESEY GDNS
WOODFIELD AVE
Pav
STANLEY PARK RD
STANLEY CT
RALEIGH CT
BURNS CT
HAWTHORN RD
LARKSPUR CT
TURPIN WAY
WILLOW RD
WOODCOTE RD
STANLEY GDNS
CRANLEY GDNS
HANNAH MEWS
BLENHEIM GDNS
Tenn Cts
Pav
COSDACH AVE
FORESTERS DR
Foresters Prim Sch
HERMES WAY
CARTER CL
SHAW WAY
DEFIANT WAY
SPARTAN CL
POWELL CL
BROWN CL
METEOR WAY
ALCOCK CL
CODY CL
BARNARD CL
MOLLISON DR
MOLLISON SQ
Tenn Cts
Pav
LINDBERGH RD
CAYLEY CL
HERACLES CL
GULL CL
BRABAZON AVE
MOORE CL
LAWFORD CL
HAWTHORNE AVE
DALMENY RD
WINDBOROUGH RD
THE AVENUE
NORTH AVE
SOUTH AVE
STANHOPE RD
STANLEY RD
NEW COLEBROOKE CT
DIANA CT
ALEXANDRA GDNS
HEATHDENE RD
WOODBOURNE GDNS
DERWENT WLK
MARLBOROUGH CT
GROSVENOR GDNS
TRINITY CT
ONSLOW GDNS
HILLSIDE GDNS
PLUMTREE CL
OAKLANDS WAY
TUDOR CL
COURT CL
SOUTHVIEW GDNS
SANDY LA S
BRAMBLEDOWN RD
PARK HILL RD
BIRDHURST CT
HOLLY CL
DINORBEN
THE NEWLANDS
INGLEBY WAY
Carshalton on the Hill
WOODCOTE AVE
AVENUE RD
ARCHMONT RD
ELYSTAN CL
NADINE CT
MOUNT PK
PINE
WOODCOTE HALL
HALL RD
Allot Gdns
CRANFIELD RD E
SANDOWN DR
SOUTHDOWN RD
GLEN ROAD END
THE WOODLANDS
MALLARD WAY
BUCKINGHAM WAY
SUNKIST WAY
28
29
30
66
6
5
65
4
3
64
2
1
63
220
A237 Coulsdon, A23
Surrey STREET ATLAS

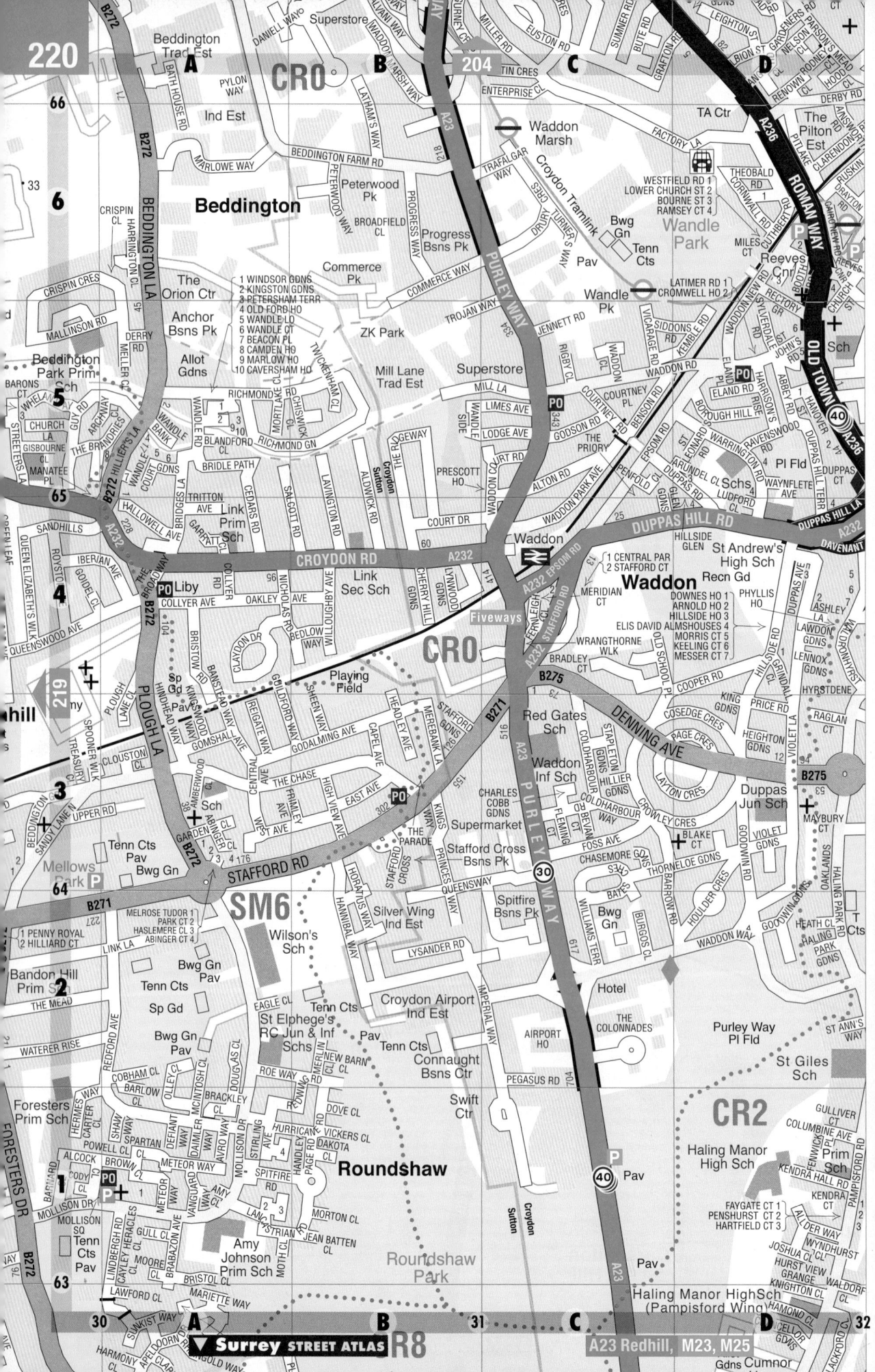

Beddington Trad Est
Superstore
CR0
204
Beddington
Ind Est
Peterwood Pk
Progress Bsns Pk
Commerce Pk
Waddon Marsh
Croydon Tramlink
Wandle Park
Wandle Pk
The Orion Ctr
Anchor Bsns Pk
ZK Park
Allot Gdns
Mill Lane Trad Est
Beddington Park Prim Sch
PURLEY WAY
CROYDON RD
DUPPAS HILL RD
ROMAN WAY
OLD TOWN
Waddon
Link Sec Sch
Link Prim Sch
St Andrew's High Sch
Fiveways
Playing Field
Red Gates Sch
Waddon Inf Sch
DENNING AVE
Duppas Jun Sch
STAFFORD RD
SM6
Wilson's Sch
Silver Wing Ind Est
Spitfire Bsns Pk
Stafford Cross Bsns Pk
Mellows Park
Bandon Hill Prim Sch
Croydon Airport Ind Est
St Elphege's RC Jun & Inf Schs
Connaught Bsns Ctr
Hotel
THE COLONNADES
Purley Way Pl Fld
St Giles Sch
CR2
Haling Manor High Sch
Roundshaw
Amy Johnson Prim Sch
Roundshaw Park
Foresters Prim Sch
Haling Manor High Sch (Pampisford Wing)
219

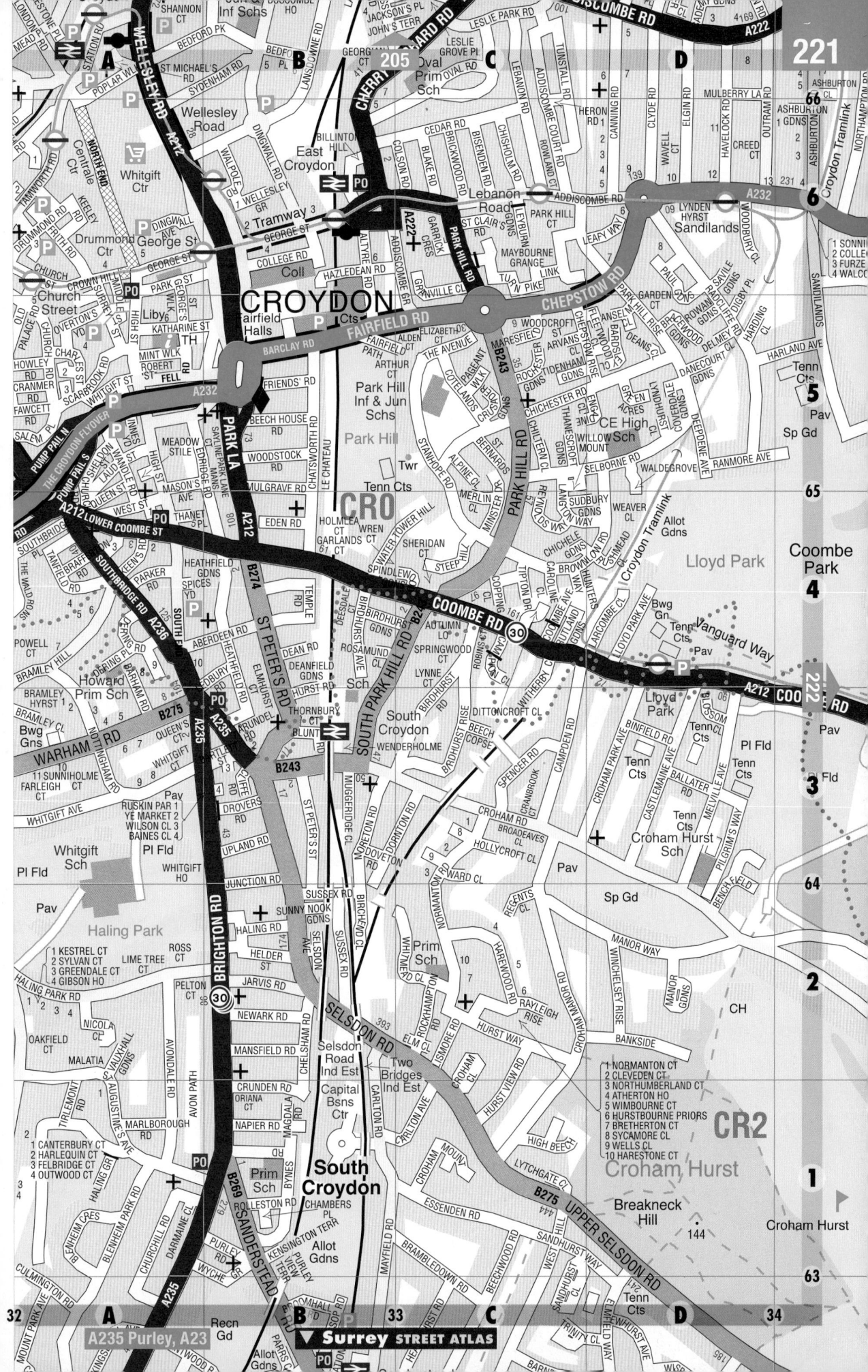

221
205
222
A
B
C
D
CROYDON
CR0
CR2
South Croydon
Wellesley Road
East Croydon
Lebanon Road
Sandilands
Whitgift Ctr
Centrale Ctr
Drummond Ctr
George St
Church Street
Fairfield Halls
Coll
Park Hill Inf & Jun Schs
Park Hill
Twr
Tenn Cts
CE High Sch
Lloyd Park
Coombe Park
Croydon Tramlink
Vanguard Way
Howard Prim Sch
Whitgift Sch
Haling Park
Selsdon Road Ind Est
Two Bridges Ind Est
Capital Bsns Ctr
Croham Hurst Sch
Croham Hurst
Breakneck Hill
Allot Gdns
Recn Gd
Oval Prim Sch
WELLESLEY RD
A212
A232
A222
A235
A236
B243
B274
B275
B269
PARK LA
PARK HILL RD
COOMBE RD
FAIRFIELD RD
BARCLAY RD
CHEPSTOW RD
ADDISCOMBE RD
CHERRY ORCHARD RD
LOWER COOMBE ST
SOUTH PARK HILL RD
ST PETER'S RD
BRIGHTON RD
SELSDON RD
UPPER SELSDON RD
WARHAM RD
SOUTHBRIDGE RD
THE CROYDON FLYOVER
HARLAND AVE
RANMORE AVE
MANOR WAY
CROHAM RD
SANDERSTEAD RD
1 KESTREL CT
2 SYLVAN CT
3 GREENDALE CT
4 GIBSON HO
1 CANTERBURY CT
2 HARLEQUIN CT
3 FELBRIDGE CT
4 OUTWOOD CT
1 NORMANTON CT
2 CLEVEDEN CT
3 NORTHUMBERLAND CT
4 ATHERTON HO
5 WIMBOURNE CT
6 HURSTBOURNE PRIORS
7 BRETHERTON CT
8 SYCAMORE CL
9 WELLS CL
10 HARESTONE CT
RUSKIN PAR 1
YE MARKET 2
WILSON CL 3
BAINES CL 4
66
65
64
63
32
33
34
A235 Purley, A23
Surrey STREET ATLAS

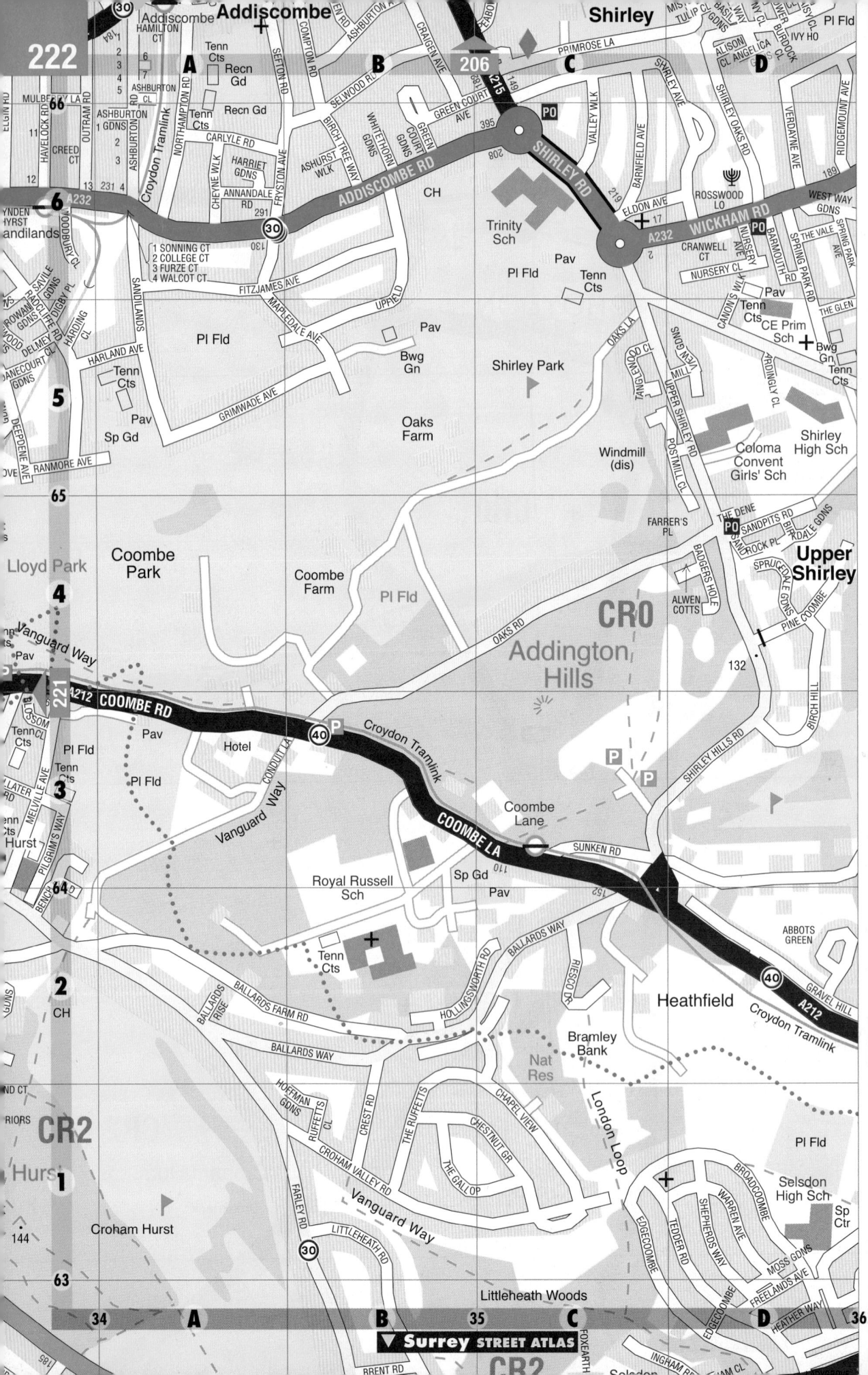
Addiscombe
Shirley
206
A
B
C
D
6
5
4
3
2
1
66
65
64
63
34
35
36
221
Recn Gd
Tenn Cts
Pl Fld
Ashburton Rd
Ashburton Gdns
Ashburton Ct
Mulberry La
Havelock Rd
Outram Rd
Creed Ct
Elgin Rd
Croydon Tramlink
Northampton Rd
Carlyle Rd
Harriet Gdns
Annandale Rd
Cheyne Wlk
Fryston Ave
Sefton Rd
Compton Rd
Ashburton Rd
Selwood Rd
Birch Tree Way
Ashurst Wlk
Whitethorn Gdns
Court Gdns
Green Court Ave
Craigen Ave
Addiscombe Rd
A232
A215
Shirley Rd
Primrose La
Valley Wlk
Barnfield Ave
Shirley Ave
Shirley Oaks Rd
Verdayne Ave
Ridgemount Ave
Tulip Cl
Alison Cl
Angelica Gdns
Burdock Cl
Ivy Ho
Eldon Ave
Rosswood Lo
Wickham Rd
West Way Gdns
Cranwell Ct
Nursery Ave
Nursery Cl
Barmouth Rd
Spring Park Rd
The Vale
Spring Park Ave
The Glen
Canon's Wlk
CE Prim Sch
Bwg Gn
Pav
CH
Trinity Sch
Shirley Park
Oaks La
Tanglewood Cl
View Gdns
Mill
Upper Shirley Rd
Postmill Cl
Ardingly Cl
Coloma Convent Girls' Sch
Shirley High Sch
Windmill (dis)
Oaks Farm
1 Sonning Ct
2 College Ct
3 Furze Ct
4 Walcot Ct
Fitzjames Ave
Mapledale Ave
Upfield
Grimwade Ave
Sandilands
Harland Ave
Sp Gd
Ranmore Ave
Deepdene Ave
Woodbury Cl
Digby Pl
Harding Cl
Savile Gdns
Radcliffe Rd
Rowan Gdns
Delmey Cl
Danecourt Gdns
Lloyd Park
Coombe Park
Coombe Farm
Farrer's Pl
The Dene
Sandpits Rd
Birdhurst Rd
Rock Pl
Kendale Gdns
Upper Shirley
Sprucedale Gdns
Badgers Hole
Alwen Cotts
Pine Coombe
CR0
Addington Hills
Oaks Rd
132
Birch Hill
Shirley Hills Rd
Vanguard Way
A212
Coombe Rd
Hotel
Conduit La
Croydon Tramlink
Coombe Lane
Coombe La
Sunken Rd
Royal Russell Sch
Blossom Cl
Melville Ave
Pilgrim's Way
Hurst
Bench
Ballards Way
Hollingsworth Rd
Riesco Dr
Ballards Farm Rd
Ballards Rise
Heathfield
Abbots Green
Gravel Hill
Bramley Bank
Nat Res
London Loop
Hoffman Gdns
Ruffetts Cl
Crest Rd
The Ruffetts
Chestnut Gr
Chapel View
The Gallop
Croham Valley Rd
Farley Rd
Littleheath Rd
Croham Hurst
144
CR2
Littleheath Woods
Edgecoombe
Tedder Rd
Shepherds Way
Warren Ave
Broadcoombe
Selsdon High Sch
Sp Ctr
Moss Gdns
Freelands Ave
Heather Way
Foxearth
Brent Rd
Ingham Rd

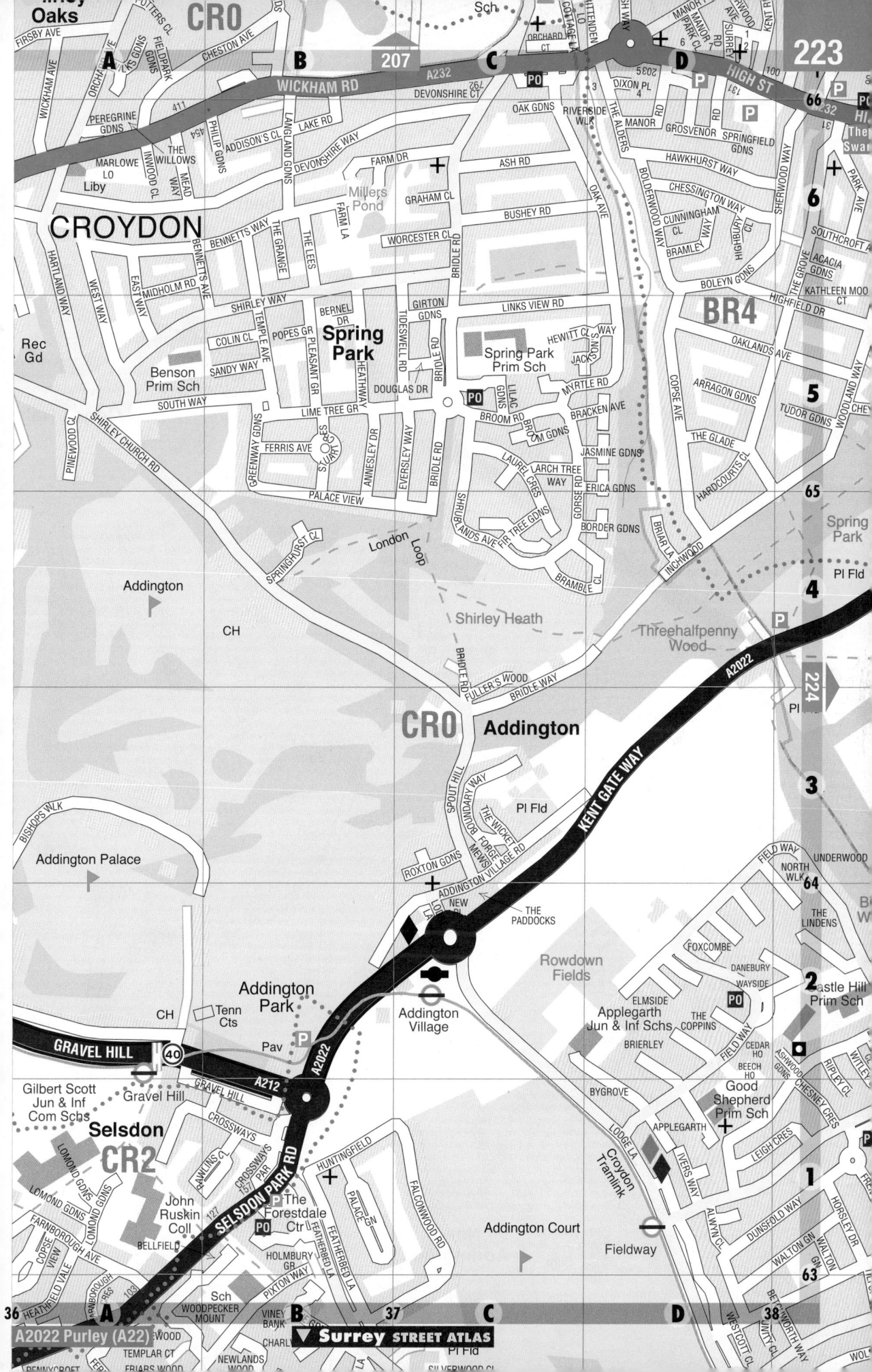

Oaks
CR0
207
FIRSBY AVE
CHESTON AVE
WICKHAM RD
A232
DEVONSHIRE CT
ORCHARD CT
HIGH ST
DIXON PL
OAK GDNS
RIVERSIDE WLK
THE ALDERS
MANOR RD
GROSVENOR RD
SPRINGFIELD GDNS
HAWKHURST WAY
WICKHAM AVE
PEREGRINE GDNS
THE WILLOWS
MARLOWE LO
Liby
INWOOD CL
MEAD WAY
PHILIP GDNS
ADDISON'S CL
LANGLAND GDNS
LAKE RD
DEVONSHIRE WAY
FARM DR
ASH RD
GRAHAM CL
Millers Pond
FARM LA
CROYDON
BENNETTS WAY
BENNETTS AVE
THE GRANGE
THE LEES
WORCESTER CL
BRIDLE RD
BUSHEY RD
OAK AVE
BOLDERWOOD WAY
CHESSINGTON WAY
CUNNINGHAM CL
BRAMLEY WAY
HIGHBURY CL
SHERWOOD WAY
PARK AVE
SOUTHCROFT AVE
ACACIA GDNS
THE GROVE
BOLEYN GDNS
KATHLEEN MOORE CT
HIGHFIELD DR
BR4
HARTLAND WAY
WEST WAY
EAST WAY
MIDHOLM RD
SHIRLEY WAY
BERNEL DR
GIRTON GDNS
LINKS VIEW RD
Rec Gd
COLIN CL
TEMPLE AVE
POPES GR
PLEASANT GR
Spring Park
TIDESWELL RD
HEWITT CL
JACKSON'S WAY
OAKLANDS AVE
Benson Prim Sch
SANDY WAY
HEATHWAY
DOUGLAS DR
Spring Park Prim Sch
MYRTLE RD
ARRAGON GDNS
WOODLAND WAY
SOUTH WAY
LIME TREE GR
LILAC GDNS
BROOM RD
BROOM GDNS
BRACKEN AVE
COPSE AVE
TUDOR GDNS
PINEWOOD CL
SHIRLEY CHURCH RD
GREENWAY GDNS
FERRIS AVE
STUART CRES
ANNESLEY DR
EVERSLEY WAY
LAUREL CRES
LARCH TREE WAY
JASMINE GDNS
THE GLADE
HARDCOURTS CL
ERICA GDNS
GORSE RD
PALACE VIEW
SHRUBLANDS AVE
FIR TREE GDNS
BORDER GDNS
BRIAR LA
INCHWOOD
Spring Park
SPRINGHURST CL
London Loop
BRAMBLE CL
Pl Fld
Addington
CH
Shirley Heath
Threehalfpenny Wood
FULLER'S WOOD
BRIDLE WAY
A2022
224
CR0
Addington
SPOUT HILL
BOUNDARY WAY
THE WICKET
FORGE MEWS
Pl Fld
KENT GATE WAY
BISHOPS WLK
Addington Palace
ROXTON GDNS
ADDINGTON VILLAGE RD
NEW PL
LOT LA
THE PADDOCKS
FIELD WAY
NORTH WLK
UNDERWOOD
THE LINDENS
FOXCOMBE
Rowdown Fields
DANEBURY
WAYSIDE
Castle Hill Prim Sch
ELMSIDE
Applegarth Jun & Inf Schs
THE COPPINS
Addington Park
Addington Village
CH
Tenn Cts
Pav
GRAVEL HILL
40
A212
BRIERLEY
CEDAR HO
BEECH HO
ASHWOOD GDNS
RIPLEY CL
WITLEY CRES
Gilbert Scott Jun & Inf Com Schs
Gravel Hill
BYGROVE
Good Shepherd Prim Sch
CHESNEY CRES
Selsdon
CROSSWAYS
APPLEGARTH
CR2
LOMOND GDNS
RAWLINS CL
CROSSWAYS PAR
HUNTINGFIELD
LODGE LA
Croydon Tramlink
LEIGH CRES
John Ruskin Coll
SELSDON PARK RD
The Forestdale Ctr
PALACE GN
FALCONWOOD RD
IVERS WAY
FARNBOROUGH AVE
COPSE VIEW
BELLFIELD
FEATHERBED LA
Addington Court
ALWYN CL
DUNSFOLD WAY
HORSLEY DR
Fieldway
WALTON GN
HOLMBURY GR
PIXTON WAY
HEATHFIELD VALE
Sch
WOODPECKER MOUNT
VINEY BANK
BETCHWORTH WAY
WESTCOTT CL
A2022 Purley (A22)
TEMPLAR CT
NEWLANDS WOOD
Pl Fld
A
B
C
D
1
2
3
4
5
6
36
37
38
63
64
65
66

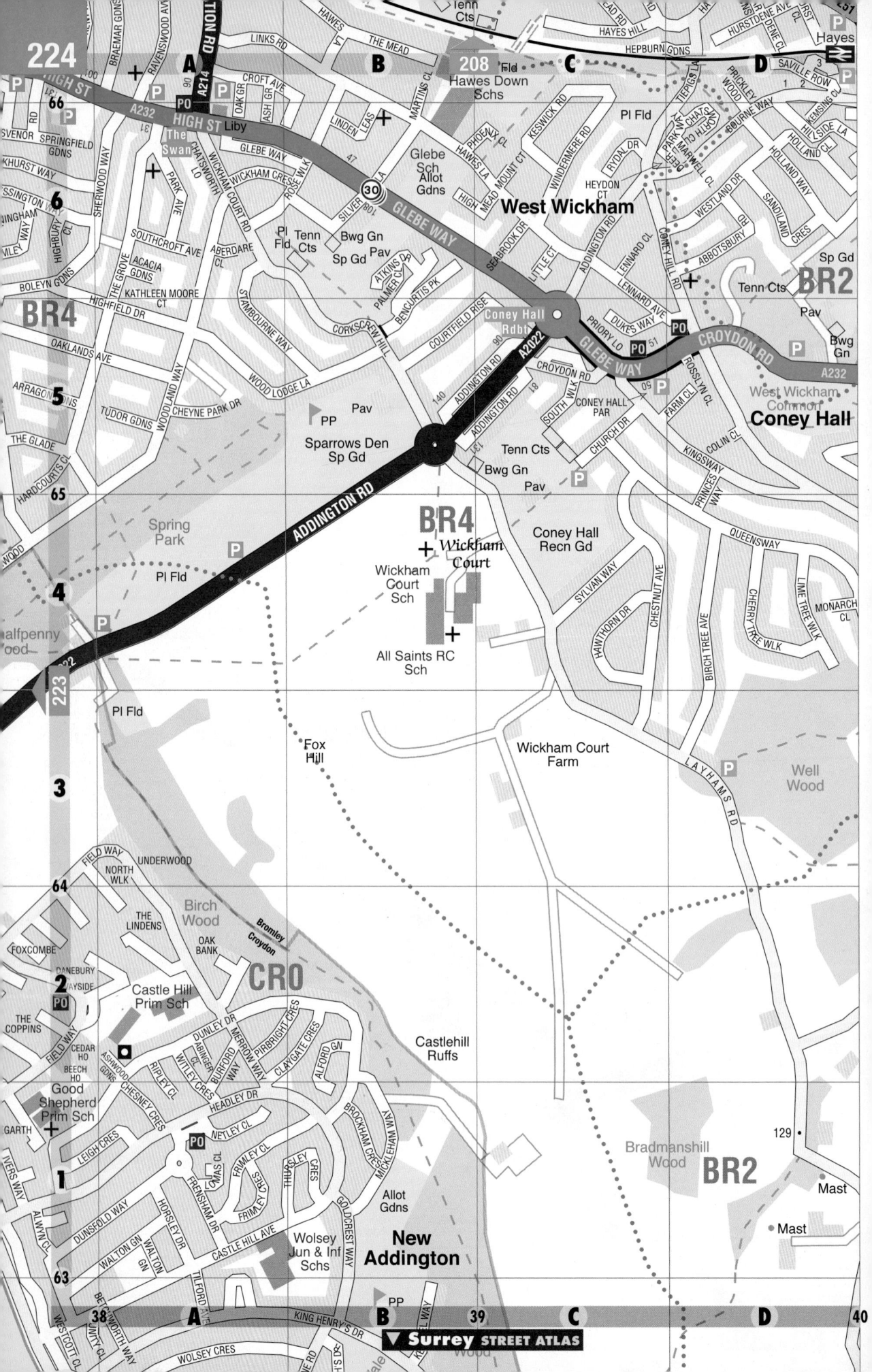
West Wickham
Coney Hall
New Addington
BR4
BR2
CR0
HIGH ST
GLEBE WAY
ADDINGTON RD
CROYDON RD
LAYHAMS RD
Coney Hall Rdbt
Wickham Court
Wickham Court Sch
All Saints RC Sch
Wickham Court Farm
Coney Hall Recn Gd
Sparrows Den Sp Gd
Spring Park
Fox Hill
Birch Wood
Castle Hill Prim Sch
Castlehill Ruffs
Good Shepherd Prim Sch
Wolsey Jun & Inf Schs
Bradmanshill Wood
Well Wood
West Wickham Common
Hawes Down Schs
Glebe Sch
Hayes
208
223
Surrey STREET ATLAS

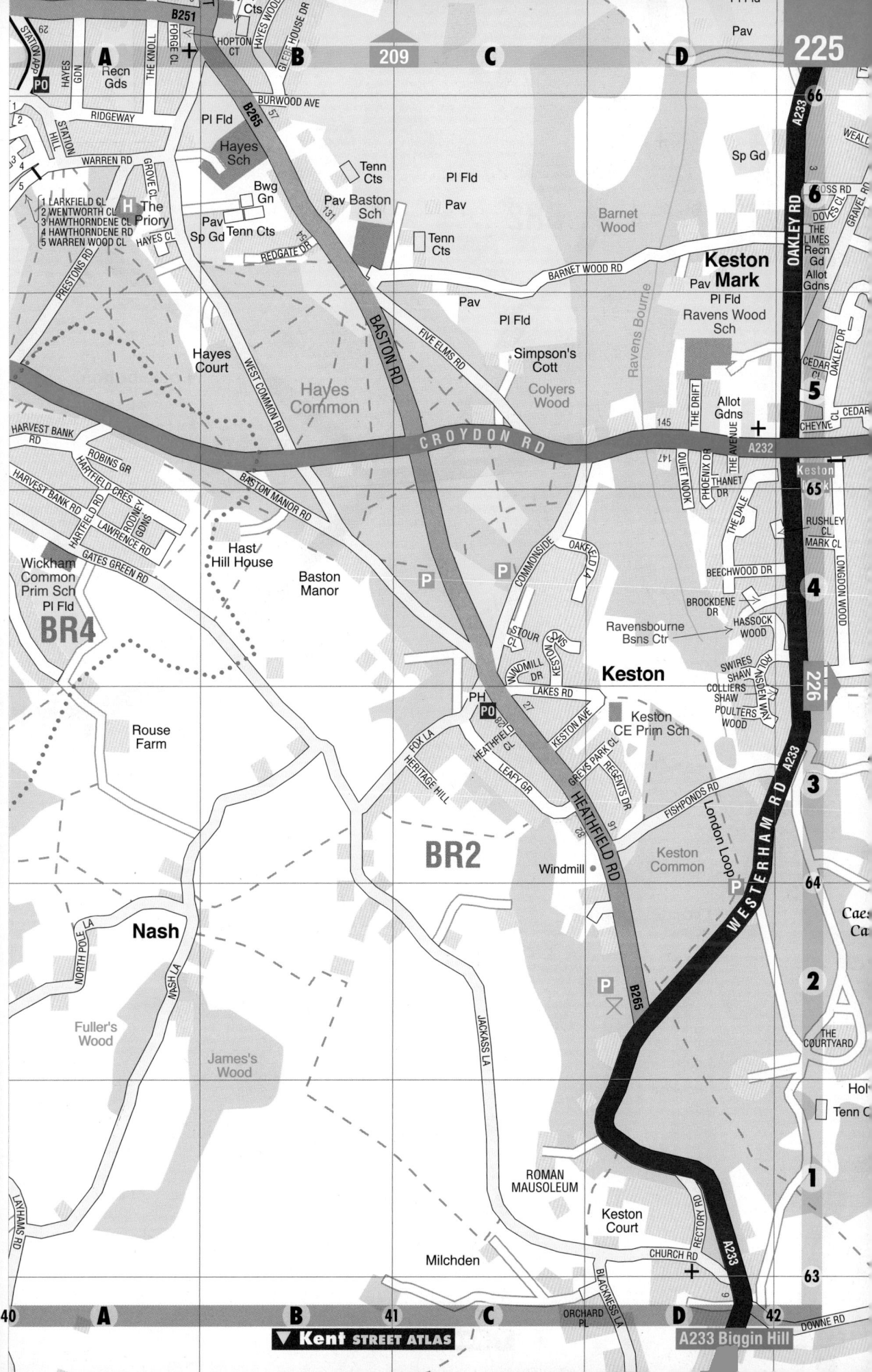
209
Recn Gds
RIDGEWAY
WARREN RD
STATION HILL
HAYES GDN
THE KNOLL
FORGE CL
HOPTON CT
HAYES WOOD
GLEBE HOUSE DR
BURWOOD AVE
B251
B265
Pl Fld
Hayes Sch
Bwg Gn
Pav
Sp Gd
Tenn Cts
REDGATE DR
1 LARKFIELD CL
2 WENTWORTH CL
3 HAWTHORNDENE CL
4 HAWTHORNDENE RD
5 WARREN WOOD CL
The Priory
GROVE CL
HAYES CL
PRESTONS RD
Pav Baston Sch
Tenn Cts
Pl Fld
Pav
Barnet Wood
BARNET WOOD RD
Keston Mark
Pav
Pl Fld
Ravens Wood Sch
Sp Gd
OAKLEY RD
A233
WEALL
ROSS RD
DOVES CL
THE LIMES
Recn Gd
Allot Gdns
GRAVEL RD
Ravens Bourne
Simpson's Cott
Colyers Wood
Hayes Court
Hayes Common
WEST COMMON RD
BASTON RD
FIVE ELMS RD
CROYDON RD
A232
THE DRIFT
Allot Gdns
THE AVENUE
QUIET NOOK
PHOENIX DR
THANET DR
CEDAR CL
OAKLEY DR
CHEYNE CL
CEDAR
Keston Park
HARVEST BANK RD
ROBINS GR
HARTFIELD CRES
HARTFIELD RD
RODNEY GDNS
LAWRENCE RD
GATES GREEN RD
BASTON MANOR RD
Wickham Common Prim Sch
Pl Fld
BR4
Hast Hill House
Baston Manor
COMMONSIDE
OAKFIELD LA
STOUR CL
KESTON GDNS
WINDMILL DR
LAKES RD
Keston
THE DALE
RUSHLEY CL
MARK CL
BEECHWOOD DR
BROCKDENE DR
HASSOCK WOOD
Ravensbourne Bsns Ctr
SWIRES SHAW
COLLIERS SHAW
POULTERS WOOD
ROLINSDEN WAY
LONGDON WOOD
226
Rouse Farm
PH
PO
FOX LA
HERITAGE HILL
HEATHFIELD CL
LEAFY GR
KESTON AVE
GREYS PARK CL
REGENTS DR
Keston CE Prim Sch
FISHPONDS RD
London Loop
WESTERHAM RD
HEATHFIELD RD
BR2
Windmill
Keston Common
Nash
NORTH POLE LA
NASH LA
Fuller's Wood
James's Wood
JACKASS LA
THE COURTYARD
Tenn C
ROMAN MAUSOLEUM
Keston Court
RECTORY RD
CHURCH RD
Milchden
BLACKNESS LA
ORCHARD PL
LAYHAMS RD
DOWNE RD
A233 Biggin Hill
Kent STREET ATLAS
A B C D
1 2 3 4 5 6
40 41 42
62 63 64 65 66

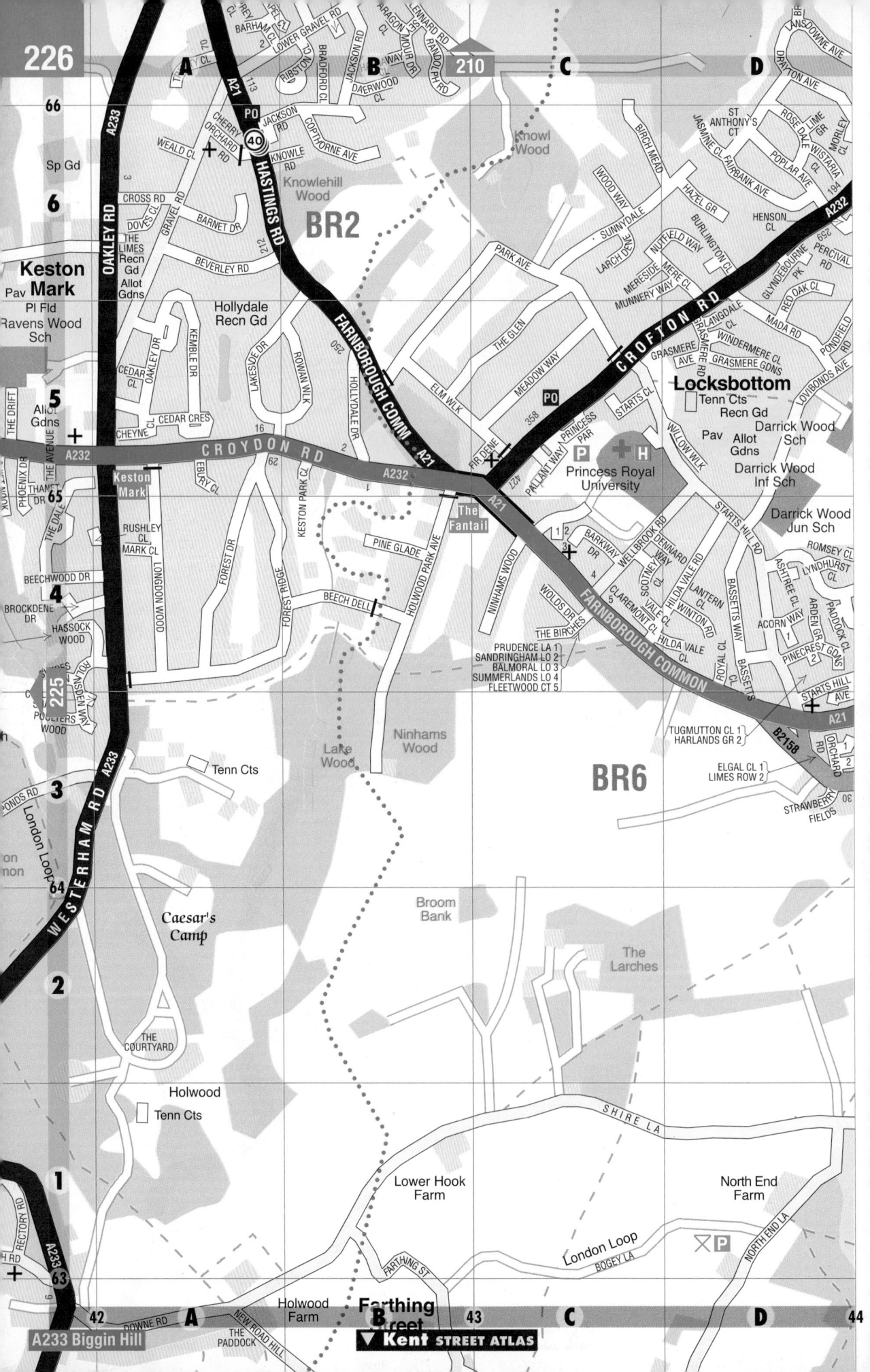

A | B | 210 | C | D

66

Sp Gd

6

Keston Mark
Pav
Pl Fld
Ravens Wood Sch

5
Allot Gdns

65

4
Beechwood Dr
Brockdene Dr
Hassock Wood

225

3
London Loop
non

64

2

1

A233 Biggin Hill

OAKLEY RD   A233
A21
113
PO
CHERRY ORCHARD RD
40
WEALD CL
Knowle RD
JACKSON RD
COPTHORNE AVE
DAERWOOD CL
WAY CL
RIBSTON CL
BRADFORD CL
LOWER GRAVEL RD
BARHAM
REY CL

BR2

CROSS RD
DOVES
GRAVEL RD
BARNET DR
BEVERLEY RD
THE LIMES Recn Gd
Allot Gdns
Hollydale Recn Gd

CEDAR CL
OAKLEY DR
KEMBLE DR
CEDAR CRES
CHEYNE
LAKESIDE DR
ROMAN WLK
HOLLYDALE DR
16
FARNBOROUGH COMM

HASTINGS RD
Knowlehill Wood

CROYDON RD   A232
A232
Keston Mark
EBURY CL
KESTON PARK CL
PINE GLADE
HOLWOOD PARK AVE
BEECH DELL
FOREST RIDGE
FOREST DR
LONGDON WOOD
RUSHLEY CL
MARK CL

THE AVENUE
THE DRIFT
PHOENIX DR
THANET DR
THE DALE

Knowl Wood

PARK AVE
LARCH DENE
SUNNYDALE
MERESIDE
MUNNERY WAY
MERE CL
NUTFIELD WAY
HAZEL GR
BIRCH MEAD
WOOD WAY
JASMINE CL FAIRBANK AVE
ST ANTHONY'S CT

CROFTON RD   A232
259
LANSDOWNE AVE
DRAYTON AVE
ROSE DALE
POPLAR AVE
WISTARIA
MORLEY CL
194
PERCIVAL RD
RED OAK CL
MADA RD
PONDFIELD
LOVIBONDS AVE
GLYNDEBOURNE PK
GRASMERE CL
WINDERMERE CL
GRASMERE GDNS
GRASMERE AVE
BURLINGTON CL
HENSON CL

THE GLEN
MEADOW WAY
ELM WLK
FIR DENE
358
PO
STARTS CL

Locksbottom
Tenn Cts
Recn Gd
Pav
Allot Gdns
Darrick Wood Sch
Darrick Wood Inf Sch
Darrick Wood Jun Sch

WILLOW WLK
PRINCESS PAR
PRINCESS WAY
P
H
Princess Royal University
PALLANT WAY
BARKWAY DR
WELLBROOK RD
1
2
3
4
SCOTNEYS WAY
DENMARD WAY
HILDA VALE CL
VALE CL
LANTERN CL
WINTON RD
CLAREMONT CL
HILDA VALE RD
ROYAL CL
BASSETTS WAY
STARTS HILL RD
ACORN WAY
1
ASHTREE CL
ARDEN GR
PINECREST GDNS
PADDOCK CL
ROMSEY CL
LYNDHURST CL
STARTS HILL AVE

The Fantail
A232
A21
FARNBOROUGH COMM   A21
NINHAMS WOOD
WOLDS DR
THE BIRCHES
PRUDENCE LA 1
SANDRINGHAM LO 2
BALMORAL LO 3
SUMMERLANDS LO 4
FLEETWOOD CT 5
THE Recn
Keston Park CL

BR6

225
RAMSDEN WAY
POOLERS WOOD

Tenn Cts
Lake Wood
Ninhams Wood

TUGMUTTON CL 1
HARLANDS GR 2
ELGAL CL 1
LIMES ROW 2
STRAWBERRY FIELDS
30
ORCHARD
1
2
B2158
FARNBOROUGH COMMON

PONDS RD

WESTERHAM RD   A233

Caesar's Camp

Broom Bank

The Larches

Holwood
Tenn Cts

63
A233

42
DOWNE RD
A
Holwood Farm
NEW ROAD HILL
THE PADDOCK
FARTHING ST
B
Farthing Street
43
C
SHIRE LA
London Loop
BOGEY LA
Lower Hook Farm
North End Farm
NORTH END LA
P
D
44

Kent STREET ATLAS

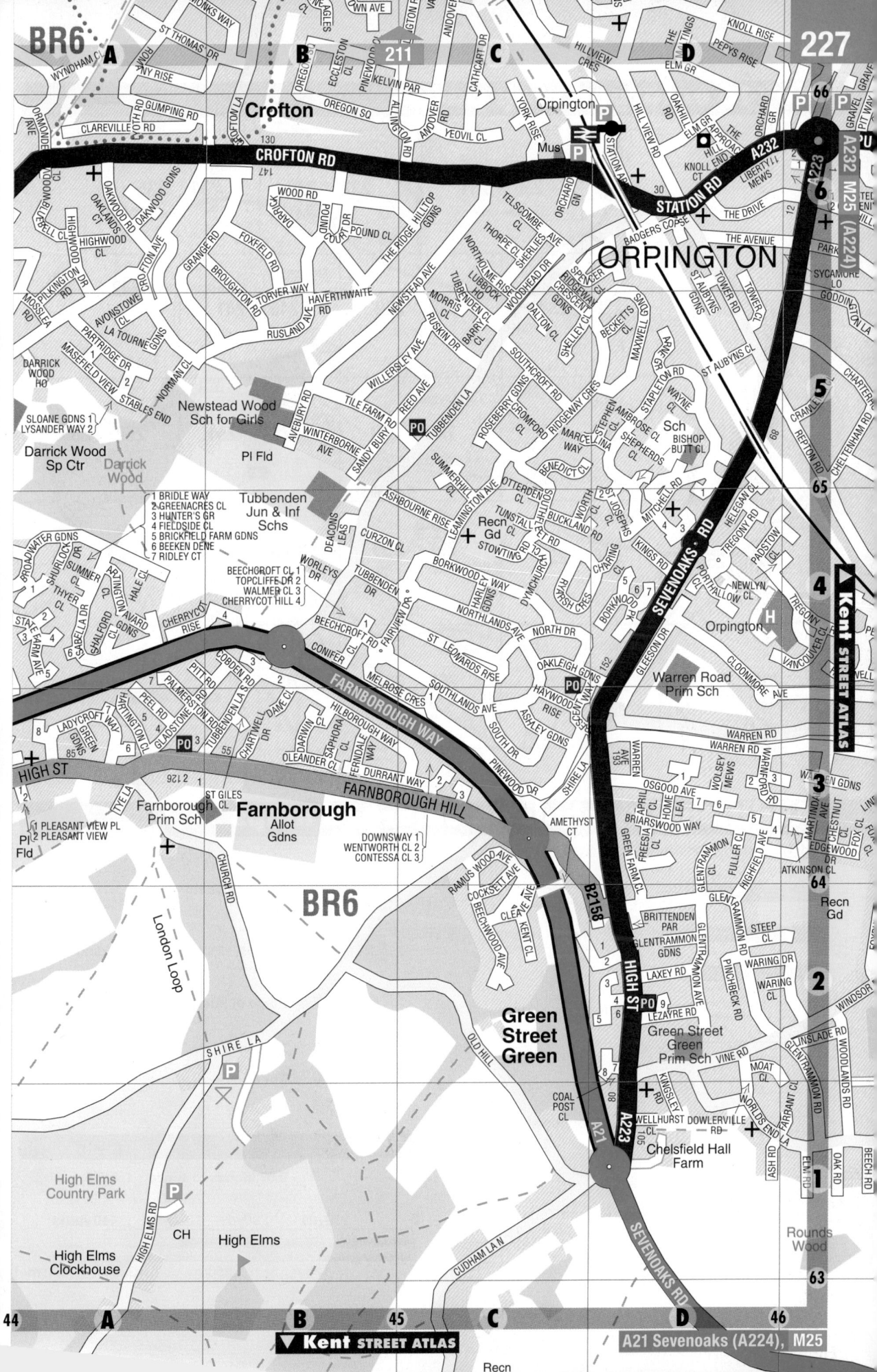

BR6
Crofton
CROFTON RD
ORPINGTON
STATION RD
Orpington
Newstead Wood Sch for Girls
Darrick Wood Sp Ctr
Tubbenden Jun & Inf Schs
FARNBOROUGH WAY
FARNBOROUGH HILL
Farnborough
Farnborough Prim Sch
Allot Gdns
Warren Road Prim Sch
Green Street Green
Green Street Green Prim Sch
Chelsfield Hall Farm
High Elms Country Park
High Elms
High Elms Clockhouse
London Loop
SEVENOAKS RD
HIGH ST
A21 Sevenoaks (A224), M25
Kent STREET ATLAS

Key to enlarged map pages

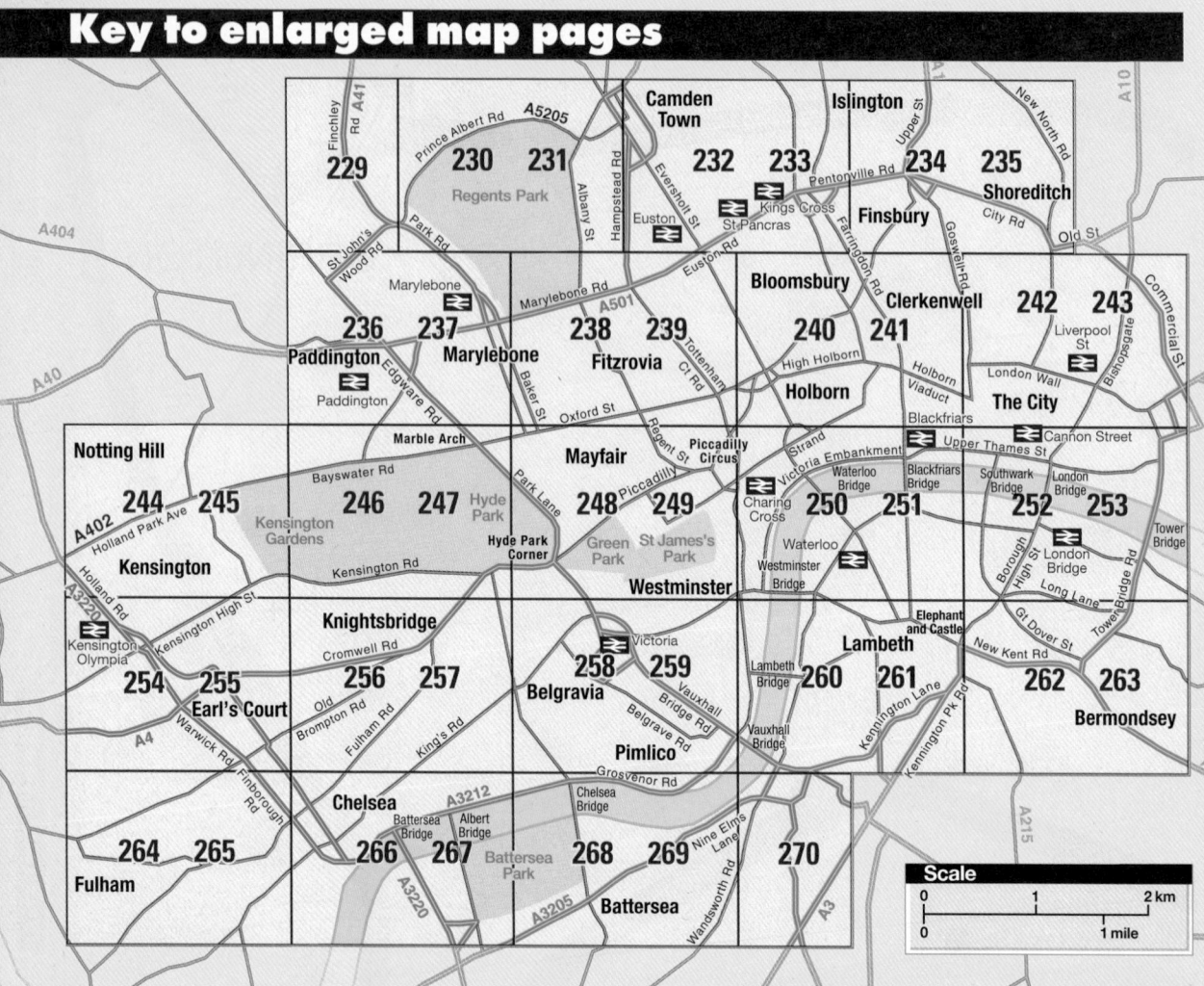

Scale

0   1   2 km

0   1 mile

Additional symbols on enlarged maps

For all other symbols see page XXVIII

Primary route – single, dual carriageway	
A road – single, dual carriageway	
B road	
Through-route	
Minor road	
One way street	
No access in direction shown	

Congestion Charge Zone boundary
Roads within the zone are outlined in green – for further information call 0845 900 1234

Public building

Railway or bus station building

Place of interest

Ⓔ Embassy

Theatre

Museum

Scale

9.67 inches to 1 mile   1:6559

0   110yds   220yds   330yds   **440 yards**

0   125m   250m   325m   **500 metre**

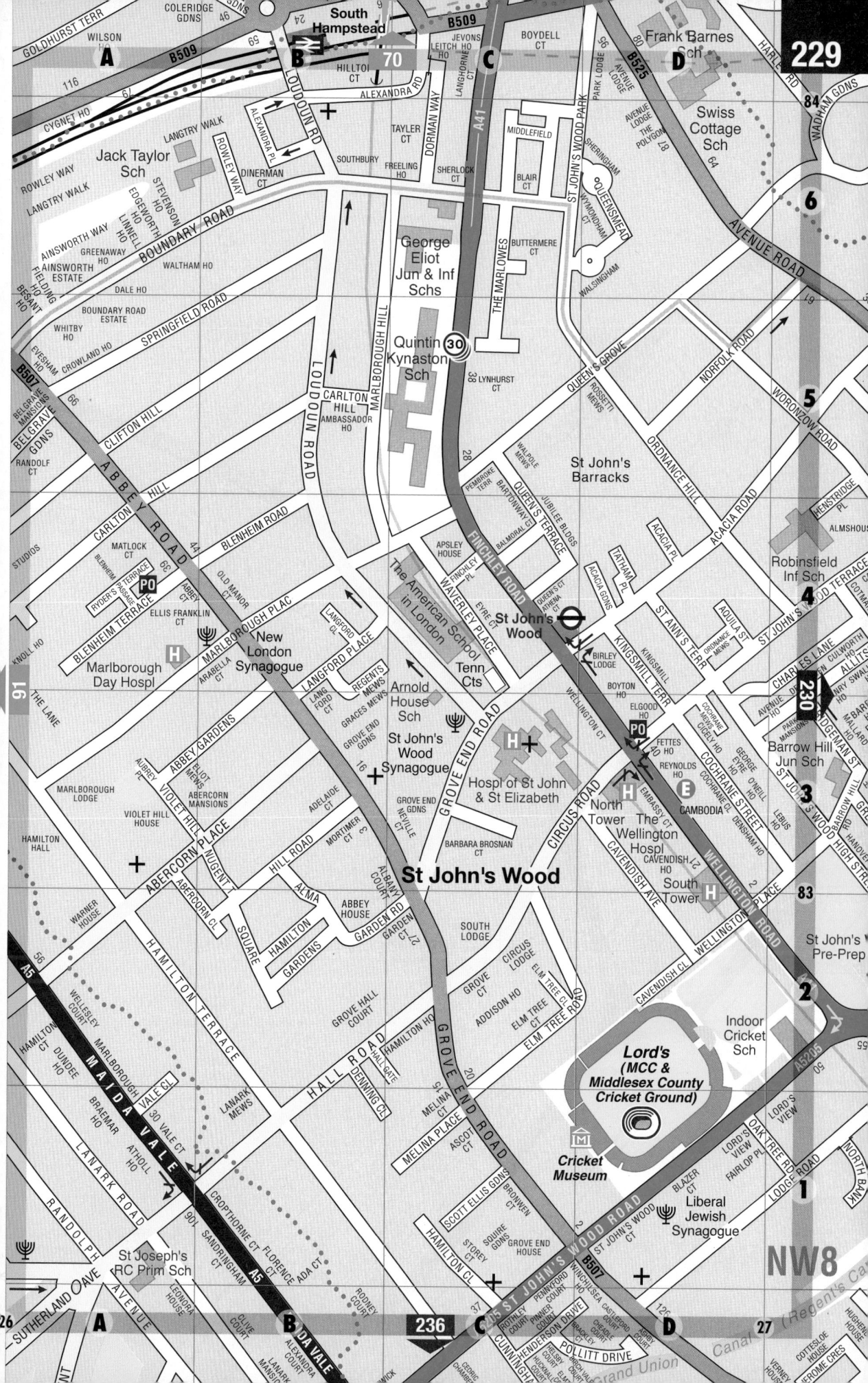
South Hampstead
Frank Barnes Sch
Swiss Cottage Sch
Jack Taylor Sch
George Eliot Jun & Inf Schs
Quintin Kynaston Sch
St John's Barracks
Robinsfield Inf Sch
The American School in London
St John's Wood
New London Synagogue
Marlborough Day Hospl
Arnold House Sch
St John's Wood Synagogue
Hospl of St John & St Elizabeth
North Tower
The Wellington Hospl
South Tower
Barrow Hill Jun Sch
St John's Pre-Prep
St John's Wood
Lord's (MCC & Middlesex County Cricket Ground)
Cricket Museum
Indoor Cricket Sch
Liberal Jewish Synagogue
St Joseph's RC Prim Sch
NW8
BOUNDARY ROAD
ABBEY ROAD
FINCHLEY ROAD
GROVE END ROAD
WELLINGTON ROAD
AVENUE ROAD
MAIDA VALE
ST JOHN'S WOOD ROAD
HALL ROAD
HAMILTON TERRACE
LOUDOUN ROAD
CARLTON HILL
QUEEN'S GROVE
ACACIA ROAD
CIRCUS ROAD
Grand Union Canal (Regent's Canal)

70
91
230
236

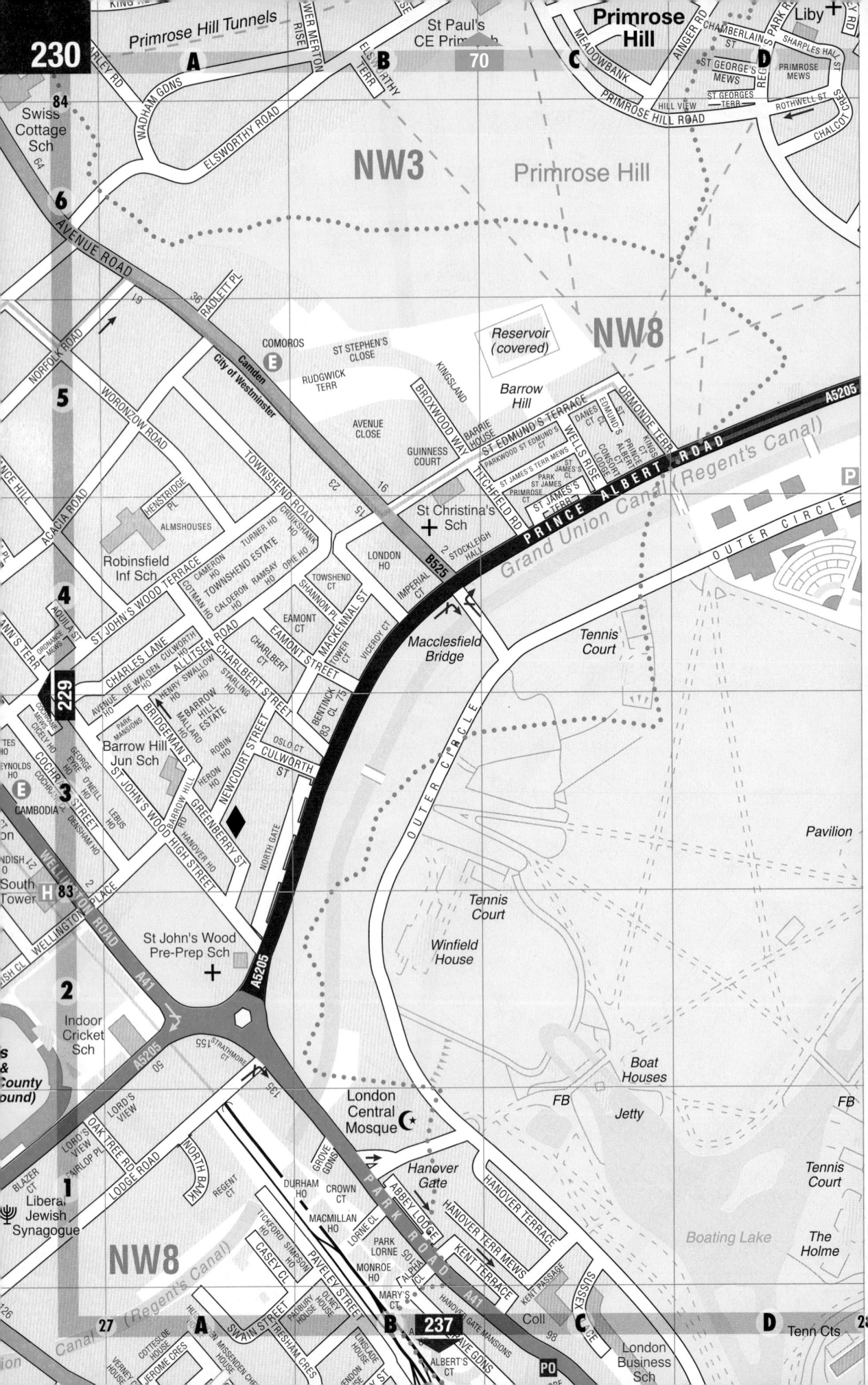

Primrose Hill Tunnels
St Paul's CE Prim Sch
Primrose Hill
NW3
Primrose Hill
NW8
Swiss Cottage Sch
WADHAM GDNS
ELSWORTHY ROAD
ELSWORTHY TERR
AVENUE ROAD
MEADOWBANK
PRIMROSE HILL ROAD
AINGER RD
CHAMBERLAIN ST
ST GEORGE'S MEWS
ST GEORGES TERR
HILL VIEW
PRIMROSE MEWS
SHARPLES HALL ST
ROTHWELL ST
CHALCOT CRES
REGENT'S PARK RD
Liby
Reservoir (covered)
Barrow Hill
COMOROS
ST STEPHEN'S CLOSE
RUDGWICK TERR
AVENUE CLOSE
GUINNESS COURT
BROXWOOD WAY
KINGSLAND
BARRIE HOUSE
ST EDMUND'S TERRACE
PARKWOOD ST EDMUND'S CT
ST JAMES'S TERR MEWS
WELLS RISE
ORMONDE TERR
PRINCE ALBERT ROAD
A5205
Grand Union Canal (Regent's Canal)
OUTER CIRCLE
Camden
City of Westminster
RADLETT PL
NORFOLK ROAD
WORONZOW ROAD
TOWNSHEND ROAD
ACACIA ROAD
HENSTRIDGE PL
ALMSHOUSES
Robinsfield Inf Sch
ST JOHN'S WOOD TERRACE
TOWNSHEND ESTATE
St Christina's Sch
STOCKLEIGH HALL
LONDON HO
IMPERIAL CT
B525
TOWSHEND CT
EAMONT CT
EAMONT STREET
MACKENNAL ST
SHANNON PL
TOWER CT
VICEROY CT
Macclesfield Bridge
Tennis Court
CHARLES LANE
ALLITSEN ROAD
CHARLBERT STREET
CHARLBERT CT
AQUILA ST
ORDNANCE MEWS
229
BENTINCK CL
BARROW HILL ESTATE
BRIDGEMAN ST
Barrow Hill Jun Sch
NEWCOURT STREET
OSLO CT
CULWORTH ST
NORTH GATE
ST JOHN'S WOOD HIGH STREET
GREENBERRY ST
HANOVER HO
COCHRANE STREET
CAMBODIA
WELLINGTON ROAD
WELLINGTON PLACE
South Tower
St John's Wood Pre-Prep Sch
Indoor Cricket Sch
A41
STRATHMORE CT
Pavilion
Tennis Court
Winfield House
Boat Houses
FB
Jetty
London Central Mosque
Hanover Gate
PARK ROAD
HANOVER TERRACE
HANOVER TERR MEWS
KENT TERRACE
KENT PASSAGE
SUSSEX PLACE
ABBEY LODGE
LORD'S VIEW
OAK TREE RD
FAIRLOP PL
LODGE ROAD
NORTH BANK
REGENT CT
DURHAM HO
CROWN CT
MACMILLAN HO
LORNE CL
PARK LORNE
MONROE HO
ALPHA CL
MARY'S CT
GROVE GDNS
Liberal Jewish Synagogue
NW8
Canal (Regent's Canal)
TICKFORD HO
SIMPSON HO
CASEY CL
PAVELEY STREET
SWAIN STREET
TRESHAM CRES
PADBURY HOUSE
OLNEY HOUSE
LINSLADE HOUSE
JEROME CRES
COTTESLOE HOUSE
VERNEY HOUSE
237
ALBERT'S CT
HANOVER GATE MANSIONS
Coll
London Business Sch
Boating Lake
The Holme
Tennis Court
Tenn Cts
PO

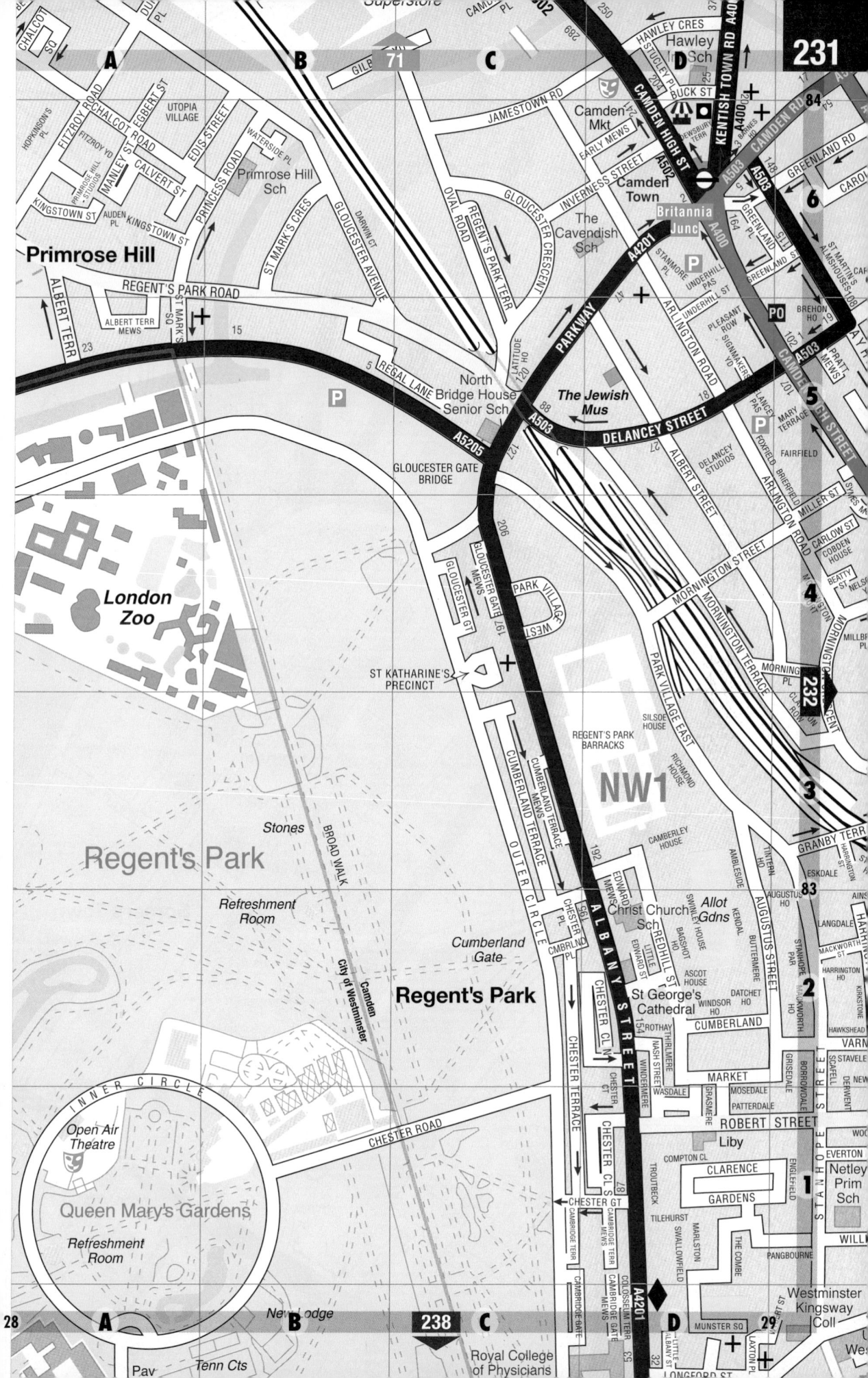
A
B
C
D
71
238
232
28
29
84
83
1
2
3
4
5
6
Primrose Hill
Regent's Park
Regent's Park
London Zoo
Camden Town
NW1
Queen Mary's Gardens
Open Air Theatre
Refreshment Room
Refreshment Room
Stones
Cumberland Gate
New Lodge
Tenn Cts
Pav
Royal College of Physicians
Primrose Hill Sch
North Bridge House Senior Sch
The Cavendish Sch
The Jewish Mus
Camden Mkt
Hawley Inf Sch
Britannia Junc
Christ Church Sch
St George's Cathedral
Allot Gdns
Liby
Netley Prim Sch
Westminster Kingsway Coll
REGENT'S PARK BARRACKS
GLOUCESTER GATE BRIDGE
ST KATHARINE'S PRECINCT
UTOPIA VILLAGE
CAMDEN HIGH ST
KENTISH TOWN RD
CAMDEN RD
PARKWAY
DELANCEY STREET
ALBANY STREET
REGENT'S PARK ROAD
GLOUCESTER AVENUE
GLOUCESTER CRESCENT
ARLINGTON ROAD
ALBERT STREET
MORNINGTON STREET
MORNINGTON TERRACE
PARK VILLAGE EAST
OUTER CIRCLE
INNER CIRCLE
CHESTER ROAD
CHESTER TERRACE
CUMBERLAND TERRACE
BROAD WALK
ROBERT STREET
AUGUSTUS STREET
STANHOPE STREET
CLARENCE GARDENS
CUMBERLAND MARKET
City of Westminster
Camden
A5205
A503
A4201
A502
A400
PO

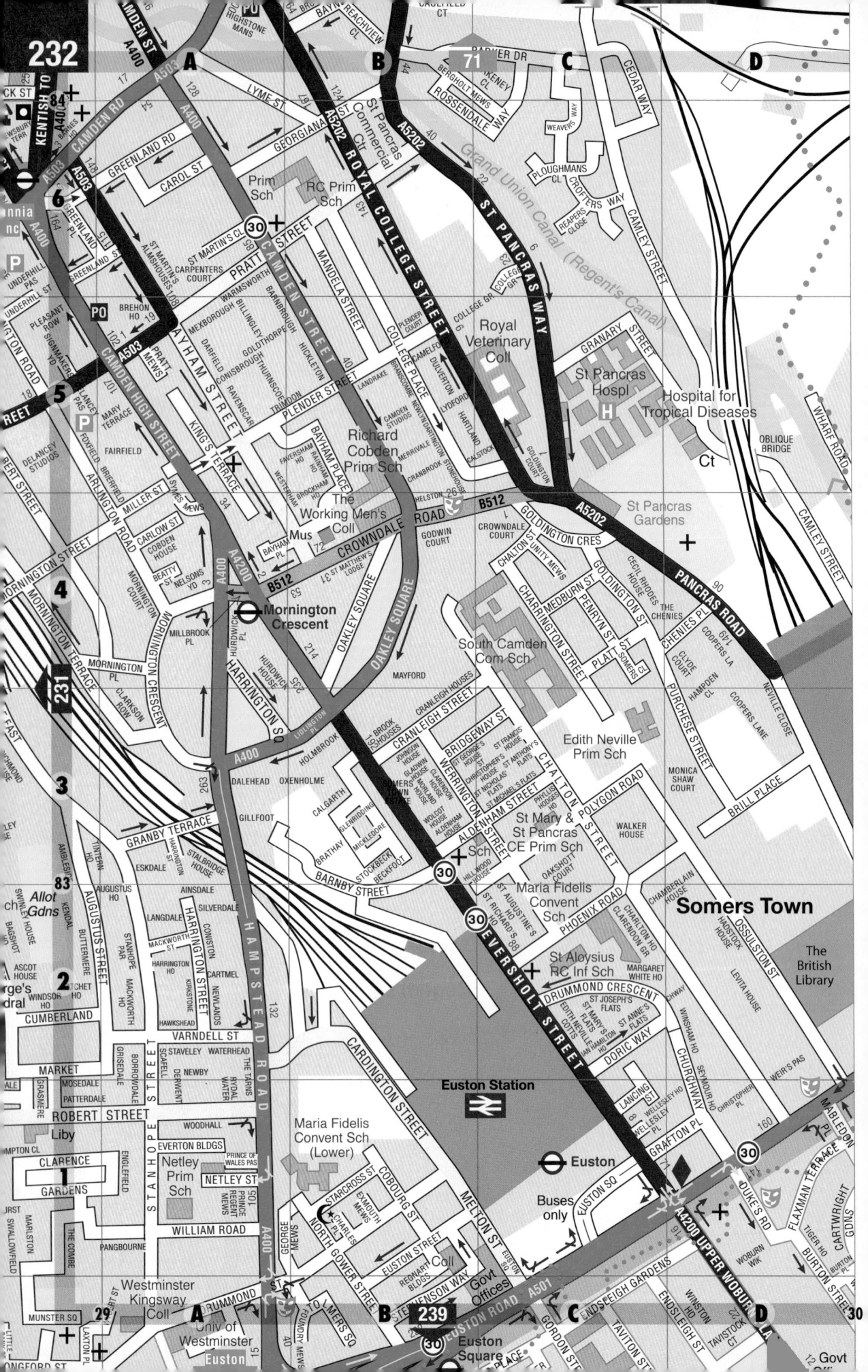

A
B
C
D
71
231
239
Camden High Street
Camden Street
Royal College Street
St Pancras Way
Grand Union Canal (Regent's Canal)
Royal Veterinary Coll
St Pancras Hospl
Hospital for Tropical Diseases
St Pancras Gardens
Pancras Road
Crowndale Road
Mornington Crescent
Oakley Square
South Camden Com Sch
Edith Neville Prim Sch
St Mary & St Pancras CE Prim Sch
Maria Fidelis Convent Sch
Somers Town
The British Library
St Aloysius RC Inf Sch
Eversholt Street
Hampstead Road
Euston Station
Euston
Euston Square
Euston Road
Maria Fidelis Convent Sch (Lower)
Cardington Street
Richard Cobden Prim Sch
The Working Men's Coll
Westminster Kingsway Coll
Univ of Westminster
Netley Prim Sch
Robert Street
Drummond Crescent
Churchway
Ossulston St
Brill Place
Camley Street
Mornington Terrace
Arlington Road
Pratt Street
Plender Street
Bayham Street
Granby Terrace
Harrington Street
Augustus Street
Stanhope Street
William Road
Euston Street
Grafton Pl
Upper Woburn Pl
Endsleigh Gardens
Mabledon Pl
Flaxman Terrace
Duke's Rd
Cartwright Gdns
Goldington Cres
Chalton Street
Polygon Road
Phoenix Road
Charrington Street
Purchese Street
Cranleigh Street
Barnby Street
Aldenham Street
Werrington Street
Harrington Sq
Buses only
Govt Offices
Allot Gdns
29
30
83

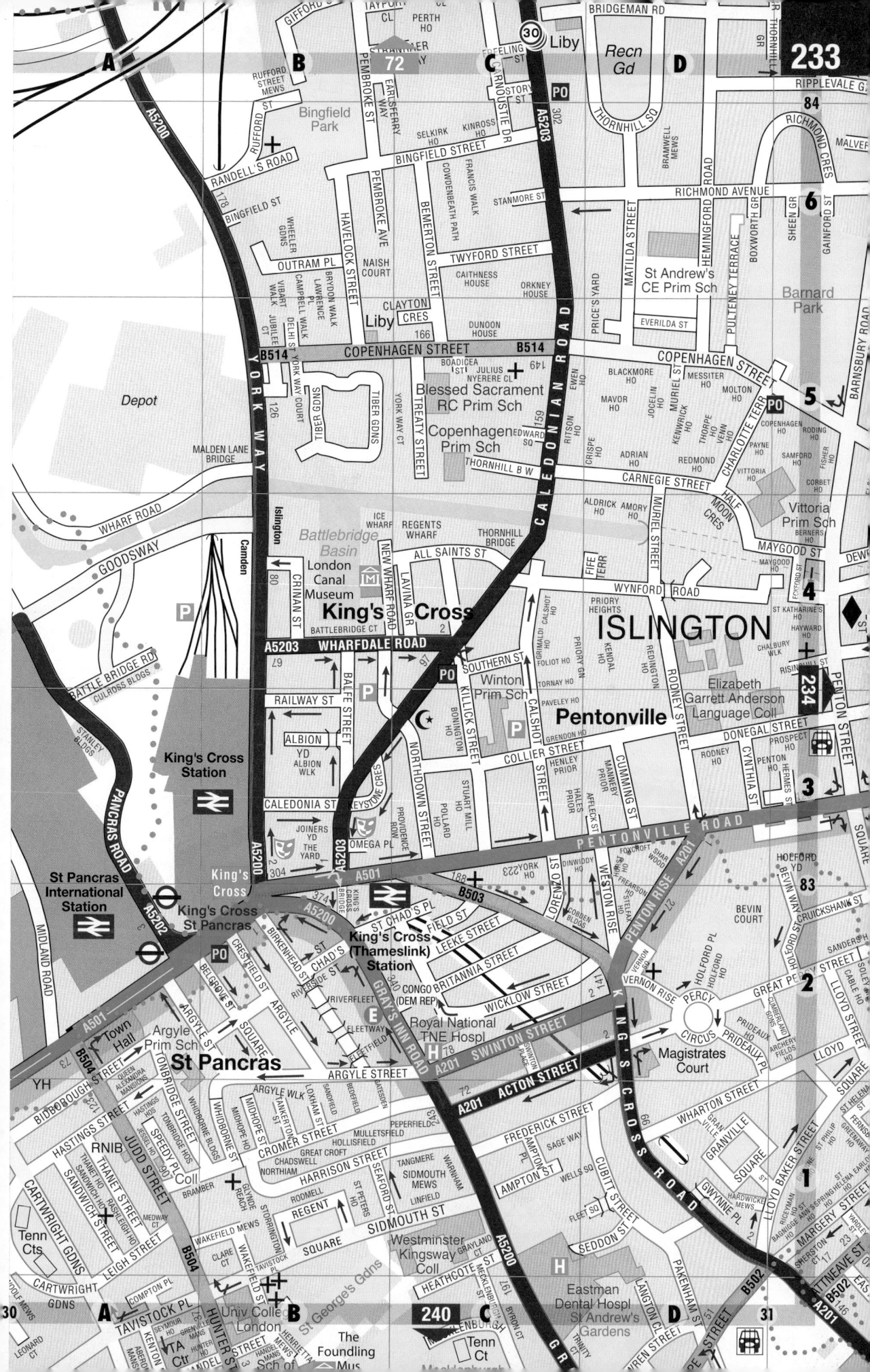
A
B
C
D
72
234
240
1
2
3
4
5
6
83
84
31
30
A5200
A5203
A5202
A501
A201
B514
B503
B504
B502
GIFFORD ST
PERTH HO
STRANRAER WAY
BRIDGEMAN RD
Liby
Recn Gd
THORNHILL GR
RIPPLEVALE GR
RUFFORD STREET MEWS
Bingfield Park
PEMBROKE ST
EARLSFERRY WAY
CARNOUSTIE DR
STORY ST
PO
THORNHILL SQ
RICHMOND CRES
MALVERN
RUFFORD ST
RANDELL'S ROAD
BINGFIELD STREET
SELKIRK HO
KINROSS HO
BRAMWELL MEWS
RICHMOND AVENUE
BINGFIELD ST
PEMBROKE AVE
COWDENBEATH PATH
FRANCIS WALK
STANMORE ST
HEMINGFORD ROAD
BOXWORTH GR
SHEEN GR
GAINFORD ST
WHEELER GDNS
HAVELOCK STREET
BEMERTON STREET
TWYFORD STREET
MATILDA STREET
PULTENEY TERRACE
OUTRAM PL
NAISH COURT
CAITHNESS HOUSE
ORKNEY HOUSE
PRICE'S YARD
St Andrew's CE Prim Sch
Barnard Park
VIBART WALK
CAMPBELL WALK
LAWRENCE PL
BRYDON WALK
CLAYTON CRES
JUBILEE CT
DELHI ST
DUNOON HOUSE
EVERILDA ST
BARNSBURY ROAD
COPENHAGEN STREET
BOADICEA ST
JULIUS NYERERE CL
BLACKMORE HO
MESSITER HO
MOLTON HO
Depot
YORK WAY
YORK WAY COURT
TIBER GDNS
YORK WAY CT
TREATY STREET
Blessed Sacrament RC Prim Sch
Copenhagen Prim Sch
EDWARD SQ
CALEDONIAN ROAD
MAVOR HO
EWEN HO
JOCELIN HO
MURIEL ST
KENWRICK HO
THORPE HO
VENN HO
CHARLOTTE TERR
COPENHAGEN HO
RODING HO
PAYNE HO
SAMFORD HO
FISHER HO
MALDEN LANE BRIDGE
THORNHILL B W
RITSON HO
CRISPE HO
ADRIAN HO
REDMOND HO
VITTORIA HO
CORBET HO
CARNEGIE STREET
HALF MOON CRES
WHARF ROAD
Islington
Camden
ICE WHARF
REGENTS WHARF
THORNHILL BRIDGE
ALDRICK HO
AMORY HO
MURIEL STREET
Vittoria Prim Sch
BERNERS HO
Battlebridge Basin
GOODSWAY
NEW WHARF ROAD
ALL SAINTS ST
MAYGOOD ST
London Canal Museum
CRINAN ST
LAVINA GR
FIFE TERR
WYNFORD ROAD
MAYGOOD HO
ECKFORD ST
King's Cross
PRIORY HEIGHTS
ISLINGTON
ST KATHARINE'S HO
HAYWARD HO
CHALBURY WLK
BATTLEBRIDGE CT
CALSHOT HO
WHARFDALE ROAD
SOUTHERN ST
GRIMALDI HO
FOLIOT HO
PRIORY GN
KENDAL HO
REDINGTON HO
RISINGHILL ST
PENTON STREET
BATTLE BRIDGE RD
CULROSS BLDGS
RAILWAY ST
BALFE STREET
Winton Prim Sch
TORNAY HO
Elizabeth Garrett Anderson Language Coll
KILLICK STREET
CALSHOT STREET
PAVELEY HO
Pentonville
RODNEY STREET
STANLEY BLDGS
ALBION YD
ALBION WLK
BONINGTON HO
GRENDON HO
DONEGAL STREET
King's Cross Station
NORTHDOWN STREET
COLLIER STREET
HENLEY PRIOR
MANNEBY PRIOR
RODNEY HO
CYNTHIA ST
PROSPECT HO
PENTON HO
HERMES ST
PANCRAS ROAD
CALEDONIA ST
KEYSTONE CRES
STUART MILL HO
POLLARD HO
HALES PRIOR
AFFLECK ST
CUMMING ST
JOINERS YD
THE YARD
PROVIDENCE ROW
OMEGA PL
PENTONVILLE ROAD
FOXCROFT
SHARWOOD
HOLFORD YD
YORK HO
DINWIDDY HO
St Pancras International Station
King's Cross
KING'S CROSS BRIDGE
ST CHAD'S PL
LORENZO ST
WESTON RISE
PENTON RISE
BEVIN WAY
CRUICKSHANK ST
BEVIN COURT
King's Cross St Pancras
FIELD ST
LEEKE STREET
COBDEN BLDGS
FREARSON HO
King's Cross (Thameslink) Station
BRITANNIA STREET
VERNON SQ
HOLFORD PL
HOLFORD HO
SANDERS HO
GREAT PERCY STREET
MIDLAND ROAD
BELGROVE ST
CRESTFIELD ST
BIRKENHEAD ST
ST CHAD'S ST
RIVERSIDE CT
CONGO (DEM REP)
WICKLOW STREET
VERNON RISE
PERCY CIRCUS
CUMBERLAND GDNS
LLOYD STREET
CABLE HO
ARGYLE ST
ARGYLE SQUARE
RIVERFLEET
GRAY'S INN ROAD
Royal National TNE Hospl
SWINTON STREET
SWINTON PLACE
PRIDEAUX PL
PRIDEAUX HO
Town Hall
Argyle Prim Sch
FLEETWAY
FLEETFIELD
Magistrates Court
ARCHERY FIELDS HO
LLOYD SQUARE
St Pancras
ARGYLE STREET
ACTON STREET
KING'S CROSS ROAD
YH
BIDBOROUGH STREET
QUEEN ALEXANDRA MANSIONS
TONBRIDGE STREET
ARGYLE WLK
LOXHAM ST
SANDFIELD
BEDEFIELD
GATESDEN
WHARTON STREET
GRANVILLE SQUARE
ST HELENA HO
FERNSBY HO
GREENAWAY HO
EARLOM HO
HASTINGS STREET
HASTINGS HOS
WHIDBORNE BLDGS
WHIDBORNE ST
MIDHOPE HO
MIDHOPE ST
TANKERTON ST
PEPPERFIELD
FREDERICK STREET
AMPTON PL
SAGE WAY
CROMER STREET
HOLLISFIELD
MULLETSFIELD
RNIB
THANET HO
SANDWICH HO
JUDD STREET
SPEEDY PL
TONBRIDGE HOS
JESSEL HO
Coll
GREAT CROFT
CHADSWELL
NORTHIAM
HARRISON STREET
TANGMERE
SIDMOUTH MEWS
WARNHAM
AMPTON ST
WELLS SQ
CUBITT STREET
HARDWICKE MEWS
GWYNNE PL
LLOYD BAKER STREET
ST PHILIP HO
SPRING HO
CARTWRIGHT GDNS
THANET STREET
RASHLEIGH HO
SANDWICH STREET
BRAMBER
GLYNDE REACH
STORRINGTON
RODMELL
REGENT SQUARE
SEAFORD ST
ST PETERS HO
LINFIELD
SIDMOUTH ST
FLEET SQ
RICEYMAN HO
BAGNIGGE HO
MARGERY STREET
YARDLEY ST
Tenn Cts
MEDWAY CT
LEIGH STREET
WAKEFIELD MEWS
CLARE CT
WAKEFIELD ST
Westminster Kingsway Coll
GRAYLAND CT
SEDDON ST
SHERSTON CT
CATTNEAVE ST
CARTWRIGHT GDNS
COMPTON PL
TAVISTOCK PL
HEATHCOTE ST
MECKLENBURGH ST
BYRON CT
Eastman Dental Hospl
LANGTON CL
PAKENHAM ST
St George's Gdns
St Andrew's Gardens
TAVISTOCK PL
HUNTER ST
Univ Coll London
The Foundling Mus
Tenn Ct
MECKLENBURGH
TRINITY CT
ACTON STREET
LEONARD CT
SEYMOUR HO
GRENVILLE MANS
HUNTER HO
TA Ctr
HANDEL MANS
HENRIETTA MEWS
KENTON CT

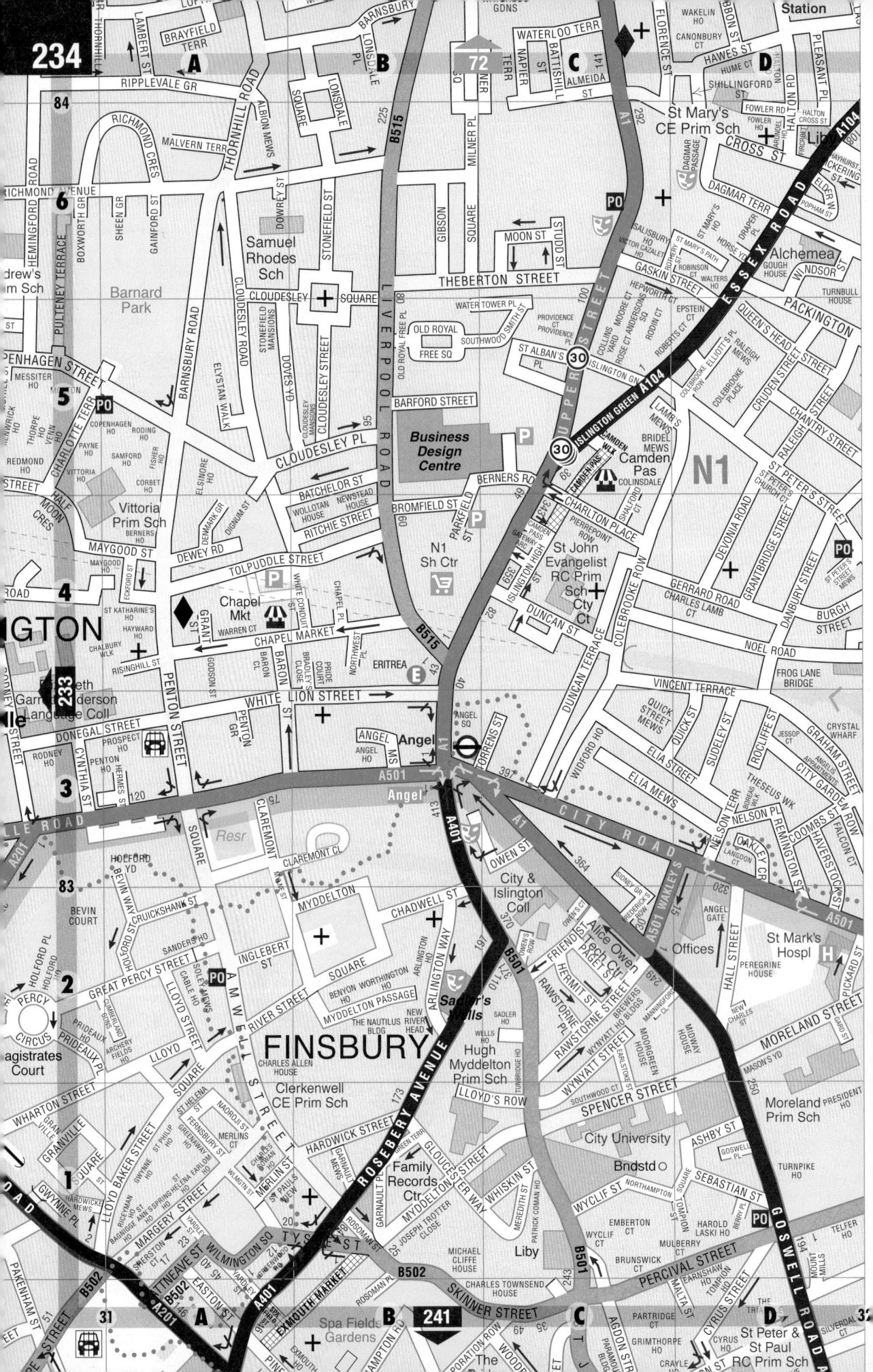

72
233
241
A
B
C
D
6
5
4
3
2
1
84
83
31
32
FINSBURY
N1
Barnard Park
Samuel Rhodes Sch
Business Design Centre
N1 Sh Ctr
Chapel Mkt
Angel
City & Islington Coll
Alice Owen Tech Ctr
Sadler's Wells
Hugh Myddelton Prim Sch
Clerkenwell CE Prim Sch
Family Records Ctr
City University
Bndstd
St Mark's Hospl
Offices
Moreland Prim Sch
St Mary's CE Prim Sch
Alchemea
Vittoria Prim Sch
St John Evangelist RC Prim Sch
Camden Pas
Spa Fields Gardens
St Peter & St Paul RC Prim Sch
Magistrates Court
Station
LIVERPOOL ROAD
UPPER STREET
ESSEX ROAD
CITY ROAD
ROSEBERY AVENUE
GOSWELL ROAD
PENTONVILLE ROAD
WHITE LION STREET
CHAPEL MARKET
THEBERTON STREET
CLOUDESLEY SQUARE
BARNSBURY ROAD
THORNHILL ROAD
RICHMOND AVENUE
PULTENEY TERRACE
COPENHAGEN STREET
ISLINGTON GREEN
PERCIVAL STREET
SKINNER STREET
SPENCER STREET
AMWELL STREET
MYDDELTON SQUARE
LLOYD BAKER STREET
GREAT PERCY STREET
MORELAND STREET
PACKINGTON STREET
ST PETER'S STREET
DUNCAN TERRACE
COLEBROOKE ROW
VINCENT TERRACE
NOEL ROAD
GRAHAM STREET
A1
A104
A501
A401
A201
B515
B501
B502

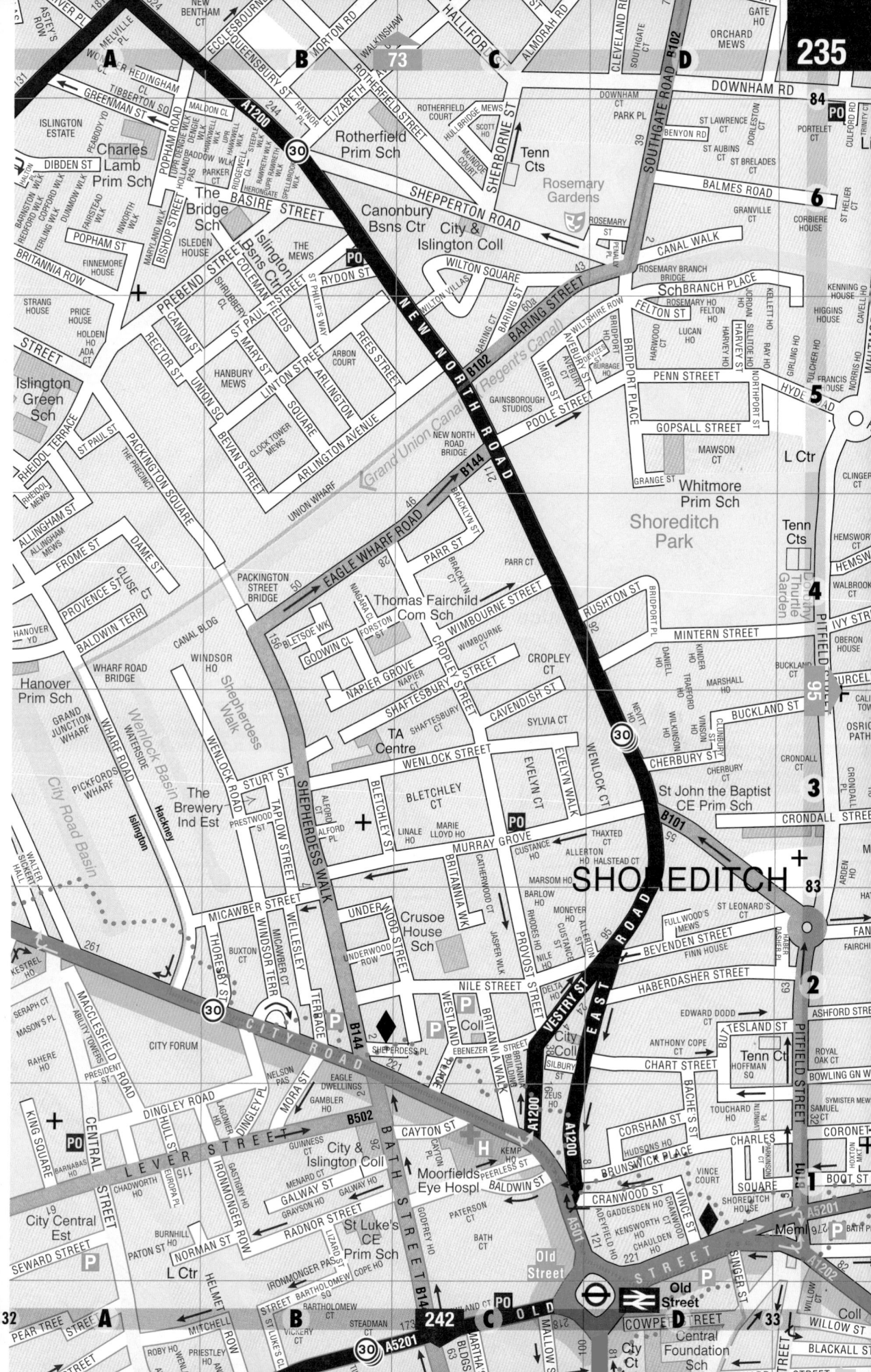
A
B
C
D
73
6
5
4
3
2
1
32
33
242
A1200
30
NEW NORTH ROAD
SHOREDITCH
Islington Estate
Charles Lamb Prim Sch
The Bridge Sch
Islington Bsns Ctr
Rotherfield Prim Sch
Canonbury Bsns Ctr
City & Islington Coll
Tenn Cts
Rosemary Gardens
Islington Green Sch
Hanover Prim Sch
Shoreditch Park
Whitmore Prim Sch
L Ctr
Dorothy Thurtle Garden
Thomas Fairchild Com Sch
TA Centre
The Brewery Ind Est
Shepherdess Walk
Wenlock Basin
City Road Basin
Grand Union Canal
Regent's Canal
St John the Baptist CE Prim Sch
Crusoe House Sch
City Forum
Moorfields Eye Hospl
St Luke's CE Prim Sch
City Central Est
Central Foundation Sch
Old Street
Islington
Hackney
SHEPPERTON ROAD
BASIRE STREET
PREBEND STREET
DOWNHAM RD
BALMES ROAD
CANAL WALK
BARING STREET
PENN STREET
GOPSALL STREET
POOLE STREET
EAGLE WHARF ROAD
WIMBOURNE STREET
MINTERN STREET
CROPLEY STREET
SHAFTESBURY STREET
WENLOCK STREET
WENLOCK ROAD
MURRAY GROVE
MICAWBER STREET
NILE STREET
HABERDASHER STREET
BEVENDEN STREET
CHART STREET
PITFIELD STREET
EAST ROAD
CITY ROAD
LEVER STREET
DINGLEY ROAD
BATH STREET
RADNOR STREET
OLD STREET
PACKINGTON SQUARE
WHARF ROAD
SOUTHGATE ROAD
ARLINGTON AVENUE
BRIDPORT PLACE
CRONDALL STREET
CHARLES SQUARE
BRUNSWICK PLACE
CENTRAL STREET
SEWARD STREET
COWPER STREET
B102
B144
B101
B502
A5201
A501

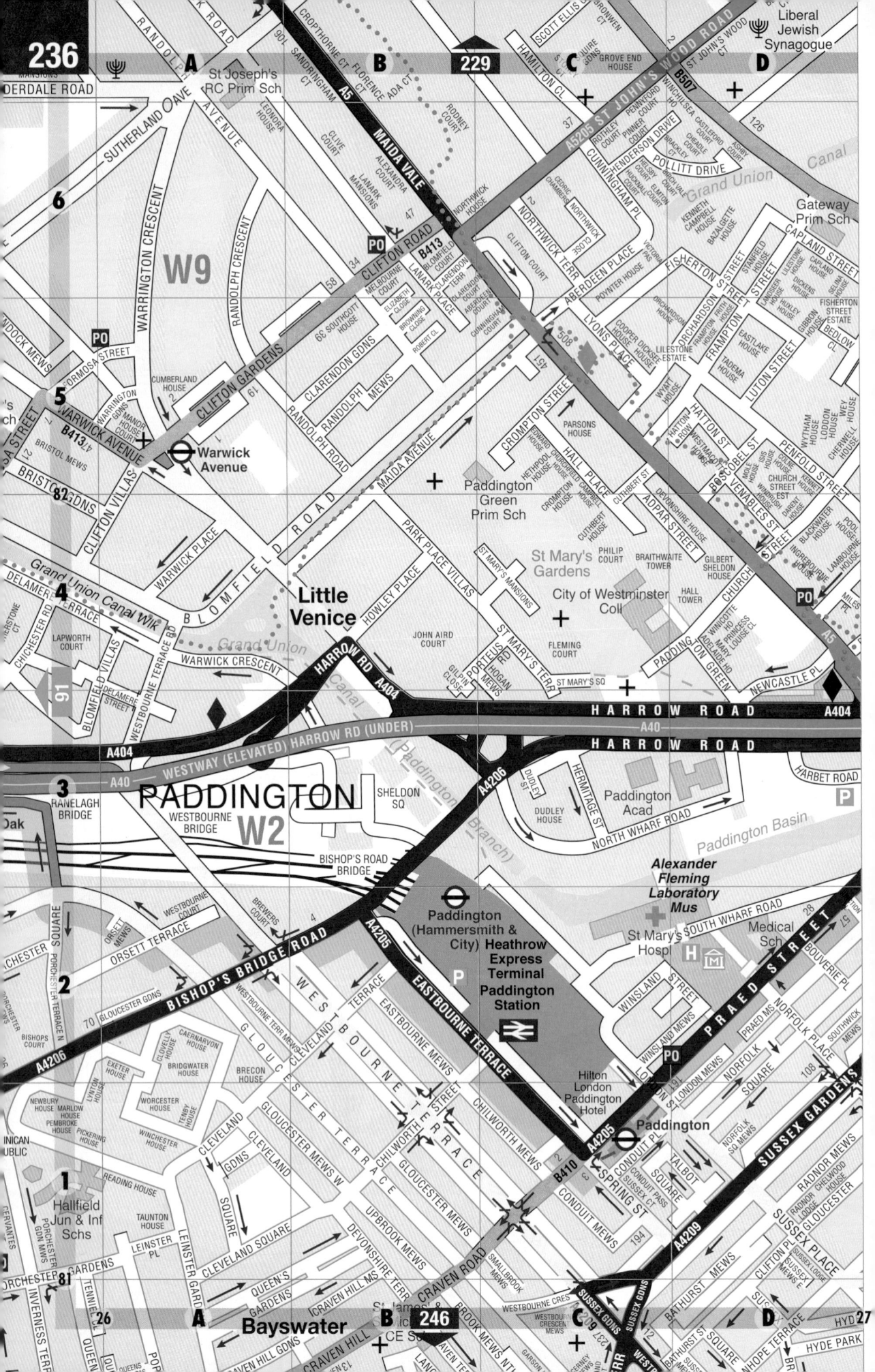
229
246
91
A
B
C
D
1
2
3
4
5
6
W9
W2
PADDINGTON
Little Venice
Bayswater
Liberal Jewish Synagogue
St Joseph's RC Prim Sch
Gateway Prim Sch
Paddington Green Prim Sch
St Mary's Gardens
City of Westminster Coll
Paddington Acad
Paddington Basin
Alexander Fleming Laboratory Mus
St Mary's Hospl
Medical Sch
Heathrow Express Terminal Paddington Station
Paddington (Hammersmith & City)
Hilton London Paddington Hotel
Paddington
Warwick Avenue
Hallfield Jun & Inf Schs
MAIDA VALE
ST JOHN'S WOOD ROAD
CLIFTON ROAD
CLIFTON GARDENS
WARWICK AVENUE
WARRINGTON CRESCENT
RANDOLPH CRESCENT
RANDOLPH AVENUE
SUTHERLAND AVE
BLOMFIELD ROAD
MAIDA AVENUE
WARWICK PLACE
WARWICK CRESCENT
HARROW ROAD
HARROW RD
WESTWAY (ELEVATED) HARROW RD (UNDER)
Grand Union Canal
Grand Union Canal Wlk
Paddington Branch
BISHOP'S BRIDGE ROAD
EASTBOURNE TERRACE
WESTBOURNE TERRACE
GLOUCESTER TERRACE
PRAED STREET
SUSSEX GARDENS
CRAVEN ROAD
NORTH WHARF ROAD
SOUTH WHARF ROAD
HERMITAGE ST
EDGWARE ROAD
CROMPTON STREET
HALL PLACE
ADPAR STREET
CHURCH STREET
ABERDEEN PLACE
NORTHWICK TERR
LYONS PLACE
FISHERTON STREET
CAPLAND STREET
PENFOLD STREET
LUTON STREET
FRAMPTON STREET
BOSCOBEL ST
HATTON ST
ST MARY'S TERR
PARK PLACE VILLAS
HOWLEY PLACE
CLEVELAND SQUARE
CLEVELAND GDNS
LEINSTER GARDENS
PORCHESTER GARDENS
ORSETT TERRACE
WESTBOURNE CRES
CONDUIT MEWS
LONDON ST
WINSLAND STREET
NORFOLK PLACE
NORFOLK SQUARE
SPRING ST
SUSSEX PLACE
BATHURST MEWS
HYDE PARK

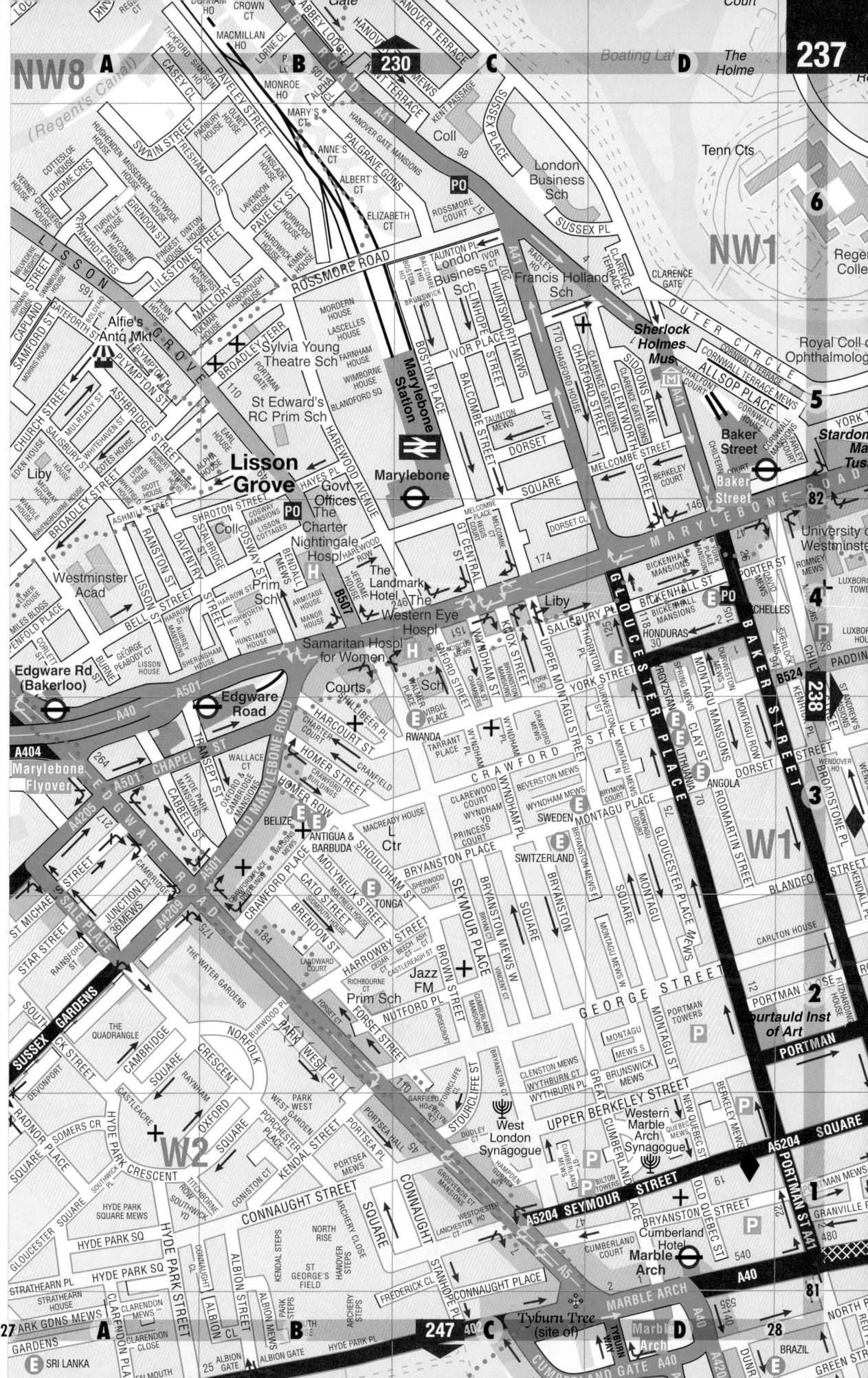
NW8
A
B
C
D
230
Boating Lake
The Holme
(Regent's Canal)
Crown Ct
Macmillan Ho
Lorne Cl
Abbey Lodge
Hanover Terrace
Park Road
A41
Kent Terrace
Kent Passage
Sussex Place
Tickford Ho
Simpson Ho
Casey Cl
Paveley Street
Monroe Ho
Mary's Ct
Anne's Ct
Albert's Ct
Elizabeth Ct
Hanover Gate Mansions
Palgrave Gdns
Coll
98
London Business Sch
PO
Rossmore Court
Sussex Pl
Tenn Cts
NW1
6
Regent's College
Swain Street
Tresham Cres
Paobury House
Olney House
Linslade House
Lavendon House
Paveley St
Horwood House
Hardwick House
Kimble House
Cotteslo House
Jerome Cres
Verney House
Chequers House
Hughenden House
Missenden House
Chetwode House
Bernhardt Cres
Turville House
Wycombe House
Grendon St
Fingest House
Dinton House
Lilestone Street
Gaydon House
Mallory St
Risborough House
Penn House
Fulmar House
Lisson Grove
Belvedere Heights
Swanbourne House
Jordans House
165
Capland Street
Gateforth St
Boldero Pl
Alfie's Antq Mkt
Samford St
Morris House
Plympton Pl
Plympton St
Broadley Terr
Rossmore Road
Taunton Pl
Boston Ho
Balcombe Ho
Brunswick Ho
London Business Sch
Ivor Ct
Francis Holland Sch
Radley Ho
Clarence Terrace
Clarence Gate
Outer Circle
Sherlock Holmes Mus
Cornwall Terrace
Cornwall Terrace Mews
Allsop Place
Chalfont Court
Royal Coll of Ophthalmologists
5
Mordern House
Lascelles House
Farnham House
Wimborne House
Blandford Sq
Sylvia Young Theatre Sch
Portman Gate
St Edward's RC Prim Sch
Marylebone Station
Boston Place
Balcombe Street
Ivor Place
Huntsworth Mews
Linhope Street
Taunton Mews
Dorset Square
147
Chagford Street
Chagford House
Clarence Gate Gdns
Glentworth Street
Siddons Lane
170
Melcombe Street
Berkeley Court
Chiltern Court
Baker Street
Cornwall Mansions
Harley House
York Terrace
Stardome Madame Tussauds
Marylebone Road
82
University of Westminster
Church Street
Ashbridge Street
Mulready St
Salisbury St
Whitehaven St
Cotes House
Eden House
Liby
Lea House
Medway House
Lyon House
Hubert House
Earl House
Alpha House
Lisson Grove
Harewood Avenue
Marylebone
Govt Offices
Hayes Pl
Broadley Street
Ravensbourne House
Wandle House
Ashmill Street
Shroton Street
Cosway Mansions
Lisson Cottages
PO
The Charter Nightingale Hospl
Coll
Ranston St
Daventry St
Stalbridge St
Cosway St
Bendall Mews
Harewood Row
Jerome House
The Landmark Hotel
B507
Gt Central St
Melcombe Place
Regis Court
Melcombe Ct
174
Dorset Cl
146
Bickenhall Mansions
York Place Mansions
Porter St
David Mews
Romney Mews
Luxborough Tower
Westminster Acad
Elmer House
Miles Bldgs
Penfold Place
Lisson St
Bell Street
Harrow St
Highworth St
Prim Sch
Armitage House
Manor House
The Western Eye Hospl
246
Samaritan Hospl for Women
Liby
Bickenhall St
Salisbury Pl
Gloucester Place
E
PO
Baker Street
Chiltern St
Sherlock Mews
Luxborough Ho
Paddington St
4
Corlett St
Burne St
George Peabody Ct
Lisson House
Sheringham House
Harrow St
Albury Mansions
Hunstanton House
151
Enford Street
Circus Mews
Wyndham St
Bryanston Mansions
Knox Street
York Ho
Upper Montagu Street
Thornton Pl
Durweston Mews
Honduras
30
118
105
Edgware Rd (Bakerloo)
A501
Edgware Road
A40
Courts
Shillibeer Pl
Harcourt St
Charter Court
Walmer Place
Virgil Place
Sch
York Street
Durweston St
Kyrgyzstan
Spring Mews
Montagu Mansions
B524
Kenrick Pl
St Andrew's Mansions
238
A404
Marylebone Flyover
264
Chapel St
Transept St
Wallace Ct
Oxford & Cambridge Mansions
Hyde Park Mansions
Cabbell St
Old Marylebone Road
Homer Street
Cranfield Ct
Rwanda
Tarrant Place
Wyndham Pl
Crawford Mews
Crawford
Montagu Mews N
Lithuania
Clay St
Montagu Row
Dorset Street
Wendover Ho
Broadstone Pl
3
Edgware Road
A4205
217
Homer Row
Crawford Buildings
Belize
Antigua & Barbuda
Macready House
L Ctr
Clarewood Court
Wyndham Yd
Princess Court
Beverston Mews
Wyndham Mews
Sweden
Montagu Place
Brymon Court
Montagu Court
Angola
Rodmartin Street
W1
Switzerland
Bryanston Square
Montagu Square
Gloucester Place Mews
Shouldham St
Molyneux Street
Cato Street
Sidmouth House
Crawford Place
Bryanston Place
Sherwood Court
Seymour Place
Bryanston Mews W
Bryanston Mews E
Tonga
Blandford Street
Kendall Pl
Street
St Michael's Street
Sale Place
Junction Mews
Cambridge Ct
A4209
175
184
Brendon St
Harrowby Street
Cedar Ct
Beech Ct
Ash Ct
Castlereagh St
Brown Street
Landward Court
Montagu Mews W
Carlton House
Star Street
Rainsford St
The Water Gardens
Richbourne Ct
Jazz FM
Prim Sch
Nutford Pl
Cumberland Mansions
Vincent Ct
George Street
Portman Towers
12
Portman Close
Fitzhardinge House
2
Courtauld Inst of Art
Sussex Gardens
The Quadrangle
Cambridge Square
Norfolk Crescent
Burwood Pl
Park West Pl
Forset Street
Forset Ct
Furscroft
Montagu Mews S
Montagu Square
Montagu St
Portman
Devonport
Radnor Place
Somers Cr
Raynham
Oxford Square
Castleacre
W2
Hyde Park Crescent
Southwick Pl
Titchborne Row
Southwick Yd
Park West
West Garden
Porchester Place
Kendal Street
Portsea Hall
Portsea Place
Portsea Mews
110
Garfield Ho
Stourcliffe St
Evelyn Ct
Bryanston Ct
Dudley Ct
Clenston Mews
Wythburn Ct
Wythburn Pl
Great Cumberland Place
Brunswick Mews
Upper Berkeley Street
Western Marble Arch Synagogue
New Quebec St
Quebec Mews
Berkeley Mews
West London Synagogue
Hampden Gurney St
Cumberland Mews
Bilton Towers
Seymour Street
A5204
Square
Portman Square
Portman Mews
Granville Pl
480
1
Hyde Park Square Mews
Gloucester Square
Hyde Park Sq
Connaught Street
Coniston Ct
Archery Close
North Rise
Connaught Square
Connaught
Grosvenor Ct Mansions
Westchester Ho
Lanchester Ct
Bryanston Street
Old Quebec St
Cumberland Hotel
Cumberland Court
Marble Arch
540
A40
A41
Portman St
Strathearn Pl
Strathearn House
Hyde Park Sq
Connaught Cl
Albion Street
Kendal Steps
St George's Field
Hanover Steps
Frederick Cl
Stanhope Pl
Connaught Place
A5
Marble Arch
81
Park Gdns Mews
Clarendon Mews
Clarendon Close
Hyde Park Street
Albion Cl
Albion Mews
Park Steps
Archery Steps
247
Tyburn Tree (site of)
Tyburn Way
Marble Arch
A40
28
North Row
Red Pl
Gardens
Sri Lanka
Clarendon Place
Falmouth House
Albion Gate
25
Hyde Park Pl
Cumberland Gate A40
A4202
Brazil
Green Street
27

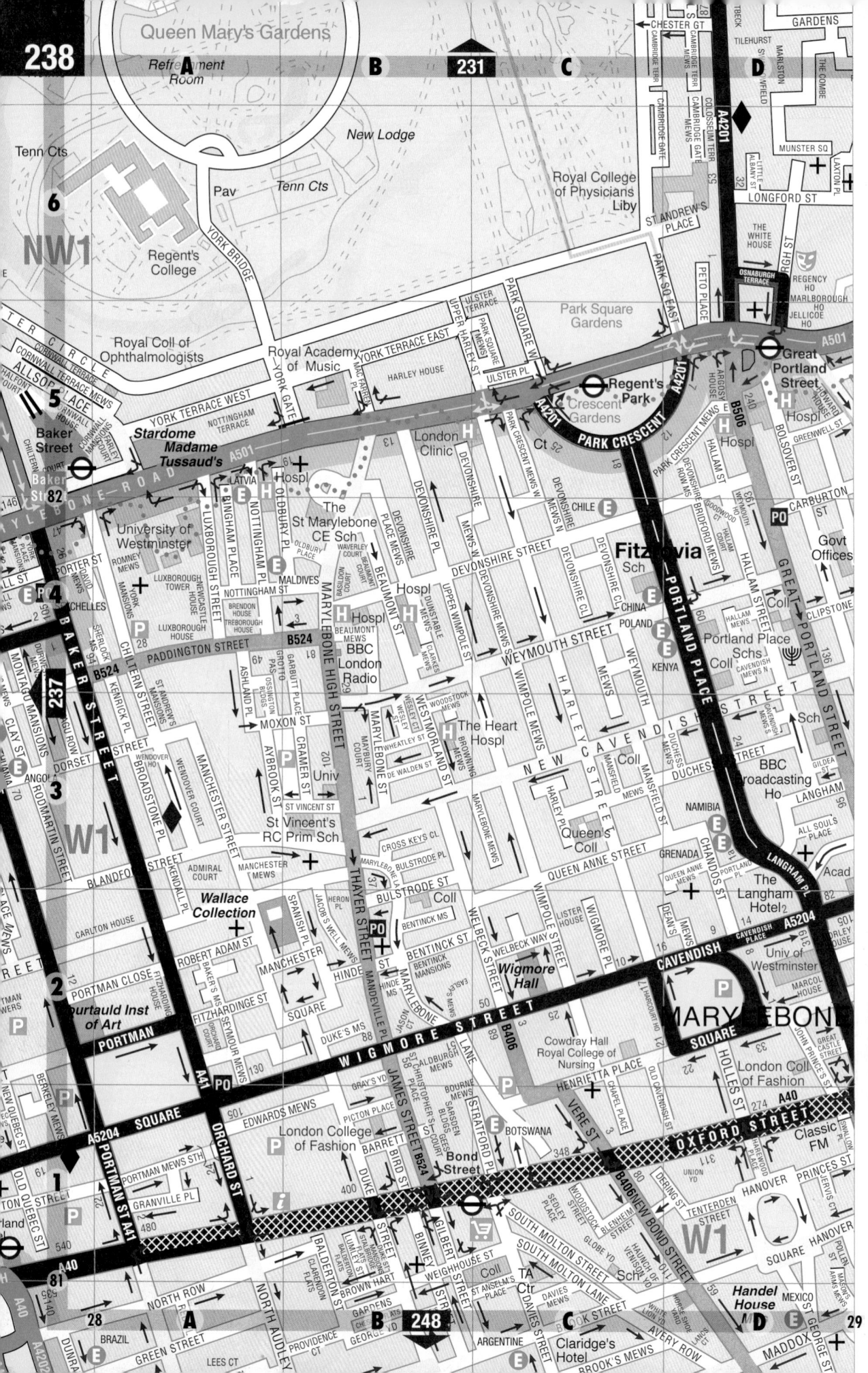
Queen Mary's Gardens
Refreshment Room
A
B
231
C
D
New Lodge
Tenn Cts
Pav
Tenn Cts
Royal College of Physicians Liby
6
NW1
Regent's College
YORK BRIDGE
Royal Coll of Ophthalmologists
Royal Academy of Music
Park Square Gardens
CHESTER GT
CAMBRIDGE TERR
CAMBRIDGE TERR MEWS
CAMBRIDGE GATE
CAMBRIDGE GATE MEWS
COLOSSEUM TERR
ST ANDREW'S PLACE
PARK SQ EAST
PETO PLACE
A4201
GARDENS
TILEHURST
MARLSTON
THE COMBE
MUNSTER SQ
LONGFORD ST
LITTLE ALBANY ST
LAXTON PL
THE WHITE HOUSE
OSNABURGH TERRACE
REGENCY HO
MARLBOROUGH HO
JELLICOE HO
A501
Great Portland Street
ULSTER TERRACE
PARK SQUARE MEWS
PARK SQUARE W
UPPER HARLEY ST
YORK TERRACE EAST
HARLEY HOUSE
ULSTER PL
MACFARREN PL
YORK GATE
YORK TERRACE WEST
NOTTINGHAM TERRACE
OUTER CIRCLE
CORNWALL TERRACE
CORNWALL TERRACE MEWS
ALLSOP PLACE
CORNWALL MANSIONS
5
Baker Street
Stardome Madame Tussaud's
MARYLEBONE ROAD
Regent's Park
Crescent Gardens
PARK CRESCENT
PARK CRESCENT MEWS W
PARK CRESCENT MEWS E
ARGOSY HOUSE
B506
Hospl
London Clinic
DEVONSHIRE MEWS W
DEVONSHIRE PL
DEVONSHIRE MEWS N
DEVONSHIRE PLACE MEWS
DEVONSHIRE ROW MS
HALLAM ST
BOLSOVER ST
GREENWELL ST
HOWARD HOUSE
CARBURTON ST
CHILE
Govt Offices
The St Marylebone CE Sch
University of Westminster
LATVIA
BINGHAM PLACE
NOTTINGHAM PL
OLDBURY PL
LUXBOROUGH STREET
LUXBOROUGH TOWER
LUXBOROUGH HOUSE
NEWCASTLE HOUSE
ROMNEY MEWS
YORK MANSIONS
PORTER ST
DAVID MEWS
MALDIVES
NOTTINGHAM ST
BRENDON HOUSE
TREBOROUGH HOUSE
WAVERLEY COURT
BEAUMONT COURT
BASILDON COURT
BEAUMONT ST
BEAUMONT MEWS
DUNSTABLE MEWS
CLARKES MEWS
UPPER WIMPOLE ST
DEVONSHIRE STREET
DEVONSHIRE CL
DEVONSHIRE MEWS S
Fitzrovia
Sch
CHINA
POLAND
KENYA
Portland Place Schs
Coll
HALLAM MEWS
CAVENDISH MEWS N
GREAT PORTLAND STREET
CLIPSTONE
PORTLAND PLACE
BRIDFORD MEWS
GOODWOOD HO
HALLAM COURT
WEYMOUTH STREET
WEYMOUTH MEWS
HARLEY STREET
MEWS
4
SEYCHELLES
BAKER STREET
PADDINGTON STREET
B524
BBC London Radio
MARYLEBONE HIGH STREET
GROTTO PAS
GARBUTT PLACE
OSSINGTON BLDGS
ASHLAND PL
MOXON ST
AYBROOK ST
CRAMER ST
CHILTERN STREET
KENRICK PL
ST ANDREW'S MANSIONS
SHERLOCK MEWS
DURWESTON MEWS
MONTAGU MANSIONS
237
CLAY ST
DORSET STREET
ANGOLA
3
RODMARTIN STREET
W1
BROADSTONE PL
WENDOVER HO
WENDOVER COURT
MANCHESTER STREET
Univ
ST VINCENT ST
St Vincent's RC Prim Sch
MARYLEBONE LANE
WESLEY ST
WHEATLEY ST
DE WALDEN ST
MAYBURY COURT
WESTMORLAND ST
WOODSTOCK MEWS
The Heart Hospl
BROWNING MEWS
WIMPOLE MEWS
NEW CAVENDISH STREET
MANSFIELD MEWS
MANSFIELD ST
DUCHESS MEWS
DUCHESS STREET
CAVENDISH MEWS S
BBC Broadcasting Ho
GILDEA ST
LANGHAM
ALL SOULS PLACE
NAMIBIA
GRENADA
CHANDOS ST
Queen's Coll
HARLEY PL
MARYLEBONE MEWS
CROSS KEYS CL
BULSTRODE PL
BULSTRODE ST
QUEEN ANNE STREET
QUEEN ANNE MEWS
PORTLAND PL
The Langham Hotel
LANGHAM PL
Acad
ADMIRAL COURT
MANCHESTER MEWS
BLANDFORD STREET
KENDALL PL
CARLTON HOUSE
Wallace Collection
SPANISH PL
JACOB'S WELL MEWS
HERON PL
THAYER STREET
BENTINCK MS
BENTINCK ST
BENTINCK MANSIONS
WELBECK STREET
WELBECK WAY
WIMPOLE STREET
LISTER HOUSE
WIGMORE PL
Wigmore Hall
DEAN'S MEWS
CAVENDISH PLACE
CAVENDISH
A5204
Univ of Westminster
MARCOL HOUSE
ROBERT ADAM ST
BAKER'S MS
PORTMAN CLOSE
FITZHARDING HOUSE
FITZHARDINGE ST
MANCHESTER SQUARE
HINDE ST
HINDE MS
MARYLEBONE LANE
MANDEVILLE PL
EASLEY'S MEWS
2
Courtauld Inst of Art
PORTMAN SQUARE
SEYMOUR MEWS
ORCHARD COURT
DUKE'S MS
JASON CT
WIGMORE STREET
B406
HARCOURT HO
Cowdray Hall Royal College of Nursing
MARYLEBONE SQUARE
HOLLES ST
JOHN PRINCE'S ST
GREAT CASTLE STREET
London Coll of Fashion
A41
PO
EDWARDS MEWS
ORCHARD ST
GRAY'S YD
ST CHRISTOPHER'S PLACE
ALDBURGH MEWS
BOURNE MEWS
SARSDEN BLDGS
GEES COURT
STRATFORD PL
HENRIETTA PLACE
CHAPEL PLACE
OLD CAVENDISH ST
VERE ST
BOTSWANA
OXFORD STREET
Classic FM
SWALLOW PL
HAREWOOD PLACE
A40
BERKELEY MEWS
NEW QUEBEC ST
A5204 SQUARE
PORTMAN ST
PORTMAN MEWS STH
GRANVILLE PL
London College of Fashion
PICTON PLACE
BARRETT ST
JAMES STREET
BIRD ST
B524
Bond Street
DUKE ST
UNION YD
DERING ST
TENTERDEN STREET
HANOVER
HANOVER SQUARE
PRINCES ST
JERVIS CT
1
OLD QUEBEC ST
UPTON STREET
NEW BOND STREET
B406
WOODSTOCK STREET
SEDLEY PLACE
BLENHEIM STREET
GLOBE YD
HAUNCH OF VENISON YD
SOUTH MOLTON STREET
SOUTH MOLTON LANE
W1
A40
NORTH ROW
NORTH AUDLEY
BALDERTON ST
BALDERTON FLATS
CLARENDON FLATS
LUMLEY ST
STREET
BINNEY
GILBERT STREET
WEIGHHOUSE ST
BROWN HART GARDENS
ST ANSELM'S PLACE
DAVIES STREET
DAVIES MEWS
TA Ctr
Sch
HORSE SHOE YARD
Handel House
MEXICO
ST GEORGE ST
MASON'S ARMS MEWS
POLLEN ST
BRAZIL
GREEN STREET
LEES CT
PROVIDENCE CT
GEORGE YD
248
ARGENTINE
Claridge's Hotel
BROOK STREET
BROOK'S MEWS
AVERY ROW
WHITE LION YD
LANCASHIRE CT
MADDOX ST
28
29
A4202
DUNRAVEN

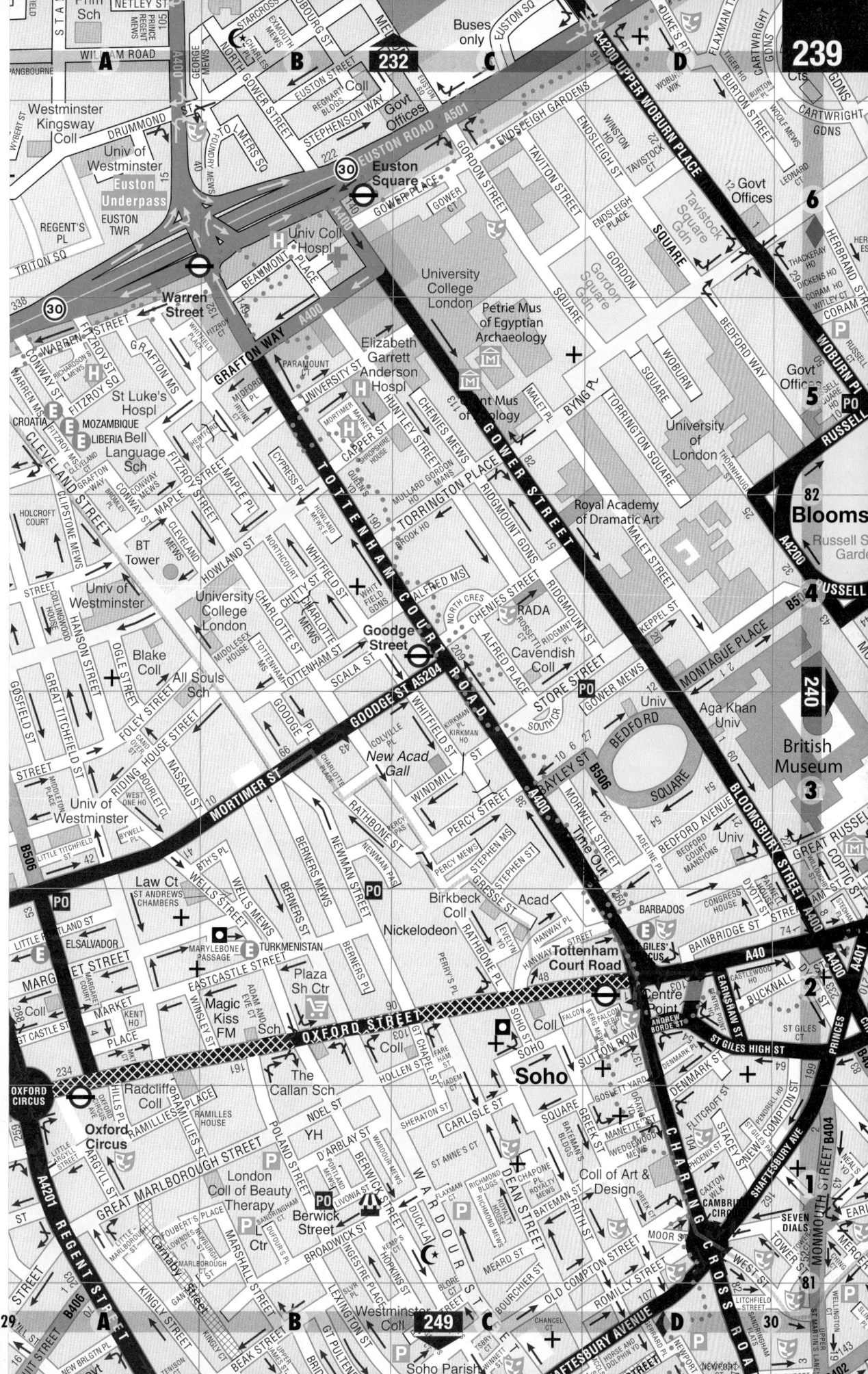
A
B
C
D
232
Euston Road
Euston Square
Euston Underpass
Warren Street
Univ Coll Hospl
University College London
Petrie Mus of Egyptian Archaeology
Grant Mus of Zoology
Elizabeth Garrett Anderson Hospl
Tavistock Square Gdn
Gordon Square Gdn
University of London
Royal Academy of Dramatic Art
Bloomsbury
Upper Woburn Place
Woburn Place
Russell Square
Bedford Square
Bedford Way
Torrington Square
Gower Street
Tottenham Court Road
Goodge Street
Goodge St A5204
Mortimer St
BT Tower
Fitzroy Sq
St Luke's Hospl
Bell Language Sch
Univ of Westminster
Westminster Kingsway Coll
Blake Coll
All Souls Sch
Cavendish Coll
RADA
Aga Khan Univ
British Museum
240
Montague Place
Bloomsbury Street
Great Russell St
New Acad Gall
Birkbeck Coll
Nickelodeon
Time Out
Law Ct
Plaza Sh Ctr
Magic Kiss FM
Oxford Street
Oxford Circus
Regent Street
A4201
Great Marlborough Street
London Coll of Beauty Therapy
Carnaby Street
Berwick Street
Wardour Street
Soho
Soho Square
Dean Street
Coll of Art & Design
Centre Point
St Giles High St
Charing Cross Road
Shaftesbury Ave
Seven Dials
Monmouth Street B404
Old Compton Street
Westminster Coll
249
Soho Parish
Shaftesbury Avenue
6
5
4
3
2
1
29
30

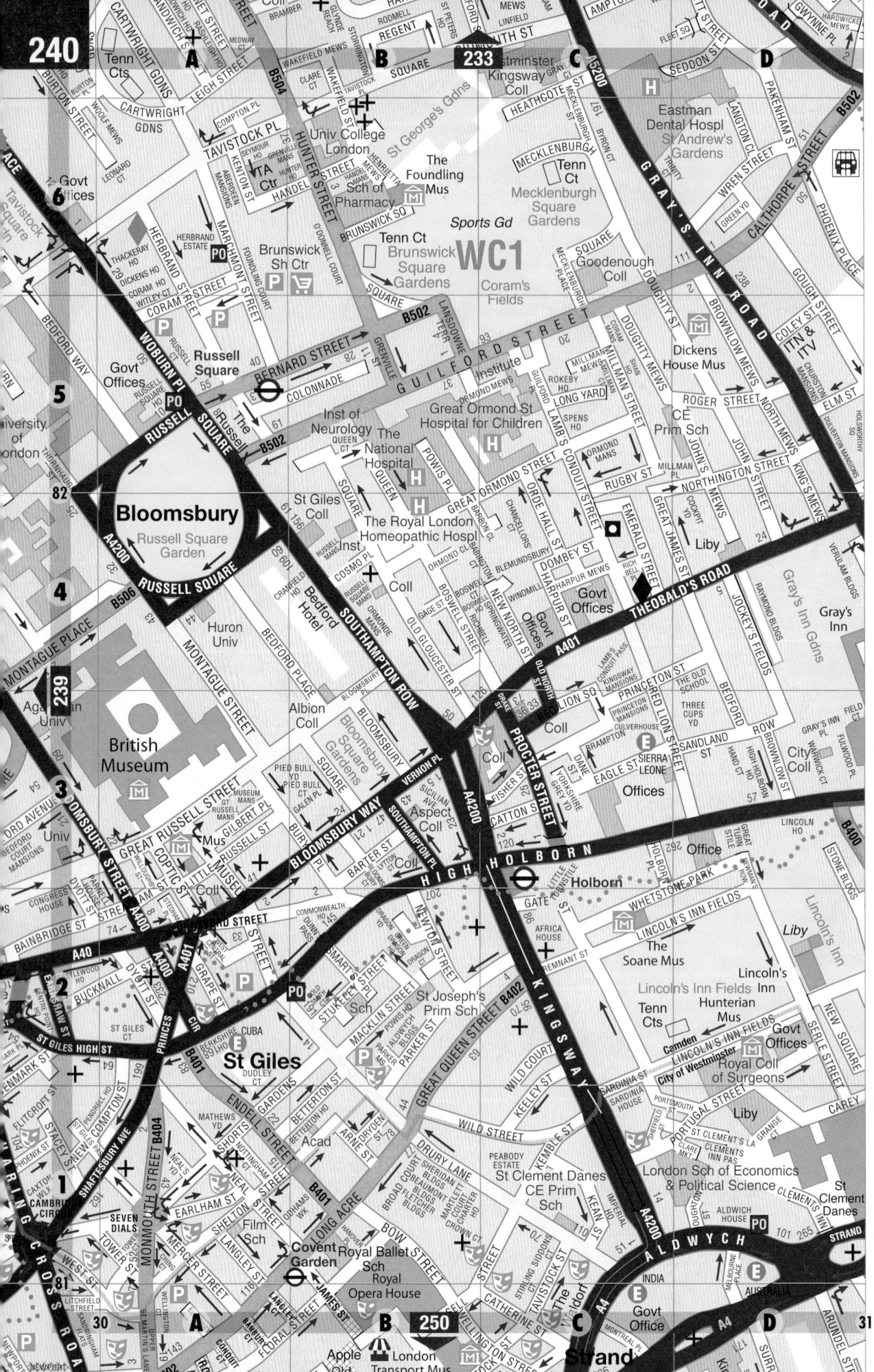

233
Bloomsbury
Russell Square Garden
British Museum
WC1
Brunswick Square Gardens
Mecklenburgh Square Gardens
Coram's Fields
St George's Gdns
The Foundling Mus
Great Ormond St Hospital for Children
The National Hospital
The Royal London Homeopathic Hospl
Dickens House Mus
Gray's Inn Gdns
Gray's Inn
Holborn
Lincoln's Inn Fields
Lincoln's Inn
The Soane Mus
Hunterian Mus
Royal Coll of Surgeons
London Sch of Economics & Political Science
St Giles
Covent Garden
Royal Opera House
Royal Ballet Sch
London Transport Mus
Strand
ALDWYCH
KINGSWAY
HIGH HOLBORN
THEOBALD'S ROAD
SOUTHAMPTON ROW
GRAY'S INN ROAD
GUILFORD STREET
RUSSELL SQUARE
WOBURN PL
BLOOMSBURY WAY
NEW OXFORD STREET
SHAFTESBURY AVE
CHARING CROSS ROAD
LONG ACRE
DRURY LANE
GREAT QUEEN STREET
Camden
City of Westminster
239
250

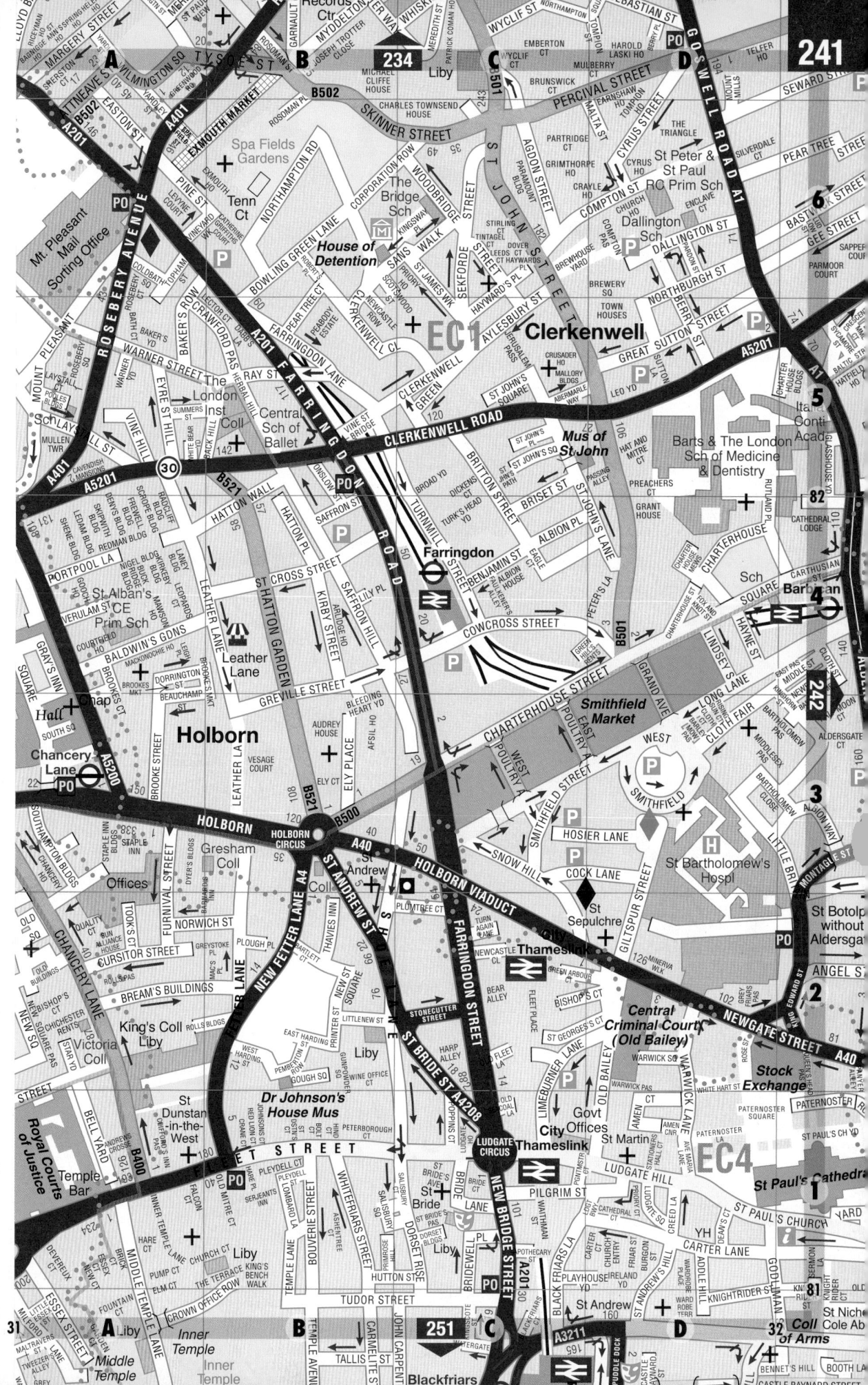
Clerkenwell
Holborn
EC1
EC4
Farringdon
Barbican
Smithfield Market
St Paul's Cathedral
Central Criminal Court (Old Bailey)
St Bartholomew's Hospl
Barts & The London Sch of Medicine & Dentistry
Royal Courts of Justice
Blackfriars
Chancery Lane
City Thameslink
Holborn Circus
Ludgate Circus
House of Detention
Mus of St John
Leather Lane
Mt. Pleasant Mail Sorting Office
Spa Fields Gardens
Dr Johnson's House Mus
Stock Exchange
Inner Temple
Middle Temple
Temple Bar
FARRINGDON ROAD
CLERKENWELL ROAD
HOLBORN VIADUCT
HOLBORN
NEWGATE STREET
FLEET STREET
GOSWELL ROAD A1
ROSEBERY AVENUE
FARRINGDON STREET
NEW BRIDGE STREET
CHANCERY LANE
ST JOHN STREET
CHARTERHOUSE STREET
LUDGATE HILL
SKINNER STREET
PERCIVAL STREET
234
242
251

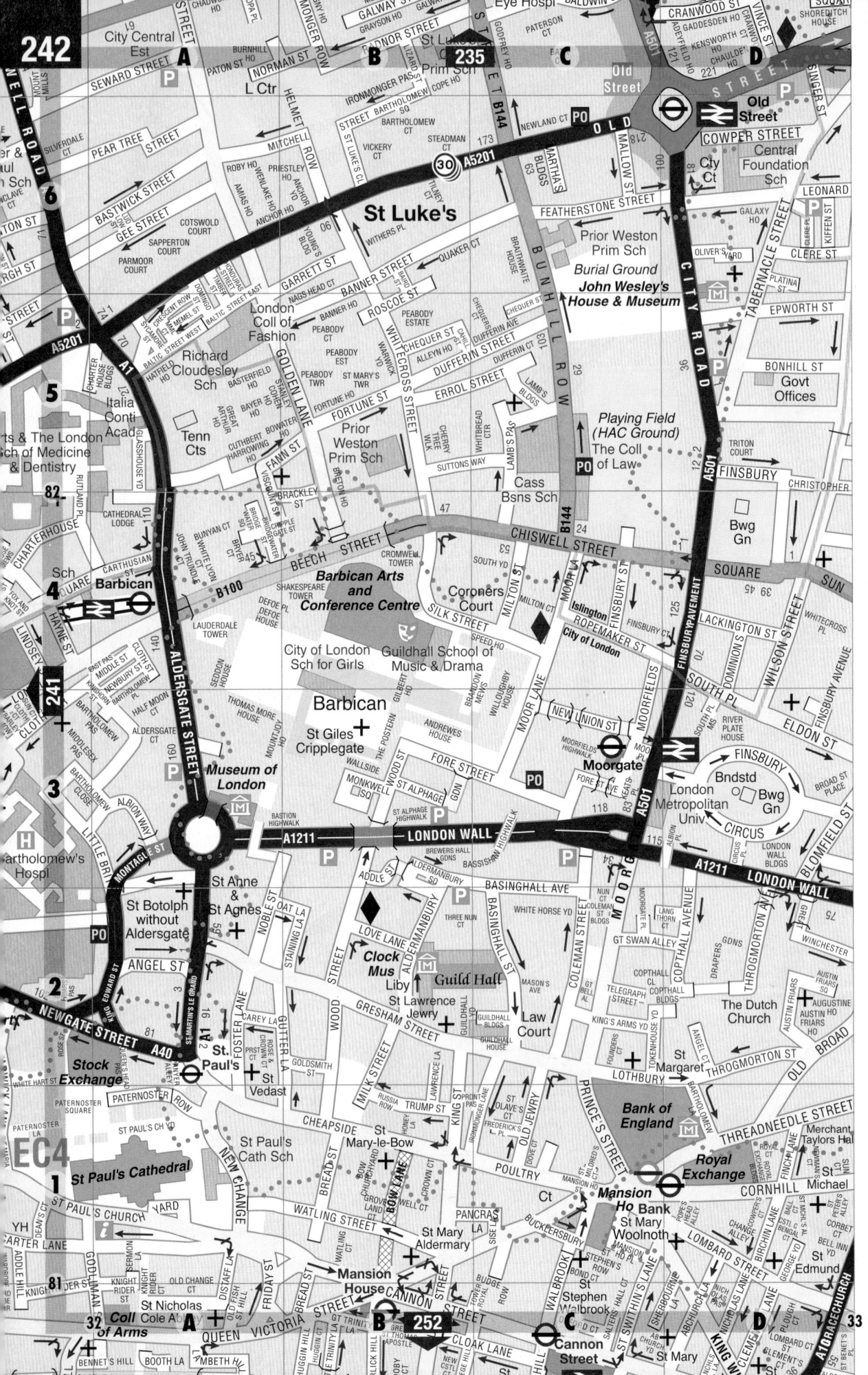

242
A
B
C
D
235
252
1
2
3
4
5
6
32
33
EC4
City Central Est
St Luke's
Old Street
Old Street
City Rd
Central Foundation Sch
Eye Hospl
Prior Weston Prim Sch
Burial Ground
John Wesley's House & Museum
Playing Field (HAC Ground)
The Coll of Law
Cass Bsns Sch
Bwg Gn
Govt Offices
London Coll of Fashion
Richard Cloudesley Sch
Tenn Cts
Italia Conti Acad
Barbican
Barbican Arts and Conference Centre
City of London Sch for Girls
Guildhall School of Music & Drama
St Giles Cripplegate
Coroners Court
Museum of London
Moorgate
London Metropolitan Univ
Bndstd
St Botolph without Aldersgate
St Anne & St Agnes
Clock Mus
Guild Hall
Liby
St Lawrence Jewry
Law Court
The Dutch Church
Bank of England
Royal Exchange
Bank
Mansion Ho
St Mary Woolnoth
St Paul's
Stock Exchange
St Paul's Cathedral
St Paul's Cath Sch
St Mary-le-Bow
St Mary Aldermary
Mansion House
Cannon Street
St Stephen Walbrook
St Nicholas Cole Abbey
Coll of Arms
St Vedast
St Margaret
St Michael
St Edmund
Merchant Taylors Hal
Islington
City of London
OLD STREET
CITY ROAD
BUNHILL ROW
ALDERSGATE STREET
LONDON WALL
CHISWELL STREET
BEECH STREET
FINSBURY PAVEMENT
MOORGATE
CHEAPSIDE
NEWGATE STREET
QUEEN VICTORIA STREET
CANNON STREET
GRESHAM STREET
THREADNEEDLE STREET
CORNHILL
LOMBARD STREET
POULTRY
WHITECROSS STREET
GOLDEN LANE
FINSBURY SQUARE
FINSBURY CIRCUS
WOOD STREET
COLEMAN STREET
BASINGHALL ST
MOOR LANE
ROPEMAKER ST
SILK STREET
FORE STREET
A501
A5201
A1
A1211
A40
B144
B100

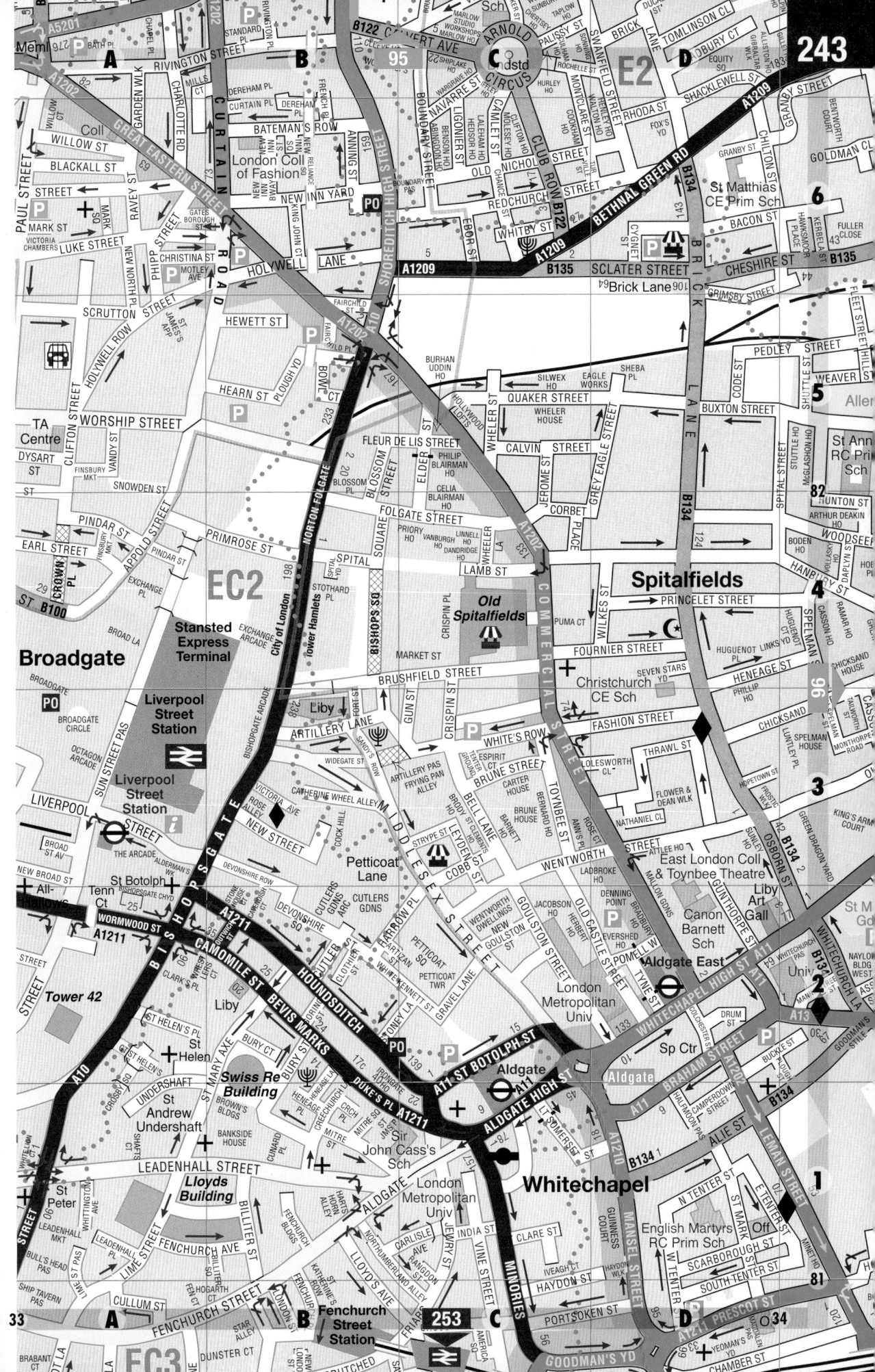
A
B
C
D
E2
EC2
EC3
95
96
253
33
34
81
82
1
2
3
4
5
6
RIVINGTON STREET
GREAT EASTERN STREET
CURTAIN ROAD
SHOREDITCH HIGH STREET
CALVERT AVE
ARNOLD CIRCUS
BOUNDARY STREET
OLD NICHOL STREET
REDCHURCH STREET
CLUB ROW
BETHNAL GREEN RD
SCLATER STREET
CHESHIRE ST
BRICK LANE
Brick Lane
London Coll of Fashion
St Matthias CE Prim Sch
HOLYWELL LANE
SCRUTTON STREET
WORSHIP STREET
HEWETT ST
HEARN ST
TA Centre
NORTON FOLGATE
FOLGATE STREET
QUAKER STREET
BUXTON STREET
PEDLEY STREET
WHELER ST
CALVIN STREET
FLEUR DE LIS STREET
PRIMROSE ST
LAMB ST
COMMERCIAL STREET
Spitalfields
PRINCELET STREET
FOURNIER STREET
HANBURY ST
Old Spitalfields
Stansted Express Terminal
Broadgate
Liverpool Street Station
BRUSHFIELD STREET
Christchurch CE Sch
FASHION STREET
ARTILLERY LANE
MIDDLESEX STREET
Petticoat Lane
WENTWORTH STREET
East London Coll & Toynbee Theatre
Canon Barnett Sch
Aldgate East
WHITECHAPEL HIGH ST
BISHOPSGATE
CAMOMILE ST
BEVIS MARKS
HOUNDSDITCH
ST BOTOLPH ST
Aldgate
ALDGATE HIGH ST
Swiss Re Building
Tower 42
St Helen
St Andrew Undershaft
LEADENHALL STREET
Lloyds Building
FENCHURCH AVE
FENCHURCH STREET
Fenchurch Street Station
St Peter
Sir John Cass's Sch
London Metropolitan Univ
MINORIES
Whitechapel
MANSELL STREET
LEMAN STREET
English Martyrs RC Prim Sch
PRESCOT ST
GOODMAN'S YD
CHAMBER ST
ALIE ST
WORMWOOD ST
LIVERPOOL STREET
NEW STREET
St Botolph
Tenn Ct
Liby
Sp Ctr
Univ

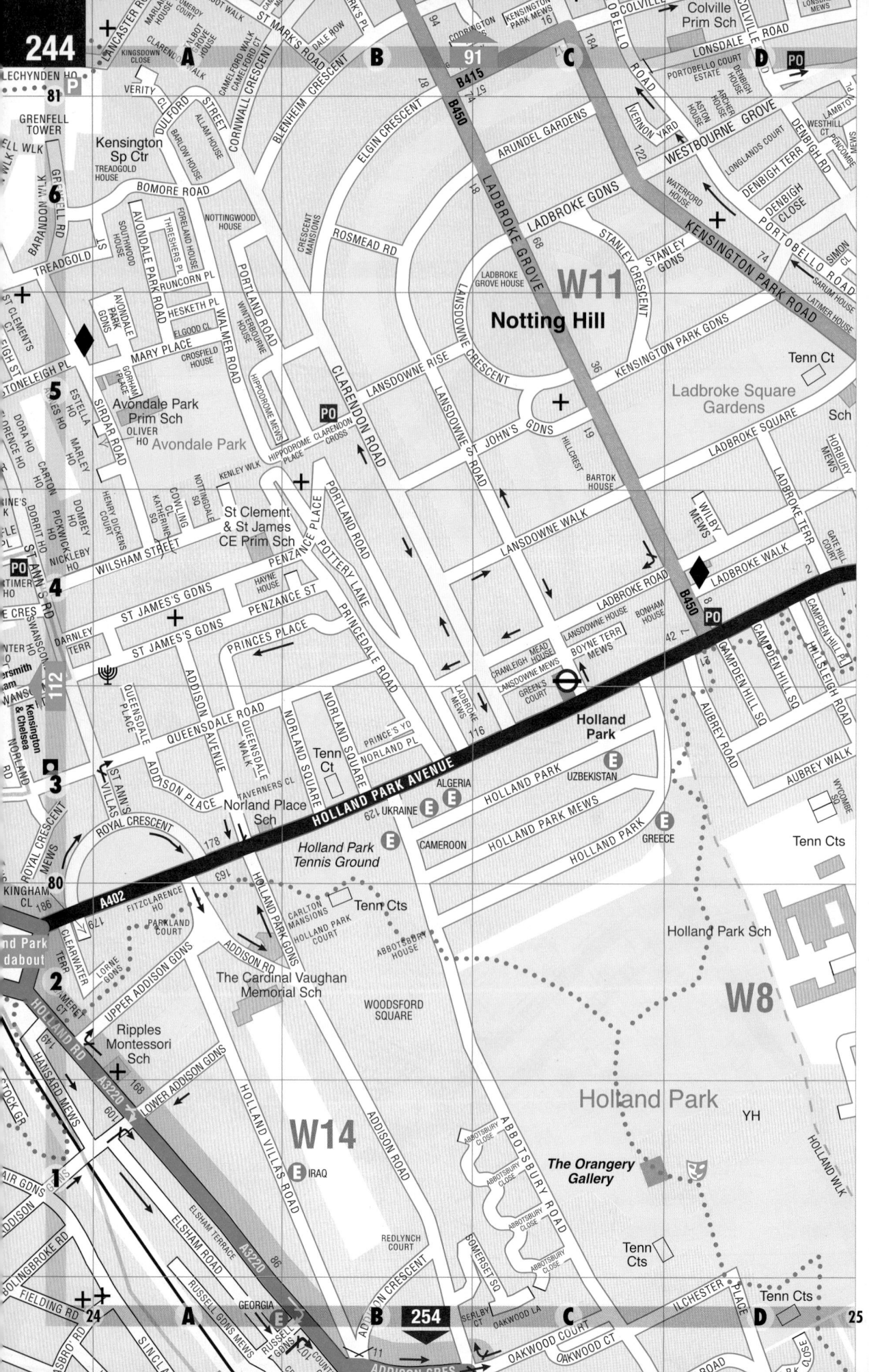

91
254
112
W11
Notting Hill
W14
W8
Holland Park
Ladbroke Square Gardens
Avondale Park
Holland Park Tennis Ground
The Orangery Gallery
Kensington Sp Ctr
Grenfell Tower
Colville Prim Sch
Avondale Park Prim Sch
St Clement & St James CE Prim Sch
Norland Place Sch
The Cardinal Vaughan Memorial Sch
Ripples Montessori Sch
Holland Park Sch
Holland Park Avenue
Ladbroke Grove
Kensington Park Road
Westbourne Grove
Portobello Road
Clarendon Road
Holland Park
Addison Road
Abbotsbury Road
Holland Villas Road
Holland Rd
A402
A3220
B450
B415

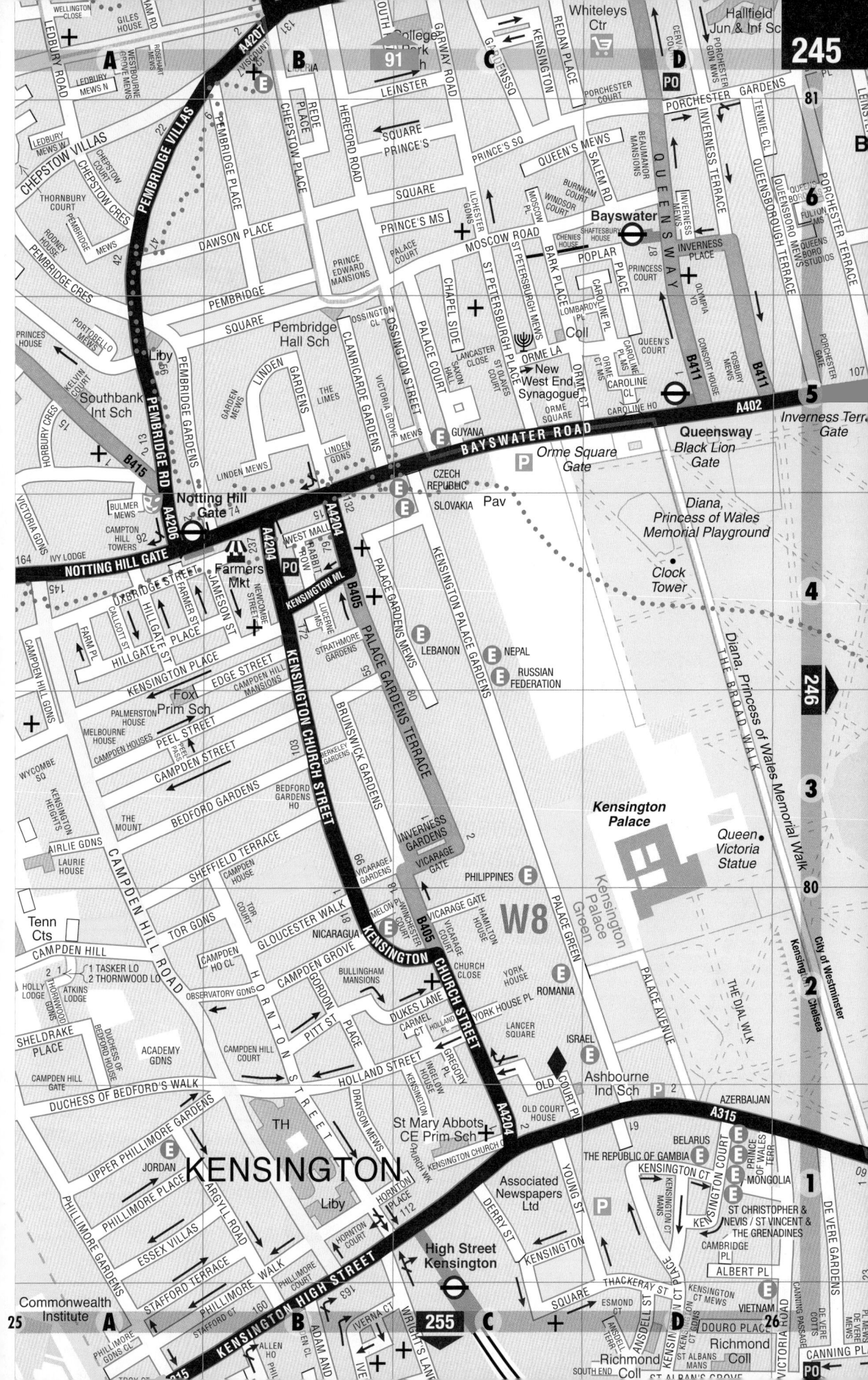
A
B
C
D
91
Whiteleys Ctr
Hallfield Jun & Inf Sch
College Park Sch
WELLINGTON CLOSE
GILES HOUSE
LEDBURY ROAD
WESTBOURNE GROVE MEWS
ROSEHART MEWS
A4207
VISCOUNT CT
LEDBURY MEWS N
LEDBURY MEWS W
CHEPSTOW VILLAS
CHEPSTOW COURT
CHEPSTOW CRES
THORNBURY COURT
RODNEY HOUSE
PEMBRIDGE MEWS
PEMBRIDGE CRES
PEMBRIDGE VILLAS
PEMBRIDGE PLACE
DAWSON PLACE
PEMBRIDGE SQUARE
REDE PLACE
CHEPSTOW PLACE
HEREFORD ROAD
LEINSTER SQUARE
PRINCE'S SQUARE
PRINCE'S MS
PRINCE EDWARD MANSIONS
PALACE COURT
GARWAY ROAD
GARDENS SQ
KENSINGTON GARDENS SQ
REDAN PLACE
PORCHESTER COURT
PORCHESTER GARDENS
PORCHESTER GDN MEWS
INVERNESS TERRACE
TENNIEL CL
QUEENSBOROUGH TERRACE
QUEENSBORO MEWS
QUEENS BORO STUDIOS
FULTON MS
PORCHESTER TERRACE
PRINCE'S SQ
QUEEN'S MEWS
BEAUMANOR MANSIONS
SALEM RD
BURNHAM COURT
WINDSOR COURT
MOSCOW PL
ILCHESTER GDNS
MOSCOW ROAD
Bayswater
SHAFTESBURY HOUSE
CHENIES HOUSE
POPLAR PLACE
BARK PLACE
INVERNESS MEWS
INVERNESS PLACE
QUEENSWAY
PRINCESS COURT
OLYMPIA YD
CAROLINE PL
LOMBARDY PL
Coll
QUEEN'S COURT
CONSORT HOUSE
FOSBURY MEWS
B411
CHAPEL SIDE
ST PETERSBURGH PLACE
ST PETERSBURGH MEWS
PALACE COURT
OSSINGTON STREET
OSSINGTON CL
CLANRICARDE GARDENS
VICTORIA GROVE MEWS
Pembridge Hall Sch
LANCASTER CLOSE
SAXON HALL
ST OLAVES COURT
ORME LA
New West End Synagogue
ORME CT
ORME CT MS
CAROLINE PL MS
CAROLINE CL
CAROLINE HO
ORME SQUARE
PRINCES HOUSE
PORTOBELLO MEWS
KELVIN COURT
Liby
Southbank Int Sch
HORBURY CRES
HORBURY MEWS
PEMBRIDGE RD
PEMBRIDGE GARDENS
GARDEN MEWS
LINDEN GARDENS
THE LIMES
LINDEN MEWS
LINDEN GDNS
GUYANA
BAYSWATER ROAD
A402
Orme Square Gate
Inverness Terr Gate
Queensway Black Lion Gate
107
5
B415
Notting Hill Gate
BULMER MEWS
CAMPTON HILL TOWERS
VICTORIA GDNS
IVY LODGE
NOTTING HILL GATE
A4206
A4204
CZECH REPUBLIC
SLOVAKIA
Pav
Diana, Princess of Wales Memorial Playground
Clock Tower
WEST MALL
RABBIT ROW
PO
Farmers Mkt
KENSINGTON ML
UXBRIDGE STREET
HILLGATE STREET
FARMER ST
JAMESON ST
NEWCOMBE STREET
CALLCOTT ST
FARM PL
HILLGATE PLACE
HILLGATE ST
LUCERNE MS
STRATHMORE GARDENS
B405
PALACE GARDENS MEWS
LEBANON
KENSINGTON PALACE GARDENS
NEPAL
RUSSIAN FEDERATION
4
KENSINGTON PLACE
EDGE STREET
CAMPDEN HILL MANSIONS
CAMPDEN HILL GDNS
Fox Prim Sch
PALMERSTON HOUSE
MELBOURNE HOUSE
CAMPDEN HOUSES
PEEL STREET
PEEL PASS
CAMPDEN STREET
KENSINGTON CHURCH STREET
BERKELEY GARDENS
BRUNSWICK GARDENS
PALACE GARDENS TERRACE
Diana, Princess of Wales Memorial Walk
THE BROAD WALK
246
WYCOMBE SQ
KENSINGTON HEIGHTS
BEDFORD GARDENS
BEDFORD GARDENS HO
THE MOUNT
3
Kensington Palace
INVERNESS GARDENS
VICARAGE GATE
Queen Victoria Statue
AIRLIE GDNS
LAURIE HOUSE
SHEFFIELD TERRACE
CAMPDEN HOUSE
VICARAGE GARDENS
PHILIPPINES
80
Tenn Cts
CAMPDEN HILL ROAD
TOR GDNS
TOR COURT
GLOUCESTER WALK
NICARAGUA
MELON PL
WINCHESTER COURT
VICARAGE COURT
HAMILTON HOUSE
W8
PALACE GREEN
Kensington Palace Green
Kensington & Chelsea
City of Westminster
CAMPDEN HILL
1 TASKER LO
2 THORNWOOD LO
HOLLY LODGE
THORNWOOD GDNS
ATKINS LODGE
CAMPDEN HO CL
CAMPDEN GROVE
HORNTON STREET
BULLINGHAM MANSIONS
GORDON PLACE
CHURCH CLOSE
YORK HOUSE
ROMANIA
PALACE AVENUE
THE DIAL WLK
2
OBSERVATORY GDNS
SHELDRAKE PLACE
DUCHESS OF BEDFORD HOUSE
ACADEMY GDNS
PITT ST
DUKES LANE
CARMEL CT
HOLLAND PL
YORK HOUSE PL
LANCER SQUARE
ISRAEL
CAMPDEN HILL COURT
HOLLAND STREET
INGELOW HOUSE
GREGORY PL
KENSINGTON HOUSE
CAMPDEN HILL GATE
DUCHESS OF BEDFORD'S WALK
OLD COURT PL
OLD COURT HOUSE
Ashbourne Ind Sch
AZERBAIJAN
A315
UPPER PHILLIMORE GARDENS
TH
DRAYSON MEWS
St Mary Abbots CE Prim Sch
KENSINGTON CHURCH CT
CHURCH WK
BELARUS
THE REPUBLIC OF GAMBIA
PRINCE OF WALES TERR
JORDAN
KENSINGTON
Associated Newspapers Ltd
YOUNG ST
KENSINGTON CT
KENSINGTON CT MANS
KENSINGTON COURT
MONGOLIA
1
PHILLIMORE PLACE
ARGYLL ROAD
Liby
HORNTON PLACE
DERRY ST
ST CHRISTOPHER & NEVIS / ST VINCENT & THE GRENADINES
CAMBRIDGE PL
DE VERE GARDENS
PHILLIMORE GARDENS
ESSEX VILLAS
HORNTON COURT
High Street Kensington
KENSINGTON SQUARE
ALBERT PL
STAFFORD TERRACE
PHILLIMORE WALK
PHILLIMORE COURT
THACKERAY ST
KENSINGTON CT PLACE
KENSINGTON CT MEWS
VIETNAM
CANNING PASSAGE
VICTORIA ROAD
Commonwealth Institute
KENSINGTON HIGH STREET
STAFFORD CT
ESMOND CT
ANSDELL ST
ANSDELL TERR
KENSINGTON CT GDNS
DOURO PLACE
DE VERE COTTS
DE VERE MEWS
PHILLIMORE GDNS CL
ALLEN HO
IVERNA CT
ADAM AND EVE
WRIGHT'S LANE
255
Richmond Coll
ST ALBANS MANS
SOUTH END
CANNING PL
25
26

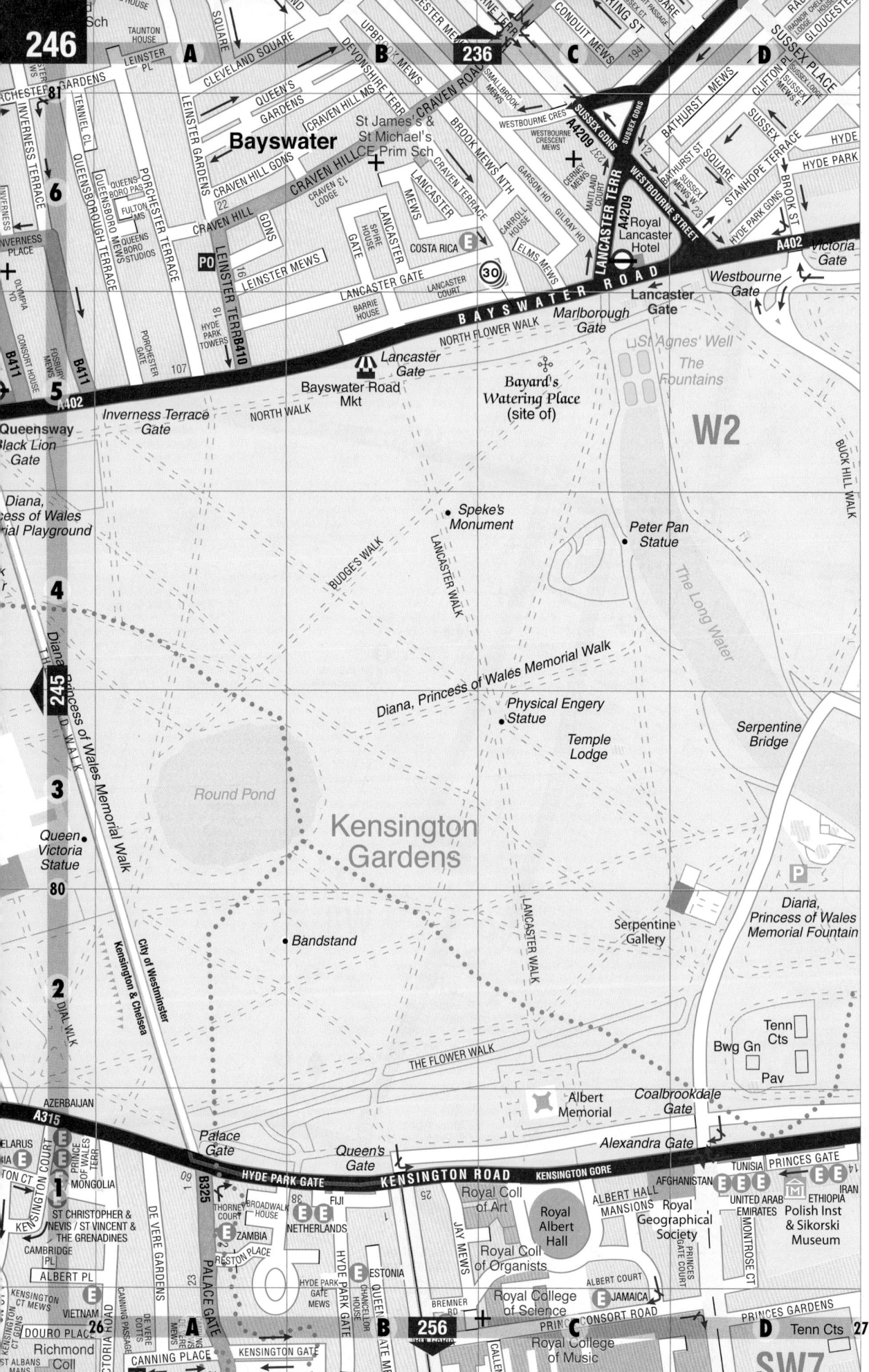

Bayswater
Kensington Gardens
W2
SW7
BAYSWATER ROAD
KENSINGTON ROAD
HYDE PARK GATE
KENSINGTON GORE
Round Pond
The Long Water
Serpentine Bridge
Serpentine Gallery
Diana, Princess of Wales Memorial Fountain
Diana, Princess of Wales Memorial Walk
Peter Pan Statue
Speke's Monument
Physical Engery Statue
Temple Lodge
Bandstand
Albert Memorial
Royal Albert Hall
Royal Coll of Art
Royal Coll of Organists
Royal College of Science
Royal College of Music
Royal Geographical Society
Polish Inst & Sikorski Museum
Queen Victoria Statue
Bayard's Watering Place (site of)
St Agnes' Well
The Fountains
Lancaster Gate
Marlborough Gate
Westbourne Gate
Victoria Gate
Palace Gate
Queen's Gate
Alexandra Gate
Coalbrookdale Gate
Inverness Terrace Gate
Royal Lancaster Hotel
Bayswater Road Mkt
St James's & St Michael's CE Prim Sch
THE FLOWER WALK
NORTH FLOWER WALK
NORTH WALK
BUDGE'S WALK
LANCASTER WALK
BUCK HILL WALK
DIAL WALK
Kensington & Chelsea
City of Westminster
CRAVEN HILL
CRAVEN ROAD
LANCASTER TERR
WESTBOURNE STREET
LEINSTER TERR
PORCHESTER TERRACE
QUEENSBOROUGH TERRACE
INVERNESS TERRACE
CLEVELAND SQUARE
LANCASTER GATE
PRINCE CONSORT ROAD
PALACE GATE
DE VERE GARDENS
HYDE PARK GATE
PRINCES GARDENS
236
245
256

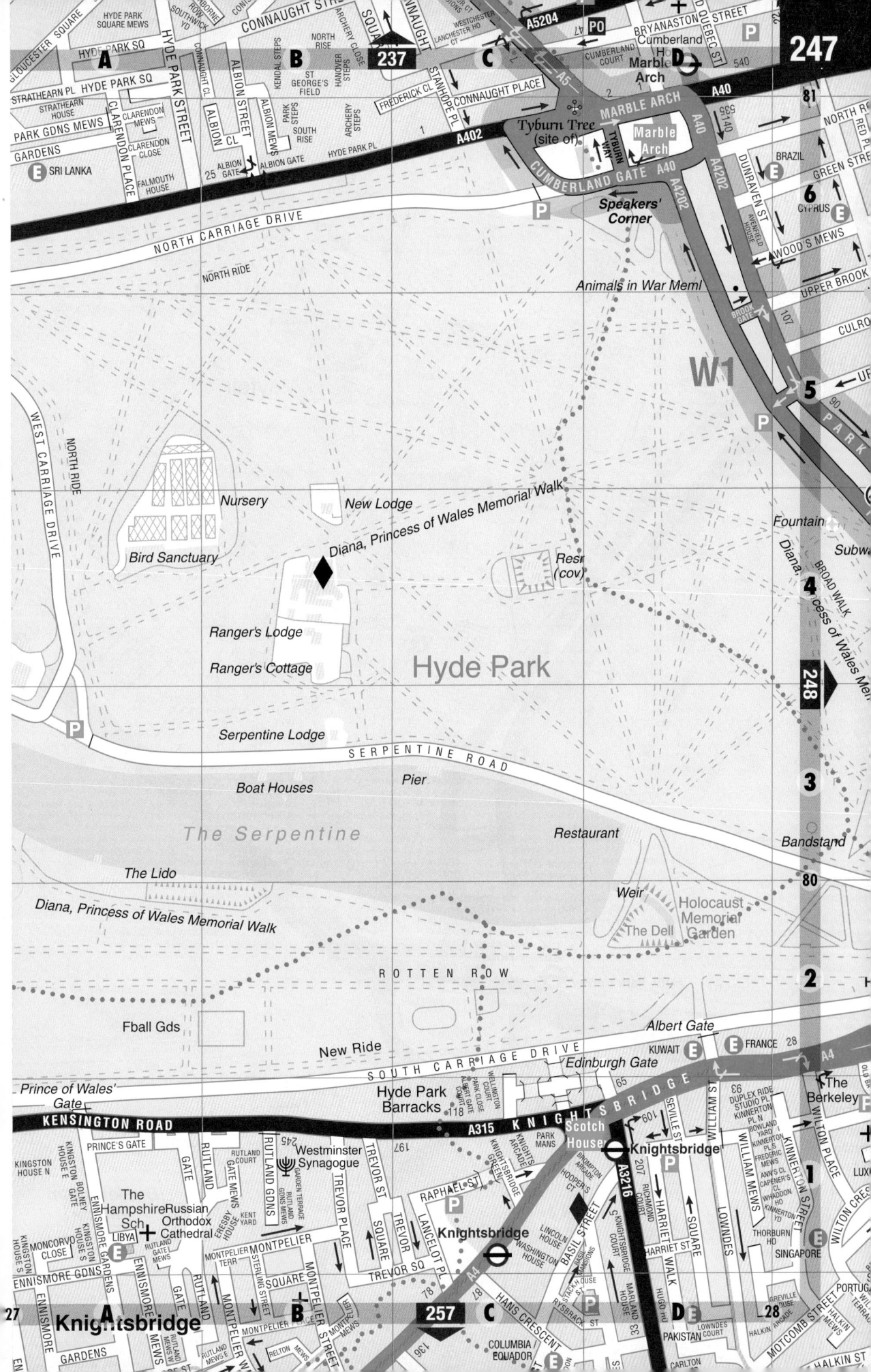

Hyde Park
W1
The Serpentine
Marble Arch
Tyburn Tree (site of)
Speakers' Corner
Animals in War Meml
Nursery
New Lodge
Bird Sanctuary
Diana, Princess of Wales Memorial Walk
Ranger's Lodge
Ranger's Cottage
Serpentine Lodge
SERPENTINE ROAD
Boat Houses
Pier
Restaurant
The Lido
Weir
Holocaust Memorial Garden
The Dell
ROTTEN ROW
Fball Gds
New Ride
SOUTH CARRIAGE DRIVE
NORTH CARRIAGE DRIVE
WEST CARRIAGE DRIVE
NORTH RIDE
Albert Gate
Edinburgh Gate
Prince of Wales' Gate
Hyde Park Barracks
KENSINGTON ROAD
KNIGHTSBRIDGE
Knightsbridge
Scotch House
Westminster Synagogue
The Hampshire Sch
Russian Orthodox Cathedral
Fountain
Bandstand
BROAD WALK
CUMBERLAND GATE
CONNAUGHT PLACE
HYDE PARK SQ
HYDE PARK STREET
ALBION STREET
CONNAUGHT ST
BRYANASTON ST
Cumberland Hotel
PARK LANE
WILTON PLACE
The Berkeley
TREVOR PLACE
MONTPELIER STREET
ENNISMORE GARDENS
HANS CRESCENT
BASIL STREET
SLOANE STREET
LOWNDES SQUARE
WILLIAM ST
KINNERTON STREET
248
237
257
Knightsbridge

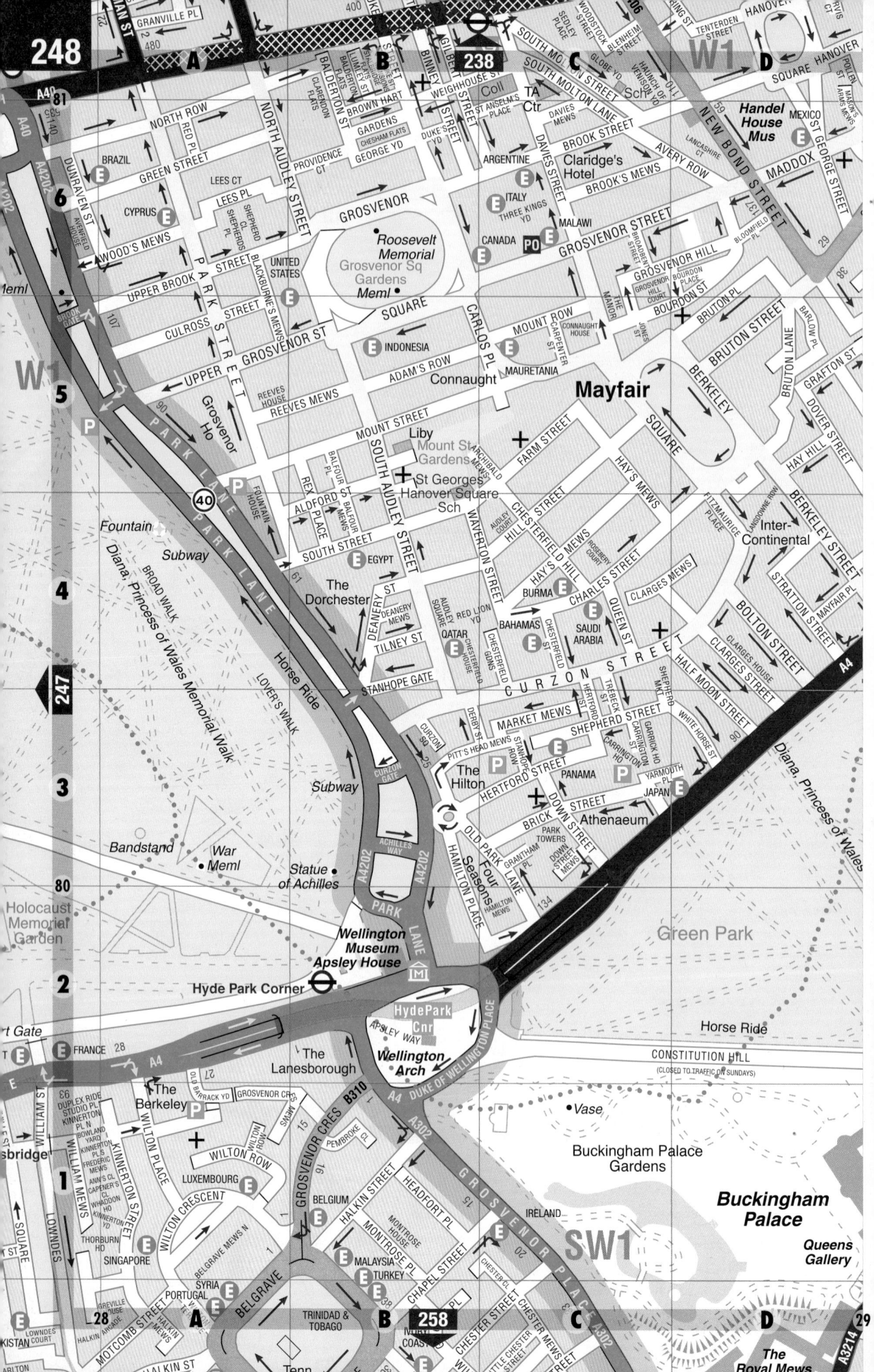
A
B
C
D
238
W1
GRANVILLE PL
NORTH ROW
RED PL
BRAZIL
GREEN STREET
DUNRAVEN ST
CYPRUS
LEES CT
LEES PL
SHEPHERD CL
WOOD'S MEWS
UPPER BROOK STREET
CULROSS STREET
PARK STREET
BLACKBURNE'S MEWS
UNITED STATES
NORTH AUDLEY STREET
BALDERTON ST
CLARENDON FLATS
BROWN HART GARDENS
CHESHAM FLATS
GEORGE YD
PROVIDENCE CT
GROSVENOR
Roosevelt Memorial
Grosvenor Sq Gardens
Meml
SQUARE
UPPER GROSVENOR ST
INDONESIA
ADAM'S ROW
Connaught
MAURETANIA
REEVES MEWS
REEVES HOUSE
Grosvenor Ho
MOUNT STREET
Liby
Mount St Gardens
St Georges Hanover Square Sch
SOUTH AUDLEY STREET
BALFOUR PL
REX PLACE
ALDFORD ST
SOUTH STREET
EGYPT
The Dorchester
DEANERY ST
DEANERY MEWS
TILNEY ST
STANHOPE GATE
AUDLEY SQUARE
QATAR
RED LION YD
CHESTERFIELD GDNS
WAVERTON STREET
CARLOS PL
MOUNT ROW
CARPENTER ST
CONNAUGHT HOUSE
BINNEY ST
GILBERT STREET
WEIGHHOUSE ST
DUKE'S YD
Coll
TA Ctr
ST ANSELM'S PLACE
ARGENTINE
ITALY
THREE KINGS YD
CANADA
PO
MALAWI
DAVIES STREET
DAVIES MEWS
SOUTH MOLTON STREET
SOUTH MOLTON LANE
BROOK STREET
Claridge's Hotel
BROOK'S MEWS
AVERY ROW
GROSVENOR STREET
BROADBENT STREET
GROSVENOR HILL
BOURDON ST
BOURDON PLACE
JONES ST
THE MANOR
Mayfair
BERKELEY SQUARE
BRUTON PL
BRUTON STREET
BRUTON LANE
BARLOW PL
GRAFTON ST
DOVER STREET
HAY HILL
FARM STREET
ARCHIBALD MEWS
HAY'S MEWS
HILL STREET
CHESTERFIELD HILL
ROSEBERY COURT
BURMA
CHARLES STREET
QUEEN ST
CLARGES MEWS
BAHAMAS
SAUDI ARABIA
CHESTERFIELD ST
CURZON STREET
FITZMAURICE PLACE
LANSDOWNE ROW
Inter-Continental
BERKELEY STREET
STRATTON STREET
MAYFAIR PL
BOLTON STREET
CLARGES STREET
HALF MOON STREET
WHITE HORSE ST
SHEPHERD MKT
TREBECK ST
HERTFORD ST
MARKET MEWS
SHEPHERD STREET
CARRINGTON ST
GARRICK HO
DERBY ST
CURZON SQ
PITT'S HEAD MEWS
STANHOPE ROW
The Hilton
HERTFORD STREET
PANAMA
YARMOUTH PL
JAPAN
BRICK STREET
DOWN STREET
Athenaeum
PARK TOWERS
GRANTHAM PL
OLD PARK LANE
HAMILTON PLACE
Four Seasons
HAMILTON MEWS
DOWN STREET MEWS
NEW BOND STREET
Handel House Mus
MEXICO
ST GEORGE STREET
MADDOX
HANOVER SQUARE
TENTERDEN STREET
WOODSTOCK STREET
BLENHEIM STREET
SEDLEY PLACE
GLOBE YD
HAUNCH OF VENISON YD
Sch
LANCASHIRE CT
BLOOMFIELD PL
PARK LANE
FOUNTAIN HOUSE
Fountain
Subway
Diana, Princess of Wales Memorial Walk
BROAD WALK
LOVER'S WALK
Horse Ride
CURZON GATE
ACHILLES WAY
Bandstand
War Meml
Statue of Achilles
Holocaust Memorial Garden
Wellington Museum
Apsley House
Hyde Park Corner
HydePark Cnr
APSLEY WAY
Wellington Arch
DUKE OF WELLINGTON PLACE
Green Park
Horse Ride
CONSTITUTION HILL
(CLOSED TO TRAFFIC ON SUNDAYS)
Vase
Buckingham Palace Gardens
Buckingham Palace
Queens Gallery
The Royal Mews
FRANCE
The Lanesborough
The Berkeley
OLD BARRACK YD
GROSVENOR CRES MEWS
WILLIAM ST
DUPLEX RIDE
STUDIO PL
KINNERTON PL N
BOWLAND YARD
KINNERTON PL S
FREDERIC MEWS
ANN'S CL
CAPENER'S CL
WHADDON HO
KINNERTON YD
WILLIAM MEWS
KINNERTON STREET
WILTON PLACE
WILTON ROW
LUXEMBOURG
WILTON CRESCENT
THORBURN HO
SINGAPORE
BELGRAVE MEWS N
SYRIA
PORTUGAL
GROSVENOR CRES
PEMBROKE CL
BELGIUM
HALKIN STREET
HEADFORT PL
MONTROSE HOUSE
MONTROSE PL
MALAYSIA
TURKEY
CHAPEL STREET
IRELAND
GROSVENOR PLACE
SW1
CHESTER CL
CHESTER STREET
CHESTER MEWS
LITTLE CHESTER STREET
BELGRAVE
TRINIDAD & TOBAGO
IVORY COAST
LOWNDES SQUARE
LOWNDES COURT
PAKISTAN
GREVILLE HOUSE
HALKIN ARCADE
MOTCOMB STREET
HALKIN MEWS
HALKIN ST
Tenn
247
258
A40
A4202
A4
A302
A3214
B310
1
2
3
4
5
6
28
29
80
81

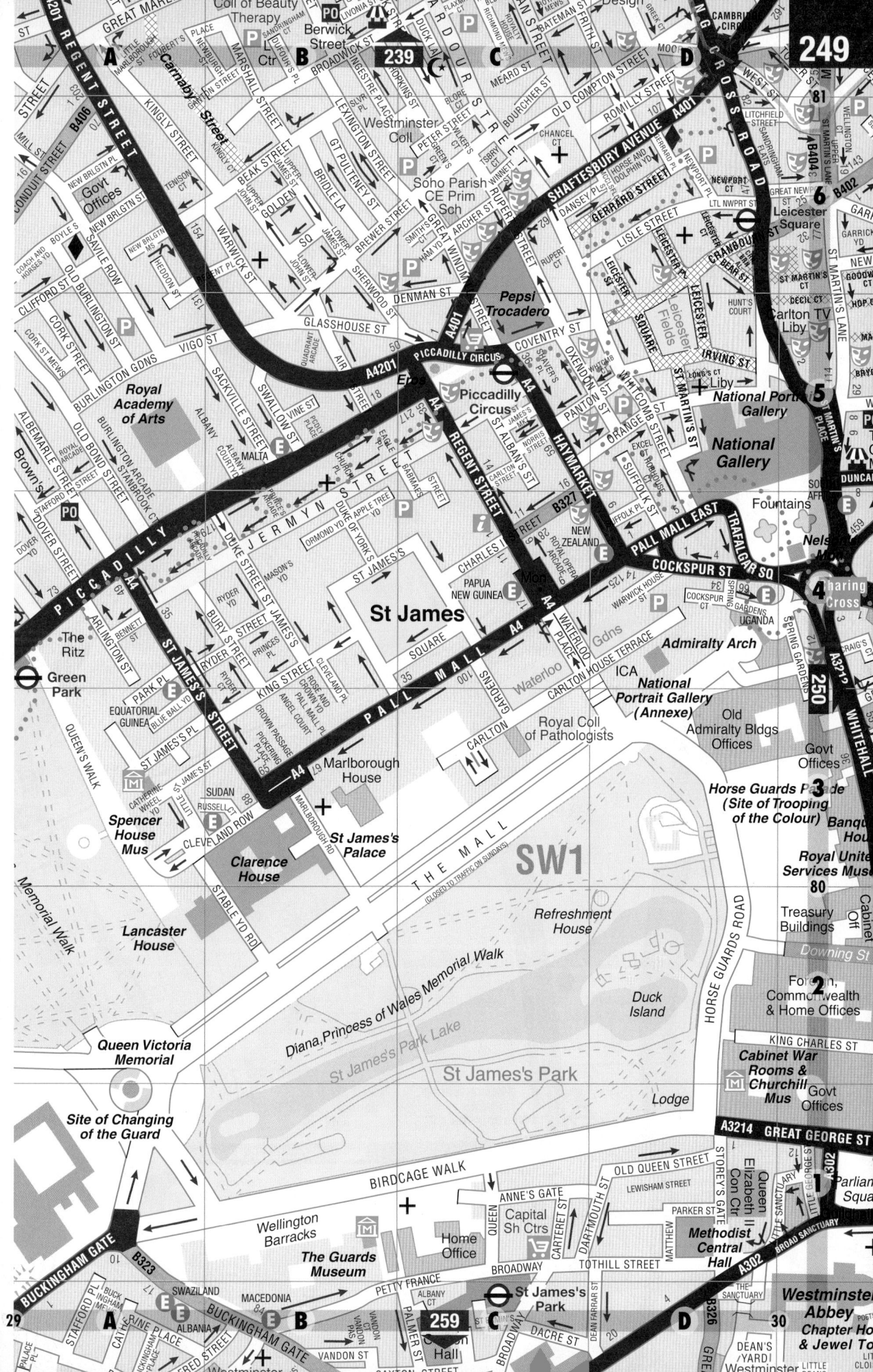
A
B
C
D
239
259
250
29
30
6
5
4
3
2
1
81
80
SW1
REGENT STREET
A4201
GREAT MARLBOROUGH ST
Coll of Beauty Therapy
Berwick Street
BROADWICK ST
WARDOUR STREET
BATEMAN ST
FRITH ST
Design
CAMBRIDGE CIRCUS
CHARING CROSS ROAD
OLD COMPTON STREET
ROMILLY STREET
MEARD ST
Carnaby Street
KINGLY STREET
MARSHALL STREET
LEXINGTON STREET
INGESTRE PLACE
HOPKINS ST
Westminster Coll
PETER STREET
BOURCHIER ST
CHANCEL CT
SHAFTESBURY AVENUE
A401
WEST ST
LITCHFIELD STREET
ST MARTIN'S LANE
B404
B402
CONDUIT STREET
B406
MILL ST
Govt Offices
NEW BRLGTN PL
BEAK STREET
GOLDEN SQ
BRIDLE LA
GT PULTENEY ST
Soho Parish CE Prim Sch
GERRARD STREET
DANSEY PL
NEWPORT PL
NEWPORT CT
Leicester Square
GARRICK YD
LISLE STREET
CRANBOURN ST
BREWER STREET
WARWICK ST
SAVILE ROW
CLIFFORD ST
OLD BURLINGTON ST
CORK STREET
BURLINGTON GDNS
VIGO ST
REGENT PL
HEDDON ST
DENMAN ST
GLASSHOUSE ST
SHERWOOD ST
Pepsi Trocadero
RUPERT ST
LEICESTER ST
LEICESTER PL
LEICESTER SQUARE
Leicester Fields
HUNT'S COURT
Carlton TV Liby
CECIL CT
ST MARTIN'S CT
IRVING ST
PICCADILLY CIRCUS
Eros
COVENTRY ST
Piccadilly Circus
OXENDON ST
WHITCOMB ST
PANTON ST
ORANGE ST
Liby
National Portrait Gallery
National Gallery
ST MARTIN'S PLACE
DUNCANNON
Royal Academy of Arts
ALBANY
SACKVILLE STREET
SWALLOW ST
VINE ST
AIR STREET
MALTA
BURLINGTON ARCADE
STANBROOK CT
ALBEMARLE STREET
OLD BOND STREET
Brown's
STAFFORD ST
DOVER STREET
JERMYN STREET
CHURCH PL
EAGLE PL
BARMAES
ST ALBAN'S ST
CARLTON STREET
HAYMARKET
B327
SUFFOLK ST
EXCEL CT
NEW ZEALAND
PALL MALL EAST
TRAFALGAR SQ
Fountains
Nelson's Mon
COCKSPUR ST
Charing Cross
PICCADILLY
A4
DUKE STREET ST JAMES'S
ORMOND YD
APPLE TREE YD
DUKE OF YORK'S ST
ST JAMES'S
CHARLES II STREET
ROYAL OPERA ARCADE
PAPUA NEW GUINEA
Mon
WARWICK HOUSE ST
COCKSPUR CT
SPRING GARDENS
UGANDA
St James
MASON'S YD
RYDER YD
BURY STREET
ST JAMES'S STREET
ARLINGTON ST
BENNETT ST
The Ritz
Green Park
RYDER STREET
PRINCES PL
KING STREET
CLEVELAND PL
ST JAMES'S SQUARE
WATERLOO PLACE
Waterloo Gdns
CARLTON HOUSE TERRACE
Admiralty Arch
ICA
National Portrait Gallery (Annexe)
Old Admiralty Bldgs Offices
PARK PL
BLUE BALL YD
EQUATORIAL GUINEA
ST JAMES'S PL
ROSE AND CROWN YD
ANGEL COURT
CROWN PASSAGE
PICKERING PLACE
PALL MALL
CARLTON GARDENS
Royal Coll of Pathologists
QUEEN'S WALK
Marlborough House
CATHERINE WHEEL YD
SUDAN
RUSSELL CT
Spencer House Mus
CLEVELAND ROW
Clarence House
MARLBOROUGH RD
St James's Palace
STABLE YD RD
THE MALL
(CLOSED TO TRAFFIC ON SUNDAYS)
Horse Guards Parade (Site of Trooping of the Colour)
Govt Offices
WHITEHALL
Royal United Services Mus
Treasury Buildings
Cabinet Off
Downing St
Foreign, Commonwealth & Home Offices
KING CHARLES ST
Memorial Walk
Lancaster House
Refreshment House
HORSE GUARDS ROAD
Diana, Princess of Wales Memorial Walk
Duck Island
St James's Park Lake
St James's Park
Queen Victoria Memorial
Cabinet War Rooms & Churchill Mus
Govt Offices
Lodge
Site of Changing of the Guard
A3214
GREAT GEORGE ST
BIRDCAGE WALK
OLD QUEEN STREET
LEWISHAM STREET
STOREY'S GATE
Queen Elizabeth II Con Ctr
ANNE'S GATE
QUEEN ANNE'S GATE
Capital Sh Ctrs
CARTERET ST
DARTMOUTH ST
PARKER ST
MATTHEW PARKER ST
Methodist Central Hall
BROAD SANCTUARY
A302
Wellington Barracks
Home Office
The Guards Museum
BROADWAY
TOTHILL STREET
BUCKINGHAM GATE
B323
SWAZILAND
MACEDONIA
PETTY FRANCE
ALBANY CT
St James's Park
DEAN FARRAR ST
THE SANCTUARY
Westminster Abbey
Chapter House & Jewel Tower
ALBANIA
CATHERINE PLACE
STAFFORD PL
PALMER ST
DACRE ST
VANDON ST
CAXTON STREET
Caxton Hall
DEAN'S YARD
Westminster
LITTLE DEANS YD

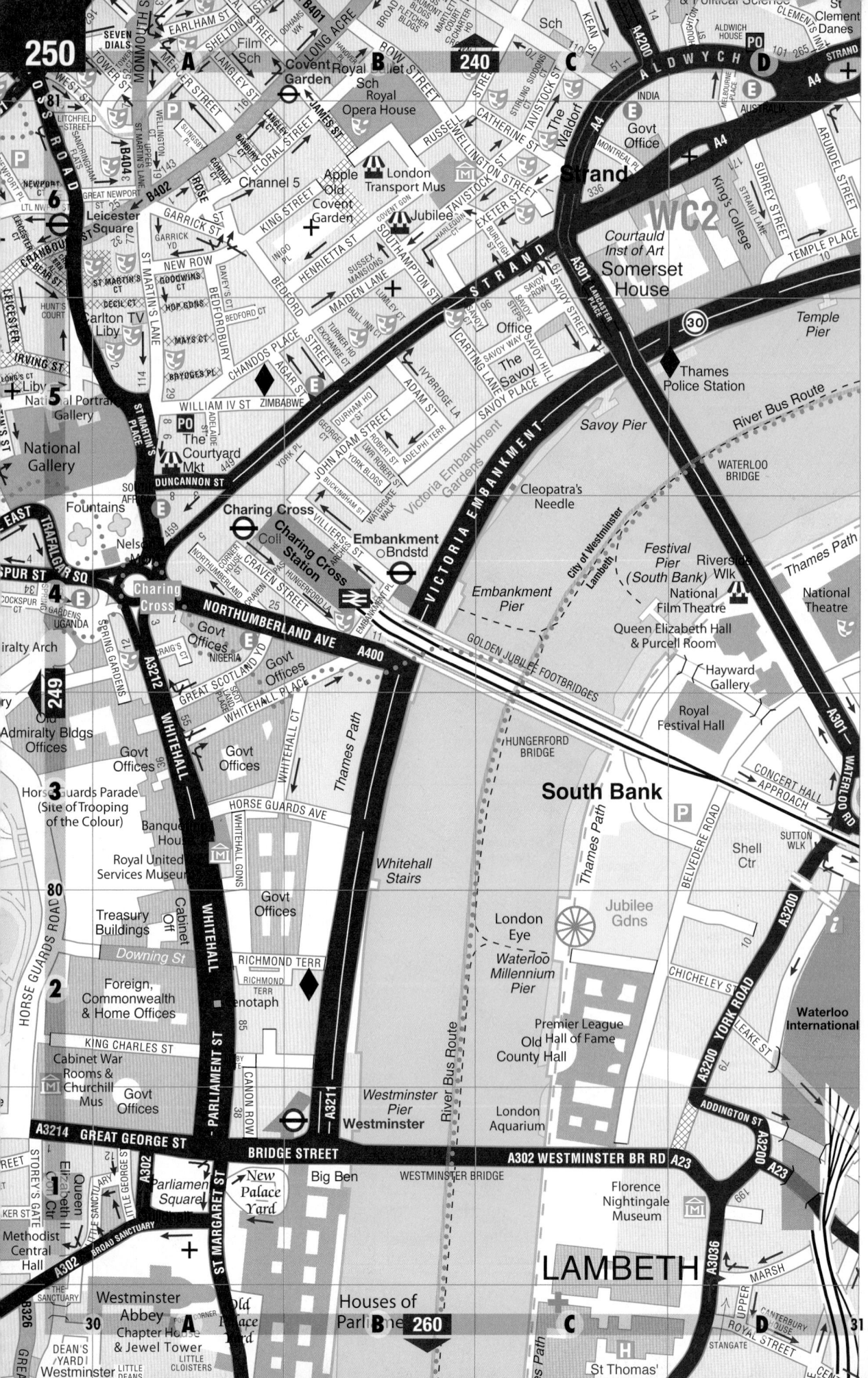

SEVEN DIALS
EARLHAM ST
SHELTON ST
Film Sch
MONMOUTH ST
LONG ACRE
B401
Covent Garden
Royal Ballet Sch
Royal Opera House
BOW STREET
240
Sch
KEAN ST
A4200
ALDWYCH
ALDWYCH HOUSE
PO
St Clement Danes
STRAND
A4
INDIA
AUSTRALIA
Govt Office
TAVISTOCK ST
The Waldorf
CATHERINE ST
WELLINGTON STREET
RUSSELL ST
London Transport Mus
Apple
Old Covent Garden
Channel 5
FLORAL STREET
JAMES ST
KING STREET
HENRIETTA ST
MAIDEN LANE
SOUTHAMPTON ST
Jubilee
EXETER ST
Strand
336
WC2
Kings College
SURREY STREET
ARUNDEL STREET
TEMPLE PLACE
Courtauld Inst of Art
Somerset House
Temple Pier
Thames Police Station
River Bus Route
WATERLOO BRIDGE
LANCASTER PLACE
A301
SAVOY STREET
Office
The Savoy
SAVOY PLACE
SAVOY HILL
Savoy Pier
Cleopatra's Needle
VICTORIA EMBANKMENT
Victoria Embankment Gardens
IVYBRIDGE LA
ADAM ST
JOHN ADAM STREET
YORK PL
VILLIERS ST
Embankment
Bndstd
Charing Cross
Charing Cross Station
CRAVEN STREET
NORTHUMBERLAND AVE
A400
GARRICK ST
NEW ROW
ST MARTIN'S LANE
BEDFORDBURY
CHANDOS PLACE
AGAR ST
BEDFORD ST
WILLIAM IV ST
ZIMBABWE
The Courtyard Mkt
DUNCANNON ST
Leicester Square
CHARING CROSS ROAD
CRANBOURN ST
IRVING ST
Carlton TV Liby
National Portrait Gallery
National Gallery
Fountains
TRAFALGAR SQ
SPUR ST
UGANDA
Admiralty Arch
249
Old Admiralty Bldgs Offices
Govt Offices
NIGERIA
GREAT SCOTLAND YD
WHITEHALL PLACE
WHITEHALL CT
A3212
WHITEHALL
Thames Path
Horse Guards Parade (Site of Trooping of the Colour)
Banqueting Hou
HORSE GUARDS AVE
Royal United Services Museum
Treasury Buildings
Cabinet Off
Downing St
RICHMOND TERR
Foreign, Commonwealth & Home Offices
Cenotaph
KING CHARLES ST
Cabinet War Rooms & Churchill Mus
PARLIAMENT ST
CANON ROW
HORSE GUARDS ROAD
80
Whitehall Stairs
A3211
Westminster Pier
Westminster
City of Westminster
Lambeth
Festival Pier (South Bank)
Riverside Wlk
Thames Path
National Film Theatre
National Theatre
Embankment Pier
Queen Elizabeth Hall & Purcell Room
GOLDEN JUBILEE FOOTBRIDGES
Hayward Gallery
Royal Festival Hall
HUNGERFORD BRIDGE
CONCERT HALL APPROACH
WATERLOO RD
South Bank
BELVEDERE ROAD
Shell Ctr
SUTTON WLK
A3200
Jubilee Gdns
London Eye
Waterloo Millennium Pier
CHICHELEY ST
YORK ROAD
Waterloo International
Premier League Hall of Fame
Old County Hall
LEAKE ST
London Aquarium
ADDINGTON ST
River Bus Route
A3214
GREAT GEORGE ST
BRIDGE STREET
A302 WESTMINSTER BR RD
A23
WESTMINSTER BRIDGE
Big Ben
New Palace Yard
Parliament Square
A302
ST MARGARET ST
Queen Elizabeth II Conf Ctr
Methodist Central Hall
BROAD SANCTUARY
Florence Nightingale Museum
LAMBETH
A3036
MARSH
Westminster Abbey
Chapter House & Jewel Tower
Old Palace Yard
Houses of Parliament
260
DEAN'S YARD
Westminster
LITTLE CLOISTERS
UPPER
ROYAL STREET
STANGATE
St Thomas'
B326
30
31
A
B
C
D
1
2
3
4
5
6

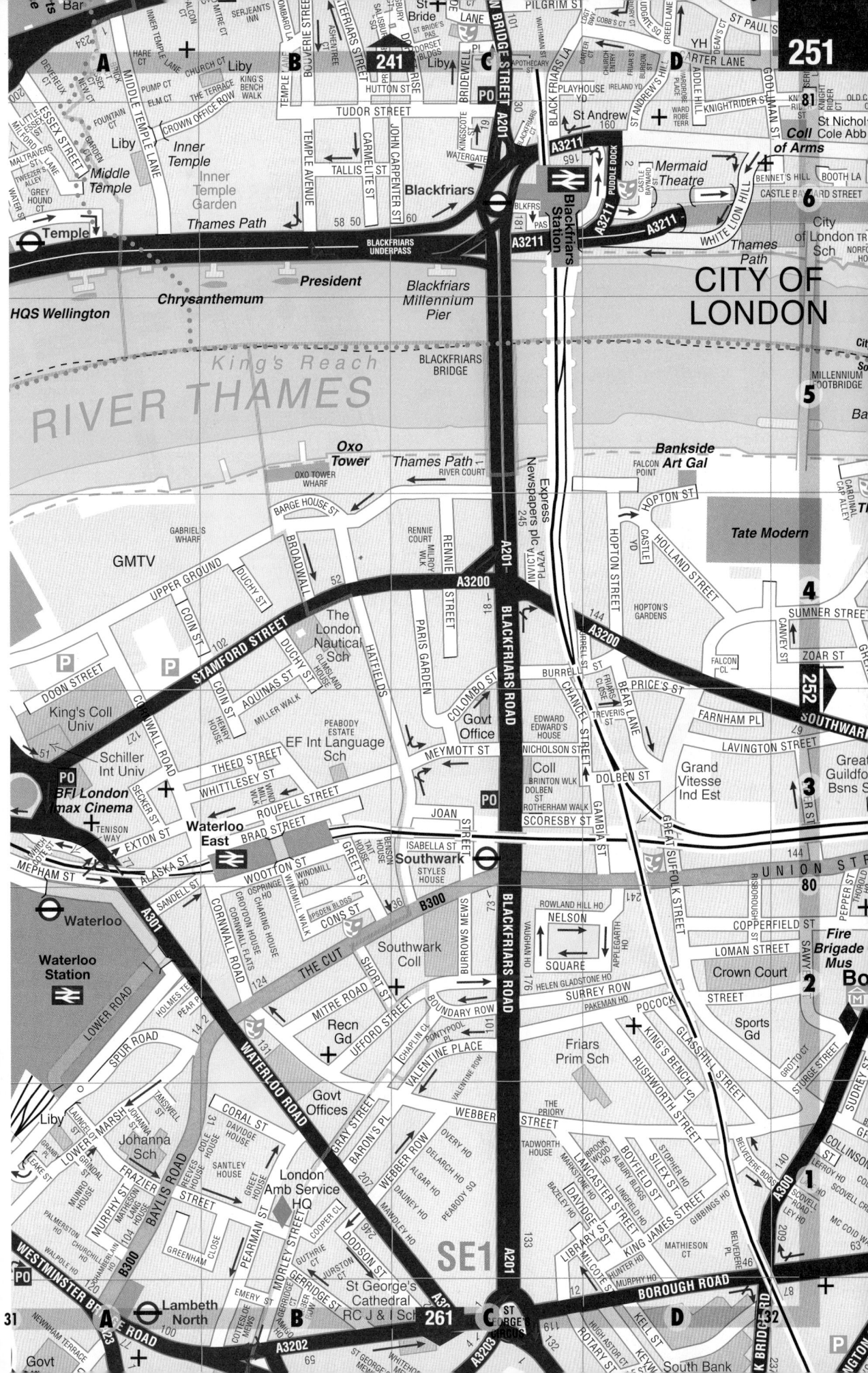

A
B
C
D
241
Liby
Inner Temple
Middle Temple
Inner Temple Garden
Temple
Thames Path
Blackfriars
Blackfriars Station
Mermaid Theatre
St Andrew
St Bride
Coll of Arms
St Nichol Cole Abb
City of London Sch
BLACKFRIARS UNDERPASS
HQS Wellington
Chrysanthemum
President
Blackfriars Millennium Pier
CITY OF LONDON
King's Reach
RIVER THAMES
BLACKFRIARS BRIDGE
MILLENNIUM FOOTBRIDGE
Oxo Tower
OXO TOWER WHARF
RIVER COURT
Bankside Art Gal
FALCON POINT
Express Newspapers plc
Tate Modern
GABRIEL'S WHARF
GMTV
BARGE HOUSE ST
UPPER GROUND
BROADWALL
HOPTON ST
HOLLAND STREET
HOPTON'S GARDENS
STAMFORD STREET
The London Nautical Sch
HATFIELDS
PARIS GARDEN
BLACKFRIARS ROAD
SUMNER STREET
ZOAR ST
DOON STREET
King's Coll Univ
Schiller Int Univ
BFI London Imax Cinema
EF Int Language Sch
Govt Office
Coll
252
SOUTHWARK
LAVINGTON STREET
FARNHAM PL
Grand Vitesse Ind Est
Great Guildford Bsns Sq
Waterloo East
Southwark
UNION ST
GREAT SUFFOLK STREET
Waterloo
Waterloo Station
THE CUT
Southwark Coll
NELSON SQUARE
SURREY ROW
COPPERFIELD ST
LOMAN STREET
Crown Court
Fire Brigade Mus
Sports Gd
Recn Gd
Friars Prim Sch
WATERLOO ROAD
Govt Offices
WEBBER STREET
London Amb Service HQ
Johanna Sch
BAYLIS ROAD
LOWER MARSH
SE1
St George's Cathedral RC J & I Sch
Lambeth North
WESTMINSTER BRIDGE ROAD
BOROUGH ROAD
KING JAMES STREET
LANCASTER STREET
ST GEORGE'S CIRCUS
261
South Bank
A201
A3200
A3211
A301
A300
B300
A3202
A3203

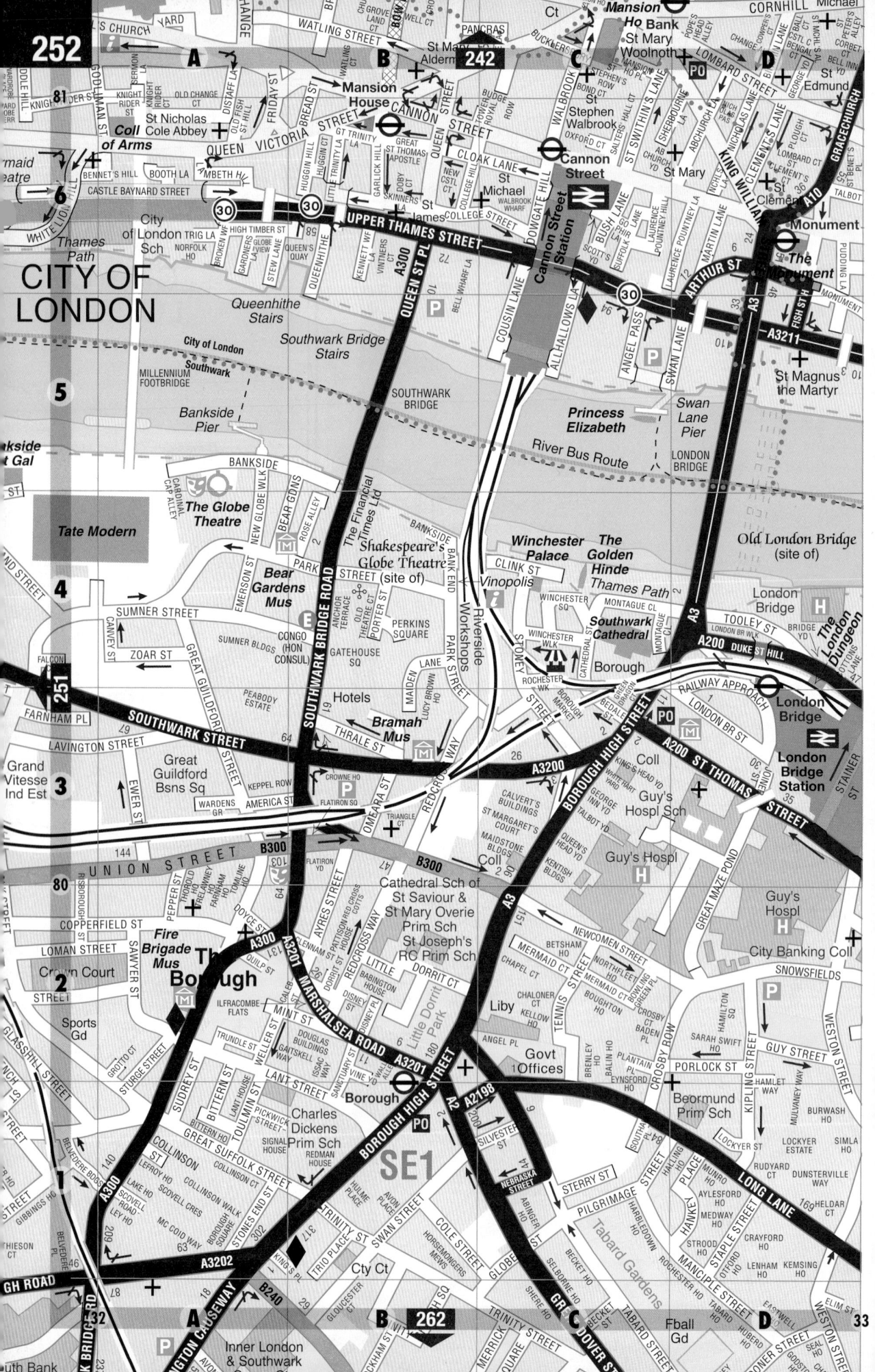
CITY OF LONDON
Mansion House
Cannon Street Station
Monument
Queenhithe Stairs
Southwark Bridge Stairs
SOUTHWARK BRIDGE
MILLENNIUM FOOTBRIDGE
Bankside Pier
Princess Elizabeth
River Bus Route
Swan Lane Pier
LONDON BRIDGE
Tate Modern
The Globe Theatre
Bear Gardens Mus
Shakespeare's Globe Theatre (site of)
The Financial Times Ltd
Winchester Palace
The Golden Hinde
Old London Bridge (site of)
Vinopolis
Southwark Cathedral
Borough
London Bridge Station
The London Dungeon
Guy's Hospl
Guy's Hospl Sch
City Banking Coll
Bramah Mus
Fire Brigade Mus
The Borough
Crown Court
Sports Gd
Cathedral Sch of St Saviour & St Mary Overie Prim Sch
St Joseph's RC Prim Sch
Little Dorrit Park
Govt Offices
Charles Dickens Prim Sch
Beormund Prim Sch
Tabard Gardens
SE1
UPPER THAMES STREET
QUEEN VICTORIA STREET
CANNON STREET
SOUTHWARK BRIDGE ROAD
SOUTHWARK STREET
UNION STREET
BOROUGH HIGH STREET
MARSHALSEA ROAD
GREAT SUFFOLK STREET
LONG LANE
TOOLEY ST
ST THOMAS STREET
KING WILLIAM ST
GRACECHURCH
LOMBARD STREET
CORNHILL
A3
A300
A3200
A3211
A200
A2
B300
242
251
262
33

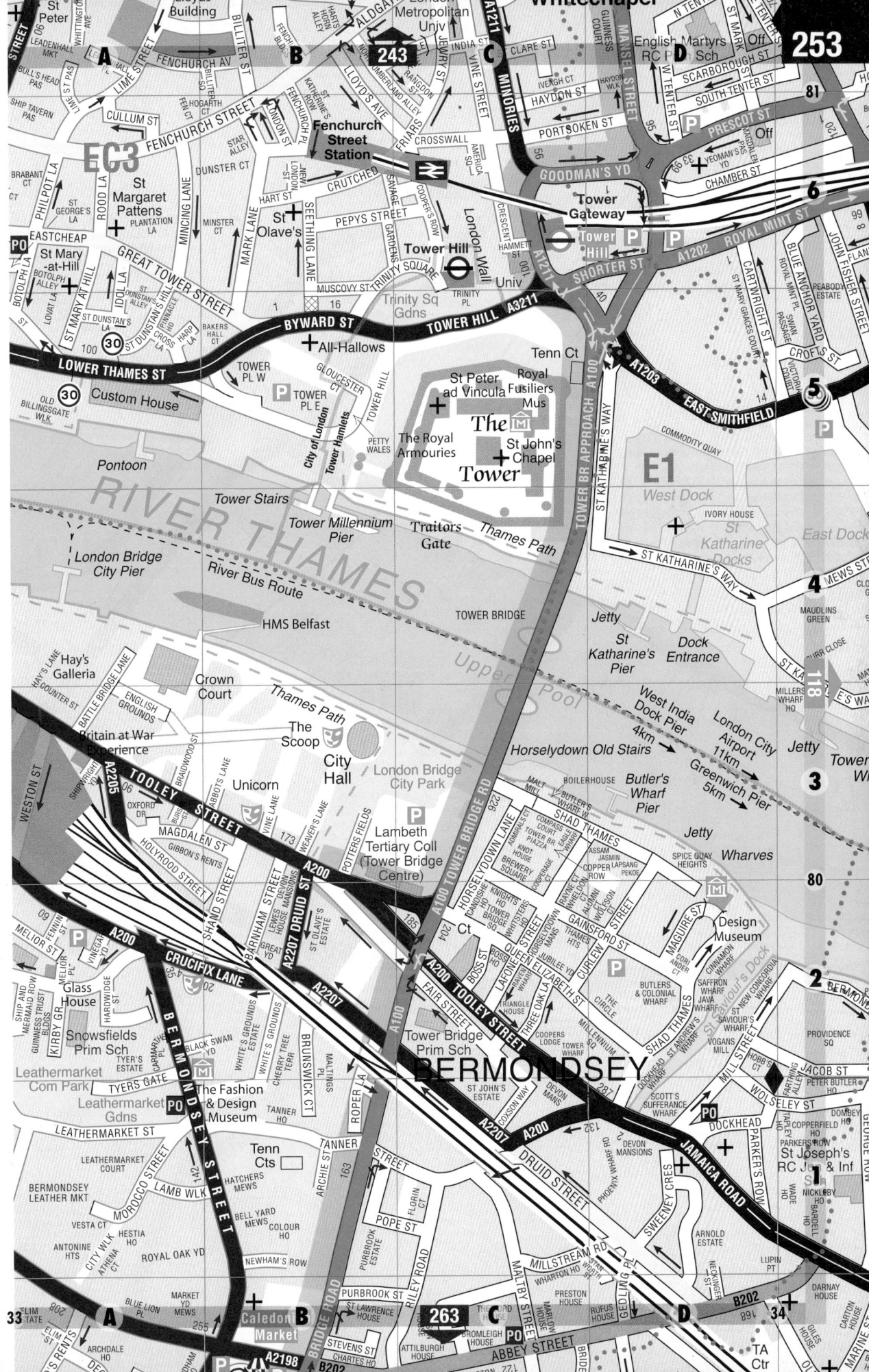

Whitechapel
EC3
St Peter
Lloyds Building
FENCHURCH AV
BILLITER ST
LIME STREET
LEADENHALL MKT
FENCHURCH STREET
Fenchurch Street Station
243
Metropolitan Univ
MINORIES
INDIA ST
CLARE ST
HAYDON ST
PORTSOKEN ST
MANSELL STREET
English Martyrs RC Prim Sch
SCARBOROUGH ST
SOUTH TENTER ST
PRESCOT ST
CHAMBER ST
GOODMAN'S YD
CRUTCHED FRIARS
CROSSWALL
St Margaret Pattens
EASTCHEAP
GREAT TOWER STREET
St Mary -at-Hill
MINCING LANE
MARK LANE
SEETHING LANE
St Olave's
PEPYS STREET
HART ST
COOPER'S ROW
Tower Hill
London Wall
TRINITY SQUARE
Trinity Sq Gdns
Tower Gateway
Tower Hill
SHORTER ST
A1202 ROYAL MINT ST
BYWARD ST
TOWER HILL A3211
LOWER THAMES ST
All-Hallows
Custom House
TOWER PL W
TOWER PL E
City of London
Tower Hamlets
Tenn Ct
St Peter ad Vincula
Royal Fusiliers Mus
The Tower
The Royal Armouries
St John's Chapel
TOWER BR APPROACH A100
ST KATHARINE'S WAY
A1203 EAST SMITHFIELD
E1
West Dock
East Dock
IVORY HOUSE
St Katharine Docks
Pontoon
RIVER THAMES
Tower Stairs
Tower Millennium Pier
Traitors Gate
Thames Path
London Bridge City Pier
River Bus Route
TOWER BRIDGE
HMS Belfast
Jetty
St Katharine's Pier
Dock Entrance
Upper Pool
Hay's Galleria
Crown Court
The Scoop
City Hall
London Bridge City Park
Britain at War Experience
West India Dock Pier 4km
London City Airport 11km
Greenwich Pier 5km
Horselydown Old Stairs
Butler's Wharf Pier
TOOLEY STREET
Unicorn
Lambeth Tertiary Coll (Tower Bridge Centre)
A100 TOWER BRIDGE RD
SHAD THAMES
Jetty
Wharves
WESTON ST
MAGDALEN ST
HOLYROOD STREET
SHAND STREET
DRUID ST
A200
Design Museum
GAINSFORD ST
QUEEN ELIZABETH ST
CRUCIFIX LANE
Glass House
Snowsfields Prim Sch
Leathermarket Com Park
Leathermarket Gdns
The Fashion & Design Museum
BERMONDSEY STREET
Tower Bridge Prim Sch
BERMONDSEY
JAMAICA ROAD
St Joseph's RC Jun & Inf
LEATHERMARKET ST
Tenn Cts
MOROCCO STREET
ROYAL OAK YD
POPE ST
MILLSTREAM RD
ABBEY STREET
Caledonian Market
263
118

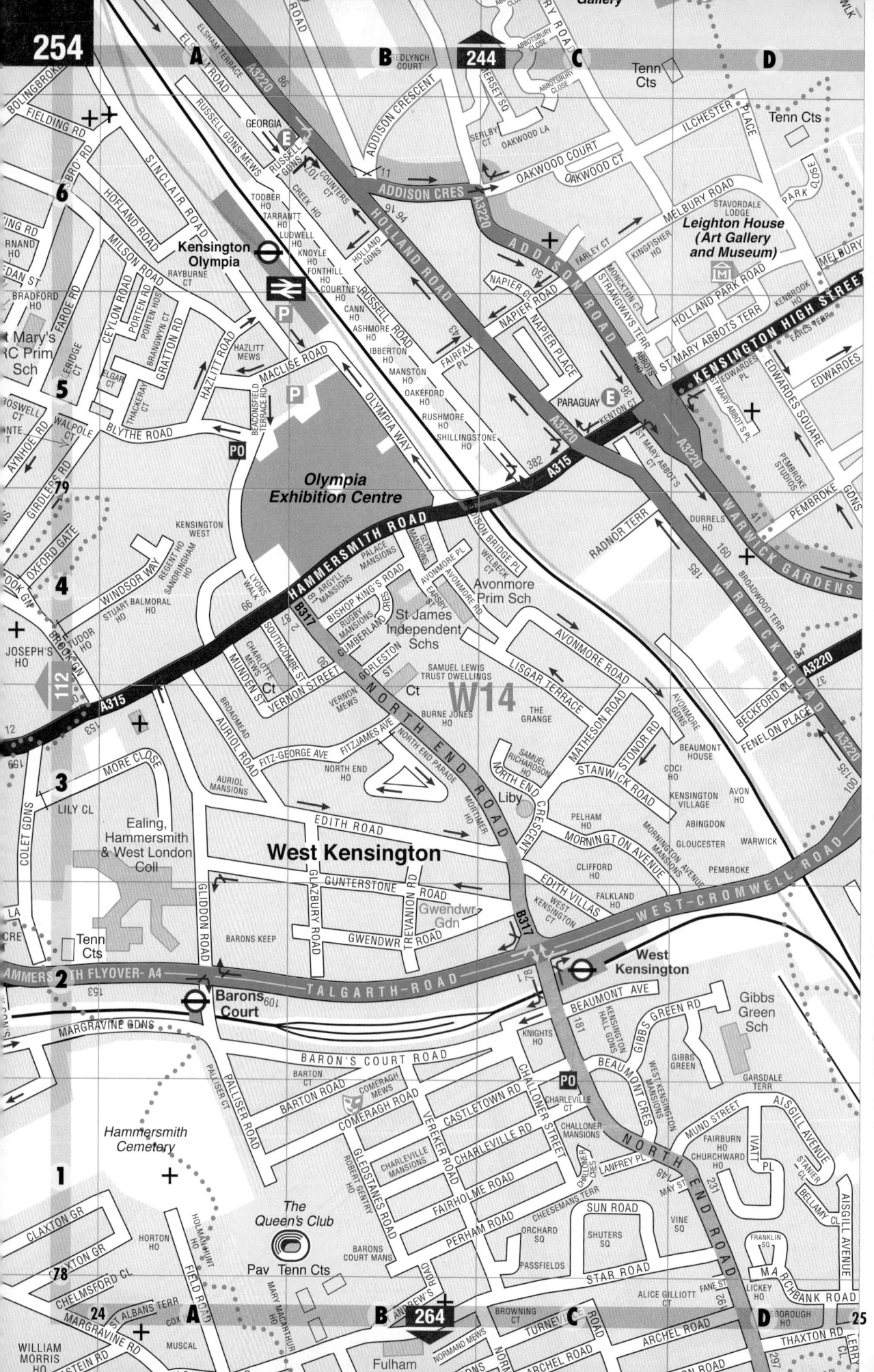
244
264
112
A
B
C
D
1
2
3
4
5
6
Kensington Olympia
Olympia Exhibition Centre
Leighton House (Art Gallery and Museum)
West Kensington
W14
Barons Court
West Kensington
Hammersmith Cemetery
The Queen's Club
Pav Tenn Cts
Ealing, Hammersmith & West London Coll
Avonmore Prim Sch
St James Independent Schs
Gibbs Green Sch
St Mary's RC Prim Sch
Tenn Cts
Liby
PO
HAMMERSMITH ROAD
A315
A3220
B317
HOLLAND ROAD
ADDISON ROAD
ADDISON CRES
ADDISON CRESCENT
RUSSELL ROAD
RUSSELL GDNS MEWS
ELSHAM ROAD
SINCLAIR ROAD
HOFLAND ROAD
MILSON ROAD
CEYLON ROAD
PORTEN RD
GRATTON RD
HAZLITT ROAD
MACLISE ROAD
BLYTHE ROAD
OLYMPIA WAY
FAROE RD
FIELDING RD
BOLINGBROKE
GIRDLERS RD
OXFORD GATE
WINDSOR WAY
BROOK GN
KENSINGTON HIGH STREET
WARWICK ROAD
WARWICK GARDENS
EDWARDES SQUARE
PEMBROKE GDNS
MELBURY ROAD
ILCHESTER PLACE
OAKWOOD COURT
HOLLAND PARK ROAD
ST MARY ABBOTS TERR
STRANGWAYS TERR
NAPIER ROAD
NAPIER PLACE
RADNOR TERR
AVONMORE ROAD
LISGAR TERRACE
MATHESON ROAD
STONOR RD
STANWICK ROAD
NORTH END ROAD
NORTH END CRESCENT
MORNINGTON AVENUE
EDITH ROAD
EDITH VILLAS
GUNTERSTONE ROAD
GWENDWR ROAD
GLAZBURY ROAD
TREVANION RD
GLIDDON ROAD
AURIOL ROAD
FITZ-GEORGE AVE
FITZJAMES AVE
VERNON STREET
MUNDEN ST
SOUTHCOMBE ST
BISHOP KING'S ROAD
GORLESTON ST
MORE CLOSE
LILY CL
COLET GDNS
HAMMERSMITH FLYOVER- A4
TALGARTH ROAD
WEST CROMWELL ROAD
BEAUMONT AVE
BEAUMONT CRES
GIBBS GREEN RD
MARGRAVINE GDNS
BARON'S COURT ROAD
BARTON ROAD
COMERAGH ROAD
PALLISER ROAD
CASTLETOWN RD
CHARLEVILLE RD
CHALLONER STREET
VEREKER ROAD
GLEDSTANES ROAD
FAIRHOLME ROAD
PERHAM ROAD
SUN ROAD
STAR ROAD
MUND STREET
AISGILL AVENUE
MARCHBANK ROAD
ARCHEL ROAD
THAXTON RD
CLAXTON GR
CHELMSFORD CL
MARGRAVINE RD
ST ALBANS TERR
FIELD ROAD
Fulham

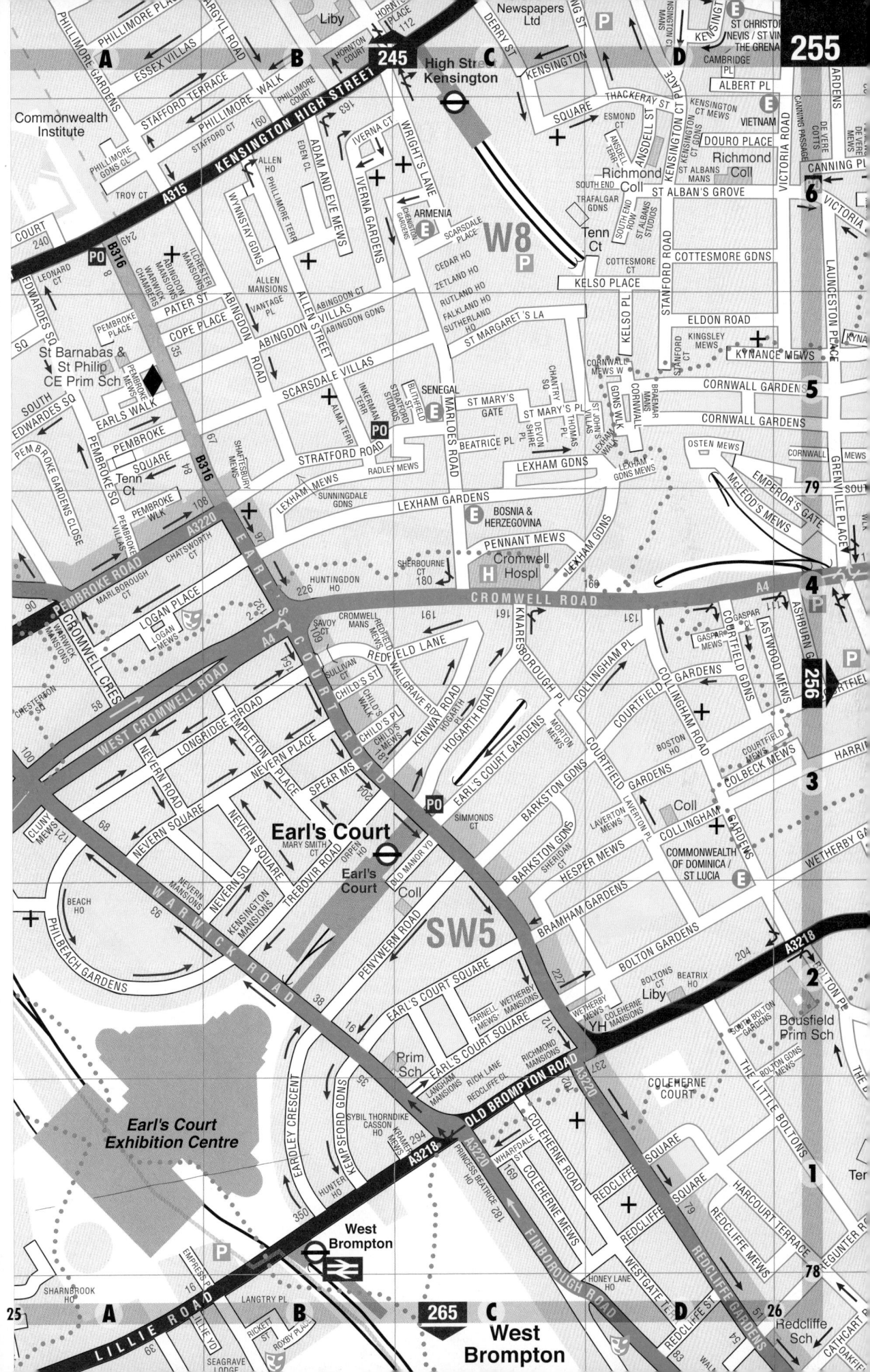

A
B
C
D
245
High Street Kensington
Newspapers Ltd
Liby
Commonwealth Institute
KENSINGTON HIGH STREET
A315
PHILLIMORE GARDENS
PHILLIMORE PLACE
ESSEX VILLAS
STAFFORD TERRACE
PHILLIMORE WALK
ARGYLL ROAD
DERRY ST
KENSINGTON SQUARE
THACKERAY ST
ANSDELL ST
KENSINGTON CT PLACE
DOURO PLACE
Richmond Coll
VICTORIA ROAD
CANNING PL
ST ALBAN'S GROVE
W8
WRIGHT'S LANE
IVERNA GARDENS
ADAM AND EVE MEWS
ALLEN STREET
ABINGDON ROAD
ABINGDON VILLAS
ARMENIA
SCARSDALE PLACE
CEDAR HO
ZETLAND HO
RUTLAND HO
FALKLAND HO
SUTHERLAND HO
ST MARGARET'S LA
KELSO PLACE
COTTESMORE GDNS
STANFORD ROAD
ELDON ROAD
KYNANCE MEWS
LAUNCESTON PLACE
CORNWALL GARDENS
B316
PATER ST
COPE PLACE
EARLS WALK
PEMBROKE SQUARE
St Barnabas & St Philip CE Prim Sch
SOUTH EDWARDES SQ
EDWARDES SQ
SCARSDALE VILLAS
STRATFORD ROAD
SENEGAL
MARLOES ROAD
ST MARY'S GATE
BEATRICE PL
LEXHAM GDNS
LEXHAM GARDENS
LEXHAM MEWS
BOSNIA & HERZEGOVINA
PENNANT MEWS
Cromwell Hospl
OSTEN MEWS
EMPEROR'S GATE
McLEOD'S MEWS
GRENVILLE PLACE
PEMBROKE ROAD
A3220
PEMBROKE VILLAS
PEMBROKE GARDENS CLOSE
EARL'S COURT ROAD
CROMWELL ROAD
A4
LOGAN PLACE
CROMWELL CRES
WEST CROMWELL ROAD
REDFIELD LANE
WALLGRAVE RD
KENWAY ROAD
HOGARTH ROAD
KNARESBOROUGH PL
COLLINGHAM PL
COURTFIELD GARDENS
COURTFIELD GDNS
COLLINGHAM ROAD
ASTWOOD MEWS
ASHBURN G
256
LONGRIDGE ROAD
TEMPLETON PLACE
NEVERN PLACE
NEVERN ROAD
NEVERN SQUARE
SPEAR MS
Earl's Court
TREBOVIR ROAD
EARL'S COURT GARDENS
BARKSTON GDNS
HESPER MEWS
COLLINGHAM GARDENS
COMMONWEALTH OF DOMINICA / ST LUCIA
COLBECK MEWS
WETHERBY GA
SW5
WARWICK ROAD
PHILBEACH GARDENS
PENYWERN ROAD
BRAMHAM GARDENS
BOLTON GARDENS
A3218
Liby
YH
Bousfield Prim Sch
EARL'S COURT SQUARE
OLD BROMPTON ROAD
Earl's Court Exhibition Centre
EARDLEY CRESCENT
KEMPSFORD GDNS
COLEHERNE ROAD
COLEHERNE MEWS
COLEHERNE COURT
THE LITTLE BOLTONS
REDCLIFFE SQUARE
HARCOURT TERRACE
REDCLIFFE MEWS
REDCLIFFE GARDENS
FINBOROUGH ROAD
West Brompton
LILLIE ROAD
265
Redcliffe Sch
1
2
3
4
5
6

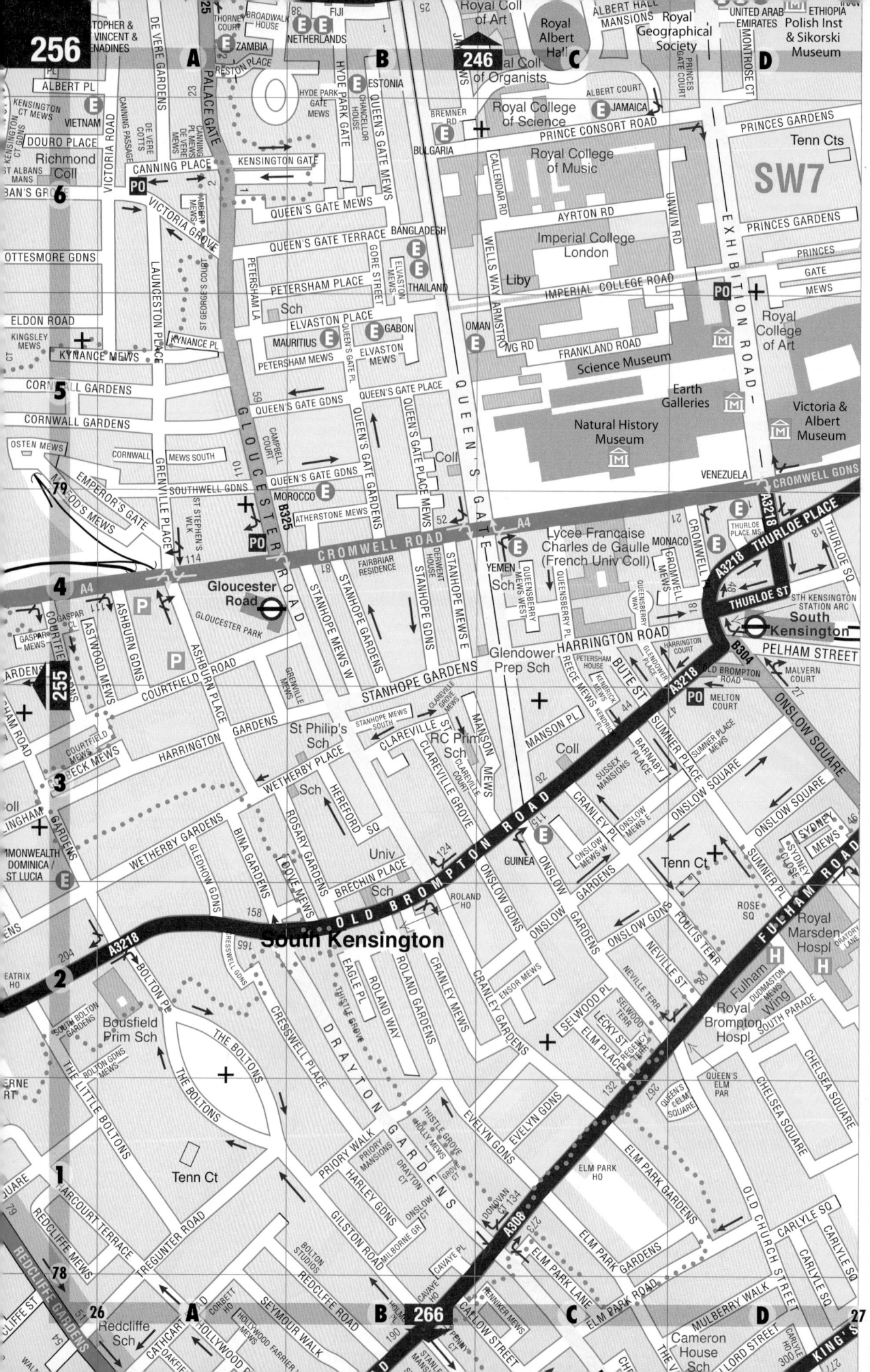

Royal Albert Hall
Royal Coll of Art
Royal Coll of Organists
Royal Geographical Society
Polish Inst & Sikorski Museum
Royal College of Science
Royal College of Music
Imperial College London
Liby
PRINCE CONSORT ROAD
IMPERIAL COLLEGE ROAD
EXHIBITION ROAD
QUEEN'S GATE
SW7
Science Museum
Earth Galleries
Natural History Museum
Victoria & Albert Museum
Royal College of Art
CROMWELL ROAD
A4
Lycee Francaise Charles de Gaulle (French Univ Coll)
Gloucester Road
GLOUCESTER ROAD
B325
South Kensington
THURLOE PLACE
A3218
HARRINGTON ROAD
Glendower Prep Sch
STANHOPE GARDENS
OLD BROMPTON ROAD
South Kensington
FULHAM ROAD
Royal Marsden Hospl
Royal Brompton Hospl
Fulham Wing
ONSLOW SQUARE
ONSLOW GARDENS
THE BOLTONS
Bousfield Prim Sch
DRAYTON GARDENS
ELM PARK GARDENS
OLD CHURCH STREET
A308
REDCLIFFE GARDENS
Redcliffe Sch
Cameron House Sch
CARLYLE SQ
CHELSEA SQUARE
Richmond Coll
VICTORIA ROAD
CANNING PLACE
KENSINGTON GATE
QUEEN'S GATE TERRACE
CORNWALL GARDENS
EMPEROR'S GATE
COURTFIELD ROAD
HARRINGTON GARDENS
WETHERBY GARDENS
St Philip's Sch
RC Prim Sch
Univ
Tenn Ct
Tenn Cts
246
255
266

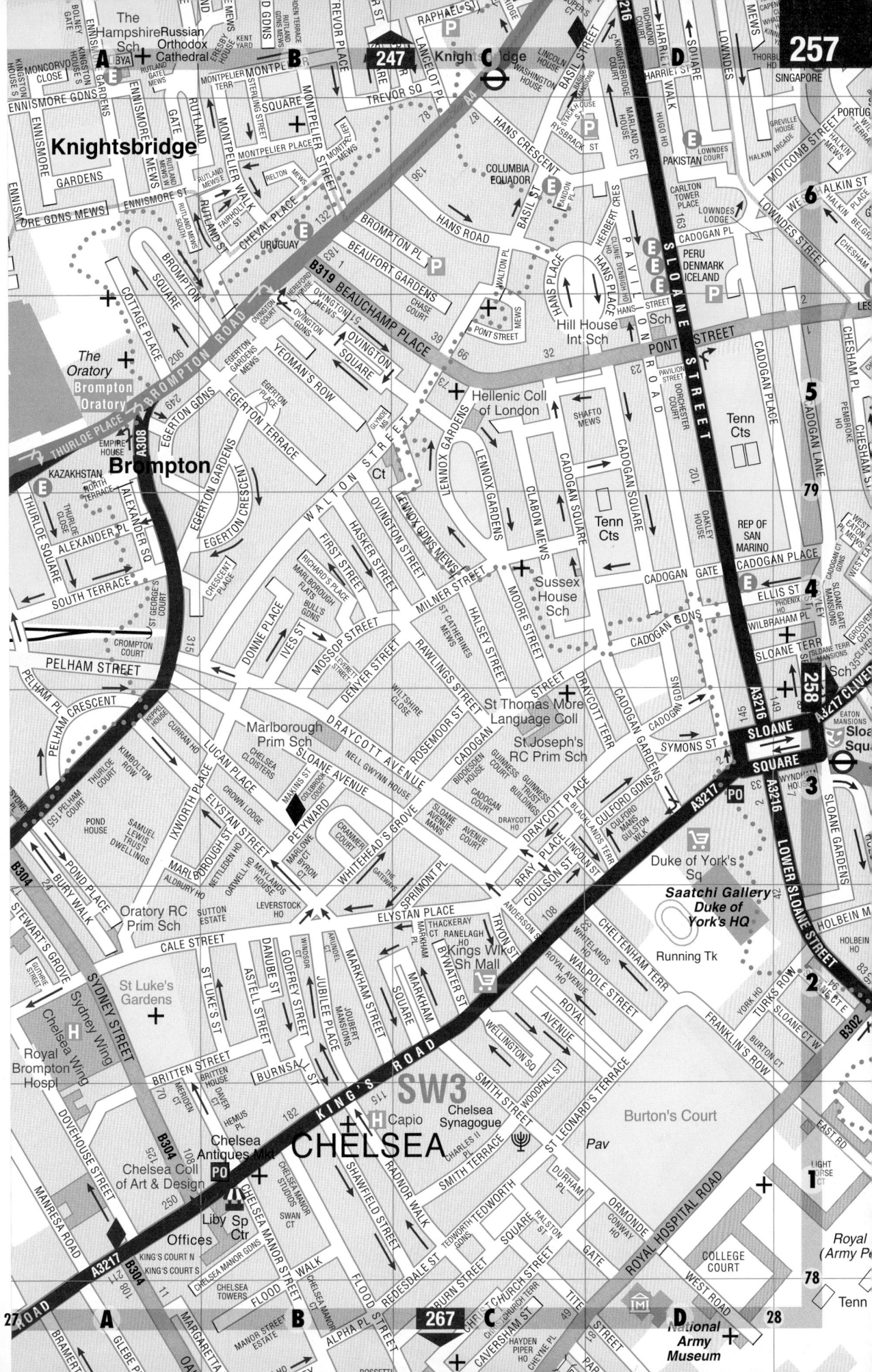
A
B
C
D
247
258
267
27
28
6
5
4
3
2
1
79
78
Knightsbridge
Brompton
CHELSEA
SW3
The Hampshire Sch
Russian Orthodox Cathedral
LIBYA
Knightsbridge
SINGAPORE
PAKISTAN
COLUMBIA / EQUADOR
URUGUAY
PERU
DENMARK
ICELAND
KAZAKHSTAN
REP OF SAN MARINO
The Oratory
Brompton Oratory
Hill House Int Sch
Hellenic Coll of London
Tenn Cts
Sussex House Sch
St Thomas More Language Coll
St Joseph's RC Prim Sch
Marlborough Prim Sch
Oratory RC Prim Sch
Duke of York's Sq
Saatchi Gallery
Duke of York's HQ
Running Tk
Kings Wlk Sh Mall
St Luke's Gardens
Royal Brompton Hospl
Sydney Wing
Chelsea Wing
Chelsea Antiques Mkt
Chelsea Coll of Art & Design
Capio
Chelsea Synagogue
Burton's Court
Pav
Liby
Sp Ctr
Offices
COLLEGE COURT
National Army Museum
Royal Army
Sloane Square
ENNISMORE GARDENS
ENNISMORE GDNS MEWS
MONTPELIER SQUARE
MONTPELIER PLACE
MONTPELIER STREET
MONTPELIER WALK
TREVOR PLACE
TREVOR SQ
LANCELOT PL
RAPHAEL ST
BASIL STREET
HANS CRESCENT
HANS ROAD
HANS PLACE
BROMPTON PL
BEAUFORT GARDENS
BEAUCHAMP PLACE
BROMPTON SQUARE
COTTAGE PLACE
CHEVAL PLACE
RUTLAND GATE
BROMPTON ROAD
THURLOE PLACE
EGERTON GDNS
EGERTON TERRACE
EGERTON CRESCENT
EGERTON GARDENS
YEOMAN'S ROW
OVINGTON SQUARE
OVINGTON GDNS
PONT STREET
SLOANE STREET
CADOGAN PLACE
CADOGAN SQUARE
CADOGAN GDNS
CADOGAN GATE
CADOGAN LANE
LENNOX GARDENS
CLABON MEWS
WALTON STREET
MILNER STREET
HASKER STREET
OVINGTON STREET
FIRST STREET
MOORE STREET
HALSEY STREET
RAWLINGS STREET
DRAYCOTT AVENUE
DRAYCOTT PLACE
DRAYCOTT TERR
SLOANE AVENUE
SLOANE SQUARE
LOWER SLOANE STREET
SLOANE GARDENS
ALEXANDER SQ
THURLOE SQUARE
SOUTH TERRACE
PELHAM STREET
PELHAM CRESCENT
FULHAM ROAD
IXWORTH PLACE
ELYSTAN STREET
ELYSTAN PLACE
LUCAN PLACE
CALE STREET
SYDNEY STREET
KING'S ROAD
JUBILEE PLACE
MARKHAM SQUARE
SMITH STREET
WALPOLE STREET
ROYAL AVENUE
CHELTENHAM TERR
FRANKLIN'S ROW
TURKS ROW
ST LEONARD'S TERRACE
ROYAL HOSPITAL ROAD
WEST ROAD
TITE STREET
TEDWORTH SQUARE
RADNOR WALK
SHAWFIELD STREET
FLOOD STREET
CHELSEA MANOR STREET
OAKLEY STREET
MANRESA ROAD
DOVEHOUSE STREET
BRITTEN STREET
ST LUKE'S ST
GODFREY STREET
MARKHAM STREET
A4
A308
A3216
A3217
B319
B304
B302

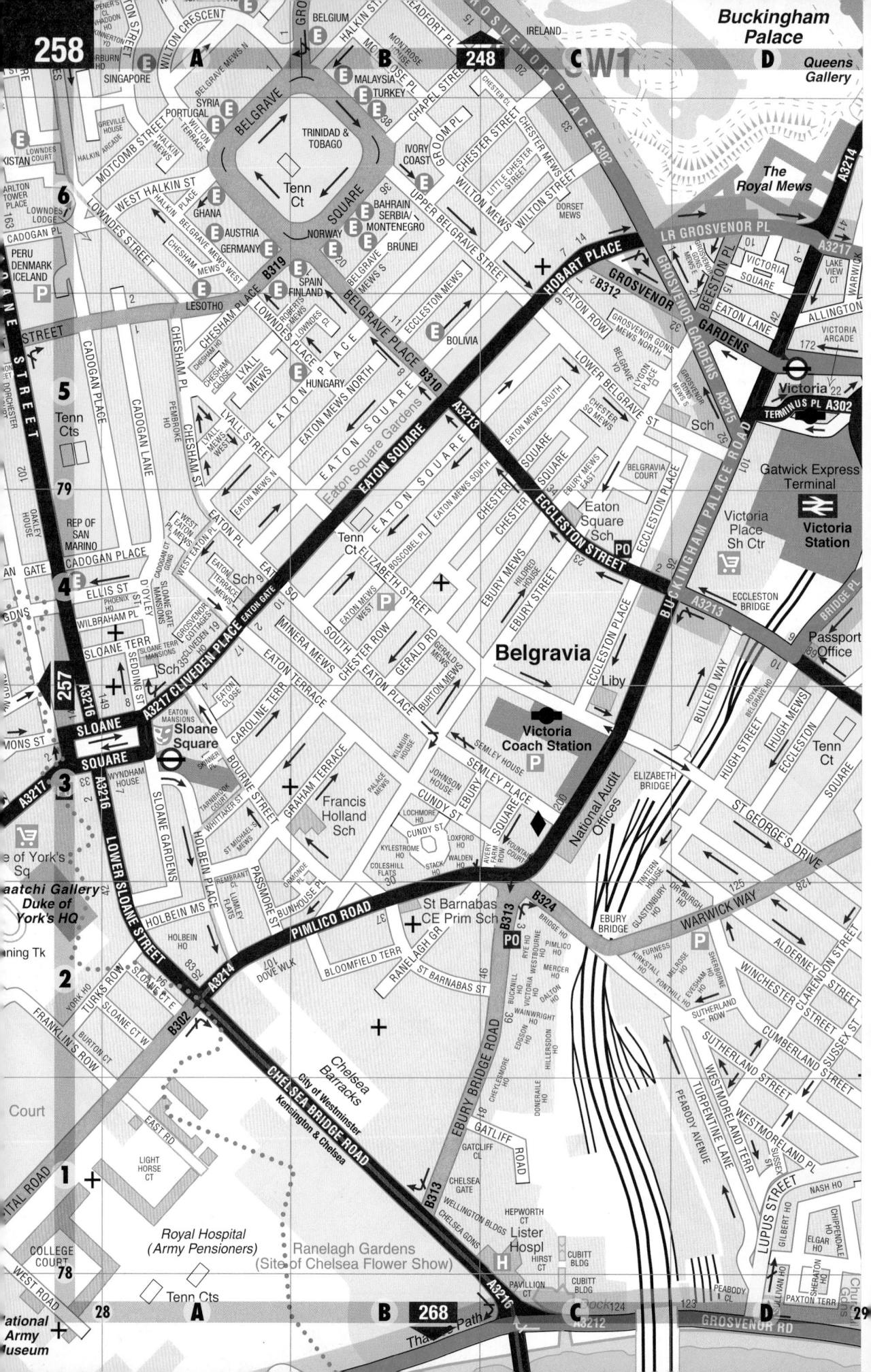
Buckingham Palace
Queens Gallery
The Royal Mews
SW1
Belgravia
Victoria Coach Station
Victoria Station
Gatwick Express Terminal
Victoria Place Sh Ctr
Passport Office
National Audit Offices
Eaton Square Gardens
Eaton Square Sch
Francis Holland Sch
St Barnabas CE Prim Sch
Chelsea Barracks
City of Westminster
Kensington & Chelsea
Royal Hospital (Army Pensioners)
Ranelagh Gardens (Site of Chelsea Flower Show)
Lister Hospl
Saatchi Gallery
Duke of York's HQ
National Army Museum
Sloane Square
Belgrave Square
Eaton Square
Eaton Place
Ebury Street
Eccleston Street
Buckingham Palace Road
Grosvenor Gardens
Grosvenor Place A302
Hobart Place
Lower Belgrave St
Chester Square
Elizabeth Street
Pimlico Road
Chelsea Bridge Road
Ebury Bridge Road
Lower Sloane Street
Sloane Street
Cliveden Place
Warwick Way
St George's Drive
Grosvenor Rd
Eccleston Bridge
Elizabeth Bridge
Ebury Bridge
Lupus Street
Sutherland Street
Cumberland Street
Winchester Street
Alderney Street
Westmoreland Terr
Turpentine Lane
Peabody Avenue
Holbein Place
Bourne Street
Graham Terrace
Cundy St
Semley Place
Gatliff Road
Franklin's Row
Turks Row
Cadogan Place
Cadogan Lane
Chesham Place
Lowndes Street
Lowndes Place
Motcomb Street
West Halkin St
Wilton Crescent
Upper Belgrave Street
Chester Street
Wilton Street
Allington St
Victoria Square
Eaton Lane
Terminus Pl A302
Royal Hospital Road
West Road
Thames Path
248
257
268
A B C D
1 2 3 4 5 6

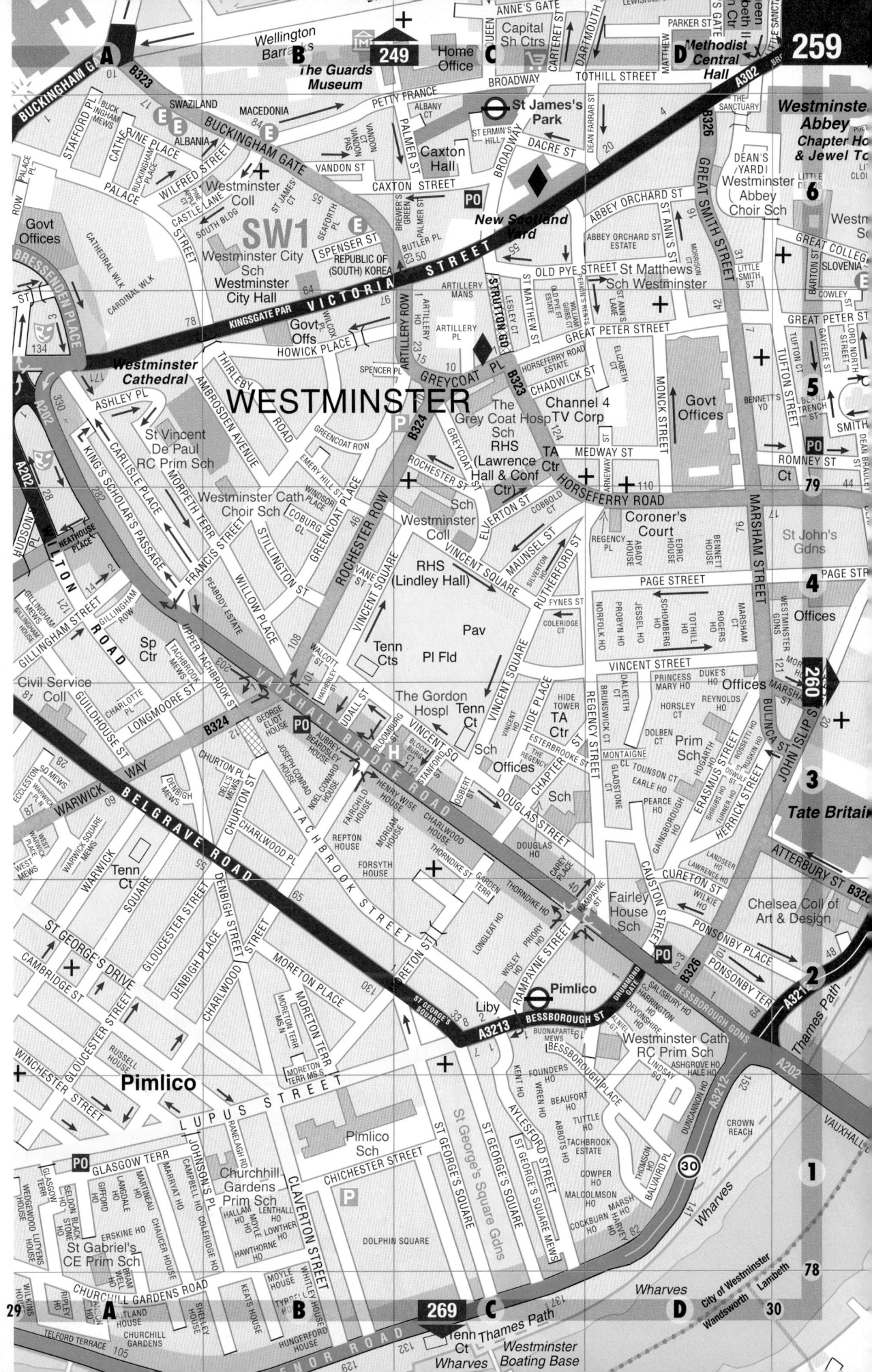

259
249
260
269
Wellington Barracks
The Guards Museum
Home Office
Capital Sh Ctrs
Methodist Central Hall
St James's Park
Westminster Abbey
Chapter House & Jewel Tower
Caxton Hall
New Scotland Yard
Westminster Coll
SW1
Westminster City Sch
Westminster City Hall
Govt Offices
Westminster Cathedral
WESTMINSTER
St Vincent De Paul RC Prim Sch
Westminster Cath Choir Sch
Grey Coat Hosp Sch
RHS (Lawrence Hall & Conf Ctr)
Channel 4 TV Corp
Westminster Abbey Choir Sch
St Matthews Sch Westminster
Coroner's Court
St John's Gdns
RHS (Lindley Hall)
Tenn Cts
Pl Fld
Pav
The Gordon Hospl
Civil Service Coll
Tate Britain
Chelsea Coll of Art & Design
Fairley House Sch
Pimlico
Westminster Cath RC Prim Sch
Pimlico Sch
Churchhill Gardens Prim Sch
St Gabriel's CE Prim Sch
St George's Square Gdns
Dolphin Square
Westminster Boating Base
Thames Path
Wharves
Crown Reach
VICTORIA STREET
VAUXHALL BRIDGE ROAD
BELGRAVE ROAD
HORSEFERRY ROAD
MARSHAM STREET
GREAT SMITH STREET
BUCKINGHAM GATE
ROCHESTER ROW
TACHBROOK STREET
WARWICK WAY
LUPUS STREET
CLAVERTON STREET
BESSBOROUGH ST
GROSVENOR ROAD
City of Westminster
Lambeth
Wandsworth

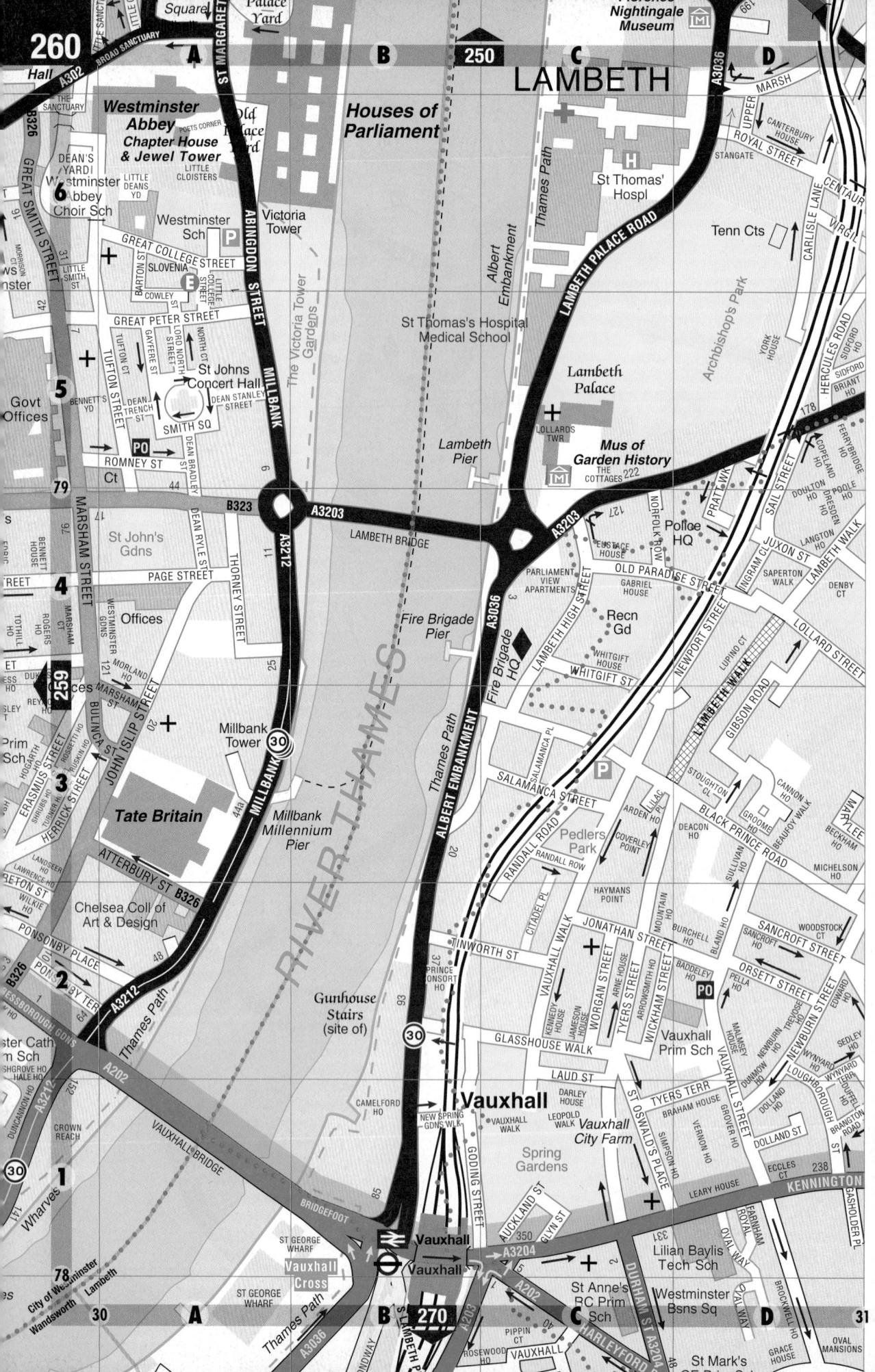

250
LAMBETH
Westminster Abbey
Chapter House & Jewel Tower
Houses of Parliament
Old Palace Yard
Palace Yard
Broad Sanctuary
The Sanctuary
St Margaret St
Florence Nightingale Museum
Great Smith Street
Dean's Yard
Little Cloisters
Westminster Abbey Choir Sch
Westminster Sch
Victoria Tower
Abingdon Street
Great College Street
Little Smith St
Barton St
Cowley St
Great Peter Street
Tufton Street
Lord North Street
North Ct
St Johns Concert Hall
Dean Stanley Street
Smith Sq
Dean Trench St
Bennett's Yd
Govt Offices
Romney St
Dean Bradley St
The Victoria Tower Gardens
Millbank
St Thomas's Hospital Medical School
Albert Embankment
Thames Path
St Thomas' Hospl
Lambeth Palace Road
Upper Marsh
Royal Street
Canterbury House
Stangate
Carlisle Lane
Centaur
Virgil
Tenn Cts
Archbishop's Park
York House
Hercules Road
Sidford Ho
Briant Ho
Lambeth Palace
Lollards Twr
Mus of Garden History
The Cottages
Lambeth Pier
Marsham Street
B323
A3203
Lambeth Bridge
A3212
A3036
St John's Gdns
Dean Ryle St
Thorney Street
Page Street
Offices
Westminster Gdns
Morland Ho
Bulinca St
John Islip Street
Parliament View Apartments
Old Paradise Street
Gabriel House
Eustace House
Norfolk Row
Pratt Wk
Police HQ
Sail Street
Juxon St
Lambeth Walk
Lambeth High Street
Recn Gd
Whitgift House
Whitgift St
Fire Brigade Pier
Fire Brigade HQ
Newport Street
Lollard Street
Gibson Road
Millbank Tower
RIVER THAMES
Tate Britain
Erasmus Street
Herrick Street
Atterbury St
B326
Chelsea Coll of Art & Design
Ponsonby Place
Ponsonby Ter
Millbank Millennium Pier
Albert Embankment
Salamanca Street
Salamanca Pl
Randall Road
Randall Row
Pedlers Park
Black Prince Road
Stoughton Cl
Cannon Ho
Groome Ho
Beaufoy Walk
Marylee
Michelson Ho
Haymans Point
Citadel Pl
Vauxhall Walk
Jonathan Street
Tinworth St
Sancroft Street
Orsett Street
Newburn Street
Worgan Street
Tyers Street
Wickham Street
Glasshouse Walk
Gunhouse Stairs (site of)
Vauxhall Prim Sch
Laud St
Vauxhall
Vauxhall City Farm
Spring Gardens
St Oswald's Place
Tyers Terr
Vauxhall Street
Loughborough St
Dolland St
Kennington Lane
Vauxhall Bridge
Bridgefoot
St George Wharf
Vauxhall Cross
Goding Street
Auckland St
Glyn St
A3204
A202
Lilian Baylis Tech Sch
St Anne's RC Prim Sch
Westminster Bsns Sq
Durham St
Harleyford Road
Oval Way
Brockwell Ho
St Mark's
Oval Mansions
Thames Path
Wharves
Crown Reach
Bessborough Gdns
City of Westminster
Wandsworth
Lambeth
259
270

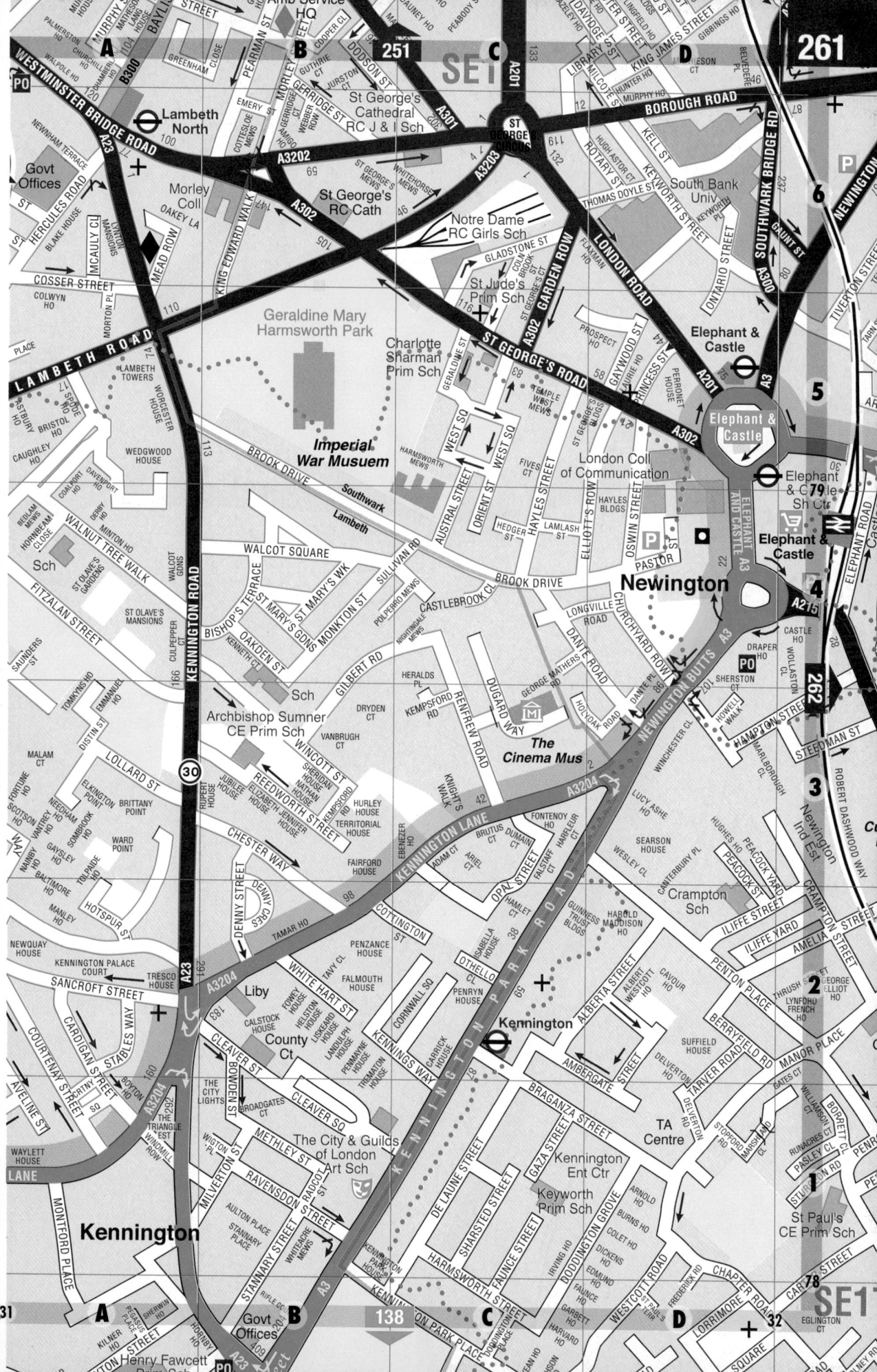
261
251
262
138
A
B
C
D
SE1
SE11
Westminster Bridge Road
Lambeth North
Lambeth Road
Borough Road
St George's Circus
St George's Cathedral RC J & I Sch
St George's RC Cath
Notre Dame RC Girls Sch
St Jude's Prim Sch
Charlotte Sharman Prim Sch
St George's Road
London Road
Southwark Bridge Rd
South Bank Univ
Elephant & Castle
Elephant & Castle Sh Ctr
Newington Butts
Newington
Newington Ind Est
Geraldine Mary Harmsworth Park
Imperial War Museum
Govt Offices
Morley Coll
Amb Service HQ
Kennington Road
Brook Drive
Southwark
Lambeth
Walcot Square
London Coll of Communication
The Cinema Mus
Archbishop Sumner CE Prim Sch
Kennington Lane
Kennington Park Road
Kennington
Crampton Sch
Liby
County Ct
The City & Guilds of London Art Sch
TA Centre
Kennington Ent Ctr
Keyworth Prim Sch
St Paul's CE Prim Sch
Henry Fawcett Prim Sch
Cosser Street
Fitzalan Street
Walnut Tree Walk
Sancroft Street
Cleaver Sq
Braganza Street
Manor Place
Penton Place
Hercules Road
Mead Row
Hayles Street
Garden Row
Keyworth Street
Ontario Street
Newington Butts
Robert Dashwood Way
Elephant Road
A3
A23
A302
A3202
A3203
A3204
A201
A301
A300
A215
B300
31
32
78
79

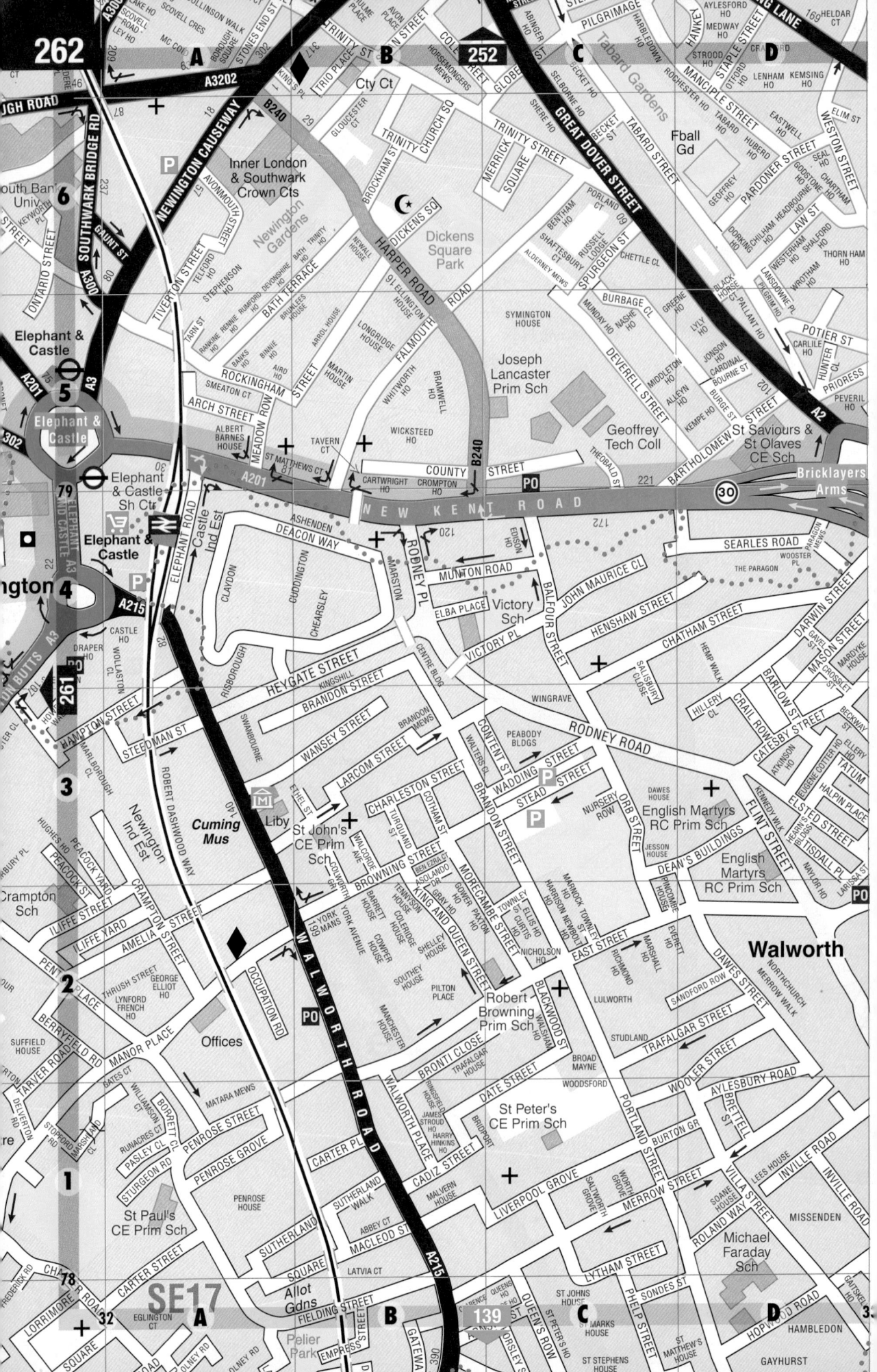
262
A
B
C
D
252
Tabard Gardens
SCOVELL CRES
ROLLINSON WALK
BOROUGH SQUARE
STONES END ST
TRINITY ST
TRIO PLACE
HORSEMONGERS MEWS
GLOBE ST
PILGRIMAGE ST
HARBLEDOWN HO
AYLESFORD HO
MEDWAY HO
STROOD HO
HELDAR CT
LENHAM HO
KEMSING HO
A3202
NEWINGTON CAUSEWAY
B240
City Ct
GLOUCESTER CT
TRINITY CHURCH SQ
TRINITY STREET
GREAT DOVER STREET
TABARD STREET
Fball Gd
MANCIPLE STREET
STAPLE STREET
WESTON STREET
ELIM ST
EASTWELL HO
PARDONER STREET
SOUTHWARK BRIDGE RD
Inner London & Southwark Crown Cts
MERRICK SQUARE
Newington Gardens
DICKENS SQ
Dickens Square Park
HARPER ROAD
BROCKHAM ST
AVONMOUTH STREET
GAUNT ST
ONTARIO STREET
KEYWORTH PL
TIVERTON STREET
BATH TERRACE
SPURGEON ST
CHETTLE CL
ALDERNEY MEWS
SHAFTESBURY CT
RUSSELL LODGE
BENTHAM HO
LAW ST
THORN HAM HO
LANSDOWNE PL
Elephant & Castle
A201
A3
5
6
4
3
2
1
SYMINGTON HOUSE
BURBAGE CL
MUNDAY HO
NASHE HO
GREENE HO
LYLY HO
POTIER ST
CARLILE HO
HUNTER CL
PRIORESS
PEVERIL HO
Joseph Lancaster Prim Sch
DEVERELL STREET
LONGRIDGE HOUSE
FALMOUTH ROAD
ROCKINGHAM STREET
SMEATON CT
ARCH STREET
MEADOW ROW
ALBERT BARNES HOUSE
ST MATTHEWS CT
TAVERN CT
WICKSTEED HO
Geoffrey Tech Coll
BARTHOLOMEW STREET
St Saviours & St Olaves CE Sch
A2
Bricklayers Arms
COUNTY STREET
CARTWRIGHT HO
CROMPTON HO
NEW KENT ROAD
30
Elephant & Castle Sh Ctr
ELEPHANT AND CASTLE
ELEPHANT ROAD
Castle Ind Est
ASHENDEN
DEACON WAY
CLAYDON
CUDDINGTON
CHEARSLEY
MARSTON
RODNEY PL
MUNTON ROAD
EDISON HO
SEARLES ROAD
THE PARAGON
PARAGON MEWS
WOOSTER PL
JOHN MAURICE CL
HENSHAW STREET
CHATHAM STREET
DARWIN STREET
Victory Sch
ELBA PLACE
VICTORY PL
BALFOUR STREET
A215
CASTLE HO
NEWINGTON BUTTS
DRAPER HO
WOLLASTON CL
261
HEYGATE STREET
KINGSHILL
BRANDON STREET
RISBOROUGH
CENTRE BLDG
SALISBURY CLOSE
HEMP WALK
WINGRAVE
MASON STREET
MARDYKE HOUSE
HAMPTON STREET
STEEDMAN ST
WANSEY STREET
SWANBOURNE
BRANDON MEWS
LARCOM STREET
PEABODY BLDGS
RODNEY ROAD
HILLERY CL
CRAIL ROW
BARLOW ST
CATESBY STREET
BECKWAY ST
ELLERY HO
TATUM
MARLBOROUGH CL
ROBERT DASHWOOD WAY
Newington Ind Est
Cuming Mus
Liby
St John's CE Prim Sch
CHARLESTON STREET
COTHAM ST
WADDING STREET
STEAD STREET
NURSERY ROW
DAWES HOUSE
English Martyrs RC Prim Sch
ORB STREET
FLINT STREET
ELSTED STREET
HALPIN PLACE
TISDALL PL
LARISSA ST
Crampton Sch
PEACOCK ST
PEACOCK YARD
ILIFFE STREET
ILIFFE YARD
CRAMPTON STREET
AMELIA STREET
BROWNING STREET
KING AND QUEEN STREET
MORECAMBE STREET
JESSON HOUSE
DEAN'S BUILDINGS
PINCOMBE HOUSE
Walworth
WALWORTH ROAD
YORK AVENUE
EAST STREET
MARSHALL HO
EVERETT HO
DAWES STREET
NORTHCHURCH
MERROW WALK
THRUSH STREET
GEORGE ELLIOT HO
LYNFORD FRENCH HO
OCCUPATION RD
PO
PILTON PLACE
Robert Browning Prim Sch
BLACKWOOD ST
LULWORTH
SANDFORD ROW
SUFFIELD HOUSE
BERRYFIELD RD
MANOR PLACE
Offices
TARVER ROAD
STUDLAND
TRAFALGAR STREET
BRONTI CLOSE
TRAFALGAR HOUSE
BROAD MAYNE
WOOLER STREET
AYLESBURY ROAD
MATARA MEWS
DATE STREET
WOODSFORD
St Peter's CE Prim Sch
BRETTELL ST
PENROSE STREET
PENROSE GROVE
PASLEY CL
STURGEON RD
CARTER PL
WALWORTH PLACE
CADIZ STREET
BURTON GR
PORTLAND STREET
INVILLE ROAD
PENROSE HOUSE
SUTHERLAND WALK
MALVERN HOUSE
LIVERPOOL GROVE
MERROW STREET
VILLA STREET
ROLAND WAY
MISSENDEN
St Paul's CE Prim Sch
SUTHERLAND SQUARE
MACLEOD ST
ABBEY CT
LATVIA CT
LYTHAM STREET
Michael Faraday Sch
CARTER STREET
SE17
Allot Gdns
FIELDING STREET
139
ST JOHNS HOUSE
SONDES ST
PHELP STREET
HOPWOOD ROAD
HAMBLEDON
LORRIMORE SQUARE
EGLINTON CT
Pelier Park
EMPRESS ST
QUEEN'S ROW
ST MARKS HOUSE
ST STEPHENS HOUSE
ST MATTHEW'S HOUSE
GAYHURST

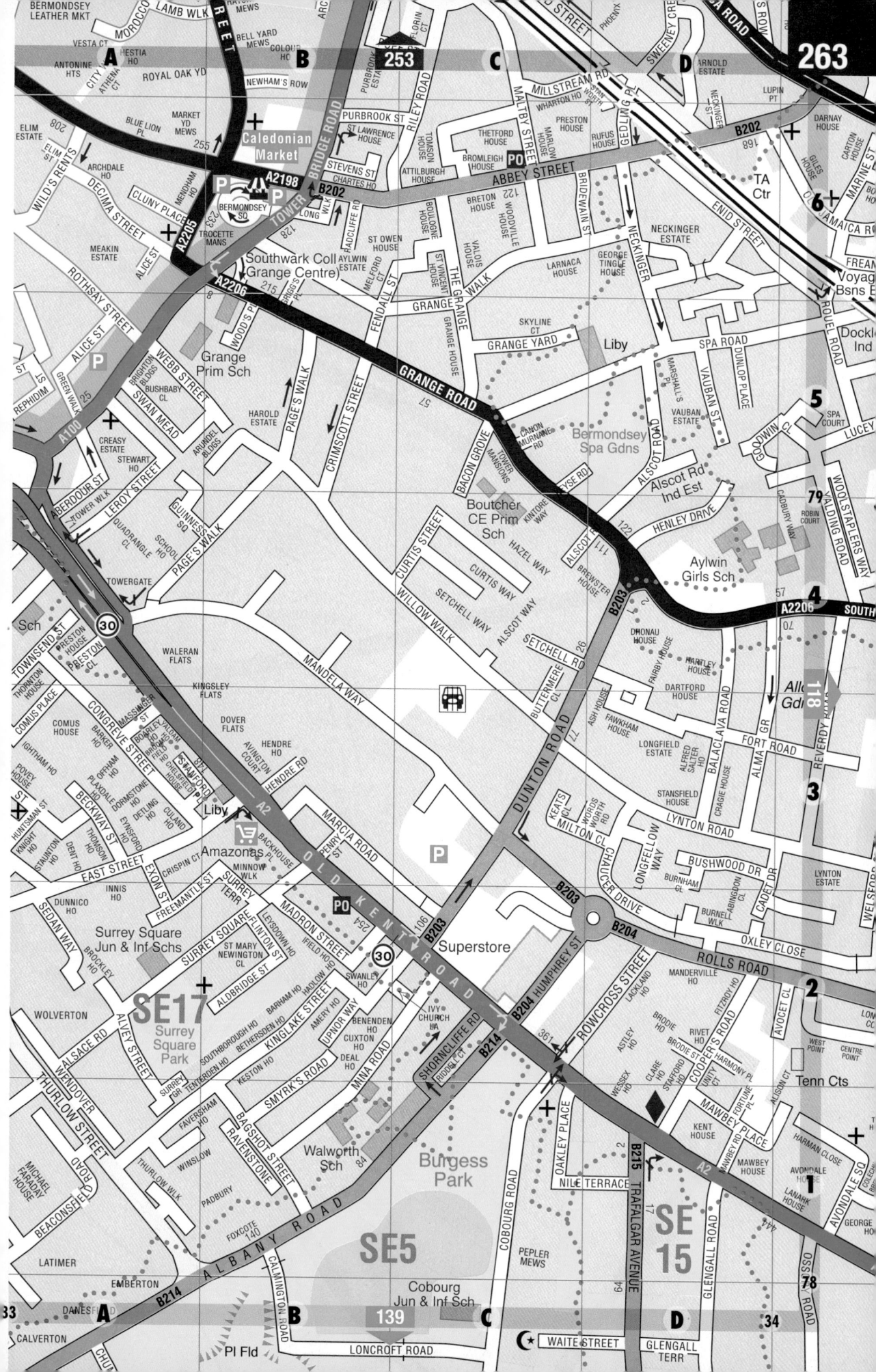
263
253
139
118
A
B
C
D
1
2
3
4
5
6
SE17
SE5
SE 15
Bermondsey Spa Gdns
Burgess Park
Surrey Square Park
Caledonian Market
Southwark Coll (Grange Centre)
Grange Prim Sch
Boutcher CE Prim Sch
Aylwin Girls Sch
Surrey Square Jun & Inf Schs
Walworth Sch
Cobourg Jun & Inf Sch
Alscot Rd Ind Est
Superstore
Amazonas
Liby
TA Ctr
Tenn Cts
Pl Fld
GRANGE ROAD
TOWER BRIDGE ROAD
ABBEY STREET
OLD KENT ROAD
ALBANY ROAD
DUNTON ROAD
ROLLS ROAD
SPA ROAD
MANDELA WAY
WILLOW WALK
PAGE'S WALK
CRIMSCOTT STREET
FENDALL ST
NECKINGER
ENID STREET
LYNTON ROAD
FORT ROAD
BALACLAVA ROAD
COBOURG ROAD
TRAFALGAR AVENUE
GLENGALL ROAD
WAITE STREET
GLENGALL TERR
LONCROFT ROAD
CALMINGTON ROAD
HUMPHREY ST
ROWCROSS STREET
COOPER'S ROAD
MAWBEY PLACE
SURREY SQUARE
CONGREVE STREET
EAST STREET
THURLOW STREET
BEACONSFIELD ROAD
ALSACE RD
MINA ROAD
SMYRK'S ROAD
KINGLAKE STREET
BAGSHOT STREET
MADRON STREET
MARCIA ROAD
DECIMA STREET
ROTHSAY STREET
ALICE ST
LEROY STREET
ABERDOUR ST
WEBB STREET
SWAN MEAD
CURTIS STREET
SETCHELL WAY
ALSCOT WAY
ALSCOT ROAD
HENLEY DRIVE
CHAUCER DRIVE
OXLEY CLOSE
ROUEL ROAD
VALDING ROAD
WOOLSTAPLERS WAY
JAMAICA RD
A2
A2206
A2198
A2205
A100
B202
B203
B204
B214
B215

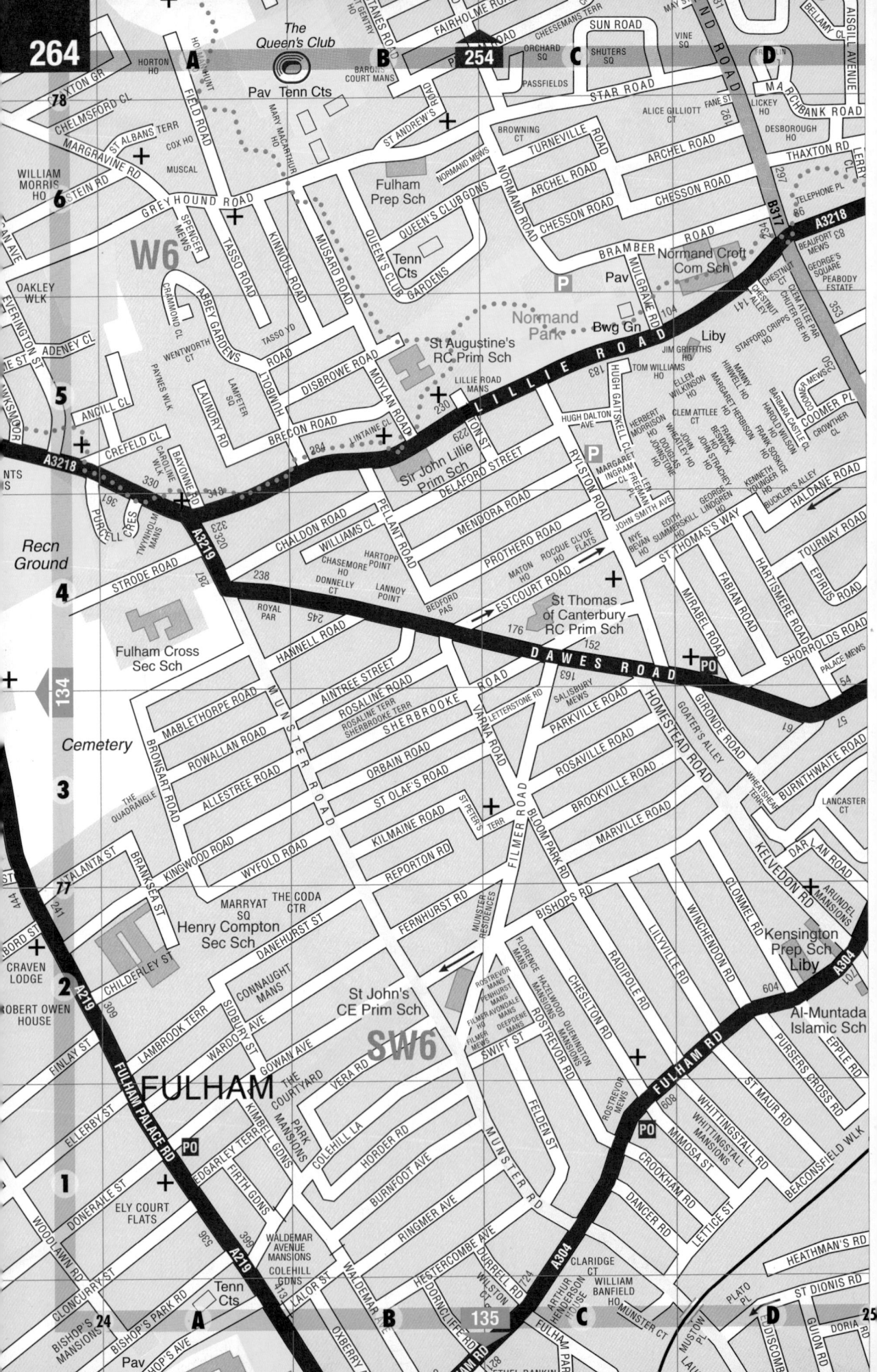
264
A
B
C
D
254
The Queen's Club
Pav Tenn Cts
HORTON HO
BARONS COURT MANS
FAIRHOLME ROAD
CHEESEMANS TERR
SUN ROAD
VINE SQ
ORCHARD SQ
SHUTERS SQ
PASSFIELDS
STAR ROAD
BELLAMY CL
AISGILL AVENUE
MARCHBANK ROAD
LICKEY HO
DESBOROUGH HO
THAXTON RD
ALICE GILLIOTT CT
FANE ST
TELEPHONE PL
78
CHELMSFORD CL
ST ALBANS TERR
COX HO
MARGRAVINE RD
MUSCAL
WILLIAM MORRIS HO
STEIN RD
6
GREYHOUND ROAD
SPENCER MEWS
FIELD ROAD
MARY MACARTHUR HO
ST ANDREW'S ROAD
BROWNING CT
TURNEVILLE ROAD
ARCHEL ROAD
CHESSON ROAD
NORMAND MEWS
Fulham Prep Sch
QUEEN'S CLUB GDNS
NORMAND ROAD
W6
TASSO ROAD
KINNOUL ROAD
MUSARD ROAD
QUEEN'S CLUB GARDENS
Tenn Cts
BRAMBER ROAD
Normand Croft Com Sch
Pav
P
MULGRAVE RD
B317
A3218
BEAUFORT MEWS
GEORGE'S SQUARE
PEABODY ESTATE
OAKLEY WLK
CRAMMOND CL
ABBEY GARDENS
TASSO YD
EVERINGTON ST
ADENEY CL
WENTWORTH CT
Normand Park
Bwg Gn
104
CHESTNUT ALLEY
CHESTNUT CT
CLEM ATLEE PAR
CHUTER EDE HO
STAFFORD CRIPPS HO
Liby
JIM GRIFFITHS HO
St Augustine's RC Prim Sch
DISBROWE ROAD
MOYLAN ROAD
HUMBOLT ROAD
PAYNES WLK
LAMPETER SQ
LAUNDRY RD
LILLIE ROAD
LILLIE ROAD MANS
TOM WILLIAMS HO
HUGH GAITSKELL CL
ELLEN WILKINSON HO
MANNY HINWELL HO
MARGARET HERBISON HO
COOMER MEWS
COOMER PL
5
ANCILL CL
CREFELD CL
BRECON ROAD
LINTAINE CL
284
230
229
183
HUGH DALTON AVE
HERBERT MORRISON HO
CLEM ATTLEE CT
BARBARA CASTLE CL
HAROLD WILSON HO
CROWTHER CL
A3218
CAROLINE WALK
BAYONNE RD
330
318
361
Sir John Lillie Prim Sch
DELAFORD STREET
RYLSTON ROAD
P
MARGARET INGRAM CL
LEN FREEMAN PL
DOUGLAS JOHNSTONE HO
JOHN WHEATLEY HO
FRANK BESWICK HO
JOHN STRACHEY HO
FRANK SOSKICE HO
KENNETH YOUNGER HO
BUCKLER'S ALLEY
HALDANE ROAD
PURCELL CRES
TWYNHOLM MANS
323
320
A3219
CHALDON ROAD
WILLIAMS CL
PELLANT ROAD
MENDORA ROAD
JOHN SMITH AVE
GEORGE LINDGREN HO
EDITH SUMMERSKILL HO
NYE BEVAN HO
ST THOMAS'S WAY
TOURNAY ROAD
Recn Ground
STRODE ROAD
287
238
CHASEMORE HO
HARTOPP POINT
PROTHERO ROAD
ROCQUE HO
CLYDE FLATS
MATON HO
4
DONNELLY CT
LANNOY POINT
ESTCOURT ROAD
BEDFORD PAS
EPIRUS ROAD
MIRABEL ROAD
FABIAN ROAD
HARTISMERE ROAD
ROYAL PAR
245
St Thomas of Canterbury RC Prim Sch
176
152
SHORROLDS ROAD
Fulham Cross Sec Sch
HANNELL ROAD
DAWES ROAD
PO
PALACE MEWS
54
134
AINTREE STREET
MUNSTER ROAD
ROSALINE ROAD
ROSALINE TERR
SHERBROOKE TERR
SHERBROOKE ROAD
163
SALISBURY MEWS
LETTERSTONE RD
HOMESTEAD ROAD
GOATER'S ALLEY
GIRONDE ROAD
61
57
MABLETHORPE ROAD
Cemetery
ROWALLAN ROAD
BRONSART ROAD
ORBAIN ROAD
VARNA ROAD
PARKVILLE ROAD
ROSAVILLE ROAD
WHEATSHEAF TERR
BURNTHWAITE ROAD
3
THE QUADRANGLE
ALLESTREE ROAD
ST OLAF'S ROAD
BROOKVILLE ROAD
LANCASTER CT
ST PETER'S TERR
KILMAINE ROAD
FILMER ROAD
BLOOM PARK RD
MARVILLE ROAD
ATALANTA ST
BRANKSEA ST
KINGWOOD ROAD
WYFOLD ROAD
REPORTON RD
DAR LAN ROAD
KELVEDON RD
ARUNDEL MANSIONS
77
241
444
MARRYAT SQ
THE CODA CTR
FERNHURST RD
BISHOPS RD
CLONMEL RD
Henry Compton Sec Sch
DANEHURST ST
MUNSTER RESIDENCES
Kensington Prep Sch
Liby
CRAVEN LODGE
CHILDERLEY ST
2
A219
CONNAUGHT MANS
FLORENCE MANS
HAZELWOOD MANSIONS
CHESILTON RD
RADIPOLE RD
LILYVILLE RD
WINCHENDON RD
A304
604
ROBERT OWEN HOUSE
309
St John's CE Prim Sch
ROSTREVOR MANS
PENHURST MANS
AVONDALE MANS
DEEPDENE MANS
FILMER MANS
FILMER MEWS
QUEENINGTON MANSIONS
ROSTREVOR RD
Al-Muntada Islamic Sch
LAMBROOK TERR
SIDBURY ST
WARDO AVE
GOWAN AVE
SW6
SWIFT ST
PURSERS CROSS RD
EPPLE RD
FINLAY ST
FULHAM
THE COURTYARD
VERA RD
FELDEN ST
ROSTREVOR MEWS
FULHAM RD
608
ST MAUR RD
ELLERBY ST
FULHAM PALACE RD
KIMBELL GDNS
PARK MANSIONS
COLEHILL LA
HORDER RD
MUNSTER RD
PO
MIMOSA ST
WHITTINGSTALL MANSIONS
WHITTINGSTALL RD
PO
EDGARLEY TERR
FIRTH GDNS
BURNFOOT AVE
CROOKHAM RD
BEACONSFIELD WLK
1
DONERAILE ST
ELY COURT FLATS
RINGMER AVE
DANCER RD
LETTICE ST
WOODLAWN RD
536
399
WALDEMAR AVENUE MANSIONS
HESTERCOMBE AVE
DURRELL RD
A304
CLARIDGE CT
HEATHMAN'S RD
COLEHILL GDNS
724
WILLIAM BANFIELD HO
ARTHUR HENDERSON HOUSE
ST DIONIS RD
CLONCURRY ST
413
LALOR ST
WALDEMAR AVE
WILSTON CL
MUNSTER CT
PLATO PL
BISHOP'S MANSIONS
24
BISHOP'S PARK RD
Tenn Cts
A
B
135
C
D
25
DORNCLIFFE RD
FULHAM PARK
MUSTOW PL
DISCOMBE
GUION RD
DORIA
OXBERRY AVE
Pav
ETHEL RANKIN

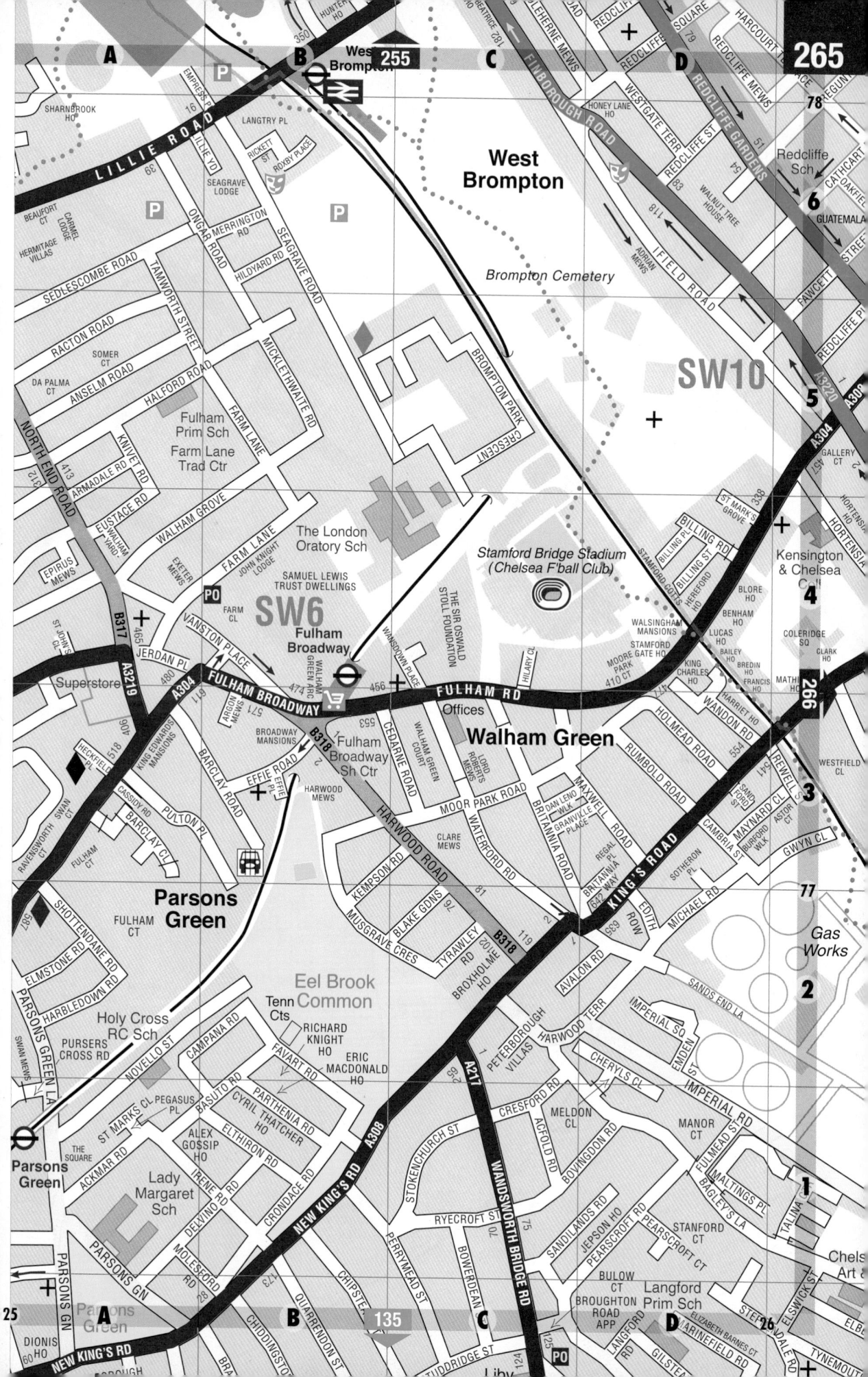
265
A
B
C
D
West Brompton
255
West Brompton
Brompton Cemetery
SW10
SW6
LILLIE ROAD
FINBOROUGH ROAD
REDCLIFFE GARDENS
REDCLIFFE SQUARE
REDCLIFFE MEWS
REDCLIFFE ST
WESTGATE TERR
HONEY LANE HO
HARCOURT TERRACE
IFIELD ROAD
ADRIAN MEWS
WALNUT TREE HOUSE
Redcliffe Sch
CATHCART
OAKFIELD
GUATEMALA
FAWCETT
REDCLIFFE PL
SHARNBROOK HO
EMPRESS PL
LANGTRY PL
RICKETT ST
ROXBY PLACE
LILLIE YD
SEAGRAVE LODGE
SEAGRAVE ROAD
ONGAR ROAD
MERRINGTON RD
HILDYARD RD
BEAUFORT CT
CARMEL LODGE
HERMITAGE VILLAS
SEDLESCOMBE ROAD
TAMWORTH STREET
RACTON ROAD
SOMER CT
DA PALMA CT
ANSELM ROAD
HALFORD ROAD
MICKLETHWAITE RD
BROMPTON PARK CRESCENT
Fulham Prim Sch
Farm Lane Trad Ctr
FARM LANE
NORTH END ROAD
KNIVET RD
ARMADALE RD
EUSTACE RD
WALHAM YARD
WALHAM GROVE
EPIRUS MEWS
EXETER MEWS
JOHN KNIGHT LODGE
The London Oratory Sch
SAMUEL LEWIS TRUST DWELLINGS
Stamford Bridge Stadium (Chelsea F'ball Club)
THE SIR OSWALD STOLL FOUNDATION
STAMFORD COTTS
ST MARK'S GROVE
BILLING RD
BILLING PL
BILLING ST
HEREFORD HO
Kensington & Chelsea Coll
BLORE HO
BENHAM HO
LUCAS HO
COLERIDGE SQ
CLARK HO
BAILEY HO
BREDIN HO
FRANCIS HO
MATHIE HO
KING CHARLES HO
HORTENSIA
GALLERY CT
WALSINGHAM MANSIONS
STAMFORD GATE HO
MOORE PARK CT
HILARY CL
PO
FARM CL
Fulham Broadway
VANSTON PLACE
JERDAN PL
ST JOHN'S CL
B317
A3219
Superstore
A304
FULHAM BROADWAY
FULHAM RD
WANSDOWN PLACE
WALHAM GREEN ARC
ARGON MEWS
BROADWAY MANSIONS
Fulham Broadway Sh Ctr
Offices
Walham Green
CEDARNE ROAD
WALHAM GREEN COURT
LORD ROBERTS MEWS
HOLMEAD ROAD
RUMBOLD ROAD
WANDON RD
HARRIET HO
266
WESTFIELD CL
KING EDWARDS MANSIONS
HECKFIELD PL
BARCLAY ROAD
EFFIE ROAD
EFFIE PL
HARWOOD MEWS
B318
HARWOOD ROAD
MOOR PARK ROAD
WATERFORD RD
CLARE MEWS
BRITANNIA ROAD
MAXWELL ROAD
DAN LENO WLK
GRANVILLE PLACE
REGAL PL
BRITANNIA WAY
KING'S ROAD
CAMBRIA ST
MAYNARD CL
SANDFORD ST
BURFORD WLK
ASTOR CT
GWYN CL
TREWELL
SOTHERON PL
MICHAEL RD
EDITH ROW
CASSIDY RD
PULTON PL
BARCLAY CL
RAVENSWORTH CT
SWAN CT
FULHAM CT
Parsons Green
KEMPSON RD
BLAKE GDNS
MUSGRAVE CRES
TYRAWLEY RD
BROXHOLME HO
SHOTTENDANE RD
ELMSTONE RD
HARBLEDOWN RD
PARSONS GREEN LA
Eel Brook Common
Tenn Cts
RICHARD KNIGHT HO
ERIC MACDONALD HO
Holy Cross RC Sch
PURSERS CROSS RD
SWAN MEWS
NOVELLO ST
CAMPANA RD
FAVART RD
PARTHENIA RD
CYRIL THATCHER HO
BASUTO RD
ELTHIRON RD
PEGASUS PL
ST MARKS CL
ALEX GOSSIP HO
IRENE RD
DELVINO RD
CRONDACE RD
THE SQUARE
ACKMAR RD
Lady Margaret Sch
Parsons Green
PARSONS GN
MOLESFORD RD
NEW KING'S RD
A308
A217
WANDSWORTH BRIDGE RD
AVALON RD
PETERBOROUGH VILLAS
HARWOOD TERR
CRESFORD RD
ACFOLD RD
MELDON CL
BOVINGDON RD
STOKENCHURCH ST
RYECROFT ST
PERRYMEAD ST
BOWERDEAN ST
SANDILANDS RD
JEPSON HO
PEARSCROFT RD
PEARSCROFT CT
STANFORD CT
BULOW CT
BROUGHTON ROAD APP
Langford Prim Sch
LANGFORD RD
ELIZABETH BARNES CT
MARINEFIELD RD
STEPHENDALE RD
SANDS END LA
IMPERIAL SQ
EMDEN ST
CHERYLS CL
IMPERIAL RD
MANOR CT
FULMEAD ST
MALTINGS PL
BAGLEY'S LA
TALINA
ELSWICK ST
Chelsea Art
Gas Works
TYNEMOUTH
A3220
25
26
135
QUARRENDON ST
CHIDDINGSTONE
DIONIS HO
TUDDRIDGE ST
PO

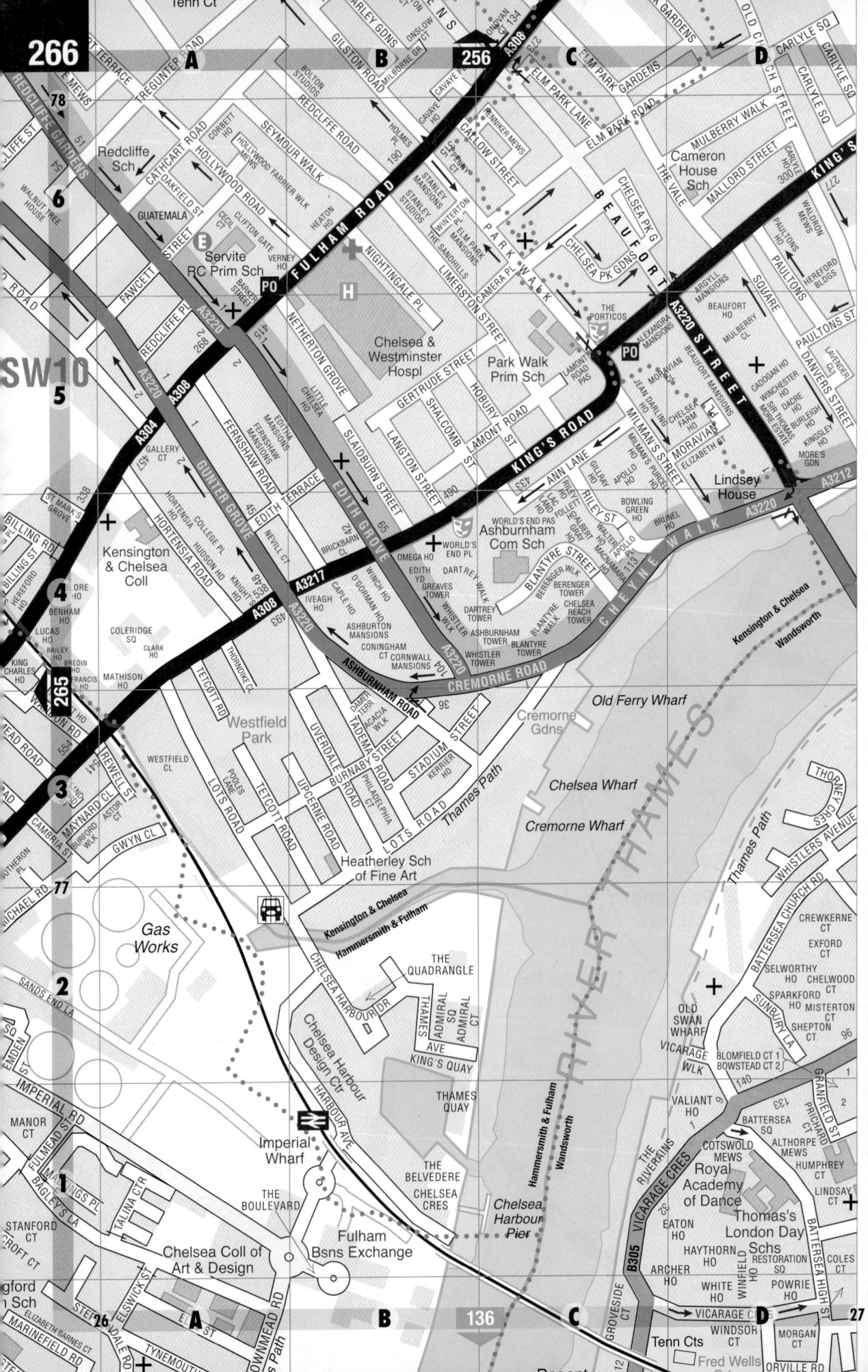

Tenn Ct
A
B
256
C
D
78
6
5
4
3
77
2
1
SW10
265
136
26
27
REDCLIFFE GARDENS
TREGUNTER ROAD
GILSTON ROAD
REDCLIFFE ROAD
SEYMOUR WALK
CATHCART ROAD
HOLLYWOOD ROAD
OAKFIELD ST
GUATEMALA
HOLLYWOOD FARRIER WALK
CLIFTON GATE
FULHAM ROAD
NIGHTINGALE PL
ELM PARK GARDENS
ELM PARK LANE
ELM PARK ROAD
CALLOW STREET
MULBERRY WALK
MALLORD STREET
THE VALE
CARLYLE SQ
OLD CHURCH STREET
BEAUFORT
PARK WALK
LIMERSTON STREET
CAMERA PL
CHELSEA PK GDNS
KING'S ROAD
PAULTONS SQUARE
PAULTONS ST
DANVERS STREET
BEAUFORT STREET
Cameron House Sch
Redcliffe Sch
Servite RC Prim Sch
PO
H
Chelsea & Westminster Hospl
Park Walk Prim Sch
THE PORTICOS
ALEXANDRA MANSIONS
MORAVIAN CL
BEAUFORT MANSIONS
GERTRUDE STREET
SHALCOMB ST
LAMONT ROAD
HOBURY ST
LANGTON STREET
SLAIDBURN STREET
NETHERTON GROVE
FERNSHAW ROAD
EDITH TERRACE
EDITH GROVE
GUNTER GROVE
MILMAN'S STREET
ANN LANE
RILEY ST
Lindsey House
CHEYNE WALK
A3220
A3212
A3217
A308
A304
REDCLIFFE PL
FAWCETT
HORTENSIA ROAD
Kensington & Chelsea Coll
COLERIDGE SQ
WORLD'S END PL
Ashburnham Com Sch
BLANTYRE STREET
DARTREY WALK
WHISTLER WALK
ASHBURNHAM ROAD
CREMORNE ROAD
Old Ferry Wharf
Cremorne Gdns
Chelsea Wharf
Cremorne Wharf
RIVER THAMES
Kensington & Chelsea
Wandsworth
Westfield Park
TETCOTT ROAD
LOTS ROAD
UVERDALE ROAD
UPCERNE ROAD
BURNABY STREET
TADEMA ROAD
STADIUM STREET
Thames Path
Heatherley Sch of Fine Art
Hammersmith & Fulham
Gas Works
SANDS END LA
IMPERIAL RD
CHELSEA HARBOUR DR
THE QUADRANGLE
ADMIRAL SQ
THAMES AVE
KING'S QUAY
Chelsea Harbour Design Ctr
HARBOUR AVE
THAMES QUAY
Imperial Wharf
THE BOULEVARD
THE BELVEDERE
CHELSEA CRES
Chelsea Harbour Pier
Fulham Bsns Exchange
Chelsea Coll of Art & Design
TYNEMOUTH
TOWNMEAD RD
BAGLEY'S LA
THORNEY CRES
WHISTLERS AVENUE
BATTERSEA CHURCH RD
SUNBURY LA
OLD SWAN WHARF
VICARAGE WLK
VICARAGE CRES
THE RIVERAINS
B305
Royal Academy of Dance
Thomas's London Day Schs
BATTERSEA HIGH ST
GROVESIDE CT
Tenn Cts
Fred Wells
ORVILLE RD

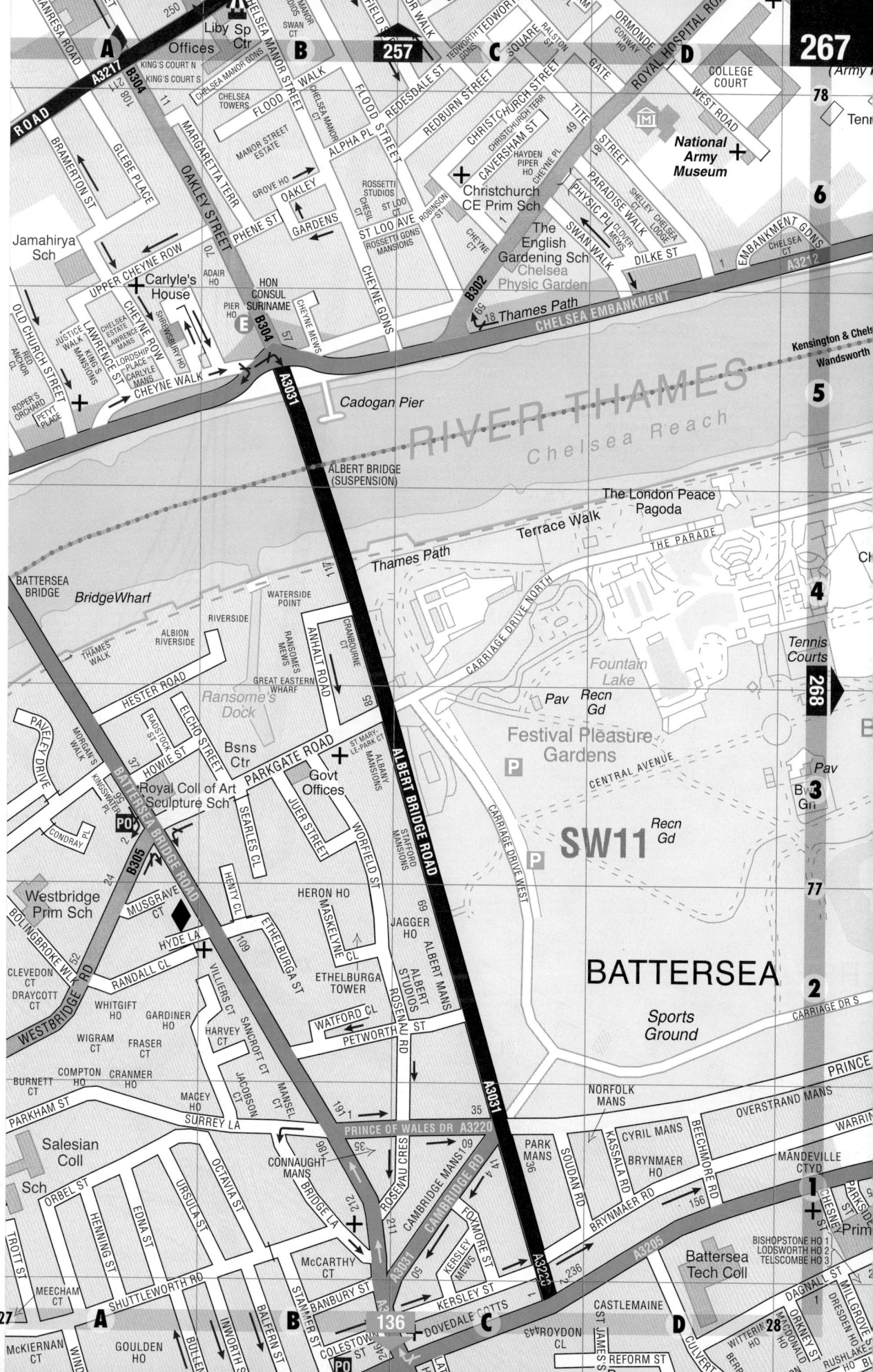

A
B
C
D
257
268
136
27
28
78
77
6
5
4
3
2
1
RIVER THAMES
Chelsea Reach
BATTERSEA
SW11
Festival Pleasure Gardens
National Army Museum
Cadogan Pier
ALBERT BRIDGE (SUSPENSION)
BATTERSEA BRIDGE
ALBERT BRIDGE ROAD
BATTERSEA BRIDGE ROAD
CHELSEA EMBANKMENT
OAKLEY STREET
CHEYNE WALK
ROYAL HOSPITAL ROAD
PRINCE OF WALES DR
Thames Path
The London Peace Pagoda
Terrace Walk
Fountain Lake
Sports Ground
Carlyle's House
Chelsea Physic Garden
The English Gardening Sch
Christchurch CE Prim Sch
Jamahiriya Sch
Royal Coll of Art Sculpture Sch
Westbridge Prim Sch
Salesian Coll
Battersea Tech Coll
Ransome's Dock
Bsns Ctr
Govt Offices
Kensington & Chelsea
Wandsworth

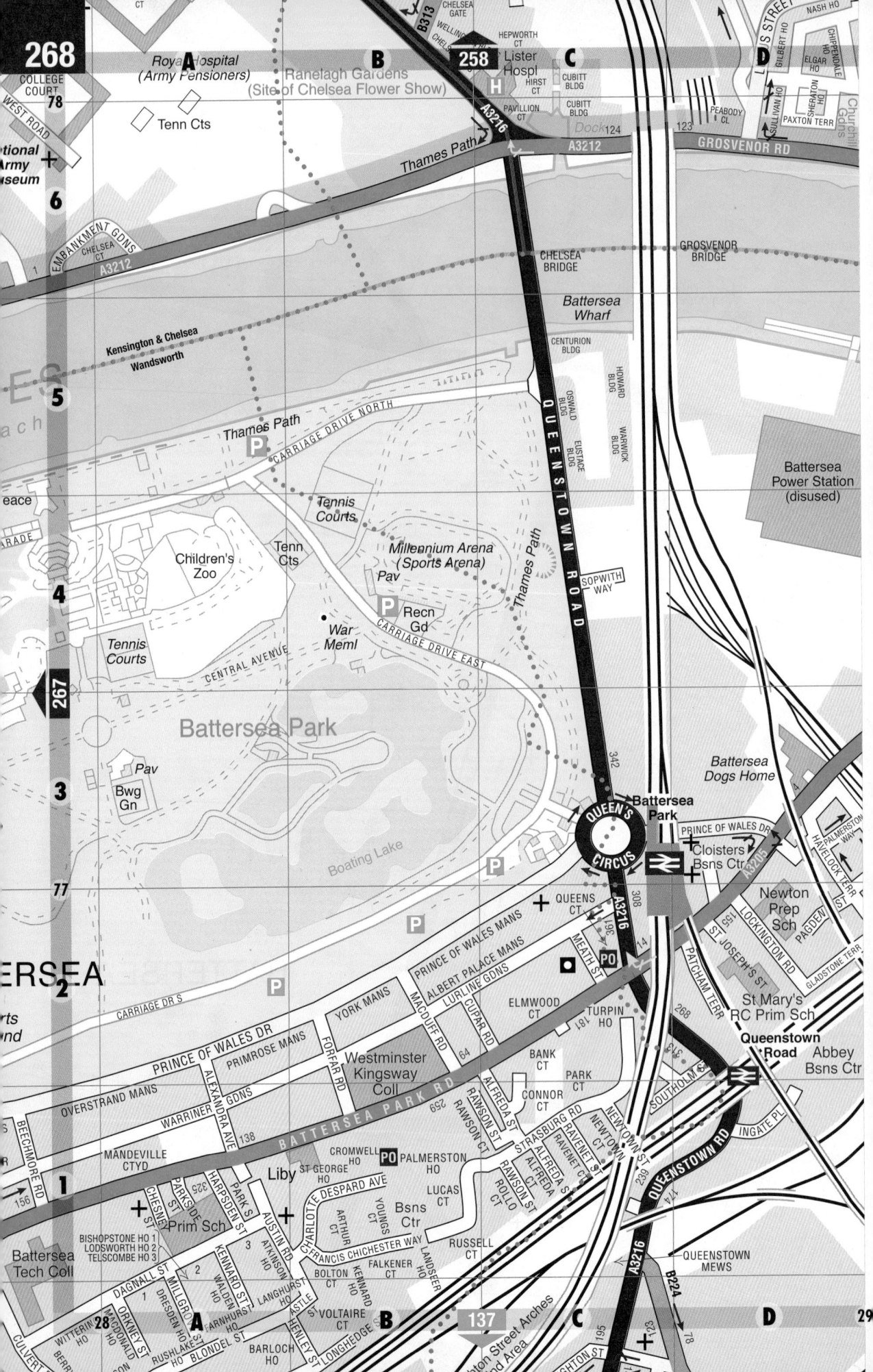
Royal Hospital (Army Pensioners)
Ranelagh Gardens (Site of Chelsea Flower Show)
Lister Hospl
Tenn Cts
COLLEGE COURT
WEST ROAD
CHELSEA GATE
HEPWORTH CT
HIRST CT
PAVILLION CT
CUBITT BLDG
PEABODY CL
GROSVENOR RD
PAXTON TERR
NASH HO
ELGAR HO
Thames Path
A3212
A3216
B313
EMBANKMENT GDNS
CHELSEA CT
CHELSEA BRIDGE
GROSVENOR BRIDGE
Battersea Wharf
Kensington & Chelsea
Wandsworth
CENTURION BLDG
HOWARD BLDG
OSWALD BLDG
EUSTACE BLDG
WARWICK BLDG
QUEENSTOWN ROAD
Battersea Power Station (disused)
CARRIAGE DRIVE NORTH
Tennis Courts
Children's Zoo
Tenn Cts
Millennium Arena (Sports Arena)
Pav
Recn Gd
War Meml
CARRIAGE DRIVE EAST
CENTRAL AVENUE
SOPWITH WAY
Battersea Park
Bwg Gn
Boating Lake
Battersea Dogs Home
Battersea Park
QUEEN'S CIRCUS
PRINCE OF WALES DR
Cloisters Bsns Ctr
PALMERSTON WAY
HAVELOCK TERR
Newton Prep Sch
QUEENS CT
PRINCE OF WALES MANS
ALBERT PALACE MANS
LURLINE GDNS
MEATH ST
LOCKINGTON RD
ST JOSEPH'S ST
PAGDEN ST
GLADSTONE TERR
PATCHAM TERR
St Mary's RC Prim Sch
Queenstown Road
Abbey Bsns Ctr
CARRIAGE DR S
YORK MANS
MACDUFF RD
CUPAR RD
ELMWOOD CT
TURPIN HO
PRIMROSE MANS
FORFAR RD
Westminster Kingsway Coll
BANK CT
PARK CT
CONNOR CT
SOUTHOLM ST
OVERSTRAND MANS
ALEXANDRA AVE
WARRINER GDNS
BATTERSEA PARK RD
RAWSON ST
ALFREDA ST
STRASBURG RD
RAVENET ST
NEWTOWN ST
NEWTOWN CT
INGATE PL
BEECHMORE RD
MANDEVILLE CTYD
CROMWELL HO
PALMERSTON HO
ST GEORGE HO
Liby
CHARLOTTE DESPARD AVE
LUCAS CT
Bsns Ctr
ARTHUR CT
YOUNGS CT
ROLLO CT
RAWSON CT
ALFREDA CT
QUEENSTOWN RD
CHESNEY ST
PARKSIDE ST
HARPSDEN ST
PARK S
AUSTIN RD
Prim Sch
BISHOPSTONE HO 1
LODSWORTH HO 2
TELSCOMBE HO 3
FRANCIS CHICHESTER WAY
RUSSELL CT
QUEENSTOWN MEWS
Battersea Tech Coll
DAGNALL ST
KENNARD ST
WALDEN HO
ATKINSON HO
BOLTON CT
KENNARD HO
FALKENER CT
LANDSEER HO
MILLGROVE ST
DRESDEN HO
FARNHURST HO
LANGHURST HO
ASTLE ST
VOLTAIRE CT
HENLEY ST
LONGHEDGE ST
ORKNEY ST
MACDONALD HO
WITTERING HO
RUSHLAKE HO
BLONDEL ST
BARLOCH HO
CULVERT
Stewarts Lane Arches Ind Area
B224
A3205
267
258
137
29

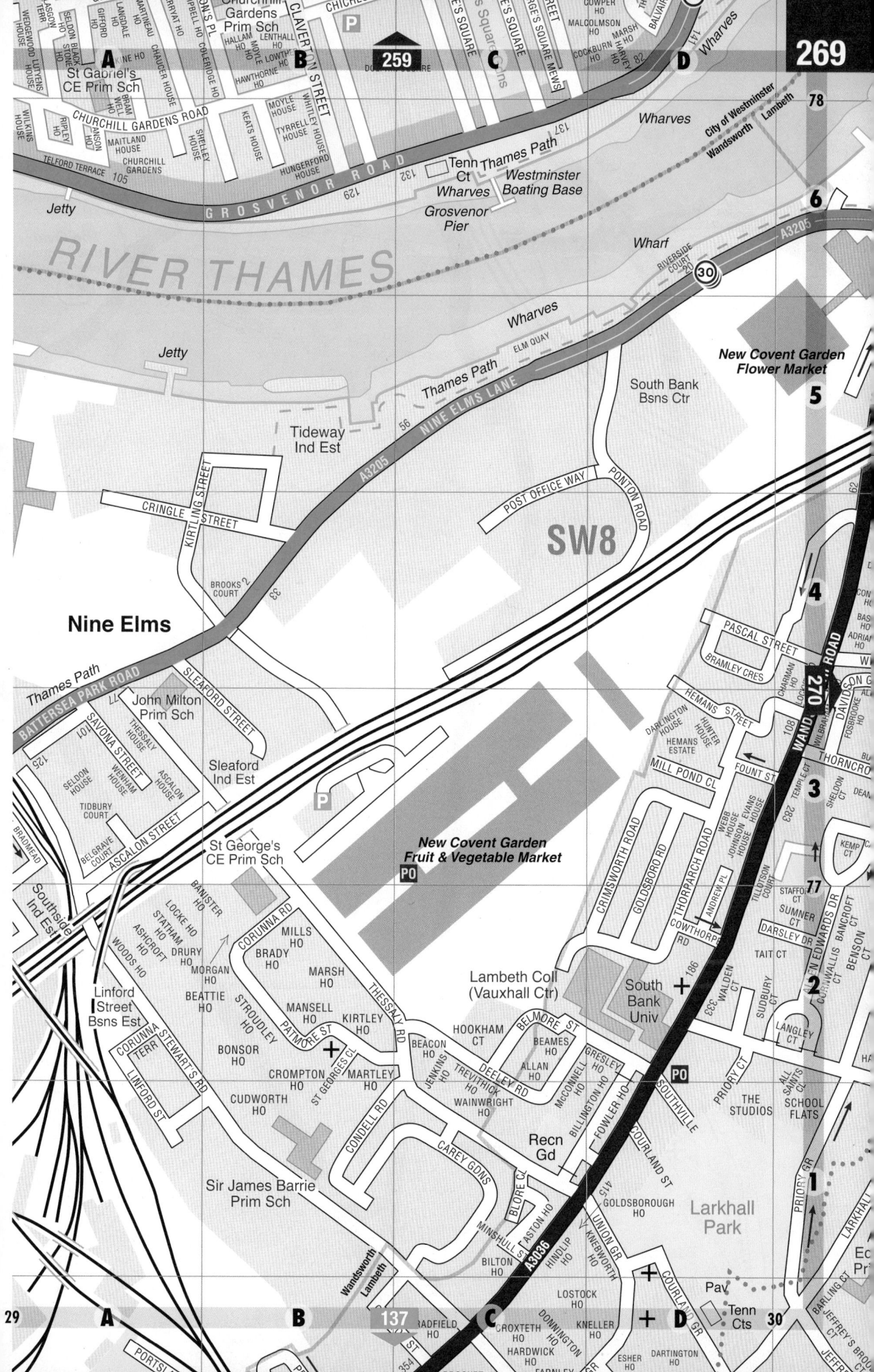

RIVER THAMES
Nine Elms
SW8
New Covent Garden Flower Market
New Covent Garden Fruit & Vegetable Market
South Bank Bsns Ctr
Tideway Ind Est
Thames Path
Wharves
Wharf
Jetty
Grosvenor Pier
Westminster Boating Base
GROSVENOR ROAD
NINE ELMS LANE
BATTERSEA PARK ROAD
A3205
A3036
CHURCHILL GARDENS ROAD
Churchill Gardens Prim Sch
St Gabriel's CE Prim Sch
CLAVERTON STREET
TELFORD TERRACE
CRINGLE STREET
KIRTLING STREET
POST OFFICE WAY
PONTON ROAD
John Milton Prim Sch
SLEAFORD STREET
Sleaford Ind Est
SAVONA STREET
ASCALON STREET
St George's CE Prim Sch
Southside Ind Est
Linford Street Bsns Est
CORUNNA RD
CORUNNA TERR
STEWART'S RD
LINFORD ST
THESSALY RD
PATMORE ST
CONDELL RD
CAREY GDNS
Sir James Barrie Prim Sch
Lambeth Coll (Vauxhall Ctr)
South Bank Univ
BELMORE ST
DEELEY RD
Recn Gd
SOUTHVILLE
COURLAND ST
Larkhall Park
PASCAL STREET
BRAMLEY CRES
HEMANS STREET
HEMANS ESTATE
MILL POND CL
FOUNT ST
CRIMSWORTH ROAD
GOLDSBORO RD
THORPARCH ROAD
COWTHORPE RD
WANDSWORTH ROAD
PRIORY GR
PRIORY CT
THE STUDIOS
SCHOOL FLATS
City of Westminster
Wandsworth
Lambeth
Tenn Cts
Pav
259
137
270

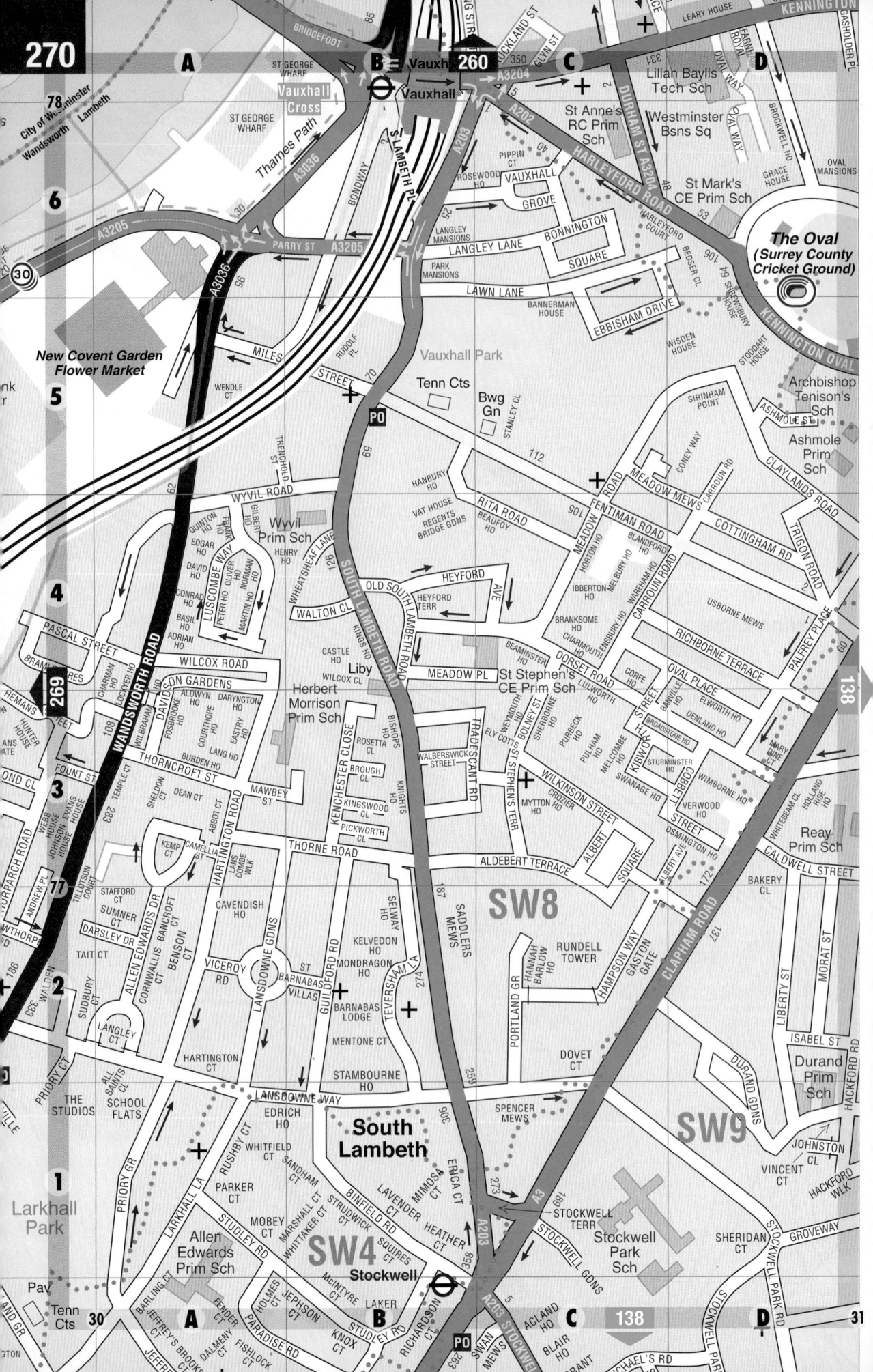

Vauxhall
Vauxhall Cross
St George Wharf
Thames Path
New Covent Garden Flower Market
Vauxhall Park
Tenn Cts
Bwg Gn
Lilian Baylis Tech Sch
St Anne's RC Prim Sch
Westminster Bsns Sq
St Mark's CE Prim Sch
The Oval (Surrey County Cricket Ground)
Archbishop Tenison's Sch
Ashmole Prim Sch
Wyvil Prim Sch
Herbert Morrison Prim Sch
Liby
St Stephen's CE Prim Sch
Reay Prim Sch
Durand Prim Sch
SW8
SW9
SW4
South Lambeth
Stockwell
Stockwell Park Sch
Allen Edwards Prim Sch
Larkhall Park
Harleyford Road
Kennington Oval
South Lambeth Road
Wandsworth Road
Clapham Road
Fentiman Road
Lansdowne Way
Wyvil Road
Parry St
Miles Street

260
269
138

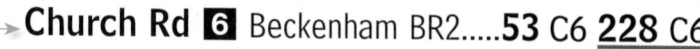

Place name May be abbreviated on the map

Location number Present when a number indicates the place's position in a crowded area of mapping

Locality, town or village Shown when more than one place has the same name

Postcode district District for the indexed place

Standard-scale reference Page number and grid reference for the standard-scale mapping on pages 1–227

Large-scale reference Page number and grid reference for the large-scale central London mapping on pages 229–270, underlined in red

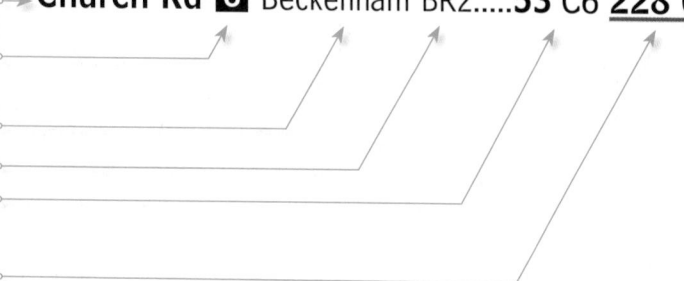

Cities, towns and villages are listed in **CAPITAL LETTERS** **Public and commercial buildings** are highlighted in **magenta**
Places of interest are highlighted in **blue** with a star★

Abbreviations used in the index

Abbreviation	Meaning	Abbreviation	Meaning	Abbreviation	Meaning	Abbreviation	Meaning	Abbreviation	Meaning
Acad	Academy	Comm	Common	Gd	Ground	L	Leisure	Prom	Promenade
App	Approach	Cott	Cottage	Gdn	Garden	La	Lane	Rd	Road
Arc	Arcade	Cres	Crescent	Gn	Green	Liby	Library	Recn	Recreation
Ave	Avenue	Cswy	Causeway	Gr	Grove	Mdw	Meadow	Ret	Retail
Bglw	Bungalow	Ct	Court	H	Hall	Meml	Memorial	Sh	Shopping
Bldg	Building	Ctr	Centre	Ho	House	Mkt	Market	Sq	Square
Bsns, Bus	Business	Ctry	Country	Hospl	Hospital	Mus	Museum	St	Street
Bvd	Boulevard	Cty	County	HQ	Headquarters	Orch	Orchard	Sta	Station
Cath	Cathedral	Dr	Drive	Hts	Heights	Pal	Palace	Terr	Terrace
Cir	Circus	Dro	Drove	Ind	Industrial	Par	Parade	TH	Town Hall
Cl	Close	Ed	Education	Inst	Institute	Pas	Passage	Univ	University
Cnr	Corner	Emb	Embankment	Int	International	Pk	Park	Wk, Wlk	Walk
Coll	College	Est	Estate	Intc	Interchange	Pl	Place	Wr	Water
Com	Community	Ex	Exhibition	Junc	Junction	Prec	Precinct	Yd	Yard

Index of towns, villages, streets, hospitals, industrial estates, railway stations, schools, shopping centres, universities and places of interest

A

Aaron Ct BR3 . . . . 207 D6
Aaron Hill Rd E6 . . . . 100 C2
Abady Ho SW1 . . . . 259 D4
Abberley Mews 9 SW8 . . . . 137 B2
Abberton IG8 . . . . 37 C5
Abbess Cl
11 Newham E6 . . . . 100 A2
Streatham SW2 . . . . 160 D3
Abbeville Mews 3 SW4 . . . . 137 D1
Abbeville Rd
Clapham Pk SW4 . . . . 159 C6
Hornsey N8 . . . . 49 D5
Abbey Ave HA0 . . . . 88 A5
Abbey Bsns Ctr SW8 . . . . 137 B4 268 D2
Abbey Cl Hayes UB3 . . . . 106 B5
Northolt UB5 . . . . 85 B4
Pinner HA5 . . . . 40 C6
Abbey Cres DA17 . . . . 125 C2
Abbey Ct
6 Bedford Pk W12 . . . . 111 C3
Camberwell SE17 . . . . 262 B1
Church End N3 . . . . 47 C6
5 Edgware HA8 . . . . 26 D5
Hampton TW12 . . . . 173 C3
St John's Wood NW8 . . 229 A4
Twickenham TW2 . . . . 152 B2
Abbeydale Rd HA0 . . . . 88 C6
Abbey Dr SW17 . . . . 181 A5
Abbeyfield Cl CR4 . . . . 180 C1
Abbeyfield Rd SE16 . . . . 118 C2
Abbeyfields Cl NW10 . . . . 88 C5
Abbey Gdns
10 Bermondsey SE16 . . . 118 A2
Chislehurst BR7 . . . . 188 C2
St John's Wood NW8 . . . . 92 A5 229 B3
West Kensington W6 . . . . 135 A6 264 A5
Abbey Gr SE2 . . . . 124 B2
Abbeyhill Rd DA15 . . . . 168 C2
Abbey Ho Newham E15 . . . 98 C5
St John's Wood NW8 . . 229 B2
Abbey Ind Est CR4 . . . . 202 D4
Abbey La
Beckenham BR3 . . . . 185 C3
Mill Meads E15 . . . . 98 B5
Abbey Lane Commercial Est 1 E15 . . . . 98 C5
Abbey Lo Bromley SE12 . . 187 B6
1 Ealing W5 . . . . 109 C6
Lisson Gr NW8 . . . . 230 B1
Abbey Manufacturing Est HA0 . . . . 88 B6
Abbey Mews
Brentford TW7 . . . . 131 B4
Walthamstow E17 . . . . 53 C4
Abbey Mount DA17 . . . . 125 B1
Abbey Orchard St SW1 . . . . 115 D3 259 D6
Abbey Orchard Street Est SW1 . . . . 259 D6
Abbey Par Ealing NW10 . . 88 B4
Merton SW19 . . . . 180 A3
Abbey Park Ind Est IG11 . . . . 101 A6
Abbey Pk BR3 . . . . 185 C3
Abbey Prim Sch SM4 . . . 201 C2
Abbey Rd Barking IG11 . . 100 D6
Bexley DA7 . . . . 147 A1
Croydon CR0 . . . . 220 D5
Enfield EN1 . . . . 17 C6
Erith DA17 . . . . 125 A3
Ilford IG2 . . . . 57 B4
Lower Halliford TW17 . . . 192 C1
Merton SW19 . . . . 180 A2
Newham E15 . . . . 98 C5
St John's Wood NW8 . . . . 92 A5 229 A4
Wembley NW10 . . . . 88 D5
Abbey Rd Motorist Ctr 4 NW6 . . . . 91 D6
Abbey St
Bermondsey SE1 . . . . 117 D3 263 C6
Newham E13 . . . . 99 A3
Abbey Terr SE2 . . . . 124 C2
Abbey Trad Est SE26 . . . 185 B5
Abbey View NW7 . . . . 11 D1
Abbey Wlk KT8 . . . . 195 D5
ABBEY WOOD 124 B3
Abbey Wood Rd SE2 . . . 124 C2
Abbey Wood Sch SE2 . . 124 A3
Abbey Wood Sta SE2 . . . 124 C3
Abbot Cl HA4 . . . . 62 D5
Abbot Ct SW8 . . . . 270 A3
Abbot Ho 14 E14 . . . . 119 D6
Abbotsbury Cl
Kensington W14 . . . . 113 B4 244 C1
Mill Meads E15 . . . . 98 A5
Abbotsbury Gdns HA5 . . . 40 C3
Abbotsbury Ho W14 . . . 244 B2
Abbotsbury Mews SE15 . . . . 140 C2
Abbotsbury Prim Sch SM4 . . . . 201 D4
Abbotsbury Rd
Coney Hall BR2, BR4 . . . . 224 D6
Kensington W14 . . . . 113 B4 244 C1
Morden SM4 . . . . 201 D5
Abbots Cl BR5 . . . . 211 A1
Abbots Ct SE25 . . . . 205 C6
Abbots Dr HA2 . . . . 63 C6
Abbotsfield Sch UB10 . . . 82 D5
Abbotsford Ave N15 . . . . 51 A5
Abbotsford Gdns IG8 . . . 37 A3
Abbotsford Rd IG3 . . . . 80 B6
Abbots Gdns N2 . . . . 48 B5
Abbots Gn CR0, CR2 . . . . 222 D2
Abbots Green CR2 . . . . 222 D2
Abbotshade Rd 15 SE16 . . . . 118 D5
Abbotshall Ave N14 . . . . 15 C1
Abbotshall Rd SE6 . . . . 164 B2
Abbots Ho
Kensington W14 . . . . 254 C5
Pimlico SW1 . . . . 259 C1
Walthamstow E17 . . . . 35 B1
Abbots La SE1 . . 117 C5 253 B3
Abbotsleigh Cl SM2 . . . . 217 D1
Abbotsleigh Rd SW16 . . 181 C5
Abbotsmede Cl TW1 . . . 152 D2
Abbots Pk SW2 . . . . 160 C3
Abbot's Pl NW6 . . . . 91 D6
Abbots Rd
Burnt Oak HA8 . . . . 27 B3
Cheam SM3 . . . . 217 A4
Abbots Rd *continued*
Newham E6 . . . . 99 D6
Abbot St E8 . . . . 73 D2
Abbots Terr N8 . . . . 50 A3
Abbotstone Ho 4 E5 . . . . 74 A6
Abbotstone Rd SW15 . . . 134 C2
Abbotsview Ct NW7 . . . . 12 A1
Abbots Way BR3 . . . . 207 A4
Abbotswell Rd SE4 . . . . 163 B6
Abbotswood Cl 7 DA17 . . . . 125 A3
Abbotswood Gdns IG5 . . 56 B6
Abbotswood Rd
London SE22 . . . . 139 C1
Streatham SW16 . . . . 159 D1
Abbotswood Way UB3 . . 106 B5
Abbott Ave SW20 . . . . 178 D2
Abbott Cl
Hampton TW12 . . . . 173 A4
Northolt UB5 . . . . 63 B2
Abbott Ho SW12 . . . . 158 D4
Abbott Rd E14 . . . . 98 B1
Abbotts Cl
Canonbury N1 . . . . 73 A2
Romford RM7 . . . . 59 D6
Woolwich SE28 . . . . 124 C6
Abbotts Cres
Chingford E4 . . . . 36 B6
Enfield EN2 . . . . 4 D3
Abbotts Ct HA2 . . . . 64 B6
Abbotts Dr HA0 . . . . 65 B6
Abbotts Park Rd E10 . . . . 54 A2
Abbotts Rd Barnet EN5 . . . . 1 D1
Mitcham CR4 . . . . 203 C5
Southall UB1 . . . . 107 A5
Abbotts Wharf 4 E14 . . . 97 C1
Abbott's Wlk DA7 . . . . 146 D5
Abchurch La EC2, EC4 . . . . 117 B6 252 D6
Abchurch Yd EC4 . . . . 252 C6
Abdale Rd W12 . . . . 112 B5
Abel Ho
7 Kennington SE11 . . . . 138 C6
Woolwich SE18 . . . . 123 A2
Abenglen Ind Est UB3 . . 105 B4
Aberavon Rd E3 . . . . 97 A4
Abercairn Rd SW16 . . . . 181 C3
Aberconway Rd SM4 . . . 201 D5
Abercorn Cl
Finchley NW7 . . . . 29 A3
St John's Wood NW8 . . . . 92 A4 229 A2
Abercorn Cres HA2 . . . . 41 D1
Abercorn Gdns
Harrow HA3 . . . . 43 D2
Ilford RM6 . . . . 58 B3
Abercorn Gr HA4 . . . . 39 B5
Abercorn Mans NW8 . . 229 B3
Abercorn Mews 10 TW10 . . . . 132 B1
Abercorn Pl NW8 . . . . 92 A5 229 A3
Abercorn Rd
Finchley NW7 . . . . 29 A3
Stanmore HA7 . . . . 25 C3
Abercorn Trad Est HA0 . . 87 D6
Abercorn Way SE1 . . . . 118 A1
Abercrombie Dr EN1 . . . . 6 A4
Abercrombie Ho 1 W12 . . . . 112 B6
Abercrombie St SW11 . . 136 C3
Aberdale Ct 22 SE16 . . . . 118 D4
Aberdare Cl BR4 . . . . 224 A6
Aberdare Gdns
Finchley NW7 . . . . 28 D3
South Hampstead NW6 . . . 69 D1
Aberdare Rd EN3 . . . . 6 C1
Aberdeen Cotts HA7 . . . . 25 C3
Aberdeen Ct
Canonbury N5 . . . . 73 A3
Paddington W2 . . . . 236 C5
Aberdeen Ctr N5 . . . . 73 A3
Aberdeen La N5 . . . . 73 A3
Aberdeen Mans WC1 . . 240 A6
Aberdeen Par N18 . . . . 34 B5
Aberdeen Pk N5 . . . . 73 A3
Aberdeen Pl NW8 . . . . 92 B3 236 C6
Aberdeen Rd
Canonbury N5 . . . . 73 A4
Croydon CR0 . . . . 221 B4
Dudden Hill NW10 . . . . 67 D3
Edmonton N18 . . . . 34 B5
Harrow HA3 . . . . 24 D1
Aberdeen Terr SE3 . . . . 142 B3
Aberdour Rd IG3 . . . . 80 B6

Aar–Abi

Aberdour St SE1 . . . . 117 C2 263 A4
Aberfeldy Ho SE5 . . . . 138 D5
Aberfeldy St E14 . . . . 98 A1
Aberford Gdns SE18 . . . 144 A4
Aberfoyle Rd SW16 . . . . 181 D4
Abergeldie Rd SE12 . . . . 165 B5
Abernethy Rd SE13 . . . . 142 C1
Abersham Rd E8 . . . . 73 D3
Abery St SE18 . . . . 123 C2
Ability Plaza 8 E8 . . . . 73 D1
Ability Twrs EC1 . . . . 235 A2
Abingdon W14 . . . . 254 D3
Abingdon Cl
Fulham SE1 . . . . 263 D2
Hillingdon UB10 . . . . 82 B6
Kentish Town NW1 . . . . 71 D2
Wimbledon SW19 . . . . 180 A4
Abingdon Ct
Earl's Ct W8 . . . . 255 B5
Edgware HA8 . . . . 26 A6
Upper Tooting SW17 . . . . 180 D4
Abingdon Gdns W8 . . . 255 B5
Abingdon Ho
Bromley BR1 . . . . 187 B3
Spitalfields E2 . . . . 243 C6
Abingdon Lo
2 Barnet EN5 . . . . 1 A1
Bromley BR2 . . . . 186 D1
Abingdon Mans W8 . . . 255 A6
Abingdon Rd
Finchley N3 . . . . 30 A1
Kensington W8 . 113 C3 255 B5
Thornton Heath SW16 . . . 182 A2
Abingdon St SW1 . . . . 116 A3 260 A6
Abingdon Villas W8 . . . . 113 C3 255 B5
Abinger Cl Barking IG11 . . 80 A4
Bickley BR1 . . . . 210 A6
New Addington CR0 . . . . 224 A2
Wallington SM6 . . . . 220 A3
Abinger Ct
3 Ealing W5 . . . . 109 C6
Thornton Heath CR0 . . . . 204 D2

Abinger Ct *continued*
Wallington SM6 .....220 A3
Abinger Gdns TW7 .....130 C2
Abinger Gr SE8 .....141 B6
Abinger Ho
Borough The SE1 .....252 C1
2 Kingston u T KT2 .....176 D3
Abinger Mews W9 .....91 C3
Abinger Rd W4 .....111 C3
Abington Ho NW11 .....48 A3
Ablett St SE16 .....118 C1
Abney Gdns 5 N16 .....73 D6
Abney Park Cemetery* N16 .....73 C6
Abney Park Ct N16 .....73 D6
Aborfield 6 NW5 .....71 C3
Aboyne Dr SW20 .....178 A1
Aboyne Rd
Neasden NW10 .....67 C5
Wandsworth SW17 .....158 B1
Abraham Cl WD19 .....22 B6
Abraham Cohen Ct IG1 .....56 C3
Abraham Fisher Ho 2 E12 .....78 C3
Abridge Way IG11 .....102 B5
Abyssinia Cl SW11 .....136 C1
Abyssinia Rd SW11 .....136 C1
Acacia Ave
Brentford TW8 .....131 B5
East Finchley N2 .....47 D6
Hayes UB3 .....83 D1
Littleton TW17 .....192 C4
Ruislip HA4 .....40 B2
Tottenham N17 .....33 B3
Wembley HA9 .....66 A3
Yiewsley UB7 .....104 B6
Acacia Bsns Ctr 1 E11 ..76 C5
Acacia Cl Penge SE20 ...184 A1
Petts Wood BR5 .....211 B4
Rotherhithe SE8 .....119 A2
Stanmore HA7 .....24 C4
Acacia Ct Harrow HA1 ....41 D3
5 West Norwood SW16 .....182 C5
Acacia Dr SM3 .....201 C1
Acacia Gdns
St John's Wood NW8 ..229 D4
West Wickham BR4 .....224 A6
Acacia Gr Dulwich SE21 .161 B2
Kingston u T KT3 .....199 C6
Acacia Ho Brockley SE4 .141 B1
1 New Malden KT3 .....199 C5
Stoke Newington N16 .....73 B6
Wood Green N22 .....32 C2
Acacia Lo 6 N3 .....29 B1
Acacia Pl NW8 ...92 B5 229 D4
Acacia Rd Acton W3 .....111 A6
Beckenham BR3 .....207 B6
Enfield EN2 .....5 B4
Hampton TW12 .....173 C4
Leyton E11 .....76 C6
Mitcham CR4 .....181 B1
St John's Wood NW8 .....92 B5 229 D4
Thornton Heath SW16 ..182 A2
Walthamstow E17 .....53 A3
Wood Green N22 .....32 C2
Acacias Lo EN4 .....14 B6
Acacias The EN4 .....14 B6
Acacia Way DA15 .....167 D3
Acacia Wlk SW10 .....266 B3
Acad at Peckham The SE15 .....139 D4
Academy Ct 13 E2 .....96 C4
Academy Gdns
Croydon CR0 .....205 D1
Kensington W8 .....245 A2
Northolt UB5 .....84 D5
Academy Pl SE18 .....144 C4
Academy Rd SE18 .....144 B5
Academy Sch The NW3 ..70 B4
Academy The 2 N19 .....49 C1
Acad of Live & Recorded Arts The SW18 .....158 B5
Acanthus Dr SE1 .....118 A1
Acanthus Rd SW11 .....137 A2
Accadia Ct NW9 .....67 A6
Accommodation Rd NW11 .....47 B1
Ace Par KT9 .....214 A5
Acer Ave UB4 .....85 A2
Acer Ct
2 Cricklewood NW2 .....68 D4
3 Enfield EN3 .....7 A2
Acers BR7 .....188 A3
Acfold Rd SW6 .....265 C1
Achilles Cl SE1 .....118 A1
Achilles Ho 16 E2 .....96 B5
Achilles Rd NW6 .....69 C3
Achilles St SE14 .....141 A5
Achilles Way W1 .....248 B3
Acklam Rd W10 .....91 B2
Acklington Dr NW9 .....27 C2
Ackmar Rd SW6 .....135 C4 265 A1
Ackroyd Dr E3 .....97 C2
Ackroyd Rd SE23 .....163 A4
Acland Burghley Sch NW5 .....71 B4
Acland Cl SE18 .....145 B5
Acland Cres SE5 .....139 B2
Acland Ho SW9 .....138 B3
Acland Rd NW2 .....68 B2
Acock Gr UB5 .....64 A4
Acol Cres HA4 .....62 B3
Acol Ct 3 NW6 .....69 C1
Acol Rd NW6 .....69 D1
Aconbury Rd RM9 .....102 B6
Acorn Cl Chingford E4 ....35 D5
Chislehurst BR7 .....189 A5
Enfield EN2 .....4 D4
1 Hampton TW12 .....173 D4
Stanmore HA7 .....25 B3
Acorn Ct 5 Bow E3 .....97 C5
Hampton TW12 .....173 B5
Ilford IG2 .....57 C4
Upton Pk E6 .....78 A1
Wood Green N11 .....31 D4
Acorn Gdns
North Acton W3 .....89 B2
South Norwood SE19 ...183 D2
Acorn Gr
Harlington UB3 .....127 D5
Ruislip HA4 .....61 D4
Acorn Par 7 SE15 .....140 B5
Acorn Production Ctr N7 .....72 A1
Acorns The 21 SW19 .....156 D3
Acorns Way KT10 .....212 A3
Acorn Way
Beckenham BR3 .....208 A4
Forest Hill SE23 .....162 D1
Orpington BR6 .....226 D4
Acorn Wharf SE15 .....140 A6
Acorn Wlk SE16 .....119 A5
Acqua Ho TW9 .....132 D5
Acre Dr SE22 .....140 A1
Acrefield Ho 4 NW4 .....46 D5
Acre La Brixton SW2 .....138 B1
Wallington SM5 .....219 A4
Acre Path UB5 .....63 A2
Acre Rd
Dagenham RM10 .....81 D1
Kingston u T KT2 .....176 B2
Mitcham SW19 .....180 B4
Acre Way HA6 .....22 A2
Acris St SW18 .....158 A6
ACS Hillingdon International Sch UB10 .....82 B6
Action Ct TW15 .....171 A2
ACTON 111 B5
Acton Bsns Ctr NW10 ...89 B3
Acton Central Ind Est 4 W3 .....110 D5
Acton Central Sta W3 ..111 B5
Acton Cl N9 .....18 A2
ACTON GREEN 111 A2
Acton High Sch W3 .....110 C4
Acton Hill Mews W3 .....110 D5
Acton Ho 5 Acton W3 .....89 A1
16 Haggerston E8 .....95 D6
Acton Hospl W3 .....110 C4
Acton La
Acton Green W4 .....111 A2
Acton W3 .....111 A4
Harlesden NW10 .....89 B5
Acton Main Line Sta W3 .....89 A1
Acton Mews E8 .....95 D6
Acton Park Ind Est W3 .....111 B4
Acton St WC1 .....94 B4 233 C1
Acton Town Sta W3 .....110 C4
Acton Vale Ind Pk W3 ..111 D5
Acuba Ho SW18 .....157 D3
Acuba Rd SW18 .....157 D2
Acworth Cl N9 .....18 C4
Acworth Ho 1 SE18 .....144 D6
Ada Ct Islington N1 .....235 A5
St John's Wood W9 .....92 A4 229 B1
Ada Gdns Plaistow E15 ...98 D6
South Bromley E14 .....98 B1
Ada Ho 23 E2 .....96 A6
Adair Cl SE25 .....206 B6
Adair Ho SW3 .....267 B6
Adair Rd W10 .....91 A3
Adair Twr 7 W10 .....91 A3
Ada Kennedy Ct 6 SE10 .....142 A5
Ada Lewis Ho HA9 .....66 B4
Adam Cl SE6 .....185 C6
Adam Ct
Newington SE11 .....261 C3
15 Sutton SM1 .....218 A4
Adam & Eve Ct W1 .....239 B2
Adam & Eve Mews W8 .....113 C3 255 B6
Adamfields NW3 .....70 B1
Adam Lo N21 .....16 B6
Adam Rd E4 .....35 B4
Adams Bridge Bsns Ctr HA9 .....66 D3
Adams Cl Finchley N3 .....29 C3
Surbiton KT5 .....198 B3
Wembley Pk NW9 .....66 D6
Adams Ct E17 .....53 A3
Adams Gardens Est 5 SE16 .....118 C4
Adams Ho
3 South Bromley E14 ...98 B1
3 Streatham SW16 .....181 C5
Adams Mews
Upper Tooting SW17 .....158 D2
Wood Green N22 .....32 B3
Adamson Ct N2 .....48 C6
Adamson Rd
Hampstead NW3 .....70 B1
Newham E16 .....99 A1
Adamson Way BR3 .....208 A4
Adams Pl N7 .....72 B3
Adams Qtr TW8 .....131 C6
Adams Rd
Beckenham BR3 .....207 A4
Tottenham N17 .....33 B1
Adamsrill Cl EN1 .....17 B5
Adamsrill Prim Sch SE26 .....163 A1
Adamsrill Rd SE26 .....185 A6
Adam's Row W1 .....115 A6 248 B5
Adams Sq DA6 .....147 A2
Adam St WC2 ...116 A6 250 B5
Adams Way CR0 .....206 A3
Adams Wlk 11 KT1 .....176 A1
Adam Wlk SW6 .....134 C5
Ada Pl E2 .....96 A6
Ada Rd Camberwell SE5 ..139 C5
Wembley HA0, HA9 .....65 D5
Adare Ctr The SW16 .....160 A1
Adare Wlk SW16, SW2 ..160 B2
Ada St E8 .....96 B6
Adcot Wlk 6 BR6 .....227 D4
Adderley Gdns SE9 .....188 C6
Adderley Gr SW11 .....159 A6
Adderley Rd HA3 .....24 D2
Adderley St E14 .....98 A1
Addey Ho SE8 .....141 B5
Addey & Stanhope Sch SE14 .....141 C4
ADDINGTON 223 C3
Addington Ct 7 SW14 .....133 B2
Addington Dr N12 .....30 B4
Addington Gr SE26 .....185 A6
Addington Ho 13 SW9 ..138 B3
Addington Rd Bow E3 .....97 C4
Newham E16 .....98 C3
Stroud Green N4 .....50 C3
Thornton Heath CR0 .....204 C1
West Wickham BR4 .....224 C6
West Wickham BR4, CR0 .....224 B4
Addington Sq SE5 .....139 B5
Addington St SE1 .....116 B4 250 D1
Addington Village Rd CR0 .....223 C3
Addington Village Sta CR0 .....223 C2
Addis Cl EN3 .....6 D4
ADDISCOMBE 206 A1
Addiscombe Ave CR0 ..206 A2
Addiscombe Cl HA3 .....43 C4
Addiscombe Court Rd CR0 .....221 C6
Addiscombe Ct UB10 .....83 A3
Addiscombe Rd CR0 .....222 B6
Addiscombe Sta CR0 .....206 A1
Addis Ho 13 E1 .....96 C2
Addison Ave
Hounslow TW3 .....130 A4
Notting Hill W11 .....113 A5 244 A3
Southgate N14 .....15 C5
Addison Bridge Pl W14 .....113 B2 254 C4
Addison Cl
Northwood HA6 .....22 A2
Orpington BR5 .....211 A3
Addison Cres W14 .....113 A3 254 B6
Addison Ct
3 Belmont SM2 .....217 D1
Ealing W5 .....110 C6
Twickenham TW1 .....153 A3
Addison Dr SE12 .....165 B6
Addison Gdns
Hammersmith W14 .....112 D3
Kingston u T KT5 .....198 B5
Addison Gr W4 .....111 C3
Addison Ho NW8 .....92 B4 229 C2
Addison Park Mans 12 W14 .....112 D4
Addison Pl
Notting Hill W11 .....113 A5 244 A3
Southall UB1 .....107 C6
Addison Prim Sch W14 .....112 D3
Addison Rd
Bromley BR2 .....209 D4
Croydon SE25 .....206 A5
Enfield EN3 .....6 D4
Kensington W14 .....113 B3 254 C6
Teddington TW11 .....175 B4
Walthamstow E17 .....54 A4
Wanstead E11 .....55 A3
Addison's Cl CR0 .....223 B6
Addison Way
Hampstead Garden Suburb NW11 .....47 C5
Hayes UB3 .....84 A1
Northwood HA6 .....22 A2
Addle Hill EC4 .....241 D1
Addle St EC2 .....242 B3
Addlestone Ho 4 W10 ..90 C2
Addy Ho SE16 .....118 C2
Adecroft Way KT8 .....196 A6
Adela Ave KT3 .....200 B5
Adela Ho 9 W6 .....112 C1
Adelaide Ave SE4 .....141 C1
Adelaide Cl
Brixton SW9 .....138 C1
Enfield EN1 .....5 C5
Stanmore HA7 .....25 A6
Adelaide Ct
15 Beckenham BR3 .....185 C3
Hackney E5 .....75 A3
Hanwell W7 .....108 D4
St John's Wood NW8 .....229 B3
Adelaide Gdns RM6 .....59 A4
Adelaide Gr W12 .....112 A5
Adelaide Ho E17 .....53 B6
Adelaide Rd
Ashford TW15 .....170 A6
Chislehurst BR7 .....188 D5
Ealing W13 .....109 A4
Heston TW5 .....129 A4
Ilford IG1 .....78 D6
Kingston u T KT6 .....198 A4
Leyton E10 .....76 A5
Primrose Hill NW3 .....70 C1
Richmond TW9 .....132 B1
Southall UB2 .....107 A2
Teddington TW11 .....174 D4
2 Wandsworth SW18 ..157 C6
Adelaide St WC2 .....250 A5
Adelaide Terr TW8 .....109 D1
Adela St W10 .....91 A3
Adelina Gr E1 .....96 C2
Adelina Mews SW12 .....159 D3
Adeline Pl WC1 ..93 D2 239 D3
Adelphi Cres UB4 .....83 D4
Adelphi Ct
10 Finchley N2 .....30 B1
20 Rotherhithe SE16 .....118 D4
Adelphi Terr WC2 .....250 B5
Adelphi Way UB4 .....83 D4
Adeney Cl W6 .....134 D6
Aden Gr N16 .....73 B4
Aden Ho 15 E1 .....96 D2
Aden Lo N16 .....73 B4
Adenmore Rd SE6 .....163 C4
Aden Rd Enfield EN3 .....7 A1
Ilford IG1 .....57 A2
Adeyfield Ho EC1 .....235 D1
Adhara Rd HA6 .....22 A5
Adie Rd W6 .....112 C3
Adine Rd E13 .....99 B3
Adisham Ho 4 E5 .....74 B3
Adler Ind Est UB3 .....105 B4
Adler St E1 .....96 A1
Adley St E5 .....75 A3
Adlington Cl N18 .....33 C5
Admaston Rd SE18 .....145 A6
Admiral Ct
Barking IG11 .....102 C5
Carshalton SM5 .....202 C1
Chelsea SW10 ..136 A4 266 B2
Hendon NW4 .....46 A4
Marylebone W1 .....238 A3
Admiral Ho TW11 .....175 A6
Admiral Hyson Ind Est SE16 .....118 B1
Admiral Mews W10 .....90 D3
Admiral Pl Harringay N8 ..50 D5
Rotherhithe SE16 .....119 A5
Admirals Cl E18 .....55 B5
Admirals Ct
Bermondsey SE1 .....253 C3
3 Newham E6 .....100 D1
32 Putney SW19 .....156 D3
Admiral Seymour Rd SE9 .....144 B1
Admirals Gate SE10 .....141 D4
Admiral Sq SW10 .....136 A4 266 B2
Admiral St SE8 .....141 C4
Admirals Way E14 .....119 C4
Admiral's Wlk NW3 .....70 A5
Admiralty Arch* SW1 ..249 D4
Admiralty Cl 1 SE8 .....141 C4
Admiralty Rd TW11 .....174 D4
Admiralty Way TW11 .....174 D4
Admiral Wlk W9 .....91 C2
Adolf St SE6 .....185 D6
Adolphus Rd N4 .....50 D1
Adolphus St SE8 .....141 B5
Adomar Rd RM8 .....81 A5
Adpar St W2 .....92 B2 236 C4
Adrian Ave NW2 .....46 B1
Adrian Bolt Ho 2 E2 .....96 B4
Adrian Cl EN5 .....12 D5
Adrian Ho Islington N1 ..233 D5
South Lambeth SW8 .....270 A4
Stratford E15 .....76 B1
Adrian Mews SW10 .....265 D6
Adriatic Bldg 18 E14 .....119 A6
Adriatic Ho 18 E1 .....96 D3
Adrienne Ave UB1 .....85 B4
Adron Ho 18 SE16 .....118 C2
Adstock Ho 5 N1 .....72 D1
ADT Coll SW15 .....157 B6
Advance Rd SE27 .....183 A6
Advent Ct IG8 .....36 D5
Adventurers Ct 17 E14 .....120 B6
Advent Way N18 .....34 D5
Adyar Ct 7 SW19 .....179 A3
Adys Lawn NW2 .....68 B2
Adys Rd SE15 .....139 D2
Aegean Apts 7 E16 .....121 A6
Aegon Ho 3 E14 .....119 D3
Aerodrome Rd NW4, NW9 .....45 D6
Aerodrome Way TW5 ..128 C6
Aeroville NW9 .....27 C1
Affleck St N1 .....233 D3
Afghan Rd SW11 .....136 C3
Africa Ho WC2 .....240 C2
Afsil Ho EC1 .....241 B3
Aga Khan Univ WC1 .....239 D3
Agamemnon Rd NW6 .....69 B3
Agar Cl KT6 .....214 B6
Agar Gr NW1 .....71 D1
Agar Ho 6 KT1 .....198 A6
Agar Pl NW1 .....71 C1
Agar St WC2 .....250 B5
Agate Cl E16 .....99 D1
Agate Ho
New Malden KT4 .....199 C1
12 Penge SE26 .....184 B5
Agate Rd W6 .....112 C3
Agatha Cl E1 .....118 C5
Agaton Rd SE9 .....167 A2
Agave Rd NW2 .....68 C4
Agdon St EC1 .....94 D3 241 C6
Agincourt E11 .....54 D3
Agincourt Rd NW3 .....70 D4
Agnes Ave IG1 .....78 D4
Agnes Cl E6 .....122 C6
Agnes Ct 11 SW18 .....136 B1
Agnesfield Cl N12 .....30 C4
Agnes Gdns RM8 .....80 D4
Agnes Ho 13 W11 .....112 D6
Agnes Rd W3 .....111 D4
Agnes St E14 .....97 B1
Agnew Rd SE23 .....162 D4
Agricola Pl EN1 .....17 D6
Aidan Cl RM8 .....81 A4
Aidans Ct N12 .....30 C5
Aigburth Mans 5 SW9 .....138 C5
Ailantus Ct HA8 .....26 B5
Aileen Wlk E15 .....76 D1
Ailsa Ave TW1 .....153 B6
Ailsa Rd TW1 .....153 B6
Ailsa St E14 .....98 A2
Ainger Rd NW3 .....70 D1
Ainsdale NW1 .....232 A2
Ainsdale Cl BR6 .....211 B1
Ainsdale Cres HA5 .....41 C6
Ainsdale Dr SE1 .....118 A1
Ainsdale Rd W5 .....87 D3
Ainsley Ave RM7 .....59 D3
Ainsley Cl N9 .....17 C3
Ainsley St E2 .....96 B4
Ainslie Ct 2 HA0 .....88 A5
Ainslie Ho 1 E4 .....35 C5
Ainslie Wlk 8 SW12 .....159 B4
Ainslie Wood Cres E4 ..35 D5
Ainslie Wood Gdns E4 ..35 D5
Ainslie Wood Prim Sch E4 .....35 D5
Ainslie Wood Rd E4 .....35 D5
Ainsty St 20 SE16 .....118 C4
Ainsworth Cl
Camberwell SE5 .....139 C3
Dollis Hill NW2 .....68 A5
Ainsworth Est NW8 .....92 A6 229 A6
Ainsworth Ho NW8 .....91 D6
Ainsworth Rd
Croydon CR0 .....220 D6
Hackney E9 .....74 C1
Ainsworth Way NW8 .....92 A6 229 A6
Aintree Ave E6 .....100 A6
Aintree Cl UB8 .....82 D2
Aintree Ho SE26 .....184 B4
Aintree Rd UB6 .....87 B5
Aintree St SW6 .135 A5 264 B4
Airborne Ho 10 SM6 .....219 B4
Aird Ct TW12 .....173 D2
Aird Ho SE1 .....262 A5
Airdrie Cl Barnsbury N1 ..72 B1
Hayes UB4 .....85 A2
Airedale Ave W4 .....111 D1
Airedale Ave S W4 .....111 D1
Airedale Rd
Balham SW12 .....158 D4
Ealing W5 .....109 D3
Airlie Gdns Ilford IG1 .....56 D1
Kensington W8 113 C5 245 A3
Airlinks Ind Est TW5 .....106 C1
Air Park Way TW13 .....150 B2
Airport Gate Bsns Ctr UB7 .....126 C5
Airport Ho CR0 .....220 C2
Airport Rdbt E16 .....121 D5
Air St W1 .....249 B5
Airthrie Rd IG3 .....80 B6
Aisgill Ave SW5 .....113 B1 254 D1
Aisher Rd SE28 .....124 C6
Aislabie Ho N21 .....17 B5
Aislibie Rd SE12 .....142 C1
Aiten Pl W6 .....112 A2
Aithan Ho 15 E14 .....97 B1
Aitken Cl
Carshalton CR4 .....202 D2
Hackney E8 .....96 A6
Aitken Rd Barnet EN5 .....12 C6
Catford SE6 .....163 D2
Aits View KT8 .....195 D6
Ajax Ave NW9 .....45 C6
Ajax Ct NW9 .....45 C6
Ajax Ho 19 E2 .....96 B5
Ajax Rd NW6 .....69 C3
Akabusi Cl SE25 .....206 A3
Akbar Ho 7 E14 .....119 D2
Akehurst St SW15 .....156 A4
Akenside Ct 3 NW3 .....70 B3
Akenside Rd NW3 .....70 B3
Akerman Rd
Brixton SW9 .....138 D4
Kingston u T KT6 .....197 C3
Akintaro Ho 7 SE8 .....141 B6
Akiva Sch N3 .....29 D1
Alabama St SE18 .....145 C5
Alacross Rd W5 .....109 D4
Aladdin Workspace UB6 .....85 D6
Alamaro Lo 5 SE10 .....120 D3
Alandale Dr HA5 .....22 B2
Aland Ct SE16 .....119 A3
Alander Mews E17 .....54 A5
Alan Dr EN5 .....13 A5
Alan Gdns RM7 .....59 C2
Alan Hocken Way E15 ...98 C5
Alan Lo N3 .....29 C2
Alan Preece Ct NW6 .....68 D1
Alan Rd SW19 .....179 A5
Alanthus Cl SE12 .....165 A5
Alaska Bldg 12 SE13 .....141 D4
Alaska St SE1 .....251 A3
Alastor Ho 10 E14 .....120 A3
Alba Cl UB4 .....84 D3
Albacore Cres SE13 .....163 D5
Alba Gdns NW11 .....47 A3
Albain Cres TW15 .....148 A2
Alba Mews SW18, SW19 .....157 C2
Alban Ho
Hampstead NW3 .....70 A2
New Cross SE14 .....141 B4
Albans Cl SW16 .....160 A1
Albany W1 .....249 A5
Albany Cl Bushey WD23 ...8 B5
Ickenham UB10 .....60 C3
Mortlake SW14 .....132 D1
Sidcup DA5 .....168 D4
West Green N15 .....51 A5
Albany Coll NW4 .....46 C4
Albany Coll Hendry Ho NW4 .....46 B4
Albany Cres
Claygate KT10 .....212 C2
Edgware HA8 .....26 C3
Albany Ct
Ashford TW15 .....171 B4
Cheam SM1 .....217 B4
Chingford E4 .....19 D5
College Pk NW10 .....90 B4
Finchley N12 .....29 D4
Grahame Pk HA8 .....27 B2
Kingston u T KT2 .....176 A4
NW8 .....229 C3
Richmond TW10 .....153 B1
Surbiton KT6 .....197 D2
Walthamstow E10 .....53 C2
Westminster SW1 .....259 C6
8 Whitechapel E1 .....96 A1
Albany Ctyd W1 .....249 B5
Albany Ho
6 Brentford TW8 .....132 A6
Edgware HA8 .....26 C3
Upper Clapton E5 .....74 C6
Albany Mans SW11 .....267 B3
Albany Mews
Camberwell SE5 .....139 A6
Islington N1 .....72 C1
Kingston u T KT2 .....175 D4
Plaistow BR1 .....187 A4
Sutton SM1 .....217 D3
Albany Par 4 TW8 .....132 A6
Albany Park Ave EN3 .....6 D4
Albany Park Rd KT2 .....176 A4
Albany Park Sta DA14 ..168 D2
Albany Pas 12 TW10 .....154 A6
Albany Pl TW8 .....131 D6
Albany Rd
Brentford TW8 .....131 D6
Camberwell SE5 .....139 C6
Chislehurst BR7 .....188 D5
Dagenham RM6 .....59 B3
Ealing W13 .....109 B6
Enfield EN3 .....6 D5
Erith DA17 .....147 B6
Leyton E10 .....53 C2
Manor Pk E12 .....77 D4
New Malden KT3 .....199 B5
Richmond TW10 .....154 A6
Sidcup DA5 .....168 C4
Stroud Green N4 .....50 C3
Upper Edmonton N18 .....34 C5
Walthamstow E17 .....53 A3
Wimbledon SW19 .....179 D5
Albany Reach KT7 .....196 D4
Albany Sch EN3 .....6 D5
Albany St NW1 ...93 B4 231 D2
Albany Terr 6 TW10 .....154 B6
Albany The
Kingston u T KT2 .....175 D4
Woodford IG8 .....36 D6
Albany View IG9 .....21 A3
Albany Wlk N15 .....50 D5
Alba Pl W11 .....91 B1
Albatross 31 NW9 .....27 D1
Albatross Cl E6 .....100 B3
Albatross St SE18 .....145 C5
Albemarle SW19 .....156 D2
Albemarle App IG2 .....56 D3
Albemarle Ave TW2 .....151 B3
Albemarle Gdns
Ilford IG2 .....56 D3
New Malden KT3 .....199 B5
Albemarle Ho
2 Brixton SW9 .....138 C2
Rotherhithe SE8 .....119 B2
Albemarle Lo SE26 .....185 A5
Albemarle Mans NW3 .....69 D4
Albemarle Pk
Beckenham BR3 .....185 D2
Stanmore HA7 .....25 C5
Albemarle Prim Sch SW19 .....157 A2
Albemarle Rd
Beckenham BR2, BR3 ...186 A2
East Barnet EN4 .....14 C4
Albemarle St W1 .....115 C6 249 A5
Albemarle Way EC1 .....241 C5
Alberon Gdns NW11 .....47 B5
Alberta Ave SM1 .....217 B3
Alberta Ct 1 TW10 .....154 B6
Alberta Ho
Blackwall E14 .....120 A5
Hayes UB4 .....84 B4
Alberta Rd EN1 .....18 A5
Alberta St SE17 .....116 D1 261 D2
Albert Ave Chingford E4 ..35 C6

Albert Ave continued
South Lambeth SW8 .... 270 C3
Albert Barnes Ho SE1 .... 262 A5
Albert Bigg Point E15 .... 98 A6
Albert Bridge Rd
SW11 .... 136 D5 267 C3
Albert Carr Gdns
SW16 .... 182 A5
Albert Cl 11 Hackney E9 .... 96 B6
Wood Green N22 .... 31 D2
Albert Cotts 2 E1 .... 96 A2
Albert Cres E4 .... 35 C6
Albert Ct
Knightsbridge SW7 .... 246 C1
9 Putney SW19 .... 157 A3
Albert Dr SW19 .... 157 A3
Albert Emb
SE1 .... 116 A2 260 B3
Albert Gate Ct SW1 .... 247 C1
Albert Gdns E1 .... 96 D1
Albert Gr SW20 .... 178 D2
Albert Gray Ho SW10 .... 266 C4
Albert Hall Mans
SW7 .... 114 B4 246 C1
Albert Ho Stanmore HA7 .... 25 B5
5 Wanstead E18 .... 55 B6
2 Woolwich SE28 .... 123 A3
Albert Mans
Battersea SW11 .... 267 C2
Hornsey N8 .... 50 A2
Albert Meml*
SW7 .... 114 B4 246 C1
Albert Mews W8 .... 256 A6
Albert Palace Mans
SW11 .... 268 B2
Albert Pl Finchley N3 .... 29 C2
Kensington
W8 .... 113 D4 245 D1
Albert Rd
Ashford TW15 .... 170 B5
Bromley Comm BR2 .... 209 D4
Buckhurst Hill IG9 .... 21 D2
Chislehurst SE9 .... 166 A1
Croydon SE25 .... 206 B5
Dagenham RM8 .... 59 C1
Ealing W5 .... 87 B3
East Barnet EN4 .... 2 A1
Erith DA17 .... 125 B1
Finsbury Pk N4 .... 50 B2
Hampton TW12 .... 174 A5
Harrow HA2 .... 42 A6
Hayes UB3 .... 105 C3
Hendon NW4 .... 46 D5
Hounslow TW3 .... 129 C1
Ilford IG1 .... 79 A5
Kilburn NW6 .... 91 B5
Kingston u T KT1 .... 176 B1
Leyton E10 .... 54 A1
Mill Hill NW7 .... 27 D5
Mitcham CR4 .... 202 D6
Newham E16 .... 122 B4
New Malden KT3 .... 199 D5
Penge SE20 .... 184 D4
Richmond TW10 .... 154 B6
Sidcup DA5 .... 169 D4
Southall UB2 .... 106 D3
South Tottenham N15 .... 51 C3
Sutton SM1 .... 218 B3
Teddington TW11 .... 174 D4
Twickenham TW1 .... 152 D3
Walthamstow E17 .... 53 C4
4 Wanstead E18 .... 55 B6
Wood Green N22 .... 31 C2
Yiewsley UB7 .... 104 A5
Albert's Ct NW1 .... 237 B6
Albert Sleet Ct N9 .... 18 B1
Albert Sq Leyton E15 .... 76 C3
South Lambeth
SW8 .... 138 B5 270 C3
Albert St
Camden Town
NW1 .... 93 B6 231 D5
North Finchley N12 .... 30 A5
Albert Starr Ho 7
SE8 .... 118 D2
Albert Studios SW11 .... 267 C2
Albert Terr
Buckhurst Hill IG9 .... 21 D2
Camden Town
NW1 .... 93 A6 231 A5
Stonebridge NW10 .... 89 A6
Albert Terr Mews
NW1 .... 231 A5
Albert Victoria Ho N22 .... 32 C2
Albert Way SE15 .... 140 B5
Albert Westcott Ho
SE17 .... 261 D2
Albert Whicher Ho 3
E17 .... 54 A5
Albert Wlk E16 .... 122 D4
Albion Ave
Clapham SW8 .... 137 D3
Muswell Hill N10 .... 31 A2
Albion Cl W2 .... 247 B6
Albion Coll WC1 94 A2 240 B3
Albion Ct
7 Hammersmith W6 .... 112 B2
Sutton SM2 .... 218 B1
2 Woolwich SE7 .... 122 A2
Albion Dr E8 .... 74 A1
Albion Est SE16 .... 118 C4
Albion Gate W2 .... 247 B6
Albion Gdns 1 W6 .... 112 B2
Albion Gr N16 .... 73 C4
Albion Hill IG10 .... 21 D6
Albion Ho
17 Deptford SE8 .... 141 C5
EC1 .... 241 C4
Newham E16 .... 122 D5
Albion Mews
Bayswater
W2 .... 114 C6 247 B6
6 Hammersmith W6 .... 112 B2
Islington N1 .... 234 A6
Albion Pk IG10 .... 21 D6
Albion Pl
Broadgate EC2 .... 242 D3
Clerkenwell EC1 .... 241 C4
Hammersmith W6 .... 112 B2
South Norwood SE25 .... 206 A6
Albion Prim Sch SE16 .... 118 C4
Albion Rd Bexley DA6 .... 147 C1
Dagenham RM10 .... 81 B3
Hayes UB3 .... 83 C1
Hounslow TW3 .... 129 C1
Kingston u T KT2 .... 177 A2
Stoke Newington N16 .... 73 B4
Sutton SM2 .... 218 B1
Tottenham N17 .... 34 A1
Twickenham TW2 .... 152 C3
Walthamstow E17 .... 54 A6
Albion Riverside SW11 267 A4
Albion Sq E8 .... 73 D1
Albion St
Bayswater
W2 .... 114 C6 247 B6
Rotherhithe SE16 .... 118 C4
Thornton Heath CR0 .... 204 D1
Albion Terr Hackney E8 .... 73 D1
Sewardstone E4 .... 7 D1
Albion Villas Rd SE23,
SE26 .... 162 C1
Albion Way
Barbican EC1 .... 242 A3
Lewisham SE13 .... 142 A1
Wembley HA9 .... 66 C5
Albion Wlk N1 .... 233 B3
Albion Works Studios 14
E8 .... 74 A3
Albion Yd N1 .... 233 B3
Albon Ho SW18 .... 157 D5
Albrighton Rd SE5,
SE22 .... 139 C2
Albuhera Cl EN2 .... 4 C4
Albury Ave
Bexleyheath DA7 .... 147 A3
Hounslow TW7 .... 130 D5
Albury Bldgs SE1 .... 251 D1
Albury Cl TW12 .... 173 D4
Albury Ct
4 Croydon CR0 .... 221 A4
Deptford SE8 .... 141 C6
Mitcham CR4 .... 180 B1
6 Northolt UB5 .... 84 C4
Ruislip HA4 .... 62 C3
Sutton SM1 .... 218 A4
Albury Dr HA5 .... 22 D3
Albury Lo 7 SW2 .... 160 B4
Albury Mews E12 .... 77 C6
Albury Rd KT9 .... 214 A3
Albury St SE8 .... 141 C6
Albyfield BR1 .... 210 B6
Albyn Rd SE8 .... 141 C4
Alcester Cres E5 .... 74 B6
Alcester Ct 4 SM6 .... 219 B4
Alcester Rd SM6 .... 219 B4
Alchemea Coll of Audio
Engineering
N1 .... 94 D6 234 D6
Alcock Cl SM6 .... 219 D1
Alcock Rd TW5 .... 128 D5
Alconbury DA6 .... 169 D6
Alconbury Rd E5 .... 74 A6
Alcorn Cl SM3 .... 217 C6
Alcott Cl W7 .... 86 D2
Aldborough Ct
Chingford E4 .... 19 D1
Ilford IG2 .... 57 D4
ALDBOROUGH HATCH
.... 57 C5
Aldborough Rd IG2 .... 57 D6
Aldborough Rd N IG2 .... 57 D4
Aldborough Rd S IG3 .... 57 C2
Aldbourne Rd W12 .... 112 A5
Aldbridge St
SE17 .... 117 C1 263 B2
Aldburgh Mews W1 .... 238 B2
Aldbury Ave HA9 .... 66 D1
Aldbury Ho SW3 .... 257 A3
Aldbury Mews N9 .... 17 B4
Aldebert Terr
SW8 .... 138 B5 270 C3
Aldeburgh Cl 16 E5 .... 74 B6
Aldeburgh Pl
Greenwich SE10 .... 121 A2
Woodford IG8 .... 37 A6
Aldeburgh St SE10 .... 121 A1
Alden Ave E15 .... 98 D4
Alden Ct
South Croydon CR0 .... 221 C5
Wimbledon SW19 .... 179 C4
Aldenham Ctry Pk WD6 .... 9 B6
Aldenham Dr UB8 .... 82 D3
Aldenham Ho NW1 .... 232 B3
Aldenham Rd WD6 .... 9 C6
Aldenham St
NW1 .... 93 D5 232 C3
Alden Ho E8 .... 96 B6
Aldensley Rd W6 .... 112 B3
Alderbrook Prim Sch
SW12 .... 159 B4
Alderbrook Rd SW12 .... 159 B5
Alderbury Rd SW13 .... 134 A6
Alder Ct East Finchley N2 .... 48 B6
3 West Norwood
SW16 .... 182 C5
Alder Gr NW2 .... 68 B6
Aldergrove Gdns TW4 .... 129 A3
Aldergrove Ho 3 E5 .... 74 B6
Alder Ho
Camberwell SE15 .... 139 D6
1 Maitland Pk NW3 .... 70 D2
St Johns SE4 .... 141 C2
Alderley Ho 36 SW8 .... 137 D3
Alder Lo SW6 .... 134 D4
Alder Lodge N9 .... 17 C3
Alderman Ave IG11 .... 102 A4
Aldermanbury
EC2 .... 95 A1 242 B2
Aldermanbury Sq EC2 .... 242 B3
Alderman Ct 13 N11 .... 30 D5
Alderman Judge Mall 6
KT1 .... 176 A1
Alderman's Hill N13 .... 32 B6
Alderman's Wlk EC2 .... 243 A3
Aldermary Rd BR1 .... 187 A2
Aldermead 2 TW3 .... 129 D1
Alder Mews 12 N19 .... 71 C6
Aldermoor Rd SE6 .... 163 B1
Alderney Ave TW5 .... 129 D5
Alderney Gdns UB5 .... 63 B1
Alderney Ho
20 Canonbury N1 .... 73 A2
Enfield EN3 .... 6 D5
Alderney Mews SE1 .... 262 C6
Alderney Rd E1 .... 96 D3
Alderney St
SW1 .... 115 B1 258 D2
Alder Rd
Mortlake SW14 .... 133 B2
Sidcup DA14 .... 167 D1
Alders Ave IG8 .... 36 C4
ALDERSBROOK 77 C6
Aldersbrook Ave EN1 .... 5 C3
Aldersbrook Dr KT2 .... 176 B4
Aldersbrook La E12 .... 78 B5
Aldersbrook Prim Sch
E12 .... 77 C6
Aldersbrook Rd E11,
E12 .... 77 C6
Alders Cl Ealing W5 .... 109 D3
Edgware HA8 .... 27 A5
Wanstead E11 .... 77 B6
Alders Ct N17 .... 52 B5
Aldersey Gdns IG11 .... 79 B2
Aldersford Cl SE4 .... 140 D1
Aldersgate Ct EC1 .... 242 A3
Aldersgate St
EC1 .... 95 A2 242 A3
Aldersgrove KT8 .... 196 B4
Aldersgrove Ave SE9,
SE12 .... 165 D1
Aldershot Rd NW6 .... 91 B6
Aldersmead Ave CR0 .... 206 D3
Aldersmead Rd BR3 .... 185 A3
Alderson Pl UB2 .... 108 A5
Alderson St W10 .... 91 A3
Alders Rd HA8 .... 27 A5
Alders The
Feltham TW13 .... 173 A6
Heston TW5 .... 129 B6
Southgate N21 .... 16 C5
Streatham SW16 .... 181 C6
West Wickham BR4 .... 223 D6
Alderton 9 KT2 .... 176 D2
Alderton Cl NW10 .... 67 B5
Alderton Cres NW4 .... 46 B4
Alderton Ct KT8 .... 195 B5
Alderton Rd
Croydon CR0 .... 206 A2
Herne Hill SE24 .... 139 A2
Alderton Way NW4 .... 46 B4
Alderville Rd SW6 .... 135 B3
Alderwick Ct N7 .... 72 B2
Alderwick Dr TW3 .... 130 B2
Alder Wlk IG11 .... 79 A2
Alderwood Mews EN4 .... 2 A5
Alderwood Prim Sch
SE9 .... 167 C5
Alderwood Rd SE9 .... 167 B5
Aldford St W1 .... 115 A5 248 B4
Aldgate EC3 .... 95 C1 243 B1
Aldgate East Sta
E1 .... 95 D1 243 D2
Aldgate High St
EC3 .... 95 D1 243 C1
Aldgate Sta EC3 .... 95 D1 243 C1
Aldham Hall 1 E11 .... 55 A3
Aldham Ho SE4 .... 141 B4
Aldine Ct W12 .... 112 C5
Aldine St W12 .... 112 C4
Aldington Cl RM8 .... 58 C1
Aldington Ct 1 E8 .... 74 A1
Aldington Rd SE18 .... 121 D3
Aldis Mews
3 Holdbrook EN3 .... 7 C6
Upper Tooting SW17 .... 180 C5
Aldis St SW17 .... 180 C5
Aldred Rd NW6 .... 69 C3
Aldren Rd SW17 .... 158 A1
Aldriche Way E4 .... 36 A4
Aldrich Gdns SM3 .... 217 B5
Aldrich Terr SW18 .... 158 A2
Aldrick Ho N1 .... 233 D4
Aldridge Ave
Edgware HA8 .... 10 D1
Holdbrook EN3 .... 7 C5
Ruislip HA4 .... 62 D6
Stanmore HA7 .... 26 A2
Aldridge Ct W11 .... 91 B2
Aldridge Rd Villas W11 .... 91 B2
Aldridge Rise KT3 .... 199 C3
Aldridge Wlk N14 .... 16 A4
Aldrington Rd SW16 .... 181 C6
Aldsworth Cl W9 .... 91 D3
Aldwich Ho WC2 .... 240 D1
Aldwick Cl SE9 .... 167 B1
Aldwick Ct N12 .... 30 A6
Aldwick Rd CR0 .... 220 B4
Aldworth Gr SE13 .... 164 A5
Aldworth Rd E15 .... 76 C1
Aldwych WC2 .... 94 B1 240 D1
Aldwych Ave IG6 .... 57 A5
Aldwych Bldgs WC2 .... 240 B2
Aldwyn Ho SW8 .... 270 A3
Alers Rd DA6 .... 168 D6
Alesia Cl N22 .... 32 A3
Alestan Beck Rd E16 .... 99 D1
Alexa Ct 4 SM2 .... 217 C2
Alexander Ave NW10 .... 68 B1
Alexander Cl Barnet EN4 .... 2 B1
Hayes BR2 .... 209 A1
Sidcup DA15 .... 167 C5
Southall UB2 .... 108 A5
Twickenham TW2 .... 152 D2
Alexander Ct
Beckenham BR3 .... 186 B2
Greenwich SE3 .... 143 B3
Stanmore HA7 .... 44 B6
14 Surbiton KT6 .... 197 D2
Wandsworth SW18 .... 158 A6
Alexander Evans Mews
SE23 .... 162 D2
Alexander Fleming
Laboratory Mus*
W2 .... 236 D2
Alexander Ho
8 Kingston u T KT2 .... 176 A2
15 Millwall E14 .... 119 C3
16 Sutton SM2 .... 218 A2
Alexander Lo SM1 .... 217 B3
Alexander McLeod Prim
Sch SE2 .... 124 B1
Alexander Mews 2
W2 .... 91 D1
Alexander Pl SW7 .... 257 A4
Alexander Rd
Bexley DA7 .... 146 D3
Chislehurst BR7 .... 188 D5
Upper Holloway N19 .... 72 A6
Alexander Sq
SW3 .... 114 C2 257 A4
Alexander St W2 .... 91 C1
Alexander Terr SE2 .... 124 B1
Alexandra Ave
Battersea SW11 .... 268 A1
Harrow HA2 .... 63 C5
Southall UB1 .... 107 B6
Sutton SM1 .... 217 C5
Wood Green N22 .... 31 D2
Alexandra Bsns Ctr EN3 .... 6 D1
Alexandra Cl
Ashford TW15 .... 171 B3
Deptford SE8 .... 141 B6
Harrow HA2 .... 63 D5
Alexandra Cotts
New Cross SE14 .... 141 B4
Penge SE20 .... 184 D4
Alexandra Cres BR1 .... 186 D4
Alexandra Ct
Ashford TW15 .... 171 B4
Ealing W5 .... 87 C2
Greenford UB6 .... 85 D5
Hounslow TW3 .... 129 D3
Paddington W9 .... 236 B6
4 Shacklewell N16 .... 73 D4
5 Shepherd's Bush
W12 .... 112 A4
Southgate N14 .... 15 C6
Wembley HA9 .... 66 B4
Alexandra Dr
Surbiton KT5 .... 198 C2
West Norwood SE19 .... 183 C5
Alexandra Gdns
Chiswick W4 .... 133 C5
Cranley Gdns N10 .... 49 B5
Hounslow TW3 .... 129 D3
Wallington SM5 .... 219 A1
Alexandra Gr
Finchley N12 .... 29 D4
Finsbury Pk N4 .... 50 D1
Alexandra Ho 13 W6 .... 112 C1
Alexandra Inf Sch
Kingston u T KT2 .... 176 C3
Penge BR3 .... 184 D3
Alexandra Jun & Inf Sch
TW3 .... 129 D3
Alexandra Jun Sch
SE26 .... 184 D4
Alexandra Mans
Chelsea SW3 .... 266 C5
Cricklewood NW2 .... 68 D3
6 Hampstead NW6 .... 69 C3
9 Shepherd's Bush
W12 .... 112 C5
Alexandra Mews N2 .... 48 D6
Alexandra National Ho
N4 .... 72 D6
Alexandra Pal* N22 .... 31 D1
Alexandra Palace Sta
N22 .... 32 A1
Alexandra Palace Way
N10 .... 49 C6
Alexandra Park Rd N10,
N22 .... 31 D2
Alexandra Park Sch
N11 .... 31 C2
Alexandra Pl
Croydon CR0 .... 205 C1
South Norwood SE25 .... 205 B4
St John's Wood
NW8 .... 92 A6 229 B6
Alexandra Prim Sch
N22 .... 32 B1
Alexandra Rd
Acton W4 .... 111 B4
Ashford TW15 .... 171 C4
10 Brentford TW8 .... 131 D6
Croydon CR0 .... 205 C2
Alexandra Rd continued
Dagenham RM6 .... 59 A3
Edmonton N9 .... 18 B4
Enfield EN3 .... 6 D1
Hampstead NW8 .... 70 B1
Hendon NW4 .... 46 D5
Hornsey N8, N22 .... 50 C6
Hounslow TW3 .... 129 D3
Kingston u T KT2 .... 176 C3
Leyton E10 .... 76 A5
Mitcham SW19 .... 180 C3
Mortlake SW14 .... 133 B2
Muswell Hill N10 .... 31 B3
Penge SE26 .... 184 D4
Richmond TW9 .... 132 B3
Thames Ditton KT7 .... 196 D4
Tottenham N15 .... 51 B4
Twickenham TW1 .... 153 C5
Wallend E6 .... 100 C4
Walthamstow E17 .... 53 B2
Wanstead E18 .... 55 B6
Wimbledon SW19 .... 179 C5
Alexandra Sch HA2 .... 63 C6
Alexandra Sq SM4 .... 201 C4
Alexandra St
5 Deptford SE14 .... 141 A5
Newham E16 .... 99 A2
Alexandra Wlk 8
SE19 .... 183 C5
Alexandria Rd W13 .... 109 B6
Alex Gossip Ho SW6 .... 265 A1
Alexis St SE16 .... 118 A2
Alfearn Rd E5 .... 74 C4
Alford Ct
18 Belmont SM2 .... 217 D1
Shoreditch N1 .... 235 B3
Alford Gn CR0 .... 224 B2
Alford Ho Crouch End N6 .... 49 C3
6 Woolwich SE18 .... 144 D6
Alford Pl N1 .... 235 B3
Alfoxton Ave N8, N15 .... 50 D5
Alfreda Ct SW11 .... 268 C1
Alfreda St
SW11 .... 137 B4 268 C1
Alfred Butt Ho SW17 .... 158 D1
Alfred Cl W4 .... 111 B2
Alfred Findley Ho N22 .... 32 D1
Alfred Gdns UB1 .... 107 A6
Alfred Ho E9 .... 75 A3
Alfred Hurley Ho
SW17 .... 180 A6
Alfred Mews W1, WC1 .... 239 C4
Alfred Nunn Ho NW10 .... 89 D6
Alfred Pl WC1 .... 93 D2 239 C4
Alfred Prior Ho 7 E12 .... 78 C4
Alfred Rd Acton W3 .... 111 A5
Buckhurst Hill IG9 .... 21 D2
Croydon SE25 .... 206 A4
Erith DA17 .... 125 B1
Feltham TW13 .... 150 C2
Kingston u T KT1 .... 198 B6
Leyton E15 .... 76 D3
Paddington W2 .... 91 C2
Sutton SM1 .... 218 A3
Alfred Salter Ho SE1 .... 263 D3
Alfred Salter Prim Sch
SE16 .... 118 D4
Alfred's Gdns IG11 .... 101 C5
Alfred St E3 .... 97 B4
Alfred's Way (East Ham &
Barking By-Pass)
IG11 .... 101 B5
Alfred's Way Ind Est
IG11 .... 102 A6
Alfred Villas 9 E17 .... 54 A5
Alfreton Cl SW19 .... 156 D1
Alfriston KT5 .... 198 B3
Alfriston Ave
Harrow HA2 .... 41 C2
Thornton Heath CR0 .... 204 A2
Alfriston Cl KT5 .... 198 B3
Alfriston Rd SW11 .... 158 D6
Algar Cl Isleworth TW7 .... 131 A2
Stanmore HA7 .... 24 D5
Algar Ct TW12 .... 173 D2
Algar Ho SE1 .... 251 C1
Algar Rd TW7 .... 131 A2
Algarve Rd SW18 .... 157 D3
Algernon Rd
Hendon NW4 .... 46 A3
Kilburn NW6 .... 91 C6
Lewisham SE13 .... 141 D1
Algers Cl IG10 .... 21 D6
Algers Rd IG10 .... 21 D6
Alghers Mead IG10 .... 21 D6
Algiers Rd SE13 .... 141 C1
Alguin Ct HA7 .... 25 C3
Alibon Gdns RM10 .... 81 C3
Alibon Rd RM10 .... 81 C3
Alice Cl 13 EN5 .... 2 A1
Alice Ct 10 N3 .... 29 C2
Alice Gilliott Ct W14 .... 264 D6
Alice La E3 .... 97 B6
Alice Mews 3 TW11 .... 174 D5
Alice Owen Tech Ctr
EC1 .... 234 C2
Alice Shepherd Ho 12
E14 .... 120 A4
Alice St SE1 .... 117 C3 263 A5
Alice Thompson Cl
SE12 .... 165 C2
Alice Walker Cl 8
SE24 .... 138 D1
Alice Way TW3 .... 129 D1
Alicia Ave HA3 .... 43 C5
Alicia Cl HA3 .... 43 C5
Alicia Gdns HA3 .... 43 C5
Alicia Ho DA16 .... 146 B4
Alie St E1 .... 95 D1 243 D1
Alington Cres NW9 .... 45 A1
Alison Cl Croydon CR0 .... 206 D1
Newham E6 .... 100 C1
Alison Ct HA8 .... 26 D5
Aliwal Rd SW11 .... 136 C1
Alkerden Rd W4 .... 111 C1
Alkham Rd N16 .... 73 D6
Allam Ho W11 .... 244 A6
Allan Barclay Cl N15 .... 51 D3
Allanbridge N16 .... 51 C2
Allan Cl KT3 .... 199 B4
Allandale Ave N3 .... 47 B6
Allan Ho SW8 .... 269 C2
Allanson Ct E10 .... 75 C6
Allan Way W3 .... 89 A2
Allard Cres WD23 .... 8 A2
Allard Gdns SW4 .... 159 D6
Allardyce St SW4, SW9 .... 138 B1
Allbrook Cl TW11 .... 174 C5
Allbrook Ho 4 SW15 .... 156 A4
Allcot Cl TW14 .... 149 D3
Allcott Ho TW7 .... 130 D2
Allcroft Rd NW5 .... 71 A2
Allder Way CR2 .... 220 D1
Allenby Cl UB6 .... 85 C4
Allenby Prim Sch UB1 .... 85 C1
Allenby Rd
Forest Hill SE23 .... 163 A1
Southall UB1 .... 85 C3
Woolwich SE28 .... 123 A3
Allen Cl Streatham CR4 .... 181 C2
Sunbury TW16 .... 172 B2
Allen Ct Greenford UB6 .... 64 D3
Walthamstow E17 .... 53 C3
Allendale Ave UB1 .... 85 C1
Allendale Cl
Camberwell SE5 .... 139 B4
Forest Hill SE26 .... 184 D5
Allendale Rd UB6 .... 65 B2
Allen Edwards Dr
SW8 .... 138 A4 270 A2
Allen Edwards Prim Sch
SW4 .... 138 A4 270 A1
Allenford Ho SW15 .... 155 D5
All England Lawn Tennis &
Croquet Club The
SW19 .... 157 A1
Allen Ho W8 .... 255 B6
Allen Mans W8 .... 255 B6
Allen Rd Old Ford E3 .... 97 B5
Penge BR3 .... 184 D1
Stoke Newington N16 .... 73 C4
Sunbury TW16 .... 172 B1
Thornton Heath CR0 .... 204 C1
Allensbury Pl
7 Camden Town NW1 .... 71 D1
Camden Town NW1 .... 72 A1
Allens Rd EN3 .... 18 C6
Allen St W8 .... 113 C3 255 B5
Allenswood 12 SW19 .... 157 A3
Allenswood Rd SE9 .... 144 B3
Allerdale Ho 7 N4 .... 51 B2
Allerford Ct
Catford SE6 .... 163 D1
Harrow HA2 .... 42 A4
Allerford Rd SE6 .... 185 D6
Allerton Ct
5 Hendon NW4 .... 28 D1
North Cheam SM3 .... 216 D6
Allerton Ho
4 Merton SW19 .... 180 A3
Shoreditch N1 .... 235 D3
Allerton Rd N16 .... 73 A6
Allerton St N1 .... 235 D2
Allerton Wlk 11 N7 .... 72 B6
Allestree Rd
SW6 .... 135 A5 264 A3
Alleyn Cres SE21 .... 161 B2
Alleyndale Rd RM8 .... 80 C6
Alleyn Ho
Bermondsey SE1 .... 262 C5
St Luke's EC1 .... 242 B5
Alleyn Pk Dulwich SE21 .... 161 C1
Southall UB2 .... 107 C1
Alleyn Rd SE21 .... 161 C1
Alleyn's Sch SE22 .... 161 C6
Allfarthing La SW18 .... 158 A5
Allfarthing Prim Sch
SW18 .... 158 A5
Allgood Cl SM4 .... 200 D3
Allgood St 10 E2 .... 95 D5
Allhallows La EC4 .... 252 C5
Allhallows Rd E6 .... 100 A1
All Hallows Rd N17 .... 33 C2
Alliance Cl
Twickenham TW4 .... 151 B6
Wembley HA0 .... 65 D4
Alliance Ct Acton W3 .... 88 D2
Ashford TW15 .... 171 A6
Alliance Rd Acton W3 .... 88 D3
East Wickham SE18 .... 146 A5
1 Newham E16 .... 99 C2
Allied Ind Est W3 .... 111 C5
Allied Way W3 .... 111 C4
Allingham Cl W7 .... 108 D6
Allingham Ct NW3 .... 70 C3
Allingham Mews N1 .... 235 A4
Allingham St
N1 .... 95 A5 235 A4
Allington Ave
Tottenham N17 .... 33 C4
Upper Halliford TW17 .... 193 C6
Allington Cl
Greenford UB6 .... 64 A1
3 Wimbledon SW19 .... 178 D5
Allington Ct
6 Clapham SW8 .... 137 C3
Croydon CR0 .... 206 C3

Allington Ct continued
Enfield EN3 18 D6
Allington Rd
Harrow HA2 42 A4
Hendon NW4 46 B3
Kensal Rise W10 91 A5
Orpington BR6 211 C1
Allington St SW1 258 D5
Allison Cl SE10 142 A4
Allison Gr SE21 161 C3
Allison Rd Acton W3 111 A6
Harringay N8 50 D4
Alliston Ho 27 E2 95 D4
Allitsen Rd NW8 92 C5 230 A4
All Nations Ho 10 E8 74 B1
Allnutt Way SW4 159 D6
Alloa Ct N14 15 C2
Alloa Rd IG3 80 A6
Allom Ct 11 SW4 138 A3
Allonby Dr HA4 38 D2
Allonby Gdns HA9 43 C1
Allonby Ho E14 97 A2
Alloway Rd E3 97 A4
Allport Ho SE5 139 B2
Allport Mews 44 E1 96 C3
All Saints' Benhilton CE Prim Sch SM1 217 D5
All Saint's CE Jun Sch SE19 183 C2
All Saints CE Prim Sch
Merton SW19 180 A3
Putney SW15 134 C2
All Saints' CE Prim Sch
Blackheath Vale SE3 142 C3
Child's Hill NW2 69 B5
East Barnet N20 14 B2
Wallington SM5 219 A3
All Saints Church 9 N19 71 D5
All Saints' Cl N9 18 A2
All Saints Ct
Heston TW5 128 D4
Lower Clapton E5 74 C4
10 Shadwell E1 118 C6
All Saints Dr SE3 142 D3
All Saints Ho 2 W11 91 B2
All Saint's Inf Sch SE19 183 C2
All Saints Mews HA3 24 C4
All Saints Pas SW18 157 C6
All Saints RC Sch BR4 224 B4
All Saints RC Sch & Tech Coll RM8 59 C1
All Saints Rd
Merton SW19 180 A3
Notting Hill W11 91 B1
Sutton SM1 218 A5
All Saints' Rd W3 111 A3
All Saints St N1 94 B5 233 C4
All Saints Sta E14 119 D6
All Saints Twr 19 E10 53 D2
Allsop Pl NW1 92 D3 237 D5
All Souls' Ave NW10 90 B6
All Souls CE Prim Sch W1 93 C2 239 A4
All Souls Pl W1 238 D3
Allum La WD6 10 A6
Allum Way N20 14 A3
Allwood Cl SE26 184 D6
Alma Ave E4 36 A3
Alma Birk Ho 1 NW6 69 B1
Almack Rd E5 74 C4
Alma Cl N10 31 B2
Alma Cres SM1 217 A3
Alma Gr SE1 117 D2 263 D3
Alma Ho
7 Brentford TW8 132 A6
2 Edmonton N9 34 A6
Alma Pl College Pk NW10 90 B4
Penge SE19 183 D3
Thornton Heath CR7 204 C4
Alma Prim Sch
Bermondsey SE16 118 A2
Enfield EN3 18 D6
Alma Rd
Carshalton SM5 218 C3
Enfield EN3 7 A1
Muswell Hill N10 31 B3
Sidcup DA14 168 A1
Southall UB1 107 A6
Thames Ditton KT10, KT7 196 C1
Wandsworth SW18 158 A6
Alma Row HA3 24 B2
Alma Sq NW8 92 A4 229 B2
Alma St
Camden Town NW5 71 B2
Stratford New Town E15 76 B2
Alma Terr Earl's Ct W8 255 B5
Wandsworth SW18 158 B4
Almeida St 10 N1 72 D1
Almeric Rd SW11 136 D1
Almer Rd SW20 178 A3
Almington St N4 50 B1
Almond Ave
Carshalton SM5 218 D6
Ealing W5 110 A3
Uxbridge UB10 60 D5
West Drayton UB7 104 C3
Almond Cl
Bromley BR2 210 C2
Charlton TW17 171 A1
Feltham TW14 150 A3
Hayes UB3 105 C6
Peckham SE15 140 A3
Ruislip HA4 61 D5
Almond Gr TW8 131 B5
Almond Ho SE4 141 B3
Almond Rd
Bermondsey SE16 118 B2
Tottenham N17 34 A3
Almonds Ave IG9 21 A2
Almond Way
Bromley BR2 210 C2
Harrow HA2 24 A1
Mitcham CR4 203 D5
Almorah Rd
De Beauvoir Town N1 73 B1
Heston TW5 128 D4
Almshouse La EN1 6 B6
Almshouses
Edmonton N9 17 D2
Leyton E10 75 D6
Southall UB1 85 C1
Sunbury TW16 171 D2
Almshouses The IG11 79 A2
Al-Muntada Islamic Sch SW6 135 B4 264 D2
Alnmouth Ct 10 UB1 86 A1
Al-Noor Muslim Prim Sch IG3 58 B1
Alnwick 8 N17 34 B3
Alnwick Gr SM4 201 D5
Alnwick Rd
Eltham SE12 165 B4
Newham E16 99 C1
Alonso Ho 4 DA17 125 C1
ALPERTON 88 A6
Alperton Com Sch HA0 66 B1
Alperton La UB6 87 D5
Alperton Lower Sch HA0 87 D6
Alperton St W10 91 B3
Alperton Sta HA0 88 A6
Alphabet Gdns SM5 202 B3
Alphabet Sq E3 97 C2
Alpha Bsns Ctr E17 53 B4
Alpha Cl NW8 92 C4 230 B1
Alpha Ct 6 NW5 71 B2
Alpha Est The UB3 105 C4
Alpha Gr E14 119 C4
Alpha Ho
19 Brixton SW4 138 B1
Kilburn NW6 91 C5
Lisson Gr NW8 237 B5
Alpha Pl
Chelsea SW3 136 C6 267 B6
Kilburn NW6 91 C5
Alpha Rd Chingford E4 19 D1
Croydon CR0 205 C1
Edmonton N18 34 A4
Enfield EN3 7 A1
Hillingdon UB10 82 D3
New Cross SE14 141 B4
Surbiton KT5 198 B3
Teddington TW12 174 B5
Alpha St SE15 140 A3
Alphea Cl SW19 180 C3
Alpine Ave KT5 215 A6
Alpine Bsns Ctr E6 100 C2
Alpine Cl CR0 221 C5
Alpine Copse BR1 188 C1
Alpine Ct SE12 142 D1
Alpine Gr 37 E9 74 C1
Alpine Rd
Deptford SE16 118 D1
Leyton E10 75 D6
Walton-on-T KT12 194 A2
Alpine View SM5 218 C3
Alpine Way E6 100 C2
Alpine Wlk HA7 8 C2
Alric Ave
Kingston u T KT3 199 D6
Willesden NW10 67 B1
Alroy Rd N4 50 C2
Alsace Rd SE17 117 C1 263 A2
Al Sadiq & Al Zahra Schs NW6 91 A6
Alscot Rd SE1 117 D3 263 D5
Alscot Road Ind Est SE1 263 D5
Alscot Way SE1 263 C4
Alsike Rd DA18 125 A3
Alsom Ave KT19, KT4 216 A4
Alston Cl KT7 197 B2
Alston Ct 2 EN5 1 A2
Alstone Ct N9 18 A2
Alston Rd Edmonton N18 34 B5
High Barnet EN5 1 A2
Upper Tooting SW17 180 B6
Altair Cl N17 33 D4
Altair Ct N1 73 B2
Altash Way SE9 166 C2
Altenburg Ave W13 109 B3
Altenburg Gdns SW11 136 D1
Alt Gr SW19 179 B3
Altham Gdns WD19 22 D6
Altham Rd HA5 23 A3
Althea St SW6 135 D2
Althorne Gdns E18 54 D5
Althorne Way RM10 81 C6
Althorp Cl EN5 12 A4
Althorpe Mews SW11 266 D1
Althorpe Rd HA1 42 A4
Althorp Rd SW17 158 D3
Altima Ct SE22 140 A1
Altior Ct N6 49 C3
Altmore Ave E6 100 B6
Altmore Inf Sch E6 100 B6
Alton Ave HA7 24 D3
Alton Cl Isleworth TW7 130 D3
Sidcup DA5 169 A3
Alton Ct 18 BR3 185 C3
Alton Gdns
Beckenham BR3 185 C3
Twickenham TW2 152 B4
Alton Ho 3 E3 97 D4
Alton Rd Croydon CR0 220 C5
Richmond TW10, TW9 132 A1
Roehampton SW15 156 A3
Tottenham N17 51 B6
Alton St E14 97 D2
Altyre Cl BR3 207 B4
Altyre Rd CR0 221 B6
Altyre Way BR3 207 B4
Alum Ct KT5 198 B3
Alumni Ct SE1 253 D2
Alvanley Ct NW3 69 D3
Alvanley Gdns NW6 69 D3
Alvanley Ho 18 SW9 138 C4
Alvernia Lo SM1 217 D5
Alverstone Ave
East Barnet EN4 14 C4
Wimbledon SW18, SW19 157 C2
Alverstone Gdns SE9 167 A3
Alverstone Ho 11 SE11 138 C6
Alverstone Rd
Little Ilford E12 78 C4
New Malden KT3 199 D5
Wembley HA9 44 B1
Willesden NW2 68 C1
Alverston Gdns SE25 205 C4
Alverton St SE8 141 B6
Alveston Ave HA3 43 B6
Alveston Sq 5 E18 37 A1
Alvey St SE17 263 A2
Alvia Gdns SM1 218 A4
Alvington Cres E8 73 D3
Alway Ave KT19 215 B3
Alwen Cotts CR0 222 D4
Alwold Cres SE12 165 C5
Alwyn Ave W4 111 B1
Alwyn Cl
Borehamwood WD6 10 B5
New Addington CR0 223 D1
Alwyne La N1 72 D1
Alwyne Mans SW19 179 B4
Alwyne Pl N1 73 A1
Alwyne Rd
Canonbury N1 73 A1
Ealing W7 108 C6
Wimbledon SW19 179 B4
Alwyne Sq N1 73 A2
Alwyne Villas N1 72 D1
Alwyn Gdns Acton W3 88 D1
Hendon NW9 46 A5
Alyn Ct N8 49 D3
Alyth Gdns NW11 47 C3
Alzette Ho 11 E2 96 D5
Amalgamated Dr TW8 131 B6
Amanda Ct
Ashford TW15 148 B2
Chingford E4 36 C4
Aman Dalvi Ho SW18 157 A4
Amar Ct SE18 123 D2
Amardeep Ct SE18 123 D1
Amazon Apartments N8 50 B6
Amazonas SE1 117 C2 263 B3
Amazon St E1 96 B1
Ambassador Cl TW3 129 A3
Ambassador Ct
9 Hampstead NW6 69 C3
Hendon NW4 46 D4
Ambassador Gdns E6 100 B2
Ambassador Ho
Harrow HA3 42 C6
St John's Wood NW8 229 B5
Ambassador Sq E14 119 D2
Amber Ave E17 35 A2
Amber Ct
Feltham TW13 149 C1
Islington N7 72 C2
Mitcham CR4 202 C5
Southall UB1 107 D5
Amberden Ave N3 47 C6
Ambergene HA7 24 D4
Ambergate St SE17 116 D1 261 D2
Amber Gr NW2 46 D1
Amber Ho HA7 25 D3
Amberley Cl
2 Orpington BR6 227 D3
Pinner HA5 41 B6
Amberley Ct
2 Brixton SW9 138 D2
Sidcup DA14 190 C5
Sutton SM2 218 A1
Amberley Gdns
Enfield EN1 17 C4
Worcester Pk KT19 215 D4
Amberley Gr
Croydon CR0 205 D2
Penge SE26 184 B5
Amberley Ho
8 Barnet EN5 1 D1
7 Ealing W7 108 C5
Amberley Rd
Buckhurst Hill IG9 21 C3
Enfield EN1 17 D5
Palmers Green N13 16 B2
Walthamstow E10 53 D2
Westbourne Green W9 91 C2
West Heath SE2 146 D6
Amberley Way
Heston TW4 150 C6
Morden SM4 201 B2
Romford RM7 59 D5
Uxbridge UB10 82 A5
Amberside Cl TW2 152 B5
Amber Wharf 29 E2 95 D6
Amberwood Cl SM6 220 A3
Amberwood Rise KT3 199 C3
Amblecote Cl SE12 165 B1
Amblecote Mdws SE12 165 B1
Amblecote Rd SE12 165 B1
Ambler Prim Sch N4 72 D6
Ambler Rd N4 72 D5
Ambleside Catford BR1 186 B4
13 Putney SW19 157 A3
Regent's Pk NW1 231 D3
Ambleside Ave
Beckenham BR3 207 A4
Streatham SW16 181 D6
Walton-on-T KT12 194 C1
Ambleside Cl
Lower Clapton E9 74 C3
5 Tottenham N17 51 D6
Walthamstow E10 53 D2
Ambleside Cres EN3 6 D2
Ambleside Dr TW14 149 D3
Ambleside Gdns
Redbridge IG4 56 A4
Streatham SW16 181 D5
Sutton SM2 218 A2
Wembley HA9 43 D1
Ambleside Ho HA8 27 A5
Ambleside Point 1 SE15 140 C5
Ambleside Rd
Bexleyheath DA7 147 C3
Willesden NW10 67 D1
Ambrook Ct SM1 218 B3
Ambrook Rd DA17 125 C3
Ambrosden Ave SW1 115 C3 259 B5
Ambrose Ave NW11 47 B3
Ambrose Cl
6 Newham E6 100 B2
Orpington BR6 227 D5
Ambrose Ho 9 E14 97 C2
Ambrose Mews 2 SW11 136 D3
Ambrose St SE16 118 B2
Ambrose Wlk E3 97 C5
AMC Bsns Ctr NW10 88 D4
Amelia Cl W3 110 D4
Amelia Ho 5 W6 112 C1
Amelia St SE17 117 A1 262 A2
Amen Cnr Holborn EC4 241 D1
Streatham SW17 181 A4
Amen Ct EC4 94 D1 241 D1
Amenity Way SM4 200 C2
American Intercontinental Univ W1 93 A2 238 B3
American Sch in London The NW8 92 B5 229 C4
American Univ in London The N7 72 B5
America Sq EC3 253 C6
America St SE1 252 A3
Amerland Rd SW18 157 B5
Amersham Ave N18 33 B4
Amersham Gr SE14 141 B5
Amersham Rd
New Cross SE14 141 B4
Thornton Heath CR0 205 B3
Amersham Vale SE14, SE8 141 B5
Amery Gdns NW10 90 B6
Amery Ho SE17 263 B2
Amery Rd HA1 65 A6
Amesbury Ave SW2 160 B2
Amesbury Cl KT4 200 C1
Amesbury Ct EN2 4 C3
Amesbury Dr E4 19 D5
Amesbury Rd
Bromley BR1 209 D6
Dagenham RM9 80 D1
Feltham TW13 150 D2
Amesbury Twr 4 SW8 137 C3
Ames Cotts 12 E3 97 A2
Ames Ho 10 E2 96 D5
Amethyest Ct 1 EN3 7 A2
Amethyst Cl N11 31 D3
Amethyst Ct BR6 227 C3
Amethyst Rd E15 76 B4
Amherst Ave W13 87 C1
Amherst Dr BR5 211 D5
Amherst Gdns 2 W13 87 C1
Amherst Rd W13 87 C1
Amhurst Ct N4 51 B2
Amhurst Gdns TW7 131 A3
Amhurst Par N16 51 D2
Amhurst Pk N4, N16 51 C2
Amhurst Rd E8, N16 74 A4
Amhurst Terr E8 74 A4
Amhurst Wlk SE28 124 A5
Amias Ho EC1 242 A6
Amidas Gdns RM8 80 B4
Amiel St 15 E1 96 C3
Amies St SW11 136 D2
Amigo Ho SE1 261 B6
Amina Way SE16 118 A3
Amis Ave KT19 214 D3
Amity Gr SW20 178 C2
Amity Rd E15 76 D1
Ammanford Gn NW9 45 C3
Ammonite Ho 3 E15 76 D1
Amner Rd SW11 159 A5
Amora 8 HA7 25 C6
Amor Rd W6 112 C3
Amory Ho N1 233 D4
Amott Rd SE15 140 A2
Amoy Pl E14 119 C6
Ampere Way CR0 204 B1
Ampleforth Rd SE2 124 C4
Ampton Pl WC1 233 C1
Ampton St WC1 94 B4 233 C1
Amroth Cl SE23 162 B3
Amroth Gn NW9 45 C3
Amstel Ct 12 SE15 139 D5
Amsterdam Rd E14 120 A3
Amundsen Ct 7 E14 119 C1
Amundsen Ho 6 NW10 67 B1
Amwell Cl EN2 17 B6
Amwell St EC1 94 C4 234 A2
Amyand Cotts 12 TW1 153 B5
Amyand Park Gdns 2 TW1 153 B4
Amyand Park Rd TW1 153 B4
Amy Cl SM6 220 A1
Amy Johnson Ct HA8 26 D1
Amy Johnson Prim Sch SM6 220 A1
Amyruth Rd SE4 163 C6
Amy Warne Cl E6 100 A3
Anarth Ct KT13 193 C1
Anatola Rd N19 71 C6
Ancaster Cres KT3 200 A3
Ancaster Mews CR0 206 D6
Ancaster Rd BR3 206 D6
Ancaster St SE18 145 C5
Anchorage Cl SW19 179 C5
Anchorage Point 1 E14 119 C4
Anchorage Point Ind Est SE7 121 C3
Anchor Bsns Pk CR0, SM6 220 A5
Anchor Cl IG11 102 B4
Anchor Ct Bexley DA7 147 A4
5 Enfield EN1 17 C6
Anchor Ho Ilford IG3 80 A5
Newham E16 99 C1
St Luke's EC1 242 A6
Anchor & Hope La SE7 121 C2
Anchor Mews SW12 159 B5
Anchor Ret Pk E1 96 C3
Anchor St SE16 118 B2
Anchor Terr SE1 252 B4
Anchor Yd EC1 242 B6
Ancill Cl W6 135 A6 264 A5
Ancona Rd
Plumstead SE18 123 B1
Willesden Green NW10 90 A5
Andace Pk BR1 187 C2
Andalus Rd SW9 138 A2
Andaman Ho 3 E1 97 A2
Ander Cl HA0 65 D4
Andersens Wharf 9 E14 97 B1
Anderson Cl
Morden SM3 201 C1
North Acton W3 89 B1
Southgate N21 16 B6
Anderson Ct NW2 46 C2
Anderson Dr TW15 171 A6
Anderson Ho
1 Barking IG11 101 B5
10 Blackwall E14 120 A6
Upper Tooting SW17 180 B5
Anderson Rd
Homerton E9 74 D2
Redbridge IG8 55 D6
Anderson's Pl TW3 129 D1
Andersons Sq N1 234 C5
Anderson St SW3 257 C2
Anderson Way
Erith DA17 125 D4
Erith DA17 125 D4
Anderton Cl SE5 139 B2
Anderton Ct N22 31 D1
Andhurst Ct KT2 176 D2
Andmark Ct UB1 107 B5
Andon Ct BR3 207 A6
Andorra Ct BR1 187 C2
Andover Ave E16 99 D1
Andover Cl
East Bedfont TW14 149 D3
Greenford UB6 85 D3
Andover Ho 5 N7 72 B6
Andover Pl NW6 91 D5
Andover Rd
Finsbury Pk N7 72 B6
Orpington BR6 211 C1
Twickenham TW2 152 B3
Andoversford Ct 2 SE15 139 C6
Andrecht Terr CR4 203 D5
Andreck Ct BR3 186 A1
Andre Malraux Sch W7 86 C2
Andre St E8 74 A3
Andrew Borde St WC2 239 D2
Andrew Ct
Beckenham BR3 207 D6
2 Forest Hill SE23 162 D2
Andrewes Ct 2 W7 108 C5
Andrewes Gdns E6 100 A1
Andrewes Ho
Barbican EC2 242 B3
Sutton SM1 217 C4
Andrew Ewing Jun & Inf Sch TW5 129 B5
Andrew Ho Enfield EN3 18 C6
New Cross SE4 141 B3
Putney SW15 156 A6
Andrew Logan's Glass Ho* SE1 253 A2
Andrew Marvell Ho 12 N16 73 C4
Andrew Pl SW8 269 D2
Andrew Reed Ho SW18 157 A4
Andrews Cl
Buckhurst Hill IG9 21 C2
Harrow HA1 42 B2
North Cheam KT4 216 D6
Sidcup BR5 190 D1
Andrews Crosse WC2 241 A1
Andrew's Rd E8 96 B6
Andrew St E14 98 A1
Andrews Wharf 14 E8 96 B6
Andrews Wlk SE17 138 D6
Andrew Wells Ho BR1 187 B3
Andrew Wilmot Ct SW18 158 A3
Andridge Ct SW19 179 B2
Andringham Lo 4 BR1 187 B2
Andrula Ct N22 32 D2
Andwell Cl SE2 124 B4
ANERLEY 184 B2
Anerley Ct SE20 184 B3
Anerley Gr SE19 183 D3
Anerley Hill SE19 183 D4
Anerley Park Rd SE20 184 B3
Anerley Pk SE20 184 B2
Anerley Rd SE20 184 B2
Anerley Sta SE20 184 B2
Anerley Station Rd SE20 184 B2
Anerley Vale SE19 184 A3
Aneurin Bevan Ct NW2 68 B6
Aneurin Bevan Ho N11 31 D3
Anfield Cl SW12 159 C4
Angel EC1 94 D5 234 D3
Angela Ct 2 SE23 162 C3
Angela Davis Ind Est 20 SW9 138 D1
Angel Cl N18 34 A6
Angel Corner Par 6 N18 34 A6
Angel Ct Broadgate EC2 242 D2
St James SW1 249 B3
5 Willesden NW2 68 A2
Angel Edmonton N18 34 A5
Angelfield TW3 151 D6
Angel Gate EC1 234 D2
Angel Hill SM1 217 D5
Angel Hill Dr SM1 217 D5
Angel Ho N1 234 B3
Angelica Cl UB7 82 B1
Angelica Dr E6 100 C2
Angelica Gdns CR0 206 D1
Angelina Ho 2 SE15 140 A4
Angelis Appartments N1 234 D3
Angel La Hayes UB3 83 B2
Stratford E15 76 B2
Angell Park Gdns 4 SW9 138 C2
Angell Rd SW9 138 D2
Angel Mews
Finsbury N1 234 B3
Putney SW15 156 A4
Stepney E1 118 B6
Angel Pas EC4 117 B6 252 C5
Angel Pl
Borough The SE1 252 C2
1 Edmonton N18 34 A5
Angel Rd Harrow HA1 42 C3
Thames Ditton KT7 197 A1
Angel Rd (North Circular Rd) N18 34 B5
Angel Rd Works N18 34 C5
Angel Road Sta N18 34 C5
Angel Sq N1 234 B3
Angel St EC1 95 A1 242 A2
Angel Sta EC1 94 C5 234 B3
Angel Wlk W6 112 C2
Angerstein Bsns Pk SE10 121 A2
Angerstein La SE3 142 D4
Anglebury 5 W2 91 C1
Angle Cl UB10 82 C6
Angle Gn RM8 58 C1
Anglers Cl TW10 175 C6
Anglers La NW5 71 B2
Anglers Reach KT6 197 D4
Anglesea Ave 4 SE18 122 D2
Anglesea Ho KT1 197 D5
Anglesea Mews 12 SE18 122 D2
Anglesea Rd
Kingston u T KT1 197 D5
Woolwich SE18 122 D2
Anglesey Cl TW15 148 C1
Anglesey Court Rd SM5 219 A2
Anglesey Ct W7 86 D3
Anglesey Gdns SM5 219 A2
Anglesey Ho 13 E14 97 C1
Anglesey Rd Enfield EN3 6 B1
South Oxhey WD19 22 C5
Anglesmede Cres HA5 41 C6
Anglesmede Way HA5 41 C6
Angles Rd SW16 182 A6
Anglia Cl N17 34 B3
Anglia Ct RM8 58 D1
Anglia Ho 13 E14 97 A1
Anglian Ind Est IG11 101 D2
Anglian Rd E11 76 B5
Anglia Wlk E6 100 C6
Anglo American Laundry SW17 158 A1
Anglo Rd 16 E3 97 B5
Angrave Ct 4 E8 95 D6
Angrave Pas 5 E8 95 D6
Angus Cl KT9 214 C3
Angus Dr HA4 62 C4
Angus Gdns NW9 27 B2
Angus Ho 2 SW12 159 D4
Angus Rd E13 99 C4
Angus St SE14 141 A5
Anhalt Rd SW11 136 C5 267 B4
Animals in War Meml* W1 247 D6
Ankerdine Cres SE18 144 D4
Anlaby Rd TW11 174 C5

Anley Rd W14 112 D4
Anmersh Gr HA7 25 D2
Annabel Cl E14 97 D1
Anna Cl E8 95 D6
Annadale N22 32 B5
Annandale Gr UB10 61 A5
Annandale Rd
Chiswick W4 111 C1
Croydon CR0 222 A6
Greenwich SE10 120 D1
Sidcup DA15 167 D4
Anna Neagle Cl 2 E7 77 A4
Anne Boleyn's Wlk
Belmont SM3 217 A1
Kingston u T KT2 176 A5
Anne Compton Mews SE12 164 D4
Anne Goodman Ho 3 E1 96 C1
Anne Kerr Ct 18 SW15 156 D5
Annemount Sch N2 48 B3
Anne's Ct NW8 237 B6
Annesley Ave NW9 45 B6
Annesley Cl NW10 67 C5
Annesley Dr CR0 223 B5
Annesley Ho
31 Brixton SW9 138 C4
15 Kennington SW9 138 C5
Annesley Rd SE3 143 B4
Annesley Wlk N19 71 C6
Annesmere Gdns SE3 143 D2
Anne St E13 99 A3
Annett Cl TW17 193 C5
Annette Cl HA3 24 C1
Annette Cres 16 N1 73 A1
Annette Ct N7 72 B5
Annette Rd N7 72 B4
Annette White Lo 20 N2 30 B1
Annett Rd KT12 194 A2
Anne Way KT8 195 D5
Annie Besant Cl E3 97 B6
Annie Taylor Ho 2 E12 78 C4
Anning St E2 243 B6
Annington Rd N2 48 D6
Annis Rd E9 75 A2
Ann La SW10 136 B6 266 C5
Ann Moss Way SE16 118 C3
Ann Parkes Ct TW5 128 D3
Ann's Cl SW1 248 A1
Ann's Pl E1 243 C3
Ann St SE18 123 B2
Ann Stroud Ct SE12 165 A6
Annsworthy Ave CR7 205 B6
Annsworthy Cres CR7 183 B1
Annunciation RC Inf Sch The HA8 27 B2
Annunciation RC Jun Sch The HA8 27 B4
Ansar Gdns E17 53 B4
Ansdell Rd SE15 140 C3
Ansdell St W8 113 D3 255 D6
Ansdell Terr W8 113 D3 255 D6
Ansell Gr SM5 203 A1
Ansell Ho E1 96 C2
Ansell Rd SW17 158 D1
Anselm Cl CR0 221 D5
Anselm Rd
Hatch End HA5 23 B3
West Brompton SW6 135 C6 265 A5
Ansford Rd BR1, SE6 186 B6
Ansleigh Pl W11 112 D6
Anson 30 NW9 27 D1
Anson Ct TW19 148 A4
Anson Ho Pimlico SW1 269 A6
6 Tower Hamlets E1 97 A3
Anson Pl SE28 123 B4
Anson Prim Sch NW2 68 D3
Anson Rd
Cricklewood NW2 68 C3
Tufnell Pk N7 71 D4
Anson Terr UB5 63 D2
Anstey Ct 6 W3 110 D4
Anstey Ho 7 E9 96 C6
Anstey Lo EN1 17 C5
Anstey Rd SE15 140 A2
Anstey Wlk N15 51 A5
Anstice Cl W4 133 C5
Anstridge Rd SE9 167 B5
Antelope Rd SE18 122 B3
Antenor Ho 11 E2 96 B5
Anthony Cl NW7 27 C6
Anthony Cope Ct N1 235 D2
Anthony Ct Harrow HA1 42 B2
Isleworth TW7 130 D2
Anthony Ho NW8 237 A5
Anthony Kendal Ho 4 E5 74 B5
Anthony Rd
Croydon SE25 206 A3
East Wickham DA16 146 A4
Greenford UB6 86 C4
Anthony St E1 96 B1
Antigua Wlk SE19 183 B5
Antilles Bay 19 E14 120 A4
Antilles Ho W3 89 B1
Antill Rd Mile End E3 97 A4
Tottenham Hale N15 52 A5
Antill Terr 5 E1 96 D1
Antlers Hill E4 19 D6
Anton Cres SM1 217 C5
Antoneys Cl HA5 22 D1
Antonine Hts SE1 253 A1
Anton Pl HA9 66 D5
Anton St E8 74 A3
Antony Ho
4 Deptford SE14 140 D5
2 Rotherhithe SE16 118 C2
Antrim Gr NW3 70 D2
Antrim Ho SW11 137 A2
Antrim Mans NW3 70 D2
Antrim Rd NW3 70 D2
Antrobus Cl SM1 217 B3
Antrobus Rd W4 111 A3
Anvil Cl SW16 181 C3
Anvil Ho 10 N9 18 A1
Anvil Rd TW16 194 A6
Anworth Cl IG8 37 B4
Apex Cl BR3 185 D2
Apex Cnr Edgware NW7 27 B6
Twickenham TW13 151 B1
Apex Ct W13 87 A1
Apex Ind Est NW10 89 D3
Apex Lo 10 EN5 14 A6
Apex Ret Pk TW13 151 B1
Aphrodite Ct 11 E14 119 C2
Aplin Ct 4 SM1 217 D2
Aplin Way TW7 130 C4
Apollo Ave
Bromley BR1 187 B2
Loughton HA6 22 A5
Apollo Bldg 2 E14 119 C2
Apollo Ho
Chelsea SW10 266 C5
32 Hackney E2 96 B5
Highgate N6 48 D2
Apollo Ind Bsns Ctr 29 SE8 140 D6
Apollo Pl Chelsea SW10 266 C4
6 Leyton E11 76 C5
Apollo Studios 16 NW5 71 C3
Apollo Way 1 SE18 123 B3
Apostle Way CR7 182 D1
Apothecary St EC4 241 C1
Appach Rd SW2 160 C5
Appin Ct HA1 42 C2
Appleby Cl Chingford E4 36 A4
Hayes UB3, UB8 83 A1
Orpington BR5 211 C2
Twickenham TW2 152 B2
West Green N15 51 B4
Appleby Ct W3 111 A4
Appleby Gdns TW14 149 D3
Appleby Rd Hackney E8 74 A1
Newham E16 99 A1
Appleby St E2 95 D5
Appledore Ave HA4 62 C5
Appledore Cl
Bromley BR2 209 A4
Edgware HA8 26 C2
Upper Tooting SW12, SW17 158 D2
Appledore Cres DA14 167 D1
Appledore Way NW7 28 D3
Appleford 8 NW5 71 C3
Appleford Ho 6 W10 91 A3
Appleford Rd W10 91 A3
Applegarth
Claygate KT10 212 D3
New Addington CR0 223 D1
Apple Garth TW8 109 D2
Applegarth Dr IG2 57 D5
Applegarth Ho
Borough The SE1 251 D2
9 Camberwell SE15 140 A5
Applegarth Inf Sch CR0 223 D2
Applegarth Jun Sch CR0 223 D2
Applegarth Rd
Hammersmith W14 112 D3
Woolwich SE28 124 C6
Apple Gr
Chessington KT9 214 A4
Enfield EN1 5 C2
Apple Lo HA0 65 C5
Apple Mkt KT1 175 D1
Apple Mkt WC2 250 B6
Apple Rd E11 76 C5
Appleshaw Ho 4 SE5 139 C2
Appleton Ct 30 E8 74 B3
Appleton Gdns KT3 200 A3
Appleton Rd SE9 144 A2
Appleton Sq CR4 180 C2
Apple Tree Ave UB7 82 B1
Appletree Cl 5 SE20 184 B2
Appletree Ct
Lewisham SE13 142 B1
Northolt UB5 85 A4
Appletree Gdns EN4 2 C1
Apple Tree Yd SW1 249 B4
Applewood Cl
Dollis Hill NW2 68 B5
Ickenham UB10 60 A4
Oakleigh Pk N20 14 C3
Applewood Dr E13 99 B3
Appold St EC2 95 C2 243 A4
Appollo Ct 7 SW9 138 C4
Apprentice Gdns UB5 85 B4
Apprentice Way 5 E5 74 B4
Approach Cl N16 73 C4
Approach La NW7 29 A5
Approach Rd
Ashford TW15 171 A4
Bethnal Green E2 96 C5
East Molesey KT8 195 C4
Edgware HA8 26 C4
Merton SW20 178 C1
New Barnet EN4, EN5 2 B1
Approach The Acton W3 89 B1
Enfield EN1 6 B3
Hendon NW4 46 D4
Orpington BR6 227 D6
Aprey Gdns NW4 46 C5
April Cl Ealing W7 108 C6
Feltham TW13 150 A1
Orpington BR6 227 D3
April Ct 20 E2 96 A5
April Glen SE23 162 D1
April St E8 73 D4
Apsley Cl HA2 42 A4
Apsley Ct SM2 218 A2
Apsley Ctr The NW2 68 A6
Apsley Ho Enfield EN1 17 C5
Hounslow TW4 129 B1
Stepney E1 96 C2
St John's Wood NW8 229 C4
Apsley Rd
Croydon SE25 206 B5
Kingston u T KT3 199 A6
Apsley Way
Dollis Hill NW2 68 A6
Mayfair W1 248 B2
Aquarius TW1 153 B3
Aquarius Bsns Pk NW2 46 A1
Aquarius Way HA6 22 A6
Aquila St NW8 92 B5 229 D4
Aquinas St SE1 116 C5 251 B3
Arabella Ct NW8 229 B4
Arabella Dr SW15 133 C1
Arabia Cl E4 20 B4
Arabian Ho 3 E1 97 A3
Arabin Rd SE4 141 B1
Aragon Ave KT7 196 D4
Aragon Cl
Ashford TW16 171 D3
Bromley BR2 210 B1
Enfield EN2 4 B5
Aragon Ct
Beckenham BR3 186 A2
East Molesey KT8 196 A5
Aragon Dr HA4 40 D1
Aragon Pl SM4 201 A2
Aragon Prim Sch SM4 200 D2
Aragon Rd
Kingston u T KT2 176 A5
West Barnes SM4 201 A2
Aragon Twr SE8 119 B2
Arakan Ho 4 N16 73 B4
Aral Ho 14 E1 96 D3
Arandora Cres RM6 58 B2
Aranya Ct 3 E17 35 A1
Arapiles Ho 6 E14 98 B1
Arbery Rd E3 97 A5
Arbon Ct N1 235 B5
Arbor Cl BR3 185 D1
Arbor Ct N16 73 B6
Arborfield Cl SW2 160 B3
Arborfield Ho 7 E14 119 C6
Arbor Rd E4 20 B1
Arbour Ho 3 E1 96 D1
Arbour Rd EN3 6 D2
Arbour Sq E1 96 D1
Arbroath Rd SE9 144 A2
Arbrook Chase KT10 212 A2
Arbrook Ct
Chessington KT9 213 D3
St Paul's Cray BR5 190 A2
Arbrook Hall KT10 212 D2
Arbrook La KT10 212 B2
Arbury Ho BR1 188 A3
Arbury Terr 3 SE26 162 B1
Arbuthnot La DA5 169 A5
Arbuthnot Rd SE14 140 D3
Arbutus St E8 95 D6
Arcade Ho 7 NW11 47 B4
Arcade The
Broadgate EC2 243 A3
2 Eltham SE9 166 C5
1 Tufnell Pk N7 72 A4
Walthamstow E17 53 C5
Arcadia Ave N3 29 C2
Arcadia Centre The W5 109 D6
Arcadia Cl SM5 219 A4
Arcadian Ave DA5 169 A5
Arcadian Cl DA5 169 A5
Arcadian Gdns N22 32 C3
Arcadian Ho SW6 136 A3
Arcadian Pl SW18 157 B4
Arcadian Rd DA5 169 A5
Arcadia St E14 97 C1
Archangel St SE16 118 D4
Archbishop Coggan Ho SE13 142 B1
Archbishop Lanfranc Sch The CR0 204 A3
Archbishop Michael Ramsey Tech Coll SE5 138 D5
Archbishop's Pl 1 SW2 160 B4
Archbishop Sumner CE Prim Sch SE11 116 C2 261 B3
Archbishop Tenison's CE High Sch CR0 221 D5
Archbishop Tenison's Sch SE11 138 B6 270 D5
Archdale Bsns Ctr HA2 64 A6
Archdale Ct W12 112 B5
Archdale Ho SE1 263 A6
Archdale Pl KT3 198 D6
Archdale Rd SE22 139 D1
Archdeacon Cambridge's CE Prim Sch TW2 152 C2
Archel Rd W14 135 B6 264 C6
Archer Cl KT2 176 A3
Archer Ct TW13 150 A3
Archer Ho
1 Battersea SW11 136 B3
Ealing W13 109 B5
24 Hoxton N1 95 C6
1 New Cross SE14 141 A4
Notting Hill W11 244 D6
Archer Mews TW12 174 A4
Archer Rd SE25 206 B5
Archers Ct 3 CR2 221 A3
Archers Dr EN3 6 C3
Archers Lo 22 SE16 118 A1
Archer Sq SE14 141 A6
Archer St W1 249 C6
Archer Terr UB7 104 A6
Archery Cl Harrow HA3 42 D6
Paddington W2 237 B1
Archery Fields Ho WC1 234 A2
Archery Rd SE9 166 B6
Archery Stps W2 247 B6
Arches Bsns Ctr The UB2 107 B4
Arches The Harrow HA2 63 D6
Strand WC2 250 B4
Archgate Bsns Ctr 1 N12 30 A5
Archibald Mews W1 248 C5
Archibald Rd N7 71 D4
Archibald St E3 97 C4
Archie Cl UB7 104 C4
Archie St SE1 253 B1
Arch St SE1 117 A3 262 A5
Archway N19 71 C6
Archway Bsns Ctr 5 N19 71 D5
Archway Cl
North Kensington W10 90 D2
2 Upper Holloway N19 71 C6
Wallington SM6 220 A5
Wimbledon SW19 179 D6
Archway Hts 5 N19 49 C1
Archway Mews SW15 135 A1
Archway Rd N6 49 B2
Archway St SW13, SW14 133 C2
Archway Sta N19 71 C6
Arcola St E8 73 D3
Arcon Dr UB5 85 A3
Arctic St NW5 71 B3
Arcus Rd BR1 186 C4
Ardbeg Rd SE24 161 B6
Arden 17 SW19 156 D3
Arden Cl
Bushey Heath WD23 8 D4
Erith SE28 102 D1
Harrow HA1 64 B5
Arden Court Gdns N2 48 B3
Arden Cres
Dagenham RM9 80 D1
Millwall E14 119 C2
Arden Gr BR6 226 D4
Arden Grange N12 30 A6
Arden Ho 21 Hoxton N1 95 C5
29 Stockwell SW9 138 A3
Vauxhall SE11 260 C3
Arden Mews E17 53 D4
Arden Mhor HA5 40 B5
Arden Rd Ealing W13 109 C6
Finchley N3 47 B6
Ardent Cl SE25 205 C6
Ardent Ho 30 E3 97 A5
Ardfern Ave SW16 204 C6
Ardfillan Rd SE6 164 B2
Ardgowan Rd SE6 164 C3
Ardilaun Rd N5 73 A4
Ardingly Cl CR0 222 D5
Ardleigh Gdns SM3 201 C2
Ardleigh Ho 5 IG11 101 A6
Ardleigh Rd
Kingsland N1 73 C2
Walthamstow E17 35 B2
Ardleigh Terr E17 35 B2
Ardley Cl
Forest Hill SE6 163 A1
Neasden NW10 67 C5
Ruislip HA4 39 A2
Ardlui Rd SE27 161 A2
Ardmay Gdns KT6 198 A4
Ardmere Rd SE13 164 B5
Ardmore La IG9 21 B4
Ardmore Pl IG9 21 B4
Ardoch Rd SE6 164 B2
Ardra Rd N9 18 D1
Ardrossan Gdns KT4 216 A5
Ardshiel Cl SW15 134 D2
Ardwell Ave IG6 57 A4
Ardwell Rd SW2 160 A2
Ardwick Rd NW2 69 C4
Arena Bsns Ctr N4 51 A3
Arena Est N4 50 D3
Arena Sta SE25 206 C4
Arena The EN3 7 B5
Ares Ct 16 E14 119 C2
Arethusa Ho 8 E14 119 D2
Argali Ho 3 DA18 125 A3
Argall Ave E10 52 D1
Argall Way E10 53 A1
Argenta Way NW10 66 D1
Argent Ct KT6 214 C5
Argent Ctr The UB3 106 A4
Argent Ho HA5 23 B4
Argo Bsns Ctr 7 NW6 91 C4
Argon Mews SW6 265 B3
Argon Rd N18 34 D5
Argos Ct 5 SW9 138 C4
Argos Ho 8 E2 96 B5
Argosy Ho Fitzrovia W1 238 D5
Rotherhithe SE8 119 A2
Argus Way UB5 85 A4
Argyle Cl W13 87 A3
Argyle Ho
Cubitt Town E14 120 A3
Richmond TW10 153 C2
Sutton SM2 218 A2
Teddington TW11 174 C5
Argyle Mans 4 NW2 68 D4
Argyle Pl W6 112 B2
Argyle Prim Sch WC1 94 A4 233 A2
Argyle Rd Ealing W13 87 A2
Edmonton N18 34 A6
Harrow HA2 41 D3
Hounslow TW3 151 D6
Ilford IG1 78 C6
Leyton E15 76 C4
Newham E16 99 B1
Stepney E1 96 D3
Tottenham N17 34 A2
Woodside Pk N12 29 C5
Argyle Sq WC1 94 A4 233 B2
Argyle St WC1 94 A4 233 B2
Argyle Way SE16 118 A1
Argyle Wlk WC1 233 B1
Argyll Ave UB1 107 D5
Argyll Cl SW9 138 B2
Argyll Ct 15 SW2 160 A4
Argyll Gdns HA8 26 D2
Argyll Mans
Chelsea SW3 266 D6
West Kensington W14 254 B4
Argyll Rd
Kensington W8 113 C4 245 B1
Woolwich SE18 123 A3
Argyll St W1 93 C1 239 A1
Aria Ct IG2 57 A3
Arica Ho SE16 118 B3
Arica Rd SE4 141 A2
Ariel Ct
5 Belvedere DA17 125 C1
5 Hammersmith W12 112 A3
Newington SE11 261 C3
Ariel Rd NW6 69 C2
Ariel Way
Hounslow TW4 128 B2
Shepherd's Bush W12 112 C5
Aristotle Rd SW4 137 D2
Arizona Bldg 10 SE13 141 D4
Arkansas Ho 21 N19 49 D2
Ark Ct N16 73 D6
Arkell Gr SW16 182 D3
Arkindale Rd SE6 164 A1
Arklay Cl UB8 82 B3
ARKLEY 12 A6
Arkley Cres E17 53 B4
Arkley Dr EN5 12 B6
Arkley Pk EN5 11 B5
Arkley Rd E17 53 B4
Arklow Ho SE17 139 B6
Arklow Mews 4 KT6 214 A6
Arklow Rd SE14 141 B6
Arklow Road Trad Est SE14 141 B6
Arkwright Ho 23 SW2 160 A4
Arkwright Mans NW3 70 A3
Arkwright Rd NW3 70 A3
Arlesey Cl SW15 157 A6
Arlesford Rd SW9 138 A2
Arless Ho 8 HA1 42 D4
Arlidge Ho EC1 241 B4
Arlingford Rd SW2 160 C5
Arlington N12 13 C1
Arlington Ave N1 95 A6 235 B5
Arlington Cl
Lewisham SE13 164 B6
Sidcup DA15 167 C4
Sutton SM1 217 C6
Twickenham TW1 153 C5
Arlington Ct
13 Acton W3 110 D5
Highgate N6 49 A3
4 Twickenham TW1 153 C5
Arlington Dr
Carshalton SM5 218 D6
Ruislip HA4 39 B3
Arlington Gdns
Acton Green W4 111 A1
Ilford IG1 56 C1
Arlington Gn NW7 28 D3
Arlington Ho
3 Deptford SE8 141 B6
Finsbury EC1 234 B2
1 Shepherd's Bush W12 112 B5
Arlington Lo SW2 138 B1
Arlington Park Mans 1 W4 111 A1
Arlington Pl 7 SE10 142 A5
Arlington Rd
Ashford TW15 170 B5
Camden Town NW1 93 B6 231 D5
Ealing W13 87 B1
Osidge N14 15 C3
Richmond TW10 153 D2
Surbiton KT6 197 D3
Teddington TW11 174 D6
Twickenham TW1 153 C5
Woodford IG8 37 B3
Arlington Sq N1 95 A6 235 B5
Arlington St SW1 115 C5 249 A4
Arlington Way EC1 94 C4 234 B2
Arliss Way UB5 84 C6
Arlow Rd N21 16 C3
Armada Ct 11 SE8 141 C6
Armadale Cl N17 52 B5
Armadale Rd
Feltham TW14 150 A6
West Brompton SW6 265 A5
Armada St 10 SE8 141 C6
Armada Way E6 101 B1
Armagh Rd E3 97 B6
Armeston KT3 199 B2
Armfield Cl KT8 195 B4
Armfield Cotts 3 SW19 180 D1
Armfield Cres CR4 180 D1
Armfield Rd EN2 5 B4
Arminger Rd W12 112 B5
Armistice Gdns SE25 206 A6
Armitage Ho NW1 92 C2 237 B4
Armitage Rd
Golders Green NW11 47 B1
Greenwich SE10 120 D1
Armour Cl N7 72 B2
Armoury Ho E3 97 A6
Armoury Rd SE8 141 D3
Armoury Way SW18 157 C6
Armsby Ho 17 E1 96 C2
Armstead Wlk RM10 81 C1
Armstrong Ave IG8 36 C4
Armstrong Cl
Bickley BR1 210 A6
Dagenham RM8 58 D2
Newham E6 100 B1
Pinner HA5 40 A3
Walton-on-T KT12 194 A3
Armstrong Cres EN4 2 B2
Armstrong Ho 8 SW15 156 D5
Armstrong Rd
East Acton W3 111 D5
Feltham TW13 173 A5
Knightsbridge SW7 256 C5
Woolwich SE18 123 A3
Armstrong Way UB2 107 D4
Armytage Rd TW5 128 D5
Arnal Cres SW18 157 A4
Arncliffe NW6 91 D6
Arncliffe Cl N11 31 A4
Arncroft Ct IG11 102 B4
Arndale Wlk 6 SW18 157 D6
Arndell Ho 16 SM1 218 A4
Arne Gr BR6 227 D5
Arne Ho SE11 260 C2
Arne St WC2 94 A1 240 B1
Arnett Sq E4 35 B4
Arneways Ave RM6 58 D6
Arneway St SW1 259 D5
Arne Wlk SE3 142 D1
Arnewood Cl SW15 156 A3
Arney's La CR4 203 A3
Arngask Rd SE6 164 B4
Arnhem Pl E14 119 C3
Arnhem Way 3 SE22 161 C6
Arnhem Wharf E14 119 C3
Arnhem Wharf Prim Sch E14 119 C3
Arnison Rd KT8 196 B5
Arnold Ave E EN3 7 C5
Arnold Ave W EN3 7 B5
Arnold Cir E2 95 D4
Arnold Cl HA3 44 B2
Arnold Cres TW7 152 B6
Arnold Ct E18 36 D2
Arnold Dr KT9 213 D2
Arnold Est SE1 253 D1
Arnold Gdns N13 32 D5
Arnold Ho
Croydon CR0 220 D4
Newington SE17 261 D1
9 Stoke Newington N16 73 C5
Arnold House Sch NW8 92 B5 229 C3
Arnold Rd Bow E3 97 C4
Dagenham RM10 81 C1
Mitcham SW17 180 D3
Northolt UB5 63 A2
Tottenham N15 51 D6
Arnos Gr N14 15 D1
Arnos Grove Ct 4 N11 31 C5
Arnos Grove Sta N11 31 C6
Arnos Rd N11 31 C6
Arnot Ho 27 SE5 139 A5
Arnott Cl
Acton Green W4 111 B2
Thamesmead SE28 124 C5
Arnould Ave SE5 139 B1
Arnsberg Way DA6, DA7 147 C1
Arnside Gdns HA9 43 D1
Arnside Ho 2 SE17 139 B6
Arnside Rd DA7 147 C4
Arnside St SE17 139 A6
Arnulf St SE6 185 D6
Arnull's Rd SW16 182 D4
Arodene Rd SW2 160 B5
Arosa Rd 8 TW1 153 D5
Arragon Gdns
Streatham SW16 182 A3
West Wickham BR4 223 D5
Arragon Rd Newham E6 99 D6
4 Twickenham TW1 153 A3
Wandsworth SW18 157 C3
Arran Cl SM6 219 C4
Arran Ct Edgware HA8 10 D2
32 Hendon NW9 27 D1
Neasden NW10 67 B5
Arrandene Ho 3 BR5 190 B1
Arran Dr Stanmore HA7 25 C6
Wanstead E12 77 D6
Arran Ho
5 Canary Wharf E14 120 A5
Stoke Newington N16 51 D1
Arran Mews W5 110 B5
Arran Rd SE6 164 A2
Arran Wlk N1 73 A1
Arras Ave SM4 202 A4
Arras Ho SE2 146 D6
Arrol Ho SE1 262 B5

Arrol Rd BR3 . . . . . 206 D6
Arrowe Ct 6 E5 . . . . . 74 B4
Arrow Ho 23 N1 . . . . . 95 C6
Arrow Rd E3 . . . . . 97 D4
Arrow Scout Wlk UB5 . . . 85 A4
Arrowsmith Ho SE11 . . 260 C2
Arsenal Rd SE9 . . . . . 144 B2
Arsenal Sta N5 . . . . . 72 C5
Arsenal Way SE18 . . . . . 123 A3
Arta Ho 26 E1 . . . . . 96 C1
Artemis Ct 14 E14 . . . . . 119 C2
Artemis Pl SW18 . . . . . 157 B4
Arterberry Rd SW20, SW19 . . . . . 178 D2
Artesian Cl NW10 . . . . . 67 B1
Artesian Gr EN5 . . . . . 2 A1
Artesian Rd W2 . . . . . 91 C1
Artesian Wlk 4 E11 . . . . . 76 C5
Arthingworth St E15 . . . . 98 C6
Arthur Ct
Battersea SW11 . . . . . 268 B1
10 North Kensington W10 . . . . . 90 D1
Paddington W2 . . . . . 91 D1
South Croydon CR0 . . . . . 221 B5
Arthur Deakin Ho 1 E1 . . . . . 96 A2
Arthurdon Rd SE4 . . . . . 163 C6
Arthur Gr SE18 . . . . . 123 A2
Arthur Henderson Ho
9 Crouch End N19 . . . . . 49 D2
9 Fulham SW6 . . . . . 135 B3
Arthur Newton Ho 20 SW11 . . . . . 136 B2
Arthur Rd
Dagenham RM6 . . . . . 58 D3
Edmonton N9 . . . . . 17 D2
6 Kingston u T KT2 . . . . 176 C3
Lower Holloway N7 . . . . . 72 B4
Newham E6 . . . . . 100 B5
West Barnes KT3 . . . . . 200 B4
Wimbledon SW19 . . . . . 179 C6
Arthur Ruxley Est DA14 . . . . . 190 D4
Arthur St EC4 . . . 117 B6 252 D6
Arthur Wade Ho 7 E2 . . . 95 D4
Arthur Walls Ho 3 E12 . . 78 C5
Artichoke Hill 8 E1 . . . . 118 B6
Artichoke Mews 5 SE5 . . . . . 139 B4
Artichoke Pl SE5 . . . . . 139 B4
Artillery Cl IG2 . . . . . 57 A3
Artillery Ho Bow E3 . . . . . 97 A6
Westminster SW1 . . . . . 259 C5
Woolwich SE18 . . . . . 122 C1
Artillery La
Broadgate E1 . . . 95 C2 243 B3
North Kensington W12 . . . 90 A1
Artillery Pas E1 . . . . . 243 B3
Artillery Pl
Harrow Weald HA3 . . . . . 24 A3
Westminster SW1 . . . . . 259 C5
Woolwich SE18 . . . . . 122 C2
Artillery Row SW1 . . . . 259 C5
Artington Cl BR6 . . . . . 227 A4
Artisan Cl E16 . . . . . 122 D6
Artisan Ct E8 . . . . . 74 A2
Artisan Mews 9 NW10 . . 90 D4
Artisan Quarter 10 NW10 . . . . . 90 D4
Artizan St E1 . . . . . 243 B2
Arton Wilson Ho 12 SW15 . . . . . 156 A6
Arts Educational Sch The W4 . . . . . 111 C2
Arundale KT1 . . . . . 197 D5
Arundel Ave SM4 . . . . . 201 B5
Arundel Bldgs SE1 . . . . 263 B5
Arundel Cl
Croydon CR0 . . . . . 220 D5
Hampton TW12 . . . . . 173 D5
Leyton E15 . . . . . 76 C4
Sidcup DA5 . . . . . 169 B5
Wandsworth SW11 . . . . . 158 C6
Arundel Ct
Barnes SW13 . . . . . 134 B6
4 Beckenham BR2 . . . . . 186 C1
2 Bexley DA6 . . . . . 147 A1
Chelsea SW3 . . . . . 257 B2
Colney Hatch N12 . . . . . 30 C4
3 Croydon CR0 . . . . . 220 D5
Harrow HA2 . . . . . 63 C4
Putney SW15 . . . . . 156 D6
Tottenham N17 . . . . . 34 A2
Arundel Dr
Borehamwood WD6 . . . . . 11 A6
Harrow HA2 . . . . . 63 C4
Woodford IG8 . . . . . 37 A3
Arundel Gdns
Burnt Oak HA8 . . . . . 27 B3
Ilford IG3 . . . . . 80 A6
Notting Hill W11 . . . . . 113 B6 244 C6
Southgate N21 . . . . . 16 C3
Arundel Gr N16 . . . . . 73 C3
Arundel Ho
Croydon CR0 . . . . . 221 B3
Islington N1 . . . 94 D6 234 D6
Richmond TW10 . . . . . 154 C6
3 South Acton W3 . . . . . 110 D4
Arundel Lo
Church End N3 . . . . . 29 B1
9 Upper Holloway N19 . . 72 A6
Arundel Mans
Barnes SW13 . . . . . 134 B6
Fulham SW6 . . . . . 264 D2
Arundel Pl N1, N7 . . . . . 72 C2
Arundel Rd
Belmont SM2 . . . . . 217 B1
Cockfosters EN4 . . . . . 2 C2
Hounslow TW4 . . . . . 128 C2
Kingston u T KT1 . . . . . 177 A1
Thornton Heath CR0 . . . . 205 B3
Arundel Sq N7 . . . . . 72 C2
Arundel St WC2 . . . . . 116 B6 250 D6
Arundel Terr SW13 . . . . 134 B6
Arun Ho 5 KT2 . . . . . 175 D2
Arvon Rd N5 . . . . . 72 C3
Asa Ct UB3 . . . . . 105 D3
Asaph Ho SE14 . . . . . 141 B4
Asbaston Terr IG11 . . . . 79 A2
Asbury Ct N21 . . . . . 16 A6
Ascalon Ct 16 SW2 . . . . 160 B4
Ascalon Ho SW8 . . . . . 269 A3
Ascalon St SW8 . . . . . 137 C5 269 A3
Ascham Dr E4 . . . . . 35 C3
Ascham End E17 . . . . . 35 A2
Ascham St NW5 . . . . . 71 C3
Aschurch Rd CR0 . . . . . 205 D2
Ascot Cl
Borehamwood WD6 . . . . . 10 C6
Northolt UB5 . . . . . 63 C3
Ascot Ct
8 Brixton SW4 . . . . . 138 A1
Bromley BR1 . . . . . 188 A1
Old Bexley DA5 . . . . . 169 B4
St John's Wood NW8 . . . 229 C1
Ascot Gdns Enfield EN3 . . . . 6 C6
Southall UB1 . . . . . 85 C2
Ascot Ho
6 Acton Green W4 . . . . . 111 A1
1 Paddington W9 . . . . . 91 C2
Penge SE26 . . . . . 184 B4
Regent's Pk NW1 . . . . . 231 D2
Ascot Lo Enfield EN1 . . . . . 17 B6
Paddington NW6 . . . . . 91 D5
Ascot Par 9 SW4 . . . . . 138 A1
Ascot Pl 12 HA7 . . . . . 25 C5
Ascot Rd
East Bedfont TW14 . . . . . 148 D2
Edmonton N18 . . . . . 34 A6
Newham E6 . . . . . 100 B4
Orpington BR5 . . . . . 211 D5
Streatham SW17 . . . . . 181 A4
Tottenham N15 . . . . . 51 B4
Ascott Ave W5 . . . . . 110 A4
Ascott Ct HA5 . . . . . 40 A5
Ashbourne Ave
East Barnet N20 . . . . . 14 D2
Erith DA7 . . . . . 147 A5
Harrow HA2 . . . . . 64 B6
Temple Fortune NW11 . . . 47 B4
Wanstead E18 . . . . . 55 B5
Ashbourne Cl Ealing W5 . . 88 C2
18 Woodside Pk N12 . . . . 29 D6
Ashbourne Ct
Beckenham BR3 . . . . . 186 A2
Clapton Pk E5 . . . . . 75 A4
13 Woodside Pk N12 . . . . 29 D6
Ashbourne Gr
Chiswick W4 . . . . . 111 C1
East Dulwich SE22 . . . . . 139 D1
Edgware NW7 . . . . . 27 B5
Ashbourne Ind Sch W8 . . . . . 113 D4 245 C1
Ashbourne Lo 2 N13 . . . 32 C6
Ashbourne Par 2 NW11 . . . . . 47 B5
Ashbourne Rd
Ealing W5 . . . . . 88 B3
Mitcham CR4 . . . . . 181 A3
Ashbourne Rise BR6 . . . 227 C4
Ashbourne Terr 1 SW19 . . . . . 179 C3
Ashbourne Way NW11 . . 47 B4
Ashbridge Ct 3 W6 . . . . 112 B3
Ashbridge Rd E11 . . . . . 54 D2
Ashbridge St NW8 . . . . . 92 C3 237 A5
Ashbrook HA8 . . . . . 26 B4
Ashbrook Rd
Dagenham RM10 . . . . . 81 D5
Upper Holloway N19 . . . . 71 D6
Ashburn Ct BR1 . . . . . 187 A3
Ashburn Gdns SW7 . . . 256 A4
Ashburnham Ave HA1 . . 42 D3
Ashburnham Cl N2 . . . . 48 B5
Ashburnham Com Sch SW10 . . . . . 266 C4
Ashburnham Gdns HA1 . . 42 D3
Ashburnham Gr SE10 . . 141 D5
Ashburnham Pk KT10 . . 212 A4
Ashburnham Pl SE10 . . . 141 D5
Ashburnham Rd
Chelsea SW10 . . . . . 136 A5 266 B3
Kensal Rise NW10 . . . . . 90 C5
Richmond TW10 . . . . . 153 B1
Ashburnham Retreat 4 SE10 . . . . . 141 D5
Ashburnham Twr SW10 . . . . . 266 C4
Ashburn Pl SW7 . . . . . 114 A2 256 A3
Ashburton Ave
Croydon CR0 . . . . . 206 B1
Ilford IG3 . . . . . 79 D4
Ashburton Cl CR0 . . . . . 206 A1
Ashburton Ct 1 HA5 . . . 40 D6
Ashburton Gdns CR0 . . . 222 A6
Ashburton Ho
Enfield EN3 . . . . . 6 D2
2 Wallington SM6 . . . . . 219 D3
Ashburton Jun & Inf Sch CR0 . . . . . 206 B3
Ashburton Learning Village CR9 . . . . . 206 B2
Ashburton Mans SW10 . . 266 B4
Ashburton Rd
Croydon CR0 . . . . . 222 A6
Newham E16 . . . . . 99 A1
Ruislip HA4 . . . . . 62 A6
Ashburton Terr 2 E13 . . 99 A5
Ashbury Dr UB10 . . . . . 60 D5
Ashbury Gdns RM6 . . . . 58 D4
Ashbury Pl SW19 . . . . . 180 A4
Ashbury Rd SW11 . . . . . 137 A2
Ashby Ave KT19, KT9 . . . 214 C2
Ashby Ct NW8 . . . . . 236 D6
Ashby Gr N1 . . . . . 73 A1
Ashby Grange 7 SM6 . . 219 C2
Ashby Ho
6 Brixton SW9 . . . . . 138 D3
13 Islington N1 . . . . . 73 A1
3 Northolt UB5 . . . . . 85 B3
14 Surbiton KT6 . . . . . 198 A3
Ashby Mews
10 Clapham Pk SW2 . . . . 160 A6
New Cross SE4 . . . . . 141 B3
Ashby Rd
New Cross SE4 . . . . . 141 B3
South Tottenham N15 . . . . 52 A4
Ashby St EC1 . . . . 94 D4 234 D1
Ashby Way UB7 . . . . . 126 C5
Ashby Wlk CR0 . . . . . 205 A3
Ashchurch Ct 2 W12 . . 112 A3
Ashchurch Gr W12 . . . . 112 A3
Ashchurch Park Villas W12 . . . . . 112 A3
Ashchurch Terr W12 . . . 112 A3
Ash Cl Carshalton SM5 . . . 218 D6
Edgware HA8 . . . . . 27 A6
Kingston u T KT3 . . . . . 177 B1
Penge SE20 . . . . . 184 C1
Petts Wood BR5 . . . . . 211 B4
Sidcup DA14 . . . . . 168 B1
Stanmore HA7 . . . . . 25 A4
Ashcombe Ave KT6 . . . . 197 D2
Ashcombe Ct 4 SW15 . . . . . 157 A6
Ashcombe Gdns HA8 . . . . 26 C6
Ashcombe Ho 38 E3 . . . . 97 D4
Ashcombe Pk NW2 . . . . . 67 C5
Ashcombe Rd
Wallington SM5 . . . . . 219 A2
Wimbledon SW19 . . . . . 179 C5
Ashcombe Sq KT3 . . . . . 199 A6
Ashcombe St SW6 . . . . . 135 D3
Ashcroft Hatch End HA5 . . 23 C4
Osidge N14 . . . . . 15 D2
Ashcroft Ave DA15 . . . . 168 A5
Ashcroft Cres DA15 . . . . 168 A5
Ashcroft Ct
5 Eltham SE9 . . . . . 166 C5
Wembley HA0 . . . . . 65 A4
3 Whetstone N20 . . . . . 14 B2
Ashcroft Ho SW8 . . . . . 269 A2
Ashcroft Rd Bow E3 . . . . 97 A4
Chessington KT9 . . . . . 214 B5
Ashcroft Sq 8 W6 . . . . 112 C2
Ash Ct Chingford E4 . . . . . 20 B4
Clapham SW11 . . . . . 159 A6
Lee SE12 . . . . . 165 A4
Marylebone W1 . . . . . 237 C2
Romford RM7 . . . . . 59 D3
6 Rotherhithe SE16 . . . . 119 A5
Upper Holloway N19 . . . . 71 C6
West Ewell KT19 . . . . . 215 A4
2 West Norwood SW16 . . . . . 182 C5
9 Wimbledon SW19 . . . 179 A3
Woodford E18 . . . . . 37 C2
Ashdale Cl
Stanwell TW19 . . . . . 148 A2
Twickenham TW2 . . . . . 152 A4
Ashdale Gr HA7 . . . . . 24 D4
Ashdale Ho N4 . . . . . 51 B2
Ashdale Rd SE12 . . . . . 165 B3
Ashdale Way TW2 . . . . . 151 D4
Ashdene
6 Deptford SE15 . . . . . 140 B5
Pinner HA5 . . . . . 40 C6
Ashdene Cl TW15 . . . . . 171 A3
Ashdon Cl IG8 . . . . . 37 B4
Ashdon Rd NW10 . . . . . 89 D6
Ashdown Ealing W13 . . . . 87 B2
Putney SW15 . . . . . 156 D6
Ashdown Cl 13 BR3 . . . . 185 D1
Ashdown Cres NW5 . . . . 71 A3
Ashdown Ct
Dulwich SE22 . . . . . 162 A3
Ilford IG1 . . . . . 78 D2
New Malden KT4 . . . . . 199 D2
Sutton SM2 . . . . . 218 A2
Ashdowne Ct N17 . . . . . 34 A2
Ashdown Ho 7 E5 . . . . . 74 A6
Ashdown Pl
Ewell KT17 . . . . . 215 D1
Thames Ditton KT7 . . . . . 197 A2
Ashdown Rd Enfield EN3 . . . 6 C3
Hillingdon UB10 . . . . . 82 C5
Kingston u T KT1 . . . . . 176 A1
Ashdown Way SW17 . . . . 159 A2
Ashdown Wlk 20 E14 . . . 119 C2
Ashe Ho 9 TW1 . . . . . 153 D5
Ashen E6 . . . . . 100 C1
Ashenden SE17 . . . . . 262 B4
Ashenden Rd E5 . . . . . 75 A3
Ashen Gr SW19 . . . . . 157 C2
Ashentree Ct EC4 . . . . . 241 B1
Asher Loftus Way N11 . . . 30 D4
Asher Way E1 . . . . . 118 A6
Ashfield Ave
Bushey WD23 . . . . . 8 A4
Feltham TW13 . . . . . 150 B3
Ashfield Cl
Beckenham BR3 . . . . . 185 C3
Richmond TW10 . . . . . 154 A3
Ashfield Ct SW9 . . . . . 138 A3
Ashfield Ho 5 N5 . . . . . 73 A3
Ashfield La BR7 . . . . . 189 A3
Ashfield Par N14 . . . . . 15 D3
Ashfield Pl BR7 . . . . . 189 B3
Ashfield Rd
East Acton W3 . . . . . 111 D5
New Southgate N14 . . . . . 15 C1
Tottenham N4 . . . . . 51 A3
Ashfield St E1 . . . . . 96 C2
Ashfield Yd 21 E1 . . . . . 96 C2
ASHFORD 170 B4
Ashford Ave
Ashford TW15 . . . . . 170 D4
Hayes UB4 . . . . . 84 D1
Hornsey N8 . . . . . 50 A5
Ashford Bsns Complex TW15 . . . . . 171 A6
Ashford CE Prim Sch TW15 . . . . . 170 D4
Ashford Cl
Ashford TW15 . . . . . 170 A6
Walthamstow E17 . . . . . 53 B3
ASHFORD COMMON . . . 171 B4
Ashford Cres EN3 . . . . . 6 C3
Ashford Ct
Cricklewood NW2 . . . . . 68 D4
Edgware HA8 . . . . . 10 D1
Ashford Gn WD19 . . . . . 22 D5
Ashford Ho
14 Brixton SW9 . . . . . 138 D1
11 Deptford SE8 . . . . . 141 B6
Ashford Hospl TW15 . . . 148 A2
Ashford Ind Est TW15 . . 171 A6
Ashford Mews N17 . . . . . 34 A2
Ashford Rd
Cricklewood NW2 . . . . . 68 D4
Feltham TW13, TW15 . . . 171 B6
Littleton TW15, TW17 . . . 171 A3
Staines TW18 . . . . . 170 A4
Wallend E6 . . . . . 78 C1
Woodford E18 . . . . . 37 B1
Ashford St N1 . . . . . 95 C4
Ash Gr Cricklewood NW2 . . 69 A4
Ealing W5 . . . . . 110 A3
East Bedfont TW14 . . . . . 149 C3
Edmonton N13 . . . . . 17 A1
Enfield EN1 . . . . . 17 C4
Hackney E8 . . . . . 96 B6
Hayes UB3 . . . . . 105 B6
Heston TW5 . . . . . 128 D5
Penge SE20 . . . . . 184 C1
Southall UB1 . . . . . 85 C2
Wembley HA0 . . . . . 65 A4
West Wickham BR4 . . . . . 208 A1
Yiewsley UB7 . . . . . 104 B6
Ashgrove SE12 . . . . . 165 A3
Ashgrove Ct 2 W9 . . . . . 91 C2
Ashgrove Ho SW1 . . . . . 259 D2
Ashgrove Rd
Ashford TW15 . . . . . 171 B5
Catford BR1 . . . . . 186 B4
Ashgrove Sch BR1 . . . . 187 B1
Ash Hill Dr HA5 . . . . . 40 C6
Ash Ho
3 Canary Wharf E14 . . . 120 A4
Fulham SE1 . . . . . 263 D3
Kenton NW9 . . . . . 45 A6
Lewisham SE12 . . . . . 165 A3
2 Teddington TW11 . . . . 175 C3
Ashingdon Cl E4 . . . . . 20 A1
Ashington 1 NW5 . . . . . 71 B2
Ashington Ho 16 E1 . . . . 96 B3
Ashington Rd SW6 . . . . . 135 B3
Ashlake Rd SW16 . . . . . 182 A6
Ashland Pl W1 . . . . . 238 A4
Ashlar Ct N2 . . . . . 48 C6
Ashlar Pl SE18 . . . . . 122 D2
Ashleigh Commercial Est SE7 . . . . . 121 D3
Ashleigh Ct Ealing W5 . . 109 D2
Osidge N14 . . . . . 15 C4
Penge SE26 . . . . . 184 B4
Ashleigh Gdns SM1 . . . . 217 D6
Ashleigh Ho
Mortlake SW14 . . . . . 133 C2
1 Streatham SW16 . . . . . 182 B6
Ashleigh Point 8 SE26 . . . . . 162 D1
Ashleigh Rd
Mortlake SW14 . . . . . 133 C2
Penge SE20 . . . . . 206 B6
Ashley Ave SM4 . . . . . 201 C4
Ashley CE Prim Sch KT12 . . . . . 194 A1
Ashley Cl Hendon NW4 . . . 28 C1
Oatlands Pk KT12, KT13 . . . . . 193 D1
Pinner Green HA5 . . . . . 22 B1
Ashley Cres
Clapham SW11 . . . . . 137 A2
Wood Green N22 . . . . . 32 C1
Ashley Ct
Hampstead NW3 . . . . . 69 D3
Hendon NW4 . . . . . 28 C1
19 Kingsland N16 . . . . . 73 C3
New Barnet EN5 . . . . . 14 A6
Northolt UB5 . . . . . 85 A6
Stanmore HA7 . . . . . 25 B1
Yiewsley UB7 . . . . . 104 A5
Ashley Dr
Borehamwood WD6 . . . . . 11 B6
Hounslow TW7 . . . . . 130 C6
Twickenham TW2 . . . . . 151 D3
Ashley Gdns
Edmonton N13 . . . . . 33 A6
Orpington BR6 . . . . . 227 C3
Ashley Gdns *continued*
Richmond TW10 . . . . . 153 D2
Wembley HA9 . . . . . 66 A6
Ashley Ho BR5 . . . . . 190 A1
Ashley La Croydon CR0 . . . 220 D4
Edgware NW7 . . . . . 28 D3
Hendon NW4 . . . . . 28 C1
Ashley Park Ave KT12 . . 193 D1
Ashley Park Cres KT12 . . . . . 194 A1
Ashley Pl
Walton-on-T KT12 . . . . . 194 A1
Westminster SW1 . . . . . 115 C3 259 A5
Ashley Rd Chingford E4 . . . 35 C4
Enfield EN3 . . . . . 6 C3
Hampton TW12 . . . . . 173 C2
Hornsey N19 . . . . . 50 A2
Richmond TW9 . . . . . 132 A2
Thames Ditton KT7 . . . . . 196 D3
Thornton Heath CR7 . . . . 204 B5
Tottenham Hale N17 . . . . . 52 A6
Upton E7 . . . . . 77 C1
Walton-on-T KT12 . . . . . 194 A1
Wimbledon SW19 . . . . . 179 D4
Ashleys Alley N15 . . . . . 51 A5
Ashley Wlk NW7 . . . . . 28 D3
Ashling Ho 2 N17 . . . . . 33 D1
Ashling Rd CR0 . . . . . 206 A1
Ashlin Rd E15 . . . . . 76 B4
Ash Lo
2 Ashford TW16 . . . . . 171 D3
Fulham SW6 . . . . . 134 D4
Ashlone Rd SW15 . . . . . 134 D2
Ashlyns Way KT9 . . . . . 213 D2
Ashmead 4 N14 . . . . . 15 C6
Ashmead Bsns Ctr 2 E16 . . . . . 98 B3
Ashmead Gate BR1 . . . . 187 C2
Ashmead Ho E9 . . . . . 75 A3
Ashmead Prim Sch SE8 . . . . . 141 C3
Ashmead Rd
East Bedfont TW14 . . . . . 150 A3
St Johns SE8 . . . . . 141 C3
Ashmere Ave BR3 . . . . . 186 B1
Ashmere Cl SM3 . . . . . 216 D3
Ashmere Gr 11 SW2, SW4 . . . . . 138 A1
Ashmere Ho 10 SW2 . . . 138 A1
Ashmill Ct CR0 . . . . . 205 A3
Ashmill St NW8 . . 92 C2 237 A4
Ashmole Prim Sch SW8 . . . . . 138 B6 270 D5
Ashmole Sch N14 . . . . . 15 C3
Ashmole St SW8 . . . . . 138 B6 270 D5
Ashmoor Lo NW7 . . . . . 27 B4
Ashmore NW1 . . . . . 71 D1
Ashmore Cl SE15 . . . . . 139 D5
Ashmore Ct
Catford SE6 . . . . . 164 C3
Colney Hatch N11 . . . . . 30 D4
Heston TW5 . . . . . 129 C6
Ashmore Gr DA16 . . . . . 145 C2
Ashmore Ho W14 . . . . . 254 B5
Ashmore Rd W9 . . . . . 91 B4
Ashmount Prim Sch N19 . . . . . 49 C2
Ashmount Rd
Crouch End N19 . . . . . 49 D2
South Tottenham N15 . . . . 51 D4
Ashmount Terr W5 . . . . 109 D2
Ashneal Gdns HA1 . . . . . 64 B5
Ashness Gdns UB6 . . . . . 65 B2
Ashness Rd SW11 . . . . . 158 D6
Ashpark Ho 4 E14 . . . . . 97 B1
Ash Rd Cheam SM3 . . . . . 201 B1
Croydon CR0 . . . . . 223 C6
Littleton TW17 . . . . . 192 C5
Orpington BR6 . . . . . 227 D1
Plashet E15 . . . . . 76 D3
Ashridge Cl HA3 . . . . . 43 C3
Ashridge Cres SE18 . . . . 145 A5
Ashridge Ct
Southall UB1 . . . . . 108 A6
Southgate N14 . . . . . 15 C6
Ashridge Dr WD19 . . . . . 22 C5
Ashridge Gdns
Bowes Pk N13 . . . . . 32 A5
Pinner HA5 . . . . . 41 A5
Ashridge Ho DA14 . . . . . 189 D6
Ashridge Way
Ashford TW16 . . . . . 172 A4
Merton SM4 . . . . . 201 B5
Ash Row BR2 . . . . . 210 C3
Ashtead Ct 15 SW19 . . . . 156 D3
Ashtead Rd E5 . . . . . 52 A2
Ash Tech Coll The TW15 . . . . . 148 A1
Ashton Cl SM1 . . . . . 217 C4
Ashton Ct
1 Beckenham BR3 . . . . . 185 B2
Chingford E4 . . . . . 20 C1
Harrow HA1 . . . . . 64 D5
Ashton Gdns
Dagenham RM6 . . . . . 59 A3
Hounslow TW4 . . . . . 129 B1
Ashton Ho
13 Kennington SW9 . . . . 138 C5
Roehampton SW15 . . . . . 156 B4
Ashton Rd E15 . . . . . 76 B3
Ashton St E14 . . . . . 120 A6
Ashtree Ave CR4 . . . . . 180 B1
Ashtree Cl BR6 . . . . . 226 D4
Ash Tree Cl
Croydon CR0 . . . . . 207 A3
1 Surbiton KT6 . . . . . 198 A1
Ashtree Ct TW15 . . . . . 170 D5
Ash Tree Dell NW9 . . . . . 45 B4
Ash Tree Villas CR0 . . . . 204 B3
Ash Tree Way CR0 . . . . . 207 A3
Ashurst Cl SE20 . . . . . 184 B2
Ashurst Dr
Ilford IG2, IG6 . . . . . 57 A4
Littleton TW17 . . . . . 192 A4
Ashurst Lo 4 N5 . . . . . 72 D3
Ashurst Rd
Cockfosters EN4 . . . . . 14 D6
Colney Hatch N12 . . . . . 30 C5
Ashurst Wlk CR0 . . . . . 222 B6
Ashvale Rd SW17 . . . . . 180 D5
Ashview Cl TW15 . . . . . 170 A5
Ashview Gdns TW15 . . . 170 A5
Ashville Rd E11 . . . . . 76 B6
Ashwater Rd SE12 . . . . . 165 A3
Ashway Ctr 5 KT2 . . . . . 176 A2
Ashwell Cl 8 E6 . . . . . 100 A1
Ashwell Ct TW15 . . . . . 148 A2
Ashwin St E8 . . . . . 73 D2
Ash Wlk HA0 . . . . . 65 C4
Ashwood Ave UB8 . . . . . 82 C1
Ashwood Ct HA9 . . . . . 66 B4
Ashwood Gdns
Hayes UB3 . . . . . 105 D2
New Addington CR0 . . . . 224 A2
Ashwood Ho 10 NW4 . . . . 46 C5
Ashwood Lo
9 New Barnet EN5 . . . . . 13 D6
Southgate N21 . . . . . 16 B5
Ashwood Pk 6 SM2 . . . 217 C1
Ashwood Rd E4 . . . . . 20 B1
Ashworth Cl SE5 . . . . . 139 B3
Ashworth Mans W9 . . . . . 91 D4
Ashworth Rd W9 . . . . . 91 D4
Aske Ho 2 N1 . . . . . 95 C4
Asker Ho N7 . . . . . 72 A4
Askern Cl DA6 . . . . . 146 D1
Aske St N1 . . . . . 95 C4
Askew Cres W12 . . . . . 112 A4
Askew Mans 14 W12 . . . 112 A4
Askew Rd W12 . . . . . 112 A4
Askham Ct W12 . . . . . 112 A5
Askham Lo 5 SE12 . . . . 165 A4
Askham Rd W12 . . . . . 112 A5
Askill Dr SW15 . . . . . 157 A6
Asland Rd E15 . . . . . 98 B6
Aslett St SW18 . . . . . 158 A4
Asmara Rd NW2 . . . . . 69 A3
Asmuns Hill NW11 . . . . . 47 C4
Asmuns Pl NW11 . . . . . 47 B4
Asolando Dr SE17 . . . . . 262 B3
Aspect Coll WC1 . . . . . 94 A2 240 B3
Aspect Ho 7 E14 . . . . . 120 A4
Aspects SM1 . . . . . 217 D3
Aspen Cl Ealing W5 . . . . . 110 B4
13 Upper Holloway N19 . . 71 C6
Yiewsley UB7 . . . . . 104 B5
Aspen Copse BR1 . . . . . 188 B1
Aspen Ct 10 Acton W3 . . . . 89 A1
12 Hackney E8 . . . . . 74 A3
Redbridge IG5 . . . . . 56 A6
Richmond TW9 . . . . . 132 C5
Aspen Dr HA0 . . . . . 65 A5
Aspen Gdns
Ashford TW15 . . . . . 171 A5
2 Hammersmith W6 . . . 112 B1
Mitcham CR4 . . . . . 203 A4
Aspen Gn DA18 . . . . . 125 B3
Aspen Gr HA5 . . . . . 39 D6
Aspen Ho
8 Deptford SE15 . . . . . 140 C6
4 Maitland Pk NW3 . . . . . 70 D2
Richmond TW9 . . . . . 132 C5
2 Sidcup DA15 . . . . . 168 A1
Southgate N21 . . . . . 16 B6
Aspen La UB5 . . . . . 85 A4
Aspenlea Rd W6 . . . . . 134 D6
Aspen Lo 1 SW19 . . . . . 179 B4
Aspen Way
Canary Wharf E14 . . . . . 120 A6
Feltham TW13 . . . . . 150 B1
Aspern Gr NW3 . . . . . 70 C3
Aspinall Ho SW12 . . . . . 160 A3
Aspinall Rd SE4 . . . . . 140 D2
Aspinden Rd SE16 . . . . . 118 B2
Aspire Bld 10 SW15 . . . . 157 B6
Aspley Rd SW18 . . . . . 157 D6
Asplins Rd N17 . . . . . 34 B2
Asprey Ho CR4 . . . . . 202 C6
Asquith Cl RM8 . . . . . 58 C1
Assam SE1 . . . . . 253 D3
Assam St E1 . . . . . 96 A1
Assata Mews N1 . . . . . 72 D2
Assembly Pas E1 . . . . . 96 C2
Assembly Wlk SM5 . . . . 202 C2
Assheton-Bennett Ho 15 KT6 . . . . . 198 A4
Ass House La HA3 . . . . . 23 D6
Assisi Ct
Upper Tooting SW12 . . . . 158 D3
Wembley HA0 . . . . . 64 D5
Astall Cl HA3 . . . . . 24 C2
Astbury Bsns Pk 5 SE15 . . . . . 140 C4
Astbury Ho SE11 . . . . . 261 A5
Astbury Rd SE15 . . . . . 140 C4
Astell St SW3 . . . 114 C1 257 B2
Aster Ct 3 HA8 . . . . . 27 A6
Aster Ho 3 SE13 . . . . . 142 A3
Aste St E14 . . . . . 120 A4
Astey's Row 1 N1 . . . . . 73 A1
Asthall Gdns IG6 . . . . . 57 A5
Astins Ho 4 E17 . . . . . 53 D5
Astleham Rd TW17 . . . . . 192 A6
Astleham Way TW17 . . . . 192 A6
Astle St SW11 . . . . . 137 A3
Astley Ave NW2 . . . . . 68 C3
Astley Ho Fulham SE1 . . 263 D2

Astley Ho *continued*
39 Paddington W2 91 C2
8 West Norwood SE27 183 A6
Aston Ave HA3 43 C2
Aston Cl Bushey WD23 8 A5
Sidcup DA14 168 A1
Aston Ct
Stoke Newington N4 73 A6
8 Wimbledon SW19 178 C3
10 Woodford IG8 37 A4
Aston Gn TW5 128 C3
Aston Ho
Notting Hill W11 244 D6
South Lambeth SW8 269 C1
Aston House Sch W5 87 D1
Aston Mews RM6 58 C2
Aston Pl SW16 182 D4
Aston Rd
Claygate KT10 212 C3
Ealing W5 87 D1
Merton SW20 178 C1
Aston St E14 97 A2
Astonville St SW18 157 C3
Astor Ave RM7 59 D3
Astor Cl KT2 176 D4
Astor Ct
Colney Hatch N12 30 C4
Newham E16 99 C1
Walham Green SW6 266 A3
Astoria Mans 13 SW16 160 A1
Astoria Par SW16 160 A1
Astoria Wlk SW9 138 C2
Astra Ct W13 109 A5
Astra Ho 4 Bow E3 97 B4
Hornsey N4 50 B2
Astrid Ho TW13 150 C2
Astrop Mews W6 112 C3
Astrop Terr W6 112 C4
Astwood Mews SW7 256 A4
Asylum Rd SE15 140 B5
Atalanta St SW6 134 D5 264 A3
Atbara Ct TW11 175 B4
Atbara Rd TW11 175 B4
Atcham Rd TW3 130 A1
Atcost Rd IG11 102 A2
Atheldene Rd SW18 158 A3
Athelney Prim Sch SE6 163 C1
Athelney St SE6 163 C1
Athelstan Ct E6 100 C5
Athelstane Gr E3 97 B5
Athelstane Mews N4 50 C1
Athelstan Gdns 8 NW6 69 A1
Athelstan Ho
Hackney Wick E9 75 B3
Kingston u T KT1 198 B5
Stoke Newington N16 73 C4
Athelstan House Sch TW12 173 C2
Athelstan Rd KT1 198 B5
Athelstan Way BR5 190 A2
Athelstone Rd HA3 24 B1
Athena Cl Harrow HA2 64 C6
Kingston u T KT1 198 B6
Athena Ct
Bermondsey SE1 253 A1
St John's Wood NW8 229 C4
Athenaeum Pl 3 N10 49 B6
Athenaeum Rd N20 14 B3
Athenia Ho 7 E14 98 B1
Athenlay Rd SE15 162 D6
Athenoeum Ct N5 73 A4
Athens Gdns W9 91 C3
Atherden Rd E5 74 C4
Atherfield Ct SW18 157 D5
Atherfold Rd SW9 138 A2
Atherley Way TW4 151 B4
Atherstone Ct W2 91 D2
Atherstone Mews SW7 114 A2 256 B4
Atherton Dr SW19 178 D6
Atherton Ho CR2 221 C2
Atherton Hts HA0 65 C2
Atherton Mews E7 77 A2
Atherton Pl Harrow HA2 42 B6
Southall UB1 107 C6
Atherton Rd
Barnes SW13 134 A5
Stratford E7 76 D2
Atherton St SW11 136 C3
Athlone KT10 212 C2
Athlone Cl 24 E5 74 B3
Athlone Ct
Lewisham SE6 164 B4
Upper Walthamstow E17 54 B6
Athlone Ho
16 Camden Town NW5 71 A2
9 Stepney E1 96 C1
Athlone House N6 48 D1
Athlone Rd SW2 160 C4
Athlone St NW5 71 A2
Athlon Ind Est HA0 87 D5
Athlon Rd HA0 87 D5
Athol Cl HA5 22 B2
Athol Ct 15 N4 72 B6
Athole Gdns EN1 17 C6
Athole Terr CR7 183 A1
Athol Gdns HA5 22 B2
Atholl Ho W9 229 A1
Atholl Rd IG3 58 A2
Athol Sq E14 98 A1
Athol Way UB10 82 C4
Atkins Ct 13 Old Ford E3 97 B6
Woolwich SE7 122 A2
Atkins Dr BR4 224 B6
Atkins Lo W8 245 A2
Atkinson Ct 3 E10 53 D2
Atkinson Ho
11 Battersea SW11 137 A3
Battersea SW11 268 A1
15 Hackney E2 96 A5
Newham E13 98 D3
Walworth SE17 262 D3
Atkinson Rd E16 99 C2
Atkinson's Almhouses HA8 26 B5
Atkins Rd
Streatham SW4, SW12 159 D4
Walthamstow E10 53 D3
Atlanta Bldg 3 SE13 141 D4
Atlanta Ct CR7 205 A6
Atlantic Ct 19 E14 120 B6
Atlantic Ho
5 Putney SW15 157 B6
4 Tower Hamlets E1 97 A2
Atlantic Rd SW2, SW9, SE24 138 C1
Atlantis Cl IG11 102 B4
Atlas Bsns Ctr NW2 68 B6
Atlas Gdns SE7 121 C2
Atlas Mews Dalston E8 73 D2
Islington N7 72 B2
Atlas Rd
Friern Barnet N11 31 A4
Newham E13 99 A5
North Acton NW10 89 C4
Wembley HA9 67 A4
Atley Rd E3 97 C6
Atlip Rd HA0 88 A6
Atney Rd SW15 135 A1
Atria Rd HA6 22 A5
Atrium 9 IG9 21 D2
Atterbury Rd N4 50 D3
Atterbury St SW1 116 A2 260 A3
Attewood Ave NW10 67 C5
Attewood Rd UB5 63 A2
Attfield Cl N20 14 B2
Attilburgh Ho SE1 263 C6
Attleborough Ct 4 SE21 162 B2
Attle Cl UB10 82 C5
Attlee Cl Hayes UB4 84 B4
Thornton Heath CR7 205 A4
Attlee Ct UB4 84 B4
Attlee Ho E1 243 D3
Attlee Rd Hayes UB4 84 B4
Thamesmead SE28 124 B6
Attlee Terr 3 E17 53 D5
Attneave St WC1 234 A1
Atwater Cl SW2 160 C3
Atwell Cl E10 53 D3
Atwell Pl KT7 197 A1
Atwell Rd 6 SE15 140 A3
Atwood Ave TW9 132 C3
Atwood Ho SE21 161 C1
Atwood Rd W6 112 B2
Aubert Ct N5 72 D4
Aubert Pk N5 72 D4
Aubert Rd N5 72 D4
Aubrey Beardsley Ho SW1 259 B3
Aubrey Mans NW1 237 A4
Aubrey Moore Point E15 98 A5
Aubrey Pl NW8 229 A3
Aubrey Rd Hornsey N8 50 A4
Kensington W14 113 B5 244 D3
Walthamstow E17 53 D6
Aubrey Wlk W14 113 B5 244 D3
Auburn Cl SE14 141 A5
Aubyn Hill SE27 183 B6
Aubyn Sq SW15 156 A6
Auckland Cl Enfield EN1 6 B6
South Norwood SE19 183 D2
Auckland Ct UB4 84 C3
Auckland Gdns SE19 183 D2
Auckland Hill SE27 183 A6
Auckland Ho 11 W12 112 B6
Auckland Rd
Clapham SW11 136 C1
Ilford IG1 57 A2
Kingston u T KT1 198 B5
Leyton E10 75 D5
South Norwood SE19 183 D2
Auckland Rise SE19 183 C2
Auckland St SE11 260 C1
Audax 20 NW9 27 D1
Auden Dr WD6 10 C6
Auden Pl NW1 231 A6
Audley Cl
8 Clapham SW11 137 A2
Muswell Hill N10 31 B3
Audley Ct Ealing W5 88 C2
Mayfair W1 248 C4
Northolt UB5 84 C4
Pinner Green HA5 22 C1
Snaresbrook E11, E18 54 D5
Surbiton KT5 198 B3
Twickenham TW2 152 B1
Audley Dr 3 E16 121 B5
Audley Gdns IG3 79 D6
Audley Ho N8 50 A5
Audley Pl SM2 217 D1
Audley Rd Ealing W5 88 B2
Enfield EN2 4 D3
Hendon NW4 46 B3
Richmond TW10 154 B6
Audley Sq W1 248 B4
Audrey Cl BR3 207 D3
Audrey Gdns HA0 65 B6
Audrey Ho EC1 241 B3
Audrey Rd IG1 78 D5
Audrey St E2 96 A5
Audric Cl KT2 176 C2
Augurs La 3 E13 99 B4
Augusta Cl KT8 195 B6
Augusta Cl NW4 28 C1
Augusta Rd TW2 152 A2
Augusta St E14 97 D1
Augustine Ho
Broadgate EC2 242 D2
New Cross SE4 141 B4
Augustine Rd
Hammersmith W14 112 D3
Harrow Weald HA3 24 A2
Augustines Ct E9 74 C3
Augustus Cl
Brentford TW8 131 D5
Hammersmith W12 112 B3
Stanmore HA7 9 D1
Augustus Ct
Feltham TW13 173 B6
Isleworth TW3 130 A1
8 Putney SW19 157 A3
South Norwood SE19 183 C3
Streatham SW16 159 D2
Augustus Ho NW1 232 A2
Augustus Rd SW19 157 A3
Augustus St NW1 93 B4 231 D2
Aulay Lawrence Ct N9 18 B1
Aultone Way
Carshalton SM5 218 D5
Sutton SM1 218 A6
Aultone Yd Ind Est SM5 218 D5
Aulton Pl SE11 261 B1
Aura Ho 3 TW9 132 D4
Aurelia Gdns CR0 204 B3
Aurelia Rd CR0 204 B3
Auriga Mews N1 73 B3
Auriol Cl KT4 215 C5
Auriol Dr Greenford UB6 64 B1
Hillingdon UB10 60 D2
Auriol Jun Sch KT19 215 D4
Auriol Mans W14 254 A3
Auriol Park Rd KT4 215 C5
Auriol Rd W14 113 A2 254 A3
Aurora Bldg 4 E14 120 A5
Aurora Ct IG8 36 D6
Aurora Ho E14 97 D1
Austell Gdns NW7 11 C1
Austell Hts NW7 11 C1
Austen Cl SE28 124 B5
Austen Ho 5 NW6 91 C4
Austen Rd Erith DA8 147 D5
Harrow HA2 63 D6
Austin Ave BR1, BR2 210 A4
Austin Cl
Forest Hill SE23 163 B4
Twickenham TW1 153 C6
Austin Ct 9 Enfield EN1 17 C6
9 Newham E6 99 C6
Austin Friars EC2 242 D2
Austin Friars Ho EC2 242 D2
Austin Friars Sq EC2 242 D2
Austin Ho
6 Brixton SW2 160 B6
19 Kingston u T KT6 198 A4
1 New Cross SE14 141 B5
Austin Rd
Battersea SW11 137 A4 268 A1
Hayes UB3 105 D4
Austins Ct SE15 140 A2
Austin's La UB10 61 A5
Austin St E2 95 D4
Austral Cl DA15 167 D1
Australia Rd W12 112 B6
Austral St SE11 116 D2 261 C4
Austyn Gdns KT5 198 D1
Autumn Cl Enfield EN1 6 A4
Wimbledon SW19 180 A4
Autumn Gr BR1 187 B4
Autumn Lo CR2 221 C4
Autumn Rise 9 W4 111 B1
Autumn St E3 97 C6
Avalon BR7 188 C1
Avalon Cl Ealing W13 87 A2
Enfield EN2 4 C3
Merton SW20 179 A1
Avalon Ct CR0 205 D2
Avalon Rd Ealing W13 87 A3
Parsons Green SW6 135 D4 265 C2
Avante Ct KT1 197 D6
Avard Gdns BR6 227 A4
Avarn Rd SW17 180 D4
Avebury Ct N1 235 C5
Avebury Rd
Leytonstone E11 54 B1
Merton SW19 179 B2
Orpington BR6 227 B5
Avebury St N1 235 C5
Aveley Ct 15 E5 74 B6
Aveley Mans 1 IG11 78 D1
Aveline St SE11 116 C1 261 A1
Aveling Ho 2 N19 71 C5
Aveling Park Rd E17 35 C1
Aveling Park Sch E17 35 C1
Ave Maria La EC4 241 D1
Avenell Mans N5 72 D4
Avenell Rd N5 72 D5
Avenfield Ho W1 247 D6
Avening Rd SW18 157 C4
Avening Terr SW18 157 C4
Avenons Rd E13 99 A3
Avenue Cl
Cranford TW5 128 B4
Avenue Cl *continued*
Primrose Hill NW8 92 C6 230 B5
Southgate N14 15 C5
Avenue Cres
Cranford TW5 128 B5
South Acton W3 110 D4
Avenue Ct Chelsea SW3 257 C3
Cricklewood NW2 69 A5
Ealing W5 87 D2
Penge SE20 184 C2
Redbridge IG5 56 A6
Southgate N14 15 C5
Avenue Elmers KT6 198 A4
Avenue Gate IG10 21 C5
Avenue Gdns
Cranford TW5 128 B5
Mortlake SW14 133 C2
South Acton W3 110 D4
South Norwood SE25 184 A1
Teddington TW11 174 D4
Avenue Hall N6 49 D3
Avenue Ho
St John's Wood NW8 230 A3
Upper Clapton N16 74 A6
Willesden Green NW10 90 B5
Avenue Ind Est E4 35 B4
Avenue Lo 12 NW8 70 B1
Avenue Mans Barnet EN5 1 B1
Clapham SW11 137 A1
Hampstead NW3 69 D3
Muswell Hill N10 31 C1
Willesden NW2 68 B2
Avenue Mews N10 49 B6
Avenue Par
Southgate N21 17 B4
Sunbury TW16 194 B6
Avenue Park Rd SE21, SE27 160 D2
Avenue Prim Sch E12 78 A3
Avenue Rd
Bexley DA6, DA7 147 A2
Brentford TW8 109 C1
Crouch End N6 49 D2
Feltham TW13 149 D1
Forest Gate E7 77 B4
Hampton TW12 173 D2
Harlesden NW10 89 D5
Hounslow TW7 130 D4
Ilford RM6 58 C2
Kingston u T KT1 198 A6
Mitcham SW16 181 D1
New Malden KT3 199 C5
North Finchley N12 30 A6
Penge BR3, SE20 184 D2
Pinner HA5 41 A6
Primrose Hill NW8 92 C6 230 A6
South Acton W3 110 D4
Southall UB1 107 B5
Southgate N14 15 C5
South Norwood SE25 184 A1
Teddington TW11 175 A4
Tottenham N15 51 B4
Wallington SM6 219 C1
Wimbledon SW20 178 B1
Woodford IG8 37 C4
Avenue Road Sta BR3 184 D1
Avenue S KT5 198 C2
Avenue Sch The NW6 69 A1
Avenue Terr Ilford IG2 57 C3
Kingston u T KT3 199 A6
Avenue The Barnet EN5 1 A2
Beckenham BR3 186 A2
Bedford Pk W4 111 C3
Bromley BR1 209 D6
Brondesbury Pk NW6 91 A6
8 Buckhurst Hill IG9 21 C2
Chingford E4 36 B5
Clapham SW4 159 A6
Claygate KT10 212 C3
Cranford TW5 128 A4
Ealing W13 87 B1
Finchley N3 29 C1
Friern Barnet N11 31 B5
Greenwich SE10 142 B5
Hampton TW12 173 B4
Harrow HA3 24 D2
Hatch End HA5 23 B4
Hornsey N8 50 C6
Hounslow TW3 151 D6
Isleworth TW1 153 B6
Keston Mark BR2 225 D5
Loughton IG10 21 D5
Muswell Hill N10 31 C1
4 New Malden KT4 200 A1
Orpington BR6 227 D6
Pinner HA5 41 B3
Richmond TW9 132 B3
Sidcup DA5 168 D4
South Croydon CR0 221 C5
Stoneleigh KT17, SM3 216 C1
St Paul's Cray BR5 190 B3
Sunbury TW16 172 B1
Surbiton KT5 198 B3
Tottenham N17 33 C1
Uxbridge UB10 60 D5
Wallington SM5 219 A1
Wandsworth SW18, SW12 158 C4
Wanstead E11 55 B4
Wembley HA9 44 B1
West Wickham BR4 208 C2
Worcester Pk KT4 215 D6
Averil Gr SW16 182 D4
Averill St W6 134 D6
Avern Gdns KT8 195 D5
Avern Rd KT8 195 D5
Avery Ct 1 SE20 184 B3
Avery Farm Row SW1 258 C3
Avery Gdns IG2 56 B4
AVERY HILL 167 B5
Avery Hill Coll (Mile End Annexe) E3 97 B3
Avery Hill Rd SE9 167 B3
Avery Row W1 115 B6 248 D6
Aviary Cl E16 98 D2
Aviemore Cl BR3 207 B4
Aviemore Way BR3 207 A4
Avignon Rd SE4 140 D2
Avingdor Ct 10 W3 111 A5
Avington Ct SE1 263 B3
Avington Gr SE20 184 C3
Avion Cres NW7, NW9 28 A2
Avis Sq E1 96 D1
Avoca Rd SW17 181 A6
Avocet Cl SE1 118 A1
Avocet Mews SE28 123 B3
Avon Cl Hayes UB4 84 C3
Sutton SM1 218 A4
Worcester Pk KT4 216 A6
Avon Ct 1 Acton W3 89 A1
13 Chingford E4 20 A3
Greenford UB6 85 D3
North Finchley N12 29 D5
11 Putney SW15 157 A6
Wembley HA0 65 A4
Avondale N22 32 A3
Avondale Ave
Barnet EN4 14 D3
Finchley N12 29 D5
Hinchley Wood KT10 213 A5
Neasden NW2 67 C5
New Malden KT4 199 D1
Avondale Cres
Enfield EN3 7 A2
Redbridge IG4 55 D4
Avondale Ct
Canning Town E16 98 C2
Leytonstone E11 54 C1
9 Sutton SM2 218 A1
Woodford E18 37 B2
Avondale Dr UB3 106 B5
Avondale Gdns TW4 151 B6
Avondale Ho
11 Bermondsey SE1 118 A1
6 Mortlake SW14 133 B2
Avondale Mans SW6 264 C2
Avondale Park Gdns W11 113 A6 244 A5
Avondale Park Prim Sch W11 113 A6 244 A5
Avondale Park Rd W11 113 A6 244 A6
Avondale Pavement 7 SE1 118 A1
Avondale Rd
Bexley DA16 146 C3
Bromley BR1 186 D4
Chislehurst SE9 166 A2
Finchley N3 30 A2
Harringay N15 50 D4
Harrow HA3 42 D6
Mortlake SW14 133 B2
Newham E16 98 C2
South Croydon CR2 221 A2
Southgate N13 16 C2
Walthamstow E17 53 C2
Wimbledon SW19 179 D5
Avondale Rise SE15 139 D2
Avondale Sq SE1 118 A1
Avonfield Ct E17 54 B6
Avon Ho 2 Islington N1 72 C1
7 Kingston u T KT2 175 D2
Northolt UB5 85 A3
Southgate N21 16 B6
14 Stoke Newington N16 73 B4
West Kensington W14 254 D3
Avon House Sch IG8 37 A6
Avonhurst Ho NW6 69 A1
Avonley Rd SE14 140 C5
Avon Mews HA5 23 B2
Avonmore Gdns W14 254 D3
Avonmore Pl W14 254 B4
Avonmore Prim Sch W14 113 A2 254 B4
Avonmore Rd W14 113 B2 254 C4
Avonmouth St SE1 262 A6
Avon Path CR0 221 A1
Avon Pl SE1 252 B1
Avon Rd Ashford TW16 171 D3
Greenford UB6 85 D3
St Johns SE4 141 C2
Upper Walthamstow E17 54 B6
Avonstowe Cl BR6 227 A5
Avon Way E18 55 A6
Avonwick Rd TW3 129 D3
Avril Way E4 36 A5
Avriol Ho W12 112 B5
Avro Ct E9 75 A3
Avro Way SM6 220 A1
Awlfield Ave N17 33 B2
Awliscombe Rd DA16 145 D3
Axeholm Ave HA8 26 D2
Axe St IG11 101 A6
Axford Ho SW2 160 D3
Axiom Apartments 5 BR2 209 B5
Axis Bsns Ctr E15 97 D6
Axis Ct
7 Bermondsey SE16 118 A4
Greenwich SE10 142 C6
Axminster Cres DA16 146 C4
Axminster Rd N7 72 B5
Axon Pl 5 IG1 79 A6
Aybrook St W1 93 A2 238 A3
Aycliffe Cl BR1 210 B5
Aycliffe Rd W12 112 A5
Ayerst Ct 1 E10 54 A2
Aylands Cl HA9 66 A6
Aylesbury Cl E7 76 D2
Aylesbury Ct SM1 218 A5
Aylesbury Ho 13 SE15 140 A6
Aylesbury Rd
Bromley BR2 209 A6
Walworth SE17 117 B1 262 D1
Aylesbury St
Clerkenwell EC1 94 D3 241 C5
Neasden NW10 67 B5
Ayles Ct UB4 84 B4
Aylesford Ave BR3 207 A4
Aylesford Ho SE1 252 D1
Aylesford St SW1 115 D1 259 C1
Aylesham Cl NW7 28 A3
Aylesham Rd BR6 211 D2
Aylesham Sh Ctr SE15 140 A4
Ayles Rd UB4 84 B4
Aylestone Ave NW6 90 D6
Aylestone Ct 10 HA0 66 A2
Aylett Rd Croydon SE25 206 B5
Isleworth TW7 130 C3
Ayley Croft EN1 18 A6
Ayliffe Cl KT1 176 C1
Aylmer Cl HA7 25 A6
Aylmer Ct N2 48 D4
Aylmer Dr HA7 25 A6
Aylmer Ho SE10 120 B1
Aylmer Par N2 48 D4
Aylmer Rd Acton W12 111 D4
Dagenham RM8 81 A5
East Finchley N2 48 C4
Leytonstone E11 54 D1
Ayloffe Rd RM9 81 B2
Aylsham Dr UB10 61 A6
Aylton Est 28 SE16 118 C4
Aylward Fst & Mid Schs HA7 25 D5
Aylward Rd
Forest Hill SE23 162 D2
Merton SW20 201 B6
Aylward Sch N18 33 B6
Aylwards Rise HA7 25 A6
Aylward St E1 96 D1
Aylwin Est SE1 263 B6
Aylwin Girls Sch SE1 117 D2 263 D4
Aynhoe Mans W14 112 D2
Aynhoe Rd W14 112 D3
Ayr Ct W3 88 C2
Ayres Cl E13 99 A4
Ayres Cres NW10 67 B1
Ayres St SE1 117 A4 252 B2
Ayrsome Rd N16 73 C5
Ayrton Gould Ho 9 E2 96 D4
Ayrton Ho HA9 65 D6
Ayrton Rd SW7 114 B3 256 C6
Aysgarth Ct SM1 217 D5
Aysgarth Rd SE21 161 C4
Ayshford Ho E1 96 B4
Ayston Ho 19 SE8 118 D2
Aytoun Ct 17 SW9 138 B3
Aytoun Pl SW9 138 B3
Aytoun Rd SW9 138 B3
Azalea Cl Ealing W7 108 D5
Ilford IG1 78 D3
Azalea Ct Chingford IG8 36 C3
Ealing W7 108 D5
Azalea Ho
Feltham TW13 150 B3
New Cross SE14 141 B5
Azalea Wlk HA5 40 B3
Azania Mews NW5 71 B2
Azenby Rd SE15 139 D3
Azhar Acad E7 77 A2
Azof St SE10 120 C2
Azov Ho 10 E1 97 A3
Aztec Ct 8 N16 73 C2
Azure Appartments HA3 24 B3
Azure Ct TW13 149 D1
Azure Ho 28 E2 96 A4

B

Baalbec Rd N5 72 D3
Babbacombe Cl KT9 213 D3
Babbacombe Gdns IG4 56 A5
Babbacombe Rd BR1 187 A2
Baber Bridge Par TW14 150 C5
Baber Dr TW14 150 C5
Babington Ct
Bloomsbury WC1 240 B4
Streatham SW16 181 D5
Babington Ho SE1 252 B2
Babington House Sch BR7 188 B4
Babington Rd
Dagenham RM8 80 C4
Hendon NW4 46 B5
Streatham SW16 181 D5
Babington Rise HA9 66 C2
Babmaes St SW1 249 C5
Bacchus Wlk 12 N1 95 C5
Bache's St N1 95 B4 235 D1
Back Church La E1 96 A1
Back Hill EC1 241 B5
Backhouse Pl SE1 263 B3
Back La Brentford TW8 131 D6
Buckhurst Hill IG9 21 D2
Burnt Oak HA8 27 A2
Dagenham RM6 59 A2

Back La *continued*
Hampstead NW3 70 A4
Hornsey N8 50 A4
Richmond TW10 153 C2
Sidcup DA5 169 C4
Backley Gdns SE25 206 A3
Back Rd Sidcup DA14 190 A6
Teddington TW11 174 C3
Bacon Gr SE1 117 D3 263 C5
Bacon La Edgware HA8 26 C2
Queensbury NW9 44 D5
Bacon's Coll SE16 119 A4
Bacon's La N6 49 A1
Bacon St E2 95 D3 243 D6
Bacon Terr RM8 80 B3
Bacton NW5 71 A3
Bacton St E2 96 C4
Baddeley Cl 11 EN3 7 C6
Baddeley Ho
East Molesey KT8 195 C4
Vauxhall SE11 260 D2
Baddow Cl
Dagenham RM10 103 C6
Woodford IG8 37 D4
Baddow Wlk N1 235 A6
Baden Ct N11 31 D3
Baden Pl SE1 252 C2
Baden Powell Cl
Dagenham RM9 103 A6
Surbiton KT6 214 B6
Baden Powell Ho 11
DA17 125 C3
Baden Powell Sch E5 74 B5
Baden Rd Hornsey N8 49 D5
Ilford IG1 78 D3
Badger Cl
Feltham TW13 150 B1
Hounslow TW4 128 C2
Ilford IG2 57 A2
Badger Ct Chingford E4 36 B6
Dollis Hill NW2 68 C5
Badgers Cl
Ashford TW15 170 B5
Enfield EN2 4 D2
Harrow HA1 42 B3
Hayes UB3 105 C6
Badgers Copse
Orpington BR6 227 D6
Worcester Pk KT4 215 D6
Badgers Croft
Barnet N20 13 A3
Chislehurst SE9 166 C1
Badgers Hole CR0 222 D4
Badgers Wlk KT3 177 C1
Badlis Rd E17 53 C6
Badma Cl N9 18 C1
Badminton KT2 176 D2
Badminton Cl
Harrow HA1 42 C5
Northolt UB5 63 C2
Badminton Ct 9 N4 51 A2
Badminton Ho SE22 139 C1
Badminton Mews 9
E16 121 A5
Badminton Rd SW12 159 A5
Badric Ct SW11 136 B3
Badsworth Rd 3 SE5 139 A4
Bagley Cl UB7 104 A4
Bagley's La
SW6 135 D4 265 D1
Bagleys Spring RM6 59 A5
Bagnigge Ho WC1 234 A1
Bagshot Ho NW1 231 D2
Bagshot Rd EN1 17 D5
Bagshot St
SE17 117 C1 263 B1
Baildon 27 E2 96 C5
Baildon St SE8 141 B5
Bailey Cl Chingford E4 36 A6
Wood Green N11 31 D3
Woolwich SE28 123 C5
Bailey Cres KT9 213 D1
Bailey Ct
4 Chingford E4 36 B5
9 Shepherd's Bush
W12 112 A4
Bailey Ho Mitcham CR4 202 C6
11 Penge SE26 184 B5
Walham Green SW10 265 D4
Bailey Mews
Brixton SW2 160 C6
Chiswick W4 132 D6
Bailey Pl SE26 184 D4
Bainbridge Cl KT2 176 A5
Bainbridge Rd RM9 81 B4
Bainbridge St WC1 239 D2
Baines Cl CR2 221 B3
Bain Ho 23 SW9 138 A3
Baird Ave UB1 108 A6
Baird Cl Kingsbury NW9 45 A3
Walthamstow E10 53 C1
Baird Gdns SE19 183 C6
Baird Ho
12 Belvedere DA17 125 C3
29 Shepherd's Bush
W12 112 B6
Baird Rd EN1 6 B1
Baird St EC1 242 B6
Bairny Wood App IG8 37 B4
Baizdon Rd SE3 142 C3
Baker Beall Ct DA7 147 D2
Baker Ct E11 76 B5
Baker Ho 12 Bromley E3 97 D4
Ealing W7 108 D5
Baker La CR4 203 A6
Baker Rd
Harlesden NW10 89 C6
Baker Rd *continued*
Kidbrooke SE18 144 A4
Bakers' Almshouses
E10 53 D3
Bakers Ave E17 53 D3
Bakers Ct RM8 59 B2
Bakers Ct SE25 205 C6
Bakers End SW20 179 A1
Bakers Field N7 72 A4
Bakers Gdns SM5 218 C6
Bakers Hall Ct EC3 253 B5
Bakers Hill Barnet EN5 1 D3
Upper Clapton E5 52 C1
Bakers Ho W5 109 D5
Baker's La N6 48 D3
Bakers Mews 9 BR6 227 D2
Baker's Mews W1 238 A2
Bakers Pas 22 NW3 70 A4
Bakers Rents 18 E2 95 D4
Bakers Row E15 98 C5
Baker's Row
EC1 94 C3 241 A5
Baker St Enfield EN1 5 B4
Marylebone W1 92 D2 237 D4
Baker Street
W1 92 D2 237 D4
Baker Street Sta
NW1 92 D3 237 D5
Baker's Yd EC1 241 A5
Bakery Cl SW9 270 D3
Bakery Mews KT6 198 C1
Bakewell Way KT3 177 C1
Balaam Ho SM1 217 C4
Balaams La N14 15 D2
Balaam St E13 99 B4
Balaclava Rd
Bermondsey
SE1 117 D2 263 D3
Kingston u T KT6 197 C2
Bala Gn NW9 45 C3
Balcaskie Rd SE9 166 B6
Balchen Rd SE3 143 D3
Balchier Rd SE22 162 B5
Balcombe Cl DA6 146 D1
Balcombe Ho
Lisson Gr NW1 237 C6
3 Streatham SW2 160 B3
Balcombe St
NW1 92 D3 237 C5
Balcon Ct W5 88 B1
Balcorne St E9 74 C1
Balder Rise SE12 165 B2
Balderton Flats W1 238 B1
Balderton St
W1 93 A1 238 B1
Baldewyne Ct N17 34 A2
Baldock Ho 31 SE5 139 A3
Baldock St E3 97 D5
Baldrey Ho 1 SE10 120 D1
Baldry Gdns SW16 182 B4
Baldwin Cres SE5 139 A4
Baldwin Gdns TW3 130 A4
Baldwin Ho
15 Streatham SW2 160 C3
Wallend E12 78 C1
Baldwin's Gdns
EC1 94 C2 241 A4
Baldwin St EC1 235 C1
Baldwin Terr
N1 95 A5 235 A4
Baldwyn Gdns W3 111 B6
Balearic Apts 3 E16 121 A6
Bale Rd E1 97 A2
Bales Coll W10 90 D4
Balfern Gr W4 111 C1
Balfern St SW11 136 C3
Balfe St N1 94 A5 233 B3
Balfour Ave W7 108 D5
Balfour Bsns Ctr UB2 106 D3
Balfour Gr N20 14 D1
Balfour Ho W10 90 D2
Balfour Mews
Edmonton N9 18 A1
Mayfair W1 248 B4
Balfour Pl Mayfair W1 248 B5
Putney SW15 134 B1
Balfour Rd
Bromley Comm BR2 209 D4
Croydon SE25 206 A5
Ealing W13 109 B4
Harrow HA1 42 B4
Highbury N5 73 A4
Hounslow TW3 129 D2
Ilford IG1 57 A1
Merton SW19 179 D3
North Acton W3 89 A2
Southall UB2 106 D3
Wallington SM5 218 D1
Balfour St
SE17 117 B2 262 C4
Balfron Twr 4 E14 98 A1
Balgonie Rd E4 20 B3
Balgowan Cl KT3 199 C5
Balgowan Prim Sch
BR3 185 A1
Balgowan Rd BR3 185 B1
Balgowan St SE18 123 D2
BALHAM 159 A3
Balham Gr SW12 159 A4
Balham High Rd SW12,
SW17 159 A3
Balham Hill SW12 159 B5
Balham New Rd SW12 159 B4
Balham Park Mans
SW12 158 D3
Balham Park Rd SW12,
SW17 159 A3
Balham Rd N9 18 A2
Balham Sta SW12 159 B3
Balham Station Rd
SW12 159 B3
Balin Ho SE1 252 C2
Balkan Wlk E1 118 B6
Balladier Wlk E14 97 D2
Ballamore Rd BR1 165 A1
Ballance Rd E9 75 A2
Ballantine St SW18 136 A1
Ballantrae Ho NW2 69 B4
Ballard Cl KT2 177 B3
Ballard Ho SE10 141 D6
Ballards Cl RM10 103 D6
Ballards Farm Rd CR0,
CR2 222 A2
Ballards La N3 29 D3
Ballards Mews HA8 26 C4
Ballards Rd
Dagenham RM10 103 D6
Dollis Hill NW2 68 A6
Ballards Rise CR2 222 A2
Ballards Way CR0, CR2 222 B2
Ballast Quay SE10 120 B1
Ballater Cl WD19 22 C6
Ballater Rd
Brixton SW2, SW4 138 A1
South Croydon CR2 221 D3
Ball Ct EC3 242 D1
Ballentyne Ct N21 16 B6
Ballina St SE23 162 D4
Ballin Ct 14 E14 120 A4
Ballingdon Rd SW11 159 A5
Ballinger Point 18 E3 97 D4
Ballinger Way UB5 85 A3
Balliol Ave E4 36 C6
Balliol Ho 11 SW15 156 D5
Balliol Rd Bexley DA16 146 B3
North Kensington W10 90 D1
Tottenham N17 33 C2
Balloch Rd SE6 164 B2
Ballogie Ave NW10 67 C4
Ballow Cl 15 SE5 139 C5
Ball's Pond Pl 3 N1 73 B2
Ball's Pond Rd N1 73 C2
Balmain Cl W5 109 D5
Balmain Ct TW3 129 D4
Balman Ho 3 SE16 118 D2
Balmer Rd E3 97 B5
Balmes Rd N1 95 B6 235 D6
Balmoral Ave
Beckenham BR3 207 A5
Friern Barnet N11 31 B5
Balmoral Cl 1 SW15 156 D5
Balmoral Cres KT8 195 C6
Balmoral Ct
18 Belmont SM2 217 C1
Ealing W5 87 D1
Edgware HA8 26 D6
Grove Pk SE12 187 B6
North Cheam KT4 216 B6
21 Rotherhithe SE16 118 D5
St John's Wood NW8 229 C4
Wembley HA9 66 B5
West Norwood SE27 183 A6
Balmoral Dr
Borehamwood WD6 11 B6
Hayes UB4 83 D3
Southall UB1 85 B3
Balmoral Gdns
Ealing W13 109 A3
Ilford IG3 57 D1
Old Bexley DA5 169 B4
Balmoral Gr N7 72 B2
Balmoral Ho
2 Isle Of Dogs E14 119 D3
Stanmore HA7 26 A1
Stoke Newington N4 51 A1
Walthamstow E17 35 B1
West Kensington W14 254 A4
Balmoral Lo BR6 226 C4
Balmoral Mews W12 111 D3
Balmoral Rd
Forest Gate E7 77 C3
Harrow HA2 63 C4
Kingston u T KT1 198 B5
Leyton E10 75 D6
North Cheam KT4 216 B6
Willesden NW2 68 B2
Balmoral Trad Est
IG11 101 D2
Balmore Cl E14 98 A1
Balmore Cres EN4 15 A6
Balmore St N19 71 B6
Balmuir Gdns SW15 134 C1
Balnacraig Ave NW10 67 C4
Balniel Gate SW1 259 D2
Balsam Ho 9 E14 119 D6
Baltic Apts 5 E16 121 A6
Baltic Cl SW19 180 B3
Baltic Ho 7 SE5 139 A3
Baltic St E EC1 95 A3 242 A5
Baltic St W EC1 95 A3 242 A5
Baltimore Ho
Clapham SW18 136 A1
Kennington SE11 261 A2
Merton SW19 179 D3
Baltimore Pl DA16 145 D3
Balvaird Pl SW1 259 D1
Balvernie Gr SW18 157 C4
Bamber Ho IG11 101 A6
Bamber Rd 5 SE15 139 D4
Bamborough Gdns 12
W12 112 C4
Bamburgh 9 N17 34 B3
Bamford Ave HA0 88 B5
Bamford Ct E15 75 D3
Bamford Rd
Barking IG11 79 A2
Catford BR1 186 B5
Bampfylde Cl SM6 219 C5
Bampton Ct W5 87 D1
Bampton Dr NW7 28 A3
Bampton Rd SE23 162 D1
Banavie Gdns BR3 186 A2
Banbury Cl EN2 4 D4
Banbury Ct
11 Belmont SM2 217 C1
Ealing W13 109 A3
Strand WC2 250 A6
Banbury Ho 5 E9 74 D1
Banbury Rd
Higham Hill E17 35 A3
Homerton E9 74 D1
Banbury St 3 SW11 136 C3
Banbury Wlk UB5 85 C5
Banchory Rd SE3 143 B5
Bancroft Ave
East Finchley N2 48 C4
Woodford IG9 21 A2
Bancroft Cl TW15 170 C5
Bancroft Ct
Northolt UB5 84 C6
South Lambeth SW8 270 A2
Bancroft Gdns
Harrow Weald HA3 24 A2
Orpington BR6 211 D1
Bancroft Ho 11 E1 96 C3
Bancroft Rd
Bethnal Green E1 96 D3
Harrow Weald HA3 24 A1
Bancrofts Sch IG8 21 A1
Bandon Cl UB10 82 B5
BANDONHILL 219 D3
Bandon Hill Prim Sch
SM6 219 D2
Bandon Rise SM6 219 D3
Banff Ho 1 NW3 70 C2
Banfield Rd SE15 140 B2
Banfor Ct SM6 219 C3
Bangabandhu Prim Sch
E2 96 C4
Bangalore St SW15 134 D2
Bangor Cl UB5 63 D3
Banim St W6 112 B2
Banister Ho Hackney E9 74 D3
Nine Elms SW8 269 B2
9 West Kilburn W10 91 A4
Banister Rd W10 90 D4
Bank Ave CR4 180 B1
Bank Bldgs 13 SW16 181 C5
Bank Ct SW11 268 C2
Bank End SE1 252 B4
Bankfoot Rd BR1 186 C6
Bankhurst Rd SE6 163 B4
Bank La
Kingston u T KT2 176 A3
Roehampton SW15 155 C6
Bank Mews SM1 218 A2
Bank of England★
EC2 95 B1 242 C1
Bank of England Mus★
EC2 95 B1 242 C1
Bank Par N11 31 B5
Banks Ho
Isleworth TW7 130 C3
Newington SE1 262 A5
Banksia Rd N18 34 D5
Bankside
Borough The
SE1 117 A6 252 A5
Borough The SE1 252 B4
Enfield EN2 4 D4
Southall UB1 106 D5
South Croydon CR2 221 D2
Bankside Art Gal★
SE1 116 D6 251 D5
Bankside Ave
1 Lewisham SE13 142 A2
Northolt UB5 84 A5
Bankside Cl
Carshalton SM5 218 C2
Isleworth TW7 130 D1
Bankside Dr KT7 213 B6
Bankside Ho EC3 243 B1
Bankside Pier
SE1 117 A6 252 A5
Bankside Pk IG11 102 A4
Bankside Rd IG1 79 B3
Bankside Way 6
SE19 183 C4
Banks La DA6 147 B1
Bank St E14 119 D5
Bank Sta EC3 95 B1 242 D1
Banks Way E12 78 C4
Bank The N6 49 B1
Bankton Rd SW2 138 C1
Bankwell Rd SE13 142 C1
Banner Ct 5 SE16 118 C2
Banner Ho EC1 242 B5
Bannerman Ho SW8 270 C5
Banner St EC1 95 A3 242 B6
Banning Ho 4 SW19 156 D3
Banning St SE10 120 C1
Bannister Cl
Greenford UB6 64 B3
Streatham SW2 160 C3
Bannister Ho
28 Deptford SE14 140 D6
Harrow HA3 42 C6
Bannister Sports Ctr The
HA3 24 A4
Bannockburn Prim Sch
SE18 123 D2
Bannockburn Rd
SE18 123 D2
Bannow Cl KT19 215 C4
Banqueting Ho★ SW1 250 A3
Banstead Ct
Stoke Newington N4 51 A1
Walthamstow E10 53 D1
Banstead Gdns N9 17 C1
Banstead Rd SM5 218 C1
Banstead St SE15 140 C2
Banstead Way SM6 220 A3
Banstock Rd HA8 26 D4
Banting Dr N21 16 B6
Banting Ho 6 NW2 68 A5
Bantock Ct 1 N20 14 D2
Bantock Ho 8 W10 91 A4
Banton Cl EN1 6 B3
Bantry Ho 18 E1 96 D3
Bantry St SE5 139 B5
Banville Ho SW8 270 D3
Banwell Rd DA5 168 D5
Banyan Ho 8 NW3 69 D2
Banyard Rd SE16 118 B3
Baptist Gdns NW5 71 A2
Barandon Wlk 6
W11 112 D6
Barbanel Ho 28 E1 96 C3
Barbara Brosnan Ct
NW8 229 C3
Barbara Castle Cl SW6 264 D5
Barbara Cl TW17 192 D4
Barbara Hucklesbury Cl
N22 32 D1
Barbara Martin Ho 1
N11 31 C5
Barbara Rudolph Ct 5
N19 50 A2
Barbara Ward Ct 3
E11 76 C6
Barbauld Rd N16 73 C5
Barber Beaumont Ho 21
E1 96 D4
Barber Cl N21 16 C4
Barberry Ct E15 76 C2
Barbers Alley 1 E13 99 B4
Barbers Rd E15 97 D5
BARBICAN 95 A2
Barbican★ EC2 95 A2 242 B3
Barbican Arts & Con Ctr★
EC2 95 A2 242 B4
Barbican Rd UB1 85 D1
Barbican Sta
EC1 95 A2 242 A4
Barb Mews W6 112 C3
Barbon Cl WC1 240 C4
Barbot Cl N9 18 A1
Barbrook Ho E9 74 C2
Barchard St SW18 157 D6
Barchester Cl W7 108 D5
Barchester Lo N12 29 D6
Barchester Rd HA3 24 B1
Barchester St E14 97 D2
Barclay Cl
SW6 135 C5 265 A3
Barclay Ct N12 30 A5
Barclay Ho 21 E9 74 C1
Barclay Oval IG8 37 A6
Barclay Prim Sch E10 54 B3
Barclay Rd
Edmonton N18 33 B4
Leyton E11 54 D1
Newham E13 99 C3
Parsons Green
SW6 135 C5 265 B3
South Croydon CR0 221 B5
Walthamstow E17 54 A4
Barcombe Ave SW2 160 B2
Barcom Trad Est 1
CR0 204 A2
Bardell Ho 17 SE1 118 A4
Barden St SE18 145 C5
Bardfield Ave RM6 58 D6
Bardney Rd SM4 201 D5
Bardolph Rd
Richmond TW9 132 B2
Tufnell Pk N7 72 A4
Bard Rd W10 112 D6
Bardsey Pl 41 E1 96 C3
Bardsey Wlk 5 N1 73 A2
Bardsley Cl CR0 221 D5
Bardsley Ho 6 SE10 142 A6
Bardsley La SE10 142 A6
Barents Ho 10 E1 96 D3
Barfett St W10 91 B3
Barfield Ave N20 14 D2
Barfield Rd
Bromley BR1, BR7 210 C6
Leytonstone E11 54 D1
Barfleur La SE8 119 B2
Barford Cl NW4 28 A2
Barford Ho 23 E3 97 B5
Barford St N1 94 C6 234 B5
Barforth Rd SE15 140 B2
Barfreston Way SE20 184 B2
Bargate Cl
New Malden KT3 200 A2
Plumstead Comm SE18 123 D1
Bargehouse Rd E16 122 D4
Barge House St SE1 251 B4
Barge La 10 E3 97 B6
Bargery Rd SE6 163 D3
Bargrove Cl 8 SE20 184 A3
Bargrove Cres SE6 163 B2
Barham Cl
Chislehurst BR7 188 D5
Keston Mark BR2 210 A1
Wembley HA0 65 C2
Barham Ct
8 Croydon CR2 221 A4
Keston Mark BR2 210 A1
Wembley HA0 65 C2
Woodside Pk N12 29 B5
Barham Ho SE17 263 B2
Barham Prim Sch HA0 65 C2
Barham Rd
Chislehurst BR7 188 D5
Croydon CR2 221 A3
Wimbledon SW20 178 A3
Baring Cl SE12 165 A2
Baring Ct N1 235 C5
Baring Ho 15 E14 97 C1
Baring Prim Sch SE12 165 A4
Baring Rd Barnet EN4 2 B2
Croydon CR0 206 A1
Grove Pk SE12 165 A2
Baring St N1 95 B6 235 C5
Barker Cl
Kingston u T KT3 198 D5
Richmond TW9 132 D3
Barker Dr NW1 71 D1
Barker Ho
Dulwich SE21 161 C1
3 Harringay N15 50 D5
Walthamstow E17 53 B2
Walworth SE17 263 A3
Barker Mews SW4 137 B1
Barker St SW10 266 A6
Barker Wlk SW16 159 D1
Barkham Rd N17 33 C3
BARKING 79 B1
Barking Abbey Comp Sch
(Sports & Humanities
Coll) IG11 79 C3
Barking Abbey Sch (Sports
& Humanities Coll)
IG11 79 D2
Barking Bsns Ctr
IG11 102 A4
Barking Flyover IG11 78 D1
Barking Hospl IG11 79 D1
Barking Ind Pk IG11 102 A6
Barking Rd
East Ham E6 100 B6
Plaistow E13 99 B4
BARKINGSIDE 57 A6
Barkingside Sta IG6 57 B6
Barking Sta IG11 79 A1
Bark Pl W2 113 D6 245 C6
Barkston Gdns
SW5 113 D2 255 C3
Barkway Cl BR6 226 C4
Barkway Ct N4 73 A6
Barkwith Ho 27 SE14 140 D6
Barkworth Rd SE16 118 C1
Barlborough St SE14 140 D5
Barlby Gdns W10 90 D3
Barlby Prim Sch W10 90 D3
Barlby Rd W10 90 D2
Barley Cl WD23 8 A6
Barleycorn Way E14 119 B6
Barley Ct Ilford IG3 58 B4
Stanwell TW19 148 A3
Barleyfields Cl RM6 58 C2
Barley La IG3 58 B3
Barley Lane Prim Sch
RM6 58 B2
Barley Mow Pas
Chiswick W4 111 B1
Clerkenwell EC1 241 D3
Barley Mow Way
TW17 192 C5
Barley Shotts Bsns Pk
W10 91 B2
Barling 6 NW1 71 B1
Barling Ct 1 SW4 138 A3
Barlings Ho 2 SE4 140 D1
Barloch Ho 14 SW11 137 A3
Barlow Cl SM6 220 A1
Barlow Dr SE18 144 A4
Barlow Ho
14 Bermondsey SE16 118 B2
Notting Hill W11 244 A6
Shoreditch N1 235 C2
Barlow Pl W1 248 D5
Barlow Rd Acton W3 110 D5
Brondesbury NW6 69 B2
Hampton TW12 173 C3
Barlow St
SE17 117 B2 262 D3
Barmeston Rd SE6 163 D2
Barmor Cl HA2 23 D1
Barmouth Ave UB6 86 D5
Barmouth Ho 6 N7 72 B6
Barmouth Rd
Croydon CR0 222 D6
Wandsworth SW18 158 A5
Barnabas Ct N21 16 D6
Barnabas Ho EC1 235 A1
Barnabas Lo SW8 270 B2
Barnabas Rd E9 74 D3
Barnaby Cl HA2 64 A6
Barnaby Ct NW9 45 C6
Barnaby Pl SW7 256 C3
Barnard Cl
Chislehurst BR7 189 B2
Sunbury TW16 172 B3
Wallington SM6 219 D1
Woolwich SE18 122 C3
Barnard Ct SW16 160 B1
Barnard Gdns
Hayes UB4 84 B3
West Barnes KT3 200 A5
Barnard Gr E15 76 D1
Barnard Hill N10 31 B2
Barnard Ho 17 E2 96 B4
Barnard Lo
New Barnet EN5 2 A1
10 Paddington W9 91 C2
Barnard Mews SW11 136 C1
Barnardo Dr IG6 57 A5
Barnardo Gdns 1 E1 118 D6
Barnardo St E1 96 D1
Barnard Rd
Clapham SW11 136 C1
Enfield EN1 6 B3
Mitcham CR4 181 A1
Barnard's Inn EC4 241 B2
Barnbrough NW1 232 A5

Barnby Sq 1 E15 98 C6
Barnby St
Somers Town NW1 93 C4 232 B2
2 West Ham E15 98 C6
Barn Cl Ashford TW15 170 D5
19 Kentish Town NW5 71 D3
Northolt UB5 84 C5
Barn Cres HA7 25 C4
Barncroft Cl UB8 82 D2
Barn Croft Prim Sch E17 53 A3
Barneby Cl TW2 152 C3
Barnehurst Rd DA7 147 D3
Barnersbury Ho N7 72 A4
BARNES 133 D4
Barnes Ave
Barnes SW13 134 A5
Southall UB2 107 B2
Barnes Bridge Sta SW13 133 C3
Barnes Cl E12 77 D4
Barnes Common* SW13 134 A2
Barnes Ct Barnet EN5 1 D1
Islington N1 72 C1
3 Newham E16 99 C2
South Norwood CR7 205 A6
Woodford IG8 37 D5
Wood Green N22 32 A3
Barnes End KT3 200 A4
Barnes High St SW13 133 D3
Barnes Ho
8 Barking IG11 101 B6
14 Bethnal Green E2 96 C5
Camden Town NW1 231 D6
26 Deptford SE14 140 D6
Hornsey N19 50 A2
Barnes Hospl SW14 133 C2
Barnes Prim Sch SW13 133 D2
Barnes Qtr 6 TW8 131 C5
Barnes Rd
Edmonton N18 34 C6
Ilford IG1 79 A3
Barnes St E14 97 A1
Barnes Sta SW13 134 A2
Barnes Terr SE8 119 B1
Barnes Wallis Ct HA9 67 A5
BARNET 13 B6
Barnet By-Pass WD6 11 C6
Barnet Coll EN5 1 B1
Barnet Coll (Grahame Park Ctr) NW9 27 D2
Barnet Coll (Montagu Rd) NW4 46 A3
Barnet Dr BR2 226 A6
BARNET GATE 11 C5
Barnet Gate La EN5 11 D4
Barnet Gr E2 96 A4
Barnet Hill EN5 1 C1
Barnet Hill JMI Sch EN5 13 B6
Barnet Ho 35 SE5 139 A3
Barnet La
Barnet EN5, N20 13 B4
Borehamwood WD6 10 B5
Barnet Mus* EN5 1 A1
Barnet Rd Barnet EN5 1 B5
Edgware EN5 11 C5
Barnett Ho E1 243 C3
Barnett Homestead NW11 47 C5
Barnet Trad Est EN5 1 B2
Barnetts Ct HA2 63 D5
Barnett St 18 E1 96 B1
Barnet Way (Barnet By-Pass) EN5, NW7, WD6 11 B3
Barnet Wood Rd BR2 225 C6
Barney Cl SE7 121 C1
Barnfield KT3 199 C3
Barn Field NW3 70 D3
Barnfield Ave
Croydon CR0 222 C6
Kingston u T KT2 176 A5
Mitcham CR4 203 B6
Barnfield Cl London N4 50 A2
Wandsworth SW17 158 A1
Barnfield Gdns
Kingston u T KT2 176 A5
Shooters Hill SE18 144 D6
Barnfield Pl E14 119 C2
Barnfield Prim Sch HA8 27 A2
Barnfield Rd
Burnt Oak HA8 27 A2
Ealing W5 87 C3
Erith DA17 147 B6
Shooters Hill SE18 144 D6
Barnfield Wood Cl BR3 208 B3
Barnfield Wood Rd BR3 208 B3
Barnham Dr SE28 123 D5
Barnham Rd UB6 86 A4
Barnham St SE1 253 B2
Barnhill HA5 40 C4
Barn Hill HA9 44 D1
Barnhill Ave BR2 208 D4
Barnhill Com High Sch UB4 84 C4
Barnhill Ct UB4 84 B4
Barnhill La UB4 84 B3
Barnhill Rd Hayes UB4 84 C3
Wembley HA9 67 A5
Barnhurst Path WD19 22 C5
Barningham Way NW9 45 B3
Barnlea Cl TW13 151 A2
Barnmead Ct RM9 81 B3
Barnmead Gdns RM9 81 B3
Barnmead Rd
Dagenham RM9 81 B3
Penge BR3 185 A2
Barn Rise HA9 66 C6
BARNSBURY 72 A1
Barnsbury Cl KT3 199 A5
Barnsbury Cres KT5 199 A1
Barnsbury Gr N7 72 B1
Barnsbury Ho 12 SW4 159 D5
Barnsbury La KT5 199 A1
Barnsbury Pk N1 72 C1
Barnsbury Rd N1 94 C6 234 A5
Barnsbury Sq N1 72 C1
Barnsbury St N1 72 C1
Barnsbury Terr N1 72 B1
Barnscroft SW20 200 B6
Barnsdale Ave E14 119 C2
Barnsdale Rd W9 91 B3
Barnsley St E1 96 B3
Barn St N16 73 C6
Barnstaple Ho SE12 164 D6
Barnstaple La SE13 142 A1
Barnstaple Rd HA4 62 C5
Barnston Wlk N1 235 A6
Barnview Lo HA3 24 C2
Barn Way HA9 66 C6
Barnwell Ho 1 SE5 139 C4
Barnwell Rd SW2 160 C6
Barnwood Cl
Barnet N20 13 B3
Ruislip HA4 61 B6
Westbourne Green W9 91 D3
Baron Cl
Friern Barnet N11 31 B5
Islington N1 234 A4
Baron Ct Barnet EN5 1 D1
Mitcham CR4 202 C5
Baroness Rd 5 E2 95 D4
Baronet Gr N17 34 A2
Baronet Rd N17 34 A2
Baron Gdns IG6 57 A6
Baron Gr CR4 202 C5
Baron Ho 6 SW19 180 B2
Baron Rd RM8 58 D1
Barons 14 BR3 185 D1
Barons Court Mans W14 254 B1
Baron's Court Rd W14 113 A1 254 B2
Barons Court Sta W14 113 A1 254 A2
Barons Ct Ilford IG1 79 B6
Kingsbury NW9 45 B3
Wallington SM6 219 D5
Baronsfield Rd TW1 153 B5
Barons Gate
East Barnet EN4 14 C5
13 South Acton W4 111 A3
Barons Keep W14 113 A1 254 A2
Barons Lo 9 E14 120 A2
Barons Mead HA1 42 C5
Baronsmead Rd SW13 134 A4
Baronsmede W5 110 B4
Baronsmere Ct 9 EN5 1 A1
Baronsmere Rd N2 48 C5
Baron's Pl SE1 116 C4 251 B1
Baron St N1 94 C5 234 A4
Barons The TW1 153 B5
Baron's Wlk CR0 207 A3
Baron Wlk E16 98 D2
Barque Mews SE8 141 C6
Barrack Rd TW4 129 A1
Barradell Ho 15 W14 112 D3
Barra Hall Cir UB3 83 C1
Barra Hall Rd UB3 105 C6
Barrass Cl 7 EN3 7 C6
Barratt Ave N22 32 B1
Barratt Ho 15 N1 72 D1
Barratt Ind Pk Poplar E3 98 A3
Southall UB1 107 C5
Barratt Way HA3 42 B6
Barr Beacon SE23 162 C4
Barrenger Rd N10 30 D1
Barret Ho NW6 91 C6
Barrett Ct 2 NW10 89 C5
Barrett Rd E17 54 A5
Barrett's Gr N16 73 C3
Barrett's Green Rd NW10 89 B5
Barrett St W1 93 A1 238 B1
Barrhill Rd SW2 160 A2
Barrie Ct EN5 14 A6
Barriedale SE14 141 A3
Barrie Ho Acton W3 111 A4
Bayswater W2 246 B5
Edmonton N9 18 B4
Primrose Hill NW8 230 B5
8 Stoke Newington N16 73 C5
Barrier Gdns Pier SE18 121 D3
Barrier Point Rd E16 121 C4
Barringers Ct HA4 39 B2
Barringer Sq SW17 181 A6
Barrington N20 14 B3
Barrington Cl NW5 71 A3
Barrington Ct
9 Acton W3 110 D4
Kentish Town NW5 71 A3
4 Muswell Hill N10 31 B1
31 South Lambeth SW9 138 A3
Barrington Prim Sch DA7 146 D3
Barrington Rd
Bexley DA7 146 D3
Brixton SW9 138 D2
Cheam SM3 201 C1
Hornsey N8 49 D4
Little Ilford E12 78 C2
Barrington Villas SE18 144 C4
Barrington Wlk 9 SE19 183 C4
Barrow Ave SM5 218 D1
Barrow Cl N21 16 D2
Barrow Ct 6 SE6 164 D3
Barrowdene Cl HA5 23 A1
Barrowell Gn N21 17 A2
Barrowfield Cl N9 18 C1
Barrowgate Ho W4 111 B1
Barrowgate Rd W4 111 B1
Barrow Hedges Cl SM5 218 C1
Barrow Hedges Prim Sch SM5 218 C1
Barrow Hedges Way SM5 218 C1
Barrow Hill KT4 215 C6
Barrow Hill Cl KT4 215 C6
Barrow Hill Est NW8 92 C5 230 A3
Barrow Hill Jun Sch NW8 92 C5 230 A3
Barrow Hill Rd NW8 230 A3
Barrow Point Ave HA5 23 A1
Barrow Point La HA5 23 A1
Barrow Rd
Croydon CR0 220 C3
Streatham SW16 181 D4
Barrow Wlk TW8 109 C1
Barrs Rd NW10 67 B1
Barry Ave Erith DA7 147 A5
South Tottenham N15 51 D3
Barry Cl BR6 227 C5
Barry Ct SW4 159 C5
Barrydene N20 14 B2
Barrydene Ct EN2 4 D2
Barry Ho 4 SE16 118 B1
Barry Lo N4 50 B2
Barrymore N12 30 A3
Barry Par SE22 140 A1
Barry Rd London SE22 162 A6
Newham E6 100 A1
Willesden NW10 67 A1
Barry Terr TW15 148 B2
Barset Rd SE15 140 C2
Barsons Cl SE20 184 C3
Barston Rd SE27 161 A1
Barstow Cres SW2 160 B3
Bartell Ho SW2 160 C5
Barter St WC1 94 A2 240 B3
Barters Wlk HA5 41 A6
Barth Mews SE18 123 C2
Bartholomew Cl
Barbican EC1 242 A3
Wandsworth SW18 136 A1
Bartholomew Ct
16 Blackwall E14 120 B6
Edgware HA8 25 D3
St Luke's EC1 242 B6
Bartholomew Ho
22 Camberwell SE5 139 A3
Enfield EN3 7 A6
Bartholomew La EC2 242 D1
Bartholomew Pas EC1 241 D3
Bartholomew Pl EC1 242 A3
Bartholomew Rd NW5 71 C2
Bartholomew Sq
18 Bethnal Green E1 96 B3
St Luke's EC1 242 B6
Bartholomew St SE1 117 B3 262 D5
Bartholomew Villas NW5 71 C2
Barth Rd SE18 123 C2
Bartle Ave E6 100 A5
Bartle Rd W11 91 A1
Bartlett Cl E14 97 C1
Bartlett Ct EC4 241 B2
Bartletts Cotts 4 EN5 1 A2
Bartletts Ho 10 RM10 81 D2
Bartlett St CR2 221 B3
Bartok Ho W11 244 C5
Barton Ave RM7 59 D1
Barton Cl Bexley DA6 169 A6
Hackney E9 74 C3
Hendon NW4 46 A5
2 Newham E6 100 B1
Peckham SE15 140 B2
Shepperton TW17 192 D3
Barton Ct
Beckenham BR2 208 B6
10 South Lambeth SW4 138 A3
3 Sutton SM1 217 D2
West Kensington W14 254 B2
Barton Gn KT3 177 B1
Barton Ho
8 Bromley E3 97 D4
Islington N1 72 D1
Sands End SW6 135 D2
Barton Mdws IG6 57 A5
Barton Rd Sidcup DA14 191 A4
West Kensington W14 113 A1 254 B1
Barton St SW1 260 A6
Bartons The WD6 9 D5
Bartonway NW8 229 C4
Bartram Cl UB8 82 D3
Bartram Ct RM9 80 B2
Bartram Rd SE4 163 A5
Bartrams La EN4 2 A5
Bartrip St E9 75 B2
Barts Cl BR3 207 C4
Barts & The London Sch of Medicine & Dentistry EC1 94 D3 241 D5
Barville Cl SE4 141 A1
Barwell Bsns Pk KT9 213 D1
Barwell Ho 7 E2 96 A3
Barwell La KT9 213 C1
Barwick Dr UB8 82 D2
Barwick Ho 7 W3 111 A4
Barwick Rd E7 77 B4
Barwood Ave BR4 207 D1
Bascome St 13 SW2 160 C5
Basden Gr TW13 151 C2
Base Apartments 8 N1 73 A1
Basedale Rd RM9 80 B1
Baseing Cl E6 122 C6
Baseline Business Studios 18 W11 112 D6
Basevi Way SE8 141 D6
Bashley Rd NW10 89 B3
Basil Ave E6 100 A4
Basil Ct 11 EN5 2 A1
Basildene Rd TW4, TW5 128 D2
Basildon Ct W1 238 B4
Basildon Rd SE2 124 A1
Basil Gdns
Croydon CR0 206 D1
West Norwood SE27 183 A5
Basil Ho
South Lambeth SW8 270 A4
22 Whitechapel E1 96 A1
Basil Mans SW1 247 C1
Basilon Rd DA7 147 A3
Basil Spence Ho N22 32 B2
Basil St
Knightsbridge SW1 114 D4 247 C1
Knightsbridge SW1, SW3 114 D3 257 C6
Basin App 20 E14 97 A1
Basing Cl KT7 196 D2
Basing Ct 13 SE15 139 D4
Basingdon Way SE5 139 B1
Basing Dr DA5 169 B5
Basingfield Rd KT7 196 D2
Basinghall Ave EC2 95 B1 242 C2
Basinghall St EC2 95 B1 242 C2
Basing Hill
London NW11 47 B1
Wembley HA9 44 C1
Basing Ho
7 Barking IG11 101 B6
Catford SE6 185 C6
Basing House Yd 22 E2 95 C4
Basing Pl E2 95 C4
Basing St W11 91 B1
Basing Way London N3 47 D6
Thames Ditton KT7 196 D2
Basire St N1 95 A6 235 B6
Baskerville Ct
South Norwood SE25 205 C4
Wandsworth SW18 158 C4
Baskerville Gdns NW10 67 C4
Baskerville Rd SW18 158 C4
Basket Gdns SE9 166 A6
Basle Ho 3 E15 76 C3
Baslow Cl HA3 24 B2
Baslow Wlk E5 74 D4
Basnett Rd 9 SW11 137 A2
Basque Ct 21 SE16 118 D4
Bassano St SE22 161 D6
Bassant Rd SE18 145 D6
Bassein Park Rd W12 111 D4
Bassett Gdns TW7 130 A5
Bassett Ho RM9 102 B6
Bassett Rd W10 90 D1
Bassetts Cl BR6 226 D4
Bassett St NW5 71 A2
Bassetts Way BR6 226 D4
Bassett Way UB1 85 D1
Bassingbourn Ho 3 N1 72 D1
Bassingham Rd
Wandsworth SW18 158 A4
Wembley HA0 65 D2
Bassishaw Highwalk EC2 242 C3
Basswood Cl 5 SE15 140 B2
Bastable Ave IG11 102 A5
Basterfield Ho EC1 242 A5
Bastion Highwalk EC2 242 A3
Bastion Rd SE18, SE2 124 A1
Baston Manor Rd BR2, BR4 225 B4
Baston Rd BR2 225 B5
Baston Sch BR2 225 B6
Bastwick St EC1 95 A3 242 A6
Basuto Rd SW6 135 C4 265 B1
Batavia Cl TW16 172 C2
Batavia Ho 1 SE14 141 A5
Batavia Mews 3 SE14 141 A5
Batavia Rd
Deptford SE14 141 A5
Sunbury TW16 172 B2
Batchelor St N1 94 C6 234 B5
Bateman Cl IG11 79 A2
Bateman Ho 8 SE17 138 D6
Bateman Rd E4 35 C4
Bateman's Bldgs W1 239 C1
Bateman's Row EC2 95 C3 243 B6
Bateman St W1 93 D1 239 C1
Bates Cres
Croydon CR0 220 C3
Streatham SW16 181 C3
Bateson St 8 SE18 123 C2
Bate St 10 E14 119 B6
Bath Cl SE15 140 B5
Bath Ct Finsbury EC1 235 C1
3 Forest Hill SE26 162 A1
Holborn EC1 241 A5
Bathgate Ho 8 SW9 138 D4
Bathgate Rd SW19 156 D1
Bath Gr E2 96 A5
Bath Ho
Bethnal Green E2 96 A3
Borough The SE1 262 B6
Bath House Rd CR0 204 A1
Bath Pas KT1 175 D1
Bath Pl Barnet EN5 1 B2
14 Hammersmith W6 112 C1
11 Shoreditch EC2 95 C4
Bath Rd Acton W4 111 C2
Cranford TW3, TW4, TW5 128 C4
Dagenham RM6 59 A3
Harlington TW6, UB7, TW5 127 B4
Harmondsworth TW6, UB7 126 B4
Lower Edmonton N9 18 C2
Upton E7 77 D2
Baths Rd BR1, BR2 209 D5
Bath St EC1 95 B4 235 C1
Bath Terr SE1 117 A3 262 A6
Bathurst Ave SW19 179 D2
Bathurst Gdns NW10 90 B5
Bathurst Ho 2 W12 112 B6
Bathurst Mews W2 114 B6 246 D6
Bathurst Rd IG1 56 D1
Bathurst St W2 246 D6
Bathway 11 SE18 122 C2
Batley Cl CR4 202 D2
Batley Pl 3 N16 73 D5
Batley Rd Enfield EN2 5 B4
Shacklewell N16 73 D5
Batman Cl W12 112 B5
Batoum Gdns W6 112 C3
Batson Ho 29 E1 96 A1
Batson St W12 112 A4
Batsworth Rd CR4 202 B6
Battenburg Wlk 10 SE19 183 C5
Batten Cl E6 100 B1
Batten Ho
7 London SW4 159 C6
8 Walthamstow E17 53 D6
10 West Kilburn W10 91 A4
Batten St SW11 136 C2
Battersby Rd SE6 164 B1
BATTERSEA 136 D4
Battersea Bridge Rd SW11 136 C5 267 A3
Battersea Bsns Ctr SW11 137 A2
Battersea Church Rd SW11 136 B4 266 D2
Battersea Dogs Home SW8 137 B5 268 D3
Battersea High St SW11 136 B3
Battersea Hts SW11 136 D2
Battersea Park* SW11 137 A5 268 A3
Battersea Park Rd SW11, SW8 267 D1
Battersea Park Sta SW8 137 B5 268 C3
Battersea Power Station(dis) SW8 137 B6 268 D6
Battersea Rise SW11 136 C1
Battersea Sq SW11 266 D1
Battery Rd SE28 123 C4
Battishill St 9 N1 72 D1
Battlebridge Ct NW1 233 B4
Battle Bridge La SE1 117 C5 253 A3
Battle Bridge Rd NW1 94 A5 233 A4
Battle Cl SW19 180 A4
Battledean Rd N5 72 D3
Battle Ho 8 SE15 140 A6
Battle House Mews 7 EN5 2 A1
Battle of Britain Mus* NW9 27 D1
Batty St E1 96 A1
Baty Ho SW2 160 B3
Baudwin Rd SE6 164 C2
Baugh Rd DA14 190 C5
Baulk The SW18 157 C4
Bavant Rd SW16 182 B1
Bavaria Rd N19 72 A6
Bavdene Mews NW4 46 B5
Bavent Rd SE5 139 A3
Bawdale Rd SE22 161 D6
Bawdsey Ave IG2 57 D5
Bawtree Rd SE14 141 A5
Bawtry Rd N20 14 D1
Baxendale N20 14 A2
Baxendale St E2 96 A4
Baxter Cl Bromley BR1 210 D6
Hillingdon UB10 82 D4
Southall UB2 107 D3
Baxter Ho 11 E3 97 D4
Baxter Rd Edmonton N18 34 B6
Ilford IG1 78 D3
Islington N1 73 B2
Newham E16 99 C1
Bayard Ct DA7 147 D1
Baycliffe Ho 8 E9 74 D2
Baycroft Cl HA5 40 C6
Bay Ct Ealing W5 110 A3
7 Stepney E1 96 D3
Baydon Ct BR2 208 D6
Bayer Ho EC1 242 A5
Bayes Ct NW3 70 D1
Bayeux Ho 10 SE7 143 C6
Bayfield Ho 3 SE4 140 D1
Bayfield Rd SE9 143 D1
Bayford Lodge HA5 23 B2
Bayford Rd NW10 90 D4
Bayford St Ind Ctr 4 E8 74 B1
Bayford St 5 E8 74 B1
Baygrove Mews KT1 175 C2
Bayham Pl NW1 93 C6 232 B5
Bayham Rd Acton W4 111 B3
Ealing W13 109 B5
Morden SM4 202 A5
Bayham St NW1 93 C6 232 A5
Bay Ho UB10 60 C4
Bayhurst Ho N4 51 A2
Bayhurst Wood Countryside Park UB9 38 B4
Bayleaf Cl TW12 174 B5
Bayley St WC1 239 C3
Bayley Wlk SE2 125 A1
Baylis Mews TW1 153 A4
Baylis Rd SE1 116 C4 251 A1
Bayliss Ave SE28 124 D6
Bayliss Cl
4 Southall UB1 85 D1
Southgate N21 16 A6
Bayne Cl E6 100 B1
Baynes Cl EN1 6 A4
Baynes Mews 2 NW3 70 B2
Baynes St NW1 71 C1
Baynham Cl DA5 169 B5
Bayon Ho 27 N19 49 D2
Bayonne Rd W6 264 A5
Bays Cl SE26 184 C5
Bays Ct HA8 26 D5
Bayshill Rise UB5 63 D2
Bayston Rd N16 73 D5
BAYSWATER 114 A6
Bayswater Rd W2 114 B6 246 C5
Bayswater Sta W2 113 D6 245 D6
Bayton Ct 2 E8 74 A1
Baytree Cl
Bromley BR1 187 D2
Sidcup DA15 167 D3
Baytree Ho E4 19 D4
Baytree Rd SW2 138 B1
Bazalgette Cl KT3 199 B4
Bazalgette Gdns KT3 199 B4
Bazalgette Ho NW8 236 D6
Bazeley Ho SE1 251 C1
Bazely St E14 120 A6
Bazile Rd N21 16 C5
BBC Television Ctr W12 112 C5
Beacham Cl SE7 143 D6
Beachborough Rd BR1 186 A6
Beachcroft Ave UB1 107 B5
Beachcroft Rd E11 76 C5
Beach Ct SE9 166 A5
Beach Gr TW13 151 C2
Beach Ho SW5 255 A2
Beachy Rd E3 75 C1
Beaconfield Terrace Rd W14 254 A5
Beacon Gate SE14 140 D2
Beacon Gr SM5 219 A4
Beacon Hill N7 72 A3
Beacon Ho
11 Camberwell SE5 139 C5
7 Isle Of Dogs E14 119 D1
10 Penge SE26 184 B5
South Lambeth SW8 269 C2
Beacon House Sch W5 110 B5
Beacon Pl CR0 220 A5
Beacon Rd
Harlington TW19, TW6 148 C5
Hither Green SE13 164 B5
Beacon Rdbt TW6 148 C5
Beacons Cl 10 E6 100 A2
Beaconsfield Cl
Acton Green W4 111 A1
Friern Barnet N11 31 A5
Greenwich SE3 143 A6
Beaconsfield Ct N11 31 A5
Beaconsfield Gdns KT10 212 C1
Beaconsfield Par 1 SE9 188 A6
Beaconsfield Prim Sch UB2 107 A5
Beaconsfield Rd
Acton W4 111 B3
Bromley BR1 209 D6
Claygate KT10 212 C1
Ealing W5 109 D4
Edmonton N9 18 A1
Elmstead SE9 188 A6
Enfield EN3 6 D6
Friern Barnet N11 31 A6
Greenwich SE3 143 A5
Hayes UB4 106 C5
Kingston u T KT3 177 B1
Leyton E10 76 A5
Newham E16 98 D3
Southall UB1 107 A5
South Tottenham N15 51 C5
Surbiton KT5 198 B2
Thornton Heath CR0 205 B3
Twickenham TW1 153 B5
Walthamstow E17 53 B3
Walworth SE17 117 C1 263 A1

Beaconsfield Rd *continued*
Willesden NW10 67 D2
Beaconsfield Wlk SW6 135 B4 264 D1
Beaconshaw BR1 186 C3
Beacontree Ave E17 36 B1
Beacontree Rd E11 54 D2
Beadle Ct CR4 202 C6
Beadlow Cl SM4 202 B3
Beadman Pl SE27 182 D6
Beadman St SE27 182 D6
Beadnell Rd SE23 162 D3
Beadon Rd
Bromley BR2 209 A4
Hammersmith W6 112 C2
Beaford Gr SW20 201 B6
Beagle Cl TW13 172 B6
Beak St W1 115 C6 249 B6
Beal Cl DA16 146 A4
Beale Cl N13 32 D5
Beale Ho 7 SW9 138 B3
Beale Pl E3 97 B5
Beale Rd E3 97 B6
Beal High Sch IG5 56 A5
Beal Rd IG1 78 C6
Beam Ave RM10 103 D6
Beames Ho SW8 269 C2
Beames Rd NW10 89 B6
Beaminster Ct N15 51 B4
Beaminster Gdns IG6 56 D6
Beaminster Ho SW8 270 C4
Beamish Dr WD23 8 A3
Beamish Ho 7 SE16 118 C2
Beamish Rd N9 18 A3
Beanacre Cl E9 75 B2
Bean Rd DA6 146 D1
Beanshaw SE9 188 C6
Beansland Gr RM6 59 A6
Bear Alley EC4 241 C2
Bear Cl RM7 59 D3
Bear Croft Ho 6 SW6 135 B3
Beardell St SE19 183 D4
Beardow Gr N14 15 C5
Beard Rd KT2 176 B5
Beardsfield E13 99 A5
Beard's Hill TW12 173 C2
Beards Hill Cl TW12 173 C2
Beardsley Terr RM8 80 B3
Beardsley Way W3 111 B4
Beard's Rd TW15, TW16 171 C4
Bearfield Rd KT2 176 A3
Bear Gardens Mus* SE1 117 A5 252 A4
Bear Gdns SE1 117 A5 252 A4
Bear La SE1 116 D5 251 D3
Bear Rd TW13 172 D6
Bear St WC2 249 D6
Bearstead Rise SE4 163 B6
Bearsted Terr 7 BR3 185 C2
Beasley's Ait TW17 193 D3
Beasley's Ait La TW16, TW17 193 D3
Beaton Cl SE15 139 D4
Beatrice Ave
Thornton Heath SW16 182 B1
Wembley HA9 66 A3
Beatrice Cl Newham E13 99 A3
Pinner HA5 40 A5
Beatrice Ct
Buckhurst Hill IG9 21 D2
Hendon NW4 46 C4
Beatrice Ho
1 Brixton SW2 160 B6
Forest Hill SE6 163 C2
4 Hammersmith W6 112 C1
2 Stepney E1 96 D2
Beatrice Lo 3 N12 30 A4
Beatrice Pl W8 255 C5
Beatrice Rd
Bermondsey SE1 118 A2
Edmonton N9 18 C4
Finsbury Pk N4 50 C2
2 Richmond TW10 154 B6
Southall UB1 107 B5
Walthamstow E17 53 C4
Beatrice Tate Sch E2 96 B4
Beatrice Webb Ho 4 E3 97 A5
Beatrix Ho SW5 255 D2
Beatrix Potter Prim Sch SW18 158 A3
Beatson Wlk 23 SE16 118 D5
Beattie Cl TW14 149 D3
Beattie Ho SW8 269 B2
Beattock Rise N10 49 B5
Beatty Ho 16 E14 119 C4
Beatty Rd Stanmore HA7 25 C4
Stoke Newington N16 73 C4
Beatty St NW1 232 A4
Beattyville Gdns IG6 56 D5
Beauchamp Cl 17 W4 111 A3
Beauchamp Ct HA7 25 C5
Beauchamp Pl SW3 114 C3 257 B5
Beauchamp Rd
Clapham SW11 136 D1
East Molesey KT8 196 A4
South Norwood SE19 183 B2
Sutton SM1 217 C4
Twickenham TW1 153 A4
Upton E7 77 B1
Beauchamp St EC1 241 A3
Beauchamp Terr SW15 134 B2
Beauclerc Inf Sch TW16 194 C6
Beauclerc Rd W6 112 B3
Beauclere Ho 1 SM2 218 A1
Beauclerk Cl TW13 150 B3
Beauclerk Ho 10 SW16 160 A1
Beaudesert Mews UB7 104 A4
Beaufort E6 100 C2
Beaufort Ave HA3 43 B6
Beaufort Cl
Chingford E4 35 D4
Ealing W5 88 B2
Putney SW19 156 B4
Beaufort Ct
Friern Barnet N11 31 B5
Harrow HA3 43 A3
3 New Barnet EN5 14 A6
Richmond TW10 175 C6
West Brompton SW6 265 A6
Beaufort Dr NW11 47 C5
Beaufort Gdns
Hendon NW4 46 C3
Heston TW5 129 A4
Ilford IG1 56 C1
Knightsbridge SW3 114 C3 257 B6
South Norwood SW16 182 B3
Beaufort Ho
Ashford TW15 170 D5
Battersea SW11 136 C3
Chelsea SW3 266 D5
Hampstead Garden Suburb NW11 48 A3
20 Millwall E14 119 C4
Pimlico SW1 259 C1
8 South Tottenham N15 51 D5
1 Wimbledon SW20 178 D2
Beaufort Mans SW3 266 D5
Beaufort Mews SW6 264 D6
Beaufort Pk NW11 47 C5
Beaufort Rd Ealing W5 88 B2
Kingston u T KT1, KT5, KT6 198 A5
Richmond TW10 175 C6
Ruislip HA4 61 B6
Twickenham TW1 153 C4
Beaufort St SW3 136 B6 266 C6
Beaufort Way KT17 216 A1
Beaufoy Ho
South Lambeth SW8 270 C4
3 West Norwood SE27 160 D1
Beaufoy Rd
11 London SW8 137 B2
Tottenham N17 33 C3
Beaufoy Wlk SE11 116 B2 260 D3
Beaulieu Ave
Forest Hill SE26 184 B6
1 Newham E16 121 B5
Beaulieu Cl
Camberwell SE5 139 B2
Colindale NW9 45 C5
Hounslow TW4 151 B6
Mitcham CR4 181 A2
14 Twickenham TW1 153 D5
Beaulieu Ct W5 88 A2
Beaulieu Dr HA5 40 D2
Beaulieu Gdns N21 17 A4
Beaulieu Ho 6 NW4 28 D1
Beaulieu Hts CR7 183 C2
Beaulieu Pl W4 111 A3
Beaumanor Gdns SE9 188 C6
Beaumanor Mans W2 245 D6
Beaumaris 5 N11 32 A4
Beaumaris Dr IG8 37 D3
Beaumaris Gn NW9 45 C3
Beaumaris Twr 2 W3 110 D4
Beaumont SW15 157 A6
Beaumont Ave
Harrow HA2 41 D3
Richmond TW9 132 B2
Wembley HA0 65 C4
West Kensington W14 113 B1 254 C2
Beaumont Bldgs WC2 240 B1
Beaumont Cl KT2 176 C3
Beaumont Cres W14 113 B1 254 C1
Beaumont Ct
10 Acton Green W4 111 A1
16 Hendon NW9 27 D1
Lower Clapton E5 74 B5
Marylebone W1 238 B4
7 Mile End E1 97 A4
6 Mitcham CR4 181 A1
Wembley HA0 65 C3
17 Wimbledon SW19 178 D3
Beaumont Dr
Ashford TW15 171 B5
New Malden KT4 200 B2
Beaumont Gdns NW3 69 C5
Beaumont Gr E1 96 D3
Beaumont Ho
12 Leyton E10 53 D2
1 Streatham SW2 160 A3
West Kensington W14 254 D3
Wimbledon SW19 157 C1
Beaumont Lo E8 74 A2
Beaumont Pl Barnet EN5 1 B4
Fitzrovia NW1, WC1, W1 93 C3 239 B6
Isleworth TW7 152 D6
Beaumont Rd
Leyton E10 53 D2
Newham E13 99 B4
Beaumont Rd *continued*
Orpington BR5 211 B3
Putney SW15, SW19 157 A4
South Acton W4 111 A3
South Norwood SE19 183 A4
Beaumont Rise N19 49 D1
Beaumont Sch The E10 53 D1
Beaumont Sq E1 96 D2
Beaumont St W1 238 B4
Beaumont Terr 1 SE13 164 C4
Beaumont Wlk NW3 70 D1
Beauvais Terr UB5 84 D4
Beauvale 6 NW1 71 A1
Beauval Rd SE22 161 D5
Beaverbank Rd SE9 167 B3
Beaver Cl
Hampton TW12 173 D2
9 Penge SE20 184 A3
West Barnes SM4 200 C2
Beaver Ctr The RM8 59 A2
Beaver Gr UB5 85 A4
Beavers Com Prim Sch TW4 128 C2
Beavers Cres TW4 128 D1
Beavers La TW4 128 C2
Beavers Lo DA14 189 D5
Beaverwood Rd BR7 189 C4
Beaverwood Sch for Girls BR7 189 C4
Beavis Ho N16 73 C5
Beavor La W6 112 A1
Bebbington Rd SE18 123 C2
Beblets Cl 4 BR6 227 D3
Bec Cl HA4 62 D5
Beccles Dr IG11 79 D2
Beccles St E14 119 B6
Bechervaise Ct 2 E10 53 D1
Beck Cl SE13 141 D4
Beck Ct BR3 206 D6
BECKENHAM 185 C1
Beckenham Bsns Ctr BR3 185 A4
Beckenham Ct BR3 185 C2
Beckenham Gdns N9 17 C1
Beckenham Gr BR2 186 B1
Beckenham Hill Rd BR3, SE6 186 A5
Beckenham Hill Sta SE6 186 A5
Beckenham Hospl BR3 185 B1
Beckenham Junction Sta BR3 185 C2
Beckenham La BR1, BR2 186 D1
Beckenham Place Pk BR3 185 D3
Beckenham Rd
Penge BR3 185 A2
West Wickham BR3, BR4 208 A2
Beckenham Rd Sta BR3 185 A2
Beckers The N16 74 A4
Becket Ave E6 100 C4
Becket Cl
Croydon SE25 206 A3
2 Merton SW19 179 D2
Becket Fold 10 HA1 42 D4
Becket Ho SE1 252 C1
Becket Rd N18 34 C6
Becket St SE1 262 C6
Beckett Cl
Abbey Wood DA17 125 B3
Streatham SW16 159 D2
Willesden NW10 67 C2
Beckett Ho
23 London SW9 138 A3
15 Stepney E1 96 C2
Becketts Cl
Feltham TW14 150 B5
Orpington BR6 227 D5
Becketts Pl KT1 175 D2
Beckett Wlk BR3 185 A4
Beckfoot NW1 232 B3
Beckford Cl W14 254 D3
Beckford Dr BR5 211 B2
Beckford Ho 16 N16 73 C3
Beckford Prim Sch NW6 69 B3
Beckford Rd CR0 205 D3
Beckham Ho SE11 260 D3
Beck Ho
4 Edmonton N18 34 A5
Stoke Newington N16 73 C5
Beckington 18 NW5 71 A2
Beck La BR3 206 D6
Beckley Ho E3 97 B3
Becklow Gdns
Chiswick W12 111 D4
1 Shepherd's Bush W12 112 A4
Becklow Mews 7 W12 112 A4
Becklow Rd W12 112 A4
Beckmead Sch BR3 207 C1
Beck Rd E8 96 B6
Beck River Pk 10 BR3 185 C2
Becks Rd DA14 168 A1
BECKTON 100 D2
Beckton Alps E6 100 B3
Beckton Alps Ski Ctr E6 100 C3
Beckton Park Sta E6 122 B6
Beckton Rd E16 98 D2
Beckton Ret Pk E6 100 C2
Beckton Sta E6 100 C2
Beckton Triangle Ret Pk E6 100 D3
Beck Way BR3 207 B6
Beckway Rd SW16 181 D1
Beckway St SE17 117 C2 263 A3
Beckwith Ho 22 E2 96 B5
Beckwith Rd SE24 161 B6
Beclands Rd SW17 181 A4
Becmead Ave
Harrow HA3 43 B4
Streatham SW16 181 D6
Becondale Rd SE19 183 C5
BECONTREE 81 A4
Becontree Ave RM8 80 C5
Becontree Day Hospl RM8 81 A6
Becontree Prim Sch RM8 80 B5
Becontree Sta RM9 80 D2
Bective Pl SW15 135 B1
Bective Rd
Forest Gate E7 77 A4
Putney SW15 135 B1
Becton Pl DA8 147 D5
Bedale Rd EN2 5 A5
Bedale St SE1 252 C3
Beddan Ct HA8 26 C4
BEDDINGTON 220 A6
BEDDINGTON CORNER 203 A2
Beddington Cross CR0 204 A2
Beddington Farm Rd CR0 204 A1
Beddington Gdns SM5, SM6 219 A2
Beddington Gn BR5 189 D2
Beddington Gr SM6 219 D3
Beddington Inf Sch SM6 219 C4
Beddington La
Wallington CR0 203 D2
Wallington CR0 220 A6
Beddington Lane Sta CR0 203 C3
Beddington Manor SM2 218 B2
Beddington Park Cotts SM6 219 D5
Beddington Park Prim Sch CR0 219 D5
Beddington Rd
Ilford IG3 57 D2
St Paul's Cray BR5 189 D2
Beddington Terr CR0 204 B2
Beddington Trad Est CR0 204 A1
Bede Cl HA5 22 D2
Bedefield WC1 233 B1
Bede Ho London SE14 141 B4
5 Putney SW15 156 D5
Bedelsford Sch KT1 198 A6
Bedens Rd DA14 191 A5
Bede Rd RM6 58 C3
Bedevere Rd N9 18 A1
Bedfont Cl
East Bedfont TW14 149 A5
Mitcham CR4 181 A1
Bedfont Green Cl TW14 149 A3
Bedfont Ind Pk TW15 149 B1
Bedfont Ind Pk N TW15 149 A1
Bedfont Jun & Inf Schs TW14 149 C5
Bedfont La TW14, TW13 149 D4
Bedfont Lakes Ctry Pk TW14 149 A2
Bedfont Rd
East Bedfont TW13, TW14 149 B2
Stanwell TW19 148 B5
Bedford Ave Barnet EN5 13 B6
Bloomsbury WC1 93 D2 239 D3
Hayes UB4 84 B1
Bedfordbury WC2 116 A6 250 A5
Bedford Cl
Chiswick W4 133 D6
Muswell Hill N10 31 A3
Bedford Cnr 3 W4 111 C2
Bedford Court Mans WC1 239 D3
Bedford Ct
6 Richmond TW9 132 B1
South Norwood SE19 183 D2
St James WC2 250 A5
Wembley HA0 65 D4
Bedford Gardens Ho W8 245 B3
Bedford Gdns W8 113 C5 245 B3
Bedford Hill SW12 159 B2
Bedford Ho
2 Acton W4 111 C2
Edgware HA8 26 B3
7 Stockwell SW4 138 A1
Bedford Mews SE6 163 D2
BEDFORD PARK 111 C3
Bedford Park Cnr 5 W4 111 C2
Bedford Park Mans 4 W4 111 B2
Bedford Pas SW6 264 B4
Bedford Pk CR0 205 A1
Bedford Pl
Bloomsbury WC1 94 A2 240 A4
Croydon CR0 205 B1
Bedford Rd Acton W4 111 C3
Barking E6 100 C6
Crouch End N8 49 D3
Ealing W13 109 B6
East Finchley N2 48 C6
Edgware NW7 11 C1
Edmonton N9 18 B4
Harrow HA1 42 A3
Ilford IG1 78 D5
North Cheam KT4 216 C6
Ruislip HA4 61 D4
Sidcup DA15 167 C1
South Tottenham N15 51 C5
Stockwell SW2, SW4 138 A1
Twickenham TW2 152 B1
Walthamstow E17 53 C6
Woodford E18 37 A1
Wood Green N22 32 A1
Bedford Row WC1 94 B2 240 D3
Bedford Sq WC1 93 D2 239 D3
Bedford St WC2 116 A6 250 B5
Bedford Terr SM2 218 A2
Bedford Villas 3 SM5 218 D5
Bedford Way WC1 93 D3 239 D5
Bedgebury Gdns SW19 157 A2
Bedgebury Rd SE9 143 D1
Bedivere Rd BR1 165 A1
Bedlam Mews SE11 261 A4
Bedlow Cl NW8 236 D5
Bedlow Way CR0 220 B4
Bedonwell Inf Sch DA17 147 A6
Bedonwell Jun Sch DA17 147 A6
Bedonwell Rd
Bexley DA17 147 A6
Erith DA7 147 C5
Bedser Cl
Kennington SE11 270 D6
South Norwood CR7 205 A6
Bedser Ct 7 SW4 138 A3
Bedser Dr UB6 64 B3
Bedster Gdns KT8 195 D6
Bedwardine Rd SE19 183 C3
Bedwell Ct 4 RM6 58 D2
Bedwell Gdns UB3 105 C2
Bedwell Ho 18 SW9 138 C3
Bedwell Rd
Belvedere DA17 125 C1
Tottenham N17 33 C2
Beeby Rd E16 99 B2
Beech Ave Acton W3 111 C5
Brentford TW8 131 B5
4 Chigwell IG9 21 B2
East Barnet N20 14 C3
Ruislip HA4 40 B1
Sidcup DA15 168 A4
Beech Cl Ashford TW15 171 B5
Carshalton SM5 218 D6
Deptford SE8 141 B6
Enfield N9 18 B5
Putney SW15 156 A4
Sunbury TW16 172 D1
West Drayton UB7 104 C3
Wimbledon SW19 178 C4
Beech Copse
Bickley BR1 188 B1
South Croydon CR2 221 C3
Beechcroft
Chislehurst West BR7 188 C3
3 Kingston u T KT2 176 D2
Beechcroft Ave
Golders Green NW11 47 B2
Harrow HA2 41 C2
Kingston u T KT1, KT3 177 A1
Beechcroft Cl
Heston TW5 129 A5
Orpington BR6 227 B4
Streatham SW16 182 B5
Beechcroft Ct
3 Golders Green NW11 47 B2
Greenwich SE3 143 A4
8 Woodside Pk N12 29 D6
Beech Croft Ct N5 72 D4
Beechcroft Gdns HA9 66 B5
Beechcroft Ho W5 88 A2
Beechcroft Lo 6 SM2 218 A1
Beechcroft Mans SW16 182 B5
Beechcroft Rd
Chessington KT9 214 B5
Mortlake SW14 133 A2
Orpington BR6 227 B4
Upper Tooting SW17 158 C2
Woodford E18 37 B1
Beechcroft Way N19 49 D1
Beech Ct
Beckenham BR3 185 B3
3 Buckhurst Hill IG9 21 D2
Child's Hill NW2 69 B6
Hayes UB3 105 D5
6 Ilford E12 78 C5
Marylebone W1 237 C2
Northolt UB5 85 A6
43 Notting Hill W2 91 C2
7 Rotherhithe SE16 119 A5
Surbiton KT6 198 A2
Teddington TW11 175 C4
Walthamstow E17 54 B6
Beech Ct *continued*
4 West Norwood SW16 182 C5
Beechdale N21 16 B2
Beechdale Rd SW2 160 B5
Beech Dell BR2, BR6 226 B4
Beechdene 4 SE15 140 B4
Beech Dr N2 48 D6
Beechen Cliff Way TW7 130 D3
Beechengrove HA5 41 B6
Beechen Pl SE23 162 C2
Beeches Ave SM5 218 C1
Beeches Cl SE20 184 C2
Beeches Ct BR1 187 A4
Beeches Prim Ctr The SE2 124 C3
Beeches Rd
Cheam SM3 201 A1
Upper Tooting SW17 158 D1
Beeches The
Ealing W7 108 D4
East Barnet N20 14 C2
East Ham E12 78 B1
Hounslow TW3 129 D4
Mitcham CR4 202 C4
1 Upper Holloway N19 50 A1
Beechey Ho 30 E1 118 B5
Beech Farm Cotts IG8 36 B3
Beechfield Cotts 5 BR1 187 C1
Beechfield Ct 7 CR2 221 A4
Beechfield Rd
Bromley BR1 187 C1
Forest Hill SE6 163 B3
Harringay N4 51 A3
Beech Gdns
Dagenham RM10 81 D1
Ealing W5 110 A3
Beech Gr
Kingston u T KT3 199 B6
Mitcham CR4 203 D5
Beech Hall Cres E4 36 B3
Beech Hall Rd E4 36 B3
Beech Hill EN4 2 C5
Beech Hill Ave EN4 2 B4
Beechhill Rd SE9 166 C6
Beech Ho Chingford E4 35 C6
Hayes UB4 84 D2
Heston TW5 129 A5
6 Maitland Pk NW3 70 D2
New Addington CR0 223 D2
22 Rotherhithe SE16 118 C4
7 Sidcup DA15 168 A1
5 Stoke Newington N16 73 B6
12 Wallington SM6 219 C2
Beech House Rd CR0 221 B5
Beech La IG9 21 B2
Beech Lawns N12 30 B5
Beechmont Cl BR1 186 C5
Beechmore Gdns SM3 216 D6
Beechmore Rd SW11 136 D4 267 D1
Beechmount Ave W7 86 C2
Beecholme 15 N12 29 D6
Beecholme Ave CR4 181 B2
Beecholme Est E5 74 B5
Beecholme Prim Sch CR4 181 B2
Beech Rd Bowes Pk N11 32 A4
East Bedfont TW14 149 C4
Thornton Heath SW16 204 B6
Beechrow KT2 176 A6
Beech St EC2 95 A2 242 B4
Beech Tree Cl
Islington N1 72 C1
Stanmore HA7 25 C5
Beech Tree Glade E4 20 D3
Beech Tree Pl SM1 217 D3
Beechvale Cl N12 30 C5
Beechway DA5 168 D5
Beech Way
Twickenham TW2 151 C1
Willesden NW10 67 B1
Beech Wlk NW7 27 C4
Beechwood Ave
Ashford TW16 172 A4
East Finchley N3 47 C6
Greenford UB6 85 D4
Harrow HA2 63 D5
Hayes UB3 105 B6
Hillingdon UB8 82 C1
Orpington BR6 227 C2
Richmond TW9 132 C4
Ruislip HA4 61 D6
Thornton Heath CR7 204 D5
Beechwood Circ HA2 63 D5
Beechwood Cl
Edgware NW7 27 C5
Fortis Green N2 48 D5
Surbiton KT6 197 D2
Beechwood Cres DA7 147 A2
Beechwood Ct
Ashford TW16 172 A5
Carshalton SM5 218 D4
Cheam SM1 217 C3
Chiswick W4 133 B6
Stamford Hill N16 51 C2
Sutton SM2 218 B2
Beechwood Dr
Keston BR2 225 D4
Woodford IG8 36 D5
Beechwood Gdns
Ealing NW10 88 B4
Harrow HA2 63 D5
Ilford IG5 56 C5
Beechwood Gr W3 111 C6
Beechwood Hall N3 47 B6
Beechwood Ho 23 E2 96 A5

Beechwood Mews 2 N9 . . . 18 A2
Beechwood Pk E18 . . . 55 A6
Beechwood Rd
Dalston E8 . . . 73 D2
London N8 . . . 50 A5
South Croydon CR2 . . . 221 C1
Beechwood Rise BR7 . . 188 D6
Beechwoods Ct 5 SE19 . . . 183 D5
Beechworth Cl NW3 . . . 69 C6
Beecroft La SE4 . . . 163 A6
Beecroft Mews SE4 . . . 163 A6
Beecroft Rd SE4 . . . 163 A6
Beehive Cl Dalston E8 . . . 73 D1
Elstree WD6 . . . 9 D5
Hillingdon UB10 . . . 60 B1
Beehive Ct IG1 . . . 56 B3
Beehive La IG1 . . . 56 B3
Beehive Pl SW9 . . . 138 C2
Beehive Prep Sch IG4 . . 56 B4
Beeken Dene BR6 . . . 227 A4
Beeleigh Rd SM4 . . . 201 D5
Beemans Row 1 SW18 . . . 158 A2
Beeston Cl
5 Dalston E8 . . . 74 A3
South Oxhey WD19 . . . 22 D6
Beeston Pl SW1 . . . 258 D6
Beeston Rd EN4 . . . 14 B5
Beeston's Ho SE15 . . . 140 B2
Beeston Way TW14 . . . 150 C5
Beethoven Rd WD6 . . . 9 D5
Beethoven St W10 . . . 91 A4
Beeton Cl HA5 . . . 23 C3
Begbie Ho SW9 . . . 138 B3
Begbie Rd SE3 . . . 143 C4
Beggars Hill KT17 . . . 215 D2
Beggar's Roost La SM1 . . . 217 C2
Begonia Cl E6 . . . 100 B3
Begonia Pl 1 TW12 . . . 173 C4
Begonia Wlk W12 . . . 89 D1
Beira St SW12 . . . 159 B4
Beis Chinuch Lebonos Girls Sch N4 . . . 51 A2
Beis Rochel d'Satmar Girls Sch N16 . . . 51 C2
Beis Soroh Schneirer (Sch) NW4 . . . 46 A3
Beis Yaakov Prim Sch NW9 . . . 45 B6
Bekesbourne St 17 E14 . . 97 A1
Belcroft Cl BR1 . . . 186 D3
Beldanes Lo NW10 . . . 68 A1
Beldham Gdns KT8 . . . 195 D6
Belenoyd Ct SW16 . . . 160 B1
Belfairs Dr RM6 . . . 58 C2
Belfairs Gn WD19 . . . 22 D5
Belfast Rd
Croydon SE25 . . . 206 B5
Stoke Newington N16 . . . 73 D6
Belfield Rd KT19 . . . 215 C1
Belfont Wlk N7 . . . 72 A4
Belford Gr SE18 . . . 122 C2
Belford Ho 7 E8 . . . 95 D6
Belfort Rd SE15 . . . 140 C3
Belfry Cl 33 SE16 . . . 118 B1
Belgrade Ho N16 . . . 73 C4
Belgrade Rd
Hampton TW12 . . . 173 D2
Stoke Newington N16 . . . 73 C4
Belgrave Cl
1 Acton W3 . . . 111 A4
Burnt Oak NW7 . . . 27 B5
Southgate N14 . . . 15 C6
Belgrave Cres TW16 . . . 172 B2
Belgrave Ct
8 Acton Green W4 . . . 111 A1
Charlton SE3 . . . 143 C5
22 Limehouse E14 . . . 119 B6
Newham E13 . . . 99 C3
Nine Elms SW8 . . . 269 A3
Belgrave Gdns
Kilburn NW8 . . . 91 D6
Southgate N14 . . . 3 D1
1 Stanmore HA7 . . . 25 C5
St John's Wood NW8 . . 229 A5
Belgrave Ho SW9 . . . 138 C5
Belgrave Hts E11 . . . 55 A1
Belgrave Mans NW8 . . 229 A5
Belgrave Market IG1 . . . 78 C6
Belgrave Mews N SW1 248 A1
Belgrave Mews S SW1 . . . 115 A3 258 B6
Belgrave Mews W SW1 . . . 258 A6
Belgrave Pl SW1 . . . 115 A3 258 B5
Belgrave Rd
Barnes SW13 . . . 133 D5
Hounslow TW4 . . . 129 B2
Leyton E10 . . . 54 A1
Mitcham CR4 . . . 202 B6
Newham E13 . . . 99 C3
Redbridge IG1 . . . 56 B1
South Norwood SE25 . . . 205 D5
Sunbury TW16 . . . 172 B2
Walthamstow E17 . . . 53 C3
Wanstead E11 . . . 55 A1
Westminster SW1 . . . 115 C2 259 A3
Belgrave Sq SW1 . . . 115 A3 258 A6
Belgrave St E1 . . . 96 D1
Belgrave Terr IG8 . . . 21 A1
Belgrave Wlk CR4 . . . 202 B6
Belgrave Wlk Sta CR4 . . 202 B5
Belgrave Yd SW1 . . . 258 C5
BELGRAVIA . . . 115 B2
Belgravia Cl EN5 . . . 1 B2
Belgravia Ct SW1 . . . 258 C5
Belgravia Gdns BR1 . . . 186 C4
Belgravia Ho
11 London SW4 . . . 159 D5
1 Teddington TW11 . . . 175 C3
Belgravia Lo N21 . . . 16 D6
Belgravia Mews KT1 . . . 197 D5
Belgrove St WC1 . . . 233 B2
Belham Wlk 13 SE5 . . . 139 B4
Belinda Rd 8 SW9 . . . 138 D2
Belitha Villas N1 . . . 72 C1
Bel La TW13 . . . 151 B1
Bellamy Cl Edgware HA8 . 11 A1
13 Millwall E14 . . . 119 C4
Uxbridge UB10 . . . 60 C5
West Kensington SW5 . 254 D1
Bellamy Ct HA7 . . . 25 B2
Bellamy Dr HA7 . . . 25 B2
Bellamy Ho Harrow HA3 . . 44 A2
Heston TW5 . . . 129 C6
Upper Tooting SW17 . . . 180 B6
Bellamy Rd Chingford E4 . 35 D4
Enfield EN2 . . . 5 B3
Bellamy's Ct 16 SE16 . . . 118 D5
Bellamy St SW12 . . . 159 B4
Bellasis Ave SW2 . . . 160 A2
Bell Ave UB7 . . . 104 B3
Bell Cl Pinner HA5 . . . 40 C6
Ruislip HA4 . . . 61 D5
Bellclose Rd UB7 . . . 104 A4
Bell Ct Hendon NW4 . . . 46 C5
Ladywell SE13 . . . 163 C6
Tolworth KT5 . . . 214 D6
Bell Dr SW18 . . . 157 A4
Bellefields Rd SW9 . . . 138 B2
Bellegrove Cl DA16 . . . 145 D3
Bellegrove Par DA16 . . . 145 D2
Bellegrove Rd DA16 . . . 145 D3
Bellenden Prim Sch SE15 . . . 140 A3
Bellenden Rd SE15 . . . 139 D3
Bellenden Rd Ret Pk SE15 . . . 140 A4
Bellendon Road Bsns Ctr SE15 . . . 139 D3
Bellerbys Coll SE8 . . . 141 C6
Bellermine Cl SE28 . . . 123 D4
Bell Estaines Pleasaunce E4 . . . 19 C2
Belleville Prim Sch SW11 . . . 158 D6
Belleville Rd SW11 . . . 158 D6
Belle Vue UB6 . . . 86 B6
Belle Vue Gdns SW9 . . . 138 A3
Belle Vue La WD23 . . . 8 B3
Bellevue Mews N11 . . . 31 A5
Bellevue Pk CR7 . . . 205 A5
Bellevue Pl E1 . . . 96 C3
Bellevue Rd
Barnes SW13 . . . 134 A3
Bexley DA6 . . . 169 B6
Ealing W13 . . . 87 B3
Friern Barnet N11 . . . 31 A5
Kingston u T KT1 . . . 198 A6
Upper Tooting SW17 . . . 158 D3
Belle Vue Rd
Chingford E17 . . . 36 B1
8 Hendon NW4 . . . 46 C5
Bellew St SW17 . . . 158 A1
Bellfield CR0 . . . 223 B1
Bellfield Ave HA3 . . . 24 B4
Bell Flats 4 NW2 . . . 68 A2
Bellflower Cl 2 E6 . . . 100 A2
Bellflower Ct SE13 . . . 141 D1
Bellgate Mews NW5 . . . 71 B5
Bell Gn SE26 . . . 185 B6
Bellgrave Lo 9 W4 . . . 110 D1
BELL GREEN . . . 163 B1
Bell Green La SE26 . . . 185 B6
Bell Ho
6 Dagenham RM10 . . . 81 D2
Greenwich SE10 . . . 142 A6
15 Streatham SW2 . . . 160 C4
Wembley HA9 . . . 66 A5
West Heath SE2 . . . 124 D1
Bellina Mews NW5 . . . 71 C4
Bell Ind Est 2 W4 . . . 111 A2
BELLINGHAM . . . 185 C5
Bellingham 10 N17 . . . 34 B3
Bellingham Ct IG11 . . . 102 B4
Bellingham Gn SE6 . . . 163 C1
Bellingham Rd SE6 . . . 164 A1
Bellingham Sta SE6 . . . 163 D1
Bellingham Trad Est SE6 . . . 163 D2
Bell Inn Yd EC3 . . . 242 D1
Bell La Enfield EN3 . . . 6 D5
Hendon NW4 . . . 46 D5
Newham E16 . . . 121 A5
Spitalfields E1 . . . 95 D2 243 C3
Twickenham TW1 . . . 153 A3
Wembley HA9 . . . 65 D6
Bell Lane Prim Sch NW4 . . . 46 D5
Bell Language Sch W1 . . . 93 C3 239 A5
Bellmaker Ct 13 E3 . . . 97 C2
Bell Mdw SE19 . . . 183 C6
Bell Moor NW3 . . . 70 A5
Bellmore Ct 5 CR0 . . . 205 D1
Bello Cl SE24, SW2 . . . 160 D3
Bellot Gdns 1 SE10 . . . 120 C1
Bellot St SE10 . . . 120 C1
Bell Rd
East Molesey KT8 . . . 196 B4
Enfield EN1 . . . 5 B4
Hounslow TW3 . . . 129 D1
Bellring Cl DA17 . . . 147 C6
Bell's Coll IG3 . . . 58 A1
Bells Hill EN5 . . . 12 D6
Bell St Kidbrooke SE18 . . . 144 A4
Paddington NW1 92 C2 237 A4
Bell The E17 . . . 53 C6
Bell View BR3 . . . 185 B3
Bellview Ct TW3 . . . 129 D1
Bell View Manor HA4 . . . 39 C2
Bell Water Gate SE18 . . 122 C3
Bell Wharf La EC4 . . . 252 B6
Bellwood Rd SE15 . . . 140 D1
Bell Yard Mews SE1 . . . 253 B1
Bell Yd WC2 . . . 94 C1 241 A1
BELMONT . . . 25 B2
Belmont Ave
Bowes Pk N13 . . . 32 B5
Cockfosters EN4 . . . 14 D6
Edmonton N9 . . . 18 A3
Falconwood DA16 . . . 145 C2
Southall UB2 . . . 107 A3
Tottenham N17 . . . 51 A6
Wembley HA0 . . . 88 B6
West Barnes KT3 . . . 200 A5
Belmont Circ HA3 . . . 25 B2
Belmont Cl Chingford E4 . . 36 B5
Clapham SW4 . . . 137 C2
Cockfosters EN4 . . . 2 D1
Totteridge N20 . . . 13 D3
Uxbridge UB8 . . . 60 A2
Woodford IG8 . . . 37 B6
Belmont Ct Highbury N5 . . 73 A4
6 Stamford Hill N16 . . . 51 C1
Temple Fortune NW11 . . . 47 B4
1 Whetstone N20 . . . 14 A1
Wood Green N11 . . . 31 D3
Belmont Fst & Mid Schs HA3 . . . 24 D1
Belmont Gr
Chiswick W4 . . . 111 B2
Lewisham SE13 . . . 142 B2
Belmont Hall Ct SE13 . . 142 B2
Belmont Hill SE13 . . . 142 B2
Belmont Jun & Inf Schs N22 . . . 51 A6
Belmont La
Chislehurst BR7 . . . 189 A5
Stanmore HA7 . . . 25 C3
Belmont Lo Harrow HA3 . . 24 B3
Stanmore HA7 . . . 25 C6
Belmont Mews SW19 . . . 156 D2
Belmont Mill Hill Jun Sch NW7 . . . 12 A1
Belmont Par
Chislehurst BR7 . . . 189 A5
2 Temple Fortune NW11 . . . 47 B4
Belmont Park Cl SE13 . . 142 C1
Belmont Park Rd E10 . . . 53 D3
Belmont Pk SE13 . . . 142 C1
Belmont Pk Sch E10 . . . 54 A3
Belmont Prim Sch
Chiswick W4 . . . 111 B2
Erith DA8 . . . 147 C5
Belmont Rd
Beckenham BR3 . . . 185 B1
Chislehurst BR7 . . . 188 D5
Clapham SW4 . . . 137 C2
Croydon SE25 . . . 206 B4
Erith DA8 . . . 147 D4
Harrow HA3 . . . 43 A6
Ilford IG1 . . . 79 A5
London W4 . . . 111 B2
Twickenham TW2 . . . 152 B2
Uxbridge UB8 . . . 60 A2
Wallington SM6 . . . 219 C3
West Green N15, N17 . . . 51 A5
Belmont Rise SM1, SM2 . . . 217 B1
Belmont St NW1 . . . 71 A1
Belmont Terr W4 . . . 111 B2
Belmor WD6 . . . 10 C5
Belmore Ave UB4 . . . 84 A1
Belmore Ho N7 . . . 71 D3
Belmore La N7 . . . 71 D3
Belmore Prim Sch UB4 . . 84 B4
Belmore St SW8 . . . 137 D4 269 C2
Beloe Cl SW15 . . . 134 A1
Belper Ct 11 E5 . . . 74 D4
Belsham St E9 . . . 74 C2
Belsize Ave
Bowes Pk N13 . . . 32 B4
Ealing W13 . . . 109 B3
Maitland Pk NW3 . . . 70 C3
Belsize Court Garages 1 NW3 . . . 70 B3
Belsize Cres NW3 . . . 70 B2
Belsize Ct NW3 . . . 70 B3
Belsize Gdns SM1 . . . 217 D4
Belsize Gr NW3 . . . 70 C2
Belsize La NW3 . . . 70 B3
Belsize Mews NW3 . . . 70 B2
Belsize Park Gdns NW3 . . . 70 C2
Belsize Park Mews 1 NW3 . . . 70 B2
Belsize Park Sta NW3 . . . 70 C3
Belsize Pk NW3 . . . 70 B2
Belsize Pl NW3 . . . 70 B3
Belsize Rd Harrow HA3 . . . 24 B3
Kilburn NW6 . . . 91 D6
Belsize Sq NW3 . . . 70 B2
Belsize Terr NW3 . . . 70 B2
Belson Rd SE18 . . . 122 B2
Beltane Dr SW19 . . . 156 D1
Belthorn Cres SW12 . . . 159 C4
Belton Rd Leyton E11 . . . 76 C4
Sidcup DA14 . . . 190 A6
Tottenham N17 . . . 51 C6
Upton E7 . . . 77 B1
Willesden NW2 . . . 68 A2
Belton Way E3 . . . 97 C2
Beltran Rd SW6 . . . 135 D3
BELVEDERE . . . 125 D2
Belvedere Ave SW19 . . . 179 A5
Belvedere Bldgs SE1 . . . 251 D1
Belvedere Cl TW11 . . . 174 C5
Belvedere Ct
Abbey Wood DA17 . . . 125 B3
Brondesbury NW2 . . . 68 D2
7 Clapham Pk SW4 . . . 159 D5
East Finchley N2 . . . 48 B4
8 Kingston u T KT2 . . . 176 C3
Putney SW15 . . . 134 C1
33 Shoreditch N1 . . . 95 C6
Southall UB1 . . . 107 D6
Southgate N21 . . . 16 C4
Belvedere Dr SW19 . . . 179 A5
Belvedere Gdns KT8 . . . 195 C4
Belvedere Gr SW19 . . . 179 A5
Belvedere Ho TW14 . . . 150 A3
Belvedere Htss NW8 . . 237 A6
Belvedere Jun & Inf Sch DA17 . . . 125 D3
Belvedere Mews
Greenwich SE3 . . . 143 B5
Nunhead SE15 . . . 140 C2
Belvedere Pl
Brixton SW2 . . . 138 B1
Lambeth SE1 . . . 251 D1
Belvedere Rd
Bexleyheath DA7 . . . 147 B3
Erith SE2, SE28 . . . 124 D5
Hanwell W7 . . . 108 D3
Lambeth SE1 . . 116 B5 250 D3
Penge SE19 . . . 183 D3
Walthamstow E10 . . . 53 A1
Belvedere Sq SW19 . . . 179 A5
Belvedere Sta DA17 . . . 125 D3
Belvedere Strand NW9 . . 27 D1
Belvedere The SW10 . . 266 B1
Belvedere Way HA3 . . . 44 A3
Belvoir Cl SE9 . . . 166 A1
Belvoir Ct HA3 . . . 43 A3
Belvoir Lo SE22 . . . 162 A4
Belvoir Rd SE22 . . . 162 A4
Belvue Bsns Ctr UB5 . . . 63 D1
Belvue Cl UB5 . . . 63 C1
Belvue Rd UB5 . . . 63 C1
Belvue Sch UB5 . . . 85 C6
Bembridge Cl NW6 . . . 69 A1
Bembridge Gdns HA4 . . . 61 B6
Bembridge Ho
9 Deptford SE8 . . . 119 B2
Wandsworth SW18 . . . 157 D5
Bemersyde Point 6 E13 . . . 99 B4
Bemerton St N1 . 94 B6 233 C6
Bemish Rd SW15 . . . 134 D2
Bempton Dr HA4 . . . 62 B5
Bemsted Rd E17 . . . 53 B6
Benabo Ct 6 E8 . . . 74 A3
Benares Rd SE18, SE2 . . 123 D2
Benbow Ct W6 . . . 112 B3
Benbow Ho 12 SE8 . . . 141 C6
Benbow Rd W6 . . . 112 B3
Benbow St SE8 . . . 141 C6
Benbury Cl BR1 . . . 186 A5
Bence Ho 13 SE8 . . . 119 A2
Bench Field CR2 . . . 221 D3
Bencroft Rd SW16 . . . 181 C3
Bencurtis Pk BR4 . . . 224 B6
Bendall Mews NW1 . . . 237 B4
Bendemeer Rd SW15 . . . 134 D2
Benden Ho SE13 . . . 164 A6
Bendish Point SE28 . . . 123 A4
Bendish Rd E6 . . . 78 A1
Bendmore Ave SE2 . . . 124 A2
Bendon Valley SW18 . . . 157 D4
Benedict Cl
9 Erith DA17 . . . 125 A3
Orpington BR6 . . . 227 C5
Benedict Ct
Dagenham RM9 . . . 59 B3
Pinner HA5 . . . 23 B2
Benedict Dr TW14 . . . 149 B4
Benedict House Prep Sch DA15 . . . 168 A1
Benedict Prim Sch CR4 . . . 202 B6
Benedict Rd
London SW9 . . . 138 B2
Mitcham CR4 . . . 202 B6
Benedict Way N2 . . . 48 A6
Benedict Wharf CR4 . . . 202 C6
Benenden Gn BR2 . . . 209 A4
Benenden Ho SE17 . . . 263 B2
Benett Gdns SW16 . . . 182 A1
Beney Ct BR3 . . . 185 C1
Ben Ezra Ct SE17 . . . 262 B3
Benfleet Cl SM1 . . . 218 A5
Benfleet Ct 6 E8 . . . 95 D6
Benfleet Way N11 . . . 15 A2
Bengal Ct EC3 . . . 242 D1
Bengal Ho E1 . . . 96 D2
Bengal Rd IG1 . . . 78 D5
Bengarth Dr HA3 . . . 24 B1
Bengarth Rd UB5 . . . 85 A6
Bengeo Gdns RM6 . . . 58 C3
Bengeworth Rd
Camberwell SE5 . . . 139 A2
Harrow HA1 . . . 65 A5
Ben Hale Cl HA7 . . . 25 B5
Benham Cl
1 Battersea SW11 . . . 136 B2
Chessington KT9 . . . 213 C2
Benham Gdns TW3, TW4 . . . 151 B6
Benham Ho SW10 . . . 265 D4
Benham Rd W7 . . . 86 C2
Benham's Pl 11 NW3 . . . 70 A4
Benhill Ave SM1 . . . 218 A4
Benhill Rd London SE5 . . 139 B4
Sutton SM1 . . . 218 B4
Benhill Wood Rd SM1 . . 218 A4
BENHILTON . . . 218 A5
Benhilton Ct SM1 . . . 218 A4
Benhilton Gdns SM1 . . . 217 D5
Benhurst Ct Ealing W5 . . 110 A6
12 Penge SE20 . . . 184 B2
West Norwood SW16 . . . 182 C5
Benhurst La SW16 . . . 182 C5
Benington Ct N4 . . . 73 A6
Benin St SE13 . . . 164 B4
Benjafield Cl N18 . . . 34 B6
Benjamin Cl E8 . . . 96 A6
Benjamin Ct
4 Ealing W7 . . . 108 C5
4 Erith DA17 . . . 147 B6
Littleton TW15 . . . 171 A3
Benjamin Ho 12 W3 . . . 110 D5
Benjamin Mews SW12 . 159 C4
Benjamin St EC1 . . . 241 C4
Ben Jonson Ct 30 N1 . . . 95 C5
Ben Jonson Prim Sch E1 . . . 97 A3
Ben Jonson Rd E1 . . . 97 A2
Benledi Rd E14 . . . 98 B1
Bennelong Cl W12 . . . 90 B1
Bennerley Rd SW11 . . . 158 D6
Bennet Cl KT1 . . . 175 C2
Bennets Ct SW19 . . . 180 A2
Bennetsfield Rd UB11 . . 104 D5
Bennet's Hill EC4 . . . 251 D6
Bennets Lo EN2 . . . 5 A2
Bennett Cl
Twickenham TW4 . . . 151 A6
Welling DA16 . . . 146 A3
Bennett Ct
Hampstead NW6 . . . 69 D2
Lower Holloway N7 . . . 72 B5
7 South Acton W3 . . . 110 D4
Bennett Gr SE13 . . . 141 D4
Bennett Ho
2 Streatham SW4 . . . 159 D4
Westminster SW1 . . . 259 D4
Bennett Pk SE3 . . . 142 D2
Bennett Rd
Brixton SW9 . . . 138 C3
Dagenham RM6 . . . 59 A2
Newham E13 . . . 99 C3
Bennetts Ave
Croydon CR0 . . . 223 A6
Greenford UB6 . . . 86 C6
Bennett's Castle La RM8 . . . 80 D5
Bennetts Cl
Mitcham CR4, SW16 . . . 181 B2
Tottenham N17 . . . 33 D4
Bennetts Copse BR7 . . . 188 A4
Bennett St
Chiswick W4 . . . 111 C1
St James SW1 . . . 249 A4
Bennetts Way CR0 . . . 223 B6
Bennett's Yd SW1 . . . 259 D5
Benn Ho
Bethnal Green E2 . . . 96 A4
7 Greenwich SE7 . . . 121 C1
Benninghholme Rd HA8 . . 27 C4
Bennington Rd
Chingford IG8 . . . 36 C3
Tottenham N17 . . . 33 C2
Benn St E9 . . . 75 A2
Benns Wlk 8 TW9 . . . 132 A1
Bensbury Cl SW15 . . . 156 C4
Bensham Cl CR7 . . . 205 A5
Bensham Gr CR7 . . . 183 A1
Bensham La CR0, CR7 . . . 204 D3
Bensham Manor Rd CR7 . . . 205 A5
Bensham Manor Sch CR7 . . . 205 A4
Bensington Ct TW14 . . . 149 B5
Bensley Cl 7 N11 . . . 30 D5
Ben Smith Way 21 SE16 . . . 118 A3
Benson Ave E13, E6 . . . 99 D5
Benson Cl
Hillingdon UB8 . . . 82 A2
Hounslow TW3 . . . 129 C1
Benson Ct Holdbrook EN3 . . 7 C5
South Lambeth SW8 . . . 270 A2
1 Tufnell Pk N19 . . . 71 C4
Benson Ho
Lambeth SE1 . . . 251 B3
1 Richmond TW10 . . . 153 C1
Shoreditch E2 . . . 243 C6
Benson Prim sch CR0 . . 223 A5
Benson Quay E1 . . . 118 C6
Benson Rd
Croydon CR0 . . . 220 C5
Forest Hill SE23 . . . 162 C3
Bentall Sh Ctr The 10 KT1 . . . 176 A1
Bentfield Gdns SE9 . . . 165 D1
Benthal Ct N16 . . . 74 A5
Benthal Prim Sch N16 . . 74 A5
Benthal Rd N16 . . . 74 A5
Bentham Ct 11 N1 . . . 73 A1
Bentham Ho SE1 . . . 262 C6
Bentham Rd
Homerton E9 . . . 74 D2
Woolwich SE28 . . . 124 B5
Bentham Wlk NW10 . . . 67 A3
Ben Tillet Cl E16 . . . 122 B5
Ben Tillet Ho N15 . . . 50 D6
Bentinck Cl NW8 . . . 230 B3
Bentinck Ho
4 Richmond TW10 . . . 153 C1
4 Shepherd's Bush W12 . . . 112 B6
Bentinck Mans W1 . . . 238 B2
Bentinck Mews W1 . . . 238 B2
Bentinck Rd UB7 . . . 104 A5
Bentinck St W1 . . 93 A1 238 B2
Bentley Cl SW19 . . . 157 C1
Bentley Ct SE13 . . . 142 A1
Bentley Dr IG2 . . . 57 A3
Bentley Ho 6 Bow E3 . . . 97 C3
4 Camberwell SE5 . . . 139 C4
Bentley Lo WD23 . . . 8 C2
Bentley Mews EN1 . . . 17 B5
Bentley Rd N1 . . . 73 C2
Bentley Way
Stanmore HA7 . . . 25 A5
Woodford IG8 . . . 21 A1
Bentley Wood High Sch HA7 . . . 24 D5
Benton Rd
Ilford IG1, IG2 . . . 57 B1
South Oxhey WD19 . . . 22 D5
Benton's La SE27 . . . 183 A6
Benton's Rise SE27 . . . 183 B5
Bentry Cl RM8 . . . 81 A6
Bentry Rd RM8 . . . 81 B6
Bentworth Ct 1 E2 . . . 96 A3
Bentworth Prim Sch W12 . . . 90 B1
Bentworth Rd W12 . . . 90 B1
Benwell Ct TW16 . . . 172 A2
Benwell Rd N7 . . . 72 C3
Benwick Cl SE16 . . . 118 B2
Benwick Ct SE20 . . . 184 C2
Benwood Ct SM1 . . . 218 A5
Benworth St E3 . . . 97 B4
Benyon Ho EC1 . . . 234 B2
Benyon Rd N1 . . . 95 B6 235 D6
Benyon Wharf 31 E8 . . . 95 C6
Beormund Prim Sch SE1 . . . 117 B4 252 D1
Bequerel Ct SE10 . . . 120 D3
Berberis Ct IG1 . . . 78 D2
Berberis Ho 17 E3 . . . 97 C2
Berberis Wlk UB7 . . . 104 A2
Berber Pl 2 E14 . . . 119 C6
Berber Rd SW11 . . . 158 D6
Berberry Cl 5 HA8 . . . 27 A6
Bercta Rd SE9 . . . 167 A2
Berebinder Ho 21 E3 . . . 97 B5
Berengers Pl RM9 . . . 80 B2
Berenger Twr SW10 . . 266 C4
Berenger Wlk SW10 . . 266 C4
Berens Ct DA14 . . . 189 D6
Berens Rd NW10 . . . 90 D4
Berens Way BR5, BR7 . . 211 D6
Beresford Ave
Ealing W7 . . . 86 C2
Friern Barnet N20 . . . 14 D2
Tolworth KT5 . . . 199 A2
Twickenham TW1 . . . 153 C5
Wembley HA0 . . . 88 C6
Beresford Ct
Homerton E9 . . . 75 A3
11 Twickenham TW1 . . . 153 C5
Beresford Dr
Bickley BR1 . . . 210 A6
Woodford IG8 . . . 37 C6
Beresford Gdns
Dagenham RM6 . . . 59 A4
Enfield EN1 . . . 5 C1
Hounslow TW4 . . . 151 B6
Beresford Ho
Dulwich SE21 . . . 161 C1
15 Stockwell SW4 . . . 138 A1
Beresford Lo N4 . . . 73 B3
Beresford Rd
Belmont SM2 . . . 217 B1
Canonbury N5 . . . 73 B3
Chingford E4 . . . 20 C3
East Finchley N2 . . . 48 C6
Harringay N8 . . . 50 D4
Harrow HA1 . . . 42 B4
Kingston u T KT2 . . . 176 B2
New Malden KT3 . . . 199 A5
Southall UB1 . . . 106 D5
Walthamstow E17 . . . 35 D2
Beresford Sq 1 SE18 . . 122 D2
Beresford Square Mkt SE18 . . . 122 D2
Beresford St SE18 . . . 122 D3
Beresford Terr 3 N5 . . . 73 A3
Bere St E1 . . . 118 D6
Berestede Rd 4 W6 . . . 111 D1
Bergen Ho 1 SE5 . . . 139 A3
Bergenia Ho TW13 . . . 150 B3
Bergen Sq SE16 . . . 119 A3
Berger Cl BR5 . . . 211 C3
Berger Prim Sch E9 . . . 74 D2
Berger Rd E9 . . . 74 D2
Berghem Mews W14 . . . 112 D3
Bergholt Ave IG4 . . . 56 A4
Bergholt Cres N16 . . . 51 C2
Bergholt Mews 4 NW1 . . . 71 D1
Berglen Ct E14 . . . 119 A6
Berica Ct IG6 . . . 57 A6
Bering Sq E14 . . . 119 C1
Bering Wlk E16 . . . 99 D1
Berisford Mews SW18 . . 158 A5
Berkeley Ave
Cranford TW4 . . . 128 A3
Erith DA16 . . . 146 D4
Northolt UB6 . . . 64 C2
Berkeley Cl
Borehamwood WD6 . . . 10 C6
Broom Hill BR5 . . . 211 C2
2 Kingston u T KT2 . . . 176 A3
Ruislip HA4 . . . 62 A5

Berkeley Cres EN4 14 B6
Berkeley Ct Ealing W5 109 C6
Edgware HA8 26 D5
Finchley N3 29 D2
1 Golders Green NW11 47 B2
Marylebone NW1 237 D5
Southgate N14 15 C5
Wallington SM6 219 C4
Willesden NW10 67 C4
Berkeley Dr KT8 195 C6
Berkeley Gdns
Claygate KT10 213 A2
Kensington W8 245 B3
Southgate N21 17 B4
Walton-on-T KT12 193 D2
Berkeley Ho 17 Bow E3 97 C4
11 Brentford TW8 131 D6
8 Deptford SE8 119 B1
Berkeley Lo Enfield EN2 4 C2
New Malden KT3 199 C5
Berkeley Mews
Marylebone W1 237 D1
Sunbury TW16 194 C6
Berkeley Pl SW19 178 D4
Berkeley Prim Sch
TW5 128 D5
Berkeley Rd
Barnes SW13 134 A4
Crouch End N8 49 D3
Hillingdon UB10 61 A1
Manor Pk E12 78 A3
Queensbury NW9 44 C4
Stamford Hill N15 51 B3
Berkeley Sq
W1 115 B6 248 D5
Berkeley St
W1 115 B5 248 D4
Berkeleys The SE25 206 A5
Berkeley The NW11 47 D2
Berkeley Waye TW5 128 D5
Berkeley Wlk 1 N7 72 B6
Berkhampstead Rd
DA17 125 C1
Berkhamsted Ave HA9 66 C2
Berkley Cl TW2 152 C1
Berkley Ct 8 TW1 153 A4
Berkley Gr NW1 71 A1
Berkley Rd NW1 70 D1
Berkshire Ct 1 W7 86 D3
Berkshire Gdns
Bowes Pk N13 32 C4
Upper Edmonton N18 34 B5
Berkshire Ho
Catford SE6 185 C6
St Giles WC2 240 A2
Berkshire Rd E9 75 B2
Berkshire Way CR4 204 A5
Bermans Way NW10 67 D4
BERMONDSEY 118 A4
Bermondsey Leather Mkt
SE1 253 A1
Bermondsey Mkt*
SE1 117 C3 263 B6
Bermondsey Sq SE1 263 B6
Bermondsey St
SE1 117 C4 253 A1
Bermondsey Trad Est
SE16 118 C1
Bermondsey Wall E
SE16 118 B4
Bermondsey Wall W SE1,
SE16 118 A4
Bermuda Ho HA1 64 B5
Bernal Cl SE28 124 D6
Bernard Angell Ho 4
SE10 142 B6
Bernard Ashley Dr
SE7 121 B1
Bernard Ave W13 109 B3
Bernard Cassidy St 2
E16 98 D2
Bernard Gdns SW19 179 B5
Bernard Ho E1 243 C3
Bernard Rd
South Tottenham N15 51 D4
Wallington SM5, SM6 219 B4
Bernard Shaw Ct 5
NW1 71 C1
Bernard Shaw Ho 2
NW10 89 B6
Bernard St WC1 94 A3 240 B5
Bernays Cl HA7 25 C4
Bernay's Gr SW9 138 B1
Bernel Dr CR0 223 B5
Berne Rd CR7 205 A4
Berners Dr W13 109 A6
Berners Ho N1 234 A4
Bernersmede SE3 143 A2
Berners Mews
W1 93 C2 239 B3
Berners Pl W1 239 B2
Berners Rd Islington N1 234 C5
Wood Green N22 32 C1
Berners St W1 93 C1 239 B2
Berner Terr 27 E1 96 A1
Berney Ho BR3 207 A4
Berney Rd CR0 205 B2
Bernhard Baron Ho 23
E1 96 A1
Bernhardt Cres NW8 237 A6
Bernhart Cl HA8 27 A3
Bernie Grant Ho 40 E9 74 C1
Bernwell Rd E4 20 C1
Bernwood Ho 6 N4 51 B2
Berridge Gn HA8 26 C3
Berridge Mews NW6 69 C3
Berridge Rd SE19 183 C5
Berriman Rd N7 72 B5
Berrite Works UB7 104 C4
Berriton Rd HA2 41 B1
Berrybank Cl 4 E4 20 A2
Berry Cl
Dagenham RM10 81 C3
Southgate N21 16 D3
Berry Cotts 2 E14 97 A1
Berry Ct TW4 151 B6
Berrydale Rd UB4 85 A3
Berryfield Cl BR1 188 A1
Berry Field Cl 8 E17 53 D5
Berryfield Rd
SE17 116 D1 261 D2
Berryhill SE9 144 D1
Berry Hill HA7 25 D6
Berryhill Gdns SE9 144 D1
Berry Ho
10 Battersea SW11 136 D3
25 Bethnal Green E1 96 B3
Berry La SE21 183 B6
BERRYLANDS 198 C3
Berrylands
Surbiton KT5 198 C3
West Barnes SW20 200 C5
Berrylands Ct 16 SM2 217 D1
Berrylands Rd KT5 198 B3
Berrylands Sta KT5 198 D5
Berryman Cl RM8 80 C5
Berryman's La SE26 184 D6
Berrymead Gdns W3 111 A4
Berrymede Inf Sch
W3 110 D4
Berrymede Jun Sch
W3 110 D4
Berrymede Rd W4 111 B3
Berry Pl EC1 234 D1
Berry St EC1 241 D5
Berry Way W5 110 A3
Bertal Rd SW17 180 B6
Bertha Hollamby Ct
DA14 190 C5
Bertha James Ct BR2 209 B5
Bertha Neubergh Ho 1
SE5 139 A4
Berthan Gdns E17 54 B4
Berthon St SE8 141 C6
Bertie Rd Penge SE26 184 D4
Willesden NW10 68 A2
Bertram Cotts SW19 179 C3
Bertram Rd Enfield EN1 6 A1
Hendon NW4 46 A3
Kingston u T KT2 176 C3
Bertram St N19 71 B6
Bertrand Ho 11 SW16 160 A1
Bertrand St SE13 141 D2
Bertrand Way SE28 124 C6
Bert Rd CR7 205 A4
Bert Reilly Ho 1 SE18 123 B1
Bertrum House Sch
SW17 159 A2
Bert Way EN1 5 D1
Berwick Ave UB4 106 D6
Berwick Cl Harrow HA7 24 D4
Twickenham TW2 151 C3
Berwick Cres DA15 167 C5
Berwick Ct 8 BR3 185 C2
Berwick Gdns SM1 218 A5
Berwick Ho 10 N2 30 B1
Berwick Rd
Newham E16 99 C1
Tottenham N22 32 D2
Welling DA16 146 B4
Berwick St W1 93 C1 239 B1
Berwyn Ave TW3 129 D4
Berwyn Ho 3 N16 51 D1
Berwyn Rd
Mortlake SW14,
TW10 132 D1
Streatham SE24 160 D3
Beryl Ave E6 100 A2
Beryl Harding Ho 3
SW19 178 D3
Beryl Ho SE18 123 D1
Beryl Rd W6 112 D1
Berystede KT2 176 D3
Besant Cl NW2 69 A5
Besant Ct Canonbury N1 73 B3
15 Thamesmead SE28 124 B6
Besant Ho NW8 229 A5
Besant Pl SE22 139 D1
Besant Rd NW2 69 A4
Besant Way NW10 67 A3
Besant Wlk N7 72 B6
Besford Ho 26 E2 96 A5
Besley St SW16 181 C4
Bessant Dr TW9 132 D4
Bessborough Gdns
SW1 115 D1 259 D2
Bessborough Pl
SW1 115 D1 259 D2
Bessborough Rd
Harrow HA1 42 B1
Roehampton SW15 156 A3
Bessborough St
SW1 115 D1 259 C2
Bessborough Wks
KT8 195 B4
Bessemer Ct 7 NW1 71 C1
Bessemer Grange Prim
Sch SE5 139 C1
Bessemer Park Ind Est 3
SE24 138 D1
Bessemer Rd SE5 139 A3
Bessie Lansbury Cl
E6 100 C1
Bessingby Rd HA4 62 B6
Bessingham Wlk SE4 162 D6
Besson St SE14 140 D4
Bessy St E2 96 C4
Bestwood St SE8 118 D2
Beswick Mews 1 NW6 69 D2
Betam Rd UB3 105 B4
Beta Pl 20 SW4 138 B1
Betchworth Cl SM1 218 B3
Betchworth Ho 8 N7 71 D3
Betchworth Rd IG3 79 C5
Betham Rd UB6 86 B4
Bethany Ct 8 DA6 147 A1
Bethany Waye TW14 149 C4
Bethecar Rd HA1 42 C4
Bethel Cl NW4 46 D4
Bethell Ave Ilford IG1 56 C2
Newham E13, E16 98 D3
Bethel Lo N11 31 C5
Bethel Rd DA16 146 C2
Bethersden Cl BR3 185 B3
Bethersden Ho SE17 263 B2
Bethesda Ct 5 SE20 184 C3
Beth Jacob Gram Sch
NW4 46 D5
Bethlehem Ho 13 E14 119 B6
Bethlem Royal Hospl
BR3 207 C2
BETHNAL GREEN 96 B4
Bethnal Green Rd
Bethnal Green E2 96 A4
Shoreditch E1,
E2 95 D3 243 D6
Bethnal Green Sta
Bethnal Green E1 96 B3
Bethnal Green E2 96 C4
Bethnal Green Tech Coll
E2 95 D4
Beths Gram Sch DA5 169 D5
Bethune Ave N11 30 D6
Bethune Rd
North Acton NW10 89 B3
Stamford Hill N16 51 C2
Bethwin Rd SE5 139 A5
Betjeman Cl HA5 41 C5
Betjeman Ct EN4 15 A6
Betony Cl CR0 206 D1
Betoyne Ave E4 36 C6
Betsham Ho SE1 252 C2
Betspath Ho 6 N11 31 C5
Betstyle Circus N11 31 B6
Betstyle Ho 2 N10 31 A3
Betstyle Rd N11 31 B6
Betterton Dr DA14 169 A2
Betterton Ho WC2 240 B1
Betterton St
WC2 94 A1 240 B1
Bettons Pk E15 98 C6
Bettridge Rd SW6 135 B3
Betts Cl BR3 185 A1
Betts Ho E1 118 B6
Betts Mews E17 53 B3
Betts Rd E16 121 B6
Betts St E1 118 B6
Betts Way
Long Ditton KT6 197 B1
Penge SE20 184 B2
Bettswood Ct 15 SE20 184 B2
Betty Brooks Ho E11 76 B5
Betty Layward Prim Sch
N16 73 B5
Betty May Gray Ho 2
E14 120 A2
Beulah Ave CR7 183 A1
Beulah Cl HA8 10 D1
Beulah Cres CR7 183 A1
Beulah Gr CR0 205 A3
Beulah Hill SE19 183 A3
Beulah Inf Sch CR7 205 A6
Beulah Jun Sch CR7 205 A6
Beulah Rd
Merton SW19 179 B3
South Norwood CR7 205 A6
Sutton SM1 217 C4
Walthamstow E17 53 D4
Beuleigh Ct E17 54 B4
Bevan Ave IG11 80 A1
Bevan Ct Croydon CR0 220 C3
10 Twickenham TW1 153 D5
Bevan Ho IG11 80 B1
Bevan Rd Cockfosters EN4 2 D1
Plumstead Comm SE2 124 B1
Bevan St N1 95 A6 235 B5
Bev Callender Cl 4
SW8 137 B2
Bevenden St N1 95 B4 235 D2
Bevercote Wlk 1
DA17 147 B6
Beveridge Ct
Southgate N21 16 A6
1 Thamesmead SE28 124 B6
Beveridge Rd 1 NW10 67 C1
Beverley DA14 190 A5
Beverley Ave
Hounslow TW4 129 B1
Sidcup DA15 167 D4
Wimbledon SW20 177 D2
Beverley Cl
Barnes SW13 134 A3
Chessington KT9 213 C4
Edmonton N21 17 A3
Enfield EN1 5 C1
6 Wandsworth SW11 136 B1
Beverley Cotts SW15 155 C1
Beverley Cres IG8 37 B2
Beverley Ct
9 Acton Green W4 111 A1
5 Acton W12 111 C4
Brockley SE4 141 B2
6 Cheam SM2 217 C2
Chingford Hatch E4 35 B6
Fortis Green N2 48 D5
Harrow HA2 42 B6
Hounslow TW4 129 B1
Beverley Ct *continued*
Islington N5 72 D2
Northolt UB5 84 C5
Oakleigh Pk N20 14 A4
Oakwood N14 15 C4
Sidcup DA14 190 B6
Wimbledon SW20 177 D2
Beverley Dr HA8 44 C6
Beverley Gdns
Barnes SW13 133 D2
Hendon NW11 47 A2
2 New Malden KT4 200 A1
Stanmore HA7 25 A2
Wembley HA9 44 C1
Beverley Ho 5 BR1 186 B5
Beverley Hyrst 10 CR0 221 D6
Beverley La KT2 177 C3
Beverley Lo 6 TW10 154 A6
Beverley Mans TW4 129 B1
Beverley Path 9
SW13 133 D3
Beverley Rd
Barnes SW13 133 D2
Chingford E4 36 B4
Chiswick W4 111 D1
Dagenham RM9 81 A4
Keston Mark BR2 226 A6
Mitcham CR4 203 D5
Newham E6 99 D4
North Cheam KT4 216 C6
Penge SE20 184 B1
Ruislip HA4 62 B6
Southall UB2 107 A3
Sunbury TW16 171 D2
Teddington KT1 175 C2
West Barnes KT3 200 A5
Beverley Trad Est
SM4 200 D2
Beverley Way KT3, SW20,
KT2 177 D2
Beverley Way (Kingston By
Pass) KT3, SW20 200 A6
Beverly Ct HA3 43 C5
Beversbrook Rd N19 71 D5
Beverstone Rd
London SW2 160 B6
Thornton Heath CR7 204 D5
Beverston Mews NW1 237 C3
Bevill Allen Cl SW17 180 D5
Bevill Cl SE25 206 A6
Bevin Cl SE16 119 A5
Bevin Ct WC1 233 D2
Bevington Prim Sch
W10 91 A2
Bevington Rd
Beckenham BR3 185 D1
Kensal Town W10 91 A2
Bevington St SE16 118 A4
Bevin Ho
35 Bethnal Green E2 96 C4
8 Bow E3 97 C4
Bevin Rd UB4 84 B4
Bevin Sq SW17 158 D1
Bevin Way WC1 234 A2
Bevis Marks
EC3 95 C1 243 B2
Bewcastle Gdns EN2 4 A1
Bew Ct SE21 162 A4
Bewdley Ho N4 51 A2
Bewdley St N1 72 C1
Bewick Mews SE15 140 B5
Bewick St SW8 137 B3
Bewley Ct SW2 160 B5
Bewley Ho 7 E1 118 B6
Bewley St Stepney E1 118 B6
Wimbledon SW19 180 A4
Bewlys Rd SE27 182 D5
Bexhill Cl TW13 151 A2
Bexhill Rd Catford SE4 163 B5
Mortlake SW14 133 A2
Wood Green N11 31 D5
Bexhill Wlk 6 E15 98 C6
BEXLEY 146 B1
Bexley Coll (Erith Rd
Campus) DA17 125 D1
Bexley Gdns
Edmonton N9 17 B1
Ilford RM6 58 B4
Bexley Gram Sch
DA16 146 B1
BEXLEYHEATH 147 B2
Bexleyheath Sch DA8 147 C2
Bexleyheath Sta DA7 147 A3
Bexley High St DA5 169 D3
Bexley Ho SE4 141 A1
Bexley La DA14 168 C1
Bexley Rd SE9 167 A6
Bexley Sta DA5 169 C3
Beynon Rd SM5 218 D3
BFI London Imax Cinema
SE1 116 C5 251 A3
Bglws The SM6 219 B3
Bianca Rd SE1, SE15 140 A6
Bibsworth Lo N3 29 B1
Bibsworth Rd N3 29 B1
Bicester Rd TW9 132 D2
Bickenhall Mans W1 237 D4
Bickenhall St
W1 92 D2 237 D4
Bickersteth Rd SW17 180 D4
Bickerton Rd N19 71 C6
BICKLEY 188 B1
Bickley Cres BR1 210 A5
Bickley Ct
10 Merton SW19 179 C3
1 Stanmore HA7 25 C6
Bickley Park Rd BR1,
BR7 210 B6
Bickley Park Sch BR1 210 A6
Bickley Prim Sch BR1 209 C6
Bickley Rd
Bromley BR1 187 D1
Leyton E10 53 D2
Bickley St SW17 180 D5
Bickley Sta BR1 210 A6
Bicknell Ho 34 E1 96 A1
Bicknell Rd SE5 139 A2
Bicknoller Rd EN1 5 D4
Bicknor Ho 2 E5 74 B3
Bicknor Rd BR6 211 D2
Bidborough Cl 3 BR2 208 D4
Bidborough St N1,
WC1 94 A4 233 A1
Biddenden Way SE9 188 C6
Biddenham Ho 18
SE16 118 D2
Bidder St E16 98 C2
Biddesden Ho SW3 257 C3
Biddestone Rd N7 72 B4
Biddulph Ho 22 SE18 122 B2
Biddulph Mans W9 91 D4
Biddulph Rd W9 91 D4
Bideford Ave UB6 87 B5
Bideford Cl
Edgware HA8 26 C2
Twickenham TW13 151 B1
Bideford Gdns EN1 17 C4
Bideford Rd
Catford BR1 164 D1
East Wickham DA16 146 B5
Enfield EN3 7 B5
Ruislip HA4 62 B5
Bidmead Ct KT6 214 A5
Bidwell Gdns N11 31 C3
Bidwell Ho
Southall UB2 107 A2
3 Willesden NW2 68 A5
Bidwell St SE15 140 B4
Big Ben* SW1 250 B1
Bigbury Cl N17 33 C3
Biggerstaff Rd E15 98 A6
Biggerstaff St N4 72 C6
Biggin Ave CR4 180 D2
Biggin Hill SE19 182 D3
Biggin Hill Cl KT2 175 C5
Biggin Way SE19 183 A3
Bigginwood Rd SW16 182 D2
Bigg's Row SW15 134 D2
Big Hill E5 52 B1
Bigland Green Prim Sch
E1 96 B1
Bigland St E1 96 B1
Bignell Rd SE18 122 D1
Bignold Rd E7 77 A4
Bigwood Ct NW11 47 D4
Bigwood Rd NW11 47 D3
Biko Ho 1 NW10 67 B1
Bilberry Ho 18 E3 97 C2
Bilberry Manor SM2 218 A1
Billet Rd Ilford RM6 58 C6
Walthamstow E17 35 B2
Billetts Hart Cl W7 108 C4
Bill Hamling Cl SE9 166 B2
Billie Holiday Ct NW10 89 B5
Billingford Cl SE4 140 D1
Billing Ho 7 E1 96 D1
Billingley NW1 232 A5
Billing Pl
SW10 135 D5 265 D4
Billing Rd
SW10 135 D5 265 D4
Billings Cl RM9 80 C1
Billingsgate Mkt E14 119 D5
Billing St
SW10 135 D5 265 D4
Billington Ho SW8 269 D1
Billington Rd SE14 140 D5
Billinton Hill CR0 221 B6
Billiter Sq EC3 243 B1
Billiter St EC3 95 C1 243 B1
Bill Nicholson Way
N17 33 D3
Billockby Cl KT9 214 B2
Billsley Ct SE25 205 C5
Billson St E14 120 A2
Bilsby Gr SE9 187 D6
Bilton Ho SW8 269 C1
Bilton Rd UB6 87 B6
Bilton Twrs W1 237 D1
Bilton Way Enfield EN3 7 B5
Hayes UB3 106 B4
Bina Gdns
SW5 114 A2 256 A3
Binbrook Ho 13 W10 90 C2
Bincote Rd EN2 4 B2
Binden Rd W12 111 D3
Bindon Gn SM4 201 D5
Binfield Ct SE5 139 A3
Binfield Rd
London SW4 138 A4 270 B1
South Croydon CR2 221 D3
Bingfield St N1 94 B6 233 C6
Bingham Cnr CR0 206 A1
Bingham Pl W1 93 A2 238 A4
Bingham Point 11
SE18 122 D2
Bingham Rd CR0 206 B1
Bingham St N1 73 B2
Bingley Rd
Ashford TW16 172 A3
Newham E16 99 C1
Southall UB6 86 A2
Binley Ho SW15 155 D5
Binney St W1 93 A1 238 B1
Binnie Ct SE10 141 D5
Binnie Ho SE1 262 A5
Binns Rd W4 111 C1
Binns Terr 3 W4 111 C1
Binsey Wlk 1 SE2 124 C4
Binstead Cl UB4 85 A2
Binstead Ho SW18 157 D5
Binyon Cres HA7 24 D5
Binyon Ho 8 N16 73 C4
Birbeck Ho 4 N19 49 D1
Birbetts Rd SE9 166 B2
Bircham Path SE4 140 D1
Birchanger Rd SE25 206 A4
Birch Ave Edmonton N13 17 A1
Hillingdon UB7 82 B1
Birch Cl Brentford TW8 131 B5
Buckhurst Hill IG9 21 D1
Hounslow TW3 130 B3
Newham E16 98 C2
Peckham SE15 140 A3
Romford RM7 59 D6
Teddington TW11 175 A5
Upper Holloway N19 71 C6
Birch Cres UB10 82 B6
Birch Ct Chingford E4 35 D4
Forest Gate E7 76 D4
Ilford RM6 58 C3
Sutton SM1 218 A4
9 Wallington SM6 219 B4
7 Woodside Pk N12 29 D6
Birchdale Gdns RM6 58 D2
Birchdale Rd E7 77 C3
Birchdene Dr SE28 124 A5
Birchdown Ho 32 E3 97 D4
Birchen Cl NW9 67 B6
Birchend Cl CR2 221 B2
Birchen Gr NW9 67 B6
Birches Cl
Mitcham CR4 202 D6
Pinner HA5 41 A4
Birches The
2 Beckenham BR2 208 D5
Bushey WD23 8 A6
Camberwell SE5 139 C3
Greenwich SE7 143 B6
Manor Pk E12 78 A4
Orpington BR6 226 C4
Southgate N21 16 B5
South Norwood SE25 183 D1
Twickenham TW4 151 B4
Birchfield Ho 3 E14 119 C6
Birchfield St E14 119 C6
Birch Gn NW9 27 C3
Birch Gr Acton W3 110 C6
Bexley DA16 146 A1
Lewisham SE12 164 D4
Leyton E11 76 C5
Upper Halliford TW17 171 C1
Birchgrove Ho TW9 132 D5
Birch Hill CR0 222 D3
Birch Ho
New Cross Gate SE14 141 B4
Teddington TW11 175 C3
8 Tulse Hill SW2 160 C5
Birchington Cl DA7 147 D4
Birchington Ct
Crouch End N8 49 D3
2 Kilburn NW6 91 D6
Birchington Ho 1 E5 74 B3
Birchington Rd
Crouch End N8 49 D3
Kilburn NW6 91 C6
Surbiton KT5 198 B2
Birchin La EC3 242 D1
Birchlands Ave SW12 158 D4
Birch Mead BR2, BR6 226 C6
Birchmead Ave HA5 40 C5
Birchmere Bsns Pk
SE2 124 A4
Birchmere Lo 18 SE16 118 B1
Birchmere Row SE3 142 D3
Birchmore Wlk N5 73 A5
Birch Pk HA3 24 A3
Birch Rd Feltham TW13 172 D5
Romford RM7 59 D6
Birch Row BR2 210 C3
Birch Tree Ave BR4 224 D4
Birch Tree Ho 16 SE7 143 C6
Birch Tree Way CR0 222 B6
Birch Vale Ct NW8 236 D6
Birchway UB3 106 A5
Birch Wlk CR4 181 B2
Birchwood Ave
Beckenham BR3 207 B5
Hackbridge SM5, SM6 219 B5
Muswell Hill N10 49 A6
Sidcup DA14 168 C1
Birchwood Cl SM4 201 D5
Birchwood Ct
Burnt Oak HA8 27 A1
Edmonton N13 32 D5
Birchwood Dr NW3 69 D5
Birchwood Gr TW12 173 C4
Birchwood Rd
Orpington BR5 211 C5
Streatham SW17 181 B5
Birdbrook Rd SE3 143 C2
Birdcage Wlk
SW1 115 D4 249 C1
Bird Coll DA14 168 A1
Birdham Cl BR1 210 A4
Birdhurst Ave CR2 221 B4
Birdhurst Ct SM6 219 C1
Birdhurst Gdns CR2 221 B4
Birdhurst Rd
London SW18 158 A6
Mitcham SW19 180 C4
South Croydon CR2 221 C3
Birdhurst Rise CR2 221 C3
Bird In Bush Rd SE15 140 A5
Bird-in-Hand La BR1 187 D1
Bird-In-Hand Pas
SE23 162 C2
Bird In Hand Yd 24
NW3 70 A4
Birdsall Ho 5 SE5 139 C2

Birdsfield La 12 E3. . . . . . . 97 B6
Bird St W1. . . . . 238 B1
Bird Wlk TW2 . . . . 151 B3
Birdwood Cl TW1. . . . . . . 174 C6
Birkbeck Ave
  Acton W3. . . . . .111 A6
  Greenford UB6 . . . . 86 A6
Birkbeck Coll
  W1. . . . . .93 D1 239 C2
Birkbeck St 13 . . . . .111 B5
Birkbeck Gdns IG8. . . . . . . 21 A2
Birkbeck Gr W3 . . . . .111 B4
Birkbeck Hill SE21 . . . . . . 160 D3
Birkbeck Mews 5 E8 . . . 73 D3
Birkbeck Pl SE21 . . . . . . .161 A2
Birkbeck Prim Sch
  DA14. . . . . .168 B1
Birkbeck Rd Acton W3 . . .111 B5
  Dalston E8. . . . . 73 D3
  Ealing W5 . . . . .109 C2
  Edgware NW7. . . . . 27 D5
  Enfield EN2 . . . . 5 B5
  Hornsey N8 . . . . 50 A5
  Ilford IG2 . . . . 57 A5
  North Finchley N12. . . . . . 30 A5
  Penge BR3. . . . . .184 D1
  Sidcup DA14. . . . . .168 A1
  Tottenham N17 . . . . 33 D2
  Wimbledon SW19 . . . . . .179 D4
Birkbeck St E2 . . . . 96 B4
Birkbeck Sta SE20 . . . . . .206 C6
Birkbeck Way UB6 . . . . . . 86 B6
Birkdale Ave
  30 Bermondsey SE16 . . .118 B1
  Crofton BR6. . . . . .211 B2
  Erith SE28 . . . . .102 C1
Birkdale Cl 3 UB1. . . . . . . 86 A1
Birkdale Gdns CR0. . . . . .222 C6
Birkdale Rd
  Abbey Wood SE2 . . . . . .124 A2
  Ealing W5 . . . . 88 A3
Birkenhead Ave KT2 . . . .176 B2
Birkenhead Ho 11 N7 . . . . 72 C3
Birkenhead St
  WC1. . . . . 94 A4 233 B2
Birkhall Rd SE6. . . . . . . .164 B2
Birkwood Cl SW12 . . . . . .159 E4
Birley Lo NW8 . . . . 229 D4
Birley Rd N20. . . . . 14 A2
Birley St SW11. . . . . .137 A3
Birnam Rd N4 . . . . 72 B6
Birnbeck Ct NW11 . . . . . . 47 B4
Birnham Ho TW1 . . . . . .153 C4
Birrell Ho 9 SW9. . . . . . .138 B3
Birse Cres NW10. . . . . 67 C4
Birstal Gn WD19 . . . . 22 D6
Birstall Rd N15 . . . . 51 C4
Birtwhistle Ho 5 E3 . . . . 97 B6
Biscay Ho 11 E1 . . . . 96 D1
Biscay Rd W6. . . . . .112 D1
Biscoe Cl TW5. . . . . .129 C6
Biscoe Ho UB2. . . . . .107 D2
Biscoe Way SE13 . . . . . .142 B2
Biscott Ho 3 E3 . . . . 97 D3
Bisenden Rd CR0 . . . . . . .221 C6
Bisham Cl CR4. . . . . .202 B1
Bisham Gdns N6. . . . . 49 A1
Bishop Butt Cl BR6. . . . . .227 D5
Bishop Challoner
  Collegiate Sch E1 . . . . 96 C1
Bishop Challoner Sch
  BR2. . . . . .186 B1
Bishop Ct 20 SW2. . . . . .160 C5
Bishop Douglass RC High
  Sch N2 . . . . 48 A6
Bishop Duppa's
  Almshouses 7
  TW10. . . . . .154 A6
Bishop Duppas Pk
  TW17. . . . . .193 C2
Bishop Fox Way KT8 . . . .195 B5
Bishop Gilpins CE Prim
  Sch SW19 . . . . .179 B5
Bishop John Robinson CE
  Prim Sch SE28 . . . . . . .124 C4
Bishop Justus CE Sch
  BR2. . . . . .210 B1
Bishop Ken Rd HA3 . . . . . 24 D2
Bishop King's Rd
  W14. . . . . .113 A2 254 B4
Bishop Perrin CE Prim Sch
  TW2. . . . . .151 B2
Bishop Ramsey CE Sch
  HA4 . . . . 40 A2
Bishop Ramsey CE Sch
  (Annexe) HA4 . . . . 39 D2
Bishop Rd N14. . . . . 15 B4
Bishop Ridley CE Prim Sch
  DA16. . . . . .145 C1
Bishops Ave
  Borehamwood WD6 . . . . 10 B6
  Bromley BR1. . . . . .209 C6
  Ilford RM6. . . . . 58 C3
  Newham E13. . . . . 99 B6
Bishop's Ave SW6 . . . . . .135 A3
Bishops Ave The N2 . . . . 48 B3
Bishopsbourne Ho
  BR1. . . . . .187 B3
Bishop's Bridge Rd
  W2. . . . . 92 A1 236 A2
Bishops Cl
  Acton Green W4 . . . . . . .111 A1
  Barnet EN5 . . . . 12 D5
  Enfield EN1 . . . . 6 B3
  New Eltham SE9 . . . . . . .167 A4
  Richmond TW10 . . . . . . .153 D1
  Sutton SM1. . . . . .217 C5
Bishop's Cl
  Dartmouth Pk N19 . . . . . . 71 C5

Bishop's Cl continued
  Hillingdon UB10 . . . . 82 C5
  Walthamstow E17 . . . . . . 53 D5
Bishopscourt 8 CR0 . . . .221 D6
Bishops Ct
  1 Ashford TW16 . . . . . .171 D3
  13 Bayswater W2 . . . . . . 91 D1
  East Finchley N2 . . . . 48 C5
  Richmond TW9 . . . . .132 A2
  Romford RM7 . . . . 59 D5
  Wembley HA0 . . . . 65 B4
Bishop's Ct Holborn EC4 . 241 C2
  Holborn WC2. . . . . 241 A2
Bishopsdale Ho 8
  NW6 . . . . 91 C6
Bishops Dr
  East Bedfont TW14 . . . . .149 B5
  Northolt UB5. . . . . 85 A6
Bishopsford Com Sch
  SM4 . . . . .202 B3
Bishopsford Ho SM4 . . . .202 B3
Bishopsford Rd SM4 . . . .202 B3
Bishopsgate
  EC2 . . . . 95 C1 243 A2
Bishopsgate Arc E1. . . . . 243 B3
Bishopsgate Churchyard
  EC2 . . . . 243 A2
Bishops Gn BR1. . . . . . . .187 C2
Bishops Gr
  East Finchley N2 . . . . 48 C3
  Feltham TW12 . . . . .173 B6
Bishop's Hall KT1. . . . . . .175 D1
Bishopshalt Sch UB8. . . . 82 B4
Bishops Hill KT12 . . . . . . .194 A2
Bishops Ho SW8 . . . . . . 270 B3
Bishop's Mans SW6 . . . .134 D3
Bishops Mead SE5 . . . . . .139 A5
Bishops Park Rd
  SW16. . . . . .182 A2
Bishop's Park Rd SW6 . . .134 D3
Bishop's Pl SM1 . . . . .218 A3
Bishops Rd
  Fulham SW6 . . .135 B4 264 C2
  Highgate N6. . . . . 49 A3
Bishop's Rd
  Hanwell W7 . . . . .108 C4
  Hayes UB3. . . . . 83 A1
  Thornton Heath CR0 . . . .204 D2
Bishops Sq E1. . . . . 243 B4
Bishop St N1 . . . 95 A6 235 A6
Bishop's Terr
  SE11 . . . . .116 C2 261 B4
Bishopsthorpe Rd
  SE26 . . . . .184 D6
Bishopstone Ho 4
  SW11. . . . . .137 A3
Bishop Stopford's Sch
  EN1. . . . . 6 B3
Bishops View TW10 . . . . . 49 B5
Bishop's Way 2 . . . 96 C5
Bishops Wlk
  Chislehurst BR7 . . . . . . .189 A2
  South Croydon CR0,
  CR9 . . . . .223 A3
Bishopswood Rd N6 . . . . 48 D2
Bishop Thomas Grant RC
  Sec Sch SW16. . . . . . . .182 B5
Bishop Wand CE Sch The
  TW16. . . . . .171 D1
Bishop Way UB1. . . . . 67 C1
Bishop Wilfred Wood Cl
  SE15 . . . . .140 A3
Bishop Wilfred Wood Ct
  3 E13. . . . . 99 C5
Bishop Winnington-
  Ingram CE Prim Sch
  HA4 . . . . 39 B2
Bisley Cl KT4 . . . . .200 C1
Bisley Ho SW19. . . . . . . .156 D2
Bispham Ho NW8 . . . . . . 88 B4
Bisson Rd E15 . . . . 98 A5
Bisterne Ave E11 . . . . 54 B6
Bittacy Bsns Ctr NW7 . . . 29 A3
Bittacy Cl NW7 . . . . 28 D4
Bittacy Ct NW7 . . . . 29 A3
Bittacy Hill NW7 . . . . 28 D4
Bittacy Park Ave NW7. . . 28 D4
Bittacy Rd NW7 . . . . 28 D4
Bittacy Rise NW7 . . . . 28 D4
Bittern Cl UB4. . . . . 84 D2
Bittern Ct Chingford E4 . . 20 B4
  7 Deptford SE8 . . . . . . .141 C6
  Hendon NW9 . . . . 27 C1
Bittern Ho SE1. . . . . 252 A1
Bittern St SE1 . . . . 252 A1
Bittoms The KT1. . . . . . . .197 D6
Bixley Cl UB2. . . . . .107 B2
Blackall St EC2 . . . . 243 A6
Blackberry Cl TW17. . . . . .193 C5
Blackberry Farm Cl
  TW5. . . . . .129 A5
Blackberry Field BR5 . . . .190 A2
Blackbird Ct NW9 . . . . . . 67 B5
Blackbird Hill NW9 . . . . . 67 B5
Blackborne Rd RM10. . . . 81 D2
Black Boy La N15 . . . . . . 51 A4
Blackbrook La BR1,
  BR2. . . . . .210 C5
Blackburn 21 NW1. . . . . . 71 D1
Blackburn St 21 SW2. . . .160 C5
Blackburne's Mews
  W1. . . . . 248 A5
Blackburn Rd NW6. . . . . . 69 D2
Blackburn Trad Est
  TW19 . . . . .148 B5
Blackburn Way UB3 . . . . .151 A4
Blackbush Ave RM6. . . . . 58 D4
Blackbush Cl SM2 . . . . . .217 D1
Blackcap Ct NW9 . . . . . . 27 C1

Blackdown Cl N2 . . . . 30 A1
Blackdown Ho E8. . . . . . . 74 A4
Blackett St SW15 . . . . . . .134 D2
Black Fan Cl EN2 . . . . 5 A4
BLACKFEN 168 A5
Blackfen Par DA15. . . . . .168 A5
Blackfen Rd DA15. . . . . . .168 B5
Blackfen Sch for Girls
  DA15. . . . . .168 B5
Blackford Rd WD19 . . . . . 22 D6
Blackfriars Bridge EC4 . . 251 C6
Blackfriars Ct EC4 . . . . . . 251 C6
Black Friars La
  EC4 . . . . .94 D1 241 C1
Blackfriars Pas EC4 . . . . . 251 C6
Blackfriars Pier EC4 . . . . . 251 C6
Blackfriars Rd
  SE1 . . . . .116 D5 251 A3
Blackfriars Sta
  EC4 . . . . .116 D6 251 C6
Blackfriars Underpass
  EC4 . . . . .116 D5 251 B6
Blackham Ho SW19 . . . . .179 A4
BLACKHEATH 142 C2
Blackheath* SE3 . . . . . . .142 D4
Blackheath Ave SE3. . . . .142 C5
Blackheath Bluecoat CE
  Sec Sch SE3 . . . . .143 B5
Blackheath Bsns Est
  SE10 . . . . .142 A4
Blackheath Gr SE3 . . . . . .142 D3
Blackheath High Sch
  Blackheath SE3. . . . . . . .142 D3
  Greenwich SE3 . . . . .143 A5
Blackheath Hill SE10 . . . .142 A4
Blackheath Hospl SE3 . . .142 C2
BLACKHEATH PARK 143 A1
Blackheath Pk SE3 . . . . . .143 A2
Blackheath Prep Sch
  SE3. . . . . .143 A4
Blackheath Rd SE10. . . . .141 D4
Blackheath Rise SE13 . . .142 A3
Blackheath Sta SE3 . . . . .142 D2
BLACKHEATH VALE 142 C3
Blackheath Vale SE3. . . . .142 C3
Blackheath Village
  SE3 . . . . .142 D3
Black Horse La
  Croydon CR0 . . . . .206 A2
  Higham Hill E17. . . . . 34 C1
Blackhorse La Sta
  CR0. . . . . .206 A2
Black Horse Mews E17. . . 52 D6
Black Horse Par HA5. . . . 40 B4
Blackhorse Rd
  Deptford SE8. . . . . .141 A6
  Walthamstow E17 . . . . . . 53 A5
Black Horse Road E17 . . . 52 D5
Blackhorse Road Sta
  E17. . . . . 52 D5
Blacklands Dr UB4. . . . . . 83 A3
Blacklands Rd SE6 . . . . . .186 A6
Blacklands Terr SW3. . . . . 257 D3
Black Lion La W6 . . . . . . .112 A2
Black Lion Mews 4
  W6. . . . . .112 A2
Blackmore Ho UB1. . . . . .108 B5
Blackmore Dr NW10 . . . . 66 D1
Blackmore Ho
  Forest Hill SE23 . . . . . . .163 B6
  Islington N1 . . . . 233 D6
  2 Wandsworth SW18 . . .157 D3
Blackmore's Gr TW11 . . . .175 A4
Blackmore Twr 1
  W3. . . . . .111 A3
Blackness La 2. . . . 225 D1
Blackpool Gdns UB4 . . . . 83 C3
Blackpool Rd SE15. . . . . .140 B3
Black Prince Intc DA6. . . .169 D5
Black Prince Rd SE1,
  SE11 . . . . .116 B2 260 D3
Black Rod Cl UB3 . . . . . . .105 D3
Black Roof Ho 9 SE5 . . .138 D4
Blackshaw Rd SW17 . . . .180 B5
Blacksmith Cl RM6. . . . . . 58 C3
Blacksmiths Ho 7 E17. . . 53 C5
Black's Rd W6 . . . . .112 C2
Blackstock Ho 2 N5. . . . . 72 B5
Blackstock Mews N4. . . . . 72 C5
Blackstock Rd N4, N5 . . . 72 D6
Blackstone Ho
  Dulwich SE21 . . . . .161 C1
  Pimlico SW1 . . . . 259 A1
Blackstone Rd NW2. . . . . 68 C4
Black Swan Yd SE1 . . . . 253 A2
Blackthorn Ave UB7. . . . .104 C3
Blackthorn Ct
  20 Camberwell SE15. . . .139 D5
  Heston TW5. . . . . .129 A5
  4 Leyton E15. . . . . 76 B4
  6 West Norwood
  SW16. . . . . .182 C5
Blackthorne Ave CR0 . . . .206 C1
Blackthorne Ct
  2 Littleton TW15. . . . . . .171 A4
  Southall UB1. . . . . .107 D5
Blackthorne Dr E4. . . . . . . 36 B6
Blackthorn Gr DA7. . . . . .147 A2
Blackthorn Rd IG1. . . . . . . 79 B3
Blackthorn St E3 . . . . 97 C3
Blacktree Mews 11
  SW9. . . . . .138 C2
BLACKWALL 120 B6
Blackwall Sta E14 . . . . . .120 A6
Blackwall Trad Est E14 . . 98 B2
Blackwall Tunnel E14,
  SE10 . . . . .120 B5

Blackwall Tunnel App
  SE10 . . . . .120 C4
Blackwall Tunnel Northern
  Approach E14, E3. . . . . . 98 A3
Blackwall Way E14. . . . . .120 A3
Blackwater Cl 7 . . . . 76 D4
Blackwater Ho NW8 . . . . 236 D4
Blackwater St SE22 . . . . .161 D6
Blackwell Cl
  10 Clapton Pk E5 . . . . . . 74 D4
  Harrow HA3 . . . . 24 B3
Blackwell Gdns HA8 . . . . 10 C1
Blackwell Ho 4 SW4. . . .159 D5
Blackwood Ho 11 E1. . . . 96 B3
Blackwood St
  SE17 . . . . .117 B1 262 C2
Blade Ho TW1. . . . . .153 D5
Blade Mews SW15 . . . . . .135 A3
Bladen Ho 4 E1. . . . . 96 D1
Blades Ct
  4 Hammersmith W6 . . . .112 B1
  Putney SW15. . . . . .135 B1
Blades Ho 12 SE11 . . . . .138 C6
Blades Lo 10 SW2 . . . . . .160 C5
Bladindon Dr DA5. . . . . . .168 D4
Bladon Ct
  Beckenham BR2 . . . . . . .208 C6
  Streatham SW16. . . . . . .182 A4
Bladon Gdns HA2. . . . . . . 41 D3
Blagden's Cl N14 . . . . 15 D2
Blagden's La N14. . . . . . . 15 D2
Blagdon Ct W7 . . . . .108 C6
Blagdon Rd
  London SE13 . . . . .163 D5
  New Malden KT3. . . . . . .199 D5
Blagdon Wlk TW11. . . . . .175 C4
Blagrove Rd 1 W10 . . . . 91 B2
Blair Ave London NW9. . . 45 C2
  Thames Ditton KT10. . . . .212 A6
Blair Cl Avery Hill DA15. . .167 C6
  Canonbury N1 . . . . 73 A2
  Hayes UB3. . . . . .106 A2
Blair Ct
  Beckenham BR3. . . . . . . .185 D2
  8 Carshalton SM5. . . . . .218 D5
  7 Catford SE6 . . . . .164 D3
  St John's Wood NW8 . . . 229 C6
Blairderry Rd SW2 . . . . . .160 A2
Blairgowrie Ct 13 E14. . . 98 B1
Blair Ho SW9 . . . . .138 B3
Blair Peach Prim Sch
  UB1. . . . . .106 D5
Blair St E14 . . . . 98 B1
Blake Apartments N8 . . . 50 B6
Blake Ave IG11 . . . . .101 D6
Blake Cl Bexley DA16. . . .145 C4
  Carshalton SM5. . . . . . . .202 D1
Blake Coll 93 C2 239 A4
Blake Ct
  8 Bermondsey SE16 . . . .118 B1
  9 Clapham SW8 . . . . . .137 C3
  Croydon CR2 . . . . .220 D3
  Kilburn NW6 . . . . 91 C4
  Southgate N11 . . . . 16 B6
Blakeden Dr KT10. . . . . . .212 D2
Blake Gdns
  SW6. . . . . .135 D4 265 C2
Blake Hall Cres E11. . . . . . 55 A1
Blakehall Rd SM5 . . . . . . .218 D2
Blake Hall Rd E11. . . . . . . 55 A2
Blake Ho
  6 Beckenham BR3. . . . . .185 D4
  2 Deptford SE8 . . . . .141 C6
  Harrow HA1 . . . . 64 C6
  Isle Of Dogs E14. . . . . . .119 D4
  2 Kentish Town N19 . . . . 71 D1
  Lambeth SE1. . . . . 261 A6
  14 Stoke Newington N16 .73 C4
Blake Lo N3 . . . . 29 B1
Blake Mews 15 TW9. . . . .132 C4
Blakemore Rd
  Streatham SW16. . . . . . .160 A1
  Thornton Heath CR7 . . . .204 B4
Blakemore Way DA17. . . .125 A3
Blakeney Ave BR3. . . . . . .185 B2
Blakeney Cl
  5 Camden Town NW1. . . 71 D1
  4 Dalston E8 . . . . 74 A3
  Whetstone N20 . . . . 14 A3
Blakeney Ct En2. . . . . 17 B6
Blakeney Rd BR3. . . . . . . .185 B2
Blakenham Rd W12 . . . . .112 A5
Blakenham Rd SW17. . . .180 D6
Blaker Ct SE7. . . . . .143 C5
Blake Rd Croydon CR0. . .221 D6
  Mitcham CR4. . . . . .202 C6
  Newham E16. . . . . 98 D3
  Wood Green N11. . . . . . . 31 C3
Blaker Rd E15 . . . . 98 A6
Blakes Ave KT3. . . . . .199 D4
Blakes Cl W10 . . . . 90 C2
Blake's Gn BR4. . . . . .208 A1
Blakes La KT3 . . . . .199 D4
Blakesley Ave W5. . . . . . . 87 C1
Blakesley Ho 4 E12 . . . . 78 C5
Blake's Rd SE15 . . . . .139 C5
Blakes Terr KT3 . . . . .200 A4
Blakesware Gdns N9. . . . . 17 B4
Blakewood Cl 5 SE20. . . .184 B3
Blanca Ho 16 N1 . . . . . . 95 C5
Blanchard Cl SE9 . . . . . . .166 A1
Blanchard Gr EN3 . . . . 7 D5
Blanchard Ho
  Chislehurst BR7 . . . . . . .189 A4
  7 Twickenham TW1. . . . .153 D5
Blanchard Way E8 . . . . . . 74 A2
Blanch Cl SE15 . . . . .140 C5
Blanchedowne SE5 . . . . .139 A1

Blanche Nevile Sch
  N10. . . . . 31 A1
Blanche St E16 . . . . 98 D3
Blanchland Rd SM4 . . . . .201 D4
Blandfield Rd SW12 . . . . .159 A4
Blandford Ave
  2 Beckenham BR3. . . . . .185 A1
  Twickenham TW2. . . . . . .151 D3
Blandford Cl London N2. . 48 A5
  Romford RM7 . . . . 59 D5
  Wallington CR0 . . . . .220 A5
Blandford Cres E4 . . . . . . 20 A4
Blandford Ct
  Brondesbury Pk NW6 . . . 69 A1
  6 De Beauvoir Town N1 . 73 C4
Blandford Ho SW8 . . . . . 270 C4
Blandford Rd
  Acton W4. . . . . .111 C3
  Ealing W5 . . . . .109 D4
  Penge BR3. . . . . .184 D1
  Southall UB2. . . . . .107 C2
  Teddington TW11 . . . . . . .174 C5
Blandford Sq NW1. . . . . . 237 B3
Blandford St
  W1. . . . . 93 A2 238 A3
Blandford Waye UB4. . . . . 84 C1
Bland Ho SE11. . . . . 260 D2
Bland St SE9 . . . . .143 D1
Blaney Cres E6 . . . . .100 D4
Blanmerle Rd SE9 . . . . . .166 D3
Blann Cl SE9 . . . . .165 D5
Blantyre St
  SW10. . . . . . . .136 B5 266 C4
Blantyre Twr SW10 . . . . . 266 C4
Blantyre Wlk
  SW10. . . . . . . .136 B5 266 C4
Blashford NW3 . . . . 70 D1
Blashford St SE13. . . . . . .164 B4
Blasker Wlk 8 E14. . . . . .119 D1
Blatchford Ct KT12. . . . . .194 A1
Blatchford Ho 8 RM10. . . 81 C5
Blawith Rd HA1. . . . . 42 D5
Blaxland Ho 12 W12. . . . .112 B6
Blaydon Cl Ha4 . . . . 39 C2
Blaydon Ct 4 UB5 . . . . . . 63 C2
Blaydon Wlk N17 . . . . 34 B3
Blazer Ct NW8 . . . . 229 D1
Bleak Hill La SE18 . . . . . .145 D6
Blean Gr SE20 . . . . .184 C3
Bleasdale Ave UB6 . . . . . 85 C6
Blechynden Ho 17 W10. . 90 D1
Blechynden St W10 . . . . .112 D6
Bledlow Cl SE28 . . . . .124 C6
Bledlow Rise UB6. . . . . . . 86 A5
Bleeding Heart Yd
  EC1 . . . . 241 B3
Blegborough Rd
  SW16. . . . . .181 C4
Blemundsbury WC1. . . . . 240 C4
Blendon Dr DA5. . . . . . . .168 C5
Blendon Path 9 BR1. . . .186 D3
Blendon Rd DA5. . . . . . . .168 C5
Blendon Terr SE18. . . . . .145 A6
Blendworth Point 4
  SW15. . . . . .156 B3
Blenheim 28 SW19 . . . . .156 D3
Blenheim Ave IG2 . . . . . . 56 C3
Blenheim Bsns Ctr
  CR4. . . . . .180 D1
Blenheim Centre 7
  SE20 . . . . .184 D3
Blenheim Cl
  Edmonton N21. . . . . 17 A3
  Eltham SE12 . . . . .165 B3
  Greenford UB6 . . . . 86 B5
  Wallington SM6. . . . . . . .219 C1
  West Barnes SW20. . . . . .200 C5
Blenheim Cres
  Notting Hill W11 . . . . 91 A1
  Notting Hill W11 . . . . 244 B6
  Ruislip HA4 . . . . 61 B6
  South Croydon CR2 . . . .221 A1
Blenheim Ct
  Barnsbury N7 . . . . 72 A2
  Beckenham BR3. . . . . . . .208 D5
  5 Hampton TW12 . . . . . .173 C2
  Harrow HA1 . . . . 43 A3
  Hendon NW4 . . . . 46 D5
  Longlands DA14. . . . . . . .167 B1
  Richmond TW9 . . . . .132 B2
  17 Rotherhithe SE16. . . .118 D5
  South Norwood SE19 . . .183 C2
  Sutton SM2. . . . . .218 A2
  Upper Holloway N19. . . . . 72 A6
  Woodford IG8 . . . . 37 B3
Blenheim Ctr TW3. . . . . . .129 D2
Blenheim Dr DA16 . . . . . .145 D4
Blenheim Gdns
  Clapham Pk SW2. . . . . . .160 B5
  Dollis Hill NW2 . . . . 68 C3
  Kingston u T KT2. . . . . . .176 D3
  Wallington SM6. . . . . . . .219 C1
  Wembley HA9 . . . . 66 A5
Blenheim Gr SE15 . . . . . .140 A3
Blenheim Ho
  6 Edmonton N9 . . . . 18 A1
  Hounslow TW3 . . . . .129 C2
  8 Woolwich SE18 . . . . . .123 A3
Blenheim Par 2 UB10. . . 82 D3
Blenheim Park Rd
  CR2 . . . . .221 A1
Blenheim Pas NW8 . . . . . 229 A4
Blenheim Pl TW11 . . . . . .174 D5
Blenheim Rd
  Acton W4. . . . . .111 C3
  Bromley BR1, BR2. . . . . .210 A5
  Harrow HA2 . . . . 41 D3
  Leyton E15. . . . . 76 C4
  Newham E6 . . . . 99 D4
  Northolt UB5 . . . . 63 D2

Blenheim Rd continued
  Penge SE20. . . . . .184 C3
  Sidcup DA15 . . . . .168 C3
  St John's Wood
  NW8. . . . . 92 A5 229 A4
  Sutton SM1. . . . . .217 D5
  Walthamstow E17 . . . . . . 53 A6
  West Barnes SW20. . . . . .200 C6
Blenheim Rise N15 . . . . . . 51 D5
Blenheim St W1 . . . . 238 C2
Blenheim Terr
  NW8 . . . . 92 A5 229 A4
Blenheim Way TW7 . . . . .131 A4
Blenkarne Rd SW11 . . . . .158 D5
Bleriot 27 NW9 . . . . 27 C1
Bleriot Rd TW5 . . . . .128 C5
Blessbury Rd HA8. . . . . . . 27 A2
Blessed Dominic RC Sch
  NW9 . . . . 27 D1
Blessed Sacrament RC
  Prim Sch N1 . . 94 B6 233 C5
Blessington Cl SE13. . . . .142 B2
Blessington Rd SE13 . . . .142 B1
Blessing Way IG11. . . . . .102 C5
Bletchingley Cl CR7. . . . . .204 D5
Bletchington Ct 2
  DA17. . . . . .125 C2
Bletchley Ct N1. . . . . 235 C3
Bletchley St N1 . . . 95 A5 235 B3
Bletchmore Cl UB3 . . . . .105 B3
Bletsoe Wlk N1. . . . . 235 B4
Blewbury Ho 3 SE2. . . . .124 C5
Blick Ho 1 SE16. . . . . . . .118 C3
Bligh Ho 2 SE17 . . . . . . .183 A6
Blincoe Cl SW19 . . . . . . .156 D2
Blissett St SE10 . . . . .142 A4
Blissland Ct 5 N12 . . . . . 30 A4
Bliss Mews 14 W10 . . . . 91 A4
Blisworth Cl UB4 . . . . 85 A3
Blisworth Ho 2 E2 . . . . . 96 A6
Blithbury Rd RM9 . . . . . . 80 B2
Blithdale Rd SE2. . . . . . . .124 A2
Blithfield St W8 . . . . 255 C5
Blockley Rd HA0. . . . . 65 B6
Bloemfontein Ave
  W12. . . . . .112 A5
Bloemfontein Rd W12. . . .112 B6
Blomfield Ct
  Battersea SW11 . . . . 266 D2
  Paddington W9 . . . . 236 B6
Blomfield Ho 4 E14 . . . .119 D6
Blomfield Mans 3
  W12. . . . . .112 C5
Blomfield Rd
  W9. . . . . 92 A2 236 A5
Blomfield St
  EC2 . . . . 95 B2 242 D3
Blomfield Villas W9. . . . . . 236 A4
Blomville Rd RM8. . . . . . . 81 A5
Blondel St SW11. . . . . . . .137 A3
Blondin Ave W5 . . . . .109 C3
Blondin St E3 . . . . 97 C5
Bloomburg St SW1 . . . . . 259 B3
Bloomfield Cres IG2. . . . . 56 D3
Bloomfield Ct N6. . . . . . . 49 A4
Bloomfield Ho 19 E1. . . . 96 A2
Bloomfield Pl W1 . . . . . . 248 D6
Bloomfield Rd
  Bromley Comm BR2 . . . .209 D4
  Highgate N6 . . . . 49 A3
  Kingston u T KT1. . . . . . .198 A6
  Woolwich SE18 . . . . .122 D1
Bloomfield Terr
  SW1. . . . . .115 A1 258 B2
Bloom Gr SE27 . . . . .160 D1
Bloomhall Rd SE19. . . . . .183 B5
Bloom Park Rd SW6 . . . . 264 C3
BLOOMSBURY 93 D2
Bloomsbury Cl
  Ealing W5 . . . . .110 B6
  Edgware NW7. . . . . 28 A3
Bloomsbury Ct
  Cranford TW5. . . . . .128 A4
  Leytonstone E11 . . . . 54 B1
  Pinner HA5 . . . . 41 B6
  St Giles WC1. . . . . 240 B3
Bloomsbury Ho 10
  SW4. . . . . .159 D5
Bloomsbury Pl
  London SW18 . . . . .158 A5
  St Giles WC1. . . . . 240 B3
Bloomsbury Sq
  WC1. . . . . 94 A2 240 B3
Bloomsbury St
  WC1. . . . . 93 D2 239 D3
Bloomsbury Way
  WC1. . . . . 94 A2 240 B3
Blore Cl SW8 . . . . 269 C2
Blore Ct W1 . . . . 249 C6
Blore Ho SW10 . . . . 265 D4
Blossom Cl
  Dagenham RM9. . . . . . . .103 B6
  Ealing W5 . . . . .110 A4
  South Croydon CR2 . . . .221 D3
Blossom La EN2 . . . . 5 A4
Blossom Pl E1. . . . . 243 B5
Blossom St E1. . 95 C3 243 B5
Blossom Way
  Hillingdon UB10 . . . . 60 B1
  West Drayton UB7 . . . . . .104 C2
Blossom Waye TW5. . . . . .129 A5
Blount St E14 . . . . 97 A1
Bloxam Gdns SE9 . . . . . .166 A6
Bloxhall Rd E10. . . . . 53 B1
Bloxham Cres TW12. . . . .173 B2
Bloxworth Cl SM6. . . . . . .219 C5
Blucher Rd SE5. . . . . .139 A5

Blue Anchor Alley 4 TW9 132 A1
Blue Anchor La SE16 118 B2
Blue Anchor Yd E1 118 A6
Blue Ball Yd SW1 249 A3
Bluebell Ave E12 78 A3
Bluebell Cl
Forest Hill SE26 183 D6
Hackbridge SM6 203 B1
10 Hackney E9 96 C6
Northolt UB5 63 B2
Orpington BR6 227 A6
Bluebell Ct 4 N12 14 A1
Bluebell Way IG1 78 D2
Blueberry Cl IG8 37 A4
Blueberry Ct
Edgware HA8 27 A5
3 Enfield EN2 4 D3
Bluebird La RM10 81 C1
Bluebird Way SE28 123 B4
Bluefield Cl TW12 173 C5
Blue Gate Fields Jun & Inf Schs E1 118 C6
Bluegate Mews E1 118 B6
Bluegates
Stoneleigh KT17 216 A1
Wimbledon SW19 179 A5
Bluehouse Rd E4 20 C1
Blue Lion Pl SE1 263 A6
Blue Point Ct 2 HA1 42 D4
Blueprint Apartments 15 SW12 159 B4
Blue Sch The TW7 131 A2
Blundell Cl E8 74 A4
Blundell Rd HA8 27 C3
Blundell St N7 72 A2
Blunden Cl RM8 58 C1
Blunt Rd CR0 221 B3
Blunts Ave UB7 126 C5
Blunts Rd SE9 166 C6
Blurton Rd E5 74 D4
Blydon Ct N21 16 B6
Blyth Cl
4 Cubitt Town E14 120 B2
Twickenham TW1 152 D5
Blythe Cl SE23 163 B4
Blythe Hill
Forest Hill SE6 163 B4
St Paul's Cray BR5 190 A2
Blythe Hill La SE6 163 B3
Blythe Ho 8 SE11 138 C6
Blythe Mews 2 W14 112 D3
Blythendale Ho 34 E2 96 A5
Blythe Rd W14 113 A3 254 A5
Blythe St E2 96 B4
Blytheswood Pl 4 SW16 182 B6
Blythe Vale SE6 163 B3
Blythewood 5 SM1 218 B3
Blyth Rd Bromley BR1 186 D2
Hayes UB3 105 C4
Walthamstow E17 53 B2
Woolwich SE28 124 C6
Blyth's Wharf E14 119 A6
Blythswood Rd IG3 58 A2
Blythwood Pk 10 BR1 186 D2
Blythwood Rd
London N4 50 A2
Pinner HA5 22 D2
Bnois Jerusalem Sch N16 51 B2
Boades Mews 3 NW3 70 B4
Boadicea St N1 233 C5
Boardman Ave E4 19 D6
Boardman Cl EN5 13 A6
Boardwalk Pl E14 120 A5
Boarhound 25 NW9 27 D1
Boarley Ho SE17 263 A3
Boatemah Wlk 21 SW9 138 C3
Boathouse Ctr The W10 90 D3
Boathouse Wlk 24 SE15 139 D5
Boat Lifter Way 19 SE16 119 A2
Bob Anker Cl 1 E13 99 A4
Bobbin Cl SW4 137 C2
Bobby Moore Bridge The HA9 66 C5
Bob Marley Way 11 SE24 138 C1
Bob Thompson Ct HA9 66 D5
Bockhampton Rd KT2 176 B3
Bocking St E8 96 B6
Boddicott Cl SW19 157 A2
Boddington Gdns W3 110 C4
Boddington Ho 2 SE14 140 C4
Bodeney Ho 10 SE5 139 C4
Boden Ho 4 E1 96 A2
Bodiam Cl EN1 5 C3
Bodiam Ct
Beckenham BR2 208 D5
Sutton SM1 218 B4
Bodiam Rd SW16 181 D3
Bodiam Way NW10 88 B4
Bodicea Mews TW4 151 C5
Bodington Ct 2 W12 112 D4
Bodley Cl KT3 199 C4
Bodley Manor Way SE24 160 C4
Bodley Rd KT3 199 C4
Bodmin 26 NW9 27 D1
Bodmin Cl HA2 63 B5
Bodmin Gr SM4 201 D4
Bodmin St SW18 157 C3
Bodnant Gdns SW20 200 B6
Bodney Rd E5, E8 74 B3
Boeing Way UB2 106 B3
Boevey Path DA17 125 B1
Bogart Ct 18 E14 119 C6
Bognor Gdns WD19 22 C5
Bognor Rd DA16 146 D4
Bohemia Pl 1 E8 74 B2
Bohn Rd E1 97 A2
Bohun Gr EN4 14 D5
Boileau Par W5 88 B1
Boileau Rd
Barnes SW13 134 B6
Ealing W5 88 B1
Boilerhouse SE1 253 C3
Boisseau Ho 31 E1 96 C2
Bolden St SE8 141 D3
Boldero Pl NW8 237 A5
Bolderwood Way BR4 223 D6
Boldmere Rd HA5 40 C2
Boleyn Ave EN1 6 B4
Boleyn Ct
Beckenham BR3 186 A2
Buckhurst Hill IG9 21 B3
East Molesey KT8 196 B5
Hayes UB3 105 D4
Walthamstow E17 53 C5
Boleyn Dr
East Molesey KT8 195 B6
Ruislip HA4 62 D6
Boleyn Gdns BR4 223 D6
Boleyn Ground(Upton Park) (West Ham Utd FC) E13, E6 99 D5
Boleyn Rd Newham E6 99 D5
Stoke Newington N16 73 C3
Upton E7 77 B1
Boleyn Way EN5 2 A2
Bolina Rd SE16 118 C1
Bolingbroke Gr SW11 158 D5
Bolingbroke Ho
Beckenham BR3 207 A4
Catford BR3 185 D5
Bolingbroke Hospl The SW11 158 C6
Bolingbroke Rd W14 112 D3
Bolingbroke Way UB3, UB11 105 B5
Bolingbroke Wlk SW11 136 C4 267 A2
Bollo Bridge Rd W3 111 A4
Bollo Ct 2 W3 111 A3
Bollo La W3 110 D3
Bolney Ct KT6 197 D4
Bolney Gate SW7 247 A1
Bolney St SW8 138 B5 270 C3
Bolsover St W1 93 B3 238 D5
Bolstead Rd CR4 181 B2
Bolster Gr N22 31 D2
Bolt Ct EC4 241 B1
Boltmore Cl NW4 46 D6
Bolton Cl
Chessington KT9 214 A2
Penge SE20 184 A1
Bolton Cres SE5 138 D5
Bolton Ct SW11 268 B1
Bolton Dr SM4 202 B2
Bolton Gdns
Bromley BR1 186 D4
Kensal Rise NW10 90 D5
South Kensington SW5 113 D1 255 D2
Teddington TW11 175 A4
Bolton Gdns Mews SW10 256 A2
Bolton Ho 4 SE10 120 C1
Bolton Pl SW5 256 A2
Bolton Rd
Chessington KT9 214 A2
Chiswick W4 133 A5
Edmonton N18 33 D5
Harlesden NW10 89 C6
Harrow HA1 42 B5
Kilburn NW8 91 D6
Stratford E15 76 D2
Boltons Ct SW5 255 D2
Bolton's La TW6, UB7 127 A5
Bolton St W1 115 B5 248 D4
Boltons The
Harrow HA1 42 A5
South Kensington SW10 114 A1 256 A2
6 Stratford E15 76 D2
Wembley HA0 64 D4
Woodford IG8 37 A6
Bolton Studios SW10 256 B1
Bolton Wlk N7 72 B6
Bombay Ct 8 SE16 118 C4
Bombay St SE16 118 B2
Bomer Cl UB7 126 C5
Bomore Rd W11 113 A6 244 A6
Bonar Pl BR7 188 A3
Bonar Rd SE15 140 A5
Bonchester Cl BR7 188 C3
Bonchurch Cl SM2 217 D1
Bonchurch Rd
Ealing W13 109 B5
Kensal Town W10 91 A2
Bond Cl UB7 82 B1
Bond Ct EC4 242 C1
Bondfield Ave UB4 84 A4
Bondfield Rd 4 E6 100 B2
Bond Gdns SM6 219 C4
Bond Ho 4 NW6 91 B5
Bonding Yard Wlk SE16 119 A3
Bond Prim Sch CR4 180 D1
Bond Rd Mitcham CR4 180 D1
Surbiton KT6 214 B6
Bond St Chiswick W4 111 B2
Ealing W5 109 D6
Stratford E15 76 C3
Bond Street Sta W1 93 A1 238 B1
Bondway SW8 138 A6 270 B6
Boneta Rd SE18 122 B3
Bonfield Rd SE13 142 A1
Bonham Gdns RM8 80 D6
Bonham Ho W11 244 C4
Bonham Rd
Brixton SW2 160 B6
Dagenham RM8 80 D5
Bonheur Rd W4 111 B4
Bonhill St EC2 95 B3 242 D5
Boniface Gdns HA3 23 D3
Boniface Rd UB10 60 D5
Boniface Wlk HA3 23 D3
Bonington Ho
Enfield EN1 18 A6
Pentonville N1 233 C3
Bonita Mews SE15 140 D2
Bonne Marche Terr Mews 18 SE27 183 C6
Bonner Hill Rd KT1 198 C6
Bonner Ho 3 SW15 156 A6
Bonner Prim Sch E2 96 C4
Bonner Rd E2 96 C5
Bonnersfield Cl HA1 43 A3
Bonnersfield La
Greenhill HA1 42 D3
Kenton HA1, HA3 43 A3
Bonner St E2 96 C5
Bonneville Gdns SW4 159 C5
Bonneville Prim Sch SW4 159 C5
Bonnington Ct 14 UB5 84 D5
Bonnington Ho 9 SM2 217 D2
Bonnington Sq SW8 138 B6 270 C6
Bonnington Twr BR2 210 A3
Bonny St NW1 71 C1
Bonser Rd TW1 152 D2
Bonsor Ho SW8 269 B2
Bonsor St SE5 139 C5
Bonthron Ho SW15 134 C3
Bonus Pastor RC Sch BR1 186 C6
Bonville Gdns 17 NW4 46 A5
Bonville Rd BR1 186 D5
Bookbinder Cotts N20 14 D1
Booker Cl 11 E3 97 B2
Booker Rd 5 N18 34 A5
Bookham Ct CR4 202 B6
Boone Ct N9 18 C1
Boones Rd SE13 142 C1
Boone St SE13 142 C1
Boord St SE10 120 C3
Boothby Ct E4 20 A1
Boothby Ho 2 SW16 181 C5
Boothby Rd N19 71 D6
Booth Cl 10 Hackney E9 96 B6
Thamesmead SE28 124 B6
Booth Ho
9 Brentford TW8 131 C5
2 Streatham SW2 160 C4
Booth La EC4 252 A6
Boothman Ho HA3 43 D6
Booth Rd Croydon CR0 220 D6
Hendon NW9 27 C1
Boothroyd Ho TW7 130 D2
Booth's Pl W1 239 B3
Boot Par HA8 26 C4
Boot St N1 95 C4
Bordars Rd W7 86 D2
Bordars Wlk W7 86 C2
Bordeaux Ho 1 E15 76 C3
Borden Ave EN1 17 B5
Border Cres SE26 184 B5
Border Gate CR4 180 D2
Border Gdns CR0 223 D4
Border Rd SE26 184 B5
Bordesley Rd SM4 201 D5
Bordeston Ct 11 TW8 131 C5
Bordley Ct 4 N20 14 D2
Bordon Wlk 5 SW15 156 A4
Boreas Wlk N1 234 D3
Boreham Ave E16 99 A1
Boreham Cl E11 54 A1
Boreham Rd N22 33 A1
BOREHAMWOOD 11 A5
Boreman Ho 11 SE10 142 A6
Borgard Rd SE18 122 B2
Borkwood Pk BR6 227 D4
Borkwood Way BR6 227 C4
Borland Rd
London SE15 140 C1
Teddington TW11 175 B3
Borneo St SW15 134 C2
Borough High St SE1 117 B5 252 C4
Borough Hill CR0 220 D5
Borough Mkt* SE1 252 C3
Borough Rd
Hounslow TW7 130 D4
7 Kingston u T KT2 176 C3
Lambeth SE1 116 D3 261 D6
Mitcham CR4 180 C1
Borough Sq SE1 252 A1
Borough Sta SE1 117 A4 252 B1
BOROUGH THE 117 A4
Borrett Cl SE17 117 A1 262 A1
Borrodaile Rd SW18 157 D5
Borrowdale NW1 232 A1
Borrowdale Ave HA3 25 A1
Borrowdale Cl IG4 56 A5
Borrowdale Ct EN2 5 A4
Borthwick Mews E15 76 C4
Borthwick Rd
Leyton E15 76 C4
London NW9 45 D3
Borthwick St SE8 119 C1
Borwick Ave E17 53 B6
Bosbury Rd SE6 164 A1
Boscastle Rd NW5 71 B5
Boscobel Cl BR1 188 B1
Boscobel Ho 4 E8 74 B2
Boscobel Pl SW1 258 B4
Boscobel St NW8 92 B3 236 D5
Boscombe Ave E10 54 B2
Boscombe Circus NW9 27 B1
Boscombe Cl E5 75 A3
Boscombe Gdns SW16 182 A4
Boscombe Ho CR0 205 B1
Boscombe Rd
Merton SW19 179 D2
North Cheam KT4 200 D1
Shepherd's Bush W12 112 A4
Streatham SW17 181 A4
Bose Cl N3 29 A2
Bosgrove E4 20 A2
Boss Ho SE1 253 C2
Boss St SE1 253 C2
Bostall Hill SE2 124 B1
Bostall La SE2 124 B1
Bostall Manorway SE2 124 B2
Bostall Park Ave DA7 147 A5
Bostall Rd BR5 190 B3
Bostock Ho TW5 129 C6
Boston Bsns Pk W7 108 C3
Boston Ct
South Norwood SE25 205 D5
Sutton SM2 218 A1
Boston Gdns
Brentford TW8 109 B2
Chiswick W4 133 C6
Boston Gr HA4 39 A3
Boston Ho
24 Camberwell SE5 139 A3
Earl's Ct SW5 255 D3
Lisson Gr NW1 237 C6
Boston Lo W13 109 C1
Boston Manor Ho TW8 109 B1
Boston Manor Rd TW8 109 B1
Boston Manor Sta TW8 109 A2
Boston Par W7 109 A2
Boston Park Rd TW8 109 C1
Boston Pl NW1 92 D3 237 C5
Boston Rd
Burnt Oak HA8 27 A3
Ealing W7 109 A3
Newham E6 100 A4
Thornton Heath CR0 204 C3
Bostonthorpe Rd W7 108 C4
Boston Vale W7 109 A2
Bosun Cl 22 E14 119 C4
Boswell Ct
Bloomsbury WC1 240 B4
9 Hammersmith W14 112 D3
Kingston u T KT2 176 C2
Boswell Ho
Bloomsbury WC1 240 B4
Bromley Comm BR2 209 D4
5 Streatham SW16 181 C5
Boswell Rd CR7 205 A5
Boswell St WC1 94 A2 240 B4
Boswood Ct TW4 129 B2
Bosworth Cl E17 35 B2
Bosworth Ho 4 W10 91 A3
Bosworth Rd Barnet EN5 1 C2
Dagenham RM10 81 C5
Kensal Town W10 91 A3
Wood Green N11 31 D4
Botany Bay La BR7 189 A1
Botany Cl EN4 2 C1
Boteley Cl E4 20 B2
Botham Cl 6 HA8 27 A3
Botha Rd E13 99 C2
Bothwell Cl E16 98 D2
Bothwell St 4 W6 134 D6
Botolph Alley EC3 253 A6
Botolph La EC3 253 A6
Botsford Rd SW20 179 A1
Bott's Mews W2 91 C1
Botwell Common Rd UB3 105 C6
Botwell Cres UB3 83 C1
Botwell House RC Prim Sch UB3 105 D4
Botwell La UB3 105 C6
Boucher Cl TW11 174 D5
Bouchier Ho 6 N2 30 B1
Bough Beech Ct EN3 6 D6
Boughton Ave BR2 208 D2
Boughton Ho
Borough The SE1 252 C2
Bromley BR1 188 A3
Boughton Rd SE28 123 C3
Boulcott St E1 96 D1
Boulevard The
Chelsea SW6 266 B1
4 Upper Tooting SW17 159 A2
Boullen Ct SM1 218 A4
Boulogne Ho SE1 263 C6
Boulogne Rd CR0 205 A3
Boulter Ho 4 SE14 140 C4
Boulters Ct HA0 65 A4
Boulton Ho TW8 110 A1
Boulton Rd RM8 81 B6
Boultwood Rd E6 100 B1
Bounces La N9 18 B2
Bounces Rd N9 18 C2
Boundaries Mans 3 SW12 159 A3
Boundaries Rd
Feltham TW13 150 C3
Upper Tooting SW12 159 A3
Boundary Ave E17 53 B2
Boundary Bsns Ct CR4 202 B6
Boundary Cl Barnet EN5 1 B4
Ilford IG3 79 C4
Kingston u T KT1 198 D6
Penge SE20 184 A1
Southall UB2 107 C1
Boundary Ct
3 Edmonton N18 33 D4
9 New Southgate N11 31 B6
Boundary Ho
Balham SW12 159 B3
1 Camberwell SE5 139 A5
Edgware HA8 44 B6
Isleworth TW1 153 B6
15 Notting Hill W11 112 D5
Boundary La
Camberwell SE17 139 A6
Newham E13, E6 99 D3
Boundary Pas E2 243 C6
Boundary Rd
Avery Hill DA15 167 C6
Barking IG11 101 A5
London N2 30 B2
Mitcham SW19 180 B4
Newham E13 99 D4
Pinner HA5 40 D2
Ponders End N9 18 C5
St John's Wood NW8 92 A6 229 B6
Tottenham N22 33 A1
Wallington SM5, SM6 219 A1
Walthamstow E17 53 C3
Boundary Road Est NW8 92 A6 229 A5
Boundary Row SE1 251 C2
Boundary St E2 95 D3 243 C6
Boundary Way CR0 223 C3
Boundfield Rd SE6 164 C2
Bounds Green Ct N11 31 D4
Bounds Green Ind Est N11 31 C4
Bounds Green Jun & Inf Schs N11 32 A3
Bounds Green Rd
London N11 31 D4
Wood Green N22 32 A3
Bounds Green Sta N11 31 D3
Bourbon Ho 9 SE6 186 A6
Bourchier St W1 249 C6
Bourdillon Ct 2 SE9 166 A2
Bourdon Pl W1 248 D6
Bourdon Rd SE20 184 C1
Bourdon St W1 115 B6 248 D5
Bourke Cl London SW4 160 A5
Willesden NW10 67 C2
Bourlet Cl W1 239 A3
Bourn Ave
Hillingdon UB8 82 C3
New Barnet EN4 14 B6
West Green N15 51 B5
Bournbrook Rd SE3, SE9 143 D2
Bourne Ave Hayes UB3 105 B3
Palmers Green N14 16 A2
Ruislip HA4 62 C3
Bourne Cir UB3 105 A3
Bourne Cl
Hinchley Wood KT7 212 D6
Isleworth TW7 130 C2
Bourne Ct Chiswick W4 133 A6
Ruislip HA4 62 B3
Wanstead E11 55 A4
Woodford IG8 37 D1
Bourne Dr CR4 180 B1
Bourne Gdns E4 35 D6
Bourne Hill N13 16 B2
Bourne Ho
4 Ashford TW15 170 C5
3 Buckhurst Hill IG9 21 D1
5 Clapham SW4 137 C1
1 Dollis Hill NW2 68 A5
Bourne Mans N13 32 C5
Bournemead Ave UB5 84 A5
Bournemead Cl UB5 84 A4
Bournemead Way UB5 84 B5
Bourne Mews W1 238 B1
Bournemouth Cl SE15 140 A3
Bournemouth Ct 6 SM1 218 A3
Bournemouth Rd
London SE15 140 A3
Merton SW19 179 C2
Bourne Par DA5 169 D4
Bourne Pl W4 111 B1
Bourne Prim Sch HA4 62 C2
Bourne Rd Bexley DA5 169 D5
Bromley BR2 209 D5
Hornsey N8 50 A3
Leyton E7, E11 76 D5
Bournes Ho 4 N15 51 C3
Bourneside 5 N14 15 D3
Bourneside Cres 6 N14 15 D3
Bourneside Gdns SE6 186 A5
Bourne St
Belgravia SW1 115 A2 258 A3
Croydon CR0 220 D6
Bourne Terr W2 91 D2
Bourne The N14 16 A3
Bourne Vale BR2 209 A2
Bournevale Rd SW16 182 A6
Bourne View UB6 64 D3
Bourne Way
Cheam SM1 217 B3
Coney Hall BR2, BR4 224 D6
West Ewell KT19 215 A4
Bournewood Rd SE18 146 A5
Bournville Rd SE6 163 C4
Bournwell Cl EN4 2 D3
Bourton Cl UB3 106 A5
Bousfield Prim Sch SW10 114 A1 256 A2
Bousfield Rd SE14 140 D3
Boutcher CE Prim Sch SE1 117 D2 263 C4
Boutflower Rd SW11 136 C1
Bouverie Ct 4 SW16 182 A5
Bouverie Gdns HA3 43 D3
Bouverie Mews N16 73 C6
Bouverie Pl W2 236 D2
Bouverie Rd
Harrow HA1 42 A3
Stoke Newington N16 73 C6
Bouverie St EC4 94 C1 241 B1
Bouvier Rd EN3 6 C5
Boveney Rd SE23 162 D4
Bovill Rd SE23 162 D4
Bovingdon Ave HA9 66 C2
Bovingdon Cl 4 N19 71 C6
Bovingdon La NW9 27 C2
Bovingdon Rd SW6 135 D4 265 D1
Bovril Ho EN1 5 C2
BOW 97 B5
Bowater Cl
Clapham Pk SW2 160 A5
Kingsbury NW9 45 B4
Bowater Gdns TW16 172 C2
Bowater Ho EC1 242 B5
Bowater Pl SE3 143 B5
Bowater Rd
Greenwich SE18 121 D3
Wembley HA9 66 D5
Bow Brook The 20 E2 96 D5
Bow Church Sta E3 97 C4
BOW COMMON 97 D2
Bow Common La E3 97 B3
Bowden Cl TW14 149 C3
Bowden Ct HA4 62 C3
Bowden Ho 29 E3 97 D4
Bowden House Hospl (Private) HA1 64 C6
Bowden St SE11 116 C1 261 B1
Bowditch SE8 119 B1
Bowdon Rd E17 53 C2
Bowen Ct 2 N5 72 D4
Bowen Dr SE21 161 C1
Bowen Rd HA1 42 A2
Bowen St E14 97 D1
Bower Ave SE3 142 C5
Bower Cl UB5 84 C5
Bowerdean St SW6 135 D3
Bower Ho SE14 140 D4
Bowerman Ave SE14 141 A6
Bowerman Ct 1 N19 71 D6
Bowers Ho 5 IG11 78 D1
Bower St E1 96 D1
Bowers Wlk 1 E6 100 B1
Bowery Ct 16 RM10 81 D2
Bowes Cl DA15 168 B5
Bowes Ho N13 32 B5
Bowes-Lyon Hall 13 E16 121 A5
Bowes Lyon Ho 2 TW10 153 C1
BOWES PARK 32 A4
Bowes Park Sta N22 32 A3
Bowes Prim Sch N11 31 D5
Bowes Rd Acton W3 111 C6
Dagenham RM8 80 C4
New Southgate N11 31 C5
Walton-on-T KT12 194 B1
Bowes Rd (North Circular Rd) N13 32 A5
Bowfell Rd W6 134 C6
Bowford Ave DA7 147 A4
Bowhill Cl SW9 138 C5
Bow Ho 1 E3 97 C4
Bowie Cl SW4 159 D4
Bow Ind Pk E15 75 C1
Bow La
Barbican EC2, EC4 95 A1 242 B1
Finchley N12 30 A3
Bowland Ho N4 51 A2
Bowland Rd
London SW4 137 D1
Woodford IG8 37 C4
Bowland Yd SW1 247 D1
Bowl Ct EC2 243 B5
Bowles Ct Finchley N12 30 C3
Harrow HA3 43 A3
Bowles Rd 1 SE1 140 A6
Bowley Cl SE19 183 D4
Bowley Ho 6 SE16 118 A3
Bowley La SE19 183 D5
Bowling Cl UB10 82 B6
Bowling Green Cl SW19 156 B4
Bowling Green Ct HA9 66 B6
Bowling Green Ho SW10 266 C4
Bowling Green La EC1 94 C3 241 B6
Bowling Green Pl SE1 252 C2
Bowling Green Row 1 SE18 122 B2

Bowling Green St SE11 138 C6
Bowling Green Wlk N1 95 C4
Bowls Cl HA7 25 B5
Bowman Ave E16 120 D6
Bowman Homes W5 109 D4
Bowman Mews
 St George in t East E1 118 A6
 Wandsworth SW18 157 B3
Bowmans Cl W13 109 B5
Bowmans Lea SE23 162 C4
Bowman's Meadow SM6 219 B5
Bowman's Mews N7 72 A5
Bowman's Pl N7 72 A5
Bowman Trad Est NW9 44 C5
Bowmar Lo 13 EN5 1 D1
Bowmead SE9 166 B2
Bowmore Wlk NW1 71 D1
Bowness Cl 5 E8 73 D2
Bowness Cres KT2, SW15 177 C5
Bowness Dr TW4 129 A1
Bowness Ho SE15 140 C5
Bowness Rd
 Catford SE6 163 D4
 Erith DA7 147 D3
Bowood Rd
 Clapham SW11 159 A6
 Enfield EN3 6 D3
Bow Rd E3 97 C4
Bowring Gn WD19 22 C5
Bow Road Sta E3 97 C4
Bowrons Ave HA0 65 D1
Bowry Ho 14 E14 97 B2
Bow Sch E3 97 C4
Bowsley Ct TW13 150 A2
Bowsprit Point 1 E14 119 C3
Bow St
 St Giles WC2 94 A1 240 B1
 Stratford E15 76 C3
Bowstead Ct SW11 266 D1
Bow Triangle Bsns Ctr 17 E3 97 C3
Bowyer Cl E6 100 B2
Bowyer Ct 4 E4 20 A3
Bowyer Ho
 Mitcham CR4 202 C6
 27 Shoreditch N1 95 C6
 Wandsworth SW18 157 D5
Bowyer Pl SE5 139 A5
Bowyer St 15 SE5 139 A5
Boxall Rd SE21 161 C5
Box Cnr TW2 152 C2
Box Elder Cl HA8 27 A5
Boxgrove Prim Sch SE2 124 C3
Boxgrove Rd SE2 124 C3
Box La IG11 102 C5
Boxley Ho 3 E5 74 B3
Boxley Rd SM4 202 A5
Boxley St E16 121 B5
Boxmoor Ho
 16 Hackney E2 96 A6
 9 Shepherd's Bush W11 112 D5
Boxmoor Rd HA3 43 B5
Boxoll Rd RM9 81 B5
Boxshall Ho 7 SE18 144 D6
Box Tree Ho SE8 119 A1
Boxtree La HA3 24 B3
Boxtree Rd HA3 24 B3
Boxwood Cl UB7 104 B4
Boxworth Cl N12 30 B5
Boxworth Gr N1 94 B6 233 D6
Boyard Rd SE18 122 D1
Boyce Ho
 Streatham SW16 181 C5
 1 West Kilburn W10 91 B4
Boyce Way E13 99 A3
Boycroft Ave NW9 45 A3
Boyd Ave UB1 107 B5
Boyd Cl KT2 176 C3
Boyd Ct SW15 156 C5
Boydell Ct NW8 70 B1
Boyden Ho 8 E17 54 A6
Boyd Rd SW19 180 B4
Boyd St E1 96 A1
Boyfield St SE1 116 D4 251 D1
Boyland Rd BR1 186 D5
Boyle Ave HA7 25 A4
Boyle Cl UB10 82 B5
Boyle Farm Rd KT7 197 A3
Boyle Ho
 13 Belvedere DA17 125 C3
 Wembley HA9 66 D5
Boyle St W1 249 A6
Boyne Ave NW4 46 D5
Boyne Ct NW10 68 A1
Boyne Ho 10 E5 74 B6
Boyne Rd
 Dagenham RM10 81 C5
 Lewisham SE13 142 B2
Boyne Terr Mews W11 113 B5 244 C4
Boyson Rd 10 SE17 139 B6
Boyton Cl London N8 50 A6
 Stepney E1 96 D3
Boyton Ho
 Kennington SE11 261 A1
 St John's Wood NW8 229 D4
Boyton Rd N8 50 A6
Brabant Ct EC3 253 A6
Brabant Rd N22 32 B1
Brabazon Ave SM6 220 A1
Brabazon Rd
 Heston TW5 128 D5
Brabazon Rd *continued*
 Northolt UB5 85 C5
Brabazon St E14 97 D2
Brabner Ho 3 E2 96 A4
Brabourne Cl 7 SE19 183 C5
Brabourne Cres DA7 147 B6
Brabourne Hts NW7 11 C1
Brabourne Rise BR3 208 B4
Brabourn Gr SE15 140 C3
Brabrook Ct SM6 219 B3
Brabstone Ho 2 UB6 86 D5
Bracer Ho 1 N1 95 C5
Bracewell Ave UB6 65 A2
Bracewell Rd W10 90 C2
Bracewood Gdns CR0 221 D5
Bracey Mews 1 N4 72 A6
Bracey St N4 72 A6
Bracken Ave
 Balham SW12 159 A4
 Croydon CR0 223 C5
Brackenbridge Dr HA4 62 D5
Brackenbury N4 50 B1
Brackenbury Gdns W6 112 B3
Brackenbury Prim Sch W6 112 B3
Brackenbury Rd
 East Finchley N2 48 A6
 Hammersmith W6 112 B3
Bracken Cl
 Ashford TW16 171 D4
 Newham E6 100 B2
 Twickenham TW4 151 C4
Brackendale
 Kingston u T KT1 176 D1
 Southgate N21 16 B2
Brackendale Cl TW5 129 D4
Brackendale Ct 2 BR3 185 C3
Bracken End TW7 152 B6
Brackenfield Cl E5 74 B5
Bracken Gdns SW13 134 A3
Brackenhill HA4 63 A4
Bracken Hill Cl 5 BR1 186 D2
Bracken Hill La BR1 186 D2
Bracken Ho 15 E3 97 C2
Bracken Mews
 Chingford E4 20 A3
 Romford RM7 59 D3
Brackens BR3 185 C3
Brackens The EN1 17 C4
Bracken The E4 20 A2
Brackenwood TW16 172 A2
Brackenwood Lo EN5 1 C1
Brackley Ave SE15 140 C2
Brackley Cl SM6 220 A1
Brackley Ct NW8 236 D6
Brackley Rd
 Beckenham BR3 185 C3
 Chiswick W4 111 C1
Brackley Sq IG8 37 D3
Brackley St EC1 242 B4
Brackley Terr 6 W4 111 C1
Bracklyn Ct N1 235 C4
Bracklyn St N1 235 C4
Bracknell Cl N22 32 C2
Bracknell Gate NW3 69 D3
Bracknell Gdns NW3 69 D4
Bracknell Way NW3 69 D4
Bracondale KT10 212 A3
Bracondale Rd SE2 124 A2
Braconhyrst HA1 42 C2
Bradbeer Ho 24 E2 96 C4
Bradbourne Ct 11 SM2 217 D2
Bradbourne Rd DA5 169 C4
Bradbourne St SW6 135 C3
Bradbury Cl UB2 107 B2
Bradbury Ct
 4 Barnet EN5 1 D1
 2 Greenwich SE3 143 A5
 Merton SW20 178 C1
Bradbury Ho E1 243 D2
Bradbury St 28 N16 73 C3
Bradby Ho NW8 91 D5
Braddock Cl TW7 130 D3
Braddon Rd TW9 132 B2
Braddyll St SE10 120 C1
Bradenham 11 SE17 139 B6
Bradenham Ave DA16 146 A1
Bradenham Cl SE17 139 B6
Bradenham Rd
 Harrow HA3 43 B5
 Hayes UB4 83 C4
Braden St W9 91 D3
Bradfield Ct 10 NW1 71 B1
Bradfield Dr IG11 80 A3
Bradfield Ho 15 SW8 137 D3
Bradfield Rd
 Newham E16 121 B4
 Ruislip HA4 63 A3
Bradford Cl
 Bromley BR2 210 B1
 Forest Hill SE26 184 B6
 Tottenham N17 33 D4
Bradford Dr KT19 215 D2
Bradford Ho 4 W14 112 D3
Bradford Rd Acton W3 111 C4
 Ilford IG1 57 C1
Bradgate Rd SE6 163 D5
Brading Cres E11 77 B6
Brading Rd
 Streatham SW2 160 B4
 Thornton Heath CR0 204 B3
Brading Terr W12 112 A3
Bradiston Rd W9 91 B4
Bradley Cl N7 72 B2
Bradley Ct CR0 220 C4
Bradley Gdns W13 87 B1
Bradley Ho
 Bermondsey SE16 118 B2
 1 Bromley E3 97 D4
 Twickenham TW1 152 D3
 Woodford IG8 37 A3
Bradley Mews SW12 158 D3
Bradley Rd Enfield EN3 7 A6
 South Norwood SE19 183 A4
 Wood Green N22 32 B1
Bradley's Cl N1 234 B4
Bradley Stone Rd E6 100 B2
Bradlord Ho SE21 161 C1
Bradman Row 7 HA8 27 A3
Bradmead SW8 137 C5 269 A3
Bradmore Ct 2 EN3 7 A2
Bradmore Park Rd W6 112 B2
Bradon 24 NW9 27 D1
Bradshaw Cl SW19 179 C4
Bradshaw Dr NW7 28 D3
Bradshawe Waye UB8 82 B2
Bradshaws Cl SE25 206 A6
Bradsole Ho 13 BR3 185 C3
Brad St SE1 116 C5 251 B3
Bradstock Ho E9 75 A1
Bradstock Rd
 Homerton E9 74 D2
 Stoneleigh KT17 216 B3
Bradwell Ave RM10 81 C6
Bradwell Cl E18 54 D5
Bradwell Ho
 8 Kilburn NW6 91 D6
 9 Walthamstow E17 53 D6
Bradwell Mews 5 N18 34 A6
Brady Ct RM8 58 D1
Brady Dr BR1 210 C6
Brady Ho London SW4 159 D6
 South Lambeth SW8 269 B2
Bradymead E6 100 D1
Brady St E1 96 B3
Braeburn Ct 1 EN4 2 C1
Brae Ct
 2 Kingston u T KT2 176 C2
 South Norwood SE25 183 C2
Braefoot Ct SW15 156 D6
Braemar SW15 156 D5
Braemar Ave
 Thornton Heath CR7 204 D6
 Welsh Harp NW10 67 B6
 Wembley HA0 66 A1
 Wimbledon SW18, SW19 157 C2
 Wood Green N22 32 A2
Braemar Ct
 4 Brentford TW8 131 D6
 5 Catford SE6 164 D3
Braemar Gdns
 Hendon NW9 27 B2
 Longlands DA15 167 B1
 West Wickham BR4 208 A1
Braemar Ho
 Richmond TW11 175 B5
 St John's Wood W9 229 A1
Braemar Mans W8 255 D5
Braemar Rd
 Brentford TW8 131 D6
 Newham E13 98 D3
 North Cheam KT4 216 B5
 South Tottenham N15 51 C4
Braemore Ct EN4 3 A1
Braeside BR3 185 D5
Braeside Ave SW19 179 A2
Braeside Cl HA5 23 C3
Braeside Rd SW16 181 C3
Braeside Sch
 Buckhurst Hill IG9 21 B3
 Buckhurst Hill IG9 21 C2
Braes St N1 72 D1
Braesyde Cl DA17 125 B2
Brafferton Rd CR0 221 A4
Braganza St SE17 116 D1 261 C1
Bragg Cl RM8 80 B2
Bragg Rd TW11 174 D4
Braham Ho SE11 260 D1
Braham St E1 243 D2
Brahma Kumaris World Spiritual Univ NW10 68 A1
Braid Ave W3 89 C1
Braid Cl TW13 151 B2
Braid Ho SE10 142 A4
Braidwood Ho 2 CR7 204 D5
Braidwood Rd SE6 164 B3
Braidwood St SE1 117 C5 253 A3
Braikenridge Ho N21 17 B5
Brailsford Cl SW19 180 C3
Brailsford Rd SW2 160 C5
Braintcroft Prim Sch NW2 67 D5
Brainton Ave TW14 150 C4
Braintree Ave IG4 56 A5
Braintree Ho 6 E1 96 C3
Braintree Ind Est HA4 62 B4
Braintree Rd
 Dagenham RM10 81 C5
 Ruislip HA4 62 B4
Braintree St E2 96 C4
Braithwaite Ave RM7 59 C2
Braithwaite Gdns HA7 25 C2
Braithwaite Ho EC1 242 C6
Braithwaite Rd EN3 7 B2
Braithwaite Twr W2 236 C4
Brake Shear Ho 1 EN5 1 B2
Bramah Gn SW9 138 C4
Bramah Mus of Tea & Coffee* SE1 252 B3
Bramalea Cl N6 49 A3
Bramall Cl E15 76 D3
Bramall Ct N7 72 B2
Bramber WC1 233 A1
Bramber Ct TW8 110 A2
Bramber Ho 9 KT2 176 A2
Bramber Rd
 Colney Hatch N12 30 C5
 Fulham W14 135 B6 264 C6
Bramble Acres Cl SM2 217 C1
Bramblebury Rd SE18 123 A1
Bramble Cl
 Beckenham BR3 208 A4
 Croydon CR0 223 D4
 Hillingdon UB8 82 B1
 South Tottenham N15 52 A5
 Stanmore HA7 25 D3
 Upper Halliford TW17 193 B6
Brambledown 8 N4 50 A2
Brambledown Cl BR2, BR4 208 C4
Brambledown Rd
 South Croydon CR2 221 C1
 Wallington SM5, SM6 219 B1
Bramble Gdns W12 111 D6
Bramble Ho 16 E3 97 C2
Bramble La TW12 173 B4
Brambles Cl TW7, TW8 131 B5
Brambles Farm Dr UB10 82 C4
Brambles The
 West Drayton UB7 104 A2
 8 Wimbledon SW19 179 B5
Bramblewood Cl SM5 202 C1
Brambling Ct
 25 Deptford SE8 141 B6
 South Norwood SE25 205 D5
Bramblings The E4 36 B6
Bramcote Ave CR4 202 D5
Bramcote Ct CR4 202 D5
Bramcote Gr SE16 118 C1
Bramcote Rd SW15 134 B1
Bramdean Cres SE12 165 A3
Bramdean Gdns SE12 165 A3
Bramerton NW6 68 D1
Bramerton Rd BR3 207 B6
Bramerton St SW3 136 C6 267 A6
Bramfield Ct N4 73 A6
Bramfield Rd SW11 158 D6
Bramford Ct N14 15 D2
Bramford Rd SW18 136 A1
Bramham Gdns
 Chessington KT9 213 D4
 South Kensington SW5 113 D1 255 D2
Bramham Ho SE22 139 C1
Bramhope La SE7 143 B6
Bramlands Cl SW11 136 C2
Bramley Ave TW17 193 C6
Bramley Cl
 Croydon CR2 221 A3
 East Barnet N14 15 B6
 Hayes UB3 106 A6
 Higham Hill E17 35 A1
 Orpington BR6 210 D1
 Pinner HA5 39 D6
 Twickenham TW2 152 A5
 Woodford IG8 37 C3
Bramley Cres Ilford IG2 56 C3
 Nine Elms SW8 137 D5 269 D4
Bramley Ct 2 Barnet EN4 2 C1
 9 Chingford E4 20 A3
 Dollis Hill NW2 68 B5
 Feltham TW14 149 C5
 Hither Green SE13 164 B6
 Mitcham CR4 180 B1
 Southall UB1 108 A6
 Wallington SM6 219 C3
 Welling DA16 146 B4
Bramley Gdns WD19 22 C5
Bramley Hill CR2 221 A4
Bramley Ho
 Hounslow TW3 129 B1
 Ilford IG1 56 C3
 1 Kingston u T KT2 176 D3
 19 North Kensington W10 90 D1
 Roehampton SW15 155 D5
Bramley House Ct EN2 5 B6
Bramleyhyrst CR2 221 A3
Bramley Lo HA0 65 D4
Bramley Rd Ealing W5 109 C3
 North Kensington W10 90 D1
 Southgate N14 15 C6
 Sutton SM1 218 B3
Bramley Way
 Hounslow TW4 151 B6
 West Wickham BR4 223 D6
Brampton WC1 240 C3
Brampton Cl 14 E5 74 B6
Brampton Coll NW4 46 C5
Brampton Ct NW4 46 B5
Brampton Gr
 Harrow HA3 43 B5
 Hendon NW4 46 C5
 Wembley HA9 44 C1
Brampton La 6 NW4 46 C5
Brampton Lo DA7 146 D5
Brampton Manor Sch E6 99 D3
Brampton Park Rd N22 50 C6
Brampton Prim Sch
 Bexley DA7 146 D3
 Newham E6 100 A4
Brampton Rd
 Bexleyheath DA7 147 A4
 Croydon CR0 205 D3
 Harringay N15 51 A4
 Hillingdon UB10 82 D5
Brampton Rd *continued*
 Newham E6 99 D4
 Queensbury NW9 44 C5
Bramshaw Gdns WD19 22 D5
Bramshaw Rd E9 74 D2
Bramshaw Rise KT3 199 C3
Bramshill Gdns NW5 71 B5
Bramshill Rd NW10 89 D5
Bramshot Ave SE7 143 B6
Bramshott Ct 3 KT6 198 A3
Bramshurst NW8 91 D6
Bramston Rd
 Harlesden NW10 90 A5
 Wandsworth SW17 158 A1
Bramwell Cl TW16 172 D1
Bramwell Ho
 Borough The SE1 262 B5
 Chelsea SW1 269 A6
Bramwell Mews N1 233 D6
Brancaster Dr NW7 28 A3
Brancaster Ho
 22 Globe Town E1 96 D4
 Islington N5 72 D3
Brancaster Rd
 Ilford E12 78 B4
 Newbury Pk IG2 57 C3
 Streatham SW16 160 A1
Brancepeth Gdns IG9 21 A2
Branch Hill NW3 70 A5
Branch Ho 13 SM1 218 A4
Branch Pl N1 95 B6 235 D6
Branch Rd E14 119 A6
Branch St SE15 139 C5
Brancker Rd HA3 43 D6
Brancroft Way EN3 7 B4
Brandan Ho 11 HA1 42 D4
Brand Cl N4 50 D1
Branden Lo 13 W4 111 A1
Brandlehow Rd SW15 135 B1
Brandon Ho BR3 185 D5
Brandon Mews
 Barbican EC2 242 C4
 Walworth SE17 262 B3
Brandon Pl N8 50 B5
Brandon Rd
 Barnsbury N7 72 A1
 Southall UB2 107 B1
 Sutton SM1 217 D4
 Walthamstow E17 54 A6
Brandon St SE17 117 A2 262 B3
Brandram Rd SE13 142 C1
Brandrams Wharf SE16 118 C4
Brandreth Ct HA1 42 D3
Brandreth Rd
 Newham E6 100 B1
 Upper Tooting SW17 159 B2
Brandries The SM6 219 D5
Brand St SE10 142 A5
Brandville Gdns IG6 56 D5
Brandville Rd UB7 104 A4
Brandy Way SM2 217 C1
Brangbourne Rd BR1 186 A5
Brangton Rd SE11 260 D1
Brangwyn Cres SW19 180 B1
Brangwyn Ct W14 254 A5
Branham Ho 11 SE18 122 D1
Branksea St SW6 135 A5 264 A3
Branksome Ave N18 33 D5
Branksome Cl
 Teddington TW11 174 B6
 Walton-on-T KT12 194 D1
Branksome Ct 6 N2 48 A6
Branksome Ho SW8 270 C4
Branksome Rd
 London SW2 160 A6
 Merton SW19 179 C2
Branksome Way
 Harrow HA3 44 B3
 Kingston u T KT3 177 B2
Bransby Ct 4 N16 73 C4
Bransby Rd KT9 214 A2
Branscombe NW1 232 B5
Branscombe Ct BR2 208 C4
Branscombe Gdns N21 16 C4
Branscombe St SE13 141 D2
Bransdale Cl NW6 91 C6
Bransgrove Rd HA8 26 B3
Branston Cres BR5 211 B1
Branstone Ct 9 TW9 132 B4
Branstone Rd TW9 132 B4
Branston Ho N7 72 C3
Brants Wlk W7 86 C3
Brantwood Ave
 Erith DA8 147 D5
 Isleworth TW7 131 A1
Brantwood Cl E17 53 D6
Brantwood Gdns
 Enfield EN2 16 A6
 Redbridge IG4 56 A5
Brantwood Ho 9 SE5 139 A5
Brantwood Rd
 Erith DA7 147 D3
 Herne Hill SE24 161 A6
 Tottenham N17 34 A4
Brasenose Dr SW13 134 C6
Brasher Cl UB6 64 B3
Brashley Road Cvn Site NW10 89 C4
Brassett Point 3 E15 98 C6
Brassey Cl TW14 150 A3
Brassey Ho
 1 Millwall E14 119 D2
 Walton-on-T KT12 194 A1
Brassey Rd NW6 69 B2
Brassey Sq SW11 137 A2
Brassie Ave W3 89 C1
Brass Talley Alley 31 SE16 118 D4
Brasted Cl Bexley DA6 168 D6
 Forest Hill SE26 184 C6
Brasted Lo 11 BR3 185 C3
Brathay NW1 232 B3
Brathway Rd SW18 157 C4
Bratley St 11 E1 96 A3
Bratten Ct CR0 205 B3
Braund Ave UB6 85 D3
Braundton Ave DA15 167 D3
Braunston Dr UB4 85 A3
Braunston Ho TW8 131 C6
Bravington Cl TW17 192 B4
Bravington Pl W9 91 B3
Bravington Rd W9 91 B4
Brawne Ho 12 SE17 138 D6
Braxfield Rd SE4 141 B1
Braxted Pk SW16 182 B4
Bray NW3 70 C1
Brayard's Rd SE15 140 B3
Braybourne Dr TW7 130 D5
Braybrooke Gdns SE19 183 C3
Braybrook St W12 89 D1
Brayburne Ave SW4 137 C3
Braycourt Ave KT12 194 C2
Bray Cres SE16 118 D4
Bray Ct
 Chessington KT9 214 B3
 Streatham SW16 182 A5
Braydon Rd N16 52 A1
Bray Dr E16 120 D6
Brayfield Terr N1 72 C1
Brayford Sq 12 E1 96 C1
Bray Pl SW3 114 D2 257 C3
Bray Rd NW7 28 D4
Brayton Gdns EN2 3 D1
Braywick Ct 9 KT2 176 C3
Braywood Rd SE9 145 B1
Brazier Cres UB5 85 B3
Brazil Cl CR0 204 A2
Breach La RM9 103 C4
Bread St EC2, EC4 242 B1
Breakspeare SE21 161 D1
Breakspear Jun & Inf Schs UB10 60 C6
Breakspear Rd HA4, UB9 38 D3
Breakspear Rd N UB9 38 B5
Breakspear Rd S UB9, UB10 38 C1
Breakspears Dr BR5 190 A2
Breakspears Mews SE4 141 C3
Breakspears Rd SE4 141 C2
Breakwell Ct 16 W10 91 A3
Bream Cl N17 52 B5
Bream Gdns E6 100 C4
Breamore Cl SW15 156 A3
Breamore Ct IG3 80 A6
Breamore Ho 21 SE15 140 A5
Breamore Rd IG3 79 D6
Bream's Bldgs EC4 94 C1 241 A2
Bream St E3 75 C1
Breamwater Gdns TW10 153 B1
Brearley Cl
 Burnt Oak HA8 27 A3
 Uxbridge UB8 60 A2
Breaside Prep Sch BR1 187 D2
Breasley Cl SW15 134 B1
Brechin Pl SW7 114 A2 256 B3
Brecknock Prim Sch N7 71 D2
Brecknock Rd N19 71 D3
Breckonmead BR1 187 C1
Brecon Cl Mitcham CR4 204 A6
 North Cheam KT4 216 C6
Brecon Ct
 7 Eltham SE9 166 C5
 Whetstone N12 14 A1
Brecon Gn NW9 45 C3
Brecon Ho
 Stamford Hill N16 51 D1
 Wandsworth SW18 157 C4
Brecon Rd Enfield EN3 6 C1
 Fulham W6 135 A6 264 B5
Brede Cl E6 100 C4
Bredel Ho 1 E14 97 C2
Bredgar SE13 163 D6
Bredgar Rd N19 71 C6
Bredhurst Cl SE20 184 C4
Bredinghurst SE22 162 A4
Bredinghurst Sch SE15 140 D1
Bredin Ho SW10 265 D4
Bredo Ho IG11 102 B4
Bredon Ct HA8 26 B6
Bredon Rd CR0 205 D2
Breer St SW6 135 D2
Breezer's Ct 22 E1 118 A6
Breezer's Hill E1 118 A6
Brehon Ho NW1 232 A5
Brember Rd HA2 64 A6
Bremer Mews E17 53 D5
Bremner Rd SW7 256 B6
Brenchley Cl
 Chislehurst BR7 188 C2
 Hayes BR2 208 D3
Brenchley Gdns SE15, SE22, SE23 162 D5
Brenchley Rd BR5 189 D1
Bren Ct 27 EN3 7 C6

Brenda Rd SW17 ... 158 D2
Brende Gdns KT8 ... 195 D5
Brendon Ave NW10 ... 67 C4
Brendon Cl Esher KT10 ... 212 A2
Harlington UB7 ... 127 A5
Brendon Ct
3 London N20 ... 14 C2
Southall UB2 ... 107 D2
Brendon Dr KT10 ... 212 A2
Brendon Gdns
Harrow HA2 ... 63 D4
Ilford IG2 ... 57 C4
Brendon Gr N2 ... 30 A1
Brendon Ho
Marylebone W1 ... 238 A4
Sutton SM2 ... 218 A2
Brendon Rd
Dagenham RM8 ... 59 C1
New Eltham SE9 ... 167 B2
Brendon St W1 ... 92 C1 237 B2
Brendon Villas N21 ... 17 A3
Brendon Way EN1 ... 17 C4
Brenley Cl CR4 ... 203 A6
Brenley Gdns SE9 ... 143 D1
Brenley Ho SE1 ... 252 C2
Brennands Ct 14 N19 ... 71 C5
Brent Adult Comm Education Service Coll NW10 ... 89 B6
Brent Cl DA5 ... 169 A3
Brentcot Cl W13 ... 87 B3
Brent Cres NW10 ... 88 B5
Brent Cross Flyover NW2, NW4 ... 46 D2
Brent Cross Gdns NW4 ... 46 D3
Brent Cross Interchange NW2, NW4 ... 46 D2
Brent Cross Sh Ctr NW4 ... 46 C2
Brent Cross Sta NW11 ... 46 D2
Brent Ct 5 Acton W12 ... 111 C3
Ealing W7 ... 108 B6
Hendon NW11 ... 46 D2
Brentfield NW10 ... 66 D1
Brentfield Cl NW10 ... 67 B2
Brentfield Gdns NW2 ... 46 D2
Brentfield Ho 7 NW10 ... 67 B1
Brentfield Prim Sch NW10 ... 67 B2
Brentfield Rd NW10 ... 67 B2
BRENTFORD ... 131 B6
Brentford Bsns Ctr TW8 ... 131 C5
Brentford Cl UB4 ... 84 D3
BRENTFORD END ... 131 C4
Brentford Fountain L Ctr W4 ... 110 C1
Brentford Ho 6 TW1 ... 153 B4
Brentford Sch for Girls TW8 ... 131 D6
Brentford Sta TW8 ... 131 C6
Brent Gn NW4 ... 46 D4
Brentham Way W5 ... 87 D3
Brent Ho
3 Catford BR1 ... 186 B5
18 Hackney E9 ... 74 C2
Wembley HA9 ... 66 B3
Brenthouse Rd E9 ... 74 C2
Brenthurst Rd NW10 ... 67 D2
Brent Knoll Sch SE26 ... 162 D1
Brent Lea TW8 ... 131 C5
Brent Mans NW4 ... 46 C4
Brentmead Cl W7 ... 108 C6
Brentmead Gdns NW10 ... 88 B5
Brentmead Pl NW11 ... 46 D3
Brent Mus* NW10 ... 68 B2
Brent New Ent Ctr NW10 ... 67 D2
Brenton Ct E9 ... 75 A3
Brenton St E14 ... 97 A1
Brent Park Ind Est UB2 ... 106 C3
Brent Park Rd NW4 ... 46 B2
Brent Pl EN5 ... 13 B6
Brent Rd
Brentford TW8 ... 131 C6
Newham E16 ... 99 A2
Southall UB2 ... 106 C3
Woolwich SE18 ... 144 D5
Brentside TW8 ... 131 C6
Brentside Cl W13 ... 87 A3
Brentside Executive Ctr TW8 ... 131 B6
Brentside High Sch W7 ... 86 C3
Brentside Prim Sch W7 ... 86 C3
Brent St NW4 ... 46 C4
Brent Trad Est NW10 ... 67 C3
Brentvale Ave
Southall UB1 ... 108 B5
Wembley HA0 ... 88 B6
Brent View Rd NW9 ... 46 A2
Brentwaters Bsns Pk TW8 ... 131 C5
Brent Way
Brentford TW8 ... 131 D5
Finchley N3 ... 29 C4
Wembley HA9 ... 66 D2
Brentwick Gdns TW8 ... 110 A2
Brentwood Cl SE9 ... 167 A3
Brentwood Ho 2 SE18 ... 143 D5
Brentwood Lo NW4 ... 46 D4
Brereton Ho 4 SW2 ... 160 C4
Brereton Rd N17 ... 33 D3
Bressenden Pl SW1 ... 115 C3 259 A6
Bressey Ave EN1 ... 6 A4
Bressey Gr E18 ... 36 D1
Bretherton Ct CR2 ... 221 C2
Breton Ho
Bermondsey SE1 ... 263 C6
St Luke's EC2 ... 242 B5
Brett Cl 15 Northolt UB5 ... 84 D4
Stoke Newington N16 ... 73 C6
Brett Cres NW10 ... 89 B6
Brett Ct N9 ... 18 C2
Brettell St SE17 ... 262 D1
Brettenham Ave E17 ... 35 C2
Brettenham Prim Sch N18 ... 34 A6
Brettenham Rd
Edmonton N18 ... 34 A6
Walthamstow E17 ... 35 C2
Brett Ho 1 SW15 ... 156 D4
Brett House Cl 2 SW15 ... 156 D4
Brettinghurst 8 SE1 ... 118 A1
Bretton Ho N19 ... 50 A1
Brett Pas 28 E8 ... 74 B3
Brett Rd Barnet EN5 ... 12 C6
Hackney E8 ... 74 B3
Brewers Bldgs EC1 ... 234 C2
Brewers Ct W2 ... 236 A2
Brewer's Gn SW1 ... 259 C6
Brewers Hall Gdns EC2 ... 242 B3
Brewers La 11 TW9 ... 153 D6
Brewer St W1 ... 115 C6 249 B6
Brewery Cl HA0 ... 65 A4
Brewery Ind Est The N1 ... 235 B3
Brewery Mews Bsns Ctr 1 TW7 ... 131 A2
Brewery Rd Islington N7 ... 72 A2
Keston Mark BR2 ... 210 A1
Plumstead SE18 ... 123 B1
Brewery Sq
Bermondsey SE1 ... 253 C3
Clerkenwell EC1 ... 241 D6
Brewhouse La
Putney SW15 ... 135 A2
Wapping E1 ... 118 B5
Brewhouse Rd 3 SE18 ... 122 B2
Brewhouse Wlk SE16 ... 119 A5
Brewhouse Yd EC1 ... 241 C6
Brewood Rd RM8 ... 80 B2
Brewster Gdns W10 ... 90 C2
Brewster Ho
Bermondsey SE1 ... 263 D4
Poplar E14 ... 119 B6
Brewster Rd E10 ... 53 D1
Brian Ct N10 ... 31 B2
Brian Rd RM6 ... 58 C4
Briant Ho SE1 ... 260 D5
Briants Cl HA5 ... 23 B1
Briant St SE14 ... 140 D5
Briar Ave SW16 ... 182 B3
Briarbank Rd W13 ... 87 A1
Briar Cl
Buckhurst Hill IG9 ... 21 D2
Edmonton N13 ... 17 A1
Finchley N2 ... 30 A1
Hampton TW12 ... 173 B5
Isleworth TW7 ... 152 D6
Briar Cres UB5 ... 63 D2
Briar Ct 7 Bow E3 ... 97 C5
Cheam SM3 ... 216 C4
Dalston E8 ... 73 D1
Hampton TW12 ... 173 D5
Leytonstone E11 ... 54 B2
Briardale Edgware HA8 ... 27 B6
Wandsworth SW19 ... 157 B3
Briardale Gdns NW3 ... 69 C5
Briardale Ho 12 N16 ... 51 C1
Briarfield Ave N3 ... 29 D1
Briarfield Cl DA7 ... 147 C3
Briar Gdns BR2 ... 208 D1
Briaris Cl 11 N17 ... 34 B3
Briar La CR0 ... 223 D4
Briar Lo E18 ... 37 C2
Briar Rd
Cricklewood NW2 ... 68 C4
Harrow HA3 ... 43 C4
Littleton TW17 ... 192 C4
Thornton Heath SW16 ... 204 B6
Twickenham TW2 ... 152 C3
Briars The WD23 ... 8 C4
Briarswood Way BR6 ... 227 D3
Briar The 11 SM1 ... 218 A4
Briarview Ct E4 ... 36 B4
Briar Way UB7 ... 104 C4
Briar Wlk Burnt Oak HA8 ... 27 A3
Putney SW15 ... 134 B1
West Kilburn W10 ... 91 A3
Briarwood Cl
Feltham TW13 ... 149 C1
Kingsbury NW9 ... 45 A3
Briarwood Ct 5 KT4 ... 200 A1
Briarwood Dr HA6 ... 22 A1
Briarwood Rd
London SW4 ... 159 D6
Stoneleigh KT17 ... 216 A2
Briary Cl NW3 ... 70 C1
Briary Ct
10 Canning Town E16 ... 98 D1
Sidcup DA14 ... 190 B5
Briary Gdns BR1 ... 187 B5
Briary Gr HA8 ... 26 D1
Briary La N9 ... 17 D1
Briary Lo BR3 ... 186 A2
Brickbarn Cl SW10 ... 266 B4
Brick Ct EC4 ... 241 A1
Brickett Cl HA4 ... 39 A4
Brick Farm Cl TW9 ... 132 D4
Brickfield Cl TW8 ... 131 C5
Brickfield Cotts SE18 ... 145 D6
Brickfield Farm Gdns BR6 ... 227 A4
Brickfield La
Edgware EN5 ... 11 D5
Harlington UB3 ... 127 B6
Brickfield Rd
South Norwood CR7, SW16 ... 182 D2
Wimbledon SW19 ... 179 D6
Brickfields HA2 ... 64 B6
Brickfields Way UB7 ... 104 B3
Brick La Enfield EN1 ... 6 B3
Northolt UB5 ... 85 B4
Shoreditch E2 ... 95 D4
Spitalfields E1 ... 95 D3 243 D5
Stanmore HA7 ... 25 D3
Bricklayers Arms SE1 ... 262 D5
Brick St W1 ... 115 B5 248 C3
Brickwall La HA4 ... 39 D1
Brickwood Cl SE26 ... 162 B1
Brickwood Rd CR0 ... 221 C6
Brickworth Ho 26 SW9 ... 138 C4
Brideale Cl SE15 ... 139 D6
Bride Ct EC4 ... 241 C1
Bride La EC4 ... 94 D1 241 C1
Bridel Mews N1 ... 234 C5
Bride St N7 ... 72 B2
Bridewain St SE1 ... 263 C6
Bridewell Pl
Holborn EC4 ... 241 C1
20 Wapping E1 ... 118 B5
Bridford Mews W1 ... 238 D4
Bridge App NW3 ... 71 A1
Bridge Ave Ealing W7 ... 86 B2
Hammersmith W6 ... 112 C1
Bridge Avenue Mans 1 W6 ... 112 C1
Bridge Bsns Ctr The UB2 ... 107 C4
Bridge Cl Enfield EN1 ... 6 B3
13 North Kensington W10 ... 90 D1
Teddington TW11 ... 174 D6
Walton-on-T KT12 ... 193 D1
Bridge Ct
9 Blackwall E14 ... 120 B6
Leyton E10 ... 53 B2
2 Walton-on-T KT12 ... 193 D1
7 Willesden NW10 ... 67 C1
Bridge Dr N13 ... 32 B6
Bridge End E17 ... 36 A2
Bridge Field Ho 7 W2 ... 91 D1
Bridgefield Rd SM1 ... 217 C2
Bridgefoot SE1 ... 116 A1 260 B1
Bridge Gate N21 ... 17 A4
Bridge Gdns
Canonbury N16 ... 73 B4
East Molesey KT8 ... 196 B5
Littleton TW15 ... 171 A3
Bridge Ho Brockley SE4 ... 141 B1
1 Camden Town NW1 ... 71 A1
Ealing TW3 ... 109 A2
Homerton E9 ... 74 D3
Woolwich SE28 ... 123 C5
Bridge Ho S TW8 ... 109 A2
Bridge House Quay E14 ... 120 A5
Bridge La
Battersea SW11 ... 136 C4 267 B1
Temple Fortune NW11 ... 47 B4
Bridgeland Rd E16 ... 121 A6
Bridgelands Cl BR3 ... 185 B3
Bridgeman Ho 19 E9 ... 74 C1
Bridgeman Rd
Islington N1 ... 72 B1
Teddington TW11 ... 175 A4
Bridgeman St NW8 ... 92 C5 230 A3
Bridge Meadows SE14 ... 140 D6
Bridgend Rd SW18 ... 136 A1
Bridgenhall Rd EN1 ... 5 D4
Bridgen Ho 9 E1 ... 96 B1
Bridgen Rd DA5 ... 169 A4
Bridge Par
7 Croydon CR0 ... 220 D5
Edmonton N21 ... 17 A4
Bridge Pk
7 London SW18 ... 157 C6
Wembley NW10 ... 66 D1
Bridge Pl
Belgravia SW1 ... 115 B2 258 D4
Croydon CR0 ... 205 B1
Bridgepoint Lofts 2 E7 ... 77 C1
Bridgeport Pl 4 E1 ... 118 A5
Bridge Rd
Beckenham BR3 ... 185 B3
Bexleyheath DA7 ... 147 A3
Chessington KT9 ... 214 A3
East Ham E6 ... 78 B1
East Molesey KT8 ... 196 C5
Isleworth TW3, TW7 ... 130 B2
Southall UB2 ... 107 C4
Stratford Marsh E15 ... 98 B6
Sutton SM2 ... 217 D2
Twickenham TW1 ... 153 B5
Wallington SM6 ... 219 C3
Walthamstow E17 ... 53 B2
Wembley HA9 ... 66 C5
Willesden NW10 ... 67 C2
Wood Green N22 ... 32 A2
Bridge Row CR0 ... 205 B1
Bridge Sch The
Clerkenwell EC1 ... 94 D3 241 C6
Shoreditch N1 ... 95 A6 235 B6
Bridges Ct SW11 ... 136 B3
Bridges Ho 15 SE5 ... 139 B5
Bridges La CR0 ... 220 A4
Bridges Rd
Stanmore HA7 ... 24 D5
Wimbledon SW19 ... 179 D4
Bridges Road Mews SW19 ... 179 D4
Bridge St Chiswick W4 ... 111 B2
Pinner HA5 ... 41 A6
Richmond TW10 ... 153 D6
Walton-on-T KT12 ... 193 D2
Westminster SW1 ... 116 A4 250 B1
Bridges The NW4 ... 46 A6
Bridge Terr E15 ... 76 B1
Bridge The HA3 ... 42 D5
Bridgetown Cl 5 SE19 ... 183 C5
Bridgeview 2 W6 ... 112 C1
Bridgewater Cl BR7 ... 211 C6
Bridgewater Ct HA0 ... 65 C2
Bridgewater Gdns HA8 ... 26 B1
Bridgewater Ho UB5 ... 85 A3
Bridgewater Rd
Ruislip HA4 ... 62 B4
Stratford Marsh E15 ... 98 A6
Wembley HA0 ... 65 C1
Bridgewater Sq EC2 ... 242 A4
Bridgewater St EC2 ... 242 A4
Bridgeway Barking IG11 ... 79 D1
Wembley HA0 ... 66 B1
Bridge Way
London NW11 ... 47 B4
Twickenham TW2 ... 152 A4
Uxbridge UB10 ... 60 D3
Bridgeway St NW1 ... 93 C5 232 B3
Bridge Wharf 18 E2 ... 96 D5
Bridge Wharf Rd TW7 ... 131 B2
Bridgewood Cl SE20 ... 184 B3
Bridgewood Rd
North Cheam KT17, KT4 ... 216 A4
Streatham SW16 ... 181 D3
Bridge Yd SE1 ... 252 D4
Bridgford St SW17, SW18 ... 158 A1
Bridgman Rd W4 ... 111 A3
Bridgnorth Ho 10 SE15 ... 140 A6
Bridgwater Ho W2 ... 236 A2
Bridle Cl Enfield EN3 ... 7 B6
Kingston u T KT1 ... 197 D5
Sunbury TW16 ... 194 A6
West Ewell KT19 ... 215 B3
Bridle La
Marylebone W1 ... 115 C6 249 B6
Twickenham TW1 ... 153 B5
Bridle Path CR0 ... 220 A5
Bridle Path The IG8 ... 36 C3
Bridlepath Way TW14 ... 149 C3
Bridle Rd
Addington CR0 ... 223 C4
Claygate KT10 ... 213 B2
Croydon CR0 ... 223 C6
Pinner HA5 ... 40 C4
Bridle Way
Addington CR0 ... 223 C3
Orpington BR6 ... 227 A4
Bridle Way The SM6 ... 219 C3
Bridlington Ho SW18 ... 136 A1
Bridlington Rd N9 ... 18 B4
Bridport SE17 ... 262 B1
Bridport Ave RM7 ... 59 D3
Bridport Ho
6 Edmonton N18 ... 34 A5
Shoreditch N1 ... 235 D5
Bridport Pl N1 ... 95 B6 235 D5
Bridport Rd
Edmonton N18 ... 33 D5
Greenford UB6 ... 85 D6
Thornton Heath CR7 ... 204 D6
Bridstow Pl W2 ... 91 C1
Brief St SE5 ... 138 D4
Brierfield NW1 ... 232 A5
Brierley CR0 ... 223 D2
Brierley Ave N9 ... 18 C3
Brierley Cl SE25 ... 206 A5
Brierley Ct W7 ... 108 C6
Brierley Rd Leyton E11 ... 76 B4
Upper Tooting SW12 ... 159 C2
Brierly Gdns E2 ... 96 C5
Brigade Cl HA2 ... 64 B6
Brigade St SE3 ... 142 D3
Brigadier Ave EN2 ... 5 A4
Brigadier Hill EN2 ... 5 A5
Briggeford Cl 5 E5 ... 74 A6
Briggs Cl CR4 ... 181 B2
Briggs Ho 20 E2 ... 95 D4
Bright Cl DA17 ... 124 D2
Bright Ct 8 SE28 ... 124 C5
Brightfield Rd SE12 ... 164 D6
Brightling Rd SE4 ... 163 B5
Brightlingsea Pl 5 E14 ... 119 B6
Brightman Rd SW18 ... 158 B3
Brighton Ave E17 ... 53 B4
Brighton Bldgs SE1 ... 263 A5
Brighton Cl UB10 ... 60 D1
Brighton Ct SW15 ... 157 B5
Brighton Dr 3 UB5 ... 63 C2
Brighton Gr SE14 ... 141 A4
Brighton Ho 7 SE5 ... 139 B4
Brighton Rd
Belmont SM2 ... 217 D1
Finchley N2 ... 30 A1
South Croydon CR2 ... 221 B2
Stoke Newington N16 ... 73 C4
Surbiton KT6 ... 197 D3
Sutton SM2 ... 218 A1
Wallend E6 ... 100 C4
Brighton Terr SW9 ... 138 B1
Brightside Rd SE13 ... 164 B5
Brightside The EN3 ... 7 A4
Bright St E14 ... 97 D2
Brightwell Cl CR0 ... 204 C1
Brightwell Cres SW17 ... 180 D5
Brightwell Ct N7 ... 72 B3
Brightwells 1 SW6 ... 135 D3
Brig Mews SE8 ... 141 C6
Brigstock Ho SE5 ... 139 A3
Brigstock Par 1 CR7 ... 204 C4
Brigstock Rd
Belvedere DA17 ... 125 D2
Thornton Heath CR7 ... 204 D4
Brill Ho NW10 ... 67 B5
Brill Pl NW1 ... 93 D5 232 D3
Brim Hill N2 ... 48 B5
Brimpsfield Cl SE2 ... 124 B3
BRIMSDOWN ... 7 B3
Brimsdown Ave EN3 ... 7 A4
Brimsdown Ho E3 ... 98 A3
Brimsdown Jun & Inf Sch EN3 ... 6 D2
Brimsdown Sta EN3 ... 7 A3
Brimstone Ho 4 E15 ... 76 C1
Brindishe Prim Sch SE12 ... 164 D6
Brindle Gate DA15 ... 167 C3
Brindley Cl
Bexleyheath DA7 ... 147 D2
Wembley HA0 ... 87 D6
Brindley Ho
Carshalton SM1 ... 218 C3
37 Notting Hill W2 ... 91 C2
22 Streatham SW12 ... 160 A4
Brindley St SE14 ... 141 B4
Brindley Way
Bromley BR1 ... 187 B5
Southall UB1 ... 107 D6
Brindwood Rd E4 ... 19 C1
Brine Ct KT6 ... 197 D4
Brine Ho 11 E3 ... 97 A5
Brinkburn Cl
Abbey Wood SE2 ... 124 A2
Edgware HA8 ... 44 D6
Brinkburn Gdns HA8 ... 44 C6
Brinkley 18 KT1 ... 176 C1
Brinkley Rd KT4 ... 216 B6
Brinklow Cres SE18 ... 144 D5
Brinklow Ho W2 ... 91 D2
Brinkworth Rd IG5 ... 56 A6
Brinkworth Way E9 ... 75 B2
Brinsdale Rd NW4 ... 46 D6
Brinsley Ho 17 E1 ... 96 C1
Brinsley Rd HA3 ... 24 B1
Brinsley St 35 E1 ... 96 B1
Brinsworth Cl TW2 ... 152 B2
Brinton Wlk SE1 ... 251 C3
Brion Pl E14 ... 98 A2
Brisbane Ave SW19 ... 179 D2
Brisbane Ct N10 ... 31 B3
Brisbane Ho 8 W12 ... 112 B6
Brisbane Rd
Ealing W13 ... 109 A4
Ilford IG1 ... 57 A1
Leyton E10 ... 75 D6
Brisbane St SE5 ... 139 B5
Briscoe Cl E11 ... 76 D6
Briscoe Rd SW19 ... 180 B4
Briset Rd SE9 ... 143 D1
Briset St EC1 ... 94 D3 241 C5
Briset Way N7 ... 72 B6
Bristol Cl
Stanwell TW19 ... 148 A5
Wallington SM6 ... 220 A1
Bristol Ct 11 TW19 ... 148 A5
Bristol Gdns
Putney SW15 ... 156 C4
Westbourne Green W9 ... 91 D3
Bristol Ho
1 Barking IG11 ... 80 A1
SE11 ... 261 A5
Bristol Mews W9 ... 91 D3
Bristol Park Rd 1 E17 ... 53 A5
Bristol Rd
Greenford UB6 ... 85 D6
Morden SM4 ... 202 A4
Upton E7 ... 77 D2
Briston Gr N8 ... 50 A3
Briston Mews NW7 ... 28 A3
Bristowe Cl 24 SW2 ... 160 C5
Bristow Rd
Bexleyheath DA7 ... 147 A4
Hounslow TW3 ... 130 A2
Wallington CR0 ... 220 A4
West Norwood SE19 ... 183 C5
Britain at War Experience* SE1 ... 253 A3
Britannia Building N1 ... 235 C2
Britannia Cl
London SW4 ... 137 D1
Northolt UB5 ... 85 A4
Britannia Gate 11 E16 ... 121 A5
Britannia Ho N20 ... 14 A1
Britannia Junc NW1 ... 231 D6
Britannia La TW2 ... 152 A4
Britannia Rd Ilford IG1 ... 78 D5
23 Millwall E14 ... 119 C2
Surbiton KT5 ... 198 B2
Walham Green SW6 ... 135 D5 265 C3
Britannia Rd *continued*
Whetstone N12 ... 14 A1
Britannia Row N1 ... 95 A6 235 A6
Britannia St WC1 ... 94 B4 233 C2
Britannia Village Prim Sch E16 ... 121 B5
Britannia Way NW10 ... 88 D3
Britannia Wlk N1 ... 235 C2
British Coll of Osteopathic Medicine NW3 ... 70 A2
British Gr W4 ... 111 D1
British Grove Pas 2 W4 ... 111 D1
British Grove S 3 W4 ... 111 D1
British Home & Hospl for Incurables SE27 ... 182 D5
British Legion Rd E4 ... 20 D2
British Library (Newspaper Library) NW9 ... 45 C6
British Library The* WC1 ... 93 D4 232 D2
British Mus* WC1 ... 94 A2 240 A3
British St E3 ... 97 B4
British Wharf Ind Est SE14 ... 140 D6
Britley Ho 16 E14 ... 97 B1
Brittain Ct SE9 ... 166 A3
Brittain Rd RM8 ... 81 B5
Brittany Ho SW15 ... 134 C1
Brittany Point SE11 ... 261 A3
Britten Cl Elstree WD6 ... 9 D5
Golders Green NW11 ... 47 D1
Brittenden Cl 1 BR6 ... 227 D2
Brittenden Par BR6 ... 227 D2
Britten Dr UB1 ... 85 C1
Britten Ho SW3 ... 257 B2
Britten St SW3 ... 114 C1 257 A2
Britton Cl SE6 ... 164 B4
Britton St EC1 ... 94 D3 241 C5
Brixham Cres HA4 ... 40 A1
Brixham Gdns IG3 ... 79 C3
Brixham Rd DA16 ... 146 D4
Brixham St E16 ... 122 C5
BRIXTON ... 138 C2
Brixton Day Coll SW9 ... 138 A2
Brixton Hill SW2 ... 160 B5
Brixton Hill Ct 5 SW2 ... 160 B6
Brixton Hill Pl SW2 ... 160 A4
Brixton Mkt SW9 ... 138 C1
Brixton Oval 7 SW2 ... 138 C1
Brixton Rd SW9 ... 138 C4
Brixton Sta SW9 ... 138 C1
Brixton Station Rd SW9 ... 138 C2
Brixton Water La SW2 ... 160 B6
Broadacre Cl UB10 ... 60 D5
Broadbent Cl N6 ... 49 B1
Broadbent St W1 ... 248 C6
Broadberry Ct N18 ... 34 B5
Broadbridge Cl SE3 ... 143 A5
Broad Common Est N16 ... 52 A1
Broadcoombe CR2 ... 222 D1
Broadcroft Ave HA7 ... 25 D1
Broadcroft Rd BR5 ... 211 B2
Broad Ct WC2 ... 240 B1
Broadeaves Cl CR2 ... 221 C3
Broadfield NW6 ... 69 D2
Broadfield Cl
Croydon CR0 ... 220 B6
Dollis Hill NW2 ... 68 C5
Broadfield Ct
Bushey WD23 ... 8 C2
Edgware HA8 ... 10 D1
Broadfield La NW1 ... 72 A1
Broadfield Rd SE6 ... 164 C3
Broadfields Harrow HA2 ... 23 D1
Thames Ditton KT8 ... 196 C3
Broadfields Ave
Edgware HA8 ... 10 D1
Southgate N21 ... 16 C4
Broadfields Hts HA8 ... 26 D6
Broadfields Prim Sch HA8 ... 10 C2
Broadfield Sq EN1 ... 6 B3
Broadfields Way NW10 ... 67 D3
Broadfield Way IG9 ... 21 C1
Broadford Ho 12 E1 ... 97 A3
BROADGATE ... 95 C2
Broadgate EC2 ... 95 C2 243 A4
Broadgate Circ EC2 ... 95 C2 243 A3
Broadgate Rd E16 ... 99 D1
Broadgates Ave EN4 ... 1 D4
Broadgates Ct SE11 ... 261 B1
Broadgates Rd SW18 ... 158 B3
BROAD GREEN ... 204 D3
Broad Green Ave CR0 ... 204 D2
Broadhead Strand NW9 ... 27 D2
Broadheath Dr BR7 ... 188 B5
Broadhinton Rd SW4 ... 137 C2
Broadhurst Ave
Edgware HA8 ... 26 D6
Ilford IG3 ... 79 D4
Broadhurst Cl
Hampstead NW6 ... 70 A2
9 Richmond TW10 ... 154 B6
Broadhurst Gdns
Hampstead NW6 ... 69 D2
Ruislip HA4 ... 62 C6
Broadhurst Mans NW6 ... 69 D2
Broad La Broadgate EC2 ... 243 A4
Hampton TW12 ... 173 C4
Hornsey Vale N8 ... 50 B4
South Tottenham N15 ... 51 D5

Broad La continued
South Tottenham N15 . . . . . . **52** A5

Broadlands
Feltham TW13 . . . . **151** C1
Highgate N6 . . . . **49** A2

Broadlands Ave
Enfield EN3 . . . . **6** B2
Shepperton TW17 . . . . . . **193** A3
Streatham SW16 . . . . **160** A2

Broadlands Cl
Enfield EN3 . . . . **6** C2
Highgate N6 . . . . **49** A2
Streatham SW16 . . . . **160** A2

Broadlands Ct TW9 . . . . . **132** C5
Broadlands Lo N6 . . . . . . **48** D2
Broadlands Mans 2
SW16 . . . . **160** A2

Broadlands Rd
Grove Pk BR1 . . . . **187** B6
Highgate N6 . . . . **48** D2

Broadlands Way KT3 . . . **199** D3
Broad Lawn SE9 . . . . . . **166** C3
Broadlawns Ct HA3 . . . . **24** D2
Broadley St
NW8 . . . . **92** C2 **237** A4
Broadley Terr
NW1 . . . . **92** C3 **237** B5
Broadmayne SE17 . . . . . **262** C2
Broadmead
Catford SE6 . . . . **163** C1
Hampton TW12 . . . . **173** C4
West Kensington W14 . . . **254** A3
Broadmead Cl
Hampton TW12 . . . . **173** C4
Pinner HA5 . . . . **23** A3
Broadmead Ct 6 IG8 . . . **37** A4
Broadmead Inf Sch
CR0 . . . . **205** B2
Broadmead Jun Sch
CR0 . . . . **205** B3
Broadmead Rd
Northolt UB5 . . . . **85** A3
Woodford IG8 . . . . **37** B3
Broad Oak
Ashford TW16 . . . . **171** D4
Woodford IG8 . . . . **37** B5
Broad Oak Cl
Chingford E4 . . . . **35** C5
St Paul's Cray BR5 . . . . . **190** A1
Broadoak Ct 8 SW9 . . . . **138** C2
Broadoak Ho 11 NW6 . . . **91** D6
Broadoaks BR7 . . . . **188** D4
Broad Oaks KT6 . . . . . . **214** D6
Broadoaks Way BR2 . . . **208** D4
Broad St Ave EC2 . . . . . **243** A3
Broad Sanctuary SW1 . . **250** A1
Broad St
Dagenham RM10 . . . . **81** C1
Teddington TW11 . . . . . . **174** D4
Broadstone Ho SW8 . . . **270** C3
Broadstone Pl W1 . . . . . **238** A3
Broad Street Health Ctr
RM10 . . . . **103** C6
Broad Street Pl EC2. . . . **242** D3
Broadview NW9 . . . . **44** C3
Broadview Est TW19 . . . **148** C4
Broadview Ho RM8 . . . . . **58** D1
Broadview Rd SW16 . . . **181** D3
Broadwalk Harrow HA2 . . **41** D4
Snaresbrook E18. . . . . **54** D6
Broadwalk Ho SW7 . . . . **246** A1
Broadwalk La NW11 . . . . **47** B2
Broadwalk Sh Ctr The
HA8 . . . . **26** D4
Broadwall SE1 . . **116** C5 **251** B4
Broadwater Farm Prim
Sch N17 . . . . **33** B1
Broadwater Gdns BR6 . . **227** A4
Broadwater Prim Sch
SW17 . . . . **180** C6
Broadwater Rd
Plumstead SE18 . . . . **123** B3
Tottenham N17 . . . . **33** C1
Upper Tooting SW17 . . . . **180** C6
Broadway
Barking IG11 . . . . **101** A6
Bexley DA6 . . . . **147** C1
Bexleyheath DA6 . . . . . . **147** B1
Hanwell W7 . . . . **108** C5
Stratford E15 . . . . **76** B1
West Ealing W13 . . . . . . **109** A5
Westminster
SW1 . . . . . **115** D3 **259** C6
Broadway Arc 3 W6. . . . **112** C2
Broadway Ave
Thornton Heath CR0 . . . . **205** B4
Twickenham TW1. . . . . . . **153** B5
Broadway Bldgs 5
W7. . . . . **108** C5
Broadway Cl IG8 . . . . **37** B4
Broadway Ct
Beckenham BR3 . . . . **208** A6
Wimbledon SW19 . . . . . . **179** C4
Broadway Ctr The 6
W6 . . . . **112** C2
Broadway Gdns
Mitcham CR4 . . . . **202** C5
Woodford IG8 . . . . **37** B4
Broadway Ho 5
SW19 . . . . **179** C3
Broadway Lofts SW17 . . **180** C6
Broadway Mans SW6. . . **265** B3
Broadway Market E8 . . . **96 B6
Broadway Market Mews 21
E8 . . . . **96** A6
Broadway Mews
Bowes Pk N13. . . . . **32** B5
Southgate N21 . . . . **16** D3

Broadway Mews continued
Stamford Hill E5 . . . . **51** D2
Broadway Par
Chingford E4 . . . . **36** A4
Hayes UB3. . . . . **106** A5
Hornsey N8 . . . . **50** A3
West Drayton UB7 . . . . . **104** A4
Broadway Pl SW19. . . . . **179** C4
Broadway Ret Pk NW2. . . **68** D4
Broadway Sh Ctr 5
DA6. . . . . **147** C1
Broadway The
Barnes SW13 . . . . **133** C3
Cheam SM3 . . . . **217** A2
Chingford E4 . . . . **36** B4
Dagenham RM8. . . . . **81** C6
Ealing W5 . . . . **109** D6
Edmonton N9. . . . . **18** A1
Friern Barnet N11. . . . . . . **31** A3
Greenford UB6 . . . . **86** A3
Harrow HA3 . . . . **24** D1
Hornsey N8 . . . . **50** A3
Merton SW19 . . . . **179** C3
Newham E13. . . . . **99** B5
Pinner HA5 . . . . **23** B3
South Acton W3. . . . . **110** C4
Southall UB1 . . . . **107** A6
2 Southgate N14. . . . . . . **15** D3
Stanmore HA7. . . . . **25** C5
Sutton SM1 . . . . **218** A4
Thames Ditton KT10 . . . . **196** C1
Tolworth KT6. . . . . **198** C1
Wallington SM6. . . . . **220** A4
Wembley HA9 . . . . **66** A5
Woodford IG8 . . . . **37** B4
Wood Green N22. . . . . **32** C1
Broadway Wlk 4 E14 . . . **119** C3
Broadwell Ct TW5 . . . . . **128** D4
Broadwick St
W1. . . . . **93** C1 **239** B1
Broad Wlk
Eltham SE3, SE18 . . . . . . **144** A3
Heston TW5. . . . . **129** A4
Mayfair W1 . . . **115** A5 **248** A4
Regent's Pk
NW1. . . . . **93** A3 **231** B3
Richmond TW9 . . . . **132** B5
Southgate N21 . . . . **16** B3
Broad Wlk The
W8. . . . . **113** D5 **245** D3
Broadwood Ave HA4 . . . . **39** C3
Broadwood Terr W14 . . . **254** A3
Broad Yd EC1. . . . . **241** C5
Brocade Ct NW9 . . . . **45** C5
Brocas Cl NW3 . . . . **70** C1
Brockbridge Ho
SW15. . . . . **155** D5
Brockdene Dr BR2 . . . . . **225** D4
Brockdish Ave IG11. . . . . **79** D3
Brockelbank Lo RM8. . . . **80** D6
Brockenhurst KT8 . . . . . **195** B3
Brockenhurst Ave
KT4 . . . . **199** C1
Brockenhurst Gdns
Edgware NW7 . . . . **27** C5
Ilford IG1 . . . . **79** A3
Brockenhurst Mews 9
N18 . . . . **34** A6
Brockenhurst Rd CR0 . . **206** B2
Brockenhurst Way
SW16. . . . . **181** D1
Brocket Ho 8 SW8 . . . . . **137** D3
Brockham Cres CR0. . . . **224** B1
Brockham Ct
17 Belmont SM2 . . . . **217** D1
8 South Croydon CR2 . . . **221** A3
Brockham Dr Ilford IG2 . . **57** A4
Streatham SW2 . . . . **160** B4
Brockham Ho
Camden Town NW1. . . . . **232** B5
11 Streatham SW2. . . . . **160** B4
Brockham St SE1 . . . . . . **262** B6
Brockhurst Cl HA1 . . . . . . **24** D4
Brockhurst Ho N4 . . . . **51** B2
Brockill Cres SE4 . . . . . **141** A1
Brocklebank Ho 7
E16 . . . . **122** C5
Brocklebank Rd
Greenwich SE7 . . . . **121** B2
Wandsworth SW18 . . . . . **158** A4
Brocklebank Road Ind Est
SE7. . . . . **121** A2
Brocklehurst St SE14. . . **140** D5
Brocklesby Rd SE25. . . . **206** B5
BROCKLEY **141** B1
Brockley Ave HA7. . . . . . . **10** A1
Brockley Cl HA7 . . . . **26** A6
Brockley Cross SE4 . . . . **141** B2
Brockley Cross Bsns Ctr
SE4. . . . . **141** A2
Brockley Gdns SE4. . . . . **141** B3
Brockley Gr SE4 . . . . **163** B6
Brockley Hall Rd SE4. . . **163** A6
Brockley Hill HA7, HA8. . . **9** D2
Brockley Hill Ho HA7. . . . . **9** C3
Brockley Ho SE17. . . . . . **263** A2
Brockley Mews SE4 . . . . **163** A6
Brockley Pk SE23 . . . . . . **163** A4
Brockley Prim Sch
SE4. . . . . **163** B6
Brockley Rd SE4. . . . . . . **163** B6
Brockley Rise SE23 . . . . **163** B4
Brockleyside HA7. . . . . . . **26** A6
Brockley Sta SE4 . . . . . . **141** A2
Brockley View SE23. . . . **163** A4
Brockley Way SE4 . . . . . **163** A6
Brockman Rise BR1. . . . **186** B6
Brockmer Ho 5 E1. . . . . **118** B6

Brock Pl E3 . . . . **97** D3
Brock Rd E13. . . . . **99** B2
Brocks Dr SM3 . . . . **217** A5
Brockshot Cl 1 TW8. . . . **131** D6
Brock St SE15 . . . . **140** C2
Brockway Cl E11. . . . . **76** C6
Brockweir 28 E2 . . . . **96** C5
Brockwell Ave BR3. . . . . **207** D4
Brockweir Cl BR5 . . . . . . **211** D4
Brockwell Ct
2 London SW2. . . . . **160** C4
Thornton Heath CR0 . . . . **204** D2
Brockwell Ho SE11. . . . . **270** A1
Brockwell Park*
SE24. . . . . **160** D5
Brockwell Park Gdns
SE24. . . . . **160** D5
Brockwell Park Row
SW2. . . . . **160** C5
Brockworth 8 KT2 . . . . . **176** D2
Broderick Ho SE21. . . . . **161** C1
Brodia Rd N16 . . . . **73** C5
Brodick Ho 12 E3 . . . . **97** B5
Brodie Ct E10 . . . . **54** B1
Brodie Ho
Bermondsey SE1. . . . . . . **263** D2
7 Wallington SM6. . . . . . **219** B4
Brodie Rd Chingford E4. . . **20** A2
Enfield EN2 . . . . **5** A5
Brodie St SE1. . . **117** D1 **263** D2
Brodlove La E1 . . . . **118** D6
Brodrick Gr SE2 . . . . **124** B2
Brodrick Rd SW17 . . . . . **158** C2
Brody Ho E1. . . . . **243** C3
Brograve Gdns BR3. . . . . **185** D1
Broken Wharf EC4 . . . . . **252** A6
Brokesley St E3 . . . . **97** B4
Broke Wlk Hackney E8 . . . **95** D6
1 Hackney E8 . . . . **96** A6
Bromar Rd SE5 . . . . **139** C2
Bromborough Gn
WD19 . . . . **22** C5
Bromefield HA7. . . . . **25** C2
Bromehead St 8 E1. . . . . **96** C1
Bromell's Rd SW4 . . . . . **137** C1
Brome Rd SE9 . . . . **144** B2
Bromfelde Rd SW4. . . . . **137** D3
Bromfield Ct 20 SE16. . . **118** A3
Bromfield St N1 . . . . **234** B4
Bromhall Rd RM8 . . . . **80** B2
Bromhedge SE9 . . . . **166** B1
Bromholm Rd SE2 . . . . . **124** B3
Bromleigh Ct 1 SE21,
SE22 . . . . **162** B2
Bromleigh Ho SE1 . . . . . **263** C6
BROMLEY BR1. . . . . **186** C2
Bromley Ave BR1. . . . . . . **186** C3
Bromley-by-Bow Sta
E3. **98** A4
Bromley Coll BR1. . . . . . . **187** A2
Bromley Coll of F & H Ed
BR2. . . . . **209** D3
Bromley Comm BR2 . . . . **209** D4
BROMLEY COMMON . . **210** A3
Bromley Cres
Beckenham BR2 . . . . **208** C6
Ruislip HA4 . . . . **61** D4
Bromley Ct BR1. . . . . **186** D3
Bromley Gdns BR2. . . . . **208** D6
Bromley Gr BR2 . . . . **208** A6
Bromley Hall Rd E14. . . . . **98** A2
Bromley High Sch
BR1. . . . . **210** C5
Bromley High St E3 . . . . . **97** D4
Bromley Hill BR1. . . . . . . **186** C4
Bromley Ho 5 BR1 . . . . . **187** A2
Bromley Ind Ctr BR1. . . . **209** D6
Bromley La BR7. . . . . **189** B3
Bromley Lo 2 W3 . . . . **89** A1
Bromley Manor Mans 3
BR1. . . . . **209** A6
Bromley North Sta
BR1. . . . . **187** A2
BROMLEY PARK **186** D2
Bromley Pk 11 BR1. . . . . **186** D2
Bromley Pl W1 . . . . **239** A4
Bromley Rd
Beckenham BR3 . . . . **185** D2
Bromley BR2, BR3. . . . . . **186** B1
Catford SE6. . . . . **163** D1
Chislehurst BR7 . . . . **188** D2
Edmonton N18. . . . . **17** B1
Leyton E10. . . . . **53** D3
Tottenham N17 . . . . **34** A2
Walthamstow E17 . . . . **53** C6
Bromley Road Inf Sch
BR3. . . . . **185** D2
Bromley Road Ret Pk
SE6. . . . . **163** D2
Bromley South Sta
BR2. . . . . **209** A6
Bromley St E1. . . . . **96** C1
BROMPTON **114** B3
Brompton Arc SW1 . . . **247** D5
Brompton Cl
Hounslow TW4 . . . . **151** B6
Penge SE20. . . . . **184** A1
Brompton Ct 4 HA7 . . . . . **25** C6
Brompton Gr SE20 . . . . . **184** B1
Brompton Ho 3 N9. . . . . . **34** A6
Brompton Oratory
SW3. . . . . **114** C3 **257** A5
Brompton Park Cres
SW6. . . . . **135** D6 **265** C5
Brompton Pl
SW3. . . . . **114** C3 **257** B5
Brompton Rd
SW3. . . . . **114** C3 **257** A5

Brompton Sq
SW3. . . . . **114** C3 **257** A6
Bromstone Ho 18
SW9. . . . . **138** C4
Bromwich Ave N6 . . . . **71** A6
Bromwich Ho 3
TW10. . . . . **154** A5
Bromyard Ave W3 . . . . . . **111** C6
Bromyard Ho
Acton W3. . . . . **111** C5
3 Peckham SE15. . . . . . **140** B5
Bron Ct NW6 . . . . **91** C6
BRONDESBURY **69** A2
Brondesbury Coll for Boys
NW6 . . . . **69** A1
Brondesbury Ct NW2. . . . **68** D2
Brondesbury Mews 11
NW6 . . . . **69** C1
BRONDESBURY PARK . . **90** D6
Brondesbury Park Sta
NW6 . . . . **91** A6
Brondesbury Pk NW2 . . . **68** D1
Brondesbury Rd NW6 . . . **91** C5
Brondesbury Sta NW6 . . . **69** B1
Brondesbury Villas
NW6 . . . . **91** C5
Bronhill Terr N17. . . . . **34** A2
Bronsart Rd
SW6. . . . . **135** A5 **264** A3
Bronson Rd SW20. . . . . . **179** A1
Bronte Cl Erith DA8. . . . . **147** D5
1 Forest Gate E7 . . . . **77** A4
Ilford IG2 . . . . **56** C5
Bronte Ct 8 W14 . . . . **112** D3
Bronte Ho Kilburn NW6. . . **91** C4
3 Stoke Newington N16 . . **73** D3
Bronti Cl SE17. . **117** A1 **262** B2
Bronwen Ct NW8 . . . . **229** C1
Bronze Age Way
DA17. . . . . **125** D4
Bronze St SE8 . . . . **141** C5
Brook Ave
Dagenham RM10. . . . . **81** D1
Edgware HA8 . . . . **26** D4
Wembley HA9 . . . . **66** C5
Brook Bank EN1 . . . . **6** B6
Brookbank Ave W7 . . . . . . **86** B2
Brookbank Rd SE13. . . . . **141** D2
Brook Cl Acton W3. . . . . . **110** C5
Finchley N12 . . . . **29** A3
Ruislip HA4 . . . . **39** C2
Stanwell TW19 . . . . **148** B4
Upper Tooting SW17 . . . . **159** A2
West Barnes SW20. . . . . **200** B6
Brook Com Prim Sch
E8. **74** A3
Brook Cres Chingford E4. . **35** D6
Edmonton N9. . . . . **34** B6
Brook Ct Barking IG11. . . **101** D6
5 Brentford TW8. . . . . . . **131** D6
Cheam SM3 . . . . **216** C4
Edgware HA8 . . . . **26** D5
2 Leyton E11. . . . . **76** C5
Mortlake SW14 . . . . **133** C2
Stratford New Town E15. . **76** A3
Walthamstow E17. . . . . . . **53** A6
Brookdale N11. . . . . **31** C6
Brookdale Rd
Catford SE6. . . . . **163** D4
Lewisham SE6. . . . . **163** D5
Sidcup DA5 . . . . **169** A5
Walthamstow E17 . . . . **35** C4
Brookdene Rd SE18,
SE2 . . . . **123** D2
Brook Dr Harrow HA1. . . . . **42** A5
Newington
SE11. . . . . **116** D2 **261** C4
Ruislip HA4 . . . . **39** C2
Brooke Ave HA2 . . . . **64** A5
Brooke Ct WD23 . . . . **8** A4
Brooke Ct Kilburn W10 . . . **91** A5
4 Kingston u T KT2 . . . . **175** D6
Brooke Ho Bushey WD23 . . **8** A4
4 New Cross Gate
SE14. . . . . **141** A4
Brookehowse Rd SE6. . . **163** D1
Brookend Rd DA15. . . . . . **167** C3
Brooke Rd
Shacklewell E5, N16. . . . . **74** A5
Walthamstow E17. . . . . . . **54** A5
Brookes Ct EC1. . . . . **241** A4
Brooke's Mkt EC1. . . . . . **241** B4
Brooke St EC1. . . **94** C2 **241** A3
Brooke Way WD23 . . . . **8** A4
Brookfield
Dartmouth Pk N6 . . . . **71** A5
1 Finsbury Pk N4 . . . . **72** C6
Brookfield Ave
Carshalton SM1, SM5. . . **218** C5
Ealing W5 . . . . **87** D3
Mill Hill NW7. . . . . **28** B4
Walthamstow E17. . . . . . . **54** A5
Brookfield Cl NW7. . . . . . . **28** B4
Brookfield Cres
Harrow HA3 . . . . **44** A4
Mill Hill NW7. . . . . **28** B4
Brookfield Ct
Greenford UB6 . . . . **86** A4
1 London N12 . . . . **29** D6
Wembley HA3 . . . . **42** C1
Brookfield Gdns KT10. . . **212** D2
Brookfield Ho 23 E2. . . . . **96** B5
Brookfield House Sch
IG8 . . . . **36** C4
Brookfield Path IG8 . . . . . **36** C4
Brookfield Pk NW5 . . . . . . **71** B5
Brookfield Prim Sch
Cheam SM3. . . . . **201** A1

Brookfield Prim Sch
continued
Dartmouth Pk N19 . . . . . . **71** B6
Brookfield Rd
Acton W4. . . . . **111** B4
Edmonton N9. . . . . **18** B1
Homerton E9 . . . . **75** A2
Brookfields EN3 . . . . **6** D1
Brookfields Ave CR4 . . . **202** C5
Brookgate N16 . . . . **73** B6
Brook Gate
W1. . . . . **114** D6 **247** D5
Brook Gdns
Barnes SW13 . . . . **133** C3
Chingford E4 . . . . **35** D6
Kingston u T KT2 . . . . **177** A2
Brook Gn NW6 . . . . **112** D2
BROOK GREEN **112** D3
Brook Green Flats 11
W14. . . . . **112** D3
Brookhill Cl
East Barnet EN4 . . . . **14** C6
Woolwich SE18. . . . . **122** C1
Brookhill Ct 2 EN4 . . . . . . **14** C5
Brookhill Rd
East Barnet EN4 . . . . **14** C6
Woolwich SE18. . . . . **122** C1
Brook Ho
3 Clapham Pk SW4 . . . . **159** C6
Ealing W3 . . . . **110** C4
6 Edmonton N9 . . . . **18** A1
4 Hammersmith W6 . . . . **112** C2
Marylebone WC1. . . . . . . **239** C4
4 Twickenham TW1. . . . . **153** A4
Brook Hos NW1. . . . . **232** B3
Brookhouse Gdns E4. . . . **36** C6
Brook House Sixth Form
Coll E5 . . . . **74** B5
Brook Ind Est UB4. . . . . . **106** C5
Brooking Cl RM8. . . . . **80** C5
Brooking Rd E7. . . . . **77** A3
Brook La Bexley DA5 . . . . **168** D5
Greenwich SE3 . . . . **143** B3
Plaistow BR1. . . . . **187** A4
Brook La N 3 TW8 . . . . . **131** D6
Brookland Cl NW11 . . . . . . **47** C5
Brookland Garth NW11. . . **47** D5
Brookland Hill NW11. . . . . **47** D5
Brookland Jun & Inf Schs
NW11. . . . . **47** D5
Brookland Rise NW11. . . . **47** C5
Brooklands Ave
New Eltham DA15. . . . . . **167** B2
Wandsworth SW18 . . . . . **157** D2
Brooklands Cl TW16 . . . . **171** C2
Brooklands Court
Apartments 3 NW6 . . . . . **69** B1
Brooklands Ct
10 Clapham SW8 . . . . . . **137** C3
Enfield N21. . . . . **17** B6
Kingston u T KT1 . . . . **197** D5
2 London NW6 . . . . **69** B1
2 Mitcham CR4 . . . . **180** B1
Brooklands Dr UB6 . . . . . . **87** D6
Brooklands Ho SE3 . . . . . **143** A2
Brooklands Pk SE3 . . . . . **143** A2
Brooklands Pl TW12 . . . . **173** D5
Brooklands Prim Sch
SE3. . . . . **143** A2
Brooklands Rd KT7 . . . . . **197** A1
Brooklands The TW7. . . . **130** B4
Brook Lane Bns Ctr
TW8 . . . . **109** D1
Brooklea Cl NW9 . . . . **27** C2
Brook Lo Crouch End N8 . . **49** D3
4 Edgware HA8 . . . . **26** D4
Hendon NW4. . . . . **46** D4
Brooklyn SW20. . . . . **184** A3
Brooklyn Ave SE25 . . . . . **206** B5
Brooklyn Cl SM5 . . . . **218** C6
Brooklyn Ct
Feltham TW13 . . . . **150** B2
Shepherd's Bush W12 . . . **112** C5
Brooklyn Gr SE25 . . . . . . **206** B5
Brooklyn Rd
Bromley BR2. . . . . **210** A4
Croydon SE25 . . . . **206** B5
Brookmarsh Ind Est
SE10. . . . . **141** D5
Brook Mdw N12 . . . . **13** D1
Brook Mead KT19 . . . . . . **215** C2
Brookmead Ave BR1,
BR2. . . . . **210** B4
Brookmead Ct N20. . . . . . **14** A2
Brookmead Ind Est
CR4. . . . . **203** C3
Brook Meadow Cl IG8. . . . **36** C4
Brookmead Rd CR0 . . . . **203** C3
Brook Mews N
W2. . . . . **114** A6 **246** B6
Brookmill Rd SE8 . . . . . . **141** C4
Brook Park Cl N21. . . . . . . **16** D6
Brook Pl EN5 . . . . **13** C6
Brook Rd
Buckhurst Hill IG9. . . . . . . **21** A3
Dollis Hill NW2 . . . . **68** A6
Finchley N12 . . . . **30** C3
Hornsey N8 . . . . **50** A5
Ilford IG2 . . . . **57** C3
South Norwood CR7 . . . . **205** A5
Surbiton KT6 . . . . **214** A6
Twickenham TW1. . . . . . . **153** A5
Wood Green N22. . . . . **50** B6
Brook Rd S TW8. . . . . . . **131** D6
Brook Ret Pk HA4 . . . . **62** D3
Brooks Ave E6. . . . . **100** B3
Brooksbank Ho 7 E9 . . . . . **74** C2
Brooksbank St 8 E9 . . . . . **74** C2
Brooksby Ho 9 N1 . . . . **72** C1
Brooksby Mews N1 . . . . . . **72** C1

Bro–Bro 287

Brooksby St N1. . . . . **72** C1
Brooksby's Wlk E9. . . . . . **74** D3
Brooks Cl SE9 . . . . **166** C2
Brookscroft E17 . . . . **53** D6
Brookscroft Rd E17 . . . . . **35** C2
Brooks Ct
3 London SW4 . . . . **138** A3
Nine Elms SW8 . . . . **269** B4
Brookshill HA3 . . . . **24** B5
Brookshill Ave HA3 . . . . . **24** C5
Brookshill Dr HA3 . . . . . . **24** B5
Brookshill Gate HA3 . . . . **24** B5
Brooks Ho 6 SW2 . . . . . . **160** C3
Brookside
Broom Hill BR6. . . . . **211** D2
East Barnet EN4 . . . . **14** C5
Hillingdon UB10 . . . . **60** B1
Southgate N21 . . . . **16** B5
Wallington SM5. . . . . **219** A3
Brookside Cl
Barnet EN5 . . . . **13** A5
Feltham TW13 . . . . **150** A1
Harrow HA3 . . . . **43** D4
South Harrow HA2, HA4. . **63** A4
Brookside Cres 1
KT4 . . . . **200** A1
Brookside Ct SW16 . . . . . **181** C3
Brookside Gdns EN1 . . . . . **6** C6
Brookside Ho N17 . . . . **33** C1
Brookside Prim Sch
UB4. . . . . **84** C4
Brookside Rd
Edmonton N9. . . . . **34** B6
Hayes UB4. . . . . **106** C6
Temple Fortune NW11 . . . **47** B3
Upper Holloway N19. . . . . **71** C6
Brookside S EN4. . . . . **15** A4
Brookside Way CR0 . . . . **206** D3
Brooks La W4 . . . . **132** C6
Brook's Mans 5 IG3 . . . . . **58** B1
Brook's Mews
W1. . . . . **115** B6 **248** C6
Brook's Par 6 IG3. . . . . . . **58** B1
Brook Sq SE18. . . . . **144** A4
Brooks Rd W4 . . . . **110** C1
Brook St
Bayswater
W2. . . . . **114** B6 **246** D6
Erith DA8. . . . . **147** D5
Kingston u T KT1. . . . . . . **176** A1
Mayfair W1 . . . **115** B6 **248** C6
7 Tottenham N17 . . . . **33** D1
Brookstone Ct SE15. . . . . **140** B1
Brooksville Ave NW6. . . . . **91** A6
Brook Vale DA8. . . . . **147** D4
Brookview Ct 11 EN1. . . . . **17** C6
Brookview Rd SW16 . . . . **181** C3
Brookville Rd
SW6. . . . . **135** B5 **264** C3
Brookway SE3. . . . . **143** A2
Brook Wlk
Burnt Oak HA8 . . . . **27** B4
Finchley N2 . . . . **30** B2
Brookwood Ave SW13. . . **133** D3
Brookwood Cl BR2. . . . . . **208** D5
Brookwood Ho SE1 . . . . **251** D1
Brookwood Rd
Hounslow TW3 . . . . **129** D4
Wandsworth SW18 . . . . . **157** C3
Broom Ave BR5. . . . . **190** B1
Broom Cl
Bromley Comm BR2 . . . . **210** A3
Teddington KT1, TW11 . . **175** D3
Broomcroft Ave UB5. . . . . **84** C4
Broome Ct 3 TW9 . . . . . . **132** C4
Broome Ho 7 E5 . . . . **74** B3
Broome Rd TW12 . . . . . . **173** B2
Broome Way SE5 . . . . . . **139** B5
Broom Farm SW6. . . . . . **135** C3
Broomfield
7 Camden Town NW1 . . . **71** A1
Sunbury TW16 . . . . **172** A2
Walthamstow E17 . . . . **53** B2
Broomfield Ave N13. . . . . . **32** B5
Broomfield Cotts N13 . . . . **32** A1
Broomfield Ct N13. . . . . . . **32** A5
Broomfield Ho
Stanmore HA7. . . . . **9** A1
4 St Paul's Cray BR5. . . . **190** B1
Walworth SE17 . . . . **263** A2
Broomfield House Sch
TW9 . . . . **132** B4
Broomfield La N13. . . . . . . **32** A5
Broomfield Pl W13 . . . . . **109** B5
Broomfield Rd
Beckenham BR3 . . . . **207** B6
Bexley DA6 . . . . **169** C6
Bowes Pk N13. . . . . **32** A5
Dagenham RM6. . . . . **58** D2
Ealing W13 . . . . **109** B5
Richmond TW9 . . . . **132** B4
Surbiton KT5 . . . . **198** B1
Teddington TW11 . . . . . . **175** C4
Broomfields KT10. . . . . . . **212** A3
Broomfield Sch N14 . . . . . **31** B5
Broomfield St E14 . . . . . . **97** D2
Broom Gdns CR0 . . . . . . **223** C5
Broomgrove Gdns HA8. . . **26** C2
Broomgrove Rd SW9. . . . **138** B3
BROOM HILL **211** D2
Broomhill Ct 2 IG8 . . . . . . **37** A4
Broomhill Rd
Broom Hill BR6. . . . . **211** D2
Ilford IG3 . . . . **80** A1
Wandsworth SW18 . . . . . **157** C5
Woodford IG8 . . . . **37** A4

Broomhill Rise DA6 169 C6
Broomhill Wlk IG8 36 D3
Broomhouse La SW6 135 C2
Broomhouse Rd SW6 135 C3
Broomleigh BR1 187 A2
Broomloan La SM1 217 C6
Broom Lock TW11 175 C4
Broom Mead DA6 169 C6
Broom Pk KT1 175 D3
Broom Rd Croydon CR0 223 C5
Teddington TW11 175 C4
Broomsleigh Bsns Pk SE26 185 B5
Broomsleigh St NW6 69 B3
Broom Water TW11 175 C5
Broom Water W TW11 175 C5
Broomwood Cl CR0 206 D4
Broomwood Hall Sch SW12 159 A4
Broomwood Rd
London SW11 159 A6
St Paul's Cray BR5 190 B1
Broseley Gr SE26 185 A5
Broster Gdns SE25 205 D6
Brougham Rd Acton W3 89 A1
Hackney E8 96 A6
Brougham St SW11 136 D3
Brough Cl
Kingston u T KT2 175 D5
South Lambeth SW8 270 B3
Broughton Ave
London N3 47 A6
Richmond TW10 175 C6
Broughton Ct W13 109 B6
Broughton Dr 19 SW9 138 D1
Broughton Gdns N6 49 C3
Broughton Ho 10 SW19 179 A3
Broughton Rd
Ealing W13 109 B6
Orpington BR6 227 B6
Sands End SW6 135 D3
Thornton Heath CR7 204 C3
Broughton Road App 2 SW6 135 D3
Broughton St SW8 137 B3
Brouncker Rd W3 111 A4
Browells La TW13 150 B2
Brown Bear Ct TW13 172 D6
Brown Cl SM6 220 A1
Browne Ho
13 Deptford SE8 141 C5
9 Penge SE26 184 B5
Brownfield St E14 98 A1
Brownflete Ho SE4 141 A1
Browngraves Rd UB7 127 A5
Brown Hart Gdns W1 248 B6
Brownhill Rd SE6 164 A4
Browning Ave
Carshalton SM1 218 C4
Ealing W7 86 D1
North Cheam KT4 200 B1
Browning Cl
Bexley DA16 145 C4
Feltham TW12 173 B6
Paddington W9 236 B5
Walthamstow E17 54 A5
Browning Ct W14 264 C6
Browning Ho
2 London SE14 141 A4
7 Shepherd's Bush W12 90 C1
10 Stoke Newington N16 73 C4
Browning Mews W1 238 B3
Browning Rd Enfield EN2 5 B5
Leytonstone E11 54 D2
Plashet E12 78 B2
Browning St SE17 117 A2 262 B3
Browning Way TW5 128 D4
Brownlea Gdns IG3 80 A6
Brownlow Cl EN4 14 B6
Brownlow Ct
2 Bowes Pk N11 32 A4
Hampstead Garden Suburb N2 48 A4
Brownlow Ho 10 SE16 118 A4
Brownlow Lo 1 N11 32 A4
Brownlow Mews WC1 94 B3 240 D5
Brownlow Rd
Bowes Pk N11 32 A4
6 Ealing W13 109 A5
Finchley N3 29 D3
3 Forest Gate E7 77 A4
Hackney E8 96 A6
South Croydon CR0 221 D4
Willesden NW10 67 C1
Brownlow St WC1 94 B2 240 D3
Brownrigg Rd TW15 170 C6
Brown's Bldgs EC3 243 B1
Brownsea Wlk NW7 28 D4
Brownspring Dr SE9 166 D1
Brown's Rd
Surbiton KT5, KT6 198 B2
Walthamstow E17 53 C6
Brown St W1 92 D1 237 C2
Brownswell Rd N2 30 B1
Brownswood Rd N4 73 A6
Broxash Rd SW11 159 A5
Broxbourne Ave E18 55 B5
Broxbourne Ho 1 E3 97 D3
Broxbourne Rd
Broom Hill BR6 211 D2
Wanstead E7 77 A5
Broxholme Ho SW6 265 C2
Broxholm Rd SE27, SW16 160 C1
Broxted Rd SE6 163 B2
Broxwood Way NW8 92 C6 230 B5
Bruce Ave TW17 193 A3
Bruce Castle Ct N17 33 C2
Bruce Castle Mus* N17 33 C2
Bruce Castle Rd N17 33 D2
Bruce Cl
North Kensington W10 90 D2
Welling DA16 146 B4
Bruce Ct DA15 189 D6
Bruce Gdns N20 14 D1
Bruce Glasier Ho 13 N19 49 D2
Bruce Gr N17 33 D1
Bruce Grove N17 33 D1
Bruce Grove Prim Sch N17 33 D1
Bruce Grove Sta N17 33 D1
Bruce Hall Mews SW17 181 A6
Bruce Ho
4 Clapham Pk SW4 159 D5
5 Greenhill HA1 42 D4
North Kensington W10 90 D2
Preston HA3 44 A2
Putney SW15 156 B6
Bruce Lawns SW17 181 A6
Bruce Rd Barnet EN5 1 A2
Bromley E3 97 D4
Harrow HA3 24 C1
Mitcham CR4 181 A3
South Norwood SE25 205 B5
Willesden NW10 67 B1
Bruckner St W10 91 B4
Brudenell Rd SW17 181 A6
Bruffs Meadow UB5 63 A2
Bruges Pl 16 NW1 71 C1
Brumfield Rd KT19 215 A3
Brune Ho E1 243 C3
Brunel Cl
Cranford TW5 128 B5
Northolt UB5 85 B4
Penge SE19 183 D4
Brunel Ct 8 SW13 133 D3
Brunel Engine House Rotherhithe* SE16 118 C4
Brunel Est W2 91 C2
Brunel Ho
Chelsea SW10 266 D4
4 Gospel Oak NW5 71 B4
Hayes UB3 105 D3
Millwall E14 119 D1
New Cross SE8 141 B5
25 Streatham SW2 160 A4
Brunel Mews NW10 90 D4
Brunel Pl 7 UB1 85 D1
Brunel Rd Acton W3 89 C2
Walthamstow E17 53 A3
Wapping SE16 118 C5
Brunel Science Pk UB8 82 A4
Brunel St E16 98 D1
Brunel Univ UB8 82 A4
Brunel Univ Coll Osterley Campus TW7 130 D5
Brunel Wlk
South Tottenham N15 51 C5
Twickenham TW4 151 C4
Brune St E1 95 D2 243 C3
Brunlees Ho SE1 262 B5
Brunner Cl NW11 48 A4
Brunner Ho 6 SE6 186 A6
Brunner Rd Ealing W5 87 D3
Walthamstow E17 53 B4
Bruno Ct 5 E8 74 A2
Bruno Pl NW9 67 A6
Brunswick Ave N11 15 A1
Brunswick Cl
Bexley DA6 146 D1
Pinner HA5 41 A3
Thames Ditton KT7 196 D1
Twickenham TW2 152 B1
Brunswick Cres N11 15 A1
Brunswick Ct
Bermondsey SE1 117 C4 253 B2
Finsbury EC1 234 C1
Kingston u T KT2 175 D4
New Barnet EN4 14 B6
2 Penge SE19 184 A3
Westminster SW1 259 D3
2 Wimbledon SW19 179 A3
Brunswick Gdns
Ealing W5 88 A3
Kensington W8 113 C5 245 B3
Brunswick Gr N11 15 A1
Brunswick Ho
Church End N3 29 B2
4 Haggerston E2 95 D5
Lisson Gr NW1 237 C6
Brunswick Lo 6 E4 20 A2
Brunswick Manor SM1 218 A4
Brunswick Mews
Marylebone W1 237 D2
Streatham SW16 181 D4
BRUNSWICK PARK 15 A1
Brunswick Park Gdns N11 15 A2
Brunswick Park Prim Sch
Brunswick Pk N14 15 A2
Camberwell SE5 139 B5
Brunswick Park Rd N11 15 A1
Brunswick Pk SE5 139 C4
Brunswick Pl
Penge SE19 184 A3
Shoreditch N1 95 B4 235 D1
Brunswick Quay SE16 118 D3
Brunswick Rd
Bexley DA6 147 A1
Ealing W5 88 A4
Holdbrook EN3 7 C5
Kingston u T KT2 176 C2
Leyton E10 54 A1
Poplar E14 98 A1
South Tottenham N15 51 C4
South Tottenham N15 51 C5
Sutton SM1 217 D4
Brunswick Sh Ctr WC1 94 A3 240 B6
Brunswick Sq
St Pancras WC1 94 A3 240 B6
Tottenham N17 33 D4
Brunswick St E17 54 A4
Brunswick Terr BR3 185 D2
Brunswick Villas 2 SE5 139 C4
Brunswick Way N11 31 B6
Brunton Pl E14 97 A1
Brushfield St E1 95 D2 243 C4
Brushwood Lo 1 DA17 125 C2
Brussels Ct N18 33 C5
Brussels Rd SW11 136 B1
Bruton Cl BR7 188 B3
Bruton La W1 115 B6 248 D5
Bruton Pl W1 115 B6 248 D5
Bruton Rd SM4 202 A5
Bruton St W1 115 B6 248 D5
Bruton Way W13 87 A2
Brutus Ct SE11 261 C3
Bryan Ave NW10 68 B1
Bryan Cl TW16 172 A3
Bryan Ct W1 237 C2
Bryan Ho SE16 119 B4
Bryan Rd SE16 119 B4
Bryanston Ave TW2 151 D3
Bryanston Cl UB2 107 B2
Bryanston Ct W1 237 C2
Bryanstone Ct SM1 218 A5
Bryanstone Rd N8 49 D4
Bryanston Ho 12 SE15 139 D4
Bryanston Mans W1 237 C4
Bryanston Mews E W1 237 C3
Bryanston Mews W W1 92 D1 237 C2
Bryanston Pl W1 92 D2 237 C3
Bryanston Sq W1 92 D1 237 C2
Bryanston St W1 92 D1 237 D1
Bryant Cl EN5 13 B6
Bryant Ct Acton W3 111 B5
Haggerston E2 95 D5
Bryant Rd UB5 84 C4
Bryant St E15 76 C1
Bryantwood Rd N5, N7 72 C3
Brycedale Cres N14 15 D1
Bryce Ho 25 SE14 140 D6
Bryce Rd RM8 80 C4
Brydale Ho 2 SE16 118 D2
Bryden Cl SE26 185 A5
Brydges Pl WC2 250 A5
Brydges Rd E15 76 B3
Brydon Wlk N1 233 B6
Bryer Ct EC2 242 A4
Bryett Rd N7 72 A5
Bryher Ho W4 111 A1
Brymay Cl E3 97 C5
Brymon Ct W1 237 D3
Brynmaer Ho SW11 267 D1
Brynmaer Rd SW11 136 D4 267 D1
Bryn-y-Mawr Rd EN1 5 D1
Bryony Cl UB8 82 B2
Bryony Rd W12 112 A6
Bryony Way TW16 172 A4
B Sky B Hq TW7 131 A6
BT Telecom Twr* W1 93 C2 239 A4
Buccleuch Ho E5 52 A2
Buchanan Cl N21 16 B6
Buchanan Ct 16 SE16 118 D2
Buchanan Gdns NW10 90 B5
Buchanan Ho
Dulwich SE21 161 C1
Wandsworth SW18 157 C4
Buchan Ho W3 110 D4
Buchan Rd SE15 140 C2
Bucharest Rd SW18 158 A4
Buckden Cl
Fortis Green N2 48 D5
Lee SE12 165 A5
Buckfast Ct W13 109 A6
Buckfast Ho N14 15 C6
Buckfast Rd SM4 201 D5
Buckfast St E2 96 A4
Buck Hill Wlk W2 114 B6 246 D5
Buckhold Rd SW18 157 C5
Buckhurst Ave CR4, SM5 202 D1
Buckhurst Ct 7 IG9 21 D2
BUCKHURST HILL 21 C2
Buckhurst Hill Ho 3 IG9 21 B2
Buckhurst Hill Sta IG9 21 D2
Buckhurst Ho 15 N7 71 D3
Buckhurst St E1 96 B3
Buckhurst Way IG9 21 D1
Buckingham Ave
East Molesey KT8 173 D1
Falconwood DA16 145 C1
Feltham TW14 150 B5
Oakleigh Pk N20 14 B4
South Norwood CR7 182 C2
Wembley UB6 87 A6
Buckingham Cl
Broom Hill BR5 211 C2
Ealing W5 87 C2
Enfield EN1 5 C3
Hampton TW12 173 B5
Buckingham College Sch HA1 42 C4
Buckingham Ct
2 Ealing W7 86 D3
Hendon NW4 46 A6
Mitcham CR4 204 A4
Northolt UB5 85 A6
Wembley HA0 65 C2
Buckingham Dr BR7 189 A5
Buckingham Gate SW1 115 C3 259 B6
Buckingham Gdns
East Molesey KT8 173 D1
Edgware HA8 26 B3
South Norwood CR7 182 C1
Buckingham Gr UB10 82 C5
Buckingham Ho
1 Acton W3 88 C1
Finsbury Pk N4 51 A1
Richmond TW10 154 C6
Buckingham La SE23 163 A4
Buckingham Lo N10 49 C5
Buckingham Mans NW6 69 D3
Buckingham Mews
Harlesden NW10 89 D5
7 Kingsland N1 73 C2
Westminster SW1 259 A6
Buckingham Pal* SW1 115 C4 249 A1
Buckingham Palace Rd SW1 115 B2 258 D4
Buckingham Par 19 HA7 25 C5
Buckingham Pl SW1 259 A6
Buckingham Prim Sch TW12 173 B5
Buckingham Rd
Edgware HA8 26 B3
Hampton TW12, TW13 173 B5
Harlesden NW10 89 D5
Harrow HA1 42 B4
Ilford IG1 79 B6
Kingsland N1 73 C2
Kingston u T KT1 198 B5
Leyton E10 75 D5
Mitcham CR4 204 A4
Richmond TW10 153 D2
Stratford E15 76 D3
Wanstead E11 55 C4
Woodford E18 36 D2
Wood Green N22 32 A2
Buckingham St WC2 250 B5
Buckingham Way SM6 219 C1
Buckingham Yd NW10 89 D5
Buck La NW9 45 B4
Buckland Cl NW7 28 A6
Buckland Cres NW3 70 B2
Buckland Ct
6 Shoreditch N1 95 C5
Uxbridge UB10 61 A6
Buckland Ho 3 N1 72 C1
Buckland Inf Sch KT9 214 B3
Buckland Rd
Chessington KT9 214 B3
Leyton E10 76 A6
Orpington BR6 227 C4
Buckland Rise HA5 22 D2
Bucklands Rd TW11 175 C4
Buckland St N1 95 B5 235 D3
Buckland Way KT4 200 C1
Buckland Wlk
2 Acton W3 111 A4
Morden SM4 202 A5
Buckle Ct HA8 27 A3
Buckleigh Ave SW20 201 B6
Buckleigh Ho SW17 180 B5
Buckleigh Rd SW16 182 A3
Buckleigh Way SE19 183 D3
Buckler Gdns SE9 166 B1
Buckler's Alley SW6 264 D4
Bucklersbury EC2, EC4 242 C1
Bucklers' Way SM5 218 D5
Buckles Ct DA17 124 D2
Buckle St
15 Whitechapel E1 96 A1
Whitechapel E1 243 D2
Buckley Cl SE23 162 B4
Buckley Ct
5 Brondesbury NW6 69 B1
London N8 49 D4
Buckley Ho W3 110 C5
Buckley Rd NW6 69 B1
Buckmaster Cl 1 SW9 138 C2
Buckmaster Ho 1 N7 72 B4
Buckmaster Rd SW11 136 C1
Bucknall St WC1 240 A2
Bucknall Way BR3 208 A5
Bucknell Cl SW2 138 B1
Buckner Rd SW2 138 B1
Buckrell Rd E4 20 B2
Buckridge Bldg EC1 241 A4
Buckshead Ho 19 W2 91 C2
Buck St NW1 71 B1
Buckstone Cl SE23 162 C5
Buckstone Rd N18 34 A5
Buckters Rents SE16 119 A5
Buckthorne Rd SE4 163 A6
Buckthorn Ho DA15 167 D1
Buckwheat Ct DA18 124 D3
Budd Cl N12 29 D6
Buddings Circ HA9 67 A5
Bude Cl E17 53 B4
Budge La CR4 202 D2
Budge Row EC4 242 C1
Budge's Wlk W2 114 A5 246 B4
Budleigh Cres DA16 146 C4
Budleigh Ho 19 SE15 140 A5
Budoch Ct IG3 80 A6
Budoch Dr IG3 80 A6
Buer Rd SW6 135 A3
Bugsby's Way SE10 120 D2
Buick Ho 4 E3 97 C3
Building 36 7 SE18 123 A3
Building 47 6 SE18 123 A3
Building 48 5 SE18 123 A3
Building 49 4 SE18 123 A3
Building 50 3 SE18 123 A3
Bulbarrow NW8 91 D6
Bulganak Rd CR7 205 A5
Bulinca St SW1 115 D2 259 D3
Bullace Row SE5 139 B4
Bull Alley DA16 146 B2
Bullard Rd TW11 174 D4
Bullards Pl 13 E2 96 D4
Bull Dog The (Juct) TW15 148 A2
Bulleid Way SW1 115 B2 258 D3
Bullen Ho 13 E1 96 B3
Bullen St SW11 136 C3
Buller Cl SE15 140 A5
Buller Rd Barking IG11 79 C1
Kensal Green NW10 90 D4
South Norwood CR7 205 B6
Tottenham N17 34 A1
Wood Green N22 32 C1
Bullers Cl DA14 191 A5
Bullers Wood Dr BR7 188 B3
Bullers Wood Sch BR7 188 A2
Bullescroft Rd HA8 10 D1
Bullfinch Ct 4 SE21 161 B2
Bullingham Mans W8 245 B2
Bull Inn Ct WC2 250 B5
Bullivant St 9 E14 120 A6
Bull La Chislehurst BR7 189 B3
Dagenham RM10 81 D5
Edmonton N18 33 C5
Bull Rd E15 98 D5
Bullrush Cl
Carshalton SM5 218 C6
Thornton Heath CR0 205 C3
Bulls Alley SW14 133 B3
Bulls Bridge Ind Est UB2 106 B2
Bulls Bridge Rd UB2 106 B2
Bullsbrook Rd UB4 106 C5
Bull's Cross EN1, EN2 6 A6
Bull's Gdns SW3 257 B4
Bulls Head Pas EC3 243 A1
Bull Yd SE15 140 A4
Bulmer Gdns HA3 43 D2
Bulmer Mews W11 113 C5 245 A4
Bulow Ct 3 SW6 135 D3
Bulstrode Ave TW3 129 C2
Bulstrode Gdns TW3 129 C2
Bulstrode Pl W1 238 B3
Bulstrode Rd TW3 129 C2
Bulstrode St W1 93 A1 238 B2
Bulwer Court Rd E11 54 B1
Bulwer Ct E11 54 B1
Bulwer Gdns EN5 2 A1
Bulwer Rd
Edmonton N18 33 C6
Leytonstone E11 54 B1
New Barnet EN5 2 A1
Bulwer St W12 112 C5
Bunbury Ho SE15 140 A5
Bunces La IG8 36 D3
Bungalow Rd SE25 205 C5
Bungalows The
Leyton E10 54 A3
Mitcham SW16 181 B3
Bunhill Row EC1 95 B3 242 C5
Bunhouse Pl SW1 258 B2
Bunkers Hill
London NW11 48 A2
North Cray DA14 169 B1
Bunker's Hill DA17 125 C2
Bunning Ho N7 72 A4
Bunning Way N7 72 B1
Bunn's La NW7 27 D4
Bunsen Ho 2 E3 97 A5
Bunsen St 3 E3 97 A5
Buntingbridge Rd IG2 57 B4
Bunting Cl London N9 18 D3
Mitcham CR4 202 D4
Bunting Ct NW9 27 C1
Bunton St SE18 122 C3
Bunyan Ct EC2 242 A4
Bunyan Rd E17 53 A6
Buonaparte Mews SW1 259 C2
BUPA Bushey Hospl WD23 8 D3
Burbage Cl
Bermondsey SE1 117 B3 262 C5
Hayes UB3 83 B1
Burbage Ho
10 Deptford SE14 140 D6
Shoreditch N1 235 D5
Burbage Rd SE21, SE24 161 B4
Burbage Sch N1 95 C5
Burbank KT3 199 D6
Burberry Cl KT3 177 C1
Burberry Ct 8 N3 29 D3
Burbidge Rd TW17 192 C5
Burbridge Way N17 34 A1
Burcham St E14 98 A1
Burcharbro Rd SE2 146 D6
Burchell Ct WD23 8 A4
Burchell Ho SE11 260 D2
Burchell Rd Leyton E10 53 D1
London SE15 140 B4
Burcher Gale Gr 5 SE15 139 D5
Burchetts Way TW17 192 D3
Burchett Way RM6 59 B3
Burcote Rd SW18 158 B4
Burden Cl TW8 109 C1
Burden Ho SW8 270 A3
Burdenshott Ave TW10 132 D1
Burden Way E11 77 B6
Burder Cl N1 73 C2
Burder Rd N1 73 C2
Burdett Ave SW20 178 A2
Burdett Cl
2 Ealing W7 108 D5
Sidcup DA14 191 A5
Burdett Coutts & Townshend CE Prim Sch SW1 115 D2 259 D3
Burdett Mews 4 W2 91 D1
Burdett Rd
Richmond TW9 132 B2
Thornton Heath CR0 205 B3
Tower Hamlets E3 97 B2
Burdetts Rd RM9 103 B6
Burdock Cl CR0 206 D1
Burdock Rd N17 52 A6
Burdon Ct 3 E8 74 A2
Burdon La SM2 217 A1
Bure Ct 17 EN5 13 D6
Burfield Cl SW17 180 B6
Burford Cl
Dagenham RM8 80 C5
Ickenham UB10 60 A4
Ilford IG6 57 A5
Burford Ct SE8 141 C6
Burford Gdns N13 16 B1
Burford Ho
1 Brentford TW8 110 A1
11 South Lambeth SW9 138 B3
Burford Rd
Brentford TW8 110 A1
Bromley BR1 210 A5
Forest Hill SE6 163 B2
Newham E6 100 A4
New Malden KT4 200 A2
5 Stratford Marsh E15 98 B6
Sutton SM1 217 C6
Burford Way CR0 224 A2
Burford Wlk SW6 265 D3
Burgate Ct 9 SW9 138 C2
Burges Gr SW13 134 B5
Burges Rd E6 78 B1
Burgess Ave NW9 45 B3
Burgess Cl 4 TW13 173 A6
Burgess Ct
2 London N20 14 D2
3 Southall UB1 85 D1
Wallend E12 78 C1
Burgess Hill NW2 69 C4
Burgess Ho 3 SE5 139 A5
Burgess Ind Pk SE5 139 B5
Burgess Mews SW19 179 D4
Burgess Park Mans NW6 69 C4
Burgess Rd Leyton E15 76 C4
Sutton SM1 217 D4
Burgess St E14 97 C2
Burge St SE1 262 D5
Burghill Rd SE26 185 A6
Burghley Ave
Borehamwood WD6 11 A6
Kingston u T KT3 177 B2
Burghley Ct SW19 179 A5
Burghley Hall Cl SW19 157 A3
Burghley Ho SW19 157 A1
Burghley Pl CR4 202 D5
Burghley Rd
Camden Town NW5 71 B4
Leytonstone E11 54 C1
London N8 50 C6
Wimbledon SW19 179 A6
Burghley Twr W3 111 D6
Burgh St N1 94 D5 234 D4
Burgon St EC4 241 D1
Burgos Cl CR0 220 C2
Burgos Gr SE10 141 D4
Burgoyne Rd
Ashford TW16 171 D4
Brixton SW9 138 B2
Harringay N4 50 D3
South Norwood SE25 205 D5
Burham Cl SE20 184 C3
Burhan Uddin Ho E1 243 C5
Burhill Gr HA5 23 A1
Buriton Ho 9 SW15 156 B3
Burke Cl SW15 133 C1
Burke Ho 1 SW11 136 B1
Burke Lodge E13 99 B4
Burke St E16 98 D2
Burket Cl UB2 107 B2
Burland Rd SW11 158 D6

Burleigh Ave
Bexley DA15 ... 167 D6
Hackbridge SM6 ... 219 B5
Burleigh Ct N17 ... 34 A4
Burleigh Gdns
Ashford TW15 ... 171 A5
Osidge N14 ... 15 C3
Burleigh Ho
Cheam SM3 ... 201 A1
Chelsea SW3 ... 266 D5
North Kensington W10 ... 90 D2
Burleigh Lo 3 SW19 ... 179 D3
Burleigh Par N14 ... 15 D3
Burleigh Pl SW15 ... 156 D6
Burleigh Rd
Cheam SM3 ... 201 A1
Enfield EN1 ... 5 C1
Hillingdon UB10 ... 82 D6
Burleigh St WC2 ... 250 C6
Burleigh Way EN2 ... 5 B2
Burleigh Wlk SE6 ... 164 A3
Burley Cl Chingford E4 ... 35 C5
Mitcham SW16 ... 181 D1
Burley Ho E1 ... 96 D1
Burley Rd E16 ... 99 C2
Burlington Apartments
SE20 ... 184 B3
Burlington Arc W1 ... 249 A5
Burlington Ave
Richmond TW9 ... 132 C4
Romford RM7 ... 59 D3
Burlington Cl
East Bedfont TW14 ... 149 B4
5 Newham E6 ... 100 A1
Orpington BR6 ... 226 D6
Paddington W9 ... 91 C3
Pinner HA5 ... 40 B6
Burlington Ct
Chiswick W4 ... 133 A5
Highgate N6 ... 49 A1
Burlington Danes Sch
W12 ... 90 B1
Burlington Gate
SW20 ... 179 A1
Burlington Gdns
Acton Green W4 ... 111 A1
Acton W3 ... 111 A5
Dagenham RM6 ... 59 A2
Fulham SW6 ... 135 A3
Marylebone
W1 ... 115 C6 249 A5
Burlington Ho NW3 ... 70 B3
Burlington Inf Sch
KT3 ... 199 D5
Burlington Jun Sch
KT3 ... 199 D5
Burlington La W4 ... 133 B5
Burlington Lo BR7 ... 188 B3
Burlington Mews
Acton W3 ... 111 A5
2 Putney SW15 ... 157 B6
Burlington Park Ho 6
HA7 ... 25 C6
Burlington Pl
Fulham SW6 ... 135 A3
Woodford IG8 ... 21 A1
Burlington Rd
Acton Green W4 ... 111 A1
Enfield EN2 ... 5 B4
Fulham SW6 ... 135 A3
Hounslow TW7 ... 130 B4
Muswell Hill N10 ... 49 A6
New Malden KT3 ... 199 D5
South Norwood CR7 ... 183 B1
Tottenham N17 ... 34 A2
Burlington Rise EN4 ... 14 D4
Burma Rd N16 ... 73 B4
Burmarsh 6 NW5 ... 71 A2
Burmarsh Ct SE20 ... 184 C2
Burma Terr 11 SE19 ... 183 C5
Burmester Ho SW17 ... 158 A1
Burmester Rd SW17 ... 158 A1
Burnaby Cres W4 ... 133 A6
Burnaby Ct 31 SE16 ... 118 A4
Burnaby Gdns W4 ... 132 D6
Burnaby St
SW10 ... 136 A5 266 B3
Burnand Ho 3 W14 ... 112 D3
Burnbrae Cl N12 ... 29 D4
Burnbury Rd SW12 ... 159 C3
Burncroft Ave EN3 ... 6 C3
Burndell Way UB4 ... 84 D2
Burne Jones Ho W14 ... 254 B3
Burnell Ave
Richmond TW10 ... 175 C5
Welling DA16 ... 146 A3
Burnell Gdns HA7 ... 25 D1
Burnell Ho 18 SW2 ... 160 C3
Burnell Rd SM1 ... 217 D4
Burnell Wlk SE1 ... 263 D2
Burnels Ave E6 ... 100 C4
Burness Cl N7 ... 72 B2
Burne St NW1 ... 237 A4
Burnett Cl E9 ... 74 C3
Burnett Ct SW11 ... 267 A1
Burnett Ho 6 SE13 ... 142 A3
Burney Ave KT5 ... 198 B4
Burney Ho 4 SW16 ... 181 C5
Burney St SE10 ... 142 A5
Burnfoot Ave
SW6 ... 135 A4 264 B1
Burnham NW3 ... 70 C1
Burnham Ave UB10 ... 61 A4
Burnham Cl
Bermondsey SE1 ... 263 D3
Enfield EN1 ... 5 C5
Harrow HA3 ... 43 A5
Hendon NW7 ... 28 A3
Burnham Cres E11 ... 55 C5
Burnham Ct
Bayswater W2 ... 245 D6
Hendon NW4 ... 46 C5
15 Stanmore HA7 ... 25 C5
Burnham Dr KT4 ... 216 D6
Burnham Est 8 E2 ... 96 C4
Burnham Gdns
Cranford TW4 ... 128 B4
Croydon CR0 ... 205 D2
Hayes UB3 ... 105 B3
Burnham Rd
Chingford Hatch E4 ... 35 B5
Dagenham RM9 ... 102 B6
Morden SM4 ... 201 D5
Sidcup DA14 ... 169 A2
Burnham St
Bethnal Green E2 ... 96 C4
Kingston u T KT2 ... 176 C2
Burnham Way
Ealing W13 ... 109 B3
Penge SE26 ... 185 B5
Burnhill Ho EC1 ... 235 A1
Burnhill Rd BR3 ... 185 C1
Burnley Cl WD19 ... 22 C5
Burnley Rd
London SW9 ... 138 B3
Willesden NW10 ... 68 A3
Burnsall St
SW3 ... 114 C1 257 B2
Burns Ave
Blackfen DA15 ... 168 B5
Feltham TW14 ... 150 A5
Ilford RM6 ... 58 C2
Southall UB1 ... 107 C6
Burns Cl Bexley DA16 ... 145 D4
Hayes UB4 ... 84 A2
Mitcham SW17 ... 180 B4
Walthamstow E17 ... 54 A5
Burns Ct Tottenham N17 ... 34 B3
Wallington SM6 ... 219 B1
Burns Ho
18 Bethnal Green E2 ... 96 C4
Bexley DA16 ... 146 C4
1 Islington N7 ... 72 B2
Kennington SE17 ... 261 D1
11 Stoke Newington N16 ... 73 C4
Burn's Ho NW10 ... 89 C6
Burnside Ave E4 ... 35 B4
Burnside Cl Barnet EN5 ... 1 C2
Rotherhithe SE16 ... 118 D5
Twickenham TW1 ... 153 A5
Burnside Cres HA0 ... 87 D6
Burnside Ct 1 SM6 ... 219 A5
Burnside Rd RM8 ... 58 D1
Burns Rd
Battersea SW11 ... 136 D3
Ealing W13 ... 109 B4
Wembley HA0 ... 88 A5
Burn's Rd NW10 ... 89 D6
Burns Way TW5 ... 128 D4
Burnt Ash Hill
Lee SE12 ... 164 D5
Lewisham SE12 ... 165 A3
Burnt Ash Hts BR1 ... 187 B5
Burnt Ash La BR1,
SE12 ... 187 B5
Burnt Ash Prim Sch
BR1 ... 187 A5
Burnt Ash Rd SE12 ... 164 D6
Burnthwaite Rd
SW6 ... 135 B5 264 D3
BURNT OAK ... 27 B3
Burnt Oak Broadway
HA8 ... 26 D2
Burnt Oak Fields HA8 ... 27 A2
Burnt Oak Jun Sch
DA15 ... 168 A3
Burnt Oak La DA15 ... 168 B3
Burnt Oak Sta HA8 ... 27 A2
Burntwood Cl SW18 ... 158 C3
Burntwood Ct SW17 ... 158 A1
Burntwood Grange Rd
SW18 ... 158 C3
Burntwood La SW17 ... 158 B2
Burntwood Sch SW17 ... 158 B2
Burntwood View 6
SE19 ... 183 D5
Buross St E1 ... 96 B1
Burpham Cl UB4 ... 84 D2
Burrage Ct 17 SE16 ... 118 D2
Burrage Gr SE18 ... 123 A2
Burrage Pl SE18 ... 122 D1
Burrage Rd SE18 ... 123 A1
Burrard Ho 11 E2 ... 96 C5
Burrard Rd Newham E16 ... 99 B1
West Hampstead NW6 ... 69 C4
Burr Cl
Bexleyheath DA7 ... 147 B2
St George in t East E1 ... 118 A5
Burrell Cl Croydon CR0 ... 207 A3
Edgware HA8 ... 10 D2
Burrell Ct HA1 ... 42 B2
Burrell Ho 4 TW1 ... 153 B4
Burrell Row BR3 ... 185 C1
Burrells 9 BR3 ... 185 D1
Burrell St SE1 ... 116 D5 251 C4
Burrell's Wharf Sq
E14 ... 119 D1
Burrell Twrs E10 ... 53 C2
Burrhill Ct SE16 ... 118 D3
Burritt Rd KT1 ... 176 C1
Burrmead Ct NW2 ... 67 D5
Burroughs Gdns NW4 ... 46 B5
Burroughs The NW4 ... 46 B5
Burrow Ho 19 SW9 ... 138 B3
Burrow Rd SE22 ... 139 C1
Burrows Mews SE1 ... 251 C2
Burrows Rd NW10 ... 90 C4
Burrow Wlk SE21 ... 161 A4
Burr Rd SW18 ... 157 C4
Bursar St SE1 ... 253 A3
Bursdon Cl DA15 ... 167 D2
Bursland Rd EN3 ... 6 D1
Burslem St E1 ... 96 A1
Bursted Wood Prim Sch
DA7 ... 147 D3
Burstock Rd SW15 ... 135 A1
Burston Rd SW15 ... 156 D6
Burstow Rd SW20 ... 179 A2
Burtenshaw Rd KT7 ... 197 A3
Burtley Cl N4 ... 51 A1
Burton Bank N1 ... 73 B1
Burton Cl
Chessington KT9 ... 213 D1
South Norwood CR7 ... 205 B6
Burton Ct Chelsea SW3 ... 257 D2
10 Friern Barnet N11 ... 30 D5
Thames Ditton KT7 ... 197 A3
Burton Dr EN3 ... 7 C6
Burton Gdns TW5 ... 129 B4
Burton Gr SE17 ... 262 C1
Burton Ho
8 Bermondsey SE16 ... 118 B4
Brixton SE5 ... 138 D4
Penge SE26 ... 184 B5
Burtonhole Cl NW7 ... 28 D6
Burtonhole La
Finchley NW7 ... 29 A6
Mill Hill NW7 ... 28 D6
Burton La 3 SW9 ... 138 C3
Burton Lo 3 SW15 ... 157 B6
Burton Mews SW1 ... 258 B3
Burton Pl WC1 ... 232 D1
Burton Rd
7 Brixton SW9 ... 138 C3
Brixton SW9 ... 138 D3
Brondesbury NW6 ... 69 B1
Kingston u T KT2 ... 176 A3
Wanstead E18 ... 55 B6
Burtons Ct E15 ... 76 B1
Burtons Rd TW12 ... 174 A6
Burton St WC1 ... 93 D3 239 D6
Burtonwood Ho N4 ... 51 B2
Burt Rd E16 ... 121 C5
Burtt Ho 6 N1 ... 95 C4
Burtwell La SE21, SE27 ... 183 B6
Burvill Ct SW20 ... 178 C2
Burwash Ho SE1 ... 252 D1
Burwash Rd SE18 ... 123 B1
Burwell 2 KT1 ... 176 C1
Burwell Ave UB6 ... 64 C2
Burwell Cl 27 E1 ... 96 B1
Burwell Rd E10 ... 53 A1
Burwell Wlk 14 E3 ... 97 C3
Burwood Ave
Hayes BR2 ... 225 B6
Pinner HA5 ... 40 C4
Burwood Cl KT6 ... 198 C1
Burwood Ct SE23 ... 162 C4
Burwood Ho 11 SW9 ... 138 D1
Burwood Lo SW19 ... 179 B6
Burwood Pl Barnet EN4 ... 2 A4
Paddington W2 ... 237 B2
Bury Ave Hayes UB4 ... 83 C5
Ruislip HA4 ... 39 A3
Bury Cl SE16 ... 118 D5
Bury Ct EC3 ... 243 B2
Buryfield Ct 23 SE8 ... 118 D2
Bury Gr SM4 ... 201 D4
Bury Hall Villas N9 ... 17 D4
Bury Pl WC1 ... 94 A2 240 B3
Bury Rd Chingford E4 ... 20 C6
Dagenham RM10 ... 81 D3
Hornsey N22 ... 50 C6
Bury St W N9 ... 17 C4
Buryside Cl IG2 ... 57 D5
Bury St Edmonton N9 ... 18 A3
Ruislip HA4 ... 39 B3
St James SW1 ... 115 C5 249 B4
Whitechapel EC3 95 C1 243 B2
Bury Wlk SW3 ... 114 C1 257 A2
Burywood Ct EN3 ... 6 C3
Busbridge Ho 24 E14 ... 97 C2
Busby Ho SW16 ... 181 C6
Busby Mews 5 NW1 ... 71 D2
Busby Pl NW5 ... 71 D2
Busch Cl TW7 ... 131 B4
Busch Cnr TW7 ... 131 B4
Bushbaby Cl SE1 ... 263 A5
Bushberry Rd E9 ... 75 A2
Bush Cl IG2 ... 57 B4
Bush Cotts 12 SW18 ... 157 C6
Bush Ct London N14 ... 15 C3
7 Shepherd's Bush
W12 ... 112 D4
Bushell Cl SW2 ... 160 B2
Bushell Gn WD23 ... 8 B2
Bushell Ho 3 SE27 ... 183 A6
Bushell Way BR7 ... 188 C5
BUSHEY ... 8 A2
Bushey Ave
Crofton BR5 ... 211 B2
Snaresbrook E18 ... 54 D6
Bushey Cl Chingford E4 ... 20 A1
Ickenham UB10 ... 60 C6
Bushey Ct SW20 ... 178 B1
Bushey Down SW12 ... 159 B2
Bushey Hall SE5 ... 139 D4
BUSHEY HEATH ... 8 C4
Bushey Heath Prim Sch
WD23 ... 8 B3
Bushey Hill Rd SE5 ... 139 D4
Bushey Ho SE12 ... 165 C1
Bushey La SM1 ... 217 C4
Bushey Lees DA15 ... 167 D5
BUSHEY MEAD ... 200 D6
Bushey Meads Sch
WD23 ... 8 A6
Bushey Rd
Croydon CR0 ... 223 C6
Bushey Rd *continued*
Hayes UB3 ... 105 C2
Ickenham UB10 ... 60 C6
Newham E13 ... 99 C5
South Tottenham N15 ... 51 C3
Sutton SM1 ... 217 C4
West Barnes SW20 ... 178 D1
Bushey Way BR3 ... 208 B4
Bush Fair Ct N14 ... 15 B5
Bushfield Cl HA8 ... 10 D2
Bushfield Cres HA8 ... 10 D2
Bushfield Ho N5 ... 73 A3
Bush Gr London NW9 ... 45 A2
Stanmore HA7 ... 25 D2
Bushgrove Rd RM8 ... 80 D5
BUSH HILL ... 17 B5
Bush Hill N21 ... 17 A5
Bush Hill Par EN1 ... 17 B4
BUSH HILL PARK ... 17 C5
Bush Hill Park Prim Sch
EN1 ... 18 A6
Bush Hill Park Sta EN1 ... 17 D5
Bush Hill Rd Enfield N21 ... 17 B5
Harrow HA3 ... 44 B3
Bush Ind Est NW10 ... 89 B3
Bush La EC4 ... 117 B6 252 C6
Bushmead Cl 7 N15 ... 51 D5
Bushmoor Cres SE18 ... 144 D5
Bushnell Rd SW17 ... 159 B1
Bush Rd
Bermondsey SE8 ... 118 D2
Hackney E8 ... 96 B6
Littleton TW17 ... 192 B4
Richmond TW9 ... 132 B6
Wanstead E11 ... 55 A2
Woodford IG9 ... 37 D6
Bushway RM8 ... 80 D5
Bushwood E11 ... 55 A1
Bushwood Dr
SE1 ... 117 D2 263 D3
Bushwood Rd TW9 ... 132 C6
Bushy Ct KT1 ... 175 C2
Bushy Park Gdns
TW12 ... 174 B5
Bushy Park Rd TW11 ... 175 B3
Bushy Rd TW11 ... 174 D3
Business Acad Bexley The
DA18 ... 125 A4
Business Design Ctr*
N1 ... 94 C6 234 B5
Buspace Studios 3
W10 ... 91 A3
Butcher Row E1 ... 96 D1
Butchers Rd E16 ... 99 A1
Bute Ave TW10 ... 154 A2
Bute Ct SM6 ... 219 C3
Bute Gardens W SM6 ... 219 C3
Bute Gdns
Hammersmith W6 ... 112 D2
Wallington SM6 ... 219 C3
Bute House Prep Sch
W6 ... 112 D2
Bute Mews NW11 ... 48 A4
Bute Rd Ilford IG6 ... 56 D4
Thornton Heath CR0 ... 204 C1
Wallington SM6 ... 219 C4
Bute St SW7 ... 114 B2 256 C4
Bute Wlk 18 N1 ... 73 B2
Butfield Ho 6 E9 ... 74 C2
Butler Ave HA1 ... 42 B2
Butler Cl HA8 ... 26 D1
Butler Ct Dagenham RM8 ... 81 C6
Wembley HA0 ... 65 A4
Butler Ho
32 Bethnal Green E2 ... 96 C4
5 Brixton SW9 ... 138 D4
11 Poplar E14 ... 97 B1
Butler Pl SW1 ... 259 C6
Butler Rd
Dagenham RM8 ... 80 B4
Harrow HA1 ... 42 A2
Willesden NW10 ... 67 D1
Butlers Cl TW3 ... 129 B1
Butlers & Colonial Wharf
SE1 ... 253 D2
Butler's Cotts DA7 ... 147 C3
Butler St
33 Bethnal Green E2 ... 96 C4
Hillingdon UB10 ... 82 D3
Butler's Wharf W SE1 ... 253 C3
Butley Ct 8 E3 ... 97 A5
Butt Ct SM4 ... 202 A3
Buttercup Cl UB5 ... 63 B2
Butterfield Cl
1 Bermondsey SE16 ... 118 B4
Tottenham N17 ... 33 A4
Twickenham TW1 ... 152 D5
Butterfield Ho 4 EN2 ... 4 D3
Butterfields E17 ... 54 A4
Butterfield Sq 10 E6 ... 100 B1
Butterfly Ct E6 ... 100 B4
Butterfly La SE9 ... 166 D5
Butterfly Wlk 2 SE5 ... 139 B4
Butter Hill SM5, SM6 ... 219 A4
Butteridges Cl RM9 ... 103 B6
Buttermere NW1 ... 231 D2
Buttermere Cl
Bermondsey SE1 ... 263 C3
East Bedfont TW14 ... 149 D3
Leyton E11 ... 76 B4
West Barnes SM4 ... 200 D3
Buttermere Ct NW8 ... 229 C6
Buttermere Dr SW15 ... 157 A6
Buttermere Ho
London N12 ... 30 C5
13 Tower Hamlets E3 ... 97 B4
Buttermere Wlk 9 E8 ... 73 D2
Butterwick W6 ... 112 C2
Butterworth Ct SW16 ... 160 A1
Butterworth Gdns IG8 ... 37 A5
Buttesland St
N1 ... 95 B4 235 D2
Buttfield Cl RM10 ... 81 D2
Buttmarsh Cl SE18 ... 122 D1
Buttsbury Rd IG1 ... 79 A3
Butts Cotts TW13 ... 151 B1
Butts Cres TW13 ... 151 C1
Butts Ho TW13 ... 151 C1
Butts Piece UB5 ... 84 B5
Butts Rd BR1 ... 186 C5
Butts The TW8 ... 131 D6
Buxhall Cres E9 ... 75 B2
Buxlow Prep Sch HA9 ... 66 A5
Buxted Rd
Camberwell SE22 ... 139 C1
Colney Hatch N12 ... 30 C5
Dalston E8 ... 73 D1
Buxton Cl London N9 ... 18 C2
Woodford IG8 ... 37 D4
Buxton Cres SM3 ... 217 A4
Buxton Ct 1 Leyton E11 ... 54 D2
Shoreditch N1 ... 235 B2
Buxton Dr
Kingston u T KT3 ... 177 B1
Leytonstone E11 ... 54 C5
Buxton Gdns W3 ... 110 D6
Buxton Ho
Leytonstone E11 ... 54 C5
3 London SW11 ... 136 B1
Buxton Lo E11 ... 77 B6
Buxton Mews SW4 ... 137 D3
Buxton Rd Chingford E4 ... 20 B4
Ilford IG2 ... 57 C3
Mortlake SW14 ... 133 C2
Newham E6 ... 100 A4
Stratford E15 ... 76 C3
Thornton Heath CR7 ... 204 D4
Upper Holloway N19 ... 49 D1
Walthamstow E17 ... 53 A5
Willesden NW2 ... 68 B2
Buxton St E1 ... 95 D3 243 D5
Buzzard Creek Ind Est
IG11 ... 102 A2
Byam Shaw Sch of Art
N19 ... 71 D6
Byam St SW6 ... 136 A3
Byards Croft SW16 ... 181 D2
Byards Ct SE16 ... 118 D3
Byas Ho 6 E3 ... 97 B4
Byatt Wlk TW12 ... 173 A4
Bychurch End 11
TW11 ... 174 D5
Bycroft Rd UB1 ... 85 C3
Bycroft St SE20 ... 184 D3
Bycullah Ave EN2 ... 4 D3
Bycullah Ct EN2 ... 4 D2
Bycullah Rd EN2 ... 4 D3
Byefield Cl SE16 ... 119 A4
Byegrove Ct SW19 ... 180 B4
Byegrove Rd SW19 ... 180 B4
Byelands Cl 12 SE16 ... 118 D5
Bye The W3 ... 89 C1
Bye Ways TW2 ... 151 D1
Byeways The KT5 ... 198 D4
Byeway The SW14 ... 133 A2
Bye Way The HA3 ... 24 D2
Byfeld Gdns SW13 ... 134 A4
Byfield Ct KT3 ... 200 A5
Byfield Rd TW7 ... 131 A2
Byford Cl E15 ... 76 C1
Bygrove CR0 ... 223 D1
Bygrove Prim Sch E14 ... 97 D1
Bygrove St E14 ... 97 D1
Byland Cl
Abbey Wood SE2 ... 124 B3
Carshalton SM4 ... 202 B2
Southgate N21 ... 16 B4
Byne Rd
Carshalton SM5 ... 218 C6
Forest Hill SE26 ... 184 C5
Bynes Rd CR2 ... 221 B1
Byng Pl WC1 ... 93 D3 239 C5
Byng St E14 ... 119 C4
Bynon Ave DA7 ... 147 B2
Byre Rd N14 ... 15 B5
Byrne Ho 11 SW2 ... 160 B6
Byrne Rd SW12 ... 159 B2
Byron Ave
Borehamwood WD6 ... 10 C6
Cranford TW4 ... 128 B3
Plashet E12 ... 78 A2
Queensbury NW9 ... 44 D6
Sutton SM1 ... 218 B4
West Barnes KT3 ... 200 A4
Woodford E18 ... 36 D1
Byron Ave E SM1 ... 218 B4
Byron Cl Feltham TW12 ... 173 B6
Forest Hill SE26 ... 185 A6
Hackney E8 ... 96 A6
Streatham SW16 ... 182 A4
Thamesmead SE28 ... 124 C5
Walton-on-T KT12 ... 195 A1
Byron Court Prim Sch
HA0 ... 65 C6
Byron Ct Chelsea SW3 ... 257 B3
Dulwich SE21 ... 162 A3
Ealing W7 ... 109 A2
Enfield EN2 ... 4 D3
3 Hampstead NW6 ... 70 A1
Harrow HA1 ... 42 C3
4 New Barnet EN5 ... 2 A1
Paddington W9 ... 91 C3
1 Richmond TW10 ... 175 D6
South Norwood CR7 ... 183 A1
St Pancras WC1 ... 240 C6
11 Wanstead E11 ... 55 A5
Woodford E18 ... 37 B2
Byron Dr
East Finchley N2 ... 48 B3
Erith DA8 ... 147 D5
Byron Gdns SM1 ... 218 B4
Byron Hill Rd HA1, HA2 ... 64 C6
Byron Ho 5 BR3 ... 185 D4
Byron Mews
Hampstead NW3 ... 70 C4
2 Maida Vale W9 ... 91 C3
Byron Par UB10 ... 83 A3
Byron Rd Dollis Hill NW2 ... 68 B6
Ealing W5 ... 110 B5
Edgware NW7 ... 28 A5
Harrow HA1 ... 42 C3
Leyton E10 ... 53 D1
Walthamstow E17 ... 53 C6
Wealdstone HA3 ... 24 D1
Wembley HA0 ... 65 C5
Byron St E14 ... 98 A1
Byron Way Hayes UB4 ... 83 D3
Northolt UB5 ... 85 A4
West Drayton UB7 ... 104 B2
Bysouth Cl N15 ... 51 B5
Bythorn St SW9 ... 138 B1
Byton Rd SW17 ... 180 D4
Byward Ave TW14 ... 150 C5
Byward St EC3 ... 117 C6 253 B5
Bywater Ho SE18 ... 122 A3
Bywater Pl SE16 ... 119 A5
Bywater St
SW3 ... 114 D1 257 C2
Byway The KT19 ... 215 D4
Bywell Pl W1 ... 239 A3
Bywood Ave CR0 ... 206 D3
Bywood Terr CR0 ... 206 C3
Byworth Ho HA7 ... 25 C4
Byworth Wlk N19 ... 50 A1

C

Cabbell St NW1 ... 92 C2 237 A3
Cabinet Off SW1 ... 250 A2
Cabinet War Rooms & Churchill Mus*
SW1 ... 115 D4 249 D2
Cabinet Way E4 ... 35 B4
Cable Ho WC1 ... 234 A2
Cable Pl SE10 ... 142 A4
Cable St E1 ... 118 B6
Cabot Ct SE16 ... 118 D3
Cabot Sq E14 ... 119 C5
Cabot Way 3 E6 ... 99 D6
Cabul Rd SW11 ... 136 C3
Cactus Cl SE5 ... 139 C3
Cactus Wlk W12 ... 89 D1
Cadbury Cl
Ashford TW16 ... 171 C3
Isleworth TW7 ... 131 A4
Cadbury Rd TW16 ... 171 C4
Cadbury Way 1 SE16 ... 118 A2
Caddington Cl EN4 ... 14 C6
Caddington Rd NW2 ... 69 A5
Caddis Cl HA7 ... 24 D3
Cadell Cl E2 ... 95 D5
Cadell Ho 12 E2 ... 95 D5
Cade Rd SE10 ... 142 B4
Cader Rd SW18 ... 158 A5
Cadet Dr SE1 ... 117 D1 263 D2
Cade Tyler Ho 10
SE10 ... 142 A4
Cadiz St SE17 ... 117 A1 262 B1
Cadley Terr SE23 ... 162 C2
Cadman Cl SW9 ... 138 D5
Cadmer Cl KT3 ... 199 C5
Cadmore Ho 4 N1 ... 72 D1
Cadmus Cl 9 SW4 ... 137 D2
Cadmus Ct 6 SW9 ... 138 C4
Cadnam Lo E14 ... 120 B3
Cadnam Point 15
SW15 ... 156 B3
Cadogan Cl
Beckenham BR3 ... 186 B1
Hackney Wick E9 ... 75 B1
Harrow HA2 ... 63 D4
Teddington TW11 ... 174 C5
Cadogan Ct
Chelsea SW3 ... 257 C3
New Malden KT3 ... 199 C5
Sutton SM2 ... 217 D2
Cadogan Ct Gdns SW1 258 A4
Cadogan Gate
SW1 ... 114 D2 257 D4
Cadogan Gdns
Chelsea
SW3 ... 114 D2 257 D3
Finchley N3 ... 29 D2
Southgate N21 ... 16 C6
Wanstead E18 ... 55 B6
Cadogan Ho SW3 ... 266 D5
Cadogan La
SW1 ... 115 A3 258 A5
Cadogan Pl
SW1 ... 114 D3 257 D5
Cadogan Rd
Kingston u T KT6 ... 197 D4
Woolwich SE18 ... 123 A3
Cadogan Sq
SW1 ... 114 D3 257 D5
Cadogan St
SW3 ... 114 D2 257 C3
Cadogan Terr E9 ... 75 B1
Cadoxton Ave 3 N15 ... 51 D3
Cadwallon Rd SE9 ... 167 A2
Caedmon Rd N7 ... 72 B4
Caerleon Cl
Claygate KT10 ... 213 B1
Sidcup DA14 ... 190 C5
Caerleon Terr SE2 ... 124 B2
Caernafon Ho HA7 ... 25 A5

Caernarvon Cl CR4 204 A6
Caernarvon Ct 3 KT5 198 B4
Caernarvon Ho W2 236 A2
Caesar Ct 25 E2 96 D5
Caesar's Way TW17 193 B3
Caesars Wlk CR4 202 D4
Cahill St EC1 242 B5
Cahir St E14 119 D2
Cain Ct 2 W5 87 C2
Caine Ho W3 110 D4
Cain's La TW14 149 C6
Caird St W10 91 B4
Cairn Ave W5 109 D5
Cairndale Cl BR1 186 D3
Cairnfield Ave NW2 67 D5
Cairnfield Ct NW2 67 C5
Cairngorm Cl 3 TW11 175 A5
Cairn Ho 3 SW19 180 C3
Cairns Ho 3 N7 72 B4
Cairns Mews SE18 144 A4
Cairns Rd SW11 158 C6
Cairn Way HA7 24 D4
Cairo New Rd CR0 220 D6
Cairo Rd E17 53 C5
Caister Ho N7 72 B2
Caistor Ho
 10 Balham SW12 159 B4
 5 West Ham E15 98 D6
Caistor Mews SW12 159 B4
Caistor Park Rd E15 98 D6
Caistor Rd SW12 159 B4
Caithness Gdns DA15 167 D5
Caithness Ho N1 233 C6
Caithness Rd
 Hammersmith W14 112 D3
 Mitcham CR4 181 B3
Calabria Rd N5 72 D3
Calais Gate SE5 138 D4
Calais St SE5 138 D4
Calbourne Rd SW12 159 A4
Calcott Wlk SE9 187 D6
Calcraft Ho 10 E2 96 C5
Caldbeck Ave KT4 200 B1
Caldecot Ct SE5 139 A3
Caldecote 3 KT1 176 C1
Caldecote Gdns WD23 8 C4
Caldecote La WD23 8 D5
Caldecot Rd SE5 139 A3
Caldecott Way E5 74 D5
Calder Ave UB6 86 D5
Calder Cl EN1 5 C2
Calder Ct SE16 119 B5
Calder Gdns HA8 44 C6
Calder Ho UB5 85 A6
Calderon Ho NW8 230 A4
Calderon Pl 20 W10 90 C2
Calderon Rd E11 76 B5
Calder Rd SM4 202 A4
Caldervale Rd SW4 159 D6
Calderwood St SE18 122 C2
Caldew Ct NW7 28 A3
Caldew St SE5 139 B5
Caldicote Gn NW9 45 C3
Caldon Ho 2 UB5 85 B3
Caldwell Rd WD19 22 D6
Caldwell St SW9 138 B5 270 D3
Caldy Rd DA17 125 D3
Caldy Wlk 13 N1 73 A2
Caleb St SE1 252 B2
Caledonia Ct
 Barking IG11 102 C5
 Hendon NW4 28 C1
Caledonia Ho 15 E14 97 A1
Caledonian Cl 1 IG3 58 B1
Caledonian Ct UB5 85 A3
Caledonian Market SE1 117 C3 263 B6
Caledonian Rd
 Islington N1 94 B6 233 C5
 Lower Holloway N7 72 B2
Caledonian Road & Barnsbury Sta N7 72 B1
Caledonian Road Sta N7 72 B2
Caledonian Sq 6 NW1 71 D2
Caledonian Wharf Rd E14 120 B2
Caledonia Rd TW19 148 A3
Caledonia St N1 233 B3
Caledon Rd East Ham E6 78 B1
 Hackbridge SM5, SM6 219 A4
Cale St SW3 114 C1 257 A2
Caletock Way SE10 120 D1
Calgarth NW1 232 B3
Calgary Ct 30 SE16 118 C4
Caliban Twr 9 N1 95 C5
Calico Ho 4 SW11 136 A2
Calico Row 5 SW11 136 A2
Calidore Cl SW2 160 B5
California Bldg 2 SE13 141 D4
California La WD23 8 B3
California Rd KT3 199 A6
Callaby Terr 11 N1 73 B2
Callaghan Cl SE13 142 C1
Callahan Cotts 8 E1 96 C2
Callander Rd SE6 164 A2
Callanders The WD23 8 C3
Callan Sch The W1 93 C1 239 B2
Callard Ave N13 32 D6
Callcott Ct NW6 69 B1
Callcott Rd NW6 69 B1
Callcott St W8 245 A4
Callendar Rd SW7 256 C6
Callingham Cl 13 E14 97 B2
Callingham Ho 1 SW4 138 A2
Callis Farm Cl TW19 148 A5
Callis Rd E17 53 B3
Callonfield 3 E17 53 A5
Callow St SW3 136 B6 266 C6
Calmington Rd SE5 139 C6
Calmont Rd BR1 186 C4
Calonne Rd SW19 178 D6
Calshot Ho N1 233 C4
Calshot Rd TW6 126 D3
Calshot St N1 94 B5 233 C3
Calshot Way Enfield EN2 4 D2
 Harlington TW6 126 C3
Calstock NW1 232 C5
Calstock Ho SE11 261 B2
Calthorpe Gdns
 Edgware HA8 26 B5
 Sutton SM1 218 A5
Calthorpe St WC1 94 B3 240 D6
Calton Ave SE21 161 C5
Calton Rd EN5 14 B5
Calumet Ct SW17 180 C4
Calver 13 NW5 71 B4
Calver Ct E17 54 B6
Calverley Cl BR3 185 D4
Calverley Cres RM10 81 C6
Calverley Gdns HA3 43 D2
Calverley Gr N19 49 D1
Calverley Rd KT17 216 A2
Calvert Ave E2 95 D4
Calvert Cl
 Belvedere DA17 125 D2
 Sidcup DA14 191 A4
Calvert Ct
 1 London N19 49 C1
 5 Richmond TW9 132 B1
Calvert Ho 9 W12 112 B6
Calverton SE5 139 C6
Calverton Prim Sch E16 99 D1
Calverton Rd E6 100 C6
Calvert Rd SE10 120 D1
Calvert's Bldgs SE1 252 C3
Calvert St NW1 93 A6 231 A6
Calvin St E1 95 D3 243 C5
Calydon Rd SE7 121 B1
Calypso Cres 6 SE15 139 D5
Calypso Way SE8, SE16 119 B2
Camac Rd TW2 152 B3
Camarthen Gn NW9 45 C3
Cambalt Ho 3 SW15 156 D6
Cambalt Rd SW15 156 D6
Cambay Ho 7 E1 97 A3
Cambell Jun & Inf Schs RM9 80 D1
Camber Ho 4 SE15 140 C6
Camberley Ave
 Enfield EN1 5 C1
 Wimbledon SW20 178 B1
Camberley Cl SM3 216 D5
Camberley Ct 15 SM2 217 D1
Camberley Ho NW1 231 D3
Camberley Rd TW6 126 C2
Cambert Way SE9 143 B1
CAMBERWELL 139 A4
Camberwell Bsns Ctr SE5 139 B5
Camberwell Church St SE5 139 B4
Camberwell Coll of Arts
 Camberwell SE5 139 C4
 Camberwell SE15 139 D5
Camberwell Glebe SE5 139 C4
Camberwell Gn SE5 139 B4
Camberwell Gr SE5 139 C3
Camberwell Green SE5 139 A4
Camberwell New Rd SW9 138 D5
Camberwell Rd SE5 139 A5
Camberwell Station Rd SE5 139 A4
Camberwell Trad Est SE5 139 A4
Cambeys Rd RM10 81 D3
Cambisgate SW19 179 A5
Camborne Ave W13 109 C4
Camborne Cl TW6 126 C2
Camborne Rd
 Belmont SM2 217 D1
 Bexley DA16 145 D3
 Croydon CR0 206 A2
 Harmondsworth TW6 126 C2
 Sidcup DA14 168 C1
 Wandsworth SW18 157 C4
 West Barnes SM4 200 D4
Camborne Way
 Harlington TW6 126 C2
 Heston TW5 129 C4
Cambourne Ave N9 18 D4
Cambourne Mews 6 W11 91 A1
Cambrai Ct N13 32 A6
Cambray Rd
 Broom Hill BR6 211 D2
 Streatham SW12 159 C3
Cambria 6 BR3 185 D1
Cambria Cl
 Hounslow TW3 129 C1
 Sidcup DA15 167 C3
Cambria Ct TW14 150 B4
Cambria Gdns TW19 148 A4
Cambria Ho
 Forest Hill SE26 184 A6
 14 Limehouse E14 97 A1
Cambria Lo 3 SW15 157 B6
Cambrian Ave IG2 57 C4
Cambrian Cl SE27 160 D1
Cambrian Ct UB2 107 D2
Cambrian Gn NW9 45 C4
Cambrian Rd Leyton E10 53 C1
 Richmond TW10 154 B5
Cambria Rd SE5 139 A2
Cambria St SW6 135 D5 265 D3
Cambridge Ave
 Falconwood DA16 145 D1
 Greenford UB6 64 D3
 Kilburn NW6 91 C5
 Kingston u T KT3, SW20 177 D1
Cambridge Barracks Rd 11 SE18 122 B2
Cambridge Cir WC2 93 D1 239 D1
Cambridge Cl
 Hounslow TW4 129 A1
 Walthamstow E17 53 B3
 Willesden NW10 67 A5
 Wimbledon SW20 178 B2
 Wood Green N22 32 C2
Cambridge Cotts TW9 132 C6
Cambridge Cres
 20 Bethnal Green E2 96 B5
 Teddington TW11 175 A5
Cambridge Ct
 4 Barnet EN5 1 B2
 26 Bethnal Green E2 96 B5
 7 Hammersmith W6 112 C2
 2 Kilburn NW6 91 C5
 Marylebone W2 237 A3
 Stamford Hill N16 51 C2
 Wembley HA0 65 D4
 Wimbledon SW20 178 B2
Cambridge Dr
 Lee SE12 165 A6
 Ruislip HA4 62 D6
Cambridge Gate NW1 238 C6
Cambridge Gate Mews NW1 238 D6
Cambridge Gdns
 Enfield EN1 6 A3
 Kilburn NW6 91 C5
 Kingston u T KT1 176 C1
 Muswell Hill N10 31 B2
 North Kensington W10 91 A1
 Southgate N21 17 B4
 Tottenham N17 33 B3
Cambridge Gn SE9 166 D3
Cambridge Gr
 Hammersmith W6 112 B2
 Penge SE20 184 B2
Cambridge Grove Rd
 13 Kingston u T KT1 176 C1
 Kingston u T KT1 198 C6
Cambridge Heath Rd E1, E2 96 B4
Cambridge Heath Sta E2 96 B5
Cambridge Ho
 Barking IG11 79 A1
 Ealing W13 87 A1
 Fulham SW6 135 A2
 2 Teddington TW11 175 A5
 8 Woolwich SE18 122 B2
Cambridge Mans SW11 267 C1
Cambridge Par EN1 6 A4
CAMBRIDGE PARK 153 C4
Cambridge Park Ct TW1 153 D4
Cambridge Park Rd E11 55 A2
Cambridge Pas 9 E9 74 C1
Cambridge Pk
 Twickenham TW1 153 D5
 Wanstead E11 55 A3
Cambridge Pl W8 245 D1
Cambridge Rd
 Barking IG11 79 A1
 Barnes SW13 133 D3
 Battersea SW11 136 D4 267 C1
 Carshalton SM5 218 C3
 3 Chingford E4 20 B3
 East Molesey KT8 195 B5
 Hampton TW12 173 B3
 Hanwell W7 108 D4
 Harrow HA2 41 C4
 Hounslow TW4 129 A1
 Ilford IG3 57 C1
 Kilburn NW6 91 C4
 Kilburn NW6 91 C5
 Kingston u T KT1 176 C1
 Leytonstone E11 54 D3
 Littleton TW15 171 A3
 Mitcham CR4 203 C6
 New Malden KT3 199 C5
 Penge SE20 206 B6
 Plaistow BR1 187 A3
 Richmond TW9 132 C5
 Sidcup DA14 189 C6
 Southall UB1 107 B5
 Teddington TW11 175 A5
 Twickenham TW1 153 D5
 Walton-on-T KT12 194 B3
 Wimbledon SW20 178 B2
Cambridge Rd N W4 110 D1
Cambridge Rd S 3 W4 110 D1
Cambridge Row SE18 122 D1
Cambridge Sch W6 112 B2
Cambridge Sq W2 92 C1 237 A2
Cambridge St SW1 115 C1 259 A2
Cambridge Terr
 Edmonton N9 17 D4
 Regent's Pk NW1 231 C1
Cambridge Terr Mews NW1 231 D1
Cambstone Cl N11 15 A2
Cambus Cl UB4 85 A2
Cambus Rd E16 99 A2
Cam Ct 2 SE15 139 D6
Camdale Rd SE18 145 D5
Camden Ave
 Feltham TW13 150 C3
 Hayes UB4 106 D6
Camden Cl BR7 189 A2
Camden Coll of English NW1 71 A1
Camden Ct 9 DA17 125 C1
Camden Gdns
 Camden Town NW1 71 B1
 Sutton SM1 217 D3
 Thornton Heath CR7 204 D6
Camden Gr BR7 188 D4
Camden High St NW1 93 C6 232 A5
Camden Hill Rd SE19 183 C4
Camden Ho
 6 Deptford SE8 119 B1
 Wallington CR6 220 A5
Camdenhurst St E14 97 A1
Camden Jun Sch SM5 218 D4
Camden Lock Pl NW1 71 B1
Camden Mews NW1 71 D2
Camden Mkt* NW1 93 B6 231 D6
Camden Park Rd
 Camden Town NW1 71 D2
 Chislehurst BR7 188 C3
Camden Pas N1 94 D6 234 C5
Camden Rd
 Camden Town NW1 93 B6 231 D6
 Carshalton SM5 218 D4
 Old Bexley DA5 169 B4
 Sutton SM1 217 D3
 Walthamstow E17 53 B3
 Wanstead E11 55 B3
Camden Road Sta NW1 71 C1
Camden Row SE3 142 C3
Camden Sch for Girls The NW5 71 C2
Camden Sq NW1 71 D2
Camden St NW1 93 C6 232 B5
Camden Studios NW1 232 B5
Camden Terr 17 NW1 71 D2
CAMDEN TOWN 71 B1
Camden Town Sta NW1 93 B6 231 D6
Camden Way
 Chislehurst West BR7 188 C3
 Thornton Heath CR7 204 D6
Camden Wlk N1 234 C5
Cameford Ct 20 SW12 160 A4
Camelford NW1 232 B5
Camelford Ct 15 W11 91 A1
Camelford Ho SE1 260 B1
Camelford Wlk 13 W11 91 A1
Camel Gr KT2 175 D5
Camelia Ct IG8 36 C4
Camellia Ct 20 BR3 185 C3
Camellia Ho
 Feltham TW13 150 A3
 New Cross SE8 141 B5
Camellia Pl TW2 151 D4
Camellia St SW8 270 A3
Camelot Cl
 Plumstead SE18 123 B4
 Wimbledon SW19 179 C6
Camelot Ho 15 NW1 71 D2
Camelot Prim Sch SE15 140 B6
Camel Rd E16 121 D5
Camera Pl SW10 266 C6
Cameret Ct 6 W11 112 D4
Cameron Cl
 East Barnet N20 14 C2
 Edmonton N18 34 B5
Cameron Ct 3 SW19 157 A3
Cameron Ho
 8 Bromley BR1 186 D2
 Camberwell SE5 139 A5
 St John's Wood NW8 230 A4
Cameron House Sch SW10 266 D6
Cameron Lo TW3 130 A1
Cameron Pl SW16 160 C2
Cameron Rd
 Bromley BR2 209 A4
 Forest Hill SE6 163 B2
 Ilford IG3 57 C1
 Thornton Heath CR0 204 D3
Cameron Sq CR4 180 C2
Camerton Cl 8 E8 73 D2
Camfrey Ct N8 50 A5
Camgate Ctr The TW19 148 B4
Camilla Cl TW16 171 D4
Camilla Ct 12 SM2 217 C1
Camilla Rd SE16 118 B2
Camille Cl SE25 206 A6
Camlan Rd BR1 186 D6
Camlet St E2 243 C6
Camlet Way EN4 1 D4
Camley St NW1 93 D5 232 D4
Camm 23 NW9 27 D1
Camm Gdns
 5 Kingston u T KT1 176 B1
 Thames Ditton KT7 196 D2
Camomile Ave CR4 180 D2
Camomile St EC3 95 C1 243 B2
Camomile Way UB7 82 A1
Campaign Ct W9 91 B3
Campana Rd SW6 135 C4 265 B2
Campasps Bsns Pk TW16 193 D4
Campbell Ave IG6 57 A5
Campbell Cl Ruislip HA4 40 A3
 Shooters Hill SE18 144 C4
 Streatham SW16 181 D6
 Twickenham TW2 152 B3
Campbell Croft HA8 26 C5
Campbell Ct
 Dulwich SE21 162 A3
 Ealing W7 108 C6
 Kingsbury NW9 45 A3
 South Kensington SW7 256 A5
 Tottenham N17 33 D2
Campbell Gordon Way NW2 68 B4
Campbell Ho
 Paddington W2 236 C5
 Pimlico SW1 259 A1
 30 Shepherd's Bush W12 112 B6
 6 Wallington SM6 219 B4
Campbell Rd Bow E3 97 C4
 Ealing W7 108 C6
 Newham E6 100 A6
 Stratford E15 76 D4
 Thornton Heath CR0 204 D3
 Tottenham N17 34 A2
 Twickenham TW2 152 B2
 Walthamstow E17 53 B5
Campbell Wlk N1 233 B6
Campdale Rd N7 71 D5
Campden Cres
 Dagenham RM8 80 C4
 Wembley HA0 65 B5
Campden Gr W8 113 C4 245 B2
Campden Hill W8 113 C4 245 A2
Campden Hill Ct W8 245 B2
Campden Hill Gate W8 245 A2
Campden Hill Gdns W8 245 A4
Campden Hill Mans W8 245 B4
Campden Hill Pl W14 244 D4
Campden Hill Rd W8 113 C4 245 A2
Campden Hill Sq W14 113 B5 244 D4
Campden Ho 4 NW6 70 B1
Campden Hos W8 245 A3
Campden House Cl W8 245 B2
Campden Rd
 Ickenham UB10 60 B4
 South Croydon CR2 221 C3
Campden St W8 113 C5 245 A3
Campden Way RM8 80 B4
Campe Ho 1 N10 31 A3
Campen Cl SW19 157 A2
Camperdown St E1 243 D1
Campfield Rd SE9 165 D4
Campion Cl Harrow HA3 44 B3
 Hillingdon UB8 82 B2
 Newham E6 122 B6
 South Croydon CR2 221 C4
Campion Ct London N12 30 C4
 10 Wembley HA0 88 A5
Campion Gdns IG8 37 A5
Campion Ho 15 N16 73 C3
Campion House (Seminary) TW7 130 B4
Campion Pl SE28 124 B5
Campion Rd
 Hounslow TW7 130 D4
 Putney SW15 156 C6
Campion Terr NW2 68 D5
Campion Way HA8 27 A6
Camplin Rd HA3 44 A4
Camplin St SE14 140 D5
Camp Rd SW19 178 C5
Campsbourne Ho 3 N8 50 A5
Campsbourne Jun & Inf Schs N8 50 A6
Campsbourne Rd
 Hornsey N8 50 A5
 Hornsey N8 50 A6
Campsbourne The N8 50 A5
Campsey Gdns RM9 80 B1
Campsey Rd RM9 80 B1
Campsfield Ho N8 50 A6
Campsfield Rd N8 50 A6
Campshill Pl SE13 164 A6
Campshill Rd SE13 164 A6
Camp Site The BR8 191 C3
Campton Hill Twrs W8 245 A4
Campus Rd E17 53 B3
Camp View SW19 178 B5
Cam Rd E15 98 B6
Camrose Ave
 Edgware HA8 26 B2
 Erith DA8 147 D6
 Feltham TW13 172 C6
Camrose Cl
 Croydon CR0 207 A2
 Morden SM4 201 C5
Camrose St SE2 124 A2
Camsey Ho 8 SW2 160 B6
Canada Ave N18 33 A4
Canada Cres W3 89 A3
Canada Gdns SE13 164 A6
Canada Rd W3 89 A2
Canada Sq E14 119 D5
Canada St SE16 118 D4
Canada Water Sta SE16 118 D3
Canada Way W12 112 B6
Canadian Ave SE6 163 D3
Canal App SE8 141 A6
Canal Bldg N1 235 A4
Canal Bridge SE15 140 A6
Canal Bvd 7 NW1 71 D2
Canal Cl Mile End E1 97 A3
 North Kensington W10 90 D3
Canal Gr SE15 140 B6
Canal Head Public Sq 1 SE15 140 A4
Canal Path 22 E2 95 D6
Canalside Studios 29 N1 95 C6
Canal St SE5 139 B6
Canal Way W10 90 D3
Canal Wlk
 Croydon CR0 205 D3
 Forest Hill SE26 184 C5
 Shoreditch N1 95 B6 235 D6
CANARY WHARF 119 D5
Canary Wharf* E14 119 D5
Canary Wharf Pier (River Bus) E14 119 B5
Canary Wharf Sta E14 119 D5
Canary Wharf Sta (DLR) E14 119 C5
Canberra Cl NW4 46 A6
Canberra Dr UB4 84 C4
Canberra Ho 7 HA4 40 C1
Canberra Prim Sch W12 112 B6
Canberra Rd
 Charlton SE7 143 D6
 Ealing W13 109 A5
 Erith DA7 146 D6
 Harlington TW6 126 C2
 Newham E6 100 B6
Canbury Ave KT2 176 B2
Canbury Bsns Pk 3 KT2 176 A2
Canbury Ct 3 KT2 176 A3
Canbury Mews SE26 162 A1
Canbury Park Rd KT2 176 B2
Canbury Sch KT2 176 D4
Cancell Rd SW9 138 C4
Candahar Rd SW11 136 C3
Candida Ct 9 NW1 71 B1
Candishe Ho SE1 253 C2
Candle Gr SE15 140 B2
Candlelight Ct 5 E15 76 D2
Candlemakers 25 SW11 136 B2
Candler Mews TW1 153 A4
Candler St N15 51 B3
Candover St W1 239 A3
Candy St E3 97 B6
Caney Mews NW2 68 D6
Canfield Dr HA4 62 B3
Canfield Gdns NW6 69 D1
Canfield Ho N15 51 C3
Canfield Pl NW6 70 A2
Canford Ave UB5 85 A6
Canford Cl EN2 4 C3
Canford Gdns KT3 199 C3
Canford Pl TW11 175 C4
Canford Rd SW11 159 A6
Canham Rd Acton W3 111 C4
 South Norwood SE25 205 C6
Canmore Gdns SW16 181 C3
Cann Hall Prim Sch E11 76 D5
Cann Hall Rd E11 76 D4
Cann Ho W14 254 B5
Canning Cres N22 32 B2
Canning Cross SE5 139 C3
Canning Ct N22 32 B2
Canning Ho 23 W12 112 B6
Canning Pas W8 114 A3 256 A6
Canning Pl W8 114 A3 256 A6
Canning Pl Mews W8 256 A6
Canning Rd
 Croydon CR0 221 D6
 Harrow HA3 42 D6
 Highbury N5 72 D5
 Walthamstow E17 53 A6
 West Ham E15 98 C5
Cannington 14 NW5 71 A2
Cannington Rd RM9 80 C2
CANNING TOWN 99 B2
Canning Town E16 98 C1
Canning Town Sta E16 98 C1
Cannizaro Rd SW19 178 D5
Cannock Ho N4 51 B2
Cannock Lo EN1 17 C5
Cannonbury Ave HA5 40 D3
Cannon Cl
 Hampton TW12 173 D4
 West Barnes SW20 200 C6
Cannon Dr 21 E14 119 C6
Cannon Hill
 Palmers Green N14 16 A1
 West Hampstead NW6 69 C3
Cannon Hill La SM4, SW20 201 A5
Cannon Hill Mews N14 16 A1
Cannon Ho
 Lambeth SE11 260 D3
 Penge SE26 184 B4
Cannon La
 Hampstead NW3 70 B5
 Pinner HA5 41 A3

Cannon Lane Fst & Mid Schs HA5 ....40 D3
Cannon Pl
Hampstead NW3........70 B5
Woolwich SE7..........122 A1
Cannon Rd Erith DA7 ...147 B4
Palmers Green N14........16 A1
Cannon St EC4. .117 A6 252 B6
Cannon Street Rd E1....96 B1
Cannon Street Sta EC4..........117 B6 252 C6
Cannon Trad Est HA9....66 D4
Cannon Way KT8 ....195 D5
Cannon (W End of General Roy's Base Line)* TW6..................126 D4
Cannon Wharf Bsns Ctr 12 SE8..................119 A2
Canon Ave RM6..........58 C4
Canon Barnett Prim Sch E1.............95 D1 243 D2
Canon Beck Rd SE16....118 C4
Canonbie Rd SE23 .....162 C4
CANONBURY 73 A2
Canonbury Bsns Ctr N1.................. 235 B6
Canonbury Cres N1.....73 A1
Canonbury Ct 21 N1.....72 D1
Canonbury Gr N1........73 A1
Canonbury Hts 6 N1 ....73 B2
Canonbury La N1........72 D1
Canonbury Pk N N1.....73 A2
Canonbury Pk S N1......73 A2
Canonbury Pl N1 ....72 D2
Canonbury Prim Sch N1...........................72 D2
Canonbury Rd
Enfield EN1.............5 C4
Islington N1 ....72 D1
Canonbury Sq N1.......72 D1
Canonbury St N1 ....73 A1
Canonbury Sta N1, N5...73 A3
Canonbury Villas N1....72 D1
Canon Mohan Cl N14......15 B5
Canon Murnane Rd SE1 .... 263 C5
Canon Palmer RC Sch IG3...........................57 C1
Canon Rd BR1.........209 D6
Canon Row SW1..........116 A4 250 A1
Canons Cl
East Finchley N2.........48 B2
Edgware HA8 ....26 B4
Canons Cnr HA8 ....26 A6
Canons Ct Edgware HA8 ..26 B4
Leyton E15.............76 C4
Canons Dr HA8 ....26 B4
Canons High Sch HA8....26 B1
Canons L Ctr The CR4 ..202 D5
Canonsleigh Rd RM9....80 B1
CANONS PARK 26 A3
Canons Park Cl HA8 .....26 A3
Canons Park Sta HA8 ....26 A3
Canon St N1.....95 A6 235 A5
Canon's Wlk CR0 ......222 D5
Canopus Way
Northwood HA6.........22 A6
Stanwell TW19 ....148 A4
Canrobert St E2 ....96 B4
Cantelowes Ho EN5......12 D6
Cantelowes Rd NW1 ....71 D2
Canterbury SE13.......164 A6
Canterbury Ave
Redbridge IG1...........56 A2
Sidcup DA15 ....168 C2
Canterbury Cl
Beckenham BR3 ....185 D2
16 Camberwell SE5.......139 A3
7 Newham E6 ....100 B1
North Cheam KT4 ......216 D6
Southall UB6 ....85 D2
Canterbury Cres SW9 ..138 C2
Canterbury Ct
Acton W3..............111 C5
4 Ashford TW15 ....170 B6
Eltham SE12 ....165 B1
15 Hendon NW9 ....27 D1
Kilburn NW6 ....91 C5
South Croydon CR2.....221 A1
Thornton Heath CR0 ....204 C2
Canterbury Gr SE27, SW16.................160 C1
Canterbury Hall KT4 ...200 B2
Canterbury Ho
2 Barking IG11 ....80 A1
6 Bromley E3 ....97 D4
Lambeth SE1........... 260 D6
Canterbury Ind Pk 15 SE15.................140 C6
Canterbury Mans NW6 ..69 D2
Canterbury Pl SE17 ... 261 D3
Canterbury Rd
Feltham TW13..........151 A2
Harrow HA1, HA2 ....42 A4
Kilburn NW6 ....91 C5
Leyton E10...............54 A3
Morden SM4 ....202 A3
Thornton Heath CR0 ....204 C2
Canterbury Terr NW6 ...91 C5
Cantium Ret Pk SE1 ...140 A6
Cantley Gdns Ilford IG2 ..57 A3
South Norwood SE19 ...183 D2
Cantley Rd W7 ....109 A3
Canton St E14 ....97 C1
Cantrell Rd E3............97 C3
Cantwell Ho SE18.......144 D5
Cantwell Rd SE18.......144 D5
Canute Ct SW16 ....160 C1
Canute Gdns SE16 .....118 D2
Canute Ho 1 TW8 .....131 C5
Canvey St SE1 .... 252 A4
Cape Cl IG11 ....78 D1
Cape Henry Ct 15 E14 ..120 B6
Capel KT5..............198 B2
Capel Ave SM6 ....220 B3
Capel Cl
Keston Mark BR2 ......210 A1
Whetstone N20..........14 A1
Capel Ct SE20 ....184 C2
Capel Gdns Ilford IG3....79 D4
Pinner HA5 ....41 B5
Capel Ho 17 Hackney E9 ..74 C1
South Oxhey WD19 ......22 D6
Capella Ho 1 SE7 .....143 B6
Capel Lo
5 Richmond TW9.......132 B4
12 Streatham SW2.......160 B4
Capel Point E7 ....77 B4
Capel Rd
East Barnet EN4 ....14 C5
Forest Gate E7, E12 .....77 C4
Capener's Cl SW1..... 248 A1
Cape Rd N17 ....52 A6
Capern Rd SW18.......158 A3
Cape Yd 6 E1..........118 A5
Capio Nightingale Hospl SW3 .... 257 B1
Capital Bsns Ctr
South Croydon CR0.....221 B1
Wembley HA0 ....87 D5
Capital City Acad NW10...................90 B6
Capital East Apts 8 E16 ....121 A6
Capital Ind Est
Belvedere DA17 ....125 D3
Mitcham CR4..........202 D4
Capital Interchange Way TW8.................110 C1
Capital Sh Ctrs SW1 .. 249 C1
Capital Wharf 15 E1....118 A5
Capitol Ind Pk NW9.....45 A6
Capitol Way NW9.......45 A6
Capland Ho NW8 ...... 236 D6
Capland St NW8 . 92 B3 236 D6
Caplan Est CR4 ....181 C2
Caple Ho SW10........ 266 B4
Caple Rd NW10 ....89 D5
Capper St WC1 .. 93 C3 239 B5
Caprea Cl UB4..........84 D2
Capricorn Ctr RM8.......59 B2
Capri Ho E17 ....35 B1
Capri Rd CR0...........205 D2
Capstan Cl RM6..........58 B3
Capstan Ho 6 E14......120 A2
Capstan Rd SE8........119 B2
Capstan Ride EN2.........4 C3
Capstan Sq E14.........120 A4
Capstan Way SE16 ......119 A5
Capstone Rd BR1 ......186 D6
Capthorne Ave HA2......41 B1
Capuchin Cl HA7.........25 B4
Capulet Mews 1 E16 ..121 A5
Capworth St E10.........53 D2
Caradoc Cl W2 ....91 C1
Caradoc Evans Cl N11...31 B5
Caradoc St SE10........120 C1
Caradon Cl 4 E11 ....76 C6
Caradon Ct 7 TW1 .....153 C5
Caradon Way N15.........51 B5
Cara Ho 10 N1 ....72 C1
Caranday Villas 5 W11.................112 D5
Caravel Cl E14.........119 C3
Caravelle Gdns 1 UB5 ..84 D4
Caravel Mews 14 SE8 ..141 C6
Caraway Cl E13.........99 B2
Caraway Hts E14.......120 A6
Caraway Pl SM6 ....219 B5
Carberry Rd 12 SE19 ..183 C4
Carbery Ave W3 ......110 B4
Carbis Cl E4.............20 B3
Carbis Rd E14 ....97 B1
Carbroke Ho 9 E9........96 C6
Carburton St W1............93 B3 238 D5
Cardale St 1 E14.......120 A3
Cardamom Ct 1 E12....78 C4
Carden Rd SE15 ....140 B2
Cardiff Ho 9 SE15.....140 A6
Cardiff Rd Ealing W7.....109 A3
Enfield EN3 ....6 B1
Cardiff St SE18 ....145 C5
Cardigan Ct 3 W7........86 D3
Cardigan Gdns IG3 .....80 A6
Cardigan Rd
Barnes SW13 ....134 A3
Bow E3 ....97 B5
Richmond TW10 ....154 A5
Wimbledon SW19 .....180 A4
Cardigan St SE11 ....116 C1 261 A2
Cardigan Wlk 19 N1.....73 A1
Cardinal Ave
Kingston u T KT2.......176 A4
West Barnes SM4.......201 A3
Cardinal Bourne St SE1 .... 262 D5
Cardinal Cap Alley SE1 .... 252 A5
Cardinal Cl
Burnt Oak HA8 ....27 B3
Chislehurst BR7 ....189 B2
West Barnes SM4.......201 A3
Worcester Pk KT19, KT4 ....216 A4
Cardinal Cres KT3 .....177 A1
Cardinal Ct KT8.........196 B5
Cardinal Dr KT12 ......194 D1
Cardinal Hinsey Cl NW10 ....90 A5
Cardinal Hinsley RC High Sch (Boys) NW10.......90 A6
Cardinal Pl SW15 ......134 D1
Cardinal Pole RC Sch
London E9 ....74 D1
London E9 ....75 A3
Cardinal Rd
Feltham TW13.........150 B3
Ruislip HA4 ....40 D1
Cardinal Road Inf Sch TW13 ....150 B3
Cardinals Way N19......49 D1
Cardinal's Wlk
Ashford TW16 ....171 C4
Hampton TW12 ....174 A3
Cardinal Vaughan Meml Sch The W14......... 244 A2
Cardinal Way HA3 ......42 C6
Cardinal Wiseman RC Sch The UB6 ....86 A2
Cardinal Wlk SW1 .... 259 A5
Cardine Mews SE15....140 B5
Cardington Sq TW4....128 D1
Cardington St NW1 .... 93 C4 232 B1
Cardozo Rd N7 ....72 A3
Cardrew Ave N12 ....30 B5
Cardrew Cl N12..........30 B5
Cardrew Ct 8 N12.......30 B5
Cardross St W6.........112 B3
Cardwell Prim Sch SE18......................122 B2
Cardwell Rd 3 N7.......72 A4
Career Ct 11 SE16......118 D4
Carew Cl N7.............72 B6
Carew Ct
15 Deptford SE14 ....140 D6
Ilford RM6...............58 B3
Carew Ho
West Norwood SW16 ...160 C1
23 Woolwich SE18 ....122 B2
Carew Manor Sch SM6 ....219 D5
Carew Rd
Ashford TW15 ....171 A4
Ealing W13 ....109 C4
Mitcham CR4...........181 A1
Thornton Heath CR7 ....204 D5
Tottenham N17 ....34 A1
Wallington SM6.........219 C2
Carew St SE5...........139 A3
Carey Ct Bexley DA6 ....169 D6
20 Camberwell SE5.....139 A5
Carey Gdns SW8............137 D4 269 C1
Carey Ho E5.............74 B5
Carey La EC2 .... 242 A2
Carey Pl SW1.......... 259 C3
Carey Rd RM9 ....81 A4
Carey St WC2....94 B1 240 D1
Carey Way HA9 ....66 D4
Carfax Pl SW4 ....137 D1
Carfax Rd UB3 ....106 A2
Carfree Cl 5 N1.........72 C1
Cargill Rd SW18 ....158 A3
Cargreen Pl SE25 ......205 D5
Cargreen Rd SE25 .....205 D5
Cargrey Ho 9 HA7.......25 C5
Carholme Rd SE23 ......163 B3
Carillon Ct W5 ....109 D6
Carinthia Ct 5 SE8 .....119 A2
Carisbrook 2 N10 ....31 B1
Carisbrook Cl EN1 ....5 D4
Carisbrooke Ave DA5 ..168 D3
Carisbrooke Cl
Stanmore HA7...........25 D1
Twickenham TW4.......151 A4
Carisbrooke Ct
Acton W3..............111 A4
Belmont SM2...........217 B1
Northolt UB5 ....85 B6
1 Streatham SW16......160 B1
Carisbrooke Gdns SE15 ....139 D5
Carisbrooke Ho
10 Kingston u T KT2 .....176 A2
Richmond TW10 ....154 C6
Carisbrooke Rd
Bromley BR2 ....209 C5
Mitcham CR4...........204 A5
Walthamstow E17 ....53 A4
Carleton Ave SM6......219 D1
Carleton Cl KT10.......196 B1
Carleton Gdns N19......71 C3
Carleton Ho 4 N8 ....50 A4
Carleton Rd N7 ....71 D4
Carley Ct 6 N12..........30 B5
Carlile Cl E3.............97 B5
Carlile Ho SE1 .... 262 D5
Carlina Gdns IG8 ....37 B5
Carling Ct TW1 ....152 D4
Carlingford DA14 ......190 A5
Carlingford Gdns CR4 ..181 A3
Carlingford Rd
Hampstead NW3..........70 B4
London N15..............50 D6
West Barnes SM4 ......200 D3
Carlisle Ave Acton W3 ....89 C1
Whitechapel EC3....... 243 C1
Carlisle Cl
Kingston u T KT2........176 C2
Pinner HA5 ....41 A2
Carlisle Gdns
Harrow HA3 ....43 D2
Redbridge IG1............56 A3
Carlisle Ho
6 Dartmouth Pk NW5 ....71 C5
Redbridge IG1............56 A3
Carlisle Inf Sch TW12 ..173 D4
Carlisle La SE1 .116 B3 260 D6
Carlisle Lo 1 N3 ....29 B1
Carlisle Pl London N11 ...31 B6
Westminster SW1....... 115 C3 259 A5
Carlisle Rd Cheam SM1..217 B2
Finsbury Pk N4 ....50 C2
Hampton TW12 ....173 D3
Hendon NW9............45 A6
Kilburn NW6 ....91 A6
Leyton E10...............53 C1
Carlisle St W1 ...93 D1 239 C1
Carlisle Way SW17.....181 A5
Carlisle Wlk 6 E8 ......73 D2
Carlos Pl W1 ...115 B6 248 C5
Carlow St NW1 .... 232 A4
Carlson Ct SW15.......135 B1
Carlton Ave
Feltham TW14..........150 C5
Harrow HA3 ....43 B4
Hayes UB3.............105 C2
South Croydon CR2.....221 C1
Southgate N14 ....15 D6
Carlton Ave E HA9 ......65 D6
Carlton Ave W HA0 .....65 B6
Carlton Cl
Chessington KT9 ....213 D2
Child's Hill NW3 ....69 C6
Edgware HA8 ....26 C5
Northolt UB5 ....64 A3
Carlton Cres SM3......217 A4
Carlton Ct Brixton SW9..138 D4
Ealing W7 ....108 D4
Finchley N3 ....29 C3
Ilford IG6 ....57 B6
Kilburn NW6 ....91 D5
11 Penge SE20 ....184 B2
South Norwood SE19 ...183 D2
8 Willesden NW2 ....68 C2
Carlton Dr Ilford IG6.....57 B6
Putney SW15...........157 A6
Carlton Gdns
Ealing W5 ....109 C6
St James SW1. 115 D5 249 C3
Carlton Gn DA14.......189 D6
Carlton Gr SE15.........140 B4
Carlton Hill NW8 ....92 A5 229 A4
Carlton Ho Cheam SM1..217 B2
Edmonton N21...........17 A3
Feltham TW14 ....149 D5
Hounslow TW4 ....151 C5
8 Kilburn NW6 ....91 B5
Kilburn NW6 ....91 C5
Marylebone W1....... 237 D2
Carlton House Terr SW1..............115 D5 249 D4
Carlton Lo N4 ....50 C2
Carlton Mans
Brixton SW9 ....138 C1
Cricklewood NW2 ....68 D3
Kensington W14 ...... 244 B2
Maida Vale W9 ....91 D4
7 South Hampstead NW6...............69 C1
Stamford Hill N16 ....51 D1
Carlton Par HA9 ....44 A1
Carlton Park Ave SW20....................178 D1
Carlton Prim Sch NW5..71 A3
Carlton Rd Acton W4...111 B4
Ashford TW16 ....171 D3
Ealing W5 ....87 C1
Erith DA8..............147 D6
Finsbury Pk N4 ....50 C2
Friern Barnet N11........31 A5
Higham Hill E17.........35 A2
Kingston u T KT3........177 C1
Leytonstone E11 ....54 D1
Manor Pk E12 ....77 D4
Mortlake SW14.........133 A1
Sidcup DA14 ....189 D6
South Croydon CR2.....221 B1
Walton-on-T KT12 ......194 B2
Welling DA16...........146 B2
Carlton Sq E1 ....96 D3
Carlton St SW1 .... 249 C5
Carltons The 5 SW15..157 A6
Carlton Terr
Edmonton N18...........33 B6
Forest Hill SE26 ....162 C1
Upton E7 ....77 C1
Wanstead E11...........55 B4
Carlton Tower Pl SW1 257 D6
Carlton Twrs SM5.......218 D5
Carlton Vale NW6.......91 C5
Carlton Vale Inf Sch NW6.....................91 B4
Carlwell St SW17 ......180 C5
Carlyle Ave
Bromley BR1...........209 D6
Southall UB1 ....107 B6
Carlyle Cl
East Molesey KT8 ......173 D1
Hampstead Garden Suburb N2 ....48 A3
Carlyle Gdns UB1 .....107 B6
Carlyle Ho
4 Camberwell SE5.....139 A5
Chelsea SW3.......... 266 D6
Ealing W5 ....109 D2
East Molesey KT8 ......195 C4
12 Stoke Newington N16 .73 C5
Carlyle Lo 6 EN5 ....14 A6
Carlyle Mans SW3 .... 267 A5
Carlyle Mews 24 E1......96 D3
Carlyle Pl SW15.........134 D1
Carlyle Rd
Croydon CR0 ....222 A6
Carlyle Rd *continued*
Ealing W5 ....109 C2
Manor Pk E12 ....78 A4
1 Stonebridge NW10 ...89 B6
Woolwich SE28 ....124 C6
Carlyle's Ho* SW3.... 267 A5
Carlyle Sq SW3..........114 B1 256 D1
Carlyon Ave HA2.........63 C4
Carlyon Cl HA0 ....88 A6
Carlyon Ct HA0 ....88 B6
Carlyon Mans 1 HA0 ...88 A5
Carlyon Rd Hayes UB4 ...84 C2
Wembley HA0 ....88 A6
Carlys Cl BR3...........184 D1
Carmalt Gdns SW15....134 C1
Carmarthen Ct 4 W7....86 D3
Carmarthen Ho 8 SW15...............156 C4
Carmarthen Pl SE1 ... 253 A2
Carmel Ct
Kensington W8 .... 245 C2
Wembley Pk HA9.........66 D6
Carmelite Cl HA3 ....24 A2
Carmelite Rd HA3 ....24 A1
Carmelite St EC4 ....116 C6 251 B6
Carmelite Way HA3 .....24 A1
Carmelite Wlk HA3 .....24 A2
Carmel Lo SW6 .... 265 A6
Carmen St E14 ....97 D1
Carmichael Cl
9 London SW11.........136 B2
Ruislip HA4 ....62 A4
Carmichael Ct 5 SW13.................133 D3
Carmichael Ho
17 Dulwich SE21........183 C6
6 Poplar E14 ....120 A6
Carmichael Mews SW18..................158 B4
Carmichael Rd SE25 ...206 A5
Carminia Rd SW17......159 B2
Carnaby St* W1............93 C1 239 A1
Carnac St SE21, SE27 ...161 B1
Carna Ct TW9 ....132 A2
Carnanton Rd E17 ......36 B2
Carnarvon Ave EN1 ......5 D3
Carnarvon Dr UB3 .....105 A3
Carnarvon Rd Barnet EN5 . 1 A2
Leyton E10...............54 A4
Stratford E15 ....76 D2
Woodford E18...........36 D2
Carnation St SE2 ....124 B1
Carnbrook Rd SE3 .....143 D2
Carnecke Gdns SE9....166 A6
Carnegie Cl
Holdbrook EN3 ....7 D5
Surbiton KT6 ....214 B6
Carnegie Ho NW3.......70 B5
Carnegie Pl SW19.......156 D1
Carnegie St N1 .. 94 B6 233 D5
Carnforth Cl KT19......214 D2
Carnforth Rd SW16 ....181 D3
Carnicot Ho 9 SE15 ...140 B4
Carnoustie Cl SE28 ...102 D1
Carnoustie Dr N1........72 B1
Carnwath Ho SW6 ......135 D2
Carnwath Rd SW6 ......135 D2
Caroe Ct N9 ....18 B3
Carol Cl NW4............46 D5
Carole Ho 18 SE20 .....184 B2
Carolina Cl E15..........76 C3
Carolina Rd CR7 ....183 A2
Caroline Cl
Bayswater W2........ 245 D5
Hounslow TW7 ....130 C5
Muswell Hill N10.........31 B1
South Croydon CR0.....221 C4
Streatham SW16.......160 B1
Caroline Ct
Ashford TW15 ....170 D4
Catford SE6.............186 B6
Stanmore HA7...........25 A4
17 Surbiton KT6 ....197 D2
23 Woodside Pk N12 ....29 D6
Caroline Gdns E2........95 C4
Caroline Ho
Bayswater W2........ 245 D5
20 Hammersmith W6 ...112 C1
Caroline Martyn Ho 8 N19 ....49 D2
Caroline Pl
Bayswater W2........ 245 D5
Clapham SW11 ....137 A3
Harlington UB3 ....127 C5
Caroline Pl Mews W2. 245 D5
Caroline Rd SW19 ......179 B3
Caroline St E1...........96 D1
Caroline Terr SW1..........115 A2 258 A3
Caroline Wlk W6 ..... 264 A5
Carol St NW1....93 C6 232 A6
Carolyn Ho IG3..........58 A1
Caronia Ct 4 SE16.....119 A2
Carpenter Gdns N21 ....16 D2
Carpenter Ho
London NW11 ....48 A3
11 Tower Hamlets E14...97 C2
5 Tufnell Pk N19 ....71 D4
Carpenters Bsns Pk E15........................75 D1
Carpenters Cl EN5 ......13 D5
Carpenters Ct
Camden Town NW1.... 232 A6
5 Dagenham RM10......81 D2
Twickenham TW2.......152 C2
Carpenter's Pl SW4....137 D1
Carpenters Prim Sch E15.......................98 A6
Carpenter's Rd E15 .....75 D1
Carpenter St W1...... 248 C5
Carradale Ho 2 E14 ....98 A1
Carrara Cl 18 SW9 .....138 D1
Carrara Wharf SW6.....135 A2
Carr Cl HA7 ....25 A4
Carr Gr SE18 ....122 A2
Carriage Dr E SW11.........137 A5 268 B4
Carriage Drive E SW11.........137 A5 268 B4
Carriage Drive N SW11, SW8.........137 A6 268 B5
Carriage Dr N
Battersea SW8, SW11....... 136 D5 267 C4
Battersea SW8, SW11.......137 A6 268 B5
Carriage Dr S SW11.........137 A4 268 A2
Carriage Dr W SW11..........136 D5 267 C3
Carriage Mews IG1 .....79 A6
Carriage Pl 14 SW16....181 C5
Carrick Cl TW7 ....131 A2
Carrick Gate KT10 .....212 A5
Carrick Gdns N17........33 C3
Carrick Ho Islington N7 ..72 B2
Kennington SE11...... 261 C2
Carrick Mews SE8 .....141 C6
Carrill Way DA17.......124 D3
Carrington Ave
Borehamwood WD6 .....10 D6
Hounslow TW3 ....151 D6
Carrington Cl
Barnet EN5 ....12 A6
Borehamwood WD6 .....11 A6
Croydon CR0 ....207 A2
Carrington Ct
London SW11 ....136 C1
3 New Malden KT3....199 C5
Southgate N21 ....16 D5
Carrington Gdns 4 E7 ..77 A4
Carrington Ho
Mayfair W1 .... 248 C3
7 Merton SW19.......179 C3
Carrington Lo
3 Richmond TW10.....154 A6
Wembley HA9 ....66 B5
Carrington Pl KT10 ....212 A4
Carrington Rd TW10 ...132 C1
Carrington Sq HA3......24 A3
Carrington St W1..... 248 C3
Carrol Cl NW5 ....71 B4
Carroll Cl E15 ....76 D3
Carroll Ct Acton W3 ....110 D3
4 Shacklewell E5.......74 A5
Carroll Ho W2........ 246 C6
Carronade Pl SE18.....123 B3
Carron Cl E14 ....97 D1
Carroun Rd SW8..........138 B5 270 C4
Carroway La UB6 ....86 B4
Carrow Rd RM9..........80 B1
Carr Rd Northolt UB5....64 A1
Walthamstow E17 ....35 C1
Carrs La N21 ....17 B6
Carr St 5 E14 ....97 A1
CARSHALTON 218 C4
Carshalton, Beddington & Wallington War Meml Hospl SM5 ....218 D2
Carshalton Beeches Sta SM5 ....218 D2
Carshalton Boys Sports Coll SM5.............218 C6
Carshalton Coll SM5 ...218 D5
Carshalton Gr SM1......218 B3
Carshalton High Sch for Girls SM5 ....218 C5
CARSHALTON ON THE HILL 219 B1
Carshalton Park Rd SM5.................218 D3
Carshalton Pl SM5 .....219 A3
Carshalton Rd
Mitcham CR4...........203 A4
Sutton SM1, SM5.......218 B3
Carshalton Sta SM5....218 D4
Carslake Rd SW15 .....156 C5
Carson Rd
Cockfosters EN4 ....2 D1
Dulwich SE21 ....161 B2
Newham E16............99 A2
Carstairs Rd SE6.......164 A1
Carston Cl SE12 ....164 D6
Carswell Cl IG4..........55 D5
Carswell Rd SE6 ....164 A4
Carter Cl Kenton NW9....45 B3
Wallington SM6.........219 D1
Carter Ct EC4......... 241 D1
Carteret Ho 8 W12 ....112 B6
Carteret St SW1 ...... 249 C1
Carteret Way SE8......119 A2
Carterhatch Jun & Inf Schs EN1 ....6 B4
Carterhatch La EN1.......6 A4
Carterhatch Rd EN3.......6 D4
Carter Ho
11 London SW2.........160 C6
Spitalfields E1......... 243 C3
Carter La EC4....94 D1 241 D1
Carter Pl SE17 ..117 A1 262 B1
Carter Rd
Mitcham SW19 ....180 B4

Carter Rd *continued*
Newham E13 ... 99 B6
Carters Cl
10 Kentish Town NW5 ... 71 D2
North Cheam KT4 ... 200 D1
Carters Hill Cl SE9 ... 165 C3
Carters La SE23 ... 163 B1
Carters Rd N2 ... 30 C3
Carter St SE17 .. 117 A1 262 A1
Carter's Yd SW18 ... 157 C6
Carthew Rd W6 ... 112 B3
Carthew Villas W6 ... 112 B3
Carthusian St EC1 ... 242 A4
Cartier Circ E14 ... 120 A5
Carting La WC2 ... 116 A6 250 B5
Cart La E4 ... 20 C3
Cartmel NW1 ... 232 A2
Cartmel Cl N17 ... 34 B3
Cartmel Ct
Beckenham BR2 ... 186 C1
Northolt UB5 ... 63 A2
Cartmel Gdns SM4 ... 202 A4
Cartmel Rd DA7 ... 147 C4
Carton Ho
4 Bermondsey SE16 ... 118 A3
2 Dollis Hill NW2 ... 68 A5
12 Shepherd's Bush W11 ... 112 D6
Cartoon Mus The* WC1 ... 94 A2 240 A3
Cartwright Gdns WC1 ... 94 A4 233 A1
Cartwright Ho SE1 ... 262 B5
Cartwright Rd RM9 ... 81 B1
Cartwright St E1 ... 117 D6 253 D5
Cartwright Way SW13 .. 134 B5
Carvel Ho E14 ... 120 A1
Carver Cl 15 W4 ... 111 A3
Carver Rd SE24 ... 161 A5
Carville Cres TW8 ... 110 A2
Caryl Ho 6 SW19 ... 156 D3
Cary Rd E11 ... 76 C5
Carysfort Rd
Canonbury N16 ... 73 B4
London N8 ... 49 D4
Casby Ho 7 SE16 ... 118 A3
Cascade Ave N10 ... 49 C5
Cascade Cl IG9 ... 21 D2
Cascade Rd IG9 ... 21 D2
Cascadia Ho 22 KT1 ... 176 C1
Casella Rd SE14 ... 140 D5
Casewick Rd SE27 ... 182 D6
Casey Cl NW8 ... 92 C4 230 B1
Casimir Rd E5 ... 74 C5
Casino Ave SE24 ... 161 B6
Caspian Ho 10 E1 ... 96 D2
Caspian St SE5 ... 139 B5
Caspian Wlk E16 ... 99 D1
Cassandra Cl UB5 ... 64 B4
Cassandra Ct 7 NW2 ... 68 C2
Cass Bsns Sch EC1 ... 95 B3 242 C5
Casselden Rd NW10 ... 67 B1
Cassel Hospl TW10 ... 175 D6
Cassell Ho 21 SW9 ... 138 A3
Casserley Ho W4 ... 111 B3
Cass Ho 23 E9 ... 74 D2
Cassidy Rd SW6 ... 265 A3
Cassilda Rd SE2 ... 124 A2
Cassilis Rd
Millwall E14 ... 119 C4
Twickenham TW1 ... 153 B5
Cassinghurst SE24 ... 161 B6
Cassiobury Ave TW14 .. 149 D4
Cassiobury Rd E17 ... 53 A4
Cassland Rd
Homerton E9 ... 74 D2
South Norwood CR7 ... 205 B5
Casslee Rd SE6 ... 163 B4
Cassocks Sq TW17 ... 193 B2
Casson Ho 11 E1 ... 96 A2
Casson St E1 ... 96 A2
Castalia Sq 6 E14 ... 120 A4
Castellain Mans W9 ... 91 D3
Castellain Rd W9 ... 91 D3
Castellane Cl HA7 ... 24 D3
Castell Ho 11 SE8 ... 141 C5
Castello Ave SW15 ... 156 C6
Castelnau SW13 ... 134 B5
Castelnau Gdns SW13 .. 134 B6
Castelnau Mans SW13 .. 134 B6
Castelnau Row SW13 .. 134 B6
Casterbridge
Kilburn NW6 ... 91 D6
3 Notting Hill W11 ... 91 C1
Casterbridge Rd SE3 ... 143 A2
Casterton St E8 ... 74 B2
Castile Rd SE18 ... 122 C2
Castilion Prim Sch SE28 ... 102 C1
Castillon Rd SE6 ... 164 C2
Castlands Rd SE6 ... 163 B2
Castleacre W2 ... 237 A1
Castle Ave Chingford E4 .. 36 B5
Yiewsley UB7 ... 104 B6
Castlebar Ct 5 W5 ... 87 C2
Castlebar Hill W5 ... 87 C2
Castlebar Mews W5 ... 87 C2
Castle Bar Park Sta W7 ... 86 D2
Castlebar Pk W5 ... 87 B2
Castlebar Rd W5 ... 87 C1
Castlebar Sch W13 ... 87 A2
Castle Baynard St EC4 ... 117 A6 252 A6
Castlebrook Cl SE11 ... 116 D2 261 C4
Castle Bsns Village TW12 ... 173 D2
Castle Cl 12 Acton W3 ... 111 A4
Ashford TW16 ... 171 C3
Beckenham BR2 ... 208 C6
Homerton E9 ... 75 A3
South Acton W3 ... 110 D4
Wimbledon SW19 ... 156 D1
Castlecombe Dr SW19 ... 156 D4
Castlecombe Prim Sch SE9 ... 188 A5
Castlecombe Rd SE9 ... 188 A6
Castle Ct Belmont SM2 .. 217 C2
City of London EC3 ... 242 D1
Dagenham RM9 ... 103 A6
Forest Hill SE26 ... 185 A6
Morden SM4 ... 202 B4
Castleden Ho NW6 ... 70 B1
Castledine Rd SE20 ... 184 B3
Castle Dr IG4 ... 56 A3
Castleford Ave SE9 ... 166 D3
Castleford Cl N17 ... 33 D4
Castleford Ct NW8 ... 236 D6
Castlefrank Ho 20 N1 ... 95 C4
Castlegate TW9 ... 132 B2
CASTLE GREEN ... 102 C6
Castleham Ct HA8 ... 26 C4
Castlehaven Rd NW1 ... 71 B1
Castle Hill Ave CR0 ... 224 A1
Castle Hill Prim Sch CR0 ... 224 A2
Castle Ho
17 Belmont SM2 ... 217 C1
3 Chingford E4 ... 36 B5
Newington SE1 ... 262 A4
South Lambeth SW8 ... 270 B4
Castle Hts RM9 ... 102 B6
Castle Ind Est SE17 ... 262 A4
Castle La SW1 .. 115 C3 259 A6
Castleleigh Ct EN2 ... 17 B6
Castlemaine 8 SW11 .. 136 D3
Castlemaine Ave CR2 .. 221 D3
Castlemaine St 2 E1 ... 96 B2
Castle Mead SE5 ... 139 A5
Castle Mews
Camden Town NW1 ... 71 B2
North Finchley N12 ... 30 A5
Castle Par KT17 ... 216 A1
Castle Pl 8 Acton W4 ... 111 C2
Camden Town NW1 ... 71 B2
Castle Point 4 E13 ... 99 C5
Castle Rd
Camden Town NW1 ... 71 B2
Dagenham RM9 ... 102 B6
Enfield EN3 ... 7 A5
Isleworth TW7 ... 130 D3
North Finchley N12 ... 30 B5
Northolt UB5 ... 63 D1
Southall UB2 ... 107 B3
Castlereagh Ho HA7 ... 25 B4
Castlereagh St W1 ... 237 C2
Castle St
Kingston u T KT2 ... 176 A1
Newham E6 ... 99 C5
Castleton Ave HA9 ... 66 A4
Castleton Cl CR0 ... 207 A3
Castleton Ct KT5 ... 198 B4
Castleton Gdns HA9 ... 66 A5
Castleton Ho 3 E14 ... 120 A2
Castleton Rd
Chingford E17 ... 36 B1
Ilford IG3 ... 58 B1
Mitcham CR4 ... 203 D5
Mottingham SE12, SE9 .. 187 D6
Ruislip HA4 ... 40 D1
Castletown Rd W14 ... 113 A1 254 B1
Castleview Cl N4 ... 73 A6
Castleview Gdns IG1 ... 56 B3
Castle Way
Feltham TW13 ... 172 C6
Wimbledon SW19 ... 156 D1
Castle Wlk TW16 ... 194 C6
Castlewood Day Hospl SE18 ... 144 C4
Castlewood Dr SE9 ... 144 B3
Castlewood Ho WC1 .. 239 D2
Castlewood Rd
Barnet EN4 ... 2 B2
Stamford Hill N16 ... 52 A3
Castle Yd Highgate N6 ... 49 A2
Lambeth SE1 ... 251 D4
18 Richmond TW10 ... 153 D6
Castor La E14 ... 119 D6
Catalina Rd TW6 ... 126 C2
Catalpa Ct SE13 ... 164 B5
Caterham Rd SE13 ... 142 B2
Catesby Ho 25 E9 ... 74 C1
Catesby St SE17 ... 117 B2 262 D3
CATFORD ... 163 C3
Catford Br SE6 ... 163 C4
Catford Bridge Sta SE6 ... 163 C4
Catford Broadway SE6 ... 163 D4
Catford Gyratory SE6 .. 163 D4
Catford High Sch SE6 .. 164 A1
Catford Hill SE6 ... 163 C3
Catford Rd SE6 ... 163 C4
Catford Sh Ctr SE6 ... 163 D4
Catford Sta SE6 ... 163 C4
Cathall Rd E11 ... 76 B5
Cathay Ho SE16 ... 118 B4
Cathay St 12 SE16 ... 118 B4
Cathay Wlk UB5 ... 85 C5
Cathcart Dr BR6 ... 211 C1
Cathcart Hill N19 ... 71 C5
Cathcart Rd SW10 ... 136 A6 266 A6
Cathcart St NW5 ... 71 B2
Cathedral Ct EC4 ... 241 D1
Cathedral Lo EC1 ... 242 A4
Cathedral Sch of St Saviour & St Mary Overie Prim Sch SE1 ... 117 A4 252 B2
Cathedral St SE1 ... 117 B5 252 C4
Cathedral Wlk SW1 ... 259 A6
Catherall Rd N5, N16 ... 73 A5
Catherine Baird Ct 12 SW12 ... 159 B4
Catherine Ct Barnet EN5 .. 1 D2
1 Ilford IG2 ... 57 A3
2 Southgate N14 ... 15 C6
3 Wimbledon SW19 ... 179 B5
Catherine Dr
Ashford TW16 ... 171 D4
Richmond TW9 ... 132 A1
Catherine Gdns TW3 ... 130 B1
Catherine Godfrey Ho RM9 ... 103 B6
Catherine Gr SE10 ... 141 D4
Catherine Griffiths Ct EC1 ... 241 B6
Catherine Ho
Isleworth TW7 ... 131 B4
16 Shoreditch N1 ... 95 C6
Catherine Lo E18 ... 37 C2
Catherine Pl
Harrow HA1 ... 42 D4
Westminster SW1 ... 115 C3 259 A6
Catherine Rd Enfield EN3 .. 7 A6
Kingston u T KT6 ... 197 D4
Catherine St WC2 ... 116 B6 250 C6
Catherine Wheel Alley E1 ... 243 B3
Catherine Wheel Rd TW8 ... 131 D5
Catherine Wheel Yd SW1 ... 249 A3
Catherwood Ct N1 ... 235 C3
Cat Hill EN4 ... 14 D6
Cathles Rd SW12 ... 159 B5
Cathnor Rd W12 ... 112 B4
Catisfield Rd EN3 ... 7 A6
Catlin Cres TW17 ... 193 B4
Catling Cl SE23 ... 162 D1
Catlin's La HA5 ... 40 B5
Catlin St SE16 ... 118 B1
Catman Ho N4 ... 50 B1
Caton Ct BR2 ... 186 C1
Cato Rd SW4 ... 137 D1
Cator La BR3 ... 185 B2
Cator Park Sch BR3 ... 185 A3
Cator Rd
Penge SE20, SE26 ... 184 D5
Wallington SM5 ... 218 D3
Cator St
Camberwell SE15 ... 139 D5
Camberwell SE15 ... 139 D6
Cato St W1 ... 92 C1 237 B2
Catsey La WD23 ... 8 A4
Catsey Wood WD23 ... 8 A4
Catterick Cl N11 ... 31 A4
Cattistock Rd SE9 ... 188 B5
Cattley Cl EN5 ... 1 A1
Catton St WC1 ... 240 C3
Caughley Ho SE11 ... 261 A5
Caulfield Ct 15 NW1 ... 71 C1
Caulfield Rd
East Ham E6 ... 78 B1
London SE15 ... 140 B3
Causeway TW14, TW4 ... 128 B1
Causeway The
Carshalton SM5 ... 219 A6
Chessington KT9 ... 214 A4
Claygate KT10 ... 212 D1
East Finchley N2 ... 48 C5
Teddington TW11 ... 174 D4
Wandsworth SW18 ... 157 D6
Wimbledon SW19 ... 178 C5
Causeyware Rd N9 ... 18 C4
Causton Cotts 3 E14 ... 97 A1
Causton Ho SE5 ... 139 A5
Causton Rd N6 ... 49 B2
Causton Sq RM10 ... 81 C1
Causton St SW1 ... 115 D1 259 D2
Cautley Ave SW4 ... 159 C6
Cavalier Cl RM6 ... 58 D5
Cavalier Gdns UB3 ... 83 B1
Cavalier Ho W5 ... 109 C6
Cavalry Cres TW4 ... 128 D1
Cavalry Gdns SW15 ... 157 B6
Cavan Pl HA5 ... 23 B2
Cavaye Ho SW10 ... 266 B6
Cavaye Pl SW10 ... 256 B1
Cavell Ct 5 N19 ... 71 C6
Cavell Dr EN2 ... 4 C3
Cavell Ho 8 N1 ... 95 C6
Cavell Rd N17 ... 33 B3
Cavell St E1 ... 96 B2
Cavendish Ave
Ealing W13 ... 87 A1
Falconwood DA16 ... 145 D2
Finchley N3 ... 29 C1
Harrow HA1 ... 64 C4
Ruislip HA4 ... 62 B3
Sidcup DA15 ... 168 A4
St John's Wood NW8 ... 92 B5 229 D3
West Barnes KT3 ... 200 B5
Woodford IG8 ... 37 B3
Cavendish Cl
Ashford TW16 ... 171 D4
Brondesbury NW6 ... 69 B2
Edmonton N18 ... 34 B5
Hayes UB4 ... 83 C2
3 Putney SW15 ... 157 A6
St John's Wood NW8 ... 92 B4 229 D2
Cavendish Coll WC1 ... 93 D2 239 C4
Cavendish Cres WD6 ... 10 C6
Cavendish Ct
Ashford TW16 ... 171 D4
Catford SE6 ... 163 D3
5 Chingford E4 ... 20 C4
Wallington SM6 ... 219 B2
Wembley HA0 ... 65 D3
Whitechapel EC2 ... 243 B2
Cavendish Dr
Claygate KT10 ... 212 C3
Edgware HA8 ... 26 B4
Leytonstone E11 ... 54 B1
Cavendish Gdns
Barking IG11 ... 79 D3
Clapham Pk SW4 ... 159 C5
Dagenham RM6 ... 59 A4
Ilford IG1 ... 56 C1
Cavendish Ho
London N12 ... 30 A6
5 Muswell Hill N10 ... 31 A3
3 Richmond TW10 ... 153 C1
South Lambeth SW8 ... 270 A2
St John's Wood NW8 ... 229 D3
Twickenham TW1 ... 153 A5
Cavendish Mans
2 Clapham Pk SW12 ... 159 C5
Hackney E5 ... 74 C3
Holborn EC1 ... 241 A5
8 West Hampstead NW6 ... 69 C3
Cavendish Mews N W1 ... 238 D4
Cavendish Mews S W1 ... 238 D3
Cavendish Par
Balham SW12 ... 159 B5
Hounslow TW4 ... 129 A3
Cavendish Pl
Balham SW4 ... 159 B5
Bromley BR1 ... 210 B6
Brondesbury NW2 ... 68 D2
Marylebone W1 ... 238 D2
Cavendish Prim Sch W4 ... 133 C5
Cavendish Rd
Ashford TW16 ... 171 D4
Brondesbury NW6 ... 69 B1
Chingford E4 ... 36 A4
Chiswick W4 ... 133 A4
Clapham Pk SW12 ... 159 C5
Edmonton N18 ... 34 B5
Harringay N4 ... 50 D3
Mitcham SW19 ... 180 C3
New Malden KT3 ... 199 D5
Sutton SM2 ... 218 A1
Thornton Heath CR0 ... 204 D1
Cavendish Sch The NW1 ... 93 B6 231 D6
Cavendish Sq W1 ... 93 B1 238 D2
Cavendish St N1 ... 95 B5 235 C3
Cavendish Terr
Feltham TW13 ... 150 A2
11 Tower Hamlets E3 ... 97 B4
Cavendish The NW11 ... 47 D2
Cavendish Way BR4 ... 207 D1
Cavenham Gdns IG1 ... 79 B5
Cave Rd Newham E13 ... 99 B4
Richmond TW10 ... 175 C6
Caverleigh Way KT4 ... 200 B2
Caversham Ave
Cheam SM3 ... 217 A6
Palmers Green N13 ... 16 C1
Caversham Ct N11 ... 15 A1
Caversham Ho
8 Kingston u T KT1 ... 176 A1
7 Peckham SE15 ... 140 A6
Wallington CR0 ... 220 A5
West Green N15 ... 51 A5
Caversham Lo N10 ... 31 C1
Caversham Rd
Kentish Town NW5 ... 71 C2
Kingston u T KT1 ... 176 B1
West Green N15 ... 51 A5
Caversham St SW3 ... 136 D6 267 C6
Caverswall St W12 ... 90 C1
Caveside Cl BR7 ... 188 C2
Cavour Ho SE17 ... 261 D2
Cawdor Cres W7 ... 109 A2
Cawnpore St SE19 ... 183 C5
Cawston Ct 8 BR1 ... 186 D3
Caxton Gr E3 ... 97 C4
Caxton Hall* SW1 ... 259 C6
Caxton Rd
Shepherd's Bush W12 ... 112 D4
Southall UB2 ... 106 D3
Wimbledon SW19 ... 180 A5
Wood Green N22 ... 32 B1
Caxton St N E16 ... 98 D1
Caxton St SW1 .. 115 D3 259 C6
Caxton Trad Est UB3 ... 105 C5
Caxton Wlk WC2 ... 239 D1
Cayford Ho 1 NW3 ... 70 D3
Caygill Cl BR2 ... 208 D5
Cayley Cl SM6 ... 220 A1
Cayley Prim Sch E14 ... 97 A1
Cayley Rd UB2 ... 107 D3
Cayton Pl EC1 ... 235 C1
Cayton Rd UB6 ... 86 C5
Cayton St EC1 ... 235 C1
Cazenove Mans 1 N16 .. 74 A6
Cazenove Rd
Stoke Newington N16 ... 74 A6
Walthamstow E17 ... 35 C2
Cearns Ho E6 ... 99 D6
Ceasors Ct TW1 ... 152 D2
Cecil Ave Barking IG11 ... 79 B1
Enfield EN1 ... 5 D1
Wembley HA9 ... 66 B3
Cecil Cl
Chessington KT9 ... 213 D4
Ealing W5 ... 87 D2
Littleton TW15 ... 171 A3
Cecil Ct Chelsea SW10 .. 266 A6
12 Croydon CR0 ... 221 D6
Ealing W5 ... 87 D2
South Hampstead NW6 ... 69 D1
St James WC2 ... 250 A5
Cecile Pk N8 ... 50 A3
Cecil Ho E17 ... 35 C2
Cecilia Cl N2 ... 48 A6
Cecilia Rd E8 ... 74 A3
Cecil Lo KT9 ... 213 D4
Cecil Mans 2 SW17 ... 159 A2
Cecil Pk HA5 ... 41 A5
Cecil Pl CR4 ... 202 D4
Cecil Rd Acton W3 ... 89 A2
Ashford TW15 ... 171 A4
Cheam SM1, SM2 ... 217 B2
Colindale NW9 ... 45 C6
Dagenham RM6 ... 58 D2
Enfield EN2 ... 5 B1
Harlesden NW10 ... 89 C6
Harrow HA3 ... 42 C6
Hounslow TW3 ... 130 A3
Ilford IG1 ... 78 D4
Leyton E11 ... 76 C5
Merton SW19 ... 179 D3
Muswell Hill N10 ... 31 B1
Newham E13 ... 99 A6
Osidge N14 ... 15 C3
Thornton Heath CR0 ... 204 B3
Walthamstow E17 ... 35 C2
Cecil Rhodes Ho NW1 ... 232 C4
Cecil Rosen Ct HA0 ... 65 B5
Cecil Way BR2 ... 209 A1
Cedar Ave
Dagenham RM6 ... 59 A4
East Barnet EN4 ... 14 C4
Enfield EN3 ... 6 C3
Hayes UB3 ... 84 A1
Ruislip HA4 ... 62 C3
Sidcup DA15 ... 168 A4
Twickenham TW2 ... 152 A5
Yiewsley UB7 ... 104 B6
Cedar Cl
Buckhurst Hill IG9 ... 21 D2
East Molesey KT8 ... 196 C5
Keston Mark BR2 ... 226 A5
Kingston u T KT2 ... 177 B6
Old Ford E3 ... 97 B6
Wallington SM5 ... 218 D2
West Norwood SE21 ... 161 A2
Cedar Copse BR1 ... 188 B1
Cedar Cres BR2 ... 226 A5
Cedarcroft Rd KT9 ... 214 B4
Cedar Ct
7 Brentford TW8 ... 131 D6
19 Charlton SE7 ... 143 C6
Edgware HA8 ... 11 A1
Eltham SE9 ... 166 A5
Finchley N3 ... 29 C3
Islington N1 ... 73 A1
Marylebone W1 ... 237 B2
Mortlake SW14 ... 133 A1
1 Muswell Hill N10 ... 31 B1
5 New Southgate N11 ... 31 C5
Oakleigh Pk N20 ... 14 B3
Stoneleigh KT17 ... 216 A1
3 Sutton SM2 ... 218 A2
6 Wanstead E11 ... 55 B4
Wembley HA0 ... 65 B4
Wimbledon SW19 ... 156 D1
5 Woodford E18 ... 37 A2
Cedar Dr London N2 ... 48 C5
Pinner HA5 ... 23 C4
Cedar Gdns SM2 ... 218 A2
Cedar Gr Ealing W5 ... 110 A3
Sidcup DA5 ... 168 D5
Southall UB1 ... 85 C2
Cedar Grange 10 EN1 ... 17 C6
Cedar Ho
Ashford TW16 ... 171 D3
5 Cubitt Town E14 ... 120 A4
Hayes UB4 ... 84 C3
Kensington W8 ... 255 C6
New Addington CR0 ... 223 D2
New Cross Gate SE14 ... 140 D4
5 Richmond TW9 ... 132 D4
16 Rotherhithe SE16 ... 118 D4
Wood Green N22 ... 32 C2
Cedar Hts TW10 ... 154 A3
Cedarhurst BR1 ... 186 C3
Cedarhurst Dr SE9 ... 165 C6
Cedar Lawn Ave EN5 ... 13 A6
Cedar Lo
Brondesbury NW2 ... 69 B2
Fulham SW6 ... 134 D4
Cedarmore Ct BR7 ... 189 A2
Cedar Mount SE9 ... 165 D3
Cedarne Rd SW6 ... 135 D5 265 C3
Cedar Park Gdns RM6 ... 58 D2
Cedar Park Rd EN2 ... 5 A5
Cedar Pl 3 SE7 ... 121 C1
Cedar Rd Bromley BR1 .. 187 C1
Cedar Rd *continued*
Cranford TW5 ... 128 C3
Cricklewood NW2 ... 68 C4
Croydon CR0 ... 221 C6
East Bedfont TW14 ... 149 B3
East Molesey KT8 ... 196 C5
Enfield EN2 ... 5 A5
Sutton SM2 ... 218 A2
Teddington TW11 ... 175 A5
Tottenham N17 ... 33 D2
Cedar Rise N14 ... 15 A4
Cedars Ave
Mitcham CR4 ... 203 A6
Walthamstow E17 ... 53 C4
Cedars Cl Hendon NW4 ... 46 D6
Lewisham SE13 ... 142 B2
Cedars Ct Edmonton N9 ... 17 D2
Putney SW15 ... 156 A5
Cedars Dr UB10 ... 82 C5
Cedars Fst & Mid Schs HA3 ... 24 A2
Cedars Ho
21 London SW2 ... 138 B1
15 Walthamstow E17 ... 53 D6
5 West Norwood SW27 ... 182 D5
Cedars Mews SW4 ... 137 B1
Cedars Prim Sch The TW5 ... 128 A5
Cedars Rd
Barnes SW13 ... 134 A3
Beckenham BR3 ... 185 B1
Clapham SW4 ... 137 B1
4 Lower Edmonton N9 .. 18 A2
Morden SM4 ... 201 C5
Stratford E15 ... 76 C2
Teddington KT8 ... 175 C2
Wallington CR0 ... 220 A4
Winchmore Hill N21 ... 16 D2
Cedars The
Buckhurst Hill IG9 ... 21 A3
Ealing W13 ... 87 C1
Hackney E9 ... 74 D1
4 Kingston u T KT2 ... 176 D2
Teddington TW11 ... 174 D4
Wallington SM6 ... 219 C4
Cedar Terr
9 Dagenham RM8 ... 58 D2
Richmond TW9 ... 132 A1
Cedar Tree Gr SE27 ... 182 D5
Cedarville Gdns SW16 .. 182 B4
Cedar Way
Ashford TW16 ... 171 C3
Camden Town NW1 ... 93 D6 232 C6
Cedar Wlk KT10 ... 212 D2
Cedarwood BR3 ... 185 B3
Cedarwood Ho EN2 ... 4 D3
Cedarwood Lo HA8 ... 26 B5
Cedra Ct N16 ... 52 A1
Cedric Chambers NW8 236 C6
Cedric Rd SE9 ... 167 A1
Celadon Cl EN3 ... 7 A2
Celandine Cl E3, E14 ... 97 C2
Celandine Ct E4 ... 19 D1
Celandine Dr
Dalston E8 ... 73 D1
Woolwich SE28 ... 124 B5
Celandine Gr N14 ... 15 C6
Celandine Way E15 ... 98 C4
Celbridge Mews W2 ... 91 D1
Celestial Gdns SE13 ... 142 B1
Celia Blairman Ho E1 .. 243 C4
Celia Ct 7 TW9 ... 132 B4
Celia Ho 10 N1 ... 95 C5
Celia Rd N19 ... 71 C4
Celtic Ave BR2 ... 208 C6
Celtic St E14 ... 97 D2
Cemetery La
Lower Halliford TW17 ... 192 D2
Woolwich SE7 ... 144 A6
Cemetery Rd
East Wickham SE2 ... 146 B5
Forest Gate E7 ... 76 D4
Tottenham N17 ... 33 C3
Cenacle Cl NW3 ... 69 C5
Cenotaph* SW1 ... 250 A2
Centaur Ct 3 TW8 ... 110 A1
Centaurs Bsns Pk TW7 ... 131 A6
Centaur St SE1 .116 B3 260 D6
Centenary Rd EN3 ... 7 B1
Centennial Ave WD6 ... 9 C4
Centennial Ct WD6 ... 9 C4
Centennial Pk HA7, WD6 .. 9 C4
Central Ave
Battersea SW11 ... 136 D5 267 D3
East Finchley N2 ... 47 D6
East Molesey KT8 ... 195 B4
Edmonton N9 ... 17 D1
Enfield EN1 ... 6 B3
Finchley N2 ... 30 B1
Hayes UB3 ... 106 A6
Isleworth TW3, TW7 ... 130 A1
Leyton E11 ... 76 B6
Pinner HA5 ... 41 B2
Wallington SM6 ... 220 A3
Welling DA16 ... 146 A3
Central Bsns Ctr NW10 .. 67 C3
Central Chambers W5 ... 109 D6
Central Cir NW4 ... 46 B4
Central Criminal Court (Old Bailey)* EC4 ... 94 D1 241 D2
Central Ct 2 SE18 ... 122 D2
Centrale Ctr CR0 ... 221 A6

Central Foundation Boys' Sch EC2.......95 B3 242 D6
Central Foundation Lower Girls Sch The E3.......97 A4
Central Foundation Upper Girls Sch The E3.......97 B4
Central Gdns SM4.....201 D4
Central Hill SE19.......183 B4
Central Ho Barking IG11..79 A1
Mill Meads E15.........98 A5
Central Mans
8 London NW4........46 B4
1 Streatham SW16....182 A6
Central Middlesex Hospl NW10.............89 A4
Central Par
Croydon CR0.........220 C4
Ealing UB6...........87 A4
Enfield EN3............6 C3
Feltham TW14........150 C4
Harrow HA1..........42 D4
Heston TW5..........129 C5
Ilford IG2............57 B3
Penge SE20..........184 D3
South Acton W3.......110 D4
2 Streatham SW16....182 A6
Surbiton KT6.........198 A3
8 Walthamstow E17....53 C5
Central Park Ave RM10..81 D5
Central Park Prim Sch E6..................99 D5
Central Park Rd E6.....99 D5
Central Par Villas BR5................190 C1
Central Pk Est TW4....128 D1
Central Public Health Laboratories NW9.....45 C6
Central Rd
Morden SM4..........201 D4
Wembley HA0..........65 B3
Worcester Pk KT4......216 A6
Central St Martins Coll EC1...........94 C3 241 B5
Central St Martin's Coll of Art & Design W1...........93 D1 239 D1
Central St Martins Coll of Art & Design (The London Inst) WC1..........94 B2 240 C3
Central Sch of Ballet EC1.............94 C3 241 B5
Central Sch of Speech & Drama The NW3.......70 B1
Central Sq
East Molesey KT8......195 B5
Hampstead Garden Suburb NW11..............47 D3
4 Wembley HA9.......66 A3
Central St EC1....95 A4 235 A1
Central Terr BR3.......206 D6
Central Way
Feltham TW14........150 B6
Lower Place NW10......89 A4
Sutton SM5...........218 C1
Thamesmead SE28.....124 B6
Centre Ave Acton W3....111 B5
Finchley N2............30 C1
Centre Bldg SE17.....262 B4
Centre Common Rd BR7.................189 A3
Centre Court Sh Ctr 8 SW19..................179 B4
Centre Ct N20.........14 B2
Centre Dr E7..........77 C4
Centre Hts 5 NW3.....70 B1
Centre Point 8 SE1....118 A1
Centre Point Ho WC2 . 239 D2
Centre Rd
Dagenham RM10.......103 D5
Wanstead E7, E11.......77 A6
Centre St E2...........96 B5
Centre The TW13......150 B3
Centreway 4 IG1......79 A6
Centre Way N9.........18 D2
Centro Ct E11..........54 C1
Centurian Way DA18....125 C3
Centurion Bldg SW8.. 268 C5
Centurion Cl N7........72 B1
Centurion Ct
Hackbridge SM6.......219 B6
7 Woolwich SE18.....122 B2
Centurion La E3.......97 B5
Centurion Lodge 2 RM10..................81 D2
Century Cl NW4.......46 D4
Century Ho
Edgware HA8..........26 C3
Harrow HA3...........42 C6
Lewisham SE13........141 D3
Wembley HA9.........66 B6
Century Rd E17........53 A6
Century Yd SE23.......162 C2
Cephas Ave E1.........96 C3
Cephas Ho 9 E1.......96 C3
Cephas St E1..........96 C3
Ceres Ct 12 KT1.......176 A1
Ceres Rd SE18.........123 D2
Cerise Rd SE15........140 A4
Cerne Cl UB4..........106 C6
Cerne Rd SM4.........202 A3
Cerney Mews W2...... 246 C6
Cervantes Ct 12 W2.....91 D1
Cester St E2...........96 A6
Ceylon Rd
6 Hammersmith W14..............112 D3
Kensington W14...... 254 A5
Chabot Dr SE15........140 B2
Chace Com Sch EN1.....5 C4
Chadacre Ave IG5......56 B6
Chadacre Ct E15.......99 A6
Chadacre Ho 10 SW9....138 D1
Chadacre Rd KT17.....216 B3
Chadbourn St E14......97 D2
Chadbury Ct NW7.......28 A2
Chad Cres N9..........18 C1
Chadd Dr BR1.........210 A6
Chadd Gn E13..........99 A6
Chaddlewood EN4.......3 A1
Chadston Ho 17 N1.....72 D1
Chadswell WC1....... 233 B1
Chadview Ct 2 RM6....58 D2
Chadville Gdns RM6.....58 D4
Chadway RM8..........58 C1
Chadwell Ave RM6......58 B2
CHADWELL HEATH 58 D4
Chadwell Heath Foundation Sch The RM6...................58 B3
Chadwell Heath Hospl RM6...................58 B4
Chadwell Heath Ind Pk RM8..................58 D1
Chadwell Heath La RM6..................58 C3
Chadwell Heath Sta RM6...................58 D2
Chadwell Prim Sch RM6...................58 C2
Chadwell St EC1. 94 C4 234 B2
Chadwick Ave
Chingford E4..........36 B6
Enfield N21.............4 B1
Wimbledon SW19......179 C4
Chadwick Cl
12 Ealing W7..........86 D2
Roehampton SW15.....155 D4
Teddington TW11......175 A4
Chadwick Ct 4 SE28...124 B5
Chadwick Pl KT6.......197 C3
Chadwick Rd
Harlesden NW10........89 D6
Ilford IG1.............78 D5
Leytonstone E11.......54 D3
Peckham SE15.........139 D3
Chadwick St SW1.........115 D3 259 C5
Chadwick Way SE28...124 D6
Chadwin Rd E13........99 B2
Chadworth Ho
Finsbury EC1......... 235 A1
Finsbury Pk N4.........51 A1
Chadworth Way KT10...212 B3
Chaffey Ho 6 SE7......121 C1
Chaffinch Ave CR0.....206 D3
Chaffinch Bsns Pk CR0...................206 D5
Chaffinch Cl
Croydon CR0..........206 D3
Edmonton N9...........18 D3
Tolworth KT6..........214 C5
Chaffinch Rd BR3......185 A2
Chafford Way RM6......58 C5
Chagford Ct SW19.....180 C3
Chagford Ho
38 Bromley E3.........97 D4
Marylebone NW1..... 237 C5
Chagford St NW1...........92 D3 237 D5
Chailey Ave EN1.........5 D3
Chailey Cl TW5........128 D4
Chailey Ind Est UB3....106 A4
Chailey St E5..........74 C5
Chalbury Ho 8 SW9....138 B1
Chalbury Wlk N1..... 234 A4
Chalcombe Rd SE2.....124 B3
Chalcot Cl SM2........217 C1
Chalcot Cres NW1..........92 D6 230 D6
Chalcot Gdns NW3......70 D2
Chalcot Mews SW16...160 A1
Chalcot Rd NW1 . 93 A6 231 A6
Chalcot Sch NW1.......71 B1
Chalcot Sq NW1........71 A1
Chalcott Gdns KT6.....197 C1
Chalcroft Rd SE13.....164 C6
Chaldon Rd SW6.........135 A5 264 B4
Chale Rd SW2.........160 A5
Chalfont Ave HA9.......66 D2
Chalfont Ct
3 Belvedere DA17.....125 C1
12 Harrow HA1.........42 D3
Hendon NW9...........45 D6
Marylebone NW1..... 237 D5
Chalfont Gn N9.........17 C1
Chalfont Ho
2 Bermondsey SE16...118 B3
Willesden NW10........67 B5
Chalfont Rd
Edmonton N9...........17 D1
Hayes UB3............106 A4
South Norwood SE25...205 D6
Chalfont Way W13.....109 B3
Chalfont Wlk 5 HA5....22 C1
Chalford 7 NW3........70 A2
Chalford Cl KT8.......195 C5
Chalford Ct Ilford IG2....56 D4
15 Putney SW15.......156 D5
Surbiton KT6..........198 B2
Chalford Rd SE21......183 B6
Chalford Wlk IG8.......37 D3
Chalgrove Ave SM4....201 C4
Chalgrove Gdns N3.....47 A6
Chalgrove Prim Sch N3...................47 A6
Chalgrove Rd
Sutton SM2...........218 B1
Tottenham N17.........34 B2
Chalice Cl SM6........219 D2
Chalice Ct N2..........48 C5
Chalkenden Cl SE20....184 B3
Chalkers Cnr TW9.....132 D2
Chalk Farm Rd NW1....71 A1
Chalk Farm Sta NW3....71 A1
Chalkhill Prim Sch HA9.66 D5
Chalkhill Rd HA9.......67 A5
Chalk Hill Rd W6......112 D2
Chalk La EN4............2 D1
Chalklands HA9.........67 A5
Chalkley Cl CR4.......181 A1
Chalkmill Dr EN1........6 B2
Chalk Pit Ave BR5.....190 C1
Chalk Pit Way SM1.....218 A3
Chalk Rd E13...........99 C2
Chalkstone Cl DA16....146 A4
Chalkwell Ho 10 E1.....96 D1
Chalkwell Park Ave EN1..5 C1
Challenge Cl NW10.....89 C6
Challenge Ct TW2.....152 C4
Challenge Rd TW15....149 B1
Challenger Ho 7 E14..119 A6
Challice Way SW2.....160 B3
Challiner Ct HA1.......43 A4
Challin St 1 SE20.....184 C2
Challis Rd TW8........109 D1
Challoner Cl N2........30 B1
Challoner Cres W14.. 254 C1
Challoner Ct BR2......186 B1
Challoner Mans W14.. 254 C1
Challoners Cl KT8......196 B5
Challoner St W14.........113 B1 254 C1
Chalmers Ho
13 London SW11.......136 A2
Walthamstow E17.......53 D4
Chalmers Rd TW15.....170 D5
Chalmers Rd E TW15...171 A5
Chalmers Way TW14...150 B6
Chalmer's Wlk 14 SE17...................138 D6
Chalner Ho SW2.......160 C3
Chaloner Ct SE1...... 252 C2
Chalsey Lodge SE4.....141 B1
Chalsey Rd SE4........141 B1
Chalton Dr N2..........48 B3
Chalton St NW1.. 93 D5 232 C3
Chamberlain Cl
Ilford IG1.............79 A5
Plumstead SE18.......123 B3
Chamberlain Cotts SE5...................139 B4
Chamberlain Cres BR4..................207 D1
Chamberlain Gdns TW3..................130 A4
Chamberlain Ho 6 E1...................118 C6
Chamberlain La HA5....40 A5
Chamberlain Pl E17.....53 A6
Chamberlain Rd
Ealing W13..........109 A4
Finchley N2............30 A1
Chamberlain St 7 NW1...................70 D1
Chamberlain Way
Pinner HA5............40 B6
Surbiton KT6..........198 A2
Chamberlain Wlk 5 TW13..................173 A6
Chamberlayne Ave HA9...................66 A6
Chamberlayne Mans 8 NW10..................90 D4
Chamberlayne Rd NW10..................90 C6
Chambers Gdns N2.....30 B2
Chambers Ho 2 SW16..................181 C6
Chambers La NW10.....68 C1
Chambers Pl CR2......221 B1
Chambers Rd N7........72 A4
Chambers St SE16.....118 A4
Chamber St E1...........117 D6 253 D6
Chambers Walk HA7....25 B5
Chambon Pl 7 W6....112 A2
Chambord Ho 24 E2.....95 D4
Chambord St E2........95 D4
Chamomile Ct E17......53 C3
Champa Cl N17.........33 D1
Champion Cres SE26...185 A6
Champion Gr SE5......139 B2
Champion Hill SE5.....139 B2
Champion Pk SE5......139 B3
Champion Rd SE26.....185 A6
Champlain Ho 28 W12..112 B6
Champness Cl 9 SE27...................183 B6
Champness Rd IG11....79 D1
Champneys Cl SM2....217 B1
Champneys Ct N21......16 A6
Chancel Ct W1....... 249 C6
Chancellor Gr SE21....161 A1
Chancellor Ho
South Kensington SW7............. 256 B6
29 Wapping E1........118 B5
Chancellor Pas E14....119 C5
Chancellor Pl NW9.....27 D1
Chancellors' Ct WC1.. 240 C4
Chancellors Loft N8....50 A3
Chancellor's Rd W6.....112 C1
Chancellors St W6.....112 C1
Chancellors Wharf 21 W6...................112 C1
Chancelot Rd SE2......124 B2
Chancel St SE1..........116 D5 251 C3
Chancery Bldgs 14 E1..118 C6
Chancerygate Bsns Ctr HA4...................63 A3
Chancery Gate Bsns Ctr CR4...................202 D4
Chancery Ho WC2 .... 241 A3
Chancery La
Beckenham BR3.......185 D1
Holborn EC4 ....94 C1 241 A2
Chancery Lane Sta WC1...........94 C2 241 A3
Chancery Mews SW17..158 C2
Chance St E2......... 243 C6
Chanctonbury Cl SE9 ..166 D1
Chanctonbury Gdns SM2...................217 D1
Chanctonbury Way N12...................29 C6
Chanderia Ct 5 CR0...221 A5
Chand Ho 7 N12.......30 A5
Chandler Ave E16.......99 A2
Chandler Cl TW12.....173 C2
Chandler Ct
Feltham TW14........150 A5
Thornton Heath CR7 ...204 D4
2 Tolworth KT5.......198 D1
8 Wallington SM6.....219 B2
Chandlers Cl TW14.....149 D4
Chandlers Field Prim Sch KT8...................195 C4
Chandlers Mews E14...119 C4
Chandler St E1........118 B5
Chandlers Way 11 SE24..................160 C4
Chandler Way SE15....139 D5
Chandlery Ho 26 E1.....96 A1
Chandon Lo SM2.......218 A1
Chandos Ave
Ealing W5............109 D2
New Southgate N14......15 C1
Oakleigh Pk N20.......14 B3
Walthamstow E17.......35 C1
Chandos Bsns Ctr 11 SM6..................219 C2
Chandos Cl IG9.........21 B2
Chandos Cres HA8......26 C3
Chandos Ct
Edgware HA8..........26 B3
Palmers Green N14......15 D2
Stanmore HA7..........25 B4
Chandos Pl WC2.........116 A6 250 A5
Chandos Rd
Cricklewood NW2.......68 C3
Finchley N2............30 C1
Harrow HA1............42 A4
Old Oak Comm NW10....89 C3
Pinner HA5............40 D2
Stratford New Town E15..76 B3
Tottenham N17.........33 C1
Chandos St W1.. 93 B2 238 D3
Chandos Way NW11.....47 D1
Change Alley EC3..... 242 D1
Channel Cl TW5.......129 C4
Channel Gate Rd NW10..89 C4
Channel Ho E14........97 A2
Channelsea Bsns Ctr E15...................98 B5
Channelsea Rd E15.....98 B6
Channing Sch N6.......49 B1
Channon Ct 8 KT6.....198 A4
Chantrey Rd SW9......138 B2
Chantries The HA7......25 A5
Chantry Cl
2 Abbey Wood SE2....124 C3
Edgware NW7..........11 D4
Enfield EN2.............5 A5
Harrow HA3...........44 B4
Sidcup DA14..........191 A5
Sunbury TW16.........172 A3
West Kilburn W9........91 B3
Chantry Cres NW10.....67 D2
Chantry Ct SM5........218 C5
Chantry Ct SW6........135 A2
Chantry La BR2........209 D4
Chantry Pl HA3.........23 D2
Chantry Rd
Chessington KT9.......214 C3
Harrow HA3............23 D2
Chantry Sch UB7......104 A6
Chantry Sq W8..........113 D3 255 C5
Chantry St N1....94 D6 234 D5
Chantry The
3 Chingford E4........20 A3
Hillingdon UB8.........82 B4
Chantry Way CR4......202 B6
Chant Sq E15...........76 B1
Chant St E15...........76 B1
Chapel Cl NW10........67 D2
Chapel Ct
Borough The SE1...... 252 C2
East Finchley N2.......48 C6
Hayes UB3............105 D6
Chapel End Ho E17.....35 D2
Chapel End Inf Sch E17...................35 D2
Chapel End Jun Sch E17...................35 D2
Chapel Farm Rd SE9...166 B2
Chapel Hill N2.........30 C1
Chapel House St E14...119 D2
Chapel La
5 Dagenham RM6.......58 D2
Hillingdon UB8.........82 C1
Pinner HA5............40 D6
Chapel Market N1...........94 C5 234 A4
Chapel Mill Rd KT1....198 B6
Chapel Pl Islington N1 . 234 B4
Chapel Pl *continued*
Marylebone W1....... 238 C1
12 Shoreditch EC2.......95 C4
Tottenham N17.........33 D3
Chapel Rd
Bexleyheath DA7......147 C1
Ealing W13...........109 B5
Hounslow TW3.........129 D2
Ilford IG1.............78 D5
Twickenham TW1......153 B4
West Norwood SE27....182 D6
Chapel Side W2...........113 D6 245 C5
Chapel St Enfield EN2.....5 B2
Paddington NW1 92 C2 237 A3
Westminster SW1........115 A4 248 B1
Chapel View CR2......222 C1
Chapel Wlk NW4........46 C5
Chapleton Ho SW2.....160 C6
Chaplin Cl Lambeth SE1 251 C2
Wembley HA0..........65 D2
Chaplin Cres TW16.....171 C4
Chaplin Ho
6 London SW9........138 C1
Sidcup DA14..........190 A6
Chaplin Rd
Dagenham RM9.........81 A1
3 Tottenham N17.......51 D6
Wembley HA0..........65 D2
West Ham E15..........98 D6
Willesden NW2.........68 A2
Chaplow Cl SW6.......136 A3
Chapman Cl UB7.......104 B3
Chapman Cres HA3......44 B4
Chapman Gn N22.......32 C2
Chapman Ho
26 Stepney E1..........96 B1
2 West Norwood SE27...............160 D1
Chapman Rd
Belvedere DA17.......125 D1
Hackney Wick E9.......75 B2
Thornton Heath CR0....204 C1
Chapmans End BR5....191 A1
Chapman's La BR5.....190 D1
Chapmans Park Ind Est NW10..................67 D2
Chapman Sq SW19.....156 D2
Chapman St E1........118 B6
Chapone Pl W1....... 239 C1
Chapter Cl
Hillingdon UB10........60 B1
16 South Acton W4.....111 A3
Chapter House & Jewel Twr* SW1.......... 260 A6
Chapter Rd
Kennington SE17...... 116 D1 261 D1
Willesden NW2.........68 A3
Chapter St SW1....... 259 C3
Chapter Way
Hampton TW12.........173 C6
Mitcham SW19.........180 B2
Chara Pl W4..........133 B6
Charcot Ho SW15......155 D5
Charcroft Ct 11 W14 ...112 D4
Charcroft Gdns EN3......6 D1
Chard Ho 7 N7.........72 B6
Chardin Ho 30 SW9....138 C4
Chardin Rd 11 W4.....111 C2
Chardmore Rd N16.....52 A1
Chardwell Cl E6.......100 B1
Charecroft Way W12...112 D4
Charfield Ct W9........91 D3
Charford Rd E16........99 A2
Chargeable La E13......99 A3
Chargeable St E16......98 D3
Chargrove Cl 24 SE16..118 D4
Charing Cl BR6........227 D4
Charing Cross SW1.........116 A5 250 A4
Charing Cross Hospl W6..................112 D1
Charing Cross Rd WC2..........93 D1 239 D1
Charing Cross Sta WC2 ....116 A5 250 B4
Charing Ct BR2........186 C1
Charing Ho SE1....... 251 B2
Chariot Cl 3 E3........97 C6
Charlbert Ct NW8..... 230 A4
Charlbert St NW8...........92 C5 230 A4
Charlbury Ave HA7......25 D5
Charlbury Gdns IG3.....79 D6
Charlbury Gr W5.......87 C1
Charlbury Ho 1 E12....78 C5
Charlbury Rd UB10.....60 B5
Charldane Rd SE9.....166 D1
Charlecote Gr SE26....162 B1
Charlecote Rd RM8.....81 A5
Charlemont Rd E6......100 C4
Charles Allen Ho EC1 . 234 A2
Charles Auffray Ho 30 E1..................96 C2
Charles Babbage Cl KT9..................213 C1
Charles Barry Cl SW4..137 C2
Charles Bradlaugh Ho 2 N17..................34 B3
Charles Burton Ct E5....75 A4
Charles Cl DA14.......190 B6
Charles Cobb Gdns CR0..................220 C3
Charles Coveney Rd 4 SE15.................139 D4
Charles Cres HA1.......42 B2
Charles Ct 5 TW11.....174 C5
Charles Darwin Ho
8 Bethnal Green E2....96 B4
Bromley BR1..........187 B3
Charles Dickens Ct SE25.................206 A5
Charles Dickens Ho 1 E2......................96 B4
Charles Dickens Prim Sch SE1..........117 A4 252 A1
Charles Edward Brooke Sch SW9............138 D4
Charles Edward Brooke Sch (Dennen Site) SE5...................138 D4
Charlesfield SE12......165 C1
Charles Flemwell Mews 7 E16.................121 A5
Charles Goddard Ho 3 HA0...................65 D3
Charles Gr N14.........15 C3
Charles Grinling Wlk SE18..................122 C2
Charles Haller St 25 SW2..................160 C4
Charles Harrod Ct SW13.................134 C6
Charles Ho
Southall UB2..........107 C4
1 Tottenham N17......33 D3
Charles Hobson Ho 4 NW10..................67 C1
Charles Hocking Ho 8 W3...................111 A4
Charles II Pl SW3..........114 D1 257 C1
Charles II St SW1..........115 D5 249 C4
Charles La NW8 . 92 C5 230 A4
Charles Lamb Ct N1 .. 234 D4
Charles Lamb Prim Sch N1.............95 A6 235 A6
Charles Lesser KT9....213 D3
Charles Mackenzie Ho 7 SE16..................118 A2
Charlesmere Gdns SE28..................123 C4
Charles Mills Ct SW16..182 A4
Charles Pl NW1...... 232 B1
Charles Rd
Dagenham RM6.........58 D3
Ealing W13............87 A1
Merton SW19.........179 C2
Upton E7..............77 C1
Charles Rowan Ho WC1................ 234 A1
Charles Sevright Dr NW7..................28 D5
Charles Sq N1....95 B4 235 D1
Charles St
Barnes SW13.........133 C3
Croydon CR0..........221 A5
Enfield EN1............17 D6
Hillingdon UB10........82 D3
Hounslow TW3........129 B3
Mayfair W1....115 B5 248 C4
Newham E16..........121 C5
Charles Staunton Ho 3 SE27..................183 B6
Charleston Cl TW13....150 A1
Charleston St SE17 ... 262 B3
Charles Townsend Ho EC1................. 241 C6
Charles Utton Ct E8.....74 A4
Charles Whincup Rd 2 E16.................121 B5
Charlesworth Ho 6 E14..................97 C1
Charleville Cir SE26....184 A5
Charleville Ct SW5.... 254 C1
Charleville Mans W14. 254 B1
Charleville Mews TW7..................131 B1
Charleville Rd W14.........113 B1 254 C1
Charlie Browns Rdbt E18..................37 C1
Charlmont Rd SW17 ...180 D4
Charlotte Cl DA6.......169 A6
Charlotte Ct
Crouch End N8.........49 D3
Esher KT10...........212 A3
10 Hammersmith W6...112 A2
Ilford IG2.............56 C3
11 Wembley HA0.......66 A2
Charlotte Despard Ave SW11.........137 A4 268 B1
Charlotte Ho 12 W6....112 C1
Charlotte Mews
Marylebone W1....... 239 B4
North Kensington W10...90 D1
West Kensington W14.. 254 A4
Charlotte Par SE23.....163 A2
Charlotte Park Ave BR1..................210 A6
Charlotte Pl
Kenton NW9...........45 A4
Marylebone W1....... 239 B3
Westminster SW1...... 259 A3
Charlotte Rd
Barnes SW13.........133 D4
Dagenham RM10........81 D2
Shoreditch EC2 ..95 C3 243 A6
Wallington SM6....... 219 C2
Charlotte Row SW4....137 C2
Charlotte Sharman Prim Sch SE11...... 116 D3 261 C5
Charlotte Sq 5 TW10...154 B5

Charlotte St W1 . 93 C2 **239** B4
Charlotte Terr
  N1 . . . . 94 B6 **233** D5
CHARLTON 143 D6
  171 B1
Charlton Church La
  SE7 . . . . 121 C1
Charlton Cl UB10 . . . . . . 60 D6
Charlton Cres IG11 . . . . 101 D5
Charlton Ct Finchley N3 . . 29 A1
  25 Hackney E2 . . . . 95 D6
  17 Kentish Town N7 . . . . 71 D3
  Newham E6 . . . . 100 B4
Charlton Dene SE7 . . . . . 143 D5
Charlton Gate Bsns Pk
  SE7 . . . . 121 C2
Charlton Ho
  5 Brentford TW8 . . . . . 132 A6
  Charlton TW17 . . . . 171 A1
  Somers Town NW1 . . . . **232** C2
Charlton King's Rd
  NW5 . . . . 71 D3
Charlton La
  Greenwich SE7 . . . . 121 C1
  Upper Halliford TW17 . . 193 B5
  Upper Halliford TW17 . . 193 C5
Charlton Lo **1** NW11 . . 47 B3
Charlton Manor Prim Sch
  SE7 . . . . 143 D5
Charlton Park La SE7 . . . 144 A6
Charlton Park Rd SE7 . . . 143 D5
Charlton Pl N1 . 94 D5 **234** C4
Charlton Rd
  Charlton TW17 . . . . 171 A1
  Edmonton N9 . . . . 18 D4
  Greenwich SE3, SE7 . . . 143 B6
  Harlesden NW10 . . . . . . 89 C6
  Harrow HA3 . . . . 43 D5
  Wembley HA9 . . . . 44 B1
Charlton Sch SE7 . . . . . . 144 A6
Charlton Way SE10,
  SE3 . . . . 142 C4
Charlwood Cl HA3 . . . . . 24 C4
Charlwood Ho
  Richmond TW9 . . . . 132 D5
  1 Streatham SW2 . . . . 160 B1
  Westminster SW1 . . . . . **259** C3
Charlwood Pl
  SW1 . . . . 115 C2 **259** B2
Charlwood Rd SW15 . . . . 134 C1
Charlwood St
  SW1 . . . . 115 C1 **259** B2
Charlwood Terr **5**
  SW15 . . . . 134 C1
Charman Ho
  18 London SW2 . . . . . . 160 C5
  South Lambeth SW8 . . . **270** A4
Charmian Ave HA7 . . . . . 25 D1
Charmian Ho **10** N1 . . . 95 C5
Charminster Ave
  SW19 . . . . 179 D1
Charminster Ct **3**
  KT6 . . . . 197 D2
Charminster Rd
  Mottingham SE12,
  SE9 . . . . 187 D6
  North Cheam KT4 . . . . . 200 D1
Charmouth Ct TW10 . . . . 154 B6
Charmouth Ho SW8 . . . . **270** C4
Charmouth Rd DA16 . . . . 146 C4
Charnock Ho **22** W12 . . 112 B6
Charnock Rd E5 . . . . 74 B5
Charnwood Ave SW19 . . . 179 D1
Charnwood Cl KT3 . . . . . 199 C5
Charnwood Dr E18 . . . . . . 55 B5
Charnwood Gdns E14 . . . 119 C2
Charnwood Ho **9** E5 . . . 74 B6
Charnwood Pl N20 . . . . . . 14 A1
Charnwood Rd
  Hillingdon UB10 . . . . . . 82 C5
  South Norwood SE25 . . . 205 B5
Charnwood St E5 . . . . 74 B6
Charolais Ho UB4 . . . . . . 83 B2
Charrington Ho **42** E1 . . 96 C3
Charrington Rd **2**
  CR0 . . . . 221 A6
Charrington St
  NW1 . . . . 93 D5 **232** C4
Charsley Rd SE6 . . . . 163 D2
Chart Cl Bromley BR2 . . . 186 C2
  Croydon CR0 . . . . 206 C3
  Mitcham CR4 . . . . 202 D5
Charter Ave IG2 . . . . 57 B2
Charter Bldgs **14**
  SE10 . . . . 141 D4
Charter Cres TW4 . . . . . . 129 A1
Charter Ct
  Finsbury Pk N4 . . . . 50 C1
  Kingston u T KT3 . . . . . 199 C6
  Marylebone W1 . . . . . . **237** B3
  Southall UB1 . . . . 107 C5
  Wood Green N22 . . . . . . 31 D2
Charter Dr DA5 . . . . 169 A4
Charter Ho WC2 . . . . **240** B1
Charterhouse Ave HA0 . . 65 C3
Charterhouse Bldgs
  EC1 . . . . **242** A5
Charterhouse Mews
  EC1 . . . . **241** D4
Charterhouse Rd E8 . . 74 A3
Charterhouse Sq
  EC1 . . . . 94 D2 **241** D4
Charterhouse Square Sch
  EC1 . . . . 94 D2 **241** D4
Charterhouse St EC1 . . **241** C3
Charterhouse Works
  SW18 . . . . 136 A1

Charteris Rd
  Finsbury Pk N4 . . . . 50 C1
  Kilburn NW6 . . . . 91 B6
  Woodford IG8 . . . . 37 B4
Charter Nightingale Hospl
  NW1 . . . . 92 C2 **237** B4
Charter Rd KT1 . . . . 198 D6
Charter Rd The IG8 . . . . . 36 D4
Charter Sch The SE24 . . . 161 B6
Charters Cl SE19 . . . . . . 183 C5
Charter Sq KT1 . . . . 176 D1
Charter Way
  London NW3 . . . . 47 B5
  Southgate N14 . . . . 15 D5
Chartes Ho SE1 . . . . . . **263** B6
Chartfield Ave SW15 . . . . 156 C6
Chartfield Sch SW15 . . . . 156 B6
Chartfield Sq SW15 . . . . 156 D6
Chartham Ct **12** SW9 . . 138 C2
Chartham Gr SE27 . . . . . 160 C1
Chartham Ho SE1 . . . . . **262** D6
Chartham Rd SE25 . . . . . 206 B6
Chart Hills Cl SE28 . . . . . 103 A1
Chart Ho **7** SW19 . . . . 180 D1
Chart House The **5**
  E14 . . . . 119 D1
Chartley Ave
  Harrow HA7 . . . . 24 D4
  Neasden NW2 . . . . 67 C5
Charton Cl **5** DA17 . . . 147 B6
Chartres Ct UB6 . . . . 86 B5
Chartridge SE17 . . . . 139 B6
Chartridge Cl
  Barnet EN5 . . . . 12 A6
  Bushey WD23 . . . . 8 A5
Chartridge Ct **6** HA7 . . 25 C5
Chart St N1 . . . . 95 B4 **235** D2
Chartwell **23** SW19 . . . 156 D3
Chartwell Bsns Ctr
  BR1 . . . . 209 D6
Chartwell Cl
  2 Croydon CR0 . . . . . . 205 B1
  Greenford UB6 . . . . 85 D6
  Sidcup SE9 . . . . 167 B2
Chartwell Ct
  10 Barnet EN5 . . . . 1 A1
  Dollis Hill NW2 . . . . 68 A5
  2 Woodford IG8 . . . . . . 37 A3
Chartwell Dr BR6 . . . . . . 227 B3
Chartwell Gdns SM3 . . . . 217 A4
Chartwell Lo **6** W5 . . . 185 C3
Chartwell Pl
  Cheam SM3 . . . . 217 B4
  Harrow HA2 . . . . 64 B6
Chartwell Way **3**
  SE20 . . . . 184 B2
Charville Ct **8** HA1 . . . 42 D3
Charville La **4** UB10 . . 82 C4
Charville La W UB10 . . . . 82 D4
Charville Prim Sch
  UB4. . . . . 83 C5
Charwood SW16 . . . . 182 C6
Chase Bridge Prim Sch
  TW2 . . . . 152 C5
Chase Court Gdns EN2 . . 5 A2
Chase Ct Chelsea SW3 . . **257** C5
  Isleworth TW7 . . . . 131 A3
  Merton SW20 . . . . 179 A1
  Southgate N14 . . . . 15 C5
  Wembley HA0 . . . . 65 D2
Chase Ctr The NW10 . . . . 89 B4
Chase Farm Hospl EN2. . . 4 C5
Chasefield Rd SW17 . . . . 180 D6
Chase Gdns
  Chingford E4 . . . . 35 C6
  Twickenham TW2. . . . . . 152 B4
Chase Gn EN2 . . . . 5 A2
Chase Green Ave EN2 . . . 5 A3
Chase Hill EN2. . . . . 5 A2
Chase La IG6 . . . . 57 A6
Chase Lane Inf Sch E4 . . 35 B6
Chase Lane Jun Sch
  E4 . . . . 35 B6
Chaseley Ct
  Gunnersbury W4 . . . . . . 110 D1
  Oatlands Pk KT13 . . . . . 193 C1
Chaseley St E14 . . . . 97 A1
Chasemore Cl CR4 . . . . . 202 D2
Chasemore Gdns CR0 . . . 220 C3
Chasemore Ho SW6 . . . . **264** B4
Chase Rd
  North Acton NW10 . . . . 89 B3
  Southgate N14 . . . . 15 D5
Chase Ridings EN2 . . . . . 4 C3
Chase Road Trad Est
  NW10 . . . . 89 B3
Chase Side
  East Barnet N14 . . . . . . 15 B4
  Enfield EN2 . . . . 5 A3
Chase Side Ave
  Enfield EN2 . . . . 5 A4
  Merton SW20 . . . . 179 A1
Chase Side Cres EN2. . . . 5 A4
Chase Side Pl EN2 . . . . . 5 A3
Chase Side Prim Sch
  EN2. . . . . 5 A3
Chase Side Works N14 . . 15 D4
Chase The
  Bromley BR1 . . . . 209 B6
  Clapham SW4 . . . . 137 B2
  Dagenham RM6. . . . . . . 59 A3
  Eastcote HA5. . . . . 40 C3
  Edgware HA8 . . . . 26 D2
  Erith DA7. . . . . 147 D2
  Ickenham UB10. . . . . . . 60 C3
  Loughton IG10 . . . . 21 D4
  Manor Pk E12 . . . . 77 D4
  Pinner HA5 . . . . 41 B5
  South Norwood SW16. . . 182 C3
  Stanmore HA7. . . . . 25 A4

Chase The *continued*
  Sunbury TW16. . . . . 172 B2
  Wallington CR0, SM6. . . 220 B1
Chaseville Par N21. . . . . . 16 B6
Chaseville Park Rd N21 . . 16 B6
Chase Way N14. . . . . 15 C3
Chasewood Ave EN2 . . . . 4 D3
Chasewood Ct **4** NW7 . . 27 B5
Chasewood Pk HA1 . . . . . 64 C5
Chateau The **4** SM5 . . . 218 B5
Chatelain Ho NW7 . . . . . . 28 C6
Chater Ho **6** E2 . . . . . . 96 D4
Chatfield Rd
  London SW11 . . . . 136 A2
  Thornton Heath CR0 . . . 204 D1
Chatham Ave BR2. . . . . . 209 A2
Chatham Cl
  Cheam SM3 . . . . 201 B2
  Hampstead Garden Suburb
  NW11. . . . . 47 C4
Chatham Ct SW11. . . . . . 158 D6
Chatham Ho
  7 London SE5 . . . . . . 139 C3
  16 Wallington SM6 . . . . 219 B3
  21 Woolwich SE18 . . . . 122 B2
Chatham Pl E9 . . . . 74 C2
Chatham Rd
  Clapham SW11 . . . . 158 D6
  Kingston u T KT1, KT2. . 176 C1
  Walthamstow E17 . . . . . 53 A6
  1 Woodford E18 . . . . . . 36 D1
Chatham St
  SE17 . . . . 117 B2 **262** D4
Chatsfield Pl W5 . . . . 88 A1
Chatsworth Ave
  Grove Pk BR1 . . . . 187 B6
  Hendon NW4 . . . . 28 C1
  Merton SW20 . . . . 179 A1
  Sidcup DA15 . . . . 168 A3
  Wembley HA9 . . . . 66 B3
Chatsworth Cl
  Coney Hall BR2, BR4. . . 224 D6
  Hendon NW4 . . . . 28 C1
Chatsworth Cres TW3,
  TW7. . . . . 130 D2
Chatsworth Ct
  Brondesbury NW2. . . . . . 68 D2
  Clapton Pk E5 . . . . 74 D4
  Earl's Ct W8 . . . . **255** A4
  5 Stanmore HA7. . . . . . 25 C5
  Thornton Heath SW16. . . 204 B6
Chatsworth Dr EN1 . . . . . 18 A5
Chatsworth Est E5 . . . . . 74 D4
Chatsworth Gdns
  Acton W3. . . . . 110 D5
  Harrow HA2 . . . . 41 D1
  New Malden KT3. . . . . . 199 D4
Chatsworth Ho
  2 Bromley BR2 . . . . . . 209 A5
  Kingston u T KT6 . . . . . 197 D4
Chatsworth Inf Sch
  Isleworth TW3 . . . . 130 A1
  Sidcup DA15 . . . . 168 A3
Chatsworth Jun Sch
  TW3 . . . . 130 A1
Chatsworth Lo
  1 Chiswick W4 . . . . . . 111 B1
  West Wickham BR4 . . . . 224 A6
Chatsworth Par BR5 . . . . 211 A4
Chatsworth Pl
  Mitcham CR4. . . . . 202 D6
  Teddington TW11 . . . . . 175 A6
Chatsworth Rd
  Brondesbury NW2. . . . . . 68 D2
  Cheam SM3 . . . . 217 A4
  Chiswick W4 . . . . 133 A6
  Clapton Pk E5 . . . . 74 D4
  Ealing W5 . . . . 88 B3
  Hayes UB4. . . . . 84 B3
  South Croydon CR0 . . . . 221 B5
  Stratford E15 . . . . 76 D3
Chatsworth Rise W5 . . . . 88 B3
Chatsworth Way SE27 . . . 161 A1
Chattenden Ho **8** N4 . . . 51 B2
Chatteris Ct NW4 . . . . . . 46 C6
CHATTERN HILL 170 D6
Chattern Hill TW15 . . . . . 170 D6
Chattern Rd TW15 . . . . . 171 A6
Chatterton Ct TW9 . . . . . 132 B3
Chatterton Rd
  Bromley Comm BR2 . . . 209 D4
  Highbury N4 . . . . 72 D5
Chatton St **5** NW9. . . . . 46 A5
Chatto Rd SW11 . . . . . . 158 D6
Chaucer Ave
  Cranford TW4 . . . . 128 B3
  Hayes UB4. . . . . 84 A2
  Richmond TW9 . . . . 132 C3
Chaucer Cl N11 . . . . 31 D5
Chaucer Ct
  14 New Barnet EN5 . . . . 13 D6
  7 Stoke Newington N16 . 73 C4
Chaucer Dr
  SE1 . . . . 117 D2 **263** D3
Chaucer Gdns SM1. . . . . 217 C5
Chaucer Gn CR0 . . . . . . 206 C2
Chaucer Ho
  Harrow HA2 . . . . 41 D4
  Pimlico SW1 . . . . **259** A1
  Sutton SM1 . . . . 217 C5
  2 West Norwood
  SE27. . . . . 183 A6
Chaucer Rd Acton W3. . . 111 A5
  Ashford TW15 . . . . 170 B6
  Bexley DA16 . . . . 145 D4
  Chingford E17 . . . . 36 A1
  Herne Hill SE24. . . . . . . 160 D6
  Sidcup DA15 . . . . 168 C3
  Sutton SM1 . . . . 217 C4
  Upton E7 . . . . 77 A2

Chaucer Rd *continued*
  Wanstead E11. . . . . 55 A3
Chaucer Way SW17 . . . . 180 B5
Chaulden Ho EC1 . . . . . **235** D1
Chauncey Cl N9 . . . . 18 A1
Chaundrye Cl SE9. . . . . . 166 B5
Chauntler Cl E16 . . . . . . 121 B6
Chaville Ct N11 . . . . 31 A6
Cheadle Ct NW8 . . . . . . **236** D6
Cheadle Ho **17** E14. . . . . 97 B1
CHEAM 217 B3
Cheam Common Inf Sch
  KT4. . . . . 216 B6
Cheam Common Jun Sch
  KT4. . . . . 216 B6
Cheam Common Rd
  KT4 . . . . 216 C5
Cheam Court Flats **1**
  SM3 . . . . 217 A2
Cheam Fields Prim Sch
  SM3 . . . . 217 A3
Cheam High Sch SM3 . . . 217 A4
Cheam Mans SM3. . . . . . 217 A2
Cheam Park Farm Inf Sch
  SM3 . . . . 217 A5
Cheam Park Farm Jun Sch
  SM3 . . . . 217 A5
Cheam Park Way SM3. . . 217 A2
Cheam Rd
  Belmont SM2, SM3 . . . . 216 D1
  Cheam SM1. . . . . 217 C2
Cheam St **6** SE15. . . . . 140 B2
Cheam Sta SM2. . . . . . . 217 A1
Cheam Village SM3 . . . . 217 A2
Cheapside
  Barbican EC2. . . 95 A1 **242** B1
  Edmonton N13. . . . . 33 A6
Chearsley SE17 . . . . . . **262** B4
Cheddar Cl **1** N11. . . . . 31 A4
Cheddar Rd TW6. . . . . . . 126 C3
Cheddar Waye UB4 . . . . . 84 B1
Cheddington Ho **9** E2 . . 96 A6
Cheddington Rd N18. . . . . 33 C6
Chedworth Cl E16 . . . . . . 98 D1
Chedworth Ho
  London N15. . . . . 51 B5
  2 Stoke Newington E5 . . 74 A6
Cheeseman Cl TW12 . . . . 173 A4
Cheeseman Ct UB1 . . . . 107 D6
Cheesemans Terr W14 . . **254** C1
Cheffrey Ct TW15 . . . . . . 170 C4
Cheldon Ave NW7 . . . . . . 28 D3
Chelford Rd BR1. . . . . . . 186 B5
Chelmer Cres IG11 . . . . . 102 B5
Chelmer Ct E18. . . . . 37 B2
Chelmer Rd E9 . . . . 74 D3
Chelmsford Cl
  Fulham W6 . . . . 134 D6
  Newham E6. . . . . 100 B1
Chelmsford Ct N14 . . . . . 15 D4
Chelmsford Gdns IG1 . . . 56 B2
Chelmsford Ho **5** N7 . . 72 B4
Chelmsford Rd
  Leytonstone E11 . . . . . . 54 B1
  London N14. . . . . 15 C4
  Walthamstow E17 . . . . . 53 C3
  Woodford E18 . . . . 36 D2
Chelmsford Sq NW10 . . . 90 C6
CHELSEA 114 C1
Chelsea Barracks*
  SW1 . . . . 115 A1 **258** B1
Chelsea Bridge
  SW1 . . . . 137 B6 **268** C6
Chelsea Bridge Rd
  SW1 . . . . 115 A1 **258** B1
Chelsea Cl Edgware HA8. . 26 C1
  Hampton TW12 . . . . 174 A5
  New Malden KT4. . . . . . 200 A2
  Stonebridge NW10 . . . . . 89 B6
Chelsea Cloisters SW3 **257** B3
Chelsea Coll of Art &
  Design
  Chelsea SW3. . . 114 C1 **257** A1
  Pimlico SW1 . . . 116 A1 **260** A2
Chelsea Cres
  Brondesbury NW2. . . . . . 69 B2
  Chelsea SW10 . . . . **266** B1
Chelsea Ct
  Chelsea SW3 . . . . **268** A6
  8 Chingford E4 . . . . 20 A3
  Sutton SM2 . . . . 217 D2
Chelsea Emb
  SW3. . . . . 136 D6 **267** C5
Chelsea Est SW3 . . . . . . **267** A5
Chelsea Farm Ho
  SW10. . . . . **266** D6
Chelsea Fields SW19. . . . 180 B2
Chelsea Gate SW1 . . . . . **258** B1
Chelsea Gdns
  Cheam SM3 . . . . 217 A4
  Chelsea SW1 . . . . **258** B1
  Ealing W13 . . . . 86 D2
Chelsea Harbour Design
  Ctr SW10 . . . . **266** B2
Chelsea Harbour Dr
  SW10. . . . . 136 A4 **266** B2
Chelsea Harbour Pier
  SW10. . . . . **266** C1
Chelsea Lo SW3 . . . . . . **267** D6
Chelsea Manor Ct
  SW3. . . . . **267** B6
Chelsea Manor Gdns
  SW3. . . . . **257** B1
Chelsea Manor St
  SW3. . . . . 114 C1 **257** B1
Chelsea Manor Studios
  SW3. . . . . **257** B1

Chelsea Physic Gdn*
  SW1 . . . . **267** C6
Chelsea Reach Twr
  SW10. . . . . **266** C4
Chelsea Sq
  SW3. . . . . 114 B1 **256** D1
Chelsea Twrs SW3 . . . . **267** B6
Chelsea & Westminster
  Hospl SW10 . . . 136 A6 **266** B5
Chelsfield Ave N9 . . . . . . 18 C4
Chelsfield Gdns SE26 . . . 162 C1
Chelsfield Gn N9 . . . . 18 C4
Chelsfield Ho SE17. . . . . **263** A3
Chelsfield Point **3** E9. . 74 D1
Chelsham Ho **1** SW4 . . 137 D2
Chelsham Rd
  London SW4 . . . . 137 D2
  South Croydon CR2 . . . 221 B2
Chelsiter Ct DA14 . . . . . 189 D6
Chelston App HA4 . . . . . . 62 A6
Chelston Ct **2** E11. . . . . 55 B4
Chelston Rd HA4. . . . . . . 40 A1
Chelsworth Dr SE18 . . . . 145 B6
Cheltenham Ave **10**
  TW1. . . . . 153 A4
Cheltenham Cl
  Kingston u T KT3. . . . . . 199 A6
  Northolt UB5. . . . . 63 D2
Cheltenham Ct **8** HA7. . 25 C5
Cheltenham Gdns E6 . . . 100 A5
Cheltenham Ho UB3 . . . . 105 A3
Cheltenham Pl
  10 Acton W3. . . . . 110 D5
  Acton W3. . . . . 111 A4
  Harrow HA3 . . . . 44 A5
  1 South Acton W3. . . . 110 D4
Cheltenham Rd
  Leyton E10. . . . . 54 A3
  London SE15 . . . . 162 C5
Cheltenham Terr
  SW3. . . . . 114 D1 **257** D2
Cheltenham Villas
  CR7. . . . . 204 C3
Chelverton Ct SW15 . . . . 134 D1
Chelverton Rd SW15 . . . . 134 D1
Chelwood
  Gospel Oak NW5. . . . . . . 71 A3
  London N20 . . . . 14 B2
Chelwood Cl E4 . . . . 19 C5
Chelwood Ct
  Battersea SW11 . . . . . . **266** D2
  9 South Croydon CR2 . . 221 A3
Chelwood Gdns TW9 . . . . 132 C3
Chelwood Ho **2** **236** D1
Chelwood Lo N12. . . . . . . 30 A4
Chenappa Ct E13 . . . . . . 99 A4
Chenduit Way HA7. . . . . . 24 D5
Chene Colline Ct KT6 . . . 198 A3
Cheney Ct SE23 . . . . 162 D3
Cheney Row E17 . . . . 35 B2
Cheneys Rd E11 . . . . 76 C5
Cheney St HA5 . . . . 40 C4
Chenies Ho **2** **245** C6
Chenies Mews WC1 . . . . **239** C5
Chenies Pl NW1 . . . . . . **232** D4
Chenies St . 93 D2 **239** C4
Chenies The
  Orpington BR6. . . . . 211 C3
  Somers Town NW1 . . . . **232** B4
Cheniston Gdns W8. . . . **255** C6
Chennestone Prim Sch
  TW16 . . . . 172 B1
Chepstow Cl SW15 . . . . . 157 A6
Chepstow Cres
  Ilford IG3 . . . . 57 C3
  Notting Hill
  W11. . . . . 113 C6 **245** A6
Chepstow Ct W11. . . . . . **245** A6
Chepstow Gdns UB1 . . . . 85 B1
Chepstow Pl
  W2. . . . . 113 C6 **245** A6
Chepstow Rd
  Croydon CR0 . . . . 221 D6
  Ealing W7 . . . . 109 A3
  Paddington W2 . . . . 91 C1
Chepstow Rise CR0 . . . . 221 D6
Chepstow Villas
  W11. . . . . 113 C6 **245** A6
Chequers IG9 . . . . 21 B3
Chequers Ct
  London NW9 . . . . 45 C6
  Orpington BR5. . . . . 211 D5
Chequers Ho **8** **237** A6
Chequers La RM9 . . . . . . 103 C5
Chequers Par
  Dagenham RM9. . . . . . . 103 C6
  Edmonton N13. . . . . 33 A5
Chequer St EC1. . . 95 A3 **242** B5
Chequers The HA5 . . . . . 40 C6
Chequers Way N13 . . . . . 32 D5
Cherbury Ct SE28 . . . . . 102 D1
Cherbury Ct N1. . . . . . . **235** D3
Cherbury St N1. . . 95 B5 **235** D3
Cherchefells Mews
  HA7. . . . . 25 B5
Cherimoya Gdns KT8. . . . 195 D6
Cherington Rd W7 . . . . . 108 D5
Cheriton Ave BR2. . . . . . 209 A4
Cheriton Cl
  Cockfosters EN4 . . . . 2 D1
  10 Ealing W5. . . . . 87 C2
Cheriton Ct
  4 Lee SE12. . . . . 165 A4
  South Norwood SE25 . . . 206 C5
  Walton-on-T KT12. . . . . 194 C1
Cheriton Dr SE18 . . . . . . 145 B6
Cheriton Ho **9** E5. . . . . 74 B3

Cheriton Sq SW17 . . . . . 159 A2
Cherry Ave UB1. . . . . . . 106 C5
Cherry Blossom Cl N13. . 32 D5
Cherry Cl
  Carshalton SM5. . . . . . . 218 D6
  Ealing W5 . . . . 109 D3
  Merton SM4 . . . . 201 A5
  Ruislip HA4 . . . . 61 D5
  7 Streatham SW2 . . . . 160 C4
  Walthamstow E17 . . . . . 53 D4
Cherrycot Hill BR6. . . . . . 227 B4
Cherrycot Rise BR6. . . . . 227 A4
Cherry Cres TW8 . . . . . . 131 B5
Cherry Croft Gdns **3**
  HA5. . . . . 23 B3
Cherry Ct Acton W3. . . . 111 C5
  Hackbridge CR4 . . . . . . 203 A1
  Ilford IG6 . . . . 56 C6
  Pinner HA5 . . . . 22 D2
  5 Rotherhithe SE16. . . . 119 A5
  Sidcup DA14 . . . . 168 B1
Cherrydeal Ct E11 . . . . . 54 B2
Cherrydown Ave E4. . . . . 19 C1
Cherrydown Cl E4 . . . . . . 19 C1
Cherrydown Rd DA14. . . . 168 D2
Cherry Garden Ho **7**
  SE16. . . . . 118 A4
Cherry Garden Sch
  SE16. . . . . 118 A2
Cherry Garden St
  SE16. . . . . 118 B4
Cherry Garth TW8 . . . . . 109 D1
Cherry Gdns
  Dagenham RM9. . . . . . . 81 B3
  Northolt UB5. . . . . 63 D1
Cherry Gr Hayes UB3 . . . 106 B5
  Hillingdon UB8 . . . . 83 A3
Cherry Hill
  New Barnet EN5 . . . . . . 13 D5
  Stanmore HA3. . . . . 24 B4
Cherry Hill Gdns CR0. . . . 220 B4
Cherry Hills WD19 . . . . . 23 A5
Cherry La UB7 . . . . 104 C2
Cherry Lane Prim Sch
  UB7. . . . . 104 B2
Cherry Laurel Wlk
  SW2. . . . . 160 B5
Cherry Orch
  Charlton SE7 . . . . 143 C6
  West Drayton UB7 . . . . 104 C4
Cherry Orchard Gdns
  2 Croydon CR0 . . . . . . 205 B3
  East Molesey KT8 . . . . . 195 B6
  5 South Croydon CR0 . . 221 B5
Cherry Orchard Prim Sch
  SE7. . . . . 143 C5
Cherry Orchard Rd
  Croydon CR0 . . . . 205 C1
  East Molesey KT8. . . . . 195 C6
  Keston Mark BR2 . . . . . 226 A6
Cherry Rd EN3. . . . . 6 C5
Cherry Tree Ave UB7. . . . 82 B1
Cherry Tree Cl
  11 Hackney E9 . . . . 96 C6
  Wembley HA0 . . . . 65 A4
Cherry Tree Ct
  1 Camden Town NW1 . . 71 C2
  17 Charlton SE7 . . . . . . 143 C6
  Kingsbury NW9. . . . . 45 A5
  1 Peckham SE15. . . . . . 140 B4
  3 Woodford E18 . . . . . . 36 D1
Cherry Tree Dr SW16 . . . 160 A1
Cherry Tree Hill N6. . . . . 48 D6
Cherrytree Ho **8** W10. . . 90 D4
Cherry Tree Ho
  London SE14 . . . . 141 B3
  Ruislip HA4 . . . . 39 C1
  Twickenham TW2. . . . . . 152 B2
  Wood Green N22. . . . . . . 32 A3
Cherry Tree Rd
  London N2. . . . . 48 D6
  Stratford E15 . . . . 76 C3
Cherry Tree Rise IG9 . . . 37 C2
Cherry Trees Sch The
  E3. . . . . 97 C4
Cherry Tree Terr SE1 . . **253** B2
Cherry Tree Way HA7 . . . 25 C2
Cherry Tree Wlk
  Beckenham BR3. . . . . . . 207 B6
  Coney Hall BR4 . . . . . . 224 D4
  St Luke's EC1 . . . . **242** B5
Cherry Way
  Upper Halliford
  TW17 . . . . 193 C3
  West Ewell KT19. . . . . . 215 B2
Cherry Wlk BR2. . . . . . . 209 A1
Cherrywood Cl Bow E3 . . 97 A4
  Kingston u T KT2. . . . . . 176 C3
Cherrywood Ct **1**
  TW11. . . . . 175 A5
Cherrywood Dr SW15 . . . 156 D6
Cherrywood La SM4,
  SW20. . . . . 201 A5
Cherry Wood Way W5. . . 88 C2
Chertsey Ct SW14. . . . . . 132 D2
Chertsey Dr SM3. . . . . . . 217 A4
Chertsey Ho
  Feltham TW13 . . . . 151 C1
  37 Shoreditch E2 . . . . . 95 D4
Chertsey Rd
  Ashford TW15, TW16 . . . 171 B5
  Feltham TW13, TW16 . . . 171 C4
  Ilford IG1 . . . . 79 B4
  Leyton E11. . . . . 76 B6
  Lower Halliford TW17. . . 192 C1
  Shepperton TW17 . . . . . 192 A2
  Twickenham TW2. . . . . . 152 B4
Chertsey St SW17 . . . . . 181 A6
Chervil Cl TW13 . . . . 150 A4

Chervil Mews SE28 ... 124 B5
Cherwell Ct
Teddington KT1 ... 175 D3
West Ewell KT19 ... 215 A4
Cherwell Ho NW8 ... 236 D5
Cherwell Way HA4 ... 39 A3
Cheryls Cl
SW6 ... 135 D4 265 D2
Cheseman St SE26 ... 162 B1
Chesfield Rd KT2 ... 176 A3
Chesham Ave BR2,
BR5 ... 210 D3
Chesham Cl SW1 ... 258 A5
Chesham Cres SE20 ... 184 C2
Chesham Ct SW18 ... 158 B4
Chesham Flats W1 ... 248 B6
Chesham Ho SW1 ... 258 A5
Chesham Mews SW1 ... 258 A6
Chesham Pl
SW1 ... 115 A3 258 A5
Chesham Rd
Kingston u T KT1,
KT2 ... 176 C1
Mitcham SW19 ... 180 B4
Penge SE20 ... 184 C2
Chesham St
Westminster
SW1 ... 115 A3 258 A5
Willesden NW10 ... 67 B5
Chesham Terr W13 ... 109 B4
Cheshire Cl
Chingford E17 ... 35 D2
Mitcham CR4, SW16 ... 204 A6
Cheshire Gdns KT9 ... 213 D2
Cheshire Ho SM4 ... 201 D2
Cheshire Rd N22 ... 32 B4
Cheshire St E2 ... 95 D3 243 D6
Cheshir Ho NW4 ... 46 C5
Chesholm Rd N16 ... 73 C5
Cheshunt Ho
Hendon NW4 ... 46 C6
9 Kilburn NW6 ... 91 D6
Cheshunt Rd
Belvedere DA17 ... 125 C1
Upton E7 ... 77 B2
Chesil Ct
17 Bethnal Green E2 ... 96 C5
Chelsea SW3 ... 267 B6
Chesil Ho BR7 ... 189 B2
Chesilton Rd
SW6 ... 135 B4 264 C2
Chesil Way UB4 ... 83 D4
Chesley Gdns E6 ... 100 A4
Chesney Cres CR0 ... 224 A1
Chesney Ct W9 ... 91 C3
Chesney Ho SE13 ... 142 B1
Chesney St SW11 ... 268 A1
Chesnut Gr N17 ... 51 D6
Chesnut Rd N17 ... 51 D6
Chessell Cl CR7 ... 204 D5
Chessholme Ct TW16 ... 171 C3
Chessholme Rd TW15 ... 171 A4
Chessing Ct N2 ... 48 D6
CHESSINGTON ... 214 A2
Chessington Ave
Church End N3 ... 47 B6
Erith DA7 ... 147 A5
Chessington Cl KT19 ... 215 A2
Chessington Com Coll
KT9 ... 213 D1
Chessington Ct
London N3 ... 47 B6
Pinner HA5 ... 41 B5
Chessington Hall Gdns
KT9 ... 213 D1
Chessington Hill Pk
KT9 ... 214 C3
Chessington Ho 19
SW8 ... 137 D3
Chessington Lo N3 ... 47 B6
Chessington Mans
Leyton E10 ... 53 C2
Leytonstone E11 ... 54 C2
Chessington North Sta
KT9 ... 214 A3
Chessington Par KT9 ... 213 D3
Chessington Pk KT9 ... 214 C4
Chessington Rd KT19 ... 215 B1
Chessington South Sta
KT9 ... 213 D1
Chessington Trade Pk
KT9 ... 214 C4
Chessington Way BR4 ... 223 D6
Chesson Rd
W14 ... 135 B6 264 D6
Chessum Ho E8 ... 74 A2
Chesswood Way HA5 ... 22 D1
Chestbrook Ct 12 EN1 ... 17 C6
Chester Ave
Richmond TW10 ... 154 B5
Twickenham TW2 ... 151 B3
Chester Cl
Ashford TW15 ... 171 B5
Barnes SW13 ... 134 B2
Hayes UB8 ... 82 D1
Knightsbridge SW1 ... 248 C1
1 Richmond TW10 ... 154 B5
Sutton SM1 ... 217 C6
Chester Close N NW1 ... 231 D2
Chester Close S NW1 ... 231 D1
Chester Cres E8 ... 73 D3
Chester Ct 2 Acton W3 ... 88 C1
Bermondsey SE8 ... 118 D1
4 Camberwell SE5 ... 139 B5
Gospel Oak NW5 ... 71 A4
Harrow HA1 ... 42 D3
Regent's Pk NW1 ... 231 D1
Chester Dr HA2 ... 41 C3
Chesterfield Ct
Ashford TW15 ... 170 A6

Chesterfield Ct *continued*
Kingston u T KT6 ... 198 A4
Lewisham SE13 ... 142 A2
Chesterfield Dr KT10 ... 213 A6
Chesterfield Flats EN5 ... 12 D6
Chesterfield Gdns
Greenwich SE10 ... 142 B5
Harringay N4 ... 50 D4
Mayfair W1 ... 248 C4
Chesterfield Gr SE22 ... 161 D6
Chesterfield Hill
W1 ... 115 B5 248 C4
Chesterfield Ho
Highgate N6 ... 49 A1
Mayfair W1 ... 248 B4
6 Streatham SW16 ... 181 C5
Chesterfield Lo N21 ... 16 B4
Chesterfield Mews
Ashford TW15 ... 170 A6
Harringay N4 ... 50 D4
Chesterfield Rd
Ashford TW15 ... 170 A5
Barnet EN5 ... 12 D6
Chiswick W4 ... 133 A6
Enfield EN3 ... 7 A6
Finchley N3 ... 29 C4
Leyton E10 ... 54 A3
West Ewell KT19 ... 215 B1
Chesterfield Sch EN3 ... 7 A6
Chesterfield St W1 ... 248 C4
Chesterfield Way
Hayes UB3 ... 106 A4
Peckham SE15 ... 140 C5
Chesterford Gdns NW3 ... 69 D4
Chesterford Ho 4
SE18 ... 143 D5
Chesterford Rd E12 ... 78 B3
Chester Gate NW1 ... 231 D1
Chester Gdns
Ealing W13 ... 87 B1
Enfield EN3 ... 18 B5
Morden SM4 ... 202 A3
Chester Ho
5 Barnet EN5 ... 1 D1
Dartmouth Pk N19 ... 71 B6
1 Deptford SE8 ... 141 B6
Kingston u T KT1 ... 176 D1
Chesterman Ct W4 ... 133 C5
Chester Mews
Belgravia SW1 ... 258 C6
Walthamstow E17 ... 35 C1
Chester Pl NW1 ... 231 C2
Chester Rd
Avery Hill DA15 ... 167 C6
Dartmouth Pk N19 ... 71 B6
Edmonton N9 ... 18 B3
Harlington TW6 ... 126 C2
Hounslow TW4 ... 128 B2
Ilford IG3 ... 57 D2
Newham E16 ... 98 C3
Regent's Pk
NW1 ... 93 B4 231 C2
Tottenham N17 ... 51 C6
Upton E7 ... 77 D1
Walthamstow E17 ... 52 D4
Wanstead E11 ... 55 B3
Wimbledon SW19,
SW20 ... 178 C4
Chester Row
SW1 ... 115 A2 258 B4
Chester Sq
SW1 ... 115 B2 258 C4
Chester Sq Mews SW1 ... 258 C5
Chester St
Bethnal Green E2 ... 96 A3
Westminster
SW1 ... 115 A3 258 B6
Chesters The KT3 ... 177 C2
Chester Terr
NW1 ... 93 B4 231 C2
Chesterton Cl
Greenford UB6 ... 85 D5
Wandsworth SW18 ... 157 C6
Chesterton Ct W3 ... 110 D3
Chesterton Dr TW19 ... 148 B3
Chesterton Ho
21 Battersea SW11 ... 136 B2
3 Kensal Town W10 ... 91 A2
3 Sutton SM1 ... 218 A4
Chesterton Prim Sch
SW11 ... 137 A4 268 A1
Chesterton Rd
Kensal Town W10 ... 91 A2
Newham E13 ... 99 A4
Chesterton Sq W8 ... 255 A3
Chesterton Terr
6 Kingston u T KT1 ... 176 C1
Newham E13 ... 99 A4
Chester Way
SE11 ... 116 C2 261 B3
Chesthunte Rd N17 ... 33 A2
Chestnut Alley SW6 ... 264 D5
Chestnut Ave
Brentford TW8 ... 109 D2
Buckhurst Hill IG9 ... 21 D1
Coney Hall BR4 ... 224 C4
Edgware HA8 ... 26 B4
Forest Gate E7 ... 77 B4
Hampton TW12 ... 173 C3
Hornsey N8 ... 50 A4
Kingston u T KT8, KT11 ... 174 D2
11 Mortlake SW14 ... 133 B2
Thames Ditton KT10 ... 196 B1
Wembley HA0 ... 65 B3
Worcester Pk KT19 ... 215 C4
Yiewsley UB7 ... 104 B6
Chestnut Ave N E17 ... 54 B5
Chestnut Ave S E17 ... 54 B4
Chestnut Cl
Buckhurst Hill IG9 ... 21 D2

Chestnut Cl *continued*
Carshalton SM5 ... 202 D1
Catford SE6 ... 186 A6
Chattern Hill TW15 ... 170 D6
Harlington UB7 ... 126 D5
Hayes UB3 ... 105 C6
New Cross Gate SE14 ... 141 B4
Sidcup DA15 ... 168 A2
Southgate N14 ... 15 D6
1 Stoke Newington N16 ... 73 B6
Sunbury Comm TW16 ... 171 D4
West Norwood SW16 ... 182 C6
Chestnut Ct
Beckenham BR3 ... 185 C3
7 Cheam SM2 ... 217 C2
5 Croydon CR0 ... 221 A4
Feltham TW13 ... 172 D5
Harrow HA1 ... 42 C2
Hornsey N8 ... 50 A4
Hounslow TW3 ... 129 C2
Kingston u T KT3 ... 199 C6
Surbiton KT6 ... 198 A2
Wembley HA0 ... 65 B3
West Brompton SW6 ... 264 D6
Chestnut Dr
Bexley DA7 ... 147 A2
Harrow HA3 ... 24 D2
Pinner HA5 ... 41 A3
Wanstead E11 ... 55 A3
Chestnut Gr
Cockfosters EN4 ... 14 D6
Ealing W5 ... 109 D3
Isleworth TW7 ... 131 A1
Kingston u T KT3 ... 199 B6
Mitcham CR4 ... 203 D5
Penge SE20 ... 184 C3
South Croydon CR2 ... 222 B1
Upper Tooting SW12 ... 159 A3
Wembley HA0 ... 65 B3
Chestnut Grove Sch
SW12 ... 159 A3
Chestnut Ho
1 Acton W4 ... 111 C2
Brockley SE4 ... 141 B2
7 Maitland Pk NW3 ... 70 D2
West Norwood SE27 ... 161 A1
Chestnut La N20 ... 13 A3
Chestnut Pl SE19 ... 183 D6
Chestnut Rd
Ashford TW15 ... 170 D6
Kingston u T KT2 ... 176 A3
Twickenham TW2 ... 152 C2
West Barnes SW20 ... 178 D1
West Norwood SE21,
SE27 ... 161 A1
Chestnut Rise SE18 ... 123 C1
Chestnut Row N3 ... 29 C3
Chestnuts Ct 3 E17 ... 54 A6
Chestnuts Prim Sch
N15 ... 51 A4
Chestnuts Royal BR7 ... 189 B3
Chestnuts The
Chislehurst BR7 ... 189 B3
Colindale NW9 ... 45 C6
East Finchley N2 ... 48 D4
7 Erith DA17 ... 125 B1
1 Highbury N5 ... 72 D4
Penge BR3 ... 206 D6
8 Pinner HA5 ... 23 B3
Shooters Hill SE18 ... 144 D4
Uxbridge UB10 ... 60 A1
Walton-on-T KT12 ... 194 B1
Chestnut Way TW13 ... 150 B1
Chestnut Wlk
Upper Halliford
TW17 ... 193 C5
Woodford IG8 ... 37 A5
Cheston Ave CR0 ... 207 B1
Chestwood Gr UB10 ... 60 B1
Chettle Cl SE1 ... 262 C6
Chettle Ct N8 ... 50 C3
Chetwode Ho NW8 ... 237 A6
Chetwode Rd SW17 ... 158 D1
Chetwood Wlk 13 E6 ... 100 A2
Chetwynd Ave EN4 ... 14 D3
Chetwynd Dr UB10 ... 82 B5
Chetwynd Rd NW5 ... 71 B5
Cheval Ct SW15 ... 134 B1
Chevalier Cl HA7 ... 26 A6
Cheval Pl SW7 ... 114 C3 257 B6
Cheval St E14 ... 119 C3
Chevender BR7 ... 188 D3
Cheveney Wlk 2 BR2 ... 209 A6
Chevening Ho BR5 ... 190 A2
Chevening Rd
Cubitt Town SE10 ... 120 D1
Kilburn NW6 ... 91 A6
South Norwood SE19 ... 183 B4
Chevenings The DA14 ... 168 C1
Cheverell Ho 25 E2 ... 96 A5
Cheverton Rd N19 ... 49 D1
Chevet St E9 ... 75 A3
Chevington NW2 ... 69 B2
Cheviot 4 N17 ... 34 B3
Cheviot Cl Bushey WD23 ... 8 A5
Enfield EN1 ... 5 B3
Harlington UB3 ... 127 B5
Cheviot Ct
16 Deptford SE14 ... 140 C5
Enfield EN2 ... 5 B3
Southall UB2 ... 107 D2
Cheviot Gate NW2 ... 69 A6
Cheviot Gdns
Cricklewood NW2 ... 69 A6
West Norwood SE27 ... 182 D6
Cheviot Ho N16 ... 51 D1
Cheviot Rd SE27 ... 182 D5
Cheviots Hostel EN1 ... 5 B3
Cheviot Way IG2 ... 57 C5
Chevron Cl E16 ... 99 A1

Chevy Rd UB2 ... 108 A4
Chewton Rd E17 ... 53 A5
Cheylesmore Ho SW1 ... 258 C2
Cheyne Ave
Snaresbrook E18 ... 54 D6
Twickenham TW2 ... 151 B3
Cheyne Cl
6 Hendon NW4 ... 46 B4
Keston Mark BR2 ... 226 A5
Cheyne Ct Chelsea SW3 ... 267 C6
1 Croydon CR0 ... 221 D6
Ruislip HA4 ... 39 C1
4 Wallington SM6 ... 219 B2
Cheyne Gdns
SW3 ... 136 C6 267 B5
Cheyne Hill KT5 ... 198 B5
Cheyne Mews
SW3 ... 136 C6 267 B5
Cheyne Park Dr BR4 ... 224 A5
Cheyne Path W7 ... 86 D1
Cheyne Pl SW3 ... 267 C6
Cheyne Rd TW15 ... 171 B4
Cheyne Row
SW3 ... 136 C6 267 A5
Cheyne Wlk
Chelsea
SW10 ... 136 B5 266 C4
Croydon CR0 ... 222 A6
Hendon NW4 ... 46 C3
Southgate N21 ... 16 D6
Cheyney Ho 2 E9 ... 74 D2
Cheyneys Ave HA8 ... 25 D4
Chichele Gdns CR0 ... 221 C4
Chichele Ho HA8 ... 26 B6
Chichele Mans NW2 ... 68 D3
Chichele Rd NW2 ... 68 D3
Chicheley Gdns HA3 ... 24 A3
Chicheley Rd HA3 ... 24 A3
Chicheley St SE1 ... 250 D2
Chichester Ave HA4 ... 61 B6
Chichester Cl
Hampton TW12 ... 173 B4
Kidbrooke SE3 ... 143 C4
Newham E6 ... 100 A1
Chichester Ct Barnet EN4 ... 2 B1
2 Camden Town NW1 ... 71 C1
Edgware HA8 ... 26 C4
Harrow HA2 ... 41 B1
Northolt UB5 ... 85 A6
3 Sidcup DA5 ... 169 C4
Stanmore HA7 ... 44 A6
Stanwell TW19 ... 148 A3
Chichester Gdns IG1 ... 56 B2
Chichester Ho
Kilburn NW6 ... 91 C5
2 Kingston u T KT2 ... 176 D2
Chichester Mews
SE27 ... 182 C6
Chichester Rd
Bayswater W2 ... 91 D2
Edmonton N9 ... 18 A3
Kilburn NW6 ... 91 C5
Leyton E11 ... 76 C5
South Croydon CR0 ... 221 C5
Chichester Rents WC2 ... 241 A2
Chichester St
SW1 ... 115 C1 259 B1
Chichester Way
Cubitt Town E14 ... 120 B2
Feltham TW14 ... 150 C4
Chicksand Ho 14 E1 ... 96 A2
Chicksand St
E1 ... 95 D2 243 D3
Chicksand Street E1 ... 96 A2
Chiddingfold N12 ... 13 C1
Chiddingstone SE13 ... 164 A6
Chiddingstone Ave
DA7 ... 147 B5
Chiddingstone St
SW6 ... 135 C3
Chieveley Par DA7 ... 147 D2
Chieveley Rd DA7 ... 147 D1
Chignell Pl 7 W13 ... 109 A5
Chigwell Ct 1 E9 ... 75 A2
Chigwell Hill E1 ... 118 B6
Chigwell Hurst Ct HA5 ... 40 D6
Chigwell Rd
Wanstead E18 ... 55 B6
Woodford IG8 ... 37 D3
Chiham Ho 5 SE15 ... 140 C6
Chilchester Ct 3 BR3 ... 207 D6
Chilcombe Ho 6
SW15 ... 156 A4
Chilcot Cl 13 E14 ... 97 D1
Chilcott Cl HA0 ... 65 C4
Child Ct E11 ... 54 B2
Childebert Rd SW17 ... 159 B2
Childeric Prim Sch
SE14 ... 141 A5
Childeric Rd SE14 ... 141 A5
Childerley St
SW6 ... 135 A4 264 A2
Childerly KT1 ... 198 C6
Childers St SE8 ... 141 B6
Child La SE10 ... 120 D3
Childs Ct UB3 ... 106 A6
CHILD'S HILL ... 69 C6
Child's Hill Prim Sch
NW2 ... 69 A5
Childs La 11 SE19 ... 183 C4
Child's Mews SW5 ... 255 B3
Child's Pl SW5 ... 255 B3
Child's St SW5 ... 255 B3
Childs Way NW11 ... 47 B4
Child's Wlk SW5 ... 255 B3
Chilham Cl
Old Bexley DA5 ... 169 B4
Wembley UB6 ... 87 A5
Chilham Ct 13 SW9 ... 138 C2
Chilham Ho SE1 ... 262 D6

Chilham Rd SE9 ... 188 A6
Chilham Way BR2 ... 209 A2
Chillerton Rd SW17 ... 181 B5
Chillingford Ho SW17 ... 180 A6
Chillington Dr SW11 ... 136 B1
Chillingworth Gdns
TW1 ... 152 D1
Chillingworth Rd N7 ... 72 C3
Chilmark Gdns KT3 ... 200 A3
Chilmark Rd SW16 ... 181 D2
Chiltern Ave
Bushey WD23 ... 8 A5
Twickenham TW2 ... 151 C3
Chiltern Cl Bus WD23 ... 8 A5
Ickenham UB10 ... 60 C6
North Cheam KT4 ... 216 C6
South Croydon CR0 ... 221 C5
Chiltern Ct
15 Deptford SE14 ... 140 C5
6 East Barnet N20 ... 14 C2
11 Eltham SE9 ... 166 C5
Harrow HA1 ... 42 B4
Hillingdon UB8 ... 82 D3
Marylebone NW1 ... 237 D5
Muswell Hill N10 ... 31 A1
1 New Barnet EN5 ... 14 A6
Chiltern Dene EN2 ... 4 B1
Chiltern Dr KT5 ... 198 D4
Chiltern Gdns
Beckenham BR2 ... 208 D5
Cricklewood NW2 ... 68 D5
Chiltern Ho
Camberwell SE17 ... 139 B6
Ealing W5 ... 88 A2
5 Edmonton N9 ... 18 A1
Harrow HA1 ... 42 C1
4 Kensal Town W10 ... 91 A2
5 Stamford Hill N16 ... 51 D1
Chiltern Rd Bow E3 ... 97 C3
Ilford IG2 ... 57 C4
Pinner HA5 ... 40 C4
Chiltern St W1 ... 93 A2 238 A4
Chilterns The BR1 ... 187 B1
Chiltern Way IG8 ... 21 A1
Chilthorne Cl SE6 ... 163 B4
Chilton Ave W5 ... 109 D2
Chilton Gr SE8 ... 119 A2
Chiltonian Ind Est
SE12 ... 164 D5
Chilton Rd Edgware HA8 ... 26 C4
Richmond TW9 ... 132 C2
Chilton St E2 ... 95 D3 243 D6
Chiltons The 1 E18 ... 37 A1
Chilvers Cl TW2 ... 152 C2
Chilver St SE10 ... 120 D1
Chilwell Gdns WD19 ... 22 C6
Chilworth Ct 8 SW19 ... 156 D3
Chilworth Gdns SM1 ... 218 A5
Chilworth Mews
W2 ... 92 B1 236 C1
Chilworth St
W2 ... 92 A1 236 B1
Chimes Ave N13 ... 32 D6
Chimney Ct 23 E1 ... 118 B5
Chimneys Ct 2 SW19 ... 178 C3
China Ct 1 E1 ... 118 B5
China Hall Mews 16
SE16 ... 118 C3
China Mews 17 SW2 ... 160 B4
Chinbrook Cres SE12 ... 165 B1
Chinbrook Rd SE12 ... 165 B1
Chinchilla Dr TW4 ... 128 C3
Chindit Ho 11 N16 ... 73 B4
Chine The London N10 ... 49 C5
Southgate N21 ... 16 D6
Wembley HA0 ... 65 B3
Ching Ct Chingford E4 ... 20 C1
St Giles WC2 ... 240 A1
Chingdale Rd E4 ... 20 C1
CHINGFORD ... 20 C3
Chingford Ave E4 ... 19 D2
Chingford CE Inf Sch
E4 ... 20 B3
Chingford CE Jun Sch
E4 ... 20 B3
Chingford Foundation Sch
E4 ... 19 D3
CHINGFORD GREEN ... 20 A4
Chingford Hall Com Prim
Sch E4 ... 35 B4
CHINGFORD HATCH ... 36 B6
Chingford Hospl E4 ... 20 A1
Chingford Ind Ctr E4 ... 35 A5
Chingford La IG8 ... 36 D5
Chingford Mount Rd
E4 ... 35 C5
Chingford Rd
Highams Pk E4 ... 35 C3
Walthamstow E17 ... 35 D1
Chingford Sta E4 ... 20 C4
Chingley Cl BR1 ... 186 C4
Ching Way E4 ... 35 B4
Chinnery Cl EN1 ... 5 D4
Chinnocks Wharf E14 ... 119 A6
Chinnor Cres UB6 ... 86 A5
Chipka St E14 ... 120 A4
Chipley St SE14 ... 141 A6
Chipmunk Gr UB5 ... 85 A4
Chippendale Ho SW1 ... 258 D1
Chippendale St E5 ... 74 D5
Chippenham 4 KT1 ... 176 B1
Chippenham Ave HA9 ... 66 D3
Chippenham Cl HA5 ... 39 D5
Chippenham Gdns
NW6 ... 91 C4
Chippenham Mews W9 ... 91 C3
Chippenham Rd W9 ... 91 C3
Chipperfield Rd BR5 ... 190 A1
CHIPPING BARNET ... 1 B1
Chipping Cl EN5 ... 1 A2

Chip St SW4 ... 137 D1
Chipstead Ave CR7 ... 204 D5
Chipstead Cl SE19 ... 183 D3
Chipstead Gdns NW2 ... 68 B6
Chipstead Ho 4 SW2 ... 160 A3
Chipstead St SW6 ... 135 C3
Chirk Cl UB4 ... 85 A3
Chirk Ct SE4 ... 141 B3
Chisenhale Prim Sch
E3 ... 97 A5
Chisenhale Rd E3 ... 97 A5
Chisholm Ct 1 W6 ... 112 A1
Chisholm Rd
Croydon CR0 ... 221 C6
13 Richmond TW10 ... 154 B5
Chisledon Wlk E9 ... 75 B2
CHISLEHURST ... 189 C3
Chislehurst Ave N12 ... 30 A3
Chislehurst High St
BR7 ... 188 D4
Chislehurst Rd
Bromley BR1, BR7 ... 188 A2
Broom Hill BR6 ... 211 D2
Orpington BR5, BR6,
BR7 ... 211 C4
Richmond TW10 ... 154 A6
Sidcup DA14 ... 190 A5
Chislehurst St Nicholas CE
Prim Sch BR7 ... 189 A3
Chislehurst & Sidcup
Gram Sch DA15 ... 168 B2
Chislehurst Sta BR7 ... 188 C1
CHISLEHURST WEST ... 188 C4
Chislet 5 NW5 ... 71 A2
Chislet Cl BR3 ... 185 C3
Chisley Rd 5 N15 ... 51 C3
Chiswell Sq SE3 ... 143 B3
Chiswell St
Barbican EC1 ... 95 B2 242 C4
Camberwell SE5 ... 139 B5
CHISWICK ... 111 D1
Chiswick & Bedford Park
Prep Sch W4 ... 111 C2
Chiswick Cl CR0 ... 220 B5
Chiswick Common Rd
W4 ... 111 B2
Chiswick Com Sch
W4 ... 133 B5
Chiswick Ct HA5 ... 41 B6
Chiswick Green Studios 1
W4 ... 111 A2
Chiswick High Rd W4 ... 111 C2
Chiswick High Road
(North Circular Rd)
W4 ... 110 C1
Chiswick Ho* W4 ... 133 B6
Chiswick La W4 ... 111 C1
Chiswick La S W4 ... 133 D6
Chiswick Mall W4 ... 111 D1
Chiswick Maternity Hospl
W4 ... 111 D1
Chiswick Park Sta
W4 ... 111 A2
Chiswick Pier W4 ... 133 D5
Chiswick Pk W4 ... 110 D2
Chiswick Plaza W4 ... 133 A6
Chiswick Quay W4 ... 133 A4
Chiswick Rd Acton W4 ... 111 A2
Edmonton N9 ... 18 A2
Chiswick Rdbt W4 ... 110 C1
Chiswick Sq W4 ... 133 C6
Chiswick Sta W4 ... 133 A5
Chiswick Staithe W4 ... 133 A4
Chiswick Terr 6 W4 ... 111 A2
Chiswick Village W4 ... 132 D6
Chiswick Wharf W4 ... 133 D6
Chitterfield Gate UB7 ... 126 C5
Chitty's La RM8 ... 80 D6
Chitty St W1 ... 93 C2 239 B4
Chivalry Rd SW11 ... 158 C6
Chivelston 27 SW19 ... 156 D3
Chivenor Gr KT2 ... 175 D5
Chivers Rd E4 ... 35 D6
Chivins Ct N3 ... 29 C3
Choats Manor Way
RM9 ... 103 B4
Choats Rd IG11 ... 102 D4
Chobham Gdns SW19 ... 156 D2
Chobham Rd E15 ... 76 B3
Cholmeley Cres N6 ... 49 B2
Cholmeley Ct N12 ... 30 A6
Cholmeley Lo N6 ... 49 B1
Cholmeley Pk N6 ... 49 B2
Cholmley Gdns NW6 ... 69 C3
Cholmley Rd KT7 ... 197 B3
Cholmondeley Ave
NW10 ... 90 A5
Cholmondeley Wlk
TW9 ... 153 C6
Chopin's Ct 13 E1 ... 118 B5
Chopwell Cl E15 ... 76 B1
Chorleywood Cres
BR5 ... 190 A1
Choumert Gr SE15 ... 140 A3
Choumert Mews SE15 ... 140 A3
Choumert Rd SE15 ... 139 D3
Choumert Sq 4 SE15 ... 140 A3
Chow Sq 2 E8 ... 73 D3
Chrisp Ho SE10 ... 142 C6
Chrisp St E14 ... 97 D1
Christabel Cl TW7 ... 130 C2
Christ Church TW9 ... 132 A2
Christchurch Ave
Brondesbury Pk NW6 ... 69 A1
Finchley N12 ... 30 A4
Harrow HA3 ... 42 D5
Harrow HA3 ... 43 A5

Christchurch Ave *continued*
5 Teddington TW11....175 A5
Wembley HA0..........66 A2
Christ Church Bentinck CE Prim Sch NW1 . 92 C2 237 B4
Christ Church CE Mid Sch W5..........109 D6
Christchurch CE Prim Sch SW3......... 136 D6 267 C6
Christ Church CE Prim Sch
Battersea SW11.......136 C2
Brondesbury NW6.......69 B1
Camberwell SW9.......138 C4
Cubitt Town SE10......120 C1
Forest Hill SE23.......162 D2
Shooters Hill SE18.....144 C4
Surbiton KT5.........198 C3
Christchurch CE Sch E1..........95 D2 243 D3
Christchurch Cl
Enfield EN2............5 A3
Finchley N12..........30 B3
Mitcham SW19........180 B3
Christchurch Ct UB4....84 C3
Christ Church Ct
1 Brondesbury Pk NW6..............69 A1
Harlesden NW10........89 C6
Christchurch Gdns HA3...........43 A5
Christchurch Gn HA0...66 A2
Christchurch Hill NW3..70 B4
Christchurch Ho 2 SW2...............160 A3
Christ Church La EN5....1 A3
Christchurch Lo EN4.....2 D1
Christ Church New Malden CE Prim Sch KT3.....199 C6
Christchurch Pas NW3..70 A5
Christchurch Pk SM2..218 A1
Christchurch Prim Sch IG1.............57 A1
Christ Church Prim Sch, Hampstead NW3......70 B5
Christchurch Rd
Ilford IG1............57 A1
Mitcham SW19........180 B3
Mortlake SW14........155 A6
Sidcup DA15.........167 D1
Streatham SW2........160 C3
Christ Church Rd
1 Beckenham BR3.....185 C1
Hornsey N8...........50 A3
Surbiton KT5.........198 B3
Christ Church Sch NW1..........93 B4 231 D2
Christchurch Sq 2 E9...96 C6
Christchurch St SW3.........136 D6 267 C6
Christ Church Streatham CE Prim Sch SW2....160 B3
Christchurch Terr SW3............. 267 C6
Christchurch Way SE10..............120 C1
Christian Ct SE16......119 B5
Christian Fields SW16..182 C3
Christian St E1.........96 A1
Christie Ct
Maitland Pk NW3.......70 C3
2 Upper Holloway N19..72 A6
Christie Dr SE25.......206 A4
Christie Gdns RM6......58 B2
Christie Ho Bexley DA6..169 D6
2 Cubitt Town SE10....120 D1
Harrow HA3...........42 D6
4 West Wickham BR4..207 D1
Christie Rd E9..........75 A2
Christina Sq N4.........50 D1
Christina St EC2...... 243 A6
Christine Worsley Cl N21...............16 D3
Christopher Ave W7...109 A3
Christopher Boone's Almshouses SE13....142 B1
Christopher Cl
Bexley DA15.........167 D6
Rotherhithe SE16......118 D4
Christopher Ct
Ashford TW15.........170 A5
12 Barnet EN5.........1 D1
6 Croydon CR0........206 A1
Hendon NW4..........28 C1
23 Surbiton KT6.......198 A4
Sutton SM1..........217 C3
Christopher France Ho 6 E1...................97 A4
Christopher Gdns RM9..80 D3
Christopher Hatton Prim Sch EC1........94 C3 241 A5
Christopher Lo 2 N6...49 D2
Christopher Pl NW1... 232 D1
Christopher Rd UB2....106 B2
Christopher St EC2...........95 B3 242 D5
Christ's Coll Finchley NW11...............47 D6
Christ's Coll Upper Sch N3....................29 B1
Christ's Sch TW10.....154 C6
Christ the King RC Fst Sch TW19...............148 A5
Christ the King RC Prim Sch N4...............72 B6
Christ the King Sixth Form Coll SE13...........142 B2

Chryssell Rd SW9......138 C5
Chubworthy St 5 SE14................141 A6
Chudleigh 1 DA14......190 B6
Chudleigh Cres IG3....79 C4
Chudleigh Gdns SM1...218 A5
Chudleigh Rd
Hampstead NW6........68 D1
London SE4..........163 C6
Twickenham TW1, TW2..152 D4
Chudleigh St E1........96 D1
Chudleigh Way HA4.....40 A1
Chulsa Rd SE26........184 B5
Chumleigh Gdns SE5...139 C6
Chumleigh St SE5.....139 C6
Chumleigh Wlk KT5....198 B5
Church App SE21......161 B1
Church Ave
Beckenham BR3.......185 C2
Camden Town NW1......71 B2
Chingford E4..........36 B4
Finchley N2...........30 B2
Mortlake SW14........133 B2
Northolt UB5..........63 B1
Pinner HA5...........41 B3
Ruislip HA4...........39 B1
Sidcup DA14.........190 B5
Southall UB2.........107 A3
Churchbank E17........53 C5
Churchbury Cl EN1......5 C3
Churchbury La EN1......5 C3
Churchbury Rd
Eltham SE9..........165 D4
Enfield EN1............5 C3
Church Cl Edgware HA8..27 A5
Friern Barnet N20......14 C1
Hayes UB4............83 B2
Hounslow TW4........129 B3
Kensington W8....... 245 C2
West Drayton UB7.....104 A3
Church Cres
Church End N3.........29 B2
Cranley Gdns N10......49 B5
Friern Barnet N20......14 C1
Hackney E9...........74 D1
Churchcroft Cl SW12...159 A4
Church Ct
East Finchley N2.......48 B6
Forest Hill SE26.......185 A5
Harmondsworth UB7....126 C6
Holborn EC4......... 241 B1
16 Richmond TW10.....153 D6
Rotherhithe SE16......119 B4
Ruislip HA4...........62 D5
5 West Norwood SE27..............182 D6
Churchdale Ct 1 W4..110 D1
Churchdown BR1.......186 C6
Church Dr
Coney Hall BR4.......224 C5
Harrow HA2...........41 C3
Welsh Harp NW9.......45 B1
Church Elm La RM10.....81 C2
Church End NW4.......46 B6
CHURCH END N3.......29 C1
NW10................67 D3
Church End E17.......53 D5
Church Entry EC4..... 241 D1
Church Estate Almshouses 8 TW9...........132 B1
Church Farm House Mus* NW4..................46 B6
Church Farm La SM3...217 A2
Churchfield Ave N12....30 B4
Churchfield Cl
Harrow HA2...........42 A5
Hayes UB3...........105 D6
Churchfield Ho W2.... 236 C5
Churchfield Mans 5 SW6..............135 B3
Churchfield Pl TW17...192 D2
Churchfield Prim Sch N9...................17 D3
Churchfield Rd
Acton W3............111 A5
Ealing W13..........109 C5
Hanwell W7..........108 C4
Walton-on-T KT12.....194 A1
Welling DA16.........146 A2
Churchfields
East Molesey KT8......195 C6
Greenwich SE10.......142 A6
Woodford E18.........37 A2
Churchfields Ave TW13...............151 C1
Churchfields Jun & Inf Sch E18.................37 A2
Churchfields Prim Sch BR3................206 D6
Churchfields Rd BR3...185 A1
Churchfield Way N12....30 A4
Church Garth 4 N19....71 D6
Church Gate SW6......135 A2
Church Gdns
Ealing W5...........109 D4
Wembley HA0..........65 A4
Church Gn
4 Brixton SW9........138 C3
Hayes UB3............83 D1
Church Gr
London SE13.........163 D6
Teddington KT1.......175 C1
Church Hill Harrow HA1..42 C1
Southgate N21.........16 C4
Wallington SM5.......218 D3
Walthamstow E17......53 D5
Wimbledon SW19......179 B5
Woolwich SE18.......122 B3
Churchhill Gardens Prim Sch SW1.....115 C1 259 B1

Church Hill Rd
Cheam SM1, SM3......217 A4
East Barnet EN4........14 D4
Kingston u T KT6......198 A4
Walthamstow E17......53 D5
Church Hill Sch EN4....14 D4
Church Hill Wood BR5...............211 D4
Church Ho EC1....... 241 D6
Church Hyde SE18.....145 C6
Churchill Ave
Harrow HA3...........43 B3
Hillingdon UB10........82 D4
Churchill Cl
East Bedfont TW14.....149 D3
Hillingdon UB10........82 D4
Churchill Ct Ealing W5...88 B3
Edmonton N9..........17 B3
4 Farnborough BR6....227 A3
Finsbury Pk N4........50 C2
Harrow HA2...........41 D4
7 Ilford IG1...........78 D5
Northolt UB5..........63 C3
Peckham SE15........140 A3
Willesden NW2........68 B3
9 Woolwich SE18......122 B2
Churchill Gdns
Acton W3.............88 C1
Pimlico SW1....137 C6 269 A6
Churchill Gdns Rd SW1.........137 C6 269 A6
Churchill Ho
Brentford TW8........109 C1
Mitcham CR4.........180 D2
Churchill Lo
Streatham SW16.......181 D5
Woodford IG8..........36 D4
Churchill Lodge IG6....57 A5
Churchill Mews IG8.....36 D4
Churchill Pl
Canary Wharf E14.....119 D5
Harrow HA1...........42 C5
Churchill Rd
Edgware HA8..........26 C4
Gospel Oak NW5.......71 B4
Newham E16...........99 C1
South Croydon CR2.....221 A1
Willesden NW2.........68 B2
Churchill Terr E4.......19 C1
Churchill Way
Ashford TW16.........172 A4
Bromley BR1.........187 A1
Churchill Wlk E9.......74 C3
Church La
Chessington KT9......214 B2
Chislehurst BR7.......189 A2
Dagenham RM10........81 D1
Ealing W5...........109 D4
East Finchley N2.......48 B6
Edmonton N9..........18 A2
Enfield EN1............5 B2
Harrow HA3...........24 D2
Hornsey N8...........50 B5
Keston Mark BR2......210 A1
Kingsbury NW9.........45 B2
Leytonstone E11.......54 C1
Merton SW19.........179 C2
Pinner HA5...........41 B6
Teddington TW11......174 D5
Thames Ditton KT7.....197 A3
Tottenham N17........33 C2
Twickenham TW1......153 A3
Upper Tooting SW17....181 A5
Wallington SM6.......219 D5
Walthamstow E17......53 D5
Churchley Rd SE26.....184 B6
Churchley Villas SE26..184 B6
Church Lo UB5.........63 B1
Church Manor Way SE18, SE2...............124 A2
Church Mdw KT6......213 C6
Church Mead SE5......139 A5
Churchmead Cl EN4....14 C5
Church Mead Inf Sch E10...................53 C1
Churchmead Rd NW10..68 A2
Churchmore Rd SW16..181 D2
Church Mount N2.......48 B4
Church Paddock Ct SM6................219 D5
Church Par
5 Ashford TW15.......170 B6
Harrow HA3...........42 C6
Church Path
Merton SW19.........179 C1
Mitcham CR4.........202 C6
South Acton W4.......111 A3
Walthamstow E17......53 D5
Wanstead E11.........55 A4
Church Pl Ealing W5...109 D4
Mitcham CR4.........202 C6
St James SW1........ 249 B5
Uxbridge UB10.........61 A5
Church Rd Acton W3....111 A4
Ashford TW15.........170 B6
Barking IG11..........79 A2
Barnes SW13.........134 A4
Beckenham BR2.......208 C6
Bexleyheath DA7......147 B2
Bromley BR1, BR2.....187 A1
Buckhurst Hill IG9......21 B3
24 Canonbury N1.......73 A2
Cheam SM3..........217 A2
Claygate KT10........212 D1
Cranford TW5.........128 B6
Croydon CR0.........221 A5
Ealing W7...........108 C6
East Molesey KT8......196 B6
Enfield EN3...........18 C6
Farnborough BR6......227 B3

Church Rd *continued*
Feltham TW13.........172 D5
Hayes UB3...........105 D6
Hendon NW4...........46 C5
Heston TW5..........129 C5
Higham Hill E17........35 A1
Highgate N6...........49 A3
Hillingdon UB8.........82 A3
Hounslow TW7........130 C5
Ilford IG2.............57 C3
Keston BR2..........225 D1
Kingston u T KT1......176 B1
Leyton E10............75 C6
Long Ditton KT6.......197 C1
Lower Halliford TW17...192 D2
Manor Pk E12..........78 A3
Mitcham CR4.........202 C6
Mitcham CR4, SW19....180 B1
New Malden KT4......199 C1
Northolt UB5..........85 A6
Richmond TW10.......176 A6
Richmond TW10, TW9...154 A6
Sidcup DA14.........190 A6
Southall UB2.........107 B3
South Norwood SE19...183 C3
Stanmore HA7.........25 B5
Teddington TW11......174 D5
Tottenham N17........33 D3
Wallington SM6.......219 D5
Welling DA16.........146 B3
West Drayton UB7.....104 A3
West Ewell KT19......215 B1
Willesden NW10........67 C1
Wimbledon SW19......179 A6
Church Rd N N2........30 B2
Church Rd S N2........30 B2
Church Rise
Chessington KT9......214 B2
Forest Hill SE23.......162 D2
Church Row
Chislehurst BR7.......189 A2
Hampstead NW3.......70 A4
Church Row Mews BR7.................189 A3
Church St N E15.......98 C6
Church St Sta CR0.....221 A6
Church Sq TW17.......192 D2
Church St Chiswick W4..133 D6
Croydon CR0.........220 D6
Croydon CR0.........221 A6
Dagenham RM10........81 D2
Edmonton N9..........17 C2
Enfield EN2............5 B2
Hampton TW12........174 A2
Isleworth TW7........131 B3
Kingston u T KT1......175 D1
Lisson Gr NW8..92 C3 237 A5
Newham E16.........122 D5
Sunbury TW16........194 B6
Twickenham TW1......153 A3
Walton-on-T KT12.....194 A2
West Ham E15.........98 D6
Church Street Est NW8................ 236 D5
Church Stretton Rd TW3................152 A6
Church Studios 16 NW1...................71 D2
Church Terr
Hendon NW4..........46 B6
Lewisham SE13.......142 C2
21 Richmond TW10....153 D6
Church Vale
Forest Hill SE23.......162 D2
Muswell Hill N2........48 D6
Churchview Rd TW2...152 B2
Church Villa TW16.....194 B6
Churchward Ho
Camberwell SE17......138 D6
West Kensington SW5 . 254 D1
Churchway NW1...... 232 D2
Church Way
Cockfosters EN4.........2 D1
Friern Barnet N20......14 C1
Church Wlk
Barnes SW13.........134 A4
Brentford TW8........131 C6
Canonbury N16........73 B4
Child's Hill NW2.......69 B5
Dartmouth Pk N6.......71 A5
Hayes UB3............83 D1
Mitcham SW16........181 C1
15 Richmond TW10.....153 D6
Thames Ditton KT7.....196 D3
Walton-on-T KT12.....194 A1
Welsh Harp NW9.......67 B6
West Barnes SW20.....200 C6
Churchwood Gdns IG8..37 A6
Churchyard Row SE11........116 D2 261 D4
Churnfield 2 N4........72 C6
Churston Ave E13.......99 B6
Churston Cl 18 SW2....160 C3
Churston Dr SM4......201 A4
Churston Gdns N11.....31 C4
Churston Mans WC1.. 240 D5
Churton Pl
Brentford W4.........132 D6
Pimlico SW1......... 259 B3
Churton St SW1.....115 C2 259 B3
Chute Ho 17 SW9......138 C3
Chuter Ede Ho SW6... 264 D5
Chyngton Cl DA15.....167 D1
Chyngton Ct HA1.......64 C6
Cibber Rd SE23.......162 D2
Cicada Rd SW18.......158 A6
Cicely Ho NW8....... 229 D3
Cicely Rd SE15........140 A4
Cinderford Way BR1...186 C6

Cinema Mus The* SE11................ 261 C3
Cinema Par RM8........81 B6
Cinnabar Wharf Central 17 E1...................118 A5
Cinnabar Wharf East 16 E1...................118 A5
Cinnabar Wharf West 18 E1...................118 A5
Cinnamon Cl
8 Camberwell SE15....139 D5
Thornton Heath CR0....204 A2
Cinnamon Row 3 SW11...............136 A2
Cinnamon St E1.......118 B5
Cinnamon Wharf SE1 . 253 D2
Cinque Cotts SW19....178 C4
Cintra Ct SE19.........183 D4
Cintra Pk SE19........183 D3
Circle Ct HA0..........65 D4
Circle Gdns SW19......179 C1
Circle Ho 14 E14........98 B1
Circle The
Bermondsey SE1...... 253 D2
Burnt Oak NW7.........27 B4
Neasden NW2..........67 C5
Circuits The HA5........40 C5
Circular Rd London N2...30 B2
Tottenham N17........51 D6
Circular Way SE18.....144 C6
Circus Lo NW8........ 229 C2
Circus Mews W1...... 237 C4
Circus Pl EC2........ 242 D3
Circus Rd NW8..92 B5 229 C3
Circus St SE10........142 A5
Cirencester St W2......91 D2
Cirrus 17 NW9..........27 D1
Cirrus Cl 6 SM6.......220 A1
Cissbury Ho 6 SE26....162 A1
Cissbury Rd N15.......51 B4
Cissbury Ring N N12....29 C5
Cissbury Ring S N12....29 B5
Citadel Pl SE11....... 260 C2
Citizen Ho N7..........72 C4
Citizen Rd N7..........72 C4
Citron Terr 4 SE15.....140 B2
Citrus Ho 10 SE8.......119 B1
City Banking Coll SE1..........117 B4 252 D2
City Bsns Ctr 33 SE16..118 C4
City Central Est EC1.. 235 A1
City Coll N1.......... 235 C2
City Coll of London The WC1................. 240 D3
City Forum EC1..95 A4 235 A2
City Garden Row N1..........94 D5 234 D3
City Gate E1...........96 C3
City & Guilds of London Art Sch The SE11.......116 C1 261 B1
City Harbour E14......119 D3
City & Islington 6th Form Coll EC1.......94 D4 234 C2
City & Islington Coll
Finsbury Pk N4........72 D6
Lower Holloway N7.....72 A4
Lower Holloway N7......72 B4
Shoreditch EC1...95 A4 235 B1
Shoreditch N1...95 B6 235 C6
City Lights The SE11.. 261 B1
CITY OF LONDON.......117 A6
City of London Sch EC4...........117 A6 252 A6
City of London Sch for Girls EC2........95 A2 242 B4
City of Westminster Coll
Paddington NW1.........92 C2 237 B4
Paddington W2..92 B2 236 C4
City of Westminster Coll, Maida Vale Ctr W9.....91 D4
City of Westminster Coll, Queens Park Ctr W9...91 C4
City Prospect 5 SE19...183 C4
City Rd EC1......95 A4 235 B2
City Thameslink Sta EC4..........94 D1 241 C1
City University EC1..........94 D4 234 C1
City View 3 IG1.........79 A6
City Wharf Ho KT7......197 B3
City Wlk SE1.......... 253 A1
Civic Way Ilford IG6......57 A5
Ruislip HA4...........62 D3
Civil Service Coll SW1.........115 C2 259 A3
Clabon Mews SW1..........114 D2 257 C4
Clack St SE16.........118 C4
Clacton Rd Newham E6...99 D4
Tottenham N17.........33 D1
Walthamstow E17......53 A3
Claigmar Gdns N3......29 D2
Claire Ct
Brondesbury NW2.......69 A2
Bushey WD23...........8 B3
4 Pinner HA5..........23 B3
Whetstone N12.........14 A1
Claire Gdns HA7........25 C5
Claire Pl E14..........119 C3
Clairvale Rd TW5.......129 A4
Clairview Rd SW16.....181 B5
Clairville Gdns W7......108 C5
Clairville Point 12 SE23...............162 D1
Clamp Hill HA7.........24 C5
Clancarty Rd SW6......135 C3
Clandon Cl
South Acton W3........110 D4

Clandon Cl *continued*
Stoneleigh KT17.......216 A2
Clandon Ct
Plaistow BR1..........187 A4
Sutton SM2...........218 B2
Clandon Gdns N3.......47 C6
Clandon Ho
East Finchley N3.......47 C6
12 Kingston u T KT2....176 D4
Clandon Rd IG3.........79 C6
Clandon St SE8........141 C3
Clanfield Ho 12 SW15..156 A3
Clanricarde Gdns W2.........113 C6 245 B5
CLAPHAM............137 B2
Clapham Common* SW4..................137 B1
Clapham Common North Side SW4............137 A1
Clapham Common South Side SW4............159 C6
Clapham Common Sta SW4..................137 C1
Clapham Common West Side
Clapham SW4, SW11...136 D1
Clapham SW11........159 A6
Clapham Computer & Secretarial Coll SW11...................158 D6
Clapham Court Terr 2 SW4................160 A6
Clapham Cres SW4....137 D1
Clapham Ct 3 SW4....160 A6
Clapham High St SW4..................137 D1
Clapham High Street Sta SW4..................137 D2
Clapham Junction Est SW11.................136 C1
Clapham Junction Sta SW11.................136 C1
Clapham Manor Ct 1 SW4..................137 C2
Clapham Manor Prim Sch SW4..................137 C2
Clapham Manor St SW4..................137 D2
Clapham Mans SW4....159 B5
Clapham North Bsns Ctr 10 SW4..............137 D2
Clapham North Sta SW4..................138 A2
CLAPHAM PARK.......159 D6
Clapham Park Rd SW4..................137 D
Clapham Park Terr 4 SW2...................160 A
Clapham Rd SW9.........138 B5 270 D
Clapham South Sta SW4..................159 B
Claps Gate La E6......100 D
Clapton Comm E5......52 A
Clapton Girls Tec Coll E5.....................74 C
CLAPTON PARK........74 D
Clapton Pas E5.........74 C
Clapton Sq E5..........74 C
Clapton Sta E5.........74 B
Clapton Terr E5........52 A
Clapton Way E5........74 A
Clara Grant Ho 10 E14..................119 C
Clara Grant Prim Sch The E3.....................97 C
Clara Pl SE18..........122 C
Clare Cl
Borehamwood WD6......10 B
East Finchley N2........48 A
Clare Cnr SE9.........166 D
Clare Ct
Chislehurst BR7.......188 B
St Pancras WC1....... 233 B
Wimbledon SW19......179 A
Claredale Ct SM2......218 A
Claredale Ho 3 E2......96 B
Claredale St E2.........96 A
Clare Gdns Barking IG11..80 A
Forest Gate E7.........77 A
Notting Hill W11........91 A
Clare Ho
Bermondsey SE1...... 263 D
4 Burnt Oak HA8.......27 A
5 Ealing W7...........108 D
6 Old Ford E3..........97 B
Clare House Prim Sch BR3...................186 A
Clare La N1............73 A
Clare Lawn Ave SW14..155 B
Clare Mews SW6...... 265 C
Clare Mkt WC2....... 240 C
Claremont
1 Putney SW15.......157 A
Shepperton TW17......192 C
Claremont Ave
Harrow HA3...........44 A
Sunbury TW16.........172 B
West Barnes KT3......200 B
Claremont Cl
Finsbury N1.....94 C5 234 B
Newham E16..........122 C
Orpington BR6.........226 C
4 Streatham SW2......160 B
Claremont Ct 1 W9......91 B
Claremont Dr TW17....192 C
Claremont Gdns
Ilford IG3.............79 C
Kingston u T KT6......198 A

Claremont Gr
Chiswick W4 133 C5
Woodford IG8 37 C4
Claremont High Sch HA3 44 A4
Claremont Ho 15 SM2 217 C1
Claremont Hts EN2 4 D1
Claremont La KT10 212 A3
Claremont Lo 12 SW19 178 D3
Claremont Pk N3 29 A2
Claremont Pl KT10 212 D2
Claremont Prim Sch NW2 68 D6
Claremont Rd
Bromley BR1 210 B5
Claygate KT10 212 C1
Croydon CR0 206 A1
Ealing W13 87 A2
Forest Gate E7 77 C3
Hadley Wood EN4 2 B6
Harrow HA3 24 C1
Hendon NW2 68 D6
Higham Hill E17 35 A1
Highgate N6 49 C2
Kingston u T KT6 198 A4
Leyton E7 76 B5
Teddington TW11 174 D6
Twickenham TW1 153 C5
West Kilburn W9 91 B5
Claremont Sq N1 94 C5 234 A3
Claremont St
Edmonton N18 34 A4
Greenwich SE10 141 D6
Newham E16 122 C4
Claremont Terr KT7 197 B2
Claremont Way NW2 46 C1
Claremont Way Ind Est NW2 46 C1
Clarence Ave
Bromley BR1, BR2 210 A5
Clapham Pk SW4 159 D5
Ilford IG2 56 C3
Kingston u T KT3 177 B1
Clarence Cl Bushey WD23 8 D4
New Barnet EN4 14 B6
Clarence Cres
Clapham Pk SW4 159 D5
Sidcup DA14 168 B1
Clarence Ct
Edgware NW7 27 D5
10 Hammersmith W6 112 B2
5 North Finchley N12 30 B5
Clarence Gate NW1 237 D6
Clarence Gate Gdns NW1 237 D5
Clarence Gdns NW1 93 B4 231 D1
Clarence Ho SE17 139 A6
Clarence Ho* SW1 115 C5 249 B3
Clarence La SW15 155 D5
Clarence Mews
Balham SW12 159 B4
Hackney E5 74 B3
1 Rotherhithe SE16 118 D5
Clarence Pl 25 E5 74 B3
Clarence Rd
Bexley DA6 147 A1
Brentford W4 110 C1
Bromley BR1, BR2 210 A6
Brondesbury NW6 69 B1
Chislehurst SE9 166 A2
Enfield EN3 18 C6
Harringay N15 51 A4
Higham Hill E17 34 D1
Lower Clapton E5 74 B4
Manor Pk E12 77 D3
Newham E16 98 C3
Richmond TW9 132 C4
Sidcup DA14 168 B1
Sutton SM1 217 D3
Teddington TW11 175 A4
Thornton Heath CR0 205 B2
Wallington SM6 219 B3
Wimbledon SW19 179 D4
Wood Green N22 32 A3
Clarence St
Kingston u T KT1, KT2 176 A1
5 Richmond TW9 132 A1
Southall UB2 106 D3
Clarence Terr
Hounslow TW3 129 D1
Lisson Gr NW1 237 D6
Clarence Way NW1 71 B1
Clarence Wlk 9 SW4 138 A3
Clarendon Cl
Bayswater W2 247 A6
38 Hackney E9 74 C1
Clarendon Cres TW2 152 B1
Clarendon Cross W11 244 B5
Clarendon Ct
London NW11 47 B5
Mitcham SM4 202 C4
Paddington W9 236 B6
1 Richmond TW9 132 C4
Willesden NW2 68 C1
Clarendon Dr SW15 134 C1
Clarendon Flats W1 238 B1
Clarendon Gdns
Hendon NW4 46 B6
Paddington W9 92 A3 236 B5
Redbridge IG1 56 B2
Wembley HA9 66 A4
Clarendon Gr
Mitcham CR4 202 D6
Somers Town NW1 232 C2
Clarendon Ho
Harrow HA2 42 B6
North Finchley N12 30 A5
Somers Town NW1 232 B3
South Oxhey WD19 22 D5
Clarendon Mews
Bayswater W2 247 A6
Old Bexley DA5 169 D3
Clarendon Pl W2 114 C6 247 A6
Clarendon Prim Sch TW15 170 B6
Clarendon Rd
Ashford TW15 170 B6
Croydon CR0 220 D6
Ealing W5 88 A3
Edmonton N18 34 A5
Harrow HA1 42 C3
Hayes UB3 105 D4
Hornsey N8 50 B6
Leytonstone E11 54 B1
Mitcham SW19 180 C3
Notting Hill W11 113 A6 244 B5
Wallington SM6 219 C2
Walthamstow E17 53 D3
Wanstead E18 55 A6
West Green N15 51 A5
Wood Green N22 32 B1
Clarendon Rise SE13 142 A1
Clarendon Sch TW12 173 D4
Clarendon St SW1 115 B1 258 D2
Clarendon Terr W9 236 B6
Clarendon Way
Enfield N21 17 A5
Orpington BR5, BR7 211 D6
Clarendon Wlk 11 W11 91 A1
Clarens St SE6 163 B2
Clare Pl SW15 155 D4
Clare Point NW2 46 D1
Clare Rd
Hounslow TW4 129 B2
Leytonstone E11 54 B3
New Cross Gate SE14 141 B4
Northolt UB6 64 B2
Stanwell TW19 148 A4
Willesden NW10 68 A1
Clare St E2 96 B5
Claret Gdns SE25 205 C5
Clareville Ct SW7 256 B3
Clareville Gr SW7 114 A2 256 B3
Clareville Grove Mews SW7 256 B3
Clareville Rd BR5 227 A6
Clareville St SW7 114 A2 256 B3
Clare Way DA7 147 A4
Clarewood Ct W1 237 C3
Clarewood Wlk SW9 138 C1
Clarges Ho W1 248 D4
Clarges Mews W1 115 B5 248 C4
Clarges St W1 115 B5 248 D4
Clariat Ct W3 110 C4
Claribel Rd SW9 138 D3
Clarice Ct NW4 46 B6
Claridge Ct SW6 264 C1
Claridge Rd RM8 58 D1
Clarinet Ct HA8 26 D3
Clarissa Ho 7 E14 97 D1
Clarissa Rd RM6 58 D2
Clarissa St E8 95 D6
Clark Ct 17 NW10 67 B1
Clarke Ho
2 London SW4 137 C2
5 Richmond TW10 153 C1
Clarke Mans 9 IG11 79 D1
Clarke Mews N9 18 B1
Clarke Path N16 52 A1
Clarke's Ave KT4, SM3 216 D6
Clarkes Dr UB8 82 A2
Clarkes Mews W1 238 B4
Clark Ho SW10 266 A4
Clark Lawrence Ct 11 SW11 136 B2
Clarks Mead WD23 8 B4
Clarkson Rd E16 98 D1
Clarkson Row NW1 232 A3
Clarkson St E2 96 B4
Clarksons The IG11 101 A5
Clark's Pl EC2 243 A2
Clark's Rd IG1 79 B6
Clark St E1 96 C2
Clark Way TW5 128 D5
Classic Mans 33 E9 74 C1
Classinghall Ho 14 SW15 156 D5
Classon Cl UB7 104 A4
Claude Rd Leyton E10 54 A1
London SE15 140 B3
Newham E13 99 B6
Claude St E14 119 C2
Claudia Jones Way SW2 160 A5
Claudia Pl SW19 157 A3
Claudius Cl HA7 9 D1
Claughton Rd E13 99 C5
Clauson Ave UB5 64 A3
Clavell St 8 SE10 142 A6
Claverdale Rd SW2 160 C4
Clavering Ave SW13 134 B6
Clavering Cl TW1 175 A6
Clavering Ho SE13 142 B1
Clavering Rd E12 77 D6
Claverings Ind Est N9 18 C2
Claverley Gr N3 29 D2
Claverley Villas N3 29 D3
Claverton St SW1 115 C1 259 B1
Clave St E1 118 C5
Claxton Gr W6 112 D1 254 A1
Clay Ave CR4 181 B1
Claybank Gr SE13 141 D2
Claybee Ct N22 32 B5
Claybourne Mews 2 SE19 183 D3
Claybridge Rd SE12 187 C6
Claybrook Cl N2 48 B6
Claybrook Rd W6 134 D6
Claybury Broadway IG5 56 A6
Clay Ct E17 54 B6
Claydon SE17 262 A4
Claydon Dr CR0 220 A4
Claydon Ho NW4 28 D1
Claydown Mews SE18 122 C1
Clayfarm Rd SE9 167 A2
CLAYGATE 212 D1
Claygate Cres CR0 224 B2
Claygate Ct SM1 218 A5
Claygate La
Hinchley Wood KT10 213 A6
Thames Ditton KT7 197 A1
Claygate Lodge Cl KT10 212 C1
Claygate Prim Sch KT10 212 C1
Claygate Rd W13 109 B3
Claygate Sta KT10 212 C2
CLAYHALL 56 B6
Clayhall Ct 20 E3 97 B5
CLAY HILL 5 A6
Clay Hill EN2 5 B6
Clayhill Cres SE12, SE9 187 D6
Clay La Bushey WD23 8 C4
Stanwell TW19 148 B4
Claylands Ct SE19 183 B5
Claylands Pl SW8 138 C5
Claylands Rd SW8 138 B6 270 D5
Claymill Ho 2 SE18 123 A1
Claymore Cl SM3, SM4 201 C2
Claymore Ct 4 E17 35 A2
Claypole Ct E17 53 C4
Claypole Dr TW5 129 A4
Claypole Rd E15 98 A5
Clayponds Ave TW8 110 A2
Clayponds Gdns W5 109 D2
Clayponds Hospl & Day Treatment Ctr TW8 110 A2
Clayponds La TW8 110 A1
Clays Ct N16 51 D1
Clays La E15 75 D3
Clays Lane Cl E15 75 D3
Clays Lane Cvn Site E15 76 A3
Clay St W1 92 D2 237 D3
Clayton 22 NW9 27 D1
Clayton Ave HA0 66 A1
Clayton Bsns Ctr UB3 105 C4
Clayton Cl 3 E6 100 B1
Clayton Cres
Brentford TW8 109 D1
Islington N1 233 C5
Clayton Ct
1 Higham Hill E17 35 A1
Stamford Hill N16 52 A2
Clayton Field NW9 27 C2
Clayton Ho
22 Hackney E9 74 C1
Long Ditton KT7 197 B1
Clayton Mews SE10 142 B4
Clayton Rd
Chessington KT10, KT9 213 D4
Hayes UB3 105 C4
Isleworth TW7 130 C2
Peckham SE15 140 A4
Clayton St SE11 138 C6
Clayton Terr UB4 84 D2
Claytonville Terr DA17 125 D4
Clay Wood Cl BR6 211 C2
Clayworth Cl DA15 168 B5
Cleanthus Cl SE18 144 D4
Cleanthus Rd SE18 144 D4
Clearbrook Way 13 E1 96 C1
Clearmont Ho UB2 107 C3
Clearwater Ho BR3 207 D4
Clear Water Ho 9 TW10 154 A6
Clearwater Pl KT6 197 C3
Clearwater Terr 4 W11 112 D4
Clearwell Dr W9 91 D3
Cleave Ave Hayes UB3 105 C2
Orpington BR6 227 C2
Cleaveland Rd KT6 197 D4
Cleaver Ho 6 NW3 70 D1
Cleaverholme Cl SE25 206 B3
Cleaver Sq SE11 116 C1 261 B1
Cleaver St SE11 116 C1 261 B2
Cleave's Almshos 1 KT2 176 A1
Cleeve Ct
East Bedfont TW14 149 C3
Muswell Hill N10 31 B3
Cleeve Hill SE23 162 B3
Cleeve Ho 15 E2 95 C4
Cleeve Park Gdns DA14 168 B2
Cleeve Park Sch DA14 168 C1
Cleeve Way
Cheam SM1 201 D1
Cleeve Way *continued*
Roehampton SW15 155 D4
Cleeve Workshops 14 E2 95 C4
Clegg Ho SE3 143 B1
Clegg St Newham E13 99 A5
16 Wapping E1 118 B5
Cleland Ho 19 E2 96 C5
Clematis Gdns IG8 37 A5
Clematis St W12 112 A6
Clem Attlee Par SW6 264 D5
Clem Attlee Ct SW6 135 B6 264 D5
Clemence St E14 97 B2
Clement Attlee Ho NW10 67 D1
Clement Ave SW4 137 D1
Clement Cl Acton W4 111 B2
Hampstead NW6 68 C1
Clement Danes Ho 2 W12 90 B1
Clement Gdns UB3 105 C2
Clement Ho
14 Deptford SE8 119 A2
17 North Kensington W10 90 C2
Clementhorpe Rd RM9 80 C2
Clementina Rd E10 53 B1
Clementine Churchill Hospl The HA1 64 D5
Clementine Cl W13 109 B4
Clementine Wlk 4 IG8 37 A3
Clement Rd Penge BR3 184 D1
Wimbledon SW19 179 A5
Clements Ave 1 E16 121 A6
Clements Cl 19 N12 29 D6
Clements Ct
Hounslow TW4 128 D1
5 Ilford IG1 78 D5
Clements Ho N17 34 A2
Clements Inn WC2 94 B1 240 D1
Clements Inn Pas WC2 240 D1
Clements La IG1 78 D5
Clement's La EC2, EC4 117 B6 252 D6
Clements Pl TW8 109 D1
Clements Rd
East Ham E6 78 B1
Ilford IG1 78 D5
Clement's Rd SE16 118 B3
Cleminson Ct DA14 190 D4
Clemson Ho 9 E8 95 D6
Clendon Way SE18 123 B2
Clennam St SE1 252 B2
Clensham Ct SM3 217 C6
Clensham La SM1 217 C6
Clenston Mews W1 237 C2
Clent Ho 4 N16 51 D1
Cleopatra's Needle* WC2 116 B6 250 C5
Clephane Rd 18 N1 73 A2
Clephane Rd N N1 73 A2
Clephane Rd S N1 73 B2
Clere Pl EC2 242 D6
Clere St EC2 95 B3 242 D6
Clerics Wlk TW17 193 B3
CLERKENWELL 94 D3
Clerkenwell Cl EC1 94 C3 241 B5
Clerkenwell Gn EC1 94 D3 241 C5
Clerkenwell Parochial CE Prim Sch EC1 94 C4 234 A1
Clerkenwell Rd EC1 94 D3 241 C5
Clermont Rd E9 96 C6
Cleveden Ct CR2 221 C3
Cleveden Ho BR1 188 A3
Clevedon Ct
Battersea SW11 267 A2
Dulwich SE21 161 B1
Clevedon Gdns
Cranford TW5 128 B4
Hayes UB3 105 B3
Clevedon Ho 4 SM1 218 A4
Clevedon Mans NW5 71 A4
Clevedon Rd
Kingston u T KT1 176 C1
Penge SE20 184 D2
Twickenham TW1 153 D5
Cleve Ho NW6 69 D1
Cleveland Ave
Chiswick W4 111 D2
Hampton TW12 173 B3
Merton SW20 179 B1
Cleveland Cres WD6 11 A6
Cleveland Ct Ealing W13 87 B2
Marylebone W1 239 B5
Southall UB2 107 D2
Cleveland Gdns
Barnes SW13 133 D3
Harringay N4, N15 51 A4
Hendon NW2 68 D6
Paddington W2 92 A1 236 A1
Worcester Pk KT4 215 D6
Cleveland Gr 39 E1 96 C3
Cleveland Ho 7 N2 30 B1
Cleveland Inf Sch IG1 78 D5
Cleveland Jun Sch IG1 78 D5
Cleveland Mans
8 Brixton SW9 138 C5
4 Brondesbury NW6 69 B1
Paddington W9 91 C3
Cleveland Mews W1 239 A4
Cleveland Park Ave E17 53 C5
Cleveland Park Cres E17 53 C5
Cleveland Pk TW19 148 A5
Cleveland Pl SW1 249 B4
Cleveland Rd
Barnes SW13 133 D3
Bexley DA16 145 D3
Ealing W13 87 B2
Edmonton N9 18 B4
Ilford IG1 78 D5
Isleworth TW7 131 A1
Islington N1 73 B1
New Malden KT3 199 C5
14 South Acton W4 111 A3
Wanstead E18 55 A6
Worcester Pk KT4 215 C6
Cleveland Rise SM4 200 D2
Cleveland Row SW1 115 C5 249 B3
Cleveland Sq W2 92 A1 236 A1
Cleveland St W1 93 C3 239 A5
Cleveland Terr W2 92 A1 236 B2
Cleveland Way E1 96 C3
Cleveley Cres W5 88 B5
Cleveleys Rd E5 74 B5
Clevely Cl SE7 121 D2
Clevendon Cl N16 73 D5
Cleve Rd Sidcup DA14 168 D1
South Hampstead NW6 69 D1
Cleverly Cotts W12 111 D5
Cleverly Est W12 112 A6
Cleves Ct KT6 198 A3
Cleves Prim Sch E6 99 D6
Cleves Rd Newham E6 99 D5
Richmond TW10 153 C1
Cleves Way
Ashford TW16 171 D4
Hampton TW12 173 B3
Ruislip HA4 40 D1
Clewer Cres HA3 24 B2
Clewer Ct 2 E10 53 C1
Clewer Ho 6 SE2 124 D4
Cley Ho SE4 140 D1
Clichy Ho 32 E1 96 C2
Clifden Centre (Richmond Adult & Com Coll) TW1 152 D3
Clifden Ho 6 TW8 131 D6
Clifden Mews E5 74 D3
Clifden Rd
Brentford TW8 131 D6
Homerton E5 74 D3
Twickenham TW1 152 D3
Cliff Ct 14 NW1 71 D2
Cliffe Ho 4 SE10 120 D1
Cliffe Rd CR2 221 B3
Cliffe Wlk 2 SM1 218 A3
Clifford Ave
Elmstead BR7 188 B4
Mortlake SW14 133 A3
Mortlake SW14, TW9 132 D2
Wallington SM6 219 C4
Clifford Cl UB5 85 A6
Clifford Ct
Bayswater W2 91 D2
Wandsworth SW18 158 B4
Willesden NW10 67 C4
Clifford Dr SW9 138 D1
Clifford Gdns
Hayes UB3 105 B2
Kensal Green NW10 90 C5
Clifford Gr TW15 170 C6
Clifford Haigh Ho SW6 134 D5
Clifford Ho
2 Beckenham BR3 185 D4
West Kensington W14 254 C3
Clifford Lo 5 N3 29 B1
Clifford Rd Barnet EN5 1 D2
Chingford E17 36 A1
Croydon SE25 206 A5
Hounslow TW4 128 D2
Newham E16 98 D3
Ponders End N9 18 C5
Richmond TW10 153 D2
Wembley HA0 87 D6
Clifford's Inn Pas EC4 241 A1
Clifford St W1 115 C6 249 A5
Clifford Way NW10 67 D4
Cliff Rd NW1 71 D2
Cliff Road Studios 13 NW1 71 D2
Cliffsend Ho 23 SW9 138 C4
Cliff Terr SE8 141 C3
Cliffview Rd SE13 141 C2
Cliff Villas NW1 71 D2
Cliff Wlk E16 98 D2
Clifton Ave
Church End N3 29 B2
Feltham TW13 150 C1
Shepherd's Bush W12 111 D5
Stanmore HA7 25 B1
Walthamstow E17 52 D6
Wembley HA9 66 B2
Clifton Cl 8 BR6 227 A3
Clifton Cres SE15 140 B5
Clifton Ct
1 Beckenham BR3 185 D2
Finsbury Pk N4 72 C6
Paddington NW8 236 C6
Peckham SE15 140 B5
Putney SW15 156 D6
South Norwood SE25 205 C4
9 Stanwell TW19 148 A5
Surbiton KT5 198 B2
3 Woodford IG8 37 A4
Clifton Gate SW10 266 A6
Clifton Gdns
Chiswick W4 111 B2
Clifton Gdns *continued*
Enfield EN2 16 A6
Hillingdon UB10 82 D5
Paddington W9 92 A3 236 A5
South Tottenham N15 51 D3
2 Temple Fortune NW11 47 B3
Clifton Gr E8 74 A2
Clifton Hill NW8 92 A6 229 A5
Clifton Ho Leyton E11 76 C6
Shoreditch E2 243 C6
Clifton Mans 4 SW9 138 C1
Clifton Mews SE25 205 C5
Clifton Par TW13 172 C6
Clifton Park Ave SW20 178 C1
Clifton Pl
Paddington W2 236 D1
Rotherhithe SE16 118 C4
Clifton Prim Sch UB2 107 A2
Clifton Rd Bexley DA16 146 C2
Crouch End N8 49 D3
Finchley N3 30 A2
Greenford UB6 86 B3
Harlesden NW10 90 A5
Harlington TW6 126 D2
Harrow HA3 44 B4
Ilford IG2 57 B3
Isleworth TW7 130 C3
Kingston u T KT2 176 B2
Newham E16 98 C2
Paddington W9 92 A3 236 B6
Sidcup DA14 189 C6
Southall UB2 107 A2
South Norwood SE25 205 C5
Teddington TW11 174 C6
Upton E7 77 D2
Wallington SM6 219 B3
Wimbledon SW19 178 D4
Wood Green N22 31 C2
Clifton Rise SE14 141 A5
Cliftons Roundabout SE9, SE12 165 C5
Clifton St EC2 95 C3 243 A5
Clifton Terr N4 72 C6
Clifton The KT6 214 A6
Clifton Villas W9 92 A2 236 A4
Cliftonville Ct SE12 165 A3
Clifton Way
Peckham SE15 140 C5
Wembley HA0 88 A6
Climsland Ho SE1 251 B4
Clinch Ct 11 E16 99 A2
Cline Ho SW15 156 A6
Cline Rd N11 31 C4
Clinger Ct N1 95 C6
Clink St SE1 117 B5 252 C4
Clinton Ave
Bexley DA16 146 A1
East Molesey KT8 196 A5
Clinton Ho
New Malden KT3 199 B1
6 Surbiton KT6 197 D2
Clinton Rd Bow E3 97 A4
Forest Gate E7 77 A4
West Green N15 51 B5
Clipper Appts 12 SE10 142 A6
Clipper Cl 3 SE16 118 D4
Clipper Ho E14 120 A1
Clipper Way SE13 142 A1
Clippesby Cl KT9 214 B2
Clipstone Ho 10 SW15 156 A6
Clipstone Mews W1 239 A4
Clipstone Rd TW3 129 C2
Clipstone St W1 93 C2 239 A4
Clissold Cl N2 48 D6
Clissold Cres N16 73 B4
Clissold Ct N4 73 A6
Clissold Ho 4 N16 73 B6
Clissold Rd N16 73 B5
Clitheroe Ave HA2 41 C1
Clitheroe Rd SW9 138 A3
Clitherow Ave W7 109 A3
Clitherow Rd TW8 109 C1
Clitterhouse Cres NW2 46 C1
Clitterhouse Rd NW2 46 C1
Clive Ave N18 34 A4
Clive Ct Paddington W9 236 B6
Streatham SW16 181 D5
Tolworth KT6 214 C6
Cliveden Cl N12 30 A6
Cliveden Ho SW1 258 A4
Cliveden Pl
Belgravia SW1 115 A2 258 A4
Shepperton TW17 193 A3
Cliveden Rd SW19 179 B2
Clivedon Ct Ealing W13 87 B2
6 New Barnet EN5 2 A1
Clivedon Rd E4 36 C5
Clive Ho
18 Clapham SW8 137 D3
3 Croydon CR0 205 D1
Greenwich SE10 142 A6
Clive Lloyd Ho N15 51 A4
Clive Lo NW4 46 D3
Clive Rd
Belvedere DA17 125 C2
Enfield EN1 6 A1
Feltham TW14 150 A5
Mitcham SW19 180 C4
Teddington TW1 175 A6
West Norwood SE21, SE27 161 B1
Clivesdale Dr UB3 106 B5
Clive Way EN1 6 A1

Cloak La EC4 ... 117 B6 252 C6
Clochar Ct NW10 ... 89 D6
Clock Ct 2 E11 ... 55 B5
Clock Ho
 Stamford Hill N16 ... 51 D2
 Walthamstow E17 ... 54 B5
Clock Ho The EN2 ... 5 D6
Clockhouse Ave IG11 ... 101 A6
Clockhouse Cl SW19 ... 156 C2
Clock House Ct 1 BR3 ... 185 A1
Clockhouse Junc N13 ... 32 C5
Clockhouse La TW14, TW15 ... 148 D2
Clockhouse Mans N13 ... 32 C5
Clockhouse Par N13 ... 32 C5
Clockhouse Par E11 ... 55 B3
Clockhouse Pl SW15 ... 157 A5
Clock House Rd BR3 ... 185 A1
Clockhouse Rdbt TW14 ... 149 A3
Clock House Sta BR3 ... 185 A2
Clockhouse The SW19 ... 156 C1
Clock Mus* EC2 ... 95 A1 242 B2
Clocktower Mews 6 W7 ... 108 C5
Clock Tower Mews
 Islington N1 ... 235 B5
 Thamesmead SE28 ... 124 B6
Clock Tower Pl N7 ... 72 A2
Clock Tower Rd TW7 ... 130 D2
Cloister Cl TW11 ... 175 B5
Cloister Gdns
 Croydon SE25 ... 206 B3
 Edgware HA8 ... 27 A5
Cloister Rd Acton W3 ... 89 A2
 Child's Hill NW2 ... 69 B6
Cloisters Ave BR1, BR2 ... 210 B4
Cloisters Ct Erith DA7 ... 147 D2
 Highgate N6 ... 49 B1
Cloisters Ho 8 SW19 ... 179 C3
Cloisters The 22 SW9 ... 138 C4
Clonard Way HA5 ... 23 C4
Clonbrock Rd N16 ... 73 C4
Cloncurry St SW6 ... 134 D3
Clone Ct 4 W12 ... 111 C3
Clone The 5 KT2 ... 176 D3
Clonmel Cl HA2 ... 42 B1
Clonmell Rd N17 ... 51 B6
Clonmel Rd
 Fulham SW6 ... 135 B4 264 D2
 Teddington TW11 ... 174 B6
Clonmore St SW18 ... 157 B3
Cloonmore Ave BR6 ... 227 D4
Clorane Gdns NW3 ... 69 C5
Close The
 Beckenham BR3 ... 207 A5
 Cheam SM3 ... 201 B2
 Chingford E4 ... 36 A3
 Cockfosters EN4 ... 14 D6
 Croydon SE25 ... 206 A3
 Dagenham RM6 ... 59 A3
 Eastcote HA5 ... 40 C2
 Harrow HA2 ... 24 A1
 Hillingdon UB10 ... 82 C6
 Hounslow TW7 ... 130 B3
 Ilford IG2 ... 57 C3
 Kingston u T KT3 ... 177 A1
 Lewisham SE3 ... 142 B3
 Mitcham CR4 ... 202 D5
 Mortlake TW9 ... 132 D2
 Muswell Hill N10 ... 31 B1
 1 Old Bexley DA5 ... 169 C4
 Palmers Green N14 ... 15 D2
 Petts Wood BR5 ... 211 C3
 Rayners La HA5 ... 41 B2
 Sidcup DA14 ... 190 B5
 Surbiton KT6 ... 198 A3
 Totteridge N20 ... 13 B2
 Wembley HA0 ... 66 A2
 Wembley Pk HA9 ... 67 A5
Cloth Ct EC1 ... 241 D3
Cloth Fair EC1 ... 94 D2 241 D3
Clothier Ho SE7 ... 122 A1
Clothier St EC3 ... 243 B2
Cloth St EC1 ... 95 A2 242 A4
Clothworkers Rd SE18 ... 145 B5
Cloudesdale Rd SW17 ... 159 B2
Cloudesley Mans N1 ... 234 B5
Cloudesley Pl N1 ... 94 C6 234 B5
Cloudesley Rd
 Erith DA7 ... 147 B4
 Islington N1 ... 94 C6 234 A5
Cloudesley Sq N1 ... 94 C6 234 B6
Cloudesley St N1 ... 94 C6 234 B5
Clouston Cl SM6 ... 220 A3
Clova Rd E7 ... 77 A3
Clove Cres E14 ... 120 B6
Clovelly Ave
 London NW9 ... 45 D5
 Uxbridge UB10 ... 61 A4
Clovelly Cl Pinner HA5 ... 40 C6
 Uxbridge UB10 ... 61 A4
Clovelly Ct NW2 ... 68 C3
Clovelly Gdns
 Enfield EN1 ... 17 C4
 South Norwood SE19 ... 183 D2
Clovelly Ho W2 ... 236 A2
Clovelly Rd Acton W4 ... 111 B4
 Ealing W5 ... 109 C4
 Erith DA7 ... 147 A6
 Hornsey N8 ... 49 D5
Clovelly Rd continued
 Hounslow TW3 ... 129 C3
Clovelly Way
 Harrow HA2 ... 63 B6
 Orpington BR6 ... 211 D3
 Stepney E1 ... 96 C1
Clover Cl E11 ... 76 B6
Clover Ct Enfield EN3 ... 7 A1
 Sutton SM2 ... 217 D2
Cloverdale Gdns DA15 ... 167 D5
Clover Ho
 Hounslow TW3 ... 130 A4
 Southgate N21 ... 16 B6
Cloverleys IG10 ... 21 D6
Clover Mews SW3 ... 267 D6
Clover Way SM6 ... 203 A1
Clove St 9 E13 ... 99 A3
Clowders Rd SE6 ... 163 B1
Clowes Ho 3 SW4 ... 138 A1
Clowser Cl 4 SM1 ... 218 A3
Cloysters Gn E1 ... 118 A5
Cloyster Wood HA8 ... 25 D4
Club Gardens Rd BR2 ... 209 A2
Club Row E2 ... 95 D3 243 C6
Clumps The TW15 ... 171 B6
Clunbury Ave UB2 ... 107 B1
Clunbury St N1 ... 235 D3
Clunie Ho SW1 ... 257 D6
Cluny Mews SW5 ... 255 A3
Cluny Pl SE1 ... 117 C3 263 A6
Cluse Ct N1 ... 235 A4
Clutton St E14 ... 97 D2
Clydach Rd EN1 ... 5 D1
Clyde Cir N15 ... 51 C5
Clyde Ct NW1 ... 232 D4
Clyde Flats SW6 ... 264 C4
Clyde Ho 9 KT2 ... 175 D2
Clyde Pl E10 ... 53 D2
Clyde Rd Croydon CR0 ... 221 D6
 South Tottenham N15 ... 51 C5
 Stanwell TW19 ... 148 A3
 Sutton SM1 ... 217 C3
 Wallington SM6 ... 219 C2
 Wood Green N22 ... 31 D2
Clydesdale EN3 ... 6 D1
Clydesdale Ave HA7 ... 43 D6
Clydesdale Cl
 Borehamwood WD6 ... 11 B6
 Isleworth TW7 ... 130 D2
Clydesdale Ct N20 ... 14 B3
Clydesdale Gdns TW10 ... 132 D1
Clydesdale Ho
 Abbey Wood DA18 ... 125 A4
 4 Notting Hill W11 ... 91 B1
Clydesdale Path WD6 ... 11 B6
Clydesdale Rd W11 ... 91 B1
Clyde St SE8 ... 141 B6
Clyde Terr SE23 ... 162 C2
Clyde Vale SE23 ... 162 C2
Clyde Works 10 SM6 ... 219 C2
Clyfford Rd HA4 ... 61 D4
Clymping Dene TW14 ... 150 B4
Clynes Ho
 6 Dagenham RM10 ... 81 C5
 3 Globe Town E2 ... 96 D4
 Hayes UB4 ... 84 A4
Clyro Ct N4 ... 50 B1
Clyston St SW8 ... 137 C3
Clytha Ct SE27 ... 183 A6
Coach Ho NW10 ... 67 A1
Coach & Horses Yd W1 ... 249 A6
Coach House La
 Highbury N5 ... 72 D4
 Wimbledon SW19 ... 156 D1
Coach House Mews SE23 ... 162 D5
Coach House Yd 5 NW3 ... 70 B4
Coachmaker Mews 5 SW9 ... 138 A2
Coachman Lo N12 ... 30 A5
Coalbrook Mans 3 SW12 ... 159 B3
Coaldale Wlk SE21 ... 161 A4
Coalecroft Rd SW15 ... 156 C6
Coalport Ho SE11 ... 261 A4
Coal Post Cl BR6 ... 227 D2
Coatbridge Ho 8 N1 ... 72 B1
Coates Ave SW18 ... 158 C5
Coates Cl CR7 ... 205 A6
Coates Ct NW3 ... 70 C3
Coates Hill Rd BR1 ... 188 C1
Coates Rd WD6 ... 9 D4
Coate St E2 ... 96 A5
Coates Wlk TW8 ... 110 A1
Cobalt SE2 ... 124 A4
Cobalt Cl CR0 ... 206 D5
Cobb Cl WD6 ... 11 A6
Cobbett Rd
 Kidbrooke SE9 ... 144 A2
 Twickenham TW2 ... 151 C3
Cobbetts Ave IG4 ... 55 D4
Cobbett St SW8 ... 138 B5 270 D3
Cobble La N1 ... 72 D1
Cobble Mews N4, N5 ... 73 A5
Cobbler's Wlk TW11 ... 174 D3
Cobblestone Pl CR0 ... 205 A1
Cobbold Ct SW1 ... 259 C4
Cobbold Ind Est NW10 ... 67 D2
Cobbold Mews W12 ... 111 D4
Cobbold Rd
 Bedford Pk W12 ... 111 D4
 Leyton E11 ... 76 D5
 Willesden NW10 ... 67 D2
Cobb's Hall 1 SW6 ... 134 D6
Cobbs Rd TW4 ... 129 B1
Cobb St E1 ... 243 C3
Cobden Bldgs WC1 ... 233 C2
Cobden Ct
 Bromley BR2 ... 209 C5
 9 Thamesmead SE28 ... 124 C5
Cobden Ho
 11 Bethnal Green E2 ... 96 A4
 Regent's Pk NW1 ... 232 A4
Cobden Mews SE26 ... 184 B5
Cobden Rd
 Croydon SE25 ... 206 A4
 Leyton E11 ... 76 C6
 Orpington BR6 ... 227 B4
Cobham 21 NW9 ... 27 D1
Cobham Ave KT3 ... 200 A4
Cobham Cl
 2 Blackfen DA15 ... 168 B5
 Bromley BR2 ... 210 A2
 Clapham SW11 ... 158 C5
 Edgware HA8 ... 26 D1
 Enfield EN1 ... 6 A2
 Wallington SM6 ... 220 A2
Cobham Ct CR4 ... 180 B1
Cobham Ho IG11 ... 101 A6
Cobham Mews 3 NW1 ... 71 D1
Cobham Pl DA6 ... 168 D6
Cobham Rd
 Chingford E17 ... 36 A2
 Harringay N22 ... 50 D6
 Heston TW5 ... 128 C5
 Ilford IG3 ... 79 C5
 Kingston u T KT1, KT2 ... 176 C1
Cobland Rd SE12 ... 187 C6
Coborn Mews 9 E3 ... 97 B4
Coborn Rd E3 ... 97 B4
Coborn St E3 ... 97 B4
Cobourg Prim Sch SE5 ... 139 D6
Cobourg Rd SE5 ... 139 D6
Cobourg St NW1 ... 93 C4 232 B1
Coburg Cl SW1 ... 259 B4
Coburg Cres SW2 ... 160 C3
Coburg Dwellings 11 E1 ... 118 C6
Coburg Gdns IG5 ... 37 D1
Coburg Rd N22 ... 32 B1
Cochrane Cl NW8 ... 229 D3
Cochrane Ct 3 E10 ... 53 C1
Cochrane Ho 15 E14 ... 119 C4
Cochrane Mews NW8 ... 92 B5 229 D3
Cochrane Rd SW19 ... 179 B3
Cochrane St NW8 ... 92 B5 229 D3
Coci Ho W14 ... 254 D3
Cockburn Ho SW1 ... 259 D1
Cockerell Rd E17 ... 53 A3
COCKFOSTERS ... 2 D1
Cockfosters Par EN4 ... 3 A1
Cockfosters Rd EN4 ... 2 D3
Cockfosters Sta EN4 ... 3 A1
Cock Hill E1 ... 243 B3
Cock La EC1 ... 94 D2 241 D3
Cockpit Yd WC1 ... 240 D4
Cocks Cres KT3 ... 199 D5
Cocksett Ave BR6 ... 227 C2
Cockspur Ct SW1 ... 249 D4
Cockspur St SW1 ... 115 D5 249 D4
Cocksure La DA14 ... 191 C6
Coda Ctr The SW6 ... 135 A4 264 B2
Code St E1 ... 95 D3 243 D5
Codicote Ho 22 SE8 ... 118 D2
Codicote Terr N4 ... 73 A6
Codling Cl 13 E1 ... 118 A5
Codling Way HA0 ... 65 D4
Codrington Ct 3 SE16 ... 119 A5
Codrington Hill SE23 ... 163 A4
Codrington Ho 7 E1 ... 96 B3
Codrington Mews W11 ... 91 A1
Cody Cl Harrow HA3 ... 43 D6
 Wallington SM6 ... 219 D1
Cody Rd E16 ... 98 B3
Coe Ave SE25 ... 206 A3
Coe's Alley EN5 ... 1 A1
Coffey St SE8 ... 141 C5
Cogan Ave E17 ... 35 A2
Cohen Ho NW7 ... 28 A6
Cohen Lo E5 ... 75 A3
Coin St SE1 ... 116 C5 251 A4
Coity Rd NW5 ... 71 A2
Cokers La SE21 ... 161 B3
Coke St E1 ... 96 A1
Colab Ct N22 ... 32 C2
Colas Mews 7 NW6 ... 91 C6
Colbeck Mews SW5 ... 113 D2 255 D3
Colbeck Rd HA1 ... 42 A2
Colberg Pl N16 ... 51 D2
Colbert 1 SE5 ... 139 D4
Colborne Ct 8 SW19 ... 179 D2
Colborne Ho 8 E14 ... 119 C6
Colborne Way KT4 ... 216 C6
Colbrook Ave UB3 ... 105 B3
Colbrook Cl UB3 ... 105 B3
Colburn Ave HA5 ... 23 A4
Colburn Way SM1 ... 218 B5
Colby Rd
 Walton-on-T KT12 ... 194 A1
 West Norwood SE19 ... 183 C5
Colchester Ave E12 ... 78 B5
Colchester Dr HA5 ... 40 D4
Colchester Ho 17 SW8 ... 137 D3
Colchester Rd
 Burnt Oak HA8 ... 27 A3
 Leyton E10 ... 54 A2
Colchester Rd continued
 Pinner HA6 ... 22 A1
 Walthamstow E17 ... 53 C3
Colchester St E1 ... 243 D2
Colchester Villas CR7 ... 204 C3
Coldbath Sq EC1 ... 241 A6
Coldbath St SE13 ... 141 D3
Cold Blow La SE14 ... 140 D6
Coldershaw Rd W13 ... 109 A4
Coldfall Ave N10 ... 31 A1
Coldfall Prim Sch N10 ... 30 D1
Coldham Ct N22 ... 32 D2
Coldham Gr EN3 ... 7 A6
Coldharbour E14 ... 120 A5
Coldharbour Crest SE9 ... 166 C1
Coldharbour Ind Est SE5 ... 139 A3
Coldharbour La
 Brixton SW9 ... 138 D2
 Bushey WD23 ... 8 A6
 Hayes UB3 ... 106 A5
Coldharbour Lane Ho UB3 ... 106 A5
Coldharbour Pl SE5 ... 139 B3
Coldharbour Rd CR0 ... 220 C3
Coldharbour Sports Ctr SE9 ... 166 C2
Coldharbour Way CR0 ... 220 C3
Coldstream Gdns SW18 ... 157 B5
Colebeck Mews N1 ... 72 D2
Colebert Ave E1 ... 96 C3
Colebert Ho 21 E1 ... 96 C3
Colebrook Cl
 Edgware NW7 ... 28 D3
 Putney SW19 ... 156 D4
Colebrook Ct SW3 ... 257 B3
Colebrooke Ave W13 ... 87 B1
Colebrooke Ct DA14 ... 190 B6
Colebrooke Dr E11 ... 55 C2
Colebrooke Pl N1 ... 234 D5
Colebrooke Row
 Islington N1 ... 94 D5 234 C4
 Islington N1 ... 234 D5
Colebrook Ho 1 E14 ... 97 D1
Colebrook Rd SW16 ... 182 A2
Colebrook Rise BR2 ... 186 C1
Colebrook Way N11 ... 31 B5
Coleby Path 21 SE5 ... 139 B5
Colechurch Ho 9 SE1 ... 118 A1
Cole Cl SE28 ... 124 B5
Cole Court Lo 9 TW1 ... 153 A4
Coledale Dr HA7 ... 25 C2
Colefax Bldg 12 E1 ... 96 A1
Coleford Rd SW18 ... 158 A6
Cole Gdns TW5 ... 128 A5
Colegrave Prim Sch E15 ... 76 B3
Colegrave Rd E15 ... 76 B3
Colegrove Rd SE15 ... 139 D6
Coleherne Ct SW10 ... 113 D1 255 D1
Coleherne Mans SW5 ... 255 D2
Coleherne Mews SW10 ... 113 D1 255 C1
Coleherne Rd SW10 ... 113 D1 255 C1
Colehill Gdns SW6 ... 264 A1
Colehill La SW6 ... 135 A4 264 B1
Cole Ho SE1 ... 251 B1
Coleman Cl SE25 ... 184 A1
Coleman Ct SW18 ... 157 C4
Coleman Fields N1 ... 95 A6 235 B6
Coleman Mans N19 ... 50 A2
Coleman Rd
 Belvedere DA17 ... 125 C2
 Camberwell SE5 ... 139 C5
 Dagenham RM9 ... 81 A2
Colemans Heath SE9 ... 166 D1
Coleman St EC2 ... 95 B1 242 C2
Coleman Street Bldgs EC2 ... 242 C2
Colenso Dr NW7 ... 28 A3
Colenso Rd Ilford IG2 ... 57 C2
 Lower Clapton E5 ... 74 C4
Cole Park Gdns TW1 ... 153 A5
Cole Park Rd TW1 ... 153 A5
Cole Park View 2 TW1 ... 153 A5
Colepits Wood Rd SE9 ... 167 B6
Coleraine Park Prim Sch N17 ... 34 B2
Coleraine Rd
 Greenwich SE3 ... 142 D6
 Hornsey N8, N22 ... 50 C6
Cole Rd TW1 ... 153 A5
Coleridge Ave
 Carshalton SM1 ... 218 C4
 Plashet E12 ... 78 A2
Coleridge Cl SW8 ... 137 B3
Coleridge Ct
 Hammersmith W14 ... 112 D3
 15 New Barnet EN5 ... 13 D6
 2 Richmond TW10 ... 175 D6
Coleridge Gdns NW6 ... 70 A1
Coleridge Ho
 Pimlico SW1 ... 259 B1
 Walworth SE17 ... 262 B2
 Wembley HA9 ... 65 D6
Coleridge Prim Sch N8 ... 49 D2
Coleridge Rd
 Ashford TW15 ... 170 B6
 Crouch End N8 ... 49 D3
 Croydon CR0 ... 206 C2
 Finsbury Pk N4, N7 ... 72 C6
Coleridge Rd continued
 North Finchley N12 ... 30 A5
 Walthamstow E17 ... 53 B5
Coleridge Sq
 Chelsea SW10 ... 266 A4
 Ealing W13 ... 87 A1
Coleridge Way
 Borehamwood WD6 ... 10 C6
 Hayes UB4 ... 84 A1
 West Drayton UB7 ... 104 B2
Coleridge Wlk NW11 ... 47 C5
Colerne Ct NW4 ... 29 A1
Colesburg Rd BR3 ... 185 B1
Coles Cres HA2 ... 63 D6
Coles Ct SW11 ... 266 D1
Coles Gn WD23 ... 8 A3
Coles Green Ct NW2 ... 68 A6
Coles Green Rd NW2 ... 68 B6
Coleshill Flats SW1 ... 258 B3
Coleshill Rd TW11 ... 174 C4
Cole St SE1 ... 117 A4 252 B1
Colestown St 4 SW11 ... 136 C3
Coleswood N20 ... 14 C3
Colesworth Ho 1 HA8 ... 27 A1
Colet Cl N13 ... 32 D4
Colet Gdns W14 ... 112 D2
Colet Ho SE17 ... 261 D1
Colette Ct 5 SE16 ... 118 D4
Coley St WC1 ... 94 B3 240 D5
Colfe & Hatchcliffe's Glebe SE13 ... 163 D6
Colfe Rd SE23 ... 163 A3
Colfe's Sch SE12 ... 165 A5
Colgate Ct EN5 ... 13 A6
Colgate Ho SE13 ... 141 D3
Colgate Pl 10 EN3 ... 7 C6
Colham Ave UB7 ... 104 A5
COLHAM GREEN ... 82 C2
Colham Green Rd UB8 ... 82 C2
Colham Manor Prim Sch UB8 ... 82 C1
Colham Rd UB8 ... 82 B3
Colina Mews N8, N15 ... 50 D5
Colina Rd N8, N15 ... 50 D4
Colin Blanchard Ho SE4 ... 141 C3
Colin Cl Colindale NW9 ... 45 C5
 Coney Hall BR4 ... 224 D5
 Croydon CR0 ... 223 B5
Colin Cres NW9 ... 45 D5
Colin Ct Forest Hill SE6 ... 163 B4
 Hendon NW9 ... 45 D5
 Streatham SW16 ... 159 D2
COLINDALE ... 45 C6
Colindale Ave NW9 ... 45 C6
Colindale Bsns Pk NW9 ... 45 A6
Colindale Hospl NW9 ... 45 C6
Colindale Prim Sch NW9 ... 45 D5
Colindale Sta NW9 ... 45 C6
Colindeep Gdns NW4 ... 46 A5
Colindeep La NW9, NW4 ... 45 D5
Colin Dr NW9 ... 45 D4
Colinette Rd SW15 ... 134 C1
Colin Gdns NW9 ... 45 D5
Colin Par NW9 ... 45 C5
Colin Park Rd NW9 ... 45 C5
Colin Pond Ct RM6 ... 58 D6
Colin Rd NW10 ... 68 A2
Colinsdale N1 ... 234 C5
Colinton Rd IG3 ... 80 B6
Colin Winter Ho 45 E1 ... 96 C3
Coliseum Apartments N8 ... 50 D4
Coliston Pas SW18 ... 157 C4
Coliston Rd SW18 ... 157 C4
Collamore Ave SW18 ... 158 C3
Collapit Cl HA1 ... 41 D3
Collard Pl NW1 ... 71 B1
Collard's Almshouses 1 E17 ... 54 A4
Collcutt Lo SW4 ... 138 A1
Collection Point N8 ... 50 A3
College App SE10 ... 142 A6
College Ave HA3 ... 24 C2
College Cl
 Edmonton N18 ... 33 D5
 Hackney E5 ... 74 C3
 Harrow HA3 ... 24 C3
 Twickenham TW2 ... 152 B3
College Cres NW3 ... 70 B2
College Cross N1 ... 72 C1
College Ct
 Chelsea SW3 ... 114 D1 257 D1
 Croydon CR0 ... 222 A6
 Ealing W5 ... 110 A6
 Enfield EN3 ... 18 C6
 3 Hammersmith W6 ... 112 C1
 Hampstead NW3 ... 70 B2
College Dr Ruislip HA4 ... 40 A2
 Thames Ditton KT7 ... 196 C2
College Fields Bsns Ctr SW19 ... 180 B2
College Gdns
 Chingford E4 ... 20 A3
 Dulwich SE21 ... 161 C3
 Edmonton N18 ... 34 A5
 Enfield EN2 ... 5 B4
 New Malden KT3 ... 199 D4
 Redbridge IG4 ... 56 A4
 Upper Tooting SW17 ... 158 C2
College Gn SE19 ... 183 C3
College Gr NW1 ... 232 C6
College Green Ct SW9 ... 138 D2
College Hill EC4 ... 252 B6
College Hill Rd HA3 ... 24 C3
College La NW5 ... 71 B4
College Mews 5 SW18 ... 157 D6
COLLEGE PARK ... 90 B4
College Park Cl SE13 ... 142 B1
College Park Rd N17 ... 33 D4
College Park Sch W2 ... 91 D1
College Pl
 Camden Town NW1 ... 93 C6 232 B5
 Chelsea SW10 ... 266 A4
 Walthamstow E17 ... 54 C5
College Pt 3 E15 ... 76 D2
College Rd
 Dulwich SE19, SE21 ... 161 C2
 Ealing W13 ... 87 B1
 Enfield EN2 ... 5 B3
 Harrow HA1 ... 42 C3
 Harrow Weald HA3 ... 24 C2
 Hounslow TW7 ... 130 D4
 Kensal Green NW10 ... 90 C5
 Mitcham SW19 ... 180 B4
 Plaistow BR1 ... 187 A3
 South Croydon CR0 ... 221 B6
 Southgate N21 ... 16 C2
 Tottenham N17 ... 33 D4
 Walthamstow E17 ... 54 A4
 Wembley HA9 ... 43 D1
College Rdbt 1 KT1 ... 198 A6
College St EC4 ... 117 A6 252 B6
College Terr Bow E3 ... 97 B4
 Church End N3 ... 29 B1
College View SE9 ... 165 D3
College Way
 Ashford TW15 ... 170 B6
 Hayes UB3 ... 106 A6
College Wlk 10 KT1 ... 198 A6
Collent Ho 12 E9 ... 74 C2
Collent St E9 ... 74 C2
Collerston Ho SE10 ... 120 D1
Colless Rd N15 ... 51 D4
Collette Ct SE25 ... 205 C4
Collette Ho N16 ... 51 D1
Collett Ho SE13 ... 141 D2
Collett Rd SE16 ... 118 A3
Collett Way UB2 ... 107 D4
Colley Ho 12 N7 ... 71 D3
Collier Cl Newham E16 ... 122 D6
 West Ewell KT19 ... 214 D2
Collier Dr HA8 ... 26 C1
Colliers Shaw BR2 ... 225 D3
Collier St N1 ... 94 B5 233 C3
Colliers Water La CR7 ... 204 C4
Colliers Wood SW19 ... 180 B3
COLLIER'S WOOD ... 180 C4
Collier's Wood Sta SW19 ... 180 B3
Collindale Ave
 Erith DA8 ... 147 D6
 Sidcup DA15 ... 168 A3
Collingbourne Rd W12 ... 112 B5
Collingham Gdns SW5 ... 113 D2 255 D3
Collingham Pl SW5 ... 113 D2 255 D4
Collingham Rd SW5 ... 113 D2 255 D3
Collingham Sixth Form Coll SW5 ... 113 D2 255 D3
Collings Cl N22 ... 32 B4
Collington Ho 2 SE7 ... 143 B6
Collington St SE10 ... 120 B1
Collingtree Rd SE26 ... 184 C6
Collingwood Ave
 London N10 ... 49 A5
 Tolworth KT5 ... 199 A1
Collingwood Cl
 2 Penge SE20 ... 184 B2
 Twickenham TW2, TW4 ... 151 C4
Collingwood Ct
 London NW4 ... 46 C4
 New Barnet EN5 ... 13 D6
 Sutton SM1 ... 217 C4
Collingwood Ho
 27 Bethnal Green E1 ... 96 B3
 Marylebone W1 ... 239 A4
Collingwood Rd
 Hillingdon UB8 ... 82 D3
 Mitcham CR4 ... 202 C6
 South Tottenham N15 ... 51 C5
 Sutton SM1 ... 217 C4
Collingwood Sch SM6 ... 219 B3
Collingwood St E1 ... 96 B3
Collins Ave HA7 ... 26 A1
Collins Ct Dalston E8 ... 74 A2
 3 Loughton IG10 ... 21 D6
Collins Dr HA4 ... 62 C6
Collins Ho
 8 Barking IG11 ... 78 D1
 6 Cubitt Town SE10 ... 120 D1
 4 Poplar E14 ... 120 A6
Collinson Ct
 Borough The SE1 ... 252 A1
 Edgware HA8 ... 26 B6
Collinson Ho 14 SE15 ... 140 A5
Collinson St SE1 ... 252 A1
Collinson Wlk SE1 ... 252 A1
Collins Rd N5, N16 ... 73 A4
Collins Sq SE3 ... 142 D3
Collins St SE3 ... 142 C3
Collins Yd N1 ... 234 C5
Collinwood Ave EN3 ... 6 C2
Collinwood Gdns IG5 ... 56 C5
Collison Pl N16 ... 51 C1
Collis Prim Sch TW11 ... 175 B4
Coll of Arms* EC4 ... 117 A6 252 A6

Coll of Central London The EC2 243 A6
Coll of Law The EC1 95 B3 242 C5
Coll of North East London The N15 51 D5
Coll of NW London NW6 91 C6
Coll of NW London (Willesden Centre) NW10 67 D3
Coll of Optometrists The SW1 250 A4
Coll Sharp Ct 42 E2 95 D4
Coll's Rd SE15 140 A4
Collyer Ave CR0 220 A4
Collyer Pl SE15 140 A4
Collyer Rd CR0 220 A4
Colman Ct London N12 30 A4
Stanmore HA7 25 B4
Colman Rd E16 99 C2
Colmans Wharf 5 E14 97 D2
Colmar Cl 3 E1 96 D3
Colmer Pl HA3 24 B3
Colmer Rd SW16 182 A3
Colmore Ct NW4 46 A6
Colmore Mews SE15 140 B4
Colmore Rd EN3 6 C1
Colnbrook Ct SW17 180 B6
Colnbrook St SE1 261 C6
Colne Ct Ealing W7 86 B1
West Ewell KT19 215 A4
Colne Ho Barking IG11 78 D2
Paddington NW8 236 D5
Colne Rd Clapton Pk E5 75 A4
Southgate N21 17 B4
Twickenham TW1, TW2 152 C3
Colne St E13 99 A4
COLNEY HATCH 30 C4
Colney Hatch N10 31 A3
Colney Hatch La N10 31 A3
Cologne Rd SW11 136 B1
Coloma Convent Girls Sch CR0 222 D5
Colombo Rd IG1 57 A2
Colombo St SE1 251 C3
Colomb St SE10 120 C1
Colonades The 4 SE5 139 B4
Colonels Wlk EN2 4 D2
Colonial Ave TW2 152 A5
Colonial Dr W4 111 A2
Colonial Rd TW14 149 C4
Colonnade WC1 240 B5
Colonnade Ho SE3 142 D3
Colonnades The
Croydon CR0 220 C2
6 Hackney E8 74 B2
Colonnade The 12 SE8 119 B2
Colorado Bldg 9 SE13 141 D4
Colosseum Ct N3 29 B1
Colosseum Ret Pk EN1 6 A1
Colosseum Terr NW1 238 D6
Colour Ho SE1 253 B1
Colroy Ct NW4 47 A4
Colson Rd CR0 221 C6
Colson Way SW16 181 C6
Colstead Ho 22 E1 96 B1
Colsterworth Rd N15 51 D5
Colston Ave SM1, SM5 218 C4
Colston Ct SM5 218 D4
Colston Rd
Mortlake SW14 133 A1
Upton E7 77 D2
Colthurst Cres N4 73 A6
Colthurst Dr N9 18 B1
Coltman Ho SE10 142 A6
Coltman St E14 97 A2
Colt Mews 5 EN3 7 C6
Coltness Cres SE2 124 B1
Colton Gdns N17 51 A6
Colton Rd HA1 42 C4
Coltsfoot Dr UB7 82 A1
Coltswood Ct N14 15 D3
Colts Yd E11 54 D2
Columba Ho SE14 141 B4
Columbas Dr NW3 48 B1
Columbia Ave
Edgware HA8 26 D2
New Malden KT4 199 D2
Ruislip HA4 40 B1
Columbia Ct
Edgware HA8 26 D2
New Malden KT3 199 D2
Columbia Ho 18 E3 97 C4
Columbia Point 7 SE16 118 C3
Columbia Prim Sch E2 95 D4
Columbia Rd
9 Hackney E2 96 A5
Newham E13 98 D3
Shoreditch E2 95 D4
Columbia Road Mkt E2 95 D4
Columbine Ave
Croydon CR2 220 D1
Newham E6 100 A2
Columbus Gdns HA6 22 A2
Colveiw Ct SE9 165 D3
Colverson Ho 14 E1 96 C2
Colvestone Cres E8 73 D3
Colvestone Prim Sch E8 73 D3
Colville Gdns W11 91 B1
Colville Ho
32 Bethnal Green E2 96 C5
Notting Hill W11 91 B1
Colville Mews W11 91 B1
Colville Pl W1 239 B3
Colville Prim Sch W11 91 B1
Colville Rd Edmonton N9 18 B3
Higham Hill E17 35 A1
Leyton E11 76 A5
Notting Hill W11 91 B1
South Acton W3 110 D3
Colville Sq W11 91 B1
Colville Terr W11 91 B1
Colvin Cl SE26 184 C5
Colvin Gdns
Chingford E4 20 A1
Wanstead E11 55 B5
Colvin Rd
Thornton Heath CR7 204 C4
Upton Pk E6 78 A1
Colwall Gdns IG8 37 A5
Colwall Ho 18 SW9 138 B3
Colwell Rd SE22 161 D6
Colwick Cl N6 49 D2
Colwith Rd W6 134 C6
Colwood Gdns SW19 180 B3
Colworth Gr SE17 262 B3
Colworth Rd
Croydon CR0 206 A1
Leytonstone E11 54 C2
Colwyn Ave UB6 86 D5
Colwyn Cl SW16 181 C5
Colwyn Cres TW3 130 A4
Colwyn Gn NW9 45 C3
Colwyn Ho SE1 261 A5
Colwyn Rd NW2 68 B5
Colyer Cl SE9 166 D2
Colyer Ho SE2 124 D1
Colyton Cl Erith DA16 146 D4
Wembley HA0 65 C2
Colyton La 14 SW16 182 C5
Colyton Rd SE22 162 B6
Colyton Way N18 34 A5
Combe Ave SE3 142 D5
Combedale Rd SE10 121 A1
Combe Ho
Mortlake SW14 133 A3
20 Paddington W2 91 C2
Combe Lane Sta CR0 222 C3
Combemartin Rd SW18 157 A3
Combe Mews 4 SE3 142 D5
Comber Cl NW2 68 B6
Comber Gr SE5 139 A5
Comber Grove Prim Sch SE5 139 A5
Comber Ho SE5 139 A5
Combermere Rd
London SW9 138 B2
Morden SM4 201 D4
Comberton 10 KT1 176 C1
Comberton Rd E5 74 B6
Combeside SE18 145 D5
Combes Rd RM9 81 B1
Combe The NW1 231 D1
Combwell Cres SE2 124 A3
Com Coll Hackney The E8 96 B6
Comely Bank Rd E17 54 A4
Comeragh Mews W14 254 B1
Comeragh Rd W14 113 A1 254 B1
Comer Cres UB2 108 A4
Comerford Rd SE4 141 B1
Comer Ho 10 EN5 2 A1
Comet Cl E12 77 D4
Comet Pl SE8 141 C5
Comet St SE8 141 C5
Comins Ho SW4 159 C6
Commerce Est E18 37 C1
Commerce Pk CR0 220 B6
Commerce Rd
Brentford TW8 131 C5
Wood Green N22 32 B2
Commerce Way CR0 220 B6
Commercial Rd
Edmonton N18 33 C4
Stepney E1 96 C1
Whitechapel E1 96 A1
Commercial St E1 95 D2 243 C4
Commercial Way
Peckham SE15 140 A5
Wembley NW10 88 D5
Commerell Pl SE10 120 D1
Commerell St SE10 120 C1
Commodity Quay E1 253 D5
Commodore Ct SE8 141 C4
Commodore Ho 7 E14 120 A6
Commodore St E1 97 A3
Commondale SW15 134 C2
Common La KT10 213 A1
Common Rd
Barnes SW13 134 A2
Claygate KT10 213 A1
Stanmore HA7 8 C1
Commonside BR2 225 C4
Commonside Ct SW16 182 A4
Commonside E CR4 203 B6
Commonside W CR4 203 A6
Common The
Ealing W5 110 A5
Southall UB2 106 D2
Stanmore HA7 8 D2
1 Stratford E15 76 D2
Common View SW15 134 C2
Commonwealth Ave
Hayes UB3 83 B1
21 Shepherd's Bush W12 112 B6
23 Shepherd's Bush W12 112 B6
Commonwealth Ho WC1 240 B2
Commonwealth Rd N17 34 A3
Commonwealth Way SE2 124 C1
Community Cl
Cranford TW5 128 B4
Uxbridge UB10 61 A5
Community Rd
Greenford UB6 86 A6
Stratford New Town E15 76 B3
Comodore Ho SW18 136 A1
Como Rd SE23 163 A2
Compania Bldg 12 E1 118 D6
Compass Cl
Edgware HA8 26 B6
Littleton TW15 171 A3
Compass Ct SE1 253 C3
Compass Hill TW10 153 D5
Compass Ho
Bayswater W2 91 D1
London SE8 141 D3
Compass Point 10 E14 119 C6
Compayne Gdns NW6 69 D1
Compton Ave
Islington N1 72 D2
London N6 48 C2
Newham E6 99 D5
Wembley HA0 65 C4
Compton Cl
5 Burnt Oak HA8 27 A3
Camberwell SE15 139 D5
Cricklewood NW11 68 D5
Ealing W13 87 A1
Esher KT10 212 B3
Regent's Pk NW1 231 D1
Compton Cres
Chessington KT9 214 A2
Chiswick W4 133 A6
Northolt UB5 84 D6
Tottenham N17 33 A3
Compton Ct London N12 30 A2
Sutton SM1 218 A4
9 West Norwood SE19 183 C5
Compton Ho SW11 267 A2
Compton Lo N21 16 D3
Compton Pas EC1 241 D6
Compton Pl
Bloomsbury WC1 240 A6
South Oxhey WD19 23 A6
Compton Rd
Croydon CR0 206 B1
Hayes UB3 105 D6
Islington N1 72 D2
Kensal Green NW10 90 D4
Southgate N21 16 D3
Wimbledon SW19 179 B4
Compton Rise HA5 41 B4
Compton Sch The N12 30 C4
Compton St EC1 94 D3 241 D6
Compton Terr
Islington N1 72 D2
Southgate N21 16 C3
Comreddy Cl EN2 4 D4
Comus Ho SE17 263 A3
Comus Pl SE17 117 C2 263 A3
Comyn Rd SW11 136 C1
Comyns Cl E16 98 D2
Comyns Rd RM9 81 C1
Comyns The WD23 8 A3
Conal Ct SW16 181 D5
Conant Ho SE11 138 D6
Conant Mews 1 E1 118 A6
Concanon Rd SW2, SW4 138 B1
Concert Hall App SE1 116 B5 250 D3
Concord Bsns Ctr W3 88 D2
Concord Cl UB5 85 A4
Concord Ct KT1 198 B6
Concorde Cl
Hounslow TW3 129 D3
Uxbridge UB10 82 A5
Concorde Dr E6 100 B2
Concorde Way SE16 118 D2
Concord Ho
Kingston u T KT3 199 C6
5 Tottenham N17 33 D3
Concordia Wharf 10 E14 120 A5
Concord Rd Acton W3 88 D3
Enfield EN3 18 C6
Concord Terr HA2 63 D6
Concourse The
32 Edgware NW9 27 D2
7 Edmonton N9 18 A2
Condell Rd SW8 137 C4 269 B1
Conder St E14 97 A1
Condor Path UB5 85 C5
Condover Cres SE18 144 D5
Condray Pl SW11 267 A3
Conduit Ct WC2 250 A6
Conduit Ho SE10 142 B4
Conduit La London N18 34 C5
South Croydon CR0 222 A3
Conduit Mews W2 92 B1 236 C1
Conduit Pas W2 236 C1
Conduit Pl W2 236 C1
Conduit Rd SE18 122 D1
Conduit St W1 115 C6 249 A6
Conduit Way NW10 67 A1
Conewood St N5 72 D5
Coney Acre SE21 161 A3
Coney Burrows E4 20 C2
Coney Gr UB8 82 C4
Coneygrove Path UB5 63 A2
CONEY HALL 224 D5
Coney Hall Par BR4 224 C5
Coney Hall Rdbt BR4 224 C5
Coney Hill Rd BR4 224 D6
Coney Way SW8 270 D5
Conference Cl 3 E4 20 A2
Conference Ho UB8 83 A1
Conference Rd SE2 124 C2
Congers Ho SE8 141 C5
Congleton Gr SE18 123 A1
Congo Dr N9 18 C1
Congo Rd SE18 123 B1
Congress Ho WC1 239 D2
Congress Rd SE2 124 C2
Congreve Ho 10 N16 73 C3
Congreve Rd SE9 144 B2
Congreve St SE17 117 C2 263 A3
Congreve Wlk 6 E16 99 D2
Conical Cnr EN2 5 A3
Conifer Cl BR6 227 B4
Conifer Ct
Ashford TW15 170 B5
Hendon NW4 28 C1
Ilford IG1 78 D2
23 Putney SW19 156 D3
Sutton SM2 218 B2
Conifer Gdns
Enfield EN1 17 C5
Streatham SW16 160 B1
Sutton SM1 217 D6
Conifer Ho SE4 141 B1
Conifers Cl TW11 175 C3
Conifer Way
Hayes UB3 106 A6
Wembley HA0 65 C5
Coniger Rd SW6 135 C3
Coningham Ct SW10 266 B4
Coningham Mews W12 112 A5
Coningham Rd W12 112 B4
Coningsby Ave NW9 27 C1
Coningsby Cotts W5 109 D4
Coningsby Ct 4 CR4 181 A1
Coningsby Gdns E4 35 D4
Coningsby Rd
Ealing W5 109 D4
Harringay N4 50 D2
Conington Rd SE13 142 A3
Conisbee Ct 3 N14 15 C6
Conisborough Cres SE6 164 A1
Conisbrough NW1 232 A5
Coniscliffe Cl BR7 188 C2
Coniscliffe Rd N13 17 A1
Coniston NW1 232 A2
Coniston Ave
Barking IG11 79 C1
Ealing UB6 87 B4
Falconwood DA16 145 C2
Coniston Cl
Barking IG11 79 C1
Barnes SW13 133 D5
Chiswick W4 133 A5
West Barnes SM4 200 D3
Whetstone N20 14 A1
Coniston Ct
Beckenham BR3 186 A2
Chessington KT9 214 A5
Edgware HA8 26 B5
4 Finchley NW7 29 A3
Marylebone W2 237 B1
Penge SE26 184 B4
6 Rotherhithe SE16 118 D4
3 Wallington SM6 219 B4
Conistone Way N7 72 A1
Coniston Gdns
Edmonton N9 18 C3
Kingsbury NW9 45 B4
Pinner HA5 40 A5
Redbridge IG4 56 A5
Sutton SM2 218 B2
Wembley HA9 43 C1
Coniston Ho 14 Bow E3 97 B4
18 Camberwell SE5 139 A5
Coniston Rd
Catford BR1 186 C4
Croydon CR0 206 A2
Muswell Hill N10 31 B1
Tottenham N17 34 A4
Twickenham TW2 151 D5
Coniston Way KT9 214 A5
Coniston Wlk E9 74 C3
Conlan St W10 91 A3
Conley Rd NW10 67 C2
Conley St SE10 120 C1
Connaught Ave
Ashford TW15 170 A6
Barnet EN4 14 D3
Chingford E4 20 B4
Enfield EN1 5 C3
Hounslow TW4 129 A1
Mortlake SW14 133 A1
Connaught Bridge E16 121 D6
Connaught Bsns Ctr
London NW9 45 D4
Mitcham CR4 202 D4
Wallington CR0 220 B2
Connaught Cl
Carshalton SM1 218 B6
Enfield EN1 5 C3
Hillingdon UB8 83 A3
Lea Bridge E10 75 A6
Marylebone W2 237 B1
Connaught Ct
1 Chingford E4 20 C4
9 Walthamstow E17 53 D5
Connaught Day Hospl E11 54 C3
Connaught Dr NW11 47 C5
Connaught Gdns
Cranley Gdns N10 49 B4
Edmonton N13 32 D6
Morden SM4 202 A5
Connaught Grange N13 32 D6
Connaught Ho
College Pk NW10 90 B4
London N10 49 B4
Mayfair W1 248 C5
Connaught Hts UB10 83 A3
Connaught La IG1 79 B6
Connaught Lo N4 50 C2
Connaught Mans
Battersea SW11 267 B1
3 Brixton SW9 138 C1
15 Canonbury N16 73 B4
Fulham SW6 264 A2
Connaught Mews
Ilford IG1 79 B6
Woolwich SE18 122 C1
Connaught Pl W2 237 C1
Connaught Rd
Barnet EN5 12 D5
Carshalton SM1 218 B6
Chingford E4 20 C3
Ealing W13 109 B6
Finsbury Pk N4 50 C2
Harlesden NW10 89 C5
Harrow HA3 24 D2
Ilford IG1 79 B6
Leytonstone E11 54 B1
Newham E16 121 D5
New Malden KT3 199 C5
5 Richmond TW10 154 B6
Teddington TW11, TW12 174 B5
Walthamstow E17 53 C4
Woolwich SE18 122 D1
Connaught Sch for Girls E11 54 C1
Connaught Sch for Girls (Annexe) E11 76 C6
Connaught Sq W2 92 D1 237 C1
Connaught St W2 92 C1 237 B1
Connaught Way N13 32 D6
Connaught Works E3 97 A6
Connections Ho N2 30 B2
Connell Cres W5 88 B3
Connell Ct 6 SE14 140 D6
Connell Ho 6 SM6 219 C2
Connemara Cl WD6 11 B5
Conniffe Ct SE9 166 D6
Connington 5 KT1 176 C1
Connington Cres E4 20 B1
Connolly Ho SW19 180 A4
Connoly Ct NW2 68 B5
Connop Rd EN3 6 D5
Connor Cl E11 54 C2
Connor Ct SW11 268 C1
Connor Rd RM9 81 B4
Connor St E9 96 D6
Conolly Rd W7 108 C5
Conrad Dr KT4 200 D1
Conrad Ho
8 Limehouse SE16 119 A6
South Lambeth SW8 270 A4
12 Stoke Newington N16 73 C3
Conrad Twr W3 110 D3
Conroy Ct 6 DA14 190 A6
Conservatory Ct SE19 183 C3
Consfield Ave KT3 200 A4
Consort Ho
Bayswater W2 245 D5
Edgware NW7 27 D5
Consort Lo NW8 230 C5
Consort Mews TW7 152 B6
Consort Rd SE15 140 B3
Cons St SE1 251 B2
Constable Ave E16 121 B5
Constable Cl
12 Friern Barnet N11 30 D5
Hampstead Garden Suburb NW11 47 D3
Hayes UB4 83 A5
Constable Cres N15 52 A4
Constable Ct 11 SE16 118 B1
Constable Gdns
Edgware HA8 26 C1
Isleworth TW7 152 B6
Constable Ho
Enfield EN1 18 A6
25 Millwall E14 119 C4
13 Northolt UB5 84 D5
Primrose Hill NW3 70 D1
Constable Mews RM8 80 B4
Constable Wlk SE21 161 C1
Constance Cres BR2 208 D1
Constance Ct N10 31 B3
Constance Rd
Enfield EN1 17 C5
Sutton SM1 218 A4
Thornton Heath CR0 204 D2
Twickenham TW2 151 D4
Constance St E16 122 A5
Constant Ho 26 E14 119 D6
Constantine Ho SW2 160 D3
Constantine Pl UB10 82 B6
Constantine Rd NW3 70 C4
Constitution Hill SW1, W1 115 B4 248 D2
Constitution Rise SE18 144 C4
Consul Ho 5 E3 97 C3
Content St SE17 117 B2 262 C3
Contessa Cl BR6 227 C3
Control Tower Rd TW6 126 D2
Convair Wlk 11 UB5 84 D4
Convent Cl BR3 186 A3
Convent Gdns
Ealing W5 109 C2
Notting Hill W11 91 B1
Convent Hill SE19 183 A4
Convent Lo TW15 170 D5
Convent of Jesus & Mary Language Coll NW10 89 D6
Convent of Jesus & Mary RC Inf Sch NW2 68 C2
Convent Rd TW15 170 D5
Convent Way UB2 106 D2
Conway Cl HA7 25 A4
Conway Cres
Dagenham RM6 58 C3
Greenford UB6 86 C5
Conway Dr
Ashford TW15 171 A4
Hayes UB3 105 A3
Sutton SM2 217 D2
Conway Gdns Enfield EN2 5 C5
Mitcham CR4 204 A5
Wembley HA9 43 C2
Conway Gr W3 89 B2
Conway Ho
Chelsea SW3 257 D1
5 Millwall E14 119 D2
6 Streatham SW2 160 A3
Conway Mews W1 239 A5
Conway Prim Sch SE18 123 C2
Conway Rd
Dollis Hill NW2 68 C6
Feltham TW13 172 D5
Harlington TW6 126 D2
Harringay N15 51 A4
Palmers Green N14 16 A1
Plumstead SE18 123 C2
Twickenham TW4 151 C4
Wimbledon SW20 178 C2
Conway St W1 93 C3 239 A5
Conway Wlk TW12 173 B4
Conybeare NW3 70 C1
Conyers Cl IG8 36 C4
Conyer's Rd SW16 181 D5
Conyer St 21 E3 97 A5
Cooden Cl BR1 187 B3
Cookes Cl E11 76 D6
Cookes La SM3 217 A2
Cooke St 3 IG11 101 A6
Cookham Cl UB2 107 D4
Cookham Cres SE16 118 D4
Cookham Dene Cl BR7 189 B2
Cookham Ho E2 243 C6
Cookham Rd BR8, DA14 191 C2
Cookhill Rd SE2 124 B3
Cooks Ferry N18 34 D5
Cook's Hole Rd EN2 5 A5
Cookson Gr DA8 147 D5
Cook's Rd
Camberwell SE17 138 D6
Stratford Marsh E15 97 D5
Coolfin Rd E16 99 B1
Coolgardie Ave E4 36 B5
Coolgardie Rd TW15 171 A5
Coolhurst Rd N8 49 D3
Cool Oak La NW9 45 D2
Coomassie Rd W9 91 B3
COOMBE 177 B3
Coombe Ave CR0 221 C4
Coombe Bank KT2, KT3 177 C2
Coombe Boys' Sch KT3 200 A4
Coombe Cl
Edgware HA8 26 B1
Hounslow TW3 129 C1
Coombe Cnr N21 16 D3
Coombe Cres TW12 173 A3
Coombe Ct 2 BR3 185 B2
Coombe Dr HA4 40 B1
Coombe End KT2 177 B3
Coombefield Cl KT3 199 C4
Coombe Gdns
New Malden KT3 199 D5
Wimbledon SW20 178 A2
Coombe Girls Sch KT3 177 B1
Coombe Hill Glade KT2 177 C3
Coombe Hill Inf Sch KT2 177 B2
Coombe Hill Jun Sch KT2 177 B2
Coombe Hill Rd KT2 177 C3
Coombe Ho 18 N7 71 D3
Coombe House Chase KT3 177 B2
Coombehurst Cl EN4 2 D3
Coombehurst (Kingston University) KT2 177 A5
Coombe La CR0 222 B3
Coombe Lane Flyover SW20 177 D2
Coombe La W KT2 177 B2
Coombe Lea BR1 210 A6
Coombe Lo SE7 143 C6
Coombe Neville KT2 177 B3
Coombe Pk KT2 177 B5
Coombe Pl KT2 177 A5
Coombe Rd Bushey WD23 8 B4
Chiswick W4 111 C1

Coombe Rd *continued*
Ealing W13 109 B3
Forest Hill SE26 184 B6
Hampton TW12 173 B4
New Malden KT3 199 C6
Norbiton KT2 176 C2
South Croydon CR0, CR2 221 C4
Willesden NW10 67 B5
Wood Green N22 32 C2
Coomber Ho SW6 135 D2
Coombe Ridings KT2 177 A5
Coombe Rise KT2 177 A2
Coomber Way CR0 203 D3
Coombes Rd RM9 103 B6
Coombe Wlk SM1 217 D5
Coombewood Dr RM6 59 B3
Coombe Wood Rd KT2 177 A5
Coombs St N1 234 D3
Coomer Mews SW6 264 D5
Coomer Pl SW6 135 B6 264 D5
Cooms Wlk HA8 27 A2
Cooperage Cl 5 N17 33 D4
Cooperage The SE1 253 C3
Cooper Ave E17 35 A2
Cooper Cl SE1 251 B1
Cooper Cres SM5 218 D5
Cooper Ct
Shooters Hill SE18 144 D6
Stratford New Town E15 76 A3
Cooper Ho
Hounslow TW4 129 B2
Paddington NW8 236 C5
Upper Tooting SW17 180 B6
7 West Norwood SW27 182 D5
Cooper Rd
Croydon CR0, CR9 220 D4
Hendon NW4 46 D3
Willesden NW10 68 A3
Coopersale Cl 3 IG8 37 C3
Coopersale Rd E9 74 D3
Coopers Cl
Bethnal Green E1 96 C3
Dagenham RM10 81 D2
Coopers Ct
9 Acton W3 111 A5
4 Friern Barnet N20 14 D1
Isleworth TW7 130 D3
Tower Hamlets E3 97 B3
Coopers La
Grove Pk SE12 165 B2
Somers Town NW1 232 D3
Cooper's La E10 54 A1
Cooper's Lane Prim Sch SE12 165 B2
Coopers Lo SE1 253 C2
Coopers Mews BR3 185 C1
Cooper's Rd SE1 117 D1 263 D2
Cooper's Row EC3 117 D6 253 C6
Cooper St 10 E16 98 D2
Coopers Tech Sch BR7 189 A2
Coopers Yd N1 72 D1
Cooper's Yd SE19 183 C4
Coote Gdns RM8 81 B5
Coote Rd
Dagenham RM8 81 B5
Erith DA7 147 B4
Cope Ho EC1 235 B1
Copeland Dr E14 119 C2
Copeland Ho
Lambeth SE11 260 D5
Upper Tooting SW17 180 B6
Copeland Rd
London SE15 140 B3
Walthamstow E17 53 D3
Copelands BR3 185 B3
Copeman Cl SE26 184 C5
Copenhagen Gdns W4 111 B4
Copenhagen Ho N1 234 A5
Copenhagen Pl E14 97 B1
Copenhagen Prim Sch N1 94 B6 233 C5
Copenhagen St N1 94 B6 233 C5
Cope Pl W8 113 C3 255 A5
Copers Cope Rd BR3 185 B3
Cope St SE16 118 D2
Copeswood Ct UB7 126 C5
Copford Wlk N1 235 A6
Copgate Path SW16 182 C4
Copinger Wlk HA8 26 D2
Copland Ave HA0 65 D3
Copland Cl HA0 65 C3
Copland Com Sch & Tech Ctr HA9 66 B3
Copland Ho UB1 107 B4
Copland Mews 8 HA0 66 A2
Copland Rd HA0 66 A2
Copleston Rd SE15 139 D2
Copley Cl
15 Camberwell SE17 138 D6
Ealing W7 86 D2
Copley Dene BR1 187 D2
Copley Pk SW16 182 B4
Copley Rd HA7 25 C5
Coppard Gdns KT9 213 C2
Coppedhall 2 SE21 161 B2
Coppelia Rd SE3 142 D1
Coppen Rd RM8 59 B2
Copperas St SE8 141 D6
Copper Beech N6 49 A2
Copperbeech Cl NW3 70 B3
Copper Beech Ct N20 14 A1
Copper Beeches TW7 130 B4
Copper Cl Penge SE19 183 D3
Tottenham N17 34 B3
Copperdale Rd UB3 106 A4
Copperfield Ave UB8 82 C3
Copperfield Ct
Blackheath SE3 142 D2
Ilford IG6 57 A6
Copperfield Dr N15 51 D5
Copperfield Ho 12 SE1 118 A4
Copperfield Mews N18 33 C5
Copperfield Rd
Stepney E3 97 A2
Thamesmead SE28 102 C1
Copperfields
5 Beckenham BR3 186 A2
Harrow HA1 42 C2
Copperfields Ct W3 110 C4
Copperfield St SE1 117 A4 252 A2
Copperfield Way
Chislehurst BR7 189 A4
Pinner HA5 41 B5
Coppergate Cl BR1 187 B2
Coppermead Cl NW2 68 C5
Copper Mews 19 W4 111 A3
Copper Mill Dr TW7 130 D3
Coppermill La E17 52 D4
Copper Mill La SW17 180 A6
Coppermill Prim Sch E17 52 D4
Copper Row SE1 253 C3
Copperwood Lo EN2 4 D3
Coppetts Cl N12 30 D3
Coppetts Ctr N12 30 D3
Coppetts Rd N10 30 D2
Coppetts Wood Hospl N10 30 D2
Coppetts Wood Prim Sch N10 31 A2
Coppice Cl
Beckenham BR3 207 D5
Harrow HA7 24 D4
Ruislip HA4 39 B3
West Barnes SW20 200 C6
Coppice Dr SW15 156 B5
Coppice The
Ashford TW15 170 D4
Enfield EN2 4 D1
Hillingdon UB7 82 A1
New Barnet EN5 13 D5
Coppice Way E18 54 D6
Coppice Wlk N20 13 C1
Coppies Gr N11 31 B6
Copping Cl CR0 221 C4
Coppin Ho SW2 160 D3
Coppins The
2 Ilford RM6 58 B2
New Addington CR0 223 D2
Stanmore HA3 24 C4
Coppock Cl SW11 136 C3
Coppsfield KT8 195 C6
Copse Ave BR4 223 D5
Copse Cl SE7 143 B6
Copse Ct SW15 157 A6
Copse Glade KT6 197 D1
COPSE HILL 178 B3
Copse Hill
Belmont SM2 217 D1
Wimbledon SW20 178 B3
Copsem Dr KT10 212 A2
Copsem La KT10 212 A1
Copsem Way KT10 212 A2
Copse The Chingford E4 20 D3
Muswell Hill N2 48 D6
Copse View CR2 223 A1
Copsewood Cl DA15 167 C5
Coptefield Dr DA17 125 A3
Copthall Ave EC2 95 B1 242 D2
Copthall Bldgs EC2 242 D2
Copthall Cl EC2 242 C2
Copthall Dr NW7 28 A4
Copthall Gdns
Hendon NW7 28 A3
Twickenham TW1 152 D3
Copthall Rd E UB10 60 C5
Copthall Rd W UB10 60 C6
Copthall Sch NW7 28 B3
Copthall Sports Ctr NW4 28 B2
Copthorne Ave
Bromley BR2 226 B6
Streatham SW12 159 D4
Copthorne Chase 3 TW15 170 B6
Copthorne Cl TW17 193 A3
Copthorne Ct SM1 218 A5
Copthorne Mews UB3 105 C2
Coptic St WC1 94 A2 240 A3
Copton Cl E3 97 C2
Copwood Cl N12 30 B6
Coral Apts 6 E16 121 A6
Coral Cl RM6 58 C6
Coral Ho 5 E1 97 A3
Coraline Cl UB1 85 B4
Coralline Wlk 4 SE2 124 C4
Coral Row 14 SW11 136 A2
Coral St SE1 116 C4 251 B1
Coram Ho
Bloomsbury WC1 240 A6
9 Chiswick W4 111 C1
Coram Mans WC1 240 C5
Coram St WC1 94 A3 240 A5
Coran Cl N9 18 D4
Corban Rd TW3 129 C2
Corbar Cl EN4 2 B4
Corbden Cl SE15 139 D4
Corbet Cl CR4, SM6 219 A6
Corbet Ct EC3 242 D1
Corbet Ho N1 234 A5
Corbet Pl E1 95 D2 243 C4
Corbett Ct SE26 185 B6
Corbett Gr N22 32 A3
Corbett Ho SW10 266 A6
Corbett Rd
Walthamstow E17 54 A6
Wanstead E11 55 C3
Corbett's La SE16 118 C2
Corbetts Pas 8 SE16 118 C2
Corbett Villas RM8 58 C1
Corbicum E11 54 C2
Corbidge Ct SE8 141 D6
Corbiere Ct SW19 178 D4
Corbiere Ho 5 N1 95 C6
Corbin Ho 7 E3 97 D4
Corbin's La HA2 63 D5
Corbridge 5 N17 34 B3
Corbridge Cres E2 96 B5
Corbridge Ho SE2 124 C3
Corby Cres EN2 4 A1
Corbylands Rd DA15 167 C3
Corbyn St N4, N19 50 A1
Corby Rd NW10 89 B5
Corby Way E3 97 C3
Cordelia Cl SE24 138 D1
Cordelia Gdns TW19 148 A4
Cordelia Ho 26 N1 95 C5
Cordelia Rd TW19 148 A4
Cordelia St E14 97 D1
Cordell Ho N15 51 D4
Cordingley Rd HA4 61 B6
Cording St E14 97 D2
Cordwainers Ct 18 E9 74 C1
Cordwainers Wlk 9 E13 99 A5
Cordwain Ho 7 N18 34 A5
Cordwell Rd SE13 164 C6
Corefield Cl N11 15 A2
Corelli Rd SE3 144 A4
Corfe Ave HA2 63 C4
Corfe Cl Hayes UB4 84 C1
Twickenham TW4 151 A3
Corfe Ho SW8 270 C4
Corfe Lodge 15 SE21 161 B2
Corfe Twr 6 W3 111 A4
Corfield Rd N21 16 B6
Corfield St E2 96 B4
Corfton Lo W5 88 A2
Corfton Rd W5 88 A2
Coriander Ave E14 98 B1
Coriander Ct SE1 253 D2
Cories Cl RM8 80 D6
Corigan Ct 6 E11 76 C6
Corinium Cl HA9 66 B4
Corinne Rd N19 71 C4
Corinth Ho IG3 58 A2
Cork St Mews W1 249 A5
Corkscrew Hill BR4 224 B5
Cork Sq E1 118 B5
Cork St W1 115 C6 249 A5
Cork Tree Ho 3 SW27 182 D5
Cork Tree Ret Pk N18 35 A4
Cork Tree Way E4 35 A5
Corlett St NW1 237 A4
Cormont Rd SE5 138 D4
Cormorant Cl E17 35 A3
Cormorant Ct
36 Deptford SE8 141 B6
13 Dulwich SE21 161 B2
Cormorant Ho EN3 18 D6
Cormorant Pl SM1 217 B3
Cormorant Rd E7 76 D3
Cornbury Ho 5 SE8 141 B6
Cornbury Rd HA8 25 D3
Cornel Ho 4 DA15 168 A1
Cornelia Dr UB4 84 C3
Cornelia St N7 72 B2
Cornelion Cotts 1 SM6 219 B3
Cornelius Ct 4 N12 30 A5
Cornell Bldg 9 E1 96 A1
Cornell Cl DA14 191 A4
Cornell Ct 4 EN3 7 A2
Cornell Ho HA2 63 B5
Corner Fielde SW2 160 B3
Corner Gn SE3 143 A3
Corner House St WC2 250 A4
Corner Mead NW9 27 D2
Cornerside TW15 171 A3
Cornerstone Ct 13 E1 96 A3
Cornerways Harrow HA1 65 A5
Putney SW15 134 A1
Corney Rd W4 133 C6
Corney Reach Way W4 133 C5
Cornflower La CR0 206 D1
Cornflower Terr SE22 162 B5
Cornford Cl BR2 209 A4
Cornford Gr SW12 159 B2
Cornhill EC3 95 B1 242 D1
Cornhill Dr EN3 7 A6
Cornick Ho 7 SE16 118 B3
Cornish Ct N9 18 B4
Cornish Gr SE20 184 B2
Cornish Ho
Brentford TW8 110 B1
7 Camberwell SE17 138 D6
Cornmill La SE13 142 A2
Cornmow Dr NW10 68 A3
Cornshaw Rd RM8 58 D1
Cornthwaite Rd E5 74 C5
Cornwall Ave
Bethnal Green E2 96 C4
Claygate KT10 212 D1
Cornwall Ave *continued*
Falconwood DA16 145 D2
Finchley N3 29 C3
Southall UB1 85 C2
Wood Green N22 32 A2
Cornwall Cl IG11 79 D2
Cornwall Cres W11 91 A1
Cornwall Ct
5 Ealing W7 86 D3
6 Pinner HA5 23 B3
Upper Tooting SW17 180 C6
Cornwall Dr BR5 190 C3
Cornwall Flats SE1 251 B2
Cornwall Gdns
Kensington SW7 113 D3 255 D5
Willesden NW10 68 B2
Cornwall Gdns Wlk SW7 255 D5
Cornwall Gr W4 111 C1
Cornwall Ho
Marylebone NW1 237 D5
3 Putney SW15 156 C4
Cornwallis Ave
London N9 18 C2
New Eltham SE9 167 B2
Cornwallis Ct SW8 270 A2
Cornwallis Gr N9 18 C2
Cornwallis Ho 24 W12 112 B6
Cornwallis Rd
Dagenham RM9 81 A4
Edmonton N9 18 B2
Upper Holloway N19 72 A6
Walthamstow E17 52 D5
Woolwich SE18 122 D3
Woolwich SE18 123 A3
Cornwallis Sq N19 72 A6
Cornwallis Wlk SE9 144 B2
Cornwall Mans
Chelsea SW10 266 B4
Marylebone NW1 237 D5
Cornwall Mews S SW7 256 A5
Cornwall Mews W SW7 255 D5
Cornwall Rd
Belmont SM2 217 B1
Croydon CR0 220 D6
Edmonton N18 34 A5
Finsbury Pk N4 50 C2
Harrow HA1 42 A3
Lambeth SE1 116 C4 251 B2
Pinner HA5 23 B3
Ruislip HA4 61 D6
Twickenham TW1 153 A3
West Green N15 51 B4
Cornwall Sq SE11 261 C2
Cornwall St 4 E1 118 B6
Cornwall Terr NW1 237 D5
Cornwall Terrace Mews NW1 237 D5
Corn Way E11 76 C5
Cornwood Cl N2 48 B5
Cornwood Dr E1 96 C1
Cornworthy Rd RM8 80 C3
Corona Rd SE12 165 A4
Coronation Ave 1 N16 73 D4
Coronation Cl
Bexley DA5 168 D5
Ilford IG6 57 A5
Coronation Ct
19 North Kensington W10 90 C2
Stratford E15 76 D2
Coronation Rd
Acton NW10 88 C3
Hayes UB3 105 D2
Newham E13 99 C4
Coronet Ho HA7 24 D4
Coronet Par 9 HA0 66 A2
Coronet St N1 95 C4
Corporation Ave TW4 129 A1
Corporation Row EC1 241 B6
Corporation St
Lower Holloway N7 72 A3
West Ham E15 98 D5
Corpus Christi RC Prim Sch
Brixton SW2 160 B6
Kingston u T KT3 199 A6
Corrance Rd SW2, SW4 138 A1
Corri Ave N14 31 D6
Corrib Ct N13 16 B1
Corrib Dr SM1 218 C3
Corrib Hts N8 49 D3
Corrigan Cl NW4 46 C6
Corringham Ct NW11 47 C2
Corringham Ho 11 E1 96 D1
Corringham Rd
London NW11 47 C2
Wembley HA9 66 C6
Corringway Ealing W5 88 C2
Golders Green NW11 47 D2
Corris Gn NW9 45 C3
Corry Dr SW9 138 D1
Corry Ho 2 E14 119 D6
Corsair Cl TW19 148 A4
Corsair Rd TW19 148 A4
Corscombe Cl KT2 177 A5
Corsehill St SW16 181 C4
Corsell Ho 5 TW8 131 C5
Corsham Ho HA9 66 C2
Corsham St N1 95 B4 235 D1
Corsica St N5 72 D2
Corsley Way E9 75 B2
Cortayne Ct TW2 152 C2
Cortayne Rd SW6 135 B3
Cortis Rd SW15 156 B5
Cortis Terr SW15 156 B5
Corunna Rd SW8 137 C4 269 B2
Corunna Terr SW8 269 A2
Corvette Sq 5 SE10 142 B6
Corwell Gdns UB8 83 A1
Corwell La UB8 83 A1
Coryton Path W9 91 B3
Cosbycote Ave SE24 161 A6
Cosdach Ave SM6 219 D1
Cosedge Cres CR0, CR9 220 D3
Cosgrove Cl
Edmonton N21 17 A2
Hayes UB4 84 D3
Cosgrove Ho 11 E2 96 A6
Cosmo Pl WC1 240 B4
Cosmur Cl W12 111 D3
Cossall Wlk SE15 140 B4
Cossar Mews 10 SW2 160 C6
Cosser St SE1 116 C3 261 A6
Costa St SE15 140 A3
Coston Prim Sch UB6 86 A4
Costons Ave UB6 86 B4
Costons La UB6 86 B4
Coston Wlk 4 SE4 140 D1
Cosway Ho NW11 48 A3
Cosway Mans NW1 237 B4
Cosway St NW1 92 C2 237 B4
Cotall St E14 97 C2
Coteford Cl HA5 40 A4
Coteford Inf Sch HA5 40 A3
Coteford Jun Sch HA5 39 D4
Coteford St SW17 181 A6
Cotelands CR0 221 C5
Cotesbach Rd E5 74 C5
Cotes Ho NW8 237 A5
Cotesmore Gdns RM8 80 C4
Cotford Rd CR7 205 A5
Cotham St SE17 262 B3
Cotherstone Rd SW2 160 B3
Cotleigh Ave DA5 168 D2
Cotleigh Rd NW6 69 C1
Cotman Cl London NW11 48 A3
Putney SW15 156 D6
Cotman Ct BR3 185 B2
Cotmandene Cres BR5 190 A1
Cotman Gdns HA8 26 C1
Cotman Ho
5 Northolt UB5 84 D5
St John's Wood NW8 230 A4
Cotman Mews RM8 80 C3
Cotmans Cl UB3 106 A5
Coton Rd DA16 146 A2
Cotrill Gdns E8 74 B2
Cotsford Ave KT3 199 B4
Cotswold Ave WD23 8 A5
Cotswold Cl
Hinchley Wood KT10 212 D6
Kingston u T KT2 177 A4
Cotswold Ct London N11 31 A6
St Luke's EC1 242 A6
3 Wembley UB6 86 D5
Cotswold Gate NW2 47 A1
Cotswold Gdns
Hendon NW2 68 D6
Ilford IG2 57 B2
Newham E6 99 D5
Cotswold Gn EN2 4 B1
Cotswold Ho N16 51 D1
Cotswold Mews SW11 266 D1
Cotswold Rd TW12 173 C4
Cotswold Rise BR6 211 D3
Cotswold St SE27 182 D6
Cotswold Way
Enfield EN2 4 B2
North Cheam KT4 216 C6
Cottage Ave BR2 210 A1
Cottage Cl Harrow HA2 64 C6
Ruislip HA4 39 B1
Cottage Field Cl DA14 168 C3
Cottage Gn SE5 139 B5
Cottage Gr
London SW9 138 A2
Surbiton KT6 197 D3
Cottage Pl SW3 114 C3 257 A5
Cottage Rd KT19 215 B1
Cottage St E14 119 D6
Cottages The
Ickenham UB10 60 A6
Lambeth SE1 260 C5
Uxbridge UB10 60 D5
Cottage Wlk 2 N16 73 D5
Cottenham Dr
London NW9 45 D6
Wimbledon SW20 178 B3
Cottenham Ho 5 N19 72 A6
Cottenham Par SW20 178 B1
COTTENHAM PARK 178 B2
Cottenham Park Rd SW20 178 C3
Cottenham Pl SW20 178 B3
Cottenham Rd E17 53 B5
Cotterill Rd KT6 198 B1
Cottesbrook St 9 SE14 141 A5
Cottesloe Ho NW8 237 A6
Cottesloe Mews SE1 261 B6
Cottesmore Ct W8 255 D6
Cottesmore Gdns W8 113 D3 255 D6
Cottimore Ave KT12 194 B1
Cottimore Cres KT12 194 B2
Cottimore La KT12 194 B2
Cottimore Terr KT12 194 B2
Cottingham Chase HA4 62 A5
Cottingham Rd
Penge SE20 184 D3
Cottingham Rd *continued*
South Lambeth SW8 138 B5 270 D4
Cottington Rd TW13 172 D6
Cottington St SE11 261 C2
Cotton Ave W3 89 B1
Cotton Cl
Dagenham RM9 80 C1
12 Leyton E11 76 C6
Cottongrass Cl 1 CR0 206 D1
Cotton Hill BR1 186 B6
Cotton Ho
Bedford Pk W12 111 D4
18 Streatham SW12 160 A4
Cotton Row SW11 136 B2
Cotton's Gdns E2 95 C4
Cottons La SE1 252 D4
Cotton St E14 120 A6
Cottrell Ct SE10 120 D2
Cotts Cl 13 W7 86 D2
Couchman Ho 8 SW4 159 C5
Couchmore Ave KT10 212 C6
Coulgate St SE4 141 A2
Coulsdon Ct 4 N8 49 D4
Coulsdon Ho 5 SW2 160 A3
Coulson Cl RM8 58 C1
Coulson St SW3 114 D1 257 C2
Coulter Cl UB4 85 A3
Coulter Rd W6 112 B3
Coulthurst Ct SW16 182 A3
Coults Cres NW5 71 A5
Councillor St SE5 139 A5
Counters Ct W14 254 B6
Counter St SE1 253 A3
Countess Rd NW5 71 C3
Countisbury Ave EN1 17 D4
Countisbury Ho SE26 162 A1
Country Way TW13, TW16 172 C5
County Gate
Longlands SE9 167 A1
New Barnet EN5 13 D5
County Gr SE5 139 A4
County Ho
22 Herne Hill SE24 138 D1
9 South Lambeth SW9 138 C4
County Par TW8 131 D5
County Rd Newham E6 100 D2
South Norwood CR7 182 D1
County St SE1 117 A3 262 B5
Coupland Pl SE18 123 A1
Courcy Rd N8, N22 50 C6
Courier Ho 12 SW2 160 C4
Courland Gr SW8 137 D3
Courland St SW8 137 D4 269 D1
Course The SE9 166 C1
Courtauld Ho 12 E2 96 A5
Courtauld Inst of Art*
Marylebone W1 237 D2
Strand WC2 250 C6
Courtauld Rd N19 50 A1
Courtaulds Cl SE28 124 A5
Court Ave DA17 125 B1
Court Cl Harrow HA3 44 A6
Twickenham TW13, TW2 151 D1
Wallington SM6 219 D1
Court Close Ave TW13, TW2 151 D1
Court Cres KT9 213 D2
Court Downs Rd BR3 185 D1
Court Dr
Carshalton SM1 218 C4
Edgware HA7 26 A6
Hillingdon UB10 82 C6
Wallington CR0 220 B4
Courtenay Ave
Harrow HA3 24 A2
Highgate N6 48 C2
Courtenay Dr BR3 186 B1
Courtenay Gdns HA3 24 A1
Courtenay Mews E17 53 A4
Courtenay Pl E17 53 A4
Courtenay Rd
Leyton E11 76 D5
North Cheam KT4, SM3 216 C5
Penge BR3, SE20 184 D4
Walthamstow E17 52 D5
Courtenay Rd HA9 65 D5
Courtenay Sq SE11 261 A1
Courtenay St SE11 116 C1 261 A1
Courtens Mews HA7 25 C3
Court Farm Ave KT19 215 B3
Court Farm Ind Est TW19 148 B4
Court Farm Rd
Chislehurst SE9 166 A1
Northolt UB5 63 C1
Courtfield W13 87 C1
Courtfield Ave HA1 42 D4
Courtfield Cres HA1 42 D4
Courtfield Gdns
Ealing W13 87 A1
Ruislip HA4 61 D6
South Kensington SW5 113 D2 255 D3
Courtfield Ho EC1 241 A4
Courtfield Mews SW7 255 D3
Courtfield Rd
Ashford TW15 170 D4
South Kensington SW7 114 A2 256 A3
Courtfield Rise BR4 224 B6
Courtgate Cl NW7 27 D4
Court Gdns N7 72 C1

Courthill Rd SE13 142 A1
Courthope Ho
14 Rotherhithe SE16 118 C3
South Lambeth SW8 270 A3
Courthope Rd
Gospel Oak NW3 70 D4
Greenford UB6 86 B5
Wimbledon SW19 179 A5
Courthope Villas SW19 179 A3
Court House Gdns N3 29 C4
Court House Rd N12 29 D4
Court La SE21 161 D4
Courtland Ave
Chingford E4 20 D2
Edgware NW7 11 C1
Redbridge IG1 78 B6
South Norwood SW16 182 B3
Courtland Gr SE28 124 D6
Courtland Rd E6 100 A6
Courtlands
11 Beckenham BR3 185 D1
8 Belmont SM2 217 D1
Ealing W5 87 C2
Richmond TW10 154 C6
5 Upper Clapton E5 52 B1
Walton-on-T KT12 194 A2
Courtlands Ave
Hampton TW12 173 B4
Hayes BR2 208 D1
Lee SE12 165 B6
Richmond TW9 132 D3
Courtland Sch NW7 11 C2
Courtlands Cl HA4 39 D2
Courtlands Dr KT19 215 D2
Courtlands Rd KT5 198 C2
Court Lane Gdns SE21 161 C4
Courtleet Dr DA8 147 D4
Courtleigh 6 NW11 47 B4
Courtleigh Ave EN4 2 B5
Courtleigh Gdns NW11 47 A5
Court Lo 11 DA17 125 C1
Courtman Rd N17 33 A3
Court Mans 8 W6 112 A2
Court Mead UB5 85 B4
Courtmead Cl SE24 161 A5
Courtnell St W2 91 C1
Courtney Cl SE19 183 C4
Courtney Cres SM5 218 D1
Courtney Ct N7 72 C3
Courtney Ho
1 Hendon NW4 46 C5
Kensington W14 254 B6
Courtney Pl CR0 220 C5
Courtney Rd
Croydon CR0 220 C5
Islington N7 72 C3
Mitcham SW19 180 C3
Courtney Twrs IG2 57 B3
Courtney Way TW6 126 C2
Court One TW15 149 A1
Court Par HA0 65 B5
Courtrai Rd SE23 163 A5
Court Rd Eltham SE9 166 B4
Southall UB2 107 B1
South Norwood SE25 205 D6
Uxbridge UB10 60 D4
Court Royal SW15 157 A6
Courtside Crouch End N8 49 D3
Forest Hill SE23 162 C1
Court St Bromley BR1 187 A1
3 Stepney E1 96 B2
Court The London N10 49 C5
Ruislip HA4 63 A4
Court Three TW15 149 A1
Court Two TW15 149 A1
Courtville Ho 12 W10 91 A4
Courtway IG8 37 C5
Court Way Acton W3 89 A2
Colindale NW9 45 C5
Ilford IG6 57 A6
Twickenham TW1, TW2 152 D4
Courtyard Apartments TW11 174 B5
Courtyard Mews BR5 190 A3
Courtyard The
Fulham SW6 135 A4 264 A1
Islington N1 72 B1
Keston BR2 226 A2
Thornton Heath CR0 204 B3
13 Wandsworth SW18 136 B1
Court Yd SE9 166 B5
Cousin La EC4 117 B6 252 C5
Cousins Cl 2 UB7 104 A6
Cousins Ct 2 NW9 46 A5
Couthurst Rd SE3 143 B5
Coutts Ave KT9 214 A3
Couzens Ho 8 E3 97 B2
Coval Gdns SW14 132 D1
Coval La SW14 132 D1
Coval Pas SW14 133 A1
Coval Rd SW14 133 A1
Covardale Ct EN3 7 A6
Covelees Wall E6 100 C1
Covell Ct 16 SE8 141 C5
Covent Garden Sta WC2 94 A1 240 B1
Covent Gdn* WC2 116 A6 250 B6
Coventry Cl Kilburn NW6 91 C6
9 Newham E6 100 B1
Coventry Rd
Bethnal Green E1 96 B3
Croydon SE25 206 A5
Ilford IG1 56 D1
Coventry St W1 249 C5
Coverack Cl
Croydon CR0 207 A2
Southgate N14 15 C5
Coverdale Cl HA7 25 B5
Coverdale Gdns CR0 221 D5
Coverdale Rd
Brondesbury NW2 69 A2
Friern Barnet N11 31 A4
Hammersmith W12 112 B4
Hampstead NW6 68 D1
Coverdales The IG11 101 B5
Coverham Ho 5 SE4 140 D1
Coverley Cl E1 96 A2
Coverley Point SE11 260 C3
Coverton Rd SW17 180 C5
Coverts Rd KT10 212 D1
Covert The BR6 211 C3
Covert Way EN4 2 A3
Covet Wood Cl BR5 211 D3
Covey Cl SW19 179 D1
Covington Gdns SW16 182 D3
Covington Way
South Norwood SW16 182 C3
South Norwood SW16 182 D3
Cowan Cl E6 100 A2
Cowan Ct 14 NW10 67 B1
Cowan Lo 6 IG8 37 C4
Cowbridge La IG11 78 D1
Cowbridge Rd HA3 44 B5
Cowcross St EC1 94 D2 241 C4
Cowdenbeath Path N1 233 C6
Cowden Rd BR6 211 D2
Cowden St SE6 185 C6
Cowdray Hall Royal Coll of Nursing W1 93 B1 238 C2
Cowdray Ho 22 SE22 139 C2
Cowdray Rd UB10 83 A6
Cowdrey Cl EN1 5 C3
Cowdrey Rd SW19 180 A5
Cowdry Rd E9 75 B2
Cowell Lo E4 36 D5
Cowen Ave HA2 64 B6
Cowen Ho 4 SE18 144 D6
Cowgate Rd UB6 86 B4
Cowick Rd SW17 180 D6
Cowings Mead UB5 63 A2
Cowland Ave EN3 6 C1
Cow Leaze E6 100 C1
Cowleaze Rd KT2 176 A2
Cowley Ct 8 E18 37 A1
Cowley La E11 76 C5
COWLEY PEACHY 82 A2
Cowley Pl NW4 46 C4
Cowley Rd
Brixton SW9 138 C4
East Acton W3 111 D5
16 Kennington SW9 138 C5
Mortlake SW14 133 C2
Redbridge IG1 56 B2
Wanstead E11 55 B4
Cowley St SW1 260 A5
Cowling Cl W11 244 A4
Cowper Ave
Sutton SM1 218 B4
Upton Pk E6 78 A1
Cowper Cl Bexley DA16 168 A6
Bromley BR2 209 D5
Cowper Gdns
Southgate N14 15 C5
Wallington SM6 219 C2
Cowper Ho
Pimlico SW1 259 D1
Walworth SE17 262 B2
Cowper Rd Acton W3 111 B5
6 Belvedere DA17 125 C2
Bromley BR2 209 D5
Ealing W7 108 D6
East Barnet N14 15 B3
Edmonton N18 34 A5
Kingston u T KT2 176 B5
Stoke Newington N16 73 C4
Wimbledon SW19 180 A4
Cowper's Ct EC3 242 D1
Cowper St EC1, EC2 95 B3 242 D6
Cowper Terr W10 90 D2
Cowslip Cl UB10 60 A1
Cowslip Rd E18 37 B1
Cowthorpe Rd SW8 269 D2
Cox Ct 3 EN4 2 C1
Coxe Pl HA3 43 A5
Cox Ho W6 264 A6
Cox La Chessington KT9 214 B4
West Ewell KT19 215 A3
Coxmount Rd SE7 121 D1
Coxs Ave TW17 193 C6
Coxson Way SE1 253 C1
Coxwell Rd
Plumstead SE18 123 B1
South Norwood SE19 183 C3
Coxwold Path KT9 214 A1
Coysh Ct 8 SW15 157 A6
Crabbs Croft Cl 7 BR6 227 A3
Crab Hill BR3 186 B3
Crabtree Ave
Dagenham RM6 58 D5
Wembley HA0 88 B5
Crabtree Cl E2 95 D5
Crabtree Ct Barnet EN5 1 D1
Temple Mills E15 75 D3
Crabtree Hall SW6 134 C5
Crabtree La SW6 134 D5
Cracknell Cl EN1 6 B6
Craddock Rd EN1 5 D2
Craddock St NW5 71 A2
Cradley Rd SE9 167 B3
Cragie Ho SE1 263 D3
Craig Dr UB8 82 D1
Craigen Ave CR0 206 B1
Craigerne Rd SE3 143 B5
Craig Gdns E18 36 D1
Craig Ho Ealing W13 109 B6
Greenwich SE3 143 B5
Craigholm SE18 144 C4
Craigie Lea N10 31 B1
Craigleith SW15 156 D5
Craigmuir Pk HA0 88 B6
Craignair Rd SW2 160 C4
Craignish Ave SW16 182 B1
Craig Park Rd N18 34 B6
Craig Rd TW10 175 C6
Craig's Ct SW1 250 A4
Craigside KT2 176 D2
Craigton Rd SE9 144 B1
Craigweil Cl HA7 25 D5
Craigweil Dr HA7 25 D5
Craigwell Ave TW13 150 A1
Craik Ct NW6 91 B5
Crail Row SE17 117 B2 262 D3
Crales Ho SE18 122 A3
Cramer Ct KT3 199 A6
Cramer St W1 93 A2 238 B3
Cramhurst Ho 3 SM1 218 B3
Crammond Cl W6 264 A5
Cramond Ct TW14 149 C3
Cramonde Ct DA16 146 A3
Crampton Rd SE20 184 C4
Crampton Sch SE17 116 D1 261 D2
Crampton St SE17 117 A1 262 A2
Cranberry Cl 2 UB5 84 D5
Cranberry La E16 98 C3
Cranborne Ave
Southall UB2 107 C2
Tolworth KT6, KT9 214 C5
Cranborne Rd IG11 101 B6
Cranborne Waye
Hayes UB4 84 B1
Hayes UB4 106 C6
Cranbourn Alley WC2 249 D6
Cranbourne Cl SW16 204 A6
Cranbourne Ct
East Finchley N2 47 D6
2 Edgware HA8 26 D5
Finchley NW7 29 A3
SW11 267 B4
Walton-on-T KT12 194 B2
Wanstead E18 55 B5
Cranbourne Dr HA5 40 D4
Cranbourne Gdns
Ilford IG6 57 A6
Temple Fortune NW11 47 B4
Cranbourne Rd
Leyton E15 76 A4
London N10 31 B1
Manor Pk E12 78 A3
Northwood HA6 39 D6
Cranbourn Ho 6 SE16 118 B4
Cranbourn Pas 5 SE16 118 B4
Cranbourn St WC2 115 D6 249 D6
CRANBROOK 56 C1
Cranbrook NW1 232 B5
Cranbrook Cl BR2 209 A3
Cranbrook Coll (Boys) IG1 78 C6
Cranbrook Ct
8 Brentford TW8 131 D6
South Croydon CR2 221 C3
Cranbrook Dr
Thames Ditton KT10 196 A1
Twickenham TW2 151 D3
Cranbrook Ho
5 Hackney E5 74 B3
South Norwood SE19 183 B2
Cranbrook La N11 31 B6
Cranbrook Mews E17 53 B4
Cranbrook Pk N22 32 C2
Cranbrook Rd
Chiswick W4 111 C1
Erith DA7 147 B4
Hounslow TW4 129 B1
Ilford IG1, IG2 56 C3
New Barnet EN4 14 B5
South Norwood CR7 183 A1
St Johns SE8 141 C4
Wimbledon SW19 179 A3
Cranbrook Rise IG1 56 B2
Cranbrook St E2 96 D5
Cranbury Rd SW6 135 D3
Crandale Ho 8 E5 74 B3
Crandley Ct SE8 119 A2
Crane Ave Acton W3 111 A6
Isleworth TW7 153 A6
Cranebank TW4 128 B2
Cranebank Mews TW1 131 A1
Cranebrook TW2 152 A2
Crane Cl
Dagenham RM10 81 C2
Harrow HA2 64 A5
Crane Ct 7 Acton W12 111 C4
Holborn EC4 241 B1
West Ewell KT19 215 A4
Craneford Cl TW2 152 D4
Craneford Way TW2 152 D4
Crane Gdns UB3 105 D2
Crane Gr N7 72 C2
Crane Ho 24 Bow E3 97 A5
9 Catford BR1 186 B5
Feltham TW13 151 C1
10 Peckham SE15 139 D4
Crane Lodge Rd TW5 128 B6
Crane Mead SE16 118 D2
Crane Mead Ct TW1 152 D4
Crane Park Prim Sch TW13 151 B2
Crane Park Rd TW2 151 D2
Crane Rd
Stanwell TW19 148 C5
Twickenham TW2 152 C3
Cranesbill Cl NW9 45 B6
Cranes Dr KT5 198 B5
Cranes Park Ave KT5, KT6 198 B5
Cranes Park Cres KT5 198 B5
Cranes Pk KT5, KT6 198 A4
Crane St
Greenwich SE10 120 B1
6 Peckham SE15 139 D4
Craneswater TW6 127 D5
Craneswater Pk UB2 107 B1
Cranes Way WD6 11 A6
Crane Way TW2 152 A4
Cranfield Ct
Marylebone NW1 237 B3
2 Woodford IG8 37 A6
Cranfield Dr NW9 27 C3
Cranfield Ho WC1 240 B4
Cranfield Rd SE4 141 B2
CRANFORD 128 C4
Cranford Ave
Bowes Pk N13 32 A5
Stanwell TW19 148 B4
Cranford Cl
Stanwell TW19 148 A4
Wimbledon SW20 178 B3
Cranford Com Coll TW5 128 B6
Cranford Cotts 8 E1 118 D6
Cranford Ct SM1 218 A4
Cranford Dr UB3 105 D2
Cranford Jun & Inf Schs TW4 128 B3
Cranford La
Harlington TW6 127 D4
Harlington UB3 127 C5
Hatton TW6 127 D2
Heston TW5 128 C5
Cranford Lo SW19 156 D2
Cranford Park Prim Sch UB3 105 D2
Cranford Park Rd UB3 105 D2
Cranford Rise KT10 212 A3
Cranford St E1 118 D6
Cranford Way N8 50 C4
Cranhurst Rd NW2 68 C3
Cranleigh W11 244 C4
Cranleigh Cl
Bexley DA5 169 D5
Penge SE20 184 B1
Cranleigh Ct
1 Barnet EN5 1 D1
Mitcham CR4 202 B6
Richmond TW9 132 C2
Southall UB1 85 B1
4 Stamford Hill N16 51 C1
Cranleigh Gardens Ind Est UB1 85 B2
Cranleigh Gdns
Barking IG11 79 B2
Harrow HA3 44 A4
Kingston u T KT2 176 B4
Southall UB1 85 B1
Southgate N21 16 C6
South Norwood SE25 205 C6
Sutton SM1 217 D6
Cranleigh Ho SW20 178 B1
Cranleigh Hos NW1 232 B3
Cranleigh Mews SW11 136 D3
Cranleigh Rd
Feltham TW13 171 D6
Harringay N15 51 A4
Merton SW19 201 C6
Thames Ditton KT10 196 A1
Cranleigh St NW1 93 C5 232 B3
Cranley Dene Ct N10 49 B5
Cranley Dr Ilford IG2 57 A2
Ruislip HA4 61 D6
CRANLEY GARDENS 49 B5
Cranley Gdns
London N10 49 B5
Palmers Green N13 16 B1
South Kensington SW7 114 B1 256 C2
Wallington SM6 219 C1
Cranley Mews SW7 114 A1 256 B2
Cranley Par 2 SE9 188 A6
Cranley Pl SW7 114 B2 256 C3
Cranley Rd Ilford IG2 57 A2
Newham E13 99 B2
Cranmer Ave W13 109 B3
Cranmer Cl Ruislip HA4 40 D1
Stanmore HA7 25 C3
West Barnes SM4 200 D3
Cranmer Ct
Chelsea SW3 257 B3
Church End N3 29 A1
Hampton TW12 173 D5
Kingston u T KT2 175 D6
Cranmere Prim Sch KT10 196 A1
Cranmer Farm Cl CR4 202 D5
Cranmer Ho SW11 267 A2
Cranmer Prim Sch CR4 202 D5
Cranmer Rd
Brixton SW9 138 C5
Croydon CR0 221 A5
Edgware HA8 10 D1
Cranmer Rd *continued*
Forest Gate E7 77 B4
Hampton TW12 173 D5
Hayes UB3 83 B1
Kingston u T KT2 176 A5
Mitcham CR4 202 D5
Cranmer Terr SW17 180 B5
Cranmore Ave TW7 130 A5
Cranmore Rd
Catford BR1 164 D1
Elmstead BR7 188 B5
Cranmore Way N10 49 C5
Cranston Cl
Hounslow TW3, TW4 129 A3
Uxbridge UB10 61 B6
Cranston Ct 6 N20 14 D2
Cranston Gdns E4 35 D4
Cranston Rd SE23 163 A2
Cranswick Rd SE16 118 B1
Crantock Rd SE6 164 A2
Cranwell Cl E3 97 D3
Cranwell Ct
Croydon CR0 222 D6
6 Hendon NW9 27 D3
Cranwell Gr TW17 192 B5
Cranwell Rd TW6 126 D3
Cranwich Ave N21 17 B4
Cranwich Rd N16 51 C2
Cranwood Ct EC1 235 D1
Cranwood St EC1 95 B4 235 D1
Cranworth Cres 7 E4 20 B3
Cranworth Gdns SW9 138 C4
Cranworth Ho 6 N7 72 B4
Craster Rd SW2 160 B4
Craston Ho 2 SE5 139 C3
Crathie Rd SE12 165 B5
Crathorne Ho N2 30 B1
Cravan Ave TW13 150 A2
Craven Ave Ealing W5 109 C6
Southall UB1 85 B2
Craven Cl Hayes UB4 84 A1
Stamford Hill N16 52 A2
Craven Cottage (Fulham FC) SW6 134 D4
Craven Ct
Dagenham RM6 59 A3
Edgware HA8 26 B6
Harlesden NW10 89 C6
Southall UB1 107 D5
Craven Gdns
Barking IG11 101 C5
Ilford IG6 57 B6
Wimbledon SW19 179 D5
Craven Hill W2 114 A6 246 B6
Craven Hill Gdns W2 114 A6 246 A6
Craven Hill Mews W2 246 B6
Craven Ho Ealing W5 109 C6
16 Finchley N2 30 B1
2 Mortlake SW14 133 B2
Craven Lo
Bayswater W2 246 B6
Fulham SW6 134 D4
Craven Mews 6 SW11 137 A2
Craven Park Mews NW10 89 C6
Craven Park Rd
Harlesden NW10 89 C6
South Tottenham N15 52 A3
Craven Pas WC2 250 A4
Craven Pk NW10 89 C6
Craven Rd Croydon CR0 206 B1
Ealing W5 109 C6
Kingston u T KT2 176 B2
Paddington W2 92 A1 236 B1
Stonebridge NW10 89 B6
Craven St WC2 116 A5 250 A4
Craven Terr W2 114 A6 246 B6
Craven Wlk E5, N16 52 A2
Crawford Ave HA0 65 D3
Crawford Bldgs NW1 237 B3
Crawford Cl TW7 130 C3
Crawford Ct SE18 146 A6
Crawford Gdns
Edmonton N13 16 D1
Northolt UB5 85 B4
Crawford Mews W1 237 C3
Crawford Pas EC1 241 B5
Crawford Pl W1 92 C2 237 B3
Crawford Place Dwellings NW1 237 B3
Crawford Point 4 E16 98 D1
Crawford Prim Sch SE5 139 A4
Crawford Rd SE5 139 A3
Crawford St
Marylebone W1 92 D2 237 C3
16 Willesden NW10 67 B1
Crawley Rd Enfield EN1 17 D4
Leyton E10 53 D1
Tottenham N22 33 A1
Crawshay Ct SW9 138 C4
Crawshay Ho 13 N16 73 B4
Crawthew Gr SE22 139 D1
Cray Bldgs DA14 190 C4
Craybrooke Rd DA14 190 B6
Craybury End SE9 167 A2
Crayfields Bsns Pk BR5 190 C2
Crayfields Ind Pk BR5 190 C1
Crayford Cl E6 100 A1
Crayford Ho
Bermondsey SE1 252 D1
5 Lower Holloway N7 72 A4
Crayford Rd N7 72 A4
Crayke Hill KT9 214 A1
Crayle Ho EC1 241 D6
Crayleigh Terr DA14 190 C4
Crayonne Cl TW16 171 C2
Cray Rd Erith DA17 147 C6
Sidcup DA14 190 C4
Crays Par The BR5 190 C1
Crealock Gr IG8 36 D5
Crealock St SW18 157 D5
Creasy Est SE1 263 A5
Crebor St SE22 162 A5
Credenhall Dr BR2 210 B1
Credenhill Ho 2 SE15 140 B5
Credenhill St SW16 181 C4
Crediton Hill NW6 69 D3
Crediton Ho EN3 6 D2
Crediton Rd
Brondesbury Pk NW10 90 D6
Newham E16 99 A1
Crediton Way KT10 213 A3
Credon Rd
Bermondsey SE16 118 B1
Newham E13 99 C5
Creechurch La EC3 243 B1
Creechurch Pl EC3 243 B1
Creed Ct 5 E1 97 A4
Creed Ho SE15 140 B2
Creed La EC4 241 D1
Creek Ho W14 254 B6
CREEKMOUTH 101 D2
Creekmouth Ind Pk IG11 101 D3
Creek Rd Barking IG11 101 D4
East Molesey KT8 196 C5
Greenwich SE10, SE8 141 D6
Creek Road Ind Est SE8 141 D6
Creekside SE8 141 D5
Creekside Foyer SE8 141 D6
Creek The TW16 194 A4
Creeland Gr SE6 163 B3
Crefeld Cl W6 135 A6 264 A5
Creffield Rd W3, W5 110 C6
Creighton Ave
London N2, N10 30 D1
Newham E6 99 D5
Creighton Cl W12 112 B6
Creighton Ho N2 48 C6
Creighton Rd
Ealing W5 109 D3
Kensal Rise NW6 90 D5
Tottenham N17 33 C3
Cremer Bsns Ctr 8 E2 95 D5
Cremer Ho 9 SE8 141 C5
Cremer St E2 95 D5
Cremorne Rd SW10 136 B5 266 C4
Creon Ct 3 SW9 138 C4
Crescent EC3 253 C6
Crescent Arc 11 SE10 142 A6
Crescent Court Bsns Ctr 1 E16 98 B3
Crescent Ct
Clapham Pk SW4 159 D6
Crouch End N8 49 D3
Kingston u T KT6 197 D4
14 Sidcup DA15 168 A1
Crescent Dr BR5 211 A3
Crescent E EN4 2 A5
Crescent Gdns
Ruislip HA4 40 B2
Wimbledon SW19 157 C1
Crescent Gr
London SW4 137 C1
Mitcham CR4 202 C5
Crescent Ho
London SE13 141 D3
5 Wimbledon SW20 178 D2
Crescent La SW4 159 D6
Crescent Mans
Islington N5 72 D3
Notting Hill W11 244 B6
Crescent Par UB10 82 C4
Crescent Pl SW3 257 B4
Crescent Rd
Beckenham BR3 185 D1
Chingford E4 20 C4
Church End N3 29 B2
Crouch End N8 49 D3
Dagenham RM10 81 D5
East Barnet EN4 14 C6
Edmonton N9 18 A3
Enfield EN2 4 D1
Friern Barnet N11 30 D6
Harringay N15 50 D6
Kingston u T KT2 176 D3
Leyton E10 75 D6
Plaistow BR1 187 A3
Shepperton TW17 193 A4
Sidcup DA15 167 D1
Upton Pk E6 99 C6
West Ham E13 99 A6
Wimbledon SW20 178 D2
Woodford E18 37 C2
Wood Green N22 31 D2
Woolwich SE18 122 D2
Crescent Rise
East Barnet EN4 14 C6
3 Finchley N3 29 C2
Wood Green N22 31 D2
Crescent Row EC1 242 A5
Crescent St N1 72 B1
Crescent Stables SW15 157 A6
Crescent The Acton W3 89 C1
Ashford TW15 170 B5
Barnes SW13 134 A3
Barnet EN5 1 D3

Crescent The continued
Beckenham BR3 ... 185 C2
Bexley DA5 ... 168 C4
Coombe KT3 ... 177 A1
Dollis Hill NW2 ... 68 B5
East Finchley N2 ... 47 D6
East Molesey KT8 ... 195 C5
Friern Barnet N11 ... 31 A6
Harlington UB7 ... 127 B5
Harrow HA2 ... 42 A1
Ilford IG2 ... 56 C3
Loughton IG10 ... 21 D5
Lower Halliford TW17 ... 193 D2
Sidcup DA14 ... 189 D6
Southall UB1 ... 107 A4
Surbiton KT6 ... 198 A4
Sutton SM1 ... 218 B3
Thornton Heath CR0 ... 205 B3
Walthamstow E17 ... 53 A4
Wembley HA0 ... 65 B6
West Wickham BR4 ... 208 C3
Wimbledon SW19 ... 157 C1
Crescent View IG10 ... 21 D6
Crescent W EN4 ... 2 A5
Crescentway N12 ... 30 C4
Crescent Way
London SE4 ... 141 C2
Orpington BR6 ... 227 C3
South Norwood SW16 ... 182 C3
Crescent Wood Rd SE21,
SE26 ... 162 A1
Cresford Rd SW6 ... 135 D4 265 C1
Crespigny Rd NW4 ... 46 B3
Cressage CI UB1 ... 85 C3
Cressage Ho 14 E14 ... 132 A6
Cressall Ho 15 E14 ... 119 C3
Crèsset Ho 8 E9 ... 74 C2
Cresset Rd E9 ... 74 C2
Cresset St SW4 ... 137 D2
Cressfield CI NW5 ... 71 A3
Cressida Rd N19 ... 49 D1
Cressingham Ct 11
DA17 ... 125 C3
Cressingham Gr SM1 ... 218 A4
Cressingham Rd
Burnt Oak HA8 ... 27 B3
Lewisham SE13 ... 142 A2
Cressington CI 4 N16 ... 73 C3
Cress Mews BR1 ... 186 B5
Cresswell Gdns SW5 ... 256 A2
Cresswell Ho HA4 ... 66 A5
Cresswell Pk SE3 ... 142 D2
Cresswell Pl
SW10 ... 114 A1 256 B2
Cresswell Rd
Croydon SE25 ... 206 A5
Feltham TW13 ... 173 A6
Twickenham TW1 ... 153 D5
Cresswell Way N21 ... 16 C4
Cressy Ct
Hammersmith W6 ... 112 B3
6 Stepney E1 ... 96 C2
Cressy Ho SW13 ... 134 B2
Cressy Hos 7 E1 ... 96 C2
Cressy Pl E1 ... 96 C2
Cressy Rd NW3 ... 70 D4
Cresta Ct W5 ... 88 B3
Cresta Ho 7 Bow E3 ... 97 C3
Hampstead NW6 ... 70 B1
Crestbrook Ave N13 ... 16 D1
Crestbrook Pl N13 ... 16 D1
Crest Ct NW4 ... 46 C4
Crest Dr EN3 ... 6 C5
Crestfield St N1, WC1 ... 233 B2
Crest Gdns HA4 ... 62 C5
Crest Ho 3 TW15 ... 170 C5
Creston Way KT4 ... 200 D1
Crest Rd Dollis Hill NW2 ... 68 A6
Hayes BR2 ... 208 D2
South Croydon CR2 ... 222 B1
Crest The Edmonton N13 ... 32 C6
Finchley N12 ... 29 D4
Hendon NW4 ... 46 C4
Surbiton KT5 ... 198 C4
10 West Norwood
SW27 ... 182 D5
Crestview NW5 ... 71 B5
Crest View HA5 ... 40 D5
Crest View Dr BR5 ... 211 A4
Crestway SW15 ... 156 B5
Crestwood Way TW4 ... 151 A6
Creswell Dr BR3 ... 207 D4
Creswick Ct W3 ... 110 D6
Creswick Rd W3 ... 110 D6
Creswick Wlk
7 Bow E3 ... 97 C4
Temple Fortune NW11 ... 47 B5
Creton St SE18 ... 122 C3
Crewdson Rd SW9 ... 138 C5
Crewe Pl NW10 ... 89 D4
Crewkerne Ct SW11 ... 266 D2
Crews St E14 ... 119 C2
Crewys Rd
Child's Hill NW2 ... 69 B6
London SE15 ... 140 B3
Crichton Ave SM6 ... 219 D4
Crichton Rd SM5 ... 218 D1
Crichton St SW8 ... 137 C3
Cricket Ct E6 ... 100 B4
Cricketers Arms Rd EN2 ... 5 A3
Cricketers CI
Chessington KT9 ... 213 D4
Oakwood N14 ... 15 C4
Cricketers Mews 4
SW18 ... 157 C6
Cricketers Terr SM5 ... 218 C5

Cricketers Wlk SE26 ... 184 C5
Cricketfield Rd E5 ... 74 B4
Cricket Gn CR4 ... 202 D5
Cricket Green Sch
CR4 ... 202 C6
Cricket Ground Rd
BR7 ... 188 D2
Cricket La BR3 ... 185 A4
Cricket Row N2 ... 48 B6
Cricklade Ave SW2 ... 160 B2
CRICKLEWOOD ... 68 C4
Cricklewood Broadway
NW2 ... 68 C4
Cricklewood La NW2 ... 69 B5
Cricklewood Sta NW2 ... 68 D4
Cridland St E15 ... 98 D6
Crieff Ct 3 TW11 ... 175 C3
Crieff Rd SW18 ... 158 A5
Criffel Ave SW2 ... 159 D3
Crimscott St
SE1 ... 117 C3 263 B5
Crimsworth Rd
SW8 ... 137 D5 269 D3
Crinan St N1 ... 94 A5 233 B4
Cringle St
SW8 ... 137 C5 269 A4
Cripplegate St EC1 ... 242 B4
Cripps Gn UB4 ... 84 B3
Crispe Ho
4 Barking IG11 ... 101 B5
Islington N1 ... 233 D5
Crispen Rd TW13 ... 173 A6
Crispian CI NW10 ... 67 C4
Crispin CI SM6 ... 220 A6
Crispin Cres SM6 ... 219 D6
Crispin Ct SE17 ... 263 A3
Crispin Pl E1 ... 243 C2
Crispin Rd HA8 ... 27 A4
Crispin St E1 ... 95 D2 243 C3
Crispin Way UB8 ... 82 B3
Crisp Rd W6 ... 112 C1
Cristowe Rd SW6 ... 135 B3
Criterion Bldgs KT7 ... 197 B2
Criterion Mews N19 ... 71 D6
Crittall's Cnr DA14 ... 190 C3
Crittenden Lo BR4 ... 207 C1
Crockerton Rd SW17 ... 158 D2
Crockham Way SE9 ... 188 C6
Crocus CI CR0 ... 206 D1
Crocus Field EN5 ... 13 B5
Croft Ave BR4 ... 208 A1
Croft CI Edgware NW7 ... 11 C1
Elmstead BR7 ... 188 B5
Erith DA17 ... 125 B1
Harlington UB7 ... 127 A5
Hillingdon UB10 ... 60 C1
Croft Ct London SE13 ... 164 A5
Ruislip HA4 ... 39 D1
Croftdown Rd NW5 ... 71 B5
Croft End CI KT9 ... 214 B5
Crofters CI TW7 ... 152 B6
Crofters St 9 SE8 ... 119 A2
Crofters Way
NW1 ... 93 D6 232 C6
Croft Gdns Ealing W7 ... 109 A4
Ruislip HA4 ... 39 D1
Croft Ho Putney SW15 ... 157 A5
11 West Kilburn W10 ... 91 A4
Croft Lodge CI IG8 ... 37 B4
Croft Mews 3 N12 ... 14 A1
CROFTON ... 227 B6
Crofton Ave
Chiswick W4 ... 133 B5
Orpington BR6 ... 227 A6
Sidcup DA5 ... 168 D4
Crofton Gate Way
SE4 ... 163 A6
Crofton Gr E4 ... 36 B6
Crofton Inf Sch BR5 ... 211 B2
Crofton Jun Sch BR5 ... 211 B2
Crofton La BR5, BR6 ... 211 B2
Crofton L Ctr SE4 ... 163 C5
Crofton Park Rd SE4 ... 163 B5
Crofton Park Sta SE4 ... 163 A6
Crofton Rd
Camberwell SE5 ... 139 C3
Locksbottom BR6 ... 226 C5
Newham E13 ... 99 B3
Crofton Roman Villa*
BR6 ... 227 C6
Crofton Sch SE4 ... 163 C5
Crofton Terr
Homerton E5 ... 75 A3
Richmond TW9 ... 132 B1
Crofton Way Enfield EN2 ... 4 C3
New Barnet EN5 ... 13 D5
Croft Rd
Carshalton SM1 ... 218 C3
Enfield EN3 ... 7 A4
Merton SW19 ... 180 A3
South Norwood SW16 ... 182 C4
Crofts Ho 21 E2 ... 96 A5
Crofts La N22 ... 32 C3
Crofts Rd HA1 ... 43 A4
Crofts St E1 ... 118 A6
Croft St SE8 ... 119 A2
Crofts The TW17 ... 193 C5
Croft The Barnet EN5 ... 1 A1
Chingford E4 ... 20 C2
Ealing W5 ... 88 A2
Edgware HA8 ... 26 D3
Harlesden NW10 ... 89 D5
Heston TW5 ... 129 A5
New Malden KT3 ... 199 C4
Pinner HA5 ... 41 B2
Ruislip HA4 ... 62 C4
Wembley HA0 ... 65 C5
Croft Villas HA1 ... 43 A4

Croft Way
Richmond TW10 ... 153 B1
Sidcup DA15 ... 167 C1
Crogsland Rd NW1 ... 71 A1
Croham CI CR2 ... 221 C1
Croham Hurst Sch
CR2 ... 221 D3
Croham Manor Rd
CR2 ... 221 C2
Croham Mount CR2 ... 221 C1
Croham Park Ave
CR2 ... 221 D3
Croham Rd CR2 ... 221 C2
Croham Valley Rd
CR2 ... 222 B1
Croindene Rd SW16 ... 182 A2
Crokesley Ho 2 HA8 ... 27 A1
Cromartie Rd N19 ... 49 D2
Cromarty Ct 7 BR1 ... 187 C1
Cromarty Ho 8 E1 ... 97 A2
Cromarty Rd HA8 ... 10 C3
Cromberdale Ct N17 ... 34 A2
Crombie CI IG4 ... 56 B4
Crombie Mews 5
SW11 ... 136 C3
Crombie Rd DA15 ... 167 B3
Cromdale Ct N16 ... 51 D2
Crome Ho UB5 ... 85 A5
Cromer CI UB8 ... 83 A1
Cromer Ct
Streatham SW16 ... 160 A1
Wandsworth SW18 ... 157 B5
Crome Rd NW10 ... 67 C2
Cromer Mans 6 SM1 ... 217 D3
Cromer Pl 15 BR6 ... 211 B1
Cromer Rd Barnet EN5 ... 2 A2
Croydon SE25 ... 206 B6
Dagenham RM6 ... 59 A3
Harlington TW6 ... 126 C3
Leyton E10 ... 54 B2
Streatham SW17 ... 181 A4
Tottenham N17 ... 34 A1
Woodford IG8 ... 37 A6
Cromer Road Prim Sch
EN5 ... 2 A2
Cromer St WC1 ... 94 A4 233 B1
Cromer Terr Dalston E8 ... 74 A3
3 Ilford RM6 ... 58 A4
Cromer Villas Rd
SW18 ... 157 B5
Cromford CI BR6 ... 227 C5
Cromford Path 11 E5 ... 74 D4
Cromford Rd SW18 ... 157 C6
Cromford Way KT3 ... 177 B2
Cromlix CI BR7 ... 188 D1
Crompton Ct SW3 ... 257 A4
Crompton Ho
Borough The SE1 ... 262 B5
Paddington W2 ... 236 C5
South Lambeth SW8 ... 269 B1
Crompton Pl EN3 ... 7 C5
Crompton St
W2 ... 92 B3 236 C5
Cromwell Ave
Bromley BR2 ... 209 B5
Hammersmith W6 ... 112 B2
Highgate N6 ... 49 B1
New Malden KT3 ... 199 D4
Cromwell CI Acton W3 ... 111 A5
Bromley BR2 ... 209 B5
East Finchley N2 ... 48 B5
2 Gunnersbury W4 ... 110 D1
Walton-on-T KT12 ... 194 B1
Cromwell Cres
SW5 ... 113 C2 255 A4
Cromwell St 16 SE18 ... 122 D1
15 Kingston u T KT2 ... 176 C3
Wembley HA0 ... 88 A3
Cromwell Ctr
Barking IG11 ... 102 A4
North Acton NW10 ... 89 B4
Cromwell Ctr The RM8 ... 59 B2
Cromwell Est E10 ... 53 A1
Cromwell Gdns
SW7 ... 114 B3 256 D5
Cromwell Gr W6 ... 112 C3
Cromwell Ho
Battersea SW11 ... 268 B1
2 Croydon CR0 ... 220 D5
Muswell Hill N10 ... 31 B3
Putney SW15 ... 134 A1
Cromwell Hospl
SW5 ... 113 D2 255 C4
Cromwell Lo
Barking IG11 ... 79 C3
40 Bethnal Green E1 ... 96 C3
Cromwell Mans 255 B4
Cromwell Mews SW7 ... 256 D4
Cromwell Pl
6 Acton W3 ... 111 A5
Highgate N6 ... 49 B1
Mortlake SW14 ... 133 A2
South Kensington
SW7 ... 114 B2 256 D4
Cromwell Rd
Beckenham BR3 ... 207 A6
Brixton SW9 ... 138 C4
Feltham TW13 ... 150 B3
Finchley N3 ... 30 A2
Hayes UB3 ... 83 B1
Hounslow TW3 ... 129 C1
Kingston u T KT2 ... 176 A2
Muswell Hill N10 ... 31 A3
South Kensington SW7 ... 256 B4
Teddington TW11 ... 175 A4
Thornton Heath CR0 ... 205 B2
Upton E7 ... 77 C1
Walthamstow E17 ... 54 A4
Walton-on-T KT12 ... 194 B1
Wembley HA0 ... 88 A5

Cromwell Rd continued
Wimbledon SW19 ... 179 D5
Worcester Pk KT4 ... 215 C5
Cromwell St TW3 ... 129 C1
Cromwell Trad Ctr
IG11 ... 101 C4
Cromwell Twr EC2 ... 242 B4
Crondace Rd
SW6 ... 135 C4 265 B1
Crondall Ct 7 N1 ... 95 C5
Crondall Ho SW15 ... 156 A3
Crondall Pl 15 N1 ... 95 C5
Crondall St N1 ... 95 B5
Crone Ct 5 NW6 ... 91 B5
Cronin St SE15 ... 139 D5
CROOKED BILLET ... 178 C4
Crooked Billet
Chingford E4 ... 35 C3
Wimbledon SW19 ... 178 C3
Crooked Billet Yd 18
E2 ... 95 C4
Crooked Usage N3 ... 47 A6
Crooke Rd SE8 ... 119 A1
Crookham Rd
SW6 ... 135 B4 264 C1
Crook Log DA6 ... 146 D1
Crook Log L Ctr DA7 ... 146 D2
Crook Log Prim Sch
DA6 ... 146 C2
Crookston Rd SE9 ... 144 C2
Croombs Rd E16 ... 99 C2
Croom's Hill SE10 ... 142 B5
Croom's Hill Gr SE10 ... 142 A5
Cropley Ct N1 ... 235 C4
Cropley St N1 ... 95 B5 235 C4
Croppath Rd RM10 ... 81 C4
Cropthorne Ct W9 ... 229 B1
Crosbie 10 NW9 ... 27 D1
Crosbie Ho 20 E17 ... 53 D6
Crosby CI TW13 ... 173 A6
Crosby Ho
18 Cubitt Town E14 ... 120 A3
Forest Gate E7 ... 77 A2
Crosby Rd
Dagenham RM10 ... 103 D6
Upton E7 ... 77 A2
Crosby Row
SE1 ... 117 B4 252 C2
Crosby Sq EC3 ... 243 A2
Crosby Wlk
3 Dalston E8 ... 73 D2
Streatham SE24 ... 160 C4
Crosfield Ct 3 W10 ... 90 D1
Crosfield Ho W11 ... 244 A5
Crosier CI SE3 ... 144 A3
Crosier Rd UB10 ... 61 A4
Crosier Way HA4 ... 61 C5
Crosland Pl 5 SW11 ... 137 A2
Crossbow Ho
Ealing W13 ... 109 B5
15 Shoreditch N1 ... 95 C6
Crossbrook Rd SE3 ... 144 A2
Cross CI SE15 ... 140 B3
11 Thamesmead SE28 ... 124 B6
Cross Deep TW1 ... 153 A2
Cross Deep Gdns
TW1 ... 152 D2
Crossfield Rd
Hampstead NW3 ... 70 B2
London N17 ... 51 A6
Crossfield St SE8 ... 141 C5
Crossford St SW9 ... 138 B3
Crossgate Edgware HA8 ... 10 C1
Wembley UB6 ... 65 B2
Crossharbour Sta E14 ... 119 D3
Cross Ho N8 ... 50 B5
Cross Keys CI
5 Edmonton N9 ... 18 A2
Marylebone W1 ... 238 B3
Cross La
City of London EC3 ... 253 A5
Hornsey N8 ... 50 B5
Old Bexley DA5 ... 169 B4
Cross Lances Rd TW3 ... 129 D1
Crossland Rd CR7 ... 204 D3
Crosslands Ave
Ealing W5 ... 110 B5
Southall UB2 ... 107 B1
Crosslands Rd KT19 ... 215 B2
Crossleigh Ct
3 New Cross SE14 ... 141 B5
Streatham SW16 ... 181 B6
Crosslet St SE17 ... 262 D4
Crosslet Vale SE10 ... 141 D4
Crossley St N7 ... 72 C2
Crossman Hos 19
SW12 ... 160 A4
Crossmead SE9 ... 166 B3
Crossmead Ave UB6 ... 85 C4
Crossmount Ho 13
SE5 ... 139 A5
Crossness Rd IG11 ... 101 D4
Cross Rd Belmont HA3 ... 25 A1
Camberwell SE5 ... 139 C3
Chingford E4 ... 20 C3
Croydon CR0 ... 205 B1
Enfield EN1 ... 5 C1
Feltham TW13 ... 173 A6
Finchley N2 ... 30 C1
Friern Barnet N11 ... 31 B5
Harrow HA1 ... 42 B4
Ilford RM6 ... 58 C2
Keston Mark BR2 ... 226 A6
Kingston u T KT2 ... 176 B3
Merton SW19 ... 179 C3

Cross Rd continued
Romford RM7 ... 59 C6
Sidcup DA14 ... 190 B6
South Harrow HA2 ... 63 D5
Sutton SM1 ... 218 B3
Wood Green N22 ... 32 C3
Cross St
2 Edmonton N18 ... 34 A5
Hampton TW12 ... 174 A5
Islington N1 ... 94 D6 234 D6
Mortlake SW13 ... 133 C2
Crossthwaite Ave SE5,
SE24 ... 139 B1
Crosstrees Ho 7 E14 ... 119 C3
Crosswall EC3 ... 117 D6 253 C6
Crossway
Dagenham RM8 ... 80 C5
Ealing W13 ... 87 A3
Enfield EN1 ... 17 C4
Finchley N12 ... 30 B4
Hayes UB3 ... 106 A5
Hendon NW9 ... 45 D5
Kingsland E8, N16 ... 73 C3
Petts Wood BR5 ... 211 B4
Ruislip HA4 ... 62 C4
Woodford IG8 ... 37 C6
Crossway Ct SE4 ... 141 A3
Crossway Par N22 ... 32 C3
Crossways
Ashford TW16 ... 171 D3
South Croydon CR2 ... 223 B1
Sutton SM2 ... 218 B1
Crossways Acad SE4 ... 141 A3
Crossways Par CR2 ... 223 B1
Crossways Rd
Beckenham BR3 ... 207 C3
Mitcham CR4 ... 203 B6
Crossways The
Heston TW5 ... 129 B5
Wembley HA9 ... 66 C5
Crossway The
Chislehurst SE9 ... 165 D2
Hillingdon UB10 ... 82 B5
Tottenham N22 ... 32 C3
Cross Way The HA3 ... 24 C1
Crosswell CI TW17 ... 171 A1
Croston St E8 ... 96 A6
Crothall CI N13 ... 16 B1
Crouch Ave IG11 ... 102 B5
Crouch CI BR3 ... 185 C4
Crouch Croft SE9 ... 166 C1
CROUCH END ... 49 D3
Crouch End Hill N8 ... 49 D2
Crouch Hall Ct N19 ... 50 A1
Crouch Hall Rd N8 ... 49 D3
Crouch Hill N4, N8, N19 ... 50 A2
Crouch Hill Sta N4 ... 50 B2
Crouchmans CI SE21,
SE26 ... 162 A1
Crouch Rd NW10 ... 67 B4
Crowborough Ct W13 ... 109 C6
Crowborough Path
WD19 ... 22 B6
Crowborough Rd
SW17 ... 181 A5
Crowden Way SE28 ... 124 C6
Crowder CI N12 ... 30 A3
Crowder St E1 ... 118 B6
Crowfield Ho N5 ... 73 A4
Crowfoot CI
Hackney Wick E9 ... 75 B3
Woolwich SE18 ... 123 C5
Crowhurst SE25 ... 206 A5
Crowhurst CI SW9 ... 138 C3
Crowhurst Ho N17 ... 34 B2
Crowhurst Ho 8 SW9 ... 138 D3
Crow La RM7, RM8 ... 59 D2
Crowland Ave UB3 ... 105 C2
Crowland Gdns N14 ... 16 A4
Crowland Ho NW8 ... 229 A5
Crowland Prim Sch
N15 ... 52 A4
Crowland Rd
South Norwood CR7 ... 205 A4
South Tottenham N15 ... 51 D4
Crowlands Ave RM7 ... 59 D3
Crowland Terr N1 ... 73 B1
Crowland Wlk SM4 ... 202 A3
Crowley Cres CR0 ... 220 C3
Crowline Wlk 1 N1 ... 73 A2
Crowmarsh Gdns
SE23 ... 162 C4
Crown Arc KT1 ... 175 C1
Crown Bldgs 4 E4 ... 20 B3
Crownbourne Ct SM1 ... 217 D4
Crown Ct Bow E3 ... 97 C6
Edgware NW7 ... 11 D2
Hampstead NW6 ... 69 D2
Hayes UB3 ... 105 D4
Walton-on-T KT12 ... 194 C2
Wood Green N22 ... 32 C2
Crown Close Bsns Ctr 12
E3 ... 97 C6
Crown Ct Bromley BR1 ... 209 D4
City of London EC4 ... 242 A1
Harrow HA2 ... 42 C1
Lee SE12 ... 165 B5
11 Muswell Hill N10 ... 31 A3
4 Putney SW15 ... 134 D1
St Giles WC2 ... 240 B1
St John's Wood NW8 ... 230 B1
3 Twickenham TW1 ... 153 B1
Crown Dale SE19 ... 183 A5
Crowndale Ct NW1 ... 232 C6
Crowndale Rd
NW1 ... 93 C5 232 B4

Crowne Ho SE1 ... 252 B3
Crownfield Ave IG2 ... 57 C4
Crownfield Rd E15 ... 76 B4
Crowngate Ho 33 E3 ... 97 B5
Crown Hill CR0 ... 221 A5
Crownhill Rd NW10 ... 89 D6
Crown Ho Ruislip HA4 ... 40 A1
Wembley HA9 ... 66 B3
Woolwich SE18 ... 123 A4
Crown La
Bromley Comm BR2 ... 209 D4
Chislehurst BR7 ... 189 A2
Merton SM4 ... 201 C6
Osidge N14 ... 15 C3
South Norwood SE19,
SW16 ... 182 C5
Crown Lane Gdns
SE27 ... 182 C5
Crown Lane Prim Sch
SE27 ... 182 C5
Crown Lane Spur BR2 ... 209 C3
Crownleigh Ct SW2 ... 160 C6
Crown Lo Chelsea SW3 ... 257 B3
Finchley N3 ... 29 B2
Crownmead Way RM7 ... 59 D5
Crown Mews
2 Newham E13 ... 99 C6
9 Stepney E1 ... 96 D2
Crown Mill CR4 ... 202 C4
Crown Office Row EC4 ... 251 A6
Crown Par London N14 ... 15 C3
Morden SM4 ... 201 D5
Crown Pas
Kingston u T KT1 ... 175 C1
St James SW1 ... 249 B1
Crown Pl
Broadgate EC2 ... 243 A4
Kentish Town NW5 ... 71 B2
Crown Point Par SE19 ... 182 D4
Crown Rd Enfield EN1 ... 6 B2
Ilford IG6 ... 57 B5
Kingston u T KT3 ... 177 A2
Morden SM4 ... 201 D5
Muswell Hill N10 ... 31 A3
Ruislip HA4 ... 62 D3
Sutton SM1 ... 217 D4
Twickenham TW1 ... 153 B5
Crown Reach SW1 ... 259 D1
Crown St Acton W3 ... 110 D5
Camberwell SE5 ... 139 A5
Dagenham RM10 ... 81 D2
Harrow HA2 ... 42 C1
Crownstone Ct 1
SW2 ... 160 C6
Crownstone Rd SW2 ... 160 C6
Crown Terr TW9 ... 132 B1
Crown Trad Ctr UB3 ... 105 C4
Crowntree CI TW7 ... 130 D6
Crown Way UB7 ... 104 B5
Crown Wlk HA9 ... 66 B5
Crown Wood La SE18 ... 144 D1
Crown Woods Sch
SE9 ... 167 A6
Crown Woods Way SE9 ... 167 B6
Crown Yard TW3 ... 130 A2
Crowshott Ave HA7 ... 25 D2
Crows Rd Barking IG11 ... 78 D2
Mill Meads E15 ... 98 B4
Crowther Ave TW8 ... 110 A3
Crowther CI
SW6 ... 135 B6 264 D6
Crowther Ct SE25 ... 206 A5
Crowthorne CI SW18 ... 157 B3
Crowthorne Rd W10 ... 90 D1
Croxall Ho KT12 ... 194 C3
Croxden CI HA8 ... 44 C6
Croxden Wlk SM4 ... 202 A3
Croxford Gdns N22 ... 32 D3
Croxley CI BR5 ... 190 B1
Croxley Gn BR5 ... 190 B2
Croxley Rd W9 ... 91 B4
Croxted CI SE21 ... 161 A4
Croxted Rd SE21, SE24 ... 161 B3
Croxteth Ho 11 SW8 ... 137 D3
Croxton 17 KT1 ... 176 C1
Croyde Ave
Greenford UB6 ... 86 A4
Hayes UB3 ... 105 C2
Croyde CI DA15 ... 167 B4
Croyden Ct HA0 ... 65 D2
CROYDON ... 221 B5
Croydon N17 ... 33 B1
Croydon Airport Ind Est
CR0 ... 220 B2
Croydon Coll CR0 ... 221 B6
Croydon Coll Annexe
CR0 ... 205 B1
**Croydon Coll (Selhurst
Tertiary Ctr)** SE25 ... 205 B4
Croydon Flyover The
CR0 ... 221 B5
Croydon Gr CR0 ... 204 C3
Croydon Ho
Lambeth SE1 ... 251 B2
Thornton Heath CR0 ... 204 B3
Croydon Rd
Bandonhill CR0, SM5,
SM6 ... 219 C5
Beckenham BR3 ... 207 A6
Coney Hall BR2, BR4 ... 224 D5
Harlington TW6 ... 126 D2
Keston Mark BR2, BR4,
BR6 ... 225 C5
Mitcham CR0, CR4 ... 203 C4
Newham E13 ... 98 D3
Penge SE20 ... 184 C2
Waddon CR0 ... 220 B4
Croydon Rd Ind Est
BR3 ... 206 D5

Croydon Valley Trade Pk
2 CR0 ... 204 A2
Croyland Rd N9 ... 18 A3
Croylands Dr KT6 ... 198 A2
Croysdale Ave TW16 ... 194 A6
Crozier Ho
Blackheath Pk SE3 ... 143 B2
South Lambeth SW8 ... 270 C3
Crozier Terr E9 ... 74 D3
Crucible Cl RM6 ... 58 B3
Crucifix La
SE1 ... 117 C4 253 A2
Cruden Ho 15 Bow E3 ... 97 B5
11 Camberwell SE17 ... 138 D6
Cruden St N1 ... 94 D6 234 D5
Cruickshank St WC1 ... 234 A2
Cruikshank Ho NW8 ... 230 B4
Cruikshank Rd E15 ... 76 C3
Crummock Gdns NW9 ... 45 C4
Crumpsall St SE2 ... 124 C2
Crundale Ave NW9 ... 44 C4
Crunden Rd CR2 ... 221 B1
Crusader Gdns CR0 ... 221 C5
Crusader Ho EC1 ... 241 C5
Crusader Ind Est N4 ... 51 A3
Crusoe Ct E11 ... 76 D5
Crusoe House Sch
N1 ... 95 B4 235 C2
Crusoe Mews N16 ... 73 B6
Crusoe Rd CR4 ... 180 D3
Crutched Friars
EC3 ... 117 C6 253 B6
Crutchfield La KT12 ... 194 B1
Crutchley Rd SE6 ... 164 C2
Crystal Ct SE19 ... 183 D5
Crystal Ctr The 1 HA1 ... 42 D4
Crystal Ho SE18 ... 123 D1
CRYSTAL PALACE ... 184 A5
Crystal Palace Mus*
SE19 ... 183 D4
Crystal Palace National
Sports Ctr SE20 ... 184 A4
Crystal Palace Par
SE19 ... 183 D5
Crystal Palace Park Rd
SE26 ... 184 B5
Crystal Palace Rd
SE22 ... 162 A6
Crystal Palace Sta
SE19 ... 184 A4
Crystal Palace Station Rd
SE19 ... 184 A4
Crystal Terr SE19 ... 183 B4
Crystal View Ct BR1 ... 186 B6
Crystal Way
Dagenham RM8 ... 58 C1
Harrow HA1 ... 42 D4
Crystal Wharf N1 ... 234 D3
Cuba Dr EN3 ... 6 C3
Cuba St E14 ... 119 C4
Cubitt Bldg SW1 ... 258 C1
Cubitt Ho 4 SW4 ... 159 C5
Cubitt Sq UB2 ... 108 A5
Cubitt St WC1 ... 94 B4 233 D1
Cubitt Terr SW4 ... 137 C2
CUBITT TOWN ... 120 A2
Cubitt Town Jun & Inf Sch
E14 ... 120 A3
Cuckoo Ave W7 ... 86 C3
Cuckoo Dene W7 ... 86 B2
Cuckoo Hall La N9 ... 18 D4
Cuckoo Hall Prim Sch
N9 ... 18 C4
Cuckoo Hill HA5 ... 40 C6
Cuckoo Hill Dr HA5 ... 40 C6
Cuckoo Hill Rd HA5 ... 40 D5
Cuckoo La W7 ... 108 C6
Cuda's Cl KT19 ... 215 D4
Cuddington SE17 ... 262 B4
Cuddington Ave KT19,
KT4 ... 215 D5
Cuddington Com Prim Sch
KT4 ... 215 D5
Cudham La N BR6 ... 227 C1
Cudham St SE6 ... 164 A4
Cudworth Ho SW8 ... 269 B1
Cudworth St E1 ... 96 B3
Cuff Cres SE9 ... 165 D5
Cuffley Ho 3 W10 ... 90 C2
Cuff Point 12 E2 ... 95 D4
Culand Ho SE17 ... 263 A3
Culford Gdns
SW3 ... 114 D2 257 D3
Culford Gr N1 ... 73 C2
Culford Mans SW3 ... 257 D3
Culford Mews N1 ... 73 C2
Culford Rd Kingsland N1 ... 73 C2
Shoreditch N1 ... 95 C6
Culgaith Gdns EN2 ... 4 A1
Culham Ho
21 Paddington W2 ... 91 C2
33 Shoreditch E2 ... 95 D4
Cullen Ho W9 ... 91 B5
Cullen Way NW10 ... 89 A3
Culling Rd SE16 ... 118 C3
Cullington Cl HA3 ... 43 A5
Cullingworth Rd NW10 ... 68 B3
Culloden Cl 21 SE16 ... 118 A1
Culloden Prim Sch E14 ... 98 A1
Culloden Rd EN2 ... 4 D3
Cullum St EC3 ... 253 A6
Culmington Mans
W13 ... 109 C6
Culmington Par W13 ... 109 C6
Culmington Rd
Ealing W13, W5 ... 109 C5
South Croydon CR2 ... 221 A1
Culmore Rd SE15 ... 140 C5
Culmstock Rd SW11 ... 159 A6
Culpepper Cl N18 ... 34 B5
Culpepper Ct SE11 ... 261 A4
Culross Bldgs NW1 ... 233 A4
Culross Cl N15 ... 51 A5
Culross St W1 ... 115 A6 248 A5
Culsac Rd KT6 ... 214 A6
Culver Ct SW18 ... 157 D5
Culverden Rd SW12 ... 159 C2
Culver Gr HA7 ... 25 C1
Culverhouse WC1 ... 240 C3
Culverhouse Gdns
SW16 ... 160 B1
Culverin Ct 1 N7 ... 72 B3
Culverlands Cl HA7 ... 25 B6
Culverley Ct N20 ... 14 B3
Culverley Rd SE6 ... 164 A3
Culvers Ave SM5 ... 218 D6
Culvers House Prim Sch
CR4 ... 203 A1
Culvers Retreat SM5 ... 218 D6
Culverstone Cl BR2 ... 208 D4
Culvers Way SM5 ... 218 D6
Culvert Ct SW11 ... 137 A3
Culverton Ct 3 DA14 ... 190 A6
Culvert Pl SW11 ... 137 A3
Culvert Rd
London SW11 ... 136 D3
South Tottenham N15 ... 51 C4
Culworth Ho NW8 ... 230 A4
Culworth St NW8 ... 230 A3
Cumber Ho SW18 ... 157 C3
Cumberland Ave
Falconwood DA16 ... 145 D1
Wembley NW10 ... 88 D4
Cumberland Bsns Pk
NW10 ... 88 D4
Cumberland Cl
Dalston E8 ... 73 D2
2 Twickenham TW1 ... 153 B5
8 Wimbledon SW20 ... 178 D3
Cumberland Cres W14 ... 254 B4
Cumberland Ct
4 Croydon CR0 ... 205 B1
7 Finchley N3 ... 29 B1
Harrow HA1 ... 42 C6
Marylebone W1 ... 237 D1
Woodford IG8 ... 37 B3
Cumberland Dr
Chessington KT9 ... 214 B5
Erith DA7 ... 147 A5
Hinchley Wood KT10 ... 213 A6
Cumberland Gate
W1 ... 114 D6 247 D6
Cumberland Gdns
Church End NW4 ... 29 A1
Finsbury WC1 ... 234 A2
Cumberland Ho
Edmonton N9 ... 18 C3
Kingston u T KT2 ... 176 D3
Paddington W9 ... 236 A5
1 Putney SW15 ... 156 C4
Woolwich SE28 ... 123 B4
Cumberland Mans
Marylebone W1 ... 237 C2
7 West Hampstead
NW6 ... 69 C3
Cumberland Market
NW1 ... 93 B4 231 D2
Cumberland Mills Sq
E14 ... 120 B1
Cumberland Park Ind Est
NW10 ... 90 A4
Cumberland Pk W3 ... 111 A6
Cumberland Pl
Catford SE6 ... 164 D3
Regent's Pk NW1 ... 231 C2
Sunbury TW16 ... 194 A5
Cumberland Rd
Acton W3 ... 111 A6
Ashford TW15 ... 148 A1
Barnes SW13 ... 134 A4
Beckenham BR2 ... 208 D6
Croydon SE25 ... 206 B3
Edmonton N9 ... 18 C3
Hanwell W7 ... 108 D4
Harrow HA1 ... 41 D4
Higham Hill E17 ... 35 A1
Manor Pk E12 ... 77 D4
Newham E13 ... 99 B3
Richmond TW9 ... 132 C5
Stanmore HA7, HA8 ... 44 B6
Wood Green N22 ... 32 B1
Cumberland Sch E13 ... 99 C3
Cumberland St
SW1 ... 115 B1 258 D2
Cumberland Terr NW1 ... 231 C3
Cumberland Terrace
Mews NW1 ... 231 C3
Cumberland Villas
W3 ... 111 A6
Cumberland Wharf 12
SE16 ... 118 C4
Cumberlow Ave SE25 ... 206 A6
Cumbernauld Gdns
TW16 ... 171 D5
Cumberton Rd N17 ... 33 B2
Cumbrae Gdns KT6 ... 213 D6
Cumbrian Gdns NW2 ... 69 A6
Cuming Mus* SE17 ... 262 A3
Cumming St N1 ... 233 D3
Cumnor Cl 23 SW9 ... 138 B3
Cumnor Gdns KT17 ... 216 A2
Cumnor Rd SM2 ... 218 A2
Cunard Cres N21 ... 17 B5
Cunard Pl EC3 ... 243 B1
Cunard Rd NW10 ... 89 B4
Cunard Wlk 3 SE16 ... 119 A2
Cundy Rd E16 ... 99 C1
Cundy St SW1 ... 115 A2 258 B3
Cunliffe Rd KT19 ... 215 D4
Cunliffe St SW16 ... 181 C4
Cunningham Cl
Dagenham RM6 ... 58 C4
West Wickham BR4 ... 223 D6
Cunningham Ct
Harrow HA1 ... 42 B4
Paddington W2 ... 236 C5
Cunningham Ho 16
SE5 ... 139 B5
Cunningham Pk HA1 ... 42 B4
Cunningham Pl
NW8 ... 92 B3 236 C6
Cunningham Rd N15 ... 52 A5
Cunnington St W4 ... 111 A2
Cupar Rd SW11 ... 268 B2
Cupola Cl BR1 ... 187 B5
Cureton St
SW1 ... 115 D2 259 D3
Curie Gdns NW9 ... 27 C1
Curie Ho 1 HA9 ... 67 A5
Curlew Cl SE28 ... 124 D6
Curlew Ct KT6 ... 214 C5
Curlew Ho
Brockley SE4 ... 141 A1
Enfield EN3 ... 18 D6
7 Peckham SE15 ... 139 D4
Curlew St SE1 ... 117 D4 253 D2
Curlew Way UB4 ... 84 D2
Curness St SE13 ... 142 A1
Curnick's La SE27 ... 183 A6
Curran Ave
Bexley DA15 ... 167 D6
Hackbridge SM6 ... 219 A5
Curran Ho SW3 ... 257 A3
Currey Rd UB6 ... 64 B2
Curricle St W3 ... 111 C5
Currie Hill Cl SW19 ... 179 B6
Currie Ho 13 SW12 ... 159 D4
Curry Rise NW7 ... 28 D4
Cursitor St EC4 ... 94 C1 241 A2
Curtain Pl EC2 ... 243 B6
Curtain Rd EC2 ... 95 C3 243 B6
Curthwaite Gdns EN2 ... 15 D6
Curtis Dr W3 ... 89 B1
Curtis Field Rd SW16 ... 182 C6
Curtis Ho 7 London N11 ... 31 C5
Walworth SE17 ... 262 C2
Curtis La HA0 ... 66 A3
Curtis Rd
Twickenham TW4 ... 151 B4
West Ewell KT19 ... 215 A4
Curtis St SE1 ... 117 D2 263 C4
Curtis Way
Bermondsey SE1 ... 263 C4
7 Thamesmead SE28 ... 124 B6
Curtlington Ho 8 HA8 ... 27 A1
Curve Bldg The SE4 ... 163 B6
Curve The Ealing W5 ... 109 D4
Shepherd's Bush W12 ... 112 A6
Curwen Ave E7 ... 77 B4
Curwen & New Acad Gall*
W1 ... 239 C3
Curwen Prim Sch E13 ... 99 A5
Curwen Rd W12 ... 112 A4
Curzon Ave Enfield EN3 ... 18 D6
Stanmore HA7 ... 25 A2
Curzon Cl BR6 ... 227 B4
Curzon Cres
Barking IG11 ... 101 D4
Willesden NW10 ... 67 C1
Curzon Ct SE9 ... 167 A1
Curzon Gate W1 ... 248 B3
Curzon Ho W5 ... 87 B3
Curzon Pl HA5 ... 40 C4
Curzon Rd Ealing W5 ... 87 B3
Muswell Hill N10 ... 31 B1
Thornton Heath CR7 ... 204 C3
Curzon Sq W1 ... 248 B3
Curzon St W1 ... 115 B5 248 C4
Cusack Cl TW1 ... 174 D6
Custance Ho N1 ... 235 C3
Custance St N1 ... 235 C2
CUSTOM HOUSE ... 121 C6
Custom House
EC3 ... 117 C6 253 A5
Custom House for ExCeL
Sta E16 ... 121 B6
Custom House Reach
SE16 ... 119 B3
Cutbush Ho N7 ... 71 D3
Cutcombe Rd SE5 ... 139 A3
Cuthberga Cl IG11 ... 79 A1
Cuthbert Gdns SE25 ... 205 C6
Cuthbert Harrowing Ho
EC1 ... 242 A5
Cuthbert Ho W2 ... 236 C4
Cuthbert Rd
Croydon CR0 ... 220 D6
8 Edmonton N18 ... 34 A6
Walthamstow E17 ... 54 A6
Cuthbert St W2 ... 236 C5
Cuthill Wlk 3 SE5 ... 139 B4
Cutlers Gdns EC2 ... 243 B2
Cutlers Gdns Arc EC2 ... 243 B2
Cutlers Sq E14 ... 119 C2
Cutler St EC2 ... 243 B2
Cut The SE1 ... 116 C4 251 B2
Cutty Sark* SE10 ... 142 A6
Cutty Sark Ho 10 E14 ... 119 D2
Cutty Sark Ret
Development SE10 ... 142 A6
Cutty Sark Sta SE10 ... 142 A6
Cuxton BR5 ... 211 A4
Cuxton Cl DA6 ... 169 A6
Cuxton Ho SE17 ... 263 B2
Cyclamen Cl 4 TW12 ... 173 C4
Cyclamen Way KT19 ... 215 A3
Cyclops Mews 12 E14 ... 119 C2
Cygnet Ave TW14 ... 150 D4
Cygnet Cl NW10 ... 67 B3
Cygnet Ct EN3 ... 7 A4
Cygnet Ho Harrow HA7 ... 24 D4
St John's Wood NW8 ... 229 A6
Cygnet House N 18 E14 ... 97 D1
Cygnet House S 19 E14 ... 97 D1
Cygnet St E1 ... 243 D6
Cygnets The TW13 ... 173 A6
Cygnet Way UB4 ... 84 D2
Cygnus Bsns Ctr NW10 ... 67 D2
Cymbeline Ct 6 HA1 ... 42 D3
Cyna Ct 5 E11 ... 55 A3
Cynthia St N1 ... 233 D3
Cyntra Pl 8 E8 ... 74 B1
Cypress Ave London N2 ... 47 D6
Twickenham TW2 ... 152 A4
Cypress Cl 9 E5 ... 74 A6
Cypress Ct Cheam SM1 ... 217 C2
5 Leyton E11 ... 76 B4
7 West Norwood
SW16 ... 182 C5
Cypress Gdns SE4 ... 163 A6
Cypress Ho SE14 ... 140 D4
Cypress Inf Sch SE25 ... 183 C1
Cypress Jun Sch SE25 ... 183 C1
Cypress Lo SE25 ... 183 C1
Cypress Pl W1 ... 239 B5
Cypress Rd Harrow HA3 ... 24 B1
South Norwood SE25 ... 183 C1
Cypress Tree Cl DA15 ... 167 D3
CYPRUS ... 122 C6
Cyprus Ave N3 ... 29 A1
Cyprus Cl N4 ... 50 C3
Cyprus Ct 9 N3 ... 29 B1
Cyprus Gdns N3 ... 29 A1
Cyprus Ho 10 N3 ... 29 B1
Cyprus Pl
23 Bethnal Green E2 ... 96 C5
Newham E6 ... 122 C6
Cyprus Rd
Church End N3 ... 29 B1
Edmonton N9 ... 17 D2
Cyprus St E2 ... 96 C5
Cyprus Sta E6 ... 122 C6
Cyrena Rd SE22 ... 161 D6
Cyril Jackson Prim Sch
(North Bldg) E14 ... 119 B6
Cyril Jackson Prim Sch
(South Bldg) E14 ... 119 B6
Cyril Lo 2 DA14 ... 190 A6
Cyril Mans SW11 ... 267 D1
Cyril Rd DA7 ... 147 A3
Cyril Smith Ho N13 ... 32 B5
Cyril Thatcher Ho
SW6 ... 265 B1
Cyrus Ho EC1 ... 241 D6
Cyrus St EC1 ... 94 D3 241 D6
Czar St SE8 ... 141 C6

D

Dabbs Hill La UB5 ... 63 C3
Dabb's La EC1 ... 241 B5
Dabin Cres SE10 ... 142 A4
Dacca St SE8 ... 141 B6
Dace Rd E3 ... 97 C6
Dacre Cl UB6 ... 85 D5
Dacre Gdns
Borehamwood WD6 ... 11 B6
Lewisham SE13 ... 142 C1
Dacre Ho SW3 ... 266 D5
Dacre Pk SE13 ... 142 C1
Dacre Pl SE13 ... 142 C2
Dacre Rd
Leytonstone E11 ... 54 D1
Newham E13 ... 99 B6
Thornton Heath CR0 ... 204 A2
Dacres Rd SE23 ... 162 D1
Dacre St SW1 ... 115 D3 259 C6
Dade Way UB2 ... 107 B1
Daerwood Cl BR2 ... 210 B1
Daffodil Cl CR0 ... 206 D1
Daffodil Gdns IG1 ... 78 D3
Daffodil Pl 7 TW12 ... 173 C4
Daffodil St W12 ... 111 D6
Dafforne Rd SW17 ... 159 A1
DAGENHAM ... 81 D1
Dagenham Ave
Dagenham RM9 ... 81 B1
Dagenham RM9 ... 103 A6
Dagenham Dock Sta
RM9 ... 103 B5
Dagenham East Sta
RM10 ... 81 D3
Dagenham Heathway Sta
RM9 ... 81 B2
Dagenham Park Com Sch
RM10 ... 103 D6
Dagenham Rd
Dagenham RM10 ... 81 D4
London E10 ... 53 B1
Dagger La WD23 ... 9 A6
Dagmar Ave HA9 ... 66 B4
Dagmar Ct
Cubitt Town E14 ... 120 A3
South Tottenham N15 ... 51 B5
Dagmar Gdns NW10 ... 90 D5
Dagmar Mews UB2 ... 107 A3
Dagmar Pas N1 ... 234 D6
Dagmar Rd
Camberwell SE5 ... 139 C4
Finsbury Pk N4 ... 50 C2
4 Kingston u T KT2 ... 176 C3
Southall UB2 ... 107 A3
South Norwood SE25 ... 205 C4
West Green N15 ... 51 B5
Wood Green N22 ... 31 D2
Dagmar Terr
N1 ... 94 D6 234 D6
Dagnall Pk SE25 ... 205 C4
Dagnall Rd SE25 ... 205 C4
Dagnall St
SW11 ... 137 A4 268 A1
Dagnan Rd SW12 ... 159 C4
Dagobert Ho 27 E1 ... 96 C2
Dagonet Gdns BR1 ... 165 A1
Dagonet Rd BR1 ... 165 A1
Dahlia Gdns Ilford IG1 ... 78 D2
Mitcham CR4 ... 203 D5
Dahlia Rd SE2 ... 124 B2
Dahomey Rd SW16 ... 181 C4
Daiglen Sch The IG9 ... 21 C2
Daimler Ho 8 E3 ... 97 C3
Daimler Way SM6 ... 220 A1
Daines Cl E12 ... 78 B5
Dainford Cl BR1 ... 186 B5
Dainton Cl 1 BR1 ... 187 B2
Dainton Ho 22 W2 ... 91 C2
Daintry Cl HA3 ... 43 A5
Daintry Way E9 ... 75 B2
Dairsie Ct 3 BR1 ... 187 C1
Dairsie Rd SE9 ... 144 C2
Dairy Cl Bromley BR1 ... 187 B3
South Norwood CR7 ... 183 A1
Willesden NW10 ... 90 A6
Dairy La SE18 ... 122 B2
Dairyman Cl NW2 ... 69 A5
Dairy Meadow Prim Sch
UB2 ... 107 B3
Daisy Cl CR0 ... 206 D1
Daisy Dormer Ct 11
SW9 ... 138 B1
Daisy Ho IG3 ... 58 A1
Daisy La SW6 ... 135 C2
Daisy Rd Newham E16 ... 98 C3
Woodford E18 ... 37 B1
Dakin Pl 9 E1 ... 97 A2
Dakota bldg 6 SE13 ... 141 D4
Dakota Cl SM6 ... 220 B1
Dakota Gdns
Newham E6 ... 100 A3
Northolt UB5 ... 85 A4
Dalberg Rd SW2 ... 160 C6
Dalberg Way SE2 ... 124 D3
Dalbury Ho 6 SW9 ... 138 B1
Dalby Rd SW18 ... 136 A1
Dalbys Cres N17 ... 33 C4
Dalby St NW5 ... 71 B2
Dalcross Rd TW4, TW5 ... 129 A3
Dale Ave Edgware HA8 ... 26 B1
Hounslow TW4 ... 129 A2
Dalebury Rd SW17 ... 158 D2
Dale Cl
Blackheath Pk SE3 ... 143 A2
New Barnet EN5 ... 13 D5
Pinner HA5 ... 22 B2
Dale Croft N4 ... 73 A5
Dale Ct Cranley Gdns N8 ... 49 C5
3 Kingston u T KT2 ... 176 B3
Northolt UB5 ... 63 B1
Wembley HA0 ... 65 D4
Woodford E18 ... 37 A1
Dale Dr UB4 ... 83 D4
Dalefield IG9 ... 21 D3
Dale Gdns IG8 ... 37 B6
Dale Gr N12 ... 30 A5
Dale Green Rd N11 ... 15 B1
Dalehaed NW1 ... 232 A3
Daleham Dr UB8 ... 82 D1
Daleham Gdns NW3 ... 70 B2
Daleham Mews NW3 ... 70 B2
Dale Ho London SE4 ... 141 A1
St John's Wood NW8 ... 229 A6
Dale Lo N6 ... 49 C3
Dalemain Ho 5 SW8 ... 137 D3
Dalemain Mews 12
E16 ... 121 A5
Dale Park Ave SM5 ... 218 D6
Dale Park Rd SE19 ... 183 B2
Dale Rd Ashford TW16 ... 171 D3
Camberwell SE17 ... 138 D6
Cheam SM1 ... 217 B4
Gospel Oak NW5 ... 71 A3
Southall UB6 ... 85 D2
Walton-on-T KT12 ... 193 D2
Dale Row W11 ... 91 A1
Daleside Rd
Streatham SW17 ... 181 B5
West Ewell KT19 ... 215 B2
Dales Path WD6 ... 11 B6
Dales Rd WD6 ... 11 B6
Dale St W4 ... 111 C1
Dale The BR2 ... 225 D4
Dale View Ave E4 ... 20 A2
Dale View Cres E4 ... 20 A1
Dale View Gdns E4 ... 20 B1
Daleview Rd N15 ... 51 C3
Dalewood Gdns KT4 ... 216 B6
Dale Wood Rd BR6 ... 211 C1
Daley Ho 6 W12 ... 90 B1
Daley St E9 ... 74 D2
Daley Thompson Way 7
SW8 ... 137 B2
Dalgarno Gdns W10 ... 90 C2
Dalgarno Way W10 ... 90 C3
Daling Way E3 ... 97 A5
Dalkeith Ct SW1 ... 259 D3
Dalkeith Gr HA7 ... 26 A5
Dalkeith Ho 6 SW9 ... 138 D4
Dalkeith Rd Ilford IG1 ... 79 A5
West Norwood SE21 ... 161 A4
Dallas Ct SM3 ... 217 A2
Dallas Rd Cheam SM3 ... 217 A2
Ealing W5 ... 88 B2
Forest Hill SE26 ... 162 B1
Hendon NW4 ... 46 A2
Dallas Terr UB3 ... 105 D3
Dallega Cl UB3 ... 105 B6
Dallinger Rd SE12 ... 164 D5
Dalling Rd W6 ... 112 B2
Dallington Sch
EC1 ... 94 D3 241 D6
Dallington St
EC1 ... 94 D3 241 D6
Dallin Rd Bexley DA6 ... 146 D1
Woolwich SE18 ... 144 D5
Dalmain Prim Sch
SE23 ... 163 A3
Dalmain Rd SE23 ... 162 D3
Dalmally Pas CR0 ... 205 D2
Dalmally Passage
CR0 ... 205 D3
Dalmally Rd CR0 ... 206 A2
Dalmeny Ave
Thornton Heath
SW16 ... 182 C1
Tufnell Pk N7 ... 71 D4
Dalmeny Avenue Est 3
N7 ... 71 D4
Dalmeny Cl HA0 ... 65 C2
Dalmeny Cres TW3 ... 130 B1
Dalmeny Ct 4 SW4 ... 138 A3
Dalmeny Rd Erith DA8 ... 147 D4
New Barnet EN5 ... 14 A5
North Cheam KT4 ... 216 B5
Tufnell Pk N7 ... 71 D4
Wallington SM5 ... 219 A1
Dalmeyer Rd NW10 ... 67 D2
Dalmore Ave KT10 ... 212 D2
Dalmore Rd SE21 ... 161 A2
Dalrymple Cl N14 ... 15 D4
Dalrymple Rd SE4 ... 141 A1
DALSTON ... 74 A2
Dalston Gdns HA7 ... 26 A1
Dalston Jct E8 ... 73 D2
Dalston Kingsland Sta
E8 ... 73 D3
Dalston La E8 ... 74 A3
Dalton Ave CR4 ... 180 C1
Dalton Cl Hayes UB4 ... 83 B3
Orpington BR6 ... 227 C5
Dalton Ho
7 Balham SW12 ... 159 B4
10 Bow E3 ... 97 A5
19 Deptford SE14 ... 140 D6
Merton SW19 ... 180 A2
Stanmore HA7 ... 25 B5
Dalton St SE27 ... 160 D1
Daltry Ho HA1 ... 42 D5
Dalwood St SE5 ... 139 C4
Daly Ct E15 ... 76 A3
Daly Dr BR1 ... 210 C6
Dalyell Rd SW9 ... 138 B2
Damascene Wlk SE21 ... 161 A3
Damask Cres E16 ... 98 C3
Damask Ct SM1 ... 201 D1
Damer Ho 9 TW10 ... 154 B5
Damer Terr SW10 ... 266 B3
Dames Rd E7 ... 77 A5
Dame St N1 ... 95 A5 235 A4
Damien Ct 12 E1 ... 96 B1
Damien St E1 ... 96 B1
Damon Cl DA14 ... 168 B1
Damon Ct DA14 ... 168 B1
Damon Ho 2 N12 ... 30 B5
Damory Ho 1 SE16 ... 118 C2
Damson Dr UB3 ... 106 A6
Damsonwood Rd UB2 ... 107 C3
Danbrook Rd SW16 ... 182 A3
Dan Bryant Ho 5
SW12 ... 159 C4
Danbury Cl RM6 ... 58 D6
Danbury Mans 3 IG11 ... 78 D1
Danbury Mews SM5,
SM6 ... 219 B4
Danbury St N1 ... 94 D5 234 D4
Danbury Way IG8 ... 37 C4
Danby Ct EN2 ... 5 A2
Danby Ho
23 Hackney E9 ... 74 C1
3 West Kilburn W10 ... 91 B4
Danby St SE15 ... 139 D2
Dancastle Ct 7 N3 ... 29 C2
Dancer Rd
Fulham SW6 ... 135 B4 264 C1
Richmond TW9 ... 132 C2
Dando Cres SE3 ... 143 B2
Dandridge Cl SE10 ... 120 D1
Dandridge Ho E1 ... 243 C4
Danebury
New Addington CR0 ... 223 D2
18 North Kensington
W10 ... 90 C2
Danebury Ave SW15 ... 155 D5
Daneby Rd SE6 ... 164 A2
Dane Cl
Farnborough BR6 ... 227 B3
Sidcup DA5 ... 169 C4
Danecourt Gdns CR0 ... 221 D5
Danecroft Rd SE24 ... 161 B6
Daneglen Ct 18 HA7 ... 25 C5
Danegrove Prim Sch
EN4 ... 14 C5
Danegrove Sch EN4 ... 14 D5
Danehill Wlk DA14 ... 168 A1
Dane Ho
15 London SE5 ... 139 A3
Upper Tooting SW17 ... 180 A6
Danehurst TW8 ... 131 C5
Danehurst Gdns IG4 ... 56 B4
Danehurst St
SW6 ... 135 A4 264 A2
Daneland EN4 ... 14 D5
Danemead Gr UB5 ... 63 D3
Danemere St SW15 ... 134 C2
Dane Pl E3 ... 97 B5
Dane Rd Ashford TW15 ... 171 B4

Dane Rd *continued*
Ealing W13 ... 109 C5
Ilford IG1 ... 79 A3
Lower Edmonton N18 ... 18 C1
Merton SW19 ... 180 A2
Southall UB1 ... 107 A6
Danesbury Rd TW13 ... 150 B3
Danescombe SE12 ... 165 A3
Danescourt Cres SM1 .. 218 A6
Danescroft Hendon NW4 . 46 D4
3 North Finchley N12 ... 30 A5
Danescroft Ave NW4 ... 46 D4
Danescroft Gdns NW4 ... 46 D4
Danes Ct
Primrose Hill NW8 ... 230 C5
Wembley HA9 ... 66 D5
Danesdale Rd E9 ... 75 A2
Danesfield SE5 ... 139 C6
Danes Gate HA1 ... 42 C6
Danes Ho 10 W10 ... 90 C2
Dane St WC1 ... 240 C3
Daneswood Ave SE6 ... 164 A1
Danethorpe Rd HA0 ... 65 D2
Danetree Cl KT19 ... 215 A1
Danetree Jun Sch
KT19 ... 215 A1
Danetree Rd KT19 ... 215 A1
Danette Gdns RM8 ... 81 B6
Daneville Rd SE5 ... 139 B4
Danford Ho 9 N11 ... 31 C5
Dangan Rd E11 ... 55 A3
Daniel Almshouse NW4 . 46 B5
Daniel Bolt Cl E14 ... 97 D2
Daniel Cl London N18 ... 34 C6
Twickenham TW4 ... 151 B4
Upper Tooting SW17 ... 180 C4
Daniel Ct Acton W3 ... 111 C6
3 Beckenham BR3 ... 185 C3
7 Edgware HA8 ... 26 D5
10 Hendon NW9 ... 27 C2
Daniel Gdns SE15 ... 139 D5
Daniel Ho 1 HA5 ... 22 C1
Daniell Ho N1 ... 235 D4
Daniell Way CR0 ... 204 B1
Daniel Pl NW4 ... 46 B2
Daniel Rd W5 ... 110 B6
Daniel's Rd SE15 ... 140 C2
Dan Leno Wlk SW6 ... 265 C3
Dansey Pl W1 ... 249 C6
Dansington Rd DA16 ... 146 A1
Danson Cres DA16 ... 146 B2
Danson House* DA6 ... 146 C1
Danson Intc DA5 ... 168 C5
Danson La DA16 ... 146 B1
Danson Mead DA16 ... 146 C2
Danson Prim Sch
DA16 ... 146 A1
Danson Rd DA5 ... 168 D6
Danson Underpass
DA5 ... 168 C5
Dante Pl SE11 ... 261 D3
Dante Rd SE11 .. 116 D2 261 C4
Danube Ct 13 SE15 ... 139 D5
Danube St
SW3 ... 114 C1 257 B2
Danvers Ho 35 E1 ... 96 A1
Danvers Rd N8 ... 49 D5
Danvers St
SW3 ... 136 B6 266 D5
Da Palma Ct SW6 ... 265 A5
Daphne Ct Ealing W5 ... 87 C1
Wembley HA0 ... 65 D3
Worcester Pk KT4 ... 215 C6
Daphne Gdns E4 ... 20 A1
Daphne Ho N22 ... 32 C2
Daphne St SW18 ... 158 A5
Daplyn St 6 E1 ... 96 A2
D'arblay St W1 .. 93 C1 239 B1
Darby Cres TW16 ... 172 C1
Darby Gdns TW16 ... 172 C1
Darcy Ave SM6 ... 219 C4
Darcy Cl N20 ... 14 B2
D'arcy Dr HA3 ... 43 D5
D'arcy Gdns
Dagenham RM9 ... 103 B6
Harrow HA3 ... 44 A5
Darcy Ho E8 ... 96 B6
D'arcy Pl BR2 ... 209 A5
Darcy Rd
Isleworth TW7 ... 131 A4
Thornton Heath SW16 .. 182 A1
D'arcy Rd SM3 ... 216 D4
Dare Ct 2 E10 ... 54 A2
Dare Gdns RM8 ... 81 A5
Darell Prim Sch TW9 .. 132 C2
Darell Rd TW9 ... 132 C2
Daren Ct N7 ... 72 A4
Darent Ho
4 Catford BR1 ... 186 B5
Lisson Gr NW8 ... 236 D4
Darenth Rd
Stamford Hill N16 ... 51 D1
Welling DA16 ... 146 A4
Darfield NW1 ... 232 A5
Darfield Rd SE4 ... 163 B6
Darfield Way W10 ... 90 D1
Darfur St SW15 ... 134 D2
Dargate Cl SE19 ... 183 D3
Darien Ho
17 London SW11 ... 136 B2
11 Stepney E1 ... 96 D2
Darien Rd SW11 ... 136 B2
Daring Ho 23 E3 ... 97 A5
Darland Ho SE9 ... 167 B5
Darlands Dr EN5 ... 12 D6
Darlan Rd SW6 . 135 B5 264 D3
Darlaston Rd SW19 ... 179 A3
Darley Cl CR0 ... 207 A3
Darley Dr KT3 ... 177 B1
Darley Gdns SM4 ... 201 D3
Darley Ho SE11 ... 260 C1
Darley Rd
Clapham SW11 ... 158 D5
Edmonton N9 ... 17 D3
Darling Ho 12 TW1 ... 153 D5
Darling Rd SE4 ... 141 C2
Darling Row E1 ... 96 B3
Darlington Ct 8 SE6 ... 164 D3
Darlington Ho
South Lambeth SW8 ... 269 D3
2 Surbiton KT6 ... 197 D2
Darlington Rd SE27 ... 182 D5
Darmaine Cl CR2 ... 221 A1
Darnall Ho 4 SE10 ... 142 A4
Darnay Ho 3 SE16 ... 118 A3
Darndale Cl E17 ... 35 B1
Darnell Ho 9 SE10 ... 142 A5
Darnley Ho 7 E14 ... 97 A1
Darnley Rd Hackney E9 ... 74 C2
Woodford IG8 ... 37 B2
Darnley Terr 12 W11 ... 112 D5
Darrell Ct BR2 ... 208 C6
Darrell Rd SE22 ... 162 A6
Darren Cl N4 ... 50 B2
Darrick Wood Ho BR6 .. 227 A5
Darrick Wood Inf Sch
BR6 ... 226 D5
Darrick Wood Jun Sch
BR6 ... 226 D4
Darrick Wood Rd BR6 .. 227 B6
Darrick Wood Sch
BR6 ... 226 D5
Darrick Wood Sports Ctr
BR6 ... 227 A5
Darris Cl UB4 ... 85 A3
Darsley Dr
SW8 ... 138 A4 270 A2
Dartford Ave N9 ... 18 D5
Dartford Gdns RM6 ... 58 B4
Dartford Ho SE1 ... 263 D4
Dartford St SE17 ... 139 A6
Dartington NW1 ... 232 B5
Dartington Ho
Bayswater W2 ... 91 D2
7 London SW8 ... 137 D3
Dartle Ct 29 SE16 ... 118 A4
Dartmoor Wlk 18 E14 ... 119 C2
Dartmouth Cl W11 ... 91 C1
Dartmouth Ct SE10 ... 142 A4
Dartmouth Gr SE10 ... 142 A4
Dartmouth Hill SE10 ... 142 A4
Dartmouth Ho
Dartmouth Pk N19 ... 71 B6
11 Kingston u T KT2 ... 176 A2
Lewisham SE10 ... 142 A3
Thornton Heath CR0 ... 204 D2
DARTMOUTH PARK ... 71 B5
Dartmouth Park Ave
NW5 ... 71 B5
Dartmouth Park Hill
N19 ... 71 B6
Dartmouth Park Rd
NW5 ... 71 B5
Dartmouth Pl
Chiswick W4 ... 133 C6
Forest Hill SE23 ... 162 C2
Dartmouth Rd
Brondesbury NW2 ... 68 D2
Forest Hill SE23, SE26 .. 162 C1
Hayes BR2 ... 209 A2
Hendon NW4 ... 46 A3
Ruislip HA4 ... 62 A5
Dartmouth Row SE10 .. 142 A4
Dartmouth St
SW1 ... 115 D4 249 D1
Dartmouth Terr SE10 .. 142 B4
Dartnell Rd CR0 ... 205 D2
Darton Ct W3 ... 111 A5
Dartrey Twr SW10 ... 266 C4
Dartrey Wlk
SW10 ... 136 A5 266 B4
Dart St W10 ... 91 B4
Darville Rd N16 ... 73 D5
Darwell Cl E6 ... 100 C5
Darwen Pl E2 ... 96 B6
Darwin Cl
Farnborough BR6 ... 227 B3
New Southgate N11 ... 15 B1
Darwin Ct Eltham SE9 .. 166 C5
Newham E13 ... 99 B4
Primrose Hill NW1 ... 231 B6
Darwin Dr UB1 ... 85 D1
Darwin Gdns WD19 ... 22 C5
Darwin Ho
8 London SE13 ... 142 A3
2 Wembley HA9 ... 67 A5
Darwin Rd Ealing W5 .. 109 C2
Falconwood DA16 ... 145 D2
Tottenham N22 ... 32 D1
Darwin St
SE17 ... 117 B2 262 D4
Daryngton Dr UB6 ... 86 C5
Daryngton Ho SW8 ... 270 A3
Dashwood Cl DA6 ... 169 C6
Dashwood Ct TW3 ... 130 A1
Dashwood Ho SE21 ... 161 D1
Dashwood Rd N8 ... 50 B3
Dassett Rd SE27 ... 182 D5
Data Point Bsns Ctr
E16 ... 98 B3
Datchelor Pl 14 SE5 ... 139 B4
Datchet Ho NW1 ... 231 D2
Datchet Rd SE6 ... 163 B2
Datchett Ho 40 E2 ... 95 D4
Datchwood Ct N4 ... 73 A5
Datchworth Ct 7 EN1 ... 17 C6
Datchworth Ho 8 N1 ... 72 D1
Date St SE17 ... 117 B1 262 C1
Daubeney Gdns N17 ... 33 A3
Daubeney Pl TW12 ... 173 D1
Daubeney Prim Sch E5 . 75 A4
Daubeney Rd
Clapton Pk E5 ... 75 A4
Tottenham N17 ... 33 A3
Daubeney Twr 2 SE8 .. 119 B1
Dault Rd SW18 ... 158 A5
Dauney Ho SE1 ... 251 C1
Dauphine Ct HA3 ... 24 C1
Dave Adams Ho 8 E3 ... 97 B5
Davenant Ho 20 E1 ... 96 A2
Davenant Rd
Croydon CR0, CR9 ... 220 D4
Upper Holloway N19 ... 71 D6
Davenant St E1 ... 96 A2
Davenport Cl TW11 ... 175 A4
Davenport Ctr IG11 ... 102 B5
Davenport Ho SE11 ... 261 A5
Davenport Lo TW3 ... 129 A5
Davenport Mews 6
W12 ... 112 B5
Davenport Rd
London SE6 ... 164 A5
Sidcup DA14 ... 169 A2
Daventer Dr HA7 ... 24 D3
Daventry Ave E17 ... 53 C3
Daventry St
NW1 ... 92 C2 237 A4
Dave Porter Hts
SW19 ... 157 A4
Dave Ramsey Ho SE18 .. 123 B2
Daver Ct Chelsea SW3 .. 257 B1
Ealing W5 ... 87 D3
Davern Cl SE10 ... 120 D2
Davey Cl Bowes Pk N13 ... 32 B5
Islington N7 ... 72 B2
Davey Ho HA9 ... 67 A6
Davey Rd E9 ... 75 C1
Davey's Ct WC2 ... 250 A6
Davey St SE15 ... 139 D6
David Ave UB6 ... 86 C5
David Beckham Acad The
SE10 ... 120 D4
David Cl UB3 ... 127 C5
David Coffer Ct DA17 .. 125 D2
David Ct N20 ... 14 A1
David Devine Ho 8 E8 .. 74 A3
David Game Coll SW7 . 256 C3
Davidge Ho SE1 ... 251 B1
Davidge St
SE1 ... 116 D4 251 D1
David Henry Waring Ct
TW14 ... 149 A3
David Hewitt Ho 2 E3 .. 97 D2
David Ho
8 Putney SW15 ... 156 A6
South Lambeth SW8 ... 270 A4
South Norwood SE25 .. 206 A6
David Lee Point 4 E15 .. 98 C6
David Livingstone Prim
Sch CR7 ... 183 A2
David Mews W1 ... 237 D4
David Rd RM8 ... 81 A6
Davidson Gdns
SW8 ... 138 A5 270 A4
Davidson Ho 7 N19 ... 71 C4
Davidson Lo CR0 ... 205 C2
Davidson Prim Sch
CR0 ... 205 D2
Davidson Rd CR0 ... 205 D3
Davidson Terrs E7 ... 77 B3
David's Rd SE23 ... 162 C3
David St E15 ... 76 B3
David Twigg Cl KT2 ... 176 A2
Davies Cl CR0 ... 206 A3
Davies La E11 ... 76 D6
Davies Laing & Dick Coll
W1 ... 93 A1 238 B2
Davies Lane Prim Sch
E11 ... 76 D6
Davies Mews W1 ... 248 C6
Davies St W1 ... 115 B6 248 C6
Davies Walk TW7 ... 130 B4
Davina Ho
Brondesbury NW2 ... 69 B2
11 Hackney E5 ... 74 B3
Da Vinci Ct 12 SE16 ... 118 B1
Davington Ct 19 SM2 .. 217 C1
Davington Gdns RM8 ... 80 B3
Davington Rd RM8 ... 80 B3
Davis Ct 1 N20 ... 14 B2
Davis Ho 35 W12 ... 112 B6
Davis Rd
Bedford Pk W3 ... 111 D4
Chessington KT9 ... 214 C4
Davis Sch The E10 ... 53 D1
Davis St E13 ... 99 B5
Davisville Rd W12 ... 112 A4
Davmor Ct TW8 ... 109 C1
Dawes Ave TW7 ... 131 A1
Dawe's Cl UB10 ... 82 A5
Dawes Ho SE17 ... 262 C3
Dawes Rd SW6 . 135 B5 264 C4
Dawe's Rd UB10 ... 82 A5
Dawes St SE17 .. 117 B1 262 D2
Dawley Ave UB8 ... 83 A1
Dawley Par UB3 ... 105 A6
Dawley Rd
Harlington UB3 ... 105 C2
Hayes UB3 ... 105 B6
Dawlish Ave
Bowes Pk N13 ... 32 A5
Wandsworth SW18 ... 157 D2
Wembley UB6 ... 87 A5
Dawlish Dr Ilford IG3 ... 79 D4
Pinner HA5 ... 41 A3
Ruislip HA4 ... 62 B6
Dawlish Prim Sch E10 .. 54 A1
Dawlish Rd
Brondesbury NW2 ... 68 D2
Leyton E10 ... 76 A6
Tottenham Hale N17 ... 52 A6
Dawnay Gdns SW18 ... 158 B2
Dawnay Rd SW17,
SW18 ... 158 B2
Dawn Cl TW4 ... 129 A2
Dawn Cres E15 ... 98 B6
Dawn Wlk BR2 ... 186 B1
Dawpool Rd NW2 ... 67 D6
Daws La NW7 ... 28 A5
Dawson Ave
Barking IG11 ... 79 D1
St Paul's Cray BR5 ... 190 B1
Dawson Cl Hayes UB3 ... 83 B2
Woolwich SE18 ... 123 A2
Dawson Gdns 10 IG11 ... 79 D1
Dawson Ho
23 Bethnal Green E2 ... 96 C4
5 Camberwell SE5 ... 139 C4
Dawson Pl W2 .. 113 C6 245 B6
Dawson Rd
Cricklewood NW2 ... 68 C4
Kingston u T KT1 ... 198 B6
Dawson St E2 ... 95 D5
Dawson Terr N9 ... 18 C4
Dax Ct TW16 ... 194 C6
Daybrook Rd SW19 ... 201 D6
Day Ho 2 SE5 ... 139 A5
Daylesford Ave SW15 .. 134 A1
Daymer Gdns HA5 ... 40 C5
Daynor Ho 4 NW6 ... 91 C6
Day's Armhouses HA8 ... 26 B5
Daysbrook Rd SW2 ... 160 B3
Days La DA15 ... 167 C4
Days Lane Prim Sch
DA15 ... 167 D5
Daytone Ho SW20 ... 178 D2
Dayton Gr SE15 ... 140 C4
Deaconess Ct 5 N15 ... 51 D5
Deacon Ho SE11 ... 260 D3
Deacon Mews N1 ... 73 B1
Deacon Rd
Kingston u T KT2 ... 176 B2
Willesden NW2 ... 68 A2
Deacons Cl HA5 ... 22 B1
DEACONS HILL ... 10 C5
Deacon's Hill Rd WD6 ... 10 C6
Deacons Hts WD6 ... 10 C5
Deacons Leas BR6 ... 227 B4
Deacons Rise N2 ... 48 B4
Deacons Wlk TW12 ... 173 C6
Deacon Way
SE17 ... 117 A2 262 B4
Deal Ct 13 Hendon NW9 .. 27 D1
7 Southall UB1 ... 86 A1
Deal Ho Deptford SE15 .. 140 D6
Walworth SE17 ... 263 B2
Deal Porters Way
SE16 ... 118 D3
Deal Rd SW17 ... 181 A4
Deal St E1 ... 96 A2
Dealtry Rd SW15 ... 134 C1
Deal Wlk 3 SW9 ... 138 C5
Dean Bradley St SW1 . 260 A5
Dean Cl Hackney E9 ... 74 C3
Hillingdon UB10 ... 60 B1
Rotherhithe SE16 ... 118 D5
Dean Coll of London
N7 ... 72 B5
Deancross St E1 ... 96 C1
Dean Ct Acton W3 ... 89 B1
Ealing W13 ... 109 B5
10 Kingston u T KT2 ... 176 C3
South Lambeth SW8 ... 270 A3
Wembley HA0 ... 65 B5
Dean Dr HA7 ... 26 A1
Deane Ave HA4 ... 62 C3
Deane Croft Rd HA5 ... 40 C3
Deanery Cl N2 ... 48 C5
Deanery Mews W1 ... 248 B4
Deanery Rd E15 ... 76 C2
Deanery St W1 . 115 A5 248 B4
Deanesfield Prim HA4 .. 62 D4
Deane Way HA4 ... 40 B3
Dean Farrar St SW1 ... 259 D6
Deanfield Gdns CR0 ... 221 B4
Dean Gdns E17 ... 54 B5
Deanhill Ct 2 SW14 ... 132 D1
Deanhill Rd SW14 ... 132 D1
Dean Ho London N4 ... 51 A2
New Cross SE14 ... 141 B5
Ruislip HA4 ... 39 B1
Stamford Hill N16 ... 51 D1
18 Stepney E1 ... 96 C1
Dean Rd Croydon CR0 .. 221 B4
Hampton TW12 ... 173 C5
Hounslow TW3 ... 151 D6
Thamesmead SE28 ... 124 A6
Willesden NW2 ... 68 C2
Dean Ryle St SW1 ... 260 A4
Dean's Bldgs
SE17 ... 117 B2 262 D3
Deansbrook Cl HA8 ... 27 A3
Deansbrook Jun & Inf
Schs NW7 ... 27 A4
Deansbrook Rd
Burnt Oak HA8 ... 27 B4
Edgware HA8 ... 26 D3
Deans Cl Burnt Oak HA8 .. 27 A4
Chiswick W4 ... 132 D6
South Croydon CR0 ... 221 D5
Deanscroft Ave NW9 ... 45 A1
Deans Ct HA8 ... 26 D4
Dean's Ct EC4 ... 241 D1
Deans Dr N13 ... 32 D4
Dean's Dr HA8 ... 27 B5
Deansfield Prim Sch
Eltham SE9 ... 144 C2
Deansfield Prim Sch
continued
Ruislip HA4 ... 62 D4
Deans Gate Cl SE23 ... 162 D1
Deanshanger Ho 21
SE8 ... 118 D2
Dean's La HA8 ... 27 A4
Dean's Mews W1 ... 238 D2
Deans Rd SM1 ... 217 D5
Dean's Rd W7 ... 108 D4
Dean St Forest Gate E7 ... 77 A3
Soho W1 ... 93 D1 239 C1
Dean Stanley St SW1 .. 260 A5
Deansway
East Finchley N2 ... 48 B5
Edmonton N9 ... 17 C1
Deans Way HA8 ... 27 A5
Deanswood N11 ... 31 D4
Dean's Yd SW1 ... 259 D6
Dean Trench St SW1 ... 260 A5
Dean Way UB2 ... 107 D4
Dean Wlk HA8 ... 27 B3
Deanwood Ct N14 ... 15 C3
Dearmer Ho 6 SW2 ... 160 C4
Dearne Cl HA7 ... 25 A5
De'arn Gdns CR4 ... 202 C6
Dearsley Rd EN1 ... 6 A2
Deason St E15 ... 98 A6
Deauville Ct
14 London SW4 ... 159 C5
4 Rotherhithe SE16 ... 118 D4
Deauville Mans 13
SW4 ... 159 C5
De Barowe Mews 1
N5 ... 72 D3
Debdale Ho 20 E2 ... 96 A6
Debden N17 ... 33 B1
Debden Cl
7 Edgware NW9 ... 27 C2
Kingston u T KT2 ... 175 D5
Woodford IG8 ... 37 D3
De Beauvoir Cres N1 ... 95 C6
De Beauvoir Ct N1 ... 73 B1
De Beauvoir Pl 5 N1 ... 73 C2
De Beauvoir Prim Sch
N1 ... 73 C2
De Beauvoir Rd N1 ... 73 C1
De Beauvoir Sq N1 ... 73 C1
DE BEAUVOIR TOWN ... 73 C1
Debenham Ct
Barnet EN5 ... 12 C6
Hackney E8 ... 96 A6
Debham Ct NW2 ... 68 C5
Debnams Rd SE16 ... 118 C2
De Bohun Ave N14 ... 15 B5
De Bohun Prim Sch
N14 ... 15 B6
Deborah Cl TW7 ... 130 C4
Deborah Cres HA4 ... 39 B2
Deborah Ct 7 E18 ... 55 B6
Deborah Lo HA8 ... 26 D2
De Broome Rd TW13 ... 150 C3
De Burgh Ho 10 SW19 .. 180 A3
Deburgh Rd SW19 ... 180 A3
Debussy 9 NW9 ... 27 D1
Decimal Ctr UB2 ... 107 C4
Decima St SE1 .. 117 C3 263 A6
Decimus Cl CR7 ... 205 B5
Deck Cl SE16 ... 118 D5
Decoy Ave NW11 ... 47 A5
De Crespigny Pk SE5 ... 139 B3
Dedham Ho 1 SE6 ... 186 A6
Dee Ct W7 ... 86 B1
Deeley Rd
SW8 ... 137 D4 269 C2
Deena Cl W3 ... 88 B1
Deepdale Highbury N4 ... 72 D5
Wimbledon SW19 ... 178 D6
Deepdale Ave BR2 ... 208 D5
Deepdale Cl N11 ... 31 A4
Deepdene N12 ... 30 C6
Deepdene Ave CR0 ... 221 D5
Deepdene Cl E11 ... 55 A5
Deepdene Ct
Beckenham BR2 ... 208 C6
Southgate N21 ... 16 D5
Deepdene Gdns SW2 ... 160 B4
Deepdene Ho N16 ... 51 B1
Deepdene Lo 5 SW2 .. 160 B4
Deepdene Mans SW6 . 264 C2
Deepdene Point 9
SE26 ... 162 D1
Deepdene Rd
London SE5, SE24 ... 139 B1
Welling DA16 ... 146 A2
Deepwell Cl TW7 ... 131 A4
Deepwood La UB6 ... 86 B4
Deerbrook Rd SE24,
SW2 ... 160 D3
Dee Rd TW9 ... 132 B1
Deerdale Rd SE24 ... 139 A1
Deerfield Cl NW9 ... 45 D4
Deerhurst
7 Kingston u T KT2 ... 176 D2
5 Streatham SW16 ... 182 A5
Deerhurst Cl TW13 ... 172 B6
Deerhurst Cres TW12 .. 174 A5
Deerhurst Ct CR0 ... 204 D1
Deerhurst Ho 6 SE15 .. 140 A6
Deerhurst Rd
Brondesbury NW2 ... 68 D2
Streatham SW16 ... 182 B5
Deerings Ct 2 N20 ... 14 B2
Deerings Dr HA5 ... 40 A4
Deerleap Gr E4 ... 19 D6
Deer Lo SW6 ... 135 A2
Deer Park Cl KT2 ... 176 D3
Deer Park Gdns CR4 ... 202 B5
Deer Park Rd SW19 ... 180 A1
Deer Park Way BR4 ... 224 D6
Deesdale Ct CR2 ... 221 B4
Deeside Rd SW17 ... 158 B1
Dee St E14 ... 98 A1
Defence Cl SE28 ... 123 C5
Defiance Wlk SE18 ... 122 B3
Defiant 18 NW9 ... 27 D1
Defiant Way SM6 ... 220 A1
Defoe Ave TW9 ... 132 C5
Defoe Cl SW17 ... 180 C4
Defoe Ho Barbican EC2 . 242 A4
5 Stoke Newington N16 . 73 C5
Defoe Pl Barbican EC2 .. 242 A4
Upper Tooting SW17 ... 180 D6
Defoe Rd
Rotherhithe SE16 ... 119 B4
Stoke Newington N16 ... 73 C5
De Frene Rd SE26 ... 163 A1
De Gama Pl 3 E14 ... 119 C1
Degema Rd BR7 ... 188 D5
Dehar Cres NW9 ... 46 A2
De Haviland Dr 8
SE18 ... 122 D1
Dehavilland Cl UB5 ... 84 D4
De Havilland Rd
Edgware HA8 ... 26 D1
Heston TW5 ... 128 C5
De Havilland Sq IG1 ... 57 B1
Dehavilland Studios E5 . 74 C6
De Havilland Way
TW19 ... 148 A5
Dekker Ho 19 SE5 ... 139 B5
Dekker Rd SE21 ... 161 C5
Delacourt Rd SE3 ... 143 B5
Delafield Ho 25 E1 ... 96 A1
Delafield Rd SE7 ... 121 C1
Delaford Rd SE16 ... 118 B1
Delaford St
SW6 ... 135 A6 264 B5
Delamare Cres CR0 ... 206 C3
Delamere Gdns NW7 ... 27 B4
Delamere Ho 4 N4 ... 51 B2
Delamere Rd
Ealing W5 ... 110 A4
Hayes UB4 ... 106 D6
Wimbledon SW20 ... 178 D2
Delamere St W2 ... 236 A3
Delamere Terr W2 ... 91 D2
Delancey Pas NW1 ... 231 D5
Delancey St
NW1 ... 93 B6 231 D5
Delancey Studios
NW1 ... 231 D5
Delany Ho SE10 ... 142 A6
Delarch Ho SE1 ... 251 C1
De Laune St
SE17 ... 116 D1 261 C1
Delaware Rd W9 ... 91 D3
Delawyk Cres SE24 ... 161 B5
Delcombe Ave KT4 ... 200 C1
Delft Ho 8 KT2 ... 176 B3
Delft Way 2 SE22 ... 161 C6
Delhi Rd EN1 ... 17 D4
Delhi St N1 ... 94 A6 233 B5
Delia St SW18 ... 157 D4
Delisle Rd SE28 ... 123 C5
Delius Cl WD6 ... 9 C5
Delius Gr E15 ... 98 A5
Dellafield N4 ... 72 C6
Della Path E5 ... 74 B5
Dellbow Rd TW14 ... 150 B6
Dell Cl
Stratford Marsh E15 ... 98 B6
Wallington SM6 ... 219 D4
Woodford IG8 ... 21 B1
Dellfield Cl BR3 ... 186 A2
Dell La KT17 ... 216 A3
Dellors Cl EN5 ... 12 D6
Dellow Cl IG2 ... 57 B2
Dellow Ho 6 E1 ... 118 B6
Dellow St E1 ... 118 B6
Dell Rd Enfield EN3 ... 6 C5
Stoneleigh KT17 ... 216 A2
West Drayton UB7 ... 104 B3
Dells Cl Chingford E4 ... 19 D4
Teddington TW11 ... 174 D4
Dell's Mews SW1 ... 259 B3
Dell The Brentford TW8 . 131 C6
Feltham TW14 ... 150 B4
Pinner HA5 ... 22 D1
Plumstead Comm SE2 .. 124 A1
South Norwood SE19 ... 183 D2
Wembley HA0 ... 65 B3
Woodford IG8 ... 21 B1
Dell Way W13 ... 87 C1
Dell Wlk KT3 ... 177 C1
Dellwood Gdns IG5 ... 56 C6
Delme Cres SE3 ... 143 B3
Delmey Cl CR0 ... 221 D5
Deloraine Ho SE8 ... 141 C4
Deloraine St SE8 ... 141 C4
Delorme St W6 ... 134 D6
Delphian Ct 5 SW16 ... 182 C6
Delroy Ct N20 ... 14 A4
Delta Bldg 7 E14 ... 98 A1
Delta Cl KT4 ... 215 D5
Delta Ct NW2 ... 68 A6
Delta Gr UB5 ... 84 D4
Delta Ho N1 ... 235 C2
Delta Pk SW18 ... 135 D1
Delta Pk Ind Est EN3 ... 7 B3
Delta Point 5 E2 ... 96 A4
Delta Rd KT4 ... 215 C5
Delta St 4 E2 ... 96 A4
De Lucy Prim Sch SE2 . 124 B4
De Lucy St SE2 ... 124 B2
Delvan Cl SE18 ... 144 C5
Delverton Ho SE17 ... 261 D2
Delverton Rd SE17 ... 261 D1
Delvino Rd
SW6 ... 135 C4 265 B1

De Mandeville Gate EN1 6 B1
Demesne Rd SM6 219 D4
Demeta Cl HA9 67 A5
De Montfort Ct 1
SW16 160 A1
De Montfort Rd SW16 160 A2
De Morgan Rd SW6 135 D2
Dempster Cl KT6 197 C1
Dempster Rd SW18 158 A6
Denberry Dr DA14 168 B1
Denbigh Cl
Cheam SM1 217 B3
Elmstead BR7 188 B4
Notting Hill
W11 113 B6 244 D6
Ruislip HA4 61 D6
Southall UB1 85 B1
Willesden NW10 67 C1
Denbigh Ct
1 Ealing W7 86 D2
Newham E6 99 D4
Denbigh Dr UB3 105 A4
Denbigh Gdns TW10 154 B6
Denbigh Ho
Knightsbridge SW1 257 D6
7 Notting Hill W11 91 B1
Notting Hill W11 244 D6
Denbigh Mews SW1 259 A3
Denbigh Pl
SW1 115 C1 259 A2
Denbigh Rd Ealing W13 87 B1
Hounslow TW3 129 D3
Newham E6 99 D4
Notting Hill
W11 113 B6 244 D6
Southall UB1 85 B1
Denbigh St
SW1 115 C1 259 B2
Denbigh Terr
W11 113 B6 244 D6
Denbridge Rd BR1,
BR7 188 B1
Denbury Ho 48 E3 97 D4
Denby Ct Barnet EN5 1 D2
Lambeth SE11 260 D4
Dence Ho 15 E2 96 A4
Denchworth Ho 14
SW9 138 C3
Den Cl BR2, BR3 208 B6
Dencliffe 2 TW15 170 C5
Dencora Centre The
EN3 7 A2
Dendridge Cl EN1 6 B6
Dene Ave
Blackfen DA15 168 B4
Hounslow TW3 129 B2
Dene Cl Brockley SE4 141 A1
Hayes BR2 208 D1
Worcester Pk KT4 215 D6
Denecroft Cres UB10 82 D6
Dene Ct Ealing W5 87 C2
Hanwell W7 108 D4
Dene Gdns
Hinchley Wood KT7 213 A6
Stanmore HA7 25 C5
Dene Ho N14 15 D4
Denehole Ho SE18 124 A1
Denehurst Gdns
Acton W3 110 D5
Hendon NW4 46 C3
Richmond TW10 132 C1
Twickenham TW2 152 B4
Woodford IG8 37 B6
Dene Mans 1 NW6 69 C2
Dene Rd
Buckhurst Hill IG9 21 D3
Friern Barnet N11 14 D2
Denesmead SE24 161 A6
Dene The Ealing W13 87 B2
East Molesey KT12,
KT8 195 B4
South Croydon CR0 222 D4
Wembley HA9 66 A4
Denewood EN5 14 A6
Denewood Ho 6 SM1 218 A4
Denewood Rd N6 48 D2
Dengie Wlk N1 235 A6
Denham Cl DA16 146 C2
Denham Cres CR4 202 D5
Denham Ct
Forest Hill SE26 162 B1
Southall UB1 108 A6
Denham Dr IG2 57 A3
Denham Ho 32 W12 112 B6
Denham Lo W5 88 A1
Denham Rd
Feltham TW14 150 C4
Friern Barnet N20 14 D1
Denham St SE10 121 A1
Denham Way IG11 101 D6
Denholme Rd W9 91 B4
Deniel Lo TW9 153 C6
Denise Ct HA0 65 C4
Denison Cl N2 48 A6
Denison Rd Ealing W5 87 C3
Feltham TW13 171 D6
Mitcham SW19 180 B4
Deniston Ave DA5 169 A3
Denland Ho SW8 270 D3
Denleigh Ct N14 15 D4
Denleigh Gdns
Southgate N21 16 C4
Thames Ditton KT7 196 C3
Denman Dr
Ashford TW15 170 D4
Claygate KT10 213 A3
Hampstead Garden Suburb
NW11 47 C4
Denman Dr N NW11 47 C4
Denman Dr S NW11 47 C4
Denman Ho N16 73 C6
Denman Rd SE15 139 D3
Denman St W1 249 C5
Denmark Ave SW19 179 A3
Denmark Ct SM4 201 C4
Denmark Gdns SM5 218 D5
Denmark Gr N1 234 A4
Denmark Hill SE5 139 B3
Denmark Hill Dr NW9 46 A6
Denmark Hill Sta SE5 139 B3
Denmark Ho 9 SE7 122 A2
Denmark Mans 14
SE5 139 A3
Denmark Pl
2 Bromley E3 97 C4
Soho WC2 239 D2
Denmark Rd
Bromley BR1 187 B2
Camberwell SE5 139 A3
Carshalton SM5 218 D5
Croydon SE25 206 B4
Ealing W13 109 B6
Hornsey N8 50 C5
Kilburn NW6 91 B5
Kingston u T KT1 198 A6
Twickenham TW2 152 B1
Wimbledon SW19 178 D4
Denmark St
8 Leyton E11 76 C5
Newham E13 99 B2
Soho WC2 239 D2
Tottenham N17 34 B3
Denmark Terr NW2 48 D6
Denmead Ho SW15 155 D5
Denmead Rd CR0 204 D1
Denmead Sch TW12 173 D3
Denmead Upper Sch
TW12 173 D3
Denmore Ct SM6 219 B3
Dennan Rd KT6 198 B1
Dennard Way BR6 226 C4
Denner Rd E4 19 C2
Dene Terr E8 95 D6
Dennett Rd CR0 204 C2
Dennett's Gr SE14 140 D3
Dennett's Rd SE14 140 C4
Denning Ave CR0 220 C3
Denning Cl
Hampton TW12 173 B5
St John's Wood
NW8 92 A4 229 B1
Denning Point E1 243 D2
Denning Rd NW3 70 B4
Dennington Cl 17 E5 74 B6
Dennington Park
Mansions 12 NW6 69 C3
Dennington Park Rd
NW6 69 C2
Denningtons The KT4 215 C6
Dennis Ave HA9 66 B3
Dennis Cl TW15 171 B3
Dennis Ct Chingford E17 36 B1
Greenford UB6 86 A1
Lewisham SE10 142 A4
Dennis Gdns HA7 25 C5
Dennis Ho 4 Bow E3 97 B5
Sutton SM1 217 C4
Dennis La HA7 25 B6
Dennison Point E15 76 A1
Dennis Par 1 N14 15 D3
Dennis Park Cres
SW20 179 A2
Dennis Rd KT8 196 A5
Dennis Reeve Cl CR4 180 D2
Dennis Way SW4 137 D2
Denny Cl 15 E6 100 A2
Denny Cres SE11 261 B2
Denny Gdns RM9 80 B1
Denny Rd N9 18 B3
Denny St SE11 116 C1 261 B2
Den Rd BR2 208 B6
Densham Ho NW8 229 D3
Densham Rd E15 98 C6
Densole Cl BR3 185 A2
Denstone Ho 5 SE15 140 A6
Densworth Gr N9 18 C2
Dent Ho SE17 263 A3
Denton NW1 71 A2
Denton Cl EN5 12 C6
Denton Ct BR2 210 C2
Denton Ho N1 72 D1
Denton Rd
Bexley DA16 146 C5
Edmonton N18 33 C6
Hornsey N8 50 B3
Twickenham TW1 153 D5
Denton St SW18 157 D5
Denton Way E5 74 D5
Dents Rd SW11 158 D5
Denvale Trade Pk
CR4 202 B5
Denver Cl BR6 211 C3
Denver Ct UB1 107 B5
Denver Rd N16 51 C2
Denwood SE23 162 D1
Denyer Ho 1 NW5 71 B4
Denyer St SW3 114 C2 257 B4
Denys Bldg EC1 241 A4
Denziloe Ave UB10 82 D4
Denzil Rd NW10 67 D3
Deodar Rd SW15 135 A1
Deodora Cl N20 14 D1
Depot App NW2 68 D4
Depot Rd
Isleworth TW3, TW7 130 B2
Shepherd's Bush W12 112 C6
Depot St SE5 139 B6
DEPTFORD 140 D6
Deptford Bridge SE8 141 C4
Deptford Bridge Sta
SE8 141 C4
Deptford Broadway SE8,
SE14 141 C4
Deptford Church St
SE8 141 C5
Deptford Ferry Rd 24
E14 119 C2
Deptford Gn SE8 141 C6
Deptford Green Sch
SE14 141 B5
Deptford Green Sch
(Annex) SE14 141 A5
Deptford High St SE8 141 C5
Deptford Park Prim Sch
SE8 119 A1
Deptford Sta SE8 141 C5
Deptford Trad Est
SE8 141 A6
Deptford Wharf SE8 119 B2
Dept of Transport &
Environment SW1 259 D5
De Quincey Mews 3
E16 121 A5
De Quincey Rd N17 33 B2
Derby Ave Harrow HA3 24 B2
North Finchley N12 30 A5
Romford RM7 59 D3
Derby Ct
8 Clapton Pk E5 74 D4
Woodford E18 36 D2
Derby Gate SW1 250 A2
Derby Hill SE23 162 C2
Derby Hill Cres SE23 162 C2
Derby Ho Hendon NW4 46 C6
Lambeth SE11 261 A4
Pinner HA5 22 D1
4 Wallington SM6 219 B3
Derby Lo N3 29 B1
Derby Rd
Cheam SM1, SM2 217 B2
Edmonton N18 34 C5
Enfield EN3 18 C6
Greenford UB6 85 D6
Hounslow TW3 129 D1
Merton SW19 179 C3
Mortlake SW14 132 D1
South Hackney E9 96 D6
Surbiton KT5, KT6 198 C1
Thornton Heath CR0 204 D1
Upton E7 77 D1
Woodford E18 36 D2
Derbyshire St E2 96 A4
Derby St W1 248 B3
Dereham Ho 7 SE4 140 D1
Dereham Pl EC2 243 B6
Dereham Rd IG11 79 D3
Derek Ave
Chessington KT19 214 D3
Wallington SM6 219 B4
Wembley HA9 66 D1
Derek Cl KT19 214 D3
Derek Walcott Cl
SE24 160 D6
Dericote St E8 96 B6
Deri Dene Cl 2 TW19 148 A5
Derifall Cl E6 100 B2
Dering Pl CR0 221 A4
Dering Rd CR0 221 A4
Dering St W1 238 D1
Derinton Rd SW17 181 A6
Derley Rd UB2 106 D3
Dermody Gdns SE13 164 B6
Dermody Rd SE13 164 B6
Deronda Rd SE24,
SW2 160 D3
Deroy Cl SM5 218 D2
Derrick Gdns SE7 121 C2
Derrick Ho 13 SW2 160 C3
Derrick Rd BR3 207 B5
Derrycombe Ho 18 W2 91 C2
Derry Rd CR0, SM6 220 A5
Derry St W8 113 D4 245 C1
Dersingham Ave E12 78 C4
Dersingham Inf Sch
E12 78 C3
Dersingham Rd NW2 69 A5
Derwent NW1 232 A1
Derwent Ave
Barnet EN4 14 D3
Burnt Oak NW7 27 B4
Edmonton N18 33 B5
Hyde The NW9 45 C4
Kingston u T SW15 177 C6
Pinner HA5 23 A4
Uxbridge UB10 60 C5
Derwent Cl
Claygate KT10 212 D2
East Bedfont TW14 149 D3
Derwent Cres
Bexleyheath DA7 147 C3
Stanmore HA7 25 C1
Whetstone N20 14 A1
Derwent Ct
2 Hammersmith W6 112 A2
Hornsey N8 50 A3
8 Rotherhithe SE16 118 D4
Derwent Dr
Crofton BR5 211 B2
Hayes UB4 83 C2
Derwent Gdns
Redbridge IG4 56 A5
Wembley HA9 43 C2
Derwent Gr SE22 139 D1
Derwent Ho
Penge SE20 184 B1
South Kensington SW7 256 B4
Tower Hamlets E3 97 B3
Derwent Lo
Hounslow TW7 130 B3
Derwent Lo *continued*
North Cheam KT4 216 B6
Derwent Rd Ealing W5 109 C3
Palmers Green N13 16 B1
Penge SE20 184 B1
Southall UB1 85 B1
Twickenham TW2 151 D5
West Barnes SM4 200 D3
Derwent Rise NW9 45 C3
Derwent St SE10 120 C1
Derwentwater Mans 2
W3 111 A5
Derwentwater Prim Sch
W3 111 A5
Derwentwater Rd W3 111 A5
Derwent Wlk SM6 219 B1
Derwent Yd W5 109 C3
De Salis Rd UB10 83 A3
Desborough Cl
Bayswater W2 91 D2
Lower Halliford TW17 192 C2
Desborough Ct SE25 206 B5
Desborough Ho W14 264 D6
Desenfans Rd SE21 161 C5
Deseret Ho 6 CR4 202 D6
Desford Rd E16 98 C3
Desford Way TW15 148 B2
Desmond Ho 4 EN4 14 C5
Desmond St SE14 141 A6
Desmond Tutu Dr
SE23 163 A3
Despard Ho SW2 160 C2
Despard Rd N19 49 C1
Dessouter 19 NW9 27 D1
Desvignes Dr SE13 164 B5
Detherick Ct TW3 130 A1
Dethick Ct E3 97 A6
Detling Ho SE17 263 A3
Detling Rd BR1 187 A5
Detmold Rd E5 74 C6
Devalls Cl E6 122 C6
Devana End SM5 218 D5
Devas Rd SW20 178 C2
Devas St E3 97 D3
Devema Cl BR7 188 C2
Devenay Rd E15 76 D1
Devenish Rd SE2 124 A4
Deventer Cres 8
SE22 161 C6
Deveraux Cl BR3 208 A4
De Vere Cotts W8 256 A6
De Vere Ct 1 E5 74 B5
De Vere Gdns
Kensington
W8 114 A4 246 A1
Redbridge IG1 56 B1
Deverell St
SE1 117 B3 262 C5
De Vere Mews W8 256 A6
Devereux Ct WC2 241 A1
Devereux Ho 7 SW15 156 A6
Devereux La SW13 134 B5
Devereux Rd SW11 158 D5
Deverill Ct SE20 184 C2
Devey Cl KT2 177 B5
Devitt Ho 5 E14 119 D6
Devizes St N1 235 D5
Devon Ave TW2 152 A3
Devon Cl Chigwell IG9 21 B2
Tottenham N17 51 D6
Wembley UB6 87 C6
Devoncroft Gdns TW1 153 A4
Devon Ct 3 Acton W3 88 C1
2 Ealing W7 86 D2
Hampton TW12 173 C3
Devon Gdns N4 50 D3
Devon Ho
9 Penge SE20 184 B3
Walthamstow E17 35 B1
6 Wanstead E11 55 A4
Devonhurst Pl 4 W4 111 B1
Devonia Gdns N18 33 A4
Devonia Rd N1 94 D5 234 D4
Devon Mans SE1 253 B2
Devon Par HA3 43 C4
Devonport W2 237 A2
Devonport Gdns IG1 56 B3
Devonport Ho
Greenwich SE10 142 A6
23 Paddington W2 91 C2
Devonport Rd W12 112 B4
Devonport St E1 96 D1
Devon Rd IG11 101 C6
Devon Rise N2 48 B5
Devonshire Ave SM2 218 A1
Devonshire Cl
Edmonton N13 32 C6
Leyton E15 76 C4
Marylebone W1 238 C4
Devonshire Cres NW7 28 D3
Devonshire Ct
14 Balham SW12 159 B4
Croydon CR0 207 C1
Feltham TW13 150 B2
Pinner HA5 23 B2
6 Richmond TW9 132 B4
Tottenham N17 33 A4
Devonshire Dr
London SE10 141 D4
Long Ditton KT6 213 D6
Devonshire Gdns
Chiswick W4 133 A5
Edmonton N21 17 A4
Tottenham N17 33 A4
Devonshire Gr SE15 140 B6
Devonshire Hall 15 E9 74 C2
Devonshire Hill La N17 33 A4
Devonshire Hill Prim Sch
N17 33 B4
Devonshire Ho
Brondesbury NW6 69 B2
Hounslow TW3 130 A2
Newington SE1 262 A6
Paddington W2 236 D4
2 Putney SW15 156 C4
10 Sutton SM2 218 A1
Westminster SW1 259 D2
Whetstone N12 14 A1
Devonshire Hospl
W1 93 A2 238 B4
Devonshire House Prep
Sch NW3 70 B3
Devonshire House Sch
NW3 70 A3
Devonshire Mews 2
W4 111 C1
Devonshire Mews N
W1 238 C4
Devonshire Mews S
W1 238 C4
Devonshire Mews W
W1 238 B4
Devonshire Pl
Child's Hill NW2 69 C5
Kensington W8 255 C5
Marylebone W1 93 A2 238 B4
Devonshire Place Mews
W1 238 B4
Devonshire Prim Sch
SM2 218 A1
Devonshire Rd
Bexley DA6 147 A1
Chislehurst SE9 166 A2
Chiswick W4 111 C1
Ealing W5 109 C3
Eastcote HA5 40 C2
Edmonton N9 18 C3
Feltham TW13 173 A6
Forest Hill SE23 162 C4
Hackbridge SM5, SM6 219 A4
Harrow HA1 42 B3
Hatch End HA5 23 B2
Ilford IG2 57 C2
Mill Hill NW7 28 D3
Mitcham SW19 180 C3
Newham E16 99 B1
Palmers Green N13 32 C6
Southall UB1 85 C2
Sutton SM2 218 A1
Thornton Heath CR0 205 B2
Tottenham N17 33 A4
Walthamstow E17 53 C3
Devonshire Row EC2 243 B3
Devonshire Row Mews
W1 238 D5
Devonshire Sq
Bromley BR2 209 B5
Whitechapel EC2 95 C1 243 B2
Devonshire St
Chiswick W4 111 C1
Marylebone W1 93 B2 238 C4
Devonshire Terr
W2 92 A1 236 B1
Devonshire Way
Croydon CR0, CR9 223 B6
Hayes UB4 84 B1
Devons Rd E3 97 D3
Devons Road Sta E3 97 D3
Devon St SE15 140 B6
Devon Way
Chessington KT9 213 C3
Ewell KT19 214 D3
Hillingdon UB10 82 B5
Devon Waye TW5 129 B5
De Walden Ho NW8 230 A4
De Walden St W1 238 B3
Dewar Ho 2 SW17 180 C5
Dewar St SE15 140 A2
Dewberry Gdns E6 100 A2
Dewberry St E14 98 A2
Dewey Rd
Dagenham RM10 81 D2
Islington N1 94 C5 234 A4
Dewey St SW17 180 D5
Dewhurst Rd W14 112 D3
Dewlands Ct 7 NW4 28 D1
Dewsbury Cl HA5 41 A3
Dewsbury Ct 5 W4 111 A2
Dewsbury Gdns KT4 216 A5
Dewsbury Rd NW10 68 A3
Dewsbury Terr NW1 231 D6
Dexter Ho 2 DA18 125 A3
Dexter Rd EN5 12 D5
Deyncourt Rd N17 33 A2
Deynecourt Gdns E11 55 C5
D'eynsford Rd SE5 139 B4
Dhonau Ho SE16 263 D4
Diadem Ct W1 239 C2
Dial Wlk The
W8 113 D4 245 D2
Diameter Rd BR5 211 A3
Diamond Cl RM8 58 C1
Diamond Ct 8 W7 108 C5
Diamond Est SW17 158 C1
Diamond Ho 22 E3 97 A5
Diamond Rd HA4 63 A4
Diamond St
18 London NW10 67 B1
SE15 139 C5
Diamond Terr SE10 142 A4
Diana Cl
27 Deptford SE8 141 B6
Sidcup DA14 169 A2
Woodford E18 37 B2
Diana Ct SM5 219 A1
Diana Gdns KT6 214 B6
Diana Ho Barnes SW13 133 D4
4 Brixton SW2 160 B6
Diana, Princess of Wales
Mml Wlk W2 114 A5 246 A3
Diana Rd E17 53 B6
Dianne Ct SE12 165 A3
Dianne Way EN4 2 C1
Dianthus Cl SE2 124 B1
Dias Ho UB5 85 A6
Dibden Ho 8 SE5 139 C5
Dibden St N1 95 A6 235 A6
Dibdin Cl SM1 217 C5
Dibdin Ho W9 91 D5
Dibdin Rd SM1 217 C6
Dicey Ave NW2 68 C4
Dickens Ave Finchley N3 30 A2
Hayes UB8 82 D1
Dickens Cl Erith DA8 147 D5
Hayes UB3 105 C2
Richmond TW10 154 A2
Dickens Ct
Clerkenwell EC1 241 C5
10 Wanstead E11 55 A5
Wembley HA0 65 C5
Dickens Dr BR7 189 A4
Dickens Ho
Bloomsbury WC1 240 A6
3 Erith DA17 125 B1
Hayes UB3 105 C2
Kennington SE17 261 D1
Kilburn NW6 91 C4
Paddington NW8 236 D6
Dickens House Mus*
WC1 94 B3 240 D5
Dickens La N18 33 C5
Dickenson Cl N9 18 A3
Dickenson Ho N8 50 B3
Dickenson Rd
Feltham TW13 172 D5
Hornsey N8 50 A2
Dickenson's La SE25 206 A3
Dickenson's Pl SE25 206 A3
Dickens Rd E6 99 D5
Dickens Sq
SE1 117 A3 262 B6
Dickens St SW8 137 B3
Dickenswood Cl SE19 182 D3
Dickerage Hill
Kingston u T KT3 177 A1
Kingston u T KT3 199 A6
Dickerage La KT3 199 A6
Dickerage Rd KT1, KT2,
KT3 177 A1
Dickinson Ho 13 E2 96 A4
Dicksee Ho NW8 236 C5
Dick Shepherd Ct 17
SW2 160 C5
Dickson Fold HA5 40 D5
Dickson Ho
3 Charlton SE18 144 A4
4 Stepney E1 96 B1
Dickson Rd SE9 144 A2
Dick Turpin Way
TW14 127 D1
Didbin Ho N7 72 B6
Didsbury Cl E6 100 B6
Digby Bsns Ctr E9 74 D2
Digby Cres N4 73 A6
Digby Gdns RM10 103 C6
Digby Mans W6 112 C1
Digby Pl CR0 221 D5
Digby Rd Barking IG11 79 D1
Homerton E9 74 D2
Digby St E2 96 C4
Diggon St E1 96 D2
Dighton Ct SE17 139 A6
Dighton Rd SW18 136 A1
Dignum St N1 234 A4
Digswell St N7 72 C2
Dilhorne Cl SE12 165 B1
Dilke St SW3 136 D6 267 D6
Dilloway Yd UB2 107 A4
Dillwyn Cl SE26 185 A6
Dilston Cl 1 UB5 84 C4
Dilston Gr SE16 118 C2
Dilton Gdns SW15 156 B3
Dilwyn Ct E17 35 A1
Dimes Pl 9 W6 112 B2
Dimmock Dr UB6 64 B3
Dimond Cl E7 77 A4
Dimsdale Dr Enfield EN1 18 A5
Welsh Harp NW9 45 A1
Dimsdale Wlk 4 E13 99 A5
Dimson Cres E3 97 C4
Dinerman Ct NW8 229 B6
Dingle Cl EN5 11 D5
Dingle Ct 16 HA7 25 C5
Dingle Gdns E14 119 C6
Dingle Rd TW15 170 D5
Dingles Ct HA5 22 D1
Dingle The UB10 82 D4
Dingley La SW16 159 D2
Dingley Pl EC1 95 A4 235 B1
Dingley Rd EC1 95 A4 235 A1
Dingwall Ave CR0 221 A6
Dingwall Gdns NW11 47 C3
Dingwall Rd
South Croydon CR0 221 B6
Wandsworth SW18 158 A4
Dinmont Ho 27 E2 96 A5
Dinmont St 1 E2 96 B5
Dinmore Ho 6 E9 96 C6
Dinnington Ho 17 E1 96 B3
Dinorben SM6 219 C1
Dinsdale Ct EN5 13 D6
Dinsdale Gdns
New Barnet EN5 13 D6
South Norwood SE25 205 C4
Dinsdale Rd SE3 142 D6

Dinsmore Rd SW12 159 B4
Dinton Ho NW8 237 A6
Dinton Rd
Kingston u T KT2 176 B3
Mitcham SW19 180 B4
Dinwiddy Ho N1 233 C3
Dionis Ho SW6 135 C3
Diploma Ave N2 48 C5
Diploma Ct N2 48 C5
Diprose Lo SW17 180 B6
Dirleton Rd E15 98 D6
Disbrowe Rd
W6 135 A6 264 B5
Discovery Bsns Pk 13
SE16 118 A3
Discovery Dock E E14 119 D4
Discovery Ho 1 E14 120 A6
Dishforth La NW9 27 C2
Disley Ct 2 UB1 85 D1
Disney Pl SE1 252 B2
Disney St SE1 252 B2
Dison Cl EN3 6 D4
Disraeli Cl
1 Acton W4 111 B2
Thamesmead SE28 124 C5
Disraeli Gdns SW15 135 B1
Disraeli Rd Acton NW10 89 B5
Ealing W5 109 D5
Putney SW15 135 A1
Upton E7 77 A1
Diss St E2 95 D4
Distaff La EC4 252 A6
Distillery La W6 112 C1
Distillery Rd W6 112 C1
Distillery Wlk 14 TW8 132 A6
Distin Ct 3 SM1 217 D3
Distin St SE11 116 C2 261 A3
District Rd HA0 65 B3
Ditchburn St E14 120 A6
Ditchfield Rd UB4 85 A3
Ditchley Ct W7 86 D2
Dittisham Rd SE9 188 A6
Ditton Cl KT7 197 A2
Dittoncroft Cl CR0 221 C4
Ditton Grange Cl KT6 197 D1
Ditton Grange Dr KT6 197 D1
Ditton Hill KT6 213 D6
Ditton Hill Rd KT6 197 C1
Ditton Ho 10 E5 74 B3
Ditton Lawn KT7 197 A1
Ditton Pl 6 SE20 184 B2
Ditton Rd Bexley DA6 169 A6
Southall UB2 107 B1
Surbiton KT6 198 B1
Ditton Reach KT7 197 B3
Divis Way SW15 156 B5
Dixon Cl 4 E6 100 B1
Dixon Clark Ct N1 72 D2
Dixon Ct N4 50 C3
Dixon Ho
20 North Kensington
NW10 90 D1
West Heath SE2 124 C1
Dixon Pl BR4 207 D1
Dixon Rd London SE14 141 A4
South Norwood SE25 205 D6
Dixon's Alley 10 SE16 118 B4
Dobbin Cl HA3 25 A1
Dobell Rd SE9 166 B6
Dobree Ave NW10 68 B1
Dobson Cl NW6 70 B1
Dobson Ho 18 SE14 140 D6
Doby Ct EC4 252 B6
Dockers Tanner Rd 26
E14 119 C2
Dockett Eddy La KT16,
TW17 192 B1
Dockett Moorings
KT16 192 B1
Dockhead SE1 117 D4 253 D1
Dockhead Wharf SE1 253 D2
Dock Hill Ave SE16 118 D4
Docklands Ct 20 E14 97 B1
Docklands Heritage Mus*
SE16 119 B5
Dockland St E16 122 C5
Dockley Rd SE16 118 A3
Dockley Road Ind Est 11
SE16 118 A3
Dock Offices 12 SE16 118 C3
Dock Rd
Brentford TW8 131 D5
Canning Town E16 120 D6
Dockside Rd E16 121 D6
Dock St E1 118 A6
Dockwell Cl TW14 128 A1
Dockwell's Ind Est
TW14 150 B6
Doctor Johnson Ho 2
SW16 181 D6
Doctors Cl SE26 184 C5
Doctor Spurstowe
Almshouses 9 E8 74 B2
Docura Ho N7 72 B6
Docwras Bldgs N1 73 C2
Dodbrooke Rd SE27 160 D1
Dodd Ho 18 SE16 118 B2
Doddington Gr
SE17 116 D1 261 D1
Doddington Pl 4
SE17 138 D6
Dodsley Pl N9 18 C1
Dodson St SE1 116 C4 251 B1
Dod St E14 97 C1
Doebury Wlk SE18 146 A6
Doel Cl SW19 180 A3
Doggett Rd SE6 163 C4
Doggetts Ct EN4 14 C6
Doghurst Ave UB3 126 D5
Doghurst Dr UB7 126 D5
Dog Kennel Hill SE22 139 C2
Dog Kennel Hill Sch
SE22 139 C2
Dog La NW10 67 C4
Dogrose Ct 14 NW9 46 A5
Doherty Rd E13 99 A3
Dokal Ind Est UB2 107 A4
Doland Ct SW17 180 D4
Dolben Ct SW1 259 D3
Dolben St SE1 116 D5 251 D3
Dolby Rd SW6 135 B3
Doleman Ho 19 SE10 141 D4
Dolland Ho SE11 260 D1
Dolland St SE11 260 D1
Dollar Bay E14 120 A4
Dollary Ct KT3 198 D6
Dolliffe Cl CR4 180 D1
Dollis Ave N3 29 B2
Dollis Brook Wlk EN5 13 A5
Dollis Cres HA4 40 C1
Dolliscroft NW7 29 A3
Dollis Ct N3 29 B2
DOLLIS HILL 68 B5
Dollis Hill Ave NW2 68 B5
Dollis Hill Est NW2 68 A5
Dollis Hill La NW2 68 A5
Dollis Hill Sta NW2 68 A3
Dollis Hts NW2 68 B5
Dollis Jun & Inf Schs
NW7 28 C3
Dollis Mews N3 29 C2
Dollis Pk N3 29 B2
Dollis Rd N3, NW7 29 B3
Dollis Valley Dr EN5 13 B6
Dollis Valley Way EN5 13 B5
Dolman Cl N3 30 A1
Dolman Rd W4 111 B2
Dolman St SW4 138 B1
Dolphin Cl
Kingston u T KT6 197 D4
2 Rotherhithe SE16 118 D4
Thamesmead SE28 102 D1
Dolphin Ct
London NW11 47 A3
Merton SW19 179 C3
Tufnell Pk N7 71 D4
2 Wallington SM6 219 B2
Dolphin Est The TW16 171 B2
Dolphin La E14 119 D6
Dolphin Rd
Charlton TW16 171 C2
Northolt UB5 85 B5
Dolphin Rd N TW16 171 C2
Dolphin Rd S TW16 171 C2
Dolphin Rd W TW16 171 C2
Dolphin Sch SW11 158 D6
Dolphin Sq
SW1 115 C1 259 B1
Dolphin St KT2 176 A2
Dolphin Twr 21 SE8 141 B6
Dombey Ho
13 Bermondsey SE1 118 A4
4 Shepherd's Bush
W11 112 D5
Dombey St WC1 240 C4
Dome Hill Pk SE26 183 D6
Domelton Ho SW18 157 D5
Domett Cl SE5 139 B1
Domfe Pl E5 74 C4
Domingo St EC1 242 A5
Dominica Cl 6 E6 99 D5
Dominion Bsns Pk N9 18 D2
Dominion Cl TW3 130 B3
Dominion Ind Est UB2 107 A4
Dominion Par HA1 42 D4
Dominion Rd
Croydon CR0 205 D2
Southall UB2 107 A3
Dominion St
EC2 95 B2 242 D4
Dominion Wks RM8 59 A1
Domonic Dr SE9 166 D1
Domville Cl N20 14 B2
Donaghue Cotts 11 E14 97 A2
Donald Dr RM6 58 C4
Donald Lynch Ho CR4 180 D1
Donald Rd Newham E13 99 B6
Thornton Heath CR0 204 B2
Donaldson Rd
Kilburn NW6 91 B6
Shooters Hill SE18 144 C4
Donald Woods Gdns
KT5 215 A6
Doncaster Dr UB5 63 B3
Doncaster Gdns
London N4 51 A3
Northolt UB5 63 B3
Doncaster Gn WD19 22 C5
Doncaster Rd N9 18 B4
Doncel Ct E4 20 B4
Donegal Ho 2 E1 96 C3
Donegal St N1 94 B5 233 D3
Doneraile Ho SW1 258 C1
Doneraile St SW6 134 D4
Dongola Rd
Newham E13 99 B4
Tottenham N17 51 C6
Tower Hamlets E1 97 A2
Dongola Rd W 5 E13 99 B4
Don Gratton Ho 23 E1 96 A2
Donington Ave IG6 57 A4
Donkey Alley SE22 162 A5
Donkey La EN1 6 A3
Donkin Ho 15 SE16 118 B2
Donne Ct SE24 161 A5
Donnefield Ave HA8 26 A3
Donne Ho
18 Canonbury N16 73 B4
19 Deptford SE14 140 D6
11 Poplar E14 97 C1
Donnelly Ct SW6 264 B4
Donne Pl
Chelsea SW3 114 C2 257 B4
Mitcham CR4 203 B5
Donne Rd RM8 80 C6
Donnington Ct
11 Camden Town NW1 71 B1
Willesden NW10 68 B1
Donnington Ho 12
SW8 137 D3
Donnington Prim Sch
NW10 90 B6
Donnington Rd
Harrow HA3 43 D3
Willesden Green NW10 90 B6
Worcester Pk KT4 216 A6
Donnybrook Rd SW16 181 D3
Donoghue Bsns Pk
NW2 68 D5
Donovan Ave N10 31 C1
Donovan Ct SW7 256 C1
Donovan Ho 4 E1 118 C6
Donovan Pl N21 16 B6
Don Phelan Cl SE5 139 B4
Doone Cl TW11 175 A4
Doon St SE1 116 C5 251 A4
Doradus Ct 20 SW19 156 D3
Dora Ho
11 Shepherd's Bush
W11 112 D6
1 Tower Hamlets E14 97 B1
Doral Way SM5 218 D3
Doran Ct E6 100 B5
Dorando Cl W12 112 B6
Doran Gr SE18 145 C5
Doran Manor N2 48 D4
Doran Wlk Stratford E15 76 A1
Stratford Marsh E15 98 A6
Dora Rd SW19 179 C6
Dora St E14 97 B1
Dora Way SW9 138 C3
Dorcas Ct 9 SW18 136 B1
Dorchester Ave
Edmonton N13 33 A6
Harrow HA2 42 A3
Sidcup DA5 168 D4
Dorchester Cl
Northolt UB5 63 D3
St Paul's Cray BR5 190 B3
Dorchester Ct
Cricklewood NW2 68 D5
1 De Beauvoir Town N1 73 C1
East Barnet N14 15 B4
Herne Hill SE24 161 A6
Knightsbridge SW1 257 D5
1 Muswell Hill N10 49 B6
5 Streatham SW16 160 A2
2 Woodford E18 36 D2
Dorchester Dr
Feltham TW14 149 C5
Herne Hill SE24 161 A6
Dorchester Gdns
Chingford E4 35 C6
East Finchley NW11 47 C5
Dorchester Gr W4 111 D1
Dorchester Ho
Richmond TW9 132 D5
Wallington SM5 218 D3
Dorchester Mews
New Malden KT3 199 B5
Twickenham TW1 153 C5
Dorchester Prim Sch
KT4 200 C1
Dorchester Rd
Cheam SM4 202 A2
North Cheam KT4 200 C1
Northolt UB5 63 D3
Dorchester Way HA3 44 B3
Dorchester Waye
Hayes UB4 84 B1
Hayes UB4 84 C1
Dorcis Ave DA7 147 A3
Dordrecht Rd W3 111 C5
Dore Ave E12 78 C3
Doreen Ave NW9 45 B1
Doreen Capstan Ho 5
E11 76 C5
Dore Gdns SM4 201 D2
Dorell Cl UB1 85 B2
Dorey Ho 7 TW8 131 C5
Doria Rd SW6 135 B3
Doric Ho 7 E2 96 D5
Doric Way NW1 93 D4 232 C2
Dorie Mews N12 29 D6
Dorien Rd SW20 178 D1
Doris Emmerton Ct
SW18 136 A1
Doris Rd Ashford TW15 171 B4
Upton E7 77 A1
Dorking Cl
Deptford SE8 141 B6
North Cheam KT4 216 D6
Dorking Ct N17 34 A2
Dorking Ho SE1 262 D6
Dorland Ct SW15 157 B5
Dorlcote Rd SW18 158 C4
Dorleston Ct N1 235 D6
Dorly Cl TW17 193 C4
Dorman Pl 6 N9 18 A2
Dorman Way
NW8 92 B6 229 C6
Dorman Wlk NW10 67 B2
Dorma Trad Pk E10 52 D1
Dormay St SW18 157 D6
Dormer Cl Barnet EN5 12 D6
Stratford E15 76 D2
Dormer's Ave UB1 85 C1
Dormers Lo EN4 2 C3
Dormers Rise UB1 85 D1
DORMER'S WELLS 107 C6
Dormer's Wells High Sch
UB1 85 C1
Dormers Wells Ho UB4 84 C2
Dormer's Wells Inf Sch
UB1 107 D6
Dormer's Wells Jun Sch
UB1 107 D6
Dormer's Wells La
UB1 107 C5
Dormstone Ho SE17 263 A3
Dormywood HA4 39 D4
Dornberg Cl SE3 143 A5
Dornberg Rd SE3 143 B5
Dorncliffe Rd SW6 135 A3
Dorney NW3 70 C1
Dorney Ct SW6 135 A2
Dorney Rise BR5 211 D5
Dorney Way TW4 151 A6
Dornfell St NW6 69 B3
Dornoch Ho 26 E3 97 B5
Dornton Rd
South Croydon CR2 221 C3
Upper Tooting SW12,
SW17 159 C2
Dorothy Ave HA0 66 A1
Dorothy Barley Schs
RM8 80 B3
Dorothy Charrington Ho
1 SE22 162 A6
Dorothy Evans Cl DA7 147 D1
Dorothy Gdns RM8 80 B4
Dorothy Pettingel Ho 1
SM1 217 D5
Dorothy Rd SW11 136 D2
Dorothy Villas UB1 107 C5
Dorrien Wlk SW16 159 D2
Dorrington Ct SE25 183 C1
Dorrington Point 20 E3 97 D4
Dorrington St EC1 241 A4
Dorrington Way BR3 208 A4
Dorrit Ho 2 W11 112 D5
Dorrit Mews N18 33 C5
Dorrit St SE1 252 B2
Dorrit Way BR7 189 A4
Dorryn Ct SE26 184 D5
Dors Cl NW9 45 B1
Dorset Ave
Falconwood DA16 145 D1
Hayes UB4 83 C4
Southall UB2 107 C2
Dorset Bldgs EC4 241 C1
Dorset Cl Hayes UB4 83 C4
Marylebone NW1 237 C4
Dorset Ct 3 Ealing W7 86 D2
3 London N1 73 C1
4 Northolt UB5 85 B4
Dorset Dr HA8 26 B4
Dorset Gdns SW16 204 B5
Dorset Hall SW19 179 C2
Dorset Ho 1 SE20 184 B2
Dorset Mans 2 W6 134 D6
Dorset Mews
Belgravia SW1 258 C6
Finchley N3 29 C2
Dorset Pl E15 76 B2
Dorset Rd
Ashford TW15 148 A1
Chislehurst SE9 166 A2
Ealing W5 109 D3
Harrow HA1 42 A3
Merton SW19 179 C1
Mitcham CR4 180 C1
Penge BR3 206 D6
South Lambeth
SW8 138 B5 270 C4
Upton E7 77 C1
West Green N15 51 B5
Wood Green N22 32 A2
Dorset Rise EC4 94 D1 241 C1
Dorset Road Inf Sch
SE9 166 A2
Dorset Sq NW1 92 D3 237 C5
Dorset St W1 92 D2 237 D3
Dorset Way
Hillingdon UB10 82 B5
Twickenham TW2 152 B3
Dorset Waye TW5 129 B5
Dorton Cl 6 SE15 139 C5
Dorton Villas UB7 126 C4
Dorville Cres W6 112 B3
Dorville Rd SE12 165 A6
Dothill Rd SE18 145 A5
Douai Gr TW12 174 A2
Douay Martyrs RC Sch
(Annexe) The UB10 60 D3
Douay Martyrs RC Sch The
UB10 60 D4
Doughty Ct 11 E1 118 B5
Doughty Mews
WC1 94 B3 240 C5
Doughty St WC1 94 B3 240 C5
Douglas 20 NW9 27 D1
Douglas Ave
Walthamstow E17 35 C2
Wembley HA0 66 A1
West Barnes KT3 200 B5
Douglas Bader Ho N3 29 D4
Douglas Bldgs SE1 252 B2
Douglas Cl
Stanmore HA7 25 A5
Wallington SM6 220 A2
Douglas Cres UB4 84 D3
Douglas Ct London N3 29 D1
5 South Hampstead
NW6 69 C1
Douglas Ct *continued*
1 Upper Tooting
SW17 180 C4
Douglas Dr CR0 223 C5
Douglas Gracey Ho
SW18 157 A4
Douglas Ho
Isleworth TW1 153 B6
Putney SW15 156 A5
Westminster SW1 259 C3
Douglas Johnstone Ho
SW6 264 C5
Douglas Mews NW2 69 A5
Douglas Path E14 120 A1
Douglas Rd
Chingford E4 20 C3
Hounslow TW3 129 D2
Ilford IG3 58 A3
Islington N1 73 A1
Kilburn NW6 91 B6
Kingston u T KT1 176 D1
5 Newham E16 99 A2
Stanwell TW19 148 A5
Surbiton KT6 198 B1
Thames Ditton KT10 212 A6
Welling DA16 146 B4
Wood Green N22 32 C2
Douglas Rd N N1 73 A2
Douglas Rd S N1 73 A2
Douglas Robinson Ct
SW16 182 A3
Douglas Sq SM4 201 C3
Douglas St
SW1 115 D2 259 C3
Douglas Terr E17 35 B2
Douglas Waite Ho
NW6 69 D1
Douglas Way SE8 141 B5
Doulton Ho SE11 260 D4
Doulton Mews 4 NW6 69 D2
Dounesforth Gdns
SW18 157 D3
Douro Pl W8 113 D3 255 D6
Douro St E3 97 C5
Douthwaite Sq 12 E1 118 A5
Dove App E6 100 A2
Dove Cl Hendon NW7 27 D3
Northolt UB5 84 D3
Wallington SM6 220 B1
Dovecot Cl HA5 40 C4
Dovecote Gdns 8
SW14 133 B2
Dove Ct
City of London EC2 242 C1
Enfield EN3 18 B6
Stanwell TW19 148 A4
Dovedale Ave HA3 43 C3
Dovedale Cl DA16 146 A3
Dovedale Cotts 6
SW11 136 D3
Dovedale Ho N16 51 B2
Dovedale Rd SE22 162 B5
Dovedale Rise CR4 180 D3
Dovedon Cl N14 16 A2
Dove House Gdns E4 19 C2
Dovehouse Mead
IG11 101 B5
Dovehouse St
SW3 114 C1 257 A1
Dove Mews
SW7 114 A1 256 B2
Dove Pk HA5 23 C3
Dover Cl NW2 68 D6
Dovercourt Ave CR7 204 C5
Dovercourt Gdns HA7 26 A5
Dovercourt La SM1 218 A5
Dovercourt Rd SE22 161 D5
Dover Ct
Clerkenwell EC1 241 C6
17 Greenwich SE10 141 D4
Sutton SM1 218 B4
Dove Rd N1 73 B2
Doverfield Rd SW2 160 A4
Dover Flats SE1 263 B3
Dover Gdns SM5 218 D5
Dover Ho
7 Beckenham BR3 185 C3
Brixton SE5 138 D4
11 Deptford SE15 140 C6
Edgware HA8 26 B3
14 Penge SE20 184 B2
Dover House Rd
SW15 156 B6
Doveridge Gdns N13 32 D6
Dover Mans 16 SW9 138 C2
Dove Row E2 96 A6
Dover Park Dr SW15 156 B5
Dover Patrol SE3 143 C3
Dover Rd
Dagenham RM6 59 A3
Lower Edmonton N9 18 C2
South Norwood SE19 183 B4
Wanstead E12 77 C6
Woolwich SE18 145 A3
Dover St W1 115 C5 249 A4
Dover Terr TW9 132 C3
Dover Yd W1 249 A4
Doves Cl BR2 226 A6
Doves Yd N1 94 C6 234 A5
Dovet Ct SW8 270 C2
Doveton Ho 7 E1 96 C3
Doveton Rd CR2 221 B3
Doveton St 8 E1 96 C3
Dove Wlk SW1 258 A2
Dovey Lo 4 N1 72 C1
Dowanhill Rd SE6 164 B3
Dowd Cl N11 15 A2
Dowdeny Cl 12 NW5 71 C3
Dowdeswell Cl SW15 133 C1
Dowding Ho N6 49 A2
Dowding Pl HA7 25 A4
Dowding Rd UB10 60 B1
Dowe Ho SE3 142 C2
Dowell Ho SE21 161 D1
Dower Ho The DA14 169 B1
Dowes Ho 13 SW16 160 A1
Dowgate Hill EC4 252 C6
Dowland Ho EN1 5 D5
Dowland St W10 91 A4
Dowlas St SE5 139 C5
Dowlen Ct 14 E14 119 C4
Dowler Ct 2 KT2 176 B2
Dowler Ho 32 E1 96 A1
Dowlerville Rd BR6 227 D2
Dowling Ho DA17 125 B3
Dowman Cl 2 SW19 179 D3
Downage NW4 46 C6
Downalong WD23 8 B3
Down Barns Rd HA4 62 D5
Downbarton Ho 11
SW9 138 C4
Downbury Mews 13
SW18 157 C6
Down Cl UB5 84 B5
Downderry Prim Sch
BR1 186 C6
Downderry Rd BR1 186 C6
Downe Cl DA16 146 C5
Downe Ho 9 SE7 143 C6
Downe Manor Prim Sch
UB5 84 B4
Downend SE18 144 D5
Downend Ct 1 SE15 139 C6
Downe Rd CR4 180 D1
Downer's Cotts SW4 137 C1
Downes Cl TW1 153 B5
Downes Ct N21 16 C3
Downes Ho CR0 220 D4
Downey Ho 6 E1 96 D3
Downfield KT4 200 A1
Downfield Cl W9 91 D3
Downfield Ho KT3 199 B1
Down Hall Rd KT2 175 D2
DOWNHAM 186 C5
Downham Ct 1 N1 73 B1
Downham Ent Ctr
SE6 164 D2
Downham La BR1 186 B5
Downham Rd N1 73 B1
Downham Way BR1 186 C6
Downhills Ave N17 51 B6
Downhills Park Rd N17 51 A6
Downhills Prim Sch
N15 51 B5
Downhills Way N17 33 A1
Downhurst Ave NW7 27 B5
Downhurst Ct NW4 46 C6
Downing Cl HA2 42 A6
Downing Ct N12 29 D5
Downing Dr UB6 86 C6
Downing Ho
9 Merton SW19 179 C3
2 North Kensington
W10 90 D1
4 Putney SW15 156 A6
Downing Rd RM9 81 B1
Downings E6 100 C1
Downing St*
SW1 116 A4 250 A2
Downland Cl N20 14 A3
Downland Ct E11 76 C6
Downleys Cl SE9 166 B2
Downman Rd SE9 144 A2
Down Pl W6 112 B1
Down Rd TW11 175 B4
Down St Mews W1 248 C3
Downs Ave
Elmstead BR7 188 B5
Pinner HA5 41 B2
Downs Bridge Rd BR3 186 B2
Downs Ct 16 Hackney E8 74 B3
13 Wimbledon SW19 178 D3
Downsell Prim Sch E15 76 B4
Downsell Rd E15 76 B4
Downsfield Rd E17 53 A3
Downshall Ave IG3 57 C3
Downshall Ct IG3 57 C3
Downshall Prim Sch
IG3 57 C2
Downs Hill BR2, BR3 186 B2
Downshire Hill NW3 70 B4
Downside
2 Putney SW15 157 A6
Sunbury TW16 172 A2
Twickenham TW1 152 D1
Downside Cl SW19 180 A4
Downside Cres
Ealing W13 87 A3
Maitland Pk NW3 70 C3
Downside Rd SM2 218 C2
Downside Wlk UB5 85 B4
Downs La 2 E5 74 B4
Downs Park Rd E5, E8 74 A3
Downs Rd
Beckenham BR3 185 D1
Enfield EN1 5 C1
Shacklewell E5, N16 74 A4
South Norwood CR7 183 A2
Down St
East Molesey KT8 195 C4
Mayfair W1 115 B5 248 C3
Downs The SW19,
SW20 178 D3
Downs View TW7 131 A4
Downsview Gdns
SE19 183 A3
Downs View Lo 9
KT6 198 A3
Downsview Prim Sch
SE19 183 A3

Downsview Rd SE19 ... 183 A3
Downsview Sch E5 ... 74 B4
Downsway BR6 ... 227 C3
Downton Ave SW2 ... 160 B2
Downtown Rd SE16 ... 119 A4
Downway N12 ... 30 C3
Down Way UB5 ... 84 B4
Dowrey St N1 ... 234 A6
Dowsett Rd N17 ... 34 A1
Dowson Cl SE5 ... 139 B1
Dowson Ct SE13 ... 142 B2
Dowson Ho 8 E1 ... 96 D1
Doyce St SE1 ... 252 A2
Doyle Gdns NW10 ... 90 B6
Doyle Ho W3 ... 110 D4
Doyle Rd SE25 ... 206 A5
D'Oyley St SW1 ... 258 A4
Doynton St N19 ... 71 B6
Draco St SE17 ... 139 A6
Dragon Ct WC2 ... 240 B2
Dragonfly Cl E13 ... 99 B4
Dragon Rd SE15 ... 139 C6
Dragon Yd WC1 ... 240 B2
Dragoon Rd SE8 ... 119 B1
Dragor Rd NW10 ... 89 A3
Drake Cl 30 SE16 ... 118 D4
Drake Cres SE28 ... 102 C1
Drake Croft N16 ... 73 B6
Drake Ct Dulwich SE19 ... 183 D5
5 Hammersmith W12 ... 112 B4
Kingston u T KT5 ... 198 B5
Drakefell Rd SE4,
SE14 ... 140 D2
Drakefield Rd SW17 ... 159 A1
Drake Hall 13 E16 ... 121 B5
Drake Ho
2 Limehouse E14 ... 119 A6
20 Stepney E1 ... 96 C2
Drakeley Ct N5 ... 72 D4
Drake Mews BR2 ... 209 C5
Drake Rd Brockley SE4 ... 141 C2
Chessington KT9 ... 214 C3
Harrow HA2 ... 63 B6
Mitcham CR4 ... 203 A3
Thornton Heath CR0 ... 204 B2
Drakes Ct SE23 ... 162 C3
Drakes Ctyd NW6 ... 69 B1
Drake St Enfield EN2 ... 5 B4
Holborn WC1 ... 240 C3
Drakes Wlk E6 ... 100 B6
Drakewood Rd SW16 ... 181 D3
Draper Cl
Belvedere DA17 ... 125 B2
Hounslow TW7 ... 130 B3
Draper Ct BR1 ... 210 A5
Draper Ho SE1 ... 261 D4
Draper Pl N1 ... 234 D6
Drapers Almhouses 5
E3 ... 97 C4
Draper's Cottage Homes
NW7 ... 28 A6
Drapers Gdns EC2 ... 242 D2
Drapers Rd Enfield EN2 ... 4 D4
Leyton E15 ... 76 B4
Tottenham N17 ... 51 D6
Drappers Way 8
SE16 ... 118 A2
Draven Cl BR2 ... 208 D2
Drawell Cl SE18 ... 123 C1
Drax Ave SW20 ... 178 A3
Draxmont SW19 ... 179 A4
Draycot Rd
Tolworth KT6 ... 198 C1
Wanstead E11 ... 55 B2
Draycott Ave
Chelsea SW3 ... 114 C2 257 B3
Harrow HA3 ... 43 C3
Draycott Cl
Camberwell SE5 ... 139 B5
Cricklewood NW2 ... 68 D5
Harrow HA3 ... 43 B3
Draycott Ct SW11 ... 267 A2
Draycott Ho SW3 ... 257 C3
Draycott Pl
SW3 ... 114 D2 257 C3
Draycott Terr
SW3 ... 114 D2 257 D3
Drayford Cl W9 ... 91 B3
Dray Gdns SW2 ... 160 B6
Draymans Ct 4 SW9 ... 138 B2
Draymans Way TW7 ... 130 D2
Drayside Mews UB2 ... 107 B4
Drayson Mews
W8 ... 113 C4 245 B1
Drayton Ave
Ealing W13 ... 109 A6
Orpington BR6 ... 210 D1
Drayton Bridge Rd
Ealing W7, W13 ... 108 D6
Ealing W13 ... 87 A1
Drayton Cl
Hounslow TW4 ... 151 B6
Ilford IG1 ... 57 B1
Drayton Ct
South Kensington
SW10 ... 256 B1
Tolworth KT5 ... 214 D6
West Drayton UB7 ... 104 B2
Drayton Gdns
Ealing W13 ... 109 A6
Southgate N21 ... 16 D4
South Kensington
SW10 ... 114 A1 256 B1
West Drayton UB7 ... 104 A4
Drayton Gn W13 ... 109 A6
Drayton Gr W13 ... 109 A6
Drayton Green Prim Sch
W13 ... 109 A6
Drayton Green Rd
W13 ... 109 B6
Drayton Green Sta W7 ... 86 D1
Drayton Ho
14 Camberwell SE5 ... 139 B5
Leytonstone E11 ... 54 B1
Drayton Lo E17 ... 35 D1
Drayton Manor High Sch
W7 ... 86 D1
Drayton Park Mews 12
N5 ... 72 C3
Drayton Park Prim Sch
N5 ... 72 C3
Drayton Park Sta N5 ... 72 C3
Drayton Pk N5, N7 ... 72 C4
Drayton Rd
Croydon CR0 ... 220 D6
Ealing W13 ... 109 B6
Harlesden NW10 ... 89 D6
Leytonstone E11 ... 54 B1
Tottenham N17 ... 33 C1
Drayton Waye HA3 ... 43 B3
Dreadnought Cl SW19 ... 180 B1
Dreadnought St SE10 ... 120 C3
Drenon Sq UB3 ... 105 D6
Dresden Cl NW6 ... 69 D2
Dresden Ho
5 Clapham SW11 ... 137 A3
Lambeth SE11 ... 260 D4
Dresden Rd N19 ... 49 D1
Dressington Ave SE4 ... 163 C5
Drew Ave NW7 ... 29 A4
Drewery Ct SE3 ... 142 C2
Drewett Ho 31 E1 ... 96 A1
Drew Gdns UB6 ... 64 D2
Drew Ho 12 SW16 ... 160 A1
Drew Prim Sch E16 ... 122 A5
Drew Rd E16 ... 122 A5
Drewstead La SW16 ... 159 D2
Drewstead Rd SW16 ... 159 D2
Driberg Ct RM9 ... 80 B2
Driffield Ct 4 NW9 ... 27 C2
Driffield Rd E3 ... 97 A5
Drift The BR2 ... 225 D5
Driftway Ho 19 E3 ... 97 B5
Driftway The CR4 ... 181 A2
Drinkwater Ho 11 SE5 ... 139 B5
Drinkwater Rd HA2 ... 63 D6
Drive Ct HA8 ... 26 C5
Drive Ho CR4 ... 202 C5
Drive Mans SW6 ... 135 A3
Drive The Acton W3 ... 89 A1
Ashford TW15 ... 171 B3
Barking IG11 ... 79 D1
Barking IG11 ... 80 A2
Barnet EN5 ... 1 A2
Beckenham BR3 ... 185 C2
Bexley DA5 ... 168 D4
Buckhurst Hill IG9 ... 21 C4
Chingford E4 ... 20 B4
Chislehurst BR7 ... 189 D2
Edgware HA8 ... 26 C5
Enfield EN2 ... 5 B4
Erith DA8 ... 147 D6
Feltham TW14 ... 150 C4
Finchley N3 ... 29 C3
Fortis Green N6 ... 48 D4
Harlesden NW10 ... 89 D6
Harrow HA2 ... 41 C2
Hendon NW11 ... 47 A2
Hounslow TW3, TW7 ... 130 B3
Ickenham UB10 ... 60 A5
Islington N7 ... 72 B2
Kingston u T KT2 ... 177 A3
Morden SM4 ... 202 B4
New Barnet EN5 ... 14 A5
Orpington BR6 ... 227 D6
Redbridge IG1 ... 56 B2
Sidcup DA14 ... 190 B6
South Norwood CR7 ... 205 B5
St Paul's Cray BR7 ... 211 D6
Surbiton KT6 ... 198 A2
Thames Ditton KT10 ... 196 A1
Walthamstow E17 ... 53 D6
Wanstead E18 ... 55 A6
Wembley Pk HA9 ... 67 A6
West Ewell KT19 ... 215 D2
West Wickham BR4 ... 208 B2
Wimbledon SW19,
SW20 ... 178 C3
Wood Green N11 ... 31 D4
Dr Johnson Ave SW17 ... 159 B1
Dr Johnson's House Mus*
EC4 ... 241 B1
Droitwich Cl SE26 ... 162 A1
Dromey Gdns HA3 ... 24 D3
Dromore Rd SW15 ... 157 A5
Dronfield Gdns RM8 ... 80 C3
Dron Ho E1 ... 96 C2
Droop St W10 ... 91 A3
Drovers Ct
3 Kingston u T KT1 ... 176 A1
Lewisham SE13 ... 142 A2
Drovers Pl SE15 ... 140 B5
Drovers Rd CR2 ... 221 B3
Dr Triplett's CE Prim Sch
UB3 ... 83 D1
Druce Rd SE21 ... 161 C5
Druid St SE1 ... 117 D4 253 C1
Druids Way BR2 ... 208 B5
Drumaline Ridge KT4 ... 215 C6
Drummer Lo N7 ... 72 B5
Drummond Castle Ct
E7 ... 76 D4
Drummond Cres
NW1 ... 93 D4 232 C2
Drummond Ct
Finchley N12 ... 30 C3
Harrow HA1 ... 42 C2
Drummond Ctr CR0 ... 221 A6
Drummond Dr HA7 ... 24 D3
Drummond Gate SW1 ... 259 D2
Drummond Ho
13 Bethnal Green E2 ... 96 A5
Finchley N2 ... 30 A1
Drummond Rd
Bermondsey SE16 ... 118 B3
Croydon CR0 ... 221 A6
Wanstead E11 ... 55 C3
Drummonds Pl TW9 ... 132 A1
Drummond St
NW1 ... 93 C3 239 A6
Drummonds The IG9 ... 21 B2
Drum St E1 ... 243 D2
Drury Cres CR0 ... 220 C6
Drury Ho SW8 ... 269 A2
Drury La WC2 ... 94 A1 240 B1
Drury Rd HA1 ... 42 A2
Drury Way NW10 ... 67 B3
Drury Way Ind Est
NW10 ... 67 B3
Dryad St SW15 ... 134 D2
Dryburgh Gdns NW9 ... 44 C6
Dryburgh Ho SW1 ... 258 D2
Dryburgh Mans SW15 ... 134 C2
Dryburgh Rd SW15 ... 134 C2
Dryden Ave W7 ... 86 D1
Dryden Bldg 10 E1 ... 96 A1
Dryden Ct
Lambeth SE11 ... 261 B3
11 Richmond TW10 ... 175 D6
Dryden Ho
Bromley Comm BR2 ... 209 D4
6 Camberwell SE5 ... 139 C4
16 Stoke Newington N16 ... 73 C5
Dryden Rd
Bexley DA16 ... 145 D4
Enfield EN1 ... 17 D5
Harrow HA3 ... 24 D2
Wimbledon SW19 ... 180 A4
Dryden St WC2 ... 240 B1
Dryer Ct 21 EN3 ... 7 C6
Dryfield Cl NW10 ... 67 A2
Dryfield Rd HA8 ... 27 A4
Dryfield Wlk 1 SE8 ... 141 C6
Dryhill Rd DA17 ... 147 B6
Dryland Ave 5 BR6 ... 227 D4
Drylands Rd N8 ... 50 A3
Drysdale Ave E4 ... 19 D5
Drysdale Flats 3 E8 ... 73 D3
Drysdale Ho 19 E2 ... 95 C4
Drysdale Pl N1 ... 95 C4
Drysdale St N1 ... 95 C4
Dublin Ave E8 ... 96 A6
Du Burstow Terr W7 ... 108 C4
Ducal St 25 E2 ... 95 D4
Ducane Cl 6 W12 ... 90 C1
Du Cane Ct SW12 ... 159 A3
Du Cane Rd W12 ... 90 A1
Ducavel Ho SW2 ... 160 B3
Duchess Cl London N11 ... 31 B5
Sutton SM1 ... 218 A4
Duchess Gr IG9 ... 21 B2
Duchess Mews W1 ... 238 D3
Duchess of Bedford Ho
W8 ... 245 A2
Duchess of Bedford's Wlk
W8 ... 113 C4 245 A1
Duchess St W1 ... 93 B2 238 D3
Duchy Rd EN4 ... 2 B5
Duchy St SE1 ... 116 C5 251 B4
Ducie Ho
8 Charlton SE7 ... 143 C6
2 Putney SW15 ... 156 C6
Ducie St SW4 ... 138 B1
Duckett Mews N4 ... 50 D3
Duckett Rd N4 ... 50 D3
Duckett St E1 ... 97 A2
Duck La W1 ... 239 C1
Duck Lees La EN3 ... 7 A1
Ducks Hill Rd HA4, HA6 ... 39 A5
DUCKS ISLAND ... 12 D5
Duck's Wlk TW1 ... 153 C6
Du Cros Dr HA7 ... 25 D4
Du Cros Rd W3 ... 111 C5
DUDDEN HILL ... 68 A3
Dudden Hill La NW10 ... 67 D3
Duddington Cl SE9 ... 187 D6
Dudley Ave HA3 ... 43 C6
Dudley Ct
Colney Hatch N12 ... 30 C5
Marylebone W1 ... 237 C1
St Giles WC2 ... 240 A2
Temple Fortune NW11 ... 47 B5
14 Wanstead E11 ... 55 A4
Wembley HA0 ... 65 D3
Dudley Dr Ruislip HA4 ... 62 B3
West Barnes SM4 ... 201 A2
Dudley Gdns
Ealing W13 ... 109 B4
Harrow HA2 ... 42 B1
Dudley Ho
18 Brixton SW9 ... 138 C3
Edgware HA8 ... 26 B3
Paddington W2 ... 236 C3
Dudley Mews 14 SW2 ... 160 C5
Dudley Pl UB3 ... 105 B2
Dudley Rd
Ashford TW15 ... 170 B6
East Bedfont TW14 ... 149 B3
Finchley N3 ... 29 D1
Harrow HA2 ... 64 A6
Ilford IG1 ... 78 D4
Kilburn NW6 ... 91 B5
Kingston u T KT1 ... 198 B6
Richmond TW9 ... 132 B3
Southall UB2 ... 106 D3
Walthamstow E17 ... 35 C1
Walton-on-T KT12 ... 194 A2
Wimbledon SW19 ... 179 C4
Dudley St W2 ... 236 C3
Dudlington Rd E5 ... 74 C6
Dudmaston Mews
SW3 ... 256 D2
Dudsbury Rd DA14 ... 190 B4
Dudset La TW5 ... 128 A4
Duett Ct TW3 ... 129 A5
Duffell Ho SE11 ... 260 D1
Dufferin Ave EC1 ... 242 C5
Dufferin Ct EC1 ... 242 C5
Dufferin St EC1 ... 95 A3 242 B5
Duffield Cl HA1 ... 42 D4
Duffield Dr N15 ... 51 D5
Duffield Ho N4 ... 51 A2
Duff St E14 ... 97 D1
Dufour's Pl W1 ... 239 B1
Dugard Way
SE11 ... 116 D2 261 C3
Dugdale Ho 10 N7 ... 71 D3
Duggan Dr BR7 ... 188 A4
Dugolly Ave HA9 ... 66 D5
Duke Gdns IG6 ... 57 B5
Duke Humphrey Rd
SE3 ... 142 C3
Duke Of Cambridge Cl
TW2 ... 152 B5
Duke Of Edinburgh Rd
SM1 ... 218 B6
Duke Of Wellington Ave
SE18 ... 123 A3
Duke of Wellington Pl SW1,
W1 ... 248 B2
Duke of York's Sq
SW3 ... 114 D2 257 D3
Duke of York St SW1 ... 249 B4
Duke Rd Chiswick W4 ... 111 B1
Ilford IG6 ... 57 B5
Duke St Hill SE1 ... 252 D4
Duke St St James's
SW1 ... 115 C5 249 B4
Dukes Ave Edgware HA8 ... 26 B5
Finchley N3 ... 29 D2
Hornsey N10 ... 49 C6
Hounslow TW4 ... 129 A1
Kingston u T KT3 ... 199 D6
Northolt UB5 ... 63 A1
Rayners La HA2, HA5 ... 41 B3
Richmond KT2, TW10 ... 175 D6
Wealdstone HA1 ... 42 C5
Duke's Ave W4 ... 111 B1
Dukes Cl Ashford TW15 ... 171 A6
Hampton TW12 ... 173 B5
Dukes Ct Barking E6 ... 100 C6
Beckenham BR3 ... 207 A6
Dulwich SE22 ... 162 A3
Ealing W13 ... 87 B2
East Dulwich SE22 ... 162 B6
Lewisham SE13 ... 142 A3
Mortlake SW14 ... 133 B3
Dukes Gate 4 W4 ... 111 A2
Dukes Green Ave
TW14 ... 150 A6
Dukes Head Yd N6 ... 49 B1
Duke's Ho SW1 ... 259 D4
Duke Shore Wharf
E14 ... 119 B6
Dukes La W8 ... 113 D4 245 C2
Dukes Mews N10 ... 49 B6
Duke's Mews W1 ... 238 B2
Duke's Pl EC3 ... 95 C1 243 B1
Dukes Point N6 ... 49 B1
Dukes Rd Acton W3 ... 88 C3
Barking E6 ... 100 C6
Duke's Rd WC1 ... 93 D4 232 D1
Dukes Ride UB10 ... 60 A4
Duke St
Marylebone
W1 ... 93 A1 238 B1
Richmond TW10, TW9 ... 153 D6
Sutton SM1 ... 218 B4
Dukesthorpe Rd SE26 ... 184 D6
Duke Street Mans W1 ... 238 B1
Dukes Way BR4 ... 224 C5
Duke's Yd W1 ... 248 B6
Dulas St N4 ... 50 B1
Dulford St
W11 ... 113 A6 244 A6
Dulka Rd SW11 ... 158 D6
Dulverton NW1 ... 232 B5
Dulverton Ct 12 KT6 ... 198 A4
Dulverton Mans WC1 ... 240 D5
Dulverton Prim Sch
SE9 ... 167 B2
Dulverton Rd
New Eltham SE9 ... 167 B2
Ruislip HA4 ... 62 A6
DULWICH ... 161 C1
Dulwich Bsns Ctr
SE23 ... 162 D3
Dulwich Coll SE21 ... 161 C2
Dulwich Coll Picture
Gall* SE21 ... 161 C4
Dulwich Coll Prep Sch
SE21 ... 161 C1
Dulwich Comm SE21 ... 161 C3
Dulwich Ct SE22 ... 162 B3
Dulwich Hamlet Jun Sch
SE21 ... 161 B5
Dulwich Hospl SE22 ... 139 C1
Dulwich Lawn Cl
SE22 ... 161 D6
Dulwich Mead SE24 ... 161 A5
Dulwich Mews
1 East Dulwich
SE22 ... 139 D1
East Dulwich SE22 ... 161 D6
Dulwich Oaks The
SE21 ... 161 D1
Dulwich Rd SE24 ... 160 D5
DULWICH VILLAGE ... 161 C4
Dulwich Village SE21 ... 161 C5
Dulwich Village CE Inf Sch
SE21 ... 161 C5
Dulwich Wood Ave
SE19 ... 183 C5
Dulwich Wood Pk
SE19 ... 183 C6
Dumain Ct SE11 ... 261 C3
Du Maurier Ho 2 NW3 ... 70 D3
Dumbarton Ct 16
SW2 ... 160 A4
Dumbarton Rd SW2 ... 160 A5
Dumbleton Cl KT2 ... 176 D2
Dumbreck Rd SE9 ... 144 C2
Dumont Rd N16 ... 73 C5
Dumphreys Ho 5
SW4 ... 159 D4
Dumpton Pl NW1 ... 71 A1
Dunally Pk TW17 ... 193 B2
Dunbar Ave
Beckenham BR3 ... 207 A5
Dagenham RM10 ... 81 C5
Thornton Heath SW16 ... 182 C1
Dunbar Cl UB4 ... 84 A2
Dunbar Ct
3 London N12 ... 29 D6
Sutton SM1 ... 218 B3
Walton-on-T KT12 ... 194 C1
Dunbar Gdns RM10 ... 81 D3
Dunbar Rd
New Malden KT3 ... 199 A5
Tottenham N22 ... 32 D2
Upton E7 ... 77 A2
Dunbar St SE27 ... 161 A1
Dunbar Wharf 20 E14 ... 119 B6
Dunblane Cl HA8 ... 10 D2
Dunblane Rd SE9 ... 144 A3
Dunboe Pl TW17 ... 193 A2
Dunboyne Rd NW3 ... 70 D3
Dunbridge Ho SW15 ... 155 D5
Dunbridge St
Bethnal Green E2 ...
Bethnal Green E2 ... 96 B3
Duncan Cl EN5 ... 2 A1
Duncan Ct
5 London N12 ... 29 D5
3 Poplar E14 ... 98 A2
Southgate N21 ... 16 D3
Duncan Gr W3 ... 89 C1
Duncan Ho Harrow HA2 ... 64 A5
3 Primrose Hill NW3 ... 70 D1
Duncannon Ho SW1 ... 259 D1
Duncannon St WC2 ... 250 A5
Duncan Rd Hackney E8 ... 96 B6
Richmond TW9 ... 132 A1
Duncan St N1 ... 94 D5 234 C4
Duncan Terr N1 ... 94 D5 234 C4
Dunch St 33 E1 ... 96 B1
Dunchurch Ho RM10 ... 81 C1
Duncombe Hill SE23 ... 163 A4
Duncombe Ho 7
SW19 ... 156 D3
Duncombe Prim Sch
N19 ... 50 A1
Duncombe Rd N19 ... 49 D1
Duncrievie Rd SE13 ... 164 B5
Duncroft SE18 ... 145 C5
Dundalk Ho 2 E1 ... 96 C1
Dundalk Rd SE4 ... 141 A2
Dundas Gdns KT8 ... 195 D6
Dundas Ho 12 E2 ... 96 C5
Dundas Mews 4 EN3 ... 7 C6
Dundas Rd SE15 ... 140 C3
Dundee Ct 36 E1 ... 118 B5
Dundee Ho W9 ... 229 A2
Dundee Rd
Croydon SE25 ... 206 B4
Newham E13 ... 99 B5
Dundee St E1 ... 118 B5
Dundee Way EN3 ... 7 A2
Dundee Wharf E14 ... 119 B6
Dundela Gdns KT17,
KT4 ... 216 B4
Dundonald Cl 6 E6 ... 100 A1
Dundonald Prim Sch
SW19 ... 179 B3
Dundonald Rd
Brondesbury Pk NW10 ... 90 D6
Merton SW19 ... 179 B3
Dundonald Road Sta
SW19 ... 179 B3
Dundry Ho 8 SE26 ... 162 A1
Duneaves HA1 ... 64 C5
Dunedin Ho E16 ... 122 B5
Dunedin Rd Ilford IG1 ... 57 A1
Leyton E10 ... 75 D5
Dunedin Way UB4 ... 84 C3
Dunelm Gr SE27 ... 161 A1
Dunelm St E1 ... 96 D1
Dunfield Gdns SE6 ... 185 D5
Dunfield Rd SE6 ... 185 D5
Dunford Ct 9 HA5 ... 23 B3
Dunford Rd N7 ... 72 B4
Dungarvan Ave SW15 ... 134 A1
Dungeness Ho SW18 ... 136 A1
Dunheved Cl CR7 ... 204 C3
Dunheved Ct 2 CR7 ... 204 C3
Dunheved Rd N CR7 ... 204 C3
Dunheved Rd S CR7 ... 204 C3
Dunheved Rd W CR7 ... 204 C3
Dunhill Point 12
SW15 ... 156 B3
Dunholme Gn N9 ... 17 D1
Dunholme La N9 ... 17 D1
Dunholme Rd N9 ... 17 D1
Dunkeld Ho 15 E14 ... 98 B1
Dunkeld Rd
Dagenham RM8 ... 80 C6
South Norwood SE25 ... 205 B5
Dunkery Rd SE9 ... 166 A1
Dunkirk St 12 SE27 ... 183 A6
Dunlace Rd E5 ... 74 D4
Dunleary Cl TW4 ... 151 B4
Dunley Dr CR0 ... 224 A2
Dunlin Ct 12 SE21 ... 161 B2
Dunlin Ho 13 SE16 ... 118 D2
Dunloe Ave N17 ... 51 B6
Dunloe Ct 7 E2 ... 95 D5
Dunloe St E2 ... 95 D5
Dunlop Pl
SE16 ... 117 D3 263 D5
Dunmore Point 15 E2 ... 95 D4
Dunmore Rd
Kilburn NW6 ... 91 A6
Wimbledon SW20 ... 178 D2
Dunmow Cl
Dagenham RM6 ... 58 C4
3 Feltham TW13 ... 173 A6
Dunmow Ho
Dagenham RM9 ... 102 B6
Vauxhall SE11 ... 260 D2
Dunmow Rd E15 ... 76 B4
Dunmow Wlk N1 ... 235 A6
Dunnage Cres SE16 ... 119 A2
Dunne Mews 11 NW5 ... 71 C3
Dunnet Ho 27 E3 ... 97 B5
Dunnico Ho SE17 ... 263 A2
Dunn Mead NW9 ... 27 D3
Dunnock Cl N9 ... 18 D3
Dunnock Ct 11 SE21 ... 161 B2
Dunnock Rd E6 ... 100 A1
Dunn's Pas WC1 ... 240 B2
Dunn St E8 ... 73 D3
Dunollie Pl NW5 ... 71 C3
Dunollie Rd NW5 ... 71 C3
Dunoon Gdns SE23 ... 162 D4
Dunoon Ho N1 ... 233 C5
Dunoon Rd SE23 ... 162 C4
Dunraven Dr EN2 ... 4 C3
Dunraven Ho 12 TW9 ... 132 B4
Dunraven Rd W12 ... 112 A5
Dunraven Sch SW16 ... 160 B1
Dunraven St
W1 ... 114 D6 247 D6
Dunrobin Ct NW3 ... 69 D3
Dunsany Rd W14 ... 112 D3
Dunsfold Ct 14 SM2 ... 217 D1
Dunsfold Ho
10 Kingston u T KT2 ... 176 D4
4 Streatham SW2 ... 160 B4
Dunsfold Way CR0 ... 223 D1
Dunsford Way SW15 ... 156 B5
Dunsmore Cl
Bushey WD23 ... 8 B5
Hayes UB4 ... 85 A3
Dunsmore Rd KT12 ... 194 B3
Dunsmore Way WD23 ... 8 B5
Dunsmure Rd N16 ... 51 C1
Dunstable Ct 3 SE3 ... 143 A5
Dunstable Mews W1 ... 238 B4
Dunstable Rd
East Molesey KT8 ... 195 B5
Richmond TW10, TW9 ... 132 A1
Dunstall Ho 9 SE15 ... 140 A4
Dunstall Rd SW19,
SW20 ... 178 C4
Dunstall Way KT8 ... 195 D6
Dunstall Welling Est
DA16 ... 146 B3
Dunstan Cl 2 N2 ... 48 A6
Dunstan Glade BR5 ... 211 B3
Dunstan Ho SE4 ... 141 B3
Dunstan Hos 5 E1 ... 96 C2
Dunstan Rd NW11 ... 47 C1
Dunstan's Gr SE22 ... 162 B5
Dunstan's Rd SE22 ... 162 A5
Dunster Ave SM4 ... 200 D1
Dunster Ct EC3 ... 253 B6
Dunster Dr NW9 ... 45 A1
Dunster Gdns NW6 ... 69 B1
Dunster Ho SE6 ... 163 D1
Dunsterville Way SE1 ... 252 D1
Dunster Way
Carshalton CR4 ... 203 A1
Harrow HA2 ... 63 A5
Dunston Rd
Clapham SW11 ... 137 A3
Hackney E8 ... 95 D6
Dunston St E8 ... 95 D6
Dunton Cl KT6 ... 198 A1
Dunton Ct 5 SE26 ... 162 B2
Dunton Ho 14 SW16 ... 160 A1
Dunton Rd
Bermondsey
SE1 ... 117 D2 263 C3
Leyton E10 ... 53 D2
Duntshill Rd SW18 ... 157 D3
Dunvegan Cl KT8 ... 195 D5
Dunvegan Rd SE9 ... 144 B1
Dunwich Ct 2 RM6 ... 58 B4
Dunwich Rd DA7 ... 147 B4
Dunworth Mews W11 ... 91 B1
Duplex Ride SW1 ... 247 D1
Dupont Rd SW20 ... 178 D1
Duppas Ave CR0 ... 220 D4
Duppas Cl TW17 ... 193 B4
Duppas Ct CR0 ... 220 D5
Duppas Hill La CR0 ... 220 D4
Duppas Hill Rd CR0 ... 220 D4
Duppas Hill Terr CR0 ... 220 D5
Duppas Jun Sch CR0 ... 220 D3
Duppas Rd CR0 ... 220 D5
Dupree Rd SE7 ... 121 B1
Dura Den Cl BR3 ... 185 D3
Durand Cl SM5 ... 202 D1
Durand Gdns
SW9 ... 138 B4 270 D1

Durand Prim Sch
SW9 138 B4 270 D2
Durand Way NW10 67 A1
Durants Lo EN3 6 D2
Durants Park Ave EN3 6 D1
Durants Rd EN3 6 D1
Durants Sch EN3 6 C4
Durant St E2 96 A4
Durban Ct E7 77 D1
Durban Ho 28 W12 112 B6
Durban Rd
Beckenham BR3 185 B1
Ilford IG2 57 C1
Newham E15 98 C4
Tottenham N17 33 D4
Walthamstow E17 35 B2
West Norwood SE27 183 B6
Durbin Ho 15 N9 18 A1
Durbin Rd KT9 214 B4
Durdan Cotts UB5 85 B1
Durdans Ho 3 NW1 71 C1
Durdans Park Prim Sch
UB1 85 B2
Durdans Rd UB1 85 B1
Durell Gdns RM9 80 D3
Durell Rd RM9 80 D3
Durfey Pl SE5 139 B5
Durford Cres SW15 156 B3
Durham Ave
Beckenham BR2 208 D5
Hounslow TW5 107 B1
Woodford IG8 37 D5
Durham Cl SW20 178 B1
Durham Ct 2 Barnet EN5 1 B2
Brockley SE4 141 C2
4 Kilburn NW6 91 C5
Teddington TW11 174 C6
Durham Hill BR1 186 D6
Durham Ho
3 Barking IG11 80 A1
7 Dartmouth Pk NW5 71 C5
Edgware HA8 26 B3
Lisson Gr NW8 230 B1
Durham House St
WC2 250 B5
Durham Pl
Chelsea SW3 257 C1
Ilford IG1 79 A4
Durham Rd
Beckenham BR2 208 D6
Ealing W5 109 D3
Edmonton N9 18 A2
Feltham TW14 150 C4
Harrow HA1 41 D4
Lower Holloway N4, N7 72 B6
Manor Pk E12 77 D4
Muswell Hill N2 48 D6
Newham E16 98 C3
Sidcup DA14 190 B5
Wimbledon SW20 178 B2
Durham Rise SE18 123 B1
Durham Row E1 97 A2
Durham St
SE11 138 B6 270 C6
Durham Terr W2 91 D1
Durham Wharf Dr
TW8 131 C5
Durley Ave HA5 41 A3
Durley Rd N16 51 C2
Durlock Ho 16 SW9 138 C4
Durlston Rd
Kingston u T KT2 176 A4
Stoke Newington E5 74 A6
Durnford Ho SE6 163 D1
Durnford St
4 Greenwich SE10 142 A6
South Tottenham N15 51 C4
Durning Rd SE19 183 B5
Durnsford Ave SW18,
SW19 157 C2
Durnsford Ct 5 EN3 7 A2
Durnsford Rd
London N11 31 D3
Wimbledon SW18,
SW19 157 C1
Durnston Ct 2 SM1 217 D2
Durrant Ct HA3 24 C2
Durrant Way BR6 227 B3
Durrell Rd SW6 264 C1
Durrell Way TW17 193 B3
Durrels Ho W14 254 D4
Durrington Ave SW20 178 C3
Durrington Park Rd
SW20 178 C2
Durrington Rd E5 75 A4
Durrington Twr 3
SW8 137 C3
Durrisdeer Ho NW2 69 B4
Dursley Cl SE3 143 C3
Dursley Gdns SE3 143 D4
Dursley Rd SE3 143 C3
Durston NW5 71 A3
Durston House
Middleton's Sch W5 87 D1
Durston House Prep Sch
W5 87 D1
Durward St E1 96 B2
Durweston Mews W1 237 D4
Durweston St W1 237 D3
Dury Rd EN5 1 B3
Dutch Gdns KT2 176 D4
Dutch Yd SW18 157 C6
Dutton Ho SW2 160 D3
Dutton St SE10 142 A4
Duxberry Cl BR2 210 A4
Duxford 21 KT1 176 C1
Duxford Ho 10 SE2 124 D4
Dwight Ct SW6 135 A3
Dycer Ho 10 E9 74 D2
Dye House La E3 97 C6
Dyer Ho
Hampton TW12 173 D2
New Cross SE4 141 A3
Dyer's Bldgs EC1 241 A3
Dyers Hall Rd
Leyton E11 76 B6
Leytonstone E11 54 C1
Dyer's La SW15 134 B1
Dykes Ct 11 SW2 160 B3
Dykes Way BR2 208 D6
Dylan Cl WD6 9 D4
Dylan Rd
Belvedere DA17 125 C3
2 Brixton SE24 138 D1
Dylways SE5 139 B1
Dymchurch Cl
Ilford IG5 56 C6
Orpington BR6 227 C4
Dymchurch Ho 12 E5 74 B3
Dymes Path SW19 156 D2
Dymock St SW6 135 D2
Dyneley Rd SE12 165 C1
Dyne Rd NW6 69 B1
Dynevor Rd
Richmond TW10 154 A6
Shacklewell N16 73 D5
Dynham Rd NW6 69 C1
Dyott St Soho WC1 239 D2
St Giles WC1,
WC2 94 A1 240 A2
Dysart Ave KT2, TW10 175 C6
Dysart Sch KT6 198 B2
Dysart St EC2 95 C3 243 A5
Dyson Ct London NW2 46 C2
Wembley HA0 65 A4
Dyson Ho 3 SE10 120 D1
Dyson Rd
Leytonstone E11 54 C3
Stratford E15 76 D2
Dyson's Rd N18 34 B4

E

Eade Rd N4 51 A2
Eagans Cl N2 48 B6
Eagle Ave RM6 59 A3
Eagle Cl
Bermondsey SE16 118 C1
Enfield EN3 6 C1
Wallington SM6 220 A2
Eagle Ct
10 Dulwich SE21 161 B2
Edmonton N18 33 D4
Holborn EC1 241 C4
6 Wanstead E11 55 A5
Eagle Dr NW9 27 C1
Eagle Dwellings EC1 235 B2
Eagle Hill SE19 183 B4
Eagle Ho
22 Bethnal Green E1 96 B3
Finsbury Pk N7 72 B5
Eagle House Sch CR4 180 D1
Eagle Hts 10 SW11 136 C2
Eagle La E11 55 A5
Eagle Lo
Leytonstone E11 54 D5
London NW11 47 B2
Eagle Mans N16 73 D3
Eagle Mews N1 73 C2
Eagle Pl
South Kensington
SW7 114 A1 256 B2
St James SW1 249 B5
Eagle Rd Hatton TW6 127 D2
Wembley HA0 65 D1
Eaglesfield Rd SE18 144 D4
Eagle St WC1 94 B2 240 C3
Eagle Star Ho SM1 217 D4
Eagle Terr IG8 37 B3
Eagle Trad Est CR4 202 D3
Eagle Wharf SE1 253 C3
Eagle Wharf Rd
N1 95 A5 235 B4
Eagle Works E1 243 D5
Eagling Cl E3 97 C4
Ealcom Ct W3 110 B5
Ealdham Prim Sch
SE9 143 C1
Ealdham Sq SE9 143 C1
EALING 109 D6
Ealing Broadway Ctr
W5 109 D6
Ealing Broadway Sta
W5 109 D6
Ealing Coll W13 87 B1
Ealing Coll of Higher Ed
W5 109 D5
Ealing Common W5 110 B6
Ealing Common Sta
W5 110 B5
Ealing Court Man W5 109 D4
Ealing Gateway W5 109 C6
Ealing Gn W5 109 D5
Ealing, Hammersmith &
West London Coll
W14 113 A1 254 A2
Ealing Hospl UB1, UB2 108 B4
Ealing Park Gdns W5 109 C2
Ealing Park Lo UB6 87 A5
Ealing Park Mans W5 109 D3
Ealing Rd
Brentford TW8 109 D2
Northolt UB5 63 C1
Wembley HA0 66 A1
Ealing Road Trad Est
TW8 109 D1
Ealing Tertiary Coll
W3 110 D5
Ealing Village W5 88 A1
Ealing & West London Coll
W5 109 D5
Eamann Casey Ho 34
SW9 138 C4
Eamont Cl HA4 38 D2
Eamont Ct NW8 230 B4
Eamont St NW8 92 C5 230 B4
Eardley Cres
SW5 113 C1 255 B1
Eardley Point 9 SE18 122 D2
Eardley Rd
Belvedere DA17 125 C1
Streatham SW16 181 C4
Eardley Sch SW16 181 C4
Earl Cl N11 31 B5
Earldom Rd SW15 134 C1
Earle Gdns KT2 176 A3
Earle Ho SW1 259 D3
Earlham Gr
Forest Gate E7 77 A3
Wood Green N22 32 B3
Earlham Prim Sch
Stratford E7 76 D3
Wood Green N22 32 C3
Earlham St WC2 94 A1 240 A1
Earl Ho NW1 237 B5
Earlom Ho WC1 234 A1
Earl Rd SW14 133 A1
Earl Rise SE18 123 B2
EARL'S COURT 113 C1
Earl's Court Ex Ctr*
SW5 113 C1 255 A1
Earl's Court Gdns
SW5 113 D2 255 C3
Earl's Court Rd SW5,
W8 113 C2 255 B4
Earl's Court Sq
SW5 113 D1 255 C2
Earl's Court Sta
SW5 113 C2 255 B3
Earls Cres HA1 42 C5
Earlsdown Ho 6 IG11 101 B5
Earlsferry Way N1 72 A1
EARLSFIELD 158 A3
Earlsfield Ho 16 KT2 175 D2
Earlsfield Prim Sch
SW18 158 A2
Earlsfield Rd SW18 158 A4
Earlsfield Sta SW18 158 A3
Earlshall Rd SE9 144 C1
Earlsmead HA2 63 B4
Earlsmead Fst & Mid Sch
HA2 63 B4
Earlsmead Prim Sch
N15 51 D5
Earlsmead Rd
Kensal Green NW10 90 C4
South Tottenham N15 51 D4
Earl St EC2 95 C2 243 A4
Earls Terr W8 254 D5
Earlsthorpe Mews 3
SW12 159 A5
Earlsthorpe Rd SE26 184 D6
Earlstoke St EC1 234 C2
Earlston Gr E9 96 B6
Earls Wlk
Dagenham RM8 80 B4
Kensington W8 113 C3 255 A5
Earlswood Ave CR7 204 C4
Earlswood Cl 10 SE10 120 C1
Earlswood Gdns IG5 56 C6
Earlswood Ho 2 SW2 160 B3
Earlswood St SE10 120 C1
Early Mews NW1 231 D6
Earnshaw Ho EC1 234 D1
Earnshaw St WC1, WC2 239 D2
Earsby St W14 254 B4
Earth Galleries*
SW7 114 B3 256 D5
Easby Cres SM4 201 D3
Easebourne Rd RM8 80 C3
Easedale Ho TW7 152 D6
Eashing Point 5
SW15 156 B3
Easleys Mews W1 238 B2
East 10 Ent Pk E10 53 A1
EAST ACTON 111 C5
East Acton Arc W3 89 D1
East Acton Ct W3 111 C6
East Acton La W3 111 C6
East Acton Prim Sch
W3 111 C6
East Acton Sta W12 89 D1
East Arbour St E1 96 D1
East Ave Croydon CR0 220 B3
East Finchley NW2 48 A6
Hayes UB3 106 A5
Plashet E12 78 A1
Southall UB1 107 B6
Walthamstow E17 53 D5
East Bank N16 51 C2
Eastbank Rd TW12 174 A5
EAST BARNET 14 D4
East Barnet Rd EN4 2 B1
East Barnet Sch
Barnet EN4 2 B2
East Barnet EN4 14 D5
East Beckton District Ctr
E6 100 B2
EAST BEDFONT 149 C3
East Block 5 E1 118 D6
Eastbourne Ave W3 89 B1
Eastbourne Gdns
SW14 133 A2
Eastbourne Mews
W2 92 A1 236 B2
Eastbourne Rd
Brentford TW8 109 D1
Chiswick W4 133 A6
Feltham TW13 150 D2
South Tottenham N15 51 C3
Streatham SW17 181 A4
Wallend E6 100 C4
West Ham E15 98 C6
Eastbourne Terr
W2 92 A1 236 B2
Eastbournia Ave N9 18 B1
Eastbrook Ave N9 18 C4
Eastbrook Rd SE3 143 B4
EASTBURY 22 A5
Eastbury Ave
Barking IG11 101 C6
Enfield EN1 5 D4
Mo Pk HA6 22 A5
Eastbury Comp Sch
IG11 79 C2
Eastbury Ct
Barking IG11 101 C6
New Barnet EN5 14 A6
Eastbury Gr W4 111 C1
Eastbury Inf Sch IG11 79 D1
Eastbury Rd
Kingston u T KT2 176 A3
Newham E6 100 C3
Orpington BR5 211 B3
Eastbury Sq IG11 101 D6
Eastbury Terr E1 96 D3
Eastcastle St
W1 93 C1 239 B2
Eastcheap EC3 117 C6 253 A6
East Churchfield Rd
W3 111 B5
Eastchurch Rd TW6 127 C2
Eastchurch Road Rdbt
TW6 127 C3
East Cl Cockfosters EN4 3 A1
Ealing W5 88 C3
Greenford UB6 86 A5
Eastcombe Ave SE7 143 B6
EASTCOTE 40 C3
Eastcote BR6 211 D1
Eastcote Ave
East Molesey KT8 195 C4
Harrow HA2 64 A6
Wembley UB6 65 A3
Eastcote Ind Est HA4 40 C2
Eastcote La Harrow HA2 63 C5
Northolt UB5 63 B2
Eastcote La N UB5 63 C2
Eastcote Pl HA5 40 B3
Eastcote Prim Sch
DA16 145 B2
Eastcote Rd
Bexley DA16 145 B3
Harrow HA2 64 A5
Pinner HA5 40 D4
Ruislip HA4 40 A3
Eastcote St SW9 138 B3
Eastcote Sta HA5 40 C2
Eastcote View HA5 40 C5
EASTCOTE VILLAGE 40 B4
Eastcourt Ind Sch IG3 58 A1
East Cres Enfield EN1 17 D6
Friern Barnet N11 30 D6
Eastcroft Rd KT19 215 C1
East Cross Ctr E15 75 C2
East Cross Route
Bow E3 97 C6
Hackney Wick E9 75 B3
East Croydon Sta CR0 221 B6
East Ct Sunbury TW16 172 C1
Wembley HA0 65 C6
Eastdown Ho E8 74 A4
Eastdown Pk SE13 142 B1
East Duck Lees La EN3 7 B1
EAST DULWICH 162 A6
East Dulwich Gr SE22 161 C6
East Dulwich Rd SE15,
SE22 140 A1
East Dulwich Sta
SE22 139 C1
East End Rd
East Finchley N2, N3 48 A6
Finchley N3 29 C1
East End Way HA5 41 A6
East Entrance RM10 103 D5
Eastern Ave
Gants Hill IG1, IG2,
IG4 56 C3
Newbury Pk IG2 57 B3
Pinner HA5 40 D2
Wanstead E11 55 C3
Eastern Avenue W RM7 59 C5
Eastern Bsns Pk
TW16 127 D3
Eastern Perimeter Rd
TW14 127 D3
Eastern Quay 15 E16 121 B5
Eastern Rd
Brockley SE4 141 C1
Fortis Green N2 48 D5
Newham E13 99 B5
Walthamstow E17 54 A4
Wood Green N22 32 A2
Easternville Gdns IG2 57 A3
Eastern Way SE28 124 B4
East Ferry Rd E14 119 D2
Eastfield Gdns RM10 81 C4
Eastfield Prim Sch EN3 6 D5
Eastfield Rd
Dagenham RM9 81 B4
Dagenham RM10 81 C4
Enfield EN3 6 D5
Hornsey N8 50 A6
Walthamstow E17 53 C5
Eastfields HA5 40 C4
Eastfields Ave SW18 135 C1
Eastfields Rd Acton W3 89 A2
Mitcham CR4 181 A1
Eastfield St E14 97 A2
EAST FINCHLEY 48 B5
East Finchley Sta N2 48 C5
Eastgate Bsns Pk E10 53 A1
Eastgate Cl SE28 102 D1
Eastgate Ct N3 29 C1
East Gdns SW17 180 C4
Eastglade HA5 41 B6
EAST HAM 100 A5
Eastham Cl EN5 13 B6
East Ham Ind Est E6 100 A2
East Ham Manor Way
E6 100 C1
East Ham Meml Hospl
E7 77 D1
East Ham Sta E6 78 A1
East Harding St EC4 241 B2
East Heath Rd NW3 70 B5
East Hill London SW18 158 A6
Wembley HA9 44 C1
Eastholm NW11 47 D5
Eastholme UB3 106 A5
East India Bldgs 9
E14 119 C6
East India Ct 7 SE16 118 C4
East India Dock Basin*
E14 120 C6
East India Dock Rd
E14 119 D6
East India Dock Road
Tunnel 18 E14 98 B1
East India Sta E14 120 B6
East India Way CR0 205 D1
East La
5 Bermondsey SE16 118 A4
Bermondsey SE16 118 A4
Kingston u T KT1 197 D6
Wembley HA0, HA9 65 D5
Eastlake Ho NW8 236 D5
Eastlake Rd SE5 139 A3
Eastland Ct 2 BR1 187 C1
Eastlands Cres SE21 161 D5
East Lane Bsns Pk HA9 65 D5
Eastlea Com Sch E16 98 C3
Eastlea Mews E16 98 C3
Eastleigh Ave HA2 63 D6
Eastleigh Cl
Belmont SM2 217 D1
Neasden NW2 67 C5
Eastleigh Rd E17 35 B1
Eastleigh Way TW14 150 A3
Eastleigh Wlk 9
SW15 156 A4
East London Coll E11 76 C6
East London Coll &
Toynbee Theatre
E1 95 D2 243 D3
East London Stad E3 97 B2
Eastman Dental Hospl
WC1 94 B3 240 C6
Eastman Ho 7 SW4 159 C5
Eastman Rd W3 111 B4
East Mascalls 15 SE7 143 C6
Eastmead IG3 58 A2
East Mead HA4 62 D5
Eastmead Ave UB6 85 D4
Eastmead Cl BR1 188 A1
Eastmearn Rd SE21,
SE27 161 A2
EAST MOLESEY 196 A4
Eastmont Rd KT10 212 D6
Eastmoor Pl SE7 121 D3
Eastmoor St SE7 121 D3
East Mount St E1 96 B2
Eastney Rd CR0 204 D1
Eastney St SE10 120 B1
Eastnor Rd SE9 167 A3
Easton Ho 4 SE27 160 D1
Easton St WC1 241 A6
East Park Cl RM6 59 A4
East Parkside SE10 120 D4
East Pas EC1 242 A4
East Pl SE27 183 A6
East Plaza E14 119 D5
East Point 4 SE1 118 A1
Eastpole Cotts N14 3 D1
East Poultry Ave EC1 241 C3
East Putney Sta SW15 157 A6
East Ramp TW6 126 D4
East Rd Burnt Oak HA8 27 A2
Chelsea SW1 115 A1 258 A1
Dagenham RM6 59 A4
East Barnet EN4 15 A3
East Bedfont TW14 149 B4
Enfield EN3 6 C5
Finchley N2 30 C2
Kingston u T KT2 176 A2
Newham E15 99 A6
Shoreditch N1 95 B4 235 D2
Welling DA16 146 B3
West Drayton UB7 104 C2
Wimbledon SW19 180 A4
East Rochester Way DA5,
DA15, SE9 168 C5
East Row
Kensal Town W10 91 A3
Wanstead E11 55 A3
Eastry Ave BR2 208 D3
Eastry Ho SW8 270 A3
Eastry Rd DA8 147 C5
EAST SHEEN 133 B1
East Sheen Ave SW14 133 B1
East Sheen Prim Sch
SW14 133 C1
Eastside Rd NW11 47 B5
East Smithfield
E1 117 D6 253 D5
East St Barking IG11 79 A1
Bexleyheath DA7 147 C1
Brentford TW8 131 C5
Bromley BR1 187 A1
Walworth SE17 117 B1 262 C2
East Surrey Gr SE15 139 D5
East Tenter St
E1 95 D1 243 D1
East Terr DA15 167 C3
East Thamesmead Bsns Pk
DA18 125 B4
East Towers HA5 40 D3
Eastvale W3 111 D5
East View Barnet EN5 1 B2
Chingford E4 36 A5
Hampstead NW3 70 B6
Eastview Ave SE18 145 C5
East View Ho 18 N2 30 B1
Eastville Ave NW11 47 B3
Eastway Hayes BR2 209 A2
Merton SM4, SW20 201 A5
South Hackney E3, E9 97 A6
Temple Mills E9, E10 75 C4
Wallington SM6 219 C4
Wanstead E11 55 B4
East Way Croydon CR0 223 A5
Hayes UB3 106 A5
Ruislip HA4 40 A1
Eastway Cres HA2 63 D6
Eastwell Cl BR3 185 A2
Eastwell Ho SE1 262 D6
Eastwick Ct 2 SW19 156 D3
EAST WICKHAM 146 A5
East Wickham Inf Sch
DA16 145 D4
East Wickham Jun Sch
DA16 146 A4
East Wlk
East Barnet EN4 15 A3
Hayes UB3 106 A5
Eastwood Cl
2 Islington N7 72 C3
7 Tottenham N17 34 B3
Woodford E18 37 A1
Eastwood Rd Ilford IG3 58 A2
Muswell Hill N10 31 A1
West Drayton UB7 104 C4
Woodford E18 37 A1
East Woodside DA5 169 A3
Eastwood St SW16 181 C4
Eatington Rd E10 54 B4
Eaton Cl Belgravia SW1 258 A3
Stanmore HA7 25 B6
Eaton Ct
Chislehurst BR7 189 A4
Ealing W5 87 D1
Edgware HA8 26 C6
Southall UB1 107 B6
Sutton SM2 218 B2
6 Woodford E18 37 A1
Eaton Dr Brixton SW9 138 D1
Kingston u T KT2 176 C3
Eaton Gate
SW1 115 A2 258 A4
Eaton Gdns RM9 81 A1
Eaton Ho
Battersea SW11 266 D1
Ealing W5 87 D1
23 Limehouse E14 119 B6
Eaton House Sch
SW1 115 A2 258 A4
Eaton House The Manor
Sch SW4 137 B1
Eaton La SW1 115 B3 258 D5
Eaton Lo SM2 218 B2
Eaton Mans SW1 258 A3
Eaton Mews N
SW1 115 A3 258 B5
Eaton Mews S
SW1 115 B3 258 C5
Eaton Mews W SW1 258 B4
Eaton Park Rd N13 16 D2
Eaton Pl SW1 115 A3 258 B5
Eaton Rd Enfield EN1 5 C1
Hendon NW4 46 C4
Isleworth TW3, TW7 130 B1
Sidcup DA14 168 D2
Sutton SM2 218 B2
Eaton Rise Ealing W5 87 D1
Wanstead E11 55 C4
Eaton Row
SW1 115 B3 258 C5
Eatons Mead E4 19 C2
Eaton Sq SW1 115 A3 258 B5
Eaton Square Sch
SW1 115 B2 258 C4
Eaton Terr
Belgravia
SW1 115 A2 258 B4
Bow E3 97 A4
Eaton Terr Mews SW1 258 A4
Eatonville Rd SW17 158 D2
Eatonville Villas
SW17 158 D2
Ebb Ct E16 123 A6
Ebbisham Dr
SW8 138 B6 270 C5
Ebbisham Rd KT4 216 C6
Ebbsfleet Rd NW2 69 A4
Ebdon Way SE3 143 B2
Ebenezer Ho SE11 261 C3
Ebenezer Mussel Ho 5
E2 96 C5
Ebenezer St N1 235 C2
Ebenezer Wlk CR4 181 C2
Ebley Cl SE15 139 D6
Ebner St SW18 157 D6
Ebony Ct NW10 67 D2
Ebony Ho
27 Bethnal Green E2 96 A4

Ebony Ho *continued*
10 West Hampstead NW3 69 D2
Ebor Cotts SW15 155 C1
Ebor St E1, E2 243 C6
Ebrington Rd HA3 43 D3
Ebsworth St SE23 162 D4
Eburne Rd N7 72 A5
Ebury Bridge Rd SW1 115 A1 258 B1
Ebury Cl BR2 226 A5
Ebury Mews
Belgravia SW1 115 B2 258 C4
West Norwood SE27 160 D1
Ebury Mews E SW1 258 C5
Ebury Sq SW1 258 B3
Ebury St SW1 115 B2 258 C4
Ecclesbourne Cl N13 32 C5
Ecclesbourne Gdns N13 32 C5
Ecclesbourne Inf Sch CR7 205 A4
Ecclesbourne Jun Sch CR7 205 A4
Ecclesbourne Rd
Islington N1 73 A1
Thornton Heath CR7 205 A4
Eccles Ct SE11 260 D1
Eccleshill 3 BR2 208 D5
Eccles Rd SW11 136 D1
Eccleston Cl
Cockfosters EN4 2 D1
Crofton BR6 211 B1
Eccleston Cres RM6 58 B2
Ecclestone Ct HA9 66 A3
Ecclestone Mews HA9 66 A3
Ecclestone Pl HA9 66 B3
Eccleston Ho 1 SW2 160 C5
Eccleston Mews SW1 115 A3 258 B5
Eccleston Pl SW1 115 B2 258 C4
Eccleston Rd W13 109 A5
Eccleston Sq SW1 115 B2 258 D3
Eccleston Sq Mews SW1 259 A3
Eccleston St SW1 115 B2 258 C4
Echelforde Dr TW15 170 C6
Echelford Prim Sch The TW15 170 D5
Echo Hts E4 19 D3
Eckford St N1 234 A4
Eckington Ho N15 51 B3
Eckstein Rd SW11 136 C1
Eclipse Ho N22 32 B1
Eclipse Rd E13 99 B2
Ector Rd SE6 164 C2
Edam Ct 11 DA14 168 A1
Edans Ct W12 111 D4
Edbrooke Rd W9 91 C3
Eddisbury Ho 7 SE26 162 A1
Eddiscombe Rd SW6 135 B3
Eddison Ct N19 72 A6
Eddy Cl RM7 59 D3
Eddystone Rd SE4 163 A6
Eddystone Twr SE8 119 A1
Eddystone Wlk TW19 148 A4
Ede Cl TW4 129 B2
Edenbridge Cl 29 SE16 118 B1
Edenbridge Rd
Enfield EN1 17 C5
Hackney E9 74 D1
Eden Cl Child's Hill NW3 69 C6
Enfield EN3 7 C5
Kensington W8 255 B6
Wembley HA0 87 D6
Edencourt W5 88 B1
Edencourt Rd SW16 181 B4
Eden Ct 3 N3 29 B1
Edendale W3 110 D6
Edenfield Gdns KT4 215 D5
Eden Gr Islington N7 72 B3
Walthamstow E17 53 D4
Edenham High Sch CR0 207 B2
Edenham Way W10 91 B2
Eden Ho
15 Battersea SW11 136 C2
Lisson Gr NW8 237 A5
Edenhurst Ave SW6 135 B2
Eden Lodge NW6 68 D1
Eden Mews SW17 158 A1
EDEN PARK 207 C5
Eden Park Ave BR3 207 C4
Eden Park Sta BR3 207 C4
Eden Rd Croydon CR0 221 B4
Penge BR3 185 A2
Walthamstow E17 53 D4
West Norwood SE27 182 D5
Edensmuir Ct SE3 143 A5
Edensor Gdns W4 133 C5
Edensor Rd W4 133 C5
Eden St KT1, KT2 176 A1
Edenvale Cl CR4 181 A3
Edenvale Rd CR4 181 A3
Edenvale St SW6 136 A3
Eden Way
Beckenham BR3 207 C3
Bow E3 97 B6
Eden Wlk 5 KT1 176 A1
Ederline Ave SW16 182 C1
Edgar Ct KT3 199 C6
Edgar Ho Homerton E9 75 A3
South Lambeth SW8 270 A4
Wanstead E11 55 A2
Edgar Kail Way SE22 139 C1
Edgarley Terr SW6 264 A1
Edgar Rd Bromley E3 97 D4
Dagenham RM6 58 D2
Twickenham TW4 151 B4
Yiewsley UB7 104 A5
Edgar Wallace Cl 4 SE15 139 C5
Edgbury Ct NW9 45 A5
Edgcott Ho 2 W10 90 C2
Edgeborough Way BR1 187 D2
Edge Bsns Ctr The NW2 68 B6
Edgebury BR7, SE9 188 D6
Edgebury Prim Sch BR7 189 A6
Edgebury Wlk BR7 167 A1
Edgecombe Ho
4 London SE5 139 C3
Putney SW19 157 A4
Edgecoombe CR2 222 C1
Edgecoombe Cl KT2 177 B3
Edgecote Cl 7 W3 111 A5
Edgecot Gr N15 51 C4
Edgecumbe Ct 2 CR0 206 A1
Edgefield Ave IG11 79 D1
Edgefield Ct 3 IG11 79 D1
Edge Hill
Shooters Hill SE18 144 D6
Wimbledon SW19 178 D3
Edge Hill Ave N3 47 C5
Edgehill Ct KT12 194 C1
Edge Hill Ct
Sidcup DA14 189 D6
Wimbledon SW19 178 D3
Edgehill Gdns RM10 81 C4
Edgehill Ho 4 SW9 138 D3
Edgehill Rd Ealing W13 87 C2
Longlands BR7 189 A6
Mitcham CR4 181 B2
Edgeley La SW4 137 D2
Edgeley Rd SW4 137 D2
Edgel St SW18 135 D1
Edge Point Cl SE27 182 D5
Edge St W8 113 C5 245 B4
Edgewood Dr BR6 227 D3
Edgewood Gn CR0 206 D1
Edgeworth Ave NW4 46 A4
Edgeworth Cl NW4 46 A4
Edgeworth Cres NW4 46 A4
Edgeworth Ct 10 EN4 2 C1
Edgeworth Ho NW8 229 A6
Edgeworth Rd
Barnet EN4 2 C1
Eltham SE9 143 D1
Edgington Rd SW16 181 D4
Edgington Way DA14 190 D3
Edgson Ho SW1 258 C2
EDGWARE 26 C6
Edgware Acad WC2 240 B1
EDGWARE BURY 10 B3
Edgwarebury Ct HA8 26 C5
Edgwarebury Gdns HA8 26 C5
Edgwarebury La
Edgware Bury HA8 10 C2
Edgware HA8 26 C5
Edgware Community Hospl HA8 26 D3
Edgware Ct HA8 26 C4
Edgware Jun & Inf Schs HA8 26 C4
Edgware Rd
Dollis Hill NW2 68 C6
Paddington W1, W2, NW1, NW8 92 C2 237 A3
Edgware Rd Burnt Oak Broadway HA8 26 D3
Edgware Rd High St HA8 26 C4
Edgware Road Sta (Bakerloo) NW1 92 C2 237 A3
Edgware Road Sta (Met, Distr, Circle) NW1 237 B3
Edgware Road The Hyde NW9 45 C5
Edgware Road West Hendon Broadway NW9 46 A2
Edgware Sta HA8 26 D4
Edgware Way (Watford By-Pass) HA8 27 A6
Edinburgh Cl
7 Bethnal Green E2 96 C5
Pinner HA5 41 A2
Uxbridge UB10 60 D4
Edinburgh Ct
1 Catford SE6 164 D3
2 Kingston u T KT1 198 A6
Newham E13 99 B5
10 Rotherhithe SE16 118 D5
West Barnes SM4 200 D4
Edinburgh Dr UB10 60 D4
Edinburgh Ho
3 Acton W3 89 B1
Carshalton SM1 218 B6
Hendon NW4 46 C6
Maida Vale W9 91 D4
Edinburgh Prim Sch E17 53 B4
Edinburgh Rd
Carshalton SM1 218 B6
Edmonton N18 34 A5
Hanwell W7 108 D4
Newham E13 99 B5
Walthamstow E17 53 C4
Edington 20 NW5 71 A2
Edington Rd
Abbey Wood SE2 124 B3
Edington Rd *continued*
Enfield EN3 6 C3
Edison Bldg 7 E14 119 C4
Edison Cl
Walthamstow E17 53 C4
West Drayton UB7 104 B4
Edison Ct SE10 120 D3
Edison Dr Southall UB1 85 D1
Wembley HA9 66 A6
Edison Gr SE18 145 D5
Edison Ho
Walworth SE1 262 C4
7 Wembley HA9 67 A5
Edison Rd Bexley DA16 145 D4
Brimsdown EN3 7 B3
Bromley BR2 187 A1
Crouch End N8 49 D3
Edis St NW1 93 A6 231 B6
Editha Mans SW10 266 A5
Edith Cavell Cl 2 N19 50 A2
Edith Cavell Way SE18 144 A4
Edith Ct TW14 149 B5
Edith Gdns KT5 198 D2
Edith Gr SW10 136 A5 266 B4
Edith Ho 6 W6 112 C1
Edithna St SW9 138 A2
Edith Neville Cotts NW1 232 C2
Edith Neville Prim Sch NW1 93 D5 232 C3
Edith Pond Ct SE9 166 D2
Edith Ramsay Ho 2 E1 97 A2
Edith Rd Dagenham RM6 58 D2
South Norwood SE25 205 B4
Stratford New Town E15 76 B3
Upton Pk E6 77 D1
West Kensington W14 113 A2 254 B3
Wimbledon SW19 179 D4
Wood Green N11 31 D3
Edith Row SW6 265 D2
Edith St E2 96 A5
Edith Summerskill Ho SW6 264 C4
Edith Terr SW10 136 A5 266 A4
Edith Villas W14 113 B1 254 C2
Edith Yd SW10 266 B4
Edmansons' Cl N17 33 D2
Edmeston Cl E9 75 A2
Edmond Ct SE14 140 C4
Edmonscote W13 87 A2
EDMONTON 33 D6
Edmonton Ct 5 SE16 118 C3
Edmonton Cty Lower Sch N9 17 C3
Edmonton Cty Upper Sch EN1 17 D4
Edmonton Green Sh Ctr N9 18 B2
Edmonton Green Sta N9 18 A2
Edmonton Wharf N18 34 D4
Edmund Gr TW13 151 B2
Edmund Halley Way SE10 120 C4
Edmund Ho
Kennington SE17 261 D1
New Cross Gate SE14 141 B4
Edmund Hurst Dr E6 100 D2
Edmund Rd
Mitcham CR4 202 C6
Welling DA16 146 A2
Edmundsbury Ct Est 16 SW9 138 B1
Edmunds Cl UB4 84 C2
Edmund St SE5 139 B5
Edmunds Wlk N2 48 C5
Edmund Waller Prim Sch SE14 140 D3
Ednam Ho SE15 140 A6
Edna Rd SW20 178 D1
Edna St SW11 136 C4 267 A1
Edred Ho E9 75 A4
Edrich Ho SW4 270 A1
Edric Ho SW1 259 D4
Edrick Rd HA8 27 A4
Edrick Wlk HA8 27 A4
Edric Rd SE14 140 D5
Edridge Cl WD23 8 A6
Edridge Ho 9 SE27 160 D1
Edridge Rd CR0 221 B5
Edward Alleyn Ho SE21 161 C4
Edward Ave
Chingford E4 35 D4
Morden SM4 202 B4
Edward Betham CE Prim Sch UB6 86 A5
Edward Cl Edmonton N9 17 D4
Hampton TW12 174 A5
Edward Ct 2 Ealing W5 87 B3
Harrow HA1 64 C6
2 Newham E16 99 A2
Edward Dodd Ct N1 235 D2
Edward Edward's Ho SE1 251 C3
Edwardes Pl W8 254 D5
Edwardes Sq W8 113 B3 254 D5
Edward Friend Ho 6 N16 73 C5
Edward Gr EN4 14 B6
Edward Harvey Ct DA17 125 B1
Edward Ho
Paddington W2 236 C5
Vauxhall SE11 260 D2
Edward Kennedy Ho 18 W10 91 A3
Edward Mann Cl 13 E1 96 D1
Edward Mans 8 IG11 79 D1
Edward Mews NW1 231 D3
Edward Pauling Ho TW14 149 D4
Edward Pauling Prim Sch TW13 149 C2
Edward Pinner Ct 5 KT6 214 A6
Edward Pl SE8 141 B6
Edward Rd
Bromley BR1 187 C3
Chislehurst BR7 188 D5
Croydon CR0 205 C2
Dagenham RM6 59 A3
Hampton TW12 174 A5
Harrow HA2 42 A6
Hatton TW14 149 C6
New Barnet EN4 14 B6
Northolt UB5 84 C5
Penge SE20 184 D4
Walthamstow E17 52 D4
Edward Robinson Ho 3 SE14 140 D5
Edward's Ave HA4 62 C2
Edwards Cl KT4 216 D6
Edward's Cotts 11 N1 72 D1
Edwards Dr N11 31 D3
Edwards Ho 7 TW10 153 C1
Edward's La N16 73 C6
Edwards Language Sch W5 110 A6
Edwards Mews
Islington N1 72 C1
Marylebone W1 93 A1 238 A1
Edward Sq Islington N1 233 C5
1 Rotherhithe SE16 119 A5
Edwards Rd DA17 125 C2
Edward St
New Cross SE14 141 B5
10 Newham E16 99 A3
Edward Temme Ave E15 76 D1
Edward Tyler Rd SE12 165 C2
Edward VII Mans NW10 90 D4
Edward Way TW15 148 B2
Edward Wilson Prim Sch W2 91 D2
Edwina Ct SM1 217 D4
Edwina Gdns IG4 56 A4
Edwin Arnold Ct DA15 189 D6
Edwin Ave E6 100 C5
Edwin Cl DA7 147 B6
Edwin Ho SE15 140 A5
Edwin Rd Burnt Oak HA8 27 B4
Twickenham TW1, TW2 152 C3
Edwin's Mead E9 75 A4
Edwin St
Bethnal Green E1 96 C3
Newham E16 99 A2
Edwin Stray Ho TW13 151 C1
Edwin Ware Ct 4 HA5 22 C1
Edwy Ho E9 75 B4
Edwyn Cl EN5 12 D5
Edwyn Ho SW18 157 D5
Eel Pie Island* TW1 153 A3
Effie Pl SW6 265 B3
Effie Rd SW6 135 C5 265 B3
Effingham Cl SM2 217 D1
Effingham Ct SW19 180 C3
Effingham Ho
37 Clapham SW8 137 D3
9 Kingston u T KT2 176 D4
Effingham Lo 1 KT6 198 A4
Effingham Rd
Hornsey N8 50 C5
Lewisham SE12 164 D6
Thames Ditton KT6, KT7 197 C2
Thornton Heath CR0 204 B2
Effort St SW17 180 C5
Effra Cl SW19 179 D4
Effra Ct London SW2 160 B6
South Norwood SE19 183 C3
Effra Mans SW2 160 C6
Effra Par SW2 160 C6
Effra Rd London SW2 160 C6
Wimbledon SW19 179 D4
Effra Road Ret Pk SW2 160 C6
EF International Language Sch SE1 251 B3
Egan Way UB3 105 C6
Egbert Ho E9 75 A3
Egbert St NW1 93 A6 231 A6
Egbury Ho SW15 155 D5
Egerton Cl HA5 40 A5
Egerton Cres SW3 114 C2 257 B4
Egerton Ct
Leytonstone E11 54 B2
5 Richmond TW10 154 A6
Egerton Dr SE10 141 D4
Egerton Gdns
Ealing W13 87 B1
Hendon NW4 46 B5
Ilford IG3 79 D5
Knightsbridge SW3 114 C3 257 A5
Willesden NW10 90 C6
Egerton Gdns Mews SW3 257 B5
Egerton Ho W4 133 A6
Egerton Pl SW3 257 B5
Egerton Rd
New Malden KT3 199 D5
South Norwood SE25 205 C6
Egerton Rd *continued*
Stamford Hill N16 51 D2
Twickenham TW2 152 C4
Wembley HA0 66 B1
Egerton Terr SW3 114 C3 257 B5
Egerton Way UB3 126 D5
Eggardon Ct UB5 64 A2
Egham Cl Cheam SM3 217 A6
Putney SW19 157 A2
Egham Cres SM3 217 A6
Egham Ct KT6 197 D4
Egham Rd E13 99 B2
Eglantine Rd SW18 158 A6
Egleston Rd SM4 201 D3
Eglington Ct SE17 139 A6
Eglington Rd E4 20 B4
Eglinton Hill SE18 144 D5
Eglinton Prim Sch SE18 144 C6
Eglinton Rd SE18 144 C6
Egliston Mews SW15 134 C2
Egliston Rd SW15 134 C2
Egmont Ave KT6 198 B1
Egmont Rd
New Malden KT3 199 D5
Sutton SM2 218 A1
Tolworth KT6 198 C1
Walton-on-T KT12 194 B2
Egmont St SE14 140 D5
Egremont Ho SE13 141 D3
Egremont Rd SE27 160 C1
Egret Ho 11 SE16 118 D2
Egret Way UB4 84 D2
Eider Cl Hayes UB4 84 D2
Stratford E7 76 D3
Eider Ct 33 SE8 141 B6
Eighteenth Rd CR4 204 A5
Eighth Ave Hayes UB3 106 A5
Ilford E12 78 B4
Eileen Ct BR7 188 C5
Eileen Rd SE25 205 B4
Eindhoven Cl SM5 203 A1
Einstein Ho HA9 67 A5
Eisenhower Dr E6 100 A2
Eisenhower Ho KT8 175 C2
Elaine Ct 13 NW3 70 D2
Elaine Gr NW5 71 A3
Elaine Ho N4 50 A1
Elam Cl SE5 138 D3
Elam St SE5 138 D3
Elan Ct E1 96 B2
Eland Pl CR0 220 D5
Eland Rd
Clapham SW11 136 D2
Croydon CR0 220 D5
Elba Pl SE17 117 A2 262 B4
Elberon Ave CR0 203 C3
Elbe St SW6 136 A3
Elborough Rd SE25 206 A4
Elborough St SW18 157 C3
Elbourne Trad Est DA17 125 D3
Elbury Dr E16 99 A1
Elcho St SW11 136 C5 267 B3
Elcot Ave SE15 140 B5
Elder Ave N8 50 A4
Elderberry Ct 2 EN2 4 D3
Elderberry Gr 10 SE27 183 A6
Elderberry Rd W5 110 A4
Elderberry Way E6 100 B4
Elder Cl Barnet N20 13 D3
Sidcup DA15 167 D3
Yiewsley UB7 104 A6
Elder Ct WD23 8 C2
Elderfield Ho 4 E14 119 C6
Elderfield Pl SW17 181 B6
Elderfield Rd E5 74 C4
Elderfield Wlk E11 55 B4
Elderflower Way E15 76 C1
Elder Gdns 9 SE27 183 A6
Elder Oak Cl SE20 184 B2
Elder Rd SE27 183 A5
Elderslie Cl BR3 207 D3
Elderslie Rd SE9 166 C6
Elder St E1 95 D3 243 C5
Elderton Rd SE26 185 A6
Eldertree Pl CR4 181 C2
Eldertree Way CR4 181 C2
Elder Wlk Islington N1 234 D6
2 Lewisham SE13 142 A2
Elderwood Pl SE27 183 A5
Eldon Ave Croydon CR0 222 C6
Heston TW5 129 C5
Eldon Ct NW6 91 C6
Eldon Gr NW3 70 B3
Eldon Ho SW9 138 D2
Eldon Jun & Inf Schs N9 18 C3
Eldon Pk SE25 206 B5
Eldon Rd Edmonton N9 18 C3
Kensington W8 113 D3 255 D5
Tottenham N22 32 D2
Walthamstow E17 53 B5
Eldon St EC2 95 B2 242 D3
Eldonwall Est RM8 59 B1
Eldon Way NW10 88 D5
Eldred Rd IG11 101 C6
Eldrick Ct TW14 149 B3
Eldridge Cl TW14 150 A3
Eldridge Ct
Bermondsey SE16 118 A3
14 Dagenham RM10 81 D2
Eleanor Cl
Rotherhithe SE16 118 D4
South Tottenham N15 51 D6
Eleanor Cres NW7 28 D6
Eleanor Ct 13 E2 96 A6
Eleanor Gdns
Barnet EN5 12 D6
Dagenham RM8 81 B6
Eleanor Gr
Mortlake SW13 133 C2
Uxbridge UB10 60 D5
Eleanor Ho
18 Hammersmith W6 112 C1
1 Kentish Town NW5 71 C3
6 Merton SW19 179 D2
Eleanor Palmer Prim Sch NW5 71 C4
Eleanor Rathbone Ho 1 N6 49 D2
Eleanor Rd
Bowes Pk N11 32 A4
Hackney E8 74 B1
Stratford E15 76 D2
Eleanor Smith Sch E13 99 B5
Eleanor Smith Sch (West Beckton Site) E16 99 C2
Eleanor St E3 97 C4
Eleanor Wlk 24 SE18 122 B2
Electra Ave TW6 127 D2
Electra Ct 6 NW2 68 C2
Electric Ave SW9 138 C1
Electric Ho 18 Bow E3 97 C4
Walthamstow E17 53 C5
Electric La 2 SW9 138 C1
Electric Mans 1 SW9 138 C1
Electric Par Ilford IG3 57 D1
Surbiton KT6 197 D3
Woodford E18 37 A1
Elenmore Ct BR1 210 A5
Elephant & Castle
Newington SE1 116 D3 261 D5
Newington SE1 261 D4
Elephant & Castle Sh Ctr SE1 117 A2 262 A4
Elephant & Castle Sta
Lambeth SE1 116 D3 261 D5
Newington SE17 117 A2 262 A4
Elephant La SE16 118 C4
Elephant Rd SE17 117 A2 262 A4
Elers Rd Ealing W13 109 C4
Hayes UB3 105 B2
Eley Rd N18 34 D5
Eley's Est N18 34 D6
Elfindale Rd SE24 161 A6
Elfin Gr TW11 174 D5
Elford Cl SE9 143 C1
Elfort Rd N5 72 C4
Elfrida Cres SE6 185 C6
Elfrida Prim Sch SE6 185 C6
Elf Row E1 118 C6
Elfwine Rd W7 86 C2
Elgal Cl BR6 226 D3
Elgar N8 50 A6
Elgar Ave Ealing W5 110 A4
Thornton Heath SW16 204 A6
Tolworth KT5, KT6 198 D2
Willesden NW10 67 B2
Elgar Cl
Buckhurst Hill IG9 21 D2
Deptford SE8 141 C5
Elstree WD6 9 D4
Ickenham UB10 60 C6
Newham E13 99 C5
Elgar Ct W14 254 A5
Elgar Ho Hayes UB4 84 C2
Isleworth TW2 152 B5
Pimlico SW1 258 D1
Southall UB1 85 C1
South Hampstead NW6 70 A1
Elgar St SE16 119 A3
Elgin Ave
Ashford TW15 171 A4
Hammersmith W12 112 B3
Harrow HA3 25 B1
Westbourne Green W9 91 D3
Elgin Cl W12 112 B4
Elgin Cres Hatton TW6 127 C3
Notting Hill W11 113 A6 244 B6
Elgin Ct
6 Croydon CR0 221 A4
Westbourne Green W9 91 C3
Elgin Ho Northolt UB5 84 B5
8 Poplar E14 97 D1
Elgin Mans W9 91 D4
Elgin Mews W11 91 A1
Elgin Mews N W9 91 D4
Elgin Mews S W9 91 D4
Elgin Rd Croydon CR0 221 D6
Ilford IG3 57 C2
Sutton SM1 218 A5
Wallington SM6 219 C2
Wood Green N22 31 C1
Elgood Ave HA6 22 A3
Elgood Cl W11 244 A3
Elgood Ho NW8 229 D3
Elham Cl BR1 187 D3
Elham Ho 13 E5 74 B3
Elia Mews N1 94 D5 234 C3
Elias Pl SW8 138 C6
Elia St N1 94 D5 234 C3
Elibank Rd SE9 144 C1
Elim Est SE1 263 A6
Elim St SE1 263 A6
Elim Way E13 98 D4
Eliot Bank SE23, SE26 162 B2
Eliot Bank Prim Sch SE26 162 B2
Eliot Cotts SE3 142 C3

Eliot Ct SW18 157 D5
Eliot Dr HA2 63 D6
Eliot Gdns SW15 134 A1
Eliot Hill SE13 142 A3
Eliot Ho 10 TW10 154 B5
Eliot Mews NW8 229 A3
Eliot Pk SE13 142 A3
Eliot Pl SE3 142 C3
Eliot Rd RM9 80 D4
Eliot Vale SE3 142 B3
Elis David Almshouses CR0 220 D4
Elizabethan Ct N3 47 A6
Elizabeth Ave Enfield EN2 4 D2
Ilford IG1 79 A3
Islington N1 73 B1
Shoreditch N1 95 A6 235 B6
Elizabeth Barnes Ct 5 SW6 135 D3
Elizabeth Blackwell Ho N22 32 C2
Elizabeth Blount Ct 4 E14 97 A1
Elizabeth Cl
Cheam SM1 217 B4
Paddington W9 236 B5
12 Poplar E14 97 D1
Elizabeth Clyde Cl N15 51 C5
Elizabeth Cooper Lo SW12 159 A5
Elizabeth Cotts 5 TW9 132 C4
Elizabeth Ct
Buckhurst Hill IG9 21 B3
Chelsea SW10 266 D5
East Dulwich SE22 140 A1
Kingston u T KT2 176 A2
Marylebone NW8 237 B6
South Croydon CR0 221 C5
Sunbury TW16 194 C6
3 Teddington TW11 174 C5
Upper Tooting SW17 181 A5
West Barnes SM4 201 A2
Westminster SW1 259 D5
6 Woodford Green E18 37 A2
2 Woodford Green IG8 37 C3
10 Woolwich SE18 122 B2
Elizabeth Finn Ho 1 W12 112 A3
Elizabeth Fry Ho UB3 105 D2
Elizabeth Fry Pl SE18 144 A4
Elizabeth Garrett Anderson Ho 9 DA17 125 C3
Elizabeth Garrett Anderson Hospl NW1 93 C3 239 B5
Elizabeth Garrett Anderson Language Coll N1 94 B5 233 D3
Elizabeth Gdns
East Acton W3 111 D5
Isleworth TW7 131 A1
Stanmore HA7 25 C5
Sunbury TW16 194 C6
Elizabeth Ho
Cheam SM3 217 A2
Friern Barnet N20 14 D1
15 Hammersmith W6 112 C1
Lambeth SE11 261 B3
Stanmore HA7 26 A1
Wembley HA9 66 B3
Elizabeth Ind Est SE14 140 D6
Elizabeth Kenny Ho N1 73 A2
Elizabeth Mews
28 Hackney E2 96 A5
Maitland Pk NW3 70 D2
Elizabeth Pl N15 51 B5
Elizabeth Rd
Newham E6 99 D6
South Tottenham N15 51 C4
Elizabeth Ride N9 18 B4
Elizabeth Selby Inf Sch E2 96 A4
Elizabeth Sq 13 SE16 119 A6
Elizabeth St SW1 115 A2 258 B4
Elizabeth Terr SE9 166 B5
Elizabeth Way
Feltham TW13 172 C6
South Norwood SE19 183 B3
Elkanette Mews N20 14 A2
Elkington Point SE11 261 A3
Elkington Rd E13 99 B3
Elkstone Rd W10 91 B2
Ella Cl BR3 185 C1
Ellacombe Ho 1 SW2 160 C4
Ellaline Rd W6 134 D6
Ella Mews NW3 70 D4
Ellanby Cres N18 34 B5
Elland Ho 18 E14 97 B1
Elland Rd SE15 140 C1
Ella Rd N4, N8 50 A2
Ellard Ct DA16 146 C2
Elle Ct N12 29 D5
Ellement Cl HA5 40 D4
Ellena Ct N14 16 A1
Ellenborough Ct N22 32 D2
Ellenborough Ho 5 W12 112 B6
Ellenborough Pl SW15 134 A1
Ellenborough Rd
Sidcup DA14 191 A5
Tottenham N22 33 A2
Ellen Cl BR1 209 D6
Ellen Ct 6 Chingford E4 20 A3
Lower Edmonton N9 18 C2
Ellen Miller Ho 2 E17 54 A4
Ellen St E1 96 A1
Ellen Webb Dr HA3 42 C6
Ellen Wilkinson Ho
12 Dagenham RM10 81 C5
7 Globe Town E2 96 D4
West Brompton SW6 264 D5
Ellen Wilkinson Prim Sch E6 100 A2
Ellen Wilkinson Sch for Girls W3 88 B1
Elleray Rd TW11 174 D4
Ellerby St SW6 134 D4
Ellerdale Cl 15 NW3 70 A4
Ellerdale Rd NW3 70 A3
Ellerdale St SE13 141 D2
Ellerdine Rd TW3 130 B1
Ellerker Gdns TW10 154 A5
Ellerman Ave TW2, TW4 151 B3
Ellerslie Ct 6 SM6 219 B2
Ellerslie Gdns NW10 90 A6
Ellerslie Ind Est SW2 160 A6
Ellerslie Rd W12 112 B5
Ellerton Ct W3 110 D4
Ellerton Gdns RM9 80 C1
Ellerton Lo N3 29 C1
Ellerton Rd
Barnes SW13 134 A4
Dagenham RM9 80 C1
Surbiton KT6 198 B1
Wandsworth SW17, SW18 158 B3
Wimbledon SW20 178 A3
Ellery Cl 5 NW10 89 D5
Ellery Ho SE17 262 D3
Ellery Rd SE19 183 B3
Ellery St SE15 140 B3
Ellesborough Cl WD19 22 C5
Ellesmere Ave
Beckenham BR3 185 D1
Edgware NW7 11 B1
Ellesmere Cl
Leytonstone E11 54 D4
Ruislip HA4 39 A2
Ellesmere Ct
Chiswick W4 133 B6
Lewisham SE12 165 A3
Penge SE20 184 B1
Ellesmere Gdns IG4 56 A3
Ellesmere Gr EN5 13 B6
Ellesmere Rd Bow E3 97 A5
Chiswick W4 133 B6
Greenford UB6 86 A3
Twickenham TW1 153 C5
Willesden NW10 68 A3
Ellesmere St E14 97 D1
Ellies Mews TW15 148 A2
Ellingfort Rd E8 74 B1
Ellingham Prim Sch KT9 213 D1
Ellingham Rd
Chessington KT9 213 D2
Leyton E15 76 B4
Shepherd's Bush W12 112 A4
Ellington Ct N14 15 D2
Ellington Ho SE1 262 B5
Ellington Rd
Cranley Gdns N10 49 B5
Feltham TW13 171 D6
Hounslow TW3 129 D3
Ellington St N7 72 C2
Elliot Cl Stratford E15 76 C1
Wembley HA9 66 C5
Woodford IG8 37 D4
Elliot Ct 6 N15 51 D5
Elliot Rd NW4 46 B3
Elliott Ave HA4 62 B6
Elliott Gdns TW17 192 C5
Elliott Ho 3 CR7 204 D5
Elliott Rd Acton W4 111 C2
Brixton SW9 138 D4
Bromley BR2 209 D5
Camberwell SW9 138 D4
Stanmore HA7 25 A4
Thornton Heath CR7 204 D5
Elliott Sch SW15 156 C5
Elliott's Pl N1 234 D5
Elliott Sq NW3 70 C1
Elliott's Row SE11 116 D2 261 D4
Ellis Cl Burnt Oak HA8 27 C4
New Eltham SE9 167 A2
Willesden NW10 68 C2
Elliscombe Mount 11 SE7 143 C6
Elliscombe Rd SE7 143 C6
Ellis Ct W7 86 D2
Ellisfield Dr SW15 156 A4
Ellis Franklin Ct NW8 229 A4
Ellis Ho
Walthamstow E17 54 A4
Walworth SE17 262 C2
Ellison Gdns UB2 107 B2
Ellison Ho 1 SE13 142 A3
Ellison Rd
Barnes SW13 133 D3
New Eltham DA15 167 B3
Streatham SW16 182 A3
Ellis Rd Mitcham CR4 202 D3
Southall UB2 108 A5
Ellis St SW1 115 A2 258 A4
Elliston Ho 8 SE18 122 C2
Ellora Rd SW16 181 D5
Ellswood Ct 18 KT6 197 D2
Ellsworth St E2 96 B4
Ellwood Ct 1 W9 91 D3
Elmar Ct SW6 135 A3
Elmar Rd N15 51 B5
Elm Ave Ealing W5 110 B5
Ruislip HA4 40 B2
Elmbank N14 16 A4
Elm Bank Dr BR1 187 D1
Elm Bank Gdns SW13 133 C3
Elm Bank Mans SW13 133 C3
Elmbank Way W7 86 B2
Elmbourne Dr DA17 125 D2
Elmbourne Rd SW17 159 B1
Elmbridge Ave KT5 199 A3
Elmbridge Cl HA4 40 A3
Elmbridge Dr HA4 40 A3
Elmbridge Wlk E8 74 A1
Elmbrook 3 E18 55 A6
Elmbrook Cl TW16 172 B2
Elmbrook Gdns SE9 144 A1
Elmbrook Rd SM1 217 B4
Elm Cl Buckhurst Hill IG9 21 D2
Carshalton SM5 202 D1
Harrow HA2 41 D3
Hayes UB3 84 A1
Hendon NW4 46 D4
South Croydon CR2 221 C2
Tolworth KT5 199 A2
Twickenham TW13, TW2 151 D2
Upper Holloway N19 71 C6
Wanstead E11 55 B3
West Barnes SW20 200 C5
Elmcote HA5 22 D1
Elmcourt Rd SE21, SE27 160 D2
Elm Court Sch SE27 161 A2
Elm Cres Ealing W5 110 A4
Kingston u T KT2 176 A2
Elmcroft Highgate N6 49 C2
Hornsey Vale N8 50 B4
Elmcroft Ave
Blackfen DA15 168 A5
Enfield N9 18 B5
Golders Green NW11 47 B2
Wanstead E11 55 B5
Elmcroft Cl
Chessington KT9 214 A5
Ealing W5 87 D1
Feltham TW14 149 D5
Wanstead E11 55 B5
Elmcroft Cres
Harrow HA2 41 C6
Hendon NW11 47 A2
Elmcroft Dr
Ashford TW15 170 C5
Chessington KT9 214 A5
Elmcroft Gdns NW9 44 C4
Elmcroft St E5 74 C4
Elmcroft Terr UB8 82 C1
Elm Ct
5 Ashford TW16 171 D3
Brixton SW9 138 C4
Catford SE6 163 D3
Chingford E4 36 A4
4 Finchley N3 29 C2
Lewisham SE13 142 B2
Mitcham CR4 180 D1
42 Notting Hill W2 91 C2
Strand EC4 251 A6
Elmdale Rd N13 32 B5
Elmdene KT5 199 A1
Elmdene Cl BR3 207 B4
Elmdene Rd SE18 122 D1
Elmdon Rd
Hatton TW6 127 D2
Hounslow TW5 129 A3
Elm Dr Harrow HA2 41 D3
Sunbury TW16 172 C1
Elmer Cl EN2 4 B2
Elmer Ct HA1 42 D3
Elmer Gdns
Edgware HA8 26 D3
Isleworth TW7 130 B2
Elmer Ho NW1 237 A4
Elmer Rd SE6 164 A4
Elmer's Dr TW11 175 B4
ELMERS END 206 D6
Elmers End Rd BR3, SE20 206 C6
Elmers End Sta BR3 206 D5
Elmerside Rd BR3 207 A5
Elmers Rd SE25 206 A2
Elmfield Ave London N8 50 A4
Mitcham CR4 181 A2
Teddington TW11 174 D5
Elmfield Cl HA1 64 C6
Elmfield Ct DA16 146 B4
Elmfield Ho
6 Canonbury N5 73 A3
22 London N2 30 B1
Paddington W9 91 C3
Elmfield Mans 5 SW17 159 A2
Elmfield Pk BR1 209 A6
Elmfield Rd
Bromley BR1 209 A6
Chingford E4 20 B2
East Finchley N2 48 B6
Southall UB2 107 A3
Upper Tooting SW17 159 B2
Walthamstow E17 52 D3
Elmfield Way
Paddington W9 91 C2
South Croydon CR2 221 D1
Elm Friars Wlk NW1 71 D1
Elmgate Ave TW13 150 C1
Elmgate Ct HA8 27 A5
Elmgate Gdns HA8 27 B6
Elm Gdns
Claygate KT10 212 D2
East Finchley N2 48 A6
Enfield EN2 5 B5
Elm Gdns *continued*
Mitcham CR4 203 D5
Elm Gn W3 89 C1
Elm Gr Cricklewood NW2 68 D4
Harrow HA2 41 C2
Hornsey N8 50 A3
Kingston u T KT2 176 A2
Orpington BR6 211 D1
Peckham SE15 140 A3
Sutton SM1 217 D4
Wimbledon SW19 179 A3
Woodford IG8 36 D5
Yiewsley UB7 104 B6
Elmgreen Cl 8 E15 98 C6
Elmgrove Cres HA1 43 A4
Elmgrove Fst & Mid Schs HA3 43 A5
Elmgrove Gdns HA1 43 A4
Elm Grove Par SM6 219 A5
Elmgrove Rd
Croydon CR0 206 B2
Harrow HA1 42 D4
Elm Grove Rd
Barnes SW13 134 A3
Ealing W5 110 A4
Elm Hall Gdns E11 55 B3
Elm Hatch HA5 23 B3
Elm Ho
4 Cubitt Town E14 120 A4
2 Kingston u T KT2 176 B3
Teddington TW11 175 C3
Elmhurst DA17 147 A6
Elmhurst Ave London N2 48 B6
Mitcham CR4 181 B3
Elmhurst Cres N2 48 B5
Elmhurst Ct
Carshalton SM5 218 B6
Croydon CR0 221 B3
Elmhurst Dr E18 37 A1
Elmhurst Lo 8 SM2 218 A1
Elmhurst Mans SW4 137 D2
Elmhurst Prim Sch E7 77 B1
Elmhurst Rd
Chislehurst SE9 166 A1
Enfield EN3 6 C6
Tottenham N17 33 D1
Upton E7 77 B1
Elmhurst Sch CR2 221 B3
Elmhurst St SW4 137 D2
Elmhurst Villas SE15 140 C1
Elmington Cl DA5 169 D5
Elmington Rd SE5 139 B5
Elmira St SE13 141 D2
Elm La SE6 163 B2
Elm Lawn Cl UB8 60 A1
Elmlea Dr UB3 83 D2
Elm Lea Trad Est N17 34 B4
Elmlee Cl BR7 188 B4
Elmley Cl 12 E6 100 A2
Elmley St SE18 123 B2
Elm Lo SW6 134 D4
Elmore Cl HA0 88 A5
Elmore Ho SW9 138 D3
Elmore Rd Enfield EN3 6 D5
Leyton E11 76 B5
Elmore St N1 73 B1
Elm Park Ave N15 52 A3
Elm Park Ct HA5 40 C6
Elm Park Gdns
Chelsea SW10 114 B1 256 C1
Hendon NW4 46 D4
Elm Park Ho SW10 256 C1
Elm Park La SW3 114 B1 256 C1
Elm Park Mans SW10 266 B6
Elm Park Rd
Chelsea SW3 136 B6 266 C6
Edmonton N21 17 A4
Finchley N3 29 B3
Pinner HA5 40 D6
South Norwood SE25 205 D6
Walthamstow E10 53 A1
Elm Pk Stanmore HA7 25 C5
Streatham SW2 160 B4
Elm Pl SW7 114 B1 256 C2
Elm Quay SW8 269 C5
Elm Rd Barnet EN5 1 B1
Beckenham BR3 185 B1
Chessington KT9 214 A4
Claygate KT10 212 D2
East Bedfont TW14 149 B4
Hackbridge SM6 203 A1
Kingston u T KT2 176 B2
Leyton E11 76 B6
Mortlake SW14 133 A1
New Malden KT3 199 B6
Sidcup DA14 190 A6
South Norwood CR7 205 B5
Stoneleigh KT17 215 D2
Stratford E7 76 D2
Tottenham N22 32 D2
Walthamstow E17 54 A4
Wembley HA9 66 A3
Elm Rd W SM4 201 B2
Elm Row NW3 70 A5
Elms Ave Hendon NW4 46 D4
Muswell Hill N10 49 B6
Elmscott Gdns N21 17 A5
Elmscott Rd BR1 186 D5
Elms Cotts 1 CR4 180 D1
Elms Cres SW4 159 D5
Elms Ct Merton SW19 179 D3
Wembley HA0 65 A4
Elmsdale Rd E17 53 B5
Elms Gdns
Dagenham RM9 81 B4
Wembley HA0 65 A4
Elmshaw Rd SW15 156 A6
Elmside CR0 223 D2
Elmside Rd HA9 66 C5
Elms La HA0 65 A5
Elmsleigh Ave HA3 43 C5
Elmsleigh Ct SM1 217 D5
Elmsleigh Ho TW2 152 B2
Elmsleigh Rd TW2 152 B2
Elmslie Ct SE9 166 C5
Elmslie Point 2 E3 97 B2
Elms Mews W2 246 C6
Elms Park Ave HA0 65 A4
Elms Rd
Clapham Pk SW4 159 C6
Harrow HA3 24 C3
Elm St WC1 94 B3 240 D5
ELMSTEAD 188 A5
Elmstead Ave
Elmstead BR7 188 B5
Wembley HA9 66 B6
Elmstead Cl
Totteridge N20 13 C2
West Ewell KT19 215 C3
Elmstead Ct HA9 44 B1
Elmstead Gdns KT4 216 A5
Elmstead Glade BR7 188 B4
Elmstead La BR7 188 B5
Elmstead Rd IG3 79 D6
Elmstead Woods Sta BR7 188 A4
Elmsted Cres DA16 146 C6
Elms The
5 Ashford TW15 170 C5
Barnes SW13 133 D2
Claygate KT10 212 D1
Croydon CR0 205 A1
3 Harlesden NW10 89 C5
Kingsbury NW9 45 A3
Plashet E12 78 A2
Wallington SM6 219 C4
Elmstone Rd SW6 265 A2
Elmsway TW15 170 C5
Elmsworth Ave TW3 129 D3
Elm Terr Child's Hill NW2 69 C5
3 Eltham SE9 166 C5
Harrow HA3 24 B2
Elmton Ct NW8 236 C6
Elm Tree Ave KT10 196 C2
Elm Tree Cl
Ashford TW15 170 D5
Northolt UB5 85 B5
St John's Wood NW8 92 B4 229 C2
Elmtree Ct HA4 40 A1
Elm Tree Ct
5 Camberwell SE5 139 A4
18 Charlton SE7 143 C6
St John's Wood NW8 229 C2
Elmtree Rd TW11 174 C5
Elm Tree Rd NW8 92 B4 229 C2
Elm View Ct UB2 107 C2
Elm Way London N11 31 A4
North Cheam KT4 216 C5
West Ewell KT19 215 B3
Willesden NW10 67 C4
Elm Wlk Child's Hill NW3 69 C6
Orpington BR6 226 B5
West Barnes SW20 200 D5
Elmwood Ave
Bowes Pk N13 32 A5
Feltham TW13 150 B1
Harrow HA3 43 B3
Elmwood Cl
Hackbridge SM6 219 B6
Stoneleigh KT17 216 A1
Elmwood Cres NW9 45 A5
Elmwood Ct
Battersea SW11 268 C2
Walthamstow E10 53 C1
Wembley HA0 65 A5
Elmwood Dr
Sidcup DA5 169 A4
Stoneleigh KT17 216 A1
Elmwood Gdns W7 86 C1
Elmwood Ho Enfield EN2 4 D1
Feltham TW13 150 B1
Elmwood Inf Sch CR0 204 D3
Elmwood Jun Sch CR0 204 D2
Elm Wood Prim Sch SE27 161 B1
Elmwood Rd
Chiswick W4 133 A6
Herne Hill SE24 161 B6
Mitcham CR4 202 D6
Thornton Heath CR0 204 D2
Elmworth Gr SE21 161 B2
Elnathan Mews W9 91 D3
Elphinstone Ct SW16 182 A4
Elphinstone Rd E17 35 B1
Elphinstone St N5 72 D4
Elrington Rd Dalston E8 74 A2
Woodford IG8 37 A5
Elsa Ct BR3 185 B2
Elsa Rd DA16 146 C3
Elsa St E1 97 A2
Elsdale Ho 14 E9 74 C2
Elsdale St E9 74 C1
Elsden Mews E2 96 C5
Elsden Rd N17 33 D2
Elsenham Rd E12 78 C3
Elsenham St SW18, SW19 157 B2
Elsfield NW5 71 B3
Elsham Rd
Kensington W14 113 A4 244 A1
Leyton E11 76 C4
Elsham Terr W14 244 A1
Elsiedene Rd N21 17 A4
Elsie Lane Ct W2 91 D2
Elsiemaud Rd SE4 163 B6
Elsie Rd SE22 139 D1
Elsinge Rd EN1 6 B6
Elsinore Ave TW19 148 A4
Elsinore Gdns NW2 69 A5
Elsinore Ho
12 Camberwell SE5 139 A3
Islington N1 234 A5
7 Woolwich SE7 122 A2
Elsinore Rd SE23 163 A3
Elsinore Way TW9 132 D2
Elsley Ct HA9 66 D2
Elsley Prim Sch HA9 66 B2
Elsley Rd SW11 137 A2
Elsley Sch SW11 137 A2
Elspeth Rd
London SW11 136 D1
Wembley HA0 66 A3
Elsrick Ave SM4 201 C4
Elstan Way CR0 207 A2
Elstead Ct SM3 201 A1
Elstead Ho 9 SW2 160 B4
Elsted St SE17 117 B2 262 D3
Elstow Cl Eltham SE9 166 B6
Ruislip HA4 40 D2
Elstow Gdns RM9 103 A6
Elstow Grange NW6 68 D1
Elstow Rd RM9 103 A6
ELSTREE 10 A5
Elstree Gdns
Abbey Wood DA17 125 A2
Edmonton N9 18 B3
Ilford IG1 79 A3
Elstree Hill BR1 186 C3
Elstree Hill N WD6 9 D6
Elstree Hill S WD6 9 D4
Elstree Ho 3 HA7 25 C6
Elstree Pk WD6 11 B5
Elstree Rd Bushey WD23 8 C4
Elstree WD6 9 A5
Elswick Rd SE13 141 D3
Elswick St SW6 136 A3
Elsworth Cl TW14 149 C3
Elsworthy KT7 196 C3
Elsworthy Rd NW3 92 C6 230 A6
Elsworthy Rise NW3 70 C1
Elsworthy Terr NW3 70 C1
Elsynge Rd SW18 158 B6
Elsynge Road Mans SW18 158 B6
ELTHAM 166 B6
Eltham CE Prim Sch SE9 166 B6
Eltham Coll SE9 165 D2
Eltham Coll Jun Sch SE9 165 D3
Eltham Green Rd SE9 165 C6
Eltham Green Specialist Sports Coll SE9 165 D5
Eltham High St SE9 166 B5
Eltham Hill SE9 166 A6
Eltham Hill Tech Coll for Girls SE9 166 A5
Eltham Pal* SE9 166 A4
Eltham Palace Rd SE9 165 D5
Eltham Park Gdns SE9 144 C1
Eltham Rd SE9, SE12 165 B6
Eltham Sta SE9 166 B6
Elthiron Rd SW6 135 C4 265 B1
Elthorne Ave W7 109 A4
Elthorne Ct
Feltham TW13 150 C3
Kingsbury NW9 45 B3
Elthorne Park High Sch W7 108 D3
Elthorne Park Rd W7 109 A4
Elthorne Rd
London NW9 45 B2
Upper Holloway N19 71 D6
Elthorne Way NW9 45 B3
Elthruda Rd SE13 164 B5
Eltisley Rd IG1 78 D4
Elton Ave Barnet EN5 13 B6
Wembley HA0 65 B3
Wembley UB6 64 D2
Elton Cl KT1 175 C3
Elton Ho 3 E3 97 B6
Elton Lo 4 W5 110 A6
Elton Pl N16 73 C3
Elton Rd KT2 176 C2
Elton St 11 N16 73 C3
Eltringham St SW18 136 A1
Elvaston Ct EN5 12 C6
Elvaston Mews SW7 256 B6
Elvaston Pl SW7 114 A3 256 B5
Elveden Ho 17 SW9 138 D1
Elveden Pl NW10 88 C5
Elveden Rd NW10 88 C5
Elvedon Rd TW13 149 D1
Elvendon Rd N13 32 A4
Elver Gdns 10 E2 96 A4
Elverson Rd SE8 141 D3
Elverson Rd Sta SE8 141 D3
Elverton St SW1 115 D2 259 C4
Elvin Ct NW9 45 A2
Elvington Gn BR2 208 D4
Elvington La NW9 27 C2
Elvin Ho 2 E9 74 C2
Elvino Rd SE26 185 A5
Elvis Rd NW2 68 C2
Elwill Way BR3 208 B5
Elwin St E2 96 A4
Elwood Ho N5 72 D5
Elwood St N4, N5 72 D5

Elworth Ho SW8 270 D3
Elwyn Gdns SE12 165 A4
Ely Cl SW20 177 D1
Ely Cotts SW8 270 C3
Ely Court Flats SW6 264 A1
Ely Ct Holborn EC1 241 B3
3 Maida Vale NW6 91 C5
Ely Gdns
Borehamwood WD6 11 B6
Redbridge IG1 56 A2
Ely Ho Barnet EN4 2 C1
Northolt UB5 85 A6
22 Peckham SE15 140 A5
Elyne Rd N4 50 C3
Ely Pl EC1 94 C2 241 B3
Ely Rd Hatton TW6 127 D3
Hounslow TW4 128 C2
Leyton E10 54 A2
Thornton Heath CR0 205 B4
Elysian Ave BR5 211 D3
Elysium Gate 7 SW6 135 B3
Elysium Pl SW6 135 B3
Elysium St SW6 135 B3
Elystan Bsns Ctr UB4 106 C6
Elystan Ct SW15 156 B6
Elystan Pl SW3 114 D1 257 C2
Elystan St SW3 114 C2 257 B3
Elystan Wlk N1 234 A5
Emanuel Ave W3 89 A1
Emanuel Ct Acton W3 89 B1
10 Leyton E10 53 D2
Emanuel Dr TW12 173 B5
Emanuel Sch SW11 158 C6
Embankment SW15 134 D3
Embankment Gdns
SW3 136 D6 267 D6
Embankment Pier
WC2 116 A5 250 B4
Embankment Pl WC2 250 B4
Embankment Sta
WC2 116 A5 250 B4
Embankment The
TW1 153 A3
Embassy Ct Ealing W5 110 B6
Kingston u T KT6 197 D4
Sidcup DA14 168 B1
St John's Wood NW8 229 D3
7 Wallington SM6 219 B2
8 Wanstead E18 55 A6
Welling DA16 146 B2
Wood Green N11 31 D4
Embassy Gdns BR3 185 B2
Embassy Ho 2 NW6 69 C1
Embassy Lo N3 29 B1
Emba St SE16 118 A4
Ember Cl BR5 211 A2
Embercourt Rd KT10, KT7,
KT8 196 C3
Ember Ct
2 Acton W12 111 C3
14 Hendon NW9 27 D1
Ember Farm Ave KT8 196 B3
Ember Farm Way KT8 196 B4
Ember Gdns KT10, KT8 196 C2
Ember Ho 8 BR1 186 B5
Ember La KT10, KT8 196 B2
Emberson Ho 7 E17 54 A5
Emberton SE5 139 C6
Emberton Ct EC1 234 C1
Embleton Rd SE13 141 D1
Embleton Wlk TW12 173 B5
Embry Cl HA7 25 A6
Embry Dr HA7 25 A4
Embry Way HA7 25 A6
Emden Cl UB7 104 C4
Emden St SW6 265 D2
Emerald Cl E16 100 A1
Emerald Ct N12 30 A6
Emerald Gdns RM8 59 C1
Emerald Rd NW10 89 B6
Emerald Sq UB2 106 D3
Emerald St WC1 94 B2 240 C4
Emerson Apartments
N8 50 B6
Emerson Ct 8 SW19 179 A4
Emerson Gdns HA3 44 B3
Emerson Ho N16 73 C3
Emerson Rd IG1 56 C2
Emerson St
SE1 117 A5 252 A4
Emerton Cl DA6 147 A1
Emery Hill St SW1 259 B5
Emery St SE1 116 C3 261 B6
Emilia Cl EN3 18 B6
Emily St 7 E16 98 D1
Emirates Stad (Arsenal
FC) N7 72 C4
Emlyn Gdns 3 W12 111 C3
Emlyn Rd W12 111 D3
Emmanual Ho SE18 123 B1
Emmanuel CE Prim Sch
NW6 69 C3
Emmanuel Ct 3 EN4 14 D3
Emmanuel Ho
Dulwich SE21 161 B1
Lambeth SE11 261 A3
Emmanuel Rd
Northwood HA6 22 A3
Streatham SW12 159 D3
Emma Rd E13 98 D5
Emma St E2 96 B5
Emmeline Ct KT12 194 C2
Emminster NW6 91 D6
Emmott Ave IG6 57 A4
Emmott Cl
London NW11 48 A3
Mile End E1 97 A3
Emperor's Gate
SW7 114 A2 256 A4
Empingham Ho 20
SE8 118 D2
Empire Ave N18 33 A4
Empire Ct HA9 66 D5
Empire Ho
Brompton SW3 257 A5
Edmonton N18 33 B4
Empire Par
Edmonton N18 33 B4
Wembley HA9 66 C5
Empire Rd UB6 65 C1
Empire Sq N19 72 A5
Empire Way HA9 66 C4
Empire Wharf E3 97 A6
Empire Wharf Rd E14 120 B2
Empress Ave
Chingford E4 35 D3
Ilford IG1 78 C6
Wanstead E12 77 D6
Woodford IG8 36 D3
Empress Dr BR7 188 D4
Empress Mews 36
SE5 139 A3
Empress Par E4 35 C3
Empress Pl
SW5 113 C1 255 A1
Empress St SE17 139 A6
Empson St E3 97 D3
Emsworth Cl N9 18 C3
Emsworth St SW2 160 B2
Emu Rd SW8 137 B3
Ena Rd SW16 204 A6
Enard Ho 28 E3 97 B5
Enbrook St W10 91 A4
Enclave Ct EC1 241 D6
Endale Cl SM5 218 D6
Endeavour Way
Barking IG11 102 A5
Thornton Heath CR0 204 A2
Wimbledon SW19 179 D6
Endell St WC2 94 A1 240 A1
Enderby St SE10 120 C1
Enderfield Ct BR7 188 C2
Enderley Cl HA3 24 C2
Enderley Ho SE19 183 D2
Enderley Rd HA3 24 C2
Endersby Rd EN5 12 C6
Endersleigh Gdns NW4 46 A5
Endlebury Ct E4 20 B2
Endlebury Rd E4 20 A2
Endlesham Ct 2
SW12 159 A4
Endlesham Rd SW12 159 A4
Endsleigh Gdns
Bloomsbury
WC1 93 D3 239 C6
Ilford IG1 56 D1
Kingston u T KT6 197 C3
Endsleigh Ind Est UB2 107 B2
Endsleigh Mans 4
SW16 160 A1
Endsleigh Pl WC1 239 D6
Endsleigh Rd
Ealing W13 109 A6
Southall UB2 107 A2
Endsleigh St
WC1 93 D3 239 D6
Endway KT5 198 D2
Endwell Rd SE4 141 A3
Endymion Rd
Harringay N4 50 D2
Tulse Hill SW2 160 B5
Energen Cl NW10 67 C2
ENFIELD 6 B2
Enfield Chase Sta EN2 5 A2
Enfield Cloisters 7 N1 95 C4
Enfield Coll EN3 6 C2
Enfield Gram Sch EN2 5 B2
Enfield Gram Sch Lower
EN1 5 B3
ENFIELD HIGHWAY 6 C3
Enfield Ho 24 SW9 138 A3
ENFIELD LOCK 7 B6
Enfield Lock Sta EN3 7 A6
Enfield Rd
Brentford TW8 109 D1
De Beauvoir Town E8,
N1 73 C1
Enfield EN2 4 A2
Hatton TW6 127 C3
South Acton W3 110 D4
Enfield Ret Pk EN1 6 A2
Enfield Road Rdbt
TW6 127 C3
Enfield Sec Tuition Ctr
PRU N9 18 C3
ENFIELD TOWN 5 B1
Enfield Town Sta EN1 5 B2
ENFIELD WASH 6 D5
Enfield Wlk TW8 109 D1
Enford St W1 92 D2 237 C4
Engadine Cl CR0 221 D5
Engadine St SW18 157 C3
Engate St SE13 142 A1
Engel Pk NW7 28 C4
Engineer Cl SE18 144 C6
Engineers Way HA9 66 C4
England's La NW3 70 D2
England Way KT3 199 A5
Englefield
Bromley BR1 188 A1
Regent's Pk NW1 232 A1
Englefield Cl Enfield EN2 4 C3
Orpington BR5 211 D5
Thornton Heath CR0 205 A3
Englefield Path BR5 211 D5
Englefield Rd N1 73 C1
Engleheart Dr TW14 149 D5
Engleheart Rd SE6 164 A4
Englewood Rd SW12 159 C5
English Gardening Sch
The SW3 136 D6 267 C6
English Grounds SE1 253 A3
English Martyrs RC Prim
Sch E1 95 D1 243 D1
English St E3 97 B3
Enid St SE16 117 D3 263 D6
Enid Stacy Ho 11 N19 49 D2
Enmore Ave SE25 206 A4
Enmore Ct SW14 155 B6
Enmore Gdns SW14 155 B6
Enmore Rd
Croydon SE25 206 A4
Putney SW15 156 C6
Southall UB1 85 C3
Ennerdale Ave HA3,
HA7 43 C6
Ennerdale Cl
Cheam SM1 217 B4
East Bedfont TW14 149 D3
Ennerdale Ct E11 55 A2
Ennerdale Dr NW9 45 C4
Ennerdale Gdns HA9 43 C1
Ennerdale Ho 3 N4 51 B2
Ennerdale Rd
Erith DA7 147 C4
Richmond TW9 132 B3
Ennersdale Rd SE13 164 B6
Ennis Ho 16 E14 97 D1
Ennismore Ave
Chiswick W4 111 D2
Greenford UB6 64 C3
Ennismore Gdns
Knightsbridge
SW7 114 C3 257 A6
Thames Ditton KT7 196 C3
Ennismore Gdns Mews
SW7 114 C3 257 A6
Ennismore Mews
SW7 114 C3 257 A6
Ennismore St
SW7 114 C3 257 A6
Ennis Rd London N4 50 C1
Shooters Hill SE18 145 A6
Ennor Ct KT4 216 C4
Ensbury Ho SW8 270 C4
Ensign Cl TW19 148 A3
Ensign Ct 12 E1 118 A6
Ensign Dr N13 17 A1
Ensign Ho 19 E14 119 C4
Ensign St E1 118 A6
Ensign Way
Stanwell TW19 148 A3
2 Wallington SM6 220 A1
Enslin Rd SE9 166 C4
Ensor Mews SW7 256 C2
Enstone Rd Enfield EN3 7 A2
Ickenham UB10 60 B5
Enterprise Cl CR0 204 C1
Enterprise Ho IG11 101 D4
Enterprise Ho E4 20 A4
Enterprise Ho
36 Hackney E9 74 C1
Walton-on-T KT12 194 B2
Enterprise Row N15 51 D4
Enterprise Way
College Pk NW10 90 A4
Teddington TW11 174 D4
Wandsworth SW18 135 C1
Enterprise Works EN3 7 B4
Enterprize Way SE8 119 B2
Enthoven Ho SE18 122 D2
Enton Pl TW3 129 D1
Enversham Ct SE23 163 A1
Epirus Mews SW6 265 A4
Epirus Rd SW6 135 B5 264 D4
Epping Cl Millwall E14 119 C2
Romford RM7 59 D6
Epping Forest* IG10 21 B6
Epping Glade E4 20 A5
Epping Ho 8 E5 74 A6
Epping New Rd IG9 21 B5
Epping Pl N1 72 C2
Epping Way E4 19 D5
Epple Rd SW6 135 B4 264 D2
Epsom Cl Erith DA7 147 D2
Northolt UB5 63 B3
Epsom & Ewell High Sch
KT19 215 A3
Epsom Ho SM1 217 D4
Epsom Rd Croydon CR0 220 C4
Ilford IG3 57 D3
Leyton E10 54 A3
Morden SM3, SM4 201 B2
Epsom Sq TW6 127 D3
Epstein Ct N1 234 D5
Epstein Rd SE28 124 B5
Epworth Rd TW7, TW8 131 B5
Epworth St EC2 95 B3 242 D5
Equity Sq 29 E2 95 D4
Erasmus St
SW1 115 D2 259 D3
Erconwald St W12 89 D1
Erebus Dr SE28 123 B4
Eresby Dr BR3 207 C1
Eresby Ho SW7 247 B1
Eresby Pl NW6 69 C1
Erica Ct SW4 270 B1
Erica Gdns CR0 223 D5
Erica Ho London SE4 141 B2
6 Wimbledon SW19 179 A3
Wood Green N22 32 C2
Erica St W12 112 A6
Eric Cl E7 77 A4
Eric Clarke La IG11 101 A4
Ericcson Cl SW18 157 C6
Eric Fletcher Ct 15 N1 73 A1
Eric Macdonald Ho
SW6 265 B1
Eric Rd Dagenham RM6 58 D2
Forest Gate E7 77 A4
Willesden NW10 67 D2
Eric Shipman Terr 2
E13 99 A3
Ericson Ho
London SE13 142 B1
Stamford Hill N16 51 D1
Eric St E3 97 B3
Eric Wilkins Ho 14
SE1 118 A1
Eridge Ho SE22 139 D2
Eridge Rd W4 111 B3
Erin Cl Bromley BR1 186 C3
Ilford IG3 58 A3
Erin Ct NW2 68 C2
Erindale SE18 145 B6
Erindale Ct 1 BR3 185 C2
Erindale Terr SE18 145 B6
ERITH 147 D6
Erith Rd
Belvedere DA17 125 D1
Erith DA7 147 D2
Erlanger Rd SE14 140 D3
Erlesmere Gdns W13 109 A3
Ermine Cl TW4 128 C3
Ermine Ho 3 N17 33 D3
Ermine Rd
London SE13 141 D1
South Tottenham N15 51 D3
Ermine Side EN1 18 A6
Ermington Rd SE9 167 A2
Ernald Ave E6 100 A5
Erncroft Way TW1 152 D5
Ernest Ave SE27 182 D6
Ernest Bevin Coll
SW17 158 C2
Ernest Cl BR3 207 C4
Ernest Cotts KT17 215 D1
Ernest Gdns W4 132 D6
Ernest Gr BR3 207 B4
Ernest Rd KT1 176 D1
Ernest Richards Twr
E17 53 B3
Ernest Simmonds Ho
SE14 140 C3
Ernest Sq KT1 176 D1
Ernest St E1 96 D3
Ernle Rd SW20 178 C3
Ernshaw Pl SW15 157 A6
Eros Ho SE6 163 D4
Eros (Shaftesbury Meml)*
W1 115 D6 249 C5
Erpingham Rd SW15 134 C2
Erridge Rd SW19 179 C1
Errington Manor 6
SM5 218 D5
Errington Rd W9 91 B3
Errol Gdns Hayes UB4 84 B3
West Barnes KT3 200 A5
Errol St EC1 95 A3 242 B5
Erskine Cl SM1 218 C5
Erskine Cres N17 52 B5
Erskine Hill NW11 47 C4
Erskine Ho
7 Charlton SE7 143 C6
Pimlico SW1 259 A1
Erskine Rd
Carshalton SM1 218 B5
Primrose Hill NW3 70 D1
Walthamstow E17 53 B5
Erwood Rd SE7 122 A1
Esam Way SW16 182 C5
Escot Rd TW16 171 C3
Escott Gdns SE9 188 A6
Escot Way EN5 12 C6
Escreet Gr SE18 122 C2
Escuan Lo N5 73 A3
ESHER 212 A4
Esher Ave Cheam SM3 216 D5
Walton-on-T KT12 194 A1
Esher CE Prim Sch
KT10 212 A3
Esher Cl DA5 169 A3
Esher Coll KT7 196 C2
Esher Cres TW6 127 D3
Esher Gdns SW19 156 D2
Esher Ho 8 SW8 137 D3
Esher Mews 4 CR4 202 D6
Esher Park Ave KT10 212 A3
Esher Rd
East Molesey KT8 196 B4
Ilford IG3 79 C5
Esher Sta KT10 212 B6
Eskdale Enfield EN1 17 C6
Regent's Pk NW1 232 A3
Eskdale Ave UB5 85 B6
Eskdale Cl HA9 65 D6
Eskdale Rd DA7 147 C4
Esk Ho E3 97 B3
Eskmont Ridge SE19 183 C3
Esk Rd E13 99 B3
Esmar Cres NW9 46 A2
Esme Ho SW15 133 D1
Esmeralda Rd SE1 118 A2
Esmond Ct Barnet EN5 1 C1
Kensington W8 255 D6
Esmond Gdns W4 111 B2
Esmond Rd Acton W4 111 B3
Kilburn NW6 91 B6
Esmond St SW15 135 A1
Esparto St SW18 157 D4
Espirit Ct E1 243 C3
Espirit Ho 6 SW15 157 A6
Essan Ho W13 87 B2
Essence Ct HA9 66 B6
Essenden Rd
Belvedere DA17 125 C1
South Croydon CR2 221 C1
Essendine Mans W9 91 C4
Essendine Prim Sch
W9 91 C4
Essendine Rd W9 91 C4
Essex Ave TW7 130 C2
Essex Cl Romford RM7 59 D5
Ruislip HA4 40 D1
Walthamstow E17 53 A5
West Barnes SM4 200 D2
Essex Ct Barnes SW13 133 D3
Hammersmith W6 112 C3
Holborn EC4 241 A1
South Norwood SE19 183 B4
Essex Gdns N4 50 D3
Essex Gr SE19 183 B4
Essex Ho 4 Acton W3 88 C1
2 Poplar E14 97 D1
Essex Lo 5 N10 31 B1
Essex Mans E11 54 B2
Essex Park Mews W3 111 C5
Essex Pk N3 29 D4
Essex Pl W4 111 A2
Essex Place Sq 5 W4 111 B2
Essex Prim Sch E12 78 A3
Essex Rd Acton W3 111 A6
Barking IG11 79 B1
Chingford E4 20 C3
Chiswick W4 111 B2
Enfield EN2 5 B1
Ilford RM6 58 C2
Islington N1 94 D6 234 D6
Leyton E10 54 A3
Plashet E12 78 A2
Romford RM7 59 D5
Walthamstow E17 53 A3
Willesden NW10 67 C1
Woodford E18 37 B1
Essex Rd S E11 54 B2
Essex Road Sta N1 73 A1
Essex St Forest Gate E7 77 A3
Strand WC2 116 C6 251 A6
Essex Twr 4 SE20 184 B2
Essex Villas
W8 113 C4 245 A1
Essian St E1 97 A2
Essington SW15 157 A5
Essoldo Way HA8 44 B6
Estate Way E10 53 B1
Estcourt Rd
Croydon SE25 206 B3
Fulham SW6 135 B5 264 C4
Estella Ave KT3 200 B5
Estella Ho 15 W11 112 D6
Estelle Rd NW3 70 D4
Esterbrooke St SW1 259 C3
Este Rd SW11 136 C2
Esther Cl N21 16 C4
Esther Doe Lo N21 16 C4
Esther Rd E11 54 C2
Estoria Cl 22 SW2 160 C4
Estreham Rd SW16 181 D4
Estridge Cl TW3 129 C1
Estuary Cl IG11 102 B4
Eswyn Rd SW17 180 D5
Etal Ho N1 72 D1
Etchingham Ct N12 30 A3
Etchingham Park Rd
N3 29 D3
Etchingham Rd E15 76 A4
Eternit Wlk SW6 134 D4
Etfield Gr DA14 190 B5
Ethelbert Cl BR1 209 A6
Ethelbert Gdns IG2 56 C4
Ethelbert Ho E9 75 A4
Ethelbert Rd
Bromley BR1, BR2 209 A6
Wimbledon SW20 178 D2
Ethelbert St SW12 159 B3
Ethel Brooks Ho SE18 144 D6
Ethelburga St
SW11 136 C4 267 B2
Ethelburga Twr SW11 267 B2
Ethel Cotts RM6 58 D6
Etheldene Ave N10 49 C5
Ethelden Rd W12 112 B5
Ethel Rankin Ct 8
SW6 135 B3
Ethel Rd Ashford TW15 170 A5
Newham E16 99 B1
Ethel St SE17 262 B3
Ethelworth Ct 4 SW2 160 C3
Etheridge Rd NW2 46 C2
Etherley Rd N15 51 A4
Etherow St SE22 162 A4
Etherstone Gn SW16 182 C6
Etherstone Rd SW16 182 C6
Ethnard Rd SE15 140 B6
Ethronvi Rd DA7 147 A2
Etienne Ho NW7 28 C6
Etloe Ho E10 53 C1
Etloe Rd E10 75 C6
Eton Ave
East Barnet EN4 14 C5
Finchley N12 30 A3
Heston TW5 129 C6
New Malden KT3 199 B5
Primrose Hill NW3 70 C1
Wembley HA0 65 C4
Eton Cl SW18 157 D4
Eton College Rd NW3 70 D2
Eton Ct Hampstead NW3 70 B1
Highgate N6 49 B3
Wembley HA0 65 C4
Eton Garages 11 NW3 70 C2
Eton Gr Lewisham SE13 142 C2
Queensbury NW9 44 C5
Eton Hall NW3 70 D2
Eton Ho Hackney E9 75 B2
Highbury N5 72 D4
Eton Manor Ct E10 75 C6
Eton Pl NW1 71 A1
Eton Rd Harlington UB3 127 D5
Ilford IG1 79 B4
Maitland Pk NW3 70 D2
Eton Rise NW3 70 D2
Eton St TW10 154 A6
Eton Villas NW3 70 D2
Etta St SE8 141 A6
Ettrick Ho 8 E5 74 B6
Ettrick St E14 98 A1
Etwell Pl KT5 198 B3
Euesden Cl N9 18 B1
Eugene Cotter Ho
SE17 262 D3
Eugenia Rd SE16 118 C2
Eugenie Mews BR7 188 D2
Eureka Rd 8 KT1 176 C1
Euro Bsns Ctr 3 E15 98 D6
Euro Cl NW10 68 A2
Eurolink Bsns Ctr
SW2 160 C6
Europa Pl EC1 235 A1
Europe Rd SE18 122 B3
Eustace Bldg SW8 268 C5
Eustace Ho SE11 260 C4
Eustace Pl SE18 122 B2
Eustace Rd
Dagenham RM6 58 D2
Newham E6 100 A4
Walham Green
SW6 135 C5 265 A4
Euston Ct 5 HA0 66 A2
Euston Rd
Fitzrovia NW1 93 C3 239 B6
Thornton Heath CR0 204 C1
Euston Sq NW1 232 C1
Euston Square Sta
WC1 93 C3 239 B6
Euston St NW1 93 C4 232 B1
Euston Sta NW1 93 D4 232 C1
Euston Underpass
NW1 239 A6
Evandale Rd SW9 138 C3
Evangelist Rd NW5 71 B4
Evans Cl E8 73 D2
Evans Gr TW13 151 C2
Evans Ho
34 Shepherd's Bush
W12 112 B6
South Lambeth SW8 269 D3
Evans Rd SE6 164 C2
Evanston Ave E4 36 A3
Evanston Gdns IG4 56 A3
Eva Rd RM6 58 D2
Eve Ct CR4 181 A1
Evelina Mans 9 SE5 139 B5
Evelina Rd
London SE15 140 C3
Penge SE20 184 D3
Eveline Ct N10 49 B4
Eveline Lowe Prim Sch
SE1 118 A1
Eveline Rd CR4 180 D2
Evelyn Ave London NW9 45 B5
Ruislip HA4 39 D2
Evelyn Cl TW2 151 D4
Evelyn Cres TW16 171 D2
Evelyn Ct
Chislehurst SE9 166 A2
Marylebone W1 237 C1
Shacklewell E8 74 A4
Shoreditch N1 235 C3
Evelyn Denington Ct 2
N1 72 D1
Evelyn Denington Rd
E6 100 A3
Evelyn Dr HA5 22 D3
Evelyn Fox Ct W10 90 C2
Evelyn Gdns
Richmond TW9 132 A1
South Kensington
SW7 114 B1 256 C1
Evelyn Gr Ealing W5 110 B5
Southall UB1 85 B1
Evelyn Ho
Bedford Pk W12 111 D4
3 Brixton SW2 160 B6
Harrow HA1 42 B4
18 Spitalfields E1 96 A2
Evelyn Rd Acton W4 111 B3
Cockfosters EN4 2 D1
Ham TW10 153 C1
Newham E16 121 B5
Richmond TW9 132 A2
Walthamstow E17 54 A5
Wimbledon SW19 179 D4
Evelyns Cl UB8 82 C1
Evelyn St SE8 119 A1
Evelyn Terr TW9 132 A2
Evelyn Way
Sunbury TW16 171 D2
Wallington SM6 219 D4
Evelyn Wlk N1 95 B5 235 C3
Evelyn Yd W1 239 C2
Evening Hill BR3 186 A3
Evenlode Ho 5 SE2 124 C4
Evenwood Cl SW15 157 A6
Everard Ave BR2 209 A1
Everard Ct N13 16 B1
Everard Ho 33 E1 96 A1
Everard Way HA9 66 A5
Everatt Cl SW18 157 B6
Eve Rd Isleworth TW7 131 A1
Leyton E11 76 C4
Tottenham N17 51 C6
West Ham E15 98 C5
Everdale Ct N2 48 C5
Everdon Rd SW13 134 A6

Everest Ct
6 Chislehurst SE9 … 166 A2
South Norwood SE19 … 183 C2
Everest Pl E14 … 98 A2
Everest Rd Eltham SE9 … 166 B6
Stanwell TW19 … 148 A4
Everett Cl Bushey WD23 … 8 C3
Pinner HA5 … 39 D6
Everett Ho Islington N7 … 72 C4
Walworth SE17 … 262 C2
Everett Wlk DA17 … 125 B1
Everglade Ho E17 … 35 B1
Everglades
Beckenham BR2 … 208 C6
Hounslow TW3 … 130 A2
Everglade Strand NW9 … 27 D2
Evergreen Cl SE20 … 184 C3
Evergreen Ct 6 SM2 … 218 A2
Evergreen Sq 3 E8 … 73 D1
Evergreen Way UB3 … 105 D6
Everilda St N1 … 233 D5
Evering Rd E5, N16 … 74 A5
Everington Rd N10 … 30 D1
Everington St W6 … 134 D6
Everitt Rd NW10 … 89 B4
Everleigh St N4 … 50 B1
Eversfield Ct SE12 … 165 B2
Eversfield Gdns HA8,
NW7 … 27 C3
Eversfield Rd TW9 … 132 B3
Evershed Ho E1 … 243 D2
Evershed Wlk W4 … 111 B2
Eversholt Ct EN5 … 14 A6
Eversholt St
NW1 … 93 D4 232 C2
Evershot Rd N4 … 50 B1
Eversleigh Ct N3 … 29 C3
Eversleigh Rd
Clapham SW11 … 137 A3
Finchley N3 … 29 B3
New Barnet EN5 … 14 A6
Newham E6 … 99 D6
Eversley Ave HA9 … 66 C6
Eversley Cl N21 … 16 B5
Eversley Cres
Hounslow TW7 … 130 B4
Ruislip HA4 … 61 D6
Southgate N21 … 16 C5
Eversley Ho 12 E2 … 96 A4
Eversley Mount N21 … 16 B5
Eversley Park Rd N21 … 16 B5
Eversley Pk SW19 … 178 B5
Eversley Prim Sch N21 … 16 B5
Eversley Rd
Greenwich SE7 … 143 B6
Kingston u T KT5 … 198 B4
South Norwood SE19 … 183 B3
Eversley Way CR0 … 223 C5
Everthorpe Rd SE15 … 139 D2
Everton Bldgs NW1 … 232 A1
Everton Ct HA0 … 65 D4
Everton Dr HA7 … 44 A6
Everton Rd CR0 … 206 A1
Evesham Ave E17 … 35 C1
Evesham Cl
Belmont SM2 … 217 C1
Greenford UB6 … 85 D5
Evesham Ct
2 Ealing W13 … 109 A5
2 Richmond TW10 … 154 B5
Evesham Gn SM4 … 201 D3
Evesham Ho
1 Bethnal Green E2 … 96 C5
Pimlico SW1 … 258 D2
St John's Wood NW8 … 229 A5
Evesham Rd
London N11 … 31 D5
Morden SM4 … 201 D3
Stratford E15 … 76 D1
Evesham St W11 … 112 D6
Evesham Way
Clapham SW11 … 137 A2
Ilford IG5 … 56 C6
Evesham Wlk
Brixton SW9 … 138 C3
Camberwell SE5 … 139 B3
Evry Rd DA14 … 190 C4
Ewald Rd SW6 … 135 B3
Ewanrigg Terr IG8 … 37 C5
Ewart Gr N22 … 32 C2
Ewart Pl 13 E3 … 97 B5
Ewart Rd SE23 … 162 D4
Ewe Cl N7 … 72 A2
EWELL … 215 C1
Ewell By-Pass KT17 … 216 A1
EWELL COURT … 215 C2
Ewell Court Ave KT19 … 215 C3
Ewell Park Gdns KT17 … 216 A1
Ewell Park Way KT17 … 216 A1
Ewell Rd
Cheam SM2, SM3 … 216 D2
Surbiton KT6 … 198 B2
Thames Ditton KT6,
KT7 … 197 B2
Tolworth KT6 … 198 D1
Ewelme Rd SE23 … 162 C3
Ewen Cres SW2 … 160 C4
Ewen Henderson Ct 10
SE14 … 141 A5
Ewen Ho N1 … 233 C5
Ewer St SE1 … 117 A5 252 A3
Ewhurst 19 SW15 … 156 D5
Ewhurst Cl E1 … 96 C2
Ewhurst Ct CR4 … 202 B6
Ewhurst Rd SE4 … 163 B5
Exbury Ho Hackney E9 … 74 C2
4 London SW9 … 138 B1
Exbury Rd SE6 … 163 C2
Excel Ct WC2 … 249 D5
Excel Ex Ctr E16 … 121 B6
Excelsior Cl KT1 … 176 C1
Excelsior Gdns SE13 … 142 A3
Excelsior Ind Est SE16 … 140 C6
Exchange Apartments 4
BR2 … 209 B5
Exchange Arc EC2 … 243 B4
Exchange Cl N11 … 15 A2
Exchange Ct WC2 … 250 B5
Exchange Mans 2
NW11 … 47 B2
Exchange Pl EC2 … 243 A4
Exchange The IG1 … 78 D6
Exchange Wlk HA5 … 41 A2
Exeforde Ave TW15 … 170 C6
Exeter Cl E6 … 100 B1
Exeter Ct Kilburn NW6 … 91 C5
Kingston u T KT6 … 198 A4
Mitcham SW19 … 180 C3
Exeter Gdns IG1 … 56 B1
Exeter Ho
7 Barking IG11 … 80 A1
Feltham TW13 … 151 C2
Paddington W2 … 236 A2
11 Peckham SE15 … 140 A6
Putney SW15 … 156 C5
Exeter Mans NW2 … 69 A2
Exeter Mews
Fulham SW6 … 265 A4
12 Hampstead NW6 … 69 D2
Exeter Rd Bexley DA16 … 145 D3
Brondesbury NW2 … 69 A2
Croydon CR0 … 205 D2
Dagenham RM10 … 81 D2
East Barnet N14 … 15 B4
Enfield EN3 … 6 D2
Harrow HA2 … 63 A6
Hatton TW6 … 127 C2
Lower Edmonton N9 … 18 C2
Newham E16 … 99 A2
Twickenham TW13 … 151 B1
Walthamstow E17 … 53 C4
Exeter St WC2 … 116 B6 250 C6
Exeter Way
Hatton TW6 … 127 C3
2 New Cross SE14 … 141 B5
Exford Ct SW11 … 266 D2
Exford Gdns SE12 … 165 B3
Exford Rd SE12 … 165 B3
Exhibition Cl W12 … 112 C6
Exhibition Rd
SW7 … 114 B3 256 D6
Exit Rd N2 … 30 B1
Exmoor Ho 25 E3 … 97 A5
Exmoor St W10 … 90 D2
Exmouth Ho
Clerkenwell EC1 … 241 B6
6 Millwall E14 … 119 D2
Exmouth Market
EC1 … 94 C3 241 B6
Exmouth Mews NW1 … 232 B1
Exmouth Pl E8 … 74 B1
Exmouth Rd
Bexley DA16 … 146 C5
Hayes UB4 … 83 C4
Ruislip HA4 … 62 C5
Walthamstow E17 … 53 B4
Exmouth St E1 … 96 C1
Exning Rd E16 … 98 D3
Exonbury NW8 … 91 D6
Exon St SE17 … 117 C2 263 A3
Explorer Ave TW19 … 148 A3
Explorers Ct 6 E14 … 120 B6
Express Dr IG3 … 58 B1
Express Wharf 10 E14 … 119 C4
Exton Cres NW10 … 67 A1
Exton Gdns RM8 … 80 C3
Exton Rd NW10 … 67 A1
Exton St SE1 … 116 C5 251 A3
Eyebright Cl 3 CR0 … 206 D1
Eyhurst Cl NW2 … 68 A6
Eylewood Rd SE27 … 183 A5
Eynella Rd SE21 … 161 D4
Eynham Rd W12 … 90 C1
Eynsford Cl BR5 … 211 A3
Eynsford Cres DA5 … 168 D3
Eynsford Ho
Borough The SE1 … 252 C2
12 Deptford SE15 … 140 C6
Walworth SE17 … 263 A3
Eynsford Rd IG3 … 79 C6
Eynsford Terr UB7 … 82 B1
Eynsham Dr SE2 … 124 B3
Eynswood Dr DA14 … 190 C5
Eyot Gdns W6 … 111 D1
Eyot Gn W4 … 111 D1
Eyre Ct NW8 … 229 C4
Eyre St Hill EC1 … 94 C3 241 A5
Eysham Ct 12 EN5 … 13 D6
Eythorne Rd SW9 … 138 C4
Ezra St E2 … 95 D4

F

Faber Gdns NW4 … 46 A4
Fabian Rd
SW6 … 135 B5 264 D4
Fabian St E6 … 100 B3
Fabyc Ho TW9 … 132 C5
Factory La
Croydon CR0 … 220 D6
Tottenham N17 … 33 D1
Factory Rd E16 … 122 A5
Factory Yd W7 … 108 C5
Fagg's Rd TW14 … 150 A6
Fairacre Hounslow TW7 … 130 B4
Kingston u T KT3 … 199 C6
Fairacre *continued*
Pinner HA5 … 40 A5
Fairacres Putney SW15 … 134 A1
Ruislip HA4 … 39 D2
Fair Acres BR2 … 209 A4
Fairbairn Gn 1 SW9 … 138 D4
Fairbairn Hall E13 … 99 A3
Fairbank Ave BR6 … 226 D6
Fairbanks Rd N17 … 52 A6
Fairbourne Ho UB3 … 105 A3
Fairbourne Rd N17 … 51 C6
Fairbriar Residence
SW7 … 256 B4
Fairbridge Rd N19 … 71 D6
Fairbrook Cl N13 … 32 C5
Fairbrook Rd N13 … 32 C4
Fairburn Ct SW15 … 157 A6
Fairburn Ho
9 Stamford Hill N16 … 51 C1
West Kensington SW5 … 254 D1
Fairby Ho SE1 … 263 D4
Fairby Rd SE12 … 165 B6
Faircharm Trad Est
SE8 … 141 D5
Fairchild Cl 6 SW11 … 136 B3
Fairchild Ho
13 Hackney E9 … 74 C1
Pimlico SW1 … 259 B3
5 Shoreditch N1 … 95 C4
Fairchild Pl EC2 … 243 B5
Fairchild St EC2 … 243 B5
Fairclough Cl UB5 … 85 B3
Fairclough St E1 … 96 A1
Faircourt 14 NW3 … 70 D2
Faircroft
6 Forest Hill SE26 … 184 C6
Stoke Newington N16 … 51 B1
FAIR CROSS … 79 D3
Fair Cross IG11 … 79 C3
Faircross Ave IG11 … 79 A2
Faircross Par IG11 … 79 C3
Fairdale Gdns
Hayes UB3 … 106 A4
Putney SW15 … 134 B1
Fairdene Ct N7 … 72 A3
Fairey Ave UB3 … 105 D3
Fairfax Cl KT12 … 194 B1
Fairfax Gdns SE3 … 143 C4
Fairfax Ho
11 Brixton SW9 … 138 C3
5 Ealing W5 … 88 A4
6 Putney SW15 … 156 A6
Fairfax Mews
London N8 … 50 D5
Newham E16 … 121 B5
Putney SW15 … 134 C1
Fairfax Pl
Kensington W14 … 254 B5
South Hampstead NW6 … 70 A1
Fairfax Rd Acton W4 … 111 C3
Hornsey N8 … 50 C5
South Hampstead NW6 … 70 A1
Teddington TW11 … 175 B3
Fairfax Way N10 … 31 A3
Fairfield
Camden Town NW1 … 232 A5
Oakleigh Pk N20 … 14 B4
Pinner HA6 … 22 A1
4 Stepney E1 … 96 C2
Fairfield Ave
Edgware HA8 … 26 D3
Hendon NW4 … 46 B3
Ruislip HA4 … 39 A2
Twickenham TW2 … 151 D3
Fairfield Cl
Blackfen DA15 … 167 D5
Enfield EN3 … 7 A1
Mitcham SW19 … 180 C3
North Finchley N12 … 30 A6
West Ewell KT19 … 215 C3
Fairfield Cres HA8 … 26 D4
Fairfield Ct
Harlesden NW10 … 90 A6
1 London SW18 … 157 D6
Ruislip HA4 … 39 B1
8 Woodford IG8 … 37 A4
Fairfield Dr Harrow HA2 … 42 A6
Wandsworth SW18 … 157 D6
Wembley UB6 … 87 C6
Fairfield E KT1 … 176 A1
Fairfield Gdns N8 … 50 A4
Fairfield Gr SE7 … 143 D6
Fairfield Ind Est KT1 … 198 B6
Fairfield N KT1, KT2 … 176 A1
Fairfield Path CR0 … 221 B5
Fairfield Pl KT1 … 198 A6
Fairfield Rd
Beckenham BR3 … 185 C1
Bexleyheath DA7 … 147 B3
Bow E3 … 97 C5
Edmonton N18 … 34 A6
Higham Hill E17 … 35 A1
Hornsey N8 … 50 A4
Ilford IG1 … 78 D2
Kingston u T KT1 … 176 A1
Petts Wood BR5 … 211 B3
Plaistow BR1 … 187 A3
Southall UB1 … 85 B1
South Croydon CR0 … 221 C5
Woodford IG8 … 37 A4
Yiewsley UB7 … 104 A6
Fairfields SE6 … 163 D4
Fairfield S KT1 … 176 B1
Fairfields Cl NW9 … 45 A4
Fairfields Cres NW9 … 45 A4
Fairfields Rd TW3 … 130 A2
Fairfield St SW18 … 157 D6
Fairfield W KT1 … 176 A1
Fairfield Way
Barnet EN5 … 13 C6
Fairfield Way *continued*
West Ewell KT19 … 215 C3
Fairfoot Rd E3 … 97 C3
Fairford SE6 … 163 C3
Fairford Ave CR0 … 206 D4
Fairford Cl CR0 … 207 A4
Fairford Ct SM2 … 217 D1
Fairford Gdns KT4 … 215 D5
Fairford Ho SE11 … 261 B3
Fairgreen EN4 … 2 D2
Fairgreen Ct EN4 … 2 D2
Fair Green Ct 1 CR4 … 202 D6
Fairgreen E EN4 … 2 D2
Fairgreen Rd CR7 … 204 D4
Fairhall Ct KT6 … 198 B2
Fairhaven Ave CR0 … 206 D3
Fairhaven Ct 7 CR2 … 221 A3
Fairhazel Gdns NW6 … 70 A1
Fairheathe SW15 … 156 D5
Fairholme TW14 … 149 C4
Fairholme Cl N3 … 47 A5
Fairholme Cres UB4 … 84 A3
Fairholme Gdns N3 … 47 A5
Fairholme Ho 4 KT3 … 199 C5
Fairholme Prim Sch
TW14 … 149 B3
Fairholme Rd
Ashford TW15 … 170 B5
Cheam SM1 … 217 B2
Harrow HA1 … 42 D4
Ilford IG1 … 56 C2
Thornton Heath CR0 … 204 C2
West Kensington
W14 … 113 A1 254 B1
Fairholt Cl N16 … 51 C1
Fairholt Rd N16 … 51 B1
Fairholt St SW7 … 257 B6
Fairhurst 4 NW6 … 70 A2
Fairland Ho BR2 … 209 B5
Fairland Rd E15 … 76 D1
Fairlands Ave
Sutton SM1 … 217 C6
Thornton Heath CR7 … 204 C4
Woodford IG9 … 21 A2
Fairlands Ct 6 SE9 … 166 C5
Fairlawn SE7 … 143 C6
Fairlawn Ave
Acton W4 … 111 A2
Bexley DA7 … 146 D3
East Finchley N2 … 48 C5
Fairlawn Cl
Claygate KT10 … 212 D2
Feltham TW13 … 173 B6
Kingston u T KT2 … 177 A4
Southgate N14 … 15 D5
Fairlawn Ct
3 Acton W4 … 111 A2
Charlton SE7 … 143 C5
Fairlawn Dr IG8 … 37 A3
Fairlawnes SM6 … 219 B3
Fairlawn Gdns UB1 … 107 B6
Fairlawn Gr W4 … 111 A2
Fairlawn Mans SE14 … 140 D4
Fairlawn Pk SE26 … 185 A5
Fairlawn Prim Sch
SE23 … 162 C4
Fairlawn Prim Sch
(Annexe) SE23 … 162 C3
Fairlawn Rd SW19 … 179 B3
Fairlawns
4 Bowes Pk N11 … 32 A4
10 Chingford E4 … 20 A2
Pinner HA5 … 22 D1
Putney SW15 … 156 D6
Sunbury TW16 … 194 A6
Twickenham TW1 … 153 C5
Fairlead Ho 6 E14 … 119 C3
Fairlea Pl W5 … 87 D3
Fair Lea Pl W5 … 87 C2
Fairleas 12 BR3 … 185 D1
Fairley Ct HA0 … 65 D3
Fairley House Sch
SW1 … 259 D2
Fairlie Ct 22 Bromley E3 … 97 D4
1 Tufnell Pk N7 … 71 D4
Fairlie Gdns SE23 … 162 C4
Fairlight TW12 … 173 D5
Fairlight Ave
Chingford E4 … 20 B2
Harlesden NW10 … 89 C5
Woodford IG8 … 37 A4
Fairlight Cl Cheam KT4 … 216 C4
Chingford E4 … 20 B2
Fairlight Ct
Greenford UB6 … 86 B5
4 Harlesden NW10 … 89 C5
Fairlight Rd SW17 … 180 B6
Fairline Ct BR3 … 186 A1
Fairlop Ct E11 … 54 C1
Fairlop Pl NW8 … 229 D1
Fairlop Rd E11 … 54 B2
Fairmark Cl UB10 … 60 C2
Fairmead Bromley BR1 … 210 B5
Tolworth KT5, KT6 … 198 D1
Fairmead Cl
Bromley BR1 … 210 B5
Heston TW5 … 128 D5
Kingston u T KT3 … 199 B6
Fairmead Cres HA8 … 11 A1
Fairmead Ct
3 Chingford E4 … 20 C4
Oakleigh Pk N20 … 14 A4
Fairmead Gdns IG4 … 56 A4
Fairmead Ho E9 … 75 A4
Fairmead Rd
Lower Holloway N7,
N19 … 72 A5
Thornton Heath CR0 … 204 C2
Fairmeadside IG10 … 21 C6
Fairmile Ave SW16 … 181 D5
Fairmile Ho
St Paul's Cray BR5 … 190 A1
Teddington TW11 … 175 A6
Fairmont Ave E14 … 120 B5
Fairmont Cl DA17 … 125 B1
Fairmont Ho 1 E3 … 97 C3
Fairmount Rd SW2 … 160 B5
Fairoak Cl BR5 … 210 D2
Fairoak Dr SE9 … 167 B6
Fairoaks Gr EN3 … 6 D6
Fairseat Cl WD23 … 8 C2
Fair St
Bermondsey
SE1 … 117 D4 253 C2
Hounslow TW3 … 130 A2
Fairstead Lo 4 IG8 … 37 A4
Fairstead Wlk N1 … 235 A6
Fairthorn Rd SE7,
SE10 … 121 A1
Fairview Ave HA0 … 65 D2
Fairview Cl SE26 … 185 A5
Fair View Cl E17 … 35 A2
Fairview Cres HA2 … 41 C1
Fairview Ct
Ashford TW15 … 170 C5
Hendon NW4 … 28 D1
Kingston u T KT2 … 176 D2
Fairview Dr
Littleton TW17 … 192 B4
Orpington BR6 … 227 B4
Fairview Gdns IG8 … 37 B2
Fairview Ho 14 SW2 … 160 B4
Fairview Pl SW2 … 160 B4
Fairview Rd
Carshalton SM1, SM5 … 218 C3
Enfield EN2 … 4 C4
South Tottenham N15 … 51 D3
Thornton Heath SW16 … 182 B2
Fairview Way HA8 … 26 C6
Fairwall Ho 9 SE5 … 139 C4
Fairwater Ave DA16 … 146 A1
Fairwater Ho TW11 … 175 A6
Fairway Bexley DA6 … 169 A6
Petts Wood BR5 … 211 B4
West Barnes SW20 … 200 C6
Woodford IG8 … 37 C5
Fairway Ave NW9 … 44 D6
Fairway Cl
Croydon CR0 … 207 A4
Heston TW4 … 150 C6
Hounslow TW4 … 150 D6
North End NW11 … 48 A2
West Ewell KT19 … 215 A4
Fairway Ct
Edgware NW7 … 11 B1
12 Eltham SE9 … 166 C5
New Barnet EN5 … 13 D5
18 Rotherhithe SE16 … 118 D4
Fairway Dr Erith SE28 … 103 A1
Greenford UB6 … 63 D1
Fairway Est TW4 … 150 C6
Fairway Gdns Ilford IG1 … 79 A3
West Wickham BR3 … 208 B3
Fairway Prim Sch NW7 … 11 B2
Fairways Ashford TW15 … 170 D4
12 Chingford E4 … 20 A3
4 Hounslow TW7 … 130 C4
Stanmore HA7 … 26 A1
Teddington TW11 … 175 D3
Walthamstow E17 … 54 A5
Fairways Bsns Pk E10 … 75 A6
Fairway The Acton W3 … 89 C1
Bromley BR1, BR2 … 210 B4
East Molesey KT8 … 195 D6
Edgware NW7 … 11 B1
Edmonton N13 … 17 B1
Hillingdon UB10 … 82 B5
Kingston u T KT3 … 177 B2
New Barnet EN5 … 13 D5
Northolt UB5 … 64 A2
Ruislip HA4 … 62 D5
Southgate N14 … 15 C5
Wembley HA0 … 65 B6
Fairweather Cl N15 … 51 C5
Fairweather Ct N13 … 32 B6
Fairweather Ho N7 … 72 A4
Fairweather Rd N16 … 52 A3
Fairwood Ct E11 … 54 B2
Fairwyn Rd SE26 … 185 A6
Faith Ct NW2 … 68 B2
Faithfull Ho N5 … 73 A3
Fakenham Cl
Hendon NW7 … 28 A3
5 Northolt UB5 … 63 C2
Fakruddin St E1 … 96 A3
Falcon Ave BR1 … 210 A5
Falconberg Ct W1 … 239 D2
Falconberg Mews W1 … 239 D2
Falconbrook Prim Sch
SW11 … 136 B2
Falcon Cl Chiswick W4 … 133 A6
Lambeth SE1 … 251 D4
Falcon Cres EN3 … 18 D6
Falcon Ct
9 Dulwich SE21 … 161 B2
Holborn EC4 … 241 A1
Islington N1 … 234 D3
New Barnet EN5 … 2 A1
Ruislip HA4 … 61 C6
6 Wanstead E18 … 55 B6
Falcon Dr TW19 … 148 A5
Falconer Ct N17 … 33 A3
Falconer Wlk 12 N7 … 72 B6
Falcon Gr SW11 … 136 C2
Falcon Ho
11 London SE15 … 139 D4
9 Merton SW19 … 179 D2
Falconhurst 4 KT6 … 198 A4
Falcon La SW11 … 136 C2
Falcon Lo
11 Paddington W9 … 91 C2
West Hampstead NW3 … 69 D4
Falcon Pk Ind Est
NW10 … 67 C3
Falcon Point SE1 … 251 D5
Falcon Rd
Battersea SW11 … 136 C2
Enfield EN3 … 18 D6
Hampton TW12 … 173 B3
Falconry Ct KT1 … 198 A6
Falcon St E13 … 99 A3
Falcon Terr SW11 … 136 C2
Falcon Way
Feltham TW14 … 150 B6
Harrow HA3 … 44 A3
Hendon NW9 … 27 C1
Millwall E14 … 119 D2
Sunbury TW16 … 171 C1
Wanstead E11 … 55 A5
FALCONWOOD … 145 C1
Falconwood Ave
DA16 … 145 C3
Falconwood Ct SE3 … 142 D3
Falconwood Par
DA16 … 145 D1
Falconwood Rd CR0 … 223 C1
Falconwood Sta SE9 … 145 B1
Falcourt Cl SM1 … 217 D3
Falkener Ct SW11 … 268 B1
Falkirk Ct 11 SE16 … 118 D5
Falkirk Gdns WD19 … 22 D5
Falkirk Ho W9 … 91 D4
Falkirk St N1 … 95 C5
Falkland Ave
Finchley N3 … 29 C3
Friern Barnet N11 … 31 B6
Falkland Ho
Catford SE6 … 186 A6
Kensington W8 … 255 C5
West Kensington W14 … 254 C2
Falkland Park Ave
SE25 … 183 C1
Falkland Pl 2 NW5 … 71 C3
Falkland Rd Barnet EN5 … 1 A3
Hornsey N8 … 50 C5
Kentish Town NW5 … 71 C3
Falkner House Sch
SW7 … 256 B2
Fallaize Ave IG1 … 78 D4
Falling La UB7 … 104 A6
Falloden Ct NW11 … 47 C5
Falloden Way NW11 … 47 C5
Fallodon Ho
6 London SW8 … 137 D3
Paddington W11 … 91 B2
Fallow Court Ave N12 … 30 A4
Fallow Ct 20 SE16 … 118 A1
Fallowfield
Lower Holloway N4 … 72 B6
Stanmore HA7 … 9 A1
Fallowfield Ct HA7 … 9 A1
Fallow Fields IG10 … 21 C4
Fallowfields Dr N12 … 30 C4
Fallows Cl N2 … 30 B1
Fallsbrook Rd SW16 … 181 C4
Falman Cl N9 … 18 A3
Falmer Rd Enfield EN1 … 5 C1
Walthamstow E17 … 53 D6
West Green N15 … 51 B4
Falmouth Ave E4 … 36 C5
Falmouth Cl
London SE12 … 164 D6
Wood Green N22 … 32 B3
Falmouth Gdns IG4 … 55 D5
Falmouth Ho
Bayswater W2 … 247 A6
Kennington SE11 … 261 B2
15 Kingston u T KT2 … 175 D2
6 Pinner HA5 … 23 B3
Falmouth Rd
SE1 … 117 A3 262 B5
Falmouth St E15 … 76 B3
Falmouth Way E17 … 53 B4
Falstaff Ct SE11 … 261 C3
Falstaff Ho 18 N1 … 95 C5
Fambridge Cl SE26 … 185 B6
Fambridge Rd RM8 … 59 C1
Fane St W14 … 264 D6
Fann St EC1 … 95 A3 242 B5
Fanshawe Ave IG11 … 79 A2
Fanshawe Cres RM9 … 81 B3
Fanshawe Rd TW10 … 175 C6
Fanshaw Ho 6 E17 … 53 D6
Fanshaw St N1 … 95 C4
Fantail Cl SE28 … 102 C1
Fantail The BR6 … 226 B5
Fanthorpe St SW15 … 134 C2
Faraday Ave DA14 … 168 B2
Faraday Cl N7 … 72 B2
Faraday Ho
2 Balham SW12 … 159 B4
4 Belvedere DA17 … 125 C3
6 Gospel Oak NW5 … 71 B4
5 Hampton TW12 … 173 D4
Kensal Town W10 … 91 A2
6 Poplar E14 … 119 B6
Wembley HA9 … 67 A5
Faraday Lo SE10 … 120 D3
Faraday Pl KT8 … 195 C5
Faraday Rd Acton W3 … 111 A6
East Molesey KT8 … 195 C5
Kensal Town W10 … 91 A2
Southall UB1 … 107 D6
Stratford E15 … 76 D2
Welling DA16 … 146 A2
Wimbledon SW19 … 179 D4
Faraday Way
Greenwich SE18 … 121 D3
Thornton Heath CR0 … 204 B1

Fareham Ho 13 SW15 156 A3
Fareham Rd TW14 150 C4
Fareham St W1 239 C2
Farendon Ho 15 SM2 218 A2
Farewell Pl CR4 180 C2
Faringdon Ave BR2 210 C3
Faringford Rd E15 76 C1
Farjeon Ho NW6 70 B1
Farjeon Rd SE3 143 D4
Farleigh Ave BR2 209 A2
Farleigh Ct CR2 221 A3
Farleigh Ho 7 KT2 176 D4
Farleigh Pl N16 73 D4
Farleigh Rd N16 73 D4
Farleycroft 1 CR0 206 A1
Farley Croft BR2 186 C1
Farley Ct
Kensington W14 254 C6
Marylebone NW1 238 A5
Farley Dr IG3 57 C1
Farley Ho SE26 162 B1
Farley Mews SE6 164 A4
Farley Pl SE25 206 A5
Farley Rd Catford SE6 164 A4
South Croydon CR2 222 B1
Farlington Pl SW15 156 B4
Farlow Rd SW15 134 D2
Farlton Rd SW18 157 D4
Farman Gr 2 UB5 84 D4
Farman Terr HA3 43 D5
Farm Ave
Child's Hill NW2 69 B5
Harrow HA2, HA5 41 C3
Streatham SW16 182 A6
Wembley HA0 65 C2
Farmborough Cl HA1 42 B2
Farm Cl Barnet EN5 12 C6
Buckhurst Hill IG9 21 C1
Coney Hall BR4 224 D5
Lower Halliford TW17 192 C2
Southall UB1 107 D6
Sutton SM2 218 B1
Uxbridge UB10 60 D6
Walham Green SW6 265 B4
Farmcote Rd SE12 165 A3
Farm Cotts E17 53 A3
Farm Ct NW4 46 A6
Farmdale Rd
Greenwich SE10 121 A1
Sutton SM5 218 C1
Farm Dr CR0 223 B6
Farm End E4 20 C6
Farmer Ho 4 SE16 118 B3
Farmer Rd E10 53 D1
Farmers Rd SE5 138 D5
Farmer St W8 245 A4
Farmfield Rd BR1 186 C5
Farm House Ct NW7 28 A3
Farmhouse Rd SW16 181 C3
Farmilo Rd E17 53 C2
Farmington Ave SM1 218 B5
Farm La Croydon CR0 223 B6
East Barnet N14 15 B5
Walham Green
SW6 135 C5 265 B4
Farmlands Enfield EN2 4 C4
Pinner HA5 40 A5
Farmlands The UB5 63 C2
Farmland Wlk BR7 188 D5
Farm Lane Trad Ctr
SW6 135 C6 265 B5
Farmleigh N14 15 C4
Farmleigh Ho SW9 160 D6
Farm Pl W8 245 A4
Farm Rd Edgware HA8 27 A5
Edmonton N21 17 A3
Morden SM4 201 D4
Stonebridge NW10 89 B6
Sutton SM2 218 B1
Thames Ditton KT10 195 C1
Twickenham TW4 151 A3
Farm St W1 115 B6 248 C5
Farmstead Ct 3 SM6 219 B3
Farmstead Rd
Catford SE6 185 D6
Harrow HA3 24 B1
Farm Vale DA5 169 D5
Farm View N3 47 B6
Farmway RM8 80 C5
Farm Way
Buckhurst Hill IG9 37 C6
North Cheam KT4 216 C5
Farm Wlk NW11 47 C4
Farnaby Ho 2 W10 91 B4
Farnaby Rd
Bromley BR1, BR2 186 C2
Kidbrooke SE9 143 C1
Farnan Ave E17 53 D6
Farnan Hall 6 SW16 182 A5
Farnan Rd SW16 182 A5
FARNBOROUGH 227 B3
Farnborough Ave
South Croydon CR2 223 A1
Walthamstow E17 53 A6
Farnborough Cl HA9 66 D6
Farnborough Comm
Keston Mark BR2,
BR6 226 B5
Orpington BR6 226 C4
Farnborough Cres
3 Hayes BR2 208 D1
South Croydon CR2 223 A1
Farnborough Ct 2
BR6 227 A3
Farnborough Hill BR6 227 C3
Farnborough Ho 1
SW15 156 A3
Farnborough Prim Sch
BR6 227 A3
Farnborough Way
BR6 227 B3
Farncombe St SE16 118 A4
Farndale Ave N13 17 A1
Farndale Cres UB6 86 A4
Farndale Ho 3 NW6 91 D6
Farnell Mews SW5 255 C2
Farnell Pl W3 110 D6
Farnell Rd TW7 130 B2
Farnell's Almshouses
TW7 130 D3
Farnfield Ho 12 SW2 160 B6
Farnham Cl N20 14 A4
Farnham Ct
2 Cheam SM3 217 A2
1 Southall UB1 86 A1
2 Stamford Hill N16 51 C1
Farnham Gdns SW20 178 B1
Farnham Green Prim Sch
IG3 58 A3
Farnham Ho
Borough The SE1 252 A3
Marylebone NW1 237 B5
Farnham Pl SE1 251 D3
Farnham Rd
Bexley DA16 146 C3
Ilford IG3 57 D2
Farnham Royal
SE11 116 B1 260 D1
Farnhurst Ho 7
SW11 137 A3
Farningham Ct SW16 181 D3
Farningham Ho 9 N4 51 B2
Farningham Rd N17 34 A3
Farnley Ho 13 SW8 137 D3
Farnley Rd Chingford E4 20 C4
South Norwood SE25 205 B5
Farnsworth Ct SE10 120 D3
Farnsworth Ho 8
SW27 182 D5
Farnworth Ho 5 E14 120 B2
Faro Cl BR1 188 C1
Faroe Rd W14 112 D3
Farorna Wlk EN2 4 C4
Farquhar Rd
Dulwich SE19 183 D5
Wimbledon SW19 157 C1
Farquharson Rd CR0 205 A1
Farrance Rd RM6 59 A2
Farrance St E14 97 C1
Farrans Ct HA3 43 B2
Farrant Ave N22 32 D1
Farrant Cl BR6 227 D1
Farrant Ho 15 SW11 136 B2
Farrants Ct BR1 188 B1
Farr Ave IG11 102 A5
Farrell Ho E1 96 C1
Farren Rd SE23 163 A2
Farrer Ho SE8 141 C5
Farrer Mews N8 49 C5
Farrer Rd Harrow HA3 44 A5
Hornsey N8 49 D5
Farrer's Pl CR0 222 D4
Farrier Cl Bromley BR1 209 D6
Hillingdon UB8 82 C1
Sunbury TW16 194 A5
Farrier Pl SM1 217 D6
Farrier Rd UB5 85 C5
Farriers Ct
Belmont SM2 217 A1
Wimbledon SW19 179 A3
Farriers Mews SE15 140 C2
Farrier St NW1 71 C1
Farriers Way WD6 11 B6
Farrier Wlk
SW10 136 A6 266 A6
Farringdon La
EC1 94 C3 241 B5
Farringdon Rd
EC1 94 C3 241 B5
Farringdon St
EC4 94 D1 241 C2
Farringdon Sta
EC1 94 D2 241 C4
Farrington Pl BR7 189 B3
Farrington & Stratford
House Sch BR7 189 B3
Farrins Rents SE16 119 A5
Farrow La SE14 140 C5
Farrow Pl SE16 119 A3
Farr Rd EN2 5 B4
Farthingale Wlk E15 76 B1
Farthing Alley 8 SE1 118 A4
Farthing Ct 3 NW7 29 A3
Farthing Fields 8 E1 118 B5
Farthings Cl
Chingford E4 20 C1
Pinner HA5 40 B3
Farthing St BR6 226 B1
Farthings The 1 KT2 176 C2
FARTHING STREET 226 B1
Farwell Rd DA14 190 C6
Farwig La BR1 187 A2
Fashion & Design Mus
The★ SE1 253 A2
Fashion Retail Acad The
W1 239 C2
Fashion St E1 95 D2 243 D3
Fashoda Rd BR2 209 D5
Fassett Rd Dalston E8 74 A2
Kingston u T KT1 198 A5
Fassett Sq E8 74 A2
Fauconberg Ct W4 133 A6
Fauconberg Rd W4 133 A6
Faulkner Cl 6 RM8 58 D2
Faulkner Ho SW15 134 C3
Faulkner's Alley EC1 241 C4
Faulkner St SE14 140 C4
Fauna Cl Dagenham RM6 58 C3
Stanmore HA7 25 D6
Faunce Ho 1 SE17 138 D6
Faunce St
SE17 116 D1 261 C1
Favart Rd SW6 135 C4 265 B2
F Ave SE18 122 D3
Faversham Ave
Chingford E4 20 D3
Enfield EN1 17 B5
Faversham Ct SE6 163 B3
Faversham Ho
Camden Town NW1 232 B5
Walworth SE17 263 A1
Faversham Rd
Beckenham BR3 185 B1
Forest Hill SE6 163 B3
Morden SM4 201 D3
Fawcett Cl
London SW11 136 B3
West Norwood SW16 182 C6
Fawcett Est E5 52 A1
Fawcett Ho 25 SW9 138 A3
Fawcett Rd
Croydon CR0 221 A5
Willesden NW10 67 D1
Fawcett St
SW10 136 A6 266 A6
Fawcus Cl KT10 212 C2
Fawe Park Rd SW15 135 B1
Fawe St E14 97 D2
Fawkham Ho SE1 263 D3
Fawley Ct SE27 160 D2
Fawley Lo 2 E14 120 B2
Fawley Rd NW6 69 D3
Fawnbrake Ave SE24 161 A6
Fawn Rd E13 99 C5
Fawns Manor Cl
TW14 149 A3
Fawns Manor Rd
TW14 149 B3
Fawood Ave NW10 67 B1
Fayetville Ho 26 N19 49 D2
Faygate Cres DA6 169 C6
Faygate Ct CR2 220 D1
Faygate Rd SW2 160 B2
Fayland Ave SW16 181 C5
Fazal Laj IG1 79 A6
Fazerley Ct 49 W2 91 C2
Fearnley Cres TW12 173 B4
Fearnley Ho SE5 139 C3
Fearon St SE10 121 A1
Featherbed La CR0 223 B1
Feathers Pl SE10 142 B6
Featherstone Ave 4
SE23 162 C2
Featherstone Ct NW7 28 A3
Featherstone High Sch
UB2 107 A3
Featherstone Ho UB4 84 C2
Featherstone Ind Est
UB2 107 A3
Featherstone Prim Sch
UB2 106 C2
Featherstone Rd
Mill Hill NW7 28 B4
Southall UB2 107 A3
Featherstone St
EC1 95 B3 242 C6
Featherstone Terr
UB2 107 A3
Featley Rd SW9 138 D2
Federal Rd UB6 87 C5
Federation Rd SE2 124 C2
Fee Farm Rd KT10 212 D1
Felbridge Ave HA7 25 B2
Felbridge Cl SW16 182 C6
Felbridge Ct
Croydon CR2 221 A1
Feltham TW13 150 B3
Harlington UB3 127 B6
Felbridge Ho 21 SE22 139 C2
Felbrigge Rd IG3 57 D1
Felday Rd SE13 163 D5
Felden Cl HA5 23 A3
Felden St SW6 135 B4 264 C1
Feldman Cl N16 52 A1
Feldspar Ct 6 EN3 7 A2
Felgate Mews 4 W6 112 B2
Felhampton Rd SE9 166 D1
Felhurst Cres RM10 81 D4
Feline Ct 1 EN4 14 C5
Felix Ave N8 50 A3
Felix Ct E17 53 D4
Felix La TW17 193 D3
Felix Manor BR7 189 C4
Felix Neubergh Ct EN1 5 C1
Felix Rd Ealing W13 109 A6
Walton-on-T KT12 194 A3
Felix St 9 E2 96 B5
Felixstowe Ct E16 122 D5
Felixstowe Rd
Abbey Wood SE2 124 B3
College Pk NW10 90 B4
Edmonton N9 34 A6
Tottenham N17 51 D6
Fellbrigg Rd SE22 161 D6
Fellbrigg St 21 E1 96 B3
Fellbrook TW10 153 B1
Fell Ho 11 N19 71 C5
Fellmongers Yd 1
CR0 221 A5
Fellowes Cl UB4 84 D3
Fellowes Ct UB3 127 B6
Fellowes Rd SM5 218 C6
Fellows Ct E2 95 D5
Fellows Rd NW3 70 C1
Fell Rd CR0 221 A5
Fells Haugh 6 W3 89 A1
Felltram Way SE7 121 A1
Fell Wlk HA8 26 D2
Felmersham Cl 2
SW4 137 D1
Felmingham Rd SE20 184 C1
Felnex Trad Est SM6 219 A6
Felpham Ct HA9 65 D4
Felsberg Rd SW2 160 A4
Fels Cl RM10 81 D5
Felsham Ho SW15 134 D2
Felsham Mews SW15 134 D2
Felsham Rd SW15 134 D2
Felspar Cl SE18 123 D1
Felstead Cl N13 32 C5
Felstead Rd E11 55 A2
Felstead St E9 75 B2
Felstead Wharf E14 120 A1
Felsted Rd E16 99 D1
FELTHAM 150 B2
Feltham Ave KT8 196 C5
Felthambrook Ind Est
TW13 150 B1
Felthambrook Way
TW13 172 B6
Feltham Bsns Complex
TW13 150 B2
Feltham Com Sch
TW13 150 C2
Feltham Corporate Ctr
TW13 150 B1
FELTHAMHILL 171 D5
Feltham Hill Jun & Inf
Schs TW13 149 D1
Feltham Hill Rd
Ashford TW15 171 A4
Feltham TW13 172 C5
Feltham Rd
Ashford TW15 171 A6
Mitcham CR4 181 A1
Feltham Sta TW13 150 B3
Felton Cl BR5 210 D3
Felton Gdns IG11 101 C5
Felton Ho
Kidbrooke SE9 143 C1
Shoreditch N1 235 D5
Felton Lea DA14 189 D5
Felton Rd Barking IG11 101 C5
Ealing W13 109 C4
Felton St N1 95 B6 235 D5
Fenchurch Ave
EC3 95 C1 243 A1
Fenchurch Bldgs EC3 243 B1
Fenchurch Pl EC3 253 B6
Fenchurch St
EC3 117 C6 253 B6
Fenchurch Street Sta
EC3 117 C6 253 B6
Fen Ct EC3 253 A6
Fendall Rd KT19 215 A3
Fendall St SE1 117 C3 263 B5
Fender Ct 5 SW4 138 A3
Fendt Cl 8 E16 98 D1
Fendyke Rd SE2, DA17 124 D3
Fenelon Pl
W14 113 B2 254 D3
Fen Gr DA15 167 D5
Fenham Rd SE15 140 B5
Fenman Ct N17 34 B2
Fenman Gdns IG3 58 B1
Fenn Cl BR1 187 A4
Fenn Ct HA1 43 A4
Fennel Cl Croydon CR0 206 D1
Newham E16 98 C3
Fennell St SE18 144 C6
Fenner Cl SE16 118 B2
Fenner Ho 20 E1 118 B5
Fenner Sq 10 SW11 136 B2
Fenn Ho TW7 131 B4
Fenning Ct CR4 202 C5
Fenning St SE1 253 A2
Fenn St E9 74 C3
Fen St E16 120 D6
Fenstanton 3 N4 50 B1
Fenstanton Ave N12 30 B5
Fenstanton Prim Sch
SW2 160 C3
Fenswood Cl DA5 169 C5
Fentiman Rd
SW8 138 B5 270 C4
Fentiman Way HA2 63 D6
Fenton Cl Dalston E8 73 D2
Elmstead BR7 188 B5
South Lambeth SW9 138 B3
Fenton Ct TW3 129 A5
Fenton Ho
Deptford SE14 141 A5
Heston TW5 129 C6
Fenton House★ NW3 70 A5
Fenton Rd N17 33 A3
Fentons SE3 142 D5
Fenton's Ave E13 99 B5
Fenton St E1 96 B1
Fenwick Cl 16 SE18 144 C6
Fenwick Gr SE15 140 A2
Fenwick Pl
Croydon CR2 220 D1
Stockwell SW9 138 A2
Fenwick Rd SE15 140 A2
Ferby Ct DA15 189 D6
Ferdinand Ho 1 NW1 71 B1
Ferdinand Pl NW1 71 A1
Ferdinand St NW1 71 A1
Ferguson Ave KT5 198 B4
Ferguson Cl BR2, BR3 208 B6
Ferguson Dr W3 89 B1
Ferguson Ho SE10 142 A4
Ferguson's Cl E14 119 C2
Fergus Rd N5 72 D3
Fermain Ct E N1 95 C6
Fermain Ct N N1 95 C6
Fermain Ct W N1 95 C6
Ferme Park Rd N4, N8 50 B3
Fermor Rd SE23 163 A3
Fermoy Rd
Greenford UB6 85 D3
West Kilburn W9 91 B3
Fern Ave CR4 203 D5
Fernbank IG9 21 B3
Fernbank Ave
Walton-on-T KT12 195 A2
Wembley HA0 64 D3
Fernbank Mews SW12 159 C5
Fernbrook Cres SE13 164 C5
Fernbrook Dr HA2 41 D2
Fernbrook Rd SE13 164 C5
Fern Cl 8 N1 95 C5
Ferncliff Rd E8 74 A3
Ferncroft Ave
London N12 30 D4
Ruislip HA4 62 C6
West Hampstead NW3 69 C4
Fern Ct
Bexleyheath DA7 147 C1
Chingford E4 36 A4
New Cross Gate SE14 140 D3
Ferndale BR1 187 C1
Ferndale Ave
Hounslow TW4 129 A2
Walthamstow E17 54 B4
Ferndale Cl DA7 147 A4
Ferndale Ct 3 SE3 142 D5
Ferndale Ho N16 51 B1
Ferndale Rd
Ashford TW15 170 A5
Brixton SW4, SW9 138 B1
Croydon SE25 206 B4
Enfield EN3 7 A6
Leyton E11 76 D6
South Tottenham N15 51 D4
Upton E7 77 B1
Ferndale St E6 100 D1
Ferndale Way BR6 227 B3
Ferndene NW9 45 A4
Fern Dene W13 87 B2
Ferndene Rd SE24 139 A1
Ferndown Way RM7 59 D3
Ferndown
5 Kingston u T KT6 198 A4
Pinner HA6 22 A1
7 Wanstead E18 55 A6
Ferndown Ave BR6 211 B1
Ferndown Cl
Pinner HA5 23 A3
Sutton SM2 218 B2
Ferndown Ct 6 UB1 86 A1
Ferndown Lo 17 E14 120 A3
Ferndown Rd
Eltham SE9 165 D4
South Oxhey WD19 22 C6
Ferney Meade Way
TW7 131 A3
Ferney Rd EN4 15 A3
Fern Gr TW14 150 B4
Fernhall N12 30 C5
Fernhall Dr IG4 55 D4
Fernham Rd CR7 205 A6
Fernhead 12 SM1 218 A4
Fernhead Rd W9 91 B4
Fernhill Ct
Chingford E17 36 B1
Kingston u T KT2 175 D5
Fernhill Gdns KT2 176 A5
Fernhill Ho E5 74 A6
Fern Hill Pl 3 BR6 227 A3
Fern Hill Prim Sch
KT2 176 A4
Fernhill St E16 122 B5
Fern Ho HA7 24 D4
Fernholme Rd SE15 162 D6
Fernhurst Gdns HA8 26 C4
Fernhurst Rd
Ashford TW15 171 A6
Croydon CR0 206 B1
Fulham SW6 135 A4 264 B2
Fernie Ho SE22 139 D2
Fern La TW5 107 B1
Fernlea Ho NW10 88 B4
Fernlea Rd
Balham SW12 159 B3
Mitcham CR4 181 A2
Fernleigh Cl
Croydon CR0 220 C4
West Kilburn W9 91 B4
Fernleigh Ct
Harrow HA2 23 D1
Wembley HA9 44 A1
Fernleigh Rd N21 16 D2
Fern Lo 13 SW16 182 C5
Fernly Cl HA5 40 A5
Fernsbury St WC1 234 A1
Fernshaw Mans SW10 266 A5
Fernshaw Rd
SW10 136 A6 266 A5
Fernside
Buckhurst Hill IG9 21 B3
Golders Green NW11 47 C1
Fernside Ave
Edgware NW7 11 B1
Feltham TW13 172 B6
Fernside Ct NW4 28 D1
Fernside Rd SW12 159 A4
Ferns Rd E15 76 D2
Fern St E3 97 C3
Fernthorpe Rd SW16 181 C4
Ferntower Rd N5 73 B3
Fernways IG1 78 D4
Fern Wlk 18 SE16 118 A1
Fernwood
Wandsworth SW19 157 B3
Wood Green N22 32 A3
Fernwood Ave
Streatham SW16 181 D6
Fernwood Ave *continued*
Wembley HA0 65 C2
Fernwood Cl BR1 187 C1
Fernwood Cres N20 14 D1
Fernwood Ct N14 15 D3
Ferny Hill EN4 3 A5
Ferranti Cl SE18 121 D3
Ferraro Cl TW5 129 C6
Ferrers Ave
Wallington SM6 219 D4
West Drayton UB7 104 A4
Ferrers Rd SW16 181 D5
Ferrestone Rd N8 50 B5
Ferrey Mews 19 SW9 138 C3
Ferriby Cl N1 72 C1
Ferrier Ind Est SW18 135 D1
Ferrier Point 6 E16 99 A2
Ferrier St SW18 135 D1
Ferring Cl HA2 42 A1
Ferrings SE21 161 C1
Ferris Ave CR0 223 B5
Ferris Rd SE22 140 A1
Ferron Rd E5 74 B5
Ferrour Ct N2 48 B6
Ferrybridge Ho SE11 260 D5
Ferrydale Lo 4 NW4 46 C5
Ferry Ho E5 52 B1
Ferry Island Ret Pk
N17 52 A6
Ferry La Barnes SW13 133 D6
Brentford TW8 132 A6
Lower Halliford TW17 192 C1
Richmond TW9 132 B6
Tottenham Hale N17 52 B5
Ferry Lane Ind Est E17 52 D5
Ferry Lane Prim Sch
N17 52 B5
Ferrymead Ave UB6 85 C5
Ferrymead Dr UB6 85 C5
Ferrymead Gdns UB6 86 A5
Ferrymoor TW10 153 B1
Ferry Quays Ctyd 13
TW8 131 D6
Ferry Rd Barnes SW13 134 A4
East Molesey KT8 195 C6
Richmond TW11 175 B5
Thames Ditton KT7 197 B3
Twickenham TW1 153 B3
Ferry Sq
1 Brentford TW8 132 A6
Lower Halliford TW17 192 D2
Ferry St E14 120 A1
Ferry Wks TW17 192 C1
Festing Rd SW15 134 D2
Festival Cl
Hillingdon UB10 82 D6
Sidcup DA5 168 D3
Festival Ct Cheam SM1 201 D1
5 Dalston E8 73 D1
Festival Pier
SE1 116 B5 250 C4
Festival Pleasure Gdns
SW11 136 D5 267 C3
Festoon Way E16 121 D6
Fetherston Ct RM6 59 B3
Fetter La EC4 94 C1 241 B2
Fettes Ho NW8 229 D3
Fews Lodge RM6 58 D5
Ffinch St SE8 141 C5
Fidgeon Cl BR1 210 C6
Field Cl Bromley BR1 187 C1
Buckhurst Hill IG9 21 C1
Chessington KT9 213 C3
Chingford E4 35 D4
Cranford TW4 128 B4
East Molesey KT8 195 D4
Harlington UB7 127 A5
Ruislip HA4 39 A1
Uxbridge UB10 60 D6
Willesden NW2 68 A6
Fieldcommon La KT12 195 B1
Field Ct Hampstead NW3 70 A3
Holborn WC1 240 D3
Lower Holloway N7 72 A3
Wimbledon SW19 157 C1
Fieldend TW11 174 D6
Field End HA4 62 C2
Field End Jun & Inf Schs
HA4 62 D6
Fieldend Rd SW16 181 C2
Field End Rd HA5, HA4 40 C1
Fielders Cl 2 Enfield EN1 5 C1
Harrow HA2 42 A1
Fieldfare Rd SE28 124 C6
Fieldgate Mans 25 E1 96 A2
Fieldgate St E1 96 A2
Field Ho
4 Edmonton N9 34 A6
Kensal Green NW10 90 D4
8 Richmond TW10 153 C1
Fieldhouse Cl E18 37 B2
Fieldhouse Rd SW12 159 C3
Fielding Ave TW2 152 A1
Fielding Ho
Chiswick W4 133 C6
6 Kilburn NW6 91 C4
St John's Wood NW8 229 A6
Fielding Mews SW13 134 B6
Fielding Prim Sch
W13 109 B3
Fielding Rd Acton W4 111 C3
Hammersmith W14 112 D3
Fielding St SE17 139 A6
Fieldings The SE23 162 C3
Fielding Terr W5 110 B6
Field La Brentford TW8 131 C5
Teddington TW11 175 A5

Field Lo NW10 . . . 67 D2
Field Mead NW9, NW7 . . . 27 D3
Fieldpark Gdns CR0 . . . 207 A1
Field Pl KT3 . . . 199 D3
Field Point E7 . . . 77 A4
Field Rd Feltham TW14 . . 150 B5
Forest Gate E7 . . . 77 A4
Fulham W6 . . . 135 A6 264 A6
Tottenham N17 . . . 51 C6
Fieldsend Rd SM3 . . . 217 A3
Fields Est E8 . . . 74 A1
Fieldside Cl BR6 . . . 227 A4
Fieldside Rd BR1 . . . 186 B5
Fields Park Cres RM6 . . . 58 D4
Field St WC1 . . . 233 C2
Fieldsway Ho N5 . . . 72 C3
Fieldview SW17, SW18 . . 158 B3
Field View TW13 . . . 171 B6
Field View Cl RM7 . . . 59 C6
Fieldview Ct
2 Islington N5 . . . 72 D3
London NW9 . . . 44 C3
Fieldway Dagenham RM8 . 80 C4
Petts Wood BR5 . . . 211 B3
Field Way
Greenford UB6 . . . 85 D6
New Addington CR0 . . . 223 D2
Ruislip HA4 . . . 39 A1
Willesden NW10 . . . 67 A1
Fieldway Cres N5, N7 . . . 72 C3
Fieldway Sta CR0 . . . 223 D1
Fieldwick Ho 14 E9 . . . 74 D2
Fiennes Cl RM8 . . . 58 C1
Fife Ct 5 W3 . . . 88 C1
Fifehead Cl TW15 . . . 170 A4
Fife Rd
Kingston u T KT2 . . . 176 A1
Mortlake SW14 . . . 155 A6
Newham E16 . . . 99 A2
Tottenham N22 . . . 32 D3
Fife Terr N1 . . . 233 D4
Fifield Path SE23 . . . 162 D1
Fifteenpenny Fields
SE9 . . . 166 C6
Fifth Ave Hayes UB3 . . . 105 D5
Ilford E12 . . . 78 B4
West Kilburn W10 . . . 91 A4
Fifth Cross Rd TW2 . . . 152 B2
Fifth Way HA9 . . . 66 D4
Figge's Rd CR4 . . . 181 A3
Fig Tree Cl NW10 . . . 89 C6
Filanco Ct W7 . . . 108 D5
Filby Rd KT9 . . . 214 B2
Filey Ave N16 . . . 52 A1
Filey Cl SM2 . . . 218 A1
Filey Ho SW18 . . . 136 A1
Filey Waye HA4 . . . 62 B6
Filigree Ct SE16 . . . 119 B5
Fillebrook Ave EN1 . . . 5 D3
Fillebrook Rd E11 . . . 54 C1
Filmer Ho SW6 . . . 264 B2
Filmer Mews SW6 . . . 264 B2
Filmer Rd SW6 . 135 B5 264 C3
Filston Rd DA8 . . . 125 D1
Filton Cl NW9 . . . 27 C1
Filton Ct 10 SE14 . . . 140 C5
Finborough Rd
Upper Tooting SW17 . . . 180 D4
West Brompton
SW10 . . . 135 D6 265 D6
Finchale Rd SE2 . . . 124 A3
Fincham Cl UB10 . . . 61 A5
Finch Ave SE27 . . . 183 B6
Finch Cl Barnet EN5 . . . 13 C6
Willesden NW10 . . . 67 B2
Finch Ct DA14 . . . 168 B1
Finchdean Ho SW15 . . . 155 D4
Finch Dr TW14 . . . 150 D4
Finch Gdns E4 . . . 35 C5
Finch Ho 1 SE8 . . . 141 D5
Finchingfield Ave IG8 . . . 37 C3
Finch La EC2, EC3 . . . 242 D1
FINCHLEY . . . 29 D3
Finchley Cath High Sch
N12 . . . 13 D1
Finchley Central Sta
N3 . . . 29 C2
Finchley Ct N3 . . . 29 D4
Finchley La NW4 . . . 46 D5
Finchley Lo N12 . . . 29 D5
Finchley Meml Hospl
N12 . . . 30 A3
Finchley Pk N12 . . . 30 B6
Finchley Pl NW8 . . . 229 C4
Finchley Rd
Hampstead NW3 . . . 70 A2
London NW11 . . . 47 B3
St John's Wood NW8 . . 229 C4
Finchley Road & Frognal
Sta NW3 . . . 70 A3
Finchley Road Sta
NW3 . . . 70 A2
Finchley Way N3 . . . 29 C3
Finch Lo 15 W9 . . . 91 C2
Finch Mews 3 SE15 . . . 139 D4
Finch's Ct 10 E14 . . . 119 D6
Finden Rd E7 . . . 77 C3
Findhorn Ave UB4 . . . 84 B2
Findhorn St 8 E14 . . . 98 A1
Findon Cl Harrow HA2 . . . 63 D5
Wandsworth SW18 . . . 157 C5
Findon Rd Edmonton N9 . . 18 B3
Shepherd's Bush W12 . . 112 A4
Fine Bush La HA4 . . . 38 D3
Fineran Ct 15 SW11 . . . 136 B1
Fingal St SE10 . . . 120 D1
Fingest Ho NW8 . . . 237 A6
Finians Cl UB10 . . . 60 B1
Finland Rd SE4 . . . 141 A2
Finland St SE16 . . . 119 A3
Finlays Cl KT9 . . . 214 C3
Finlay St SW6 . . . 134 D4
Finley Ct 21 SE5 . . . 139 A5
Finmere Ho 1 N4 . . . 51 A2
Finnemore Ho N1 . . . 235 A6
Finney La TW7 . . . 131 A4
Finn Ho N1 . . . 235 D2
Finnis St E2 . . . 96 B3
Finnymore Rd RM9 . . . 81 A1
FINSBURY . . . 94 C4
Finsbury Ave EC2 . . . 242 D3
Finsbury Cir
EC2 . . . 95 B2 242 D3
Finsbury Coll N4 . . . 72 C6
Finsbury Cotts N22 . . . 32 A3
Finsbury Ct EC2 . . . 242 C4
Finsbury Ho N22 . . . 32 A2
Finsbury Market EC2 . . 243 A4
Finsbury Mkt EC2 . . . 243 A5
FINSBURY PARK . . . 72 C6
Finsbury Park Ave N4 . . . 51 A3
Finsbury Park Rd N4,
N5 . . . 72 D6
Finsbury Park Sta N4 . . . 72 C6
Finsbury Pavement
EC2 . . . 95 B2 242 D4
Finsbury Rd N22 . . . 32 B2
Finsbury Sq EC2 . 95 B2 242 D4
Finsbury St EC2 . . . 242 C4
Finsbury Way DA5 . . . 169 B5
Finsen Rd SE5 . . . 139 A2
Finstock Rd W10 . . . 90 D1
Finton House Sch
SW17 . . . 158 D2
Finucane Ct TW9 . . . 132 B2
Finucane Rise WD23 . . . 8 A2
Finwhale Ho E14 . . . 119 D3
Fiona Ct Enfield EN2 . . . 4 D2
9 Kilburn NW6 . . . 91 B5
Firbank Cl Enfield EN2 . . . 5 A1
Newham E16 . . . 99 D2
Firbank Rd SE15 . . . 140 B3
Fir Cl KT12 . . . 194 A2
Fircroft N1 . . . 94 D6 234 D6
Fircroft Gdns HA1 . . . 64 C5
Fircroft Prim Sch
SW17 . . . 158 D1
Fircroft Rd
Chessington KT9 . . . 214 B4
Upper Tooting SW17 . . . 158 D1
Firdene KT5 . . . 199 A1
Fir Dene BR6 . . . 226 C5
Fire Bell Alley KT6 . . . 198 A3
Firebell Mews KT6 . . . 198 A3
Fire Brigade Cotts HA5 . . 41 C5
Fire Brigade Pier SE1 . . 260 B4
Firecrest Dr NW3 . . . 69 D5
Firefly 7 NW9 . . . 27 D1
Firefly Gdns E6 . . . 100 A3
Firemans Cotts N10 . . . 49 A6
Fireman's Flats N22 . . . 32 A2
Firepower (The Royal
Artillery Mus)*
SE18 . . . 122 D3
Fire Station Alley EN5 . . . 1 A3
Fire Station Flats
TW7 . . . 130 C3
Fire Station Mews 4
BR3 . . . 185 D2
Firethorn Cl 4 HA8 . . . 27 A6
Fir Gr KT3 . . . 199 D3
Fir Grove Rd 25 SW9 . . . 138 C3
Firhill Rd SE6 . . . 163 C1
Fir Island NW7 . . . 28 C5
Firle Ho 7 W10 . . . 90 C2
Fir Lo SW15 . . . 134 B1
Firmans Ct E17 . . . 54 B5
Firmston Ho 9 SW14 . . 133 B2
Fir Rd Cheam SM3 . . . 201 B1
Feltham TW13 . . . 172 D5
Firs Ave
Fortis Green N10 . . . 49 A5
Friern Barnet N11 . . . 31 A4
Mortlake SW14 . . . 133 A1
Firsby Ave CR0 . . . 207 A1
Firsby Rd N16 . . . 52 A1
Firs Cl Claygate KT10 . . . 212 C2
Forest Hill SE23 . . . 163 A4
Mitcham CR4 . . . 181 B2
Muswell Hill N10 . . . 49 A6
Firscroft N13 . . . 17 A1
Firs Dr TW5 . . . 128 B5
Firs Farm Prim Sch
N13 . . . 17 B1
Firs Ho N22 . . . 32 C2
Firside Gr DA15 . . . 167 D3
Firs La N21, N13 . . . 17 A2
Firs Park Ave N21 . . . 17 B3
Firs Park Gdns N21 . . . 17 B3
First Ave Bexley DA7 . . . 146 C5
Chadwell Heath RM6 . . . 58 C4
Dagenham RM10 . . . 103 D5
East Acton W3 . . . 111 D5
East Molesey KT8 . . . 195 C5
Edmonton N18 . . . 34 C6
Enfield EN1 . . . 17 D6
Hayes UB3 . . . 105 D5
Hendon NW4 . . . 46 C5
Manor Pk E12 . . . 78 A3
Mortlake SW14 . . . 133 C2
Newham E13 . . . 99 A4
Walthamstow E17 . . . 53 D4
Walton-on-T KT12 . . . 194 B3
Wembley HA9 . . . 65 D6
West Kilburn W10 . . . 91 B3
First Cl KT8 . . . 196 A6
First Cross Rd TW2 . . . 152 C2
First Dr NW10 . . . 67 A1
Firs The Belmont SM2 . . . 217 D1
Claygate KT10 . . . 212 C2
Ealing W5 . . . 87 D2
Forest Hill SE26 . . . 184 C5
Oakleigh Pk N20 . . . 14 B3
2 Penge SE26 . . . 184 B5
Sidcup DA15 . . . 167 D1
Upton Pk E6 . . . 78 A1
Wimbledon SW20 . . . 178 A3
Woodford IG8 . . . 37 C3
First St SW3 . . . 114 C2 257 B4
Firstway SW20 . . . 178 C1
First Way HA9 . . . 66 D4
Firs Wlk IG8 . . . 37 A5
Firswood Ave KT19 . . . 215 D3
Firth Gdns
SW6 . . . 135 A4 264 A1
Firtree Ave CR4 . . . 181 A1
Fir Tree Ave UB7 . . . 104 C3
Fir Tree Cl Ealing W5 . . . 88 A1
Esher KT10 . . . 212 A3
5 Orpington BR6 . . . 227 D3
Streatham SW16 . . . 181 C5
Worcester Pk KT19 . . . 215 D4
Firtree Ct BR2 . . . 208 D6
Fir Tree Gdns CR0 . . . 223 C4
Fir Tree Gr SM5 . . . 218 D1
Firtree Ho SE13 . . . 164 B4
Fir Tree Ho 11 SE14 . . . 140 C5
Firtree Lodge N21 . . . 17 A2
Fir Tree Rd TW4 . . . 129 A1
Fir Trees Cl SE16 . . . 119 A5
Fir Tree Wlk EN1 . . . 5 B2
Fir Wlk KT17, SM3 . . . 216 D2
Fisher Cl Croydon CR0 . . 205 D1
Holdbrook EN3 . . . 7 C6
Southall UB6 . . . 85 C4
Fisherdene KT10 . . . 213 A1
Fisher Ho Islington N1 . . 234 A5
9 Shadwell E1 . . . 118 C6
2 Tufnell Pk N19 . . . 71 C5
Fisherman Cl TW10 . . . 175 C6
Fishermans Dr SE16 . . . 118 D4
Fishermans Wlk SE28 . . 123 C4
Fisherman's Wlk E14 . . 119 C5
Fisher Rd HA3 . . . 24 D1
Fishers Cl SW16 . . . 159 D1
Fishers Ct London SE14 . . 140 D4
6 Teddington TW11 . . . 174 D5
Fisher's La W4 . . . 111 B2
Fisher St Holborn WC1 . . 240 C3
Newham E16 . . . 99 A2
Fisherton St
NW8 . . . 92 B3 236 D6
Fisherton Street Est
NW8 . . . 92 B3 236 D5
Fishguard Way E16 . . . 122 D5
Fishlock Ct 6 SW4 . . . 138 A3
Fishponds Rd
Keston BR2 . . . 225 D3
Upper Tooting SW17 . . . 180 C6
Fish St Hill EC3 . . . 252 D5
Fisk Cl TW16 . . . 171 D4
Fiske Ct Barking IG11 . . . 101 B5
1 Merton SW19 . . . 180 A3
Sutton SM2 . . . 218 A1
Tottenham N17 . . . 34 A2
Fitch Ct London SW2 . . . 160 C6
8 Mitcham CR4 . . . 181 A1
Fitzalan Rd
Church End N3 . . . 47 B6
Claygate KT10 . . . 212 C1
Fitzalan St
SE11 . . . 116 C2 261 A4
Fitzclarence Ho W11 . . 244 A2
Fitzgeorge Ave KT2,
KT3 . . . 177 B2
Fitz-George Ave W14 . 254 A3
Fitzgerald Ave SW14 . . . 133 C2
Fitzgerald Ct 1 E10 . . . 53 D1
Fitzgerald Ho
15 Brixton SW9 . . . 138 C3
Hayes UB3 . . . 106 B5
14 Poplar E14 . . . 97 D1
Fitzgerald Rd
Mortlake SW14 . . . 133 B2
Thames Ditton KT7 . . . 197 A3
Wanstead E11 . . . 55 A4
Fitzhardinge Ho
Beckenham BR3 . . . 185 D1
Marylebone W1 . . . 238 A2
Fitzhardinge St W1 . . . 238 A2
Fitzherbert Ho 11
TW10 . . . 154 B5
Fitzhugh Gr SW18 . . . 158 B5
Fitzjames Ave
Croydon CR0 . . . 222 A6
West Kensington W14 . . 254 B3
Fitzjohn Ave EN5 . . . 1 B1
Fitzjohn's Ave NW3 . . . 70 B3
Fitzjohns Mans NW3 . . . 70 A2
Fitzjohns Prim Sch
NW3 . . . 70 B3
Fitzmaurice Ho 17
SE16 . . . 118 B2
Fitzmaurice Pl W1 . . . 248 D4
Fitzneal St W12 . . . 89 D1
FITZROVIA . . . 93 C2
Fitzroy Cl N6 . . . 48 D1
Fitzroy Cres W4 . . . 133 B5
Fitzroy Ct London N6 . . . 49 C3
Marylebone W1 . . . 239 B5
Fitzroy Gdns SE19 . . . 183 C3
Fitzroy Ho
Bermondsey SE1 . . . 263 D2
12 Tower Hamlets E14 . . . 97 B1
Fitzroy Lo N21 . . . 16 D6
Fitzroy Mews W1 . . . 239 A5
Fitzroy Pk N6 . . . 48 D1
Fitzroy Rd NW1 . . 93 A6 231 A6
Fitzroy Sq W1 . . . 239 A5
Fitzroy St W1 . . . 93 C3 239 A5
Fitzroy Yd NW1 . . . 231 A6
Fitzstephen Rd RM8 . . . 80 C3
Fitzwarren Gdns N19 . . . 49 C1
Fitzwilliam Ave TW9 . . . 132 B3
Fitzwilliam Ho
4 Higham Hill E17 . . . 35 A1
Richmond TW9 . . . 131 D1
Fitzwilliam Hts 1
SE23 . . . 162 C2
Fitzwilliam Mews E16 . . 121 A5
Fitzwilliam Rd SW4 . . . 137 C2
Fitzwygram Cl TW12 . . . 174 A5
Five Acre NW9 . . . 27 D1
Fiveacre Cl CR7 . . . 204 C3
Five Arch Bridge
DA14 . . . 191 A6
Five Arches Bsns Pk
DA14 . . . 190 D4
Five Elms Prim Sch
RM8 . . . 81 B5
Five Elms Rd
Dagenham RM9 . . . 81 B5
Keston Mark BR2 . . . 225 C5
Five Oaks Mews BR1 . . . 165 A1
Fives Ct SE11 . . . 261 C5
Fiveways
Chislehurst SE9 . . . 166 D2
Croydon CR0 . . . 220 C4
Ruislip HA4 . . . 39 B1
Five Ways Cnr NW4 . . . 28 A2
Fiveways Rd SW9 . . . 138 C3
Flack Ct 15 E10 . . . 53 D2
Fladbury Rd N15 . . . 51 B3
Fladgate Rd E11 . . . 54 C3
Flag Cl CR0 . . . 206 D1
Flag Wlk HA5 . . . 40 A3
Flambard Rd HA1, HA3 . . 43 A3
Flamborough Ho 12
SE15 . . . 140 A4
Flamborough Rd HA4 . . . 62 A5
Flamborough St E14 . . . 97 A1
Flamingo Ct 2 SE8 . . . 141 C5
Flamingo Gdns UB5 . . . 85 A4
Flamstead Gdns RM9 . . . 80 C1
Flamstead Rd RM9 . . . 80 C1
Flamsted Ave HA9 . . . 66 C2
Flamsteed Ct 15 SE13 . . 141 D4
Flamsteed Ho* SE10 . . . 142 B5
Flamsteed Rd SE7 . . . 122 A1
Flanchford Rd W12 . . . 111 D3
Flanders Cres SW17 . . . 180 D4
Flanders Ct E17 . . . 53 A3
Flanders Ho N16 . . . 73 C5
Flanders Mans 1 W4 . . . 111 D2
Flanders Rd Acton W4 . . 111 C2
Wallend E6 . . . 100 C5
Flanders Way E9 . . . 74 D2
Flandrian Cl EN3 . . . 7 D5
Flank St 9 E1 . . . 118 A6
Flansham Ho 2 E14 . . . 97 B1
Flash La EN2 . . . 5 A6
Flask Cotts 4 NW3 . . . 70 B4
Flask Wlk NW3 . . . 70 B4
Flatford Ho 2 SE6 . . . 186 A6
Flather Cl 12 SW16 . . . 181 C5
Flatiron Sq SE1 . . . 252 B3
Flatiron Yd SE1 . . . 252 B3
Flavell Mews SE10 . . . 120 C1
Flaxen Cl E4 . . . 19 D1
Flaxen Rd E4 . . . 19 D1
Flaxley Rd SM4 . . . 201 D2
Flaxman Ct
12 Belvedere DA17 . . . 125 C1
Soho W1 . . . 239 C1
Flaxman Ho
10 Chiswick W4 . . . 111 C1
Newington SE1 . . . 261 D6
Flaxman Rd SE5 . . . 138 D3
Flaxman Terr
WC1 . . . 93 D4 232 D1
Flaxman Villas N2 . . . 48 A6
Flaxmore Ct Erith DA7 . . 147 D2
South Norwood CR7 . . . 183 B1
Flaxton Rd SE18 . . . 145 C5
Flecker Cl HA7 . . . 24 D5
Flecker Ho 6 SE5 . . . 139 B5
Fleece Dr N9 . . . 34 A6
Fleecefield Prim Sch
N18 . . . 34 A6
Fleece Rd KT6 . . . 197 C1
Fleece Wlk N7 . . . 72 A2
Fleeming Cl E17 . . . 35 B1
Fleeming Rd E17 . . . 35 B1
Fleet Cl
East Molesey KT8 . . . 195 B4
Ruislip HA4 . . . 39 A3
Fleet Ct 1 W12 . . . 111 C3
Fleetfield WC1 . . . 233 B2
Fleet Ho
6 Brixton SW2 . . . 160 C6
4 Limehouse E14 . . . 119 A6
Fleet Pl EC4 . . . 241 C2
Fleet Prim Sch NW3 . . . 70 D3
Fleet Rd NW3 . . . 70 D3
Fleetside KT8 . . . 195 C4
Fleet Sq WC1 . . . 233 D1
Fleet St EC4 . . . 94 C1 241 B1
Fleet Street Hill 10 E1 . . 96 A3
Fleet Terr SE6 . . . 164 A4
Fleetway WC1 . . . 233 B2
Fleetway West Bsns Pk
UB6 . . . 87 B5
Fleet Wood 6 N16 . . . 73 D6
Fleetwood Cl
Chessington KT9 . . . 213 D1
Newham E16 . . . 99 D2
South Croydon CR0 . . . 221 D5
Fleetwood Ct
1 Newham E6 . . . 100 B2
Orpington BR6 . . . 226 C4
8 Stanwell TW19 . . . 148 A5
Fleetwood Rd
Kingston u T KT3 . . . 198 D6
Willesden NW10 . . . 68 A3
Fleetwood Sq KT3 . . . 198 D6
Fleetwood St N16 . . . 73 C6
Fleetwood Way WD19 . . . 22 C6
Fleming Cl 4 W9 . . . 91 C3
Fleming Ct
Croydon CR0 . . . 220 C3
Paddington W2 . . . 236 C4
Fleming Dr N21 . . . 16 B6
Fleming Ho
14 Bermondsey SE16 . . . 118 A4
Finsbury Pk N4 . . . 51 A1
5 Wembley HA9 . . . 67 A5
Fleming Mead CR4 . . . 180 D3
Fleming Rd
Camberwell SE17 . . . 138 D6
Southall UB1 . . . 86 A1
Fleming Way
Isleworth TW7 . . . 130 D1
Thamesmead SE28 . . . 124 D6
Fleming Wlk NW9 . . . 27 C1
Flemming Ave HA4 . . . 62 B6
Flempton Rd E10 . . . 53 A1
Fletcher Bldgs WC2 . . . 240 B1
Fletcher Cl E16 . . . 122 D6
Fletcher Ct 9 NW5 . . . 71 B4
Fletcher Ho 16 N16 . . . 73 C4
Fletcher La E10 . . . 54 A2
Fletcher Path 7 SE8 . . . 141 C5
Fletcher Rd W4 . . . 111 A3
Fletchers Cl BR2 . . . 209 B5
Fletcher St 16 E1 . . . 118 A6
Fletching Rd
Charlton SE7 . . . 143 D6
Lower Clapton E5 . . . 74 C5
Fletton Rd N11 . . . 32 A3
Fleur De Lis St E1 . . . 243 C5
Fleur Gates 7 SW19 . . . 156 D4
Flexmere Rd N17 . . . 33 C2
Flimwell Cl BR1 . . . 186 C5
Flinders Ho 23 E1 . . . 118 B5
Flint Cl
8 Green Street Green
BR6 . . . 227 D2
1 Stratford E15 . . . 76 D1
Flint Ct CR0 . . . 204 B3
Flint Down Cl BR5 . . . 190 A2
Flintmill Cres SE3, SE9 . . 144 A3
Flinton St SE17 . 117 C1 263 B2
Flint St SE17 . . . 117 B2 262 D3
Flitcroft St WC2 . . . 239 D1
Flitton Ho 7 N1 . . . 72 D1
Floathaven Cl SE28 . . . 124 A5
Flock Mill Pl SW18 . . . 157 D3
Flockton St
20 Bermondsey SE16 . . . 118 A4
3 Bermondsey SE16 . . . 118 A4
Flodden Rd SE5 . . . 139 A4
Flood La 5 TW1 . . . 153 A3
Flood St SW3 . . . 136 C6 267 B6
Flood Wlk
SW3 . . . 136 C6 267 B6
Flora Cl E14 . . . 97 D1
Flora Gardens Prim Sch
W6 . . . 112 B2
Flora Gdns
Dagenham RM6 . . . 58 C3
2 Hammersmith W6 . . . 112 B2
Floral St WC2 . . . 116 A6 250 A6
Flora St DA17 . . . 125 B1
Florence Ave Enfield EN2 . . 5 A2
Morden SM4 . . . 202 A4
Florence Cl KT12 . . . 194 B2
Florence Ct
18 New Barnet EN5 . . . 13 D6
St John's Wood W9 . . . 229 B1
Wanstead E11 . . . 55 C5
5 Wimbledon SW19 . . . 179 A4
Florence Dr EN2 . . . 5 A2
Florence Elson Cl E12 . . . 78 C4
Florence Gdns
Chiswick W4 . . . 133 A6
Ilford RM6 . . . 58 C2
Florence Ho
20 Bermondsey SE16 . . . 118 B1
2 Brixton SW2 . . . 160 B6
Kidbrooke SE18 . . . 144 B4
5 Kingston u T KT2 . . . 176 B3
10 Shepherd's Bush
W11 . . . 112 D6
7 Wandsworth SW18 . . 136 B1
Florence Mans
Fulham SW6 . . . 264 C2
4 Hendon NW4 . . . 46 B4
Florence Nightingale Ho
14 N1 . . . 73 A2
Florence Nightingale
Mus* SE1 . . . 250 D1
Florence Rd
Abbey Wood SE2 . . . 124 C2
Acton W4 . . . 111 B3
5 Beckenham BR3 . . . 185 A1
Bromley BR1 . . . 187 A2
Ealing W5 . . . 110 A6
Feltham TW13 . . . 150 B3
Finsbury Pk N4 . . . 50 C2
6 Kingston u T KT2 . . . 176 B3
New Cross Gate SE14 . . . 141 B4
Southall UB2 . . . 106 D3
7 Upton Pk E6 . . . 99 C6
Walton-on-T KT12 . . . 194 B2
West Ham E13 . . . 99 A5
Wimbledon SW19 . . . 179 D4
Florence Root Ho 3
IG4 . . . 56 B4
Florence St Islington N1 . . 72 D1
London NW4 . . . 46 C5
Newham E16 . . . 98 D3
Florence Terr
Kingston u T SW15 . . . 155 C1
New Cross Gate SE14 . . . 141 B4
Florence Way SW12 . . . 158 D3
Florence White Ct N9 . . . 18 B1
Florentine Ho 3 IG1 . . . 78 D6
Flores Ho 13 E1 . . . 96 D2
Florey Sq N21 . . . 16 B6
Florfield Rd E8 . . . 74 B2
Florian SE5 . . . 139 C4
Florian Ave SM1 . . . 218 B4
Florian Rd SW15 . . . 135 A1
Florida Cl WD23 . . . 8 B2
Florida Ct BR2 . . . 208 D5
Florida Rd CR7 . . . 182 D2
Florida St E2 . . . 96 A4
Florida State Univ
WC1 . . . 93 D2 239 D3
Florin Ct
Bermondsey SE1 . . . 253 C1
Edmonton N18 . . . 33 C6
8 St George in t East
SE1 . . . 118 A6
Floris Pl 7 SW4 . . . 137 C2
Floriston Ave UB10 . . . 61 A1
Floriston Cl HA7 . . . 25 B2
Floriston Ct UB5 . . . 63 D3
Floriston Gdns HA7 . . . 25 B2
Florys Ct 7 SW19 . . . 157 A3
Floss St SW15 . . . 134 C3
Flower & Dean Wlk
E1 . . . 243 D3
Flower La NW7 . . . 27 D4
Flower Mews NW11 . . . 47 A3
Flower Pot Cl N15 . . . 51 D3
Flowers Cl NW2 . . . 68 A5
Flowersmead SW17 . . . 159 A2
Flowers Mews 1 N19 . . . 71 C6
Flower Wlk The
SW7 . . . 114 A4 246 B2
Floyd Rd SE7 . . . 121 C1
Floyer Cl TW10 . . . 154 B6
Fludyer St SE13 . . . 142 C1
Flynn Ct 13 E14 . . . 119 C6
Fogerty Cl EN3 . . . 7 D6
Foley Cotts KT10 . . . 212 D2
Foley Ct N12 . . . 30 A5
Foley Ho 19 E1 . . . 96 C1
Foley Mews KT10 . . . 212 C2
Foley Rd KT10 . . . 212 C1
Foley St W1 . . . 93 C2 239 A3
Folgate St E1 . . . 95 D2 243 C4
Foliot Ho N1 . . . 233 C4
Foliot St W12 . . . 89 D1
Folkestone Ct UB5 . . . 63 D3
Folkestone Rd
Edmonton N18 . . . 34 A6
Wallend E6 . . . 100 C4
Walthamstow E17 . . . 53 D5
Folkingham La 6 NW9 . . 27 C2
Folkington Cnr N12 . . . 29 B5
Folland 6 NW9 . . . 27 D1
Follett Ho SW10 . . . 266 C4
Follett St E14 . . . 98 A1
Folly La Higham Hill E17 . . 35 A2
Walthamstow E4 . . . 35 B3
Folly Wall E14 . . . 120 A4
Fonda Ct 14 E14 . . . 119 C6
Fontaine Ct
3 Beckenham BR3 . . . 185 B2
Southgate N14 . . . 15 D2
Fontaine Rd SW16 . . . 182 B3
Fontarabia Rd SW11 . . . 137 A1
Fontenelle SE5 . . . 139 C4
Fontenoy Ho SE11 . . . 261 C3
Fontenoy Rd SW12,
SW17 . . . 159 C2
Fonteyne Gdns IG8 . . . 37 D1
Fonthill Cl SE20 . . . 184 A1
Fonthill Ct SE23 . . . 162 C4
Fonthill Ho
Kensington W14 . . . 254 B6
Pimlico SW1 . . . 258 D2
Fonthill Mews N4 . . . 72 B6
Fonthill Rd N4 . . . 72 C6
Font Hills N2 . . . 30 A1
Fontley Way SW15 . . . 156 A4
Fontmell Cl TW15 . . . 170 C5
Fontmell Pk TW15 . . . 170 C5
Fontwell Cl Harrow HA3 . . 24 C3
Northolt UB5 . . . 63 C2
Fontwell Dr BR2 . . . 210 C4
Football La HA1 . . . 42 C1
Footpath The SW15 . . . 156 A6
FOOTS CRAY . . . 190 B4
Foots Cray High St
DA14 . . . 190 D4
Foots Cray La DA14 . . . 168 C3
Footscray Rd SE9 . . . 166 D3
Forber Ho 25 E2 . . . 96 C4
Forbes Cl NW2 . . . 68 A5
Forbes Ct SE19 . . . 183 C5
Forbes Ho 2 W4 . . . 110 C1
Forbes St E1 . . . 96 A1
Forbes Way HA4 . . . 62 B6
Forburg Rd N16 . . . 52 A1
Fordbridge Ct TW15 . . . 170 A4
Fordbridge Rd
Ashford TW15 . . . 170 B5
Lower Halliford TW16,
TW17 . . . 193 D3
Sunbury TW16 . . . 194 A5
Fordbridge Rdbt
TW15 . . . 170 A4
Ford Cl Ashford TW15 . . . 170 A4

Ford Cl *continued*
12 Bow E3 97 A5
Harrow HA1 42 B2
Littleton TW17 192 C4
Thornton Heath CR7 204 D4
Fordcombe 13 NW5 71 A2
Forde Ave BR1 209 C6
Fordel Rd SE6 164 B3
Ford End IG8 37 B4
Fordham 4 KT1 176 C1
Fordham Cl EN4 2 C2
Fordham Ho 11 SE14 141 A5
Fordham Rd EN4 2 C2
Fordham St 13 E1 96 A1
Ford Ho
2 New Barnet EN5 13 D6
2 Woolwich SE18 122 D1
Fordhook Ave W5 110 C6
Fordingley Rd W9 91 B4
Fordington Ho 2
SE26 162 B1
Fordington Rd N6 48 D5
Fordmill Rd SE6 163 C2
Ford Rd Ashford TW15 170 B6
Bow E3 97 B5
Dagenham RM10 81 C1
Ford's Gr N21 17 A3
Fords Park Rd E16 99 A1
Ford Sq E1 96 B2
Ford St Bow E3 97 A5
Canning Town E16 98 D1
Fordwich Cl BR6 211 D2
Fordwych Ct NW2 69 A2
Fordwych Rd NW2 69 A3
Fordyce Ho 3 SW16 181 C6
Fordyce Rd SE13 164 A6
Fordyke Rd RM8 81 B6
Forecastle Ct E14 119 C4
Foreign, Commonwealth & Home Offices SW1 250 A2
Foreland Ct NW4 29 A2
Foreland Ho W11 244 A6
Foreland St SE18 123 B2
Foreshore SE8 119 B2
Fore St
Barbican EC2 95 A2 242 B3
Edmonton N18 34 A6
Pinner HA5 40 A4
Forest App Chingford E4 20 C4
Woodford IG8 37 A3
Forest Ave E4 20 C4
Forest Bsns Pk E17 52 D2
Forest Cl
Brondesbury NW6 69 A1
Chislehurst BR7 188 C2
Wanstead E11 55 A4
Woodford IG8 37 B6
Forest Croft SE23 162 B2
Forest Ct Chingford E4 20 D3
Leytonstone E11 54 C5
14 Woodside Pk N12 29 D6
Forestdale N14 31 D6
Forestdale Ctr The
CR0 223 B1
Forest Dene Ct 2
SM2 218 A2
Forest Dr
Ashford TW16 171 D3
Chingford IG8 36 C3
Keston Mark BR2 226 A4
Wanstead E12 77 D5
Forest Dr E E11 54 B3
Forest Dr W E11 54 B2
Forest Edge IG9 21 D1
Forester Rd SE15 140 B2
Foresters Cl SM6 219 D1
Foresters Cres DA7 147 D1
Foresters Dr
Wallington SM6 219 D1
Walthamstow E17 54 B5
Foresters Homes The
DA7 147 D1
Foresters Prim Sch
SM6 219 D1
FOREST GATE 77 A3
Forest Gate NW9 45 C4
Forest Gate Com Sch
E7 77 A3
Forest Gate Sta E7 77 A3
Forest Gdns N17 33 D1
Forest Glade
Chingford E4 36 C5
Leytonstone E11 54 C3
Forest Gr E8 73 D2
FOREST HILL 163 A3
Forest Hill SE23 162 C3
Forest Hill Bsns Ctr
SE23 162 C2
Forest Hill Ct 6 SE26 162 B1
Forest Hill Ind Est
SE23 162 C2
Forest Hill Rd SE22 162 B5
Forest Hill Sec Sch
SE23 162 D1
Forest Hill Sta SE23 162 C2
Forest Ho 9 E4 20 C4
Forestholme Cl SE23 162 C2
Forest Ho The SE23 163 A3
Forest Hts IG9 21 A2
Forest La E7, E15 76 D3
Forest Lawns BR1 187 C2
Forest Lea 3 E11 54 D2
Forest Lo 1 SE23 162 C1
Forest Mount Rd IG8 36 B3
Forest Point E7 77 B3
Forest Rd Dalston E8 73 D2
Edmonton N9 18 B3
Feltham TW13 150 C1
Forest Gate E7 77 A4
Leytonstone E11 54 B2
Forest Rd *continued*
Morden SM3, SM4 201 C2
Richmond TW9 132 C5
Romford RM7 59 D6
Walthamstow E17 53 C6
Woodford IG8 21 A1
Fore Street Ave EC2 242 C3
Forest Ridge
Beckenham BR3 207 C6
Bromley BR2 226 B4
Forest Rise E17 54 B5
Forest Sch E17 54 C5
Forest Side
Buckhurst Hill IG9 21 C3
Chingford E4 20 D3
Forest Gate E7 77 B4
New Malden KT4 199 D1
Forest St E7 77 A3
Forest The E11 54 C5
Forest Trad Est E17 52 D6
Forest View
Chingford E4 20 B4
Leytonstone E11 54 D2
Forest View Ave E10 54 B4
Forest View Rd
Chingford E17 36 A2
Manor Pk E12 78 A4
Forest Way
Orpington BR5 211 D4
Sidcup DA15 167 B4
9 Upper Holloway N19 71 C6
Woodford IG8 37 B6
Forest Wlk N10 31 B2
Forfar Rd
London
SW11 137 A4 268 B2
Tottenham N22 32 D2
Forge Cl
Harlington UB3 127 B6
Hayes BR2 209 A1
Forge Cotts W5 109 D5
Forge Dr KT10 213 A1
Forge La Belmont SM3 217 A1
Feltham TW13 173 A5
Richmond TW10 154 A3
Sunbury TW16 194 A6
Forge Lane Prim Sch
TW13 173 A5
Forge Lo 2 TW7 131 A2
Forge Mews
Addington CR0 223 C3
Sunbury TW16 194 A6
Forge Pl NW1 71 A2
Forlong Path UB5 63 A2
Forman Ct TW1 152 D3
Forman Ho SE4 140 D1
Forman Pl N16 73 D4
Formby Ave HA3, HA7 43 C6
Formby Ct 9 N7 72 C3
Formosa Ho 1 E1 97 A3
Formosa St W9 91 D3
Formunt Cl E16 98 D2
Forres Gdns NW11 47 C3
Forrest Ct N7 72 C2
Forrester Path SE26 184 C6
Forresters The HA5 40 B3
Forrest Gdns SW16 204 B6
Forrest Ho SW15 134 C3
Forris Ave UB3 105 D5
Forset Ct W1 237 B2
Forset St W1 92 C1 237 B2
Forstal Cl BR2 209 A6
Forster Cl IG8 36 B3
Forster Ho SE6 164 B1
Forster Park Prim Sch
SE6 164 C1
Forster Rd
Beckenham BR3 207 A6
Streatham SW2 160 A4
Thornton Heath CR0 205 A2
Tottenham N17 51 D6
Walthamstow E17 53 A3
Forsters Cl RM6 59 B3
Forsters Way UB4 84 B1
Forston St N1 95 A5 235 B4
Forsyte Cres SE19 183 C2
Forsyte Ct KT2 176 D2
Forsyth Ct
13 Dagenham RM10 81 D2
Harrow HA1 42 B3
Kingston u T KT3 177 C1
Forsythe Shades BR3 186 A2
Forsyth Gdns SE17 138 D6
Forsyth Ho
14 Hackney E9 74 C1
Pimlico SW1 259 B3
Forsythia Cl IG1 78 D3
Forsythia Ho SE4 141 A2
Forsyth Pl EN1 17 C6
Forterie Gdns IG3 80 A4
Fortescue Ave
1 Hackney E8 74 B1
Twickenham TW2 152 A1
Fortescue Rd
Burnt Oak HA8 27 B3
Mitcham SW19 180 B3
Fortess Gr NW5 71 C3
Fortess Rd NW5 71 C4
Fortess Wlk NW5 71 B3
Forthbridge Rd SW11 137 A1
Forth Ho 30 E3 97 B5
Forties The 9 NW5 71 C3
Fortior Ct N6 49 C2
Fortis Cl E16 99 C1
Fortis Ct N10 49 A6
Fortis Gn N2, N10 48 D6
FORTIS GREEN 48 D5
Fortis Green Ave N2 48 D5
Fortis Green Cotts N2 48 D6
Fortismere Ave N10 49 A6
Fortismere Sch N10 30 D1
Fortismere Sch (South Wing) N10 49 A6
Fortnam Rd N19 71 D6
Fortnums Acre HA7 24 D4
Fort Rd
Bermondsey
SE1 117 D2 263 D3
Northolt UB5 63 C1
Fortrose Cl E14 98 B1
Fortrose Gdns SW12,
SW2 160 A3
Fort St Broadgate E1 243 B3
Newham E16 121 B5
Fortuna Cl N7 72 B2
Fortune Ct
Barking IG11 102 B5
6 Dalston E8 73 D1
Fortune Gate Rd NW10 89 C6
Fortune Green Rd NW6 69 C4
Fortune Ho
Lambeth SE11 261 A3
St Luke's EC1 242 B5
Fortune La WD6 9 D5
Fortunes Mead UB5 63 A2
Fortune St EC1 95 A3 242 B5
Fortune Way NW10 90 A4
Fortune Wlk 4 SE28 123 B3
Forty Acre La E16 99 A2
Forty Ave HA9 66 B6
Forty Cl HA9 66 B5
Forty Hall* EN2 5 D6
FORTY HILL 5 D4
Forty Hill EN2 5 D5
Forty Hill CE Prim Sch
EN2 6 A6
Forty Hill Ho EN1 5 D5
Forty La HA9 66 D6
Forum Cl 7 E3 97 C6
Forumside HA8 26 C4
Forum The KT8 195 D5
Forum Way HA8 26 C4
Forval Cl CR4 202 D4
Forward Bsns Ctr The 3
E16 98 B3
Forward Dr HA3 42 D5
Fosbrooke Ho SW8 270 A3
Fosbury Ho 7 SW9 138 B1
Fosbury Mews W2 245 D5
Foscote Mews W9 91 C2
Foscote Rd NW4 46 B3
Foskett Ho 21 N2 30 B1
Foskett Rd SW6 135 B3
Foss Ave CR0, CR9 220 C3
Fossdene Prim Sch
SE7 121 B1
Fossdene Rd SE7 121 B1
Fossdyke Cl UB4 85 A2
Fosse Way W13 87 A2
Fossil Rd SE13 141 C2
Fossington Rd DA17 124 D2
Foss Rd SW17 180 B6
Fossway RM8 80 C6
Foster Ct
6 Camden Town NW1 71 C1
Canning Town E16 120 D6
Hendon NW4 46 C5
Foster Ho SE14 141 B4
Foster La EC2 95 A1 242 A2
Foster Rd Acton W3 111 C6
Chiswick W4 111 B1
Newham E13 99 A3
Fosters Cl
Elmstead BR7 188 B5
Woodford E18 37 B2
Fosters Old Sch DA16 146 B3
Foster's Prim Sch
DA16 146 C2
Foster St NW4 46 C5
Foster Wlk NW4 46 C5
Fothergill Cl E13 99 A5
Fothergill Dr N21 16 A6
Fotheringham Ct EN1 5 D1
Fotheringham Rd EN1 5 D1
Foubert's Pl W1 239 A1
Foulden Rd N16 73 D4
Foulden Terr N16 73 D4
Foulis Terr
SW7 114 B1 256 D2
Foulser Rd SW17 159 A1
Foulsham Rd CR7 205 B6
Foundary Ho 6 E14 97 D2
Founder Cl 2 E6 100 D1
Founders Cl UB5 85 B4
Founders Ct EC2 242 C2
Founders Gdns SE19 183 A3
Founders Ho SW1 259 C2
Foundling Ct WC1 240 A6
Foundling Mus The*
WC1 94 A3 240 B6
Foundry Cl SE16 119 A5
Foundry Mews NW1 239 B6
Foundry Pl Stepney E1 96 C2
Wandsworth SW18 157 D4
Fountain Cl UB8 83 A2
Fountain Ct
Belgravia SW1 258 C3
Blackfen DA15 168 B5
New Malden KT3 199 A5
5 Penge SE26 184 C4
14 Shepherd's Bush
W11 112 D4
Strand EC4 251 A6
Fountain Dr
Dulwich SE19 183 D6
Wallington SM5 218 D1
Fountain Green Sq 32
SE16 118 A4
Fountain Ho
33 Bermondsey SE16 118 A4
Fountain Ho *continued*
3 Brondesbury Pk NW6 69 A1
Mayfair W1 248 A4
5 Mitcham SW19 180 D1
Fountain Mews
1 Highbury N5 73 A4
Maitland Pk NW3 70 D2
Fountain Pl SW9 138 C4
Fountain Rd
South Norwood CR7 183 A1
Upper Tooting SW17 180 B6
Fountains Ave TW13 151 B1
Fountains Cl TW13 151 B1
Fountains Cres N14 16 A4
Fountains The
London N3 29 D3
Loughton IG10 21 D4
Fountayne Bsns Ctr
N15 52 A5
Fountayne Rd
South Tottenham N15 52 A5
Stoke Newington N16 74 A6
Fount St SW8 137 D5 269 D3
Fouracres EN3 7 A4
Four Acres N12 29 D6
Fourland Wlk HA8 27 A4
Fournier St E1 95 D2 243 D4
Fourscore Mans E8 74 A1
Four Seasons Cl E3 97 C5
Four Seasons Cres
SM3 217 B6
Four Square Ct TW4 151 C5
Fourth Ave Hayes UB3 105 D5
Ilford E12 78 B4
West Kilburn W10 91 A4
Fourth Cross Rd TW2 152 B2
Fourth Way
Wembley HA9 66 D4
Wembley HA9 67 A4
Four Tubs The WD23 8 B4
Fourways 2 CR0 221 D6
Four Wents The E4 20 B2
Fovant Ct 5 SW8 137 C3
Fowey Ave IG4 55 D4
Fowey Cl E1 118 B5
Fowey Ho SE11 261 B2
Fowler Cl
London SW11 136 B2
Sidcup DA14 191 A5
Fowler Ho
5 Camberwell SE5 139 C3
Islington N1 94 D6 234 D6
South Lambeth SW8 269 D1
West Green N15 51 B4
Fowler Rd
Forest Gate E7 77 A4
Islington N1 94 D6 234 D6
Mitcham CR4 181 A1
Fowler's Wlk W5 87 D3
Fownes St SW11 136 C2
Fox and Knot St EC1 241 D4
Foxberry Ct SE4 141 B1
Foxberry Rd SE4 141 A2
Foxborough Gdns
SE4 163 C6
Foxbourne Rd SW17 159 A2
Foxbury Ave BR7 189 B4
Foxbury Cl BR1 187 B4
Foxbury Rd BR1 187 B4
Fox Cl Bethnal Green E1 96 C3
Elstree WD6 9 D5
Newham E16 99 A2
Foxcombe CR0 223 D2
Foxcombe Cl 1 E6 99 D5
Foxcombe Rd 6
SW15 156 A3
Foxcote SE5 263 B1
Foxcroft N1 233 D3
Foxcroft Rd SE18 144 D4
Foxes Dale
Beckenham BR2 208 B6
Blackheath Pk SE3 143 A2
Foxfield NW1 231 D5
Foxfield Prim Sch
SE18 123 A1
Foxfield Rd BR6 227 B6
Foxglove Cl
Bexley DA15 168 A5
Edmonton N9 18 C3
Southall UB1 107 A6
Foxglove Ct 11 HA0 88 A5
Foxglove Gdns E11 55 C5
Foxglove La KT9 214 C4
Foxglove Path SE28 123 C5
Foxglove St W12 111 D6
Foxglove Way SM6 203 B1
Fox Gr KT12 194 B2
Foxgrove N14 16 A1
Foxgrove Ave BR3 185 D3
Foxgrove Path WD19 22 D5
Foxgrove Rd BR3 186 A3
Foxham Rd N19 71 D5
Fox Hill SE19 183 D3
Fox Hill Gdns SE19 183 D3
Fox Ho
2 London SW11 136 B1
Northolt UB5 85 A6
Foxhole Rd 2 SE9 166 A6
Fox Hollow Cl 1
SE18 123 C1
Fox Hollow Dr DA7 146 D2
Foxholt Gdns NW10 67 A1
Foxhome Cl BR7 188 C4
Fox House Rd DA17 125 D1
Fox La Ealing W5 88 A3
Keston BR2 225 C3
Palmers Green N13 16 B1
Foxlees HA0 65 A4
Foxley Cl E8 74 A3
Foxley Ct SM2 218 A1
Foxley Ho 4 E3 97 D4
Foxley Rd
Camberwell SW9 138 D5
Thornton Heath CR7 204 D5
Foxley Sq 3 SW9 138 D4
Foxmead Cl EN2 4 B2
Foxmore St SW11 267 C1
Fox Prim Sch
W8 113 C5 245 A3
Fox Rd E16 98 D2
Foxs Path CR4 180 C1
Fox's Yd E2 243 D6
Foxtail Ho TW3 130 A4
Foxton KT1 198 C6
Foxton Gr CR4 180 B1
Foxton Ho E16 122 C4
Foxwarren KT10 212 D1
Foxwell Mews SE4 141 A2
Foxwell St SE4 141 A2
Foxwood Cl
Edgware NW7 27 C6
Feltham TW13 150 B1
Foxwood Green Cl EN1 17 C5
Foxwood Rd SE3 142 D1
Foyle Rd
Greenwich SE3 142 D6
Tottenham N17 34 A2
Fradel Lo N16 51 B1
Framfield Cl N12 13 C1
Framfield Ct EN1 17 C5
Framfield Rd Ealing W7 86 D1
Islington N5 72 D3
Mitcham CR4 181 A3
Framlingham Cl 2 E5 74 C6
Framlingham Cres
SE9 188 B6
Framlingham Ct 5
RM6 58 B4
Frampton NW1 71 D1
Frampton Cl SM2 217 C1
Frampton Ct 3 W3 111 A4
Frampton Ho NW8 236 D5
Frampton Park Rd E9 74 C1
Frampton Rd TW4 151 A6
Frampton St
NW8 92 B3 236 D5
Francemary Rd SE4 163 C6
Frances Ct
South Norwood SE25 183 D1
Walthamstow E17 53 C3
Frances & Dick James Ct
2 NW7 29 A3
Frances Rd E4 35 C4
Frances St SE18 122 B2
Franche Court Rd
SW17 158 A1
Francis Ave
Bexleyheath DA7 147 C3
Feltham TW13 150 A1
Ilford IG1 79 B6
Francis Barber Cl
SW16 182 B6
Franciscan Prim Sch
SW17 181 A5
Franciscan Rd SW17 181 A6
Francis Chichester Way
SW11 137 A4 268 B1
Francis Cl
6 Cubitt Town E14 120 B2
Littleton TW17 192 C5
West Ewell KT19 215 B4
Francis Ct
12 Deptford SE14 140 D6
Ealing W5 110 B6
Edgware NW7 27 D5
Kingston u T KT5 198 A5
Francis Gr SW19 179 B4
Francis Ho
Harlesden NW10 89 D6
11 Shoreditch N1 95 C6
Walham Green SW10 265 D4
Francis Holland Sch
Belgravia
SW1 115 A2 258 B3
Marylebone
NW1 92 D3 237 C6
Francis Rd
Fortis Green N2 48 D5
Harrow HA1 43 A4
Hounslow TW4 128 D3
Ilford IG1 79 B6
Leyton E10 76 A6
Pinner HA5 40 C4
Thornton Heath CR0 204 D2
Wallington SM6 219 C2
Wembley UB6 87 C6
Francis Snary Lo 11
SW18 157 C6
Francis St Ilford IG1 79 B6
Stratford E15 76 C3
Westminster
SW1 115 C2 259 B4
Francis Terr N19 71 C5
Francis Terrace Mews 16
N19 71 C5
Francis Wlk N1 233 C6
Francklyn Gdns HA8 10 C1
Franconia Rd SW4 159 D6
Frank Bailey Wlk E12 78 C2
Frank Barnes Sch NW3 70 B1
Frank Beswick Ho
SW6 264 D5
Frank Burton Cl 4
SE7 121 B1
Frank Dixon Cl SE21 161 C3
Frank Dixon Way
SE21 161 C3
Frankfurt Rd SE24 161 A6
Frank Godley Ct DA14 190 B5
Frankham Ho 8 SE8 141 C5
Frankham St SE8 141 C5
Frank Ho SW8 270 A4
Frankland Cl
Bermondsey SE16 118 B2
Woodford IG8 37 C5
Frankland Ho 4
SW12 159 B4
Frankland Rd
Brompton
SW7 114 B3 256 C5
Chingford E4 35 C5
Franklin Bldg 5 E14 119 C4
Franklin Cl
Greenwich SE13 141 D4
Kingston u T KT1 198 C6
Oakleigh Pk N20 14 A4
West Norwood SE27 160 D1
Franklin Cres CR4 203 C5
Franklin Ho
Beckenham BR2 208 C6
New Cross SE4 141 A3
26 Wapping E1 118 B5
West Hendon NW9 45 D2
Franklin Ind Est SE20 184 C2
Franklin Pas SE9 144 A2
Franklin Pl SE13 141 D4
Franklin Rd
Bexleyheath DA7 147 A4
Penge SE20 184 C3
Walton-on-T KT12 194 A3
Franklins Mews HA2 64 A6
Franklin Sq SW5 254 D1
Franklin's Row
SW3 114 D1 257 D2
Franklin St
43 Bromley E3 97 D4
South Tottenham N15 51 C3
Franklin Way CR0 204 A2
Franklyn Rd
Walton-on-T KT12 194 B3
Willesden NW10 67 D2
Franks Ave KT3 199 A5
Franks Ho TW7 131 B1
Frank Slater Ho 4 IG3 58 B1
Frank Soskice Ho
SW6 264 D5
Frank St 5 E13 99 A3
Frankswood Ave
Hillingdon UB7 82 B1
Petts Wood BR2, BR5 211 A4
Frank Towell Ct TW14 150 A3
Frank Welch Ct HA5 40 C5
Frank Whymark Ho 4
SE16 118 C4
Franlaw Cres N13 33 A6
Frans Ct HA4 40 A1
Fransfield Gr SE26 162 B1
Frans Hals Ct E14 120 B3
Franshams WD23 8 C2
Frant Cl SE20 184 C3
Franthorne Way SE6 163 D1
Frant Rd CR7 204 D4
Fraserburgh Ho 29 E3 97 B5
Fraser Cl 3 E6 100 A1
Fraser Ct
Battersea SW11 267 A2
Heston TW3 129 A5
Fraser Ho
Brentford TW8 110 B1
40 Clapham SW8 137 D3
3 Woolwich SE18 122 C2
Fraser Rd Edmonton N9 18 B1
Walthamstow E17 53 D3
Wembley UB6 87 C6
Fraser Regnart Ct 12
NW5 70 D3
Fraser St W4 111 C1
Frating Cres IG8 37 B4
Frazer Ave HA4 62 C3
Frazier St SE1 116 C4 251 A1
Freame Ho N21 17 B5
Frean St SE16 118 A3
Frearson Ho WC1 233 D2
Freda Corbett Cl 10
SE15 140 A5
Frederica Rd E4 20 B4
Frederica St 4 N7 72 B1
Frederick Blg N1 73 C2
Frederick Charrington Ho
4 E1 96 C3
Frederick Cl
Cheam SM1 217 B3
Marylebone
W2 114 D6 247 C6
Frederick Cres
Camberwell SW9 138 D5
Enfield EN3 6 C3
Frederick Ct SW6 135 A2
Frederick Gdns
Cheam SM1 217 B3
Thornton Heath CR0 204 D3
Frederick Ho
Ashford TW15 170 A6
Southall UB1 107 B6
Woolwich SE7 122 A3
Frederick Pl SE18 122 D1
Frederick Rd SM1 217 B3
Frederick's Pl
City of London EC2 242 C1
North Finchley N12 30 A6
Frederick Sq 11 SE16 119 A6
Frederick's Row EC1 234 C2
Frederick St
WC1 94 B4 233 C1
Frederick Terr E8 73 D1
Frederic Mews SW1 248 A1
Frederic St E17 53 A4

Fredora Ave UB4 ... 83 D3
Fred Styles Ho SE7 ... 143 C6
Fred Tibble Ct RM9 ... 81 A4
Fred Wigg Twr E11 ... 76 D6
Freedom Cl E17 ... 53 A5
Freedom St SW11 ... 136 D3
Freegrove Rd N7 ... 72 A3
Freehold Ind Ctr TW4 ... 150 C6
Freeland Ct Ealing W5 ... 110 B6
15 Sidcup DA14 ... 168 A1
Freeland Pk N3 ... 29 A1
Freeland Rd W5 ... 110 B6
Freelands Ave CR2 ... 222 D1
Freelands Gr BR1 ... 187 B2
Freelands Rd BR1 ... 187 B2
Freeling Ho NW8 ... 229 C6
Freeling St 7 N1 ... 72 B1
Freeman Cl
Northolt UB5 ... 63 A1
Upper Halliford TW17 ... 193 C5
Freeman Ct SW16 ... 182 A1
Freeman Dr KT8 ... 195 B5
Freeman Ho 13 SW2 ... 160 A4
Freeman Rd SM4 ... 202 B4
Freemans La UB3 ... 105 C6
Freemantle Ave EN3 ... 18 D6
Freemantle St
SE17 ... 117 C1 263 A2
Freemasons Rd E16 ... 99 B1
Freemason's Rd CR0 ... 205 C1
Freemens Hos 1
SW9 ... 138 B1
Freesia Cl BR6 ... 227 D3
Freethorpe Cl SE19 ... 183 C2
Freezeland Way UB10 ... 60 D2
Freke Rd SW11 ... 137 A2
Fremantle Ho 14 E1 ... 96 B3
Fremantle Rd
Belvedere DA17 ... 125 C2
Ilford IG6 ... 57 A6
Fremont St E9 ... 96 C6
French Gdns KT12 ... 195 B1
French Pl E1 ... 243 B6
French St TW16 ... 172 C1
Frendsbury Rd SE4 ... 141 A1
Frensham Cl UB1 ... 85 B4
Frensham Ct
Canonbury N5 ... 73 A3
4 London NW9 ... 46 A5
Mitcham CR4 ... 202 B6
Frensham Dr
New Addington CR0 ... 224 A1
Roehampton SW15 ... 156 A2
Frensham Ho 7 KT6 ... 198 A4
Frensham Rd SE9 ... 167 B2
Frensham St SE15 ... 140 A6
Frere St 6 SW11 ... 136 C3
Fresham Ho BR2 ... 208 D6
Freshfield Ave E8 ... 73 D1
Freshfield Cl SE13 ... 142 B1
Freshfield Dr N14 ... 15 B4
Freshfields CR0 ... 207 B1
Freshford St SW17,
SW18 ... 158 A1
Freshwater Cl SW17 ... 181 A4
Freshwater Ct UB1 ... 85 C4
Freshwater Rd
Dagenham RM8 ... 59 A1
Streatham SW17 ... 181 A4
Freshwell Ave RM6 ... 58 C5
Fresh Wharf Est IG11 ... 100 D6
Fresh Wharf Rd IG11 ... 100 D5
Freshwood Cl BR3 ... 185 D2
Freston Gdns EN4 ... 15 A6
Freston Pk N3 ... 29 B1
Freston Rd W10, W11 ... 112 D6
Freswick Ho 6 SE8 ... 119 A2
Freta Rd DA6 ... 169 B6
Freud Mus The* NW3 ... 70 A2
Frewell Bldg EC1 ... 241 A4
Frewing Cl BR7 ... 188 C5
Frewin Rd SW18 ... 158 B3
Friar Mews SE27 ... 160 D1
Friar Rd UB4 ... 84 D3
Friars Ave London N20 ... 30 C6
Roehampton SW15 ... 155 D1
Friars Cl Chingford E4 ... 20 A1
Ilford IG1 ... 57 B1
Lambeth SE1 ... 251 D3
16 Northolt UB5 ... 84 D4
Friars Ct
5 Wallington SM6 ... 219 B4
Walthamstow E17 ... 35 B2
Friars Gate Cl IG8 ... 37 A6
Friars Gdns W3 ... 89 B1
Friars La TW9 ... 153 D6
Friars Mead E14 ... 120 A3
Friars Mews SE9 ... 166 C6
Friars Place La W3 ... 111 B6
Friars Prim Sch
SE1 ... 116 D4 251 D1
Friar's Rd E6 ... 99 D6
Friars Stile Pl 9
TW10 ... 154 A5
Friars Stile Rd TW10 ... 154 A5
Friar St EC4 ... 241 D1
Friars Way W3 ... 89 B1
Friars Wlk London N14 ... 15 B4
West Heath SE2 ... 124 D1
Friary Cl N12 ... 30 C5
Friary La IG8 ... 37 A6
Friary Park Ct 12 W3 ... 89 A1
Friary Rd Acton W3 ... 89 B1
London N12 ... 30 C6
Peckham SE15 ... 140 A5
Friary Way N12 ... 30 C6
Friday Grove Mews 11
SW12 ... 159 C4
FRIDAY HILL ... 20 C1
Friday Hill E4 ... 20 C1
Friday Hill E E4 ... 20 C1
Friday Hill W E4 ... 20 C2
Friday Rd CR4 ... 180 D3
Friday St EC4 ... 117 A6 252 A6
Frideswide Pl NW5 ... 71 C3
Friendly Pl 16 SE13 ... 141 D4
Friendly St SE8 ... 141 C4
Friendly Street Mews
SE8 ... 141 C3
Friendship Way E15 ... 98 A6
Friendship Wlk UB5 ... 84 D4
Friends' Rd CR0 ... 221 B5
Friend St EC1 ... 94 D4 234 C2
FRIERN BARNET ... 31 A6
Friern Barnet La N20 ... 30 C6
Friern Barnet Rd N11 ... 31 A5
Friern Barnet Sch N11 ... 30 D5
Friern Bridge Ret Pk
N11 ... 31 B4
Friern Ct N20 ... 14 B1
Friern Mount Dr N20 ... 14 A4
Friern Pk N12 ... 30 B5
Friern Rd SE22 ... 162 A5
Friern Watch Ave N12 ... 30 B6
Frigate Ho 7 E14 ... 120 A2
Frigate Mews SE8 ... 141 C6
Frimley Ave SM6 ... 220 B3
Frimley Cl
New Addington CR0 ... 224 A1
Putney SW19 ... 157 A2
Frimley Cres CR0 ... 224 A1
Frimley Ct DA14 ... 190 C5
Frimley Gdns CR4 ... 202 C6
Frimley Ho CR4 ... 202 C6
Frimley Rd
Chessington KT9 ... 214 A3
Ilford IG3 ... 79 C5
Frimley Way E1 ... 96 D3
Frinstead Ho 1 W10 ... 112 D6
Frinton Ct W13 ... 87 B2
Frinton Dr IG8 ... 36 B3
Frinton Mews IG2 ... 56 C3
Frinton Rd Newham E6 ... 99 D4
Sidcup DA14 ... 169 A2
South Tottenham N15 ... 51 C3
Streatham SW17 ... 181 A4
Friston St SW6 ... 135 D3
Friswell Pl 1 DA6 ... 147 C1
Fritham Cl KT3 ... 199 C3
Frith Ct NW7 ... 29 A3
Frith Ho
Bethnal Green E2 ... 96 A4
Paddington NW8 ... 236 D5
Frith La NW7 ... 29 A4
Frith Manor Cotts N12 ... 29 B5
Frith Manor Prim Sch
N12 ... 29 B5
Frith Rd Croydon CR0 ... 221 A6
Leyton E11 ... 76 B4
Frith St W1 ... 93 D1 239 C1
Frithville Ct 2 W12 ... 112 C5
Frithville Gdns W12 ... 112 C5
Frizlands La RM10 ... 81 D5
Frobisher Cl HA5 ... 40 D2
Frobisher Cres TW19 ... 148 A4
Frobisher Ct
Belmont SM2 ... 217 B1
6 Forest Hill SE23 ... 162 B2
1 Greenwich SE10 ... 142 B6
Hendon NW9 ... 27 C1
3 Shepherd's Bush
W12 ... 112 C4
Frobisher Gdns TW19 ... 148 A4
Frobisher Ho
3 Ealing W5 ... 88 A4
27 Wapping E1 ... 118 B5
Frobisher Mews EN2 ... 5 B1
Frobisher Pas E14 ... 119 C5
Frobisher Pl SE14 ... 140 C4
Frobisher Rd London N8 ... 50 C5
Newham E6 ... 100 B1
Frobisher St SE10 ... 142 C6
Froghall Cotts EN5 ... 11 B5
Frogley Rd SE22 ... 139 D1
Frogmore SW18 ... 157 C6
Frogmore Ave UB4 ... 83 C3
Frogmore Cl SM3 ... 217 A5
Frogmore Ct UB2 ... 107 B2
Frogmore Est NW10 ... 89 A4
Frogmore Gdns
Cheam SM3 ... 217 A4
Hayes UB4 ... 83 C3
Frogmore Ind Est
Hayes UB3 ... 105 D4
Highbury N5 ... 73 A4
Frognal NW3 ... 70 A3
Frognal Ave
Harrow HA1 ... 42 D5
Sidcup DA14 ... 190 A4
Frognal Cl NW3 ... 70 A3
Frognal Cnr BR7 ... 189 D4
Frognal Ct NW3 ... 70 A2
Frognal Gdns NW3 ... 70 A4
Frognal La NW3 ... 69 D3
Frognal Par NW3 ... 70 A2
Frognal Pl DA14 ... 190 A5
Frognal Rise NW3 ... 70 A4
Frognal Way NW3 ... 70 A4
Froissart Rd SE9 ... 166 A6
Frome Ho SE15 ... 140 C1
Frome Rd N22 ... 50 D6
Frome St N1 ... 95 A5 235 A4
Fromondes Rd SM3 ... 217 A3
Fromow's Cnr 14 W4 ... 111 A1
Frontenac NW10 ... 68 B1
Frontier Works N17 ... 33 C4
Frosbery Ct 23 EN3 ... 7 C6
Frostic Wlk E1 ... 243 D3
Froude St SW8 ... 137 B3
Fruen Rd TW14 ... 149 D4
Fryatt Rd N17 ... 33 B3
Frye Ct 5 E3 ... 97 B4
Fryent Cl NW9 ... 44 C3
Fryent Cres NW9 ... 45 C3
Fryent Ctry Park HA3, HA9,
NW9 ... 44 C2
Fryent Fields NW9 ... 45 C3
Fryent Gr NW9 ... 45 C3
Fryent Prim Sch NW9 ... 45 A2
Fryent Way HA9, NW9 ... 44 D2
Fry Ho E6 ... 77 C1
Frying Pan Alley E1 ... 243 C3
Fry Rd Harlesden NW10 ... 89 D6
Upton Pk E6 ... 77 D1
Fryston Ave CR0 ... 222 A6
Fuchsia St SE2 ... 124 B1
Fulbeck Dr NW9 ... 27 C2
Fulbeck Ho N7 ... 72 B2
Fulbeck Way HA2 ... 24 A1
Fulbourn 9 KT1 ... 176 C1
Fulbourne Rd E17 ... 36 A1
Fulbourne St E1 ... 96 B2
Fulbrook Rd N19 ... 71 C4
Fulcher Ct SE8 ... 141 B6
Fulcher Ho
13 Deptford SE8 ... 119 B1
10 Shoreditch N1 ... 95 C6
Fulford Mans 3 N19 ... 72 A5
Fulford Rd KT19 ... 215 B1
Fulford St SE16 ... 118 B4
FULHAM ... 134 D3
Fulham Broadway
SW6 ... 135 C5 265 B3
Fulham Broadway Sh Ctr
SW6 ... 265 B3
Fulham Broadway Sta
SW6 ... 135 C5 265 B4
Fulham Bsns Exchange
SW6 ... 266 B1
Fulham Cl UB10 ... 83 A3
Fulham Cross Sec Sch
SW6 ... 135 A5 264 A3
Fulham Ct
SW6 ... 135 C4 265 A2
Fulham High St SW6 ... 135 A3
Fulham Pal* SW6 ... 135 A3
Fulham Palace Rd SW6,
W6 ... 134 D6
Fulham Park Gdns
SW6 ... 135 B3
Fulham Park Rd SW6 ... 135 B3
Fulham Prep Sch
Fulham SW6 ... 135 A3
Fulham W14 ... 135 A6 264 B6
Fulham Prim Sch
SW6 ... 135 C6 265 A5
Fulham Rd
Chelsea
SW10 ... 136 A6 266 B6
Fulham SW6 ... 135 B4 264 D2
Fulke Ho E5 ... 74 B5
Fullbrooks Ave KT4 ... 199 D1
Fuller Cl
4 Bethnal Green E2 ... 96 A3
Bushey WD23 ... 8 B4
Orpington BR6 ... 227 D3
Fuller Rd RM8 ... 80 C4
Fullers Ave KT6 ... 214 B6
Fuller's Ave IG8 ... 36 D3
Fullers Ho 6 SW18 ... 157 C6
Fuller's Rd E18 ... 36 D3
Fuller St NW4 ... 46 C5
Fullers Way N KT6 ... 214 B5
Fullers Way S KT9 ... 214 A5
Fuller's Wood CR0 ... 223 C3
Fuller Terr IG1 ... 79 B3
Fullerton Ct TW11 ... 175 A4
Fullerton Rd
Croydon CR0 ... 205 D2
Wandsworth SW18 ... 158 A6
Fuller Way UB3 ... 105 D1
Fullwood Prim Sch
IG6 ... 57 A5
Fullwood's Mews N1 ... 235 D2
Fulmar Ct
6 Dulwich SE21 ... 161 B2
10 Ealing W13 ... 86 D3
Surbiton KT5 ... 198 B3
Fulmar Ho
12 Bermondsey SE16 ... 118 D2
Marylebone NW8 ... 237 B5
Fulmead St SW6 ... 265 D1
Fulmer Cl TW12 ... 173 A5
Fulmer Rd E16 ... 99 D2
Fulmer Way W13 ... 109 B3
Fulneck 1 E1 ... 96 C2
Fulready Rd E10 ... 54 B4
Fulstone Cl TW4 ... 129 B1
Fulthorp Rd SE3 ... 143 A3
Fulton Ct EN3 ... 7 C5
Fulton Mews W2 ... 246 A6
Fulton Rd HA9 ... 66 C5
Fulwell Ct Southall UB1 ... 108 A6
Teddington TW11 ... 174 C6
Fulwell Park Ave TW2 ... 152 A2
Fulwell Rd TW11,
TW12 ... 174 B6
Fulwell Sta TW11 ... 174 B6
Fulwood Ave HA0 ... 88 B5
Fulwood Cl UB3 ... 83 D1
Fulwood Ct Harrow HA3 ... 43 A3
Stanwell TW19 ... 148 B5
Fulwood Gdns TW1 ... 153 A5
Fulwood Pl WC1 ... 240 D3
Fulwood Wlk SW19 ... 157 A3
Furber St W6 ... 112 B3
Furham Field HA5 ... 23 C3
Furley Ho 7 SE15 ... 140 A5
Furley Rd SE15 ... 140 A5
Furlong Cl SM6 ... 203 B1
Furlong Rd N7 ... 72 C2
Furmage St SW18 ... 157 D4
Furneaux Ave SE27 ... 182 D5
Furness Ho SW1 ... 258 C2
Furness Lo 4 SW14 ... 132 D1
Furness Prim Sch The
NW10 ... 90 A5
Furness Rd
Harlesden NW10 ... 90 A5
Harrow HA2 ... 41 D1
Morden SM4 ... 201 D3
Sands End SW6 ... 135 D3
Furnival St EC4 ... 94 C1 241 A2
Furrow La E9 ... 74 C3
Furrows The KT12 ... 194 C1
Fursby Ave N3 ... 29 C4
Fursecroft W1 ... 237 C2
Further Acre NW9 ... 27 D1
Furtherfield Cl CR0 ... 204 C3
Further Green Rd SE6 ... 164 C3
Furze Cl WD19 ... 22 C5
Furze Ct CR0 ... 222 A6
FURZEDOWN ... 181 B6
Furzedown Dr SW17 ... 181 B5
Furzedown Prim Sch
SW17 ... 181 A4
Furzedown Rd SW17 ... 181 B5
Furzefield Cl BR7 ... 188 D4
Furzefield Rd SE3 ... 143 B5
Furzeground Way
UB11 ... 105 A5
Furzeham Rd UB7 ... 104 A4
Furzehill Rd WD6 ... 11 A6
Furze Inf Sch RM6 ... 59 A3
Furzeland Ho 2 KT3 ... 199 C2
Furze Rd CR7 ... 205 A6
Furze St E3 ... 97 C2
Furzewood TW16 ... 172 A2
Fuschia Ct IG8 ... 36 C4
Fuscia Ct TW13 ... 149 D1
Fusion Ct SW15 ... 155 C1
Futters Ct 1 NW10 ... 89 C5
Fyfe Way BR1 ... 187 A1
Fyfield N4 ... 72 C6
Fyfield Cl BR2, BR3 ... 208 B5
Fyfield Ct E7 ... 77 A2
Fyfield Ho RM9 ... 80 B1
Fyfield Rd
5 Brixton SW9 ... 138 C2
Enfield EN1 ... 5 C2
Walthamstow E17 ... 54 B6
Woodford IG8 ... 37 C3
Fynes St SW1 ... 259 C4

G

Gable Cl HA5 ... 23 C3
Gable Ct SE26 ... 184 B6
Gable Ho 12 W4 ... 111 C2
Gable Lo
Hadley Wood EN4 ... 2 A5
5 North Finchley N12 ... 30 A5
West Wickham BR4 ... 208 A1
Gables Ave TW15 ... 170 B5
Gables Cl
Camberwell SE5 ... 139 C4
Lewisham SE12 ... 165 A3
Gables The
Barking IG11 ... 79 A2
Bromley BR1 ... 187 B3
3 Clapham SW4 ... 137 C2
Ealing W13 ... 87 B1
Hampstead NW3 ... 70 B6
Heston TW5 ... 129 C6
Mitcham CR4 ... 203 B6
Muswell Hill N10 ... 49 A6
North Finchley N12 ... 29 D5
Wembley HA9 ... 66 B5
Gabriel Cl 1 TW13 ... 173 A6
Gabriel Ho SE11 ... 260 C4
Gabrielle Cl HA9 ... 66 B5
Gabrielle Ct NW3 ... 70 B2
Gabriel Mews NW2 ... 69 B6
Gabriel St SE23 ... 163 A4
Gabriel's Wharf SE1 ... 251 A4
Gad Cl E13 ... 99 B4
Gaddesden Ave HA9 ... 66 B2
Gaddesden Ho EC1 ... 235 D1
Gade Cl UB3 ... 106 B5
Gadesden Rd KT19 ... 215 A2
Gadsbury Cl NW9 ... 45 D3
Gadsden Ho
6 Homerton E9 ... 74 D2
8 Kensal Town W10 ... 91 A3
Gadwall Cl E16 ... 99 B1
Gadwall Way SE28 ... 123 B4
Gagarin Ho SW11 ... 136 B2
Gage Rd E16 ... 98 C2
Gage St WC1 ... 240 B4
Gainford Ho 18 E2 ... 96 B4
Gainford St N1 ... 94 C6 234 A6
Gainsboro Gdns UB6 ... 64 C3
Gainsborough Ave E12 ... 78 C3
Gainsborough Cl
Beckenham BR3 ... 185 C3
Thames Ditton KT10 ... 196 C1
Gainsborough Ct
11 Barnet EN5 ... 1 D1
6 Bermondsey SE16 ... 118 B1
Bromley BR2 ... 209 C5
Dulwich SE21 ... 161 C2
North Finchley N12 ... 29 D5
Shepherd's Bush W12 ... 112 C4
Gainsborough Gdns
Edgware HA8 ... 26 C1
Gainsborough Gdns
continued
Golders Green NW11 ... 47 B2
Hampstead NW3 ... 70 B5
Isleworth TW7 ... 152 B6
Gainsborough Ho
Dagenham RM8 ... 80 B4
Enfield EN1 ... 18 A6
Finsbury Pk N4 ... 50 B1
3 Hampstead NW3 ... 70 A4
5 Limehouse E14 ... 119 A6
Westminster SW1 ... 259 D3
Gainsborough Lodge
HA1 ... 42 C4
Gainsborough Mews 5
SE26 ... 162 B1
Gainsborough Prim Sch
Hackney Wick E9 ... 75 C2
Newham E15 ... 98 C4
Gainsborough Rd
Bedford Pk W4 ... 111 D2
Dagenham RM8 ... 80 B5
Hayes UB4 ... 83 B5
Leytonstone E11 ... 54 C2
Newham E15 ... 98 C4
New Malden KT3 ... 199 B2
North Finchley N12 ... 29 D5
Richmond TW9 ... 132 B2
Gainsborough Sq
DA6 ... 146 D2
Gainsborough St 3 E9 ... 75 B2
Gainsborough Studios
N1 ... 235 C5
Gainsborough Twr 7
UB5 ... 84 D5
Gainsfield Ct 3 E11 ... 76 C5
Gainsford Rd E17 ... 53 B5
Gainsford St
SE1 ... 117 D4 253 D2
Gairloch Ho 2 NW1 ... 71 D1
Gairloch Rd SE5 ... 139 C3
Gaisford St NW5 ... 71 C2
Gaitskell Ct SW11 ... 136 C3
Gaitskell Ho
Camberwell SE17 ... 139 B6
2 Newham E6 ... 99 D6
3 Walthamstow E17 ... 53 D6
Gaitskell Rd SE9 ... 167 A3
Gaitskell Way SE1 ... 252 A2
Galahad Rd
Edmonton N9 ... 18 A1
Grove Pk BR1 ... 187 A6
Galata Rd SW13 ... 134 A5
Galatea Sq SE15 ... 140 B2
Galaxy Bldg 6 E14 ... 119 C2
Galaxy Ho EC2 ... 242 D6
Galba Ct 1 TW8 ... 131 D5
Galbraith St E14 ... 120 A3
Galdana Ave EN5 ... 2 A2
Galeborough Ave IG8 ... 36 B3
Gale Cl Hampton TW12 ... 173 A4
Mitcham CR4 ... 202 B6
Gale Ho
10 Brixton SW2 ... 160 B6
Carshalton SM5 ... 218 C3
Galena Ho
5 Hammersmith W6 ... 112 B2
Plumstead Comm SE18 ... 123 D1
Galena Rd W6 ... 112 B2
Galen Pl WC1 ... 240 B3
Galesbury Rd SW18 ... 158 A5
Gales Gdns E2 ... 96 B4
Gale St Dagenham RM9 ... 80 D1
Tower Hamlets E3 ... 97 C2
Galgate Cl 4 SW19 ... 157 A3
Gallants Farm Rd EN4 ... 14 C3
Galleon Cl SE16 ... 118 D4
Galleon Ho 8 E14 ... 120 A2
Galleons Dr IG11 ... 102 A4
Gallery Ct SW10 ... 266 A5
Gallery Gdns UB5 ... 84 D5
Gallery Rd SE21 ... 161 B3
Galleywall Rd SE16 ... 118 B2
Galleywall Road Trad Est
12 SE16 ... 118 B2
Galleywood Ho 1 W10 ... 90 C2
Gallia Rd N5 ... 72 D3
Galliard Cl N9 ... 18 C5
Galliard Ct N9 ... 18 A5
Galliard Prim Sch N9 ... 18 A4
Galliard Rd N9 ... 18 A5
Gallica Ct SM1 ... 201 D1
Gallions Cl IG11 ... 102 A4
Gallions Mount Prim Sch
SE18 ... 123 D1
Gallions Prim Sch E6 ... 100 D1
Gallions Rd E16 ... 122 D6
Gallions Reach Shp Pk
IG11 ... 101 A2
Gallions Reach Sta
E16 ... 122 D6
Gallions View Rd
SE28 ... 123 C4
Gallon Cl SE7 ... 121 C2
Gallop The
South Croydon CR2 ... 222 B1
Sutton SM2 ... 218 A1
Gallosson Rd SE18 ... 123 C2
Galloway Rd W12 ... 112 A5
Gallus Cl N21 ... 16 B5
Gallus Sq SE3 ... 143 B2
Galpin's Rd CR4, CR7 ... 204 B5
Galsworthy Ave
Ilford RM6 ... 58 B2
Tower Hamlets E14 ... 97 A2
Galsworthy Cl SE28 ... 124 B5
Galsworthy Cres SE3 ... 143 C4
Galsworthy Ct W3 ... 110 D3
Galsworthy Ho 4 W11 ... 91 A1
Galsworthy Rd
Cricklewood NW2 ... 69 A4
Kingston u T KT2 ... 176 D2
Galton Ho SE18 ... 144 B4
Galton St W10 ... 91 A4
Galva Cl EN4 ... 3 A1
Galvani Way CR0 ... 204 B1
Galveston Ho 2 E1 ... 97 A3
Galveston Rd SW15 ... 157 B6
Galway Cl 28 SE16 ... 118 B1
Galway Ho Finsbury EC1 ... 235 B1
7 Stepney E1 ... 96 D2
Galway St EC1 ... 95 A4 235 B1
Galy 5 NW9 ... 27 D1
Gambetta St 3 SW8 ... 137 B3
Gambia St SE1 ... 116 D5 251 D3
Gambler Ho EC1 ... 235 B1
Gambole Rd SW17 ... 180 C6
Games Ho 6 SE7 ... 143 C6
Games Rd EN4 ... 2 D2
Gamlen Rd SW15 ... 134 D1
Gamma Ct 9 CR0 ... 205 B1
Gamuel Cl E17 ... 53 C3
Gander Green Cres
TW12 ... 173 C2
Gander Green La KT4, SM1,
SM3 ... 217 B5
Gandhi Cl E17 ... 53 C3
Gandolfi St 5 SE15 ... 139 C6
Ganley Ct 10 SW11 ... 136 B2
Gannet Ct 5 SE21 ... 161 B2
Gannet Ho SE15 ... 139 D4
Ganton St W1 ... 239 B1
Ganton Wlk WD19 ... 22 D6
GANTS HILL ... 56 C3
Gants Hill IG2 ... 56 C3
Gantshill Cres IG2 ... 56 C4
Gants Hill Sta IG2 ... 56 C3
Gap Rd SW19 ... 179 D5
Garage Rd W3 ... 88 C1
Garand Ct 2 N7 ... 72 B3
Garbett Ho 2 SE17 ... 138 D6
Garbutt Pl W1 ... 238 B3
Garden Ave
Bexleyheath DA7 ... 147 C2
Mitcham CR4 ... 181 B3
Garden City HA8 ... 26 C4
Garden Cl
Ashford TW15 ... 171 A4
Chingford E4 ... 35 C5
Grove Pk SE12 ... 165 B1
Hampton TW12 ... 173 B5
Northolt UB5 ... 85 A6
Roehampton SW15 ... 156 B4
Ruislip HA4 ... 61 D6
Wallington SM6 ... 220 A3
Garden Cotts BR5 ... 190 C1
Garden Ct
5 Belmont SM2 ... 217 C1
10 Eltham SE9 ... 166 C5
Hampton TW12 ... 173 B5
North Finchley N12 ... 29 D5
4 Richmond TW9 ... 132 B4
12 South Acton W4 ... 111 A3
South Croydon CR0 ... 221 D5
4 Stanmore HA7 ... 25 C5
St John's Wood NW8 ... 229 C2
Strand EC4 ... 251 A6
Wembley HA0 ... 65 C5
Wimbledon SW20 ... 178 D2
Gardeners Cl SE9 ... 166 A1
Gardeners Rd CR0 ... 204 D1
Garden Flats SW16 ... 160 A1
Garden Ho
2 Finchley N2 ... 30 B1
12 South Lambeth SW9 ... 138 A3
Garden Hospl The
NW4 ... 46 C6
Gardenia Ct 1 BR3 ... 185 C3
Gardenia Rd
Bromley BR1 ... 210 C6
Enfield EN1 ... 17 C5
Gardenia Way IG8 ... 37 A5
Garden La Bromley BR1 ... 187 B4
Streatham SW2 ... 160 B3
Garden Lodge Ct N2 ... 48 B6
Garden Mews W2 ... 245 B5
Garden Pl 28 E2 ... 95 D6
Garden Prim Sch CR4 ... 203 D6
Garden Rd
Bromley BR1 ... 187 B4
Penge SE20 ... 184 C2
Richmond TW9 ... 132 C2
St John's Wood
NW8 ... 92 A4 229 B2
Walton-on-T KT12 ... 194 B2
Garden Row
SE1 ... 116 D3 261 C6
Garden Royal 16
SW15 ... 156 D5
Garden St E1 ... 96 D2
Gardens The
Beckenham BR3 ... 186 A2
East Bedfont TW14 ... 149 B5
East Dulwich SE22 ... 140 A1
Harrow HA1, HA2 ... 42 A3
Pinner HA5 ... 41 B3
Stamford Hill N16 ... 51 D2
Garden Suburb Jun & Inf
Schs NW11 ... 47 B4
Garden Terr
Knightsbridge SW7 ... 247 B1
Pimlico SW1 ... 259 C2
Garden Way NW10 ... 67 A2
Garden Wlk
Beckenham BR3 ... 185 B2
Shoreditch EC2 ... 95 C3 243 A6
Gardiner Ave NW2 ... 68 C3
Gardiner Cl
Chislehurst BR5 ... 190 C1

Gardiner Cl *continued*
Dagenham RM8 . . . . 80 D4
Enfield EN3 . . . . 18 D5
Gardiner Ct NW10 . . . . . . 89 B6
Gardiner Ho SW11 . . . . 267 A2
Gardner Cl E11 . . . . 55 B3
Gardner Ct Highbury N5 . . 73 A4
Hounslow TW3 . . . . 129 C2
Tottenham N22 . . . . 32 D1
Gardner Ho
Feltham TW13 . . . . 151 B2
Southall UB1 . . . . 106 D6
Gardner Ind Est SE26 . . 185 B5
Gardner Pl TW14 . . . . . . 150 B5
Gardner Rd E13 . . . . 99 B3
Gardners Cl N11 . . . . 15 A2
Gardners La EC4 . . . . . . 252 A6
Gardnor Mans 14 NW3 . . 70 A4
Gardnor Rd NW3 . . . . 70 B4
Gard St EC1 . . . . 234 D2
Garendon Gdns SM4 . . . 201 D2
Garendon Rd SM4 . . . . . 201 D2
Garenne Ct 10 E4 . . . . 20 A3
Gareth Cl KT4 . . . . 216 D6
Gareth Ct SW16 . . . . 159 D1
Gareth Gr BR1 . . . . 187 A6
Garfield Edmonton N9 . . . . 18 B3
Enfield EN2 . . . . 17 B6
Garfield Ho W2 . . . . 237 C1
Garfield Mews 7
SW11 . . . . 137 A2
Garfield Prim Sch
London N11 . . . . 31 C5
Wimbledon SW19 . . . . . . 180 A4
Garfield Rd Chingford E4 . 20 B3
Clapham SW11 . . . . 137 A2
Enfield EN3 . . . . 6 C1
Newham E13 . . . . 98 D3
3 Twickenham TW1 . . . . 153 A3
Wimbledon SW19 . . . . . . 180 A4
Garford St E14 . . . . 119 C6
Garganey Ct NW10 . . . . . . 67 B2
Garganey Wlk SE28 . . . . 124 C6
Garibaldi St SE18 . . . . . . 123 C2
Garland Ct 12 E14 . . . . . . 119 C6
Garland Dr TW3 . . . . 130 A3
Garland Ho
12 Kingston u T KT2 . . . . 176 A2
Stoke Newington N16 . . . . 73 B5
Garland Rd
Plumstead Comm
SE18 . . . . 145 B5
Stanmore HA7 . . . . 26 A2
Garlands Ct CR0 . . . . 221 B4
Garlands Ho NW8 . . . . 91 D5
Garlands La HA1 . . . . 42 D1
Garlands The HA1 . . . . . . 42 D2
Garlick Hill
EC4 . . . . 117 A6 252 B6
Garlies Rd SE23 . . . . 163 A1
Garlinge Ho 12 SW9 . . . . 138 C4
Garlinge Rd NW2 . . . . 69 B2
Garman Cl N18 . . . . 33 B5
Garman Rd N17 . . . . 34 C3
Garnault Mews EC1 . . . 234 B1
Garnault Pl EC1 . . . . 234 B1
Garnault Rd EN1 . . . . 5 D5
Garner Cl RM8 . . . . 58 D1
Garner Rd E17 . . . . 36 A2
Garner St E2 . . . . 96 A5
Garnet Ct TW13 . . . . 149 C1
Garnet Ho KT4 . . . . 199 B1
Garnet Rd
South Norwood CR7 . . . . 205 B5
Willesden NW10 . . . . 67 C2
Garnet St E1 . . . . 118 C6
Garnett Cl SE9 . . . . 144 B2
Garnett Ho 5 NW3 . . . . . 70 D3
Garnett Rd NW3 . . . . 70 D3
Garnett Way 3 E17 . . . . . . 35 A2
Garnet Wlk 3 E6 . . . . 100 A2
Garnham Cl 2 N16 . . . . . . 73 D6
Garnham St 1 N16 . . . . . . 73 D6
Garnies Cl SE15 . . . . 139 D5
Garrad's Rd SW16 . . . . . . 159 D1
Garrard Cl
Bexleyheath DA7 . . . . 147 C2
Chislehurst BR7 . . . . 188 D5
Garrard Ho BR2 . . . . 209 C5
Garrard Wlk NW10 . . . . . . 67 C2
Garratt Cl CR0 . . . . 220 A4
Garratt Ho 8 N16 . . . . 51 C1
Garratt La
Upper Tooting SW17,
SW18 . . . . 180 C6
Wandsworth SW18 . . . . . 157 D3
Garratt Park Sch
SW18 . . . . 158 A1
Garratt Rd HA8 . . . . 26 C3
Garratts Rd WD23 . . . . 8 A4
Garratt Terr SW17 . . . . . 180 C6
Garraway Ct SW13 . . . . . 134 C5
Garraway Ho SE21 . . . . . 161 D1
Garrett Cl W3 . . . . 89 B2
Garrett Ho
8 Shepherd's Bush
W12 . . . . 90 B1
Teddington TW11 . . . . . . 175 B4
Garrett St EC1 . . . . 95 A3 242 B6
Garrick Ave NW11 . . . . 47 A3
Garrick Cl Ealing W5 . . . . . 88 A3
1 Richmond TW9 . . . . . . 153 D6
Wandsworth SW18 . . . . . 136 A1
Garrick Cres CR0 . . . . . . 221 C6
Garrick Ct HA8 . . . . 26 B6
Garrick Dr Hendon NW4 . . 28 C1
Plumstead SE18 . . . . 123 B3
Garrick Gdns KT8 . . . . . . 195 C6
Garrick Ho
Chiswick W4 . . . . 133 C6
Garrick Ho *continued*
2 Kingston u T KT1 . . . . 198 A5
Mayfair W1 . . . . 248 C3
7 Streatham SW16 . . . . . 181 C5
Garrick Ind Ctr NW9 . . . . 45 D4
Garrick Pk NW4 . . . . 28 D1
Garrick Rd
Greenford UB6 . . . . 85 D3
Richmond TW9 . . . . 132 C3
West Hendon NW9 . . . . . . 45 D3
Garrick's Ait KT8 . . . . . . 174 A1
Garricks Ho KT1 . . . . 175 D1
Garrick St
WC2 . . . . 116 A6 250 A6
Garrick's Villa TW12 . . . 174 A1
Garrick Way NW4 . . . . 46 D5
Garrick Yd WC2 . . . . . . 250 A6
Garrison Cl
Hounslow TW4 . . . . 151 B6
Shooters Hill SE18 . . . . . 144 C5
Garrison La KT9 . . . . 214 A1
Garrowsfield EN5 . . . . 13 B6
Garsdale Cl N11 . . . . 31 A4
Garsdale Terr SW5 . . . . 254 D2
Garside Cl
Hampton TW12 . . . . 173 D4
Plumstead SE28 . . . . 123 B3
Garside Ct 5 N20 . . . . 14 D2
Garsington Mews SE4 . . 141 B2
Garson Ho W2 . . . . 246 C6
Garston Ho 6 N1 . . . . 72 D1
Garter Way SE16 . . . . 118 D4
Garth Cl
Kingston u T KT2 . . . . . . 176 B5
Ruislip HA4 . . . . 40 D1
West Barnes SM4 . . . . . . 200 D2
Garth Ct Chiswick W4 . . . 133 B6
11 Harrow HA1 . . . . 42 D3
Garth Dr N9 . . . . 18 A2
Garth Ho NW2 . . . . 69 B6
Garthland Dr EN5 . . . . 12 C6
Garth Mews W5 . . . . 88 A3
Garthorne Rd SE23 . . . . . 162 D4
Garth Rd Child's Hill NW2 . 69 B6
8 Chiswick W4 . . . . 111 B1
Kingston u T KT2 . . . . . . 176 B5
West Barnes SM4 . . . . . . 200 D2
Garth Road Ind Ctr The
SM4 . . . . 200 D1
Garthside TW10 . . . . 176 A5
Garth The
Hampton TW12 . . . . 173 D4
Harrow HA3 . . . . 44 B3
North Finchley N12 . . . . . . 29 D5
Garthway N12 . . . . 30 C4
Gartmoor Gdns SW19 . . 157 B3
Gartmore Rd IG3 . . . . 79 D6
Garton Ho 6 N6 . . . . 49 D2
Garton Pl SW18 . . . . 158 A5
Gartons Cl EN3 . . . . 6 C1
Gartons Way SW11 . . . . . 136 A2
Garvary Rd E16 . . . . 99 B1
Garvens SE19 . . . . 183 C5
Garway Rd W2 . . . . 91 D1
Garwood Cl N17 . . . . 34 B2
Garwood Lo N22 . . . . 32 B3
Gascoigne Gdns IG8 . . . . 36 C3
Gascoigne Pl 17 E2 . . . . . 95 D4
Gascoigne Prim Sch
IG11 . . . . 101 A6
Gascoigne Rd IG11 . . . . . 101 A5
Gascony Ave NW6 . . . . 69 C1
Gascoyne Ho 2 E9 . . . . . . 74 D1
Gascoyne Rd E9 . . . . 74 D1
Gaselee St E14 . . . . 120 A6
Gasholder Pl
SE11 . . . . 116 B1 260 D1
Gaskarth Rd
Balham SW12 . . . . 159 B5
Burnt Oak HA8 . . . . 27 A1
Gaskell Rd N6 . . . . 48 D3
Gaskell St SW4 . . . . 138 A3
Gaskin Ho N16 . . . . 73 B5
Gaskin St N1 . . . . 94 D6 234 C6
Gaspar Cl SW7 . . . . 255 D4
Gaspar Mews SW5 . . . . 255 D4
Gassiot Rd SW17 . . . . . . 180 D6
Gassiot Way SM1 . . . . . . 218 B5
Gasson Ho 24 SE14 . . . . 140 D6
Gastein Rd W6 . . . . 134 D6
Gastigny Ho EC1 . . . . . . 235 B1
Gaston Bell Cl TW9 . . . . 132 B2
Gaston Bridge Rd
TW17 . . . . 193 B3
Gaston Gate SW8 . . . . . 270 C2
Gaston Rd CR4 . . . . 203 A6
Gaston Way TW17 . . . . . 193 B4
Gataker Ho 5 SE16 . . . . 118 B3
Gataker St 6 SE16 . . . . . 118 B3
Gatcliff Cl SW1 . . . . 258 B1
Gatcombe Ct BR3 . . . . . . 185 C3
Gatcombe Ho 20 SE22 . . 139 C2
Gatcombe Mews W5 . . . . 110 B6
Gatcombe Rd
8 Newham E16 . . . . 121 A5
Tufnell Pk N19 . . . . 71 D5
Gatcombe Way EN4 . . . . . . 2 D2
Gateacre Ct DA14 . . . . . . 190 B6
Gate End HA6 . . . . 22 A3
Gatefield Ct SE15 . . . . . . 140 A2
Gateforth St NW8 . . . . . 237 A5
Gate Hill Ct W11 . . . . . . 244 D4
Gatehill Rd HA6 . . . . 22 A3
Gate Ho 4 KT6 . . . . 198 A1
Gatehouse Cl KT2 . . . . . 177 A3
Gatehouse Sch E2 . . . . 96 D5
Gatehouse Sq SE1 . . . . . 252 B4
Gateley Ho 6 SE4 . . . . . 140 D1
Gateley Rd SW9 . . . . 138 B2
Gate Mews
SW7 . . . . 114 C4 247 B1
Gater Dr EN2 . . . . 5 B4
Gates 4 NW9 . . . . 27 D1
Gatesborough St EC2 . 243 A6
Gates Ct SE17 . . . . 262 A2
Gatesden WC1 . . . . 233 B1
Gates Green Rd BR2,
BR4 . . . . 225 A4
Gateside Rd SW17 . . . . . 158 D1
Gate St WC2 . . . . . 94 B1 240 C2
Gatestone Ct 10 SE19 . . 183 C4
Gatestone Rd SE19 . . . . 183 C4
Gateway SE17 . . . . 139 A6
Gateway Arc N1 . . . . . . 234 C4
Gateway Bsns Ctr
SE28 . . . . 123 B3
Gateway Ho
Balham SW12 . . . . 159 B5
4 Barking IG11 . . . . 101 A6
3 Upper Tooting
SW17 . . . . 180 C4
Gateway Mews 4 E8 . . . . 73 D3
Gateway Prim Sch
NW8 . . . . 92 B3 236 D6
Gateway Ret Pk E6 . . . . 100 D3
Gateways KT6 . . . . 198 A4
Gateways Ct SM6 . . . . . . 219 B3
Gateways The
Chelsea SW3 . . . . 257 B3
Richmond TW9 . . . . 131 D1
Gateway Trad Est
NW10 . . . . 89 D4
Gatfield Gr TW13 . . . . . . 151 C2
Gatfield Ho TW13 . . . . . . 151 C2
Gathorne Rd N22 . . . . 32 C2
Gathorne St 19 E2 . . . . . . 96 D5
Gatley Ave KT19 . . . . 214 D3
Gatliff Rd SW1 . . 115 B1 258 C1
Gatling Rd SE18, SE2 . . . 124 A1
Gatonby St SE15 . . . . 139 D4
Gatting Cl HA8 . . . . 27 A3
Gatting Way UB8 . . . . 60 A2
Gatton Prim Sch
SW17 . . . . 180 C6
Gatton Rd SW17 . . . . 180 C6
Gattons Way DA14 . . . . . 191 B6
Gatward Cl N21 . . . . 16 D5
Gatward Gn N9 . . . . 17 D2
Gatwick Ho 3 E14 . . . . . . 97 B1
Gatwick Rd SW18 . . . . . . 157 B4
Gauden Cl SW4 . . . . 137 D2
Gauden Rd SW4 . . . . 137 D2
Gaugin Ct 18 SE16 . . . . . 118 B1
Gauntlet 1 NW9 . . . . 27 D1
Gauntlet Cl UB5 . . . . 63 A1
Gauntlett Ct HA0 . . . . 65 B3
Gauntlett Rd SM1 . . . . . . 218 B3
Gaunt St SE1 . . . . 262 A6
Gautrey Rd SE15 . . . . . . 140 C3
Gautrey Sq 5 E6 . . . . . . 100 B1
Gavel St SE17 . . . . 262 D4
Gaven Ho N17 . . . . 33 C1
Gaverick Mews 3
E14 . . . . 119 C2
Gavestone Cres SE12 . . . 165 B4
Gavestone Rd SE12 . . . . 165 B4
Gavestone Terr SE12 . . . 165 B4
Gaviller Pl 3 E5 . . . . 74 B4
Gavina Cl SM4 . . . . 202 C4
Gavin Ho 1 SE18 . . . . . . 123 C2
Gawain Wlk N9 . . . . 18 A1
Gawber St E2 . . . . 96 C4
Gawsworth Cl E15 . . . . . . 76 D3
Gawthorne Ave NW7 . . . . 29 A5
Gawthorne Ct E3 . . . . 97 C5
Gay Cl NW2 . . . . 68 B3
Gaydon Ho W2 . . . . 91 D2
Gaydon La NW9 . . . . 27 C2
Gayfere Rd
Redbridge IG5 . . . . 56 B6
Stoneleigh KT17 . . . . 216 A3
Gayfere St
SW1 . . . . 116 A3 260 A5
Gayford Rd W12 . . . . 111 D4
Gay Ho N16 . . . . 73 C3
Gayhurst SE17 . . . . 139 B6
Gayhurst Ct 9 UB5 . . . . . . 84 C4
Gayhurst Ho NW8 . . . . . 237 B6
Gayhurst Prim Sch E8 . . 74 A1
Gayhurst Rd E8 . . . . 74 A1
Gaylor Rd UB5 . . . . 63 B3
Gaymead NW8 . . . . 91 D6
Gaynesford Rd
Forest Hill SE23 . . . . 162 D2
Wallington SM5 . . . . 218 D1
Gay Rd E15 . . . . 98 B5
Gaysham Ave IG2 . . . . 56 D4
Gaysham Hall IG5 . . . . . . 56 D6
Gaysley Ho SE11 . . . . . . 261 A3
Gay St SW15 . . . . 134 D2
Gayton Cres NW3 . . . . 70 B4
Gayton Ct
3 Harrow HA1 . . . . 42 D3
New Malden KT3 . . . . 199 D4
Gayton Ho E3 . . . . 97 C3
Gayton Rd
Abbey Wood SE2 . . . . 124 C3
Hampstead NW3 . . . . 70 B4
Harrow HA1 . . . . 43 A3
Gayville Rd SW11 . . . . . . 158 D5
Gaywood Cl SW2 . . . . . . 160 C3
Gaywood Rd E17 . . . . 53 C6
Gaywood St SE1 . . . . . . 261 D5
Gaza St SE17 . . . 116 D1 261 C1
Gaze Ho 11 E14 . . . . 98 B1
Gean Ct 3 E11 . . . . 76 B4
Gearies Inf Sch IG2 . . . . . 56 D4
Gearies Jun Sch IG2 . . . . 56 D4
Geariesville Gdns IG6 . . . 56 D5
Gearing Cl SW17 . . . . 181 A6
Geary Ho N7 . . . . 72 B3
Geary Rd NW10 . . . . 68 A3
Geary St N7 . . . . 72 B3
GEC Est HA9 . . . . 65 D6
Geddes Pl 3 DA6 . . . . . . 147 C1
Gedeney Rd N17 . . . . 33 A2
Gedge Ct CR4 . . . . 202 C5
Gedling Ho SE22 . . . . 139 D2
Gedling Pl SE1 . . . . 263 D6
Geere Rd E15 . . . . 98 D6
Gees Ct W1 . . . . 238 B1
Gee St EC1 . . . . . . 95 A3 242 A6
Geffrey's Ct SE9 . . . . . . 166 A1
Geffrye Ct N1 . . . . 95 C5
Geffrye Mus* E2 . . . . 95 D5
Geffrye St E2 . . . . 95 D5
Geldart Rd SE15 . . . . 140 B5
Geldeston Rd E5 . . . . 74 A6
Gellatly Rd SE14 . . . . 140 D3
Gell Cl UB10 . . . . 60 B5
Gemima Ct SM1 . . . . 217 C3
Gemini Bsns Ctr E16 . . . . 98 B3
Gemini Gr UB5 . . . . 85 A4
Gemini Ho 11 E3 . . . . 97 C6
Gemma Ct BR3 . . . . 185 B1
General Gordon Pl
SE18 . . . . 122 D2
Generals Wlk The EN3 . . . 7 A6
General Wolfe Rd
SE10 . . . . 142 B4
Genesis Bsns Pk NW10 . . 88 D5
Genesis Cl TW19 . . . . 148 B3
Genesis Ho KT6 . . . . 197 D1
Genesta Rd SE18 . . . . 145 A6
Geneva Cl TW17 . . . . 171 C1
Geneva Ct Hendon NW9 . . 45 D4
1 Putney SW15 . . . . 156 D6
Stoke Newington N16 . . . . 51 B1
Geneva Dr SW9 . . . . 138 C1
Geneva Gdns RM6 . . . . 59 A4
Geneva Rd
Kingston u T KT1 . . . . 198 A5
Thornton Heath CR7 . . . . 205 A4
Genever Cl E4 . . . . 35 C5
Genista Rd N18 . . . . 34 B5
Genoa Ave SW15 . . . . 156 C6
Genoa Ho 19 E1 . . . . 96 D3
Genoa Rd SE20 . . . . 184 C2
Genotin Rd EN1 . . . . 5 B2
Genotin Terr EN1 . . . . 5 B2
Gentleman's Row EN2 . . . 5 A2
Gentry Gdns E13 . . . . 99 A4
Geoffrey Chaucer Tech
Coll SE1 . . . . 117 B3 262 D5
Geoffrey Cl SE5 . . . . 139 A3
Geoffrey Ct SE4 . . . . 141 B2
Geoffrey Gdns E6 . . . . . . 100 A5
Geoffrey Ho SE1 . . . . . . 262 D6
Geoffrey Jones Ct
NW10 . . . . 90 A6
Geoffrey Rd SE4 . . . . 141 B2
George Akass Ho 5
SE18 . . . . 123 A1
George Beard Rd 11
SE8 . . . . 119 B2
George Beare Lo 9
SW4 . . . . 159 C6
George Belt Ho 8 E2 . . . . 96 D4
George Carver Ho E7 . . . . 77 A3
George Comberton Wlk 4
E12 . . . . 78 C3
George Cres N10 . . . . 31 A3
George Ct
Buckhurst Hill IG9 . . . . 21 D2
St James WC2 . . . . 250 B5
George Davies Lodge
IG6 . . . . 57 A4
George Downing Est
N16 . . . . 73 D6
George Eliot Ho SW1 . . 259 B3
George Eliot Jun & Inf
Schs NW8 . . . . . . 92 B6 229 C6
George Elliot Ho SE17 . . 262 A2
George Elliston Ho 13
SE1 . . . . 118 A1
George Eyre Ho NW8 . . 229 D3
George Gange Way
HA3 . . . . 42 D6
George Green's Sec Sch
E14 . . . . 120 A1
George Groves Rd
SE20 . . . . 184 A2
George Ho 3 SE26 . . . . . 184 B5
George Inn Yd SE1 . . . . 252 C3
George La Hayes BR2 . . . 209 B1
Lewisham SE13 . . . . 164 A5
Wanstead E18 . . . . 55 B6
Woodford E18 . . . . 37 A1
George Lansbury Ho
7 Bow E3 . . . . 97 B4
3 Willesden NW10 . . . . . . 67 C1
Wood Green N22 . . . . 32 C2
George Lashwood Ct 12
SW9 . . . . 138 B1
George Leybourne Ho 15
E1 . . . . 118 A6
George Lindgren Ho
SW6 . . . . 264 D4
George Loveless Ho 4
E2 . . . . 95 D4
George Lovell Dr EN3 . . . . 7 C6
George Mathers Rd
SE11 . . . . 261 C4
George Mews NW1 . . . . 232 A1
George Mitchell Sch
E10 . . . . 53 D1
George Parr Ho N21 . . . . . 16 D4
George Peabody Ct
NW1 . . . . 237 A4
George Rd Chingford E4 . . 35 C4
Kingston u T KT2 . . . . 177 A3
New Malden KT3 . . . . 199 D4
George Row SE16 . . . . . . 118 A4
Georges Mead WD6 . . . . . 10 A5
George Spicer Prim Sch
EN1 . . . . 5 D2
George Sq SW19 . . . . 201 C6
George's Rd N7 . . . . 72 B3
George's Sq SW6 . . . . . 264 D6
George St Barking IG11 . . 79 A1
6 Canning Town E16 . . . . 98 D1
Ealing W7 . . . . 108 C5
Hounslow TW3, TW5 . . . . 129 B3
Marylebone W1 . . 92 D1 237 D2
Richmond TW10 . . . . 153 D6
Southall UB2 . . . . 107 A2
South Croydon CR0 . . . . . 221 B6
George Street Sta
CR0 . . . . 221 A6
George Taylor Ct N9 . . . 18 B1
George Tingle Ho SE1 . 263 D6
George Tomlinson Prim
Sch E11 . . . . 54 C1
Georgetown Cl 4
SE19 . . . . 183 C5
Georgette Pl SE10 . . . . . 142 A5
George Vale Ho 35 E2 . . . 96 A5
George V Ave HA2, HA5 . . 41 C6
Georgeville Gdns IG6 . . . 56 D5
George V Way UB6 . . . . . . 87 B6
George Walter Ho 11
SE16 . . . . 118 C2
George Wyver Cl
SW18 . . . . 157 A4
George Yd
City of London EC3 . . . . 242 D1
Mayfair W1 . . . . 115 A6 248 B6
Georgiana St
NW1 . . . . 93 C6 232 B6
Georgian Cl Hayes BR2 . . 209 B1
Ickenham UB10 . . . . 60 A4
Stanmore HA7 . . . . 25 A3
Georgian Ct
Croydon CR0 . . . . 205 B1
12 Hackney E9 . . . . 96 C6
3 Hendon NW4 . . . . 46 B4
Wembley HA9 . . . . 66 D2
Georgian Ho HA0 . . . . 65 A5
Georgian Lo HA5 . . . . 40 B4
Georgian Village The
E17 . . . . 54 A6
Georgian Way HA1 . . . . . . 64 B6
Georgia Rd
New Malden KT3 . . . . 199 A5
South Norwood CR7 . . . . 182 D2
Georgina Ct 5 TW1 . . . . 153 C5
Georgina Gdns 10 E2 . . . . 95 D4
Geraint Rd BR1 . . . . 187 A6
Geraldine Ct 6 NW9 . . . . 46 A5
Geraldine Rd
Brentford W4 . . . . 132 C6
Wandsworth SW18 . . . . . 158 A6
Geraldine St SE11 . . . . . 261 C5
Gerald Mews SW1 . . . . . 258 B4
Gerald Rd
Belgravia
SW1 . . . . 115 A2 258 B4
Dagenham RM8 . . . . 59 B1
Newham E16 . . . . 98 D3
Gerard Ave TW4 . . . . 151 C4
Gerard Ct NW2 . . . . 68 D3
Gerard Rd
Barnes SW13 . . . . 133 D4
Harrow HA1 . . . . 43 A3
Gerards Cl SE16 . . . . 118 C1
Gerboa Ct 6 E4 . . . . 36 B5
Gerda Rd SE9 . . . . 167 A2
Germander Way E15 . . . . 98 C4
German Sch The
TW10 . . . . 153 D3
Gernigan Ho SW18 . . . . . 158 B5
Gernon Rd E3 . . . . 97 A5
Geron Way NW2 . . . . 68 C6
Gerrard Gdns HA5 . . . . . . 40 A4
Gerrard Ho 5 SE14 . . . . . 140 D5
Gerrard Pl W1 . . . . 249 D6
Gerrard Rd N1 . . . . 94 D5 234 D4
Gerrards Cl N14 . . . . 15 C6
Gerrard's Ct W5 . . . . 109 D3
Gerrard St W1 . . 115 D6 249 D6
Gerridge Ct SE1 . . . . . . 261 B6
Gerridge St
SE1 . . . . 116 C3 261 B6
Gerry Raffles Sq E15 . . . . 76 B2
Gertrude Rd DA17 . . . . . . 125 C2
Gertrude St
SW10 . . . . 136 A6 266 B5
Gervase Cl HA9 . . . . 67 A5
Gervase Rd HA8 . . . . 27 B2
Gervase St SE15 . . . . 140 B5
Getters Talmud Torah
N16 . . . . 51 B2
Ghent St SE6 . . . . 163 C2
Ghent Way E8 . . . . 73 D2
Giant Arches Rd SE24 . . 161 A5
Giant Tree Hill WD23 . . . . . 8 B3
Gibbards Cott 1 IG11 . . . 79 D1
Gibbfield Cl RM6 . . . . 59 A6
Gibbings Ho SE1 . . . . . . 251 D1
Gibbins Rd E15 . . . . 76 A1
Gibbon Ho NW8 . . . . 236 D5
Gibbon Rd Acton W3 . . . . 111 C6
Kingston u T KT2 . . . . 176 A3
Nunhead SE15 . . . . 140 C3
Gibbons Mews NW11 . . . . 47 B4
Gibbons Rd NW10 . . . . 67 C2
Gibbon's Rents SE1 . . . 253 A3
Gibbon Wlk SW15 . . . . . . 134 A1
Gibbs Ave SE19 . . . . 183 B5
Gibbs Cl SE19 . . . . 183 B5
Gibbs Gn Edgware HA8 . . 27 A6
West Kensington
W14 . . . . 113 B1 254 D2
Gibbs Green Rd
W14 . . . . 113 B1 254 C2
Gibbs Green Sch
W14 . . . . 113 B1 254 D2
Gibbs Ho
6 Balham SW12 . . . . 159 B4
2 Bromley BR1 . . . . 186 D2
Gibbs Rd N18 . . . . 34 C6
Gibbs Sq SE19 . . . . 183 B5
Gibraltar Ho NW10 . . . . . . 89 C5
Gibraltar Wlk 28 E2 . . . . . 95 D4
Gibson Bsns Ctr 10
N17 . . . . 33 D3
Gibson Cl
Bethnal Green E1 . . . . 96 C3
Chessington KT9 . . . . 213 C3
Isleworth TW7 . . . . 130 B2
Southgate N21 . . . . 16 C5
Gibson Ct
9 Friern Barnet N11 . . . . . 30 D5
Hinchley Wood KT10 . . . . 212 D5
Gibson Gdns N16 . . . . 73 D6
Gibson Ho
South Croydon CR2 . . . . . 221 A2
Sutton SM1 . . . . 217 C4
Gibson Rd
Dagenham RM8 . . . . 58 C1
Ickenham UB10 . . . . 60 B4
Lambeth SE11 . . . . 260 D3
Sutton SM1 . . . . 217 D3
Gibson's Hill SW16 . . . . . 182 C3
Gibson Sq N1 . . . . 94 C6 234 B6
Gibson St SE10 . . . . 120 C1
Gideon Cl DA17 . . . . 125 D2
Gideon Mews W5 . . . . . . 109 D4
Gideon Rd SW11 . . . . 137 A2
Giesbach Rd N19 . . . . 71 D6
Giffard Rd N18 . . . . 33 C4
Giffen Square Mkt
SE8 . . . . 141 C5
Giffin St SE8 . . . . 141 C5
Gifford Gdns W7 . . . . 86 C2
Gifford Ho
5 Clapham SW4 . . . . 137 D1
Greenwich SE10 . . . . 120 B1
Pimlico SW1 . . . . 259 A1
Gifford Prim Sch UB5 . . . 85 B5
Gifford St N1 . . . . 72 A1
Gift La E15 . . . . 98 D6
Giggs Hill BR5 . . . . 190 A2
Giggs Hill Gdns KT7 . . . . 197 A1
Giggs Hill Rd KT7 . . . . . . 197 A2
Gilbert Cl
Kidbrooke SE18 . . . . 144 B4
1 Merton SW19 . . . . 179 D2
Gilbert Ct W5 . . . . 88 B1
Gilbert Gr HA8 . . . . 27 B2
Gilbert Ho Barbican EC2 . 242 B3
Deptford SE8 . . . . 141 C6
5 Globe Town E2 . . . . 96 D4
Pimlico SW1 . . . . 258 D1
South Lambeth SW8 . . . . 270 A4
5 Walthamstow E17 . . . . . 54 A6
Gilbert Pl WC1 . . . 94 A2 240 A3
Gilbert Rd
Belvedere DA17 . . . . 125 C3
Lambeth SE11 . . 116 C2 261 B4
Merton SW19 . . . . 180 A3
Pinner HA5 . . . . 40 D5
Plaistow BR1 . . . . 187 A3
Gilbert Scott Inf Com Sch
CR2 . . . . 223 A1
Gilbert Scott Jun Com Sch
CR2 . . . . 223 A1
Gilbert Sheldon Ho
W2 . . . . 236 D4
Gilbertson Ho 11 E14 . . . 119 C3
Gilbert St Enfield EN3 . . . . . 6 C6
Hounslow TW3 . . . . 130 A2
Leyton E15 . . . . 76 C4
Marylebone W1 . . 93 A1 238 B1
Gilbey Cl UB10 . . . . 60 D4
Gilbey Rd SW17 . . . . 180 C5
Gilbeys Yd NW1 . . . . 71 A1
Gilbourne Rd SE18 . . . . . 145 D6
Gilby Ho 5 E9 . . . . 74 D2
Gilda Ave EN3 . . . . 19 A6
Gilda Cres N16 . . . . 52 A1
Gilda Ct NW7 . . . . 28 A2
Gildea Cl HA5 . . . . 23 C3
Gildea St W1 . . . . 238 D3
Gilden Cres NW5 . . . . 71 A3
Gildersome St SE18 . . . . 144 C6
Gilders Rd KT9 . . . . 214 B2
Giles Coppice SE19 . . . . 183 D6
Giles Ho
5 Bermondsey SE16 . . . . 118 A3
Notting Hill W11 . . . . 91 C1
Gilesmead SE5 . . . . 139 B4
Gilfrid Cl UB8 . . . . 82 D1
Gilkes Cres SE21 . . . . 161 C5
Gilkes Pl SE21 . . . . 161 C5
Gillam Ho 9 SE16 . . . . . . 118 C2
Gillan Ct SE12 . . . . 165 B1
Gillan Gn WD23 . . . . 8 A2
Gillards Mews 6 E17 . . . . 53 C5
Gillards Way E17 . . . . 53 C5
Gill Ave E16 . . . . 99 A1
Gill Ct SE18 . . . . 123 A2
Gillender St E3 . . . . 98 A3
Gillespie Prim Sch N5 . . 72 D5
Gillespie Rd N4, N5 . . . . . 72 D5
Gillett Ave E6 . . . . 100 A5

Gillette Cnr TW7 131 A5
Gillett Ho N8 50 A6
Gillett Pl 27 E8 73 C3
Gillett Rd CR7 205 B5
Gillett St E8, N16 73 C3
Gillfoot NW1 232 A3
Gillham Terr N17 34 A3
Gillian Ho HA3 24 C4
Gillian Park Rd SM3 201 B1
Gillian St SE13 163 D6
Gillies Ct Sidcup DA14 189 C6
Southgate N21 16 B6
Gillies St NW5 71 A3
Gilling Ct 5 NW3 70 C2
Gillingham Ho SW1 259 A4
Gillingham Mews SW1 259 A4
Gillingham Rd NW2 69 A5
Gillingham Row SW1 259 A4
Gillingham St
SW1 115 C2 259 A4
Gillings Ct EN5 1 A1
Gillison Wlk 19 SE16 118 A3
Gillman Dr E15 98 D6
Gillman Ho 24 E2 96 A5
Gillray Ho
Chelsea SW10 266 C5
2 Sutton SM1 218 B3
Gills Ct 2 EN5 14 A6
Gill St E14 119 B6
Gillum Cl EN4 14 D3
Gilmore Cl UB10 60 C5
Gilmore Cres TW15 170 C4
Gilmore Ct N11 30 D5
Gilmore Ho SW4 136 D1
Gilmore Rd SE13 142 B1
Gilpin Ave SW14 133 B1
Gilpin Cl Mitcham CR4 180 C1
Paddington W2 236 B4
Gilpin Cres
Edmonton N18 33 D5
Twickenham TW2 151 D4
Gilpin Ho
9 Edmonton N9 18 A1
New Malden KT3 199 C4
Gilpin Rd E5 75 A4
Gilpin Way UB3 127 B5
Gilray Ho W2 246 C6
Gilsland Rd CR7 205 B5
Gilstead Ho IG11 102 B5
Gilstead Rd SW6 135 D3
Gilston Rd
SW10 114 A1 256 B1
Gilton Rd SE6 164 C1
Giltspur St EC1 94 D1 241 D2
Gilwell Cl E4 7 D1
Gilwell Ct 7 E5 74 B4
Gippeswyck Cl HA5 22 D2
Gipsy Cnr W3 89 B2
Gipsy Hill SE19 183 C5
Gipsy Hill Sta SE19 183 C5
Gipsy La SW15 134 B2
Gipsy Moth IV* SE10 142 A6
Gipsy Rd Bexley DA16 146 D3
West Norwood SE27 183 B6
Gipsy Road Gdns
SE27 183 A6
Giralda Cl E16 99 D2
Giraud St E14 97 D1
Girdlers Rd W14 112 D2
Girdlestone Wlk N19 71 C6
Girdwood Rd SW18,
SW19 157 A4
Girling Ho 9 N1 95 C6
Girling Way TW14 128 A2
Gironde Rd
SW6 135 B5 264 D3
Girtin Ho
6 Belmont SM2 217 D1
4 Northolt UB5 84 D5
Girton Ave NW9 44 C6
Girton Cl UB5 64 A2
Girton Gdns CR0 223 C5
Girton Ho SW15 156 D5
Girton Rd
Forest Hill SE26 184 D5
Northolt UB5 64 A2
Girton Villas 6 W10 90 D1
Gisbourne Cl SM6 219 D5
Gisburn Ho 23 SE15 140 A5
Gisburn Mans N8 50 B5
Gisburn Rd N8 50 B5
Gissing Wlk N1 72 C1
Gittens Cl BR1 186 D6
Given-Wilson Wlk E13 98 D5
Glacier Way HA0 87 D5
Gladbeck Way EN2 4 D1
Gladding Rd E12 77 D4
Gladebury Ct 2 SW19 179 B4
Glade Cl KT6 213 D6
Glade Gdns CR0 207 A2
Glade La UB2 107 D4
Gladeside Croydon CR0 206 D3
Southgate N21 16 B4
Gladeside Cl KT9 213 D1
Gladesmore Com Sch
N15 52 A4
Gladesmore Rd N15 51 D3
Glades Sh Ctr The
BR1 187 A1
Gladeswood Rd DA17 125 D2
Glade The
Bromley BR1 187 D1
Charlton SE7 143 C5
Croydon CR0 206 D3
Enfield EN2 4 C3
Hammersmith W12 112 B4
Southgate N21 16 B4
Glade The *continued*
Stoneleigh KT17 216 A2
West Wickham BR4 223 D5
Woodford IG8 21 B1
Gladiator St SE23 163 A4
Glading Terr N16 73 D5
Gladioli Cl 6 TW12 173 C4
Gladsdale Dr HA5 40 B5
Gladsmuir Rd Barnet EN5 1 A3
Upper Holloway N19 49 C1
Gladstone Ave
Feltham TW14 150 B5
Plashet E12 78 A1
Tottenham N22 32 D1
Twickenham TW2 152 B4
Gladstone Ct
12 Merton SW19 179 C3
Ruislip HA4 61 C6
Westminster SW1 259 D3
Willesden NW2 68 B3
Gladstone Gdns TW3 130 A4
Gladstone Ho
6 Mitcham SW19 180 D1
16 Poplar E14 97 C1
Gladstone Mews
3 Penge SE20 184 C3
Wood Green N22 32 C1
Gladstone Par NW2 68 C5
Gladstone Park Gdns
NW2 68 B5
Gladstone Park Sch
NW10 68 B3
Gladstone Pl KT8 196 C4
Gladstone Rd
Acton W4 111 B3
Buckhurst Hill IG9 21 C3
Farnborough BR6 227 A3
Kingston u T KT1 198 C6
Merton SW19 179 C3
Southall UB2 107 A4
Surbiton KT6 214 A6
Thornton Heath CR0 205 B2
Gladstone St SE1 261 C6
Gladstone Terr
SW8 137 B4 268 D2
Gladstone Way HA3 42 C6
Gladwell Rd London N8 50 B3
Plaistow BR1 187 A4
Gladwin Ho NW1 232 B3
Gladwyn Rd SW15 134 D2
Gladys Dimson Ho E7 76 D3
Gladys Rd NW6 69 C1
Glaisdale Sch SM2 217 B1
Glaisher St SE8 141 D6
Glamis Cres UB3 105 A3
Glamis Ct W3 110 D4
Glamis Est 3 E1 118 D6
Glamis Pl E1 118 C6
Glamis Rd E1 118 C6
Glamis Way UB5 64 A2
Glamorgan Cl CR4,
SW16 204 A6
Glamorgan Ct 4 W7 86 D2
Glamorgan Rd KT1 175 C3
Glandford Way RM6 58 B4
Glanfield Rd BR3 207 B5
Glanleam Rd HA7 25 D6
Glanville Ho 4 SW12 159 C4
Glanville Mews HA7 25 A5
Glanville Rd
Bromley BR2 209 B6
Clapham Pk SW2 160 A6
Glasbrook Ave TW2 151 B3
Glasbrook Rd SE9 165 D4
Glasbury Ho 5 SW9 138 B1
Glaserton Rd N16 51 C2
Glasford St SW17 180 D4
Glasfryn Ct HA2 64 B6
Glasgow Ho W9 91 D5
Glasgow Rd
Edmonton N18 34 B5
Newham E13 99 B5
Glasgow Terr
SW1 115 C1 259 A1
Glasier Ct 6 E15 76 C1
Glasse Cl W13 109 A6
Glasshill St
SE1 116 D4 251 D2
Glasshouse Cl UB8 82 D2
Glasshouse Fields E1 118 D6
Glasshouse St
W1 115 C6 249 B5
Glasshouse The SE13 142 A1
Glasshouse Wlk
SE11 116 B1 260 C2
Glasshouse Yd EC1 242 A5
Glasslyn Rd N8 49 D4
Glassmill La BR2 186 D1
Glass St 4 E2 96 B3
Glass Yd SE18 122 C3
Glastonbury Ave IG8 37 D4
Glastonbury Ct
12 Deptford SE14 140 C5
1 Ealing W13 109 A5
Glastonbury Ho
London SE12 164 D6
Pimlico SW1 258 C2
Glastonbury Pl 22 E1 96 C1
Glastonbury Rd
Edmonton N9 18 A3
Morden SM4 201 C2
Glastonbury St NW6 69 B3
Glaston Ct W5 109 D5
Glaucus St E3 97 D2
Glazbury Rd
W14 113 A1 254 B2
Glazebrook Cl SE21 161 B2
Glazebrook Rd TW11 174 D3
Gleave Ct 7 N20 14 D2
Glebe Ave Enfield EN2 4 D2
Glebe Ave *continued*
Harrow HA3 44 A6
Mitcham CR4 180 C1
Ruislip HA4 62 B2
Uxbridge UB10 61 A4
Woodford IG8 37 A4
Glebe Cl
1 Chiswick W4 111 C1
Uxbridge UB10 61 A4
Glebe Cotts
Feltham TW13 151 C1
Sutton SM1 217 D4
Glebe Cres Harrow HA3 44 A6
Hendon NW4 46 C5
Glebe Ct 15 Bromley E3 97 D4
Ealing W5 109 D5
Hanwell W7 108 B6
Lewisham SE3 142 C2
Mitcham CR4 202 D6
Palmers Green N13 16 C1
Ruislip HA4 39 B2
Stanmore HA7 25 C5
Glebe Fst & Mid Sch
HA3 44 A5
Glebe Gdns KT3 199 C2
Glebe Ho
8 Bermondsey SE16 118 B3
Feltham TW13 151 C1
7 Woolwich SE18 122 C2
Glebe House Dr BR2 209 B1
Glebehyrst SE19 183 C6
Glebe La Barnet EN5 12 A5
Harrow HA3 44 A5
Glebeland Gdns TW17 193 A3
Glebelands
East Molesey KT8 195 D5
Leyton E10 75 D6
Mitcham CR4 202 C6
Glebelands Ave
Ilford IG2 57 B2
Woodford E18 37 A1
Glebelands Cl
Camberwell SE5 139 C2
Finchley N2 30 B2
Glebelands Rd TW14 150 A4
Glebe Path CR4 202 D6
Glebe Pl SW3 136 C6 267 A6
Glebe Prim Sch UB10 61 B4
Glebe Rd Barnes SW13 134 A3
Belmont SM2 217 A1
Bromley BR1 187 A2
Dagenham RM10 81 D2
Dalston E8 73 D1
Finchley N3 30 A2
Hayes UB3 105 D5
Hornsey N8 50 B5
Stanmore HA7 25 C5
Wallington SM5 218 D2
Willesden NW10 68 A2
Glebe Sch BR4 224 B6
Glebe Side TW1 152 D5
Glebe Sq CR4 202 D6
Glebe St W4 111 C1
Glebe The
Chislehurst BR7 189 A2
Lewisham SE3 142 C2
New Malden KT4 199 D1
Streatham SW16 181 D6
West Drayton UB7 104 B2
Glebeway IG8 37 C5
Glebe Way
Feltham TW13 151 C1
West Wickham BR4 224 B6
Gledhow Gdns SW5 256 A3
Gledstanes Rd
W14 113 A1 254 B1
Gledwood Ave UB4 84 A2
Gledwood Cres UB4 83 D2
Gledwood Ct UB4 83 D2
Gledwood Dr UB4 83 D2
Gledwood Gdns UB4 84 A2
Gleed Ave WD23 8 B2
Gleeson Dr BR6 227 D4
Glegg Pl 3 SW15 134 D1
Glenaffric Ave E14 120 B2
Glen Albyn Rd SW19 156 D2
Glenalla Rd HA4 39 D2
Glenalmond Ho
Ashford TW15 148 A1
2 Putney SW15 156 D5
Glenalmond Rd HA3 44 A5
Glenalvon Way 5
SE7 122 A2
Glena Mount SM1 218 A4
Glenarm Coll IG1 78 D6
Glenarm Rd E5 74 D4
Glen Ave TW15 170 C6
Glenavon Cl KT10 213 A1
Glenavon Ct KT4 216 B6
Glenavon Lo 5 E18 55 A6
Glenavon Rd E15 76 C1
Glenbarr Cl SE9 144 D2
Glenbow Rd BR1 186 C5
Glenbrook N EN2 4 B1
Glenbrook Prim Sch
SW4 159 D5
Glenbrook Rd NW6 69 C3
Glenbrook S EN2 4 B1
Glenbuck Ct 6 KT6 198 A3
Glenbuck Rd KT6 198 A3
Glenburnie Rd SW17 158 D1
Glencairn Dr W5 87 C3
Glencairne Cl E16 99 D2
Glencairn Rd SW16 182 A3
Glen Cl TW17 192 C5
Glencoe Ave IG2 57 C2
Glencoe Dr RM10 81 C4
Glencoe Mans 6
SW9 138 C5
Glencoe Rd UB4 84 D3
Glencorse Gn WD19 22 D6
Glen Cres IG8 37 B4
Glencroft Ct SM1 217 C3
Glen Ct
6 Bromley BR1 186 D3
9 Penge SE20 184 B2
Sidcup DA14 190 A6
Glendale Ave
Edgware HA8 26 C6
Ilford RM6 58 C2
Wood Green N22 32 C3
Glendale Cl SE9 144 C2
Glendale Dr SW19 179 B5
Glendale Gdns HA9 44 A1
Glendale Mews BR3 185 D2
Glendale Way SE28 124 C6
Glendall St SW9 138 B1
Glendarvon St SW15 134 D2
Glendevon Cl HA8 10 D1
Glendish Rd N17 34 B2
Glendor Gdns NW7 27 B6
Glendower Gdns 10
SW14 133 B2
Glendower Pl SW7 256 C4
Glendower Prep Sch
SW7 114 B2 256 C4
Glendower Rd
Chingford E4 20 B3
Mortlake SW14 133 B2
Glendown Ho 2 E8 74 A3
Glendown Rd SE2 124 A1
Glendun Ct W3 111 C6
Glendun Rd W3 111 C6
Gleneagle Lo BR3 185 C2
Gleneagle Mews
SW16 181 D5
Gleneagle Rd SW16 181 D5
Gleneagles Ealing W13 87 B2
Stanmore HA7 25 B4
Gleneagles Cl
21 Bermondsey SE16 118 B1
Crofton BR6 211 B1
South Oxhey WD19 22 D6
Gleneagles Ct 4
TW11 175 A5
Gleneagles Gn 1 BR6 211 B1
Gleneagles Twr 2 UB1 86 A1
Gleneldon Mews
SW16 182 A6
Gleneldon Rd SW16 182 A6
Glenelg Rd SW2 160 A6
Glenesk Rd SE9 144 D1
Glenfarg Rd SE6 164 B3
Glenfield Cres HA4 39 B2
Glenfield Rd
Ashford TW15 171 A4
Ealing W13 109 B4
Streatham SW12 159 C3
Glenfield Terr W13 109 B5
Glenfinlas Way SE5 138 D5
Glenforth St SE10 120 D1
Glengall Ct SE23 163 A4
Glengall Gr E14 120 A3
Glengall Pass 2 NW6 91 C6
Glengall Rd
Bexley DA7 147 A2
Camberwell SE15 139 D6
Edgware HA8 10 D1
Kilburn NW6 91 B6
Woodford IG8 37 B4
Glengall Terr SE15 139 D6
Glengarnock Ave E14 120 A2
Glengarry Rd SE22 161 D6
Glen Gdns CR0 220 C4
Glenham Dr IG2 56 D4
Glenhead Cl SE9 144 D2
Glenhill Cl N3 29 C1
Glen Ho
6 Newham E16 122 C5
Wallington SM6 219 C4
Glenhouse Rd SE9 166 C6
Glenhurst 4 BR3 186 A2
Glenhurst Ave
Gospel Oak NW5 71 A4
Ruislip HA4 39 A1
Sidcup DA5 169 B3
Glenhurst Ct 1 SE19 183 D5
Glenhurst Rd
Brentford TW8 109 C1
North Finchley N12 30 B5
Glenhurst Rise SE19 183 A3
Glenilla Rd NW3 70 C2
Glenister Ho UB3 106 B5
Glenister Park Rd
SW16 181 D3
Glenister Rd SE10 120 D1
Glenister St E16 122 C5
Glenkerry Ho 1 E14 98 A1
Glenlea Rd SE9 166 C6
Glenloch Ct 2 NW3 70 C2
Glenloch Rd Enfield EN3 6 C3
Maitland Pk NW3 70 C3
Glenluce Rd SE3 143 A6
Glenlyon Rd SE9 166 C6
Glenmead IG9 21 C3
Glenmere Ave NW7 28 A4
Glen Mews E17 53 B4
Glenmill TW12 173 B5
Glenmore SW15 156 D5
Glenmore Ho 6
TW10 154 A5
Glenmore Lawns W13 87 A1
Glenmore Rd
Bexley DA16 145 D4
Maitland Pk NW3 70 C2
Glenmore Way IG11 102 A5
Glenmount Path 1
SE18 123 A1
Glennie Ct SE21 162 A3
Glennie Ho SE10 142 A4
Glennie Rd SE27,
SW16 160 C1
Glenny Rd IG11 79 A2
Glenorchy Cl UB4 85 A2
Glenpark Ct W13 109 A6
Glenparke Rd E7 77 B2
Glen Rd
Chessington KT9 214 A5
Newham E13 99 C3
Walthamstow E17 53 B4
Glenridding NW1 232 B3
Glen Rise IG8 37 B4
Glenrosa St SW6 136 A3
Glenrose Ct DA14 190 B5
Glenrose Ho 9 SM1 218 A4
Glenroy St W12 90 C1
Glensdale Rd SE4 141 B2
Glenshaw Mans 7
SW9 138 C5
Glenshiel Rd SE9 166 C6
Glentanner Way
SW17 158 B1
Glen Terr E14 120 A4
Glentham Gdns SW13 134 B6
Glentham Rd SW13 134 B6
Glen The
Beckenham BR2 186 C1
Eastcote Village HA5 40 B4
Enfield EN2 4 D1
Locksbottom BR6 226 C5
Rayners La HA5 41 A2
Southall UB2 107 B1
South Croydon CR0 222 D5
Wembley HA9 65 D4
Glenthorne Ave CR0 206 C1
Glenthorne Cl SM3 201 C1
Glenthorne Gdns
Cheam SM3 201 C1
Ilford IG6 56 D5
Glenthorne High Sch
SM3 201 C1
Glenthorne Mews W6 112 B2
Glenthorne Rd
Friern Barnet N11 31 A5
Hammersmith W6 112 B2
Kingston u T KT1 198 B5
Walthamstow E17 53 A4
Glenthorpe SW15 134 A1
Glenthorpe Rd SM4 200 D4
Glenton Rd SE13 142 C1
Glentrammon Ave
BR6 227 D2
Glentrammon Cl BR6 227 D3
Glentrammon Gdns
BR6 227 D2
Glentrammon Rd BR6 227 D2
Glentworth Ct HA8 26 B5
Glentworth St
NW1 92 D3 237 D5
Glenure Rd SE9 166 C6
Glenview SE2 146 D6
Glen View Rd BR1 187 D1
Glenville Ave EN2 5 A5
Glenville Gr SE8 141 B5
Glenville Mews SW18 157 C4
Glenville Rd KT2 176 C2
Glen Wlk TW7 152 B6
Glenwood Ave NW9 45 C1
Glenwood Cl HA1 42 D4
Glenwood Ct
7 Sidcup DA14 190 A6
6 Wanstead E18 55 A6
Glenwood Gdns IG2 56 C4
Glenwood Gr NW9 45 A1
Glenwood Ho 3 EN5 13 D6
Glenwood Rd
Edgware NW7 11 C1
Forest Hill SE6 163 C3
Harringay N15 50 D4
Hounslow TW3 130 B2
Stoneleigh KT17 216 A2
Glenwood Way CR0 206 D3
Glenworth Ave E14 120 B2
Gliddon Dr E5 74 B4
Gliddon Rd
W14 113 A1 254 A2
Glimpsing Gn DA18 125 A3
Glisson Rd UB10 82 C5
Globe Ct SE18 145 A6
Globe Pond Rd SE16 119 A5
Globe Prim Sch E2 96 C4
Globe Rd
Bethnal Green E1, E2 96 C3
Stratford E15 76 D3
Woodford IG8 37 C4
Globe St SE1 117 B4 252 C1
Globe Terr 9 E2 96 C4
Globe Theatre The*
SE1 252 A5
GLOBE TOWN 96 D4
Globe View EC4 252 A6
Globe Yd W1 238 C1
Glossop Ho TW7 131 A1
Gloster Rd KT3 199 C5
Gloucester W14 254 D3
Gloucester Ave
Camden Town
NW1 93 A6 231 B6
Falconwood DA16 145 D1
Sidcup DA15 167 C2
Gloucester Cir SE10 142 A5
Gloucester Cl
Thames Ditton KT7 197 A1
Willesden NW10 67 B1
Gloucester Cres
Camden Town
NW1 93 B6 231 C6
Staines TW18 170 A4
Gloucester Ct
6 Acton W3 88 C1
Gloucester Ct *continued*
10 Belmont SM2 217 C1
Borough The SE1 262 B6
City of London EC3 253 B5
Dulwich SE22 162 A3
5 Ealing W7 86 D2
Golders Green NW11 47 B2
Harrow HA1 42 C6
Redbridge IG1 56 B2
Richmond TW9 132 C5
8 Surbiton KT6 197 D2
Gloucester Dr
Finsbury Pk N4 72 D6
London NW11 47 C5
Gloucester Gate NW1 231 C4
Gloucester Gate Mews
NW1 231 C4
Gloucester Gdns
Cockfosters EN4 15 A6
Golders Green NW11 47 B2
Paddington W2 236 A2
Redbridge IG1 56 A2
Sutton SM1 217 D6
Gloucester Gr HA8 27 B2
Gloucester Ho
Kilburn NW6 91 C5
Richmond TW10 154 C6
Gloucester Lo 9 CR0 221 D6
Gloucester Mews
Paddington W2 236 B1
Walthamstow E17 53 C2
Gloucester Mews W
W2 236 B1
Gloucester Par
Bexley DA15 168 A6
Hayes UB3 105 A3
Gloucester Pk SW7 256 A4
Gloucester Pl
W1 92 D2 237 D4
Gloucester Pl Mews
W1 92 D2 237 D3
Gloucester Prim Sch
SE15 139 C5
Gloucester Rd
Acton W3 111 A4
Croydon CR0 205 C2
Ealing W5 109 C4
Edmonton N18 33 D5
Enfield EN2 5 A5
Erith DA17 125 B1
Feltham TW13 150 C3
Hampton TW12 173 D3
Harrow HA1 41 D4
Higham Hill E17 34 D1
Hounslow TW4 129 A1
Ilford E12 78 B4
Kingston u T KT1, KT2 176 D1
Leyton E10 53 C2
New Barnet EN5 14 A6
Richmond TW9 132 C5
South Kensington
SW7 114 A2 256 A4
Teddington TW11 174 C5
Tottenham N17 51 B6
Twickenham TW2 152 A3
Wanstead E11 55 C4
Gloucester Road Sta
SW7 114 A2 256 A4
Gloucester Sq
6 Hackney E2 96 A6
Paddington W2 92 C1 237 A1
Gloucester St
SW1 115 C1 259 A2
Gloucester Terr
W2 92 A1 236 B1
Gloucester Way EC1 234 B1
Gloucester Wlk
W8 113 C4 245 B2
Glover Cl SE2 124 C2
Glover Dr N18 34 C4
Glover Ho London SE15 140 B1
2 South Hampstead
NW6 70 A1
Glover Rd HA5 40 D3
Glovers Gr HA4 38 D2
Glovers Lo 24 TW10 153 D6
Glowhill Ct N12 30 A3
Gloxinia Wlk TW12 173 C4
Glycena Rd SW11 136 D2
Glyn Ave EN4 2 B1
Glyn Cl SE25 183 C2
Glyn Ct Stanmore HA7 25 B4
West Norwood SE27 160 C1
Glyndale Grange SM2 217 D2
Glyndebourne Ct 5
UB5 84 C4
Glyndebourne Pk BR6 226 D6
Glynde Mews SW3 257 B5
Glynde Rd DA7 147 A2
Glynde Reach WC1 233 B1
Glynde St SE4 163 B5
Glyndon Rd SE18 123 B2
Glyn Dr DA14 190 B6
Glynfield Rd NW10 67 C1
Glyn Mans W14 254 B4
Glynne Rd N22 32 C1
Glyn Rd Clapton Pk E5 74 D4
Enfield EN3 6 C1
North Cheam KT4, SM3 216 D6
Glyn St SE11 260 C1
Glynwood Ct 7 SE23 162 C2
Goater's Alley SW6 264 D3
Goat La EN1 5 D5
Goat Rd CR4 202 D2
Goat Wharf TW8 132 A6
Godalming Ave SM6 220 B3
Godalming Rd E14 97 D2
Godbold Rd E15 98 C4
Goddard Cl TW17 192 B6
Goddard Ct HA3 25 A1

Goddard Ho SW19 156 D2
Goddard Pl N19 71 C5
Goddard Rd BR3 207 A5
Goddards Way IG1 57 B1
Goddarts Ho E17 53 C6
Godfrey Ave
Northolt UB5 85 A6
Twickenham TW2 152 B4
Godfrey Hill SE18 122 A2
Godfrey Ho EC1 235 C1
Godfrey Rd SE18 122 B2
Godfrey St
Chelsea SW3 114 C1 257 B2
Mill Meads E15 98 A5
Godfrey Way TW4 151 B4
Goding St
SE11 116 A1 260 B1
Godley Rd SW18 158 B3
Godliman St EC4 252 A6
Godman Rd SE15 140 B3
Godolphin Cl N13 32 D4
Godolphin Ho
Primrose Hill NW3 70 C1
7 Streatham SW2 160 C3
Godolphin & Latymer Sch
W6 112 B2
Godolphin Pl W3 111 B6
Godolphin Rd W12 112 B4
Godson Rd CR0 220 C5
Godson St N1 234 A4
Godstone Ct 1 N16 51 C1
Godstone Ho
Borough The SE1 262 D6
1 Kingston u T KT2 176 D4
Godstone Rd
Sutton SM1 218 A4
Twickenham TW1 153 B5
Godstow Rd SE2 124 C4
Godwin Cl
Shoreditch N1 235 B4
West Ewell KT19 215 A2
Godwin Ct NW1 232 B4
Godwin Ho
2 Haggerston E2 95 D5
Kidbrooke SE18 144 B4
Kilburn NW6 91 D5
Godwin Jun Sch E7 77 B4
Godwin Prim Sch RM9 81 A1
Godwin Rd
Bromley BR1, BR2 209 C6
Forest Gate E7 77 B4
Godwyn Ho 13 KT6 198 A3
Goffers Ho SE3 142 C3
Goffers Rd SE3, SE13 142 C3
Goffs Rd TW15 171 B4
Goffton Ho 14 SW9 138 B3
Goidel Cl SM6 219 D4
Golborne Gdns
5 Kensal Town W10 91 A3
West Kilburn W10 91 B3
Golborne Mews 9
W10 91 A2
Golborne Rd W10 91 A2
Golda Cl EN5 12 D5
Golda Ct N3 29 B1
Goldbeaters Gr HA8 27 C3
Goldbeaters Prim Sch
HA8 27 B2
Goldcliff Cl SM4 201 C2
Goldcrest Cl
Newham E16 99 D2
Woolwich SE28 124 C6
Goldcrest Mews W5 87 D2
Goldcrest Way
Bushey WD23 8 A3
New Addington CR0 224 B1
Golden Cres UB3 105 D5
Golden Cross Mews 2
W11 91 B1
Golden Ct 4 Barnet EN4 2 C1
Ealing W7 108 C6
Hounslow TW3 130 B3
10 Richmond TW9 153 D6
Golden Hinde The*
SE1 252 C4
Golden Hind Pl 5
SE8 119 B2
Golden La EC1 95 A3 242 B5
Golden Manor W7 108 C6
Golden Mews SE20 184 C2
Golden Par 2 E17 54 A6
Golden Plover Cl E16 99 A1
Golden Sq W1 115 C6 249 B6
Golders Cl HA8 26 D5
Golders Ct NW11 47 B2
Golders Gdns NW11 47 B2
GOLDERS GREEN 47 B2
Golders Green Coll
NW11 47 C1
Golders Green Cres
NW11 47 C2
Golders Green Rd
NW11 47 A2
Golders Green Sta
NW11 47 C1
Golders Hill Sch NW11 47 C2
Golderslea NW11 47 C1
Golders Manor Dr
NW11 47 A3
Golders Park Cl NW11 47 C1
Golders Rise NW4 46 D4
Golders Way NW11 47 B2
Golderton 2 NW4 46 C5
Goldfinch Rd SE28 123 B3
Goldhawk Ind Est The
W6 112 B3
Goldhawk Mews 2
W12 112 B4
Goldhawk Rd W12 112 A3
Goldhawk Road Sta
W12 112 C4
Goldhaze Cl IG8 37 D3
Gold Hill HA8 27 B4
Goldhurst Terr NW6 70 A1
Goldie Ho N19 49 D2
Goldie Leigh Hospl
SE2 146 C6
Golding Cl KT9 213 C2
Golding Ct 7 IG1 78 C5
Golding St E1 96 A1
Goldington Cres NW1 232 C4
Goldington Ct NW1 232 C5
Goldington St
NW1 93 D5 232 C4
Gold La HA8 27 B4
Goldman Cl E2 96 A3
Goldmark Ho SE3 143 B2
Goldney Rd W9 91 C3
Goldrill Dr N11 15 A2
Goldsboro Rd
SW8 137 D5 269 D3
Goldsborough Cres E4 20 A2
Goldsborough Ho
SW8 269 D1
Goldsdown Cl EN3 7 A3
Goldsdown Rd EN3 7 A3
Goldsmid St 2 SE18 123 C1
Goldsmith Ave
Acton W3 111 B6
Dagenham RM7 59 C2
Hyde The NW9 45 C3
Plashet E12 78 A2
Goldsmith Cl HA2 41 D1
Goldsmith Ct
Edgware HA8 26 B6
St Giles WC1 240 B2
Goldsmith Ho W3 111 B6
Goldsmith La NW9 45 A5
Goldsmith Rd
Acton W3 111 B5
Friern Barnet N11 30 D5
Higham Hill E17 34 D1
Leyton E10 53 D1
Peckham SE15 140 A4
Goldsmiths Bldgs W3 111 B5
Goldsmiths Cl W3 111 B5
Goldsmiths Coll, Univ of
London SE14 141 A4
Goldsmith's Ct N6 49 B3
Goldsmith's Pl 6 NW6 91 D6
Goldsmith's Row E2 96 A5
Goldsmith's Sq 17 E2 96 A5
Goldsmith St EC2 242 B2
Goldthorpe NW1 232 A5
Goldwell Ho SE22 139 C1
Goldwell Rd CR7 204 B5
Goldwin Cl SE14 140 C4
Goldwing Cl E16 99 A1
Golf Cl
South Norwood
SW16 182 C2
Stanmore HA7 25 C3
Golf Club Dr KT2 177 B3
Golfe Ho IG1 79 B5
Golfe Rd IG1 79 B5
Golfers View N12 30 B6
Golf Rd Bromley BR1 210 C6
Ealing W5 88 B1
Golf Side TW2 152 B1
Golfside Cl N20 14 C1
Golf Side Cl KT3 177 C1
Gollogly Terr 9 SE7 121 C1
Gomer Gdns TW11 175 A4
Gomer Pl TW11 175 A4
Gomm Rd SE16 118 C3
Gomshall Ave SM6 220 A3
Gondar Gdns NW6 69 B3
Gondar Mans NW6 69 B3
Gonson St SE8 141 D6
Gonston Cl SW19 157 A2
Gonville Cres UB5 63 D2
Gonville Ct 6 EN4 14 D3
Gonville Ho 6 SW15 156 D5
Gonville Prim Sch
CR7 204 B4
Gonville Rd CR7 204 B4
Gonville St SW6 135 A2
Gooch Ho Holborn EC1 241 A4
Lower Clapton E5 74 B5
Goodall Ho 10 SE4 140 D1
Goodall Rd E11 76 A5
Goodbehere Ho 7
SE27 183 A6
Gooden Ct HA1 64 C5
Goodenough Coll
WC1 94 B3 240 C6
Goodenough Rd
SW19 179 B3
Goodey Rd IG11 79 D1
Goodfaith Ho 18 E14 119 D6
Goodge Pl W1 239 B3
Goodge St W1 93 C2 239 B3
Goodge Street Sta
W1 93 D2 239 C4
Goodhall Cl HA7 25 B4
Goodhall St NW10 89 D4
Good Hart Pl E14 119 A6
Goodhart Way BR4 208 C3
Goodhew Rd CR0 206 A3
Goodhope Ho 17 E14 119 D6
Gooding Cl KT3 199 A4
Goodinge Cl N7 72 A2
Goodinge Rd N7 72 A2
Gooding Ho 4 SE7 121 C1
Goodison Cl WD23 8 A6
Goodland Ho 1 KT3 199 C2
Goodman Cres SW2 159 D2
Goodman Rd E10 54 A2
Goodmans Ct HA0 65 D4
Goodman's Stile 17 E1 96 A1
Goodman's Yd E1,
EC3 117 D6 253 C6
GOODMAYES 58 B1
Goodmayes Ave IG3 58 A1
Goodmayes Hospl IG3 58 A4
Goodmayes La IG3 80 A5
Goodmayes Lodge
RM8 80 A4
Goodmayes Prim Sch
IG3 58 B1
Goodmayes Rd IG3 58 A1
Goodmayes Ret Pk
RM6 58 B2
Goodmayes Sta IG3 58 A1
Goodrich Com Sch
SE22 162 A5
Goodrich Ct 9 W10 90 D1
Goodrich Ho
20 Bethnal Green E2 96 C5
Stamford Hill N16 51 C2
Goodrich Rd SE22 162 A5
Goodridge Ho E17 36 A3
Good Shepherd RC Prim
Sch
Catford BR1 186 D6
New Addington CR0 223 D1
Good Shepherd RC Prim
Sch The W12 111 D4
Goodson Ho SM4 202 A2
Goodson Rd NW10 67 C1
Goodspeed Ho 20 E14 119 D6
Goodsway NW1 94 A5 233 A4
Goodway Gdns E14 98 B1
Goodwill Ho 22 E14 119 D6
Goodwin Cl
Bermondsey
SE16 117 D3 263 D5
Mitcham CR4 202 B6
Goodwin Ct
East Barnet EN4 14 C5
Hornsey N8 50 A6
2 Mitcham SW19 180 C3
Goodwin Dr DA14 168 D2
Goodwin Gdns CR0,
CR2 220 D2
Goodwin Ho
Edmonton N9 18 C3
2 Peckham SE15 140 B2
Goodwin Rd
Croydon CR0 220 D3
Edmonton N9 18 D3
Shepherd's Bush W12 112 A4
Goodwins Ct WC2 250 A6
Goodwin St N4 72 C6
Goodwood Ave EN3 6 C6
Goodwood Cl
Morden SM4 201 C5
11 Stanmore HA7 25 C5
Goodwood Ct W1 238 D4
Goodwood Dr UB5 63 C2
Goodwood Ho
3 Acton Green W4 111 A1
Penge SE26 184 B4
Goodwood Lo 1 SM6 219 D5
Goodwood Mans 3
SW9 138 C2
Goodwood Par BR3 207 A5
Goodwood Rd SE14 141 A5
Goodwyn Ave NW7 27 C5
Goodwyn Sch NW7 28 A5
Goodwyn's Vale N10 31 B2
Goodyear Ho 8 N2 30 B1
Goodyers Gdns NW4 46 D4
Goosander Ct 34 NW9 27 D1
Goosander Way SE18,
SE28 123 B3
Gooseacre La HA3 43 D4
Goose Green Cl BR5 190 A1
Goose Green Prim Sch
SE22 139 D1
Goose Green Trad Est
SE22 140 A1
Gooseley La E6 100 C4
Goose Sq 8 E6 100 B1
Goossens Cl 1 SM1 218 A3
Gophir La EC4 252 C6
Gopsall St N1 95 B6 235 D5
Gordon Ave
Chingford E4 36 C4
Isleworth TW1 153 B6
Mortlake SW14 133 C1
Stanmore HA7 25 A4
Gordonbrock Prim Sch
SE4 163 C6
Gordonbrock Rd SE4 163 C6
Gordon Cl E17 53 C3
Gordon Cres
Croydon CR0 205 D1
Hayes UB3 106 A2
Gordon Ct Edgware HA8 26 B5
Hampton TW12 174 A5
5 Shepherd's Bush
W12 90 C1
18 Wimbledon SW20 178 D3
Gordondale Rd SW18,
SW19 157 C2
Gordon Dr TW17 193 B2
Gordon Gdns HA8 26 D1
Gordon Gr SE5 138 D3
Gordon Hill EN2 5 A4
Gordon Hill Sta EN2 4 D4
Gordon Ho
2 Ealing W5 88 A4
Lee SE12 165 A4
17 Shadwell E1 118 C6
Gordon Hospl The
SW1 115 D2 259 C3
Gordon House Rd NW5 71 A4
Gordon Inf Sch IG1 79 B5
Gordon Lo N16 51 B1
Gordon Mans
3 Barnet EN5 1 B1
Marylebone WC1 239 C5
Gordon Pl W8 113 C4 245 B2
Gordon Prim Sch SE9 144 B1
Gordon Rd
Ashford TW15 148 A1
Avery Hill DA15 167 C6
Barking IG11 101 C6
Beckenham BR3 207 B6
Chingford E4 20 C4
Chiswick W4 132 D6
Claygate KT10 212 C1
Dagenham RM6 59 B3
Ealing W13 109 C6
Edmonton N9 18 B2
Enfield EN2 5 B3
Finchley N3 29 B3
Harrow HA3 42 C6
Ilford IG1 79 B5
Isleworth TW3 130 A1
Kingston u T KT2 176 B2
Leyton E15 76 A4
Peckham SE15 140 B3
Richmond TW9 132 B3
Shepperton TW17 193 B3
Southall UB2 107 A2
Surbiton KT5 198 B2
Wallington SM5 218 D2
Wanstead E11 55 A3
Woodford E18 37 B2
Wood Green N11 31 D3
Yiewsley UB7 104 A6
Gordon Sq WC1 93 D3 239 D6
Gordon St
Bloomsbury
WC1 93 D3 239 C6
Newham E13 99 A4
Gordon Way Barnet EN5 1 B1
Bromley BR1 187 A2
Gore Ct NW9 44 C4
Gorefield Ho NW6 91 C5
Gorefield Pl NW6 91 C5
Gore Rd Hackney E9 96 C6
Merton SW20 178 C1
Goresbrook Rd RM9 102 D6
Gore St SW7 114 A3 256 B6
Gorham Ho 12 SW4 159 C5
Gorham Pl W11 244 A5
Goring Gdns RM8 80 C4
Goring Rd N11 32 A4
Goring St EC3 243 B2
Goring Way UB6 86 A5
Gorleston Rd N15 51 B4
Gorleston St
W14 113 A2 254 B4
Gorman Rd SE18 122 B2
Gorringe Park Ave
CR4 181 A3
Gorringe Park Prim Sch
CR4 181 A2
Gorse Cl E16 99 A1
Gorsefield Ho 6 E14 119 C6
Gorse Rd CR0 223 C5
Gorse Rise SW17 181 A5
Gorse Wlk UB7 82 A1
Gorst Rd London SW11 158 D5
North Acton NW10 89 B3
Gorsuch Pl 1 E2 95 D4
Gorsuch St E2 95 D4
Gosberton Rd SW12 159 A3
Gosbury Hill KT9 214 A4
Gosfield Rd RM8 59 C1
Gosfield St W1 93 C2 239 A3
Gosford Gdns IG4 56 B4
Gosford Ho 25 E3 97 B5
Goshawk Gdns UB4 83 C5
Goslett Yd WC2 239 D2
Gosling Cl UB6 85 C4
Gosling Ho 2 E1 118 C6
Gosling Way SW9 138 C4
Gosmore Ct N9 18 B2
Gospatric Home Ho
SW14 133 C2
Gospatrick Rd N17 33 A2
GOSPEL OAK 71 A4
Gospel Oak Prim Sch
NW5 71 A4
Gospel Oak Sta NW5 71 A4
Gosport Ho 9 SW15 156 A3
Gosport Rd E17 53 B4
Gosport Wlk N17 52 B5
Gossage Rd
Hillingdon UB10 60 B1
Plumstead SE18 123 B1
Gosset St E2 96 A4
Gosshill Rd BR7 188 C1
Gossington Cl BR7 188 D6
Gosterwood St SE8 141 A6
Gostling Rd TW2 151 C3
Goston Gdns CR7 204 C6
Goswell Pl EC1 234 D1
Goswell Rd EC1 94 D4 234 D2
Gothic Ct
17 Camberwell SE5 139 A5
Harlington UB3 127 B6
Gothic Rd TW2 152 B2
Gottfried Mews NW5 71 C4
Goudhurst Ho 7
SE20 184 C3
Goudhurst Rd BR1 186 D5
Gough Ho Islington N1 234 D6
4 Kingston u T KT1 176 A1
Gough Rd Enfield EN1 6 B3
Stratford E15 76 D4
Gough Sq EC4 94 C1 241 B2
Gough St WC1 94 B3 240 D5
Gough Wlk 14 E14 97 C1
Gould Ct SE19 183 C5
Goulden Ho SW11 136 C3
Goulding Gdns CR7 183 A1
Gouldman Ho 33 E1 96 C3
Gould Rd
East Bedfont TW14 149 C4
Twickenham TW2 152 C3
Gould's Gn UB8 104 D6
Gould Terr 26 E8 74 B3
Goulston St E1 95 D1 243 C2
Goulton Rd E5 74 B4
Gourley Pl N15 51 C4
Gourley St N15 51 C4
Gourock Rd SE9 166 C6
Govan St E2 96 A6
Gover Ct 8 SW4 138 A3
Government Row EN3 7 C6
Govett Ave TW17 193 A4
Govier Cl E15 76 C1
Gowan Ave
SW6 135 A4 264 A2
Gowan Ho 22 E2 95 D4
Gowan Lea 4 E18 55 A5
Gowan Rd NW10 68 B2
Gower Cl SW4 159 C5
Gower Ct WC1 239 C6
Gower Ho Barking IG11 79 A1
Hayes UB3 105 C6
Upper Tooting SW17 180 B6
12 Walthamstow E17 53 D6
Walworth SE17 262 B2
Gower House Sch NW9 67 A6
Gower Mews WC1 239 D4
Gower Pl NW1,
WC1 93 D3 239 C6
Gower Rd
Hounslow TW7 130 D6
Upton E7 77 A2
Gower Sch The N7 72 A2
Gower St WC1 93 D3 239 C5
Gower's Wlk E1 96 A1
Gowland Pl BR3 185 B1
Gowlett Rd SE15 140 A2
Gowlland Cl CR0 206 A2
Gowrie Rd SW11 137 A2
Graburn Way KT8 196 B6
Grace Ave DA7 147 B3
Grace Bsns Ctr CR4 202 D3
Gracechurch St EC2,
EC4 252 D6
Grace Cl Burnt Oak HA8 27 A3
Mottingham SE9 165 D1
Grace Ct
5 Croydon CR0 220 D5
Twickenham TW2 152 C2
Gracedale Rd SW16 181 B5
Gracedyer Ho N22 32 A3
Gracefield Gdns
SW16 160 A1
Gracehill 2 E1 96 C2
Grace Ho
Kennington SE11 270 D6
Penge SE26 184 B5
Grace Jones Cl E8 74 A2
Grace Path 2 SE26 184 C6
Grace Pl E3 97 D4
Grace Rd CR0 205 A3
Graces Alley 14 SE1 118 A6
Graces Mews NW8 229 B3
Grace's Mews SE5 139 C3
Grace's Rd SE5 139 C3
Grace St E3 97 D4
Gradient The SE26 184 A6
Graeme Ct UB6 85 D4
Graeme Rd EN1 5 C3
Graemesdyke Ave
SW14 132 D1
Grafton Cl Ealing W13 87 A1
Twickenham TW4 151 B3
Worcester Pk KT4 215 C5
Grafton Cres NW1 71 B2
Grafton Ct
10 Dalston E8 74 A3
East Bedfont TW14 149 B3
Grafton Gdns
Dagenham RM8 81 A6
Harringay N4 51 A3
Grafton Ho 16 Bow E3 97 C4
12 Deptford SE8 119 B1
Grafton Jun & Inf Schs
RM8 81 B6
Grafton Mans SW4 137 C1
Grafton Mews W1 239 A5
Grafton Park Rd KT4 215 C6
Grafton Pl NW1 93 D4 232 D1
Grafton Prim Sch N7 72 A5
Grafton Rd Acton W3 111 A6
Dagenham RM8 81 A6
Enfield EN2 4 B2
Gospel Oak NW5 71 A3
Harrow HA1 42 A4
Kingston u T KT3 199 C6
Thornton Heath CR0 204 C1
Worcester Pk KT4 215 C5
Grafton Sq SW4 137 C2
Grafton St W1 115 B6 248 D5
Grafton Terr NW5 71 A3
Grafton Way
East Molesey KT8 195 B5
Marylebone W1 239 B5
Grafton Yd NW5 71 B2
Graham Ave
Ealing W13 109 B4
Mitcham CR4 181 A2
Graham Cl CR0 223 C6
Graham Ct
Bromley BR1 187 B3
5 Deptford SE14 140 D6
Northolt UB5 63 B3
GRAHAME PARK 27 C2
Grahame Park Way NW7,
NW9 27 D2
Grahame White Ho
HA3 43 D6
Graham Gdns KT6 198 A1
Graham Ho
5 Balham SW12 159 B4
6 Barnet EN5 1 D1
Edmonton N9 18 C3
6 Tufnell Pk N19 71 D4
Woolwich SE18 144 D5
Graham Lo Edgware HA8 26 B4
Hendon NW4 46 B3
Graham Mans
11 Barking IG11 80 A1
2 Hackney E8 74 B2
Graham Rd Acton W4 111 B3
Bexleyheath DA6 147 C1
Dalston E8 74 A2
Hampton TW12 173 C6
Harringay N15 50 D6
Harrow HA3 42 C6
Hendon NW4 46 B3
Merton SW19 179 B3
Mitcham CR4 181 A2
Newham E13 99 A3
Graham St N1 94 D5 234 D3
Graham Terr
SW1 115 A2 258 B3
Graham Twr W3 110 D3
Grainger Cl UB5 64 A3
Grainger Ct 22 SE5 139 A5
Grainger Rd
Isleworth TW7 130 D3
Tottenham N22 33 A2
Gramer Cl E11 76 B6
Grampian Cl
Harlington UB3 127 B5
Orpington BR6 211 D3
15 Sutton SM2 218 A1
Grampian Gdns NW2 47 A1
Grampians The 10
W14 112 D4
Gramsci Way SE6 163 D1
Granada St SW17 180 D5
Granard Ave SW15 156 B6
Granard Bsns Ctr NW7 27 C4
Granard Ho 20 E9 74 D2
Granard Prim Sch
SW15 156 B5
Granard Rd SW11,
SW12 158 D4
Granary Cl N9 18 C4
Granary Ct 3 RM6 58 D2
Granary Mans SE28 123 A4
Granary Rd E1 96 B3
Granary Sq N1 72 C2
Granary St NW1 93 D6 232 C5
Granary The SE8 141 C5
Granby Ho 13 SE18 122 B2
Granby Pl SE1 251 A1
Granby Rd Eltham SE9 144 B2
Woolwich SE18 122 D3
Granby St
Bethnal Green E2 96 A3
Shoreditch E2 243 D6
Granby Terr
NW1 93 C5 232 A3
Grand Arc N12 30 A5
Grand Ave
Clerkenwell EC1 241 D4
Fortis Green N10 49 A5
Tolworth KT5 198 D3
Wembley HA9 66 C3
Grand Ave E HA9 66 D3
Grand Avenue Prim Sch
KT5 199 A3
Grand Ct RM8 81 A5
Grand Depot Rd SE18 122 C1
Grand Dr Southall UB2 108 A4
West Barnes SM4,
SW20 200 C5
Granden Rd SW16 182 A1
Grandfield Ct W4 133 B6
Grandison Rd
London SW11 158 D6
North Cheam KT4 216 C5
Grand Junction Wharf
N1 235 A3
Grand Par London N4 50 D3
Mortlake SW14 133 A1
Tolworth KT6 198 C1
Wembley HA9 66 C6
Grand Union Cl W9 91 B2
Grand Union Cres E8 96 A6
Grand Union Ind Est
NW10 88 D5
Grand Union Way
UB2 107 C4
Grand Vitesse Ind Est
SE1 251 D3
Granfield St SW11 266 D1
Grange Ave
East Barnet EN4 14 D3
North Finchley N12 30 A5
South Norwood SE25 183 C1
Stanmore HA7 25 C1
Totteridge N20 13 A4
Twickenham TW2 152 C2
Woodford IG8 37 A3
Grange Cl
East Molesey KT8 195 D5
Edgware HA8 27 A5
Hayes UB3 83 C2
Heston TW5 129 B6
Sidcup DA15 168 A1
Woodford IG8 37 A3

Grangecliffe Gdns
SE25 . . . .**183** C1
Grangecourt Rd N16 . . . **51** C1
Grange Cres SE28. . . . . .**102** C1
Grange Ct
Belmont SM2. . . . . . .**217** D1
4 Finchley N12 . . . .**30** A4
Hackbridge SM6 . . . . .**219** B5
Harrow HA1 . . . .**64** D5
Ilford IG6 . . . .**57** A6
Littleton TW17. . . . . . .**192** C5
Loughton IG10 . . . .**21** D6
Northolt UB5. . . . .**84** C5
Peckham SE15. . . . . . .**139** D3
Pinner HA5 . . . .**41** A6
Strand WC2 . . . . **240** D1
Wembley HA0 . . . .**65** C3
1 Willesden NW10 . . . .**67** C4
Grange Dr BR7 . . . .**188** B4
Grange Farm Cl HA2 . . .**64** A6
Grange Farm Est
TW17. . . . .**193** C6
Grangefield NW1 . . . .**72** A1
Grange Fst & Mid Schs
HA2 . . . .**41** D1
Grange Gdns
London N14. . . . .**15** D3
Pinner HA5 . . . .**41** A5
South Norwood SE25 . .**183** C1
West Hampstead NW3 . .**69** D5
Grange Gr N1 . . . .**73** A2
Grange Hill
Edgware HA8 . . . .**27** A5
South Norwood SE25 . .**183** C1
Grangehill Pl SE9 . . . . . .**144** B2
Grangehill Rd SE9 . . . . .**144** B1
Grange Ho
6 Barking IG11 . . . . . .**101** B6
Bermondsey SE1. . . . . **263** C5
Willesden NW10 . . . . . .**68** B1
Grange La SE21. . . . .**161** D2
Grange Lo SW19 . . . .**178** C4
Grange Mans KT17. . . . .**215** D1
Grangemill 11 NW5 . . . . .**71** B4
Grangemill Rd SE6 . . . . .**163** C2
GRANGE MILLS **113** C3
Grange Mills SW12 . . . .**159** C3
Grangemill Way SE6 . . .**163** C2
GRANGE PARK **16** C6
Grange Park Ave N21 . . .**17** A5
Grange Park Jun & Inf
Schs UB4 . . . .**83** D3
Grange Park Pl SW20 . .**178** B3
Grange Park Prep Sch
N21. . . . .**16** D5
Grange Park Prim Sch
N21. . . . .**4** C1
Grange Park Rd
Leyton E10. . . . .**53** D1
South Norwood CR7 . . .**205** B6
Grange Park Sta N21 . . .**16** D5
Grange Pk W5 . . . .**110** A5
Grange Pl NW6 . . . .**69** C1
Grange Prim Sch
Bermondsey
SE1. . . . . **117** C3 **263** A5
Ealing W5 . . . .**109** D4
Newham E13 . . . .**98** D4
Grange Rd
Barnes SW13 . . . .**134** A4
Belmont SM2. . . . . . .**217** C1
Bermondsey
SE1. . . . . **117** D3 **263** C5
Borehamwood WD6 . . . .**10** B6
Burnt Oak HA8 . . . .**27** B4
Chessington KT9 . . . . .**214** A4
Ealing W5 . . . .**110** A5
East Molesey KT8 . . . .**195** D5
Greenhill HA1 . . . .**43** A4
Gunnersbury W4 . . . . .**110** D1
Hayes UB3. . . . .**83** C1
Highgate N6 . . . .**49** A3
Ilford IG1 . . . .**79** A4
Kingston u T KT1 . . . . .**198** A6
Leyton E10. . . . .**53** C1
Newham E13 . . . .**98** D4
Orpington BR6. . . . . . .**227** A6
Roxeth HA2 . . . .**64** B6
Southall UB1 . . . .**107** A4
South Norwood SE19,
SE25. . . . .**183** B1
Tottenham N17 . . . .**34** A4
Walthamstow E17. . . . . .**53** A4
Willesden NW10 . . . . . .**68** B2
Grange St N1. . . . . **235** D5
Grange The
Bermondsey
SE1. . . . . **117** D3 **263** C5
Cockfosters EN4 . . . .**2** D2
Croydon CR0 . . . .**223** B6
Ealing W13 . . . .**87** C2
7 Gunnersbury W4 . . .**110** D1
Hammersmith W12 . . . .**112** B3
19 Maitland Pk NW3. . . .**70** D2
South Acton W3. . . . . .**110** D4
3 Walthamstow E17 . . .**53** A4
4 Wanstead E18 . . . . . .**55** A6
Wembley HA0 . . . .**66** C1
West Barnes KT3 . . . . .**200** A4
West Ewell KT19. . . . . .**215** B4
West Kensington
W14. . . . .**113** B2 **254** C3
Wimbledon SW19 . . . .**178** C4
Grange Vale SM2. . . . . .**217** C1
Grange View Rd N20. . . .**14** A3
Grangeway London N12 . .**29** D6

Grangeway continued
South Hampstead NW6. . .**69** C1
Woodford IG8 . . . .**37** C6
Grangeway Gdns IG4 . . .**56** A4
Grangeway The N21 . . . .**16** D5
Grange Wlk
SE1. . . . . **117** D3 **263** C5
Grangewood DA5. . . . . .**169** B3
Grangewood Cl HA5 . . . .**40** A4
Grangewood Ind Sch
E7. . . . .**77** D1
Grangewood La BR3 . . .**185** B4
Grangewood Sch HA5. . .**40** A4
Grangewood St E6. . . . . .**99** D6
Grange Yd SE1 . **117** D3 **263** C5
Granham Gdns N9 . . . . . .**17** D2
Granite Apts E15. . . . . . .**76** B2
Granite St SE18. . . . . . .**123** D1
Granleigh Rd E11. . . . . . .**76** C6
Grannary The TW16 SE16 .**118** C4
Gransden Ave E8 . . . .**74** B1
Gransden Ho 1 SE8 . . . .**119** B1
Gransden Rd W12 . . . . . .**111** D4
Grantbridge St
N1. . . . . **94** D5 **234** D4
Grantchester 12 KT1 . . .**176** C1
Grantchester Cl HA1 . . . .**64** D5
Grant Cl London N14 . . . . .**15** C4
Shepperton TW17 . . . . .**192** D3
Tottenham N17 . . . .**33** C1
Grant Ct 2 Chingford E4. .**20** A3
11 Hendon NW4 . . . .**27** D1
Grantham Cl HA8 . . . .**10** A1
Grantham Ct
Dagenham RM6. . . . . . .**59** B2
Kingston u T KT2 . . . . .**175** D5
9 Rotherhithe SE16. . . .**118** D4
Grantham Gdns RM6 . . . .**59** B2
Grantham Ho
Ashford TW16. . . . . . .**171** C3
12 Peckham SE15. . . . . .**140** A6
Grantham Pl W1 . . . . **248** C3
Grantham Rd
Chiswick W4 . . . .**133** C5
Little Ilford E12. . . . . . .**78** C4
South Lambeth SW9 . . .**138** A3
Grant Ho
38 Clapham SW8 . . . . .**137** D3
Clerkenwell EC1 . . . . . **241** D4
Grantley Ho
2 Deptford SE14 . . . . .**140** D6
5 Putney SW19 . . . . . .**156** A3
Grantley Pl KT10. . . . . . .**212** A3
Grantley Rd TW4, TW5 . .**128** C3
Grantley St E1. . . . .**96** D3
Grant Mus of Zoology &
*Comparative Anatomy**
WC1 . . . .**93** D3 **239** C5
Grantock Rd E17. . . . .**36** B2
Granton Prim Sch
SW16 . . . .**181** C3
Granton Rd Ilford IG3. . . . .**58** A1
Sidcup DA14 . . . .**190** C4
Streatham SW16. . . . . .**181** C2
Grant Pl 2 CR0. . . . .**205** D1
Grant Rd
Battersea SW11 . . . . . .**136** C2
Croydon CR0 . . . .**205** D1
Harrow HA3 . . . .**42** D6
Grants Cl NW7. . . . .**28** D3
Grant St Islington N1. . . **234** A4
Newham E13 . . . .**99** A4
Grantully Rd W9. . . . .**91** D4
Grant Way TW7 . . . .**131** A6
Granville Ave
Feltham TW13 . . . .**150** A2
Hounslow TW3, TW4. . .**151** C6
Lower Edmonton N9 . . . .**18** C1
Granville Cl CR0 . . . .**221** C6
Granville Ct
8 Deptford SE14 . . . . .**141** A5
Hornsey N4 . . . .**50** B3
Shoreditch N1 . . . . **235** D6
Granville Gdns
Ealing W5 . . . .**110** B5
South Norwood SW16. . .**182** B3
Granville Gr SE13 . . . . . .**142** A2
Granville Ho 18 E14 . . . . .**97** C1
Granville Ind Est NW2. . .**69** B6
Granville Mans 8
W12. . . . .**112** C4
Granville Mews DA14 . . .**190** A6
Granville Pk SE13 . . . . . .**142** B2
Granville Pl London N12. .**30** A3
Marylebone W1. . . **93** A1 **238** A1
Pinner HA5 . . . .**40** D6
Walham Green SW6 . . . **265** C3
Granville Point NW2 . . . .**69** B6
Granville Rd
Bexley DA16 . . . .**146** C2
Bowes Pk N13. . . . .**32** B4
Child's Hill NW2 . . . .**69** B4
Finchley N12 . . . .**30** A3
Hayes UB3. . . . .**105** D2
Hornsey N4, N8. . . . . . .**50** B3
Ilford IG1 . . . .**78** D6
Kilburn NW6 . . . .**91** C5
Merton SW19 . . . .**179** C3
Sidcup DA14 . . . .**190** B6
Tottenham N22 . . . .**32** D2
Walthamstow E17. . . . . .**53** D3
Wandsworth SW18 . . . .**157** B4
Woodford E18 . . . .**37** B1
Granville Sq
3 Camberwell SE15. . . .**139** C5
Finsbury WC1 . . . **94** B4 **233** D1
Granville St WC1 . . . . . **233** D1

Granwood Ct 5 TW7. . . .**130** C4
Grape St WC2 . . . . **240** A2
Grapsome Cl KT9 . . . . . .**213** C1
Grasdene Rd SE18. . . . . .**146** A5
Grasmere NW1 . . . . **231** D1
Grasmere Ave
Acton W3. . . . .**111** B6
Kingston u T SW15 . . . .**177** C6
Locksbottom BR6 . . . . .**226** D5
Merton SW19 . . . .**201** C6
Ruislip HA4 . . . .**39** A2
Twickenham TW3 . . . . .**151** D5
Wembley HA9 . . . .**43** D1
Grasmere Cl TW14 . . . . .**149** D3
Grasmere Ct
Barnes SW13 . . . .**134** A6
Bowes Pk N22. . . . .**32** B4
Forest Hill SE26 . . . . . .**184** A5
7 Sutton SM2 . . . .**218** A2
Grasmere Gdns
Harrow HA3 . . . .**25** A1
Locksbottom BR6 . . . . .**226** D5
Redbridge IG4. . . . .**56** B4
Grasmere Ho 20 N16. . . .**73** B4
Grasmere Point 2
SE15 . . . .**140** C5
Grasmere Prim Sch
N16. . . . .**73** B4
Grasmere Rd
Bromley BR1. . . . .**186** D3
Croydon SE25 . . . .**206** B4
Locksbottom BR6 . . . . .**226** D5
Muswell Hill N10. . . . . . .**31** B2
3 Newham E13 . . . .**99** A5
Streatham SW16. . . . . .**182** B5
Tottenham N17 . . . .**34** A4
Grasshaven Way SE28. .**123** D5
Grassington Cl N11 . . . . . .**31** A4
Grassington Rd DA14 . .**190** A6
Grassmere Ct 5 EN1. . . .**17** C6
Grassmount SE23 . . . . . .**162** B2
Grass Pk N3 . . . .**29** B2
Grassway SM6. . . . .**219** C4
Grasvenor Ave EN5 . . . . .**13** C5
Grasvenor Avenue Inf Sch
EN5. . . . .**13** C5
Grateley Ho 10 SW15. . .**156** B3
Gratton Rd
W14. . . . .**113** A3 **254** A5
Gratton Terr NW2. . . . . . .**68** D5
Graveley 16 KT1 . . . .**176** C1
Graveley Ave WD6 . . . . . .**11** A6
Graveley Ho 7 SE8 . . . . .**119** A2
Gravel Hill Bexley DA6 . .**169** B6
Church End N3 . . . .**29** B1
South Croydon CR0,
CR2 . . . .**223** B1
Gravel Hill Cl DA6. . . . . .**169** D5
Gravel Hill Prim Sch
DA6. . . . .**169** D6
Gravel Hill Sta CR0 . . . . .**223** A2
Gravel La E1 . . . **95** D1 **243** C2
Gravel Rd
Keston Mark BR2 . . . . .**226** A6
Twickenham TW2 . . . . .**152** C3
Gravelwood Cl BR7 . . . . .**167** A1
Gravenel Gdns 5
SW17. . . . .**180** C5
Graveney Gr SE20. . . . . .**184** C3
Graveney Rd SW17. . . . . .**180** C4
Graveney Sch SW17. . . . .**181** B5
Gravesend Rd W12. . . . . .**112** A6
Graves Est DA16 . . . . . .**146** B3
Gray Ave RM8 . . . .**59** B1
Gray Ct 8 KT2. . . . .**175** D6
Grayfriars Pas EC1. . . . . **241** C2
Grayham Cres KT3. . . . . .**199** B5
Grayham Rd KT3. . . . . . .**199** B5
Gray Ho SE17 . . . . **262** B2
Grayland Cl BR1. . . . . . .**187** D2
Grayland Ct WC1 . . . . . . **233** C1
Grayling Cl E16 . . . .**98** C3
Grayling Ct Ealing W5. . .**109** D5
Tottenham Hale N17 . . . .**52** B5
Grayling Rd N16 . . . .**73** B6
Grayling Sq E2 . . . .**96** A4
Grays Cotts UB9 . . . .**38** C1
Grays Court Hospl
RM10 . . . .**81** D1
Grayscroft Rd SW16. . . .**181** D3
Grays Farm Prim Sch
BR5. . . . .**190** B2
Grays Farm Production
Village BR5. . . . .**190** B2
Grays Farm Rd BR5 . . . .**190** B2
Grayshott Ct 10 SM2 . . .**217** D1
Grayshott Rd SW11 . . . .**137** A2
*Gray's Inn**
WC1. . . . .**94** B3 **240** D4
Gray's Inn Pl WC1. . . . . **240** D3
Gray's Inn Rd
WC1. . . . .**94** B3 **240** D6
Gray's Inn Sq
WC1. . . . .**94** C2 **241** A4
Grays La TW15. . . . .**170** D6
Grayson Ho EC1 . . . . . . **235** B1
Gray's Rd UB10 . . . .**60** A1
Gray St SE1 . . . . **116** C4 **251** B1
Grayswood Gdns
SW20. . . . .**178** B3
Grayswood Point 14
SW15. . . . .**156** A3
Gray's Yd W1. . . . . **238** B2
Graywood Ct N12 . . . .**30** A3
Grazebrook Prim Sch
N16. . . . .**73** C6
Grazebrook Rd N16 . . . . .**73** B6
Grazeley Ct SE19. . . . . . .**183** C5
Great Arthur Ho EC1 . . . **242** A5

Great Bell Alley EC2 . . . **242** C2
Great Benty UB7. . . . . . .**104** A2
Great Brownings
SE21 . . . .**183** D6
Great Bushey Dr N20. . . .**13** D3
Great Cambridge Ind Est
EN1. . . . .**18** B6
Great Cambridge Junction
N13, N18. . . . .**33** B6
Great Cambridge Rd
Edmonton N9, N18 . . . . .**17** C3
Enfield EN1 . . . .**6** A3
Great Castle St W1 . . . **239** A2
Great Central Ave HA4 . .**62** C3
Great Central St
NW1 . . . . **92** D2 **237** C4
Great Central Way
NW10 . . . .**67** B4
Great Chapel St
W1. . . . . **93** D1 **239** C2
Great Chart St SW11 . . .**136** A1
Great Chertsey Rd
Chiswick SW14, W4 . . . .**133** B4
Feltham TW13, TW2 . . .**151** C1
Great Church La W6. . . .**112** D1
Great College St
SW1. . . . .**116** A3 **260** A6
Great Croft WC1 . . . . . . **233** D1
Great Cross Ave SE3 . . .**142** C5
Great Cumberland Mews
W1. . . . . **237** C1
Great Cumberland Pl
W1. . . . . **92** D1 **237** D1
Great Dover St
SE1 . . . .**117** B3 **262** C6
Greatdown Rd W7 . . . .**86** D2
Great Eastern Bldgs 10
E8 . . . .**74** B2
Great Eastern Ent Ctr
E14 . . . .**119** D4
Great Eastern Pier
E14. . . . .**119** C1
Great Eastern Rd E15 . . .**76** B2
Great Eastern St
EC2 . . . .**95** C3 **243** A6
Great Eastern Wharf
SW11 . . . . **267** B3
Great Elms Rd BR2. . . . .**209** C5
Great Field
Hendon NW9. . . . .**27** D2
7 Kentish Town NW5 . . .**71** C3
Greatfield Ave E6. . . . . .**100** B3
Greatfield Cl
London SE4 . . . .**141** C1
4 Tufnell Pk N19 . . . . . .**71** C4
Greatfields Dr UB8. . . . . .**82** C2
Greatfields Rd IG11. . . . .**101** B5
Great Fleete Way
IG11. . . . .**102** C5
Great Galley Cl IG11 . . . .**102** C4
Great Gatton Cl CR0 . . .**207** A2
Great George St
SW1. . . . .**116** A4 **250** A1
Great Guildford Bsns Sq
SE1. . . . . **252** A3
Great Guildford St
SE1 . . . .**117** A5 **252** A3
Great Hall The 1 E11 . . . .**55** B5
Greatham Wlk 8
SW15. . . . .**156** A3
Great Harry Dr SE9 . . . . .**166** C1
Great James St WC1 . . . **240** C4
Great Marlborough St
W1. . . . . **93** C1 **239** A1
Great Maze Pond
SE1 . . . .**117** B4 **262** D2
Great Newport St WC2 . **250** A4
Great North Rd
Barnet EN5 . . . .**1** A2
East Finchley N2 . . . . . .**48** C5
New Barnet EN5 . . . .**13** D4
Great North Way (Barnet
By-Pass) NW4 . . . .**46** D6
Greatorex Ho 13 E1 . . . . .**96** A2
Greatorex St E1 . . . .**96** A2
Great Ormond St Hospl for
Children WC1 . . **94** B3 **240** C5
Great Ormond St
WC1. . . . .**94** B3 **240** C5
Great Percy St
WC1. . . . .**94** C4 **234** A2
Great Peter St
SW1. . . . .**115** D3 **259** D5
Great Portland St
W1. . . . . **93** B2 **238** D4
Great Portland Street Sta
W1 . . . . **93** B3 **238** D5
Great Pulteney St W1. . **249** B6
Great Queen St
WC2. . . . . **94** A1 **240** B2
Great Russell Mans
W1. . . . . **240** A3
Great Russell St
WC1. . . . .**94** A2 **240** A3
Great St Helen's EC3. . . **243** A2
Great St Thomas Apostle
EC4 . . . . **252** B6
Great Scotland Yd SW1,
WC2. . . . .**116** A5 **250** A4
Great Smith St
SW1. . . . .**115** D3 **259** D6
Great South West Rd TW6,
TW14, TW4 . . . .**148** B6
Great South-West Rd
TW5. . . . .**128** B2
Great Spilmans SE22. . .**161** C6
Greatstone Ho 10
SE20 . . . .**184** C3
Great Strand NW9 . . . . . .**27** D1

Great Suffolk St
SE1. . . . .**116** D5 **251** D3
Great Sutton St
EC1 . . . .**94** D3 **241** D5
Great Swan Alley EC2. . **242** C2
Great Thrift BR5 . . . .**211** A5
Great Titchfield St
W1. . . . . **93** C2 **239** A3
Great Tower St
EC3 . . . .**117** C6 **253** A6
Great Trinity La EC4 . . . **252** B6
Great Turnstile WC2 . . . **240** D3
Great Western Ind Pk
UB2. . . . .**108** A4
Great Western Rd W2,
W9. . . . .**91** B2
Great West Ho TW8. . . .**131** C6
Great West Rd
Brentford TW7, TW8 . . .**131** B6
Chiswick W4, W6. . . . . .**133** B6
Heston TW5, TW7 . . . . .**129** B4
Hounslow TW5, TW7 . . .**130** B5
Great West Road Cedars
Rd W4 . . . .**133** A6
Great West Road Hogarth
La W4. . . . .**133** C6
Great West Trad Est
TW8 . . . .**131** B6
Great Winchester St
EC2. . . . . **95** B1 **242** D2
Great Windmill St
W1. . . . .**115** D6 **249** C6
Greatwood BR7. . . . .**188** C3
Great Yd SE1 . . . . **253** B2
Greaves Cl IG11 . . . .**79** C1
Greaves Cotts E14. . . . . .**97** A2
Greaves Ct N8 . . . .**50** C5
Greaves Pl SW17. . . . . . .**180** C6
Greaves Twr SW10. . . . . **266** B4
Grebe 3 NW9 . . . .**27** D1
Grebe Ave UB4 . . . .**84** D1
Grebe Cl Barking IG11. . .**102** A3
Higham Hill E17. . . . . . .**35** A3
Stratford E7. . . . .**76** D3
Grebe Ct Cheam SM1. . .**217** B3
16 Cubitt Town E14. . . . .**120** A4
Grebe Terr 4 KT1 . . . . .**198** A6
Grecian Cres SE19 . . . . .**182** D4
Greek Ct W1 . . . . **239** D1
Greek St W1 . . . **93** D1 **239** D1
Greenacre Cl Barnet EN5 . .**1** B5
Northolt UB5. . . . .**63** B3
Greenacre Ct E8 . . . .**74** A1
Greenacre Gdns E17 . . . .**54** A5
Greenacre Pl SM6 . . . . . .**219** B6
Greenacres Bushey WD23 . .**8** B2
Church End N3 . . . .**29** A1
Eltham SE9 . . . .**166** C5
Green Acres Hayes UB4 . . .**84** B3
Sidcup DA14 . . . .**189** D6
South Croydon CR0 . . . .**221** D5
Greenacres Ave UB10 . . .**60** C5
Greenacres Cl BR6. . . . .**227** A4
Greenacres Dr HA7 . . . . .**25** B3
Greenacres Prim Sch
SE9 . . . .**166** C5
Greenacre Sq 28 SE16. .**118** C4
Greenacre Wlk N14. . . . . .**15** D1
Green Arbour Ct EC1. . . **241** C2
Green Ave Ealing W13. . .**109** B3
Edgware NW7 . . . .**27** C2
Greenaway Gdns NW3 . . .**69** D4
Greenaway Ho
Finsbury WC1 . . . . **234** A1
St John's Wood NW8 . . **229** A6
Greenaway Terr
TW19. . . . .**148** A3
Green Bank London N12. . .**29** D6
Wapping E1. . . . .**118** B5
Greenbank Ave HA0. . . . . .**65** A3
Greenbank Cl E4 . . . .**20** A2
Greenbank Cres NW4 . . . .**47** A5
Greenbank Lo 2 BR7 . . .**188** C2
Greenbanks HA1. . . . .**64** C4
Greenbay Rd SE7 . . . . . .**143** D5
Greenberry St NW8 . . . . **230** A3
Greenbrook Ave EN4 . . . . .**2** A3
Green CE Prim Sch The
N17. . . . .**51** D6
Green CE Sch Holy Trinity
(Inf Annexe) The N15 . .**51** D5
Green Cl
Beckenham BR2 . . . . . .**208** C6
Carshalton SM5. . . . . . .**218** D6
Feltham TW13 . . . .**173** A5
Kingsbury NW9 . . . .**45** A3
North End NW11. . . . . . .**48** A2
Greencoat Pl
SW1. . . . .**115** C2 **259** B4
Greencoat Row SW1 . . . **259** B5
Greencourt Ave HA8 . . . . .**26** D2
Greencourt Ho BR5 . . . . .**211** C4
Greencourt Rd BR5 . . . . .**211** C4
Greencroft HA8. . . . .**27** A5
Greencroft Ave HA4. . . . . .**62** C6
Greencroft Cl E16 . . . .**99** D2
Greencroft Gdns
Enfield EN1 . . . .**5** C2
South Hampstead NW6. . .**70** A1
Greencroft Rd TW5 . . . . .**129** B4
Green Ct Ashford TW16. .**171** D4
2 Willesden NW10 . . . . .**67** C4
Green Dale SE22 . . . .**161** C6
Greendale Cl SE22 . . . . . .**161** C6
Greendale Ct CR2. . . . . .**221** D2
Green Dr UB1 . . . .**107** C5

Green Dragon Ct SE1 . **252** C2
Green Dragon Ho
WC1. . . . . **240** A2
Green Dragon La
Brentford TW8 . . . .**110** B1
Southgate N21 . . . .**16** D5
Green Dragon Prim Sch
TW8 . . . .**132** A6
Green Dragon Yd 24
E1 . . . .**96** A2
Greene Ct 20 SE14 . . . . .**140** D6
Greene Ho SE1 . . . . **262** C5
Green Elms IG6. . . . .**57** A6
Green End
Chessington KT9 . . . . . .**214** A4
Edmonton N21. . . . .**16** D2
Greenend Rd W4 . . . .**111** C4
Greener Ct 26 EN3 . . . .**7** C5
Greener Ho 3 SW4 . . . . .**137** D2
Green Farm Cl BR6 . . . . .**227** D3
Greenfell Mans SE8 . . . .**141** D6
Greenfield Ave KT5 . . . .**198** D3
Greenfield Cl SE9 . . . . . .**166** A1
Greenfield Dr
Bromley BR1. . . . .**187** C1
Fortis Green N2 . . . .**48** D5
Greenfield Gdns
Cricklewood NW2 . . . . . .**69** A5
Crofton BR5. . . . .**211** B2
Dagenham RM9. . . . . . .**102** D6
Greenfield Ho 28
SW19. . . . .**156** D3
Greenfield Rd
Dagenham RM9. . . . . . .**102** C6
South Tottenham N15 . . .**51** C4
Whitechapel E1 . . . .**96** A1
Greenfields UB1. . . . .**85** C1
Greenfields Prim Sch
WD19 . . . .**22** C5
Greenfield Way HA2 . . . . .**41** D6
GREENFORD **86** A4
Greenford Ave
Ealing W7 . . . .**86** C1
Southall UB1. . . . .**107** B6
Greenford Gdns UB6. . . . .**86** A4
Greenford High Sch
UB6. . . . .**85** C4
Greenford Rd
Greenford UB6. . . . .**86** A3
Sudbury HA1, UB6. . . . . .**64** C3
Sutton SM1 . . . .**217** D4
Greenford Rdbt UB6. . . . .**86** B5
Greenford Sta UB6. . . . . .**86** B6
Greengate UB6 . . . .**65** B2
Greengate St E13 . . . .**99** B4
Green Gdns BR6. . . . .**227** A3
Greenhalgh Wlk N2. . . . . .**48** A5
Greenham Cl SE1. . . . . . **251** A1
Greenham Cres E4. . . . . . .**35** B4
Greenham Ho
5 Hackney E9 . . . .**96** C6
Isleworth TW7 . . . .**130** B2
Greenham Rd N10 . . . .**31** A1
Greenhaven Dr SE28 . . . .**102** B1
Greenheath Bsns Ctr 3
E2. . . . .**96** B3
Green Hedges 8
TW1. . . . .**153** C5
Greenheys Dr E18 . . . .**54** D6
GREENHILL **42** D4
Greenhill
Buckhurst Hill IG9. . . . . .**21** C3
Hampstead NW3. . . . . . .**70** B4
Sutton SM1 . . . .**218** A4
Wembley Pk HA9. . . . . . .**66** D6
Green Hill SE18. . . . .**122** B1
Greenhill Cts SE7 . . . . . .**122** B1
Greenhill Gdns UB5 . . . . .**85** B5
Greenhill Gr E12. . . . .**78** A4
Greenhill Par EN5 . . . .**13** C6
Greenhill Pk
Harlesden NW10 . . . . . .**89** C6
New Barnet EN5 . . . .**13** D6
Greenhill Rd
Harlesden NW10 . . . . . .**89** C6
Harrow HA1 . . . .**42** C3
Greenhill's Rents EC1 . . **241** C4
Greenhills Terr 16 N1 . . . .**73** B2
Greenhill Terr
Northolt UB5 . . . .**85** B5
Woolwich SE18 . . . .**122** B1
Greenhill Way
Harrow HA1 . . . .**42** C3
Wembley Pk HA9. . . . . . .**66** D6
Greenhithe Cl DA15. . . . .**167** C4
Green Ho TW7 . . . .**130** D3
Greenholm Rd SE9 . . . . .**166** D6
Green Ho The 5
SW19. . . . .**157** A2
Green Hundred Rd
SE15 . . . .**140** A6
Greenhurst Rd SE27. . . .**182** C5
Greening Ho SE13 . . . . . .**142** B1
Greening St SE2 . . . .**124** C2
Green La
Ashford TW16. . . . .**171** D4
Chessington KT9 . . . . . .**214** A4
Chislehurst SE9. . . . . . .**166** D1
Dagenham RM8. . . . . . .**81** B6
East Molesey KT8 . . . . .**195** D4
Edgware HA8 . . . .**26** C5
Feltham TW13 . . . .**173** A5
Hanwell W7 . . . .**108** C4
Hendon NW4. . . . .**46** D4
Hillingdon UB8 . . . .**83** A2
Hounslow TW4 . . . .**128** C1
Ilford IG1, IG3. . . . .**79** C6
Morden SM4 . . . .**201** D3
New Malden KT3. . . . . .**199** A4
New Malden KT4. . . . . .**200** D4

Green La *continued*
Penge SE20 184 D3
Shepperton TW17 193 A4
South Norwood CR7, SW16 182 C2
Stanmore HA7 25 B5
Greenland Cres UB2 106 D3
Greenland Ho
Bermondsey SE8 118 D1
4 Mile End E1 97 A3
Greenland Mews SE8 118 D1
Greenland Pl NW1 231 D6
Greenland Quay SE16 118 D2
Greenland Rd
Barnet EN5 12 C5
Camden Town NW1 93 C6 232 A6
Greenlands
Borehamwood WD6 11 B5
Chessington KT19 214 D3
Greenland St NW1 231 D6
Greenland Way CR0 203 D2
Green Lane Bsns Pk SE9 166 C2
Green Lane Cotts HA7 25 B6
Green Lane Gdns CR7 183 A1
Green Lane Mews SM4 201 D3
Green Lane Prim Sch KT4 200 B2
Green Lanes
London N4, N8, N15 50 D2
Palmers Green N13 16 C1
West Ewell KT19 215 C1
Greenlaw Ct W5 87 D1
Greenlaw Gdns KT3 199 D2
Greenlaw La TW8 109 D2
Greenlawns N12 29 D4
Green Lawns
Ruislip HA4 40 C1
8 Woolwich SE18 122 D2
Greenlaw St SE18 122 C3
Green Leaf Ave SM6 219 D4
Greenleaf Cl 8 SW2 160 C4
Greenleaf Ct N20 14 B3
Greenleafe Dr IG6 56 D6
Greenleaf Prim Sch E17 53 B6
Greenleaf Rd
5 Newham E6 99 C6
Walthamstow E17 53 B6
Greenleaf Way HA3 42 D6
Greenlea Pk SW19 180 C2
Green Leas
Ashford TW16 171 D4
Kingston u T KT1 198 A6
Green Leas Cl TW16 171 D4
Greenleaves Ct TW15 170 D4
Green Link Wlk TW9 132 D4
Green Man Gdns W13 109 A6
Green Man Intc E11 54 D2
Green Man La
Ealing W13 109 A5
Hatton TW14 128 A1
Greenman St N1 95 A6 235 A6
Greenmead Cl SE25 206 A4
Greenmead Sch SW15 156 B6
Green Moor Link N21 16 D4
Greenmoor Rd EN3 6 C3
Greenoak Pl EN4 2 D3
Green Oaks UB2 106 D2
Greenoak Way SW19 178 D6
Greenock Rd
Mitcham SW16 181 D2
11 South Acton W3 111 A3
Greeno Cres TW17 192 C4
Green Park* SW1, W1 115 B4 248 D2
Greenpark Ct HA0 65 C1
Green Park Sta W1 115 C5 249 A4
Green Park Way UB6 86 C6
Green Pond Cl E17 53 B6
Green Pond Rd E17 53 A6
Green Pt E15 76 C2
Green Rd
East Barnet N14 15 B5
Whetstone N20 14 A1
Green Ride IG10, E4 21 A6
Greenroof Way SE10 120 D3
Green Sch (Girls) The TW7 131 A4
Greens Ct Soho W1 249 C6
Wembley HA9 65 D5
Green's Ct W11 244 C3
Greens End SE18 122 D2
Greenshank Cl E17 35 A3
Greenshaw High Sch SM1 218 A6
Greenshields Ind Est E16 121 B5
Greenside
Dagenham RM8 58 C1
Sidcup DA5 169 A3
Greenside Cl
Catford SE6 164 B2
Whetstone N20 14 B2
Greenside Prim Sch W12 112 A4
Greenside Rd
Shepherd's Bush W12 112 A4
Thornton Heath CR0 204 C2
Greenslade Prim Sch SE18 145 B6
Greenslade Rd IG11 79 B1
Greensleeves Ho UB2 107 D2
Greensleeves Manor SM2 217 D2

Green St Enfield EN3 6 D3
Mayfair W1 115 A6 248 A6
Newham E13 99 C6
Sunbury TW16 172 A1
Upton E7 77 C1
Greenstead Ave IG8 37 C4
Greenstead Cl IG8 37 C4
Greenstead Gdns
Putney SW15 156 B6
Woodford IG8 37 C4
Greenstone Mews E11 55 A3
GREEN STREET GREEN 227 C2
Green Street Green Prim Sch BR6 227 D2
Greenstreet Hill SE4 140 D2
Greensward Ho SW6 136 A3
Green Terr EC1 234 B1
Green The Acton W3 89 C1
Buckhurst Hill IG9 21 B3
Chingford E4 20 B3
Claygate KT10 212 D2
Ealing W5 109 D6
Edmonton N9 18 A2
Erith DA7 147 C4
Falconwood DA16 145 C1
Feltham TW13 150 B2
Grove Pk BR1 165 A1
Hackbridge SM6 219 A6
Hayes BR2 209 A2
Heston TW5 129 C6
Kingston u T KT3 177 A1
Merton SM4 201 A5
Palmers Green N14 15 D1
Richmond TW9 131 D1
7 Richmond TW9 153 D6
Sidcup DA14 190 A5
Southall UB2 107 B4
Southgate N21 16 C4
St Paul's Cray BR5 190 B3
Stratford E15 76 D2
Sutton SM1 217 D5
Tottenham N17 33 A4
Twickenham TW2 152 C2
Upper Halliford TW17 193 C5
Uxbridge UB10 61 A6
Wallington SM5 219 A4
Wanstead E11 55 B3
Wembley HA0 65 A6
Wimbledon SW19 178 D5
Woodford IG8 37 A5
Green Vale Bexley DA6 168 D6
Ealing W5 88 B1
Greenvale Rd SE9 144 C1
Greenvale Sch SE23 163 A1
Green Verges HA7 25 D3
Green View KT9 214 B1
Greenview Ave CR0 207 A3
Greenview Cl W3 111 C5
Greenview Ct
Ashford TW15 170 B6
East Dulwich SE22 140 A1
Oakleigh Pk N20 14 A4
Wandsworth SW18 158 C4
Greenway
Chislehurst BR7 188 D5
Dagenham RM8 58 C1
Harrow HA3 44 A4
Hayes UB4 84 B3
Palmers Green N14 16 A2
Pinner HA5 22 B1
Totteridge N20 13 C2
Wallington SM6 219 C4
West Barnes SW20 200 C5
Woodford IG8 37 C5
Green Way
Bromley Comm BR2 210 A3
Eltham SE9 165 D6
Sunbury TW16 194 A5
Greenway Ave E17 54 B5
Greenway Cl
Finsbury Pk N4 73 A6
Friern Barnet N11 31 A4
Hendon NW9 27 B1
2 South Tottenham N15 51 D5
Totteridge N20 13 C2
Greenway Ct Hayes UB4 84 B3
Ilford IG1 56 D1
2 Newham E15 98 C5
Greenway Gdns
Croydon CR0 223 B5
Greenford UB6 85 D4
Hendon NW9 27 B1
Green Way Gdns HA3 24 C1
Greenways
Beckenham BR3 185 C1
5 Forest Hill SE26 184 C6
Hinchley Wood KT10 212 C4
Greenways The 1 TW1 153 A5
Greenway The
Harrow HA3 24 C2
Hendon NW9 27 B1
Hounslow TW4 129 B1
Pinner HA5 41 B3
Uxbridge UB8 82 A5
West Ruislip UB10 61 A6
Greenwell St W1 238 D5
GREENWICH 142 C6
Greenwich Acad SE10 141 D4
Greenwich Borough Mus* SE18 123 D1
Greenwich Bsns Ctr SE10 141 D5
Greenwich Bsns Pk SE10 141 D5
Greenwich Church St SE10 142 A6
Greenwich Coll SE10 142 A5

Greenwich Com Coll Plumstead Ctr SE18 123 A2
Greenwich Cres E6 100 A2
Greenwich Ct 11 E1 96 B1
Greenwich High Rd SE10 141 D5
Greenwich Ho SE13 164 B5
Greenwich Hts SE18 144 A5
Greenwich Ind Est SE10 141 D5
Greenwich London Coll SE18 122 D2
Greenwich Mkt SE10 142 A6
Greenwich Mkt 2 SE10 142 A6
Greenwich Park* SE10 142 C5
Greenwich Park St SE10 142 B6
Greenwich Quay SE8 141 D6
Greenwich Sh Pk SE7 121 B2
Greenwich South St SE10 142 A4
Greenwich Sta SE10 141 D5
Greenwich View Pl E14 119 D3
Green Wlk
Bermondsey SE1 263 A5
Hampton TW12 173 B4
Hendon NW4 46 D4
Ruislip HA4 39 D1
Southall UB2 107 C1
Green Wlk The E4 20 B3
Greenwood
8 Putney SW19 156 D4
3 Woodford IG8 37 A3
Green Wood NW5 71 C3
Greenwood Ave
Dagenham RM10 81 D4
Enfield EN3 7 A4
Greenwood Cl
Bushey WD23 8 C3
Merton SM4 201 A5
Orpington BR5 211 C3
Sidcup DA15 168 A2
Thames Ditton KT7 197 A1
Greenwood Dr E4 36 B5
Greenwood Gdns N13 16 D1
Greenwood Ho
Finsbury WC1 234 A1
8 Nunhead SE4 140 D1
Wood Green N22 32 C2
Greenwood La TW12 173 D5
Greenwood Mans 9 IG11 80 A1
Greenwood Pk KT2 177 C3
Greenwood Pl NW5 71 B3
Greenwood Prim Sch UB5 64 A3
Greenwood Rd
Dalston E8 74 A2
Hinchley Wood KT7 213 A6
Isleworth TW7 130 D2
Mitcham CR4 203 D6
Thornton Heath CR0 205 A2
West Ham E13 98 D5
Greenwoods The HA2 64 A5
Greenwood Terr NW10 89 B5
Green Wrythe Cres SM5 202 C1
Green Wrythe La SM5 202 C2
Green Wrythe Prim Sch SM5 202 B3
Green Yd WC1 240 D6
Greer Rd HA3 24 A2
Greet Ho SE1 251 B1
Greet St SE1 116 C5 251 B3
Greg Cl E10 54 A3
Gregor Mews SE3 143 A5
Gregory Cres SE9 165 D4
Gregory Ho SE3 143 B3
Gregory Pl W8 245 C2
Gregory Rd
Dagenham RM6 58 D5
Southall UB2 107 C3
Greig City Acad N8 50 A5
Greig Cl N8 50 A4
Greig Ho 9 TW10 153 C1
Greig Terr SE17 138 D6
Grenaby Ave CR0 205 B2
Grenaby Rd CR0 205 B2
Grenada Ho 18 E14 119 B6
Grenada Rd SE7 143 C5
Grenade St E14 119 B6
Grenadier St E16 122 C5
Grena Gdns TW9 132 B1
Grena Rd TW10, TW9 132 B1
Grenard Cl SE15 140 A5
Grendon Gdns HA9 66 C6
Grendon Ho
29 Hackney E9 74 C1
Pentonville N1 233 C3
Grendon St NW8 92 C3 237 A6
Grenfell Ct NW7 28 B4
Grenfell Gdns
Harrow HA3 44 A2
Ilford IG2 57 D4
Grenfell Ho SE5 139 A5
Grenfell Rd
Mitcham CR4, SW17 180 D4
Shepherd's Bush W11 112 D6
Grenfell Twr 5 W11 112 D6
Grenfell Wlk 4 W11 112 D6
Grengate Lodge 2 E13 99 B4
Grenier Apartments 11 SE15 140 B5
Grennell Cl SM1 218 B6
Grennell Rd SM1 218 A6
Grenoble Gdns N13 32 C4

Grenville Cl
Church End N3 29 B2
Tolworth KT5 199 A1
Grenville Ct
3 Dulwich SE19 183 D5
Ealing W13 87 B2
Edgware HA8 26 D6
Grenville Gdns IG8 37 C3
Grenville Ho 28 Bow E3 97 A5
4 Deptford SE8 141 C6
Grenville Lo N6 49 C2
Grenville Mans WC1 240 A6
Grenville Mews
Hampton TW12 173 D5
South Kensington SW7 256 A3
Grenville Pl
Burnt Oak NW7 27 B5
South Kensington SW7 114 A2 256 A4
Grenville Rd N19 50 A1
Grenville St WC1 240 B5
Gresham Almshouses 3 SW9 138 B1
Gresham Ave N20 30 D6
Gresham Cl Enfield EN2 5 A2
Sidcup DA5 169 B5
Gresham Coll EC1 94 C2 241 B3
Gresham Ct TW3 130 A4
Gresham Dr RM6 58 B3
Gresham Gdns NW11 47 A1
Gresham Ho
4 Teddington TW11 174 D5
3 Thames Ditton KT7 197 A2
West Barnes KT3 200 B5
Gresham Lo E17 53 D4
Gresham Pl 2 N19 71 D6
Gresham Rd
Beckenham BR3 185 A1
Brixton SW9 138 C2
Canning Town E16 99 B1
Croydon SE25 206 A5
East Ham E6 100 B5
Edgware HA8 26 B4
Hampton TW12 173 C4
Hillingdon UB10 82 C5
Hounslow TW3, TW5 130 A4
Willesden NW10 67 B3
Gresham St EC2 95 A1 242 B2
Gresham Way SW19 157 C1
Gresham Way Est SW19 157 D1
Gresley Cl London N15 51 B5
Walthamstow E17 53 A3
Gresley Ho SW8 269 D2
Gresley Rd N19 49 C2
Gressenhall Rd SW18 157 B4
Gressenham Ct 7 HA7 25 C6
Gresse St W1 93 D1 239 C2
Gresswell Cl DA14 168 A1
Greswell St SW6 134 D4
Greta Ho SE3 142 D6
Gretton Ho 2 E2 96 C4
Gretton Rd N17 33 D3
Greville Cl TW1 153 B4
Greville Ct Harrow HA1 64 C4
3 Lower Clapton E5 74 B5
Greville Hall NW6 91 D5
Greville Ho Harrow HA2 42 B1
Knightsbridge SW1 258 A6
Putney SW15 134 D2
Greville Lo
5 Bayswater W2 91 D1
16 London N12 29 D6
Greville Mews 5 NW6 91 D6
Greville Pl W9 91 D5
Greville Rd Kilburn NW6 91 D5
Richmond TW10 154 B5
Walthamstow E17 54 A5
Greville St EC1 94 C2 241 B4
Grey Cl NW11 48 A3
Grey Coat Hospital Sch (St Michaels) The SW1 115 D2 259 C3
Grey Coat Hospital Sch The SW1 115 D3 259 C5
Greycoat Pl SW1 115 D3 259 C5
Greycoat St SW1 115 D3 259 C5
Greycot Rd BR3 185 C5
Grey Court Sch TW10 153 C1
Grey Eagle St E1 95 D3 243 D5
Greyfell Cl HA7 25 B5
Greyfriars 16 SE26 162 A1
Greyfriars Ho SE3 142 D6
Grey Ho 27 W12 112 B6
Greyhound Ct WC2 251 A6
Greyhound Hill NW4 46 B6
Greyhound La SW16 181 D4
Greyhound Rd
College Pk NW10 90 B4
Fulham W6 135 A6 264 A6
Sutton SM1 218 A3
Tottenham N17 51 C6
Greyhound Terr SW16 181 C2
Greyladies Gdns SE10 142 A3
Greys Park Cl BR2 225 D3
Greystead Rd SE23 162 C4
Greystoke Ave HA5 41 C6
Greystoke Ct W5 88 B3
Greystoke Dr HA4 38 D3
Greystoke Gdns
Ealing W5 88 B3
Enfield EN2 3 D1
Greystoke Ho Ealing W5 88 A3
Peckham SE15 140 A6
Greystoke Lo W5 88 B3

Greystoke Park Terr W5 88 A4
Greystoke Pl EC4 241 B2
Greystone Gdns HA3 43 C3
Greystones TW2 152 A2
Greyswood St SW16 181 B4
Greytiles TW11 174 D4
Grey Turner Ho W12 90 A1
Grice Ct N1 73 A2
Grierson Ho SW16 181 C6
Grierson Rd
Forest Hill SE23 162 D4
Forest Hill SE23 163 A5
Griffin Cl NW10 68 B3
Griffin Ct
8 Brentford TW8 132 A6
Chiswick W4 111 D1
Shepherd's Bush W12 112 B5
Griffin Ctr TW14 150 B5
Griffin Ctr The KT1 175 D1
Griffin Gate SW15 134 D2
Griffin Lo N12 30 A6
Griffin Manor Way SE28 123 B3
Griffin Park (Brentford FC) TW8 131 D6
Griffin Rd
Plumstead SE18 123 B1
Tottenham N17 33 C1
Griffins Cl N21 17 B4
Griffin Way
Sunbury TW16 172 A1
Woolwich SE28 123 C3
Griffith Cl RM8 58 C1
Griffiths Cl KT4 216 B6
Griffiths Ho 2 SE18 144 D6
Griffiths Rd SW19 179 D3
Griffon Ho 3 SW11 136 C2
Griggs App IG1 79 A6
Grigg's Pl SE1 263 B5
Griggs Rd E10 54 A3
Grilse Cl N9 34 B6
Grimaldi Ho N1 233 C4
Grimsby Gr E16 122 D5
Grimsby St
8 Bethnal Green E2 96 A3
Shoreditch E2 243 D6
Grimsdyke Fst & Mid Sch HA5 23 B4
Grimsdyke Rd HA5 23 A3
Grimsel Path SE5 138 D5
Grimshaw Cl N6 49 A2
Grimston Rd SW6 135 B3
Grimthorpe Ho EC1 241 C6
Grimwade Ave CR0 222 A5
Grimwade Cl SE15 140 C2
Grimwood Rd TW1 152 D4
Grindall Cl CR0 220 D4
Grindall Ho 26 E1 96 B3
Grindal St SE1 251 A1
Grindleford Ave N11 15 A2
Grindley Gdns CR0 205 D3
Grindley Ho 3 E3 97 B2
Grinling Gibbons Prim Sch SE8 141 B6
Grinling Ho 6 SE18 122 C2
Grinling Pl SE8 141 C6
Grinstead Rd SE8 119 A1
Grisedale NW1 232 A2
Grittleton Ave HA9 66 D2
Grittleton Rd W9 91 C3
Grizedale Terr 8 SE23 162 B2
Grogan Cl TW12 173 B4
Groombridge Cl DA16 168 A6
Groombridge Ho 1 SE20 184 D3
Groombridge Rd E9 74 D1
Groom Cl BR2 209 B5
Groom Cres SW18 158 B4
Groome Ho SE11 260 D3
Groomfield Cl SW17 181 A6
Groom Pl SW1 115 A3 258 B6
Grooms Dr HA5 40 A4
Grosmont Rd SE18 123 D1
Grosse Way SW15 156 B5
Grosslea SM4 202 B4
Grosvenor Ave
Canonbury N5 73 A3
Harrow HA2 41 D3
Hayes UB4 83 D5
Mortlake SW14 133 C2
Richmond TW10 154 A6
Wallington SM5, SM6 219 A2
Grosvenor Bridge SW1 137 B6 268 D6
Grosvenor Cotts SW1 258 A4
Grosvenor Court Mans W2 237 C1
Grosvenor Cres
Hillingdon UB10 82 D6
Queensbury NW9 44 C5
Westminster SW1 115 A4 248 B1
Grosvenor Cres Mews SW1 248 A1
Grosvenor Ct
4 Acton W3 110 C5
Brondesbury Pk NW6 90 D6
3 Ealing W5 110 A6
3 Edgware NW7 27 B5
Gunnersbury W4 110 D1
Leyton E10 53 D1
Morden SM4 201 C5
Oakwood N14 15 C4
Penge SE19 183 D4
22 Poplar E14 97 B1
Putney SW15 157 A6
1 Sutton SM2 218 A2
Teddington TW11 175 A4

Grosvenor Ct *continued*
3 Wanstead E11 55 B4
2 Wimbledon SW19 179 A4
Grosvenor Gdns
Cricklewood NW2 68 C3
Hornsey N10 49 C6
Kingston u T KT2 175 D4
Mortlake SW14 133 C2
Newham E6 99 D4
Southgate N14 15 D6
Temple Fortune NW11 47 B4
Wallington SM6 219 C1
Westminster SW1 115 B3 258 D5
Woodford IG8 37 B4
Grosvenor Gdns Mews E SW1 258 D6
Grosvenor Gdns Mews N SW1 258 C5
Grosvenor Gdns Mews S SW1 258 D5
Grosvenor Hill
Mayfair W1 115 B6 248 C6
Wimbledon SW19 179 A4
Grosvenor Hill Ct W1 248 C6
Grosvenor Ho
5 Sutton SM1 217 D3
Upper Clapton E5 52 A1
Grosvenor Hts E4 20 C4
Grosvenor Lo
London N20 14 A1
4 Woodford E18 36 D1
Grosvenor Par 1 W5 110 C5
Grosvenor Park SE5 139 A5
Grosvenor Park Rd E17 53 D4
Grosvenor Pier SW1 269 C6
Grosvenor Pk SE5 139 A6
Grosvenor Pl SW1 115 B4 248 C1
Grosvenor Rd
Acton Green W4 111 A1
Bexley DA6 169 A6
Brentford TW8 131 D6
Croydon SE25 206 A5
Dagenham RM8 59 B1
Ealing W7 109 A5
Edmonton N9 18 B3
Erith DA17 147 C6
Finchley N3 29 C3
Hounslow TW3, TW4 129 B2
Ilford IG1 79 A5
Leyton E10 54 A1
Muswell Hill N10 31 B2
Newham E6 99 D6
Orpington BR6 211 C3
Pimlico SW1 137 C6 269 B6
Richmond TW10 154 A6
Southall UB2 107 B3
Twickenham TW1 153 A3
Upton E7 77 B2
Wallington SM6 219 B3
Wanstead E11 55 B4
West Wickham BR4 223 D6
Grosvenor Residences 1 W14 112 D3
Grosvenor Rise E E17 53 D4
Grosvenor Sq W1 115 A6 248 B6
Grosvenor St W1 115 B6 248 C6
Grosvenor Terr SE5 139 A6
Grosvenor The NW11 47 D2
Grosvenor Vale HA4 61 D6
Grosvenor Way E5 74 C6
Grosvernor Wharf Rd E14 120 B2
Grote's Bldgs SE3 142 C3
Grote's Pl SE3 142 C3
Groton Rd SW18 157 D2
Grotto Ct SE1 252 A2
Grotto Pas W1 238 A4
Grotto Rd TW1 152 D2
Grove Ave Cheam SM1 217 C2
Ealing W7 86 C1
Finchley N3 29 C3
Pinner HA5 41 A5
Twickenham TW1 152 D3
Wood Green N10 31 C1
Grovebury Ct
Bexley DA6 169 D6
Southgate N14 15 D4
Grovebury Rd SE2 124 B4
Grove Cl East Barnet N14 15 B4
Forest Hill SE23 163 A3
Hayes BR2 225 A6
Ickenham UB10 60 C3
Kingston u T KT1 198 B5
Grove Cres
Feltham TW13 173 A6
Kingsbury NW9 45 B5
Kingston u T KT1 198 A6
Walton-on-T KT12 194 B2
Woodford E18 36 D1
Grove Crescent Rd E15 76 B2
Grove Ct Barnet EN5 1 B2
Camberwell SE5 139 C3
Clapham SW4 137 C2
Ealing W5 110 A5
East Molesey KT8 196 B4
3 Forest Hill SE26 185 A6
8 Kingston u T KT1 198 A6
New Malden KT3 199 C6
Penge SE20 184 B3
Seething Wells KT6 197 D4
South Kensington SW10 256 B1

Grove Ct continued
St John's Wood NW8 ... 229 C2
Grovedale Rd N19 ... 71 D6
Grove Dwellings E1 ... 96 C2
Grove End
Gospel Oak NW5 ... 71 B4
Woodford E18 ... 36 D1
Grove End Gdns NW8 ... 229 B3
Grove End Ho NW8 ... 229 C1
Grove End La KT10 ... 196 B1
Grove End Rd
NW8 ... 92 B4 229 C1
Grove Farm Ct CR4 ... 202 D4
Grovefield 1 N11 ... 31 B6
Grove Footpath KT5 ... 198 A5
Grove Gdns Enfield EN3 ... 6 D5
Hendon NW4 ... 46 A5
Lisson Gr NW8 ... 92 C4 230 B1
Teddington TW11 ... 175 A6
Grove Glade Shop Hall
W13 ... 109 A5
Grove Green Rd E11 ... 76 B6
Grove Hall Ct Bow E3 ... 97 C5
St John's Wood
NW8 ... 92 A4 229 B2
Grove Hill Harrow HA1 ... 42 C2
Woodford E18 ... 36 D1
Grovehill Ct BR1 ... 186 D4
Grove Hill Rd
Camberwell SE5 ... 139 C2
Harrow HA1 ... 42 D2
Grove Ho
Blackheath SE3 ... 142 D3
Chelsea SW3 ... 267 B6
Hendon N3 ... 46 D6
Grove House Rd N8 ... 50 A5
Grove La
Camberwell SE5 ... 139 C2
Hillingdon UB8 ... 82 B3
Kingston u T KT1 ... 198 A5
Groveland Ave SW16 ... 182 B3
Groveland Ct EC4 ... 242 B1
Groveland Rd BR3 ... 207 B6
Grovelands
East Molesey KT8 ... 195 C5
Kingston u T KT1 ... 197 D5
Grovelands Cl
Camberwell SE5 ... 139 C3
Harrow HA2 ... 63 D5
Grovelands Ct N14 ... 15 D4
Grovelands Inf Sch
KT12 ... 194 B3
Grovelands Priory (Private
Hospl) N14 ... 16 A3
Grovelands Rd
Palmers Green N13 ... 16 B1
South Tottenham N15 ... 52 A3
St Paul's Cray BR5 ... 190 A3
Groveland Way KT3 ... 199 B4
Grove Lane Terr SE5 ... 139 B3
Groveley Ho 7 N4 ... 51 A2
Groveley Rd TW13,
TW16 ... 171 D5
Grove Lo Clapham SW4 ... 137 C1
Cranley Gdns N10 ... 49 C5
Grove Mans
London SW4 ... 136 D1
2 Shepherd's Bush
W6 ... 112 C4
3 Stamford Hill N16 ... 52 A1
Grove Market Pl SE9 ... 166 B5
Grove Mews W6 ... 112 C3
Grove Mill CR4 ... 202 C4
Grove Mill Pl SM5 ... 219 A5
GROVE PARK SE9 ... 165 B1
W4 ... 133 A4
Grove Park Ave E4 ... 35 D3
Grove Park Bridge
W4 ... 133 A5
Grove Park Gdns W4 ... 133 A5
Grove Park Mews W4 ... 133 A5
Grove Park Prim Sch
W4 ... 133 A6
Grove Park Rd
Chiswick W4 ... 132 D5
Mottingham SE9, SE12 ... 165 D2
South Tottenham N15 ... 51 C5
Grove Park Sch NW9 ... 45 A5
Grove Park Sta SE12 ... 165 B1
Grove Park Terr W4 ... 132 D6
Grove Pk
Camberwell SE5 ... 139 C3
Kingsbury NW9 ... 45 B5
Wanstead E11 ... 55 B4
Grove Pl Acton W3 ... 111 A5
Balham SW12 ... 159 B5
Hampstead NW3 ... 70 B5
Grove Prim Sch RM6 ... 58 C4
Grover Ct SE13 ... 141 D3
Grove Rd Acton W3 ... 111 A5
Barnes SW13 ... 133 D3
Belmont SM2 ... 217 C2
Bow E3 ... 97 A5
Brentford TW8 ... 109 C1
Chingford E4 ... 20 A1
Cockfosters EN4 ... 2 C2
Dagenham RM6 ... 58 C3
Ealing W5 ... 109 D6
East Molesey KT8 ... 196 B5
Edgware HA8 ... 26 C4
8 Erith DA17 ... 147 B6
Friern Barnet N11 ... 31 B5
Hounslow TW3 ... 129 C1
Kingston u T KT6 ... 197 D4
Leytonstone E11 ... 54 D2
Merton SW19 ... 180 A3
Mitcham CR4 ... 181 B1
Grove Rd continued
North Finchley N12 ... 30 B5
Pinner HA5 ... 41 B4
Richmond TW10 ... 154 B5
Shepperton TW17 ... 193 A3
South Tottenham N15 ... 51 C4
Spring Gr TW7 ... 130 C4
Thornton Heath CR7 ... 204 C5
Twickenham TW2 ... 152 B1
Uxbridge UB8 ... 60 A1
Walthamstow E17 ... 53 D4
Willesden NW2 ... 68 C2
Woodford E18 ... 36 D1
Grove Rd Prim Sch
TW3 ... 129 C1
Grove Rd W EN3 ... 6 C6
Grover Ho
4 London SW4 ... 159 C6
Vauxhall SE11 ... 260 D1
Groves Ho UB4 ... 84 B4
Groveside Cl Acton W3 ... 88 C1
Carshalton SM5 ... 218 C6
Groveside Ct SW11 ... 136 B3
Groveside Rd E4 ... 20 C1
Grove St Deptford SE8 ... 119 B1
Edmonton N18 ... 33 D4
Grovestile Waye
TW14 ... 149 B4
Grove Terr
Gospel Oak NW5 ... 71 B4
Southall UB1 ... 107 C6
Teddington TW11 ... 175 A6
Grove Terrace Mews
NW5 ... 71 B5
Grove The Bexley DA6 ... 146 D1
Dulwich SE21 ... 162 A3
Ealing W5 ... 110 A5
Edgware HA8 ... 26 D6
Edmonton N13 ... 32 C6
Enfield EN2 ... 4 C3
Finchley N3 ... 29 C3
Hendon NW11 ... 47 A2
Highgate N6 ... 49 A1
Hornsey N8 ... 49 D4
Hounslow TW7 ... 130 C4
Ickenham UB10 ... 60 C3
Kingsbury NW9 ... 45 B4
Sidcup DA14 ... 191 A6
Southall UB6 ... 86 A1
Stratford E15 ... 76 C2
Stroud Green N4 ... 50 B2
Teddington TW11 ... 175 A6
1 Twickenham TW1 ... 153 B5
Walton-on-T KT12 ... 194 B2
West Wickham BR4 ... 224 A6
Grove Vale
Chislehurst West
BR7 ... 188 C4
East Dulwich SE22 ... 139 D1
Groveway
Dagenham RM8 ... 80 D4
South Lambeth
SW9 ... 138 B4 270 D1
Grove Way
Thames Ditton KT10 ... 196 A1
Wembley HA9 ... 67 A3
Grovewood 9 TW9 ... 132 C4
Grovewood Ct 6
TW7 ... 130 C4
Grovewood Ho NW2 ... 69 B6
Grummant Rd SE15 ... 139 D4
Grundy St E14 ... 97 D1
Gruneisen Rd N3 ... 29 D3
Guardian Angels RC Prim
Sch E3 ... 97 A4
Guardian Ct SE12 ... 164 C6
Guards Mus The*
SW1 ... 115 C4 249 B1
Gubyon Ave SE24 ... 160 D6
Guerin Sq E3 ... 97 B4
Guernsey Cl TW5 ... 129 C5
Guernsey Gr SE24 ... 161 A4
Guernsey Ho
10 Canonbury N1 ... 73 A2
Enfield EN3 ... 6 D5
Guernsey Rd
11 Canonbury N1 ... 73 A2
Leytonstone E11 ... 54 B1
Guibal Rd SE12 ... 165 B3
Guildersfield Rd
SW16 ... 182 A3
Guildford Ave TW13 ... 150 A2
Guildford Gr SE10 ... 141 D4
Guildford Ho 23 SE5 ... 139 A3
Guildford Rd
Chingford E17 ... 36 A2
Ilford IG3 ... 79 C6
Newham E6 ... 100 B1
South Lambeth
SW8 ... 138 A4 270 B2
Thornton Heath CR0 ... 205 B3
Guildford Way SM6 ... 220 A3
Guild Hall* EC2 ... 95 A1 242 B2
Guildhall Bldgs EC2 ... 242 C2
Guildhall Ho EC2 ... 242 C2
Guildhall Sch Music &
Drama EC2 ... 95 A2 242 B4
Guildhall Yd EC2 ... 242 B2
Guild Ho SW19 ... 179 B4
Guildhouse St
SW1 ... 115 C2 259 A3
Guildown Ave N12 ... 29 D6
Guild Rd SE7 ... 143 D6
Guildsway E17 ... 35 B2
Guilford Ave KT5 ... 198 B4
Guilford Pl WC1 ... 240 C5
Guilford St WC1 ... 94 A3 240 B5
Guilfoyle 2 NW9 ... 27 D1
Guillemot Ct 28 SE8 ... 141 B6
Guilsborough Cl NW10 ... 67 C1
Guinness Cl Hayes UB3 ... 105 B3
Homerton E9 ... 75 A1
Guinness Ct
Chelsea SW3 ... 257 C3
6 Croydon CR0 ... 221 D6
Finsbury EC1 ... 235 B1
Primrose Hill NW8 ... 230 B5
Whitechapel E1 ... 243 D1
Guinness Sq SE1 ... 263 A4
Guinness Trust Bldgs
Bermondsey SE1 ... 253 A2
7 Bethnal Green E2 ... 96 A5
Chelsea SW3 ... 257 C3
Hammersmith W6 ... 112 C1
Kennington SE11 ... 261 C2
Guion Rd SW6 ... 135 B3
Gujarat Ho 1 N16 ... 73 C5
Gulland Cl WD23 ... 8 A6
Gulland Wlk 21 N1 ... 73 A2
Gullane Ho 24 E3 ... 97 B5
Gull Cl SM6 ... 220 A1
Gulliver Cl UB5 ... 85 B6
Gulliver Ct CR2 ... 220 D1
Gulliver Rd DA15 ... 167 C2
Gulliver St SE16 ... 119 B3
Gulston Wlk SW3 ... 257 D3
Gumleigh Rd W5 ... 109 C2
Gumley Gdns TW7 ... 131 A2
Gumley House RC Convent
Sch (Girls) TW7 ... 131 A2
Gumping Rd BR5 ... 227 A6
Gundulph Rd BR2 ... 209 C6
Gunmakers La E3 ... 97 A6
Gunnel Cl SE26 ... 184 A6
Gunnell Cl SE25 ... 206 A3
Gunnell Ct 3 CR4 ... 180 C2
Gunnels Ct & Hastingwood
Ct 6 IG9 ... 21 C2
Gunner Dr 9 EN3 ... 7 C6
Gunner La SE18 ... 122 C1
GUNNERSBURY ... 110 D2
Gunnersbury Avenue
(North Circular Rd)
W3 ... 110 C3
Gunnersbury Cl 8
W4 ... 110 D1
Gunnersbury Cres
W3 ... 110 C4
Gunnersbury Ct 8
W3 ... 110 D4
Gunnersbury Dr W5 ... 110 B4
Gunnersbury Gdns
W3 ... 110 C4
Gunnersbury La W3 ... 110 C4
Gunnersbury Manor
W5 ... 110 B5
Gunnersbury Mews 6
W4 ... 110 D1
Gunnersbury Park
W3 ... 110 C3
Gunnersbury Park Mus*
W3 ... 110 C3
Gunnersbury RC Sch
TW8 ... 109 C1
Gunnersbury Sta W4 ... 110 D1
Gunners Gr E4 ... 20 A1
Gunners Rd SW18 ... 158 B2
Gunnery Terr SE18 ... 123 A3
Gunning St SE18 ... 123 C2
Gunpowder Sq EC4 ... 241 B2
Gun St E1 ... 243 C3
Gunstor Rd N16 ... 73 C4
Gunter Gr
Chelsea SW6 ... 136 A5 266 A4
Hendon HA8 ... 27 B2
Gunterstone Rd
W14 ... 113 A1 254 B2
Gunthorpe St
E1 ... 95 D1 243 D2
Gunton Rd
Streatham SW17 ... 181 A4
Upper Clapton E5 ... 74 B6
Gunwhale Cl SE16 ... 118 D5
Gun Wharf Old Ford E3 ... 97 A6
Wapping E1 ... 118 C5
Gurdon Ho 7 E14 ... 97 C1
Gurdon Rd SE7 ... 121 A1
Gurnell Gr W13 ... 86 D3
Gurney Cl Barking IG11 ... 78 D2
Higham Hill E17 ... 34 D2
Stratford E15 ... 76 C3
Gurney Cres CR0 ... 204 B1
Gurney Dr N2 ... 48 A5
Gurney Ho
3 Bayswater W2 ... 91 D1
14 Bethnal Green E2 ... 96 A5
Hayes UB3 ... 105 C2
Gurney Rd
London SW6 ... 136 A2
Northolt UB5 ... 84 C4
Stratford E15 ... 76 C3
Wallington SM5 ... 219 A4
Guru Nanak Sikh Prim &
Sec Schs UB4 ... 106 C5
Guthrie Ct SE1 ... 251 B1
Guthrie St SW3 ... 257 A2
Gutter La EC2 ... 95 A1 242 A2
Guyatt Gdns CR4 ... 181 A1
Guy Barnett Gr SE3 ... 143 A2
Guy Rd SM6 ... 219 D5
Guyscliff Rd SE13 ... 164 A6
Guy's Hospl
SE1 ... 117 B4 252 D2
Guy's Hospl Sch
SE1 ... 117 B5 252 D3
Guy's Retreat IG9 ... 21 C4
Guy St SE1 ... 117 B4 252 D2
Gwalior Ho N14 ... 15 C5
Gwalior Rd SW15 ... 134 D2
Gwendolen Ave SW15 ... 156 D6
Gwendolen Cl SW15 ... 156 D6
Gwendolen Ho TW19 ... 148 A3
Gwendoline Ave E13 ... 99 B6
Gwendoline Ct TW15 ... 170 A6
Gwendwr Rd
W14 ... 113 A1 254 B2
Gwent Ct 13 SE16 ... 118 D5
Gwillim Cl DA15 ... 168 A6
Gwilym Maries Ho 11
E2 ... 96 B4
Gwydor Rd BR3 ... 206 D6
Gwydyr Rd BR2 ... 208 D6
Gwyn Cl SW6 ... 136 A5 266 A3
Gwyn Jones Prim Sch
E11 ... 54 B2
Gwynne Ave CR0 ... 206 D2
Gwynne Cl W4 ... 133 D6
Gwynne Ho
Finsbury WC1 ... 234 A1
6 Streatham SW2 ... 160 B3
3 Wanstead E11 ... 55 A4
Whitechapel E1 ... 96 B2
Gwynne Pl WC1 ... 233 D1
Gwynne Rd SW11 ... 136 B3
Gye Ho 2 SW4 ... 138 A1
Gylcote Cl SE5 ... 139 B1
Gyles Pk HA7 ... 25 C2
Gyllyngdune Gdns IG3 ... 79 D5

H

Haarlem Rd 12 W14 ... 112 D3
Haberdasher Pl 4 N1 ... 95 C4
Haberdashers' Aske's
Hatcham Coll SE4 ... 141 A3
Haberdashers' Aske's
Knights Acad BR1 ... 187 A6
Haberdasher St
N1 ... 95 B4 235 D2
Haccombe Rd SW19 ... 180 A4
HACKBRIDGE ... 219 B6
Hackbridge Park Gdns
SM5 ... 218 D6
Hackbridge Prim Sch
SM5 ... 203 A1
Hackbridge Rd SM5,
SM6 ... 219 A6
Hackbridge Sta SM6 ... 219 B6
Hackford Rd
SW9 ... 138 B4 270 D2
Hackford Wlk SW9 ... 138 C4
Hackforth Cl EN5 ... 12 B6
Hackington Cres BR3 ... 185 C4
HACKNEY ... 74 B2
Hackney Central Sta
E8 ... 74 B2
Hackney Cl WD6 ... 11 B6
Hackney Coll (Poplar Ctr)
E3 ... 97 D3
Hackney Com Coll N1 ... 95 C4
Hackney Downs Sta E8 ... 74 B3
Hackney Free & Parochial
CE Sec Sch E9 ... 74 C2
Hackney Gr E8 ... 74 B2
Hackney Hospl E9 ... 75 A3
Hackney Rd E2 ... 96 A5
Hackney Stadium Mkt*
E15 ... 75 C2
HACKNEY WICK ... 75 C2
Hackney Wick E9 ... 75 B2
Hackney Wick Sta E9 ... 75 C2
Hackworth Point 24 E3 ... 97 D4
Hacon Sq 12 E8 ... 74 B1
Hadar Cl N20 ... 13 D3
Haddenham Ct SW17 ... 180 B6
Hadden Rd SE28 ... 123 C3
Hadden Way UB6 ... 64 B2
Haddington Rd BR1 ... 186 B6
Haddo Ho
Gospel Oak NW5 ... 71 B4
Greenwich SE10 ... 141 D6
Haddon Cl Enfield EN1 ... 18 A5
New Malden KT3 ... 199 D4
Haddon Ct
East Acton W3 ... 111 D6
Hendon NW4 ... 46 C6
Haddon Gr DA15 ... 168 A4
Haddon Rd SM1 ... 217 D4
Haddo St SE10 ... 142 A6
Haden Ct N4 ... 72 C6
Hadfield Cl UB1 ... 85 B4
Hadfield Ho
Edgware NW7 ... 28 C6
37 Whitechapel E1 ... 96 A1
Hadleigh Cl
17 Bethnal Green E1 ... 96 C3
Merton SW20 ... 179 B1
Hadleigh Ct 8 E4 ... 20 C4
Hadleigh Ho 16 E1 ... 96 C3
Hadleigh Lo 5 IG8 ... 37 A4
Hadleigh Rd N9 ... 18 B4
Hadleigh St E2 ... 96 C4
Hadleigh Wlk 1 E6 ... 100 A1
HADLEY ... 1 B2
Hadley Cl
Borehamwood WD6 ... 10 B5
Southgate N21 ... 16 C5
Hadley Ct 1 London N3 ... 29 D3
Stamford Hill N16 ... 52 A1
Hadley Gdns
Chiswick W4 ... 111 B1
Southall UB2 ... 107 B1
Hadley Gn EN5 ... 1 B3
Hadley Gn W EN5 ... 1 B3
Hadley Gr EN5 ... 1 A3
Hadley Green Rd EN5 ... 1 B3
Hadley Hall N21 ... 16 C3
Hadley Highstone EN5 ... 1 B4
Hadley Ho BR5 ... 189 D1
Hadley Hts EN5 ... 1 D3
Hadley Rd Barnet EN5 ... 1 D2
Belvedere DA17 ... 125 B2
Enfield EN2 ... 4 A5
Mitcham CR4 ... 203 D5
Hadley Ridge EN5 ... 1 B2
Hadley St NW1 ... 71 B2
Hadleyvale Ct EN5 ... 1 D2
Hadley View 9 EN5 ... 1 D1
Hadley Way N21 ... 16 C5
HADLEY WOOD ... 2 B5
Hadley Wood Prim Sch
EN4 ... 2 A5
Hadley Wood Rd
Barnet EN4 ... 2 A3
Barnet EN5 ... 1 C3
Hadley Wood Sta EN4 ... 2 A5
Hadlow Coll (Mottingham
Ctr) SE12 ... 165 C3
Hadlow Coll Nature
Reserve* SE12 ... 165 C3
Hadlow Ho SE17 ... 263 B2
Hadlow Pl SE19 ... 184 A3
Hadlow Rd
Bexley DA16 ... 146 C5
Sidcup DA14 ... 190 A6
Hadrian Cl
5 Old Ford E3 ... 97 C6
Stanwell TW19 ... 148 A4
Hadrian Ct Barnet EN5 ... 1 D1
11 Belmont SM2 ... 217 D1
Brockley SE4 ... 141 C2
Hadrian Est 33 E2 ... 96 A5
Hadrian's Ride EN1 ... 17 D6
Hadrian St SE10 ... 120 C1
Hadrian Way TW19 ... 148 A4
Hadstock Ho NW1 ... 232 D2
Hadyn Park Ct 13
W12 ... 112 A4
Hadyn Park Rd W12 ... 112 A4
Hafer Rd SW11 ... 136 D1
Hafton Rd SE6 ... 164 C2
Haggard Rd TW1 ... 153 B4
Hagger Ct E17 ... 54 B6
HAGGERSTON ... 95 D5
Haggerston Rd E8 ... 95 D6
Haggerston Sch E2 ... 95 D5
Haggerston Studios 30
E8 ... 95 D6
Hague Prim Sch E2 ... 96 B3
Hague St 30 E2 ... 96 A4
Ha-Ha Rd SE7, SE18 ... 144 B6
Haig Ct BR7 ... 188 D5
Haig Ho 4 E2 ... 96 A5
Haig Pl SM4 ... 201 C3
Haig Rd Hillingdon UB8 ... 83 A2
Stanmore HA7 ... 25 C5
Haig Rd E E13 ... 99 C5
Haig Rd W E13 ... 99 C4
Haigville Gdns IG6 ... 56 D5
Hailes Cl SW19 ... 180 A4
Haileybury Ave EN1 ... 17 D5
Hailey Rd DA18 ... 125 C4
Hailey Rd Bsns Pk
DA18 ... 125 C4
Hailing Mews BR2 ... 209 B6
Hailsham Ave SW2 ... 160 B2
Hailsham Cl KT6 ... 197 D2
Hailsham Dr HA1 ... 42 B6
Hailsham Rd SW17 ... 181 A4
Hailsham Terr N18 ... 33 B5
Haimo Prim Sch SE9 ... 165 D6
Haimo Rd SE9 ... 165 D6
Hainault Bldgs E10 ... 54 A1
Hainault Bridge Par 5
IG1 ... 78 D6
Hainault Ct E17 ... 54 B5
Hainault Gore RM6 ... 59 A4
Hainault Rd
Dagenham RM6 ... 59 B3
Ilford RM6 ... 58 B6
Leytonstone E11 ... 54 B2
Hainault St Ilford IG1 ... 78 D6
New Eltham SE9 ... 166 D3
Haines Wlk SM4 ... 201 D2
Hainford Cl SE4 ... 140 D1
Haining Cl 3 W4 ... 110 C1
Hainthorpe Rd SE27 ... 182 D6
Hainton Cl E1 ... 96 B1
Halberd Mews E5 ... 74 B6
Halbutt Gdns RM9 ... 81 B5
Halbutt St RM9 ... 81 B4
Halcomb St N1 ... 95 C6
Halcot Ave DA6 ... 169 D6
Halcroft Ct SM1 ... 218 B4
Halcrow St E1 ... 96 B2
Halcyon Ho 8 EN1 ... 17 C6
Halcyon Wharf 19 E1 ... 118 A5
Haldane Cl
Holdbrook EN3 ... 7 D5
Muswell Hill N10 ... 31 B3
Haldane Pl SW18 ... 157 D3
Haldane Rd
Fulham SW6 ... 135 B6 264 D5
Newham E6 ... 100 A4
Southall UB1 ... 86 A1
Thamesmead SE28 ... 124 D6
Haldan Rd E4 ... 36 A4
Haldon Rd SW18 ... 157 B5
Hale Cl Chingford E4 ... 20 A1
Edgware HA8 ... 27 A5
Orpington BR6 ... 227 A4
Hale Ct HA8 ... 27 A5
Hale Dr NW7 ... 27 B4
HALE END ... 36 C4
Hale End Cl HA4 ... 40 A3
Hale End Rd E17 ... 36 B2
Halefield Rd N17 ... 34 B2
Hale Gdns Acton W3 ... 110 C5
Tottenham Hale N17 ... 52 A6
Hale Grove Gdns NW7 ... 27 C5
Hale Ho Enfield EN3 ... 6 D6
Westminster SW1 ... 259 D2
Hale La NW7, HA8 ... 27 B5
Hale Lo HA1 ... 42 C2
Hale Rd Newham E6 ... 100 A3
Tottenham Hale N17 ... 52 A6
Hales Ct 6 TW11 ... 175 A5
Hales Ho 3 SW12 ... 159 B4
Halesowen Rd SM4 ... 201 D2
Hales Prior N1 ... 233 C3
Hales St SE8 ... 141 C5
Hale St E14 ... 119 D6
Halesworth Cl 3 E5 ... 74 C6
Halesworth Rd SE13 ... 141 D2
Hale The Chingford E4 ... 36 B3
Tottenham Hale N17 ... 52 A6
Hale Wlk W7 ... 86 C2
Haley Rd NW4 ... 46 C3
Halfacre 2 HA7 ... 25 C5
Half Acre
Brentford TW8 ... 131 D6
2 Wanstead E18 ... 55 A6
Half Acre Mews TW8 ... 131 D6
Half Acre Rd W7 ... 108 C5
Half Moon Cres N1 ... 233 D4
Half Moon Ct EC1 ... 242 A3
Half Moon La SE24 ... 161 A5
Halfmoon Pas E1 ... 243 D1
Half Moon St
W1 ... 115 B5 248 D3
Halford Cl HA8 ... 26 D1
Halford Ct KT9 ... 214 A1
Halford Ho 9 SW15 ... 156 D6
Halford Rd
Ickenham UB10 ... 60 C3
Leyton E10 ... 54 B4
Richmond TW10 ... 154 A6
West Brompton
SW6 ... 135 C6 265 A5
Halfway St DA15 ... 167 C3
Haliburton Rd TW1,
TW7 ... 131 A1
Haliday Ho N1 ... 73 B2
Haliday Wlk 4 N1 ... 73 B2
Halidon Cl E9 ... 74 C3
Halifax 8 NW9 ... 27 D1
Halifax Cl TW11 ... 174 C4
Halifax Rd Enfield EN2 ... 5 B3
Greenford UB6 ... 85 D6
Halifax St SE26 ... 162 B1
Halifield Dr DA17 ... 125 A3
Haling Gr CR2 ... 221 A1
Haling Manor High Sch
CR2 ... 220 D1
Haling Park Gdns
CR2 ... 220 D2
Haling Park Rd
Croydon CR2 ... 220 D3
South Croydon CR2 ... 221 A2
Haling Rd CR2 ... 221 B2
Haliwel Ho 10 NW6 ... 91 D6
Halkett Ho 1 E2 ... 96 C6
Halkin Arc
SW1 ... 114 D3 257 D6
Halkin Mews SW1 ... 258 A6
Halkin Pl SW1 ... 258 A6
Halkin St SW1 ... 115 A4 248 B1
Hallam Cl BR7 ... 188 B5
Hallam Ct W1 ... 238 D4
Hallam Gdns HA5 ... 23 A3
Hallam Ho
17 London SW9 ... 138 C4
Pimlico SW1 ... 259 B1
Hallam Mews W1 ... 238 D4
Hallam Rd
Barnes SW13 ... 134 B2
Harringay N15 ... 50 D5
Hallam St W1 ... 93 B2 238 D4
Hallane Ho SE27 ... 183 A5
Hall Cl W5 ... 88 A2
Hall Ct TW11 ... 174 D5
Hall Dr Ealing W7 ... 86 C1
Forest Hill SE26 ... 184 C5
Halley Gdns SE13 ... 142 B1
Halley Ho
16 Bethnal Green E2 ... 96 A5
8 Cubitt Town SE10 ... 120 D1
Halley Prim Sch E14 ... 97 A2
Halley Rd E7, E12 ... 77 D2
Halley St E14 ... 97 A2
Hall Farm Cl HA7 ... 25 B6
Hall Farm Dr TW2 ... 152 B4
Hallfield Jun & Inf Schs
W2 ... 91 D1
Hallgate SE3 ... 143 A2
Hall Gate NW8 ... 92 A4 229 B2
Hall Gdns E4 ... 35 B6
Halliards The KT12 ... 194 A3
Halliday Ho 40 E1 ... 96 A1
Halliday Sq UB2 ... 108 B5
Halliford Cl TW17 ... 193 C6
Halliford Rd
Sunbury TW16 ... 194 A5
Upper Halliford TW16,
TW17 ... 193 D5
Halliford Sch TW17 ... 193 A2
Halliford St N1 ... 73 B1
Hallingbury Ct 1 E17 ... 55 D6
Halling Ho SE1 ... 252 D1
Hallings Wharf Studios 2
E15 ... 98 B6
Halliwell Ct 4 SE22 ... 162 A6
Halliwell Rd SW2 ... 160 B5
Halliwick Court Par 2
N12 ... 30 D5
Halliwick Ct 1 N12 ... 30 D5
Halliwick Ho N21 ... 17 B5
Halliwick Rd N10 ... 31 A2

Hall La
Chingford Hatch E4 . . . . . . .35 B5
Harlington UB3 . . . . .127 B5
Hendon NW4 . . . . .28 A1
Hall Lane E4 . . . . .35 A5
Hallmark Trad Ctr HA9 . .67 A4
Hallmead Rd SM1 . . . . . .217 D5
Hall Oak Wlk NW6 . . . . . .69 B2
Hallowell Ave CR0 . . . . . .220 A4
Hallowell Cl CR4 . . . . . . .203 A6
Hallowfield Way CR4 . . . .202 C6
Hallows Gr TW16 . . . . . . .171 D5
Hall Pl W2 . . . . .92 B3 236 C5
Hall Rd Dagenham RM6 . . .58 D3
Isleworth TW7 . . . . .152 B6
Leyton E15 . . . . .76 B4
Newham E6 . . . . .100 B6
St John's Wood
NW8 . . . . .92 A4 229 B2
Halls Bsns Ctr UB3 . . . . .106 A3
Hall Sch SW20 . . . . .178 D2
Hall Sch The NW3 . . . . . . .70 B2
Hall Sch Wimbledon
SW19 . . . . .156 A1
Hall St
Finsbury EC1 . . . .94 C4 234 D2
North Finchley N12 . . . . . .30 A5
Halls Terr UB10 . . . . .82 B2
Hallside Rd EN1 . . . . .5 D5
Hallsville Prim Sch E16 . .99 A1
Hallsville Rd E16 . . . . .98 D1
Hallswelle Par 11
NW11 . . . . .47 B4
Hallswelle Rd NW11 . . . . .47 B4
Hall The SE3 . . . . .143 A2
Hall Twr W2 . . . . .236 D4
Hall View SE9 . . . . .165 D2
Hallywell Cres E6 . . . . . . .100 B2
Halons Rd SE9 . . . . .166 C4
Halpin Pl SE17 . .117 B2 262 D3
Halsbrook Rd SE3 . . . . . .143 D2
Halsbury Cl HA7 . . . . .25 B6
Halsbury Ct HA7 . . . . .25 B6
Halsbury Ho 4 N7 . . . . . . .72 B4
Halsbury Rd W12 . . . . . . .112 B5
Halsbury Rd E UB5 . . . . . .64 A4
Halsbury Rd W UB5 . . . . . .63 D3
Halsend UB3 . . . . .106 B5
Halsey St SW3 . .114 D2 257 C4
Halsham Cres IG11 . . . . . .79 D3
Halsmere Rd SE5 . . . . . . .138 D4
Halstead Cl 2 CR0 . . . . . .221 A5
Halstead Ct
Shoreditch N1 . . . . .235 D3
Walthamstow E17 . . . . . . .53 B2
Halstead Gdns N21 . . . . . .17 B3
Halstead Rd
Edmonton N21 . . . . .17 B3
Enfield EN1 . . . . .5 C1
Wanstead E11 . . . . .55 B4
Halston Cl SW11 . . . . . . .158 D5
Halstow 12 NW5 . . . . .71 A2
Halstow Prim Sch
SE10 . . . . .121 A1
Halstow Rd
Greenwich SE3, SE10 . . .121 A1
Kensal Green NW10 . . . . . .90 D4
Halsway UB3 . . . . .106 A5
Halter Cl WD6 . . . . .11 B6
Halton Cl N11 . . . . .30 D4
Halton Cross St
N1 . . . . .94 D6 234 D6
Haltone Ho 1 SW4 . . . . .137 D3
Halton Ho 22 N1 . . . . .72 D1
Halton Mans N1 . . . . .72 D1
Halton Pl N1 . . . . .235 A6
Halton Rd N1 . . . .94 D6 234 D6
Halt Robin La DA17 . . . . .125 D2
Halt Robin Rd DA17 . . . . .125 D2
Halyard Ho E14 . . . . .120 A3
HAM 153 C1
Hamara Ghar 4 E13 . . . . .99 C6
Hambalt Rd SW4 . . . . . . .159 C6
Hamble Cl HA4 . . . . .61 C6
Hamble Ct KT1 . . . . .175 D3
Hambledon SE17 . . . . . . .139 B6
Hambledon Chase N4 . . . . .50 A2
Hambledon Cl UB8 . . . . . .82 D3
Hambledon Ct
5 Ealing W5 . . . . .110 A6
9 Wallington SM6 . . . . . .219 B2
Hambledon Gdns
SE25 . . . . .205 D6
Hambledon Ho
2 Kingston u T KT2 . . . . .176 D4
Lower Clapton E5 . . . . . . .74 B4
Hambledon Pl SE21 . . . . .161 D3
Hambledon Rd SW18 . . . .157 B4
Hambledown Rd
DA15 . . . . .167 C4
Hamble St SW6 . . . . .135 D2
Hambleton Cl KT4 . . . . . .216 C6
Hamble Wlk UB5 . . . . .85 C5
Hambley Ho 5 SE16 . . . . .118 B2
Hamblin Ho UB1 . . . . .107 A6
Hambly Mans SW16 . . . . .182 A4
Hamblyn Ct N16 . . . . .51 D2
Hambridge Way SW2 . . . .160 C4
Hambro Ave BR2 . . . . . . .209 A4
Hambrook Ct 12 NW5 . . . . .71 B4
Hambrook Rd SE25 . . . . . .206 B6
Hambro Rd SW16 . . . . . . .181 D5
Hambrough Ho 4 UB4 . . . .84 C2
Hambrough Prim Sch
UB1 . . . . .107 B5
Hambrough Rd UB1 . . . . . .107 A5
Ham Cl TW10 . . . . .153 C1
Ham Comm TW10 . . . . . .153 D1
Ham Croft Cl TW13 . . . . .150 A1
Ham Ct 12 NW9 . . . . .27 D1

Hamden Cres RM10 . . . . . .81 D5
Hamel Cl HA3 . . . . .43 D5
Hamers Ho 15 SW2 . . . . .160 C4
Hameway E6 . . . . .100 C4
Ham Farm Rd KT2,
TW10 . . . . .176 A6
Hamfrith Rd E15 . . . . .76 D2
Ham Gate Ave TW10 . . . .176 A6
Ham Ho* TW10 . . . . .153 C2
Hamilton Ave
Cheam SM3 . . . . .217 A6
Edmonton N9 . . . . .18 A4
Ilford IG6 . . . . .57 A4
Tolworth KT6, SM3 . . . . .214 C6
Hamilton Cl
Ashford TW13 . . . . .171 D5
Cockfosters EN4 . . . . .2 D1
Rotherhithe SE16 . . . . . .119 A4
St John's Wood
NW8 . . . . .92 B4 229 C1
Teddington TW11 . . . . . .175 B4
Tottenham N17 . . . . .51 D6
Hamilton Cres
Edmonton N13 . . . . .32 C6
Harrow HA2 . . . . .63 B5
Hounslow TW3 . . . . .151 D6
Hamilton Ct
9 Catford SE6 . . . . .164 D3
Croydon CR0 . . . . .206 A1
Ealing W5 . . . . .110 B6
St John's Wood W9 . . . . .229 A2
Hamilton Gdns
NW8 . . . . .92 A4 229 B2
Hamilton Hall
NW8 . . . . .92 A5 229 A3
Hamilton Ho 28 Bow E3 . . .97 B4
Chiswick W4 . . . . .133 C6
Kensington W8 . . . . .245 C2
Oakleigh Pk N20 . . . . .14 A4
1 Poplar E14 . . . . .119 B6
Putney SW15 . . . . .156 A6
10 Richmond TW9 . . . . . .132 C4
St John's Wood NW8 . . . .229 C2
Hamilton La N5 . . . . .72 C3
Hamilton Lo 7 E1 . . . . . . .96 C3
Hamilton Mews W1 . . . . .248 C2
Hamilton Par TW14 . . . . .172 A6
Hamilton Pk N5 . . . . .72 C3
Hamilton Pk W N5 . . . . . . .72 C3
Hamilton Pl
Mayfair W1 . . . .115 A5 248 B5
Sunbury TW16 . . . . .172 B3
Tottenham N17 . . . . .33 D1
Hamilton Rd Acton W4 . . .111 C4
Barnet EN4 . . . . .2 C1
Bexleyheath DA7 . . . . . . .147 A3
Brentford TW8 . . . . .131 D6
Ealing W5 . . . . .110 A6
East Finchley N2 . . . . .48 A6
Edmonton N9 . . . . .18 A4
Feltham TW13 . . . . .171 D6
Harrow HA1 . . . . .42 C4
Hayes UB3 . . . . .106 B6
Hendon NW11 . . . . .47 A2
Higham Hill E17 . . . . .35 A1
Ilford IG1 . . . . .78 D4
Merton SW19 . . . . .179 D5
Newham E15 . . . . .98 C4
Sidcup DA15 . . . . .190 A6
South Norwood CR7 . . . . .205 B6
West Norwood SE27 . . . . .183 B6
Willesden NW10 . . . . .68 A3
Hamilton Road Ind Est
SE27 . . . . .183 B6
Hamilton Road Mews 11
SW19 . . . . .179 D3
Hamilton Sq
Bermondsey SE1 . . . . . . .252 C2
Finchley N12 . . . . .30 A4
Hamilton St SE8 . . . . .141 C6
Hamilton Terr
NW8 . . . . .92 A4 229 B2
Hamilton Way
Edmonton N13 . . . . .32 D6
Finchley N3 . . . . .29 C4
Hamlea Cl SE12 . . . . .165 A6
Hamlet Cl SE13 . . . . .142 C1
Hamlet Ct
14 Enfield EN1 . . . . .17 C6
1 Hammersmith W6 . . . . .112 A2
Kennington SE11 . . . . . . .261 C2
Hamlet Gdns W6 . . . . .112 A2
Hamlet Ho SE9 . . . . .166 C6
Hamlet Ind Est 9 E5 . . . . .75 C1
Hamleton Terr RM9 . . . . . .80 C1
Hamlet Rd SE19 . . . . .184 A3
Hamlet Sq NW2 . . . . .69 A5
Hamlets The SE5 . . . . . . .139 B2
Hamlet Way SE1 . . . . . . .252 D2
Hamlin Cres HA5 . . . . .40 C4
Hamlyn Cl HA8 . . . . .10 A1
Hamlyn Gdns SE19 . . . . .183 C3
Hamlyn Ho TW13 . . . . . . .150 A3
Hammelton Ct 4 BR1 . . . .186 D2
Hammelton Gn 2
SW9 . . . . .138 C4
Hammelton Rd BR1 . . . . .187 A2
Hammers La NW7 . . . . . . .28 A4
Hammersley Ho 8
SE14 . . . . .140 C5
HAMMERSMITH 112 C2
Hammersmith Bridge Rd
W6, SW13 . . . . .112 C1
Hammersmith Broadway
W6 . . . . .112 C2
Hammersmith W6 . . . . . .112 C1
5 Hammersmith W6 . . . . .112 C2

Hammersmith Flyover
W6 . . . . .112 C1
Hammersmith Hospl
W12 . . . . .90 B1
Hammersmith Rd
Hammersmith W6 . . . . . .112 D2
Kensington W14 . . . . . . .254 B4
Hammersmith Sta
W6 . . . . .112 C2
Hammersmith Terr 6
W6 . . . . .112 A1
Hammet Cl UB4 . . . . .84 D2
Hammett St EC3 . . . . . . .253 C6
Hammond Ave CR4 . . . . . .181 B1
Hammond Cl
Barnet EN5 . . . . .13 B6
Greenford UB6 . . . . .64 B3
Hampton TW12 . . . . .173 C2
Hammond Ct
1 Leyton E10 . . . . .75 D6
1 Walthamstow E17 . . . . .53 A4
Hammond Ho
10 Deptford SE14 . . . . . .140 C5
Millwall E14 . . . . .119 D3
Hammond Lo 6 W9 . . . . . .91 C2
Hammond Rd Enfield EN1 . .6 B3
Southall UB2 . . . . .107 A3
Hammonds Cl RM8 . . . . . .60 B5
Hammonds Ho TW19 . . . .148 B3
Hammond St NW5 . . . . . . .71 C2
Hammond Way 2
SE28 . . . . .124 B6
Hamonde Cl HA8 . . . . .10 D2
Hamond Sq N1 . . . . .95 C5
Ham Park Rd E15 . . . . .76 D1
Hampden Ave BR3 . . . . . .185 A1
Hampden Cl NW1 . . . . . . .232 D4
Hampden Ct
Harrow HA1 . . . . .42 C6
10 Muswell Hill N10 . . . . .31 A3
Hampden Gurney CE Prim
Sch W1 . . . . . . .92 C1 237 B2
Hampden Gurney St
W1 . . . . .237 C1
Hampden La N17 . . . . .34 A2
Hampden Rd
Beckenham BR3 . . . . . . .185 A1
Harrow HA3 . . . . .24 A1
Hornsey N8 . . . . .50 C5
Kingston u T KT1 . . . . . .198 C6
Muswell Hill N10 . . . . . . .31 A3
Tottenham N17 . . . . .34 A2
Upper Holloway N19 . . . . .71 D6
Hampden Sq N14 . . . . . . .15 B3
Hampden Way N14 . . . . . .15 B2
Hampshire Cl N18 . . . . . . .34 B1
Hampshire Ct
6 Barnes SW13 . . . . . . .133 D3
Hendon NW4 . . . . .46 D4
Hampshire Ho HA8 . . . . . .26 B3
Hampshire Hog La
3 Hammersmith W6 . . . . .112 B1
11 Hammersmith W6 . . . .112 B2
Hampshire Rd N22 . . . . . . .32 B3
Hampshire Sch The
SW7 . . . . .114 C4 247 A1
Hampshire St NW5 . . . . . .71 D2
Hampson Way
SW8 . . . . .138 B4 270 C2
HAMPSTEAD 70 B3
Hampstead Cl SE28 . . . . .124 B5
Hampstead Coll of Fine
Arts & Humanities
NW3 . . . . .70 C2
HAMPSTEAD GARDEN
SUBURB 47 D4
Hampstead Garden
Suburb Inst NW11 . . . . . .47 D4
Hampstead Gate NW3 . . . .70 A3
Hampstead Gdns NW11 . . .47 C3
Hampstead Gn NW3 . . . . . .70 C3
Hampstead Gr NW3 . . . . . .70 A5
Hampstead Heath* NW3 . . .70 B6
Hampstead Heath Sta
NW3 . . . . .70 C4
Hampstead High St
NW3 . . . . .70 B4
Hampstead Hill Gdns
NW3 . . . . .70 C4
Hampstead Hill Sch
NW3 . . . . .70 C3
Hampstead Hts N2 . . . . . . .48 A6
Hampstead La N6 . . . . .48 C5
Hampstead Parochial CE
Prim Sch NW3 . . . . .70 A4
Hampstead Rd
NW1 . . . . .93 C4 232 A2
Hampstead Sch NW2 . . . . .69 A4
Hampstead Sq 1 NW3 . . . .70 A5
Hampstead Way NW11 . . . .47 A3
Hampstead West 4
NW6 . . . . .69 C2
Hampstead Wlk 1 E3 . . . . .97 B6
HAMPTON 173 C1
Hampton Cl
Borehamwood WD6 . . . . . .11 A6
Friern Barnet N11 . . . . . . .31 B5
Kilburn NW6 . . . . .91 C4
Wimbledon SW20 . . . . . .178 D3
Hampton Com Coll
TW12 . . . . .173 C1
Hampton Court Ave
KT8 . . . . .196 C4
Hampton Court Cres
KT8 . . . . .196 B6
Hampton Court Landing
Stage KT8 . . . . .196 D4

Hampton Court Pal*
KT8 . . . . .196 D6
Hampton Court Par
KT8 . . . . .196 C5
Hampton Court Rd KT1,
KT8 . . . . .197 B6
Hampton Court Sta
KT8 . . . . .254 B4
Hampton Court Way KT10,
KT7, KT8 . . . . .196 C5
Hampton Ct
Hampton KT8 . . . . .196 C6
5 Islington N1 . . . . .72 D2
19 Rotherhithe SE16 . . . .118 D5
Wood Green N22 . . . . .31 C2
Hampton Farm Ind Est
TW13 . . . . .151 A1
HAMPTON HILL 174 A5
Hampton Hill Bsns Pk
TW12 . . . . .174 A4
Hampton Hill Jun Sch
TW12 . . . . .174 A5
Hampton Ho DA7 . . . . . . .147 D3
Hampton Inf Sch
TW12 . . . . .173 C3
Hampton Jun Sch
TW12 . . . . .173 C3
Hampton La TW13 . . . . . .173 A6
Hampton Rd
Chingford Hatch E4 . . . . . .35 B5
Forest Gate E7 . . . . .77 C3
Ilford IG1 . . . . .79 A4
Leytonstone E11 . . . . .54 B1
North Cheam KT4 . . . . . .216 B6
Teddington TW11,
TW12 . . . . .174 C5
Thornton Heath CR0 . . . . .205 A3
Twickenham TW2 . . . . . . .152 B1
Hampton Rd E TW13 . . . . .151 B1
Hampton Rd W TW13 . . . .151 A1
Hampton Rise HA3 . . . . . . .44 A3
Hampton Road Ind Pk
CR0 . . . . .205 A3
Hampton Sch TW12 . . . . .173 C5
Hampton St
SE1 . . . . .116 D2 261 D3
Hampton Sta TW12 . . . . .173 C2
HAMPTON WICK 175 D3
Hampton Wick Inf Sch
TW11 . . . . .175 D3
Hampton Wick Sta
KT1 . . . . .175 C2
Ham Ridings TW10 . . . . . .176 B5
Ham Shades Cl 1
DA15 . . . . .168 A1
Hamson Ct HA2 . . . . .64 B6
Ham St TW10 . . . . .153 C1
Hamstead Gates 11
NW5 . . . . .71 B2
Ham The TW8 . . . . .131 C5
Ham View CR0 . . . . .207 A3
Ham Yd W1 . . . . .249 C6
Hanameel St E16 . . . . . . .121 B5
Hana Mews E5 . . . . .74 B4
Hanbury Cl NW4 . . . . .46 C6
Hanbury Ct HA1 . . . . .42 D3
Hanbury Dr
2 Leyton E11 . . . . .54 D2
Southgate N21 . . . . .16 B3
Hanbury Ho
8 Bethnal Green E1 . . . . .96 A2
South Lambeth SW8 . . . .270 B5
Hanbury Mews N1 . . . . . .235 B3
Hanbury Rd
South Acton W3 . . . . .110 D4
Tottenham N17 . . . . .34 B1
Hanbury St E1 . . .95 D2 243 D4
Hancock Ho 4 E17 . . . . . .53 D6
Hancock Nunn Ho 1
NW3 . . . . .70 D1
Hancock Rd Bromley E3 . . .98 A4
South Norwood SE19 . . . .183 B4
Handa Wlk 3 N1 . . . . .73 A2
Handcroft Rd CR0 . . . . . .204 D1
Hand Ct WC1 . . . . .240 D3
Handel Cl HA8 . . . . .26 A4
Handel Ho TW2 . . . . .152 B6
Handel Mans
Barnes SW13 . . . . .134 C5
Bloomsbury WC1 . . . . . . .240 B6
Handel Par HA8 . . . . .26 C3
Handel Pl NW10 . . . . .67 B2
Handel St WC1 . .94 A3 240 B6
Handel Way HA8 . . . . .26 C3
Handen Rd SE12 . . . . .164 D6
Handforth Rd
Brixton SW9 . . . . .138 C5
6 Ilford IG1 . . . . .78 D5
Handley Gr NW2 . . . . .69 D5
Handley Page Rd SM6 . . .220 B1
Handley Rd E9 . . . . .96 C6
Handowe Cl NW4 . . . . .46 A5
Handside Cl KT4 . . . . .200 D1
Hands Wlk E16 . . . . .99 A1
Handsworth Ave E4 . . . . . .36 B4
Handsworth Prim Sch
E4 . . . . .36 B4
Handsworth Rd N17 . . . . . .51 B6
Handtrough Way
IG11 . . . . .100 D5
Hanford Cl SW18 . . . . . . .157 C3
Hanford Row SW19 . . . . .178 C4
Hanger Gn W5 . . . . .88 C1
Hanger La (North Circular
Rd) W5 . . . . .88 B2
Hanger Vale La W5 . . . . . .88 B1
Hanger View Way W3 . . . . .88 C2
Hangmans Cnr BR7 . . . . .188 D2

Hankey Pl SE1 . .117 B4 252 D1
Hankins La NW7 . . . . .11 C1
Hanley Ct N4 . . . . .50 B1
Hanley Gdns N4 . . . . .50 B1
Hanley Pl BR3 . . . . .185 C3
Hanley Rd N4, N19 . . . . . .50 A1
Hanmer Wlk N7 . . . . .72 B6
Hannah Cl
Beckenham BR3 . . . . . . .208 A6
Wembley NW10 . . . . .67 A4
Hannah Ct
Palmers Green N13 . . . . . .16 B3
5 Sutton SM1 . . . . .217 D2
Wimbledon SW19 . . . . . .178 B3
Hannah Mary Way 17
SE1 . . . . .118 A2
Hannah Mews SM6 . . . . .219 C1
Hannay La N8 . . . . .49 D2
Hannay Wlk SW16 . . . . . .159 D2
Hannell Rd
SW6 . . . . .135 A5 264 B4
Hannen Ho SE5 . . . . .139 B2
Hannen Rd SE27 . . . . . . .160 D1
Hannibal Rd
Stanwell TW19 . . . . .148 A4
Stepney E1 . . . . .96 C2
Hannibal Way CR0 . . . . . .220 B2
Hanning Lo TW3 . . . . .130 A1
Hannington Rd SW4 . . . . .137 B2
Hanover Ave
Feltham TW13 . . . . .150 A2
Newham E16 . . . . .121 A5
Hanover Circ UB3 . . . . . . .83 B1
Hanover Cl Cheam SM3 . . .217 B4
Richmond TW9 . . . . .132 C5
Hanover Ct
Colindale NW9 . . . . .45 C6
Harrow HA1 . . . . .42 B2
1 Penge SE19 . . . . .184 A3
11 Pinner HA5 . . . . .23 B3
Shepherd's Bush W12 . . . .112 A5
Stamford Hill N16 . . . . . . .51 D2
Hanover Dr BR7 . . . . .189 A6
Hanover Gate Mans
NW1 . . . . .237 B6
Hanover Gdns SE11 . . . . .138 C6
Hanover Ho
1 New Barnet EN5 . . . . . .2 A1
St John's Wood NW8 . . . .230 A3
Tolworth KT6 . . . . .198 C1
Hanover Lo N21 . . . . .16 D6
Hanover Mans 5
SW2 . . . . .160 C6
Hanover Mead NW11 . . . . .47 A3
Hanover Pk SE15 . . . . . . .140 A4
Hanover Pl 16 Bow E3 . . . .97 B4
St Giles WC2 . . . . .240 B1
Hanover Prim Sch
N1 . . . . .95 A5 235 A4
Hanover Rd
Merton SW19 . . . . .180 A3
South Tottenham N15 . . . . .51 D5
Willesden NW10 . . . . .90 C6
Hanover Sq W1 . . .93 B1 238 D1
Hanover St
Croydon CR0 . . . . .220 D5
Marylebone W1 . .93 B1 238 D1
Hanover Stps W2 . . . . . . .237 B1
Hanover Terr
Isleworth TW7 . . . . .131 A4
Lisson Gr NW1 . .92 C4 230 C1
Hanover Terrace Mews
NW1 . . . . .92 C4 230 B1
Hanover Way DA6 . . . . . . .146 D2
Hanover West Ind Est
NW10 . . . . .89 B4
Hansard Mews W14 . . . . .112 D4
Hansart Way EN2 . . . . .4 C1
Hanscomb Mews
SW4 . . . . .137 C1
Hans Cres
SW1 . . . . .114 D3 257 C5
Hanselin Cl HA7 . . . . .24 D5
Hansen Dr N21 . . . . .16 B6
Hanshaw Dr HA8 . . . . .27 B2
Hansler Ct 14 SW19 . . . . .157 A3
Hansler Gr KT8 . . . . .196 B5
Hansler Rd SE22 . . . . .161 D6
Hansol Rd DA6 . . . . .169 A6
Hanson Cl
Balham SW12 . . . . .159 B4
Beckenham BR3 . . . . . . .185 C5
Mortlake SW14 . . . . .133 A2
West Drayton UB7 . . . . . .104 B3
Hanson Ct E17 . . . . .53 D3
Hanson Gdns UB1 . . . . . . .107 A4
Hanson Ho 2 E1 . . . . . . .118 A6
Hanson St W1 . . .93 C2 239 A4
Hans Pl SW1 . . .114 D3 257 C5
Hans Rd SW3 . . .114 D3 257 C6
Hans St SW1 . . .114 D3 257 D5
Hanway Ho 25 SW9 . . . . .138 C4
Hanway Pl W1 . . . . .239 C2
Hanway Rd W7 . . . . .86 C1
Hanway St W1 . . . . .239 C2
HANWELL 108 D5
Hanwell Sta W7 . . . . .108 C6
HANWORTH 172 D6
Hanworth Ho SE5 . . . . . . .138 C5
Hanworth Rd
Ashford TW16 . . . . .172 A3
Feltham TW13 . . . . .150 B3
Hampton TW12 . . . . .173 C3
Hounslow TW3, TW4 . . . .129 D1
Twickenham TW4 . . . . . .151 B4
Hanworth Terr TW3 . . . . .129 D1
Hanworth Trad Est
TW13 . . . . .151 A1
Hapgood Cl UB6 . . . . .64 B3

Harben Rd NW6 . . . . .70 A1
Harberson Rd
Balham SW12 . . . . .159 B3
West Ham E15 . . . . .98 D6
Harberton Rd N19 . . . . . . .49 C1
Harbet Rd
Highams Pk N18 . . . . .35 A4
Paddington W2 . .92 B2 236 D3
Harbex Cl DA5 . . . . .169 D4
Harbinger Prim Sch
E14 . . . . .119 D2
Harbinger Rd E14 . . . . . . .119 D2
Harbin Ho 5 SW2 . . . . . . .160 C3
Harbledown Ho SE1 . . . . .252 C1
Harbledown Rd SW6 . . . . .265 A2
Harbord Cl SE5 . . . . .139 B3
Harbord Ho 5 SE16 . . . . .118 D2
Harbord St SW6 . . . . .134 D4
Harborne Cl WD19 . . . . . . .22 C5
Harborough Ave
DA15 . . . . .167 D4
Harborough Rd SW16 . . . .182 B6
Harborough Sch N19 . . . . .71 D1
Harbour Ave
SW10 . . . . .136 A4 266 B1
Harbour Exchange Sq
E14 . . . . .119 D4
Harbour Rd SE5 . . . . .139 A2
Harbridge Ave SW15 . . . . .156 A4
Harbury Rd SM5 . . . . .218 C1
Harbut Rd SW11 . . . . .136 B1
Harcombe Rd N16 . . . . . . .73 C5
Harcourt Ave
Edgware HA8 . . . . .11 A1
Little Ilford E12 . . . . .78 B3
Sidcup DA15 . . . . .168 C4
Wallington SM6 . . . . .219 B4
Harcourt Cl TW7 . . . . .131 A2
Harcourt Field SM6 . . . . . .219 B4
Harcourt Ho
5 Chingford E4 . . . . .36 B5
27 Clapham SW8 . . . . . . .137 D3
Marylebone W1 . . . . .238 C2
4 Willesden NW10 . . . . . .68 C2
Harcourt Lo 2 SM6 . . . . . .219 B4
Harcourt Rd
Bexley DA6 . . . . .147 A1
Brockley SE4 . . . . .141 B2
Bushey WD23 . . . . .8 A6
Merton SW19 . . . . .179 C5
Thornton Heath CR7 . . . . .204 C3
Wallington SM6 . . . . .219 B4
West Ham E15 . . . . .98 D5
Wood Green N22 . . . . .31 C2
Harcourt St W1 . . .92 C2 237 B3
Harcourt Terr
SW10 . . . . .113 D1 255 D1
Hardcastle Cl SE25 . . . . . .206 A3
Hardcastle Ho
3 New Cross Gate
SE14 . . . . .141 A4
8 Peckham SE15 . . . . . .140 A4
Hardcourts Cl BR4 . . . . . .223 D5
Hard Ct IG8 . . . . .37 C4
Hardel Rise SW2 . . . . .160 D3
Hardel Wlk SE24, SW2 . . .160 C4
Harden Ct 1 SE7 . . . . . . .122 A2
Harden Ho SE5 . . . . .139 C3
Harders Rd SE15 . . . . .140 B3
Hardess St SE24 . . . . .139 A2
Hardham Ho 5 SW2 . . . . .160 C4
Hardie Cl NW10 . . . . .67 B3
Harding Cl
Camberwell SE17 . . . . . . .139 A6
South Croydon CR0 . . . . .221 D5
Harding Ct SE25 . . . . .183 D1
Hardinge Cl UB8 . . . . .82 D1
Hardinge Cres SE18 . . . . .123 A3
Hardinge Rd
Edmonton N18 . . . . .33 C4
Willesden NW10 . . . . .90 C6
Hardinge St Stepney E1 . . .96 C1
Woolwich SE18 . . . . .122 D1
Harding Ho
Barnes SW13 . . . . .134 B6
Hayes UB3 . . . . .84 B1
14 Woolwich SE18 . . . . .122 B2
Harding Pl SE23 . . . . .163 A4
Harding Rd DA7 . . . . .147 B3
Hardings Cl KT2 . . . . .176 B2
Hardings La SE20 . . . . . . .184 D4
Hardington 2 NW1 . . . . . . .71 A2
Hardman Rd
Greenwich SE7 . . . . .121 D1
Kingston u T KT2 . . . . . .176 A2
Hardwick Cl HA7 . . . . .25 C5
Hardwick Ct 8 E11 . . . . . . .55 A3
Hardwicke Ave TW5 . . . . .129 C4
Hardwicke Ho 14 E3 . . . . . .97 C4
Hardwicke Mews WC1 . . . .233 D1
Hardwicke Rd
Acton W4 . . . . .111 B2
Bowes Pk N13 . . . . .32 A4
Richmond TW10 . . . . . . .175 C6
Hardwicke St IG11 . . . . . .101 A6
Hardwick Ho
14 London SW8 . . . . . . .137 D4
Marylebone NW8 . . . . . . .237 B6
Hardwick St
EC1 . . . . .94 C4 234 B1
Hardwick's Way SW18 . . .157 C6
Hardwidge St SE1 . . . . . . .253 A2
Hardy Av
1 Newham E16 . . . . .121 A5
Ruislip HA4 . . . . .62 B3
Hardy Cl Barnet EN5 . . . . .13 A6

Hardy Cl *continued*
Pinner HA5 ... 40 D2
Rotherhithe SE16 ... 118 D4
Hardy Cotts 2 SE10 ... 142 B6
Hardy Ct
Greenwich SE3 ... 142 D6
9 Wanstead E11 ... 55 A5
Hardyng Ho 4 E17 ... 53 A5
Hardy Pas N22 ... 32 C1
Hardy Rd
Greenwich SE3 ... 142 D6
Merton SW19 ... 179 D3
Walthamstow E4 ... 35 B4
Hardys Mews KT8 ... 196 C5
Hardy Way EN2 ... 4 C4
Hare and Billet Rd
SE3 ... 142 B3
Harebell Dr E6 ... 100 C2
Harecastle Cl UB4 ... 85 A3
Harecourt Rd N1 ... 73 A2
Hare Ct EC4 ... 241 A1
Haredale Ho 23 SE16 ... 118 A4
Haredale Rd SE24 ... 139 A1
Haredon Cl SE23 ... 162 D4
Harefield KT10 ... 212 C5
Harefield Cl EN2 ... 4 C4
Harefield Ct 4 SW19 ... 179 C3
Harefield Mews SE4 ... 141 B2
Harefield Rd
Brockley SE4 ... 141 B2
Hornsey N8 ... 49 D4
Sidcup DA14 ... 168 D1
South Norwood SW16 ... 182 B3
Uxbridge UB8 ... 60 A3
Hare La KT10 ... 212 C2
Hare Marsh E2 ... 96 A3
Harenc Sch Trust
DA14 ... 190 C5
Hare Pl EC4 ... 241 B1
Hare Row E2 ... 96 B5
Haresfield Rd RM10 ... 81 C2
Hare St SE18 ... 122 C3
Harestone Ct CR2 ... 221 C2
Hare Wlk N1 ... 95 C5
Harewood Ave
Lisson Gr
NW1 ... 92 C3 237 B5
Northolt UB5 ... 63 B1
Harewood Cl UB5 ... 63 B1
Harewood Ct HA3 ... 24 C2
Harewood Pl W1 ... 238 D1
Harewood Rd
Hounslow TW7 ... 130 D4
Mitcham SW19 ... 180 C4
South Croydon CR2 ... 221 C2
Harewood Row NW1 ... 237 B4
Harewood Terr UB2 ... 107 B2
Harfield Gdns 1 SE5 ... 139 C2
Harfield Rd TW16 ... 172 D1
Harfleur Ct SE11 ... 261 C3
Harford Cl E4 ... 19 D4
Harford Ho
Camberwell SE5 ... 139 A6
Notting Hill W11 ... 91 B2
Harford Mews 6 N19 ... 71 D5
Harford Rd E4 ... 19 D4
Harford St E1 ... 97 A3
Harford Wlk N2 ... 48 B5
Hargood Cl HA3 ... 44 A3
Hargood Rd SE3 ... 143 C4
Hargrave Mans 3 N19 ... 71 D6
Hargrave Park Prim Sch
N19 ... 71 C6
Hargrave Pk N19 ... 71 C6
Hargrave Pl N7 ... 71 D3
Hargrave Rd N19 ... 71 C6
Hargraves Ho 14 W12 ... 112 B6
Hargwyne St SW9 ... 138 B2
Haringey Pk N8 ... 50 A3
Haringey Rd N8 ... 50 A5
Harington Terr N18 ... 17 B1
Harkett Cl HA3 ... 24 D1
Harkett Ct HA3 ... 24 D1
Harkness Ct SM1 ... 201 D1
Harkness Ho 30 E1 ... 96 A1
Harland Ave
Sidcup DA15 ... 167 C2
South Croydon CR0 ... 222 A5
Harland Cl SW19 ... 201 D6
Harland Rd SE12 ... 165 A3
Harlands Gr BR6 ... 226 D4
Harlech Ct 1 SE23 ... 162 C3
Harlech Gdns TW5 ... 128 C5
Harlech Rd N14 ... 16 A1
Harlech Twr 5 W3 ... 111 A4
Harlequin Ave TW8 ... 131 A6
Harlequin Cl Hayes UB4 ... 84 D2
Isleworth TW7 ... 152 C6
Harlequin Ct
Croydon CR2 ... 221 A1
Ealing W5 ... 109 C6
Willesden NW10 ... 67 B2
Harlequin Ho 1 DA18 ... 125 A3
Harlequin Rd TW11 ... 175 B3
Harlescott Rd SE15 ... 140 D1
HARLESDEN ... 89 D6
Harlesden Gdns NW10 ... 89 D6
Harlesden Plaza 2
NW10 ... 89 D5
Harlesden Prim Sch
NW10 ... 89 C5
Harlesden Rd NW10 ... 90 A6
Harlesden Sta NW10 ... 89 B5
Harleston Cl 4 E5 ... 74 C6
Harley BR7 ... 189 B2
Harley Cl HA0 ... 65 D2
Harley Cres HA1 ... 42 B5
Harley Ct Harrow HA1 ... 42 B5
Wanstead E11 ... 55 A2
Whetstone N20 ... 14 A1
Harleyford BR1 ... 187 C2
Harleyford Ct
Kennington SW8 ... 270 C6
Wembley HA0 ... 65 A4
Harleyford Manor 8
W3 ... 111 A5
Harleyford Rd
SE11 ... 138 B6 270 C6
Harleyford St SE11 ... 138 C6
Harley Gdns
Orpington BR6 ... 227 C4
South Kensington
SW10 ... 114 A1 256 B1
Harley Gr E3 ... 97 B4
Harley Ho
Leytonstone E11 ... 54 B2
Marylebone NW1 ... 238 B5
Harley Pl W1 ... 93 B2 238 C3
Harley Rd
Hampstead NW3 ... 70 B1
Harlesden NW10 ... 89 C5
Harrow HA1 ... 42 B5
Harley St W1 ... 93 B2 238 C3
Harley Villas NW10 ... 89 C5
Harling Ct 3 SW11 ... 136 D3
Harlinger St SE18 ... 122 A3
HARLINGTON ... 127 A6
Harlington Cl UB7 ... 127 A5
Harlington Cnr UB3 ... 127 B4
Harlington Com Sch
UB3 ... 105 B2
Harlington Rd
Bexley DA7 ... 147 A2
Hillingdon UB8 ... 82 C3
Harlington Rd E TW13,
TW14 ... 150 C3
Harlington Rd W
TW14 ... 150 B5
Harlowe Ho 13 E8 ... 95 D6
Harlow Mans 2 IG11 ... 78 D1
Harlow Rd N13 ... 17 B1
Harlyn Dr HA5 ... 40 B6
Harlyn Prim Sch HA5 ... 40 B6
Harlynwood 19 SE5 ... 139 A5
Harman Ave IG8 ... 36 D4
Harman Cl
10 Bermondsey SE1 ... 118 A1
Chingford E4 ... 36 B6
Cricklewood NW2 ... 69 A5
Harman Dr
Blackfen DA15 ... 167 D5
Cricklewood NW2 ... 69 A4
Harman Rd EN1 ... 17 D6
HARMONDSWORTH ... 126 A6
Harmondsworth La
UB7 ... 126 B6
Harmondsworth Rd
UB7 ... 104 A2
Harmon Ho 7 SE8 ... 119 B2
Harmony Cl NW11 ... 47 A4
Harmony Way
Bromley BR1 ... 187 A1
Hendon NW4 ... 46 C5
Harmood Gr NW1 ... 71 B1
Harmood Ho 2 NW1 ... 71 B1
Harmood St NW1 ... 71 B1
Harmsworth St
SE17 ... 116 D1 261 C1
Harmsworth Way N20 ... 13 C3
Harnage Ho TW8 ... 110 A1
Harness Rd SE28 ... 124 A4
Harney Ct SE14 ... 141 A4
Harold Ave Erith DA17 ... 125 B1
Hayes UB3 ... 105 D3
Harold Ct
14 Rotherhithe SE16 ... 118 D4
6 Teddington TW11 ... 174 C5
Harold Est SE1 ... 263 B5
Harold Gibbons Ct 12
SE7 ... 143 C6
Harold Ho 16 E2 ... 96 D5
Harold Laski Ho EC1 ... 234 D1
Harold Maddison Ho
SE17 ... 261 D2
Harold Rd Chingford E4 ... 20 A1
Hornsey N8 ... 50 B5
Leytonstone E11 ... 54 C1
Newham E13 ... 99 B6
North Acton NW10 ... 89 B4
South Norwood SE19 ... 183 B3
South Tottenham N15 ... 51 D4
Sutton SM1 ... 218 B4
Woodford IG8 ... 37 A2
Haroldstone Rd E17 ... 53 A4
Harold Wilson Ho
SW6 ... 264 D5
Haronton Ct E10 ... 76 A6
Harp Alley EC4 ... 241 C2
Harp Bsns Ctr The
NW2 ... 68 A6
Harpenden Rd
Wanstead E12 ... 77 C6
West Norwood SE27,
SW16 ... 160 D2
Harpenmead Point
NW2 ... 69 B6
Harper Cl N14 ... 15 C6
Harper Ho 3 SW9 ... 138 D2
Harper Mews SW17 ... 158 A1
Harper Rd
Bermondsey
SE1 ... 117 A3 262 B6
Newham E6 ... 100 B1
Harper's Yd N17 ... 33 D2
Harp Island Cl NW10 ... 67 B6
Harp La EC3 ... 253 A5
Harpley Sq E1 ... 96 D3
Harpour Rd IG11 ... 79 A2
Harp Rd W7 ... 86 D3
Harpsden St SW11 ... 268 A1
Harpur Mews WC1 ... 240 C4
Harpur St WC1 ... 94 B2 240 C4
Harraden Rd SE3 ... 143 C4
Harrier Ave E11 ... 55 B3
Harrier Ct TW4 ... 129 A3
Harrier Ho 9 SW11 ... 136 C2
Harrier Mews SE28 ... 123 B4
Harrier Rd NW9 ... 27 C1
Harriers Cl W5 ... 110 A6
Harrier Way E6 ... 100 B2
Harries Rd UB4 ... 84 C3
Harriet Cl E8 ... 96 A6
Harriet Gdns CR0 ... 222 A6
Harriet Ho
Walham Green SW6 ... 265 D3
Walthamstow E17 ... 53 D4
Harriet St
SW1 ... 114 D4 247 D1
Harriet Tubman Cl 21
SW2 ... 160 C4
Harriet Way WD23 ... 8 B4
Harriet Wlk
SW1 ... 114 D4 247 D1
HARRINGAY ... 50 D4
Harringay Gdns N8 ... 50 D5
Harringay Green Lanes Sta
N4 ... 50 D3
Harringay Rd N15 ... 50 D5
Harringay Sta N4 ... 50 C3
Harrington Cl
Wallington CR0 ... 220 A6
Willesden NW10 ... 67 B5
Harrington Ct
6 South Croydon
CR0 ... 221 B6
South Kensington SW7 ... 256 D4
9 West Kilburn W9 ... 91 B4
Harrington Gdns
SW7 ... 114 A2 256 A3
Harrington Hill E5 ... 52 B1
Harrington Hill Prim Sch
E5 ... 52 B1
Harrington Ho
2 Bromley BR1 ... 187 A2
Regent's Pk NW1 ... 232 A2
Upper Clapton E5 ... 52 C1
Westminster SW1 ... 259 D2
Harrington Rd
Croydon SE25 ... 206 B5
Leytonstone E11 ... 54 C1
South Kensington
SW7 ... 114 B2 256 C4
Harrington Road Sta
SE25 ... 206 C6
Harrington Sq
NW1 ... 93 C5 232 A3
Harrington St
NW1 ... 93 C4 232 A2
Harrington Way SE18 ... 121 D3
Harriott Cl SE10 ... 120 D2
Harriott Ho 11 E1 ... 96 C1
Harris Acad CR4 ... 203 D6
Harris City Tech Coll
SE19 ... 183 D2
Harris Cl Enfield EN2 ... 4 D4
Heston TW5 ... 129 C4
Harris Cotts 1 E15 ... 98 D6
Harris Ct HA9 ... 66 B5
Harris Girl's Acad
SE15 ... 162 C6
Harris Ho 11 Bow E3 ... 97 C4
7 Brixton SW9 ... 138 C2
Harris Lo SE6 ... 164 A3
Harrison Cl N20 ... 14 C3
Harrison Ho SE17 ... 262 C2
Harrison Rd
Dagenham RM10 ... 81 D2
Stonebridge NW10 ... 89 B6
Harrisons Ct 1 SE14 ... 140 D6
Harrison's Rise CR0 ... 220 D5
Harrison St
WC1 ... 94 A4 233 B1
Harrison Way TW17 ... 192 D4
Harris Rd
Dagenham RM9 ... 81 B3
Erith DA7 ... 147 B4
Harris St
Camberwell SE5 ... 139 B5
Walthamstow E17 ... 53 B2
Harris Way TW16 ... 171 C2
Harrodian Sch The
SW13 ... 133 D5
Harrogate Ct
2 Forest Hill SE26 ... 162 A1
9 New Southgate N11 ... 31 A4
Harrold Ho 1 NW3 ... 70 A1
Harrold Rd RM8 ... 80 B3
HARROW ... 42 B3
Harrow Ave EN1 ... 17 D5
Harroway Rd SW11 ... 136 B3
Harrowby St
W1 ... 92 C1 237 B2
Harrow Cl KT9 ... 213 D1
Harrow Coll HA1 ... 42 C2
Harrow Coll (Harrow
Weald Campus) HA3 ... 24 C4
Harrowdene Cl HA0 ... 65 D4
Harrowdene Ct SW19 ... 179 A5
Harrowdene Gdns
TW11 ... 175 A3
Harrowdene Rd HA0 ... 65 D4
Harrow Dr N9 ... 17 D3
Harrowes Meade HA8 ... 10 C1
Harrow Fields Gdns
HA1 ... 64 C5
Harrowgate Ho 22 E9 ... 74 D2
Harrowgate Rd E9 ... 75 A1
Harrow Gn E11 ... 76 C5
Harrow High Sch & Sports
Coll HA1 ... 43 A3
Harrow La E14 ... 120 A6
Harrow Lo SM2 ... 218 B2
Harrow Manor Way
SE2 ... 124 C3
Harrow Mus & Her Ctr*
HA2 ... 42 A6
HARROW ON THE HILL
... 42 C1
Harrow-on-the-Hill Sta
HA1 ... 42 C3
Harrow Pk HA1 ... 64 C6
Harrow Pl E1 ... 95 C1 243 B2
Harrow Rd
Ashford TW15 ... 148 C2
Barking IG11 ... 101 C6
Carshalton SM5 ... 218 C2
Ilford IG1 ... 79 A4
Leyton E11 ... 76 D5
Little Venice W2 ... 92 A2 236 B3
2 Newham E6 ... 100 A6
Sudbury HA0 ... 65 A4
Tokyngton HA9 ... 66 C2
Wembley HA0 ... 65 D3
Westbourne Green W2,
W9 ... 91 C3
Harrow Sch HA1 ... 42 C1
Harrow St NW1 ... 237 A4
Harrow View
Harrow HA1, HA2 ... 42 B5
Hayes UB3 ... 84 A1
Hillingdon UB10 ... 83 A4
Harrow View Rd W5 ... 87 B3
Harrow Way
Charlton TW17 ... 171 A1
South Oxhey WD19 ... 23 A6
HARROW WEALD ... 24 B2
Harrow Weald Pk HA3 ... 24 B4
Harrow & Wealdstone Sta
HA1 ... 42 C5
Harry Ct 15 NW9 ... 46 A5
Harry Gosling Prim Sch
E1 ... 96 A1
Harry Hinkins Ho SE17 ... 262 B1
Harry Lambourn Ho 10
SE15 ... 140 B5
Harston 15 KT1 ... 176 C1
Harston Dr EN3 ... 7 C5
Hart Ct E12 ... 78 C1
Harte Rd TW3 ... 129 B3
Hartfield Ave
Borehamwood WD6 ... 10 C6
Northolt UB5 ... 84 B5
Hartfield Cl WD6 ... 10 C6
Hartfield Cres
Coney Hall BR4 ... 225 A5
Merton SW19 ... 179 B3
Hartfield Ct CR2 ... 220 D1
Hartfield Gr SE20 ... 184 C2
Hartfield Ho UB5 ... 84 B5
Hartfield Rd
Chessington KT9 ... 213 D3
Hayes BR4 ... 225 A4
Merton SW19 ... 179 C3
Hartfield Terr E3 ... 97 C5
Hartford Ave HA3 ... 43 B6
Hartford Rd
Old Bexley DA5 ... 169 C5
West Ewell KT19 ... 214 D2
Hart Gr Ealing W5 ... 110 C5
Southall UB1 ... 85 C2
Hartgrove Ct NW9 ... 45 A5
Hart Grove Ct 3 W5 ... 110 C5
Hartham Cl
Isleworth TW7 ... 131 A4
Lower Holloway N7 ... 72 A3
Hartham Rd
Isleworth TW7 ... 131 A4
Lower Holloway N7 ... 72 A3
Tottenham N17 ... 33 D1
Hart Ho Hayes UB4 ... 83 B2
Streatham SW2 ... 160 C3
Harting Rd SE9 ... 166 A1
Hartington Cl
Farnborough BR6 ... 227 A3
Harrow HA1 ... 64 C4
Hartington Ct
Chiswick W4 ... 132 D5
South Lambeth SW8 ... 270 A2
Hartington Rd
Chiswick W4 ... 133 A4
Ealing W13 ... 109 B6
Newham E16 ... 99 B1
Southall UB2 ... 107 A3
South Lambeth
SW8 ... 138 A5 270 A3
Twickenham TW1 ... 153 B5
Walthamstow E17 ... 53 A3
Hartismere Rd
SW6 ... 135 B5 264 D4
Hartlake Rd E9 ... 75 A2
Hartland NW1 ... 232 B5
Hartland Cl
Edgware HA8 ... 10 C2
Enfield N21 ... 17 A5
Hartland Ct 5 N11 ... 30 D5
Hartland Dr
Edgware HA8 ... 10 C2
Ruislip HA4 ... 62 B4
Hartland Rd
Camden Town NW1 ... 71 B1
Cheam SM4 ... 201 D2
Friern Barnet N11 ... 30 D5
Hampton TW12 ... 173 D6
Isleworth TW7 ... 131 A2
Kilburn NW6 ... 91 B6
Stratford E15 ... 76 D1
Hartlands Cl DA5 ... 169 B5
Hartlands The TW5 ... 128 B6
Hartland Way
Croydon CR0 ... 223 A6
Morden SM4 ... 201 B2
Hartlepool Ct E16 ... 122 D5
Hartley Ave
Edgware NW7 ... 27 D5
Newham E6 ... 100 A6
Hartley Cl Bickley BR1 ... 188 B1
Edgware NW7 ... 27 D5
Hartley Ct Ealing W5 ... 110 C5
5 Mitcham CR4 ... 180 C2
Hartley Ho
Bermondsey SE1 ... 263 D4
Finchley N3 ... 29 D4
Putney SW15 ... 156 A6
Hartley Prim Sch E6 ... 100 A6
Hartley Rd
Bexley DA16 ... 146 C5
Leytonstone E11 ... 54 D1
Thornton Heath CR0 ... 205 A2
Hartley St E2 ... 96 C4
Hart Lo EN5 ... 1 A2
Hartmann Rd E16 ... 122 A5
Hartmoor Mews EN3 ... 6 D6
Hartnoll Ho 4 N7 ... 72 C3
Hartnoll St N7 ... 72 B3
Harton Cl BR1 ... 187 D2
Harton Lodge 2 SE8 ... 141 C4
Harton Rd N9 ... 18 B2
Harton St SE8 ... 141 C4
Hartopp Ct 20 N16 ... 73 C5
Hartopp Point SW6 ... 264 B4
Hartsbourne Ave WD23 ... 8 B2
Hartsbourne Cl WD23 ... 8 B2
Hartsbourne Ct 5 UB1 ... 86 A1
Hartsbourne Pk WD23 ... 8 C2
Hartsbourne Prim Sch
WD23 ... 8 B2
Hartsbourne Rd WD23 ... 8 B2
Harts Gr IG8 ... 37 A5
Hartshill Cl UB10 ... 60 D2
Hartshorn Alley EC3 ... 243 B1
Hartshorn Gdns E6 ... 100 C3
Harts La IG11 ... 78 D2
Hart's La SE14 ... 141 A4
Hartslock Dr SE2 ... 124 D4
Hartsmead Rd SE9 ... 166 B2
Hart Sq SM4 ... 201 C3
Hart St EC3 ... 253 B6
Hartsway EN3 ... 6 C1
Hartswood Gn WD23 ... 8 B2
Hartswood Ho 10
SW2 ... 160 A3
Hartswood Rd W12 ... 111 D3
Hartsworth Cl E13 ... 98 D5
Hartville Rd SE18 ... 123 C2
Hartwell Ct SE22 ... 140 A1
Hartwell Dr E4 ... 36 A4
Hartwell Ho 2 SE7 ... 121 B1
Hartwell St E8 ... 73 D2
Harvard Ct
9 Eltham SE9 ... 166 C5
West Hampstead NW6 ... 69 D3
Harvard Hill W4 ... 132 D6
Harvard Ho
3 Camberwell SE17 ... 138 D6
Putney SW15 ... 156 D5
Harvard Mans 18
SW11 ... 136 B1
Harvard Rd
11 Acton Green W4 ... 111 A1
Gunnersbury W4 ... 110 D1
Hounslow TW7 ... 130 C4
Lewisham SE13 ... 164 A6
Harvel Cres SE2 ... 124 D1
Harvel Ct SE2 ... 125 A1
Harvest Bank Rd BR4 ... 225 A5
Harvest Ct
Beckenham BR3 ... 185 C3
Littleton TW17 ... 192 C5
Harvesters Cl TW7 ... 152 B6
Harvest La
Loughton IG10 ... 21 D4
Thames Ditton KT7 ... 197 A3
Harvest Rd TW13 ... 150 A1
Harvey Ct
Battersea SW11 ... 267 B2
Walthamstow E17 ... 53 C4
Harvey Dr TW12 ... 173 C2
Harvey Gdns
Greenwich SE7 ... 121 C1
Leytonstone E11 ... 54 D1
Harvey Ho Barking IG11 ... 79 A1
10 Bethnal Green E1 ... 96 B3
Brentford TW8 ... 110 A1
Dagenham RM6 ... 58 D5
Hornsey N8 ... 50 A6
Pimlico SW1 ... 259 D1
Shoreditch N1 ... 235 D5
Wembley Pk HA9 ... 66 D6
Harvey Lo 8 W9 ... 91 C2
Harvey Mews N8 ... 50 B4
Harvey Point 7 E16 ... 99 A2
Harvey Rd
15 Camberwell SE5 ... 139 B4
Hillingdon UB10 ... 82 C5
Hornsey Vale N8 ... 50 B4
Ilford IG1 ... 78 D3
Leytonstone E11 ... 54 D1
Ruislip UB5 ... 62 C1
Twickenham TW4 ... 151 B4
Walton-on-T KT12 ... 194 A2
Harvey St N1 ... 235 D5
Harvill Rd
Newyears Green UB9 ... 38 A2
Sidcup DA14 ... 191 A5
Harvil Rd UB9, UB10 ... 38 A2
Harvington Sch W5 ... 87 D1
Harvington Wlk E8 ... 74 A1
Harvist Rd NW6 ... 91 A5
Harwell Cl HA4 ... 39 B1
Harwood Ave
Bromley BR1 ... 187 B1
Mitcham CR4 ... 202 C6
Harwood Cl London N12 ... 30 C4
Wembley HA0 ... 65 D4
Harwood Ct
Putney SW15 ... 134 C1
Shoreditch N1 ... 235 D5
Harwood Dr UB10 ... 82 B6
Harwood Point SE16 ... 119 B4
Harwood Rd
SW6 ... 135 D5 265 C3
Harwoods Yd N21 ... 16 C4
Harwood Terr
SW6 ... 135 D4 265 C2
Hascombe Ho 11
SW15 ... 156 B3
Hascombe Terr 2
SE5 ... 139 B3
Haselbury Rd N9 ... 17 C1
Haseley End SE23 ... 162 C4
Haselrigge Rd SW4 ... 137 D1
Haseltine Prim Sch
SE26 ... 185 B6
Haseltine Rd SE26 ... 185 B6
Haselwood Dr EN2 ... 4 D1
Haskard Rd RM9 ... 80 B4
Hasker St SW3 ... 114 C2 257 B4
Haslam Ave SM3 ... 201 A1
Haslam Cl Islington N1 ... 72 C1
Uxbridge UB10 ... 61 A6
Haslam Ct N11 ... 31 B6
Haslam Ho 12 N1 ... 73 A1
Haslam St SE15 ... 139 D4
Haslemere Ave
Barnet EN4 ... 14 D3
Cranford TW5 ... 128 C3
Ealing W13 ... 109 A3
Hendon NW4 ... 46 D3
Mitcham CR4, SW19 ... 180 B1
Wandsworth SW18 ... 157 D2
Haslemere Bsns Ctr
EN1 ... 18 B6
Haslemere Cl
Hampton TW12 ... 173 B5
Wallington SM6 ... 220 A3
Haslemere Ct 5 N16 ... 51 C1
Haslemere Gdns N3 ... 47 B5
Haslemere & Heathrow
Est The TW4 ... 128 B3
Haslemere Ind Est
Feltham TW14 ... 150 A6
Wandsworth SW18 ... 157 D2
Haslemere Prim Sch
CR4 ... 180 B1
Haslemere Rd
Bexleyheath DA7 ... 147 C3
Hornsey N8 ... 50 A2
Ilford IG3 ... 79 D6
Southgate N21 ... 16 D3
Thornton Heath CR7 ... 204 D4
Hasler Cl SE28 ... 124 C6
Hasler Ct E12 ... 78 A4
Haslett Rd TW17 ... 171 C1
Hasluck Gdns EN5 ... 14 A5
Hasmonean High Sch
(Boys) NW4 ... 28 D1
Hasmonean High Sch
(Girls) NW7 ... 28 A2
Hasmonean Prim Sch
NW4 ... 46 D4
Hassard St E2 ... 95 D5
Hassendean Rd SE3 ... 143 B5
Hassett Rd E9 ... 75 A2
Hassocks Cl SE23,
SE26 ... 162 B1
Hassocks Rd SW16 ... 181 D2
Hassock Wood BR2 ... 225 D4
Hassop Rd NW2 ... 68 D4
Hassop Wlk SE9 ... 188 A6
Hasted Rd SE7 ... 121 D1
Hasting Ct TW11 ... 174 B5
Hastings Ave IG6 ... 57 A5
Hastings Cl
New Barnet EN5 ... 2 A1
17 Peckham SE15 ... 140 A5
Wembley HA0 ... 65 C4
Hastings Dr KT6 ... 197 C3
Hastings Ho
Ealing W13 ... 109 B6
Enfield EN3 ... 6 C3
18 Shepherd's Bush
W12 ... 112 B6
Tottenham N17 ... 34 A2
6 Woolwich SE18 ... 122 B2
Hastings Hos WC1 ... 233 A1
Hastings Pl 1 CR0 ... 205 D1
Hastings Rd
Croydon CR0 ... 205 D1
Ealing W13 ... 109 B6
Keston Mark BR2 ... 226 A6
Tottenham N17 ... 51 B6
Wood Green N11 ... 31 D5
Hastings St
St Pancras
WC1 ... 94 A4 233 A1
Woolwich SE18 ... 123 A3
Hastingwood Ct
Newham E6 ... 100 B5
Walthamstow E17 ... 53 D4
Hastingwood Trad Est
N18 ... 35 A4
Hastoe Cl UB4 ... 85 A3
Hasty Cl CR4 ... 181 A2
Hatcham Mews Bsns Ctr
SE14 ... 140 D4
Hatcham Park Mews
SE14 ... 140 D4

Hat–Hea 325

Hatcham Park Rd SE14 140 D4
Hatcham Rd SE15 140 C6
Hatchard Rd N19 72 A6
Hatchcroft NW4 46 B6
HATCH END 23 A3
Hatch End High Sch HA3 23 D2
Hatch End Sta HA5 23 C3
Hatchers Mews SE1 253 B1
Hatchett Rd TW14 149 A3
Hatchfield Ho 8 N15 51 C3
Hatch Gr RM6 59 A5
Hatch Ho
 9 Muswell Hill N10 31 A3
 14 Richmond TW10 153 C1
Hatch La E4 20 C1
Hatch Pl KT2 176 B5
Hatch Rd SW16 182 A1
Hatch The EN3 6 D4
Hatchwoods IG8 36 D6
Hatcliffe Almshouses 8 SE10 120 C1
Hatcliffe Cl SE3 142 D2
Hatcliffe St SE10 120 D1
Hatfield Cl
 Deptford SE14 140 D5
 Ilford IG6 56 D6
 Mitcham CR4 202 B5
Hatfield Ct
 Greenwich SE3 143 A5
 8 Northolt UB5 84 C4
Hatfield Ho
 16 Kingston u T KT6 198 A4
 Leytonstone E11 54 D2
 St Luke's EC1 242 A5
Hatfield Mead SM4 201 C4
Hatfield Mews RM9 81 A1
Hatfield Prim Sch SM4 201 A3
Hatfield Rd Acton W4 111 B4
 Dagenham RM9 81 A1
 10 Ealing W13, W7 109 A5
 Stratford E15 76 C3
Hatfields SE1 116 C5 251 B4
Hathaway Cl
 Bromley BR2 210 B1
 Ruislip HA4 61 D4
 Stanmore HA7 25 A5
Hathaway Cres E12 78 C2
Hathaway Gdns
 Ealing W13 87 A2
 Ilford RM6 58 D4
Hathaway Ho 3 N1 95 C4
Hathaway Prim Sch W13 86 D2
Hathaway Rd CR0 204 D2
Hatherleigh Cl
 Barnet EN4 1 D4
 Chessington KT9 213 D3
 Edgware NW7 28 D3
 Morden SM4 201 C5
Hatherleigh Ho SM4 201 C5
Hatherleigh Rd HA4 62 A6
Hatherley Cres DA14 168 A2
Hatherley Ct 6 W2 91 D1
Hatherley Gdns
 London N8 50 A3
 Newham E6 99 D4
Hatherley Gr W2 91 D1
Hatherley Ho 2 E17 53 C5
Hatherley Mews E17 53 C5
Hatherley Rd
 Richmond TW9 132 B4
 Sidcup DA14 168 A1
 Walthamstow E17 53 C5
Hatherley St SW1 259 B3
Hathern Gdns SE9 188 C6
Hatherop Rd TW12 173 B3
Hathersage Ct N1 73 B3
Hathersley Ho 3 SW2 160 C4
Hathorne Cl 3 SE15 140 B3
Hathway Ho 3 SE15 140 C3
Hathway St 4 SE15 140 C3
Hatley Ave IG6 57 A5
Hatley Cl N11 30 D5
Hatley Rd N4, N7 72 B6
Hat & Mitre Ct EC1 241 D5
Hatstone Ct NW3 70 A3
Hatteraick St 6 SE16 118 C4
Hattersfield Cl DA17 125 B2
HATTON 127 D1
Hatton Cl SE18 145 B5
Hatton Cross Rdbt TW6 127 D2
Hatton Cross Sta TW6 127 D1
Hatton Ct BR7 188 B3
Hatton Gdn EC1 94 C2 241 B4
Hatton Gdns CR4 202 D4
Hatton Gn TW14 128 A1
Hatton Ho 17 E1 118 A6
Hatton Pl EC1 241 B4
Hatton Rd
 Hatton TW14, TW6 149 C6
 Thornton Heath CR0 204 C1
Hatton Rd N TW6 127 B4
Hatton Row NW8 236 D5
Hatton Sch IG8 55 D6
Hatton St NW8 236 D5
Hatton Wall EC1 94 C2 241 B4
Haughmond 4 N12 29 D6
Haunch of Venison Yd W1 238 C1
Hauteville Court Gdns 2 W6 111 D3
Havana Rd SW18, SW19 157 C2
Havannah St E14 119 C4
Havant Rd E17 54 A6
Havelock Cl 13 W12 112 B6
Havelock Ct
 8 Peckham SE15 140 B5
 Southall UB2 107 B3
Havelock Hall 8 CR0 205 D1
Havelock Ho
 4 Croydon CR0 205 D1
 Forest Hill SE23 162 C3
Havelock Pl HA1 42 C3
Havelock Prim Sch UB2 107 B3
Havelock Rd
 Belvedere DA17 125 B2
 Bromley BR2 209 C5
 Croydon CR0 221 D6
 Harrow HA3 42 C6
 Southall UB2 107 C3
 Tottenham N17 34 A1
 Wimbledon SW19 180 A5
Havelock St Ilford IG1 78 D6
 Islington N1 94 A6 233 B6
Havelock Terr SW8 137 B5 268 D3
Havelock Wlk SE23 162 C2
Haven Cl
 Chislehurst SE9 166 B1
 Hayes UB4 83 C3
 Hinchley Wood KT10 212 C6
 Sidcup DA14 190 C4
 Wimbledon SW19 156 D1
Haven Ct
 Beckenham BR3 186 A1
 Hinchley Wood KT10 212 C6
 Thornton Heath CR7 204 C6
Haven Gn W5 87 D1
Haven Green Ct W5 87 D1
Havenhurst Rise EN2 4 C3
Haven La W5 88 A1
Haven Lo 15 Enfield EN1 17 C6
 Temple Fortune NW11 47 B4
 7 Woolwich SE18 122 D2
Haven Pl Ealing W5 109 D6
 Hinchley Wood KT10 212 C6
Havenpool NW8 91 D6
Haven Rd TW15 148 D1
Haven St 18 NW1 71 B1
Haven The
 Ashford TW16 172 A3
 East Barnet N14 15 B5
 Richmond TW9 132 C2
Havenwood HA9 66 D5
Havercourt 3 NW3 70 C2
Haverfield Gdns TW9 132 C5
Haverfield Rd E3 97 A4
Haverford Way HA8 26 B2
Havergal Villas N15 50 D6
Haverhill Rd
 Chingford E4 20 A3
 Streatham SW12 159 C3
Havering 8 NW1 71 B1
Havering Gdns RM6 58 D4
Havering Ho N4 51 A2
Havering St E1 96 D1
Havering Way IG11 102 B4
Haverley 15 SW20 178 D3
Haversham Cl TW1 153 D5
Haversham Ct UB6 64 D2
Haversham Lo NW2 68 D3
Haversham Pl N6 70 D6
Haverstock Ct 2 BR5 190 B1
Haverstock Hill NW3 70 D2
Haverstock Rd NW5 71 A3
Haverstock Sch NW1 71 A2
Haverstock St N1 94 D5 234 D3
Haverthwaite Rd BR6 227 B5
Havilland Ct HA8 26 B6
Havil St SE5 139 C4
Havisham Ho 25 SE16 118 A4
Havisham Pl SW16 182 D3
Hawarden Gr SE24 161 A4
Hawarden Hill NW2 68 A5
Hawarden Rd E17 52 D5
Hawberry Lo N7 72 A2
Hawbridge Rd E11 54 B1
Hawes Down Inf Sch BR4 208 B1
Hawes Down Jun Sch BR4 208 B1
Hawes La BR4 224 C6
Hawes Rd Bromley BR1 187 B2
 Edmonton N18 34 B4
Hawes St N1 72 D1
Haweswater Ho TW1 152 D6
Hawfinch 29 NW9 27 D2
Hawgood St E3 97 C2
Hawkdene E4 20 A5
Hawke Ct UB4 84 C3
Hawkedale Inf Sch TW16 193 D6
Hawke Ho 20 E1 96 D3
Hawke Park Rd N22 50 D6
Hawke Pl 29 SE16 118 D4
Hawker 28 NW9 27 D2
Hawker Ct 14 KT2 176 C3
Hawke Rd SE19 183 C4
Hawkesbury Rd SW15 156 B6
Hawkesfield Rd SE23 163 B2
Hawkesley Cl TW1 175 A6
Hawkes Rd
 Feltham TW14 150 A4
 Mitcham CR4 180 D2
Hawkesworth Ho 5 SW4 159 C5
Hawke Twr 4 SE14 141 A6
Hawkewood Rd TW16 194 A6
Hawkfield Ct TW7 130 C3
Hawk Ho 7 SW11 136 C2
Hawkhurst Gdns KT9 214 A4
Hawkhurst Rd SW16 181 D2
Hawkhurst Way
 New Malden KT3 199 B4
 West Wickham BR4 223 D6
Hawkinge N17 33 B1
Hawkins Cl
 Burnt Oak NW7 27 B5
 Harrow HA1 42 B2
Hawkins Ho
 3 Deptford SE8 141 C6
 10 Richmond TW10 153 C1
Hawkins Rd
 Teddington TW11 175 B4
 Willesden NW10 67 C1
Hawkins Way SE6 185 C5
Hawkley Gdns SE27 160 D2
Hawkridge 19 NW5 71 A2
Hawkridge Cl RM6 58 C3
Hawksbrook La BR3 208 A3
Hawkshaw Cl 28 SW2 160 A4
Hawkshead NW1 232 A2
Hawkshead Cl BR1 186 C3
Hawkshead Rd
 Acton W4 111 C4
 Willesden NW10 67 D1
Hawkslade Rd SE15 162 D6
Hawksley Rd N16 73 C5
Hawks Mews 10 SE10 142 A5
Hawksmoor Cl
 2 Newham E6 100 A1
 Plumstead Comm SE18 123 C1
Hawksmoor Mews E1 118 B6
Hawksmoor Pl 2 E2 96 A3
Hawksmoor Sch SE28 124 B6
Hawksmoor St 5 W6 134 D6
Hawksmouth E4 20 A4
Hawks Rd KT1 176 B1
Hawkstone Rd SE16 118 C2
Hawkwell Ct E4 20 A1
Hawkwell Ho RM8 81 C6
Hawkwell Wlk N1 235 B6
Hawkwood Cres E4 19 D5
Hawkwood La BR7 189 A2
Hawkwood Mount 1 E5 52 B1
Hawlands Dr HA5 41 A2
Hawley Cl TW12 173 B4
Hawley Cres NW1 71 B1
Hawley Inf Sch NW1 71 B1
Hawley Mews 4 NW1 71 B1
Hawley Rd
 3 Camden Town NW1 71 B1
 London N18 34 D5
Hawley St NW1 71 B1
Hawley Way TW15 170 D5
Haworth Ho 7 SW2 160 C5
Hawstead Rd SE6 163 D5
Hawsted IG9 21 B4
Hawthorn Ave
 Bowes Pk N13 32 A5
 Old Ford E3 97 B6
 South Norwood CR7 182 D2
Hawthorn Cl
 Cranford TW5 128 B5
 Hampton TW12 173 C5
 Petts Wood BR5 211 B3
Hawthorn Cres SW17 181 A5
Hawthorn Ct
 Littleton TW15 171 A3
 2 Pinner HA5 22 C1
 Putney SW15 134 B2
 Redbridge IG5 56 B6
 Richmond TW9 132 D4
 Sutton SM1 217 C4
 8 West Norwood SW16 182 C5
Hawthorn Ctr HA1 43 A4
Hawthorndene Cl N12 30 C4
Hawthorndene Cl BR2 225 A6
Hawthorndene Rd BR2 225 A6
Hawthorn Dr
 Coney Hall BR4 224 C4
 Harrow HA2 41 C3
Hawthorne Ave
 Harrow HA3 43 A3
 Mitcham CR4 180 B1
 Ruislip HA4 40 B2
 Wallington SM5 219 A1
Hawthorne Cl
 Bickley BR1 210 B6
 Kingsland N1 73 C2
 Sutton SM1 218 A6
Hawthorne Cres UB7 104 B4
Hawthorne Ct
 Chingford E4 35 D4
 Ealing W5 110 A5
 Pinner HA6 22 A1
Hawthorne Gr NW9 45 A2
Hawthorne Ho SW1 259 B1
Hawthorne Mews UB6 86 A1
Hawthorne Rd
 Bickley BR1 210 B6
 Edmonton N18 33 D5
 Walthamstow E17 53 C6
Hawthorne Way N9 17 D2
Hawthorn Farm Ave UB5 85 A6
Hawthorn Gdns W5 109 D3
Hawthorn Gr
 Edgware EN5 11 D5
 Enfield EN2 5 B5
 Penge SE20 184 B2
Hawthorn Hatch TW8 131 B5
Hawthorn Ho SE14 141 B4
Hawthorn Mews NW7 29 A2
Hawthorn Pl UB3 105 D6
Hawthorn Rd
 Bexleyheath DA6 147 B1
 Brentford TW8 131 B5
 Carshalton SM1 218 C2
Hawthorn Rd *continued*
 Feltham TW14 150 A3
 Hornsey N8 50 A6
 Wallington SM5, SM6 219 B1
 Willesden NW10 68 A1
 Woodford IG9 37 D6
Hawthorns IG8 21 A1
Hawthorns The
 2 Cheam SM2 217 C2
 Edgware NW7 27 B4
 Stoneleigh KT17 216 A1
Hawthorn Terr DA15 167 D6
Hawthorn Way TW17 193 B5
Hawthorn Wlk W10 91 A3
Hawtrey Ave UB5 84 D5
Hawtrey Dr HA4 40 A2
Hawtrey Rd NW3 70 C1
Haxted Rd BR1 187 B2
Haybridge Ho 1 E5 74 C6
Hay Cl E15 76 D1
Haycroft Gdns NW10 90 B6
Haycroft Mans NW10 90 A6
Haycroft Rd
 London SW2 160 A6
 Surbiton KT6 214 A6
Hay Currie St E14 97 D1
Hayday Rd E16 99 A2
Hayden Piper Ho SW3 267 C6
Hayden's Pl W11 91 B1
Haydock Ave UB5 63 C2
Haydock Gn UB5 63 C2
Haydock Green Flats 2 UB5 63 C2
Haydock Lo 2 SM6 219 D5
Haydon Cl Enfield EN1 17 C6
 Kingsbury NW9 45 A5
Haydon Ct NW9 45 A5
Haydon Dr HA5 40 A5
Haydon Ho W7 108 D5
Haydon Park Rd SW19 179 D5
Haydon Rd RM8 80 C6
Haydon Sch HA5 39 D6
Haydon's Rd SW19 180 A4
Haydons Road Sta SW19 180 A5
Haydon St E1, EC3 117 D6 253 C6
Haydon Way SW11 136 B1
Haydon Wlk E1 243 D1
HAYES BR2 209 A2
 UB3 83 C1
Hayes Bridge Ret Pk UB4 106 D6
Hayes Chase BR4 208 C3
Hayes Cl BR2 225 A6
Hayes Cres
 Cheam SM3 216 D4
 Temple Fortune NW11 47 B4
Hayes Ct
 23 Camberwell SE5 139 A5
 Streatham SW12 160 A3
 Wimbledon SW19 179 A4
HAYES END 83 B3
Hayes End Cl UB4 83 B2
Hayes End Dr UB4 83 B3
Hayesend Ho SW17 180 A6
Hayes End Rd UB4 83 B3
Hayesford Park Dr BR2 208 D4
Hayes Gdn BR2 209 A1
Hayes Gr SE15, SE22 139 D1
Hayes & Harlington Sta UB3 105 D3
Hayes Hill BR2 208 C1
Hayes Hill Rd BR2 208 D1
Hayes La
 Beckenham BR2, BR3 208 B5
 Hayes BR2 209 A4
Hayes Mead Rd BR2 208 C1
Hayes Park Sch UB4 83 D3
Hayes Pl NW1 237 B5
Hayes Prim Sch BR2 209 B1
Hayes Rd Bromley BR2 209 A5
 Southall UB2 106 B2
Hayes Sch BR2 225 B6
Hayes St BR2 209 B1
Hayes Sta BR2 208 D1
HAYES TOWN 106 B5
Hayes Way BR3 208 B5
Hayes Wood Ave BR2 209 B1
Hayfield Pas E1 96 C3
Hayfield Yd 43 E1 96 C3
Hayford Ct NW2 68 D5
Haygarth Pl 2 SW19 178 D5
Haygreen Cl KT2 176 D4
Hay Hill W1 115 B6 248 D5
Hayhurst N1 234 D6
Hay La NW9 45 B5
Hayland Cl NW9 45 B5
Hay Lane Sch NW9 45 A5
Hayles Bldgs SE11 261 D4
Hayles St SE11 116 D2 261 C4
Haylett Gdns KT1 197 D5
Hayley Ho DA17 147 C6
Hayling Ave TW13 150 A1
Hayling Cl 20 N16 73 C3
Hayling Ct SM3 216 C4
Haymaker Cl UB10 60 B1
Hayman Cres UB4 83 B5
Haymans Point SE11 260 C2
Haymarket SW1 115 D6 249 C5
Haymeads Dr KT10 212 A2
Haymer Gdns KT4 216 A5
Haymerle Ho 6 SE15 140 A5
Haymerle Rd SE15 140 A6
Haymerle Sch SE15 140 A6
Haymill Cl UB6 86 D4
Haymills Ct W5 88 B3
Hayne Ho W11 244 A4
Hayne Rd BR3 185 B2
Haynes Cl
 Friern Barnet N11 15 A1
 Lewisham SE3 142 C2
 Tottenham N17 34 B3
Haynes Dr N9 18 B1
Haynes Ho 3 E9 74 D2
Haynes La SE19 183 C4
Haynes Rd HA0 66 A1
Hayne St EC1 94 D2 241 D4
Haynt Wlk SW20 201 A6
Hay's Galleria* SE1 253 A4
Hay's La SE1 253 A4
Haysleigh Gdns SE20 184 A1
Haysleigh Ho SE20 184 B1
Hay's Mews W1 115 B5 248 C4
Hay St E2 96 A6
Haystall Cl UB4 83 C5
Hayter Ct E11 77 B6
Hayter Ho W12 112 A6
Hayter Rd SW2 160 B6
Haythorn Ho SW11 136 B4 266 D1
Hayton Cl 11 E8 73 D2
Hayward Cl SW19 179 D2
Hayward Ct
 14 London SW4 138 A3
 Mitcham CR4 180 B1
Hayward Gallery* SE1 116 B5 250 D4
Hayward Gdns SW15 156 C5
Hayward Ho
 Islington N1 234 A4
 Lower Clapton E5 74 B5
Hayward Rd London N20 14 A2
 Thames Ditton KT7 196 D1
Haywards Cl RM6 58 C4
Haywards Pl EC1 241 C6
Hayward's Pl EC1 241 C6
Haywood Cl HA5 22 D1
Haywood Ct N11 31 D4
Haywood Lo 23 N7 71 D3
Haywood Rd BR2 209 D5
Haywood Rise BR6 227 C3
Hazel Ave UB7 104 C3
Hazelbank KT5 199 A1
Hazel Bank SE25 183 C1
Hazelbank Rd SE6 164 C2
Hazelbourne Rd SW12 159 B5
Hazelbury Cl SW19 179 C1
Hazelbury Gn N9 17 C1
Hazelbury Inf Sch N9 17 C1
Hazelbury Jun Sch N9 17 C1
Hazelbury La N9 17 C1
Hazel Cl Brentford TW8 131 B5
 Croydon CR0 206 D1
 Edmonton N13 17 B1
 Hendon NW9 27 D1
 Mitcham CR4 203 D5
 Peckham SE15 140 A3
 Twickenham TW2 152 A4
 Upper Holloway N19 71 C6
Hazelcroft HA5 23 D4
Hazelcroft Cl UB10 60 B1
Hazel Ct Ealing W5 110 A6
 8 Rotherhithe SE16 119 A5
 9 West Norwood SW16 182 C5
Hazeldean Rd NW10 67 B1
Hazeldene Dr HA5 40 C6
Hazeldene Gdns UB10 83 A6
Hazeldene Rd
 Bexley DA16 146 C3
 Ilford IG3 80 B6
Hazeldon Rd SE4 163 A6
Hazel Gdns HA8 26 D6
Hazel Gr Dagenham RM6 59 A6
 Enfield EN1 18 A5
 Feltham TW14 150 A3
 Forest Hill SE26 184 D6
 Orpington BR6 226 D6
 Wembley HA0 88 A6
Hazelgreen Cl N21 16 D3
Hazel Ho London SE4 141 B2
 12 Maitland Pk NW3 70 D2
Hazelhurst BR3 186 B2
Hazelhurst Ct SE6 186 A5
Hazelhurst Rd SW17 180 B6
Hazellville Rd N19 49 D1
Hazel Mead EN5 12 B6
Hazelmere Cl
 Feltham TW14 149 C5
 Northolt UB5 85 B5
Hazelmere Ct 10 SW2 160 B3
Hazelmere Dr UB5 85 B5
Hazelmere Rd
 Kilburn NW6 91 B6
 Northolt UB5 85 B5
 Petts Wood BR5 211 B5
Hazelmere Way BR2 209 A3
Hazelmere Wlk UB5 85 B5
Hazel Rd
 Kensal Green NW10 90 C4
 Stratford E15 76 C3
Hazeltree La UB5 85 A4
Hazel Way
 Bermondsey SE1 263 C4
 Walthamstow E4 35 B4
Hazel Wlk BR2 210 C3
Hazelwood IG10 21 D6
Hazelwood Ave SM4 201 D5
Hazelwood Cl
 Clapton Pk E5 75 A5
 Ealing W5 110 A4
 Harrow HA2 41 D5
Hazelwood Cres N13 32 C6
Hazelwood Ct
 1 Edmonton N13 32 C6
Hazelwood Ct *continued*
 Surbiton KT6 198 A3
 1 Willesden NW10 67 C5
Hazelwood Dr HA5 22 B1
Hazelwood Ho
 Beckenham BR2 208 C6
 Chingford E4 20 B4
 11 Deptford SE8 119 A2
 Edmonton N13 32 D6
 2 Sutton SM1 218 A4
Hazelwood Jun & Inf Schs N13 32 C6
Hazelwood La N13 32 C6
Hazelwood Lo BR4 208 A2
Hazelwood Mans SW6 264 C2
Hazelwood Rd
 Enfield EN1 17 D5
 Walthamstow E17 53 A4
Hazlebury Rd SW6 135 D3
Hazledean Rd CR0 221 B6
Hazledene Rd W4 133 A6
Hazlemere 3 DA14 190 A6
Hazlemere Gdns KT4 200 A1
Hazlewell Rd SW15 156 C6
Hazlewood Cres W10 91 A3
Hazlewood Twr W10 91 B3
Hazlitt Cl TW13 173 A6
Hazlitt Ct 4 SE28 124 C5
Hazlitt Mews W14 254 A5
Hazlitt Rd W14 113 A3 254 A5
Heacham Ave UB10 61 A5
Headbourne Ho SE1 262 D6
Headcorn 10 NW5 71 A2
Headcorn Pl CR7 204 B5
Headcorn Rd
 Plaistow BR1 187 A5
 Thornton Heath CR7 204 B5
 Tottenham N17 33 D3
Headfort Pl SW1 115 A4 248 B1
Headington Rd SW18 158 A2
Headlam Rd SW4 159 D4
Headlam St E1 96 B3
Headley App IG2 56 D4
Headley Ave CR0, SM6 220 B3
Headley Cl KT19 214 C2
Headley Ct SE26 184 C5
Headley Dr Ilford IG2 56 D3
 New Addington CR0 224 A1
Headley Ho 5 BR5 190 B1
Heads Mews W11 91 C1
Head St E1 96 D1
Headstart Montessori Sch SW17 180 A6
HEADSTONE 41 D5
Headstone Dr HA1, HA3 42 C6
Headstone Gdns HA2 42 A5
Headstone La
 Harrow HA2, HA3 23 D2
 Headstone HA2 41 D5
Headstone Lane Sta HA3 23 D2
Headstone Rd HA1 42 C3
Headway Cl TW10 175 C6
Heald St SE8, SE14 141 C4
Healey Ho RM6 59 A5
Healey St NW1 71 B2
Healy Ct EN5 12 D5
Healy Dr 1 BR6 227 D4
Healy Ho
 12 Kennington SW9 138 C5
 2 Tower Hamlets E3 97 C3
Heanor Ct 4 E5 74 D4
Hearne Rd W4 132 C6
Hearn Rise UB5 84 D6
Hearn's Bldgs SE17 262 D3
Hearnshaw St 1 E14 97 A1
Hearn St EC2 95 C3 243 B5
Hearnville Rd SW12 159 A3
Heart Hospl The W1 93 A2 238 B3
Heart Raido W11 112 D6
Heart The KT12 193 D1
Heatham Pk TW2 152 D4
Heath Ave DA7 146 D6
Heathbourne Rd WD23 8 D3
Heathbrook Prim Sch SW4 137 C3
Heath Brow NW3 70 A5
Heath Bsns Ctr The TW3 130 A1
Heath Cl Croydon CR2 220 D2
 Ealing W5 88 B3
 Golders Green NW11 47 D2
 Harlington UB3 127 B5
Heathcote Gr E4 20 A2
Heathcote Point 25 E9 74 D2
Heathcote Rd TW1 153 B6
Heathcote Sch E4 20 C2
Heathcote St WC1 94 B4 233 C1
Heathcroft Ealing W5 88 B3
 Golders Green NW11 47 D1
Heathcroft Ave TW16 171 D3
Heathcroft Gdns E4 36 B2
Heath Ct
 Carshalton SM5 218 B6
 Eltham SE9 167 A3
 2 Hampstead NW3 70 A2
 Leytonstone E11 54 D3
 Stoke Newington N16 51 B1
 Uxbridge UB8 60 A1
Heathdale Ave TW4 129 A2
Heathdene N14 15 C4
Heathdene Dr DA17 125 D2

Heathdene Rd
 South Norwood
  SW16 . . . . .182 B3
 Wallington SM5, SM6 . .219 B1
Heath Dr SW20 . . . . .200 C5
Heathedge SE23, SE26 . .162 B2
Heath End St WD23 . . . . . 8 C2
Heatherbank
 Chislehurst BR7 . . . . . .188 C1
 Eltham SE9 . . . . .144 B3
Heather Cl
 Clapham SW8 . . . . .137 B2
 Hampton TW12 . . . . . . .173 B2
 Hillingdon UB8 . . . . .82 B2
 Hither Green SE13 . . . . .164 B4
 Isleworth TW7 . . . . . . .152 B6
 Newham E16 . . . . .100 C5
Heather Ct
 South Lambeth SW4 . . . 270 B1
 6 West Norwood
  SW16 . . . . .182 C6
Heatherdale Cl KT2 . . . .176 D3
Heatherdene Cl
 London N12 . . . . .30 A2
 Mitcham CR4 . . . . .202 C5
Heatherdene Ct CR4 . . . .202 B5
Heatherdene Mans 2
 TW1 . . . . .153 D5
Heather Dr EN2 . . . . 4 D3
Heatherfold Way HA5,
 HA6 . . . . .39 D6
Heather Gdns
 Belmont SM2 . . . . .217 C2
 Hendon NW11 . . . . .47 A3
Heather Ho 11 E14 . . . . . .98 A1
Heather La UB7 . . . . .82 A1
Heatherlands TW16 . . . .172 A4
Heatherley Ct N16 . . . . . .74 A5
Heatherley Dr IG5 . . . . . .56 B6
Heatherley Sch of Fine Art
 SW10 . . . . .266 B3
Heather Lo N1 . . . . .51 C1
Heather Park Dr HA0 . . . .66 C1
Heather Park Par HA0 . . .66 B1
Heather Rd
 Dollis Hill NW2 . . . . .67 D6
 Lewisham SE12 . . . . . . .165 A3
 Walthamstow E4 . . . . . .35 B4
Heatherset Cl KT10 . . . .212 A3
Heatherset Gdns
 SW16 . . . . .182 B3
Heatherside Rd
 Sidcup DA14 . . . . .168 C1
 West Ewell KT19 . . . . . .197 A1
Heathers The TW19 . . . .148 B4
Heather Way HA7 . . . . . .24 D4
Heather Wlk
 Edgware HA8 . . . . .26 D5
 Twickenham TW4 . . . . .151 C4
 West Kilburn W10 . . . . . .91 A3
Heatherwood Cl E12 . . . .77 C6
Heatherwood Dr UB4 . . . .83 B5
Heathfield Chingford E4 . .20 A1
 Chislehurst BR7 . . . . . .189 A4
Heathfield Ave SW18 . . .158 B4
Heathfield Cl
 Keston BR2 . . . . .225 C3
 Newham E16 . . . . .99 D2
Heathfield Ct
 Ashford TW15 . . . . . . .148 A1
 3 Bow E3 . . . . .97 C5
 5 Chiswick W4 . . . . . . .111 B1
 Penge SE20 . . . . .184 C3
 Sidcup DA14 . . . . .190 B5
 8 Sutton SM2 . . . . .218 A2
 Wandsworth SW18 . . . .158 B4
Heathfield Dr CR4 . . . . .180 C2
Heathfielde N2 . . . . .48 A4
Heathfield Gdns
 Acton Green W4 . . . . . .111 A1
 Blackheath SE3 . . . . . .142 C3
 Croydon CR0 . . . . .221 B4
 Hendon NW11 . . . . .46 D3
 Wandsworth SW18 . . . .158 B5
Heathfield Ho SE3 . . . . .142 C3
Heathfield Inf Sch
 TW2 . . . . .151 C1
Heathfield Jun Sch
 TW2 . . . . .151 C1
Heathfield La BR7 . . . . .189 A4
Heathfield N TW1,
 TW2 . . . . .152 D4
Heathfield Park Dr
 RM6 . . . . .58 B4
Heathfield Pk NW2 . . . . .68 C2
Heathfield Rd
 Bexleyheath DA6 . . . . .147 B1
 Bromley BR1 . . . . .186 D3
 Croydon CR0 . . . . .221 B4
 Keston BR2 . . . . .225 D3
 South Acton W3 . . . . . .110 D4
 Wandsworth SW18 . . . .158 B5
Heathfield Rise HA4 . . . .39 A2
Heathfield S TW1,
 TW2 . . . . .152 D4
Heathfield Sch HA5 . . . . .40 D2
Heathfield Sq SW18 . . . .158 B4
Heathfield Terr
 Chiswick W4 . . . . .111 B1
 Plumstead SE18 . . . . . .123 B1
Heathfield Vale CR2 . . . .223 A1
Heathgate NW11 . . . . . . .47 B3
Heathgate Pl NW3 . . . . . .70 D4
Heath Gdns TW1 . . . . . .152 D2
Heath Gr
 Ashford TW16 . . . . . . .171 D3
 Penge SE20 . . . . .184 C3

Heath Ho Sidcup DA15. . .189 D6
 Thornton Heath CR7 . . .204 C4
 Uxbridge UB10 . . . . .60 D4
Heath Hurst Rd NW3 . . . .70 C4
Heathland Rd N16 . . . . . .51 C1
Heathland Sch The
 TW4 . . . . .151 B5
Heathlands Cl
 Sunbury TW16 . . . . . . .172 A1
 Twickenham TW1 . . . . .152 D3
Heathlands Ct
 Hounslow TW4 . . . . . . .151 A6
 Mitcham CR4 . . . . .203 A6
Heathlands Way TW4 . . .151 A6
Heathlee Rd SE3 . . . . . .142 D1
Heathley End BR7 . . . . .189 A4
Heath Lo WD23 . . . . 8 B3
Heath Mans
 5 Hampstead NW3 . . . . .70 A4
 Putney SW15 . . . . .156 D5
Heathman's Rd
 SW6 . . . . .135 B4 264 D1
Heath Mead SW19 . . . . .156 D1
Heathmere Prim Sch
 SW15 . . . . .156 A3
Heath Park Dr BR1 . . . . .210 A6
Heath Park Gdns NW3 . .69 D5
Heath Park Ind Est
 RM8 . . . . .59 A1
Heathpool Ct 8 E1 . . . . .96 B3
Heath Rd Clapham SW8. .137 B3
 Dagenham RM6 . . . . . . .59 A2
 Harrow HA1 . . . . .42 A2
 Hillingdon UB10 . . . . . . .83 A3
 Isleworth TW3, TW7 . . .130 A1
 South Norwood CR7 . . .205 A6
 Twickenham TW1 . . . . .152 D3
Heath Rise Hayes BR2. . .209 A3
 Putney SW15 . . . . .156 D5
Heathrow Airport London
 TW6 . . . . .126 D3
Heathrow Bvd UB7 . . . . .126 B5
Heathrow Causeway Est
 TW4 . . . . .128 B2
Heathrow International
 Trad Est TW4 . . . . . . .128 B2
Heathrow Prim Sch
 UB7 . . . . .126 B6
Heathrow Terminal 4 Sta
 TW6 . . . . .149 A5
Heathrow Terminals 1, 2,
 3 TW6 . . . . .126 D2
Heath Royal SW15 . . . . .156 D5
Heath's Cl EN1 . . . . 5 C3
Heathshott 8 TW10 . . . .154 A5
Heathside
 Hampstead NW3 . . . . . .70 B4
 Hinchley Wood KT10 . . .212 C5
 Twickenham TW4 . . . . .151 B4
Heath Side BR5 . . . . . . .211 A2
Heathside Ave DA7 . . . .147 A3
Heathside Cl
 Hinchley Wood KT10 . . .212 C5
 Ilford IG2 . . . . .57 B4
Heathside Prep Sch
 NW3 . . . . .70 A4
Heath St NW3 . . . . .70 A5
Heathstan Rd W12 . . . . .90 A1
Heath Terr RM6 . . . . .58 D2
Heath The W7 . . . . .108 C5
Heath View
 Gospel Oak NW5 . . . . . .71 A4
 London N2 . . . . .48 A5
Heath View Cl N2 . . . . . .48 A5
Heathview Ct SW19 . . . .156 D2
Heath View Dr SE2 . . . . .146 D6
Heathview Gdns
 SW15 . . . . .156 C4
Heathview Rd CR7 . . . . .204 C5
Heath Villas
 Hampstead NW3 . . . . . .70 B5
 Plumstead Comm SE18 . .123 D1
Heathville Rd N4, N19 . . .50 A2
Heathwall St SW11 . . . . .136 D2
Heathway Croydon CR0. . .223 B5
 Dagenham RM10 . . . . . .81 C2
 Dagenham RM10 . . . . . .103 C6
 Greenwich SE3 . . . . . .143 A5
 Woodford IG8 . . . . .37 C5
Heathway Ct NW3 . . . . . .69 C6
Heathway Ind Est
 RM10 . . . . .81 D4
Heathwood
 1 Hounslow TW3 . . . . .129 D1
 Streatham SW12 . . . . . .159 C3
Heathwood Gdns SE7 . . .122 A1
Heathwood Point 7
 SE26 . . . . .162 D1
Heaton Cl E4 . . . . .20 A1
Heaton Ct 3 N20 . . . . . .14 D2
Heaton Ho
 Chelsea SW10 . . . . . . .266 B6
 6 Peckham SE15 . . . . .140 B4
Heaton Rd
 London SE15 . . . . .140 B3
 Mitcham CR4 . . . . .181 A3
Heaven Tree Cl N1 . . . . .73 A3
Heaver Rd 24 SW11 . . . .136 B2
Heavers Farm Prim Sch
 SE25 . . . . .205 D4
Heavitree Cl SE18 . . . . .123 B1
Heavitree Ct E17 . . . . . . .35 D2
Heavitree Rd SE18 . . . . .123 B1
Hebble Ho UB5 . . . . .85 A6
Hebden Ct 24 E2 . . . . . . .95 D6
Hebden Terr N17 . . . . . . .33 C4
Hebdon Rd SW17 . . . . . .158 C1
Hebe Ct SM1 . . . . .218 A4
Heber Prim Sch SE22 . . .161 D5

Heber Rd
 Cricklewood NW2 . . . . . .68 D4
 East Dulwich SE22 . . . .161 D5
Hebron Rd W6 . . . . .112 B3
Hecham Cl E17 . . . . .35 A2
Heckfield Pl
 SW6 . . . . .135 C5 265 A3
Heckford Ho E14 . . . . . . .97 D1
Heckford St E1 . . . . .118 D6
Hector 11 NW9 . . . . .27 D2
Hector Ct
 1 London SW9 . . . . . . .138 C4
 Putney SW15 . . . . .156 D6
Hector Ho 14 E2 . . . . . . .96 B5
Hector St SE18 . . . . .123 C2
Heddington Gr N7 . . . . . .72 B3
Heddon Cl TW7 . . . . . . .131 A1
Heddon Court Ave EN4 . .14 C6
Heddon Court Par EN4 . .15 A6
Heddon Ct EN4 . . . . .15 A6
Heddon Rd EN4 . . . . . . .14 D6
Heddon St W1 . . . . .249 A6
Hedge Hill EN2 . . . . 4 D4
Hedge La N13 . . . . .17 A1
Hedgeley IG4 . . . . .56 B5
Hedgemans Rd RM9 . . . .81 A1
Hedgemans Way RM9 . . .81 A2
Hedgemoor Ct 1 E4 . . . .36 B5
Hedgerley Gdns UB6 . . . .86 A5
Hedgerow La EN5 . . . . . .12 B6
Hedger's Gr E9 . . . . .75 A2
Hedger St SE11 . . . . . . .261 C4
Hedge Wlk SE6 . . . . . . .185 D6
Hedgewood Gdns IG5 . . .56 C4
Hedgewood Specl Sch
 UB4 . . . . .83 C4
Hedgley Mews SE12 . . . .164 D6
Hedgley St SE12 . . . . . .164 D6
Hedingham Cl 6 N1 . . . .73 A1
Hedingham Ho 7
 KT2 . . . . .176 A2
Hedingham Rd RM8 . . . .80 B3
Hedley Ct SW15 . . . . . . .156 D5
Hedley Ho E14 . . . . .120 A3
Hedley Rd TW4 . . . . . . .151 C4
Hedley Row N5, N16 . . . .73 B3
Hedsor Ho E2 . . . . .243 C6
Heenan Cl IG11 . . . . .79 A2
Heene Rd EN2 . . . . 5 B4
Heidegger Cres SW13 . .134 B5
Heigham Rd E6 . . . . .78 A1
Heighton Gdns CR0 . . . .220 D3
Heights Cl SW20 . . . . . .178 B3
Heights The
 Beckenham BR3 . . . . . .186 A3
 Greenwich SE7 . . . . . . .121 C1
 Hampstead NW3 . . . . . .70 A4
 Northolt UB5 . . . . .63 C3
 Stroud Green N4 . . . . . .50 C3
Heiron St SE17 . . . . .138 D6
Helby Rd SW4 . . . . .159 D5
Heldar Ct SE12 . . . . . . .164 D4
Helder Gr SE12 . . . . . . .164 C4
Helder St CR2 . . . . .221 B2
Heldmann Cl TW7 . . . . .130 B1
Helegan Cl BR6 . . . . . . .227 D4
Helena Cl EN4 . . . . 2 B5
Helena Ct W5 . . . . .87 D2
Helena Pl 3 E9 . . . . .96 C6
Helena Rd Ealing W5 . . . .87 D2
 Newham E13 . . . . .99 A5
 Walthamstow E17 . . . . .53 C4
 Willesden NW10 . . . . . . .68 B3
Helena Sq 12 SE16 . . . .119 A6
Helen Ave TW14 . . . . . .150 B4
Helen Cl
 East Finchley N2 . . . . . .48 A6
 East Molesey KT8 . . . . .195 D5
Helen Clare Ct EN2 . . . . .4 D2
Helen Ct N1 . . . . .233 A6
Helen Gladstone Ho
 SE1 . . . . .251 C2
Helen Ho 9 E2 . . . . .96 B5
Helen Mackay Ho 10
 E14 . . . . .98 B1
Helen Peele Cotts 10
 SE16 . . . . .118 C3
Helenslea Ave NW11 . . . .47 C1
Helen's Pl E2 . . . . .96 C4
Helen St SE18 . . . . .122 D2
Helen Taylor Ho 5
 SE16 . . . . .118 A2
Helford Cl HA4 . . . . .61 C6
Helgiford Gdns TW16 . . .171 C3
Helios Rd CR4 . . . . .203 A1
Heliport Est The
 SW11 . . . . .136 B3
Helix Ct 17 W11 . . . . . . .112 D5
Helix Gdns SW2 . . . . . . .160 B5
Helix Ho TW7 . . . . .131 B3
Helix Rd SW2 . . . . .160 B5
Helix The SW19 . . . . . . .156 D5
Hellenic Coll of London
 SW1 . . . . .114 D3 257 C5
Hellen Way WD19 . . . . . .22 D6
Hellings St E1 . . . . .118 A5
Helme Cl SW19 . . . . . . .179 B5
Helmet Row EC1 . . . . . . .242 B6
Helmore Rd IG11 . . . . . . .79 D1
Helmsdale Cl UB4 . . . . . .85 A3
Helmsdale Ho NW6 . . . . .91 D5
Helmsdale Rd SW16 . . . .181 D2
Helmsley 11 E18 . . . . . . .55 A6
Helmsley Pl E8 . . . . .74 B1
Helmsley St 7 E8 . . . . . .74 B1
Helperby Rd NW10 . . . . .67 C1
Helsby Ct NW8 . . . . .236 C6
Helsby Rd SW16 . . . . . .159 A3
Helsinki Sq 5 SE16 . . . .119 A3
Helston Cl HA5 . . . . .23 B3

Helston Ct N15 . . . . .51 C4
Helston Ho SE11 . . . . . . .261 B2
Helvetia St SE6 . . . . . . .163 B2
Helwys Ct E4 . . . . .36 A4
Hemans Est
 SW8 . . . . .137 D5 269 D3
Hemans St
 SW8 . . . . .137 D5 269 D3
Hemberton Rd SW9 . . . .138 A2
Hemery Rd UB6 . . . . .64 B3
Hemingford Ct N12 . . . . .30 D5
Hemingford Rd
 Cheam SM3 . . . . .216 C4
 Islington N1 . . . .94 B6 233 D6
Heming Rd HA8 . . . . .26 D3
Hemington Ave N11 . . . . .30 D5
Hemlock Rd W12 . . . . . .111 D6
Hemmen La UB3 . . . . . . .83 D1
Hemming Cl 6 TW12 . . .173 C2
Hemmings Cl DA14 . . . .168 B2
Hemmings Ct HA8 . . . . . .27 A3
Hemming St E1 . . . . .96 A4
Hemmings Mead
 KT19 . . . . .215 A2
Hemming St E1 . . . . .96 A3
Hemmingway Cl NW5 . . . .71 A4
Hempstead Cl IG9 . . . . . .21 A2
Hempstead Rd E17 . . . . . .36 B1
Hemp Wlk SE17 . . . . . . .262 D4
Hemsby Rd KT9 . . . . . . .214 B2
Hemstal Rd NW6 . . . . . . .69 C1
Hemswell Dr NW9 . . . . . .27 C2
Hemsworth St N1 . . . . . . .95 C5
Hemsworth St N1 . . . . . . .95 C5
Hemus Pl SW3 . . . . .257 B1
Henchman St W12 . . . . . .89 D1
Hendale Ave NW4 . . . . . .46 B6
Hendale Ho 13 E6 . . . . . .74 B6
Henderson Cl NW10 . . . .67 A2
Henderson Ct
 8 Deptford SE14 . . . . .140 D6
 Hampstead NW3 . . . . . .70 B3
 Wandsworth SW18 . . . .158 C4
 Woodside Pk N12 . . . . . .14 B1
Henderson Dr
 NW8 . . . . .92 B3 236 C6
Henderson Ho 7 RM10. .81 C5
Henderson Rd
 Edmonton N9 . . . . .18 B3
 Forest Gate E7 . . . . . . .77 C2
 Hayes UB4 . . . . .84 A4
 Thornton Heath CR0 . . .205 B3
 Wandsworth SW18 . . . .158 C4
Hendfield Ct 5 SM6 . . . .219 B2
Hendham Rd SW17 . . . .158 D2
HENDON 46 C3
Hendon Ave N3 . . . . .29 A2
Hendon Central NW4 . . . .46 B4
Hendon Central Sta
 NW4 . . . . .46 B4
Hendon Hall Ct NW4 . . . .46 B6
Hendon Ho NW4 . . . . . . .46 D4
Hendon La N3 . . . . .29 B1
Hendon Lo NW4 . . . . . . .46 B6
Hendon Park Mans
 NW4 . . . . .46 C4
Hendon Park Row
 NW11 . . . . .47 B3
Hendon Pk Cotts NW7 . .47 D5
Hendon Prep Sch NW4. .46 D6
Hendon Rd N9 . . . . .18 A2
Hendon Sch NW4 . . . . . .46 A4
Hendon Sta NW4 . . . . . .46 A3
Hendon Terr TW15 . . . . .171 B4
Hendon Way NW2, NW4 . .46 C3
Hendon Wood La NW7 . . .12 A3
Hendre Ho E2 . . . . .263 B3
Hendren Cl UB6 . . . . . . .64 B3
Hendre Rd SE1 . 117 C2 263 B3
Hendrick Ave SW12 . . . .158 C4
Heneage La EC3 . . . . . . .243 B1
Heneage Pl EC3 . . . . . . .243 B1
Heneage St E1 . . .95 D2 243 D4
Henfield Cl London N19 . .49 C1
 Old Bexley DA5 . . . . . .169 C5
Henfield Rd SW19 . . . . .179 B2
Hengelo Gdns CR4 . . . . .202 B5
Hengist Rd
 Eltham SE12 . . . . .165 B4
 Erith DA8 . . . . .147 D4
Hengist Way BR2, BR3 . .208 C5
Hengrave Rd SE23 . . . . .162 B4
Hengrove Ct DA5 . . . . . .169 A3
Henley Ave SM3 . . . . . . .217 A5
Henley Cl Greenford UB6 . .86 A5
 Hounslow TW7 . . . . . . .130 D4
 Rotherhithe SE16 . . . . .118 C4
Henley Ct
 Brondesbury NW2 . . . . .68 D2
 Hendon NW4 . . . . .46 A6
 Ilford IG1 . . . . .78 D4
 Mitcham CR4 . . . . .203 A6
 Oakwood N14 . . . . .15 C4
 Peckham SE15 . . . . . . .140 A2
 Sidcup DA5 . . . . .169 B4
Henley Dr
 Bermondsey
  SE1 . . . . .117 D2 263 D4
 Kingston u T KT2 . . . . .177 D3
Henley Gdns
 Dagenham RM6 . . . . . . .59 A4
 Pinner HA5 . . . . .40 B6
Henley Ho London N12 . .30 B5
 Shoreditch E2 . . . . .243 D6
Henley Lo
 South Norwood SE25 . . .205 D5
 Walthamstow E17 . . . . .53 B4
Henley Prior N1 . . . . . . .233 C3
Henley Rd
 Edmonton N18 . . . . .33 C4
 Ilford IG1 . . . . .79 B4

Henley Rd continued
 Newham E16 . . . . .122 B4
 Willesden NW10 . . . . . . .90 C6
Henleys Cnr NW11 . . . . .47 B5
Henleys Rdbt TW5 . . . . .128 C3
Henley St SW11 . . . . . . .137 A3
Henley Way TW13 . . . . .172 D5
Henlow Pl TW10 . . . . . . .153 D2
Hennel Cl SE23 . . . . . . .162 C1
Hennessy Rd N9 . . . . . . .18 C2
Henniker Gdns E6 . . . . .100 A4
Henniker Mews SW3 . . .266 C6
Henniker Point E15 . . . . .76 C3
Henniker Rd E15 . . . . . . .76 B3
Henningham Rd N17 . . . .33 B2
Henning St
 SW11 . . . . .136 C4 267 A1
Henrietta Barnett Sch
 NW11 . . . . .47 D3
Henrietta Cl SE8 . . . . . .141 C6
Henrietta Ho
 11 Hammersmith W6 . . .112 C1
 3 New Barnet EN5 . . . . . 2 A1
 3 South Tottenham N15 .51 B2
Henrietta Mews WC1 . . .240 B6
Henrietta Pl W1 . 93 B1 238 C2
Henrietta St
 Strand WC2 . . . .116 A6 250 B6
 Stratford New Town E15 . .76 A3
Henriques St E1 . . . . .96 A1
Henry Addlington Cl
 E6 . . . . .100 D2
Henry Cavendish Prim Sch
 SW12 . . . . .159 C3
Henry Cl EN2 . . . . 5 C5
Henry Compton Sec Sch
 SW6 . . . . .135 A4 264 A2
Henry Cooper Way
 SE12 . . . . .187 D6
Henry Darlot Dr NW7 . . . .29 A5
Henry Dent Cl SE5 . . . . .139 B2
Henry Dickens Ct W11 . .244 A4
Henry Doulton Dr
 SW17 . . . . .181 B6
Henry Fawcett Prim Sch
 SE11 . . . . .138 C2
Henry Green Prim Sch
 RM8 . . . . .80 D6
Henry Hatch Ct SM2 . . . .218 A1
Henry Ho London SE1 . . .251 B3
 South Lambeth SW8 . . .270 A4
 St John's Wood NW8 . . .230 A4
Henry Jackson Ho
 SW15 . . . . .134 D2
Henry Jackson Rd
 SW15 . . . . .134 D2
Henry Macaulay Ave 13
 KT2 . . . . .175 D2
Henry Maynard Inf Sch
 E17 . . . . .54 A4
Henry Maynard Jun Sch
 E17 . . . . .54 A4
Henry Peters Dr
 TW11 . . . . .174 C5
Henry Rd London N4 . . . .51 A1
 New Barnet EN4 . . . . . .14 B6
 Newham E6 . . . . .100 A4
Henry's Ave IG8 . . . . .36 D5
Henryson Rd SE4 . . . . . .163 C6
Henry St BR1 . . . . .187 B2
Henry Tate Mews
 SW16 . . . . .182 C5
Henry Wise Ho SW1 . . . .259 B3
Hensford Gdns SE26 . . .184 B6
Henshall Point E3 . . . . . .97 D4
Henshall St N1 . . . . .73 B2
Henshaw Rd RM8 . . . . . .80 D5
Henshaw St
 SE17 . . . . .117 B2 262 C4
Hensley Point 28 E9 . . . .74 D2
Henslowe Rd SE22 . . . . .162 A6
Henslow Ho 12 SE15 . . .140 A5
Henson Ave NW2 . . . . . .68 C3
Henson Cl BR6 . . . . .226 D6
Henson Ct 3 N5 . . . . . . .73 A4
Henson Path HA3 . . . . . .43 D6
Henson Pl UB5 . . . . .84 C6
Henstridge Pl NW8 . . . . .230 A5
Henty Cl SW11 . 136 C4 267 B2
Henty Wlk SW15 . . . . . .156 B6
Henville Rd BR1 . . . . . . .187 B2
Henwick Prim Sch
 SE9 . . . . .144 A2
Henwick Rd SE9 . . . . . . .144 A2
Hepburn Gdns BR2 . . . .208 D1
Hepburn Mews SW11 . . .158 D6
Hepple Cl TW7 . . . . .131 B3
Hepplestone Cl SW15 . . .156 B5
Hepscott Rd E9 . . . . .75 C1
Hepworth Ct
 Barking IG11 . . . . .80 A3
 Cheam SM3 . . . . .201 C1
 Chelsea SW1 . . . . .258 C1
 Islington N1 . . . . .234 C6
Hepworth Gdns IG11 . . . .80 A3
Hepworth Ho IG8 . . . . . . .21 A1
Hepworth Rd SW16 . . . .182 A3
Hepworth Way KT12 . . . .193 D1
Heracles 30 NW9 . . . . . . .27 D2
Heracles Cl SM6 . . . . . . .220 A1
Hera Ct 15 E14 . . . . .119 C2
Herald Gdns SM6 . . . . . .219 B5
Heralds Pl SE11 . . . . . . .261 C4
Herald St 5 E2 . . . . .96 B3
Herbal Hill EC1 . . . . .241 B5
Herbert Chapman Ct
 N5 . . . . .72 D4
Herbert Cres SW1 . . . . .257 D6
Herbert Ct 4 KT5 . . . . . .198 B3

Herbert Gdns
 Chiswick W4 . . . . .132 D6
 Dagenham RM6 . . . . . . .58 D2
 Willesden Green NW10 . .90 B3
Herbert Ho E1 . . . . .243 C6
Herbert Mews 15
 SW2 . . . . .160 C5
Herbert Morrison Ho
 SW6 . . . . .264 C5
Herbert Morrison Prim
 Sch SW8 . . . . .138 A5 270 A1
Herbert Pl
 Hounslow TW3 . . . . . . .130 B3
 Shooters Hill SE18 . . . .144 D6
Herbert Rd
 Bexleyheath DA7 . . . . .147 A3
 Bromley BR2 . . . . .210 A4
 Hendon NW9 . . . . .46 A3
 Ilford IG3 . . . . .79 C6
 Kingston u T KT1 . . . . .198 B6
 Manor Pk E12 . . . . .78 A4
 Merton SW19 . . . . .179 B3
 Shooters Hill SE18 . . . .144 D6
 South Tottenham N15 . . .51 D4
 Southall UB1 . . . . .107 B5
 Walthamstow E17 . . . . .53 B2
 Wood Green N11 . . . . . .32 A3
Herbert St
 Camden Town NW5 . . . . .71 A2
 Newham E13 . . . . .99 A5
Herbrand Est
 WC1 . . . . .94 A3 240 A6
Herbrand St
 WC1 . . . . .94 A3 240 A6
Hercies Rd UB10 . . . . . . .60 C2
Hercules Ct 5 SE14. . . . .141 A6
Hercules Pl N7 . . . . .72 A5
Hercules Rd
 SE1 . . . . .116 B3 260 D5
Hercules St N7 . . . . .72 A5
Hereford Ave EN4 . . . . . .14 C1
Hereford Bldgs SW3 . . . .266 D6
Hereford Ct
 20 Belmont SM2 . . . . . .217 C1
 6 Croydon CR0 . . . . . . .205 D1
 6 Ealing W7 . . . . .86 D1
 Harrow HA1 . . . . .42 C2
Hereford Gdns
 London SE13 . . . . .164 C6
 Pinner HA5 . . . . .41 A4
 Redbridge IG1 . . . . .56 A3
 Twickenham TW2 . . . . .152 A4
Hereford Ho
 7 Acton W3 . . . . .88 C2
 5 Brixton SW2 . . . . . . .138 C1
 23 Camberwell SE5 . . . .139 A2
 Edgware HA8 . . . . .26 B2
 Knightsbridge SW3 . . . .257 B6
 Walham Green SW10 . . .265 D2
Hereford Mans 10 W2 . . .91 C1
Hereford Mews 11 W2 . . .91 C1
Hereford Pl SE14 . . . . . .141 B5
Hereford Rd Acton W3 . . .111 A4
 Bayswater W2 . .113 C1 245 B4
 Ealing W5 . . . . .109 C6
 Feltham TW13 . . . . . . .150 C2
 Wanstead E11 . . . . .55 B3
Hereford Retreat 5
 SE15 . . . . .140 A5
Hereford Sq
 SW7 . . . . .114 A2 256 B4
Hereford St E2 . . . . .96 A4
Hereford Way KT9 . . . . .213 D6
Herent Dr IG5 . . . . .56 B4
Hereward Gdns N13 . . . .32 C5
Hereward House Sch
 NW3 . . . . .70 B4
Hereward Rd SW17 . . . .180 D6
Herga Ct HA1 . . . . .64 C6
Herga Rd HA3 . . . . .42 D5
Heriot Rd NW4 . . . . .46 C6
Heriot Ave E4 . . . . .19 C6
Heriots Cl HA7 . . . . .25 A4
Heritage Cl
 London SW9 . . . . .138 D2
 Sunbury TW16 . . . . . . .172 A4
Heritage Ct SE8 . . . . . . .118 C6
Heritage Hill BR2 . . . . . .225 C4
Heritage Ho
 22 Putney SW19 . . . . . .156 D6
 3 Twickenham TW1 . . . .153 A4
Heritage View HA1. . . . . .64 D6
Herlwyn Ave HA4 . . . . . .61 C6
Herlwyn Gdns SW17 . . . .180 D6
Herm Cl TW7 . . . . .130 A4
Hermes Cl 5 W9 . . . . . . .91 C1
Hermes Ct 4 SW9 . . . . .138 C2
Hermes St N1 . . . . .234 A4
Hermes Way SM6 . . . . . .219 D6
Hermes Wlk UB5 . . . . . . .85 C1
Herm Ho EN3 . . . . 6 D1
Hermiston Ave N8 . . . . . .50 A4
Hermiston Ct
 3 Hornsey N8 . . . . .50 A4
 7 North Finchley N12 . . .30 B6
Hermitage Cl
 1 Abbey Wood SE2 . . . .124 C2
 Claygate KT10 . . . . . . .212 C3
 Enfield EN2 . . . . 4 D3
 Littleton TW17 . . . . . . .192 C1
 Snaresbrook E18 . . . . . .54 D2
Hermitage Ct
 2 Child's Hill NW2 . . . . .69 C2
 Colney Hatch N11 . . . . .30 D2
 3 Wanstead E18 . . . . . .55 A4
 14 Wapping E1 . . . . . . .118 A4
Hermitage Gdns
 Child's Hill NW2 . . . . . .69 C2
 South Norwood SE19 . . .183 A4

Hermitage La
Child's Hill NW2 69 C5
Croydon CR0 206 A3
South Norwood SW16 182 B3
Hermitage Prim Sch
E1 118 A5
Hermitage Rd
London N4, N15 51 A3
South Norwood SE19 183 B4
Hermitage Row 9 E8 74 A3
Hermitage St W2 236 C3
Hermitage The
Barnes SW13 133 D4
Feltham TW13 149 D1
Forest Hill SE23 162 C3
Kingston u T KT1 197 D5
Richmond TW10 154 A6
Uxbridge UB8 60 A2
Hermitage Villas SW6 265 A6
Hermitage Wall E1 118 A5
Hermitage Way HA7 25 A2
Hermitage Wlk E18 54 D5
Hermit Pl NW6 91 D6
Hermit Rd E16 98 D3
Hermit St EC1 234 C2
Hermon Gr UB3 106 A5
Hermon Hill E11 55 A5
Herndon Rd SW18 158 A6
Herne Cl Hayes UB3 83 D1
Willesden NW10 67 B3
Herne Ct WD23 8 A4
HERNE HILL 161 A6
Herne Hill SE24 139 A1
Herne Hill Ho SE24 160 D5
Herne Hill Mans SE24 161 A5
Herne Hill Rd SE24 139 A1
Herne Hill Sch SE24 161 A6
Herne Hill Sta SE24 160 D5
Herne Hill Stad SE24 161 B5
Herne Mews N18 34 A6
Herne Pl SE24 160 D6
Herne Rd KT6 214 A6
Heron Cl
Buckhurst Hill IG9 21 A3
Cheam SM1 217 B3
Walthamstow E17 35 B1
Willesden NW10 67 C2
Heron Cres DA14 189 C6
Heron Ct Bromley BR2 209 C5
16 Cubitt Town E14 120 A3
7 Dulwich SE21 161 B2
9 Forest Hill SE23 162 C3
Ilford IG1 78 D6
5 Kingston u T KT1 198 A6
Merton SW20 178 C1
Mitcham CR4 180 C2
Ruislip HA4 61 B6
Stanwell TW19 148 A3
Herondale Ave SW18 158 C3
Heron Dr N4 73 A6
Herongate N1 235 B6
Herongate Rd E12 77 C6
Heron Hill DA17 125 B2
Heron Ho
Battersea SW11 267 B2
Ealing W13 87 A3
Peckham SE15 139 D4
Sidcup DA14 168 B1
St John's Wood NW8 230 A3
Teddington KT1 175 C2
Heron Ind Est E15 97 D5
Heron Mead EN3 7 C5
Heron Mews IG1 78 D6
Heron Pl
Marylebone W1 238 B2
Rotherhithe SE16 119 A5
Heron Quays E14 119 C5
Heron Quays Sta E14 119 C5
Heron Rd Croydon CR0 221 C6
Herne Hill SE24 139 A1
Isleworth TW1 131 B1
Heronsforde W13 87 C1
Heronsgate HA8 26 C5
Heronsgate Prim Sch
SE28 123 B3
Heron's Lea N6 48 D3
Heronslea Dr HA7 26 A5
Herons Pl TW7 131 B2
Heron Sq 27 TW10 153 D6
Herons Rise EN4 2 C1
Herons The E11 54 D3
Heron Trad Est W3 88 D2
Heronway IG8 37 C6
Heron Way TW14 128 A1
Herrick Ct 4 TW10 175 D6
Herrick Ho
18 Camberwell SE5 139 B5
17 Canonbury N16 73 B4
Herrick Rd N5 73 A5
Herrick St
SW1 115 D2 259 D3
Herries St W10 91 A5
Herringham Rd SE7 121 C3
Herrongate Cl EN1 5 D3
Hersant Cl NW10 90 A6
Herschell Rd SE23 163 A4
Herschell's Mews SE5 139 A2
Hersham Cl SW15 156 A4
Hersham Rd KT12 194 A1
Hershell Ct 1 SW14 132 D1
Hertford Ave SW14 133 C1
Hertford Cl EN4 2 B2
Hertford Ct
16 London SW11 136 C2
Newham E6 100 B4
Palmers Green N13 16 C1
Hertford Ho 5 UB5 85 B3
Hertford Lo 10 SW19 157 A3
Hertford Pl W1 239 B5
Hertford Rd
Barking IG11 78 D1
Barnet EN4 2 A2
East Finchley N2 48 C6
Edmonton N9 18 B3
Enfield EN3 6 C5
Ilford IG2 57 C3
Shoreditch N1 95 C6
Hertford Rd High St
EN3 18 C6
Hertford St
W1 115 B5 248 C3
Hertford Way CR4 204 A5
Hertford Wlk 13 DA17 125 C1
Hertmitage The 5
SE13 142 A3
Hertslet Rd N7 72 B5
Hertsmere Rd E14 119 C6
Hertswood Ct 1 EN5 1 A1
Hervey Cl N3 29 C2
Hervey Park Rd E17 53 A5
Hervey Rd SE3 143 B4
Hesa Rd UB3 106 A6
Hesewall Cl SW4 137 C3
Hesketh Pl W11 244 A5
Hesketh Rd E7 77 A5
Heslop Ct 1 SW12 159 A3
Heslop Rd SW12 158 D3
Hesper Mews
SW5 113 D2 255 C3
Hesperus Cres E14 119 D2
Hessel Rd W13 109 B4
Hessel St E1 96 B1
Hestercombe Ave
SW6 135 A4 264 B1
Hester Ct SW16 181 C5
Hesterman Way CR0 204 B1
Hester Rd
Battersea
SW11 136 C5 267 A3
Edmonton N18 34 A5
Hester Terr TW9 132 C2
Hestia Ho SE1 253 A1
HESTON 129 B5
Heston Ave TW5 129 A5
Heston Com Sch TW5 129 C5
Heston Ctr The TW5 106 C1
Heston Grange TW5 129 B6
Heston Grange La
TW5 129 B6
Heston Ho
Gunnersbury W4 110 D1
5 St Johns SE8 141 C4
Heston Ind Mall TW5 129 B5
Heston Inf Sch TW5 129 C5
Heston Jun Sch TW5 129 C5
Heston Phoenix
Distribution Pk TW5 128 C6
Heston Rd TW5 129 C5
Heston St SE14 141 C4
Hetherington Rd
Charlton TW17 171 A1
Stockwell SW2, SW4 138 A1
Hetherington Way
UB10 60 A4
Hethpool Ho W2 236 C5
Hetley Gdns 1 SE19 183 D3
Hetley Rd W12 112 B4
Heton Gdns NW4 46 A5
Hetty Rees Ct 6 N19 50 A2
Hevelius Cl SE10 120 D1
Hever Croft SE9 188 C6
Heverfield Ct CR4 180 D3
Hever Gdns BR1 188 C1
Heverham Rd SE18 123 C2
Hever Ho SE15 140 D6
Heversham Ho SE15 140 C6
Heversham Rd DA7 147 C4
Hevingham Dr RM6 58 C4
Heward Ct SE13 142 A3
Hewens Rd UB4 83 A3
Hewer Ho 6 SW4 159 C6
Hewer St W10 90 D2
Hewes Ho E17 52 D5
Hewett Cl HA7 25 B6
Hewett Ho
Putney SW15 134 C3
7 Woolwich SE18 122 D1
Hewett Rd RM8 80 D4
Hewetts Quay 7 IG11 101 A6
Hewett St EC2 95 C3 243 B5
Hewish Rd N18 33 C6
Hewison St E3 97 B5
Hewitt Ave N22 32 D1
Hewitt Cl CR0 223 C5
Hewitt Ho 2 E4 36 B5
Hewitt Rd N8 50 D4
Hewlett Rd E3 97 A5
Hewling Ho 1 N16 73 C3
Hexagon Bsns Ctr
UB4 106 C6
Hexagon The N6 48 D1
Hexal Rd SE6 164 C1
Hexham Gdns TW7 131 A5
Hexham Rd Barnet EN5 1 D1
Cheam SM4 201 D1
West Norwood SE27 161 A2
Hexton Ct N4 73 A6
Heybourne Rd N17 34 B3
Heybridge 9 NW1 71 B2
Heybridge Ave SW16 182 B4
Heybridge Dr IG6 57 B6
Heybridge Way E10 53 B1
Heydon Ct BR4 224 C6
Heydon Ho 3 SE14 140 C4
Heyford Ave
Merton SW20 201 B6
South Lambeth
SW8 138 A5 270 B4
Heyford Rd CR4 180 C1
Heyford Terr SW8 270 B4
Heygate St
SE17 117 A2 262 B4
Heylyn Sq E3 97 B4
Heynes Rd RM8 80 C4
Heysham Dr WD19 22 D5
Heysham La NW3 69 D5
Heysham Rd N15 51 B3
Heythorp St SW18 157 B2
Heythrop Dr UB10 60 B4
Heyward Ct SM2 217 C2
Heywood Ave NW9 27 C2
Heywood Ct 2 HA7 25 C5
Heywood Ho
11 Deptford SE14 140 D6
6 Tulse Hill SW2 160 C5
Heyworth Rd
Lower Clapton E5 74 B4
Stratford E15 76 D4
Hibbert Ho 13 E14 119 C3
Hibbert Rd Harrow HA3 24 D1
Walthamstow E17 53 B2
Hibbert St SW11 136 B2
Hibernia Gdns TW3 151 C6
Hibernia Point 9 SE2 124 D4
Hibernia Rd TW3 129 C1
Hibiscus Cl 6 HA8 27 A6
Hibiscus Lo 5 E15 76 C1
Hichisson Rd SE15 162 C6
Hickes Ho 6 NW6 70 B1
Hickey's Almshouses 7
TW9 132 B1
Hickin Cl SE7 121 D2
Hickin St 2 E14 120 A3
Hickleton NW1 232 B5
Hickling Ho 10 SE16 118 B3
Hickling Rd IG1 78 D3
Hickman Ave E4 36 A4
Hickman Cl E16 99 D2
Hickman Rd RM6 58 C2
Hickmore Wlk SW4 137 C2
Hickory Cl N9 18 A4
Hicks Ave UB6 86 C4
Hicks Cl SW11 136 C2
Hicks Ct RM10 81 D5
Hicks St SE8 119 A1
Hidaburn Ct 7 SW16 181 C6
Hidcote Gdns SW20 200 B6
Hidcote Ho 11 SM2 218 A1
Hide E6 100 C1
Hide Pl SW1 115 D2 259 C3
Hider Ct SE3 143 C5
Hide Rd HA1 42 B5
Hide Twr SW1 259 C3
Hieover SE21 161 A2
Higgins Ho 7 N1 95 C6
Higginson Ho 2 NW3 70 D1
Higgins Wlk TW12 173 A4
Higgs Ind Est 9 SE24 138 D2
High Acre EN2 4 D2
Higham Ct 9 IG8 37 A4
HIGHAM HILL 35 A2
Higham Hill Ho E17 34 D2
Higham Hill Rd E17 35 A1
Higham Ho E4 35 C4
Higham Mews UB5 85 B3
Higham Pl E17 53 A6
Higham Rd
Tottenham N17 51 B6
Woodford IG8 37 A4
Highams Lodge Bsns Ctr
E17 52 D6
HIGHAMS PARK 36 A3
Highams Park Sch E4 36 B4
Highams Park Sta E4 36 B4
Higham St E17 53 A6
Higham Station Ave E4 35 D4
Highams The E17 36 A2
High Ashton 11 KT2 176 D3
Highbanks Cl DA16 146 B5
Highbanks Rd HA5 23 D4
Highbank Way N8 50 C3
HIGH BARNET 1 B2
High Barnet Sta EN5 1 C1
Highbarrow Rd CR0 206 A1
High Beech
South Croydon CR2 221 C1
Southgate N21 16 B5
High Beeches DA14 191 A5
High Birch Ct 7 EN4 2 C1
Highbridge Ct 13
SE14 140 C5
Highbridge Rd IG11 100 D6
High Bridge Wharf
SE10 120 B1
Highbrook Rd SE3 143 D2
High Broom Cres BR4 207 D2
Highburty Mans 24 N1 72 D1
HIGHBURY 72 D4
Highbury Ave CR7 182 D1
Highbury Cl
New Malden KT3 199 A4
West Wickham BR4 223 D6
Highbury Cnr N5 72 D2
Highbury Corner N5 72 D2
Highbury Cres N5 72 C3
Highbury Fields Sch
N5 72 D3
Highbury Gdns IG3 79 C6
Highbury Gr N5 72 D3
Highbury Grange N5 73 A4
Highbury Grove Ct N5 72 D2
Highbury Grove Sch
N5 73 A3
Highbury Hill N5 72 D4
Highbury & Islington Sta
N1 72 D2
Highbury New Pk N5 73 A4
Highbury Pk N5 72 D4
Highbury Pl N5 72 D3
Highbury Quadrant N5 73 A5
Highbury Quadrant Prim
Sch N5 73 A4
Highbury Rd SW19 179 A5
Highbury Sq N14 15 C3
Highbury Station Rd
N1 72 C2
Highbury Terr N5 72 D3
Highbury Terrace Mews
N5 72 D3
High Cedar Dr SW20 178 B3
Highclears 6 IG9 21 B2
Highclere Rd KT3 199 B6
Highclere St SE26 185 A6
Highcliffe
Beckenham BR3 185 D2
Ealing W13 87 B2
Highcliffe Dr SW15 155 D5
Highcliffe Gdns IG4 56 A4
Highcombe SE7 143 B6
Highcombe Cl SE9 166 A3
High Coombe Pl KT2 177 B3
Highcroft Highgate N6 49 A3
Hyde The NW9 45 C4
2 Kingston u T KT5 198 B4
Highcroft Ave HA0 88 C6
Highcroft Gdns NW11 47 B3
Highcroft Point E17 35 D2
Highcroft Rd N19 50 A2
High Cross Ctr The
N15 52 A5
High Cross Rd N17 52 A6
Highcross Way 4
SW15 156 A3
Highdaun Dr SW16 204 B5
High Dene EN2 4 D2
Highdown KT4 215 D6
Highdown Rd SW15 156 B5
High Dr KT2, KT3 177 A1
High Elms IG8 37 A5
High Elms Ctry Pk*
BR6 227 A1
High Elms Rd BR6 227 A1
Highfield WD23 8 C2
Highfield Ave
Erith DA8 147 D6
Greenford UB6 64 D3
Hendon NW11 47 A2
Kingsbury NW9 45 A4
Orpington BR6 227 D3
Pinner HA5 41 B4
Wembley HA9 66 B5
Highfield Cl
Hither Green SE13 164 B5
Kingsbury NW9 45 A4
Long Ditton KT6 197 C1
Wood Green N22 32 C2
Highfield Ct
7 Barnet EN5 1 D1
Hendon NW11 47 A3
Mitcham CR4 202 C5
Southgate N14 15 C5
Wanstead E12 77 C6
Highfield Dr
Beckenham BR2 208 D5
Ickenham UB10 60 A5
West Ewell KT19 215 D2
West Wickham BR4 224 A5
Highfield Gdns NW11 47 A3
Highfield Hill SE19 183 C3
Highfield Ho N21 16 D3
Highfield Inf Sch BR2 208 C5
Highfield Jun Sch
BR2 208 C5
Highfield Mews NW6 69 D1
Highfield Prim Sch
Edmonton N21 17 A3
Hillingdon UB10 82 D4
Highfield Rd Acton W3 89 A2
Bexley DA6 169 B6
Bromley BR1 210 B5
Carshalton SM1 218 C3
Edmonton N21 16 D2
Feltham TW13 150 A2
Hendon NW11 47 A3
Hounslow TW7 130 D4
Orpington BR5, BR7 211 D6
St Paul's Cray BR5, BR7 211 D6
Tolworth KT5 199 A2
Upper Halliford TW16 193 D4
Walton-on-T KT12 194 A1
Highfields SM1 217 C6
Highfield Sch SW18 158 C4
Highfields Gr N6 48 D1
High Foleys KT10 213 B1
High Gables
Beckenham BR2 186 C1
Loughton IG10 21 D6
High Garth KT10 212 A2
HIGHGATE 49 A2
Highgate Archway N6 49 C1
Highgate Ave N6 49 B2
Highgate Ballet Sch
NW11 47 D5
Highgate Cemetery*
N19 71 B6
Highgate Cl N6 49 A2
High Gate Edge N2 48 C4
Highgate High St N6 49 B1
Highgate Hill N19 49 C1
Highgate Ho 11 SE26 162 A1
Highgate Hts N6 49 C3
Highgate Prim Sch N6 48 D3
Highgate Private Hospl
N6 48 D3
Highgate Rd NW5 71 B4
Highgate Sch
Highgate N6 48 D2
Highgate N6 49 A2
Highgate Spinney N8 49 D3
Highgate Sta N6 49 B3
Highgate West Hill N6 71 A6
Highgate Wlk SE23 162 C2
Highgate Wood Sec Sch
N8 49 C4
High Gr Bromley BR1 187 D2
Woolwich SE18 145 B4
Highgrove Cl
London N11 31 A5
Widmore BR7 188 A2
Highgrove Ct BR3 185 C3
Highgrove Ho HA4 40 A3
Highgrove Mews SM5 218 D5
Highgrove Point 2
NW3 70 A4
Highgrove Rd RM8 80 C4
Highgrove Way HA4 40 A2
High Hill Ferry 3 E5 52 B1
High Holborn
WC1 94 B2 240 C3
High Holborn Ho WC1 240 D3
High La W7 86 B1
Highland Ave W7 86 C1
Highland Cotts SM6 219 C4
Highland Croft BR3 185 D4
Highland Ct E18 37 B2
Highland Dr WD23 8 A4
Highland Lo 3 SE19 183 D3
Highland Pk TW13 171 D6
Highland Rd
Bexley DA6 147 C1
Bromley BR1 186 D2
Pinner HA6 22 A1
West Norwood SE19 183 C4
Highlands N20 14 B2
Highlands Ave
Acton W3 111 A6
Southgate N21 16 B6
Highlands Cl
Hornsey N4 50 A2
Hounslow TW3 129 D4
Highlands Ct SE19 183 C4
Highlands Gdns IG1 56 B1
Highlands Heath
SW15 156 C4
Highlands Prim Sch
IG1 56 B1
Highlands Rd EN5 13 C6
Highlands Sch N21 4 C1
Highlands The
Barnet EN5 1 D1
Edgware HA8 26 D1
Highlawn Hall HA1 64 C5
Highlea Cl NW9 27 C2
High Level Dr SE26 184 A6
Highlever Rd W10 90 C2
High Limes 2 SE19 183 C4
High London 5 N6 49 D2
Highmead
9 Edmonton N18 34 A5
Plumstead Comm SE18 145 D5
High Mead Harrow HA1 42 D4
West Wickham BR4 224 C6
Highmead Cres HA0 66 B1
High Meadow Cl HA5 40 C5
High Meadow Cres
NW9 45 B4
High Meads Rd E16 99 D1
Highmore Rd SE3 142 C5
High Mount
Hendon NW4 46 A3
11 Hornsey N4 50 A2
High Oaks EN2 4 B5
High Oaks Lo 9 E18 37 A1
High Park Ave TW9 132 C4
High Park Rd TW9 132 C4
High Par The SW16 160 A1
High Path SW19 180 A2
Highpoint EN5 14 A6
High Point
Chislehurst SE9 166 D1
Highgate N6 49 A2
High Range SW20 178 C3
High Rd
Buckhurst Hill IG9,
IG10 21 C5
Bushey WD23 8 B3
Chadwell Heath RM6 58 C2
East Finchley N2 48 C6
Finchley N2, N12 30 A3
Friern Barnet N11 31 B5
Harrow HA3 24 C3
Ilford IG1 78 D6
Leyton E10 53 D3
Oakleigh Pk N20 14 A4
Seven Kings IG1, IG3 79 C6
South Tottenham N15,
N17 51 D5
Tottenham N17 33 D2
Wembley HA0, HA9 66 A3
Willesden NW10 68 A2
Woodford E18 37 A2
Wood Green N22 32 B3
High Ridge N10 31 B2
Highridge Pl EN2 4 B5
High Road Buckhurst Hill
5 IG9 21 B2
High Road Eastcote
HA5 40 B4
High Road, Ickenham
UB10 61 A6
High Road Leyton E10 75 D6
High Road Leytonstone
E11 76 C6
High Road Woodford Gn
IG8 37 A6
High St Mews SW19 179 A5
High St N Newham E6 100 A6
Plashet E12 78 A2
High St S E6 100 B4
High Sheldon N6 48 D3
Highshore Rd SE15 139 D3
Highshore Sch SE15 139 D4
High Silver IG10 21 D6
High St Acton W3 110 D5
Barnet EN5 1 B1
Beckenham BR3 185 C1
Brentford TW8 132 A6
Bromley BR1 187 A1
Cheam SM1, KT17 217 A2
Claygate KT10 212 D2
Cranford TW5 128 B5
Croydon CR0 221 A5
Ealing W5 109 D6
East Molesey KT8 195 C5
Elstree WD6 9 D5
Farnborough BR6 227 A3
Feltham TW13 150 A2
Green Street Green
BR6 227 D2
Hampton TW12 174 A4
Harlington UB3 127 B6
Harrow on t H HA1 42 C1
Hornsey N8 50 B5
Hounslow TW3 129 D2
Ilford IG6 57 A6
Kingston u T KT1 175 D2
Kingston u T KT1 197 D6
Mill Hill NW7 28 B5
Newham E13 99 A5
New Malden KT3 199 C5
Palmers Green N14 15 D2
Penge SE20 184 D3
Pinner HA5 41 A6
Ruislip HA4 39 C1
Shepperton TW17 193 A3
Sidcup DA14 190 A6
Southall UB1 107 B5
South Norwood CR7 205 B5
South Norwood SE25 206 A5
Stratford Marsh E15 98 A6
Sutton SM1 217 D4
Sutton SM1, SM2 217 D3
Teddington TW11 175 A5
Thames Ditton KT7 197 A3
Twickenham TW2 152 A4
Wallington SM5 219 A4
Walthamstow E17 53 B5
Walton-on-T KT12 194 A1
Wanstead E11 55 A4
Wealdstone HA3 24 C1
Wealdstone HA3 42 C6
Wembley HA9 66 B4
West Wickham BR4 207 D1
Wimbledon SW19 178 D5
Yiewsley UB7 104 A6
Highstone Ave E11 55 A3
Highstone Ct E11 54 D3
High Street Collier's Wood
SW17, SW19 180 B4
High Street Harlesden
NW10 89 D5
High Street Harlington
TW6 127 B5
High Street Kensington
Sta W8 113 D4 245 C1
High The SW16 160 A1
High Timber St EC4 252 A6
High Tor Cl BR1 187 B3
High Tor View SE28 123 C5
High Trees Cheam SM3 201 B2
Croydon CR0 207 A1
East Barnet EN4 14 C6
Streatham SW2 160 C3
Uxbridge UB10 61 A6
Whetstone N20 14 A1
Hightrees Ct W7 108 C6
Hightrees Ho SW12 159 A5
Highview Crouch End N6 49 C3
Hornsey N8 50 A2
Northolt UB5 85 A4
Woolwich SE18 144 D5
High View
6 Penge SE19 183 D3
Pinner HA5 40 C6
Highview Ave HA8 27 A6
High View Ave CR0,
SM6 220 B3
High View Cl
Loughton IG10 21 C6
South Norwood SE19 183 D1
Highview Ct
2 Loughton IG10 21 D6
2 Putney SW19 157 A3
High View Ct HA3 24 C3
Highview Gdns
Edgware HA8 27 A6
Hendon N3 47 A6
New Southgate N11 31 C5
Highview Ho
2 Buckhurst Hill IG9 21 D1
1 Buckhurst Hill IG9 21 D1
High View Ho RM6 59 A5
High View Par 1 IG4 56 B4
High View Prim Sch
London SW11 136 B1
Wallington SM6 220 A3
Highview Rd Ealing W13 87 A1
Sidcup DA14 190 B6
High View Rd
London N10 30 D2
Snaresbrook E18 54 D6
South Norwood SE19 183 B4
Highway Bsns Pk The 7
E1 118 D6
Highway The
Shadwell E1 118 C6

Highway The *continued*
Stanmore HA7 .... 25 A3
Highway Trad Ctr The 6
E1 .... 118 D6
High Wigsell TW11 ..... 175 A5
Highwood IG8 .... 36 D6
Highwood Ave N12 ..... 30 A6
Highwood Cl
Dulwich SE22 .... 162 A3
Orpington BR6 .... 227 A6
Highwood Ct
Barnet EN5 .... 13 C6
Whetstone N12 .... 14 A1
Highwood Dr BR6 ...... 227 A6
Highwood Gdns IG5 ..... 56 B5
Highwood Gr NW7 ...... 27 B5
Highwood Hill NW7 ..... 11 D2
Highwood Rd N19 ...... 72 A5
High Worple HA2 .... 41 B1
Highworth Rd N11 ...... 31 D5
Highworth St NW1 .... 237 B4
Hilary Ave CR4 .... 203 A6
Hilary Cl Bexley DA8 .... 147 D4
Walham Green SW6 ... 265 C4
Hilary Ct N9 .... 18 D3
Hilary Rd W12 .... 111 D6
Hilbert Rd SM3 .... 216 D5
Hilborough Cl SW19 ... 180 A3
Hilborough Ct 1 E8 .... 95 D6
Hilborough Rd 1 E8 .... 73 D1
Hilborough Way BR6 ... 227 B3
Hilda Lockert Wlk
SW9 .... 138 D3
Hilda Rd Newham E16 .... 98 C3
Upton Pk E6 .... 77 D1
Hilda Terr 2 SW9 ..... 138 C3
Hilda Vale Cl BR6 ..... 226 D4
Hilda Vale Rd BR6 ..... 226 D4
Hildenborough Gdns
BR1 .... 186 D4
Hildenbrough Ho BR3 .. 185 B3
Hildenlea Pl BR2 .... 186 C1
Hilditch Ho 7 TW10 .... 154 B5
Hildred Ho SW1 ...... 258 C4
Hildreth St SW12 ...... 159 B3
Hildreth Street Mews 2
SW12 .... 159 B3
Hildyard Rd SW6 ..... 265 B6
Hiley Rd NW10 .... 90 C4
Hilfield La WD23 .... 8 C6
Hilgrove Rd NW6 .... 70 A1
Hiliary Gdns HA7 .... 25 C1
Hillary Cres KT12 ...... 194 C1
Hillary Ct
3 Chislehurst SE9 ..... 166 A2
13 Shepherd's Bush
W12 .... 112 C4
Stanwell TW19 .... 148 A3
Hillary Dr TW7 .... 152 D6
Hillary Rd UB2 .... 107 C3
Hillary Rise EN5 .... 1 C1
Hillbeck Cl
Deptford SE15 .... 140 C5
Deptford SE15 .... 140 C6
Hillbeck Way UB6 .... 86 B6
Hillborne Cl UB3 .... 106 A1
Hillboro Ct
Leytonstone E11 .... 54 B2
1 Woodford E18 .... 36 D2
Hillborough Ct HA1 ..... 42 C2
Hillbrook Rd SW17 ..... 181 A6
Hillbrook Sch SW17 .... 181 A6
Hillbrow
Kingston u T KT3 ...... 199 D6
7 Richmond TW10 ..... 154 A5
Hill Brow BR1 .... 187 D2
Hillbrow Ct KT10 ...... 212 A4
Hillbrow Rd
Catford BR1 .... 186 C4
Esher KT10 .... 212 A4
Hill Bunker's DA17 ..... 125 C2
Hillbury Ave HA3 .... 43 B4
Hillbury Rd SW17 ...... 159 B1
Hill Cl Barnet EN5 .... 12 C6
Chislehurst BR7 .... 188 D5
Dollis Hill NW2 .... 68 B5
Hampstead Garden Suburb
NW11 .... 47 C3
Harrow HA1 .... 64 C5
Stanmore HA7 .... 25 B6
Hillcote Ave SW16 ..... 182 C3
Hillcourt N6 .... 49 C3
Hillcourt Ave N12 .... 29 D4
Hillcourt Rd SE22 ...... 162 B5
Hill Cres Harrow HA1 .... 43 A4
Kingston u T KT5 ...... 198 B4
North Cheam KT4 ..... 216 C6
Totteridge N20 .... 13 D2
Hillcrest
Camberwell SE24 ...... 139 B1
Highgate N6 .... 49 A2
Notting Hill W11 ..... 244 C5
Southgate N21 .... 16 C4
Hill Crest DA15 .... 168 B4
Hillcrest Ave
Edgware HA8 .... 26 D6
Pinner HA5 .... 40 D5
Temple Fortune NW11 ... 47 B4
Hillcrest Cl
Beckenham BR3 .... 207 B3
Forest Hill SE26 .... 184 A6
Hillcrest Ct
Brondesbury NW2 ...... 69 A3
8 Edgware HA8 .... 26 D5
Lewisham SE6 .... 164 B4
Sutton SM2 .... 218 B2
Hillcrest Gdns
Dollis Hill NW2 .... 68 A5
Hendon N3 .... 47 A5
Hinchley Wood KT10 ... 212 D5
Hillcrest Hts W5 .... 88 A3
Hillcrest Rd Acton W3 .. 110 D5
Chingford E17 .... 36 B1
Ealing W5 .... 88 A2
Grove Pk BR1 .... 187 A6
Loughton IG10 .... 21 D5
Woodford E18 .... 37 A1
Hillcrest View BR3 ..... 207 B3
Hillcroft Ave HA5 .... 41 B3
Hillcroft Coll KT6 ...... 198 A3
Hillcroft Cres Ealing W5 .. 87 D1
Ruislip HA4 .... 62 D5
Wembley HA9 .... 66 B4
Hillcroft Rd E6 .... 100 D2
Hillcroome Rd SM2 .... 218 B2
Hillcross Ave SM4 ..... 201 A4
Hillcross Prim Sch
SM4 .... 201 B5
Hill Ct Barnet EN4 .... 2 C1
Ealing W5 .... 88 B3
Hampstead NW3 .... 70 C4
8 Norbiton KT2 .... 176 D3
Northolt UB5 .... 63 C3
Putney SW15 .... 156 D6
14 Surbiton KT6 .... 198 A4
Wembley HA0 .... 65 A4
9 Wimbledon SW19 .... 179 A4
Hilldale Rd SM1 .... 217 B4
Hilldown Ct SW16 ...... 182 A3
Hilldown Rd
Hayes BR2 .... 208 D1
South Norwood SW16 .. 182 B3
Hill Dr London NW9 ..... 45 A1
Thornton Heath SW16 .. 204 B6
Hilldrop Cres N7 .... 71 D3
Hilldrop La N7 .... 71 D3
Hilldrop Rd
Bromley BR1 .... 187 B4
Kentish Town N7 ...... 71 D3
Hill End Orpington BR6 .. 227 D6
Shooters Hill SE18 ..... 144 C4
Hillersdon Ave
Barnes SW13 .... 134 A3
Edgware HA8 .... 26 B5
Hillersdon Ho SW1 .... 258 C2
Hillery Cl SE17 .... 262 D3
Hill Farm Rd W10 ...... 90 D2
Hillfield Ave
Colindale NW9 .... 45 C5
Hornsey N8 .... 50 A5
Mitcham SM4 .... 202 C4
Wembley HA0 .... 66 B1
Hillfield Cl HA2 .... 42 A5
Hillfield Ct NW3 .... 70 C3
Hillfield Ho N5 .... 73 A3
Hillfield La S WD23 ...... 8 D5
Hillfield Lo SW17 ...... 180 D5
Hillfield Mans NW3 ..... 70 C3
Hillfield Par SM4 ...... 202 B3
Hillfield Park Mews
N10 .... 49 B5
Hillfield Pk London N10 .. 49 B5
Southgate N21 .... 16 C2
Hillfield Rd
Hampton TW12 .... 173 B2
West Hampstead NW6 ... 69 C3
Hillgate Pl
Balham SW12 .... 159 B4
Kensington W8 113 C5 245 A4
Hillgate St W8 .... 245 A4
Hill Gate Wlk N6 .... 49 C3
Hill Gr TW13 .... 151 B2
Hill Ho Southall UB1 ..... 85 C1
Stanmore HA7 .... 9 A1
Upper Clapton E5 ...... 52 B1
Woolwich SE28 .... 123 C5
Hill House Ave HA7 ..... 24 D3
Hill House Cl N21 ...... 16 C4
Hill House Dr TW12 .... 173 C2
Hill House Rd SW16 .... 182 B5
Hill House Sch
SW1 .... 114 D3 257 D5
Hilliard Ct SM6 .... 219 D2
Hilliard Ho 15 E1 ...... 118 B5
Hilliard's Ct E1 .... 118 C5
Hillier Cl EN5 .... 13 D5
Hillier Gdns CR0 ...... 220 C3
Hillier Ho 1 NW1 .... 71 D1
Hillier Lo TW12 .... 174 B5
Hillier Pl KT9 .... 213 D2
Hillier Rd SW11 .... 158 D5
Hilliers Ave UB8 .... 82 C4
Hillier's La CR0, SM6 ... 220 A5
HILLINGDON 82 D5
Hillingdon Ave TW19 ... 148 A3
Hillingdon Circus UB10 .. 60 D2
HILLINGDON HEATH ... 82 D2
Hillingdon Hill UB10 .... 82 B4
Hillingdon Hospl UB8 ... 82 B2
Hillingdon Manor Sch
UB8 .... 82 D2
Hillingdon Par 6 UB10 .. 82 D3
Hillingdon Prim Sch
UB10 .... 82 D4
Hillingdon Rd UB10 ..... 82 A5
Hillingdon St SE17 ..... 138 D6
Hillingdon Sta UB10 .... 60 D3
Hillington Gdns IG8 ..... 37 D1
Hill La HA4 .... 39 A1
Hill Lo SW11 .... 136 B1
Hillman Cl UB8 .... 60 A3
Hillman Dr 12 NW10 .... 90 C3
Hillman St E8 .... 74 B2
Hillmarton Rd N7 .... 72 A3
Hillmead Dr SW9 ...... 138 D1
Hill Mead Prim Sch
SW9 .... 138 D1
Hillmont Rd KT10 ...... 212 C5
Hillmore Ct SE13 ...... 142 B2
Hillmore Gr SE26 ...... 185 A5
Hill Rd Carshalton SM5 .. 218 C2
Finchley N10 .... 30 D2
Harrow HA1 .... 43 A4
Mitcham CR4 .... 181 B3
Pinner HA5 .... 41 A3
St John's Wood
NW8 .... 92 A5 229 B3
Sutton SM1 .... 217 D3
Wembley HA0 .... 65 B5
Hillreach SE7, SE18 .... 122 B1
Hillrise KT12 .... 193 D2
Hill Rise
East Finchley NW11 ..... 47 D5
Enfield N9 .... 18 B5
Forest Hill SE23 ...... 162 B3
Greenford UB6 .... 86 A6
Hinchley Wood KT10 ... 213 B6
Richmond TW10 ...... 153 D6
Ruislip HA4 .... 39 B1
Hillrise Mans N19 ...... 50 A2
Hillrise Rd N19 .... 50 A2
Hillsboro Rd SE22 ..... 161 C6
Hillsborough Ct 13
NW6 .... 91 D6
Hillsde 6 SM1 .... 218 B3
Hillsgrove Cl DA16 .... 146 C5
Hillsgrove Prim Sch
DA16 .... 146 C5
Hillside Barnet EN5 ..... 14 A6
Crouch End N8 .... 49 D3
Greenwich SE10 ...... 142 B5
Kingsbury NW9 .... 45 B5
Stonebridge NW10 ..... 89 B6
Wimbledon SW19 ..... 178 D4
Hill Side EN5 .... 14 A6
Hillside Ave London N11 .. 30 D4
Wembley HA9 .... 66 B4
Woodford IG8 .... 37 C5
Hillside Cl Merton SM4 .. 201 A5
St John's Wood NW8 .... 91 D5
Woodford IG8 .... 37 C5
Hillside Cres Enfield EN2 .. 5 B5
Harrow HA2 .... 42 A1
Northwood HA6 .... 22 A2
Hillside Ct
Hampstead NW3 .... 69 D3
7 Kingston u T KT2 .... 176 D3
Hillside Dr HA8 .... 26 C5
Hillside Gdns
Chipping Barnet EN5 ..... 1 A1
Edgware HA8 .... 26 B6
Friern Barnet N11 ...... 31 C4
Harrow HA3 .... 44 A2
Highgate N6 .... 49 B3
Northwood HA6 .... 22 B2
Streatham SW2 .... 160 C2
Wallington SM6 ...... 219 C1
Walthamstow E17 ...... 54 B6
Hillside Glen CR0 ..... 220 D4
Hillside Gr Hendon NW7 .. 28 A3
Southgate N14 .... 15 D4
Hillside Ho CR0 .... 220 D4
Hillside Jun & Inf Schs
HA6 .... 22 A3
Hillside La BR2 .... 224 D6
Hillside Mans EN5 .... 1 B1
Hillside Rd
Beckenham BR2 ...... 208 D6
Belmont SM2 .... 217 B1
Croydon CR0 .... 220 D4
Ealing W5 .... 88 A2
Northwood HA6, HA5 ... 22 B3
Southall UB1 .... 85 C3
South Tottenham N15 ... 51 C3
Streatham SW2 .... 160 C2
Surbiton KT5 .... 198 C4
Hillside Rise HA6 ...... 22 A3
Hillsleigh Rd
W14 .... 113 B5 244 D4
Hillsley DA14 .... 190 A6
Hills Mews 2 W5 ...... 110 A6
Hills Pl W1 .... 239 A1
Hill's Rd IG9 .... 21 B3
Hill St
Mayfair W1 .... 115 B5 248 C4
Richmond TW10 ...... 153 D6
Hillstone Ct 5 E3 .... 97 D3
Hillstowe St E5 .... 74 C5
Hilltop 7 E17 .... 53 D6
Hill Top Cheam SM3 .... 201 B2
East Finchley NW11 .... 47 D5
Hilltop Ave NW10 ...... 67 A1
Hilltop Ct
12 London SW18 ...... 136 B1
South Hampstead NW8 .. 70 A1
South Norwood SE19 ... 183 B2
Hilltop Gdns
Hendon NW4 .... 28 B1
Orpington BR6 .... 227 C6
Hilltop Ho 7 N6 .... 49 D2
Hilltop Rd NW6 .... 69 C1
Hilltop Way HA7 .... 9 A1
Hillview SW20 .... 178 B3
Hill View Mitcham CR4 .. 204 A5
Primrose Hill NW1 .... 230 D6
Hillview Ave HA3 .... 44 A4
Hillview Cl Pinner HA5 ... 23 B4
Wembley HA9 .... 66 B6
Hillview Cres
Orpington BR6 .... 211 D1
Redbridge IG1 .... 56 B3
Hillview Ct SE19 ...... 183 C6
Hill View Dr
Bexley DA16 .... 145 C3
Woolwich SE28 ...... 123 C5
Hillview Gdns
Harrow HA2 .... 41 C5
Hendon NW4 .... 46 D5
Hill View Gdns NW9 .... 45 B4
Hillview Rd
Carshalton SM1 ...... 218 B5
Chislehurst BR7 ...... 188 D6
Mill Hill NW7 .... 28 D6
Pinner HA5 .... 23 B4
Hill View Rd
Claygate KT10 .... 213 A1
Orpington BR6 .... 227 D6
Twickenham TW1 ..... 153 A5
Hillway Highgate N6 ..... 71 A6
London NW9 .... 45 C1
Hill Wood Ho NW1 .... 232 C3
Hillworth 7 BR3 ...... 185 D1
Hillworth Rd SW2 ..... 160 C4
Hillyard Rd W7 .... 86 C2
Hillyard St SW9 .... 138 C4
Hillyfield E17 .... 35 A1
Hillyfield Cl E9 .... 75 A3
Hillyfield Prim Sch E17 . 53 A6
Hilly Fields Cres SE4 ... 141 C2
Hilly Mead SW19 ...... 179 A3
Hilsea Point 7 SW15 .. 156 B3
Hilsea St E5 .... 74 C4
Hilton Ave N12 .... 30 B5
Hilton Ho 4 Ealing W13 .. 87 C1
12 Finchley N2 .... 30 B1
Lower Holloway N7 ..... 72 A4
9 Nunhead SE4 ...... 140 D1
Hilversum Cres 10
SE22 .... 161 C6
Himley Rd SW17 ...... 180 D4
Hinchlay Manor KT10 .. 212 D5
Hinchley Cl KT10 ...... 212 D5
Hinchley Dr KT10 ...... 212 D5
Hinchley Way KT10 .... 213 A5
HINCHLEY WOOD 212 D6
Hinchley Wood Prim Sch
KT10 .... 213 A6
Hinchley Wood Sch &
Sixth Form Ctr KT10 .. 213 A6
Hinchley Wood Sta
KT10 .... 212 D5
Hinckley Rd SE15 ..... 140 A1
Hind Ct EC4 .... 241 B1
Hinde Mews W1 ..... 238 B2
Hindes Rd HA1 .... 42 C4
Hinde St W1 .... 93 A1 238 B2
Hind Gr E14 .... 97 C1
Hindhead Cl UB8 .... 82 D2
Hindhead Gdns UB5 .... 85 A6
Hindhead Gn WD19 .... 22 C5
Hindhead Point 6
SW15 .... 156 B3
Hindhead Way SM6 .... 220 A3
Hind Ho
13 Deptford SE14 ..... 140 D6
Islington N7 .... 72 C4
Hindhurst Ct NW9 ...... 45 A5
Hindle Ho E8 .... 73 D3
Hindley Ho N7 .... 72 B5
Hindlip Ho SW8 ...... 269 C1
Hindmans Rd SE22 .... 162 A6
Hindmans Way RM9 ... 103 B3
Hindmarsh Cl E1 ...... 118 A6
Hindrey Rd E5 .... 74 B3
Hindsley's Pl SE23 .... 162 C2
Hines Ct HA1 .... 43 A4
Hinkler Rd HA3 .... 43 D6
Hinksey Path SE2 ..... 124 D3
Hinstock NW6 .... 91 D6
Hinstock Rd SE18 ..... 145 A5
Hinton Ave TW4 ...... 128 D1
Hinton Cl SE9 .... 166 A3
Hinton Ct 3 E10 .... 75 D6
Hinton Rd Brixton SE24 .. 138 D2
Edmonton N18 .... 33 C6
Wallington SM6 ...... 219 C2
Hippisley Ct TW7 ..... 130 D2
Hippodrome Mews
W11 .... 244 A5
Hippodrome Pl W11 .. 244 B5
Hirst Cres HA9 .... 66 A5
Hirst Ct SW1 .... 258 C1
Hispano Mews 17 EN3 .... 7 C6
Hitcham Rd E17 .... 53 B2
Hitchcock Cl TW17 .... 192 B6
Hitchin Sq E3 .... 97 A5
Hithe Gr 15 SE16 ..... 118 C3
Hitherbroom Rd UB3 ... 106 A6
Hither Farm Rd SE3 ... 143 C2
Hitherfield Prim Sch
SW16 .... 160 C2
Hitherfield Rd
Dagenham RM8 .... 81 A6
Streatham SW16,
SW27 .... 160 C1
HITHER GREEN 164 C5
Hither Green La SE13 .. 164 B5
Hither Green Prim Sch
SE13 .... 164 B5
Hither Green Sta
SE13 .... 164 C5
Hitherlands SW12 ..... 159 B2
Hitherwell Dr HA3 ...... 24 B2
Hitherwood Ct SE21 ... 183 D6
Hitherwood Dr SE19 ... 183 D6
Hive Cl WD23 .... 8 B2
Hive Rd WD23 .... 8 C2
Hive Wood Ho E7 ...... 77 A2
HM Prison Wormwood
Scrubs W12 .... 90 A1
HMS Belfast* SE1 ..... 253 B4
Hoadly Rd SW16 ...... 159 D2
Hobart Cl
East Barnet N20 .... 14 C2
Hayes UB4 .... 84 D3
Hobart Ct Harrow HA1 ... 42 C2
Woodford IG8 .... 36 D6
Hobart Dr UB4 .... 84 D3
Hobart Gdns CR7 ..... 205 B6
Hobart Ho 24 KT6 .... 198 A4
Hobart La UB4 .... 84 D3
Hobart Pl
Richmond TW10 ...... 154 B4
Westminster
SW1 .... 115 B3 258 C6
Hobart Rd
Dagenham RM9 .... 80 D4
Hayes UB4 .... 84 D3
North Cheam KT4 ..... 216 B5
Hobbayne Prim Sch
W7 .... 86 D1
Hobbayne Rd W7 ...... 86 B1
Hobbes Wlk SW15 .... 156 B6
Hobb's Ct SE1 .... 253 D2
Hobbs Gn N2 .... 48 A6
Hobbs Mews IG3 ...... 79 D6
Hobbs' Pl N1 .... 95 C6
Hobbs Rd 5 SE27 ..... 183 A6
Hobby St EN3 .... 18 D6
Hobday St E14 .... 97 D1
Hobhouse Ct SW1 ... 249 D5
Hobill Wlk KT5 .... 198 B3
Hoblands End BR7 .... 189 C4
Hobsons Pl 7 E1 ...... 96 A2
Hobury St
SW10 .... 136 B6 266 C5
Hockenden La BR5,
BR8 .... 191 D1
Hocker St 41 E2 ...... 95 D4
Hockett Cl SE8 .... 119 B2
Hockington Ct 7 EN5 ... 13 D6
Hockley Ave E6 .... 100 A5
Hockley Ct 2 E18 ...... 37 A2
Hockley Ho 4 E9 ...... 74 C2
Hockley Mews IG11 ... 101 C5
Hockliffe Ho 5 W10 ... 90 C2
Hockney Ct 1 SE16 ... 118 B1
Hockworth Ho 7 N16 ... 51 C1
Hocroft Ave NW2 ...... 69 B5
Hocroft Ct NW2 .... 69 B5
Hocroft Rd NW2 .... 69 B5
Hocroft Wlk NW2 ...... 69 B5
Hodder Dr UB6 .... 86 D5
Hoddesdon Rd DA17 ... 125 C1
Hodford Lo NW11 ...... 69 C6
Hodford Rd NW11 ..... 47 B1
Hodgkins Cl SE28 ..... 124 D6
Hodgkins Mews HA7 ... 25 B5
Hodister Cl 26 SE5 ... 139 A5
Hodson Cl HA2 .... 63 B5
Hodson Pl EN3 .... 7 C5
Hoecroft Ct EN3 .... 6 C5
Hoe La EN1 .... 6 B5
Hoe St E17 .... 53 C4
Hoffman Gdns CR2 .... 222 B1
Hoffman Sq N1 ...... 235 D2
Hofland Rd
W14 .... 113 A3 254 A6
Hogan Mews W2 ..... 236 C4
Hogan Way E5 .... 74 A6
Hogarth Ave TW15 .... 171 A4
Hogarth Bsns Pk W4 ... 133 C6
Hogarth Cl Ealing W5 ... 88 A2
Newham E16 .... 99 D2
Hogarth Cres
Mitcham SW19 ...... 180 B2
Thornton Heath CR0 ... 205 A2
Hogarth Ct
8 Camden Town NW1 ... 71 C1
City of London EC3 ... 253 B6
Dulwich SE19 .... 183 D6
Heston TW5 .... 129 A5
24 Whitechapel E1 ..... 96 A1
Hogarth Gdns TW5 .... 129 C5
Hogarth Hill NW11 ..... 47 B5
Hogarth Ho Enfield EN1 .. 18 A6
12 Northolt UB5 .... 84 D5
1 Sutton SM1 .... 218 B3
Westminster SW1 .... 259 D3
6 West Norwood
SE27 .... 183 A6
Hogarth Ind Est NW10 .. 90 A3
Hogarth La W4 .... 133 C6
Hogarth Pl SW5 ..... 255 C3
Hogarth Rd Barking RM8 .. 80 B3
Earl's Ct SW5 . 113 D2 255 C3
Edgware HA8 .... 26 C1
Hogarth Roundabout
W4 .... 133 C6
Hogarth's House*
W4 .... 133 C6
Hogarth Way TW12 .... 174 A2
Hogsmill Way KT19 ... 215 A4
Holbeach Cl 8 NW9 .... 27 C2
Holbeach Gdns DA15 .. 167 D5
Holbeach Mews 1
SW12 .... 159 B3
Holbeach Prim Sch
SE6 .... 163 C4
Holbeach Rd SE6 ..... 163 D4
Holbeck Row SE15 .... 140 A5
Holbein Ho
Chelsea SW1 .... 258 A2
10 Stanmore HA7 ...... 25 C5
Holbein Mews
SW1 .... 115 A1 258 A2
Holbein Pl
SW1 .... 115 A2 258 A3
Holberry Ho 5 SE21 ... 183 C6
Holberton Gdns NW10 .. 90 B4
HOLBORN 94 C2
Holborn EC1 .... 94 C2 241 B3
Holborn Cir EC1 . 94 C2 241 B3
Holborn Ho 1 W12 ..... 90 B1
Holborn Pl WC1 ..... 240 C3
Holborn Rd E13 .... 99 B3
Holborn Sta
WC1 .... 94 B2 240 C3
Holborn Viaduct
EC1 .... 94 D2 241 C3
Holborn Way CR4 ..... 180 D1
Holbrook Cl Enfield EN1 .. 6 A5
Highgate N19 .... 49 B1
Holbrook Ct W7 ...... 108 C6
Holbrooke Ct N7 ...... 72 A4
Holbrooke Pl 25
TW10 .... 153 D6
Holbrook Ho Acton W3 .. 89 B2
Chislehurst BR7 ..... 189 B2
5 Streatham SW2 .... 160 B3
Holbrook La BR7 ..... 189 B3
Holbrook Rd E15 ...... 98 D5
Holbrook Way BR2 .... 210 B4
Holburne Cl SE3 ..... 143 C4
Holburne Gdns SE3 ... 143 D4
Holburne Rd SE3 ..... 143 D4
Holcombe Hill NW7 ... 12 A1
Holcombe Ho SW9 .... 138 A2
Holcombe Pl SE4 ..... 141 A2
Holcombe Rd Ilford IG1 .. 56 C2
Tottenham Hale N17 ... 52 A6
1 Tottenham N17 ..... 51 D6
Holcombe St W6 ..... 112 B2
Holcote Cl DA17 ..... 125 A3
Holcroft Ct W1 ...... 239 A4
Holcroft Ho
Battersea SW11 ...... 136 B2
Lewisham SE10 ...... 142 A4
Holcroft Rd E9 .... 74 C1
Holden Ave
North Finchley N12 ..... 29 D5
Welsh Harp NW9 ...... 45 A1
Holdenby Rd SE4 ..... 163 A6
Holden Cl RM8 .... 80 B5
Holden Ho
12 Deptford SE8 ..... 141 C5
Islington N1 .... 235 A5
Holden Hts N12 .... 13 D1
Holdenhurst Ave N12 ... 30 A3
Holden Lo N11 .... 31 C5
Holden Point E15 ...... 76 B2
Holden Rd N12 .... 29 D6
Holden St SW11 ...... 137 A3
Holdernesse Rd
Isleworth TW7 .... 131 A4
6 Upper Tooting
SW17 .... 159 A2
Holderness Ho SE5 ... 139 C2
Holderness Way SE27 .. 182 D5
Holders Hill Ave NW4 ... 46 D6
Holders Hill Cres NW4 .. 28 D1
Holders Hill Dr NW4 ... 28 D1
Holders Hill Gdns NW4 .. 29 A1
Holders Hill Par NW7 ... 29 A2
Holders Hill Rd
Church End NW4, NW7 .. 29 A2
Hendon NW4 .... 28 D1
Holdsworth Ho 5
SW2 .... 160 C4
Holford Ho
6 Bermondsey SE16 ... 118 B2
Finsbury WC1 .... 233 D2
Holford Pl WC1 ..... 233 D2
Holford Rd NW3 .... 70 A5
Holford St WC1 ..... 234 A2
Holford Yd WC1 ..... 234 A3
Holgate Ave SW11 .... 136 B2
Holgate Ct HA8 .... 26 B6
Holgate Gdns RM10 ... 81 C2
Holgate Rd RM10 ..... 81 C3
Holgate St SE7 ...... 121 D3
Holkham Ho 6 EN5 ..... 1 A2
Holland Ho N8 .... 50 B5
Holland Ave
Belmont SM2 .... 217 C1
Wimbledon SW20 .... 177 D2
Holland Cl
Coney Hall BR2 ...... 224 D6
New Barnet EN5 ...... 14 B6
Stanmore HA7 .... 25 B5
Holland Ct
Ashford TW15 .... 170 B6
Hendon NW7 .... 28 A4
6 Walthamstow E17 ... 54 A5
Holland Dr SE23 ..... 163 A1
Holland Gdns
Brentford TW8 .... 132 A6
Kensington W14 ..... 254 B6
Holland Gr SW9 ...... 138 C5
Holland Ho E4 .... 36 A6
Holland House Sch
HA8 .... 26 D6
Holland Park
W11 .... 113 B5 244 C3
Holland Park Ave
Ilford IG3 .... 57 D4
Notting Hill
W11 .... 113 A5 244 B3
Holland Park Ct W14 .. 244 B2
Holland Park Gdns
W14 .... 113 A4 244 A2
Holland Park Mews
W11 .... 113 B5 244 C3
Holland Park Rd
W14 .... 113 B3 254 D5
Holland Park Rdbt
W12 .... 112 D4
Holland Park Sch
W8 .... 113 B4 244 D2
Holland Park Sta
W11 .... 113 B5 244 C3
Holland Pas N1 ...... 235 A6
Holland Pl W8 ...... 245 C2
Holland Rd
Croydon SE25 ...... 206 A4

Holland Rd *continued*
Newham E15 ... 98 C4
Wallend E6 ... 78 C1
Wembley HA0 ... 65 D2
West Kensington W14 ... 113 A3 254 B6
Willesden Green NW10 ... 90 B5
Holland Rise Ho SW9 . 270 D3
Holland St
Kensington W8 ... 113 C4 245 B2
Lambeth SE1 .. 116 D5 251 D4
Hollands The
Feltham TW13 ... 172 D6
New Malden KT4 ... 199 D1
Holland Villas Rd W14 ... 113 A4 244 A1
Holland Way BR2 ... 224 D6
Holland Wlk
Kensington W14 ... 113 B4 244 D1
Stanmore HA7 ... 25 A5
Upper Holloway N19 ... 49 D1
Hollar Rd N16 ... 73 D5
Hollen St W1 ... 239 C2
Holles Cl TW12 ... 173 C5
Holles Ho 8 SW9 ... 138 C3
Holles St W1 ... 93 B1 238 D2
Holley Rd W3 ... 111 C4
Hollickwood Ave N12 ... 30 D4
Hollickwood Prim Sch N10 ... 31 B3
Holliday Sq 7 SW11 ... 136 B2
Hollidge Way RM10 ... 81 D1
Hollies Ave DA15 ... 167 D3
Hollies Cl
South Norwood SW16 ... 182 C4
Twickenham TW1 ... 152 D2
Hollies End NW7 ... 28 B5
Hollies Rd W5 ... 109 C2
Hollies The Harrow HA3 .. 43 A5
Oakleigh Pk N20 ... 14 B3
Upper Tooting SW12 ... 159 C2
9 Wanstead E11 ... 55 A4
Wood Green N11 ... 31 D4
Hollies Way 1 SW12 ... 159 A4
Holligrave Rd BR1 ... 187 A2
Hollingbourne Ave DA7 ... 147 B4
Hollingbourne Gdns W13 ... 87 B2
Hollingbourne Rd SE24 ... 161 A6
Hollingsworth Ct 7 KT6 ... 197 D2
Hollingsworth Rd CR0 .. 222 B2
Hollington Cres KT3 ... 199 D3
Hollington Ct BR7 ... 188 D4
Hollington Rd
Newham E6 ... 100 B4
Tottenham N17 ... 34 A1
Hollingworth Cl KT8 ... 195 B5
Hollingworth Rd BR2, BR5 ... 210 D2
Hollins Ho N7 ... 72 A4
Hollisfield WC1 ... 233 B1
Hollman Gdns SW16 .. 182 D4
Holloway Cl UB7 ... 104 A1
Holloway La UB7 ... 104 B1
Holloway Rd Leyton E11 .. 76 B5
Lower Holloway N7 ... 72 B4
Newham E6 ... 100 B4
Upper Holloway N19 ... 71 D6
Holloway Road Sta N7 .. 72 B3
Holloway Sch N7 ... 71 D3
Holloway St TW3 ... 129 D2
Hollow Combe SE20 .. 184 B6
Hollowfield Wlk UB5 ... 63 A2
Hollow The IG8 ... 36 D6
Holly Ave London N2 ... 47 D6
Stanmore HA7 ... 26 A1
Walton-on-T KT12 ... 194 D1
Hollybank Cl TW12 ... 173 C5
Holly Berry La 8 NW3 .. 70 A4
Hollybrake Cl BR7 ... 189 B3
Hollybush Cl
Harrow HA3 ... 24 C2
Wanstead E11 ... 55 A4
Hollybush Gdns E2 ... 96 B4
Hollybush Hill E11 ... 54 D3
Holly Bush Hill 4 NW3 .. 70 A4
Hollybush Ho 23 E2 ... 96 B4
Holly Bush La TW12 ... 173 C3
Hollybush Pl E2 ... 96 B4
Hollybush Rd KT2 ... 176 A4
Hollybush St E13 ... 99 B4
Holly Bush Steps 6 NW3 ... 70 A4
Holly Bush Vale 10 NW3 ... 70 A4
Holly Cl
Beckenham BR3 ... 208 A5
Buckhurst Hill IG9 ... 21 D1
Feltham TW13 ... 173 A5
Wallington SM6 ... 219 B1
Holly Cottage Mews UB8 ... 82 C2
Holly Cotts KT7 ... 197 A1
Holly Cres
Beckenham BR3 ... 207 B4
Chingford IG8 ... 36 B3
Hollycroft Ave
Child's Hill NW3 ... 69 C5
Wembley HA9 ... 66 B5
Hollycroft Cl
Harmondsworth UB7 ... 126 C6
South Croydon CR2 ... 221 C3
Hollycroft Gdns UB7 ... 126 C6
Holly Ct
16 Belmont SM2 ... 217 C1
Catford SE6 ... 164 A1
4 Sidcup DA14 ... 190 B6
South Tottenham N15 ... 51 C5
Hollydale Cl UB5 ... 63 D4
Hollydale Dr BR2 ... 226 B5
Hollydale Prim Sch SE15 ... 140 C3
Hollydale Rd SE15 ... 140 C3
Hollydene
Bromley BR1 ... 186 D2
Hither Green SE13 ... 164 B5
5 Peckham SE15 ... 140 B4
Hollydown Way E11 ... 76 B5
Holly Dr E4 ... 19 D4
Holly Farm Rd UB2 ... 107 A1
Hollyfield Ave N11 ... 30 D5
Hollyfield Rd KT5 ... 198 B2
Hollyfield Sch & Sixth Form Ctr The KT6 ... 198 A4
Holly Gdns UB7 ... 104 B4
Holly Gr Kingsbury NW9 .. 45 A2
Peckham SE15 ... 140 A3
Pinner HA5 ... 23 A2
Hollygrove WD23 ... 8 B4
Hollygrove Cl TW3 ... 129 B1
Hollyhedge Ho SE3 ... 142 B3
Holly Hedge Terr SE13 ... 164 B6
Holly Hill
Hampstead NW3 ... 70 A4
Southgate N21 ... 16 B5
Holly Hill Rd DA8, DA17 ... 125 D1
Holly Ho
Brentford TW8 ... 131 C6
Ilford IG3 ... 58 A1
Holly House Hospl IG9 .. 21 B2
Holly Lo
Cottenham Pk SW20 ... 178 B1
Harrow HA1 ... 42 B4
Kensington W8 ... 245 A2
Southgate N21 ... 16 C3
4 Wimbledon SW19 ... 179 A4
Holly Lodge
Lewisham SE13 ... 142 B1
Southall UB2 ... 107 B2
Holly Lodge Gdns N6 ... 49 A1
Holly Lodge Mans N6 ... 71 A6
Hollymead SM5 ... 218 D5
Holly Mews SW10 ... 256 B1
Holly Mount NW3 ... 70 A4
Hollymount Cl 9 SE10 ... 142 A4
Hollymount Sch SW20 ... 178 C2
Holly Park Est N4 ... 50 B2
Holly Park Gdns N3 ... 47 C6
Holly Park Prim Sch N11 ... 31 A5
Holly Park Rd
Ealing W7 ... 108 D5
Friern Barnet N11 ... 31 A5
Holly Pk East Finchley N3 . 47 C6
Hornsey N4 ... 50 B2
Holly Pl NW3 ... 70 A4
Holly Rd
6 Chiswick W4 ... 111 B2
Hampton TW12 ... 174 A4
Hounslow TW3 ... 129 D1
Leytonstone E11 ... 54 D2
Twickenham TW1 ... 153 A3
Holly St E8 ... 73 D1
Holly Terr N6 ... 49 A1
Hollytree Cl SW19 ... 156 D3
Holly Tree Ho SE4 ... 141 B2
Holly Tree Lo EN2 ... 4 D3
Hollyview Cl NW4 ... 46 A3
Holly Village N6 ... 71 B6
Holly Way CR4 ... 203 D6
Holly Wlk Enfield EN2 ... 5 B2
Hampstead NW3 ... 70 A4
Hollywood Ct W5 ... 110 B6
Hollywood Gdns UB4 ... 84 B1
Hollywood Lofts E1 ... 243 C5
Hollywood Mews SW10 ... 266 A6
Hollywood Rd
Chelsea SW10 ... 136 A6 266 A6
Highams Pk E4 ... 35 A5
Hollywood Way IG8 ... 36 B4
Holman Ho 2 E2 ... 96 D4
Holman Hunt Ho W14. 254 A1
Holman Rd
London SW11 ... 136 B3
West Ewell KT19 ... 215 A3
Holmbank Dr TW17 ... 193 C5
Holmbridge Gdns EN3 ... 6 D1
Holmbrook NW1 ... 232 B3
Holmbrook Dr NW4 ... 46 D4
Holmbury Cl WD23 ... 8 C2
Holmbury Ct
Mitcham SW19 ... 180 C3
Upper Tooting SW17 ... 158 D1
Holmbury Gdns UB3 ... 105 D5
Holmbury Gr CR0 ... 223 B1
Holmbury Ho SW9 ... 160 D6
Holmbury Manor 9 DA14 ... 190 A6
Holmbury Pk BR7 ... 188 A3
Holmbury View 2 E5 ... 52 B1
Holmbush Ct NW4 ... 46 D4
Holmbush Rd SW15 ... 157 A5
Holmcote Gdns N5 ... 73 A3
Holmcroft Ho 10 E17 ... 53 D5
Holmcroft Way BR2 ... 210 B4
Holm Ct SE12 ... 165 B1
Holmdale Gdns NW4 ... 46 D4
Holmdale Rd
Chislehurst BR7 ... 189 A5
South Hampstead NW6 .. 69 C3
Holmdale Terr N15 ... 51 C3
Holmdene N12 ... 29 D5
Holmdene Ave
Harrow HA2 ... 41 D6
Hendon NW7 ... 28 A4
Herne Hill SE24 ... 161 A6
Holmdene Cl BR3 ... 186 A1
Holmdene Ct BR1 ... 210 A6
Holmead Rd SW6 ... 135 D5 265 D3
Holme Ct 12 TW7 ... 131 A2
Holmefield Ct 4 NW3 .. 70 C2
Holmefield Ho W10 ... 91 A3
Holme Lacey Rd SE12 .. 164 D5
Holmeleigh Ct EN3 ... 6 C1
Holme Rd E6 ... 100 A6
Holmes Ave
Mill Hill NW7 ... 29 A5
Walthamstow E17 ... 53 B6
Holmes Cl SE22 ... 140 A1
Holmes Ct Chingford E4 .. 20 B2
18 South Acton W4 ... 111 A3
18 South Lambeth SW4 . 138 A3
Holmesdale Ave SW14 ... 132 D1
Holmesdale Cl SE25 ... 205 D6
Holmesdale Ho 12 NW6 ... 91 C6
Holmesdale Rd
Bexley DA7 ... 146 D3
Highgate N6 ... 49 B2
Richmond TW9 ... 132 B4
South Norwood SE25 ... 205 C5
Teddington TW11 ... 175 C4
Thornton Heath CR0 ... 205 B4
Holmesley Rd SE23 ... 163 A5
Holmes Pl SW10 ... 266 B6
Holmes Rd
Kentish Town NW5 ... 71 B3
Merton SW19 ... 180 A3
Twickenham TW1 ... 152 D2
Holmes Terr SE1 ... 251 A2
Holmeswood 1 SM2 ... 217 D1
Holmeswood Ct 3 N22 . 32 C1
Holme Way HA7 ... 24 D4
Holmewood Gdns SW2 ... 160 B4
Holmewood Rd
South Norwood SE25 ... 205 C6
Streatham SW2 ... 160 B4
Holmfield Ave NW4 ... 46 D4
Holmfield Ho E17 ... 54 B5
Holm Gr UB10 ... 60 C1
Holmhurst
London SE13 ... 164 B5
Wimbledon SW19 ... 178 C3
Holmhurst Rd DA17 ... 125 D1
Holmlea Ct CR0 ... 221 B4
Holmleigh Prim Sch N16 ... 51 C1
Holmleigh Rd N16 ... 51 C1
Holm Oak Cl SW15 ... 157 B5
Holmoaks Ho BR3 ... 186 A1
Holmsbury Ho 6 N7 ... 71 D3
Holmsdale Ho
6 London N11 ... 31 B6
24 Poplar E14 ... 119 D6
Holmshaw Cl SE26 ... 185 A6
Holmside Ct SW12 ... 159 A5
Holmside Rd SW12 ... 159 A5
Holmsley Cl KT3 ... 199 D2
Holmsley Ho SW15 ... 155 D4
Holmstall Ave HA8 ... 27 A1
Holmstall Par HA8 ... 27 A1
Holm Wlk SE3 ... 143 A3
Holmwood 2 KT5 ... 198 B3
Holmwood Cl
Cheam SM2 ... 216 D1
Harrow HA2 ... 42 A6
Northolt UB5 ... 63 D2
Holmwood Ct
Kingston u T KT3 ... 199 B6
Sidcup DA14 ... 189 D5
3 Stamford Hill N16 ... 51 D2
Holmwood Gdns
London N3 ... 29 C1
Wallington SM6 ... 219 B2
Holmwood Gr NW7 ... 27 B5
Holmwood Mans W3 ... 110 C5
Holmwood Rd
Chessington KT9 ... 214 A3
Ilford IG3 ... 79 C6
Holne Chase London N2 .. 48 A3
Morden SM4 ... 201 C3
Holne Lo N6 ... 49 C3
Holness Rd E15 ... 76 D2
Holocaust Meml Gdn* W2 ... 114 D4 247 D2
Holroyd Rd SW15 ... 156 C6
Holsgrove Ct W3 ... 111 C5
Holstein Way 6 DA18 .. 125 A3
Holst Mans SW13 ... 134 C5
Holstock Rd IG1 ... 79 A6
Holsworth Cl HA2 ... 42 A4
Holsworthy Ho 49 E3 ... 97 D4
Holsworthy Sq WC1 ... 240 D5
Holsworthy Way KT9 ... 213 C3
Holt Cl London N10 ... 49 A5
Woolwich SE28 ... 124 C6
Holt Ct Greenwich SE10 .. 142 A6
Stratford New Town E15 .. 76 A3
Holt Ho SW2 ... 160 C5
Holtoake Ct 1 W5 ... 87 C3
Holtoake Ho 3 W5 ... 87 C3
Holton St E1 ... 96 D3
Holt Rd Newham E16 ... 122 A5
Wembley HA0 ... 65 C5
Holt The Morden SM4 ... 201 C5
Wallington SM6 ... 219 C4
Holtwhite Ave EN2 ... 5 A3
Holtwhite's Hill EN2 ... 4 D4
Holwell Pl HA5 ... 41 A5
Holwood Park Ave BR2, BR6 ... 226 B4
Holwood Pl 7 SW4 ... 137 D1
Holybourne Ave SW15 ... 156 A4
Holy Cross Prep Sch KT2 ... 177 A3
Holy Cross RC Prim Sch SE6 ... 164 A3
Holy Cross RC Sch SW6 ... 135 C4 265 A2
Holy Cross Sch The KT3 ... 199 C4
Holy Family RC Coll The
Walthamstow E17 ... 54 A5
Walthamstow E17 ... 54 A6
Holy Family RC Prim Sch
Kidbrooke SE9 ... 143 C1
Poplar E14 ... 119 C6
Holy Ghost RC Prim Sch SW12 ... 159 A4
Holyhead Cl Bow E3 ... 97 C4
3 Newham E6 ... 100 B2
Holyhead Ct KT1 ... 197 D5
Holy Innocents RC Prim Sch BR6 ... 227 D5
Holyoake Ct SE16 ... 119 B4
Holyoake Wlk
Ealing W5 ... 87 C3
East Finchley N2 ... 48 A6
Holyoak Rd SE11 ... 116 D2 261 D3
Holyport Rd SW6 ... 134 D5
Holyrood Ave HA2 ... 63 B4
Holyrood Gdns HA8 ... 26 D1
Holyrood Ho N4 ... 51 A1
Holyrood Mews 10 E16 ... 121 A5
Holyrood Rd EN5 ... 14 B5
Holyrood St SE1 ... 117 C5 253 A3
Holy Trinity CE Jun Sch SM6 ... 219 C4
Holy Trinity CE Prim Sch
Belgravia SW1 ... 115 A2 258 A4
Dalston E8 ... 73 D2
East Finchley N2 ... 48 B6
Forest Hill SE26 ... 162 C2
Hampstead NW3 ... 70 A2
Richmond TW10 ... 132 C1
Streatham SW2 ... 160 B4
Wimbledon SW19 ... 179 D4
Holy Trinity Coll Prep Sch BR1 ... 187 C2
Holy Trinity Lamorbey CE Prim Sch DA15 ... 168 A3
Holy Trinity & Saint Silas CE Prim Sch NW1 ... 71 B1
Holywell Cl
35 Bermondsey SE16 ... 118 B1
2 Greenwich SE3 ... 143 A6
Stanwell TW19 ... 148 A3
Holywell La EC2 ... 243 B6
Holywell Lo EN2 ... 4 B5
Holywell Row EC2 ... 95 C3 243 A5
Holywell Way TW19 ... 148 A3
Homan Ct N12 ... 30 A6
Homan Ho 6 SW4 ... 159 D4
Homebush Ho E4 ... 19 D4
Homecedars Ho WD23 ... 8 B3
Homecherry Ho 5 IG10 ... 21 D6
Home Cl
Carshalton SM5 ... 218 D6
Northolt UB5 ... 85 B4
Homecoppice Ho 1 BR1 ... 186 D3
Homecroft Rd
Forest Hill SE26 ... 184 C5
Tottenham N22 ... 33 A2
Homecross Ho 7 W4 .. 111 B2
Home Ct KT6 ... 197 D4
Homedale Ho SM1 ... 217 D4
Home Farm Cl
Thames Ditton KT7 ... 196 D2
Upper Halliford TW17 ... 193 C5
Home Farm Cotts BR5 ... 190 D2
Homefarm Rd W7 ... 86 D1
Homefield SM4 ... 201 C5
Home Field EN5 ... 13 B6
Homefield Ave IG2 ... 57 C4
Homefield Cl
Hayes UB4 ... 84 D3
Willesden NW10 ... 67 A2
Homefield Ct NW4 ... 46 C5
Homefield Gdns
London N2 ... 48 B6
Mitcham CR4, SW19 ... 180 B1
Homefield Ho SE23 ... 162 D1
Homefield Pk SM1, SM2 ... 217 D2
Homefield Pl 4 SW19 ... 178 D5
Homefield Prep Sch SM1 ... 217 C3
Homefield Rd
Bromley BR1 ... 187 C2
Burnt Oak HA8 ... 27 B4
Chiswick W4 ... 111 D1
Walton-on-T KT12 ... 195 A2
Homefield Rd *continued*
Wembley HA0 ... 65 B4
Wimbledon SW19 ... 179 A4
Homefield St 14 N1 ... 95 C5
Homefirs Ho HA9 ... 66 B5
Homeheather Ho 5 IG4 ... 56 B4
Homelands Dr SE19 ... 183 C3
Home Lea BR6 ... 227 D3
Homeleigh Ct 8 SW16 ... 160 A1
Homeleigh Rd SE15 ... 162 D6
Homemead SW12 ... 159 B2
Home Mead HA7 ... 25 C2
Homemead Rd
Bromley BR2 ... 210 B4
Wallington CR0 ... 203 C3
Home Office SW1 ... 249 C1
Home Park Rd SW19 ... 157 B1
Home Park Terr KT1 ... 175 D1
Home Park Wlk KT1 ... 197 D5
Home Rd SW11 ... 136 C3
Homer Dr E14 ... 119 C2
Homer Rd
Croydon CR0 ... 206 D3
Homerton E9 ... 75 A2
Homer Row W1 ... 237 B3
Homersham Rd KT1 ... 176 D1
Homer St W1 ... 92 C2 237 B3
HOMERTON ... 74 D1
Homerton Coll of Technology E9 ... 74 C3
Homerton Ct 2 EN4 ... 14 D3
Homerton Gr E9 ... 74 D3
Homerton High St E9 ... 74 D3
Homerton Rd E9 ... 75 B3
Homerton Row E9 ... 74 C3
Homerton Sta E9 ... 74 D2
Homerton Terr E9 ... 74 C2
Homerton University Hospl E9 ... 74 D3
Homesdale Cl E11 ... 55 A4
Homesdale Rd
Bromley BR1, BR2 ... 209 C6
Orpington BR5 ... 211 C2
Homesfield NW11 ... 47 C4
Homes Of Rest (CE Temperance Society) IG1 ... 79 B5
Homestall Rd SE22 ... 162 C6
Homestead Ct EN5 ... 13 C6
Homestead Gdns KT10 ... 212 C3
Homestead Paddock N14 ... 15 B6
Homestead Pk NW2 ... 67 D5
Homestead Rd
Dagenham RM8 ... 81 B6
Fulham SW6 .. 135 B5 264 D3
Homesteads The BR3 .. 185 D4
Homestead The N11 ... 31 B6
Homewalk Ho 1 SE26 ... 184 C6
Homewaters Ave TW16 ... 171 D2
Homewillow Cl N21 ... 16 D5
Homewood Cl TW12 ... 173 B4
Homewood Cres BR7 .. 189 C4
Homewood Gdns SE25 ... 205 C4
Homewoods 2 SW12 ... 159 C4
Homildon Ho 10 SE26 .. 162 A1
Homington Ct KT2 ... 176 A3
Honduras St EC1 ... 242 A6
Honeybourne Rd NW6 .. 69 D3
Honeybourne Way BR5 ... 211 B1
Honeybrook Rd SW12, SW4 ... 159 C4
Honey Cl RM10 ... 81 D2
Honeycroft Hill UB10 ... 60 A1
Honeyden Rd DA14 ... 191 A4
Honeyfield N4 ... 72 C6
Honey Hill UB10 ... 60 B1
Honey La EC2 ... 242 B1
Honey Lane Ho SW10 . 265 D6
Honeyman Cl NW6 ... 68 D1
Honeypot Bsns Ctr HA7 ... 26 A2
Honeypot Cl NW9 ... 44 B5
Honeypot La HA3, HA7, NW9 ... 44 B6
Honeysett Rd 3 N17 ... 33 D1
Honeysuckle Cl UB1 ... 107 A6
Honeysuckle Ct
Ilford IG1 ... 78 D2
2 Lee SE12 ... 165 A4
6 Sutton SM2 ... 217 D2
Honeysuckle Gdns CR0 ... 206 D1
Honeywell Jun & Inf Schs SW11 ... 158 D5
Honeywell Rd SW11 ... 158 D5
Honeywood Heritage Ctr* SM5 ... 218 D4
Honeywood Ho 5 SE15 ... 140 A4
Honeywood Rd
Harlesden NW10 ... 89 D5
Isleworth TW7 ... 131 A1
Honeywood Wlk SM5 .. 218 D4
Honister Cl HA7 ... 25 B2
Honister Gdns HA7 ... 25 B2
Honister Pl HA7 ... 25 B2
Honiton Gdns
Edgware NW7 ... 28 D3
1 Nunhead SE15 ... 140 C3
Honiton Ho 29 SE5 ... 139 A3
Honiton Rd
Bexley DA16 ... 145 D3
Honiton Rd *continued*
Kilburn NW6 ... 91 B5
Honley Rd SE6 ... 163 D4
Honnor Gdns TW7 ... 130 B3
HONOR OAK ... 162 C6
Honor Oak Park Sta SE23 ... 162 D5
Honor Oak Pk SE23 ... 162 D5
Honor Oak Rd SE23 ... 162 C4
Honor Oak Rise SE23 ... 162 C5
Honwell Ho 24 W2 ... 91 C2
Hood Ave
East Barnet N14 ... 15 B5
Mortlake SW14 ... 155 A6
Hood Cl CR0 ... 204 D1
Hoodcote Gdns N21 ... 16 D4
Hood Ct N7 ... 72 B5
Hood Ho 17 SE5 ... 139 B5
Hood Lo E11 ... 77 B6
Hood Rd SW20 ... 177 D3
HOOK ... 214 A4
Hook KT6 ... 214 A5
Hooke Ct SE10 ... 142 A4
Hooke Ho 32 E3 ... 97 A5
Hooker's Rd E17 ... 52 D6
Hook Farm Rd BR2 ... 209 D4
Hookham Ct SW8 ... 269 C2
Hook Ho 9 SW27 ... 182 D5
Hooking Gn HA2 ... 41 D4
Hook La DA16 ... 146 A1
Hook Lane Prim Sch DA16 ... 146 A2
Hook Rd KT19, KT17 ... 215 A1
Hook Rise N
Surbiton KT6 ... 214 A5
Tolworth KT6 ... 214 D6
Hook Rise S KT6, KT9 .. 214 D6
Hook Rise South KT6 ... 214 A5
Hook Rise South Ind Pk KT6 ... 214 C5
Hooks Cl SE15 ... 140 B4
Hookstone Way IG8 ... 37 D3
Hook The EN5 ... 14 B5
Hook Underpass KT6 ... 214 A5
Hook Wlk HA8 ... 27 A4
Hooper Dr UB8 ... 82 D2
Hooper Ho 9 SW18 ... 157 B6
Hooper Rd E16 ... 99 A1
Hooper's Ct SW1 ... 247 C1
Hooper's Mews 4 W3 ... 111 A5
Hooper St E1 ... 96 A1
Hoop La NW11 ... 47 C2
Hoover Ho 5 SE6 ... 186 A6
Hope Cl
2 Brentford TW8 ... 110 A1
Canonbury N1 ... 73 A2
Dagenham RM6 ... 58 D5
Grove Pk SE12 ... 165 B1
Sutton SM1 ... 218 A3
1 Woodford IG8 ... 37 C4
Hope Ct 1 SE1 ... 118 A1
Hopedale Rd SE7 ... 143 B6
Hopefield 3 W7 ... 108 D5
Hopefield Ave NW6 ... 91 A5
Hope Gdns 10 W3 ... 110 D4
Hope Pk BR1 ... 186 D3
Hopes Cl TW5 ... 129 C6
Hope St SW11 ... 136 B2
Hopetown St E1 ... 243 D3
Hopewell St SE5 ... 139 B5
Hop Gdns WC2 ... 250 A5
Hopgood St 5 W12 ... 112 C5
Hopkins Cl N10 ... 31 A3
Hopkins Ho 17 E14 ... 97 C1
Hopkins Mews E15 ... 98 D6
Hopkinson Ho 1 SW11 ... 137 A3
Hopkinson's Pl NW1 .. 231 A6
Hopkins St W1 .. 93 D1 239 C1
Hopley Ho W13 ... 109 B6
Hoppers Rd N21 ... 16 C2
Hoppett Rd E4 ... 20 C2
Hopping La N1 ... 72 D2
Hoppingwood Ave KT3 ... 199 C6
Hoppner Rd UB4 ... 83 B5
Hop St SE10 ... 120 D2
Hopton Ct BR2 ... 209 A1
Hopton Gdns KT3 ... 200 A3
Hopton Ho 5 SW9 ... 138 D3
Hopton Par 2 SW16 ... 182 A5
Hopton Rd
Streatham SW16 ... 182 A5
Woolwich SE18 ... 122 D3
Hopton's Gdns SE1 ... 251 D4
Hopton St SE1 .. 116 D5 251 D4
Hoptree Cl N12 ... 29 D6
Hopwood Cl SW17 ... 158 A1
Hopwood Rd SE17 ... 139 B6
Hopwood Wlk E8 ... 74 A1
Horace Rd
Forest Gate E7 ... 77 B4
Ilford IG6 ... 57 A6
Kingston u T KT1 ... 198 B6
Horatio Ho
13 Haggerston E2 ... 95 D5
4 Merton SW19 ... 179 D3
Horatio Pl
9 Canary Wharf E14 ... 120 A5
Merton SW19 ... 179 C2
Horatio St 11 E2 ... 95 D5
Horatius Way CR0 ... 220 B2
Horbury Cres W11 ... 113 C6 245 A5
Horbury Lo TW12 ... 173 C3

Horbury Mews W11 113 B6 244 D5
Horder Rd SW6 135 A4 264 B1
Hordle Prom E 15 SE15 139 D5
Hordle Prom N 4 SE15 139 D5
Hordle Prom S 7 SE15 139 D5
Horizon Bldg 22 E14 119 C6
Horizon Sch N16 73 C4
Horle Wlk SE5 138 D3
Horley Cl DA6 169 C6
Horley Rd SE9 188 A6
Hormead Rd W9 91 B3
Hornbeam Cl
Barking IG11 102 B3
Buckhurst Hill IG9 21 D1
Edgware NW7 11 D1
Ilford IG1 79 B3
Lambeth SE11 261 A4
Northolt UB5 63 B3
Hornbeam Cres TW8 131 B5
Hornbeam Gdns KT3 200 A3
Hornbeam Gr E4 20 D1
Hornbeam Ho
1 Buckhurst Hill IG9 21 D1
2 Maitland Pk NW3 70 D2
6 Penge SE20 184 D3
6 Sidcup DA15 168 A1
Hornbeam La E4 20 C6
Hornbeam Rd
Buckhurst Hill IG9 21 D1
Hayes UB4 84 C2
Hornbeam Sq 8 E3 97 B6
Hornbeams Rise N11 31 A4
Hornbeam Terr SM5 202 C1
Hornbeam Way BR2 210 C3
Hornblower Cl 2 SE16 119 A2
Hornbuckle Cl HA2 64 B6
Hornby Cl NW3 70 B1
Hornby Ho
6 Kennington SE11 138 C6
13 Richmond TW10 153 C1
Horncastle Cl SE12 165 A4
Horncastle Rd SE12 165 A4
Hornchurch N17 33 B1
Hornchurch Cl KT2 175 D6
Horndean Cl 3 SW15 156 A3
Horne Ho 4 SE18 144 A4
Horner Ct E11 76 B5
Horne Rd TW17 192 C5
Horner Hos 18 N1 95 C6
Horner La 3 CR4 180 B1
Horne Way SW15 134 C3
Hornfair Rd SE7 143 D5
Horniman Dr SE23 162 C4
Horniman Grange 7 SE23 162 C3
Horniman Mus & Gdns* SE23 162 B3
Horniman Sch SE23 162 B3
Horning Cl SE9 188 A6
Horn La Acton W3 89 A1
Greenwich SE10 121 A2
Woodford IG8 37 A3
Horn Link Way SE10 121 A2
Horn Park Cl SE12 165 B6
Horn Park La SE12 165 B5
Horn Park Prim Sch SE12 165 B4
Hornsby House Sch SW12 159 A3
Horns Croft IG11 79 C1
Horns End Pl HA5 40 C4
HORNSEY 50 A5
Hornsey Central Hospl N8 49 D4
Hornsey La N6 49 C2
Hornsey Lane Gdns N6 49 C2
Hornsey Park Rd N8 50 B6
Hornsey Rd N7, N19 72 B6
Hornsey Rise Gdns N19 50 A2
Hornsey Sch for Girls N8 50 B4
Hornsey St N7 72 B3
Hornsey Sta N8 50 B5
HORNSEY VALE 50 B4
Hornshay St SE15 140 C6
Horns Rd IG2, IG6 57 A4
Hornton Ct W8 245 B1
Hornton Pl W8 245 B1
Hornton St W8 113 C4 245 B2
Horrocks Ho SW15 156 B6
Horsa Rd Eltham SE12 165 C4
Erith DA8 147 D5
Horsebridge Cl RM9 103 A6
Horsecroft Rd HA8 27 B3
Horse & Dolphin Yd W1 249 D6
Horse Fair KT1 175 D1
Horseferry Pl SE10 142 A6
Horseferry Rd
Limehouse E14 119 A6
Westminster SW1 115 D2 259 D4
Horseferry Rd Est SW1 259 C5
Horse Guards Ave SW1 116 A5 250 A3
Horse Guards Par* SW1 115 D5 249 D3
Horse Guards Rd SW1 115 D4 249 D2
Horse Leaze E6 100 C1
Horsell Rd Islington N5 72 C3
St Paul's Cray BR5 190 B2
Horselydown La SE1 117 D5 253 C3
Horselydown Mans SE1 253 C2
Horsemongers Mews SE1 252 B1
Horsenden Ave UB6 64 D3
Horsenden Cres UB6 64 D3
Horsenden La N UB6 64 D1
Horsenden La S UB6 87 A6
Horsenden Prim Sch UB6 64 C2
Horsendon Ho 11 N7 71 D3
Horseshoe Cl
Cubitt Town E14 120 A1
Dollis Hill NW2 68 B6
Horse Shoe Cres UB5 85 C5
Horseshoe Dr UB8 82 C1
Horse Shoe Gn SM1 217 D6
Horseshoe La
Barnet N20 12 D3
Enfield EN2 5 A2
Horse Yd N1 234 D6
Horsfeld Gdns 1 SE9 166 A6
Horsfeld Rd SE9 165 D6
Horsfield Ho 13 N1 73 A1
Horsford Rd SW2 160 B6
Horsham Ave N12 30 C5
Horsham Ct N17 34 A2
Horsham Rd
Bexley DA6 169 C6
East Bedfont TW14 149 A5
Horsley Ct SW1 259 D3
Horsley Dr
Kingston u T KT2 175 D5
New Addington CR0 224 A1
Horsley Ho 11 SE4 140 D1
Horsley Rd
Bromley BR1 187 B2
Chingford E4 20 A2
Horsley St 3 SE17 139 B6
Horsman Ho SE5 139 A6
Horsman St SE5 139 A6
Horsmonden Cl BR6 211 D2
Horsmonden Rd SE4 163 B5
Horston Ho N4 51 A2
Hortensia Ho SW10 266 A4
Hortensia Rd SW10 136 A5 266 A4
Horticultural Pl 6 W4 111 B1
Horton Ave NW2 69 A4
Horton Bridge Rd UB7 104 B5
Horton Cl UB7 104 B5
Horton Ctry Pk KT19 214 C1
Horton Ho
13 Deptford SE15 140 C6
South Lambeth SW8 270 C4
West Kensington W14 254 A1
Horton Ind Pk UB7 104 B5
Horton La KT19 215 A1
Horton Par UB7 104 A5
Horton Rd Hackney E8 74 B2
Yiewsley UB7 104 B5
Horton Road Ind Est UB7 104 B5
Horton St SE13 141 D2
Horton Way CR0 206 D4
Hortus Rd Chingford E4 20 A2
Southall UB2 107 B4
Horwood Ho
24 Bethnal Green E2 96 B4
Marylebone NW8 237 B6
Hosack Rd SW12, SW17 159 A2
Hoser Ave SE12 165 A2
Hosier La EC1 94 D2 241 D3
Hoskins Cl UB3 105 D1
Hoskin's Cl E16 99 C1
Hoskins St SE10 120 B1
Hospital Bridge Rd TW2 151 D3
Hospital Bridge Rdbt TW2 151 D2
Hospital of the Holy Trinity (Almshouses) 5 CR0 221 A6
Hospital Rd TW3 129 C2
Hospital Way SE13 164 B4
Hospl for Tropical Diseases
Fitzrovia WC1 93 C3 239 B5
Somers Town NW1 232 D5
Hospl of St John & St Elizabeth NW8 92 B5 229 C3
Hotham Cl KT8 195 C6
Hotham Prim Sch SW15 134 D1
Hotham Rd
Merton SW19 180 A3
Putney SW15 134 C2
Hotham Road Mews 12 SW19 180 A3
Hotham St E15 98 C6
Hothfield Pl SE16 118 C3
Hotspur Ind Est N17 34 B4
Hotspur Rd UB5 85 C5
Hotspur St SE11 116 C1 261 A2
Houblon Rd TW10 154 A6
Houghton Cl
10 Dalston E8 73 D2
Hampton TW12 173 A4
Houghton Rd N15 51 D5
Houghton Sq SW9 138 A2
Houghton St WC2 240 D1
Houlder Cres CR0 220 D2
Houndsden Rd N21 16 C5
Houndsditch EC3 95 C1 243 B2
Houndsfield Prim Sch N9 18 B4
Houndsfield Rd N9 18 B4
HOUNSLOW 129 C3
Hounslow Ave TW3 151 D6
Hounslow Bsns Pk TW3 129 D1
Hounslow Central Sta TW3 129 D2
Hounslow Ctr The TW3 129 D2
Hounslow East Sta TW3 130 A3
Hounslow Gdns TW3 151 D6
Hounslow Heath Jun & Inf Schs TW4 129 A2
Hounslow Heath Nature Reserve TW4 151 A5
Hounslow Manor Sch TW3 130 A2
Hounslow Rd
Feltham TW14 150 B4
Hanworth TW13 151 A2
Twickenham TW2, TW3 152 A5
Hounslow Sta TW3 151 D6
Hounslow Town Prim Sch TW3 130 B2
HOUNSLOW WEST 128 D2
Hounslow West Sta TW3 129 A3
Houseman Way 20 SE5 139 B5
House of Detention* EC1 94 C3 241 B6
Houses of Parliament* SW1 116 A3 260 B6
Houston Ct 3 CR0 205 C1
Houston Pl KT10 196 C1
Houston Rd
Forest Hill SE23 163 A1
Thames Ditton KT6 197 B3
Houstoun Ct TW5 129 B5
Hove Ave E17 53 B4
Hoveden Rd NW2 69 A3
Hove Gdns SM1 201 D1
Hovenden Ho 6 SE21 183 C6
Hoveton Rd SE28 102 C1
Howard Ave DA5 168 C4
Howard Bldg SW8 268 C5
Howard Cl Acton W3 88 D1
Ashford TW16 171 D4
Brunswick Pk N11 15 A2
Bushey WD23 8 C4
Cricklewood NW2 69 A4
Hampton TW12 174 A4
Howard Ct
12 Barking IG11 101 B6
Beckenham BR3 186 A1
Lewisham SE10 142 A4
Peckham SE15 140 A2
Howard Ho
6 Brixton SW9 138 C2
14 Deptford SE8 141 B6
Fitzrovia W1 238 D5
Penge SE20 184 C2
6 Upper Clapton E5 74 C6
Howard Mans E17 53 D6
Howard Mews N5 72 D4
Howard Prim Sch CR0 221 A4
Howard Rd
Barking IG11 101 B6
Canonbury N16 73 B4
Cricklewood NW2 68 D4
Croydon SE25 206 A3
Ilford IG1 78 D4
Isleworth TW7 130 D2
Leyton E11 76 C5
Newham E6 100 B5
New Malden KT3 199 D5
Penge SE20 184 C2
Plaistow BR1 187 A3
Southall UB1 85 D1
South Tottenham N15 51 C3
Surbiton KT5 198 B3
Walthamstow E17 53 D6
Howards Cl HA5 22 B1
Howards Crest Cl BR3 186 A1
Howard's La SW15 134 B1
Howard's Rd E13 99 A4
Howard St KT7 197 B3
Howard Way EN5 12 D6
Howard Wlk N2 48 B5
Howarth Ct E15 76 A3
Howarth Rd SE2 124 A2
Howberry Cl HA8 25 D4
Howberry Rd
South Norwood CR7 183 B1
Stanmore HA7, H8 25 D4
Howbury Rd SE15 140 C2
Howcroft Cres N3 29 C3
Howcroft Ho 3 E3 97 B4
Howcroft La UB6 86 B4
Howden Cl SE28 124 D6
Howden Ct SE25 183 D1
Howden Rd SE25 183 D1
Howden St SE15 140 A2
Howell Cl RM6 58 D4
Howell Ct 2 E10 53 D2
Howell Ho 5 N7 71 D3
Howell Wlk SE1 261 D3
Howe Lo TW1 153 A4
Howerd Way SE18 144 A4
Howes Cl N3 47 C6
Howeth Ct 7 N11 31 A4
Howfield Pl N17 51 D6
Howgate Rd SW14 133 B2
Howick Mans SE18 122 A3
Howick Pl SW1 115 C3 259 B5
Howie St SW11 136 C5 267 A3
Howitt Cl
6 Maitland Pk NW3 70 C2
Stoke Newington N16 73 C4
Howitt Rd NW3 70 C2
Howland Ho 9 SW16 160 A1
Howland Mews E W1 239 B4
Howland St W1 93 C2 239 B4
Howland Way SE16 119 A4
Howletts La HA4 39 A3
Howletts Rd SE24 161 A5
Howley Pl W2 92 A2 236 B4
Howley Rd CR0 221 A5
Howmic Ct 1 TW1 153 C5
Howsman Rd SW13 134 A6
Howson Rd SE4 141 A1
Howson Terr TW10 154 A5
How's St E2 95 D5
Howton Pl WD23 8 B3
HOXTON 95 C5
Hoxton Mkt 10 N1 95 C4
Hoxton Point EC1 95 C4
Hoxton Sq N1 95 C4
Hoxton St N1 95 C5
Hoylake Cres UB10 60 D6
Hoylake Gdns
Mitcham CR4 203 C6
Ruislip HA4 40 B1
South Oxhey WD19 22 D6
Hoylake Rd W3 89 C1
Hoyland Cl 4 SE15 140 B5
Hoyle Rd SW17 180 C5
Hoy St E16 98 D1
Hubbard Dr KT9 213 D2
Hubbard Rd SE27 183 A6
Hubbards Cl UB8 82 D1
Hubbard St E15 98 C6
Hub Buildings The 4 SW12 159 B3
Huberd Ho SE1 262 D6
Hubert Gr SW9 138 A2
Hubert Ho NW8 237 A5
Hubert Rd E6 99 D4
Hucknall Ct NW8 236 C6
Huddart St 6 E3 97 B2
Huddleston Cl E2 96 C5
Huddlestone Rd
Forest Gate E7 76 D4
Willesden NW2 68 B2
Huddleston Rd N7 71 C4
Hudson 27 NW9 27 D2
Hudson Cl Newham E15 99 A6
15 Shepherd's Bush W12 112 B6
Hudson Ct
Croydon SE25 206 A5
1 Isle Of Dogs E14 119 C1
4 Merton SW19 179 D2
Hudson Ho
Chelsea SW10 266 A4
5 Notting Hill W11 91 A1
Hudson Pl SE18 123 A1
Hudson Rd Erith DA7 147 B4
Harlington UB7 127 B6
Hudsons Ho N1 235 D1
Hudson's Pl SW1 115 C2 259 A4
Hudson Way N9 18 C2
Huggin Ct EC4 252 B6
Huggin Hill EC4 252 B6
Huggins Ho 9 E3 97 C4
Huggins Pl SW2 160 B3
Hughan Rd E15 76 B3
Hugh Astor Ct SE1 261 D6
Hugh Clark Ho 13 W13 109 A5
Hugh Dalton Ave SW6 264 C5
Hughenden Ave HA3 43 B4
Hughenden Gdns UB5 84 C4
Hughenden Ho NW8 237 A6
Hughenden Rd KT4 200 A2
Hughendon EN5 1 D1
Hughendon Terr E15 76 A4
Hughes Cl N12 30 A5
Hughes Ho
26 Bethnal Green E2 96 C4
Camberwell SE5 139 A4
15 Deptford SE8 141 C6
Newington SE17 261 D3
Hughes Mans E1 96 A3
Hughes Rd
Ashford TW15 171 A4
Hayes UB3 106 B6
Hughes Terr 6 E16 98 D2
Hughes Wlk CR0 205 A2
Hugh Gaitskell Cl SW6 264 C5
Hugh Gaitskell Ho
Stoke Newington N16 73 D6
Willesden NW10 67 D1
Hugh Herland KT1 198 A6
Hugh Mews SW1 258 D3
Hugh Morgan Ho 5 SW4 137 D2
Hugh Myddelton Prim Sch EC1 94 C4 234 B1
Hugh Platt Ho 29 E2 96 B5
Hugh St SW1 115 B2 258 D3
Hugo Ho SW1 257 D6
Hugon Rd SW6 135 D2
Hugo Rd N19 71 C4
Huguenot Ct 9 E1 96 A2
Huguenot Pl
London SW18 158 A6
Spitalfields E1 243 D4
Huguenot Sq SE15 140 B2
Hullbridge Mews N1 235 C6
Hull Cl SE16 118 D5
Hull Ct SE5 139 B3
Hull Pl E16 123 A5
Hull St EC1 235 A1
Hulme Pl SE1 252 B1
Hulse Ave IG11 79 C2
Humber Ct W7 86 B1
Humber Dr W10 90 D3
Humber Rd
Dollis Hill NW2 68 B6
Greenwich SE3 142 D6
Humberstone Rd E13 99 C4
Humberton Cl E9 75 A3
Humber Trad Est NW2 68 B6
Humbolt Rd W6 135 A6 264 A5
Hume Ct N1 72 D1
Hume Ho 14 W11 112 D5
Humes Ave W7 108 D4
Hume Terr E16 99 B1
Hume Way HA4 40 A3
Humphrey Ct SW11 266 D1
Humphrey St SE1 117 D1 263 C2
Humphries Cl RM9 81 B4
Humphry Ho 10 SW15 156 D6
Hundred Acre NW9 27 D1
Hungerdown E4 20 A3
Hungerford Bridge WC2 250 C4
Hungerford Ho SW1 269 B6
Hungerford La WC2 250 B4
Hungerford Prim Sch N7 71 D2
Hungerford Rd
12 Camden Town N7 71 D2
Lower Holloway N7 72 A3
Hungerford St 21 E1 96 B1
Hunsdon Cl RM9 81 A2
Hunsdon Ho E5 74 B5
Hunsdon Rd SE14 140 D5
Hunslett St 28 E2 96 C5
Hunstanton Ho NW1 237 B4
Hunston Rd SM4 201 D1
Hunt Cl W11 112 D5
Hunt Ct London N14 15 B4
10 Northolt UB5 84 D5
Hunter Cl
Borehamwood WD6 11 A6
Borough The SE1 262 D5
Upper Tooting SW12 159 A3
3 Wallington SM6 220 A1
Huntercombe Roehampton Hospl The SW15 156 A4
Huntercrombe Gdns WD19 22 C5
Hunter Ct
8 London SE5 139 B1
27 Streatham SW2 160 C4
11 Wanstead E11 55 A4
Hunter Ho
Bloomsbury WC1 240 B6
Feltham TW14 150 A3
Lambeth SE1 251 D1
South Lambeth SW8 269 D3
1 Tufnell Pk N19 71 C5
West Brompton SW5 255 B1
Hunterian Mus* WC2 94 B1 240 D2
Hunter Lo 9 W9 91 C2
Hunter Rd
South Norwood CR7 205 B6
Wimbledon SW20 178 C2
Hunters Ct 5 TW9 153 D6
Hunters Gr Harrow HA3 43 C5
Hayes UB3 106 A4
Hunter's Gr BR6 227 A4
Hunters Hall Prim Sch RM10 81 D3
Hunters Hall Rd RM10 81 C3
Hunters Hill HA4 62 D5
Hunters Lo
9 Edgware HA8 26 D5
10 Sidcup DA15 168 A1
Hunters Mdw SE19 183 C6
Hunters Rd
Chessington KT9 214 A4
Ilford IG1 78 D3
Hunters Sq RM10 81 C4
Hunter St WC1 94 A3 240 B6
Hunters The 2 BR3 186 A2
Hunters Way Enfield EN2 4 C4
South Croydon CR0 221 C4
Hunter Wlk
Borehamwood WD6 11 B6
Newham E13 99 A5
Huntingdon Cl
Mitcham CR4, SW16 204 A5
Northolt UB5 63 C2
Huntingdon Ct
3 Barnet EN5 1 B2
Mortlake SW14 133 A2
Huntingdon Gdns
Chiswick W4 133 A5
North Cheam KT4 216 C5
Huntingdon Ho SW5 255 B4
Huntingdon Rd
East Finchley N2 48 C6
Edmonton N9 18 C3
Huntingdon St
Canning Town E16 98 D1
Islington N1 72 B1
Huntingfield CR0 223 B1
Huntingfield Rd SW15 156 A6
Huntingford Ho SW15 134 C3
Hunting Gate Cl EN2 4 C2
Hunting Gate Dr KT9 214 A1
Hunting Gate Mews
Sutton SM1 217 D5
Twickenham TW2 152 C3
Huntings Farm IG1 79 C6
Huntings Rd RM10 81 C2
Huntington Ho NW2 68 C2
Huntley Cl TW19 148 A4
Huntley Ho 7 SE21 183 C6
Huntley St WC1 93 D3 239 C5
Huntley Way SW20 178 A1
Huntly Dr N3 29 C4
Huntly Rd SE25 205 C5
Hunton St E1 96 A2
Hunt Rd UB2 107 C3
Hunts Cl SE3 143 A3
Hunt's Ct WC2 249 D5
Huntshaw Ho 37 E3 97 D4
Hunt's La E15 98 A5
Huntsmans Cl TW13 172 B6
Huntsman St SE17 263 A3
Hunts Mead EN3 6 D2
Hunts Mead Cl BR7 188 B3
Huntsmoor Rd KT19 215 B3
Huntspill St SW17 158 A1
Hunts Slip Rd SE21 161 C2
Huntsworth Ct SE6 163 C3
Huntsworth Mews NW1 92 D3 237 C5
Huon Ct N20 14 C2
Hurdwick Ho NW1 232 A4
Hurdwick Pl NW1 232 A4
Hurleston Ho 11 SE8 119 B1
Hurley Cres SE16 118 D4
Hurley Ct 1 W5 87 C1
Hurley Ho
Lambeth SE11 261 B3
34 Shoreditch E2 95 D4
Hurley Lo SE22 162 C5
Hurley Rd UB6 85 D2
Hurlingham Bsns Pk SW6 135 C2
Hurlingham & Chelsea Sec Sch SW6 135 C2
Hurlingham Court Mans SW6 135 C3
Hurlingham Ct SW6 135 B2
Hurlingham Gdns SW6 135 B2
Hurlingham Rd
Erith DA7 147 B5
Fulham SW6 135 B3
Hurlingham Sch SW15 135 B1
Hurlingham Sq SW6 135 D2
Hurlock Ho 1 N5 72 D5
Hurlock St N5 72 D5
Hurlstone Rd SE25 205 C4
Hurn Court Rd TW5 128 D3
Hurn Ct TW5 128 D3
Huron Cl 5 BR6 227 D2
Huron Rd SW17 159 A1
Huron Univ WC1 94 A2 240 A4
Hurren Cl SE3 142 C2
Hurricane Rd SM6 220 B1
Hurricane Trad Ctr NW9 28 A2
Hurry Cl E15 76 C1
Hursley Ct 11 KT6 197 D2
Hurst Ave Chingford E4 19 C1
Highgate N6 49 C3
Hurstbourne KT10 212 D2
Hurstbourne Cotts DA5 169 D4
Hurstbourne Gdns IG11 79 C2
Hurstbourne Ho SW15 155 D5
Hurstbourne Priors CR2 221 C2
Hurstbourne Rd SE23 163 A3
Hurst Cl
Chessington KT9 214 C3
Chingford E4 19 C1
Hampstead Garden Suburb NW11 47 D3
Hayes BR2 208 D1
Northolt UB5 63 B3
Hurstcombe IG9 21 A2
Hurstcourt Rd SM1 217 D6
Hurst Ct
Beckenham BR3 185 C3
Newham E6 99 D2
South Norwood SE25 205 D5
Woodford IG8 37 B4
Hurstdene Ave BR2 208 D1
Hurstdene Gdns N15 51 C2
Hurstfield BR2 209 A4
Hurstfield Cres UB4 83 C2
Hurstfield Rd KT8 195 C6
Hurst Gr KT12 193 D1
Hurst Ho
7 Penge SE26 184 B5
Pentonville N1 233 D3
West Heath SE2 124 D1
Hurst La
East Molesey KT8 196 A6
West Heath SE2 124 D1
Hurst Lo London N8 49 D3
Wembley HA0 66 B1
Hurstmead Ct HA8 26 D6
Hurstmere Foundation Sch for Boys DA15 168 C3
HURST PARK 174 A1
Hurst Park Prim Sch KT8 195 C6
Hurst Pl Erith SE2 146 D6
Woolwich SE2 124 C1
Hurst Prim Sch DA5 168 D3

Hurst Rd
Buckhurst Hill IG9. . . . . .21 D3
Croydon CR0 . . . . .221 B3
East Molesey KT8,
KT12. . . . . .195 C6
Sidcup DA5, DA15. . . . . .168 C3
Southgate N21 . . . . .16 C3
Walthamstow E17. . . . . . .53 D6
Walton-on-T KT8&KT12. .194 D5
Hurst Rise EN5 . . . . .1 C2
Hurst Springs DA5. . . . . .169 A3
Hurst St SE24. . . . . .160 D5
Hurst View Grange
CR2. . . . . .220 D1
Hurst View Rd CR2. . . . . .221 C1
Hurst Way CR2 . . . . .221 C2
Hurstway Wlk 2 W11. .112 D6
Hurstwood Ave
Sidcup DA5. . . . . .169 A3
Wanstead E18. . . . . .55 B5
Hurstwood Ct
Colney Hatch N12 . . . . . . .30 C4
Temple Fortune NW11 . . .47 B5
Hurstwood Dr BR1. . . . . .210 B6
Hurstwood Rd NW11. . . .47 B5
Hurtwood Rd KT12. . . . . .195 B2
Husbourne Ho 8 SE8 . .119 A2
Huson Cl NW3. . . . . .70 C1
Hussain Cl HA1. . . . . . . .64 D4
Hussars Cl TW4. . . . . . . .129 A2
Husseywell Cres BR2. . . .209 A1
Hutching's St E14. . . . . . .119 C4
Hutching's Wharf 11
E14. . . . . .119 C4
Hutchins Wlk NW11. . . . .47 D5
Hutchins Cl E15 . . . . .76 A1
Hutchins Ho 8 SW4 . . .159 D4
Hutchinson Ct RM6 . . . . .58 D5
Hutchinson Ho 9
SE14. . . . . .140 C5
Hutchinson Terr HA9 . . . .65 D5
Hutchins Rd SE28. . . . . .124 A5
Hutton 1 Greenford UB6 . .64 B3
Woodford IG8. . . . . .37 B4
Hutton Ct 1 Ealing W5. . .87 C2
Edmonton N9. . . . . .18 C4
4 Finsbury Pk N4 . . . . . .50 B1
Hutton Gdns HA3. . . . . . .24 A3
Hutton Gr N12. . . . . .29 D5
Hutton Ho 19 E2 . . . . . . .96 A4
Hutton La HA3. . . . . .24 A3
Hutton Row 4 HA8 . . . . .27 A3
Hutton St EC4. . . . . .241 B1
Hutton Wlk HA3. . . . . . . .24 A3
Huxbear St SE4. . . . . . . .163 B6
Huxley Cl UB5 . . . . .85 A6
Huxley Dr RM6. . . . . .58 B2
Huxley Gdns NW10. . . . . .88 B5
Huxley Ho
4 London SW9. . . . . . .138 B3
Paddington NW8. . . . . .236 D5
West Heath SE2 . . . . . . .124 C1
Huxley Par N18. . . . . .33 B5
Huxley Pl N13 . . . . .16 D1
Huxley Rd
Edmonton N18. . . . . . . .33 C6
Falconwood DA16. . . . . .145 D2
Leyton E10. . . . . .76 A6
Huxley Sayze N18. . . . . . .33 B5
Huxley South N18. . . . . . .33 B5
Huxley St W10. . . . . .91 A4
Hyacinth Cl
3 Hampton TW12. . . . .173 C4
Ilford TW16 . . . . .78 D2
Hyacinth Ct 2 HA5 . . . . .40 C6
Hyacinth Dr UB10. . . . . . .60 A1
Hyacinth Rd SW15. . . . . .156 A3
Hyde Cl Ashford TW16. . . .171 C4
Barnet EN5 . . . . .1 B2
Newham E13. . . . . .99 A5
Hyde Cres NW9. . . . . . . .45 C4
Hyde Ct
Forest Hill SE23 . . . . . .163 A2
Hounslow TW4. . . . . . . .151 B6
Kingsbury NW9 . . . . . . .45 B2
Whetstone N20 . . . . . . .14 B1
Hyde Estate Rd NW9 . . . .45 D4
Hyde Farm Mews
SW12. . . . . .159 D3
Hydefield Cl N21. . . . . . . .17 B3
Hydefield Ct N9 . . . . .17 C2
Hyde Ho 12 Ealing W13. .109 A5
Hounslow TW3. . . . . . . .130 A2
Hyde Ind Est The NW9 . . .45 D4
Hyde La SW11 . .136 C4 267 A2
Hyde Park*
W2. . . . . .114 D5 247 C3
Hyde Park Ave N21. . . . . .17 B3
Hyde Park Cnr SW1. . . . .248 B2
Hyde Park Corner Sta
SW1. . . . . .115 A4 248 B2
Hyde Park Cres
W2. . . . . .92 C1 237 A1
Hyde Park Gate Mews
SW7. . . . . .246 B1
Hyde Park Gdns
Bayswater
W2. . . . . .114 B6 246 D6
Edmonton N21. . . . . . . .17 A3
Hyde Park Gdns Mews
W2. . . . . .114 C6 247 A6
Hyde Park Mans NW1. . .237 A3
Hyde Park Pl W2 . . . . . . .247 B6
Hyde Park Sq
W2. . . . . .92 C1 237 A1
Hyde Park Square Mews
W2. . . . . .237 A1
Hyde Park St
W2. . . . . .92 C1 237 A1
Hyde Park Twrs W2. . . . .246 A5

Hyderabad Way E15 . . . .76 C1
Hyde Rd
Bexleyheath DA7. . . . . .147 B3
Richmond TW10 . . . . . .154 B6
Shoreditch N1. . . . . .95 C6
Hyde Sch The NW9 . . . . .45 D4
Hydeside Gdns N9. . . . . . .17 D2
Hyde's Pl 12 N1. . . . . . . .72 D1
Hyde St SE8 . . . . .141 C6
Hyde Terr TW15, TW16. .171 C4
HYDE THE 45 D4
Hydethorpe Ave N9. . . . . .17 D2
Hydethorpe Rd SW12 . . .159 C3
Hyde Vale SE10. . . . . . .142 A5
Hyde Way Edmonton N9 . .17 D2
Hayes UB3. . . . . .105 D2
Hyde Wlk SM4. . . . . . . .201 C2
Hydon Ct N11. . . . . .30 D5
Hyh Ho E17. . . . . .35 D2
Hyland House Sch E17. . .36 B1
Hylands Rd E17. . . . . .36 B1
Hylda Ct NW5. . . . . .71 A5
Hylton St SE18. . . . . . . .123 D2
Hynewood 14 SE23. . . . .162 D1
Hyndman Ho
5 Dagenham RM10. . . . .81 C5
4 Tufnell Pk N19 . . . . . .71 D4
Hyndman St SE15. . . . . .140 B6
Hynton Rd RM8. . . . . . . .80 C6
Hyperion Ho 27 Bow E3. .97 A5
Streatham SW2. . . . . . .160 B4
Hyrstdene CR0 . . . . .220 D4
Hyrst The CR0 . . . . .207 A1
Hyson Rd SE16. . . . . . . .118 B1
Hythe Ave DA7. . . . . . . .147 B5
Hythe Cl N18. . . . . .34 A6
Hythe Ho 14 SE16. . . . . .118 C4
Hythe Rd
College Pk NW10 . . . . . .90 A3
South Norwood CR7 . . . .183 B1
Hythe Road Ind Est
NW10. . . . . .90 A3
Hyver Hill NW7 . . . . .11 B4

I

Ian Ct SE23. . . . . .162 C2
Ian Hamilton Ho NW1. . .232 C2
Ian Mikardo Sch E3. . . . .97 D4
Ian Sq EN3 . . . . .6 D4
Ibberton Ho
Kensington W14 . . . . . .254 B5
South Lambeth SW8 . . .270 C4
Ibbotson Ave E16. . . . . . .98 D1
Ibbott St 22 E1. . . . . . . .96 C3
Iberia Ho 11 N19. . . . . . .49 D2
Iberian Ave CR0, SM6. . .220 A4
Ibex Ho E15 . . . . .76 C3
Ibis Ct 16 SE8. . . . . . . .141 B6
Ibis Ho E12. . . . . .78 B4
Ibis La W4. . . . . .133 A4
Ibrox Ct 3 IG9 . . . . .21 C2
Ibsley Gdns SW15. . . . . .156 A3
Ibsley Way EN4 . . . . .2 C1
Ibstock Place Sch
SW15. . . . . .155 C5
Icarus Ho 21 E3. . . . . . . .97 B4
Iceland Rd E3. . . . . .97 C6
Iceland Wharf SE16. . . . .119 A2
Iceni Ct 28 Bow E3. . . . . .97 B6
Ice Wharf NW1. . . . . . . .233 B4
Ickburgh Est E5 . . . . .74 B6
Ickburgh Rd E5. . . . . . . .74 B5
Ickburgh Sch E5. . . . . . . .74 B5
ICKENHAM 60 C4
Ickenham Cl HA4 . . . . . . .61 B6
Ickenham Rd HA4. . . . . . .39 B1
Ickenham Sta UB10. . . . .61 A4
Ickleton Rd SE9. . . . . . . .188 A6
Icknield Dr IG2. . . . . .56 D4
Ickworth Park Rd E17. . . .53 A5
Icough Ct SE3 . . . . .143 B5
Idaho Bldg 7 SE13. . . . .141 D4
Ida Ho N15. . . . . .51 B5
Ida St E14. . . . . .98 A1
Iden Cl BR2. . . . . .208 C6
Idlecombe Rd SW17. . . . .181 A4
Idmiston Rd
New Malden KT4. . . . . .199 D2
Stratford E15. . . . . .76 D3
West Norwood SE21,
SE27. . . . . .161 A2
Idmiston Sq KT4. . . . . . .199 D2
Idol La EC3 . . . . .117 C6 253 A5
Idonia St SE8. . . . . .141 C5
Iffley Rd 47 E2. . . . . .95 D4
Iffley Rd W6. . . . . .112 B3
Ifield Ho SE17 . . . . .263 B2
Ifield Rd SW10. .135 D6 265 D6
Ifor Evans Pl E1 . . . . .96 D3
Ightham Ho
Beckenham BR3. . . . . .185 B3
Walworth SE17. . . . . . .263 A3
Ightham Rd DA8. . . . . . .147 C5
Ikon Ho 21 E1 . . . . .118 C6
Ikra Prim Sch N16. . . . . .73 D4
Ilbert St W10. . . . . .91 A4
Ilchester Gdns W2. . . . . .245 C6
Ilchester Mans W8. . . . .255 A6
Ilchester Pl
W14. . . . . .113 B3 254 D6
Ilchester Rd RM8 . . . . . .80 A5
Ildersly Gr SE21. . . . . . .161 B2
Ilderton Prim Sch
SE16. . . . . .118 C1
Ilderton Rd SE15, SE16. .140 C6
Ilex Cl TW16. . . . . .172 C1

Ilex Rd NW10. . . . . .67 D2
Ilex Way SW16. . . . . . . .182 C5
ILFORD 78 D6
Ilford Chambers 10
IG1. . . . . .78 D5
Ilford Hill IG1 . . . . .78 C5
Ilford Ho 14 N1 . . . . .73 B2
Ilford Interchange IG1. . . .78 C5
Ilford Jewish Prim Sch
IG6. . . . . .57 B6
Ilford La IG1 . . . . .78 C4
Ilford Prep Sch IG3. . . . . .58 A1
Ilford Ret Pk IG1 . . . . . . .79 A4
Ilford Sta IG1. . . . . .78 D6
Ilford Ursuline High Sch
IG1. . . . . .78 B6
Ilfracombe Flats SE1. . . .252 B2
Ilfracombe Gdns RM6. . . .58 B2
Ilfracombe Rd BR1. . . . . .164 D1
Iliffe St SE17 . . . .116 C3 261 D2
Iliffe Yd SE17. . . .116 C3 261 D2
Ilkeston Ct 7 E5. . . . . . . .74 D4
Ilkley Cl SE19 . . . . .183 B4
Ilkley Ct N11 . . . . .31 A4
Ilkley Rd Newham E16. . . .99 C2
South Oxhey WD19 . . . . .22 D5
Illingworth Cl SW3. . . . .202 B6
Illingworth Way EN1 . . . . .17 C6
Ilmington Rd HA3. . . . . . .43 D3
Ilminster Gdns SW11. . . .136 C1
Ilsley Ct 8 SW8 . . . . . . .137 C3
Imber Cl London N14. . . . .15 C4
Thames Ditton KT7. . . . .196 B1
Imber Court Trad Est
KT8. . . . . .196 B3
Imber Cross KT7. . . . . . .196 B3
Imber Ct 4 SE9. . . . . . . .166 C5
Imber Gr KT10 . . . . .196 B2
Imber Park Rd KT10. . . . .196 B1
Imber St N1. . . . . .235 C5
Immanuel Coll WD23. . . . .8 C4
Immanuel & St Andrew CE
Prim Sch SW16. . . . . .182 A4
Impact Ct SE20. . . . . . . .184 B1
Imperial Ave 5 N16. . . . .73 C4
Imperial Ho 2 HA2. . . . . .41 C3
Imperial College Rd
SW7. . . . . .114 B3 256 C6
Imperial College London
SW7. . . . . .114 B3 256 C6
Imperial Cres SW6. . . . . .136 A3
Imperial Ct
Chislehurst BR7. . . . . . .188 D4
Harrow HA2 . . . . .41 C2
St John's Wood NW8 . . .230 B4
Wembley HA9 . . . . .66 C5
Whetstone N20. . . . . . . .14 A1
Imperial Dr HA2 . . . . . . .41 C3
Imperial Gdns CR4. . . . . .203 B6
Imperial Ho 1 Bow E3. . .97 A4
2 Poplar E14. . . . . . . .119 B6
Strand WC2. . . . . .240 C1
Imperial Mews 8 E6. . . . .99 D5
Imperial Pl BR7. . . . . . . .188 C2
Imperial Rd
East Bedfont TW14 . . . .149 C4
Walham Green SW6 . . . .265 C4
Wood Green N22. . . . . . .32 A2
Imperial Sq SW6. . . . . . .265 D2
Imperial St E3 . . . . .98 A4
Imperial Twrs 3 NW3. . . .70 A2
Imperial Way
Croydon CR0, CR9. . . . .220 C2
Harrow HA3 . . . . .44 A3
Longlands BR7. . . . . . . .167 A1
Imperial Wharf Sta
SW10. . . . . . . .136 A4 266 B3
Impington 19 KT1. . . . . .176 C1
Imre Cl W12. . . . . .112 B5
Inca Dr SE9. . . . . .166 D4
Ince Terr 3 N15. . . . . . . .50 D6
Inchmery Rd SE6. . . . . . .164 A3
Inchwood BR4, CR0. . . . .223 D4
Independant Jewish Day
Sch NW4. . . . . .46 D4
Independence Ho 4
N19. . . . . .180 B2
Independent Ind Est
UB7. . . . . .104 C5
Independent Pl E8. . . . . . .73 D3
Independents Rd SE3 . . .142 D2
Inderwick Rd N8. . . . . . . .50 B4
Indescon Ct E14. . . . . . .119 C4
Indiana Bldg 7 SE8. . . . .141 C4
India St EC3. . . . . .243 C1
India Way W12. . . . . . . .112 B6
Indigo Ct TW13. . . . . . . .149 D1
Indigo Mews N16. . . . . . .73 B5
Indus Ct 18 SE15. . . . . .139 D5
Indus Rd SE7. . . . . .143 C5
Ingal Rd E13. . . . . .99 A3
Ingate Pl SW8 . . .137 B4 268 C1
Ingatestone Rd
Croydon SE25. . . . . . . .206 B5
Wanstead E12. . . . . .55 C1
Woodford IG8 . . . . .37 B3
Ingelow Ho W8. . . . . . . .245 C2
Ingelow Rd SW8. . . . . . .137 B3
Ingersoll Rd
Enfield EN3 . . . . .6 C5
Shepherd's Bush W12. . .112 B3
Ingestre Pl W1 . . . . .239 B1
Ingestre Rd
Forest Gate E7 . . . . .77 A4
Gospel Oak NW5. . . . . . .71 B4
Ingham Rd NW6. . . . . . . .69 C4
Inglebert St EC1 . .94 C4 234 A2
Ingleborough EN2 . . . . . . .4 C3

Ingleborough St SW9 . . .138 C3
Ingleby Ct N21. . . . . .16 D3
Ingleby Dr HA1 . . . . .64 B5
Ingleby Rd
Dagenham RM10. . . . . . .81 D2
Ilford IG1. . . . . .56 D1
Lower Holloway N7. . . . .72 A5
Ingleby Way
Chislehurst West
BR7. . . . . .188 C5
Wallington SM6. . . . . . .219 C1
Ingle Cl HA5. . . . . .41 B6
Ingledew Rd SE18. . . . . .123 B1
Inglefield Sq 12 E1. . . . .118 B5
Ingle Ho 3 SW12. . . . . . .159 D3
Inglehurst Gdns IG4 . . . . .56 B4
Inglemere Ct CR4,
SW17. . . . . .180 D3
Inglemere Rd
Forest Hill SE23 . . . . . .162 D1
Mitcham CR4, SW17. . . .180 D3
Inglesham Wlk E9 . . . . . .75 B2
Ingleside Cl BR3. . . . . . . .185 C3
Ingleside Gr SE3. . . . . . .142 D6
Inglethorpe Ho 6 E5. . . .74 A4
Inglethorpe St SW6. . . . .134 D4
Ingleton Ave DA16. . . . . .168 A6
Ingleton Rd N18. . . . . . . .34 A4
Ingleton St SW9 . . . . . . .138 C3
Ingleway N12. . . . . .30 C4
Inglewood BR7. . . . . . . .189 B4
Inglewood Cl E14 . . . . . .119 C2
Inglewood Copse BR1. . .188 B1
Inglewood Ct 4 BR1. . . .186 D3
Inglewood Mans 11
NW6. . . . . .69 C3
Inglewood Rd NW6 . . . . .69 C3
Inglis Ho W5. . . . . .110 B6
Inglis Rd Croydon CR0. . .205 D1
Ealing W5 . . . . .110 B6
Inglis St SE5. . . . . .138 C4
Ingram Ave NW11. . . . . .48 A2
Ingram Cl
Lambeth SE11. . . . . . . .260 C4
Stanmore HA7. . . . . . . .25 C5
Ingram Ct EN1. . . . . .17 D5
Ingram Ho
7 Harrow HA1. . . . . . . .42 D4
Old Ford E3 . . . . .97 A6
Teddington KT8. . . . . . .175 C2
Ingram Lo 8 SW4 . . . . . .159 D5
Ingram Rd London N2. . . .48 C5
South Norwood CR7 . . . .183 A2
Ingram Way UB6. . . . . . .86 B6
Ingrave Ho RM9. . . . . . .102 B6
Ingrave St SW11. . . . . . .136 C2
Ingrebourne Ct E4 . . . . . .19 D2
Ingrebourne Ho
2 Catford BR1. . . . . . .186 B5
Lisson Gr NW8. . . . . . .236 D4
Ingress St 4 W4. . . . . . .111 C1
Inigo Jones Rd SE7 . . . . .144 A5
Inigo Pl WC2 . . . . .250 A6
Inkerman Rd NW5 . . . . . .71 B2
Inkerman Terr W8 . . . . . .255 B5
Inks Gn E4 . . . . .36 A5
Inkster Ho 9 SW11 . . . . .136 C2
Inkwell Cl N12. . . . . .14 A1
Inman Rd
Harlesden NW10. . . . . . .89 C6
Wandsworth SW18. . . . .158 A4
Inmans Row IG8 . . . . . . .37 A6
Inner Circ NW1 . .93 A4 231 A2
Inner Park Rd SW19. . . . .156 D2
Inner Ring E TW6. . . . . . .126 D2
Inner Ring W TW6. . . . . .126 C2
Inner Temple* EC4. . . . . .251 A6
Inner Temple La EC4. . . .241 A1
Innes Cl SW20. . . . . . . .179 A1
Innes Gdns SW15. . . . . .156 B5
Innes Lo SE23. . . . . .162 B3
Innes Yd CR0. . . . . .221 A5
Innisfree Ho NW2. . . . . . .68 D2
Innis Ho SE17. . . . . .263 A2
Inniskilling Rd E13. . . . . .99 C5
Innova Bsns Pk EN3. . . . .7 B3
Innovation Cl HA0. . . . . . .88 A6
Inskip Cl E10 . . . . .75 D6
Inskip Rd RM8 . . . . .58 D1
Insley Ho 13 E3. . . . . . . .97 D4
Inst for Child Health
WC1. . . . . .94 B3 240 C5
Institute Pl E8 . . . . .74 B3
Instituto Espanol Vicente
Canada Blanch W10 . . . .91 A2
Inst of Neurology
Bloomsbury
WC1. . . . . .94 A2 240 B4
St Pancras WC1 . .94 A3 240 B6
Int Coll of Accountancy
The SW17. . . . . .158 D1
Integer Gdns E11. . . . . . .54 B2
Interchange The
Kentish Town NW5. . . . .71 B3
Thornton Heath CR0 . . .204 D2
International Ave
TW5. . . . . .106 C1
International House
Language Sch
WC2. . . . . .94 A1 240 B2
International Sch of
London W3 . . . . .110 C2
International Trad Est
UB2. . . . . .106 B3
International Way
TW16. . . . . .171 C2
Inverary Pl SE18 . . . . . . .145 B6
Inver Cl E5. . . . . .74 C6

Inverclyde Gdns RM6 . . .58 D5
Inver Ct
11 Bayswater W2. . . . . .91 D1
4 Hammersmith W6. . . .112 A1
Inveresk Gdns KT4. . . . . .216 A5
Inverey Ho N12. . . . . .29 D5
Inverforth Cl NW3. . . . . . .70 A6
Inverforth Ho NW3. . . . . .70 A6
Inverforth Rd N11. . . . . . .31 B5
Invergarry Ct 11 EN5. . . .13 C6
Invergarry Ho NW6. . . . . .91 D5
Inverine Rd SE7 . . . . . . .121 B1
Invermead Cl 4 W6. . . . . .112 A2
Invermore Pl SE18. . . . . .123 A2
Inverness Ave EN1 . . . . . .5 C4
Inverness Ct
8 Acton W3 . . . . .88 C1
10 Catford SE6 . . . . . .164 D3
Inverness Gdns W8. . . . .245 C3
Inverness Mews
Bayswater W2. . . . . . . .245 D6
Newham E16. . . . . .122 D5
North Woolwich E16. . . .123 A5
Inverness Pl W2 . . . . . . .245 D6
Inverness Rd
Edmonton N18. . . . . . . .34 B5
Hounslow TW3. . . . . . . .129 C1
North Cheam KT4. . . . . .200 C3
Southall UB2. . . . . .107 A2
Inverness St NW1. . . . . .231 D6
Inverness Terr
W2. . . . . .113 D6 245 D6
Inverton Rd SE15. . . . . . .140 D1
Invicta Cl
Chislehurst West
BR7. . . . . .188 C5
East Bedfont TW14. . . . .149 D3
21 Tower Hamlets E3. . .97 C2
Invicta Ct KT9. . . . . .214 B3
Invicta Ctr The IG11. . . . .102 A6
Invicta Gr UB5. . . . . .85 B4
Invicta Plaza SE1. . . . . .251 C4
Invicta Prim Sch SE3. . . .143 A5
Invicta Rd SE3, SE7. . . . .143 A6
Inville Rd SE17 . .117 B1 262 D1
Inwen Ct SE8 . . . . .119 A1
Inwood Ave TW3. . . . . . .130 A2
Inwood Bsns Pk TW3. . . .129 C1
Inwood Cl CR0. . . . . .223 A6
Inwood Ct 12 NW1 . . . . .71 C1
Inwood Ho 19 SE22. . . . .139 C2
Inwood Rd TW3. . . . . . . .130 A1
Inworth St SW11. . . . . . .136 C3
Inworth Wlk N1. . . . . . . .235 A6
Io Ctr Barking IG11. . . . .101 D3
Woolwich SE18. . . . . . .123 A3
Iona Cl Catford SE6 . . . . .163 C4
Morden SM4. . . . . .201 D2
Ion Ct 8 E2 . . . . .96 A5
Ionian Bldg 18 E14. . . . . .119 A6
Ionian Ho 22 E1. . . . . . . .96 D3
Ipsden Bldgs SE1. . . . . .251 B2
Ipswich Ho SE4 . . . . . . .162 B6
Ipswich Rd SW17 . . . . . .181 A4
Irby Ho SW2. . . . . .160 C5
Ireland Cl E16 . . . . .100 B2
Ireland Pl N22. . . . . .32 A3
Ireland Yd EC4. . . . . . . .241 D1
Irene Rd
Broom Hill BR6. . . . . . .211 D2
Parsons Green
SW6. . . . . .135 C4 265 B1
Ireton Ho 22 SW9 . . . . . .138 C3
Ireton St 12 E3 . . . . .97 C3
Iris Ave DA5. . . . . .169 A5
Iris Cl Croydon CR0. . . . .206 D1
Newham E6. . . . . .100 A3
Surbiton KT6. . . . . .198 B2
Iris Cres DA7. . . . . .147 B6
Iris Ct Dagenham IG11. . . .80 B1
8 Peckham SE15. . . . . .140 B3
4 Pinner HA5. . . . . .40 C6
Iris Rd KT19 . . . . .214 D3
Iris Way E4. . . . . .35 B4
Iris Wlk 1 HA8 . . . . .27 A6
Irkdale Ave EN1 . . . . .5 D4
Iroko Ho 7 NW3. . . . . . . .69 D2
Iron Bridge Cl
Southall UB2. . . . . .108 A5
Willesden NW10. . . . . . .67 C3
Iron Bridge Ho NW3. . . . .70 D1
Iron Bridge Rd N
UB11. . . . . .104 C5
Iron Bridge Rd S UB7. . . .104 C4
Irongate Ho EC3 . . . . . . .243 B2
Iron Mill Pl SW18. . . . . . .157 D5
Iron Mill Rd SW18. . . . . .157 D5
Ironmonger La
EC2. . . . . .95 B1 242 C1
Ironmonger Pas EC1. . . .235 B1
Ironmonger Row
EC1. . . . . .95 A4 235 B1
Ironmonger's Pl 22
E14. . . . . .119 C2
Ironside Cl SE16. . . . . . .118 D4
Ironside Ho E9. . . . . .75 A4
Ironworks 1 E3 . . . . .97 C6
Irvine Ave HA3. . . . . .43 B6
Irvine Cl N20 . . . . .14 C2
Irvine Ct
Marylebone W1. . . . . . .239 B5
Thornton Heath CR7 . . .204 C3
Irvine Ho N7. . . . . .72 B2
Irvine Way BR6. . . . . . . .211 D2
Irving Ave UB5. . . . . .84 D6
Irving Ct N20 . . . . .32 D2
Irving Gr SW9 . . . . .138 B3
Irving Ho SE17. . . . . . . .261 C1
Irving Mews N1. . . . . .73 A2

Irving Rd W14 . . . . .112 D3
Irving St WC2. . . . . .249 D5
Irwell Ct W7. . . . . .86 B1
Irwell Est 31 SE16. . . . . .118 C4
Irwin Ave SE18 . . . . .145 C5
Irwin Cl UB10. . . . . .60 C5
Irwin Gdns NW10. . . . . . .90 B6
Isabel Hill Cl TW12. . . . .173 C2
Isabella Cl N14 . . . . .15 C4
Isabella Ct 8 TW10. . . . .154 B5
Isabella Dr BR6. . . . . . . .227 A4
Isabella Ho
19 Hammersmith W6. . .112 C1
Kennington SE11. . . . . .261 C2
Isabella Pl KT2 . . . . .176 B5
Isabella Rd E9. . . . . .74 C3
Isabella St SE1. . . . . . . .251 C3
Isabel St SW9. . . . . .270 D2
Isambard Mews E14. . . .120 A3
Isambard Pl SE16. . . . . .118 C5
Iseldon Ct N7. . . . . .72 A4
Isel Way 4 SE22. . . . . . .161 C6
Isham Rd SW16. . . . . . . .182 A1
Isis Cl Putney SW15. . . . .134 C1
Ruislip HA4 . . . . .39 A3
Isis Ct W4. . . . . .132 D4
Isis Ho 2 Edmonton N18. .33 D4
Paddington NW8. . . . . .236 D5
Isis St SW18. . . . . .158 A2
Islamia Girls' High Sch
NW6. . . . . .91 A6
Islamia Prim Sch NW6. . .91 A6
Islamic Coll for Advanced
Studies NW10. . . . . . . .68 B2
Island Centre Way 16
EN3. . . . . .7 C6
Island Farm Ave KT8. . . .195 B4
Island Farm Rd KT8. . . . .195 B4
Island Gardens Sta
E14. . . . . .120 A1
Island Ho Bromley E14 . . .98 A4
Morden SW19. . . . . . . .202 A5
Island Rd
Deptford SE16. . . . . . . .118 D2
Mitcham CR4. . . . . .180 D3
Island Row E14. . . . . . . .97 B1
Isla Rd SE18 . . . . .145 A6
Islay Gdns TW4. . . . . . . .150 D6
Islay Wlk 17 N1. . . . . . . .73 A2
Isleden Ho N1. . . . . .235 A6
Isledon Rd N4, N7. . . . . . .72 C5
Islehurst Cl BR7. . . . . . . .188 C2
ISLE OF DOGS 120 A2
ISLEWORTH 131 B2
Isleworth Bsns Complex
TW7. . . . . .130 D3
Isleworth Sta TW7 . . . . .130 D3
Isleworth & Syon Sch for
Boys TW7 . . . . .130 C4
Isleworth Town Prim Sch
TW7. . . . . .131 A3
ISLINGTON 72 D2
Islington Arts & Media Sch
N4. . . . . .50 B1
Islington Bsns Ctr N1. . .235 B6
Islington Est 1 . .95 A6 235 A6
Islington Gn N1. .94 D6 234 C5
Islington Green Sch
N1. . . . . .95 A6 235 A6
Islington High St
N1. . . . . .94 D5 234 C4
Islington Park Mews 1
N1. . . . . .72 D1
Islington Park St N1. . . . .72 D1
Islington Sixth Form Ctr
N7. . . . . .72 C4
Islip Gdns Burnt Oak HA8 .27 B3
Northolt UB5. . . . . .63 A1
Islip Manor Rd UB5 . . . . .63 A1
Islip St NW5. . . . . .71 C3
Ismailia Rd E7. . . . . .77 B1
Isobel Ho
10 Ashford TW16 . . . . .171 D3
Harrow HA1. . . . . .42 D4
Isokon Flats 3 NW3. . . . .70 D1
Isom Cl E13 . . . . .99 B4
Issac Way SE1. . . . . . . .252 B2
Italia Conti Acad of
Theatre Arts EC1 . . . . .242 A5
Ithell Ct HA0. . . . . .65 D3
Ivanhoe Dr HA3 . . . . . . .25 B1
Ivanhoe Ho
1 Balham SW12. . . . . .159 B4
34 Bow E3. . . . . .97 A5
Hounslow TW4. . . . . . .128 C2
Peckham SE5. . . . . . . .139 D2
Ivatt Pl W14. . . . .113 B1 254 D1
Ivatt Way N17. . . . . .50 D6
Iveagh Ave NW10. . . . . . .88 C5
Iveagh Cl Ealing NW10. . .88 C5
South Hackney E9 . . . . . .96 C6
Iveagh Ct
4 Beckenham BR3. . . . .207 D6
Whitechapel EC3. . . . . .243 C1
Iveagh Ho
2 Brixton SW9. . . . . . .138 D3
Chelsea SW10 . . . . . . .266 B4
Ivebury Ct 9 W10. . . . . . .90 C1
Ivedon Rd DA16. . . . . . . .146 C3
Ive Farm Cl E10. . . . . . . .75 C5
Ive Farm La E10 . . . . . . .75 C5
Iveley Rd SW4 . . . . .137 C3
Iver Ct N1. . . . . .73 A2
Ivere Dr EN5. . . . . .13 D5
Iverhurst Cl DA6. . . . . . .168 C3
Iverna Ct W8 . . . . .255 B6

Iverna Gdns
Hatton TW14 ... 149 B6
Kensington W8 . 113 C3 255 B6
Iverson Rd NW6 ... 69 C2
Ivers Way CR0 ... 223 D1
Ives Rd E16 ... 98 C2
Ives St SW3 ... 114 C2 257 B4
Ivestor Terr SE23 ... 162 C4
Ivimey St E2 ... 96 A4
Ivinghoe Cl EN1 ... 5 C4
Ivinghoe Ho 14 N7 ... 71 D3
Ivinghoe Rd
Barking RM8 ... 80 B3
Bushey WD23 ... 8 B4
Ivor Ct Hendon N3 ... 47 A6
Hornsey N8 ... 50 A3
Lisson Gr NW1 ... 237 C6
Ivor Gr SE9 ... 166 D3
Ivor Ho DA14 ... 190 C5
Ivories The N1 ... 73 A1
Ivor Mayor Lo SW12 ... 159 A5
Ivor Pl NW1 ... 92 D3 237 C5
Ivor St NW1 ... 71 C1
Ivory Ct TW13 ... 150 A3
Ivorydown BR1 ... 187 A6
Ivory Ho
9 London SW11 ... 136 A2
St George in t East E1 .. 253 D4
Ivory Sq 15 SW18 ... 136 A2
Ivybridge Cl
2 Twickenham TW1 ... 153 A4
Uxbridge UB8 ... 82 A4
Ivybridge Ct 1 BR7 ... 188 C2
Ivybridge Ho 18 SE22 ... 139 C2
Ivybridge La WC2 ... 250 B5
Ivybridge Prim Sch
TW1 ... 152 D5
Ivybridge Ret Pk TW7 .. 152 D6
Ivychurch Cl SE20 ... 184 C3
Ivy Church La SE1,
SE17 ... 263 C2
Ivy Cl Harrow HA2 ... 63 B4
Pinner HA5 ... 40 C2
Sunbury TW16 ... 172 C1
Ivy Cotts UB10 ... 82 C4
Ivy Cres W4 ... 111 A2
Ivy Ct
19 Bermondsey SE16 ... 118 A1
Lewisham SE3 ... 142 D1
Ivydale Prim Sch
SE15 ... 140 D1
Ivydale Rd
Carshalton SM5 ... 218 D6
Nunhead SE15 ... 140 D1
Ivyday Gr SW16 ... 160 B1
Ivydene KT12, KT8 ... 195 B4
Ivydene Cl SM1 ... 218 A4
Ivy Gdns London N8 ... 50 A3
Mitcham CR4 ... 203 D6
Ivy Ho Croydon CR0 ... 206 D1
6 Upper Clapton E5 ... 52 B1
Ivyhouse Rd RM9 ... 81 A2
Ivy House Rd UB10 ... 60 D5
Ivy La TW4 ... 129 B1
Ivy Lo W8 ... 245 A4
Ivymount Rd SE27 ... 160 C1
Ivy Rd Brockley SE4 ... 141 C1
Cricklewood NW2 ... 68 C4
Hounslow TW3 ... 129 D1
Newham E16 ... 99 A1
Southgate N14 ... 15 D4
Tolworth KT6 ... 198 C1
Upper Tooting SW17 ... 180 C5
Walthamstow E17 ... 53 C3
Ivy St N1 ... 95 C5
Ivy Terr 3 IG2 ... 57 A3
Ivy Wlk RM9 ... 81 A2
Ixworth Pl
SW3 ... 114 C2 257 A3
Izane Rd DA6 ... 147 B1

J

Jacaranda Cl KT3 ... 199 C6
Jacaranda Gr E8 ... 73 D1
Jack Ashley Ct 5 NW9 .. 27 C2
Jackass La BR2 ... 225 C2
Jack Barnett Way N22 .. 32 B1
Jack Clow Rd E15 ... 98 C5
Jack Cook Ho 9 IG11 ... 78 D1
Jack Cornwell St E12 ... 78 C4
Jack Goodchild Way
KT3 ... 198 D6
Jack & Jill Sch TW12 .. 173 C4
Jacklin Gn IG8 ... 37 A6
Jackman Ho 24 E1 ... 118 B5
Jackman Mews NW2 ... 67 C5
Jackman St E8 ... 96 B6
Jackson Cl Hackney E9 .. 74 D1
Uxbridge UB10 ... 60 A1
Jackson Ct
Forest Gate E7 ... 77 B2
Wanstead E11 ... 55 B1
Jackson Ho
16 London SW11 ... 136 B2
13 New Southgate N11 ... 31 C5
Jackson Rd
Barking IG11 ... 101 B6
Bromley BR2 ... 226 B6
East Barnet EN4 ... 14 C5
Lower Holloway N7 ... 72 B4
Uxbridge UB10 ... 60 A1
Jackson's La N6 ... 49 B2
Jackson's Pl CR0 ... 205 C1
Jackson St SE18 ... 144 C6
Jackson's Way CR0 ... 223 C5
Jackson Way UB2 ... 107 D4
Jack Taylor Sch
NW8 ... 92 A6 229 A6
Jack Tizard Sch W12 ... 112 B5
Jack Walker Ct N5 ... 72 D4
Jacob Ct 24 EN3 ... 7 C6
Jacob Ho 14 DA18 ... 124 D4
Jacobin Lo N7 ... 72 A3
Jacob Mans 15 E1 ... 96 B1
Jacobs Cl RM10 ... 81 D4
Jacobs Ho E13 ... 99 C4
Jacobson Ct SW11 ... 267 B1
Jacobson Ho E1 ... 243 C2
Jacob St SE1 ... 118 A4
Jacob's Well Mews
W1 ... 238 B2
Jacotts Ho W10 ... 90 C3
Jacqueline Cl UB5 ... 85 A6
Jacqueline Ho 8 E1 ... 96 D2
Jade Cl Dagenham RM8 ... 58 C1
Hendon NW2 ... 46 D2
Newham E16 ... 99 D1
Jaffe Rd IG1 ... 57 B1
Jaffray Rd BR2 ... 209 D5
Jaggard Way SW12 ... 158 D4
Jagger Ho SW11 ... 267 C2
Jago Cl SE18 ... 145 A6
Jago Wlk SE5 ... 139 B5
Jamahirya Sch
SW3 ... 136 C6 267 A6
Jamaica Rd
Bermondsey SE1 ... 253 D1
Bermondsey SE16 ... 118 B3
Thornton Heath CR7 ... 204 D3
Jamaica St E1 ... 96 C2
James Allen's Girls' Sch
SE22 ... 161 C6
James Allens Pre-Prep
Sch SE21 ... 161 B5
James Anderson Ct 29
E2 ... 95 C5
James Ave
Cricklewood NW2 ... 68 C3
Dagenham RM8 ... 59 B1
James Bedford Cl HA5 .. 22 C1
James Boswell Cl 1
SW16 ... 182 C6
James Brine Ho 6 E2 ... 95 D4
James Campbell Ho 2
E2 ... 96 C5
James Cl London NW11 ... 47 A3
8 Newham E13 ... 99 A5
James Collins Cl W9 ... 91 B3
James Ct Chingford E4 ... 20 B2
Finchley N12 ... 30 C3
Hendon NW9 ... 27 C1
Northolt UB5 ... 85 A5
3 Woodford E18 ... 37 B1
James Dixon Prim Sch
SE20 ... 184 B3
James Docherty Ho 4
E2 ... 96 C5
James Dudson Ct
NW10 ... 67 A1
James Est CR4 ... 180 D1
James Gdns N22 ... 32 D3
James Hammett Ho 9
E2 ... 95 D5
James Ho Mile End E1 ... 97 A3
33 Rotherhithe SE16 ... 118 D4
James Joyce Wlk 7
SE24 ... 138 D1
James La E10, E11 ... 54 B3
James Lee Sq EN3 ... 7 C5
James Leicester Hall of
Residence N7 ... 72 A2
James Lind Ho 6 SE8 .. 119 B2
James Middleton Ho 20
E2 ... 96 B4
James Newman Ct
SE9 ... 166 C1
Jameson Ct 6 E2 ... 96 C5
Jameson Ho SE11 ... 260 C2
Jameson Lo N6 ... 49 C3
Jameson Pl 11 W3 ... 111 A4
Jameson St W8 ... 245 B4
James Pl N17 ... 33 D2
James's Cotts TW9 ... 132 C5
James St Barking IG11 ... 79 A1
Enfield EN1 ... 17 D6
Hounslow TW3 ... 130 B2
Marylebone W1 .. 93 A1 238 B1
Strand WC2 ... 116 A6 250 B6
James Stewart Ho
NW6 ... 69 B1
James Stroud Ho SE17 262 B1
Jamestown Rd
NW1 ... 93 B6 231 C6
Jamestown Way E14 ... 120 B6
James Way WD19 ... 22 D6
James Wolfe Prim Sch
SE10 ... 142 A5
Jamieson Ho TW4 ... 151 B5
Jamuna Cl E14 ... 97 A2
Jane Austen Hall 14
E16 ... 121 B5
Jane St E1 ... 96 B1
Janet Ct
4 Bexleyheath DA7 ... 147 C1
Wood Green N22 ... 32 B2
Janet St E14 ... 119 C3
Janeway Pl 2 SE16 ... 118 B4
Janeway St SE16 ... 118 A4
Janice Mews 3 IG1 ... 78 D5
Jansen Ho 8 SW15 ... 156 A6
Jansen Wlk SW11 ... 136 B1
Janson Cl Stratford E15 .. 76 C3
Willesden NW10 ... 67 C5
Janson Rd E15 ... 76 C3
Jansons Rd N15 ... 51 C6
Japan Cres N4 ... 50 B1
Japanese Sch The
W3 ... 110 C6
Japan Rd RM6 ... 58 D3
Jaquets Ct DA5 ... 169 C2
Jardine Ho HA1 ... 42 C2
Jardine Rd E1 ... 118 D6
Jarman Ho
Bermondsey SE16 ... 118 D2
16 Stepney E1 ... 96 C2
Jarrett Cl SW2 ... 160 D3
Jarrow Cl SM4 ... 201 D4
Jarrow Rd
Bermondsey SE16 ... 118 C1
Dagenham RM6 ... 58 C3
Tottenham Hale N17 ... 52 B5
Jarrow Way E9 ... 75 A4
Jarvis Cl
1 Barking IG11 ... 101 B6
Barnet EN5 ... 12 D6
Jarvis Ho 3 SE15 ... 140 A4
Jarvis Rd London SE22 .. 139 C1
South Croydon CR2 ... 221 B2
Jasmin SE1 ... 253 D3
Jasmine Cl Ilford IG1 ... 78 D3
Orpington BR6 ... 226 D6
Southall UB1 ... 107 A6
Jasmine Ct Lee SE12 ... 165 A5
11 Wallington SM6 ... 219 B2
Wimbledon SW19 ... 179 C5
Jasmine Gdns
Harrow HA2 ... 63 C6
West Wickham CR0 ... 223 D5
Jasmine Gr SE20 ... 184 B2
Jasmine Sq 15 E3 ... 97 B6
Jasmine Terr UB7 ... 104 C4
Jasmine Way KT7 ... 196 C5
Jasmin Ho SE4 ... 141 B2
Jasmin Lo 17 SE16 ... 118 B1
Jasmin Rd KT19 ... 214 D3
Jason Ct
2 London SW9 ... 138 C4
Marylebone W1 ... 238 B2
Jason Ho UB5 ... 84 B4
Jason Wlk SE9 ... 188 C6
Jasper Cl EN3 ... 6 C5
Jasper Ho KT4 ... 199 B1
Jasper Rd Newham E16 .. 99 D1
Penge SE19 ... 183 D4
Jasper Wlk N1 ... 235 C2
Java Wharf SE1 ... 253 D2
Javelin Ct HA7 ... 25 B5
Javelin Way UB5 ... 84 D4
Jawahar Bagh SW16 ... 182 D4
Jaycroft EN2 ... 4 C4
Jay Gdns BR7 ... 188 B6
Jay Ho SW15 ... 134 C3
Jay Mews SW7 . 114 A4 246 B1
Jayson Ct 7 CR0 ... 206 A1
Jazzfern Terr HA0 ... 65 A3
Jean Batten Cl SM6 ... 220 B1
Jean Darling Ho SW10 266 C5
Jean Ho 3 SW17 ... 180 C5
Jean Humbert Ho 2
SE27 ... 183 B6
Jean Pardies Ho 23 E1 .. 96 C2
Jebb Ave SW2 ... 160 A5
Jebb St E3 ... 97 C5
Jedburgh Rd E13 ... 99 C4
Jedburgh St SW11 ... 137 A1
Jeddo Mews W12 ... 111 D4
Jeddo Rd W12 ... 111 D4
Jefferies Ho 13 NW10 ... 67 B1
Jefferson Bldg 3 E14 .. 119 C4
Jefferson Cl
Ealing W13 ... 109 B3
Ilford IG2 ... 56 D4
Jefferson Wlk 13
SE18 ... 144 C6
Jeffrey Row SE12 ... 165 B6
Jeffrey's Ct 2 SW4 ... 138 A3
Jeffrey's Pl NW1 ... 71 C1
Jeffreys Rd EN3 ... 7 B1
Jeffrey's Rd SW4 ... 138 A3
Jeffrey's St NW1 ... 71 C1
Jeffs Cl TW12 ... 173 D4
Jeffs Rd SM1 ... 217 B4
Jeff Wooller Coll
WC1 ... 94 A2 240 B4
Jefton Ct SM6 ... 219 C3
Jeger Ave E2 ... 95 D6
Jeken Rd SE9 ... 143 C1
Jelf Rd SW2 ... 160 C6
Jellicoe Ct E4 ... 36 B4
Jellicoe Gdns HA7 ... 25 A4
Jellicoe Ho
5 Bethnal Green E2 ... 96 A5
Fitzrovia NW1 ... 238 D5
11 Putney SW15 ... 156 D6
Jellicoe Rd
4 Newham E13 ... 99 A3
Tottenham N17 ... 33 B3
Jemmett Cl KT2 ... 176 D2
Jemotts Ct 9 SE14 ... 140 D6
Jem Paterson Ct HA1 ... 64 C4
Jengar Cl SM1 ... 217 D4
Jenkins Ho SW8 ... 269 C2
Jenkins La IG11 ... 101 A4
Jenkinson Ho 12 E2 ... 96 D4
Jenkins Rd E13 ... 99 B3
Jenner Ave W3 ... 89 B2
Jenner Cl DA14 ... 190 A6
Jenner Ct N21 ... 16 A6
Jenner Ho
5 Belvedere DA17 ... 125 C3
Greenwich SE3 ... 142 C6
Jenner Pl SW13 ... 134 B6
Jenner Rd N16 ... 73 D5
Jennett Rd CR0 ... 220 C5
Jennifer Ho SE11 ... 261 B3
Jennifer Rd BR1 ... 164 D1
Jennings Cl KT6 ... 197 C2
Jennings Ho SE10 ... 120 B1
Jennings Rd SE22 ... 161 D5
Jenny Hammond Cl
E11 ... 76 D5
Jenny Hammond Prim Sch
E11 ... 76 C4
Jensen Ho 10 E3 ... 97 C3
Jenson Way SE19 ... 183 D3
Jenton Ave DA7 ... 147 A3
Jephson Ct 17 SW4 ... 138 A3
Jephson Ho 6 SE17 ... 138 D6
Jephson Rd E7 ... 77 C1
Jephson St SE5 ... 139 B4
Jephtha Rd SW18 ... 157 C5
Jeppo's La CR4 ... 202 D5
Jerdan Pl SW6 ... 265 A4
Jeremiah St 11 E14 ... 97 D1
Jeremy Bentham Ho 24
E2 ... 96 A4
Jeremy's Gn N18 ... 34 C6
Jermyn St
SW1 ... 115 C5 249 B4
Jernigham Ct SE14 ... 141 A4
Jerningham Rd SE14 ... 141 A4
Jerome Cres
NW8 ... 92 C3 237 A6
Jerome Ct 2 N11 ... 31 C5
Jerome Ho
Kingston u T KT1 ... 175 D1
Lisson Gr NW1 ... 237 B4
Jerome Pl KT1 ... 175 D1
Jerome St E1 ... 95 D3 243 C5
Jerome Twr 5 W3 ... 110 D4
Jerrard St SE13 ... 141 D2
Jerrold Lo SW15 ... 134 C2
Jerrold St 24 N1 ... 95 C5
Jersey Ave HA7 ... 25 C1
Jersey Ct UB2 ... 107 B3
Jersey Dr BR5 ... 211 B3
Jersey Ho
15 Canonbury N1 ... 73 A2
Enfield EN3 ... 6 D5
Jersey Rd Canonbury N1 .. 73 A2
Ealing W7 ... 109 A4
Hounslow TW5, TW7 ... 130 B5
Ilford IG1 ... 78 D4
Leytonstone E11 ... 54 B1
Mitcham SW17 ... 181 B4
Newham E16 ... 99 C1
Jersey St E2 ... 96 B4
Jerusalem Pas EC1 ... 241 C5
Jervis Bay Ho 9 E14 ... 98 B1
Jervis Ct
9 Dagenham RM10 ... 81 D2
2 Greenwich SE10 ... 142 A4
Marylebone W1 ... 238 D1
Jerviston Gdns SW16 .. 182 C4
Jesmond Ave HA9 ... 66 B2
Jesmond Cl CR4 ... 203 B6
Jesmond Ct HA9 ... 66 C2
Jesmond Rd CR0 ... 205 D2
Jesmond Way HA7 ... 26 A5
Jessam Ave E5 ... 52 B1
Jessamine Rd W7 ... 108 D5
Jessel Ho
St Pancras WC1 ... 233 A1
Westminster SW1 ... 259 D4
Jesse Rd E10 ... 54 A1
Jessica Rd SW18 ... 158 A6
Jessie Blythe La 4
N19 ... 50 A2
Jessie Duffett Ho 11
SE5 ... 139 A5
Jessie's Cotts E17 ... 53 A3
Jessiman Terr TW17 ... 192 C4
Jesson Ho SE17 ... 262 C3
Jessop Ave UB2 ... 107 B2
Jessop Ct N1 ... 234 D3
Jessop Ho 9 W4 ... 111 B2
Jessop Pl CR4 ... 202 C5
Jessop Prim Sch
SE24 ... 139 A1
Jessop Sq E14 ... 119 C5
Jessops Way CR0 ... 203 C3
Jessops Wharf 4
TW8 ... 131 C5
Jessup Cl SE18 ... 123 A2
Jeston Ho 10 SE27 ... 160 D1
Jethou Ho 16 N1 ... 73 A2
Jetstar Way UB5 ... 85 A4
Jevington Way SE12 ... 165 B3
Jevons Ho 9 NW8 ... 70 B1
Jewell Ho 3 SW12 ... 159 C4
Jewel Rd E17 ... 53 C6
Jewish Mus The*
Camden Town
NW1 ... 93 B6 231 D5
Finchley N3 ... 29 D1
Jewry St EC3 ... 95 D1 243 C1
Jews Row SW18 ... 136 A1
Jews Wlk SE26 ... 184 B6
Jeymer Ave NW2 ... 68 C3
Jeymer Dr UB6 ... 86 A6
Jeypore Rd SW18 ... 158 A5
JFS Sch HA3 ... 44 C3
Jillian Cl TW12 ... 173 C3
Jim Bradley Cl 10
SE18 ... 122 C2
Jim Griffiths Ho SW6 .. 264 D5
Joan Cres SE9 ... 165 D4
Joan Gdns RM8 ... 81 A6
Joanna Ho 7 W6 ... 112 C1
Joanne Ct EN1 ... 17 C5
Joan Player Ho EN3 ... 6 D6
Joan Rd RM8 ... 81 A6
Joan St SE1 ... 116 D5 251 C3
Joan Villas IG2 ... 57 A2
Jocelin Ho N1 ... 233 D5
Jocelyn Rd TW9 ... 132 A2
Jocelyn St SE15 ... 140 A4
Jockey's Fields
WC1 ... 94 B2 240 D4
Jodane Rd SE8 ... 119 B2
Jodrell Cl TW7 ... 131 A4
Jodrell Rd E3 ... 75 B1
Joe Hunte Ct 2
SW27 ... 182 D5
Joel St HA5, HA6 ... 40 A5
Johanna Prim Sch
SE1 ... 116 C4 251 A1
Johanna St SE1 ... 251 A1
John Adam St
WC2 ... 116 A6 250 B5
John Aird Ct
W2 ... 92 A2 236 B4
John Aldis Ho N22 ... 32 B1
John Archer Way
SW18 ... 158 B5
John Ashby Cl SW2 ... 160 A5
John Austin Cl KT2 ... 176 B2
John Baird Ct SE26 ... 184 D6
John Baird Ho 11
SE20 ... 184 C3
John Ball Prim Sch
SE3 ... 142 C3
John Barker Ct NW6 ... 69 A1
John Barker Ho IG1 ... 79 B6
John Barnes Wlk E15 ... 76 D2
John Barter Ho TW3 ... 129 B3
John Betts' Ho W12 ... 112 A3
John Betts Prim Sch
W6 ... 112 B3
John Bond Ho 2 E3 ... 97 B5
John Bradshaw Rd
N14 ... 15 D3
John Brent Ho 8 SE8 .. 118 D2
John Buck Ho NW10 ... 89 D6
John Burns Dr IG11 ... 79 C1
John Burns Prim Sch
SW11 ... 137 A3
Johnby Cl EN3 ... 7 A6
John Campbell Rd 26
N16 ... 73 C3
John Carpenter St
EC4 ... 251 C6
John Cartwright Ho 7
E2 ... 96 B4
John Chilton Sch UB5 ... 63 A1
John Clifford Ho N8 ... 50 A3
John Clynes Ct SW15 .. 134 B1
John Conwey Ho 23
SW2 ... 160 C5
John Cornwell VC Ho 6
E12 ... 78 C4
John Day Ho TW7 ... 131 B2
John Dee Ho 3 SW14 .. 133 B2
John Donne Prim Sch
SE15 ... 140 B4
John Drinkwater Cl
E11 ... 54 D2
John Dwight Ho SW6 .. 135 D2
John Fearon Wlk 5
W10 ... 91 A4
John Felton Rd 19
SE16 ... 118 A4
John Fielden Ho 10 E2 .. 96 B4
John Fisher St E1 ... 118 A6
John F. Kennedy Specl
Sch E15 ... 98 B6
John Gooch Dr EN2 ... 4 D4
John Harris Ho SE15 ... 140 A2
John Harrison Way
SE10 ... 120 D3
John Hunt Ct 5 SE9 ... 166 A2
John Islip St
SW1 ... 116 A2 260 A3
John Kaye Ct TW17 ... 192 C4
John Keall Ho SW15 ... 134 D2
John Keats Ho N22 ... 32 B2
John Keats Lo EN2 ... 5 B4
John Keble CE Prim Sch
NW10 ... 89 D6
John Kelly Tech Colls
NW2 ... 67 D5
John Kennedy Ct 1
N1 ... 73 B2
John Kennedy Ho 1
SE16 ... 118 D2
John Kennedy Lo 2
N1 ... 73 B2
John King Ct 5 N19 ... 71 D6
John Kirk Ho
22 Battersea SW11 ... 136 B2
Beckenham BR3 ... 207 A5
5 Streatham SW16 ... 160 A1
John Knight Lo SW6 .. 265 B4
John Lamb Ct HA3 ... 24 C2
John Loughborough Sch
N17 ... 33 D1
John Lyon Sch The
HA2 ... 42 B1
John McDonald Ho 3
E14 ... 120 A3
John McKenna Wlk 17
SE16 ... 118 A3
John & Mary Sch NW5 .. 71 D3
John Masefield Ho N15 . 51 B3
John Maurice Cl
SE17 ... 117 B2 262 C4
John Milton Prim Sch
SW8 ... 137 C5 269 A3
John Nettleford Ho 14
E2 ... 96 B4
John Newton Ct DA16 .. 146 B2
John Orwell Sports Ctr
E1 ... 118 B5
John Parker Cl RM10 ... 81 D1
John Parker Sq 8
SW11 ... 136 B2
John Parry Ct 28 N1 ... 95 C5
John Paul II Sch
SW19 ... 156 D4
John Penn Ho SE8 ... 141 B5
John Penn St SE13 ... 141 D4
John Perrin Pl HA3 ... 44 A2
John Perryn Prim Sch
W3 ... 89 C1
John Prince's St W1 .. 238 D2
John Pritchard Ho 16
E1 ... 96 A3
John Ratcliffe Ho 8
NW6 ... 91 C4
John Rennie Wlk 1
E1 ... 118 C5
John Roan Sch The
SE3 ... 142 C5
John Roll Way SE16 ... 118 A3
John Ruskin Coll CR2 .. 223 A1
John Ruskin Prim Sch
SE5 ... 139 A6
John Ruskin St SE5 ... 139 A6
John's Ave NW4 ... 46 C5
Johns Cl TW15 ... 171 A6
John Scurr Ho 18 E14 ... 97 A1
John Scurr Prim Sch
E1 ... 96 C3
John Silkin La SE8 ... 118 D1
Johns La SM4 ... 202 A4
John's Mews
WC1 ... 94 B3 240 D5
John Smith Ave
SW6 ... 135 B5 264 C4
John Smith Mews
E14 ... 120 B6
Johnson Cl E8 ... 96 A6
Johnson Ct
Hendon NW4 ... 46 A6
10 Wandsworth SW18 .. 136 B1
Johnson Ho
Belgravia SW1 ... 258 B3
23 Bethnal Green E2 ... 96 A4
Somers Town NW1 ... 232 B3
South Lambeth SW8 ... 269 D3
Johnson Lo 12 W9 ... 91 C2
Johnson Rd
Bromley Comm BR2 ... 209 D4
Heston TW5 ... 128 C5
Stonebridge NW10 ... 89 B6
Thornton Heath CR0 ... 205 B2
Johnson's Cl SM5 ... 218 D5
Johnsons Ct EC4 ... 241 B1
Johnsons Dr TW12 ... 174 A2
Johnson's Ind Est
UB3 ... 106 A3
Johnson's Pl
SW1 ... 115 C1 259 A1
Johnson St
Southall UB2 ... 106 D3
Stepney E1 ... 96 C1
Johnsons Way NW10 ... 88 D3
John Spencer Sq N1 ... 72 D2
John's Pl E1 ... 96 B1
John St Croydon SE25 ... 206 A5
Enfield EN1 ... 17 D6
Finsbury WC1 .. 94 B3 240 D5
Hounslow TW3, TW5 ... 129 A3
West Ham E15 ... 98 D6
John Stainer Com Prim
Sch SE4 ... 141 A2
John's Terr CR0 ... 205 C1
Johnston Cl SW9 ... 270 D1
Johnstone Ho SE13 ... 142 B2
Johnstone Rd E6 ... 100 B4
Johnston Rd IG8 ... 37 A5
Johnston Terr NW2 ... 68 D5
John Strachey Ho
SW6 ... 264 D5
John Strype Ct E10 ... 53 D1
John Trundle Ct EC2 .. 242 A4
John Tucker Ho 3
E14 ... 119 C3
John Walsh Twr E11 ... 76 D6
John Wesley Ct 6
TW1 ... 153 A3
John Wesley's House &
Mus* EC1 ... 242 D6
John Wheatley Ho
14 London N19 ... 49 D2
West Brompton SW6 ... 264 D5
John William Cl 12
KT2 ... 175 D2
John Williams Cl
SE14 ... 140 D6
John Wilson St SE18 ... 122 C2
John Wooley Cl SE13 .. 142 C1
Joiners Arms Yd 1
SE5 ... 139 B4
Joiners Ct 5 N20 ... 14 D1
Joiner St SE1 ... 252 D3
Joiners Yd N1 ... 233 B3
Joint Rd N10 ... 30 C2
Jolles Ho 9 E3 ... 97 D4
Jollys La Harrow HA2 ... 42 B1
Hayes UB4 ... 84 D2
Jonathan Ct 9 W4 ... 111 C2
Jonathan St
SE11 ... 116 B1 260 C2
Jones Ho
4 South Bromley E14 ... 98 B1
Stamford Hill N16 ... 51 C1
Jones Rd E13 ... 99 B3
Jones St W1 ... 248 C5
Jones Wlk 6 TW10 ... 154 B5
Jonquil Gdns 5
TW12 ... 173 C4
Jonson Cl Hayes UB4 ... 84 A2
Mitcham CR4 ... 203 B6

Jonson Ho
Borough The SE1 262 D5
16 Canonbury N16 73 B4
Jordan Cl HA2 63 B5
Jordan Ct SW15 134 D1
Jordan Hill N10 30 C2
Jordan Ho
12 London SE4 140 D1
Shoreditch N1 235 D5
Jordan Lo SW17 180 C5
Jordan Rd UB6 87 C6
Jordans Cl
Dagenham RM10 81 D4
Hounslow TW7 130 C4
Jordans Ho NW8 237 A5
Jordans Mews TW11 152 C2
Jo Richardson Comm Sch
RM9 102 D6
Jo Richardson Com Sch
RM9 80 C2
Joscoyne Ho 5 E1 96 B1
Josef Perrin Ho 1
SE27 183 B6
Joseph Ave W3 89 B1
Joseph Clarke Sch E4 36 B4
Joseph Conrad Ho
SW1 259 B3
Joseph Ct N16 51 C2
Joseph Hardcastle Cl
SE14 140 D5
Joseph Hood Prim Sch
SW20 201 A6
Josephine Ave SW2 160 B6
Joseph Irwin Ho 11
E14 119 B6
Joseph Lancaster Prim
Sch SE1 117 B3 262 C5
Joseph Lister Ct E7 77 A1
Joseph Lister Lo E11 55 B1
Joseph Powell Cl 1
SW12 159 C5
Joseph Priestley Ho 12
E2 96 B4
Joseph Ray Rd E11 76 C6
Joseph St E3 97 B3
Joseph Trotter Cl EC1 234 B1
Joshua Cl Croydon CR2 220 D1
Muswell Hill N10 31 B3
Joshua St E14 98 A1
Joslings Cl W12 112 A6
Joslyn Cl EN3 7 C5
Josseline Ct 9 E3 97 A5
Joubert Mans SW3 257 B2
Joubert St SW11 136 D3
Jowett Ho 27 SW9 138 A3
Jowett St SE15 139 D5
Joyce Ave N18 33 D5
Joyce Butler Ho N22 32 B2
Joyce Dawson Way
SE28 124 A6
Joyce Lattimore Ct N9 18 B1
Joyce Page Cl SE7 143 D6
Joy Ct NW2 68 D5
Joydon Dr RM6 58 B3
Joyner Ct UB1 107 B6
Joyners Cl RM9 81 B4
Joystone Ct 8 EN4 2 C1
Jubb Powell Ho N15 51 C3
Jubet Ho 9 N16 73 B4
Jubilee Ave
Chingford E4 36 A4
Romford RM7 59 D4
Twickenham TW2 152 A3
Jubilee Bldgs NW8 229 C4
Jubilee Cl
4 Harlesden NW10 89 D5
Kingsbury NW9 45 B3
Pinner HA5 22 C1
Romford RM7 59 D4
Teddington KT1 175 C2
Jubilee Cres
Cubitt Town E14 120 A3
Edmonton N9 18 A3
Jubilee Ct Harrow HA3 44 A2
Hounslow TW3 129 D2
Islington N1 233 B6
Muswell Hill N10 49 A6
12 Sutton SM2 218 A2
Thornton Heath CR7 204 C5
Jubilee Dr HA4 63 A4
Jubilee Gdns UB1 85 C1
Jubilee Ho
3 Hampton TW12 173 C2
Lambeth SE11 261 B3
Jubilee Hts NW2 69 B2
Jubilee Lo HA7 25 A5
Jubilee Mans 10 E1 96 C1
Jubilee Mkt WC2 250 B6
Jubilee Par IG8 37 C4
Jubilee Park Ctry Pk
BR2 210 C4
Jubilee Pl SW3 114 C1 257 B2
Jubilee Prim Sch
London SW2 160 C5
Stamford Hill N16 52 A1
Woolwich SE28 124 C6
Jubilee Rd Cheam SM3 216 D1
Wembley UB6 87 B6
Jubilee St E1 96 C2
Jubilee The 2 SE10 141 D5
Jubilee Villas KT10 196 C1
Jubilee Way
East Bedfont TW14 150 A3
Merton SW19 179 D2
Sidcup DA14 168 A2
Tolworth KT4, KT9 214 D5
Jubilee Wks SW19 180 A1
Jubilee Wlk WD19 22 B6
Jubilee Yd SE1 253 C2
Judd St WC1 94 A4 233 A1
Jude St E16 98 D1
Judge Heath La UB3 83 B1
Judges' Wlk NW3 70 A5
Judge Wlk KT10 212 C2
Juer St SW11 136 C5 267 B3
Jules Thorn Ave EN1 6 A1
Julia Ct E17 53 D4
Julia Garfield Mews 4
E16 121 B5
Julia Gdns IG11 102 D5
Juliana Cl N2 48 A6
Julian Ave W3 110 D6
Julian Cl EN5 1 D2
Julian Ct SW13 133 D4
Julian Hill HA1 64 C6
Julian Ho SE21 183 C6
Julian Pl E14 119 D1
Julian's Prim Sch
SW16 182 C6
Julian Taylor Path 7
SE23 162 B2
Julia St NW5 71 A3
Julien Rd W5 109 C3
Juliet Ho 11 N1 95 C5
Juliette Rd E13 99 A5
Julius Caesar Way HA7 9 D1
Julius Ct TW8 132 A5
Julius Ho 8 E14 98 B1
Julius Nyerere Cl N1 233 C5
Junction App
Battersea SW11 136 C2
Lewisham SE13 142 A2
Junction Mews W2 237 A2
Junction Pl W2 236 D2
Junction Rd
Ashford TW15 171 B5
Brentford TW8 109 D2
Croydon CR2 221 B3
Dartmouth Pk N19 71 C5
Edmonton N9 18 A3
Harrow HA1 42 C3
Newham E13 99 B5
Tottenham Hale N17 52 A6
Junction Rd E RM6 59 A2
Junction Rd W RM6 59 A2
Junction Wembley Ret Pk
The HA9 66 D4
Juniper Cl Barnet EN5 12 D6
Chessington KT9 214 B3
Wembley HA9 66 C3
Juniper Cres NW1 71 A1
Juniper Ct
Dagenham RM6 58 C3
Harrow HA3 24 D2
Hounslow TW3 129 D1
Stoke Newington N16 73 B6
Thornton Heath CR0 204 C3
Juniper Dr SW18 136 A1
Juniper Gdns
Ashford TW16 171 D4
Streatham CR4 181 C2
Juniper Ho
12 Ealing W5 87 C2
6 Peckham SE14,
SE15 140 C5
9 Richmond TW9 132 D4
Juniper La E6 100 A2
Juniper Rd IG1 78 D4
Juniper St 16 E1 118 C6
Juniper Way UB3 105 C6
Juno Ct 11 SW9 138 C5
Juno Ho 2 E3 97 C6
Juno Way SE14 140 D6
Juno Way Ind Est
SE14 140 D6
Jupiter Ct
10 Brixton SW9 138 C5
8 Northolt UB5 84 D4
Jupiter Hts UB10 82 B6
Jupiter Way N7 72 B2
Jupp Rd E15 76 B1
Jupp Rd W E15 98 B6
Jura Ho SE16 119 A2
Jurston Ct SE1 251 B1
Justice Wlk SW3 267 A5
Justin Cl TW8 131 D5
Justin Ct 3 CR7 204 C4
Justines Pl E2 96 D4
Justin Plaza CR4 202 C5
Justin Rd E4 35 B4
Jute La EN3 7 A2
Jutland Cl N19 50 A1
Jutland Ho
4 London SE5 139 A3
10 Woolwich SE7 122 A2
Jutland Rd Catford SE6 164 A4
Newham E13 99 A3
Jutsums Ave RM7 59 D3
Jutsums Ct RM7 59 D3
Jutsums La RM7 59 D3
Juxon Cl HA3 23 D2
Juxon St SE11 116 B2 260 D4
JVC Bsns Pk NW2 46 A1

K

Kaduna Cl HA5 40 B4
Kaizen Prim Sch E13 99 B3
Kale Rd DA18 125 A4
Kambala Rd SW11 136 B2
Kangley Bridge Ctr
SE26 185 B5
Kangley Bridge Rd
SE26 185 B5
Kaplan Dr N21 16 B6
Karachi Ho E15 76 C2
Kara Way NW2 68 D4
Karen Ct Bromley BR1 186 D2
2 Camberwell SE5 139 C2
Karen Ct *continued*
Forest Hill SE23 163 A5
Karen Ho 7 N16 73 B4
Karens Ct EN3 6 D6
Karen Terr Ilford IG2 57 B4
Leyton E11 76 D6
Karenza Ct HA9 43 C2
Kariba Cl N9 18 C1
Karman Ct HA3 42 C6
Karma Way HA2 41 C1
Karoline Gdns UB6 86 B5
Karyatis Ct EN1 17 D6
Kashgar Rd SE18 123 D2
Kashmir Rd SE7 143 D5
Kasmin Ct NW10 68 A1
Kassala Rd
SW11 136 D4 267 D1
Katella Trad Est IG11 101 C4
Kates Cl EN5 12 A6
Katharine Ho 1 TW1 153 A3
Katharine St CR0 221 A5
Katherine Cl 3 SE16 118 D5
Katherine Ct
10 Forest Hill SE23 162 C3
Penge SE20 184 C2
Katherine Gdns SE9 143 D1
Katherine Ho
15 Kensal Town W10 91 A3
6 South Croydon CR0 221 A5
South Norwood SE19 183 C4
Katherine Rd E6, E7 77 C1
Katherine Sq W11 244 A4
Kathleen Ave Acton W3 89 A2
Wembley HA0 66 A1
Kathleen Ferrier Ct 4
N17 33 D3
Kathleen Godfree Ct
SW19 179 C5
Kathleen Moore Ct
BR4 224 A6
Kathleen Rd SW11 136 D2
Katrine Ct NW2 68 C5
Kayemoor Rd SM2 218 C2
Kay Rd SW9 138 B3
Kays Ct EN3 6 D1
Kay St Bethnal Green E2 96 A5
Welling DA16 146 B4
Keadby Ho 2 UB5 85 B4
Kean Ho 5 SE17 138 D6
Kean St WC2 94 B1 240 C1
Keates Est N16 73 D6
Keatley Gn E4 35 B4
Keats Ave E16 121 B5
Keats Cl
Bermondsey SE1 263 C3
Enfield EN3 18 D6
Hampstead NW3 70 C4
Hayes UB4 84 A2
Mitcham SW19 180 B4
Wanstead E11 55 B4
Keats Ct HA0 65 C5
Keats Gr NW3 70 C4
Keats Ho
7 Beckenham BR3 185 D4
22 Bethnal Green E2 96 C4
30 Camberwell SE5 139 A5
Chelsea SW1 269 B6
Harrow HA2 64 C6
Keats House Mus*
NW3 70 C4
Keats Par 3 N9 18 A2
Keats Pl EC2 242 C3
Keats Rd DA16 145 D4
Keats Way
Croydon CR0 206 C3
Southall UB6 85 D2
West Drayton UB7 104 B2
Kebbell Terr E7 77 B3
Keble Cl
New Malden KT4 199 D1
Northolt UB5 64 A3
Keble Ct SW19 179 C4
Keble Ho 4 SW15 156 D5
Keble Pl SW13 134 B6
Keble Prep Sch N21 16 C4
Keble St SW17 180 A6
Kechill Gdns BR2 209 A2
Kedelston Ct E5 75 A4
Kedeston Ct SM1 201 D1
Kedge Ho 16 E14 119 C3
Kedleston Dr BR5 211 D4
Kedleston Wlk 21 E2 96 B4
Kedyngton Ho 5 HA8 27 A1
Keeble Cl SE18 144 D6
Keedonwood Rd BR1 186 D5
Keel Cl Barking IG11 102 C5
Rotherhithe SE16 118 D5
Keel Ct 8 E14 120 B6
Keeley Rd CR0 221 A6
Keeley St WC2 94 B1 240 C1
Keeling 2 TW11 174 C5
Keeling Ct CR0 220 D4
Keeling Ho 4 E2 96 B5
Keeling Rd SE9 165 D6
Keelson Ho 9 E14 119 C3
Keely Cl EN4 14 C6
Keemor Cl SE18 144 C5
Keens Cl SW16 181 D5
Keen's Rd CR0 221 A4
Keen's Yd N1 72 D2
Keepers Ct 4 CR2 221 A3
Keepers Mews TW11 175 C4
Keeper Wharf E1 118 D6
Keepier Wharf 15 E1 118 D6
Keep The
Forest Hill SE6 163 C3
Kidbrooke SE3 143 A3
Kingston u T KT2 176 B3
Keeton's Rd SE16 118 B3
Keevil Dr SW19 157 A4
Keighley Cl N7 72 A4
Keightley Dr SE9 167 A3
Keilder Cl UB10 82 C5
Keildon Rd SW11 136 D1
Keir Hardie Est E5 52 B1
Keir Hardie Ho
6 Belvedere DA17 125 C3
Fulham W6 134 D6
15 Upper Holloway N19 49 D2
Willesden NW10 67 D1
Keir Hardie Way
Barking IG11 80 A1
Hayes UB4 84 A4
Keir Hardy Prim Sch
E16 99 A2
Keir The SW19 178 C5
Keith Connor Cl 5
SW8 137 B2
Keith Gr W12 112 A5
Keith Ho NW6 91 D5
Keith Park Rd UB10 60 B1
Keith Rd Barking IG11 101 B5
Hayes UB3 105 C3
Walthamstow E17 35 B2
Keith Sutton Ho 3
SE9 167 A2
Kelbrook Rd SE3 144 A2
Kelby Ho N7 72 B2
Kelceda Cl NW2 68 A6
Kelf Gr UB3 83 D1
Kelfield Ct 1 W10 90 D1
Kelfield Gdns W10 90 D1
Kelfield Mews W10 90 D1
Kelham Ho 10 SE18 144 D6
Kelland Cl 1 N8 49 D4
Kelland Rd E13 99 A3
Kellaway Rd SE3 143 D3
Keller Cres E12 77 D4
Kellerton Rd SE13 164 C6
Kellett Ho N1 235 D5
Kellett Rd SW2 138 C1
Kelling Gdns CR0 204 D2
Kellino St SW17 180 D6
Kellner Rd SE28 123 D3
Kellow Ho SE1 252 C2
Kell St SE1 116 D3 261 D6
Kelly Ave SE15 139 D4
Kelly Cl
Upper Halliford
TW17 171 C1
Willesden NW10 67 B5
Kelly Ct 18 E14 119 C6
Kelly Mews 4 W9 91 B3
Kelly Rd NW7 29 A4
Kelly St NW1 71 B2
Kelly Way RM6 59 A3
Kelman Cl SW4 137 D3
Kelmore Gr SE22 140 A1
Kelmscott 5 SE23 162 D1
Kelmscott Cl E17 35 B2
Kelmscott Ct 2 HA7 25 C6
Kelmscott Gdns W12 112 A3
Kelmscott L Ctr E17 53 B3
Kelmscott Rd SW11 158 D6
Kelmscott Sch E17 53 B3
Kelross Rd N5 73 A4
Kelsall Cl SE3 143 B3
Kelsall Mews TW9 132 D4
Kelsey Gate 8 BR3 185 D1
Kelsey La BR3 207 C6
Kelsey Park Ave BR3 185 D1
Kelsey Park Man BR3 207 D6
Kelsey Park Rd BR3 185 C1
Kelsey Park Sp Coll
BR3 207 C6
Kelsey Rd BR5 190 B1
Kelsey Sq BR3 185 C1
Kelsey St E2 96 A3
Kelsey Way BR3 207 C6
Kelshall Ct N4 73 A6
Kelso Ct SE20 184 B3
Kelso Lo E18 37 B1
Kelson Ho E14 120 A3
Kelso Pl W8 113 D3 255 D6
Kelso Rd SM5 202 A2
Kelvedon Cl KT2 176 C4
Kelvedon Ct HA4 62 C4
Kelvedon Ho SW8 270 B2
Kelvedon Rd
SW6 135 B5 264 D3
Kelvin Ave N13 32 B4
Kelvinbrook KT8 195 D6
Kelvin Cl KT19 214 C2
Kelvin Cres HA3 24 C3
Kelvin Ct Chiswick W4 133 A5
Harrow HA2 42 A1
Isleworth TW7 130 C3
Notting Hill W11 245 A5
7 Penge SE20 184 B2
8 Twickenham TW1 153 B5
Kelvin Dr TW1 153 B5
Kelvin Gdns
Southall UB1 85 C1
Thornton Heath CR0 204 A2
Kelvin Gr
Forest Hill SE26 162 B1
Surbiton KT6 214 A5
Kelvin Grove Prim Sch
SE26 162 B1
Kelvington Cl CR0 207 A2
Kelvington Rd SE15 162 D6
Kelvin Ho 3 DA17 125 C3
Kelvin Par BR6 211 C1
Kelvin Rd Highbury N5 73 A4
Welling DA16 146 A2
Kelyway Ho 20 SW2 160 C4
Kember St N1 72 B1
Kemble Dr BR2 226 A5
Kemble Ho
London SW9 138 D2
Kemble Ho *continued*
Stanmore HA7 24 D5
Kemble Rd
Croydon CR0 220 D5
Forest Hill SE23 162 D3
Tottenham N17 34 A2
Kemble St WC2 94 B1 240 C1
Kemerton Rd
Beckenham BR3 185 D1
Camberwell SE5 139 A2
Croydon CR0 205 D2
Kemey's St E9 75 A3
Kemnal Rd BR7 189 B5
Kemnal Tech Coll
DA14 190 B3
Kemnal Warren BR7 189 B4
Kemp 24 NW9 27 D2
Kemp Ct SW8 270 A3
Kempe Ho SE1 262 D5
Kempe Rd NW6 90 D5
Kemp Gdns CR0 205 A3
Kemp Ho Finsbury EC1 235 C1
1 Globe Town E2 96 D5
Wallend E6 78 C2
Kempis Way 5 SE22 161 C6
Kemplay Rd NW3 70 B4
Kemp Rd RM8 58 D1
Kemps Ct NW2 68 D5
Kemp's Ct W1 239 C1
Kemps Dr E14 119 C6
Kempsford Gdns
SW5 113 C1 255 B1
Kempsford Rd
Lambeth SE11 261 B3
Newington SE11 261 C3
Kemps Gdns SE13 164 A6
Kempshott Rd SW16 182 A3
Kempson Rd
SW6 135 C5 265 B3
Kempthorne Rd SE8 119 B2
Kempton Ave
Northolt UB5 63 C3
Sunbury TW16 172 B2
Kempton Cl UB10 61 A4
Kempton Ct Stepney E1 96 B2
Sunbury TW16 172 B2
Kempton Ho 13 N1 95 C6
Kempton Lo 3 SM6 219 D5
Kempton Park Race
Course TW16 172 C3
Kempton Park Sta
TW16 172 B3
Kempton Rd E6 100 B6
Kempton Wlk CR0 207 A3
Kempt St SE18 144 C6
Kemsing Cl
Coney Hall BR2 224 D6
Sidcup DA5 169 A4
South Norwood CR7 205 A5
Kemsing Ho SE1 252 D1
Kemsing Rd SE10 121 A1
Kemsley SE13 163 D6
Kemsley Ct Ealing W13 109 C5
St Paul's Cray BR5 190 B2
Kenbrook Ho
Kensington W14 254 D5
5 Kentish Town NW5 71 C3
Kenbury Cl UB10 60 C5
Kenbury Gdns 10 SE5 139 A3
Kenbury Mans 13 SE5 139 A3
Kenbury St SE5 139 A3
Kenchester Cl
SW8 138 A5 270 B3
Kencot Cl DA18 125 B4
Kendal NW1 231 D2
Kendal Ave Acton W3 88 D2
Barking IG11 101 C6
Edmonton N18 33 B6
Kendal Cl
Camberwell SE5 138 D5
East Bedfont TW14 149 D3
Hayes UB4 83 C5
Woodford IG8 20 D2
Kendal Ct Acton W3 88 C2
Brondesbury NW2 69 A3
11 Chingford E4 20 A3
Kendale Rd BR1 186 C5
Kendal Gdns
Edmonton N18 33 B6
Sutton SM1 218 A6
Kendal Ho Edgware HA8 27 A6
Forest Hill SE23 163 B3
32 Hackney E9 74 C1
Islington N1 233 D4
Penge SE20 184 B1
Kendall Ave BR3 185 A1
Kendall Ct
3 London SE22 162 A6
Mitcham SW19 180 B4
5 Penge SE19 183 D3
Sidcup DA15 168 A1
Kendall Ho SE12 164 D4
Kendall Lo 5 BR1 187 B2
Kendall Pl W1 238 A3
Kendall Rd
Beckenham BR3 185 A1
Isleworth TW7 131 A3
Kidbrooke SE18 144 A4
Kendalmere Cl N10 31 B2
Kendal Par N18 33 B6
Kendal Pl SW15 157 B6
Kendal Rd NW10 68 A4
Kendal St W2 92 C1 237 B1
Kendal Stps W2 237 B1
Kender Prim Sch
SE14 140 C4
Kender St SE14 140 C4
Kendoa Rd 1 SW4 137 D1
Kendon Cl E11 55 B4
Kendon Ho E15 76 B1
Kendra Ct CR2 220 D1
Kendra Hall Rd CR2 220 D1
Kendrey Gdns TW2 152 C4
Kendrick Ct 12 SE15 140 B4
Kendrick Mews SW7 256 C3
Kendrick Pl SW7 256 C3
Kenelm Cl HA1 65 A5
Kenerne Dr EN5 13 A6
Kenilford Rd SW12 159 B4
Kenilworth Ave
Harrow HA2 63 B4
Walthamstow E17 53 C6
Wimbledon SW19 179 C6
Kenilworth Cres EN1 5 C4
Kenilworth Ct
7 Chingford E4 20 A2
Fulham SW6 135 A2
Twickenham TW2 152 C2
Kenilworth Gdns
Hayes UB4 83 D2
Ilford IG3 79 D6
Southall UB1 85 B4
South Oxhey WD19 22 C5
Woolwich SE18 144 D3
Kenilworth Ho HA7 25 B3
Kenilworth Rd
Ashford TW15, TW19 148 A1
Bow E3 97 A5
Ealing W5 110 A5
Edgware HA8 11 A1
Kilburn NW6 91 B6
Orpington BR5 211 A3
Penge SE20 184 D2
Stoneleigh KT17 216 A3
Kenilworth Terr 3
SM2 217 C1
Kenley N17 33 B1
Kenley Ave NW9 27 C2
Kenley Cl Barnet EN4 2 C1
Sidcup DA5 169 C4
St Paul's Cray BR7 211 C6
Kenley Gdns CR7 204 D5
Kenley Ho
5 Croydon CR0 206 A1
6 St Paul's Cray BR5 190 B1
Kenley Rd
Kingston u T KT1,
KT3 176 D1
Merton SW19 201 C6
Twickenham TW1 153 B5
Kenley Wlk
Cheam SM3 216 D4
Notting Hill W11 244 A5
Kenlor Ct 6 HA8 26 D5
Kenlor Rd SW17 180 B5
Kenmare Ct 5 HA7 25 C6
Kenmare Dr
Mitcham CR4 180 D3
1 Tottenham N17 33 D1
Kenmare Gdns N13 33 A6
Kenmare Rd CR7 204 C3
Kenmere Gdns HA0 88 C6
Kenmere Rd DA16 146 C3
Kenmont Gdns NW10 90 B4
Kenmont Prim Sch
NW10 90 B4
Kenmore Ave HA3 43 A6
Kenmore Cl TW9 132 C5
Kenmore Cres UB4 83 D4
Kenmore Ct NW6 69 C1
Kenmore Gdns HA8 26 D1
Kenmore Park Fst & Mid
Schs HA3 44 A6
Kenmore Rd HA3 43 D5
Kenmure Mans W5 87 C3
Kenmure Rd E8 74 B3
Kenmure Yd E8 74 B3
Kennacraig Cl 6 E16 121 A5
Kennard Ho 12 SW11 137 A3
Kennard Mans 6 N11 30 D5
Kennard Rd London N11 30 D5
Stratford E15 76 B1
Kennard St
9 London SW11 137 A3
Newham E16 122 B5
Kennedy Ave EN3 18 C5
Kennedy Cl
Crofton BR5 211 B1
1 Mitcham CR4 181 A1
Newham E13 99 A5
Pinner HA5 23 B4
Kennedy Cox Ho 9
E16 98 D2
Kennedy Ct
Ashford TW15 171 A5
Bushey WD23 8 B2
Kennedy Ho SE11 260 C2
Kennedy Path W7 86 D3
Kennedy Rd
Barking IG11 101 C6
Ealing W7 86 C2
Kennedy Wlk SE17 262 D3
Kennet Cl SW11 136 B1
Kennet Ct 47 W2 91 C2
Kennet Dr UB4 85 A2
Kenneth Ave IG1 78 D4
Kenneth Campbell Ho
NW8 236 D6
Kenneth Cres NW2 68 B3
Kenneth Ct SE11 261 B4
Kenneth Gdns HA7 25 A4
Kenneth More Rd 4
IG1 78 D5
Kennet Ho NW8 236 D5
Kenneth Rd RM6 59 A2
Kenneth Robbins Ho 1
N17 34 B3

Kenneth Younger Ho SW6 . . . 264 D5
Kennet Rd
Isleworth TW7 . . . 130 D2
West Kilburn W9 . . . 91 B3
Kennet Sq CR4 . . . 180 C2
Kennet St E1 . . . 118 A5
Kennett Ho HA1 . . . 64 D6
Kennett Wharf La EC4. 252 B6
Kenninghall N18 . . . 34 C5
Kenninghall Rd
London N18 . . . 34 C5
Lower Clapton E5 . . . 74 B5
Kenning Ho 6 N1 . . . 95 C6
Kenning St 18 SE16 . . . 118 C4
Kennings Way SE11 . . . 116 C1 261 B2
KENNINGTON . . . 116 C1
Kennington Ent Ctr SE17 . . . 261 C1
Kennington La SE11 . . . 116 B1 260 D1
Kennington Oval SE11 . . . 138 B6 270 D5
Kennington Palace Ct SE11 . . . 261 A2
Kennington Park Gdns SE17 . . . 138 D6
Kennington Park Ho SE11 . . . 261 B1
Kennington Park Pl SE11 . . . 138 D6
Kennington Park Rd SE11 . . . 116 D1 261 C2
Kennington Rd SE11 . . . 116 C2 261 A3
Kennington Sta SE17 . . . 116 D1 261 C2
Kennoldes SE21 . . . 161 B2
Kennyland Ct NW4 . . . 46 B3
Kenny Rd NW7 . . . 29 A5
Kenrick Pl W1 . . . 238 A3
KENSAL GREEN . . . 90 C4
Kensal Green Cemy (All Souls)* NW10 . . . 90 C4
Kensal Green Sta NW10 . . . 90 C4
Kensal Ho W10 . . . 90 D3
Kensal Rd W10 . . . 91 A3
KENSAL RISE . . . 90 D5
Kensal Rise Prim Sch NW6 . . . 90 D5
Kensal Rise Sta NW10 . . . 90 D5
KENSAL TOWN . . . 91 A3
KENSINGTON . . . 113 C4
Kensington Ave
Plashet E12 . . . 78 B2
South Norwood CR7 . . . 182 C2
Kensington Avenue Prim Sch CR7 . . . 182 C2
Kensington & Chelsea Coll
Chelsea SW10 . . . 136 A5 266 A4
Kensal Town W10 . . . 91 A2
Kensington Church Ct W8 . . . 245 C1
Kensington Church St W8 . . . 113 C5 245 B3
Kensington Church Wlk W8 . . . 245 C1
Kensington Cl N11 . . . 31 A4
Kensington Court Mans W8 . . . 245 D1
Kensington Court Mews W8 . . . 255 D6
Kensington Court Pl W8 . . . 113 D3 255 D6
Kensington Ct
2 Burnt Oak NW7 . . . 27 B5
Enfield EN2 . . . 5 C5
Hendon NW4 . . . 28 C1
Kensington W8 . . . 113 D4 245 D1
Kensington Ct Gdns W8 . . . 255 D6
Kensington Dr IG8 . . . 37 D1
Kensington Gardens* W2 . . . 114 A5 246 B3
Kensington Gate W8 . . . 114 A3 256 A6
Kensington Gdns
Kingston u T KT1 . . . 197 D6
Redbridge IG1 . . . 56 B1
Kensington Gdns Sq W2 . . . 91 D1
Kensington Gore SW7 . . . 114 B4 246 C1
Kensington Hall Gdns W14 . . . 254 C2
Kensington High St W8 . . . 113 C3 255 B6
Kensington Ho 3 NW5 . . 71 C3
Kensington Hts
Harrow HA1 . . . 42 D3
Kensington W8 . . . 245 A3
Kensington Lodge UB5 . . 85 C5
Kensington Mall W8 . . 245 B4
Kensington Mans SW5 255 B2
Kensington Olympia Sta W14 . . . 113 A3 254 A6
Kensington Pal* W8 . . . 113 D5 245 D3
Kensington Palace Gdns W8 . . . 113 D5 245 C4
Kensington Park Gdns W11 . . . 113 B6 244 D5
Kensington Park Mews W11 . . . 91 B1
Kensington Park Rd W11 . . . 113 B6 244 D6
Kensington Pl W8 . . . 113 C5 245 A4
Kensington Prep Sch SW6 . . . 135 B4 264 D2
Kensington Prim Sch E12 . . . 78 B2
Kensington Rd
Kensington SW7 . . . 114 A4 246 B1
Northolt UB5 . . . 85 C5
Kensington Sports Ctr W11 . . . 244 A6
Kensington Sq W8 . . . 113 D4 245 C1
Kensington Terr CR2 . . . 221 B1
Kensington Village W14 . . . 113 B2 254 D3
Kensington W W14 . . . 254 A4
Kensit Meml Coll N3 . . . 29 A1
Kensworth Ho EC1 . . . 235 D1
Kent Ave Bexley DA16 . . . 167 D6
Dagenham RM9 . . . 103 C3
Ealing W13 . . . 87 B2
Kent Cl
Mitcham CR4, SW16 . . . 204 A5
Orpington BR6 . . . 227 C2
Kent Ct Acton W3 . . . 88 B1
3 Haggerston E2 . . . 95 D5
Hendon NW9 . . . 27 C1
Kent Dr Cockfosters EN4 . . 15 A6
Teddington TW11 . . . 174 C5
Kentford Way UB5 . . . 85 A6
Kent Gate Way CR0 . . . 223 D3
Kent Gdns Ealing W13 . . . 87 B2
Ruislip HA4 . . . 40 B3
Kent Ho
Camberwell SE1 . . . 263 D1
13 Chiswick W4 . . . 111 C1
Edgware HA8 . . . 26 B3
Marylebone W1 . . . 239 A2
Pimlico SW1 . . . 259 C1
Richmond TW10 . . . 154 C6
Kent House La BR3 . . . 185 A5
Kent House Rd BR3 . . . 185 A4
Kent House Sta BR3 . . . 185 A2
Kent House Station App BR3 . . . 184 D2
Kentish Bldgs SE1 . . . 252 C3
Kentish Rd DA17 . . . 125 C2
KENTISH TOWN . . . 71 C3
Kentish Town CE Prim Sch NW5 . . . 71 C3
Kentish Town Rd NW1 . . 71 B2
Kentish Town Sta NW5 . . 71 C3
Kentish Town West Sta NW5 . . . 71 B2
Kentish Way BR1, BR2 . . 209 B6
Kentlea Rd SE28 . . . 123 C4
Kent Lo 9 SW19 . . . 156 D3
Kentmere Ho SE15 . . . 140 C6
Kentmere Rd SE18 . . . 123 C2
KENTON . . . 43 C3
Kenton Ave Harrow HA1 . . 42 D2
Southall UB1 . . . 107 C6
Sunbury TW16 . . . 173 A1
Kenton Ct
2 Forest Hill SE26 . . . 185 A6
Harrow HA3 . . . 43 B3
3 Richmond TW10 . . . 153 D5
West Kensington W14 . . 254 C5
Kenton Gdns HA3 . . . 43 C4
Kenton Grove Ho HA3 . . . 44 B4
Kenton Ho
20 Globe Town E1 . . . 96 C3
Highbury N5 . . . 72 C5
Kenton La Harrow HA3 . . . 24 D3
Kenton HA3 . . . 43 C6
Kenton Park Ave HA3 . . . 43 D5
Kenton Park Cl HA3 . . . 43 C4
Kenton Park Cres HA3 . . 43 D5
Kenton Park Mans HA3 . . 43 C4
Kenton Park Par HA3 . . . 43 D4
Kenton Park Rd HA3 . . . 43 C5
Kenton Rd Harrow HA3 . . . 43 C4
Homerton E9 . . . 74 D2
Kenton St WC1 . . . 240 A6
Kenton Sta HA3 . . . 43 B3
Kenton Way UB4 . . . 83 C4
Kent Pas NW1 . . . 237 C6
Kent Pk Ind Est SE15 . . . 140 B6
Kent Rd
Dagenham RM10 . . . 81 D3
East Molesey KT8 . . . 196 A5
Kingston u T KT1 . . . 197 D6
Richmond TW9 . . . 132 C5
South Acton W4 . . . 111 A3
Southgate N21 . . . 17 B4
West Wickham BR4 . . . 207 D1
Kent St Haggerston E2 . . . 95 D5
Newham E13 . . . 99 B4
Kent Terr NW1 . . 92 C4 230 B1
Kent Twr SE20 . . . 184 B3
Kent View Gdns IG3 . . . 79 C6
Kent Way KT6 . . . 214 B6
Kentwell Cl SE4 . . . 141 A1
Kentwins N14 . . . 15 B6
Kentwode Gn SW13 . . . 134 A5
Kent Yard SW7 . . . 247 B1
Kenver Ave N12 . . . 30 B4
Kenward Rd SE9 . . . 165 D6
Ken Way HA9 . . . 67 A5
Kenway Rd SW5 . . . 113 D2 255 C3
Ken Wilson Ho 19 E2 . . . 96 A5
Kenwood Ave N14 . . . 15 D6
Kenwood Cl
North End NW3 . . . 48 B1
Sipson UB7 . . . 126 C6
Kenwood Ct NW9 . . . 45 A5
Kenwood Dr BR3 . . . 208 A6
Kenwood Gdns
Ilford IG2 . . . 56 C4
2 Wanstead E18 . . . 55 B6
Kenwood Ho
15 Brixton SW9 . . . 138 D1
Enfield EN1 . . . 17 C5
Kenwood Ho* NW3 . . . 48 C1
Kenwood Rd
Edmonton N9 . . . 18 A3
Highgate N6 . . . 48 D3
Kenworthy Rd E9 . . . 75 A2
Kenwrick Ho N1 . . . 233 D5
Kenwyn Dr NW2 . . . 67 D5
Kenwyn Rd
Clapham SW4 . . . 137 D1
Wimbledon SW20 . . . 178 C2
Kenya Rd SE7 . . . 143 D5
Kenyngton Dr TW16 . . . 172 A5
Kenyngton Manor Prim Sch TW16 . . . 172 A4
Kenyngton Pl HA3 . . . 43 C4
Kenyon Ho 31 SE5 . . . 139 A5
Kenyon St SW6 . . . 134 D4
Keogh Rd E15 . . . 76 D2
Kepler Ho 9 SE10 . . . 120 D1
Kepler Rd SW2, SW4 . . . 138 A1
Keppel Ho
Brompton SW3 . . . 257 A3
5 Deptford SE8 . . . 119 B1
Keppel Rd
Dagenham RM9 . . . 81 A4
Newham E6 . . . 100 B6
Keppel Row SE1 . . . 252 A3
Keppel St WC1 . . . 239 D4
Kerala Ct N17 . . . 33 D2
Kerbela St 3 E2 . . . 96 A3
Kerbey St E14 . . . 97 D1
Kerem Sch N2 . . . 48 B4
Kerfield Cres SE5 . . . 139 B4
Kerfield Pl SE5 . . . 139 B4
Kerridge Ct N1 . . . 73 C2
Kerrier Ho SW10 . . . 266 B3
Kerrington Ct 7 W12 . . 112 C4
Kerrison Pl W5 . . . 109 D5
Kerrison Rd
Battersea SW11 . . . 136 C2
Ealing W5 . . . 109 D5
Mill Meads E15 . . . 98 B6
Kerrison Villas W5 . . . 109 D5
Kerry N7 . . . 72 A2
Kerry Ave HA7 . . . 25 D6
Kerry Cl Newham E16 . . . 99 B1
Palmers Green N13 . . . 16 B2
Kerry Ct HA7 . . . 25 D6
Kerry Ho 5 E1 . . . 96 C1
Kerry Path SE8 . . . 141 B6
Kerry Rd SE8 . . . 141 B6
Kerscott Ho 30 E3 . . . 97 D4
Kersey Gdns SE9 . . . 188 A6
Kersfield Ho SW15 . . . 156 D5
Kersfield Rd SW15 . . . 156 D5
Kershaw Cl SW18 . . . 158 B5
Kershaw Ho 7 SE27 . . . 160 D1
Kershaw Rd RM10 . . . 81 C5
Kersley Mews SW11 . . . 267 C1
Kersley Rd N16 . . . 73 C5
Kersley St SW11 . . . 136 D3
Kerstin Cl UB3 . . . 105 D6
Kerswell Cl N15 . . . 51 C4
Kerwick Cl 1 N7 . . . 72 B1
Keslake Mans NW10 . . . 90 D5
Keslake Rd NW6 . . . 90 D5
Kessock Cl N17 . . . 52 B4
Kestlake Rd DA5 . . . 168 C5
KESTON . . . 225 D4
Keston Ave BR2 . . . 225 C3
Keston CE Prim Sch BR2 . . . 225 D3
Keston Cl Bexley DA16 . . 146 C5
Edmonton N18 . . . 17 B1
Keston Ct DA5 . . . 169 B4
Keston Gdns BR2 . . . 225 C4
Keston Ho SE17 . . . 263 B2
KESTON MARK . . . 225 D6
Keston Mark BR2 . . . 226 A5
Keston Park Cl BR2 . . . 226 B5
Keston Rd
East Dulwich SE15 . . . 140 A2
Thornton Heath CR7 . . . 204 C3
West Green N17 . . . 51 B5
Kestrel Ave
East Ham E6 . . . 100 A2
Herne Hill SE24 . . . 161 A6
Kestrel Cl
Grahame Pk NW9 . . . 27 C1
Kingston u T KT2 . . . 175 D6
Neasden NW10 . . . 67 B3
Kestrel Ct
Higham Hill E17 . . . 34 D1
Ruislip HA4 . . . 61 B6
South Croydon CR2 . . . 221 A2
Wallington SM6 . . . 219 C3
Kestrel Ho
4 Battersea SW11 . . . 136 C2
Enfield EN3 . . . 19 A6
Finsbury EC1 . . . 235 A2
Kestrel Pl SE14 . . . 141 A6
Kestrel Way UB3 . . . 105 B4
Keswick Apartments 4 N17 . . . 51 D6
Keswick Ave
Kingston u T KT2, SW15 . . . 177 C5
Merton SW19 . . . 179 C1
Upper Halliford TW17 . . . 193 C6
Keswick Broadway 1 SW15 . . . 157 B6
Keswick Cl SM1 . . . 218 A4
Keswick Ct
13 Catford SE6 . . . 164 D3
2 East Dulwich SE22 . . . 162 A6
Keswick Dr EN3 . . . 6 C6
Keswick Gdns
Redbridge IG4 . . . 56 A5
Ruislip HA4 . . . 39 B3
Wembley HA9 . . . 66 A4
Keswick Ho 8 SE5 . . . 139 A4
Keswick Hts 9 SW15 . . . 157 A6
Keswick Lo E8 . . . 73 D2
Keswick Mews W5 . . . 110 A5
Keswick Rd
Bexleyheath DA7 . . . 147 C4
Broom Hill BR6 . . . 211 D1
Putney SW15 . . . 157 A6
Twickenham TW2 . . . 152 A5
West Wickham BR4 . . . 224 C6
Kettering Ct CR7 . . . 205 A5
Kettering Rd EN3 . . . 6 D6
Kettering St SW16 . . . 181 C4
Kett Gdns SW2 . . . 160 B6
Kettlebaston Rd E10 . . . 53 B1
Kettleby Ho SW9 . . . 138 D2
Kettlewell Cl N11 . . . 31 A4
Ketton Ho 11 W10 . . . 90 C3
Kevan Ct 6 E17 . . . 53 D5
Kevan Ho SE5 . . . 139 A5
Kevelioc Rd N17 . . . 33 A2
Kevin Cl TW4 . . . 128 D3
Kevington Cl BR5 . . . 211 D5
Kevington Dr BR5, BR7 . . . 211 D5
KEW . . . 132 C6
Kew Bridge TW8 . . . 110 B1
Kew Bridge Ct 8 W4 . . . 110 C1
Kew Bridge Distribution Ctr TW8 . . . 110 B1
Kew Bridge Rd TW8 . . . 110 B1
Kew Bridge Sta TW8 . . . 110 B1
Kew Bridge Steam Mus* TW8 . . . 110 B1
Kew Coll TW9 . . . 132 C5
Kew Cres SM3 . . . 217 B5
Kew Ct KT2 . . . 176 A2
Kew Foot Rd TW9 . . . 132 A2
Kew Gardens Rd TW9 . . 132 C4
Kew Gardens (Royal Botanic)* TW9 . . . 132 A4
Kew Gardens Sta TW9 . . . 132 C4
Kew Gn TW9 . . . 132 B6
Kew Green TW9 . . . 132 C6
Kew Green Prep Sch TW9 . . . 132 B6
Kew Lo 11 TW9 . . . 132 B4
Kew Montessori Sch TW9 . . . 132 C4
Kew Obsy* TW9 . . . 131 C2
Kew Pal* TW9 . . . 132 A5
Kew Pier TW9 . . . 132 C6
Kew Rd Finchley N2 . . . 30 C2
Richmond TW9, W4 . . . 132 B4
Kew Ret Pk TW9 . . . 132 D4
Kew Riverside Prim Sch TW9 . . . 132 D3
Key Cl E1 . . . 96 B3
Keyes Ct SE22 . . . 162 A6
Keyes Rd NW2 . . . 68 D3
Keyham Ho 31 W2 . . . 91 C2
Key Ho 9 SE11 . . . 138 C6
Keymer Rd SW2 . . . 160 B2
Keynes Cl N2 . . . 48 D6
Keynes Ct 9 SE28 . . . 124 B6
Keynsham Ave IG8 . . . 36 C6
Keynsham Gdns SE9 . . . 166 A6
Keynsham Ho 2 N4 . . . 51 A2
Keynsham Rd
Cheam SM4 . . . 201 D1
Eltham SE9 . . . 166 A6
Keynsham Wlk SM4 . . . 201 D1
Keyse Rd SE1 . . 117 D3 263 C5
Keysham Ave TW5 . . . 128 A4
Keysham Ct HA9 . . . 66 A6
Keystone Cres N1 . . . 233 B3
Keywood Dr TW16 . . . 172 A4
Keyworth Cl E5 . . . 75 A4
Keyworth Pl SE1 . . . 261 D6
Keyworth Prim Sch SE17 . . . 116 D1 261 C2
Keyworth St SE1 . . . 116 D3 261 D6
Kezia St SE8 . . . 119 A1
Khalsa Ct N22 . . . 32 D2
Khama Rd SW17 . . . 180 C6
Khartoum Rd Ilford IG1 . . 78 D3
Newham E13 . . . 99 B4
Upper Tooting SW17 . . . 180 B6
Khyber Rd SW11 . . . 136 C3
Kibworth St SW8 . . . 138 B5 270 C3
KIDBROOKE . . . 143 C3
Kidbrooke Gdns SE3 . . . 143 A4
Kidbrooke Gr SE3 . . . 143 B4
Kidbrooke Interchange SE3 . . . 143 C2
Kidbrooke La SE9 . . . 144 A1
Kidbrooke Park Cl SE3 . . . 143 B4
Kidbrooke Park Prim Sch SE3 . . . 143 C4
Kidbrooke Park Rd SE12, SE3 . . . 143 B2
Kidbrooke Sch SE3 . . . 143 D3
Kidbrooke Sta SE3 . . . 143 B2
Kidbrooke Way SE3 . . . 143 B3
Kiddens BR8 . . . 191 D1
Kidderminster Pl CR0 . . 204 D1
Kidderminster Rd CR0 . . . 205 A2
Kidderpore Ave NW3 . . . 69 C4
Kidderpore Gdns NW3 . . 69 C4
Kidd Ho RM9 . . . 81 B4
Kidd Pl SE7 . . . 122 A1
Kidlington Way NW9 . . . 27 C2
Kierbeck Bsns Complex E16 . . . 121 B4
Kiffen St EC2 . . . 242 D6
Kilberry Cl TW7 . . . 130 B4
Kilbrennan Ho 9 E14 . . . 98 A1
KILBURN . . . 91 C6
Kilburn Bridge 14 NW6 . . 91 C6
Kilburn Gate NW6 . . . 91 D5
Kilburn High Rd NW6 . . . 91 C6
Kilburn High Road Sta NW6 . . . 91 D6
Kilburn Ho 11 W9 . . . 91 B4
Kilburn La W10 . . . 91 A5
Kilburn Park Foundation Sch The NW6 . . . 91 B5
Kilburn Park Rd NW6 . . . 91 C4
Kilburn Park Sta NW6 . . 91 C5
Kilburn Pl NW6 . . . 91 C6
Kilburn Priory NW6 . . . 91 D6
Kilburn Sq NW6 . . . 91 C6
Kilburn Sta NW2 . . . 69 B2
Kilburn Vale NW6 . . . 91 D6
Kilburn Vale Est 13 NW6 . . . 91 C6
Kilby Ct SE10 . . . 120 D3
Kildare Cl HA4 . . . 40 C1
Kildare Ct W2 . . . 91 C1
Kildare Gdns W2 . . . 91 C1
Kildare Rd E16 . . . 99 A2
Kildare Terr W2 . . . 91 C1
Kildare Wlk E14 . . . 97 C1
Kildoran Rd SW2 . . . 160 A6
Kildowan Rd IG3 . . . 58 A1
Kilgour Rd SE23 . . . 163 A5
Kilkie St SW6 . . . 136 A3
Killarney Rd SW18 . . . 158 A5
Killburns Mill Cl SM6 . . 219 B6
Killearn Rd SE6 . . . 164 B3
Killester Gdns KT17, KT4 . . . 216 B4
Killick Ho SM1 . . . 217 D4
Killick St N1 . . . 94 B5 233 C3
Killieser Ave SW2 . . . 160 A2
Killigrew Ho TW16 . . . 171 C3
Killip Cl E16 . . . 98 D1
Killoran Ho 9 E14 . . . 120 A3
Killowen Ave UB5 . . . 64 A3
Killowen Rd E9 . . . 74 D2
Killyon Rd SW8 . . . 137 C3
Kilmaine Rd SW6 . . . 135 A5 264 B3
Kilmarnock Gdns RM8 . . 80 C5
Kilmarnock Rd WD19 . . . 22 D6
Kilmarsh Rd W6 . . . 112 C2
Kilmartin Ave SW16 . . . 204 C6
Kilmartin Rd IG3 . . . 80 A6
Kilmington Rd SW13 . . . 134 A6
Kilmiston Ave TW17 . . . 193 A3
Kilmiston Ho TW17 . . . 193 A3
Kilmore Ho 17 E14 . . . 97 D1
Kilmorey Gdns TW1 . . . 131 B1
Kilmorey Rd TW1 . . . 131 B1
Kilmorie Prim Sch SE23 . . . 163 A2
Kilmorie Rd SE23 . . . 163 A2
Kilmuir Ho SW1 . . . 258 B3
Kiln Cl UB3 . . . 127 B6
Kiln Ct E14 . . . 119 B6
Kilner Ho 3 SE11 . . . 138 C6
Kilner St E14 . . . 97 C2
Kiln Mews SW17 . . . 180 B5
Kiln Pl NW5 . . . 71 A3
Kilnsey Ct 8 N11 . . . 31 A4
Kilnside KT10 . . . 213 A1
Kiloh Ct 1 SW11 . . . 136 C2
Kilpatrick Ct N16 . . . 51 D1
Kilpatrick Way UB4 . . . 85 A2
Kilpeck Ho 3 N4 . . . 51 A2
Kilravock Ho SE25 . . . 205 C6
Kilravock St W10 . . . 91 A4
Kilronan 5 W3 . . . 89 B1
Kilross Rd TW14 . . . 149 C3
Kilsby Wlk RM9 . . . 80 B2
Kilsha Rd KT12 . . . 194 C3
Kilvinton Dr EN2 . . . 5 B5
Kimbell Gdns SW6 . . . 135 A4 264 A1
Kimbell Pl SE9 . . . 143 C1
Kimber Ctr The SW18 . . 157 C4
Kimber Ho 11 SE18 . . . 144 D6
Kimberley Ave
Ilford IG2 . . . 57 C2
Newham E6 . . . 100 A5
Nunhead SE15 . . . 140 C2
Kimberley Ct
Belvedere DA17 . . . 125 B2
Kilburn NW6 . . . 91 A6
Kimberley Dr DA14 . . . 168 D2
Kimberley Gate 3 BR1 . . . 186 D3
Kimberley Gdns
Enfield EN1 . . . 5 D2
Harringay N4 . . . 50 D4
Kimberley Ho 7 E14 . . . 120 A3
Kimberley Ind Est E17 . . 35 B2
Kimberley Rd
Chingford E4 . . . 20 C3
Edmonton N18 . . . 34 B4
Kilburn NW6 . . . 91 A6
Leyton E11 . . . 76 B6
Newham E16 . . . 98 D3
Penge BR3 . . . 184 D1
Kimberley Rd *continued*
Stockwell SW9 . . . 138 A2
Thornton Heath CR0 . . . 204 D3
Tottenham N17 . . . 34 A1
Walthamstow E17 . . . 35 B2
Kimberley Way E4 . . . 20 C3
Kimberley Wlk KT12 . . . 194 B2
Kimber Rd SW18 . . . 157 D4
Kimble Cres WD23 . . . 8 A4
Kimble Ho
Lisson Gr NW8 . . . 237 B6
1 Lower Holloway N7 . . . 72 A3
Kimble Rd SW17 . . . 180 B4
Kimbolton Cl SE12 . . . 164 D5
Kimbolton Row SW3 . . . 257 A3
Kimmeridge Gdns 3 SE9 . . . 188 A6
Kimmeridge Rd SE9 . . . 188 A6
Kimm Ho 16 E17 . . . 53 D6
Kimpton Ct 12 SE5 . . . 139 B4
Kimpton Ho SW15 . . . 156 A4
Kimpton Link Bsns Ctr SM3 . . . 217 B6
Kimpton Park Way SM3 . . . 217 B6
Kimpton Rd
Camberwell SE5 . . . 139 B4
Cheam SM3 . . . 217 B6
Kimpton Trade & Bsns Ctr SM3 . . . 217 B6
Kinburn St SE16 . . . 118 D4
Kincaid Rd SE15 . . . 140 B5
Kincardine Gdns W9 . . . 91 C3
Kinch Gr HA3, HA9 . . . 44 B2
Kincraig BR7 . . . 188 C2
Kindell Ho 4 SW14 . . . 133 B2
Kinder Cl SE28 . . . 124 D6
Kinder Ho N1 . . . 235 D4
Kindersley Ho 38 E1 . . . 96 A1
Kinder St 19 E1 . . . 96 B1
Kinderton Cl N14 . . . 15 C3
Kinefold Ho N7 . . . 72 A2
Kinfauns Rd Ilford IG3 . . . 58 B1
Streatham SW2 . . . 160 C2
King Alfred Ave
Catford SE6 . . . 163 C1
Catford SE6 . . . 185 C6
King Alfred Sch NW11 . . 47 D1
King Arthur Cl SE15 . . . 140 C5
King Athelstan Prim Sch KT1 . . . 198 B6
King Charles Cres KT5 . . . 198 B2
King Charles Ct 16 SE17 . . . 138 D6
King Charles Ho SW6 . 265 D4
King Charles' Rd KT5, KT6 . . . 198 B3
King Charles St SW1 . . . 116 A4 250 A2
King Charles Terr 11 E1 . . . 118 B6
King Charles Wlk 6 SW19 . . . 157 A3
King Ct 16 E10 . . . 53 D2
Kingcup Cl CR0 . . . 206 D1
King David La E1 . . . 118 C6
Kingdon Ho 8 E14 . . . 120 A3
Kingdon Rd NW6 . . . 69 C2
Kingdown Cl W10 . . . 90 D1
King Edward Dr KT6 . . . 214 A5
King Edward Mans 12 E8 . . . 96 B6
King Edward Mews SW13 . . . 134 A4
King Edward Rd
Barnet EN5 . . . 1 D1
Leytonstone E10 . . . 54 A1
Walthamstow E17 . . . 53 A6
King Edward's Gdns W3 . . . 110 C5
King Edward's Gr TW11 . . . 175 C4
King Edwards Mans SW6 . . . 265 A3
King Edward's Rd
Barking IG11 . . . 101 B5
Edmonton N9 . . . 18 B4
Enfield EN3 . . . 6 D1
Ruislip HA4 . . . 39 B1
South Hackney E9 . . . 96 C6
King Edward St EC1 . . . 242 A2
King Edward The Third Mews 11 SE16 . . . 118 B4
King Edward VII Hospl-Sister Agnes W1 . . . 93 A2 238 B4
King Edward Wlk SE1 . . . 116 C3 261 B6
King Fahad Acad The W5 . . . 109 C2
King Fahed Acad W3 . . 111 D6
Kingfield Rd W5 . . . 87 D3
Kingfield St E14 . . . 120 A2
Kingfisher Ave E11 . . . 55 B3
Kingfisher Cl
Harrow HA3 . . . 24 D3
Woolwich SE28 . . . 124 C6
Kingfisher Ct
11 Battersea SW11 . . . 136 C2
Cheam SM1 . . . 217 B3
17 Cubitt Town E14 . . . 120 A4
East Molesey KT8 . . . 196 C5
Enfield EN2 . . . 4 D5
Hounslow TW3 . . . 151 D6
Merton SW19 . . . 179 B3
Putney SW19 . . . 157 A2
Spring Gr TW3 . . . 130 B3
Kingfisher Dr TW10 . . . 175 B6

Kingfisher Ho
16 Battersea SW18 136 A2
Peckham SE15 139 D4
West Kensington W14 254 C6
Kingfisher Lo TW11 175 A6
Kingfisher Mews
SE13 163 D6
Kingfisher Sq 19 SE8 141 B6
Kingfisher St E6 100 A2
Kingfisher Way
Croydon CR0 206 D4
Neasden NW10 67 B3
Kingfisher Wlk NW9 27 C1
King Frederick IX Twr
SE16 119 B3
King Garth Mews
SE23 162 C2
King Gdns CR0 220 D3
King George Ave
Ilford IG2 57 B3
Newham E16 99 D1
Walton-on-T KT12 194 D1
King George Cl TW16 171 C5
King George Hospl IG3 58 A4
King George Sq TW10 154 B5
King George St SE10 142 A5
King George's Trad Est
KT9 214 C4
King George VI Ave
CR4 202 D5
King George V Sta
E16 122 C5
Kingham Cl
3 Shepherd's Bush
W11 112 D4
Wandsworth SW18 158 A4
Kingham Ind Est NW10 89 B4
King Harolds Way
DA7 147 A5
King Henry Mews
Harrow HA2 42 C1
7 Orpington BR6 227 D3
King Henry's Mews EN3 7 C6
King Henry's Rd
Kingston u T KT1,
KT3 198 D6
Primrose Hill NW3 70 C1
King Henry's Reach
W6 134 C6
King Henry St N16 73 C3
King Henry's Wlk N1 73 C2
King Henry's Yd 5 N16 73 C3
King Henry Terr 10
E1 118 B6
King Ho 5 W12 90 B1
Kinghorn St EC1 242 A3
King James St
SE1 116 D4 251 D1
King John Ct EC2 243 B6
King John St E1 96 D2
King John's Wlk SE9 166 A5
Kinglake St
SE17 117 C1 263 B2
Kinglet Cl E7 77 A2
Kingly Ct W1 249 B6
Kingly St W1 115 C6 249 A6
King & Queen Cl 4
SE9 188 A6
King & Queen St
SE17 117 A1 262 B2
Kingsand Rd SE12 165 A2
Kings Arbour UB2 107 A1
King's Arms Ct E1 96 A2
King's Arms Yd EC2 242 C2
Kingsash Dr UB4 85 A3
Kings Ave Bromley BR1 186 D4
Clapham Pk SW4 160 A5
Dagenham RM6 59 B3
Ealing W5 87 D1
Muswell Hill N10 49 A6
New Malden KT3 199 D5
Wallington SM5 218 D1
King's Ave
Ashford TW16 171 D4
Buckhurst Hill IG9 21 D2
Hounslow TW3, TW5 129 D4
Southall UB1 85 D1
Southgate N21 16 D3
Woodford IG8 37 C5
Kings Avenue Sch
SW4 160 A6
King's Bench St
SE1 116 D4 251 D2
King's Bench Wlk EC4 241 B1
Kingsbridge N16 51 B1
Kingsbridge Ave W3 110 B4
Kingsbridge Cres UB1 85 B2
Kingsbridge Ct
Edmonton N21 16 D2
Millwall E14 119 C2
Kingsbridge Dr NW7 28 D3
Kingsbridge Ho 10
SE20 184 B2
Kingsbridge Ind Est
IG11 101 C4
Kingsbridge Rd
Barking IG11 101 B5
North Kensington W10 90 C1
Southall UB2 107 B2
Walton-on-T KT12 194 B2
West Barnes SM4 200 D2
Kingsbridge Way UB4 83 C4
KINGSBURY 45 B3
Kingsbury Green Prim Sch
NW9 44 D4
Kingsbury High Sch
(Lower Sch) NW9 45 A5
Kingsbury High Sch
(Upper Sch) NW9 44 D5
Kingsbury Hospl NW9 44 C5
Kingsbury Rd
Kingsbury NW9 44 D4
Kingsland N1 73 C2
Kingsbury Sta NW9 44 C4
Kingsbury Terr N1 73 C2
Kingsbury Trad Est
NW9 45 B3
Kings Chase KT8 196 A6
Kings Chase View EN2 4 C3
Kings Cl Hendon NW4 46 D5
Walton-on-T KT12 194 B1
King's Cl
Thames Ditton KT7 197 A2
Walthamstow E10 53 D2
Kingsclere Cl SW15 156 A4
Kingsclere Ct
Colney Hatch N12 30 C5
New Barnet EN5 14 A6
Kingsclere Pl EN2 5 A3
Kingscliffe Gdns
SW19 157 B3
King's Coll
Dulwich Village SE24 161 B5
Strand WC2 116 B6 250 D6
Kings College Ct NW3 70 C1
King's College Hospl
SE5 139 B3
Kings College Rd
Primrose Hill NW3 70 B1
Ruislip HA4 39 D3
King's Coll London
(Hampstead) NW3 69 C4
King's Coll Sch SW19 178 D4
King's Coll Univ
SE1 116 C5 251 A3
Kingscote NW11 47 B1
Kingscote Rd
Bedford Pk W4 111 B3
Croydon CR0 206 B2
Kingston u T KT3 199 B6
Kingscote St EC4 251 C6
Kings Court Mews
KT8 196 B4
King's Court N SW3 257 A1
Kingscourt Rd SW16 160 A1
King's Court S SW3 257 A1
King's Cres N4, N5 73 A5
Kingscroft SW4 160 A5
Kingscroft Rd NW2 69 B2
KING'S CROSS 94 A5
King's Cross
WC1 94 A4 233 B2
King's Cross Bridge
WC1 233 B2
King's Cross Rd
WC1 94 B4 233 D1
King's Cross, St Pancras
N1 94 A4 233 A2
King's Cross Sta
N1 94 A5 233 B3
King's Cross (Thames
Link) Sta WC1 94 A4 233 B2
Kings Ct
6 Barnsbury N7 72 B1
2 Buckhurst Hill IG9 21 D2
Chiswick W6 112 A2
East Dulwich SE22 140 A1
16 Kingston u T KT2 176 C3
Newham E13 99 B6
Primrose Hill NW8 230 C5
10 Putney SW15 156 A4
3 Wallington SM6 219 B2
Wembley Pk HA9 66 D6
King's Ct
Beckenham BR3 207 D6
9 Ealing W5 87 C2
Wimbledon SW19 179 C4
Kingsdale Ct EN4 2 D3
Kingsdale Gdns W11 112 D5
Kingsdale Rd
Penge SE20 184 D3
Plumstead Comm SE18 145 D6
Kingsdale Sec Sch
SE21 161 C1
Kingsdown SW19 178 D3
Kingsdown Ave
East Acton W3 111 C6
West Ealing W13 109 B4
Kingsdown Cl
26 Deptford SE16 118 B1
8 Notting Hill W11 91 A1
Kingsdown Ct SW11 158 C5
Kingsdowne Rd KT6 198 B2
Kingsdown Ho 1 E8 74 A3
Kingsdown Rd
Cheam SM3 217 A3
Leyton E11 76 C5
4 Upper Holloway N19 72 A6
Kingsdown Way BR2 209 A3
Kings Dr Edgware HA8 26 B6
Surbiton KT5 198 C3
Wembley Pk HA9 66 D6
King's Dr KT7 197 B2
Kingsend HA4 39 C1
Kingsend Ct HA4 39 C1
Kings Farm E17 35 D2
Kings Farm Ave TW10 132 C1
Kingsfield Ave HA1,
HA2 42 A4
Kingsfield Ct HA1 42 B2
Kingsfield Ho
Mottingham SE9 165 D1
7 Muswell Hill N10 31 A3
18 Stoke Newington N16 73 C5
Kingsfield Rd HA1 42 B2
Kingsford Com Sch
E6 100 B1
Kingsford St NW5 70 D3
Kingsford Way E6 100 B2
Kingsgate HA9 67 A5
Kingsgate Ave N3 47 C6
Kingsgate Bsns Ctr
KT2 176 A2
Kingsgate Cl Erith DA7 147 A4
Sidcup BR5 190 C1
Kingsgate Est N1 73 C2
Kingsgate Ho 29 SW9 138 C4
Kingsgate Par SW1 259 B5
Kingsgate Pl NW6 69 C1
Kingsgate Prim Sch
NW6 69 C1
Kingsgate Rd
Hampstead NW6 69 C1
Kingston u T KT2 176 A2
Kings Gdns IG1 57 B1
King's Gdns 6 NW6 69 C1
King's Gr
Peckham SE15 140 B4
Peckham SE15 140 B5
Kings Grange HA4 39 D1
Kingsground SE9 166 A5
Kingshall Mews SE13 142 A2
Kings Hall Rd BR3 185 A2
Kings Head Hill E4 19 D4
King's Head Yd SE1 252 C3
King's Highway SE18 145 D6
Kingshill SE17 262 B4
Kingshill Ave
Harrow HA3 43 B5
Hayes UB4 83 D4
New Malden KT4 200 B2
Northolt UB5 84 B4
Kingshill Cl UB4, UB5 84 A4
Kingshill Ct 8 EN5 1 A1
Kingshill Dr HA3 43 B6
Kings Ho
19 Limehouse E14 119 B6
South Lambeth SW8 270 B4
Kingshold Rd E9 74 C1
Kingsholm Gdns SE9 144 A1
King's House Sch
TW10 154 B6
King's House Sch (Jun)
TW10 154 B6
Kingshurst Rd SE12 165 A4
Kings Keep KT6 198 A5
King's Keep 6 SW15 156 D6
King's La SM1 218 B3
KINGSLAND 73 C2
Kingsland NW8 92 C6 230 B5
Kingsland Gn 1 E8, N1 73 C2
Kingsland High St E8 73 D3
Kingsland Pas 2 E8 73 C2
Kingsland Rd Hoxton E2 95 C5
Newham E13 99 C4
Kingsland Sh Ctr 12 E8 73 D2
Kingslawn Cl SW15 156 B6
Kingslee Ct 4 SM2 217 D1
Kingsleigh Cl TW8 131 D6
Kingsleigh Pl CR4 202 D6
Kingsleigh Wlk BR2 208 D5
Kingsley Ave
Ealing W13 87 A1
Hounslow TW3 130 A3
Southall UB1 107 C6
Sutton SM1 218 B4
Kingsley Cl
Dagenham RM10 81 D4
East Finchley N2 48 A4
Kingsley Ct Bexley DA6 147 C1
Edgware HA8 10 D2
Snaresbrook E11 54 D3
1 Thamesmead SE28 124 C5
Willesden NW2 68 B2
Wood Green N22 32 B3
Worcester Pk KT4 215 D6
Kingsley Dr KT4 215 D6
Kingsley Flats SE1 263 B3
Kingsley Gdns E4 35 C5
Kingsley Grange 1
E11 55 A4
Kingsley High Sch HA3 24 A3
Kingsley Ho
Chelsea SW3 266 D5
3 Clapham SW4 137 D3
East Finchley NW11 48 A3
8 Kingston u T KT6 198 A4
Kingsley Mews
Chislehurst West
BR7 188 D4
Dagenham RM9 80 D4
4 Ilford IG1 78 D6
Kensington W8 255 D5
15 St George in t East
E1 118 B6
Kingsley Pl N6 49 A2
Kingsley Prim Sch
CR9 204 C1
Kingsley Rd
Chingford E17 36 A1
Edmonton N13 32 D6
Harrow HA2 64 A5
Hounslow TW3 130 A3
Kilburn NW6 91 B6
Orpington BR6 227 D1
Pinner HA5 41 B5
Thornton Heath CR0 204 C1
Upton E7 77 A1
Wimbledon SW19 179 D5
Kingsley St SW11 136 D2
Kingsley Way N2 48 A4
Kingsley Wood Dr
SE9 166 B1
Kings Lo HA4 39 C1
Kingslyn Cres SE19 183 C2
Kings Mall Sh Ctr W6 112 C2
Kingsman Par SE18 122 B3
King's Mans SW3 267 A5
Kingsman St SE18 122 B2
Kingsmead Barnet EN5 1 C1
Kingsmead *continued*
Richmond TW10 154 B5
Kingsmead Ave
Edmonton N9 18 B3
Kingsbury NW9 45 B2
Mitcham CR4 203 C6
North Cheam KT4 216 B5
Sunbury TW16 172 C1
Tolworth KT6 214 C6
Kingsmead Cl
Sidcup DA15 168 A2
Teddington TW11 175 B4
West Ewell KT19 215 B1
Kingsmead Cotts BR2 210 A1
Kingsmead Ct
Bromley BR1 186 D3
Crouch End N6 49 D2
Kingsmead Dr UB5 63 B1
Kingsmead Ho E9 75 A4
Kingsmead Lo
9 Chingford E4 20 A2
Sutton SM2 218 B2
Kings Mead Pk KT10 212 C1
Kingsmead Prim Sch
E9 75 A4
Kingsmead Rd SW2 160 C2
Kingsmead Sch EN1 6 A2
King's Mead Way E5,
E9 75 A4
Kingsmere Catford SE6 163 D3
Widmore BR7 188 A2
Kingsmere Cl SW15 134 D2
Kingsmere Ct NW9 44 D1
Kingsmere Pk NW9 45 A1
Kingsmere Pl N16 51 B1
Kingsmere Rd SW19 156 D2
King's Mews
1 Clapham Pk SW4 160 A6
Gray's Inn WC1 94 B3 240 D5
Kingsmill NW8 92 B5 229 D4
Kingsmill Bsns Pk
KT1 198 B6
Kingsmill Gdns RM9 81 B3
Kingsmill Rd RM9 81 B3
Kingsmill Terr
NW8 92 B5 229 D4
Kingsmount Ct SM1 217 D4
Kingsnorth Ho 12 W10 90 D1
Kingsnympton Pk
KT2 176 D4
Kings Oak RM7 59 C6
Kings Oak Hospl (Private)
The EN2 4 C5
King's Orch SE9 166 A5
King's Paddock TW12 174 A2
King's Par
3 Hammersmith
W12 112 A3
Willesden NW10 90 C6
Kingspark Bsns Ctr
KT3 199 A6
Kingspark Ct E18 55 A6
King's Pas KT2 175 D2
King's Penny Ho 4
KT2 176 A3
Kings Pl
Acton Green W4 111 A2
Buckhurst Hill IG9 21 D2
Loughton IG10 21 D4
King's Pl SE1 252 A1
King Sq EC1 95 A4 235 A1
King's Quay SW10 266 B2
Kings Rd Ealing W5 87 D2
Feltham TW13 150 C3
Harrow HA2 63 B6
Mitcham CR4 203 A6
Orpington BR6 227 D4
Richmond TW10, TW9 154 B6
Walton-on-T KT12 194 B1
West Drayton UB7 104 B4
Willesden NW10 68 B1
Wood Green N22 32 B2
King's Rd Barking IG11 79 A1
Chelsea SW3 257 B1
Chelsea SW10 136 B6 266 C5
Chingford E4 20 B3
Edmonton N18 34 A6
Kingston u T KT2 176 B3
Leytonstone E11 54 C2
Long Ditton KT6 197 C1
Mortlake SW14 133 B2
Newham E6 99 C6
South Norwood SE25 206 A6
Teddington TW11,
TW12 174 B5
Tottenham N17 33 D2
Twickenham TW1 153 B5
Wimbledon SW19 179 C4
Kings Ride Gate
TW10 132 C1
Kingsridge SW19 157 A2
Kings Road Bglws HA2 63 B5
King's Scholars' Pas
SW1 259 A4
King St Acton W3 111 A5
East Finchley N2 48 B6
Hammersmith W6 112 A2
Newham E13 98 D3
Newham E13 99 A3
Richmond TW9 153 D6
Southall UB2 107 A3
St James SW1 115 C5 249 B4
Strand WC2 250 A6
Tottenham N17 33 D2
Twickenham TW1 153 A3
Whitechapel EC2 95 A1 242 B1
King Stairs Cl SE16 118 B4
King's Terr
Camden Town
NW1 93 C6 232 A5
King's Terr *continued*
10 Isleworth TW7 131 A2
Kingsthorpe Rd SE26 184 D6
Kingston Ave
Cheam SM3 217 A5
Feltham TW14 149 D5
Yiewsley UB7 104 B6
Kingston Bsns Ctr
KT9 214 B5
Kingston By-Pass KT6, KT7,
KT9 213 C5
Kingston By - Pass
KT6 214 C5
Kingston Cl
Dagenham RM6 59 A6
Northolt UB5 85 B6
Teddington TW11 175 B4
Kingston Coll of F Ed
KT1 197 D6
Kingston Coll of F Ed (M V
Annex) KT2 176 A2
Kingston Cres BR3 185 B2
Kingston Ct HA3 44 B4
Kingston Gdns CR0 220 A5
Kingston Gram Sch
KT2 176 B1
Kingston Hall Rd KT1 197 D6
Kingston Hill KT2 177 A5
Kingston Hill Ave RM6 59 A6
Kingston Hill Pl KT2,
TW10 177 A6
Kingston Ho 4 NW6 69 A1
Kingston Ho E SW7 247 A1
Kingston Ho N SW7 247 A1
Kingston Ho S SW7 247 A1
Kingston Hospl KT2 176 D2
Kingston House Est
KT6 197 B3
Kingston La
Teddington TW11 175 B4
Uxbridge UB8 82 A4
West Drayton UB7 104 B4
Kingston Lo 2 KT3 199 C5
Kingston Mus* KT1 176 A1
Kingston Pl HA3 24 D3
Kingston Rd
Ashford TW15 170 A4
Ashford TW15 170 B4
Edmonton N9 18 A2
Ewell KT17 215 D1
Ilford IG1 79 A4
Kingston u T KT1, KT3 199 A5
Merton SW19, SW20 179 B1
New Barnet EN4 14 B6
Roehampton SW15,
SW19 156 B3
Southall UB2 107 B4
Teddington TW11 175 B4
Kingston Sq SE19 183 B5
Kingston Sta KT2 176 A2
Kingston Univ
Kingston u T KT1 198 A6
Kingston Vale KT2 177 B5
Kingston Univ Annex
KT1 176 B1
Kingston Univ
Roehampton Vale
Campus SW15 155 D1
KINGSTON UPON THAMES
197 C6
KINGSTON VALE 177 B6
Kingston Vale SW15 155 C1
Kingstown St
NW1 93 A6 231 A6
King Street Cloisters 8
W6 112 B2
King Street Coll W12 112 C4
King Street Par 7
TW1 153 A3
Kings View Ct 1
SW20 178 D3
Kingswater Pl SW11 267 A3
Kingsway
Coney Hall BR4 224 D5
Enfield EN3 18 B6
Hayes UB3 83 A2
Mortlake SW14, TW9 132 D2
North Finchley N12 30 A4
Petts Wood BR5 211 B4
Stanwell TW19 148 A3
St Giles WC2 94 B1 240 C2
Wembley HA9 66 A4
West Barnes KT3 200 C4
Woodford IG8 37 C5
Kings Way
Croydon CR0 220 B3
Harrow HA1 42 C5
Kingsway Bsns Pk
TW12 173 B2
Kingsway Coll NW5 71 B2
Kingsway Cres HA2 42 A5
Kingsway Est N18 34 D4
Kingsway Mans WC1 240 C4
Kingsway Pl EC1 241 C6
Kingsway Rd SM3 217 A1
Kingswear Ho 5
SE23 162 C2
Kingswear Rd
Dartmouth Pk NW5 71 B5
Ruislip HA4 62 A6
Kings Well 25 NW3 70 A4
Kings Wlk Sh Mall
SW3 114 D1 257 C2
Kingswood 31 E2 96 C5
Kingswood Ave
Beckenham BR2, BR3 208 C5
Belvedere DA17 125 B2
Hampton TW12 173 D4
Hounslow TW3, TW5 129 B3
Kensal Rise NW6 91 A5
Kingswood Ave *continued*
Thornton Heath CR7 204 C4
Kingswood Cl
Ashford TW15 171 B5
Crofton BR6 211 B2
East Barnet N20 14 A4
Enfield EN1 17 D6
New Malden KT3 199 D3
South Lambeth SW8 270 B3
Surbiton KT6 198 A2
Kingswood Ct
Chingford E4 35 C5
Hither Green SE13 164 B5
7 Richmond TW10 154 B6
Kings Wood Ct 4 NW6 69 C1
Kingswood Dr
Carshalton SM5 202 D1
Dulwich SE19, SE21 183 D6
Kingswood Ho 3 KT2 176 D4
Kingswood Mans 14
SM2 217 C1
Kingswood Pk N3 29 B1
Kingswood Pl SE13 142 C1
Kingswood Prim Sch
SE27 183 B5
Kingswood Rd
Beckenham BR2 208 C6
Ilford IG3 58 A2
Leytonstone E11 54 C2
Merton SW19 179 B2
Penge SE20 184 C4
South Acton W4 111 A3
Streatham SW2 160 A4
Wembley HA9 66 C5
Kingswood Terr W4 111 A3
Kingswood Way SM6 220 A3
Kingsworth Cl BR3 207 A4
Kingsworthy Cl KT1 198 B6
Kings Yd E15 75 C2
Kingthorpe Rd NW10 67 B1
Kingthorpe Terr 2
NW10 67 B1
Kington Ho 18 NW6 91 D6
Kingward Ho E1 96 A2
Kingwell Rd EN4 2 B5
Kingweston Cl NW2 69 A5
King William IV Gdns
SE20 184 C4
King William La 3
SE10 120 C1
King William St
EC4 117 B6 252 D6
King William Wlk
SE10 142 A6
Kingwood Rd
SW6 135 A5 264 A3
Kinlet Rd SE18 145 A4
Kinloch Dr NW9 45 C2
Kinloch St N7 72 B5
Kinloss Ct NW3 47 B5
Kinloss Gdns NW3 47 B5
Kinloss Rd SM5 202 A2
Kinnaird Ave
Bromley BR1 186 D4
Chiswick W4 133 A5
Kinnaird Cl BR1 186 D4
Kinnear Ct 2 SW20 178 D2
Kinnear Rd W12 111 D4
Kinnerton Pl N SW1 247 D1
Kinnerton Pl S SW1 247 D1
Kinnerton St
SW1 115 A4 248 A1
Kinnerton Yd SW1 248 A1
Kinnoull Mans 10 E5 74 B4
Kinnoul Rd
W6 135 A6 264 A6
Kinross Ave KT4 216 A6
Kinross Cl
Ashford TW16 171 D5
Edgware HA8 10 D2
Harrow HA3 44 B4
Kinross Ct 1 SE6 164 D2
Kinross Dr TW16 171 D5
Kinross Ho N1 233 C6
Kinross Terr E17 35 B1
Kinsale Grange 10
SM2 218 A2
Kinsale Rd SE15 140 A2
Kinsella Gdns SW19 178 B5
Kinsey Ho SE21 183 C6
Kinsham Ho 5 E2 96 A3
Kintore Way SE1 263 C4
Kintyre Cl SW16 204 B6
Kintyre Ct 17 SW2 160 A4
Kintyre Ho 6 E14 120 A5
Kinveachy Gdns SE7 122 A1
Kinver Ho N4 51 B2
Kinver Rd SE26 184 C6
Kipling Ct W7 108 D6
Kipling Dr SW17 180 B4
Kipling Ho 29 SE5 139 A5
Kipling Pl HA7 24 D4
Kipling Rd DA7 147 A4
Kipling St SE1 117 B4 252 D2
Kipling Terr N9 17 B2
Kipling Twr 3 W3 111 A3
Kippington Dr SE9 165 D3
Kirby Cl KT19 215 D3
Kirby Est SE16 118 B3
Kirby Gr SE1 117 C4 253 A2
Kirby St EC1 94 C2 241 B4
Kirby Way
Hillingdon UB8 82 B3
Walton-on-T KT12 194 C3
Kirchen Rd W13 109 B6
Kirkby Cl N11 31 A4
Kirkdale SE26 162 B1

Kirkdale Rd E11 54 C2
Kirkeby Bldg EC1 241 A4
Kirkfield Cl W13 109 B5
Kirkham Rd E6 100 A1
Kirkham St SE18 145 C6
Kirk Ho HA9 66 A5
Kirk La SE18 145 A6
Kirkland Cl DA15 167 C5
Kirkland Dr EN2 5 A4
Kirkland Terr BR3 185 C4
Kirkland Wlk [4] E8 73 D2
Kirkleas Rd KT6 198 A1
Kirklees Rd
 Dagenham RM8 80 C3
 Thornton Heath CR7 204 C4
Kirkley Ho N16 51 C1
Kirkley Rd SW19 179 C2
Kirkman Ho W1 239 C3
Kirkman Pl W1 239 C3
Kirkmichael Rd E14 98 A1
Kirk Rd E17 53 B3
Kirk Rise SM1 217 D5
Kirkside Rd SE3 143 A6
Kirkstall Ave N17 51 B5
Kirkstall Gdns SW2 160 A3
Kirkstall Ho SW1 258 C2
Kirkstall Rd SW2 160 A3
Kirkstead Ct E5 75 A4
Kirksted Rd SM4 201 D1
Kirkstone NW1 232 A2
Kirkstone Way BR1 186 C3
Kirkton Rd N15 51 C5
Kirkwall Pl E2 96 C4
Kirkwood Rd SE15 140 B3
Kirn Rd W13 109 B6
Kirrane Cl KT3 199 D4
Kirtley Ho SW8 269 B2
Kirtley Rd SE26 185 A6
Kirtling St
 SW8 137 C5 269 A4
Kirton Cl W4 111 B2
Kirton Gdns [23] E2 95 D4
Kirton Rd E13 99 C5
Kirton Wlk HA8 27 A3
Kirwin Way SE5 138 D5
Kisharon Day Sch
 NW11 47 B3
Kitcat Terr E3 97 C4
Kitchener Rd
 Dagenham RM10 81 D2
 East Finchley N2 48 C6
 South Norwood CR7 205 B6
 Tottenham N17 51 C6
 Upton E7 77 B2
 Walthamstow E17 35 D2
Kite Ho [5] SW11 136 C2
Kite Pl [9] E2 96 A4
Kitley Gdns SE19 183 D2
Kitson Rd
 Barnes SW13 134 A4
 Camberwell SE5 139 A5
Kittiwake Ct [26] SE8 141 B6
Kittiwake Pl SM1 217 B3
Kittiwake Rd UB5 84 D4
Kittiwake Way UB4 84 D2
Kitto Rd SE14 140 D3
KITTS END 1 A5
Kitt's End Rd EN5 1 A6
Kiver Rd N19 72 A6
Klea Ave SW4 159 C5
Kleffens Ct [2] SE3 142 D5
Kleine Wharf [30] N1 95 C6
Knaggs Ho [1] TW11 174 C5
Knapdale Cl SE23 162 B2
Knapmill Rd SE6 163 D2
Knapmill Way SE6 163 D2
Knapp Cl NW10 67 C2
Knapp Rd
 Ashford TW15 170 B6
 Bow E3 97 C3
Knapton Mews SW17 181 A4
Knaresborough Dr
 SW18 157 D3
Knaresborough Ho [4]
 N4 51 A2
Knaresborough Pl
 SW5 113 D2 255 C4
Knatchbull Rd
 Brixton SE5 138 D4
 Stonebridge NW10 89 B6
Knebworth Ave E17 35 C2
Knebworth Ho
 South Lambeth SW8 269 D1
 [2] Stoke Newington N16 73 C4
 Walthamstow E17 35 C2
Knebworth Rd [3] N16 73 C4
Knee Hill SE2 124 C1
Knee Hill Cres SE2 124 C2
Kneller Gdns TW7 152 B5
Kneller Ho [9] SW8 137 D3
Kneller Rd
 Brockley SE4 141 A1
 Isleworth TW2 152 B5
 New Malden KT3 199 C2
Knevett Terr TW3 129 C1
Knight Cl RM8 80 C6
Knight Ct
 [1] Chingford E4 20 A3
 Stamford Hill N15 51 C4
Knighten St E1 118 B5
Knighthead Point [26]
 E14 119 C4
Knight Ho
 Walworth SE17 263 A3
 Worcester Pk KT4 216 A6
Knightland Ho E5 74 B6
Knightland Rd E5 74 B6
Knightleas Ct NW2 68 C2
Knightleys Ct E10 53 A1
Knighton Cl
 Croydon CR2 220 D1
 Woodford IG8 37 B6
Knighton Dr IG8 37 B6
Knighton Gn IG9 21 B2
Knighton La IG9 21 B2
Knighton Park Rd
 SE26 184 D5
Knighton Rd E7 77 A4
Knightrider Ct EC4 252 A6
Knightrider St EC4 251 D6
Knights Arc SW1 247 C1
Knight's Ave W5 110 A4
KNIGHTSBRIDGE 114 C4
Knightsbridge SW1,
 SW7 114 D4 247 C1
Knightsbridge Ct SW1 247 D1
Knightsbridge Gn SW1 247 C1
Knightsbridge Mews
 BR7 188 B3
Knightsbridge Under Sch
 SW7 256 B3
Knights Cl
 East Molesey KT8 195 B4
 Lower Clapton E9 74 C3
Knights Ct Bushey WD23 8 B3
 [11] Friern Barnet N11 30 D5
 Kingston u T KT1 198 A6
 Penge BR3 185 A2
Knight's Ct BR1 164 D1
Knightshayes Ho [8]
 NW4 28 D1
Knight's Hill SE19,
 SE27 182 D6
Knight's Hill Sq SE27 182 D6
Knights Ho
 Bermondsey SE1 253 C2
 South Lambeth SW8 270 B3
 West Kensington SW5 254 C2
Knight's Ho SW10 266 A4
Knight's Pk KT1 198 A6
Knight's Pl TW2 152 C3
Knights Rd
 Newham E16 121 A4
 Stanmore HA7 25 C6
Knight's Wlk SE11 261 C3
Knightswood Cl HA8 11 A2
Knightswood Ct N6 49 D2
Knightswood Ho N12 30 A4
Knightwood Cres KT3 199 C3
Knivet Rd SW6 135 C6 265 A5
Knobs Hill Rd E15 97 D6
Knockholt Rd SE9 165 D6
Knole Cl CR0 206 C3
Knole Ct UB5 84 C4
Knole Gate DA15 167 C1
Knole The SE9 188 C6
Knoll Ct Dulwich SE19 183 D5
 Orpington BR6 227 D6
Knoll Dr N14 15 A4
Knoll Ho NW8 229 A4
Knoll Lo EN5 14 A6
Knollmead KT4, KT5 199 A1
Knollmead Prim Sch
 KT5 215 A6
Knoll Rd Bexley DA5 169 C5
 Sidcup DA14 190 B6
 Wandsworth SW18 158 A6
Knoll Rise BR6 211 D1
Knolls Cl KT4 216 B5
Knoll The
 Beckenham BR3 185 D2
 Ealing W13 87 C2
 Hayes BR2 209 A1
Knolly's Cl SE27, SW16 160 C1
Knolly's Rd SE27,
 SW16 160 C1
Knot Ho SE1 253 C3
Knottisford St E2 96 C4
Knotts Green Mews
 E10 54 A3
Knotts Green Rd E10 54 A3
Knowlden Ho [5] E1 118 C6
Knowle Ave DA7 147 B5
Knowle Cl SW9 138 C2
Knowledge Point Sch
 N7 72 B2
Knowle Lo BR7 188 B4
Knowle Rd
 Bromley BR2 226 A6
 Twickenham TW2 152 C3
Knowles Cl UB7 104 A5
Knowles Ct [7] HA1 42 D3
Knowles Hill Cres
 SE13 164 B6
Knowles Ho
 Wandsworth SW18 157 D5
 Willesden Green NW10 90 A6
Knowles Wlk SW4 137 C2
Knowl Pk WD6 10 A6
Knowlton Gn [1] BR2 208 D4
Knowlton Ho [32] SW9 138 C4
Knowl Way WD6 10 B6
Knowsley Ave UB1 107 D5
Knowsley Rd SW11 136 D3
Knox Ct [16] SW4 138 A3
Knox Ho SW15 134 C3
Knox Rd E7 77 A2
Knox St W1 92 D2 237 C4
Knoyle Ho W14 254 B6
Knoyle St SE14 141 A6
Kobi Nazrul Prim Sch
 E1 96 A1
Koblenz Ho N8 50 A6
Kohat Rd SW19 179 D5
Korda Cl TW17 192 B6
Kossuth St SE10 120 C1
Kotree Way [16] SE1 118 A2
Kramer Mews SW5 255 C1
Kreedman Wlk [8] E8 74 A3
Kreisel Wlk TW9 132 B6
Kristina Ct [5] SM2 217 C2
Kuala Gdns SW16 182 B2
Kubrick Bsns Est E7 77 B4
Kuhn Way E7 77 A3
Kwesi Johnson Ct [4]
 N22 32 C1
Kydbrook Cl BR5 211 A2
Kyle Ho TW12 174 A2
Kylemore Cl [3] E6 99 D5
Kylemore Ct [4] W12 112 A4
Kylemore Rd NW6 69 C1
Kylestrome Ho SW1 258 B3
Kymberley Rd HA1 42 C3
Kynance Gdns HA7 25 C2
Kynance Mews
 SW7 113 D3 255 D5
Kynance Pl SW7 256 A5
Kynaston Ave CR7 205 A4
Kynaston Cl HA3 24 B3
Kynaston Cres CR7 205 A4
Kynaston Ho [7] SW2 160 B3
Kynaston Rd Enfield EN2 5 B4
 Plaistow BR1 187 A5
 Stoke Newington N16 73 C5
 Thornton Heath CR7 205 A4
Kynaston Wood HA3 24 B3
Kynersley Cl [1] SM5 218 D5
Kynoch Rd N18 34 D6
Kyrle Rd SW11 159 A5
Kyverdale Rd N16 51 D1

L

Laburnam Ct [12] SW16 182 C5
Laburnham Cl HA0 88 C6
Laburnham Ct
 Child's Hill NW2 69 B6
 Sutton SM1 217 C3
Laburnham Pl SE9 166 C6
Laburnum Ave
 Carshalton SM1 218 C5
 Edmonton N9 17 D2
 Tottenham N17 33 B3
 Yiewsley UB7 104 B6
Laburnum Cl
 Friern Barnet N11 31 A4
 [5] Nunhead SE15 140 C5
 Walthamstow E4 35 B4
Laburnum Cres TW16 172 B2
Laburnum Ct
 [26] Haggerston E2 95 D6
 Harrow HA1 41 D3
 [5] Mitcham CR4 181 A1
 Stanmore HA7 25 C6
Laburnum Gdns
 Croydon CR0 206 D1
 Edmonton N21 17 A2
Laburnum Gr
 Edmonton N21 17 A2
 Hounslow TW3 129 B1
 Kingsbury NW9 45 A2
 Kingston u T KT3 177 B1
 Ruislip HA4 39 B3
 Southall UB1 85 B3
Laburnum Ho
 Dagenham RM10 81 C6
 New Cross SE4 141 B3
 [6] Stoke Newington N16 73 B6
Laburnum JMI Sch E2 95 D6
Laburnum Lo [2] N3 29 B1
Laburnum Rd
 Hayes UB3 105 D2
 Merton SW19 180 A3
 Mitcham CR4 181 A1
Laburnum St E2 95 D6
Laburnums The E6 100 A3
Laburnum Way
 Southborough BR2 210 D2
 Stanwell TW19 148 B3
Lacebark Cl DA15 167 D4
Lacewing Cl E13 99 A4
Lacey Cl N9 18 A2
Lacey Dr Dagenham RM8 80 C5
 Edgware HA8 26 B6
 Hampton TW12 173 B2
Lacey Ho [7] SE13 142 A3
Lacine Ct [12] SE16 118 D4
Lackington St EC2 242 D4
Lackland Ho SE1 263 D2
Lacland Ho SW10 266 C4
Lacock Cl SW19 180 A4
Lacock Ct [3] W13 109 A5
Lacon Rd SE22 140 A1
Lacrosse Way SW16 181 D2
Lacy Rd SW15 134 D1
Ladas Rd SE27 183 A5
Ladbroke Cres W11 91 A1
Ladbroke Gdns
 W11 113 B6 244 C6
Ladbroke Gr
 Kensal Town W10 91 A2
 Notting Hill
 W11 113 B6 244 C6
Ladbroke Grove Ho
 W11 244 C6
Ladbroke Grove Sta
 W10 91 A1
Ladbroke Ho E1 243 D3
Ladbroke Mews W11 244 B3
Ladbroke Rd
 Enfield EN1 17 D5
 Notting Hill
 W11 113 B5 244 C4
Ladbroke Sq
 W11 113 B6 244 D5
Ladbroke Terr
 W11 113 B5 244 D4
Ladbroke Wlk
 W11 113 B5 244 D4
Ladbrook Cl HA5 41 B4
Ladbrooke Cres DA14 168 D1
Ladbrook Rd SE25 205 B5
Ladderstile Ride KT2,
 TW10 176 D5
Ladderswood Way N11 31 C5
Ladlands SE22 162 A4
Lady Alesford Ave HA7 25 B5
Lady Bankes Jun & Inf
 Schs HA4 62 A6
Lady Booth Rd [7] KT1 176 A1
Ladybower Ct [6] E5 74 D4
Ladycroft Gdns [6]
 BR6 227 A3
Ladycroft Rd SE13 141 D2
Ladycroft Way BR6 227 A3
Ladycroft Wlk HA7 25 D1
Lady Eleanor Holles Sch
 The (Jun Girls)
 TW12 173 D5
Lady Eleanor Holles Sch
 The (Senior Girls)
 TW12 173 D5
Lady Elizabeth Ho
 SW14 133 A2
Ladyfern Ho [19] E3 97 C2
Lady Florence Ctyd [15]
 SE8 141 C5
Ladygate La HA4 39 A3
Lady Hay KT4 215 D6
Lady Helen Seymour Ho [14]
 E13 99 A5
Lady Margaret Prim Sch
 UB1 85 B2
Lady Margaret Rd
 Kentish Town NW5 71 C3
 Southall UB1 85 B2
Lady Margaret Sch
 SW6 135 C4 265 A1
Lady Shaw Ct N13 16 B1
Ladysmith Ave
 Ilford IG2 57 C2
 Newham E6 100 A5
Ladysmith Cl NW7 28 A3
Ladysmith Rd
 Edmonton N18 34 B5
 Eltham SE9 166 C5
 Enfield EN1 5 D3
 Harrow HA3 24 C1
 Newham E16 98 D4
 Tottenham N17 34 A1
Lady Somerset Rd
 NW5 71 B4
LADYWELL 163 C6
Ladywell Cl SE4 141 C1
Ladywell Ho [7] BR5 190 B1
Ladywell Hts SE4 163 B5
Ladywell Rd SE13 163 D6
Ladywell St [4] E15 98 D6
Ladywell Sta SE13 163 D6
Ladywell Water Twr
 SE4 163 C6
Ladywood Ave BR5 211 C4
Ladywood Rd KT6 214 C6
Lafitte Ho [22] N19 49 D2
Lafone Ave TW13 150 C2
Lafone Ho [11] SW2 160 A4
Lafone St SE1 117 D4 253 C2
Lagado Mews SE16 118 D5
Lagonda Ho [11] E3 97 C3
Lagonier Ho EC1 235 B1
Laidlaw Dr N21 16 B6
Laindon Ho [6] N16 51 D1
Laing Dean UB5 84 C6
Laing Ho SE5 139 A5
Laings Ave CR4 180 D1
Laings Cnr CR4 180 D2
Lainlock Pl TW3 129 D4
Lainson St SW18 157 C4
Lairdale Cl SE21 161 A4
Laird Ho SE5 139 A5
Lairs Cl N7 72 A2
Lait Ho [1] BR3 185 D2
Laitwood Rd SW12 159 B3
Lakanal [14] SE5 139 C4
Lake Ave BR1 187 A4
Lake Bsns Ctr N17 34 A3
Lake Cl Dagenham RM8 80 D5
 [6] Wimbledon SW19 179 B5
Lakedale Ct IG11 102 A3
Lakedale Rd SE18 123 C1
Lake Dr WD23 8 B2
Lake Farm Ctry Pk
 UB3 105 C5
Lakefield Cl SE20 184 B3
Lakefield Rd N22 32 D1
Lake Gdns
 Dagenham RM10 81 C3
 Hackbridge SM6 219 B5
 Richmond TW10 153 B2
Lakehall Gdns CR7 204 D4
Lakehall Rd CR7 204 D4
Lake Ho
 Borough The SE1 252 A1
 [4] West Norwood
 SW27 182 D5
Lake House Rd E11 77 A6
Lakehurst Rd KT19 215 C3
Lakeland Cl HA3 24 B4
Lakeman Ct CR7 183 A1
Lakenheath N14 15 D6
Laker Ct SW4 138 A3
Lake Rd Croydon CR0 223 B6
 Dagenham RM6 58 D5
 Wimbledon SW19 179 B5
Laker Pl SW15 157 A5
Lakeside
 Beckenham BR3 207 D6
 Deacons Hill WD6 10 C6
 Ealing W13 87 C1
 Enfield EN2 3 D1
 Finchley N3 29 D1
 [10] Kingston u T KT2 176 D3
 Wallington SM6 219 B4
 West Ewell KT19 215 C2
Lakeside Ave
 Redbridge IG4 55 D5
 Thamesmead SE28 124 A5
Lakeside Cl Ruislip HA4 39 B5
 Sidcup DA15 168 C6
 South Norwood SE25 184 A1
Lakeside Complex The
 SE2 124 D5
Lakeside Cres EN4 14 D6
Lakeside Ct N4 51 A1
Lakeside Dr Acton NW10 88 B4
 Esher KT10 212 A2
 Keston Mark BR2 226 A5
Lakeside Lo NW4 47 A5
Lakeside Rd
 Brook Green W14 112 D3
 Palmers Green N13 16 B1
Lakeside Way HA9 66 C4
Lakes Rd BR2 225 C3
Lakeswood Rd BR5 211 A3
Lake The WD23 8 B3
Lakeview [23] E3 96 D5
Lake View HA8 26 B5
Lakeview Ct E4 36 B4
Lake View Ct SW1 258 D6
Lakeview Rd
 Bexley DA16 146 B1
 West Norwood SE27 182 D5
Lake View Terr N18 33 D6
Lakis Cl NW3 70 A4
Laleham Ave NW7 11 B1
Laleham Ho E2 243 C6
Laleham Rd
 Catford SE6 164 A4
 Littleton TW17 192 C4
Lalor St SW6 135 A3
Lambarde Ave SE9 188 C6
Lambard Ho [4] SE10 142 A5
Lamb Cl UB5 85 A4
Lamb Ct [16] E14 119 A6
Lamberhurst Ho [14]
 SE15 140 C6
Lamberhurst Rd
 Dagenham RM8 59 B1
 West Norwood SE27 182 C5
Lambert Ave TW9 132 D2
Lambert Ho
 [16] Brixton SW9 138 C3
 [19] Crouch End N19 49 D2
Lambert Lo TW8 109 D1
Lambert Rd
 Clapham Pk SW2 160 B6
 Newham E16 99 B1
 North Finchley N12 30 B5
Lambert's Pl CR0 205 B1
Lambert's Rd KT6 198 B4
Lambert St N1 72 C1
Lambert Way N12 30 A5
Lambert Wlk HA9 65 D5
LAMBETH 116 B4
Lambeth Acad SW4 159 C6
Lambeth Coll (Brixton Ctr)
 SW2 160 B6
Lambeth Coll (Clapham
 Ctr) SW4 159 C6
Lambeth Coll (Tower
 Bridge Ctr)
 SE1 117 C5 253 B3
Lambeth Coll (Vauxhall
 Ctr) SW8 137 D4 269 C2
Lambeth Ct [8] SW18 157 C6
Lambeth High St
 SE1 116 B2 260 C4
Lambeth Hill EC4 252 A6
Lambeth Hospl SW9 138 B2
Lambeth North Sta
 SE1 116 C3 261 A6
Lambeth Pal*
 SE1 116 B3 260 C5
Lambeth Palace Rd
 SE1 116 B3 260 C6
Lambeth Pier SE1 260 B5
Lambeth Prospect
 SE19 183 B4
Lambeth Rd
 Lambeth SE1 116 C3 261 B5
 Thornton Heath CR0 204 D1
Lambeth Towers SE11 261 A5
Lambeth Wlk
 SE11 116 B2 260 D4
Lambfold Ho N7 72 A2
Lamb Ho
 [28] Camberwell SE5 139 A5
 [11] Camberwell SE5 139 B4
 Greenwich SE10 142 A6
Lamb La E8 74 B1
Lamble St NW5 71 A4
Lambley Rd RM9 80 B2
Lambolle Pl NW3 70 C2
Lambolle Rd NW3 70 C2
Lambourn Cl
 Hanwell W7 108 D4
 [9] Kentish Town NW5 71 C4
Lambourne Ave SW19 179 B6
Lambourne Ct [5] IG8 37 C3
Lambourne Gdns
 [5] Barking IG11 79 D1
 Chingford E4 19 C2
 Enfield EN1 5 D3
Lambourne Gr
 Deptford SE16 118 D1
Lambourne Gr *continued*
 Kingston u T KT1 176 D1
Lambourne Ho NW8 236 D4
Lambourne Pl SE3 143 B4
Lambourne Rd
 Barking IG11 79 D1
 Ilford IG3 79 C6
 Leytonstone E11 54 A2
Lambourn Ho BR1 188 A3
Lambourn Rd SW4 137 B2
Lambrook Ho [13] SE15 140 A4
Lambrook Terr
 SW6 135 A4 264 A2
Lamb's Bldgs EC1 242 C5
Lamb's Cl N9 18 A2
Lamb's Conduit Pas
 WC1 240 C4
Lamb's Conduit St
 WC1 94 B3 240 C5
Lambscroft Ave SE9,
 SE12 165 D1
Lambs Mdw IG8 37 D1
Lamb's Mews N1 234 C5
Lamb's Pas EC1 95 B3 242 C5
Lamb St E1 95 D2 243 C4
Lamb's Terr N9 17 B2
Lambs Wlk EN2 5 A3
Lambton Ct [2] N19 50 A1
Lambton Mews [4] N19 50 A1
Lambton Pl W11 244 D6
Lambton Rd
 Finsbury Pk N19 50 A1
 Wimbledon SW20 178 C2
Lamb Wlk SE1 253 A1
Lamerock Rd BR1 186 D6
Lamerton Lo [10] TW9 132 B4
Lamerton St [8] SE8 141 C6
Lamford Cl N17 33 B3
Lamington St [3] W6 112 B2
Lamlash St SE11 261 C4
Lamley Ho SE10 141 D5
Lammas Ave CR4 181 A1
Lammas Gn SE26 162 B1
Lammas Park Gdns
 W5 109 C5
Lammas Park Rd W5 109 D4
Lammas Rd
 Homerton E9 74 D1
 Richmond TW10 175 C6
 Walthamstow E10 53 A1
Lammas Sch The E10 53 B1
Lammermoor Rd
 SW12 159 B4
Lamont Rd
 SW10 136 B6 266 C5
Lamont Rd Pas SW10 266 C5
Lamorbey Cl DA15 167 D2
Lamorna Cl E17 36 A2
Lamorna Gr HA7 25 D1
Lampard Gr N16 51 D1
Lampern Sq [8] E2 96 A4
Lampeter Cl NW9 45 C3
Lampeter Sq W6 264 A5
Lamplighter Cl [31] E1 96 C3
Lampmead Rd SE12 142 D1
Lamport Cl SE18 122 B2
Lampson Ho [6] N19 71 C4
LAMPTON 129 D4
Lampton Ave TW5 129 D4
Lampton Ct TW5 129 D4
Lampton House Cl
 SW19 178 D6
Lampton Park Rd
 TW3 129 D3
Lampton Rd TW3,
 TW5 129 D3
Lampton Sch TW5 129 C4
Lanacre Ave NW9 27 C2
Lanain Ct SE12 164 D4
Lanark Cl W5 87 C2
Lanark Ct UB5 63 C3
Lanark Ho [12] SE1 118 A1
Lanark Mans
 Paddington W9 236 B6
 [15] Shepherd's Bush
 W12 112 C4
Lanark Mews NW8 229 B1
Lanark Pl W9 92 A3 236 B6
Lanark Rd W9 92 A4 229 A1
Lanark Sq E14 119 D3
Lanata Wlk UB4 84 D3
Lanbury Rd SE15 140 D1
Lancashire Ct W1 248 D6
Lancaster Ave
 Barking IG11 101 C6
 Croydon CR4 204 A5
 Hadley Wood EN4 2 B5
 Wanstead E18 55 B5
 West Norwood SE21,
 SE27 161 A2
 Wimbledon SW19 178 D5
Lancaster Cl
 Ashford TW15 170 A6
 Beckenham BR2 208 D5
 [10] De Beauvoir Town N1 73 C1
 Grahame Pk NW9 27 D3
 Kensington W2 245 C5
 Kingston u T KT2 175 D5
 New Malden KT4 200 B2
 Stanwell TW19 148 A5
 Tottenham N17 34 A3
Lancaster Cotts [1]
 TW10 154 A5
Lancaster Ct
 Bayswater W2 246 B6
 [1] Belmont SM2 217 C1
 Parsons Green SW6 264 D3
 Stanwell TW19 148 A3
 Walton-on-T KT12 194 B2
 West Norwood SE27 160 D2

Lancaster Dr
Canary Wharf E14......120 A5
Maitland Pk NW3.......70 C2
Lancaster Gate W2...........114 A6 246 B6
Lancaster Gate Sta W2...........114 B6 246 C6
Lancaster Gdns
Bromley BR1..........210 A4
Kingston u T KT2.......175 D5
West Ealing W13.......109 B4
Wimbledon SW19.......179 A5
Lancaster Gr NW3......70 C2
Lancaster hall 14 E16..121 A5
Lancaster Ho Enfield EN2.. 5 B4
Putney SW15...........134 C3
Stanmore HA7........... 9 A1
Lancaster Ho SW1.... 249 A2
Lancaster Ho SW18....157 D4
Lancasterian Prim Sch N17.................33 D2
Lancaster Lo 2 W11.... 91 A1
Lancaster Mews
Bayswater W2.........114 A6 246 B6
2 Richmond TW10.....154 A5
3 Wandsworth SW18..157 D6
Lancaster Pk TW10....154 A6
Lancaster Pl
Hounslow TW5........128 D3
Ilford IG1............79 A4
Strand WC2....116 B6 250 C5
Twickenham TW1.......153 A4
1 Wimbledon SW19....178 D5
Lancaster Rd
Bowes Pk N11..........31 D4
Dudden Hill NW10.......68 A3
Edmonton N18..........33 D5
Enfield EN2............. 5 B4
Finsbury Pk N4.........50 C2
Harrow HA2...........41 C4
Higham Hill E17.........34 D1
Leytonstone E11.........76 C6
New Barnet EN4.........14 B6
Northolt UB5...........64 A2
Notting Hill W11........91 A1
Southall UB1..........107 A6
South Norwood SE25...206 A6
Upton E7..............77 A1
Wimbledon SW19......178 D5
Lancaster Road Ind Est 2 EN4.................14 B6
Lancaster St SE1.........116 D4 251 D1
Lancaster Stables 10 NW3................70 C2
Lancaster Terr W2...........114 B6 246 C6
Lancaster Wlk
Hayes UB3.............83 A1
Knightsbridge W2.........114 A5 246 B4
Lancastrian Rd SM6....220 B1
Lancefield Ho SE15....140 B2
Lancefield St W10......91 B4
Lancell St N16..........73 C6
Lancelot Ave HA0.......65 D4
Lancelot Cres HA0......65 D4
Lancelot Gdns EN4......15 A4
Lancelot Ho SM5......202 C1
Lancelot Pl SW7..........114 D4 247 C1
Lancelot Rd
Welling DA16..........146 A2
Wembley HA0..........65 D3
Lance Rd HA1..........42 A2
Lancer Sq W8........ 245 C2
Lancey Cl SE7........122 A2
Lanchester Ct W2.... 237 C1
Lanchester Rd N6.......48 D4
Lanchester Way SE14..140 D4
Lancing Gdns N9.......17 D3
Lancing Rd Ealing W13..109 B6
Feltham TW13.........149 D2
Ilford IG2.............57 B2
Thornton Heath CR0....204 B2
Lancing St NW1...... 232 C1
Lancresse Ct N1........95 C6
Landale Ct SE10.......142 A4
Landale Ho 13 SE16....118 C3
Landau Ct 11 CR2.....221 A3
Landcroft Rd SE22.....161 D5
Landells Rd SE22......162 A5
Lander Ct EN5..........14 A6
Landford Rd SW15.....134 C2
Landgrove Rd SW19....179 C5
Landin Ho 1 E14.......97 C1
Landleys Field 21 N7....71 D3
Landmann Ho 16 SE16..118 B2
Landmann Way SE14...118 D1
Landmark Commercial Ctr N18...................33 C4
Landmark Hts E5.......75 A4
Landon Pl SW1....... 257 C6
Landons Cl E14.........120 A5
Landon Way TW15.....170 D4
Landon Wlk 16 E14.....119 D6
Landor Ct N16..........73 C3
Landor Ho 7 SE5......139 B5
Landor Rd SW9........138 A2
Landor Wlk 11 W12....112 A4
Landra Gdns N21.......16 D5
Landrake NW1........ 232 B5
Landridge Dr EN1.........6 B5
Landridge Rd SW6.....135 B3
Landrock Rd N8........50 B3
Landscape Rd IG8......37 B3
Landsdown Cl 9 EN5....2 A1
Landseer Ave E12.......78 C3
Landseer Cl
Edgware HA8..........26 C1
Mitcham SW19........180 B2
Landseer Ct Hayes UB4.. 83 B5
10 Upper Holloway N19..72 A6
Landseer Ho
Battersea SW11...... 268 B1
16 Northolt UB5........84 D5
Paddington NW8....... 236 D6
Westminster SW1...... 259 D3
Landseer Rd
Cheam SM1...........217 C2
Enfield EN1............18 A6
New Malden KT3.......199 B2
Upper Holloway N19.....72 A6
Lands' End WD6.........9 D5
Landstead Rd SE18....145 B5
Landulph Ho SE11.... 261 B2
Landward Ct W1...... 237 B2
Lane Cl NW2...........68 B5
Lane Ct SW11..........158 D4
Lane End DA7.........147 D2
Lane Gdns
Bushey Heath WD23......8 C4
Claygate KT10.........212 D1
Lane Mews E12.........78 B5
Lanercost Cl SW2.......160 C2
Lanercost Gdns N14....16 A4
Lanercost Rd SW2.....160 C2
Laneside
Chislehurst BR7.......189 A5
Edgware HA8..........27 A5
Laneside Ave RM8......59 B2
Lane The
Blackheath Pk SE3.....143 A2
St John's Wood NW8.........92 A5 229 A3
Laneway SW15........156 B6
Laney Bldg EC1....... 241 A4
Lanfranc Ct HA1........64 D5
Lanfranc Rd E3.........97 A5
Lanfrey Pl W14....... 254 C1
Langbourn Ct E17......53 A3
Langbourne Ave N6.....71 A6
Langbourne Ho 7 SW2.................160 C6
Langbourne Mans N6...71 A6
Langbourne Pl E14....119 D1
Langbourne Prim Sch SE21.................161 C1
Langbourne Way KT10................213 A2
Langbrook Rd SE3.....143 D3
Langcroft Cl SM5......218 D5
Langdale NW1........ 232 A2
Langdale Ave CR4.....202 D6
Langdale Cl
Camberwell SE17......139 A6
Dagenham RM8.........58 C1
Locksbottom BR6......226 D5
Mortlake SW14.........132 D1
Langdale Cres DA7....147 C4
Langdale Ct
3 Ealing W5...........87 C2
9 Ilford IG1...........78 D5
Ruislip HA4............62 B3
Langdale Dr UB4.......83 C5
Langdale Gdns UB6.....87 B4
Langdale Ho SW1..... 259 A1
Langdale Par 8 CR4...202 D6
Langdale Rd
Greenwich SE10.......142 A5
Thornton Heath CR7....204 C5
Langdale St 25 E1......96 B1
Langdon Cres E6......100 C5
Langdon Ct
Finsbury EC1......... 234 D3
Harlesden NW10.........89 C6
Langdon Dr NW9.......45 A1
Langdon Ho 3 E14......98 A1
Langdon Park Rd N6.....49 C2
Langdon Park Sec Sch E14..................98 A1
Langdon Pk TW11.....175 C3
Langdon Pl SW14......133 A2
Langdon Rd
Barking E6...........100 C6
Bromley BR2..........209 B6
Morden SM4..........202 A4
Langdon Sch E6........100 D6
Langdons Ct UB2......107 C3
Langdon Shaw DA14...189 D5
Langdon Way 18 SE1...118 A2
Langdon Wlk SM4.....202 A4
Langford Cl
Shacklewell E8.........74 A3
1 South Tottenham N15.51 C3
St John's Wood NW8.. 229 B4
Langford Cres EN4.......2 D1
Langford Ct NW8..... 229 B3
Langford Gn SE5.......139 C2
Langford Ho 5 SE8....141 C6
Langford Pl
Sidcup DA14..........168 A1
St John's Wood NW8.........92 A5 229 B4
Langford Prim Sch SW6..................135 D3
Langford Rd
Cockfosters EN4.........2 D1
4 Sands End SW6......135 D3
Woodford IG8..........37 C4
Langfords IG9...........21 D2
Langham Cl 1 N15.....50 D6
Langham Ct
Hendon NW4...........46 D4
Merton SW20.........178 C1
4 Putney SW15........156 D6
Ruislip HA4............62 B3
12 Twickenham TW1....153 C5
Langham Dr RM6.......58 B3
Langham Gdns
Burnt Oak HA8.........27 A3
Ealing W13...........109 B6
Richmond TW10.......175 C6
Southgate N21.........16 D6
Wembley HA0..........65 C6
Langham Ho
Clapham Pk SW4.......159 C6
3 Wanstead E11.......55 B5
Langham House Cl TW10.................175 D6
Langham Mans SW5.. 255 C1
Langham Park Pl BR2..208 D5
Langham Pl
Chiswick W4..........133 C6
Fitzrovia W1....93 B2 238 D3
Noel Pk N15...........50 D6
Langham Rd
Burnt Oak HA8.........27 A4
Teddington TW11......175 B4
West Green N15.........51 A6
Wimbledon SW20......178 C2
Langham St W1. 93 B2 238 D3
Langhedge Cl N18......33 D4
Langhedge La N18......33 D4
Langhedge Lane Ind Est N18...................33 D4
Lang Ho
South Lambeth SW8... 270 A3
Stanwell TW19........148 A3
3 Tufnell Pk N19.......71 C5
Langholm Cl SW12.....159 D4
Langholme WD23........8 A3
Langhorn Dr TW2......152 C4
Langhorne Ct 10 NW8...70 B1
Langhorne Ho 5 SE7..143 C6
Langhorne Rd RM10....81 C1
Langhurst Ho 10 SW11................137 A3
Langland Cres HA7.....25 D1
Langland Dr HA5.......23 A3
Langland Gdns
Croydon CR0..........223 B6
West Hampstead NW3...69 D3
Langland Ho 10 SE5....139 B5
Upper Tooting SW17....180 B5
Langland Mans NW3....69 D3
Langler Rd NW10.......90 C5
Langley Ave
North Cheam KT4, SM3...............216 D6
Ruislip HA4............62 B6
Surbiton KT6..........198 A1
Langley Cres
Dagenham RM9.........80 D1
Edgware HA8..........11 A1
Harlington UB3........127 D5
Wanstead E11..........55 C2
Langley Ct
South Lambeth SW8... 270 A2
Strand WC2.......... 250 A6
13 Sutton SM2........218 A2
Langley Dr
South Acton W3........110 D4
Wanstead E11..........55 B2
Langley Gdns
Bromley BR2..........209 C5
Dagenham RM9.........80 D1
Southborough BR5.....210 D3
Langley Gr KT3........177 C1
Langley Ho
11 Lower Clapton E5....74 B3
36 Paddington W2......91 C2
Langley La SW8.........138 A6 270 B6
Langley Lawns SM2....218 B1
Langley Manor BR3....208 A4
Langley Mans SW8.... 270 B6
Langley Park Rd SM1, SM2..................218 A1
Langley Park Sch for Boys BR3..................207 D3
Langley Park Sch for Girls BR3..................208 A3
Langley Pk NW7........27 C4
Langley Rd
Beckenham BR3.......207 A5
Isleworth TW7.........130 D3
Merton SW19.........179 C2
Surbiton KT6..........198 A2
West Heath DA16......146 C6
Langley Row EN5........1 B4
Langley St WC2.. 94 A1 240 A1
Langley Way BR4......208 C2
Langmead Dr WD23......8 B3
Langmead Ho 34 E3....97 D4
Langmead St SE27.....183 A6
Langmore Ct DA6......146 D2
Langmore Ho 39 E1.....96 A1
Langport Ct KT12......194 C1
Langport Ho 1 SW9...138 D3
Langridge 15 NW5......71 A2
Langridge Mews TW12.................173 B4
Langroyd Rd SW17.....158 D2
Langside Ave SW15....134 A1
Langside Cres N14......15 D1
Lang St E1.............96 C3
Langstone Way NW7....28 D3
Langston Hughes Cl 5 SE24..................138 D1
Langthorn Ct EC2..... 242 D2
Langthorne Ct 3 SE6..186 A6
Langthorne Ho UB3....105 C2
Langthorne Hospl E11..76 B5
Langthorne Lo 30 SW2.................160 C4
Langthorne Rd E11.....76 B5
Langthorne St SW6....134 D5
Langton Ave
Oakleigh Pk N20........14 B4
Wallend E6...........100 C4
Langton Cl WC1. 94 B3 240 D6
Langton Ct SW15......157 B5
Langton Ho Harrow HA2.. 64 C6
Lambeth SE11....... 260 D4
5 Streatham SW16....181 C6
Langton Pl SW18......157 C3
Langton Rd
Camberwell SW9.......138 D5
Cricklewood NW2.......68 C5
East Molesey KT8......196 A5
Harrow Weald HA3......24 A3
Langton Rise SE22, SE23.................162 B4
Langton St SW10.........136 A6 266 B5
Langton Way
Greenwich SE3........143 A5
South Croydon CR0.....221 C4
Langtry Ho BR1........187 B3
Langtry Pl SW6....... 265 B6
Langtry Rd Northolt UB5.. 84 D5
Paddington NW8........91 D6
Langtry Wlk NW8..........92 A6 229 A6
Langwood Chase TW11..................175 C4
Langworth Dr UB4......84 B1
Langworthy HA5........23 C4
Lanherne Ho 7 SW19..178 D3
Lanhill Rd W9..........91 C3
Lanier Rd SE13........164 B5
Lanigan Dr TW3.......151 D6
Lankaster Gdns N2.....30 B2
Lankers Dr HA2.........41 B3
Lankton Cl BR3........186 A2
Lanner Ho 2 SW11.....136 C2
Lannock Ct 2 SW17...180 C4
Lannock Rd UB3.......105 D5
Lannoy Point SW6.... 264 B4
Lannoy Rd SE9........167 A3
Lanrick Rd E14.........98 C1
Lanridge Rd SE2.......124 D3
Lansan Ct E11..........76 D6
Lansbury Ave
Barking IG11...........80 A1
Dagenham RM6.........59 A4
Edmonton N18..........33 C5
Feltham TW14.........150 B5
Lansbury Cl NW10......67 A3
Lansbury Ct 4 SE28...124 B6
Lansbury Dr UB4........83 D3
Lansbury Gdns 1 E14...98 B1
Lansbury Ho 5 DA17...125 B1
Lansbury Lawrence Prim Sch E14................97 D1
Lansbury Rd EN3........6 D4
Lansbury Way N18......33 C5
Lanscombe Wlk SW8.. 270 A3
Lansdell Ho 9 SW2.....160 C5
Lansdell Rd CR4.......181 A1
Lansdown Cl KT12.....194 C1
Lansdowne Ave
Orpington BR6.........210 D1
West Heath DA7.......146 D5
Lansdowne Cl
Tolworth KT5..........214 D6
Twickenham TW1.......152 D3
Wimbledon SW20......178 D3
Lansdowne Coll W2.. 245 C5
Lansdowne Copse 1 KT4..................216 A6
Lansdowne Cres W11..........113 A6 244 B5
Lansdowne Ct
Redbridge IG5..........56 A6
2 Worcester Pk KT4...216 A6
Lansdowne Dr E8........74 A1
Lansdowne Gdns SW8..........138 A4 270 A2
Lansdowne Gr NW10...67 C4
Lansdowne Hill SE27...160 D1
Lansdowne Ho
19 Belmont SM2.......217 D1
Enfield EN2.............4 C3
Notting Hill W11..... 244 C4
Lansdowne Int Coll Ltd SW7................. 256 B5
Lansdowne La SE7.....121 D1
Lansdowne Mews
Greenwich SE7........121 D1
Notting Hill W11..... 244 C4
Lansdowne Pl
Borough The SE1...... 262 D6
Penge SE19...........183 D3
Lansdowne Rd
Chingford E4..........19 C2
Croydon CR0.........205 B1
Finchley N3...........29 C3
Harrow HA1...........42 C2
Hayes UB8.............83 A1
Hounslow TW3........129 D2
Ilford IG3.............57 D2
Leytonstone E11.......76 D6
Muswell Hill N10........31 C1
Notting Hill W11........113 A6 244 B5
Stanmore HA7..........25 C4
Sundridge BR1........187 B3
Tottenham N17.........34 A2
Walthamstow E17.......53 C3
Wanstead E18...........55 A6
West Ewell KT19.......215 B1
Wimbledon SW19, SW20...............178 C3
Lansdowne Rise W11.........113 A6 244 B5
Lansdowne Row W1.. 248 D4
Lansdowne Sch SW9...138 B2
Lansdowne Terr WC1. 240 B5
Lansdowne Way SW4, SW8.........138 A4 270 B1
Lansdowne Wlk W11.........113 B5 244 C4
Lansdowne Wood Cl 11 SE27...............160 D1
Lansdowne Workshops SE7..................121 D1
Lansdown Ho 28 SE5...139 A3
Lansdown Rd
Sidcup DA14..........168 B1
Upton E7..............77 C1
Lansfield Ave N18......34 A6
Lanson Ho HA8.........26 C4
Lantern Cl
Orpington BR6.........226 D4
Putney SW15...........134 A1
Wembley HA0..........65 D3
Lantern Ct
Southgate N14.........15 D3
4 Wimbledon SW20...178 D2
Lantern Ho
Millwall E14...........119 C4
Woolwich SE18........122 C1
Lanterns Ct E14.......119 C3
Lanterns The N12.......29 D4
Lantern Way UB7......104 B4
Lant Ho SE1.......... 252 A1
Lantry Ct 1 W3.......110 D5
Lant St SE1.....117 A4 252 B1
Lanvanor Rd SE15.....140 C3
Lanyard Ho 4 SE8......119 B2
Lapford Cl W9.........91 B3
Lapponum Wlk UB4.....84 D2
Lapsang SE1......... 253 D3
Lapse Wood Wlk SE22..162 B3
Lapstone Gdns HA3.....43 C3
Lapwing Ct
Grahame Pk NW9.......27 C1
Tolworth KT6..........214 C5
Lapwing Terr E7........77 D3
Lapwing Twr 31 SE8...141 B6
Lapwing Way UB4......84 D1
Lapworth 2 N11.........31 B6
Lapworth Ct W2.........91 D2
Lara Cl
Chessington KT9.......214 A1
Lewisham SE13........164 A5
Lara Lo SM1...........217 C3
Larbert Rd SW16.......181 C3
Larch Ave W3..........111 C5
Larch Cl Balham SW12..159 B2
Colney Hatch N11.......31 A3
15 Deptford SE8.......141 B6
Newham E13............99 C3
10 Upper Holloway N19..71 C6
Larch Cres Hayes UB4...84 D2
West Ewell KT19.......214 D2
Larch Ct 41 W2.........91 C2
Larch Dene BR6.......226 C6
Larches Ave SW14.....133 B1
Larches The
Edmonton N13..........17 A1
Hillingdon UB10........82 D5
Larchfield Ho 2 N5.....73 A3
Larch Gn NW9..........27 C2
Larch Gr DA15.........167 D3
Larch Ho Hayes UB4.....84 C2
23 Rotherhithe SE16....118 C4
Larchmont HA4.........39 B2
Larchmore Ct N19......72 A6
Larch Rd
Criclewood NW2........68 C4
Leyton E10.............75 C6
Larch Tree Way CR0...223 C5
Larchvale Ct 20 SM2...217 D1
Larch Way BR2........210 C2
Larchwood Rd SE9......166 D2
Larcombe Cl CR0......221 D4
Larcom St SE17.........117 A2 262 B3
Larden Rd W3..........111 C4
La Retraite RC Girls Sch SW12.................159 C4
Largewood Ave KT6....214 C6
Larissa St SE17...... 262 D3
Larix Ct NW10..........90 A6
Larkbere Rd SE26.......185 A6
Larken Cl WD23.........8 A3
Larken Dr WD23.........8 A3
Larkfield Ave HA3.....43 B6
Larkfield Cl BR2......225 A6
Larkfield Rd
Longlands DA14.......167 D1
Richmond TW9........132 A1
Larkhall La SW4..........138 A4 270 A1
Lark Hall Prim Sch SW4..................137 D3
Larkhall Rise SW4.....137 D3
Larkham Cl TW13.......149 C1
Lark Row E2...........96 C6
Larksfield Gr EN1........6 B4
Larks Gr IG11..........79 C1
Larkshall Bsns Ctr E4...20 B2
Larkshall Cres E4.......36 A6
Larkshall Ct E4.........36 A5
Larkshall Rd E4.........36 B6
Larkspur Cl
Kingsbury NW9.........44 D4
4 Newham E6.........100 A2
Ruislip HA4...........39 A2
Tottenham N17.........33 B3
Larkspur Ct SM6......219 B1
Larkspur Gr HA8.......27 A6
Larkspur Way KT19....215 A3
Larkswood Ct E4.......36 B5
Larkswood Prim Sch E4...................35 D6
Larkswood Rd E4.......35 D6
Larkswood Rise HA5....40 C5
Lark Way SM5.........202 C2
Larkway Cl NW9.........45 B5
Larmenier & Sacred Heart RC Prim Sch W6.....112 D2
Larnaca Ho SE1....... 263 C6
Larnach Rd W6........134 D6
Larne Rd HA4...........39 D2
Larpent Ave SW15.....156 C6
Larwood Cl UB6........64 B3
La Saint Union RC Sec Sch NW5...................71 A5
Lascelles Ave HA1......42 B2
Lascelles Cl E11........76 B6
Lascelles Ho NW1.... 237 B5
Lascott's Rd N22........32 B4
Laseron Ho 1 N15......51 D5
Lashford Ho HA8.......27 A4
Lassa Rd SE9.........166 B6
Lassell St SE10........120 B1
Lasseter Pl SE3........142 D6
Latchett Rd E18.........37 B2
Latchingdon Ct E17.....52 D5
Latchmere Cl KT2, TW10................176 A5
Latchmere Jun & Inf Schs KT2.................176 B4
Latchmere La KT2, TW10.................176 B5
Latchmere Rd
Battersea SW11.......136 D3
Kingston u T KT2.......176 B4
Latchmere St 5 SW11.................136 D3
Lateward Rd TW8......131 D6
Latham Cl Newham E6..100 A1
6 Twickenham TW1....153 A4
Latham Ct
3 Bowes Pk N11.......32 A4
7 Northolt UB5.........84 D4
Latham Ho Stepney E1...96 D1
18 Walthamstow E17....53 D6
Latham Rd
Bexleyheath DA6.......169 C6
Twickenham TW1.......152 D4
Latham's Way CR0.....220 B6
Lathkill Cl EN1..........18 A4
Lathkill Ct BR3........185 B2
Lathom Jun Sch E6.....78 A1
Lathom Rd E6...........78 B1
Lathwood Ho 6 SE26..184 B5
Latimer SE17......... 263 A1
Latimer Ave E6.........100 B6
Latimer Cl
North Cheam KT4......216 B4
Pinner Green HA5.......22 C2
Latimer Gdns HA5......22 C2
Latimer Ho
11 Homerton E9........74 D2
Notting Hill W11...... 244 D5
Latimer Ind Est 1 NW10..................90 C1
Latimer Pl W10.........90 C1
Latimer Rd Barnet EN5.... 1 D2
1 Croydon CR0.......220 D5
Forest Gate E7.........77 B4
North Kensington W10...90 C1
South Tottenham N15....51 C3
Teddington TW11......174 D5
Wimbledon SW19......179 D4
Latimer Road Sta W10...................112 D6
Latitude Ho NW1..... 231 C5
Latona Rd SE15........140 A6
La Tourne Gdns BR6...227 A5
Lattimer Pl W4........133 C6
Latton Cl KT12.........195 A2
Latvia Ct SE17....... 262 B1
Latymer All Saints CE Prim Sch N9...............17 D2
Latymer Ct W6.........112 D2
Latymer Rd N9.........17 D3
Latymer Sch The N9....17 C2
Latymer Upper Sch W6...................112 A1
Latymer Way N9.........17 C2
Laubin Cl TW1.........131 B1
Lauder Cl UB5..........84 D5
Lauder Ct N14..........16 A4
Lauderdale Dr TW10...153 D1
Lauderdale Mans W9...91 D4
Lauderdale Rd W9......91 D4
Lauderdale Twr EC2... 242 A4
Laud St Croydon CR0....221 A5
Vauxhall SE11..116 B1 260 C2
Laughton Ho 11 SW2...160 C5
Laughton Rd UB5.......84 D6
Launcelot Prim Sch BR1...................187 A6
Launcelot Rd BR1, SE12..................187 A6
Launcelot St SE1..... 251 A1
Launceston Ct CR7.....204 C3
Launceston Gdns UB6...65 C1
Launceston Pl W8.........114 A3 256 A5
Launceston Rd UB6.....87 C6
Launch St E14.........120 A3
Laundress La N16.......74 A5
Laundry La 7 N1.......73 A1
Laundry Mews SE23....162 D4
Laundry Rd W6.........135 A6 264 A5
Launton Dr DA6.......146 D1

Laura Cl Enfield EN1 17 C6
Wanstead E11 55 C4
Laura Ct HA2 24 A1
Lauradale Rd N2 48 D5
Laura Pl E5 74 C4
Laurel Ave TW1 152 D3
Laurel Bank Gdns 3
SW6 135 B3
Laurel Bank Rd EN2 5 B4
Laurel Cl Sidcup DA14 168 A1
8 Upper Holloway N19 71 C6
Upper Tooting SW17 180 C5
Laurel Cres CR0 223 C5
Laurel Ct Dalston E8 73 D1
2 Putney SW15 156 D6
9 Rotherhithe SE16 119 A5
South Norwood SE25 205 C4
8 Wembley HA0 88 A5
Laurel Dr N21 16 C4
Laurel Gdns
Bromley BR1 210 A5
Chingford E4 19 D4
Ealing W7 108 C5
Edgware NW7 11 B1
Hounslow TW4 129 A1
Laurel Gr
Forest Hill SE26 185 A6
Penge SE20 184 C3
Laurel Ho
Brentford W5 109 C2
9 Deptford SE8 141 B6
5 Hamstead NW3 69 D2
Morden SM4 201 D4
Laurel La UB7 104 A2
Laurel Manor SM2 218 A1
Laurel Mead Ct 8 E18 37 A2
Laurel Pk HA3 24 D3
Laurel Rd
Barnes SW13 134 A3
Teddington TW12 174 B5
Wimbledon SW20 178 B2
Laurel St E8 73 D2
Laurels The
8 Belvedere DA17 125 C1
2 Buckhurst Hill IG9 21 C3
Bushey WD23 8 C2
Finchley N3 29 D4
Shortlands BR2 209 A5
9 Sundridge BR1 187 B2
Laurel View N12 13 D1
Laurel Way
Snaresbrook E18 54 D5
Woodside Pk N20 13 C1
Laurence Ct E10 53 D2
Laurence Mews 12
W12 112 A4
Laurence Pountney Hill
EC4 252 C6
Laurence Pountney La
EC4 252 D6
Laurie Gr SE14 141 A4
Laurie Ho
Newington SE1 261 D5
Notting Hill W8 113 C5 245 A3
Laurie Rd W7 86 C2
Laurier Rd
Croydon CR0 205 D2
Dartmouth Pk NW5 71 B5
Laurimel Cl HA7 25 B4
Laurino Pl WD23 8 A2
Lauriston Apartments 6
N17 51 D6
Lauriston Ho 6 E9 74 D1
Lauriston Lo NW6 69 B2
Lauriston Rd
Homerton E9 74 D1
Wimbledon SW19 178 D4
Lauriston Sch E9 96 D6
Lausanne Rd
Hornsey N8 50 C5
St Johns SE15 140 C4
Lavehham Ho E17 35 D2
Lavell St N16 73 B4
Lavender Ave
Mitcham CR4 180 C2
North Cheam KT4, SM3 216 C5
Welsh Harp NW9 45 A1
Lavender Cl
Bromley Comm BR2 210 A3
South Kensington SW3 266 D5
Wallington SM5 219 B4
Lavender Ct
Colney Hatch N12 30 C4
East Molesey KT8 195 D6
Edgware HA8 27 A5
Feltham TW14 150 B5
South Lambeth SW4 270 B1
Sutton SM2 218 A1
Lavender Gdns
Clapham SW11 136 D1
Enfield EN2 4 D4
Stanmore HA3 24 C4
Lavender Gr Dalston E8 74 A1
Mitcham CR4 180 C2
Lavender Hill
Clapham SW11 137 A2
Enfield EN2 4 D4
Lavender Ho
8 Richmond TW9 132 D4
14 Rotherhithe SE16 118 D5
Lavender Pl IG1 78 D3
Lavender Prim Sch EN2 5 C5
Lavender Rd
Battersea SW11 136 B2
Enfield EN2 5 B4
Hillingdon UB8 82 B2
Rotherhithe SE16 119 A5

Lavender Rd *continued*
Sutton SM1 218 B4
Thornton Heath CR0 204 B3
Wallington SM5 219 A4
West Ewell KT19 214 D2
Lavender Rise UB7 104 C4
Lavender St E15 76 C2
Lavender Sweep
SW11 136 D1
Lavender Terr 12
SW11 136 C2
Lavender Vale SM6 219 D2
Lavender Way CR0 206 D3
Lavender Wlk SW11 136 D1
Lavendon Ho NW8 237 B6
Lavengro Rd SE27 161 A2
Lavenham Rd SW18 157 C3
Lavernock Rd DA7 147 C3
Lavers Rd N16 73 C5
Laverstoke Gdns
SW15 156 A4
Laverton Mews SW5 255 D3
Laverton Pl SW5 255 D3
Lavidge Rd SE9 166 B2
Lavina Gr N1 233 C4
Lavington Cl E9 75 B2
Lavington Rd
Ealing W13 109 B5
Wallington CR0 220 B4
Lavington St
SE1 116 D5 251 D3
Lavinia Ct BR1 186 C3
Lavisham Ho BR1 187 B5
Lawdale Jun Sch E2 96 A4
Lawdon Gdns CR0 220 D4
Lawford Rd
Chiswick W4 133 A5
De Beauvoir Town N1 73 C1
Kentish Town NW5 71 C2
Lawfords Wharf 18
NW1 71 C1
Law Ho IG11 102 A5
Lawless Ho 5 E14 120 A6
Lawless St 12 E14 119 D6
Lawley Ho 11 TW1 153 D5
Lawley Rd N14 15 B4
Lawley St E5 74 C4
Lawman Ct 2 TW9 132 B4
Lawn Cl Edmonton N9 17 D4
Kingston u T KT3 177 C1
Ruislip HA4 61 D5
Sundridge BR1 187 B3
Lawn Cres TW9 132 C3
Lawn Farm Gr RM6 59 A5
Lawnfield Ct NW6 68 D1
Lawn Gdns W7 108 C5
Lawn House Cl E14 120 A4
Lawn La SW8 138 B6 270 C6
Lawn Mans EN5 1 B1
Lawn Rd
Beckenham BR3 185 B3
Maitland Pk NW3 70 D3
Lawns Ct HA9 66 C6
Lawnside SE3 142 D1
Lawns The
Belmont SM2 217 A1
Blackheath SE3 142 D2
Chingford E4 35 C5
Harrow HA5 23 D3
Sidcup DA14 190 B6
South Norwood SE19 183 B2
Stoke Newington N16 73 C3
1 Wimbledon SW19 179 B5
Lawn Terr SE3 142 C2
Lawn The UB2 107 C1
Lawn Vale HA5 23 A1
Lawrence Ave
Edmonton N13 32 D6
Higham Hill E17 34 D2
Little Ilford E12 78 C4
Mill Hill NW7 27 D6
New Malden KT3 199 C2
Stonebridge NW10 89 B6
Lawrence Bldgs 1
N16 73 D5
Lawrence Camp Cl N20 14 B1
Lawrence Cl Bow E3 97 C5
6 Shepherd's Bush
W12 112 B6
West Green N15 51 C5
Lawrence Cres
Dagenham RM10 81 D5
Edgware HA8 26 C1
Lawrence Ct
Hornsey N10 49 C6
Mill Hill NW7 27 C5
4 South Acton W3 111 A3
Stoke Newington N16 73 D5
5 Woodford IG8 37 C4
Lawrence Dr UB10 61 A4
Lawrence Est TW4 128 C1
Lawrence Gdns NW7 11 D1
Lawrence Hall E13 99 B3
Lawrence Hill E4 19 C2
Lawrence Ho
Bowes Pk N22 32 B4
20 Camden Town NW1 71 B1
Westminster SW1 259 D3
Lawrence La EC2 242 B2
Lawrence Mans SW3 267 A5
Lawrence Pl N1 233 B6
Lawrence Rd
Coney Hall BR4 225 A4
Ealing W5 109 D2
Edmonton N18 34 B6
Erith DA8 147 D5
Hampton TW12 173 B3
Hillingdon UB4 83 A5
Hounslow TW4 128 C1
Pinner HA5 40 D4

Lawrence Rd *continued*
Richmond TW10 175 C6
South Norwood SE25 205 D5
Tottenham N15 51 C5
Upton Pk E6 100 A6
West Ham E13 99 B6
Lawrence St
Canning Town E16 98 D2
Chelsea SW3 136 C6 267 A5
Mill Hill NW7 27 D6
Lawrence Trad Est
SE10 120 C2
Lawrence Univ SW7 256 B3
Lawrence Way NW10 67 B5
Lawrence Weaver Cl
SM4 201 C3
Lawrence Yd N15 51 C5
Lawrie Ct HA3 24 D3
Lawrie Park Ave SE26 184 B5
Lawrie Park Cres
SE26 184 B5
Lawrie Park Gdns
SE26 184 B5
Lawrie Park Rd SE26 184 C5
Laws Cl SE25 205 B5
Lawson Cl Ilford IG1 79 B3
Newham E16 99 C2
Wimbledon SW19 156 D1
Lawson Ct
1 Finsbury Pk N4 50 B1
13 Surbiton KT6 197 D2
Lawson Gdns HA5 40 B6
Lawson Ho
17 Shepherd's Bush
W12 112 B6
1 Woolwich SE18 144 C6
Lawson Rd Enfield EN3 6 C4
Southall UB1 85 C3
Law St SE1 117 B3 262 D6
Lawton Rd Barnet EN4 2 B2
Bow E3 97 A4
Leytonstone E10 54 A1
Laxcon Cl NW10 67 B3
Laxey Rd BR6 227 D2
Laxfield Ct E8 96 A6
Laxley Cl SE5 138 D5
Laxmi Ct N3 29 B2
Laxton Ct CR7 205 A5
Laxton Path 1 SE4 140 D1
Laxton Pl NW1 238 D6
Layard Rd Enfield EN1 5 D4
Rotherhithe SE16 118 B2
South Norwood CR7 183 B1
Layard Sq SE16 118 B2
Laybourne Ho 18 E14 119 C4
Laycock Prim Sch N1 72 D2
Laycock St N1 72 C2
Layer Gdns W3 110 C6
Layfield Cl NW4 46 B2
Layfield Cres NW4 46 B2
Layfield Ho 1 SE10 121 A1
Layfield Rd NW4 46 B2
Laymarsh Cl DA17 125 B3
Laymead Cl UB5 63 A2
Laystall Ct EC1 241 A5
Laystall St EC1 241 A5
Layton Cres CR0 220 D3
Layton Ct TW8 109 D1
Layton Pl TW9 132 C4
Layton Rd
Brentford TW8 109 D1
Hounslow TW3 129 D1
Layton's La TW16 171 D1
Layzell Wlk SE9 165 D3
Lazar Wlk 2 N7 72 B6
Leabank Cl HA1 64 C5
Leabank Sq E9 75 C2
Leabank View N15 52 A3
Leabourne Rd N16 52 A2
LEA BRIDGE 74 D5
Lea Bridge Rd E10 53 C2
Lea Cl TW2 151 B4
Lea Cotts 10 CR4 181 A1
Lea Cres HA4 61 D4
Leacroft Ave SW12 158 D4
Leacroft Cl
Southgate N21 16 D2
3 Yiewsley UB7 104 A6
Lea Ct
3 Bedford Pk W12 111 C4
1 Chingford E4 20 A2
3 Hillingdon UB10 82 D3
2 Newham E13 99 A4
Leadale Ave E4 19 C2
Leadale Rd N16 52 A3
Leadbeaters Cl 8 N11 30 D5
Leadbetter Ct 12 NW10 67 B1
Leadenhall Mkt EC3 243 A1
Leadenhall Pl EC3 243 A1
Leadenhall St
EC3 95 C1 243 A1
Leadenham Ct 15 E3 97 C3
Leader Ave E12 78 C3
Leadings The HA9 67 A5
Leaf Cl KT7, KT8 196 C4
Leaf Gr SE27 182 C5
Leaf Ho Barnet EN5 1 D1
9 Harrow HA1 42 D4
Leafield Cl SW16 182 D4
Leafield La DA14 169 B1
Leafield Rd
Merton SW19, SW20 201 B6
Sutton SM1 217 C6
Leafy Gr BR2 225 C3
Leafy Oak Rd SE12 165 C1
Leafy Way CR0 221 D6
Lea Gdns HA9 66 B4
Leagrave St E5 74 C5
Lea Hall Gdns E10 53 C1
Lea Hall Rd E10 53 C1

Lea Ho 2 Edmonton N9 18 A1
Lisson Gr NW8 237 A5
Upper Clapton E5 52 C1
Leaholme Waye HA4 39 A3
Leahurst Rd SE13 164 B6
Lea Int E9 75 C3
Leake St Lambeth SE1 251 A1
South Bank
SE1 116 B4 250 D2
Lealand Rd N15 51 D3
Leamington Ave
Bromley BR1 187 C5
Farnborough BR6 227 C4
Merton SM4 201 B5
Walthamstow E17 53 C4
Leamington Cl
Bromley BR1 187 C5
Hounslow TW3 152 A6
Plashet E12 78 A3
Leamington Cres HA2 63 B5
Leamington Ct
4 Forest Hill SE26 162 A1
North Acton W3 89 B2
Leamington Gdns IG3 79 D6
Leamington Ho
Edgware HA8 26 B5
4 Kensal Town W11 91 B2
Leamington Pk W3 89 B2
Leamington Pl UB4 83 D3
Leamington Rd UB2 106 D2
Leamington Rd Villas
W11 91 B2
Leamington Villas
SE13 164 C6
Leamore St W6 112 C2
Leamouth Rd
Newham E6 100 A2
South Bromley E14 98 B1
Leander Ct
11 Edgware NW9 27 C2
27 Hackney E9 74 C1
St Johns SE8 141 C4
5 Surbiton KT6 197 D2
Leander Rd
Northolt UB5 85 C5
Thornton Heath CR7 204 B5
Tulse Hill SW2 160 C5
Lea Park Trad Est E10 53 B1
Lea Rd
2 Beckenham BR3 185 C1
Enfield EN2 5 B4
Southall UB2 107 A2
Learner Dr HA2 63 C6
Learoyd Gdns E6 122 C6
Leary Ho SE11 260 D1
Leas Cl KT9 214 B1
Leas Dale SE9 166 C1
Leas Gn BR7 189 D4
Leaside Ave N10 49 A5
Leaside Bsns Ctr EN3 7 B3
Leaside Ct UB10 82 D4
Leaside Ho 4 E5 52 B1
Leaside Mans N10 49 A6
Leaside Rd E5 52 C1
Leasowes Rd E10 53 C1
Lea Sq 22 E3 97 B6
Leas The SE18 144 D4
Leatherbottle Gn
DA18 125 B3
Leather Cl CR4 181 A1
Leatherdale St
32 Bethnal Green E1 96 C3
19 Globe Town E1 96 D4
Leather Gdns E15 98 C6
Leatherhead Cl N16 51 D1
Leatherhead Rd KT9 213 D1
Leather La EC1 94 C2 241 B4
Leathermarket Ct SE1 253 A1
Leathermarket St
SE1 117 C4 253 A1
Leather Rd SE16 118 D2
Leathersellers Cl 5 EN5 1 A2
Leathsale Rd HA2 63 D5
Leathwaite Rd SW11 158 D6
Leathwell Rd SE8 141 D3
Lea Valley Prim Sch
N17 34 A3
Lea Valley Rd EN3 19 B5
Lea Valley Technopark
N17 52 A6
Lea Valley Trad Est
N18 34 D5
Leaveland Cl BR3 207 C5
Leaver Gdns UB6 86 C5
Leavesden Rd HA7 25 A4
Lea View Ho E5 52 B1
Lebanon Ave TW13 172 D5
Lebanon Ct 10 TW1 153 B4
Lebanon Gdns SW18 157 C5
Lebanon Park Mans
TW1 153 B4
Lebanon Pk TW1 153 B4
Lebanon Rd
Croydon CR0 205 C1
Wandsworth SW18 157 C6
Lebanon Road Sta
CR0 221 C6
Lebrun Sq SE3 143 B2
Lebus Ho NW8 230 A3
Le Chateau CR0 221 B5
Lechmere App IG8 37 D1
Lechmere Ave IG8 37 D1
Lechmere Rd NW2 68 B2
Leckford Rd SW18 158 A3
Leckhampton Pl 23
SW2 160 C4
Leckwith Ave DA7 147 A6
Lecky Ho NW2 68 A5
Lecky St SW7 114 B1 256 C2
Leclair Ho SE3 143 B2

L'Ecole des Petits Sch
SW6 135 D3
Leconfield Ave SW13,
SW15 133 D2
Leconfield Ho SE5 139 C2
Leconfield Rd N5 73 B4
Lector Ct EC1 241 B5
Leda Ave EN3 6 D5
Leda Ct 9 SW9 138 C5
Ledalle Ho NW2 68 B5
Ledam Bldg EC1 241 A4
Leda Rd SE18 122 B3
Ledbury Ho 12 SE22 139 C2
Ledbury Mews N W11 91 C1
Ledbury Mews W W11 245 A6
Ledbury Pl 10 CR0 221 A4
Ledbury Rd
Croydon CR0 221 B4
Kensington W11 91 C1
Ledbury St SE15 140 A5
Ledo Ho 1 N16 73 B4
Ledrington Rd SE19 184 A4
Ledway Dr HA9 44 B2
LEE 164 D5
Lee Ave RM6 59 A3
Leechcroft Ave DA15 167 D6
Leechcroft Rd SM6 219 A5
Lee Church St SE13 142 C1
Lee Cl Higham Hill E17 34 D2
New Barnet EN5 2 A1
Lee Conservancy Rd
E9 75 B3
Leecroft Rd EN5 1 A1
Lee Ct SE13 142 B1
Leeds Ct
7 Carshalton SM5 218 D5
Catford SE6 163 D1
Clerkenwell EC1 241 C6
Leeds Rd IG1 57 B1
Leeds St N18 34 A5
Leegate SE12 164 D6
Lee Green SE12 142 D1
Lee High Rd SE12,
SE13 142 C1
Lee Ho
3 Kentish Town N19 71 D3
Wimbledon SW19 179 D4
Leeke St WC1 94 B4 233 C2
Leeland Mans 15 W13 109 A5
Leeland Rd W13 109 A5
Leeland Terr W13 109 A5
Leeland Way NW10 67 D4
Lee Manor Sch SE13 164 C5
Lee Mews BR3 207 A6
Lee Park Way N9, N18 19 A1
Lee Pk SE3 142 D2
Lee Rd Enfield EN1 18 A5
Lewisham SE3 142 D1
Merton SW19 179 D2
Mill Hill NW7 28 D3
Wembley UB6 87 C6
Leerdam Dr E14 120 A3
Lees Ct W1 248 A6
Lees Ho SE17 262 D1
Leeside EN5 13 A5
Leeside Cres NW11 47 C3
Leeside Ind Est N17 34 B3
Leeside Rd N17 34 B4
Leeside Trad Est N17 34 C3
Leeside Works N17 34 C3
Leeson Ho 7 TW1 153 B4
Leeson Rd 12 SE24 138 C1
Leesons Hill BR5, BR7 211 D6
Leesons Way BR5 189 D1
Lees Par UB10 82 D3
Lees Pl W1 115 A6 248 A6
Lees Rd UB8 82 D3
Lee St E8 95 D6
Lee Sta SE12 165 A5
Lees The CR0 223 B6
Leet Ct N16 73 B4
Lee Terr SE3 142 C2
Lee Valley Country Pk
EN3 7 C4
Lee Valley L Ctr N9 19 A3
Lee Valley Riding Ctr
E10 52 D1
Lee Valley Sp Ctr E10 75 D4
Leeve Ho 7 W9 91 B4
Lee View EN2 4 D4
Leeview Ct 7 E4 20 A3
Leeward Ct 3 E1 118 A5
Leeward Gdns SW19 179 B5
Leeway SE8 119 B1
Leeway Cl HA5 23 B3
Leewood Cl SE12 165 A5
Lefevre Wlk E3 97 C6
Leffern Rd W12 112 A4
Leff Ho 9 NW6 69 A1
Lefroy Ho SE1 252 A1
Lefroy Rd W12 111 D4
Legard Rd N5 72 D5
Legat Ct N4 51 A4
Legatt Rd SE9 165 D6
Leggatt Rd E15 98 A5
Legge St SE13 164 A6
Leghorn Rd
Plumstead SE18 123 B1
Willesden Green NW10 90 A5
Legion Cl N1 72 C1
Legion Ct SM4 201 C3
Legion Rd UB6 86 A5
Legion Terr E3 97 C6
Legion Way N12 30 C3
Legrace Ave TW4,
TW5 128 D3
Leicester Ave CR4 204 A5
Leicester Cl KT4 216 C4
Leicester Ct
46 Paddington W2 91 C2

Leicester Ct *continued*
St James WC2 249 D6
5 Twickenham TW1 153 D5
Leicester Gdns IG3 57 C2
Leicester Ho
4 Brixton SW9 138 D2
Carshalton SM5 218 C5
5 Putney SW15 156 C4
2 Thames Ditton KT7 197 A2
Leicester Mews N2 48 C6
Leicester Pl WC2 249 D6
Leicester Rd Barnet EN5 1 D1
Croydon CR0 205 C2
East Finchley N2 48 C6
Stonebridge NW10 67 B1
Wanstead E11 55 B4
Leicester Sq★
WC2 115 D6 249 D5
Leicester Square Sta
WC2 115 D6 249 D6
Leicester St WC2 249 D6
Leigham Ave SW16 160 A1
Leigham Cl
Streatham SW16 182 B6
9 Wallington SM6 219 C2
Leigham Court Rd
SW16 182 C6
Leigham Dr TW7 130 C5
Leigham Hall 3
SW16 160 A1
Leigham Hall Par 2
SW16 160 A1
Leigham Vale SE27, SW16,
SW2 160 C2
Leigh Ave IG4 55 D5
Leigh Cl KT3 199 B5
Leigh Close Ind Est
KT3 199 B5
Leigh Cres CR0 223 D1
Leigh Ct Harrow HA2 42 C1
22 Tulse Hill SW2 160 C5
3 Woodford E18 37 A1
Leighfield Ho 5 N4 51 A2
Leigh Gdns NW10 90 C5
Leigh Ho
4 Kingston u T KT2 176 D4
9 Putney SW15 156 A6
Leigh Hunt Dr N14 15 D3
Leigh Orchard Cl
SW16 160 B1
Leigh Pl Feltham TW13 150 C3
Holborn EC1 241 A4
Welling DA16 146 A3
Leigh Rd Highbury N5 72 D4
Isleworth TW3 130 B1
Leytonstone E10 54 A2
Wallend E6 78 C2
Leigh St WC1 94 A4 233 A1
Leigh The KT2 177 C3
Leighton Ave
Little Ilford E12 78 C3
Pinner HA5 41 A6
Leighton Cl HA8 26 C1
Leighton Cres NW5 71 C3
Leighton Ct NW7 28 D3
Leighton Gdns
Thornton Heath CR0 204 D1
Willesden Green NW10 90 C5
Leighton Gr NW5 71 C3
Leighton Ho 7 KT6 198 A3
Leighton House (Art Gall
& Mus)★ W14 254 D6
Leighton Pl NW5 71 C3
Leighton Rd
Ealing W13 109 A4
Enfield EN1 18 A6
Harrow HA3 24 B1
Kentish Town NW5 71 C3
Leighton St CR0 204 D1
Leila Parnell Pl 14
SE7 143 C6
Leinster Ave SW14 133 A1
Leinster Gdns
W2 114 A6 246 A6
Leinster Mews
7 Barnet EN5 1 A2
Bayswater W2 246 A6
Leinster Pl W2 236 A1
Leinster Rd N10 49 B5
Leinster Sq W2 91 D1
Leinster Terr W2 246 A6
Leisure Way N12 30 B3
Leitch Ho 8 NW8 70 B1
Leith Cl NW9 45 B1
Leithcote Gdns SW16 182 B6
Leithcote Path SW16 160 B1
Leith Hill BR5 190 A2
Leith Hill Gn BR5 190 A2
Leith Ho
7 Kentish Town N7 71 D3
13 Streatham SW2 160 B4
Leith Mans W9 91 D4
Leith Rd N22 32 D2
Leith Towers 7 SM2 217 D1
Leith Yd 3 NW6 91 C6
Lela Ave TW4, TW5 128 C3
Lelitia Cl E8 96 A6
Lely Ho 3 UB5 84 D5
Leman St E1 96 A1
Lemark Cl HA7 25 C4
Le May Ave SE12 165 B1
Lemmon Rd SE10 142 C6
Lemna Ct E11 54 C2
Lemna Rd E11 54 C2
Le Moal Ho 28 E1 96 C2
Lemon Gr TW14 150 A3
Lemonwell Ct SE9 167 A6
Lemonwell Dr SE9 167 A6
Lemsford Cl N15 52 A4
Lemsford Ct N4 73 A6

Lena Cres N9 ... 18 C2
Lena Gardens Prim Sch W6 ... 112 C3
Lena Gdns W6 ... 112 C3
Lena Kennedy Cl E4 ... 36 A4
Lenan Ct W13 ... 109 C5
Len Clifton Ho 12 SE18 ... 122 B2
Lendal Terr 7 SW4 ... 137 D2
Lenelby Rd KT6 ... 198 C1
Len Freeman Pl SW6 ... 264 C5
Lenham 11 NW5 ... 71 A2
Lenham Ho SE1 ... 252 D1
Lenham Rd Erith DA7 ... 147 B6
Lewisham SE12 ... 142 D1
South Norwood CR7 ... 183 B1
Sutton SM1 ... 218 A3
Lennard Ave BR4 ... 224 C6
Lennard Cl BR4 ... 224 C6
Lennard Rd
Bromley BR2 ... 210 B1
Croydon CR0 ... 205 A1
Penge BR3 ... 185 A4
Lennon Rd NW2 ... 68 C2
Lennox Gdns
Croydon CR0 ... 220 D4
Knightsbridge SW1 ... 114 D3 257 C5
Redbridge IG1 ... 56 B1
Willesden NW10 ... 67 D4
Lennox Gdns Mews SW1 ... 257 C4
Lennox Ho
7 Belvedere DA17 ... 125 C3
10 Hackney E9 ... 74 C2
4 Twickenham TW1 ... 153 D5
Lennox Rd
Finsbury Pk N4, N7 ... 72 C6
Walthamstow E17 ... 53 C3
Lenor Cl DA6 ... 147 A1
Lensbury Way SE2 ... 124 D3
Lens Rd E7 ... 77 C1
Lenthall Ho SW1 ... 259 B1
Lenthall Rd E8 ... 74 A1
Lenthorp Rd SE10 ... 120 D2
Lentmead Rd BR1 ... 164 D1
Lenton Rise TW9 ... 132 A2
Lenton St SE18 ... 123 B2
Len Williams Ct NW6 ... 91 C5
Leo Ct 4 TW8 ... 131 D5
Leof Cres SE6 ... 185 D5
Leominster Rd SM4 ... 202 A3
Leominster Wlk SM4 ... 202 A3
Leonard Ave SM4 ... 202 A4
Leonard Ct
Bloomsbury WC1 ... 240 A6
Harrow HA3 ... 24 C3
Kensington W8 ... 255 A6
Leonard Day Ho 3 NW5 ... 71 B2
Leonard Ho 17 E17 ... 54 A5
Leonard Pl 6 N16 ... 73 C4
Leonard Rd
Chingford E4 ... 35 C4
Edmonton N9 ... 18 A1
Forest Gate E7 ... 77 A4
Mitcham CR4, SW16 ... 181 C2
Southall UB2 ... 106 D2
Leonard Robbins Path 3 SE28 ... 124 B6
Leonard St
Broadgate EC2 ... 95 B3 242 D6
Newham E16 ... 122 A5
Leonora Ho W9 ... 236 A6
Leontine Cl SE15 ... 140 A5
Leopards Ct EC1 ... 241 A4
Leopold Ave SW19 ... 179 B5
Leopold Bldgs 14 E2 ... 95 D4
Leopold Ct 12 SW19 ... 179 B5
Leopold Mews E9 ... 96 C6
Leopold Prim Sch NW10 ... 67 D1
Leopold Rd Ealing W5 ... 110 B5
East Finchley N2 ... 48 B6
Edmonton N18 ... 34 B5
Walthamstow E17 ... 53 C4
Willesden NW10 ... 67 C1
Wimbledon SW19 ... 179 B5
Leopold St E3 ... 97 B2
Leopold Terr SW19 ... 179 C5
Leopold Wlk SE11 ... 260 C1
Leo St SE15 ... 140 B5
Leo Yd EC1 ... 241 D5
Leppoc Rd SW4 ... 159 D6
Leroy St SE1 ... 117 C2 263 A4
Lerry Cl W14 ... 264 D6
Lerwick Ct 4 EN1 ... 17 C6
Lerwick Ho SW18 ... 136 A1
Lescombe Cl SE23 ... 163 A1
Lescombe Rd SE23, SE6 ... 163 A1
Lesley Cl DA5 ... 169 D4
Lesley Ct
8 Wallington SM6 ... 219 B4
Westminster SW1 ... 259 C5
Leslie Gdns SM2 ... 217 C1
Leslie Gr CR0 ... 205 C1
Leslie Grove Pl CR0 ... 205 C1
Leslie Park Rd CR0 ... 205 C1
Leslie Prince Ct 8 SE5 ... 139 B5
Leslie Rd
East Finchley N2 ... 48 B6
Leyton E11 ... 76 B4
Newham E16 ... 99 B1
Leslie Smith Sq 7 SE18 ... 144 C6
Lessar Ave SW4 ... 159 C5
Lessar Ct SW4 ... 159 C5
Lessingham Ave
Ilford IG5 ... 56 C6
Upper Tooting SW17 ... 181 A6
Lessing St SE23 ... 163 A4
Lessness Ave DA7 ... 146 D5
LESSNESS HEATH ... 125 D1
Lessness Heath Prim Sch DA17 ... 125 C1
Lessness Pk DA17 ... 125 C1
Lessness Rd
Belvedere DA17 ... 125 C1
Morden SM4 ... 202 A4
Lester Ave E16 ... 98 C3
Lester Ct 42 E3 ... 97 D4
Lester Ho IG8 ... 36 B3
Lestock Cl 2 SE25 ... 206 A6
Lestock Ho SE3 ... 143 D4
Lestor Ct TW7 ... 130 D2
Leswin Pl N16 ... 73 D5
Leswin Rd N16 ... 73 D5
Letchford Gdns NW10 ... 90 A4
Letchford Mews NW10 ... 90 A4
Letchmore Ho 7 W10 ... 90 C3
Letchworth Ave TW14 ... 149 D4
Letchworth Cl
Bromley BR2 ... 209 A4
South Oxhey WD19 ... 22 D5
Letchworth Dr BR2 ... 209 A4
Letchworth St SW17 ... 180 D6
Lethaby Ho 15 SW4 ... 138 B1
Lethbridge Cl SE13 ... 142 A3
Letterstone Rd SW6 ... 264 C3
Lettice St SW6 ... 135 B4 264 D1
Lett Rd E15 ... 76 B1
Lettsom St SE5 ... 139 C3
Lettsom Wlk 1 E13 ... 99 A5
Leucha Rd E17 ... 53 A4
Levana Cl SW19 ... 157 A3
Levant Ho 17 E1 ... 96 D3
Levehurst Ho SE27 ... 183 A5
Levehurst Way SW4, SW9 ... 138 A3
Leven Cl WD19 ... 22 D5
Levendale Rd SE23 ... 163 B2
Leven Rd E14 ... 98 B1
Leven Way UB3 ... 83 C1
Lever Ct 15 E9 ... 74 D2
Leverett St SW3 ... 257 B4
Leverholme Gdns SE9 ... 188 C6
Leverington Pl N1 ... 235 D1
Leverson St SW16 ... 181 C4
Lever St EC1 ... 95 A4 235 A1
Leverstock Ho SW3 ... 257 B2
Leverton Pl NW5 ... 71 C3
Leverton St NW5 ... 71 C3
Levett Gdns IG3 ... 80 A5
Levett Ho 8 SW16 ... 181 C5
Levett Rd IG11 ... 79 C2
Levine Gdns IG11 ... 102 D5
Levison Way 2 N19 ... 49 D1
Levita Ho NW1 ... 232 D2
Levyne Ct EC1 ... 241 A6
Lewes Cl UB5 ... 63 C2
Lewes Ct 3 CR4 ... 202 D6
Lewesdon Cl 13 SW19 ... 156 D3
Lewes Ho
Bermondsey SE1 ... 253 B2
Peckham SE15 ... 140 A6
Lewes Rd Bromley BR1 ... 187 D1
Colney Hatch N12 ... 30 C5
Leweston Pl N16 ... 51 D2
Lewey Ho E3 ... 97 B3
Lewgars Ave NW9 ... 45 A3
Lewin Ct
2 Plumstead SE18 ... 123 C2
Streatham SW16 ... 182 A4
Lewing Cl BR6 ... 211 C1
Lewington Ct EN3 ... 6 D6
Lewin Rd Bexley DA6 ... 147 A1
Mortlake SW14 ... 133 B2
Streatham SW16 ... 181 D4
Lewin Terr TW14 ... 149 B4
Lewis Ave E17 ... 35 C2
Lewis Cl N14 ... 15 C4
Lewis Cres NW10 ... 67 B3
Lewis Ct 5 SE16 ... 118 B1
Lewis Gdns N2 ... 30 B1
Lewis Gr SE13 ... 142 A2
LEWISHAM ... 142 A1
Lewisham Bridge Prim Sch SE13 ... 141 D2
Lewisham Bsns Ctr SE14 ... 140 D6
Lewisham Coll SE4 ... 141 C3
Lewisham Ct EN3 ... 7 C5
Lewisham Ctr SE13 ... 142 A2
Lewisham High St SE13 ... 163 D6
Lewisham Hill SE13 ... 142 A3
Lewisham Hospl SE13 ... 163 D6
Lewisham Pk SE13 ... 164 A5
Lewisham Rd SE13 ... 142 A3
Lewisham St SW1 ... 249 D1
Lewisham Sta SE13 ... 142 A2
Lewisham Way SE4, SE14 ... 141 B4
Lewis Ho 2 E4 ... 35 C5
Lewis King Ho BR1 ... 187 B3
Lewis Pl E8 ... 74 A3
Lewis Rd Bexley DA16 ... 146 C2
Mitcham CR4 ... 180 C1
10 Richmond TW10 ... 153 D6
Sidcup DA14 ... 168 C1
Southall UB1 ... 107 A4
Sutton SM1 ... 217 D4
Lewis Silkin Ho 9 SE15 ... 140 C6
Lewis Sports & L Ctr SE19 ... 183 D2
Lewis St NW1 ... 71 B2
Lewiston Cl KT4 ... 200 B2
Lewis Way RM10 ... 81 D2
Lexden Dr RM6 ... 58 B3
Lexden Rd Acton W3 ... 110 D5
Mitcham CR4 ... 203 D5
Lexdon Ct RM6 ... 58 B3
Lexfield Ho N5 ... 73 A4
Lexham Ct UB6 ... 86 B6
Lexham Gardens Mews W8 ... 255 D5
Lexham Gdns W8 ... 113 D2 255 C4
Lexham Ho 9 IG11 ... 101 B6
Lexham Mews W8 ... 113 C2 255 B4
Lexham Wlk W8 ... 255 D5
Lexington Pl KT1 ... 175 D2
Lexington St W1 ... 115 C6 249 B6
Lexton Gdns SW12 ... 159 D3
Leyborne Ave W13 ... 109 C4
Leyborne Pk TW9 ... 132 C4
Leybourne Cl BR2 ... 209 A3
Leybourne Ct 1 SE25 ... 206 A6
Leybourne Ho 20 SE15 ... 140 C6
Leybourne Rd
17 Camden Town NW1 ... 71 B1
Hillingdon UB10 ... 83 A6
Leytonstone E11 ... 54 D1
Queensbury NW9 ... 44 C4
Leybourne St 5 NW1 ... 71 B1
Leybridge Ct SE12 ... 165 A6
Leyburn Cl E17 ... 53 D5
Leyburn Gdns CR0 ... 221 C6
Leyburn Gr N18 ... 34 A4
Leyburn Ho SE18 ... 144 A5
Leyburn Rd N18 ... 34 B4
Leyden Mans 7 N19 ... 50 A2
Leyden St E1 ... 95 D2 243 C3
Leydon Cl SE16 ... 118 D5
Leyes Rd E16 ... 99 D1
Leyfield KT4 ... 199 D1
Ley Ho SE1 ... 252 A1
Leyland Ave EN3 ... 7 A3
Leyland Ct 8 N11 ... 31 B6
Leyland Gdns IG8 ... 37 C5
Leyland Ho
6 Canary Wharf E14 ... 119 D6
12 Richmond TW10 ... 153 C1
Leyland Rd SE12 ... 165 A6
Leylands SW18 ... 157 B5
Leylang Rd SE14 ... 140 D5
Leys Cl Finchley N12 ... 30 C3
Harrow HA1 ... 42 B4
Leys Ct 9 SW9 ... 138 C3
Leysdown 9 NW5 ... 71 A2
Leysdown Ho SE17 ... 263 B2
Leysdown Rd SE9 ... 166 B2
Leysfield Rd W12 ... 112 A4
Leys Gdns EN4 ... 15 A6
Leyspring Rd E11 ... 54 D1
Leys Rd E EN3 ... 7 A4
Leys Rd W EN3 ... 7 A4
Ley St Ilford IG1 ... 78 D6
Newbury Pk IG1, IG2 ... 57 B1
Leys The
East Finchley N2 ... 48 A5
Harrow HA3 ... 44 B3
Leyswood Dr IG2 ... 57 C4
Leythe Rd W3 ... 111 A4
LEYTON ... 76 B5
Leyton Bsns Ctr E10 ... 75 C6
Leyton Ct SE23 ... 162 C3
Leyton Grange E10 ... 53 C1
Leyton Green Rd E10 ... 54 A3
Leyton Green Twrs E10 ... 54 A3
Leyton Ind Village E10 ... 52 D2
Leyton Link Est E10 ... 53 A2
Leyton Midland Road Sta E10 ... 54 A1
Leyton Mills E10 ... 76 A4
Leyton Park Rd E10 ... 76 A5
Leyton Rd
Merton SW19 ... 180 A3
Stratford E15 ... 76 B2
Leyton Sixth Form Coll E10 ... 54 B3
Leyton Sta E11 ... 76 A5
Leyton Stadium (Leyton Orient FC) E10 ... 75 D5
LEYTONSTONE ... 54 D1
Leytonstone Bsns & Spec Sch E11 ... 54 C3
Leytonstone High Road Sta E11 ... 76 C6
Leytonstone Rd E15 ... 76 C3
Leytonstone Sta E11 ... 54 C1
Leyton Town Ctr E10 ... 76 A5
Leywick St E15 ... 98 C5
Lezayre Rd BR6 ... 227 D2
Liardet St SE14 ... 141 A6
Liberia Rd N5 ... 72 D2
Libert Cl N18 ... 33 D6
Liberty Ave SW19 ... 180 B2
Liberty Ct IG11 ... 102 C5
Liberty Ctr HA0 ... 88 B6
Liberty Ho 11 E1 ... 118 A6
Liberty Mews
Balham SW12 ... 159 B5
Orpington BR6 ... 227 D6
Liberty Sch CR4 ... 180 C1
Liberty St SW9 ... 138 B4 270 D2
Libra Rd 7 Bow E3 ... 97 B5
Newham E13 ... 99 A5
Library Ct N17 ... 51 D6
Library Mans 4 W12 ... 112 C4
Library Par NW10 ... 89 C6
Library Pl E1 ... 118 B6
Library St SE1 ... 116 D4 251 D1
Libro Ct E4 ... 35 C6
Lichen Ct IG6 ... 56 D6
Lichfield Cl EN4 ... 2 D2
Lichfield Ct
Kingston u T KT6 ... 198 A4
Richmond TW9 ... 132 A1
Lichfield Gdns TW10, TW9 ... 154 A6
Lichfield Gr N3 ... 29 C1
Lichfield Ho 27 SE5 ... 139 A3
Lichfield Rd
Dagenham RM8 ... 80 C5
Edmonton N9 ... 18 A2
Hounslow TW4 ... 128 C2
Mile End E3 ... 97 A4
Newham E6 ... 99 D4
Northwood HA6 ... 40 A6
Richmond TW9 ... 132 B4
West Hampstead NW2 ... 69 A4
Woodford IG8 ... 36 C6
Lichfield Terr 1 TW9 ... 154 A6
Lichlade Cl 7 BR6 ... 227 D4
Lichport Ct N4 ... 50 D1
Lickey Ho W14 ... 264 D6
Lidbury Rd NW7 ... 29 A4
Lidcote Gdns 22 SW9 ... 138 B3
Liddall Way UB7 ... 104 B5
Liddell Cl HA3 ... 43 D6
Liddell Gdns NW10 ... 90 C5
Liddell Rd NW6 ... 69 C2
Lidding Rd HA3 ... 43 D4
Liddington Rd E15 ... 98 D6
Liddlesdale Ho E 6 KT2 ... 176 D2
Liddlesdale Ho W 5 KT2 ... 176 D2
Liddon Rd
Bromley BR1 ... 209 D6
Newham E13 ... 99 B4
Liden Cl E10, E17 ... 53 B1
Lidfield Rd N16 ... 73 B4
Lidgate Rd 22 SE15 ... 139 D5
Lidiard Rd SW18 ... 158 A2
Lidlington Pl NW1 ... 232 B3
Lido Sq N17 ... 33 B1
Lidyard Rd N19 ... 49 C1
Liffey Ct Edmonton N9 ... 18 C1
Willesden NW10 ... 68 A1
Liffler Rd SE18 ... 123 C1
Liffords Pl SW13 ... 133 D3
Lifford St SW15 ... 134 D1
Lightcliffe Rd N13 ... 16 C1
Lighter Cl 10 SE16 ... 119 A2
Lighterman Mews 15 E1 ... 96 D1
Lighterman's Rd E14 ... 119 D4
Lighterman's Wlk SW18 ... 135 C1
Lightfoot Rd N8 ... 50 A4
Light Horse Ct SW1 ... 258 A1
Lightley Cl HA0 ... 88 B6
Ligonier St E2 ... 243 C6
Lilac Cl E4 ... 35 B4
Lilac Ct
Colney Hatch N12 ... 30 C4
3 Newham E13 ... 99 C6
Teddington TW11 ... 174 D6
Lilac Gdns
Croydon CR0 ... 223 C5
Ealing W5 ... 109 D3
Hayes UB3 ... 83 C1
Lilac Ho SE4 ... 141 B2
Lilac Pl
Vauxhall SE11 ... 116 B2 260 C3
Yiewsley UB7 ... 104 B6
Lilac St W12 ... 112 A6
Lilah Mews BR2 ... 186 D1
Lilburne Gdns SE9 ... 166 A6
Lilburne Rd SE9 ... 166 A6
Lilburne Wlk NW10 ... 67 A2
Lile Cres W7 ... 86 C2
Lilestone Est NW8 ... 236 D5
Lilestone Ho NW8 ... 236 D6
Lilestone St NW8 ... 92 C3 237 A6
Lilford Ho 21 SE5 ... 139 A3
Lilford Rd SE5 ... 138 D3
Lilian Barker Cl SE12 ... 165 A6
Lilian Baylis Ho N1 ... 73 A2
Lilian Baylis Tech Sch SE11 ... 116 B1 260 D1
Lilian Board Way UB6 ... 64 B3
Lilian Gdns IG8 ... 37 B2
Lilian Rd SW16 ... 181 C2
Lilian Rolfe Ho 5 SE27 ... 183 B6
Lillechurch Rd RM8 ... 80 C2
Lilleshall Rd SM4 ... 202 B3
Lilley Cl E1 ... 118 A5
Lillian Ave W3 ... 110 C4
Lillian Cl 14 N16 ... 73 C5
Lillian Rd SW13 ... 134 B6
Lillie Ho N5 ... 72 C3
Lillie Rd SW6 ... 135 B6 264 C5
Lillie Road Mans SW6 ... 264 B5
Lillieshall Rd SW4 ... 137 C2
Lillie Yd SW6 ... 135 C6 265 A6
Lillingston Ho N7 ... 72 C4
Lilliput Ave UB5 ... 85 B6
Lillywhite 21 NW9 ... 27 D2
Lily Albon Ct RM9 ... 81 B4
Lily Cl W14 ... 112 D2
Lily Gdns HA0 ... 87 C5
Lily Ho 7 HA9 ... 66 A3
Lily Pl EC1 ... 241 B4
Lily Rd E17 ... 53 C3
Lilyville Rd SW6 ... 135 B4 264 C2
Limavady Ho 12 SE18 ... 122 C2
Limborough Ho 5 E14 ... 97 C2
Limbourne Ave RM8 ... 59 B2
Limburg Rd SW11 ... 136 C1
Lime Ave UB7 ... 104 B6
Limeburner La EC4 ... 94 D1 241 C2
Lime Cl Bromley BR1 ... 210 A5
Buckhurst Hill IG9 ... 21 D2
Carshalton SM5 ... 218 D6
Harrow HA3 ... 25 A1
Pinner HA5 ... 39 D6
Wapping E1 ... 118 A5
Lime Cres TW16 ... 172 C1
Limecroft Cl KT19 ... 215 B1
Lime Ct 9 Harrow HA1 ... 42 D3
Hendon NW4 ... 28 C1
Kingston u T KT3 ... 198 D6
9 Leyton E11 ... 76 C6
Mitcham CR4 ... 180 B1
Putney SW15 ... 134 B2
Limedene Cl HA5 ... 22 D2
Lime Gr Barnet N20 ... 13 B3
Blackfen DA15 ... 167 D5
Hayes UB3 ... 105 B6
Kingston u T KT3 ... 199 C6
Orpington BR6 ... 226 D6
Ruislip HA4 ... 40 B2
Shepherd's Bush W12 ... 112 C4
Twickenham TW1 ... 153 A5
Walthamstow E4 ... 35 B4
Limeharbour E14 ... 119 D4
Lime Ho 7 TW9 ... 132 D4
LIMEHOUSE ... 119 A6
Limehouse Cswy E14 ... 119 B6
Limehouse Ct 5 E14 ... 97 C1
Lime House Ct 23 E14 ... 97 B1
Limehouse Cut 4 E14 ... 97 D2
Limehouse Fields Est 14 E14 ... 97 A2
Limehouse Link (Tunnel) E14 ... 119 B6
Limehouse Sta E14 ... 97 A1
Lime Kiln Dr SE7 ... 143 B6
Limekiln Pl SE19 ... 183 D3
Limekiln Wharf 21 E14 ... 119 B6
Limeleaf Ct HA8 ... 27 A6
Lime Lo 3 TW16 ... 171 D3
Limerick Cl SW12 ... 159 C4
Limerick Ct 1 SW12 ... 159 C4
Lime Row DA18 ... 125 B3
Limerston St SW10 ... 136 A6 266 B5
Lime St Pas EC3 ... 253 A6
Limes Ave
Barnes SW13 ... 133 D3
Carshalton SM5 ... 202 D1
Croydon CR0 ... 220 C5
Edgware NW7 ... 27 C4
Golders Green NW11 ... 47 A2
North Finchley N12 ... 30 A6
Penge SE20 ... 184 B3
Wanstead E11 ... 55 B5
Limes Ave The N11 ... 31 C5
Limes Cl Ashford TW15 ... 170 C5
3 Friern Barnet N11 ... 31 C5
Limes Ct
Beckenham BR3 ... 185 D1
Willesden NW6 ... 68 D1
Limesdale Gdns HA8 ... 27 A2
Limes Field Rd SW14 ... 133 C2
Limesford Rd SE15 ... 140 D1
Limes Gdns SW18 ... 157 C5
Limes Gr SE13 ... 142 A1
Limes Rd
Beckenham BR3 ... 185 D1
Thornton Heath CR0 ... 205 B2
Limes Row BR6 ... 226 D3
Lime St
Walthamstow E17 ... 53 A5
Whitechapel EC3 ... 95 C1 243 A1
Limes The
Camberwell SE5 ... 139 C2
3 Cheam SM2 ... 217 C2
East Molesey KT8 ... 195 D5
Kensington W2 ... 245 B5
Keston Mark BR2 ... 226 A6
Stanmore HA7 ... 9 B2
Limestone Wlk 12 DA18 ... 124 D4
Limes Wlk Ealing W5 ... 109 D4
Nunhead SE15 ... 140 C1
Lime Terr W7 ... 108 C6
Lime Tree Ave KT10, KT7 ... 196 C1
Limetree Cl SW2 ... 160 B3
Lime Tree Ct E11 ... 55 C5
Limetree Ct HA5 ... 23 C3
Lime Tree Ct
East Barnet EN4 ... 14 C6
East Finchley N2 ... 47 D6
14 Poplar E3 ... 97 C2
South Croydon CR2 ... 221 A2
Lime Tree Gr CR0 ... 223 B5
Limetree Pl CR4 ... 181 B2
Lime Tree Rd TW5 ... 129 D4
Limetree Wlk 2 SW17 ... 181 A5
Lime Tree Wlk
Bushey WD23 ... 8 C2
Coney Hall BR4 ... 224 D4
Enfield EN2 ... 5 A5
Lime Wlk 11 E15 ... 98 C6
Limewood Cl
Beckenham BR3 ... 208 A4
Ealing W13 ... 87 B1
Walthamstow E17 ... 53 B5
Limewood Ct IG4 ... 56 B4
Limpsfield Ave
Putney SW19 ... 156 D2
Thornton Heath CR7 ... 204 B4
Limscott Ho 35 E3 ... 97 D4
Linacre Cl SE15 ... 140 B2
Linacre Ct W6 ... 112 D1
Linacre Rd NW2 ... 68 B2
Linale Ho N1 ... 235 C3
Linberry Wlk 3 SE8 ... 119 B2
Linchmere Rd SE12 ... 164 D4
Lincoln Ave Osidge N14 ... 15 C2
Twickenham TW2 ... 152 A2
Wimbledon SW19 ... 156 D1
Lincoln Cl
Croydon SE25 ... 206 B3
Greenford UB6 ... 86 A6
Harrow HA2 ... 41 B4
Lincoln Cres EN1 ... 17 D6
Lincoln Ct
Borehamwood WD6 ... 11 B6
Enfield EN2 ... 5 B1
Grove Pk SE12 ... 165 C1
Hampton TW12 ... 173 B5
Hendon NW4 ... 46 B5
2 Ilford IG2 ... 57 A3
Mitcham CR4 ... 204 A4
Redbridge IG1 ... 56 B2
5 South Croydon CR2 ... 221 A3
Stoke Newington N16 ... 51 B2
Lincoln Gdns IG1 ... 56 A2
Lincoln Green Rd BR5 ... 211 D4
Lincoln Ho
Bloomsbury WC1 ... 240 D3
9 Dartmouth Pk NW5 ... 71 C5
2 Islington N1 ... 73 A1
Knightsbridge SW1 ... 247 C1
10 Putney SW15 ... 157 A6
Lincoln Lo 10 BR3 ... 185 D1
Lincoln Mews NW6 ... 91 B6
Lincoln Rd
Croydon SE25 ... 206 B6
East Finchley N2 ... 48 C6
Enfield EN1, EN3 ... 18 B6
Harrow HA2, HA5 ... 41 B4
Kingston u T KT3 ... 199 A6
Mitcham CR4 ... 204 A4
Newham E13 ... 99 B3
North Cheam KT4 ... 200 B1
Northwood HA6 ... 39 D6
Plashet E7 ... 77 D2
Sidcup DA14 ... 190 B5
Twickenham TW13 ... 151 B1
Wembley HA0 ... 65 D2
Woodford E18 ... 37 A2
Lincoln's Inn* WC2 ... 94 B1 240 D2
Lincoln's Inn Fields WC2 ... 94 B1 240 D2
Lincoln St Chelsea SW3 ... 257 C3
Leyton E11 ... 76 C6
Lincolns The NW7 ... 11 D1
Lincoln Terr 4 SM2 ... 217 C1
Lincoln Way
Charlton TW16 ... 171 C2
Enfield EN1 ... 18 B6
Lincombe Rd BR1 ... 164 D1
Linda Ct KT9 ... 213 D4
Lindal Cres EN2 ... 4 B1
Lindal Ct 1 E18 ... 37 A2
Lindale SW19 ... 157 A2
Lindales The N17 ... 33 D4
Lindal Rd SE4 ... 163 B6
Lindbergh Rd SM6 ... 220 A1
Linden Ave Enfield EN1 ... 6 A4
Hounslow TW3 ... 151 D6
Kensal Rise NW10 ... 90 D5
Ruislip HA4 ... 40 A1
Thornton Heath CR7 ... 204 D5
Wembley HA9 ... 66 B3
Linden Bridge Sch KT4 ... 215 C5
Linden Cl Ruislip HA4 ... 40 A1
Southgate N14 ... 15 C5
Stanmore HA7 ... 25 B5
Thames Ditton KT7 ... 197 A2
Linden Cotts 6 SW19 ... 179 A4
Linden Cres
Kingston u T KT1 ... 176 B1
Wembley UB6 ... 64 D2
Woodford IG8 ... 37 B4
Linden Ct
8 Battersea SW18 ... 136 B1
1 Beckenham BR3 ... 207 D6
2 Bromley BR1 ... 186 D3
Edgware NW7 ... 27 B5
Penge SE20 ... 184 B3
1 Shepherd's Bush W12 ... 112 C5
Sidcup DA14 ... 189 C6
11 Sutton SM2 ... 218 A2
Lindenfield BR7 ... 188 D1
Linden Gate SW20 ... 200 C6
Linden Gdns
Chiswick W4 ... 111 B1
Enfield EN1 ... 6 A4
Notting Hill W2 ... 113 C6 245 B5
Linden Gr
Kingston u T KT3 ... 199 C6
Nunhead SE15 ... 140 C2
Penge SE20 ... 184 C4
Teddington TW11 ... 174 D5
Linden Ho Bromley BR1 ... 187 B3
10 Deptford SE8 ... 141 B6
Hampton TW12 ... 173 D4
Walthamstow E17 ... 35 B1
Linden Lawns HA9 ... 66 B4
Linden Lea N2 ... 48 A4

Lindenlea Ct E17 53 B5
Linden Leas BR4 224 B6
Linden Lo N21 16 B4
Linden Lodge Sch
SW19 157 A3
Linden Mans N6 49 B1
Linden Mews
Kensington W2 245 B5
Stoke Newington N1 73 B3
Linden Pl CR4 202 C5
Linden Rd
Brunswick Pk N11 15 A2
Cranley Gdns N10 49 B5
Hampton TW12 173 C2
Tottenham N15 51 A5
Lindens The
Chiswick W4 133 A4
New Addington CR0 224 A2
North Finchley N12 30 B5
5 Walthamstow E17 53 D5
Linden Way
Shepperton TW17 193 A4
Southgate N14 15 C5
Lindeth Cl HA7 25 B4
Lindfield Gdns NW3 70 A3
Lindfield Hts NW3 70 A3
Lindfield Rd
Croydon CR0 205 D3
Ealing W5 87 C3
Lindfield St E14 97 C1
Lindford Christie Stadium
The W12 90 B2
Lindhill Cl EN3 6 D3
Lindholme Ct 3 NW9 27 C2
Lindisfarne Rd
Dagenham RM8 80 C5
Wimbledon SW20 178 A3
Lindisfarne Way E9 75 A4
Lindley Ct KT1 175 C2
Lindley Ho
13 Peckham SE15 140 A5
9 Stepney E1 96 C2
Lindley Pl TW9 132 C4
Lindley Rd E10 76 A6
Lindley St E1 96 C2
Lindon Bennett Sch
TW13 172 D5
Lindop Ho 8 E1 97 A3
Lindore Rd SW11 136 D1
Lindores Rd SM5 202 A1
Lindo St SE15 140 C3
Lind Rd SM1 218 A3
Lindrop St SW6 136 A3
Lindsay Cl KT9 214 A1
Lindsay Ct
Battersea SW11 266 D1
Sutton SM1 217 C3
Lindsay Dr Harrow HA3 44 B4
Shepperton TW17 193 B3
Lindsay Ho 2 SE18 122 C2
Lindsay Rd
Hampton TW12 173 D6
North Cheam KT4 216 B6
Lindsay Sq
SW1 115 D1 259 D2
Lindsell St 6 SE10 142 A4
Lindsey Cl Bickley BR1 210 A6
Mitcham CR4, SW16 204 A5
Lindsey Ct N13 16 C1
Lindsey Gdns TW14 149 B4
Lindsey Ho W5 109 D2
Lindsey Ho* SW10 266 D4
Lindsey Mews 18 N1 73 A1
Lindsey Rd RM8 80 C4
Lindsey St EC1 94 D2 241 D4
Lind St SE8 141 D3
Lindum Rd TW11 175 C3
Lindums The BR3 185 B4
Lindway SE27 182 D5
Lindwood Cl 8 E6 100 B2
Linear View HA9 66 D6
Linfield WC1 233 C1
Linfield Cl NW4 46 B5
Linford Ct 1 CR4 180 C2
Linford Ho 17 E2 96 A6
Linford Rd E17 54 A6
Linford St SW8 137 C4 269 A1
Linford Street Bsns Est
SW8 269 A2
Lingard Ho 11 E14 120 A3
Lingards Rd SE13 142 A1
Lingey Cl DA15 167 D2
Lingfield Ave KT1, KT5 198 B5
Lingfield Cl EN1 17 C5
Lingfield Cres SE9 145 B1
Lingfield Ct
Northolt UB5 85 C5
Wimbledon SW19 178 D4
Lingfield Gdns N9 18 B4
Lingfield Ho
5 Acton Green W4 111 A1
Lambeth SE1 251 D1
Penge SE26 184 B4
Lingfield Rd
North Cheam KT4 216 C5
Wimbledon SW19 178 D4
Lingham St SW9 138 B3
Lingholm Way EN5 12 D6
Ling Rd E16 99 A2
Lingrove Gdns IG9 21 B2
Ling's Coppice SE21 161 B2
Lingwell Rd SW17 158 C1
Lingwood DA7 147 D3
Lingwood Gdns TW7 130 C5
Lingwood Rd E5 52 A2
Linhope St NW1 92 D3 237 C5
Linkenholt Mans 3
W6 111 D2
Linkfield KT8 195 D6
Link Field BR2 209 A3
Linkfield Rd TW7 130 D3
Link La SM6 220 A2
Linklea Cl NW9 27 C3
Link Prim Sch CR0 220 A4
Link Rd Dagenham RM9 103 D5
East Bedfont TW14 149 D4
Friern Barnet N11 31 A6
Hackbridge SM6 203 A1
Links Ave SM4 201 C5
Linkscroft Ave TW15 170 D4
Links Ct N20 14 B1
Links Dr N20 13 D3
Link Sec Sch CR0 220 B4
Links Gdns SW16 182 C3
Linkside Finchley N12 29 C4
Kingston u T KT3 177 C1
Linkside Cl EN2 4 C2
Linkside Gdns EN2 4 B2
Links Ind Est TW13 151 A1
Links Prim Sch SW17 181 A4
Links Rd Acton W3 88 C1
Ashford TW15 170 A5
Mitcham SW16, SW17 181 A4
West Wickham BR4 208 A1
Willesden NW2 67 D6
Woodford IG8 37 A5
Links Side EN2 4 C2
Link St E9 74 C3
Links The E17 53 A5
Linksview N2 48 D4
Links View Finchley N3 29 B3
Shooters Hill SE18 144 D4
Links View Cl HA7 25 A4
Links View Rd
Croydon CR0 223 C5
Hampton TW12 174 A6
Linksway NW4 28 D1
Links Way
Beckenham BR3 207 C3
Streatham SW17 181 A4
Links Yd
10 Spitalfields E1 96 A2
Spitalfields E1 243 D4
Link The Acton W3 88 D1
Chislehurst SE9 166 C1
Enfield EN3 7 A4
Hendon NW2 46 A1
Northolt UB5 63 B3
Pinner HA5 40 C2
Teddington TW11 174 D4
Wembley HA0 43 C1
Linkway Dagenham RM8 80 C4
Pinner HA5 22 D2
Stoke Newington N4 51 A2
West Barnes SW20 200 B5
Link Way Bromley BR2 210 A2
Richmond TW10 153 B2
Linkway The EN5 13 D5
Linkwood Wlk NW1 71 D1
Linley Cres RM7 59 D6
Linley Ct
1 Dulwich SE21 183 C6
Sutton SM1 218 A4
Linley Rd N17 33 C1
Linnell Cl NW11 47 D3
Linnell Dr NW11 47 D3
Linnell Ho
Spitalfields E1 243 C4
St John's Wood NW8 229 A6
Linnell Rd
Camberwell SE5 139 C3
Edmonton N18 34 A5
Linnet Cl Bushey WD23 8 A3
Lower Edmonton N9 18 D3
Woolwich SE28 124 C6
Linnet Ct CR4 180 C2
Linnet Mews SW12 159 A4
Linnett Cl E4 36 A6
Linom Rd SW4 138 A1
Linscott Rd E5 74 C4
Linsdell Rd IG11 101 A6
Linsey St
Bermondsey SE16 118 A2
Bermondsey SE16 118 A3
Linslade Cl
Hounslow TW4 151 A6
Pinner HA5 40 B6
Linslade Ho
10 Hackney E2 96 A6
Marylebone NW8 237 B6
Linstead St 1 NW6 69 C1
Linstead Way SW18,
SW19 157 A4
Linsted Ct SE9 167 C5
Linster Gr WD6 11 A6
Lintaine Cl W6 264 B5
Linthorpe Ave HA0 65 C2
Linthorpe Rd
Cockfosters EN4 2 C2
Stamford Hill N16 51 C2
Linton Cl
Carshalton CR4 202 D2
2 Greenwich SE7 121 C1
Welling DA16 146 B4
Linton Gdns E6 100 A1
Linton Gr SE27 183 A5
Linton Ho
Lower Holloway N7 72 B4
2 Tower Hamlets E3 97 C2
Linton Mead Prim Sch
SE28 124 B6
Linton Rd IG11 79 A1
Linton St N1 95 A6 235 B5
Lintons The
Barking IG11 79 A1
Finchley N3 29 B2
Linver Rd SW6 135 C3
Linwood Cl SE5 139 D3
Linwood Cres EN1 6 A4
Linzee Rd N8 50 A5
Lion Ave TW1 152 D3
Lion Cl Ladywell SE4 163 C5
Littleton TW17 192 A6
Lion Ct 12 NW9 46 A5
Lion Ctr The TW13 151 A1
Lionel Gdns SE9 165 D6
Lionel Ho Bowes Pk N22 32 B4
5 Kensal Town W10 91 A2
Lionel Mans 14 W14 112 D3
Lionel Mews 15 W10 91 A2
Lionel Rd SE9 165 D6
Lionel Road N TW8 110 A2
Lionel Road Prim Sch
TW8 110 A2
Lionel Road S TW8 110 B1
Lion Gate Gdns TW9 132 B2
Lion Gate Mews
SW18 157 C4
Lion House Sch SW15 134 D1
Lion Mills 36 E2 96 A5
Lion Park Ave KT9 214 C4
Lion Rd
Bexleyheath DA6 147 B1
Edmonton N9 18 A2
Newham E6 100 B2
Thornton Heath CR0 205 A4
Twickenham TW1, TW2 152 D3
Lions Cl SE12 165 D1
Lion Way TW8 131 D5
Lion Wharf Rd TW7 131 B2
Lion Yd SW4 137 D1
Liphook Cres SE23 162 C4
Liphook Rd WD19 22 D6
Lipton Cl SE28 124 C6
Lipton Ct N14 15 C4
Lipton Rd 9 E1 96 D1
Lisa Lo 5 EN5 13 D6
Lisbon Ave TW2 152 A2
Lisbon Cl E17 35 B1
Lisburne Rd NW3 70 D4
Lisford St SE15 139 D4
Lisgar Terr
W14 113 B2 254 C4
Liskeard Cl BR7 189 A4
Liskeard Gdns SE3 143 A4
Liskeard Ho SE11 261 B2
Lisle Cl SW17 181 B6
Lisle Ct NW2 69 A5
Lisle St WC2 115 D6 249 D6
Lismirrane Ind Pk WD6 9 B5
Lismore 9 SW19 179 B5
Lismore Cir NW5 71 A3
Lismore Cl TW7 131 A3
Lismore Rd
South Croydon CR2 221 C2
Tottenham N17 51 B6
Lismore Wlk 4 N1 73 A2
Lissant Cl KT6 197 D2
Lisselton Ho 3 NW4 46 D5
Lissenden Gdns NW5 71 A4
Lissenden Mans NW5 71 A4
Lisson Cotts NW1 237 B4
Lisson Gr NW1,
NW8 92 C3 237 A6
LISSON GROVE 92 B3
Lisson Ho NW1 237 A4
Lisson St NW1 92 C2 237 A4
Lister Cl Dagenham W3 89 B2
Mitcham SW19 180 C2
Lister Com Sch E13 99 B5
Lister Cotts WD6 9 A6
Lister Ct Hendon NW9 27 C1
Stoke Newington N16 73 C6
Lister Gdns N18 33 A5
Lister Ho
Greenwich SE3 142 C6
Hayes UB3 105 C2
Marylebone W1 238 C2
Spitalfields E1 96 A2
6 Wembley HA9 67 A5
West Heath SE2 124 D1
Lister Hospl
SW1 115 B1 258 C1
Lister Mews N7 72 B4
Lister Rd E11 54 D1
Lister Wlk SE28 124 D6
Liston Ho N21 16 B6
Liston Rd
Clapham SW4 137 C2
Tottenham N17 34 A2
Liston Way 1 IG8 37 C3
Listowel Cl 2 SW9 138 C5
Listowel Rd RM10 81 C5
Listria Lo N16 73 D6
Listria Pk N16 73 D6
Litcham Ho 28 E1 96 D4
Litchfield Ave
Morden SM4 201 B2
Stratford E15 76 C2
Litchfield Ct E17 53 C3
Litchfield Gdns NW10 68 A2
Litchfield Rd SM1 218 A4
Litchfield St WC2 249 D6
Litchfield Way NW11 48 A4
Lithgow's Rd TW14,
TW6 127 D1
Lithos Rd NW3 70 A2
Little Acre BR3 207 C6
Little Albany St NW1 238 D6
Little Argyll St W1 239 A1
Little Birches DA15 167 C2
Little Boltons The
SW10 255 D1
Little Bornes SE21 183 C6
Littlebourne 2 SE13 164 C4
Little Britain EC1 242 A3
Littlebrook Cl CR0 206 D3
Little Brownings SE23 162 B2
Littlebury Rd SW4 137 D2
Little Bury St N9 17 C4
Little Bushey La WD23 8 B5
Little Cedars N12 30 A6
Little Chelsea Ho
SW10 266 B5
Little Chester St SW1 258 C6
Little Cloisters SW1 260 A6
Little College St SW1 260 A6
Littlecombe SE7 143 B6
Little Combe Cl 13
SW15 156 D5
Little Common HA7 9 A1
Littlecote Cl SW19 157 A4
Littlecote Pl HA5 23 B2
Little Cottage Pl SE10 141 D5
Littlecroft SE9 144 C2
Little Ct Harrow HA1 42 C2
West Wickham BR4 224 C6
Littledale SE2 146 A6
Little Deans Yd SW1 260 A6
Little Dell Lo 8 N3 29 B1
Little Dimocks SW12 159 B2
Little Dorrit Ct SE1 252 B2
Little Ealing La W5 109 C2
Little Ealing Prim Sch
W5 109 C3
Little Edward St NW1 231 D2
Little Elms UB3 127 B5
Little Essex St WC2 251 A6
Little Ferry Rd TW1 153 B3
Littlefield Cl
9 Kingston u T KT1 176 A1
Tufnell Pk N19 71 C4
Littlefield Ct UB7 126 A5
Littlefield Ho KT1 176 A1
Littlefield Rd HA8 27 A3
Little Friday Rd E4 20 C2
Little Gearies IG6 56 D5
Little George St SW1 250 A1
Little Gn TW9 131 D1
Little Grange UB6 87 A4
Little Green St NW5 71 B4
Littlegrove EN4 14 C5
Littlegrove Ct 3 EN4 14 C5
Little Halliards KT12 194 A3
LITTLE HEATH 58 B5
Little Heath Ilford RM6 58 B5
Woolwich SE7 122 A1
Littleheath Rd CR2 222 B1
Little Heath Rd DA7 147 B5
Little Heath Sch RM6 58 B5
Little Holt 10 E11 55 A4
LITTLE ILFORD 78 C3
Little Ilford La E12 78 B4
Little Ilford Sch E12 78 B3
Littlejohn Rd W7 86 D1
Little Larkins EN5 13 A5
Little London Cl UB8 82 D2
Little Marlborough St
W1 239 A1
Littlemead KT10 212 B4
Littlemede SE9 166 B1
Littlemoor Rd IG1 79 B5
Littlemore Rd SE2 124 A4
Little Moss La HA5 23 A1
Little Newport St WC2 249 D6
Little New St EC4 241 B2
Little Oak Cl TW17 192 B5
Little Orchard Cl HA5 23 A1
Little Oxhey La WD19 23 A6
Little Park Dr TW13 151 A2
Little Park Gdns EN2 5 B2
Little Pluckett's Way
IG9 21 D3
Little Portland St W1 239 A2
Little Potters WD23 8 C4
Little Queens Rd
TW11 174 D4
Little Rd UB3 105 D4
Little Redlands BR1 188 A1
Littlers Cl SW19 180 B2
Little Russell St WC1 240 A3
Little St James's St
SW1 249 A3
Little St Leonards
SW14 133 A2
Little Sanctuary SW1 250 A1
Little Smith St SW1 259 D6
Little Somerset St E1 243 C1
LITTLE STANMORE 26 B2
Littlestone Cl BR3 185 C4
Little Strand NW9 27 D1
Little Thrift BR5 211 A5
Little Titchfield St W1 239 A3
LITTLETON 192 C6
Littleton Ave E4 20 D3
Littleton CE Inf Sch
TW17 192 C6
LITTLETON COMMON
171 B3
Littleton Cres HA1 64 D6
Littleton Ho TW15 171 A3
Littleton La TW17,
TW18 192 A4
Littleton Rd
Harrow HA1 64 D6
Littleton TW15, TW17 171 A3
Littleton St SW18 158 A2
Little Trinity La EC4 252 B6
Little Turnstile WC1 240 C3
LITTLE VENICE 92 A2
Little Venice*
W9 92 A2 236 A4
Littlewood SE13 164 A5
Littlewood Cl W13 109 B3
Little Wood Cl BR5 190 A2
Littleworth Ave KT10 212 B3
Littleworth Common Rd
KT10 212 B5
Littleworth La KT10 212 B4
Littleworth Pl KT10 212 B4
Littleworth Rd KT10 212 C5
Livermere Ct 3 E8 95 D6
Livermere Rd E8 95 D6
Liverpool Gr
SE17 117 B1 262 C1
Liverpool Ho N7 72 C2
Liverpool Rd
Ealing W5 109 D4
Islington N1 234 B5
Islington N1, N7 72 C1
Kingston u T KT2 176 C3
Leytonstone E10 54 A3
Newham E16 98 C2
South Norwood CR7 205 A6
Liverpool St
EC2 95 C2 243 A3
Liverpool Street Sta
EC2 95 C2 243 A3
Livesey Cl
Kingston u T KT1 198 B6
Woolwich SE28 123 A3
Livesey Mus* SE15 140 B6
Livesey Pl SE15 140 A6
Livingstone Ct
Barnet EN5 1 A3
Leytonstone E10 54 A3
Stanwell TW19 148 A3
Livingstone Ho 16
SE5 139 A5
Livingstone Lo
13 Paddington W9 91 C2
Walthamstow E17 35 C1
Livingstone Pl E14 120 A1
Livingstone Prim Sch
EN4 2 B2
Livingstone Rd
14 Battersea SW11 136 B2
Bowes Pk N13 32 A5
Isleworth TW3 130 A1
Mill Meads E15 98 A6
Southall UB1 106 D6
South Norwood CR7 183 B1
Walthamstow E17 53 D3
Livity Sch The SW2 160 A6
Livonia St W1 239 B1
Lizard St EC1 95 A4 235 B1
Lizban St SE3 143 B5
Llandovery Ho 1 E14 120 A4
Llanelly Rd NW2 69 B6
Llanover Rd
Shooters Hill SE18 144 C5
Wembley HA9 65 D4
Llanthony Rd SM4 202 B4
Llanvanor Rd NW2 69 B6
Llewellyn Ct SE20 184 C2
Llewellyn Ho 10 N19 71 C5
Llewellyn St SE16 118 A4
Lloyd Ave SW16 182 A2
Lloyd Baker St
WC1 94 C4 234 A1
Lloyd Ct Ladywell SE13 163 D6
Pinner HA5 40 D4
6 West Norwood
SE27 160 D1
Lloyd Ho
3 Beckenham BR3 185 D4
Bromley BR1 187 B5
Stoke Newington N16 73 B5
Lloyd Mews EN3 7 C5
Lloyd Park Ave CR0 221 D4
Lloyd Park Ho E17 53 C6
Lloyd Park Sta CR0 221 D4
Lloyd Rd Dagenham RM9 81 B1
Newham E6 100 B6
North Cheam KT4, SM3 216 D5
Walthamstow E17 52 D5
Lloyd's Ave EC3 243 B1
Lloyd's Bldg*
EC3 95 C1 243 A1
Lloyd's Pl SE3 142 C3
Lloyd Sq WC1 94 C4 234 A2
Lloyd's Row EC1 94 D4 234 C1
Lloyd St WC1 94 C4 234 A2
Lloyds Way BR3 207 B4
Lloyd Villas SE4 141 C3
Loampit Hill SE13 141 D3
Loampit Vale SE13 142 A2
Loanda Cl 17 E8 95 D6
Loats Rd SW2 160 A5
Lobelia Cl 5 E6 100 A2
Locarno Cl 15 SW16 181 C5
Locarno Rd
6 Acton W3 111 A5
Greenford UB6 86 B3
Lochaber Rd SE13 142 C1
Lochaline St W6 134 C6
Lochan Cl UB4 85 A3
Lochbie 9 N4 50 A2
Lochinvar St SW12 159 B4
Lochleven Ho 9 N2 30 B1
Lochmere Cl DA8 147 D6
Lochmore Ho SW1 258 B3
Lochnagar St E14 98 A2
Lockbridge Ct 3 W9 91 C2
Lock Chase SE3 142 C2
Lock Cl UB2 108 A4
Locke Ho
Nine Elms SW8 269 A2
Stamford Hill N16 51 D1
Lockesfield Pl E14 119 D1
Lockesley Dr BR5 211 D3
Lockesley Sq KT6 197 D3
Locket Rd HA3 24 D1
Lockfield Ave EN3 7 B4
Lockgate Cl E9 75 B3
Lockhart Cl
Barnsbury N7 72 B2
Enfield EN3 18 B6
Lockhart Lo 4 E4 20 C4
Lockhart St E3 97 B3
Lockhurst St E5 74 D4
Lockier Wlk HA9 65 D5
Lockington Rd
SW8 137 B4 268 D2
Lockmead Rd
Lewisham SE13 142 A2
South Tottenham N15 52 A3
Lock Mews 9 NW1 71 D2
Lock Rd TW10 175 C6
LOCKSBOTTOM 226 D5
Lockside 17 E14 119 A6
Lock's La CR4 181 A1
Locksley St E14 97 B2
Locksmeade Rd TW10 175 C6
Lock View Ct 9 E14 119 A6
Lockwell Rd RM10 81 C5
Lockwood Cl SE26 184 D6
Lockwood Ct KT3 199 A5
Lockwood Ho 10 SE11 138 C6
Lockwood Ind Pk N17 52 B6
Lockwood Pl E4 35 C4
Lockwood Sq SE16 118 B3
Lockwood Way
Chessington KT9 214 C3
Higham Hill E17 34 D1
Lockyer Cl EN3 7 D5
Lockyer Est SE1 252 D1
Lockyer Ho
7 Greenwich SE10 120 D1
Putney SW15 134 D2
South Lambeth SW8 270 A4
Lockyer St SE1 252 D1
Locomotive Dr TW14 150 A3
Locton Gn 4 E3 97 B6
Lodden Lo 18 SM2 218 A1
Loddiges Ho 5 E9 74 C1
Loddiges Rd E9 74 C1
Loddon Ho NW8 236 D5
Loder St SE15 140 C5
Lodge Ave
Borehamwood WD6 10 B6
Croydon CR0 220 C5
Dagenham RM8, RM9,
IG11 80 B3
Harrow HA3 44 A5
Mortlake SW14 133 C2
Lodge Cl Edgware HA8 26 C4
Edmonton N18 33 A5
Hackbridge SM6 203 A1
Isleworth TW7 131 B4
Lodge Ct 3 HA0 66 A3
Lodge Dr N13 32 C6
Lodge Gdns BR3 207 B4
Lodge Hill
East Wickham DA16 146 B5
Redbridge IG4 56 A5
Lodgehill Park Cl HA2 63 D6
Lodge La Bexley DA5 168 D5
New Addington CR0 223 D1
North Finchley N12 30 A5
Lodge Mead Ct 5 N3 29 D3
Lodge Pl SM1 217 D3
Lodge Rd Bromley BR1 187 C3
Hendon NW4 46 C5
Lisson Gr NW8 92 C4 230 A1
Sutton SM1 217 D3
Thornton Heath CR0 204 D2
Wallington SM6 219 B3
Lodge The
9 Chiswick W4 111 C3
1 Sutton SM1 218 A4
Lodge Villas IG8 36 D4
Lodge Way
Charlton TW17 171 A1
Stanwell TW15 148 A2
Lodore Gdns NW9 45 C4
Lodore Gn UB10 60 A5
Lodore St E14 98 A1
Lodsworth Ho SW11 268 A1
Lofthouse Pl KT9 213 C2
Loftie St SE16 118 A4
Lofting Ho 8 N1 72 C1
Lofting Rd N1 72 C1
Lofts on the Park 24
E9 74 D2
Loftus Rd Barking IG11 79 A2
Shepherd's Bush W12 112 B5
Loftus Rd (Queens Park
Rangers FC) W12 112 B5
Logan Cl Enfield EN3 6 D4
Hounslow TW4 129 B2
Logan Mews W8 255 A4
Logan Pl W8 113 C2 255 A4
Logan Rd Edmonton N9 18 B2
Wembley HA9 66 A6
Loggetts SE21 161 C2
Logs Hill BR1, BR7 188 A2
Logs Hill Cl BR7 188 A2
Lohmann Ho 5 SE11 138 C6
Lois Dr TW17 192 D4
Lolesworth Cl E1 243 D3
Lolland Ho 8 SE7 122 A2
Lollard St
SE11 116 C2 261 A3
Lollards Twr SE1 260 C5
Loman St SE1 116 D4 251 D2
Lomas Cl CR0 224 A1
Lomas St E1 96 A2
Lombard Ave Enfield EN3 6 C4
Ilford IG3 57 C1
Lombard Bsns Pk
Merton SW19 179 D1
Thornton Heath CR0 204 B2
Lombard Ct
14 Acton W3 110 D5

Lombard Ct *continued*
City of London EC3 252 D6
Lombard La EC4 241 B1
Lombard Rd
Battersea SW11 136 B3
Friern Barnet N11 31 B5
Merton SW19 179 D1
Lombard Rdbt CR0 204 B2
Lombard St EC3 95 B1 242 D1
Lombard Trad Est
SE7 121 B2
Lombard Wall SE7 121 B2
Lombardy Pl W2 245 D5
Lombardy Ret Pk UB3 106 B6
Lomley Ho 10 SW2 160 C5
Lomond Cl
Tottenham N15 51 C4
Wembley HA0 66 B1
Lomond Ct HA3 42 D6
Lomond Gdns CR2 223 A1
Lomond Gr SE5 139 B5
Lomond Ho 10 SE5 139 B4
Loncroft Rd SE5 139 C6
Londesborough Ho 1
N16 73 C4
Londesborough Rd
N16 73 C4
London Academy HA8 26 B6
London Acad of
Computing & Electronics
SW17 158 D1
London Aquarium*
SE1 250 C1
London Bridge EC4,
SE1 117 B6 252 D5
London Bridge City Pier
SE1 117 C5 253 A4
London Bridge Hospl
SE1 117 B5 252 D4
London Bridge St
SE1 117 B5 252 D3
London Bridge Sta
SE1 117 B5 252 D3
London Bridge Wlk
SE1 252 D4
London Britannia Coll
N1 95 B4 235 C2
London Business Sch
NW1 92 D3 237 C6
London Butterfly Ho*
TW8 131 B4
London Canal Mus*
N1 94 A5 233 B4
London Central Mosque*
NW8 92 C4 230 B1
London Chest Hospl
E2 96 C5
London City Airport
E16 122 B5
London City Airport Sta
E16 122 A5
London Clinic
NW1 93 A3 238 B5
London Coll of Advanced
Studies SE1 252 C3
London Coll of Beauty
Therapy W1 93 C1 239 B1
London Coll of Bsns &
Computer Studies
SW4 137 D1
London Coll of
Communication (Sch of
Printing & Publishing)
SE11 116 D3 261 D5
London Coll of Economics
& Science NW10 89 A3
London Coll of Fashion
Broadgate EC2 95 C3 243 B6
Marylebone W1 238 D2
Marylebone W1 238 B1
Marylebone W1 238 C1
St Luke's EC1 95 A3 242 A5
London Coll of Fashion
(Mare St) E8 74 B1
London Coll of
International Business
Studies WC1 240 B3
London Ct 3 SW18 157 C6
London Docklands Visitor
Ctr* E14 120 A4
London Dungeon The*
SE1 117 B5 252 D4
London Electronics Coll
SW5 113 D1 255 C2
London Eye (Millennium
Wheel)* SE1 116 B4 250 C2
London Fields East Side
E8 74 B1
London Fields Prim Sch
E8 96 B6
London Fields Sta E8 74 B1
London Fields West Side
E8 74 A1
London Fire Brigade
Mus* SE1 252 A2
London Gas Mus The* E3,
E16 98 B3
London Group Bsns Pk
NW2 46 A1
London Ho
Edgware HA8 26 A6
13 Hammersmith W6 112 A2
London Ho TW9 132 B2
London Ho NW8 230 B4
London Hospital Dental
Inst E1 96 B2
London Independent
Hospl The E1 96 D2
London Inst The
SW17 181 B5
London Int Coll N7 72 B5
London International Film
Sch WC2 94 A1 240 A1
London IT Coll IG2 56 C3
London La
Bromley BR1 186 D3
Hackney E8 74 B1
London Metropolitan
Univ
Islington N7 72 C3
Whitechapel E1 95 D1 243 C2
Whitechapel E1 95 D1 243 C1
Whitechapel
EC3 117 D6 253 C6
London Metropolitan Univ
(Central Ho) E1 96 A1
London Metropolitan Univ
(Commercial Rd) E1 96 A1
London Metropolitan Univ
(Ladbrook Ho) N5 72 D3
London Metropolitan Univ
(Moorgate)
EC2 95 B2 242 D3
London Metropolitan Univ
(Spring Ho) N7 72 C2
London Mews W2 236 D2
London Motorcycle Mus*
UB6 86 A4
London Nautical Sch The
SE1 116 C5 251 B4
London Oratory Sch The
SW6 135 C5 265 B4
London Pavilion SW1 249 C5
London Peace Pagoda*
SW3 267 D4
London Rd
Ashford TW15, TW18, TW19,
TW14 148 B2
Brentford TW7, TW8 131 B4
Bromley BR1 186 D3
Carshalton CR4 203 A2
Enfield EN2 5 B1
Forest Hill SE22, SE23 162 C3
Hackbridge SM6, CR4 219 B6
Harrow HA1 64 C6
Hounslow TW3, TW7, TW1,
TW8 130 B3
Kingston u T KT1, KT2 176 B1
Lambeth SE1 116 D3 261 D6
Mitcham CR4 180 D2
Morden SM4 201 C5
Newham E13 99 A5
Romford RM7, RM8 59 C5
Stanmore HA7 25 D6
Stoneleigh KT17, KT4,
SM3 216 B3
Thornton Heath CR0, CR7,
SW16 204 C3
Twickenham TW1 153 A4
Wembley HA9 66 A2
London Road Rdbt
TW1 153 A5
London Sch of Economics
& Political Science
WC2 94 B1 240 D1
London Sch of Jewish
Studies NW4 46 D5
London St
City of London EC3 253 B6
Paddington W2 92 B1 236 C1
London Stile 5 W4 110 C1
London Stock Exchange*
EC2 242 A2
London Stone Bsns Est 15
SW11 137 A3
London Terr 1 E2 96 A5
London Tottenham Coll
N17 33 D3
London Transport Mus*
WC2 250 B6
London Wall
EC2 95 B2 242 D3
London Wall Bldgs
EC2 242 D3
London Wetland Ctr*
SW13 134 B5
London Wetland Visitor
Ctr* SW13 134 B4
London Wharf 4 E2 96 B6
London Xtra Tuition Coll
N4 72 D6
London Zoo*
NW1 93 A5 231 A4
Lonesome Prim Sch
CR4 181 B1
Lonesome Way CR4 181 C2
Long Acre WC2 94 A1 240 B1
Long Acre Ct W13 87 A2
Longacre Pl SM5 219 A2
Longacre Rd E17 36 B2
Longbeach Rd SW11 136 D2
Longberrys NW2 69 B5
Longboat Row UB1 85 B6
Longbridge Ho RM8 80 B4
Longbridge Rd
Barking IG11 79 C3
Dagenham RM8 80 B4
Longbridge Way SE13 164 A6
Longbury Dr BR5 190 B1
Longchamp Ct 13 HA7 25 C5
Longcliffe Ho SW18 157 D6
Longcroft SE9 166 C1
Longcrofte Rd HA8 25 D3
Long Deacon Rd E4 20 C3
LONG DITTON 197 C1
Long Ditton Inf Sch
KT6 197 C1
Longdon Wood BR2 226 A4
Longdown Rd SE6 185 C6
Long Dr Dagenham W3 89 C1
Long Dr *continued*
Greenford UB6 85 D6
Ruislip HA4 62 D4
Long Elmes HA3 24 A2
Longfellow Rd
North Cheam KT4 200 B1
Walthamstow E17 53 B3
Longfellow Way SE1 263 D3
Longfield
3 Bromley BR1 186 D2
Loughton IG10 21 C6
Long Field NW9 27 D3
Longfield Ave
Ealing W5 109 C6
Enfield EN3 6 C5
Hackbridge SM6 203 A1
Hendon NW7 28 A3
Walthamstow E17 53 A5
Wembley HA9 44 A1
Longfield Cres SE23,
SE26 162 C1
Longfield Ct 4 N2 48 A6
Longfield Dr
Mitcham SW19 180 C2
Mortlake SW14 154 D6
Longfield Est SE1 263 D3
Longfield Fst & Mid Schs
HA2 41 C3
Longfield Ho
Ealing W5 109 C6
Walthamstow E17 53 B4
Longfield Rd W5 87 C1
Longfield St SW18 157 C4
Longford Ave
Feltham TW14 149 D5
Southall UB1 107 D6
Stanwell TW19 148 A3
Longford Cl
Feltham TW13 151 A1
Hampton TW12 173 C6
Hayes UB4 106 D6
Longford Com Sch
TW14 149 D4
Longford Ct
1 Bedford Pk W12 111 C4
2 Clapton Pk E5 74 D4
Hampton TW12 173 D4
9 Hendon NW4 46 C5
Southall UB1 107 C5
West Ewell KT19 215 A4
Longford Gdns
Hayes UB4 106 D6
Sutton SM1 218 A6
Longford Ho
1 Catford BR1 186 B5
Hampton TW12 173 C6
7 Stepney E1 96 C1
Longford Ind Est
TW12 173 D4
Longford Rd TW2 151 D3
Longford St
NW1 93 B3 238 D6
Longford Way TW19 148 A3
Longford Wlk 9 SW2 160 C4
Longhayes Ave RM6 58 D5
Longhayes Ct RM6 58 D5
Longheath Gdns CR0 206 C4
Longhedge Ho SE26 184 A6
Longhedge St SW11 137 A3
Longhill Rd SE6 164 B1
Long Ho SM5 218 C6
Longhook Gdns UB5 84 B4
Longhope Cl SE15 139 D6
Longhurst Ho 8 W9 91 B4
Longhurst Rd
Croydon CR0 206 B3
Lewisham SE13 164 C6
Long La
Bermondsey
SE1 117 B4 252 D1
Croydon CR0 206 C3
East Finchley N2 48 B6
Erith DA7 147 B4
Finchley N3 29 D2
Hillingdon UB10 82 D6
Holborn EC1 94 D2 241 D4
Stanwell TW15, TW19 148 B3
Longland Ct
Bermondsey SE1 118 A1
Hackney E9 75 A3
Longland Dr N20 13 D2
LONGLANDS 167 B1
Longlands Ct
Higham Hill E17 35 A2
Mitcham CR4 181 A2
Notting Hill W11 244 D6
Sidcup DA15 167 D1
Longlands Park Cres
DA15 167 C2
Longlands Prim Sch
DA15 167 C1
Longlands Rd DA15 167 D1
Longleat Ct 3 DA6 147 A1
Longleat Ho SW1 259 C2
Longleat Rd EN1 17 C6
Longleat Way TW14 149 B4
Longleigh Ho 8 SE5 139 C4
Longleigh La SE2, DA7 146 C6
Longlents Ho 3 NW10 89 B6
Longley Ave HA0 88 B6
Longley Ho 5 N19 71 C4
Longley Rd Harrow HA1 42 B5
Thornton Heath CR0 204 D2
Upper Tooting SW17 180 D4
Long Leys E4 36 A4
Longley St SE1 118 A2
Longley Way NW2 68 C5
Longman Ho
9 Globe Town E2 96 D5
10 Shoreditch E8 95 D6
Long Mark Rd 5 E16 99 D2
Longmarsh La SE28 123 C5
Longmead BR7 188 C1
Long Mead NW9 27 D2
Longmead Dr DA14 168 D2
Longmead Ho SE27 183 A5
Long Meadow 20 N7 71 D3
Long Meadow Cl BR3,
BR4 208 A2
Longmeadow Rd
DA15 167 C3
Longmead Prim Sch
UB7 104 A2
Longmead Rd
Hayes UB3 105 D6
Thames Ditton KT7 196 D2
Upper Tooting SW17 180 D5
Longmoor Point 14
SW15 156 B3
Longmore Ave EN4, EN5 14 B5
Longmore St
SW1 115 C2 259 A3
Longnor Rd E1 96 D4
Long Pond Rd SE3 142 C4
Long Rd SW4 137 C1
Longreach Ct IG11 101 B5
Long Reach Rd IG11 101 D3
Longridge Ho SE1 262 B5
Longridge La UB1 85 D1
Longridge Rd
SW5 113 C2 255 B3
Long Ridges N2 49 A6
Longs Ct 2 TW9 132 B1
Long's Ct W1 249 D5
Longshaw Prim Sch E4 20 B1
Longshaw Rd E4 20 B1
Longshore SE8 119 B2
Long St E2 95 D4
Longstaff Cres SW18 157 C4
Longstaff Rd SW18 157 C5
Longstone Ave NW10 89 D6
Longstone Rd SW17 181 B5
Longthorne Ho 18 E3 97 B4
Longthornton Rd
SW16 181 D1
Longthorpe Ct 9 W6 112 A2
Longton Ave SE26 184 A6
Longton Gr SE26 184 B6
Longville Rd SE11 261 D4
Longwalk Rd UB11 104 D5
Long Wlk
Bermondsey SE1 263 B6
Kingston u T KT3 199 A6
Shooters Hill SE18 144 D6
Longwood Bsns Pk
TW16 193 D4
Longwood Dr SW15 156 A5
Longwood Gdns IG2, IG6,
IG5 56 C6
Longwood Par IG6 56 D6
Longworth Cl SE28 102 D1
Long Yd WC1 94 B3 240 C5
Loning The Enfield EN3 6 C5
Hyde The NW9 45 D5
Lonsdale Ave
Newham E6 100 A3
Wembley HA9 66 A3
Lonsdale Cl
Edgware HA8 26 B5
Hillingdon UB8 83 A2
Mottingham SE12 165 D1
Newham E6 100 A3
Pinner HA5 23 A2
Lonsdale Cres IG2 56 D3
Lonsdale Dr EN2 16 A6
Lonsdale Dr N EN2 4 A1
Lonsdale Gdns CR7,
SW16 204 B5
Lonsdale Ho
Fulham SW6 135 C2
6 Stoke Newington N4 51 A2
Lonsdale Mews
Notting Hill W11 91 B1
4 Richmond TW9 132 C4
Lonsdale Pl N1 72 C1
Lonsdale Rd
Barnes SW13 133 D5
Bexley DA7 147 B3
Chiswick W4 111 D2
Croydon SE25 206 B5
Kilburn NW6 91 B6
Leytonstone E11 54 D2
Notting Hill W11 91 B1
Southall UB2 106 D3
Lonsdale Sq
Islington N1 72 C1
Islington N1 234 B6
Loobert Rd N15 51 C6
Looe Gdns IG6 56 D6
Loop Rd BR7 189 A4
Lopen Rd N18 33 C6
Lopen Works N18 33 C6
Lopez Ho 4 SW9 138 A2
Lorac Ct 13 SM2 217 C1
Loraine Cl EN3 18 C6
Loraine Ct BR7 188 D5
Loraine Ho 1 SM5 219 B4
Loraine Rd
Chiswick W4 132 D6
Islington N7 72 B4
Lord Ave IG5 56 B6
Lord Chancellor Wlk
KT2 177 A2
Lord David Pitt Ho 8
SE24 138 C1
Lordell Pl SW19 178 C4
Lorden Wlk 13 E2 96 A4
Lord Gdns IG5 56 B5
Lord Hills Rd W2 91 D2
Lord Holland La 5
SW9 138 C3
Lord Knyvetts Ct 3
TW19 148 A5
Lord Napier Pl W6 112 A1
Lord North St SW1 260 A5
Lord Roberts Mews
SW6 265 C3
Lord Roberts Terr
SE18 122 C1
Lords Cl Feltham TW13 151 A2
West Norwood SE21 161 A2
Lord's Cricket Mus*
NW8 92 B4 229 D1
Lords Ct 3 HA8 27 A3
Lordship Gr N16 73 B6
Lordship Ho 3 N16 73 B6
Lordship La
Dulwich Village SE22 161 D5
Tottenham N22 33 B2
Lordship Lane Prim Sch
N22 33 A2
Lordship Park Mews
N16 73 A6
Lordship Pk N16 73 B6
Lordship Pl SW3 267 A5
Lordship Rd
Northolt UB5 63 A1
Stoke Newington N16 73 B6
Lordship Terr N16 73 B6
Lord's Indoor Cricket Sch
NW8 230 A2
Lord's (MCC & Middlesex
Cty Cricket Ground)*
NW8 92 B4 229 D2
Lordsmead Rd N17 33 C1
Lord St E16 122 A5
Lord's View NW8 229 D1
Lord Warwick St SE18 122 B3
Loreburn Ho 2 N7 72 B4
Lorenzo St N1, WC1 233 C2
Loretto Gdns HA3 44 A5
Lorian Cl N12 29 D6
Loring Rd
East Barnet N20 14 C2
Isleworth TW7 130 D3
Loris Rd W6 112 C3
Lorn Ct SW9 138 C3
Lorne Ave CR0 206 D2
Lorne Cl NW8 92 C4 230 B1
Lorne Ct Harrow HA1 42 C2
Putney SW15 156 D5
Lorne Gdns
Croydon CR0 206 D2
5 Hammersmith W11 112 D4
Wanstead E11 55 C5
Lorne Ho
Friern Barnet N11 31 B5
Hornsey N4 50 B2
7 Tower Hamlets E1 97 A2
Lorne Rd Finsbury Pk N4 50 B1
Forest Gate E7 77 C4
Harrow HA3 24 D1
3 Richmond TW10 154 B6
Walthamstow E17 53 C4
Lorn Rd SW9 138 C3
Lorraine Ct
Beckenham BR3 186 A2
9 Belmont SM2 217 C1
10 Camden Town NW1 71 B1
Lorraine Pk HA3 24 C3
Lorrimore Rd SE17 138 D6
Lorrimore Sq SE17 138 D6
Lorton Ho 9 NW6 91 C6
Loseberry Rd KT10 212 B3
Lostock Ho 10 SW8 137 D3
Lothair Rd W5 109 D4
Lothair Rd N N4 50 D3
Lothair Rd S N4 50 D2
Lothbury EC2 95 B1 242 C2
Lothian Ave UB4 84 B2
Lothian Cl HA0 65 A5
Lothian Rd SW9 138 D4
Lothrop St W10 91 A4
Lots Rd SW10 136 A5 266 B3
Loubet St SW17 180 D4
Loudoun Ave IG6 56 D4
Loudoun Rd
NW8 92 A6 229 B5
Loudwater Cl TW16 194 A5
Loudwater Rd TW16 194 A5
Loughborough Ct 7
SW9 138 D2
Loughborough Junction
Sta SW9 138 D2
Loughborough Pk
SW9 138 D1
Loughborough Prim Sch
SW9 138 D3
Loughborough Rd SE5,
SW9 138 D3
Loughborough St
SE11 116 B1 260 D1
Lough Rd N7 72 B2
LOUGHTON 21 D5
Loughton Way IG9 21 D3
Louie Black Ho 4
SW19 179 A3
Louisa Cl E9 96 D6
Louisa Ct
Twickenham TW2 152 C2
Wood Green N11 31 D3
Louisa Gdns E1 96 D3
Louisa Ho SW15 133 D1
Louisa St E1 96 D3
Louis Ct 3 RM10 81 D2
Louise Bennett Cl 9
SE24 138 D1
Louise Ct
7 Bexley DA6 147 A1
Louise Ct *continued*
4 Wanstead E11 55 B4
Wood Green N22 32 C2
Louise De Marillac Ho 26
E1 96 C2
Louise Graham Ho 5
IG11 101 B6
Louise Rd E15 76 C2
Louise White Ho 1
N19 49 D1
Louis Gdns BR7 188 B6
Louis Mews N10 31 B2
Louisville Rd SW17 159 A1
Lousada Lo N14 15 C5
Louvaine Rd SW11 136 B1
Lovage App E6 100 A2
Lovat Cl NW2 67 D5
Lovat La EC3 253 A5
Lovatt Cl HA8 26 D4
Lovatt Ct SW12 159 B3
Lovatt Dr HA4 39 D4
Lovat Wlk TW5 129 A5
Loveday Ho 2 SW2 160 C3
Loveday Rd W13 109 B5
Lovegrove St SE1 140 A6
Lovegrove Wlk E14 120 A5
Lovekyn Cl KT2 176 B1
Love La Cheam SM3 217 A2
City of London
EC2 95 A1 242 B2
Croydon SE25 206 B6
Long Ditton KT6 213 D6
Mitcham CR4 202 C6
Morden SM4 201 D2
Old Bexley DA5 169 C5
Pinner HA5 41 A6
Tottenham N17 33 D3
Woolwich SE18 122 D2
Lovelace Ave BR2 210 C3
Lovelace Gdns
Barking IG11 80 A4
Surbiton KT6 197 D2
Lovelace Gn SE9 144 B2
Lovelace Ho 12 E8 95 D6
Lovelace Prim Sch
KT9 213 C3
Lovelace Rd
East Barnet EN4 14 C4
Surbiton KT6 197 D2
West Norwood SE21 161 A3
Loveland Mans 7 IG11 79 D1
Lovel Ave DA16 146 A3
Lovelinch Cl SE15 140 C6
Lovell Ho Hackney E8 96 A6
4 Merton SW19 180 A2
Lovell Pl SE16 119 A3
Lovell Rd
Richmond TW10 153 C1
Southall UB1 85 D1
Loveridge Mews NW6 69 B2
Loveridge Rd NW6 69 B2
Lover's Wlk
W1 115 A5 248 A3
Lovett Dr SM5 202 B2
Lovette Ho 4 E3 97 C4
Lovetts Pl SW18 135 D1
Lovett Way NW10 67 A3
Love Wlk SE5 139 B3
Lovibonds Ave
Hillingdon UB7 82 B1
Locksbottom BR6 226 D5
Lowbrook Rd IG1 78 D4
Lowdell Cl UB7 82 A1
Lowden Rd
Edmonton N9 18 B3
Herne Hill SE24 139 A1
Southall UB1 107 A6
Lowder Ho 6 E1 118 B5
Lowe Ave E16 99 A2
Lowell Ho 10 SE5 139 A5
Lowell St E14 97 A1
Lower Addiscombe Rd
CR0 205 C1
Lower Addison Gdns
W14 113 A4 244 A1
Lower Belgrave St
SW1 115 B3 258 C5
Lower Boston Rd W7 108 C4
Lower Broad St RM10 103 C6
Lower Camden BR7 188 B2
Lower Church St CR0 220 D6
LOWER CLAPTON 74 C4
Lower Clapton Rd E5 74 C4
Lower Clarendon Wlk 9
W11 91 A1
Lower Comm S SW15 134 B2
Lower Coombe St
CR0 221 A4
Lower Downs Rd
SW20 178 D2
LOWER EDMONTON 18 B1
LOWER FELTHAM 149 D1
Lower Fosters NW4 46 C4
Lower George St 13
TW10 153 D6
Lower Gn W CR4 202 C6
Lower Gravel Rd BR2 210 B1
LOWER GREEN 195 C1
Lower Green Gdns
KT4 200 A1
Lower Green Rd KT10 212 A6
Lower Grosvenor Pl
SW1 115 B3 258 D6
Lower Grove Rd TW10 154 B6
LOWER HALLIFORD 193 C3
Lower Hall La E4 35 A6

Lower Hampton Rd TW12, TW16 . . . 172 D1
Lower Ham Rd KT2 . . . 175 D4
LOWER HOLLOWAY . . . 72 A3
Lower James St W1 . . 249 B6
Lower John St W1 . . . 249 B6
Lower Kenwood Ave
EN2 . . . 16 A6
Lower Kings Rd KT2 . . . 176 A3
Lower Lea Crossing E14, E16 . . . 120 C6
Lower Maidstone Rd
N11 . . . 31 C4
Lower Mall W6 . . . 112 B1
Lower Marsh
SE1 . . . 116 C4 251 A1
Lower Marsh La KT1, KT5 . . . 198 C5
Lower Merton Rise
NW3 . . . 70 C1
LOWER MORDEN . . . 201 A2
Lower Morden La
SM4 . . . 201 A3
Lower Mortlake Rd
TW9 . . . 132 B2
Lower Park Rd
Belvedere DA17 . . . 125 C2
Friern Barnet N11 . . . 31 C5
4 Loughton IG10 . . . 21 D6
Lower Pk Acton W3 . . . 89 A3
5 Putney SW15 . . . 156 D6
LOWER PLACE . . . 89 A5
Lower Place Bsns Ctr
NW10 . . . 89 A5
Lower Queen's Rd IG9 . . 21 D2
Lower Rd
Belvedere DA17 . . . 125 D3
Finchley N2 . . . 30 B2
Harrow HA2 . . . 42 B1
Rotherhithe SE16 . . . 118 C4
Sutton SM1 . . . 218 A4
Lower Richmond Rd
Mortlake SW14, TW9 . . . 132 D2
Putney SW15 . . . 134 C2
Lower Robert St WC2 . 250 B5
Lower Sand Hills KT6 . . 197 C2
Lower Sloane St
SW1 . . . 115 A1 258 A2
Lower Sq TW7 . . . 131 B2
Lower Strand NW9 . . . 27 D1
Lower Sunbury Rd
TW12 . . . 173 C1
LOWER SYDENHAM . . . 185 A6
Lower Sydenham Sta
SE26 . . . 185 B5
Lower Teddington Rd
KT1 . . . 175 D2
Lower Terr NW3 . . . 70 A5
Lower Thames St
EC3 . . . 117 C6 253 A5
Lower Tub WD23 . . . 8 B4
Lowerwood Ct W11 . . . 91 A1
Lower Wood Rd KT10 . . 213 B2
Lowestoft Cl 5 E5 . . . 74 C6
Lowestoft Mews E16 . . . 122 D4
Loweswater Cl HA9 . . . 65 D6
Loweswater Ho E3 . . . 97 B3
Lowfield Rd
Dagenham W3 . . . 89 A1
Hampstead NW6 . . . 69 C1
Low Hall Cl E4 . . . 19 D4
Low Hall La E17 . . . 53 A3
Lowick Rd HA1 . . . 42 C4
Lowland Gdns RM7 . . . 59 D3
Lowlands NW3 . . . 70 C2
Lowlands Ct NW7 . . . 27 D5
Lowlands Rd
Harrow HA1 . . . 42 C2
Pinner HA5 . . . 40 C3
Lowman Rd N7 . . . 72 B4
Lowndes Cl SW1 . . . 258 B5
Lowndes Ct
Knightsbridge SW1 . . . 257 D6
Marylebone W1 . . . 239 A1
Lowndes Lo Barnet EN5 . . . 1 D2
SW1 . . . 257 D6
Lowndes Pl
SW1 . . . 115 A3 258 A5
Lowndes Sq
SW1 . . . 114 D4 247 D1
Lowndes St
SW1 . . . 115 A3 258 A6
Lownds Ct BR1 . . . 187 A1
Lowood Ct SE19 . . . 183 D5
Lowood Ho 12 E1 . . . 118 C6
Lowood St E1 . . . 118 B6
Lowry Cres CR4 . . . 180 C1
Lowry Ct 3 SE16 . . . 118 B1
Lowry Ho N17 . . . 33 D2
Lowry Lo 1 HA0 . . . 65 D3
Lowry Rd RM8 . . . 80 B3
Lowther Cl WD6 . . . 10 B6
Lowther Dr EN2 . . . 4 A1
Lowther Hill SE23 . . . 163 A4
Lowther Ho
Pimlico SW1 . . . 259 B1
11 Shoreditch E8 . . . 95 D6
Lowther Prim Sch
SW13 . . . 134 A6
Lowther Rd
Barnes SW13 . . . 133 D4
Higham Hill E17 . . . 35 A1
Islington N7 . . . 72 C3
Kingston u T KT2 . . . 176 B2
Stanmore HA7 . . . 44 B6
Lowth Rd SE5 . . . 139 A3
Lowton Lo E17 . . . 53 A6
LOXFORD . . . 79 A3
Loxford Ave E6 . . . 99 D5
Loxford Ho SW1 . . . 258 B3
Loxford La IG1 . . . 79 B3
Loxford Rd IG11 . . . 78 D2
Loxford Sch of Science & Tech IG1 . . . 79 B3
Loxham Rd E4 . . . 35 D3
Loxham St WC1 . . . 233 B1
Loxley Cl SE26 . . . 184 D5
Loxley Hall E11 . . . 54 C2
Loxley Ho HA9 . . . 66 A5
Loxley Rd
Feltham TW12 . . . 173 B6
Wandsworth SW18 . . . 158 B3
Loxton Rd SE23 . . . 163 A3
Loxwood Cl TW14 . . . 149 B3
Loxwood Rd N17 . . . 51 C6
Loyola Prep Sch IG9 . . . 21 C3
LTC Coll London W1 . . 239 A2
Lubavitch House Sch (Jun Boys) E5 . . . 51 D2
Lubbock Ct BR7 . . . 188 B3
Lubbock Ho
21 Canary Wharf
E14 . . . 119 D6
Orpington BR6 . . . 227 C6
Lubbock Rd BR7 . . . 188 B3
Lubbock St SE14 . . . 140 C5
Lucan Ho N1 . . . 235 D5
Lucan Pl SW3 . . 114 C2 257 B3
Lucan Rd EN5 . . . 1 A2
Lucas Ave Harrow HA2 . . . 63 C6
Newham E13 . . . 99 B6
Lucas Ct
Battersea SW11 . . . 268 B1
Forest Hill SE26 . . . 185 A5
Lucas Gdns N2 . . . 30 A1
Lucas Ho
2 Clapham SW8 . . . 137 C3
Walham Green SW10 . . 265 D4
Lucas Rd SE20 . . . 184 C4
Lucas Sq NW11 . . . 47 C3
Lucas St SE4, SE8 . . . 141 C4
Lucas Vale Prim Sch
SE8 . . . 141 C4
Lucerne Cl N14 . . . 16 A1
Lucerne Ct
5 Abbey Wood
DA18 . . . 125 A3
8 Beckenham BR3 . . . 185 C3
Lucerne Gr E17 . . . 54 B5
Lucerne Mews W8 . . . 245 B4
Lucerne Rd Highbury N5 . . 72 D4
Orpington BR6 . . . 211 D1
South Norwood CR7 . . . 205 A5
Lucey Rd SE16 . . . 118 A3
Lucey Way SE16 . . . 118 A2
Lucie Ave TW15 . . . 170 D4
Lucien Rd
Upper Tooting SW17 . . . 181 A6
Wandsworth SW18 . . . 157 D2
Lucille Ho SE26 . . . 184 B4
Lucknow St SE18 . . . 145 C5
Lucorn Cl SE12 . . . 164 D5
Lucraft Ho 12 SW2 . . . 160 A4
Luctons Ave IG9 . . . 21 C3
Lucy Ashe Ho SE17 . . . 261 D3
Lucy Brown Ho SE1 . . . 252 B3
Lucy Cres W3 . . . 89 A3
Lucy Gdns RM8 . . . 81 A5
Luddesdon Rd DA8 . . . 147 C5
Ludford Cl
Croydon CR0 . . . 220 D4
Edgware NW9 . . . 27 C1
Ludgate Broadway
EC4 . . . 241 D1
Ludgate Cir EC4 . 94 D1 241 C1
Ludgate Hill
EC4 . . . 94 D1 241 D1
Ludgate Ho EC4 . . . 241 C1
Ludgate Sq EC4 . . . 241 D1
Ludgrove Ct EN4 . . . 2 C1
Ludgrove Hall EN4 . . . 2 C2
Ludham NW5 . . . 70 D3
Ludham Cl SE28 . . . 102 C1
Lud Lo TW15 . . . 148 A2
Ludlow Cl Bromley BR2 . . 209 A6
Harrow HA2 . . . 63 B4
Ludlow Ct Acton W3 . . . 111 A4
East Barnet EN4 . . . 14 C6
Ludlow Rd Ealing W5 . . . 87 C3
Feltham TW13 . . . 172 A6
Ludlow St EC1 . . . 242 A6
Ludlow Way N2 . . . 48 A5
Ludovick Wlk SW15 . . . 133 C1
Ludwell Ho W14 . . . 254 B6
Ludwick Mews SE14 . . . 141 A5
Luffield Rd SE2 . . . 124 B3
Luffman Rd SE12 . . . 165 B1
Lugard Ho 2 W12 . . . 112 B5
Lugard Rd SE15 . . . 140 B4
Lugg App E12 . . . 78 C5
Luke Ho 32 E1 . . . 96 B1
Lukes Ct N3 . . . 47 C6
Luke St EC2 . . . 95 C3 243 A6
Lukin Cres E4 . . . 20 B1
Lukin St E1 . . . 96 C1
Lullingstone Cl BR5 . . . 190 B3
Lullingstone Cres BR5 . . 190 B3
Lullingstone Ho 21
SE15 . . . 140 C6
Lullingstone La SE13 . . . 164 B5
Lullingstone Rd 3
DA17 . . . 147 B6
Lullington Garth
Borehamwood WD6 . . . 10 D6
Bromley BR1 . . . 186 C3
Finchley N12 . . . 29 B5
Lullington Rd
Dagenham RM9 . . . 81 A1
Penge SE20 . . . 184 A3
Lulot Gdns N19 . . . 71 B6
Lulworth
Camden Town NW1 . . . 71 D1
Walworth SE17 . . . 262 C2
Lulworth Ave
Hounslow TW5, TW7 . . . 130 A5
Wembley HA9 . . . 43 C2
Lulworth Cl HA2 . . . 63 B5
Lulworth Cres CR4 . . . 180 C1
Lulworth Ct N14 . . . 16 A1
Lulworth Dr HA5 . . . 41 A2
Lulworth Gdns HA2 . . . 63 B6
Lulworth Ho SW8 . . . 270 C3
Lulworth Rd
Bexley DA16 . . . 145 D3
Chislehurst SE9 . . . 166 A2
Peckham SE15 . . . 140 B3
Lulworth Waye UB4 . . . 84 B1
Lumen Rd HA9 . . . 65 D6
Lumiere Bldg The E7 . . . 77 D3
Lumiere Ct 7 SW17 . . . 159 A2
Lumina Bldg 1 E14 . . . 120 A5
Lumley Cl DA17 . . . 125 C1
Lumley Ct WC2 . . . 250 B5
Lumley Flats SW1 . . . 258 A2
Lumley Gdns SM3 . . . 217 A3
Lumley Ho KT3 . . . 199 B1
Lumley Rd SM1, SM3 . . . 217 A3
Lumley St W1 . . . 238 B1
Lumsdon NW8 . . . 91 D6
Luna Ho 6 SE16 . . . 118 A4
Lunan Ho 14 E3 . . . 97 B5
Luna Rd CR7 . . . 205 A6
Lundin Wlk WD19 . . . 22 D6
Lund Point E15 . . . 98 A6
Lundy Dr UB3 . . . 105 C2
Lunham Rd SE19 . . . 183 C4
Lupin Cl Croydon CR0 . . . 206 D1
Streatham SW2 . . . 160 D2
Lupin Cres IG11 . . . 78 D2
Lupino Ct SE11 . . . 260 D4
Lupin Point SE1 . . . 253 D1
Lupton Cl SE12 . . . 187 B6
Lupton St NW5 . . . 71 C4
Lupus Ct SE19 . . . 183 B2
Lupus St SW1 . . . 115 C1 259 B1
Luralda Gdns E14 . . . 120 B1
Lurgan Ave W6 . . . 134 D6
Lurline Gdns
SW11 . . . 137 A4 268 B2
Luscombe Ct BR2 . . . 186 C1
Luscombe Ho SW18 . . . 157 B6
Luscombe Way
SW8 . . . 138 A5 270 A4
Lusher Ho SW15 . . . 156 D5
Lushington Ho KT12 . . . 194 C3
Lushington Rd
Catford SE6 . . . 185 D5
Willesden Green NW10 . . . 90 B5
Lushington Terr 11 E8 . . . 74 A3
Lutea Ho SM2 . . . 218 A1
Luther Cl HA8 . . . 11 A2
Luther King Cl E17 . . . 53 A3
Luther Mews 2 TW11 . . 174 D5
Luther Rd TW11 . . . 174 D5
Luton Pl SE10 . . . 142 A5
Luton Rd Newham E13 . . . 99 A3
Sidcup DA14 . . . 168 C1
Walthamstow E17 . . . 53 B6
Luton St NW8 . . . 92 B3 236 D5
Luttrell Ave SW15 . . . 156 B6
Lutwyche Rd SE6 . . . 163 B2
Lutyens Ho SW1 . . . 259 A1
Luxborough Ho W1 . . . 238 A4
Luxborough St
W1 . . . 93 A2 238 A4
Luxborough Twr W1 . . 238 A4
Luxembourg Mews 2
E15 . . . 76 C3
Luxemburg Gdns W6 . . . 112 D2
Luxfield Rd SE9 . . . 166 A3
Luxford St SE16 . . . 118 D2
Luxmore St SE4 . . . 141 B4
Luxor St SE5 . . . 139 A2
Lyall Ave SE21 . . . 183 D6
Lyall Mews
SW1 . . . 115 A3 258 A5
Lyall Mews W SW1 . . . 258 A5
Lyall St SW1 . . . 115 A3 258 A5
Lyal Rd E3 . . . 97 A5
Lyce e Francais Charles de Gaulle (French Univ Coll) SW7 . . . 114 B2 256 C4
Lycee The
SE11 . . . 116 C1 261 B1
Lycett Ho 10 SW2 . . . 160 A4
Lycett Pl 3 W12 . . . 112 A4
Lychgate Ct 4 N12 . . . 30 B5
Lychgate Manor HA1 . . . 42 C2
Lych Gate Wlk UB3 . . . 105 D6
Lyconby Gdns CR0 . . . 207 A2
Lydd Cl DA14 . . . 167 C1
Lydden Ct SE9 . . . 167 C5
Lydden Gr SW18 . . . 157 D4
Lydden Rd SW18 . . . 157 D4
Lydd Rd DA7 . . . 147 B5
Lydeard Rd E6 . . . 78 B1
Lydford NW1 . . . 232 B5
Lydford Cl 22 N16 . . . 73 C3
Lydford Rd
Brondesbury NW2 . . . 68 D2
Paddington W9 . . . 91 B3
Tottenham N15 . . . 51 B4
Lydgate Ho 8 N16 . . . 73 C3
Lydhurst Ave SW2 . . . 160 B2
Lydia Ct 2 N12 . . . 30 A4
Lydia Lodge HA1 . . . 64 C4
Lydney Cl
Camberwell SE15 . . . 139 C5
Putney SW19 . . . 157 A2
Lydon Rd SW4 . . . 137 C2
Lydstep Rd BR7 . . . 188 C6
Lydwell Ho 29 SW8 . . . 137 D3
Lyford Rd SW18 . . . 158 C3
Lyford St SE7 . . . 122 A2
Lygoe Ho 18 N6 . . . 49 D2
Lygoe Rd N2 . . . 30 B2
Lygon Ho 2 E2 . . . 96 A4
Lygon Pl SW1 . . . 258 C5
Lyham Cl SW2 . . . 160 A5
Lyham Rd SW2 . . . 160 A5
Lyle Cl CR4 . . . 203 A2
Lyle Ct SM4 . . . 202 B3
Lyle Pk SW15 . . . 156 D5
Lyly Ho SE1 . . . 262 D5
Lyme Farm Rd SE12 . . . 143 B1
Lyme Gr E9 . . . 74 C1
Lyme Grove Ho 2 E9 . . . 74 C1
Lymer Ave SE19 . . . 183 D5
Lyme Rd DA16 . . . 146 B4
Lymescote Gdns SM1 . . 217 C6
Lyme St NW1 . . . 93 C6 232 A6
Lyminge Cl DA14 . . . 189 D6
Lyminge Gdns SW17, SW18 . . . 158 C3
Lymington Ave N22 . . . 32 D1
Lymington Cl
Mitcham SW16 . . . 181 D1
2 Newham E6 . . . 100 B2
Lymington Ct SM1 . . . 218 A5
Lymington Dr HA4 . . . 61 B6
Lymington Gdns KT19 . . 215 D3
Lymington Mans NW6 . . . 69 D2
Lymington Rd
Dagenham RM8 . . . 58 D1
Hampstead NW6 . . . 69 D2
Lyminster Cl UB4 . . . 85 A2
Lympne N17 . . . 33 B1
Lympstone Gdns SE15 . . 140 A5
Lynbridge Gdns N13 . . . 32 D6
Lynbrook Gr SE15 . . . 139 C5
Lynchen Cl TW5 . . . 128 B4
Lynch Wlk 2 SE8 . . . 141 B6
Lyncott Cres SW4 . . . 137 B1
Lyncourt SE3 . . . 142 B3
Lyncroft Ave HA5 . . . 41 A4
Lyncroft Gdns
Ealing W13 . . . 109 C5
Hampstead NW6 . . . 69 C3
Hounslow TW3 . . . 152 A6
Lyncroft Mans 4 NW6 . . 69 C3
Lyndale NW2 . . . 69 B5
Lyndale Ave NW2 . . . 69 B5
Lyndale Cl SE3 . . . 142 D6
Lyndean Ind Est SE2 . . . 124 C3
Lynde Ho
2 Clapham SW4 . . . 137 D2
Walton-on-T KT12 . . . 194 C3
Lynden Gate SW15 . . . 156 B4
Lyndenhurst SE3 . . . 142 D2
Lynden Hyrst CR0 . . . 221 D6
Lyndhurst BR7 . . . 188 D4
Lyndhurst Ave
Colney Hatch N12 . . . 30 D4
Edgware NW7 . . . 27 C4
Mitcham SW16 . . . 181 D1
Pinner HA5 . . . 22 B2
Southall UB1 . . . 107 D5
Sunbury TW16 . . . 194 A6
Tolworth KT5 . . . 198 D1
Twickenham TW2, TW4 . . 151 C3
Lyndhurst Cl
Bexleyheath DA7 . . . 147 D2
Neasden NW10 . . . 67 B5
Orpington BR6 . . . 226 D4
South Croydon CR0 . . . 221 D5
Lyndhurst Ct
8 Belmont SM2 . . . 217 C1
11 Woodford E18 . . . 37 A2
Lyndhurst Dr
Leytonstone E10 . . . 54 A2
New Malden KT3 . . . 199 D2
Lyndhurst Gdns
Barking IG11 . . . 79 C2
Enfield EN1 . . . 5 C1
Hampstead NW3 . . . 70 B3
Hendon N3 . . . 29 A2
Ilford IG2 . . . 57 B3
Pinner HA5 . . . 22 B2
Lyndhurst Gr SE5, SE15 . . . 139 D3
Lyndhurst Ho 2
SW15 . . . 156 A4
Lyndhurst House Prep Sch
NW3 . . . 70 B3
Lyndhurst Lo 3 E14 . . . 120 B2
Lyndhurst Rd
Bexleyheath DA7 . . . 147 D2
Chingford E4 . . . 36 A3
Edmonton N18 . . . 34 A6
Greenford UB6 . . . 85 D3
Hampstead NW3 . . . 70 B3
Thornton Heath CR7 . . . 204 C5
Tottenham N22 . . . 32 C4
Lyndhurst Sch SE5 . . . 139 B3
Lyndhurst Sq SE15 . . . 139 D4
Lyndhurst Terr NW3 . . . 70 B3
Lyndhurst Way
Belmont SM2 . . . 217 C1
Camberwell SE15 . . . 139 D3
Lyndon Ave
Bexley DA15 . . . 167 D6
Hackbridge SM6 . . . 219 A5
Pinner HA5 . . . 23 A4
Lyndon Rd DA17 . . . 125 C2
Lyndon Yd SW17 . . . 179 D6
Lyndum Ct N22 . . . 32 C2
Lyne Cres E17 . . . 35 B2
Lyne Ct NW9 . . . 45 B2
Lynegrove Ave TW15 . . . 171 A5
Lyneham Wlk
Hackney E5 . . . 75 A3
Pinner HA5 . . . 39 D6
Lynette Ave SW4 . . . 159 C5
Lynfield Ct SE23 . . . 162 D4
Lynford Cl
Barnet Gate EN5 . . . 11 D6
Burnt Oak HA8 . . . 27 A2
Lynford French Ho
SE17 . . . 262 A2
Lynford Gdns
Edgware HA8 . . . 10 D1
Ilford IG3 . . . 79 D6
Lynford Terr N9 . . . 17 D3
Lyngham Ct 10 N4 . . . 50 A2
Lynhurst Cres UB10 . . . 61 B1
Lynhurst Ct NW8 . . . 229 C5
Lynhurst Rd UB10 . . . 61 A1
Lynmere Rd DA16 . . . 146 B3
Lyn Mews 12 E3 . . . 97 B4
Lynmouth Ave
Enfield EN1 . . . 17 D5
West Barnes SM4 . . . 200 D2
Lynmouth Dr HA4 . . . 62 B5
Lynmouth Gdns
Heston TW5 . . . 128 D4
Wembley UB6 . . . 65 B1
Lynmouth Rd
Fortis Green N2 . . . 48 D5
Stamford Hill N16 . . . 51 D1
Walthamstow E17 . . . 53 A4
Wembley UB6 . . . 87 B6
Lynn Cl Ashford TW15 . . . 171 B5
Harrow HA3 . . . 24 B1
Lynn Ct SW16 . . . 181 D5
Lynne Cl 7 BR6 . . . 227 D2
Lynne Ct
Forest Hill SE23 . . . 163 B4
Hampstead NW6 . . . 69 D1
South Croydon CR2 . . . 221 C4
Wimbledon SW20 . . . 178 B2
Lynnett Ct E9 . . . 75 A2
Lynnett Rd RM8 . . . 58 D1
Lynne Way UB5 . . . 84 D5
Lynne Wlk KT10 . . . 212 A3
Lynn Ho SE15 . . . 140 A6
Lynn Mews E11 . . . 76 C6
Lynn Rd Balham SW12 . . . 159 B4
Ilford IG2 . . . 57 B2
Leyton E11 . . . 76 C5
Lynn St EN2 . . . 5 B4
Lynsted Cl Bexley DA6 . . . 169 D6
Bromley BR1 . . . 187 C1
Lynsted Ct 4 BR3 . . . 185 A1
Lynsted Gdns SE9 . . . 143 D2
Lynton KT7 . . . 197 A2
Lynton Ave Ealing W13 . . . 87 A1
Hyde The NW9 . . . 45 D5
North Finchley N12 . . . 30 B6
Lynton Cl
Chessington KT9 . . . 214 A4
Isleworth TW7 . . . 130 D1
Willesden NW10 . . . 67 D3
Lynton Cres IG2 . . . 56 D3
Lynton Ct Bowes Pk N13 . . 32 A5
9 Dagenham W3 . . . 89 A1
Penge SE20 . . . 184 B2
Sutton SM2 . . . 218 A2
Lynton Est SE1 . . . 118 A2
Lynton Gdns Enfield EN1 . 17 C4
Friern Barnet N11 . . . 31 D4
Lynton Grange N2 . . . 48 D6
Lynton Ho 16 W2 . . . 91 D1
Lynton Lo N5 . . . 72 D3
Lynton Mans SE1 . . . 261 A6
Lynton Mead N20 . . . 13 D2
Lynton Rd Acton W3 . . . 110 D6
Bermondsey SE1 . . . 117 D2
Chingford E4 . . . 35 D5
Harrow HA2 . . . 63 A6
Hornsey N8 . . . 50 A4
New Malden KT3 . . . 199 B4
Paddington NW6 . . . 91 B5
Thornton Heath CR0 . . . 204 C3
Lynton Terr 4 W3 . . . 89 A1
Lynton Wlk UB4 . . . 83 C4
Lynwood Cl Harrow HA2 . . 63 A5
Woodford E18 . . . 37 C2
Lynwood Ct TW15 . . . 170 B5
Lynwood Dr KT4 . . . 216 A6
Lynwood Gdns
Southall UB1 . . . 85 B1
Wallington CR0 . . . 220 B4
Lynwood Gr
Orpington BR6 . . . 211 C1
Southgate N21 . . . 16 C3
Lynwood Rd Ealing W5 . . . 88 A3
Thames Ditton KT7 . . . 196 D1
Upper Tooting SW17 . . . 180 D6
Lynx Terr SW19 . . . 157 C1
Lynx Way E16 . . . 121 D6
Lyon Bsns Pk IG11 . . . 101 C5
Lyon Ct HA4 . . . 39 D1
Lyon Ho NW8 . . . 237 A5
Lyon Meade HA7 . . . 25 C2
Lyon Park Ave HA0 . . . 66 B2
Lyon Park Jun & Inf Schs
HA0 . . . 66 B1
Lyon Rd Harrow HA1 . . . 42 D3
Merton SW19 . . . 180 A2
Lyonsdown Ave EN5 . . . 14 A5
Lyonsdown Ct EN5 . . . 14 A6
Lyonsdown Rd EN5 . . . 14 A6
Lyonsdown Sch EN5 . . . 14 A6
Lyons Pl NW8 . . . 92 B3 236 C5
Lyon St N1 . . . 72 B1
Lyons Wlk W14 . . . 254 A4
Lyon Way UB6 . . . 86 C6
Lyoth Rd BR5 . . . 227 A6
Lyric Dr UB6 . . . 85 D3
Lyric Mews SE26 . . . 184 C6
Lyric Rd SW13 . . . 133 D4
Lysander 20 NW9 . . . 27 D2
Lysander Ct 8 EN5 . . . 13 D6
Lysander Gdns KT5 . . . 198 B3
Lysander Gr N19 . . . 49 D1
Lysander Ho 10 E2 . . . 96 B5
Lysander Rd Ruislip HA4 . . 61 B6
Wallington CR0 . . . 220 B2
Lysander Way BR6 . . . 227 A5
Lysia Ct SW6 . . . 134 D5
Lysias Rd SW12 . . . 159 B5
Lysia St SW6 . . . 134 D5
Lysons Wlk SW15 . . . 156 A6
Lytchet Rd BR1 . . . 187 B3
Lytchet Way EN3 . . . 6 C4
Lytchgate Cl CR2 . . . 221 C1
Lytcott Dr KT8 . . . 195 B6
Lytcott Gr SE22 . . . 161 D6
Lytham Ave WD19 . . . 22 D5
Lytham Cl SE28 . . . 103 A1
Lytham Ct 5 UB1 . . . 85 D1
Lytham Gr W5 . . . 88 B4
Lytham St
SE17 . . . 117 B1 262 C1
Lyttelton Cl NW3 . . . 70 C1
Lyttelton Ct N2 . . . 48 A4
Lyttelton Rd
Hampstead Garden Suburb
N2 . . . 48 A4
Leyton E10 . . . 76 A5
Lytten Ct 6 W12 . . . 112 A4
Lyttleton Ct UB4 . . . 84 C3
Lyttleton Ho 10 E9 . . . 74 C1
Lyttleton Rd N8 . . . 50 C6
Lytton Ave Enfield EN3 . . . 7 A5
Southgate N13 . . . 16 C2
Lytton Cl
Hampstead Garden Suburb
N2 . . . 48 B4
Northolt UB5 . . . 63 B1
Lytton Ct WC1 . . . 240 B3
Lytton Gdns SM6 . . . 219 D4
Lytton Gr SW15 . . . 157 A5
Lytton Ho 3 TW12 . . . 173 D4
Lytton Rd
Leytonstone E11 . . . 54 C2
New Barnet EN5 . . . 2 A1
Pinner HA5 . . . 23 A3
Lytton Strachey Path 8
SE28 . . . 124 B6
Lyveden Rd
Greenwich SE3 . . . 143 B5
Mitcham SW17, SW19 . . 180 D4

M

Mabbett Ho 2 SE18 . . . 144 C6
Mabel Crout Ct SE9 . . . 145 B1
Mabel Evetts Ct UB3 . . . 106 B6
Mabel Thornton Ho 12
N16 . . . 73 B4
Maberley Cres SE19 . . . 184 A3
Maberley Ct SE19 . . . 184 A3
Maberley Rd SE19 . . . 182 C2
Mabledon Pl NW1, WC1 . . . 232 D1
Mablethorpe Rd SW6 . 264 A3
Mabley St E9 . . . 75 A3
Mablin Lo 3 IG9 . . . 21 C3
McAdam Dr EN2 . . . 4 D3
MacAllister Ho 8
SE18 . . . 144 D6
Macaret Cl N20 . . . 14 A4
MacArthur Cl E7 . . . 77 A2
MacArthur Ho 4
SW2 . . . 160 A4
Macartney Ho SE10 . . . 142 B5
MacAulay Ave KT10 . . . 212 C6
Macaulay CE Prim Sch
SW4 . . . 137 B1
MacAulay Ct SW4 . . . 137 B2
MacAulay Ho
2 Kensal Town W10 . . . 91 A2
10 Stoke Newington N16 . 73 C5
MacAulay Rd
Clapham SW4 . . . 137 B2
Newham E6 . . . 99 D5
MacAulay Sq SW4 . . . 137 B1
MacAulay Way 2
SE28 . . . 124 B5
McAuley Cl Eltham SE9 . . 166 C6
Lambeth SE1 . . 116 C3 261 A6
MacAuley Mews SE13 . . . 142 A3
McAusland Ho 5 E3 . . . 97 B5
Macbean St SE18 . . . 122 D3
Macbeth Ho 4 N1 . . . 95 C5
Macbeth St W6 . . . 112 B1
McBride Ho 6 E3 . . . 97 B5
McCall Cl SW4 . . . 138 A3
McCall Cres SE7 . . . 122 A1
McCall Ho N7 . . . 72 A4
Mccarthy Ct SW11 . . . 267 B1
McCarthy Rd TW13 . . . 172 D5
Macclesfield Rd
Croydon SE25 . . . 206 C4
Shoreditch EC1 . . 95 A4 235 A2
Macclesfield St W1 . . . 249 D6
McClintock Pl EN3 . . . 7 D6
McCoid Way SE1 . . . 252 A1
McConnell Ho SW8 . . . 269 C1
McCormick Ho 9
SW2 . . . 160 C3
McCrone Mews 3
NW3 . . . 70 B2

McCullum Rd E3 97 B6
McDermott Cl SW11 136 C2
McDermott Rd SE15 140 A2
MacDonald Ave RM10 81 D5
McDonald Ct TW3 130 A1
McDonald Ho 1 KT2 176 B3
MacDonald Ho 2
SW11 137 A3
MacDonald Rd
Chingford E17 36 A1
Dartmouth Pk N19 71 C6
Forest Gate E7 77 A4
Friern Barnet N11 30 D5
McDonough Cl KT9 214 A4
McDougall Ct TW9 132 C3
Mcdougall Ho E2 96 A4
McDowall Cl E16 98 D2
McDowall Rd SE5 139 A4
Macduff Rd
SW11 137 A4 268 B2
Mace Cl E1 118 B5
Mace Ho 2 E17 53 D6
McEntee Ave E17 35 A2
Mace St E2 96 D5
McEwan Way E15 98 B6
Macey Ho
Battersea SW11 267 A1
10 Greenwich SE10 142 A6
Macfarlane La TW7 131 A6
Macfarlane Rd W12 112 C5
Macfarren Ho 7 W10 91 A4
MacFarren Pl NW1 238 B5
McGlashon Ho 15 E1 96 A3
McGrath Rd E15 76 D2
McGregor Ct 8 N1 95 C4
MacGregor Ho 2
SW12 159 D3
McGregor Rd W11 91 B2
MacGregor Rd E16 99 C2
Mcguffie Ct E17 53 B6
Machell Rd SE15 140 C2
McIndoe Ct N1 235 C6
McIntosh Cl SM6 220 A1
McIntosh Ho 14 SE16 118 C2
McIntyre Ct 19 SW4 138 A3
Mackay Ho 33 W12 112 B6
McKay Rd SW20 178 C4
Mackay Rd SW4 137 B2
McKellar Cl WD23 8 A2
McKenna Ho 3 E3 97 B5
Mackennal St
NW8 92 C5 230 B4
Mackenzie Cl 7 W12 112 B6
Mackenzie Ho
5 Dollis Hill NW2 68 A5
1 Hornsey N8 50 A5
Mackenzie Rd
Barnsbury N7 72 B2
Penge BR3 184 D1
Mackenzie Wlk E14 119 C5
McKerrell Rd SE15 140 A4
Mackeson Rd NW3 70 D4
Mackie Ho 18 SW2 160 C4
Mackie Rd SW2 160 C4
McKiernan Ct 2
SW11 136 C3
Mc Killop Way DA14 190 C3
McKinlay Ct
Beckenham BR3 185 B1
Bexley DA16 146 C2
McKinnon Wood Ho 16
E2 96 A4
Mackintosh La E9 74 D3
Macklin Ho SE23 162 B2
Macklin St WC2 94 A1 240 B2
Mackonochie Ho EC1 241 A4
Mackrow Wlk 11 E14 120 A6
Macks Rd SE16 118 A2
Mackworth Ho NW1 232 A2
Mackworth St NW1 232 A2
Mac Laren Mews
SW15 134 C1
Maclean Rd SE23 163 A5
McLeod Ct SE21 162 A3
McLeod Ho 3 SE23 162 C2
McLeod Rd SE2 124 B2
MacLeod Rd N21 16 A6
McLeod's Mews
SW7 113 D2 255 D4
MacLeod St
SE17 117 A1 262 B1
Maclise Rd
W14 113 A3 254 A5
McManus Ho 3 SW11 136 B2
McMillan Ct 2 SE6 164 D3
Macmillan Ct HA2 41 C1
McMillan Ho SE4 141 A2
Macmillan Ho
Cricklewood NW4 68 B4
Lisson Gr NW8 230 B1
McMillan St SE8 141 C6
Macmillan Way SW17 181 B6
Mcmorran Ho 4 N7 72 A4
McNair Rd UB2 107 D3
Macnamara Ho SW10 266 C4
McNeil Rd SE5 139 C3
McNicol Dr NW10 89 A5
Macoma Rd SE18 145 B6
Macoma Terr SE18 145 B6
Maconochies Rd 9
E14 119 D1
Macquarie Way E14 119 D2
McRae La CR4 202 D2
Macready Ho W1 237 B3
Macready Pl 2 N7 72 A4
Macroom Ho W9 91 B4
Macroom Rd W9 91 B4
Mac's Pl EC4 241 B2
Madame Tussaud's*
NW1 93 A3 238 A5
Mada Rd BR6 226 D5
Maddams St E3 97 D3
Madderfields Ct N11 31 D2
Maddison Cl
Finchley N2 30 A1
Teddington TW11 174 D4
Maddison Ct NW4 28 C1
Maddocks Cl DA14 191 A5
Maddocks Ho 8 E1 118 B6
Maddock Way SE17 138 D6
Maddox Ct 1 E4 20 B3
Maddox St W1 248 D6
Madeira Ave BR1 186 C3
Madeira Gr IG8 37 C4
Madeira Rd
Edmonton N13 16 D1
Leytonstone E11 54 C1
Mitcham CR4 202 D5
Streatham SW16 182 A5
Madeleine Cl RM6 58 C3
Madeley Ct W5 88 A1
Madeley Rd W5 88 A1
Madeline Gr IG1 79 B3
Madeline Rd SE20 184 A3
Madge Gill Way 4 E6 100 A6
Madge Hill W7 108 C6
Madinah Rd E8 74 A3
Madingley 11 KT1 176 C1
Madingley Ct TW1 153 C6
Madison Apartments
N11 31 D3
Madison Cres DA7 146 C5
Madison Ct 15 RM10 81 D2
Madison Gdns
Beckenham BR2 208 D6
Bexley DA7 146 C5
Madison Ho E3 98 A4
Madras Ho IG1 78 D4
Madras Pl N7 72 C2
Madras Rd IG1 78 D4
Madrid Rd SW13 134 A5
Madron St
SE17 117 C1 263 B2
Mafeking Ave
Brentford TW8 132 A6
Ilford IG2 57 B2
Newham E6 100 A5
Mafeking Rd Enfield EN1 5 D2
Newham E16 98 D3
Tottenham N17 34 A1
Magdala Ave N19 71 C6
Magdala Rd
Isleworth TW7 131 A2
South Croydon CR2 221 B1
Magdalen Ct SE25 206 A4
Magdalene Cl 7 SE15 140 B3
Magdalene Gdns E6 100 C3
Magdalene Ho 7
SW15 156 D5
Magdalene Rd TW17 192 B6
Magdalen Pas E1 253 D6
Magdalen Rd SW18 158 B3
Magdalen St SE1 253 A3
Magee St SE11 138 C6
Magellan Ct 11 NW10 67 B1
Magellan Ho 16 E1 96 D3
Magellan Pl 25 E14 119 C2
Magna Ct UB6 86 B4
Magnaville Rd WD23 8 D4
Magnet Rd HA9 65 D6
Magnin Cl 5 E8 96 A6
Magnolia Cl
Kingston u T KT2 176 D4
Leyton E10 75 C6
Magnolia Ct
13 Belmont SM2 217 D1
Feltham TW14 150 A3
2 Finchley N12 29 D6
Forest Hill SE26 184 C5
Harrow HA3 44 B2
Hillingdon UB10 60 D2
Northolt UB5 85 A3
Richmond TW9 132 D4
Wallington SM6 219 B3
Wandsworth SW11 158 D5
Magnolia Gdns HA8 27 A6
Magnolia Ho 13 SE8 141 B6
Magnolia Lo E4 19 D1
Magnolia Pl
Clapham Pk SW4 160 A6
Ealing W5 87 D2
Magnolia Rd W4 132 D6
Magnolia Way KT19 215 A3
Magnolia Wharf W4 132 D6
Magpie Cl Edgware NW9 27 C1
Enfield EN1 6 A4
Forest Gate E7 76 D3
Magpie Hall Cl BR2 210 A3
Magpie Hall La BR2 210 B3
Magpie Hall Rd WD23 8 C2
Magpie Ho 7 E3 97 B6
Magpie Pl SE14 141 A6
Magri Wlk 22 E1 96 C2
Maguire Dr TW10 175 C6
Maguire St
SE1 117 D4 253 D2
Mahatma Gandhi Ind Est
1 SE24 138 D1
Mahlon Ave HA4 62 B2
Mahogany Cl SE16 119 A5
Mahon Cl EN1 5 D4
Mahoney Ho SE14 141 B4
Maida Ave Chingford E4 19 D4
Little Venice W2 92 A3 236 B5
Maida Rd DA17 125 C3
MAIDA VALE 91 D4
Maida Vale W9 92 A4 229 A1
Maida Vale Sta W9 91 D4
Maida Way E4 19 D4
Maiden Erlegh Ave
DA5 169 A3
Maiden La
Borough The
SE1 117 A5 252 B4
Camden Town NW1 71 D1
Strand WC2 116 A6 250 B6
Maiden Rd E15 76 C1
Maidenstone Hill
SE10 142 A4
Maids of Honour Row 4
TW9 153 D6
Maidstone Bldgs SE1 252 C3
Maidstone Ct N11 31 D4
Maidstone Ho 4 E14 97 D1
Maidstone Rd
Friern Barnet N11 31 D4
Ruxley DA14 191 C3
Mail Coach Yd 23 E2 95 C4
Main Ave EN1 17 D6
Main Dr HA9 65 D5
Main Rd
Chislehurst BR5 190 C1
Sidcup DA14 167 C1
Mainridge Rd BR7,
SE9 188 C6
Main St TW13 172 D5
Mainwaring Ct 3
CR4 181 A1
Main Yd E9 75 C2
Mais Ho SE26 162 B2
Maismore St SE15 140 A6
Maison Alfort HA3 24 C2
Maisonettes The SM1 217 B3
Maitland Cl
3 Greenwich SE10 141 D5
Hounslow TW4 129 B2
Maitland Ct W2 246 C6
Maitland Ho
Chelsea SW1 269 A6
16 South Hackney E2 96 C5
MAITLAND PARK 70 D2
Maitland Park Rd NW3 70 D2
Maitland Park Villas
NW3 70 D2
Maitland Pl E5 74 C4
Maitland Rd
Penge SE26 184 D4
Stratford E15 76 D2
Majendie Rd SE18 123 B1
Majestic Ct N4 50 D1
Majestic Way CR4 180 D1
Major Cl SW9 138 D2
Majorie Mews 6 E1 96 D1
Major Rd
22 Bermondsey SE16 118 A3
Stratford New Town E15 76 B3
Makepeace Ave N6 71 A6
Makepeace Mans N6 71 A6
Makepeace Rd
Northolt UB5 85 A6
Wanstead E11 55 A5
Makinen Ho 5 IG9 21 C3
Makins St SW3 257 B3
Malabar Ct 20 W12 112 B6
Malabar St E14 119 C4
Malam Ct SE11 261 A3
Malam Gdns 3 E14 119 D6
Malatia CR2 221 A2
Malay Ho 2 E1 118 C5
Malborough Ho 3 N20 14 D1
Malbrook Rd SW15 134 B1
Malbury Ct N22 32 A3
Malcolm Cl SE20 184 C3
Malcolm Cres NW4 46 A3
Malcolm Ct Ealing W5 88 B3
Hendon NW4 46 A3
Stanmore HA7 25 C5
Stratford E7 76 D2
Malcolm Dr KT6 198 A1
Malcolm Ho 18 N1 95 C5
Malcolm Pl E2 96 C3
Malcolm Prim Sch
SE20 184 C3
Malcolm Rd
Bethnal Green E1 96 C3
Croydon SE25 206 A3
Ickenham UB10 60 B4
Penge SE20 184 C3
Wimbledon SW19 179 A4
Malcolmson Ho SW1 259 D1
Malcolms Way N14 15 C6
Malcolm Way E11 55 A5
Malden Ave
Croydon SE25 206 B6
Northolt UB6 64 C2
Malden CE Prim Sch
KT4 199 C1
Malden Cres NW1 71 A2
Malden Ct
Stoke Newington N4 51 A3
West Barnes KT3 200 B6
Malden Green Ave
KT4 200 A1
Malden Hill KT3 199 D6
Malden Hill Gdns KT3 199 D6
Malden Junc KT3 199 D4
Malden Manor Prim Sch
KT3 199 C2
Malden Manor Sta
KT3 199 C2
Malden Pk KT3 199 D3
Malden Pl NW5 71 A3
Malden Rd
Camden Town NW5 71 A2
Cheam KT4, SM3 216 D4
New Malden KT3, KT4 199 D2
Malden Way KT3 200 A5
Malden Way (Kingston By
Pass) KT3, KT5 199 C4
Maldon Cl
Camberwell SE5 139 C2
Shoreditch N1 235 B6
Stratford New Town E15 76 B3
Maldon Ct Barking E6 100 C6
Wallington SM6 219 C3
Maldon Rd Acton W3 111 A6
Edmonton N9 17 D1
Wallington SM6 219 B3
Maldon Wlk IG8 37 C4
Malet Pl WC1 239 C5
Malet St WC1 93 D2 239 D4
Maley Ave SE27 160 D2
Malford Ct E18 37 A1
Malford Gr E18 54 D6
Malfort Rd SE5 139 C2
Malham Cl N11 31 A4
Malham Rd SE23 162 D3
Malham Road Ind Est
SE23 162 D3
Malindi Ct N8 49 D4
Malins Cl EN5 12 C6
Malins Ct SW12 159 A5
Mallaig Ct HA8 10 D2
Mallams Mews 1
SW9 138 D2
Mallard Cl
1 Hackney E9 75 B2
Hanwell W7 108 C4
Kilburn NW6 91 C6
New Barnet EN5 14 B5
Twickenham TW4 151 C4
Mallard Ct Chingford E4 20 B4
Ilford IG1 79 A6
Kingsbury NW9 45 A2
Little Ilford E12 78 B3
16 Richmond TW10 153 D5
Walthamstow E17 54 B6
Mallard Ho
8 Camberwell SE15 139 D4
St John's Wood NW8 230 A3
Mallard Path 3 SE28 123 B3
Mallard Pl TW1 153 A1
Mallard Point 6 E3 97 C4
Mallards E11 55 A2
Mallards Rd
Barking IG11 102 A3
Woodford IG8 37 B3
Mallard Way NW9 45 A2
Mallard Wlk
Beckenham BR3 206 D4
Sidcup DA14 190 C4
Mall Ct W5 110 A6
Mallet Dr UB5 63 B3
Mallet Ho 11 SW15 156 A6
Mallet Rd SE13 164 B5
Malling SE13 163 D6
Malling Cl CR0 206 C3
Malling Gdns SM4 202 A3
Malling Ho 9 BR3 185 C3
Malling Way BR2 208 D2
Mallinson Ct 2 E11 76 C6
Mallinson Rd
Wallington SM6 219 D5
Wandsworth SW11 158 D6
Mallon Gdns E1 243 D3
Mallord St
SW3 136 B6 266 D6
Mallory Bldgs EC1 241 C5
Mallory Cl SE4 141 A1
Mallory Gdns EN4 15 A4
Mallory St NW8 92 C3 237 B6
Mallow Cl CR0 206 D1
Mallow Ct
Colney Hatch N12 30 C4
Lewisham SE13 142 A3
Mallow Mead NW7 29 A3
Mallow St EC1 242 C6
Mallows The UB10 60 D5
Mall Rd W6 112 B1
Mall Studios 9 NW3 70 D3
Mall The
6 Bexley DA6 147 C1
Brentford TW8 131 D6
4 Bromley BR1 209 A6
Ealing W5 110 A6
Harrow HA3 44 B3
Kingston u T KT6 197 D4
Mortlake SW14 155 A6
Palmers Green N14 16 A1
St James SW1 115 D5 249 C3
Mall The (Prep Sch)
TW2 152 B1
Malmains Cl BR3 208 B5
Malmains Way BR3 208 B5
Malmesbury 30 E2 96 C5
Malmesbury Cl HA5 40 A5
Malmesbury Prim Sch
Morden SM4 202 A3
Tower Hamlets E3 97 B4
Malmesbury Rd Bow E3 97 B5
Morden SM4 202 A3
Newham E16 98 C2
Woodford E18 36 D2
Malmesbury Terr E16 98 D2
Malmsey Ho SE11 260 D2
Malmsmead Ho E9 75 A3
Malorees Jun & Inf Schs
NW6 68 D1
Malory Cl BR3 185 A1
Malpas Dr HA5 40 D4
Malpas Rd
Dagenham RM9 80 D2
Hackney E8 74 B2
New Cross SE4 141 B3
Malta Rd E10 53 C2
Malta St EC1 241 D6
Maltby Dr EN1 6 B5
Maltby Rd KT9 214 C2
Maltby St SE1 117 D3 263 C6
Maltham Terr N18 34 B4
Malthouse Dr
Chiswick W4 133 D6
Feltham TW13 172 D5
Malthouse Pas SW13 133 C3
Malthus Path 7 SE28 124 C5
Malting Ho E14 119 B6
Maltings W4 110 C1
Maltings Cl SW13 133 C3
Maltings Lo W4 133 C5
Maltings Pl
Bermondsey SE1 253 B2
Parsons Green SW6 265 D1
Maltings The BR6 211 D1
Malting Way TW7 130 D2
Malt Mill SE1 253 C3
Malton Ho SE25 205 C5
Malton Mews
1 Notting Hill W10 91 A1
Plumstead Comm SE18 145 C6
Malton Rd W10 91 A1
Malton St SE18 145 C6
Maltravers St WC2 251 A6
Malt St SE1 140 A6
Malva Cl SW18 157 D6
Malvern Ave
Chingford E4 36 B3
Erith DA7 147 A5
Harrow HA2 63 B5
Malvern Cl Bushey WD23 8 A5
Ickenham UB10 60 C6
Mitcham CR4 203 C6
Notting Hill W10 91 B2
Penge SE20 184 A1
Surbiton KT6 198 A1
Malvern Ct
Belmont SM2 217 C1
5 East Barnet N20 14 C2
15 Shepherd's Bush
W12 112 A4
South Kensington SW7 256 D4
3 Surbiton KT6 198 A1
Malvern Dr
Feltham TW13 172 D5
Ilford IG3 79 D4
Woodford IG8 37 C6
Malvern Gdns
Cricklewood NW2 69 A6
Harrow HA3 44 A5
Malvern Ho London N16 51 D1
SE17 262 B1
Malvern Lo N12 30 B6
Malvern Mews NW6 91 C4
Malvern Pl NW6 91 B4
Malvern Rd Dalston E8 74 A1
Enfield EN3 7 A6
Hampton TW12 173 C3
Harlington UB3 127 C5
Hornsey N8 50 C6
Leytonstone E11 76 D6
Maida Vale NW6 91 C4
Newham E6 100 A6
Surbiton KT6 198 A1
Thornton Heath CR7 204 C5
Tottenham Hale N17 52 A6
Upper Holloway N19 49 D1
Malvern Terr
Edmonton N9 17 D3
Islington N1 234 A6
Malvern Way W13 87 B2
Malwood Rd SW12 159 B5
Malyons Rd SE13 163 D6
Malyons Terr SE13 163 D6
Malyons The TW17 193 B3
Managers St 8 E14 120 A5
Manatee Pl SM6 219 D5
Manaton Cl SE15 140 B2
Manaton Cres UB1 85 C1
Manbey Gr E15 76 C2
Manbey Park Rd E15 76 C2
Manbey Rd E15 76 C2
Manbey St E15 76 C2
Manbre Rd W6 134 C6
Manbrough Ave E6 100 C4
Manchester Ct E16 99 B1
Manchester Dr W10 91 A3
Manchester Gr E14 120 A1
Manchester Ho SE17 262 B2
Manchester Mans N19 49 D2
Manchester Mews W1 238 A3
Manchester Rd
Cubitt Town E14 120 A3
South Norwood CR7 205 A6
Tottenham N15 51 B3
Manchester Sq
W1 93 A1 238 B2
Manchester St
W1 93 A2 238 A3
Manchester Way RM10 81 D4
Manchuria Rd SW11 159 A5
Manciple St
SE1 117 B3 262 D6
Mandalay Ho 6 N16 73 B4
Mandalay Rd SW4 159 C6
Mandarin Ct
6 Deptford SE8 141 C6
Willesden NW10 67 B2
Mandarin Way UB4 84 D1
Mandela Cl
36 Shepherd's Bush
W12 112 B6
Stonebridge NW10 67 A1
Mandela Ho
Plumstead Comm
SE18 145 B6
18 Spitalfields E2 95 D4
Mandela Rd E16 99 A1
Mandela St
Camden Town
NW1 93 C6 232 B6
Mandela St *continued*
Kennington SW9 138 C5
Mandela Way
SE1 117 C2 263 B4
Manderville Ho SE1 263 D2
Mandeville Cl
5 Greenwich SE3 142 D5
Merton SW19 179 A2
Mandeville Ct
Hampstead NW3 69 D3
Highams Pk E4 35 A6
Mandeville Ctyd SW11 268 A1
Mandeville Dr KT6 197 D1
Mandeville Ho 8
SW4 159 C6
Mandeville Pl W1 238 B2
Mandeville Prim Sch
E5 74 D5
Mandeville Rd
Enfield EN3 7 A6
Isleworth TW7 131 A3
Littleton TW17 192 C4
Northolt UB5 63 C1
Osidge N14 15 C2
Mandeville Sch UB5 63 B2
Mandeville St E5 75 A5
Mandrake Rd SW17 158 D1
Mandrake Way 7 E15 76 C1
Mandrell Rd SW2 160 A6
Manesty Ct N14 15 D4
Manette St W1 239 D1
Manfred Ct 7 SW15 157 B6
Manfred Rd SW15 157 B6
Manger Rd N7 72 A2
Mangold Way 4
DA18 125 A3
Manilla Ct RM6 58 B3
Manilla St E14 119 C4
Manister Rd SE2 124 A3
Manitoba Ct 29 SE16 118 C4
Manitoba Gdns 6
BR6 227 D2
Manley Ct N16 73 D5
Manley Ho SE11 261 A2
Manley St NW1 231 A6
Manly Dixon Dr EN3 7 A6
Mann Cl 3 CR0 221 A5
Manneby Prior N1 233 D3
Mannering Ho 16
SW2 160 B6
Manning Ct 3 SE28 124 B5
Manningford Cl EC1 234 C2
Manning Gdns HA3 43 D2
Manning Ho
3 Notting Hill W11 91 A1
6 Walthamstow E17 54 A6
Manning Pl TW10 154 B5
Manning Rd
Dagenham RM10 81 C1
Walthamstow E17 53 A4
Manningtree Cl SW19 157 A3
Manningtree Rd HA4 62 B4
Manningtree St 2 E1 96 A1
Mannin Rd RM6 58 B2
Mannock Mews IG8 37 B2
Mannock Rd N22 50 D6
Mann's Cl TW7 152 D6
Manns Rd HA8 26 C4
Manny Shinwell Ho
SW6 264 D5
Manoel Rd TW2 152 A2
Manor Ave
Hounslow TW4 128 D3
New Cross SE4 141 B3
Northolt UB5 63 B1
Manorbrook SE12, SE3 143 A1
Manor Circus TW9 132 C2
Manor Cl Barnet EN5 1 A1
Edgware NW7 27 B5
Higham Hill E17 35 A1
Kingsbury NW9 44 D4
New Malden KT4 199 C1
Ruislip HA4 39 D1
Thamesmead SE28 102 C1
Manor Cottages App
N2 30 A1
Manor Cotts N2 30 A1
Manor Court Lo 12 E18 37 A2
Manor Court Rd W7 108 C6
Manor Cres KT5 198 C3
Manor Croft HA8 26 C4
Manor Ct
4 Barking IG11 79 D1
7 Brixton SW2 160 B6
Camberwell SE15 139 D4
Chingford E4 20 C3
Fortis Green N2 48 D4
Friern Barnet N20 14 D1
Gunnersbury W3 110 C2
5 Hackbridge SM6 219 A5
Harrow HA1 42 D3
Kingston u T KT2 176 C2
Osidge N14 15 D2
Parsons Green SW6 265 D1
Streatham SW16 160 A1
Surbiton KT5 198 C3
8 Sutton SM1 218 A4
Twickenham TW2 152 A2
Walthamstow E10 53 D1
5 Wembley HA9 66 A3
Manordene Cl KT7 197 A1
Manordene Rd SE28 102 D1
Manor Dr
East Barnet N14 15 B3
Edgware NW7 27 B5
Feltham TW13 172 D5
Friern Barnet N20 14 D1

Manor Dr *continued*
Hinchley Wood KT10 213 A5
Sunbury TW16 172 A1
Surbiton KT5 198 C3
Wembley HA9 66 B4
West Ewell KT19 215 C2
Manor Dr N KT3, KT4 199 B2
Manor Dr The KT4 199 D1
Manor Farm Ave
TW17 192 D3
Manor Farm Cl KT4 199 C1
Manor Farm Ct E6 100 B4
Manor Farm Dr E4 20 C1
Manor Farm Rd
Thornton Heath CR7,
SW16 182 C1
Wembley HA0 87 D5
Manorfield Cl 3 N19 71 C4
Manorfield Prim Sch
E14 97 D2
Manorfields Cl BR7 211 D6
Manor Gate UB5 63 A1
Manorgate Rd KT2 176 C2
Manor Gdns
8 Chiswick W4 111 C1
Clapham SW4 137 C3
Gunnersbury W3 110 C2
Hampton TW12 174 A3
Merton SW20 179 B1
Richmond TW10, TW9 132 B1
Ruislip HA4 62 C3
South Croydon CR2 221 D2
Sunbury TW16 172 A1
Upper Holloway N7 72 A5
Manor Gr
Beckenham BR3 185 D1
Deptford SE15 140 C6
Richmond TW9 132 C2
Manor Gt SW15 157 A6
Manor Hall Ave NW4 28 D1
Manor Hall Dr NW4 28 D1
Manor Hall Gdns E10 53 C1
Manor Ho
Brentford TW8 109 C1
Manor Pk E12 77 D4
Osidge N14 15 D3
Paddington NW1 237 B4
Twickenham TW2 152 C2
Wallington SM6 219 B3
Manor Ho The
Bexley DA5 169 D3
Chislehurst SE9 188 A5
Manor House Ct
Lower Halliford
TW17 192 D2
Paddington W9 236 A5
Manor House Dr NW6 68 D1
Manor House Est HA7 25 B5
Manor House Gdns E11 55 B3
Manor House Sta N4 50 D1
Manor House Way
TW7 131 B2
Manor Jun & Inf Schs
IG11 79 D2
Manor La
Feltham TW13 150 A2
Harlington UB3 127 B6
Hither Green SE12 164 C5
Sunbury TW16 172 B1
Sutton SM1 218 A3
Manor Lane Terr
SE13 164 C6
Manor Lo NW2 68 D2
Manor Mans
7 Hampstead NW3 70 C2
Tufnell Pk N7 72 A5
Manor Mead Sch
TW17 192 D4
Manor Mews
New Cross SE4 141 B3
Paddington NW6 91 C5
Manor Mount SE23 162 C3
Manor Oak Mans
SE22 162 B5
Manor Par Harrow HA1 42 D3
Stoke Newington N16 73 D6
MANOR PARK 78 A4
Manor Park Cl BR4 207 D1
Manor Park Cres HA8 26 C4
Manor Park Dr HA2 41 D6
Manor Park Gdns HA8 26 C4
Manor Park Par SE13 142 B1
Manor Park Prim Sch
SM1 218 A3
Manor Park Rd
Chislehurst BR7 189 B2
Dagenham NW10 89 D6
East Finchley N2 48 B6
Manor Pk E12 77 D4
Sutton SM1 218 A3
West Wickham BR4 207 D1
Manor Park Sta E12 77 D4
Manor Pk
Chislehurst BR7 189 B2
Lewisham SE13 164 C6
Richmond TW9 132 B1
Manor Pl
Chislehurst BR7 189 B1
East Bedfont TW14 150 A3
Mitcham CR4 203 C6
Newington
SE17 117 A1 262 A2
Sutton SM1 217 D4
Walton-on-T KT12 194 A2
Manor Prim Sch E15 98 C5
Manor Rd
Ashford TW15 170 C5

Manor Rd *continued*
Barking IG11 79 D2
Barnet EN5 1 A1
Beckenham BR3 185 D1
Belmont SM2 217 B1
Bowes Pk N22 32 A4
Dagenham RM6 58 D3
Ealing W13 109 A6
East Molesey KT8 196 B5
Enfield EN2 5 B3
Harrow HA1 43 A3
Hayes UB3 84 A1
Higham Hill E17 35 A1
Loughton IG10 21 B5
Merton SW20 179 B1
Mitcham CR4 203 C6
Newham E15, E16 98 C4
Old Bexley DA5 169 D3
Richmond TW10, TW9 132 B1
Ruislip HA4 39 B1
Sidcup DA15 168 A1
South Norwood SE25 206 A6
Stamford Hill N16 51 C1
Teddington TW11 175 B5
Tottenham N17 34 B2
Twickenham TW2 152 B2
Wallington SM5, SM6 219 B3
Walthamstow E10 53 C2
Walton-on-T KT12 193 D2
West Wickham BR4 223 D6
Manor Rd N
Hinchley Wood KT7 213 A6
Wallington SM5, SM6 219 B4
Manor Rd S KT10 212 C4
Manor Road Ho HA1 43 A3
Manor Sch NW10 90 C6
Manorside EN5 1 A1
Manorside Cl SE2 124 D2
Manorside Prim Sch
N3 30 A2
Manor Sq RM8 80 C6
Manor Street Est SW3 267 B6
Manor The
Dulwich SE23 162 C4
Mayfair W1 248 C5
Manor Vale TW8 109 C1
Manor View N3 29 D1
Manorway Enfield EN1 17 C4
Woodford IG8 37 C5
Manor Way
Beckenham BR3 207 C6
Bromley BR2 210 A3
Chingford E4 36 B6
Colindale NW9 45 C5
Greenwich SE3 143 A1
Gunnersbury W3 110 C2
Harrow HA2 41 D5
Mitcham CR4 203 C6
New Malden KT4 199 D1
Orpington BR5 211 A5
Ruislip HA4 39 D1
Sidcup DA5 169 C3
Southall UB2 106 D2
South Croydon CR2 221 D2
Manor Waye UB8 82 A6
Manor Way The SM6 219 B4
Manpreet Ct E12 78 B3
Manray Ct 2 N8 50 A4
Manresa Rd
SW3 114 C1 257 A1
Mansard Beeches
SW17 181 A5
Mansard Cl HA5 40 D6
Mansard Manor 4
SM2 218 A1
Manse Cl UB3 127 B6
Manse Ct DA14 190 C5
Mansel Ct SW11 267 B1
Mansel Gr E17 35 C2
Mansell Ho SW8 269 B2
Mansell Rd Acton W3 111 B4
Southall UB6 85 D2
Mansell St E1 95 D1 243 D1
Mansel Rd SW19 179 B4
Manse Rd N16 73 D5
Mansergh Cl SE18 144 A5
Mansfield Ave
East Barnet EN4 15 A5
Ruislip HA4 40 B1
Tottenham N15 51 B5
Mansfield Cl N9 18 A5
Mansfield Ct 27 E2 95 D6
Mansfield Dr UB4 83 C3
Mansfield Hill E4 19 D3
Mansfield Ho SW15 156 D5
Mansfield Hts N2 48 D4
Mansfield Mews W1 238 C3
Mansfield Pl 28 NW3 70 A4
Mansfield Rd Acton W3 88 D3
Chessington KT9 213 D3
Ilford IG1 78 C6
Maitland Pk NW3 70 D4
South Croydon CR2 221 B2
Walthamstow E17 53 B5
Wanstead E11 55 B3
Mansfield St
W1 93 B2 238 C3
Mansford St E2 96 A5
Manship Rd CR4 181 A2
Mansion Cl SW9 138 C4
Mansion Gdns NW3 69 D5
Mansion Ho★ EC4 242 C1
Mansion House Pl EC3,
EC4 242 C1
Mansion House St EC2 242 C1
Mansion House Sta
EC4 117 A6 252 B6
Mansions The NW6 69 B3
Manson Mews
SW7 114 B2 256 C3

Manson Pl
SW7 114 B2 256 C3
Manstead Gdns RM6 58 C2
Manston
Camden Town NW1 71 C1
Tottenham N17 33 B1
Manston Ave UB2 107 C2
Manston Cl SE20 184 C2
Manstone Rd NW2 69 A3
Manston Gr KT2 175 D5
Manston Ho W14 254 B5
Mantell Ho SW4 159 C6
Manthorpe Rd SE18 123 A1
Mantilla Rd SW17 181 A6
Mantle Rd SE4 141 A2
Mantlet Cl SW16 181 C3
Mantle Way E15 76 C1
Manton Ave W7 109 A4
Manton Cl UB3 105 C6
Manton Ho N16 73 B5
Manton Rd Holdbrook EN3 7 C5
Plumstead SE2 124 A2
Mantua St 23 SW11 136 B2
Mantus Cl
Bethnal Green E1 96 C3
19 Stepney E1 96 C3
Mantus Rd E1 96 C3
Manus Way N20 14 A3
Manville Gdns SW17 159 B1
Manville Rd SW17 159 B1
Manwood Rd SE4 163 B5
Manwood St E16 122 B5
Manygate La TW17 193 A3
Many Gates SW12 159 B2
Mapesbury Ct NW2 69 A3
Mapesbury Mews 1
NW9 46 A3
Mapesbury Rd NW2 69 A2
Mapeshill Pl NW2 68 C2
Mapes Ho 7 NW6 69 A1
Mape St E2 96 B3
Maple Ave
East Acton W3 111 C5
Harrow HA2 63 D6
Walthamstow E4 35 B4
Yiewsley UB7 104 B6
Maple Cl
Buckhurst Hill IG9 21 D1
Clapham Pk SW4 159 D5
Finchley N3 29 C4
Hampton TW12 173 B4
Hayes UB4 84 D4
Mitcham CR4 181 B2
Petts Wood BR5 211 B4
Ruislip HA4 40 B3
South Tottenham N16 52 A3
Maple Cres DA15 168 A5
Maplecroft Cl E6 100 A1
Maple Ct Ashford TW15 171 B3
Catford SE6 163 D3
2 Croydon CR0 221 A4
7 Dagenham RM8 58 D2
Kingston u T KT3 199 B6
Newham E6 100 C2
6 Pinner HA5 22 C1
Sidcup DA14 190 B5
11 West Norwood
SW16 182 C5
3 Willesden NW2 68 D4
Mapledale Ave CR0 222 A5
Mapledene BR7 189 A5
Mapledene Est E8 74 A1
Mapledene Rd E8 74 A1
Mapledown Sch NW2 46 C2
Mapledurham Ct 3
N13 32 C6
Maple Gdns
Grahame Pk HA8 27 C3
Stanwell TW19 148 A2
Maple Gr
Brentford TW8 131 B5
Ealing W5 109 D3
Kingsbury NW9 45 A2
Southall UB1 85 B2
Maple Gr Bsns Ctr
TW4 128 C1
Maple Ho
2 Kingston u T KT6 198 A4
11 Maitland Pk NW3 70 D2
5 New Cross SE8 141 B5
4 Richmond TW9 132 D4
Teddington KT1 175 C3
13 Walthamstow E17 53 D6
Maplehurst 2 BR2 186 C1
Maplehurst Cl KT1 198 A5
Maple Ind Est TW13 150 A1
Maple Inf Sch KT6 197 D4
Maple Leaf Dr DA15 167 D3
Mapleleafe Gdns IG6 56 D6
Maple Leaf Sq 27
SE16 118 D4
Maple Lo
Buckhurst Hill IG9 21 D3
Putney SW15 157 A5
Welsh Harp NW9 67 B6
Maple Mews
Paddington NW6 91 D5
Streatham SW16 182 B5
Maple Pl
Marylebone W1 239 B5
Tottenham N17 34 A3
Yiewsley UB7 104 B6
Maple Rd Hayes UB4 84 D4
Kingston u T KT6 197 D4
Leytonstone E11 54 C3
Penge SE20 184 C2
Maples Pl E1 96 B2
Maple St
5 Bethnal Green E2 96 B5
Fitzrovia W1 93 C3 239 B5

Maplestead Rd
Dagenham RM9 102 B6
Streatham SW2 160 B4
Maples The 4 KT1 175 C3
Maplethorpe Rd CR7 204 D5
Mapleton Cl BR2 209 A3
Mapleton Cres
Enfield EN3 6 C5
Wandsworth SW18 157 D5
Mapleton Rd
Chingford E4 20 A1
Enfield EN1 6 B3
Wandsworth SW18 157 D5
Maple Tree Pl 7 SE3 144 A4
Maple Way TW13 150 B1
Maple Wlk W10 90 D3
Maplin Cl N21 16 B5
Maplin Ho 7 SE2 124 D4
Maplin Rd E16 99 B1
Maplin St E3 97 B4
Mapperley Cl 3 E11 55 A3
Mapperley Dr IG8 36 C3
Marabou Cl E12 78 A3
Marada Ho NW6 69 A1
Marais W4 133 A5
Maran Way DA18 124 D3
Marathon Way SE28 123 D4
Marban Rd W9 91 B4
Marble Arch★
W1 114 D6 247 D6
Marble Arch Sta
W1 92 D1 237 D1
Marble Cl W3 110 D5
Marble Dr NW2 46 D2
Marbleford Ct 4 N6 49 D2
Marble Hill★ TW1 153 C4
Marble Hill Cl TW1 153 B4
Marble Hill Gdns TW1 153 B4
Marble Ho
Paddington W9 91 B3
Plumstead Comm SE18 123 D1
Marble Quay SE1 118 A5
Marbrook Ct SE12 165 C1
Marcella Rd SW9 138 C3
Marcellina Way BR6 227 D5
March 23 NW9 27 D2
Marchant Ho 13 SW2 160 B6
Marchant Rd E11 76 B6
Marchant St SE14 141 A6
Marchbank Rd
W14 135 B6 264 D6
March Ct SW15 134 B1
Marchmont Ho 10
SW16 181 C5
Marchmont Rd
Richmond TW10 154 B6
Wallington SM6 219 C1
Marchmont St
WC1 94 A3 240 A6
March Rd 7 TW1 153 A4
Marchside Cl TW5 128 D4
Marchwood Cl 9 SE5 139 C5
Marchwood Cres W5 87 D1
Marcia Rd SE1 117 C2 263 B3
Marcilly Rd SW18 158 B6
Marcol Ho W1 238 D2
Marcon Ct 29 E8 74 B3
Marconi Pl N11 31 B6
Marconi Rd E10 53 C1
Marconi Way UB1 85 D1
Marcon Pl E8 74 B3
Marco Rd W6 112 C3
Marcourt Lawns W5 88 A3
Marcus Ct
Brentford TW8 132 A5
Newham E15 98 C6
Marcus Garvey Mews
SE22 162 B6
Marcus Garvey Way 9
SE24 138 C1
Marcus Ho 14 SE15 139 D4
Marcus St
Wandsworth SW18 157 D5
West Ham E15 98 D6
Marcus Terr SW18 157 D5
Mardale Ct NW7 28 A3
Mardale Dr NW9 45 B4
Mardell Rd CR0 206 D4
Marden Ave BR2 209 A3
Marden Cres CR0 204 B3
Marden Ho 6 E8 74 B3
Marden Rd
Thornton Heath CR0 204 B3
Tottenham N17 33 C1
Marden Sq SE16 118 B3
Marder Rd W13 109 A4
Mardon HA5 23 B3
Mardyke Ho SE17 262 D4
Marechal Niel Ave
DA15 167 B1
Marechal Niel Par
DA15 167 B1
Maresby Ho E4 19 D2
Maresfield CR0 221 C5
Maresfield Gdns NW3 70 A2
Mare St E8 74 B1
Marey Ct 10 CR2 221 A3
Marfleet Cl SM5 218 C6
Margaret Ave E4 19 D5
Margaret Bondfield Ave
IG11 80 A1
Margaret Bondfield Ho
5 Bow E3 97 A5
22 Kentish Town N7 71 D3
Margaret Ct Barnet EN4 2 B1
Marylebone W1 239 A2
Margaret Gardner Dr
SE9 166 B2
Margaret Herbison Ho
SW6 264 D5

Margaret Hill Ho 1 N8 50 A4
Margaret Ho
16 Hammersmith W6 112 C1
2 Sutton SM1 217 D5
Margaret Ingram Cl
SW6 264 C5
Margaret Lockwood Cl
KT5 198 B5
Margaret Mcmillan Ho 10
N19 49 D2
Margaret Rd Barnet EN4 2 B1
Bexley DA5 168 D5
Stamford Hill N16 51 D1
Margarets Ct HA8 26 D5
Margaret's Ct E11 54 B2
Margaret St W1 93 C1 239 A2
Margaretta Terr
SW3 136 C6 267 B6
Margaretting Rd E12 55 C1
Margaret Way IG4 56 A3
Margaret White Ho
NW1 232 C2
Margate Rd SW2 160 A6
Margery Fry Ct N7 72 A5
Margery Park Rd E7 77 A2
Margery Rd RM8 80 D5
Margery St WC1 94 C4 234 A1
Margin Dr SW19 178 D6
Margravine Gdns
Hammersmith W6 112 D1
West Kensington W14 254 A2
Margravine Rd
W6 135 A6 264 A6
Marham Gdns
Morden SM4 202 A3
Wandsworth SW17,
SW18 158 C3
Mar Ho 4 SE7 143 C6
Maria Cl 13 SE1 118 A2
Maria Fidelis Convent Sch
(Lower) NW1 93 C4 232 B1
Maria Fidelis Convent Sch
(Upper) NW1 93 D4 232 C2
Marian Cl UB4 84 D3
Marian Ct Hackney E9 74 C3
1 Sutton SM1 217 D3
Marian Lo 5 SW20 178 D3
Marian Pl E2 96 B5
Marian Rd SW16 181 C2
Marian Sq E2 96 B5
Marian St 2 E2 96 B5
Marian Vian Prim Sch
BR3 207 A4
Marian Way NW10 67 D1
Maria Terr E1 96 D3
Maria Theresa Cl KT3 199 B4
Maribor 13 SE10 142 A5
Maricas Ave HA3 24 B2
Marie Curie SE5 139 C4
Marie Lloyd Ct 13
SW9 138 B1
Marie Lloyd Gdns 1
N19 50 A2
Marie Lloyd Ho N1 235 C3
Marien Ct E4 36 B5
Marie Stopes Ct 3
N19 50 A2
Marigold Cl UB1 107 A6
Marigold Rd N17 34 C3
Marigold St SE16 118 B4
Marigold Way CR0 206 D1
Marilea Ct W5 109 D4
Marillic Ho NW7 28 C6
Marina App UB4 85 A2
Marina Ave KT3 200 B4
Marina Cl 1 BR2 209 A6
Marina Ct 12 Bow E3 97 C4
Greenford UB6 85 D5
Marina Dr DA16 145 C3
Marina Gdns RM7 59 D4
Marina Pl KT1 175 D2
Marina Point 4 E14 119 D3
Marina Way TW11 175 D3
Marine Dr
Barking IG11 102 B4
5 Woolwich SE18 122 B2
Marinefield Rd SW6 135 D3
Marinel Ho 25 SE5 139 A5
Mariner Gdns TW10 153 C1
Mariner Rd E12 78 C4
Mariners Mews E14 120 B2
Marine St SE16 118 A3
Marine Twr 20 SE8 141 B6
Marion Ave TW17 192 D4
Marion Ct 4 SW17 180 C5
Marion Gr IG8 36 C6
Marion Rd Mill Hill NW7 28 A5
Thornton Heath CR0 205 B4
Marion Richardson Prim
Sch E1 96 D1
Marischal Rd SE13 142 B2
Maritime Ho
5 Clapham SW4 137 C2
14 Woolwich SE18 122 D2
Maritime Ind Est SE7 121 B2
Maritime Quay 5 E14 119 C1
Maritime St E3 97 B3
Marius Mans 3 SW17 159 A2
Marius Rd SW17 159 A2
Marjorie Gr SW11 136 D1
Marjorie McClure Sch
BR7 189 A2
Marjory Kinnon Sch
TW14 149 C6
Markab Rd HA6 22 A5
Mark Ave E4 19 D5
Mark Cl
Bexleyheath DA7 147 A4
Keston Mark BR2 226 A4
Southall UB1 107 D5

Markeston Gn WD19 22 D6
Market Ct W1 239 A2
Market Ctr The UB2 106 B2
Market La
Burnt Oak HA8 27 A2
Shepherd's Bush W12 112 C4
Market Mews
W1 115 B5 248 C3
Market Par
Croydon SE25 206 A5
1 Edmonton N9 18 A2
Feltham TW13 151 A2
Leyton E10 53 D3
Walthamstow E17 53 B6
Market Pavilion E10 75 C5
Market Pl 3 Acton W3 111 A5
1 Bermondsey SE16 118 B2
2 Bexleyheath DA6 147 C1
Brentford TW8 131 C5
East Finchley N2 48 C6
Enfield EN2 5 B2
Kingston u T KT1 175 D1
Marylebone W1 239 A2
Market Pl The NW11 47 D5
Market Rd Barnsbury N7 72 A2
Richmond TW9 132 C2
Market Sq
Bromley BR1 187 A1
Poplar E14 97 D1
Market Sq The N9 18 B2
Market St
Spitalfields E1 243 C4
Wallend E6 100 C5
Woolwich SE18 122 C2
Market Studios 14
W12 112 C4
Market The SM1, SM5 202 A1
Market Way Poplar E14 97 D1
2 Wembley HA0 66 A3
Market Yd Mews SE1 263 A6
Markfield Beam Engine &
Mus★ N15 52 A4
Markfield Gdns E4 19 D4
Markfield Ho N15 52 A4
Markfield Rd N15 52 A4
Markham Ct NW4 46 C6
Markham Ho
1 Dagenham RM10 81 C5
9 Dulwich SE21 183 C6
Markham Pl SW3 257 C2
Markham Sq
SW3 114 D1 257 C2
Markham St
SW3 114 C1 257 B2
Mark Ho 3 E2 96 D5
Markhole Cl TW12 173 B3
Markhouse Ave E17 53 A3
Markhouse Pas E17 53 B3
Markhouse Rd E17 53 B3
Mark La EC3 117 C6 253 B6
Markland Ho W10 112 D6
Mark Lo 3 EN4 2 C1
Markmanor Ave E17 53 B2
Mark Mans W12 112 A4
Mark Rd N22 32 D1
Marksbury Ave TW9 132 C2
Marks Gate Jun & Inf Schs
RM6 59 A6
Mark Sq EC2 243 A6
Mark St Broadgate EC2 243 A6
Stratford E15 76 C1
Markstone Ho SE1 251 C1
Mark Wade Cl E12 55 D1
Markway The TW16 172 C1
Markwell Cl SE26 184 B6
Markyate Ho 6 W10 90 C3
Markyate Rd RM8 80 B3
Marland Ho SW1 257 D6
Marlands Rd IG5 56 B6
Marlang Ct BR3 186 B2
Marlborough
11 Putney SW19 156 D3
St John's Wood W9 229 A2
Marlborough Ave
Edgware HA8 10 D1
3 Hackney E8 96 A6
New Southgate N14 15 C1
Ruislip HA4 39 B3
Marlborough Cl
Broom Hill BR6 211 D3
Friern Barnet N20 14 D1
Mitcham SW19 180 C4
Newington SE17 261 D3
Marlborough Cres
Bedford Pk W4 111 C3
Harlington UB3 127 B5
Marlborough Ct
6 Beckenham BR3 185 C2
7 Bromley BR1 186 D3
7 Buckhurst Hill IG9 21 C2
Harrow HA1 42 B5
Kensington W8 255 A4
Marylebone W1 239 A1
Wallington SM6 219 C1
Marlborough Day Hospl
NW8 92 A5 229 A4
Marlborough Dr IG5 56 A6
Marlborough Flats
SW3 257 B4
Marlborough Fst & Mid
Sch HA1 42 C5
Marlborough Gdns
Friern Barnet N20 14 D1
Surbiton KT6 197 D2
Marlborough Gr SE1 118 A1
Marlborough Hill
Harrow HA1 42 C5
St John's Wood
NW8 92 A6 229 B5

Mar–May 345

Marlborough Ho
Marylebone NW1 ..... 238 D6
Richmond TW10 .... 154 C6
Stoke Newington N4 ..... 51 A1
Marlborough Ho SW1 . 249 B3
Marlborough Ho
SW19 .... 156 D1
Marlborough La SE7 ... 143 C5
Marlborough Lo
36 Stepney E1 .... 96 C3
St John's Wood NW8 .. 229 A3
Marlborough Mans 5
NW6 .... 69 C3
Marlborough Mews 18
SW2 .... 138 B1
Marlborough Par 1
UB10 .... 82 D3
Marlborough Park Ave
DA15 .... 168 A3
Marlborough Pl
NW8 .... 92 A5 229 B4
Marlborough Prim Sch
Chelsea SW3 .. 114 C2 257 B3
Isleworth TW7 .... 131 A4
Marlborough Rd
Acton Green W4 .... 111 A1
Ashford TW15 .... 170 A5
Bexley DA7 .... 146 D2
Bowes Pk N22 .... 32 B4
Brentford TW7 .... 131 B5
Bromley BR2 .... 209 C5
Chingford E4 .... 35 D4
Dagenham RM8 .... 80 C4
Ealing W5 .... 109 D4
Edmonton N9 .... 18 A3
Feltham TW13 .... 150 D2
Hampton TW12 .... 173 C4
Hillingdon UB10 .... 82 D4
Leyton E15 .... 76 C4
Mitcham SW19 .... 180 C4
Richmond TW10 .... 154 B5
Romford RM7 .... 59 D5
Southall UB2 .... 106 C3
South Croydon CR2 ..... 221 A1
St James SW1 .. 115 C5 249 B3
Sutton SM1 .... 217 C6
Upper Holloway N19 ..... 72 A6
Upton E7 .... 77 C1
Wanstead E18 .... 55 A6
Woolwich SE18 .... 123 A3
Marlborough Sch
DA15 .... 168 A4
Marlborough St
SW3 .... 114 C2 257 B3
Marlborough Trad Est
TW9 .... 132 D4
Marlborough Yd N19 .... 71 D6
Marlbury NW8 .... 91 D6
Marler Rd SE23 .... 163 B3
Marlesford Ct SM6 ..... 219 C4
Marlex Lo N3 .... 29 D2
Marley Ave DA7 .... 146 D6
Marley Cl Harringay N15 .. 50 D5
Southall UB6 .... 85 C4
Marley Ho 14 W11 ..... 112 D6
Marley Wlk NW2 .... 68 C3
Marl Field Cl KT4 ...... 200 A1
Marlfield Ct KT3 .... 199 D2
Marlin Cl TW16 .... 171 C4
Marlin Ct 5 DA14 ...... 190 A6
Marling Ct TW12 .... 173 B4
Marlingdene Cl TW12 .. 173 C4
Marlings Cl BR7 .... 211 C5
Marlings Park Ave
BR7 .... 211 C6
Marlin Ho SW15 .... 157 A6
Marlins Cl 3 SM1 ...... 218 A3
Marloes Cl HA0 .... 65 D4
Marloes Rd
W8 .... 113 D3 255 C5
Marlow Cl SE20 .... 206 B6
Marlow Cres TW1 ...... 152 D5
Marlow Ct
Colindale NW9 .... 45 D6
1 Ealing W7 .... 108 C5
6 Finchley N3 .... 29 C2
Harrow HA1 .... 42 A3
Osidge N14 .... 15 C4
Willesden NW6 .... 68 D1
Marlow Dr SM3 .... 216 D5
Marlowe Bsns Ctr 2
SE14 .... 141 A5
Marlowe Cl BR7 .... 189 B4
Marlowe Ct
Chelsea SW3 .... 257 B3
2 Dulwich SE19 .... 183 D5
6 Kingston u T KT2 .... 175 D6
Marlowe Gdns SE9 ..... 166 C5
Marlowe Ho
Kingston u T KT1 ...... 197 D5
15 Stoke Newington N16 . 73 C4
Marlowe Lo CR0 .... 223 A6
Marlowe Rd E17 .... 54 A5
Marlowe Sq CR4 .... 203 C5
Marlowes The
NW8 .... 92 B6 229 C6
Marlowe Way CR0 ..... 220 A6
Marlow Gdns UB3 ...... 105 B3
Marlow Ho
Bermondsey SE1 ...... 263 C6
15 Kensington W2 ...... 91 D1
44 Spitalfields E2 ...... 95 D4
Teddington TW11 ...... 175 A6
Wallington CR0 .... 220 A5
Marlow Rd Newham E6 .. 100 B4
Penge SE20 .... 184 B1
Southall UB2 .... 107 B3
Marlow Studio Workshops
48 E2 .... 95 D4
Marlow Way SE16 ...... 118 D4
Marl Rd SW18 .... 136 A1
Marlston NW1 .... 231 D1
Marlton St SE10 .... 120 D1
Marlwood Cl DA15 ..... 167 C2
Marmadon Rd SE18,
SE2 .... 123 D2
Marmara Apts 4 E16 .. 121 A6
Marmion App E4 .... 35 C6
Marmion Ave E4 .... 35 B6
Marmion Cl E4 .... 35 B6
Marmion Ho 13 SW12 .. 159 B4
Marmion Mews 4
SW11 .... 137 A2
Marmion Rd SW11 ..... 137 A1
Marmont Rd SE15 ...... 140 A5
Marmora Ho E1 .... 97 A2
Marmora Rd SE22 ...... 162 C5
Marmot Rd TW4 .... 128 D2
Marncrest Ct KT5 ...... 198 B4
Marne Ave
Friern Barnet N11 .... 31 B6
Welling DA16 .... 146 A2
Marnell Way TW4 ...... 128 D2
Marner Prim Sch E3 .... 97 D3
Marne St W10 .... 91 A4
Marney Rd SW11 ...... 137 A1
Marnfield Cres SW2 ... 160 B3
Marnham Ave NW2 ...... 69 A4
Marnham Cres UB6 ..... 85 D5
Marnham Ct HA0 .... 65 C3
Marnie Ct 11 E11 .... 76 C6
Marnock Ho SE17 ...... 262 C2
Marnock Rd SE4 .... 163 B6
Maroon St E14 .... 97 A2
Maroons Way SE6 ..... 185 C5
Marqueen Twrs 1
SW16 .... 182 B3
Marquess Rd N1 .... 73 B2
Marquess Rd N N1 ...... 73 B2
Marquess Rd S 22 N1 ... 73 A2
Marquis Cl HA0 .... 66 B1
Marquis Ct Barking IG11 . 79 C3
Finsbury Pk N4 .... 50 B1
1 Kingston u T KT1 .... 198 A5
Stanwell TW19 .... 148 A3
Marquis Rd
Bowes Pk N22 .... 32 B4
Finsbury Pk N4 .... 50 C1
Kentish Town NW1 ...... 71 D2
Marrabon Cl DA15 ..... 168 A3
Marrick Cl SW15 ...... 134 A1
Marrick Ho 19 NW6 ..... 91 D6
Marrilyne Ave EN3 .... 7 B5
Marriner Ct UB3 .... 105 C6
Marriott Cl TW14 ...... 149 B5
Marriott Ho 8 SE6 ..... 186 A6
Marriott Rd
Finsbury Pk N4 .... 50 B1
Muswell Hill N10 .... 30 D2
Newham E15 .... 98 C6
Marriotts Cl NW9 .... 45 D3
Marryat Cl TW3 .... 129 B1
Marryat Ct 12 W6 ..... 112 B2
Marryat Ho SW1 ...... 259 A1
Marryat Pl SW19 ...... 179 A6
Marryat Rd SW19 ...... 179 A6
Marryat Sq SW6 ...... 264 A2
Marryatt Ct W5 .... 88 B1
Marsala Rd SE13 ...... 141 D1
Marsalis Ho 3 E3 ...... 97 C4
Marsden Rd
Camberwell SE15 ...... 139 D2
Edmonton N9 .... 18 B2
Marsden St NW5 .... 71 A2
Marsden Way 2 BR6 ... 227 D4
Marshall Cl
Brunswick Pk N11 .... 15 B1
Harrow HA1 .... 42 B2
Hounslow TW4 .... 151 B6
Wandsworth SW18 ..... 158 A5
Marshall Ct SW4 ...... 270 B1
Marshall Dr UB4 .... 83 D2
Marshall Ho
5 New Malden KT3 .... 199 C5
Paddington NW6 .... 91 B5
Shoreditch N1 .... 235 D4
Walworth SE17 .... 262 C2
Marshall Path 10 SE28 . 124 B6
Marshall Rd Leyton E10 .. 75 D4
Tottenham N17 .... 33 B2
Marshalls Gr SE18 ..... 122 A2
Marshall's Pl SE16 .... 263 D5
Marshall's Rd SM1 ..... 217 D4
Marshall St W1 .. 93 C1 239 B1
Marshalsea Rd
SE1 .... 117 A4 252 B2
Marsham Cl BR7 ...... 188 D5
Marsham Ct
19 Putney SW19 ...... 156 D3
Westminster SW1 ..... 259 D4
Marsham St
SW1 .... 115 D2 259 D4
Marsh Ave CR4 .... 181 A1
Marshbrook Cl SE3 .... 143 D2
Marsh Cl NW7 .... 11 D1
Marsh Ct Dalston E8 ..... 74 A2
3 Merton SW19 .... 180 A2
Marsh Dr NW9 .... 45 D3
Marsh Farm Rd TW2 ... 152 D3
Marshfield St E14 ..... 120 A3
Marsh Gate Bsns Ctr
E15 .... 98 A5
Marshgate Ctr The E15 . 97 D6
Marshgate La E15 ...... 75 D1
Marshgate Prim Sch
TW10 .... 154 B6
Marsh Green Prim Sch
RM10 .... 103 C5
Marsh Green Rd
RM10 .... 103 C6
Marsh Hall HA9 .... 66 B5
Marsh Hill E9 .... 75 A3
Marsh Ho
Nine Elms SW8 .... 269 B2
Pimlico SW1 .... 259 D1
Marsh La Edgware NW7 .. 11 C1
Leyton E10 .... 75 C6
Stanmore HA7 .... 25 C4
Tottenham N17 .... 34 B2
Marsh Point HA5 .... 41 B5
Marsh Rd Pinner HA5 .... 41 A5
Wembley HA0 .... 87 D5
Marshside Cl N9 .... 18 C3
Marsh St E14 .... 119 D2
Marsh Wall E14 .... 119 D4
Marshwood Ho 10
NW6 .... 91 C6
Marsland Cl SE17 ..... 261 D1
Marsom Ho N1 .... 235 C3
Marston SE17 .... 262 B4
Marston Ave
Chessington KT9 .... 214 A2
Dagenham RM10 .... 81 C5
Marston Cl
Dagenham RM10 .... 81 C5
South Hampstead NW6 ... 70 A1
Marston Ct Barnet EN5 ... 13 C6
Sidcup DA14 .... 189 D6
Walton-on-T KT12 ..... 194 C1
Marston Ho 23 SW9 .... 138 C3
Marston Rd TW11 ...... 175 B5
Marston Way SE19 .... 183 A3
Marsworth Ave HA5 ..... 22 D2
Marsworth Cl UB4 ...... 85 A2
Marsworth Ho 8 E2 ..... 96 A6
Martaban Rd N16 .... 73 D6
Martello St E8 .... 74 B1
Martello Terr E8 .... 74 B1
Martell Rd SE21 .... 161 B1
Martel Pl E8 .... 73 D2
Marten Rd E17 .... 35 C1
Martens Ave DA7 ...... 147 D1
Martham Cl SE28 ...... 124 D6
Martha Rd E15 .... 76 C2
Martha's Bldgs EC1 ... 242 C6
Martha St E1 .... 96 C1
Marthorne Cres HA3 .... 24 B1
Martin Bowes Rd SE9 .. 144 B2
Martinbridge Trad Est
EN1 .... 18 A6
Martin Cl
Lower Edmonton N9 ..... 18 D3
Uxbridge UB10 .... 82 A5
Martin Cres CR0 ...... 204 C1
Martin Ct
15 Cubitt Town E14 ..... 120 A4
Lewisham SE12 .... 164 D4
Merton SW19 .... 179 C3
Southall UB2 .... 107 B4
Martindale SW14 ...... 155 A6
Martindale Ave 2
E16 .... 121 A6
Martindale Ho 23 E14 .. 119 D6
Martindale Rd
Balham SW12 .... 159 B4
Hounslow TW4 .... 129 A2
Martin Dene DA6 ...... 169 B6
Martin Dr UB5 .... 63 B3
Martineau Cl KT10 .... 212 B4
Martineau Dr TW1 ..... 131 B1
Martineau Ho SW1 .... 259 A1
Martineau Mews N5 .... 72 D4
Martineau Rd N5 .... 72 D4
Martingale Cl TW16 ... 194 A5
Martingales Cl TW10 .. 153 D1
Martin Gdns RM8 .... 80 D4
Martin Gr SM4 .... 201 C6
Martin Ho
Newington SE1 .... 262 B5
7 New Malden KT3 .... 199 C5
South Lambeth SW8 ... 270 A4
Martini Dr EN3 .... 7 C6
Martin Jun & Inf Schs
N2 .... 30 C1
Martin La EC4 .... 252 D6
Martin Rd RM8 .... 80 D4
Martin Rise DA6 ...... 169 B6
Martins Cl BR4 .... 224 B6
Martins Mount EN5 ...... 1 D1
Martins Pl SE28 .... 123 C5
Martin's Rd BR2 ...... 186 D1
Martin St SE28 .... 123 C5
Martins The
Penge SE26 .... 184 B5
Wembley HA9 .... 66 B5
Martins Wlk
Muswell Hill N10 .... 31 A2
Woolwich SE28 .... 123 C5
Martin Way SW20,
SM4 .... 201 B6
Martlesham N17 .... 33 C1
Martlesham Wlk NW9 ... 27 C2
Martlet Gr 5 UB5 .... 84 D4
Martlett Ct WC2 ...... 240 B1
Martlett Lo NW3 .... 69 D4
Martley Dr IG2 .... 56 D4
Martley Ho SW8 ...... 269 B2
Martock Cl HA3 .... 43 A5
Martock Ct 10 SE15 ... 140 B4
Martock Gdns N11 ...... 31 A5
Marton Cl SE6 .... 163 C1
Marton Rd 2 N16 .... 73 C5
Martyn Ct HA8 .... 26 B6
Martyn Ho SE2 .... 146 D6
Martynside 22 NW9 ..... 27 D2
Marvel Ho 5 SE5 ..... 139 B5
Marvell Ave UB4 .... 84 A2
Marvels Cl SE12 ...... 165 B2
Marvels La SE12 ...... 165 C1
Marvels Lane Prim Sch
SE12 .... 187 C6
Marville Rd
SW6 .... 135 B5 264 C3
Marvin Ho 9 SE18 ..... 144 D6
Marvin St 3 E8 .... 74 B2
Marwell Cl BR4 .... 224 D6
Marwell Ct SE3 .... 142 B3
Marwick Rd UB7 ...... 104 B4
Marwood Cl DA16 ..... 146 B2
Marwood Ct N3 .... 29 D3
Marwood Dr NW7 .... 28 D3
Mary Adelaide Cl
Kingston u T SW15 .... 155 C1
Kingston u T SW15 .... 177 C6
Mary Adelaide Ho W2 . 236 D4
Mary Ann Bldgs SE8 .. 141 C6
Maryatt Ave HA2 .... 63 D6
Marybank SE18 .... 122 B2
Mary Cl HA7 .... 44 B5
Mary Datchelor Cl
SE5 .... 139 B4
Mary Dine Ct SW8 .... 270 D3
Mary Gn NW8 .... 91 D6
Marygold Ho TW3 ..... 130 A4
Mary Ho
8 Hammersmith W6 ... 112 C1
6 Stockwell SW9 ..... 138 B3
Mary James Ho 32 E2 ... 96 A5
Mary Jones Ho 20
E14 .... 119 C6
Maryland Ct KT1 ..... 176 D1
Maryland Pk E15 .... 76 C3
Maryland Point E15 .... 76 C2
Maryland Prim Sch
E15 .... 76 C3
Maryland Rd
Paddington W9 .... 91 C3
South Norwood CR7 ... 182 D2
Stratford New Town E15 .. 76 B3
Tottenham N22 .... 32 C4
Marylands Ind Est E15 .. 76 C3
Maryland Sq E15 .... 76 C3
Marylands Rd W9 .... 91 D3
Maryland St E15 .... 76 C3
Maryland Sta E15 ...... 76 C2
Maryland Way TW16 ... 172 A1
Maryland Wlk N1 ..... 235 A6
Mary Lawrenson Pl 1
SE3 .... 143 A5
MARYLEBONE 93 B1
Marylebone Ct 3 HA0 .. 66 A2
Marylebone Flyover
NW1 .... 92 C2 237 A3
Marylebone High St
W1 .... 93 A2 238 B4
Marylebone La
W1 .... 93 A1 238 B2
Marylebone Mews W1 238 C3
Marylebone Pas W1 .. 239 B2
Marylebone Rd
NW1 .... 92 D2 237 D4
Marylebone St
W1 .... 93 A2 238 B3
Marylebone Sta
NW1 .... 92 D3 237 C5
Marylee Way
SE11 .... 116 B2 260 D3
Mary McArthur Ho 12
N19 .... 49 D2
Mary Macarthur Ho
8 Belvedere DA17 .... 125 C3
11 Dagenham RM10 ..... 81 C5
15 Globe Town E2 ...... 96 D4
W14 .... 264 A6
Marymount International
Sch KT2 .... 177 A3
Maryon Gr SE7 .... 122 A2
Maryon Mews NW3 ..... 70 C4
Maryon Rd SE7 .... 122 A2
Mary Peters Dr UB6 .... 64 B3
Mary Pl W11 ... 113 A6 244 A5
Mary Rose Cl TW12 ... 173 C2
Mary Rose Mall E6 .... 100 B2
Maryrose Way N20 ..... 14 B3
Mary's Ct NW8 .... 237 B6
Mary Seacole Villas 19
NW10 .... 67 B1
Mary Secole Cl 21 E8 ... 95 D6
Mary Smith Ct SW5 ... 255 B3
Mary St
5 Canning Town E16 .... 98 D2
Shoreditch N1 ... 95 A6 235 B5
Mary's Terr TW1 ...... 153 A4
Mary Tates Cotts CR4 . 202 D5
Mary Terr NW1 .... 232 A5
Maryville DA16 .... 145 D3
Mary Way WD19 .... 22 C6
Mary Wharrie Ho 4
NW3 .... 70 D1
Marzena Ct TW2 ...... 152 A6
Masbro' Rd W14 ...... 112 D3
Mascalls Ct 13 SE7 ... 143 C6
Mascalls Rd SE7 ..... 143 C6
Mascotte Rd 2 SW15 .. 134 D1
Mascotts Cl NW2 .... 68 B5
Masefield Ave
Borehamwood WD6 ..... 10 D6
Southall UB1 .... 107 C6
Stanmore HA7 .... 24 D5
Masefield Cres N14 .... 15 C5
Masefield Ct
New Barnet EN5 .... 2 A1
Stoke Newington N5 .... 73 B3
19 Surbiton KT6 ...... 197 D2
Masefield Gdns E6 .... 100 C3
Masefield Ho 4 NW6 ... 91 C4
Masefield La UB4 ...... 84 C3
Masefield Rd TW13 ... 173 B6
Masefield View BR6 ... 227 A5
Masefield Way TW19 ... 148 B3
Masham Ho 13 DA18 ... 124 D4
Mashie Rd W3 .... 89 C1
Maskall Cl SW2 .... 160 C3
Maskani Wlk SW16 .... 181 C3
Maskell Rd SW17 ..... 158 A1
Maskelyne Cl
SW11 .... 136 C4 267 B2
Mason Cl
Bermondsey SE16 ..... 118 A1
Bexleyheath DA7 ..... 147 D2
Hampton TW12 .... 173 B2
Newham E16 .... 121 A6
Wimbledon SW20 ..... 178 D2
Mason Ct
1 Penge SE19 .... 183 D3
Wembley HA9 .... 66 C6
Mason Ho
12 Bermondsey SE1 .. 118 A2
8 Friern Barnet N11 .... 31 C5
16 Hackney E9 .... 74 C1
Mason Rd Sutton SM1 . 217 D3
Woodford IG8 .... 36 C6
Mason's Arms Mews
W1 .... 248 D6
Masons Ave HA3 .... 42 D5
Mason's Ave
City of London EC2 ... 242 C2
Croydon CR0 .... 221 A5
Masons Hill
Bromley BR2 .... 209 B5
13 Woolwich SE18 .... 122 D2
Masons Ho NW9 .... 44 D4
Mason's Pl
Finsbury EC1 .... 235 A2
Mitcham CR4 .... 180 D2
Mason St SE17 .. 117 B2 262 D4
Mason's Yd
Finsbury EC1 .... 234 D2
St James SW1 .... 249 B4
Wimbledon SW19 ..... 178 D5
Massey Cl N11 .... 31 B5
Massey Ct 6 E6 .... 99 C6
Massie Rd E8 .... 74 A2
Massingberd Way
SW17 .... 181 B6
Massinger St SE1, SE17 263 A3
Massingham St E1 ..... 96 D3
Masson Ave HA4 .... 62 C2
Mast Ct 17 SE16 ..... 119 A2
Master Gunner's Pl 1
SE18 .... 144 A4
Masterman Ho 1 SE5 .. 139 B5
Masterman Rd E6 ..... 100 A4
Masters Cl SW16 ..... 181 C4
Masters Ct HA4 .... 61 C6
Masters Dr SE16 ..... 118 B1
Masters Lo 24 E1 ...... 96 C1
Master's St 16 E1 ..... 96 D2
Mast House Terr E14 .. 119 C2
Mastin Ho SW18 ..... 157 C3
Mastmaker Rd E14 .... 119 C4
Maswell Park Cres
TW3 .... 152 A6
Maswell Park Rd TW3 . 130 A1
Matara Mews SE17 ... 262 A1
Matcham Rd E11 .... 76 D5
Matching Ct 14 E3 ..... 97 C4
Matchless Dr SE18 ... 144 C5
Matfield Cl BR2 ...... 209 A4
Matfield Rd DA17 .... 147 C6
Matham Gr SE22 ..... 139 D1
Matham Rd KT8 ...... 196 B4
Mathart Ct E4 .... 36 B4
Matheson Lang Ho
SE1 .... 251 A1
Matheson Rd
W14 .... 113 B2 254 C3
Mathews Ave E6 ..... 100 C5
Mathews Park Ave E15 .. 76 D2
Mathews Yd WC2 .... 240 A1
Mathieson Ct SE1 ... 251 D1
Mathieson Ho 10 E4 ... 20 C4
Mathilda Marks-Kennedy
Jewish Prim Sch
NW7 .... 27 B5
Mathison Ho SW10 ... 266 A4
Matilda Cl SE19 ..... 183 B3
Matilda Ho E1 .... 118 A5
Matilda St N1 .... 94 B6 233 D6
Matlock Cl Barnet EN5 ... 12 D6
Herne Hill SE24 ...... 139 A1
Matlock Cres SM3 ... 217 A4
Matlock Ct
7 Herne Hill SE5 ..... 139 B1
St John's Wood NW8 .. 229 A4
Woodford IG8 .... 36 D2
Matlock Gdns SM1,
SM3 .... 217 A4
Matlock Pl SM1, SM3 .. 217 A4
Matlock Rd E10 .... 54 A3
Matlock St E14 .... 97 A1
Matlock Way KT3 .... 177 B2
Maton Ho SW6 ...... 264 C4
Matson Ct IG8 .... 36 C3
Matson Ho
9 Bermondsey SE16 .. 118 B3
16 Homerton E9 .... 74 D2
Matthew Cl W10 .... 90 D3
Matthew Ct
Mitcham CR4 .... 203 D4
4 Walthamstow E17 .... 54 A6
Matthew Parker St
SW1 .... 249 D1
Matthews Ct N5 .... 73 A4
Matthews Ho 3 E14 .... 97 C2
Matthews Rd UB6 ...... 64 B3
Matthews St SW11 ... 136 D3
Matthias Ct 12 TW10 .. 154 A5
Matthias Ho 2 N16 .... 73 C3
Matthias Rd N16 .... 73 C3
Mattingly Way 3
SE15 .... 139 D5
Mattison Rd N4 .... 50 D3
Mattock La W5, W13 ... 109 C5
Maud Cashmore Way
SE18 .... 122 B3
Maude Ho 3 E2 .... 96 A5
Maude Rd
Camberwell SE5 ...... 139 C4
Walthamstow E17 ...... 53 A4
Maudesville Cotts W7 .. 108 C5
Maude Terr E17 .... 53 A5
Maud Gdns
Barking IG11 .... 101 D5
Newham E13 .... 98 D5
Maudlins Gn E1 ...... 118 A5
Maud Rd Leyton E10 .... 76 A5
Newham E13 .... 98 D5
Maudslay Rd SE9 ..... 144 B2
Maudsley Ho TW8 ..... 110 A1
Maudsley Hospl The
SE5 .... 139 B3
Maud St E16 .... 98 D2
Maud Wilkes Cl 10
NW5 .... 71 C3
Maugham Ct 5 W3 .... 111 A3
Mauleverer Rd SW2 ... 160 A6
Maultway Ct KT19 .... 215 B3
Maundeby Wlk NW10 ... 67 C2
Maunder Rd 4 W7 .... 108 D5
Maunsel St
SW1 .... 115 D2 259 C4
Maureen Campbell Ct
TW17 .... 192 D4
Maurer Ct 2 SE10 .... 120 D3
Mauretania Bldg 11
E1 .... 118 D6
Maurice Ave N22 ...... 32 D1
Maurice Browne Cl
NW7 .... 28 D4
Maurice Ct
3 Brentford TW8 .... 131 D5
4 Mile End E1 .... 97 A4
Wood Green N22 .... 32 C2
Maurice Ho
Hither Green SE12 ... 164 D5
1 Stockwell SW9 ..... 138 B3
Maurice St W12 .... 90 B1
Maurice Wlk NW11 ..... 48 A5
Maurier Cl UB5 .... 84 C6
Mauritius Rd SE10 ... 120 C2
Maury Rd N16 .... 74 A5
Mauveine Gdns TW3 .. 129 C1
Mavelstone Cl BR1 ... 188 A2
Mavelstone Rd BR1 ... 188 A2
Maverton Rd E3 .... 97 C6
Mavery Ct 5 BR1 .... 186 D3
Mavis Ave KT19 ...... 215 C3
Mavis Cl KT19 .... 215 C3
Mavis Ct 33 NW9 ...... 27 D1
Mavis Wlk 8 E6 ..... 100 A2
Mavor Ho N1 .... 233 D5
Mawbey Ho SE1 ..... 263 D1
Mawbey Pl
SE1 .... 117 D1 263 D1
Mawbey Rd SE1 ..... 263 D1
Mawbey St SW8 ..... 270 A3
Mawdley Ho SE1 .... 251 B1
Mawney Cl RM7 .... 59 D6
Mawney Rd RM7 .... 59 D6
Mawson Cl SW20 .... 179 A1
Mawson Ct N1 ...... 235 D5
Mawson Ho EC1 ..... 241 A4
Mawson La W4 .... 133 D6
Maxden Ct SE15 .... 140 A2
Maxey Gdns RM9 ...... 81 A4
Maxey Rd
Dagenham RM9 .... 81 A4
Plumstead SE18 ..... 123 A2
Maxfield Cl N20 .... 14 A4
Maxim Apartments 3
BR2 .... 209 B5
Maxim Rd N21 .... 16 C5
Maxted Pk HA1 .... 42 C2
Maxted Rd SE15 .... 139 D2
Maxwell Cl
Croydon CR0 .... 204 A1
Hayes UB3 .... 106 A6
Maxwell Ct SE21 ... 162 A3
Maxwell Gdns BR6 ... 227 D5
Maxwell Ho
Bowes Pk N22 .... 32 B4
Chislehurst BR7 .... 188 D3
12 Shooters Hill SE18 .. 144 D6
Maxwell Rd
Ashford TW15 ...... 171 A4
Fulham SW6 .. 135 D5 265 D3
Welling DA16 ...... 146 A2
West Drayton UB7 .. 104 B2
Maxwelton Ave NW7 ... 27 B5
Maxwelton Cl NW7 .... 27 B5
Maya Angelou Ct E4 ... 36 A6
Maya Cl SE15 ...... 140 B3
Mayall Cl EN3 .... 7 C5
Mayall Rd SE24 .... 160 D6
Maya Pl N11 .... 31 D3
Maya Rd N2 .... 48 A5
Maybank Ave
Wembley HA0 .... 65 A3
Woodford E18 .... 37 B1
Maybank Gdns HA5 ... 40 A4
Maybank Rd E18 ..... 37 C2
May Bate Ave KT2 ... 175 D2
Maybells Commercial Est
IG11 .... 102 D5
Mayberry Pl KT5 .... 198 B2

Maybourne Cl SE26 ....184 B5
Maybourne Grange
CR0 ....221 C6
Maybrook Ct E11 ....77 B6
Maybury Cl Enfield EN1....6 B5
Petts Wood BR5 ....210 D4
Maybury Ct
Beckenham BR3 ....185 B3
Croydon CR2 ....220 D3
Harrow HA1 ....42 B3
Marylebone W1 ....238 B3
Maybury Gdns NW10....68 B2
Maybury Mews N6....49 C2
Maybury Rd
Barking IG11....102 A5
Newham E13....99 C3
Maybury St SW17....180 C5
Maychurch Cl HA7....25 D3
May Cl KT9....214 B2
Maycroft
2 Hayes BR2....208 D1
Pinner HA5....22 B1
Maycross Ave SM4....201 C5
May Ct 2 SW19....180 A2
Mayday Gdns SE3....144 A3
Mayday Rd CR0, CR7....204 D3
Mayday University Hospl
CR7....204 D3
Maydeb Ct RM6....59 B3
Maydew Ho SE16....118 C2
Maydwell Ho 6 E14....97 C2
Mayerne Rd SE9....165 D6
Mayesbrook Rd
Barking IG11....101 D6
Dagenham RM8, IG3....80 B5
Mayesford Rd RM6....58 C2
Mayespark Prim Sch
IG3....80 A5
Mayes Rd N22....32 B1
Mayeswood Rd SE12....187 C6
MAYFAIR....115 B6
Mayfair Ave
Bexley DA7....146 D4
Dagenham RM6....58 D3
Ilford IG1....56 C1
New Malden KT4....200 A1
Twickenham TW2....152 A4
Mayfair Cl
Beckenham BR3....185 D2
Surbiton KT6....198 A1
Mayfair Ct
2 Beckenham BR3....185 D2
7 Croydon CR0....221 D6
Edgware HA8....26 B5
13 Wimbledon SW19....179 A3
Mayfair Gdns
Tottenham N17....33 B4
Woodford IG8....37 A3
Mayfair Ho 11 SE1....118 A2
Mayfair Pl W1....248 D4
Mayfair Terr N14....15 D4
Mayfield DA7....147 B2
Mayfield Ave
Broom Hill BR6....211 D2
Chiswick W4....111 C2
Harrow HA3....43 B4
North Finchley N12....30 B6
Osidge N14....15 D2
West Ealing W13....109 B4
Woodford IG8....37 A4
Mayfield Cl
Ashford TW15....170 D4
Clapham Pk SW4....159 D6
Dalston E8....73 D2
Hillingdon UB10....82 D4
Long Ditton KT7....197 B1
Penge SE20....184 B2
Mayfield Cres
Enfield N9....18 B5
Thornton Heath CR7....204 B4
Mayfield Ct SM2....218 A1
Mayfield Dr HA5....41 B5
Mayfield Gdns
Ealing W7....86 C2
Hendon NW4....46 D3
Mayfield Ho
31 Bethnal Green E2....96 B5
Stamford Hill N16....51 C2
Mayfield Mans SW15....157 B6
Mayfield Prim Sch W7....86 B1
Mayfield Rd Acton W3....110 D6
Bedford Pk W12....111 C4
Bromley BR1....210 A4
Chingford E4....20 B2
Dagenham RM8....58 C1
Dalston E8....73 D1
Enfield EN3....6 D3
Higham Hill E17....35 A1
Hornsey Vale N8....50 B3
Merton SW19....179 B2
Newham E13....98 D3
South Croydon CR2....221 B1
Sutton SM2....218 B2
Thornton Heath CR7....204 B4
Mayfields HA9....66 C6
Mayfield Sch & Coll
RM8....58 C1
Mayfields Cl HA9....66 C6
Mayfield Villas DA14....190 C4
Mayflower Cl
Bermondsey SE16....118 D2
Ruislip HA4....39 A3
Mayflower Ho 2 IG11....101 B6
Mayflower Lo
Hendon N3....47 B6
Muswell Hill N10....31 A2
Mayflower Prim Sch
E14....97 D1
Mayflower Rd SW9....138 A2
Mayflower St 1 SE16....118 C4
Mayfly Cl HA5....40 C2
Mayfly Gdns 12 UB5....84 D4
Mayford NW1....232 B4
Mayford Cl
Balham SW12....158 D4
Penge BR3....206 D6
Mayford Rd SW12....159 A4
May Gdns Elstree WD6....9 D5
Wembley HA0....87 C4
Maygood Ho N1....234 A4
Maygood St N1....94 C5 234 A4
Maygrove Rd NW6....69 B2
Mayhew Cl E4....19 C1
Mayhew Ct 2 SE5....139 B1
Mayhill Rd Barnet EN5....13 A5
Greenwich SE7....143 B6
Mayland Mans 4 IG11....78 D1
Maylands Dr DA14....168 D1
Maylands Ho SW3....257 B3
Maylands Rd WD19....22 C6
Maylie Ho 4 SE16....118 B4
Maynard Cl
Fulham SW6....135 D5 265 D3
Tottenham N15....51 C4
Maynard Ct EN3....7 C5
Maynard Ho Mile End E1....97 A4
Plumstead SE18....123 A2
Maynard Rd E17....54 A4
Maynards Quay E1....118 C6
Mayne Ct E8....74 A4
Maynooth Gdns CR4....202 D2
Mayo Ct W13....109 B3
Mayo Ho 10 E1....96 C2
Mayola Rd E5....74 C4
Mayo Rd
Thornton Heath CR0....205 B4
Walton-on-T KT12....194 A2
Willesden NW10....67 C2
Mayow Rd SE23, SE26....184 D6
Mayplace Cl DA7....147 D2
Mayplace La SE18....144 D6
Mayplace Rd W DA7....147 C1
Maypole Ct UB2....107 B4
May Rd Chingford E4....35 C4
Newham E13....99 A5
Twickenham TW2....152 C3
Mayroyd Ave KT6....214 C6
May's Buildings Mews
SE10....142 B5
Mays Ct WC2....250 A5
May's Ct SE10....142 B5
May's Hill Rd BR2....208 C6
Mays La EN5....12 C5
Maysoule Rd SW11....136 B1
Mays Rd TW11, TW12....174 B5
May St W14....254 D1
Maystocks E18....55 C6
Mayston Mews 3
SE10....121 A1
May Terr IG1....78 D4
Maythorne Cotts SE13....164 B5
Maytime Prep Sch IG1....78 C5
Mayton St N7....72 B5
Maytree Cl HA8....11 A1
Maytree Ct
Mitcham CR4....203 A6
Northolt UB5....85 A4
May Tree Ho SE4....141 B2
Maytree La HA7....24 D3
Maytree Wlk SW2....160 C2
Mayville Prim Sch E11....76 C6
Mayville Rd Ilford IG1....78 D3
Leyton E11....76 C6
Mayward Ho 7 SE5....139 C4
May Wlk E13....99 B5
Maywood Cl BR3....185 D3
May Wynne Ho E16....99 B1
Maze Hill SE10, SE3....142 C6
Maze Hill Lodge 7
SE10....142 B6
Maze Hill Sta SE10....142 C6
Mazenod Ave NW6....69 C1
Maze Rd TW9....132 C5
Mead Cl
3 Camden Town NW1....71 A1
Harrow HA3....24 B2
Mead Cres
Carshalton SM1....218 C4
Chingford E4....36 A6
Meadcroft Ho 4 KT3....199 C2
Meadcroft Rd SE17....138 D6
Mead Ct NW9....45 B4
Meade Cl W4....132 C6
Meader Ct SE14....140 D5
Meadfield HA8....10 D2
Mead Field HA2....63 B5
Meadfield Gn HA8....10 D2
Meadfoot Rd SW16....181 C2
Mead Gr RM6....58 D6
Mead Ho W11....244 C4
Mead House La UB4....83 B3
Meadhurst Pk TW16....171 C4
Mead Inf Sch The
KT19....215 D4
Meadlands Dr TW10....153 D2
Meadlands Prim Sch
TW10....175 C6
Mead Lo W4....111 B4
Meadow Ave CR0....206 D3
Meadowbank
Lewisham SE3....142 D2
Primrose Hill NW3....70 D1
Southgate N21....16 B5
Surbiton KT5....198 B3
Meadow Bank 8
SW15....157 B6
Meadowbank Cl SW6....134 C5
Meadowbank Gdns
TW5....128 B4
Meadowbank Rd NW9....45 B2
Meadowbanks EN5....12 A6
Meadowbrook Ct
TW7....130 D2
Meadow Cl Barnet EN5....13 B5
Bexley DA6....169 B6
Catford SE6....185 C5
Chingford E4....19 D3
Chislehurst BR7....188 D5
Enfield EN3....7 A5
Hackney E9....75 B3
Hinchley Wood KT10....212 D5
Hounslow TW4....151 C5
Northolt UB5....85 C5
Richmond TW10....154 A3
Ruislip HA4....39 D3
Sutton SM1....218 A6
West Barnes SW20....200 C5
Meadowcourt Rd SE3....142 D1
Meadowcroft 9 W4....110 C1
Meadow Croft BR1....210 B6
Meadowcroft Rd N13....16 C2
Meadow Dr
Hendon NW4....28 C1
Muswell Hill N10....49 B6
Meadowford Cl SE28....124 A6
Meadow Garth NW10....67 B2
Meadow Gate HA2....63 D5
Meadowgate Cl NW7....27 D5
Meadowgate Sch SE4....141 A2
Meadow Gdns HA8....27 A4
Meadow High Sch UB8....82 A2
Meadow Hill KT3....199 C3
Meadow La SE12....165 B1
Meadow Mews SW8....270 C5
Meadow Pl
Chiswick W4....133 C5
South Lambeth
SW8....138 A5 270 B4
Meadow Rd
Ashford TW15....171 B5
Barking IG11....80 A1
Beckenham BR2....186 C1
Carshalton SM1....218 C3
Claygate KT10....212 C2
Dagenham RM9....81 B2
Feltham TW13....151 A2
Merton SW19....180 A3
Pinner HA5....41 A5
Southall UB1....107 B6
South Lambeth
SW8....138 B5 270 C4
Meadow Row SE1....262 A5
Meadows Cl E10....75 C6
Meadows Ct DA14....190 B4
Meadows End TW16....172 A2
Meadowside
Eltham SE9....143 C1
Twickenham TW1....153 D4
Meadow Stile CR0....221 A5
Meadowsweet Cl
3 Newham E16....99 D2
West Barnes KT3....200 C5
Meadow The BR7....189 A4
Meadowview TW17....193 A2
Meadow View
Blackfen DA15....168 B4
Harrow HA1....42 C1
Meadowview Rd
Catford SE6....185 C5
Sidcup DA5....169 B5
West Ewell KT19....215 C1
Meadow View Rd
Hayes UB4....83 B3
Thornton Heath CR7....204 D4
Meadow Way
Kingsbury NW9....45 B4
Locksbottom BR6....226 C5
Ruislip HA4....40 B3
Wembley HA9....65 D4
Meadow Waye TW5....129 A5
Meadow Way The HA3....24 C2
Meadow Wlk
Dagenham RM9....81 B2
Hackbridge SM6....219 B5
Wanstead E18....55 A5
West Ewell KT17, KT19....215 D1
Meadow Wood Sch
WD23....8 A6
Mead Pl Croydon CR0....205 A1
Hackney E9....74 C2
Mead Plat NW10....67 A2
Mead Rd
Chislehurst BR7....189 A4
Edgware HA8....26 C4
Richmond TW10....153 C1
Mead Road Inf Sch
BR7....189 A4
Mead Row SE1....116 C3 261 A6
Meads Ct E15....76 D2
Meadside Cl BR3....185 A2
Meads La IG3....57 D2
Meads Rd Enfield EN3....7 A4
Tottenham N22....32 D1
Meads The Cheam SM3....217 A5
Edgware HA8....27 B4
Hillingdon UB8....82 A3
Mead The
Beckenham BR3....186 A2
Ealing W13....87 B2
Finchley N2....30 A1
Ickenham UB10....60 C6
Wallington SM6....219 D2
West Wickham BR4....208 B1
Meadvale Rd
Croydon CR0....206 A3
Ealing W5....87 C3
Meadway
Ashford TW15....170 C6
Barnet EN5....1 C1
Beckenham BR3....186 A2
Enfield EN3....6 D6
Esher KT10....212 A1
Hampstead Garden Suburb
NW11....47 D3
Ilford IG3....79 C4
Palmers Green N14....16 A2
Tolworth KT5....199 A1
Twickenham TW2....152 B3
West Barnes SW20....200 C5
Woodford IG8....37 C5
Mead Way
Croydon CR0....223 A6
Hayes BR2....209 A3
Ruislip HA4....39 B3
Meadway Cl Barnet EN5....1 C1
Hampstead Garden Suburb
NW11....47 D3
Pinner HA5....23 D4
Meadway Ct
Dagenham RM8....81 B6
Ealing W5....88 B2
Hampstead Garden Suburb
NW11....47 D3
Meadway Gate NW11....47 C3
Meadway Gdns HA4....39 B3
Meadway The
Buckhurst Hill IG9....21 D3
Lewisham SE3....142 B3
Meaford Way SE20....184 B3
Meakin Est SE1....263 A6
Meakin Ho N7....72 B3
Meanley Rd E12....78 A3
Meard St W1....239 C1
Meath Ho SE24....160 D5
Meath Rd Ilford IG1....79 A5
Newham E15....98 D5
Meath St SW11....137 B4 268 C2
Mecklenburgh Pl WC1....240 C6
Mecklenburgh Sq
WC1....94 B3 240 C6
Mecklenburgh St WC1....240 C6
Medburn St NW1....232 C4
Medcalf Rd EN3....7 B6
Medcroft Gdns SW14....133 A1
Medebourne Cl SE3....143 A2
Mede Ho BR1....187 B5
Medesenge Way N13....32 D4
Medfield St SW15....156 B4
Medhurst Cl 19 E3....97 A5
Median Rd E5....74 C3
Medina Ave KT10....212 C5
Medina Ct N7....72 C5
Medina Gr N7....72 C5
Medina Ho SE15....140 C1
Medina Rd N7....72 C5
Medland Cl CR4....203 A1
Medlar Cl 1 UB5....84 D5
Medlar Ho 3 DA15....168 A1
Medlar St SE5....139 A4
Medley Rd NW6....69 C2
Medora Rd SW2....160 B4
Medresco Ho NW3....70 B3
Medusa Rd SE6, SE13....163 D5
Medway Bldgs E3....97 A5
Medway Cl
Croydon CR0....206 C3
Ilford IG1....79 A3
Medway Ct
South Norwood SE25....205 C4
St Pancras WC1....233 A1
Medway Dr UB6....86 D5
Medway Gdns HA0....65 A4
Medway Ho
Bermondsey SE1....252 D1
6 Kingston u T KT2....175 D2
Paddington NW8....237 A4
Stoke Newington N16....73 B4
Medway Mews 35 E3....97 A5
Medway Par 1 UB6....86 D5
Medway Rd E3....97 A5
Medway St
SW1....115 D3 259 D5
Medwin St SW4....138 B1
Meecham Ct 1 SW11....136 C3
Meerbrook Rd SE3....143 C2
Meers Ct SW20....178 C2
Meeson Rd E15....76 D1
Meeson St E5....75 A4
Meeting House Alley 7
E1....118 B5
Meeting House La
SE15....140 B5
Mehetabel Rd E9....74 C3
Meister Cl IG1....57 B1
Melanda Cl BR7....188 B5
Melanie Cl DA7....147 A4
Melba Way SE13....141 D4
Melbourne Ave
Bowes Pk N13....32 B4
Ealing W13....109 A5
Pinner HA2, HA5....41 D6
Melbourne Cl
Broom Hill BR6....211 C2
Ickenham UB10....60 C4
Wallington SM6....219 C3
Melbourne Ct
Hackney E5....75 A4
Muswell Hill N10....31 B3
Paddington W9....236 B6
Penge SE20....184 A3
Twickenham TW2....152 C2
Melbourne Gdns RM6....59 A4
Melbourne Gr SE22....139 D1
Melbourne Ho
Hayes UB4....84 C3
Kensington W8....245 A3
Melbourne Ho *continued*
South Norwood SE25....205 D5
Melbourne Mews
Brixton SW9....138 C4
Catford SE6....164 A4
Melbourne Pl WC2....240 D1
Melbourne Rd
Ilford IG1....56 D1
Leyton E10....53 D2
Merton SW19....179 C2
Newham E6....100 B5
Teddington TW11....175 C4
Wallington SM6....219 C3
Walthamstow E17....53 A5
Melbourne Sq 21
SW9....138 C4
Melbourne Way EN1....17 D5
Melbray Mews 11
SW6....135 B3
Melbreak Ho 11 SE22....139 C2
Melbury Ave UB2....107 D3
Melbury Cl
Claygate KT10....213 B2
Elmstead BR7....188 B4
Melbury Ct W8....113 B3 254 D6
Melbury Dr SE5....139 C5
Melbury Gdns SW20....178 B2
Melbury Grange BR1....188 A2
Melbury Ho
South Lambeth SW8....270 C4
Twickenham TW2....152 B2
Melbury Rd Harrow HA3....44 B4
Kensington
W14....113 B3 254 D6
Melchester 5 W11....91 B1
Melchester Ho 1 N19....71 D5
Melcombe Ct NW1....237 C4
Melcombe Gdns HA3....44 B3
Melcombe Ho SW8....270 C3
Melcombe Pl NW1....237 C4
Melcombe Prim Sch
W6....134 D6
Melcombe St
NW1....92 D3 237 D5
Meldex Cl NW7....28 C4
Meldon Cl SW6....265 D2
Meldone KT3....199 B1
Meldone Cl KT5....198 D3
Meldrum Rd IG3....80 A6
Melfield Gdns SE6....186 A5
Melford Ave IG11....79 D2
Melford Cl KT9....214 B3
Melford Ct
Bermondsey SE1....263 B6
Dulwich SE22....162 A4
Hackney E5....74 B5
2 Sutton SM2....218 A1
Melford Rd
Dulwich SE21, SE22....162 A3
Ilford IG1....79 B6
Leyton E11....76 C6
Newham E6....100 B4
Walthamstow E17....53 B5
Melfort Ave CR7....204 D6
Melfort Rd CR7....204 D6
Melgund Rd N5....72 C3
Melina Cl UB3....83 B2
Melina Ct Putney SW15....134 A2
St John's Wood NW8....229 C1
Melina Pl NW8....92 B4 229 C1
Melina Rd W12....112 B4
Melior Ct N6....49 C3
Melior Pl SE1....253 A2
Melior St SE1....117 C4 253 A2
Meliot Rd SE6....164 B2
Melisa Ct N6....49 D2
Meller Cl SM6....220 A5
Melling Dr EN1....6 A4
Melling St SE18....145 C6
Mellington Ct 2 N16....74 A5
Mellis Ave TW9....132 D4
Mellish Cl IG11....101 D6
Mellish Ct KT6....198 A3
Mellish Flats E10....53 C2
Mellish Gdns IG8....37 A5
Mellish Ho 2 E1....96 B1
Mellish Ind Est SE18....121 D3
Mellish St E14....119 C3
Mellison Rd SW17....180 C5
Mellitus St W12....89 D1
Mellor Cl KT12....195 B2
Mellor Ct 2 SW19....180 A3
Mellor Ho 2 SE21....183 C6
Mellow La E UB4....83 A3
Mellow Lane Sch UB4....83 A3
Mellow La W UB10....83 A4
Mellows Rd
Redbridge IG5....56 B6
Wallington SM6....219 D3
Mells Cres SE9....188 B6
Mell St 6 SE10....120 C1
Melody La N5....73 A3
Melody Rd SW18....158 A6
Melon Pl W8....245 B2
Melon Rd Leyton E11....76 C5
Peckham SE15....140 A4
Melrose Ave
Borehamwood WD6....10 D6
Cricklewood NW2....68 C3
Greenford UB6....85 D5
Mitcham CR4....181 B3
Thornton Heath SW16....204 C6
Tottenham N22....32 D2
Twickenham TW2....151 D4
Wimbledon SW19....157 C1
Melrose Cl
Greenford UB6....85 D5
Grove Pk SE12....165 B3
Hayes UB4....84 A2
Melrose Cres BR6....227 B3
Melrose Ct
5 Ealing W13....109 A5
Wandsworth SW18....157 B5
Melrose Dr UB1....107 C5
Melrose Gdns
Edgware HA8....26 D1
Hammersmith W6....112 C3
Kingston u T KT3....199 B6
Melrose Ho
Maida Vale NW6....91 C4
Pimlico SW1....258 D2
Melrose Rd
1 Barnes SW13....133 D3
Merton SW19....179 C2
Pinner HA5....41 B5
Wandsworth SW18....157 B5
Melrose Sch CR4....202 C6
Melrose Terr W6....112 C3
Melrose Tudor SM6....220 A3
Melsa Rd SM4....202 A3
Melthorne Dr HA4....62 C5
Melthorpe Gdns SE3....144 A4
Melton Cl HA4....40 C1
Melton Ct
11 Croydon CR0....221 D6
South Kensington SW7....256 D3
Sutton SM2....218 A1
1 Twickenham TW1....153 B4
Melton Ho E5....74 A6
Melton St NW1....93 D4 232 C1
Melville Ave
Greenford UB6....64 D3
South Croydon CR2....221 D3
Wimbledon SW20....178 A3
Melville Cl UB10....61 B5
Melville Court Flats 8
W12....112 B4
Melville Ct
4 Brentford W4....110 C1
Rotherhithe SE8....119 A2
Melville Gdns N13....32 D5
Melville Ho
Lewisham SE10....142 A4
New Barnet EN5....14 B5
Melville Pl 4 N1....73 A1
Melville Rd
Barnes SW13....134 A4
Sidcup DA14....168 C2
Stonebridge NW10....67 B1
Walthamstow E17....53 B6
Melville Villas Rd W3....111 B5
Melvin Ct 11 TW9....132 C4
Melvin Rd SE20....184 C2
Melwood Ho 23 E1....96 B1
Melyn Cl N7....71 C4
Memel Ct EC1....242 A5
Memel St EC1....242 A5
Memess Path 4 SE18....144 C6
Memorial Ave E15....98 C4
Memorial Cl TW5....129 B6
Memorial Hospl SE18....144 C3
Memorial Hts IG2....57 B3
Menai Pl 2 E3....97 C5
Menard Ct EC1....235 B1
Mendham Ho SE1....263 A6
Mendip Cl
Forest Hill SE26....184 C6
Harlington UB3....127 B5
North Cheam KT4....216 C6
Mendip Ct
12 Battersea SW11....136 A2
Deptford SE14....140 C6
1 East Barnet N20....14 C2
Mendip Dr NW2, NW11....69 A6
Mendip Ho Harrow HA3....43 A3
2 Stoke Newington N4....51 B2
Mendip Hos 12 E2....96 C4
Mendip Rd
Battersea SW11....136 A2
Bushey WD23....8 A5
Ilford IG2....57 C4
Mendora Rd
SW6....135 B5 264 C4
Menelik Rd NW2....69 B4
Menin Wks CR4....180 D1
Menlo Gdns SE19....183 B3
Mennie Ho SE18....144 B4
Mennis Ho SM5....218 C6
Menon Dr N9....18 B1
Menorah Foundation Sch
HA8....27 A3
Menorah Prim Sch
NW11....47 A2
Menotti St 6 E2....96 A3
Menteath Ho 9 E14....97 C1
Mentmore Cl HA3....43 C3
Mentmore Terr E8....74 B1
Mentone Ct SW8....270 B2
Meon Ct TW7....130 C3
Meon Rd W3....111 A4
Meopham Rd CR4,
SW16....181 C2
Mepham Cres HA3....24 A3
Mepham Gdns HA3....24 A3
Mepham St
SE1....116 C5 251 A3
Mera Dr DA7....147 D1
Merantun Way SW19....180 A2
Merbury Cl
Lewisham SE13....164 B6
Woolwich SE28....123 B5
Merbury Rd SE28....123 C4
Mercator Pl 4 E14....119 C1
Mercator Rd SE13....142 B1
Mercer Cl KT7....196 D2
Merceron Ho 3 E2....96 C4
Merceron St E1....96 B3
Mercer Pl HA5....22 C1
Mercers Cl SE10....120 D2
Mercer's Cotts 8 E3....97 A1

Mercers Mews N7 71 D4
Mercers Pl W6 112 D2
Mercers Rd N19 71 D5
Mercer St WC2 94 A1 240 A1
Merchant Ct E1 118 C5
Merchants Cl SE25 206 A5
Merchants Ho SE10 120 B1
Merchants Lo 5 E17 53 C5
Merchant St E3 97 B4
Merchant Taylors' Almshouses SE13 142 C1
Merchant Taylors Hall★ EC3 242 D1
Merchiston Rd SE6 164 B2
Merchland Rd SE9 167 A3
Merchon Ho N7 71 C4
Mercia Gr SE13 142 A1
Mercia Ho
9 Camberwell SE5 139 A3
Charlton TW15 171 A2
Mercie Ct SE22 162 A3
Mercier Rd SW15 157 A6
Mercury 25 NW9 27 D2
Mercury Ct
8 Brixton SW9 138 C4
10 Millwall E14 119 C2
Mercury Ctr TW14 150 A6
Mercury Ho
Brentford TW8 109 D1
6 Old Ford E3 97 C6
Mercury Rd TW8 109 C1
Mercury Way SE14 140 D6
Mercy Terr SE13 163 D6
Merebank La CR0, SM6 220 B3
Mere Cl Orpington BR6 226 D6
Putney SW15, SW19 156 D4
Meredith Ave NW2 68 C3
Meredith Cl HA5 22 D3
Meredith Ho 17 N16 73 C3
Meredith Mews SE4 141 B1
Meredith St
Finsbury EC1 234 C1
Newham E13 99 A4
Meredith Twr W3 110 D3
Meredyth Rd SW13 134 A3
Mere End CR0 206 D2
Mere Rd TW17 192 D3
Mereside BR6 226 C6
Mereside Pk TW15 171 A6
Meretone Cl SE4 141 A1
Mereton Mans 6 SE8 141 C4
Meretune Ct SM4 201 B6
Merevale Cres SM4 202 A3
Mereway Industry TW2 152 C4
Mereway Rd TW2 152 C3
Merewood Cl BR1 188 C1
Merewood Gdns CR0 206 D2
Mereworth Cl BR2 208 D4
Mereworth Dr SE18 145 A5
Mereworth Ho 3 SE15 140 C6
Merganser Ct 17 SE8 141 B6
Merganser Gdns SE28 123 B3
Meridan Ct SE13 142 B1
Meriden Cl BR1 187 D3
Meriden Ct SW3 257 A1
Meriden Ho
4 Barnet EN5 1 A1
25 Hoxton N1 95 C6
Meridian Building★ SE10 142 B5
Meridian Ct
4 Bermondsey SE16 118 A4
4 Catford SE6 164 D3
Croydon CR0 220 C4
Meridian Ho SE10 120 C2
Meridian Pl E14 120 A4
Meridian Prim Sch SE10 142 B6
Meridian Rd SE7 143 D5
Meridian Sq E15 76 B1
Meridian Trad Est SE7 121 B2
Meridian Way
Enfield EN3 19 A5
Lower Edmonton N9, N18 18 D1
Meridian Wlk N17 33 C4
Merifield Rd SE9 143 C1
Merino Cl E11 55 C5
Merino Pl DA15 168 A6
Merioneth Ct 7 W7 86 D2
Merivale Rd
Harrow HA1 42 A2
Putney SW15 135 A1
Merlewood Dr BR7 188 B2
Merley Ct NW9 45 A1
Merlin 26 NW9 27 D2
Merlin Cl Mitcham CR4 202 C6
4 Northolt UB5 84 C4
South Croydon CR0 221 C4
Wallington SM6 220 B2
Merlin Cres HA8 26 B2
Merlin Ct
Beckenham BR2 208 D5
6 Ealing W7 86 D3
Mitcham CR4 180 C2
Ruislip HA4 61 B6
Stanmore HA7 25 B5
Wood Green N22 32 C2
Merling Cl KT9 213 D3
Merlin Gdns BR1 165 A1
Merlin Gr BR3 207 C4
Merlin Ho
7 Chiswick W4 111 B1
Enfield EN3 18 D6
West Hampstead NW3 69 D4
Merlin Prim Sch BR1 165 A1
Merlin Rd Bexley DA16 146 A1
Wanstead E12 77 D6
Merlin Rd N DA16 146 A1
Merlins Ave HA2 63 B5
Merlin Sch SW15 157 A6
Merlins Ct WC1 234 A1
Merlin St EC1 94 C4 234 A1
Mermaid Ct
Bermondsey SE1 117 B4 252 C2
Rotherhithe SE16 119 B5
Stroud Green N4 50 C3
Mermaid Ho 8 E14 120 A6
Mermaid Twr 22 SE8 141 B6
Meroe Ct N16 73 C6
Merredene St SW2 160 B5
Merriam Ave 2 E9 75 B2
Merriam Cl E4 36 A5
Merrick Rd UB2 107 B3
Merricks Ct 5 SW14 132 D1
Merrick Sq SE1 117 B3 262 C6
Merridale SE12 164 D6
Merridene N21 16 D5
Merrielands Cres RM9 103 B5
Merrielands Ret Pk RM9 103 B5
Merrilands Rd KT4 200 C1
Merrilees Rd DA15 167 C4
Merrilyn Cl KT10 213 A2
Merriman Rd SE3 143 C4
Merrington Rd SW6 265 B6
Merrion Ave HA7 25 D5
Merritt Gdns KT9 213 C2
Merritt Rd SE4 163 B6
Merrivale
Camden Town NW1 232 B5
Southgate N14 15 D6
Merrivale Ave IG4 55 D5
Merrow Ct CR4 180 B1
Merrow St SE17 117 B1 262 C1
Merrow Way CR0 224 A2
Merrow Wlk SE17 262 D2
Merrydown Way BR7 188 B2
Merry Fiddlers RM8 81 B6
Merryfield SE3 142 D3
Merryfield Gdns HA7 25 C5
Merryfield Ho SE12 165 C1
Merryhill Cl E4 19 D4
Merry Hill Rd WD23 8 A3
Merryhills Ct N14 15 C6
Merryhills Dr EN2 4 A1
Merryhills Prim Sch EN2 4 B1
Merryweather Ct
13 Dartmouth Pk N19 71 C5
1 New Malden KT3 199 C4
Mersea Ho IG11 78 D2
Mersey Ct 10 KT2 175 D2
Mersey Ho 10 N7 72 C3
Mersey Rd E17 53 B6
Mersey Wlk UB5 85 C5
Mersham Dr NW9 44 D4
Mersham Pl
Penge SE20 184 B2
South Norwood CR7 183 B1
Mersham Rd CR7 183 B1
Merstone Ho SW18 157 D5
Merten Rd RM6 59 A2
Merthyr Terr SW13 134 B6
MERTON 179 C2
Merton Abbey Mills SW19 180 A2
Merton Abbey Prim Sch SW19 179 D2
Merton Ave
Chiswick W4 111 D2
Hillingdon UB10 60 D1
Northolt UB5 64 A3
Merton Cl SM4 201 B4
Merton Court Sch DA14 190 C6
Merton Ct Barnet EN5 1 D1
Welling DA16 146 B3
Merton Gdns BR5 210 D4
Merton Hall Gdns SW20 179 A2
Merton Hall Rd SW19 179 A2
Merton High St SW19 180 A3
Merton Ho SW18 157 C3
Merton Ind Pk SW19 180 A2
Merton La N6 70 D6
Merton Lo
New Barnet EN5 14 A6
3 Streatham SW16 182 A5
Merton Mans SW20 178 D1
MERTON PARK 179 C1
Merton Park Par SW19 179 B2
Merton Park Prim Sch SW19 179 C1
Merton Park Sta SW19 179 C2
Merton Pl 9 SW19 180 A3
Merton Rd Barking IG11 79 D1
Croydon SE25 206 A4
Enfield EN2 5 B5
Harrow HA2 42 A1
Ilford IG3 57 D2
Leytonstone E17 54 A3
Merton SW19 179 D3
Wandsworth SW18 157 C4
Merton Rise NW3 70 C1
Merton Road Ind Est SW18 157 C4
Merton Way
East Molesey KT8 196 A6
Hillingdon UB10 60 D1
Merttins Rd SE15 162 D6
Meru Cl NW5 71 A3
Mervan Rd SW2 138 C1
Mervyn Ave SE9 167 A2
Mervyn Ct SE18 145 C6
Mervyn Rd
Brentford W13 109 A3
Shepperton TW17 193 A2
Mervyn Stockwood Ho 1 SE9 167 A2
Messaline Ave W3 89 A1
Messent Rd SE9 165 D6
Messer Ct CR0 220 D4
Messeter Pl SE9 166 C5
Messina Ave NW6 69 C1
Messiter Ho N1 233 D5
Met Appts The SE12 164 D6
Metcalfe Ho 23 SW8 137 D3
Metcalfe Wlk 2 TW13 173 A6
Metcalf Rd TW15 170 D5
Meteor St SW11 137 A1
Meteor Way SM6 220 A1
Metford Cres EN3 7 C5
Metherell Ho N21 17 B5
Metheringham Way NW9 27 C2
Methley Ho 8 N7 72 B6
Methley St SE11 116 C1 261 B1
Methodist Central Hall★ SW1 115 D4 249 D1
Methuen Cl HA8 26 C3
Methuen Pk N10 49 B6
Methuen Rd
Belvedere DA17 125 D2
Bexleyheath DA6 147 B1
Edgware HA8 26 C3
Methwold Rd W10 90 D2
Metro Bsns Ctr The SE26 185 B5
Metro Ctr UB4 106 C6
Metro Ho E7 77 B2
Metro Ind Ctr TW7 130 C3
Metropolis Apartments 5 SW12 159 B3
Metropolitan Benefit Societies Almshouses 3 N1 73 C2
Metropolitan Bsns Ctr 9 N1 73 C1
Metropolitan Cl 23 E14 97 C2
Metropolitan Ctr The UB6 85 D6
Metro Trad Ctr HA9 66 D4
Meudon Ct KT6 197 D4
Mews Pl IG8 37 A6
Mews St E1 118 A5
Mews The
Beckenham BR3 185 C2
Hampton TW12 174 A4
Hornsey N8 50 C5
Redbridge IG4 55 D4
Shoreditch N1 235 B6
Thornton Heath SW16 182 B2
Tottenham N15 51 C5
5 Upper Holloway N19 50 A1
Woolwich SE18 122 D1
Mexborough NW1 232 A5
Mexfield Rd SW15 157 B6
Meyer Gn EN1 6 A5
Meyer Ho 1 SW12 159 B4
Meymott St SE1 116 D5 251 C3
Meynell Cres E9 74 D1
Meynell Gdns E9 74 D1
Meynell Rd E9 74 D1
Meyrick Ct CR7 204 C3
Meyrick Ho 8 E14 97 C2
Meyrick Rd
Battersea SW11 136 C2
Willesden NW10 68 A2
Miah Terr 10 E1 118 A5
Miall Wlk SE26 185 A6
Micawber Ave UB8 82 C3
Micawber Ct N1 235 B2
Micawber Ho 27 SE16 118 A4
Micawber St N1 95 A4 235 B2
Michael Cliffe Ho EC1 234 B1
Michael Faraday Ho SE17 262 D1
Michael Faraday Sch SE17 117 B1 262 D1
Michael Gaynor Cl W7 108 D5
Michael Marshall Ho 2 SE9 167 A2
Michaelmas Cl SW20 200 C6
Michael Rd
Leytonstone E11 54 D1
Parsons Green SW6 135 D4 265 D2
South Norwood SE25 205 C6
Michaels Cl SE13 142 C1
Michael Sobell Sinai Sch HA3 44 C3
Michaelson Ho 4 SE21 183 C6
Michael Tippet Sch SE27 161 A2
Michael Tippett Sch The SE11 116 C2 261 B3
Michelangelo Ct 14 SE16 118 B1
Micheldever Rd SE12 164 D5
Michelham Gdns TW1 152 D1
Michelle Ct Acton W3 111 B6
North Finchley N12 30 A5
Michell Ho TW1 152 D3
Michels Almshouses 11 TW10 154 A6
Michelsdale Dr 3 TW9 132 A1
Michelson Ho SE11 260 D3
Michel's Row 2 TW9 132 A1
Michel Wlk SE18 122 D1
Michigan Ave E12 78 B4
Michigan Ho E14 119 C3
Michleham Down N12 29 B6
Mickledore NW1 232 B3
Micklefield Ct CR0 204 D3
Mickleham Cl BR5 190 A1
Mickleham Gdns SM3 217 A2
Mickleham Rd BR5 190 A1
Mickleham Way CR0 224 B1
Micklethwaite Rd SW6 135 C6 265 B5
Mickleton Ho 30 W2 91 C2
Midas Bsns Ctr RM10 81 D4
Midas Metro Ctr SM4 200 D2
Midcroft HA4 39 C1
Middle Dene NW7 11 B1
Middlefield NW8 92 B6 229 C6
Middlefielde W13 87 B2
Middlefield Gdns IG2 56 D3
Middle Green Cl 3 KT5 198 B3
Middleham Gdns N18 34 A4
Middleham Rd N18 34 A4
Middle La Hornsey N8 50 A4
Teddington TW11 174 D4
Middle Lane Mews N8 50 A4
Middle Mill KT5 198 B6
Middle Park Ave SE9 165 D4
Middle Park Prim Sch SE9 165 D4
Middle Rd
East Barnet EN4 14 C5
Finchley N10 30 C2
Harrow HA2 42 B1
Mitcham SW16 181 D1
12 Newham E13 99 A5
Middle Row W10 91 A3
Middle Row Prim Sch W10 91 A3
Middlesborough Rd N18 34 A4
Middlesex Bsns Ctr UB2 107 B4
Middlesex Cl UB6 85 D3
Middlesex Coll of Computing & Tech HA0 66 A3
Middlesex Ct
5 Chiswick W4 111 D2
6 Harrow HA1 42 D4
Middlesex Cty Cricket Sch N3 29 D1
Middlesex Ho
Marylebone W1 239 B4
4 Penge SE20 184 C3
Wembley HA0 87 D6
Middlesex Pas EC1 241 D3
Middlesex Pl 13 E9 74 C2
Middlesex Rd CR4 204 A5
Middlesex St E1 95 D1 243 C2
Middlesex Univ N17 33 D4
Middlesex Univ (Cat Hill) EN4 15 A6
Middlesex Univ (Enfield Campus) EN3 18 C6
Middlesex Univ (Hendon Campus) NW4 46 B5
Middlesex Univ Trent Park EN4 3 C3
Middle St Croydon CR0 221 A5
Holborn EC1 242 A4
Middle Temple★ EC4 116 C6 251 A6
Middle Temple La EC4 116 C6 251 A6
Middleton Ave
Chingford Green E4 19 B1
Greenford UB5 86 B5
Sidcup DA14 190 C5
Middleton Cl E4 19 B1
Middleton Ct
Bromley BR1 187 B3
New Barnet EN5 2 A1
Middleton Dr
Bermondsey SE16 118 D4
Pinner HA5 40 A6
Middleton Gdns IG2 56 D3
Middleton Gr N7 72 A3
Middleton Ho
Dalston E8 73 D1
Newington SE1 262 C5
Middleton Mews N7 72 A3
Middleton Pl W1 239 A3
Middleton Rd
Carshalton CR4, SM5 202 B2
Dalston E8 73 D1
Golders Green NW11 47 C2
Hayes UB3 83 B2
Middleton St E2 96 B4
Middleton Way SE13 142 B1
Middleway NW11 47 D4
Middle Way Hayes UB4 84 C3
Mitcham SW16 181 D1
Middle Way The HA3 24 D1
Middlewich Ho 7 UB5 85 B3
Midfield Prim Sch BR5 190 A3
Midfield Way BR5 190 B2
Midford Ho 1 NW4 46 D5
Midford Pl W1 239 B5
Midholm
East Finchley NW11 47 D5
Wembley HA9 44 C1
Midholm Cl NW11 47 D5
Midholm Rd CR0 223 A6
Midhope Ho WC1 233 B1
Midhope St WC1 233 B1
Midhurst 1 SE26 184 C4
Midhurst Ave
Muswell Hill N10 49 A6
Thornton Heath CR0 204 C2
Midhurst Ct N8 50 A2
Midhurst Gdns UB10 61 A1
Midhurst Hill DA6 169 C6
Midhurst Ho 6 E14 97 B1
Midhurst Par N10 49 A6
Midhurst Rd W13 109 A3
Midhurst Way E5 74 A4
Midland Mainline Terminal NW1 93 D5 232 D3
Midland Pl E14 120 A1
Midland Rd
Leytonstone E10 54 A2
St Pancras NW1 94 A4 233 A2
Midland Terr
Cricklewood NW2 68 D5
Dagenham NW10 89 C3
Midlea Ho EN3 6 C4
Midleton Rd KT3 177 A1
Midlothian Ho NW2 68 B4
Midlothian Rd E3 97 B3
Midmoor Rd
Merton SW19 179 A2
Streatham SW12 159 C3
Midship Cl SE16 118 D5
Midship Point E14 119 C4
Midstrath Rd NW10 67 C4
Midsummer Apartments 7 SM2 217 C1
Midsummer Ave TW4 129 B1
Midsummer Ct
Blackheath Pk SE12 143 A1
Edgware HA8 10 D1
Harrow HA1 42 B4
Midway SM3 201 B2
Midway Ho EC1 234 D2
Midwinter Cl 3 DA16 146 A2
Midwood Cl NW2 68 B5
Mighell Ave IG4 55 D4
Milan Ct N11 31 D2
Milan Rd UB1 107 B4
Milborne Gr SW10 256 B1
Milborne Ho 11 E9 74 C2
Milborne St E9 74 C2
Milborough Cres SE12 164 C5
Milbourne La KT10 212 A3
Milbourne Lodge Jun Sch KT10 212 A2
Milbourne Lodge Sen Sch KT10 212 B2
Milbrook KT10 212 A2
Milbrook Ct NW3 48 A1
Milburn Dr 1 UB7 104 A6
Milburn Ho SW20 178 B1
Milcote St SE1 251 D1
Mildenhall Rd E5 74 C5
Mildmay Ave N1 73 B2
Mildmay Ct N1 73 B3
Mildmay Gr N N1 73 B3
Mildmay Gr S N1 73 B3
Mildmay Ho 6 SW15 156 C6
Mildmay Mission Hospl E2 95 D4
Mildmay Pk N1 73 B3
Mildmay Rd Ilford IG1 78 D5
Stoke Newington N1 73 C3
Mildmay St N1 73 B2
Mildon Ho EN3 6 C3
Mildred Ave
Hayes UB3 105 B3
Northolt UB5 63 D3
Mildura Ct N8 50 B5
MILE END 97 A3
Mile End Pl E1 96 D3
Mile End Rd E1, E3 96 D3
Mile End Sta E3 97 B4
Mile End The E17 34 D2
Mile Rd
Hackbridge SM6 203 A1
Wallington CR0, CR4, CR9 203 D1
Miles Bldgs NW1 237 A4
Miles Cl SE28 123 B5
Miles Coverdale Prim Sch W12 112 C4
Miles Ct Croydon CR0 220 D6
Stepney E1 96 B1
Miles Dr SE28 123 C5
Miles Ho 5 SE10 120 C1
Miles Lo Harrow HA1 42 B4
Stratford New Town E15 76 B3
Milespit Hill NW7 28 C5
Miles Pl NW8 236 D4
Miles Rd Hornsey N8 50 A6
Mitcham CR4 202 C6
Miles St SW8 138 A6 270 B5
Milestone Cl
Edmonton N9 18 A2
Sutton SM2 218 B1
Milestone Ct TW7 131 A4
Milestone Green SW14 133 B1
Milestone Ho KT1 197 D5
Milestone Rd SE19 183 D4
Miles Way N20 14 C2
Milfoil St W12 112 A6
Milford Cl SE2 147 A6
Milford Ct
Southall UB1 107 C5
3 Stamford Hill N16 51 C1
Milford Gdns
Croydon CR0 206 D4
Edgware HA8 26 C3
Milford Gdns *continued*
Wembley HA0 65 D3
Milford Gr SM1 218 A4
Milford La WC2 116 C6 251 A6
Milford Mews SW16 160 B1
Milford Rd Ealing W13 109 B5
Southall UB1 107 C6
Milk St Bromley BR1 187 B4
City of London EC2 95 A1 242 B2
Newham E16 122 D5
Milkwell Gdns IG8 37 B3
Milkwell Yd 7 SE5 139 A4
Milkwood Rd SE24 138 D1
Milk Yd E1 118 C6
Millais Ave E12 78 C3
Millais Cres KT19 215 C3
Millais Ct 9 UB5 84 D5
Millais Gdns HA8 26 C1
Millais Rd Enfield EN1 17 D6
Leyton E11 76 B4
New Malden KT3 199 C2
Millais Way KT19 215 A4
Milland Ho 11 SW15 156 A3
Millard Cl 21 N16 73 C3
Millard Terr RM10 81 C2
Millars Meadow Cl SE12 165 A6
Millbank
Wallington SM6 219 D3
Westminster SW1 116 A2 260 A3
Millbank Ho KT6 198 B2
Millbank Prim Sch SW1 115 D2 259 D3
Millbank Way SE12 165 A6
Millbourne Rd TW13 173 A6
Mill Bridge EN5 13 B5
Millbrook 1 E18 55 A6
Millbrook Ave DA16 145 B1
Millbrooke Ct 7 SW15 157 A6
Millbrook Gdns RM6 59 A3
Millbrook Ho 4 SE15 140 A6
Millbrook Pl NW1 232 A4
Millbrook Rd
Brixton SW9 138 D2
Edmonton N9 18 B3
Mill Cl SM5 219 A6
Mill Cnr EN5 1 B4
Millcroft Ho SE6 185 D6
Mill Ct Hendon NW7 29 A2
Leyton E10 76 A5
14 Thamesmead SE28 124 B6
Millender Wlk SE16 118 C2
Millennium Bridge★ SE1, EC4 252 A5
Millennium Bsns Ctr NW2 68 B6
Millennium City Acad W1 238 D3
Millennium Cl E16 99 B1
Millennium Dr E14 120 B2
Millennium Harbour E14 119 C4
Millennium Ho E17 52 D4
Millennium Pl 27 E2 96 B5
Millennium Prim Sch SE10 120 D3
Millennium Sq SE1 253 D2
Millennium Way SE10 120 C3
Miller Ave EN3 7 C5
Miller Cl Bromley BR1 187 B5
Carshalton CR4 202 D2
Pinner HA5 22 C1
Miller Ct
Bexleyheath DA7 147 D2
8 Hendon NW9 46 A5
Miller Ho Harringay N15 50 D5
9 Streatham SW2 160 A4
Miller Rd
Mitcham SW19 180 B4
Thornton Heath CR0 204 C1
Miller's Ave E8, N16 73 D3
Millers Cl NW7 28 A6
Millers Ct 3 HA0 88 A5
Miller's Ct 1 W4 111 D1
Millers Green Cl EN2 4 D2
Miller's House Visitor Ctr★ 1 E3 98 A4
Millers Mead Ct SW19 180 B3
Miller St NW1 232 A4
Miller's Terr 1 E8 73 D3
Miller's Way W6 112 C4
Millers Wharf Ho E1 118 A5
Millers Yd N3 29 D3
Miller Wlk SE1 251 B3
Millet Rd UB6 85 D5
Mill Farm Ave TW16 171 C3
Millfarm Bsns Pk TW4 151 A4
Mill Farm Cl HA5 22 C1
Mill Farm Cres TW4 151 A3
Millfield Charlton TW16 171 B2
Finsbury Pk N4 72 C6
Kingston u T KT1 198 B6
Millfield Ave E17 35 B2
Millfield La N6 70 D6
Millfield Pl N6 71 A6
Millfield Rd Hendon HA8 27 A1
Twickenham TW4 151 B3
Millfields Com Sch E5 74 C4
Millfields Rd E5 74 C5
Mill Gdns SE26 162 B1
Mill Gn CR4 203 A2

Mill Green Bsns Pk CR4 203 A2
Mill Green Rd CR4 203 A2
Millgrove St 6 SW11 137 A3
Millharbour E14 119 D4
Millhaven Cl RM6 58 B3
MILL HILL 28 B5
Mill Hill SW13 134 A2
Mill Hill Broadway Sta NW7 27 C4
Mill Hill Circus NW7 27 D5
Mill Hill Cty High Sch NW7 11 C2
Mill Hill East Sta NW7 29 A3
Mill Hill Gr 11 W3 110 D5
Mill Hill Ind Est NW7 27 D4
Mill Hill Rd
  Barnes SW13 134 A3
  South Acton W3 110 D4
Mill Hill Sch NW7 28 B6
Mill Hill Terr 9 W3 110 D5
Mill Ho
  4 Lewisham SE13 142 A2
  Morden SM4 202 A5
  Woodford IG8 36 D5
Millhouse Pl SE27 182 D6
Millicent Fawcett Ct N17 33 D2
Millicent Preston Ho 4 IG11 101 B6
Millicent Rd E10 53 B1
Milligan Ho SE23 163 B3
Milligan St E14 119 B6
Milliners Ho SW18 135 C1
Milling Rd HA8 27 B3
Millington Ho N16 73 B5
Millington Rd UB3 105 D3
Mill La Brondesbury NW6 69 B3
  Carshalton SM5 219 A5
  Croydon CR0 220 C5
  Dagenham RM6 59 A3
  Sewardstone E4 7 D2
  Woodford IG8 36 D5
  Woolwich SE18 122 C1
Mill Lane Trad Est CR0 220 B5
Millman Ct
  Bloomsbury WC1 240 C5
  Greenwich SE3 143 B5
Millman Mews WC1 240 C5
Millman Pl WC1 240 D5
Millman St WC1 94 B3 240 C5
Millmark Gr SE14 141 A3
Millmarsh La EN3 7 B3
Millmead Bsns Ctr N17 52 B6
Millmead Ind Ctr N17 52 B6
Mill Mead Rd N17 52 B6
MILL MEADS 98 B5
Millner Ct SE4 141 B3
Mill Pl Chislehurst BR7 188 D2
  Kingston u T KT1 198 B6
  Limehouse E14 97 A1
Mill Plat TW7 131 A3
Mill Plat Ave TW7 131 A3
Mill Pond Cl SW8 137 D5 269 D3
Millpond Est SE16 118 B4
Millpond Pl 2 SM6 219 A5
Mill Rd Ilford IG1 78 C5
  Merton SW19 180 A3
  Newham E16 121 B5
  Twickenham TW2 152 A2
Mill Ridge HA8 26 C5
Mill River Trad Est EN3 7 A1
Mill Row N1 95 C6
Mills Cl UB10 82 C5
Mills Ct 9 Leyton E11 76 C5
  Shoreditch EC2 95 C4
Mills Gr Hendon NW4 46 D6
  1 South Bromley E14 98 A2
Mills Ho Nine Elms SW8 269 B2
  Walthamstow E17 54 B6
Millshott Cl SW6 134 C4
Millside SM5 218 D6
Millside Pl TW7 131 B3
Millson Cl N20 14 B2
Mills Row W4 111 B2
Mill St
  Bermondsey SE1 117 D4 253 D2
  Kingston u T KT1 198 A6
  Mayfair W1 249 A6
Millstream Cl N13 32 C5
Millstream Ho 14 SE16 118 B4
Millstream Rd SE1 117 D4 253 C1
Mill Trad Est The NW10 89 A4
Mill Vale BR2 186 D1
Mill View Cl KT17 215 D1
Mill View Gdns CR0 222 D5
MILLWALL 119 C3
Millwall Dock Rd E14 119 C3
Mill Way Edgware NW7 27 C5
  Feltham TW14 150 B6
Millway Gdns UB5 63 B2
Millwood Rd TW3, TW7 152 A6
Millwood St 10 W10 91 A2
Mill Yd E1 118 A6
Milman Cl HA5 40 D6
Milman Rd NW6 91 A5
Milman's Ho SW10 266 C5
Milman's St SW10 136 B6 266 C5
Milne Ct Enfield EN2 4 C3
Milne Ct *continued*
  4 Woodford E18 37 A2
Milne Field HA5 23 C3
Milne Gdns SE9 166 A6
Milne Ho 18 SE18 122 B2
Milner Bldg N16 73 B5
Milner Dr TW2 152 B4
Milner Ho
  2 Battersea SW11 136 B2
  Hayes UB4 84 B4
Milner Pl N1 94 C6 234 B6
Milner Rd
  Dagenham RM8 80 C6
  Kingston u T KT1 197 D6
  Merton SW19 179 D2
  Morden SM4 202 B4
  Newham E15 98 C4
  South Norwood CR7 205 B6
Milner Sq N1 72 D1
Milner St SW3 114 D2 257 C4
Milner Wlk SE9 167 B3
Milnthorpe Rd W4 133 B6
Milo Rd SE22 161 D5
Milrood Ho 5 E1 96 D2
Milroy Wlk SE1 251 C4
Milson Rd W14 113 A3 254 A6
Milsted Ho 23 E5 74 B3
Milton Ave Barnet EN5 13 B6
  Becontree NW10 89 B6
  Carshalton SM1 218 C4
  Crouch End N6 49 C2
  Kingsbury NW9 45 A6
  Plashet E6 78 A1
  Thornton Heath CR0 205 B2
Milton Cl
  Bermondsey SE1 117 D2 263 C3
  Carshalton SM1 218 B5
  Hampstead Garden Suburb N2 48 A3
  Hayes UB4 84 A1
Milton Court Rd SE14 141 A6
Milton Cres IG2 57 A3
Milton Ct Fulham SW6 135 A2
  Ilford RM6 58 C2
  Kingston u T KT2 176 A6
  St Luke's EC2 242 C4
  Twickenham TW2 152 C1
  Uxbridge UB10 60 D5
  9 Wandsworth SW18 157 C6
Milton Dr
  Borehamwood WD6 10 D6
  Littleton TW17 192 A5
Milton Gdns TW19 148 B3
Milton Gr
  Friern Barnet N11 31 D5
  Stoke Newington N16 73 C4
Milton Ho
  12 Beckenham BR3 185 C3
  19 Bethnal Green E2 96 C4
  2 Camberwell SE5 139 B5
  5 Kingston u T KT2 176 D4
  Sutton SM1 217 C5
Milton House Mans E8 73 D4
Milton Lo
  4 Sidcup DA14 190 A6
  Southgate N21 16 D3
  Twickenham TW1 152 D4
Milton Pk N6 49 C2
Milton Pl 3 N7 72 C3
Milton Rd Acton W3 111 B5
  Belvedere DA17 125 C2
  Bexley DA16 145 D4
  Crouch End N6 49 C2
  Ealing W7 108 D6
  Hampton TW12 173 C3
  Harrow HA1 42 C5
  1 Hendon NW9 46 A2
  Mill Hill NW7 28 A5
  Mitcham CR4 181 A3
  Mortlake SW14 133 B2
  Sutton SM1 217 C4
  Thornton Heath CR0 205 B2
  Tottenham N15 50 D6
  Tulse Hill SE24 160 D6
  Uxbridge UB10 60 D4
  Wallington SM6 219 D2
  Walthamstow E17 53 C5
  Wimbledon SW19 180 A4
Milton St EC1, EC2 95 B2 242 C4
Milton Way UB7 104 B2
Milverton NW5 71 A3
Milverton Dr UB10 61 A4
Milverton Gdns IG3 79 D6
Milverton Ho SE23 163 A1
Milverton Rd NW6 68 C1
Milverton St SE11 116 C1 261 B1
Milverton Way SE9 188 C6
Milward St E1 96 B2
Milward Wlk 14 SE18 144 C6
Mimosa N15 51 B4
Mimosa Ct
  Colney Hatch N12 30 C4
  South Lambeth SW4 270 B1
Mimosa Ho UB4 84 C2
Mimosa Rd UB4 84 C2
Mimosa St SW6 135 B4 264 D1
Mina Rd Merton SW19 179 C2
  Walworth SE17 117 C1 263 B2
Minard Rd SE6 164 C3
Minchenden Cres N14 15 D1
Minchenden Ct N14 15 D2
Minchin Ho 10 E14 97 C1
Mincing La EC3 117 C6 253 A6
Minden Rd Cheam SM3 217 B6
Minden Rd *continued*
  Penge SE20 184 B2
Minehead Ct HA2 63 C6
Minehead Rd
  Harrow HA2 63 C5
  Streatham SW16 182 B5
Mineral Cl EN5 12 C6
Mineral St SE18 123 C2
Minera Mews SW1 258 B4
Minerva Cl
  Kennington SW9 138 C5
  Sidcup DA14 189 C6
Minerva Rd
  Becontree NW10 89 B4
  Chingford E4 35 D3
  Kingston u T KT1 176 B1
Minerva St E2 96 B5
Minerva Wlk EC1 241 D2
Minet Ave NW10 89 C5
Minet Ctry Pk UB2, UB3, UB4 106 C4
Minet Dr UB3 106 A5
Minet Gdns
  Dagenham NW10 89 C5
  Hayes UB3 106 B5
Minet Ho 20 E1 96 A1
Minet Jun & Inf Schs UB3 106 B5
Minet Rd SE5, SW9 138 D3
Minetta Ct 19 EN5 13 D6
Minford Gdns W14 112 D4
Mingard Wlk N7 72 B5
Ming St E14 119 C6
Minimax Cl TW14 150 A5
Ministry Way SE9 166 B2
Mink Ct TW4 128 C3
Minnie Bennett Ho SE3 143 C5
Minniedale KT5 198 B4
Minnow Wlk SE17 263 B3
Minories EC3 117 D6 253 C6
Minshaw Ct DA14 189 D6
Minshull Pl 23 BR3 185 C3
Minshull St SW8 269 C1
Minson Rd E9 96 D6
Minstead Gdns SW15 155 D4
Minstead Way KT3 199 C3
Minster Ave SM1 217 C6
Minster Ct EC3 253 B6
Minster Dr CR0 221 C4
Minster Gdns KT8 195 B5
Minsterley Ave TW16, TW17 193 C5
Minster Rd
  Bromley BR1 187 B3
  Brondesbury NW2 69 A3
Minster Wlk N8 50 A5
Minstrel Ct HA3 24 C1
Minstrel Gdns KT5 198 B5
Mint Bsns Pk 12 E16 99 A2
Mint Cl UB10 82 D4
Mintern Cl N13 16 D1
Minterne Ave UB2 107 C2
Minterne Rd HA3 44 B4
Minterne Way UB4 84 C1
Mintern St N1 95 B5 235 D4
Minton Ho SE11 261 A4
Minton Mews 3 NW6 69 D2
Mint Rd SM5, SM6 219 B4
Mint St SE1 252 B2
Mint Wlk CR0 221 A5
Mirabel Rd SW6 135 B5 264 D4
Mirage Ctr The HA9 66 D4
Miranda Cl 19 E1 96 C2
Miranda Ct W3 88 B1
Miranda Ho
  6 Belvedere DA17 125 C1
  17 Hoxton N1 95 C5
Miranda Rd N19 49 C1
Mirfield Ct SE20 184 A1
Mirfield St SE7 121 D3
Miriam Ct DA14 190 B6
Miriam Rd SE18 123 C1
Mirravale Ct 11 IG9 21 C2
Mirravale Trad Est RM8 59 A2
Mirren Cl HA2 63 B5
Mirror Path SE12 165 C1
Misbourne Rd UB10 82 C6
Missenden SE17 262 D1
Missenden Cl TW14 149 D3
Missenden Gdns SM4 202 A3
Missenden Ho NW8 237 A6
Mission Gr E17 53 A4
Mission Grove Prim Sch E17 53 B5
Mission Pl SE15 140 A4
Mission Sq 13 TW8 132 A6
Mission The
  13 Bermondsey SE16 118 B4
  14 Poplar E14 97 B1
Missouri Ct HA5 40 C3
Misterton Ct SW11 266 D2
Mistletoe Cl CR0 206 D1
Mistley Thorn IG1 56 C2
Mistral SE5 139 C4
Mistral Ct E4 19 D1
Mistys Field KT12 194 C1
Mitali Pas 21 E1 96 A1
MITCHAM 202 D5
Mitcham Garden Village CR4 203 A4
Mitcham Ho 9 SE5 139 A4
Mitcham Ind Est CR4 181 A2
Mitcham Junction Sta CR4 203 A4
Mitcham La SW16 181 C5
Mitcham Pk CR4 202 C5
Mitcham Rd Ilford IG3 57 D2
Mitcham Rd *continued*
  Newham E6 100 A4
  Upper Tooting SW17 180 D5
Mitcham Sta CR4 202 C5
Mitchell 19 NW9 27 D2
Mitchell Brook Prim Sch NW10 67 C2
Mitchellbrook Way NW10 67 B2
Mitchell Cl
  Abbey Wood SE2 124 C2
  Belvedere DA17 125 D3
Mitchell Ct SW14 133 C1
Mitchell Ho
  Gunnersbury W4 110 D1
  6 Islington N1 72 C1
  31 Shepherd's Bush W12 112 B6
Mitchell Rd
  Edmonton N13 33 A5
  Orpington BR6 227 D4
Mitchell's Pl SE21 161 C4
Mitchell St EC1 95 A3 242 B6
Mitchell Way
  1 Bromley BR1 187 A2
  Tokyngton NW10 67 A2
Mitchell Wlk E6 100 B2
Mitchison Rd N1 73 B2
Mitchley Rd N17 52 A6
Mitford Cl KT9 213 C2
Mitford Rd N19 72 A6
Mitre Bridge Ind Pk W10 90 B3
Mitre Cl
  Shepperton TW17 193 B3
  Sutton SM2 218 B1
Mitre Ct
  Belvedere DA17 125 C1
  1 Ilford RM6 58 B2
  9 Woodford E18 37 A2
Mitre Ho RM7 59 D5
Mitre Rd
  Lambeth SE1 116 C4 251 B2
  Newham E15 98 C5
Mitre Sq EC3 243 B1
Mitre St EC3 95 C1 243 B1
Mitre The 9 E14 119 B6
Mitre Way W10 90 B2
Mizzen Ct E14 119 C4
Moatbridge Sch SE9 165 D5
Moat Cl BR6 227 D2
Moat Cres N3 47 D6
Moat Croft DA16 146 C2
Moat Ct Eltham SE9 166 B5
  Sidcup DA15 167 D1
Moat Dr Harrow HA1 42 B5
  5 Newham E13 99 C5
  Ruislip HA4 39 C2
Moat Farm Rd UB5 63 B1
Moatfield NW6 69 A1
Moat Lodge The HA1 64 C6
Moat Pl Acton W3 88 D1
  Stockwell SW9 138 B2
Moat Sch The SW6 135 A3
Moat Side Enfield EN3 6 D1
  Feltham TW13 172 C6
Moat The KT3 177 C2
Moberly Rd SW4 159 D4
Mobey Ct SW4 270 A1
Moby Dick RM6 59 B5
Mocatta Ho 9 E1 96 B3
Modbury Gdns NW5 71 A2
Modder Pl SW15 134 D1
Model Cotts SW14 133 A2
Model Farm Cl SE9 166 A1
Modling Ho 8 E2 96 D5
Modoc Ho EN3 18 D6
Moelwyn Hughes Ct N7 71 D3
Moelyn Mews HA1 43 A4
Moffat Ct
  Upper Tooting SW17 180 C6
  Wimbledon SW19 179 C5
Moffat Ho 24 SE5 139 A5
Moffat Rd Bowes Pk N13 32 A4
  South Norwood CR7 183 B1
  Upper Tooting SW17 180 D6
Mogden La TW7 152 D6
Mohammedi Pk Complex UB5 85 C6
Mohawk Ho 33 E3 97 A5
Mohmmad Khan Rd E11 54 D1
Mohr Ct N22 32 B3
Moidart Ct HA8 10 D2
Moineau 18 NW9 27 D2
Moira Cl N17 33 C1
Moira Ct SW17 159 A2
Moira Ho 13 SW9 138 C4
Moira Rd SE9 144 B1
Molasses Ho 1 SW11 136 A2
Molasses Row 2 SW11 136 A2
Mole Abbey Gdns KT8 195 D6
Mole Ct
  2 Bedford Pk W12 111 C4
  West Ewell KT19 215 A4
Mole Ho NW8 236 D5
Molember Ct KT7 196 C5
Molember Rd KT8 196 C4
Molescroft SE9 167 A1
Molesey Ave KT12, KT8 195 B4
Molesey Bsns Ctr KT8 195 B4
Molesey Dr SM3 217 A5
Molesey Ho E2 243 C6
Molesey Hospl KT8 195 C4
Molesey Park Ave KT8 195 D4
Molesey Park Cl KT8 196 A4
Molesey Park Rd KT8 196 A4
Molesey Rd KT12 195 A2
Molesford Rd SW6 265 A1
Molesham Cl KT8 195 D6
Molesham Way KT8 195 D6
Molesworth Ho 9 SE17 138 D6
Molesworth St SE13 142 A2
Moliner Ct 4 BR3 185 C3
Mollie Davis Ct SE19 183 D4
Mollison Ave EN3 7 B5
Mollison Dr SM6 220 A1
Mollison Sq SM6 219 D1
Mollison Way HA8 26 C1
Molly Huggins Cl SW12 159 C4
Molton Ho N1 233 D5
Molvic Ct BR3 185 B1
Molyneux Dr SW17 181 B6
Molyneux Ho W1 237 B2
Molyneux St W1 92 C2 237 B3
Monarch Cl
  Coney Hall BR4 224 D4
  East Bedfont TW14 149 C4
Monarch Ct Ealing W5 87 C2
  Hampstead Garden Suburb N2 48 A4
Monarch Dr E16 99 D2
Monarch Mews
  Walthamstow E17 53 D3
  West Norwood SW16 182 C5
Monarch Par CR4 180 D1
Monarch Pl
  Buckhurst Hill IG9 21 C2
  Sutton SM1 218 B3
Monarch Rd DA17 125 C3
Monarchs Ct
  1 Edgware NW7 27 B5
  Harrow HA2 41 C2
Monarch's Way HA4 39 C1
Monarch Way IG2 57 B3
Mona Rd SE15 140 C3
Mona St E16 98 D2
Monastery Gdns EN2 5 B3
Monaveen Gdns KT8 195 D6
Monck's Row SW18 157 B5
Monck St SW1 115 D3 259 D5
Monckton Ct W14 254 C6
Monclar Rd SE5 139 B1
Moncorvo Cl SW7 114 C4 247 A1
Moncrieff Cl 4 E6 100 A1
Moncrieff St SE15 140 A3
Mondial Way UB7 127 A5
Mondragon Ho SW8 270 B2
Monega Prim Sch E12 77 D2
Monega Rd E7, E12 77 D2
Monet Ct 15 SE16 118 B1
Moneyer Ho N1 235 C2
Monica Ct SW16 181 D4
Monica James Ho 12 DA14 168 A1
Monica Shaw Ct NW1 232 D3
Monier Rd E3 75 C1
Monivea Rd BR3 185 B3
Monkbretton Ho E2 96 A4
Monk Ct W12 112 A5
Monk Dr E16 121 A6
MONKEN HADLEY 1 A3
Monken Hadley CE Prim Sch EN4 1 C4
Monkfrith Ave N14 15 B5
Monkfrith Cl N14 15 B4
Monkfrith Prim Sch N14 15 A4
Monkfrith Way N14 15 B4
Monkham's Ave IG8 37 B5
Monkham's Dr IG8 37 B5
Monkham's La IG8 37 B6
Monkleigh Rd SM4, SW20 201 A5
Monkridge 3 N8 49 D2
Monks Ave
  East Molesey KT8 195 B4
  New Barnet EN5 14 A5
Monks Cl
  Abbey Wood SE2 124 D2
  Enfield EN2 5 A3
  Harrow HA2 63 D6
  Ruislip HA4 62 D4
Monks Cres KT12 194 B1
Monksdene Gdns SM1 217 D5
Monks Dr W3 88 C1
Monksfield N4 72 C6
MONKS ORCHARD 207 A3
Monks Orchard Rd BR3, CR0 207 C2
Monks Orchard Sch CR0 206 D4
Monks Park Gdns HA9 66 D1
Monks Pk HA9 67 A2
Monks Rd EN2 5 A3
Monk St SE18 122 C2
Monks Way
  Beckenham BR3 207 C3
  Crofton BR5 211 B1
  Harmondsworth UB7 126 A6
  Temple Fortune NW11 47 B5
Monkswell Ct N10 31 A2
Monkswell Ho E2 96 A4
Monkswood Gdns
  Borehamwood WD6 11 B6
  Ilford IG5 56 C6
Monk Terr SE23 163 B2
Monkton Ho
  32 Bermondsey SE16 118 D4
  22 Hackney E5 74 B3
Monkton Rd DA16 145 D3
Monkton St SE11 116 C2 261 B4
Monkville Ave NW11 47 B5
Monkville Par 1 NW11 47 B5
Monkwell Sq EC2 242 B3
Monmouth Ave
  Teddington KT1 175 C3
  Wanstead E18 55 B6
Monmouth Cl
  Bedford Pk W4 111 B3
  Bexley DA16 146 A1
  Mitcham CR4, SW16 204 A5
Monmouth Ct 9 W7 86 D2
Monmouth Gr TW8 110 A2
Monmouth Ho
  5 Camden Town NW5 71 B2
  Wandsworth SW18 157 C5
Monmouth Pl W2 91 D1
Monmouth Rd
  Dagenham RM9 81 B3
  Hayes UB3 105 D2
  Lower Edmonton N9 18 C2
  Newham E6 100 B4
  Notting Hill W2 91 C1
Monmouth St WC2 94 A1 240 A1
Monnery Rd N19 71 C5
Monnow Rd SE1 118 A2
Mono La TW13 150 B2
Monoux Almshouses E17 53 D5
Monoux Gr E17 35 C2
Monroe Cres EN1 6 B4
Monroe Dr SW14 154 D6
Monroe Ho
  16 Crouch End N19 49 D2
  Lisson Gr NW8 230 B1
Monro Gdns HA3 24 C3
Monro Ho
  16 Hampstead NW3 70 A4
  Putney SW15 156 B6
Monro Way E5 74 A4
Monsal Ct E5 75 A4
Monsell Ct 4 N4 72 D5
Monsell Rd N4, N5 72 D5
Monson Prim Sch SE14 140 D5
Monson Rd
  Deptford SE14 140 D5
  Willesden Green NW10 90 B5
Mons Way BR2 210 A3
Montacute Rd
  Bushey WD23 8 C4
  Carshalton SM4 202 B3
  Forest Hill SE6 163 B4
Montagu Cres N18 34 B6
Montagu Ct W1 237 D3
Montague Ave
  Brockley SE4 141 C1
  Ealing W7 108 D5
Montague Cl
  Borough The SE1 252 C4
  Walton-on-T KT12 194 A2
Montague Ct 16 DA14 168 A1
Montague Fell HA0 64 D4
Montague Gdns W3 110 C6
Montague Pl WC1 93 D2 239 D4
Montague Rd
  Ealing W13 87 B1
  Hanwell W7 108 D4
  Hornsey Vale N8 50 B4
  Hounslow TW3 129 D2
  Leytonstone E11 76 D6
  Merton SW19 179 D3
  Richmond TW10 154 A5
  Shacklewell E8 74 A3
  Southall UB2 107 A2
  Thornton Heath CR0 204 D1
  Tottenham Hale N15 52 A5
  Uxbridge UB8 60 A1
Montague Sq SE15 140 C5
Montague St
  Bloomsbury WC1 94 A2 240 A4
  City of London EC1 242 A3
Montague Terr 1 BR2 209 A5
Montague Waye UB2 107 A3
Montague Works HA0 88 B5
Montagu Gdns
  Edmonton N18 34 B6
  Wallington SM6 219 C4
Montagu Ind Est N18 34 C6
Montagu Mans W1 92 D2 237 D3
Montagu Mews N W1 237 D3
Montagu Mews S W1 237 D2
Montagu Mews W W1 237 D2
Montagu Pl W1 92 D2 237 D3
Montagu Rd
  Hendon NW4 46 A3
  Lower Edmonton N9, N18 18 C1
Montagu Row W1 237 D3
Montagu Sq W1 92 D1 237 D2
Montagu St W1 92 D1 237 D2
Montaigne Cl SW1 259 D3
Montalt Ho IG8 36 D6
Montalt Rd IG8 36 D5
Montana Bldg 4 SE13 141 D4
Montana Gdns
  Penge SE26 185 B5
  5 Sutton SM1 218 A3
Montana Rd
  Upper Tooting SW17 159 A1
  Wimbledon SW20 178 C2
Montbelle Prim Sch SE9 188 C6
Montbelle Rd SE9 166 D1

Montcalm Cl
Hayes BR2 209 A3
Yeading UB4 84 B4
Montcalm Ho E14 119 C3
Montcalm Rd SE7 143 D5
Montclair Ct 21 N12 29 D6
Montclare St E2 95 D3 243 C6
Monteagle Ave IG11 79 A2
Monteagle Ct
Barking IG11 79 A1
27 Hoxton N1 95 C5
Monteagle Prim Sch RM9 102 B6
Monteagle Way
Nunhead SE15 140 B2
Shacklewell E5 74 A5
Montefiore Ct 2 N16 51 D1
Montefiore St 2 SW8 137 B3
Montego Cl 10 SW2 138 C1
Montem Prim Sch N7 72 B5
Montem Rd
Forest Hill SE23 163 B4
New Malden KT3 199 C5
Montem St N4 50 B1
Montenotte Rd N8 49 C4
Monteray Studios W10 91 A5
Monterey Cl NW7 27 C5
Montesole Ct 7 HA5 22 C1
Montesquieu Terr 3 E16 98 D1
Montford Pl
Kennington SE11 138 C6
Kennington SE11 261 A1
Montford Rd TW16 194 A5
Montfort Ho
4 Bethnal Green E2 96 C4
Cubitt Town E14 120 A3
Montfort Pl SW19 156 D3
Montgolfier Wlk UB5 85 A4
Montgomerie Ct 2 BR3 185 C2
Montgomery Ave KT10 212 C6
Montgomery Cl
Blackfen DA15 167 D5
Mitcham CR4 204 A5
Montgomery Ct W4 133 A6
Montgomery Gdns SM2 218 B1
Montgomery Ho 5 SW14 133 B2
Montgomery Lo 38 E1 96 C3
Montgomery Rd
Acton W4 111 A2
Edgware HA8 26 B4
Montholme Rd SW11 158 D5
Monthope Rd 17 E1 96 A2
Montolieu Gdns SW15 156 B6
Montpelier Ave
Ealing W5 87 C2
Sidcup DA5 168 D4
Montpelier Cl UB10 82 C6
Montpelier Ct
5 Beckenham BR2 208 D5
Ealing W5 87 D2
Montpelier Gdns
Ilford RM6 58 C2
Newham E6 99 D4
Montpelier Gr NW5 71 C3
Montpelier Mews SW7 257 B6
Montpelier Pl
Knightsbridge SW7 257 B6
21 Stepney E1 96 C1
Montpelier Prim Sch W5 87 D2
Montpelier Rd
Ealing W5 87 D2
Finchley N3 30 A2
Peckham SE15 140 B4
Sutton SM1 218 A4
Montpelier Rise
Golders Green NW11 47 A2
Wembley HA9 43 D1
Montpelier Row
Blackheath Vale SE3 142 D3
Twickenham TW1 153 C4
Montpelier Sq SW7 114 C4 247 B1
Montpelier St SW7 114 C3 257 B6
Montpelier Terr SW7 247 B1
Montpelier Vale SE3 142 D3
Montpelier Way NW11 47 A2
Montpelier Wlk SW7 114 C3 257 B6
Montpellier Ct KT12 194 B3
Montrave Rd SE20 184 C3
Montreal Ho
Catford SE6 163 D3
Hayes UB4 84 B4
Montreal Pl WC2 250 C6
Montreal Rd IG1 57 A2
Montrell Rd SW2 160 A3
Montrose Ave
Falconwood DA16 145 C2
Hendon HA8 27 B2
Kensal Rise NW6 91 A5
Sidcup DA15 168 A4
Twickenham TW2 151 D4
Montrose Cl
Ashford TW15 171 A5
Falconwood DA16 145 D2
Woodford IG8 37 A6
Montrose Cres
Finchley N12 30 A4
1 Wembley HA0 66 A2
Montrose Ct
2 Catford SE6 164 D2
Hendon NW9 27 A1
Montrose Ct *continued*
Knightsbridge SW7 114 B4 246 D1
Temple Fortune NW11 47 B5
Montrose Gdns
Mitcham CR4 180 D1
Sutton SM1 217 D6
Montrose Ho
Belgravia SW1 248 B1
Millwall E14 119 C3
Twickenham TW2 151 D4
Montrose Pl SW1 115 A4 248 B1
Montrose Rd
East Bedfont TW14 149 B5
Harrow HA3 24 D1
Montrose Villas 5 W6 112 A1
Montrose Way SE23 162 D3
Montserrat Ave IG8 36 B3
Montserrat Cl SE19 183 B5
Montserrat Rd SW15 135 A1
Montway Hts SW19 179 D3
Monument Gdns SE13 164 A6
Monument St EC3 117 B6 252 D6
Monument Sta EC3 117 B6 252 D6
Monument The* EC3 252 D6
Monument Way N17 51 D6
Monza Bldg The E1 118 C6
Monza St E1 118 C6
Moodkee St SE16 118 C3
Moody Rd SE15 139 D4
Moody St E1 96 D4
Moon Ct SE12 143 A1
Moon Ho HA1 42 D5
Moon La EN5 1 B2
Moon St N1 94 D6 234 C6
Moorcroft HA8 26 D2
Moorcroft Ct 4 N3 29 B1
Moorcroft Gdns BR1 210 A4
Moorcroft La UB8 82 C2
Moorcroft Rd SW16 160 A1
Moorcroft Sch UB8 82 B1
Moorcroft Way HA5 41 A4
Moordown SE18 144 D4
Moore Cl Mitcham CR4 181 B1
Mortlake SW14 133 A2
Wallington SM6 220 A1
Moore Cres RM9 102 B6
Moore Ct N1 234 C5
Moorefield Rd N17 33 D1
Moore Ho
16 Bethnal Green E2 96 C4
5 Greenwich SE10 120 D1
Hornsey N8 50 A5
7 Shadwell E1 118 C6
Wandsworth SW17 158 B1
1 West Norwood SE27 183 A6
Mooreland Rd BR1 187 A2
Moore Park Ct SW6 265 D4
Moore Park Rd SW6 135 D5 265 C3
Moore Rd SE19 183 A4
Moore St SW3 114 D2 257 C4
Moore Wlk E7 77 A4
Moorey Cl 2 E15 98 D6
Moorfield Ave W5 87 D3
Moorfield Rd
Chessington KT9 214 A3
Enfield EN3 6 C4
Moorfields EC2 95 B2 242 C3
Moorfields Ct 6 SW16 181 C6
Moorfields Eye Hospl EC1 95 B4 235 C1
Moorfields Highwalk EC2 242 C3
Moorgate EC2 95 B2 242 C3
Moorgate Pl EC2 242 C2
Moorgate Sta EC2 95 B2 242 C3
Moorgreen Ho EC1 234 C2
Moorhead Way SE3 143 B2
Moorhouse 17 NW9 27 D2
Moorhouse Rd
Harrow HA3 43 D6
Notting Hill W2 91 C1
Moorings Ho 3 TW8 131 C5
Moorings The 5 E16 99 C2
Moor La
Broadgate EC2 95 B2 242 C3
Chessington KT9 214 A3
Moorland Cl TW4 151 C4
Moorland Ct N21 16 B5
Moorland Rd SW9 138 D1
Moorlands
Chislehurst BR7 188 D3
Northolt UB5 85 A6
17 Wallington SM6 219 B2
Moorlands Ave NW7 28 B4
Moor Lane Jun Sch KT9 214 B3
Moormead Dr KT19 215 C3
Moor Mead Rd TW1 153 A5
Moor Park Gdns KT2 177 C3
Moor Park Ho N21 16 D4
Moor Pl EC2 242 C3
Moorside Ct W13 109 C5
Moorside Rd BR1 186 D6
Moor St W1 239 D1
Moortown Rd WD19 22 C6
Moot Ct NW9 44 C4
Morant Ho SW9 138 B3
Morant Pl N22 32 B2
Morant St E14 119 C6
Mora Prim Sch NW2 68 C4
Mora Rd NW2 68 C4
Mora St EC1 95 A4 235 B1
Morat St SW9 138 B4 270 D2
Moravian Cl SW3 266 D5
Moravian Pl SW10 136 B6 266 D5
Moravian St 10 E2 96 C4
Moray Ave UB3 105 D5
Moray Cl HA8 10 D2
Moray Ho
11 Kingston u T KT6 198 A4
9 Mile End E1 97 A3
Moray Mews N4, N7 72 B6
Moray Rd N4, N7 72 B6
Mordaunt Gdns RM9 81 A1
Mordaunt Ho
4 Becontree NW10 89 B6
34 Clapham SW8 137 D3
Mordaunt Rd NW10 89 B6
Mordaunt St SW9 138 B2
MORDEN 201 D3
Morden Court Par SM4 201 D5
Morden Ct SM4 201 D5
Morden Gdns
Greenford UB6 64 D3
Mitcham CR4 202 B5
Morden Hall SW19 201 D6
Morden Hall Rd SM4 202 A5
Morden Hill SE13 142 A3
Morden Ho
Morden SM4 201 C5
19 Tulse Hill SW2 160 C5
Morden La SE13 142 A4
Morden Lo BR2 186 B1
Morden Mount Prim Sch SE13 141 D3
MORDEN PARK 201 A3
Morden Park Sch Sports Ctr SM4 201 B4
Morden Prim Sch SM4 201 C4
Morden Rd
Dagenham RM6 59 A2
Kidbrooke SE3 143 A3
Merton SW19 179 D1
Mitcham CR4, SM4 202 B5
Morden Road Mews SE3 143 A3
Morden Road Sta SW19 179 D1
Morden South Sta SM4 201 C4
Morden St SE13 141 D4
Morden Sta SW19 201 D6
Morden Way SM3 201 C2
Morden Wharf Rd SE10 120 C3
Mordern Ho NW1 237 B5
Mordon Rd IG3 57 D2
Mordred Rd SE6 164 C2
Morecambe Cl 3 E1 96 D2
Morecambe Gdns HA7 25 D6
Morecambe St SE17 117 A1 262 B2
Morecambe Terr N18 33 B6
More Cl
Canning Town E16 98 D1
West Kensington W14 113 A2 254 A3
Morecoombe Cl KT2 176 D3
Morecroft TW2 152 A2
Moredown Ho 3 E8 74 A3
Moree Way N18 34 A6
More House Sch SW1 114 D3 257 D5
Moreland Ct 3 NW2 69 C5
Moreland Prim Sch EC1 94 D4 234 D1
Moreland St EC1 94 D4 234 D2
Moreland Way E4 20 A1
Morella Rd SW11, SW12 158 D4
Morell Ho 5 SW9 138 B3
Morello Ave UB8 82 D2
Morello Ct HA9 66 B5
Moremead Rd SE6 185 C6
Morena St SE6 163 D4
Moresby Ave KT5 198 D2
Moresby Rd E5 52 B1
Moresby Wlk 6 SW8 137 B3
More's Gdn SW3 266 D5
Moreton Ave TW7 130 C4
Moreton Cl Mill Hill NW7 28 C4
Tottenham N15 51 B3
Upper Clapton E5 52 C1
Moreton Ho
Bermondsey SE16 118 B3
Upper Tooting SW17 180 B6
Moreton Pl SW1 115 C1 259 B2
Moreton Rd
Croydon CR2 221 B3
North Cheam KT4 216 B6
Tottenham N15 51 B3
Moreton St SW1 115 D1 259 C2
Moreton Terr SW1 115 C1 259 B2
Moreton Terr Mews N SW1 259 B2
Moreton Terr Mews S SW1 259 B2
Moreton Twr 3 W3 110 D5
Morford Cl HA4 40 B2
Morford Way HA4 40 B2
Morgan Ave E17 54 B5
Morgan Cl RM10 81 C1
Morgan Ct
Ashford TW15 170 D5
Morgan Ct *continued*
5 Battersea SW11 136 B3
Carshalton SM5 218 D4
Morgan Ho
Nine Elms SW8 269 B2
Pimlico SW1 259 B3
Morgan Rd Islington N7 72 C3
Notting Hill W10 91 B2
Plaistow BR1 187 A3
Morgan's La UB3 83 B2
Morgan St
Canning Town E16 98 D2
Globe Town E3 96 D4
Morgan's Wlk SW11 267 A3
Morgan Terr RM6 58 C4
Moriah Jewish Day Sch The HA5 41 A1
Moriatry Cl N7 72 A4
Morie St SW18 157 D6
Morieux Rd E10 53 B1
Moring Rd SW17 181 A6
Morkyns Wlk SE21 161 C1
Morland Ave CR0 205 C1
Morland Cl
Golders Green NW11 47 D1
Hampton TW12 173 B5
Mitcham CR4 202 C6
Morland Ct W12 112 B4
Morland Est E8 74 A1
Morland Gdns
Southall UB1 107 D5
Stonebridge NW10 67 B1
Morland Ho
Kilburn NW6 91 C6
Notting Hill W11 91 A1
Somers Town NW1 232 B3
Westminster SW1 260 A4
Morland Mews N1 72 C1
Morland Rd
Croydon CR0 205 D2
Dagenham RM10 81 C1
Harrow HA3 44 A5
Ilford IG1 78 D6
Penge SE20 184 D4
Sutton SM1 218 A3
Walthamstow E17 52 D4
Morley Ave Chingford E4 36 B3
Edmonton N18 34 A6
Tottenham N22 32 D1
Morley Cl BR6 226 D6
Morley Coll SE1 116 C3 261 B6
Morley Cres
Edgware HA8 11 A2
Ruislip HA4 62 C6
Morley Cres E HA7 43 D6
Morley Cres W HA7 43 C6
Morley Ct Bromley BR3 186 B2
Chingford Hatch E4 35 B5
Lewisham SE13 142 A1
Shortlands BR2 208 D5
Morley Hill EN2 5 B5
Morley Ho
Stoke Newington N16 74 A6
Streatham SW2 160 A4
W1 238 D2
Morley Rd
Barking IG11 101 B6
Cheam SM3 201 B1
Chislehurst BR7 189 A2
Dagenham RM6 59 A4
Lewisham SE13 142 A1
Leytonstone E10 54 A1
Newham E15 98 D5
Twickenham TW1 153 D5
Morley St SE1 116 C4 251 B1
Morna Rd SE5 139 A3
Morning La E9 74 C2
Morningside Prim Sch E9 74 C2
Morningside Rd KT4 216 C6
Mornington Ave
Bromley BR1 209 D6
Ilford IG1 56 C2
West Kensington W14 113 B2 254 C3
Mornington Avenue Mans W14 254 C3
Mornington Cl IG8 37 A6
Mornington Cres
Camden Town NW1 93 C5 232 A4
Cranford TW5 128 B4
Mornington Crescent Sta NW1 93 C5 232 A4
Mornington Ct NW1 232 A4
Mornington Gr E3 97 C4
Mornington Lo EN1 17 C6
Mornington Mews 2 SE5 139 A4
Mornington Pl
4 New Cross SE8 141 B5
Regent's Pk NW1 232 A4
Mornington Rd
Ashford TW15 171 A5
Chingford E4 20 B4
Greenford UB6 85 D3
Leytonstone E11 54 D1
New Cross SE14, SE8 141 B5
Woodford IG8 36 D6
Mornington St NW1 93 B5 231 D4
Mornington Terr NW1 93 B5 231 D4
Mornington Wlk TW10 175 C6
Morocco St SE1 117 C4 253 A1
Morpeth Gr E9 96 D6
Morpeth Rd E9 96 D6
Morpeth Sec Sch E2 96 C4
Morpeth St E2 96 D4
Morpeth Terr SW1 115 C2 259 A4
Morpeth Wlk N17 34 B3
Morrab Gdns IG3 79 D5
Morrel Cl EN5 2 A2
Morrel Ct 11 E2 96 A5
Morris Ave E12 78 B3
Morris Blitz Ct 2 N16 73 D4
Morris Cl Croydon CR0 207 A4
Orpington BR6 227 C5
Morris Ct Chingford E4 19 D1
Croydon CR0 220 D4
3 Herne Hill SE5 139 B1
Morris Gdns SW18 157 C4
Morris Ho
17 Bethnal Green E2 96 C4
Lisson Gr NW8 237 A5
1 Stockwell SW4 138 A1
10 Tufnell Pk N19 71 C4
Morrish Rd SW2 160 A4
Morrison Ave
Chingford E4 35 C4
Tottenham N17 51 C6
Morrison Bldgs 5 E1 96 A1
Morrison Ct
7 Barnet EN5 1 A1
Finchley N12 30 C3
Morrison Ho SW2 160 C3
Morrison Rd
Barking IG11 103 A5
24 Brixton SW9 138 C3
Hayes UB4 84 B4
Morrison St SW11 137 A2
Morrison Yd N17 33 D1
Morris Pl N4 72 C6
Morris Rd
Bow Comm E14 97 D2
Dagenham RM8 81 B6
Isleworth TW7 130 D2
Leyton E15 76 C4
Morriss Ho
9 Bermondsey SE16 118 B4
5 Upper Clapton E5 74 B6
Morris St E1 96 B1
Morris Stephany Ho 4 SE27 182 D6
Morriston Cl WD19 22 C5
Morritt Ho 2 HA0 65 D3
Morse Cl E13 99 A4
Morshead Mans W9 91 C4
Morshead Rd W9 91 C4
Morson Rd EN3 19 A5
Morston Gdns SE9 188 B6
Mortain Ho 9 SE16 118 B2
Morten Cl SW4 159 D5
Morteyne Rd N17 33 B2
Mortgramit Sq SE18 122 C3
Mortham St E15 98 C6
Mortimer Cl
1 Child's Hill NW2 69 B5
Streatham SW16 159 D2
Mortimer Cres
Paddington NW6 91 D6
Worcester Pk KT4 215 B5
Mortimer Ct
St John's Wood NW8 229 B3
4 Whetstone N20 14 A2
Mortimer Dr EN1 17 C6
Mortimer Est NW6 91 D6
Mortimer Ho
6 Shepherd's Bush W11 112 D5
West Kensington W14 254 B3
Mortimer Lo 11 SW19 157 A3
Mortimer Market WC1 239 B5
Mortimer Pl NW6 91 D6
Mortimer Rd
De Beauvoir Town N1 73 C1
Ealing W13 87 C1
Kensal Green NW10 90 C4
Mitcham CR4 180 D2
Newham E6 100 B4
Mortimer Sq W11 112 D6
Mortimer St W1 93 C2 239 B3
Mortimer Terr NW5 71 B4
MORTLAKE 133 A2
Mortlake Cl CR0 220 A5
Mortlake Dr CR4 180 C2
Mortlake High St SW14 133 B2
Mortlake Ho 7 W4 111 A2
Mortlake Rd Ilford IG1 79 B4
Newham E16 99 B1
Richmond SW14, TW9 132 C4
Mortlake Sta SW14 133 A2
Mortlake Terr TW9 132 C5
Mortlock Cl SE15 140 B4
Mortlock Ct E12 77 D4
Morton Cl
Hillingdon UB8 82 B3
Stepney E1 96 C1
Wallington SM6 220 B1
Morton Cres N14 31 D6
Morton Ct UB5 64 A3
Morton Gdns SM6 219 C3
Morton Ho
Kennington SE17 138 D6
West Norwood SE27 183 B5
Morton Mews SW5 255 C3
Morton Pl SE1 261 A5
Morton Rd Islington N1 73 A1
Morden SM4 202 B4
Stratford E15 76 D1
Morton Way N14 31 D6
Morvale Cl DA17 125 B2
Morval Rd SW2 160 C6
Morven Rd SW17 158 D1
Morville Ho SW18 158 B5
Morville St E3 97 C5
Morwell St WC1 239 D3
Moscow Pl W2 245 C6
Moscow Rd W2 113 D6 245 C6
Mosedale NW1 231 D1
Moseley Row SE10 120 D2
Moselle Ave N22 32 C1
Moselle Cl N8 50 B6
Moselle Ct N9 18 C1
Moselle Ho 2 N17 33 D3
Moselle Pl N17 33 D3
Moselle Sch (main site) N17 33 C1
Moselle Sch (Upper) N17 51 A6
Moselle St N17 33 D3
Mosque Tower 26 E1 96 A2
Mossborough Cl N12 29 D4
Mossbourne Com Acad E8 74 A3
Mossbury Rd SW11 136 C2
Moss Cl Pinner HA5 23 A1
Spitalfields E1 96 A2
Mossdown Cl DA17 125 C2
Mossford Ct IG6 56 D6
Mossford Gn IG6 57 A6
Mossford St E3 97 B3
Moss Gdns
Feltham TW13 150 A2
South Croydon CR2 222 D1
Moss Hall Cres N12 30 A4
Moss Hall Ct N12 29 D4
Moss Hall Gr N12 29 D4
Moss Hall Inf Sch N12 29 D4
Moss Hall Jun Sch N3 29 D4
Mossington Gdns SE16 118 C2
Moss La HA5 23 A1
Mosslea Rd
Bromley Comm BR2 209 D4
Orpington BR6 227 A5
Penge SE20 184 C4
Mossop St SW3 114 C2 257 B4
Moss Rd RM10 81 C1
Mossville Gdns SM4 201 B5
Mosswell Ho 4 N10 31 A3
Moston Cl UB3 105 D1
Mostyn Ave HA9 66 B3
Mostyn Gdns NW10 90 D5
Mostyn Gr E3 97 C5
Mostyn Lo N5 73 A4
Mostyn Rd
Brixton SW9 138 C4
Bushey WD23 8 A6
Grahame Pk HA8 27 C3
Merton SW19 179 B1
Mosul Way BR2 210 A3
Motcomb St SW1 115 A3 258 A6
Moth Cl SM6 220 A1
Mothers Sq The 18 E5 74 B4
Motley Ave EC2 243 A6
Motley St SW8 137 C3
MOTSPUR PARK 200 A3
Motspur Park Sta KT3 200 B4
Motspur Pk KT3 200 A3
MOTTINGHAM 165 D2
Mottingham Ct SE9 166 B3
Mottingham Gdns SE9 165 D3
Mottingham La SE9 165 C3
Mottingham Prim Sch SE9 166 B1
Mottingham Rd
Chislehurst SE9 166 B1
Ponders End N9 18 D4
Mottingham Sta SE9 166 B3
Mottisfont Rd SE2 124 B2
Moules Ct SE5 139 A5
Moulins Rd E9 74 C1
Moulsford Ho
6 Lower Holloway N7 72 A3
32 Paddington W2 91 C2
Moulton Ave TW3, TW5 129 B3
Moundfield Rd N16 52 A3
Mound The SE9 166 C1
Mounsey Ho 18 W10 91 A4
Mountacre Cl SE26 183 D6
Mount Adon Pk SE21, SE22 162 A4
Mountague Pl 2 E14 120 A6
Mountain Ho SE11 260 C2
Mountaire Ct NW9 45 B4
Mount Angelus Rd SW15 155 D4
Mount Ararat Rd TW10 154 A6
Mount Arlington 3 BR2 186 C1
Mount Ash Rd SE26 162 B1
Mount Ave Chingford E4 19 D1
Ealing W5 87 D2
Southall UB1 85 C1
Mountbatten Cl
Plumstead Comm SE18 145 C6
6 West Norwood SE19 183 C5
Mountbatten Ct 8 IG9 21 D2
Mountbatten Gdns BR3 207 A5
Mountbatten Ho N6 49 A2
Mountbatten Mews SW18 158 A3

Mountbel Rd HA7 25 A1
Mount Carmel 3 N7 72 B3
Mount Carmel RC Tech Coll for Girls N19 49 D1
Mount Cl Bromley BR1 188 A2
Cockfosters EN4 3 A1
Ealing W5 87 C2
Mountcombe Cl KT6 198 A2
Mountcombe Ho SW17 180 B5
Mount Ct
6 Kingston u T KT2 176 D3
West Wickham BR4 224 C6
Mount Culver Ave DA14 190 D4
Mount Dr Bexley DA6 169 A6
Harrow HA2, HA5 41 B4
Welsh Harp HA9 67 A6
Mountearl Gdns SW16, SW2 160 B1
Mount Eaton Ct W5 87 C2
Mount Echo Ave E4 19 D3
Mount Echo Dr E4 19 D3
Mount Ephraim La SW16 159 D1
Mount Ephraim Rd SW16 159 D1
Mount Felix KT12 193 D1
Mountfield NW2 69 B6
Mountfield Cl SE6 164 B4
Mountfield Ct SE13 164 B5
Mountfield Rd
Ealing W5 88 A1
East Finchley N3 47 C6
Wallend E6 100 C4
Mountford Ho EN2 4 D1
Mount Ford St E1 96 A1
Mountfort Cres N1 72 C1
Mountfort Terr 1 N1 72 C1
Mount Gdns SE26 162 B1
Mount Gr HA8 27 B6
Mountgrove Rd N5 73 A5
Mounthurst Rd BR2 208 D2
Mountier Ct 12 E11 55 A4
Mountington Park Cl HA3 43 D3
Mountjoy Cl SE2 124 B4
Mountjoy Ho EC2 242 A3
Mount Lo N6 49 C3
Mount Lodge SW4 137 D1
Mount Mews TW12 173 D2
Mount Mills EC1 234 D1
Mount Nod Rd SW16, SW2 160 B1
Mount Olive Ct W7 108 C4
Mount Par EN4 2 C1
Mount Park Ave HA1 64 C6
Mount Park Cres W5 87 D1
Mount Park Rd
Ealing W5 87 D1
Harrow HA1 64 B5
Pinner HA5 40 A4
Mount Pk SM5 219 A1
Mount Pl 7 W3 110 D5
Mount Pleasant
Cockfosters EN4 2 D1
Finsbury WC1 94 C3 241 A5
Ilford IG1 79 A3
Ruislip HA4 62 D6
Wembley HA0 88 B6
West Norwood SE27 183 A6
Mount Pleasant Cotts
Osidge N14 15 D4
Southall UB1 85 C1
Mount Pleasant Cres N4 50 B2
Mount Pleasant Hill E5 74 C6
Mount Pleasant La E5 52 B1
Mount Pleasant Pl SE18 123 B2
Mount Pleasant Rd
Ealing W5 87 C3
Higham Hill E17 35 A1
Kingston u T KT3 199 A6
Lewisham SE13 164 A5
Tottenham N17 33 C1
Willesden NW10 90 C6
Mount Pleasant Villas N4 50 B2
Mount Prim Sch The KT3 199 A6
Mount Rd Bexley DA6 169 A6
Chessington KT9 214 B3
Dagenham RM8 59 B1
Dollis Hill NW2 68 C5
East Barnet EN4 14 C6
Feltham TW13 151 A1
Hayes UB3 106 A4
Hendon NW4 46 A3
Kingston u T KT3 199 B6
Mitcham CR4 180 C1
South Norwood SE19 183 B4
Wimbledon SW18, SW19 157 D2
Mount Row W1 115 B6 248 C5
Mount Sch NW7 28 C5
Mountside HA7 25 A2
Mounts Pond Rd SE3, SE13 142 B3
Mount Sq The 3 NW3 70 A5
Mount St W1 115 A6 248 B5
Mount Stewart Ave HA3 43 D2
Mount Stewart Jun & Inf Schs HA3 43 D2
Mount Terr E1 96 B2
Mount The Bexley DA6 169 D6
Cheam SM1 217 C2
Chislehurst BR7 188 C2
Finchley N2 30 C1
Hampstead NW3 70 A5
Harrow HA1 64 C6
Kensington W8 245 A3
Kingston u T KT3 199 D6
North Cheam KT4 216 B4
Northolt UB5 63 D3
6 South Croydon CR2 221 A3
Upper Clapton E5 74 B6
Welsh Harp HA9 67 A6
Whetstone N20 14 A2
Mount Tyndal NW3 48 B1
Mount Vernon NW3 70 A4
Mountview
Edgware NW7 11 B1
Northwood HA6 22 A4
5 Streatham SW16 160 B1
Mount View Ealing W5 87 D3
Enfield EN2 4 B5
Southall UB2 106 D2
Mountview Cl NW11 48 A1
Mountview Cotts EN5 11 D5
Mountview Ct
Harringay N8 50 D5
3 Whetstone N20 14 A2
Mount View Rd
Chingford E4 20 B4
Claygate KT10 213 B1
Hornsey Vale N4 50 B3
Kingsbury NW9 45 B4
Mount Villas SE27 160 D1
Mountwood KT8 195 D6
Mountwood Ho W5 87 D3
Mourne Ho NW3 70 A2
Movers La IG11 101 C6
Movers Lane (Flyover) IG11 101 C5
Mowat Ct KT4 215 D6
Mowatt Cl N19 49 D1
Mowbray Ct
South Norwood SE19 183 D2
Wood Green N22 32 C2
Mowbray Gdns UB5 85 C6
Mowbray Ho 5 N2 30 B1
Mowbray Rd
Brondesbury NW6 69 A1
Edgware HA8 26 C6
New Barnet EN5 14 A6
Richmond TW10 153 C1
South Norwood SE19 183 D2
Mowlem Prim Sch E2 96 C5
Mowlem St E2 96 B5
Mowlem Trad Est N17 34 C3
Mowll St SW9 138 C5
Moxon Cl E13 98 D5
Moxon St Barnet EN5 1 B2
Marylebone W1 93 A2 238 A3
Moye Cl 10 E2 96 A5
Moyers Rd E10 54 A2
Moylan Rd W6 135 A6 264 B5
Moyle Ho SW1 269 B6
Moyne Ho 16 SW9 138 D1
Moyne Pl NW10 88 C5
Moynihan Dr N21 16 A6
Moys Cl CR0 204 A3
Moyser Rd SW16 181 B5
Mozart St W10 91 B4
Mt Carmel RC Prim Sch W5 109 C3
Muchelney Rd SM4 202 A3
Mudchute Sta E14 119 D2
Mudie Ho 8 SW2 160 A4
Mudlarks Blvd 3 SE10 120 D3
Muggeridge Cl CR2 221 B3
Muggeridge Rd RM10 81 D4
Muirdown Ave SW14 133 B1
Muir Dr SW18 158 C5
Muirfield W3 89 C1
Muirfield Cl
23 Bermondsey SE16 118 B1
South Oxhey WD19 22 C6
Muirfield Cres E14 119 D3
Muirfield Gn WD19 22 C6
Muirfield Rd WD19 22 C6
Muirhead Quay IG11 101 A5
Muirkirk Rd SE6 164 A3
Muir Rd E5 74 A5
Muir St E16 122 A5
Mulbarton Ct BR7 189 B4
Mulberry Ave TW19 148 A3
Mulberry Bsns Ctr SE16 118 D4
Mulberry Cl Barnet EN4 2 B1
Charlton SE7 143 D6
Chelsea SW3 266 D5
Chingford E4 19 C2
East Dulwich SE22 162 A5
Hampstead NW3 70 B4
Hendon NW4 46 C6
Hornsey N8 50 A4
Northolt UB5 85 A5
Streatham SW16 181 C6
Mulberry Cres
Brentford TW8 131 C5
West Drayton UB7 104 C4
Mulberry Ct
Barking IG11 79 D1
Bexley DA16 145 D3
Finchley N2 48 C6
Finsbury EC1 234 D1
Islington N5 72 D3
1 Leyton E11 76 B4
10 Paddington W9 91 B4
4 Surbiton KT6 197 D2
Twickenham TW1 152 D1
Willesden NW10 67 B2
Mulberry Ho
1 Bethnal Green E2 96 C4
8 Deptford SE8 141 B6
Mulberry House Sch The NW2 69 A3
Mulberry La CR0 205 D1
Mulberry Mews
New Cross SE14 141 B4
2 Wallington SM6 219 C2
Mulberry Par UB7 104 C4
Mulberry Pl
Chiswick W6 112 A1
Greenwich SE9 143 D1
Mulberry Prim Sch N17 34 A1
Mulberry Rd E8 73 D1
Mulberry Sch for Girls
Stepney E1 96 B1
St George in t East E1 118 B6
Mulberry St 7 E1 96 A1
Mulberry Trees TW17 193 B2
Mulberry Way
Ilford IG6 57 A5
Woodford E18 37 B1
Mulberry Wlk SW3 136 B6 266 D6
Mulgrave Chambers SM2 217 D2
Mulgrave Hall SM2 217 D2
Mulgrave Ho 19 SE18 122 B2
Mulgrave Manor SM2 217 D2
Mulgrave Prim Sch SE18 122 C2
Mulgrave Rd
Belmont SM2 217 C2
Ealing W5 87 D3
Harrow HA1 65 A6
South Croydon CR0 221 B5
West Kensington W14 264 C6
Willesden NW10 67 D4
Woolwich SE18 122 C2
Mulholland Cl CR4 181 B1
Mulkern Rd N19 49 D1
Mullard Ho WC1 239 C4
Mullards Cl CR4 202 D1
Mullens Ho 7 SW15 156 C6
Mullen Twr EC1 241 A5
Muller Ho SE18 122 C1
Muller Rd SW4 159 D5
Mullet Gdns 7 E2 96 A4
Mulletsfield WC1 233 B1
Mull Ho 17 E3 97 B5
Mullins Path SW14 133 B2
Mullion Cl HA3 23 D2
Mullion Wlk WD19 22 D6
Mulready St NW8 237 A5
Multi Way W3 111 C4
Multon Ho E9 74 C1
Multon Rd SW18 158 B4
Mulvaney Way SE1 252 D1
Mumford Rd SE24 160 D6
Muncaster Cl TW15 170 C6
Muncaster Rd
Ashford TW15 170 D5
Balham SW11 159 A6
Muncies Mews SE6 164 A2
Mundania Ct SE22 162 B5
Mundania Rd SE22 162 C5
Munday Ho SE1 262 C5
Munday Rd E16 121 A6
Munden Ho 5 E3 97 D4
Munden St W14 113 A2 254 A4
Mundesley Cl WD19 22 C6
Mundford Rd E5 74 C6
Mundon Gdns IG1 57 B1
Mund St W14 113 B1 254 D1
Mundy Ho 6 W10 91 A4
Mundy St N1 95 C4
Mungo-Park Cl WD23 8 A2
Munnery Way BR6 226 D6
Munning Ho 12 E16 121 B5
Munnings Gdns TW7 152 B6
Munro Ho
Bermondsey SE1 252 D1
Lambeth SE1 251 A1
Munro Mews W10 91 A2
Munro Rd WD23 8 A6
Munslow Gdns SM1 218 B4
Munstead Ct 12 SM2 218 A1
Munster Ave TW4 151 A6
Munster Ct
Fulham SW6 135 B3
Teddington TW11 175 C4
Munster Gdns N13 33 A6
Munster Ho N17 33 D2
Munster Rd
Fulham SW6 135 A5 264 B4
Teddington TW11 175 C4
Munster Residences SW6 264 B2
Munster Sq NW1 93 B3 238 D6
Munton Rd SE1, SE17 117 A2 262 B4
Murchison Ave DA5 169 A3
Murchison Ho 1 W10 91 A2
Murchison Rd E10 76 A6
Murdoch Ho 4 SE16 118 C3
Murdock Cl E16 98 D1
Murdock St SE15 140 B6
Murfett Cl SW19 157 A2
Muriel Ct 18 E10 53 D2
Muriel St N1 94 B6 233 D6
Murillo Rd SE13 142 C1
Murley Ct N21 17 A4
Murphy Ho SE1 261 D6
Murphy St SE1 116 C4 251 A1
Murray Ave
Bromley BR1 187 B1
Murray Ave *continued*
Hounslow TW3 151 D6
Murray Cl SE28 123 C5
Murray Cres HA5 22 D2
Murray Ct
5 Harrow HA1 42 D3
Southall TW7 108 C3
Twickenham TW2 152 A2
Murray Gr N1 95 B5 235 C3
Murray Grey Ho UB4 83 B2
Murray Ho
1 North Finchley N12 30 B5
20 Woolwich SE18 122 B2
Murray Mews NW1 71 D1
Murray Rd
Brentford W5 109 C2
Richmond TW10 153 C2
Wimbledon SW19 178 D4
Murray Sq E16 121 B6
Murray St NW1 71 D1
Murray Terr NW3 70 B4
Musard Rd W6 135 A6 264 B6
Musbury St E1 96 C1
Muscal W6 264 A6
Muscatel Pl SE5 139 C4
Muschamp Prim Sch SM5 218 C6
Muschamp Rd
Camberwell SE15 139 D2
Carshalton SM5 218 C6
Muscott Ho 15 E2 96 A6
Muscovy Ho DA18 125 A4
Muscovy St EC3 253 B6
Museum Ho 7 E2 96 C4
Museum in Docklands* E14 119 C6
Museum Mans WC1 240 A3
Museum of Brands* W11 91 B1
Museum of Domestic Design & Architecture* EN4 15 A6
Museum St WC1 94 A1 240 A2
Musgrave Cl EN4 2 A4
Musgrave Cres SW6 135 C4 265 B2
Musgrave Ct SW11 267 A2
Musgrave Rd TW7 130 D4
Musgrove Ho 1 E9 74 D2
Musgrove Rd SE14 141 A4
Musical Mus The* TW8 132 A6
Musjid Rd 7 SW11 136 B3
Muslim Coll The W5 110 C6
Mus of Childhood (V&A)* E2 96 C4
Mus of Culinary History & Alimentation* NW1 232 B4
Mus of Garden History* SE1 260 C5
Mus of London* EC2 95 A2 242 A3
Mus of Richmond* TW10 153 D6
Mus of the Great Eastern Rly* E16 122 C4
Mus of the Order of St John* EC1 94 D3 241 C5
Musquash Way TW4 128 C3
Muston Rd E5 74 B6
Mustow Pl 2 SW6 135 B3
Muswell Ave N10 31 B1
MUSWELL HILL 49 A6
Muswell Hill N10 49 C6
Muswell Hill Broadway N10 49 B6
Muswell Hill Pl N10 49 B5
Muswell Hill Prim Sch N10 49 B6
Muswell Hill Rd N10 49 A4
Muswell Mews N10 49 B6
Muswell Rd N10 31 B1
Mutrix Rd NW6 91 C6
Mutton Pl NW1 71 A2
Muybridge Rd KT3 177 A1
Myatt Garden Prim Sch SE4 141 B3
Myatt Ho SE5 138 D3
Myatt Rd SW9 138 D4
Myatts Field Ct SE5 139 A4
Mycenae Rd SE3 143 A6
Mychell Ho 8 SW19 180 A3
Myddelton Ave EN1 5 C5
Myddelton Cl EN1 5 D4
Myddelton Gdns N21 17 A4
Myddelton Ho N8 50 A6
Myddelton Pas EC1 94 C4 234 B2
Myddelton Pk N20 14 B2
Myddelton Rd N8 50 A5
Myddelton Sq EC1 94 C4 234 B2
Myddelton St EC1 94 C4 234 B1
Myddleton Ave N4 73 A6
Myddleton Ho 14 N2 30 B1
Myddleton Mews N22 32 A3
Myddleton Rd N22 32 B3
Myers Ho 5 SE5 139 A5
Myers La SE14 140 D6
Myherin Ct SE23 163 B2
Mylius Cl SE26 184 B6
Mylius Cl SE14 140 C4
Mylne Cl W6 112 A1
Mylne Ho N21 17 B5
Mylne St EC1 234 A3
Mynterne Ct 16 SW19 156 D3
Myra St SE2 124 A2
Myrdle Ct 14 E1 96 A1
Myrdle St E1 96 A1
Myrna Cl SW19 180 C3
Myron Pl SE13 142 A2
Myrtle Alley SE18 122 C3
Myrtle Ave
Hatton TW14 149 C6
Ruislip HA4 40 B2
Myrtle Cl Barnet EN4 14 D3
Hillingdon UB8 82 B2
West Drayton UB7 104 B3
Myrtledene Rd SE2 124 A1
Myrtle Gdns W7 108 C5
Myrtle Gr Enfield EN2 5 B5
Kingston u T KT3 177 A1
Myrtle Ho SE14 140 D4
Myrtle Rd Acton W3 111 A5
Croydon CR0 223 C5
Edmonton N13 17 B1
Hampton TW12 174 A4
Hounslow TW3 130 A3
Ilford IG1 78 D6
Newham E6 100 A6
Sutton SM1 218 A3
Walthamstow E17 53 A3
Myrtle Wlk 20 N1 95 C5
Mysore Rd SW11 136 D1
Myton Rd SE21 161 B1
Mytton Ho SW8 270 C3

N

N1 Shopping Ctr N1 94 C5 234 B4
Nacton Ct 2 RM6 58 C4
Nadine St SE7 121 C1
Nadir Ct E11 55 A2
Naffenton Rise IG10 21 D6
Nagle Cl E17 36 B1
Nags Head N7 72 B4
Nags Head Ct EC1 242 B5
Nag's Head La DA16 146 B2
Nags Head Rd EN3 6 D1
Nags Head Sh Ctr The N7 72 B4
Naima Jewish Prep Sch NW6 91 D5
Nainby Ho SE11 261 A3
Nairn Ct
3 Wallington SM6 219 C2
Wimbledon SW19 179 D4
Nairne Gr SE5, SE24 139 B1
Nairn Rd HA4 62 C2
Nairn St E14 98 A2
Naish Ct N1 233 B6
Naish Ho SW19 201 D6
Naldera Gdns SE3 143 A6
Nallhead Rd TW13 172 C5
Nalton Ho 4 NW6 70 A1
Namba Roy Cl SW16 182 B6
Namton Dr CR7, SW16 204 B5
Nan Clark's La NW7 11 D2
Nankin St E14 97 C1
Nansen Ct 1 E11 76 C6
Nansen Ho 16 NW10 67 B1
Nansen Rd SW11 137 A2
Nansen Village 5 N12 29 D6
Nant Ct NW2 69 B6
Nantes Cl SW18 136 A1
Nant Rd NW2 69 B6
Nant St E2 96 B4
Naomi Watts Ho 11 SW19 179 A3
Naoroji St WC1 234 A1
Napier 15 NW9 27 D2
Napier Ave
Deptford E14 119 C1
Fulham SW6 135 B2
Napier Cl
New Cross SE14, SE8 141 B5
West Drayton UB7 104 B3
West Kensington W14 254 C6
Napier Ct
13 Croydon CR0 221 D6
Fulham SW6 135 B2
Grove Pk SE12 165 B1
Hayes UB4 84 C3
Shoreditch N1 235 C4
1 Surbiton KT6 197 D2
12 Wallington SM6 219 B2
Wembley HA0 65 D2
Napier Gr N1 95 A5 235 B4
Napier Ho Eltham SE12 165 B1
Kennington SE17 138 D6
Napier Lo TW15 171 B4
Napier Pl W14 113 B3 254 C5
Napier Rd
Ashford TW15 171 B3
Belvedere DA17 125 B2
Bromley BR2 209 B5
College Pk NW10 90 B4
Croydon SE25 206 B5
Enfield EN3 18 D6
Isleworth TW7 131 A1
Kensington W14 113 B3 254 C5
Leyton E11 76 C5
Newham E15 98 C5
South Croydon CR2 221 B1
Tottenham N17 51 C6
Wallend E6 100 C5
Wembley HA0 65 D2
Napier Terr N1 72 D1
Napier Wlk TW15 171 B3
Napoleon Rd
Hackney E5 74 B5
Twickenham TW1 153 B4
Napton Cl UB4 85 A3
Narbonne Ave SW4 159 C6
Narborough Cl UB10 61 A6
Narborough St SW6 135 D3
Narcissus Rd NW6 69 C3
Nardini 12 NW9 27 D2
Naresby Fold HA7 25 C4
Narford Rd E5 74 A6
Narrow Boat Cl SE28 123 B4
Narrow St
6 Acton W3 110 D5
Limehouse E14 119 A6
Narrow Way BR2 210 A3
Nascot St W12 90 C1
Naseby Cl
Hounslow TW7 130 C4
South Hampstead NW6 70 A1
Naseby Ct DA14 189 D6
Naseby Rd
Dagenham RM10 81 C5
South Norwood SE19 183 B4
NASH 225 A2
Nash Cl SM1 218 B5
Nash Ct HA3 43 B3
Nashe Ho SE1 262 C5
Nash Gn BR1 187 A4
Nash Ho
5 Millwall E14 119 C3
Pimlico SW1 258 D1
1 Walthamstow E17 53 D5
Nash La BR2 225 A2
Nash Rd Brockley SE4 163 A6
Dagenham RM6 58 D5
Lower Edmonton N9 18 C2
Nash St NW1 231 D2
Nash Way HA3 43 B3
Nasmyth St W6 112 B3
Nassau Path 6 SE28 124 C5
Nassau Rd SW13 133 D4
Nassau St W1 239 A3
Nassington Rd NW3 70 D4
Natalie Cl TW14 149 B4
Natalie Mews TW2 152 B1
Natal Rd Bowes Pk N11 32 A4
Ilford IG1 78 D4
South Norwood CR7 205 B6
Streatham SW16 181 D4
Nathan Ct N9 18 C4
Nathan Ho SE11 261 B3
Nathaniel Cl E1 243 D3
Nathaniel Ct E17 53 A3
Nathans Rd HA0 65 C6
Nathan Way SE28, SE18 123 D3
National Army Mus* SW3 136 D6 267 D6
National Fan Mus* SE10 142 A5
National Film Theatre* SE1 250 D4
National Gallery* W1 115 D6 249 D5
National Hospl The WC1 94 A3 240 B5
National Maritime Mus* SE10 142 B6
National Physical Laboratory TW11 174 C4
National Portrait Gallery* W1 115 D6 249 D5
National Portrait Gallery (Annexe)* SW1 115 D5 249 D4
National Theatre* SE1 116 B5 250 D4
National Wks TW4 129 B2
Nation Way E4 20 A3
Natural History Mus* SW7 114 B3 256 C5
Nat West Twr* EC2 243 A2
Nautilus Bldg The EC1 234 B2
Naval Row E14 120 A6
Navarino Gr E8 74 A2
Navarino Mans E8 74 A2
Navarino Rd E8 74 A2
Navarre Rd E6 100 A5
Navarre St E2 243 C6
Navenby Wlk 18 E3 97 C3
Navestock Cl E4 20 A1
Navestock Cres IG8 37 C3
Navestock Ho IG11 102 B5
Navigation Ct E16 123 A6
Navigator Dr UB2 108 A4
Navy St SW4 137 D2
Naxos Bldg 9 E14 119 C4
Nayland Ho SE6 186 A6
Naylor Bldg W 4 E1 96 A1
Naylor Gr EN3 18 D6
Naylor Ho
33 Clapham SW8 137 D3
Walworth SE17 262 D2
5 West Kilburn W10 91 B4
Naylor Rd
Peckham SE15 140 B5
Whetstone N20 14 A2
Nayor Bldg E 6 E1 96 A1
Nazareth Cl SE15 140 B3
Nazrul St E2 95 D4
Neal Ave UB1 85 B3
Neal Cl HA6 22 A2
Nealden St SW9 138 B2
Neale Cl N2 48 A6
Neale Ct Dagenham RM9 80 B2
Muswell Hill N10 31 B3
Neal St WC2 94 A1 240 A1
Neal's Yd WC2 240 A1
Near Acre NW9 27 D2
NEASDEN 67 B4
Neasden Cl NW10 67 C3
Neasden Junc NW10 67 C4
Neasden La
Church End NW10 67 C3
Neasden NW10 67 B5

Neasden La N NW10 .... 67 C5
Neasden Sta NW10 .... 67 C3
Neasham Rd RM8 .... 80 B3
Neate St SE5 .... 139 D6
Neath Gdns SM4 .... 202 A3
Neathouse Pl SW1 .... 259 A4
Neats Acre HA4 .... 39 B2
Neatscourt Rd E16 .... 99 D2
Nebraska Bldg 11
SE13 .... 141 D4
Nebraska St
SE1 .... 117 B4 252 C1
Neckinger
SE16 .... 117 D3 263 D6
Neckinger Est SE16 .... 263 D6
Neckinger St SE1 .... 263 D6
Nectarine Way SE13 .... 141 D3
Nedahall Ct 4 NW11 .... 47 B2
Needham Ct 20 EN3 .... 7 C6
Needham Ho SE11 .... 261 A3
Needham Rd W11 .... 91 C1
Needham Terr NW2 .... 68 D5
Needleman St SE16 .... 118 D4
Needwood Ho N4 .... 51 A1
Neela Cl UB10 .... 60 D4
Neeld Cres Hendon NW4 .... 46 B4
Wembley HA9 .... 66 C3
Neeld Ct HA9 .... 66 C3
Neeld Par HA9 .... 66 B3
Neil Cl TW15 .... 171 A5
Neilson-Terry Ct 9
SW9 .... 138 B1
Neil Wates Cres 17
SW2 .... 160 C3
Nelgarde Rd SE6 .... 163 C4
Nella Rd W6 .... 134 D6
Nelldale Rd SE16 .... 118 C2
Nellgrove Rd UB10 .... 82 D3
Nell Gwynn Ave TW17 .... 193 B3
Nell Gwynn Ho SW3 .... 257 B3
Nello James Gdns
SE27 .... 183 B6
Nelson Cl
East Bedfont TW14 .... 149 D3
Hillingdon UB10 .... 82 D4
2 Paddington NW6 .... 91 C4
Thornton Heath CR0 .... 204 D1
Walton-on-T KT12 .... 194 B1
Nelson Ct
5 Carshalton SM5 .... 218 D5
Rotherhithe SE16 .... 119 B5
Nelson Dock Pier
SE16 .... 119 B5
Nelson Gdns
Bethnal Green E2 .... 96 A4
Twickenham TW3, TW4 .... 151 C5
Nelson Grove Rd
SW19 .... 180 A2
Nelson Ho 1 W5 .... 88 A4
Nelson Hospl SW20 .... 179 B1
Nelson La UB10 .... 82 D4
Nelson Mandela Cl
N10 .... 31 A1
Nelson Mandela Rd
SE3 .... 143 C2
Nelson Pas EC1 .... 235 B2
Nelson Pl N1 .... 234 D3
Nelson Prim Sch
Twickenham TW2 .... 151 D5
Wallend E6 .... 100 C5
Nelson Rd
Ashford TW15 .... 170 A5
Bromley BR2 .... 209 C5
Chingford E4 .... 35 D4
Edmonton N9 .... 18 B2
Enfield EN3 .... 18 D5
Erith DA17 .... 125 B1
Greenwich SE10 .... 142 A6
Harmondsworth TW6 .... 126 B4
Harrow HA1 .... 42 C1
Hillingdon UB10 .... 82 D4
Hornsey Vale N8 .... 50 B3
Merton SW19 .... 180 A3
New Malden KT3 .... 199 B4
Sidcup DA14 .... 190 A6
Stanmore HA7 .... 25 C4
Tottenham N15 .... 51 C5
Twickenham TW2, TW4 .... 151 C5
Wanstead E11 .... 55 B5
Nelson's Monument★
WC2 .... 250 A4
Nelson Sq SE1 .... 116 D4 251 C2
Nelsons Row SW4 .... 137 D1
Nelson St Barking E6 .... 100 C6
Canning Town E16 .... 120 D6
Newham E6 .... 100 B5
Stepney E1 .... 96 B1
Nelsons Yd NW1 .... 232 A4
Nelson Terr N1 .... 234 D3
Nelson Trad Est
SW19 .... 179 D2
Nemoure Rd W3 .... 111 A6
Nene Gdns TW13 .... 151 B2
Nene Rd TW6, UB7 .... 126 D4
Nene Road Rdbt TW6 .... 126 D4
Nepaul Rd 17 SW11 .... 136 C2
Nepean St SW15 .... 156 A4
Neptune Ct
Dagenham IG11 .... 102 B4
13 Millwall E14 .... 119 C2
Neptune Ho
2 Rotherhithe SE16 .... 118 C3
14 Stoke Newington N16 .... 73 C3
Neptune Rd
Harlington TW6 .... 127 A4
Harrow HA1 .... 42 B3
Neptune St SE16 .... 118 C3
Nero Ct 6 TW8 .... 131 D5
Nesbit Cl SE3 .... 142 C2
Nesbit Rd SE9 .... 143 D1
Nesbitt Ho DA6 .... 169 D6
Nesbitt Sq SE19 .... 183 C3
Nesham Ho 14 N1 .... 95 C6
Nesham St E1 .... 118 A5
Ness St 9 SE16 .... 118 A3
Nesta Rd IG8 .... 36 D4
Nestle's Ave UB3 .... 105 D3
Nestor Ave N21 .... 16 D5
Nestor Ho 18 E2 .... 96 B5
Netheravon Rd
Chiswick W4 .... 111 D1
Ealing W7 .... 108 D5
Netheravon Rd S W4 .... 111 D1
Netherbury Rd W5 .... 109 D3
Netherby Gdns EN2 .... 4 A1
Netherby Ho 23 SW8 .... 137 D3
Netherby Rd SE23 .... 162 C4
Nether Cl N3 .... 29 C3
Nethercombe Ho 1
SE3 .... 143 A6
Nethercott Ho 27 E3 .... 97 D4
Nethercourt Ave N3 .... 29 C4
Netherfield Gdns IG11 .... 79 B1
Netherfield Rd
Finchley N12 .... 29 D5
Upper Tooting SW17 .... 159 A1
Netherford Rd SW4 .... 137 C3
Netherhall Gdns NW3 .... 70 A3
Netherhall Way NW3 .... 70 A3
Netherlands Rd EN5 .... 14 B5
Netherleigh Cl N6 .... 49 B1
Nether St Finchley N3 .... 29 D4
North Finchley N12 .... 30 A5
Netherton Gr
SW10 .... 136 A6 266 B5
Netherton Ho 1 UB5 .... 85 B4
Netherton Rd
Isleworth TW1 .... 153 B6
Tottenham N15 .... 51 B3
Netherwood 24 N2 .... 30 B1
Netherwood Rd W14 .... 112 D4
Netherwood St NW6 .... 69 C2
Nethewode Ct DA17 .... 125 D3
Netley Cl Cheam SM3 .... 216 D3
Netley 18 SE5 .... 139 C4
New Addington CR0 .... 224 A1
Netley Ct IG2 .... 57 B4
Netley Dr KT12 .... 195 B2
Netley Gdns SM4 .... 202 A2
Netley Prim Sch
NW1 .... 93 C4 232 A1
Netley Rd
Brentford TW8 .... 132 A6
Cheam SM4 .... 202 A2
Ilford IG2 .... 57 B4
Walthamstow E17 .... 53 B4
Netley St NW1 .... 93 C4 232 A1
Nettlecombe NW1 .... 71 D1
Nettleden Ave HA9 .... 66 C2
Nettleden Ho SW3 .... 257 B3
Nettlefold Pl SE27 .... 160 D1
Nettlestead Cl 16 BR3 .... 185 C3
Nettleton Rd
Harlington TW6 .... 126 D4
Ickenham UB10 .... 60 B4
New Cross Gate SE14 .... 140 D4
Nettlewood Rd SW16 .... 181 D3
Neuchatel Rd SE6 .... 163 B2
Nevada Cl KT3 .... 199 A5
Nevada St SE10 .... 142 A6
Nevena Ct 3 SW2 .... 160 C6
Nevern Mans SW5 .... 255 A2
Nevern Pl SW5 .... 113 C2 255 B3
Nevern Rd SW5 .... 255 A3
Nevern Sq
SW5 .... 113 C2 255 B3
Nevil Ho 7 SW9 .... 138 D3
Nevill Ct SW10 .... 266 A4
Neville Ave KT3 .... 177 B2
Neville Cl Acton W3 .... 111 A4
Hounslow TW3 .... 129 D3
Leyton E11 .... 76 D5
Paddington NW6 .... 91 B5
Peckham SE15 .... 140 A4
Sidcup DA15 .... 189 D6
Somers Town NW1 .... 232 D3
Neville Ct 10 SW12 .... 159 C4
Neville Dr N2 .... 48 A3
Neville Gdns RM8 .... 80 D5
Neville Gill Cl SW18 .... 157 D5
Neville Ho
Friern Barnet N11 .... 31 A6
5 Twickenham TW1 .... 153 A4
Neville Pl N22 .... 32 B2
Neville Rd
Dagenham RM8 .... 80 D5
Ealing W5 .... 87 D3
Forest Gate E7 .... 77 B1
Kingston u T KT1 .... 176 C1
Paddington NW6 .... 91 B5
Richmond TW10 .... 153 C2
Thornton Heath CR0 .... 205 B2
Neville's Ct NW2 .... 68 A5
Neville St SW7 .... 114 B1 256 C2
Neville Terr SW7 .... 256 C2
Neville Wlk SM5 .... 202 C2
Nevill Rd N16 .... 73 C5
Nevin Dr E4 .... 19 D3
Nevin Ho UB3 .... 105 A6
Nevinson Cl SW18 .... 158 B5
Nevis Rd SW17 .... 159 A2
Nevitt Ho N1 .... 235 D3
New Acres Rd SE28 .... 123 C5
NEW ADDINGTON 224 B1
Newall Ho SE1 .... 262 B6
Newall Rd TW6 .... 127 A4
Newark Cres NW10 .... 89 B4
Newark Ct KT12 .... 194 C1
Newark Ho 3 SW9 .... 138 D3
Newark Knok E6 .... 100 C2
Newark Rd CR2 .... 221 B2
Newark St E1 .... 96 B2
Newark Way NW4 .... 46 A6
New Ash Cl N2 .... 48 B6
New Atlas Wharf E14 .... 119 C3
New Barn Cl SM6 .... 220 B2
NEW BARNET 14 A6
New Barnet Sta EN5 .... 14 B6
New Barns Ave CR4 .... 203 D5
New Barn St E13 .... 99 B3
NEW BECKENHAM 185 A4
New Beckenham Sta
BR3 .... 185 B3
New Belmont Ho 4
SE23 .... 162 C3
New Bentham Ct 10 N1 .... 73 A1
Newbery Ho N1 .... 73 A1
Newbiggin Path WD19 .... 22 C6
Newbold Cotts 4 E1 .... 96 C1
Newbolt Ave SM3 .... 216 D3
Newbolt Ho SE17 .... 262 C2
Newbolt Rd HA7 .... 24 D5
New Bond St
W1 .... 115 B6 248 D6
Newborough Gn KT3 .... 199 B5
Newborough Ho
SW19 .... 180 B3
New Brent St NW4 .... 46 C4
Newbridge Ct SW17 .... 180 A6
Newbridge Point 3
SE23 .... 162 D1
Newbridge Sch RM6 .... 58 B4
New Bridge St
EC4 .... 94 D1 241 C1
New Broad St
EC2 .... 95 C2 243 A3
New Broadway
Ealing W5 .... 109 D6
7 Hillingdon UB10 .... 82 D3
Teddington TW12 .... 174 B5
New Bsns Ctr The
NW10 .... 89 D4
Newburgh Rd W3 .... 111 A5
Newburgh St W1 .... 239 B1
New Burlington Mews
W1 .... 249 A6
New Burlington Pl W1 .... 249 A6
New Burlington St W1 .... 249 A6
Newburn Ct N12 .... 30 A3
Newburn Ho SE11 .... 260 D2
Newburn St
SE11 .... 116 B1 260 D2
Newbury Ave EN3 .... 7 B6
Newbury Cl UB5 .... 63 B2
Newbury Cotts 4 IG2 .... 57 A3
Newbury Ct Hackney E5 .... 75 A3
Sidcup DA14 .... 189 D6
7 Wanstead E11 .... 55 A5
Newbury Gdns KT19 .... 215 D4
Newbury Ho Barnet EN4 .... 2 B1
Brixton SW9 .... 138 D3
14 Kensington W2 .... 91 D1
Wood Green N22 .... 32 A2
Newbury Mews NW5 .... 71 A2
NEWBURY PARK 57 B3
Newbury Park Prim Sch
IG2 .... 57 B3
Newbury Park Sta IG2 .... 57 B3
Newbury Rd
Bromley BR2 .... 209 A6
Chingford E4 .... 36 A4
Harmondsworth TW6 .... 126 B4
Ilford IG2 .... 57 C3
Newbury St EC1 .... 242 A4
Newbury Way UB5 .... 63 B2
New Butt La SE8 .... 141 C5
Newby NW1 .... 232 A2
Newby Cl EN1 .... 5 C3
Newby Pl E14 .... 120 A6
Newby St SW8 .... 137 B2
New Caledonian Wharf
SE16 .... 119 B3
New Campden Ct 9
NW3 .... 70 A4
Newcastle Cl EC4 .... 241 C2
Newcastle Ct EC4 .... 252 B6
Newcastle Ho W1 .... 238 A4
Newcastle Pl
W2 .... 92 B2 236 D4
Newcastle Row EC1 .... 241 B5
New Cavendish St
W1 .... 93 B2 238 C3
New Change
EC4 .... 95 A1 242 A1
New Chapel Sq TW13 .... 150 B3
New Charles St EC1 .... 234 D2
NEW CHARLTON 121 C2
New Church Ct 3
SE19 .... 184 A3
New Church Rd
32 Camberwell SE5 .... 139 A5
Camberwell SE5 .... 139 B6
New City Prim Sch E13 .... 99 C4
New City Rd E13 .... 99 C4
New Cl Feltham TW13 .... 173 A5
Morden SW19 .... 202 A6
New Colebrooke Ct
SM5 .... 219 A1
New College Ct 6
NW3 .... 70 A2
New College Mews 7
N1 .... 72 C1
New College Par 1
NW3 .... 70 B1
Newcombe Gdns TW3 .... 129 B1
Newcombe Ho N5 .... 73 A3
Newcombe Pk
Edgware NW7 .... 27 C5
Wembley HA0 .... 88 B6
Newcombe Rise UB7 .... 82 A1
Newcombe St W8 .... 245 B4
Newcome Gdns SW16 .... 182 A6
Newcome Ho E5 .... 74 B5
Newcomen Ho 5 NW5 .... 71 B4
Newcomen Rd
Battersea SW11 .... 136 B2
Leyton E11 .... 76 D5
Newcomen St
SE1 .... 117 B4 252 C2
New Compton St
WC2 .... 94 A1 240 A1
New Concordia Wharf
SE1 .... 253 D2
Newcourt Ho 26 E2 .... 96 B4
Newcourt St
NW8 .... 92 C5 230 A3
New Covent Garden
Flower Market
SW8 .... 138 A6 270 A5
New Covent Garden Fruit
& Vegetable Mkt
SW8 .... 137 D5 269 C3
New Crane Pl E1 .... 118 C5
New Crescent Yd 1
NW10 .... 89 D5
Newcroft Cl UB8 .... 82 B2
Newcroft Ho 10 NW10 .... 67 B1
NEW CROSS 141 B4
New Cross SE14 .... 141 B5
NEW CROSS GATE 140 D4
New Cross Gate SE14 .... 140 D4
New Cross Gate Sta
SE14 .... 141 A5
New Cross Hospl
SE14 .... 140 C5
New Cross Rd SE14 .... 141 A4
New Cross Sta SE14 .... 141 B5
New Ct
City of London EC4 .... 241 A1
26 Hampstead NW3 .... 70 A4
Northolt UB5 .... 63 D3
Stoke Newington N16 .... 51 B1
Newdales Cl N9 .... 18 A2
Newdene Ave UB5 .... 84 D5
New Den (Millwall FC) The
SE16 .... 118 C1
Newdigate Ho
6 Kingston u T KT2 .... 176 D4
5 Poplar E14 .... 97 B1
Newell St E14 .... 97 B1
NEW ELTHAM 167 A2
New Eltham Sta SE9 .... 166 D3
New End NW3 .... 70 A5
New End Prim Sch
NW3 .... 70 A4
New End Sq NW3 .... 70 B4
New England Est
IG11 .... 101 A5
Newent Cl
Camberwell SE15 .... 139 C5
Carshalton SM5 .... 202 D1
New Farm Ave BR2 .... 209 A5
New Ferry App SE18 .... 122 C3
New Fetter La
EC4 .... 94 C1 241 B2
Newfield Cl TW12 .... 173 C2
Newfield Prim Sch
NW10 .... 67 D1
Newfield Rise NW2 .... 68 B5
Newgale Gdns HA8 .... 26 B2
New Garden Dr UB7 .... 104 A4
Newgate CR0 .... 205 A1
Newgate Cl TW13 .... 151 A1
Newgate St
Chingford E4 .... 20 C1
Holborn EC1 .... 94 D1 241 D2
New Globe Wlk SE1 .... 252 A4
New Goulston St E1 .... 243 C2
New Green Pl SE19 .... 183 C4
NEWHAM 98 D4
Newham Acad of Music
E6 .... 100 A6
Newham Coll of FE
E6 .... 100 B5
Newham Coll (Stratford
Campus) E15 .... 76 C1
Newham Ctr for Mental
Health E16 .... 99 D3
Newham General Hospl
E13 .... 99 C3
Newham Gn N22 .... 32 C2
Newham Sch of Nursing
E3 .... 97 D3
Newham Sixth Form Coll
E13 .... 99 B3
Newham Sixth Form Coll
(Stratford Ctr) E15 .... 76 B1
Newham's Row SE1 .... 253 B1
Newham Way
Beckton E6 .... 100 B3
Canning Town E13 .... 99 B2
Newhaven Cl UB3 .... 105 D2
Newhaven Cres TW15 .... 171 B5
Newhaven Gdns SE9 .... 143 D1
Newhaven La 3 E16 .... 99 A2
Newhaven Rd SE25 .... 205 B4
New Heston Rd TW5 .... 129 B5
New Horizons Ct TW8 .... 131 A6
Newhouse 5 KT3 .... 199 C2
Newhouse Ave RM6 .... 58 D6
Newhouse Cl KT3 .... 199 C2
Newhouse Wlk SM4 .... 202 A2
Newick Cl DA5 .... 169 D5
Newick Rd E5 .... 74 C5
Newing Gn BR1 .... 187 D3
NEWINGTON 116 D2
Newington Barrow Way
N7 .... 72 B5
Newington Butts SE1,
SE11 .... 116 D2 261 D3
Newington Cswy
SE1 .... 117 A3 262 A6
Newington Gn N16 .... 73 B3
Newington Green Mans
N16 .... 73 B3
Newington Green Prim
Sch N16 .... 73 B3
Newington Green Rd
N1 .... 73 B3
Newington Ind Est
SE17 .... 262 A3
New Inn Broadway
EC2 .... 243 B6
New Inn Ct The KT8 .... 196 B4
New Inn Sq EC2 .... 243 B6
New Inn St EC2 .... 243 B6
New Inn Yd EC2 .... 95 C3 243 B6
New James Ct SE15 .... 140 B2
New Jubilee Ct 1 IG8 .... 37 A3
New Kelvin Ave TW11 .... 174 C4
New Kent Rd
SE1 .... 117 A2 262 B4
New King's Prim Sch
SW6 .... 135 B3
New King's Rd
SW6 .... 135 C4 265 B1
New King St SE8 .... 141 C6
Newland Cl HA5 .... 23 B4
Newland Ct
St Luke's EC1 .... 242 C6
Wembley HA9 .... 66 C6
Newland Dr EN1 .... 6 B4
Newland Gdns W13 .... 109 A4
Newland Ho
17 Deptford SE14 .... 140 D6
Hornsey N8 .... 50 A6
Newland House Sch
TW1 .... 174 D6
Newland House Sch Annex
TW1 .... 174 D6
Newland Rd N8 .... 50 A6
Newlands NW1 .... 232 A2
Newlands Ave KT7 .... 196 C1
Newlands Cl
Edgware HA8 .... 10 A1
Southall UB2 .... 107 A1
Wembley HA0 .... 65 C2
Newlands Croft SE20 .... 184 D4
Newlands Ct
8 Eltham SE9 .... 166 C5
6 Penge SE26 .... 184 C4
Streatham SW16 .... 182 A5
Newlands Pk SE26 .... 184 D5
Newlands Pl EN5 .... 12 D6
Newlands Quay E1 .... 118 C6
Newlands Rd
Thornton Heath
SW16 .... 182 A1
Woodford IG8 .... 20 D2
Newland St E16 .... 122 B5
Newlands The
Thames Ditton KT7 .... 196 C1
Wallington SM6 .... 219 D1
Newlands Way KT9 .... 213 C3
Newling Cl E6 .... 100 B1
New London St EC3 .... 253 B6
New Lydenburg
Commercial Est SE7 .... 121 C3
New Lydenburg St
SE7 .... 121 C3
Newlyn NW1 .... 232 B5
Newlyn Cl
Hillingdon UB8 .... 82 C2
Orpington BR6 .... 227 D4
Newlyn Gdns HA2 .... 41 B2
Newlyn Ho
7 Pinner HA5 .... 23 B3
7 Sutton SM1 .... 218 A4
Newlyn Rd Barnet EN5 .... 1 B1
Bexley DA16 .... 145 D3
Tottenham N17 .... 33 D2
NEW MALDEN 199 D5
New Malden Sta KT3 .... 199 C6
Newman Ct
3 Bromley BR1 .... 187 A2
8 Finchley N3 .... 29 C2
Newman Ho 11 TW10 .... 153 C1
Newman Pas W1 .... 239 B3
Newman Rd
Bromley BR1 .... 187 A2
Hayes UB3 .... 106 B6
Newham E13 .... 99 B4
Thornton Heath CR0 .... 204 B2
Walthamstow E17 .... 52 D4
Newman's Ct EC3 .... 242 D1
Newman's Row WC2 .... 240 D3
Newman St W1 .... 93 C2 239 B3
Newman's Way EN4 .... 2 A4
Newman Terr 9 CR4 .... 202 D6
Newmarket Ave UB5 .... 63 D3
Newmarket Gn SE9 .... 165 D4
Newmarsh Rd SE28 .... 123 D5
Newmill Ho E3 .... 98 A3
New Mill Rd BR5 .... 190 C2
Newminster Rd SM4 .... 202 A3
Newmount NW3 .... 70 B3
New Mount St E15 .... 76 B1
Newnes Path SW15 .... 134 B1
Newnham Ave HA4 .... 40 C1
Newnham Cl
Loughton IG10 .... 21 D5
Northolt UB5 .... 64 A2
South Norwood CR7 .... 183 A1
Newnham Gdns UB5 .... 64 A2
Newnham Ho
Catford SE6 .... 164 A1
Loughton IG10 .... 21 D5
9 Putney SW15 .... 156 D5
Newnham Jun & Inf Schs
HA4 .... 40 C1
Newnham Lo 10 DA17 .... 125 C1
Newnham Mews N22 .... 32 C2
Newnham Rd N22 .... 32 C2
Newnhams Cl BR1 .... 210 B6
Newnham Terr SE1 .... 261 A6
Newnham Way HA3 .... 44 A4
New North Com Sch The
N1 .... 73 B1
New North Pl EC2 .... 243 A6
New North Rd
N1 .... 95 B6 235 C5
New North Road Bridge
N1 .... 235 C5
New North St
WC1 .... 94 B2 240 C4
Newnton Cl N4 .... 51 B2
New Oak Rd N2 .... 30 A1
New Oxford St
WC1 .... 94 A1 240 A2
New Palace Yd
SW1 .... 116 A4 250 A1
New Par Ashford TW15 .... 170 B6
Yiewsley UB7 .... 104 A5
New Park Ave N13 .... 17 B1
New Park Cl UB5 .... 63 A2
New Park Ct 26 SW2 .... 160 A4
New Park Est N18 .... 34 C5
New Park Ho N13 .... 32 B6
New Park Par 14 SW2 .... 160 A4
New Park Rd
Ashford TW15 .... 171 A5
Streatham SW2 .... 160 A4
New Pl CR0 .... 223 C2
New Place Sq SE16 .... 118 B3
New Plaistow Rd E15 .... 98 C6
New Pond Par HA4 .... 62 A5
Newport Ave
Blackwall E14 .... 120 B6
Newham E13 .... 99 B3
Newport Cl EN3 .... 7 A6
Newport Ct WC2 .... 249 D6
Newport Ho 2 E3 .... 97 A4
Newport Lo 2 EN1 .... 17 C6
Newport Mead WD19 .... 22 D6
Newport Pl WC2 .... 249 D6
Newport Rd
Barnes SW13 .... 134 A4
Harmondsworth TW6 .... 126 C4
Hayes UB4 .... 83 B2
Leyton E10 .... 76 B6
Walthamstow E17 .... 53 A5
Newport Sch E10, E11 .... 76 A6
Newport St
SE11 .... 116 B2 260 D4
New Priory Ct 9 NW6 .... 69 C1
New Providence Wharf
E14 .... 120 B5
Newquay Cres HA2 .... 63 A6
Newquay Ho SE11 .... 261 A2
Newquay Rd SE6 .... 164 A2
New Quebec St W1 .... 237 D1
New Rd Brentford TW8 .... 109 D1
Carshalton CR4 .... 203 A1
Chingford E4 .... 36 A6
Dagenham RM10 .... 103 D5
East Bedfont TW14 .... 149 B5
East Molesey KT8 .... 195 C6
Edmonton N9 .... 18 B2
Elstree WD6 .... 9 D5
Esher KT10 .... 212 A4
Feltham TW14 .... 150 B3
Finchley N10 .... 30 C2
Hanworth TW13 .... 173 A5
Harlington TW6, UB7 .... 127 A5
Harrow HA1 .... 64 D4
Hendon NW7 .... 29 A3
Hillingdon UB8 .... 83 A2
Hornsey N8 .... 50 A4
Hounslow TW3 .... 129 D1
Ilford IG3 .... 79 C6
Kingston u T KT2 .... 176 C3
Littleton TW17 .... 192 D6
Richmond TW10 .... 175 C6
Stepney E1 .... 96 B2
Tottenham N22 .... 33 A2
Welling DA16 .... 146 B3
West Heath SE2 .... 124 D1
New River Cres N13 .... 32 D6
New River Ct N5 .... 73 B4
New River Sports &
Recreation Ctr N22 .... 32 D3
New River Way N4 .... 51 B2
New Row WC2 .... 116 A6 250 A6
New Rush Hall Sch IG1 .... 79 A6
Newry Rd TW1 .... 153 A6
New St Sq EC4 .... 94 C1 241 B2
Newsam Ave N15 .... 51 B4
New Scotland Yard★
SW1 .... 115 D3 259 C6
New Shepherd's Bush
Mkt★ 6 W12 .... 112 C4
Newsholme Dr N21 .... 16 B6
NEW SOUTHGATE 31 C6
New Southgate Ind Est 10
N11 .... 31 C5
New Southgate Sta
N11 .... 31 B5
New Spitalfields Mkt
E10 .... 75 C5
New Spring Gdns Wlk
SE11 .... 260 B1
New Sq
East Bedfont TW14 .... 149 A3
St Giles WC2 .... 94 B1 240 D2
New Square Pas WC2 .... 241 A2
New St EC2 .... 95 C2 243 B3
Newstead Ave BR6 .... 227 C6

Newstead Cl N12 .... 30 C4
Newstead Ct UB5 .... 85 A4
Newstead Ho
Edmonton N9.......... 17 D1
Islington N1 .... 234 B4
Newstead Rd SE12..... 164 D4
Newstead Way SW19... 178 D6
Newstead Wlk SM5 .... 202 A2
Newstead Wood Sch for Girls BR6 .... 227 B5
New Street Hill BR1.... 187 C5
Newton Ave Acton W3 .. 111 A4
Muswell Hill N10........ 31 B2
Newton Cl Harrow HA2.. 63 C6
Walthamstow E17 .... 53 A3
Newton Farm Fst & Mid Sch HA2 .... 63 B6
Newton Gr W4......... 111 C2
Newton Ho
22 Clapham SW8 ...... 137 D3
Paddington NW8........ 91 D6
1 Stepney E1......... 118 B6
10 Walthamstow E17 .... 54 A6
Newton Ind Est RM6 .... 58 D5
Newton Pl E14......... 119 C2
Newton Point 1 E16.... 98 D1
Newton Prep Sch SW8 .... 137 B4 268 D2
Newton Rd Acton W3 ... 111 A4
Cricklewood NW2......... 68 C5
Harrow HA3 .... 24 C1
Isleworth TW7 .... 130 D3
Kensington W2 .... 91 D1
South Tottenham N15 .... 52 A4
Stratford New Town E15.. 76 B3
Welling DA16.......... 146 A2
Wembley HA0 .... 66 B1
Wimbledon SW19 ...... 179 A3
Newton St WC2.. 94 A1 240 B2
Newton's Yd 14 SW18 .. 157 C6
Newton Terr BR2 ...... 209 D3
Newton Way N18 .... 33 A5
Newton Wlk HA8 .... 26 D2
New Tower Bldgs 21 E1 .... 118 B5
Newtown Ct
Battersea SW11 ...... 268 C1
Clapham SW4 .... 159 B6
New Trinity Rd 1 N2 ... 30 B1
New Union Cl E14 ..... 120 A3
New Union St EC2 .... 242 C3
New Victoria Hospl KT3.................. 177 C2
New Wanstead E11 ..... 55 A3
New Way Rd NW9....... 45 C5
New Wharf Rd N1............ 94 A5 233 B4
New Woodlands Sch BR1................. 186 C6
NEWYEARS GREEN 38 B3
Newyears Green La UB9 .... 38 B3
New Zealand Ave KT12 .... 193 D1
Nexus Ct E11 .... 54 C2
Niagara Ave W5 .... 109 C2
Niagara Cl N1 .... 235 B4
Niagara Ct 6 SE16..... 118 C3
Niagara Ho W5 .... 109 C2
Nibthwaite Rd HA1..... 42 C4
Nicholas Cl UB6 .... 85 D5
Nicholas Ct
Chiswick W4 .... 133 C5
Golders Green NW11 .... 47 C2
Lewisham SE12........ 165 A3
Newham E13 .... 99 B4
Nicholas Gdns W5 ..... 109 D4
Nicholas Ho Ealing W13.. 87 C1
Penge SE26........... 184 B4
2 Putney SW15........ 156 A6
Nicholas La EC2, EC4 .. 252 D6
Nicholas Pas EC3 ..... 252 D6
Nicholas Rd
Bethnal Green E1 .... 96 C3
Borehamwood WD6 ..... 10 B6
Dagenham RM8......... 81 B5
Wallington CR0 .... 220 A4
Nicholas Stacey Ho 3 SE7 .... 121 B1
Nicholay Rd N19......... 49 D1
Nichol Cl N14.......... 15 D3
Nicholes Rd TW3 ...... 129 C1
Nichol La BR1 .... 187 A3
Nicholl Ho N4 .... 51 A1
Nicholls Almshouses NW7 .... 28 B5
Nicholls Ave UB8 .... 82 C3
Nicholls Point E15...... 99 A6
Nicholl St E2 .... 96 A6
Nichols Cl
Chessington KT9....... 213 C2
Finsbury Pk N4 .... 50 C1
Nichols Ct E2.......... 95 D5
Nichols Gn W5 .... 88 A2
Nicholson Ct 9 N17 .... 51 D6
Nicholson Ho SE17.... 262 C2
Nicholson Mews KT1... 198 A5
Nicholson Rd CR0...... 205 D1
Nicholson St SE1 ..... 251 C3
Nickelby Cl SE28....... 102 C1
Nickleby Cl UB8 .... 82 D1
Nickleby Ho
18 Bermondsey SE1 .... 118 A4
7 Shepherd's Bush W11.............. 112 D5
Nickols Wlk SW18 ..... 135 D1
Nicola Cl Harrow HA3.... 24 B1
Nicola Cl *continued*
South Croydon CR2..... 221 A2
Nicola Terr DA7 .... 147 A4
Nicol Cl 6 TW1........ 153 B5
Nicole Ho SE25 .... 206 A6
Nicoll Ct
Dagenham NW10 .... 89 C6
Muswell Hill N10......... 31 B3
Nicoll Pl NW4 .... 46 B2
Nicoll Rd NW10......... 89 C6
Nicoll Way WD6 .... 11 B6
Nicolson 18 NW9 .... 27 D2
Nicolson Dr WD23 .... 8 A2
Nicosia Rd SW18....... 158 C4
Niederwald Rd SE26 ... 185 A6
Nield Rd UB3 .... 105 D4
Nigel Bldg EC1 .... 241 A4
Nigel Cl UB5........... 85 A5
Nigel Ct N3............ 29 D3
Nigel Fisher Way KT9 .. 213 D1
Nigel Mews IG1 .... 78 D3
Nigel Playfair Ave W6.. 112 B1
Nigel Rd Forest Gate E7 .. 77 C3
Peckham SE15......... 140 A2
Nigeria Rd SE7 .... 143 D5
Nighthawk 16 NW9..... 27 D2
Nightingale Ave
Chingford E4 .... 36 C5
Harrow HA1 .... 43 B1
Nightingale Cl
Carshalton SM5........ 219 A6
Chingford E4........... 36 C6
Chiswick W4 .... 133 A6
Pinner HA5 .... 40 C4
Nightingale Ct
14 Cubitt Town E14..... 120 A3
Finsbury Pk N4 .... 72 B6
1 Harrow HA1......... 42 D3
Penge SE19........... 183 D4
Sutton SM1 .... 218 A3
1 Wanstead E11 .... 55 B4
Nightingale Dr KT19 ... 214 D2
Nightingale Gr SE13 ... 164 B6
Nightingale Ho
Hayes UB3............ 105 D2
21 Hoxton E1 .... 95 C6
4 North Kensington W12.............. 90 C1
7 St George in t East E1.................. 118 A5
Woolwich SE18 .... 122 C1
Nightingale La
Balham SW11, SW12 ... 159 A5
Bromley BR1.......... 187 D1
Hornsey N8............ 50 A6
Richmond TW10 ...... 154 A4
Wanstead E11.......... 55 B4
Nightingale Lo
Edgware HA8 .... 27 A4
5 Paddington W9 ...... 91 C2
Nightingale Mans 4 SW12................ 159 A5
Nightingale Mews
1 Bow E3............. 97 A5
Newington SE11 ...... 261 C4
8 Wanstead E11 .... 55 B4
Nightingale Pl
Shooters Hill SE18 ..... 144 D6
West Brompton SW10....... 136 A6 266 B6
Nightingale Prim Sch
Shacklewell E5 .... 74 A4
Wanstead E18.......... 55 C5
Wood Green N22........ 32 B2
Woolwich SE18 .... 122 D1
Nightingale Rd
Carshalton SM5....... 219 A6
Dagenham NW10 .... 89 D5
Ealing W7 .... 108 D5
East Molesey KT8 ..... 195 D4
Hackney E5 .... 74 B5
Hampton TW12 .... 173 C4
Orpington BR5......... 211 A3
Ponders End N9 .... 18 C4
Walton-on-T KT12...... 194 B2
Wood Green N22........ 32 B3
Nightingale Sch SW17................ 158 C2
Nightingale Sq SW12... 159 A4
Nightingales The TW19................. 148 B3
Nightingale Vale SE18 . 144 C6
Nightingale Way E6.... 100 A2
Nightingale Wlk SW18, SW4.................. 159 B5
Nile Cl N16............ 73 D5
Nile Ct N12............ 30 C4
Nile Dr N9............. 18 C2
Nile Ho N1 .... 235 C2
Nile Path 6 SE18 ..... 144 C6
Nile Rd E13............ 99 C5
Nile St N1....... 95 B4 235 C2
Nile Terr SE1, SE15 .... 117 D1 263 D1
Nimegen Way 9 SE22 .... 161 C6
Nimmo Dr WD23......... 8 B4
Nimrod 12 NW9......... 27 C2
Nimrod Cl UB5 .... 84 D4
Nimrod Pas 4 N1 ...... 73 C2
Nimrod Rd SW16 ...... 181 B5
Nina Mackay Cl 10 E15 .. 98 C6
Nine Acres Cl E12....... 78 A3
NINE ELMS 137 C5
Nine Elms Cl TW14..... 149 D3
Nine Elms La SW8.......... 137 D6 269 C5
Nineteenth Rd CR4 .... 204 A5
Ninhams Wood BR6..... 226 C4
Ninth Ave UB3......... 106 A6
Nisbet 13 NW9.......... 27 C2
Nisbet Ho E9 .... 74 D3
Nisbett Wlk DA14 ..... 190 A6
Nita Ct SE12.......... 165 A3
Nithdale Rd SE18 ..... 145 A5
Nithsdale Gr UB10 ...... 61 A5
Niton Cl EN5 .... 12 D5
Niton Rd TW9 .... 132 C2
Niton St SW6 .... 134 D5
No 1 St SE18 .... 122 D3
No 2 Willow Rd* NW3.. 70 C4
Noam Prim Sch N12 .... 29 D6
Nobel Dr TW6 .... 127 C5
Nobel Ho 8 SE5 ...... 139 A3
Nobel Rd N18 .... 34 C6
Noble Cnr TW5 .... 129 C4
Noble Ct Mitcham CR4... 180 B1
Stepney E1 .... 118 B6
Noblefield Hts N2 ...... 48 D4
Noble Ho 18 E1........ 118 A6
Noble St EC2 .... 95 A1 242 A2
Noel 13 NW9 .... 27 D2
Noel Baker Ct 5 E11.... 76 C6
Noel Coward Ho SW1 . 259 B3
Noel Ct TW4.......... 129 B2
Noel Dene W5......... 109 C1
Noel Ho 3 NW3 .... 70 B1
NOEL PARK 32 D1
Noel Park Prim Sch N22.................. 32 C1
Noel Park Rd N22....... 32 C1
Noel Rd Acton W3 ...... 88 D1
Islington N1 ... 94 D5 234 D4
Newham E6........... 100 A3
Noel Sq RM8 .... 80 C4
Noel St W1...... 93 C1 239 B1
Noel Terr
Forest Hill SE23 .... 162 C2
Sidcup DA14 .... 190 B6
Noko NW10............ 90 D4
Nolan Way E5 .... 74 A4
Noll Ho N7 .... 72 B6
Nolton Pl HA8 .... 26 B2
Nonsuch Ct SM3....... 217 A2
Nonsuch High Sch for Girls SM3 .... 216 D1
Nonsuch Ho 5 SW19 .. 180 B2
Nonsuch Prim Sch KT17................. 216 B3
Nook The SW19........ 180 A1
Noor Ul Islam Prim Sch E10.................. 76 A6
Nora Gdns NW4 .... 46 D5
NORBITON 176 C1
Norbiton Ave KT1, KT2.. 176 C1
Norbiton Common Rd KT1, KT3 .... 198 D6
Norbiton Hall KT2 ..... 176 B1
Norbiton Rd E14........ 97 B1
Norbiton Sta KT1 ...... 176 C2
Norbreck Gdns NW10 ... 88 B4
Norbreck Par NW10..... 88 B4
Norbroke St W12 ...... 111 D6
Norburn St W10 .... 91 A2
NORBURY 182 C2
Norbury Ave
Isleworth TW3 .... 130 B1
Thornton Heath CR7, SW16................ 182 C1
Norbury Cl SW16 ..... 182 D2
Norbury Court Rd SW16................. 182 A1
Norbury Cres SW16 .... 182 C1
Norbury Cross SW16 ... 204 A6
Norbury Ct N12......... 30 A6
Norbury Gdns RM6...... 58 D4
Norbury Gr NW7........ 11 C1
Norbury Hill SW16 ..... 182 D3
Norbury Manor Bsns & Enterprise Coll For Girls CR7................ 182 C2
Norbury Manor Prim Sch SW16 .... 182 A2
Norbury Rd
Chingford E4 .... 35 C5
Feltham TW13......... 149 D1
South Norwood CR7 ... 205 A6
Norbury Rise SW16 .... 204 A6
Norbury Sch HA1 .... 42 C4
Norbury Sta SW16 ..... 182 B2
Norbury Trad Est SW16................. 182 B1
Norcombe Gdns HA3.... 43 C4
Norcombe Ho 2 N19 ... 71 D5
Norcott Cl UB4 .... 84 C3
Norcott Rd N16......... 74 A5
Norcroft Gdns SE22 ... 162 A4
Norcutt Rd TW2 .... 152 C3
Norden Ho 25 E2 .... 96 B4
Norden Point NW2...... 46 C1
Nore Ct NW10 .... 68 A1
Norfolk Ave
Edmonton N13.......... 32 D4
South Tottenham N15 .... 51 D3
Norfolk Cl
Cockfosters EN4 .... 3 A1
East Finchley N2 .... 48 C6
Edmonton N13.......... 32 D4
5 Twickenham TW1.... 153 B5
Norfolk Cres
Paddington W2.......... 92 C1 237 B2
Sidcup DA15 .... 167 C4
Norfolk Ct 5 Barnet EN5.. 1 A1
4 Ilford RM6........... 58 B4
Surbiton KT5.......... 198 B3
Wembley HA0 .... 65 C2
Norfolk Gdns DA7..... 147 B4
Norfolk Ho 13 Acton W3.. 88 C1
Beckenham BR2 .... 208 D5
Norfolk Ho *continued*
City of London EC4 .... 252 A6
Edgware HA8 .... 26 B3
Greenwich SE3 .... 142 C6
11 Merton SW19....... 180 A3
Penge SE20........... 184 C2
4 Putney SW15....... 156 C4
Richmond TW10 ...... 154 C6
Shacklewell E8 .... 73 D4
2 South Croydon CR0 .. 221 B6
3 Stanmore HA7 .... 25 C5
St Johns SE8.......... 141 C4
Westminster SW1..... 259 D4
Norfolk House Rd SW16................. 160 A1
Norfolk House Sch N10 . 31 B1
Norfolk Mans
Battersea SW11 ...... 267 D1
10 Wandsworth SW18 .. 157 C6
Norfolk Mews 12 W10... 91 A2
Norfolk Pl
Paddington W2.......... 92 B1 236 D2
Welling DA16.......... 146 A3
Norfolk Rd Barking IG11.. 79 C1
Barnet EN5 .... 1 C2
Claygate KT10......... 212 C3
Dagenham RM10......... 81 D3
Enfield EN3 .... 18 B6
Feltham TW13......... 150 C3
Harrow HA1 .... 41 D4
Higham Hill E17......... 34 D1
Ilford IG3 .... 57 C2
Mitcham SW19 .... 180 C4
Newham E6........... 100 B6
South Norwood CR7 ... 205 A6
St John's Wood NW8......... 92 B6 229 D5
Willesden NW10........ 67 C1
Norfolk Row SE1, SE11 .... 116 B2 260 C4
Norfolk Sq W2 .. 92 B1 236 D2
Norfolk Sq Mews W2 . 236 D1
Norfolk St E7........... 77 A3
Norgrove St SW12 ..... 159 A4
Norhyrst Ave SE25 ..... 205 D6
Norland Ho 18 W11 .... 112 D5
Norland Pl W11.......... 113 A5 244 B3
Norland Place Sch W11 .... 113 A5 244 A3
Norland Rd 16 W11 .... 112 D5
Norlands Cres BR7..... 188 D2
Norland Sq W11.......... 113 A5 244 B3
Norley Vale SW15...... 156 A3
Norlington Rd E10, E11 .. 54 B1
Norlington Sch for Boys E10.................. 54 B1
Norman Ave
Feltham TW13......... 151 B2
Southall UB1 .... 107 A6
Tottenham N22 .... 33 A2
Twickenham TW1....... 153 C4
Norman Butler Ho 10 W10................. 91 A3
Normanby Cl SW15 .... 157 B6
Normanby Rd NW10..... 67 D4
Norman Cl
Orpington BR6......... 227 A5
Tottenham N22 .... 33 A2
Norman Cres
Heston TW5.......... 128 D5
Pinner HA5 .... 22 C2
Norman Ct
Dulwich SE22 .... 162 A4
5 Finchley N3 .... 29 C2
Finsbury Pk N4 .... 50 C2
8 Hampton TW12 ..... 173 C2
Ilford IG2 .... 57 B2
West Norwood SW16 .. 182 C5
Willesden NW10........ 68 A1
Woodford IG8 .... 37 B5
Normand Croft Com Sch W14 .... 135 B6 264 D6
Normand Mews W14.. 264 B6
Normand Rd W14.......... 135 B6 264 C6
Normandy Ave EN5 ...... 1 B1
Normandy Cl SE26...... 163 A1
Normandy Dr UB3 ...... 83 A1
Normandy Ho
8 Cubitt Town E14..... 120 A4
4 Hendon NW4 .... 28 D1
Normandy Rd SW9..... 138 C4
Normandy Terr E16..... 99 B1
Norman Gr E3.......... 97 A5
Norman Ho
1 Cheam SM1......... 217 C2
Feltham TW13......... 151 B2
7 Leyton E11.......... 76 C6
Lower Halliford TW17.. 192 C2
South Lambeth SW8 ... 270 A4
Normanhurst TW15..... 170 C5
Normanhurst Ave DA7................. 146 D4
Normanhurst Dr TW1 .. 153 B6
Normanhurst Rd
St Paul's Cray BR5 ..... 190 B1
Streatham SW2 .... 160 B2
Walton-on-T KT12...... 194 D1
Normanhurst Sch E4.... 20 B4
Norman Par DA14....... 168 D2
Norman Rd
Ashford TW15......... 171 B4
Belvedere DA17 .... 125 D3
Greenwich SE10 .... 141 D5
Ilford IG1 .... 78 D3
Leyton E11............. 76 C6
Merton SW19 .... 180 A3
Norman Rd *continued*
Newham E6........... 100 B3
South Tottenham N15 .... 51 D4
Sutton SM1 .... 217 C3
Thornton Heath CR7 ... 204 D4
Normans Cl
Hillingdon UB8 .... 82 A2
Willesden NW10......... 67 B2
Normansfield Ave KT1, KT8 .... 175 C3
Normanshire Dr E4...... 35 D6
Normans Mead NW10... 67 B2
Norman St EC1 .. 95 A4 235 B1
Normanton Ave SW18, SW19................ 157 C2
Normanton Ct CR2..... 221 C3
Normanton Ho 6 SW4.................. 159 C5
Normanton Pk E4....... 20 C2
Normanton Rd CR2 .... 221 C2
Normanton St SE23 .... 162 D2
Norman Way Acton W3 .. 88 D1
Palmers Green N14..... 16 A2
Normington Cl SW16... 182 C5
Norrice Lea N2 .... 48 B4
Norris 11 NW9.......... 27 D2
Norris Ho 12 Hoxton N1 .. 95 C6
15 South Hackney E9 ... 96 C6
Norris St SW1 .... 249 C5
Norroy Rd SW15 .... 134 D1
Norrys Cl EN4 .... 2 D1
Norrys Rd EN4........... 2 D1
Norse Ho 13 SE5 ...... 139 A3
Norseman Cl 3 IG3..... 58 B1
Norseman Way UB6..... 85 D6
Norstead Pl SW15 ..... 156 A2
North Access Rd E17.... 52 D3
North Acre NW9 .... 27 C2
NORTH ACTON 89 B4
North Acton Rd NW10... 89 B4
North Acton Sta W3 .... 89 B2
Northampton Gr N1..... 73 B3
Northampton Pk N1 .... 73 B2
Northampton Rd
Croydon CR0 .... 222 A6
Enfield EN3 .... 7 A1
Finsbury EC1.... 94 C3 241 B6
Northampton Sq EC1 .... 94 D4 234 C1
Northampton St N1..... 73 A1
Northanger Rd SW16... 182 A4
North Audley St W1............ 115 A6 248 A6
North Ave Ealing W13.... 87 B2
Edmonton N18.......... 34 A6
Harrow HA2 .... 41 D3
Hayes UB3............ 106 A6
8 Richmond TW9...... 132 C4
Southall UB1 .... 107 B6
Wallington SM5........ 219 A1
Northaw Ho 4 W10..... 90 C3
North Bank NW8 .... 92 C4 230 A1
Northbank Rd E17 ...... 36 A1
North Beckton Prim Sch E6.................. 100 B2
North Birkbeck Rd E11.. 76 B5
North Block 19 E1 ..... 118 C6
Northborough Rd SW16................. 182 A1
Northbourne BR2 ...... 209 A2
Northbourne Ho
21 Hackney E5 .... 74 B3
Osidge N14............ 15 D4
Northbourne Rd SW4 .. 159 D6
North Bridge House Sch NW3................... 70 A2
North Bridge House Senior Sch NW1.......... 93 B6 231 C5
Northbrook CE Sch SE12................. 164 D6
Northbrook Rd
Barnet EN5 .... 13 A5
Ilford IG1 .... 78 C6
Lewisham SE13........ 164 C6
Thornton Heath CR0 ... 205 B4
Wood Green N22........ 32 A3
Northburgh St EC1 .... 94 D3 241 D6
Northbury Jun & Inf Schs IG11.................. 79 A2
North Carriage Dr W2........... 114 C6 247 B6
NORTH CHEAM 216 C6
Northchurch SE17 .... 262 D2
Northchurch Ho 19 E2 .. 96 A6
Northchurch Rd
De Beauvoir Town N1 .... 73 B1
Wembley HA9 .... 66 C2
Northchurch Terr N1 ... 73 C1
North Circular Rd
Edmonton N13.......... 32 C5
Finchley N2 .... 30 B2
Highams Pk E17 .... 35 D2
Ilford IG1, E12 .... 78 C4
Neasden NW2, NW10.... 67 C3
Temple Fortune N3, NW2, NW4.................. 47 A4
Woodford E18.......... 37 C1
North Cl Barnet EN5 .... 12 C6
Bexley DA6 .... 146 D1
Dagenham RM10....... 103 C6
East Bedfont TW14 .... 149 B5
Merton SM4 .... 201 A5
Northcliffe Cl KT4 ..... 215 C5
Northcliffe Dr N20...... 13 B3
North Colonnade The E14 .... 119 D5
North Common Rd
Ealing W5 .... 110 A6
Uxbridge UB8 .... 60 A3
Northcote 3 HA5....... 22 C1
Northcote Ave
Ealing W5 .... 110 A6
Isleworth TW7 .... 153 A6
Southall UB1.......... 107 A6
Tolworth KT5.......... 198 D2
Northcote Ho UB4 ...... 84 D2
Northcote Lodge Sch SW11................. 158 D5
Northcote Rd
Isleworth TW7 .... 153 A6
Kingston u T KT3....... 199 B6
Sidcup DA14 .... 189 C6
Thornton Heath CR0 .... 205 B3
Walthamstow E17........ 53 A5
Wandsworth SW11..... 158 D6
Willesden NW10......... 67 C1
Northcott Ave N22...... 32 A2
North Countess Rd E17 . 35 B2
Northcourt W1 .... 239 B4
NORTH CRAY 169 B1
North Cray Rd DA14.... 191 A5
North Cres Finchley N3... 29 B1
Marylebone WC1....... 239 C4
Newham E16........... 98 B3
Northcroft Ct 8 W12 .. 112 A4
Northcroft Rd
Brentford W13 .... 109 B3
West Ewell KT19....... 215 C1
North Crofts SE21..... 162 B3
North Cross Rd
East Dulwich SE22 ..... 162 A6
Ilford IG6 .... 57 A5
North Ct SW1......... 260 A5
North Dene
Edgware NW7.......... 11 B1
Hounslow TW5 .... 129 D4
Northdene Gdns N15.... 51 D3
Northdown Cl HA4...... 61 D5
Northdown Gdns IG2 ... 57 C4
Northdown Rd DA16 ... 146 C3
Northdown St N1............ 94 B5 233 C3
North Dr
Beckenham BR3 .... 207 D5
Hounslow TW3, TW7.... 130 A3
Orpington BR6.......... 227 C4
Ruislip HA4 .... 39 C2
Streatham SW16....... 181 C6
North Dulwich Sta SE21.................. 161 B6
North Ealing Prim Sch W5 .... 87 B3
North Ealing Sta W3.... 88 B1
NORTH END 70 A6
North End
Buckhurst Hill IG9....... 21 C4
Croydon CR0 .... 221 A6
North End NW3......... 70 A6
North End Ave NW3..... 70 A6
North End Cres W14.......... 113 B2 254 C3
North End Ho W14.......... 113 A2 254 B3
North End La BR6...... 226 D1
Northend Lodge 2 HA5.................. 40 D6
North End Par W14 ... 254 B3
North End Rd
Golders Green NW11 .... 47 D1
Wembley HA9 .... 66 D5
West Kensington W14....... 113 B1 254 D1
North End Way NW3 .... 70 A6
Northern Ave N9 .... 17 D2
Northernhay Wlk SM4.. 201 A5
Northern Hts N8........ 49 D2
Northern Perimeter Rd TW6................. 127 C4
Northern Perimeter Rd (W) TW6 .... 126 B4
Northern Rd E13........ 99 B5
Northern Relief Rd IG11 .... 79 A2
Northern Star Ho N11... 31 B5
Northesk Ho 6 E1...... 96 B3
North Eyot Gdns 5 W6................. 111 D1
Northey St E14 .... 119 A6
NORTH FELTHAM 150 B6
North Feltham Trad Est TW14 .... 128 B1
Northfield IG10......... 21 D6
Northfield Ave
Pinner HA5 .... 40 D6
West Ealing W13, W5... 109 B4
Northfield Cl
Bromley BR1.......... 188 A2
Hayes UB3............ 105 D3
Northfield Cres SM3... 217 A4
Northfield Gdns RM9.... 81 B4
Northfield Hall N6...... 49 A2
Northfield Ho
2 Newham E13 .... 99 C5
3 Peckham SE15....... 140 A6
Northfield Ind Est HA0.. 88 C6
Northfield Par UB3 .... 105 D3
Northfield Path RM9 .... 81 B4
Northfield Pk UB3 .... 105 D3
Northfield Rd
Cockfosters EN4 .... 2 C2
Dagenham RM9......... 81 B4
Enfield EN3 .... 18 D6
Heston TW5........... 128 D5
Plashet E6............. 78 B1
Stamford Hill N16 .... 51 C2
West Ealing W13....... 109 B4

Northfields SW18 135 C1
Northfields Prospect SW18 135 C1
Northfields Rd W3 89 A2
Northfields Sta W5 109 C3
NORTH FINCHLEY 30 A6
Northfleet Ho SE1 252 C2
North Flower Wlk W2 114 B6 246 C5
North Gate NW8 92 C5 230 A3
Northgate Bsns Ctr EN1 6 B1
Northgate Ct 14 SW9 138 C2
Northgate Dr NW9 45 C3
North Gates N12 30 A2
North Gdns SW19 180 B3
North Glade The DA5 169 B3
North Gn NW9 27 C3
North Gower St NW1 93 C4 232 B1
North Gr Highgate N6 49 A2
Tottenham N15 51 B4
North Greenwich Sta SE10 120 C4
North Harringay Prim Sch N8 50 C5
NORTH HARROW 41 D2
North Harrow Sta HA2 41 D4
North Hill N6 49 A3
North Hill Ave N6 48 D3
North Hill Ct N6 49 A2
NORTH HILLINGDON 61 A2
North Ho 3 SE8 119 B1
NORTH HYDE 107 A1
North Hyde Gdns UB2, UB3 106 A3
North Hyde La UB2 107 A1
North Hyde Rd UB3 105 D3
Northiam Finchley N12 29 C6
St Pancras WC1 233 B1
Northiam St E9 96 B6
Northington St WC1 94 B3 240 D5
NORTH KENSINGTON 90 D2
North La TW11 174 D4
Northlands 4 BR1 187 C1
Northlands Ave BR6 227 C4
Northlands St SE5 139 A3
Northleigh Ho 36 E3 97 D4
North Lo Clapham SW4 137 B1
Muswell Hill N22 31 D1
New Barnet EN5 14 A6
North Lodge Cl SW15 156 D6
North London Bsns Pk N11 15 A1
North London Collegiate Sch The HA7, HA8 26 A5
North London Nuffield Hospl EN2 4 C3
North Mall The N9 18 B2
North Mews WC1 94 B3 240 D5
North Middlesex University Hospl N18 33 C5
Northmoor 4 SE23 162 D1
North Mount N20 14 A2
Northolm HA8 27 B6
Northolme Gdns HA8 26 C2
Northolme Rd N5 73 A4
Northolme Rise BR6 227 C6
NORTHOLT 63 C1
Northolt N17 33 C1
Northolt Ave HA4 62 B3
Northolt Gdns UB6 64 D3
Northolt High Sch UB5 63 B2
Northolt Park Inf Sch UB5 63 D3
Northolt Park Sta HA2 63 D4
Northolt Rd HA2 64 A5
Northolt Sta UB5 63 C2
Northolt Trad Est UB5 63 D1
Northover BR1 164 D1
North Par
Chessington KT9 214 B3
Edgware HA8 26 C1
Southall UB1 85 C1
North Pas SW18 157 C6
North Pk SE9 166 C5
North Pl
Mitcham SW19 180 D3
Teddington TW11 174 D4
Northpoint BR1 187 A2
North Point UB7 104 A5
Northpoint Cl SM1 218 A5
Northpoint Sq 8 NW1 71 D2
North Pole La BR2 225 A2
North Pole Rd W10 90 C2
Northport St N1 235 D5
North Prim Sch UB1 107 B6
North Rd Barnsbury N7 72 A2
Brentford TW8 132 A6
Bromley BR1 187 B2
Dagenham RM6 59 A4
Ealing W5 109 D3
East Bedfont TW14 149 B5
Edgware HA8 26 D2
Edmonton N9 18 B3
Erith DA17 125 D4
Finchley N2 30 C2
Hayes UB3 83 B2
Heston TW5 128 C6
Highgate N6 49 A2
Ilford IG3 79 C6
Plumstead SE18 123 C2
Richmond TW9 132 C3
Southall UB1 107 C6
Surbiton KT6 197 D3
West Drayton UB7 104 B3
1 West Wickham BR4 207 D1
Wimbledon SW19 180 A4
North Residence IG3 58 B4
North Ride W2 114 C6 247 A5
North Rise W2 237 B1
Northrop Rd TW6 127 C4
North Row W1 115 A6 248 A6
NORTH SHEEN 132 C3
North Sheen Sta TW10 132 C1
Northside Prim Sch N12 30 A5
Northside Rd BR1 187 A2
North Side Wandsworth Comm SW18 158 B6
Northspur Rd SM1 217 C5
North Sq Edmonton N9 18 B2
Hampstead Garden Suburb NW11 47 C4
North St Barking IG11 79 A1
Bexleyheath DA7 147 C1
Bromley BR1 187 A2
Carshalton SM5 218 D4
Clapham SW4 137 C2
Hendon NW4 46 C4
Isleworth TW7 131 A2
Newham E13 99 B5
Northstead Rd SW2 160 C2
North Tenter St E1 243 D1
North Terr SW3 257 A5
Northumberland Alley EC3 243 B1
Northumberland Ave
Enfield EN1 6 B4
Falconwood DA16 145 C2
Hounslow TW7 130 D4
Wanstead E12 55 C1
Westminster WC2 116 A5 250 A4
Northumberland Cl TW19 148 A5
Northumberland Cres TW14 149 C5
Northumberland Ct
3 Hounslow TW3 129 D1
South Croydon CR2 221 C3
Northumberland Gdns
Brentford TW7 131 A5
Bromley BR1 210 C5
Edmonton N9 17 D1
Mitcham CR4 203 D4
Northumberland Gr N17 34 B3
Northumberland Heath Prim Sch DA8 147 D5
Northumberland Ho
Finchley N12 29 D4
Kentish Town NW5 71 C2
Northumberland Mans E5 74 C4
Northumberland Park Com Sch N17 34 A3
Northumberland Park Ind Est N17 34 B3
Northumberland Park Sports Ctr N17 34 A3
Northumberland Park Sta N17 34 B3
Northumberland Pk
Erith DA8 147 D5
Tottenham N17 34 A3
Northumberland Pl
Notting Hill W2 91 C1
26 Richmond TW10 153 D6
Northumberland Rd
Harrow HA2 41 C4
New Barnet EN5 14 A4
Newham E6 100 A1
Walthamstow E17 53 C2
Northumberland St WC2 250 A4
Northumbria Ct 10 TW9 132 A1
Northumbria St E14 97 C1
North Verbena Gdns 2 W6 112 A1
Northview 1 N7 72 A5
North View Ealing W5 87 C3
Pinner HA5 40 C2
Wimbledon SW19 178 C5
Northview Cres NW10 67 D4
Northview Dr IG8 37 D1
Northview Prim Sch NW10 67 D4
North View Rd N8 49 D6
North Villas NW1 71 D2
Northway
Hampstead Garden Suburb NW11 47 D4
Merton SM4 201 A5
Wallington SM6 219 C4
North Way
Friern Barnet N11 31 C4
Lower Edmonton N9 18 D2
Pinner HA5 40 D5
Queensbury NW9 44 D6
Uxbridge UB10 60 A1
Northway Cir NW7 27 B6
Northway Cres NW7 27 C6
Northway Ct NW7 27 B6
Northway Rd
Camberwell SE5 139 A2
Croydon CR0 205 D2
Northway Sch NW7 11 B1
Northways Par 2 NW3 70 B1
Northweald La KT2 175 D5
NORTH WEMBLEY 65 C6
North Wembley Sta HA0, HA9 65 D5
North Western Ave (Tylers Way) WD23 8 C6
North Western Ave (Watford By-Pass) WD6 9 B4
Northwest Pl N1 234 B4
North Wharf Rd W2 92 B2 236 C3
Northwick Ave HA3 43 B3
Northwick Circ HA3 43 C3
Northwick Cl
Harrow HA1 43 B1
Lisson Gr NW8 92 B3 236 C6
Northwick Ho NW8 236 B6
Northwick Park Hospl HA1 43 A2
Northwick Park Rd HA1 42 D3
Northwick Park Sta HA3 43 B2
Northwick Rd
South Oxhey WD19 22 C6
Wembley HA0 87 D6
Northwick Terr NW8 92 B3 236 C6
North Wlk
Bayswater W2 114 A6 246 A5
New Addington CR0 224 A3
Northwold Dr HA5 40 C6
Northwold Prim Sch E5 74 A6
Northwold Rd E5, N16 74 A6
NORTHWOOD 22 A3
Northwood Gdns
Greenford UB6 64 D3
Ilford IG5 56 C5
North Finchley N12 30 B5
NORTHWOOD HILLS 22 A1
Northwood Hills Cir HA6 22 A2
Northwood Hills Sta HA6 22 A1
North Wood Lo NW3 69 D4
Northwood & Pinner Com Hospl HA6 22 A2
Northwood Pl DA18 125 B3
Northwood Prim Sch DA18 125 B3
Northwood Rd
Forest Hill SE23 163 B3
Highgate N6 49 B2
South Norwood CR7 183 A1
Wallington SM5 219 A2
Northwood Sch HA6 22 A2
Northwood Twr 1 E17 54 A5
Northwood Way
Northwood HA6 22 A3
1 West Norwood SE19 183 C4
NORTH WOOLWICH 122 D4
North Woolwich Rd E16 121 B5
North Woolwich Rdbt E16 121 D5
North Worple Way SW14 133 B2
Norton Ave KT5 198 D2
Norton Cl Chingford E4 35 C5
Enfield EN1 6 B3
Norton Ct
Beckenham BR3 185 B2
Ilford IG2 57 B3
Norton Folgate E1 243 B4
Norton Gdns SW16 182 A1
Norton Ho
14 Globe Town E2 96 D5
6 New Malden KT3 199 C5
30 Stepney E1 96 B1
16 Stockwell SW9 138 B3
Norton Rd
Walthamstow E10 53 B1
Wembley HA0 65 D2
Norval Gn 1 SW9 138 C3
Norval Rd HA0 43 B1
Norvic Ho 5 SE5 139 A3
Norway Gate SE16 119 A3
Norway Pl E14 97 B1
Norway St SE10 141 D6
Norwegian Sch The SW20 178 C3
Norwich Cres RM6 58 B4
Norwich Ho 6 E14 97 D1
Norwich Mews IG3 58 A1
Norwich Pl 7 DA6 147 C1
Norwich Rd
Forest Gate E7 77 A3
Greenford UB6 85 D6
Northwood HA6 39 D6
South Norwood CR7 205 A6
Norwich St EC4 94 C1 241 A2
Norwich Wlk HA8 27 A3
Norwood Ave HA0 88 B5
Norwood Cl
Cricklewood NW2 69 A5
Southall UB2 107 C2
Twickenham TW2 152 B2
Norwood Dr HA2 41 C3
Norwood Gdns
Hayes UB4 84 C3
Southall UB2 107 B2
NORWOOD GREEN 107 C2
Norwood Green Inf Sch UB2 107 B1
Norwood Green Jun Sch UB2 107 A1
Norwood Green Rd UB2 107 C2
Norwood Heights Sh Ctr 18 SE19 183 C4
Norwood High St SE27 183 A6
Norwood Ho 25 E14 119 D6
Norwood Hospl SE19 183 B4
Norwood Junction Sta SE25 206 A5
NORWOOD NEW TOWN 183 A4
Norwood Park Rd SE27 183 A5
Norwood Rd
Southall UB2 107 C2
West Norwood SE24, SE27 160 D3
Norwood Sch SE19 183 A5
Norwood Terr UB2 107 D2
Notley St SE5 139 B5
Notre Dame RC Girls Sch SE1 116 D3 261 D5
Notre Dame RC Prim Sch SE18 144 D6
Notson Rd SE25 206 B5
Notting Barn Rd W10 90 D3
Nottingdale Sq W11 244 A4
Nottingham Ave E16 99 C1
Nottingham Ct WC2 240 A1
Nottingham Ho
33 Camberwell SE5 139 A3
Stoke Newington N4 51 A1
Nottingham Pl W1 93 A2 238 A4
Nottingham Rd
Croydon CR2 221 A3
Isleworth TW7 130 D3
Leytonstone E10 54 A3
Upper Tooting SW17 158 D3
Nottingham St W1 238 A4
Nottingham Terr NW1 238 A5
NOTTING HILL 113 B6
Notting Hill & Ealing High Sch W13 87 B2
Notting Hill Gate W11 113 C5 245 A4
Notting Hill Gate Sta W11 113 C5 245 A4
Nottingwood Ho W11 244 A6
Nova Bldg 1 E14 119 C2
Nova Ct E 3 E14 120 A5
Nova Ct W 2 E14 120 A5
Nova Mews SM4 201 A2
Novar Cl BR6 211 D2
Nova Rd CR0 205 A2
Novar Rd SE9 167 A3
Novello St SW6 135 C4 265 A2
Nowell Rd SW13 134 A6
Nower Ct HA5 41 B5
NOWER HILL 41 B6
Nower Hill HA5 41 B5
Nower Hill High Sch HA5 41 C5
Noyna Rd SW17 158 D1
Nubia Way SE6 164 C1
Nucleus NW10 89 A4
Nuding Cl SE13 141 C2
Nuffield Ct TW5 129 B5
Nuffield Lo 14 W9 91 C2
Nugent Ct
Streatham SW16 181 C6
3 Upper Holloway N19 50 A1
Nugent Rd
Finsbury Pk N19 50 A1
South Norwood SE25 205 D6
Nugents Ct HA5 23 B3
Nugent's Pk HA5 23 B2
Nugent Terr NW8 92 A5 229 B3
Numa Ct TW8 131 D5
Nun Ct EC2 242 C2
Nuneaton Rd RM9 81 A1
Nuneham SW16 181 D6
NUNHEAD 140 C1
Nunhead Cres SE15 140 B2
Nunhead Gn SE15 140 B2
Nunhead Gr SE15 140 C2
Nunhead La SE15 140 B2
Nunhead Sta SE15 140 C3
Nunnington Cl SE9 166 A1
Nunn's Rd EN2 5 A3
Nupton Dr EN5 12 C5
Nursery Cl HA8 27 A2
Nursery Ave
Bexleyheath DA7 147 B2
Croydon CR0 222 D6
Finchley N3 30 A1
Nursery Cl
Broom Hill BR6 211 D2
Croydon CR0 222 D6
Dagenham RM6 58 D3
Enfield EN3 6 D4
Feltham TW14 150 B4
New Cross SE4 141 B3
Putney SW15 134 D1
Woodford IG8 37 B5
Nursery Ct Ealing W13 87 A2
8 Tottenham N17 33 D3
Nursery Gdns
Chislehurst BR7 188 D4
Enfield EN3 6 D4
Hampton TW13 173 B6
Hounslow TW4 151 B6
Sunbury TW16 171 D1
Nursery La
Forest Gate E7 77 A2
Hillingdon UB8 82 A3
North Kensington W10 90 C2
Shoreditch E2 95 D6
Nurserymans Rd N11 15 A2
Nursery Rd Finchley N2 30 B2
Hackney E9 74 C2
Loughton IG10 21 C6
Merton SW19 179 D1
Nursery Rd *continued*
Mitcham CR4 202 C6
Osidge N14 15 C4
Pinner HA5 40 C6
South Norwood CR7 205 B5
Stockwell SW9 138 B1
Sunbury TW16 171 D1
Sutton SM1 218 A4
Wimbledon SW19 179 A3
Nursery Row SE17 262 C3
Nursery St N17 33 D3
Nursery Walk Ct NW4 46 B6
Nursery Wlk NW4 46 C6
Nurstead Rd DA8 147 C5
Nutborn Ho SW19 178 D4
Nutbourne St W10 91 A4
Nutbrook St SE15 140 A2
Nutbrowne Rd RM9 103 B6
Nutchford EN1 17 C5
Nutcroft Rd SE15 140 B5
Nutfield Cl
Carshalton SM5 218 C5
Edmonton N18 34 A4
Nutfield Gdns Ilford IG3 80 A6
Northolt UB5 84 C5
Nutfield Pl 1 CR7 204 D5
Nutfield Rd
Dollis Hill NW2 68 A5
East Dulwich SE22 139 D1
Leyton E15 76 A4
Thornton Heath CR7 204 D5
Nutfield Way BR6 226 D6
Nutford Pl W1 92 D1 237 C2
Nuthatch Cl TW19 148 B3
Nuthatch Gdns SE28 123 B4
Nuthurst Ave SW2 160 B2
Nutkin Wlk UB8 60 A1
Nutley Terr NW3 70 B2
Nutmeg Cl E16 98 C3
Nutmeg La E14 98 B1
Nuttall St N1 95 C5
Nutter La E11 55 C4
Nutt Gr HA8 9 D2
Nutt St SE15 139 D5
Nutty La TW17 193 A6
Nutwell St SW17 180 C5
Nuxley Rd DA17 125 C1
NW London Jewish Day Sch NW6 69 A1
Nyanza St SE18 145 B6
Nye Bevan Est E5 74 D5
Nye Bevan Ho SW6 264 C4
Nye's Wharf SE1, SE15 140 A6
Nylands Ave TW9 132 C3
Nymans Gdns SW20 200 B6
Nynehead St SE14 141 A5
Nyon Gr SE6 163 B2
Nyton Cl N19 50 A1

O

O2 Millennium Dome The* SE10 120 C5
Oak Apple Ct SE12 165 A3
Oak Ave Croydon CR0 223 D6
Enfield EN2 4 B5
Hampton TW12, TW13 173 A4
Heston TW5 129 A5
Hornsey N8 50 A5
Muswell Hill N10 31 B3
Tottenham N17 33 C3
Uxbridge UB10 60 D6
West Drayton UB7 104 C3
Oak Bank CR0 224 A2
Oakbank Ave KT12 195 B2
Oakbank Gr SE24 139 A1
Oakbark Ho 10 TW8 131 C5
Oakbrook 3 BR3 185 D1
Oakbrook Cl BR1 187 B6
Oakbury Rd SW6 135 D3
Oak Cl East Barnet N14 15 B4
Sutton SM1 218 A6
Oakcombe Cl KT3 177 C2
Oak Cottage Cl 11 SE6 164 D3
Oak Cotts W7 108 C4
Oakcourt 17 SE15 139 D5
Oak Cres E16 98 C2
Oakcroft SE12 165 B1
Oakcroft Bsns Ctr KT9 214 B4
Oakcroft Cl HA5 22 B1
Oakcroft Ct SE3 143 A4
Oakcroft Ho 3 KT3 199 C2
Oakcroft Rd
Chessington KT9 214 B4
Lewisham SE13 142 B3
Oakcroft Villas KT9 214 B4
Oak Ct Bickley BR1 188 B1
Chingford E4 35 D4
Oakdale
Beckenham BR3 186 A1
East Barnet N14 15 B3
Oakdale Ave
Harrow HA3 44 A4
Pinner HA6 22 A1
Oakdale Cl WD19 22 C6
Oakdale Ct Chingford E4 36 A5
Upper Holloway N19 72 A6
Oakdale Gdns E4 36 A5
Oakdale Inf Sch E18 37 B1
Oakdale Jun Sch E18 37 B1
Oakdale Lo NW4 29 A2
Oakdale Rd Leyton E11 76 B6
Nunhead SE15 140 C2
South Oxhey WD19 22 C6
Streatham SW16 182 A5
Tottenham N4 51 B3
Upton E7 77 B1
Woodford E18 37 B1
Oakdale Way CR4 203 A2
Oakdene
8 Peckham SE15 140 B4
1 West Norwood SE19 183 C5
Oak Dene W13 87 B2
Oakdene Ave
Chislehurst West BR7 188 C5
Thames Ditton KT7 197 A1
Oakdene Cl HA5 23 B3
Oakdene Ct
Feltham TW12 173 B6
1 Streatham SW16 182 A5
Oakdene Dr KT5 199 A1
Oakdene Ho Enfield EN2 4 D2
11 Stamford Hill N16 51 C1
Oakdene Lo 3 SE20 184 B3
Oakdene Mews SM3 201 B1
Oakdene Pk N3 29 B3
Oakdene Rd
Hillingdon UB10 82 D5
Orpington BR5 211 D4
Oakden St SE11 116 C2 261 B4
Oake Ct SW15 157 A6
Oakeford Ho W14 254 B5
Oakend Ho 10 N4 51 B2
Oaken Dr KT10 212 D2
Oakenholt Ho 1 SE2 124 D4
Oaken La KT10 212 C3
Oakenshaw Cl KT6 198 A2
Oakes Cl E6 100 B1
Oakeshott Ave N6 71 A6
Oakey La SE1 261 A6
Oak Farm WD6 11 A6
Oak Farm Jun & Inf Schs UB10 82 D6
Oakfield E4 35 D5
Oakfield Ave HA3 43 B6
Oakfield Cl
New Malden KT3 199 D4
Ruislip HA4 39 D3
Oakfield Ct
Clapham Pk SW4 160 A5
2 Ealing W5 110 C5
Finchley N3 29 D2
Finsbury Pk N8 50 A2
Hendon NW2 46 D2
South Croydon CR2 221 A2
Oakfield Gdns
Beckenham BR3 207 C4
Carshalton SM5 202 D1
Edmonton N18 33 C6
Greenford UB6 86 B4
3 West Norwood SE19 183 C5
Oakfield Ho 2 IG1 78 D5
Oakfield La BR2 225 C4
Oakfield Lo 8 IG1 78 D5
Oakfield Prep Sch SE21 161 B3
Oakfield Rd
Ashford TW15 170 D5
Croydon CR0 205 A1
Finchley N3 29 D2
Finsbury Pk N4 50 C2
Higham Hill E17 35 A1
Ilford IG1 78 D5
Newham E6 100 A6
Palmers Green N14 16 A2
Penge SE20 184 B3
Wimbledon SW19 156 D1
Oakfield Road Ind Est 11 SE20 184 B3
Oakfields KT12 194 A1
Oakfields Rd NW11 47 A3
Oakfield St SW10 136 A6 266 A6
Oakford Rd NW5 71 C4
Oak Gdns Croydon CR0 223 C6
Hendon HA8 27 A1
Oak Gr Ruislip HA4 40 B1
Sunbury TW16 172 B3
West Hampstead NW2 69 A4
West Wickham BR4 208 A1
Oak Grove Rd SE20 184 C1
Oakhall Ct
Ashford TW16 171 D5
Wanstead E11 55 B3
Oakhall Dr TW16 171 D5
Oak Hall Rd E11 55 B3
Oakham Cl
Cockfosters EN4 2 D2
Forest Hill SE6 163 B2
Oakham Dr BR2 208 D5
Oakham Ho 5 W10 90 C3
Oakhampton Rd NW7 28 D3
Oakhill KT10 213 A2
Oak Hill Chingford IG8 36 C3
Surbiton KT6 198 A2
Oakhill Ave Pinner HA5 23 A1
West Hampstead NW3 69 D4
Oak Hill Cl IG8 36 B3
Oakhill Coll N14 15 A5
Oak Hill Cres
Chingford IG8 36 C3
Surbiton KT6 198 A2
Oakhill Ct
Honor Oak SE23 162 C5
Putney SW15 157 B6
8 Surbiton KT6 198 A3
Wimbledon SW19 178 D3
Oak Hill Ct IG8 36 C3
Oak Hill Gdns E4 36 C2
Oak Hill Gr KT6 198 A3
Oakhill Ho BR5 190 A2

Oak Hill Lo NW3 . . . 69 D4
Oakhill Mans EN4 . . . 14 C5
Oak Hill Park Mews
NW3 . . . 70 A4
Oak Hill Pk NW3 . . . 69 D4
Oakhill Pl SW15 . . . 157 C6
Oakhill Prim Sch IG8 . . . 36 C4
Oakhill Rd
Beckenham BR3 . . . 186 A1
Orpington BR6 . . . 227 D6
Putney SW15 . . . 157 B6
Sutton SM1 . . . 218 A5
Thornton Heath SW16 . . . 182 B2
Oak Hill Rd KT6 . . . 198 A3
Oak Hill Way NW3 . . . 70 A4
Oak Ho
13 Cubitt Town E14 . . . 120 A4
11 Finchley N2 . . . 30 B1
8 Maitland Pk NW3 . . . 70 D2
Penge SE20 . . . 184 B1
2 Richmond TW9 . . . 132 D4
13 Sidcup DA15 . . . 168 A1
9 Stoke Newington N16 . . 73 B6
Teddington TW11 . . . 175 C4
Wood Green N22 . . . 32 A3
Oakhouse Rd DA6 . . . 169 C6
Oakhurst Ave
East Barnet EN4 . . . 14 C4
Erith DA7 . . . 147 A5
Oakhurst Cl
Chislehurst BR7 . . . 188 B2
Snaresbrook E17 . . . 54 C5
4 Teddington TW11 . . . 174 C5
Oakhurst Ct E17 . . . 54 C5
Oakhurst Gdns
Chingford E4 . . . 20 D3
Erith DA7 . . . 147 A5
Snaresbrook E11, E17 . . . 54 C5
Oakhurst Gr SE22 . . . 140 A1
Oakhurst Rd KT19 . . . 215 A2
Oakington 14 KT1 . . . 176 C1
Oakington Ave
Harrow HA2 . . . 41 C2
Hayes UB3 . . . 105 B2
Wembley HA9 . . . 66 B5
Oakington Cl TW16 . . . 172 C1
Oakington Ct 1 EN2 . . . 4 D3
Oakington Dr TW16 . . . 172 C1
Oakington Manor Dr
HA9 . . . 66 C3
Oakington Manor Prim
Sch HA9 . . . 66 D3
Oakington Rd W9 . . . 91 C3
Oakington Way N8 . . . 50 A2
Oak La Finchley N2 . . . 30 B1
Friern Barnet N11 . . . 31 D4
Isleworth TW7 . . . 130 C1
Limehouse E14 . . . 119 B6
Twickenham TW1 . . . 153 A4
Woodford IG8 . . . 36 D6
Oakland Pl IG9 . . . 21 A2
Oakland Rd E15 . . . 76 C4
Oaklands
Chislehurst BR7 . . . 189 B4
Croydon CR0 . . . 220 D3
Ealing W13 . . . 87 A2
Southgate N21 . . . 16 B2
Twickenham TW2 . . . 152 A4
Oaklands Ave Enfield N9 . . 18 B5
Hounslow TW7 . . . 130 D6
Sidcup DA15 . . . 167 D4
Thames Ditton KT10 . . . 196 B1
Thornton Heath CR7 . . . 204 C5
West Wickham BR4 . . . 223 D5
Oaklands Cl
Bexley DA6 . . . 169 B6
Chessington KT9 . . . 213 C4
Orpington BR5 . . . 211 C3
Oaklands Ct
Beckenham BR3 . . . 186 A1
Dagenham NW10 . . . 89 C6
Orpington BR6 . . . 227 A6
5 Shepherd's Bush
W12 . . . 112 B5
Wembley HA0 . . . 65 D3
Oaklands Dr TW2 . . . 152 A4
Oaklands Gr W12 . . . 112 A5
Oaklands Ho SE4 . . . 141 B2
Oaklands Mews 1
NW2 . . . 68 D4
Oaklands Park Ave IG1 . . 79 A6
Oaklands Pas NW2 . . . 68 D4
Oaklands Pl 8 SW4 . . . 137 D1
Oaklands Prim Sch
W7 . . . 108 D4
Oaklands Rd Barnet N20 . 13 B4
Bexley DA6 . . . 169 B6
Bromley BR1 . . . 186 C3
Cricklewood NW2 . . . 68 D4
Ealing W7 . . . 108 D4
Mortlake SW14 . . . 133 B2
West Ealing W7, W13 . . . 109 A4
Oaklands Sch
Hounslow TW3 . . . 130 B2
Loughton IG10 . . . 21 D6
Oaklands Sec Sch E2 . . . 96 B4
Oaklands Way SM6 . . . 219 D1
Oakland Way KT19 . . . 215 C2
Oaklawn Ct HA7 . . . 25 B4
Oakleafe Gdns IG6 . . . 56 D6
Oaklea Pas KT1 . . . 197 D6
Oakleigh Ave
East Barnet N20 . . . 14 C3
Edgware HA8 . . . 26 D2
Tolworth KT6 . . . 214 D6
Oakleigh Cl N20 . . . 14 D1
Oakleigh Cres N20 . . . 14 C1
Oakleigh Ct
East Barnet EN4 . . . 14 C5
Hendon HA8 . . . 27 A1
7 Penge SE20 . . . 184 B3
Southall UB1 . . . 107 B5
Surbiton KT6 . . . 214 B6
Oakleigh Gdns
Edgware HA8 . . . 26 B5
Oakleigh Pk N20 . . . 14 B3
Orpington BR6 . . . 227 C4
Oakleigh Lodge IG3 . . . 80 A5
Oakleigh Mews 2 N20 . . 14 A2
OAKLEIGH PARK . . . 14 B3
Oakleigh Park Ave
BR7 . . . 188 C2
Oakleigh Park Sta EN4 . . 14 C4
Oakleigh Pk N N20 . . . 14 B3
Oakleigh Pk S N20 . . . 14 C3
Oakleigh Rd
Hillingdon UB10 . . . 61 A1
Pinner HA5 . . . 23 B4
Oakleigh Rd N N20 . . . 14 C2
Oakleigh Rd S N11 . . . 31 A6
Oakleigh Sch N20 . . . 14 D1
Oakleigh Way
Mitcham CR4 . . . 181 B2
1 Tolworth KT6 . . . 198 D1
Oakley Ave Barking IG11 . 79 D1
Ealing W5 . . . 110 C6
Wallington CR0 . . . 220 A4
Oakley Cl Chingford E4 . . 20 A1
Ealing W7 . . . 108 C6
Hounslow TW7 . . . 130 B4
7 Newham E6 . . . 100 A1
Oakley Cres EC1 . . . 234 D3
Oakley Ct
Carshalton CR4 . . . 203 A2
Harlington UB7 . . . 127 A5
Wembley HA0 . . . 65 A4
Oakley Dr
Keston Mark BR2 . . . 226 A5
Lewisham SE13 . . . 164 B5
New Eltham SE9 . . . 167 B3
Oakley Gdns
Chelsea SW3 . . 136 C6 267 B6
Hornsey Vale N8 . . . 50 B4
Oakley Ho Chelsea SW1 257 D4
Ealing W5 . . . 110 C6
Oakley Pk DA5 . . . 168 C4
Oakley Pl SE1 . . 117 D1 263 C1
Oakley Rd
Croydon SE25 . . . 206 B4
De Beauvoir Town N1 . . . 73 B1
Harrow HA1 . . . 42 C3
Keston Mark BR2 . . . 226 A6
Oakley Sq NW1 . . 93 C5 232 B4
Oakley St SW3 . . 136 C6 267 A6
Oakley Wlk W6 . . . 134 D6
Oak Lo
4 Ashford TW16 . . . 171 D3
Southgate N21 . . . 16 B5
10 Sutton SM1 . . . 218 A4
Wanstead E11 . . . 55 A2
6 Wembley HA0 . . . 65 D3
Oak Lodge 14 SE21 . . . 161 B2
Oak Lodge Cl HA7 . . . 25 C5
Oak Lodge Dr BR4 . . . 207 D2
Oak Lodge Sch
Balham SW12 . . . 159 A4
East Finchley N2 . . . 48 A5
Oaklodge Way NW7 . . . 27 D4
Oakman Ho 29 SW19 . . . 156 D3
Oakmead HA1 . . . 64 B5
Oakmead Ave BR2 . . . 209 A3
Oakmead Ct HA7 . . . 25 C6
Oakmeade HA5 . . . 23 C4
Oakmead Gdns HA8 . . . 27 B6
Oakmead Pl CR4 . . . 180 C2
Oakmead Rd
Balham SW12 . . . 159 B3
Wallington CR0 . . . 203 D3
Oakmere Rd SE2 . . . 146 A6
Oakmont Pl 6 BR6 . . . 211 B1
Oak Park Gdns SW19 . . . 156 D3
Oak Park Mews N16 . . . 73 D5
Oak Rd Ealing W5 . . . 109 D6
Kingston u T KT3 . . . 177 B1
Oakridge Dr N2 . . . 48 B6
Oakridge La BR1 . . . 186 B5
Oakridge Rd BR1 . . . 186 C6
Oak Rise IG9 . . . 21 D1
Oak Row CR4 . . . 181 C1
Oaks Ave
Feltham TW13 . . . 151 A2
North Cheam KT4 . . . 216 B4
West Norwood SE19 . . . 183 C5
Oaksford Ave SE26 . . . 162 B1
Oaks Gr E4 . . . 20 C2
Oakshade Rd BR1 . . . 186 B6
Oakshaw Rd SW18 . . . 157 D4
Oakshott Ct NW1 . . . 232 C3
Oaks La Ilford IG2 . . . 57 C5
South Croydon CR0 . . . 222 C5
Oaks Park High Sch
IG2 . . . 57 C4
Oaks Rd CR0 . . . 222 C4
Oaks Sh Ctr The W3 . . . 111 A5
Oaks The
Brondesbury Pk NW6 . . . 68 D1
Chingford IG8 . . . 36 C3
Enfield EN2 . . . 4 D2
Finchley N12 . . . 29 D6
Hayes UB4 . . . 83 A5
Long Ditton KT6 . . . 213 C5
Ruislip HA4 . . . 39 C2
Southborough BR2 . . . 210 C3
Wallington SM6 . . . 219 C4
Willesden NW10 . . . 68 B1
Wimbledon SW19 . . . 179 A4
Woolwich SE18 . . . 123 A1
Oaks Way Surbiton KT6 . . 197 D1
Wallington SM5 . . . 218 D1
Oakthorpe Ct N13 . . . 33 A5
Oakthorpe Prim Sch
N13 . . . 33 A5
Oakthorpe Rd N13 . . . 32 C5
Oaktree Ave N13 . . . 16 D1
Oak Tree Ave N2 . . . 47 D6
Oak Tree Cl Ealing W5 . . 87 C1
Stanmore HA7 . . . 25 C3
Oak Tree Ct Acton W3 . . 110 D6
8 Clapham Pk SW4 . . . 160 A6
Elstree WD6 . . . 9 D5
Oak Tree Dell NW9 . . . 45 B4
Oak Tree Dr N20 . . . 13 D3
Oak Tree Gdns BR1 . . . 187 B5
Oaktree Gr IG1 . . . 79 B3
Oak Tree Ho W9 . . . 91 D3
Oak Tree Rd
NW8 . . . 92 C4 230 A1
Oaktree Sch EN4 . . . 15 A5
Oaktrees Hostel HA8 . . . 11 A2
Oakview Gdns N2 . . . 48 B5
Oakview Gr CR0 . . . 207 A1
Oakview Lo NW11 . . . 47 B2
Oakview Rd SE6 . . . 185 D5
Oak Village NW5 . . . 71 A4
Oakway
Beckenham BR2 . . . 186 B1
West Barnes SW20 . . . 200 C5
Oak Way Croydon CR0 . . . 206 D3
East Acton W3 . . . 111 C5
East Barnet N14 . . . 15 B4
East Bedfont TW14 . . . 149 C3
Oakway Cl DA5 . . . 169 A5
Oakways SE9 . . . 166 D5
Oakwell Ho 24 SW8 . . . 137 D3
Oak Wlk CR4 . . . 203 A1
OAKWOOD . . . 15 D6
Oakwood Ave
Beckenham BR2, BR3 . . . 186 A1
Bromley BR2 . . . 209 B6
Mitcham CR4 . . . 180 B1
Osidge N14 . . . 15 D4
Southall UB1 . . . 107 C6
Oakwood Cl
Chislehurst West
BR7 . . . 188 C4
Lewisham SE13 . . . 164 B5
Southgate N14 . . . 15 C5
Oakwood Cres
Southgate N21 . . . 16 B5
Wembley UB6 . . . 65 B2
Oakwood Ct
Beckenham BR3 . . . 186 A1
6 Chingford E4 . . . 20 C4
Kensington
W14 . . . 113 B3 254 C6
1 Newham E6 . . . 100 A6
17 Sutton SM1 . . . 218 A4
Oakwood Dr
Burnt Oak HA8 . . . 27 A4
West Norwood SE19 . . . 183 C4
Oakwood Gdns
Ilford IG3 . . . 79 D6
Orpington BR6 . . . 227 A6
Sutton SM1 . . . 217 C6
Oakwood La
W14 . . . 113 B3 254 C6
Oakwood Park Rd N14 . . 16 A5
Oakwood Pl CR0 . . . 204 C3
Oakwood Rd
Hampstead Garden Suburb
NW11 . . . 47 D4
Orpington BR6 . . . 227 A6
Pinner HA5 . . . 22 B1
Thornton Heath CR0 . . . 204 C3
Wimbledon SW20 . . . 178 A2
Oakwood Sta N14 . . . 15 C6
Oakwood View N14 . . . 15 D4
Oakworth Rd W10 . . . 90 D2
Oarsman Pl KT8 . . . 196 C5
Oasis The 6 BR1 . . . 187 C1
Oast Ct 8 E14 . . . 119 B6
Oast Lo W4 . . . 133 C5
Oates Cl BR2 . . . 208 B6
Oatfield Ho 11 N15 . . . 51 C3
Oatfield Rd BR6 . . . 211 D1
Oat La EC2 . . . 95 A1 242 B2
Oatland Rise E17 . . . 35 A1
Oatlands Ct 3 SW19 . . . 156 D3
Oatlands Dr KT13 . . . 193 C1
Oatlands Rd EN3 . . . 6 C4
Oatwell Ho SW3 . . . 257 B3
Oban Cl E13 . . . 99 C3
Oban Ct HA8 . . . 10 D2
Oban Ho
5 Barking IG11 . . . 101 B5
South Bromley E14 . . . 98 B1
Oban Rd Newham E13 . . . 99 C4
South Norwood SE25 . . . 205 B5
Oban St E14 . . . 98 B1
Oberon Ho 5 N1 . . . 95 C5
Oberon Way TW17 . . . 192 A6
Oberstein Rd 15 SW11 . . . 136 B1
Oborne Cl SE24 . . . 160 D6
O'Brian Ho 10 E1 . . . 96 D4
Observatory Gdns W8. 245 B2
Observatory Mews
E14 . . . 120 B2
Observatory Rd SW14 . . . 133 A1
Occupation La
Brentford W5 . . . 109 D2
Shooters Hill SE18 . . . 144 D4
Occupation Rd
Newington
SE17 . . . 117 A1 262 A2
West Ealing W13 . . . 109 B4
Ocean St E1 . . . 96 D2
Ocean Wharf E14 . . . 119 C4
Ochre Ct TW13 . . . 149 D1
Ockbrook 3 E1 . . . 96 C2
Ockendon Rd N1 . . . 73 B2
Ockham Dr BR5 . . . 190 A3
Ockley Ct Sidcup DA14 . . 167 C1
Sutton SM1 . . . 218 A4
Ockley Ho 8 KT2 . . . 176 D4
Ockley Rd
Streatham SW16 . . . 160 A1
Thornton Heath CR0 . . . 204 B2
Octagon Arc EC2 . . . 243 A3
Octagon The NW3 . . . 69 C4
Octavia Cl CR4 . . . 202 C4
Octavia Ho Catford SE6 . . 163 D4
Kensal Town W10 . . . 91 A3
Octavia Mews 1 W9 . . . 91 B3
Octavia Rd TW7 . . . 130 D2
Octavia St
SW11 . . . 136 C4 267 B1
Octavia Way 12 SE28 . . . 124 B6
Octavius St SE8 . . . 141 C5
October Ct BR2 . . . 208 D6
October Pl NW4 . . . 46 D6
Odard Rd KT8 . . . 195 C5
Odell Cl IG11 . . . 79 D1
Odell Wlk SE13 . . . 142 A2
Odeon Ct
Dagenham NW10 . . . 89 C6
1 Newham E16 . . . 99 A2
Odeon Par Eltham SE9 . . 144 A1
Wembley UB6 . . . 65 B2
Odeon The IG11 . . . 79 B1
Odessa Inf Sch E7 . . . 77 A3
Odessa Rd Leyton E7 . . . 76 D4
Willesden Green NW10 . . . 90 A5
Odessa St SE16 . . . 119 B3
Odette Ct N20 . . . 14 A1
Odette Duval Ho 29 E1 . . 96 C2
Odette Ho 6 SE27 . . . 183 B6
Odger St SW11 . . . 136 D3
Odhams Wlk WC2 . . . 240 B1
Odin Ho 6 SE5 . . . 139 A3
O'Donnell Ct WC1 . . . 240 B6
O'Driscoll Ho 4 W12 . . . 90 B1
Odyssey Bsns Pk HA4 . . . 62 B3
Offa's Mead E9 . . . 75 A4
Offenbach Ho 12 E2 . . . 96 D5
Offenham Rd BR7, SE9 . . 188 B6
Offers Ct KT1 . . . 198 B6
Offerton Rd SW4 . . . 137 C2
Offham Ho SE17 . . . 263 A3
Offham Slope N12 . . . 29 B5
Offley Ho 10 E9 . . . 74 D2
Offley Pl TW7 . . . 130 B3
Offley Rd SW9 . . . 138 C5
Offord Cl N17 . . . 34 A4
Offord Rd N1 . . . 72 B1
Offord St N1 . . . 72 B1
Ogden Ho TW13 . . . 173 A6
Ogilby St SE18 . . . 122 B2
Ogilvie Ho 12 E1 . . . 96 D1
Oglander Rd SE15 . . . 139 D2
Ogle St W1 . . . 93 C2 239 A4
Oglethorpe Rd RM10 . . . 81 C5
O'Gorman Ho SW10 . . . 266 B4
O'Grady Ct 17 W13 . . . 109 A5
O'Grady Ho 17 E17 . . . 53 D6
Ohio Bldg 13 SE13 . . . 141 D4
Ohio Rd E13 . . . 98 D3
Oil Mill La W6 . . . 112 A1
Okeburn Rd SW17 . . . 181 A5
Okehampton Cl N12 . . . 30 B5
Okehampton Cres
DA16 . . . 146 C4
Okehampton Rd NW10 . . 90 D6
Okeover Manor SW4 . . 137 B1
Olaf Palme Ho TW13 . . . 150 B1
Olaf St W11 . . . 112 D6
Old Bailey EC4 . . 94 D1 241 D1
Old Barn Cl SM2 . . . 217 A1
Old Barrack Yd SW1 . . 248 A1
Old Barrowfield 7 E15 . . 98 C6
Old Bellgate Wharf
E14 . . . 119 C3
Oldberry Rd HA8 . . . 27 B4
Old Bethnal Green Rd
E2 . . . 96 B4
OLD BEXLEY . . . 169 D4
Old Bexley Bsns Pk
DA5 . . . 169 D4
Old Bexley CE Prim Sch
DA5 . . . 169 B3
Old Billingsgate Wlk
EC3 . . . 253 A5
Old Bldgs WC2 . . . 241 A2
Old Bond St
W1 . . . 115 C6 249 A5
Oldborough Rd HA0 . . . 65 C5
Old Brewery Mews
NW3 . . . 70 B4
Old Bridge Cl UB5 . . . 85 C5
Old Bridge St KT1 . . . 175 D1
Old Broad St
EC2 . . . 95 B1 242 D2
Old Bromley Rd BR1 . . . 186 B5
Old Brompton Rd SW5,
SW7 . . . 114 A2 256 B3
Old Burlington St
W1 . . . 115 C6 249 A5
Oldbury Ct E9 . . . 75 A3
Oldbury Pl W1 . . 93 A2 238 B4
Oldbury Rd EN1 . . . 6 A3
Old Castle St
E1 . . . 95 D1 243 D2
Old Cavendish St W1 . 238 C1
Old Change Ct EC4 . . . 242 A1
Old Chapel Pl 2 N10 . . . 49 B6
Old Charlton Rd
TW17 . . . 193 A4
Old Chiswick Yd W4 . . . 133 C6
Old Church Ct N11 . . . 31 B5
Old Church La
Ealing UB6 . . . 87 A4
Stanmore HA7 . . . 25 C4
Welsh Harp NW9 . . . 67 B6
Old Church Path KT10 . . 212 A4
Old Church Rd
Chingford E4 . . . 19 C1
Stepney E1 . . . 96 D1
Old Church St SW3 . . . 256 D1
Old Claygate La KT10 . . 213 A3
Old Clem Sq 12 SE18 . . . 144 C6
Old College Ct DA17 . . . 125 D1
Old Compton St
W1 . . . 93 D1 239 C1
Old Cote Dr TW5 . . . 129 C6
Old Court Ho W8 . . . 245 C1
Old Court (Mus & Liby)*
HA0 . . . 65 C3
Old Court Pl
W8 . . . 113 D4 245 C1
Old Covent Gdn*
WC2 . . . 250 B6
Old Ctyd The BR1 . . . 187 B2
Old Cty H* SE1 . . . 250 C2
Old Dairy Mews
5 Balham SW12 . . . 159 A3
4 Camden Town NW5 . . . 71 B2
Old Dairy Sq The N21 . . . 16 C4
Old Deer Park Gdns
TW9 . . . 132 A2
Old Devonshire Rd
SW12 . . . 159 B4
Old Dock Cl TW9 . . . 132 C6
Old Dover Rd SE3 . . . 143 B5
Oldegate Ho 1 E6 . . . 99 D6
Old Farm Ave
Osidge N14 . . . 15 C4
Sidcup DA15 . . . 167 C2
Old Farm Cl TW4 . . . 129 B1
Old Farm Ct UB2 . . . 107 D2
Old Farm Rd
Hampton TW12 . . . 173 C4
London N2 . . . 30 B2
Old Farm Rd E DA15 . . . 168 A2
Old Farm Rd W DA15 . . . 167 D2
Oldfield Cl
Bromley BR1 . . . 210 B5
Greenford UB6 . . . 64 C2
Stanmore HA7 . . . 25 A5
Oldfield Farm Gdns
UB6 . . . 86 B6
Oldfield Gr SE16 . . . 118 D2
Oldfield Ho
14 Chiswick W4 . . . 111 C1
Streatham SW16 . . . 181 B6
Oldfield House Unit
TW12 . . . 173 B2
Oldfield La N UB6 . . . 64 B1
Oldfield La S UB6 . . . 86 A4
Oldfield Mews N6 . . . 49 C2
Oldfield Prim Sch UB6 . . 86 B5
Oldfield Rd
Bedford Pk W3, W12 . . . 111 D4
Bexleyheath DA7 . . . 147 A3
Bromley BR1 . . . 210 B5
Hampton TW12 . . . 173 B2
Stoke Newington N16 . . . 73 C5
Willesden NW10 . . . 67 D1
Wimbledon SW19 . . . 179 A4
Oldfields Cir UB5 . . . 64 A2
Oldfields Rd SM1, SM3 . . 217 C6
Oldfields Trad Est
SM1 . . . 217 C5
Old Fire Station The
SE18 . . . 144 D5
Old Fish St Hill EC4 . . . 252 A6
Old Fleet La EC4 . . . 241 C2
Old Fold Cl EN5 . . . 1 B4
Old Fold La EN5 . . . 1 B4
OLD FORD . . . 97 B6
Old Ford Ho CR0 . . . 220 A5
Old Ford Prim Sch E3 . . . 97 B5
Old Ford Rd E2, E3 . . . 96 D5
Old Ford Trad Ctr 13
E3 . . . 97 C6
Old Forge Cl HA7 . . . 25 A6
Old Forge Cres TW17 . . . 192 D3
Old Forge Mews W12 . . 112 B4
Old Forge Rd Enfield EN1 . . 5 D5
Upper Holloway N19 . . . 71 D6
Old Forge Way DA14 . . . 190 B6
Old Gloucester St
WC1 . . . 94 A2 240 B4
Old Hall Cl HA5 . . . 23 A2
Old Hall Dr HA5 . . . 23 A2
Oldham Ho 10 SE21 . . . 183 C6
Oldham Terr W3 . . . 111 A5
Old Hatch Manor HA4 . . . 40 A2
Old Hill Chislehurst BR7 . . 188 C2
Orpington BR6 . . . 227 C2
Oldhill St N16 . . . 52 A1
Old Homesdale Rd
BR2 . . . 209 C5
Old Hospital Cl SW12,
SW17 . . . 158 D3
Old Ho The BR7 . . . 189 B2
Old House Cl SW19 . . . 179 A5
Old House Gdns 9
TW1 . . . 153 C5
Old Howlett's La HA4 . . . 39 B3
Olding Ho 6 SW12 . . . 159 C4
Old Jamaica Bsns Est 23
SE16 . . . 118 A3
Old Jamaica Rd SE16 . . . 118 A3
Old James St SE15 . . . 140 B2
Old Jewry EC2 . . 95 B1 242 C1
Old Kenton La NW9 . . . 44 D4
Old Kent Rd
Deptford SE1, SE15 . . . 140 B6
Old Kent Rd *continued*
Walworth SE1 . . 117 C1 263 B2
Old Kingston Rd KT4 . . . 215 A5
Old Laundry The 14
SW18 . . . 136 B1
Old Lodge Pl 7 TW1 . . . 153 B5
Old Lodge Way HA7 . . . 25 A5
Old London Rd KT2 . . . 176 A1
Old Maidstone Rd BR8,
DA14 . . . 191 B3
OLD MALDEN . . . 199 C1
Old Malden La KT4 . . . 215 C6
Oldman Ct SE12 . . . 165 B2
Old Manor Ct NW8 . . . 229 B4
Old Manor Dr TW7 . . . 152 A5
Old Manor House Mews
TW17 . . . 192 C6
Old Manor Rd UB2 . . . 106 D2
Old Manor Way BR7,
SE9 . . . 188 B5
Old Manor Yd SW5 . . . 255 C3
Old Market Ct SM1 . . . 217 D4
Old Market Sq 11 E2 . . . 95 D4
Old Marylebone Rd
NW1 . . . 92 C2 237 B3
Oldmead Ho 8 RM10 . . . 81 D2
Old Mill Ct E18 . . . 55 C6
Old Mill Rd SE18 . . . 145 B6
Old Mitre Ct EC4 . . . 241 B1
Old Montague St E1 . . . 96 A2
Old Nichol St
E2 . . . 95 D3 243 C6
Old North St WC1 . . . 240 C4
Old Nursery Pl TW15 . . . 170 D5
OLD OAK COMMON . . . 89 D3
Old Oak Common La
NW10 . . . 89 C3
Old Oak La NW10 . . . 89 D4
Old Oak Prim Sch W12 . . 89 D1
Old Oak Rd W3 . . . 111 D6
Old Orch TW16 . . . 172 C1
Old Orchard Cl
Hadley Wood EN4 . . . 2 B5
Hillingdon UB8 . . . 82 C1
Old Orch The NW3 . . . 70 D4
Old Palace La TW9 . . . 153 C6
Old Palace Prim Sch
E3 . . . 97 D4
Old Palace Rd CR0 . . . 221 A5
Old Palace Sch of John
Whitgift CR9 . . . 220 D5
Old Palace Terr 8
TW9 . . . 153 D6
Old Palace Yd 2
TW9 . . . 153 D6
Old Paradise St
SE11 . . . 116 B2 260 C4
Old Park Ave
Balham SW12 . . . 159 A5
Enfield EN2 . . . 5 A1
Old Park Gr EN2 . . . 5 A1
Old Park Ho N13 . . . 32 B6
Old Park La
W1 . . . 115 B5 248 C3
Old Park Mews TW5 . . . 129 B5
Old Park Rd Enfield EN2 . . 4 D2
Palmers Green N13 . . . 32 B6
Plumstead Comm SE2 . . . 124 A1
Old Park Rd S EN2 . . . 4 D1
Old Park Ridings N21 . . . 17 A6
Old Park View EN2 . . . 4 D2
Old Perry St BR7 . . . 189 C3
Old Post Office La
SE3 . . . 143 B2
Old Pound Cl TW7 . . . 131 A4
Old Priory UB9 . . . 38 D2
Old Pye St SW1 . . . 259 C6
Old Pye Street Est
SW1 . . . 259 C5
Old Quebec St W1 . . . 237 D1
Old Queen St
SW1 . . . 115 D4 249 D1
Old Rd Enfield EN3 . . . 6 C4
Lewisham SE13 . . . 142 C1
Old Rectory Gdns HA8 . . . 26 C4
Old Redding HA3 . . . 24 A6
Oldridge Rd SW12 . . . 159 B4
Old Royal Free Pl N1 . . 234 B5
Old Royal Free Sq
N1 . . . 94 C6 234 B5
Old Ruislip Rd UB5 . . . 84 C5
Old St Andrews Mans
NW9 . . . 67 B6
Old School Cl
3 Beckenham BR3 . . . 185 A1
Merton SW19 . . . 179 C1
Old School Cres E7 . . . 77 A2
Old School Ct 8 N17 . . . 51 D6
Old School Ho CR4 . . . 202 C6
Old School Ho The EN2 . . 4 D2
Old School Pl CR0 . . . 220 C4
Old School Rd UB8 . . . 82 B3
Old School Sq
12 Poplar E14 . . . 97 C1
Thames Ditton KT7 . . . 196 D3
Old School The
Bloomsbury WC1 . . . 240 D4
Merton SW19 . . . 179 C1
Old Seacoal La EC4 . . . 241 C1
Old South Cl HA5 . . . 22 D2
Old South Lambeth Rd
SW8 . . . 138 A5 270 B4
Old Spitalfields Mkt
E1 . . . 95 D2 243 D4
Old Sq WC2 . . . 241 A2
Old St
Broadgate
EC1 . . . 95 B3 242 D6
Newham E13 . . . 99 B5
Old Stable Mews N5 . . . 73 A5

Old Station Rd UB3 ....105 D3
Old Station Yard The 11 E17 ....54 A5
Oldstead Rd BR1 ....186 B6
Old Street Sta EC1 ....95 B3 242 D6
Old Studio Cl CR0 ....205 B2
Old Sun Wharf E14 ....119 A6
Old Swan Wharf SW11 266 D2
Old Swan Yd SM5 ....218 D4
Old Theatre Ct SE1 ... 252 B4
Old Town
Clapham SW4 ....137 C2
Croydon CR0 ....220 D5
Old Tramyard SE18 ....123 C2
Old Twelve Cl W7 ....86 C3
Old Vicarage Sch TW10 ....154 A5
Old Vicarage The CR4 ..202 C6
Old Woolwich Rd SE10 ....120 B1
Old York Rd SW18 ....157 D6
Oleander Cl BR6 ....227 B3
O'Leary Sq E1 ....96 C2
Oleastor Ct IG5 ....56 A6
Olga Prim Sch E3 ....97 A5
Olga St 20 E3 ....97 A5
Olinda Rd N16 ....51 D3
Oliphant St W10 ....91 A4
Olive Blythe Ho 14 W10 ....91 A3
Oliver Ave SE25 ....205 D6
Oliver Bsns Pk NW10 ....89 A5
Oliver Cl W4 ....132 D6
Oliver Ct
Isleworth TW7 ....130 D2
2 Penge SE26 ....184 C4
Plumstead SE18 ....123 A2
Olive Rd
Cricklewood NW2 ....68 C4
Ealing W5 ....109 D3
3 Merton SW19 ....180 A3
Newham E13 ....99 C4
Oliver Gdns E6 ....100 A2
Oliver Goldsmith Prim Sch
Camberwell SE5 ....139 D4
Kingsbury NW9 ....45 B4
Oliver Gr SE25 ....205 D5
Oliver Ho
22 Bermondsey SE16 ...118 A4
Notting Hill W11 ....244 A5
South Lambeth SW8 ... 270 A4
Oliver House Prep Sch SW4 ....159 B5
Oliver Mews SE15 ....140 A3
Oliver Rd
Kingston u T KT3 ....177 A1
Leyton E10 ....75 D5
Sutton SM1 ....218 B4
Walthamstow E17 ....54 A4
Oliver's Yd EC1 ....242 D6
Olive Tree Ho
7 Deptford SE15 ....140 C6
Stroud Green N4 ....50 C3
Olive Tree Sch The SE13 ....163 D5
Olivette St 1 SW15 ....134 D1
Olive Waite Ho NW6 ....69 D1
Olivia Ct 1 EN5 ....1 B1
Ollard's Gr IG10 ....21 D6
Ollerton Gn E3 ....97 B6
Ollerton Rd N11 ....31 D5
Olley Cl SM6 ....220 A2
Ollgar Cl W12 ....111 D5
Olliffe St E14 ....120 A3
Olmar St SE1 ....140 A6
Olney Ho NW8 ....237 B6
Olney Rd SE17 ....139 A6
Olron Cres DA6 ....169 A6
Olven Rd SE18 ....145 A6
Olveston Wlk SM5 ....202 B3
Olwen Mews HA5 ....22 D1
Olyffe Ave DA16 ....146 A3
Olyffe Dr BR3 ....186 A2
Olympia Ex Ctr* W14 ....113 A3 254 B5
Olympia Ind Est N22 ....50 B6
Olympian Ct 8 E14 ....119 C2
Olympia Way W14 ....113 A3 254 B5
Olympia Yd W2 ....245 D5
Olympic Ho 10 W10 ....90 C1
Olympic Ret Pk HA9 ....66 D4
Olympic Way
Greenford UB6 ....85 D6
Wembley HA9 ....66 C4
Olympus Gr N22 ....32 C2
Olympus Sq E5 ....74 A5
Oman Ave NW2 ....68 C4
Oman Ct NW4 ....68 B4
Ombersley Ho N4 ....51 A2
Omeara St SE1 ....252 B3
Omega Cl E14 ....119 D3
Omega Ho SW10 ....266 B4
Omega Pl N1 ....233 B3
Omega St SE14 ....141 C4
Omega Works E3 ....75 C1
Ommaney Rd SE14 ....141 A4
Omnibus Bsns Ctr N7 ...72 A3
Omnibus Way E17 ....35 C1
Ondine Rd SE15 ....139 D1
Onedin Point 10 E1 ....118 A6
Onega Gate SE16 ....119 A3
O'Neill Ho NW8 ....229 D3
O'Neill Path 11 SE18 ...144 C6
One Tree Cl SE23 ....162 C5
Ongar Cl RM6 ....58 C4
Ongar Ho 15 N1 ....73 B2
Ongar Rd SW6 ..135 C6 265 B6
Onra Rd E17 ....53 C2
Onslow Ave TW10 ....154 A6
Onslow Avenue Mans 10 TW10 ....154 A6
Onslow Cl Chingford E4 ...20 B2
Notting Hill W9 ....91 B4
Thames Ditton KT7 ....196 C1
Onslow Cres BR7 ....188 D2
Onslow Ct SW10 ....256 B1
Onslow Dr DA14 ....168 D2
Onslow Gdns
Chelsea SW7 ...114 B1 256 C2
Cranley Gdns N10 ....49 B4
Southgate N21 ....16 C6
Thames Ditton KT7 ....196 C1
Wallington SM6 ....219 C1
Wanstead E18 ....55 C6
Onslow Ho 1 KT2 ....176 B2
Onslow Lo 28 SW2 ....160 C4
Onslow Mews E SW7 ..256 C3
Onslow Mews W SW7 ..256 C3
Onslow Par N14 ....15 B3
Onslow Rd
Richmond TW10 ....154 A5
Thornton Heath CR0 ....204 C1
West Barnes KT3 ....200 A5
Onslow Sq SW7 ....114 B2 256 D3
Onslow St EC1 ....241 B5
Onslow Way KT7 ....196 C1
Ontario St SE1 ..116 D3 261 D6
Ontario Way E14 ....119 C6
Onyx Ct N11 ....31 D3
Onyx Ho KT4 ....199 B1
Onyx Mews 4 E15 ....76 D2
Opal Cl E16 ....99 D1
Opal Ct N11 ....31 D3
Opal Ho KT4 ....199 B1
Opal Mews 2 IG1 ....78 D6
Opal St SE11 ...116 D1 261 C2
Open Air Theatre, Regent's Pk* NW1 ....231 A1
Openshaw Rd SE2 ....124 B2
Openview SW17, SW18 ..158 B2
Opera Ct 7 N19 ....71 D5
Operating Theatre Mus & Herb Garret* SE1 ....117 B5 252 D3
Ophelia Gdns NW2 ....69 A5
Ophir Terr SE15 ....140 A4
Opie Ho NW8 ....230 B4
Opossum Way TW4 ....128 C2
Oppenheim Rd SE13 ....142 A3
Oppidan Apartments NW6 ....69 C2
Oppidans Rd NW3 ....70 D1
Opus Studios E13 ....99 A5
Orange Gr E11 ....76 C5
Orange Hill Rd HA8 ....27 A3
Orange Pl SE16 ....118 C3
Orangery Gallery The* W8 ....113 B4 244 C1
Orangery La SE9 ....166 B6
Orangery The TW10 ....153 C2
Orange St WC2 ....115 D6 249 D5
Orange Yd WC2 ....239 D1
Oransay Rd 25 N1 ....73 A2
Oratory La SW3 ....256 D2
Oratory RC Prim Sch SW3 ....114 C1 257 A2
Oratory The* SW7 ....114 C3 257 A5
Orbain Rd SW6 .135 A5 264 B3
Orbel St SW11 ..136 C4 267 A1
Orb St SE17 ...117 B2 262 C3
Orchard Ave
Ashford TW15 ....171 A4
Carshalton CR4 ....203 A1
Croydon CR0 ....207 A1
East Finchley N3 ....47 C6
Erith DA17 ....147 B6
Hatton TW14 ....149 B6
Heston TW5 ....129 A5
Hinchley Wood KT7 ....213 A6
Kingston u T KT3 ....199 C6
Osidge N14 ....15 C4
Southall UB1 ....107 B5
Whetstone N20 ....14 B2
Orchard Bsns Ctr SE26 ....185 B5
Orchard Cl
Ashford TW15 ....171 A4
Bexleyheath DA7 ....147 A4
Bushey WD23 ....8 B3
Chingford E4 ....35 C6
Dollis Hill NW2 ....68 A5
Edgware HA8 ....26 A4
Honor Oak SE23 ....162 C5
Islington N1 ....73 A1
Kensal Town W10 ....91 A2
Northolt UB5 ....64 A2
Ruislip HA4 ....39 A2
Thames Ditton KT7 ....197 B2
Walton-on-T KT12 ....194 B2
Wanstead E11 ....55 B5
Wembley HA0 ....88 A6
West Barnes SW20 ....200 C5
West Ewell KT19 ....214 D2
Orchard Cotts
Chislehurst BR7 ....189 C4
Hayes UB3 ....105 C4
Orchard Cres
Edgware HA8 ....27 A5
Enfield EN1 ....5 D4
Orchard Ct
Barnes SW13 ....133 D2
Barnet EN5 ....1 D2
Croydon BR3 ....207 C1
Edgware HA8 ....26 B5
Orchard Ct *continued*
Hounslow TW7 ....130 B5
Marylebone W1 ....238 A2
New Malden KT4 ....200 A1
Penge SE26 ....184 D5
Southgate N14 ....15 C5
Wallington SM6 ....219 B3
Walthamstow E10 ....53 D1
1 Walton-on-T KT12 ....193 D1
Wood Green N22 ....32 A3
Orchard Dr
Blackheath Vale SE3 ....142 C3
Edgware HA8 ....26 B5
Upper Halliford TW17 ...193 C6
Orchard Gate
Colindale NW9 ....45 C5
Thames Ditton KT10 ....196 B1
Wembley UB6 ....65 B2
Orchard Gdns
Chessington KT9 ....214 A4
Sutton SM1 ....217 C3
Orchard Gn
Bromley BR1 ....187 C2
Orpington BR6 ....227 C6
Orchard Gr BR6 ....227 D6
Croydon CR0 ....207 A2
Edgware HA8 ....26 D2
Harrow HA3 ....44 B4
Orpington BR6 ....211 D1
Penge SE20 ....184 A3
Orchard Hill SE13 ....141 D4
Orchard Hill Coll SM6 ..219 B2
Orchard Ho
Camberwell SE5 ....139 A4
11 Rotherhithe SE16 ....118 C3
Shepherd's Bush W12 ....112 A5
Orchard Inf Sch The KT8 ....196 B5
Orchard Jun & Inf Sch The TW3 ....151 C6
Orchard La
Thames Ditton KT8 ....196 B3
Wimbledon SW20 ....178 B2
Woodford IG8 ....37 C6
Orchardleigh Ave EN3 ....6 C3
Orchard Lo N12 ....14 A1
Orchard Mead Ho NW11 ....69 C6
Orchardmede N21 ....17 B5
Orchard Mews N1 ....73 B1
Orchard Pl
Canning Town E14 ....120 C6
Tottenham N17 ....33 D3
Orchard Prim Sch E9 ...74 C1
Orchard Rd Barnet EN5 ...1 B1
Belvedere DA17 ....125 C2
Brentford TW8 ....131 C6
Bromley BR1 ....187 C2
Carshalton CR4 ....203 A1
Chessington KT9 ....214 A4
Dagenham RM10 ....103 C6
Enfield EN3 ....18 C6
Farnborough BR6 ....226 D3
Feltham TW14 ....150 A3
Hampton TW12 ....173 B3
Hayes UB3 ....106 A6
Highgate N6 ....49 B2
Hounslow TW4 ....151 C6
Isleworth TW1 ....153 B6
Kingston u T KT1 ....176 A1
Richmond TW9 ....132 C2
Sidcup DA14 ....189 C6
Sunbury TW16 ....172 B3
Sutton SM1 ....217 C4
Welling DA16 ....146 B2
Orchard Rise
Croydon CR0 ....207 B1
Kingston u T KT2 ....177 A2
Mortlake TW10 ....132 D1
Pinner HA5 ....39 D6
Orchard Rise E DA15 ...167 D6
Orchard Rise W DA15 ..167 C6
Orchard Sch DA14 ....190 B5
Orchard School Sports Ctr SE20 ....184 A2
Orchardson Ho NW8 ..236 D5
Orchardson St NW8 ....92 B3 236 D5
Orchard Sq W14 ....254 C1
Orchard St
Marylebone W1 ....238 B2
Walthamstow E17 ....53 A5
Orchard Terr EN1 ....18 A5
Orchard The
Acton Green W4 ....111 B2
Ealing W5 ....87 D2
East Barnet N14 ....15 B6
Edgware HA8 ....26 C5
Enfield N21 ....17 B5
Ewell KT17 ....215 D1
Hampstead Garden Suburb NW11 ....47 C4
Hounslow TW3 ....130 A3
Lewisham SE3 ....142 B3
Totteridge N20 ....13 D3
Orchard Villas BR7 ....189 C4
Orchard Way
Ashford TW15 ....148 B2
Croydon BR3, CR0 ....207 A3
Enfield EN1 ....5 C2
Esher KT10 ....212 A2
Sutton SM1 ....218 B4
Orchard Way Prim Sch CR0 ....207 A2
Orchestra Ct HA8 ....26 D3
Orchid Cl
Chessington KT9 ....213 C1
1 Newham E6 ....100 A2
Southall UB1 ....85 A1
Orchid Ct Catford BR1 ...164 B1
Orchid Ct *continued*
Harrow HA3 ....24 C2
Wembley HA9 ....66 A6
Orchid Gdns TW3 ....129 B1
Orchid Grange N14 ....15 C4
Orchid Lo N14 ....15 C4
Orchid Rd N14 ....15 C4
Orchid St W12 ....112 A6
Orde 6 NW9 ....27 D2
Orde Hall St WC1 ....94 B2 240 C4
Orde Ho 10 N16 ....73 B4
Ordell Ct 36 E3 ....97 B5
Ordell Rd E3 ....97 B5
Ordnance Cl TW13 ....150 A2
Ordnance Cres SE10 ...120 C4
Ordnance Hill NW8 ....92 B6 229 D5
Ordnance Mews NW8 . 229 D4
Ordnance Rd
Canning Town E16 ....98 D2
Enfield EN3 ....7 B6
Shooters Hill SE18 ....144 C6
Oregano Cl UB7 ....104 B6
Oregano Dr E14 ....98 B1
Oregon Ave E12 ....78 B4
Oregon Bldg 5 SE13 ...141 D4
Oregon Cl KT3 ....199 A5
Oregon Sq BR6 ....211 B1
Orestes Ct 9 E18 ....55 A6
Orestes Mews 1 NW6 ..69 C3
Orford Ct Stanmore HA7 ..25 C4
Wallington SM6 ....219 C3
West Norwood SE27 ...160 D2
Orford Gdns TW1 ....152 D2
Orford Rd Catford SE6 ..163 D1
Walthamstow E17 ....53 D4
Wanstead E18 ....55 B6
Organ Crossroads KT17 ....216 A1
Oriana Ct CR0 ....221 B1
Oriana Ho 3 E14 ....119 B6
Oriel Cl CR4 ....203 D6
Oriel Ct
6 Croydon CR0 ....205 B1
Hampstead NW3 ....70 A4
Oriel Dr SW13 ....134 C6
Oriel Gdns IG5 ....56 B6
Oriel Jun & Inf Sch TW13 ....151 A1
Oriel Rd Hackney E9 ....75 A2
Homerton E9 ....74 D2
Oriel Way UB5 ....63 D1
Oriental City NW9 ....45 B6
Oriental Rd E16 ....121 D5
Orient Ind Pk E10 ....75 C6
Orient St SE11 ..116 D2 261 C4
Orient Way
Lea Bridge E5 ....74 D5
Leyton E10 ....75 B6
Oriole Way SE28 ....124 B6
Orion Bsns Ctr SE14 ...118 D1
Orion Ct 10 HA8 ....26 D5
Orion Ctr The CR0 ....220 A6
Orion Ho 20 E1 ....96 B3
Orion Mews SM4 ....201 C5
Orion Point 5 E14 ....119 C2
Orion Prim Sch The NW9 ....27 D2
Orion Rd N11 ....31 A4
Orion Way HA6 ....22 A6
Orissa Rd SE18 ....123 C1
Orkney Ho N1 ....233 C6
Orkney St SW11 ....137 A3
Orlando Rd SW4 ....137 C2
Orleans Cl KT10 ....212 B6
Orleans Ct 9 TW1 ....153 B4
Orleans House Gallery* TW1 ....153 B3
Orleans Inf Sch TW1 ....153 B4
Orleans Park Sch TW1 ....153 B4
Orleans Rd
South Norwood SE19 ...183 B4
Twickenham TW1 ....153 C4
Orleston Mews N7 ....72 C2
Orleston Rd N7 ....72 C2
Orley Farm Rd HA1 ....64 C5
Orley Farm Sch HA1 ....64 B5
Orlop St SE10 ....120 C1
Ormanton Rd SE26 ....184 A6
Orme Ct W2 ....113 D6 245 C5
Orme Ct Mews W2 ....245 D5
Orme Ho 8 E8 ....95 D6
Orme La W2 ....113 D6 245 C5
Ormeley Rd SW12 ....159 B3
Orme Rd
Kingston u T KT1, KT3 ....176 D1
Sutton SM1 ....217 D2
Ormerod Gdns CR4 ....181 A2
Ormerod Ho 3 SW9 ....138 A2
Ormesby Cl SE28 ....124 D6
Ormesby Way HA3 ....44 B4
Orme Sq W2 ....245 C5
Ormiston Gr W12 ....112 B5
Ormiston Rd SE10 ....121 A1
Ormond Ave
Hampton TW12 ....173 D2
23 Richmond TW10 ....153 D6
Ormond Cl WC1 ....240 B4
Ormond Cres TW12 ....173 D2
Ormond Dr TW12 ....173 D3
Ormonde Ave BR6 ....227 A6
Ormonde Ct
Hendon NW4 ....46 D6
Putney SW15 ....134 C1
Ormonde Gate SW3 ....114 D1 257 D1
Ormonde Mans WC1 ..240 B4
Ormonde Pl SW1 ....258 B3
Ormonde Rd SW14 ....133 A2
Ormonde Rise IG9 ....21 C3
Ormonde Terr NW8 ....92 D6 230 C5
Ormond Ho 7 N16 ....73 B6
Ormond Mans WC1 ....240 C5
Ormond Mews WC1 ....240 B5
Ormond Rd
Finsbury Pk N4, N19 ....50 A1
Richmond TW10 ....153 D6
Ormond Yd SW1 ....249 B4
Ormrod Ct W11 ....91 B1
Ormsby SM2 ....217 D1
Ormsby Gdns UB6 ....86 A5
Ormsby Lo 7 W4 ....111 C3
Ormsby Pl N16 ....73 D5
Ormsby Point 6 SE18 ..122 D2
Ormsby St E2 ....95 D5
Ormside St SE15 ....140 C6
Ormskirk Rd WD19 ....22 D5
Ornan Rd NW3 ....70 C3
Orpen Ho SW5 ....255 B3
Orpen Wlk N16 ....73 C5
Orpheus Ho 25 N19 ....49 D2
Orpheus St SE5 ....139 B4
ORPINGTON 227 D6
Orpington Gdns N18 ....17 C1
Orpington Hospl BR6 ..227 D4
Orpington Mans N21 ....16 C3
Orpington Rd
Southgate N21 ....16 D3
St Paul's Cray BR7 ....211 C6
Orpington Sta BR6 ....227 C6
Orpwood Cl TW12 ....173 B4
Orsett Mews W2 ....92 A1 236 A2
Orsett St SE11 ..116 B1 260 D2
Orsett Terr
Bayswater W2 ...92 A1 236 A2
Woodford IG8 ....37 C3
Orsman Rd N1 ....95 C6
Orton Gr EN1 ....6 A4
Orton St E1 ....118 A5
Orville Rd SW11 ....136 B3
Orwell Cl UB3 ....105 C6
Orwell Ct Hackney E8 ....96 A6
Highbury N5 ....73 A4
Northolt UB5 ....85 A6
Orwell Ho W12 ....112 A6
Orwell Lo 2 E18 ....55 A5
Orwell Rd E13 ....99 C6
Osbaldeston Rd N16 ....52 A1
Osberton Rd SE12 ....165 A6
Osbert St SW1 ....259 C3
Osborn Cl E8 ....96 A6
Osborne Ave TW19 ....148 B3
Osborne Cl
Beckenham BR3 ....207 A5
Cockfosters EN4 ....2 D2
Feltham TW13 ....172 D5
Osborne Ct Ealing W5 ....88 A2
10 Surbiton KT6 ....198 A3
17 Walthamstow E10 ....53 D2
Osborne Gdns CR7 ....183 A1
Osborne Gr E17 ....53 B5
Osborne Mews E17 ....53 B5
Osborne Pl SM1 ....218 B3
Osborne Rd
Buckhurst Hill IG9 ....21 B3
Dagenham RM9 ....81 B3
Enfield EN3 ....7 A3
Erith DA17 ....147 B6
Finsbury Pk N4 ....50 C1
Forest Gate E7 ....77 B3
Hackney E9 ....75 B2
Hounslow TW3, TW4 ....129 B2
Kingston u T KT2 ....176 A3
Leyton E10 ....75 D6
Palmers Green N13 ....16 C1
South Acton W3 ....110 D4
Southall UB1 ....86 A1
South Norwood CR7 ....183 A1
Walton-on-T KT12 ....194 A1
Willesden NW2 ....68 B2
Osborne Sq RM9 ....81 B4
Osborne Terr 1 SW17 ....181 A5
Osborne Way KT9 ....214 B3
Osborn Gdns NW7 ....28 D3
Osborn La SE23 ....163 A4
Osborn St E1 ....95 D2 243 D4
Osborn Terr SE3 ....142 D1
Osbourne Ct HA2 ....41 D5
Osbourne Ho
Richmond TW10 ....154 C6
Twickenham TW2 ....152 A2
Oscar Faber Pl 8 N1 ....73 C1
Oscar St SE8 ....141 C3
Oseney Cres NW5 ....71 D2
Osgood Ave BR6 ....227 D3
Osgood Gdns 1 BR6 ...227 D3
OSIDGE 15 B2
Osidge Ct N14 ....15 B3
Osidge La N14 ....15 B3
Osidge Prim Sch N14 ..15 C3
Osier Cres N10 ....30 D2
Osier Ct E1 ....96 D3
Osier La SE10 ....120 D3
Osier Mews W4 ....133 D6
Osiers Ct 3 KT1 ....175 D2
Osiers Rd SW18 ....135 C1
Osier St E1 ....96 C3
Osier Way Leyton E10 ....75 D5
Mitcham CR4 ....202 D4
Oslac Rd SE6 ....185 D5
Oslo Ct Mitcham SW19 ..180 B3
St John's Wood NW8 ..230 A3
Oslo Ho 2 SE5 ....139 A3
Oslo Sq SE16 ....119 A3
Osman Cl N15 ....51 B3
Osmani Prim Sch E1 ....96 A2
Osman Rd Edmonton N9 ..18 A1
Hammersmith W6 ....112 C3
Osmington Ho SW8 ....270 D3
Osmond Cl HA2 ....64 A6
Osmond Gdns SM6 ....219 C3
Osmund St W12 ....89 D2
Osnaburgh St NW1 ....93 B3 238 D6
Osnaburgh Terr NW1 . 238 D6
Osney Ho 4 SE2 ....124 D4
Osney Wlk SM5 ....202 B3
Osprey 7 NW9 ....27 D2
Osprey Cl Cheam SM1 ...217 B3
Higham Hill E17 ....35 A3
Keston Mark BR2 ....210 A1
Newham E6 ....100 A2
Wanstead E11 ....55 A5
West Drayton UB7 ....104 A4
Osprey Ct 7 Ealing W7 ..86 D3
Hampstead NW3 ....69 D3
Thornton Heath SW16 ...182 B1
Osprey Ho
Camberwell SE15 ....139 D4
Isleworth TW7 ....131 B2
3 Limehouse E14 ....119 A6
Walthamstow E4 ....35 B4
Osprey Mews EN3 ....18 B6
Ospringe Cl 6 SE20 ....184 C3
Ospringe Ct SE9 ....167 B5
Ospringe Ho SE1 ....251 B3
Ospringe Rd NW5 ....71 C4
Osram Ct W6 ....112 C3
Osram Rd HA9 ....65 D5
Osric Path 8 N1 ....95 C5
Ossian Mews N4 ....50 B2
Ossian Rd N4 ....50 B2
Ossie Garvin Rdbt UB4 ....106 C6
Ossington Bldgs W1 ..238 A3
Ossington Cl W2 ....245 B5
Ossington St W2 ....113 D6 245 C5
Ossory Rd SE1 ....140 A6
Ossulston St NW1 ....93 D5 232 D4
Ossultan Pl N2 ....48 A6
Ossulton Way N2 ....48 A5
Ostade Rd SW2 ....160 B4
Ostell Cres EN3 ....7 C5
Osten Mews SW7 ....113 D3 255 D5
OSTERLEY 130 B5
Osterley Ave TW7 ....130 B5
Osterley Cl BR5 ....190 A2
Osterley Cres TW7 ....130 D4
Osterley Ct
Hounslow TW7 ....130 B4
7 Northolt UB5 ....84 C4
Osterley Gdns
Southall UB2 ....108 A4
South Norwood CR7 ....183 A1
Osterley Ho 5 E14 ....97 D1
Osterley La
Isleworth TW7 ....108 C1
Southall UB2, TW7 ....107 D1
Osterley Lo 1 TW7 ....130 C4
Osterley Park* TW7 ....108 B1
Osterley Park Rd UB2 ..107 B3
Osterley Park View Rd W7 ....108 C4
Osterley Rd
Hounslow TW7 ....130 C4
Stoke Newington N16 ...73 C4
Osterley Sta TW7 ....130 B5
Osterley Views UB2 ....108 B4
Osterly Lodge UB2 ....107 B3
Oster Terr E17 ....52 D4
Ostlers Dr TW15 ....171 A5
Ostliffe Rd N13 ....33 A5
Oswald Bldg SW8 ....268 C5
Oswald Rd UB1 ....107 A5
Oswald's Mead E9 ....75 A4
Oswald St E5 ....74 D5
Oswald Terr NW2 ....68 C5
Osward Pl N9 ....18 A2
Osward Rd SW12, SW17 ....158 D2
Oswell Ho 9 E1 ....118 B5
Oswin St SE11 ..116 D2 261 D4
Oswyth Rd SE5 ....139 C3
Otford Cl Bexley DA5 ....169 D5
Bromley BR1 ....210 C6
Penge SE20 ....184 C2
Otford Cres SE4 ....163 B5
Otford Ho
Bermondsey SE1 ....252 D1
6 Deptford SE15 ....140 C6
Otha Ho 13 SW9 ....138 A3
Othello Cl SE11 ....261 C2
Otho Ct 5 TW8 ....131 D5
Otis St E3 ....98 A4
Otley App IG2 ....56 D3
Otley Ct N11 ....31 A4
Otley Dr IG2 ....56 D3
Otley Ho N5 ....72 D5
Otley Rd E16 ....99 C1
Otley Terr E5 ....74 D5
Ottawa Ho 4 HA4 ....40 C1
Ottaway Ct E5 ....74 A5
Ottaway St E5 ....74 A5
Otterbourne Rd
Chingford E4 ....20 B1
1 Croydon CR0 ....221 A6
Otterburn Gdns TW7 ...131 A5
Otterburn Ho 12 SE5 ...139 A5

Otterburn St SW17......**180** A6
Otter Cl E15 ....**98** A6
Otterden Cl BR6 ......**227** C4
Otterden St SE6 ......**185** C6
Otterfield Rd UB7....**104** A6
Ottershaw Ho BR5 ....**190** B2
Otto Cl SE26.........**162** B1
Ottoman Ct W5......**109** D2
Otto St SE17.........**138** D6
Otway Ct N4..........**50** B3
Otway Gdns WD23 .....**8** C4
Oulton Cl Erith SE28 ....**102** C1
  Upper Clapton E5 ....**74** C6
Oulton Cres IG11......**79** D3
Oulton Rd N15........**51** B4
Oulton Way WD19 ....**23** B6
Oundle Ave WD23 .....**8** A5
Our Lady Immaculate RC
  Prim Sch KT6........**198** D1
Our Lady of Dolours RC
  Prim Sch W2.........**91** D2
Our Lady of Grace RC Inf
  Sch NW2.............**68** C6
Our Lady of Grace RC Jun
  Sch NW2.............**68** B5
Our Lady of Grace RC
  Prim Sch SE7 ....**143** B6
Our Lady of Lourdes RC
  Prim Sch
  Finchley N12........**30** A2
  Friern Barnet N11.....**31** C5
  Lewisham SE13......**142** B2
Our Lady of Lourdes RC
  Sch NW10...........**89** A6
Our Lady of Lourds RC
  Prim Sch E11 ......**55** A3
Our Lady of Muswell Prim
  Sch N10............**49** A6
Our Lady of Muswell RC
  Prim Sch N10.......**31** A1
Our Lady of the Rosary RC
  Prim Sch DA15......**167** C5
Our Lady of the Visitation
  RC Prim Sch UB6....**86** A3
Our Lady of Victories RC
  Prim Sch
  Putney SW15........**134** D4
  South Kensington
  SW7........**114** A2 **256** B3
Our Lady Queen of Heaven
  RC Sch SW19.......**156** D4
Our Lady RC Prim Sch
  Camden Town
  NW1......**93** C6 **232** B6
  Poplar E14...........**97** B1
Our Lady & St John's RC
  Jun & Inf Sch TW8...**109** C1
Our Lady & St Joseph RC
  Prim Sch N1.........**73** C2
Our Lady & St Philip Neri
  RC Prim Sch SE26....**185** A6
Our Lady's Convent RC
  High Sch N15........**51** C2
Ouseley Rd SW12......**158** D3
Outer Circ NW8...**92** D5 **230** D3
Outgate Rd SW6.......**67** D1
Outram Pl N1 ....**94** A6 **233** B6
Outram Rd
  Croydon CR0........**221** D6
  Muswell Hill N22......**31** D2
  Newham E6..........**100** A6
Outwich St EC3.......**243** B2
Outwood Ct CR2......**221** A1
Outwood Ho **3** SW2 ..**160** B4
Oval Burnt Oak HA8....**27** A3
  8 Teddington TW11....**174** D5
Oval Mans SE11.......**270** D6
Oval Pl SW8....**138** B5 **270** D4
Oval Prim Sch CR0....**205** C1
Oval Rd
  Camden Town
  NW1......**93** B6 **231** C6
  Croydon CR0.........**205** C1
Oval Rd N RM10.......**103** D6
Oval Rd S RM10.......**103** D5
Oval Sta SE11........**138** C6
Oval The Hackney E2 ...**96** B5
  Sidcup DA15........**168** A4
Oval The (Surrey Cnty Crkt
  Gd) SE11...........**138** C6
Oval Way SE11...**116** B1 **260** D1
Overbrae BR3 ....**185** C5
Overbrook Wlk HA8....**26** C3
Overbury **3** BR3.....**208** A6
Overbury Ave BR3 .....**208** A6
Overbury Ho **3** E5....**74** D4
Overbury Rd N4, N15....**51** B3
Overbury St E5 ....**74** D4
Overcliff Rd SE13......**141** C2
Overcourt Cl DA15.....**168** B5
Overdale Ave KT3......**177** B1
Overdale Rd W5.......**109** C3
Overdown Rd SE6......**185** D6
Overhill Rd SE21, SE22..**162** A4
Overhill Way BR3......**208** B4
Overlea Rd E5 ....**52** A2
Overmead DA15.......**167** B4
Oversley Ho **17** W2....**91** C2
Overstand Ct BR3......**207** C4
Overstone Gdns CR0...**207** B2
Overstone Ho **19** E14...**97** C1
Overstone Rd W6......**112** C2
Overstrand Mans
  SW11..............**268** A1

Overton Cl
  Hounslow TW7.......**130** D4
  Tokyngton NW10......**67** A2
Overton Ct E11 ....**55** A2
Overton Dr Ilford RM6...**58** C2
  Wanstead E11........**55** B2
Overton Grange Sch
  SM2...............**217** D1
Overton Ho SW15.....**155** D4
Overton Rd
  Abbey Wood SE2.....**124** D3
  Belmont SM2........**217** C1
  Brixton SW9........**138** C3
  Southgate N14.......**16** A4
  Walthamstow E10....**53** A1
Overton's Yd CR0.....**221** A5
Overy Ho SE1 ....**251** C1
Ovesdon Ave HA2......**41** B1
Ovett Cl SE19........**183** C4
Ovex Cl E14..........**120** A4
Ovington Ct SW3 .....**257** B5
Ovington Gdns SW3...**257** B5
Ovington Mews SW3...**257** B5
Ovington Sq
  SW3........**114** C3 **257** B5
Ovington St
  SW3........**114** C2 **257** B4
Owen Cl Hayes UB4 ....**84** B4
  Northolt UB5.........**63** A2
  Thamesmead SE28....**124** C5
  Thornton Heath CR0..**205** B3
Owen Ct UB4.........**84** B4
Owen Ho
  Feltham TW14.......**150** A4
  11 Tufnell Pk N19.....**71** C4
  5 Twickenham TW1...**153** B4
Owenite St SE2.......**124** B2
Owen Rd Edmonton N13 ..**33** A5
  Hayes UB4..........**84** B4
Owens Ct **13** E11....**76** C6
Owen's Ct EC1......**234** C2
Owens Mews **13** E11...**76** C6
Owen's Row EC1.....**234** C2
Owen St EC1 ....**234** C3
Owens Way SE23......**163** A4
Owen Way NW10 ......**67** A3
Owen Wlk **7** SE20...**184** A3
Owgan Cl SE5 ....**139** B5
Oxberry Ave SW6 .....**135** A3
Oxbridge Ct **4** W4....**110** D1
Oxendon St SW1,
  W1...........**115** D6 **249** C5
Oxenford St SE15.....**139** D3
Oxenham Ho **13** SE8...**141** C6
Oxenholme NW1......**232** B3
Oxenpark Ave HA9......**44** A2
Oxestalls Rd SE8......**119** A1
Oxford Ave
  Harlington TW6......**127** D5
  Hounslow TW5......**107** C1
  Merton SW20.......**179** A1
  Southgate N14.......**15** C3
Oxford & Cambridge Mans
  NW1...............**237** B3
Oxford Cir W1....**93** C1 **239** A1
Oxford Circus Ave W1..**239** A1
Oxford Circus Sta
  W1...........**93** C1 **239** A1
Oxford Cl Edmonton N9...**18** B2
  Littleton TW15, TW17..**171** A3
  Mitcham CR4.......**203** C6
Oxford Cres KT3......**199** B3
Oxford Ct **15** Acton W3...**88** C1
  City of London EC4 ...**252** C6
  8 Ealing W7.........**86** D2
  Gunnersbury W4.....**110** D1
  17 Kingston u T KT6 ..**198** A4
  45 Paddington W2 ....**91** C2
  Sidcup DA14........**189** D6
Oxford Dr
  Bermondsey SE1.....**253** A3
  Ruislip HA4...........**62** C2
Oxford Gardens Prim Sch
  W10................**90** D1
Oxford Gate W6......**112** D2
Oxford Gdns
  Brentford W4........**132** C6
  Edmonton N21........**17** A4
  North Kensington W10...**90** D1
  Oakleigh Pk N20......**14** B3
Oxford Ho HA4........**50** C1
Oxford Mews DA5.....**169** C4
Oxford Rd
  Carshalton SM5.....**218** C3
  Ealing W5..........**109** D6
  Edmonton N9........**18** B2
  Enfield EN3 ....**18** B6
  Finsbury Pk N4.......**50** C1
  Harrow HA1.........**42** A3
  Ilford IG1............**79** A3
  Paddington NW6......**91** C5
  Putney SW15........**135** A1
  Sidcup DA14........**190** B5
  South Norwood SE19..**183** B4
  Stratford E15.........**76** B2
  Teddington TW11,
  TW12..............**174** B5
  Wallington SM6......**219** C3
  Wealdstone HA3......**42** D6
  Woodford IG8.........**37** D5
Oxford Rd N W4......**110** C1
Oxford Rd S W4 ......**110** D1
Oxford Sq W2 ...**92** C1 **237** B1
Oxford St W1....**93** B1 **238** D1
Oxford Way TW13.....**172** D6
Oxford Wlk UB1......**107** B5
Oxgate Cl NW2.......**68** A6
Oxgate Ct Par NW2 ....**68** A6
Oxgate Gdns NW2.....**68** B6
Oxgate La NW2 ....**68** B6

Oxhawth Cres BR2...**210** D3
Oxhey Dr WD19 ....**22** B6
Oxhey Dr S HA6.......**22** B5
Oxhey La HA3.........**23** C5
Oxhey Ridge Cl HA6....**22** B5
Oxhey Wood Prim Sch
  WD19...............**22** C6
Oxleas E6 ....**100** D1
Oxleas Cl DA16......**145** B3
Oxleay Rd HA2........**41** C1
Oxleigh Cl KT3.......**199** C4
Oxley Cl SE1.........**118** A1
Oxleys Rd NW2 ....**68** B5
Oxlip Cl **2** CR0......**206** D1
Oxlow La RM10 ....**81** C4
Oxonian St SE22......**139** D1
Oxo Tower Wharf SE1..**251** B5
Oxo Twr * SE1........**251** B5
Oxted Cl CR4 ....**202** B6
Oxted Ct N16.........**51** C1
Oxtoby Way SW16....**181** D2
OYH Prim Sch NW4.....**46** D5
Oyster Catchers Cl E16..**99** B1
Oyster Catcher Terr
  IG5..................**56** C6
Oyster Row E1.........**96** C1
Ozolins Way E16.......**99** A1

Pablo Neruda Cl **4**
  SE24..............**138** D1
Pace Pl E1 ....**96** B1
Pacific Ct TW14.......**149** D3
Pacific Ho **15** E1.......**96** D2
Pacific Hts BR3.......**185** C3
Pacific Rd E16.........**99** A1
Pacific Wharf IG11......**78** D1
Pacific Wharf SE16...**118** D5
Packenham Ho
  24 Crouch End N19....**49** D2
  2 Spitalfields E2 ....**95** D4
Packham Ct KT4......**216** C5
Packington Sq
  N1...........**95** A6 **235** A6
Packington St
  N1.........**94** D6 **234** D5
Packmores Rd SE9....**167** B6
Padbury SE17.......**263** B1
Padbury Cl TW14.....**149** B3
Padbury Ct E2 ....**95** D4
Padbury Ho NW8 .....**237** B6
Padden Ct NW7.......**28** D3
Paddenswick Ct **2**
  W6................**112** B3
Paddenswick Rd W6...**112** A3
PADDINGTON **92** A2
Paddington Acad
  Paddington
  W2.........**92** B2 **236** C3
  Wembley HA0........**91** C3
Paddington Cl UB4....**84** D3
Paddington Com Hospl
  W9................**91** C2
Paddington Ct
  10 Ealing W7.........**86** D2
  7 Wembley HA0 ......**66** A2
Paddington Gn
  W2.........**92** B2 **236** C4
Paddington Green Prim
  Sch NW8...**92** B3 **236** C5
Paddington St W1.....**238** A4
Paddington Sta
  W2.........**92** B1 **236** C2
Paddock Cl
  Forest Hill SE26......**184** D6
  Kidbrooke SE3......**143** A3
  New Malden KT4......**199** C1
  Northolt UB5.........**85** C5
  Orpington BR6.......**226** D4
Paddock Ct SW20....**200** C5
Paddock Gdns SW15..**183** C4
Paddock Lo **13** EN1....**17** C6
Paddock Rd
  Bexley DA6.........**147** A1
  Dollis Hill NW2.......**68** A6
  Ruislip HA4...........**62** D5
Paddocks Cl HA2......**63** A6
Paddocks Gn NW9.....**44** D1
Paddocks The
  Addington CR0......**223** C2
  Cockfosters EN4 ......**2** D2
  Preston HA9..........**66** D6
Paddock The
  Muswell Hill N10......**49** B6
  Uxbridge UB10........**60** D4
Paddock Way
  Chislehurst BR7......**189** B3
  1 Putney SW15......**156** C4
Padfield Ct HA9.......**66** B5
Padfield Rd SE5......**139** A2
Padley Cl KT9.......**214** B3
Padnall Ct RM6.......**58** D6
Padnall Rd RM6.......**58** D6
Padstone Ho **50** E3....**97** D4
Padstow Cl BR6......**227** D5
Padstow Ho **12** E14..**119** B6
Padstow Rd EN2.......**4** D4
Padstow Wlk TW14...**149** D3
Padua Rd SE20......**184** C2
Pagden St SW8......**268** D2
Pageant Ave NW9.....**27** C2
Pageant Cres SE16....**119** B6
Pageantmaster Ct EC4..**241** C1
Pageant Wlk CR0....**221** C5
Page Cl Dagenham RM9...**81** A3
  Hampton TW12......**173** A4
  Harrow HA3..........**44** B3

Page Cres CR0........**220** D3
Page Ct NW7 ....**28** A3
Page Green Rd N15.....**52** A4
Page Green Terr N15....**51** D4
Page Heath La BR1 ...**209** D6
Page Heath Villas
  BR1................**209** D6
Page High N22 ....**50** C6
Page Ho SE10 ....**142** A6
Pagehurst Rd CR0 ....**206** B2
Page Mdw NW7 ....**28** A3
Page Rd TW14........**149** B5
Page's Ct N11.........**31** A1
Page's Hill N10........**31** A1
Page's La N10.........**31** A1
Page St Hendon NW7....**28** A3
  Westminster
  SW1........**115** D2 **259** D4
Page's Wlk
  SE1........**117** C3 **263** B5
Page's Yd W4........**133** C6
Paget Ave SM1......**218** B5
Paget Cl TW12.......**174** B6
Paget Ct SE20.......**184** C3
Paget Ct UB7........**104** A4
Paget Gdns BR7......**188** D2
Paget Ho **15** E2......**96** C5
Paget La **7** TW7.....**130** C2
Paget Pl
  Kingston u T KT2.....**177** A4
  Thames Ditton KT7...**196** D1
Paget Rd
  Hillingdon UB10.......**83** A3
  Ilford IG1............**78** D4
  Stoke Newington N16...**51** B1
Paget Rise SE18......**144** C5
Paget St EC1.......**234** C2
Paget Terr SE18......**144** D6
Pagham Ho **8** W10....**90** C3
Pagin Ho N15.........**51** C4
Pagitts Gr EN4.........**1** D4
Pagnell St SE14......**141** B5
Pagoda Ave TW9......**132** B2
Pagoda Gdns SE3.....**142** B3
Pagoda Ho SE27.....**161** A2
Paignton Rd Ruislip HA4..**62** A5
  Tottenham N15........**51** C3
Paine Ct SE3........**142** D6
Paines Cl HA5.........**41** A6
Paine's La HA5........**23** A1
Pain's Cl CR4........**181** B1
Painsthorpe Rd **3** N16..**73** C5
Painswick Ct **1** SE15..**139** D5
Painters Mews SE16...**118** A2
Painters Rd IG2, RM6...**58** A6
Paisley Rd
  Carshalton SM5......**202** B1
  Tottenham N22........**32** D2
Paisley Terr SM5.....**202** B2
Pakeman Ho SE1.....**251** D4
Pakeman Prim Sch N7...**72** B5
Pakeman St N7.......**72** B5
Pakenham Cl SW12...**159** A3
Pakenham St
  WC1..........**94** B3 **240** D6
Pakington Ho **22** SW9..**138** A3
Palace Ave
  W8.........**113** D4 **245** D2
Palace Court Gdns N10...**49** C6
Palace Ct Bromley BR1...**187** B2
  Eltham SE9.........**166** B5
  Hampstead NW3......**69** D3
  Harrow HA3..........**44** A3
  Kensington W2 **113** D6 **245** C5
  South Norwood CR7...**205** B5
  Streatham SW2......**160** C2
Palace Garden Mews
  W8................**245** B4
Palace Gate
  Hampton KT8.......**196** C6
  Knightsbridge
  W8.........**114** A4 **246** A1
Palace Gate Mews **4**
  N8.................**50** A5
Palace Gates Rd N22....**31** D2
Palace Gdns IG9........**21** D3
Palace Gdns Mews
  W8.........**113** D5 **245** D3
Palace Gdns Sh Ctr EN2..**5** B1
Palace Gn
  Kensington
  W8.........**113** D5 **245** C3
  New Addington CR0...**223** B1
Palace Gr Bromley BR1..**187** B2
  Penge SE19.........**183** D3
Palace Mans W14.....**254** B4
Palace Mews
  Belgravia SW1......**258** B3
  Fulham SW6........**264** D4
  Walthamstow E17.....**53** B5
Palace of Ind HA9......**66** C4
Palace Par E17........**53** C5
Palace Pl SW1.......**259** A6
Palace Rd Bromley BR1..**187** B2
  East Molesey KT8....**196** B6
  Hornsey N8..........**49** D4
  Kingston u T KT1.....**197** D5
  Penge SE19.........**183** D3
  Ruislip HA4...........**63** A4
  Streatham SE27, SW16,
  SW2...............**160** C2
  Wood Green N11......**32** A3
Palace Sq SE19......**183** D3
Palace View E10.....**53** C1
Palace View SE1..**115** C3 **259** A6
Palace View
  Bromley BR1........**209** B6
  Croydon CR0........**223** B4
  Grove Pk SE12......**165** A2
Palace View Rd E4.....**35** D5
Palamos Rd E10......**53** C1
Palatine Ave N16......**73** C4

Palatine Rd N16 ....**73** C4
Palazzo Apartments **11**
  N1................**73** C1
Palemead Cl SW6....**134** D4
Palermo Rd NW10 .....**90** A5
Palestine Gr SW19...**180** B2
Palewell Common Dr
  SW14.............**155** B6
Palewell Pk SW14....**133** B1
Palfrey Pl SW8 .**138** B5 **270** D4
Palgrave Ave UB1....**107** C6
Palgrave Gdns
  NW1........**92** C3 **237** B6
Palgrave Ho
  7 Camberwell SE5...**139** A5
  4 Maitland Pk NW3...**70** D3
  Twickenham TW2....**152** A4
Palgrave Rd W12.....**111** D3
Palissy St **35** E2......**95** D4
Palladino Ho **6** SW17..**180** C5
Pallant Ho SE1 ......**262** D5
Pallant Way BR6......**226** C5
Pallester Ct NW11 .....**47** A1
Pallet Way SE18......**144** A4
Palliser Ct W14.......**254** A1
Palliser Ho
  3 Greenwich SE10 ...**142** B6
  21 Stepney E1........**96** D3
Palliser Rd
  W14........**113** A1 **254** A1
Pallister Terr SW15...**155** D1
Pall Mall SW1 ...**115** D5 **249** C3
Pall Mall E
  SW1........**115** D5 **249** B3
Pall Mall Pl SW1.....**249** B3
Palmar Cres DA7.....**147** C3
Palmar Rd DA7.......**147** C3
Palm Ave DA14.......**190** D4
Palm Cl E10..........**75** D5
Palm Ct
  Beckenham BR3.....**207** B6
  18 Camberwell SE15...**139** D5
  Stoke Newington N16...**73** B6
  Wood Green N22.......**32** B3
Palmeira Rd DA7.....**146** D2
Palmer Ave KT4, SM3...**216** C4
Palmer Cl Hendon TW5..**129** C4
  Northolt UB5.........**63** A2
  West Wickham BR4....**224** B6
Palmer Cres KT1.....**198** A6
Palmer Gdns EN5......**12** C6
Palmer Ho
  6 Deptford SE14....**140** D5
  6 Kentish Town NW5 ...**71** C4
  5 Tufnell Pk N19.....**71** C5
Palmer Pl N7..........**72** C3
Palmer Rd
  Dagenham RM8......**58** D1
  Newham E13.........**99** B3
Palmer's Ct **11** N11....**31** C5
Palmers Gr SE18......**195** C5
PALMERS GREEN **16** A1
Palmers Green High Sch
  N21................**16** C2
Palmers Green Sta N13..**32** B6
Palmers La EN3.........**6** C4
Palmers Rd
  Globe Town E2.......**96** D5
  Mortlake SW14......**133** A2
  Thornton Heath SW16..**182** B1
Palmer's Rd N11......**31** C5
Palmer St SW1......**259** C6
Palmerston Cres
  Bowes Pk N13........**32** B5
  Woolwich SE18......**145** A6
Palmerston Ct
  2 Buckhurst Hill IG9...**21** C2
  22 Globe Town E2....**96** D5
  3 Surbiton KT6......**197** D2
  3 Sutton SM1.......**218** A3
  Walthamstow E17.....**53** B5
Palmerston Ctr HA3 ....**42** D6
Palmerston Gr **11**
  SW19.............**179** C3
Palmerston Ho
  Battersea SW11.....**268** B1
  Kensington W8......**245** A4
Palmerston Rd
  Acton Green W3......**111** A3
  Bowes Pk N22........**32** A4
  Brondesbury NW6......**69** B1
  Buckhurst Hill IG9.....**21** C2
  Farnborough BR6....**227** A3
  Hampstead NW6......**69** C1
  Harrow HA3..........**42** D6
  Hounslow TW3......**130** A4
  Merton SW19.......**179** C3
  Mortlake SW14......**133** A1
  Sutton SM1........**218** A3
  Thornton Heath CR0...**205** B4
  Twickenham TW2....**152** C2
  Upton E7............**77** B2
  Wallington SM5......**219** A4
  Walthamstow E17.....**53** B5
Palmerston Way SW8..**268** D3
Palm Gr W5..........**110** A3
Palm Tree Ho **5** N17...**33** C1
Palm Tree Ho **2**
  SE14..............**140** D5
Pamela Ct Finchley N12...**29** C4
  Willesden NW10......**68** A1
Pamela Gdns HA5......**40** B4
Pamela Ho **14** E8......**95** C6
Pamir Ct **10** SM2....**217** D2
Pamlion Ct N4.........**50** A2
Pams Way KT19......**215** B3
Panama Ho **6** E1......**96** D2
Panbro Ho SE18......**144** B4
Pancras La EC2......**242** C1

Pancras Rd
  NW1 ....**93** D5 **232** D4
Pandian Way **4** NW5 ...**71** D2
Pandora Ct **4** KT6....**198** A3
Pandora Rd NW6 ......**69** C2
Panfield Mews IG2 .....**56** C3
Panfield Rd SE2 ......**124** A3
Pangbourne NW1......**232** A1
Pangbourne Ave W10...**90** C2
Pangbourne Ct
  Oakleigh Pk N20 ......**14** A4
  Upper Tooting SW17...**180** A6
Pangbourne Ho N7 .....**72** A3
Panhard Pl UB1......**107** D6
Pank Ave EN5 ....**14** A6
Pankhurst Ave **8** E16..**121** B5
Pankhurst Cl
  7 Deptford SE14....**140** D5
  Isleworth TW7 ......**130** D2
Pankhurst Ho
  2 Kensington NW10 ...**90** B2
  Streatham SW16.....**181** D5
Pankhurst Rd KT12 ...**194** C2
Panmuir Rd SW20....**178** B2
Panmure Cl N5........**72** D4
Panmure Ct **11** UB1....**86** A1
Panmure Rd SE26....**162** B1
Panorama Ct N6.......**49** C3
Pansy Gdns W12.....**112** A6
Panther Dr NW10 ......**67** B3
Pantiles Cl N13........**32** C5
Pantiles The
  Bickley BR1........**210** A6
  Bushey WD23 ....**8** B3
  Erith DA7...........**147** B5
  Temple Fortune NW11...**47** B4
Panton Cl CR0.......**204** D1
Panton St SW1......**249** C5
Panyer Alley EC2 .....**242** A2
Papermill Cl SM5.....**219** A4
Paper Mill Wharf E14..**119** A6
Papillons Wlk SE3 ....**143** A2
Papworth Gdns N7 .....**72** B3
Papworth Way SW2...**160** C4
Parade Mans
  19 Camberwell SE5...**139** A4
  2 Hendon NW4......**46** B4
Parade Mews SE27,
  SW2..............**160** D2
Parade The
  Ashford TW16.......**171** D3
  Battersea
  SW11......**136** D5 **267** D4
  Claygate KT10......**212** C2
  Ilford IG2............**57** B3
  Thornton Heath CR0...**204** A3
  Thornton Heath CR7...**204** C6
  Waddon CR0........**220** B3
  Wembley UB6.........**65** B3
Paradise Pas N7.......**72** C3
Paradise Pl **15** SE7...**122** A2
Paradise Rd
  Richmond TW10 .....**154** A6
  South Lambeth SW4...**138** A3
Paradise Row E2 ......**96** B4
Paradise St SE16.....**118** B4
Paradise Wlk
  SW3........**136** D6 **267** D6
Paragon N8...........**50** C5
Paragon Cl E16.......**99** A1
Paragon Ct NW4.......**29** A2
Paragon Gr KT5......**198** B3
Paragon Ho SE3......**142** D3
Paragon Mews SE1...**262** D4
Paragon Pl
  Blackheath Vale SE3...**142** D3
  Surbiton KT5........**198** B3
Paragon Rd E9........**74** C2
Paragon The
  Kidbrooke SE3......**143** A3
  Walworth SE17......**262** D4
Paramount Bldg EC1...**241** C6
Paramount Ct WC1....**239** B5
Paramount Ho **10** E11...**76** C5
Parbury Rd SE23.....**163** A5
Parbury Rise KT9....**214** A2
Parchment Rd CR7....**205** A6
Parchmore Way CR7...**182** C5
Pardes House Gram
  N3................**29** B1
Pardes House Prim N3...**29** B1
Pardoner St
  SE1.........**117** B3 **262** D6
Pardon St EC1.......**241** D6
Parfett St E1..........**96** A1
Parfew Ct **2** SE22....**162** B2
Parfitt Cl NW11.......**48** A1
Parfrey St W6........**134** C6
Pargraves Ct HA9......**66** C6
Parham Dr IG2........**56** D4
Paris Gdn SE1 ...**116** D5 **251** C4
Parish CE Prim Sch
  BR1...............**187** A3
Parish Church CE Inf Sch
  CR0...............**221** D5
Parish Church CE Jun Sch
  CR0...............**220** D5
Parish Ct KT6........**198** A3
Parish Gate Dr DA15...**167** C5
Parish La SE20.......**184** D3
Paris Ho **12** E2........**96** B5
Parish Wharf **6** SE7..**122** A2
Park App Barking IG11...**79** A4
Park Ave Barking IG11 ...**79** A6
  Bromley BR6........**226** C6
  Edmonton N18........**34** A6
  Enfield EN1..........**17** C2
  Finchley N3..........**29** D2
  Golders Green NW11..**69** D3

Park Ave continued
Ilford IG1 56 C1
Mitcham CR4 181 B3
Mortlake SW14 133 B1
Palmers Green N13 16 C1
Plaistow BR1 187 A4
Ruislip HA4 39 C3
Southall UB1 107 C5
Stratford E15 76 C2
Twickenham TW3 151 D5
Upper Halliford TW17 193 C6
Wallend E6 100 C5
Wallington SM5 219 A2
West Wickham BR4 224 A6
Willesden NW2 68 C2
Woodford IG8 37 B5
Wood Green N22 32 B2
Park Ave E KT17 216 A2
Park Ave N
Dudden Hill NW10 68 B3
Hornsey N8 49 D5
Park Avenue Mews
CR4 181 B3
Park Avenue Rd N17 34 B3
Park Ave S N8 49 D5
Park Ave W KT17 216 A2
Park Chase HA9 66 B4
Park Cl Dollis Hill NW2 68 B5
Ealing NW10 88 B4
Hampton TW12 174 A2
Harrow HA3 24 C2
Isleworth TW3, TW7 152 A6
Kensington
W14 113 B3 254 D6
Kingston u T KT2 176 C2
Knightsbridge SW1 247 C1
North Finchley N12 30 B6
13 South Hackney E9 96 C6
Wallington SM5 219 A2
Park Cotts 10 TW1 153 B5
Park Cres Enfield EN2 5 B1
Finchley N3 30 A3
Harrow HA3 24 C2
Regent's Pk W1 93 B3 238 C5
Twickenham TW2 152 B3
Park Crescent Mews E
W1 238 D5
Park Crescent Mews W
W1 238 C5
Park Croft HA8 27 A2
Parkcroft Rd SE12 164 D4
Park Ct Battersea SW11 268 C2
2 Beckenham BR3 207 D6
2 Chingford E4 20 A2
Clapham Pk SW4 159 D6
Dulwich SE21 161 B1
12 Hammersmith W6 112 A2
New Barnet EN5 14 B4
New Malden KT3 199 B5
North Finchley N12 30 B5
Teddington KT1 175 C2
Twickenham TW4 151 D6
Upper Tooting SW12 159 A3
Wallington SM6 220 A3
Walthamstow E17 53 D4
Wembley HA9 66 A3
Wood Green N11 31 D3
Parkdale N11 31 D4
Parkdale Cres KT4 215 B5
Parkdale Rd SE18 123 C1
Park Dr Acton W3 110 C3
Enfield N21 17 A5
Golders Green NW11 47 D1
Harrow HA2 41 C2
Mortlake SW14 133 B1
Stanmore HA3 24 C4
Woolwich SE7 144 A6
Park Dwellings 7
NW3 70 D3
Park End Bromley BR1 186 D2
Hampstead NW3 70 C4
Parker Cl Newham E16 122 A5
Wallington SM5 218 D2
Parker Ct Shoreditch N1 235 B6
South Lambeth SW4 270 A1
Wimbledon SW19 179 A3
Parke Rd Barnes SW13 134 A4
Sunbury TW16 194 A5
Parker Ho 4 SE18 122 D1
Parker Mews WC2 240 B2
Parker Rd CR0 221 A4
Parkers Rd N10 30 C2
Parkers Row 15 SE16 118 A4
Parker's Row SE1 253 D1
Parker St Newham E16 122 A5
St Giles WC2 94 A1 240 B2
Park Farm Cl
East Finchley N2 48 A6
Pinner HA5 40 B4
Park Farm Ct UB3 105 C6
Park Farm Rd
Bromley BR1 187 D2
Kingston u T KT2 176 A3
Parkfield 3 TW7 130 C4
Parkfield Ave
Feltham TW13 150 A1
Harrow HA2 24 A1
Hillingdon UB10 82 D4
Mortlake SW14 133 C1
Northolt UB5 84 D5
Parkfield Cl
Edgware HA8 26 D4
Northolt UB5 85 A5
Parkfield Cres
Feltham TW13 150 A1
Harrow HA2 24 A1
Ruislip HA4 63 A5
Parkfield Ct SE14 141 B4
Parkfield Dr UB5 84 D5
Parkfield Gdns HA2 41 D6
Parkfield Ho HA2 23 D2
Parkfield Ind Est
SW11 137 A3
Parkfield Par TW13 150 A1
Parkfield Prim Sch
NW4 46 B2
Parkfield Rd
Feltham TW13 150 A1
Harrow HA2 64 A5
New Cross SE14 141 B4
Northolt UB5 85 A5
Uxbridge UB10 60 D6
Willesden NW10 68 B1
Parkfields Croydon CR0 207 B1
Putney SW15 134 C1
Parkfields Ave
Welsh Harp NW9 45 B1
Wimbledon SW20 178 B1
Parkfields Cl SM5 219 A4
Parkfields Rd KT2 176 B5
Parkfield St N1 94 C5 234 B4
Parkfield Way BR2 210 B4
Park Flats N6 48 C2
Parkgate SE3 142 D2
Park Gate Ealing W5 87 D2
East Finchley N2 48 B6
Southgate N21 16 B4
Parkgate Ave EN4 2 A4
Parkgate Cl KT2 176 D4
Parkgate Cres EN4 2 A4
Park Gate Ct TW12 174 A5
Parkgate Gdns SW14 155 B6
Parkgate House Sch
SW11 137 A1
Parkgate Mews N6 49 C2
Parkgate Rd
Battersea
SW11 136 C5 267 B3
Wallington SM5, SM6 219 B3
Park Gates HA2 63 C4
Park Gdns
Kingston u T KT2 176 B5
Queensbury NW9 44 D6
Park Gr Bromley BR1 187 B2
Edgware HA8 26 B5
Newham E15 99 A6
Wood Green N11 31 D3
Park Grove Rd E11 76 C6
Park Hall SE10 142 B5
Park Hall Rd
Dulwich SE21 161 B1
East Finchley N2 48 C5
Park Hall Road Trad Est
SE21 161 B1
Parkham Ct BR2 186 C1
Parkham St
SW11 136 C4 267 A1
Parkham Way N10 31 C1
Park Heights Ct 21 E14 97 B1
Park High Sch HA7 25 D1
Park Hill Bromley BR1 210 B5
Clapham Pk SW4 159 D6
Ealing W5 87 D2
Forest Hill SE23 162 C3
Loughton IG10 21 D6
Richmond TW10 154 B5
Wallington SM5 218 D2
Park Hill Cl SM5 218 C3
Park Hill Ct
Croydon CR0 221 C6
Ealing W5 87 D2
Upper Tooting SW17 158 D1
Parkhill Ho 1 SW16 182 C5
Parkhill Inf Sch IG5 56 C6
Park Hill Inf Sch CR0 221 C5
Parkhill Jun Sch IG5 56 C6
Park Hill Jun Sch CR0 221 C5
Parkhill Rd Chingford E4 20 A4
Maitland Pk NW3 70 D3
Old Bexley DA5 169 B4
Sidcup DA15 167 C1
Park Hill Rd
Beckenham BR2 186 C1
South Croydon CR0 221 C5
Wallington SM6 219 B1
Park Hill Rise CR0 221 D5
Park Hill Sch KT2 176 C3
Park Hill Wlk 10 NW3 70 D3
Park Ho
8 Camberwell SE5 139 B4
Finsbury Pk N4 72 D6
Forest Hill SE26 184 A5
35 Hackney E9 74 C1
Richmond TW10 154 A5
Sidcup DA14 190 A5
Southgate N21 16 B4
Parkholme Rd E8 74 A2
Park House Gdns
TW1 153 C6
Parkhouse St SE5 139 B5
Park Hts NW4 46 B6
Parkhurst Ct N7 72 A4
Parkhurst Gdns 2
DA5 169 C4
Parkhurst Rd
Bowes Pk N22 32 B4
Friern Barnet N11 31 A5
Little Ilford E12 78 C4
Lower Holloway N7 72 A4
Sidcup DA5 169 C4
Sutton SM1 218 B4
Tottenham N17 34 A1
Walthamstow E17 53 A5
Parkin Ho SE20 184 D3
Parkinson Ct
Finsbury N1 235 C1
Shoreditch EC1 235 D2
Parkinson Ho 6 E9 74 C1
Park La Cheam SM3 217 A2
Cranford TW5 128 A5
Park La continued
Dagenham RM6 58 D3
Edmonton N9 17 D1
Harrow HA2 63 D5
Hayes UB4 83 C3
Mayfair W1 115 A6 248 A5
Mill Meads E15 98 B6
Richmond TW9 131 D1
South Croydon CR0 221 B5
Stanmore HA7 9 A1
Teddington TW11 174 D4
Tottenham N17 34 A3
Wallington SM5, SM6 219 A3
Wembley HA9 66 A4
Parkland Ct
Kensington W14 244 A2
Stratford E15 76 C3
Parkland Gdns 12
SW19 156 D3
Parkland Gr
Ashford TW15 170 C6
Hounslow TW7 130 D4
Parkland Mead BR1 210 D6
Parkland Rd
Ashford TW15 170 C6
Woodford IG8 37 B3
Wood Green N22 32 B1
Parklands Bushey WD23 8 A5
East Dulwich SE22 162 B6
Highgate N6 49 B2
Kingston u T KT5 198 B4
5 Whetstone N20 14 A2
Parklands Cl
Hadley Wood EN4 2 B5
Ilford IG2 57 A2
Mortlake SW14 155 A6
Parklands Ct TW5 128 D3
Parklands Dr N3 47 A6
Parklands Par TW5 128 D3
Parklands Pl HA8 26 B6
Parklands Rd SW16 181 B5
Parklands Way KT4 215 C6
Park Lane Cl N17 34 A3
Park Lane Mans CR0 221 B5
Park Lane Prim Sch
HA9 66 A4
PARK LANGLEY 208 B4
Park Lawn CR7 183 A1
Parklea Cl NW9 27 C2
Park Lea Ct N16 51 C2
Parkleigh Ct SW19 179 D1
Parkleigh Rd SW19 179 D1
Parkleys KT2, TW10 175 D6
Park Lo 3 Ealing W5 87 B3
North Finchley N12 30 A5
1 South Hampstead
NW8 70 B1
10 Wapping E1 118 B5
Willesden NW2 68 C4
Park Lofts 9 SW4 160 A6
Park Lorne NW8 230 B1
Park Mans
Battersea SW11 267 C1
Bedford Pk W6 111 D3
Forest Hill SE26 162 C1
Fulham SW6 264 B1
5 Hendon NW4 46 B4
Knightsbridge SW1 247 C1
St John's Wood NW8 230 A3
Vauxhall SW8 270 B6
Parkmead SW15 156 B5
Park Mead
Blackfen DA15 168 B5
Harrow HA2 63 D5
Parkmead Gdns NW7 27 D4
Park Mews
Chislehurst BR7 188 D4
Greenwich SE10 120 D1
Kensal Rise W10 91 A5
Stanwell TW19 148 B4
Parkmore BR7 188 D3
Parkmore Cl IG8 37 A6
Park Nook Gdns EN2 5 B6
Park Par Acton W3 110 C3
Dagenham NW10 89 D5
Hayes UB3 83 C1
Kingsbury NW9 45 B6
Park Pl
Canary Wharf E14 119 C5
Ealing W5 109 D5
Gunnersbury W3 110 C2
Hampton TW12 174 A4
Shoreditch N1 235 D6
St James SW1 115 C5 249 A4
Wembley HA9 66 B4
Park Place Dr W3 110 C3
Park Place Ho 8
SE10 142 B6
Park Place Villas W2 236 B4
Park Prim Sch E15 76 D1
Park Rd Ashford TW15 170 D5
Beckenham BR3 185 C3
Bromley BR1 187 B2
Cheam SM3 217 A2
Chipping Barnet EN5 1 B1
Chislehurst BR7 188 D4
Chiswick W4 133 B6
Cockfosters EN4 2 C1
Dagenham NW10 89 C6
Ealing W7 108 D6
East Finchley N2 48 B6
East Molesey KT8 196 A5
Edmonton N18 34 A6
Feltham TW13 172 D6
Hackbridge SM6 219 B6
Hampton TW12 174 A5
Hampton Wick KT1 175 C2
Harringay N8, N15 50 D5
Hayes UB4 83 C2
Hendon NW4 46 B3
Park Rd continued
Hornsey N8 49 D4
Hounslow TW3, TW7 152 A6
Ilford IG1 79 B5
Isleworth TW7 131 B3
Kingsbury NW9 45 B2
Kingston u T KT2,
TW10 176 C3
Leyton E10 53 C1
Lisson Gr NW1,
NW8 92 C3 237 B6
Lower Halliford TW17 192 C1
Mitcham SW19 180 C4
Newham E15 99 A6
New Malden KT3 199 B5
Osidge N14 15 D4
Richmond TW10 154 B5
South Norwood SE25 205 C5
Sunbury TW16 172 B3
Teddington TW11 174 D4
Twickenham TW1 153 C5
Upton Pk E6 99 C6
Uxbridge UB8 60 A2
Wallington SM6 219 B3
Walthamstow E17 53 B4
Wanstead E12 77 B6
Wembley HA0 66 A2
Wood Green N11 31 D3
Park Rd E Acton W3 111 A4
Uxbridge UB10 82 A5
Park Rd N Chiswick W4 111 B1
South Acton W3 110 D4
Park Ridings N8 50 C6
Park Rise
Forest Hill SE23 163 A3
Harrow HA3 24 C2
Park Rise Rd SE23 163 A3
Park Road E 11 W3 110 D4
Park Road Ho 3 KT2 176 C3
Park Row SE10 142 B6
PARK ROYAL 88 D4
Park Royal NW10 88 D6
Park Royal Bsns Ctr
NW10 89 A3
Park Royal Metro Ctr
NW10 88 D3
Park Royal Rd NW10,
W3 89 A3
Park Royal Sta W5 88 C3
Park S SW11 268 A1
Park St James NW8 230 C5
Park Sch IG1 56 D1
Park Sheen 3 SW14 132 D1
Parkshot TW9 132 A1
Parkside
1 Beckenham BR3 185 D1
Cheam SM3 217 A2
Ealing W5 110 A6
East Acton W3 111 C5
Finchley N3 29 D3
Greenwich SE3 142 D5
Hampton TW12 174 A5
Hayes UB3 105 C6
Hendon NW7 28 A4
Sidcup DA14 168 B2
Wimbledon SW19 178 D6
Park Side Chigwell IG9 21 B2
Dollis Hill NW2 68 B4
Parkside Ave
Bromley BR1 210 A5
Wimbledon SW19 178 D5
Parkside Bsns Est
SE8 141 A6
Parkside Cl SE20 184 C3
Parkside Cres
Highbury N7 72 C5
Tolworth KT5 199 A3
Parkside Ct
Bowes Pk N22 32 B4
2 Wanstead E11 55 A3
Parkside Dr HA8 10 C1
Parkside Est E9 96 D6
Parkside Gdns
East Barnet EN4 15 A4
Wimbledon SW19 178 D6
Parkside Lo DA17 125 D1
Parkside Prep Sch N17 33 C2
Parkside (private) Hospl
SW19 156 D1
Parkside Rd
Belvedere DA17 125 D2
Hounslow TW3 151 D6
Parkside St SW11 268 A1
Parkside Terr N18 33 B6
Parkside Way HA2 42 A5
Park Sq E NW1 93 B3 238 D6
Park Square Mews
NW1 238 C5
Park Sq W NW1 93 B3 238 C5
Park St
Borough The
SE1 117 A5 252 B4
Croydon CR0 221 A6
Mayfair W1 115 A6 248 A5
Teddington TW11 174 C4
Parkstead Rd SW15 156 B6
Parkstone Ave N18 33 D5
Parkstone Rd
5 Peckham SE15 140 A3
Walthamstow E17 54 A6
Park Stps W2 247 B6
Park Terr
Carshalton SM5 218 C5
Enfield EN3 7 A5
New Malden KT4 200 A1
Park The Ealing W5 109 D5
Forest Hill SE23 162 C3
Golders Green NW11 47 D1
Highgate N6 49 A3
Sidcup DA14 190 A5
Park The continued
Wallington SM5 218 D3
Parkthorne Cl HA2 41 D3
Parkthorne Dr HA2 41 D3
Parkthorne Rd SW12 159 D4
Park Twrs W1 248 C3
Parkview UB6 87 A4
Park View
Dagenham W3 89 A2
Highbury N5 73 A4
Kingston u T KT3 199 D6
Morden SM4 202 B4
Pinner HA5 23 B2
Southgate N21 16 B4
Wembley HA9 66 D3
Willesden NW2 68 C4
Yiewsley UB7 104 A6
Park View Acad N15 51 A5
Park View Cres N11 31 B6
Parkview Ct
Fulham SW6 135 A3
Harrow HA3 24 C3
Ilford IG2 57 C3
Penge SE20 184 B2
Twickenham TW1 153 C4
Park View Ct
Colney Hatch N12 30 C6
Kingsbury NW9 45 A5
Wandsworth SW18 157 C5
Park View Dr CR4 180 B1
Park View Gdns
Hendon NW4 46 D4
Redbridge IG4 56 B5
Wood Green N22 32 C2
Park View Ho
Chingford E4 35 C5
Hampton TW12 174 A5
Streatham SE24 160 D5
Parkview Lo BR3 207 D6
Park View Mans N4 50 D2
Park View Mews 24
SW9 138 B3
Parkview Rd
Chislehurst SE9 166 D2
Croydon CR0 206 A1
Park View Rd
Bexley DA16 146 C2
Ealing W5 88 A2
Finchley N3 29 D2
Hillingdon UB8 82 C1
Pinner HA5 22 B3
Southall UB1 107 C5
Tottenham N17 34 A1
Willesden NW10 67 D4
Park Village E
NW1 93 B5 231 D3
Park Village W
NW1 93 B5 231 C4
Park Villas RM6 58 D3
Parkville Rd
SW6 135 B5 264 C3
Park Vista SE10 142 B6
Park Vista Apartments
E13 98 D4
Park Walk Prim Sch
SW10 136 B6 266 C5
Parkway
Abbey Wood DA18 125 A3
Camden Town
NW1 93 B6 231 C5
Hillingdon UB10 60 D1
Ilford IG3 79 D5
Palmers Green N14 16 A2
West Barnes SW20 200 D5
Woodford IG8 37 C5
Park Way
East Molesey KT8 195 D6
Edgware HA8 26 D2
Enfield EN2 4 C3
Feltham TW14 150 B4
Friern Barnet N20 30 D6
Gunnersbury W3 110 C2
Ruislip HA4 40 A1
Temple Fortune NW11 47 A4
Park Way Ct HA4 39 D1
Parkway Ho SW14 133 B1
Parkway Prim Sch
DA18 125 A3
Parkway The
Cranford TW5 128 B5
Hayes UB2, UB3, UB4,
TW5 106 B3
Yeading UB4 84 D2
Parkway Trad Est
TW5 128 C6
Park West W2 92 C1 237 B1
Park West Pl W1,
W2 92 C1 237 B2
Park Wlk
Chelsea
SW10 136 B6 266 C6
Highgate N6 49 A2
Parkwood
Beckenham BR3 185 C3
Primrose Hill NW8 230 C5
Parkwood Ave KT10 196 A1
Parkwood Gr TW16 194 A6
Parkwood Mews N6 49 B3
Parkwood Prim Sch
N4 72 D6
Parkwood Rd
Hounslow TW7 130 D4
Old Bexley DA5 169 B4
Wimbledon SW19 179 B5
Parliament Ct NW3 70 C4
Parliament Hill NW3 70 C4
Parliament Hill Mans
NW5 71 A4
Parliament Hill Sch
NW5 71 A4
Parliament Mews
SW14 133 A3
Parliament Sq*
SW1 116 A4 250 A1
Parliament St
SW1 116 A4 250 A2
Parliament View
Apartments SE11 260 C4
Parma Cres SW11 136 D1
Parminter Ind Est 24
E2 96 B5
Parmiter St E2 96 B5
Parmoor Ct EC1 242 A6
Parnall Ho 11 SE19 183 C6
Parnell Cl Edgware HA8 27 A6
Hammersmith W12 112 B3
Parnell Ho WC1 239 D2
Parnell Rd E3 97 B6
Parnham Cl BR1 210 D6
Parnham St E14 97 A1
Parolles Rd N19 49 C1
Paroma Rd DA17 125 C3
Parr Cl N9 34 B6
Parr Ct Feltham TW13 172 C6
Shoreditch N1 235 C4
Parrington Ho 1
SW4 159 D5
Parr Pl W4 111 D2
Parr Rd Newham E6 99 D6
Stanmore HA7 26 A2
Parr's Pl TW12 173 C3
Parr St N1 95 B5 235 C4
Parry Ave E6 100 B1
Parry Cl KT17 216 A1
Parry Ho 32 E1 118 B5
Parry Pl SE18 122 D2
Parry Rd
South Norwood SE25 205 C6
West Kilburn W10 91 A4
Parry St SW8 138 A6 270 B6
Parsifal Coll NW3 69 C4
Parsifal Ho NW3 69 C4
Parsifal Rd NW6 69 C3
Parsley Gdns CR0 206 D1
Parsloes Ave RM9 81 A3
Parsloes Prim Sch RM9 81 B2
Parsonage Cl UB3 83 D1
Parsonage Ct WD6 11 A6
Parsonage Gdns EN2 5 A3
Parsonage La Enfield EN2 5 B3
Sidcup DA14 191 B6
Parsonage Manorway
DA17 147 C6
Parsonage St E14 120 A2
Parsons Cl SM1 217 D5
Parsons Cres HA8 10 C1
Parsons Gn
SW6 135 C4 265 A1
PARSONS GREEN 135 C4
Parsons Green La
SW6 135 C4 265 A2
Parsons Green Sta
SW6 135 C4 265 A1
Parsons Hill SE18 122 C3
Parsons Ho
Paddington W2 236 C5
21 Streatham SW12 160 A4
Parsons Lo NW6 69 D1
Parsons Mead KT8 196 A6
Parson's Mead CR0 204 D1
Parsons Rd
Edgware HA8 10 C1
Newham E13 99 C5
Parson St NW4 46 C6
Parthenia Rd
SW6 135 C4 265 B1
Partingdale La NW7 28 D5
Partington Cl N19 49 D1
Parton Lo 14 E8 73 D2
Partridge Cl Barnet EN5 12 C5
Bushey WD23 8 A3
1 Newham E16 99 D2
Stanmore HA7 26 A6
Partridge Ct EC1 241 C6
Partridge Dr BR6 227 A5
Partridge Gn SE9 166 C1
Partridge Ho 22 E3 97 B5
Partridge Rd
8 Hampton TW12 173 C4
Sidcup DA14 189 C6
Partridge Sq 3 E6 100 A2
Partridge Way N22 32 A2
Pasadena Cl UB3 106 B4
Pascall Ho SE17 139 A6
Pascal St SW8 137 D5 269 D4
Pascoe Rd SE13 164 B6
Pasley Cl SE17 262 A1
Pasquier Rd E17 53 A6
Passey Pl SE9 166 B5
Passfield Dr E14 97 D2
Passfield Ho SE18 123 B2
Passfield Path 13
SE28 124 B6
Passfields Catford SE6 164 A1
West Kensington W14 254 C1
Passing Alley EC1 241 D5
Passingham Ho TW5 129 C6
Passmore Edwards Ho
N11 31 D3
Passmore Gdns N11 31 D4
Passmore Ho 12 N9 18 A1
Passmore St
SW1 115 A1 258 A2
Pasters Ct EN1 17 D5
Pasteur Cl NW9 27 C1
Pasteur Gdns N18 33 A5
Paston Cl SM6 219 C5

Paston Cres SE12 165 B4
Pastor Ct N6 49 C3
Pastor St SE1, SE11 116 D2 261 D4
Pasture Cl Bushey WD23 8 A4
Wembley HA0 65 B5
Pasture Rd
Catford SE6 164 D3
Dagenham RM9 81 B3
Wembley HA0 65 B5
Pastures Mead UB10 60 C2
Pastures The N20 13 B3
Patcham Terr SW8 268 D2
Patch Cl UB10 82 B6
Patching Way UB4 85 A2
Pat Drew Ho BR1 187 C2
Patent Ho E14 97 D2
Paternoster La EC4 94 D1 241 D2
Paternoster Row EC2, EC4 95 A1 242 A1
Paternoster Sq EC4 94 D1 241 D2
Pater St W8 113 C3 255 A5
Pates Manor Dr TW14 149 B4
Pathfield Rd SW16 181 D4
Path The SW19 179 D2
Pathway Ho SW17 180 D4
Pathway Lo CR4 180 D2
Patience Rd SW11 136 C3
Patience Villas SE13 142 B2
Patio Cl SW4 159 D5
Patmore Ho 9 N16 73 C3
Patmore St SW8 137 C4 269 B2
Patmos Rd SW9 138 D4
Paton Cl E3 97 C4
Paton Ho 3 SW9 138 B3
Paton St EC1 235 A1
Patricia Ct
Chislehurst BR7 189 B2
Woolwich DA16 146 B5
Patrick Coman Ho EC1 234 C1
Patrick Connolly Gdns 41 E3 97 D4
Patrick Rd E13 99 C4
Patriot Sq E2 96 B5
Patrol Pl SE6 163 D5
Pat Shaw Ho 2 E1 96 D3
Patshull Pl NW5 71 C2
Patshull Rd NW5 71 C2
Patson Cl E5 74 D5
Pattenden Rd SE6 163 B3
Patten Ho N4 51 A1
Patten Rd SW18 158 C4
Patterdale NW1 231 D1
Patterdale Cl BR1 186 C4
Patterdale Rd SE15 140 C5
Patterson Ct SE19 183 D4
Patterson Rd SE19 183 D4
Pattina Wlk SE16 119 A5
Pattinson Point 10 E16 99 A2
Pattison Ho
Borough The SE1 252 B2
1 Stepney E1 96 D1
Pattison Rd NW2 69 C5
Pattison Wlk SE18 123 A1
Pat Williams Ho SE27 161 A1
Paul Byrne Ho 3 N2 48 A6
Paul Cl E15 76 C1
Paul Ct
7 Edmonton N18 34 A6
Hendon N3 29 A1
Paul Daisley Ct 2 NW6 69 A1
Paulet Rd SE5 138 D4
Paul Gdns CR0 221 D6
Paulhan Rd HA3 43 D5
Paul Ho 18 W10 91 A3
Paulin Dr N21 16 C4
Pauline Cres TW2 152 A3
Pauline Ho 21 E1 96 A2
Paulinus Cl BR5 190 C1
Paul Julius Cl E14 120 B6
Paul Robeson Cl E6 100 C4
Paulson Ho 7 IG11 78 D1
Paul St
Broadgate EC2 95 C3 243 A6
Newham E15 98 C6
Paultons Ho SW3 266 D6
Paultons Sq SW3 136 B6 266 D6
Paultons St SW3 136 B6 266 D5
Pauntley Ho 6 N19 49 C1
Pauntley St 4 N19 49 C1
Pavan Ct 23 E2 96 C4
Paved Ct 8 TW9 153 D6
Paveley Ct NW7 28 D3
Paveley Dr SW11 136 C5 267 A3
Paveley Ho N1 233 C3
Paveley St NW8 92 C3 237 B6
Pavement Mews 1 RM6 58 D2
Pavement Sq CR0 206 A1
Pavement The
Brentford W5 110 A3
Clapham SW4 137 C1
Leytonstone E11 54 A1
11 West Norwood SE27 183 A6
Pavet Cl RM10 81 D2
Pavilion Ct
Dagenham RM9 103 A6
7 Hampstead NW3 70 A4
Pavilion Ct *continued*
Hampstead NW3 70 B3
3 Paddington NW6 91 C4
5 South Norwood SW16 182 B3
3 Wimbledon SW19 179 A3
Pavilion L Ctr The BR1 187 A1
Pavilion Lo HA2 42 B1
Pavilion Mans 10 SW9 138 B1
Pavilion Mews N3 29 C1
Pavilion Rd
Knightsbridge SW1 114 D3 257 D5
Redbridge IG1 56 B2
Pavilion Sq SW17 158 D1
Pavilion St SW1 257 D5
Pavilions The BR3 185 C4
Pavilion Terr Ilford IG2 57 C4
8 North Kensington W12 90 C1
Pavilion Way
Burnt Oak HA8 27 A3
Ruislip HA4 62 C6
Pavillion Ct SW1 268 C6
Pavitt Ct NW10 68 A1
Pawleyne Cl SE20 184 C3
Pawsey Cl E13 99 A6
Pawson's Rd CR0 205 A4
Paxford Rd HA0 65 B6
Paxton Cl
Richmond TW9 132 B3
Walton-on-T KT12 194 C2
Paxton Ct
1 Forest Hill SE26 185 A6
Grove Pk SE9 165 C1
Mitcham CR4 180 D1
Paxton Ho SE17 262 B2
Paxton Pl SE27 183 C6
Paxton Prim Sch SE19 183 C4
Paxton Rd Chiswick W4 133 C6
Forest Hill SE23 163 A1
Plaistow BR1 187 A3
Tottenham N17 34 A3
Paxton Terr SW1 268 D6
Paymal Ho 33 E1 96 C2
Payne Cl IG11 79 D1
Payne Ho N1 233 D5
Paynell Ct SE3 142 C2
Payne Rd E3 97 D5
Paynesfield Ave SW14 133 B2
Paynesfield Rd WD23 8 D4
Payne St SE8 141 B6
Paynes Wlk W6 135 A6 264 A5
Payzes Gdns IG8 36 D5
Peabody Ave SW1 115 B1 258 D1
Peabody Bldgs
6 Camberwell SE5 139 B4
Walworth SE17 262 C3
Peabody Cl
Croydon CR0 206 C1
SW1 268 D6
Peabody Cotts N17 33 C2
Peabody Ct
9 Camberwell SE5 139 B4
25 Enfield EN3 7 C6
St Luke's EC1 242 B5
Peabody Est
18 Bethnal Green E2 96 B5
Borough The SE1 252 A3
Fulham SW6 135 B6 264 D6
17 Hammersmith W6 112 C1
Holborn EC1 241 B5
Lambeth SE1 251 B3
North Kensington W10 90 C2
4 Ratcliff E1 118 D6
7 St George in t East E1 118 A6
St Luke's EC1 242 B5
Strand WC2 240 C1
Streatham SE24 161 A4
Westminster SW1 259 B4
Peabody Hill SE21 161 A3
Peabody Sq SE1 251 C1
Peabody Twr EC1 242 B5
Peabody Yd N1 235 A6
Peace Cl
East Barnet N14 15 B6
Greenford UB6 86 B6
South Norwood SE25 205 C5
Peace Ct 10 NW9 46 A5
Peace Gr HA9 66 D5
Peacehaven Ct 8 N10 31 A3
Peace St SE18 144 C6
Peach Ct E4 35 C6
Peaches Cl SM2 217 A1
Peaches Ct SM2 217 A1
Peach Gr E11 76 B5
Peach Rd
Feltham TW14 150 A3
London W10 91 A4
Peach Tree Ave UB7 82 B1
Peachum Rd SE3 142 D6
Peach Walk Mews 24 E3 96 D5
Peacock Ave TW14 149 B3
Peacock Cl
Dagenham RM8 80 C6
Walthamstow E4 35 B3
Peacock Ct EN1 17 C5
Peacock Ind Est N17 33 D3
Peacock St SE17 116 D2 261 D3
Peacock Wlk E16 99 B1
Peacock Yd SE17 261 D3
Peaketon Ave IG4 55 D4
Peak Hill SE26 184 C6
Peak Hill Ave SE26 184 C6
Peak Hill Gdns SE26 184 C6
Peak Ho N4 51 A1
Peak The SE26 162 C1
Peal Gdns W13 87 A3
Peall Rd CR0 204 B3
Peall Rd Ind Est CR0 204 B3
Pear Ave TW17 193 C6
Pearce Cl 2 CR4 181 A1
Pearcefield Ave 5 SE23 162 C3
Pearce Ho
Camden Town N19 71 C5
7 Streatham SW2 160 A4
Westminster SW1 259 D3
Pear Cl Kingsbury NW9 45 B5
New Cross Gate SE14 141 A5
Pearcroft Rd E11 76 B6
Pear Ct 21 SE15 139 D5
Peardon St SW8 137 B3
Peareswood Gdns HA7 25 D2
Pearfield Ho 1 N5 73 A3
Pearfield Rd SE23 163 A1
Pearl Cl Hendon NW2 46 D2
Newham E6 100 C1
Pearl Ct 18 NW9 46 A5
Pearl Rd E17 53 C6
Pearl St E1 118 B5
Pearlstones Ct RM10 103 C6
Pearmain Cl TW17 192 D4
Pearmain Ho 9 SE13 142 A3
Pearman St SE1 116 C4 251 B1
Pear Pl SE1 251 A2
Pear Rd E11 76 C5
Pearscroft Ct SW6 135 D4 265 D1
Pearscroft Rd SW6 135 D4 265 D1
Pearse St 3 SE15 139 C6
Pearson Cl Barnet EN5 1 D2
4 Camberwell SE5 139 A4
Pearson Ct SM4 201 D4
Pearson Ho SW15 134 C3
Pearson's Ave SE8, SE14 141 C4
Pearson St E2 95 D5
Pearson Way CR4 181 A2
Pears Rd TW3 130 A2
Peartree Ave SW17 158 A1
Pear Tree Ave UB7 82 B1
Pear Tree Cl
Bromley BR2 209 D4
Chessington KT9 214 C3
Mitcham CR4 180 C1
23 Shoreditch E2 95 D6
Pear Tree Ct
Holborn EC1 241 B5
Putney SW15 134 B1
Woodford IG8 37 B2
Peartree Gdns RM8 80 B4
Pear Tree Ho
Brockley SE4 141 B1
Hayes UB8 83 A1
Peartree La E1 118 C6
Peartree Rd EN1 5 C2
Pear Tree Rd TW15 171 A5
Peartree St EC1 95 A3 242 A6
Peartree Way SE10 121 A2
Peary Ho 4 NW10 67 B1
Peary Pl E2 96 C4
Peaslake Ct SM2 218 A1
Peas Mead Terr E4 36 A6
Peatfield Cl DA15 167 C1
Pebworth Lo
2 Belmont SM2 217 D1
South Norwood SE25 205 D5
Pebworth Rd HA1 65 A6
Peckarmans Wood SE21, SE26 162 A1
Peckett Sq 3 N5 72 D4
Peckford Pl SW9 138 C3
PECKHAM 140 A4
Peckham Gr SE15 139 C5
Peckham High St SE15 140 A4
Peckham Hill St SE15 140 A5
Peckham Park Prim Sch SE15 140 A5
Peckham Park Rd SE15 140 A5
Peckham Rd SE5 139 C4
Peckham Rye
East Dulwich SE22 140 A1
Peckham SE15, SE22 140 B1
Peckham Rye Sta SE15 140 A3
Peckwater Ho 2 NW5 71 D2
Peckwater St NW5 71 C3
Pedlars Wlk N7 72 A3
Pedley Rd RM8 58 C1
Pedley St E1 95 D3 243 D5
Pedro St E5 74 D4
Pedworth Gdns 4 SE16 118 C2
Peebles Ct UB1 86 A1
Peek Cres SW19 178 D5
Peel Centre (Metropolitan Police Training Establishment) NW9 45 D6
Peel Cl Chingford E4 19 D2
Edmonton N9 18 A1
Peel Ct UB6 86 A4
Peel Dr Colindale NW9 45 D6
Redbridge IG5 56 A6
Peel Gr E2 96 C5
Peel Pass W8 245 A3
Peel Pl IG5 37 D1
Peel Prec NW6 91 C5
Peel Rd
Farnborough BR6 227 A3
Harrow HA3 42 D6
Wembley HA0, HA9 65 D5
Woodford E18 36 D2
Peel St W8 113 C5 245 A3
Peel Way UB8 82 A2
Peel Yates Ho 13 SE7 122 A2
Peerglow Est EN3 18 C6
Peerless St EC1 95 B4 235 C1
Pegamoid Rd N18 18 C1
Pegasus Cl N16 73 B4
Pegasus Ct 11 Acton W3 89 A1
Brentford TW8 110 B1
6 Buckhurst Hill IG9 21 D2
College Pk NW10 90 B4
Edmonton N21 17 A4
Harrow HA3 43 D4
Kingston u T KT1 197 D6
Sutton SM1 217 D6
Pegasus Ho 9 E1 96 D3
Pegasus Lo N21 17 A4
Pegasus Pl 2 SE11 138 C6
Pegasus Rd CR0, CR9 220 C2
Pegasus Way N11 31 B4
Peggotty Way UB8 82 D1
Pegg Rd TW5 128 D5
Peggy Quirke Ct 2 HA0 66 A2
Pegley Gdns SE12 165 A2
Pegwell Ho 19 E5 74 B3
Pegwell St SE18 145 C5
Pekin St E14 97 C1
Pekoe SE1 253 D3
Peldon Ct TW10 154 B6
Pele Ct N17 33 B3
Pelham Ave IG11 101 D6
Pelham Cl SE5 139 C2
Pelham Cotts DA5 169 D3
Pelham Cres SW7 257 A3
Pelham Ct SW3 257 A3
Pelham Ho W14 254 C3
Pelham Pl Chelsea SW7 257 A3
8 Ealing W7 86 D3
Pelham Prim Sch
Bexleyheath DA7 147 C2
Merton SW19 179 C3
Pelham Rd
Bexleyheath DA7 147 C2
Ilford IG1 79 B6
Merton SW19 179 C3
Penge BR3, SE20 184 C1
Tottenham N15 51 D5
Wanstead E18 55 B6
Wood Green N22 32 C1
Pelham St SW7 114 B2 256 D4
Pelican Ho 8 SE8 119 B2
Pelican Pas 3 E1 96 C3
Pelier St SE17 139 A6
Pelinore Rd SE6 164 C2
Pella Ho SE11 260 D2
Pellant Rd SW6 135 A5 264 B4
Pellatt Gr N22 32 C2
Pellatt Rd
East Dulwich SE22 161 D6
Wembley HA9 66 A6
Pellerin Rd N16 73 C3
Pellew Ho 15 E1 96 B3
Pellings Cl BR2 208 C6
Pelling St E14 97 C1
Pellipar Cl N13 16 C1
Pellipar Gdns SE18 122 B1
Pellipar Rd SE18 122 B1
Pelly Ct 4 E17 54 A5
Pelly Rd E13 99 A5
Pelter St E2 95 D4
Pelton Ct CR2 221 A2
Pelton Rd SE10 120 C1
Pembar Ave E17 53 A6
Pemberley Chase KT19 214 D3
Pemberley Cl KT19 214 D3
Pemberley Ho KT19 214 D3
Pember Rd NW10 90 D4
Pemberton Ct 18 E1 96 D4
Pemberton Gdns
Camden Town N19 71 C5
Dagenham RM6 59 A4
Pemberton Ho SE26 184 A6
Pemberton Pl
Esher KT10 212 A5
2 Hackney E8 74 B1
Pemberton Rd
East Molesey KT8 196 A5
Harringay N4 50 D4
Pemberton Row EC4 241 B2
Pemberton Terr N19 71 C5
Pembridge Ave TW4 151 B3
Pembridge Cres W11 113 C6 245 A6
Pembridge Gdns W2 113 C6 245 A5
Pembridge Hall Sch W2 113 C6 245 B5
Pembridge Mews W11 113 C6 245 A6
Pembridge Pl
Notting Hill W2 113 C6 245 B6
1 Wandsworth SW15 157 C6
Pembridge Rd W11 113 C6 245 A5
Pembridge Sq W2 113 C6 245 B5
Pembridge Villas W11 113 C6 245 A6
Pembroke W14 254 D3
Pembroke Ave
Enfield EN1 6 B4
Harrow HA3 43 B6
Islington N1 94 A6 233 B6
Surbiton KT5 198 D4
Pembroke Bldgs NW10 90 A4
Pembroke Cl SW1 248 B1
Pembroke Ct 11 W7 86 D2
Pembroke Gdns
Dagenham RM10 81 D5
West Kensington W8 113 B2 254 D4
Pembroke Gdns Cl W8 255 A5
Pembroke Hall NW4 46 C6
Pembroke Ho
Acton W3 111 A4
Chelsea SW1 258 A5
5 Clapham Pk SW2 160 A6
17 Kensington W2 91 D1
Putney SW15 156 A6
Upper Tooting SW17 180 B5
Pembroke Lo 2 SW16 160 B1
Pembroke Mews
8 Bow E3 97 A4
Bromley BR1 187 D1
Kensington W8 255 A5
Muswell Hill N10 31 A2
Pembroke Pl
Edgware HA8 26 C3
Isleworth TW7 130 C3
Kensington W8 255 A5
Pembroke Rd
Bromley BR1 187 D1
Edmonton N13 17 A1
Greenford UB6 85 D3
Hornsey N8 50 A5
Ilford IG3 79 D6
Kensington W8 113 C2 255 A4
Mitcham CR4 181 A1
Muswell Hill N10 31 A3
Newham E6 100 B2
Ruislip HA4 39 D1
South Norwood SE25 205 C5
South Tottenham N15 51 D4
Walthamstow E17 53 D4
Wembley HA9 65 D5
Pembroke Sq W8 113 C3 255 A5
Pembroke St N1 94 A6 233 B6
Pembroke Studios W8 254 D5
Pembroke Terr NW8 229 C5
Pembroke Villas
Kensington W8 255 A4
Richmond TW9 131 D1
Pembroke Way UB3 105 A3
Pembroke Wlk W8 255 A4
Pembry Cl SW9 138 C4
Pembury Ave KT4 200 A2
Pembury Cl Hackney E5 74 B3
Hayes BR2 208 D2
Pembury Cres DA14 169 A2
Pembury Ct UB3 127 B6
Pembury Ho
Camberwell SE5 139 C3
Keston Mark BR2 210 A1
Pembury Pl 15 E5, E8 74 B3
Pembury Rd
Croydon SE25 206 A5
Erith DA7 147 A6
Hackney E5 74 B3
Tottenham N17 33 D1
Pemdevon Rd CR0 204 C2
Pemell Cl 30 E1 96 C3
Pemell Ho 31 E1 96 C3
Pemerich Cl UB3 105 D1
Pempath Pl HA9 65 D6
Penair Lodge HA1 64 C5
Penally Pl N1 235 D6
Penang St E1 118 B5
Penard Rd UB2 107 D3
Penarth Ct SM2 218 A1
Penarth Ctr The SE15 140 C6
Penarth St SE15 140 C6
Penates KT10 212 B4
Penberth Rd SE6 164 A3
Penbury Rd UB2 107 B1
Penceat Ct SE20 184 C1
Pencombe Mews W11 244 D6
Pencraig Way SE15 140 B6
Pendall Cl EN4 2 C1
Penda Rd DA8 147 D5
Pendarves Rd SW20 178 C2
Penda's Mead E9 75 A4
Pendell Ave UB3 127 D5
Pendennis Ho 15 SE8 119 A2
Pendennis Rd
Streatham SW16 182 A6
Tottenham N17 51 B6
Penderel Rd TW3 151 C6
Penderry Rise SE6 164 B2
Penderyn Way N7 71 D4
Pendlebury Ho 5 SE18 144 A4
Pendle Ho 13 SE26 162 A1
Pendle Rd SW16 181 B5
Pendlestone Rd E17 53 D4
Pendley Ho 18 E2 96 A6
Pendolino Way NW10 66 D1
Pendragon Rd BR1 165 A1
Pendragon Sch BR1 165 A1
Pendragon Wlk NW9 45 C3
Pendrell Ho WC2 239 D1
Pendrell Rd SE4 141 A3
Pendrell St SE18 145 B6
Pendula Dr UB4 84 D3
Penelope Ho 20 SW9 138 C4
Penerley Rd SE6 163 D3
Penfield Lo 7 W9 91 C2
Penfields Ho N7 72 A2
Penfold Cl CR0 220 C5
Penfold Ct 7 CR4 181 A1
Penfold Ho 14 SE18 144 D6
Penfold La DA5 168 D3
Penfold Pl NW1 92 C2 237 A4
Penfold Rd N9 18 D3
Penfold St NW8 92 B3 236 D5
Penford Gdns SE9 143 D2
Penford St SE5 138 D3
Pengarth Rd DA5 168 D5
PENGE 184 D4
Penge East Sta SE20 184 C4
Penge La SE20 184 D3
Penge Rd Newham E13 99 C6
South Norwood SE25 206 A6
Penge West Sta SE20 184 B4
Penhall Rd SE7 121 D2
Penhill Rd DA5 168 C4
Penhurst Mans SW6 264 C2
Penifather La UB6 86 B4
Peninsula Ct E14 119 D3
Peninsular Cl TW14 149 C5
Peninsular Park Rd SE7 121 A2
Penistone Rd SW16 182 A3
Penketh Dr HA1 64 B5
Penmayne Ho SE11 261 B2
Penmon Rd SE2 124 A3
Pennack Rd SE15 139 D6
Penn Almshouses 1 SE10 142 A4
Pennant Mews W8 113 D2 255 C4
Pennant Terr E17 35 B1
Pennard Mans 5 W12 112 C4
Pennard Rd W12 112 C4
Pennards The TW16 194 C6
Penn Cl Greenford UB6 85 D5
Harrow HA3 43 C5
Penn Ct NW9 45 B6
Pennefather Ho N1 73 B2
Pennells Ct TW5 129 C6
Penner Cl SW19 157 A2
Penners Gdns KT6 198 A2
Pennethorne Cl E9 96 C6
Pennethorne Ho SW11 136 B2
Pennethorne Rd SE15 140 B5
Penn Gdns BR7 188 D1
Penn Ho
7 Edmonton N9 18 A1
Lisson Gr NW8 237 A5
Pennine Dr NW2 68 D6
Pennine La NW2 69 A6
Pennine Mans NW2 69 A6
Pennine Par NW2 69 A6
Pennine Way UB7 127 B5
Pennington Cl 10 SE27 183 B6
Pennington Ct
4 Rotherhithe SE16 119 A5
23 St George in t East E1 118 A6
Pennington Dr N21 16 A6
Pennington Lo 18 KT5 198 A4
Pennington St E1 118 B6
Pennington Way SE12 165 B2
Penniston Cl N17 33 A1
Penn La Bexley DA5 168 D5
Sidcup DA5 169 A5
Penn Rd N7 72 A4
Penn St N1 95 B6 235 D5
Penny Ct SW10 266 B6
Pennyfields E14 119 C6
Pennyford Ct NW8 236 C6
Penny La TW17 193 C2
Penny Mews SW12 159 B4
Pennymore Wlk W9 91 B3
Penny Rd NW10 88 D4
Penny Royal SM6 219 D2
Pennyroyal Ave E6 100 C1
Penpoll Rd E8 74 B2
Penpool La DA16 146 B2
Penray EN5 1 A2
Penrhyn Ave E17 35 C2
Penrhyn Cres
Mortlake SW14 133 A1
Walthamstow E17 35 C2
Penrhyn Gdns KT1 197 D5
Penrhyn Gr E17 35 C2
Penrhyn Rd KT1 198 A6
Penrith Cl
Beckenham BR3 185 C2
Putney SW15 157 A6
Penrith Pl SE27 160 D2
Penrith Rd
New Malden KT3 199 B5
South Norwood CR7 183 A1
Tottenham N15 51 B4
Penrith St SW16 181 C4
Penrose Gr SE17 117 A1 262 A1
Penrose Ho
Camberwell SE17 262 A1
Southgate N21 16 B6
Penrose St SE17 117 A1 262 A1
Penryn Ho SE11 261 C2
Penryn St NW1 93 D5 232 C4
Penry St SE1 263 B3
Pensbury Pl SW8 137 C3
Pensbury St SW8 137 C3
Pensford Ave TW9 132 C3
Penshurst 2 NW5 71 A2
Penshurst Ave DA15 168 A5
Penshurst Ct
Croydon CR2 220 D1

Penshurst Ct *continued*
1 Edgware HA8 26 D5
Penshurst Gdns HA8 26 D5
Penshurst Gn BR2 208 D4
Penshurst Ho 1 SE15 140 C6
Penshurst Rd
Erith DA7 147 B4
Homerton E9 74 D1
Thornton Heath CR7 204 D4
Tottenham N17 33 D3
Penshurst Way SM2 217 C1
Penshurst Wlk 4 BR2 208 D4
Pensilver Cl EN4 2 C1
Penstemon Cl N3 29 C4
Pentavia Retail Pk NW7 27 D3
Pentelow Gdns TW14 150 A5
Pentire Rd E17 36 B2
Pentland Ave
Edgware HA8 10 D2
Littleton TW17 192 C4
Pentland Cl
Cricklewood NW11 69 A6
Lower Edmonton N9 18 C2
Pentland Gdns SW18 158 A5
Pentland Ho
17 Camden Town NW5 71 A2
7 Stamford Hill N16 51 D1
Pentland Pl UB5 85 A6
Pentland Rd
Bushey WD23 8 A5
1 Maida Vale NW6 91 C4
Pentlands BR3 186 A2
Pentlands Cl CR4 203 B6
Pentland St SW18 158 A5
Pentland Way UB10 61 A5
Pentlow St SW15 134 C2
Pentney Rd
5 Chingford E4 20 B3
Merton SW19, SW20 179 A2
Streatham SW12 159 C3
Penton Gr N1 234 A3
Penton Ho
3 Abbey Wood SE2 124 D4
Islington N1 234 A3
Sutton SM2 218 A1
Penton Pl SE17 116 D1 261 D2
Penton Rise WC1 94 B4 233 D2
Penton St N1 94 C5 234 A3
PENTONVILLE 94 B5
Pentonville Rd N1 94 B5 233 C3
Pentrich Ave EN1 6 A5
Pentridge St SE15 139 D5
Pentyre Ave N18 33 B5
Penwerris Ave TW5, TW7 130 A5
Penwerris Ct TW7 130 A5
Penwith Rd SW18 157 D2
Penwood Ct HA5 41 B5
Penwood Ho SW15 155 D5
Penwortham Ct 1 N22 32 C1
Penwortham Prim Sch SW17 181 B4
Penwortham Rd SW16 181 C4
Penylan Pl HA8 26 C3
Penywern Rd SW5 113 C1 255 B2
Penzance Ho SE11 261 B2
Penzance Pl W11 113 A5 244 B4
Penzance St W11 113 A5 244 A4
Peony Ct IG8 36 C3
Peony Gdns W12 112 A6
Peperfield WC1 233 C1
Pepler Ho 17 W10 91 A3
Pepler Mews SE1 263 C1
Peploe Rd NW6 90 D5
Pepper Cl E6 100 B2
Peppercorn Cl CR7 183 B1
Peppermead Sq SE13 163 C6
Peppermint Cl CR0 204 A2
Peppermint Pl 7 E11 76 C5
Pepper St
Borough The SE1 252 A2
Millwall E14 119 D3
Peppie Cl N16 73 C6
Pepsi Trocadero* W1 249 C5
Pepys Cl UB10 60 D4
Pepys Cres Barnet EN5 12 C6
2 Newham E16 121 A5
Pepys Ct SW20 178 C1
Pepys Ent Ctr 11 SE8 119 B2
Pepys Ho
14 Bethnal Green E2 96 C4
Clapham Pk SW4 159 D6
Pepys Rd
New Cross Gate SE14 140 D3
Wimbledon SW20 178 C2
Pepys Rise BR6 211 D1
Pepys St EC3 117 C6 253 B6
Perak Ct KT5 199 A2
Peralte Terr CR4 204 A5
Perceval Ave NW3 70 C3
Perceval Ct UB5 63 C3
Percheron Cl TW7 130 D2
Percheron Ct 3 SW9 138 B2
Percheron Rd WD6 11 B5
Perch St E8 73 D4
Percival Ct N17 33 D3
Percival Gdns RM6 58 C3
Percival Ho 3 IG8 37 A6
Percival Rd Enfield EN1 5 D1
Feltham TW13 149 D2
Percival Rd *continued*
Mortlake SW14 133 A1
Orpington BR6 226 D6
Percival St EC1 94 D4 234 D1
Percival Way KT19 215 B4
Percy Ave TW15 170 C5
Percy Bilton Ct TW5 129 D4
Percy Bryant Rd TW16 171 C3
Percy Bush Rd UB7 104 B3
Percy Cir WC1 94 B4 233 D2
Percy Ct 1 KT5 198 B3
Percy Gdns Enfield EN3 18 D6
Hayes UB4 83 C4
5 Isleworth TW7 131 A2
New Malden KT4 199 C1
Percy Ho 4 SW16 181 C6
Percy Laurie Ho 6 SW15 134 D1
Percy Mews W1 239 C3
Percy Pas W1 239 C3
Percy Rd
Bexleyheath DA7 147 A3
Carshalton CR4 203 A2
Croydon SE25 206 A4
Edmonton N21 17 A4
Hampton TW12 173 C3
Ilford IG3 58 A2
Isleworth TW7 131 A1
Leytonstone E11 54 C2
Newham E16 98 C2
North Finchley N12 30 A5
Penge SE20 184 D2
Romford RM7 59 D6
Shepherd's Bush W12 112 A4
Twickenham TW2 152 A3
Percy St W1 93 D2 239 C3
Percy Terr BR1 210 D6
Percy Way TW2 152 A3
Peregrine Cl NW10 67 B3
Peregrine Ct
Bexley DA16 145 D4
Streatham SW16 182 B6
Peregrine Gdns CR0 223 A6
Peregrine Ho
6 Battersea SW11 136 C2
Finsbury EC1 234 D2
Peregrine Rd
Sunbury TW16 171 D1
Tottenham N17 33 B3
Peregrine Way SW19, SW20 178 C3
Performing Arts & Tech Sch SE25 205 B3
Perham Rd W14 113 A1 254 B1
Peridot St E6 100 A2
Perifield SE21 161 A3
Perimeade Rd UB6 87 C5
Period Wks E10 53 A1
Periton Rd SE9 143 D1
PERIVALE 87 B5
Perivale UB6 86 D5
Perivale Gdns W13 87 B3
Perivale Grange UB6 87 A4
Perivale Ind Pk UB6 87 B5
Perivale La UB6 87 A4
Perivale Lo UB6 87 A4
Perivale New Bsns Ctr UB6 87 C5
Perivale Prim Sch UB6 87 B4
Perivale Sta UB6 87 A5
Perkin Cl
Hounslow TW3 129 D1
Wembley HA0 65 B3
Perkins Ct TW15 170 B5
Perkins Ho 15 E14 97 B2
Perkins Rd IG2 57 B4
Perkins Rents SW1 259 C5
Perkins Sq SE1 252 B4
Perks Cl SE3 142 C2
Perley Ho 9 E3 97 B2
Perotti Ho SW6 135 D2
Perpins Rd SE9 167 C5
Perran Rd SE24, SW2 160 D2
Perren St NW5 71 B2
Perrers Rd W6 112 B2
Perrin Cl TW15 170 B5
Perrin Ct TW15 170 C6
Perring Est E3 97 C2
Perrin Grange HA9 66 B6
Perrin Rd HA0 65 B4
Perrins Ct HA3 44 B2
Perrin's Ct 20 NW3 70 A4
Perrin's La NW3 70 A4
Perrin's Wlk NW3 70 A4
Perronet Ho SE1 261 D5
Perry Ave W3 89 B1
Perry Cl UB8 82 D1
Perry Ct
6 Isle of Dogs E14 119 C1
2 Kingston u T KT2 176 A1
Sutton SM1 217 C3
2 Tottenham N15 51 C3
Perryfield Way
Richmond TW10 153 B2
West Hendon NW9 45 D3
Perry Garth UB5 84 C6
Perry Gdns N9 17 C1
Perry Hall Prim Sch BR6 211 D3
Perry Hill SE6 163 B1
Perry Ho 24 SW2 160 A4
Perry How KT4 199 D1
Perryman Ho
Barking IG11 101 A6
Tottenham N17 34 B3
Perrymans Farm Rd IG2 57 B4
Perry Mead Bushey WD23 8 A5
Perry Mead *continued*
Enfield EN2 4 D3
Perrymead St SW6 135 D4 265 C1
Perrymount Prim Sch SE23 162 D2
Perryn Ct 1 TW1 153 A4
Perryn Ho W3 111 C6
Perryn Rd Acton W3 111 B6
1 Bermondsey SE16 118 B3
Perry Rise SE23 163 A1
Perry's Pl W1 239 C2
Perry St BR7 189 C4
Perry Street Gdns BR7 189 C4
Perry Vale SE23 162 D2
Perrywood Ho 17 E5 74 B3
Persant Rd SE6 164 C2
Perseverance Pl SW9 138 C5
Perseverance Works 17 E2 95 C4
Pershore Cl IG2 56 D4
Pershore Gr SM5 202 B3
Pershore Ho 11 W13 109 A5
Pert Cl N10 31 B4
Perth Ave Hayes UB4 84 C3
Kingsbury NW9 45 B2
Perth Cl Northolt UB5 63 C3
Wimbledon SW20 178 A1
Perth Ct 5 SE5 139 B1
Perth Ho 12 Acton W3 88 C1
Barnsbury N1 72 B1
Perth Rd Barking IG11 101 B6
Beckenham BR3 186 A1
Finsbury Pk N4 50 C1
Ilford IG2 56 D3
Newham E13 99 B5
Tottenham N22 32 D2
Walthamstow E10 53 B1
Perth Terr IG2 57 A2
Perwell Ave HA2 41 B1
Perystreete SE23 162 C2
Petavel Rd TW11 174 C4
Petchey Acad The E8 73 D3
Peter Ave NW10 68 B1
Peter Best Ho 1 E1 96 B1
Peterboat Cl SE10 120 C2
Peterborough Ct EC4 241 B1
Peterborough Gdns IG1 56 A2
Peterborough Mews SW6 135 C3
Peterborough Prim Sch SW6 135 C3
Peterborough Rd
Carshalton SM5 202 C3
Fulham SW6 135 C2
Harrow HA1 42 D2
Leytonstone E10 54 B3
Peterborough Villas SW6 265 C2
Peter Bradley Ct RM9 81 B1
Peter Butler Ho 9 SE1 118 A4
Peterchurch Ho SE15 140 B6
Peter Fagan Ho UB3 105 C3
Petergate SW11 136 A1
Peterhead Ct 12 UB1 86 A1
Peter Heathfield Ho 4 E15 98 B6
Peter Hills Ho 6 SE16 118 A2
Peter Hills with St Mary's & St Paul's CE Prim Sch SE16 118 D5
Peter Ho SW8 270 A4
Peter James Bsns Ctr UB3 106 A4
Peter James Ent Ctr NW10 89 A4
Peter Kennedy Ct CR0 207 B3
Peterley Bsns Ctr 21 E2 96 B5
Peter Lyell Ct HA4 62 B6
Peters Cl Bexley DA16 145 C3
Dagenham RM8 58 D1
Stanmore HA7 25 D4
Peters Ct 9 W2 91 D1
Peter's Ct SW4 160 A5
Petersfield Cl N18 33 A5
Petersfield Rd W3 111 A4
Petersfield Rise SW15 156 B3
PETERSHAM 154 A3
Petersham Cl
Richmond TW10 153 D2
Sutton SM1 217 C3
Petersham Dr BR5 190 A1
Petersham Gdns BR5 189 D1
Petersham Ho SW7 256 C4
Petersham La SW7 256 A4
Petersham Mews SW7 114 A3 256 B5
Petersham Pl SW7 114 A3 256 B6
Petersham Rd TW10 154 A3
Petersham Terr CR0 220 A5
Peter's La EC1 241 D4
Peter's Lo HA8 26 B4
Peter's Path SE26 184 B6
Peter St W1 115 D6 249 C6
Peterstone Rd SE2 124 B4
Peterstow Cl SW19 157 A2
Peterwood Pk CR9 220 B6
Peterwood Way CR0 220 B6
Petherton Ct
Brondesbury Pk NW10 90 D6
10 Harrow HA1 42 D3
Petherton Ho N4 51 A1
Petherton Rd N5 73 A3
Petiver Cl 26 E9 74 C1
Petley Rd W6 134 D5
Peto Pl NW1 238 D6
Peto St N E16 98 D1
Petrel Ct 8 SE21 161 B2
Petrie Cl NW2 69 A2
Petrie Ho 8 SE18 144 C6
Petrie Mus of Egyptian Archaeology* WC1 93 D3 239 C5
Petros Gdns 1 NW3 70 A2
Pettacre Cl SE28 123 A3
Petticoat Lane Mkt* EC2 95 D2 243 C3
Petticoat Sq E1 243 C2
Petticoat Twr E1 243 C2
Pettit's Pl RM10 81 C3
Pettit's Rd RM10 81 C3
Pettiward Cl SW15 134 C1
Pettman Cres SE18, SE28 123 B3
Pettsgrove Ave HA0 65 C3
Pett's Hill UB5 63 D3
Petts La TW17 192 C5
Pett St SE7 122 A2
PETTS WOOD 211 B5
Petts Wood Rd BR5 211 B4
Petts Wood Sta BR5 211 A4
Petty France SW1 115 D3 259 C6
Petty Wales EC3 253 B5
Petworth Cl UB5 63 B1
Petworth Gdns
Hillingdon UB10 83 A6
West Barnes SW20 200 B6
Petworth Ho 16 SE22 139 C2
Petworth Rd
Bexley DA6 169 C6
Colney Hatch N12 30 C5
Petworth St SW11 136 C4 267 B2
Petyt Pl SW3 136 C6 267 A5
Petyward SW3 114 C2 257 B3
Pevensey Ave Enfield EN1 5 C3
Friern Barnet N11 31 D5
Pevensey Cl TW7 130 A5
Pevensey Ct
4 South Acton W3 110 D4
West Norwood SW16 160 C1
10 Woodford E18 37 A2
Pevensey Ho 5 E1 97 A2
Pevensey Rd
Feltham TW13 151 A3
Forest Gate E7 77 A4
Upper Tooting SW17 180 B6
Peverel E6 100 C1
Peverel Ho RM10 81 C6
Peverett Cl N11 31 B5
Peveril Dr TW11 174 B5
Peveril Ho SE1 262 D5
Pewsey Cl E4 35 C5
Pewsham Ho N4 51 A1
Pewterers Ct N3 29 B2
Peyton Ho N11 31 A6
Peyton Pl SE10 142 A5
Pharamond NW2 68 D2
Pharaoh Cl CR4 202 D2
Pheasant Cl E16 99 B1
Phelps Ho SW15 134 D2
Phelp St SE17 139 B6
Phelps Way UB3 105 D2
Phene St SW3 136 C6 267 B6
Philadelphia Ct SW10 266 B3
Philbeach Gdns SW5 113 C1 255 A2
Phil Brown Pl 3 SW8 137 B2
Philchurch Pl 36 E1 96 A1
Philia Ho 4 NW1 71 C1
Philimore Cl SE18 123 C1
Philip Blairman Ho E1 243 C5
Philip Ct Enfield EN2 5 B4
Paddington W2 236 C4
Philip Gdns CR0 223 B6
Philip Ho
East Barnet N20 14 D2
12 Paddington NW6 91 D6
Philip La N15 51 C6
Philipot Almshouse SE9 166 B5
Philipot Path SE9 166 B5
Philippa Gdns SE9 165 D6
Philips Cl CR4 203 A1
Philip St E13 99 A3
Philip Turner Est 28 E9 74 C1
Philip Wlk SE15 140 A2
Phillimore Ct W8 245 B1
Phillimore Gardens Cl W8 113 C3 255 A6
Phillimore Gdns
Kensington W8 113 C4 245 A1
Willesden NW10 90 C6
Phillimore Pl W8 113 C4 245 A1
Phillimore Terr W8 255 B6
Phillimore Wlk W8 113 C3 255 B6
Phillip Ho E1 243 D3
Phillipp St N1 95 C6
Phillips Ct Edgware HA8 26 C4
Hayes UB4 84 B4
Phillipson Ho 6 N12 29 D5
Philpot La EC3 253 A6
Philpot Sq SW6 135 D2
Philpot St E1 96 B1
Philson Mans 18 E1 96 B1
Phineas Pett Rd SE9 144 A2
Phipp's Bridge Rd CR4, SW19 202 B6
Phipps Bridge Sta CR4 202 B6
Phipps Hatch La EN2 5 A5
Phipps Ho
1 Greenwich SE7 121 B1
16 Shepherd's Bush W12 112 B6
Phipp St EC2 95 C3 243 A6
Phoebeth Rd SE4 163 C6
Phoenix Bsns Ctr 22 E3 97 C2
Phoenix Cl
18 Shoreditch E8 95 D6
Walthamstow E17 35 B1
West Wickham BR4 224 C6
Phoenix Ct
4 Brentford TW8 110 A1
Chingford E4 19 D1
Croydon SE25 206 A4
2 Deptford SE14 141 A6
Enfield EN3 6 C5
Feltham TW13 171 C6
Millwall E14 119 C2
8 New Barnet EN5 2 A1
Phoenix Ctr The 1 SM6 220 A1
Phoenix Dr BR2 225 D5
Phoenix High Sch W12 112 A6
Phoenix Ho
Chelsea SW1 258 A4
Kingston u T KT3 199 D6
Phoenix Ind Est HA1 42 D5
Phoenix Lodge Mans 1 W6 112 C2
Phoenix Pk NW2 68 A6
Phoenix Pl WC1 94 B3 240 D6
Phoenix Rd
Penge SE20 184 C4
Somers Town NW1 93 D4 232 C2
Phoenix Sch E3 97 B4
Phoenix Sch The NW3 70 A2
Phoenix St WC2 239 D1
Phoenix Trad Est UB6 87 D6
Phoenix Trad Pk TW8 109 D1
Phoenix Way TW5 128 D6
Phoenix Wharf Rd SE1 253 D1
Phyllis Ave KT3 200 B4
Phyllis Ho CR0 220 D4
Phyllis Hodges Ho NW1 93 D5 232 C3
Physic Pl SW3 136 D6 267 C6
Picador Ho 1 RM10 81 D2
Picardy Manorway DA17 125 D4
Picardy Rd DA17 125 C2
Picardy St DA17 125 C3
Piccadilly W1 115 C5 249 A4
Piccadilly Arc SW1 249 A4
Piccadilly Cir* W1 115 D6 249 C5
Piccadilly Circus Sta SW1 115 D6 249 C5
Piccadilly Ct 5 N7 72 B2
Piccadilly Pl W1 249 B5
Pickard Cl N14 15 D3
Pickard St EC1 234 D2
Pickering Ave E6 100 C4
Pickering Cl E9 74 D1
Pickering Ct N22 32 D2
Pickering Gdns
Croydon SE25 205 D3
Friern Barnet N11 31 A4
Pickering Ho
Brentford W5 109 C2
18 Kensington W2 91 D1
Stoke Newington N4 51 B2
4 Woolwich SE18 122 C2
Pickering Mews 9 W2 91 D1
Pickering Pl SW1 249 B3
Pickering St N1 234 D6
Pickets Cl WD23 8 C3
Pickets St SW12 159 B4
Pickett Croft HA7 25 D2
Pickett's Lock La N9 18 D2
Pickford Cl DA7 147 A3
Pickford La DA7 147 A3
Pickford Rd DA7 147 A2
Pickfords Wharf N1 235 A3
Pickhurst Gn BR2 208 D2
Pickhurst Inf Sch BR2 208 D3
Pickhurst Jun Sch BR2 208 D3
Pickhurst La BR2, BR3, BR4 208 C2
Pickhurst Mead BR2 208 D2
Pickhurst Pk BR2 208 D4
Pickhurst Rise BR4 208 B1
Pickwick Cl TW4 151 A6
Pickwick Ct SE9 166 B3
Pickwick Ho
21 Bermondsey SE16 118 A4
3 Shepherd's Bush W11 112 D5
Pickwick Mews N18 33 C5
Pickwick Pl HA1 42 C2
Pickwick Rd SE21 161 C4
Pickwick St SE1 252 A1
Pickwick Way BR7 189 A4
Pickworth Cl SW8 270 B3
Picton Ho 1 SW4 160 A4
Picton Pl
Marylebone W1 238 B1
Tolworth KT6 198 C1
Picton St SE5 139 B5
Picture Ho 6 SW16 160 A2
Pied Bull Ct WC1 240 B3
Pied Bull Yd WC1 240 B3
Piedmont Rd SE18 123 B1
Pield Heath Ave UB8 82 C3
Pield Heath House Sch UB8 82 A3
Pield Heath Rd UB8 82 B3
Pier Head E1 118 B5
Pierhead Wharf 37 E1 118 B5
Pier Ho SW3 267 B5
Piermont Pl BR1 188 A1
Piermont Rd SE22 162 B6
Pier Par 3 E16 122 C5
Pierpoint Bldg 4 E14 119 C4
Pier Rd Feltham TW14 150 B6
Newham E16 122 C4
Pierrepoint SE25 205 C6
Pierrepoint Rd W3 110 D6
Pierrepoint Row N1 234 C4
Pierson Ho 12 SE19 183 C6
Pier St E14 120 A2
Pier Terr SW18 136 A1
Pier Way SE18 123 B3
Pigeon Ct E4 36 A4
Pigeon La TW12 173 C6
Piggott Ho 2 E2 96 D5
Pigott St E14 97 C1
Pike Cl Bromley BR1 187 B5
Hillingdon UB10 82 B6
Pike Rd NW7 27 B6
Pike's End HA5 40 B5
Pikestone Cl UB4 85 A3
Pikethorne 1 SE23 162 D2
Pilgrimage St SE1 117 B4 252 C1
Pilgrim Cl SM4 201 D2
Pilgrim Hill SE27 183 A6
Pilgrim Ho SE1 262 D5
Pilgrims Cl Northolt UB5 64 A3
Palmers Green N13 32 B6
Pilgrims Cloisters 10 SE5 139 C5
Pilgrims Ct Enfield EN1 5 B3
Greenwich SE3 143 A4
Pilgrim's La NW3 70 B4
Pilgrims Mews 12 E14 120 B6
Pilgrim's Pl 6 NW3 70 B4
Pilgrim's Rise EN4 14 C6
Pilgrim St EC4 241 C1
Pilgrims Way
5 Newham E6 100 A6
Upper Holloway N19 49 D1
Wembley HA9 44 D1
Pilgrim's Way CR2 221 D3
Pilgrims Way Prim Sch SE15 140 C6
Pilkington Ct 1 NW9 46 A5
Pilkington Rd
Orpington BR6 227 A6
4 Peckham SE15 140 B3
Pillions La UB4 83 B3
Pilot Ind Ctr NW10 89 C3
Pilsden Cl SW19 156 D3
Piltdown Rd WD19 22 D6
Pilton Est The CR0 220 D6
Pilton Pl SE17 262 B2
Pimento Ct W5 109 D3
Pimlico Sta SW1 115 D1 259 C2
PIMLICO 115 C1
Pimlico Rd SW1 115 A1 258 B2
Pimlico Sch SW1 115 C1 259 B1
Pimlico Wlk 1 N1 95 C4
Pinchbeck Rd BR6 227 D2
Pinchin St E1 118 A6
Pincombe Ho SE17 262 C2
Pincott Pl SE4 140 D2
Pincott Rd
8 Bexley DA6 147 C1
Merton SW19 180 A2
Pindar St EC2 95 C2 243 A4
Pindock Mews W9 91 D3
Pine Apple Ct SW1 259 A6
Pine Ave
Stratford New Town E15 76 B3
West Wickham BR4 207 D1
Pine Cl
11 Dartmouth Pk N19 71 C6
London E10 75 D6
Osidge N14 15 C4
3 Penge SE20 184 C2
Stanmore HA7 25 B6
Pine Coombe CR0 222 D4
Pinecrest Gdns BR6 226 D4
Pinecroft
East Wickham DA16 146 A5
Harrow HA3 44 B4
Pinecroft Cres EN5 1 A1
Pine Ct UB5 85 A4
Pinedene 2 SE15 140 B4
Pinefield Cl E14 119 C6
Pine Gdns Ruislip HA4 62 B6
Surbiton KT5 198 C3
Pine Glade BR6 226 B4
Pine Gr
Finsbury Pk N4, N19 72 B6
Totteridge N20 13 C3
Wimbledon SW19 179 B5
Pine Ho Bow E3 97 A6
21 Rotherhithe SE16 118 C4
Pinehurst
Chislehurst BR7 188 D4
Stanmore HA7 25 A5
Pinehurst Ct 6 W11 91 B1
Pinehurst Wlk 4 BR6 211 B1
Pinelands Cl 7 SE3 142 D5
Pine Lo SW15 157 A5
Pinemartin Cl NW2 68 C5
Pine Pl UB4 83 D3

Pine Rd
Brunswick Pk N11 15 A2
Cricklewood NW2 68 D4
Pine Ridge SM5 219 A1
Pines Ct 14 SW19 156 D3
Pines Rd BR1 188 A1
Pine St EC1 94 C3 241 A6
Pines The
Southgate N14 15 C6
South Norwood SE19 182 D4
Sunbury TW16 194 A6
Surbiton KT6 214 A5
Woodford IG8 21 A1
Pine Tree Cl TW5 128 B4
Pine Tree Ho SE14 140 D5
Pine Tree Lo BR2 208 D5
Pine Trees Dr UB10 60 A4
Pineview Ct 5 E4 20 A3
Pine Wlk KT5 198 C3
Pinewood BR7 188 C4
Pine Wood TW16 172 A2
Pinewood Ave
Hillingdon UB8 82 B1
Pinner HA5 23 D4
Sidcup DA15 167 C3
Pinewood Cl
Crofton BR6 211 B1
Croydon CR0 223 A5
Pinner HA5 23 D4
South Oxhey HA6 22 B5
Pinewood Ct
Clapham Pk SW4 159 D5
Enfield EN2 4 D2
Merton SW19 179 D3
Pinewood Dr BR6 227 C3
Pinewood Gr W5 87 C1
Pinewood Lo WD23 8 B3
Pinewood Pl KT19 215 B4
Pinewood Rd
Bromley BR2 209 A5
Feltham TW13 150 B1
West Heath SE2 146 D6
Pinfold Rd SW16 182 A6
Pinglestone Cl UB7 126 A5
Pinkcoat Cl TW13 150 B1
Pinkerton Ct KT2 176 D1
Pinkerton Pl SW16 181 D6
Pinkham Mans W4 110 C1
Pinkham Way (North Circular Rd) N12 31 A4
Pinkwell Ave UB3 105 B2
Pinkwell La UB3 105 B2
Pinkwell Prim Sch UB3 105 A2
Pinley Gdns RM9 102 B6
Pinnace Ho E14 120 A3
Pinnacle Hill DA7 147 D1
Pinnacle Hill N DA7 147 D1
Pinnacle Ho EC3 253 A5
Pinnacle The
Dagenham RM6 59 A3
7 Kingsland N1 73 B2
Pinnell Rd SE9 143 D1
PINNER 41 A6
Pinner Ct
Paddington NW8 236 C6
Pinner HA5 41 C5
Pinner Gn HA5 22 C1
Pinner Gr HA5 41 A4
PINNER GREEN 22 C1
Pinner Hill HA5 22 B3
Pinner Hill Rd HA5 22 C1
Pinner Ho
30 Camberwell SE5 139 A3
Pinner HA5 41 A6
Pinner Park Ave HA2 24 A1
Pinner Park Fst & Mid Schs HA5 41 D6
Pinner Park Gdns HA2 24 A1
Pinner Rd
Harrow HA1, HA2 42 A3
Northwood HA6 22 A1
Pinner HA2, HA5 41 C5
Pinner Sta HA5 41 A5
Pinner View HA1, HA2 42 A4
PINNERWOOD PARK 22 C3
Pinner Wood Sch HA5 22 C2
Pinn Way HA4 39 C2
Pintail Cl E6 100 A2
Pintail Ct 33 SE8 141 B6
Pintail Rd IG8 37 B3
Pintail Way UB4 84 D2
Pinter Ho 30 SW9 138 A3
Pinto Cl WD6 11 B5
Pinto Way SE3 143 B1
Pioneer Cl W12 90 B1
Pioneers Ind Pk CR0 204 A1
Pioneer St SE15 140 A4
Pioneer Way W12 90 C1
Piper Cl N7 72 B3
Piper Rd KT1 198 C6
Pipers Gdns CR0 207 A2
Pipers Gn NW9 45 A4
Pipers Green La HA8 10 A1
Pipers Ho SE10 120 B1
Piper Way IG1 57 B1
Pipewell Rd SM5 202 C3
Pippenhall SE9 166 D5
Pippin Cl Croydon CR0 207 B1
Dollis Hill NW2 68 B5
Pippin Ct 5 EN4 2 C1
Pippin Ho 17 W10 112 D6
Pippins Ct TW15 170 D4
Piquet Rd SE20 184 C1
Pirbright Cres CR0 224 A2
Pirbright Ho 11 KT2 176 D4
Pirbright Rd SW18 157 C3
Pirie St 6 E16 121 B5
Pitcairn Cl RM7 59 C5
Pitcairn Ct CR4 180 D3
Pitcairne Ct N21 16 B6
Pitcairn Ho 1 E9 74 C1
Pitcairn Rd CR4 180 D3
Pitchford St E15 76 C1
Pitfield Cres SE28 124 A5
Pitfield Ho N5 73 A3
Pitfield St N1 95 C5
Pitfield Way Enfield EN3 6 C4
Tokyngton NW10 67 A2
Pitfold Cl SE12 165 B5
Pitfold Rd SE12 165 A4
Pit Ho NW10 67 B5
Pitlake CR0 220 D6
Pitman Ho
Southgate N21 16 B6
4 St Johns SE8 141 C4
Pitman St SE5 139 A5
Pitmaston Ho 2 SE13 142 A3
Pitsea Pl E1 96 D1
Pitsea St E1 96 D1
Pitshanger Ct 2 W5 87 C3
Pitshanger La W5 87 C3
Pitshanger Manor Mus & Art Gallery* W5 109 D5
Pitt Cres SW19 179 D6
Pitt Ho 4 SW11 136 B1
Pittman Gdns IG1 79 A3
Pitt Rd Harrow HA2 64 A6
Orpington BR6 227 A4
Thornton Heath CR0, CR7 205 A4
Pitt's Head Mews W1 248 B3
Pittsmead Ave BR2 209 A2
Pitt St W8 113 C4 245 B2
Pittville Gdns SE25 206 A6
Pixfield Ct BR2 186 D1
Pixham Ct 5 SW19 179 B5
Pixley St E14 97 B1
Pixton 14 NW9 27 C2
Pixton Way CR2 223 B1
Place Farm Ave BR5, BR6 211 B1
Plains The 7 E4 20 C4
PLAISTOW BR1 187 A4
E13 99 B4
Plaistow Gr
Bromley BR1 187 B3
West Ham E15 98 D6
Plaistow Hospl E13 99 C5
Plaistow La BR1 187 C2
Plaistow Park Rd E13 99 B5
Plaistow Prim Sch E13 99 B5
Plaistow Rd E13, E15 98 D5
Plaistow Sta E13 98 D5
Plane St SE26 162 B1
Plane Tree Cres TW13 150 B1
Planetree Ct W6 112 D2
Plane Tree Ho
Deptford SE8 141 A6
Greenwich SE7 121 D1
Plane Tree Wlk 4
SE19 183 C4
Plantagenet Cl KT19 215 B4
Plantagenet Gdns RM6 58 D2
Plantagenet Ho SE18 122 B3
Plantagenet Pl RM6 58 D2
Plantagenet Rd EN5 2 A1
Plantain Gdns E11 76 B5
Plantain Pl SE1 252 C2
Plantation La EC3 253 A6
Plantation The SE3 143 A3
Plasel Ct E13 99 B6
PLASHET 78 A2
Plashet Gr E6 77 D1
Plashet Rd E13 77 B1
Plashet Sch E6 78 A1
Plassy Rd SE6 163 D4
Platehouse The 3
E14 119 D1
Platina St EC2 242 D6
Platinum Ct RM7 59 D6
Plato Pl 1 SW6 135 B3
Plato Rd SW2 138 A1
Platt Halls (a) 35 NW9 27 D1
Platt Halls (b) 37 NW9 27 D1
Platt Halls (c) 38 NW9 27 D1
Platt's Eyot TW12 173 C1
Platt's La NW3 69 C5
Platts Rd EN3 6 C4
Platt St NW1 232 C4
Plaxdale Ho SE17 263 A3
Plaxtol Cl BR1 187 C2
Plaxtol Rd DA8 147 C5
Plaxton Ct E11 76 D5
Playfair St W6 112 C1
Playfield Cres SE22 161 D6
Playfield Rd HA8 27 A1
Playford Rd
Finsbury Pk N4 72 B6
Finsbury Pk N4 72 C6
Playgreen Way SE6 185 C6
Playground Cl BR3 184 D1
Playhouse Yd EC4 241 C1
Plaza Bsns Ctr EN3 7 B3
Plaza Hts E10 76 A5
Plaza Sh Ctr W1 93 C1 239 B2
Plaza Wlk NW9 45 A6
Pleasance Rd
Putney SW15 156 B6
St Paul's Cray BR5 190 B1
Pleasance The SW15 134 B1
Pleasant Gr CR0 223 B5
Pleasant Pl N1 72 D1
Pleasant Row NW1 231 D5
Pleasant View BR6 227 A3
Pleasant View Pl BR6 227 A3
Pleasant Way HA0 87 C5
Pleasaunce Ct SE9 144 B1
Plender Ct NW1 232 B5
Plender St NW1 93 C6 232 B5
Pleshey Rd N7 71 D4
Plevna Cres N15 51 C3
Plevna Ho 1 N9 18 A1
Plevna Rd Edmonton N9 18 B1
Hampton TW12 173 D2
Plevna St E14 120 A3
Pleydell Ave
Chiswick W6 111 D2
Penge SE19 183 D3
Pleydell Ct EC4 241 B1
Pleydell Gdns SE19 183 D4
Pleydell St EC4 241 B1
Plimsoll Cl E14 97 D1
Plimsoll Rd N4 72 D5
Plough Ct EC3 252 D6
Plough Farm Cl HA4 39 B3
Plough La
Dulwich Village SE22 161 D5
7 Teddington TW11 175 A5
Wallington CR0, SM6 220 A3
Wimbledon SW17, SW19 180 A6
Plough Lane Cl CR0, SM6 220 A3
Ploughmans Cl NW1 232 C6
Ploughmans End TW7 152 B6
Plough Mews 19 SW11 136 B1
Plough Pl EC4 241 B2
Plough Rd
Battersea SW11 136 B1
West Ewell KT19 215 B1
Plough St 16 E1 96 A1
Plough Terr SW11 136 B1
Plough Way SE16 119 A2
Plough Yd EC2 243 B5
Plover Ho 4 SW9 138 C5
Plover Way Hayes UB4 84 D2
Rotherhithe SE16 119 A3
Plowman Cl N18 33 B5
Plowman Ho SW19 156 D2
Plowman Way RM8 58 C1
Plumbers Row E1 96 A1
Plumbridge St 7
SE10 142 A4
Plum Cl TW14 150 A3
Plumcroft Prim Sch
SE18 145 A6
Plume Ho SE10 141 D6
Plum Garth TW8 109 D2
Plum La SE18 145 A5
Plummer Ct SE13 163 D5
Plummer La CR4 180 D1
Plummer Rd SW4 159 D4
Plumpton Cl UB5 63 C2
Plumpton Ct SE23 163 A4
Plumpton Lo E5 74 D5
Plumpton Way SM5 218 C5
PLUMSTEAD 123 C2
PLUMSTEAD COMMON 145 D6
Plumstead Common Rd
SE18 145 A6
Plumstead High St SE18, SE2 123 C2
Plumstead Manor/Negus Sch SE18 145 B6
Plumstead Rd SE18, SE28 123 A2
Plumstead Road Covered Mkt SE18 122 D2
Plumstead Sta SE18 123 B2
Plumtree Cl
Dagenham RM10 81 D2
Wallington SM6 219 D1
Plumtree Ct EC4 241 C2
Plymen Ho KT8 195 C4
Plymouth Ho
10 Barking IG11 80 A1
20 Lewisham SE10 141 D4
Plymouth Rd
Bromley BR1 187 B2
Newham E16 99 A2
Plymouth Wharf E14 120 B2
Plympton Ave NW6 69 B1
Plympton Cl 8 DA17 125 A3
Plympton Pl NW1 237 A5
Plympton Rd NW6 69 B1
Plympton St NW8 237 A5
Plymstock Rd DA16 146 C5
Pocklington Cl NW9 27 C1
Pocklington Ct SW15 156 A3
Pocklington Lo 6
W12 112 A3
Pocock Ave UB7 104 B3
Pocock St SE1 116 D4 251 D2
Podmore Rd SW18 136 A1
Poets Cnr* SW1 260 A6
Poet's Rd N5 73 B3
Poets Way HA1 42 C5
Pointalls Cl N3 30 A1
Point Cl SE10 142 A4
Pointer Cl SE28 102 D1
Pointer Sch The SE3 143 A5
Pointers Cl E14 119 D1
Point Hill SE10 142 A4
Point Ho SE10 142 A4
Point Pl HA9 66 D1
Point Pleasant SW18 135 C1
Point Terr E7 77 B3
Point The HA4 62 A4
Point Wharf La TW8 132 A5
Poland Ho 3 E15 98 B6
Poland St W1 93 C1 239 B1
Polaris Ct EN4 14 B6
Polebrook Rd SE3 143 C2
Polecroft La SE6 163 B2
Polehamptons The
TW12 174 A2
Pole Hill Rd
Chingford E4 20 A4
Hillingdon UB4 83 A4
Polesden Gdns SW20 178 B1
Polesworth Ho 16 W2 91 C2
Polesworth Rd RM9 80 D1
Polish Inst & Sikorski Mus* SW7 246 D1
Polish Univ Abroad
W6 112 A2
Polish War Meml HA4 62 C2
Pollard Cl Islington N7 72 B4
Newham E16 121 A6
Pollard Ct SM4 202 C4
Pollard Ho Cheam KT4 216 C4
Islington N1 233 C3
Pollard Rd
East Barnet N20 14 C2
Morden SM4 202 B4
Pollard Row E2 96 A4
Pollards Cl IG10 21 C6
Pollards Cres SW16 204 A6
Pollards Hill E SW16 204 B6
Pollards Hill N SW16 204 B6
Pollards Hill S SW16 204 B6
Pollards Hill W SW16 204 B6
Pollard St E2 96 A4
Pollards Wood Rd
SW16 204 A6
Pollard Wlk DA14 190 C4
Pollen St W1 238 D1
Pollitt Dr NW8 92 B3 236 D6
Pollock Ho W10 91 A3
Polperro Cl BR6 211 D3
Polperro Mans 3 NW6 69 C3
Polperro Mews SE11 261 C4
Polsted Rd SE6 163 B4
Polsten Mews 2 EN3 7 C6
Polthorne Gr SE18 123 B2
Polworth Rd SW16 182 A5
Polygon Rd
NW1 93 D5 232 C3
Polygon The
1 Clapham SW4 137 C1
St John's Wood NW8 229 D6
Polytechnic St SE18 122 C2
Pomell Way E1 243 D2
Pomeroy Cl TW1 131 B1
Pomeroy Ct W11 91 A1
Pomeroy Ho 5 E2 96 D5
Pomeroy St SE14 140 C4
Pomfret Rd SE5 138 D2
Pomoja La N19 72 A6
Pomona Ho 10 SE8 119 A2
Pond Cl
Colney Hatch N12 30 C4
Kidbrooke SE3 143 A3
Pond Cottage La BR3, BR4 207 C1
Pond Cotts SE21 161 C3
PONDERS END 18 D6
Ponders End Ind Est
EN3 19 A6
Ponders End Sta EN3 19 A6
Ponder St 5 N7 72 B1
Pond Farm Est E5 74 C5
Pondfield End IG10 21 C4
Pondfield Ho
4 Islington N5 73 A3
West Norwood SE27 183 A5
Pondfield Rd
Dagenham RM10 81 D3
Locksbottom BR6 226 D5
West Wickham BR2 208 C1
Pond Gn HA4 61 C6
Pond Hill Gdns SM3 217 A2
Pond Ho Chelsea SW3 257 A3
Stanmore HA7 25 B4
Pond Mead SE21 161 B5
Pond Path BR7 188 D4
Pond Pl SW3 114 C2 257 A3
Pond Rd
Blackheath Vale SE3 142 D3
Newham E15 98 C5
Pondside Cl UB3 127 B6
Pond Sq N6 49 A1
Pond St NW3 70 C3
Pond Way TW11 175 C4
Pondwood Rise BR6 211 C2
Ponler St E1 96 B1
Ponsard Rd NW10 90 B4
Ponsford St E9 74 C2
Ponsonby Ho 13 E2 96 C5
Ponsonby Pl
SW1 115 D1 259 D2
Ponsonby Rd SW15 156 B4
Ponsonby Terr SW1 259 D2
Pontefract Ct UB5 63 D3
Pontefract Rd BR1 186 D5
Ponton Ho SW2 160 C3
Ponton Rd
SW8 137 D6 269 D5
Pontoon Dock Sta
E16 121 C5
Pont St Mews SW1 257 C5
Pont St SW1 114 D3 257 D5
Pontypool Pl SE1 251 C2
Pool Cl Beckenham BR3 185 C5
East Molesey KT8 195 B4
Pool Ct SE6 163 C2
Poole Cl HA4 61 C6
Poole Court Rd TW5 129 A3
Poole Ct
De Beauvoir Town N1 73 C1
Hounslow TW5 129 A3
Poole Ho SE11 260 D5
Pool End Cl TW17 192 C4
Poole Rd Homerton E9 74 D2
Poole Rd *continued*
West Ewell KT19 215 B2
Pooles Bldgs EC1 241 A5
Pooles Ct IG3 80 A5
Pooles La SW10 266 A3
Pooles Park Prim Sch
N4 72 B6
Pooles Pk N4 72 C6
Poole St N1 95 B6 235 C5
Poole Way UB4 83 C4
Pooley Ho E1 96 D4
Pool Ho NW8 236 D4
Poolmans St SE16 118 D4
Pool Rd
East Molesey KT12, KT8 195 B4
Harrow HA1 42 B2
Poolsford Rd NW9 45 C5
Poonah St E1 96 C1
Pope Cl
East Bedfont TW14 149 D3
Mitcham SW17, SW19 180 B4
Pope Ct 10 KT2 175 D6
Pope Ho
7 Bermondsey SE16 118 B2
3 Camberwell SE5 139 B5
Pope John RC Prim Sch
W12 112 B6
Pope Rd BR2 209 D4
Pope's Ave TW2 152 C2
Popes Ct TW2 152 C2
Popes Dr N3 29 C2
Popes Gr CR0 223 B5
Pope's Gr TW1, TW2 152 D2
Pope's Head Alley EC3 242 D1
Pope's La W5 110 A3
Pope's Rd SW9 138 C2
Pope St SE1 253 B1
Pope Street Ct SE9 166 B3
Popham Cl TW13 151 B1
Popham Ct N16 73 C5
Popham Gdns TW9 132 D2
Popham Rd N1 95 A6 235 A6
Popham St Islington N1 234 D6
Shoreditch N1 95 A6 235 A6
Pop In Bsns Ctr HA9 66 D3
POPLAR 97 C1
Poplar Ave
Mitcham CR4 180 D2
Orpington BR6 226 D6
Southall UB2 107 D3
Yiewsley UB7 104 B6
Poplar Bath St 11 E14 119 D6
Poplar Bsns Pk E14 120 A6
Poplar Cl Hackney E9 75 B3
Pinner HA5 22 D2
Poplar Cres KT19 215 A2
Poplar Ct Chingford E4 35 D4
Northolt UB5 84 C5
4 Streatham SW16 160 B1
18 Twickenham TW1 153 C5
Wimbledon SW19 179 C5
Poplar Farm Cl KT19 215 A2
Poplar Gdns KT3 177 B1
Poplar Gr
Friern Barnet N11 31 A4
Hammersmith W6 112 C4
Kingston u T KT3 199 B6
Wembley HA9 67 A5
Poplar High St E14 119 D6
Poplar Ho Brockley SE4 141 B1
19 Rotherhithe SE16 118 D4
Poplar Mews 4 W12 112 C5
Poplar Mount DA17 125 D2
Poplar Pl Hayes UB3 106 A6
Kensington
W2 113 D6 245 D6
Woolwich SE28 124 C6
Poplar Prim Sch
SW19 201 C6
Poplar Rd
Ashford TW15 171 A5
Cheam SM3 201 B1
Herne Hill SE24 139 A1
Merton SW19 179 C1
Poplar Rd S SW19 201 C6
Poplars Cl HA4 39 C1
Poplars Ho 14 E17 53 D6
Poplars Rd E17 53 D3
Poplar Sta E14 119 D6
Poplars The
East Barnet N14 15 B6
Kentish Town NW5 71 C3
Poplar View HA9 65 D6
Poplar Way
Feltham TW13 150 B1
Ilford IG6 57 A5
Poplar Wlk
Croydon CR0 205 A1
Herne Hill SE24 139 A1
Poppins Ct EC4 241 C1
Poppleton Rd E11 54 C3
Poppy Cl
Belvedere DA17 125 D4
Hackbridge SM6 203 A1
Northolt UB5 63 B2
Poppy Ct HA3 42 C6
Poppy La CR0 206 C1
Porchester Ct W2 91 D1
Porchester Gate W2 246 A5
Porchester Gdn Mews
W2 91 D1
Porchester Gdns
W2 113 D6 245 D6
Porchester Ho 3 E1 96 B1
Porchester Mead BR3 185 D4
Porchester Mews W2 91 D1
Porchester Pl W2 237 B1
Porchester Rd
Kensington W2 91 D1
Porchester Rd *continued*
Kingston u T KT1 176 D1
Porchester Sq W2 91 D1
Porchester Terr
W2 114 A6 246 A6
Porchester Terr N W2 91 D1
Porch Way N20 14 D1
Porcupine Cl SE9 166 A2
Porden Rd SW2 138 B1
Porland Ct SE1 262 C6
Porlock Ave HA1, HA2 42 A1
Porlock Ho 5 SE26 162 A1
Porlock Rd EN1 17 D4
Porlock St SE1 117 B4 252 D2
Porrington Cl BR7 188 C2
Porson Ct SE13 141 D2
Portal Cl Hillingdon UB10 60 B1
Ruislip HA4 62 B4
West Norwood SE27 160 C1
Portal Way W3 89 B2
Portbury Cl 17 SE15 140 A4
Portchester Cl SE24 139 B1
Port Cres E13 99 B3
Portcullis Lodge Rd EN1 5 B2
Porte 10 NW9 27 D2
Portelet Ct 1 N1 95 C6
Portelet Rd E1 96 D4
Porten Hos W14 254 A5
Porten Rd W14 254 A5
Porter Rd E6 100 B1
Porters Ave RM8, RM9 80 C3
Porter Sq N19 50 A1
Porter St
Borough The
SE1 117 A5 252 B4
Marylebone W1 237 D4
Porters & Walters Almshouses N22 32 B3
Porters Way UB7 104 B4
Porteus Rd W2 236 B4
Portfleet Pl 34 N1 95 C6
Portgate Cl W9 91 B3
Porthallow Cl BR6 227 D4
Porthcawe Rd SE26 185 B6
Porthkerry Ave DA16 146 A1
Port Ho 6 SW11 136 A2
Port House The 6
E14 119 D1
Portia Ct 12 IG11 80 A1
Portia Way E3 97 B3
Porticos The SW3 266 C5
Portinscale Rd SW15 157 B6
Portishead Ho 28 W2 91 C2
Portland Ave
Blackfen DA15 168 A5
New Malden KT3 199 D2
Stamford Hill N16 51 D2
Portland Cl
Dagenham RM6 59 A4
New Malden KT4 200 B2
Portland Commercial Est
IG11 102 C5
Portland Cotts
Feltham TW13 173 A5
Wallington CR0 203 D2
Portland Cres
1 Chislehurst SE9 166 A2
Feltham TW13 171 B6
Southall UB6 86 A2
Stanmore HA7 25 D1
Portland Cres W HA7 43 D6
Portland Ct
7 De Beauvoir Town N1 73 C1
1 Deptford SE14 141 A6
1 Sutton SM2 217 D2
Portland Dr EN2 5 C5
Portland Gdns
Harringay N4 50 D3
Ilford RM6 58 D4
Portland Gr
SW8 138 B4 270 C2
Portland Ho 19 SW2 160 C3
Portland Hospl for Women & Children The W1 238 D5
Portland Mans SE25 206 B4
Portland Mews W1 239 B1
Portland Pl
Croydon SE25 206 A5
Marylebone W1 93 B2 238 D3
Portland Place Sch
W1 93 B2 238 D3
Portland Place Schs
W1 93 B2 238 D4
Portland Rd
Ashford TW15 148 A1
Bromley BR1 187 C5
Chislehurst SE9 166 A2
Croydon SE25 206 B4
Hayes UB4 83 C4
Kingston u T KT1 198 B6
Mitcham CR4 180 C1
Notting Hill
W11 113 A5 244 B4
Notting Hill
W11 113 A6 244 A5
Southall UB2 107 B3
Tottenham N15 51 D5
Portland Rise N4 51 A1
Portland Sq 4 E1 118 B5
Portland St
SE17 117 B1 262 C1
Portland Terr
Edgware HA8 26 C3
Richmond TW9 131 D1
Portland Village W6 112 C3
Portman Ave SW14 133 B2
Portman Cl Bexley DA7 147 A2
Marylebone W1 93 A1 238 A2
Portman Dr IG8 37 D1

Portman Gate NW1 . . . 237 B5
Portman Gdns
Hendon NW9 . . . . 27 B1
Hillingdon UB10 . . . . 60 C1
Portman Hall HA3 . . . . . . 24 B5
Portman Hts 1 NW3 . . . . 69 C5
Portman Lo N21 . . . . 16 D6
Portman Mews S W1 . . 238 A1
Portman Pl E2 . . . . 96 C4
Portman Rd KT1 . . . . 176 B1
Portman Sq W1 . 93 A1 238 A2
Portman St W1 . . 93 A1 238 A1
Portman The NW11 . . . . . 47 C2
Portman Twrs W1 . . . . 237 D2
Portmeadow Wlk SE2 . . 124 D4
Portmeers Cl E17 . . . . 53 C3
Portnall Rd W9 . . . . 91 B4
Portobello Ct Est W11 . . 91 B1
Portobello Ho 6
SW27 . . . . 182 D5
Portobello Mews W11 245 A5
Portobello Rd
W11 . . . . 113 B6 244 D6
Portobello Road Mkt*
W10 . . . . 91 A2
Porton Ct KT6 . . . . 197 C3
Portpool La EC1 . 94 C2 241 A4
Portree Cl N22 . . . . 32 B3
Portree St E14 . . . . 98 B1
Port Royal Pl 3 N16 . . . . 73 C3
Portrush Ct 9 UB1 . . . . . 86 A1
Portsdown HA8 . . . . 26 C5
Portsdown Ave NW11 . . . 47 B3
Portsdown Mews
NW11 . . . . 47 B3
Portsea Hall W2 . . . . . . 237 B1
Portsea Ho 3 SW15 . . . 156 B3
Portsea Mews W2 . . . . . 237 B1
Portsea Pl W2 . . . . 237 B1
Portslade Rd SW8 . . . . . 137 C3
Portsmouth Ave KT7 . . . 197 A2
Portsmouth Rd
Esher KT10 . . . . 212 A5
Putney SW15 . . . . 156 C4
Thames Ditton KT6,
KT7 . . . . 197 C3
Portsmouth St WC2 . . . 240 D1
Portsoken St E1, EC3 . . 253 C6
Portswood Pl SW15 . . . . 155 D5
Portugal Gdns TW2 . . . . 152 A2
Portugal St
WC2 . . . . 94 B1 240 D1
Portway E15 . . . . 98 D6
Portway Gdns SE18 . . . . 143 D5
Portway Prim Sch E13 . . 98 D6
Poseidon Ct
Dagenham IG11 . . . . 102 B4
9 Millwall E14 . . . . 119 C2
Postern Gn EN2 . . . . 4 C2
Postern The EC2 . . . . . . 242 B3
Post La TW2 . . . . 152 B3
Postmasters Lodge
HA5 . . . . 41 A2
Postmill Cl CR0 . . . . 222 D5
Post Office App E7 . . . . . 77 B3
Post Office Way
SW8 . . . . 137 D5 269 C4
Post Rd UB2 . . . . 107 D3
Postway Mews 1 IG1 . . . 78 D5
Potier St SE1 . . . . 262 D5
Potter Cl CR4 . . . . 181 B1
Potteries The EN5 . . . . . . 13 C6
Potterill Ct TW11 . . . . . . 175 B3
Potterne Cl 5 SW19 . . . 156 D4
Potters Cl
5 Camberwell SE15 . . . . 139 C5
Croydon CR0 . . . . 207 A1
Pottersfield EN1 . . . . 5 C1
Potters Fields
SE1 . . . . 117 C5 253 B3
Potters Gr KT3 . . . . 199 A5
Potters Heights Cl HA5 . . 22 B3
Potter's La Barnet EN5 . . . . 1 C1
Streatham SW16 . . . . 181 D4
Potters Lo E14 . . . . 120 A1
Potters Mews 4 WD6 . . . . 9 D5
Potters Rd SW6 . . . . 136 A3
Potter's Rd EN5 . . . . 1 D1
Potter St HA5 . . . . 22 B2
Potter Street Hill HA5 . . . 22 B3
Pottery La
W11 . . . . 113 A5 244 B4
Pottery Rd TW8 . . . . 132 A6
Pottery St SE16 . . . . 118 B4
Pott St E2 . . . . 96 B4
Poulett Gdns TW1 . . . . . 153 A3
Poulett Rd E6 . . . . 100 B5
Poullett Ho SW2 . . . . 160 D3
Poulters Wood BR2 . . . . 225 D3
Poulton Ave SM1 . . . . 218 B5
Poulton Cl E8 . . . . 74 B2
Poultry EC2 . . . . . 95 B1 242 C1
Pound Cl
Long Ditton KT6 . . . . 197 C1
Orpington BR6 . . . . 227 B6
Pound Court Dr BR6 . . . 227 B6
Pound Farm Cl KT10 . . . . 196 B1
Pound Green Ct 4
DA5 . . . . 169 C4
Pound La NW10 . . . . 68 A2
Pound Park Rd SE7 . . . . 121 D2
Pound Pl SE9 . . . . 166 C5
Pound St SM5 . . . . 218 D3
Pountney Rd SW11 . . . . . 137 A2
Poverest Rd BR5 . . . . 211 D4
Povey Ho
Tulse Hill SW2 . . . . 160 C5
Walworth SE17 . . . . 263 A3
Powder Mill La TW2,
TW4 . . . . 151 C3
Powell Cl
Chessington KT9 . . . . 213 D3
Edgware HA8 . . . . 26 B4
Wallington SM6 . . . . 220 A1
Powell Ct Croydon CR2 . . 221 A4
19 Walthamstow E17 . . . . 53 D6
Powell Gdns RM10 . . . . . . 81 C4
Powell Ho 10 SW19 . . . . 179 A4
Powell Rd
Buckhurst Hill IG9 . . . . 21 C4
Hackney E5 . . . . 74 B5
Powell's Wlk W4 . . . . 133 D6
Powell Terr CR4 . . . . 204 A5
Powergate Bsns Pk
NW10 . . . . 89 B4
Power Ho 13 TW9 . . . . . . 132 C4
Power Ho The W4 . . . . . 111 D2
Power Rd W4 . . . . 110 C2
Powerscroft Rd
Lower Clapton E5 . . . . 74 C4
Sidcup DA14 . . . . 190 C4
Powers Ct TW1 . . . . 153 D4
Powis Ct Bushey WD23 . . . . 8 B3
Edgware HA8 . . . . 26 B6
Powis Gdns
Golders Green NW11 . . . . 47 B2
Notting Hill W11 . . . . 91 B1
Powis Ho WC2 . . . . 240 B2
Powis Mews W11 . . . . 91 B1
Powis Pl WC1 . . . 94 A3 240 B5
Powis Rd E3 . . . . 97 D4
Powis Sq W11 . . . . 91 B1
Powis St SE18 . . . . 122 D2
Powis Terr W11 . . . . 91 B1
Powlesland Ct 21 E14 . . . 97 A1
Powle Terr IG1 . . . . 79 B3
Powlett Ho NW1 . . . . 71 B2
Powlett Pl NW1 . . . . 71 B1
Pownall Gdns TW3 . . . . . 129 D1
Pownall Rd Hackney E8 . . 96 A6
Hounslow TW3 . . . . 129 D1
Pownsett Terr IG1 . . . . . . 79 A3
Powrie Ho 4 SW11 . . . . . 136 B3
Powster Rd BR1 . . . . 187 B5
Powys Cl DA7 . . . . 146 D6
Powys Ct N11 . . . . 32 A5
Powys La Bowes Pk N13 . . 32 A5
Palmers Green N14 . . . . . . 32 A6
Poynder Ct 3 N7 . . . . 72 A3
Poynder Lo TW7 . . . . 131 A4
Poynders Ct 9 SW4 . . . 159 C5
Poynders Gdns SW12 . . 159 C4
Poynders Rd SW12,
SW4 . . . . 159 D4
Poynings Rd N19 . . . . 71 C5
Poynings Way N12 . . . . . . 29 C5
Poyntell Cres BR7 . . . . . 189 B2
Poynter Ct 11 UB5 . . . . . 84 D5
Poynter Ho
Paddington NW8 . . . . . . 236 C6
10 Shepherd's Bush
W11 . . . . 112 D5
Poynter Rd EN1 . . . . 18 A6
Poynton Rd N17 . . . . 34 A1
Poyntz Rd SW11 . . . . 136 D3
Poyser St E2 . . . . 96 B5
Praed Mews W2 . . . . . . 236 D2
Praed St W2 . . . . 92 B1 236 D2
Pragel St E13 . . . . 99 C5
Pragnell Rd SE12 . . . . . . 165 B2
Prague Pl SW2 . . . . 160 A6
Prah Rd N4 . . . . 72 C6
Prairie St SW8 . . . . 137 B3
Pratt Mews NW1 . . . . . . 232 A5
Pratt St NW1 . . . . 93 C6 232 A6
Pratt Wlk SE1,
SE11 . . . . 116 B2 260 D4
Prayle Gr NW2 . . . . 46 D1
Preachers Ct EC1 . . . . . 241 D5
Prebend Gdns W4,
W6 . . . . 111 D2
Prebend Mans 4 W4 . . 111 D2
Prebend St N1 . . . 95 A6 235 A6
Precinct Rd UB3 . . . . 106 A6
Precincts The SM4 . . . . . 201 C3
Precinct The
Islington N1 . . . . 235 A5
Islington N5 . . . . 72 D3
Premier Corner NW6 . . . . 91 B5
Premier Ct EN3 . . . . 6 D5
Premier Ho 25 N1 . . . . 72 D1
Premier League Hall of Fame* SE1 . . . . 250 C2
Premier Lo N3 . . . . 29 C2
Premier Park Rd NW10 . . 88 D5
Premier Pk NW10 . . . . 88 D5
Premier Pl 17 E14 . . . . . 119 C6
Prendergast Ho 7
SW4 . . . . 159 D4
Prendergast Rd SE3 . . . 142 C2
Prendergast Sch SE4 . . 141 C1
Prentice Ct 2 SW19 . . . 179 B5
Prentis Rd SW16 . . . . . . 181 D6
Prentiss Ct SE7 . . . . 121 D2
Presburg Rd KT3 . . . . . . 199 C4
Prescelly Pl HA8 . . . . 26 B2
Prescot St E1 . . . 117 D6 253 D6
Prescott Ave BR5 . . . . . . 210 D3
Prescott Ho
Croydon CR0 . . . . 220 C5
13 Kennington SE17 . . . . 138 D6
Prescott Pl
Clapham SW4 . . . . 137 D1
Streatham SW16 . . . . 182 A3
Presentation Mews
SW2 . . . . 160 B3
Preshaw Cres CR4 . . . . . 202 C6
President Dr E1 . . . . 118 B5
President Ho EC1 . . . . . . 234 D1
President St EC1 . . . . . . 235 A2
Prespa Cl N9 . . . . 18 C2
Press Ho NW10 . . . . 67 B5
Press Rd NW10 . . . . 67 B5
Prestage Way 13 E14 . . 120 A6
Prestbury Rd E7 . . . . 77 C1
Prestbury Sq SE9 . . . . . . 188 B6
Prested Rd SW11 . . . . . . 136 C1
PRESTON 44 A1
Preston Ave E4 . . . . 36 B4
Preston Cl
Twickenham TW2 . . . . 152 C1
Walworth SE1 . . . . 263 A4
Preston Ct
5 New Barnet EN5 . . . . . . 2 A1
Northwood Hills HA6 . . . . . 22 A1
Sidcup DA14 . . . . 189 D6
Walton-on-T KT12 . . . . . . 194 C1
Preston Dr Bexley DA7 . . 146 D4
Wanstead E11 . . . . 55 C4
West Ewell KT19 . . . . 215 D2
Preston Gdns Enfield EN3 . 7 A6
Redbridge IG1 . . . . 56 A3
Willesden NW10 . . . . 67 C2
Preston Hill HA3 . . . . 44 B3
Preston Ho
Bermondsey SE1 . . . . . . 263 C6
3 Dagenham RM10 . . . . . 81 C5
Walworth SE1 . . . . 263 A4
1 Woolwich SE18 . . . . . . 122 C2
Preston Manor High Sch
HA9 . . . . 66 B6
Preston Park Prim Sch
HA9 . . . . 43 D1
Preston Pl
Richmond TW10 . . . . 154 A6
Willesden NW2 . . . . 68 A2
Preston Rd
Leytonstone E11 . . . . 54 C3
Littleton TW17 . . . . 192 C4
South Norwood SE19 . . . 182 D4
Wembley HA3, HA9 . . . . . . 66 A6
Wimbledon SW20 . . . . . . 177 D3
Preston Road Sta HA3 . . 44 A1
Prestons Rd BR2 . . . . 225 A6
Preston's Rd E14 . . . . . . 120 A5
Preston Waye HA3 . . . . . . 44 A1
Prestwich Terr SW4 . . . . 159 D6
Prestwick Cl UB2 . . . . . . 107 A1
Prestwick Ct
Southall UB1 . . . . 108 A6
Tottenham N17 . . . . 34 A3
Prestwick Rd WD19 . . . . . 22 D6
Prestwood Ave HA3 . . . . . 43 B5
Prestwood Cl
East Wickham SE18 . . . . . 146 A6
Harrow HA3 . . . . 43 B5
Prestwood Gdns CR0 . . 205 A2
Prestwood Ho 3
SE16 . . . . 118 B3
Prestwood St N1 . . . . . 235 B3
Pretoria Ave E17 . . . . 53 A5
Pretoria Cres E4 . . . . 20 A3
Pretoria Ho 3 HA4 . . . . . 40 C1
Pretoria Rd Chingford E4 . 20 B3
Ilford IG1 . . . . 78 D3
Leytonstone E11 . . . . 54 B1
Newham E16 . . . . 98 D3
Streatham SW16 . . . . 181 C5
Tottenham N17 . . . . 33 D4
Pretoria Rd N N18 . . . . . . 33 D4
Pretty Cnr HA6 . . . . 22 A5
Prevost Rd N11 . . . . 15 A2
Priam Ho 17 E2 . . . . 96 B5
Price Cl Finchley NW7 . . . . 29 A4
Upper Tooting SW17 . . . . 158 D1
Price Ct HA1 . . . . 43 A4
Price Ho N1 . . . . 235 A5
Price Rd CR0 . . . . 220 D3
Prices Ct SW11 . . . . 136 B2
Price's St SE1 . . . . 251 D4
Price's Yd N1 . . . . 233 D5
Price Way TW12 . . . . 173 A4
Prichard Ct
Battersea SW11 . . . . 266 D1
Islington N7 . . . . 72 B3
Pricklers Hill EN5 . . . . 13 D5
Prickley Wood BR2 . . . . 208 D1
Priddy's Yd 4 CR0 . . . . . 221 A6
Prideaux Ho WC1 . . . . . 233 D2
Prideaux Pl Acton W3 . . . 111 B6
St Pancras WC1 . 94 B4 233 D2
Prideaux Rd SW9 . . . . . . 138 A2
Pride Ct N1 . . . . 234 B4
Pridham Rd CR7 . . . . 205 B5
Priestfield Rd SE23 . . . . 163 A1
Priestlands Park Rd
DA15 . . . . 167 D1
Priestley Cl N16 . . . . 51 D2
Priestley Gdns RM6 . . . . . 58 B3
Priestley Ho
2 Camden Town NW5 . . . 71 B2
St Luke's EC1 . . . . 242 B6
3 Wembley HA9 . . . . 67 A5
Priestley Rd CR4 . . . . 181 A1
Priestley Way
Hendon NW2 . . . . 46 A1
Walthamstow E17 . . . . 52 D6
Priestman Point 25 E3 . . 97 D4
Priestmead Fst & Mid Schs HA3 . . . . 43 B6
Priest Park Ave HA2 . . . . 63 C6
Priests Bridge SW14 . . . 133 C2
Priest's Ct EC2 . . . . 242 A2
Prima Rd SW9 . . . . 138 C5
Primrose Ave Enfield EN2 . 5 C4
Ilford RM6 . . . . 58 B2
Primrose Cl 6 Bow E3 . . . 97 C5
Catford SE6 . . . . 186 A5
Finchley N3 . . . . 29 D1
Hackbridge SM6 . . . . 203 B1
Primrose Cl *continued*
Harrow HA2 . . . . 63 B5
Primrose Ct
2 Child's Hill NW2 . . . . . . 69 B5
New Malden KT4 . . . . 200 A2
Primrose Hill NW8 . . . . . 230 C5
11 Streatham SW12 . . . . 159 D4
Primrose Gdns
Hampstead NW3 . . . . 70 C2
Ruislip HA4 . . . . 62 C3
PRIMROSE HILL 70 D1
Primrose Hill EC4 . . . . . . 241 B1
Primrose Hill Ct NW3 . . . 70 D1
Primrose Hill Rd
Primrose Hill NW1,
NW3 . . . . 70 D1
Primrose Hill NW1,
NW3 . . . . 230 C6
Primrose Hill Sch
NW1 . . . . 93 A6 231 B6
Primrose Hill Studios
NW1 . . . . 231 A6
Primrose Ho
7 Peckham SE15 . . . . . . 140 A4
1 Richmond TW9 . . . . . . 132 B4
Primrose La CR0 . . . . 206 D1
Primrose Mans SW11 . . 268 A2
Primrose Mews 9
NW1 . . . . 70 D1
Primrose Pl TW7 . . . . 130 D3
Primrose Rd
Walthamstow E10 . . . . 53 D1
Woodford E18 . . . . 37 B1
Primrose Sq E9 . . . . 96 C6
Primrose St EC2 . 95 C2 243 B4
Primrose Way HA0 . . . . . . 87 D5
Primrose Wlk
Ewell KT17 . . . . 215 D1
6 New Cross Gate
SE14 . . . . 141 A5
Primula St W12 . . . . 90 A1
Prince Albert Ct
Primrose Hill NW8 . . . . . 230 C5
Sunbury TW16 . . . . 171 C3
Prince Albert Rd
NW8 . . . . 92 D6 230 C5
Prince Arthur Ct 18
NW3 . . . . 70 A4
Prince Arthur Mews 17
NW3 . . . . 70 A4
Prince Arthur Rd NW3 . . 70 A3
Prince Charles Dr NW2 . 46 C2
Prince Charles Rd
SE3 . . . . 142 D4
Prince Charles Way
SM6 . . . . 219 B5
Prince Consort Dr
BR7 . . . . 189 B2
Prince Consort Ho
SE1 . . . . 260 B2
Prince Consort Rd
SW7 . . . . 114 B3 256 C6
Princedale Rd
W11 . . . . 113 A5 244 B4
Prince Edward Mans
W2 . . . . 245 B6
Prince Edward Rd E9 . . . 75 B2
Prince George Ave
N14 . . . . 15 D6
Prince George Rd N16 . . 73 C4
Prince George's Ave
SW20 . . . . 178 C1
Prince Georges Rd
SW19 . . . . 180 B2
Prince Henry Rd SE7 . . . 143 D5
Prince Imperial Rd
Chislehurst BR7 . . . . 188 D3
Kidbrooke SE18 . . . . 144 B4
Prince John Rd SE9 . . . . 166 A6
Princelet St E1 . . 95 D2 243 D4
Prince of Orange La 3
SE10 . . . . 142 A5
Prince Of Wales Cl
NW4 . . . . 46 B5
Prince of Wales Dr
SW11 . . . . 137 A4 268 A2
Prince of Wales Mans
Battersea SW11 . . . . 268 B2
Clapham SW4 . . . . 159 B6
Prince of Wales Pas
NW1 . . . . 232 A1
Prince of Wales Prim Sch
EN3 . . . . 7 B6
Prince of Wales Rd
Blackheath Vale SE3 . . . . 142 D4
Camden Town NW5 . . . . . 71 A2
Newham E16 . . . . 99 C1
Prince Of Wales' Rd
SM1 . . . . 218 B6
Prince Of Wales Terr
Chiswick W4 . . . . 111 C1
Kensington W8 . . . . 245 D1
Prince Rd SE25 . . . . 205 C4
Prince Regent E16 . . . . . . 99 C2
Prince Regent Ct 2
SE16 . . . . 119 A5
Prince Regent La E13 . . . 99 C3
Prince Regent Mews
NW1 . . . . 232 A1
Prince Regent Rd
TW3 . . . . 130 A2
Prince Regent Sta
E16 . . . . 121 C6
Prince Rupert Rd SE9 . . 144 B1
Princes Arc SW1 . . . . . . 249 B4
Princes Ave Acton W3 . . 110 C3
Edmonton N13 . . . . 32 C5
Finchley N3 . . . . 29 D2
Muswell Hill N10 . . . . 49 B6
Orpington BR5 . . . . 211 C4
Princes Ave *continued*
Queensbury NW9 . . . . 44 D5
Tolworth KT6 . . . . 214 C6
Wallington SM5 . . . . 218 D1
Woodford IG8 . . . . 37 C6
Wood Green N22 . . . . 31 D2
Prince's Ave UB1 . . . . 85 D1
Princes Cir WC2 . 94 A1 240 A2
Princes Cl Edgware HA8 . . 26 C5
Finsbury Pk N4 . . . . 50 D1
Queensbury NW9 . . . . 44 C5
Sidcup DA14 . . . . 168 D1
Prince's Cl TW11,
TW12 . . . . 174 B6
Princes Coll WC1 . . . . . 240 A2
Princes Court Bsns Ctr 14
E1 . . . . 118 B6
Princes Ct
Brondesbury NW2 . . . . 69 A3
Hampstead NW3 . . . . 70 B4
Kingston u T KT3 . . . . 199 D6
Stepney E1 . . . . 118 B6
Wembley HA9 . . . . 66 A3
Prince's Ct SE16 . . . . 119 B3
Princes Dr HA1 . . . . 42 C6
Princes Gate
SW7 . . . . 114 B4 246 D1
Prince's Gate
SW7 . . . . 114 C4 247 A1
Princes Gate Ct SW7 . . 246 D1
Princes Gate Mews
SW7 . . . . 114 B3 256 D6
Princes Gdns Acton W3 . . 88 C2
Brompton SW7 114 B3 256 D6
Ealing W5 . . . . 87 C3
Princes Ho W11 . . . . . . 245 A5
Princes La N10 . . . . 49 B6
Princes Mews TW3 . . . . 129 C1
Prince's Mews
1 Hammersmith W6 . . . 112 B1
Kensington W2 113 D6 245 C6
Princes Par NW11 . . . . . . 47 A3
Princes Park Ave
Hayes UB3 . . . . 105 B6
Temple Fortune NW11 . . . 47 A4
Princes Park Circ
UB3 . . . . 105 B6
Princes Park Cl UB3 . . . 105 B6
Princes Park La UB3 . . . 105 B6
Princes Park Par UB3 . . 105 B6
Princes Pl
Notting Hill
W11 . . . . 113 A5 244 A4
St James SW1 . . . . 249 B4
Prince's Plain BR2 . . . . . 210 A1
Princes Plain Prim Sch
BR2 . . . . 210 A2
Princes Rd
Ashford TW15 . . . . 170 B5
Buckhurst Hill IG9 . . . . 21 C2
Ealing W13 . . . . 109 B5
Edmonton N18 . . . . 34 C6
Feltham TW13 . . . . 149 D1
Ilford IG6 . . . . 57 B5
Kew TW9 . . . . 132 B4
Kingston u T KT2 . . . . 176 C3
Penge SE20 . . . . 184 D4
Richmond TW10 . . . . 154 B6
Prince's Rd
Mortlake SW14 . . . . 133 B2
Teddington TW11,
TW12 . . . . 174 B6
Wimbledon SW19 . . . . . . 179 C4
Princes Rise SE13 . . . . . . 142 A3
Princes Riverside Rd 7
SE16 . . . . 118 D5
Princessa Ct EN2 . . . . 17 B6
Princess Alexandra School of Nursing The E1 . . . . . 96 B2
Princess Alice Ho 1
W10 . . . . 90 C3
Princess Alice Way
SE28 . . . . 123 B4
Princess Ave HA9 . . . . 66 A6
Princess Beatrice Ho
SW10 . . . . 255 C1
Princess Cl SE28 . . . . 102 D1
Princess Cres N4 . . . . 72 D6
Princess Ct
Catford BR1 . . . . 186 C4
3 Croydon CR0 . . . . 221 D6
Hampstead NW6 . . . . 69 D1
Hounslow TW4 . . . . 128 C2
Kensington W2 . . . . 245 D6
Marylebone W1 . . . . 237 C3
11 Wimbledon SW19 . . . 178 D3
Princess Frederica CE Prim Sch NW10 . . . . 90 C5
Princess Grace Hospl The
W1 . . . . 93 A3 238 A5
Princess La HA4 . . . . 39 C1
Princess Louise Cl W2 236 D4
Princess Louise Hospl
W10 . . . . 90 C2
Princess Mary Ho
SW1 . . . . 259 D3
Princess May Prim Sch
N16 . . . . 73 D4
Princess May Rd N16 . . . 73 C4
Princess Mews
Hampstead NW3 . . . . 70 B2
Kingston u T KT1 . . . . 198 B6
Princess Par
Dagenham RM10 . . . . 103 C5
Locksbottom BR6 . . . . 226 C5
Princess Park Manor
N11 . . . . 31 A5
Prince's Sq
W2 . . . . 113 D6 245 C6
Princess Rd
Camden Town
NW1 . . . . 93 A6 231 B6
Paddington NW6 . . . . 91 C5
Thornton Heath CR0 . . . . 205 A3
Princess Royal University Hospl BR6 . . . . 226 C5
Princess St Bexley DA7 . . 147 B2
Newington SE1 . . . . 261 D5
Princes St
Bexleyheath DA7 . . . . 147 B1
Marylebone W1 . . . . 238 D1
Sutton SM1 . . . . 218 B4
Tottenham N17 . . . . 33 C4
Prince's St
City of London
EC2 . . . . 95 B1 242 C1
Richmond TW10, TW9 . . . 154 A6
Prince St SE8 . . . . 141 B6
Prince's Terr E13 . . . . 99 B6
Princes Way Acton W3 . . 110 C3
Buckhurst Hill IG9 . . . . 21 C2
Coney Hall BR4 . . . . 224 D5
Croydon CR0 . . . . 220 B3
Putney SW15, SW19 . . . . 157 A3
Ruislip HA4 . . . . 63 A4
Princes Yd W11 . . . . 244 B3
Princethorpe Ho W2 . . . . 91 D2
Princethorpe Rd SE26 . . 184 D6
Princeton Ct SW15 . . . . 134 D2
Princeton Mans WC1 . . 240 C3
Princeton Mews 3
KT2 . . . . 176 C2
Princeton St
WC1 . . . . 94 B2 240 C4
Prince William Ct
TW15 . . . . 170 B5
Principal Cl N14 . . . . 15 C3
Principal Sq E9 . . . . 74 D3
Pringle Gdns SW16 . . . . 181 C6
Pringle Ho N21 . . . . 16 B6
Printers Mews E3 . . . . 97 A6
Printer St EC4 . . . . 241 B2
Printinghouse La UB3 . . 105 C4
Printing House Yd 16
E2 . . . . 95 C4
Printon Ho 16 E3 . . . . 97 B2
Print Village Ind Est
SE15 . . . . 139 D3
Priolo Rd SE7 . . . . 121 C1
Prior Ave SM2, SM5 . . . . 218 C1
Prior Bolton St N1 . . . . . . 72 D2
Prioress Ho 2 E3 . . . . 97 D4
Prioress Rd SE27 . . . . . . 160 D1
Prioress St SE1 . . . . 262 D5
Prior Rd IG1 . . . . 78 C5
Priors Croft E17 . . . . 35 B1
Priors Field UB5 . . . . 63 A2
Priors Gdns HA4 . . . . 62 C3
Priors Lo 4 TW10 . . . . . 154 A5
Priors Mead EN1 . . . . 5 C4
Prior St SE10 . . . . 142 A5
Priors Wood KT10 . . . . . 212 D6
Prior Weston Prim Sch
Broadgate EC1 . . 95 B3 242 C6
St Luke's EC1 . . . . 95 A3 242 B5
Priory Ave
Bedford Pk W4 . . . . 111 C3
Cheam SM3 . . . . 216 D4
Chingford E4 . . . . 19 C1
Hornsey N8 . . . . 49 D5
Petts Wood BR5 . . . . 211 B3
Walthamstow E17 . . . . 53 C4
Wembley HA0 . . . . 64 D4
Priory CE Prim Sch
SW19 . . . . 179 D5
Priory Cl Ashford TW16 . . 172 A3
Barnet N20 . . . . 13 B4
Beckenham BR3 . . . . 207 A6
Chingford Green E4 . . . . . . 19 B1
Chislehurst BR7 . . . . 188 B2
East Barnet N14 . . . . 15 B6
Finchley N3 . . . . 29 B2
Hampton TW12 . . . . 173 B2
Hayes UB3 . . . . 106 B6
3 Merton SW19 . . . . 179 D2
Ruislip HA4 . . . . 39 D1
Stanmore HA7 . . . . 8 D1
Wembley HA0 . . . . 64 D4
Woodford E18 . . . . 37 A2
Priory Cres
Cheam SM3 . . . . 216 D4
South Norwood SE19 . . . 183 A3
Wembley HA0 . . . . 65 A5
Priory Ct Bushey WD23 . . . . 8 A3
Cheam SM3 . . . . 217 A4
City of London EC4 . . . . . 241 D1
Hampton TW12 . . . . 173 C3
Highgate N6 . . . . 49 B3
Homerton E9 . . . . 74 D3
Hounslow TW3 . . . . 129 D2
Ilford RM6 . . . . 58 B3
Newham E6 . . . . 99 D6
Nunhead SE15 . . . . 140 C1
Roehampton SW15 . . . . . . 133 D1
South Lambeth
SW8 . . . . 137 D4 269 D2
Walthamstow E17 . . . . 35 B1
4 Wembley HA0 . . . . 88 A5
Priory Dr Stanmore HA7 . . . 8 D1
West Heath SE2 . . . . 124 D1
Priory Field Dr HA8 . . . . . . 26 D6
Priory Gdns
Ashford TW15 . . . . 171 B5
Barnes SW13 . . . . 133 D2
6 Chiswick W4 . . . . 111 C2
Ealing W5 . . . . 88 A4

Priory Gdns *continued*
Hampton TW12 173 B2
Highgate N6 49 B3
South Norwood SE25 205 D5
Wembley HA0 65 A4
Priory Gn N1 233 C4
Priory Gr Barnet EN5 13 C6
South Lambeth SW8 138 A4 270 A1
Priory Grange N2 48 D6
Priory Hill HA0 65 A4
Priory Ho
3 Charlton SE7 143 C6
Clerkenwell EC1 241 C6
Pimlico SW1 259 C2
Spitalfields E1 243 C4
Priory Hospl Hayes Grove The BR2 225 A6
Priory Hospl The SW15 133 D1
Priory House Ct SE6 163 D3
Priory Htss N1 233 D4
Priory La
East Molesey KT8 195 D5
Roehampton SW15 155 D6
Priory Leas SE9 166 A3
Priory Lo
7 Brentford W4 110 C1
Coney Hall BR4 224 C5
Ealing W5 87 C1
Priory Mans
17 Maitland Pk NW3 70 D2
South Kensington SW10 256 B1
Priory Park Rd
Kilburn NW6 91 B6
Wembley HA0 65 A4
Priory Pk SE3 142 D2
Priory Rd Barking IG11 79 B1
Bedford Pk W4 111 B3
Cheam SM3 216 D4
Chessington KT9 214 A5
Hampstead NW6 69 D1
Hampton TW12 173 C3
Hornsey N8 49 D5
Hounslow TW3 152 A6
Mitcham SW19 180 B3
Newham E6 99 D5
Richmond TW9 132 C5
Thornton Heath CR0 204 C2
Priory Ret Pk SW19 180 B3
Priory Sch SE25 205 D5
Priory St 16 E3 97 D4
Priory Terr NW6 91 D6
Priory The
Croydon CR0 220 C5
Hornsey N8 49 D5
21 Kingston u T KT6 198 A4
Lambeth SE1 251 C1
Lewisham SE3 142 D1
Priory View WD23 8 C4
Priory Villas N11 30 D5
Priory Way
Harmondsworth UB7 126 A6
Harrow HA2 41 D5
Southall UB2 106 D3
Priory Wlk
South Kensington SW10 114 A1 256 B1
Sunbury TW16 172 A3
Priscilla Cl N15 51 A4
Priscilla Ho 8 TW16 171 D3
Pritchard Ho 38 E2 96 A5
Pritchard's Rd E2 96 A5
Pritchett Cl 13 EN3 7 C6
Priter Rd SE16 118 A3
Priter Road Hostel 14 SE16 118 A3
Private Rd EN1 17 C6
Probert Rd SW2 160 C6
Probyn Ho SW1 259 D4
Probyn Rd SW2 160 D2
Procter Ho 12 SE5 139 B5
Procter St WC1 94 B2 240 C3
Proctor Cl CR4 181 A2
Proctor Ho 5 SE1 118 A1
Proctors Cl TW14 150 A3
Prodger 8 NW9 27 D2
Progress Bsns Pk CR9 220 B6
Progress Way
Croydon CR0 220 B6
Enfield EN1 18 A6
Wood Green N22 32 C2
Prologis Pk
Hounslow TW4 128 C1
Wallington CR0 203 D2
Prome Ho 3 N16 73 B4
Promenade Approach Rd W4 133 C5
Promenade Mans HA8 26 C5
Promenade The W4 133 C4
Pronto Trad Est UB4 83 C2
Prospect Cl
Belvedere DA17 125 C2
Forest Hill SE26 184 B6
Hounslow TW5 129 B4
Ruislip HA4 40 D2
Prospect Cotts SW18 135 C1
Prospect Cres TW2 152 A5
Prospect Hill E17 53 D5
Prospect Ho
1 Dalston E8 73 D2
Islington N1 234 A3
3 Mitcham SW19 180 B2
Newington SE1 261 D5
14 North Kensington W10 90 D1
9 Walthamstow E17 54 A6
Prospect House Sch SW15 156 D4
Prospect Pl
Bromley BR2 209 B6
5 Child's Hill NW2 69 B5
2 Chiswick W4 111 B1
6 Deptford SE8 141 B6
East Finchley N2 48 B5
12 Hampstead NW3 70 A4
7 Lower Holloway N7 72 A4
Tottenham N17 33 C3
Wapping E1 118 C5
Wimbledon SW20 178 B3
Prospect Quay SW18 135 C1
Prospect Rd Barnet EN5 1 D1
Child's Hill NW2 69 C5
Kingston u T KT6 197 C3
Woodford IG8 37 C5
Prospect Ring N2 48 B6
Prospect St SE16 118 B4
Prospect Vale SE7, SE18 122 A2
Prospect Wharf E1 118 C6
Prospero Ho 7 DA17 125 C1
Prospero Rd N19 49 D1
Protea Cl E16 98 D3
Protheroe Ho 11 N17 51 D6
Prothero Gdns NW4 46 B4
Prothero Ho 15 NW10 67 B1
Prothero Rd SW6 135 B5 264 C4
Proud Ho 16 E1 96 B1
Prout Gr NW10 67 D4
Prout Rd E5 74 B5
Provence St N1 235 A4
Providence 1 SE16 118 A4
Providence Ave HA2 41 C1
Providence Cl E9 96 D6
Providence Ct
Harlington UB3 127 B5
Islington N1 234 C5
Mayfair W1 248 B6
Providence La UB3 127 B5
Providence Pl N1 234 C5
Providence Rd UB7 104 B5
Providence Row N1 233 C3
Providence Row Cl 30 E1 96 B4
Providence Sq 36 SE1 118 A4
Providence Yd 1 E2 96 A4
Provident Ind Est UB3 106 A4
Provincial Terr 2 SE20 184 D3
Provost Ct NW3 70 D2
Provost Rd NW3 70 D1
Provost St N1 95 B4 235 C2
Prowse Ave WD23 8 A2
Prowse Pl NW1 71 C1
Prudence La BR6 226 C4
Pruden Cl N14 15 C2
Prudent Pas EC2 242 B1
Prusom's Island 8 E1 118 C5
Prusom St E1 118 B5
Pryors The NW3 70 B5
Public Record Office TW9 132 D5
Puccinia Ct TW19 148 A3
Pudding La EC3 252 D6
Pudding Mill La E15 97 D6
Pudding Mill Lane Sta E15 97 D6
Puddle Dock EC4 116 D6 251 D6
Puffin Cl Barking IG11 102 B4
Beckenham BR3 206 D4
Puffin Ct 9 W13 86 D3
Puffin Terr IG5 56 C6
Puget Ct N12 30 A5
Pugin Ct N1 72 C1
Pulborough Rd SW18 157 B4
Pulborough Way TW4 128 C1
Pulford Rd N15 51 B3
Pulham Ave N2 48 B5
Pulham Ho SW8 270 C3
Puller Rd EN5 1 A3
Pulleyns Ave E6 100 A4
Pullman Ct SW2 160 B3
Pullman Gdns SW15 156 C5
Pullman Mews SE12 165 B1
Pullman Pl SE9 166 A6
Pulross Rd SW9 138 B2
Pulteney Cl
3 Isleworth TW7 131 A2
20 Old Ford E3 97 B6
Pulteney Gdns 9 E18 55 B6
Pulteney Rd E18 55 B6
Pulteney Terr N1 94 B6 233 D6
Pulton Ho SE4 141 A1
Pulton Pl SW6 135 C5 265 A3
Puma Ct E1 243 C4
Puma Trade Pk CR4 202 B5
Pump Alley 8 TW8 131 D5
Pump Cl UB5 85 C5
Pump Ct EC4 241 A1
Pump House Cl
Bromley BR2 186 D1
Rotherhithe SE16 118 C4
Pumphouse Educational Mus The★ SE16 119 A5
Pumping Ho 3 E14 120 B6
Pumping Station Rd W4 133 C6
Pump La Deptford SE14 140 C5
Hayes UB3 106 A4
Pump Pail N CR0 221 A5
Pump Pail S CR0 221 A5
Punchard Cres EN3 7 D5
Punderson's Gdns E2 96 B4
Puran Ho E13 99 C5
Purbeck Ave KT3 199 D3
Purbeck Ct 2 N20 14 C2
Purbeck Dr NW2 68 D6
Purbeck Ho SW8 270 C3
Purbrook Est SE1 253 B1
Purbrook Ho 2 SW15 156 B3
Purbrook St SE1 263 B6
Purcell Cres SW6 135 A5 264 A4
Purcell Ho
Chelsea SW10 266 C5
Isleworth TW2 152 B5
Southall UB1 85 C1
Purcell Mews 2 NW10 67 C1
Purcell Rd UB6 85 D2
Purcells Ave HA8 26 C5
Purcell St N1 95 C5
Purchese St NW1 93 D5 232 D3
Purday Ho 4 W10 91 B4
Purdey Ct 3 KT4 200 A1
Purdon Ho 11 SE15 140 A4
Purdy St E3 97 D3
Purkis Cl UB3 105 A6
Purland Cl RM8 59 B1
Purland Rd SE28, SE18 123 D4
Purley Ave NW2 69 A6
Purley Oaks Prim Sch CR2 221 B1
Purley Pl N1 72 D1
Purley Rd Edmonton N9 17 C1
South Croydon CR2 221 B1
Purley View Terr CR2 221 B1
Purley Way
Croydon CR0, CR9 220 C3
Thornton Heath CR0 204 B1
Purley Way Cres CR0 204 B2
Purneys Rd SE9 143 D1
Purrett Rd SE18 123 D1
Purser Ho 3 SW2 160 C5
Pursers Cross Rd SW6 135 B4 264 D2
Pursewardens Cl W13 109 C5
Pursley Rd NW7 28 B3
Purves Rd NW10 90 C5
Purvis Ho CR0 205 B2
Pusey Ho 20 E14 97 C1
Puteaux Ho 6 E2 96 D5
PUTNEY 156 C6
Putney Bridge App SW6 135 A2
Putney Bridge Rd SW15 135 B1
Putney Bridge Sta SW6 135 B2
Putney Comm SW15 134 C2
Putney Exchange Shopping Ctr SW15 134 D1
Putney Gdns RM6 58 B4
PUTNEY HEATH 156 C4
Putney Heath SW15 156 C5
Putney Heath La SW15 156 D5
Putney High Sch SW15 156 D6
Putney High St SW15 135 A1
Putney Hill SW15 156 D6
Putney Park Ave SW15 134 A1
Putney Park La SW15 156 B6
Putney Park Sch SW15 134 B1
Putney Pier SW15 135 A2
Putney School of Art & Design SW15 135 A1
Putney Sta SW15 135 A1
PUTNEY VALE 156 A1
Putney Wharf Twr SW15 135 A2
Pycombe Cnr N12 29 B6
Pycroft Way N9 34 A6
Pykewell Lo 8 E8 74 A3
Pylbrook Rd SM1 217 D5
Pylon Trad Est E16 98 B2
Pylon Way CR0 204 A1
Pym Cl EN4 14 B6
Pymers Mead SE21 161 A3
Pymmes Brook Dr EN4 2 C1
Pymmes Brook Ho 3 N10 31 A3
Pymmes Cl
Bowes Pk N13 32 B5
Tottenham N17 34 B2
Pymmes Gdns N N9 17 D1
Pymmes Gdns S N9 17 D1
Pymmes Green Rd N11 15 C1
Pymmes Mews N13 32 A5
Pymmes Rd N13 32 A5
Pynchester Cl UB10 60 C6
Pyne Rd KT6 198 C1
Pynfolds SE16 118 B4
Pynham Cl SE2 124 B3
Pynnacles Cl HA7 25 B5
Pynnersmead SE24 161 A6
Pyramid Ho N12 30 A6
Pyrford Ho 12 SW9 138 D1
Pyrland Rd
Richmond TW10 154 B5
Stoke Newington N5 73 B3
Pyrmont Gr SE27 160 D1
Pyrmont Rd W4 132 C6
Pytchley Cres SE19 183 A4
Pytchley Rd SE22 139 C2

Q

Quadrangle Cl SE1 263 A4
Quadrangle Ho The E15 76 C2
Quadrangle Lo SW19 179 C4
Quadrangle The
Chelsea SW10 266 B2
Fulham SW6 264 A3
Herne Hill SE24 161 A6
3 North Kensington W12 90 C1
Paddington W2 237 A2
Stanmore HA7 25 C3
Walthamstow E17 35 B1
Quadrant Arc W1 249 B5
Quadrant Bsns Ctr NW6 91 A6
Quadrant Cl NW4 46 B4
Quadrant Gr NW5 70 D3
Quadrant Ho E15 98 C4
Quadrant Rd
Richmond TW9 131 D1
Thornton Heath CR7 204 D5
Quadrant The
4 Kensal Green W10 90 D4
Richmond TW9 132 A1
Sutton SM2 218 A2
West Heath DA7 146 D5
Wimbledon SW20 179 A2
Quad Rd HA9 65 D5
Quaggy Wlk SE3 143 A1
Quainton Hall Sch HA1 42 C4
Quainton St NW10 67 B5
Quaker Ct EC1 242 B6
Quaker La UB2 107 C3
Quakers Course NW9 27 D2
Quaker's Pl E7 77 D3
Quaker St E1 95 D3 243 C5
Quakers Wlk N21 17 B5
Quality Ct WC2 241 A2
Quantock Cl UB3 127 B5
Quantock Ct
4 East Barnet N20 14 C2
Greenford UB6 64 C3
Quantock Dr KT4 216 C6
Quantock Gdns NW2 68 D6
Quantock Ho N16 51 D1
Quantock Mews 3 SE15 140 A3
Quarles Park Rd RM6 58 C3
Quarrendon St SW6 135 C3
Quarr Rd SM5 202 C3
Quarry Park Rd SM1 217 B2
Quarry Rd SW18 158 A5
Quarry Rise SM1 217 B2
Quarterdeck The E14 119 C4
Quartermain Ho SM4 202 A4
Quartermile La E10, E15 75 D4
Quayside Ct 6 SE16 118 D5
Quay West Ct TW11 175 B5
Quebec & Crown Wharves E14 97 B1
Quebec Ind Est SE16 119 A3
Quebec Mews W1 237 D1
Quebec Rd Hayes UB4 84 C1
Ilford IG1 57 A2
Quebec Way SE16 119 A4
Quebec Wharf 32 E8 95 C6
Quedgeley Ct 3 SE15 139 D6
Queen Adelaide Ct SE20 184 C4
Queen Adelaide Rd SE20 184 C3
Queen Alexandra Mans WC1 233 A1
Queen Alexandra's Ct SW19 179 B5
Queen Anne Ave BR2 208 D6
Queen Anne Dr KT10 212 C1
Queen Anne Gate DA7 146 D2
Queen Anne Mews W1 238 D3
Queen Anne Rd E9 74 D2
Queen Annes Cl TW2 152 B1
Queen Anne's Gate SW1 115 D4 249 C1
Queen Anne's Gdns
Bedford Pk W4 111 C3
Ealing W5 110 A4
Enfield EN1 17 C5
Mitcham CR4 202 D6
Queen Anne's Gr
Bedford Pk W4 111 C3
Ealing W5 110 A4
Enfield EN1 17 C5
Queen Anne's Pl EN1 17 C5
Queen Anne St W1 93 B2 238 C3
Queen Anne Terr 9 E1 118 B6
Queenborough Gdns
Chislehurst BR7 189 B4
Ilford IG2 56 C5
Queen Caroline St W6 112 C1
Queen Charlotte's & Chelsea Hospl W12 90 A1
Queen Ct WC1 240 B5
Queen Elizabeth Ct
Barnet EN5 1 B1
5 Kingsland N1 73 B2
Queen Elizabeth Gdns SM4 201 C5
Queen Elizabeth Hall & Purcell Room★ SE1 250 D4
Queen Elizabeth Ho SW12 159 A4
Queen Elizabeth Hospl SE18 144 A5
Queen Elizabeth II Con Ctr SW1 249 D1
Queen Elizabeth II Jubilee Sch W9 91 B3
Queen Elizabeth II Pier SE10 120 D5
Queen Elizabeth Rd
Kingston u T KT2 176 B1
Walthamstow E17 53 A6
Queen Elizabeth's Cl N16 73 B6
Queen Elizabeth's Coll 15 SE10 142 A5
Queen Elizabeth's Dr N14 16 A3
Queen Elizabeth's Girls Sch EN5 1 B1
Queen Elizabeth's Hunting Lodge Mus★ E4 20 D4
Queen Elizabeth St SE1 117 D4 253 C2
Queen Elizabeth's Wlk
Stoke Newington N16 73 B6
Wallington SM6 219 D4
Queen Elizabeth Wlk SW13 134 B4
Queenhithe EC4 252 B6
Queen Margaret Flats 22 E2 96 B4
Queen Margarets Ct N1 73 C3
Queen Margaret's Gr N1 73 C3
Queen Mary Ave SM4 200 D4
Queen Mary Cl KT9 214 C5
Queen Mary Ct TW19 148 A3
Queen Mary Rd
Charlton TW17 171 A1
South Norwood SE19 182 D4
Queen Mary's Ave SM5 218 D1
Queen Mary's Gdns★ NW1 231 A1
Queen Mary's Hospl
Hampstead NW3 70 A5
Sidcup DA14 190 A4
Queen Mary's Univ Hospl SW15 156 A5
Queen Mary, Univ of London E1 97 A3
Queen of Denmark Ct SE16 119 B3
Queens Acre SM3 217 A1
Queen St Pl EC4 252 B6
Queens Ave
Feltham TW13 172 C6
Muswell Hill N10 49 B6
Stanmore HA7 25 C1
Whetstone N20 14 B2
Queen's Ave Finchley N3 30 A2
Southall UB1 86 A1
Southgate N21 16 D3
Woodford IG8 37 B5
Queensberry Ho 6 TW9 153 D6
Queensberry Mews W SW7 256 C4
Queensberry Pl
Chelsea SW7 114 B2 256 C4
Plashet E12 78 A3
Queensberry Way SW7 256 C4
Queensborough Ct N3 47 B5
Queensborough Mews W2 246 A6
Queensborough Pas W2 246 A6
Queensborough Terr W2 113 D6 245 D6
Queensbridge Ct 1 E2 95 D5
Queensbridge Inf Sch E8 73 D1
Queensbridge Pk TW7 152 C6
Queensbridge Rd
Dalston E8 73 D1
Shoreditch E2, E8 95 D6
QUEENSBURY 44 B6
Queensbury IG9 21 B3
Queensbury Circ Par HA3 44 A6
Queensbury Ct CR7 183 A1
Queensbury Rd
Kingsbury NW9 45 B2
Wembley HA0 88 B5
Queensbury St N1 73 A1
Queensbury Sta HA7, HA8 44 B6
Queensbury Station Par HA8 44 B6
Queen's CE Prim Sch The TW9 132 C5
Queen's Cir SW11 137 B5 268 C3
Queen's Cl Edgware HA8 26 C5
Wallington SM6 219 B3
Queen's Club Gdns W14 135 A6 264 B6
Queen's Club The W14 113 A1 254 B1
Queen's Coll W1 93 B2 238 C3
Queenscourt HA9 66 A4
Queens Cres TW10 154 B6
Queen's Cres NW5 71 A2
Queenscroft Rd SE9 165 D5
Queens Ct
Battersea SW11 268 C2
Beckenham BR3 185 D3
Camberwell SE5 139 C3
Leyton E10 53 C2
4 Limehouse E14 119 B6
Sidcup DA14 190 A6
Stanmore HA7 25 B1
8 Temple Fortune NW11 47 B4
Walthamstow E17 53 C4
Queen's Ct
Barnes SW13 134 A2
Beckenham BR3 185 C2
Croydon CR2 221 A3
8 Ealing W5 87 C2
Hampstead Garden Suburb NW11 47 C4
Kensington W2 245 D5
1 Kingston u T KT2 176 C3
Leytonstone E11 54 C2
3 Richmond TW10 154 B5
St John's Wood NW8 229 C4
Thornton Heath CR7 204 C4
Queensdale W11 112 D5
Queensdale Cres W11 112 D5
Queensdale Pl W11 244 A3
Queensdale Rd
Notting Hill W11 112 D5
Notting Hill W11 113 A5 244 A3
Queensdale Wlk W11 244 A3
Queensdown Rd E5 74 B4
Queens Dr
Surbiton KT5 198 C3
Walthamstow E10 53 C2
Queen's Dr Acton W3 88 C1
Finsbury Pk N4 72 D6
Thames Ditton KT7 197 A3
Queen's Elm Par SW3 256 D2
Queen's Elm Sq SW3 256 D1
Queensferry Wlk N17 52 B5
Queensfield Ct SM3 216 C4
Queen's Gallery★ SW1 115 B4 248 D1
Queens Gate IG4 56 B5
Queen's Gate SW7 114 A3 256 B5
Queensgate Ct N12 29 D5
Queensgate Gdns SW15 134 B1
Queens Gate Gdns BR7 189 B2
Queen's Gate Gdns SW7 114 A3 256 B5
Queensgate Ho 34 E3 97 B5
Queen's Gate Mews SW7 114 A3 256 B6
Queensgate Pl 10 NW6 69 C1
Queen's Gate Pl SW7 114 A3 256 B5
Queen's Gate Pl Mews SW7 114 A3 256 B5
Queen's Gate Sch SW7 256 C4
Queen's Gate Terr SW7 114 A3 256 B6
Queens Gate Villas E9 75 A1
Queens Gdns NW4 46 C4
Queen's Gdns
Bayswater W2 114 A6 246 A6
Ealing W5 87 C3
Heston TW5 129 A4
Queen's Gr NW8 92 B6 229 D5
Queen's Grove Rd E4 20 B3
Queen's Head Pas EC2 242 A2
Queen's Head St N1 94 D6 234 D5
Queen's Head Yd SE1 252 C3
Queens Ho 1 SE17 139 B6
Queen's Ho TW11 174 D4
Queen's House The★ SE10 142 B6
Queens Keep 10 TW1 153 C5
Queens La
2 Ashford TW15 170 B6
Muswell Hill N10 49 B6
Queensland Ave
Edmonton N18 33 A4
Merton SW19 179 D2
Queensland Cl E17 35 B1
Queensland Ct N10 31 B3
Queensland Ho 2 E16 122 C5
Queensland Rd N7 72 C4
Queens Lo HA7 25 A5
Queens Manor Sch SW6 134 D5
Queens Mans
Hampstead NW6 69 D3
Hendon NW4 46 B4
Queen's Mans
Brook Green W6 112 D2
Muswell Hill N10 49 A6
Queensmead
Ashford TW15 170 B5
St John's Wood NW8 92 B6 229 D6
Queens Mead HA8 26 B4
Queen's Mead Rd BR2 186 D1
Queensmead Sch HA4 62 D4
Queensmere 4 SM1 217 D3
Queensmere Cl SW19 156 D2
Queensmere Ct SW13 134 A6
Queensmere Rd SW19 156 D2
Queens Mews 5 IG9 21 C2
Queen's Mews W2 113 D6 245 C6

Queensmill Rd SW6 134 D5
Queensmill Sch SW6 135 C3
Queen's Mkt E13 99 C6
Queens Par Ealing W5 88 B1
7 Hendon NW4 46 B4
3 Willesden NW2 68 C2
Queen's Par
3 Friern Barnet N11 30 D5
Wood Green N11 32 A3
Queens Parade Cl N11 30 D5
Queens Park Com Sch NW6 90 D6
Queens Park Ct 5 W10 90 D4
Queens Park Gdns TW13 149 D1
Queen's Park Prim Sch W10 91 A3
Queen's Park Sta NW6 91 B5
Queen's Pas BR7 188 D4
Queen's Pl SM4 201 C5
Queen Sq WC1 94 A2 240 B4
Queen's Quay EC4 252 B6
Queens Rd Hayes UB3 83 C1
Morden SM4 201 C5
Twickenham TW1 153 A3
West Drayton UB7 104 B4
Queen's Rd
Barking IG11 79 A2
Beckenham BR3 185 A1
Bowes Pk N11 32 A4
Bromley BR1 187 A1
Buckhurst Hill IG9 21 C2
Chislehurst BR7 188 D4
Ealing W5 88 A1
Edmonton N9 18 B2
Enfield EN1 5 C1
Feltham TW13 150 B3
Finchley N3 30 A2
Hampton TW12 173 D6
Hendon NW4 46 C4
Hounslow TW3 129 D2
Kingston u T KT2 176 C3
Leytonstone E11 54 C2
Mitcham CR4 202 B6
Mortlake SW14 133 B2
New Cross Gate SE14, SE15 140 C4
Newham E13 99 C6
New Malden KT3 199 D4
Richmond KT2, TW10 176 C5
Richmond TW10 154 B5
Southall UB2 107 A4
Teddington TW11 174 D4
Thames Ditton KT7 196 D4
Thornton Heath CR0 205 A3
Wallington SM6 219 B3
Walthamstow E17 53 C3
Welling DA16 146 B3
Wimbledon SW19 179 C4
Queen's Rd W E13 99 B5
Queens Reach KT8 196 C5
Queen's Ride SW13 134 B2
Queen's Rise TW10 154 B5
Queen's Road Sta SE15 140 C4
Queen's Row SE17 139 B6
Queen St
Bexleyheath DA7 147 B2
City of London EC4 117 A6 252 B6
Croydon CR0 221 A4
Mayfair W1 115 B5 248 C4
Tottenham N17 33 C4
Queens Terr
Harrow HA3 24 C1
Newham E13 99 B6
St John's Wood NW8 92 B5 229 C4
Queen's Terr TW7 131 A1
Queens Terr Cotts W7 108 C4
Queensthorpe Rd SE26 184 D6
Queenstown Mews SW8 268 C1
Queenstown Rd SW8 137 B5 268 C4
Queenstown Road Sta SW8 137 B4 268 D2
Queensville Rd SW12, SW4 159 D4
Queens Walk Ho W5 87 C2
Queensway
Coney Hall BR4 224 D4
Croydon CR0 220 B3
Enfield EN3 6 C1
Kensington W2 113 D6 245 D6
Orpington BR5 211 A3
Sunbury TW16 172 B1
Queens Way
Feltham TW13 172 C6
Hendon NW4 46 C4
Queensway Bsns Ctr EN3 6 C1
Queensway Sta W2 113 D6 245 D5
Queens Well Ave N20 30 C6
Queenswell Jun & Inf Schs N20 14 B2
Queens Wlk
Ashford TW15 170 A6
Chingford E4 20 B3
Harrow HA1 42 C5
Ruislip HA4 62 C5
Welsh Harp NW9 67 A6
Queen's Wlk Ealing W5 87 C2
St James SW1 115 C5 249 A3
Queenswood Ave
Chingford E17 36 A2
Hampton TW12 173 D4
Hounslow TW3, TW5 129 B3
Thornton Heath CR7 204 C4
Wallington CR0, SM6 219 D4
Queenswood Ct
7 Clapham Pk SW4 160 A6
11 West Norwood SE27 183 B6
Queenswood Gdns E11 55 B1
Queenswood Pk N3 29 A2
Queenswood Rd
Blackfen DA15 167 D5
Forest Hill SE23 163 A1
Queen's Wood Rd N6 49 B3
Queens Yd E9 75 C2
Queen's Yd W1 239 B5
Queen Victoria Ave HA0 65 D1
Queen Victoria Meml* SW1 249 A2
Queen Victoria St EC4 117 A6 252 A6
Queen Victoria Terr 12 E1 118 B6
Quelch Ho 2 N19 71 D3
Quemerford Rd N7 72 B3
Quendon Ho 9 W10 90 C3
Quenington Ct 5 SE15 139 D6
Quenington Mans SW6 264 C2
Quennel Ho 7 SW12 159 C4
Quentin Pl SE13 142 C2
Quentin Rd SE13 142 C2
Quernmore Cl BR1 187 A4
Quernmore Rd
Plaistow BR1 187 A4
Stroud Green N4 50 C3
Querrin St SW6 136 A3
Quested Ct 27 E8 74 B3
Quex Mews NW6 91 C6
Quex Rd NW6 91 C6
Quick Rd W4 111 C1
Quicks Rd SW19 179 D3
Quick St N1 94 D5 234 D3
Quick Street Mews N1 234 C3
Quickswood NW3 70 C1
Quiet Nook BR2 225 D5
Quill La SW15 134 D1
Quill St Ealing W5 88 A5
Highbury N4 72 C5
Quilp St SE1 252 A2
Quilter St
Bethnal Green E2 96 A4
Plumstead Comm SE18 123 D1
Quilting Ct 23 SE16 118 D4
Quince Ho TW13 150 A3
Quince Rd SE13 141 D3
Quinta Dr EN5 12 C6
Quintin Ave SW20 179 B2
Quintin Cl HA5 40 B4
Quintin Ct W4 133 A5
Quintin Kynaston Sch NW8 92 B6 229 C5
Quintock Ho 2 TW9 132 C4
Quinton Cl
Beckenham BR3 208 A6
Cranford TW5 128 B5
Wallington SM6 219 B4
Quinton Ho SW8 270 A4
Quinton Rd KT7 197 A1
Quinton St SW18 158 A2
Quixley St 1 E14 120 B6
Quorn Rd SE22 139 C2
Quwwat-Ul-Islam Girls Sch E7 77 B2

R

Rabbit Row W8 245 B4
Rabbits Rd E12 78 A4
Rabbs Farm Prim Sch UB7 104 A6
Rabinal Ho EN3 18 D6
Rabournmead Dr UB5 63 A3
Raby Rd KT3 199 B5
Raby St E14 97 A1
Raccoon Way TW4 128 C3
Rachel Cl IG6 57 B6
Rachel Ct SM2 218 B1
Racine 15 SE5 139 C4
Rackham Cl DA16 146 B3
Rackham Mews SW16 181 C4
Racs Flats 9 SE1 118 A2
Racton Rd SW6 135 C6 265 A5
Radbourne Ave W5 109 C2
Radbourne Cl E5 74 D4
Radbourne Cres E17 36 B1
Radbourne Ct HA3 43 B3
Radbourne Rd SW12 159 D3
Radcliff Bldg EC1 241 A4
Radcliffe Ave Enfield EN2 5 A4
Willesden Green NW10 90 A5
Radcliffe Coll
Marylebone W1 93 C1 239 A1
Soho W1 93 D1 239 C2
Radcliffe Gdns SM5 218 C1
Radcliffe Ho 10 SE16 118 B2
Radcliffe Path 5 SW8 137 B3
Radcliffe Rd
Bermondsey SE1 263 B6
Harrow HA3 25 A1
South Croydon CR0 221 D5
Southgate N21 16 D3
Radcliffe Sq SW15 156 D5
Radcliffe Way UB5 84 D4
Radcliff Mews TW12 174 A5
Radcot Point 2 SE23 162 D1
Radcot St SE11 261 B1
Raddington Rd W10 91 A2
Radfield Way DA15 167 B4
Radford Ho
7 Bow Comm E14 97 D2
Islington N7 72 B3
Radford Rd SE13 164 A5
Radford Way IG11 101 D4
Radipole Rd SW6 135 B4 264 C2
Radius Pk TW6 127 D1
Radland Rd E16 99 A1
Radlet Ave SE23 162 B2
Radlett Cl E7 76 D2
Radlett Pl NW8 92 C6 230 A6
Radley Ave IG3 80 A4
Radley Cl TW14 149 D3
Radley Ct
4 Catford BR1 186 A6
25 Rotherhithe SE16 118 D4
Radley Gdns HA3 44 A5
Radley Ho
11 Abbey Wood SE2 124 D4
Marylebone NW1 237 C6
Radley Lo 30 SW19 156 D3
Radley Mews W8 255 B5
Radley Rd N17 33 C1
Radley's La E18 37 A1
Radleys Mead RM10 81 D2
Radley Sq E5 74 C6
Radley Terr 1 E16 98 D2
Radlix Rd E10 53 C1
Radnor Ave
Bexley DA16 168 B6
Harrow HA1 42 C4
Radnor Cl
Chislehurst BR7 189 C4
Mitcham CR4 204 A5
Radnor Cres
Redbridge IG4 56 B4
Woolwich SE18 146 A5
Radnor Ct Ealing W7 86 D1
6 Forest Hill SE23 162 D1
Harrow HA3 24 D2
Radnor Gdns Enfield EN1 5 C4
Twickenham TW1 152 D2
Radnor Gr UB10 82 C5
Radnor Ho
East Molesey KT8 196 B5
Thornton Heath SW16 182 B1
Radnor Lo W2 236 D1
Radnor Mews W2 92 B1 236 D1
Radnor Pl W2 92 C1 237 A1
Radnor Rd Harrow HA1 42 C4
Kensal Rise NW6 91 A6
Peckham SE15 140 A5
Twickenham TW1 152 D2
Radnor St EC1 95 A4 235 B1
Radnor Terr W14 113 B2 254 C4
Radnor Way NW10 88 D3
Radnor Wlk
Chelsea SW3 114 D1 257 C1
Croydon CR0 207 A3
21 Millwall E14 119 C2
Radstock Ave HA3 43 B6
Radstock Cl N11 31 A4
Radstock St SW11 267 A3
Radway Ho 38 W2 91 C2
Radwell Ho SW2 160 C6
Raebarn Ct 6 SW16 160 A1
Raebarn Gdns EN5 12 B6
Raeburn Ave KT5 198 D3
Raeburn Cl
Hampstead Garden Suburb NW11 48 A3
Teddington KT1 175 D3
Raeburn Ho
5 Belmont SM2 217 D1
6 Northolt UB5 84 D5
Raeburn Rd
Edgware HA8 26 C2
Hayes UB4 83 B5
Sidcup DA15 167 C5
Raeburn St SW2 138 A1
Raffles Ct HA8 26 B6
Raffles Ho NW4 46 B5
Rafford Way BR1 209 B6
RAF Mus* NW9 28 A1
Ragged School Mus The* E3 97 A2
Raggleswood BR7 188 C2
Raglan Cl TW4 151 B6
Raglan Ct Brixton SW9 138 C2
Croydon CR0, CR2 220 D3
Lee SE12 165 A6
Wembley HA9 66 C5
Raglan Jun & Inf Schs EN1 17 C4
Raglan Prim Sch BR2 209 D5
Raglan Rd
Belvedere DA17 125 B2
Bromley BR2 209 C5
Enfield EN1 17 D4
Walthamstow E17 54 B4
Woolwich SE18 123 A1
Raglan St NW5 71 B2
Raglan Terr HA2 63 D4
Raglan Way UB5 64 A2
Ragley Cl W3 111 A4
Ragwort Ct 1 SE26 184 B5
Rahere Ho EC1 235 A2
Railey Mews NW5 71 C3
Railshead Rd TW1, TW7 131 B1
Railton Rd SE24 160 D6
Railway App
Bermondsey SE1 252 D4
Harrow HA1, HA3 42 D5
Stroud Green N4 50 C3
11 Twickenham TW1 153 A4
Wallington SM6 219 B3
Railway Ave SE16 118 C4
Railway Cotts
Hammersmith W6 112 C4
Ilford IG6 57 B6
Railway Gr SE14 141 B5
Railway Pl DA17 125 C3
Railway Rd TW11 174 D6
Railway Rise SE22 139 C1
Railway Side SW13 133 C2
Railway St Ilford RM6 58 C2
King's Cross N1 233 B3
Railway Terr
Chingford E17 36 A2
Feltham TW13, TW14 150 A3
Ladywell SE13 163 D6
Rainborough Cl NW10 67 A2
Rainbow Ave E14 119 D1
Rainbow Ct 3 SE14 141 A6
Rainbow Ind Est SW20 178 B1
Rainbow Quay SE16 119 A3
Rainbow Sch The SW17 158 A2
Rainbow St SE5 139 C5
Rainbow Works N15 52 A4
Raine Gdns 4 IG8 37 A6
Raines Ct N16 73 D6
Raine's Foundation Lower Sch E2 96 B5
Raine's Foundation Sch E2 96 C5
Raine St E1 118 B5
Rainford Ho 9 N7 72 B6
Rainham Cl Sidcup SE9 167 C5
Wandsworth SW11 158 C5
Rainham Ho NW1 232 B5
Rainham Rd NW10 90 C4
Rainham Rd N RM10 81 D6
Rainham Rd S RM10 81 D4
Rainhill Way E3 97 C4
Rainsborough Ave SE8 119 A2
Rainsford Cl HA7 25 C5
Rainsford Ct NW10 88 D5
Rainsford Ho 14 SW2 160 B6
Rainsford Rd NW10 88 D5
Rainsford St W2 237 A2
Rainstar Est N18 34 C6
Rainton Rd SE7 121 A1
Rainville Rd W6 134 C6
Raisins Hill HA5 40 C6
Raith Ave N14 15 D1
Raleigh Ave Hayes UB4 84 B2
Wallington SM6 219 D4
Raleigh Cl Hendon NW4 46 C4
Pinner HA5 40 D2
Ruislip HA4 61 D6
Raleigh Ct
Beckenham BR3 185 D2
4 Dulwich SE19 183 D5
Ealing W13 87 B2
7 Hammersmith W12 112 B4
2 Rotherhithe SE16 118 D5
Wallington SM6 219 B2
Raleigh Dr
East Barnet N20 14 C1
Esher KT10 212 B3
Tolworth KT5 199 A1
Raleigh Gdns
Mitcham CR4 202 D6
Tulse Hill SW2 160 B5
Raleigh Ho
30 Clapham SW8 137 D3
Isle of Dogs E14 119 D4
1 Thames Ditton KT7 197 A2
Raleigh Mews
Islington N1 234 D5
6 Orpington BR6 227 D3
Raleigh Rd Enfield EN2 5 B1
Feltham TW13 149 D2
Finchley N10 30 C2
Hornsey N8 50 C5
Penge SE20 184 D3
Richmond TW9 132 B2
Southall UB2 107 A1
Raleigh St N1 94 D6 234 D5
Raleigh Way
Feltham TW13 172 C5
Southgate N14 16 A3
Ralph Ct 8 W2 91 D1
Ralph Perring Ct BR3 207 C5
Ralston St SW3 257 C1
Ramac Ind Est SE7 121 B1
Rama Cl SW16 182 A3
Rama Ct HA1 64 C6
Ramac Way SE7 121 B2
Rama La SE19 183 D3
Ramar Ho 12 E1 96 A2
Rambler Cl SW16 181 C6
Rambler Ct 11 NW9 46 A5
Rame Cl SW17 181 A5
Ramilles Cl SW2 160 A5
Ramillies Ho W1 239 B1
Ramillies Pl W1 93 C1 239 A1
Ramillies Rd
Bedford Pk W4 111 B3
Blackfen DA15 168 B5
Edgware NW7 11 C2
Ramillies St W1 239 A1
Ramney Dr EN3 7 A6
Rampart St E1 96 B1
Ram Pas KT1 175 D1
Rampayne St SW1 259 C2
Rampton Cl E4 19 C1
Ramsay Ho NW8 230 A4
Ramsay Rd Acton W3 111 A4
Leyton E7 76 D4
Ramscroft Cl N9 17 C4
Ramsdale Rd SW17 181 A5
Ramsdean Ho 1 SW15 156 B3
Ramsden Rd
Balham SW12 159 A4
Friern Barnet N11 30 D5
Ramsey Cl
Greenford UB6 64 B3
West Hendon NW9 45 D3
Ramsey Ct
Croydon CR0 220 D6
Hornsey N8 49 D4
Putney SW15 156 C5
6 Upper Holloway N19 71 D6
Ramsey Ho
5 Battersea SW11 136 B1
14 Kennington SW9 138 C5
7 Merton SW19 179 D2
Ramsey Rd CR7 204 B3
Ramsey St E2 96 A3
Ramsey Way N14 15 C4
Ramsfort Ho 4 SE16 118 B2
Ramsgate Cl 10 E16 121 B5
Ramsgate St E8 73 D2
Ramsgill App IG2 57 D5
Ramsgill Dr IG2 57 D5
Rams Gr RM6 59 A5
Ram St SW18 157 D6
Ramulis Dr UB4 84 D3
Ramus Wood Ave BR6 227 C3
Rance Ho 12 SE7 122 A2
Rancliffe Gdns SE9 144 A1
Rancliffe Rd E6 100 A5
Randal Cremer JMI Sch E2 95 D5
Randall 9 NW9 27 D2
Randall Ave NW2 67 D5
Randall Cl SW11 136 C4 267 A2
Randall Ct NW7 28 A3
Randall Pl SE10 142 A5
Randall Rd SE11 116 B2 260 C3
Randall Row SE11 260 C3
Randell's Rd N1 94 A6 233 B6
Randisbourne Gdns SE6 163 D1
Randle Rd TW10 175 C6
Randlesdown Rd SE6 163 D1
Randmore Ct 6 BR3 185 C3
Randolf Ct
Paddington NW6 91 D5
St John's Wood NW8 229 A5
Randolph App E16 99 C1
Randolph Ave W9 92 A4 229 A1
Randolph Cl KT2 177 A5
Randolph Cres W9 92 A3 236 A6
Randolph Ct HA5 23 C3
Randolph Gdns NW6 91 D5
Randolph Gr RM6 58 C4
Randolph Mews W9 92 A3 236 B5
Randolph Rd
Bromley BR2 210 B1
Paddington W9 92 A3 236 B5
Southall UB1 107 B4
Walthamstow E17 53 D4
Randolph St NW1 71 C1
Randon Cl HA2 23 D1
Ranelagh Ave
Barnes SW13 134 A3
Fulham SW6 135 B2
Ranelagh Cl HA8 26 C6
Ranelagh Ct HA8 26 C6
Ranelagh Dr
Edgware HA8 26 C6
Twickenham TW1 153 C6
Ranelagh Gardens Mans SW6 135 A2
Ranelagh Gardens (site of Chelsea Flower Show)* SW1 115 A1 258 B1
Ranelagh Gdns
3 Bedford Pk W6 111 D3
Chiswick W4 133 A5
Fulham SW6 135 B2
Ilford IG1 56 C1
Wanstead E11 55 C4
Ranelagh Gr SW1 115 A1 258 B2
Ranelagh Ho SW3 257 C2
Ranelagh Mans 4 SW6 135 B3
Ranelagh Pl KT3 199 C4
Ranelagh Prim Sch E15 98 C5
Ranelagh Rd
Dagenham NW10 89 D5
Ealing W5 109 D4
Leyton E11 76 C4
Newham E15 98 C5
Pimlico SW1 115 C1 259 B1
Southall UB1 106 D5
Tottenham N17 51 C6
Wallend E6 100 C5
Wembley HA0 65 D2
Wood Green N22 32 B2
Ranfurly Rd SM1 217 C6
Rangdon St EC3 243 C1
Rangefield Prim Sch BR1 186 C5
Rangefield Rd BR1 186 D5
Rangemoor Rd N15 51 D4
Ranger's House (The Wernher Collection)* SE10 142 B4
Ranger's Rd
Buckhurst Hill IG9, IG10 21 A4
Chingford E4 20 D4
Rangers Sq SE10 142 B4
Range Villas TW17 192 A2
Range Way TW17 192 C2
Rangeworth Pl DA15 167 D1
Rangoon Ho 5 N16 73 B4
Rankin Cl NW9 45 C6
Rankine Ho SE1 262 A5
Ranleigh Gdns DA7 147 B5
Ranmere St SW12 159 B3
Ranmoor Cl HA1 42 B5
Ranmoor Gdns HA1 42 C5
Ranmore Ave CR0 221 D5
Ranmore Ct
Kingston u T KT6 197 D4
3 Wimbledon SW20 178 D2
Rann Ho 1 SW14 133 B2
Rannoch Cl HA8 10 D2
Rannoch Ct 9 KT6 198 A4
Rannoch Rd W6 134 D6
Rannock Ave NW9 45 C2
Ransford Ho 16 SE21 183 C6
Ransomes Dock Bsns Ctr SW11 267 B3
Ransomes Mews SW11 267 B4
Ransom Rd 1 SE7 121 C1
Ranston St NW1 237 A4
Ranulf Rd NW2 69 B4
Ranwell Cl 18 E3 97 B6
Ranwell Ho 17 E3 97 B6
Ranworth Rd N9 18 C2
Ranyard Cl KT9 214 B5
Raphael Ct 9 SE16 118 B1
Raphael Dr KT7 196 D2
Raphael St SW7 247 C1
Rapide 15 NW9 27 C2
Rapley Ho 14 E2 96 A4
Rashleigh Ct 8 SW8 137 B2
Rashleigh Ho WC1 233 A1
Rasper Rd N20 14 A2
Rastell Ave SW12 159 D3
RATCLIFF 118 D6
Ratcliffe Cl SE12 165 A4
Ratcliffe Cross St E1 96 D1
Ratcliffe Ho 10 E14 97 A1
Ratcliffe La 16 E14 97 A1
Ratcliffe Orch 9 E1 118 D6
Ratcliff Rd E7 77 C3
Rathbone Ho
5 Canning Town E16 98 D1
Kilburn NW6 91 C6
10 Wimbledon SW19 178 D3
Rathbone Mkt 3 E16 98 D2
Rathbone Pl W1 93 D1 239 C2
Rathbone St
Canning Town E16 98 D1
Fitzrovia W1 93 C2 239 B3
Rathcoole Ave N8 50 B4
Rathcoole Gdns N8 50 B4
Rathfern Prim Sch SE6 163 B3
Rathfern Rd SE6 163 B3
Rathgar Ave W13 109 C5
Rathgar Cl N3 29 B1
Rathgar Rd SW9 138 D2
Rathmell Dr SW4 159 D5
Rathmore Rd SE7 121 B1
Ratier 16 NW9 27 C2
Rattray Ct 3 SE6 164 D2
Rattray Rd SW2 160 C6
Raul Rd SE15 140 A4
Raveley St NW5 71 C4
Raven Cl NW9 27 C1
Ravendale Rd TW16 171 D1
Ravenet Ct
Battersea SW11 268 C1
Clapham SW4 159 B6
Ravenet St SW11 137 B4 268 C1
Ravenfield Rd SW17 158 D1
Ravenhill Rd E13 99 C5
Raven Ho 10 SE16 118 D2
Ravenings Par IG3 58 A1
Ravenna Rd SW15 156 D6
Ravenor Ct UB6 85 D3
Ravenor Park Rd UB6 86 A4
Ravenor Prim Sch UB6 85 C4
Raven Rd E18 37 C1
Raven Row E1 96 B2
Ravensbourne Ave
Bromley BR2, BR3 186 C2
Catford BR2 186 B3
Stanwell TW19 148 A3
Ravensbourne Bsns Ctr BR2 225 D4
Ravensbourne Coll of Design & Communication BR7 188 B5
Ravensbourne Ct SE6 163 C4
Ravensbourne Gdns W13 87 B2
Ravensbourne Ho
10 Catford BR1 186 B5
Paddington NW8 237 A4

Ravensbourne Ho *continued*
3 Twickenham TW1 .... 153 C5
Ravensbourne Mans 9
SE8 .... 141 C6
Ravensbourne Park Cres
SE6 .... 163 B4
Ravensbourne Pk SE6 .. 163 C4
Ravensbourne Pl
SE13 .... 141 D3
Ravensbourne Rd
Bromley BR1, BR2 .... 209 A6
Forest Hill SE23 .... 163 B3
Twickenham TW1 .... 153 C5
Ravensbourne Sch The
BR2 .... 209 B5
Ravensbourne Sta
BR3 .... 186 B3
Ravensbury Ave SM4 .. 202 A4
Ravensbury Ct CR4 .... 202 B5
Ravensbury Gr CR4 .... 202 B5
Ravensbury La CR4 .... 202 B5
Ravensbury Rd
Orpington BR5 .... 211 D5
Wandsworth SW18 .... 157 D2
Ravensbury Terr
SW18 .... 157 D2
Ravenscar NW1 .... 232 A5
Ravenscar Lo 14
SW19 .... 178 D3
Ravenscar Rd
Catford BR1 .... 186 C6
Surbiton KT6 .... 214 B6
Ravens Cl Bromley BR2 .. 186 D1
Enfield EN1 .... 5 C3
Kingston u T KT6 .... 197 D3
Ravenscourt
1 Shacklewell N16 .... 74 A5
Sunbury TW16 .... 171 D2
Ravenscourt Ave W6 .. 112 A2
Ravenscourt Cl HA4 .... 39 A2
Ravenscourt Gdns
W6 .... 112 A2
Ravenscourt Ho 13
W6 .... 112 B2
Ravenscourt Park Mans 1
W6 .... 112 B3
Ravenscourt Park Prep
Sch W6 .... 112 A2
Ravenscourt Park Sta
W6 .... 112 B2
Ravenscourt Pk W6 .... 112 A2
Ravenscourt Pl W6 .... 112 B2
Ravenscourt Rd
Hammersmith W6 .... 112 B2
St Paul's Cray BR5 .... 190 B1
Ravenscourt Sq W6 .... 112 A3
Ravenscourt Theatre Sch
W6 .... 112 B2
Ravenscraig Rd N11 .... 31 C6
Ravenscroft Ave
Golders Green NW11 .... 47 B2
Wembley HA9 .... 44 B2
Ravenscroft Cl 4 E16 ... 99 A2
Ravenscroft Cres SE9 .. 166 B1
Ravenscroft Ct NW11 ... 47 B2
Ravenscroft Pk EN5 .... 1 A1
Ravenscroft Point 26
E9 .... 74 D2
Ravenscroft Prim Sch
E16 .... 99 A3
Ravenscroft Rd
Acton W4 .... 111 A2
Newham E16 .... 99 A2
Penge BR3 .... 184 D1
Ravenscroft Sch a Tech
Coll The N20 .... 13 B4
Ravenscroft St E2 .... 95 D4
Ravensdale Ave N12 .... 30 B6
Ravensdale Commercial
Est N16 .... 52 A3
Ravensdale Gdns
Hounslow TW4 .... 129 A2
South Norwood SE19 ... 183 B3
Ravensdale Mans N8 .... 50 A3
Ravensdale Rd
Hounslow TW4 .... 129 A2
South Tottenham N16 .... 51 D3
Ravensdon St
SE11 .... 116 C1 261 B1
Ravensfield Cl RM9 .... 80 D4
Ravensfield Gdns
KT19 .... 215 C4
Ravenshaw St NW6 .... 69 B3
Ravenshill BR7 .... 188 D2
Ravens Ho KT1 .... 175 D1
Ravenshurst Ave NW4 ... 46 C5
Ravenside KT6 .... 197 D4
Ravenside Cl N18 .... 34 D5
Ravenside Ret Pk N18 .. 34 D5
Ravenslea Rd SW11,
SW12 .... 158 D4
Ravensleigh Gdns
BR1 .... 187 B5
Ravensmead Rd BR2 ... 186 B3
Ravensmede Way W4 .. 111 D2
Ravensroost SE19 .... 183 B2
Ravenstone
SE17 .... 117 C1 263 B1
Ravenstone Prim Sch
SW12 .... 159 A2
Ravenstone Rd
Hornsey N8 .... 50 C6
West Hendon NW9 .... 45 D3
Ravenstone St SW12 ... 159 A3
Ravensview Ct KT6 .... 197 D4
Ravens Way SE3, SE12 .. 165 A6
Ravenswood
Bowes Pk N22 .... 32 B4
Sidcup DA5 .... 169 A3
Ravenswood Ave
Tolworth KT6 .... 214 C6
West Wickham BR4 .... 208 A1
Ravenswood Cres
Harrow HA2 .... 63 B6
West Wickham BR4 .... 208 A1
Ravenswood Gdns
TW7 .... 130 C4
Ravenswood Ind Est 5
E17 .... 54 A5
Ravenswood Pk HA6 .... 22 A4
Ravenswood Rd
Balham SW12 .... 159 B4
Croydon CR0 .... 220 D5
Walthamstow E17 .... 54 A5
Ravens Wood Sch
BR2 .... 225 D5
Ravensworth Ct SW6 .. 265 A3
Ravensworth Rd
Chislehurst SE9 .... 188 B6
College Pk NW10 .... 90 B4
Raven Wharf SE1 .... 253 C2
Ravey St EC2 .... 95 C3 243 A6
Ravine Gr SE18 .... 145 C6
Rav Pinter Cl N16 .... 51 C2
Rawlings Cl
Beckenham BR3 .... 208 A4
3 Orpington BR6 .... 227 D3
Rawlings Cres HA9 .... 66 D5
Rawlings St
SW3 .... 114 D2 257 C4
Rawlins Cl Hendon N3 .... 47 A6
South Croydon CR2 .... 223 B1
Rawlinson Ct NW2 .... 46 C2
Rawlinson Ho SE13 .... 142 B1
Rawlinson Point 8
E16 .... 98 D2
Rawnsley Ave CR4 .... 202 C4
Rawreth Wlk N1 .... 235 B6
Rawson Ct SW11 .... 268 B1
Rawson St
SW11 .... 137 B4 268 C1
Rawsthorne Cl E16 .... 122 B5
Rawstone Wlk 5 E13 .... 99 A5
Rawstorne Pl EC1 .... 234 C2
Rawstorne St
EC1 .... 94 D4 234 C2
Raybell Ct TW7 .... 130 D3
Rayburne Ct
1 Buckhurst Hill IG9 .... 21 C3
West Kensington W14 .. 254 A6
Ray Cl KT9 .... 213 C2
Ray Ct Ealing W13 .... 109 B5
Stanmore HA7 .... 25 B5
Woodford IG8 .... 37 D4
Raydean Rd EN5 .... 13 D6
Raydons Gdns RM9 .... 81 A3
Raydons Rd RM9 .... 81 A3
Raydon St N19 .... 71 B6
Rayfield Cl BR2 .... 210 A3
Rayford Ave SE12 .... 164 D4
Ray Gdns Barking IG11 .. 102 A5
Stanmore HA7 .... 25 B5
Ray Ho
7 North Kensington
W10 .... 90 D1
Shoreditch N1 .... 235 D5
Rayleas Cl SE18 .... 144 D4
Rayleigh Ave TW11 .... 174 C4
Rayleigh Cl N13 .... 17 B1
Rayleigh Ct
2 Kingston u T KT1 .... 176 B1
Tottenham N22 .... 33 A2
Rayleigh Rd
Edmonton N13 .... 17 B1
Merton SW19 .... 179 B2
5 Newham E16 .... 121 B5
Woodford IG8 .... 37 C3
Rayleigh Rise CR2 .... 221 C2
Ray Lodge Prim Sch
IG8 .... 37 D4
Ray Lodge Rd IG8 .... 37 D4
Ray Massey Way 3
E6 .... 100 A6
Raymead Ave CR7 .... 204 C4
Raymede Twr W10 .... 90 D2
Raymere Gdns SE18 .... 145 C5
Raymond Ave
Brentford W13 .... 109 A3
Woodford E18 .... 36 D1
Raymond Bldgs WC1 .. 240 D4
Raymond Cl SE26 .... 184 C5
Raymond Ct N10 .... 31 A3
Raymond Postgate Ct 5
SE28 .... 124 B6
Raymond Rd
Beckenham BR3 .... 207 A5
Ilford IG2 .... 57 B2
Newham E13 .... 99 C6
Wimbledon SW19 .... 179 A4
Raymond Way KT10 .... 213 A2
Raymouth Rd SE16 .... 118 B2
Raynald Ho 15 SW16 .... 160 A1
Rayne Ct
Bermondsey SE1 .... 253 C2
Snaresbrook E18 .... 54 D5
Rayne Ho
1 Balham SW12 .... 159 A5
Paddington W9 .... 91 D3
Rayner Ct 12 W12 .... 112 C4
Rayners Cl HA0 .... 65 D3
Rayners Cres UB5 .... 84 B4
Rayners Gdns UB5 .... 84 B4
Rayners La Harrow HA2 .. 63 D6
Pinner HA5 .... 41 B3
RAYNERS LANE 41 B1
Rayners Lane Sta HA5 .. 41 B2
Rayner's Rd SW15 .... 157 A6
Rayner Twrs E10 .... 53 C2
Raynes Ave E11 .... 55 C2
Raynes Ct NW2 .... 69 A4
Raynesfield SW20 .... 200 C6
RAYNES PARK 200 C6
Raynes Park High Sch
SW20 .... 200 B6
Raynes Park Sta
SW20 .... 178 C1
Raynham W2 .... 237 A2
Raynham Ave N18 .... 34 A5
Raynham Ho 1 E1 .... 96 D3
Raynham Prim Sch
N18 .... 34 A5
Raynham Rd
Edmonton N18 .... 34 A5
Hammersmith W6 .... 112 B2
Raynham Terr N18 .... 34 A5
Raynor Cl UB1 .... 107 B5
Raynor Pl N1 .... 235 B6
Raynton Cl Harrow HA2 .. 41 A2
Hayes UB4 .... 83 D3
Raynton Dr Hayes UB4 ... 83 C5
Hayes UB4 .... 83 D3
Raynton Rd EN3 .... 6 D6
Ray Rd KT8 .... 195 D4
Rays Ave N18 .... 34 C6
Rays Rd Edmonton N18 .... 34 C6
West Wickham BR4 .... 208 A2
Ray St EC1 .... 241 B5
Ray Wlk N7 .... 72 B6
Raywood Cl UB7 .... 127 A5
Reachview Cl 17 NW1 ... 71 C1
Read Cl KT7 .... 197 A2
Read Ct E17 .... 53 D3
Reade Ct 6 W3 .... 111 A3
Reade Wlk 5 NW10 .... 67 C1
Read Ho
Friern Barnet N11 .... 30 D6
4 Kennington SE11 .... 138 C6
Reading Ho
Paddington W2 .... 236 A1
Peckham SE15 .... 140 A6
Reading La E8 .... 74 B2
Reading Rd
Northolt UB5 .... 64 A3
Sutton SM1 .... 218 A3
Reading Way NW7 .... 29 A5
Readman Ct 8 SE20 .... 184 B2
Reads Cl IG1 .... 78 D5
Reapers Cl NW1 .... 232 C6
Reapers Way TW7 .... 152 B6
Reardon Ho 5 E1 .... 118 B5
Reardon Path 31 E1 .... 118 B5
Reardon St E1 .... 118 B5
Reaston St SE14 .... 140 D5
Reay Prim Sch
SW9 .... 138 B5 270 D3
Rebecca Ct
3 Beckenham BR3 .... 185 C2
Sidcup DA14 .... 190 B6
Rebecca Ho 12 N12 .... 29 D6
Reckitt Rd W4 .... 111 C1
Record St SE16 .... 140 C6
Recovery St SW17 .... 180 C5
Recreation Rd
Bromley BR2 .... 186 D1
Forest Hill SE26 .... 184 D6
Southall UB2 .... 107 A2
Recreation Way CR4,
SW16 .... 204 A6
Rector St N1 .... 95 A6 235 A5
Rectory Bsns Ctr 5
DA14 .... 190 B6
Rectory Cl Chingford E4 .. 19 C1
Finchley N3 .... 29 B2
Littleton TW17 .... 192 C6
Long Ditton KT6 .... 197 C1
Sidcup DA14 .... 190 B6
Stanmore HA7 .... 25 B5
West Barnes SW20 .... 200 C6
Rectory Cres E11 .... 55 C3
Rectory Ct
Cranford TW5 .... 128 C3
Feltham TW13 .... 172 C6
Leyton E11 .... 76 D5
Wallington SM6 .... 219 C4
West Drayton UB7 .... 104 A4
Woodford E18 .... 36 D2
Rectory Field Cres
SE7 .... 143 C5
Rectory Gdns
Beckenham BR3 .... 185 C2
6 Clapham SW4 .... 137 C2
Hornsey N8 .... 50 A5
Northolt UB5 .... 85 B6
Rectory Gn BR3 .... 185 B2
Rectory Gr
Clapham SW4 .... 137 C2
Croydon CR0 .... 220 D6
Hampton TW12, TW13 ... 173 B6
Rectory La Edgware HA8 .. 26 A4
Long Ditton KT6 .... 197 C1
Sidcup DA14 .... 190 C6
Stanmore HA7 .... 25 B5
Upper Tooting SW17 .... 181 A5
Wallington SM6 .... 219 C4
Rectory Orch SW19 .... 179 A6
Rectory Paddock Sch
BR5 .... 190 C1
Rectory Park Ave UB5 ... 85 B4
Rectory Pl SE18 .... 122 C2
Rectory Rd
Barnes SW13 .... 134 A3
Beckenham BR3 .... 185 C2
Cranford TW5 .... 128 C3
Dagenham RM10 .... 81 D1
Hayes UB3 .... 84 A1
Keston BR2 .... 225 D1
Rectory Rd *continued*
Little Ilford E12 .... 78 B3
1 London W3 .... 111 A5
Shacklewell N16 .... 73 D5
Southall UB2 .... 107 B3
Sutton SM1 .... 217 D5
Walthamstow E17 .... 53 D5
Rectory Road Sta N16 ... 73 D5
Rectory Sq E1 .... 96 D2
Rectory Way UB10 .... 60 D5
Reculver Ho 2 SE15 .... 140 C6
Reculver Mews N18 .... 34 A6
Reculver Rd SE16 .... 118 D1
Red Anchor Cl SW3 .... 267 A5
Redan Pl W2 .... 91 D1
Redan St W14 .... 112 D3
Redan Terr SE5 .... 138 D3
Red Barracks Rd 4
SE18 .... 122 B2
Redberry Gr SE23,
SE26 .... 162 C1
Redbourne Ave N3 .... 29 C2
Redbourne Dr SE28 .... 102 D1
Redbourne Ho
Finchley N3 .... 29 C2
7 Poplar E14 .... 97 B1
Redbourn Ho 10 W10 ... 90 C3
REDBRIDGE 55 C3
Redbridge Coll RM6 .... 58 B4
Redbridge Ct IG1 .... 55 D3
Redbridge Ent Ctr IG1 .. 79 A6
Redbridge Foyer IG1 .... 79 A6
Redbridge Gdns SE5 .... 139 C5
Redbridge La E IG4 .... 56 A4
Redbridge La W E11 .... 55 C3
Redbridge Prim Sch
IG4 .... 56 A4
Redbridge Rdbt IG4 .... 55 D3
Redbridge Sta IG4 .... 55 D3
Redburn St
SW3 .... 136 D6 267 C6
Redburn Trad Est EN3 ... 18 D5
Redcar Cl UB5 .... 63 D2
Redcar Ho SE26 .... 184 B4
Redcar St SE5 .... 139 A5
Redcastle Cl E1 .... 118 C6
Red Cedars Rd BR6 .... 211 C2
Redchurch St
E2 .... 95 D3 243 C6
Redcliffe Cl SW5 .... 255 C1
Redcliffe Ct 2 E5 .... 74 B5
Redcliffe Gdns
Chiswick W4 .... 132 D5
Fulham SW10 . 135 D6 265 D6
Ilford IG1 .... 56 C1
Redcliffe Mews SW10 .. 255 D1
Redcliffe Pl SW10 .... 266 A5
Redcliffe Rd
SW10 .... 136 A6 266 B6
Redcliffe Sch
SW10 .... 136 A6 266 A6
Redcliffe Sq
SW10 .... 113 D1 255 D1
Redcliffe St SW10 .... 265 D6
Redclose Ave SM4 .... 201 C4
Redclyffe Rd E6 .... 99 C6
Redclyffe Terr 2
SM2 .... 217 C1
Redclyf Ho 13 E1 .... 96 C3
Redcroft 5 NW6 .... 69 C2
Redcroft Rd UB1 .... 86 A1
Red Cross Cotts SE1 .. 252 B2
Redcross Way
SE1 .... 117 A5 252 B3
Redding Ho SE18 .... 122 A3
Reddings Ave WD23 .... 8 A6
Reddings Cl NW7 .... 27 D6
Reddings The NW7 .... 11 D1
Reddins Rd SE15 .... 140 A6
Reddons Rd BR3 .... 185 A3
Rede Pl W2 .... 113 C6 245 B6
Redesdale Gdns TW7 .. 131 A5
Redesdale St SW3 .... 267 C6
Redfern Ave TW2,
TW4 .... 151 C4
Redfern Ho 6 E13 .... 98 D6
Redfern Rd
Catford SE6 .... 164 A4
Willesden NW10 .... 67 C1
Redfield La
SW5 .... 113 D2 255 C4
Redfield Mews SW5 ... 255 B4
Redfiff Est SE16 .... 119 B3
Redford Ave
Thornton Heath CR7 .... 204 B5
Wallington SM6 .... 220 A2
Redford Cl TW13 .... 149 D2
Redford Wlk N1 .... 235 A6
Redgate Dr BR2 .... 225 B6
Red Gates Sch CR9 .... 220 D2
Redgate Terr SW15 .... 156 D5
Redgrave Cl SE25 .... 205 D3
Redgrave Rd SW15 .... 134 D2
Red Hill BR7 .... 188 D5
Redhill Ct SW2 .... 160 C2
Redhill Dr HA8 .... 27 A1
Red Hill Prim Sch
BR7 .... 188 D5
Redhill St NW1 .. 93 B4 231 D2
Red House* DA6 .... 147 A1
Red House La DA6 .... 147 A1
Red House Rd CR0 .... 203 D3
Red House Sq 20 N1 .... 73 A1
Redif Ho RM10 .... 81 D4
Redington Gdns NW3 ... 69 D4
Redington Ho N1 .... 233 D4
Redington Rd NW3 .... 69 D4
Redknap Ho TW10 .... 153 C1
Red La KT10 .... 213 A2
Redland Gdns KT8 .... 195 B5
Redlands
Teddington TW11 .... 175 A4
Tottenham N15 .... 51 B5
Redlands Ct BR1 .... 186 D3
Redlands Prim Sch E1 .. 96 C2
Redlands Rd EN3 .... 7 A4
Redlands The 5 BR3 ... 185 D1
Redlands Way SW2 .... 160 B4
Redleaf Cl DA17 .... 147 C6
Redleaves Ave TW15 .... 170 D4
Redlees Cl TW7 .... 131 A1
Red Leys UB8 .... 60 A1
Red Lion Bsns Ctr
KT6 .... 214 B5
Red Lion Cl 9 SE17 .... 139 B6
Red Lion Ct
Holborn EC4 .... 241 B1
Hounslow TW3 .... 129 D2
Red Lion Hill N2 .... 30 B1
Red Lion La SE18 .... 144 C4
Red Lion Pl SE18 .... 144 C4
Red Lion Rd KT6 .... 214 C6
Red Lion Row SE17 .... 139 A6
Red Lion Sq
WC1 .... 94 B2 240 C3
Red Lion St
Gray's Inn
WC1 .... 94 B2 240 C3
Richmond TW10 .... 153 D6
Red Lion Yd W1 .... 248 B4
Red Lo Ealing W5 .... 88 A2
West Wickham BR4 .... 208 A2
Red Lodge Rd BR3,
BR4 .... 208 B2
Redlynch Ct
W14 .... 113 A4 244 B1
Redlynch Ho 27 SW9 ... 138 C4
Redman Bldg EC1 .... 241 A4
Redman Cl UB5 .... 84 C5
Redman Ho SE1 .... 252 B1
Redman's Rd E1 .... 96 C2
Redmayne Ho 15 SW9 .. 138 B3
Redmead La E1 .... 118 A5
Redmead Rd UB3 .... 105 C2
Redmill Ho 24 E1 .... 96 B3
Redmond Ho N1 .... 233 D5
Redmore Rd W6 .... 112 B2
Red Oak Cl BR6 .... 226 D6
Redo Ho 3 E12 .... 78 C3
Red Pl W1 .... 248 A6
Redpoll Way DA18 .... 124 D3
Red Post Hill SE21,
SE24 .... 161 B6
Red Post Ho E6 .... 77 D1
Redriffe Rd E13 .... 98 D6
Redriff Prim Sch
SE16 .... 119 A4
Redriff Rd SE16 .... 119 A3
Redroofs Cl BR3 .... 185 D2
Redrose Trad Ctr 1
EN4 .... 14 B6
Red Rover SW13 .... 134 A2
Redrup Ho 21 SE14 .... 140 D6
Redruth Cl N22 .... 32 B3
Redruth Gdns KT10 .... 212 D1
Redruth Ho SM2 .... 217 D1
Redruth Rd E9 .... 96 C6
Red Sq The N16 .... 73 B5
Redstart Cl
New Cross Gate
SE14 .... 141 A5
Newham E6 .... 100 A2
Redston Rd N8 .... 49 D5
Redvers Rd N22 .... 32 C1
Redvers St E2 .... 95 C4
Redwald Rd E5 .... 74 D4
Redway Dr TW2 .... 152 A4
Redwing Path SE28 .... 123 B4
Redwing Rd SM6 .... 220 B1
Redwood Cl 4 Bow E3 ... 97 C5
Chigwell IG9 .... 21 B2
Hillingdon UB10 .... 82 D5
Osidge N14 .... 15 D4
Rotherhithe SE16 .... 119 A5
Sidcup DA15 .... 168 A3
South Oxhey WD19 .... 22 D6
Redwood Ct
Brondesbury NW6 .... 69 A1
Crouch End N19 .... 49 D2
Northolt UB5 .... 85 A4
10 Surbiton KT6 .... 197 D2
Redwood Est TW5 .... 128 B6
Redwood Gdns E4 .... 19 D5
Redwood Gr W5 .... 109 B2
Redwood Mews
Ashford TW15 .... 171 B3
2 Clapham SW4 .... 137 B2
Redwoods SW15 .... 156 A3
Redwood Way EN5 .... 12 D6
Redwood Wlk KT6 .... 197 D1
Reece Mews SW7 .... 256 C4
Reed Ave BR6 .... 227 C5
Reed Cl Lee SE12 .... 165 A6
Newham E16 .... 99 A2
Reede Gdns RM10 .... 81 D3
Reede Rd RM10 .... 81 D2
Reede Way RM10 .... 81 D2
Reedham Cl N17 .... 52 B5
Reedham St SE15 .... 140 A2
Reed Ho SW15 .... 156 A5
Reedholm Villas N16 .... 73 B4
Reed Mans 6 E11 .... 55 A3
Reed Pl Clapham SW4 .... 137 D1
Lower Halliford TW17 .... 192 B1
Reed Rd N17 .... 33 D1
Reedsfield Cl TW15 .... 148 D1
Reedsfield Rd TW15 .... 170 D6
Reed's Pl NW1 .... 71 C1
Reedworth St
SE11 .... 116 C2 261 B3
Reef Ho E14 .... 120 A3
Reenglass Rd HA7 .... 25 D6
Rees Dr HA7 .... 26 A6
Rees Gdns CR0 .... 205 D3
Rees Ho 6 N17 .... 33 D3
Reesland Cl E12 .... 78 C2
Rees St N1 .... 95 A6 235 B5
Reets Farm Cl NW9 .... 45 C3
Reeves Ave NW9 .... 45 B2
Reeves Cnr CR0 .... 220 D6
Reeves Cnr Sta CR0 .... 220 D6
Reeves Ho Lambeth SE1 251 A1
Mayfair W1 .... 248 A5
Reeves Mews
W1 .... 115 A6 248 B5
Reeves Rd Bromley E3 .... 97 D3
Shooters Hill SE18 .... 144 D6
Reflection Ho 9 E2 .... 96 A3
Reflection The E16 .... 122 D4
Reflex Apartments 1
BR2 .... 209 B5
Reform Row N17 .... 33 D1
Reform St SW11 .... 136 D3
Regal Cl Ealing W5 .... 87 D2
Spitalfields E1 .... 96 A2
Regal Cres SM6 .... 219 B5
Regal Ct Edmonton N18 ... 33 D5
2 Mitcham CR4 .... 202 D6
Wembley HA0 .... 65 D4
Regal Dr N11 .... 31 B5
Regal Ho IG2 .... 57 B3
Regal La NW1 .... 231 B5
Regal Pl
8 Tower Hamlets E3 .... 97 B4
Walham Green SW6 .... 265 D3
Regal Way HA3 .... 44 A3
Regan Ho 1 N18 .... 33 D4
Regan Way N1 .... 95 C5
Regatta Ho TW11 .... 175 A6
Regatta Point TW8 .... 132 B6
Regel Ct NW7 .... 29 A2
Regency Cl Ealing W5 .... 88 A1
Hampton TW12 .... 173 B5
Regency Cres 3 NW4 .... 28 D1
Regency Ct 9 Bow E3 .... 97 B5
Enfield EN1 .... 17 B6
4 Kingston u T KT5 .... 198 B4
4 Penge SE19 .... 184 A3
14 South Hackney E9 .... 96 C6
Sutton SM1 .... 217 D5
Wimbledon SW19 .... 179 B3
7 Woodford E18 .... 37 A1
Regency Dr HA4 .... 39 C1
Regency Gdns KT12 .... 194 C1
Regency Ho Finchley N3 ... 29 B1
Marylebone NW1 .... 238 D6
Regency Lo
1 Buckhurst Hill IG9 .... 21 D2
Harrow HA3 .... 42 C6
South Hampstead NW3 ... 70 B1
Regency Mews
Beckenham BR3 .... 186 A2
Camberwell SW9 .... 138 D5
Isleworth TW7 .... 152 C6
1 Willesden NW10 .... 68 A2
Regency Pl SW1 .... 259 D4
Regency St
SW1 .... 115 D2 259 D3
Regency Terr SW7 .... 256 C2
Regency Way DA6 .... 147 A2
Regency Wlk
Croydon CR0 .... 207 B3
8 Richmond TW10 .... 154 A6
Regeneration Rd
SE16 .... 118 D1
Regent Ave UB10 .... 60 D1
Regent Bsns Ctr UB3 ... 106 A4
Regent Cl
Cranford TW4 .... 128 B4
Harrow HA3 .... 44 A3
North Finchley N12 .... 30 A5
Regent Ct
4 Finchley N3 .... 29 D3
Lisson Gr NW8 .... 230 A1
South Norwood SE19 .... 182 D4
1 Stamford Hill N16 .... 51 D2
Regent Gdns IG3 .... 58 A2
Regent Ho W14 .... 254 A4
Regent Pl Croydon CR0 .. 205 D1
St James W1 .... 249 B6
Wimbledon SW19 .... 180 A5
Regent Rd
Surbiton KT5 .... 198 C4
Tulse Hill SE24 .... 160 D6
Regents Ave N13 .... 32 C5
Regents Bridge Gdns
SW8 .... 270 B4
Regents Canal Ho 19
E14 .... 97 A1
Regents Cl Hayes UB4 .... 83 C2
South Croydon CR2 .... 221 C2
Regent's Coll
NW1 .... 93 A3 238 A6
Regents Ct
22 Beckenham BR3 .... 185 C3
Bromley BR1 .... 186 D3
Edgware HA8 .... 26 A6
Hackney E8 .... 96 A6
1 Kingston u T KT2 .... 176 A2
Regent's Ct HA5 .... 22 D1
Regents Dr BR2 .... 225 D3
Regents Gate Ho 20
E14 .... 119 A6
Regents Lo 9 SW2 .... 160 B3
Regents Mews
NW8 .... 92 A5 229 B4
REGENT'S PARK 93 B4
Regent's Park*
NW1 .... 93 A5 231 A3

Regent's Park Barracks NW1 231 D3
Regent's Park Rd
Camden Town NW1 93 A6 231 A6
Hendon N3 47 B6
Primrose Hill NW3 71 A1
Regent's Park Sta NW1 93 B3 238 C5
Regent's Park Terr NW1 231 C6
Regents Pl IG10 21 D4
Regent's Pl SE3 143 A3
Regents Plaza 2 NW6 91 D5
Regent Sq
Belvedere DA17 125 D2
23 Bromley E3 97 D4
St Pancras WC1 94 A4 233 B1
Regent's Row E8 96 A6
Regent St
Brentford W4 110 C1
7 Kensal Green NW10 90 D4
Mayfair W1 115 C6 249 A6
Regents Wharf
3 Hackney E2 96 B6
Islington N1 233 C4
Regina Coeli RC Prim Sch CR2 220 D1
Regina Ct TW11 174 C5
Reginald Ct BR3 186 A2
Reginald Pl 6 SE8 141 C5
Reginald Rd
Deptford SE8 141 C5
Forest Gate E7 77 A2
Reginald Sorenson Ho E11 54 B2
Reginald Sq SE8 141 C5
Regina Point SE16 118 C3
Regina Rd Ealing W13 109 A5
Finsbury Pk N4 50 B1
Southall UB2 107 A2
South Norwood SE25 206 A6
Regina Terr W13 109 B5
Regis Ct
East Bedfont TW14 149 B5
Hornsey N8 50 B5
Marylebone NW1 237 C4
Mitcham SW19 180 C2
Regis Pl 17 SW2 138 B1
Regis Rd NW5 71 B3
Regnart Bldgs NW1 232 B1
Regnolruf Ct KT12 194 A2
Reid Cl Hayes UB3 83 C1
Pinner HA5 40 A5
Reid Ct SW14 133 A3
Reidhaven Rd SE18 123 C2
Reigate Ave SM1 201 D1
Reigate Rd
Catford BR1 164 D1
Grove Pk BR1, SE12 165 A2
Ilford IG3 79 D6
Reigate Way SM6 220 A3
Reighton Rd E5 74 A6
Reizel Cl N16 51 D1
Relay Rd W12 112 C5
Relf Rd SE15 140 A2
Reliance Sq E2 243 B6
Relko Gdns SM1 218 B3
Relton Ct W3 110 C4
Relton Mews SW7 257 B6
Rembrandt Cl E14 120 B3
Rembrandt Ct
10 Bermondsey SE16 118 B1
Harrow HA3 43 A3
West Ewell KT19 215 D2
Rembrandt Rd
Edgware HA8 26 C1
Lewisham SE13 142 C1
Rembrant Cl SW1 258 A3
Remembrance Ave N2 47 D6
Remington Rd
Newham E6 100 A1
Tottenham N15 51 B3
Remington St N1 94 D5 234 D3
Remnant St WC2 240 C2
Remsted Ho 7 NW6 91 D6
Remus Rd E3 75 C1
Renaissance Ct SM1 202 A1
Renaissance Wlk 4 SE10 120 D3
Renbold Ho 5 SE10 142 A4
Rendlebury Ho 17 SE18 122 B2
Rendle Cl CR0 206 A4
Rendlesham Ho 3 E5, N16 74 A5
Rendlesham Rd
Enfield EN2 4 D4
Shacklewell E5 74 A5
Renforth St SE16 118 C4
Renfree Way TW17 192 C2
Renfrew Cl E6 122 C6
Renfrew Ct TW5 129 A3
Renfrew Ho
Paddington NW6 91 D5
Walthamstow E17 35 B1
Renfrew Rd
Hounslow TW5 129 A3
Kingston u T KT2 177 A3
Newington SE11 116 D2 261 C3
Renmuir St SW17 180 D4
Rennell Ho 18 E9 74 D2
Rennell St SE13 142 A2
Renness Rd E17 53 A6
Rennets Cl SE9 167 C6
Rennets Wood Ho SE9 167 B6
Rennets Wood Rd SE9 167 B6
Rennie Cotts 29 E1 96 C3
Rennie Ct Holdbrook EN3 7 C5
Lambeth SE1 251 C4
Rennie Ho SE1 262 A5
Rennie St SE1 116 D5 251 C4
Renoir Ct 7 SE16 118 B1
Renovation The E16 122 D4
Renown Cl CR0 204 D1
Rensburg Rd E17 52 D3
Rensburg Villas E17 52 D4
Renshaw Cl 7 DA17 147 B6
Renshaw Cnr CR4 181 A2
Renshaw Ct SW19 179 A6
Renshaw Ho 11 SW27 182 D5
Renters Ave NW4 46 C3
Renton Cl SW2 160 B5
Renwick Rd IG11 102 B4
Repens Way UB4 84 D3
Rephidim St SE1 263 A5
Replingham Rd SW18 157 C3
Reporton Rd SW6 135 A5 264 B3
Repository Rd SE7, SE18 122 B1
Repton Ave Hayes UB3 105 B2
Wembley HA0 65 C4
Repton Cl SM5 218 C3
Repton Ct
Beckenham BR3 185 D2
Southgate N21 16 C3
Repton Ho SW1 259 B3
Repton Rd Harrow HA3 44 B5
Orpington BR6 227 D5
Repton St E14 97 A1
Reservoir Cl CR7 205 B5
Reservoir Rd
New Cross Gate SE4 141 A3
Ruislip HA4 39 B5
Southgate N14 15 C6
Reservoir Studios 14 E1 96 D1
Resham Cl UB2 106 C3
Resolution Way 14 SE8 141 C5
Resolution Wlk SE18 122 B3
Restell Cl SE3 142 C6
Restmor Way SM5, SM6 219 A6
Reston Pl SW7 246 A1
Restons Cres DA15, SE9 167 C5
Restoration Sq SW11 266 D1
Restormel Cl TW3 151 C6
Retcar Pl N19 71 B6
Retford St E2 95 C5
Retingham Way E4 19 D2
Retlas Ct HA1 42 B2
Retreat Cl HA3 43 C4
Retreat Cvn Site The IG9 21 A3
Retreat Ho 5 E9 74 C2
Retreat Pl E9 74 C2
Retreat Rd TW9 153 D6
Retreat The Harrow HA2 41 C2
Kingsbury NW9 45 B4
Mortlake SW14 133 C2
North Cheam KT4 216 B6
South Norwood CR7 205 B5
Surbiton KT5 198 B3
Reunion Row E1 118 B6
Reveley Sq SE16 119 A4
Revell Rd Cheam SM1 217 B2
Kingston u T KT1 176 D2
Revell Rise SE18 145 D6
Revelon Rd SE4 141 A2
Revelstoke Rd SW18, SW19 157 C2
Reventlow Rd SE9 167 A3
Reverdy Rd SE1 118 A2
Reverend Cl HA2 63 D5
Revesby Rd SM5 202 C3
Review Lo RM10 103 D5
Review Rd
Dagenham RM10 103 D6
Willesden NW2 67 D6
Rewell St SW6 136 A5 266 A3
Rewley Rd SM4 202 B3
Rew Lo 25 N2 30 B1
Rex Ave TW15 170 C5
Rex Ho TW13 151 A1
Rex Par 2 IG8 37 C4
Rex Pl W1 115 A5 248 B4
Reydon Ave E11 55 C3
Reygate Ct N4 51 A3
Reynard Cl
Brockley SE4 141 A2
Bromley BR1 210 C6
Reynard Dr SE19 183 D3
Reynard Mills Trad Est TW8 109 C1
Reynard Pl SE14 141 A6
Reynardson Rd N17 33 A3
Reynardson's Ct 10 N17 51 D6
Reynolah Gdns SE7 121 B1
Reynolds Ave
Chessington KT9 214 A1
Ilford RM6 58 C2
Little Ilford E12 78 C3
Reynolds Cl
Carshalton SM5 202 D1
Golders Green NW11 47 D2
Mitcham SW19 180 B2
Reynolds Ct Ilford RM6 58 D6
Leyton E11 76 D5
Reynolds Dr HA8 44 B6
Reynolds Ho Enfield EN1 18 A6
Finsbury Pk N4 50 A1
Reynolds Ho *continued*
18 South Hackney E2 96 C5
St John's Wood NW8 229 D3
Westminster SW1 259 D3
Reynolds Pl
Greenwich SE3 143 B5
12 Richmond TW10 154 B5
Reynolds Rd
Acton Green W4 111 A3
Hayes UB4 84 C3
New Malden KT3 199 B2
Nunhead SE15 140 C1
Reynolds Way CR0 221 C4
Rheidol Mews N1 235 A4
Rheidol Terr N1 95 A6 235 A5
Rhein Ho N8 50 A6
Rheola Cl N17 33 D2
Rhoda St E2 95 D3 243 D6
Rhodes Ave N22 31 C2
Rhodes Avenue Prim Sch N22 31 C2
Rhodes Ho
Shepherd's Bush W12 112 B5
Shoreditch N1 235 C2
Rhodesia Rd Leyton E11 76 B6
Stockwell SW9 138 A3
Rhodes-Moorhouse Ct SM4 201 C3
Rhodes St N7 72 B3
Rhodeswell Rd E14 97 B1
Rhodrons Ave KT9 214 A3
Rhondda Gr E3 97 B4
Rhyl Prim Sch NW5 71 A2
Rhyl Rd UB6 86 D5
Rhyl St NW5 71 A2
Rhys Ave N11 31 D3
Rialto Rd CR4 181 A1
Ribble Cl IG8 37 C4
Ribblesdale Ave
Friern Barnet N11 31 A4
Northolt UB5 63 D2
Ribblesdale Ho 11 NW6 91 C6
Ribblesdale Rd
Hornsey N8 50 B5
Streatham SW16 181 B5
Ribbon Dance Mews SE5 139 B4
Ribchester Ave UB6 86 D4
Ribston Cl BR2 210 B1
Ribstone Ho 12 E9 74 D2
Ricardo Path 5 SE28 124 C5
Ricardo St E14 97 D1
Ricards Lodge High Sch SW19 179 B5
Ricards Rd SW19 179 B5
Riccall Ct 2 NW9 27 C2
Riceyman Ho WC1 234 A1
Richard Alibon Prim Sch RM10 81 C3
Richard Anderson Ct 1 SE14 140 D5
Richard Atkins Prim Sch SW2 160 A4
Richard Burbidge Mans SW13 134 C6
Richard Burton Ct 4 IG9 21 C2
Richard Challoner Sch KT3 199 B2
Richard Cl SE18 122 A2
Richard Cloudesley Sch EC1 95 A3 242 A5
Richard Cobden Prim Sch NW1 93 C6 232 B5
Richard Ct
Ashford TW15 170 B5
1 Barnet EN5 1 A2
Richard Fell Ho 3 E12 78 C4
Richard Fox Ho N4 73 A5
Richard Ho 10 SE16 118 C2
Richard House Dr E16 100 A1
Richard Knight Ho SW6 265 B2
Richard Neale Ho 2 E1 118 B6
Richard Neve Ho 2 SE18 123 C2
Richards Cl Bushey WD23 8 B4
Harlington UB3 127 B6
Harrow HA1 43 A4
Hillingdon UB10 82 C6
Richards Ct BR3 184 D2
Richard Sharples Ct 16 SM2 218 A1
Richardson Cl 19 E8 95 D6
Richardson Ct 20 SW4 138 A3
Richardson Gdns 12 RM10 81 D2
Richardson Ho
Isleworth TW7 130 D2
10 Poplar E14 97 C2
Richardson Rd E15 98 C5
Richardson's Mews W1 239 A5
Richards Pl E17 53 C6
Richard's Pl SW3 257 B4
Richard St 20 E1 96 B1
Richbell WC1 240 B4
Richbell Pl WC1 240 C4
Richborne Terr SW8 138 B5 270 D4
Richborough Ho
10 Deptford SE15 140 C6
14 Hackney E5 74 B4
Richborough Rd NW2 69 A4
Richbourne Ct W1 237 B2
Richens Cl TW3 130 B3
Riches Rd IG1 79 A6
Richfield Ct
4 Beckenham BR3 185 B2
Wembley HA0 66 A2
Richfield Rd WD23 8 A4
Richford Gate W6 112 C3
Richford Rd E15 98 D6
Richford St W6 112 C3
Richings Ho BR5 190 A2
Rich La SW5 255 C2
Richland Ho 4 SE15 140 A4
Richlands Ave KT17 216 A4
Richman Ho 10 SE8 119 B1
RICHMOND 131 C1
Richmond Adult Com Coll TW9 131 D1
Richmond Ave
Chingford E4 36 B5
Feltham TW14 149 C5
Hillingdon UB10 60 D2
Islington N1 94 B6 233 D6
Willesden NW10 68 C2
Wimbledon SW20 179 A2
Richmond Bldgs W1 239 C1
Richmond Bridge TW1 153 D5
Richmond Bridge Mans 1 TW1 153 D5
Richmond Circus TW9 132 A1
Richmond Cl
Borehamwood WD6 11 B6
Walthamstow E17 53 B3
Richmond Coll
Kensington W8 113 D3 255 D6
Richmond TW10 154 A4
Richmond Cres
Chingford E4 36 B5
Edmonton N9 18 A3
Islington N1 94 C6 234 A6
Richmond Ct
Bromley BR1 187 B3
12 Kingston u T KT2 176 C3
Knightsbridge SW1 247 D1
1 Loughton IG10 21 D6
Mitcham CR4 202 B6
4 New Southgate N11 31 A4
Wembley HA9 66 B6
Wimbledon SW20 178 B1
Richmond Dr TW17 193 B3
Richmond Gate TW10 154 B4
Richmond Gdns
Harrow HA3 24 D3
Hendon NW4 46 A4
Richmond Gn CR0 220 A5
Richmond Gr
Islington N1 72 D1
Surbiton KT5 198 B3
Richmond Healthcare Hamlet Hospl TW9 132 A2
RICHMOND HILL 154 A5
Richmond Hill TW10 154 A5
Richmond Hill Ct 5 TW10 154 A5
Richmond Ho
12 Forest Hill SE26 162 A1
Regent's Pk NW1 231 D3
Walworth SE17 262 C2
Richmond Ho (Hampton Com Coll) TW12 173 B5
Richmond International Bsns Ctr 9 TW9 132 B1
Richmond Mans
Earl's Ct SW5 255 C2
Putney SW15 135 A2
13 Twickenham TW1 153 D5
Richmond Mews W1 239 C1
Richmond Park* TW10 155 A3
Richmond Park Rd
Kingston u T KT2 176 A3
Mortlake SW14 133 B1
Richmond Pk IG10 21 D4
Richmond Pl SE18 123 A2
Richmond Rd
Bowes Pk N11 32 A4
Chingford E4 20 B3
Dalston E8 74 A1
Ealing W5 110 A4
Finchley N2 30 A1
Forest Gate E7 77 B3
Ilford IG1 79 A5
Isleworth TW7 131 A2
Kingston u T KT2 176 A4
Leyton E11 76 B6
New Barnet EN5 14 A6
Thornton Heath CR7 204 D5
Tottenham N15 51 C3
Twickenham TW1 153 C4
Wallington CR0 220 A5
Wimbledon SW20 178 B2
Richmond St E13 99 A5
Richmond Sta TW9 132 A1
Richmond Terr SW1 116 A4 250 A2
Richmond upon Thames Coll TW2 152 C4
Richmond Way
Hammersmith W12, W14 112 D4
Wanstead E11 77 A6
Richmount Gdns SE3 143 A2
Rich St E14 119 B6
Rickard Cl Hendon NW4 46 A5
Streatham SW2 160 C3
Rickards Cl KT6 214 A6
Rickett St SW6 265 B6
Rickman Ho 23 E2 96 C3
Rickman St 24 E1 96 C3
Rickmansworth Rd HA5 22 C1
Rick Roberts Way E15 98 B5
Rickthorne Rd 7 N19 72 A6
Rickyard Path SE9 144 A1
Riddell Ct SE1 263 C2
Riddell Lo EN2 4 D3
Ridding La UB6 64 D3
Riddons Rd SE12 187 C6
Rideout St SE18 122 B2
Rider Cl DA15 167 C5
Ride The
Brentford TW8 109 C1
Enfield EN3 6 D2
Ridgdale St E3 97 D5
Ridge Ave N21 17 B4
Ridgebrook Rd SE3, SE9 143 D2
Ridge Cl Hendon NW4 28 D1
Kingsbury NW9 45 B5
Plumstead SE28 123 B4
Ridge Crest EN2 4 B4
Ridge Hill NW11 47 A1
Ridge Ho 4 KT2 176 D3
Ridgeleigh Ct 3 EN5 1 A2
Ridgemead Cl N13, N14 16 A2
Ridgemont Gdns HA8 27 A6
Ridgemount Ave CR0 222 D6
Ridgemount Cl 4 SE20 184 B3
Ridgemount Gdns EN2 4 D3
Ridgeon Ct N22 32 B4
Ridge Rd Cheam SM3 201 B1
Child's Hill NW2 69 B5
Edmonton N21 17 B3
Hornsey Vale N8 50 B3
Mitcham CR4 181 B3
Ridges The E4 35 C6
Ridge Terr N21 17 A4
Ridge The Barnet EN5 13 B6
Old Bexley DA5 169 B4
Orpington BR6 227 B6
Surbiton KT5 198 C4
Twickenham TW2 152 B4
Ridgeview Cl EN5 12 D5
Ridgeview Ct EN4 15 C6
Ridgeview Rd N20 14 A1
Ridgeway Hayes BR2 225 A6
11 Richmond TW10 154 A5
Walton-on-T KT12 193 D1
Woodford IG8 37 C6
Ridge Way
Feltham TW13 151 A1
7 West Norwood SE19 183 C4
Ridgeway Ave EN4 14 D5
Ridgeway Cres BR6 227 C5
Ridgeway Crescent Gdns BR6 227 C5
Ridgeway Ct HA5 23 C3
Ridgeway Dr Acton W3 110 C3
Grove Pk BR1 187 B6
Ridgeway E DA15 167 D6
Ridgeway Gdns
Crouch End N6 49 C2
Redbridge IG4 56 A4
Ridgeway Rd TW7 130 C4
Ridgeway Rd N TW7 130 C5
Ridgeway The
Acton W3 110 C3
Chingford E4 20 A3
Enfield EN2 4 B5
Finchley N3 29 D3
Friern Barnet N11 30 D6
Golders Green NW11 47 B1
Kenton HA3 43 C3
Kingsbury NW9 45 B5
Mill Hill NW7 28 B6
North Harrow HA2 41 D3
Palmers Green N14 16 A2
Pinner HA2 41 B4
Ruislip HA4 40 A2
Stanmore HA7 25 C4
Wallington CR0 220 B5
Ridgeway W DA15 167 C6
Ridgeway Wlk UB5 63 A2
Ridgewell Cl
Dagenham RM10 103 D6
Forest Hill SE26 185 B6
Shoreditch N1 235 B6
Ridgmount Gdns WC1 93 D2 239 C4
Ridgmount Pl WC1 239 C4
Ridgmount Rd SW18 157 D6
Ridgmount St WC1 93 D2 239 C4
Ridgway SW19, SW20 178 D4
Ridgway Ct SW19 178 D4
Ridgway Gdns SW19 178 D3
Ridgway Pl SW19 179 A4
Ridgway Rd SW9 138 D2
Ridgway The SM2 218 B1
Ridgwell Rd E16 99 C2
Riding House St W1 93 C2 239 A3
Ridings Ave N21 17 A6
Ridings Cl N6 49 C2
Ridings The Ealing W5 88 B3
Oakleigh Pk EN4 14 B4
Sunbury TW16 172 A2
Surbiton KT5 198 C4
Riding The NW11 47 B2
Ridler Rd EN1 5 C5
Ridley Ave W13 109 B3
Ridley Cl IG11 79 D1
Ridley Ct
Orpington BR6 227 A4
Streatham SW16 182 A4
Ridley Ho 14 SW11 136 C2
Ridley Rd
Beckenham BR2 208 D6
Dalston E8 73 D3
Forest Gate E7 77 C4
Merton SW19 179 D3
Welling DA16 146 B4
Willesden Green NW10 90 A5
Ridley Road Mkt E8 73 D3
Ridsdale Rd SE20 184 B2
Riefield Rd SE9 167 A6
Riesco Dr CR0 222 C2
Riffel Rd NW2 68 C3
Rifle Ct SE11 138 C6
Rifle Pl W11 112 D5
Rifle St E14 97 D2
Riga Ho 12 E1 96 D2
Rigault Rd SW6 135 A3
Rigby Cl CR0 220 C5
Rigby Ho 2 N17 51 D6
Rigby La UB3 105 A4
Rigby Mews IG1 78 C6
Rigby Pl 8 EN3 7 C6
Rigden St E14 97 D1
Rigeley Rd NW10 90 A4
Rigg App E10 53 A1
Rigge Pl SW4 137 D1
Rigg Ho 2 SW4 160 A4
Riggindale Rd SW16 181 D6
Rignold Ho 6 SE5 139 C3
Riley Ho 9 Bow E3 97 C3
Chelsea SW10 266 C5
1 Streatham SW4 159 D4
Riley Rd
Bermondsey SE1 117 D3 263 C6
Enfield EN3 6 C5
Riley St SW10 136 B5 266 C4
Rill Ho 16 SE5 139 C5
Rimini Ct SW12 158 D3
Rinaldo Rd SW12 159 B4
Ring Cl BR1 187 B3
Ringcroft St N7 72 C3
Ringer's Rd BR1 209 A6
Ringford Ho SW18 157 B6
Ringford Rd SW18 157 C5
Ring Ho 15 E1 118 C6
Ringlet Cl E16 99 B2
Ringlewell Cl EN1 6 B3
Ringmer Ave SW6 135 A4 264 B1
Ringmer Gdns 3 N19 72 A6
Ringmer Ho 15 SE22 139 C2
Ringmer Pl N21 17 B6
Ringmer Way BR1 210 B4
Ringmore Rise SE23 162 B4
Ring Rd W12 112 C5
Ringsfield Ho SE17 262 B1
Ringslade Rd N22 32 B1
Ringstead Bldgs SE6 163 D4
Ringstead Ct SM1 218 B3
Ringstead Rd
Catford SE6 163 D4
Sutton SM1 218 B3
Ringway UB2 107 A1
Ring Way N11 31 C4
Ringwold Cl BR3 185 A3
Ringwood Ave
Muswell Hill N2 48 D6
Thornton Heath CR0 204 A2
Ringwood Cl HA5 40 C6
Ringwood Gdns
17 Millwall E14 119 C2
Roehampton SW15 156 A3
Ringwood Rd E17 53 B3
Ringwood Way
Hampton TW12 173 C6
Southgate N21 16 D4
Ripley Cl Bromley BR1 210 B4
New Addington CR0 224 A2
Ripley Ct 1 CR4 180 B1
Ripley Gdns
Mortlake SW14 133 B2
Sutton SM1 218 A4
Ripley Ho
13 Kingston u T KT2 176 D4
Mortlake SW14 133 C2
Nine Elms SW1 269 A6
5 Penge SE26 184 B5
Ripley Mews E11 54 C3
Ripley Rd
Belvedere DA17 125 C2
Enfield EN2 5 A4
Hampton TW12 173 C3
Ilford IG3 79 D6
Newham E16 99 C1
Riplington Ct SW15 156 B4
Ripon Cl UB5 63 C2
Ripon Ct 10 N11 31 A4
Ripon Gdns
Chessington KT9 213 D3
Redbridge IG1 56 A2
Ripon Rd Edmonton N9 18 B4
Shooters Hill SE18 144 D6
Tottenham N17 51 B6
Ripon Way WD6 11 B6
Rippersley Rd DA16 146 A4
Ripple Ct 10 IG11 101 B6
Ripple Jun & Inf Schs IG11 79 C1
Ripple Rd Barking IG11 79 A1
Barking IG11 101 C6
Castle Green RM9 102 A6
Rippleside Commercial Est IG11 102 C5
Ripplevale Gr N1 72 B1
Rippolson Rd SE18 123 D1

Ripston Rd TW15 ...... 171 B5
Risborough SE17 ..... 262 A4
Risborough Cl 4 N10 ... 49 B6
Risborough Ct 5 N10 ... 49 B6
Risborough Dr KT4 .... 200 A2
Risborough Ho NW8 .. 237 B6
Risborough St SE1 .... 251 D2
Risdon Ho 26 SE16 ..... 118 C4
Risdon St 27 SE16 ...... 118 C4
Risedale Rd DA7 .... 147 D2
Riseholme Ct E9 .... 75 B2
Riseholme Ho 14 SE22 ... 139 C2
Riseldine Rd SE23 ..... 163 A5
Rise The
Borehamwood WD6 ..... 10 B6
Buckhurst Hill IG9 .... 21 D4
Chingford E4 .... 20 C3
Edgware HA8 .... 26 D5
Edmonton N13 .... 32 C6
Harrow HA2 .... 24 A1
Hendon NW7 .... 27 D4
Hillingdon UB10 .... 82 B5
Neasden NW10 .... 67 B5
Sidcup DA5 .... 168 C4
Wanstead E11 .... 55 A4
Wembley HA0, UB6 ...... 65 A3
Risinghill St N1 .... 234 A4
Risingholme Cl HA3 ..... 24 C2
Risingholme Rd HA3 .... 24 C1
Risings The E17 .... 54 B5
Rising Sun Ct EC1 ...... 241 D3
Risley Ave N17 .... 33 B2
Risley Avenue Prim Sch N17 ... 33 C2
Risley Ho 7 E9 .... 74 D2
Rita Rd SW8 ... 138 B5 270 C4
Ritches Rd N15 .... 51 A4
Ritchie Ho
Crouch End N19 .... 49 D2
8 Rotherhithe SE16 .... 118 C3
12 South Bromley E14 ... 98 B1
Ritchie Rd CR0 .... 206 B3
Ritchie St N1 .... 94 C5 234 B4
Ritchings Ave E17 .... 53 A5
Ritherdon Rd SW17 .... 159 B2
Ritson Ho N1 .... 233 C5
Ritson Rd E8 .... 74 A2
Ritter St SE18 .... 144 C6
Ritz Par W5 .... 88 B3
Rivaz Pl E9 .... 74 C2
Riven Ct 10 W2 .... 91 D1
Rivenhall Gdns E11, E18 ... 54 D5
Riverains The SW11 ... 266 C1
River Ave Southgate N13 .. 16 D1
Thames Ditton KT7 ..... 197 A2
Riverbank KT8 .... 196 C5
River Bank
Edmonton N21 .... 17 A4
Thames Ditton KT7 ..... 196 D4
Riverbank Rd BR1 ..... 165 A1
Riverbank Way TW8 .... 131 C6
River Barge Cl E14 ..... 120 A4
River Brent Bsns Pk W7 ... 108 C3
River Cl Ruislip HA4 ...... 39 D3
Southall UB2 .... 108 A4
Wanstead E11 .... 55 C3
River Cotts BR5 .... 190 C1
Rivercourt Rd W6 ...... 112 B1
River Crane Way TW13 ... 151 B2
River Ct
Kingston u T KT6 .... 197 D4
Lambeth SE1 .... 251 C5
Shepperton TW17 ...... 193 A2
Wanstead E11 .... 55 C3
Riverdale Cl IG11 ...... 102 B3
Riverdale Ct N21 .... 17 B6
Riverdale Dr SW18 ..... 157 D3
Riverdale Gdns TW1 ... 153 C6
Riverdale Rd Erith DA8 .. 125 D1
Feltham TW13 .... 173 B6
Plumstead Comm SE18 .. 123 D1
Sidcup DA5 .... 169 B5
Twickenham TW1 ...... 153 C5
Riverdene HA8 .... 11 A1
Riverdene Rd IG1 .... 78 D5
Riverfleet WC1 .... 233 B2
Riverford Ho 28 W2 ..... 91 C2
River Front EN1 .... 5 C2
River Gdns
Carshalton SM5 .... 219 A5
Feltham TW14 .... 150 B6
River Gdns Bsns Ctr TW14 ... 128 B1
River Grove Pk BR3 .... 185 B2
Riverhead Cl E17 .... 34 D1
River Ho Barnes SW13 .. 133 C3
1 Forest Hill SE26 ..... 162 B1
Riverholme KT8 .... 196 C6
Riverhope Mans SE18 .. 122 A3
Riverine Lo HA7 .... 25 A5
River La TW10 .... 153 D3
Riverleigh Ct E4 .... 35 A5
Rivermead
East Molesey KT8 ...... 196 A6
Kingston u T KT6 ...... 197 D4
Rivermead Cl TW11 .... 175 B5
Rivermead Ct
Ealing UB6 .... 87 A4
Fulham SW6 .... 135 B2
Rivermead Ho
Hackney E9 .... 75 A3
Sunbury TW16 .... 194 C6
River Meads Ave TW13, TW2 ... 151 D1
River Mount KT12 ..... 193 D2
Rivernook Cl KT12 ..... 194 C4
River Park Gdns BR2 ... 186 B3
River Park Rd N22 ...... 32 B1
River Pl N1 .... 73 A1
River Plate Ho EC2 .... 242 D3
River Rd Barking IG11 ... 101 D3
Buckhurst Hill IG9 .... 21 D3
River Reach TW11 ..... 175 C5
River Road Bsns Pk IG11 ... 101 D4
Riversdale Gdns N22 .... 32 C2
Riversdale Prim Sch SW18 ... 157 C3
Riversdale Rd
Highbury N5 .... 73 A5
Thames Ditton KT7 ..... 197 A3
Riversdene N5 .... 73 A5
Riversfield Rd EN1 .... 5 C2
Rivers Ho 11 TW8 ...... 110 C1
Riverside
Battersea SW11 ...... 267 B4
Forest Hill SE6 .... 185 B6
Greenwich SE7 .... 121 B3
Hendon NW4 .... 46 B2
Oatlands Pk TW17 ...... 193 C2
11 Rotherhithe SE16 .... 118 C4
St Pancras WC1 ...... 233 B2
Sunbury TW16 .... 172 D1
Twickenham TW1 ...... 153 B3
Riverside Apartments N13 ... 32 B5
Riverside Ave KT8 ..... 196 B4
Riverside Bsns Ctr SW18 ... 157 D3
Riverside Bsns Pk SW19 ... 180 A2
Riverside Cl
Chislehurst BR5 .... 190 C1
Ealing W7 .... 86 C3
Hackbridge SM6 .... 219 B5
Kingston u T KT1 .... 197 D5
Upper Clapton E5 .... 74 C6
Riverside Ct
Chingford E4 .... 19 D5
Lewisham SE12 .... 142 D1
Nine Elms SW8 .... 269 D6
Richmond TW11 .... 175 C5
Riverside Dr
Chiswick W4 .... 133 C4
Mitcham CR4 .... 202 C4
Richmond TW10 .... 153 B1
Temple Fortune NW11 ... 47 A3
Riverside Est EN3 .... 19 A5
Riverside Gdns
Enfield EN2 .... 5 A3
Hammersmith W6 ...... 112 B1
Hendon N3 .... 47 A6
Wembley HA0 .... 88 A5
Riverside Ho
Finchley N12 .... 29 D6
14 Islington N1 .... 73 A1
Morden SW19 .... 202 A5
30 Richmond TW10 ..... 153 D6
Riverside Ind Est IG11 ... 102 A4
Riverside Mans 4 E1 .. 118 C5
Riverside Pl
New Southgate N11 ..... 15 C1
Stanwell TW19 .... 148 A5
Riverside Prim Sch SE16 ... 118 A4
Riverside Rd
Mill Meads E15 .... 98 A5
Sidcup DA14 .... 169 A2
South Tottenham N15 .... 52 A3
Stanwell TW19 .... 148 A5
Wandsworth SW17, SW19 ... 158 A1
Riverside The KT8 ..... 196 B6
Riverside Wlk
Isleworth TW7 .... 130 C2
3 West Wickham BR4 .. 207 D1
Riverside Works IG11 ... 78 D1
Riverside Workshops SE1 ... 252 B4
River St EC1 ..... 94 C4 234 A2
Riverstone Cl HA2 ...... 64 B6
Riverstone Ct KT2 ..... 176 B2
Riverston Sch SE12 .... 165 A6
River Terr W6 .... 112 C1
Riverton Cl W9 .... 91 B4
Riverview TW17 .... 193 B2
River View EN2 .... 5 A2
Riverview CE Prim Sch KT19 ... 215 B4
Riverview Ct 14 DA17 ... 125 C1
Riverview Gdns SW13 .. 134 B6
River View Gdns TW1 .. 152 D2
Riverview Gr W4 ...... 132 D6
Riverview Hts SE18 .... 144 D5
Riverview Lo NW9 ...... 67 B6
Riverview Pk SE6 ...... 163 C2
Riverview Rd
Chiswick W4 .... 132 D6
West Ewell KT19 ...... 215 B4
Riverway N13 .... 32 C6
River Way
Canning Town SE10 .... 120 D3
Twickenham TW13, TW2 ... 151 D2
West Ewell KT19 ...... 215 C3
River Wlk KT12 .... 194 A3
Riverwood La BR7 ..... 189 B2
Rivet Ho SE1 .... 263 D2
Rivington Ave IG8 ...... 37 D1
Rivington Cres NW7 .... 27 D3
Rivington Ct
17 Dagenham RM10 ...... 81 D2
Willesden Green NW10 ... 90 A6
Rivington Pl EC2 .... 95 C4
Rivington St EC2 .... 95 C4
Rivington Wlk 4 E8 .... 96 A6
Rivulet Rd N17 .... 33 A3
Rixon Ho SE18 .... 144 D6
Rixon St N7 .... 72 C5
Rixsen Rd E12 .... 78 A3
Roach Rd E3 .... 75 C1
Roads Pl N19 .... 72 A6
Roan Ind Est CR4 ..... 180 D2
Roan St SE10 .... 142 A6
Robart Ho 2 N12 .... 30 A5
Robarts Cl HA5 .... 40 B4
Robbins Hall EN3 .... 18 D5
Robb Rd HA7 .... 25 A4
Robert Adam St W1 ... 238 A2
Roberta St E2 .... 96 A4
Robert Bell Ho 2 SE16 ... 118 A2
Robert Blair Prim Sch N7 ... 72 A2
Robert Browning Prim Sch SE17 ... 117 B1 262 C2
Robert Burns Ho N17 ... 34 B3
Robert Cl Barking IG11 ... 79 A2
Paddington W9 .... 236 B5
Robert Clack Lower Sch RM8 ... 81 B6
Robert Clack Upper Sch RM8 ... 59 C1
Robert Dashwood Way SE17 ... 262 A3
Robert Gentry Ho W14 254 B1
Robert Gerard Ho 7 SE27 ... 183 B6
Robert Ho 12 HA1 ...... 42 D4
Robert Jones Ho 3 SE16 ... 118 A2
Robert Keen Cl 18 SE15 ... 140 A4
Robert Lowe Cl SE14 ... 140 D5
Roberton Dr BR1 ...... 187 C2
Robert Owen Ho
Fulham SW6 .... 134 D4
8 Spitalfields E2 .... 95 D4
Robert Owen Lo 4 E5 .. 74 B4
Robertsbridge Rd SM5 ... 202 B2
Roberts Cl Cheam SM3 .. 216 D1
New Eltham SE9 .... 167 B3
South Norwood CR7 .... 205 B6
Yiewsley UB7 .... 104 A5
Roberts Ct
Chessington KT9 ...... 213 D3
Ealing W5 .... 88 A1
Islington N1 .... 234 D5
Penge SE20 .... 184 C2
Willesden NW10 .... 67 C2
Roberts Ho
Dagenham RM10 .... 81 D1
Friern Barnet N11 ...... 31 B5
6 Kidbrooke SE18 ...... 144 A4
5 West Norwood SE27 ... 160 D1
Roberts Mews SW1 ... 258 A5
Robertson Ho
Kidbrooke SE18 .... 144 B4
11 Lewisham SE10 ..... 142 A4
1 Upper Tooting SW17 ... 180 C5
Robertson Rd E15 ...... 98 A6
Robertson St SW8 ..... 137 B3
Roberts Pl RM10 .... 81 C2
Robert's Pl EC1 ...... 241 B6
Roberts Rd
Belvedere DA17 .... 125 C1
Finchley NW7 .... 29 A4
Highams Pk E17 .... 35 D2
Robert St Croydon CR0 .. 221 A5
Newham E16 .... 122 D5
Plumstead SE18 .... 123 B2
Regent's Pk NW1 ..... 93 B4 231 D1
Strand WC2 .... 250 B5
Robert Sutton Ho 20 E1 ... 96 C1
Robeson St 7 E3 .... 97 B2
Robina Cl DA6 .... 146 D1
Northwood HA6 .... 22 A2
Robin Cl Edgware NW7 ... 11 C1
Hampton TW12 .... 173 A5
Robin Cres E16 .... 99 D2
Robin Ct
15 Cubitt Town E14 ..... 120 A3
Wallington SM6 .... 219 C2
Wood Green N22 .... 32 B3
Robin Gr
Brentford TW8 .... 131 C6
Dartmouth Pk N6 .... 71 A6
Harrow HA3 .... 44 B3
Robin Hill Dr BR7 ...... 188 A4
Robin Ho NW8 .... 230 A3
Robin Hood SW15 ..... 155 C1
Robinhood Cl CR4 ..... 203 C6
Robin Hood Ct 2 SM1 ... 217 D3
Robin Hood Dr HA3 ..... 24 D3
Robin Hood Gdns 12 E14 ... 120 A6
Robin Hood Inf Sch SM1 ... 217 C3
Robin Hood Jun Sch SM1 ... 217 D3
Robinhood La CR4 ..... 203 C6
Robin Hood La
Bexley DA6 .... 169 A6
Blackwall E14 .... 120 A6
Robin Hood La *continued*
Kingston u T SW15 ..... 177 C6
Sutton SM1 .... 217 D3
Robin Hood Prim Sch SW15 ... 177 C5
Robin Hood Way UB6 ... 64 D2
Robin Hood Way (Kingston By Pass) KT2, SW15, SW20 ... 177 C5
Robinia Cl SE20 .... 184 A2
Robinia Cres E10 .... 75 D6
Robin La NW4 .... 46 D6
Robinscroft Mews 18 SE10 ... 141 D4
Robins Ct
Grove Pk SE12 .... 165 C1
Richmond TW10 .... 154 A5
South Croydon CR2 .... 221 C4
Robin's Ct
Beckenham BR3 .... 186 B1
Clapham Pk SW4 ...... 160 A5
Robinsfield Inf Sch NW8 ... 92 C5 230 A4
Robins Gr BR4 .... 225 A5
Robinson Cl Enfield EN2 ... 5 A2
11 Leyton E11 .... 76 C5
Robinson Cres WD23 ..... 8 A3
Robinson Ct
5 Barnet EN4 .... 14 D3
Islington N1 .... 234 D6
4 Richmond TW9 ...... 132 B1
Thornton Heath CR0 .... 204 D3
Robinson Ho
4 North Kensington W10 ... 90 D1
12 Tower Hamlets E14 ... 97 C2
Robinson Rd
Dagenham RM10 .... 81 C4
Mitcham SW19 .... 180 C4
South Hackney E2 .... 96 C5
Robinson's Cl W13 ...... 87 A2
Robinson St SW3 ..... 267 C6
Robinwood Gr UB8 ..... 82 B3
Robinwood Pl SW15 ... 177 B6
Robsart St SW9 .... 138 C3
Robson Ave NW10 ...... 68 A1
Robson Cl Enfield EN2 ..... 4 D3
Newham E6 .... 100 A1
Robson Ct N12 .... 30 A5
Robson Rd SE21, SE27 .. 161 A1
Roby Ho EC1 .... 242 A6
Roch Ave HA8 .... 26 B1
Rochdale 8 SE19 ...... 183 C4
Rochdale Rd
Abbey Wood SE2 ...... 124 B2
Walthamstow E17 ...... 53 C2
Rochdale Way 4 SE8 .. 141 C5
Roche Ho 15 E14 ...... 119 B6
Rochelle Cl SW11 ..... 136 B1
Rochelle Ct
Beckenham BR3 .... 185 D3
14 Stepney E1 .... 96 C1
Rochelle St 31 E2 .... 95 D4
Rochemont Wlk 2 E8 ... 96 A6
Roche Rd SW16 .... 182 B2
Roche Sch The SW18 .. 157 C6
Rochester Ave
Bromley BR1 .... 187 B1
Feltham TW13 .... 149 D2
Newham E13 .... 99 C6
Rochester Cl
1 Blackfen DA15 ...... 168 B5
Enfield EN1 .... 5 C4
Streatham SW16 ...... 182 A3
Rochester Ct
1 Bethnal Green E2 ..... 96 B3
9 Camden Town NW1 ... 71 C1
Finchley N3 .... 29 A1
Kingsbury NW9 .... 45 B4
South Norwood SE25 ... 184 A1
Rochester Dr
Old Bexley DA5 .... 169 C5
Pinner HA5 .... 40 D4
Rochester Gdns
Redbridge IG1 .... 56 B2
South Croydon CR0 .... 221 C5
Rochester Ho
Bermondsey SE1 ...... 252 D1
18 Deptford SE15 ..... 140 C6
Rochester Mews NW1 ... 71 C1
Rochester Par TW13 ... 150 A1
Rochester Pl NW1 ...... 71 C1
Rochester Rd
Carshalton SM5 .... 218 D4
Kentish Town NW1 ..... 71 C2
Northwood HA6 .... 39 D6
Rochester Row SW1 ..... 115 C2 259 B4
Rochester Sq NW1 ...... 71 C1
Rochester St SW1 .... 259 C5
Rochester Terr NW1 ... 71 C2
Rochester Way
Eltham SE9 .... 144 C2
Kidbrooke SE3, SE9 ... 143 D2
Rochester Wlk SE1 ... 252 C4
Roche Wlk SM5 .... 202 B3
Rochford N17 .... 33 C1
Rochford Ave RM6 ..... 58 C4
Rochford Cl 2 E6 ...... 99 D5
Rochford Way CR0 ..... 204 A3
Rochford Wlk 3 E8 .... 74 A1
Rochfort Ho 4 SE8 .... 119 B1
Rock Ave 13 SW14 ..... 133 B2
Rockbourne Rd SE23 ... 162 D3
Rock Cl CR4 .... 180 B1
Rockell's Pl SE22 ..... 162 B5
Rockfield Ho
Greenwich SE10 ...... 142 A6
2 Hendon NW4 .... 46 D5
Rockford Ave UB6 ...... 87 B5
Rock Gdns RM10 .... 81 D3
Rock Grove Way SE16 .. 118 A2
Rockhall Rd NW2 .... 68 D4
Rockhampton Cl 4 SE27 ... 182 C6
Rockhampton Rd
South Croydon CR2 .... 221 C2
West Norwood SE27, SW16 ... 182 C6
Rock Hill SE19 .... 183 D6
Rockingham Cl SW15 .. 133 D1
Rockingham Ct 10 BR3 ... 185 C3
Rockingham Gate WD23 .. 8 A5
Rockingham St SE1 .... 117 A3 262 A5
Rockland Rd SW15 ..... 135 A1
Rocklands N3 .... 29 B3
Rocklands Dr HA7 ...... 25 C1
Rockley Ct 9 W14 ..... 112 D4
Rockley Rd W14 ...... 112 D4
Rockliffe Manor Prim Sch SE18 ... 145 D6
Rockmount Prim Sch SE19 ... 183 B4
Rockmount Rd
Plumstead Comm SE18, SE2 ... 123 D1
South Norwood SE19 ... 183 B4
Rocks La SW13 .... 134 A2
Rock St N4 .... 72 C6
Rockstraw Ho 5 NW3 ... 70 D1
Rockware Ave UB6 ..... 86 C6
Rockware Bsns Ctr UB6 ... 86 B6
Rockways EN5 .... 11 D5
Rockwell Gdns SE19 .. 183 C6
Rockwell Rd RM10 ...... 81 D3
Rockwood Ct N16 ...... 52 A2
Rocliffe St N1 ... 94 D5 234 D3
Rocombe Cres SE23 ... 162 C4
Rocque Ho SW6 ...... 264 C4
Rocque La SE3 .... 142 D2
Rodborough Rd NW11 .. 47 C1
Rodd Est TW17 .... 193 B4
Roden Gdns CR0 ...... 205 C3
Rodenhurst Ct SW4 ... 159 D6
Rodenhurst Rd SW4 ... 159 D5
Roden St Ilford IG1 ..... 78 C5
Upper Holloway N7 ..... 72 B5
Roderick Ho 3 SE16 ... 118 C2
Roderick Rd NW3 ...... 70 D4
Rodgers Cl WD6 .... 9 D5
Rodgers Ho 4 SW4 .... 159 D4
Rodin Ct N1 .... 234 C5
Roding Ct 6 W12 ...... 111 C4
Roding Ho N1 .... 234 A5
Roding Hospl IG4 ...... 55 D6
Roding La IG9 .... 21 D3
Roding La N IG8 .... 37 D1
Roding La S IG4 .... 55 D5
Roding Lo IG1 .... 55 D3
Roding Mews E1 ...... 118 A5
Roding Prim Sch RM8 .. 80 C3
Roding Rd Hackney E5 ... 75 A3
Newham E6 .... 100 D2
Rodings Ct E4 .... 36 B5
Rodings Row EN5 .... 1 A1
Rodings The 4 IG8 .... 37 C4
Roding Valley Sta IG9 ... 37 D6
Roding View IG9 .... 21 D3
Rodmarton St W1 .... 92 D2 237 D3
Rodmell WC1 .... 233 B1
Rodmell Cl UB4 .... 85 A3
Rodmell Slope N12 ..... 29 B5
Rodmere St SE10 ..... 120 C1
Rodmill La SW2 ...... 160 A4
Rodney Cl
New Malden KT3 ...... 199 C4
Pinner HA5 .... 41 A2
Thornton Heath CR0 ... 204 D1
Walton-on-T KT12 ..... 194 C1
Rodney Ct NW8 ...... 236 B6
Rodney Gdns
Hayes BR4 .... 225 A4
Pinner HA5 .... 40 C4
Rodney Ho
4 Cubitt Town E14 .... 119 D2
Islington N1 .... 233 D3
Notting Hill W11 ...... 245 A6
Rodney Pl
Merton SW19 .... 180 A2
Newington SE17 .... 117 A2 262 B4
Walthamstow E17 ...... 35 B1
Rodney Rd
Mitcham CR4 .... 202 C6
New Malden KT3 ...... 199 C4
Twickenham TW4 ...... 151 C4
Walton-on-T KT12 ..... 194 C1
Walworth SE17 117 B2 262 C3
Wanstead E11 .... 55 B3
Rodney St N1 ... 94 B5 233 D3
Rodwall Pl HA8 .... 26 C3
Rodway Rd
Bromley BR1 .... 187 B2
Putney SW15 .... 156 A4
Rodwell Cl 2 HA4 ...... 40 C1
Rodwell Rd SE22 ..... 161 D5
Roe 5 NW9 .... 27 D2
Roebourne Way E16 ... 122 C4
Roebuck Cl
Feltham TW13 .... 172 B6
Tottenham N17 .... 33 D4
Roebuck Ct
Chingford E4 .... 36 A3
2 New Malden KT3 .... 199 C4
Roebuck Hts IG10 ...... 21 C4
Roebuck La IG9 .... 21 C3
Roebuck Rd KT9 .... 214 C3
Roedean Ave EN3 .... 6 C5
Roedean Cl EN3 .... 6 C4
Roedean Cres SW15 ... 155 C6
Roe End NW9 .... 45 A5
Roe Gn NW9 .... 45 A4
Roe Green Jun & Inf Schs NW9 ... 44 D5
ROEHAMPTON 155 C4
Roehampton CE Prim Sch SW15 ... 156 B4
Roehampton Cl SW15 .. 134 A1
Roehampton Ct SW13 .. 134 A2
Roehampton Dr BR7 ... 189 A4
Roehampton Gate SW15 ... 155 C5
Roehampton High St SW15 ... 156 A4
Roehampton La
Putney SW15 .... 156 A5
Roehampton SW15 ..... 156 B3
Roehampton Univ (Digby Stuart Coll) SW15 .... 156 A6
Roehampton Univ (Froebel Coll) SW15 .. 155 D5
Roehampton Univ (Southlands Coll) SW15 ... 156 A6
Roehampton Univ (Whitelands Coll) SW15 ... 156 A4
Roehampton Vale SW15 ... 155 D2
Roe La NW9 .... 45 A5
Roe Way SM6 .... 220 A2
Roffey Ct 9 NW9 ...... 46 A5
Roffey St E14 .... 120 A4
Rogate Ho E5 .... 74 A5
Roger Ascham Prim Sch E17 ... 35 B2
Roger Dowley Ct 8 E2 .. 96 C5
Roger's Almshouses 2 SW9 ... 138 B1
Rogers Ct 16 E14 ...... 119 C6
Rogers Est 28 E2 .... 96 C4
Rogers Gdns RM10 ..... 81 C3
Rogers Ho
9 Dagenham RM10 ..... 81 C5
Westminster SW1 ..... 259 D4
Rogers Rd
Canning Town E16 ...... 98 D1
Dagenham RM10 .... 81 C3
Upper Tooting SW17 ... 180 C6
Roger St WC1 ... 94 B3 240 D5
Roger Stone Ct NW10 ... 67 B6
Rogers Wlk N12 .... 13 D1
Rohan Pl 4 IG4 .... 56 B4
Rojack Rd SE23 .... 162 D3
Rokeby Gdns IG8 .... 37 A2
Rokeby Ho
9 Balham SW12 ...... 159 B4
Bloomsbury WC1 ..... 240 C5
Rokeby Pl SW20 ...... 178 B3
Rokeby Rd SE4 .... 141 B3
Rokeby Sch
Kingston u T KT2 ...... 177 A3
Stratford E15 .... 76 B1
Rokeby St E15 .... 98 C6
Rokeland Ho SE4 ..... 141 A1
Rokell Ho BR3 .... 185 D5
Roker Park Ave UB10 ... 60 A4
Rokesby Cl DA16 ..... 145 B3
Rokesby Pl HA0 .... 65 D3
Rokesly Ave N8 .... 50 A4
Rokesly Jun & Inf Schs N8 ... 50 A4
Roland Ct SE19 .... 183 D2
Roland Gdns SW7 .... 114 A1 256 B2
Roland Ho SW7 .... 256 B2
Roland Mews 1 E1 ..... 96 D2
Roland Rd E17 .... 54 B5
Roland Way
South Kensington SW7 .... 114 A1 256 B2
Walworth SE17 ...... 262 D1
Worcester Pk KT4 ..... 215 D6
Roles Gr RM6 .... 59 A5
Rolfe Cl EN4 .... 2 C1
Rolfe Ho N11 .... 30 D6
Rolinsden Way BR2 ... 225 D4
Rolland Ho W7 .... 86 C2
Rollesby Rd KT19, KT9 .. 214 C2
Rollesby Way SE28 .... 102 C1
Rolleston Ave BR5 .... 210 D3
Rolleston Cl BR5 ...... 210 D2
Rolleston Rd CR2 ..... 221 B1
Roll Gdns IG2 .... 56 C4
Rollins St SE15 .... 140 C6
Rollit Cres TW3 ...... 151 C6
Rollit Ho N7 .... 72 C3
Rollit St N7 .... 72 C3
Rollo Ct SW11 .... 268 C1
Rolls Bldgs EC4 ...... 241 B2
Rollscourt Ave SE24 ... 161 A6
Rolls Ct The E4 .... 36 A5
Rolls Park Ave E4 ...... 35 D5
Rolls Park Rd E4 .... 35 D5
Rolls Pas EC4 .... 241 A2
Rolls Rd SE1 ... 117 D1 263 D2
Rolt St SE8 .... 141 A6
Rolvenden Gdns BR1 .. 187 D3
Rolvenden Pl N17 ...... 34 A2
Roman Cl
Feltham TW14 .... 150 C6
South Acton W3 ...... 110 D4
Roman Ct 4 N7 .... 72 B2
Romanfield Rd SW2 ... 160 B4
Romanhurst Ave BR2 .. 208 C5

Romanhurst Gdns BR2, BR3 208 C5
Roman Ind Est CR0 205 C2
Roman Lo 6 IG9 21 C3
Roman Rd
Chiswick W4 111 D2
Finchley N12 30 C2
Globe Town E2, E3 96 D5
Ilford IG1 78 D2
Muswell Hill N10 31 B3
Newham E6 100 A3
25 Old Ford E3 97 B6
Willesden NW2 68 C5
Roman Rise SE19 183 B4
Roman Road Prim Sch E6 99 D3
Roman Sq SE28 124 A5
Roman Square Mkt 1 E3 97 B5
Roman Way
Barnsbury N7 72 B2
Croydon CR0 220 D6
4 Deptford SE15 140 C5
Enfield EN1 17 D6
Romany Gdns
Cheam SM3 201 C2
1 Higham Hill E17 35 A2
Romany Ho 8 N9 18 A1
Romany Prospect SE19 183 B4
Romany Rise BR5 211 A1
Roma Rd E17 53 A6
Roma Read Cl SW15 156 B4
Romayne Ho SW4 137 D2
Romberg Rd SW17 159 A1
Romborough Gdns SE13 164 A6
Romborough Way SE13 164 A6
Romeland WD6 9 D5
Romeland Ct WD6 9 D5
Romer Ho 9 SW2 160 B6
Romero Cl SW9 138 B2
Romero Sq SE9 143 C1
Romeyn Rd SW16 160 B1
ROMFORD 59 D4
Romford Ho 17 N1 73 B2
Romford Rd
Forest Gate E7, E12 77 C3
Stratford E15 76 D2
Romford St E1 96 B2
Romilly Dr WD19 23 A6
Romilly Rd N4 72 D6
Romilly St W1 249 D6
Romily Ct SW6 135 A3
Rommany Ct SE27 183 B6
Rommany Rd SE27 183 B6
Romney Cl
Ashford TW15 171 A5
Chessington KT9 214 A4
7 Deptford SE14 140 C5
Harrow HA2 41 C2
North End NW11 48 A1
Tottenham N17 34 B2
Romney Ct
9 Hammersmith W12 112 C4
8 Hampstead NW3 70 C2
15 Northolt UB5 84 D5
Romney Dr
Bromley BR1 187 D3
Harrow HA2 41 C2
Romney Gdns DA7 147 B4
Romney Ho
2 Blackwall E14 120 B6
Enfield EN1 18 A6
Sutton SM2 217 D2
Romney Mews W1 238 A4
Romney Par UB4 83 B5
Romney Rd
Greenwich SE10 142 B6
Hayes UB4 83 B5
New Malden KT3 199 B3
Romney Row NW2 68 D6
Romney St SW1 116 A3 260 A5
Romola Rd SE24, SW2 160 D3
Romsey Cl BR6 226 D4
Romsey Gdns RM9 102 D6
Romsey Rd
Dagenham RM9 102 D6
Ealing W13 109 A6
Romulus Ct 7 TW8 131 D5
Ronald Ave E15 98 C4
Ronald Cl BR3 207 B4
Ronald Ct EN5 1 D2
Ronald Ho Eltham SE9 143 C1
4 Sutton SM1 218 B3
Ronald Ross Prim Sch SW19 157 A4
Ronaldshay N4 50 C1
Ronalds Rd
Bromley BR1 187 A2
Islington N5 72 C3
Ronald St E1 96 C1
Ronaldstone Rd DA15 167 C5
Rona Rd NW3 71 A4
Ronart St HA3 42 D6
Rona Wlk 20 N1 73 B2
Rondu Rd NW2 69 A3
Ronelean Rd KT6 214 B5
Ron Leighton Way E6 100 A6
Ronnie La E12 78 C4
Ron Todd Cl RM10 103 C6
Ronver Lo E4 20 C1
Ronver Rd SE12 164 D3
Rood La EC3 117 C6 253 A6
Rookby Ct N21 16 D2
Rook Cl HA9 66 D5
Rookeries Cl TW13 150 C1
Rookery Cl NW9 45 D4
Rookery Cotts EN4 3 B2
Rookery Cres RM10 81 D1
Rookery Dr BR7 188 C2
Rookery La BR2 209 D3
Rookery Rd SW4 137 C1
Rookery Way NW9 45 D4
Rooke Way SE10 120 D1
Rookfield Ave N10 49 C5
Rookfield Cl N10 49 C5
Rook Lo IG1 55 D3
Rooks Heath High Sch HA2 63 C5
Rooksmead Rd TW16 172 A1
Rooks Terr UB7 104 A4
Rookstone Rd SW17 180 D5
Rook Wlk E6 100 A1
Rookwood Ave
Wallington SM6 219 D4
West Barnes KT3 200 A5
Rookwood Gdns E4 20 D2
Rookwood Ho 2 IG11 101 B5
Rookwood Rd N16 52 A2
Roosevelt Ct 15 SW19 157 A3
Rootes Dr W10 90 D2
Ropemaker Rd SE16 119 A3
Ropemaker's Fields 7 E14 119 B6
Ropemaker St EC2 95 B2 242 C4
Roper Ho 13 SE21 183 C6
Roper La SE1 117 C4 253 B1
Ropers Ave E4 36 A5
Roper's Orch SW3 267 A5
Roper St 1 SE9 166 C5
Ropers Wlk 13 SE24 160 C4
Roper Way CR4 181 A1
Ropery Bsns Pk SE7 121 C2
Ropery St E3 97 B3
Rope St SE16 119 A3
Ropewalk Gdns 18 E1 96 A1
Rope Yard Rails SE18 122 D3
Ropley St 6 E2 96 A5
Rosa Alba Mews N5 73 A4
Rosa Ave TW15 170 C6
Rosa Freedman Ctr NW2 46 C1
Rosalind Ct 6 IG11 80 A1
Rosalind Ho 25 N1 95 C5
Rosaline Rd SW6 135 A5 264 B3
Rosaline Terr SW6 264 B3
Rosamond St SE26 162 B1
Rosamund Cl CR2 221 B4
Rosamun St UB2 107 A2
Rosa Parks Ho 8 SW9 138 B3
Rosary Cl TW3, TW5 129 A3
Rosary Ct 17 E1 96 D2
Rosary Gdns
Ashford TW15 170 D6
Bushey WD23 8 C4
South Kensington SW7 114 A2 256 B3
Rosary RC Inf Sch TW5 129 C6
Rosary RC Jun Sch TW5 129 C6
Rosary RC Prim Sch NW3 70 C3
Rosaville Rd SW6 135 B5 264 C3
Rosbury SW15 157 A5
Roscastle Rd SE4 163 A6
Roscoe St EC1 95 A3 242 B5
Roscoff Cl HA8 27 A2
Roscommon Ho 2 NW3 70 B3
Roseacre Cl Ealing W13 87 B2
Littleton TW17 192 C4
Roseacre Lo EN3 6 C1
Roseacre Rd DA16 146 B2
Rose Alley
Borough The SE1 252 B4
Broadgate EC2 243 B3
Rose Ave Mitcham CR4 180 D2
Morden SM4 202 A4
Woodford E18 37 B1
Rosebank
2 Dagenham W3 89 B1
Fulham SW6 134 C5
Penge SE20 184 B3
Rosebank Ave HA0 64 D4
Rosebank Cl
Colney Hatch N12 30 C5
Teddington TW11 175 A4
Rosebank Gdns Bow E3 97 B5
1 Dagenham W3 89 B1
Rosebank Gr E17 53 B6
Rosebank Rd
Hanwell W7 108 C4
Walthamstow E17 53 D3
Rosebank Villas E17 53 C5
Rosebank Way W3 89 B1
Rosebank Wlk
Camden Town NW1 71 D1
14 Woolwich SE7 122 A2
Rose Bates Dr NW9 44 C5
Rosebay Ho 20 E3 97 C2
Roseberry Gdns
Harringay N4 50 D3
Orpington BR6 227 C5
Roseberry Pl E8 73 D2
Roseberry St SE16 118 B2
Rosebery Ave
Finsbury EC1 94 C4 234 B1
Harrow HA2 63 B4
Kingston u T KT3 199 D6
Plashet E12 78 B2
Sidcup DA15 167 C4
Rosebery Ave *continued*
South Norwood CR7 183 A1
Tottenham N17 34 A1
Rosebery Cl SM4 200 D3
Rosebery Ct
Chessington KT9 214 B3
Holborn EC1 241 A6
Mayfair W1 248 C4
Rosebery Gdns
Ealing W13 87 A1
Hornsey N8 50 A4
Sutton SM1 217 D4
Rosebery Ho 21 E2 96 C5
Rosebery Ind Pk N17 34 B1
Rosebery Mews N10 31 C1
Rosebery Rd
Cheam SM1, SM2 217 B2
Clapham Pk SW2 160 A5
Isleworth TW3, TW7 152 A6
Kingston u T KT1 176 D1
Muswell Hill N10 31 C1
Rosebery Sq
Holborn EC1 241 A5
Kingston u T KT1 176 D1
Rosebine Ave TW2 152 B4
Rosebriars KT10 212 A3
Rose Bruford Coll DA15 168 B3
Rosebury Ct SW16 182 B2
Rosebury Rd SW6 135 D3
Rosebury Vale HA4 62 A6
Rose Bush Ct NW3 70 D3
Rose Cotts KT10 212 B3
Rosecourt Rd CR0 204 B3
Rosecroft N22 32 B2
Rosecroft Ave NW3 69 C5
Rosecroft Gdns
Dollis Hill NW2 68 A5
Twickenham TW2 152 B3
Rosecroft Rd UB1 85 C3
Rosecroft Wlk
Pinner HA5 40 D4
Wembley HA0 65 D3
Rose & Crown Ct EC2 242 A2
Rose & Crown Yd SW1 249 B3
Rose Ct 7 Dalston E8 73 D1
Harrow HA2 64 A6
Ilford IG1 78 D2
Islington N1 234 C5
Muswell Hill N10 31 B3
3 Pinner HA5 40 C6
Spitalfields E1 243 D3
7 Wembley HA0 88 A5
10 Wimbledon SW19 179 B5
Rose Dale BR6 226 D6
Rosedale Ave UB3 83 B2
Rosedale Cl
Abbey Wood SE2 124 B3
Hanwell W7 108 D4
Stanmore HA7 25 B4
Rosedale Cnr BR7 188 B2
Rosedale Coll UB3 83 C1
Rosedale Ct N5 72 D4
Rosedale Dr RM9 80 B1
Rosedale Gdns RM9 80 B1
Rosedale Ho N16 51 B1
Rosedale Lo N14 15 B4
Rosedale Pl CR0 206 D2
Rosedale Rd
Dagenham RM9 80 B1
Forest Gate E7 77 C3
Richmond TW9 132 A1
Stoneleigh KT17 216 A3
Rosedale Terr W6 112 B3
Rosedene NW6 90 D6
Rosedene Ave
Morden SM4 201 C4
Southall UB6 85 C4
Streatham SW16 160 B1
Thornton Heath CR0 204 A2
Rosedene Ct HA4 39 C1
Rosedene Gdns IG2 56 C5
Rosedene Terr E10 75 D6
Rosedew Rd W6 134 D6
Rose End KT4 200 D1
Rosefield Cl SM5 218 C3
Rosefield Ct EN4 2 D1
Rosefield Gdns E14 119 C6
Roseford Ct 16 W12 112 D4
Rose Garden Cl HA8 26 A4
Rosegate Ho 32 E3 97 B5
Rose Gdns Ealing W5 109 D3
Feltham TW13 150 A2
Southall UB1 85 C3
Rose Glen NW9 45 B5
Rosehart Mews 8 W11 91 C1
Rosehatch Ave RM6 58 D6
Roseheath Rd TW4 151 B6
ROSEHILL 202 A1
Rosehill Claygate KT10 213 A2
Hampton TW12 173 C2
Rose Hill
Carshalton SM4, SM5 202 A2
Cheam SM1 201 D1
Rosehill Ave SM1, SM5 202 A1
Rosehill Ct SM4 202 A2
Rosehill Gdns
Greenford UB6 64 D3
Sutton SM1 218 A6
Rose Hill Park W SM1 218 A6
Rosehill Rd SW18 158 A6
Rose La RM6 59 A5
Roseland Cl N17 33 B3
Roseland Ho SW6 135 A2
Rose Lawn WD23 8 A3
Roseleigh Ave N5 72 D4
Roseleigh Cl 15 TW1 153 D5
Roselle Ct W5 88 A1
Rosemary Ave
East Finchley N2 47 D5
East Molesey KT8 195 C5
Edmonton N9 18 B3
Enfield EN2 5 C4
Finchley N3 29 D1
Hounslow TW4 128 D3
Rosemary Branch Bridge N1 235 D6
Rosemary Cl
Hillingdon UB8 82 C2
Thornton Heath CR0 204 A3
Rosemary Cotts 4 SW19 178 C3
Rosemary Ct 35 SE8 141 B6
Rosemary Dr
Redbridge IG4 55 D4
16 South Bromley E14 98 B1
Rosemary Gdns
Chessington KT9 214 A4
Dagenham RM8 59 B1
Mortlake SW14 133 A2
Rosemary Ho
Shoreditch N1 235 D5
Willesden NW10 90 B6
Rosemary La SW14 133 A2
Rosemary Rd
Bexley DA16 145 D4
Camberwell SE15 139 D5
Wandsworth SW17 158 A1
Rosemary St N1 235 D6
Rosemary Works Sch N1 95 B6 235 D5
Rosemead NW9 46 A2
Rosemead Ave
Feltham TW13 149 D2
Mitcham CR4 181 C1
Wembley HA9 66 A3
Rosemead Prep Sch SE27 161 A2
Rose Mews N18 34 B6
Rosemont Ave N12 30 A4
Rosemont Mans 11 NW3 69 D2
Rosemont Rd
Acton W3 110 D6
Kingston u T KT3 199 A6
Richmond TW10 154 A5
South Hampstead NW3 70 A2
Wembley HA0 88 A6
Rosemoor Ho 14 W13 109 A5
Rosemoor St SW3 114 D2 257 C3
Rosemount Ct
2 Acton W3 110 D5
South Norwood SE25 205 C6
Rosemount Dr BR1 210 B5
Rosemount Lo W3 110 D6
Rosemount Point 10 SE23 162 D1
Rosemount Rd W13 87 A1
Rosemount Twrs 5 SM6 219 C2
Rosenau Cres SW11 267 C1
Rosenau Rd SW11 136 D4 267 C2
Rosendale Prim Sch SE21 161 A4
Rosendale Rd SE21, SE24 161 A3
Roseneath Ave N21 16 D3
Roseneath Pl 2 SW16 182 B6
Roseneath Rd SW11 159 A5
Roseneath Wlk EN1 5 C1
Rosens Wlk HA8 10 D1
Rosenthal Ho SE6 163 D5
Rosenthal Rd SE6 164 A5
Rosenthorpe Rd SE15 162 D6
Roserton St E14 120 A4
Rosery The CR0 206 D3
Rose Sq SW7 256 D2
Rose St Holborn EC4 241 D2
Strand WC2 116 A6 250 A6
Roses The IG8 36 D3
Rosethorn Cl SW12 159 D4
Rosetta Cl SW8 270 B3
Rosetta Ct SE19 183 C3
Rosetta Prim Sch E16 99 B2
Rosetti Terr RM8 80 B4
Roseveare Rd SE12 187 C6
Roseville N21 16 C3
Roseville Ave TW3, TW4 151 C6
Roseville Rd UB3 106 A2
Rosevine Rd SW20 178 C2
Rosewall Ct SW19 179 D5
Roseway SE21 161 B5
Rose Way Edgware HA8 27 A6
Lee SE12 165 A6
Rosewell Cl SE20 184 B3
Rose Wlk Surbiton KT5 198 D4
West Wickham BR4 224 B6
Rosewood Ave UB6 65 A2
Rosewood Cl DA14 168 C1
Rosewood Ct
Bromley BR1 187 D2
Dagenham RM6 58 C4
Kingston u T KT2 176 C3
2 Leyton E11 76 B4
Rosewood Dr TW17 192 B4
Rosewood Gdns SE13 142 A3
Rosewood Gr SM1 218 A6
Rosewood Ho 9 NW3 69 D2
Rosewood Sq W12 90 A1
Rosher Cl E15 76 B1
Roshni Ho SW17 180 C4
Rosh Pinah Prim Sch
Edgware HA8 10 D1
Edgware HA8 26 C6
Rosina Ct SW17 180 C5
Rosina St E9 74 D2
Roskeen Ct 1 SW19 178 C3
Roskell Rd SW15 134 D2
Roskild Ct HA9 66 B4
Roslin Ho 2 E1 118 D6
Roslin Rd W3 110 D3
Roslin Way BR1 187 A5
Roslyn Cl CR4 180 B1
Roslyn Rd N15 51 C4
Rosmead Rd W11 113 A6 244 B6
Rosoman Pl EC1 241 B6
Rosoman St EC1 234 B1
Rossal Ct 2 SE20 184 B3
Rossall Cres NW10 88 B4
Rossanne Ho N3 29 D3
Ross Ave Dagenham RM8 59 B4
Finchley NW7 29 A5
Ross Cl Harrow HA3 24 A3
Hayes UB3 105 B2
Northolt UB5 64 B4
Ross Ct Chislehurst BR7 188 B3
Colindale NW9 45 C6
Ealing W13 87 B2
Edgware HA8 10 D2
1 Hackney E5 74 B4
4 Putney SW15 156 D4
South Croydon CR2 221 A2
Rossdale SM1 218 C3
Rossdale Dr
Ponders End N9 18 C5
Welsh Harp NW9 45 A1
Rossdale Rd SW15 134 C1
Rosse Gdns SE13 164 B5
Rosse Mews SE3 143 B4
Rossendale Cl EN2 4 D6
Rossendale Ho 7 E5 74 B6
Rossendale St E5 74 B6
Rossendale Way NW1 93 C6 232 B6
Rossendon Ct 1 SM6 219 C2
Rossetti Ct WC1 239 C4
Rossetti Gdns Mans SW3 267 C6
Rossetti Ho SW1 259 D3
Rossetti Mews NW8 229 D5
Rossetti Rd SE16 118 B1
Rossetti Studios SW3 267 B6
Ross Ho
2 Kidbrooke SE18 144 A4
Twickenham TW2 151 D2
18 Wapping E1 118 B5
Rossignol Gdns SM5 219 A6
Rossindel Rd TW3 151 C6
Rossington Cl EN1 6 B5
Rossington St E5 74 A6
Rossiter Fields EN5 13 B5
Rossiter Rd SW12 159 B3
Rossland Cl DA6 169 D6
Rosslyn Ave
Barnes SW13 133 D2
Chingford E4 20 D2
Dagenham RM8 59 C2
East Barnet EN4 14 C5
Feltham TW14 150 A5
Rosslyn Cl
Ashford TW16 171 C4
Coney Hall BR4 224 D5
Hayes UB3 83 B2
Rosslyn Cres
Harrow HA1 42 D5
Wembley HA9 66 A4
Rosslyn Ct NW3 70 C3
Rosslyn Hill NW3 70 B3
Rosslyn Ho 8 TW9 132 B4
Rosslyn Mans
8 Hampstead NW3 70 A2
South Hampstead NW6 70 A2
Rosslyn Mews 7 NW3 70 B4
Rosslyn Park Mews NW3 70 B3
Rosslyn Rd Barking IG11 79 B1
Twickenham TW1 153 C5
Walthamstow E17 54 A5
Rossmore Cl EN3 6 D1
Rossmore Ct NW1 237 C6
Rossmore Rd NW1 92 C3 237 B6
Ross Par SM6 219 B2
Ross Rd
South Norwood SE25 205 C6
Twickenham TW2 152 A3
Wallington SM6 219 C3
Ross Way SE9 144 A2
Rossway Dr WD23 8 B6
Rosswood Gdns SM6 219 C2
Rosswood Ho 13 SM6 219 B2
Rosswood Lo CR0 222 D6
Rostella Rd SW17 180 B6
Rostrever Gdns UB3 105 C5
Rostrevor Ave N15 51 D3
Rostrevor Gdns UB2 107 A1
Rostrevor Mans SW6 264 C2
Rostrevor Mews SW6 264 C1
Rostrevor Rd
Fulham SW6 135 B4 264 C2
Wimbledon SW19 179 C5
Rotary Ct KT8 196 C6
Rotary Lo 12 SE27 160 D1
Rotary St SE1 261 D6
Rothay NW1 231 D2
Rothbury Gdns TW7 131 A5
Rothbury Rd E9 75 C1
Rothbury Wlk N17 34 A3
Rotheley Ho 39 E9 74 C1
Rotherfield Ct
De Beauvoir Town N1 73 B1
Shoreditch N1 95 B6 235 C6
Rotherfield Prim Sch N1 95 A6 235 B6
Rotherfield Rd
Enfield EN3 6 D6
Wallington SM5 219 A3
Rotherfield St
Islington N1 73 A1
Shoreditch N1 95 A6 235 B6
Rotherham Wlk SE1 251 C3
Rotherhill Ave SW16 181 D4
ROTHERHITHE 118 D3
Rotherhithe Bsns Est 6 SE16 118 C2
Rotherhithe New Rd SE16 118 B1
Rotherhithe Old Rd SE16 118 D2
Rotherhithe Prim Sch SE16 118 D2
Rotherhithe St SE16 118 C4
Rotherhithe Sta SE16 118 C4
Rotherhithe Tunnel SE16 118 D5
Rother Ho SE15 140 B1
Rotherwick Hill W5 88 B3
Rotherwick Rd NW11 47 C2
Rotherwood Cl SW20 179 A2
Rotherwood Rd SW15 134 D2
Rothery St N1 234 D6
Rothesay Ave
Merton SW20 179 A1
Mortlake SW14, TW10 132 D1
Northolt UB6 64 B2
Rothesay Ct
4 Catford SE6 164 D2
Grove Pk SE12 165 B1
13 Kennington SE11 138 C6
Rothesay Rd SE25 205 C5
Rothley Ct NW8 236 C6
Rothsay Rd E7 77 C2
Rothsay St SE1 117 C3 263 A5
Rothsay Wlk 19 E14 119 C2
Rothschild Rd W4 111 A3
Rothschild St SE27 182 D6
Rothwell Ct
2 Bromley BR1 187 B2
4 Harrow HA1 42 D4
Rothwell Gdns RM9 102 C6
Rothwell Ho TW5 129 C6
Rothwell Rd RM9 102 C6
Rothwell St
10 Hampstead NW1 70 D1
Primrose Hill NW1 230 D6
Roth Wlk N7 72 B6
Rotten Row SW1 114 D4 247 C2
Rotterdam Dr E14 120 A3
Rouel Rd
Bermondsey SE16 118 A2
Bermondsey SE16 118 A3
Rougemont Ave SM4 201 C3
Roundabout Ho HA6 22 A2
Roundacre SW19 156 D2
Roundel Cl SE4 141 B1
Roundell Ho 10 SE21 183 C6
Rounders Ct 7 RM10 81 D2
Round Gr CR0 206 D2
Roundhay Cl SE23 162 D2
Roundhedge Way EN2 4 B5
Round Hill SE23 162 C1
Roundhill Dr EN2 4 B1
ROUNDSHAW 220 B1
Roundshaw Ctr SM6 220 A1
Roundtable Rd BR1 164 D1
Roundtree Rd HA0 65 B3
Roundways HA4 61 D5
Roundway The
Claygate KT10 212 D2
Tottenham N17 33 B2
Roundwood BR7 188 D1
Roundwood Ave UB11 105 A5
Roundwood Cl HA4 39 B2
Roundwood Rd NW10 67 D1
Rounton Rd E3 97 C3
Rountree Ct 9 UB1 85 D1
Roupell Ho 7 KT2 176 B3
Roupell Rd SW2 160 B3
Roupell St SE1 116 C5 251 B3
Rousden St NW1 71 C1
Rouse Gdns SE21 183 C6
Routemaster Cl E13 99 B4
Routh Ct TW14 149 B3
Routh Rd SW18 158 C4
Routh St E6 100 B2
Rover Ho 26 N1 95 C6
Rowallan Ct 3 SE6 164 D3
Rowallan Rd SW6 135 A5 264 A3
Rowallen Par RM8 58 C1
Rowan N10 31 B1
Rowan Ave E4 35 B4
Rowan Cl Ealing W5 110 A4
Harrow HA7 24 D4
Ilford IG1 79 B3
Kingston u T KT3 177 C1
Streatham SW16 181 C2
Wembley HA0 65 A5
Rowan Cres SW16 181 C2
Rowan Ct
19 Camberwell SE15 139 D5
Forest Hill SE26 184 C6
11 Kingston u T KT2 176 C3
Newham E13 99 B5
Twickenham TW4 151 D6
Wandsworth SW11 158 D5
Wimbledon SW20 178 B1
Rowan Dr NW9 46 A6

Rowan Gdns CR0 ... 221 D5
Rowan Ho 9 Bow E3 ... 97 B6
Dagenham NW10 ... 89 C3
East Bedfont TW14 ... 149 B5
Ilford IG1 ... 79 B3
5 Maitland Pk NW3 ... 70 D2
Sidcup DA14 ... 167 D1
Rowan Pl UB3 ... 105 D6
Rowan Rd
Brentford TW8 ... 131 B5
Brook Green W6 ... 112 D2
DA7 ... 147 A2
Mitcham SW16 ... 181 C1
West Drayton UB7 ... 104 A2
Rowans The
Ashford TW16 ... 171 D5
Edmonton N13 ... 17 A1
7 Sutton SM2 ... 217 D2
Rowan Terr W6 ... 112 D2
Rowantree Cl N21 ... 17 B3
Rowantree Rd
Edmonton N21 ... 17 B3
Enfield EN2 ... 4 D3
Rowan Way RM6 ... 58 C6
Rowan Wlk BR2 ... 226 B5
7 Dartmouth Pk N19 ... 71 C6
Hampstead Garden Suburb N2 ... 48 A4
Kensal Town W10 ... 91 A3
1 New Barnet EN5 ... 13 D6
Rowanwood Ave DA15 ... 168 A3
Rowanwood Mews EN2 .. 4 D3
Rowben Cl N20 ... 13 D3
Rowberry Cl SW6 ... 134 C5
Rowcross St SE1 ... 117 D1 263 D2
Rowdell Rd UB5 ... 85 C6
Rowden Par E4 ... 35 C4
Rowden Park Gdns E4 .. 35 C4
Rowden Rd
Beckenham BR3 ... 185 B2
Chingford E4 ... 35 D4
West Ewell KT19 ... 215 A4
Rowditch La SW11 ... 137 A3
Rowdon Ave NW10 ... 68 B1
Rowdowns Rd RM9 ... 81 B1
Rowe Gdns IG11 ... 102 A5
Rowe Ho E9 ... 74 C2
Rowe La E9 ... 74 C3
Rowena Cres SW11 ... 136 C3
Rowe Wlk HA2 ... 63 C5
Rowfant Rd SW12, SW17 ... 159 A2
Rowhill Mans 11 E5 ... 74 B4
Rowhill Rd E5 ... 74 B4
Rowington Cl W2 ... 91 D2
Rowland Ave HA3 ... 43 C6
Rowland Ct E16 ... 98 D3
South Croydon CR0 ... 221 C6
Rowland Gr SE26 ... 162 B1
Rowland Hill Almshouses 7 TW15 ... 170 C5
Rowland Hill Ave N17 ... 33 B4
Rowland Hill Ho SE1 .. 251 C2
Rowland Hill St NW3 ... 70 C3
Rowlands Ave HA5 ... 23 D4
Rowlands Cl
Hendon NW7 ... 28 A3
Highgate N6 ... 49 A3
Rowlands Rd RM8 ... 81 B6
Rowland Way
Ashford TW15 ... 171 B3
Merton SW19 ... 179 D2
Rowley Ave DA15 ... 168 B4
Rowley Cl HA0 ... 66 B1
Rowley Ct EN1 ... 17 C6
Rowley Gdns N4 ... 51 A2
Rowley Green Rd EN5 ... 12 A6
Rowley Ho SE8 ... 141 C6
Rowley Ind Pk W3 ... 110 D3
Rowley La EN5 ... 11 D6
Rowley Rd N15 ... 51 A4
Rowley Way NW8 ... 229 A6
Rowlheys Pl UB7 ... 104 A3
Rowlls Rd KT1 ... 198 B6
Rowney Gdns RM9 ... 80 C2
Rowney Rd RM9 ... 80 B2
Rowntree Cl NW6 ... 69 C2
Rowntree Clifford Cl 7 E13 ... 99 B4
Rowntree Path 1 SE28 ... 124 B5
Rowntree Rd TW2 ... 152 C3
Rowse Cl E15 ... 98 A6
Rowsham Ct HA1 ... 64 C5
Rowsley Ave NW4 ... 46 C6
Rowstock 1 NW5 ... 71 D2
Rowstock Gdns N7 ... 71 D3
Rowton Rd SE18 ... 145 A5
Roxborough Ave
Harrow HA1 ... 42 C2
Hounslow TW7 ... 130 D5
Roxborough Pk HA1 ... 42 C2
Roxborough Rd HA1 ... 42 B3
Roxbourne Cl UB5 ... 62 D2
Roxbourne Fst & Mid Schs HA2 ... 63 A6
Roxburgh Rd SE27 ... 182 D5
Roxburn Way HA4 ... 61 D5
Roxby Pl SW6 .. 135 C6 265 B6
ROXETH ... 64 A6
Roxeth Ct 6 TW15 ... 170 C5
Roxeth Fst & Mid Sch HA2 ... 64 B6
Roxeth Gr HA2 ... 63 D4
Roxeth Green Ave HA2 .. 63 D6
Roxeth Hill HA2 ... 64 C6
Roxeth Manor Fst & Mid Schs HA2 ... 63 C5
Roxeth Mead Sch HA2 .. 64 B6
Roxford Cl TW17 ... 193 C4
Roxford Ho 8 E3 ... 97 D3
Roxley Rd SE13 ... 163 D5
Roxton Gdns CR0 ... 223 C3
Roxwell 10 NW1 ... 71 B2
Roxwell Rd
Barking IG11 ... 102 A5
Shepherd's Bush W12 ... 112 A4
Roxwell Trad Pk E10 ... 53 A2
Roxwell Way IG8 ... 37 C3
Roxy Ave RM6 ... 58 C2
Royal Academy of Dramatic Art* WC1 ... 93 D2 239 C4
Royal Acad of Arts* W1 ... 115 C6 249 A5
Royal Acad of Dance SW11 ... 266 D1
Royal Acad of Music NW1 ... 238 B5
Royal Albert Hall* SW7 ... 114 B4 246 C1
Royal Albert Sta E16 ... 122 A6
Royal Albert Way E6 ... 122 B6
Royal Arc W1 ... 249 A5
Royal Armouries The* E1 ... 253 C5
Royal Ave SW3 .114 D1 257 C2
Worcester Pk KT4 ... 215 C6
Royal Avenue Ho SW3. 257 C2
Royal Ballet Sch The
Hammersmith W14 ... 112 D1
St Giles WC2 ... 94 A1 240 B1
Royal Ballet Sch (White Lodge) The TW10 ... 155 B3
Royal Brompton Hospl
Chelsea SW3 ... 114 B1 256 C2
Chelsea SW3 .. 114 C1 257 A2
Royal Cir SE27 ... 160 D1
Royal Cl Deptford SE8 ... 141 B6
Hillingdon UB7 ... 82 B1
Ilford IG3 ... 58 A2
Locksbottom BR6 ... 226 D4
Putney SW19 ... 156 D2
Stamford Hill N16 ... 51 C1
Worcester Pk KT4 ... 215 C6
Royal College of Physicians Liby NW1 ... 93 B3 238 D6
Royal College St NW1 ... 93 C6 232 B6
Royal Coll of Anaesthetists WC1 ... 240 C3
Royal Coll of Art SW7 ... 114 B4 246 C1
Royal Coll of Art Sculpture Sch SW11 ... 136 C5 267 A3
Royal Coll of Midwives W1 ... 93 B2 238 C3
Royal Coll of Music SW7 ... 114 B3 256 C6
Royal Coll of Obstetricians & Gynaecologists NW1 ... 92 D3 237 C6
Royal Coll of Ophthalmologists NW1 ... 238 A5
Royal Coll of Paediatrics & Child Health W1 ... 238 D4
Royal Coll of Pathologists SW1 ... 115 D5 249 C3
Royal Coll of Physicians NW1 ... 93 B3 238 D6
Royal Coll of Radiologists W1 ... 238 D4
Royal Coll of Science SW7 ... 114 B3 256 C6
Royal Coll of Speech Language Therapists SE1 ... 252 C3
Royal Coll of Surgeons WC2 ... 94 B1 240 D2
Royal Connaught Apts E16 ... 121 D5
Royal Courts of Justice WC2 ... 94 C1 241 A1
Royal Cres Ilford IG2 ... 57 B3
Ruislip HA4 ... 63 A5
W11 ... 113 A5 244 A3
Royal Crescent Mews W11 ... 112 D5
Royal Crest Ho SM2 ... 217 A1
Royal Ct
City of London EC3 ... 242 D1
Enfield EN1 ... 17 C5
9 Kingston u T KT2 ... 176 D3
Mottingham SE9 ... 166 B3
Rotherhithe SE16 ... 119 B3
Ruislip HA4 ... 40 A2
Royal Docks Com Sch The E16 ... 99 C1
Royal Docks Rd E6 ... 100 D2
Royal Dr N11 ... 31 A5
Royal Duchess Mews SW12 ... 159 B4
Royal Exchange* EC3. 242 D1
Royal Exchange Bldgs EC3 ... 242 D1
Royal Festival Hall* SE1 ... 116 B5 250 D3
Royal Free Hospl NW3 .. 70 C3
Royal Fusiliers Mus* E1 ... 253 C5
Royal Gdns W7 ... 109 A3
Royal Geographical Society SW7 ... 246 D1
Royal Hill SE10 ... 142 A5
Royal Hill Ct 2 SE10 ... 142 A5
Royal Horticultural Society (Lawrence Hall & Conf Ctr) SW1 ... 259 C5
Royal Horticultural Society (Lindley Hall) SW1 ... 259 C4
Royal Hospital (Army Pensioners)* SW1 ... 115 A1 258 A1
Royal Hospital Rd SW3 ... 114 D1 257 D1
Royal Hospl and Home SW15 ... 157 A5
Royal La Hillingdon UB7 ... 82 B1
Hillingdon UB8 ... 82 B3
Royal Langford Apartments 3 NW6 ... 91 D5
Royal London Est N17 ... 34 B4
Royal London Est The NW10 ... 89 B5
Royal London Homeopathic Hospl The WC1 ... 94 A2 240 B4
Royal London Hospl Archives & Mus* E1 ... 96 B2
Royal London Hospl (Mile End) The E2 ... 96 D4
Royal London Hospl (St Clements) The E3 ... 97 B4
Royal London Hospl (Whitechapel) The E1 ... 96 B2
Royal Marsden Hospl SW3 ... 114 B1 256 D2
Royal Mews KT8 ... 196 C6
Royal Mews The* SW1 ... 115 B3 258 D6
Royal Military Sch of Music (Kneller Hall) TW2 ... 152 B5
Royal Mint Pl 6 E1 ... 118 A6
Royal Mint St E1 ... 117 D6 253 D6
Royal National Orthopaedic Hospl
Regent's Pk W1 ... 93 B3 238 D5
Stanmore HA7 ... 9 C2
Royal National TNE Hospl The WC1 ... 94 B4 233 C2
Royal Nat TN&E Hospl The W5 ... 87 C2
Royal Naval Pl SE14 ... 141 B5
Royal Oak Ct
Dagenham RM8 ... 80 C6
9 Shoreditch N1 ... 95 C4
Royal Oak Mews 9 TW11 ... 175 A5
Royal Oak Pl SE22 ... 162 B5
Royal Oak Rd
Bexley DA6 ... 147 C1
DA6 ... 169 B6
5 Hackney E8 ... 74 B2
Royal Oak Sta W2 ... 91 D2
Royal Oak Yd SE1 ... 253 A1
Royal Obsy The* SE10 ... 142 B5
Royal Opera Arc SW1 . 249 C4
Royal Orchard Cl SW18 ... 157 A4
Royal Par
Blackheath Vale SE3 ... 142 D3
Chislehurst BR7 ... 189 A3
11 Dagenham RM10 ... 81 D2
Ealing W5 ... 88 A4
Fulham SW6 ... 264 A4
12 Richmond TW9 ... 132 C4
Royal Park Prim Sch DA14 ... 169 A1
Royal Pl 11 SE10 ... 142 A5
Royal Rd
Kennington SE17 ... 138 D6
Newham E16 ... 99 D1
Sidcup DA14 ... 168 D1
Teddington TW11 ... 174 B5
Royal Route HA9 ... 66 B4
Royal Russell Sch CR0 ... 222 B3
Royal Sch Hampstead The NW3 ... 70 B4
Royal St SE1 ... 116 B3 260 D6
Royal Tower Lo 3 E1 ... 118 A6
Royalty Ho W1 ... 239 C1
Royalty Mews W1 ... 239 C1
Royalty Studios W11 ... 91 A1
Royal United Services Mus* SW1 ... 250 A3
Royal Veterinary Coll NW1 ... 93 D6 232 C5
Royal Victoria Pl 7 E16 ... 121 B5
Royal Victoria Sq E16 .. 121 B6
Royal Victoria Sta E16 ... 121 A6
Royal Victor Pl E3 ... 96 D5
Royal Wlk SM6 ... 219 B5
Roycraft Ave IG11 ... 101 D5
Roycroft Cl
Streatham SW2 ... 160 C3
Woodford E18 ... 37 B2
Roydene Rd SE18 ... 123 C1
Roydon Cl 7 SW11 ... 136 D3
Roy Gdns IG2 ... 57 D4
Roy Gr TW12 ... 173 D4
Royle Cres W13 ... 87 A3
Roymount Ct TW2 ... 152 C1
Roy Ridley Ho 6 SW4 .. 137 D2
Roy Sq E14 ... 119 A6
Royston Ave
Carshalton SM1 ... 218 B5
Chingford E4 ... 35 D5
Wallington SM6 ... 219 D4
Royston Cl
Cranford TW5 ... 128 B4
Walton-on-T KT12 ... 194 A1
Royston Ct
Hinchley Wood KT10 ... 212 D6
New Cross SE4 ... 141 B3
1 Newham E13 ... 99 A6
Redbridge IG1 ... 55 D3
3 Richmond TW9 ... 132 B4
Ruislip HA5 ... 40 C2
Tolworth KT6 ... 214 C6
Royston Gdns IG1 ... 55 D3
Royston Gr HA5 ... 23 C4
Royston Ho
Friern Barnet N11 ... 31 A6
14 SE15 ... 140 A6
Royston Lo SW19 ... 180 A4
Royston Par IG1 ... 55 D3
Royston Park Rd HA5 ... 23 C5
Royston Prim Sch SE20 ... 184 D2
Royston Rd
Penge SE20 ... 184 D2
Richmond TW10 ... 154 A6
Royston St 24 E2 ... 96 C5
Roystons The KT5 ... 198 D4
Rozel Ct 3 N1 ... 95 C6
Rozelle Ct 1 CR7 ... 204 C3
Rozel Rd SW4 ... 137 C2
Rubastic Rd UB2 ... 106 C3
Rubens Rd UB5 ... 84 D5
Rubens St SE6 ... 163 B2
Rubin Pl 14 EN3 ... 7 C6
Ruby Ct TW13 ... 149 D1
Ruby Rd E17 ... 53 C6
Ruby St SE15 ... 140 B6
Stonebridge NW10 ... 67 A1
Ruby Triangle SE15 ... 140 B6
Ruckholt Cl E10 ... 75 D5
Ruckholt Rd E10 ... 75 D5
Rucklidge Ave NW10 ... 90 A5
Rudall Cres NW3 ... 70 B4
Rudbeck Ho 11 SE15 ... 140 A5
Ruddington Cl E5 ... 75 A4
Ruddock Cl HA8 ... 27 A3
Ruddstreet Cl SE18 ... 123 A2
Rudge Ho 1 SE16 ... 118 A3
Rudgwick Terr NW8 ... 92 C6 230 B5
Rudhall Ho 4 SW2 ... 160 C5
Rudland Rd DA7 ... 147 D2
Rudloe Rd SW12 ... 159 C4
Rudolf Pl SW8 ... 270 B5
Rudolph Ct SE22 ... 162 B4
Rudolph Rd E13 ... 98 D5
Paddington NW6 ... 91 C5
Rudstone Ho 10 E3 ... 97 D4
Rudyard Ct SE1 ... 252 D1
Rudyard Gr NW7 ... 27 A4
Ruegg Ho 5 SE18 ... 144 C6
Ruffetts Cl CR2 ... 222 B1
Ruffetts The CR2 ... 222 B1
Ruffle Cl UB7 ... 104 B4
Rufford Cl HA3 ... 43 A3
Rufford St N1 ... 94 A6 233 B6
Rufford Street Mews N1 ... 72 A1
Rufford Twr 5 W3 ... 110 D5
Rufforth Ct 1 NW9 ... 27 C2
Rufus Bsns Ctr SW18 .. 157 D2
Rufus Cl HA4 ... 63 A5
Rufus Ho SE1 ... 263 D6
Rufus St N1 ... 95 C4
Rugby Ave Edmonton N9 .. 17 D3
Northolt UB6 ... 64 B2
Wembley HA0 ... 65 C4
Rugby Cl HA1 ... 42 C5
Rugby Gdns RM9 ... 80 C2
Rugby Mans W14 ... 254 B4
Rugby Rd
Bedford Pk W4 ... 111 C4
Dagenham RM9 ... 80 C2
Queensbury NW9 ... 44 D5
Twickenham TW1, TW2, TW7 ... 152 C5
Rugby St WC1 ... 94 B3 240 C5
Rugg St E14 ... 119 C6
Rugless Ho 2 E14 ... 120 A4
Rugmere 4 NW1 ... 71 A1
RUISLIP ... 39 B2
Ruislip Cl UB6 ... 85 D3
RUISLIP COMMON ... 39 B4
Ruislip Ct HA4 ... 61 D6
RUISLIP GARDENS ... 61 D5
Ruislip Gardens Prim Sch HA4 ... 61 D4
Ruislip Gardens Sta HA4 ... 62 A4
Ruislip Lido* HA4, HA5 .. 39 B5
Ruislip Lido Rly* HA4 ... 39 B5
RUISLIP MANOR ... 40 A1
Ruislip Manor Sta HA4 .. 40 A1
Ruislip Rd UB6, UB5 ... 85 C4
Ruislip Rd E
Ealing UB6, W7 ... 86 D3
Greenford UB6 ... 86 B3
Ruislip St SW17 ... 180 D6
Ruislip Sta HA4 ... 39 D1
Rumball Ho 14 SE5 ... 139 C5
Rumbold Rd SW6 ... 135 D5 265 D3
Rum Cl E1 ... 118 C6
Rumford Ho SE1 ... 262 A5
Rumsey Cl TW12 ... 173 B4
Rumsey Rd SW9 ... 138 B2
Runacres Ct SE17 ... 262 A1
Runbury Circ NW9 ... 67 B6
Runcorn Cl N17 ... 52 B5
Runcorn Pl W11 ... 244 A6
Rundell Cres NW4 ... 46 B4
Rundell Twr SW8 ... 270 C2
Runes Cl CR4 ... 202 C5
Runnelfield HA1 ... 64 C5
Running Horse Yd 12 TW8 ... 132 A6
Runnymede SW19 ... 180 B2
Runnymede Cl TW2 ... 151 D4
Runnymede Cres SW16 ... 182 A2
Runnymede Ct
Roehampton SW15 ... 156 A3
1 Wallington SM6 ... 219 B2
Runnymede Gdns
Greenford UB6 ... 86 C5
Twickenham TW2 ... 151 D4
Runnymede Ho
Hackney E9 ... 75 A4
Richmond TW10 ... 154 C6
Runnymede Rd TW2 ... 151 D5
Runway The HA4 ... 62 C3
Rupack St 8 SE16 ... 118 C4
Rupert Ave 6 HA9 ... 66 A3
Rupert Ct W1 ... 249 C6
Rupert Gdns SW9 ... 138 D3
Rupert Ho SE11 ... 261 B3
8 Upper Holloway N19 .. 71 D5
Rupert Rd
Bedford Pk W4 ... 111 C3
Paddington NW6 ... 91 B5
Upper Holloway N19 ... 71 D6
Rupert St W1 ... 115 D6 249 C6
Rural Way SW16 ... 181 B3
Rusbridge Cl E8 ... 74 A3
Ruscoe Ho 12 SW27 ... 182 D5
Ruscoe Rd E16 ... 98 D1
Ruscombe Way TW14 .. 149 D4
Rusham Rd SW12 ... 158 D4
Rushbrook Cres E17 ... 35 B2
Rushbrook Ho 20 SW8 ... 137 D3
Rushbrook Rd SE9 ... 167 A2
Rushbury Ct 4 TW12 .. 173 C2
Rushby Ct SW4 ... 270 A1
Rush Common Mews 18 SW2 ... 160 B4
Rushcroft Rd
Brixton SW2, SW9 ... 138 C1
Chingford E4 ... 35 D3
Rush Croft Sch E4 ... 35 D3
Rushcutters Ct 18 SE16 ... 119 A2
Rushden Cl SE19 ... 183 B3
Rushdene SE2 ... 124 D3
Rushdene Ave EN4 ... 14 C4
Rushdene Cl UB5 ... 84 C5
Rushdene Cres UB5 ... 84 C4
Rushdene Rd HA5 ... 40 D3
Rushden Gdns
Ilford IG5 ... 56 C6
Mill Hill NW7 ... 28 C4
Rushen Wlk SM5 ... 202 B1
Rushet Rd BR5 ... 190 A1
Rushett Cl KT7 ... 197 B1
Rushett Rd KT7 ... 197 B2
Rushey Cl KT3 ... 199 B5
Rushey Gn SE6 ... 163 D4
Rushey Green Prim Sch SE6 ... 163 D3
Rushey Hill EN2 ... 4 B1
Rushey Mead SE4 ... 163 C6
Rushford Rd SE4 ... 163 B5
Rush Green Rd RM7, RM8, RM10 ... 59 D1
Rushgrove Ave NW9 ... 45 D5
Rushgrove Ct NW9 ... 45 C4
Rushgrove St SE18 ... 122 B2
Rush Hill Mews 3 SW11 ... 137 A2
Rush Hill Rd SW11 ... 137 A2
Rushlake Ho 3 SW11 .. 137 A3
Rushley Cl BR2 ... 226 A4
Rushman Villas KT3 ... 199 D5
Rushmead
5 Bethnal Green E2 ... 96 B4
Richmond TW10 ... 153 B1
Rushmead Cl CR0 ... 221 D4
Rushmere Ct KT4 ... 216 A6
Rushmere Ho 2 SW15 ... 156 A3
Rushmere Pl SW19 ... 178 D5
Rushmon Pl SM3 ... 217 A2
Rushmoor Cl HA5 ... 40 B5
Rushmore Cl BR1 ... 210 A6
Rushmore Cres 9 E5 ... 74 D4
Rushmore Ho
9 Kentish Town N7 ... 71 D3
W14 ... 254 B5
Rushmore Prim Sch E5 ... 74 D4
Rushmore Rd
Clapton Pk E5 ... 74 D4
Hackney E5 ... 75 A4
Rusholme Ave RM10 ... 81 C5
Rusholme Gr SE19 ... 183 C5
Rusholme Rd SW15 ... 157 A5
Rushout Ave HA3 ... 43 B3
Rush The SW20 ... 179 B2
Rushton Ho 26 SW8 ... 137 D3
Rushton St N1 ... 95 B5 235 D4
Rushworth St SE1 ... 116 D4 251 D1
Rushy Meadow La SM5 ... 218 C5
Rushy Meadow Prim Sch SM5 ... 218 C5
Ruskin Ave DA16 ... 146 A3
Feltham TW14 ... 149 D5
Plashet E12 ... 78 A2
Richmond TW9 ... 132 C5
Ruskin Cl NW11 ... 47 D3
Ruskin Ct
Herne Hill SE5 ... 139 B2
SE9 ... 166 B5
Southgate N21 ... 16 B4
Ruskin Dr
North Cheam KT4 ... 216 C6
Orpington BR6 ... 227 C5
Welling DA16 ... 146 A2
Ruskin Gdns Ealing W5 ... 87 D3
Harrow HA3 ... 44 B5
Ruskin Gr DA16 ... 146 A3
Ruskin Ho SW1 ... 259 D3
Ruskin Par CR0 ... 221 B3
Ruskin Park Ho SE5 ... 139 B2
Ruskin Rd
Belvedere DA17 ... 125 C2
Croydon CR0 ... 220 D6
Isleworth TW7 ... 130 D2
Southall UB1 ... 107 A6
Tottenham N17 ... 33 D2
Wallington SM5 ... 219 A3
Ruskin Way SW19 ... 180 B2
Ruskin Wlk BR2 ... 210 B3
Edmonton N9 ... 18 A2
Herne Hill SE24 ... 161 A6
Rusland Ave BR6 ... 227 B5
Rusland Hts HA1 ... 42 C5
Rusland Park Rd HA1 ... 42 C5
Rusper Cl
Cricklewood NW2 ... 68 C5
Stanmore HA7 ... 25 C6
Rusper Ct SW9 ... 138 A3
Rusper Rd
Dagenham RM9 ... 80 C2
Tottenham N17, N22 ... 51 A6
Russel Cl BR3 ... 208 A6
Russel Ct N14 ... 15 D6
Russell Ave N22 ... 32 D1
Russell Cl
Bexleyheath DA7 ... 147 C1
Chiswick W4 ... 133 D6
Greenwich SE7 ... 143 C5
Ruislip HA4 ... 62 C6
Stonebridge NW10 ... 67 A1
Russell Ct
Battersea SW11 ... 268 B1
Bloomsbury WC1 ... 240 A5
Bromley BR1 ... 186 D3
12 New Barnet EN5 ... 2 A1
5 Peckham SE15 ... 140 B3
St James SW1 ... 249 B3
Streatham SW16 ... 182 B5
Surbiton KT6 ... 198 A2
Wallington SM6 ... 219 C3
4 Walthamstow E10 ... 53 D2
Wembley HA0 ... 66 A1
Russell Gdns
East Barnet N20 ... 14 C2
Ilford IG2 ... 57 B2
Richmond TW10 ... 153 C2
Temple Fortune NW11 ... 47 A3
W14 ... 113 A3 254 A6
West Drayton UB7 ... 104 C1
Russell Gdns Mews W14 ... 113 A3 254 A6
Russell Gr
33 Brixton SW9 ... 138 C4
Edgware NW7 ... 27 C6
Russell Ho
21 Poplar E14 ... 97 C1
SW1 ... 259 A2
Russell Kerr Cl W4 ... 133 A5
Russell La N20 ... 14 D2
Russell Lo
5 Chingford E4 ... 20 A2
SE1 ... 262 C6
Russell Mans WC1 ... 240 B4
Russell Mead HA3 ... 24 D2
Russell Par NW11 ... 47 A3
Russell Pickering Ho 2 SW4 ... 138 A2
Russell Pl
Hampstead NW3 ... 70 C3
Rotherhithe SE16 ... 119 A3
Russell Rd
Bowes Pk N13 ... 32 B4
Buckhurst Hill IG9 ... 21 C3
Chingford Hatch E4 ... 35 B6
Crouch End N8 ... 49 D3
East Barnet N20 ... 14 C2
Enfield EN1 ... 5 D5
Leyton E10 ... 53 D3
Merton SW19 ... 179 C3
Mitcham CR4 ... 202 C6
Newham E16 ... 99 B1
Northolt UB5 ... 64 A3
Shepperton TW17 ... 193 A2
Tottenham N15 ... 51 C4
Twickenham TW1, TW2 .. 152 D5
W14 ... 113 A3 254 B5
Walthamstow E17 ... 53 B6
Walton-on-T KT12 ... 194 A3
West Hendon NW9 ... 45 D3
Russell Sch The TW10 ... 153 D3
Russell Sq WC1 .. 94 A3 240 A5
Russell Square Ho WC1 ... 240 A5
Russell Square Mans WC1 ... 240 B4
Russell Square Sta WC1 ... 94 A3 240 A5
Russell St WC2 . 116 A6 250 B6

Russell's Wharf 2 W9 91 B3
Russell Way SM1 217 D3
Russell Wlk 4 TW10 154 B5
Russet Ave TW16,
TW17 193 C6
Russet Cl UB10 83 A3
Russet Cres N7 72 B3
Russet Ct 6 Barnet EN4 2 C1
Dollis Hill NW2 68 B5
Feltham TW13 149 C1
Russet Dr CR0 207 A1
Russet Ho TW3 129 B1
Russet House Sch EN1 6 B4
Russets Cl E4 36 B6
Russettings 1 HA5 23 B3
Russett Way SE13 141 D3
Russia Dock Rd SE16 119 A5
Russia La E2 96 C5
Russia Row EC2 242 B1
Russington Rd TW17 193 B3
Rusthall Ave W4 111 B3
Rusthall Cl CR0 206 C3
Rusthall Mans 3 W4 111 B2
Rustic Ave SW16 181 B3
Rustic Pl HA0 65 D4
Rustic Wlk E16 99 B1
Rustington Wlk SM4 201 B2
Ruston Ave KT5 198 D2
Ruston Gdns N14 15 A5
Ruston Mews W11 91 A1
Ruston Rd SE18 122 A3
Ruston St E3 97 B6
Rust Sq SE5 139 B5
Rutford Rd SW16 182 A5
Ruth Cl HA7 44 B5
Ruth Ct 16 E3 97 A5
Rutherford Cl
Hillingdon UB8 82 B3
Sutton SM2 218 B2
Rutherford Ct
Mitcham SW19 180 B3
Southgate N21 16 B6
Rutherford Ho
12 Bethnal Green E1 96 B3
Teddington TW11 174 D5
4 Wembley HA9 67 A5
Rutherford St
SW1 115 D2 259 C4
Rutherford Twr 8 UB1 85 D1
Rutherford Way
Bushey WD23 8 C3
Wembley HA9 66 C4
Rutherglen Rd SE2 146 A6
Rutherwyke Cl KT17 216 A2
Ruth Ho W10 91 A3
Ruthin Cl NW9 45 C3
Ruthin Rd SE3 143 A6
Ruthven St E9 96 D6
Rutland Ave DA15 168 A4
Rutland Cl
Chessington KT9 214 B2
DA5 168 D3
Mitcham SW19 180 C3
Mortlake SW14 133 A2
Rutland Ct 15 Acton W3 88 C1
Chislehurst BR7 188 C2
Enfield EN3 18 B6
Herne Hill SE5 139 B1
Sidcup SE9 167 A2
SW7 247 B1
Twickenham TW2 152 C1
Rutland Dr
Morden SM4 201 C2
Richmond TW10 154 A3
Rutland Gate
Beckenham BR2 208 D5
Belvedere DA17 125 D1
SW7 114 C4 247 B1
Rutland Gate Mews
SW7 247 A1
Rutland Gdns
Dagenham RM8 80 C3
Ealing W13 87 A2
South Croydon CR0 221 C4
Stoke Newington N4 51 A3
SW7 114 C4 247 B1
Rutland Gdns Mews
SW7 247 B1
Rutland Gr W6 112 B1
Rutland Ho
Edgware HA8 26 B4
6 Northolt UB5 63 C2
2 Penge SE20 184 C2
10 Putney SW15 156 C4
Tolworth KT6 198 C1
W8 255 C5
15 Woolwich SE18 122 B2
Rutland Lo
Forest Hill SE6 163 B2
Teddington TW11 174 C5
Rutland Mews E SW7 257 B6
Rutland Mews S SW7 257 A6
Rutland Mews W SW7 257 A6
Rutland Park Gdns 1
NW2 68 C2
Rutland Park Mans 2
NW2 68 C2
Rutland Pk
Forest Hill SE6 163 B2
Willesden NW2 68 C2
Rutland Pl Bushey WD23 8 B3
EC1 241 D4
Rutland Rd
Forest Gate E7 77 D1
Harrow HA1 42 A3
Hayes UB3 105 B2
Ilford IG1 78 D5
Mitcham SW19 180 C3
Southall UB1 85 C2
South Hackney E9 96 D6
Rutland Rd *continued*
Twickenham TW2 152 B2
Walthamstow E17 53 C3
Wanstead E11 55 B4
Rutland St SW7 257 B6
Rutland Studios NW10 90 A4
Rutland Wlk SE6 163 B2
Rutley Cl SE11 138 D6
Rutlish Rd SW19 179 C2
Rutlish Sch SW20 179 B1
Rutter Gdns CR4 202 B5
Rutters Cl UB7 104 C4
Rutt's Terr SE14 140 D4
Rutts The WD23 8 B3
Ruvigny Gdns SW15 134 D2
Ruvigny Mans SW15 134 D2
Ruxbury Ct TW15 148 A1
RUXLEY 191 A3
Ruxley Cl
Chessington KT19 214 D3
Sidcup DA14 191 A4
Ruxley Cnr DA14 191 A4
Ruxley Corner Ind Est
DA14 190 D4
Ruxley Cres KT10 213 B1
Ruxley Ct KT19 215 A3
Ruxley Gdns TW17 193 A4
Ruxley La KT19 215 B3
Ruxley Mews KT19 214 D3
Ruxley Ridge KT10 213 A1
Ryall's Ct N20 14 D1
Ryan Cl Ruislip HA4 40 B1
SE9 143 C1
Ryan Ct SW16 182 A3
Ryan Dr TW8 131 A6
Ryan Ho 8 HA1 42 D4
Ryarsh Cres BR6 227 C4
Rycott Path SE22 162 A4
Rycroft Way N17 51 D6
Rycullf Sq SE3 142 D3
Rydal Cl NW4 29 A2
Rydal Cres UB6 87 C5
Rydal Ct Edgware HA8 26 B5
Wembley HA9 44 A2
Rydal Dr DA7 147 C4
West Wickham BR4 224 C6
Rydal Gdns
Kingsbury NW9 45 C4
Kingston u T SW15 177 C5
Twickenham TW2, TW3 151 D5
Wembley HA9 43 C1
Rydal Ho 25 SW8 137 D3
Rydal Lo N17 34 A3
Rydal Rd SW16 181 D6
Rydal Water NW1 232 A1
Rydal Way Enfield EN3 18 C5
Ruislip HA4 62 C4
Ryde Ho 1 NW6 91 C6
Rydens Ho SE9 165 C1
Rydens Rd KT12 194 D1
Ryde Pl TW1 153 D5
Ryder Cl BR1 187 B5
Ryder Ct Leyton E10 75 D6
SW1 249 B4
Ryder Dr SE16 118 B1
Ryder Ho
18 Bethnal Green E1 96 C3
5 Merton SW19 179 D2
Ryder St SW1 249 B4
Ryder's Terr
NW8 92 A5 229 A4
Ryder Yd SW1 249 B4
Ryde Vale Rd SW12 159 C2
Rydon Mews SW19 178 C3
Rydons Cl SE9 144 A2
Rydon St N1 235 B6
Rydston Cl 2 N7 72 B1
Rye Cl DA5 169 D5
Ryecotes Mead SE21 161 C3
Ryecroft Ave TW2 151 D3
Ryecroft Cres EN5 12 B6
Ryecroft Rd BR5 211 B3
Lewisham SE13 164 A6
South Norwood SW16 182 C4
Ryecroft St
SW6 135 D4 265 C1
Rye Ct BR3 185 B2
Ryedale SE22 162 B5
Ryedale Ct 7 TW12 173 C2
Ryefield Ave UB10 60 D1
Ryefield Cres HA5, HA6 22 A1
Ryefield Ct HA6 22 A1
Ryefield Path 7
SW15 156 A3
Ryefield Prim Sch
UB10 83 B6
Ryefield Rd SE19 183 A4
Ryegates 2 SE15 140 B3
Ryehill Ct KT3 199 D2
Rye Hill Pk SE15 140 C1
Rye Ho 17 SE16 118 C4
Rye La SE15 140 A3
Ryeland Cl UB7 82 A1
Ryelands Cres SE12 165 C5
Ryelands Prim Sch
SE25 206 B4
Rye Lane Mkt SE15 140 A3
Rye Oak Sch SE15 140 B2
Rye Rd SE15 140 D1
Rye The N14 15 C4
Rye Way HA8 26 B4
Rye Wlk SW15 156 D6
Ryfold Rd SW19 157 C1
Ryhope Rd N11 31 B6
Ryland Cl TW13 171 D6
Rylandes Rd NW2 68 A5
Ryland Ho 11 SW16 181 C5
Ryland Rd NW5 71 B2
Rylett Cres W12 111 D3
Rylett Rd W12 111 D3
Rylston Rd
Edmonton N13 17 B1
SW6 135 B6 264 C5
Rylton Ho KT12 194 A1
Rymer Rd CR0 205 C2
Rymer St SE24 160 D5
Rymill St E16 122 C5
Rysbrack St SW1 257 C6
Rythe Cl KT9 213 C1
Rythe Ct KT7 197 A2
Rythe Ho 7 BR1 186 B5
Rythe Rd KT10 212 C3

S

Saatchi Gallery Duke of York's HQ*
SW3 114 D1 257 D2
Sabah Ct TW15 170 C6
Sabbarton St 9 E16 98 D1
Sabella Ct E3 97 B5
Sabine Rd SW11 137 A2
Sable Cl TW4 128 C2
Sable Ct 3 KT3 199 C4
Sable St N1 72 D1
Sach Rd E5 74 B6
Sacketts Ho 24 SW9 138 C4
Sackville Ave BR2 209 A1
Sackville Cl HA2 64 B5
Sackville Gdns IG1 56 B1
Sackville Ho
Hornsey N8 50 A5
16 Streatham SW16 160 A1
Sackville Rd SM2 217 C1
Sackville St
W1 115 C6 249 B5
Sacred Heart High Sch
W6 112 C2
Sacred Heart Jun Sch
W6 112 D2
Sacred Heart Language Coll The HA3 24 C1
Sacred Heart Prim Sch, Battersea SW11 136 C3
Sacred Heart RC Prim Sch
East Barnet N20 14 C2
Islington N7 72 B3
Putney SW15 156 A6
Ruislip HA4 61 C6
Teddington TW11 175 B3
West Barnes KT3 200 A5
Sacred Heart RC Sec Sch
SE5 139 A4
Saddlebrook Pk TW16 171 C3
Saddlers Cl Barnet EN5 12 B6
Borehamwood WD6 11 B5
Pinner HA5 23 C5
Saddlers Mews SW8 270 B2
Teddington KT1 175 C2
Wembley HA0 64 D4
Saddlers Path WD6 11 B6
Saddlescombe Way
N12 29 C5
Sadler Cl CR4 180 D1
Sadler Ho
17 Bromley E3 97 D4
EC1 234 C2
Sadlers Ho EN1 17 C6
Sadlers Ride KT8 174 A1
Saffron Ave E14 120 B6
Saffron Cl
Temple Fortune NW11 47 B3
Thornton Heath CR0 204 A3
Saffron Ct
East Bedfont TW14 149 A4
10 Kingsland N1 73 B2
Stratford E15 76 C3
Saffron Hill EC1 94 C2 241 B4
Saffron Ho 6 TW9 132 D4
Saffron St EC1 241 B4
Saffron Way KT6 197 D1
Saffron Wharf SE1 253 D2
Sage Cl 7 E6 100 B2
Sage Mews SE22 161 D6
Sage St E1 118 C6
Sage Way WC1 233 C1
Sage Yd KT6 198 B1
Sahara Ct UB1 107 A6
Saigasso Cl E16 99 D1
Sailacre Ho 10 SE10 120 D1
Sail Ct 10 E14 120 B6
Sailmakers Ct SW6 136 A2
Sail St SE11 116 B2 260 D4
Saimet 3 NW9 27 D2
Sainfoin Rd SW17 159 A2
Sainsbury Rd SE19 183 C5
St Agatha's Dr KT2 176 B4
St Agatha's Gr SM5 202 D1
St Agatha's RC Prim Sch
KT2 176 B4
St Agnes Cl E9 96 C6
St Agnes Pl SE11 138 D6
St Agnes RC Prim Sch
E3 97 D4
St Agnes RC Sch NW2 69 A5
St Aidans Ct IG11 102 B5
St Aidan's Prim Sch N4 50 C2
St Aidan's RC Prim Sch
IG1 57 B1
St Aidan's Rd
East Dulwich SE22 162 B6
West Ealing W13 109 B4
St Aiden's Ct W13 109 C4
St Albans Ave
Bedford Pk W4 111 B3
Feltham TW13 172 D5
St Alban's Ave E6 100 C4
St Alban's CE Prim Sch
EC1 94 C2 241 A4
St Alban's Cl NW11 47 C1
St Albans Cres N22 32 C2
St Alban's Cres IG8 37 A3
St Alban's Gdns TW11 175 A5
St Alban's Gr
Carshalton SM5 202 C2
W8 113 D3 255 D6
St Albans Ho 2 SW16 182 C6
St Albans La NW11 47 C1
St Albans Mans W8 255 D6
St Alban's Pl N1 94 D6 234 C5
St Alban's RC Prim Sch
KT8 196 A4
St Albans Rd Barnet EN5 1 A3
Cheam SM1 217 B4
Ilford IG3 57 D2
Kingston u T KT2 176 A4
St Alban's Rd
Dagenham NW10 89 C6
Dartmouth Pk NW5 71 B5
Woodford IG8 37 A3
St Alban's St SW1 249 C5
St Albans Studios W8 255 D6
St Albans Terr W6 264 A6
St Alban's Villas NW5 71 A5
St Alfege Pas SE10 142 A6
St Alfege Rd SE7 143 D6
St Alfege with St Peter's CE Prim Sch SE10 142 A6
St Aloysius RC Coll
N19 49 C1
St Aloysius RC Inf Sch
NW1 93 D4 232 C2
St Aloysius RC Jun Sch
NW1 93 D5 232 C3
St Alphage Ct NW9 45 B6
St Alphage Gdn EC2 242 B3
St Alphage Highwalk
EC2 242 B3
St Alphage Wlk HA8 27 A1
St Alphege Rd N9 18 C4
St Alphonsus Rd SW4 137 D1
St Amunds Cl SE6 185 C6
St Andrew & St Francis CE Prim Sch NW2 68 A2
St Andrews Ave HA0 65 A4
St Andrew's (Barnsbury) CE Prim Sch
N1 94 B6 233 D6
St Andrew's CE Prim Sch
Enfield EN1 5 C3
Osidge N14 15 D3
Stockwell SW9 138 A3
St Andrew's CE Sch
N20 13 B2
St Andrews Chambers
W1 239 B2
St Andrews Cl
25 Bermondsey SE16 118 B1
Erith SE28 102 D1
Long Ditton KT7 197 B1
Ruislip HA4 62 D6
Stanmore HA7 25 C1
Wimbledon SW19 179 D4
St Andrew's Cl
Dollis Hill NW2 68 B5
2 Hounslow TW7 130 C4
North Finchley N12 30 A6
Upper Halliford TW17 193 B5
St Andrews Ct W4 133 A4
St Andrew's Ct
Carshalton SM5 218 C5
2 Higham Hill E17 35 A1
Kingston u T KT3 199 D6
2 Wandsworth SW18 158 A2
St Andrews Dr HA7 25 C2
St Andrew's Gr N16 51 B1
St Andrew's Greek Sch
NW1 71 C2
St Andrew's High Sch
CR0 220 D4
St Andrew's Hill
EC4 94 D1 241 D1
St Andrews Ho
11 Bermondsey SE16 118 B3
Bromley BR1 187 B4
St Andrew's Hospl E3 97 D3
St Andrews Mans 9
E5 74 B4
St Andrew's Mans W1 238 A3
St Andrews Mews
Greenwich SE3 143 A5
4 Streatham SW12 159 D3
St Andrew's Mews N16 51 C1
St Andrew's Pl NW1 238 D6
St Andrews RC Prim Sch
SW16 182 A5
St Andrews Rd
Carshalton SM5 218 C5
DA14 168 D1
Higham Hill E17 35 A1
Ponders End N9 18 C4
Uxbridge UB10 60 B1
Welsh Harp NW9 45 B1
St Andrew's Rd
3 Croydon CR0 221 A4
Dagenham W3 89 C1
Enfield EN1 5 B2
Hanwell W7 108 C4
Hillingdon UB10 82 B6
Leytonstone E11 54 C3
Newham E13 99 B4
Redbridge IG1 56 B2
Surbiton KT6 197 D3
Temple Fortune NW11 47 B3
W14 264 B6
Willesden NW2 68 B2
St Andrew's & St Mark's CE Jun Sch KT6 197 D4
St Andrew's Sq
Notting Hill W11 91 A1
Surbiton KT6 197 D3
St Andrew St EC4 241 B3
St Andrews Terr WD19 22 C5
St Andrew's Twr UB1 108 A6
St Andrews Way E3 97 D3
St Andrew's Wharf
SE1 253 D2
St Angela's Ursuline Convent Sch E7 77 B2
St Anna Rd EN5 12 D6
St Anne RC Prim Sch
E1 96 A3
St Annes Catholic High Sch for Girls (Upper)
N13 32 C6
St Anne's CE Prim Sch
SW18 157 D6
St Annes Cl WD19 22 C6
St Anne's Cl N6 71 A5
St Annes Ct 8 SM2 217 D2
St Anne's Ct
Kensal Rise NW6 91 A6
W1 239 C1
St Anne's Flats NW1 232 C2
St Annes Gdns NW10 88 B4
St Anne's Pas E14 97 B1
St Anne's RC High Sch for Girls EN2 5 B1
St Anne's RC Prim Sch
SE11 138 B6 270 C6
St Anne's Rd Leyton E11 76 B6
Wembley HA0 65 D3
St Anne's Row E14 97 B1
St Anne St E14 97 B1
St Anne's Trad Est 25
E14 97 B1
St Ann's IG11 101 A6
St Ann's CE Prim Sch
N15 51 B4
St Ann's Cres SW18 158 A5
St Ann's Ct NW4 46 B6
St Ann's Ctr HA1 42 C3
St Ann's Gdns NW5 71 A2
St Ann's General Hospl N4,
N15 51 A4
St Ann's Hill SW18 158 A5
St Ann's Ho WC1 234 A1
St Ann's La SW1 259 D5
St Ann's Park Rd
SW18 158 A5
St Anns Rd SW13 133 D4
St Ann's Rd
2 Barking IG11 101 A6
Edmonton N9 17 D3
Harrow HA1 42 C3
Shepherd's Bush W11 112 D6
Tottenham N15 51 B4
St Ann's Sch Ealing W7 108 C5
Morden SM4 201 D4
St Ann's St
SW1 115 D3 259 D6
St Ann's Terr
NW8 92 B5 229 D4
St Ann's Villas
W11 113 A5 244 A3
St Ann's Way CR2 220 D2
St Anselm RC Prim Sch
UB2 107 B3
St Anselm's Ct SW16 182 A5
St Anselm's Pl W1 248 C6
St Anselm's RC Prim Sch
Harrow HA1 42 C2
Upper Tooting SW17 159 A1
St Anselms Rd UB3 105 D4
St Anthony's Ave IG8 37 C3
St Anthonys Cl SW17 158 C2
St Anthony's Cl 8 E1 118 A5
St Anthony's Ct
2 Balham SW12 159 A5
Orpington BR6 226 D6
Upper Tooting SW17 159 A2
St Anthony's Flats
NW1 232 C3
St Anthony's Hospl
KT4 200 D1
St Anthony's RC Prim Sch
East Dulwich SE22 162 A5
Penge SE20 184 B2
Upton E7 77 B1
St Anthony's Way
TW14 127 D1
St Antony's RC Prim Sch
IG8 37 A6
St Antony's Rd E7 77 B1
St Arvans Cl CR0 221 C5
St Asaph Ct SE4 140 D2
St Asaph Rd SE4 140 D2
St Aubins Ct N1 235 D6
St Aubyns E18 54 D5
St Aubyn's Ave
Hounslow TW3, TW4 151 C6
Wimbledon SW19 179 B5
St Aubyns Cl BR6 227 D5
St Aubyn's Ct SW19 179 A4
St Aubyns Gdns BR6 227 D6
St Aubyn's Rd SE19 183 D4
St Aubyn's Sch IG8 36 D3
St Audrey Ave DA7 147 C3
St Augustine of Canterbury CE Prim Sch
DA17 125 B2
St Augustine's Ave
BR1, BR2 210 A4
Ealing W5 88 A4
St Augustine's Ave *continued*
South Croydon CR2 221 A1
Wembley HA9 66 A5
St Augustine's CE High Sch NW6 91 C5
St Augustine's CE Prim Sch NW6 91 D5
St Augustines Ct
Beckenham BR3 185 A1
4 New Barnet EN5 14 A6
St Augustine's Ct E11 54 D1
St Augustine's Ho
NW1 232 C2
Upper Tooting SW17 180 D6
St Augustine's RC Prim Sch
Ilford IG2 56 D4
W6 135 A6 264 B5
St Augustine's Rd
Camden Town NW1 71 D1
DA17 125 B2
St Augustines's RC Prim Sch SE6 186 A5
St Austell Cl HA8 26 B1
St Austell Rd SE13 142 B3
St Awdry's Rd IG11 79 B1
St Barnabas CE Prim Sch
SW1 115 A1 258 B2
St Barnabas Cl
Beckenham BR3 186 A1
11 Dulwich Village SE22 161 C6
St Barnabas Ct HA3 24 A2
St Barnabas' Gdns
KT8 195 C4
St Barnabas Ho CR4 181 A3
St Barnabas Rd
Mitcham CR4 181 A3
Sutton SM1 218 B3
Walthamstow E17 53 C3
Woodford IG8 37 C3
St Barnabas & St Philip's CE Prim Sch
W8 113 C3 255 A5
St Barnabas St SW1 258 B2
St Barnabas Terr E9 74 D3
St Barnabas Villas
SW8 138 A4 270 B2
St Bartholomews CE Prim Sch SE26 162 C1
St Bartholomew's CE Prim Sch SE26 184 C6
St Bartholomew's Cl
SE26 184 C6
St Bartholomews Ct 6
E6 100 A6
St Bartholomew's Hospl
EC1 94 D2 241 D3
St Bartholomew's Rd
E6 100 B5
St Bede's RC Inf Sch
SW12 159 D3
St Bede's RC Prim Sch
RM6 58 C4
St Benedict's Cl SW17 181 A5
St Benedict's Jun Sch
W5 87 C2
St Benedict's Sch W5 87 D2
St Benets Cl SW17 158 C2
St Benet's Gr SM5 202 A2
St Benet's Pl EC3 252 D6
St Bernadette RC Jun Sch
SW12 159 C4
St Bernadette's Prim Sch
HA3 44 B5
St Bernadette's RC Prim Sch UB10 82 D6
St Bernard Ho 6 E14 120 A3
St Bernards CR0 221 C5
St Bernards Cl 8
SE27 183 B6
St Bernards Ho 1
KT6 214 A6
St Bernard's Rd E6 99 D6
St Blaise Ave BR1 187 B1
St Bonaventure's RC Sch
E7 77 A1
St Boniface RC Prim Sch
SW17 180 D5
St Botolph St E1,
EC3 95 D1 243 C2
St Brelades Ct N1 235 D6
St Bride's Ave EC4 241 C1
Edgware HA8 26 B2
St Brides Cl DA18 124 D4
St Bride's Pas EC4 241 C1
St Bride St EC4 94 D1 241 C2
St Catherines Cl
Chessington KT9 213 D2
Upper Tooting SW17 158 C2
St Catherines Ct
TW13 150 A3
St Catherine's Ct 8
W4 111 C3
St Catherine's Dr
SE14 140 D3
St Catherines Farm Ct
HA4 39 A3
St Catherines Mews
SW3 257 C4
St Catherine's RC Sch
EN5 1 C1
St Catherine's RC Sch for Girls DA6 169 D6
St Catherines Rd
Chingford E4 19 C2

St Catherines Rd *continued*
 Ruislip HA4 . . . . .39 B3
St Catherine's Sch
 TW1 . . . . .153 A2
St Catherines Twr **5**
 E10 . . . . .53 D2
St Cecilia's CE Sch
 SW18 . . . . .157 B3
St Cecilia's Cl SM3. . . . .201 A1
St Cecilia's RC Prim Sch
 SM3 . . . . .216 D6
St Chads Cl KT6 . . . . . . .197 C2
St Chad's Gdns RM6 . . . .59 A2
St Chad's Pl WC1 . . . . .233 C2
St Chad's RC Prim Sch
 SE25 . . . . .205 C4
St Chad's Rd RM6. . . . . . .59 A2
St Chad's St WC1 . . . . .233 B2
St Charles' Hospl W10 . .90 D2
St Charles Pl W10 . . . . . .91 A2
St Charles RC Prim Sch
 W10 .90 D2
St Charles RC Sixth Form
 Coll W10. . . . . .90 D2
St Charles Sq W10 . . . . .90 D2
St Christina's Sch
 NW8 . . . . .92 C5 230 B4
St Christopher's Cl
 TW7. . . . . .130 C4
St Christophers Ct **15**
 N19 .71 C5
St Christophers Dr
 UB3 . . . . .106 B6
St Christophers Gdns
 CR7. . . . . .204 C6
St Christopher's Ho
 NW1 . . . . .232 C3
St Christopher's Mews
 SM6 . . . . .219 C3
St Christopher's Pl
 W1. . . . . .238 C2
St Christopher's Sch
 Beckenham BR3 . . . . .186 A1
 Hampstead NW3. . . . . .70 B3
 Wembley HA9 . . . . .66 B5
St Clair Dr KT4 . . . . . . .216 B4
St Clair Ho **17** E3 . . . . . .97 B4
St Clair Rd E13 . . . . .99 B5
St Clair's Rd CR0 . . . . . .221 C6
St Clare Bsns Pk
 TW12 . . . . .174 A4
St Clare St EC3 . . . . . . .243 C1
St Clement Danes CE Prim
 Sch WC2. . . . . . .94 B1 240 C1
St Clement & St James CE
 Prim Sch
 W11 . . . . .113 A5 244 A4
St Clements Ct
 Barnsbury N7 . . . . .72 B2
 7 SE14. . . . . .140 D6
 8 Shepherd's Bush
 W11. . . . . .112 B6
St Clement's Ct EC3. . . .252 D6
St Clements Ho E1. . . . .243 C3
 Walton-on-T KT12 . . . . . .194 A2
St Clement's Hts SE26. .184 A6
St Clement's La WC2. . .240 D1
St Clements Mans **3**
 SW6. . . . . .134 D6
St Clements St N7 . . . . . .72 C1
St Cloud Rd SE27 . . . . . .183 B6
St Columba's CE E15 . . .76 C4
St Columbas Ho **2**
 E17 .53 D5
St Columba's RC Boys Sch
 DA6. . . . . .169 D4
St Columb's Ho **11** W10 . .91 A2
St Crispins Cl NW3. . . . . .70 C4
St Crispin's Cl UB1. . . . . .85 B1
St Crispins Ct **1** UB1. . . .85 B1
St Cross St EC1. . .94 C2 241 B4
St Cuthberts Gdns **2**
 HA5 .23 B3
St Cuthberts Rd N13 . . . .32 C4
St Cuthbert's Rd NW2. . . .69 D2
St Cuthbert with St
 Matthias Prim Sch
 SW5 . . . . .113 D1 255 C2
St Cyprian's Greek
 Orthodox Prim Sch
 CR7. . . . . .183 A2
St Cyprian's St SW17. . .180 D6
St Davids Cl **2**
 Bermondsey SE16 . . . . . .118 B3
 Wembley HA9 . . . . .67 A5
St David's Cl BR4 . . . . . .207 D2
St David's Coll BR4 . . . .207 D2
St David's Ct **5** E11 . . . .55 B4
St David's Ct
 Bromley BR1. . . . . .210 D6
 8 Southall UB1. . . . . . . .86 A1
 1 Walthamstow E17 . . . .54 A6
St David's Dr HA8. . . . . . .26 B2
St David's Pl NW4 . . . . . .46 B2
St David's Sch TW15 . . .148 B1
St David's Sq E14. . . . . .119 C1
St Denis Rd SE27 . . . . . .183 B6
St Dionis Rd SW6. . . . . .135 B3
St Domingo Ho SE18. . . .122 B3
St Dominic RC Prim Sch
 NW5. . . . . .70 D2
St Dominics RC Prim Sch
 E9. .75 A2
St Dominic's Sixth Form
 Coll (RC) HA1. . . . . .64 C4
St Donatt's Rd SE14. . . .141 B4
St Dunstans SM1 . . . . . .217 B2

St Dunstan's Alley EC3 .253 A5
St Dunstan's Ave W3. . . .111 B6
St Dunstan's CE Prim Sch
 SM3. . . . . .217 A1
St Dunstans Cl UB3 . . . . .105 C2
St Dunstan's Coll SE6. .163 C3
St Dunstan's Ct EC4. . . .241 B1
St Dunstan's Gdns W3 . .111 B6
St Dunstan's Hill
 Cheam SM1, SM3 . . . . . .217 A3
 EC3. . . . . .253 A5
St Dunstan's La
 Beckenham BR3 . . . . .208 A4
 EC3. . . . . .253 A5
St Dunstans Rd E7. . . . . .77 C2
St Dunstan's Rd
 Cranford TW5 . . . . .128 B3
 Feltham TW13 . . . . .149 D1
 Hammersmith W6 . . . . . . .112 D1
 Hanwell W7. . . . . .108 C4
 South Norwood SE25 . . . . .205 D5
St Edmund RC Sch
 E14. . . . . .119 C2
St Edmunds Ave HA4. . . .39 B3
St Edmunds Cl DA18 . . . .124 D4
 Upper Tooting SW17 . . . . .158 C2
St Edmund's Cl NW8. . . .230 C5
St Edmund's Ct NW8. . .230 C5
St Edmund's Dr HA7. . . . .25 A2
St Edmund's La TW2. . . .151 D4
St Edmund's RC Prim
 Sch
 Edmonton N9. . . . . .18 B3
 Twickenham TW2. . . . . . . .151 D4
St Edmund's Rd N9. . . . . .18 A4
St Edmund's Rd IG1 . . . . .56 B3
St Edmund's Sq SW13. .134 C6
St Edmund's Terr
 NW8 . . . . .92 D6 230 C5
St Edward's CE Comp Sch
 RM7. . . . . .59 C3
St Edward's Cl NW11. . . .47 C3
St Edwards Ct **3** E10 . . .54 A2
St Edward's Ct NW11. . . .47 C3
St Edwards RC Prim Sch
 E6. .99 C6
St Edward's RC Prim Sch
 NW1. . . . . .92 C3 237 B5
St Egberts Way E4. . . . . .20 A3
St Elizabeth Ct
 North Finchley N12 . . . . . .30 A6
 4 Walthamstow E10 . . .53 D2
St Elizabeth RC Prim Sch
 E2. .96 C5
St Elizabeth's RC Prim Sch
 TW10. . . . . .154 B5
St Elmo Rd W12 . . . . . . .111 D4
St Elmos Rd SE16. . . . . .119 A4
St Elphege's RC Inf Sch
 SM6. . . . . .220 A1
St Elphege's RC Jun Sch
 SM6. . . . . .220 A1
SS Peter & Paul's RC
 Prim Sch
 Ilford IG1 . . . . .79 B5
 Mitcham CR4. . . . . .202 D5
St Erkenwald Mews
 IG11 . . . . .101 B6
St Erkenwald Rd IG11. . .101 B6
St Ermin's Hill SW1 . . . .259 C6
St Ervan's Rd W10 . . . . . .91 B2
St Eugene de Mazenod Rc
 Prim Sch NW6 . . . . .69 C1
St Faith's CE Prim Sch
 SW18 . . . . .158 A6
St Faith's Cl EN2. . . . . . . .5 A4
St Faith's Rd SE24 . . . . .160 D3
St Fillans Rd SE6 . . . . . .164 A4
St Francesca Cabrini Prim
 Sch SE23. . . . . .162 C5
St Francis Cl BR5 . . . . . .211 C3
St Francis de Sales RC Jun
 & Inf Sch N17 . . . . .33 D3
St Francis' Ho NW1 . . . .232 C3
St Francis Lodge HA0. . . .64 D5
St Francis of Assisi RC
 Prim Sch W11. . . . . . . .112 D6
St Francis Pl SW12. . . . .159 B5
St Francis RC Prim Sch
 SE15 . . . . .140 A5
 Stratford E15 . . . . .76 C3
St Francis Rd SE22. . . . .139 C1
St Francis Way IG1 . . . . . .79 B4
St Francis Xavier Sixth
 Form Coll SW12. . . . . . .159 B5
St Frideswides Mews **5**
 E14 .98 A1
St Gabriel's CE Prim Sch
 SW1 . . . . .115 C1 259 A1
St Gabriels Cl **3** E14. . . .97 D2
St Gabriel's Cl E11. . . . . .55 B1
St Gabriels Ct N11. . . . . . .31 D3
St Gabriel's Rd NW2. . . . .69 B3
St George Ho SW11. . . . .268 B1
ST GEORGE IN THE EAST
 . . . . .118 A6
St George's Ave
 Ealing W5 . . . . .109 C4
 Kingsbury NW9 . . . . .45 B5
 Southall UB1 . . . . .107 B6
 Tufnell Pk N7. . . . . .71 D4
 Upton E7. . . . . .77 B1
St George's Battersea CE
 Prim Sch
 SW8 . . . . .137 C5 269 B3
St George's Bickley CE
 Prim Sch BR1. . . . . . . .187 D1
St George's Bldgs
 SE11 . . . . .261 D5
St George's Cath NW1 .231 D2

St George's Cath RC Jun &
 Inf Sch SE1 . . . .116 D3 261 C6
St George's CE Prim Sch
 SE5. . . . . .139 C5
St George's Circ
 SE1 . . . . .116 D3 261 C6
St Georges Cl
 Erith DA8. . . . . .102 D1
 Nine Elms SW8 . . . . . . .269 B2
 Wembley HA0 . . . . .65 A5
St George's Cl NW11. . . . .47 B3
St Georges Coll N7 . . . . . .72 C5
St Georges Ct
 Harrow HA3 . . . . .43 A3
 Newham E6. . . . . .100 B3
 Penge SE20. . . . . .184 B2
 Putney SW15. . . . . .135 B1
 Walthamstow E17. . . . . . . .54 B4
St George's Ct
 Brompton SW3 . . . . .257 A4
 Kensington SW7 . . . . . . .256 A5
 Newington SE1 . . . . .261 C5
St George's Dr
 Ickenham UB10. . . . . .60 B6
 South Oxhey WD19 . . . . . .23 A4
 SW1. . . . . .115 C2 259 A2
St George's Field
 W2. . . . . .92 C1 237 B1
St George's Gdns KT6. .214 D6
St George's Gr SW17. . .158 B1
St Georges Hanover Sq
 Sch W1. . . . . .115 A6 248 B5
St George's Ho NW1. . . .232 B3
St George's Hospl
 SW17 . . . . .180 B5
St Georges Ind Est N22 .32 D3
St George's Ind Est
 KT2. . . . . .175 D5
St George's La EC3 . . . .253 A6
St Georges Lo N10. . . . . .49 C5
St Georges Mews **11**
 NW1 .70 D1
St George's Mews
 2 Rotherhithe SE8. . . . .119 B2
 SE1 . . . . .261 B6
St Georges Pl N7 . . . . . . .71 D4
St George's RC Cath
 SE1. . . . . .116 C3 261 B6
St George's RC Prim Sch
 Enfield EN2 . . . . .5 B3
 Harrow HA1 . . . . .64 D5
St George's RC Sec Sch
 W9 .91 D5
St Georges Rd
 Acton W4. . . . . .111 B4
 Bickley BR1. . . . . .210 B6
 Dagenham RM9. . . . . .81 A4
 Petts Wood BR5 . . . . .211 B3
St George's Rd
 Beckenham BR3 . . . . .185 D2
 Ealing W7 . . . . .108 C5
 Enfield EN1 . . . . .5 D5
 Feltham TW13 . . . . .172 D6
 Isleworth TW1 . . . . .153 B6
 2 Kingston u T KT2 . . .176 C3
 Leyton E10. . . . . .76 A5
 Mitcham CR4. . . . . .203 B6
 Newington SE1 116 D3 261 C5
 Palmers Green N13. . . . . . .16 B2
 Redbridge IG1. . . . . .56 B2
 Richmond TW9 . . . . .132 B2
 Sidcup DA14 . . . . .190 D4
 Temple Fortune NW11 . . . .47 B3
 Upton E7 . . . . .77 B2
 Wallington SM6. . . . . .219 B3
 Wimbledon SW19 . . . . . . .179 B4
St Georges Rd Ctr RM9. .81 B4
St Georges Rd W BR1. .188 A1
St George's Residences **2**
 SW2. . . . . .160 C6
St Georges's Ct EC4. . . .241 C2
St Georges Sh & L Ctr
 HA1 .42 C3
St Georges Sq **1** E14 . .119 A6
St George's Sq
 Kingston u T KT3 . . . . . . .199 C6
 Rotherhithe SE8. . . . . .119 B2
 SW1. . . . . .115 D1 259 C1
 Upton E7. . . . . .77 B1
St George's Square Mews
 SW1. . . . . .259 C1
St George St
 W1. . . . . .115 B6 248 D6
St Georges Terr
 Hampstead NW1. . . . . .70 D1
 NW1 . . . . .230 D1
St George's Way SE15. .139 C6
St George's Wlk CR0. . .221 A5
St George the Martyr CE
 Prim Sch WC1. . .94 B3 240 D5
St George Wharf SW8. .270 A4
St Gerards Cl SW4 . . . . .159 C6
St German's Pl SE3. . . . .143 A4
St German's Rd SE23. . .163 A3
St Gildas' RC Jun Sch
 N8. .50 A2
ST GILES 94 A1
St Giles Ave
 Dagenham RM10. . . . . .81 D1
 Uxbridge UB10 . . . . .61 A4
St Giles Cir
 WC1. . . . . .93 D1 239 D2
St Giles Cl BR6 . . . . .227 B3
 Dagenham RM10. . . . . .81 D1
 Heston TW3. . . . . .129 A5
St Giles Coll
 WC1. . . . . .94 A2 240 B4
St Giles CE Ealing W13 .109 C5
 WC2. . . . . .240 A1

St Giles High St
 WC2. . . . . .93 D1 239 D2
St Giles Ho
 2 New Barnet EN5 . . . .2 A1
 Streatham SW16. . . . . . . .160 A1
St Giles Hospl SE5. . . . . .139 C4
St Giles Pas WC2 . . . . . .239 D1
St Giles Rd SE5. . . . . .139 C4
St Giles' Sch CR2 . . . . . .220 D2
St Giles Twr **3** SE5 . . . .139 C4
St Gilles Ho **15** E2. . . . . .96 D5
St Gothard Rd SE21,
 SE27. . . . . .183 B6
St Gregory Cl HA4 . . . . . .62 C4
St Gregory RC High Sch
 HA3 .43 D4
St Gregory's RC Prim Sch
 W5 .87 D2
St Helena Ho **7** WC1 . . .234 A1
St Helena Pier TW9. . . . .153 D6
St Helena Rd SE16 . . . . .118 D2
St Helena St WC1. . . . . .234 A1
St Helena Terr **31**
 TW9. . . . . .153 D6
St Helens KT7 . . . . .196 D2
St Helens Coll UB10. . . . .60 C1
St Helen's Cres SW16. .182 B2
St Helen's Gdns W10. . . .90 D1
St Helen's Pl EC3 . . . . . .243 A2
St Helen's RC Inf Sch
 E17 .54 A4
St Helen's RC Prim Sch
 E13. .99 A3
St Helen's RC Sch
 SW9 . . . . .138 C2
St Helens Rd **5** DA18 . .124 D4
St Helen's Rd
 Ealing W13 . . . . .109 C5
 Redbridge IG1. . . . . .56 B3
 Thornton Heath SW16. . . .182 B2
St Helier Ave SM4 . . . . . .202 A3
St Helier Ct **4** N1. . . . . . .95 C6
St Helier Hospl SM5 . . . .202 A1
St Heliers Ave TW3,
 TW4. . . . . .151 C6
St Helier's Rd E10 . . . . . .54 A3
St Helier Sta SM4. . . . . .201 C3
St Hilary's Ct BR1. . . . . .210 D6
St Hilda's Ave TW15. . . .170 A5
St Hilda's Cl SW17. . . . .158 C2
St Hilda's Cl NW6. . . . . . .68 D1
St Hilda's Rd SW13 . . . .134 B6
St Hildas Wharf E1. . . . .118 C5
St Hubert's Ho **2** E14. .119 C3
St Hughes Cl SW17 . . . .158 C2
St Hugh's Rd SE20 . . . . .184 B3
St Ignatius Coll EN1 . . . . .6 B6
St Ignatius RC Prim Sch
 TW16. . . . . .172 A2
St Ignatius' RC Prim Sch
 N15. .51 D3
St Ives Ct NW2. . . . . .69 A2
St Ivian Ct **3** N10. . . . . . .31 B1
ST JAMES 115 C5
St James Apartments **7**
 E17 .53 A4
St James Ave
 East Barnet N20 . . . . .14 C1
 Sutton SM1 . . . . .217 C3
St James' Ave W13 . . . . .109 A5
St James CE Jun Sch
 E7. .77 A3
St James CE Prim Sch
 EN3. .5 B1
St James' CE Prim Sch
 SE16 . . . . .118 A3
St James Cl Barnet EN4 . .2 B1
 East Barnet N20 . . . . .14 C1
St James' Cl
 New Malden KT3. . . . . . . .199 D4
 Ruislip HA4 . . . . .62 C6
St James Ct
 26 Bethnal Green E2 . . .96 A4
 10 Brentford W4. . . . . . .110 C1
 1 Bromley BR2. . . . . . . .187 A1
 Forest Hill SE23 . . . . .163 A3
 SE3 . . . . .143 B4
 Thornton Heath CR0 . . . . .204 D2
 Wanstead E12. . . . . .77 C6
St James' Ct
 Bedford Pk W4 . . . . .111 B3
 7 Kingston u T KT1 . . .198 A6
 SW1. . . . . .259 B6
St James Gate IG9. . . . . .21 B3
St James Gdns IG6 . . . . . .58 B5
St James' Gdns HA0 . . . .66 A1
St James Ho N5 . . . . .72 C3
St James Hts **3** SE18 . .123 A1
St James Independent
 Schs W14. . . . . .113 A2 254 B4
St James Ind Mews **16**
 SE1. . . . . .118 A1
St James Ind Sch for Boys
 TW1 . . . . .153 A2
St James' Mans NW6 . . . .69 C1
St James Mews E14. . . .120 A3
St James' Rd High Sch
 NW9 .27 D2
St James Rd
 Carshalton SM5. . . . . .218 C5
 1 Kingston u T KT1. . . .175 D1
 Sutton SM1, SM2. . . . . . .217 C3
St James' Rd
 Edmonton N9. . . . . .18 B2
 Forest Gate E15 . . . . .76 D3
 Mitcham CR4. . . . . .181 A3

St James's SE14 . . . . . .141 A4
St James's App EC2. . . .243 A5
St James's Ave
 Beckenham BR3 . . . . .207 A6
 Hampton TW12 . . . . .174 A5
 South Hackney E2 . . . . . . .96 C5
St James's CE Prim Sch
 N10. .49 C5
St James School Flats **5**
 N7 .72 C3
St James's Cl NW8. . . . .230 C5
 Upper Tooting SW17 . . . . .158 D2
 Woolwich SE18 . . . . .123 A1
St James's Cloisters **2**
 SE22 . . . . .139 D1
St James's Cotts **14**
 TW10. . . . . .153 D6
St James's Cres SW9 . . .138 C2
St James's Ct
 Balham SW12, SW17 . . .158 A4
 Upper Tooting SW17 . . . . .158 D3
St James's Dr
 Balham SW12, SW17 . . .158 A4
 Upper Tooting SW17 . . . . .158 D3
St James's Gdns
 W11. . . . . .113 A3 244 A4
St James's Gr SW11. . . .136 C3
St James's Hatcham CE
 Prim Sch SE14 . . . . . . .141 A4
St James's La N10 . . . . . .49 B5
St James's Market
 SW1. . . . . .249 C5
St James's Mews E17. . . .53 A4
St James's Pal * . . . .
St James's Park Sta
 SW1. . . . . .115 D3 259 C6
St James's Pas EC3 . . . .243 B1
St James's Pk CR0 . . . . .205 A2
St James's Pl
 SW1. . . . . .115 C5 249 A4
St James's RC Prim Sch
 TW2 . . . . .152 C1
St James's Rd
 Bermondsey SE1,
 SE16. . . . . .118 A2
 Hampton TW12 . . . . .173 D5
 Peckham SE15. . . . . .140 A6
 Thornton Heath CR0 . . . . .205 A2
St James's Sq
 SW1. . . . . .115 C5 249 A4
 Walthamstow E17. . . . . . . .53 A4
St James St **6** SW1 . . .112 C1
St James's Terr NW8. . . .230 C6
 2 Upper Tooting
 SW12 . . . . .159 A3
St James's Terrace Mews
 NW8 . . . . .230 C5
St James Street Sta
 E17. . . . . .53 A4
St James The Great RC
 Prim Sch
 Camberwell SE15 . . . . . . .139 C4
 South Norwood CR7 . . . . .182 D1
St James Way DA14. . . .191 A5
St James Wlk EC1 . . . . .241 C6
St Jerome's Gr UB3 . . . . . .83 A1
St Joachim's RC Prim Sch
 E16. .99 C1
St Joan of Arc RC Prim
 Sch N5 . . . . .73 A4
St Joan's Rd N9 . . . . .17 D2
St John Baptist CE Prim
 Sch BR1 . . . . .186 A6
St John Evangelist RC
 Prim Sch N1 . .94 D5 234 C4
St John Fisher RC Fst &
 Mid Sch HA5 . . . . .41 C5
St John Fisher RC Prim
 Sch
 DA18 . . . . .125 A3
 Wembley UB6 . . . . .87 C4
 West Barnes SW20. . . . . .200 D4
St John of Jerusalem CE
 Prim Sch E9 . . . . .74 C1
ST JOHNS 141 C1
St John & St James CE
 Prim Sch
 Edmonton N18. . . . . .33 D3
 Hackney E9. . . . . .74 C3
St John's Angell Town CE
 Prim Sch SW9. . . . . . . .138 C3
St John's Ave
 Dagenham NW10 . . . . .89 D6
 Friern Barnet N11. . . . . . . .30 D5
 Putney SW15. . . . . .156 D6
St John's CE First Sch
 HA7 .25 A4
St John's CE JMI Sch
 N11. .30 B6
St John's CE Prim Sch
 Buckhurst Hill IG9. . . . . . .21 B3
 Croydon CR0 . . . . .222 D5
 Enfield EN2 . . . . .4 D4
 Fulham SW6 . . . .135 A4 264 B2
 Kingston u T KT1. . . . . . . .198 A6
 Penge SE20. . . . . .184 C3
 South Hackney E2 . . . . . . .96 C5
 Whetstone N20. . . . . .14 A2
St John's CE Sch
 Stanmore HA7. . . . . .25 A6

St John's Church Rd
 E9. .74 C3
St Johns Cl N14 . . . . .15 C5
St John's Cl SW6 . . . . . .265 A4
 Wembley HA9 . . . . .66 A3
St Johns Concert Hall *
 SW1 . . . . .260 A1
St John's Cotts **2**
 SE20 . . . . .184 C3
St Johns Cres SW9 . . . .138 C2
St Johns Ct **39** E1. . . . .118 B5
St John's Ct
 Buckhurst Hill IG9. . . . . . .21 B3
 Finsbury Pk N4 . . . . .72 B6
 Hammersmith W6 . . . . . . .112 B2
 2 Harrow HA1. . . . . .42 D3
 Isleworth TW7 . . . . .130 D3
 Kingston u T KT1. . . . . . . .198 A5
 Lewisham SE13. . . . . .142 A3
 Leytonstone E11. . . . . .54 C1
 5 South Hampstead
 NW3. . . . . .70 A2
Saint John's Ct N5. . . . . .72 C4
St Johns Dr KT12 . . . . . .194 C1
St John's Dr SW18. . . . . .157 D3
St John's Est **5** 253 A4
St John's Gdns
 W11. . . . . .113 B6 244 B6
St John's Gr
 3 Barnes SW13. . . . . . .133 C4
 1 Richmond TW9. . . . . .132 A1
 Upper Holloway N19. . . . . .71 C4
St John's Highbury Vale
 CE Prim Sch N5. . . . . . .72 C5
St John's Hill SW11 . . . .136 B3
St John's Hill Gr
 SW11. . . . . .136 B3
St Johns Ho **6** SE17 . . .139 B6
 Streatham SW16. . . . . . . .182 A4
St John's Ho **1** E14. . . .120 A2
St John's La
 EC1 . . . . .94 D2 241 B6
St John's Lodge **8**
 SE8 . . . . .141 B4
St John's Mans E5. . . . . .74 C3
St John's Par
 Ealing W13 . . . . .109 B5
 3 Sidcup DA14 . . . . . . .190 B6
St John's Park Mans
 N19. .71 C5
St John's Path EC1 . . . . .241 C6
St John's Pk SE3. . . . . . .143 A5
St John's Pl EC1. . . . . . .241 C6
St John's Prim Sch
 W13 . . . . .109 A5
St John's RC Prim Sch
 SE16. . . . . .119 A4
St Johns Rd Ilford IG2. . .57 C2
 Kingston u T KT3. . . . . . . .199 A6
St John's Rd
 Barking IG11. . . . . .101 C4
 Battersea SW11 . . . . .136 C1
 Canning Town E16. . . . . . . .99 A1
 Carshalton SM5. . . . . .218 C5
 Chingford E4. . . . . .35 C6
 Croydon CR0 . . . . .220 D5
 DA16. . . . . .146 B2
 East Ham E6 . . . . .100 A6
 East Molesey KT8 . . . . . . .196 B5
 Feltham TW13 . . . . .173 B6
 Harrow HA1. . . . . .42 D3
 Isleworth TW7 . . . . .130 D3
 Orpington BR5. . . . . .211 C3
 Penge SE20. . . . . .184 C4
 Richmond TW9 . . . . .132 A1
 Sidcup DA14 . . . . .190 B6
 Southall UB2 . . . . .107 A3
 Sutton SM1 . . . . .217 D6
 Teddington KT1. . . . . .175 C1
 Temple Fortune NW11 . . . .47 B3
 Tottenham N15. . . . . .51 C3
 Walthamstow E17. . . . . . . .36 A1
 Wembley HA9 . . . . .66 B3
 Wimbledon SW19 . . . . . . .179 A4
St John's & St Clements
 CE Prim Sch SE15. . . .140 A2
St John's Sch HA6. . . . . .22 B4
St John's Sq
 EC1 . . . . .94 D3 241 C6
St Johns Sta SE8 . . . . . .141 C3
St John's St EC1. . .94 D3 241 C6
St John's Terr Enfield EN2. 5 B6
 North Kensington W10. . . . .90 D3
 SE18 . . . . .145 B6
 Upton E7. . . . . .77 B2
St Johnstone Ho **17**
 N12. .29 D6
St John's Upper Holloway
 CE Prim Sch N19. . . . . .71 C5
St John's Vale SE8. . . . . .141 C3
St John's Villas
 4 Friern Barnet N11. . . .30 D5
 Upper Holloway N19. . . . . .71 D6
 W8. . . . . .255 D5
St John's Way N19. . . . . .71 C5
ST JOHN'S WOOD 92 B5
St John's Wood Ct
 NW8 . . . . .229 D2
St John's Wood High St
 NW8 . . . . .92 C5 230 A3
St John's Wood Park
 NW8 . . . . .92 B6 230 C6
St John's Wood Pre-Prep
 Sch NW8. . . . . . .92 C4 230 A2
St John's Wood Rd
 NW8 . . . . .92 B4 229 D1
St John's Wood Sta
 NW8 . . . . .92 B5 229 C4
St John's Wood Terr
 NW8 . . . . .92 C5 230 A4

St John the Baptist CE Jun Sch KT1 . . . . . . 175 D3
St John the Baptist CE Prim Sch N1 . . . 95 B5 235 D3
St John the Divine CE Jun & Inf Sch SE5 . . . . . . 138 C1
St John Vianney RC Prim Sch W7 . . . . 50 D5
St Joseph RC Prim Sch W7 . . . . 108 C5
St Josephs Acad SE3 . . 142 C2
St Josephs CI BR6 . . . . 227 D4
St Joseph's CI W10 . . . . 91 A2
St Joseph's Coll Mill Hill Missionaries NW7 . . 27 D6
St Joseph's Convent Sch E11 . . . . 55 A3
St Josephs Ct
  3 Dagenham NW10 . . . . 89 D5
  20 Walthamstow E10 . . . . 53 D2
St Joseph's Dr UB1 . . 107 B5
St Josephs Flats NW1 232 C2
St Josephs Gr NW4 . . . . 46 B5
St Joseph's Ho W6 . . . . 112 D2
St Joseph's Hospice E9, E8 . . . . 96 B6
St Joseph's RC Coll SW16 . . . . 182 D4
St Joseph's RC Fst & Mid Sch HA3 . . . . 25 A1
St Joseph's RC Inf & Jun Schs
  Hendon NW4 . . . . 46 B5
  SE5 . . . . 139 A5
St Joseph's RC Inf Sch
  Leyton E10 . . . . 75 C6
  South Norwood SE19 . . . . 183 A4
St Joseph's RC Jun & Inf Schs HA9 . . . . 66 B3
St Joseph's RC Jun Sch
  South Norwood SE19 . . . 183 A4
  Walthamstow E10 . . . . . . 53 D1
St Joseph's RC Prim Sch
  Barking IG11 . . . . 101 A4
  Bermondsey SE16 . . . . . . 118 A4
  Bromley BR1 . . . . 187 B3
  Chelsea SW3 . . 114 D2 257 C3
  Dagenham RM9 . . . . 81 B4
  Deptford SE8 . . . . 141 C5
  Greenwich SE10 . . . . . . 120 C1
  Kingston u T KT1 . . . . . . 196 B5
  Paddington W9 . . 92 A4 229 A1
  Rotherhithe SE16 . . . . . 118 C3
  St Giles WC2 . . . 94 A1 240 B2
  Upper Holloway N19 . . . . 49 B1
  Wandsworth SW18 . . . . . . 157 C4
  Willesden NW10 . . . . 67 C1
St Joseph's St SW8 . . . . 268 C2
St Joseph's Vale SE3 . . 142 B2
St Jude & St Paul's CE Prim Sch N1 . . . . 73 C2
St Jude's CE Prim Sch SE24 . . . . 160 D6
St Judes Ho 6 W10 . . . . 91 B4
St Jude's Prim Sch SE1 . . . . 116 D3 261 C5
St Jude's Rd E2 . . . . 96 B5
St Jude St N16 . . . . 73 C3
St Julian's CI SW16 . . . 182 C6
St Julian's Farm Rd SE27, SW16 . . . . 182 C6
St Julian's Rd NW6 . . . . 91 C6
St Katharine's Ho N1 . . 234 A4
St Katharine's Prec NW1 . . . . 231 C6
St Katharine's Way E1 . . . . 117 D5 253 D4
St Katherines Rd DA18 . . . . 124 C4
St Katherine's Row EC3 . . . . 243 B1
St Katherine's Wlk 1 W11 . . . . 112 D5
St Keverne Rd SE9 . . . . 188 A6
St Kilda Rd BR6 . . . . . . 211 D1
  Ealing W13 . . . . 109 A4
St Kilda's Rd
  Harrow HA1 . . . . 42 C3
  Stamford Hill N16 . . . . . . 51 C1
St Kitts Terr SE19 . . . . 183 C5
St Laurence's CI NW6 . . . 90 D6
St Lawrence CE Jun Sch KT8 . . . . 196 B5
St Lawrence CI HA8 . . . . 26 B3
St Lawrence CI N1 . . . . 235 D6
St Lawrence Dr HA5 . . . . 40 B4
St Lawrence Ho SE1 . . . 263 B6
St Lawrence RC Prim Sch TW13 . . . . 150 B2
St Lawrence St E14 . . . 120 A5
St Lawrence Terr W10 . . 91 A2
St Lawrence Way SW9 . . . . 138 C3
St Leonards Ave HA3 . . . 43 C4
St Leonard's Ave E4 . . . 36 B4
St Leonard's CE Prim Sch SW16 . . . . 181 D5
St Leonards CI 4 DA16 . . . . 146 A2
St Leonards CI SW14 . . . 133 A2
St Leonards Ct N1 . . . . 235 D2
St Leonards Gdns IG1 . . . 79 A3
St Leonard's Gdns TW5 . . . . 129 A4
St Leonard's Hospl N1 . . . 95 C5
St Leonard's Rd SW14 . . 133 A2
St Leonard's Rd Becontree NW10 . . . . 89 B3

St Leonard's Rd continued
  Claygate KT10 . . . . . . 212 D2
  Croydon CR0 . . . . 220 D5
  Ealing W13 . . . . 109 C6
  Kingston u T KT6 . . . . . 197 D4
  South Bromley E14 . . . . . 98 A2
  Thames Ditton KT7 . . . . 197 A2
St Leonards Rise BR6 . . . 227 C4
St Leonard's Sq
  Camden Town NW5 . . . . . . 71 A2
  Kingston u T KT6 . . . . . 197 D4
St Leonard's St E3 . . . . . 97 D4
St Leonard's Terr SW3 . . . . 114 D1 257 D1
St Leonard's Wlk SW16 . . . . 182 B3
St Loo Ave SW3 . . . . 136 C6 267 C6
St Loo Ct SW3 . . . . 267 C6
St Louis Rd SE27 . . . . 183 B6
St Loy's Rd N17 . . . . 51 D6
St Lucia Dr E15 . . . . 98 D6
St Luke Prim Sch E16 . . . 98 D1
ST LUKE'S 95 A3
St Luke's Ave
  Clapham SW4 . . . . 137 D1
  Enfield EN2 . . . . 5 B5
  Ilford IG1 . . . . 78 D3
St Luke's CE Prim Sch
  Cubitt Town E14 . . . . . 120 B2
  Kingston u T KT2 . . . . . 176 B2
  Paddington W9 . . . . 91 B4
  Shoreditch EC1 . . 95 A4 235 B1
  West Norwood SE27 . . . . 183 A5
St Luke's CI
  Croydon SE25 . . . . 206 B3
St Luke's EC1 . . . 95 A3 242 B6
St Lukes Ct 6 E10 . . . . 53 D2
St Luke's Ct W11 . . . . . . 91 B1
St Luke's Hospl W1 . . . . 93 C3 239 A5
St Luke's Mews W11 . . . . 91 B1
St Luke's Path 1 IG1 . . . 78 D3
St Luke's RC Sixth Form Coll DA14 . . . . 189 D5
St Luke's Rd
  Notting Hill W11 . . . . . . 91 B2
  Uxbridge UB10 . . . . 60 A1
St Luke's Sq E16 . . . . . . 98 D1
St Luke's St SW3 . . . . . 257 B2
St Luke's Woodside Hospl N10 . . . . 49 A5
St Malo Ave N9 . . . . 18 C1
St Margaret Clitherow RC Prim Sch
  Neasden NW28 . . . . 67 B4
  Woolwich SE28 . . . . . . 124 B5
ST MARGARETS 153 A5
St Margarets IG11 . . . . 101 B6
St Margarets Ave
  Ashford TW15 . . . . 170 D5
  DA15 . . . . 167 B1
  Hillingdon UB8 . . . . 82 C3
  Whetstone N20 . . . . 14 A3
St Margaret's Ave
  Cheam SM3 . . . . 217 A5
  Harringay N8, N15 . . . . . 50 D5
  Harrow HA2 . . . . 44 C4
St Margarets Bsns Ctr 11 TW1 . . . . 153 B5
St Margaret's CE Prim Sch
  Barking IG11 . . . . 79 A1
  Woolwich SE18 . . . . . . 123 A1
St Margaret's Cres SW15 . . . . 156 B6
St Margaret's Ct
  Leyton E15 . . . . 76 C4
  Putney SW15 . . . . 134 B1
  SE1 . . . . 252 C3
  9 Twickenham TW1 . . . 153 B5
St Margaret's Dr TW1 . . 153 B6
St Margaret's Gr
  Leyton E11 . . . . 76 D5
  SE18 . . . . 145 A6
  Twickenham TW1 . . . . . 153 A5
St Margaret's La W8 . . . . 113 D3 255 C5
St Margaret's Lee CE Prim Sch SE13 . . . . 142 C1
St Margarets Lo W3 . . . 110 D4
St Margaret's Pass SE13 . . . . 142 C2
St Margaret's Path 4 SE18 . . . . 123 A1
St Margarets Rd
  Edgware HA8 . . . . 26 D5
  Ruislip HA4 . . . . 39 B3
St Margaret's Rd
  Brockley SE4 . . . . 141 B1
  Hanwell W7 . . . . 108 C4
  Isleworth TW1 . . . . . . 153 B6
  Kensal Green NW10 . . . . 90 C4
  Tottenham N17 . . . . 51 C6
  Wanstead E12 . . . . 77 C6
St Margarets Rdbt TW1 . . . . 153 B6
St Margaret's Sch NW3 . . 69 D4
St Margaret's Sta TW1 . . . . 153 A5
St Margaret St SW1 . . . 250 A1
St Margaret's Terr SE18 . . . . 123 A1
St Margret's Ct N11 . . . 31 A1
St Mark's CE Acad CR4 . . . . 181 B1
St Mark's CE Prim Sch
  Bromley BR2 . . . . 209 A4
  Croydon SE25 . . . . 206 A5

St Mark's CE Prim Sch continued
  Kennington SE11 . . . . . . 138 B6 270 D6
St Marks CI 5 SE10 . . . 142 A5
St Mark's CI Barnet EN5 . . . 1 D2
  Harrow HA1 . . . . 43 B1
St Mark's Cres NW1 . . . . 93 A4 231 B6
St Mark's Ct
  Hanwell W7 . . . . 108 C4
  8 Walthamstow E10 . . . . 53 D2
St Marks Gate E9 . . . . . . 75 B1
St Mark's Gr SW10 . . . . 135 D5 265 D4
St Marks Hill KT6 . . . . 198 A3
St Marks Ho 6 SE17 . . 139 B6
St Mark's Ho 6 E17 . . . 54 A5
St Mark's Hospl EC1 . . . . 94 D4 234 D2
St Mark's Hts 25 KT6 . . 198 A4
St Marks Ind Est E16 . . 121 D5
St Mark's Mans 14 N4 . . 72 B6
St Mark's Pl
  Notting Hill W11 . . . . . . 91 A1
  Wimbledon SW19 . . . . . 179 B4
St Mark's Prim Sch
  Hanwell W7 . . . . 108 C4
  Mitcham CR4 . . . . 180 D1
  Upper Holloway N19 . . . . 72 A6
St Mark's RC Sch TW3 . . . . 129 C2
St Marks Rd 8 NW10 . . . 90 D1
St Mark's Rd
  Bromley BR2 . . . . 209 B6
  Croydon SE25 . . . . 206 A5
  Ealing W5 . . . . 110 A5
  Enfield EN1 . . . . 17 D6
  Hanwell W7 . . . . 108 C4
  Mitcham CR4 . . . . 181 A1
  North Kensington W10 . . 90 D2
  Notting Hill W11 . . . . . . 91 A1
  Teddington TW11 . . . . . 175 B3
St Mark's Sq NW1 . . . . 231 A5
St Mark St E1 . . . 95 D1 243 D1
St Martha's Convent Jun Sch EN5 . . . . 1 A1
St Martha's Senior Sch EN4 . . . . 1 C4
St Martin-in-the-Fields High Sch for Girls SW2 . . . . 160 C3
St Martin of Porres RC Prim Sch N11 . . . . 31 C4
St Martin's Almshouses NW1 . . . . 232 A6
St Martin's App HA4 . . . 39 C2
St Martin's Ave E6 . . . . 99 D5
  South Oxhey WD19 . . . . . 22 D6
St Martins CI DA18 . . . 124 C4
  NW1 . . . . 232 A6
St Martin's Ct N1 . . . . . 95 C6
  West Norwood SE27 . . . 160 D2
St Martins La BR3 . . . . 207 D4
St Martin's La WC2 . . . . 116 A4 250 A5
St Martin's Le Grand EC1 . . . . 242 A2
St Martin's Pl WC2 . . . 250 A5
St Martin's Rd
  Edmonton N9 . . . . 18 B2
  Finchley N2 . . . . 30 B2
  Stockwell SW9 . . . . 138 B3
St Martin's St SW7 . . . . 27 B5
St Martin's St WC2 . . . 249 D5
St Martin's Way SW17 . . 158 A1
St Mary Abbots CE Prim Sch W8 . . . . . . 113 D4 245 C1
St Mary Abbot's Ct W14 . . . . 254 C5
St Mary Abbot's Pl W8 . . 254 D5
St Mary Abbots Terr W14 . . . . 254 D5
St Mary at Hill EC3 . . . . 117 C4 253 A5
St Mary Ave SM3 . . . . 219 B5
St Mary Axe EC3 . . 95 C1 243 B2
Marychurch St SE16 . . . . 118 C4
St Mary Graces Ct E1 . . 253 D5
St Mary Magdalene CE Prim Sch
  Islington N7 . . . . 72 C2
  Paddington W2 . . . . 91 B3
  Peckham SE15 . . . . 140 B4
  Woolwich SE18 . . . . . . 122 C4
St Mary Magdalen's RC Prim Sch
  Brockley SE4 . . . . 141 A1
  Mortlake SW14 . . . . . . 133 B2
St Mary Magdalen's RC Jun Sch NW2 . . . . 68 B2
St Mary Newington CI SE17 . . . . 263 B2
St Mary of the Angels RC Prim Sch W10 . . . . 91 C1
St Mary RC Prim Sch W1 . . . . 91 A1
St Mary Rd E17 . . . . 53 D5
St Marys IG11 . . . . . . 101 B6

St Mary & St Joseph's RC Sch DA14 . . . . 189 D5
St Mary & St Michael Prim Sch E1 . . . . 96 C1
St Mary & St Pancras CE Prim Sch NW1 . . . . 93 D5 232 C3
St Marys Ave UB2 . . . . 107 D2
St Mary's Ave
  Beckenham BR2 . . . . . . 208 C6
  Finchley N3 . . . . 29 B1
  Teddington TW11 . . . . . 174 D4
  Wanstead E11 . . . . 55 B2
St Mary's Bryanston Square CE Sch W1 . . . . 92 D2 237 C4
St Mary's CE High Sch (Lower & Upper) NW4 . . . . 46 C6
St Mary's CE High Sch (Middle) NW4 . . . . . . 46 C6
St Mary's CE Inf Sch N8 . . . . 50 B5
St Mary's CE Jun Sch N8 . . . . 50 A5
St Mary's CE Prim Sch
  Chessington KT9 . . . . 214 B2
  East Barnet EN4 . . . . . 14 C5
  Finchley N3 . . . . 29 B3
  Islington N1 . . . 94 D6 234 D6
  Long Ditton KT7 . . . . 197 B1
  Putney SW15 . . . . 134 D2
  Walthamstow E17 . . . . . 53 D5
  Willesden NW10 . . . . . . 67 C2
St Mary's Church Ho 11 E17 . . . . 53 D5
St Mary's CI BR5 . . . . . 190 B1
  Chessington KT9 . . . . 214 B1
  Ewell KT17 . . . . 215 D1
  Sunbury TW16 . . . . . . 194 A5
  Tottenham N17 . . . . 34 A2
St Mary's Coll TW1 . . . 152 D1
St Mary's Cottage Hospl TW12 . . . . 173 B2
St Mary's Cres
  Hayes UB3 . . . . 105 D6
  Hendon NW4 . . . . 46 B6
  Hounslow TW7 . . . . . . 130 C5
St Marys Ct
  Abbey Wood SE2 . . . . . 124 D2
  Newham E6 . . . . 100 B3
  SE7 . . . . 143 D5
St Mary's Ct
  Bedford Pk W6 . . . . 111 D3
  Ealing W5 . . . . 109 D4
  Finchley N12 . . . . 30 A3
  Kingston u T KT3 . . . . 199 C6
  Leytonstone E11 . . . . . . 54 D1
St Mary's Dr TW14 . . . 149 A4
St Mary's Est 2 SE16 . . 118 C4
St Mary's Flats NW1 . . 232 C2
St Mary's Gate W8 . . . 255 C5
St Mary's Gdns SE11 . . 261 B6
St Mary's Gn 1 N2 . . . . 48 A6
St Mary's Gr
  Barnes SW13 . . . . 134 B2
  Chiswick W4 . . . . 132 D6
  Islington N1 . . . . 72 D2
  Richmond TW10, TW9 . . 132 B1
St Mary's Ho
  Ealing W5 . . . . 109 D3
  N1 . . . . 234 D6
St Mary's Hospl W2 . . . . 92 B1 236 D2
St Mary's Hospl Medical Sch W2 . . . . . . 92 B1 236 D2
St Mary's Kilburn CE Prim Sch NW6 . . . . 91 C1
St Mary's Lewisham CE Prim Sch SE13 . . . . . . 163 D6
St Mary's Lo E11 . . . . . . 55 B3
St Mary's Mans
  Dagenham NW10 . . . . . . 89 C6
  Paddington W2 . . 92 B2 236 C4
St Mary's Mews NW6 . . . 69 D1
St Mary's Path N1 . . . . 234 D6
St Mary's Pl Ealing W5 . . 109 D4
  Eltham SE9 . . . . 166 C5
  Kensington W8 113 D3 255 C5
St Mary's RC High Sch CR0 . . . . 205 A1
St Mary's RC Inf Sch Carshalton SM5 . . . . . . 218 D4
  Croydon CR0 . . . . 205 B1
St Mary's RC Jun & Inf Schs N15 . . . . 51 B4
St Mary's RC Jun Sch
  Croydon CR0 . . . . 205 B1
  Wallington SM5 . . . . . . 218 D3
  Walthamstow E17 . . . . . 54 A6
St Mary's RC Prim Sch
  Beckenham BR3 . . . . . . 186 A3
  Chingford E4 . . . . 20 B3
  Chiswick W4 . . . . 133 C6
  Clapham Pk SW4 . . . . . 159 C6
  Clapham SW8 . . 137 B4 268 D2
  Enfield EN3 . . . . 6 D1
  Hammersmith W14 . . . . 112 D3
  Isleworth TW7 . . . . . . 131 A2
  Merton SW19 . . . . 179 C3
  Paddington NW6 . . . . . . 91 C5
  SE9 . . . . 166 C6

St Mary's Rd
  Dagenham NW10 . . . . 89 C6
  Ealing W5 . . . . 109 D5
  East Barnet EN4 . . . . . . 14 C4
  East Molesey KT8 . . . . 196 B4
  Finchley N2 . . . . 30 B2
  Golders Green NW11 . . . 47 A2
  Hayes UB3 . . . . 105 D6
  Hornsey N8 . . . . 50 A5
  Leyton E10 . . . . 76 A6
  Long Ditton KT6 . . . . 197 C1
  Lower Edmonton N9 . . . . 18 C3
  Newham E13 . . . . 99 B5
  Nunhead SE15 . . . . 140 C3
  South Norwood SE25 . . 205 C6
  Surbiton KT6 . . . . 197 D3
  Wimbledon SW19 . . . . . 179 B5
  Worcester Pk KT4 . . . . 215 C6
St Mary's & St John's CE Prim Sch NW4 . . . . . . 46 B6
St Mary's & St Peter's CE Prim Sch NW1 . . . . 174 D5
St Mary's Sch Hampstead NW3 . . . . 70 B3
St Mary's Sq Ealing W5 . . 109 D4
  W2 . . . . 236 D2
St Mary's Stoke Newington CE Prim Sch N16 . . . . . . 73 C6
St Mary St SE18 . . . . 122 C2
St Mary's Terr W2 . . . . 236 C4
St Mary's Twr EC1 . . . . 242 B5
St Marys View HA3 . . . . 43 C4
St Mary's Wlk
  Hayes UB3 . . . . 105 D6
  SE11 . . . . 261 B4
St Matthew's Ave KT6 . . 198 B3
St Matthew's CE Prim Sch
  Enfield EN3 . . . . 18 C4
  Surbiton KT6 . . . . 198 A2
  Wimbledon SW20 . . . . 178 A2
  Yiewsley UB7 . . . . 104 A5
St Matthews Ct
  Muswell Hill N10 . . . . . 31 A1
  SE1 . . . . 262 A5
  2 Stratford E15 . . . . . . 76 D1
  7 Walthamstow E10 . . . 53 D2
St Matthew's Ct 1 TW15 . . . . 170 C5
St Matthews Dr BR1 . . 210 B1
St Matthew's Ho 8 SE17 . . . . 139 B6
St Matthew's Lo NW1 . . 232 B4
St Matthew's Rd
  Clapham Pk SW2 . . . . 160 B6
  Ealing W5 . . . . 110 A5
St Matthew's Row E2 . . 96 A3
St Matthews Row Westminster SW1 . . . 115 D3 259 D6
St Matthew St SW1 . . . 259 C5
St Matthias CE Prim Sch E2 . . . . 95 D3 243 D6
St Matthias CI NW9 . . . . 45 D4
St Matthias's CE Prim Sch N16 . . . . 73 C6
St Mauritius Ho SE13 . . 164 A6
St Maur Rd SW6 . . . . 135 B4 264 D1
St Mellion CI SE28 . . . 102 D1
St Merryn CI SE18 . . . 145 B5
St Merryn Ct BR3 . . . . 185 C3
St Michael-at-Bowes CE Jun Sch N13 . . . . 32 C4
St Michael RC Prim Sch TW15 . . . . 170 C5
St Michael & St Martin RC Prim Sch TW4 . . . . 129 B2
St Michael's Alley EC3 . . 242 D1
St Michaels Ave N1 . . . 118 A2
St Michael's Ave HA9 . . . 66 C2
St Michael's CE Prim Sch
  Camden Town NW1 . . . 93 C6 232 A6
  Enfield EN2 . . . . 5 A4
  Forest Hill SE26 . . . . 185 A6
  Highgate N6 . . . . 49 A2
  Wandsworth SW18 . . . . 157 B4
  Wood Green N22 . . . . . . 32 B2
St Michaels CI BR1 . . . 210 A6
  4 Newham E16 . . . . 99 D2
  Worcester Pk KT4 . . . 215 D6
St Michael's CI
  Colney Hatch N12 . . . . . 30 C5
  DA18 . . . . 124 D4
  Finchley N3 . . . . 29 B1
St Michael's Cres HA5 . . . 41 A3
St Michaels CI 2 E14 . . . 98 A2
St Michael's Ct
  Brunswick Pk N11 . . . . . 15 A1
  Golders Green NW11 . . . 47 A2
St Michael's East Wickham CE Prim Sch DA16 . . 146 C4
St Michael's Flats NW1 . . . . 232 C3
St Michael's Gdns W10 . . 91 A2
St Michaels Ho SE26 . . . 5 B6
St Michael's Hospl EN2 . . . 5 B4
St Michael's RC Gram Sch N12 . . . . 30 A4
St Michael's RC Prim Sch E6 . . . . 100 B5
St Michael's RC Sch SE16 . . . . 118 A4
St Michaels Rd TW15 . . 170 C5
St Michael's Rd
  Cricklewood NW2 . . . . . 68 C4
  Croydon CR0 . . . . 205 A1

St Michael's Rd continued
  DA16 . . . . 146 B2
  Stockwell SW9 . . . . 138 B3
  Wallington SM6 . . . . . 219 C2
St Michael's Rise DA16 . . . . 146 B4
St Michael's St W2 . . . . 92 C1 237 A2
St Michael Steiner Sch The SW18 . . . . 157 C6
St Michael's Terr N22 . . . 32 A2
St Mildred's Ct EC2 . . . 242 C1
St Mildreds Rd SE12, SE6 . . . . 164 D4
St Mirren Ct 8 EN5 . . . . 14 A6
St Monica's RC Prim Sch
  Palmers Green N14 . . . . 16 A1
  Shoreditch N1 . . . . 95 C4
St Nicholas CE Prim Sch TW17 . . . . 192 D3
St Nicholas CI WD6 . . . . 9 D5
St Nicholas CI E4 . . . . . . 36 A4
St Nicholas Ctr 7 SM1 . . . . 217 D3
St Nicholas Dr TW17 . . 192 C2
St Nicholas Elstree CE Prim Sch WD6 . . . . . . 9 D5
St Nicholas' Flats NW1 232 C3
St Nicholas Glebe SW17 . . . . 181 A4
St Nicholas Ho SE8 . . . 141 C6
St Nicholas Mans SW17 . . . . 158 D2
St Nicholas Rd
  Plumstead SE18 . . . . . 123 D2
  Sutton SM1 . . . . 217 D3
  Thames Ditton KT7 . . . 196 D3
St Nicholas Sch NW9 . . . 67 A6
St Nicholas St SE8 . . . 141 C4
St Nicholas Way SM1 . . 217 D3
St Nicolas La BR7 . . . . 188 A2
St Ninian's CE Prim Sch N20 . . . . 14 D1
St Norbert Gn SE4 . . . . 141 A1
St Norbert Rd SE4 . . . . 141 A1
St Olaf's Rd SW6 . . . . 135 A5 264 B3
St Olaves Ct W2 . . . . . 245 C5
St Olave's Ct EC2 . . . . 242 C1
St Olave's Est SE1 . . . 253 B2
St Olave's Gdns SE11 . . 261 A4
St Olave's Mans SE11 . . 261 A4
St Olaves Prep Sch SE9 . . . . 166 D2
St Olave's Rd E6 . . . . 100 C6
St Olave's Wlk SW16 . . 181 D1
St Olav's Sq 32 SE16 . . 118 C4
St Osmund's RC Prim Sch SW13 . . . . 133 D4
St Oswald's Pl SE11 . . . . 116 B1 260 C1
St Oswald's Rd SW16 . . 182 D2
St Oswulf St SW1 . . . . 259 D3
St Owen Ho SE1 . . . . . 263 B6
ST PANCRAS 94 A4
St Pancras Almshouses 13 NW5 . . . . 70 D3
St Pancras Commercial Ctr NW1 . . . . 232 B6
St Pancras Ct
  Finchley N2 . . . . 30 B1
  6 Wembley HA0 . . . . . . 66 A2
St Pancras Hospl NW1 . . . . 93 D6 232 C5
St Pancras International Sta WC1 . . . . . . 94 A4 233 A2
St Pancras Way NW1 . . . . 93 D6 232 C6
St Patrick's Coll W1 . . . . 93 D1 239 C2
St Patricks Ct IG8 . . . . 36 C3
St Patrick's RC Prim Sch
  Camden Town NW5 . . . . . 71 B3
  Plumstead SE18 . . . . . 123 B2
  Walthamstow E17 . . . . . 53 A5
St Paul's Acad SE2 . . . 146 A6
St Paul's & All Hallows CE Jun & Inf Schs N17 . . . 34 A3
St Paul's Ave
  Harrow HA3 . . . . 44 B5
  Rotherhithe SE16 . . . . 118 D5
  Willesden NW2 . . . . 68 C2
St Paul's Cath EC4 . . . . 95 A1 242 A1
St Paul's Cath Sch EC4 . . . . 95 A1 242 A1
St Paul's CE Jun Sch KT2 . . . . 176 C3
St Pauls CE Prim Sch TW8 . . . . 131 D6
St Paul's CE Prim Sch
  Chessington KT9 . . . . 214 A4
  Friern Barnet N11 . . . . 31 B5
  Hammersmith W6 . . . . 112 C1
  Hampstead NW3 . . . . . . 70 D1
  Mill Hill NW7 . . . . 28 B6
  SE17 . . . . 117 A1 262 D2
  Southgate N21 . . . . 16 D4
St Paul's Church Yd EC4 . . . . 95 A1 242 A1
St Pauls CI Ealing W5 . . 110 B4
  Hayes UB3 . . . . 105 B1
St Paul's CI
  Ashford TW15 . . . . . . 171 A5
  Borehamwood WD6 . . . . 11 A1
  Carshalton SM5 . . . . . 202 D3
  Chessington KT9 . . . . 213 D4

St Paul's Cl *continued*
Greenwich SE7 ... 121 D1
Hounslow TW3, TW4 ... 129 A3
ST PAUL'S CRAY ... 190 A1
St Paul's Cray Rd BR7 ... 189 B2
St Pauls Cres NW1 ... 71 D1
St Paul's Ct
Clapham SW4 ... 137 D1
Hounslow TW4 ... 129 A2
6 Upper Holloway N19 ... 72 A6
St Paul's Dr E15 ... 76 B3
St Paul's Girls' Sch W6 ... 112 D2
St Pauls Ho N17 ... 34 A3
St Pauls Mews NW1 ... 71 D1
St Paul's Pl N1 ... 73 B2
St Paul's RC Coll TW16 ... 172 A2
St Paul's RC Prim Sch
Thames Ditton KT7 ... 196 C2
Wood Green N22 ... 32 B1
St Pauls Rd
Barking IG11 ... 101 A6
Richmond TW9 ... 132 B2
St Paul's Rd
Brentford TW8 ... 131 D6
Canonbury N1 ... 73 A2
South Norwood CR7 ... 205 A6
Tottenham N17 ... 34 A2
St Pauls Rise N13 ... 32 D4
St Paul's Sch SW13 ... 112 A1
St Paul's Sq BR2 ... 187 A1
St Paul's Sta EC2 ... 95 A1 242 A2
St Paul St N1 ... 235 B5
St Paul's Terr SE17 ... 138 D6
St Paul's Twr 14 E10 ... 53 D2
St Pauls View WC1 ... 234 A1
St Paul's Way
Finchley N3 ... 29 D3
Tower Hamlets E3 ... 97 C2
St Paul's Way Com Sch E3 ... 97 C2
St Paul's Whitechapel CE Prim Sch E1 ... 118 A6
St Paul's with St Michael's Prim Sch E8 ... 96 A6
St Paul's Wood Hill BR5 ... 189 D1
St Paul with St Luke CE Prim Sch E3 ... 97 B2
St Peter Chanel RC Prim Sch DA14 ... 190 C5
St Peter in Chains RC Inf Sch N8 ... 50 A3
St Peter & Paul RC Prim Sch BR5 ... 189 C1
St Peter & St Paul RC Prim Sch EC1 ... 94 D3 241 D6
St Peter's Alley EC3 ... 242 D1
St Peters Ave N12 ... 30 C3
St Peter's Ave
Edmonton N18 ... 34 A6
37 Hackney E2 ... 96 A5
Walthamstow E17 ... 54 C5
St Petersburgh Mews W2 ... 245 C6
St Petersburgh Pl W2 ... 113 D6 245 C5
St Peter's CE Prim Sch
Chiswick W6 ... 112 A1
Paddington W9 ... 91 C3
SE17 ... 117 B1 262 C1
St Peter's Church Ct N1 ... 234 D5
St Peters Cl BR7 ... 189 B3
Ilford IG2 ... 57 D5
Upper Tooting SW17 ... 158 C2
St Peter's Cl Barnet EN5 ... 12 B6
Bushey WD23 ... 8 B3
Hackney E2 ... 96 A5
Ruislip HA4 ... 62 D6
St Peters Ct
East Molesey KT8 ... 195 C5
New Cross SE4 ... 141 B3
28 Stepney E1 ... 96 C3
St Peter's Ct
Hendon NW4 ... 46 C4
Lewisham SE12 ... 164 D6
St Peter's Eaton Square Prim Sch SW1 ... 115 B3 258 D5
St Peter's Gdns SE27 ... 160 C1
St Peter's Gr W6 ... 112 A2
St Peters Ho
Tottenham Hale N15 ... 52 A5
WC1 ... 233 B1
St Peter's Ho 4 SE17 ... 139 B6
Stamford Hill N16 ... 51 C2
St Peters La BR5 ... 190 A1
St Peter's London Docks CE Prim Sch E1 ... 118 C5
St Peters Mews N4 ... 50 D4
St Peter's Pl W9 ... 91 D3
St Peter's Prim Sch CR2 ... 221 C2
St Peter's RC Prim Sch
Dagenham RM9 ... 103 B6
Woolwich SE18 ... 122 D2
St Peters Rd KT1 ... 176 C1
St Peter's Rd
Chiswick W6 ... 112 A1
Croydon CR0 ... 221 B4
East Molesey KT8 ... 195 C5
Edmonton N9 ... 18 B3
Isleworth TW1 ... 153 B6
Southall UB1 ... 85 C2
St Peter's Sq
Chiswick W6 ... 111 D1
Hackney E2 ... 96 A5
St Peter's St
Croydon CR2 ... 221 B3
Islington N1 ... 94 D6 234 D5
St Peter's Street Mews N1 ... 234 D4
St Peter's Terr SW6 ... 264 B3
St Peter's Villas 5 W6 ... 112 A2
St Peters Way UB3 ... 105 B1
St Peter's Way
De Beauvoir Town N1 ... 73 C1
Ealing W5 ... 87 D2
St Peter's Wharf 8 W6 ... 112 A1
St Philip Ho WC1 ... 234 A1
St Philip's Ave KT4 ... 216 B6
St Philips Gate KT4 ... 216 B6
St Philip Sq 1 SW8 ... 137 B3
St Philip's Rd
Dalston E8 ... 74 A2
Surbiton KT6 ... 197 D3
St Philip's Sch
Chessington KT9 ... 213 D2
SW7 ... 114 A2 256 B3
St Philip St SW8 ... 137 B3
St Philip's Way N1 ... 235 B5
St Philomena's Sch SM5 ... 218 C3
St Quentin Ho SW18 ... 158 B5
St Quentin Rd DA16 ... 145 D2
St Quintin Ave W10 ... 90 D2
St Quintin Gdns 21 W10 ... 90 C2
St Quintin Rd E13 ... 99 B5
St Raphaels Ho W13 ... 109 C5
St Raphael's RC Prim Sch UB5 ... 84 B5
St Raphael's Way NW10 ... 67 A3
St Regis Cl N10 ... 31 B1
St Regis Hts NW3 ... 69 D5
St Richards Ct TW10 ... 153 B1
St Richard's Ho NW1 ... 232 C2
St Richard's with St Andrew's CE Prim Sch TW10 ... 153 B1
St Robert Southwell RC Prim Sch NW9 ... 45 A3
St Ronan's 2 N3 ... 29 C2
St Ronans Cl EN4 ... 2 B5
St Ronans Cres IG8 ... 37 A3
St Rule St SW8 ... 137 C3
St Savior's CE Inf Sch W5 ... 109 D6
St Saviours SW4 ... 137 B1
St Saviour's CE Prim Sch
Bow Comm E14 ... 97 D2
Camberwell SE24 ... 139 A2
Paddington W9 ... 91 D3
Walthamstow E17 ... 53 B2
St Saviour's Coll SE27 ... 183 B6
St Saviours Ct
Harrow HA1 ... 42 C4
Muswell Hill N22 ... 31 D1
St Saviours Ho 35 SE1 ... 118 A4
St Saviour's RC Prim Sch SE13 ... 142 A1
St Saviour's Rd
Clapham Pk SW2 ... 160 B6
Thornton Heath CR0 ... 205 A3
St Saviours & St Olaves CE Sch SE1 ... 117 B3 262 D5
St Saviour's Wharf SE1 ... 253 D2
St Scholastica's RC Prim Sch E5 ... 74 A5
Saints Cl SE27 ... 182 D6
Saints Dr E7 ... 77 D3
St Silas Pl NW5 ... 71 A2
St Simon's Ave SW15 ... 156 C6
St Stephen's Ave
Ealing W13 ... 87 B1
Shepherd's Bush W12 ... 112 B4
Walthamstow E17 ... 54 A4
St Stephen's CE Jun Sch TW1 ... 153 B5
St Stephen's CE Prim Sch
Paddington W2 ... 91 C2
Shepherd's Bush W12 ... 112 C4
St Johns SE8 ... 141 C3
SW8 ... 138 B5 270 C4
St Stephen's Cl
Maitland Pk NW5 ... 70 D3
NW8 ... 230 B5
Southall UB1 ... 85 C2
Walthamstow E17 ... 53 D4
St Stephen's Cres
Notting Hill W2 ... 91 C1
Thornton Heath CR7 ... 204 C6
St Stephens Ct
Ealing W13 ... 87 B1
Enfield EN1 ... 17 C5
Hornsey Vale N8 ... 50 B3
St Stephen's Gdns
Notting Hill W2 ... 91 C1
4 Putney SW15 ... 157 B6
Twickenham TW1 ... 153 C5
St Stephen's Gr SE13 ... 142 A2
St Stephens Ho 7 SE17 ... 139 B6
St Stephen's Mews 38 W2 ... 91 C2
St Stephens Par E6 ... 77 C1
St Stephens Prim Sch E6 ... 77 C1
St Stephen's RC Prim Sch DA16 ... 146 A3
St Stephens Rd
Barnet EN5 ... 12 D6
Upton E6 ... 77 C1
St Stephen's Rd Bow E3 ... 97 B5
Ealing W13 ... 87 C1
Enfield EN3 ... 6 D6
Hounslow TW3, TW4 ... 151 C6
Walthamstow E17 ... 53 D4
Yiewsley UB7 ... 104 A5
St Stephen's Row EC4 ... 242 C1
St Stephen's Terr SW8 ... 270 C3
St Stephen's Wlk SW7 ... 256 A4
St Swithin's La EC4 ... 117 B6 252 C6
St Swithun's Rd SE13 ... 164 B6
St Swithun Wells RC Prim Sch HA4 ... 62 D5
St Teresa's RC Fst & Mid Sch HA3 ... 24 A2
St Teresa's RC Prim Sch SM4 ... 202 B3
St Teresa's RC Prim Sch The RM8 ... 80 C4
St Theresa Ct E4 ... 20 B4
St Theresa's RC Sch N3 ... 47 D6
St Theresa's Rd TW14 ... 127 D1
St Thomas a Beckett RC Prim Sch SE2 ... 124 A3
St Thomas Becket RC Prim Sch SE25 ... 206 A3
St Thomas' CE Prim Sch W10 ... 91 A3
St Thomas' Cl KT6 ... 198 B1
St Thomas Ct
14 Camden Town NW1 ... 71 C1
Sidcup DA5 ... 169 C4
11 Walthamstow E10 ... 53 D2
St Thomas' Ct HA5 ... 23 A2
St Thomas' Dr BR5 ... 211 A1
Pinner HA5 ... 23 A2
St Thomas Gdns IG1 ... 79 A2
St Thomas Ho 2 E1 ... 96 D1
St Thomas More Language Coll SW3 ... 114 D2 257 C3
St Thomas More RC Comp Sch SE9 ... 166 C5
St Thomas More RC Prim Sch
Bexley DA7 ... 147 B3
SE9 ... 144 A2
St Thomas More Sch N22 ... 32 C3
St Thomas of Canterbury RC Prim Sch
Mitcham CR4 ... 203 A6
SW6 ... 135 B5 264 C4
St Thomas Rd
Newham E16 ... 99 A1
Osidge N14 ... 15 D4
St Thomas' Rd W4 ... 133 A6
St Thomas's Gdns NW5 ... 71 A2
St Thomas's Hospl SE1 ... 116 B3 260 C6
St Thomas's Hospl Medical Sch SE1 ... 116 B3 260 C5
St Thomas's Pl 20 E9 ... 74 C1
St Thomas's Rd
Dagenham NW10 ... 89 C6
Highbury N4, N5 ... 72 C5
St Thomas's Sq E9 ... 74 C1
St Thomas St SE1 ... 117 B5 252 D3
St Thomas's Way SW6 ... 135 B5 264 D4
St Thomas the Apostle Coll The SE15 ... 140 C4
St Timothy's Mews 3 BR1 ... 187 B2
St Ursula Gr HA5 ... 41 A4
St Ursula Rd UB1 ... 85 C1
St Ursula's Convent Sch SE10 ... 142 B5
St Vincent Cl SE27 ... 182 D5
St Vincent De Paul Ho 24 E1 ... 96 C2
St Vincent De Paul RC Prim Sch SW1 ... 115 C3 259 B6
St Vincent Ho SE1 ... 263 C6
St Vincent Rd TW2 ... 152 A5
St Vincent's Hospl HA5 ... 39 D6
St Vincents La NW7 ... 28 C6
St Vincents RC Prim Sch SE9 ... 188 A6
St Vincent's RC Prim Sch
Acton W3 ... 110 D6
Dagenham RM8 ... 80 C6
Marylebone W1 ... 93 A2 238 B3
St Vincent's RC Sch NW7 ... 28 C5
St Vincent St W1 ... 238 B3
St Wilfrid's Cl EN4 ... 14 C6
St Wilfrid's Rd EN4 ... 14 C6
St William of York RC Prim Sch SE23 ... 163 A3
St Winefride's Ave E12 ... 78 B3
St Winefride's RC Prim Sch E12 ... 78 B3
St Winifred's RC Inf Sch SE12 ... 164 C6
St Winifred's RC Jun Sch SE12 ... 164 D4
St Winifred's Rd TW11 ... 175 B4
Sakura Dr N22 ... 31 D2
Sala Ho SE3 ... 143 B1
Salamanca Pl SE1 ... 260 C3
Salamanca St SE1, SE11 ... 116 B2 260 C3
Salamander Cl KT2 ... 175 C5
Salamander Quay KT1 ... 175 D2
Salcombe Dr
Dagenham RM6 ... 59 B3
North Cheam SM4 ... 200 D1
Salcombe Gdns
Clapham SW4 ... 137 B1
Mill Hill NW7 ... 28 C4
Salcombe Ho 6 SE23 ... 162 C2
Salcombe Lo NW5 ... 71 A4
Salcombe Pk IG10 ... 21 D6
Salcombe Rd
Ashford TW15 ... 148 A1
23 Stoke Newington N16 ... 73 C3
Walthamstow E17 ... 53 B2
Salcombe Sch N14 ... 15 B4
Salcombe Villas 13 TW10 ... 154 A6
Salcombe Way
Hayes UB4 ... 83 C4
Ruislip HA4 ... 62 A6
Salcot N4 ... 72 B6
Salcott Rd
Wallington CR0 ... 220 B4
Wandsworth SW11 ... 158 D6
Salehurst Cl HA3 ... 44 A4
Salehurst Rd SE4 ... 163 B5
Salem Ho 13 E9 ... 74 D2
Salem Pl CR0 ... 221 A5
Salem Rd W2 ... 113 D6 245 D6
Sale Pl W2 ... 92 C1 237 A2
Salesian Coll SW11 ... 136 C4 267 A1
Sale St E2 ... 96 A3
Salford Ho 5 E14 ... 120 A2
Salford Rd SW12, SW2 ... 159 D3
Salhouse Cl SE28 ... 102 C1
Salisbury Ave
Barking IG11 ... 79 C1
Cheam SM1, SM2 ... 217 B2
Hendon N3 ... 47 B6
Salisbury Cl SE17 ... 262 C4
Worcester Pk KT4 ... 215 D5
Salisbury Ct
15 Bermondsey SE16 ... 118 A3
Chiswick W4 ... 111 C2
EC4 ... 241 C1
Edgware HA8 ... 26 B6
Enfield EN2 ... 5 B1
Finchley N3 ... 29 B1
Hackney E9 ... 75 A3
Northolt UB5 ... 63 D3
Salisbury Gdns
5 Buckhurst Hill IG9 ... 21 D2
Wimbledon SW19 ... 179 A3
Salisbury Hall Gdns E4 ... 35 C4
Salisbury Ho
2 Islington N1 ... 72 D2
Islington N1 ... 234 C6
3 Poplar E14 ... 97 D1
1 Ruislip HA4 ... 40 C1
Stanmore HA7 ... 25 A4
5 Wallington SM6 ... 219 B3
Westminster SW1 ... 259 D2
Wimbledon SW19 ... 156 D1
Salisbury Lower Sch N9 ... 18 C4
Salisbury Mans
Edmonton N9 ... 18 A1
Harringay N4, N15 ... 50 D4
Salisbury Mews
Bromley Comm BR2 ... 210 A4
Fulham SW6 ... 264 C3
Salisbury Pl
Camberwell SW9 ... 138 D5
Marylebone W1 ... 237 C4
Salisbury Prim Sch E12 ... 78 A3
Salisbury Rd Barnet EN5 ... 1 A2
Bromley Comm BR2 ... 210 A4
Chingford E4 ... 19 C1
Croydon SE25 ... 206 A3
Dagenham RM10 ... 81 D2
East Bedfont TW6 ... 149 A5
Enfield EN3 ... 7 B6
Feltham TW13 ... 150 C3
Forest Gate E7 ... 77 A2
Harringay N4 ... 50 D4
Harrow HA1 ... 42 B4
Hounslow TW4 ... 128 C2
Ilford IG3 ... 79 C6
Kingston u T KT3 ... 199 B6
Leyton E10 ... 76 A6
Old Bexley DA5 ... 169 C3
Pinner HA5 ... 40 A5
Plashet E12 ... 77 D3
Richmond TW9 ... 132 A1
Southall UB2 ... 107 A2
Tottenham N22 ... 32 D1
Wallington SM5 ... 218 D2
Walthamstow E17 ... 54 A4
West Ealing W13 ... 109 B4
Wimbledon SW19 ... 179 A3
Worcester Pk KT4 ... 215 C5
Salisbury Sq EC4 ... 241 B1
Salisbury St
10 Acton W3 ... 111 A4
NW8 ... 237 A5
Salisbury Terr SE15 ... 140 C2
Salisbury Upper Sch N9 ... 18 C4
Salisbury Wlk N19 ... 71 C6
Salix Cl TW16 ... 172 B3
Salix Ct N3 ... 29 C4
Salliesfield TW2 ... 152 B5
Sally Murray Cl E12 ... 78 C4
Salmen Rd E13 ... 98 D5
Salmond Cl HA7 ... 25 A4
Salmon La E14 ... 97 A1
Salmon Rd DA17 ... 125 C1
Salmons Brook Ho EN2 ... 4 D2
Salmons Rd
Chessington KT9 ... 214 A2
Edmonton N9 ... 18 A3
Salmon St
Kingsbury NW9 ... 45 A2
13 Poplar E14 ... 97 B1
Salomons Rd 2 E13 ... 99 C2
Salop Rd E17 ... 52 D3
Saltash Cl SM1 ... 217 B4
Saltash Rd DA16 ... 146 C4
Saltcoats Rd W4 ... 111 C4
Saltcroft Cl HA9 ... 44 D1
Saltdene N4 ... 50 B1
Salter Cl HA2 ... 63 B4
Salterford Rd SW17 ... 181 A4
Salter Ho 8 SW16 ... 181 C6
Saltern Ct IG11 ... 102 B4
Salter Rd SE16 ... 119 A5
Salters' Hall Ct EC4 ... 252 C6
Salter's Hill SE19 ... 183 B5
Salters Rd
North Kensington W10 ... 90 D3
Walthamstow E17 ... 54 B5
Salter St
College Pk NW10 ... 90 A4
11 Poplar E14 ... 119 C6
Salterton Rd N7 ... 72 B5
Salt Hill Cl UB8 ... 60 A3
Saltley Cl E6 ... 100 A1
Saltoun Rd SW2, SW9 ... 138 C1
Saltram Cl N15 ... 51 D5
Saltram Cres W9 ... 91 C4
Saltwell St E14 ... 119 C6
Saltwood Gr SE17 ... 262 C1
Saltwood Ho 19 SE15 ... 140 C6
Salusbury Prim Sch NW6 ... 91 B6
Salusbury Rd NW6 ... 91 A6
Salutation Rd SE10 ... 120 C2
Salvador SW17 ... 180 D5
Salvatorian RC Coll HA3 ... 24 C1
Salvia Gdns UB6 ... 87 A5
Salvin Rd SW15 ... 134 D2
Salway Cl IG8 ... 37 A3
Salway Ho E10 ... 75 D6
Salway Pl E15 ... 76 C2
Salway Rd E15 ... 76 B2
Salween Ho 2 N16 ... 73 B4
Samantha Cl E17 ... 53 B2
Samantha Ct E11 ... 54 C2
Samaritan Hospl for Women NW1 ... 237 C4
Sam Bartram Cl SE7 ... 121 C1
Sambrooke Ct EN1 ... 17 D6
Sambrook Ho 25 E1 ... 96 C2
Sambruck Mews SE6 ... 163 D3
Samels Ct W6 ... 112 A1
Samford Ho N1 ... 234 A5
Samford St NW8 ... 237 A5
Samira Cl E17 ... 53 C3
Sam Manners Ho 7 SE10 ... 120 C1
Sam March Ho 5 E14 ... 98 B1
Samos Rd SE20 ... 184 B1
Sampson Ave EN5 ... 12 D6
Sampson Cl DA17 ... 125 A3
Sampson Ct TW17 ... 193 A4
Sampson St E1 ... 118 A5
Samson Ct 5 DA17 ... 125 C2
Samson Ho SE18 ... 123 A2
Samson St E13 ... 99 C5
Samuel Cl SE14 ... 140 D6
Shoreditch E8 ... 95 D6
Woolwich SE18 ... 122 A2
Samuel Ct
Beckenham BR3 ... 207 D6
Shoreditch N1 ... 95 C4
Samuel Gray Gdns KT2 ... 175 D2
Samuel Ho
15 Shoreditch E8 ... 95 D6
3 West Norwood SE27 ... 182 D6
Samuel Johnson Cl SW16 ... 182 B6
Samuel Jones Ind Est 7 SE15 ... 139 C5
Samuel Lewis Bldgs N1 ... 72 C2
Samuel Lewis Trust Dwellings
6 Camberwell SE5 ... 139 A4
Chelsea SW3 ... 257 A3
Walham Green SW6 ... 135 C5 265 B4
West Kensington W14 ... 254 B4
Samuel Lewis Trust Est N15 ... 51 C3
Samuel Lo N3 ... 29 B1
Samuel Rhodes Sch N1 ... 94 C6 234 A6
Samuel Richardson Ho W14 ... 254 C3
Samuel's Cl 2 W6 ... 112 C2
Samuel St SE15 ... 139 D5
Woolwich SE18 ... 122 B2
Sancroft Cl NW2 ... 68 B5
Sancroft Ct SW11 ... 267 B2
Sancroft Ho SE11 ... 260 D2
Sancroft Rd HA3 ... 25 A1
Sancroft St SE11 ... 116 B1 260 D2
Sanctuary Mews 15 E8 ... 73 D2
Sanctuary Rd TW19, TW6 ... 148 C5
Sanctuary St SE1 ... 252 B2
Sanctuary The
Morden SM4 ... 201 C3
Sidcup DA5 ... 168 D5
35 Wapping E1 ... 118 B5
Westminster SW1 ... 115 D3 259 D6
Sandale Cl N16 ... 73 B5
Sandall Cl W5 ... 88 A3
Sandall Ho 7 E3 ... 97 A5
Sandall Rd Ealing W5 ... 88 A3
Kentish Town NW5 ... 71 C2
Sandal Rd
Edmonton N18 ... 34 A5
New Malden KT3 ... 199 C5
Sandal St E15 ... 98 C6
Sandalwood Cl 11 E1 ... 97 A3
Sandalwood Dr HA4 ... 39 A2
Sandalwood Ho DA15 ... 167 D1
6 Hampstead NW3 ... 69 D2
Sandalwood Rd TW13 ... 150 B1
Sandbach Pl SE18 ... 123 A1
Sandbourne
4 Kensington W11 ... 91 C1
14 Paddington NW8 ... 91 D6
Sandbourne Ave SW19 ... 179 D1
Sandbourne Rd SE4 ... 141 A3
Sandbrook Cl NW7 ... 27 B4
Sandbrook Rd N16 ... 73 C5
Sandby Ct BR3 ... 185 B2
Sandby Gn SE9 ... 144 A2
Sandby Ho
11 Camberwell SE5 ... 139 C4
6 Kilburn NW6 ... 91 C6
Sandcroft Cl N13 ... 32 D4
Sandells Ave
Ashford TW15 ... 171 A6
Ashford TW15 ... 171 A6
Sandell St SE1 ... 251 A2
Sanderling Ct 20 SE8 ... 141 B6
Woolwich SE28 ... 124 C6
Sanders Cl TW12 ... 174 A5
Sanders Ho
Streatham SW16 ... 182 A4
WC1 ... 234 A2
Sanders La NW7 ... 28 C3
Sanderson Cl NW5 ... 71 B4
Sanderson Ho 7 SE8 ... 119 B1
Sanderson Sq BR1 ... 210 C6
Sanderstead Ave NW2 ... 69 A6
Sanderstead Cl SW12 ... 159 C4
Sanderstead Rd
South Croydon CR2 ... 221 B1
Walthamstow E10 ... 53 A1
Sanders Way 3 N19 ... 49 D1
Sandfield WC1 ... 233 B1
Sandfield Gdns CR7 ... 204 D6
Sandfield Pl CR7 ... 205 A6
Sandfield Rd CR7 ... 204 D6
Sandford Ave N22 ... 33 A2
Sandford Cl E6 ... 100 B3
Sandford Ct Barnet EN5 ... 1 D2
Stamford Hill N16 ... 51 C1
Sandford Rd
Bexley DA7 ... 147 A2
BR2 ... 209 A5
Newham E6 ... 100 B4
Sandford Row SE17 ... 262 D2
Sandford St SW6 ... 265 D3
Sandgate Ho
14 Beckenham BR3 ... 185 C3
Ealing W5 ... 87 C2
15 Hackney E5 ... 74 B4
Sandgate La SW17, SW18 ... 158 C3
Sandgate Rd DA16 ... 146 C5
Sandgate St SE15 ... 140 B6
Sandgate Trad Est SE15 ... 140 B6
Sandham Ct SW4 ... 270 B1
Sandham Point 10 SE18 ... 122 D2
Sandhills CR0, SM6 ... 219 D4
Sandhills Mdw TW17 ... 193 A2
Sandhills The SW10 ... 266 B6
Sandhurst Ave
Harrow HA2 ... 41 D3
Tolworth KT5 ... 198 D2
Sandhurst Cl
Queensbury NW9 ... 44 C6
South Croydon CR2 ... 221 C1
Sandhurst Ct SW2 ... 138 A1
Sandhurst Dr IG3 ... 79 D4
Sandhurst Ho 12 E1 ... 96 C2
Sandhurst Jun & Inf Schs SE6 ... 164 C3
Sandhurst Mkt SE6 ... 164 A3
Sandhurst Rd
Bexley DA5 ... 168 D6
Catford SE6 ... 164 B3
DA15 ... 168 A1
Ponders End N9 ... 18 D5
Queensbury HA8, NW9 ... 44 C6
Sandhurst Way CR2 ... 221 C1
Sandifer Dr NW2 ... 68 D5
Sandiford Rd SM3 ... 217 B6
Sandiland Cres BR2 ... 224 D6
Sandilands CR0 ... 222 A5
Sandilands Rd SW6 ... 135 D4 265 C1
Sandilands Sta CR0 ... 221 D6
Sandison St SE15 ... 140 A2
Sandland St WC1 ... 240 D3
Sandling Rise SE9 ... 166 C1
Sandlings Cl SE15 ... 140 B3

Sandlings The
Tottenham N22 50 D6
5 Wood Green N22 32 C1
Sandmartin Way CR4 203 A1
Sandmere Rd SW4 138 A1
Sandon Cl KT10 196 B1
Sandon Ct IG3 80 A5
Sandon Ho 5 SW2 160 A4
Sandow Commercial Est
UB3 105 D3
Sandow Cres UB3 105 D3
Sandown Ave KT10 212 A3
Sandown Cl TW5 128 A4
Sandown Ct 12 SM2 217 D1
Sandown Gate KT10 212 B5
Sandown Ho
2 Acton Green W4 111 A1
Esher KT10 212 A4
Penge SE26 184 B4
Sandown Park KT10 212 A6
Sandown Rd
Croydon SE25 206 B4
Esher KT10 212 A4
Sandown Way UB5 63 B3
Sandpiper Cl
Higham Hill E17 34 D3
Rotherhithe SE16 119 B4
Sandpiper Ct
13 Cubitt Town E14 120 A3
1 SE8 141 C5
Sandpiper Rd SM1 217 B3
Sandpiper Terr IG5 56 D6
Sandpit Pl SE7 122 A1
Sandpit Rd BR1 186 C5
Sandpits Rd
Richmond TW10 153 D2
South Croydon CR0 222 D4
Sandra Cl
Hounslow TW3 151 D6
Tottenham N17 33 A2
Sandra Ho KT8 196 B4
Sandridge Cl
Hadley Wood EN4 2 C6
Harrow HA1 42 C5
Sandridge St 3 N19 71 C6
Sandringham Ave
SW20 179 A1
Sandringham Cl
Enfield EN1 5 C3
Ilford IG6 57 A6
1 Putney SW19 156 D3
Sandringham Cres
HA2 63 D6
Sandringham Ct
3 Beckenham BR3 186 A2
Edgware HA8 26 D6
Hillingdon UB10 83 A3
Kingston u T KT2 176 A2
Marylebone W1 239 B1
Putney SW15 156 D5
18 Rotherhithe SE16 118 D5
St John's Wood W9 229 B1
2 Twickenham TW1 153 A3
Sandringham Dr
Ashford TW15 170 A6
DA16 145 C3
Sandringham Flats
WC2 249 D6
Sandringham Gdns
Cranford TW5 128 A4
East Molesey KT8 195 C5
Finchley N12 30 B4
Hornsey Vale N8 50 A3
Ilford IG6 57 A6
Sandringham Ho
Richmond TW10 154 C6
W14 254 A4
Sandringham Lo BR6 226 C4
Sandringham Mews
TW12 173 B2
Sandringham Prim Sch
E7 77 C3
Sandringham Rd
Barking IG11 79 D2
BR1 187 A5
Dalston E8 73 D3
Forest Gate E7 77 C3
Golders Green NW11 47 A2
Leytonstone E10 54 B3
Northolt UB5 63 C1
Stanwell TW19, TW6 148 A6
Thornton Heath CR0 205 A4
Tottenham N22 33 A1
Willesden NW2 68 B2
Worcester Pk KT4 216 A5
Sandrock Pl CR0 222 D4
Sandrock Rd SE13 141 C2
SANDS END 136 A2
Sands End La
SW6 135 D4 265 D2
Sandstone TW9 132 C5
Sandstone La E16 121 B6
Sandstone Pl N19 71 B6
Sandstone Rd SE12 165 B2
Sandtoft Rd SE7 143 B6
Sandways 6 TW9 132 C4
Sandwell Cres 2 NW6 69 C2
Sandwell Mans 3
NW6 69 C2
Sandwich Ho
15 Rotherhithe SE16 118 C4
WC1 233 A1
Sandwich St
WC1 94 A4 233 A1
Sandwick Cl NW7 28 A3
Sandy Bury BR6 227 B5
Sandycombe Ctr TW9 132 C2
Sandycombe Rd
East Bedfont TW14 150 A3
Richmond TW9 132 C3
Sandycoombe Rd
TW1 153 C5
Sandycroft SE2 146 A6
Sandy Dr TW14 149 C3
Sandy Hill Ave SE18 122 D1
Sandy Hill La SE18 122 D2
Sandyhill Rd IG1 78 D4
Sandy Hill Rd SE18 122 D1
Sandy La Belmont SM2 217 A1
BR5 190 D2
Eastbury HA6 22 A6
Harrow HA3 44 C3
Mitcham CR4 181 A2
Richmond TW10 153 D2
Teddington KT8, TW11 175 B3
Walton-on-T KT12 194 C3
Sandy Lane N SM6 219 D3
Sandy Lane S SM6 219 C1
Sandy Lo N6 49 C2
Sandymount Ave HA7 25 D5
Sandy Rd NW3 69 D6
Sandy Ridge BR7 188 C4
Sandy's Row E1 243 B3
Sandy Way
Croydon CR0 223 B5
Walton-on-T KT12 193 D1
Sanford La 3 N16 73 D6
Sanford St SE14, SE8 141 A6
Sanford Terr N16 73 D5
Sanford Wlk SE14 141 A6
4 Stoke Newington N16 73 D6
Sangam Cl UB2 107 A3
Sanger Ave KT9 214 B4
Sangley Rd
Catford SE6 164 A3
South Norwood SE25 205 C5
Sangora Rd 17 SW11 136 B1
San Ho 29 E9 74 D2
Sankey Ho 22 E2 96 C5
Sansom Rd E11 76 D6
Sansom St
Camberwell SE5 139 B4
SE5 139 B5
Sans Wlk EC1 94 D3 241 C6
Santana SE18 144 D5
Santley Ho SE1 251 B1
Santley St SW4 138 B1
Santos Rd SW18 157 C6
Sapcote Trad Ctr
NW10 67 D2
Saperton Wlk SE11 260 D4
Saphora Cl BR6 227 B3
Sapperton Ct EC1 242 A6
Sapphire Cl
Dagenham RM8 58 C1
Newham E6 100 C1
Sapphire Ct 13 E1 118 A6
Sapphire Rd
Rotherhithe SE8 119 A2
Willesden NW10 67 A1
Saracen Cl CR0 205 B3
Saracen St E14 97 C1
Sarah Bonnell Sch E15 76 C2
Sarah Ct UB5 85 B6
Sarah Ho
Roehampton SW15 133 D1
8 Stepney E1 96 B1
Sarah Swift Ho SE1 252 D2
Sarah Turnbull Ho 2
SE18 122 B2
Sara Lane Ct 31 N1 95 C5
Saratoga Rd E5 74 C4
Sardeson Ho 13 SW27 182 D5
Sardinia Ho WC2 240 C1
Sardinia St WC2 240 C2
Sargents Hill N2 30 C2
Sarita Cl HA3 24 B1
Sarjant Path SW19 156 D2
Sark Cl TW5 129 C5
Sark Ho
9 Canonbury N1 73 A2
Enfield EN3 6 D5
Sark Twr SE28 123 A4
Sark Wlk E16 99 B1
Sarnersfield Ho SE15 140 B6
Sarnes Ct 4 N11 31 B6
Sarnesfield Rd EN2 5 B2
Sarratt Ho 6 W10 90 C2
Sarre Rd NW2 69 B3
Sarsden Bldgs W1 238 B1
Sarsen Ave TW3 129 C3
Sarsfeld Rd SW12,
SW17 158 D3
Sarsfield Rd UB6 87 C5
Sartor Rd SE15 140 D1
Sarum Hall Sch NW3 70 C1
Sarum Ho W11 244 D5
Sarwan Ho 1 E7 77 C1
Sassoon 4 NW9 27 D2
Sassoon Ho SE15 140 C3
Satanita Cl E16 99 D1
Satchell Mead NW9 27 D2
Satchwell Rd 17 E2 96 A4
Satin Ct NW9 45 D5
Saturn Ho 4 E3 97 C6
Saul Ct 4 SE15 139 D6
Sauls Gn E11 76 C5
Saunders Cl Ilford IG1 57 B1
14 Limehouse E14 119 B6
Saunders Ho 11 SW2 160 C3
Saunders Ness Rd
E14 120 B2
Saunders Rd
Hillingdon UB10 82 B6
Plumstead Comm SE18 123 D1
Saunders St SE11 261 A4
Saunders Way SE28 124 B6
Saunderton Rd HA0 65 B3
Saunton Ave UB3 127 D5
Saunton Ct UB1 108 A6
Savage Gdns EC3 253 B6
Newham E6 100 B1
Savana N16 73 C6
Savannah Cl 9 SE15 139 D5
Savernake Ct HA7 25 B4
Savernake Ho N4 51 B2
Savernake Rd
Enfield N9 18 A5
Maitland Pk NW3 70 D4
Savery Dr KT6 197 C2
Savile Cl
New Malden KT3 199 C4
Thames Ditton KT7 197 A1
Savile Gdns CR0 221 D6
Savill Ct IG8 36 D4
Saville Cres TW15 171 B4
Saville Ho E16 122 D5
Saville Rd
Bedford Pk W4 111 B3
Dagenham RM6 59 B2
Newham E16 122 A5
Twickenham TW1 152 D3
Saville Row Enfield EN3 6 D3
Hayes BR2 208 D1
W1 115 C6 249 A6
Savill Gdns SW20 200 A6
Savill Ho 2 SW4 159 D5
Savill Row IG8 36 D4
Savin Lo 7 SM2 218 A1
Savona Cl 16 SW19 178 D3
Savona Ct SW20 178 D2
Savona St SW8 137 C5 269 A3
Savoy Ave UB3 105 C1
Savoy Circus W3 111 D6
Savoy Cl Edgware HA8 26 C5
Newham E15 98 C6
Savoy Ct Earl's Ct SW5 255 B4
Strand WC2 250 B5
Savoy Hill WC2 250 C5
Savoy Mews SW9 138 A2
Savoy Par EN1 5 C2
Savoy Pier WC2 250 C5
Savoy Pl WC2 116 B6 250 C5
Savoy Row WC2 250 C6
Savoy St WC2 116 B6 250 C5
Savoy Stps WC2 250 C5
Savoy Way WC2 250 C5
Sawbill Cl UB4 84 D2
Sawkins Cl SW19 157 A2
Sawley Rd W12 112 A5
Sawmill Yd E3 97 A6
Sawtry Cl SM5 202 C2
Sawyer Cl N9 18 A2
Sawyer Ho 15 SE21 183 C6
Sawyer's Hill TW10 154 B4
Sawyers Lawn W13 87 A1
Sawyer St SE1 117 A4 252 A2
Saxby Rd SW2 160 A4
Saxham Rd IG11 101 D5
Saxlingham Rd E4 20 B1
Saxon Ave TW13 151 B2
Saxon Bsns Ctr SW19 180 A2
Saxonbury Ave TW16 172 B1
Saxonbury Cl CR4 202 B6
Saxonbury Ct
16 Kentish Town N7 71 D3
2 Lower Holloway N7 72 A3
Saxonbury Gdns KT6 197 C1
Saxon Cl Hillingdon UB8 82 A2
Surbiton KT6 197 D3
Walthamstow E17 53 C2
Saxoncroft Ho SW16 159 D1
Saxon Ct
Colney Hatch N12 30 C5
4 Edgware HA8 26 D5
Saxon Dr W3 88 D2
Saxonfield Cl SW2 160 B4
Saxon Gdns UB1 107 A6
Saxon Hall W2 245 C5
Saxon Ho
4 Clapham SW4 137 D1
Feltham TW13 151 B2
Saxon Prim Sch TW17 192 C4
Saxon Rd
Ashford TW15 171 B4
Bow E3 97 B5
Bromley BR1 186 D3
Ilford IG1 78 D3
Kingston u T KT2 176 A2
Newham E6 100 B3
Southall UB1 107 A6
South Norwood SE25 205 B4
Tottenham N22 32 D2
Wembley HA9 67 A5
Saxon Terr SE6 163 B2
Saxon Way N14 15 D5
Saxon Wlk DA14 190 C4
Saxony Par UB3 83 A2
Saxton Cl SE13 142 B2
Saxville Rd BR5 190 B1
Sayer Ho SE4 141 A1
Sayers Ho 4 N2 30 B1
Sayer's Wlk TW10 154 B4
Sayesbury La N18 34 A5
Sayes Court St SE8 141 B6
Sayes Ct SE8 141 B6
Sayline Ct CR0 221 B5
Scadbury Gdns BR5 190 A1
Scadbury Park Nature
Reserve* BR7 189 D4
Scads Hill Cl BR6 211 D3
Scafell NW1 232 A2
Scala St W1 239 B4
Scales Rd N17 52 A6
Scampston Mews 5
W10 90 D1
Scandrett St 38 E1 118 B5
Scarba Wlk N1 73 B2
Scarborough Rd
East Bedfont TW6 149 A5
Scarborough Rd *continued*
Finsbury Pk N4 50 C1
Leytonstone E11 54 B1
Ponders End N9 18 C4
Scarborough St E1 243 D1
Scarbrook Rd CR0 221 A5
Scardale Ho 12 E5 74 B6
Scarle Rd HA0 65 D2
Scarlet Rd SE6 164 C1
Scarlette Manor Wlk 10
SE24 160 C4
Scarsbrook Ho 2
SW2 160 C5
Scarsbrook Rd SE3 143 D2
Scarsdale Pl W8 255 C6
Scarsdale Rd HA2 64 A5
Scarsdale Villas
W8 113 C3 255 B5
Scarth Rd SW13 133 D2
Scawen Cl SM5 219 A4
Scawen Rd SE8 119 A1
Scawfell St E2 95 D5
Scaynes Link N12 29 C6
Sceptre Ho 10 E1 96 C3
Sceptre Rd E2 96 C4
Schiller International Univ
SE1 116 C5 251 A3
Schofield Wlk SE3 143 A5
Sch of Pharmacy
WC1 94 A3 240 B6
Scholars Cl EN5 1 A1
Scholars Ct 5 N19 49 D1
Scholars Ho 6 E4 20 B3
Scholars Rd
Chingford E4 20 B3
Streatham SW12 159 C3
Scholefield Rd N19 71 D6
Scholey Ho SW11 136 C2
Schomberg Ho SW1 259 D4
Schonfeld Sq N16 51 B1
School App 21 E2 95 C4
Schoolbank Rd SE10 120 D2
School Bell Cloisters 17
E3 97 A5
Schoolbell Mews 18 E3 97 A5
School Cotts
Bromley BR1 187 A3
Sidcup DA14 190 C5
School Flats SW8 270 A1
School Ho SE1 263 A4
Schoolhouse La E1 118 D6
School House La
TW11 175 C3
Schoolhouse Yd 9
SE18 122 D1
School La DA16 146 B2
Lower Halliford TW17 192 D4
Pinner HA5 41 A5
Surbiton KT6 198 B1
Teddington KT1 175 C2
School Pas
3 Kingston u T KT1 176 B1
Southall UB1 107 B6
School Rd
Ashford TW15 170 D4
Becontree NW10 89 B3
BR7 189 A3
Dagenham RM10 103 D6
East Molesey KT8 196 B5
Hampton TW12 174 A4
Hounslow TW3 130 A2
Ilford E12 78 B4
Littleton TW15 170 D3
Teddington KT1 175 C2
School Road Ave
TW12 174 A4
School Sq SE10 120 D3
Schoolway N12 30 B4
School Way RM8 80 C5
School Wlk TW16 193 D6
Schooner Cl
Barking IG11 102 B4
Cubitt Town E14 120 B3
1 Rotherhithe SE16 118 D4
Schubert Rd Elstree WD6 9 D5
Putney SW15 157 B6
Science Mus*
SW7 114 B3 256 C5
Scilly Isles KT10 212 C6
Sclater St E1 243 D6
Scoles Cres SW2 160 C3
Scope Way KT1 198 A5
Scoresby St SE1 251 C3
Scoresdale SE19 183 C2
Scorton Ave UB6 87 A5
Scorton Ho 2 N1 95 C5
Scotch Comm W13 87 B2
Scotch Ho
SW1 114 D4 247 C1
Scoter Cl IG8 37 B3
Scoter Ct 23 SE8 141 B6
Scot Gr HA5 22 D3
Scotia Bldg 10 E1 118 D6
Scotia Ct 3 SE16 118 C3
Scotia Rd 24 SW2 160 C4
Scotland Gn N17 33 D1
Scotland Green Rd
EN3 18 D6
Scotland Green Rd N
EN3 7 A1
Scotland Pl SW1 250 A3
Scotland Rd IG9 21 C3
Scotney Cl BR6 226 C4
Scotney Ho E9 74 C2
Scots Cl TW19 148 A3
Scotsdale Cl
Belmont SM3 217 A1
BR5 211 C5
Scotsdale Rd SE12 165 B6
Scotson Ho SE11 261 A3
Scotswood St
EC1 94 C3 241 B6
Scotswood Wlk N17 34 A3
Scott Cl
Thornton Heath
SW16 182 B2
West Drayton UB7 104 B2
West Ewell KT19 215 A3
Scott Ct Acton W4 111 B4
4 Clapham SW11 137 B3
17 Stoke Newington N16 73 C5
Scott Ellis Gdns
NW8 92 B4 229 C1
Scottes La RM8 58 D1
Scott Farm Cl KT7 197 B1
Scott Gdns TW5 128 D5
Scott Ho
2 Barnsbury N7 72 B2
3 Edmonton N18 34 A5
4 Erith DA17 125 B1
Islington N1 235 C6
Lisson Gr NW8 237 A5
17 Millwall E14 119 C4
6 Newham E13 99 A5
Richmond TW10 153 C2
3 Stonebridge NW10 67 B1
Scott Lidgett Cres
SE16 118 A4
Scott Rd HA8 26 D1
Scott's Ave
Ashford TW16 171 C3
Beckenham BR2 186 B1
Scotts Ct 6 W12 112 B4
Scotts Dr TW12 173 D3
Scotts Farm Rd KT19 215 A2
Scotts Ho DA16 146 C4
Scott's La BR2, BR3 186 B1
Scotts Park Prim Sch
BR1 187 C2
Scotts Rd BR1 187 A3
Southall UB2 106 D3
Scott's Rd
Leytonstone E10 54 A1
Shepherd's Bush W12 112 B4
Scott's Sufferance Wharf
SE1 253 D1
Scott St E1 96 B3
Scott's Way TW16 171 C3
Scott's Yd EC4 252 C6
Scott Trimmer Way
TW3 129 A3
Scottwell Dr NW9 45 D4
Scott Wilkie Prim Sch
E16 99 C1
Scoulding Ho 12 E14 119 C3
Scoulding Rd E16 99 A1
Scouler St E14 120 B6
Scout App NW10 67 C4
Scout La SW4 137 C2
Scout Way NW7 27 B6
Scovell Cres SE1 252 A1
Scovell Rd SE1 252 A1
Scratchwood Nature
Trail* NW7 11 B4
Scrattons Terr IG11 103 A5
Scriven Ct 2 E8 95 D6
Scriven St E8 95 D6
Scrooby St SE6 163 D5
Scrope Bldg EC1 241 A4
Scrubs La NW10, W10,
W12 90 B3
Scrutton Cl SW12 159 D4
Scrutton St EC2 95 C3 243 A5
Scudamore La NW9 45 A5
Scutari Rd SE22 162 C6
Scylla Cres
TW6&TW14 148 D4
Scylla Rd
East Bedfont TW14,
TW6 148 D5
Nunhead SE15 140 B2
Seabright St 27 E2 96 B4
Seabrook Dr BR4 224 C6
Seabrook Gdns RM7 59 C2
Seabrook Rd RM8 80 D5
Seacole Cl W3 89 B2
Seacole Ct N15 51 D4
Seacole Lo N21 16 B6
Seacon Twr 8 E14 119 C4
Seacourt Rd SE2 124 D4
Seacroft Gdns WD19 22 D6
Seafield Rd N11 31 D6
Seaford Cl HA4 61 B6
Seaford Ho 18 SE16 118 C4
Seaford Rd Ealing W13 109 B5
Enfield EN1 5 C1
Tottenham N15 51 C4
Walthamstow E17 53 D6
Seaford St WC1 233 B1
Seaforth Ave KT3 200 B5
Seaforth Cres N5 73 A3
Seaforth Gdns
Southgate N21 16 C3
Woodford IG8 37 C5
Worcester Pk KT19 215 D3
Seaforth Lo 2 SW13 133 D3
Seaforth Pl SW1 259 B6
Seagrave Lo SW6 265 B6
Seagrave Rd
SW6 135 C6 265 B6
Seagrove Cl E1 96 D2
Seagry Rd E11 55 B2
Seagull Cl IG11 102 A4
Seagull La E16 121 A6
Sealand Rd TW6 148 C5
Sealand Wlk UB5 85 A4
Seal Ho SE1 262 D6
Seal St E8 73 D4
Searle Ct 2 CR4 180 C2
Searle Pl N4 50 B1
Searles Cl
SW11 136 C5 267 B3
Searles Dr E6 100 D2
Searles Rd SE1 262 D4
Searson Ho SE17 261 D3
Sears Ret Pk UB6 86 C6
Sears St SE5 139 B5
Seasalter Ho 10 SW9 138 C4
Seasprite Cl 10 UB5 84 D4
Seath Ho 4 SE26 184 B5
Seaton Ave IG3 79 D3
Seaton Cl
Isleworth TW2 152 B5
6 Newham E13 99 A3
Roehampton SW15 156 B4
Seaton Dr TW15 148 A2
Seaton Gdns HA4 62 A6
Seaton Point E5 74 A4
Seaton Rd Bexley DA16 146 C5
Hayes UB3 105 B3
Mitcham CR4 180 C1
Twickenham TW2 152 A5
Wembley HA0 88 A5
Seaton Sq NW7 28 D3
Seaton St N18 34 A5
Seavington Ho 3 SE5 139 C2
Sebastian Ct 11 IG11 79 D1
Sebastian Ho 22 N1 95 C5
Sebastian St
EC1 94 D4 234 D1
Sebastopol Rd N9 34 A6
Sebbon St N1 72 D1
Sebergham Gr NW7 28 A3
Sebert Rd E7 77 B4
Sebright Ho 22 E2 96 A5
Sebright Pas 29 E2 96 A5
Sebright Rd EN5 1 A2
Sebright Sch E2 96 A5
Secker Cres HA3 24 A2
Secker Ho SW9 138 D3
Secker St SE1 251 A3
Second Ave
Chadwell Heath RM6 58 C4
Dagenham RM10 103 D5
East Acton W3 111 D5
Edmonton N18 34 C6
Enfield EN1 17 D6
Hayes UB3 105 D5
Hendon NW4 46 D5
Kensal Town W10 91 A3
Manor Pk E12 78 A3
Mortlake SW14 133 C2
Newham E13 99 A4
Walthamstow E17 53 C4
Walton-on-T KT12 194 B3
Wembley HA9 65 D6
Second Cl KT8 196 A5
Second Cross Rd
TW2 152 C2
Second Way HA9 66 D4
Secrett Ho 6 TW10 153 C1
Sedan Way
SE17 117 C1 263 A2
Sedcombe Cl DA14 190 C6
Sedcote Rd EN3 18 D6
Sedding St SW1 258 A4
Seddon Ho EC2 242 A4
Seddon Rd SM4 202 B4
Seddon St WC1 94 B4 233 D1
Sedgebrook Rd SE3 143 D2
Sedgecombe Ave HA3 43 C4
Sedgefield Ct UB5 63 D3
Sedgeford Rd W12 111 D5
Sedgehill Rd SE6 185 D5
Sedgehill Sch SE6 185 D5
Sedgemere Ave N2 48 A6
Sedgemere Rd SE2 124 C3
Sedgemoor Dr RM10 81 C4
Sedge Rd N17 34 C3
Sedgeway SE6 164 D3
Sedgewick Ho SW19 156 D2
Sedgewood Cl BR2 208 D2
Sedgley Ho N4 72 B6
Sedgmoor Pl SE5 139 C5
Sedgwick Ave UB10 60 D1
Sedgwick Rd E10 76 A6
Sedgwick St E9 74 D3
Sedleigh Rd SW18 157 B5
Sedlescombe Rd
SW6 135 C6 265 A6
Sedley Cl EN1 6 B5
Sedley Ct SE26 162 B2
Sedley Ho SE11 260 D2
Sedley Pl W1 238 C1
Sedum Cl NW9 44 D4
Seeley Dr SE21 183 C6
Seelig Ave NW9 46 A2
Seely Rd SW17 181 A4
Seething La
EC3 117 C6 253 B6
SEETHING WELLS 197 D3
Seething Wells Halls of
Residence KT6 197 C3
Seething Wells La
KT6 197 C3
Sefton Ave
Edgware NW7 27 B5
Harrow HA3 24 B2
Sefton Cl BR5 211 D5
Sefton Ct TW5 129 D4
Sefton Lo 2 TW1 153 C5
Sefton Rd Croydon CR0 206 A1
Orpington BR5 211 D5
Sefton St SW15 134 C2
Segal Cl SE23 163 A4
Sekforde St EC1 94 D3 241 C6
Sekhon Terr TW13 151 C1

Selan Gdns UB4 84 B2
Selbie Ave NW10 67 D3
Selborne 2 SW11 137 A2
Selborne Ave DA5 169 A3
Little Ilford E12 78 C4
Walthamstow E17 53 B5
Selborne Gdns
Hendon NW4 46 A5
Wembley UB6 87 A5
Selborne Ho SE1 252 C1
Selborne Prim Sch
UB6 86 D5
Selborne Rd
1 Camberwell SE5 139 B3
Ilford IG1 78 C6
Kingston u T KT3 177 C1
Palmers Green N14 16 A1
Sidcup DA14 190 B6
South Croydon CR0 221 D5
Walthamstow E17 53 C4
Wood Green N22 32 B2
Selborne Wlk E17 53 B5
Selborne Wlk Sh Ctr
E17 53 B5
Selbourne Ave KT6 214 C5
Selbridge Ct SW19 179 C4
Selby Chase HA4 62 B6
Selby Cl BR7 188 C4
Chessington KT9 214 A1
14 Newham E6 100 A2
Selby Ct TW2 152 B2
Selby Gdns UB1 85 C3
Selby Gn SM5 202 C2
Selby Ho 10 SW4 159 C5
Selby Rd Ashford TW15 171 A4
Carshalton SM5 202 C2
Ealing W5 87 C3
Leyton E11 76 C5
Newham E13 99 B2
Penge SE20 184 A1
Tottenham N17 33 C4
Selby Sq 1 W10 91 A4
Selby St E1 96 A3
Selden Ho 2 SE15 140 C3
Selden Rd SE15 140 C3
Selden Wlk N7 72 B6
Seldon Ho
Nine Elms SW8 269 A3
Pimlico SW1 259 A1
Selena Ct N20 14 D1
SELHURST 205 B4
Selhurst Cl SW19 156 D3
Selhurst New Ct SE25 205 C3
Selhurst New Rd
SE25 205 C3
Selhurst Park (Crystal Palace FC) SE25 205 C5
Selhurst Pl SE25 205 C3
Selhurst Rd
Edmonton N9 17 C1
South Norwood SE25 205 C4
Selhurst Sta SE25 205 C4
Selina Ho NW8 236 D6
Selinas La RM8 59 B2
Selkirk Ct N17 33 C1
Selkirk Ho N1 233 C6
4 Stoke Newington N16 73 C5
Selkirk Rd
Twickenham TW2 152 A3
Upper Tooting SW17 180 C6
Sellers Hall Cl N3 29 C3
Sellincourt Prim Sch
SW17 180 C4
Sellincourt Rd SW17 180 C4
Sellindge Cl BR3 185 B3
Sellons Ave NW10 89 D6
Sellsby Ct N11 31 B5
Sellwood Dr EN5 12 D6
Selma Ho 7 W12 90 B1
Selman Ho 3 E9 75 A2
SELSDON 223 A1
Selsdon Ave CR2 221 B2
Selsdon Cl KT6 198 A4
Selsdon High Sch
CR2 222 D1
Selsdon Park Rd CR0,
CR2 223 B1
Selsdon Rd
Newham E13 99 C5
South Croydon CR2 221 B2
Wanstead E11 55 A2
West Norwood SE27 182 D6
Willesden NW2 67 D6
Selsdon Road Ind Est
CR2 221 B2
Selsdon Way E14 119 D3
Selsea Pl N16 73 C3
Selsey Cres DA16 146 D4
Selsey St E14 97 C2
Selvage La NW7 27 B6
Selway Cl HA5 40 B6
Selway Ho SW8 270 B2
Selwood Ho
Chislehurst BR7 189 A4
1 Stoke Newington N4 51 B2
Selwood Pl
SW7 114 B1 256 C2
Selwood Rd
Cheam SM3 201 B1
Chessington KT9 213 D4
Croydon CR0 206 B1
Selwood Terr SW7 256 C2
Selworthy Cl E11 55 A4
Selworthy Ho SW11 266 D2
Selworthy Rd SE6 163 B1
Selwyn Ave Chingford E4 36 A4
Ilford IG3 57 D3
Selwyn Ave *continued*
Richmond TW9 132 B2
Selwyn Cl TW4 129 A1
Selwyn Cres DA16 146 B1
Selwyn Ct Edgware HA8 26 D3
Lewisham SE3 142 D2
8 Richmond TW10 154 B6
Walthamstow E17 53 C4
Wembley HA9 67 A5
Selwyn Ho 3 SW15 156 D5
Selwyn Inf Sch E4 36 A4
Selwyn Jun Sch E4 36 A4
Selwyn Prim Sch E13 99 A6
Selwyn Rd Bow E3 97 B5
Newham E13 99 B6
New Malden KT3 199 B4
Willesden NW10 67 C1
Semley Gate E9 75 B2
Semley Ho SW1 258 C3
Semley Pl SW1 115 B2 258 C3
Thornton Heath SW16 182 B1
Semley Rd SW16 182 A1
Senate St SE15 140 C3
Senators Lo 31 E3 97 A5
Senator Wlk 2 SE28 123 B3
Sencler Ho SE2 146 D6
Sendall Ct 13 SW11 136 B2
Seneca Rd CR7 205 A5
Senga Rd SM6 203 A1
Senhouse Rd SM3 216 D5
Senior St W2 91 D2
Senlac Rd SE12 165 B3
Sennen Rd EN1 17 D4
Sennen Wlk SE9 166 A1
Senrab St E1 96 D1
Sentinel Cl UB5 85 A3
Sentinel Ho NW4 46 C5
Sentinel Sq NW4 46 C5
September Ct UB1 107 D5
September Way HA7 25 B4
Sequoia Cl WD23 8 B3
Sequoia Gdns BR6 211 D2
Sequoia Pk HA5 23 D4
Seraph Ct EC1 95 A4 235 A2
Serbin Cl E10 54 A2
Serenaders Rd 20
SW9 138 C3
Sergeant Ind Est The
SW18 157 D5
Serica Ct 14 SE10 142 A5
Serjeants' Inn EC4 241 B1
Serlby Ct W14 254 C6
Serle St WC2 94 B1 240 D2
Sermon La EC4 242 A1
Serpentine Ct 10
SE16 118 D4
Serpentine Gallery*
W2 114 B4 246 D2
Serpentine Rd
W2 114 D5 247 C3
Serpentine The*
W2 114 C5 247 B3
Service Route No 1
E15 76 B1
Service Route No 2 1
E15 76 B1
Service Route No 3 2
E15 76 B1
Serviden Dr BR1 187 D2
Servite Ho
Beckenham BR3 185 B2
Bromley BR1 188 B1
East Barnet N14 15 B6
Lewisham SE13 141 D4
Penge SE26 184 C4
Worcester Pk KT4 215 D6
Servite RC Prim Sch
SW10 136 A6 266 A6
Servius Ct 2 TW8 131 D5
Sessions Terr CR4 180 D2
Setchell Rd
SE1 117 D2 263 C4
Setchell Way SE1 263 C4
Seth St 25 SE16 118 C4
Seton Ct 3 NW9 46 A5
Seton Gdns RM9 80 C1
Settle Point 11 E13 99 A5
Settlers Ct 11 E14 120 B6
Settles St E1 96 A1
Settrington Rd SW6 135 D3
Seven Acres
Carshalton SM5 218 C6
Northwood HA6 22 A4
Seven Dials
WC2 94 A1 240 A1
SEVEN KINGS 57 D2
Seven Kings High Sch
IG2 57 B2
Seven Kings Rd IG3 79 D6
Seven Kings Sta IG3 57 C1
Seven Kings Way KT2 176 A2
Seven Mills Prim Sch
E14 119 C4
Sevenoaks Rd BR6 227 D4
Catford SE4 163 B5
Sevenoaks Way BR5 190 C1
Seven Sisters N15 51 D4
Seven Sisters Prim Sch
N15 51 B4
Seven Sisters Rd
Finsbury Pk N4 72 D6
Stoke Newington N4, N7,
N15 51 A2
Seven Sisters Sta N15 51 C4
Seven Stars Cnr W12 112 A3
Seven Stars Yd E1 243 D4
Seventh Ave
Hayes UB3 106 A5
Ilford E12 78 B4
Seven Ways Par IG2 56 C4
Severnake Cl E14 119 C2
Severn Ave 2 W10 91 A4
Severn Ct 11 KT2 175 D2
Severn Dr Enfield EN1 6 A5
Hinchley Wood KT10 213 A6
Severn Way NW10 67 D3
Severus Rd SW11 136 C1
Seville Ho 11 E1 118 A5
Seville Mews N1 73 C1
Seville St SW1 247 D1
Sevington Rd NW4 46 B3
Sevington St W9 91 D3
Seward Rd Penge BR3 184 D1
West Ealing W7 109 A4
Seward St EC1 95 A4 235 A1
SEWARDSTONEBURY 20 C6
Sewardstone Gdns E4 19 D6
Sewardstone Rd
Chingford E4 19 D6
South Hackney E2 96 C5
Sewdley St E5 74 D5
Sewell Ho 7 N16 73 C3
Sewell Rd SE2 124 B4
Sewell St E13 99 A4
Sextant Ave E14 120 B2
Sexton Ct 7 E14 120 B6
Sexton's Ho 5 SE13 142 A6
Seychelle Ct BR3 185 D3
Seymour Ave
Tottenham N17 34 A1
West Barnes SM4 200 D2
Seymour Cl
East Molesey KT8 196 A4
Pinner HA5 23 B2
Seymour Ct
Chingford E4 20 D2
Dollis Hill NW2 68 B6
Muswell Hill N10 31 A1
Putney SW15 134 B1
Southgate N21 16 B5
Upper Clapton N16 52 A1
Seymour Dr BR2 210 B1
Seymour Gdns
Brockley SE4 141 A2
Feltham TW13 172 C6
Kingston u T KT5 198 B4
Redbridge IG1 56 B1
Ruislip HA4 40 D1
Twickenham TW1 153 B4
Seymour Ho
Bloomsbury WC1 240 A6
1 Clapham SW8 137 C3
Ruislip HA4 40 A5
Somers Town NW1 232 D1
Seymour Lo 14 KT1 175 D2
Seymour Mews W1 238 A2
Seymour Pl
Croydon SE25 206 B5
Paddington W1 92 D1 237 C2
Seymour Rd Acton W4 111 A2
Carshalton CR4 203 A2
Chingford E4 19 D3
East Molesey KT8 196 A4
Edmonton N9 18 B2
Finchley N3 29 D3
Hampton TW12 174 A5
Harringay N8 50 D4
Newham E6 99 D6
Teddington KT1 175 D2
Wallington SM5 219 A3
Walthamstow E10 53 B1
Wandsworth SW18 157 B5
Wimbledon SW19 156 D1
Seymour St
Paddington
W1 92 D1 237 D1
Woolwich SE18 123 A3
Seymour Terr SE20 184 B2
Seymour Villas SE20 184 A2
Seymour Way TW16 171 C3
Seymour Wlk
SW10 136 A6 266 A6
Seyssel St E14 120 A2
Shaa Rd W3 111 B6
Shabana Ct 3 W12 112 B5
Shacklegate La TW11 174 C6
Shackleton Cl SE23 162 B2
Shackleton Ct
3 Dulwich SE21 161 B2
2 Isle of Dogs E14 119 C1
4 Shepherd's Bush
W12 112 B4
7 Stanwell TW19 148 A5
Shackleton Ho
5 Stonebridge NW10 67 B1
6 Wapping E1 118 C5
Shackleton Lo SW16 181 D5
Shackleton Rd UB1 107 B6
SHACKLEWELL 73 D4
Shacklewell Ho 3 E8 73 D4
Shacklewell La E8 73 D3
Shacklewell Prim Sch
E8 73 D4
Shacklewell Rd N16 73 D4
Shacklewell Row E8 73 D4
Shacklewell St 30 E2 95 D4
Shadbolt Ave E4 35 A5
Shadbolt Cl KT4 215 D6
Shad Thames
SE1 117 D4 253 D2
SHADWELL 118 C6
Shadwell Ct UB5 85 B5
Shadwell Dr UB5 85 B4
Shadwell Gdns E1 118 C6
Shadwell Pierhead
E1 118 C6
Shadwell Pl 1 E1 118 C6
Shadwell Sta E1 118 B6
Shady Bush Cl WD23 8 A4
Shaef Way TW11 175 A3
Shaftesbury Ave
Enfield EN3 6 D3
Feltham TW14 150 A5
Kenton HA3 44 A3
New Barnet EN5 2 A1
Southall UB2 107 C3
W1 115 D6 249 D6
West Harrow HA1, HA2 42 A1
Shaftesbury Circ HA2 42 A1
Shaftesbury Ct
Borough The SE1 262 C6
1 Herne Hill SE5 139 B1
Ilford RM6 58 C2
Newham E6 100 C1
Shoreditch N1 235 C3
Streatham SW16 159 D1
3 Thamesmead SE28 124 C5
Shaftesbury Ctr NW10 90 D3
Shaftesbury Gdns
NW10 89 C3
Shaftesbury High Sch
HA3 23 D2
Shaftesbury Ho
11 Canning Town E16 98 D1
Croydon SE25 206 A3
13 Stoke Newington N16 73 C5
Upper Tooting SW17 180 B6
W2 245 D6
Shaftesbury Lo 9 E14 97 D1
Shaftesbury Mews
2 Clapham Pk SW4 159 C6
W8 255 B5
Shaftesbury Park
Chambers 1 SW11 137 A2
Shaftesbury Point E13 99 B5
Shaftesbury Prim Sch
E7 77 C1
Shaftesbury Rd
Beckenham BR3 185 B1
Carshalton SM5 202 C2
Chingford E4 20 B3
Edmonton N18 33 D4
Finsbury Pk N4, N19 50 A1
Leyton E10 53 C1
Richmond TW9 132 A2
Upton E7 77 C1
Walthamstow E17 53 D3
Shaftesbury St N1 235 C3
Shaftesburys The
IG11 101 A5
Shaftesbury Way TW2 152 B1
Shaftesbury Waye UB4 84 C1
Shafteswood Ct SW17 158 D1
Shafto Mews SW1 257 D5
Shafton Rd E9 96 D6
Shaftsbury Park Prim Sch
SW11 137 A3
Shafts Ct EC3 243 A1
Shahjalal Ho 18 E2 96 A5
Shakespeare Ave
7 Becontree NW10 89 B6
Feltham TW14 150 A5
Friern Barnet N11 31 C5
Hayes UB4 84 B2
Shakespeare Cl HA3 44 C2
Shakespeare Cres E12 78 B2
Shakespeare Ct EN5 1 D2
Shakespeare Dr HA3 44 B3
Shakespeare Gdns N2 48 D5
Shakespeare Ho
1 Erith DA17 125 B1
3 Hackney E9 74 C1
Osidge N14 15 D2
Shakespeare Rd
Acton W3 111 A5
Brixton SE24 138 D1
DA7 147 A4
Ealing W7 108 D6
Finchley N3 29 C2
Higham Hill E17 34 D1
Mill Hill NW7 28 A6
Shakespeare's Globe
Theatre (site of)*
SE1 252 B4
Shakespeare Twr EC2 242 B4
Shakespeare Way
TW13 172 C6
Shakspeare Mews 7
N16 73 C4
Shakspeare Wlk N16 73 C4
Shalbourne Sq E9 75 B2
Shalcomb St
SW10 136 A6 266 B5
Shalden Ho SW15 155 D5
Shaldon Dr Ruislip HA4 62 C5
West Barnes SM4 201 A4
Shaldon Rd HA8 26 B1
Shalfleet Dr W10 112 D6
Shalford
Willesden Green
NW10 90 A6
3 Woodford IG8 37 C4
Shalford Cl BR6 227 A4
Shalford Ct N1 234 C4
Shalford Ho SE1 262 D6
Shalimar Gdns W3 111 A6
Shalimar Lo W3 111 A6
Shalimar Rd W3 111 A6
Shallons Rd SE9 188 D6
Shalstone Rd SW14,
TW9 132 D2
Shalston Villas KT5,
KT6 198 B3
Shamrock Ct E7 77 D3
Shamrock Ho
East Barnet N14 15 B4
Forest Hill SE26 184 A6
Shamrock Rd CR0 204 B3
Shamrock St SW4 137 D2
Shamrock Way N14 15 B3
Shandon Ct SE4 141 A3
Shandon Rd SW4 159 C5
Shand St SE1 117 C4 253 B2
Shandy St E1 96 D3
Shane Ct EN2 5 A3
Shan Ho WC1 240 C5
Shanklin Gdns WD19 22 C6
Shanklin Ho E17 35 B1
Shanklin Rd Hornsey N8 49 D4
Tottenham Hale N15 52 A5
Shannon Cl
Cricklewood NW2 68 D5
Southall UB2 106 D1
Shannon Cnr KT3 200 A5
Shannon Cnr Ret Pk
KT3 200 A5
Shannon Commercial Ctr
KT3 200 A5
Shannon Ct
Croydon CR0 205 A1
11 Peckham SE15 139 D5
Stoke Newington N16 73 C5
Willesden NW10 68 A2
Shannon Gr SW9 138 B1
Shannon Pl
NW8 92 C5 230 B4
Shannon Way BR3 185 D4
Shanti Ct SW18 157 C3
Shap Cres SM5 202 D1
Shapland Way N13 32 B5
Shapla Prim Sch E1 118 A6
Shapwick Cl N11 30 D5
Shardcroft Ave SE24 160 D6
Shardeloes Rd SE14 141 B3
Shard's Sq SE15 140 A6
Sharebourne Ho SW2 160 C6
Sharland Cl CR7 204 C3
Sharman Ct DA14 190 A6
Sharman Ho 13 E14 98 A1
Sharnbrooke Cl DA16 146 C2
Sharnbrook Ho W6 265 A6
Sharon Cl KT6 197 C1
Sharon Ct 1 N12 30 A4
Sharon Gdns E9 96 C6
Sharon Rd
Chiswick W4 111 B1
Enfield EN3 7 A3
Sharpe Cl W7 86 D2
Sharp Ho SW8 137 B2
Sharples Hall St 8
NW1 70 D1
Sharpness Cl UB4 85 A2
Sharpness Ct 2 SE15 139 D5
Sharps La HA4 39 B2
Sharratt St SE15 140 C6
Sharsted St
SE17 116 D1 261 C1
Sharvel La UB5 84 B6
Sharwood WC1 233 D3
Shaver's Pl SW1 249 C5
Shaw Ave IG11 103 A5
Shawbrooke Rd SE9 143 D1
Shawbury Cl 9 NW9 27 C2
Shawbury Ct SE22 161 D6
Shawbury Rd SE22 161 D6
Shaw Cl Bushey WD23 8 C2
Woolwich SE28 124 B5
Shaw Cotts SE23 163 A1
Shaw Cres 6 E14 97 A1
Shaw Ct
8 Acton Green W3 111 A3
12 Battersea SW11 136 B2
Cheam SM4 202 A2
Upper Holloway N19 72 A6
Shaw Dr KT12 194 C2
Shawfield Ct UB7 104 A3
Shawfield Pk BR1 187 D1
Shawfield St
SW3 114 C1 257 B1
Shawford Ct 8 SW15 156 A4
Shawford Rd KT19 215 B2
Shaw Gdns IG11 103 A5
Shaw Ho 6 Erith DA17 125 B1
5 Newham E16 122 C5
Shaw Path BR1 164 D1
Shaw Rd
Camberwell SE22 139 C1
Catford BR1 164 D1
Enfield EN3 6 D4
Shaw Sq E17 35 A2
Shaws Wood Cotts EN4 3 C3
Shaw Way SM6 220 A1
Shearing Dr SM4 202 A2
Shearling Way N7 72 A2
Shearman Rd SE3 142 D2
Shears Ct TW16 171 C3
Shearsmith Ho 19 E1 118 A6
Shears The TW16 171 C3
Shears Way TW16 171 C2
Shearwater Cl IG11 102 A4
Shearwater Ct 24 SE8 141 B6
Shearwater Rd SM1 217 B3
Shearwater Way UB4 84 D1
Sheaveshill Ave NW9 45 C5
Sheaveshill Ct NW9 45 C5
Sheaveshill Par NW9 45 C5
Sheba Ct N17 34 A4
Sheba Pl E1 243 D5
Sheen Common Dr SW14,
TW10 154 C6
Sheen Court Rd TW10 132 C1
Sheen Ct TW10 132 C1
Sheendale Rd TW9 132 B1
Sheenewood SE26 184 B6
Sheen Gate Gdns
SW14 133 A1
Sheengate Mans
SW14 133 B1
Sheen Gr N1 94 C6 234 A6
Sheen La SW14 133 A1
Sheen Mount Prim Sch
SW14 154 D6
Sheen Pk TW10, TW9 132 A1
Sheen Rd
Orpington BR5 211 D5
Richmond TW10, TW9 132 B1
Sheen Way SM6 220 B3
Sheen Wood SW14 155 A6
Sheepcote Cl TW5 128 A5
Sheepcote La SW11 136 D3
Sheepcote Rd HA1 42 D3
Sheepcotes Rd RM6 59 A5
Sheephouse Way KT3 199 C2
Sheep La E8 96 B6
Sheepwalk TW17 192 B3
Sheep Walk Mews 7
SW19 179 A4
Sheerness Mews E16 122 D4
Sheerwater Rd E16 99 D2
Sheffield Ho 15 SE15 139 D4
Sheffield Rd TW14,
TW6 149 A6
Sheffield Sq 2 E3 97 B4
Sheffield St WC2 240 C1
Sheffield Terr
W8 113 C5 245 B3
Sheffield Way TW14,
TW6 149 B6
Shefton Rise HA6 22 A3
Shelbey Ct BR1 186 D2
Shelbourne Cl HA5 41 B6
Shelbourne Ho 20 N19 49 D2
Shelbourne Rd N17 34 B2
Shelburne Ct SW15 156 D6
Shelburne Dr TW4 151 C5
Shelburne Ho 9
SW16 181 C5
Shelburne Rd N7 72 B4
Shelbury Cl DA14 168 A1
Shelbury Rd SE22 162 B6
Sheldon Ave N6 48 D3
Sheldon Cl Penge SE20 184 B2
SE12 165 B6
Sheldon Ct Barnet EN5 1 D1
SW8 270 A3
Sheldon Ho
Chingford E4 36 C4
9 Homerton E9 74 D2
Teddington TW11 175 A4
Sheldon Pl E2 96 B5
Sheldon Rd
Cricklewood NW2 68 D4
DA7 147 B4
Dagenham RM9 81 A1
Edmonton N18 33 C6
Sheldon Sq W2 236 B3
Sheldon St CR0 221 A5
Sheldrake Cl E16 122 B5
Sheldrake Ho 15 SE16 118 D2
Sheldrake Pl
W8 113 C4 245 A2
Sheldrick Cl CR4 180 B1
Shelduck Cl E15 76 D3
Shelduck Ct 37 SE8 141 B6
Sheldwich Terr BR2 210 A3
Shelford 20 KT1 176 C1
Shelford Ct 7 E5 52 B1
Shelford Pl N16 73 B5
Shelford Rd EN5 12 C5
Shelford Rise SE19 183 D3
Shelgate Rd SW11 158 D6
Shell Cl BR2 210 A3
Shell Ctr SE1 250 D3
Shellduck Cl NW9 27 C1
Shelley N8 50 A6
Shelley Ave
Greenford UB6 86 B4
Plashet E12 78 A2
Shelley Cl BR6 227 C5
Edgware HA8 26 C6
Greenford UB6 86 B4
Hayes UB4 84 A2
Peckham SE15 140 B3
Shelley Cres
Heston TW5 128 D4
Southall UB1 85 B1
Shelley Ct
Finsbury Pk N4 50 B1
9 Kingston u T KT2 175 D6
SW3 267 D6
13 Walthamstow E10 53 D2
8 Wanstead E11 55 A5
Wembley HA0 65 C4
West Barnes KT3 200 A4
Shelley Dr DA16 145 C4
Shelley Gdns HA0 65 C6
Shelley Ho
21 Bethnal Green E2 96 C4
Chelsea SW1 269 A6
9 Stoke Newington N16 73 C4
Walworth SE17 262 B2
Shelley Rd NW10 89 B6
Shelley Way SW17 180 B4
Shellgrove Rd N16 73 C3
Shellness Rd E5 74 B3
Shell Rd SE13 141 D2
Shellwood Rd SW11 136 D3
Shelly Lo EN2 5 B4
Shelmerdine Cl E3 97 C2
Shelson Ave TW13 171 D6
Shelton Ct N21 16 C4
Shelton Rd SW19 179 C2
Shelton St WC2 94 A1 240 A1
Shene Bldg EC1 241 A4
Shene Sch SW14 133 C1
Shenfield Ho 3 SE18 143 D5
Shenfield Rd IG8 37 B3
Shenfield St N1 95 C5
Shenley Ave HA4 39 D1
Shenley Ho 3 SW16 182 B6

Shenley Rd
Camberwell SE5 ... 139 C4
Heston TW5 ... 129 A4
Shenstone W13 ... 109 C5
Shenstone Gdns IG2 ... 57 D4
Shenstone Ho SW16 ... 181 C5
Shepard Ho 18 SW11 ... 136 B2
Sheperdess Pl N1 ... 235 B2
Shepherd Cl
Feltham TW13 ... 173 A6
W1 ... 248 A6
Shepherdess Wlk
N1 ... 95 A5 235 B3
Shepherd Ho
Barnsbury N7 ... 72 A2
10 Poplar E14 ... 97 D1
Shepherd Mkt W1 ... 248 C3
SHEPHERD'S BUSH ... 112 B5
Shepherd's Bush (Central Line) Sta W12 ... 112 D4
Shepherd's Bush Gn W12 ... 112 C4
Shepherd's Bush (Hamm & City) Sta W12 ... 112 C5
Shepherd's Bush Market W12 ... 112 C4
Shepherd's Bush Pl W12 ... 112 D4
Shepherd's Bush Rd W6 ... 112 C3
Shepherds Cl
Dagenham RM6 ... 58 D5
Orpington BR6 ... 227 D5
Shepperton TW17 ... 192 D3
Stanmore HA7 ... 25 A5
Shepherd's Cl N6 ... 49 B3
Shepherds Ct
8 Hammersmith W12 ... 112 D4
13 Harrow HA1 ... 42 D3
Shepherds Gn BR7 ... 189 B3
Shepherd's Hill N6 ... 49 C3
Shepherds La SE28 ... 123 C5
Shepherd's La E9 ... 74 D2
Shepherds Leas SE9 ... 145 B1
Shepherds Path UB5 ... 63 A2
Shepherds Pl W1 ... 248 A6
Shepherd St
W1 ... 115 B5 248 C3
Shepherds Way CR2 ... 222 D1
Shepherds Wlk
Bushey WD23 ... 8 B2
Dollis Hill NW2 ... 68 A6
Shepherd's Wlk NW3 ... 70 B4
Shepiston La UB3 ... 105 A1
Shepley Cl SM5 ... 219 A5
Shepley Ct SW16 ... 181 C6
Shepley Mews EN3 ... 7 C6
Sheppard Cl Enfield EN1 ... 6 B5
Kingston u T KT6 ... 198 A5
Sheppard Dr SE16 ... 118 B1
Sheppard Ho
31 Hackney E2 ... 96 A5
8 Streatham SW2 ... 160 C3
Sheppard's Ct
Harrow HA1 ... 42 C2
Wembley UB6 ... 64 D2
Sheppard St E16 ... 98 D3
SHEPPERTON ... 193 A3
Shepperton Bsns Park TW17 ... 193 A4
Shepperton Court Dr TW17 ... 192 D4
Shepperton Ct TW17 ... 192 D3
SHEPPERTON GREEN ... 192 D5
Shepperton Rd
Littleton TW17, TW18 ... 192 A5
Orpington BR5 ... 228 A5
Shoreditch N1 ... 95 B6 235 C6
Shepperton Sta TW17 ... 193 A4
Shepperton Studios TW17 ... 192 B6
Sheppey Gdns RM9 ... 80 C1
Sheppey Ho 16 E5 ... 74 B4
Sheppey Rd RM9 ... 80 C1
Shepton Ct SW11 ... 266 D2
Shepton Hos 11 E2 ... 96 C4
Sherard Ct N19 ... 72 A5
Sherard Ho 24 E9 ... 74 C1
Sherard Rd SE9 ... 166 A6
Sheraton Bsns Ctr UB6 ... 87 C5
Sheraton Cl WD6 ... 10 B6
Sheraton Ho SW1 ... 268 D6
Sheraton Lo HA3 ... 42 C6
Sheraton St W1 ... 239 C1
Sheraton The 22 KT6 ... 198 A4
Sherborne Ave
Enfield EN3 ... 6 C3
Southall UB2 ... 107 C2
Sherborne Cl UB4 ... 84 C1
Sherborne Cres SM5 ... 202 C2
Sherborne Ct SE20 ... 184 C1
Sherborne Gdns
Ealing W13 ... 87 B2
Queensbury NW9 ... 44 C6
Sherborne Ho
Pimlico SW1 ... 258 D2
South Lambeth SW8 ... 270 C3
Sherborne La EC4 ... 252 D6
Sherborne Rd BR5 ... 211 D4
Cheam SM3 ... 201 C1
Chessington KT9 ... 214 A3
East Bedfont TW14 ... 149 B3
Sherborne St
N1 ... 95 B6 235 C6
Sherboro Rd 1 N15 ... 51 D3
Sherbourne Ct
1 Hampton TW12 ... 173 C2
Sherbourne Ct *continued*
9 Sutton SM2 ... 218 A2
SW5 ... 255 C4
Sherbourne Gdns
TW17 ... 193 C2
Sherbourne Pl HA7 ... 25 A4
Sherbrooke Cl DA7 ... 147 C1
Sherbrooke Ho 9 E2 ... 96 C5
Sherbrooke Rd
SW6 ... 135 A5 264 B3
Sherbrooke Terr SW6 ... 264 B3
Sherbrooke Way KT4 ... 200 B2
Sherbrook Gdns N21 ... 16 D4
Sherbrook Ho 2 N3 ... 29 D3
Shere Cl KT9 ... 213 D3
Sheredan Rd E4 ... 36 C5
Shere Ho SE1 ... 262 C6
Shere Lo 1 SW19 ... 180 C3
Shere Rd IG2 ... 56 C4
Sherfield Cl KT3 ... 198 D5
Sherfield Gdns SW15 ... 155 D5
Sheridan N8 ... 50 C5
Sheridan Bldgs WC2 ... 240 B1
Sheridan Cl UB10 ... 83 A3
Sheridan Cres BR7 ... 188 D1
Sheridan Ct Ealing W7 ... 108 D6
Earl's Ct SW5 ... 255 C3
Harrow HA1 ... 42 B3
Hounslow TW4 ... 151 A6
South Hampstead NW6 ... 70 A1
South Lambeth SW9 ... 270 D1
Sheridan Gdns HA3 ... 43 D3
Sheridan Ho SE11 ... 261 B3
7 Stoke Newington N16 ... 73 C5
Sheridan Lo Barnet EN5 ... 1 D1
Bromley BR2 ... 209 C5
East Barnet N14 ... 15 B4
Sheridan Mews E11 ... 55 B3
Sheridan Pl
Barnes SW13 ... 133 D2
Hampton TW12 ... 174 A2
Harrow HA1 ... 42 C2
Sheridan Rd
Belvedere DA17 ... 125 C2
DA7 ... 147 A2
Leyton E7 ... 76 D5
Little Ilford E12 ... 78 B3
Merton SW19 ... 179 B2
Richmond TW10 ... 153 C1
Sheridan St 34 E1 ... 96 B1
Sheridan Terr UB5 ... 63 D3
Sheridan Way 5 BR3 ... 185 B2
Sheridan Wlk
Golders Green NW11 ... 47 C3
Wallington SM5 ... 218 D3
Sheringdale Prim Sch
SW18 ... 157 B3
Sheringham NW8 ... 229 D6
Sheringham Ave
Feltham TW13 ... 150 A1
Little Ilford E12 ... 78 B3
Southgate N14 ... 15 D5
Twickenham TW2 ... 151 C3
Sheringham Ct 1 N3 ... 29 C2
Sheringham Dr IG11 ... 80 A3
Sheringham Ho NW1 ... 237 B4
Sheringham Jun Sch
E12 ... 78 B4
Sheringham Mews 4
SW18 ... 158 A2
Sheringham Rd
Islington N7 ... 72 C2
Penge SE20 ... 206 C6
Sheringham Twr UB1 ... 107 D6
Sherington Ave HA5 ... 23 C3
Sherington Prim Sch
SE7 ... 143 B6
Sherington Rd SE7 ... 143 B6
Sheriton Ct SM1 ... 217 C5
Sherland Rd TW1 ... 152 D3
Sherleys Ct HA4 ... 61 C6
Sherlies Ave BR6 ... 227 C6
Sherlock Ct NW8 ... 229 C6
Sherlock Holmes Mus*
NW1 ... 92 D3 237 D5
Sherlock Mews W1 ... 238 A4
Sherman Gdns RM6 ... 58 C3
Sherman Rd BR1 ... 187 A2
Shernhall St E17 ... 54 A5
Shernwood Ho 1 E18 ... 55 A5
Sherrard Rd E7, E12 ... 77 D2
Sherrards Way EN5 ... 13 D5
Sherren Ho 35 E1 ... 96 C3
Sherrick Green Rd
NW10 ... 68 B3
Sherriff Ct NW6 ... 69 C2
Sherriff Rd NW6 ... 69 C2
Sherringham Ave N17 ... 34 A1
Sherrin Rd E10 ... 75 D4
Sherrock Gdns NW4 ... 46 A5
Sherry Mews IG11 ... 79 B1
Sherston Ct
Finsbury WC1 ... 234 A1
Newington SE1 ... 261 D4
Sherwin Ho 1 SE11 ... 138 C6
Sherwin Rd SE14 ... 140 D4
Sherwood 3 Barnet EN5 ... 1 D1
Brondesbury NW6 ... 69 A1
Long Ditton KT6 ... 213 D6
Sherwood Ave
Greenford UB6 ... 64 C3
Hayes UB4 ... 84 B3
Mitcham SW16 ... 181 D2
Ruislip HA4 ... 39 C3
Wanstead E18 ... 55 B6
Sherwood Cl
Barnes SW13 ... 134 B2
DA5 ... 168 C5
Ealing W13 ... 109 B5
Walthamstow E17 ... 35 B1
Sherwood Ct
11 Battersea SW11 ... 136 A2
Colney Hatch N12 ... 30 C5
2 South Croydon CR2 ... 221 A3
St Johns SE13 ... 141 D3
Sutton SM1 ... 217 C3
W1 ... 237 C3
6 West Wickham BR4 ... 207 D1
Sherwood Gdns
Barking IG11 ... 79 B1
Bermondsey SE16 ... 118 B1
Millwall E14 ... 119 C2
Sherwood Hall 7 N2 ... 48 A6
Sherwood Ho N4 ... 51 A2
Sherwood Park Ave
DA15 ... 168 B5
Sherwood Park Prim Sch
DA15 ... 168 B5
Sherwood Park Rd
Mitcham CR4 ... 203 D5
Sutton SM1 ... 217 C3
Sherwood Park Sch
SM6 ... 219 D5
Sherwood Rd
Croydon CR0 ... 206 B1
DA16 ... 145 C2
Hampton TW12 ... 174 A5
Harrow HA2 ... 64 A6
Hendon NW4 ... 46 C6
Ilford IG6 ... 57 B5
Merton SW19 ... 179 B3
Sherwood Sch The
CR4 ... 203 C5
Sherwood St W1 ... 249 B6
Whetstone N20 ... 14 B1
Sherwood Terr N20 ... 14 B1
Sherwood Way BR4 ... 224 A6
Shetland Cl WD6 ... 11 B5
Shetland Rd Bow E3 ... 97 B5
East Bedfont TW6 ... 149 A5
Shield Dr TW8 ... 131 A6
Shieldhall St SE2 ... 124 C2
Shield Rd TW15 ... 171 B6
Shifford Path SE23 ... 162 D1
Shillaker Ct W3 ... 111 D5
Shillibeer Ct N18 ... 34 B5
Shillibeer Pl W1 ... 237 B3
Shillingford Cl NW7 ... 28 D3
Shillingford Ho 40 E3 ... 97 D4
Shillingford St 23 N1 ... 72 D1
Shilling Pl TW8 ... 109 A5
Shillingstone Ho W14 ... 254 B5
Shine Ho 3 N3 ... 29 D3
Shinfield St W12 ... 90 C1
Shinglewell Rd DA8 ... 147 C5
Shinners Cl SE25 ... 206 A4
Shipka Rd SW12 ... 159 B3
Ship La SW14 ... 133 A3
Shiplake Ct SW17 ... 180 B6
Shiplake Ho 45 E2 ... 95 D4
Shipley Ct SE20 ... 184 A1
Shipley Ho 32 SW8 ... 137 D3
Shipman Rd
Forest Hill SE23 ... 162 D2
Newham E16 ... 99 C1
Ship & Mermaid Row
SE1 ... 253 A2
Ship St SE8 ... 141 C4
Ship Tavern Pas EC3 ... 253 A6
Shipton Cl RM8 ... 80 D5
Shipton Ho
7 Camden Town NW5 ... 71 A2
14 Haggerston E2 ... 95 D5
Shipton Rd UB8 ... 60 B4
Shipton St E2 ... 95 D4
Shipwright Rd SE16 ... 119 A4
Shipwright Yd SE1 ... 253 A3
Shirburn Cl SE23 ... 162 C4
Shirbutt St E14 ... 119 D6
Shirebrook Rd SE3 ... 143 D2
Shire Ct DA18 ... 124 D3
Ewell KT17 ... 215 D1
Shirehall Cl NW4 ... 46 D3
Shirehall Gdns NW4 ... 46 D3
Shirehall La NW4 ... 46 D3
Shirehall Pk NW4 ... 46 D3
Shire Ho E11 ... 76 D5
Shire Horse Way TW7 ... 130 D2
Shire La BR6 ... 227 B2
Shiremeade WD6 ... 10 B6
Shire Mews TW2 ... 152 A5
Shire Pl
12 Brentford TW8 ... 131 C5
Wandsworth SW18 ... 158 A4
Shires The TW10 ... 176 A6
Shirland Mews W9 ... 91 B4
Shirland Rd W9 ... 91 C3
SHIRLEY ... 206 C1
Shirley Ave
Carshalton SM1 ... 218 C4
Croydon CR0 ... 206 D1
DA5 ... 168 D3
Shirley Church Rd
CR0 ... 223 A5
Shirley Cl
Hounslow TW3 ... 152 A6
Walthamstow E17 ... 53 D4
Shirley Cres BR3 ... 207 A5
Shirley Ct
8 Ealing W13 ... 109 A5
Ilford IG2 ... 57 B4
Kingsbury NW9 ... 45 B4
2 South Norwood
SW16 ... 182 B3
Thornton Heath SW16 ... 204 B6
Shirley Dr TW3 ... 152 A6
Shirley Gdns
Barking IG11 ... 79 C2
Ealing W7 ... 108 D5
Shirley Gr
Clapham SW11 ... 137 A2
Ponders End N9 ... 18 D4
Shirley High Sch
Performing Arts Coll
CR0 ... 222 D5
Shirley Hills Rd CR0 ... 222 D3
Shirley Ho 13 SE5 ... 139 B5
Shirley House Dr SE7 ... 143 C5
Shirley Hts 6 DA6 ... 147 A1
Shirley Lo 4 SE26 ... 185 A6
SHIRLEY OAKS ... 207 A1
Shirley Oaks Hospl
CR0 ... 206 C2
Shirley Oaks Rd CR0 ... 222 D6
Shirley Park Rd CR0 ... 206 C1
Shirley Rd Acton W4 ... 111 B4
Croydon CR0 ... 206 B1
Enfield EN2 ... 5 A2
Sidcup DA15 ... 167 C1
Stratford E15 ... 76 C1
Shirley St E16 ... 98 D1
Shirley Way CR0 ... 223 B5
Shirlock Rd NW3 ... 70 D4
Shirwell Cl NW7 ... 28 D3
Shobden Rd N17 ... 33 B2
Shobroke Cl NW2 ... 68 C5
Shoebury Rd E6 ... 78 B1
Shoe La EC4 ... 94 C1 241 B2
Shoelands Ct NW9 ... 45 B6
Shona Ho E16 ... 99 C2
Shooters Ave HA3 ... 43 C5
SHOOTERS HILL ... 145 A4
Shooters Hill SE18 ... 144 C4
Shooters Hill Rd
Blackheath Vale SE3,
SE10 ... 142 C4
SE18, SE3, SE7 ... 143 D5
Shooters Rd EN2 ... 4 D4
Shoot-Up Hill NW2 ... 69 A2
Shopstop SW11 ... 136 C1
Shore Bsns Ctr 31 E9 ... 74 C1
Shore Cl Feltham TW14 ... 150 A4
Hampton TW12 ... 173 A5
Shorediche Cl UB10 ... 60 B5
SHOREDITCH ... 95 B5
Shoreditch Ct 2 E8 ... 73 D1
Shoreditch High St
E2 ... 95 C3 243 B6
Shoreditch Ho N1 ... 235 D1
Shore Gr TW13 ... 151 C2
Shoreham Cl
Croydon CR0 ... 206 C3
DA5 ... 168 D3
Wandsworth SW18 ... 157 D6
Shoreham Rd BR5 ... 190 B1
Shoreham Rd (E)
TW6 ... 148 A6
Shoreham Rd (W)
TW6 ... 148 A6
Shoreham Way BR2 ... 209 A3
Shore Ho SW8 ... 137 B2
Shore Mews 30 E9 ... 74 C1
Shore Pl E9 ... 74 C1
Shore Point 2 IG9 ... 21 B2
Shore Rd E9 ... 74 C1
Shore Way 26 SW9 ... 138 C3
Shorncliffe Rd
SE1 ... 117 D1 263 C2
Shorndean St SE6 ... 164 A3
Shorne Cl 3 DA15 ... 168 B5
Shornefield Cl BR1 ... 210 C6
Shornells Way SE2 ... 124 C1
Shorrolds Rd
SW6 ... 135 B5 264 D4
Shortcroft Mead Ct
NW10 ... 68 A3
Shortcroft Rd KT17 ... 215 D1
Shortcrofts Rd RM9 ... 81 B2
Shorter St EC3 ... 117 D6 253 D6
Shortgate N12 ... 29 B6
Short La TW15, TW19 ... 148 B3
SHORTLANDS ... 208 C6
Shortlands
Brook Green W6 ... 112 D2
Harlington UB3 ... 127 B6
Shortlands Cl DA17 ... 125 B3
Edmonton N18 ... 17 B1
Shortlands Gdns BR2 ... 186 C1
Shortlands Gr BR2 ... 208 B6
Shortlands Rd
Beckenham BR2, BR3 ... 208 C6
Kingston u T KT2 ... 176 B3
Walthamstow E10 ... 53 D2
Shortlands Sta BR2 ... 186 C1
Short Path SE18 ... 144 D6
Short Rd Chiswick W4 ... 133 C6
Leyton E11 ... 76 C6
Stanwell TW19 ... 148 A5
Shorts Croft NW9 ... 44 D5
Shorts Gdns
WC2 ... 94 A1 240 A1
Shorts Rd SM5 ... 218 C3
Short St 7 Hendon NW4 ... 46 C5
SE1 ... 251 B2
Shortway SE9 ... 144 A2
Short Way
Colney Hatch N12 ... 30 C4
Twickenham TW2 ... 152 A4
Shotfield SM6 ... 219 B2
Shott Cl SM1 ... 218 A3
Shottendane Rd
SW6 ... 135 C4 265 A2
Shottery Cl SE9 ... 166 A1
Shottfield Ave SW14 ... 133 C1
Shottsford 1 W11 ... 91 C1
Shoulder of Mutton Alley
10 E14 ... 119 A6
Shouldham St
W1 ... 92 C2 237 B3
Showers Way UB3 ... 106 A5
Shrapnel Cl SE18 ... 144 A5
Shrapnel Rd SE9 ... 144 B2
Shreveport Ho 23 N19 ... 49 D2
Shrewsbury Ave
Harrow HA3 ... 44 A5
Mortlake SW14 ... 133 B1
Shrewsbury Cl KT6 ... 214 A6
Shrewsbury Ho
Chelsea SW3 ... 267 A5
Kennington SE11 ... 270 D5
Shrewsbury House Sch
KT6 ... 214 A6
Shrewsbury La SE18 ... 144 D4
Shrewsbury Mews 33
W2 ... 91 C2
Shrewsbury Rd
Beckenham BR3 ... 207 A6
Carshalton SM5 ... 202 C2
Friern Barnet N11 ... 31 D4
Harlington TW14, TW6 ... 149 B5
Notting Hill W2 ... 91 C1
Plashet E7 ... 77 D2
Shrewsbury St W10 ... 90 C3
Shrewsbury Wlk 9
TW7 ... 131 A2
Shrewton Rd SW17 ... 180 D3
Shri Swaminarayan
Mandir* NW10 ... 67 B2
Shroffold Rd BR1 ... 164 D1
Shropshire Cl CR4 ... 204 A5
Shropshire Ct W7 ... 86 D1
Shropshire Ho WC1 ... 239 B5
Shropshire Rd N22 ... 32 B3
Shroton St NW1 ... 92 C2 237 B4
Shrubberies The
Ilford IG2 ... 57 D4
Woodford E18 ... 37 A1
Shrubbery Cl N1 ... 235 B5
Shrubbery Gdns N21 ... 16 D4
Shrubbery Rd
Edmonton N9 ... 18 A1
Southall UB1 ... 107 C5
Streatham SW16 ... 182 A6
Shrubbery The
2 Surbiton KT6 ... 198 A1
7 Wanstead E11 ... 55 B4
Shrub Ct 5 SM2 ... 218 A2
Shrubland Gr KT4 ... 216 C5
Shrubland Rd
Hackney E8 ... 96 A6
Leyton E10 ... 53 C2
Walthamstow E17 ... 53 C4
Shrublands Ave CR0 ... 223 C4
Shrublands Cl
Forest Hill SE26 ... 162 C1
Whetstone N20 ... 14 B2
Shrubsall Cl SE9 ... 166 A3
Shrubs Ho SW1 ... 259 D3
Shurland Ave EN4 ... 14 B5
Shurland Gdns SE15 ... 139 D5
Shurlock Dr BR6 ... 227 A4
Shuters Sq W14 ... 254 C1
Shuttle Cl DA15 ... 167 D4
Shuttlemead DA5 ... 169 B4
Shuttle St E1 ... 96 A3
Shuttleworth Rd
SW11 ... 136 C3
Sibella Rd SW4 ... 137 D3
Sibford Ct 5 CR4 ... 202 D6
Sibley Cl Bexley DA6 ... 169 A6
Bromley BR1 ... 210 A4
Sibley Ct
Beckenham BR3 ... 186 C1
Hillingdon UB8 ... 83 A2
Sibley Gr E12 ... 78 A1
Sibthorpe Rd SE12 ... 165 C4
Sibthorp Rd 2 CR4 ... 180 D1
Sibton Rd SM5 ... 202 C2
Sicilian Ave WC1 ... 240 B3
Sidbury St
SW6 ... 135 A4 264 A2
SIDCUP ... 190 A5
Sidcup By Pass Rd
Sidcup DA14 ... 189 C6
St Paul's Cray BR5, BR7 ... 190 B3
Sidcup Hill DA14 ... 190 B5
Sidcup Hill Gdns
DA14 ... 190 C5
Sidcup Pl DA14 ... 190 A5
Sidcup Rd SE9 ... 166 A3
Sidcup Sta DA15 ... 168 A2
Sidcup Tech Ctr DA14 ... 190 D4
Siddeley Dr TW4 ... 129 A3
Siddons Ct WC2 ... 240 C1
Siddons Ho 8 NW3 ... 70 D3
Siddons La
NW1 ... 92 D3 237 D5
Siddons Rd
Croydon CR0 ... 220 D5
Forest Hill SE23 ... 163 A2
Tottenham N17 ... 34 A2
Side Rd E17 ... 53 B4
Sidewood Rd SE9 ... 167 B3
Sidford Ho SE1 ... 260 D5
Sidford Pl SE1 ... 116 B3 260 D5
Sidgwick Ho 26 SW9 ... 138 A3
Sidi Ct 2 N15 ... 50 D6
Sidings Mews N7 ... 72 C4
Sidings The E11 ... 54 A1
Sidlaw Ho N16 ... 51 D1
Sidmouth Ave TW7 ... 130 C3
Sidmouth Dr HA4 ... 62 A5
Sidmouth Ho
18 Camberwell SE15 ... 140 A5
Marylebone W1 ... 237 B2
26 Streatham SW2 ... 160 C4
Sidmouth Mews WC1 ... 233 C1
Sidmouth Par NW2 ... 68 C1
Sidmouth Rd
Bexley DA16 ... 146 C5
Leyton E10 ... 76 A5
Willesden NW2 ... 68 C1
Sidmouth St
WC1 ... 94 B4 233 C1
Sidney Ave N13 ... 32 B5
Sidney Boyd Ct NW6 ... 69 C1
Sidney Elson Way E6 ... 100 C5
Sidney Gdns TW8 ... 131 D6
Sidney Godley (VC) Ho 31
E2 ... 96 C4
Sidney Gr EC1 ... 234 C3
Sidney Ho
4 Globe Town E2 ... 96 D5
SE18 ... 144 B4
Sidney Miller Ct 8
W3 ... 110 D5
Sidney Rd
Beckenham BR3 ... 185 A1
Croydon SE25 ... 206 A4
Harrow HA2 ... 42 A6
Stockwell SW9 ... 138 B3
Twickenham TW1 ... 153 B5
Walton-on-T KT12 ... 194 B1
Wanstead E7 ... 77 A5
Wood Green N22 ... 32 B3
Sidney Sq E1 ... 96 C2
Sidney St E1 ... 96 C2
Sidworth St 5 E8 ... 74 B1
Siebert Rd SE3 ... 143 A6
Siedle Ho 9 SE18 ... 144 C6
Siege Ho 14 E1 ... 96 B1
Siemens Rd SE18 ... 121 D3
Sienna SE28 ... 123 D3
Sienna Ct TW13 ... 149 D1
Sierra Dr RM9 ... 103 D5
Sigdon Rd E8 ... 74 A3
Sigers The HA5 ... 40 B3
Signal Ho 9 London E8 ... 74 B1
SE1 ... 252 A1
Signmakers Yd NW1 ... 231 D5
Sigrist Sq 4 KT2 ... 176 A2
Silbury Ave CR4 ... 180 C2
Silbury Ho 9 SE26 ... 162 A1
Silbury St N1 ... 235 C2
Silchester Ct
Stanwell TW15 ... 148 A2
Thornton Heath CR7 ... 204 C5
Silchester Rd W10 ... 90 D1
Silecroft Rd DA7 ... 147 C4
Silesia Bldgs E8 ... 74 B1
Silex St SE1 ... 116 D4 251 D1
Silicone Bsns Ctr UB6 ... 87 C5
Silk Cl SE12 ... 165 A5
Silkfield Rd NW9 ... 45 C4
Silk Ho NW9 ... 45 B6
Silk Mills Path SE13 ... 142 A2
Silk Mills Sq E9 ... 75 B2
Silks Ct E11 ... 54 C1
Silk St EC2 ... 95 A2 242 B4
Silkstream Par HA8 ... 27 A2
Silkstream Rd HA8 ... 27 A2
Sillitoe Ho N1 ... 235 D5
Silsoe Ho NW1 ... 231 D3
Silsoe Rd N22 ... 50 B6
Silverbell Ct 1 N12 ... 29 D5
Silver Birch Ave E4 ... 35 B4
Silver Birch Cl
Forest Hill SE6 ... 163 B1
Friern Barnet N11 ... 31 A4
Ickenham UB10 ... 60 A4
SE28 ... 124 A5
Silver Birch Ct EN3 ... 18 D6
Silver Birch Gdns E6 ... 100 B3
Silverbirch Wlk 1
NW3 ... 71 A2
Silverburn Ho 4 SW9 ... 138 D4
Silver Cl Harrow HA3 ... 24 B3
SE14 ... 141 A5
Silvercliffe Gdns EN4 ... 2 C1
Silver Cres W4 ... 110 D2
Silver Ct N19 ... 71 C5
Silverdale Enfield EN2 ... 4 A1
Forest Hill SE26 ... 184 C6
NW1 ... 232 A2
Silverdale Ave IG3 ... 57 D4
Silverdale Cl
Cheam SM1 ... 217 B4
1 Ealing W7 ... 108 D5
Northolt UB5 ... 63 B3
Silverdale Ct EC1 ... 241 D6
Silverdale Dr
Chislehurst SE9 ... 166 A2
Sunbury TW16 ... 172 B1
Silverdale Factory Ctr
UB3 ... 106 A3
Silverdale Gdns UB3 ... 106 A4
Silverdale Ind Est
UB3 ... 106 A4
Silverdale Par IG3 ... 57 D4
Silverdale Rd
Bexleyheath DA7 ... 147 D3
Chingford E4 ... 36 B4
Hayes UB3 ... 106 A4
Petts Wood BR5 ... 211 A5
Silverhall St TW7 ... 131 A2
Silverholme Cl HA3 ... 44 A2
Silver Ind Est N17 ... 33 D1
Silver Jubilee Way
TW4 ... 128 B3
Silver La BR4 ... 224 B6
Silverland St E16 ... 122 B5
Silverleigh Rd CR7 ... 204 B4
Silvermead 7 E18 ... 37 A2
Silvermere Rd SE6 ... 163 D5
Silver Pl W1 ... 249 B6

Silver Rd
Shepherd's Bush
W12 112 D6
St Johns SE13 141 D2
Silvers 4 IG9 21 C3
Silver Spring Cl DA8 147 D6
Silver St Edmonton N18 33 C6
Enfield EN1 5 B2
Silverstone Ct 8 BR1 187 C1
Silverston Way HA7 25 C4
Silver Street Sta N18 33 D5
Silverthorn 17 NW6 91 D6
Silverthorne Lo EN1 17 C6
Silverthorne Rd SW8 137 B3
Silverthorn Gdns E4 19 C2
Silverton Lo SE19 183 C3
Silverton Rd W6 134 D6
SILVERTOWN 121 B4
Silvertown Way E16 121 A5
Silvertree La UB6 86 B4
Silver Way
Hillingdon UB10 82 D5
Romford RM7 59 D6
Silver Wing Ind Est
CR0 220 B2
Silver Wlk SE16 119 B5
Silverwood Cl BR3 185 C3
Silvester Ho
27 Bethnal Green E2 96 C4
1 Notting Hill W11 91 B1
Pinner HA5 40 A5
6 Stepney E1 96 B1
Silvester Rd SE22 161 D6
Silvester St SE1 252 C1
Silwex Ho E1 243 C5
Silwood St SE16 118 C1
Simba Ct TW1 152 D3
Simla Ho SE1 252 D1
Simmil Rd KT10 212 C3
Simmonds Ct SW5 255 C3
Simmons Cl
Chessington KT9 213 C2
East Barnet N20 14 C3
Simmons Dr RM8 81 A5
Simmons Gate KT10 212 A3
Simmons Ho
20 Bethnal Green E2 96 A4
Finsbury Pk N7 72 B6
Simmons La E4 20 B2
Simmons Rd SE18 122 D1
Simmons' Way N20 14 C2
Simms Cl SM5 218 C6
Simms Ct SW6 135 A2
Simms Gdns N2 30 A1
Simms Rd SE1 118 A2
Simnel Rd SE12 165 B4
Simon Cl W11 113 B6 244 D6
Simon Ct Paddington W9 91 C4
5 Woolwich SE28 124 B5
Simonds Rd E10 75 C6
Simone Cl BR1 187 D2
Simon Lo 31 SW19 156 D3
Simon Marks Jewish Prim
Sch N16 73 D6
Simons Wlk E15 76 B3
Simpson Cl N21 16 B6
Simpson Dr W3 89 B1
Simpson Ho
Lisson Gr NW8 230 A1
Vauxhall SE11 260 C1
Wembley HA9 65 D6
Simpson Rd
Hounslow TW4 151 B5
Richmond TW10 175 C6
Simpson's Rd BR2 209 A6
Poplar E14 119 D6
Simpson St SW11 136 C3
Simpson Way KT6 197 C3
Sim's Cotts KT10 212 D2
Sims Wlk SE3 142 D1
Sinclair Ct
21 Beckenham BR3 185 C3
Canonbury N5 73 A2
5 Croydon CR0 221 D6
Sinclair Gdns W14 112 D4
Sinclair Gr NW11 46 D3
Sinclair Ho Harrow HA7 24 D4
3 South Norwood
SW16 182 B3
1 Streatham SW12 159 D3
Sinclair Mans 13 W12 112 D4
Sinclair Pl SE4 163 C5
Sinclair Rd
Chingford Hatch E4 35 B5
W14 113 A3 254 A6
Sinclairs Ho 18 E3 97 B5
Sinclare Cl EN1 5 D4
Singapore Rd W13 109 A5
Singer St EC2 235 D1
Singlegate Prim Sch
SW19 180 B3
Singleton Cl
Mitcham SW17 180 D3
Thornton Heath CR0 205 A2
Singleton Rd RM9 81 B3
Singleton Scarp N12 29 C5
Sinnott Rd E17 34 D2
Sion Ct TW1 153 B3
Sion Ho SE13 142 A1
Sion-Manning RC Sch
for Girls
Kensal Town W10 91 A2
North Kensington W10 90 D2
Sion Rd TW1 153 B3
Sippetts Ct IG1 57 B1
SIPSON 126 C6
Sipson Cl UB7 126 C6
Sipson La UB3, UB7 126 D6
Sipson Rd
Harmondsworth UB7 126 C6
West Drayton UB7 104 B2
West Drayton UB7 104 C1
Sipson Way UB7 126 C5
Sir Abraham Dawes Cotts
SW15 135 A1
Sir Alexander Cl W3 111 D5
Sir Alexander Rd W3 111 D5
Sir Arthur Bliss Ct 4
SW19 180 D1
Sir Cyril Black Way 2
SW19 179 C3
Sirdar Rd Mitcham CR4 181 A4
Tottenham N22 33 A1
W11 113 A6 244 A5
Sir Francis Drake Prim
Sch SE8 119 A1
Sir George Monoux Sixth
Form Coll E17 35 D1
Sir Henry Floyd Ct HA7 9 B2
Sirinham Point SW8 270 D5
Sirius Bldg 18 E1 118 D6
Sir James Barrie Prim Sch
SW8 137 C4 269 B1
Sir John Cass Foundation
& Redcoat CE Sec Sch
E1 96 D2
Sir John Cass's
Foundation Prim Sch
EC3 95 C1 243 B1
Sir John Heron Prim Sch
E12 78 B4
Sir John Kirk Cl 33
SE5 139 A5
Sir John Lillie Prim Sch
SW6 135 A6 264 B5
Sir Martin Bowes Ho 9
SE18 122 C2
Sir Oswald Stoll
Foundation The SW6 265 C4
Sir Thomas Abney Sch
N16 51 B1
Sir Thomas More Est
SW3 136 B6 266 D5
Sirus Rd HA6 22 A5
Sir William Burrough Prim
Sch E14 97 A1
Sir William Powell's
Almshos SW6 135 A2
Sise La EC4 242 C1
Siskin Ho Edmonton N9 18 D3
14 Rotherhithe SE16 118 D2
Sisley Rd IG11 101 D6
Sispara Gdns SW18 157 B5
Sissinghurst Cl BR1 186 C5
Sissinghurst Ho 17
SE15 140 C6
Sissinghurst Rd CR0 206 A2
Sissulu Ct 8 E6 99 C6
Sister Mabel's Way 15
SE15 140 A5
Sisters Ave SW11 136 D1
Sistova Rd SW12 159 B3
Sisulu Pl SW9 138 C2
Sitarey Ct 4 W12 112 B5
Site of Changing of the
Guard* SW1 249 A1
Sittingbourne Ave EN1 17 B5
Sitwell Gr HA7 24 D5
Siverst Cl UB5 63 D2
Sivill Ho 9 E2 95 D4
Siviter Way RM10 81 D1
Siward Rd
Bromley BR2 209 C6
Tottenham N17 33 B2
Wandsworth SW17 158 A1
Six Bridges Ind Est 15
SE1 118 A1
Sixpenny Ct IG11 79 A2
Sixth Ave Hayes UB3 105 D5
Ilford E12 78 B4
West Kilburn W10 91 A4
Sixth Cross Rd TW2 152 A1
Skardu Rd NW2 69 A3
Skeena Hill SW18,
SW19 157 A4
Skeffington Rd E6 100 B6
Skeffington St SE18 123 A3
Skeggs Ho 5 E14 120 A3
Skegness Ho 3 N7 72 B1
Skelbrook St SW18 158 A2
Skelgill Rd SW15 135 B1
Skelley Rd E15 76 D1
Skelton Cl 7 E8 73 D2
Skelton Ho N16 73 C3
Skelton Rd E7 77 A2
Skelton's La E10 53 D2
Skelwith Rd W6 134 C6
Skenfrith Ho SE15 140 B6
Skerne Rd KT2 175 D2
Skerne Wlk KT2 175 D2
Sketchley Gdns SE16 118 D1
Sketty Rd EN1 5 D2
Skiers St E15 98 C6
Skiffington Cl SW2 160 C3
Skillen Lodge HA5 22 D2
Skinner Ct E17 53 C4
Skinner Pl SW1 258 A3
Skinners Almshouses
N13 16 C1
Skinners Company Sch
(Upper) N16 51 D2
Skinner's Company's
Lower Sch E5 52 B1
Skinners La EC4 252 B6
Hounslow TW5 129 D4
Skinner St EC1 94 C3 241 B6
Skipper Ct 6 IG11 101 A6
Skipsea Ho SW18 158 B5
Skipsey Ave E6 100 B4
Skipton Cl N11 31 A4
Skipton Dr UB3 105 A3
Skipton Ho SE4 141 A1
Skipwith Bldg EC1 241 A4
Skipworth Rd E9 96 C6
Skua Ct 33 SE8 141 B6
Skyline Ct SE1 263 C5
Skyline Plaza Bldg 19
E1 96 A1
Skylines E14 120 A4
Sky Peals Rd IG8 36 B3
Sky Studios E16 122 C4
Sladebrook Rd SE3 143 D2
Slade Ct Barnet EN5 1 D2
Brondesbury NW2 69 A3
Muswell Hill N10 31 B3
Sladedale Rd SE18 123 C1
Slade Ho TW4 151 B5
Sladen Pl 12 E5 74 B4
Slades Cl EN2 4 C2
Slades Dr BR7 189 A6
Slades Gdns EN2 4 C2
Slades Hill EN2 4 C2
Slades Rise EN2 4 C2
Slade The SE18 145 C6
Slade Twr E10 75 C6
Slade Way CR4 181 A2
Slagrove Pl SE13 163 D6
Slaidburn St
SW10 136 A6 266 B5
Slaithwaite Rd SE13 142 A1
Slaney Ct NW10 68 C1
Slaney Pl 1 N7 72 C3
Slater Cl 18 SE18 122 C2
Slatter 1 NW9 27 D2
Slattery Rd TW13 150 C3
Sleaford Ho 16 E3 97 C3
Sleaford Ind Est
SW8 137 C5 269 B3
Sleaford St
SW8 137 C5 269 B3
Sleat Ho 11 E3 97 B5
Sledmere Ct TW14 149 C3
Slievemore Cl 8 SW4 137 D2
Sligo Ho 8 E1 96 D3
Slingsby Pl WC2 250 A6
Slippers Pl SE16 118 B3
Slipway Ho 1 E14 119 D1
Sloane Ave
SW3 114 C2 257 B3
Sloane Avenue Mans
SW3 257 C3
Sloane Ct E SW3 258 A2
Sloane Ct W SW3 258 A2
Sloane Gate Mans
SW1 258 A4
Sloane Gdns
Belgravia
SW1 115 A2 258 A3
Orpington BR6 227 A5
Sloane Ho 7 E9 74 C1
Sloane Hospl BR3 186 B2
Sloane Sq SW1 257 D3
Sloane Square Sta
SW1 115 A2 258 A3
Sloane St SW1 114 D3 257 D5
Sloane Terr SW1 258 A4
Sloane Terr Mans
SW1 258 A4
Sloane Wlk CR0 207 B3
Sloan Ho RM10 81 D1
Slocum Cl SE28 124 C6
Slough La NW9 45 A3
Sly St 17 E1 96 B1
Smaldon Cl UB7 104 C3
Smallberry Ave TW7 130 D3
Smallberry Green Prim
Sch The TW7 131 A4
Smallbrook Mews W2 236 C1
Smallbugh Mans HA0 65 B4
Smalley Cl N16 73 D5
Smallwood Prim Sch
SW17 180 B6
Smallwood Rd SW17 180 B6
Smarden Cl DA17 125 C1
Smarden Gr SE9 188 B6
Smart's Pl
Edmonton N18 34 A5
WC1, WC2 240 B2
Smart St E2 96 D4
Smeaton Cl KT9 213 D2
Smeaton Ct SE1 262 A5
Smeaton Rd
Holdbrook EN3 7 C6
Wandsworth SW18 157 C4
Smeaton St E1 118 B5
Smedley St SW4 137 D3
Smeed Rd E3 75 C1
Smiles Pl SE13 142 A3
Smith Cl SE16 118 D5
Smithers Ho 3 SE20 184 D3
Smithfield Mkt EC1 241 D3
Smithfield St
EC1 94 D2 241 C3
Smithies Ct E15 76 A3
Smithies Rd SE2 124 B2
Smith's Ct W1 249 C6
Smithson Rd N17 33 B2
Smiths Point E13 99 A6
Smith Sq SW1 116 A3 260 A5
Smith St Surbiton KT5 198 B3
SW3 114 D1 257 C1
Smith's Yd SW18 158 A2
Smith Terr
SW3 114 D1 257 C1
Smithwood Cl SW19 157 A2
Smithy St E1 96 C2
Smithy Street Sch E1 96 C2
Smock Wlk CR0 205 A3
Smoothfield TW3 129 C1
Smugglers Way SW18 135 D1
Smyrk's Rd
SE17 117 C1 263 B1
Smyrna Mans 8 NW6 69 C1
Smyrna Rd NW6 69 C1
Smythe St E14 119 D6
Snakes La EN4, N14 3 C1
Snakes La E IG8 37 C4
Snakes La W IG8 37 B4
Snakey La TW13 172 B6
SNARESBROOK 54 D6
Snaresbrook Coll E18 37 A1
Snaresbrook Dr HA7 26 A6
Snaresbrook Hall 12
E18 55 A6
Snaresbrook Ho E18 54 D5
Snaresbrook Prim Sch
E18 55 A5
Snaresbrook Rd E11 54 D5
Snaresbrook Sta E11 55 A4
Snarsgate St W10 90 C2
Sneath Ave NW11 47 B2
Snell's Pk N18 33 D4
Sneyd Rd NW2 68 C4
Snowberry Cl E11 76 B4
Snowbury Rd 6 SW6 135 D3
Snow Ct 4 HA0 65 D3
Snowden Ave UB10 82 D5
Snowden St
EC2 95 C3 243 A5
Snowdon Cres UB3 105 A3
Snowdon Dr NW9 45 C3
Snowdon Rd TW6 149 A5
Snowdown Cl SE20 184 D2
Snowdrop Cl 2 TW12 173 C4
Snowe Ho SE27 160 D1
Snow Hill EC1 94 D2 241 C3
Snowman Ho NW6 91 D6
Snowsfields
SE1 117 B4 252 D2
Snowsfields Prim Sch
SE1 117 C4 253 A2
Snowshill Rd E12 78 A3
Snowy Fielder Waye
TW7 131 B3
Soames St SE15 139 D2
Soames Wlk KT3 177 C2
Soane Cl W5 109 D4
Soane Ct 10 NW1 71 C1
Soane Ho SE17 262 D1
Soane Mus The*
WC2 94 B1 240 C2
Soaphouse La TW8 132 A5
Soham Rd EN3 7 B6
SOHO 93 D1
Soho* W1 93 D1 239 C2
Soho Mills SM6 203 B1
Soho Parish CE Prim Sch
W1 115 D6 249 C6
Soho Sq W1 93 D1 239 C2
Soho St W1 239 C2
Sojourner-Truth Cl 11
E8 74 B2
Sola Ct 8 CR0 205 B1
Solander Gdns
13 Shadwell E1 118 C6
Stepney E1 118 B6
Solar Ct N3 29 D3
Soldene Ct N7 72 B2
Solebay St E1 97 A3
Solent Ct SW16 182 B1
Solent Ho 6 E1 97 A2
Solent Rd NW6 69 C3
Solent Rise E13 99 A4
Soley Mews WC1 234 A2
Solidarity Ho 5 NW10 68 C2
Solna Ave SW15 156 C6
Solna Rd N21 17 B4
Solomon Ave N9 34 A6
Solomons Ct N12 30 A3
Solomon's Pas SE15 140 B1
Solon New Rd SW4 138 A1
Solon Rd SW2 138 A1
Solway Cl TW4 129 A2
Solway Ho 12 E1 96 D3
Solway Rd
East Dulwich SE22 140 A1
Tottenham N22 32 D2
Somaford Gr EN4 14 B5
Somali Rd NW2 69 B3
Somborne Ho 11
SW15 156 A4
Sombrook Ho SE11 261 A3
Somerby Rd IG11 79 B1
Somercoates Cl EN4 2 C2
Somer Ct SW6 265 A5
Somerfield Rd N4 72 D6
Somerfield St SE16 118 D1
Somerford Cl HA5 40 A5
Somerford Gr
Shacklewell N16 73 D4
Tottenham N17 34 A3
Somerford Grove Est
N16 73 D4
Somerford St E1 96 B3
Somerford Way SE16 119 A4
Somerhill Ave DA15 168 B4
Somerhill Rd DA16 146 B3
Somerleyton Rd SW9 138 C1
Somersby Est SE20 184 C3
Somersby Gdns IG4 56 B4
Somers Cl NW1 232 C4
Somers Cres W2 237 A1
Somerset Ave
Chessington KT9 213 D4
DA16 145 D1
Wimbledon SW20 178 B1
Somerset Cl
New Malden KT3 199 C3
Tottenham N17 33 B1
Woodford IG8 37 A2
Somerset Ct
10 Buckhurst Hill IG9 21 C2
Ealing W7 86 D1
2 Hampton TW12 173 C2
Somerset Gdns
Highgate N6 49 A2
St Johns SE13 141 D3
Teddington TW11 174 C5
Thornton Heath SW16 204 B6
Tottenham N17 33 C3
Somerset Hall N17 33 C3
Somerset Ho
WC2 116 B6 250 D6
Somerset Ho SW19 157 A1
Somerset Lo
9 Brentford TW8 131 D6
5 New Barnet EN5 14 A6
Putney SW15 134 B1
Somerset Rd
Bedford Pk W4 111 B3
Brentford TW8 131 C6
Ealing W13 109 C5
Edmonton N18 33 D5
Harrow HA1 42 A4
Hendon NW4 46 C5
Holdbrook EN3 7 C5
Kingston u T KT1 176 B1
New Barnet EN5 14 A6
Southall UB1 85 C2
Teddington TW11 174 C5
Tottenham N17 51 D6
Walthamstow E17 53 C3
Wimbledon SW19 157 A1
Somerset Sq
W14 113 B4 244 C1
Somerset Waye TW5 129 A5
Somersham Rd DA7 147 A3
Somers Pl SW2 160 B4
Somers Rd
Tulse Hill SW2 160 B5
Walthamstow E17 53 B5
SOMERS TOWN 93 D4
Somers Town Est
NW1 93 C5 232 B3
Somers Way WD23 8 A4
Somerton Ave TW9 132 D2
Somerton Rd
Cricklewood NW2 69 A5
Nunhead SE15 140 B1
Somertrees Ave SE12 165 B2
Somervell Rd HA2 63 C3
Somerville Ave SW13 134 C6
Somerville Ct SW16 181 D4
Somerville Ho 10
SW15 156 D5
Somerville Point SE16 119 B4
Somerville Rd
Dagenham RM6 58 C4
Penge SE20 184 D3
Sonderburg Rd 13 N7 72 B6
Sondes St SE17 139 B6
Songhurst Cl CR0 204 B3
Sonia Ct Edgware HA8 26 B3
North Finchley N12 30 A6
Sonia Gdns
Heston TW5 129 C5
North Finchley N12 30 A6
Willesden NW10 67 D4
Sonning Ct CR0 222 A6
Sonning Gdns TW12 173 A4
Sonning Ho 32 E2 95 D4
Sonning Rd CR0 206 A3
Soper Cl
Chingford Hatch E4 35 B5
4 Forest Hill SE23 162 D2
Soper Mews EN3 7 C5
Sophia Cl N7 72 B2
Sophia Ho
10 Hammersmith W6 112 C1
Tottenham N15 51 D5
Sophia Rd Newham E13 99 B2
Walthamstow E10 53 D1
Sophia Sq 14 SE16 119 A6
Sopwith 2 NW9 27 D2
Sopwith Ave KT9 214 A3
Sopwith Cl KT2 176 B5
Sopwith Rd TW5 128 C5
Sopwith Way
Battersea
SW8 137 B5 268 C4
Kingston u T KT2 176 A2
Sorbus Ct EN2 4 D3
Sorensen Ct 2 E10 75 D6
Sorrel Cl SE28 124 A5
Sorrel Gdns E6 100 A2
Sorrel Ho TW3 130 A4
Sorrel La 17 E14 98 B1
Sorrell Cl
6 Brixton SW9 138 C3
SE14 141 A5
Sorrento Rd SM1 217 D5
Soseki Mus* SW4 137 B2
Sotheby Rd N5 73 A4
Sotheran Cl E8 96 A6
Sotheron Pl SW6 265 D3
Soudan Rd
SW11 136 D4 267 C1
Souldern Rd 10 W14 112 D3
South Access Rd E17 53 A3
Southacre NW9 27 D1
Southacre Way HA5 22 C2
SOUTH ACTON 110 D3
South Acton Sta W3,
W4 111 A3
South Africa Rd W12 112 B6
SOUTHALL 107 A5
Southall Ct UB1 107 B6
Southall Ent Ctr UB2 107 C4
Southall La TW5 106 B1
Southall Norwood Hospl
UB2 107 B3
Southall Pl SE1 252 C1
Southall Sta UB1 107 B4
Southall & West London
Coll UB1 107 A5
Southam Ho 9 W10 91 A3
Southampton Bldgs
WC2 241 A3
Southampton Gdns
CR4 204 A4
Southampton Mews
E16 121 B5
Southampton Pl WC1 240 B3
Southampton Rd
Maitland Pk NW5 70 D3
Stanwell TW19, TW6 148 B5
Southampton Row
WC1 94 A2 240 B4
Southampton St WC2 250 B6
Southampton Way
SE5 139 C5
Southam St W10 91 A3
South Audley St
W1 115 A5 248 B4
South Ave Chingford E4 20 A4
East Finchley NW11 47 D5
Richmond TW9 132 C3
Southall UB1 107 B6
Wallington SM5 219 A1
South Avenue Gdns
UB1 107 B6
Southbank KT7 197 B2
SOUTH BANK 116 B4
South Bank KT6 198 A3
South Bank Bsns Ctr
SW8 137 D6 269 D5
Southbank International
Sch NW3 70 A2
Southbank International
Sch (Westminster
Campus) W1 93 B2 238 C4
Southbank Int Sch
W11 113 C6 245 A5
South Bank Lo 2 KT6 198 A3
South Bank Terr KT6 198 A3
South Bank Univ
London SW8 137 D4 269 D2
SE1 116 D3 261 D6
SOUTH BEDDINGTON
219 C2
South Bermondsey Sta
SE16 118 C1
South Birkbeck Rd E11 76 B5
South Black Lion La 7
W6 112 A1
South Bldg SW1 259 B6
South Block 20 E1 118 C6
South Bolton Gdns
SW10 255 D2
SOUTHBOROUGH 197 D1
210 B3
Southborough Cl KT6 197 D1
Southborough High Sch
KT6 214 A5
Southborough Ho
SE17 263 B2
Southborough La BR1,
BR2 210 B4
Southborough Prim Sch
BR2 210 C4
Southborough Rd
Bromley BR1, BR2 210 A5
South Hackney E9 96 D6
Surbiton KT6 198 A1
Southborough Rd (The
Lane) KT6 198 A1
Southbourne BR2 209 A2
Southbourne Ave NW9 27 B1
Southbourne Cl HA5 41 A2
Southbourne Cres
NW4 47 A5
Southbourne Ct NW9 27 A1
Southbourne Gdns
Ilford IG1 79 A3
Ruislip HA4 40 B1
SE12 165 B6
Southbridge Pl CR0 221 A4
Southbridge Rd CR0 221 A4
Southbridge Way UB2 107 A4
SOUTH BROMLEY 98 B2
Southbrook Mews
SE12 164 D5
Southbrook Rd
Hither Green SE12 164 D5
Thornton Heath SW16 182 A2
South Building* SE10 142 B5
Southbury NW8 229 B6
Southbury Ave EN1 6 A1
Southbury Prim Sch
EN3 6 C1
Southbury Rd Enfield EN1 5 D2
Enfield EN1, EN3 6 B1
Southbury Sta EN3 6 B1
South Camden Com Sch
NW1 93 D5 232 C4
South Carriage Dr SW1,
SW7 114 D4 247 C2
South Chelsea Coll
SW9 138 B1
Southchurch Ct
Bowes Pk N13 32 B5
Newham E6 100 B5
Southchurch Rd E6 100 B5
South Cl Barnet EN5 1 B2
DA6 146 D1
Dagenham RM10 103 C6

South Cl *continued*
Highgate N6 49 B3
Morden SM4 201 C3
Pinner HA5 41 B2
Twickenham TW2 151 C1
West Drayton UB7 104 C3
South Colonnade The
E14 119 D5
Southcombe St W14 254 A4
South Common Rd
UB8 60 A2
Southcote Ave
Feltham TW13 150 A2
Tolworth KT5 198 D2
Southcote Rd
Croydon SE25 206 B3
Tufnell Pk N19 71 C4
Walthamstow E17 53 A4
Southcote Rise HA4 39 B2
Southcott Ho
31 Bromley E3 97 D4
W9 236 B5
South Countess Rd E17 53 B6
South Cres Newham E16 98 B3
WC1 239 C3
Southcroft SM1 218 C3
Southcroft Ave DA16 145 C2
West Wickham BR4 224 A6
Southcroft Rd BR6 227 C5
Streatham SW17 181 A4
South Cross Rd IG6 57 A4
South Croxted Rd
SE21 183 B6
SOUTH CROYDON 221 B1
South Croydon Sta
CR2 221 B3
South Ct 17 SW15 156 D5
Southdean Gdns
SW19 157 B2
South Dene NW7 11 B1
Southdene Ct N11 15 C1
Southdown N7 72 A2
Southdown Ave W7 109 A3
Southdown Cres
Harrow HA2 42 A1
Ilford IG2 57 C4
Southdown Dr SW20 178 D3
Southdown Rd SW20 178 D2
South Dr
Orpington BR6 227 C3
Ruislip HA4 39 C1
South Ealing Cemy
W5 109 D2
South Ealing Rd W5 109 D3
South Ealing Sta W5 109 D3
South Eastern Ave N9 17 D1
South Eastern Univ N7 72 B5
South Eaton Pl
SW1 115 A2 258 B4
South Eden Park Rd
BR3 207 D4
South Edwardes Sq
W8 255 A5
SOUTHEND 186 B6
South End
Croydon CR0 221 A4
W8 113 D3 255 D6
Southend Cl SE9 166 D5
South End Cl NW3 70 C4
Southend Cres SE9 166 D5
South End Gn NW3 70 C4
Southend Ho SE9 166 C4
Southend La SE6 185 C6
Southend Rd
Beckenham BR3 185 C2
Plashet E6 78 B1
Woodford IG8 37 D1
South End Rd NW3 70 C4
Southend Road (North
Circular Rd) E17, E18 36 C2
South End Row
W8 113 D3 255 D6
Southern Ave
East Bedfont TW14 150 A3
South Norwood SE25 205 D6
Southerngate Way
SE14 141 A5
Southern Gr E3 97 B3
Southernhay IG10 21 D6
Southern Perimeter Rd
Hatton TW14, TW6 149 B6
West Bedfont TW19,
TW6 148 C5
Southern Rd
Fortis Green N2 48 D5
Newham E13 99 B5
Southern Road Prim Sch
E13 99 B5
Southern Row W10 91 A3
Southern St N1 233 C4
Southern Way
Greenwich SE10 120 D3
Romford RM7 59 C3
Southerton Rd W6 112 C2
South Esk Rd E7 77 C2
Southey Ho SE17 262 B2
Southey Mews E16 121 A5
Southey Rd
Brixton SW9 138 C4
Merton SW19 179 C3
Tottenham N15 51 C4
Southey St SE20 184 D3
Southfield EN5 12 D5
Southfield Cl UB8 82 C4
Southfield Cotts W7 108 D4
Southfield Ct E11 76 D5
Southfield Gdns TW1,
TW2 174 D6
Southfield Lo W4 111 B4
Southfield Pk HA2 41 D5
Southfield Prim Sch
W4 111 C4
Southfield Rd
Acton W4 111 B4
Enfield EN3 18 C5
St Paul's Cray BR7 211 D6
SOUTHFIELDS 157 D3
Southfields
Hendon NW4 46 B6
Thames Ditton KT8 196 C3
Southfields Ave TW15 170 D4
Southfields Com Coll
SW18 157 C3
Southfields Ct SM3 217 C6
Southfields Rd SW18 157 C5
Southfields Sta SW18 157 B3
Southfleet Rd BR6 227 C4
SOUTHGATE 16 B4
South Gate Ave TW13 171 B6
Southgate Cir 3 N14 15 D3
Southgate Coll N14 15 D2
Southgate Ct N1 73 B1
Southgate Gr N1 73 B1
Southgate Ho 7 E17 54 A6
Southgate Rd
N1 95 B6 235 D6
Southgate Sch EN4 15 B6
Southgate Sta N14 15 D3
Southgate Way N2 30 C2
South Gdns
Mitcham SW19 180 B3
Wembley HA9 66 C6
South Gipsy Rd DA16 146 D2
South Glade The DA5 169 B3
South Gn NW9 27 C2
South Gr Highgate N6 49 A1
Tottenham N15 51 B4
Walthamstow E17 53 B4
South Greenford Sta
UB6 86 C4
South Grove Ho N6 49 A1
South Grove Prim Sch
E17 53 B3
SOUTH HACKNEY 96 C6
SOUTH HAMPSTEAD 70 A1
South Hampstead High
Sch NW3 70 B2
South Hampstead High
Sch Jun Dept NW3 70 A2
South Hampstead Sta
NW8 70 A1
South Harringay Jun & Inf
Schs N4 50 D4
SOUTH HARROW 63 D5
South Harrow Sta HA2 64 A5
South Hill BR7 188 B4
South Hill Ave HA1, HA2 64 B5
South Hill Gr HA1 64 C4
South Hill Pk NW3 70 C4
South Hill Pk Gdns
NW3 70 C4
South Hill Rd BR2 208 C5
Southholme Cl SE19 183 C2
Southill La HA5 40 B5
Southill Rd BR7 188 B3
Southill St E14 97 D1
South Island Pl SW9 138 C5
SOUTH KENSINGTON
114 A1
South Kensington Sta
SW7 114 B2 256 D4
South Kensington Station
Arc SW7 256 D4
South Kenton Sta HA9 43 C1
South La
Kingston u T KT1 197 D6
New Malden KT3 199 B4
SOUTH LAMBETH 138 A4
South Lambeth Pl
SW8 270 B6
South Lambeth Rd
SW8 138 A5 270 B4
Southland Rd SE18 145 D5
Southlands Ave BR6 227 C3
Southlands Ct BR2 209 D5
Southlands Dr SW19 156 D2
Southlands Gr BR1 210 A6
Southlands Rd BR1,
BR2 209 D5
Southland Way TW7 152 B6
South La W KT3 199 B5
South Lo
6 New Barnet EN5 13 D6
NW8 229 C2
Twickenham TW2 152 A5
South Lodge Ave CR4, CR7,
SW16 204 A5
South Lodge Cres EN2 3 D1
South Lodge Dr N14 15 D6
South London Montessori
Sch SW11 267 A1
South Mall The N9 18 A1
South Mead
Grahame Pk NW9 27 D2
West Ewell KT19 215 D1
Southmead Prim Sch
SW19 157 A3
Southmead Rd SW19 157 A3
South Merton Sta
SW20 201 B6
South Molton La
W1 93 B1 238 C1
South Molton Rd E16 99 A1
South Molton St
W1 93 B1 238 C1
Southmont Rd KT10 212 C5
Southmoor Way E9 75 B3
South Mount N20 14 A2
SOUTH NORWOOD 205 C6
South Norwood Ctry Pk*
SE25 206 C5
South Norwood Hill SE19,
SE25 183 D1
South Norwood Prim Sch
SE25 206 A5
South Oak Rd SW16 182 B6
Southold Rise SE9 166 B1
Southolm St
SW11 137 B4 268 D1
South Ordnance Rd EN3 7 C5
Southover BR1 187 A5
Finchley N12 29 C6
SOUTH OXHEY 22 B6
South Par
Acton Green W4 111 B2
Edgware HA8 26 C1
Wallington SM6 219 C2
South Parade
SW3 114 B1 256 D2
South Park Bsns Ctr
IG3 79 C6
South Park Cres
Catford SE6 164 D3
Ilford IG1 79 C5
Southpark Ct SW19 179 C4
South Park Ct 24 BR3 185 C3
South Park Dr IG3 79 C4
South Park Gr KT3 199 A5
South Park Hill Rd
CR2 221 B4
South Park Mews
SW6 135 D2
South Park Prim Sch
IG3 79 C5
South Park Rd
Ilford IG1 79 B5
Wimbledon SW19 179 D4
South Park Terr IG1 79 C5
South Park Villas IG3 79 C4
South Park Way HA4 62 C3
South Pl
Broadgate
EC2 95 B2 242 D3
Enfield EN3 18 C6
Surbiton KT5 198 B2
South Pl Mews EC2 242 D3
Southport Rd SE18 123 B2
South Quay Plaza E14 119 D4
South Quay Sta E14 119 D4
South Rd Brentford W5 109 D2
Edgware HA8 26 D2
Edmonton N9 18 A3
Feltham TW13 172 D5
Forest Hill SE23 162 D2
Hampton TW12 173 B4
Heston TW5 128 D6
Mitcham SW19 180 B4
Southall UB1 107 B5
Twickenham TW2 152 B1
West Drayton UB7 104 C3
South Residence IG3 58 B4
South Ridge BR2 209 C5
Southridge Pl SW20 178 D3
South Rise W2 247 B6
South Rise Prim Sch
SE18 123 B1
South Rise Way SE18 123 B2
South Row SE3 142 D3
SOUTH RUISLIP 62 D4
South Ruislip Sta HA4 62 C3
Southsea Rd KT1 198 A5
South Sea St SE16 119 B3
Southside N7 71 D4
South Side W6 111 D3
Southside Comm
SW19 178 D4
Southside Ind Est SW8 269 A2
Southside Quarter 4
SW11 136 D3
Southside Sh Ctr
SW18 157 D5
Southspring DA15 167 B4
South Sq
Hampstead Garden Suburb
NW11 47 D3
WC1 241 A3
South St Bromley BR1 187 A1
Enfield EN3 18 D6
Isleworth TW7 131 A2
Mayfair W1 115 A5 248 B4
South Tenter St
E1 95 D1 243 D1
South Terr
Muswell Hill N22 31 D1
Surbiton KT6 198 A3
SW7 114 C2 257 A4
South Thames Coll
(Battersea Ctr)
SW11 136 D4 267 D1
South Thames Coll
(Putney Ctr) SW15 156 D6
South Thames Coll
(Roehampton Ctr)
SW15 156 A5
South Thames Coll
(Tooting Ctr) SW17 180 C5
South Thames Coll
(Wandsworth Ctr)
SW18 157 D6
SOUTH TOTTENHAM 51 D3
South Tottenham Sta
N15 51 D4
South Vale Harrow HA1 64 C4
West Norwood SE19 183 C4
Southvale Rd SE3 142 C3
South View BR1 187 C1
Wimbledon SW19 178 D4
Southview Ave NW10 67 D3
Southview Cl SW17 181 A5
South View Cl DA5 169 B5
South View Cres IG2 56 D3
South View Ct
8 Forest Hill SE23 162 C3
South Norwood SE19 183 A3
Southview Dr E18 55 B6
Southview Gdns SM6 219 C1
Southview Rd BR1 186 B6
South View Rd
Hornsey N8 50 A6
Pinner HA5 22 B4
South Villas NW1 71 D2
Southville
SW8 137 D4 269 D1
Southville Cl
East Bedfont TW14 149 C3
West Ewell KT19 215 B1
Southville Cres TW14 149 C3
Southville Jun & Inf Schs
TW14 149 D3
Southville Rd
East Bedfont TW14 149 C4
Thames Ditton KT7 197 B2
SOUTHWARK 117 B5
Southwark Bridge SE1,
EC4 117 A6 252 B5
Southwark Bridge Rd
SE1 117 A5 252 B3
Southwark Cath*
SE1 117 B5 252 C4
Southwark Coll
SE1 116 D4 251 C2
Southwark Coll
(Blackfriars Ctr) SE1 251 C3
Southwark Coll
(Camberwell Ctr)
SE5 139 C5
Southwark Coll (Grange
Ctr) SE1 263 B5
Southwark Coll (Surrey
Docks Ctr) SE16 118 B3
Southwark Park Est 11
SE16 118 B2
Southwark Park Prim Sch
SE16 118 B3
Southwark Park Rd
SE16 118 A2
Southwark Pl BR1 210 B6
Southwark St
SE1 117 A5 252 A3
Southwater Cl
Beckenham BR3 185 D3
8 Poplar E14 97 B1
Southway
Hampstead Garden Suburb
NW11 47 D4
Hayes BR2 209 A2
Totteridge N20 13 C2
Wallington SM6 219 C4
West Barnes SW20 200 D5
South Way
Croydon CR0 223 A5
Friern Barnet N11 31 C4
Harrow HA2 41 C5
Lower Edmonton N9 18 C2
Wembley HA9 66 C3
Southway Cl 9 W12 112 B4
Southwell Ave UB5 63 C2
Southwell Gdns SW7 256 A3
Southwell Grove Rd
E11 76 C6
Southwell Ho
8 Bermondsey SE16 118 B2
13 Stoke Newington N16 73 C3
Southwell Rd
Camberwell SE5 139 A2
Harrow HA3 43 D3
Thornton Heath CR0 204 C3
South Western Rd
TW1 153 B5
Southwest Rd E11 54 B1
South Wharf Rd
W2 92 B1 236 D2
Southwick Mews W2 236 D2
Southwick Pl W2 237 A1
Southwick St
W2 92 C1 237 A2
Southwick Yd W2 237 A1
SOUTH WIMBLEDON 179 D4
South Wimbledon Sta
SW19 179 D3
South Wlk
Coney Hall BR4 224 C5
Hayes UB3 83 B2
Southwold Dr IG11 80 A3
Southwold Mans W9 91 C4
Southwold Prim Sch
E5 74 B6
Southwold Rd DA5 169 D5
Upper Clapton E5 74 C6
Southwood Ave
Highgate N6 49 B2
Kingston u T KT2, KT3 177 A2
Southwood Cl BR1 210 B5
North Cheam KT4 200 D1
Southwood Ct EC1 234 C1
Hampstead Garden Suburb
NW11 47 D4
Southwood Dr KT5 199 A1
South Woodford Sta
E18 37 B1
Southwood Gdns
Hinchley Wood KT10 213 A5
Ilford IG2 56 D5
Southwood Hall N6 49 B3
Southwood Ho
New Eltham SE9 166 D2
Notting Hill W11 244 A6
Southwood Hospl
(Geriatric) N6 49 A2
Southwood Hts N6 49 B2
Southwood La N6 49 A2
Southwood Lawn Rd
N6 49 B2
Southwood Mans N6 49 B2
Southwood Park N6 49 A2
Southwood Prim Sch
RM9 81 A4
Southwood Rd SE9 166 D2
Woolwich SE28 124 B5
Southwood Smith Ho 4
E2 96 B4
Southwood Smith St
N1 234 C5
South Worple Ave
SW14 133 C2
Southwyck Ho SW9 138 C1
South Yd EC1 242 C4
Sovereign Bsns Ctr EN3 7 B2
Sovereign Cl Ealing W5 87 C2
Ruislip HA4 39 C1
Stepney E1 118 B6
Sovereign Cres SE16 119 A6
Sovereign Ct BR2 210 B3
East Molesey KT8 195 B5
Harlington UB7 126 D5
6 Richmond TW9 132 B1
13 Stepney E1 118 B6
Sovereign Gr HA0 65 D5
Sovereign Ho
Ashford TW15 170 A6
23 Bethnal Green E1 96 B3
Chislehurst BR7 189 B3
Edgware NW7 27 B6
3 Wimbledon SW19 179 A4
Woolwich SE18 122 B3
Sovereign Mews
Barnet EN4 2 D2
6 Haggerston E2 95 D5
Sovereign Pk NW10 88 D3
Sovereign Pl HA1 42 D4
Sovereign Rd IG11 102 C4
Sovreign Ct HA6 22 A2
Sowerby Cl SE9 166 B6
Space Apartments N22 32 B3
Space Bsns Pk NW10 88 D4
Spa Central 1 SW16 182 A3
Space Waye TW14 150 B6
Spa Cl SE19 183 C2
Spa Ct
12 Bermondsey SE16 118 A3
Streatham SW16 182 B6
Spafield St EC1 241 A6
Spa Hill CR7, SE19 183 B2
Spalding Cl HA8 27 C3
Spalding Ct HA8 26 B6
Spalding Ho SE4 163 A6
Spalding Rd
Hendon NW4 46 C3
Streatham SW17 181 B5
Spanby Rd E3 97 C3
Spangate SE3 142 D2
Spaniards Cl NW11 48 B1
Spaniards End NW3 48 B1
Spaniards Rd NW3 70 A6
Spanish Pl W1 238 B2
Spanish Rd SW18 158 A6
Spanswick Lo 2 N15 50 D5
Spa Rd SE16 117 D3 263 D5
Sparkbridge Rd HA1 42 C5
Sparkes Cl BR2 209 B5
Sparke Terr 2 E16 98 D1
Sparkford Gdns N11 31 A5
Sparkford Ho SW11 266 D2
Sparks Cl Acton W3 89 B1
Dagenham RM8 80 D6
Hampton TW12 173 A4
Sparrow Cl TW12 173 A4
Sparrow Ct E4 36 A4
Sparrow Dr BR5 211 B1
Sparrow Farm Com Jun
Sch KT17 216 B4
Sparrow Farm Dr
TW14 150 D4
Sparrow Farm Inf Sch
TW14 150 C4
Sparrow Farm Jun Sch
TW14 150 C4
Sparrow Farm Rd KT17,
KT4 216 B4
Sparrow Gn RM10 81 D5
Sparrow's Farm L Ctr
SE9 167 A4
Sparrows Herne WD23 8 A4
Sparrows La SE9 167 A3
Sparrows Way WD23 8 A4
Sparsholt Rd
Barking IG11 101 C6
Finsbury Pk N19 50 B1
Sparta St SE10 142 A4
Spa Sch SE1 118 A2
Spa View 6 SW16 160 B1
Speakers' Corner*
W1 114 D6 247 D6
Speaker's Ct 3 CR0 205 B1
Speakman Ho SE4 141 A2
Spearman St 8 SE18 144 C6
Spear Mews
SW5 113 C2 255 B3
Spearpoint Gdns IG2 57 D5
Spears Rd N19 50 A1
Speart La TW5 129 A5
Spectacle Works E13 99 C4
Spectrum Ho NW5 71 A4
Spectrum Twr 1 IG1 79 A6
Spedan Cl NW3 70 A5
Speechly Mews E8 73 D3
Speed Ho EC2 242 C4
Speedwell Ct 9 N12 29 D6
Speedwell Ho 11 N12 29 D6
Speedwell St 5 SE8 141 C5
Speedy Pl WC1 233 A1
Speer Rd KT7 196 D3
Speirs Cl KT3 199 D3
Spekehill SE9 166 B1
Speke Rd CR7 183 B1
Speldhurst Cl 2 BR2 208 D4
Speldhurst Rd
Bedford Pk W4 111 B3
Homerton E9 74 D1
Spellbrook Wlk N1 235 B6
Spelman Ho 15 E1 96 A2
Spelman St E1 96 A2
Spelthorne Coll TW15 170 B6
Spelthorne Gr TW16 171 D3
Spelthorne Inf Sch
TW15 171 B4
Spelthorne Jun Sch
TW15 171 B4
Spelthorne La TW15,
TW17 171 A2
Spence Cl SE16 119 B4
Spencer Ave
Bowes Pk N13 32 B4
Hayes UB4 84 A2
Spencer Cl BR6 227 D6
Church End N3 29 C1
Ealing NW10 88 B4
Woodford IG8 37 C5
Spencer Ct 5 BR6 227 A3
6 Finchley N3 29 D3
Wimbledon SW20 178 B2
Spencer Dr N2 48 A3
Spencer Gdns SW14 155 A6
Spencer Hill SW19 179 A3
Spencer Hill Rd SW19 179 A3
Spencer Ho
31 Clapham SW8 137 D3
Hendon NW4 46 B4
24 Putney SW19 156 D3
Vale of Health NW3 70 B5
Wimbledon SW19 156 D1
Spencer House Mus*
SW1 115 C5 249 A3
Spencer Mews
Fulham W6 264 A6
South Lambeth SW9 270 C1
Spencer Park Ct
SW18 158 B6
Spencer Pk
East Molesey KT8 196 A4
Wandsworth SW18 158 B6
Spencer Pl
16 Islington N1 72 D1
SW1 259 B5
Thornton Heath CR0 205 B2
Spencer Rd Acton W3 111 A5
Bromley BR1 186 D3
Carshalton CR4 203 A2
Chingford E17 36 A1
Chiswick W4 133 A5
East Molesey KT8 196 A4
Friern Barnet N11 31 B6
Harrow HA3 24 C1
Hornsey Vale N8 50 B4
Hounslow TW3, TW5,
TW7 130 A4
Ilford IG3 57 D1
Mitcham CR4 203 A6
Newham E6 99 D6
South Croydon CR2 221 C3
Tottenham N17 34 A2
Twickenham TW2 152 C2
Wandsworth SW18 158 B6
Wembley HA0 65 C6
Wimbledon SW20 178 B2
Spencer Rise NW5 71 B5
Spencer St
Finsbury EC1 94 D4 234 C1
Southall UB2 106 D4
Spencer Wlk
23 Hampstead NW3 70 A4
Putney SW15 134 D1
Spencer Yd SE3 142 D3
Spenlow Ho 2 SE16 118 A3
Spenser Ct 5 TW10 175 D6
Spenser Gr N16 73 C4
Spenser Mews SE21 161 B3
Spenser Rd SE24 160 D6
Spenser St SW1 259 B6
Spens Ho WC1 240 C5
Spensley Wlk N16 73 B5
Speranza St SE18 123 D1
Sperling Rd N17 33 C1
Spert St E14 119 A6
Speyside N14 15 C5
Spey St E14 98 A2
Spezia Rd NW10 90 A5
Spice Ct
10 Battersea SW11 136 A2
2 St George in t East
E1 118 A5
Spice Quay Htss SE1 253 D3
Spicer Cl
Brixton SE5, SW9 138 D3
Walton-on-T KT12 194 C3
Spicer Ct EN1 5 C2
Spicer Ho E2 96 A4
Spices Yd CR0 221 A4
Spigurnell Rd N17 33 B2
Spikes Bridge Rd UB1 107 A6
Spilsby Cl NW9 27 C1
Spindle Cl SE18 122 A3
Spindle Ho 8 DA15 168 A1
Spindlewood Gdns
CR0 221 C4
Spindrift Ave E14 119 D2

Spinel Cl SE18 123 D1
Spinnaker Cl IG11 102 B4
Spinnaker Ct 2 KT1 175 D2
Spinnaker Ho 21 E14 119 C4
Spinnells Rd HA2 41 B1
Spinney Cl
Beckenham BR3 207 D5
New Malden KT3 199 C4
Worcester Pk KT4 215 D6
Yiewsley UB7 104 A6
Spinney Dr TW14 149 A4
Spinney Gdns
Dagenham RM9 81 A3
Dulwich SE19 183 D5
Spinney Oak BR1 188 A1
Spinneys The BR1 188 B1
Spinney The
Barnes SW13 134 B6
Barnet EN5 1 D3
Cheam SM3 216 C4
DA14 191 A5
Edgware HA7 26 A6
Southgate N21 16 C4
Streatham SW16 159 D1
Sunbury TW16 172 A2
Wembley HA0 65 A5
Spire Ct 10 TW10 154 A5
Spire Ho W2 246 B6
Spires The EN5 1 A2
Spirit Quay E1 118 B5
SPITALFIELDS 95 D2
Spital Sq E1 95 C2 243 B4
Spital St E1 96 A2
Spital Yd E1 243 B4
Spitfire Bsns Pk CR0 220 C2
Spitfire Est The TW5 106 C1
Spitfire Rd SM6 220 A1
Spitfire Way TW5 106 C1
Splendour Wlk SE16 118 C1
Spode Ho SE11 261 A5
Spode Wlk NW3 69 D3
Spondon Rd N15 52 A5
Spoonbill Way UB4 84 D2
Spooner 8 NW9 27 D3
Spooner Ho TW5 129 C6
Spooner Wlk SM6 219 D3
Sporle Ct 6 SW11 136 B2
Sportsbank St SE6 164 A4
Spottons Gr N17 33 A2
Spout Hill CR0 223 C3
Spratt Hall Rd E11 55 A3
Spray St SE18 122 D2
Spreighton Rd KT8 195 D5
Sprewell SW15 157 A5
Spriggs Ho 14 N1 72 D1
Sprimont Pl
SW3 114 D1 257 C2
Springall St 9 SE15 140 B5
Springalls Wharf 2
SE16 118 A4
Springbank N21 16 B5
Springbank Rd SE13 164 C5
Springbank Wlk NW1 71 D1
Springbourne Ct BR3 186 A2
Spring Bridge Rd W5 109 D6
Spring Cl Barnet EN5 12 D6
Dagenham RM8 58 D1
Springclose La SM3 217 A2
Spring Cnr TW13 149 D1
Spring Cott 10 W12 112 A4
Spring Cotts KT6 197 D4
Spring Court Rd EN2 4 C5
Springcroft Ave N2 48 D5
Spring Ct
Brondesbury NW2 69 B2
Ealing W7 108 B6
Edgware HA8 26 B5
10 Wanstead E18 55 B6
Springdale Rd N16 73 B4
Spring Dr HA5 40 A3
Springett Ho 15 SW2 160 B6
Springfield Bushey WD23 8 B3
South Norwood SE25 206 A6
Upper Clapton E5 52 B1
Springfield Ave
Hampton TW12 173 D4
Hornsey N10 49 C6
Merton SW20 201 B6
Springfield Cl
Finchley N12 29 D5
Stanmore HA7 9 A1
Springfield Com Prim Sch
N16 52 A3
Springfield Ct
7 Dagenham W3 89 A1
1 Friern Barnet N20 14 D1
Hampstead NW3 70 C1
2 Ilford IG1 78 D3
9 Kingston u T KT1 198 A6
Upper Clapton E5 52 B1
Wallington SM6 219 B3
Springfield Dr IG2 57 A3
Springfield Gdns BR1 210 B5
Kingsbury NW9 45 B4
Ruislip HA4 40 B1
Upper Clapton E5 52 B1
West Wickham BR4 223 D6
Woodford IG8 37 C3
Springfield Gr SE7 143 C6
Sunbury TW16 172 A2
Springfield Ho
Acton W3 111 A5
1 Camberwell SE5 139 C3
13 Dalston E8 73 D2
Springfield Hospl
SW17 158 C1
Springfield La NW6 91 D6
Springfield Mount
NW9 45 C4
Springfield Pl KT3 199 A5
Springfield Prim Sch
TW16 171 D1
Springfield Rd
Ashford TW15 170 B5
Bexleyheath DA7 147 D1
Bromley BR1 210 B5
Chingford E4 20 C4
Ealing W7 108 C5
Friern Barnet N11 31 C5
Harrow HA1 42 C3
Hayes UB4 106 C5
Kingston u T KT1 198 A6
Newham E15 98 C4
Penge SE26 184 B5
Plashet E6 78 B1
South Norwood CR7 183 A2
St John's Wood
NW8 92 A6 229 B5
8 Teddington TW11 175 A5
Tottenham Hale N15 52 A5
Twickenham TW2 151 C3
Wallington SM6 219 B3
Walthamstow E17 53 B3
Welling DA16 146 B2
Wimbledon SW19 179 B5
Springfield Rise SE26 162 B1
Springfields 16 EN5 13 D6
Springfield Wlk
3 BR6 211 B1
Paddington NW6 91 D6
Spring Gdns
East Molesey KT8 196 A5
Islington N5 73 A3
SW1 116 A5 250 A4
Wallington SM6 219 C3
Woodford IG8 37 C3
Spring Gr
Brentford W4 132 C6
Hampton TW12 173 D2
Loughton IG10 21 D5
Mitcham CR4 181 A2
SPRING GROVE 130 C3
Spring Grove Cres TW3,
TW5 130 A4
Spring Grove Prim Sch
TW7 130 B3
Spring Grove Rd
Hounslow TW3, TW5,
TW7 130 A4
Richmond TW10 154 B6
Springhallow Sch W13 87 A1
Spring Hill
Forest Hill SE26 184 C6
Upper Clapton E5 52 A2
Springhill Cl SE5 139 B2
Spring Ho
Merton SW19 179 B2
WC1 234 A1
Springhurst Cl CR0 223 B4
Spring La
Croydon SE25 206 B3
Muswell Hill N10 49 A6
Upper Clapton E5 52 B1
Spring Lake HA7 25 B6
Spring Mews W1 237 D4
SPRING PARK 223 B5
Spring Park Ave CR0 222 D6
Springpark Dr
Beckenham BR3 208 A6
Stoke Newington N4 51 A1
Spring Park Prim Sch
CR0 223 C5
Spring Park Rd CR0 222 D6
Spring Pl
Camden Town NW5 71 B3
Church End N3 29 C1
Springpond Rd RM9 81 A3
Spring Rd TW13 149 D1
Springrice Rd SE13 164 B5
Spring Shaw Rd BR5 190 A2
Spring St W2 92 B1 236 C1
Spring Terr TW10 154 A6
Springtide Cl 10 SE15 140 A4
Spring Vale DA7 147 D1
Springvale Ave TW8 110 A1
Springvale Ct SE12 143 A1
Springvale Terr 5
W14 112 D3
Spring Villa Rd HA8 26 C3
Springwater WC1 240 C4
Springwater Cl SE18 144 C4
Springway HA1 42 B2
Springwell Ave NW10 89 D6
Springwell Cl SW16 182 B6
Springwell Ct TW5 128 D3
Springwell Jun & Inf Schs
TW5 129 A5
Springwell Rd
Heston TW5 128 D4
West Norwood SW16 182 C5
Spring Wlk E1 96 A2
Springwood Cl 8 E3 97 C5
Springwood Cres HA8 11 A2
Springwood Ct CR2 221 C4
Sprowston Mews E7 77 A3
Sprowston Rd E7 77 A3
Spruce Ct W5 110 A3
Sprucedale Gdns CR0 222 D4
Spruce Hills Rd E17 36 A1
Spruce Ho
2 Brentford TW8 131 C5
15 Rotherhithe SE16 118 D4
Spruce Pk BR2 208 D5
Sprules Rd SE4 141 A3
Spurfield KT8 195 D6
Spurgeon Ave SE19 183 B2
Spurgeon Rd SE19 183 B3
Spurgeon's Coll SE25 183 C1
Spurgeon St
SE1 117 B3 262 C6
Spur Ho 10 SW19 179 D2
Spurling Rd
Dagenham RM9 81 B2
East Dulwich SE22 139 D1
Spur Rd Brentford TW7 131 B5
Edgware HA8 26 A6
Feltham TW14 128 B1
SE1 116 C4 251 A2
Tottenham N15 51 B5
Wallend IG11 101 A4
Spurstowe Rd E8 74 B2
Spurstowe Terr E8 74 B3
Spurway Par 2 IG2 56 B4
Square Rigger Row 7
SW11 136 A2
Square The
Hammersmith W6 112 C1
Hayes UB11 105 B5
Ilford IG1 56 C2
Leyton E10 76 A5
12 Richmond TW10 153 D6
SW6 265 A1
Wallington SM5 219 A3
Woodford IG8 37 A5
Squarey St SW17 158 A1
Squire Ct 2 CR0 205 C1
Squire Gdns NW8 229 C1
Squire's Almshouses 7
E17 53 D5
Squires Bridge Rd
KT17 192 B5
Squires Ct Finchley N3 30 A2
SW4 270 B1
Wimbledon SW19 179 C6
Squires Ho 3 SE18 144 D6
Squires La N3 30 A2
Squire's Mount NW3 70 B5
Squire's Rd TW17 192 C5
Squires The RM7 59 D3
Squires Wlk TW15 171 B3
Squires Wood Dr BR7 188 B3
Squirrel Cl TW4 128 C2
Squirrel Mews W13 109 A6
Squirrels Cl
Hillingdon UB10 60 C1
North Finchley N12 30 A6
Orpington BR6 211 C1
Squirrels Ct KT4 215 D6
Squirrels Gn KT4 216 A6
Squirrel's La IG9 21 D1
Squirrels The
Bushey WD23 8 B5
Lewisham SE13 142 B2
Pinner HA5 41 B6
Squirrels Trad Est
UB3 105 D3
Squirries St E2 96 A4
Stable Cl
Kingston u T KT2 176 B4
Northolt UB5 85 C5
Stable Ct 4 SM6 219 A5
Stable Ho 9 SE16 118 C4
Stable Mews
Twickenham TW1 152 D3
West Norwood SE27 183 A5
Stables End BR6 227 A5
Stables The IG9 21 C4
Stables Way
SE11 116 C1 261 A2
Stable Way W10 90 C1
Stable Wlk N2 30 B2
Stable Yd Rd
SW1 115 C4 249 B2
Staburn Ct HA8 27 A1
Stacey Ave N18 34 C6
Stacey Cl E10 54 B4
Stacey St Highbury N7 72 C5
Soho WC2 93 D1 239 D1
Stack Ho SW1 258 B3
Stackhouse St SW1 257 C6
Stacy Path 13 SE5 139 C5
Staddon Cl BR3 207 A5
Stadium Bsns Ctr HA9 66 D5
Stadium Rd
Hendon NW2 46 C2
SE7, SE18 144 B6
Stadium Rd E NW2 46 C2
Stadium Ret Pk HA9 66 C5
Stadium St
SW10 136 A5 266 B3
Stadium Way HA9 66 C4
Staffa Rd E10 53 A1
Stafford Cl Cheam SM3 217 A2
Maida Vale NW6 91 C4
Southgate N14 15 C6
Walthamstow E17 53 B3
Stafford Cripps Ho
30 Bethnal Green E2 96 C4
SW6 264 D5
Stafford Cross CR0 220 B3
Stafford Cross Bsns Pk
CR0 220 B3
Stafford Ct
Croydon CR0 220 C4
Ealing W7 86 D1
Kensington W8 255 B6
South Lambeth SW8 270 A2
Stafford Gdns CR0 220 B3
Stafford Ho SE1 263 D2
Stafford Mans
13 Hammersmith
W14 112 D3
14 Stockwell SW4 138 A1
SW11 267 C3
Stafford Morris Ho 9
E15 98 C6
Stafford Pl
Richmond TW10 154 B4
SW1 115 C3 259 A6
Stafford Rd Bow E3 97 B5
Harrow HA3 24 A3
Kingston u T KT3 199 A6
Maida Vale NW6 91 C4
Plashet E7 77 D2
Ruislip HA4 61 D4
Sidcup DA14 189 C6
Wallington CR0, SM6 220 A3
Staffordshire Ho N3 47 A6
Staffordshire St
Peckham SE15 140 A4
Peckham SE15 140 B4
Stafford St W1 249 A4
Stafford Terr
W8 113 C3 255 A6
Stag Cl HA8 27 A1
Stag Ct 16 SM6 219 B2
Stagg Hill EN4 2 C6
Stag Hts 1 IG9 21 B2
Stag La Chigwell IG9 21 B2
Edgware HA8, NW9 45 A6
Roehampton SW15 155 D2
Stag Lane Fst & Mid Schs
HA8 26 C1
Stags Ct KT7 197 A2
Stagshaw Ho 17 SE22 139 C2
Stags Way TW7 130 D6
Stainbank Rd CR4 203 B6
Stainby Cl UB7 104 A3
Stainby Rd N15 51 D5
Staincliffe Ho 5 SM1 218 A4
Stainer Ho SE9 143 C1
Stainer St SE1 252 D3
Staines Ave SM3 216 D6
Staines By-Pass
TW15 170 A4
Staines Rd
East Bedfont TW14 149 B4
Feltham TW14, TW3 150 C6
Hounslow TW3 129 C1
Ilford IG1 79 B4
Twickenham TW2 152 A1
Twickenham TW13,
TW2 151 D1
Staines Rd E TW12,
TW16 172 C2
Staines Rd W TW15 171 B3
Staines Wlk DA14 190 C4
Stainford Cl TW15 171 B5
Stainforth Rd Ilford IG2 57 B2
Walthamstow E17 53 C5
Staining La EC2 242 B2
Stainmore Cl BR7 189 B2
Stainsbury St 25 E2 96 C5
Stainsby Rd E14 97 C1
Stainton Rd Enfield EN3 6 C4
Lewisham SE13 164 B4
Stalbridge Flats W1 238 B1
Stalbridge Ho NW1 232 A3
Stalbridge St NW1 237 B4
Stalham St SE16 118 B3
Stambourne Ho SW8 270 B2
Stambourne Way
Penge SE19 183 D3
West Wickham BR4 224 A5
Stamford Bridge Stadium
(Chelsea FC)
SW6 135 D5 265 C4
Stamford Brook Ave
W6 111 D3
Stamford Brook Gdns 1
W6 111 D3
Stamford Brook Mans 2
W6 111 D2
Stamford Brook Rd
W6 111 D3
Stamford Brook Sta
W6 111 D2
Stamford Cl
Harrow HA3 24 C3
2 London NW3 70 A5
Southall UB1 107 C6
Tottenham Hale N15 52 A5
Stamford Cotts SW10 265 D4
Stamford Ct
Chiswick W6 112 A2
Edgware HA8 26 B6
Stamford Dr BR2 208 D5
Stamford Gdns RM9 80 C1
Stamford Gr E 1 N16 52 A1
Stamford Gr W 4 N16 52 A1
STAMFORD HILL 51 C1
Stamford Hill N16 51 D1
Stamford Hill Mans 1
N16 51 D1
Stamford Hill Prim Sch
N15 51 B3
Stamford Hill Sta N16 51 C2
Stamford Ho N15 52 A4
Stamford Hospl W6 112 A2
Stamford Lo 2 N16 51 D2
Stamford Mans 2 N16 52 A1
Stamford Rd
Dagenham RM9 80 C1
Kingsland N1 73 C2
Newham E6 100 A6
South Tottenham N15 52 A4
Stamford St
SE1 116 C5 251 B4
Stamp Pl E2 95 D4
Stanard Cl N16 51 C2
Stanborough Cl TW12 173 B4
Stanborough Ho 4 E3 97 D3
Stanborough Pas E8 73 D2
Stanborough Rd TW3,
TW7 130 B2
Stanbridge Mans
SW15 134 C2
Stanbridge Pl N21 16 D2
Stanbridge Rd SW15 134 C2
Stanbrook Ct W1 249 A4
Stanbrook Rd SE2 124 B4
Stanburn Fst & Mid Schs
HA7 25 C3
Stanbury Ct 18 NW3 70 D2
Stanbury Rd
Nunhead SE15 140 C3
Peckham SE15 140 B3
Stancroft NW9 45 C4
Standale Gr HA4 39 A4
Standard Ind Est E16 122 B4
Standard Pl 13 EC2 95 C4
Standard Rd
Becontree NW10 89 B3
Belvedere DA17 125 C1
DA6 147 A1
Enfield EN3 7 A6
Hounslow TW4 129 A2
Standen Rd SW18 157 C4
Standfield Gdns RM10 81 C2
Standfield Rd RM10 81 C3
Standish Ho
6 Chiswick W6 112 A2
SE9 143 B1
Standish Rd W6 112 A2
Standlake Point 1
SE23 162 D1
Standor Ho 7 CR4 202 D6
Stane Cl SW19 179 D3
Stanedge Ct SW16 182 A5
Stane Gr SW4 138 A3
Stanesgate Ho 20
SE15 140 A5
Stanetta Ct 3 RM6 58 B2
Stane Way SE18 144 A5
Stanfield Ho
8 Northolt UB5 84 D5
NW8 236 D6
Stanfield Rd 14 E3 97 A5
Stanford Cl
Hampton TW12 173 B4
Romford RM7 59 D3
Ruislip HA4 39 A3
Stanford Ct
Friern Barnet N11 31 A5
Kensington W8 255 D5
Walham Green SW6 265 D1
Stanford Ho IG11 102 B5
Stanford Pl
SE1 117 C2 263 A3
Stanford Prim Sch
SW16 181 D2
Stanford Rd
Friern Barnet N11 30 D5
Thornton Heath SW16 182 A1
W8 113 D3 255 D6
Stanford St SW1 259 C3
Stanford Way SW16 181 D1
Stangate SE1 260 D6
Stangate Cres WD6 11 C6
Stangate Gdns HA7 25 B6
Stangate Lo N21 16 B4
Stangate Mansi TW1 152 D1
Stanger Rd SE25 206 A5
Stanhope Ave
Harrow HA3 24 B2
Hayes BR2 209 A1
Hendon N3 47 B6
Stanhope Cl 28 SE16 118 D4
Stanhope Ct N3 29 B1
Stanhope Gate W1 248 B4
Stanhope Gdns
Crouch End N6 49 C3
Dagenham RM8 81 B5
Edgware NW7 27 D5
Redbridge IG1 56 B1
Stoke Newington N4 51 A3
SW7 114 A2 256 B4
Stanhope Gr BR3 207 B5
Stanhope Ho
Crouch End N6 49 C3
5 Friern Barnet N11 31 B6
4 Putney SW15 156 C6
SE8 141 B5
Stanhope Mews E
SW7 114 A2 256 B4
Stanhope Mews S
SW7 256 B3
Stanhope Mews W
SW7 114 A2 256 B4
Stanhope Par NW1 232 A2
Stanhope Park Rd UB6 86 A3
Stanhope Pl W2 237 C1
Stanhope Prim Sch
UB6 86 A3
Stanhope Rd
Barnet EN5 12 D5
Crouch End N6 49 C2
DA7 147 A3
Dagenham RM8 81 B5
North Finchley N12 30 A5
Sidcup DA15 190 A6
Southall UB6 86 A2
South Croydon CR0 221 C5
Wallington SM5 219 A1
Walthamstow E17 53 D4
Stanhope Row W1 248 C3
Stanhope St
NW1 93 C4 232 A1
Stanhope Terr
W2 114 B6 246 D6
Stanier Cl SW5 254 D1
Stanlake Mews 7
W12 112 C5
Stanlake Rd W12 112 C5
Stanlake Villas 8
W12 112 C5
Stanley Ave
Barking IG11 101 D5
Beckenham BR2, BR3 208 A6
Dagenham RM8 59 B2
Greenford UB6 86 A6
Wembley HA0 66 A1
West Barnes KT3 200 A4
Stanley Bldgs NW1 233 A3
Stanley Cl Eltham SE9 167 A3
SW8 270 C5
Wembley HA0 66 A1
Stanley Cohen Ho EC1 242 A5
Stanley Cres
W11 113 B6 244 C6
Stanleycroft Cl TW7 130 C4
Stanley Ct
Belmont SM2 217 D1
11 Ealing W5 87 C2
Wallington SM5 219 A1
Wimbledon SW19 179 C4
Stanley Gardens Rd
TW11 174 C5
Stanley Gdns
Bedford Pk W3 111 C4
Cricklewood NW2 68 C3
Mitcham CR4 181 A4
W11 244 C6
Wallington SM6 219 C2
Stanley Glynn Ct BR7 188 C5
Stanley Gr
Clapham SW11 137 A3
Thornton Heath CR0 204 C3
Stanley Ho
35 Clapham SW8 137 D3
Leytonstone E11 54 C3
22 Poplar E14 97 C1
Wembley HA0 66 A1
Stanley Holloway Ct
E16 99 A1
Stanley Inf Sch KT11 174 C6
Stanley Jun Sch KT11 174 C6
Stanley Mans SW10 266 B6
Upper Tooting SW17 158 D2
Stanley Park Dr HA0 88 B6
Stanley Park High Sch
SM5 219 A2
Stanley Park Inf Sch
SM5 218 D1
Stanley Park Jun Sch
SM5 218 D1
Stanley Park Rd SM5,
SM6 219 A1
Stanley Rd
Acton Green W3 111 A3
Ashford TW15 170 A5
Belmont SM2 217 D1
BR6 211 D1
Bromley BR2 209 C5
Chingford E4 20 B3
East Finchley N2 48 B6
Edmonton N9 17 D2
Enfield EN1 5 C2
Friern Barnet N11 31 D5
Harringay N15 50 D5
Harrow HA2 64 A6
2 Hendon NW9 46 A2
Ilford IG1 79 B6
Isleworth TW3 130 A1
Mill Meads E15 98 B6
Mitcham CR4 181 A3
Morden SM4 201 C5
Mortlake SW14 132 D1
Muswell Hill N10 31 B3
Northwood HA6 22 A2
Plashet E12 78 A3
Sidcup DA14 168 A1
Southall UB1 107 A6
Teddington TW11, TW2 174 C5
Thornton Heath CR0 204 C3
Twickenham TW2 152 B1
Wallington SM5 219 A1
Walthamstow E10 53 D3
Wembley HA9 66 B2
Wimbledon SW19 179 C4
Woodford E18 36 D2
Stanley St SE14, SE8 141 B5
Stanley Studios SW10 266 B6
Stanley Tech High Sch for
Boys SE25 205 D6
Stanley Terr 8 N19 72 A6
Stanliff Ho 8 E14 119 C3
Stanmer St SW11 136 C3
STANMORE 25 A5
Stanmore Coll HA7 25 C4
Stanmore Gdns
Richmond TW9 132 B2
Sutton SM1 218 A5
Stanmore Hill HA7 25 A6
Stanmore Ho 21 SW8 137 D3
Stanmore Lo HA7 25 B6
Stanmore Pl NW1 231 D6
Stanmore Rd
Harringay N15 50 D5
Leytonstone E11 54 D1
Richmond TW9 132 B2
Stanmore St N1 94 B6 233 C6
Stanmore Sta HA7 25 D6
Stanmore Terr 3
BR3 185 C1
Stanmuir Lo NW9 45 A4
Stannard Cotts 27 E1 96 C3
Stannard Ct SE6 163 D3
Stannard Mews E8 74 A2
Stannard Rd E8 74 A2
Stannary Pl SE11 261 B1
Stannary St
SE11 116 C1 261 B1
Stannet Way SM6 219 C4

Stansbury Sq **3** W10 . . . 91 A4
Stansfeld Ho SE1 . . . . 263 D3
Stansfeld Ho E6 . . . . . . 99 D1
Stansfield Rd
Cranford TW4, TW5 . . . . 128 B3
Stockwell SW9 . . . . . . 138 B2
Stansgate Rd RM10 . . . . 81 C5
Stanstead Cl BR2 . . . . . 208 D3
Stanstead Gr SE23 . . . . 163 B3
Stanstead Ho E3 . . . . . . 98 A3
Stanstead Manor SM1 . 217 C2
Stanstead Rd
Forest Hill SE23, SE6 . . 163 A4
Wanstead E11 . . . . 55 B4
Stansted Cres 168 D3
Stansted Express Terminal
EC2 . . . . 243 A4
Stansted Rd TW6 . . . . . 148 B5
Stanswood Gdns SE5 . 139 C5
Stanthorpe Cl SW16 . . 182 A5
Stanthorpe Rd SW16 . . 182 A5
Stanton Ave TW11 . . . . 174 C4
Stanton Cl
Chessington KT19 . . . . 214 D3
North Cheam KT4 . . . . 200 D5
Stanton Ct **5** DA15 . . 168 A1
Finchley N3 . . . . 29 C2
Stoke Newington N16 . . 51 B2
Stanton Ho **9** SE10 . 142 A6
Stanton Rd
Barnes SW13 . . . . 133 D3
Thornton Heath CR0 . . 205 A4
Wimbledon SW20 . . . . 178 D2
Stanton Sq SE26 . . . . . 185 B6
Stanton Way SE26 . . . . 185 B6
Stanway Ct **23** N1 . . . . 95 C5
Stanway Gdns
Acton W3 . . . . 110 C5
Edgware HA8 . . . . 27 A5
Stanway St N1 . . . . 95 C5
STANWELL 148 A3
Stanwell Fields CE Prim
Sch TW19 . . . . 148 A4
Stanwell Rd
Ashford TW15 . . . . 170 A6
East Bedfont TW14, TW19,
TW6 . . . . 148 D4
Stanwell TW15 . . . . . . 148 A1
Stanwick Rd
W14 . . . . 113 B2 254 C3
Stanworth Ct TW5 . . . . 129 C5
Stanworth St SE1 . . . . 253 D1
Stanyhurst SE23 . . . . . 163 A3
Stapenhill Rd HA0 . . . . 65 B5
Staplefield Cl
Pinner HA5 . . . . 23 A3
3 Streatham SW2 . . . 160 A3
Stapleford N17 . . . . 33 C1
Stapleford Ave IG2 . . . . 57 C4
Stapleford Cl
Chingford E4 . . . . 20 A1
Kingston u T KT1 . . . . 198 C6
Putney SW19 . . . . 157 A4
Stapleford Rd HA0 . . . . 65 D1
Stapleford Way IG11 . . 102 B6
Staplehurst Ct SW11 . . 158 D5
Staplehurst Ho **18** E5 . 74 B3
Staplehurst Rd
Lewisham SE13 . . . . . . 164 C6
Sutton SM5 . . . . 218 C1
Staple Inn WC2 . . . . . . 241 A2
Staple Inn Bldgs WC2 . 241 A2
Staples Cl SE16 . . . . . . 119 A5
Staples Corner Bsns Pk
NW2 . . . . 46 B1
Staples Corner (East)
NW2 . . . . 46 B1
Staples Corner Ret Pk
NW2 . . . . 46 B1
Staples Corner (West)
NW2 . . . . 46 B1
Staple St SE1 . . 137 B4 252 D1
Stapleton Gdns CR0 . . 220 A5
Stapleton Hall N4 . . . . . 50 B2
Stapleton Hall Rd N4 . . 50 B2
Stapleton Ho **15** E2 . . 96 B4
Stapleton Rd DA7 . . . . 147 B6
Orpington BR6 . . . . . . 227 D5
Upper Tooting SW17 . . 159 A1
Stapley Rd DA17 . . . . . 125 C1
Stapylton Rd EN5 . . . . . . 1 A2
Star Alley EC3 . . . . 253 B6
Star and Garter Hill
TW10 . . . . 154 A4
Starboard Way E14 . . . 119 C3
Starbuck Cl SE9 . . . . . . 166 C4
Star Cl EN3 . . . . 18 C5
Starcross St
NW1 . . . . 93 C4 232 B1
Star Ct UB10 . . . . 83 A3
Stardome* NW1 . . . . . . 238 A5
Starfield Rd W12 . . . . . 112 A4
Star & Garter Mans
SW15 . . . . 134 C2
Star La E16 . . . . 98 C3
Starliner Ct N7 . . . . 72 C2
Starling Cl
Beckenham BR3 . . . . . 207 A3
Buckhurst Hill IG9 . . . . . 21 A3
Pinner HA5 . . . . 40 C6
Starling Ct E13 . . . . 99 B6
Starling Ho NW8 . . . . . 230 A4
Starling Wlk TW12 . . . . 173 A5
Starmans Cl RM9 . . . . 103 A6
Star Path UB5 . . . . 85 C5
Star Pl E1 . . . . 118 A6
Star Prim Sch E16 . . . . . 98 C3
Star Rd Hillingdon UB10 . 83 A3
Hounslow TW7 . . . . . . 130 D3
W14 . . . . 113 B1 254 C1

Star St W2 . . . . 92 C1 237 A2
Starts Cl BR6 . . . . 226 C5
Starts Hill Ave BR6 . . . 226 C4
Starts Hill Rd BR6 . . . . 226 C4
Starveall Cl UB7 . . . . . 104 B3
Star Works NW10 . . . . . 90 A4
Star Yd WC2 . . . 94 C1 241 A2
State Farm Ave BR6 . . 227 A4
Stateland Ct **10** N11 . . 31 B6
Staten Gdns TW1 . . . . 152 D3
Statham Ct N7 . . . . 72 A5
Statham Gr
Edmonton N18 . . . . 33 C5
Stoke Newington N16 . . 73 B5
Statham Ho SW8 . . . . 269 A2
Station App
Ashford TW15 . . . . . . 170 B6
Belmont SM2 . . . . 217 A1
Bexleyheath DA7 . . . . 147 A3
Chislehurst BR7 . . . . . 188 C1
Dagenham NW10 . . . . 89 D4
Elmstead BR7 . . . . . . 188 A4
20 Finchley N12 . . . . . 29 D6
Forest Gate E7 . . . . 77 B4
Friern Barnet N11 . . . . 31 B5
Fulham SW6 . . . . 135 A2
Greenford UB6 . . . . 64 B1
Hampton TW12 . . . . . 173 C2
Hayes BR2 . . . . 209 A1
Hayes Town UB3 . . . . 105 D3
Hinchley Wood KT10 . 212 D5
4 Kingston u T KT1,
KT2 . . . . 176 C2
Lewisham SE3 . . . . . . 143 B2
Mottingham SE9 . . . . 166 B3
New Barnet EN5 . . . . . . 2 A1
6 New Malden KT4 . . 200 A4
Orpington BR6 . . . . . . 227 D6
Penge SE26 . . . . 185 B5
Pinner HA5 . . . . 41 A6
Richmond TW9 . . . . . . 132 C4
Ruislip HA4 . . . . 39 D1
Shepperton TW17 . . . 193 A4
3 South Croydon CR0 . 221 B6
South Ruislip HA4 . . . . 62 B3
Streatham SW16 . . . . 181 D5
Sunbury TW16 . . . . . . 172 A2
1 Surbiton KT6 . . . . . 198 A3
Walthamstow E17 . . . . 53 C4
Wanstead E11 . . . . 55 A4
West Drayton UB7 . . . 104 A4
2 Woodford E18 . . . . 37 B1
Woodford IG8 . . . . 37 B4
Woodford IG9 . . . . 37 D6
Worcester Pk KT19 . . 216 A3
Yiewsley UB7 . . . . 104 A5
Station Approach Rd
W4 . . . . 133 A5
Station Ave
5 Brixton SW9 . . . . . 138 D2
Kingston u T KT3 . . . . 199 C6
14 Richmond TW9 . . . 132 C4
West Ewell KT19 . . . . 215 D1
Station Bldgs
Catford SE6 . . . . 163 C4
Merton SW20 . . . . . . 178 C1
Station Blgs W5 . . . . . 110 B5
Station Cl Finchley N3 . 29 C2
Hampton TW12 . . . . . 173 D2
Station Cres
Ashford TW15 . . . . . . 170 A6
Greenwich SE3 . . . . . 121 A1
Tottenham N15 . . . . . . 51 B5
Wembley HA0 . . . . 65 B2
Station Ct
Mitcham CR4 . . . . 202 C5
5 Nunhead SE15 . . . 140 C3
South Tottenham N15 . 51 D4
Wembley HA9 . . . . 43 C1
Stationers Hall Ct EC4 241 D1
Station Est E18 . . . . . . 37 B1
Station Est **1** E18 . . . 37 B1
Station Estate Rd
TW14 . . . . 150 B3
Station Gdns W4 . . . . 133 A5
Station Gr HA0 . . . . 66 A2
Station Hill BR2 . . . . . 225 A6
Station House Mews
N9 . . . . 34 A6
Station Mans **9** N3 . . 29 C2
Station Mews Terr **4**
SE3 . . . . 121 A1
Station Par Acton W3 . . 88 C1
1 Ashford TW15 . . . . 170 B6
Barking IG11 . . . . 79 A1
Belmont HA3 . . . . 25 A1
Cockfosters EN4 . . . . . . 3 A1
Cricklewood NW2 . . . . 68 C2
Dagenham RM10 . . . . 81 C2
Ealing W5 . . . . 110 B5
Edgware HA8 . . . . 26 A3
Feltham TW14 . . . . . . 150 B4
Northolt UB5 . . . . 63 D4
4 Osidge N14 . . . . 15 D3
Richmond TW9 . . . . . . 132 C4
Ruislip HA4 . . . . 61 B6
South Harrow HA2 . . . 63 D4
Station Pas
New Cross Gate
SE15 . . . . 140 C4
Woodford E18 . . . . . . 37 B1
Station Pl N4 . . . . 72 D4
Station Rd
Ashford TW15 . . . . . . 170 B6
Barkingside IG6 . . . . . 57 B6

Station Rd continued
Barnes SW13 . . . . 133 D3
Beckenham BR2 . . . . . 186 C1
Belvedere DA17 . . . . . 125 C3
Bexleyheath DA7 . . . . 147 A2
Bromley BR1 . . . . 187 A2
Camden Town N19 . . . 71 C5
Carshalton SM5 . . . . . 218 D4
Chadwell Heath RM6 . . 58 D2
Chessington KT9 . . . . 214 A3
Chingford E4 . . . . 20 B3
Church End N3 . . . . . . 29 C1
Claygate KT10 . . . . . . 212 C3
Croydon CR0 . . . . 205 A1
Edgware HA8 . . . . 26 C4
Edgware NW7 . . . . 27 C4
Esher KT10 . . . . 212 B6
Forest Gate E7 . . . . 77 A4
Friern Barnet N11 . . . . 31 B5
Greenhill HA1 . . . . 42 D4
Hampton TW12 . . . . . 173 D2
Hampton Wick KT1 . . 175 D3
Hanwell W7 . . . . 108 C5
Harlesden NW10 . . . . 89 D5
Hayes UB3 . . . . 105 C5
Hendon NW4 . . . . 46 A4
Hounslow TW3 . . . . . . 129 D1
Ilford IG1 . . . . 78 D5
Kingston u T KT2 . . . . 176 C2
Lewisham SE13 . . . . . 142 A2
Leyton E10 . . . . 76 A5
Manor Pk E12 . . . . 78 A4
Merton SW19 . . . . . . 180 A2
New Barnet EN5 . . . . . 13 D6
New Malden KT3 . . . . 200 B4
North Harrow HA1, HA2 . 41 D4
Orpington BR6 . . . . . . 227 D6
Penge SE20 . . . . 184 C4
Shepperton TW17 . . . 193 A4
Sidcup DA14, DA15 . . 168 A1
South Norwood SE25 . 205 D5
Sunbury TW16 . . . . . . 172 A3
Teddington TW11 . . . . 175 A4
Thames Ditton KT7 . . 196 D2
Tottenham Hale N17 . . 52 A6
Twickenham TW1 . . . . 152 D4
Walthamstow E17 . . . . 53 A4
West Acton W5 . . . . . . 88 B1
West Barnes KT3 . . . . 200 B4
West Drayton UB7 . . . 104 A4
West Wickham BR4 . . 208 A1
Wood Green N22 . . . . . 32 B1
Station Rd N DA17 . . . 125 D3
Station Rise SE27 . . . . 160 D2
Station Sq BR5 . . . . . . 211 A4
Station St
Newham E16 . . . . 122 D5
Stratford E15 . . . . 76 B1
Station Terr
Camberwell SE5 . . . . . 139 A4
Kensal Rise NW10 . . . . 90 D5
Station View UB6 . . . . . 86 B6
Station Way
Cheam SM2, SM3 . . . 217 A1
Claygate KT10 . . . . . . 212 C2
Woodford IG9 . . . . 37 D6
Station Yd TW1 . . . . . . 153 A4
Staton Ct **1** E10 . . . . 53 D2
Staunton Ho SE17 . . . 263 A3
Staunton Rd KT2 . . . . 176 B3
Staunton St SE8 . . . . . 141 B6
Staveley NW1 . . . . 232 A2
Staveley Cl Hackney E9 . 74 C3
Lower Holloway N7 . . . 72 A4
New Cross Gate SE15 . 140 C4
8 Peckham SE15 . . . 140 B4
Staveley Ct **4** E11 . . 55 A4
Staveley Gdns W4 . . . 133 B4
Staveley Ho SE4 . . . . . 163 A4
Staveley Rd
Ashford TW15 . . . . . . 171 B4
Chiswick W4 . . . . 133 B4
Stavers Ho **31** E3 . . . 97 B5
Staverton Rd NW2 . . . . 68 C1
Stave Yard Rd SE16 . . 119 A5
Stavordale Lo W14 . . . 254 D6
Stavordale Rd
Carshalton SM5 . . . . . 202 A2
Highbury N5 . . . . 72 D4
Stayner's Rd E1 . . . . . . 96 D3
Stayton Rd SM1 . . . . . 217 C5
Steadfast Rd KT1 . . . . 175 D2
Steadman Ct EC1 . . . . 242 B6
Steadman Ho **4** RM10 . 81 C5
Stead St SE17 . . 117 B2 262 C3
Steam Farm La TW14 . 127 D1
Stean St E8 . . . . 95 D6
Stebbing Ho **8** W11 . 112 D5
Stebbing Way IG11 . . . 102 A5
Stebondale St E14 . . . 120 A2
Stebon Prim Sch E14 . 97 C2
Stedham Pl WC1 . . . . 240 A2
Stedman Cl UB10 . . . . 60 C5
Steedman St
SE17 . . . . 117 A2 262 A3
Steeds Rd N10 . . . . . . 30 D2
Steele App IG11 . . . . . 102 B5
Steele Wlk
Acton Green W4 . . . . 111 A3
Becontree NW10 . . . . 89 A5
Isleworth TW7 . . . . . . 131 A1
Leyton E11 . . . . 76 C4
Tottenham N17 . . . . . . 51 C6
Steele's Mews N NW3 . 70 D2
Steele's Mews S NW3 . 70 D2
Steele's Rd NW3 . . . . . 70 D2
Steele Wlk DA8 . . . . . . 147 A6
Steel's La **23** E1 . . . . 96 C1
Steen Way **7** SE22 . . 161 C6
Steep Cl BR6 . . . . 227 D2

Steep Hill
South Croydon CR0 . . 221 C4
Streatham SW16 . . . . 159 D1
Steeple Cl Fulham SW6 . 135 A3
Wimbledon SW19 . . . . 179 A5
Steeple Ct
19 Bethnal Green E1 . 96 B3
Wimbledon SW19 . . . . 179 A5
Steeplestone Cl N18 . . 33 A5
Steepleton Ct E11 . . . . 54 A1
Steerforth St SW18 . . . 158 A2
Steering Cl N9 . . . . 18 C3
Steers Mead CR4 . . . . 180 D2
Steers Way SE16 . . . . 119 A4
Steetley Ct **14** SM2 . 218 A1
Steinman Ct TW7 . . . . 130 D2
Stelfax Ho WC1 . . . . . 233 D2
Stella Cl UB8 . . . . 82 D2
Stella Rd SW17 . . . . . 180 D5
Stellar Ho **4** N17 . . . . 33 D4
Stellman Cl E5 . . . . 74 A5
Stembridge Rd SE20 . . 184 B1
Sten Cl **12** EN3 . . . . . . 7 C6
Stephan Ct E8 . . . . 96 A6
Stephen Cl BR6 . . . . . . 227 D5
Stephen Ct **18** SW19 . 156 D3
Stephendale Rd SW6 . 136 A3
Stephen Fox Ho **7**
W4 . . . . 111 C1
Stephen Hawking Sch
E14 . . . . 97 A1
Stephen Mews W1 . . . 239 C3
Stephen Pl SW4 . . . . . 137 C2
Stephen Saunders Ct
SW11 . . . . 158 C6
Stephens Ct
Brockley SE4 . . . . 141 A2
E16 . . . . 98 D3
Stephens Lo N12 . . . . . 14 A1
Stephenson Ct SM2 . . 217 B1
Stephenson Ho
2 Gospel Oak NW5 . . 71 B4
6 Maitland Pk NW3 . . 70 D3
Newington SE1 . . . . . 262 A6
West Heath SE2 . . . . . 124 D1
Stephenson Rd
Ealing W7 . . . . 86 D1
Twickenham TW4 . . . . 151 D4
Walthamstow E17 . . . . 53 A4
Stephenson St
Dagenham NW10 . . . . 89 D4
Newham E16 . . . . 98 C2
Stephenson Way
NW1 . . . . 93 C3 239 B6
Stephen's Rd E15 . . . . . 98 C6
Stephen St W1 . . . . . . 239 C3
STEPNEY 96 D2
Stepney City E1 . . . . . . 96 C2
Stepney Cswy E1 . . . . . 96 D1
Stepney Gn E1 . . . . 96 D2
Stepney Greencoat CE
Prim Sch The E14 . . . . 97 B1
Stepney Green Ct **4**
E1 . . . . 96 D2
Stepney Green Sch E1 . 96 D2
Stepney Green Sta E1 . 96 D2
Stepney High St E1 . . . 96 D2
Stepney Way
Mitcham CR4 . . . . 181 A2
Stepney E1 . . . . 96 C2
Sterling Ave HA8 . . . . . 26 B6
Sterling Cl NW10 . . . . . 68 A1
Sterling Gdns SE14 . . 141 A6
Sterling Ho SE3 . . . . . 143 B1
Sterling Ind Est RM10 . 81 D4
Sterling Pl W5 . . . . . . 110 A2
Sterling Rd EN2 . . . . . . 5 B5
Sterling St SW7 . . . . . 257 B6
Sterling Way (North
Circular Rd) N18 . . . . 33 C5
Stern Cl IG11 . . . . 102 C5
Sterndale Rd W14 . . . 112 D3
Sterne St W12 . . . . . . 112 D4
Sternhall La SE15 . . . . 140 A2
Sternhold Ave SW12,
SW2 . . . . 159 D2
Sterry Cres RM10 . . . . 81 C3
Sterry Dr
Thames Ditton KT7 . . 196 C3
Worcester Pk KT19 . . 215 D4
Sterry Gdns RM10 . . . . 81 C2
Sterry Rd Barking IG11 . 101 D6
Dagenham RM10 . . . . 81 C3
Sterry St SE1 . . . . 252 C1
Steucers La SE23 . . . . 163 A3
Stevanne Ct **1** DA17 . 125 C1
Steve Biko Ct W10 . . . . 90 D3
Steve Biko La SE6 . . . 185 C6
Steve Biko Lodge **13**
E13 . . . . 99 A5
Steve Biko Rd N7 . . . . . 72 C5
Steve Biko Way TW3 . . 129 C2
Stevedale Rd DA16 . . . 146 C3
Stevedore St **3** E1 . . 118 B5
Stevenage Rd
Fulham SW6 . . . . 134 D4
Wallend E6 . . . . 78 C2
Stevens Ave E9 . . . . . . 74 C2
Stevens Cl
Beckenham BR3 . . . . . 185 C4
Hampton TW12 . . . . . 173 B4
Pinner HA5 . . . . 40 C4
Stevens Ct BR3 . . . . . 185 C4
Stevens Ho **4**
SW1 . . . . 259 B3
Stevens Rd RM8 . . . . . 80 C5
Stevens St SE1 . . . . . . 263 B6
Steventon Rd W12 . . . 111 D6
Stevens Ho WD23 . . . . . 8 A3
Stevens Ho KT1 . . . . . 175 D1
Stevens' La KT10 . . . . 213 A2
Stevenson Cl EN5 . . . . 14 B4
Stevenson Cres SE16 . 118 B3

Stevenson Ho
1 Battersea SW11 . . 136 D3
6 Clapham Pk SW2 . 160 A6
NW8 . . . . 229 A6
Wembley HA9 . . . . 65 D6
Stevens Rd RM8 . . . . . 80 C5
Stevens St SE1 . . . . . . 263 B6
Steventon Rd W12 . . . 111 D6
Stewards Holte Wlk **3**
N11 . . . . 31 B6
Stewart Ave TW17 . . . 192 C5
Stewart Cl BR7 . . . . . . 188 D6
Hampton TW12 . . . . . 173 A4
Kingsbury NW9 . . . . . . 45 A3
Stewart Fleming Prim Sch
SE20 . . . . 206 C6
Stewart Headlam Prim
Sch E1 . . . . 96 B3
Stewart Ho SE1 . . . . . 263 A5
Stanmore HA7 . . . . 25 B5
Stewart Quay UB3 . . . 105 C4
Stewart Rainbird Ho **1**
E12 . . . . 78 C3
Stewart Rd E15 . . . . . . 76 B4
Stewartsby Cl N18 . . . . 33 A5
Stewart's Gr
SW3 . . . . 114 C1 257 A2
Stewart's Rd
SW8 . . . . 137 C4 269 A2
Stewart St E14 . . . . . . 120 A4
Stew La EC4 . . . . 252 A6
Steyne Ho
15 Acton W3 . . . . . . 110 D5
11 Acton W3 . . . . . . 111 A5
Steyne Rd W3 . . . . . . 110 D5
Steyning Gr SE9 . . . . . 188 B6
Steynings Way N12 . . . 29 C5
Steyning Way TW4 . . . 128 C1
Steynton Ave DA5 . . . 168 C2
Stickland Rd DA17 . . . 125 C2
Stickleton Cl UB6 . . . . 85 D4
Stifford Ho E1 . . . . 96 C2
Stilecroft Gdns HA0 . . 65 B5
Stile Hall Gdns W4 . . . 110 C5
Stile Hall Par **6** W4 . 110 C1
Stileman Ho **4** E3 . . . 97 B2
Stile Path TW16 . . . . . 194 A5
Stiles Cl BR2 . . . . 210 B3
Erith DA8 . . . . 125 D1
Stillingfleet Rd SW13 . 134 A6
Stillington St
SW1 . . . . 115 C2 259 B4
Stillness Jun & Inf Schs
SE23 . . . . 163 A5
Stillness Rd SE23 . . . . 163 B5
Stilwell Dr UB8 . . . . . . 82 B3
Stilwell Rdbt UB8 . . . . 104 D6
Stipularis Dr UB4 . . . . . 84 D3
Stirling Ave Pinner HA5 . 41 A2
Upper Halliford TW17 . 193 C6
Wallington SM6 . . . . . 220 A1
Stirling Cl Sidcup DA14 . 189 D6
Streatham SW16 . . . . 181 C2
Stirling Cnr EN5, WD6 . 11 B5
Stirling Ct
Clerkenwell EC1 . . . . . 241 C6
Ealing W13 . . . . 109 B6
Strand WC2 . . . . 240 C1
Stirling Gr TW3 . . . . . . 130 A3
Stirling Ho **5** SE18 . . 122 C1
Stirling Ind Ctr WD6 . . 11 B6
Stirling Lo **7** EN5 . . . . 14 A6
Stirling Mans NW6 . . . . 78 C2
Stirling Rd Harrow HA3 . 42 C6
Hayes UB3 . . . . 106 B6
Newham E13 . . . . 99 B5
South Acton W3 . . . . 110 D4
Stanwell TW19, TW6 . 148 B5
Stockwell SW9 . . . . . 138 A3
Tottenham N17 . . . . . . 34 A2
Twickenham TW2 . . . . 151 D4
Walthamstow E17 . . . . 53 A6
Wood Green N22 . . . . . 32 D2
Stirling Ret Pk WD6 . . . 11 B5
Stirling Way
Borehamwood WD6 . . 11 B6
Thornton Heath CR0 . . 204 A2
Stiven Cres HA2 . . . . . . 63 B5
Stoatley Ho **10** SW15 . 156 A3
Stockbeck NW1 . . . . . 232 B3
Stockbury Rd CR0 . . . 206 C3
Stockdale Rd RM8 . . . . 81 B6
Stockdove Way UB6 . . 86 D4
Stocker Gdns RM9 . . . . 80 C1
Stockfield Rd
Claygate KT10 . . . . . . 212 C3
Streatham SW16 . . . . 160 B1
Stockford Ave NW7 . . . 28 D3
Stockholm Ho E1 . . . . 118 A6
Stockholm Rd SE16 . . 118 C1
Stockholm Way **9** E1 . 118 A5
Stockhurst Cl SW15 . . 134 D1
Stockingswater La EN3 . 7 B2
Stockleigh Hall NW8 . . 230 B4
Stockley Acad UB8 . . . . 82 B1
Stockley Cl UB7 . . . . . 104 C4
Stockley Ctry Pk UB7 . 104 C4
Stockley Farm Rd
UB7 . . . . 104 D4
Stockley Park Bsns Pk
UB11 . . . . 105 A5
Stockley Rd UB7, UB8,
UB11 . . . . 104 D4
Stock Orchard Cres N7 . 72 B3
Stock Orchard St N7 . . 72 B3
Stockport Rd SW16 . . 181 D2
Stocks Ct **5** E1 . . . . . 96 D1
Stocksfield Rd E17 . . . 54 A6

Stocks Pl
Hillingdon UB10 . . . . . 82 C6
16 Limehouse E14 . . 119 B6
Stock St E13 . . . . 99 A5
Stockton Cl EN5 . . . . . . 2 A1
Stockton Gdns
Edgware NW7 . . . . 11 C1
Tottenham N17 . . . . . . 33 A3
Stockton Ho **18** E2 . . 96 B4
Harrow HA2 . . . . 41 C1
Stockton Rd
Edmonton N18 . . . . 34 B4
Tottenham N17 . . . . . . 33 A3
STOCKWELL 138 A2
Stockwell Ave SW9 . . 138 B2
Stockwell Cl BR1 . . . . 187 B1
Stockwell Gdns
SW9 . . . . 138 B4 270 C1
Stockwell Gn SW9 . . . 138 B3
Stockwell La SW9 . . . 138 B3
Stockwell Park Cres
SW9 . . . . 138 B3
Stockwell Park Rd
SW9 . . . . 138 B4 270 D1
Stockwell Park Sch
SW9 . . . . 138 B4 270 C1
Stockwell Park Wlk
SW9 . . . . 138 C2
Stockwell Prim Sch
SW9 . . . . 138 B2
Stockwell Rd SW9 . . . 138 B3
Stockwell St SE10 . . . 142 A6
Stockwell Sta SW4 . . . 138 C3
Stockwell Terr SW9 . . 270 C1
Stodart Rd SE20 . . . . 184 C2
Stoddart Ho SW8 . . . . 270 D5
Stodmarsh Ho **28**
SW9 . . . . 138 C4
Stofield Gdns SE9 . . . 165 D1
Stoford Cl SW19 . . . . 157 A4
Stokenchurch St
SW6 . . . . 135 D4 265 C1
STOKE NEWINGTON . . 73 C6
Stoke Newington Church
St N16 . . . . 73 C6
Stoke Newington Comm
N16 . . . . 73 C5
Stoke Newington High St
N16 . . . . 73 D5
Stoke Newington Rd
N16 . . . . 73 D4
Stoke Newington Sch
N16 . . . . 73 B5
Stoke Newington Sta
N16 . . . . 73 D6
Stoke Pl NW10 . . . . . . 89 D4
Stoke Rd KT2 . . . . 177 A3
Stokesby Rd KT9 . . . . 214 B2
Stokes Ct N2 . . . . 48 C5
Stokesley St W12 . . . . 89 D1
Stokes Rd Croydon CR0 . 206 A3
Newham E6 . . . . 100 A3
Stokley Ct N8 . . . . 50 A5
Stoll Cl NW2 . . . . 68 C5
Stoms Path SE6 . . . . . 185 C5
Stonard Rd
Dagenham RM8 . . . . . 80 B4
Palmers Green N13 . . 16 C1
Stondon Pk SE23 . . . . 163 A5
Stondon Wlk E6 . . . . . 99 D5
Stonebanks KT12 . . . . 194 A2
Stone Bldgs
WC2 . . . . 94 B2 240 D3
STONEBRIDGE 89 A6
Stonebridge Ct **9**
NW10 . . . . 67 B1
Stonebridge Ctr **6**
NW10 . . . . 89 B6
Stonebridge Ctr The
N15 . . . . 52 A4
Stonebridge Park HA9 . 66 C6
Stonebridge Park Sta
NW10 . . . . 66 B1
Stonebridge Pk NW10 . 67 B1
Stonebridge Rd N15 . . 51 B4
Stonebridge Sch The
NW10 . . . . 89 B6
Stonebridge Way HA9 . 66 D2
Stonechat Sq **6** E6 . 100 A2
Stone Cl Clapham SW4 . 137 C3
Dagenham RM8 . . . . . 81 B6
Yiewsley UB7 . . . . . . 104 B5
Stonecot Cl SM3 . . . . 201 A1
Stonecot Hill SM3 . . . 201 A1
Stonecroft Way CR0 . . 204 A2
Stonecrop Cl NW9 . . . . 45 B6
Stone Ct Southgate N21 . 16 B6
4 Stratford E15 . . . . . 76 D1
Stonecutter St EC4 . . 241 C2
Stonefield N4 . . . . 72 B6
Stonefield Cl DA7 . . . . 147 C2
Ruislip HA4 . . . . 62 D1
Stonefield Mans N1 . . 234 A5
Stonefield St
N1 . . . . 94 C6 234 B6
Stonefield Way
Ruislip HA4 . . . . 63 A3
SE7 . . . . 143 D5
Stonegate **8** NW5 . . . 71 A2
Stone Gr HA8 . . . . 26 B5
Stonegrove Gdns HA8 . 26 A5
Stonegrove Ho HA8 . . 26 B5
Stonehall Ave IG1 . . . . 56 A3
Stone Hall Rd N21 . . . . 16 C4
Stoneham Rd N11 . . . . 31 C5

Stonehaven BR3 185 D1
Stonehill Bsns Pk N18 34 D5
Stonehill Cl SW14 155 B6
Stonehill Ct E4 19 D4
Stonehill Rd
Brentford W4 110 C1
Mortlake SW14 155 B6
Stonehills Ct SE21 161 C1
Stonehill's Mans 3
SW16 160 A2
Stonehill Woods Pk
DA14 191 D4
Stonehorse Rd EN3 18 C6
Stonehouse NW1 232 B5
Stonehouse Ct EC2 243 B2
Stonehouse Ho 27 W2 91 C2
Stone Lake Ind Pk
SE7 121 C2
Stone Lake Ret Pk
SE7 121 C2
STONELEIGH 216 A3
Stoneleigh Ave
Enfield EN1 6 B4
North Cheam KT17,
KT4 216 A5
Stoneleigh Broadway
KT17 216 A3
Stoneleigh Cres KT19 215 D3
Stoneleigh Ct
Redbridge IG5 56 A6
6 Tottenham N17 33 D1
Stoneleigh Fst Sch
KT17 216 B4
Stoneleigh Lo 13 TW9 132 B4
Stoneleigh Mews 15
E3 97 A5
Stoneleigh Park Ave
CR0 206 D3
Stoneleigh Park Rd KT19,
KT4 216 A3
Stoneleigh Pl W11 112 D6
Stoneleigh Rd
Bromley BR1 210 D6
Carshalton SM5 202 C2
Redbridge IG5 56 B6
Tottenham N17 33 D1
Stoneleigh St W11 112 D6
Stoneleigh Sta KT19 216 A3
Stoneleigh Terr N19 71 B6
Stonell's Rd SW11 158 D6
Stonemasons Cl N15 51 B5
Stonenest St N4 50 B1
Stone Park Ave BR3 207 D5
Stone Pl KT4 216 A6
Stone Rd BR2 208 D4
Stones End St SE1 252 A1
Stonewall E6 100 C2
Stoneworth Ct SE25 206 A3
Stoney Alley SE18 144 C3
Stoneyard La E14 119 D6
Stoneycroft Cl SE12 164 D4
Stoney Deep TW11 175 A6
Stoneydown E17 53 A5
Stoneydown Ave E17 53 A5
Stoneydown Ho 2 E17 53 A5
Stoneydown Park Sch
E17 53 A5
Stoneyfields Gdns HA8 27 A6
Stoneyfields La HA8 27 A6
Stoney La E1 243 B2
Penge SE19 183 D4
Stoney St SE1 117 B5 252 C4
Stonhouse St SW4 137 D1
Stonor Rd W14 113 B2 254 C3
Stonycroft Cl EN3 7 A3
Stopes St SE15 139 D5
Stopford Rd
Newham E13 99 A6
SE17 261 D1
Stopher Ho SE1 251 D1
Storace Ho 6 SW4 138 A1
Store Rd E16 122 C4
Storers Quay E14 120 B2
Store St
Bloomsbury
WC1 93 D2 239 C4
Stratford New Town E15 76 B3
Storey Ct NW8 229 C1
Storey Ho 13 E14 119 D6
Storey Prim Sch E16 122 D5
Storey Rd Highgate N6 48 D3
Walthamstow E17 53 B5
Storey's Gate
SW1 115 D4 249 D1
Storey St E16 122 C4
Stories Rd SE5 139 C2
Stork Rd E7 77 A2
Storksmead Rd HA8 27 C3
Storks Rd SE16 118 A3
Stormont House Sch
E5 74 B4
Stormont Rd
Clapham SW11 137 A1
Highgate N6 48 D2
Stormont Way KT9 213 C3
Stormount Dr UB3 105 A4
Storrington WC1 233 B1
Storrington Rd CR0 205 D1
Story St N1 72 B1
Stotfold BR1 188 A2
Stothard Ho 25 E1 96 C3
Stothard Pl E1 243 B4
Stothard St 12 E1 96 C3
Stott Cl SW18 158 B5
Stoughton Ave SM3 217 A3
Stoughton Cl
Roehampton SW15 156 A3
Stoughton Cl *continued*
SE11 260 D3
Stour Ave UB2 107 C3
Stourbridge Ho 8 UB5 85 B3
Stour Cl BR2 225 C4
Stourcliffe Cl W1 237 C2
Stourcliffe St W1 237 C1
Stour Ct UB1 86 B1
Stourhead Cl 6
SW19 156 D4
Stourhead Gdns
SW20 200 A6
Stour Rd
Dagenham RM10 81 C6
Hackney Wick E3 75 C1
Stourton Ave TW13 173 B6
Stowage SE8 141 D6
Stow Cres E17 35 A3
Stowe Cres HA4 39 A3
Stowe Gdns N9 17 D3
Stowe Ho
Hampstead Garden Suburb
NW11 48 A3
11 Stoke Newington N16 73 C5
Stowell Ho 2 N8 50 A5
Stowe Pl N15 51 C6
Stowe Rd W12 112 B4
Stowford Coll SM2 218 A1
Stowting Rd BR6 227 C4
Stox Mead HA3 24 B2
Stracey Rd
Becontree NW10 89 B6
Forest Gate E7 77 A4
Strachan Pl SW19,
SW20 178 C4
Stradbroke Gr
Buckhurst Hill IG9 21 D3
Redbridge IG5 56 C6
Stradbroke Rd N5 73 A4
Stradbrook Cl HA2 63 B5
Stradella Rd SE24 161 A5
Straffan Lo 8 NW3 70 C2
Strafford Ho 9 SE8 119 B1
Strafford Rd Acton W3 111 A4
Barnet EN5 1 A2
Hounslow TW3 129 B2
Twickenham TW1 153 A4
Strafford St E14 119 C4
Strahan Rd E3 97 A4
Straightsmouth SE10 142 A5
Straight The UB2 107 A4
Strait Rd E6 122 B6
Straker's Rd SE15 140 B1
Strale Ho 17 N1 95 C6
STRAND 116 B6
Strand
Strand WC2 116 B6 250 C6
Strand WC2 240 D1
Strand Ct SE18 123 D1
Strand Dr TW9 132 D5
Strandfield Cl SE18 123 C1
Strand Ho SE28 123 B5
Strand La WC2 250 D6
STRAND ON THE GREEN
132 C6
Strand-on-the-Green
W4 132 C6
Strand-on-the-Green
Schs W4 132 C6
Strand Pl N18 33 C6
Strang Ho N1 235 A5
Strangways Terr W14 254 C5
Stranraer Way
Barnsbury N1 72 A1
1 Stanwell TW6 148 A5
Strasburg Rd
SW11 137 B4 268 C1
Stratfield Ho SE12 165 A2
Stratfield Park Cl N21 16 D4
STRATFORD 76 A2
Stratford Ave UB10 82 B5
Stratford Bus Sta E15 76 B1
Stratford Cir (Newham 6th
Form Coll) E15 76 B2
Stratford Cl IG11 80 A1
Stratford Ct KT3 199 B5
Stratford Gr SW15 134 D1
Stratford House Ave
BR1 210 A6
Stratford International
Sta E15 76 A2
STRATFORD MARSH 97 D6
STRATFORD NEW
TOWN 76 A3
Stratford Office Village
The 4 E15 76 C1
Stratford Pl W1 238 C1
Stratford Rd
Harlington TW6 149 A6
Hayes UB4 84 B3
Hendon NW4 46 D5
Newham E13 99 A6
Southall UB2 107 A2
Thornton Heath CR7 204 D6
W8 113 C3 255 B5
Stratford Sch E7 77 A1
Stratford Sch (Annexe)
E7 77 B2
Stratford Sh Ctr E15 76 B1
Stratford Sta E15 76 B1
Stratford Studios W8 255 C5
Stratford Villas NW1 71 D1
Stratford Workshops
E15 98 B6
Strathan Cl SW18 157 A5
Strathaven Rd SE12 165 B5
Strathblaine Rd SW11 136 B1
Strathbrook Rd SW16 182 B3
Strathcona Rd HA9 65 D6
Strathdale SW16 182 B5
Strathdon Dr SW17 158 B1
Strathearn Ave
Harlington UB3 127 D5
Twickenham TW2 152 A3
Strathearn Ho W2 247 A6
Strathearn Pl
W2 114 C6 247 A6
Strathearn Rd
Sutton SM1 217 C3
Wimbledon SW19 179 C6
Stratheden Par SE3 143 A5
Stratheden Rd SE3 143 A5
Strathfield Gdns IG11 79 B2
Strathleven Rd SW2 160 A6
Strathmore Ct NW8 230 A2
Strathmore Gdns
Edgware HA8 26 D1
Finchley N3 29 D2
W8 245 B4
Strathmore Rd
Teddington TW11,
TW2 174 C6
Thornton Heath CR0 205 B2
Wimbledon SW19 157 C1
Strathmore Sch TW10 153 D2
Strathnairn St SE1 118 A2
Strathray Gdns NW3 70 C2
Strath Terr SW11 136 C1
Strathville Rd SW18 157 D2
Strathyre Ave SW16 204 C6
Stratton Ave EN2 5 B6
Stratton Cl DA7 147 A2
Edgware HA8 26 B4
Heston TW5 129 C4
Merton SW19 179 C1
Walton-on-T KT12 194 C1
Stratton Ct
4 De Beauvoir Town
N1 73 C1
10 Kingston u T KT6 198 A4
10 Pinner HA5 23 B3
Strattondale St E14 120 A3
Stratton Dr IG11 79 D2
Stratton Gdns UB1 85 C1
Stratton Ho HA8 26 B6
Stratton Lo 10 EN5 1 D1
Stratton Rd DA7 147 A2
Merton SW19 179 C1
Sunbury TW16 171 D1
Stratton St W1 115 B5 248 D4
Strauss Rd W4 111 B4
Strawberry Fields
BR6 226 D3
STRAWBERRY HILL 152 D1
Strawberry Hill Cl
TW1 152 D1
Strawberry Hill Rd
TW1 152 D1
Strawberry Hill Sta
TW2 152 D1
Strawberry La SM5 219 A5
Strawberry Terr N10 30 D2
Strawberry Vale
Finchley N2 30 B2
Twickenham TW1 153 A1
Strayfield Rd EN2 4 D6
Streakes Field Rd NW2 68 A6
Streamdale SE2 146 B6
Stream La HA8 26 D5
Streamline Mews
SE22 162 A3
Streamside Cl BR2 209 A5
Edmonton N9 17 D3
Stream Way DA17 147 C6
Streatfeild Ave E6 100 B6
Streatfield Rd HA3, HA7 43 D6
STREATHAM 182 A4
Streatham Cl SW16 160 A2
Streatham & Clapham
High Sch SW16 159 D1
Streatham Common N
SW16 182 B5
Streatham Common S
SW16 182 B4
Streatham Common Sta
SW16 181 D3
Streatham Ct SW16 160 A1
Streatham High Rd SW16,
SW2 182 A5
STREATHAM HILL 160 A3
Streatham Hill SW2 160 A3
Streatham Hill & Clapham
High Sch SW2 160 B3
Streatham Hill Sta
SW2 160 A2
STREATHAM PARK 181 C6
Streatham Pl SW2 160 A4
Streatham Rd CR4 181 A2
Streatham St WC1 240 A2
Streatham Sta SW16 181 D5
STREATHAM VALE 181 D3
Streatham Vale SW16 181 D3
Streathbourne Rd
SW17 159 A1
Streathem Wells Prim Sch
SW2 160 C2
Streatleigh Par 4
SW16 160 A2
Streatley Pl
27 Hampstead NW3 70 A4
Hampstead NW3 70 B4
Streatley Rd NW6 69 B1
Streeters La SM6 219 D5
Streetfield Mews SE3 143 A2
Streimer Rd E15 98 A5
Strelley Way W3 111 C6
Stretford Ct 1 SW19 179 A3
Strethan Lo W13 109 B6
Stretton Mans 16 SE8 141 C6
Stretton Rd
Croydon CR0 205 C2
Richmond TW10 153 C2
Strickland Ct SE15 140 A2
Strickland Ho 26 E2 95 D4
Strickland Row SW18 158 B4
Strickland St SE8 141 C4
Strickland Way 4
BR6 227 D4
Stride Rd E13 98 D5
Strimon Cl N9 18 C2
Stringer Hos 19 N1 95 C6
Strode Cl N10 31 A3
Strode Ho 3 SW2 160 C3
Strode Rd
Forest Gate E7 77 A4
SW6 135 A5 264 A4
Tottenham N17 33 C1
Willesden NW10 68 A2
Strome Ho NW6 91 D5
Strone Rd E7, E12 77 D2
Strone Way UB4 85 A3
Strongbow Cres SE9 166 B6
Strongbow Rd SE9 166 B6
Strongbridge Cl HA2 41 C1
Stronsa Rd W12 111 D4
Strood Ho
9 Penge SE20 184 C3
SE1 252 D1
Stroud Cres SW15 156 A1
Stroudes Cl KT4 199 D2
Stroud Field UB5 63 A2
Stroud Gate HA2 63 D4
STROUD GREEN 50 C3
Stroud Green Gdns
CR0 206 C2
Stroud Green Prim Sch
N4 50 C1
Stroud Green Rd N4 50 C1
Stroud Green Way
CR0 206 C3
Stroudley Ho SW8 269 B2
Stroudley Wlk E3 97 D4
Stroud Rd
Croydon SE25 206 A3
Wimbledon SW19 157 C1
Strouds Cl RM6 58 B4
Stroud Way TW15 171 A4
Strout's Pl 2 E2 95 D4
Struan Ho 15 E11 55 A4
Strudwick Ct SW4 270 B1
Strutton Ground
SW1 115 D3 259 C5
Strype St E1 243 C3
Stuart Ave Ealing W5 110 B4
Harrow HA2 63 B5
Hayes BR2 209 A1
Hendon NW9 46 A2
Walton-on-T KT12 194 B1
Stuart Cl UB10 60 C2
Stuart Cres
Croydon CR0 223 B5
Hayes UB3 83 A1
Wood Green N22 32 B2
Stuart Ct Chingford E4 20 D2
6 Croydon CR0 220 D5
2 Elstree WD6 9 D5
Stuart Evans Cl DA16 146 C2
Stuart Gr TW11 174 C5
Stuart Ho
Hammersmith W6 112 C3
1 Homerton E9 74 D1
Queensbury NW9 44 C5
5 Stockwell SW4 138 A1
W14 254 A4
Stuart Lo SE25 183 C1
Stuart Mill Ho N1 233 C3
Stuart Pl CR4 180 D2
Stuart Rd Acton W3 111 A5
Barking IG11 79 D1
DA16 146 B4
East Barnet EN4 14 D4
Harrow HA3 42 D6
Maida Vale NW6 91 C4
Nunhead SE15 140 C1
Richmond TW10 153 B1
South Norwood CR7 205 A5
Wimbledon SW19 157 C1
Stubbs Cl NW9 45 A4
Stubbs Dr SE16 118 B1
Stubbs Ho
Finsbury Pk N4 50 B1
1 Globe Town E2 96 D4
Stubbs Mews RM8 80 B4
Stubbs Point E13 99 B3
Stubbs Way SW19 180 B2
Stucley Pl 19 NW1 71 B1
Stucley Rd TW5, TW7 130 A5
Studdridge St SW6 135 C3
Studd St N1 94 D6 234 C6
Studholme Ct NW3 69 C4
Studholme St SE15 140 B5
Studio Mews 5 NW4 46 C5
Studio Pl SW1 247 D1
Studios NW8 229 A4
Studios Rd TW17 192 B6
Studios The
4 Clapham SW4 137 C1
SW8 269 D1
Studland SE17 262 C2
Studland Cl DA15 167 D1
Studland Ho E14 97 A1
Studland Rd Ealing W7 86 C1
Forest Hill SE26 184 D5
Kingston u T KT2 176 A4
Studland St W6 112 B2
Studley Ave E4 36 B3
Studley Cl E5 75 A3
Studley Ct
13 Blackwall E14 120 B6
Studley Ct *continued*
DA14 190 B5
Redbridge IG4 55 D3
Studley Dr IG4 55 D3
Studley Grange Rd
W7 108 D4
Studley Rd
Dagenham RM9 80 D1
South Lambeth SW4 138 A3
Upton E7 77 B2
Study Prep Sch The
SW19 178 C5
Study Sch The KT3 199 C4
Stukeley Rd E7 77 B1
Stukeley St
WC2 94 A1 240 B2
Stumps Hill La BR3 185 C4
Stunell Ho 23 SE14 140 D6
Sturdee Ho 2 E2 96 A5
Sturdy Ho 28 E3 97 A5
Sturdy Rd SE15 140 B3
Sturge Ave E17 35 D1
Sturgeon Rd
SE17 117 A1 262 A1
Sturges Field BR7 189 B4
Sturgess Ave NW4 46 B2
Sturge St SE1 117 A4 252 A2
Sturmer Way N7 72 B3
Sturminster Cl UB4 84 C1
Sturminster Ho SW8 270 D3
Sturrock Cl N15 51 B5
Sturry St E14 97 D1
Sturt St N1 235 B3
Stutfield St E1 96 A1
Stuttle Ho 14 E1 96 A3
Styles Gdns SW9 138 D2
Styles Ho SE1 251 C3
Styles Way BR3 208 A5
Stylus Apartments 25
E1 96 C1
Sudbourne Prim Sch
SW2 160 B6
Sudbourne Rd SW2 160 B6
Sudbrooke Rd SW12 159 A5
Sudbrook Gdns TW10 154 A1
Sudbrook La TW10 154 A2
SUDBURY 65 A4
Sudbury E6 100 C1
Sudbury Ave HA0 65 D4
Sudbury Court Dr HA1 65 A5
Sudbury Court Rd HA1 65 A5
Sudbury Cres BR1 187 A5
Wembley HA0 65 B3
Sudbury Croft HA0 64 D4
Sudbury Ct
1 Ilford RM6 58 B4
SW8 269 D2
Sudbury Gdns CR0 221 C4
Sudbury & Harrow Road
Sta HA0 65 B3
Sudbury Heights Ave
UB6 65 A3
Sudbury Hill HA1 64 C5
Sudbury Hill Cl HA0 64 D5
Sudbury Hill Harrow Sta
HA1 64 C4
Sudbury Hill Sta HA1 64 C4
Sudbury Ho SW18 157 D6
Sudbury Prim Sch HA0 65 B4
Sudbury Rd IG11 79 D3
Sudbury Town Sta UB6 65 B2
Sudeley St N1 94 D5 234 D3
Sudlow Rd SW18 157 C6
Sudrey St SE1 252 A1
Suez Ave UB6 86 D5
Suez Rd EN3 7 A2
Suffield Ho SE17 261 D2
Suffield Rd Chingford E4 35 D6
Penge SE20 184 C1
2 South Tottenham N15 51 D4
Suffolk Cl WD6 11 B6
Suffolk Ct
3 Dagenham RM6 58 C4
Ilford IG3 57 C3
Walthamstow E17 53 C2
3 West Norwood
SW16 182 C6
Suffolk Ho 11 Acton W3 88 C1
Beckenham BR2 208 D5
8 Dartmouth Pk NW5 71 C5
Edgware HA8 26 B4
Penge SE20 184 C2
4 South Croydon CR0 221 B6
Suffolk La EC4 252 C6
Suffolk Park Rd E17 53 A5
Suffolk Pl SW1 249 D4
Suffolk Rd Barking IG11 79 B1
Barnes SW13 134 A5
Dagenham RM10 81 D3
Enfield EN3 18 B6
Harrow HA2 41 C4
Ilford IG3 57 C3
4 Newham E13 99 A4
Sidcup DA14 190 C4
South Norwood SE25 205 D5
Tottenham N15 51 B3
Willesden NW10 67 C1
Worcester Pk KT4 215 D6
Suffolks Prim Sch EN1 6 B3
Suffolk St
Forest Gate E7 77 A4
SW1 115 D5 249 D4
Sugar House La E15 98 A5
Sugar Loaf Wlk 6 E2 96 C4
Sugden Rd
Clapham SW11 137 A1
Long Ditton KT7 197 B1
Sugden Way IG11 101 D5
Sulby Ho SE4 141 A1
Sulgrave Gdns 11 W6 112 C4
Sulgrave Rd W6 112 C3
Sulina Rd SW2 160 A4
Sulivan Ct SW6 135 C3
Sulivan Ent Ctr SW6 135 C2
Sulivan Prim Sch
SW6 135 C3
Sulivan Rd SW6 135 C2
Sulkin Ho 11 E2 96 D4
Sullivan Ave E16 99 D2
Sullivan Cl
Battersea SW11 136 C2
Hayes UB4 84 C2
Sullivan Ct
4 Croydon CR0 206 A1
Stamford Hill N16 51 D1
SW5 255 B4
Sullivan Ho
Chelsea SW1 268 D6
Isleworth TW2 152 B5
Vauxhall SE11 260 D3
Sullivan Rd
SE11 116 C2 261 B4
Sullivans Reach KT12 193 D2
Sullivan Way WD6 9 C5
Sultan Ho SE1 118 A1
Sultan Rd E11 55 B5
Sultan St Penge BR3 184 D1
SE5 139 A5
Sumal Ct E9 76 B6
Sumatra Rd NW6 69 C2
Sumburgh Rd SW12 159 A5
Summer Ave KT8 196 C4
Summercourt Rd E1 96 C1
Summer Crossing
KT7 196 C4
Summerene Cl SW16 181 C3
Summerfield 6 BR1 187 B2
Summerfield Ave
Colney Hatch N12 30 C4
Kensal Rise NW6 91 A5
Summerfield Ho RM9 80 D4
Summerfield La KT6 213 D6
Summerfield Rd
Ealing W5 87 B3
Loughton IG10 21 D5
Summerfield St SE12 164 D4
Summer Gdns KT8 196 C4
Summer Gr WD6 9 D5
Summer Hill
Borehamwood WD6 10 C6
BR7 188 C1
Summerhill Cl BR6 227 C5
Summerhill Gr EN1 17 C5
Summerhill Rd N15 51 B5
Summerhill Villas
BR7 188 D2
Summerhill Way CR4 181 A2
Summer Ho SE13 142 B1
Summerhouse Ave
TW5 129 A4
Summerhouse Rd N16 73 C6
Summerland Gdns N10 49 B6
Summerland Grange
N10 49 B6
Summerlands Ave
W3 111 A6
Summerlands Lo BR6 226 C4
Summerlee Ave N2 48 D5
Summerlee Gdns N2 48 D5
Summerley St SW18 157 D2
Summer Rd
East Molesey KT8 196 B4
Thames Ditton KT7,
KT8 196 D4
Summersby Rd N6 49 B3
Summers Cl
Belmont SM2 217 C1
Wembley HA9 44 D1
Summersell Ho SE27 183 B5
Summerside Prim Sch
N12 30 B4
Summerskille Cl N9 18 B2
Summers La N12 30 B3
Summers Row N12 30 C4
Summers St EC1 241 A5
SUMMERSTOWN 158 A1
Summerstown SW17 180 A6
Summerton Way
SE28 102 D1
Summer Trees TW16 172 B2
Summerville Gdns
SM1 217 B2
Summerwood Rd TW1,
TW7 152 D5
Summit Ave NW9 45 B4
Summit Bsns Pk The
TW16 172 A3
Summit Cl Edgware HA8 26 C3
Kingsbury NW9 45 B5
Osidge N14 15 C2
Summit Ct 5 Barnet EN5 1 B2
Brondesbury NW2 69 A3
Summit Dr IG8 37 D1
Summit Est N16 52 A2
Summit Rd Northolt UB5 63 C1
Walthamstow E17 53 D5
Summit Way
Brunswick Pk N14 15 B2
South Norwood SE19 183 C3
Sumner Ave SE15 139 D4
Sumner Bldgs SE1 252 A4
Sumner Cl BR6 227 A4
Sumner Ct SW8 270 A2
Sumner Gdns CR0 204 C1
Sumner Ho 1 E3 97 D2
Sumner Pl
SW7 114 B2 256 D3
Sumner Place Mews
SW7 256 D3
Sumner Rd Harrow HA1 42 A2

Sumner Rd *continued*
SE15 139 D5
Thornton Heath CR0 204 D1
Sumner Rd S CR0 204 C1
Sumner St SE1 117 A5 252 A4
Sumpter Cl NW3 70 A2
Sun Alley 6 TW9 132 A1
Sun Alliance Ho WC2 241 A2
Sunbeam Cres W10 90 C3
Sunbeam Rd NW10 89 B3
SUNBURY 194 B6
Sunbury Ave
Edgware NW7 27 B6
Mortlake SW14 133 B1
Sunbury Cl KT12 194 A3
SUNBURY COMMON 171 D3
Sunbury Court Island
TW16 194 D6
Sunbury Court Mews
TW16 172 D1
Sunbury Court Rd
TW16 172 C1
Sunbury Cres TW13 171 D6
Sunbury Cross TW16 172 A3
Sunbury Cross Ctr 9
TW16 171 D3
Sunbury Ct
3 Barnet EN5 1 A1
3 SE14 140 D6
Sunbury TW16 172 D1
Sunbury Ct (Con Ctr)
TW16 172 D1
Sunbury Gdns NW7 27 B5
Sunbury Ho 33 E2 95 D4
Sunbury Int Bsns Ctr
TW16 171 C2
Sunbury La
Battersea
SW11 136 B4 266 D2
Walton-on-T KT12 194 A3
Sunbury Manor Sch
TW16 171 D2
Sunbury Rd
Cheam SM3 217 A5
Feltham TW13 171 D6
Sunbury St SE18 122 B3
Sunbury Sta TW16 172 A2
Sunbury Way TW13 172 C5
Sunbury Workshops 39
E2 95 D4
Suncroft Pl SE26 162 C1
Sun Ct EC3 242 D1
Sunderland Ct
Dulwich SE22 162 A4
12 Stanwell TW19 148 A5
Sunderland Ho 26 W2 91 C2
Sunderland Mount
SE23 162 D2
Sunderland Point E16 123 A5
Sunderland Rd
Ealing W5 109 D3
Forest Hill SE23 162 D2
Sunderland Terr W2 91 D1
Sunderland Way E12 77 D6
Sundew Ave W12 112 A6
Sundew Ct 9 HA0 88 A5
Sundial Ave SE25 205 D6
Sundial Ct KT5 214 D6
Sundorne Rd SE7 121 C1
Sundown Rd TW15 171 A5
Sundra Wlk 28 E1 96 D3
SUNDRIDGE 187 C4
Sundridge Ave
Bromley BR1, BR7 188 A3
DA16 145 B2
Sundridge Ho
Bromley BR1 187 B5
4 Homerton E9 74 D1
Sundridge Par BR1 187 B3
Sundridge Park Sta
BR1 187 B3
Sundridge Rd CR0 206 A1
Sunfields Pl SE3 143 B5
Sun in the Sands SE3 143 B5
Sunken Rd CR0 222 C3
Sun La SE3 143 B5
Sunland Ave DA6 147 A1
Sunleigh Ct HA0 88 A6
Sunleigh Rd HA0 88 A6
Sunley Gdns UB6 87 A6
Sunley Ho E1 243 D3
Sun Life Trad Est
TW14 128 A2
Sunlight Cl SW19 180 A4
Sunlight Sq 29 E2 96 B4
Sunmead Rd TW16 194 A6
Sunna Gdns TW16 172 B1
Sunna Lo TW16 171 D3
Sunniholme Ct CR2 221 A3
Sunningdale Ealing W13 87 B2
Friern Barnet N14 31 D5
Sunningdale Ave
Barking IG11 79 B1
East Acton W3 111 C6
Feltham TW13 151 A2
Ruislip HA4 40 C1
Sunningdale Cl
22 Bermondsey SE16 118 B1
Erith SE28 103 A1
Newham E6 100 B4
Stanmore HA7 25 A3
3 Surbiton KT6 214 A6
Sunningdale Ct
13 Kingston u T KT2 176 C3
13 Southall UB1 86 A1
Sunningdale Gdns
Kingsbury NW9 45 A4
W8 255 B5
Sunningdale Lo HA8 26 B5
Sunningdale Rd
BR1, BR2 210 A4
Cheam SM1 217 B4
Sunningfields Cres
NW4 28 B1
Sunningfields Rd NW4 46 B6
Sunninghill Ct 9 W3 111 A4
Sunninghill Gdns IG2 57 D4
Sunninghill Rd SE13 141 D3
Sunny Bank SE25 206 A6
Sunny Cres NW10 67 A1
Sunnycroft Rd
Hounslow TW3 129 D3
Southall UB1 85 C2
South Norwood SE25 206 A6
Sunnydale BR6 226 C6
Sunnydale Gdns NW7 27 C4
Sunnydale Rd SE12 165 B6
Sunnydene Ave
Chingford E4 36 B5
Ruislip HA4 62 A6
Sunnydene Gdns HA0 65 C2
Sunnydene St SE26 185 A6
Sunnyfield NW7 27 D6
Sunnyfields Prim Sch
NW4 46 B6
Sunny Gardens Par
NW4 28 B1
Sunny Gardens Rd
NW4 46 C6
Sunny Hill NW4 46 B6
Sunnyhill Cl E5 75 A4
Sunny Hill Ct NW4 28 B1
Sunnyhill Prim Sch
SW16 182 B6
Sunnyhill Rd SW16 182 A6
Sunnyhurst Cl SM1 217 C5
Sunnymead Ave CR4 203 D6
Sunnymead Ct W5 109 D6
Sunnymead Rd
Kingsbury NW9 45 B2
Putney SW15 156 B6
Sunnymede Ave KT19 215 C1
Sunnymede Dr IG6 56 D5
Sunny Nook Gdns
CR2 221 B2
Sunny Pl NW4 46 C5
Sunny Rd The EN3 6 D4
Sunnyside
4 Child's Hill NW2 69 B5
Walton-on-T KT12 194 C4
Wimbledon SW19 179 A4
Sunnyside Dr E4 20 A4
Sunnyside Ho 3 NW2 69 B5
Sunnyside Pl SW19 179 A4
Sunnyside Rd
Crouch End N19 49 D2
Ealing W5 109 D5
Ilford IG1 79 B5
Teddington TW11 174 B6
Walthamstow E10 53 C1
Sunnyside Rd E N9 18 A1
Sunnyside Rd N N9 18 A1
Sunnyside Rd S N9 18 A1
Sunny View NW9 45 B4
Sunny Way N12 30 C3
Sun Pas 8 SE16 118 A3
Sunray Ave BR2 210 B3
Herne Hill SE5, SE24 139 B1
Tolworth KT5 214 D6
Sun Rd W14 113 B1 254 C1
Sunrise Cl TW13 151 B1
Sunrise View NW7 27 D4
Sun St Pas EC2 95 C2 243 A3
Sunset Ave Chingford E4 19 D3
Woodford IG8 36 D6
Sunset Ct 4 IG8 37 C3
Sunset Gdns SE25 183 D1
Sunset Ho HA3 42 C6
Sunset Rd
Herne Hill SE5 139 B1
SE28 124 A5
Wimbledon SW19 178 B5
Sunset View EN5 1 A3
Sunshine Way CR4 180 D1
Sun St EC2 95 B2 242 D4
Sunwell Cl SE15 140 B4
Superior Dr 4 BR6 227 D2
Suraj Ho 6 N22 32 C1
SURBITON 198 A2
Surbiton Boys Prep Sch
KT6 198 A4
Surbiton Cres KT1,
KT6 198 A5
Surbiton Ct KT6 197 D3
Surbiton Hall Cl KT1 198 A5
Surbiton High Sch
KT1 198 A5
Surbiton High Sch Jun
Girls Sch KT1 198 A5
Surbiton Hill Pk KT5 198 C4
Surbiton Hill Rd KT6 198 A4
Surbiton Hospl KT6 198 A3
Surbiton Par 11 KT6 198 A3
Surbiton Rd KT1 198 A5
Surbiton Sta KT6 198 A3
Surcot Ho 2 SW4 137 D3
Surlingham Cl SE28 124 D6
Surma Cl E1 96 A3
Surmans Cl RM9 102 C6
Surrendale Pl W9 91 C3
Surrey Canal Rd SE14, SE16,
SE8 140 D6
Surrey Cl N3 47 A6
Surrey Cres 1 W4 110 C1
Surrey Ct 15 SM6 219 B2
Surrey Gdns N4 51 A3
Surrey Gr
Carshalton SM1 218 B5
SE17 263 A1
Surrey Ho Edgware HA8 26 B4
8 Rotherhithe SE16 118 D5
Surrey La
SW11 136 C4 267 B1
Surrey Lo SW20 178 C1
Surrey Mews SE27 183 C6
Surrey Mount SE23 162 B3
Surrey Quays Rd SE16 118 D4
Surrey Quays Sh Ctr
SE16 118 D3
Surrey Quays Sta
SE16 118 D2
Surrey Rd Barking IG11 79 C1
Dagenham RM10 81 D3
Harrow HA1 42 A4
Honor Oak SE15 162 D6
West Wickham BR4 207 D1
Surrey Row
SE1 116 D4 251 D2
Surrey Sq SE17 117 C1 263 B2
Surrey Square Inf Sch
SE17 117 C1 263 A2
Surrey Square Jun Sch
SE17 117 C1 263 A2
Surrey St Croydon CR0 221 A5
4 Newham E13 99 B4
WC2 116 B6 250 D6
Surrey Terr SE17 263 B2
Surrey Water Rd
SE16 118 D5
Surrey Wharf SE1 140 A6
Surridge Ct 15 SW9 138 A3
Surridge Gdns SE19 183 B4
Surr St N7 72 A3
Sury Basin KT2 176 A2
Susan Constant Ct 18
E14 120 B6
Susan Lawrence Ho 4
E12 78 C4
Susannah St E14 98 A1
Susan Rd SE3 143 B3
Susan Wood BR7 188 C2
Sussex Ave TW7 130 C2
Sussex Cl
New Malden KT3 199 C5
Redbridge IG4 56 B4
4 Twickenham TW1 153 B5
Upper Holloway N19 72 A6
Sussex Cres UB5 63 C2
Sussex Ct
4 Barnes SW13 133 D3
Greenwich SE10 142 A6
Mitcham CR4 204 A4
Paddington W2 236 C1
Sussex Gate N6 48 D4
Sussex Gdns
Chessington KT9 213 D2
Fortis Green N6 48 D4
Harringay N4 51 A4
Paddington W2 92 B1 236 D1
Sussex Ho Edgware HA8 26 B4
Hampstead NW3 70 C2
Richmond TW9 132 B3
Sussex House Sch
SW3 114 D2 257 C4
Sussex Lo W2 236 D1
Sussex Mans
South Kensington
SW7 256 C3
Strand WC2 250 B6
Sussex Mews SE6 163 C3
Sussex Mews E W2 236 D1
Sussex Mews W W2 246 D6
Sussex Pl
22 Hammersmith W6 112 C1
Lisson Gr NW1 92 D3 237 C6
New Malden KT3 199 C5
Paddington W2 92 B1 236 D1
Sussex Rd Barking E6 100 C6
Erith DA8 147 D5
Harrow HA1 42 A4
Mitcham CR4 204 A4
New Malden KT3 199 C5
Sidcup DA14 190 B5
Southall UB2 106 D3
South Croydon CR2 221 B2
Uxbridge UB10 61 A3
Wallington SM5 218 D2
2 West Wickham BR4 207 D1
Sussex Ring N12 29 C5
Sussex Sq W2 114 B6 246 D6
Sussex St Newham E13 99 B4
SW1 258 D2
Sussex Way
Cockfosters EN4 15 B6
Upper Holloway N7 72 B5
Upper Holloway N7, N19 72 A6
Upper Holloway N19 49 D1
Sutcliffe Cl NW11 47 D4
Sutcliffe Ho UB3 84 A1
Sutcliffe Rd
Bexley DA16 146 C3
SE18 145 C6
Sutherland Ave
Ealing W13 87 B1
Falconwood DA16 145 C1
Hayes UB3 106 A2
Orpington BR5 211 D4
Paddington W9 92 A3 236 A6
Sunbury TW16 171 D1
Sutherland Cl EN5 1 A1
Sutherland Ct
Kingsbury NW9 44 D4
3 Paddington W9 91 C3
Stoke Newington N16 73 B5
Sutherland Dr SW19 180 B2
Sutherland Gdns
Mortlake SW14 133 C2
North Cheam KT4 200 B1
Sunbury TW16 171 D1
Sutherland Gr
Putney SW18, SW19 157 B4
Teddington TW11 174 C5
Sutherland Ho
Ealing W13 109 A6
Kensington W8 255 C5
Kidbrooke SE18 144 B4
7 Putney SW15 156 C4
Richmond TW10 153 C2
9 South Hampstead
NW6 70 A2
Sutherland Pl W2 91 C1
Sutherland Rd
Belvedere DA17 125 C3
Chiswick W4 133 C6
Ealing W13 87 A1
Edmonton N9 18 B3
Enfield EN3 18 D6
Southall UB1 85 B1
Thornton Heath CR0 204 C2
Tottenham N17 34 A2
Walthamstow E17 53 A6
Sutherland Row SW1 258 D2
Sutherland Sq
SE17 117 A1 262 A1
Sutherland St
SW1 115 B1 258 D2
Sutherland Wlk SE17 262 B1
Sutlej Rd SE7 143 C5
Sutterton St N7 72 B2
SUTTON 218 A2
Sutton Cl
Beckenham BR3 185 D2
Pinner HA5 40 A4
Sutton Coll of Liberal Arts
SM1 217 D3
Sutton Common Rd
Cheam SM3 201 C1
Sutton SM1, SM3 217 D6
Sutton Common Sta
SM1 217 D6
Sutton Courtenay Ho
SW17 180 B6
Sutton Court Mans
W4 133 A6
Sutton Court Rd
Chiswick W4 133 A6
Hillingdon UB10 82 D6
Newham E13 99 C4
Sutton SM1 218 A2
Sutton Cres EN5 12 D6
Sutton Ct Chiswick W4 133 A6
Ealing W5 110 A5
East Molesey KT8 195 B4
8 Hackney E5 74 B4
Penge SE19 183 D3
Sutton SM2 218 A2
Sutton Dene TW3 129 D4
Sutton Est
SW3 114 C1 257 B2
Sutton Est The 8 W10 90 C2
Sutton Gdns
Barking IG11 101 C5
Croydon CR0 205 D4
Sutton Gn IG11 101 C6
Sutton Gr SM1 218 B3
Sutton Gram Sch For Boys
SM1 218 A3
Sutton Hall Rd TW5 129 C5
Sutton High Sch SM1 217 D2
Sutton Ho N21 16 B6
Sutton House★ E9 74 C3
Sutton Hts SM2 218 B1
Sutton La EC1 241 D5
Hounslow TW3, TW4,
TW5 129 B3
Sutton La N W4 111 A1
Sutton La S W4 133 A6
Sutton Par NW4 46 C5
Sutton Park Rd SM1,
SM2 217 D2
Sutton Pl E9 74 C3
Sutton Rd
Barking IG11 101 C6
E13 98 D3
Heston TW5 129 C4
Higham Hill E17 34 D2
Muswell Hill N10 31 A2
Sutton Row W1 239 D2
Sutton Sq Hackney E9 74 C3
Hounslow TW5 129 B4
Sutton St E1 96 C1
Sutton Sta SM2 218 A2
Suttons Way EC1 242 B5
Sutton Way
Hounslow TW5 129 B4
North Kensington W10 90 C2
Sutton Wlk
SE1 116 B5 250 D3
Swaby Rd SW17, SW18 158 A2
Swaffham Ct 1 RM6 58 C4
Swaffield Prim Sch
SW18 158 A4
Swaffield Rd SW18 158 A4
Swain Cl SW16 181 B4
Swain Ho CR4 180 D3
Swain Rd CR7 205 A4
Swains Cl UB7 104 A4
Swain's La N6 71 B6
Swainson Ho N7 72 C4
Swainson Rd W3 111 D4
Swains Rd CR4, SW17 180 D3
Swain St NW8 92 C3 237 A6
Swakeleys Dr UB10 60 C3
Swakeleys Rd UB10 60 C5
Swakeleys Rdbt UB8,
UB10 60 A4
Swakeleys Sch UB10 82 D5
Swaledale Cl N11 31 A4
Swallands Rd SE6 163 C1
Swallowbrook Bsns Ctr
UB4 106 D5
Swallow Cl Bushey WD23 8 A3
New Cross Gate SE14 140 D4
Swallow Ct
Chingford IG8 36 B3
Ilford IG2 56 D4
4 Paddington W9 91 C2
5 Ruislip HA4 40 C1
1 SE12 165 A4
Swallow Dr
Northolt UB5 85 C5
Willesden NW10 67 B2
Swallowfield NW1 231 D1
Swallowfield Rd SE7 121 B1
Swallowfield Way
UB3 105 B4
Swallow Gdns SW16 181 D5
Swallow Ho Hornsey N8 50 B6
NW8 230 A4
Swallow Pk KT6 214 B5
Swallow Pl
24 Poplar E14 97 B1
W1 238 D1
Swallows Ct 5 SE20 184 D3
Swallow St
Newham E6 100 A2
W1 115 C6 249 B5
Swaminarayan Sch The
NW10 67 B2
Swanage Ct 5 N1 73 C1
Swanage Ho SW8 270 C3
Swanage Rd
Chingford E4 36 A3
Wandsworth SW18 158 A5
Swanage Waye UB4 84 C1
Swan And Pike Rd EN3 7 C5
Swan App E6 100 A2
Swanbourne SE17 262 A3
Swanbourne Ho NW8 237 A6
Swanbridge Rd DA7 147 C4
Swan Bsns Ctr 8 W4 111 B2
Swan Cl Croydon CR0 205 C2
Feltham TW13 173 A6
Higham Hill E17 35 A3
Swan Ct Chelsea SW3 257 B1
Parsons Green SW6 265 A3
Poplar E14 97 B1
Whetstone N20 14 A2
Swan Ctr SW17 158 A1
Swandon Way SW18 135 D1
Swan Dr NW9 27 C1
Swanfield St E2 95 D4
Swan Ho
De Beauvoir Town N1 73 B1
Enfield EN3 18 C6
Swan La EC4 117 B6 252 D5
Loughton IG10 21 C4
Whetstone N20 14 A1
Swan Lane Pier
EC4 117 B6 252 C5
Swanlea Sec Sch E1 96 B3
Swanley Ho SE17 263 B2
Swanley Rd DA16 146 C4
Swan Mead
SE1 117 C3 263 A5
Swan Mews
Stockwell SW9 138 B3
SW6 265 A2
Swanmore Ct SW18 158 A5
Swann Ct 8 TW7 131 A2
Swanne Ho 12 SE10 142 A5
Swan Pas 5 E1 118 A6
Swan Pl SW13 133 D3
Swan Rd Feltham TW13 173 A6
Greenwich SE18 121 D3
Rotherhithe SE16 118 C4
Southall UB1 85 D1
West Drayton UB7 104 A4
Swanscombe Ho
1 BR5 190 B1
11 Shepherd's Bush
W11 112 D5
Swanscombe Point 7
E16 98 D2
Swanscombe Rd
5 Chiswick W4 111 C1
Shepherd's Bush W11 112 D5
Swansea Ct E16 122 D5
Swansea Rd Enfield EN3 6 C1
Harlington TW14, TW6 149 B5
Swansland Gdns 2
E17 35 A2
Swan St Isleworth TW7 131 B2
SE1 117 A4 252 B1
Swanston Ct TW1 152 D4
Swan The BR4 224 A6
Swanton Gdns SW19 156 D3
Swanton Rd DA8 147 D5
Swan Way EN3 6 D3
Swanwick Cl SW15 155 D4
Swan Wlk
Oatlands Pk TW17 193 C2
SW3 136 D6 267 C6
Swan Yd N1 72 D2
Swaton Rd E3 97 C3
Swaylands Rd DA17 147 C6
Swaythling Cl N18 34 B6
Swaythling Ho SW15 155 D5
Swedenborg Gdns E1 118 B6
Sweden Gate SE16 119 A2
Swedish Quays SE16 119 A3
Swedish Sch The
SW13 134 A6
Sweeney Cres SE1 253 D1
Sweet Briar Gn N9 17 D1
Sweet Briar Gr N9 17 D1
Sweet Briar Wlk N18 33 D6
Sweetcroft La UB10 60 C1
Sweetmans Ave HA5 40 D6
Sweets Way N20 14 B2
Swell Ct E17 53 D3
Swetenham Wlk SE18 123 A1
Swete St E13 99 A5
Sweyn Pl SE3 143 A3
Swift Cl Harrow HA2 63 D6
Hayes UB3 83 D1
Higham Hill E17 35 A3
Thamesmead SE28 124 B6
Swift Ct SM2 217 D1
Swift Ctr CR0 220 B1
Swift Ho 16 Stepney E1 96 C1
15 Stoke Newington N16 73 C5
1 SW9 138 C5
8 Wanstead E18 55 B6
Swift Rd Feltham TW13 173 A6
Southall UB2 107 B3
Swiftsden Way BR1 186 C4
Swift St SW6 135 B4 264 C2
Swinbrook Rd W10 91 A2
Swinburne Cres CR0 206 C3
Swinburne Ct 4 SE5 139 B1
Swinburne Ho 15 E2 96 C4
Swinburne Rd SW15 134 A1
Swinderby Rd HA0 66 A2
Swindon Cl IG3 57 C1
Swindon Rd TW6 149 A6
Swindon St W12 112 C5
Swinfield Cl TW13 173 A6
Swinford Gdns SW9 138 D2
Swingate La SE18 145 C5
Swingfield Ct BR2 209 D4
Swingfield Ho 4 E9 96 C6
Swinley Ho NW1 231 D2
Swinnerton St E9 75 A3
Swinson Ho 12 N11 31 C5
Swinton Cl HA9 44 D1
Swinton Ho 21 E2 96 A4
Swinton Pl WC1 233 C2
Swinton St WC1 94 B4 233 C2
Swires Shaw BR2 225 D4
Swiss Cottage NW3 70 B1
Swiss Cottage Sch
South Hampstead NW3 70 B1
St John's Wood
NW8 92 B6 229 D6
Swiss Cottage Sta NW3 70 B1
Swiss Re Building★
EC2 95 C1 243 B2
Swiss Terr 7 NW3 70 B1
Switch Ho 4 E14 120 B6
Swithland Gdns SE9 188 C6
Swyncombe Ave W5 109 B2
Swynford Gdns 7
NW4 46 A5
Sybil Elgar Sch UB2 107 B3
Sybil Mews N4 50 D3
Sybil Phoenix Cl SE8 118 D1
Sybil Thorndike Casson Ho
SW5 255 B1
Sybil Thorndike Ho 12
N1 73 A2
Sybourn Inf Sch Annexe
E10 53 A1
Sybourn Jun & Inf Schs
E17 53 B2
Sybourn St E17 53 B2
Sycamore Ave DA15 167 D5
Ealing W5 109 D3
East Finchley N3 47 D6
Hayes UB3 105 C6
Old Ford E3 97 B6
Sycamore Cl
Carshalton SM5 218 D4
Chislehurst SE9 166 A2
East Acton W3 111 C5
2 Edgware HA8 27 A6
Edmonton N9 34 A6
Feltham TW13 150 A1
New Barnet EN4 14 B5
Newham E16 98 C3
Northolt UB5 85 A6
South Croydon CR2 221 C3
Yiewsley UB7 104 B6
Sycamore Ct
4 Beckenham BR3 185 C2
Forest Gate E7 77 A2
3 Forest Hill SE26 184 C6
Golders Green NW11 47 A3
Hendon NW4 28 C1
Hillingdon UB8 82 C3
Hither Green SE12 164 D5
Hounslow TW4 129 A1
Kilburn NW6 91 C6
Surbiton KT6 198 A2
Tufnell Pk N19 71 D5
10 West Norwood
SW16 182 C5
Sycamore Gdns
Hammersmith W6,
W12 112 B3
Mitcham CR4 180 B1
Tottenham N15 51 D5
Sycamore Gr
Kingsbury NW9 45 A2
Kingston u T KT3 199 C6
Lewisham SE6 164 A5
Penge SE20 184 A2
Sycamore Hill N11 31 A4
Sycamore Ho
4 Buckhurst Hill IG9 21 D2
23 Finchley N2 30 B1
10 Maitland Pk NW3 70 D2
Penge SE20 184 D4
17 Rotherhithe SE16 118 D4

Sycamore Ho continued
  🔳 Shepherd's Bush
    W6 . . . . 112 B4
  🔳 Stoke Newington N16 . 73 B6
    Teddington TW11 . . . . . 175 C3
    Twickenham TW1 . . . . . 152 D2
Sycamore Lo
  🔳 Ashford TW16 . . . . . 171 D3
    Putney SW15 . . . . 134 B2
Sycamore Lodge HA2 . . 64 B6
Sycamore Mews 🔳
    SW4 . . . . 137 C2
Sycamore Rd SW19,
    SW20 . . . . 178 C4
Sycamore St EC1 . . . . . 242 B4
Sycamore Way TW11 . . 175 C4
Sycamore Wlk
    Ilford IG6 . . . . 57 A5
  🔳 Kensal Town W10 . . . 91 A3
Sydcote SE21 . . . . 161 A3
Sydenham Ave
    Penge SE26 . . . . 184 B5
    Southgate N21 . . . . 16 B6
Sydenham High Sch
    SE26 . . . . 162 B1
Sydenham High Sch GDST
    SE26 . . . . 184 B5
Sydenham Hill SE21, SE22,
    SE23, SE19 . . . . 162 A1
Sydenham Hill Sta
    SE21 . . . . 161 D1
Sydenham Ho 🔳 KT6 . . 197 D2
Sydenham Ind Est
    SE26 . . . . 185 B5
Sydenham Park Mans 🔳
    SE26 . . . . 162 C1
Sydenham Park Rd SE23,
    SE26 . . . . 162 C1
Sydenham Pk SE26 . . . 162 C1
Sydenham Rd
    Forest Hill SE26 . . . . . . 185 A6
    Thornton Heath CR0 . . . 205 B2
    Sydenham SE26 . . . . . 162 B2
Sydenham Rise SE23 . . 162 B2
Sydenham Sta SE26 . . . 184 C6
Sydenham Station App 🔳
    SE26 . . . . 184 C6
Sydmons Ct SE23 . . . . . 162 C4
Sydner Mews N16 . . . . . 73 C4
Sydner Rd N16 . . . . 73 C4
Sydney Chapman Way
    EN5 . . . . 1 B3
Sydney Cl SW3 . . . . . . 256 D3
Sydney Cotts KT10 . . . . 212 D2
Sydney Cres TW15 . . . . 170 D4
Sydney Ct Hayes UB4 . . 84 C3
    Surbiton KT6 . . . . 214 A6
Sydney Gr NW4 . . . . 46 C4
Sydney Ho
  🔳 Chiswick W4 . . . . . . 111 C2
    Muswell Hill N10 . . . . . 31 B3
Sydney Mews SW3 . . . 256 D3
Sydney Pl SW7 . . . . . . 257 A3
Sydney Rd
    Abbey Wood SE2 . . . . . 124 D3
    Bexley DA6 . . . . 146 D1
    Ealing W13 . . . . 109 A4
    East Bedfont TW14 . . . . 150 A3
    Enfield EN2 . . . . 5 B1
    Hornsey N8 . . . . 50 C5
    Muswell Hill N10 . . . . . 31 B3
    Richmond TW10, TW9 . . 132 A1
    Sidcup DA14 . . . . 189 C6
    Sutton SM1 . . . . 217 C4
    Teddington TW11 . . . . . 174 D5
    Wanstead E11 . . . . 55 B3
    West Barnes SW20 . . . . 178 D1
    Woodford IG8 . . . . 37 A6
Sydney Russell Sch The
    RM9 . . . . 80 D3
Sydney St SW3 . 114 C1 257 A2
Sydney Terr KT10 . . . . 212 D2
Sylva Cotts 🔳 SE8 . . . 141 C4
Sylva Ct 🔳 SW15 . . . . 156 D4
Sylvana Cl UB10 . . . . . . 82 B6
Sylvan Ave
    Church End N3 . . . . 29 C1
    Dagenham RM6 . . . . . . 59 B3
    Edgware NW7 . . . . 27 D4
    Wood Green N22 . . . . . 32 C3
Sylvan Ct Finchley N12 . 29 D6
  🔳 Kilburn NW6 . . . . 91 D6
    South Croydon CR2 . . . 221 A4
Sylvan Gdns KT6 . . . . 197 D2
Sylvan Gr
    Hampstead NW2 . . . . . 68 D4
    SE15 . . . . 140 B6
Sylvan Hill SE19 . . . . . 183 C4
Sylvan Ho N21 . . . . 16 B6
Sylvan Rd Ilford IG1 . . . 79 A6
    South Norwood SE19 . . 183 D2
    Upton E7 . . . . 77 B2
    Walthamstow E17 . . . . . 53 C4
    Wanstead E11 . . . . 55 A4
Sylvan Way
    Coney Hall BR4 . . . . . . 224 C4
    Dagenham RM8 . . . . . . 80 B5
Sylvan Wlk BR1 . . . . . . 210 B6
Sylverdale Rd CR0 . . . . 220 D5
Sylvester Ave BR7 . . . . 188 B4
Sylvester Ct HA0 . . . . . . 65 D3
Sylvester Ho 🔳 E8 . . . . 74 B2
Sylvester Path 🔳 E8 . . . 74 B2
Sylvester Rd Finchley N2 . 30 B1
    Hackney E8 . . . . 74 B2
    Walthamstow E17 . . . . . 53 B2
    Wembley HA0 . . . . 65 C3
Sylvestrus Cl KT1 . . . . 176 C1

Sylvia Ave HA5 . . . . 23 B4
Sylvia Ct N1 . . . . 235 C3
    Wembley HA9 . . . . 66 D1
Sylvia Gdns HA9 . . . . . . 66 D1
Sylvia Lawla Ct N22 . . . . 32 B1
Sylvia Pankhurst Ho
  🔳 Dagenham RM10 . . . . 81 C5
  🔳 Globe Town E2 . . . . . 96 D4
Sylvia Young Theatre Sch
    NW1 . . . . 237 B5
Symes Mews NW1 . . . . 232 A4
Symington Ho SE1 . . . . 262 C5
Symington Mews E9 . . . 74 D3
Symister Mews N1 . . . . . 95 C4
Symons St
    SW3 . . . . 114 D2 257 D3
Symphony Ho HA8 . . . . . 26 D3
Symphony Mews 🔳
    W10 . . . . 91 A4
Syon Gate Way TW7,
    TW8 . . . . 131 B5
Syon Ho & Pk * TW8 . . 131 C4
Syon La
    Brentford TW7, TW8 . . . 131 B5
    Hounslow TW7 . . . . . . 130 D4
Syon Lane Sta TW7 . . . 131 A5
Syon Lo 🔳 SE12 . . . . . 165 A4
Syon Park Cotts TW8 . . 131 C4
Syon Park Gdns TW7 . . 130 D5
Syon Park Sch TW7 . . . 131 B4
Syringa Ho SE4 . . . . . . 141 B2

T

Tabard Ct 🔳 E14 . . . . . 98 A1
Tabard Ho SE1 . . . . . . 262 D6
    Teddington KT1 . . . . . . 175 C2
Tabard St E1 . . 117 B3 262 C6
Tabernacle Ave 🔳 E13 . . 99 A3
Tabernacle St
    EC2 . . . . 95 B3 242 D6
Tableer Ave SW4 . . . . . 159 D6
Tabley Rd N7 . . . . 72 A4
Tabor Ct 🔳 SM3 . . . . . 217 A2
Tabor Gdns SM2, SM3 . . 217 B1
Tabor Gr SW19 . . . . . . 179 B3
Tabor Rd W6 . . . . 112 B3
Tachbrook Est
    SW1 . . . . 115 D1 259 D1
Tachbrook Mews SW1 . . 259 A4
Tachbrook Rd
    East Bedfont TW14 . . . . 149 D4
    Southall UB2 . . . . 106 D2
Tachbrook St
    SW1 . . . . 115 C2 259 B3
Tack Mews SE4 . . . . . . 141 C2
Tadbourne Ct 🔳 HA8 . . . 27 A3
Tadema Ho NW8 . . . . . 236 D5
Tadema Rd
    SW10 . . . . . . 136 A5 266 B3
Tadlow KT1 . . . . 198 C6
Tadmor Cl TW16 . . . . . 193 D5
Tadmor St W12 . . . . . . 112 D5
Tadworth Ave KT3 . . . . 199 D4
Tadworth Ct 🔳 N11 . . . . 31 A4
Tadworth Ho SE1 . . . . . 251 C1
Tadworth Rd NW2 . . . . . 68 A6
Taeping St E14 . . . . . . 119 D2
Taffrail Ho 🔳 E14 . . . . 119 D1
Taffy's How CR4 . . . . . 202 C6
Taft Way 🔳 E3 . . . . 97 D4
Taggs Ho KT1 . . . . 175 D1
Tailors Ct 🔳 SW16 . . . . 181 C6
Tailworth St 🔳 E1 . . . . . 96 A2
Tait 🔳 NW9 . . . . 27 D3
Tait Ct 🔳 Old Ford E3 . . 97 B6
    SW8 . . . . 269 D2
  🔳 Tufnell Pk N19 . . . . . 71 C4
Tait Ho SE1 . . . . 251 B3
Tait Rd CR0 . . . . 205 D2
Tait Rd Ind Est CR0 . . . 205 C2
Takhar Mews SW11 . . . 136 C3
Talacre Rd NW5 . . . . . . 71 A2
Talbot Ave N2 . . . . 48 B6
Talbot Cl N15 . . . . 51 D5
Talbot Cres NW4 . . . . . . 46 A4
Talbot Ct EC3 . . . . 252 C6
    Neasden NW9 . . . . 67 B5
Talbot Gdns IG3 . . . . . . 80 A6
Talbot Grove Ho 🔳
    W11 . . . . 91 A1
Talbot Ho Highbury N7 . . 72 C5
    Poplar E14 . . . . 97 D1
Talbot Pl SE3 . . . . 142 C3
Talbot Rd
    Ashford TW15 . . . . . . 170 A3
    Camberwell SE22 . . . . 139 C1
    Dagenham RM9 . . . . . . 81 B1
    Ealing W13 . . . . 109 A5
    Forest Gate E7 . . . . 77 A4
    Harrow HA3 . . . . 24 D1
    Highgate N6 . . . . 49 A3
    Isleworth TW1, TW7 . . . 131 A1
    Notting Hill W2 . . . . 91 C1
    Notting Hill W11 . . . . . . 91 B1
    Southall UB2 . . . . 107 A2
    South Norwood CR7 . . . 205 B5
    Tottenham N15 . . . . 51 D5
    Twickenham TW2 . . . . . 152 D3
    Wallend E6 . . . . 100 C1
    Wallington SM5 . . . . . . 219 A3
    Wembley HA0 . . . . 65 D2
    Wood Green N22 . . . . . 31 C2
Talbot Sq W2 . . . 92 B1 236 C1
Talbot Wlk
    Notting Hill W11 . . . . . . 91 A1
    Willesden NW10 . . . . . . 67 C2
Talbot Yd SE1 . . . . 252 C3
Talcott Path 🔳 SW2 . . . 160 C1

Talfourd Pl SE15 . . . . . 139 D4
Talfourd Rd SE15 . . . . . 139 D4
Talgarth Rd
    Hammersmith W6 . . . . 112 C1
    W14 . . . . 113 A1 254 B2
Talgarth Wlk NW9 . . . . . 45 C4
Talia Ho E14 . . . . 120 A3
Talina Ctr SW6 . . . . . . 266 A1
Talisman Cl 🔳 IG3 . . . . . 58 B1
Talisman Sq SE26 . . . . 184 A6
Talisman Way HA9 . . . . . 66 B5
Tallack Cl HA3 . . . . 24 C3
Tallack Rd E10 . . . . 53 B1
Tall Elms Cl BR2 . . . . . 208 D4
Talleyrand Ho SE5 . . . . 139 A3
Tallis Cl E16 . . . . 99 B1
Tallis Gr SE7 . . . . 143 B6
Tallis St EC4 . . . . 251 B6
Tallis View NW10 . . . . . 67 B2
Tallow Rd TW8 . . . . 131 C5
Tall Trees SW16 . . . . . 204 B6
Talma Gdns TW2 . . . . . 152 C4
Talmage Cl SE23 . . . . . 162 C4
Talman Gr HA7 . . . . 25 D4
Talma Rd SW2 . . . . 138 C1
Talmud Torah Chaim
    Meirim Sch N16 . . . . . . 51 D1
Talmud Torah Machzikei
    Hadass Sch E5 . . . . . . 52 A2
Talmud-Torah Yetev-Lev
    N16 . . . . 52 A1
Talwin St E3 . . . . 97 D4
Tamar Cl 🔳 E3 . . . . 97 B6
Tamar Ho
  🔳 Cubitt Town E14 . . . . 120 A4
    SE11 . . . . 261 B2
Tamarind Ct 🔳 W3 . . . . 89 A1
Tamarind Ho 🔳 SE15 . . 140 A5
Tamarind Yd 🔳 E1 . . . . 118 A5
Tamarisk Sq W12 . . . . 111 D6
Tamar Sq IG8 . . . . 37 B4
Tamar St SE7 . . . . 122 A2
Tame Way N17 . . . . 52 A6
Tame Ho 🔳 UB5 . . . . . . 85 B4
Tamesa Ho TW1 . . . . . 192 C2
Tamesis Gdns KT4 . . . . 215 C6
Tamian Ind Est TW4 . . . 128 C1
Tamian Way TW4 . . . . . 128 C1
Tamil Ho SE6 . . . . 163 C2
Tamworth N7 . . . . 72 A2
Tamworth Ave IG8 . . . . . 36 C4
Tamworth La CR4 . . . . . 203 B6
Tamworth Pk CR4 . . . . . 203 B6
Tamworth Pl 🔳 CR0 . . . 221 A6
Tamworth Rd CR0 . . . . 221 A6
Tamworth St
    SW6 . . . . 135 C6 265 A5
Tancred Rd N4 . . . . 50 D3
Tandem Ctr SW19 . . . . 180 B2
Tandridge Ct SM2 . . . . 217 D2
Tandridge Dr BR6 . . . . 211 B1
Tandridge Pl 🔳 BR6 . . . 211 B1
Tanfield Ave NW2 . . . . . 67 D4
Tangier Rd TW10 . . . . . 132 D2
Tangleberry Cl BR1 . . . 210 B5
Tangle Tree Cl N3 . . . . . 29 D1
Tanglewood Cl
    Hillingdon UB10 . . . . . . 82 C3
    South Croydon CR0 . . . 222 C5
    Stanmore HA7 . . . . 9 A3
Tanglewood Lo HA8 . . . . 27 A4
Tanglewood Way
    TW13 . . . . 150 B1
Tangley Gr SW15 . . . . . 155 D4
Tangley Park Rd
    TW12 . . . . 173 B4
Tanglyn Ave TW17 . . . . 192 D4
Tangmere
    Tottenham N17 . . . . 33 B1
    WC1 . . . . 233 C1
Tangmere Gdns UB5 . . . 84 C5
Tangmere Gr KT2 . . . . . 175 D5
Tangmere Way NW9 . . . 27 C1
Tanhurst Ho 🔳 SW2 . . 160 A4
Tanhurst Wlk SE2 . . . . 124 D3
Tankerton Rd KT6 . . . . 214 B6
Tankerton St WC1 . . . . 233 B1
Tankerton Terr CR0 . . . 204 B3
Tankerville Rd SW16 . . 182 A3
Tankridge Rd NW2 . . . . 68 B6
Tanner Ho
  🔳 Merton SW19 . . . . . 180 A2
    SE1 . . . . 253 B1
Tanner Point E13 . . . . . 99 A6
Tanners Cl KT12 . . . . . 194 B3
Tanners End La N18 . . . 33 C5
Tanners La IG6 . . . . 57 A6
Tanners Mews SE8 . . . 141 B4
Tanner St Barking IG11 . 79 A2
    SE1 . . . . 117 C4 253 B1
Tanners Yd 🔳 E2 . . . . . 96 B5
Tannery Cl
    Beckenham BR3, CR0 . . 206 D4
    Dagenham RM10 . . . . . 81 D5
Tannery Ho 🔳 E1 . . . . . 96 A2
Tannington Terr N5 . . . . 72 C5
Tannsfeld Rd SE26 . . . 184 D5
Tansley Cl N7 . . . . 71 D3
Tanswell St SE1 . . . . . 251 A1
Tansy Cl E6 . . . . 100 C1
Tantallon Rd SW12 . . . 159 A3
Tant Ave E16 . . . . 98 D1
Tantony Gr RM6 . . . . . . 58 D6
Tanworth Gdns HA5 . . . 22 C1
Tanyard Ho 🔳 E3 . . . . . 98 C1
Tan Yard La DA5 . . . . . 169 C4
Tanza Rd NW3 . . . . 70 D4
Tapestry Cl SM2 . . . . . 217 D1

Tapley Ho 🔳 SE1 . . . . 118 A4
Taplow NW3 . . . . 70 B1
Taplow Ct CR4 . . . . 202 C5
Taplow Ho 🔳 E2 . . . . . . 95 D4
Taplow Rd N13 . . . . 33 A6
Taplow St N1 . . . 95 A5 235 B3
Tappesfield Rd SE15 . . 140 C2
Tapping Cl 🔳 KT2 . . . . 176 B1
Tapp St E1 . . . . 96 B3
Tapster St EN5 . . . . 1 B2
Tara Ct 🔳 BR3 . . . . . . 185 D1
Taranto Ho 🔳 E1 . . . . . . 96 D2
Tarati Ct HA0 . . . . 65 D1
Tarbert Rd SE22 . . . . . 161 C6
Tarbert Wlk E1 . . . . 118 C6
Target Cl TW14 . . . . . . 149 C5
Target Ho W13 . . . . . . 109 B5
Target Rdbt UB5 . . . . . . 85 B6
Tariff Rd N17 . . . . 34 A4
Tarleton Ct 🔳 N22 . . . . 32 C1
Tarleton Gdns SE23 . . . 162 B3
Tarling Cl DA14 . . . . . . 168 B1
Tarling Rd
    Canning Town E16 . . . . 98 D1
    Finchley N2 . . . . 30 A1
Tarling St E1 . . . . 96 C1
Tarnbank EN2 . . . . 16 A6
Tarnbrook Ct SW1 . . . . 258 A3
Tarn St SE1 . . . 117 A3 262 A5
Tarns The NW1 . . . . . . 232 A2
Tarnwood Pk SE9 . . . . . 166 B3
Tarplett Ho 🔳 SE14 . . . 140 D6
Tarquin Ho SE26 . . . . . 184 A6
Tarragon Cl SE14 . . . . . 141 A5
Tarragon Gr SE26 . . . . 184 D4
Tarranbrae NW6 . . . . . . 69 A1
Tarrant Ho E2 . . . . 96 C4
Tarrant Pl W1 . . . . 237 C3
Tarrantt Ho W14 . . . . . 254 A6
Tarriff Cres SE8 . . . . . . 119 B2
Tarrington Cl SW16 . . . 159 C1
Tartan Ho 🔳 E14 . . . . . 98 A1
Tarver Rd
    SE17 . . . . 116 D1 261 D2
Tarves Way SE10 . . . . . 141 D5
Tash Pl N11 . . . . 31 B5
Tasker Cl UB7 . . . . 127 A5
Tasker Ho
  🔳 Barking IG11 . . . . . 101 B5
  🔳 Poplar E14 . . . . 97 B2
Tasker Lo W8 . . . . 245 A2
Tasker Rd NW3 . . . . 70 D3
Tasman Ct
    Ashford TW16 . . . . . . 171 C3
  🔳 Cubitt Town E14 . . . . 119 D2
Tasman Ho 🔳 E1 . . . . . 118 B5
Tasmania Terr N18 . . . . 33 A4
Tasman Rd SW9 . . . . . 138 A2
Tasman Wlk E16 . . . . . . 99 D1
Tasso Rd W6 . . 135 A6 264 A6
Tasso Yd W6 . . . . 264 A5
Tatam Rd NW10 . . . . . . 67 B1
Tatchbury Ho SW15 . . . 155 D5
Tate Britain *
    SW1 . . . . 116 A2 260 A3
Tate Gdns WD23 . . . . . . 8 C4
Tate Ho 🔳 E2 . . . . 96 D5
Tate Modern *
    EC4 . . . . 116 B5 251 D4
Tate Rd Newham E16 . . 122 B5
    Sutton SM1 . . . . 217 C3
Tatham Pl NW8 . . 92 B5 229 D4
Tattersall Cl SE9 . . . . . 166 A6
Tatton Cres E5, N16 . . . 51 D2
Tatum St SE17 . . 117 B2 262 D3
Tauheed Cl N4 . . . . 73 A6
Taunton Ave
    Hounslow TW3 . . . . . . 130 A3
    Wimbledon SW20 . . . . 178 B1
Taunton Cl SM3 . . . . . . 201 C1
Taunton Dr Enfield EN2 . . 4 C2
    Finchley N2 . . . . 30 A1
Taunton Ho W2 . . . . . . 236 A1
Taunton Mews NW1 . . . 237 C5
Taunton Pl
    NW1 . . . . 92 D3 237 C6
Taunton Rd
    Greenford UB6 . . . . 85 D6
    Lewisham SE12 . . . . . 164 D6
Taunton Way HA7 . . . . . 26 A1
Tavern Cl SM5 . . . . 202 C2
Tavern Ct SE1 . . . . 262 B5
Taverner Ho N16 . . . . . . 73 B5
Taverner Sq 🔳 N5 . . . . 73 A4
Taverners Cl W11 . . . . . 244 A3
Taverners Ct HA9 . . . . . 66 B6
Taverners Lo EN4 . . . . . 15 A6
Taverners Way E4 . . . . . 20 C3
Tavern La SW9 . . . . . . 138 C3
Tavistock Ave
    Mill Hill NW7 . . . . 28 D3
    Walthamstow E17 . . . . . 53 A6
    Wembley UB6 . . . . 87 A5
Tavistock Cl N16 . . . . . . 73 C3
Tavistock Cres
    Mitcham CR4 . . . . 204 A5
    Notting Hill W11 . . . . . . 91 B2
Tavistock Ct
  🔳 Croydon CR0 . . . . . 205 B1
    WC1 . . . . 239 D6
Tavistock Gdns IG3 . . . . 79 C4
Tavistock Gr CR0 . . . . . 205 B2
Tavistock Ho 🔳 W11 . . . 91 B2
Tavistock Mews 🔳
    W11 . . . . 91 B1
Tavistock Pl
    Bloomsbury
      WC1 . . . . . 94 A3 240 A6
    East Barnet N14 . . . . . . 15 B5

Tavistock Rd
  🔳 Beckenham BR2 . . . 208 D5
    Carshalton SM5 . . . . . 202 B1
    Croydon CR0 . . . . 205 B1
    DA16 . . . . 146 C4
    Dagenham NW10 . . . . . 89 D5
    Edgware HA8 . . . . 26 C2
    Leyton E7 . . . . 76 D4
    Notting Hill W11 . . . . . . 91 B2
    Stratford E15 . . . . 76 D2
    Tottenham N4, N15 . . . . 51 B3
    Uxbridge UB10 . . . . . . 61 A3
    Wanstead E18 . . . . 55 A6
Tavistock Sq
    WC1 . . . . 93 D3 239 D6
Tavistock St
    WC2 . . . . 116 A6 250 B6
Tavistock Terr N19 . . . . 71 D5
Tavistock Twr SE16 . . . 119 A3
Tavistock Wlk SM5 . . . . 202 B1
Taviton St WC1 . . 93 D3 239 C6
Tavy Bridge SE2 . . . . . 124 C4
Tavy Cl SE11 . . . . 261 B2
Tawney Rd SE28 . . . . . 124 B6
Tawny Cl Ealing W13 . . . 109 B5
    Feltham TW13 . . . . . . 150 A1
Tawny Way SE16 . . . . . 118 D2
Tayben Ave TW2 . . . . . 152 C5
Taybridge Rd SW11 . . . 137 A1
Tayburn Cl E14 . . . . 98 A1
Tayfield Cl UB10 . . . . . . 61 A5
Tay Ho 🔳 E3 . . . . 97 B5
Tayler Ct NW8 . . . . 229 C6
Taylor Ave TW9 . . . . . . 132 D3
Taylor Cl Deptford SE8 . 141 B6
    Hampton TW12 . . . . . . 174 A5
    Hounslow TW3 . . . . . . 130 A4
  🔳 Orpington BR6 . . . . 227 D4
    Tottenham N17 . . . . . . 34 A3
Taylor Ct Ealing W13 . . . 109 C5
    Penge SE26 . . . . 184 C1
    Stratford New Town E15 . 76 A3
Taylor Ho
  🔳 Streatham SW2 . . . 160 C3
Taylor Rd Mitcham CR4 . 180 C3
    Wallington SM6 . . . . . . 219 B3
Taylor's Bldgs SE18 . . . 122 D2
Taylors Cl DA14 . . . . . . 167 D1
Taylors Ct TW13 . . . . . 150 A2
Taylor's Gn W3 . . . . 89 C1
Taylor's La Barnet EN5 . . 1 B4
    Forest Hill SE26 . . . . . 184 B6
    Willesden NW10 . . . . . . 67 C1
Taylorsmead NW7 . . . . . 28 A5
Taymount Grange 🔳
    SE23 . . . . 162 C2
Taymount Rise SE23 . . . 162 C2
Tayport Cl N1 . . . . 72 A1
Tayside Ct 🔳 SE5 . . . . 139 B1
Tayside Dr HA8 . . . . 10 D2
Taywood Rd UB5 . . . . . . 85 B3
Teak Cl SE16 . . . . 119 A5
Tealby Ct N7 . . . . 72 B2
Teal Cl Enfield EN3 . . . . . 6 C6
    Newham E16 . . . . 99 D2
Teal Ct 🔳 SE8 . . . . 141 B6
    Wallington SM6 . . . . . . 219 C3
    Willesden NW10 . . . . . . 67 B2
Teale St E2 . . . . 96 A5
Tealing Dr KT19 . . . . . . 215 B4
Teal Pl SM1 . . . . 217 B3
Teal St 🔳 SE10 . . . . . . 120 D3
Teasel Cl CR0 . . . . 206 D1
Teasel Cres SE28 . . . . . 123 C5
Teasel Way E15 . . . . . . 98 C4
Teather St 🔳 SE5 . . . . . 139 C5
Tebbs Ho 🔳 SW2 . . . . . 160 C4
Tebworth Rd N17 . . . . . . 33 D3
Technology Pk NW9 . . . . 45 C6
Teck Cl TW7 . . . . 131 A3
Tedder Cl
    Chessington KT9 . . . . . 213 C3
    Hillingdon UB10 . . . . . . 60 B1
Tedder Rd CR2 . . . . . . 222 D1
TEDDINGTON 175 C5
Teddington Meml Hospl
    TW11 . . . . 174 C4
Teddington Park Rd
    TW11 . . . . 174 D6
Teddington Pk TW11 . . . 174 D5
Teddington Sch TW11 . . 175 C4
Teddington Sta TW11 . . 175 A4
Ted Hennem Ho RM10 . . 81 D5
Tedman Ct SE13 . . . . . 142 A1
Ted Roberts Ho 🔳 E2 . . 96 B5
Tedworth Gdns SW3 . . . 257 C1
Tedworth Sq
    SW3 . . . . 114 D1 257 C1
Tees Ave UB6 . . . . 86 D5
Tees Ct W7 . . . . 86 B1
Teesdale Ave TW7 . . . . 131 A4
Teesdale Cl E2 . . . . 96 B5
Teesdale Gdns
    Isleworth TW7 . . . . . . 131 A4
    South Norwood SE25 . . 183 C1
Teesdale Rd E11 . . . . . . 54 D2
Teesdale St E2 . . . . 96 B5
Teesdale St 🔳 E2 . . . . . 96 B5
Teeswater Ct DA18 . . . . 124 D3
Tee The W3 . . . . 89 C1
Teevan Cl CR0 . . . . 206 A2
Teevan Rd CR0 . . . . . . 206 A2
Teign Mews SE9 . . . . . 166 A2
Teignmouth Cl
  🔳 Clapham SW4 . . . . 137 D1
    Edgware HA8 . . . . 26 B1
Teignmouth Gdns UB6 . . 87 A4
Teignmouth Par UB6 . . . 87 B5

Teignmouth Rd
    Bexley DA16 . . . . 146 C3
    Brondesbury NW2 . . . . 68 D2
Tejas Ct N3 . . . . 47 A5
Tej Ct E7 . . . . 77 D3
Telcote Way HA4 . . . . . . 40 C2
Telegraph Hill NW3 . . . . 69 D5
Telegraph La KT10 . . . . 212 D3
Telegraph Mews
    Ilford IG3 . . . . 58 A1
    Seven Kings IG3 . . . . . . 57 D1
Telegraph Pl E14 . . . . . 119 D2
Telegraph Rd SW15 . . . 156 C4
Telegraph St EC2 . . . . . 242 C2
Telemann Sq SE3 . . . . 143 B2
Telephone Pl SW6 . . . . 264 D6
Telfer Cl 🔳 W3 . . . . 111 A4
Telfer Ho
  🔳 Dulwich SE21 . . . . . 183 C6
    EC1 . . . . 234 D1
Telferscot Prim Sch
    SW12 . . . . 159 D3
Telferscot Rd SW12 . . . 159 D3
Telford Ave SW12,
    SW2 . . . . 160 A3
Telford Avenue Mans 🔳
    SW2 . . . . 160 A3
Telford Cl Penge SE19 . . 183 D4
    Walthamstow E17 . . . . . 53 A2
Telford Ct EN5 . . . . 13 C6
Telford Dr KT12 . . . . . . 194 C2
Telford Ho
  🔳 Belvedere DA17 . . . 125 C3
  🔳 Kensal Town W10 . . . 91 A2
    SE1 . . . . 262 A6
Telford Parade Mans 🔳
    SW2 . . . . 160 A3
Telford Rd
  🔳 Hendon NW9 . . . . . . 46 A3
    Kensal Town W10 . . . . . 91 A2
    Sidcup SE9 . . . . 167 B2
    Southall UB1 . . . . 85 D1
    Twickenham TW2 . . . . . 151 C4
Telford Rd (North Circular
    Rd) N11 . . . . 31 C5
Telford's Yd 🔳 E1 . . . . . 118 A6
Telford Terr SW1 . . . . . 269 A6
Telford Way
    Dagenham W3 . . . . 89 C2
    Hayes UB4 . . . . 85 A2
Telham Rd E6 . . . . 100 C5
Tell Gr SE22 . . . . 139 D1
Tellson Ave SE18 . . . . . 144 A4
Telscombe Cl BR6 . . . . 227 C6
Telscombe Ho SW11 . . . 268 A1
Temair Ho 🔳 SE10 . . . . 142 A5
Temeraire Pl TW8 . . . . 110 B1
Temeraire St SE16 . . . . 118 C4
Tempelhof Ave NW2 . . . . 46 C2
Temperley Rd SW12 . . . 159 A4
Templar Ct RM7 . . . . . . 59 D5
Templar Dr SE28 . . . . . 102 D1
Templar Ho
    Hampstead NW2 . . . . . 69 B2
  🔳 Upper Clapton E5 . . . 74 C6
Templar Pl TW12 . . . . . 173 C3
Templars Ave NW11 . . . . 47 B3
Templars Cres N3 . . . . . 29 C1
Templars Dr HA3 . . . . . . 24 B4
Templars Ho E15 . . . . . . 75 D3
Templar St SE5 . . . . . . 138 D3
Temple Ave
    Croydon CR0 . . . . 223 B5
    Dagenham RM8 . . . . . . 59 C1
    EC4 . . . . 116 C5 251 B6
    Oakleigh Pk N20 . . . . . . 14 B4
Temple Cl Finchley N3 . . 29 B1
    Leytonstone E11 . . . . . . 54 C2
    Woolwich SE18 . . . . . . 123 A3
Templecombe Rd E9 . . . . 96 C6
Templecombe Way
    SM4 . . . . 201 A4
Templecroft TW15 . . . . 171 B4
Temple Ct Stepney E1 . . . 96 C2
    SW8 . . . . 270 A3
Templedene BR2 . . . . . 186 B1
Temple Dwellings 🔳
    E2 . . . . 96 B5
TEMPLE FORTUNE 🔳 . . 47 A4
Temple Fortune Ct 🔳
    NW11 . . . . 47 B4
Temple Fortune Hill
    NW11 . . . . 47 C4
Temple Fortune Ho 🔳
    NW11 . . . . 47 B4
Temple Fortune La
    NW11 . . . . 47 C3
Temple Fortune Par 🔳
    NW11 . . . . 47 B4
Temple Gdns
    Dagenham RM8 . . . . . . 80 D5
    Edmonton N21 . . . . 16 C2
    Temple Fortune NW11 . . 47 B3
Temple Gr Enfield EN2 . . . 4 D2
    Golders Green NW11 . . . 47 C3
Temple Hall Ct E4 . . . . . 20 B2
Temple Ho
  🔳 Battersea SW11 . . . 136 C2
  🔳 Tufnell Pk N7 . . . . . 71 C5
  🔳 Walthamstow E17 . . . 53 D6
Temple La EC4 . . 94 C1 241 B1
Temple Lo EN5 . . . . 14 B4
Templeman Rd W7 . . . . . 86 D2
Templemead Cl W3 . . . . 89 C1
Temple Mead Cl HA7 . . . 25 B4
Templemead Ho E9 . . . . 75 A4
Temple Mill La E10, E15 . 76 A4
Temple Mills Rd E9 . . . . 75 C4
TEMPLE MILLS 75 C3
Templemore DA14 . . . . 190 B5

Temple Par EN5 . . . . 14 B4
Temple Pk UB8 . . . . 82 C4
Temple Pl
WC2. . . . . .116 B6 250 D6
Temple Rd
Acton Green W4 . . . . . . .111 A3
Cricklewood NW2 . . . . . . .68 C5
Croydon CR0 . . . . .221 B4
Ealing W5 . . . . .109 D3
Hornsey N8. . . . . .50 B5
Isleworth TW3 . . . . .130 A1
Newham E6. . . . . .100 A6
Richmond TW9 . . . . .132 B2
Temple Sheen SW14 . . .155 A6
Temple Sheen Rd
SW14. . . . . .133 A1
Temple St E2. . . . . 96 B5
Temple Sta
WC2 . . . . .116 C6 251 A6
Temple Terr N22 . . . . . . .32 C1
Templeton Ave E4 . . . . . .35 D6
Templeton Cl
South Norwood SE19 . . .183 B2
25 Stoke Newington N16 . 73 C3
Templeton Ct Enfield EN3 . 6 C5
Walthamstow E10 . . . . . . .53 D1
Templeton Pl
SW5. . . . . .113 C2 255 B3
Templeton Rd N4, N15. . . 51 B3
Temple Way SM1 . . . . . .218 B5
Temple West Mews
SE11 . . . . 261 C5
Templewood W13 . . . . . . 87 B2
Templewood Ave NW3 . . 69 D5
Templewood Gdns
NW3 . . . . .69 D5
Templewood Point
NW2 . . . . .69 B6
Tempsford Cl EN2 . . . . 5 A2
Tempsford Ct HA1 . . . . . . .42 D3
Temsford Cl HA2 . . . . . . .24 A1
Tenbury Cl E7 . . . . .77 D3
Tenbury Ct SW12 . . . . . . .159 D3
Tenby Ave HA3 . . . . .25 B1
Tenby Cl Dagenham RM6. . 59 A3
Tottenham N15 . . . . .51 D5
Tenby Ct E17 . . . . .53 A4
Tenby Gdns UB5 . . . . .63 C2
Tenby Ho Hayes UB3. . . .105 A3
Islington N7 . . . . .72 C4
W2. . . . . 236 A1
Tenby Rd DA16 . . . . .146 D4
Dagenham RM6. . . . . .59 A3
Edgware HA8 . . . . .26 B1
Enfield EN3 . . . . .6 C1
Walthamstow E17. . . . . . . .53 A4
Tench St E1 . . . . .118 B5
Tenda Rd SE16 . . . . .118 B2
Tendring Ho SW2. . . . . . .160 C5
Tendring Way RM6 . . . . . .58 C4
Tenham Ave SW2. . . . . . .159 D2
Tenison Ct W1 . . . . 249 A6
Tenison Way SE1 . . . . . . 251 A3
Tenniel Cl W2 . . . . 245 D6
Tennison Ave WD6. . . . . . .10 D6
Tennison Rd SE25. . . . . .205 D4
Tennis St SE1. . .117 B4 252 C2
Tenniswood Rd EN1 . . . . . 5 C4
Tennyson Ave
Kingsbury NW9. . . . . .45 A6
Plashet E12. . . . . .78 A1
Twickenham TW1. . . . . . .152 D3
Wanstead E11. . . . . .55 A2
West Barnes KT3 . . . . . .200 B4
Tennyson Cl DA16 . . . . . .145 D4
Enfield EN3 . . . . .18 D6
Feltham TW14. . . . . .150 A5
Tennyson Ct 3 TW10 . .175 D6
Tennyson Ho
2 Erith DA17. . . . . .125 B1
SE17 . . . . 262 B2
Southall UB1 . . . . .85 C1
Tennyson Rd
Ashford TW15 . . . . .170 A5
Ealing W7 . . . . .108 D6
Hounslow TW3 . . . . .130 A3
Kilburn NW6 . . . . .91 B6
Leyton E10. . . . . .75 D6
Mill Hill NW7. . . . . .28 A5
Penge SE20. . . . . .184 D3
Stratford E15 . . . . .76 C1
Walthamstow E17. . . . . . . .53 B3
Wimbledon SW19 . . . . . .180 A4
Tennyson St SW8 . . . . . . .137 B3
Tensing Ct TW19. . . . . . .148 A3
Tensing Ho N1 . . . . .72 D2
Tensing Rd UB2 . . . . . . .107 C3
Tentelow La UB2 . . . . . .107 D3
Tenterden Cl
Hendon NW4. . . . . .46 D6
SE9 . . . . .188 B6
Tenterden Dr NW4. . . . . . .46 D6
Tenterden Gdns
Croydon CR0 . . . . .206 A2
Hendon NW4. . . . . .46 D6
Tenterden Gr NW4. . . . . . .46 D6
Tenterden Ho SE17 . . . 263 B2
Tenterden Rd
Croydon CR0 . . . . .206 A2
Dagenham RM8. . . . . .81 B6
Tottenham N17 . . . . .33 D3
Tenterden St W1 . . . . . 238 D1
Tenter Ground E1 . . . . 243 C3
Tent Peg La BR5. . . . . . .211 A4
Tent St E1. . . . . .96 B3
Tenzing Ct 4 SE9. . . . . .166 A2
Tequila Wharf E14. . . . . . .97 A1
Terborch Way 6
SE22 . . . . .161 C6
Tercelet Terr NW3 . . . . . .70 A4
Teredo St SE16 . . . . .118 D3
Terence Ct 6 DA17 . . . .147 B6
Teresa Mews E17. . . . . . . .53 C5
Teresa Wlk N10. . . . . .49 B4
Terling Cl E11 . . . . .76 D5
Terling Ho 9 W10 . . . . . .90 C2
Terling Rd RM8. . . . . .81 C6
Terling Wlk N1 . . . . 235 A6
Terminal Four Rdbt
TW6. . . . . .149 A5
Terminus Pl SW1 . . . . . 258 D5
Tern Ho 9 SE15 . . . . . . .139 D4
Terrace Gdns SW13. . . .133 D3
Terrace Ho 2 N20. . . . . . .14 A1
Terrace La TW10. . . . . . .154 A5
Terrace Rd Hackney E9. . .74 C1
Newham E13 . . . . .99 B6
Walton-on-T KT12 . . . . . .194 B3
Terraces The 6
SW20. . . . . .178 D3
Terrace The
Barnes SW13, SW14. . . .133 C3
Chingford E4 . . . . .20 C1
Cranley Gdns N2. . . . . . . .49 A5
EC4 . . . . 241 B1
Kilburn NW6 . . . . .91 C6
10 Rotherhithe SE8. . . . .119 B2
1 Woodford IG8 . . . . . . .37 A4
Terrace Wlk RM9 . . . . . . .81 A3
Terrall Apartments 7
N17 . . . . .51 D6
Terrano Ho 1 TW9 . . . .132 D4
Terrapin Ct SW17 . . . . . .159 B1
Terrapin Rd SW17 . . . . .159 B1
Terrapins KT6 . . . . .197 D2
Terrick Rd N22 . . . . .32 A2
Terrick St W12 . . . . .90 B1
Territands HA5 . . . . .41 B6
Territorial Ho SE11 . . . 261 B3
Terront Rd N15. . . . . .51 A5
Terry Ct 8 SM6. . . . . . . .219 C2
Terry Ho SW2 . . . . .160 C3
Terry Lodge 2 CR7 . . . .204 C4
Tersha St TW9. . . . . .132 B1
Tessa Sanderson Pl 6
SW8. . . . . .137 B2
Tessa Sanderson Way
UB6 . . . . .64 B3
Testerton Wlk 3
W11. . . . . .112 D6
Testwood Ct W7. . . . . . . .108 C6
Tetcott Rd
SW10. . . . . .136 A5 266 A3
Tetherdown N10. . . . . .49 A6
Tetherdown Prim Sch
N10. . . . . .49 A5
Tetty Way BR1, BR2. . . . .187 A1
Teversham La
SW8. . . . . .138 A4 270 B2
Teviot Cl DA16. . . . . .146 B4
Teviot St E14 . . . . .98 A2
Tewkesbury Ave
Forest Hill SE23 . . . . . . .162 B4
Pinner HA5 . . . . .41 A4
Tewkesbury Cl
Barnet EN4 . . . . .2 B1
Tottenham N15 . . . . .51 B3
Tewkesbury Ct N11. . . . . .31 D4
Tewkesbury Gdns NW9. . 44 D5
Tewkesbury Rd
Carshalton SM5. . . . . . . .202 B1
Ealing W13 . . . . .109 A6
Tottenham N15 . . . . .51 B3
Tewkesbury Terr N11 . . . 31 D4
Tewson Rd SE18 . . . . . . .123 C1
Teyham Ct SW11. . . . . . .158 D5
Teynham Ave EN1 . . . . . . .17 B5
Teynham Ct N12 . . . . .30 B4
Teynham Gn BR2 . . . . . . .209 A4
Teynham Ho SE9 . . . . . . .167 B5
Teynton Terr N17. . . . . . . .33 A2
Thackeray Ave N17 . . . . . .34 A1
Thackeray Cl
Hayes UB8. . . . . .82 D1
Isleworth TW7 . . . . .131 A3
Wimbledon SW19 . . . . . .178 D3
Thackeray Ct
Chelsea SW3. . . . . 257 C2
Ealing W5 . . . . .88 B1
West Kensington W14. . 254 A5
Thackeray Dr RM6 . . . . . .58 B2
Thackeray Ho
College Pk NW10 . . . . . . .90 A4
WC1. . . . . 240 A6
Thackeray Manor
SM1. . . . . .218 A3
Thackeray Mews E8 . . . . 74 A2
Thackeray Rd
Clapham SW8 . . . . .137 B3
Newham E6. . . . . .99 D5
Thackeray's Almshouses
SE6 . . . . .163 D5
Thackeray St W8 . . . . . 255 D6
Thackery Lo TW14 . . . . .149 B5
Thackrah Cl N2. . . . . .30 A1
Thakeham Cl SE26. . . . . .184 B5
Thalia Cl SE10 . . . . .142 B6
Thame Rd SE16. . . . . . . .118 D4
Thames Ave
Dagenham RM9. . . . . . . .103 D3
Sands End
SW10. . . . . . .136 A4 266 B2
Wembley UB6 . . . . .86 D5
Thames Bank SW14. . . . .133 A3
Thamesbank Pl SE28. . .102 C1
Thames Barrier Visitor
Ctr* SE18. . . . . .121 D3
Thames Christian Coll
SW11 . . . . .136 B2
Thames Circ E14. . . . . . .119 C2
Thames Cl TW12. . . . . . .173 D1
Thames Cnr TW16 . . . . .194 C6
Thames Cres W4 . . . . . . .133 C5
Thames Ct Ealing W7 . . . . 86 C1
Edmonton N9. . . . . .18 C1
10 SE15. . . . . .139 D5
West Molesey KT8 . . . . .173 D1
THAMES DITTON 197 B2
Thames Ditton Fst Sch
KT7. . . . . .196 D3
Thames Ditton Island
KT7 . . . . .197 A3
Thames Ditton Jun Sch
KT7. . . . . .196 D2
Thames Ditton Sta
KT7. . . . . .196 D2
Thames Dr HA4. . . . . .39 A3
Thames Eyot 8 TW1. . . .153 A3
Thamesfield Ct TW17 . .193 A2
Thamesfield Ho TW17 . .193 A2
Thamesfield Mews
TW17. . . . . .193 A2
Thamesgate Cl TW10. . .175 B6
Thames Gateway Pk
RM9 . . . . .103 B4
Thames Haven KT6 . . . .197 D4
Thames Hts SE1 . . . . . . 253 C2
Thameside TW11 . . . . . .175 D3
Thameside Ctr TW8. . . .132 B6
Thameside Ind Est
E16. . . . . .121 D4
Thameside Pl KT1 . . . . .175 D2
Thames Link Ho 7
TW9. . . . . .132 A1
Thames Mdw KT12,
TW17. . . . . .193 C1
THAMESMEAD 124 A5
Thames Mead KT12 . . . .194 A3
Thames Meadow KT8 . .195 C6
Thamesmead Sec Sch
TW17 . . . . .193 B3
Thamesmead Sh Ctr
SE28. . . . . .124 A6
Thamesmere Dr SE28 . .124 A6
Thames Pl SW15. . . . . . .134 D2
Thamespoint TW11 . . . .175 D3
Thames Quay
Millwall E14. . . . . .119 D4
SW10. . . . . 266 B1
Thames Rd
Barking IG11. . . . . .102 A4
Chiswick W4 . . . . .132 D6
Newham E16. . . . . .121 D5
Thames Reach
Fulham W6 . . . . .134 C6
Woolwich SE28 . . . . . . .123 C4
Thames Road Ind Est
E16. . . . . .121 D4
Thames Row TW9. . . . . .132 B6
Thames Side
Teddington KT1 . . . . .175 D2
Thames Ditton KT7 . . . . .197 B3
Thames St
Hampton TW12 . . . . .173 D1
Kingston u T KT1, KT2. . .175 D1
SE10 . . . . .141 D6
Sunbury TW16. . . . . .194 B6
Walton-on-T KT12 . . . . . .193 D2
Thamesvale Cl TW3. . . .129 C3
Thames Valley Univ
W5 . . . . .109 D5
Thames View 2 IG1 . . . . 79 A6
Thames View Ho
TW12. . . . . .194 A3
Thames View Inf Sch
IG11. . . . . .102 A5
Thames View Jun Sch
IG11. . . . . .101 D5
Thames View Lo IG11. . 101 C4
Thames Village W4 . . . .133 A4
Thames Wlk
SW11. . . . . .136 C5 267 A4
Thane Mans N7. . . . . .72 B5
Thanescroft Gdns
CR0 . . . . .221 C5
Thanet Ct 14 W3. . . . . . . .88 C1
Thanet Dr BR2. . . . . .225 D5
Thanet Ho WC1. . . . . . . 233 A1
1 West Norwood
SE27. . . . . .160 D1
Thanet Lo NW2 . . . . .69 A2
Thanet Pl CR0 . . . . .221 A4
Thanet Rd DA5 . . . . .169 C4
Thanet St WC1 . . 94 A4 233 A1
Thane Villas N7 . . . . .72 B5
Thane Works N7. . . . . .72 B5
Thanington Ct DA15. . . . .167 C5
Thant Cl E10 . . . . .75 D5
Tharp Rd SM6 . . . . .219 D3
Thatcham Ct N20 . . . . . . .14 A4
Thatcham Gdns N20 . . . . .14 A4
Thatcher Cl UB7 . . . . . . .104 A4
Thatchers Way TW7. . . .152 B6
Thatches Gr RM6 . . . . . . .59 A5
Thavies Inn EC4 . . . . . . 241 B2
Thaxted Ct N1. . . . . 235 D3
Thaxted Ho
Bermondsey SE16. . . . . .118 C2
Dagenham RM10. . . . . . . .81 D1
Thaxted Lo 3 E18 . . . . . .55 B6
Thaxted Pl 9 SW20. . . .178 D3
Thaxted Rd
Buckhurst Hill IG9. . . . . . .21 D4
SE9 . . . . .167 A2
Thaxton Rd
W14. . . . . .135 B6 264 D6
Thayers Farm
Rd BR3. . . . . .185 A2
Thayer St W1. . . . 93 A1 238 B2
Theatre Sq E15. . . . . .76 B2
Theatre St SW11. . . . . . .136 D2
Theberton St
N1. . . . . .94 D6 234 C6
Theed St SE1. . .116 C5 251 B3
Thelbridge Ho 28 E3 . . . .97 D4
Thelma Gdns SE3 . . . . . .144 A4
Thelma Gr TW11. . . . . . .175 A4
Theobald Cres HA3 . . . . . 24 A2
Theobald Rd
Croydon CR0 . . . . .220 D6
Walthamstow E17. . . . . . .53 C2
Theobalds Ave N12 . . . . . 30 A6
Theobalds Ct N4. . . . . . . .73 A6
Theobalds Park Rd EN2 . . 4 D6
Theobald's Rd
WC1. . . . . 94 B2 240 C4
Theobald St SE1. . . . . . 262 C5
Theodora Way HA5 . . . . .39 D6
Theodore Ct SE13. . . . . .164 B5
Theodore Ho 1 SW15. .156 A6
Theodore Rd SE13 . . . . .164 B5
Therapia La
Thornton Heath CR0 . . . .204 A2
Thornton Heath CR0 . . . .204 A3
Wallington CR0 . . . . .203 D2
Therapia Lane Sta
CR0. . . . . .204 A2
Therapia Rd SE22. . . . . .162 C5
Theresa Rd W6. . . . . . . .112 A2
Therfield Ct N4. . . . . .73 A6
Thermopylae Gate
E14 . . . . .119 D2
Theseus Ho
2 South Bromley E14 . . . 98 B1
2 E14. . . . . .98 B1
Theseus Wlk N1 . . . . . . 234 D3
Thesiger Rd SE20 . . . . . .184 D3
Thessaly Ho SW8 . . . . . 269 A3
Thessaly Rd
SW8. . . . . .137 C4 269 B2
Thetford Cl N13 . . . . .32 D4
Thetford Ct
3 Dulwich SE21. . . . . . . .162 B2
New Malden KT3. . . . . . .199 C4
Thetford Gdns RM9 . . . .103 A6
Thetford Ho SE1. . . . . . 263 C6
Thetford Rd
Ashford TW15 . . . . .148 A1
Dagenham RM9. . . . . .80 D1
New Malden KT3. . . . . . .199 C4
Thetis Terr TW9 . . . . . . .132 C6
Theydon Gr IG8 . . . . 37 C4
Theydon Rd E5 . . . . .74 C6
Theydon St E17. . . . . .53 B2
Thicket Cres SM1. . . . . .218 A4
Thicket Ct 14 SM1 . . . . .218 A4
Thicket Gr
Dagenham RM9. . . . . .80 C2
Penge SE20. . . . . .184 A3
Thicket Rd Penge SE20. .184 B3
Sutton SM1 . . . . .218 A4
Thicket The UB7. . . . . . . .82 A1
Third Ave
Chadwell Heath RM6. . . . .58 C3
Dagenham RM10. . . . . . .103 D5
East Acton W3. . . . . .111 D5
Enfield EN1 . . . . .17 D6
Hayes UB3. . . . . .105 D5
Little Ilford E12. . . . . .78 B3
3 Newham E13 . . . . .99 A4
Walthamstow E17. . . . . . .53 C4
Wembley HA9 . . . . .65 D6
West Kilburn W10. . . . . . .91 A4
Third Cl KT8. . . . . .196 A5
Third Cross Rd TW2. . . . .152 B2
Third Way HA9 . . . . .66 D4
Thirleby Rd Hendon HA8. . 27 B2
SW1. . . . . .115 C3 259 B5
Thirlestane Ct N10. . . . . .31 A1
Thirlestane Ho TW12. . .173 D6
Thirlmere NW1 . . . . 231 D2
Thirlmere Ave UB6. . . . . .87 C4
Thirlmere Gdns HA9 . . . .43 D1
Thirlmere Ho
Isleworth TW1 . . . . .152 D6
19 Stoke Newington N16 . 73 B4
Thirlmere Rd
Muswell Hill N10. . . . . . . .31 B2
Streatham SW16. . . . . . .181 D6
Thirlmere Rise BR1 . . . . .186 D4
Thirsk Cl UB5. . . . . .63 C2
Thirsk Rd
Clapham SW11 . . . . .137 A1
Mitcham CR4. . . . . .181 A3
South Norwood SE25 . . .205 B5
Thistlebrook SE2 . . . . . .124 C3
Thistlebrook Ind Est
SE2. . . . . .124 C4
Thistlecroft Gdns HA7. . . 25 D1
Thistle Ct N17 . . . . .52 B5
Thistledene KT7 . . . . . . .196 C3
Thistledene Ave HA2. . . . .63 A5
Thistledown Ct SE25 . . .205 C6
Thistlefield Cl DA5. . . . .168 D3
Thistle Gr SW7 . . . . 256 B1
Thistle Ho 10 E14 . . . . . . .98 A1
Thistlemead BR7 . . . . . .188 D1
Thistlewaite Rd E5. . . . . . .74 B5
Thistlewood Cl 3 N7 . . . .72 B6
Thistleworth Cl TW7 . . .130 B5
Thistley Cl N12 . . . . .30 C4
Thistly Ct SE8 . . . . .141 D6
Thomas a' Beckett Cl
HA0 . . . . .64 D4
Thomas Arnold Prim Sch
RM9 . . . . .81 B1
Thomas Baines Rd
SW11. . . . . .136 B2
Thomas Burt Ho 9 E2 . . 96 B4
Thomas Buxton Jun & Inf
Sch E1. . . . . .96 A3
Thomas Cribb Mews
E6 . . . . .100 B1
Thomas Crowell Ct 23
N1 . . . . .73 C3
Thomas Ct RM8. . . . . .80 C6
Thomas Dean Rd
SE26 . . . . .185 B6
Thomas Dinwiddy Rd
SE12 . . . . .165 B2
Thomas Doyle St SE1 . . 261 D6
Thomas Fairchild Com Sch
N1. . . . . .95 A5 235 B4
Thomas Gamuel Prim Sch
E17. . . . . .53 C3
Thomas Hardy Ho N22 . . 32 B2
Thomas Hewlett Ho
HA1. . . . . .64 C4
Thomas Ho
9 Belmont SM2. . . . . . .217 D1
3 Hackney E9 . . . . .74 C2
4 Stockwell SW4. . . . . . .138 A1
Thomas Hollywood Ho 3
E2 . . . . .96 C5
Thomas Jones Prim Sch
W11 . . . . .91 A1
Thomas' La SE6 . . . . . . .163 C4
Thomas Lo E17 . . . . .53 D4
Thomas Milner Ho 8
SE15 . . . . .140 A5
Thomas More Bldg The
HA4. . . . . .39 C1
Thomas More Ho EC2 . 242 A3
Thomas More Sq E1 . . . .118 A6
Thomas More St E1. . . .118 A5
Thomas More Way N2 . . 48 A6
Thomas North Terr 4
E16 . . . . .98 D2
Thomas Pl W8. . . . . 255 C5
Thomas Pooley Ct
KT6 . . . . .198 A2
Thomas Rd E14. . . . . .97 C2
Thomas Road Ind Est 2
E14. . . . . .97 C1
Thomas Shearley Ct
DA5 . . . . .169 D4
Thomas's London Day
Schs SW11. . . .136 B4 266 D1
Thomas's Prep Sch
Clapham SW11 . . . . . . .158 D6
Thomas St SE18 . . . . . . .122 D2
Thomas Tallis Sch
SE3. . . . . .143 B2
Thomas Wall Cl SM1 . . .217 D3
Thomas Watson Cottage
Homes The EN5. . . . . . . .13 A6
Thompson Ave
Richmond TW9 . . . . .132 C2
6 SE5. . . . . .139 A5
Thompson Cl Ilford IG1 . . 79 A6
Morden SM3 . . . . .201 C1
Thompson Ho
11 Kensal Town W10 . . . .91 A3
SE14 . . . . .140 D6
Southall UB1 . . . . .107 A6
Thompson Rd
Dagenham RM9. . . . . .81 B5
Dulwich Village SE22. . . .161 D5
Hounslow TW3 . . . . .129 D1
Uxbridge UB10 . . . . .60 A1
Thomson Cres CR0. . . . .204 C1
Thomson Ct 4 E8 . . . . . .74 A2
Thomson Ho
Pimlico SW1 . . . . 259 D1
Walworth SE17 . . . . 263 A3
Thomson Rd HA3 . . . . . . .42 C6
Thorburn Ho SW1 . . . . . 248 A1
Thorburn Sq SE1 . . . . . .118 A2
Thorburn Way SW19 . . .180 B2
Thoresby Ho N16 . . . . . . .73 B5
Thoresby St N1 . . 95 A4 235 B2
Thorkhill Gdns KT7 . . . .197 B1
Thorkhill Rd KT7. . . . . . .197 B2
Thornaby Gdns N18. . . . . 34 B5
Thornaby Ho 15 E2. . . . . 96 B4
Thorn Ave WD23. . . . . 8 A3
Thornbill Ho 1 SE15 . . .140 A5
Thornbridge Ct 10 EN5 . . 13 D6
Thornbury 3 NW4. . . . . .46 C5
Thornbury Ave TW7. . . .130 B5
Thornbury Cl
Edgware NW7. . . . . .28 D3
Stoke Newington N16. . . .73 C3
Thornbury Ct
Croydon CR2 . . . . .221 B3
Hounslow TW7 . . . . .130 C5
W11. . . . . 245 A6
Thornbury Ho N6 . . . . . . .49 C1
Thornbury Lo EN2 . . . . . . .4 D2
Thornbury Rd
Clapham Pk SW2. . . . . . .160 A5
Hounslow TW7 . . . . .130 B4
Thornbury Sq N6 . . . . 49 C1
Thornby Rd E5 . . . . 74 C5
Thorn Cl BR2 . . . . .210 C3
Northolt UB5. . . . . .85 B4
Thorncliffe Ct SW2 . . . . .160 A5
Thorncliffe Rd
Clapham Pk SW2. . . . . . .160 A5
Southall UB2 . . . . .107 B1
Thorncombe Rd SE22 . .161 C6
Thorncroft HA2. . . . . .64 A5
Thorncroft Rd SM1 . . . .217 D4
Thorncroft St
SW8. . . . . .138 A5 270 A3
Thorndale BR7 . . . . .188 B3
Thorndale Ho 10 N16. . . .51 C1
Thorndean St SW18. . . . .158 A2
Thorndene Ave N11. . . . . .15 A3
Thorndike Ave UB5 . . . . . 84 D6
Thorndike Cl
SW10. . . . . . . .136 A5 266 A4
Thorndike Ho SW1. . . . 259 C2
Thorndike Rd 21 N1. . . . . 73 B2
Thorndike St
SW1. . . . . .115 D2 259 C3
Thorndon Cl BR5 . . . . . .189 D1
Thorndon Gdns KT19. . .215 C4
Thorndon Rd BR5. . . . . .189 D1
Thorndyke Ct HA5 . . . . . . 23 B3
Thorne Cl
Claygate KT10. . . . . .213 A1
DA8 . . . . .147 D6
Leyton E11. . . . . .76 C4
Littleton TW15. . . . . .171 A3
Newham E16. . . . . .99 A1
Thorne Ho
34 Bethnal Green E2 . . . . 96 C4
4 Cubitt Town E14. . . . .120 A3
Thorneloe Gdns CR0,
CR9 . . . . .220 D3
Thorne Pas 7 SW13 . . .133 D3
Thorne Rd
SW8. . . . . .138 A5 270 B3
Thorne's Cl BR3 . . . . . . .208 A6
Thorness Ct SW18 . . . . .158 A5
Thorne St SW13, SW14. . 133 C2
Thornet Wood Rd
BR1. . . . . .210 C6
Thornewill Ho 8 E1 . . .118 C6
Thorney Cres
SW11. . . . . .136 B5 266 D3
Thorneycroft Cl KT12 . .194 C3
Thorneycroft Dr EN3. . . . . 7 C6
Thorneycroft Ho 11
W4. . . . . .111 C1
Thorney Ct W8 . . . . 246 A1
Thorney Hedge Rd
W4. . . . . .110 D2
Thorney St
SW1. . . . . .116 A2 260 A4
Thornfield Ave NW7 . . . . 29 A2
Thornfield Ct NW7 . . . . . .29 A2
Thornfield Ho 5 E14. . .119 C6
Thornfield Par NW7. . . . . 29 A3
Thornfield Rd W12. . . . .112 B4
Thornford Rd SE13. . . . .164 A6
Thorngate Rd W9. . . . . . . 91 C3
Thorngrove Rd E13 . . . . . 99 B6
Thornham Gr E15. . . . . . .76 B3
Thorn Ham Ho SE1. . . . 262 D6
Thornham St SE10 . . . . .141 D6
Thornhaugh St WC1 . . . 239 D5
Thornhill Ave SE18. . . . .145 C5
Surbiton KT6. . . . . .214 A6
Thornhill Bridge Wharf
N1. . . . . 233 C5
Thornhill Cres N1. . . . . . .72 B1
Thornhill Ct N8. . . . . .49 D3
Thornhill Gdns
Barking IG11. . . . . .79 C1
Leyton E10. . . . . .75 D6
Thornhill Gr N1. . . . . .72 C1
Thornhill Ho
12 Chiswick W4 . . . . . . .111 C1
Islington N1 . . . . .72 C1
Thornhill Mews SW15. . .135 B1
Thornhill Prim Sch N1 . . 72 C1
Thornhill Rd
Ickenham UB10. . . . . .60 C4
Islington N1 . . . .94 C6 234 A6
Leyton E10. . . . . .75 D6
Surbiton KT6. . . . . .214 B6
Thornton Heath CR0 . . . .205 A2
Thornhill Sq N1 . . . . .72 B1
Thornhill Way TW17 . . .192 C4
Thornicroft Ho 12
SW9. . . . . .138 B3
Thornlaw Rd SE27 . . . . .182 D6
Thornley Cl N17 . . . . .34 A3
Thornley Dr HA2. . . . . . . .63 D6
Thornley Pl 2 SE10. . . .120 C1
Thornsbeach Rd SE6 . . .164 A2
Thornsett Pl SE20. . . . . .184 B1
Thornsett Rd
Penge SE20. . . . . .184 B1
Wandsworth SW18. . . . .157 D3
Thornsett Terr SE20 . . . 184 B1
Thornton Ave
Chiswick W4 . . . . .111 C2
Streatham SW2. . . . . . . .159 D3
Thornton Heath CR0 . . . .204 B3
West Drayton UB7 . . . . .104 B3
Thornton Cl UB7. . . . . . .104 B3
Thornton Ct
Lower Holloway N7. . . . . .72 A3
West Barnes SW20. . . . .200 D4
Thornton Dene BR3. . . . .185 C1
Thornton Gdns SW12 . .159 D3
Thornton Gr HA5 . . . . 23 C4
THORNTON HEATH . . .204 D3
Thornton Heath Pond
CR7 . . . . .204 C4
Thornton Heath Sta
CR7. . . . . .205 A5
Thornton Hill SW19 . . . .179 A3
Thornton Ho SE17 . . . . 263 A3
7 Wanstead E11. . . . . . . .55 A3
Thornton Lo
South Norwood CR7 . . . .205 A6
8 Wimbledon SW19 . . . .179 A3
Thornton Pl W1 . . . . . . 237 D4
Thornton Rd Barnet EN5 . . 1 A2
Belvedere DA17 . . . . . . .125 D2
BR1. . . . . .187 A5
Carshalton SM5. . . . . . . .202 B1

Thornton Rd continued
Ilford IG1 78 D4
Leyton E11 76 B6
Lower Edmonton N18 18 C1
Mortlake SW14 133 B2
Streatham SW12, SW2 159 D3
Thornton Heath CR0, CR7 204 B3
Wimbledon SW19 178 D3
Thornton Rd E SW19 178 D4
Thornton Rd Ind Est CR0 204 B3
Thornton Row CR7 204 C4
Thornton St SW9 138 C3
Thornton Way NW11 47 D4
Thorntree Ct W5 88 A2
Thorntree Prim Sch SE7 121 D1
Thorntree Rd SE7 121 D1
Thornville Gr CR4 180 B1
Thornville St SE8 141 C4
Thornwell Ct W7 108 C4
Thornwood Cl E18 37 B1
Thornwood Gdns W8 245 A2
Thornwood Lo W8 245 A2
Thornwood Rd SE13 164 C6
Thornycroft Ct TW9 132 B3
Thorogood Gdns E15 76 C3
Thorold Ho SE1 252 A2
6 Streatham SW2 160 A4
Thorold Rd Ilford IG1 57 A1
Wood Green N22 32 A3
Thorparch Rd SW8 137 D5 269 D3
Thorpebank Rd W12 112 A5
Thorpe Cl BR6 227 C6
Forest Hill SE26 184 D6
Notting Hill W10 91 A1
Thorpe Coombe Hospl E17 54 A6
Thorpe Cres E17 35 B1
Thorpe Ct Enfield EN2 4 D2
Upper Tooting SW17 180 C6
Thorpedale Gdns IG6 56 D5
Thorpedale Rd N4 50 B1
Thorpe Hall W5 87 D2
Thorpe Hall Prim Sch E17 36 B2
Thorpe Hall Rd E17 36 A2
Thorpe Ho N1 233 D5
Thorpe Rd Barking IG11 79 B1
Chingford E17 36 A1
Kingston u T KT2 176 A3
Leyton E7 76 D4
Newham E6 100 B6
Tottenham N15 51 C3
Thorpewood Ave SE23, SE26 162 B2
Thorpland Ave UB10 61 A5
Thorsden Way 2 SE19 183 C5
Thorverton Rd NW2 69 A5
Thoydon Rd E3 97 A5
Thrale Almshouses SW16 182 A5
Thrale Rd SW16 181 C5
Thrale St SE1 252 B3
Thrasher Cl 20 E8 95 D6
Thrawl St E1 95 D2 243 D3
Thrayle Ho 2 SW9 138 B2
Threadgold Ho 8 N1 73 B2
Threadneedle St EC2, EC3 95 B1 242 D1
Three Bridges Bsns Ctr UB2 108 A4
Three Bridges Prim Sch UB2 107 D3
Three Colts La E2 96 B3
Three Colt St E14 119 B6
Three Corners DA7 147 D3
Three Cups Yd WC1 240 D3
Three Kings Yd W1 248 C6
Three Meadows Mews HA7 24 D2
Three Mill La E3 98 A4
Three Mills Studios E14 98 A4
Three Nun Ct EC2 242 B2
Three Oak La SE1 253 C2
Three Oaks Cl UB10 60 B5
Threshers Pl W11 244 A6
Thriffwood SE23, SE26 162 D1
Thrigby Rd KT9 214 B2
Thring Ho 2 SW9 138 B3
Throckmorten Rd E16 99 B1
Throgmorton Ave EC2 95 B1 242 D2
Throgmorton St EC2 95 B1 242 D2
Throwley Cl SE2 124 C3
Throwley Rd SM1 217 D3
Throwley Way SM1 217 D3
Thrupp Cl CR4 181 B1
Thrush Gn HA2 41 C5
Thrush St SE17 262 A2
Thunderer Rd RM9 103 B3
Thurbarn Rd SE6 185 D5
Thurbin Ho UB4 83 B2
Thurland Ho 3 SE16 118 B2
Thurland Rd SE16 118 A3
Thurlby Cl HA1 43 A3
Thurlby Croft NW4 46 C6
Thurlby Rd Wembley HA0 65 D2
West Norwood SE27 182 C6
Thurleigh Ave SW12 159 A5
Thurleigh Ct SW12 159 A5
Thurleigh Rd SW12 159 A5
Thurleston Ave SM4 201 A4
Thurlestone Ave Colney Hatch N12 30 D4
Ilford IG3 79 D4
Thurlestone Cl TW17 193 A3
Thurlestone Ct 1 UB1 85 D1
Thurlestone Par TW17 193 A3
Thurlestone Rd SE27 182 C6
Thurloe Cl SW7 257 A4
Thurloe Ct SW3 257 A3
Thurloe Pl SW7 114 B2 256 D4
Thurloe Place Mews SW7 256 D4
Thurloe Sq SW7 114 C2 257 A4
Thurloe St SW7 114 B2 256 D4
Thurlow Cl E4 35 D4
Thurlow Ct 5 E11 55 A4
Thurlow Gdns HA0 65 D3
Thurlow Hill SE21 161 A2
Thurlow Ho 17 SW16 160 A1
Thurlow Park Rd SE21, SE24 161 A2
Thurlow Rd Hampstead NW3 70 B3
West Ealing W7 109 A4
Thurlow St SE17 117 C1 263 A1
Thurlow Terr NW5 71 A3
Thurlow Twrs SE27 160 C1
Thurlow Wlk SE17 263 A1
Thurlston Rd HA4 62 A5
Thurnby Ct TW2 152 C1
Thurnscoe NW1 232 A5
Thursland Rd DA14 191 A5
Thursley Cres CR0 224 B1
Thursley Gdns SW19 156 D2
Thursley Ho 3 Kingston u T KT2 176 D3
10 Streatham SW2 160 B4
Thursley Rd SE9 166 B1
Thurso Ho NW6 91 D5
Thurso St SW17 180 B6
Thurstan Rd SW20 178 B3
Thurston Ho 4 BR3 185 D4
Thurston Ind Est SE13 141 D2
Thurston Rd Southall UB1 85 B1
St Johns SE8, SE13 141 D3
Thurtle Rd E2 95 D5
Thurza Ct TW7 130 D3
Thyer Cl BR6 227 A4
Thyme Cl SE3 143 C2
Thyme Ct NW7 29 A3
Thyra Gr N12 29 D4
Tibbatt's Rd E3 97 D3
Tibbenham Pl SE6 163 C2
Tibbenham Wlk E13 98 D5
Tibberton Sq N1 235 A6
Tibbets Cl SW19 156 D3
Tibbet's Corner SW19 156 D4
Tibbet's Ride SW19 156 D4
Tiber Cl 10 E3 97 C6
Tiber Gdns N1 233 B5
Ticehurst Cl BR5 190 A3
Ticehurst Rd SE23 163 A2
Tickford Cl SE2 124 C4
Tickford Ho NW8 230 A1
Tidal Basin Rd E16 120 D6
Tidbury Ct SW8 269 A3
Tideham Ho SE28 123 B5
Tidelock Ho SE28 123 B4
Tidemill Prim Sch SE8 141 C5
Tidenham Gdns CR0 221 C5
Tideside Ct SE18 122 A3
Tideslea Path SE28 123 B5
Tideslea Twr SE28 123 A4
Tideswell 10 NW5 71 B4
Tideswell Rd Croydon CR0 223 C5
Putney SW15 134 C1
Tideway Cl TW10 175 C6
Tideway Ct 9 SE16 118 D5
Tideway Ho E14 119 C4
Tideway Ind Est SW8 137 C6 269 B5
Tideway Wharf SW13 133 C3
Tideway Yd SW13 133 C3
Tidey St E3 97 C2
Tidford Rd DA16 145 D3
Tidworth Ho 18 SE22 139 C2
Tidworth Rd E3 97 C3
Tiepigs La BR2, BR4 208 D1
Tierney Ct 4 CR0 221 D6
Tierney Rd SW2 160 A3
Tierney Terr SW2 160 A3
Tiffin Girls' Sch The KT2 176 A4
Tiffin Sch KT2 176 B1
Tiger Ho WC1 232 D1
Tiger La BR2 209 B5
Tiger Way E5 74 B4
Tignel Ct W3 110 C4
Tigris Cl N9 18 C2
Tilbrook Rd SE3 143 C2
Tilbury Cl 14 Camberwell SE15 139 D5
St Paul's Cray BR5 190 B1
Tilbury Ho 4 SE14 140 D6
Tilbury Rd Leytonstone E10 54 A2
Newham E6 100 B5
Tildesley Rd SW15 156 C5
Tile Farm Rd BR6 227 B5
Tilehurst NW1 231 D1
Tilehurst Point 2 SE2 124 C4
Tilehurst Rd Cheam SM3 217 A3
Wandsworth SW17, SW18 158 B3
Tile Kiln La Edmonton N13 33 A5
Harefield UB9 38 D2
Upper Holloway N6 49 C1
Tileyard Rd N7 72 A1
Tilford Ave CR0 224 A1
Tilford Gdns SW19 156 D3
Tilford Ho 8 SW2 160 B4
Tilia Cl SM1 217 B3
Tilia Rd E5 74 B4
Tilia Wlk 21 SW9 138 D1
Tiller Ho 28 N1 95 C6
Tiller Rd E14 119 C3
Tillet Sq SE16 119 A4
Tillett Cl NW10 67 A2
Tillet Way 6 E2 96 A4
Tilley Rd TW14 150 A3
Tillingbourne Gdns N3 47 B6
Tillingbourne Way N3 47 B5
Tillingham Way N12 29 D6
Tilling Ho 1 SE15 140 B2
Tilling Rd NW2 46 C2
Tilling Way HA9 65 D6
Tillman Ho 8 SW2 160 B3
Tillman St E1 96 B1
Tilloch St 9 N1 72 B1
Tillotson Ct SW8 269 D3
Tillotson Rd Edmonton N9 17 D2
Harrow HA3 23 D3
Ilford IG1 56 C2
Tilney Ct EC1 242 B6
Kingston u T KT6 197 D4
Woodford IG9 21 A2
Tilney Dr IG9 21 A2
Tilney Gdns 12 N1 73 B2
Tilney Rd Dagenham RM9 81 B2
Southall UB2 106 C2
Woodford IG9 21 A2
Tilney St W1 248 B4
Tilson Cl 2 SE15 139 C5
Tilson Gdns SW2, SW4 160 A4
Tilson Ho SW2 160 A4
Tilson Rd N17 34 A2
Tilston Cl E11 76 D5
Tilton St SW6 264 B5
Tiltwood The W3 111 A6
Tilt Yard App SE9 166 B5
Timber Cl BR7 188 C1
Timbercroft KT19 215 C4
Timbercroft La SE18 145 C5
Timbercroft Prim Sch SE18 145 C5
Timberdene NW4 28 D1
Timberland Cl 16 SE15 140 A5
Timberland Rd E1 96 B1
Timber Mill Way SW4 137 D2
Timber Pond Rd SE16 118 D4
Timber St EC1 242 A6
Timberwharf Rd N16 52 A3
Time Sq E8 73 D3
Times Sq SM1 217 D3
Timor Ct UB1 107 D5
Timothy Cl Bexley DA6 169 A6
1 Clapham Pk SW4 159 C6
Timothy Ho DA18 125 A4
Timsbury Wlk 5 SW15 156 A3
Tina Ct Forest Hill SE6 163 B4
West Norwood SW16 160 C1
Tindal St SW9 138 D4
Tinniswood Cl N5 72 C3
Tinsley Cl SE25 206 B6
Tinsley Rd E1 96 C2
Tintagel Cres SE22 139 D1
Tintagel Ct EC1 241 C6
Tintagel Dr HA7 25 D6
Tintagel Ho SE20 184 A3
Tintern Ave NW9 44 D6
Tintern Cl Putney SW15 157 A6
Wimbledon SW19 180 A4
Tintern Ct W13 109 A6
Tintern Gdns N14 16 A4
Tintern Ho Belgravia SW1 258 C3
Regent's Pk NW1 231 D3
Tintern Path NW9 45 C3
Tintern Rd Carshalton SM5 202 B1
Tottenham N22 33 A2
Tintern St SW4 138 A1
Tintern Way HA2 41 D1
Tinto Rd E16 99 A3
Tinwell Mews WD6 11 B6
Tinworth St SE11 116 A1 260 B2
Tippett Ct E6 100 B5
Tippetts Cl EN2 5 A4
Tipthorpe Rd SW11 137 A2
Tipton Dr CR0 221 C4
Tiptree 7 NW1 71 B1
Tiptree Cl E4 20 A1
Tiptree Cres IG5 56 C6
Tiptree Ct EN2 5 B1
Tiptree Dr EN2 5 B1
Tiptree Rd HA4 62 B4
Tirlemont Rd CR2 221 A1
Tirrell Rd CR0 205 A3
Tisbury Ct W1 249 C6
Tisbury Rd SW16 182 A1
Tisdall Pl SE17 117 B2 262 D3
Tissington Ct 4 SE16 118 D2
Titan Bsns Est 3 SE8 141 C5
Titan Ct TW8 110 B1
Titchborne Row W2 237 B1
Titchfield Rd Carshalton SM5 202 B1
Enfield EN3 7 A6
Paddington NW8 92 D6 230 C6
Titchfield Wlk SM5 202 B2
Titchwell Rd SW18 158 B3
Tite St SW3 136 D6 267 C6
Tithe Barn Cl KT2 176 B2
Tithe Barn Way UB5 84 B5
Tithe Cl Hayes UB4 83 D2
Hendon NW7 28 A2
Walton-on-T KT12 194 B3
Tithe Ct NW4 28 A2
Tithe Farm Ave HA2 63 C5
Tithe Farm Cl HA2 63 C5
Tithe Wlk NW7 28 A2
Titian Ave WD23 8 C4
Titley Cl E4 35 C5
Titmus Cl UB8 83 A1
Titmuss Ave SE28 124 B6
Titmuss St W12 112 C4
Tivendale N8 50 A6
Tiverton Ave IG5 56 C6
Tiverton Cl CR0 205 D2
Tiverton Dr SE9 167 A3
Tiverton Prim Sch N15 51 B3
Tiverton Rd Brondesbury Pk NW6, NW10 90 D6
Edgware HA8 26 B1
Edmonton N18 33 C5
Hounslow TW3 130 A3
Ruislip HA4 62 A5
Tottenham N4, N15 51 B3
Wembley HA0 88 A5
Tiverton St SE1 117 A3 262 A6
Tiverton Way Chessington KT9 213 D3
Edgware NW7 28 D3
Tivoli Ct SE16 119 B5
Tivoli Gdns 11 SE7 122 A2
Tivoli Rd Hornsey N8 49 D4
Hounslow TW4 129 A1
West Norwood SE27 183 A5
Toad La TW4 129 B1
Tobago St 12 E14 119 C4
Tobin Cl NW3 70 C1
Toby Ct N9 18 C4
Toby La E1 97 A3
Toby Way KT5, KT6 214 D6
Todber Ho W14 254 A6
Todd Ho 3 N2 30 B1
Todds Wlk N7 72 B6
Tokenhouse Yd EC2 242 C2
TOKYNGTON 66 D2
Tokyngton Ave HA9 66 C2
Toland Sq SW15 156 A6
Tolcairn Ct 2 DA17 125 C1
Tolcarne Dr HA5 40 B6
Tolchurch 2 W11 91 C1
Toldos Yakov Yosef sch N16 51 C1
Toley Ave HA3, HA9 44 A2
Tolhurst Dr 4 W10 91 A4
Tollbridge Cl W10 91 A3
Tollesbury Gdns IG6 57 B6
Tollet St E1 96 D3
Tollgate Dr Dulwich SE21 161 C2
Hayes UB4 106 D6
Tollgate Ho 1 NW6 91 D5
Tollgate Prim Sch Croydon CR0 206 C3
Newham E13 99 C3
Tollgate Rd E6 100 A2
Tollhouse Way N19 71 C6
Tollington Ct N4 72 B6
Tollington Ho 4 N19 72 A5
Tollington Pk N4 72 B6
Tollington Pl N4 72 B6
Tollington Rd N7 72 B4
Tollington Way N7 72 A5
Tolmers Sq NW1 93 C3 239 B6
Tolpaide Ho SE11 261 A3
Tolpuddle Ave 1 E13 99 C6
Tolpuddle St N1 94 C5 234 A4
Tolsford Rd E5 74 B3
Tolson Ho 4 TW7 131 A2
Tolson Rd TW7 131 A2
Tolverne Rd SW20 178 C2
TOLWORTH 214 C6
Tolworth Broadway KT6 198 D1
Tolworth Cl KT6 198 D1
Tolworth Gdns RM6 58 D4
Tolworth Girls' Sch KT6 214 B5
Tolworth Hospl KT6 214 C6
Tolworth Inf Sch KT6 198 B1
Tolworth Junc KT6 214 D6
Tolworth Jun Sch KT6 198 B1
Tolworth Par RM6 59 A4
Tolworth Park Rd KT6 214 B6
Tolworth Rd KT6 214 A6
Tolworth Rise N KT5 198 D1
Tolworth Rise S KT5 198 D1
Tolworth Sta KT5 214 D6
Tolworth Underpass KT5, KT6 214 D6
Tomahawk Gdns 4 UB5 84 D4
Tom Coombs Cl SE9 144 A1
Tom Cribb Rd SE18, SE28 123 B3
Tom Groves Cl E15 76 B3
Tom Hood Cl E15 76 B3
Tom Hood Sch E11 76 D5
Tom Jenkinson Rd 5 E16 121 A5
Tomkyns Ho SE11 261 A3
Tomline Ho SE1 252 A3
Tomlin's Gr E3 97 C4
Tomlinson Cl 5 Gunnersbury W4 110 D1
Spitalfields E2 95 D4
Tomlins Orch IG11 101 A6
Tomlin's Terr E14 97 A1
Tomlins Wlk 4 N7 72 B6
Tom Mann Cl IG11 101 C6
Tom Nolan Cl E15 98 C5
Tompion Ho EC1 241 D6
Tompion St EC1 234 D1
Tom Smith Cl SE10 142 C6
Tom Smith Ho 3 E17 54 A4
Tomson Ho SE1 263 C6
Tom Williams Ho SW6 264 C5
Tonbridge Cres HA3 44 A5
Tonbridge Hos WC1 233 A1
Tonbridge Rd KT12, KT8 195 B5
Tonbridge St WC1 94 A4 233 A1
Toneborough 16 NW8 91 D6
Tonfield Rd SM3 201 B1
Tonge Cl BR3 207 C4
Tonsley Hill SW18 157 D6
Tonsley Pl SW18 157 D6
Tonsley Rd SW18 157 D6
Tonsley St SW18 157 D6
Tonstall Rd CR4 181 A1
Tony Law Ho SE12 165 A6
Tooke Cl HA5 23 A2
Tookey Cl HA3 44 B2
Took's Ct EC4 241 A2
Tooley St SE1 117 C5 253 A3
Toorack Rd HA3 24 B1
Tooting Bec Gdns SW16 181 D6
Tooting Bec Lido SW16 181 C6
Tooting Bec Rd Furzedown SW17 181 B6
Streatham SW16 181 C5
Tooting Bec Sta SW17 159 A1
Tooting Broadway SW17 180 D5
Tooting Broadway Sta SW17 180 C5
Tooting Gr SW17 180 C5
TOOTING GRAVENEY 180 B5
Tooting High St SW17, SW19 180 C5
Tooting Mkts SW17 180 D6
Tooting Sta SW17 180 D4
Tootswood Rd BR2, BR3 208 C5
Topaz Ct TW13 149 D1
Topaz Ho KT4 199 B1
Topaz Wlk NW2 46 D4
Topcliffe Dr BR6 227 B4
Topham Ho 8 SE10 142 A5
Topham Sq N17 33 A2
Topham St EC1 241 A6
Top House Rise E4 20 A4
Topiary Sq TW9 132 B2
Topley St SE9 143 D1
Topmast Point 23 E14 119 C4
Top Pk BR3 208 C4
Topsfield Cl N8 49 D4
Topsfield Par N8 50 A3
Topsfield Rd N8 50 A4
Topsham Rd SW17 181 A6
Tora Ct 9 IG9 21 C2
Torbay Ct 13 NW1 71 B1
Torbay Mans NW6 91 B6
Torbay Rd Brondesbury NW6 69 B1
Harrow HA2 63 A6
Torbay St 15 NW1 71 B1
Torbitt Way IG2 57 D4
Torbridge Cl HA8 26 A3
Torbrook Cl DA5 169 A5
Torcross Dr SE23 162 C2
Torcross Rd HA4 62 C5
Tor Ct W8 245 B2
Torfell 5 E18 36 D1
Tor Gdns W8 113 C4 245 A2
Tor Gr SE28 123 C5
Tor Ho N6 49 B3
Tormead Cl SM1 217 C2
Tormount Rd SE18 145 C6
Tornay Ho Hackney E9 74 C1
N1 233 C4
Toronto Ave E12 78 B4
Toronto Rd IG1 57 A1
Torquay Gdns IG4 55 D5
Torquay Ho 1 SM6 219 D3
Torquay St W2 91 D2
Tor Rd DA16 146 C4
Torrence Ho 6 N19 71 C6
Torrens Ct SE5 139 B2
Torrens Rd Clapham Pk SW2 160 B6
Stratford E15 76 D2
Torrens Sq E15 76 D2
Torrens St EC1 94 D5 234 C3
Torres Sq E14 119 C1
Torre Wlk SM5 202 C1
Torrey Dr SW9 138 C3
Torriano Ave NW5 71 D3
Torriano Cotts NW5 71 C3
Torriano Jun & Inf Schs NW5 71 D3
Torriano Mews NW5 71 C3
Torridge Gdns SE15 140 C1
Torridge Rd CR7 204 D4
Torridon Ct HA8 10 D2
Torridon Ho NW6 91 D5
Torridon Jun & Inf Schs SE6 164 B2
Torridon Rd SE13, SE6 164 B3
Torrington Ave N12 30 B5
Torrington Cl Claygate KT10 212 C2
North Finchley N12 30 B6
Torrington Ct Forest Hill SE26 184 A5
Harrow HA2 63 D5
North Finchley N12 30 B6
Torrington Dr HA2 63 D5
Torrington Gdns Friern Barnet N11 31 C4
Wembley UB6 65 C1
Torrington Gr N12 30 C5
Torrington Pk N12 30 B6
Torrington Pl Bloomsbury WC1 93 D2 239 C4
St George in t East E1 118 A5
Torrington Rd Claygate KT10 212 C2
Dagenham RM8 59 B1
Ruislip HA4 62 A5
Wanstead E18 55 A6
Wembley UB6 87 C6
Torrington Sq Bloomsbury WC1 93 D3 239 D5
Thornton Heath CR0 205 B2
Torrington Way SM4 201 C3
Torr Rd SE20 184 D3
Tortington Ho 1 SE15 140 B5
Torver Rd HA1 42 C5
Torver Way BR6 227 B5
Torwood Rd SW15 156 A6
Totham Lo SW20 178 B2
Tothill Ho SW1 259 D4
Tothill St SW1 115 D4 249 D1
Totland Ho SW18 157 D5
Totnes Rd DA16 146 C5
Totnes Villas N11 31 C5
Totnes Wlk N2 48 B5
Tottan Terr E1 96 D1
Tottenhall 5 NW1 71 A1
Tottenhall Inf Sch N13 32 C4
Tottenhall Rd N13 32 D4
TOTTENHAM 33 D1
Tottenham Court Rd W1 93 C2 239 B4
Tottenham Court Road Sta W1 93 D1 239 D2
Tottenham Gn E 3 N15 51 D5
Tottenham Gn E South Side 4 N15 51 D5
TOTTENHAM HALE 52 A6
Tottenham Hale N15 52 A5
Tottenham Hale Ret Pk N15 52 A5
Tottenham Hale Sta N17 52 B6
Tottenham La N8 50 B4
Tottenham Mews W1 239 B4
Tottenham Rd N1 73 C2
Tottenham St W1 93 C2 239 B4
Totterdown St SW17 180 D5
TOTTERIDGE 13 C3
Totteridge Comm N20 12 C3
Totteridge Gn N20 13 C2
Totteridge Ho Barnet N20 13 B3
Battersea SW11 136 B3
Totteridge La N20 13 D3
Totteridge Pk N20 12 D3
Totteridge Rd EN3 6 D6
Totteridge Village N20 13 B3
Totteridge & Whetstone Sta N20 14 A2
Totternhoe Cl HA3 43 C4
Totton Rd CR7 204 C6
Toucan Cl NW10 88 C4
Touchard Ho N1 235 D1
Toulmin St SE1 117 A4 252 A1
Toulon St SE5 139 A5
Toulouse Ct 2 SE16 118 B1
Tounson Ct SW1 259 D3
Tournay Rd SW6 135 B5 264 D4
Toussaint Wlk 18 SE16 118 A3
Tovil Cl SE20 184 B1
Tovy Ho 6 SE1 118 A1
Towcester Rd E3 98 A3
Tower 42* EC2 95 C1 243 A2
Tower Bldgs 22 E1 118 B5
Tower Br App E1, EC3 253 C5
Tower Bridge* E1, EC3, SE1 117 D5 253 C4
Tower Bridge Bsns Complex SE16 118 B3
Tower Bridge Bsns Sq SE16 118 B2
Tower Bridge Mews HA0 64 D4
Tower Bridge Piazza SE1 253 C3

Tower Bridge Prim Sch SE1 117 D4 253 C2
Tower Bridge Rd SE1 117 C4 253 A1
Tower Bridge Sq SE1 253 C2
Tower Bridge Wharf SE1 118 A5
Tower Cl
Hampstead NW3 70 B3
Orpington BR6 227 D5
Penge SE20 184 B3
Tower Ct Brockley SE4 141 A1
Stamford Hill E5 51 D2
St Giles WC2 240 A1
St John's Wood NW8 230 B4
Tower Gardens Rd N17 33 B2
Towergate SE1 263 A4
Towergate Cl UB8 60 A3
Towergate Ho 35 E3 97 B5
Tower Gateway Sta EC3 117 D6 253 C6
Tower Gdns KT10 213 A1
Tower Gr KT13 193 C1
TOWER HAMLETS 97 B2
Tower Hamlets Coll
Poplar E14 97 D1
Poplar E14 119 D6
Stepney E1 96 D1
Tower Hamlets Rd
Forest Gate E7 76 D3
Walthamstow E17 53 C6
Tower Hill EC3 117 D6 253 D5
Tower Hill Sta EC3 117 D6 253 C6
Tower La HA9 65 D5
Tower Mans SE1 263 C5
Tower Mews
Hackney E5 75 A3
Walthamstow E17 53 C5
Tower Millennium Pier EC3 117 C5 253 B4
Tower Mill Rd 1 SE15 139 C5
Tower Pl E EC3 253 B5
Tower Pl W EC3 253 B5
Tower Rd DA7 147 D1
Orpington BR6 227 D5
Twickenham TW1, TW2 152 D1
Willesden NW10 68 A1
Tower Rise TW9 132 A2
Tower Royal EC4 252 C6
Towers Ave UB10 83 A4
Towers Bsns Pk HA9 66 D4
Towers Ct UB10 83 A4
Towers Pl TW10 154 A6
Towers Rd Pinner HA5 23 A2
Southall UB1 85 C3
Tower St WC2 240 A1
Towers The
Dartmouth Pk NW5 71 B5
1 Richmond TW9 132 B1
Tower Terr
Brockley SE4 141 A1
Wood Green N22 32 B1
Tower The★ EC3 117 D6 253 C5
Towerview SE13 163 C6
Tower View
Bushey WD23 8 C4
Croydon CR0 207 A2
Tower Wharf SE1 253 C2
Tower Wlk SE1 263 A4
Towfield Ct TW13 151 B2
Towfield Rd TW13 151 B2
Towncourt Cres BR5 211 B5
Towncourt La BR5 211 B2
Towncourt Path N4 51 A1
Townend Ct 6 BR1 186 D2
Towney Mead UB5 85 B5
Towney Mead Ct UB5 85 B5
Townfield Rd UB3 105 D5
Townfield Sq UB3 105 D6
Town Field Way TW7 131 A3
Town Hall Approach Rd N15 51 D5
Townhall Ave 3 W4 111 B1
Town Hall Rd SW11 136 D2
Townholm Cres W7 108 D3
Town Hos EC1 241 D5
Town La TW19 148 A2
Townley Ct E15 76 D2
Townley Gram Sch for Girls DA6 169 B6
Townley Rd DA6 169 B6
Dulwich Village SE22 161 C6
Townley St SE17 117 B1 262 C2
Townmead Bsns Ctr SW6 136 A2
Town Meadow TW8 131 D5
Townmead Rd
Richmond TW9 132 D3
Sands End SW6 136 A3
Town Quay IG11 100 D6
Town Quay Wharf IG11 100 D6
Town Rd N9 18 B2
Townsend Ave N14 31 D6
Townsend Ct NW9 45 B2
Townsend Ho 14 SE1 118 A2
Townsend Ind Est NW10 89 A5
Townsend La NW9 45 B3
Townsend Mews 3 SW18 158 A2
Townsend Prim Sch SE17 117 C2 263 A4
Townsend Rd
Ashford TW15 170 A5
Southall UB1 107 A5
Townsend Rd *continued*
South Tottenham N15 51 D4
Townsend St SE1, SE17 117 C2 263 A4
Townsend Way HA6 22 A3
Townsend Yd N6 49 B1
Townshend Cl DA14 190 C4
Townshend Ct NW8 230 B4
Townshend Est NW8 92 C5 230 A4
Townshend Ho 16 SE18 122 B2
Townshend Rd
Chislehurst BR7 188 D5
Primrose Hill NW8 92 C6 230 A5
Richmond TW9 132 B1
Townshend Terr TW9 132 B1
Towns Ho 4 SW4 137 D2
Townson Ave UB5 84 B5
Townson Way UB5 84 A5
Town The EN2 5 B2
Town Tree Rd TW15 170 C5
Towpath TW17 192 B1
Towpath Way CR0 205 D4
Towpath Wlk E9 75 B3
Towton Rd SE27 161 A2
Toxteth Ho N4 51 A2
Toynbec Cl BR7 188 D6
Toynbee Rd SW19, SW20 179 A2
Toynbee St E1 95 D2 243 C3
Toyne Way N6 48 D3
Tracey Ave NW2 68 C3
Tracy Ct HA7 25 C3
Tracy Ho 15 E3 97 B4
Trade Cl N13 32 C6
Trader Rd E6 100 D1
Tradescant Ho 15 E9 74 C1
Tradescant Rd SW8 138 A5 270 B3
Trade Twr 8 SW11 136 A2
Trade Winds Ct 1 E1 118 A5
Trading Estate Rd NW10 89 A3
Traemore Ct SW16 160 C1
Trafalgar Ave
North Cheam KT4, SM3, SM4 200 D1
SE15 139 D6
Tottenham N17 33 C4
Trafalgar Bsns Ctr IG11 101 D3
Trafalgar Cl 1 SE16 119 A2
Trafalgar Ct
Barking E6 100 C6
Hounslow TW3 129 B2
West Barnes KT3 200 B6
Trafalgar Gdns
Stepney E1 96 D2
W8 255 D6
Trafalgar Gr SE10 142 B6
Trafalgar Ho
Barking IG11 102 B4
SE17 262 B2
Trafalgar Inf Sch TW2 152 B2
Trafalgar Jun Sch TW2 152 B2
Trafalgar Mews E9 75 B2
Trafalgar Pl
Edmonton N18 34 A5
Wanstead E11 55 A5
Trafalgar Point 2 N1 73 B1
Trafalgar Rd
Greenwich SE10 120 C1
Merton SW19 180 A3
Twickenham TW2 152 B2
Trafalgar Sq★ SW1 115 D5 249 D4
Trafalgar St SE17 117 B1 262 D2
Trafalgar Terr HA1 42 C1
Trafalgar Trad Est EN3 7 A1
Trafalgar Way
Canary Wharf E14 120 A5
Croydon CR0 220 C6
Trafford Cl E15 75 D3
Trafford Ho N1 235 D4
Trafford Rd CR7 204 B4
Trafford Villas CR0 204 B4
Tragail SW15 157 A6
Traherne Lo 5 TW11 174 D5
Trahorn Cl E1 96 B3
Traitors Gate★ EC3 117 D5 253 C4
Tralee Ct 31 SE16 118 B1
Tramsheds Ind Est The CR0, CR4 203 D2
Tramway Ave
Ponders End N9 18 C4
Stratford E15 76 B1
Tramway Cl SE20 184 C2
Tramway Path CR4 202 C5
Trance Way W3 110 C3
Tranmere Ct 5 SM2 218 A1
Tranmere Ho 7 N7 72 C3
Tranmere Rd
Edmonton N9 17 D4
Twickenham TW2 151 D4
Wandsworth SW17, SW18 158 A2
Tranquil Pas SE3 142 D3
Tranquil Vale SE3 142 C3
Transept St NW1 237 B3
Transmere Cl BR5 211 A3
Transmere Rd BR5 211 A3
Transom Cl SE16 119 A2
Transom Sq E14 119 D1
Transport Ave TW8 131 B6
Tranton Rd SE16 118 B3
Trappes Ho 2 SE16 118 B2
Traps La KT2, KT3 177 C2
Travellers Way TW5 128 C3
Travers Cl E17 34 D2
Travers Ho 6 SE10 142 B6
Travers Rd N7 72 C5
Travis Ho SE10 142 A4
Treacy Cl WD23 8 A2
Treadgold Ho 7 W11 112 D6
Treadgold St W11 112 D6
Treadway St E2 96 B5
Treasury Bldgs SW1 250 A2
Treasury Cl SM6 219 D3
Treaty Ctr TW3 129 D2
Treaty St N1 94 B6 233 C5
Trebeck St W1 248 C3
Treborough Ho W1 238 A4
Trebovir Rd SW5 113 C2 255 B3
Treby St E3 97 B3
Trecastle Way 2 N7 71 D4
Tredegar Mews 10 E3 97 B4
Tredegar Rd Bow E3 97 B5
Wood Green N11 31 D3
Tredegar Sq E3 97 B4
Tredegar Terr E3 97 B4
Trederwen Rd E8 96 A6
Tredown Rd SE26 184 C5
Tredwell Cl BR2 210 A5
Tredwell Rd SE27 182 D6
Tree Cl TW10 153 D3
Treehouse Sch N10 49 A5
Treen Ave SW13 133 D2
Tree Rd E16 99 C1
Trees The N16 51 B2
Tree Tops 1 IG8 37 A6
Treetops Cl SE2 125 A1
Treetops Ct CR7 205 A4
Treetops View IG10 21 D4
Treeview Cl SE19 183 C2
Treewall Gdns BR1 187 B6
Trefgarne Rd RM10 81 C6
Trefil Wlk N7 72 A4
Trefoil Ho DA18 125 A4
Trefoil Rd SW18 158 A6
Trefusis Ct TW5 128 B4
Tregaron Ave N8 50 A3
Tregaron Gdns KT3 199 C5
Tregarvon Rd SW11 137 A1
Tregenna Ave HA2 63 C4
Tregenna Cl 1 N14 15 C6
Tregenna Ct HA2 63 C4
Tregony Rd BR6 227 D4
Trego Rd E9 75 C1
Tregothnan Rd SW9 138 A2
Tregunter Rd SW10 114 A1 256 A1
Treherne Ct
Brixton SW9 138 D4
Upper Tooting SW17 181 A6
Trehern Rd 12 SW14 133 B2
Trehurst St E5 75 A3
Trelawney Cl E17 53 D5
Trelawney Est E9 74 C2
Trelawney Ho SE1 252 A2
Trelawn Rd Leyton E10 76 A5
Tulse Hill SW2 160 C6
Trellis Ho SW19 180 A3
Trellis Sq 1 E3 97 B4
Treloar Gdns SE19 183 B4
Tremadoc Rd SW4 137 D1
Tremaine Cl SE4 141 C3
Tremaine Rd SE20 184 B1
Trematon Ho SE11 261 B2
Trematon Pl TW11 175 C3
Tremlett Gr N19 71 C5
Tremlett Mews N19 71 C5
Trenance Gdns IG3 80 A5
Trenchard Ave HA4 62 B4
Trenchard Cl
Grahame Pk NW9 27 C2
Stanmore HA7 25 B4
Trenchard Ct SM4 201 C3
Trenchard St SE10 120 B1
Trenchold St SW8 138 A6 270 A5
Trend Ct W13 109 B5
Trendell Ho 8 E14 97 C1
Trenholme Cl 6 SE20 184 B3
Trenholme Rd SE20 184 B3
Trenholme Terr SE20 184 B3
Trenmar Gdns NW10 90 B4
Trent Ave W5 109 C3
Trent CE Prim Sch EN4 2 D1
Trent Ct
1 South Croydon CR2 221 A3
Wanstead E11 55 A4
Trent Ctry Pk★ EN4 3 A3
Trent Gdns N14 15 B5
Trentham Ct W3 89 B2
Trentham Lo 8 EN1 17 C6
Trentham St SW18 157 C3
Trent Ho
4 Kingston u T KT2 175 D2
Nunhead SE15 140 C1
Trent Rd
Buckhurst Hill IG9 21 B3
Clapham Pk SW2 160 B6
Trent Way Hayes UB4 83 C4
North Cheam KT4 216 C5
Trentwood Side EN2 4 B2
Treport St SW18 157 D4
Tresco Cl BR1 186 C4
Trescoe Gdns HA2 41 A2
Tresco Gdns IG3 80 A6
Tresco Ho SE11 261 A2
Tresco Rd SE15 140 B1
Tresham Cres NW8 92 C3 237 A6
Tresham Rd IG11 79 D1
Tresham Wlk E9 74 C3
Tresidder Ho 10 SW4 159 D4
Tresilian Ave N21 16 B6
Tressel Cl 20 N1 72 D1
Tressillian Cres SE4 141 C2
Tressillian Rd SE4 141 C2
Trestis Cl UB4 84 D2
Treswell Rd RM9 103 A6
Tretawn Gdns NW7 11 C1
Tretawn Pk NW7 27 C6
Trevallyn Lo 1 KT2 176 D2
Trevanion Rd W14 254 B2
Treve Ave HA1 42 B2
Trevelyan Ave E12 78 B4
Trevelyan Cres HA3 43 D2
Trevelyan Ct KT3 199 D2
Trevelyan Gdns NW10 90 C6
Trevelyan Ho
16 Globe Town E2 96 D4
SE5 138 D5
6 Twickenham TW1 153 C5
Trevelyan Rd
Leyton E15 76 D4
Upper Tooting SW17 180 D4
Trevenna Ho 13 SE23 162 D1
Trevera Ct EN3 19 A6
Treveris St SE1 251 D3
Traversh Ct 7 BR1 186 D2
Treverton St W10 90 D3
Treverton Twr W10 90 D2
Treves Cl N21 16 B6
Treves Ho E1 96 A3
Treville St SW15 156 B4
Treviso Rd SE23 163 A2
Trevithick Cl TW14 149 D3
Trevithick Ho
13 Bermondsey SE16 118 B2
3 Gospel Oak NW5 71 B4
SW8 269 C2
Trevithick St SE8 141 C6
Trevone Gdns HA5 41 A3
Trevor Cl Harrow HA3 24 D3
Hayes BR2 209 A2
Isleworth TW7 152 D6
New Barnet EN4 14 B5
Northolt UB5 84 C5
Trevor Cres HA4 61 D4
Trevor Gdns
Hendon HA8 27 B2
Northolt UB5 84 C5
Ruislip HA4 62 A4
Trevor Pl SW7 114 C4 247 B1
Trevor Rd Hayes UB3 105 C4
Hendon HA8 27 B2
Wimbledon SW19 179 A3
Woodford IG8 37 A3
Trevor Roberts Tutorial Coll NW8 70 B1
Trevor Sq SW7 114 C4 247 B1
Trevor St SW7 114 C4 247 B1
Trevose Ho SE11 260 D2
Trevose Rd E17 36 B2
Trewenna Dr KT9 213 D3
Trewince Rd SW20 178 C2
Trewint St SW18 158 A2
Trewsbury Ho 2 SE2 124 D4
Trewsbury Rd SE26 184 D5
Triandra Way UB4 84 D2
Triangle Ct
4 Newham E16 99 C2
SE1 252 B3
Triangle Ctr UB1 108 B5
Triangle Est The SE11 261 A1
Triangle Ho SE1 253 C2
Triangle Pl SW4 137 D1
Triangle Rd 7 E8 96 B6
Triangle The
Barking IG11 79 A2
Crouch End N19 49 D2
EC1 241 D6
Hackney E8 96 B6
Kingston u T KT3 177 A1
Tribune Ct 16 NW9 46 A5
Tricorn Ho SE28 123 B5
Trident Bsns Ctr SW17 180 D5
Trident Gdns 6 UB5 84 D4
Trident Ho
14 South Bromley E14 98 A1
Woolwich SE28 123 B5
Trident St SE16 118 D2
Trident Way UB2 106 B3
Trieste Ct SW12 158 D3
Trig La EC4 252 A6
Trigon Rd SW8 138 B5 270 D4
Trilby Rd SE23 162 D2
Trillington Ho W12 112 A5
Trillo Ct IG1 57 C2
Trimdon NW1 232 B5
Trimmer Ct TW7 130 D2
Trimmer Wlk 11 TW8 132 A6
Trim St SE8 141 B6
Trinder Gdns N19 50 A1
Trinder Mews 10 TW11 175 A5
Trinder Rd Barnet EN5 12 C6
Finsbury Pk N4, N19 50 A1
Tring Ave Ealing W5 110 B5
Southall UB1 85 B1
Wembley HA9 66 C2
Tring Cl IG2 57 B4
Tring Ct TW1 175 A6
Trinidad Ho 17 E14 119 B6
Trinidad St E14 119 B6
Trinity Ave
East Finchley N2 48 B6
Enfield EN1 17 D5
Trinity Church Rd SW13 134 B6
Trinity Church Sq SE1 117 A3 262 B6
Trinity Cl
3 Clapham SW4 137 C1
Hounslow TW4 129 A1
Keston Mark BR2 210 A1
Lewisham SE13 142 B1
Leyton E11 76 C6
Trinity Cotts TW9 132 B2
Trinity Cres SW17 159 A2
Trinity Ct
8 Chingford E4 20 A2
Edmonton N18 33 D4
Eltham SE9 166 D5
Finsbury WC1 240 C6
Forest Hill SE23 162 C1
Greenwich SE7 121 D2
2 Hoxton N1 95 C6
Rotherhithe SE16 119 A4
Southgate N21 16 D3
Thornton Heath SE25 205 C3
Twickenham TW2 152 C2
Wallington SM6 219 C1
Willesden NW2 68 C3
Wimbledon SW19 179 C4
Trinity Dr UB8 83 A1
Trinity Gdns E16 98 D2
Stockwell SW2, SW9 138 B1
11 Wanstead E18 55 B6
Trinity Gn E1 96 C2
Trinity Gr 8 SE10 142 A4
Trinity Ho SE1 262 B6
5 Walthamstow E17 53 D6
Trinity Homes 14 SW2 138 B1
Trinity Mews
Penge SE20 184 B2
SE9 167 B5
Wandsworth SW18 157 C3
Trinity Par TW3 129 D2
Trinity Pl
Bexleyheath DA6 147 B1
City of London EC3 253 C5
Trinity RC High Sch (Lower) IG8 37 A6
Trinity RC High Sch (Upper) IG8 37 A6
Trinity RC High Sch (Upper Sch) IG8 36 D6
Trinity Rd
East Finchley N2 48 B6
Ilford IG6 57 A6
Richmond TW9 132 B2
Southall UB1 107 A5
Wandsworth SW17, SW18 158 C4
Wimbledon SW19 179 C4
Wood Green N22 32 A3
Wood Green N22 32 B2
Trinity Rise SE24, SW2 160 D4
Trinity St Mary's CE Prim Sch SW12 159 A3
Trinity Sch
Croydon CR0 222 C6
Dagenham RM10 81 C4
Trinity Sq EC3 117 C6 253 B6
Trinity St Enfield EN2 5 A3
9 Newham E16 99 A2
SE1 117 B3 262 C6
Trinity Terr IG9 21 B4
Trinity Way
East Acton W3 111 D6
Walthamstow E4 35 B4
Trio Pl SE1 117 A4 252 B1
Triscott Ho UB3 106 A5
Tristan Ct 34 SE8 141 B6
Tristan Sq SE3 142 C2
Tristram Cl E17 54 B6
Tristram Dr N9 18 A1
Tristram Rd BR1 186 D6
Triton Ct EC2 242 D5
Woodford IG9 21 A2
Triton Ho 2 E14 119 D2
Triton Sq NW1 239 A6
Tritton Ave CR0 220 A4
Tritton Ho N21 17 B5
Tritton Rd SE21, SE27 161 B1
Triumph Cl UB7 127 A4
Triumph Ho IG11 102 A4
Triumph Rd E6 100 B1
Triumph Trad Est N17 34 A4
Trocette Mans SE1 263 B6
Trojan Ct
Brondesbury NW6 69 A1
9 Ealing W7 109 A5
Trojan Ind Est NW10 67 D2
Trojan Way CR0 220 B5
Troon Cl
34 Bermondsey SE16 118 B1
Erith SE28 102 D1
Troon Ct UB1 108 A6
Troon Ho 9 E14 97 A1
Troon St E1 97 A1
Tropical Ct 2 W10 90 D4
Trosley Rd DA17 147 C6
Trossachs Rd SE22 161 C6
Trothy Rd SE1 118 A2
Trotman Ho 1 SE14 140 C4
Trott Rd N10 31 A3
Trott St SW11 136 C4 267 A1
Trotwood Ho 3 SE16 118 B4
Troubridge Ct 12 W4 111 A1
Troughton Rd SE7 121 B1
Troutbeck NW1 231 D1
Troutbeck Rd SE14 141 A4
Trouville Rd SW4 159 C5
Trowbridge Rd E9 75 B2
Trower Ho 5 E9 75 A2
Trowlock Ave TW11 175 C4
Trowlock Island TW11 175 D4
Trowlock Way TW11 175 D4
Troy Ct W8 255 A6
5 Woolwich SE18 122 D2
Troyes Ho NW3 70 D3
Troy Rd SE19 183 B4
Troy Town SE15 140 A2
Troy Town Flats SE15 140 A2
Trubshaw Rd UB2 107 D3
Trulock Ct N17 34 A3
Trulock Rd N17 34 A3
Truman Cl 2 HA8 27 A3
Truman's Rd 24 N16 73 C3
Trumpers Way W7 108 D3
Trumpeters Inn TW9 153 C6
Trumpington Rd E7 76 D4
Trump St EC2 242 B1
Trundlers Way WD23 8 C3
Trundle St SE1 252 A2
Trundleys Rd SE8 141 A6
Trundley's Rd SE8 118 D1
Trundley's Terr SE8 118 D2
Truro Ct 2 N8 49 D4
Truro Gdns IG1 56 A2
Truro Ho
25 Paddington W2 91 C2
Pinner HA5 23 B2
Truro Rd
Walthamstow E17 53 B5
Wood Green N22 32 B3
Truro St NW5 71 A2
Truro Way UB4 83 C4
Truscott Ho 3 CR7 204 C3
Trusedale Rd E6 100 B1
Truslove Rd SE27 182 D5
Trussley Rd W6 112 C3
Trust Wlk SE21 160 D3
Tryfan Cl IG4 55 D4
Tryon Cres E9 96 C6
Tryon St SW3 114 D1 257 C2
Trystings Cl KT10 213 A2
Tuam Rd SE18 145 B6
Tubbenden Cl BR6 227 C5
Tubbenden Dr BR6 227 B4
Tubbenden Jun & Inf Schs BR6 227 B4
Tubbenden La BR6 227 C5
Tubbenden La S BR6 227 B3
Tubbs Rd NW10 89 D5
Tudor Ave
Hampton TW12 173 C3
North Cheam KT4 216 B4
Tudor Cl Ashford TW15 170 A6
BR7 188 B2
Cheam SM3 217 A2
Chessington KT9 214 A3
Crouch End N6 49 C2
Hampstead NW3 70 C2
Hampton TW12 174 A5
Hendon NW7 28 A4
Pinner HA5 40 A4
Tulse Hill SW2 160 B5
Wallington SM6 219 C1
Welsh Harp NW9 67 A6
Woodford IG8 37 B5
Tudor Coll WC1 233 A1
Tudor Court N HA9 66 C3
Tudor Court S HA9 66 C3
Tudor Cres EN2 5 A4
Tudor Ct 2 Barnet EN5 1 B1
3 Ealing W13 87 C1
Feltham TW13 172 C6
Kingsland N1 73 C2
5 Rotherhithe SE16 118 D5
Sidcup DA14 168 A1
South Acton W5 110 C4
4 Stanwell TW19 148 A5
Teddington TW11 174 D4
Walthamstow E17 53 B2
Tudor Dr
Kingston u T KT2 176 A5
Walton-on-T KT12 194 D1
West Barnes SM4 201 A3
Tudor Ent Pk HA3 42 B6
Tudor Est NW10 88 D5
Tudor Gables NW7 27 D6
Tudor Gdns Acton W3 88 C1
Harrow HA3 24 B1
Mortlake SW14 133 C2
Twickenham TW1 152 D3
Welsh Harp NW9 67 A6
West Wickham BR4 224 A5
Tudor Gr E9 74 C1
Tudor Ho
Brook Green W14 112 D2
Feltham TW13 172 C6
34 Hackney E9 74 C1
Mitcham CR4 181 A2
6 Muswell Hill N10 31 A3
Queensbury NW9 44 C5
Tolworth KT6 198 C1
Tudor Lo 4 N12 29 D5
Tudor Mews
Walthamstow E17 53 B5
2 Willesden NW10 68 A2
Tudor Par
Dagenham RM6 58 D2
SE9 144 A1
Tudor Pl SW19 180 C3
Tudor Prim Sch
Finchley N3 30 A2
Southall UB1 107 A6
Tudor Rd
Ashford TW15 171 B4
Barking IG11 101 D6
Barnet EN5 1 D2
Beckenham BR3 208 A6
Chingford E4 35 D4

Tudor Rd *continued*
Croydon SE25 206 B4
Hackney E9 96 B6
Hampton TW12 173 C3
Harrow HA3 24 B1
Hayes UB3 83 B1
Isleworth TW3 130 B1
Kingston u T KT2 176 C3
Newham E6 99 C6
Penge SE19 183 D3
Pinner HA5 22 C1
Ponders End N9 18 C4
Southall UB1 107 A6
Tudor Sq UB3 83 B2
Tudor St EC4 116 C6 251 B6
Tudors The 2 BR3 185 D1
Tudor Way BR5 211 B3
Hillingdon UB10 60 C2
Osidge N14 15 D3
South Acton W3 110 C4
Tudor Well Cl HA7 25 B5
Tudor Wlk DA5 169 A5
Tudway Rd SE3, SE9 143 C1
Tufnell Ct 19 E3 97 B6
Tufnell Mans 7 N7 71 D4
TUFNELL PARK 71 D4
Tufnell Park Mans 2 N7 72 A5
Tufnell Park Prim Sch N7 71 D4
Tufnell Park Rd N19, N7 71 D4
Tufnell Park Sta N19 71 C4
Tufton Ct SW1 260 A5
Tufton Gdns KT8 173 D1
Tufton Rd E4 35 C6
Tufton St SW1 116 A3 260 A5
Tugboat St SE28 123 C4
Tugela Rd CR0 205 B3
Tugela St SE6 163 B2
Tugmutton Cl BR6 226 D4
Tuke Sch SE15 140 B4
Tulip Cl Croydon CR0 226 D1
Hampton TW12 173 B4
5 Newham E6 100 B2
Southall UB2 108 A4
Tulip Ct 1 HA5 40 C6
Tulip Gdns Chingford E4 20 B1
Ilford IG1 78 D2
Tullis Ho 12 E9 74 C1
Tull St CR4 202 D2
Tulse Cl BR3 208 A6
TULSE HILL 160 D4
Tulse Hill
Tulse Hill SW2 160 C4
Tulse Hill SW27 160 D2
Tulse Hill Sta SE27 160 D2
Tulse Ho SW2 160 C5
Tulsemere Rd SE21, SE27 161 A2
Tumbling Bay KT12 194 A3
Tummons Gdns SE25 183 C1
Tump Ho SE28 123 C5
Tunbridge Ct 1 SE26 162 A1
Tunbridge Ho EC1 234 C2
Tuncombe Rd N18 33 C6
Tunis Rd W12 112 B5
Tunley Gn 12 E14 97 B2
Tunley Rd
Dagenham NW10 89 C6
Upper Tooting SW12, SW17 159 A2
Tunmarsh La E13 99 C4
Tunnan Leys E6 100 C1
Tunnel Avenue Trad Est SE10 120 B4
Tunnel Gdns N11 31 C3
Tunnel Link Rd TW6 148 C5
Tunnel Rd SE16 118 C4
Tunnel Rd E TW6 126 D3
Tunnel Rd W TW6 126 D4
Tunstall Cl BR6 227 C4
Tunstall Ct 14 TW9 132 B4
Tunstall Rd
Croydon CR0 205 C1
Stockwell SW9 138 B1
Tunstall Wlk 10 TW8 132 A6
Tunstock Way DA17 125 A3
Tunworth Cl NW9 45 A3
Tunworth Cres SW15 155 D5
Tun Yd SW8 137 B2
Tupelo Rd E10 75 D6
Tupman Ho 26 SE16 118 A4
Tuppy St SE28 123 A3
Turberville Ho 1 SW9 138 B2
Turenne Cl SW18 136 A1
Turin Rd N9 18 C4
Turin St E2 96 A4
Turkey Oak Cl SE19 183 C2
Turkey St EN1, EN3 6 C6
Turkey Street Sta EN3 6 C6
Turks Cl UB8 82 C4
Turk's Head Yd EC1 241 C4
Turks Row SW3 114 D1 257 D2
Turle Rd Finsbury Pk N4 72 B6
Thornton Heath SW16 182 A1
Turlewray Cl N4 50 B1
Turley Cl E15 98 C6
Turnagain La EC4 241 C2
Turnage Rd RM8 59 A1
Turnant Rd N17 33 A2
Turnberry Cl
24 Bermondsey SE16 118 B1
Hendon NW4 28 D1
Turnberry Quay 1 E14 119 D3
Turnberry Way BR6 211 B1
Turnbull Ho N1 234 D6
Turnbury Cl SE28 102 D1
Turnchapel Mews 1 SW4 137 B2
Turner Ave
Mitcham CR4 180 D2
Tottenham N15 51 C5
Twickenham TW2 152 A1
Turner Cl
7 Brixton SW9 138 D4
Hampstead Garden Suburb NW11 47 D3
Hillingdon UB4 83 A4
Wembley HA0 65 D2
Turner Ct
9 Herne Hill SE5 139 B1
24 Rotherhithe SE16 118 C4
Turner Dr NW11 47 D3
Turner Ho
Finsbury Pk N4 50 B1
24 Millwall E14 119 C4
St John's Wood NW8 230 A4
Strand WC2 250 B5
6 Twickenham TW1 153 D5
Westminster SW1 259 D3
Turner Lo 10 SW19 156 D3
Turner Mews SM2 217 D1
Turner Pl SW11 158 C6
Turner Rd Edgware HA8 26 B1
New Malden KT3 199 B2
Walthamstow E17 54 A6
Turners Cl N20 14 D1
Turners Ct Leyton E15 76 A4
New Barnet EN5 13 D5
Tottenham N15 51 B4
Turners Meadow Way BR3 185 B2
Turner's Rd E3 97 B2
Turner St
Canning Town E16 98 D1
Stepney E1 96 B2
Turners Way CR0 220 C6
Turneville Rd W14 135 B6 264 C6
Turney Prim & Sec Specl Sch SE21 161 A4
Turney Rd SE21 161 B4
Turnham Green Sta W4 111 C2
Turnham Green Terr W4 111 C2
Turnham Ho SE4 141 A1
Turnham Prim Sch SE4 141 A1
Turnham Rd SE4 141 A1
Turnmill Ho 8 SW2 160 C6
Turnmill St EC1 94 D2 241 C4
Turnour Ho 31 E1 96 B1
Turnpike Cl SE8 141 B5
Turnpike Ct DA6 146 D1
Turnpike Ho EC1 234 D1
Turnpike La Hornsey N8 50 C6
Sutton SM1 218 A3
Uxbridge UB10 82 A5
Turnpike Lane Sta N15 50 D6
Turnpike Link CR0 221 C6
Turnpike Mews N8 50 C6
Turnpike Way TW7 131 A4
Turnpin La 3 SE10 142 A6
Turnstone Cl
Edgware NW9 27 C1
Newham E13 99 A4
Uxbridge UB10 60 D3
Turnstone Terr 11 W13 86 D3
Turpentine La SW1 115 B1 258 D1
Turpin Cl 15 EN3 7 C6
Turpington Cl BR2 210 A2
Turpington La BR2 210 A3
Turpin Ho SW11 268 C2
Turpin Rd TW14 149 D5
Turpin Way
Upper Holloway N19 49 D1
Wallington SM6 219 B1
Turquand St SE17 262 B3
Turret Gr SW4 137 C2
Turret Ho KT2 176 A4
Turton Ho 5 SE18 144 D6
Turton Rd HA0 66 A3
Turville Ho NW8 237 A6
Turville St E2 243 C6
Tuscan Ho 36 E2 96 C4
Tuscan Rd SE18 123 B1
Tuscany Ho E17 35 B1
Tuskar St SE10 120 C1
Tutorial Coll of West London UB1 107 B5
Tuttlebee La IG9 21 A2
Tuttle Ho SW1 259 D1
Tweedale Ct E15 76 A3
Tweed Ct W7 86 C1
Tweeddale Gr UB10 61 A5
Tweeddale Prim Sch SM5 202 B2
Tweeddale Rd SM5 202 B1
Tweed Ho E14 98 A3
Tweedmouth Rd E13 99 B5
Tweedy Cl EN1 17 D6
Tweedy Rd BR1 187 A2
Tweezer's Alley WC2 251 A6
Twelve Acre Ho 5 E12 78 C5
Twelvetrees Bsns Pk E16 98 B3
Twelvetrees Cres E3 98 A3
Twentyman Cl IG8 37 A5
Twice Times Montessori Sch SW6 135 C3
TWICKENHAM 152 D4
Twickenham Bridge TW9 153 C6
Twickenham Cl CR0 220 B5
Twickenham Gdns
Harrow HA3 24 C3
Wembley UB6 65 A3
Twickenham Pl KT7 212 D6
Twickenham Prep Sch TW12 174 A2
Twickenham Rd
Isleworth TW1, TW7 131 A2
Leyton E11 76 B6
Richmond TW1, TW9 131 C1
Teddington TW11 175 A6
Twickenham TW13 151 B1
Twickenham Rugby Football Union Ground TW2 152 C5
Twickenham Sta TW1 153 A4
Twickenham Trad Ctr TW1 152 D5
Twig Folly Cl 21 E2 96 D5
Twilley St SW18 157 D4
Twine Cl IG11 102 B4
Twine Ct E1 118 C6
Twineham Gn N12 29 C6
Twining Ave TW2 152 B1
Twinn Rd NW7 29 A4
Twin Tumps Way SE28 124 A6
Twisden Rd NW5 71 B4
Twiss Ho 6 SE18 122 D1
Twist Ho E10 75 D6
Two Bridges Ind Est CR0 221 B2
Twybridge Way NW10 67 A1
Twyford Abbey Rd NW10 88 B4
Twyford Ave Acton W3 110 C6
Muswell Hill N2 48 D6
Twyford CE High Sch W3 110 D5
Twyford Cres W3 110 C5
Twyford Ct Acton W3 110 C6
Muswell Hill N10 49 A6
6 Wembley HA0 88 A5
Twyford Ho Highbury N5 72 D5
6 Tottenham N15 51 C3
Twyford Par KT6 198 C1
Twyford Rd
Carshalton SM5 202 B1
Harrow HA2 41 D2
Ilford IG1 79 A3
Twyford St N1 94 B6 233 C6
Twynholm Mans SW6 264 A4
Tyas Rd E16 98 D3
Tybenham Rd SW19 201 C6
Tyberry Rd EN3 6 C2
Tyburn La HA1 42 D2
Tyburn Tree (site of)* W2 247 C6
Tyburn Way W1 247 D6
Tye La BR6 227 A3
Tyer's Est SE1 253 A2
Tyers Gate SE1 117 C4 253 A1
Tyers Ho 1 SW16 181 C5
Tyers St SE11 116 B1 260 C2
Tyers Terr SE11 116 B1 260 D1
Tyeshurst Cl SE2 125 A1
Tylecroft Rd SW16 182 A1
Tylehurst Gdns IG1 79 A3
Tyler Cl Erith DA8 147 D5
Haggerston E2 95 D5
Tyler Ho SE3 142 B3
Tyler Rd UB2 107 D3
Tylers Ct
4 Walthamstow E17 53 C5
5 Wembley HA0 88 A5
Tylers Gate HA3 44 A3
Tylers Path SM5 218 D4
Tyler St
Greenwich SE10 120 C1
SE10 142 C6
Tylney Ave SE19 183 D5
Tylney Ho 10 E1 96 B1
Tylney Rd BR1 187 D1
Forest Gate E7 77 C4
Tymperley Ct SW19 157 A3
Tynamara KT1 197 D5
Tynan Cl TW14 150 A3
Tyndale La N1 72 D1
Tyndale Mans N1 72 D1
Tyndale Terr 13 N1 72 D1
Tyndall Gdns E10 76 A6
Tyndall Rd DA16 145 D2
Leyton E10 76 A6
Tyne Ct W7 86 C1
Tyneham Cl 10 SW11 137 A2
Tyneham Rd SW11 137 A2
Tyne Ho 8 KT2 175 D2
Tynemouth Cl E6 100 D1
Tynemouth Dr EN1 6 A5
Tynemouth Rd
Mitcham CR4 181 A3
Plumstead Comm SE18 123 C1
Tottenham N15 51 D5
Tynemouth St SW6 136 A3
Tynemouth Terr 9 N15 51 D5
Tyne St E1 243 D2
Tynsdale Rd NW10 67 C2
Tynte Ct E9 75 A3
Tynwald Ho 14 SE26 162 A1
Type St E2 96 D5
Tyrawley Rd SW6 265 C2
Tyrell Cl HA1 64 C4
Tyrell Ct SM5 218 D4
Tyrells Ct 3 SE15 140 B2
Tyrols Rd SE23 162 D3
Tyrone Ct SW16 181 D5
Tyrone Rd E6 100 B4
Tyron Way DA14 189 D5
Tyrrell Ave DA16 168 B6
Tyrrell Ho Catford BR3 185 D5
SW1 269 B6
Tyrrell Rd SE22 140 A1
Tyrrell Sq CR4 180 C2
Tyrrel Way NW9 46 A2
Tyrwhitt Rd SE4 141 C2
Tysoe Ave EN3 7 B6
Tysoe St EC1 234 B1
Tyson Rd SE23 162 C4
Tyssen Com Prim Sch N16 52 A1
Tyssen Rd N16 73 D5
Tyssen St Dalston E8 73 D2
Hoxton N1 95 C5
Tysson Ho E9 75 A1
Tytherton 29 E2 96 C5
Tytherton Rd N19 71 D5

U

Uamvar St E14 97 D2
Uckfield Gr CR4 181 A2
Uckfield Rd EN3 6 D6
Udall St SW1 259 B3
Udimore Ho 11 W10 90 C2
Udney Park Rd TW11 175 A4
Uffington Rd
West Norwood SE27 182 C6
Willesden Green NW10 90 B6
Ufford Cl HA3 23 D3
Ufford Rd HA3 23 D3
Ufford St SE1 116 C4 251 B2
Ufton Ct UB5 84 D4
Ufton Gr N1 73 B1
Ufton Rd N1 73 C1
Uhura Sq 19 N16 73 C5
Ujima Ct
Finsbury Pk N19 50 A1
Streatham SW16 182 A6
Ujima Ho SW16 182 A6
UK Coll of Bsns & Computing IG2 56 C3
Uk Cotts UB3 105 B4
Ullathorne Rd SW16 181 C6
Ulleswater Rd N14 16 B1
Ullin St E14 98 A2
Ullswater SW15 156 D5
Ullswater Cl
Bromley BR1 186 C3
Hayes UB4 83 C5
Kingston u T KT2, SW15 177 B6
Ullswater Cres SW15 177 B6
Ullswater Ct
Harrow HA2 41 C2
2 Woodford E18 37 A1
Ullswater Ho SE15 140 C6
Ullswater Rd
Barnes SW13 134 A5
West Norwood SE27, SW16 160 D2
Ulster Ct KT2 175 D4
Ulster Gdns N13 33 A6
Ulster Pl NW1 238 C5
Ulster Terr NW1 238 C6
Ulundi Rd SE3 142 C6
Ulva Rd SW15 134 D1
Ulverscroft Rd SE22 162 A6
Ulverstone Rd SE27 160 D2
Ulverston Rd E17 36 B1
Ulysses Rd NW6 69 B3
Umberston St E1 96 B1
Umbria St SW15 156 A5
Umfreville Rd N4 50 D3
Umoja Ho N22 32 B1
Una Ho 7 NW5 71 B2
Undercliff SE10 142 A4
Undercliff Rd SE13 141 D2
UNDERHILL 13 C6
Underhill EN5 13 C6
Underhill Ct EN5 13 C6
Underhill Ho 7 E14 97 C2
Underhill Jun & Inf Schs EN5 13 A6
Underhill Pas NW1 231 D6
Underhill Rd SE21, SE22 162 B4
Underhill St NW1 231 D5
Underne Ave N14 15 B2
Undershaft EC3 95 C1 243 A1
Undershaw Rd BR1 164 D1
Underwood CR0 224 A3
Underwood Ct 3 E10 53 D1
Underwood Ho
East Molesey KT8 195 C4
Hammersmith W6 112 B3
Underwood Rd
Bethnal Green E1 96 A3
Chingford E4 35 D5
Woodford IG8 37 D3
Underwood Row N1 235 B2
Underwood St N1 95 A4 235 B2
Underwood The SE9 166 B2
Undine Rd E14 119 D2
Undine St SW17 180 D5
Uneeda Dr UB6 86 B6
Unicorn Bldg 14 E1 118 D6
Unicorn Prim Sch BR3 207 D4
Unicorn Sch TW9 132 B4
Unicorn Works N17 34 C3
Union Cl E11 76 B4
Union Ct
45 Paddington W2 91 C2
2 Richmond TW10 154 A6
South Lambeth SW4 138 A3
Union Dr E1 97 A3
Union Gr SW8 137 D3
Union Mews 32 SW9 138 A3
Union Pk 11 SE10 120 D1
Union Rd BR2 209 D4
Clapham SW8 137 D3
Friern Barnet N11 31 D4
Northolt UB5 85 C5
Thornton Heath CR0 205 A2
Wembley HA0 66 A2
Union Sq N1 95 A6 235 B5
Union St Barnet EN5 1 A2
Kingston u T KT1 175 D1
Mill Meads E15 98 B6
SE1 117 A5 252 A3
Union Terr HA2 41 C1
Union Wharf N1 235 B4
Union Wlk E2 95 C4
Union Yd W1 238 D1
Unity Cl
West Norwood SE19 183 A5
Willesden NW10 68 A2
Unity Mews NW1 232 C4
Unity Rd EN3 6 C6
Unity Terr HA2 63 D6
Unity Way SE18 121 D3
Univ Coll Jun Sch NW3 70 A4
Univ Coll London
Bloomsbury WC1 93 D3 239 C6
Bloomsbury WC1 94 A3 240 B6
Univ Coll London (Windeyer Inst) W1 93 C2 239 B4
Univ Coll London (Wolfson Ho) NW1 93 C4 232 B1
University Cl NW7 27 D3
University Coll Hospl WC1 93 C3 239 B6
University Coll Sch NW3 70 A3
University Gdns DA5 169 B4
University Mans SW15 134 D2
University Pl DA8 147 D5
University Rd SW19 180 B4
University St WC1 93 C3 239 B5
University Way E16 122 D6
Univ of California WC1 93 D2 239 D3
Univ of East London
Barking RM8 80 A4
Newham E16 122 C6
Stratford E15 76 C2
Univ of East London (Duncan Ho) E15 98 B6
Univ of East London (Holbrook Ctr) E15 98 D5
Univ of Greenwich SE10 142 B6
Univ of Greenwich Avery Hill Campus Mansion Site SE9 167 A5
Univ of Greenwich Avery Hill Campus Southwood Site SE9 167 B4
Univ of Greenwich Rachel Mcmillan Campus SE8 141 C6
Univ of Greenwich Riverside Ho Annexe SE18 122 C3
Univ of London WC1 93 D3 239 D5
Univ of London (King's Coll Hall) SE5 139 B2
Univ of London Obsy NW7 27 D4
Univ of London (Queen Mary & Westfield Coll) E1 97 A3
Univ of Westminster NW1 93 C3 239 A6
Univ of Westminster (Cavendish Campus) W1 93 C2 239 A4
Univ of Westminster (Harrow Campus) HA1 43 A2
Univ of Westminster (Marylebone Campus) W1 93 A2 238 A4
Univ of Westminster (Regent Campus) W1 93 C2 239 A3
Univ of Westminster (Regent Campus, Univ HQ) W1 93 B1 238 D2
Uno Apartments 4 BR1 187 A2
Unwin Ave TW14 149 B6
Unwin Cl SE15 140 A6
Unwin Rd
Isleworth TW7 130 C2
SW7 114 B3 256 D6
Upbrook Mews W2 92 A1 236 B1
Upcerne Rd SW10 136 A5 266 B3
Upchurch Cl 8 SE20 184 B3
Upcott Ho
33 Bromley E3 97 D4
4 Hackney E9 74 C1
Upcroft Ave HA8 27 A6
Updale Rd DA14 189 D6
Upfield CR0 222 B5
Upfield Rd W7 86 D2
Upgrove Manor Way 12 SE24 160 C4
Uphall Prim Sch IG1 78 D3
Uphall Rd IG1 78 D3
Upham Park Rd W4 111 C2
Uphill Dr Edgware NW7 27 C5
Kingsbury NW9 45 A4
Uphill Gr NW7 27 C6
Uphill Rd NW7 27 C6
Upland Ct SE23 162 C2
Upland Prim Sch DA7 147 B2
Upland Rd
Croydon CR2 221 B3
DA7 147 B2
East Dulwich SE22 162 A5
8 Newham E13 99 A3
Sutton SM2 218 B1
Uplands
Beckenham BR3 185 C1
Woolwich SE18 122 D1
Uplands Ave E17 34 D1
Uplands Bsns Pk E17 52 D6
Uplands Cl SW14 154 D6
Uplands Ct N21 16 C4
Uplands Park Rd EN2 4 C3
Uplands Rd
East Barnet EN4 15 A3
Hornsey Vale N8 50 B4
Ilford RM6 58 D6
Woodford IG8 37 D3
Uplands The HA4 40 A1
Uplands Way N21 16 C6
Upnall Ho 16 SE15 140 C6
Upney Ct 2 IG11 79 D1
Upney La IG11 79 D1
Upney Sta IG11 79 D1
Upnor Way SE17 263 B2
Uppark Dr IG2 57 A3
Upper Abbey Rd DA17 125 C2
Upper Addison Gdns W14 113 A4 244 A2
Upper Bank St E14 119 D5
Upper Bardsey Wlk 7 N1 73 A2
Upper Belgrave St SW1 115 A3 258 B6
Upper Berkeley St W1 92 D1 237 D1
Upper Beulah Hill SE19 183 C2
Upper Brighton Rd KT6 198 A2
Upper Brockley Rd SE4 141 B3
Upper Brook St W1 115 A6 248 A6
Upper Butts TW8 131 C6
Upper Caldy Wlk 18 N1 73 A2
Upper Camelford Wlk 14 W10 91 A1
Upper Cavendish Ave N3 47 C6
Upper Cheyne Row SW3 136 C6 267 A6
UPPER CLAPTON 52 B1
Upper Clapton Rd E5 74 B6
Upper Clarendon Wlk 12 W11 91 A1
Upper Dengie Wlk N1 235 A6
UPPER EDMONTON 34 B5
UPPER ELMERS END 207 B3
Upper Elmers End Rd BR3 207 A4
Upper Farm Rd KT8 195 B5
Upper Fosters NW4 46 C5
Upper Gn W CR4 180 D1
Upper Gr SE25 205 D5
Upper Grosvenor St W1 115 A6 248 A5
Upper Grotto Rd TW1 152 D2
Upper Ground SE1 116 C5 251 A4
Upper Grove Rd DA17 147 B6
Upper Gulland Wlk 23 N1 73 A2
UPPER HALLIFORD 193 B5
Upper Halliford Rd TW17 193 C6
Upper Halliford Sta TW16 171 C1
Upper Hampstead Wlk 29 NW3 70 A4
Upper Ham Rd KT2, TW10 175 D6
Upper Handa Wlk 2 N1 73 A2
Upper Harley St NW1 238 B5
Upper Hawkwell Wlk N1 235 B6
UPPER HOLLOWAY 71 D6
Upper Holloway Sta N19 71 D6
Upper Holly Hill Rd DA17 125 D1
Upper James St W1 249 B6
Upper John St W1 249 B6
Upper Lismore Wlk 8 N1 73 A2
Upper Lodge Mews TW12 174 A4
Upper Mall W6 112 B1
Upper Marsh SE1 116 B3 260 D6
Upper Montague St W1 92 D2 237 C3

Upper Mulgrave Rd
SM2 ... 217 A1
Upper North St E3, E14 .. 97 C2
UPPER NORWOOD 183 C3
Upper Park Rd
Belvedere DA17 ... 125 D2
BR1 ... 187 C2
Friern Barnet N11 ... 31 C5
Kingston u T KT2 ... 176 C4
Maitland Pk NW3 ... 70 D3
Upper Phillimore Gdns
W8 ... 113 C4 245 A1
Upper Pk IG10 ... 21 D6
Upper Ramsey Wlk 19
N1 ... 73 B2
Upper Rawreth Wlk
N1 ... 235 B6
Upper Rd Finchley N2 ... 30 C2
Newham E13 ... 99 A4
Wallington SM6 ... 219 D3
Upper Richmond Rd
SW15 ... 134 C1
Upper Richmond Rd W
TW10, SW14, SW15 ... 133 A1
UPPER RUXLEY ... 191 C3
Upper St Martin's La
WC2 ... 250 A6
Upper Selsdon Rd
CR2 ... 221 D1
Upper Sheridan Rd 3
DA17 ... 125 C2
UPPER SHIRLEY ... 222 D4
Upper Shirley Rd CR0 .. 222 D5
Upper Sq TW7 ... 131 A2
Upper St N1 ... 94 D6 234 C5
Upper Sunbury Rd
TW12 ... 173 C2
Upper Sutton La TW5 .. 129 C4
UPPER SYDENHAM ... 184 A6
Upper Tachbrook St
SW1 ... 259 B4
Upper Talbot Wlk 7
W10 ... 91 A1
Upper Teddington Rd KT1,
KT8 ... 175 C2
Upper Terr NW3 ... 70 A5
Upper Thames St
EC4 ... 117 A6 252 B6
Upper Tollington Pk
N4 ... 50 C1
Upperton Rd DA14 ... 189 D5
Upperton Rd E E13 ... 99 C4
Upperton Rd W E13 ... 99 C4
UPPER TOOTING ... 158 D1
Upper Tooting Park Mans
1 SW17 ... 159 A2
Upper Tooting Pk
SW17 ... 158 D2
Upper Tooting Rd
SW17 ... 158 D1
Upper Town Rd UB6 ... 85 D3
Upper Tulse Hill SW2 .. 160 B3
Upper Vernon Rd
SM1 ... 218 B3
UPPER WALTHAMSTOW
... 54 C6
Upper Walthamstow Rd
E17 ... 54 B6
Upper Wickham La
DA16 ... 146 B4
Upper Wimpole St
W1 ... 93 A2 238 B4
Upper Woburn Pl NW1,
WC1 ... 93 D4 232 D1
Uppingham Ave HA7 ... 25 C1
Upsdell Ave N13 ... 32 C4
Upshire Ho E17 ... 35 B1
Upstall St SE5 ... 138 D4
UPTON ... 77 B1
Upton Ave E7 ... 77 A1
Upton Cl
Cricklewood NW2 ... 69 A5
Sidcup DA5 ... 169 B5
Upton Cross E13 ... 99 A6
Upton Cross Prim Sch
E13 ... 99 B6
Upton Ct Penge SE20 ... 184 C3
Southall UB1 ... 107 D5
4 Wimbledon SW19 .. 178 D3
Upton Day Hospl DA6 .. 147 A1
Upton Dene SM2 ... 217 D1
Upton Gdns HA3 ... 43 C3
Upton Hts E7 ... 77 A1
Upton La E7 ... 77 A1
Upton Lo E7 ... 77 A2
Upton Lodge Cl WD23 ... 8 A4
UPTON PARK ... 99 D6
Upton Park Rd E7 ... 77 B1
Upton Park Sta E13 ... 99 C6
Upton Prim Sch DA5 ... 169 B6
Upton Rd Bexley DA6 ... 169 A6
Edmonton N18 ... 34 A5
Hounslow TW3 ... 129 C2
SE18 ... 145 A6
South Norwood CR7 ... 183 B1
Upton Rd S DA5 ... 169 B5
Upton Villas 4 DA6 ... 147 A1
Upway N12 ... 30 C4
Upwood Rd SE12 ... 165 A5
Thornton Heath SW16 ... 182 A2
Urban Mews N4 ... 50 D2
Urlwin St SE5 ... 139 A6
Urlwin Wlk SW9 ... 138 D4
Urmston Dr SW19 ... 157 A3
Urmston Ho 4 E14 ... 120 A2
Urquhart Ct BR3 ... 185 B3
Ursula Lo DA14 ... 190 B5
Ursula Mews N4 ... 51 A1
Ursula St
SW11 ... 136 C4 267 A1
Ursuline High Sch
SW20 ... 178 D2
Ursuline Prep Sch
SW19 ... 178 D3
Urswick Gdns RM9 ... 81 A1
Urswick Rd
Dagenham RM9 ... 81 A1
Hackney E5, E9 ... 74 C3
Usborne Mews SW8 ... 270 D4
Usher Hall NW4 ... 46 B5
Usher Rd E3 ... 97 B5
Usk Rd SW11 ... 136 A1
Usk St E2 ... 96 D4
Utah Bldg 8 SE13 ... 141 D4
Utopia Ho 3 NW2 ... 68 A2
Utopia Village
NW1 ... 93 A6 231 A6
Uvedale Rd
Dagenham RM10 ... 81 C5
Enfield EN2 ... 17 B6
Uverdale Rd
SW10 ... 136 A5 266 B3
UXBRIDGE ... 82 A6
Uxbridge Coll
Hayes UB3 ... 106 A6
Uxbridge UB8 ... 60 A2
Uxbridge High Sch
UB8 ... 82 A5
Uxbridge Rd
Acton W3, W5 ... 110 C5
Ealing W13 ... 109 C6
Feltham TW13 ... 150 D2
Hampton TW12, TW13 .. 173 D5
Hayes UB4 ... 106 C6
Hillingdon UB10, UB4 ... 83 C2
Kingston u T KT1, KT6 .. 197 D4
Shepherd's Bush W12 .. 112 B5
Southall UB1, UB2, W5,
W7 ... 108 B5
Stanmore HA7 ... 25 A5
Uxbridge Road (Harrow
Weald) HA3 ... 24 B3
Uxbridge Road (Hatch
End) HA5 ... 23 B3
Uxbridge Road (Pinner)
HA5 ... 22 D1
Uxbridge St
W8 ... 113 C5 245 A4
Uxendon Cres HA3, HA9 .. 44 A1
Uxendon Hill HA9 ... 44 B2
Uxendon Manor Prim Sch
HA3 ... 44 A4

V

Vadnie Bish Ho NW5 ... 71 C2
Vaine Ho 4 E9 ... 75 A2
Valance Ave E4 ... 20 D3
Valan Leas BR2 ... 208 C6
Vale Ave WD6 ... 10 D6
Vale Cl Muswell Hill N2 ... 48 D6
Orpington BR6 ... 226 C4
St John's Wood
W9 ... 92 A4 229 A1
Twickenham TW1 ... 153 A1
Vale Cres SW15 ... 177 C6
Vale Croft
Claygate KT10 ... 212 D1
Pinner HA5 ... 41 A4
Vale Ct Barnet EN5 ... 1 D1
East Acton W3 ... 111 D5
St John's Wood
W9 ... 92 A4 229 A1
Wembley HA0 ... 65 C5
Vale Dr EN5 ... 13 C6
Vale End SE22 ... 139 D1
Vale Est The W3 ... 111 C5
Vale Farm Sports Ctr
HA0 ... 65 B4
Vale Gr Acton W3 ... 111 B5
Stoke Newington N4 ... 51 A2
Vale La W3 ... 88 C2
Vale Lo SE23 ... 162 C2
Valence Ave RM8 ... 80 D6
Valence Cir RM8 ... 81 A5
Valence House Mus*
RM8 ... 81 A6
Valence Jun & Inf Schs
RM8 ... 80 D6
Valence Wood Rd RM8 .. 81 A5
Valencia Rd HA7 ... 25 C6
Valens Ho 1 SW2 ... 160 C3
Valentia Pl SW9 ... 138 C1
Valentine Ave DA5 ... 169 A3
Valentine Ct Elstree WD6 .. 9 D5
3 Forest Hill SE23 ... 162 D2
Valentine Ho
11 Clapham Pk SW4 ... 159 C5
26 Old Ford E3 ... 97 B6
Valentine Pl
SE1 ... 116 D4 251 C2
Valentine Rd
Harrow HA2 ... 64 A5
Homerton E9 ... 74 D2
Valentine Row SE1 ... 251 C1
Valentines High Sch
IG2 ... 56 C3
Valentines Rd IG1 ... 56 D1
VALE OF HEALTH ... 70 B5
Vale of Health NW3 ... 70 B5
Vale Rd BR1 ... 188 C1
Claygate KT10 ... 212 D1
Mitcham CR4 ... 203 D5
Stoke Newington N4 ... 51 A2
Sutton SM1 ... 217 D4
Upton E7 ... 77 B2
Worcester Pk KT19,
KT4 ... 215 D5
Vale Rd N KT6 ... 214 A6
Vale Rd S KT6 ... 214 A6
Valerian Way E15 ... 98 C4
Valerie Ct
Belmont SM2 ... 217 D1
Bushey WD23 ... 8 A4
Vale Rise NW11 ... 47 B1
Vale Row N5 ... 72 D5
Vale Royal N7 ... 72 A1
Valery Pl TW12 ... 173 C3
Vale Sch The SW7 ... 256 A5
Valeside Ct 2 EN5 ... 1 D1
Valeswood Rd BR1 ... 186 D5
Vale Terr N4 ... 51 A3
Vale The Ashford TW16 .. 172 A4
Cricklewood NW11 ... 69 A6
Croydon CR0 ... 222 D6
East Acton W3 ... 111 C5
Feltham TW14 ... 150 B5
Heston TW5 ... 129 A6
Muswell Hill N10 ... 31 A2
Ruislip HA4 ... 62 C4
Southgate N14 ... 16 A4
SW3 ... 136 B6 266 D6
Woodford IG8 ... 37 A3
Valetta Gr E13 ... 99 A5
Valetta Rd W3 ... 111 D4
Valette Ct N10 ... 49 B5
Valette Ho E9 ... 74 C2
Valette St E8 ... 74 B2
Valiant Cl 13 UB5 ... 84 D4
Valiant Ho
9 Cubitt Town E14 ... 120 A4
5 Greenwich SE7 ... 121 C1
SW11 ... 266 D1
Valiant Way E6 ... 100 B2
Vallance Rd
Bethnal Green E1 ... 96 A3
Muswell Hill N22 ... 31 C1
Vallentin Rd E17 ... 54 A5
Valley Ave N12 ... 30 B6
Valley (Charlton Athletic
FC) The SE7 ... 121 C1
Valley Cl HA5 ... 22 B1
Valley Ct IG8 ... 37 B3
Valley Dr NW9 ... 44 D3
Valleyfield Rd SW16 ... 182 B5
Valley Fields Cres EN2 ... 4 C3
Valley Gdns
Mitcham SW19 ... 180 B3
Wembley HA0 ... 66 B1
Valley Gr SE7 ... 121 C1
Valley Ho
4 Edmonton N9 ... 18 A1
Upper Clapton E5 ... 52 C1
Valleylink Est EN3 ... 19 A5
Valley Mews TW1 ... 153 A2
Valley Pl KT6 ... 198 A3
Valley Point Ind Est
CR0 ... 204 A2
Valley Prim Sch BR2 ... 186 D1
Valley Prospect 3
SE19 ... 183 C4
Valley Rd
Beckenham BR2 ... 186 C1
BR5 ... 190 B2
Streatham SW16 ... 182 B6
Uxbridge UB10 ... 82 A5
Valleyside SE7 ... 121 D1
Valley Side E4 ... 19 C3
Valley Side Par E4 ... 19 C2
Valley View EN5 ... 13 A5
Valley Wlk CR0 ... 222 C6
Valliere Rd NW10 ... 90 A4
Valliers Wood Rd
DA15 ... 167 C3
Vallis Way
Chessington KT9 ... 213 D4
Ealing W13 ... 87 A2
Val McKenzie Ave N7 ... 72 C5
Valmar Rd SE5 ... 139 A4
Valmar Trad Est SE5 ... 139 A4
Valnay St SW17 ... 180 D5
Valognes Ave E17 ... 35 A2
Valois Ho SE1 ... 263 C6
Valonia Gdns SW18 ... 157 B5
Vambery Rd SE18 ... 145 A6
Vanbern Ho NW5 ... 71 A2
Vanborough Ct 4
SM2 ... 218 A2
Vanbrough Cres UB5 ... 84 C6
Vanbrugh Cl 2 E16 ... 99 D2
Vanbrugh Ct SE11 ... 261 B3
Vanbrugh Dr KT12 ... 194 C3
Vanbrugh Fields SE3 ... 142 D5
Vanbrugh Hill SE10,
SE3 ... 142 D6
Vanbrugh Ho 8 E9 ... 74 C1
Vanbrugh Mews KT12 .. 194 C2
Vanbrugh Park Rd
SE3 ... 142 D5
Vanbrugh Park Rd W
SE3 ... 142 D5
Vanbrugh Pk SE3 ... 142 D5
Vanbrugh Rd W4 ... 111 B3
Vanbrugh Terr SE3 ... 142 D4
Vanburgh Cl BR6 ... 211 C1
Vanburgh Ct 6 EN5 ... 1 A1
Vanburgh Ho E1 ... 243 C4
Vancouver Rd
Edgware HA8 ... 26 D2
Forest Hill SE23 ... 163 B2
Hayes UB4 ... 84 B3
Richmond TW10 ... 175 C6
Vancover Ho 33 E1 ... 118 B5
Vanderbilt Rd SW18 ... 158 A3
Vanderbilt Villas 1
W12 ... 112 D4
Vanderville Gdns N2 ... 30 B1
Vandome Cl E16 ... 99 B1
Vandon Ct SW1 ... 259 B6
Vandon Pas SW1 ... 259 B6
Vandon St SW1 ... 259 B6
Van Dyck Ave KT3 ... 199 B2
Vandyke Cl SW15 ... 156 D5
Vandyke Cross SE9 ... 166 A6
Vandy St EC2 ... 243 A5
Vane Cl Hampstead NW3 .. 70 B4
Harrow HA3 ... 44 B3
Vane Ho 18 N2 ... 30 B1
Vanessa Cl DA17 ... 125 C1
Vane St SW1 ... 259 B4
Vanfame Ct KT3 ... 199 D6
Vange Ho 12 W10 ... 90 C2
Van Gogh Cl 11 TW7 ... 131 A2
Van Gogh Ct E14 ... 120 B3
Vanguard Bldg 6
E14 ... 119 C4
Vanguard Cl
Newham E16 ... 99 B2
Thornton Heath CR0 ... 204 D1
Vanguard Ho
11 Hackney E8 ... 74 B1
7 Merton SW19 ... 180 A3
6 Stanwell TW19 ... 148 A5
Vanguard St SE8 ... 141 C4
Vanguard Trad Ctr E15 .. 98 A6
Vanguard Way
Hatton TW6 ... 127 C3
Wallington SM6 ... 220 A1
Van Lang Ho EN3 ... 18 D6
Vanneck Sq SW15 ... 156 A6
Vanner Point 27 E9 ... 74 D2
Vanoc Gdns BR1 ... 187 A6
Vansittart Rd E7 ... 77 A4
Vansittart St 7 SE14 ... 141 A5
Vanston Pl
SW6 ... 135 C5 265 B4
Vantage Ct
Harlington UB3 ... 127 C5
4 South Norwood
SW16 ... 182 B3
Vantage Mews 7 E14 .. 120 A5
Vantage Pl W8 ... 255 B5
Vant Rd SW17 ... 180 D5
Vantrey Ho SE11 ... 261 A3
Varcoe Rd SE16 ... 118 C1
Vardens Rd SW11 ... 136 B1
Varden St E1 ... 96 B1
Vardon Cl W3 ... 89 B1
Vardon Ho SE10 ... 142 A4
Vardy Ho HA7 ... 25 B5
Varey Ho E1 ... 97 A4
Varley Ho 5 NW6 ... 91 C6
Varley Par NW9 ... 45 C5
Varley Rd E16 ... 99 B1
Varley Way CR4 ... 180 B1
Varma Ct SE3 ... 143 A4
Varna Rd
Hampton TW12 ... 173 D2
SW6 ... 135 B5 264 C3
Varndell St
NW1 ... 93 C4 232 A2
Varsity Dr TW1, TW7 ... 152 D5
Varsity Row SW14 ... 133 A3
Vartry Rd N15 ... 51 C3
Vascroft Est NW10 ... 88 D3
Vassall Ho 3 E3 ... 97 A4
Vassall Rd SW9 ... 138 C5
Vat Ho SW8 ... 270 B4
Vauban Est SE16 ... 263 D5
Vauban St
SE16 ... 117 D3 263 D5
Vaudeville Ct N4 ... 72 C6
Vaughan Almshouses
TW15 ... 170 D5
Vaughan Ave
Chiswick W6 ... 111 D2
Hendon NW4 ... 46 A4
Vaughan Cl TW12 ... 173 A4
Vaughan Est 3 E2 ... 95 D4
Vaughan Fst & Mid Sch
HA1 ... 42 A3
Vaughan Gdns IG1 ... 56 B2
Vaughan Ho SE1 ... 251 C2
Vaughan Rd
Camberwell SE5 ... 139 A2
DA16 ... 145 D3
Harrow HA1 ... 42 B3
Stratford E15 ... 76 D2
Thames Ditton KT7 ... 197 B2
Vaughan St SE16 ... 119 B4
Vaughan Way E1 ... 118 A5
Vaughan Williams Cl
SE8 ... 141 C5
VAUXHALL ... 116 A1
Vauxhall Bridge Rd
SW1 ... 115 C2 259 B3
Vauxhall Cross SE1,
SW8 ... 116 A1 260 B1
Vauxhall Gdns CR2 ... 221 A2
Vauxhall Gr
SW8 ... 138 B6 270 C6
Vauxhall Prim Sch
SE11 ... 116 B1 260 D2
Vauxhall St
SE11 ... 116 B1 260 D2
Vauxhall Sta
SE11 ... 116 A1 260 B1
Vauxhall Wlk SE11 ... 260 C2
Vawdrey Cl E1 ... 96 C3
Vaynor Ho N7 ... 72 A4
Veals Mead CR4 ... 180 C2
Vectis Ct SW18 ... 157 D5
Vectis Gdns SW17 ... 181 B4
Vectis Rd SW17 ... 181 B4
Veda Rd SE13 ... 141 C1
Vega Cres HA6 ... 22 A5
Vega Rd WD23 ... 8 A4
Veitch Cl TW14 ... 149 D4
Veldene Way HA2 ... 63 B5
Velde Way 1 SE22 ... 161 C6
Vellacott Ho 3 W12 ... 90 B1
Velletri Ho 17 E2 ... 96 D5
Vellum Dr SM5 ... 219 A5
Venables Cl RM10 ... 81 D4
Venables St
NW8 ... 92 B2 236 D4
Vencourt Pl W6 ... 112 A2
Venetian Rd SE5 ... 139 A3
Venetia Rd Ealing W5 ... 109 D4
Harringay N4 ... 50 D3
Venice Ct 14 SE5 ... 139 A5
Venita Manor SE27 ... 182 C5
Venmead Ct 7 DA17 ... 125 C2
Venner Rd SE26 ... 184 C5
Venn Ho N1 ... 233 D5
Venn St SW4 ... 137 C1
Ventnor Ave HA7 ... 25 B1
Ventnor Dr N20 ... 13 D2
Ventnor Gdns IG11 ... 79 C2
Ventnor Mans IG11 ... 79 C2
Ventnor Rd
Belmont SM2 ... 217 D1
SE14 ... 140 D5
Ventnor Terr N15 ... 52 A5
Ventura Ho 12 SW2 ... 138 A1
Venture Cl DA5 ... 169 A4
Venture Ct 3 SE12 ... 165 A4
Venue St E14 ... 98 A2
Venus Ho
7 Millwall E14 ... 119 C2
8 Old Ford E3 ... 97 C6
Venus Mews CR4 ... 202 C6
Venus Rd SE18 ... 122 B3
Vera Ave N21 ... 16 C6
Vera Ct
1 Kensington W2 ... 91 D1
Tottenham N22 ... 32 D2
Vera Lynn Cl 5 E7 ... 77 A4
Vera Rd SW6 ... 135 A4 264 B2
Verbena Cl E16 ... 98 D3
Verbena Gdns 4 W6 ... 112 A1
Verdant Ct 3 SE6 ... 164 C4
Verdant La SE6 ... 164 C3
Verdayne Ave CR0 ... 222 D6
Verdi Cres W10 ... 91 A5
Verdun Rd
Barnes SW13 ... 134 A5
SE18 ... 146 A6
Vere Bank SW19 ... 157 B3
Vereker Dr TW16 ... 194 A6
Vereker Rd W14 ... 254 B1
Vere St W1 ... 93 B1 238 C1
Verity Cl W11 ... 91 A1
Verity Ct N9 ... 18 D3
Verity Ho 20 E3 ... 97 B4
Vermeer Ct E14 ... 120 B3
Vermillion Ct TW13 ... 149 D1
Vermont Cl EN2 ... 4 D1
Vermont Ho E17 ... 35 B1
Vermont Rd
Sutton SM1 ... 217 D5
Wandsworth SW18 ... 157 D5
West Norwood SE19 ... 183 C4
Verne Ct 9 W3 ... 111 A3
Verneer Gdns SE15 ... 140 C1
Verney Gdns RM9 ... 81 A4
Verney Ho
Isleworth TW3 ... 130 A1
Lisson Gr NW8 ... 237 A6
South Kensington SW10 266 A6
Verney Rd
Bermondsey SE16 ... 118 B1
Dagenham RM9 ... 81 A4
Verney St NW10 ... 67 B5
Verney Way SE16 ... 118 B1
Vernham Rd SE18 ... 145 A6
Vernon Ave Ilford E12 ... 78 B4
West Barnes SW20 ... 178 D1
Woodford IG8 ... 37 B3
Vernon Cl
Stanwell TW19 ... 148 A3
West Ewell KT19 ... 215 A2
Vernon Cres EN4 ... 15 A5
Vernon Ct
Child's Hill NW2 ... 69 B5
Ealing W5 ... 109 C6
Stanmore HA7 ... 25 B2
Vernon Dr HA7 ... 25 A2
Vernon Ho
Hyde The NW9 ... 45 D4
SE11 ... 260 D1
Vernon House Sch
NW10 ... 67 B3
Vernon Mews W14 ... 254 B3
Vernon Pl WC1 ... 240 B3
Vernon Rd Bow E3 ... 97 B5
Feltham TW13 ... 149 D2
Hornsey N8 ... 50 C6
Ilford IG3 ... 57 D1
Leytonstone E11 ... 54 C1
Mortlake SW14 ... 133 B2
Stratford E15 ... 76 C1
Sutton SM1 ... 218 B3
Walthamstow E17 ... 53 B4
Vernon Rise
Greenford UB6 ... 64 B3
WC1 ... 233 D2
Vernon Sq WC1 ... 233 D2
Vernon St W14 .. 113 A2 254 B3
Vernon Yd
W11 ... 113 B6 244 C6
Veroan Rd DA7 ... 147 A3
Verona Ct Chiswick W4 .. 111 C1
10 SE14 ... 140 D6
Verona Dr KT6 ... 214 A6
Verona Rd E7 ... 77 A1
Veronica Gdns CR4,
SW16 ... 181 C2
Veronica Ho
Brockley SE4 ... 141 B2
46 Bromley E3 ... 97 D4
Veronica Rd SW17 ... 159 B2
Veronique Gdns IG6 ... 57 A4
Verran Rd SW12 ... 159 B4
Versailles Rd SE20 ... 184 A3
Verulam Ave E17 ... 53 B2
Verulam Bldgs WC1 ... 240 D4
Verulam Ct
Hendon NW9 ... 46 A2
4 Southall UB1 ... 86 A1
Verulam Ho 1 W6 ... 112 C4
Verulam Rd UB6 ... 85 C3
Verulam St EC1 .. 94 C2 241 A4
Vervain Ho 2 SE15 ... 140 A5
Verwood Dr EN4 ... 2 D2
Verwood Ho SW8 ... 270 D3
Verwood Lo 1 E14 ... 120 B2
Verwood Rd HA2 ... 24 A1
Veryan Ct 3 N8 ... 49 D4
Vesage Ct EC1 ... 241 B3
Vesey Path 15 E14 ... 97 D1
Vespan Rd W12 ... 112 A4
Vesta Ct SE1 ... 253 A1
Vesta Ho 9 E3 ... 97 C6
Vesta Rd SE4, SE14 ... 141 A3
Vestris Rd SE23 ... 162 D2
Vestry House (Mus)*
E17 ... 53 D5
Vestry Mews 12 SE5 ... 139 C4
Vestry Rd
Camberwell SE5 ... 139 C4
Walthamstow E17 ... 53 D5
Vestry St N1 ... 95 B4 235 C2
Veysey Gdns RM10 ... 81 C5
Viaduct Pl 28 E2 ... 96 B4
Viaduct Rd N2 ... 30 C1
Viaduct St E2 ... 96 B4
Viaduct The
Harrow HA2 ... 64 A5
Woodford E18 ... 37 B1
Vian St SE13 ... 141 D2
Vibart Gdns SW2 ... 160 B4
Vibart Wlk N1 ... 233 B6
Vicarage Ave SE3 ... 143 A5
Vicarage Cl
New Malden KT4 ... 199 C1
Northolt UB5 ... 63 B1
Ruislip HA4 ... 39 B2
Vicarage Cres
SW11 ... 136 B4 266 C1
Vicarage Ct
Beckenham BR3 ... 207 A6
East Bedfont TW14 ... 149 A4
Finchley N12 ... 29 D5
7 Putney SW15 ... 156 A4
W8 ... 245 C2
Vicarage Dr
Barking IG11 ... 79 A1
Beckenham BR3 ... 185 C2
Mortlake SW14 ... 155 B6
Vicarage Farm Ct
TW5 ... 129 B5
Vicarage Farm Rd TW3,
TW4, TW5 ... 129 A4
Vicarage Fields KT12 .. 194 C3
Vicarage Field Sh Ctr The
IG11 ... 79 A1
Vicarage Gate
W8 ... 113 D5 245 C3
Vicarage Gdns
Mitcham CR4 ... 202 C6
Mortlake SW14 ... 155 B6
W8 ... 245 B3
Vicarage Gr SE5 ... 139 B4
Vicarage Ho 1 KT1 ... 176 B1
Vicarage La Ilford IG1 ... 57 B1
Stratford E15 ... 76 D1
Wallend E6 ... 100 C4
Vicarage Mans N15 ... 51 A5
Vicarage Pk SE18 ... 123 A1
Vicarage Prim Sch E6 .. 100 B4
Vicarage Rd
Ashford TW16 ... 171 D4
Croydon CR0 ... 220 C5
DA5 ... 169 D3
Dagenham RM10 ... 81 D1
Hampton Wick KT1 ... 175 C2
Hendon NW4 ... 46 A3
Kingston u T KT1 ... 175 D1
Mortlake SW14 ... 155 B6
Stratford E15 ... 76 D1
Sutton SM1 ... 217 D5
Teddington TW11 ... 175 A5
Tottenham N17 ... 34 A2
Walthamstow E10 ... 53 D1
Woolwich SE18 ... 123 A1
Vicarage The N8 ... 50 B3
Vicarage Way
Harrow HA2 ... 41 C2
Neasden NW10 ... 67 B5
Vicarage Wlk
SW11 ... 136 B4 266 D2
Vicars Bridge Cl HA0 ... 88 A5
Vicar's Cl Enfield EN1 ... 5 C3
Newham E15 ... 99 A6
South Hackney E9 ... 96 C6
Vicar's Green Prim Sch
HA0 ... 87 C5
Vicars Hill SE13 ... 141 D1
Vicar's Moor La N21 ... 16 D4
Vicars Oak Rd SE19 ... 183 C4
Vicar's Rd NW5 ... 71 A3
Vicar's Wlk RM8 ... 80 B5
Viceroy Cl N2 ... 48 C6

Viceroy Ct
5 Croydon CR0 205 B1
NW8 230 B4
Viceroy Lo 6 KT6 198 A4
Viceroy Par N2 48 C6
Viceroy Rd
SW8 138 A4 270 A2
Vic Johnson Ho 21 E3 97 B6
Vickers Cl SM6 220 B1
Vickers Ct 10 TW19 148 A5
Vickery Ct EC1 242 B6
Vickery Ho 13 SW4 138 A1
Vickery's Wharf 3 E14 97 C1
Victor Cazalet Ho N1 234 C6
Victor Gr HA0 66 A1
Victor Ho 2 N20 14 D1
Victoria & Albert Mus*
SW7 114 B3 256 D5
Victoria Arc SW1 258 D5
Victoria Ave Barnet EN4 2 B1
East Molesey KT8 195 D6
EC2 243 B3
Finchley N3 29 B2
Hackbridge SM5, SM6 219 A5
Hillingdon UB10 60 D1
Hounslow TW3, TW4 151 C6
Newham E6 99 D6
Surbiton KT6 197 D3
Wembley HA9 66 D2
Victoria Bglws DA14 191 B3
Victoria Bldgs 13 E8 96 B6
Victoria Bsns Ctr
DA16 146 B3
Victoria Chambers
EC2 243 A6
Victoria Cl Barnet EN4 2 B1
East Molesey KT8 195 C6
Harrow HA1 42 D3
Hayes UB3 83 B1
Victoria Coach Sta
SW1 115 B2 258 C3
Victoria Coll WC2 241 A2
Victoria Cotts Ilford IG6 57 A4
Muswell Hill N10 31 A1
7 Richmond TW9 132 C4
3 Spitalfields E1 96 A2
Victoria Cres
Tottenham N15 51 C4
West Norwood SE19 183 C4
Victoria Ct
5 Clapham Pk SW4 159 D5
3 Penge SE26 184 C4
South Acton W3 110 C4
4 St George in t East
E1 118 A6
1 Wanstead E18 55 B6
Wembley HA9 66 C2
Victoria Dock Rd E16 121 B6
Victoria Dr SW19 156 D3
Victoria Emb
WC2 116 C6 251 A5
Victoria Gdns
Heston TW5 129 A4
W11 113 C5 245 A4
Victoria Gr
North Finchley N12 30 B5
W8 114 A3 256 A6
Victoria Gr Mews W2 245 C5
Victoria Hall 15 E16 121 A5
Victoria Ho
6 Clapham Pk SW4 159 D5
Edgware HA8 26 D4
2 Shepherd's Bush
W12 112 A4
SW1 258 C2
Victoria Ind Est W3 89 C2
Victoria Jun Sch
TW13 150 B3
Victoria La Barnet EN5 1 B1
Hayes UB3 105 B1
Victoria Lo 5 SW19 178 C3
Victoria Mans
8 Islington N7 72 C3
Willesden NW10 68 B1
Victoria Mews
Kilburn NW6 91 C6
Wandsworth SW18 158 A3
Victoria Mills 1 E15 98 B6
Victorian Gr N16 73 C5
Victorian Hts 7 SW8 137 B3
Victorian Rd N16 73 D5
Victoria Park Ct 11 E9 74 C1
Victoria Park Ind Ctr
E9 75 B1
Victoria Park Lofts E9 96 D6
Victoria Park Rd E9 74 D1
Victoria Park Sq E2 96 C4
Victoria Pas NW8 236 C6
Victoria Pl 17 TW10 153 D6
Victoria Place Sh Ctr
SW1 115 B2 258 D4
Victoria Point 10 E13 99 A5
Victoria Rd
Barking IG11 78 D2
Barnet EN4 2 B1
Bexley DA6 147 C1
Bromley Comm BR2 209 D4
Buckhurst Hill IG9 21 D2
Chingford E4 20 C3
Chislehurst West BR7 188 C5
Dagenham RM10 81 D3
Ealing W5 87 B2
Edgware NW7 27 D5
Edmonton N9 17 D1
Feltham TW13 150 B3
Finsbury Pk N4 50 B1
Hendon NW4 46 D5
Victoria Rd *continued*
Kensington W8 114 A3 256 A6
Kilburn NW6 91 B6
Kingston u T KT1 176 B1
Leyton E11 76 C4
Mitcham CR4 180 D3
Mortlake SW14 133 B2
Muswell Hill N22 31 D2
Newham E13 99 A5
North Acton NW10 89 C3
Ruislip HA4 62 B4
Sidcup DA15 168 A1
Southall UB2 107 B3
Surbiton KT6 197 D3
Sutton SM1 218 B3
Teddington TW11 175 A4
Tottenham Hale N15 52 A5
Twickenham TW1 153 B4
Walthamstow E17 36 A1
Wanstead E18 55 B6
Victoria Ret Pk HA4 62 D3
Victoria Rise SW4 137 B2
Victoria Sq SW1 258 D6
Victoria St Erith DA17 125 B1
Stratford E15 76 C1
SW1 115 C3 259 B5
Victoria Sta
SW1 115 B2 258 D4
Victoria Terr
Dagenham NW10 89 C3
Finsbury Pk N4 50 C1
Harrow HA1 42 C1
Victoria (Underground)
SW1 115 B3 258 D5
Victoria Villas TW9 132 B1
Victoria Way SE7 143 C6
Victoria Wharf E14 119 A6
Victoria Yd 28 E1 96 A1
Victor Mills Cotts BR8 191 C3
Victor Rd
College Pk NW10 90 B4
Harrow HA2 42 A6
Penge SE20 184 D3
Teddington TW11 174 C6
Victors Dr TW12 173 A4
Victor Seymour Inf Sch
SM5 218 D4
Victors Way EN5 1 B2
Victor Villas N9 17 B1
Victory Ave SM4 202 A4
Victory Bsns Ctr The
TW7 130 D1
Victory Cl TW19 148 A3
Victory Ct IG11 102 B4
Victory Pl
6 Limehouse E14 119 A6
SE17 117 B2 262 C4
West Norwood SE19 183 C4
Victory Rd
Merton SW19 180 A3
Wanstead E11 55 B5
Victory Road Mews 5
SW19 180 A3
Victory Sch
SE17 117 A2 262 B4
Victory Way
Hounslow TW5 106 C1
Rotherhithe SE16 119 A4
Victory Wlk SE8 141 C4
Video Ct N4 50 A2
Vidler Cl KT9 213 C2
Vienna Cl IG5 37 D1
View Cl Harrow HA1 42 B5
Highgate N6 48 D2
View Cres N8 49 D4
Viewfield Cl HA3 44 A2
Viewfield Rd DA5 168 C3
Wandsworth SW18 157 B5
Viewland Rd SE18 123 D1
Viewpoint Ealing W5 110 B6
3 Islington N5 72 D3
Lewisham SE3 142 D2
View Point N20 14 A4
Viewpoint Ct 8 HA5 22 C1
View Rd N6 48 D3
Viewside Lo N6 49 C3
View The SE2 125 A1
Viga Rd N21 16 C5
Vigilant Cl SE26 184 A6
Vignoles Rd RM7 59 C2
Vigo St W1 115 C6 249 A5
Vi & John Rubens Ho
IG2 56 C3
Viking Cl 18 E3 97 A5
Viking Ct
Hampton TW12 173 D2
New Barnet EN4 14 B6
Viking Gdns E6 100 A3
Viking Ho
3 Camberwell SE5 139 A3
3 Woolwich SE7 122 A2
Viking Pl E10 53 B1
Viking Prim Sch UB5 84 D4
Viking Rd UB1 107 A6
Villacourt Rd SE18 146 A6
Village Arc The 2 E4 20 B3
Village Cl Chingford E4 36 A5
Hampstead NW3 70 B3
Village Ct
Blackheath SE3 142 C2
Walthamstow E17 53 D4
Village Gate TW17 192 D4
Village Home The IG6 57 A6
Village Hts IG8 36 D5
Village Inf Sch RM10 81 C1
Village Mount 19 NW3 70 A4
Village Park Cl EN1 17 C5
Village Rd Enfield EN1 17 C6
Hendon N3 29 A1
Village Row SM2 217 C1
Village Sch The NW3 70 D2
Village The
Battersea SW11 136 D2
SE7 143 D6
Village Way
Ashford TW15 170 C6
Beckenham BR3 207 C6
Dulwich Village SE21 161 B5
Ilford IG6 57 A6
Pinner HA5 41 B2
Willesden NW10 67 B4
Village Way E HA2 41 C2
Villa Rd SW9 138 C2
Villas On The Heath
NW3 70 A5
Villas Rd SE18 123 A2
Villa St SE17 117 B1 262 D1
Villiers Ave
Kingston u T KT5 198 B5
Twickenham TW2 151 B3
Villiers Cl
Kingston u T KT5 198 B5
Leyton E10 75 C6
Villiers Ct
Oakleigh Pk N20 14 A4
SW11 267 B2
Villiers High Sch UB1 107 B5
Villiers Ho W5 109 D6
Villiers Rd
Isleworth TW7 130 C3
Kingston u T KT1 198 B6
Penge BR3 184 D1
Southall UB1 107 B5
Willesden NW2 68 A2
Villiers St WC2 250 B4
Vincam Cl TW2 151 C4
Vince Ct N1 235 D1
Vincent Ave KT5 215 A6
Vincent Cl
Avery Hill DA15 167 C3
Barnet EN5 1 D2
Bromley BR2 209 B5
Harmondsworth UB7 126 C6
Vincent Ct
Finsbury Pk N4 50 A1
Hendon NW4 46 D5
Marylebone W1 237 C2
Ruislip HA4 62 B3
South Lambeth SW9 270 D1
Vincent Dr
Hillingdon UB10 82 B6
Upper Halliford TW17 193 C6
Vincent Gdns NW2 67 D5
Vincent Ho KT3 199 D5
Vincent Mews 1 E3 97 C5
Vincent Rd
Acton Green W3 111 A3
Chingford E4 36 B4
Croydon CR0 205 C2
Dagenham RM9 81 A1
Hounslow West TW4 128 D2
Kingston u T KT1 198 C6
Osterley TW7 130 B4
Tottenham N15 51 A5
Wembley HA0 66 B1
Wood Green N22 32 C1
Woolwich SE18 122 D2
Vincent Row TW12 174 A5
Vincents Cl SE16 119 A4
Vincents Path UB5 63 A2
Vincent Sq
SW1 115 D2 259 C4
Wood Green N22 32 C1
Vincent St
Canning Town E16 98 D2
Westminster
SW1 115 D2 259 D4
Vincent Terr N1 94 D5 234 D4
Vince St EC1 95 B4 235 D1
Vine Cl Surbiton KT5 198 B3
Sutton SM1 218 A5
West Drayton UB7 104 C2
Vine Cotts
3 Ealing W7 108 C5
Southall UB2 107 D2
Vine Ct Harrow HA3 44 A3
Spitalfields E1 96 A2
Vinegar St E1 118 B5
Vinegar Yd SE1 253 A2
Vine Gdns IG1 79 A3
Vine Gr UB10 60 C1
Vine Hill EC1 241 A5
Vine La Hillingdon UB10 82 B6
SE1 117 C5 253 B3
Uxbridge UB10 60 B1
Vine Lo N12 30 A4
Vine Pl Ealing W5 110 A5
Hounslow TW3 129 D1
Vine Rd Barnes SW13 133 D2
BR6 227 D2
East Molesey KT8 196 A5
Stratford E15 76 D1
Vineries Bank NW7 28 B5
Vineries Cl
Dagenham RM9 81 B2
Harmondsworth UB7 126 C6
Vineries The Enfield EN1 5 C2
Southgate N14 15 C5
Viners Cl KT12 194 C3
Vine St Bridge EC1 241 B5
Vines Ave N3 29 D2
Vine Sq W14 254 D1
Vines Sch The SW11 137 A1
Vine St W1 249 B5
Whitechapel
EC3 95 D1 243 C1
Vinewood Ct E17 54 B4
Vineyard Ave NW7 29 A3
Vineyard Cl
Forest Hill SE6 163 C3
Vineyard Cl *continued*
Kingston u T KT1 198 B6
Vineyard Gr N3 29 D2
Vineyard Hill Rd
SW19 179 C6
Vineyard Path SW14 133 B2
Vineyard Rd TW13 150 A1
Vineyard Row KT1,
KT8 175 C2
Vineyard Sch The
TW10 154 A5
Vineyards The TW13 150 A1
Vineyard Studios 3 E7 77 C1
Vineyard The TW10 154 A6
Vineyard Wlk EC1 241 A6
Viney Ct 9 SW4 159 D5
Vine Yd SE1 252 B2
Viney Rd SE13 141 D2
Vining St SW2, SW9 138 C1
Vinlake Ave UB10 60 C5
Vinson Ho N1 235 D3
Vinter Ct TW17 192 C4
Vintners Ct EC4 252 B6
Vintry Mews 3 E17 53 C5
Viola Ave
Feltham TW14 150 C5
SE2 124 B1
Stanwell TW19 148 A3
Viola Ct HA8 26 D3
Viola Sq W12 111 D6
Violet Ave Enfield EN2 5 B5
Hillingdon UB8 82 B2
Violet Cl Cheam SM3 201 A1
Hackbridge SM6 203 A1
Newham E16 98 C3
32 SE8 141 B6
Violet Ct 2 E15 76 C1
Violet Gdns CR0 220 D3
Violet Hill NW8 92 A5 229 A3
Violet Hill Ho NW8 229 A3
Violet La CR0 220 D3
Violet Rd Bromley E3 97 D3
Walthamstow E17 53 C3
Woodford E18 37 B1
Violet St E2 96 B3
Violet Terr UB8 82 C2
Violette Szabo Ho 4
SE27 183 B6
VIP Trad Est SE7 121 C2
Virgil Pl W1 237 C3
Virgil St SE1 116 B3 260 D6
Virginia Cl KT3 199 A5
Virginia Ct
Ashford TW15 170 A6
7 Rotherhithe SE16 118 D4
Virginia Ho
3 Blackwall E14 120 A6
Teddington TW11 175 A5
Virginia Prim Sch E2 95 D4
Virginia Rd
South Norwood CR7 182 D2
19 Spitalfields E2 95 D4
Virginia St E1 118 A6
Virginia Wlk SW2 160 B5
Viridian Ct TW13 149 D1
Viscount Cl N11 31 B5
Viscount Ct
9 Kensington W11 91 C1
1 Littleton TW15 171 A3
Viscount Dr E6 100 B2
Viscount Gr 3 UB5 84 D4
Viscount Point 6
SW19 179 C3
Viscount Rd TW19 148 A3
Viscount St EC1 242 A4
Viscount Way TW6 127 C1
Vista Ave EN3 6 D3
Vista Bldgs 19 E3 97 B4
Vista Bldg The 14
SE18 122 C2
Vista Dr IG4 55 D4
Vista Ho 2 SW19 180 B2
Vista Hts SE23 163 A4
Vista The Chingford E4 20 B4
SE9 165 D4
Sidcup DA14 189 D5
Vista Way HA3 44 A3
Vitae Apartments 7
W6 112 A3
Vita Et Pax Sch N14 15 B6
Vittoria Ho N1 233 D5
Vittoria Prim Sch
N1 94 C5 234 A4
Viveash Cl UB3 105 D3
Vivian Ave Hendon NW4 46 B4
Wembley HA9 66 C2
Vivian Comma Cl 3
N4 72 D5
Vivian Ct Finchley N12 29 D5
Paddington NW6 91 D5
Vivian Gdns HA9 66 C3
Vivian Ho N4 51 B2
Vivian Mans 1 NW4 46 B4
Vivian Rd E3 97 A5
Vivian Sq SE15 140 B2
Vivian Way N2 48 B4
Vivien Cl KT9 214 A1
Vivienne Cl TW1 153 D5
Voce Rd SE18 145 B5
Voewood Cl KT3 199 D3
Vogans Mill SE1 253 D2
Vogler Ho 3 E1 118 C6
Vogue Ct 8 BR1 187 B2
Vollasky Ho 5 E1 96 A2
Volta Cl N9 18 C1
Voltaire
2 Camberwell SE5 139 D4
15 Richmond TW9 132 B4
Voltaire Ct 13 SW11 137 A3
Voltaire Rd SW4 137 D2
Voltaire Way UB3 105 C6
Volt Ave NW10 89 C4
Volta Way CR0 204 B1
Voluntary Pl E11 55 A3
Vora Ho HA0 65 D2
Vorley Rd N19 71 C6
Voss Ct SW16 182 A4
Voss St E2 96 A4
Voyager Bsns Est 10
SE16 118 A3
Voyagers Cl IG11 102 C1
Voysey Cl N3 47 A6
Vulcan Cl E6 100 C1
Vulcan Gate EN2 4 C3
Vulcan Rd SE4 141 B3
Vulcan Sq E14 119 C2
Vulcan Terr SE4 141 B3
Vulcan Way N7 72 B2
Vyne Ho SM5 218 D2
Vyner Ct E5 74 A6
Vyner Rd W3 111 B6
Vyners Sch UB10 60 B4
Vyner St E2 96 B6
Vyners Way UB10 60 C3
Vyne The DA7 147 D2
Vyvyan Ho SE18 144 C4

W

Wadbrook St KT1 175 D1
Wadcroft Ct SE4 141 B2
Waddesdon Lo HA3 43 A3
Wadding St
SE17 117 B2 262 C3
Waddington Cl EN1 5 C1
Waddington Rd E15 76 B2
Waddington St E15 76 B2
Waddington Way
SE19 183 B2
WADDON 220 C4
Waddon Cl CR0 220 C5
Waddon Court Rd
CR0 220 C5
Waddon Inf Sch CR9 220 C3
Waddon Marsh Sta
CR0 220 C6
Waddon Marsh Way
CR0 204 B1
Waddon New Rd CR0 220 D6
Waddon Park Ave
CR0 220 C5
Waddon Rd CR0 220 D5
Waddon Sta CR0 220 C4
Waddon Way CR0, CR2,
CR9 220 D2
Wade Ct
Muswell Hill N10 31 B3
Wembley HA0 65 D5
Wade Ho
16 Bermondsey SE1 118 A4
1 Enfield EN1 17 C6
Wade's Gr N21 16 C4
Wade's Hill N21 16 C4
Wade's La TW11 175 A5
Wadeson St E2 96 B5
Wade's Pl E14 119 D6
Wadeville Ave RM6 59 B2
Wadeville Cl DA17 125 C1
Wadham Ave E17 35 D3
Wadham Cl TW17 193 A2
Wadham Gdns
Greenford UB6 64 B2
Primrose Hill
NW3 92 C6 230 A6
Wadham Ho N18 33 D5
Wadham Rd
Highams Pk E17 35 D2
Putney SW15 135 A1
Wadhurst Cl SE20 184 B1
Wadhurst Ct E6 100 C5
Wadhurst Rd W4 111 B3
Wadley Rd E11 54 C2
Wadsworth Bsns Ctr
UB6 87 C5
Wadsworth Cl
Enfield EN3 18 D6
Wembley UB6 87 C5
Wadsworth Ct E10 54 A3
Wadsworth Rd UB6 87 C5
Wager St E3 97 B3
Waggoners Rdbt TW5 128 B4
Waggon Mews N14 15 C3
Waggon Rd EN4 2 B6
Waghorn Rd
Harrow HA3 43 D6
Newham E13 99 C6
Waghorn St SE15 140 A2
Wagner St SE15 140 C5
Wagon Rd EN4, EN5 1 D6
Wagstaff Gdns RM9 80 C1
Wagtail Cl NW9 27 C1
Wagtail Wlk BR3 208 A4
Waights Ct KT2 176 A2
Waikato Lo IG9 21 C3
Wainford Cl SW19 156 D3
Wainwright Gr TW7 130 B1
Wainwright Ho 3 E1 118 C5
Waite Davies Rd SE12 164 D4
Waitelands Ho KT3 199 B5
Waite St SE15 139 D6
Waithman St EC4 241 C1
Wakefield Ct 4 SE26 184 C4
Wakefield Gdns
Redbridge IG1 56 A3
South Norwood SE19 183 C3
Wakefield Ho
Dulwich SE22 162 B3
6 Peckham SE15 140 A4
Wakefield Mews WC1 233 B1
Wakefield Rd
Friern Barnet N11 31 D5
20 Richmond TW10 153 D6
South Tottenham N15 51 D4
Wakefield St
Edmonton N18 34 A5
Newham E6 100 A6
St Pancras WC1 94 A4 233 B1
Wakeford Cl SW4 159 C6
Wakehams Hill HA5 41 B6
Wakeham St 9 N1 73 B2
Wakehurst Rd SW11 158 D6
Wakeling Ct E7 77 C2
Wakeling Ho 8 SE27 160 D1
Wakeling La HA0 65 B5
Wakeling Rd W7 86 D2
Wakeling St 11 E14 97 A1
Wakelin Ho
Forest Hill SE23 163 A4
19 Islington N1 72 D1
Wakelin Rd E15 98 C5
Wakeman Ho HA8 26 A6
Wakeman Rd NW10 90 D4
Wakemans Hill Ave
NW9 45 B4
Wakering Rd IG11 79 A1
Wakerley Cl 6 E6 100 B1
Wakley St EC1 94 D4 234 C2
Walberswick St SW8 270 B3
Walbrook EC4 252 C6
10 Wanstead E18 55 A6
Walbrook Ct 32 N1 95 C5
Walbrook Ho N9 18 C2
Walbrook Wharf EC4 252 C6
Walburgh St E1 96 B1
Walcorde Ave SE17 262 B3
Walcot Ct CR0 222 A6
Walcot Gdns SE11 261 A4
Walcot Ho 9 SE22 139 C2
Walcot Rd EN3 7 B3
Walcot Sq
SE11 116 C2 261 B4
Walcott St SW1 259 B4
Waldair Ct E16 122 D4
Waldeck Gr SE27 160 D1
Waldeck Rd
Brentford W4 132 C6
Ealing W13 87 B1
Mortlake SW14 133 A2
Tottenham N15 50 D6
Waldeck Terr SW14 133 A2
Waldegrave Ct
11 Barking IG11 101 B6
1 Teddington TW11 174 D5
Waldegrave Gdns
TW1 152 D1
Waldegrave Ho 5
SW15 156 C6
Waldegrave Pk TW1 174 D6
Waldegrave Rd BR1 210 B5
Dagenham RM8 80 C6
Ealing W5 110 B6
Hornsey N8 50 C6
Penge SE19 183 D3
Teddington TW11 174 D6
Waldegrave Sch TW2 152 B1
Waldegrove CR0 221 D5
Waldemar Ave
Ealing W13 109 C5
Fulham SW6 135 A3
Waldemar Avenue Mans
SW6 264 A1
Waldemar Rd SW19 179 C5
Walden Ave BR7 188 B6
Edmonton N13 33 A6
Walden Cl DA17 125 B1
Walden Ct SW8 269 D2
Walden Gdns CR7,
SW16 204 B5
Walden Ho Barnet EN4 2 C1
8 Clapham SW11 137 A3
SW1 258 B3
Walden Rd BR7 188 B4
Tottenham N17 33 B2
Waldenshaw Rd SE23 162 C3
Walden St E1 96 B1
Walden Way NW7 28 D4
Waldo Cl SW4 159 C6
Waldo Ind Est BR1 209 D6
Waldo Pl SW19 180 C3
Waldo Rd BR1 209 D6
College Pk NW10 90 B4
Waldorf Cl CR2 220 D1
Waldram Cres SE23 162 C3
Waldram Park Rd
SE23 162 D3
Waldram Pl 6 SE23 162 C3
Waldrist Way DA18 125 B4
Waldron Gdns BR2 208 B6
Waldron Ho 17 SW2 160 B6
Waldronhyrst CR0,
CR2 220 D4
Waldron Mews SW3 266 D6
Waldron Rd
Harrow HA1, HA2 42 C1
Wandsworth SW18 158 A1
Waldrons The CR0 221 A4
Waldron's Yd HA2 64 B6
Waldstock Rd SE28 124 A6
Waleran Cl HA7 24 D4
Walerand Rd SE13 142 A3
Waleran Flats SE1 263 A4
Wales Ave SM5 218 C3
Wales Cl SE15 140 B6
Wales Farm Rd W3 89 B2
Waleton Acres SM6 219 C2
Waley St 1 E1 97 A2
Walfield Ave N20 13 D4
Walfield Ho N20 14 A4
Walford Ho 28 E1 96 B1

Walford Rd N16 .... 73 C4
Walfrey Gdns RM9 .... 81 A1
Walham Ct 15 NW3 .... 70 D2
Walham Gr
SW6 .... 135 C5 265 A4
WALHAM GREEN 135 D5
Walham Green Arc
SW6 .... 265 B4
Walham Rise 1 SW19 .. 179 A4
Walham Yd SW6 .... 265 A4
Walkden Rd BR7 .... 188 C5
Walker Cl Ealing W7 .... 108 C5
East Bedfont TW14 .... 149 D4
Friern Barnet N11 .... 31 C6
Hampton TW12 .... 173 B4
Plumstead SE18 .... 123 A2
Walker Ho NW1 .... 232 C3
Walker Mews 9 SW2 .. 160 C6
Walker Prim Sch N14 ... 15 D2
Walkerscroft Mead
SE21 .... 161 A3
Walker's Ct W1 .... 249 C6
Walkers Lo 18 E14 .... 120 A4
Walker's Pl SW15 .... 135 A1
Walkinshaw Ct 9 N1 ... 73 A1
Walks The N2 .... 48 B6
Walk The
Ashford TW16 .... 171 D3
Palmers Green N13 .... 16 C1
Walkynscroft 1 SE15 .. 140 B3
Wallace Cl SE28 .... 124 D6
Upper Halliford TW17 .. 193 B5
Uxbridge UB10 .... 82 A5
Wallace Collection*
W1 .... 238 A2
Wallace Cres SM5 .... 218 D3
Wallace Ct 19 Enfield EN3 . 7 C6
NW1 .... 237 B3
Wallace Ho N7 .... 72 B2
Wallace Lo N4 .... 50 C1
Wallace Rd N1, N5 .... 73 A2
Wallasey Cres UB10 .... 60 C5
Wallbrook Bsns Ctr
TW4 .... 128 B2
Wallbutton Rd SE4 .... 141 A3
Wallcote Ave NW2 .... 46 D1
Wall Ct N4 .... 50 B1
Walled Garden Cl
BR3 .... 207 D5
Walled Gdn The*
TW16 .... 194 B6
WALLEND 100 C6
Wall End Ct E6 .... 100 C6
Wall End Rd E6 .... 78 C1
Waller Dr HA6 .... 22 A2
Waller Rd SE14 .... 140 D3
Wallers Cl RM9 .... 103 B6
Wallett Ct 11 NW1 .... 71 C1
Wallflower St W12 .... 111 D6
Wallgrave Rd SW5 .... 255 C3
Wallingford Ave W10 ... 90 D1
WALLINGTON 219 A2
Wallington Cl HA4 .... 39 A3
Wallington Ct 10 SM6 .. 219 B2
Wallington Cty Gram Sch
SM6 .... 219 B5
Wallington Green
SM6 .... 219 B4
Wallington Rd IG3 .... 57 D2
Wallington Sq 4 SM6 .. 219 C2
Wallington Sta SM6 .... 219 B2
Wallis Alley SE1 .... 252 B2
Wallis Cl SW11 .... 136 B2
Wallis Ho
5 New Cross Gate
SE14 .... 141 A4
Ruislip HA4 .... 39 A1
Ruislip HA4 .... 39 B1
Wallis Rd
Hackney Wick E9 .... 75 C2
Southall UB1 .... 85 D1
Wallorton Gdns SW14 .. 133 B1
Wallside EC2 .... 242 B3
Wall St N1 .... 73 B2
Wallwood Rd E11 .... 54 B2
Wallwood St E14 .... 97 B2
Walmar Cl EN4 .... 2 B4
Walmer Cl BR6 .... 227 B4
Chingford E4 .... 19 D2
Walmer Gdns W13 .... 109 A4
Walmer Ho
8 North Kensington
W10 .... 90 D1
8 Penge SE20 .... 184 C3
Walmer Pl W1 .... 237 C4
Walmer Rd
North Kensington W10 ... 90 C1
W11 .... 113 A6 244 A5
Walmer Terr SE18 .... 123 B2
Walmgate Rd UB6 .... 87 B6
Walmington Fold N12 ... 29 C4
Walm La NW2 .... 68 C2
Walmsley Ho 1 SW16 .. 181 C6
Walney Wlk 6 N1 .... 73 A2
Walnut Ave UB7 .... 104 C3
Walnut Cl Hayes UB3 ... 105 C6
Ilford IG6 .... 57 A5
SE8 .... 141 B6
Wallington SM5 .... 218 D3
Walnut Ct 2 E17 .... 54 A5
Walnut Gdns E15 .... 76 C3
Walnut Gr EN1 .... 17 B6
Walnut Ho 11 E3 .... 97 B6
Walnut Mews SM2 .... 218 A1
Walnut Rd E10 .... 75 D6
Walnut Tree Ave CR4 .. 202 C6
Walnut Tree Cl
Barnes SW13 .... 133 D4
Chislehurst BR7 .... 189 A2
Walnut Tree Cotts
SW19 .... 179 A5
Walnut Tree Ho SW10 . 265 D6
Walnut Tree Rd
Brentford TW8 .... 132 A6
Charlton TW17 .... 171 A1
Dagenham RM8 .... 81 A6
Greenwich SE10 .... 120 C1
Heston TW5 .... 129 B6
Walnut Tree Walk Prim
Sch SE11 .... 116 C2 261 A4
Walnut Tree Wlk
SE11 .... 116 C2 261 A4
Walnut Way
Buckhurst Hill IG9 .... 21 D1
Ruislip HA4 .... 62 C2
Walpole Ave TW9 .... 132 B3
Walpole Cl Pinner HA5 ... 23 C4
West Ealing W13 .... 109 C4
Walpole Cres 10
TW11 .... 174 D5
Walpole Ct Ealing W5 ... 109 D5
7 Hammersmith W14 .. 112 D3
South Hampstead NW6 .... 70 A1
Twickenham TW2 .... 152 C2
2 Wallington SM6 .... 219 B3
Walpole Gdns
Acton Green W4 .... 111 A1
Twickenham TW2 .... 152 C1
Walpole Ho
Chislehurst BR7 .... 189 B2
East Molesey KT8 .... 195 C4
Walpole Lo W13 .... 109 C5
Walpole Mews NW8 .... 229 C5
Walpole Pl
9 Teddington TW11 .... 174 D5
3 Woolwich SE18 .... 122 D2
Walpole Rd BR2 .... 209 D4
Mitcham SW19 .... 180 B4
South Croydon CR0 .... 221 B6
Surbiton KT6 .... 198 A3
Teddington TW11 .... 174 D5
Tottenham N17 .... 33 A1
Tottenham N17 .... 51 A6
Twickenham TW2 .... 152 C2
Upton E6 .... 77 C1
Walthamstow E17 .... 53 A5
Woodford E18 .... 36 D2
Walpole St
SW3 .... 114 D1 257 D2
Walrond Ave HA9 .... 66 A3
Walsham Cl SE28 .... 124 D6
Upper Clapton N16 .... 52 A1
Walsham Ho
New Cross Gate
SE14 .... 140 D3
SE17 .... 262 C2
Walsham Rd
Feltham TW14 .... 150 B4
New Cross Gate SE14 ... 140 D3
Walsh Lodge HA4 .... 40 B3
Walsingham NW8 .... 229 D6
Walsingham Gdns
KT19 .... 215 D3
Walsingham Ho
Chingford E4 .... 20 B4
Twickenham TW2 .... 152 B2
Walsingham Lo SW13 .. 134 A4
Walsingham Mans
SW6 .... 265 D4
Walsingham Pk BR7 ... 189 B1
Walsingham Pl SW4,
SW11 .... 159 A5
Walsingham Rd BR5 .... 190 B2
Ealing W13 .... 109 A5
Enfield EN2 .... 17 B6
Mitcham CR4 .... 202 D4
Shacklewell E5 .... 74 A5
Walsingham Wlk
DA17 .... 147 C6
Walter Besant Ho 20
E1 .... 96 D4
Walter Ct 3 W3 .... 89 A1
Walter Green Ho
SE15 .... 140 C4
Walter Ho SW10 .... 266 C4
Walter Hurford Par 5
E12 .... 78 C4
Walter Northcott Ho 2
NW6 .... 69 C3
Walter Rodney Cl E12 ... 78 B2
Walter Savill Twr E17 ... 53 C3
Walters Cl Hayes UB3 ... 105 D4
SE17 .... 262 B3
Walters Ho
3 Camberwell SE5 .... 139 C3
Islington N1 .... 234 D6
10 Kennington SE17 .... 138 D6
Walter Sickert Hall N1 235 A3
Walters Rd EN3 .... 6 C1
Walter's Rd SE25 .... 205 C5
Walter St Globe Town E2 .. 96 D4
2 Kingston u T KT2 .... 176 A2
Walters Way SE23 .... 162 D5
Walters Yd BR1 .... 187 A1
Walter Taylor Ct SE4 ... 141 B1
Walter Terr E1 .... 96 D1
Walterton Rd W9 .... 91 C3
Walter Wlk HA8 .... 27 A4
Waltham Ave
Hayes UB3 .... 105 B3
Preston NW9 .... 44 C3
Waltham Ct
Chingford E17 .... 36 A2
Whetstone N20 .... 14 B1
Waltham Dr HA8 .... 44 C6
Waltham Forest Coll
E17 .... 35 D1
Waltham Gdns EN3 .... 6 C6
Waltham Green Ct
SW6 .... 265 C3
Waltham Ho NW8 .... 229 A6
10 Stockwell SW9 .... 138 B3
Waltham Park Way
E17 .... 35 C3
Waltham Pk E17 .... 35 C2
Waltham Rd
Carshalton SM5 .... 202 C1
Southall UB2 .... 107 A3
WALTHAMSTOW 53 D6
Walthamstow Acad
E17 .... 35 B2
Walthamstow Ave E4 ... 35 C3
Walthamstow Ave (North
Circular Rd) E4 .... 35 B4
Walthamstow Bsns Ctr
E17 .... 36 A1
Walthamstow Central Sta
E17 .... 53 C4
Walthamstow Mkt E17 .. 53 C5
Walthamstow Queens
Road Sta E17 .... 53 C4
Walthamstow Sch for Girls
E17 .... 53 D5
Waltham Way E4 .... 19 C2
Waltheof Ave N17 .... 33 B2
Waltheof Gdns N17 .... 33 B2
Walton Ave
Cheam SM3 .... 217 B5
Harrow HA2 .... 63 B4
New Malden KT3 .... 199 D5
Wembley HA9 .... 66 D5
Walton Bridge Rd KT12,
TW17 .... 193 C2
Walton Cl
Dollis Hill NW2 .... 68 B6
Harrow HA1 .... 42 B5
Lea Bridge E5 .... 74 D5
SW8 .... 138 A5 270 B4
Walton Croft HA1 .... 64 C4
Walton Ct EN5 .... 14 A6
Walton Dr Harrow HA1 ... 42 B5
Willesden NW10 .... 67 B2
Walton Gdns Acton W3 .. 88 D2
Feltham TW13 .... 171 D6
Wembley HA9 .... 66 A6
Walton Gn CR0 .... 224 A1
Walton Ho E2 .... 243 D6
Ealing W5 .... 109 D2
1 Edmonton N9 .... 34 A6
1 Kingston u T KT2 .... 176 A3
Upper Holloway N7 .... 72 B5
10 Walthamstow E17 .... 53 D6
Wandsworth SW18 .... 157 C5
Walton La
Oatlands Pk KT13,
TW17 .... 193 B1
Shepperton TW17 .... 193 B2
Walton Oak Prim Sch
KT12 .... 194 C1
WALTON-ON-THAMES
.... 194 C2
Walton Pl SW3 .... 257 C6
Walton Rd
East Molesey KT8,
KT12 .... 195 C5
Harrow HA1 .... 42 B5
Little Ilford E12 .... 78 C4
Newham E13 .... 99 C5
Sidcup DA14 .... 168 C1
Tottenham N15 .... 51 D5
Walton-on-T KT12&KT8 . 194 D4
Walton St Enfield EN2 .... 5 B4
SW3 .... 114 C3 257 B5
Walton Way Acton W3 ... 88 D2
Mitcham CR4 .... 203 C5
Walt Whitman Cl 6
SE24 .... 138 D1
WALWORTH 117 B1
Walworth Pl
SE17 .... 117 A1 262 B1
Walworth Rd
SE17 .... 117 A1 262 B2
Walworth Sch
SE17 .... 117 C1 263 B1
Walwyn Ave BR1 .... 209 D6
Wanborough Dr SW15 . 156 B3
Wanderer Dr IG11 .... 102 C4
Wandle Bank
Mitcham SW19 .... 180 B3
Wallington CR0 .... 220 A5
Wandle Court Gdns
CR0 .... 220 A5
Wandle Ct
4 Bedford Pk W12 .... 111 C4
Wallington CR0 .... 220 A5
West Ewell KT19 .... 215 A4
Wandle Ho
6 Catford BR1 .... 186 B5
NW8 .... 237 A4
Wandsworth SW18 .... 157 D4
Wandle Lo CR0 .... 220 A5
Wandle Lodge SM6 .... 219 B6
Wandle Pk Sta CR0 .... 220 C6
Wandle Rd
Croydon CR0 .... 221 A5
Hackbridge SM6 .... 219 B6
Morden SM4 .... 202 B4
Upper Tooting SW17 .... 158 C2
Wallington CR0 .... 220 A5
Wandle Side
Hackbridge SM6 .... 219 B5
Wallington CR0 .... 220 B5
Wandle Tech Pk CR4 ... 202 D2
Wandle Trad Est CR4 ... 202 D2
Wandle Valley Sch
SM5 .... 202 C2
Wandle Way
Mitcham CR4 .... 202 D4
Wandle Way *continued*
Wandsworth SW18 .... 157 D3
Wandon Rd
SW6 .... 135 D5 265 D3
WANDSWORTH 157 C5
Wandsworth Bridge Rd
SW6 .... 135 D4 265 C1
Wandsworth Common Sta
SW12 .... 158 D4
Wandsworth Common
West Side SW18 .... 158 A6
Wandsworth Gyratory
SW18 .... 157 D6
Wandsworth High St
SW18 .... 157 D6
Wandsworth Mus*
SW18 .... 157 D6
Wandsworth Plain
SW18 .... 157 D6
Wandsworth Rd
SW8 .... 138 A5 270 A3
Wandsworth Road Sta
SW4 .... 137 C3
Wandsworth Town Sta
SW18 .... 135 D1
Wangey Rd RM6 .... 58 D2
Wangford Ho 15 SW9 .. 138 D1
Wanless Rd SE24 .... 139 A2
Wanley Rd SE5 .... 139 B1
Wanlip Rd E13 .... 99 B3
Wansbeck Ct EN2 .... 4 D2
Wansbeck Rd E3, E9 .... 75 B1
Wansdown Pl
SW6 .... 135 D5 265 C4
Wansey St
SE17 .... 117 A2 262 B3
Wansford Rd IG8 .... 37 C2
WANSTEAD 55 C3
Wanstead Church Sch
E11 .... 55 A4
Wanstead Cl BR1 .... 187 C1
Wanstead High Sch
E11 .... 55 C3
Wanstead Hospl E11 .... 55 B5
Wanstead Hts 8 E11 .... 55 A4
Wanstead La IG1 .... 56 A3
Wanstead Park Ave
E12 .... 77 D6
Wanstead Park Rd IG1 .. 56 A1
Wanstead Park Sta E7 .. 77 B4
Wanstead Pl E11 .... 55 A4
Wanstead Rd BR1 .... 187 C1
Wanstead Sta E11 .... 55 B3
Wantage Rd SE12 .... 164 D6
Wantz Rd RM10 .... 81 D3
WAPPING 118 B5
Wapping Dock St 19
E1 .... 118 B5
Wapping High St E1 ... 118 B5
Wapping La E1 .... 118 B5
Wapping Sta E1 .... 118 C5
Wapping Wall E1 .... 118 C5
Warbank La KT2 .... 177 D3
Warbeck Rd W12 .... 112 B4
Warberry Rd N22 .... 32 B1
Warboys App KT2 .... 176 D4
Warboys Cres E4 .... 36 A5
Warboys Rd KT2 .... 176 D4
Warburg Ho E2 .... 96 A4
Warburton Cl
6 Kingsland N1 .... 73 C2
Stanmore HA3 .... 24 B4
Warburton Ct
Peckham SE15 .... 140 A2
Ruislip HA4 .... 62 A6
Warburton Ho 5 E8 .... 96 B6
Warburton Rd
8 Hackney E8 .... 96 B6
Twickenham TW2 .... 151 D3
Warburton St 6 E8 .... 96 B6
Warburton Terr E17 .... 35 D1
Wardalls Ho 12 SE8 .... 141 B6
Ward Cl CR2 .... 221 C3
Wardell Cl NW7 .... 27 C3
Wardell Ct N2 .... 48 B6
Wardell Ho 7 SE10 .... 142 A6
Warden Ave HA2 .... 41 B1
Warden Rd NW5 .... 71 A2
Wardens Field Cl 2
BR6 .... 227 D2
Wardens Gr SE1 .... 252 A3
Wardle St E9 .... 74 D3
Wardley Lo E11 .... 54 D3
Wardley St SW18 .... 157 D4
Wardlow 8 NW5 .... 71 B4
Wardo Ave
SW6 .... 135 A4 264 A2
Wardour Mews W1 .... 239 B1
Wardour St W1 .. 93 D1 239 C1
Ward Point SE11 .... 261 A3
Ward Rd
Camden Town N19 .... 71 C5
Mill Meads E15 .... 98 B6
Wardrew Ct 9 EN5 .... 14 A6
Wardrobe Pl EC4 .... 241 D1
Wardrobe Terr EC4 .... 251 D6
Wardrobe The 3
TW9 .... 153 D6
Wards Cotts TW19 .... 148 B4
Wards Rd IG2 .... 57 B2
Wards Wharf App
E16 .... 121 D4
Ware Ct Cheam SM1 .... 217 B4
Edgware HA8 .... 26 A6
Wareham Cl TW3 .... 129 D1
Wareham Ct 2 N1 .... 73 C1
Wareham Ho SW8 .... 270 C4
Warehouse W E16 .... 121 B6
Waremead Rd IG2 .... 56 D4
Ware Point Dr SE28 .... 123 B4
Warfield Rd
East Bedfont TW14 .... 149 C4
Hampton TW12 .... 173 D2
Kensal Green NW10 .... 90 D4
Warfield Yd 6 NW10 .... 90 D4
Wargrave Ave N15 .... 51 D3
Wargrave Ho 46 E2 .... 95 D4
Wargrave Rd HA2 .... 64 A5
Warham Rd
Croydon CR2 .... 221 A3
Harringay N4 .... 50 D4
Harrow HA3 .... 24 D1
Warham St SE5 .... 138 D5
Waring Cl BR6 .... 227 D2
Waring Dr BR6 .... 227 D2
Waring Ho 25 E2 .... 96 A4
Waring Rd DA14 .... 190 C4
Waring St SE27 .... 183 A6
Warkworth Gdns TW7 .. 131 A5
Warkworth Rd N17 .... 33 B3
Warland Rd SE18 .... 145 C5
Warley Ave
Dagenham RM8 .... 59 B2
Hayes UB4 .... 84 A1
Warley Cl E10 .... 53 B1
Warley Ho N1 .... 73 B2
Warley Rd Hayes UB4 ... 84 A2
Lower Edmonton N9 .... 18 C2
Woodford IG8 .... 37 B3
Warley St E2 .... 96 D4
Warlingham Rd CR7 .... 204 D5
Warlock Rd W9 .... 91 C3
Warlow Cl 6 EN3 .... 7 C6
Warlters Cl N7 .... 72 A4
Warlters Rd N7 .... 72 A4
Warltersville Mans
N19 .... 50 A2
Warltersville Rd N4, N8,
N19 .... 50 A2
War Meml Homes W4 .. 133 B5
Warming Cl E5 .... 74 D5
Warmington Rd SE24 .. 161 A5
Warmington St 3 E13 .. 99 A3
Warminster Gdns
SE25 .... 184 A1
Warminster Rd SE25 ... 184 A1
Warminster Sq SE25 ... 184 A1
Warminster Way CR4 .. 181 B1
Warmsworth NW1 .... 232 A6
Warmwell Ave NW9 .... 27 C2
Warndon St SE16 .... 118 C2
Warneford Rd HA3 .... 44 A6
Warneford St E9 .... 96 B6
Warne Pl 4 DA15 .... 168 B5
Warner Ave SM3 .... 217 A6
Warner Cl
Hampton TW12 .... 173 B5
Harlington UB3 .... 127 B5
Hendon NW9 .... 46 A2
Stratford E15 .... 76 C3
Warner Ct SM3 .... 217 A6
Warner Ho
1 Beckenham BR3 .... 185 D4
Harrow HA1 .... 42 B2
4 Homerton E9 .... 74 D2
Lewisham SE13 .... 141 D3
NW8 .... 229 A2
Warner Pl E2 .... 96 A4
Warner Rd
Bromley BR1 .... 186 D3
Camberwell SE5 .... 139 A4
Hornsey N8 .... 49 D5
Walthamstow E17 .... 53 A5
Warners Cl IG8 .... 37 A5
Warner St EC1 ... 94 C3 241 A5
Warner Yd EC1 .... 241 A5
Warnford Ho SW15 .... 155 C5
Warnford Ind Est UB3 .. 105 C4
Warnford Rd BR6 .... 227 D3
Warnham WC1 .... 233 C1
Warnham Court Rd
SM5 .... 218 D1
Warnham Ho 6 SW2 ... 160 B4
Warnham Rd N12 .... 30 C5
Warple Mews W3 .... 111 C4
Warple Way W3, W12 ... 111 C4
Warren Ave
Bromley BR1 .... 186 C3
Leyton E11 .... 76 B5
Mortlake SW14, TW10 .. 132 D1
Orpington BR6 .... 227 D3
South Croydon CR2 .... 222 D1
Warren Cl DA6 .... 169 C6
Esher KT10 .... 212 A4
Hayes UB4 .... 84 C2
Ponders End N9 .... 18 D4
Wembley HA9 .... 65 D6
West Norwood SE21 .... 161 A4
Warren Comp Sch The
RM6 .... 59 B4
Warren Cres N9 .... 17 D4
Warren Ct
17 Beckenham BR3 .... 185 C3
5 Croydon CR0 .... 205 C1
6 Ealing W5 .... 87 C2
Greenwich SE7 .... 143 C6
N1 .... 234 A4
Tottenham Hale N17 .... 52 A6
Warren Cutting KT2 .... 177 B3
Warrender Prim Sch
HA4 .... 39 D2
Warrender Rd N19 .... 71 C4
Warrender Way HA4 .... 40 A2
Warren Dr
Greenford UB6 .... 86 A3
Ruislip HA4 .... 40 D2
Warren Dr N KT5, KT6 .. 198 D1
Warren Dr S KT5 .... 199 A1
Warren Dr The E11 .... 55 C2
Warren Farm Cotts
RM6 .... 59 B5
Warren Fields HA7 .... 25 C6
Warren Gdns E15 .... 76 B3
Warren Hill IG10 .... 21 C6
Warren Ho 21 E3 .... 97 D4
Warren Jun Sch RM6 ... 59 B4
Warren La Stanmore HA7 .. 9 A2
Woolwich SE18 .... 122 D3
Warren Mews W1 .... 239 A5
Warren Park Rd SM1 ... 218 C2
Warren Pk KT2 .... 177 A4
Warren Pond Rd E4 .... 20 D4
Warren Rd
Ashford TW15 .... 171 C3
Bexleyheath DA6 .... 169 C6
Bushey WD23 .... 8 B3
Chingford E4 .... 20 A2
Croydon CR0 .... 205 D1
Hayes BR2 .... 225 A6
Ickenham UB10 .... 60 B4
Ilford IG6 .... 57 B4
Isleworth TW2 .... 152 B5
Kingston u T KT2 .... 177 A4
Leyton E10 .... 76 A5
Mitcham SW19 .... 180 C4
Sidcup DA14 .... 168 C1
Wanstead E11 .... 55 C2
Willesden NW2 .... 67 D6
Warren Rise KT3 .... 177 B2
Warren Road Prim Sch
BR6 .... 227 D4
Warrens Shawe La
HA8 .... 10 D2
Warren St W1 ... 93 C3 239 A5
Warren Street Sta
NW1 .... 93 C3 239 B6
Warren Terr RM6 .... 58 D5
Warren The Hayes UB4 .. 84 A1
Heston TW5 .... 129 B5
Manor Pk E12 .... 78 A4
Worcester Pk KT19 .... 215 B5
Warren Way
Edgware HA8 .... 26 D1
Finchley NW7 .... 29 A4
Warren Wlk 1 SE7 .... 143 C6
Warren Wood Cl BR2 .. 225 A6
Warriner Dr N9 .... 18 A1
Warriner Gdns
SW11 .... 137 A4 268 A1
Warrington Cres
W9 .... 92 A3 236 A6
Warrington Ct
4 Croydon CR0 .... 220 D5
13 Merton SW19 .... 179 C3
Warrington Gdns W9 . 236 A5
Warrington Rd
Croydon CR0 .... 220 D5
Dagenham RM8 .... 81 A6
Harrow HA1 .... 42 C4
22 Richmond TW10 .... 153 D6
Warrington Sq RM8 .... 80 D6
Warrior Cl SE28 .... 123 C5
Warrior Sq E12 .... 78 C4
Warsaw Cl HA4 .... 62 B2
Warspite Ho 3 E14 .... 119 D2
Warspite Rd SE18 .... 122 A3
Warton Rd E15 .... 98 A6
Warwall E6 .... 100 D1
Warwick W14 .. 113 B2 254 D3
Warwick Ave
Edgware HA8 .... 11 A1
Harrow HA2 .... 63 B4
Paddington W9 .. 92 A3 236 A5
Warwick Avenue Sta
W9 .... 92 A3 236 A5
Warwick Bldg SW8 .... 268 C5
Warwick Chambers
W8 .... 255 A6
Warwick Cl Bushey WD23 . 8 C4
DA5 .... 169 B4
Hampton TW12 .... 174 A3
New Barnet EN4 .... 14 B6
Warwick Cres
Hayes UB4 .... 83 D3
Little Venice W2 .92 A2 236 A4
Warwick Ct
1 Beckenham BR2 .... 186 C1
Ealing W7 .... 86 D1
5 East Finchley N2 .... 48 A6
Friern Barnet N11 .... 31 D4
Harrow HA1 .... 42 C6
Merton SW19 .... 179 B2
18 New Barnet EN5 .... 13 D6
Northolt UB5 .... 63 C3
Surbiton KT6 .... 214 A6
3 Upper Clapton E5 .... 74 B6
WC1 .... 240 D3
Warwick Dene W5 .... 110 A5
Warwick Dr SW15 .... 134 B2
Warwick Gdns
Harringay N4 .... 51 A4
Ilford IG1 .... 56 D1
Thames Ditton KT7 .... 196 D4
Thornton Heath CR7 .... 204 C5
W14 .... 113 B2 254 D4
Warwick Gr
Surbiton KT5 .... 198 B2
Upper Clapton E5 .... 52 B1
Warwick Ho
9 Acton W3 .... 88 C1
10 Brixton SW9 .... 138 C3
8 Kingston u T KT2 .... 176 A2
6 Putney SW15 .... 156 C4
Stoke Newington N4 .... 51 A1
5 Wimbledon SW19 .... 179 A3

Warwick House St
SW1 ... 249 D4
Warwick La EC4 . 94 D1 241 D1
Warwick Lo
Brondesbury NW2 ... 69 A3
Cheam SM1 ... 217 B4
Twickenham TW2 ... 151 D1
Warwick Mans SW5 ... 255 A4
Warwick Par HA7 ... 25 B1
Warwick Pas EC4 ... 241 D2
Warwick Pl Ealing W5 ... 109 D4
Little Venice W9 .92 A2 236 A4
Warwick Pl N SW1 ... 259 A3
Warwick Rd
Ashford TW15 ... 170 A5
Barnet EN5 ... 1 D1
Bexley DA16 ... 146 C2
Chingford E4 ... 35 C5
Ealing W5 ... 110 A5
Edmonton N18 ... 33 D6
Enfield EN3 ... 7 B6
Friern Barnet N11 ... 31 D4
Hounslow TW4 ... 128 B2
Kingston u T KT3 ... 199 A6
Penge SE20 ... 206 B6
Plashet E12 ... 78 A3
Sidcup DA14 ... 190 B5
Southall UB2 ... 107 B3
Stratford E15 ... 76 D2
Sutton SM1 ... 218 A3
Teddington KT1 ... 175 C2
Thames Ditton KT7 ... 196 D4
Thornton Heath CR7 ... 204 C6
Twickenham TW2 ... 152 C3
Walthamstow E17 ... 35 B1
Wanstead E11 ... 55 B4
West Kensington W14,
SW5 ... 113 B2 254 D4
Yiewsley UB7 ... 104 A5
Warwick Row
SW1 ... 115 B3 258 D6
Warwick Sch for Boys
E17 ... 54 A5
Warwickshire Path
SE8 ... 141 B5
Warwick Sq
Holborn EC4 ... 241 D2
Pimlico SW1 .. 115 C1 259 A2
Warwick Sq Mews
SW1 ... 259 A3
Warwick St
W1 ... 115 C6 249 B6
Warwick Terr
Leytonstone E17 ... 54 B4
SE18 ... 145 B6
Warwick Way
SW1 ... 115 B2 258 D4
Warwick Yd EC1 ... 242 B5
Wasdale NW1 ... 231 D1
Washbourne Ct N9 ... 18 A2
Washbrook Ho SW2 ... 160 C5
Washington Ave E12 ... 78 B4
Washington Bldg 1
SE13 ... 141 D4
Washington Cl 45 E3 ... 97 D4
Washington Ct SW17 ... 180 D4
Washington Ho SW1 .. 247 C1
Walthamstow E17 ... 35 B1
Washington Rd
Barnes SW13 ... 134 A5
Kingston u T KT1 ... 176 C1
North Cheam KT4 ... 200 B1
Upton E6 ... 77 C1
2 Woodford E18 ... 36 D1
Wastdale Rd SE23 ... 162 D3
Watchfield Ct 7 W4 ... 111 A1
Watcombe Cotts TW9 .. 132 C6
Watcombe Rd SE25 ... 206 B4
Waterbank Rd SE6 ... 186 A6
Waterbeach Rd RM9 ... 80 C2
Water Brook La NW4 ... 46 C4
Watercress Pl N1 ... 73 C1
Waterdale Rd SE2 ... 146 A6
Waterden Cres E9 ... 75 C3
Waterden Rd E15 ... 75 C2
Waterer Ho 7 SE6 ... 186 A6
Waterer Rise SM6 ... 219 D2
Waterfall Cl N14 ... 15 C1
Waterfall Cotts SW19 .. 180 B4
Waterfall Rd
Mitcham SW19 ... 180 B4
New Southgate N11, N14 . 15 C1
Waterfall Terr SW17 ... 180 C4
Waterfield Cl
Belvedere DA17 ... 125 C3
Woolwich SE28 ... 124 B5
Waterfield Gdns SE25 .. 205 C4
Waterford Ct 16 W13 ... 109 A5
Waterford Rd
SW6 ... 135 D5 265 C3
Waterford Way NW10 ... 68 A3
Watergardens The
Kingston u T KT2 ... 177 A4
Woodford IG8 ... 37 A5
Water Gardens The
W2 ... 92 C1 237 B2
Watergate EC4 ... 251 C6
Watergate Ho 5
SE18 ... 122 C2
Watergate Sch SE6 ... 185 D5
Watergate St SE8 ... 141 C6
Watergate Wlk WC2 .. 250 B4
Water Gdns HA7 ... 25 B4
Waterglade Ctr The
W5 ... 109 D6
Waterhall Ave E4 ... 36 C6
Waterhall Cl E17 ... 34 D2
Waterhead NW1 ... 232 A2
Waterhedge Mews
EN1 ... 17 D6
Waterhouse Cl
Hammersmith W6 ... 112 D1
Hampstead NW3 ... 70 B3
Newham E16 ... 99 D2
Waterhouse Ct 7
TW11 ... 174 D5
Wateridge Cl E14 ... 119 C3
Wateringbury Cl BR5 ... 190 B1
Water La
16 Camden Town NW1 ... 71 B1
Edmonton N9 ... 18 B4
Ilford IG3 ... 79 D5
Richmond TW10, TW9 ... 153 D6
SE14 ... 140 C5
Sidcup DA14 ... 169 B2
Stratford E15 ... 76 C2
Teddington KT1 ... 175 D2
Twickenham TW1 ... 153 A3
Water Lane Ho 29
TW10 ... 153 D6
Water Lily Cl UB2 ... 108 A4
Waterloo Bridge SE1,
WC2 ... 116 B6 250 D5
Waterloo Cl
East Bedfont TW14 ... 149 D3
Hackney E9 ... 74 C3
Waterloo Ct 4 HA0 ... 66 A2
Waterloo East Sta
SE1 ... 116 C5 251 B3
Waterloo Gdns
26 Islington N1 ... 72 D1
South Hackney E2 ... 96 C5
Waterloo Int Sta
SE1 ... 116 B4 250 D2
Waterloo Pier SE1 ... 250 C2
Waterloo Pl Kew TW9 .. 132 C6
9 Richmond TW9 ... 132 A1
SW1 ... 115 D5 249 C4
Waterloo Rd
Dollis Hill NW2 ... 68 A6
Forest Gate E7 ... 76 D3
SE1 ... 116 C4 251 B2
Sutton SM1 ... 218 B3
Upton E6 ... 77 C1
Walthamstow E10 ... 53 C2
Waterloo Sta
SE1 ... 116 C4 251 A2
Waterloo Terr N1 ... 72 D1
Waterlow Ct NW11 ... 47 D2
Waterlow Rd N19 ... 49 C1
Waterman Bldg 2
E14 ... 119 C4
Watermans Ct
12 Brentford TW8 ... 131 D6
2 Brentford TW8 ... 132 A6
Watermans Mews 1
W5 ... 110 A6
Waterman St SW15 ... 134 D2
Waterman Way E1 ... 118 B5
Watermark Ct RM6 ... 58 B3
Watermead TW14 ... 149 C3
Watermead Ho E9 ... 75 B3
Watermead La CR4 ... 202 D2
Watermeadow La
SW6 ... 136 A3
Watermead Rd SE6 ... 186 A6
Watermead Way N17 ... 34 B1
Watermen's Sq 1
SE20 ... 184 C3
Water Mews SE15 ... 140 C1
Watermill Bsns Ctr EN3 .. 7 B3
Watermill Cl TW10 ... 153 C1
Watermill Ct SE13 ... 141 D2
Watermill La N18 ... 33 C5
Watermill Way SW19 .. 180 A2
Water Mill Way TW13 .. 151 C2
Watermint Quay N16 ... 52 A2
Water Rd HA0 ... 88 B6
Watersedge KT19 ... 215 A4
Water's Edge SW6 ... 134 C4
Watersfield Way HA8 ... 26 A3
Waters Gdns RM10 ... 81 C3
Watershipdown Ho 4
E11 ... 54 D2
Waterside
11 Beckenham BR3 ... 185 C2
N1 ... 235 A3
Walthamstow E17 ... 52 C3
Waterside Ave BR3 ... 207 D4
Waterside Cl
Barking IG11 ... 80 A4
30 Bermondsey SE16 ... 118 A4
Northolt UB5 ... 85 B4
Old Ford E3 ... 97 B6
Surbiton KT6 ... 214 A6
Woolwich SE28 ... 123 D5
Waterside Ct
3 Hackbridge SM6 ... 219 A5
Lewisham SE13 ... 142 B1
Waterside Dr KT12 ... 194 B4
Waterside Pl NW1 ... 231 B6
Waterside Point SW11 267 B4
Waterside Rd UB2 ... 107 C3
Waterside Sch SE18 ... 123 B1
Waterside Trad Ctr
W7 ... 108 C3
Waterside Way SW17 .. 180 A5
Watersmeet Way
SE28 ... 102 D1
Waterson St E2 ... 95 D4
Waters Pl SW15 ... 134 C3
Watersplash Cl KT1 ... 198 A6
Watersplash La
Hayes UB3 ... 106 A2
Southall TW5 ... 106 B1
Watersplash Rd TW17 .. 192 C5
Waters Rd Catford SE6 .. 164 C1
Waters Rd *continued*
Kingston u T KT1 ... 176 D1
Waters Sq KT1 ... 198 D6
Water St WC2 ... 251 A6
Water View Cl DA6 ... 168 D6
Waterview Ho 13 E14 ... 97 A2
Waterville Lo 6 N12 ... 30 A5
Waterways Bsns Ctr EN3 . 7 C5
Waterworks Cnr E17 ... 36 C1
Waterworks La E5 ... 74 D6
Waterworks Rd SW2 ... 160 B5
Waterworks Yd 4
CR0 ... 221 A5
Watery La DA14 ... 190 B4
Hayes UB3 ... 105 B1
Merton SW19, SW20 ... 179 B1
Northolt UB5 ... 84 C5
Wates Way CR4 ... 202 D3
Wateville Rd N17 ... 33 A2
Watford Cl SW11 ... 267 B2
Watford Rd Elstree WD6 ... 9 C5
Harrow HA1 ... 43 A1
Newham E16 ... 99 A2
Northwood HA6 ... 22 A4
Sudbury HA0, HA1 ... 65 B4
Watford Way NW4 ... 46 A5
Watford Way (Barnet By-Pass) NW9 ... 27 D3
Watkin Mews 18 EN3 ... 7 C6
Watkin Rd HA9 ... 66 D5
Watkins Ho
11 Cubitt Town E14 ... 120 A4
Harrow HA1 ... 42 D4
Watkinson Rd N7 ... 72 B2
Watling Ave HA8 ... 27 B2
Watling Ct EC4 ... 242 B1
1 Elstree WD6 ... 9 D5
Watling Gate NW9 ... 45 C5
Watling Gdns NW2 ... 69 A2
Watling Ho 10 SE18 ... 144 C6
Watlings Cl CR0 ... 207 A3
Watling St
Bexleyheath DA7 ... 147 D1
4 Camberwell SE15 ... 139 C6
City of London
EC4 ... 95 A1 242 B1
Watlington Gr SE26 ... 185 A5
Watney Cotts SW14 ... 133 A2
Watney Mkt* E1 ... 96 B1
Watney Rd SW14 ... 133 A2
Watneys Rd CR4 ... 203 D4
Watney St E1 ... 96 B1
Watson Ave
Cheam SM3 ... 217 A6
Wallend E6 ... 78 C1
Watson Cl
Mitcham SW19 ... 180 C3
Stoke Newington N16 ... 73 B3
Watson Ho 3 SW2 ... 160 A4
Watsons Lo 4 RM10 ... 81 D2
Watsons Mews W1 ... 237 B3
Watsons Rd N22 ... 32 B2
Watson's St SE8 ... 141 C5
Watson St E13 ... 99 B5
Wattisfield Rd E5 ... 74 C5
Watts Cl N15 ... 51 C4
Wattsdown Cl E13 ... 99 A6
Watts Gr E3 ... 97 D2
Watts Ho 6 W10 ... 91 A2
Watt's La
Chislehurst BR7 ... 189 A2
Teddington TW11 ... 175 A5
Watts Rd KT7 ... 197 A2
Watts St SE15 ... 139 D4
Wapping E1 ... 118 B5
Wat Tyler Ho N8 ... 50 A6
Wat Tyler Rd SE10 ... 142 B4
Wauthier Cl N13 ... 32 D5
Wavel Ct
7 Streatham SW16 ... 160 A1
2 Wapping E1 ... 118 C5
Wavell Dr DA15 ... 167 C5
Wavell Ho N6 ... 49 A3
Wavel Mews
Hampstead NW6 ... 69 D1
Hornsey N8 ... 49 D5
Wavel Pl SE26 ... 183 D6
Wavendon Ave W4 ... 111 B1
Waveney Ave SE15 ... 140 B1
Waveney Cl E1 ... 118 A5
Waveney Ho SE15 ... 140 B1
Waverley Ave
Chingford Hatch E4 ... 35 B6
Sutton SM1 ... 217 D6
Tolworth KT5 ... 199 A3
Twickenham TW2, TW4 .. 151 C3
Walthamstow E17 ... 54 B6
Wembley HA9 ... 66 B3
Waverley Cl BR2 ... 209 D4
East Molesey KT8 ... 195 C4
Hayes UB3 ... 105 B2
Woodford E18 ... 37 C1
Waverley Cres SE18 ... 123 B1
Waverley Ct
5 Brondesbury NW6 ... 69 A1
Enfield EN2 ... 5 A2
North Finchley N12 ... 30 B6
W1 ... 238 B4
Waverley Gdns
Barking IG11 ... 101 C5
Ealing NW10 ... 88 B5
Ilford IG6 ... 57 B6
Newham E6 ... 100 A2
Northwood HA6 ... 22 A2
Waverley Gr N3 ... 47 A6
Waverley Ind Pk HA1 ... 42 B6
Waverley Pl
Finsbury Pk N4 ... 50 D1
St John's Wood
NW8 ... 92 B5 229 C4
Waverley Rd
Croydon SE25 ... 206 B6
Enfield EN2 ... 4 D2
Finsbury Pk N8 ... 50 A2
Harrow HA2 ... 41 A1
Plumstead SE18 ... 123 B1
Southall UB1 ... 107 C6
Stoneleigh KT17, KT4 ... 216 B3
Tottenham N17 ... 34 B3
Walthamstow E17 ... 54 A6
Woodford E18 ... 37 C2
Waverley Sch EN3 ... 6 C1
Waverley Way SM5 ... 218 C2
Waverly Ct NW3 ... 70 D2
Waverton Ho 2 E3 ... 97 B6
Waverton Rd SW18 ... 158 A4
Waverton St
W1 ... 115 B5 248 C4
Wavertree Ct 9 SW2 .. 160 A3
Wavertree Rd
Streatham SW2 ... 160 B3
Woodford E18 ... 37 A1
Waxham NW5 ... 70 D3
Waxlow Cres UB1 ... 85 C1
Waxlow Ho UB4 ... 84 C2
Waxlow Rd NW10 ... 89 B5
Waxlow Way UB5 ... 85 B3
Waxwell Cl HA5 ... 22 D1
Waxwell La HA5 ... 22 D1
Wayatt Point 1 SE28 .. 123 A3
Wayborne Gr HA4 ... 39 A3
Waye Ave TW5 ... 128 A4
Wayfarer Rd UB5 ... 85 A4
Wayfield Link SE9 ... 167 B5
Wayford St SW11 ... 136 C3
Wayland Ave E8 ... 74 A3
Wayland Ho 12 SW9 ... 138 C3
Waylands UB3 ... 83 B2
Waylands Ct IG1 ... 79 B4
Waylands Mead BR3 ... 185 D2
Waylett Ho SE11 ... 261 A1
Waylett Pl Wembley HA0 . 65 D4
West Norwood SE27 ... 160 D1
Wayman Ct E8 ... 74 B2
Wayne Cl BR6 ... 227 D5
Waynflete Ave CR0 ... 220 D5
Waynflete Sq
18 North Kensington
W10 ... 90 D1
16 Shepherd's Bush
W10 ... 112 D6
Waynflete St SW18 ... 158 A2
Wayside
Chislehurst BR7 ... 189 B2
Golders Green NW11 ... 47 A1
Mortlake SW14 ... 155 A6
New Addington CR0 ... 223 D2
Wayside Ave WD23 ... 8 B5
Wayside Cl N14 ... 15 C5
Wayside Commercial Est
IG11 ... 102 A5
Wayside Ct
Isleworth TW7 ... 130 C3
Twickenham TW1 ... 153 C5
Wembley HA9 ... 66 C5
Wayside Gdns RM10 ... 81 C3
Wayside Gr BR7, SE9 ... 188 B6
Wayside Mews IG2 ... 56 C4
Weald Cl
16 Bermondsey SE16 ... 118 B1
BR2 ... 226 A6
Weald Fst & Mid Schs
HA3 ... 24 D3
Weald La HA3 ... 24 B2
Weald Rd UB10 ... 82 C5
Weald Rise HA3 ... 24 D2
Weald Sq E5 ... 74 B6
WEALDSTONE ... 42 D6
Wealdstone Rd SM3 ... 217 B6
Weald The BR7 ... 188 B4
Weald Way Hayes UB4 ... 83 C4
Romford RM7 ... 59 D3
Wealdwood Gdns HA5 .. 23 D4
Weale Rd E4 ... 20 B1
Weall Ct HA5 ... 41 A5
Weardale Ct EN5 ... 12 C6
Weardale Gdns EN2 ... 5 B4
Weardale Ho N4 ... 51 A2
Weardale Rd SE13 ... 142 B1
Wearmouth Ho 1 E3 ... 97 B2
Wear Pl 18 E2 ... 96 B4
Wearside Rd SE13 ... 141 D1
Weatherbury 6 W2 ... 91 C1
Weatherbury Ho 3
N19 ... 71 D5
Weatherill Ct SE25 ... 206 B3
Weatherley Cl E3 ... 97 B2
Weathersfield Ct SE9 .. 166 B5
Weaver Cl
Newham E16 ... 122 D6
South Croydon CR0 ... 221 D4
Weaver Ct 2 E2 ... 96 B3
Weaver Ho
12 Bethnal Green E1 ... 96 A3
1 Northolt UB5 ... 85 B3
Weavers Cl TW7 ... 130 C1
Weavers Ho 4 E11 ... 55 A3
Weaver's La
SE1 ... 117 C5 253 B3
Weaver St E1 ... 96 A3
Weavers Way
6 Camden Town NW1 ... 71 D1
NW1 ... 232 C6
Weaver Wlk SE27 ... 182 D6
Webb Cl NW10 ... 90 C3
Webb Ct 6 SE28 ... 124 B6
South Acton W3 ... 110 D4
Webber Cl WD6 ... 9 D5
Webber Ho 6 IG11 ... 78 D1
Webber Row
SE1 ... 116 D4 251 C1
Webber St SE1 .116 D4 251 C1
Webb Est E5 ... 52 A2
Webb Gdns 1 E13 ... 99 A3
Webb Ho
2 Dagenham RM10 ... 81 C5
Feltham TW13 ... 151 A1
SW8 ... 269 D3
Webb Pl NW10 ... 89 D4
Webb Rd SE3 ... 142 D6
Webbscroft Rd RM10 ... 81 D4
Webbs Rd UB4 ... 84 B4
Webb's Rd SW11 ... 158 D6
Webb St SE1 ... 117 C3 263 A5
Webheath 6 NW6 ... 69 B1
Webley Ct 22 EN3 ... 7 C6
Webster Gdns W5 ... 109 D5
Webster Ho 16 N16 ... 73 C3
Webster Rd
Bermondsey SE16 ... 118 A3
Leyton E11 ... 76 A5
Weddell Ho 23 E1 ... 96 D3
Wedderburn Rd
Barking IG11 ... 101 C6
Hampstead NW3 ... 70 B3
Wedgewood Ct
1 Beckenham BR2 ... 208 D5
DA5 ... 169 B4
Wedgewood Ho SW1 .. 259 A1
Thames Ditton KT7 ... 196 D1
Wedgewood Mews
W1 ... 239 D1
Wedgewood Wlk NW3 .. 69 D3
Wedgwood Ho
17 Globe Town E2 ... 96 D4
SE11 ... 261 A5
Wedgwood Way SE19 .. 183 A3
Wedlake St W10 ... 91 A3
Wedmore Gdns N19 ... 71 D6
Wedmore Rd UB6 ... 86 B4
Wedmore St N19 ... 71 D5
Weech Rd NW6 ... 69 C4
Weedington Rd NW5 ... 71 A3
Weedon Ho W12 ... 90 A1
Weekley Sq SW11 ... 136 B2
Weeks Ho TW10 ... 175 C6
Weigall Rd SE12, SE3 ... 143 A1
Weighhouse St W1 ... 238 B1
Weighton Rd
Harrow HA3 ... 24 B2
Penge SE20 ... 184 B1
Weihurst Ct SM1 ... 218 C3
Weihurst Gdns SM1 ... 218 B3
Weimar St SW15 ... 135 A2
Weirdale Ave N20 ... 14 D2
Weir Hall Ave N18 ... 33 B4
Weir Hall Gdns N18 ... 33 B5
Weir Hall Rd N18 ... 33 B4
Weir Ho 8 SW12 ... 159 C4
Weir Rd Sidcup DA5 ... 169 D4
Streatham SW12 ... 159 C4
Walton-on-T KT12 ... 194 A3
Wimbledon SW18,
SW19 ... 157 D1
Weir's Pas NW1 ... 232 D2
Weiss Rd SW15 ... 134 D2
Welbeck Ave
Grove Pk BR1 ... 187 B6
Hayes UB4 ... 84 B3
Sidcup DA15 ... 168 A3
Welbeck Cl
New Malden KT3 ... 199 D4
North Finchley N12 ... 30 B5
Stoneleigh KT17 ... 216 A1
Welbeck Ct Hayes UB4 ... 84 B3
W14 ... 254 C4
Welbeck Mans 10 NW6 .. 69 C3
Welbeck Rd
Carshalton SM1 ... 218 B6
Carshalton SM5 ... 202 C1
East Barnet EN4 ... 14 C5
Harrow HA2 ... 41 D1
Newham E6 ... 99 D4
Welbeck St W1 .. 93 B1 238 C2
Welbeck Villas N21 ... 17 A3
Welbeck Way W1 ... 238 C2
Welbeck Wlk SM5 ... 202 B1
Welbourne Prim Sch
N17 ... 52 A6
Welbury Ct E8 ... 73 C1
Welby Ho N19 ... 49 D2
Welby St SE5 ... 138 D4
Welch Pl HA5 ... 22 C2
Welcome Ct E17 ... 53 C2
Weldon Cl HA4 ... 62 B2
Weldon Ct
Southgate N21 ... 16 B6
St Johns SE8 ... 141 C3
7 Sutton SM1 ... 218 B3
Thornton Heath CR7 ... 204 D4
Weldon Dr KT8 ... 195 B5
Weld Pl N11 ... 31 B5
Welfare Rd E15 ... 76 C1
Welford Cl E5 ... 74 D5
Welford Ct
12 Camden Town NW1 ... 71 B1
7 Clapham SW8 ... 137 C3
Welford Ho 4 UB5 ... 85 B3
Welford Pl SW19 ... 179 A6
Welham Rd SW16,
SW17 ... 181 B4
Welhouse Rd SM5 ... 202 C1
Wellacre Rd HA3 ... 43 B3
Wellan Cl DA15, DA16 ... 168 B6
Welland Ct SE6 ... 163 B2
Welland Gdns UB6 ... 86 D5
Welland Ho SE15 ... 140 C1
Welland Mews E1 ... 118 A5
Wellands Cl BR1 ... 188 B1
Welland St SE10 ... 142 A6
Well App EN5 ... 12 C6
Wellbrook Rd BR6 ... 226 C4
Wellby Cl N9 ... 18 A3
Wellby Ct 1 E13 ... 99 C5
Well Cl Ruislip HA4 ... 63 A5
Streatham SW16 ... 182 B6
Wellclose Sq E1 ... 118 A6
Wellclose St 20 E1 ... 118 A6
Well Cottage Cl E11 ... 55 C2
Well Ct EC4 ... 242 B1
Wellday Ho 2 E9 ... 75 A2
Welldon Cres HA1 ... 42 C3
Welldon Ct Harrow HA1 .. 42 C4
1 West Dulwich SE21 .. 161 B2
Welldon Park Fst Sch
HA2 ... 64 A4
Welldon Park Mid Sch
HA2 ... 64 A4
Weller Ho 23 SE16 ... 118 A4
Weller Mews 6 BR2 ... 209 B5
Weller St SE1 ... 252 A2
Welles Ct 15 E14 ... 119 C6
Wellesley Ave W6 ... 112 B3
Wellesley Cl 8 SE7 ... 121 C1
Wellesley Court Rd 1
CR0 ... 221 B6
Wellesley Cres TW2 ... 152 C1
Wellesley Ct
Cheam SM3 ... 201 A1
St John's Wood
W9 ... 92 A4 229 A2
Twickenham TW2 ... 152 C1
Wellesley Gr CR0 ... 221 B6
Wellesley Ho NW1 ... 232 C1
12 Wimbledon SW19 ... 179 A3
Wellesley Park Mews
EN2 ... 4 D3
Wellesley Pl
Camden Town NW5 ... 71 A3
NW1 ... 232 C1
Wellesley Rd
Croydon CR0 ... 205 A1
Gospel Oak NW5 ... 71 A3
Gunnersbury W4 ... 110 D1
Harrow HA1 ... 42 C4
Ilford IG1 ... 57 A1
Sutton SM2 ... 218 A2
Twickenham TW2 ... 152 C1
Walthamstow E17 ... 53 C3
Wanstead E11 ... 55 A4
Wood Green N22 ... 32 C1
Wellesley Road Sta
CR0 ... 221 B6
Wellesley St E1 ... 96 D2
Wellesley Terr
N1 ... 95 A4 235 B2
Wellfield Ave N10 ... 49 B6
Wellfield Rd SW16 ... 182 B6
Wellfit St 6 SE24 ... 138 D2
Wellgarth UB6 ... 65 B2
Wellgarth Rd NW11 ... 47 D1
Well Gr N20 ... 14 B3
Wellgrove Sch N20 ... 14 B3
Well Hall Par SE9 ... 144 B1
Well Hall Pleasaunce*
SE9 ... 144 A1
Well Hall Rd SE9 ... 144 B1
Well Ho 11 N9 ... 18 A1
Wellhouse Rd BR3 ... 207 C5
Wellhurst Cl BR6 ... 227 D1
WELLING ... 146 B2
Wellingfield Ct 1
DA16 ... 146 A2
Welling High St DA16 .. 146 B2
Welling Sch DA16 ... 146 B4
Wellings Ho UB3 ... 106 B5
Welling Sta DA16 ... 146 A3
Wellington
1 Grahame Pk NW9 ... 27 D3
Hornsey N8 ... 50 A5
Wellington Arch*
SW1 ... 248 B2
Wellington Ave
Chingford E4 ... 19 D2
DA15 ... 168 A5
Edmonton N9 ... 18 B1
Hounslow TW3, TW4 ... 151 C6
North Cheam KT4 ... 216 C5
Pinner HA5 ... 23 B2
South Tottenham N15 ... 52 A3
Wellington Bldgs
15 Bow E3 ... 97 C4
SW1 ... 258 B1
Wellington Cl
Kensington W11 ... 91 C1
New Cross Gate SE14 .. 140 D4
Walton-on-T KT12 ... 193 D1
Wellington Cres KT3 ... 199 A6
Wellington Ct
Ashford TW15 ... 170 A6
Knightsbridge SW1 ... 247 C1
Stanwell TW19 ... 148 A4
St John's Wood NW8 ... 229 D3
Strand WC2 ... 250 A6
5 Surbiton KT6 ... 198 A3
Teddington TW12 ... 174 B5
4 Upper Tooting
SW17 ... 180 C4
Wandsworth SW18 ... 158 C6
Wellington Gdns
Greenwich SE7 ... 121 C1
Teddington TW12, TW2 .. 174 B6
Wellington Gr SE10 ... 142 B5
Wellington Ho
4 Ealing W5 ... 88 A4
18 Maitland Pk NW3 ... 70 D2
Northolt UB5 ... 63 C1
6 Ruislip HA4 ... 40 C1
Stanmore HA7 ... 9 A1

Wellington Hospl The
NW8 92 B5 229 D3
Wellington Mans
Shacklewell N16 73 D4
1 Walthamstow E10 53 C1
Wellington Mews
East Dulwich SE22 140 A1
3 Islington N7 72 B2
SE7 143 C6
Streatham SW16 159 D1
Wellington Mus (Apsley Ho)* SW1 115 A4 248 B2
Wellington Par DA15 168 A6
Wellington Park Est
NW2 68 A6
Wellington Pas 7 E11 55 A4
Wellington Pl
East Finchley N2 48 C4
St John's Wood
NW8 92 B4 229 D2
Wellington Prim Sch
Bow E3 97 C4
Chingford E4 19 D2
Hounslow TW3 129 B3
Wellington Rd
Ashford TW15 170 A5
Bexley DA5 168 D6
Brentford W5 109 C3
Bromley BR2 209 C5
Enfield EN1 17 C6
Erith DA17 125 B1
Harrow HA3 42 C6
Hatton TW14 149 C6
Kensal Green NW10 90 D4
Leyton E7 76 D4
Newham E6 100 B5
Pinner HA5 23 B2
St John's Wood
NW8 92 B5 229 D3
Teddington TW12, TW2 174 B6
Thornton Heath CR0 204 D2
Walthamstow E10 53 A1
Walthamstow E17 53 A5
Wanstead E11 55 A4
Wimbledon SW19 157 C2
Wellington Rd N TW4 129 B2
Wellington Rd S TW4 151 B6
Wellington Row E2 96 A4
Wellington Sq
SW3 114 D1 257 C2
Wellington St
1 Barking IG11 101 A6
WC2 116 B6 250 C6
Woolwich SE18 122 C2
Wellington Terr
Harrow HA1 42 B1
2 Wapping E1 118 B5
Wellington Way E3 97 C4
Welling Way DA16 145 B2
Well La SW14 155 A6
Wellmead IG3 58 A2
Wellmeadow Rd
Brentford W7 109 A2
Catford SE13, SE6 164 C3
Wellow Wlk SM5 202 B1
Well Rd Barnet EN5 12 C6
Vale of Health NW3 70 B5
Wells Cl 2 Northolt UB5 84 C4
South Croydon CR2 221 C3
Wells Ct
21 Hampstead NW3 70 A4
4 Mitcham CR4 180 C2
1 Paddington NW6 91 C5
Stoke Newington N1 73 C3
Wells Dr NW9 45 B1
Wells Gdns
Dagenham RM10 81 D3
Redbridge IG1 56 A2
Wells Ho
4 Barking IG11 80 A1
Ealing W5 109 D6
Finsbury EC1 234 C2
12 Kensal Town W10 91 A3
New Cross Gate SE4 141 A3
Plaistow BR1 187 B5
9 Rotherhithe SE16 118 C3
Wells Ho The 2 NW3 70 B4
Wells House Rd NW10 89 C2
Wellside Gdns SW14 155 A6
Wells Mews W1 239 B2
Wellsmoor Gdns BR1 210 C6
Wells Park Ct SE26 184 B6
Wells Park Rd SE26 184 B6
Wells Pl SW18 158 A4
Wells Prim Sch IG8 37 A6
Wellspring Cres HA9 66 D5
Wells Rd BR1 188 B1
Hammersmith W12 112 C4
Wells Rise NW8 92 D6 230 C5
Wells Sq WC1 233 D1
Wells St W1 93 C1 239 B2
Well St Hackney E9 74 C1
Stratford E15 76 C2
Wellstead Ave N9 18 D4
Wellstead Rd E6 100 C5
Wells Terr N4 72 C6
Wells The N14 15 D4
Wells Way
Brompton
SW7 114 B3 256 C6
Camberwell SE5 139 C6
Well Wlk NW3 70 B5
Wellwood Ct SW15 134 C1
Wellwood Rd IG3 58 A2
Welmar Works SW4 137 D1
Welsby Ct W5 87 C2
Welsford St SE1 118 A2
Welsh Cl E13 99 A4
WELSH HARP 45 C1
Welsh Harp Field Centre
NW9 45 B1
Welsh Ho 14 E1 118 B5
Welshpool Ho 22 E8 96 A6
Welshpool St 1 E8 96 B6
Welshside NW9 45 C3
Welshside Wlk NW9 45 C3
Welstead Ho 29 E1 96 B1
Welstead Way W4 111 D2
Weltje Rd W6 112 A1
Welton Ct SE5 139 C4
Welton Ho E1 96 D2
Welton Rd SE18 145 C5
Welwyn Ave TW14 149 D5
Welwyn St E2 96 C4
Welwyn Way UB4 83 C3
WEMBLEY 65 D2
Wembley HA0 65 D2
Wembley Arena HA9 66 C4
Wembley Central Sta
HA9 66 A3
Wembley Commercial Ctr
HA9 65 D6
Wembley Conference Ctr
HA9 66 C4
Wembley Exhibition Halls
HA9 66 C4
Wembley High Tech Coll
HA0 65 C5
Wembley Hill Rd HA9 66 B4
Wembley Hospl HA0 65 D2
Wembley Mkt
1 Wembley HA0 66 A3
1 Wembley Pk HA9 66 C4
WEMBLEY PARK 66 C5
Wembley Park Bsns Ctr
HA9 66 D5
Wembley Park Dr HA9 66 B5
Wembley Park Sta HA9 66 C5
Wembley Prim Sch
HA9 66 A5
Wembley Rd TW12 173 C2
Wembley Stadium HA9 66 C3
Wembley Stadium Ind Est
Wembley HA9 66 C5
Wembley HA9 66 D4
Wembley Stadium Sta
HA9 66 B3
Wembley Way HA9 66 D2
Wemborough Rd HA7 25 C3
Wembury Mews N6 49 C2
Wembury Rd N6 49 B2
Wemyss Rd SE3 142 D3
Wendela Ct HA1 64 C6
Wendell Park Prim Sch
W12 111 D4
Wendell Rd W12 111 D4
Wenderholme CR2 221 B3
Wendle Ct SW8 270 A5
Wendling NW5 70 D3
Wendling Rd SM1 218 B6
Wendon Ct 13 SM6 219 C2
Wendon St E3 97 B6
Wendover
SE17 117 C1 263 A1
Wendover Cl UB4 85 A3
Wendover Ct Acton W3 88 D3
Becontree W3 89 A3
Bromley BR2 209 B6
4 Child's Hill NW2 69 C5
W1 238 A3
Wendover Dr KT3 199 D3
Wendover Ho
Bowes Pk N22 32 B5
W1 238 A3
Wendover Lo NW9 45 D3
Wendover Rd
Blackheath SE9 143 D2
Bromley BR1, BR2 209 B6
Dagenham NW10 89 D5
Wendover Way
Bexley DA16 146 A1
Bushey WD23 8 A5
Wendy Cl EN1 17 D5
Wendy Ho 3 N12 30 B5
Wendy Way HA0 88 A6
Wengham Ho W12 112 A6
Wenham Ho SW8 269 A3
Wenlake Ho EC1 242 A6
Wenlock Ct N1 235 D3
Wenlock Gdns 13 NW4 46 A5
Wenlock Rd
Burnt Oak HA8 27 A4
Shoreditch N1 95 A5 235 B3
Wenlock St N1 95 B5 235 C3
Wennington Rd E3 96 D5
Wensdale Ho E5 74 A6
Wensley Ave IG8 37 A3
Wensley Cl
6 Barnet N11 31 A4
SE9 166 B5
Wensleydale Gdns
TW12 173 D3
Wensleydale Ho 8 N4 51 A2
Wensleydale Rd
TW12 173 D3
Wensley Rd N18 34 B4
Wentland Cl SE6 164 B2
Wentland Rd SE6 164 B2
Wentway Ct W13 87 A3
Wentwood Ho 1 E5 74 B6
Wentworth Ave
Borehamwood WD6 10 B6
Finchley N3 29 C3
Wentworth Cl
Ashford TW15 170 D6
Finchley N3 29 D3
Hayes BR2 225 A6
Long Ditton KT6 213 D6
Wentworth Cl *continued*
Morden SM4 201 C2
Orpington BR6 227 C3
Thamesmead SE28 102 D1
Wentworth Cres
Hayes UB3 105 B3
SE15 140 A5
Wentworth Ct
Barnet EN5 1 A2
7 Chingford E4 36 B5
20 Kingston u T KT6 198 A4
Southall UB2 106 C2
2 Surbiton KT6 214 A6
Twickenham TW2 152 C1
W6 264 A5
Wandsworth SW18 157 D5
Wentworth Dr HA5 40 A4
Wentworth Dwellings
E1 243 C2
Wentworth Gdns N13 16 D1
Wentworth Hall NW7 28 C5
Wentworth Hill HA9 44 B1
Wentworth Ho
Enfield EN1 17 C5
4 Greenwich SE3 143 A5
Wentworth Lo N3 29 D3
Wentworth Mews E3 97 B4
Wentworth Pk N3 29 D3
Wentworth Pl HA7 25 B4
Wentworth Rd
Manor Pk E12 77 D4
Southall UB2 106 D2
Temple Fortune NW11 47 B3
Thornton Heath CR0 204 C2
Wentworth St
E1 95 D2 243 D3
Wentworth Tutorial Coll
NW11 46 D3
Wentworth Way HA5 41 A5
Wenvoe Ave DA7 147 D3
Wepham Cl UB4 84 D2
Wernbrook St SE18 145 A6
Werndee Rd SE25 206 A5
Werneth Hall Rd IG5 56 C6
Werrington St
NW1 93 C5 232 B3
Werter Rd SW15 135 A1
Wesleyan Pl NW5 71 B4
Wesley Ave
Becontree NW10 89 B4
Hounslow TW3 129 B3
Newham E16 121 B5
Wesley Cl
Finsbury Pk N7 72 B6
Harrow HA2 64 A6
SE17 261 D3
Wesley Ct W1 238 B3
Wesley Ho SE24 161 B5
Wesley Rd
Becontree NW10 89 A6
Finchley N10 30 C2
Hayes UB3 84 A1
Leytonstone E10 54 A2
Wesley Sq W11 91 A1
Wesley St W1 238 B3
Wessex Ave SW19 201 C6
Wessex Cl
Hinchley Wood KT10,
KT7 212 D6
Ilford IG3 57 C3
Kingston u T KT1, KT2 176 D2
Wessex Ct
Putney SW15 156 D6
5 Stanwell TW19 148 A5
Wembley HA9 66 B6
Wessex Dr HA5 23 A3
Wessex Gardens Prim Sch
NW11 47 A1
Wessex Gdns NW11 47 A1
Wessex Ho SE1 263 D1
4 Tufnell Pk N19 71 D5
Wessex La UB6 86 B5
Wessex St E2 96 C4
Wessex Way NW11 47 A1
Wesson Ho 3 CR0 206 A1
West 12 Sh Ctr W12 112 D4
Westacott UB4 83 C2
Westacott Cl N19 49 D1
WEST ACTON 88 C1
West Acton Prim Sch
W3 88 D1
West Acton Sta W3 88 C1
West App BR5 211 A4
West Arbour St E1 96 D1
West Ave
East Finchley N2 47 D6
Finchley N3 29 C4
Hayes UB3 105 D6
Hendon NW4 46 D4
Pinner HA5 41 B2
Southall UB1 107 B6
Wallington SM6 220 A3
Walthamstow E17 53 D4
West Avenue Rd E17 53 D5
West Bank
Barking IG11 100 D6
Enfield EN2 5 A3
Stamford Hill N16 51 C2
Westbank Rd TW12 174 A4
WEST BARNES 200 C4
West Barnes La KT3,
SW20 200 B5
WEST BEDFONT 148 B4
Westbeech Rd N22 50 C6
Westbere Ct HA7 25 D5
Westbere Dr HA7 25 D5
Westbere Rd NW2 69 A3
West Block 18 E1 118 C6
Westbourne Ave
Cheam SM3 217 A6
Westbourne Ave *continued*
Dagenham W3 89 B1
Westbourne Cl UB4 84 C3
Westbourne Cres W2 246 C6
Westbourne Ct
Cheam SM3 217 A6
W2 236 A2
Westbourne Dr SE23 162 D2
Westbourne Gdns W2 91 D1
Westbourne Gr
Notting Hill W2, W11 91 C1
W11 113 B6 244 D6
WESTBOURNE GREEN
91 D3
Westbourne Gr Mews 7
W11 91 C1
Westbourne Gr Terr
W2 91 D1
Westbourne Ho
Heston TW5 129 C6
SW1 258 C2
8 Twickenham TW1 153 B4
Westbourne Par 4
UB10 82 D3
Westbourne Park Rd
Notting Hill W2 91 C1
Notting Hill W11 91 B1
Westbourne Park Sta
W11 91 B2
Westbourne Park Villas
W2 91 D2
Westbourne Pl N9 18 B1
Westbourne Prim Sch
SM1 217 C5
Westbourne Rd
Barnsbury N7 72 B2
Croydon CR0 205 D3
DA7 147 A5
Feltham TW13 149 D1
Hillingdon UB8 82 D3
Penge SE26 184 D4
Westbourne St
W2 114 B6 246 C6
Westbourne Terr
W2 92 A1 236 B2
Westbourne Terrace Mews
W2 236 A2
Westbourne Terrace Rd
W2 92 A2 236 A3
Westbridge Cl W12 112 A5
Westbridge Prim Sch
SW11 267 A2
Westbridge Rd
SW11 136 C4 267 A2
WEST BROMPTON 135 D6
West Brompton Sta
SW5 113 C1 255 B1
Westbrook Ave TW12 173 B3
Westbrook Cl EN4 2 B2
Westbrook Cres EN4 2 B2
Westbrook Ct SE3 143 B4
Westbrooke Cres
DA16 146 C2
Westbrooke Rd
Bexley DA16 146 C2
DA15 167 B2
Westbrooke Sch
DA16 146 D2
Westbrook Ho
5 Bethnal Green E2 96 C4
5 Clapham Pk SW4 159 C6
Westbrook Rd
Heston TW5 129 B5
SE3 143 B4
South Norwood CR7 183 B1
Westbrook Sq EN4 2 B2
West Brow BR7 188 D5
Westbury Ave
Claygate KT10 212 D2
Southall UB1 85 C3
Tottenham N22 32 D1
Wembley HA0 66 A1
Westbury Cl Ruislip HA4 40 A2
Shepperton TW17 192 D3
Westbury Ct
3 Barking IG11 101 B6
Beckenham BR3 185 D2
1 Buckhurst Hill IG9 21 C2
Clapham SW4 159 B5
11 New Barnet EN5 14 A6
Tottenham N22 33 A1
Westbury Gr N12 29 C4
Westbury Ho
1 Walthamstow E17 53 C5
6 Willesden NW10 67 C1
Westbury House Sch
KT3 199 B4
Westbury La IG9 21 C2
Westbury Lodge Cl
HA5 40 D6
Westbury Pl 2 TW8 131 D6
Westbury Rd
Barking IG11 101 B6
Beckenham BR3 207 A6
Bowes Pk N11 32 A4
Bromley BR1 187 D2
Buckhurst Hill IG9 21 C3
Ealing W5 88 A1
Feltham TW13 150 D3
Finchley N12 29 D5
Ilford IG1 78 C6
New Malden KT3 199 B4
Penge SE20 184 D2
Thornton Heath CR0 205 B3
Upton E7 77 B2
Walthamstow E17 53 C5
Wembley HA0 66 A1
Westbury Terr E7 77 B2
Westbush Ct 1 W12 112 B4
West Carriage Dr
W2 114 C5 247 A4
West Central St WC1 240 A2
West Chantry HA3 23 D2
Westchester Ct NW4 46 D6
Westchester Dr NW4 46 D6
Westchester Ho W2 237 C1
West Cl Ashford TW15 170 A6
Barnet EN5 12 B6
Cockfosters EN4 3 A1
Edmonton N9 17 D1
Greenford UB6 86 A5
Hampton TW12 173 A4
Wembley HA9 44 B1
Westcliff Ho 13 N1 73 B2
Westcombe Ave CR0 204 B2
Westcombe Ct 1 SE3 142 D5
Westcombe Dr EN5 13 C6
Westcombe Hill SE3,
SE10 143 A6
Westcombe Lodge Dr
UB4 83 B2
Westcombe Park Rd
SE3 142 D5
Westcombe Park Sta
SE3 121 A1
West Common Rd
BR2 225 B5
Westcoombe Ave
SW20 177 D2
Westcote Rd SW16 181 C5
Westcote Rise HA4 39 A2
Westcott Cl BR1 210 A4
2 South Tottenham N15 51 D3
Westcott Cres W7 86 C2
Westcott Ho 1 E14 119 D6
Westcott Rd SE17 138 D6
West Cotts NW6 69 C3
Westcroft 1 SM5 219 A4
Westcroft Cl Enfield EN3 6 C5
West Hampstead NW2 69 A4
Westcroft Ct
3 Chiswick W6 112 A2
Kingsbury NW9 44 D4
Westcroft Gdns SM4 201 B5
Westcroft Ho 2 SM5 219 A4
Westcroft Rd SM5,
SM6 219 A4
Westcroft Sq W6 112 A2
Westcroft Way NW2 69 A4
West Cromwell Rd
W14 113 B1 254 D2
West Cross Ctr TW8 131 B6
West Cross Route W10,
W11 112 D6
West Cross Way TW8 131 B6
West Croydon Sta
CR9 205 A1
West Ct Hounslow TW7 130 A5
Sunbury TW16 172 B1
Walthamstow E17 53 D5
Wembley HA0 65 C6
Westdale Rd SE18 144 D6
Westdean Ave SE12 165 C3
Westdean Cl SW18 157 D5
Westdown Rd
Catford SE6 163 C4
Leyton E15 76 A4
West Dr Stanmore HA3 24 B4
Streatham SW16 181 C6
WEST DRAYTON 104 B4
West Drayton Park Ave
UB7 104 A3
West Drayton Prim Sch
UB7 104 A4
West Drayton Rd UB8 82 D1
West Drayton Sta
UB7 104 A5
West Drive Gdns HA3 24 B4
WEST DULWICH 161 A2
West Dulwich Sta
SE21 161 B3
WEST EALING 109 B5
West Ealing Bsns Ctr
W13 109 A6
West Ealing Sta W13 109 B6
West Eaton Pl SW1 258 A4
West Eaton Pl Mews
SW1 258 A4
West Ella Rd NW10 67 C1
West End Ave
Leytonstone E10 54 B4
Pinner HA5 40 D5
West End Cl
Stonebridge NW10 67 A1
Willesden NW10 67 A1
West End Ct
Hampstead NW6 69 D1
Pinner HA5 40 D5
West End Gdns UB5 84 C5
West End La
Hampstead NW6 69 D2
Harlington UB7 127 A5
Pinner HA5 40 D5
West End Rd
Ruislip HA4, UB5 62 A4
Ruislip UB5 62 C1
Southall UB1 107 A5
Westerdale Ct N5 72 D4
Westerdale Rd 2
SE10 121 A1
Westerfield Rd 1 N15 51 D4
Westergate W5 88 A2
Westergate Rd SE2 147 A6
Westerham
13 Kingston u T KT6 198 A4
NW1 232 A5
Westerham Ave N9 17 C1
Westerham Dr DA15 168 C5
Westerham Ho SE1 262 D6
Westerham Lo 10 BR3 185 C3
Westerham Rd
Keston BR2 225 D2
Walthamstow E10 53 D2
Westerley Cres SE26 185 B5
Westerley Ct HA4 62 B3
Western Ave
Dagenham W3 89 B1
Hendon NW11 46 D3
Hillingdon HA4, UB4, UB5,
UB10 61 C1
Northolt UB5, UB6 85 B6
Ruislip UB8, UB9, UB10 60 B3
Wembley UB6 87 C4
Western Avenue Bsns Pk
W3 88 D3
Western Beach Apts
E16 121 A5
Western Ct
4 Dagenham W3 89 B1
Finchley N3 29 C4
3 Kilburn W9 91 B5
Southall UB2 107 A3
Western Dr TW17 193 B3
Western Eye Hospl The
NW1 92 D2 237 C4
Western Gateway E16 121 A6
Western Gdns W5 110 C6
Western Ho 3 W9 91 B3
Western Hts SM1 217 C3
Western International
Market UB2 106 B2
Western La SW12 159 A4
Western Mews W9 91 B3
Western Par EN5 13 D6
Western Pl 19 SE16 118 C4
Western Rd
Becontree NW10 89 A3
Brixton SW9 138 C2
Ealing W5 109 D6
Fortis Green N2 48 D5
Mitcham CR4, SW19 180 C1
Newham E13 99 C5
Southall UB2 106 D2
Sutton SM1 217 C3
Walthamstow E17 54 A4
Wood Green N22 32 B1
Western Terr 3 W6 112 A1
Western View UB3 105 D4
Westernville Gdns IG2 57 A2
Western Way
New Barnet EN5 13 D5
Plumstead SE28 123 C4
Western Wharf 2
SE15 140 A6
WEST EWELL 215 C1
West Ewell Inf Sch
KT19 215 B3
West Farm Ct EN4 2 D2
Westferry Cir E14 119 C5
Westferry Rd E14 119 C3
Westferry Sta E14 119 C6
Westfield 1 BR6 227 A3
Loughton IG10 21 C6
West Hampstead NW3 69 C4
Westfield Cl
Cheam SM1 217 B4
Enfield EN3 7 A2
Kingsbury NW9 45 A6
SW10 266 A3
Westfield Ct
1 Kensal Green W10 90 D4
Kingston u T KT6 197 D4
Westfield Dr HA3 43 D5
Westfield Gdns
Harrow HA3 43 D5
Ilford RM6 58 C3
Westfield Ho 6 SE16 118 D2
Westfield La HA3 43 D5
Westfield Pk HA5 23 B3
Westfield Rd
Beckenham BR3 185 B1
Cheam SM1 217 B4
Croydon CR0 220 D6
Dagenham RM9 81 B4
Ealing W13 109 A5
Edgware NW7 11 C1
Kingston u T KT6 197 D4
Mitcham CR4 180 D1
Walton-on-T KT12 195 A2
Westfields SW13 133 D2
Westfields Ave SW13 133 C2
Westfields Rd W3 88 D2
Westfield St SE18 121 D3
Westfield Way
Mile End E1 97 A3
Ruislip HA4 61 D5
West Finchley Sta N3 29 D4
West Garden Pl W2 237 B1
West Gate W5 88 A4
Westgate Bsns Ctr
2 Kensal Town W10 91 A3
North Kensington W10 90 D3
Westgate Ct
6 Beckenham BR3 186 A2
15 Brixton SW9 138 C2
Lewisham SE12 165 A3
Westgate Est TW14 148 D3
Westgate Rd
Beckenham BR3 186 A2
Croydon SE25 206 B5
Westgate St E8 96 B6
Westgate Terr
SW10 135 D6 265 D6
West Gdns
Mitcham SW19 180 C4
Stepney E1 118 B6

Westglade Ct HA3 43 D4
West Gr
Lewisham SE10 142 B4
Woodford IG8 37 C5
WEST GREEN 51 A5
West Green Pl UB6 86 B6
West Green Prim Sch N15 51 A5
West Green Rd N15 51 B5
Westgrove La SE10 142 A4
West Grove Prim Sch N14 15 D4
West Halkin St SW1 115 A3 258 A6
West Hallowes SE9 166 A3
West Hall Rd TW9 132 D4
WEST HAM 99 B6
West Ham Church Prim Sch E15 98 D6
West Ham La E15 76 C1
WEST HAMPSTEAD 69 C4
West Hampstead Mews NW6 69 D2
West Hampstead Sta NW6 69 C2
West Hampstead Thameslink Sta NW6 69 C2
West Ham Sta E15 98 C4
West Harding St EC4 241 B2
WEST HARROW 42 A2
West Harrow Sta HA1 42 A3
West Hatch Manor HA4 39 D2
Westhaven SM1 217 C3
Westhay Gdns SW14 154 D6
WEST HEATH 146 D6
West Heath Ave NW11 47 C1
West Heath Cl NW3 69 C5
West Heath Ct NW11 47 C1
West Heath Dr NW11 47 C1
West Heath Gdns NW3 69 C5
West Heath Rd
SE2, DA7 146 D6
West Hampstead NW3 69 D5
WEST HENDON 45 D3
WEST HILL 157 B5
West Hill Harrow HA2 64 C6
Highgate N6 49 A1
Putney SW15 157 A5
South Croydon CR2 221 C1
Wembley HA9 44 B1
Westhill Ct W11 244 D6
West Hill Ct N6 71 A5
West Hill Hall HA2 64 C6
Westhill Pk
Dartmouth Pk N6 71 A6
Highgate N6 70 D6
West Hill Prim Sch SW18 157 C6
West Hill Rd SW18 157 B5
West Hill Way N20 13 D3
West Ho Barking IG11 78 D2
4 Penge SE20 184 D3
9 Streatham SW12 159 C4
Westholm NW11 47 D5
Westholme BR6 211 D2
Westholme Gdns HA4 40 A1
Westhope Ho 29 E2 96 A4
Westhorne Ave SE9, SE12 165 C5
Westhorpe Gdns NW4 46 C6
Westhorpe Rd SW15 134 C2
West House Cl SW19 157 A3
Westhurst Dr BR7 188 D5
West India Ave E14 119 C5
West India Dock Rd E14 119 C6
West India Ho 1 E14 119 C6
West India Quay Sta E14 119 C6
WEST KENSINGTON 113 A2
West Kensington Ct W14 254 C2
West Kensington Mans W14 254 C1
West Kensington Sta W14 113 B1 254 C2
WEST KILBURN 91 A4
West La SE16 118 B4
Westlake 12 SE16 118 C2
Westlake Cl Hayes UB4 85 A3
Palmers Green N13 16 C1
Westlake Rd HA9 65 D6
Westland Cl TW19 148 A5
Westland Ct 9 UB5 84 D4
Westland Dr BR2, BR4 224 D6
Westland Ho 1 E16 122 C5
Westland Lo 1 BR1 187 C1
Westland Pl N1 235 C2
Westlands Cl UB3 106 A2
Westlands Ct KT8 196 C5
Westlands Terr 3 SW12 159 C5
Westlea Rd W7 109 A3
West Lea Sch N9 17 C1
Westleigh Ave SW15 156 C6
Westleigh Ct
Finchley N12 29 D4
16 Wanstead E11 55 A4
Westleigh Dr BR1 188 A2
Westleigh Gdns HA8 26 C1
West Links HA0 87 D4
Westlinton Cl NW7 29 A4
West Lodge Ave W3 110 C5
West Lodge Ct W3 110 C5
West Lodge Fst & Mid Schs HA5 40 D5
West Lodge Sch DA15 168 A1
West London Acad
Northolt UB5 63 A1
Northolt UB5 85 A6
West London Shooting Grounds UB5 84 B5
Westly Ct NW2 68 D2
Westly Ho N9 18 B3
Westmacott Dr TW14 149 D3
Westmacott Ho NW8 236 D5
West Mall W11 245 B4
Westmark Point 13 SW15 156 B3
Westmead SW15 156 B5
West Mead
Ruislip HA4 62 C4
West Ewell KT19 215 C2
Westmead Cnr SM5 218 C4
Westmead Rd SM1 218 B4
Westmeath Ho NW2 68 A5
Westmere Dr NW7 11 B1
West Mersea Cl 9 E16 121 B5
West Mews SW1 259 A3
West Middlesex Univ Hosp TW7 131 A3
Westmill Ct N4 73 A6
WESTMINSTER 115 C4
Westminster Abbey* SW1 116 A3 260 A6
Westminster Abbey Choir Sch SW1 115 D3 259 D6
Westminster Acad NW1 92 C2 237 A4
Westminster Acad (Sch of English) W1 93 C1 239 B2
Westminster Ave CR7 182 D1
Westminster Boating Base SW1 269 C6
Westminster Bridge SE1, SW1 116 A4 250 B1
Westminster Bridge Rd SE1 116 B4 250 C1
Westminster Cath* SW1 115 C3 259 A5
Westminster Cath Choir Sch SW1 115 C2 259 B4
Westminster Cath RC Prim Sch SW1 115 D1 259 D2
Westminster City Hall SW1 259 B6
Westminster City Sch SW1 259 B6
Westminster Cl
East Bedfont TW14 150 A3
Teddington TW11 175 A5
Westminster Coll of Computing HA9 66 A3
Westminster Ct
22 Rotherhithe SE16 118 D5
South Norwood CR7 183 A1
5 Wandsworth SW18 157 C6
Wanstead E11 55 B3
Westminster Dr N13 32 A5
Westminster Gdns
Barking IG11 101 C5
Chingford E4 20 C3
SW1 260 A4
Westminster Ind Est SE18 121 D3
Westminster Kingsway Coll
Battersea SW11 137 A4 268 B2
St Pancras WC1 94 B4 233 C1
Westminster Kingsway Coll (Regent's Park Ctr) NW1 93 C3 239 A6
Westminster Pier SW1 250 B1
Westminster Rd
Carshalton SM1 218 B6
Ealing W7 108 C5
Edmonton N9 18 B3
Westminster Sch SW1 116 A3 260 A6
Westminster Sta SW1 116 A4 250 B1
Westminster Under Sch SW1 115 D2 259 C3
Westmoat Cl BR3 186 A3
WEST MOLESEY 195 C5
Westmont Rd KT10 212 C6
Westmoor Gdns EN3 6 D3
Westmoor Rd EN3 6 D3
Westmoor St SE7 121 D3
Westmore Ct SW15 157 A6
Westmoreland Ave DA16 145 C1
Westmoreland Dr SM2 217 D1
Westmoreland Ho NW10 90 A4
Westmoreland Pl
5 Bromley BR1 209 A6
Ealing W5 87 D2
Pimlico SW1 258 D1
Westmoreland Rd
Barnes SW13 134 A4
Beckenham BR2, BR3 208 D5
Bromley BR2 209 A5
Camberwell SE17 139 B6
Queensbury NW9 44 B5
Westmoreland St W1 238 B3
Westmoreland Terr
10 Penge SE20 184 B3
SW1 115 B1 258 D1
Westmorland Cl
3 Twickenham TW1 153 B5
Westmorland Cl *continued*
Wanstead E12 77 D6
Westmorland Ct
12 Surbiton KT6 197 D2
Sutton SM1 218 A5
Westmorland Rd BR2 209 A5
Harrow HA1 41 D4
Walthamstow E17 53 C3
Westmorland Way CR4 203 D4
Westmount Ct W5 88 B2
Westmount Rd SE9 144 C1
WEST NORWOOD 161 A1
West Norwood Sta SE27 160 D1
West Oak BR3 186 B2
Westoe Rd N9 18 B2
Weston Ave
East Molesey KT8 195 B5
Thames Ditton KT10, KT7 196 C2
Westonbirt Ct 6 SE15 139 D6
Weston Ct Highbury N4 73 A5
3 Kingston u T KT1 198 A6
Oakleigh Pk N20 14 A4
Weston Dr HA7 25 B2
Weston Ed Ctr The SE5 139 A3
West One Ho W1 239 A3
Westone Mans 6 IG11 79 D1
West One Sh Ctr W1 93 B1 238 C1
Weston Gdns TW7 130 C4
Weston Gn
Dagenham RM9 81 B4
Thames Ditton KT7 196 C1
Weston Gr 1 BR1 186 D2
WESTON GREEN 196 D1
Weston Green Prep Sch KT7 196 C1
Weston Green Rd KT7 196 C2
Weston Ho
6 Brondesbury NW6 69 A1
8 South Hackney E9 96 C6
Weston Lo KT7 196 D1
Weston Park Cl KT7 196 C1
Weston Park Prim Sch N8 50 B4
Weston Pk
Hornsey Vale N8 50 B3
Kingston u T KT1 176 A1
Thames Ditton KT10, KT7 196 C1
Weston Rd
Acton Green W4 111 A3
Bromley BR1 186 D3
Dagenham RM9 81 A4
Enfield EN2 5 B3
Thames Ditton KT7 196 C1
Weston Rise N1, WC1 94 B4 233 D2
Weston St SE1 117 B4 252 D2
Weston Wlk 3 E8, E9 74 B1
Westover Hill NW3 69 C6
Westover Rd SW18 158 A5
Westow Hill SE19 183 D4
Westow St SE19 183 C4
Westpark W5 87 D1
West Park Ave TW9 132 D4
West Park Cl
Heston TW5 129 B6
Ilford RM6 58 D4
West Park Rd
Richmond TW9 132 C4
Southall UB2 108 B5
West Parkside
Greenwich SE10 120 D3
Greenwich SE10 121 A2
West Pk SE9 166 A3
West Pl SW19 178 C5
West Plaza E14 119 D5
Westpoint
Beckenham BR2 208 B6
Putney SW15 156 D5
West Point 2 SE1 118 A1
Westpoint Apartments N8 50 B5
Westpoint Trad Est W3 88 D2
Westpole Ave EN4 3 B1
Westport Ct UB4 84 C3
Westport Rd E13 99 B3
Westport St E1 96 D1
West Poultry Ave EC1 241 C3
West Quarters W12 90 A1
West Quay Dr UB4 85 A2
West Ramp TW6 126 C4
West Rd
Chelsea SW3 136 D6 267 D6
Clapham Pk SW4 159 D6
Dagenham RM6 59 A3
Ealing W5 88 A2
East Barnet EN4 15 A3
East Bedfont TW14 149 B4
Finchley N2 30 B2
Kingston u T KT2, KT3 177 A2
Tottenham N17 34 B4
West Drayton UB7 104 B3
West Ham E15 98 D6
West Ridge Gdns UB6 86 A5
Westrow SW15 156 C5
West Row W10 91 A3
Westrow Dr IG11 80 A2
Westrow Gdns IG3 79 D5
WEST RUISLIP 61 B6
West Ruislip Ct HA4 61 B6
West Ruislip Elementary Sch UB10 61 A5
West Ruislip Sta HA4 61 A6
West Sheen Vale TW9 132 B1
Westside
11 Hammersmith W6 112 A2
Hendon NW4 28 B1
Muswell Hill N2 48 D6
West Side Comm SW19 178 C5
Westside Ct 1 W9 91 C3
West Silvertown Sta E16 121 A5
West Smithfield EC1 94 D2 241 D3
West Sq SE11 116 D3 261 C5
West St
30 Bethnal Green E2 96 B5
Bexleyheath DA7 147 B2
Bromley BR1 187 A1
Carshalton SM5 218 D4
Croydon CR0 221 A4
Harrow HA1 42 C1
Leyton E11 76 C5
Soho WC2 93 D1 239 D1
Sutton SM1 217 D3
Walthamstow E17 53 D4
West Street La SM5 218 D4
West Street Pl 1 CR0 221 A4
West Surrey Est TW15 171 A2
West Sutton Sta SM1 217 C4
West Temple Sheen SW14 154 D6
West Tenter St E1 95 D1 243 D1
West Terr DA15 167 C3
West Thames Coll TW7 130 C4
West Thamesmead Bsns Pk SE28 123 D3
West Thornton Prim Sch CR0 204 B3
West Towers HA5 40 D3
West Twyford Prim Sch NW10 88 C5
Westvale Mews W3 111 C4
Westview W7 86 C1
West View
Dagenham RM6 58 C4
East Bedfont TW14 149 A4
Westview Cl
North Kensington W10 90 C1
Willesden NW10 67 D3
Westview Cres N9 17 C4
Westview Ct
3 Elstree WD6 9 D5
1 Whetstone N20 14 A2
Westview Dr IG8 37 D1
West View Gdns WD6 9 D5
Westville Rd
Shepherd's Bush W12 112 A4
Thames Ditton KT7 197 A2
Westward Rd E4 35 B5
Westward Way HA3 44 A3
West Warwick Pl SW1 259 A3
Westway
Shepherd's Bush W10, W12 112 A6
West Barnes SW20 200 C5
West Way BR5 211 B4
Burnt Oak HA8 27 A4
Croydon CR0 223 A5
Edmonton N18 33 B6
Hounslow TW5 129 B4
Neasden NW10 67 B5
Pinner HA5 40 D5
Ruislip HA4 39 D1
Shepperton TW17 193 B3
West Wickham BR4 208 C3
Westway Cl SW20 200 B6
Westway Ct UB5 85 C6
Westway (Elevated Rd) W10 91 B2
West Way Gdns CR0 222 D6
Westway Lo 35 W2 91 C2
Westways KT19 215 D4
West Ways HA6 22 A1
Westwell 4 NW5 71 A2
Westwell Rd SW16 182 A4
Westwell Road App SW16 182 A4
Westwick 7 KT1 176 C1
Westwick Gdns
Cranford TW4, TW5 128 B3
Hammersmith W14 112 D4
WEST WICKHAM 224 C6
West Wickham Sta BR3 208 A2
West Wimbledon Prim Sch SW20 200 B6
West Wlk
East Barnet EN4 15 A3
Hayes UB3 106 A5
Westwood Ave
Harrow HA2 63 D4
South Norwood SE19 183 A2
Westwood Bsns Ctr NW10 89 C3
Westwood Cl BR1 209 D6
Esher KT10 212 A5
Ruislip HA4 38 D3
Westwood Coll DA16 145 C1
Westwood Ct
Enfield EN1 17 C5
3 Forest Hill SE23 162 C3
7 Wimbledon SW19 179 B5
Westwood Gdns SW13 133 D2
Westwood Hill SE26 184 B6
Westwood Ho
6 Shepherd's Bush W12 112 C5
Westwood Ho *continued*
5 Stoke Newington N4 51 B2
Westwood La DA16 145 D1
Westwood Language College for Girls SE19 183 B3
Westwood Lo N12 30 C5
Westwood Park Trad Est W3 88 D3
Westwood Pk SE23 162 B4
Westwood Pl SE26 184 A6
Westwood Rd
Barnes SW13 133 D2
Ilford IG3 58 A2
Westwood Sch WD23 8 B2
West Woodside DA5 169 A3
Wetheral Ct SW17 180 B6
Wetheral Dr HA7 25 C1
Wetherby Cl UB5 63 D2
Wetherby Ct SE25 183 C1
Wetherby Gdns SW5 114 A2 256 A3
Wetherby Mans SW5 255 C2
Wetherby Mews SW5 255 D2
Wetherby Pl SW7 114 A2 256 B3
Wetherby Rd EN2 5 A4
Wetherby Way KT9 214 A1
Wetherden St E17 53 B2
Wetherell Rd E9 96 D6
Wetherill Rd N10 31 A2
Wevco Wharf SE15 140 B6
Wexford Ho 11 E1 96 C2
Wexford Rd SW12 158 D4
Weybourne St SW18 158 A2
Weybridge Ct 19 SE16 118 B1
Weybridge Ho N4 51 A2
Weybridge Point 11 SW11 136 D3
Weybridge Rd CR7 204 C5
Wey Ct KT19 215 A4
Weydown Cl SW19 157 A3
Weyhill Ho 26 SE5 139 A3
Weyhill Rd 11 E1 96 A1
Wey Ho 6 Northolt UB5 85 B3
NW8 236 D5
Weylands Cl KT12 195 B1
Weylond Rd RM8 81 B5
Weyman Rd SE3 143 C4
Weymarks The N17 33 B4
Weymouth Ave
Brentford W5 109 C3
Edgware NW7 27 C5
Weymouth Cl 1 E6 100 D1
Weymouth Ct
Belmont SM2 217 C1
5 Haggerston E2 95 D5
15 Streatham SW2 160 B4
Weymouth Ho
Bromley BR2 186 D1
Edgware HA8 26 B4
Fitzrovia W1 238 D4
South Lambeth SW8 270 C3
Weymouth Mews W1 93 B2 238 C4
Weymouth Rd UB4 83 C4
Weymouth St W1 93 B2 238 C4
Weymouth Terr E2 95 D5
Weymouth Wlk HA7 25 A4
Whadcoat St N4 72 C6
Whaddon Ho
10 Camberwell SE5 139 C2
SW1 247 D1
Whalebone Ave RM6 59 B3
Whalebone Gr RM6 59 B3
Whalebone La E15 76 C1
Whalebone Lane N RM6 59 A6
Whalebone Lane S RM6, RM8 59 B2
Whales Yd E15 76 C1
Wharfdale Cl N11 31 A4
Wharfdale Rd N1 94 A5 233 B4
Wharfedale Ct 5 E5 74 D4
Wharfedale Gdns CR7, SW16 204 B6
Wharfedale St SW10 255 C1
Wharf La 10 Poplar E14 97 B1
Twickenham TW1 153 A3
Wharf Pl E2 96 B6
Wharf Rd Enfield EN3 19 A5
King's Cross NW1 93 D6 232 D5
Shoreditch N1 95 A5 235 A3
Wharf Road NW1 94 A5 233 A4
Wharfside HA0 88 A6
Wharfside Rd E16 98 C2
Wharf St E16 98 C2
Wharf View Ct 15 E14 98 A1
Wharncliffe Dr UB1 108 B5
Wharncliffe Gdns SE25 183 C1
Wharncliffe Ho 3 SW15 156 C6
Wharncliffe Rd SE25 183 C1
Wharton Cl NW10 67 C2
Wharton Ho SE1 263 C6
Wharton Rd BR1 187 B2
Wharton St WC1 94 B4 233 D1
Whateley Rd
East Dulwich SE22 161 D6
Penge SE20 184 D3
Whatley Ave SW20 201 A6
Whatman Ho 10 E14 97 B1
Whatman Rd SE23 162 D4
Wheatcroft Ct SM1 201 D1
Wheatfields Enfield EN3 7 A3
Newham E6 100 D1
Wheatfield Way KT1 176 A1
Wheathill Ho SE20 184 B1
Wheathill Rd SE20 206 B6
Wheat Ho TW19 148 A3
Wheatland Ho 7 SE22 139 C2
Wheatlands TW5 129 C6
Wheatlands Rd SW17 159 A1
Wheatley Cl NW4 28 A1
Wheatley Cres UB3 106 A6
Wheatley Gdns N9 17 C2
Wheatley Ho
Gospel Oak NW5 71 B4
3 Putney SW15 156 A4
Wheatley Mans 8 IG11 80 A1
Wheatley Rd TW7 130 D2
Wheatley St W1 238 B3
Wheatsheaf Cl UB5 63 A3
Wheat Sheaf Cl E14 119 D2
Wheatsheaf La
Fulham SW6 134 C5
SW8 270 B4
Wheatsheaf Par 7 BR4 207 D1
Wheatsheaf Terr SW6 264 D3
Wheatstone Cl SW19 180 C2
Wheatstone Ho 7 W10 91 A2
Wheatstone Rd W10 91 A2
Wheeler 2 NW9 27 D3
Wheeler Ct 5 SW11 136 B2
Wheeler Gdns N1 233 B6
Wheeler La E1 243 C4
Wheeler Pl 2 BR2 209 B5
Wheelers Cross IG11 101 B5
Wheelers Dr HA4 39 A3
Wheeler's St SM1 217 C5
Wheelhouse The 4 E14 119 D1
Wheelock Cl DA8 147 D5
Wheelwright St N7 72 B1
Whelan Way SM6 219 D5
Wheldon Ct SE1 253 C2
Wheler Ho E1 243 C5
Wheler St E1 95 D3 243 C5
Whellock Rd W4 111 C3
Whernside Cl SE28 124 C6
WHETSTONE 14 A2
Whetstone Cl N20 14 B2
Whetstone Park WC2 94 B1 240 C2
Whetstone Rd SE3 143 D4
Whewell Rd N19 72 A6
Whichcote St SE1 251 A3
Whidborne Bldgs WC1 233 A1
Whidborne Cl SE8 141 C3
Whidborne St WC1 233 B1
Whimbrel Cl SE28 124 C6
Whimbrel Way UB4 84 D2
Whinchat Rd SE18, SE28 123 B3
Whinfell Cl SW16 181 D5
Whinyates Rd SE9 144 A2
Whippendell Cl BR5 190 B2
Whippendell Way BR5 190 B1
Whippingham Ho 22 E3 97 B4
Whipps Cross E17 54 B4
Whipps Cross Ho E17 54 B4
Whipps Cross Hospl E10, E11 54 B3
Whipps Cross Rd E11 54 C3
Whiskin St EC1 94 D4 234 C1
Whisperwood Cl HA3 24 C3
Whistler Gdns HA8 26 B1
Whistler Mews
Dagenham RM8 80 B3
23 SE15 139 D5
Whistlers Ave SW11 136 B5 266 D3
Whistler St N5 72 D3
Whistler Twr SW10 266 A3
Whistler Wlk SW10 266 B4
Whiston Ho 18 N1 72 D1
Whiston Rd E2 96 A6
Whitakers Lo EN2 5 B4
Whitbread Cl N17 34 A2
Whitbread Ctr EC1 242 C5
Whitbread Rd SE4 141 B1
Whitburn Rd SE13 142 A1
Whitby Ave NW10 88 D4
Whitby Ct
6 Lower Holloway N7 72 A4
3 New Southgate N11 31 A4
Whitby Gdns
Carshalton SM1 218 B6
Queensbury NW9 44 C6
Whitby Ho NW8 229 A5
Whitby Par HA4 62 C6
Whitby Rd
Carshalton SM1 218 B6
Harrow HA2 64 A5
Ruislip HA4 62 C6
Woolwich SE18 122 B2
Whitby St E1 243 C6
Whitcher Cl SE14 141 A6
Whitcher Pl NW1 71 C2
Whitchurch Ave HA8 26 B3
Whitchurch Cl HA8 26 B4
Whitchurch Ct SW17 180 B6
Whitchurch Fst & Mid Schs HA7 25 D3
Whitchurch Gdns HA8 26 B4
Whitchurch Ho
Catford SE6 164 A1
16 North Kensington W10 90 D1
Whitchurch La HA8 26 B3

Whitchurch Par HA8 ... 26 C3
Whitchurch Rd W11 ... 112 D6
Whitcomb Ct WC1 ... 249 D5
Whitcomb St
WC2 ... 115 D6 249 D5
Whitcome Mews TW9 .. 132 D4
Whiteacre Mews SE11 261 B1
Whiteadder Way E14 ... 119 D2
Whitear Wlk E15 ... 76 B2
Whitebarn La RM10 ... 103 C6
Whitebeam Ave BR2 ... 210 C3
Whitebeam Cl SW9 ... 270 D3
Whitebeam Ho 3 NW3 .. 70 D2
White Bear Pl 1 NW3 ... 70 B4
White Bear Yd EC1 ... 241 A5
White Bridge Ave CR4 .. 202 B6
White Bridge Cl
TW14 ... 149 D5
White Butts Rd HA4 ... 62 D5
WHITECHAPEL ... 95 D1
Whitechapel High St
E1 ... 95 D1 243 D2
Whitechapel Mkt E1 ... 96 A2
Whitechapel Rd E1 ... 96 B2
Whitechapel Sta E1 ... 96 B2
Whitechurch La 3 E1 ... 96 A1
Whitechurch Pas 1 E1 . 96 A1
White City W10 ... 90 C1
White City Cl W12 ... 112 C6
White City Est W12 ... 112 B6
White City Rd W12 ... 112 C6
White City Sta W12 ... 112 C6
Whitecliff Ho SW18 ... 157 D5
White Conduit St N1 .. 234 B4
Whitecote Rd UB1 ... 86 A1
White Craig Cl HA5 ... 23 C5
Whitecroft Cl BR3 ... 208 B5
Whitecroft Way BR3 ... 208 B5
Whitecross Pl EC2 ... 242 D4
Whitecross St
EC1 ... 95 A3 242 B5
White Cube The, Art Gallery* N1 ... 95 C4
Whitefield Ave NW2 ... 46 C1
Whitefield Cl SW15 ... 157 A5
Whitefield Sch
Chingford E17 ... 36 A1
Hendon NW2 ... 46 D2
Whitefoot La BR1 ... 164 B1
Whitefoot Terr BR1 ... 164 D1
Whitefriars Ave HA3 ... 24 C1
Whitefriars Ct 9 N12 ... 30 B5
Whitefriars Dr HA3 ... 24 C1
Whitefriars Fst & Mid Sch
HA3 ... 24 C1
Whitefriars St
EC4 ... 94 C1 241 B1
Whitefriars Trad Est
HA3 ... 24 B1
White Gate Gdns HA3 ... 24 D3
Whitegates 4 EN5 ... 13 D6
White Gdns RM10 ... 81 C2
Whitehall SW1 ... 250 A2
Whitehall Cres KT9 ... 213 D3
Whitehall Ct
SW1 ... 116 A5 250 B3
Whitehall Gdns
Acton W3 ... 110 C5
Chingford E4 ... 20 C3
Chiswick W4 ... 132 D6
SW1 ... 250 A3
Whitehall La IG9 ... 21 A2
Whitehall Lo
Muswell Hill N10 ... 49 A6
Woodford IG8 ... 21 A1
Whitehall Mans 3 N19 .. 49 C1
Whitehall Park Rd
W4 ... 132 D6
Whitehall Pk N19 ... 49 C1
Whitehall Pl
Wallington SM5 ... 219 B4
WC2, SW1 ... 116 A5 250 A3
Whitehall Prim Sch E4 .. 20 C2
Whitehall Rd
Bromley BR2 ... 209 D5
Chingford E4 ... 20 C2
Harrow HA1 ... 42 C2
Thornton Heath CR7 ... 204 C4
West Ealing W7 ... 109 A4
Woodford IG8 ... 21 A1
Whitehall St N17 ... 33 D3
White Hart Ave SE28,
SE18 ... 123 D3
White Hart La
Mortlake SW13 ... 133 C2
Willesden NW10 ... 67 D2
White Hart Lane Sec Sch
N22 ... 32 D3
White Hart Lane Sta
N17 ... 33 D3
White Hart Lane (Tottenham Hotspur FC)
N17 ... 34 A3
Whitehart Lo SW19 ... 180 A4
White Hart Rd SE18 ... 123 C2
White Hart Rdbt UB5 ... 84 D5
White Hart St
Holborn EC4 ... 241 D2
Kennington
SE11 ... 116 C1 261 B2
White Hart Terr N17 ... 33 D3
White Hart Yd SE1 ... 252 C3
Whitehaven Cl BR2 ... 209 A5
Whitehaven Ct 5
DA6 ... 147 A1
Whitehaven St NW8 ... 237 A5
Whitehead Cl
Edmonton N18 ... 33 B5
Wandsworth SW18 ... 158 A4
Whitehead Ct
Muswell Hill N10 ... 31 A2
Twickenham TW1 ... 152 D4
Whitehead Ho 8
SW15 ... 156 D6
Whitehead's Gr
SW3 ... 114 C2 257 B3
White Heart Ave UB8 ... 83 A2
Whiteheath Ave HA4 ... 39 A2
Whiteheath Inf Sch
HA4 ... 39 A3
Whiteheath Jun Sch
HA4 ... 39 A2
White Heron Mews
TW11 ... 174 D4
White Ho
2 Battersea SW11 ... 136 B3
Lower Edmonton N9 ... 18 C2
3 Streatham SW4 ... 159 D4
Whitehorn Ho 6 E1 ... 118 C5
White Horse Hill BR7,
SE9 ... 188 C6
Whitehorse La SE25 ... 205 C5
White Horse La E1 ... 96 D2
Whitehorse Manor Inf Sch
CR7 ... 205 B5
Whitehorse Manor Jun Sch CR7 ... 205 B5
Whitehorse Mews SE1 261 C6
Whitehorse Rd
South Norwood CR0,
CR7 ... 205 B3
Tower Hamlets E1 ... 97 A2
White Horse Rd
Limehouse E1 ... 97 A1
Newham E6 ... 100 B4
White Horse St
W1 ... 115 B5 248 D3
White Horse Yd EC2 .. 242 C2
White Ho The NW1 ... 238 D6
Tottenham N17 ... 51 C6
Upper Tooting SW17 ... 180 D5
White House Ct
1 Beckenham BR3 ... 186 A2
Osidge N14 ... 15 D2
White House Dr HA7 ... 25 C6
Whitehouse Est E10 ... 54 A3
White House La EN2 ... 5 A4
Whitehouse Way N14 ... 15 B1
White Kennett St E1 .. 243 B2
Whitelands Cres
SW18 ... 157 A4
Whitelands Ho SW3 ... 257 D2
Whiteledges W13 ... 87 C1
Whitelegg Rd E13 ... 98 D5
Whiteley Ho 9 SW4 ... 159 D4
Whiteley Rd SE19 ... 183 B5
Whiteleys Ctr 19 W2 ... 91 D1
Whiteleys Ho TW13 ... 151 C1
Whiteleys Par 5 UB10 .. 82 D3
Whiteleys Way TW13 ... 151 C1
White Lion Ct EC3 ... 243 A1
White Lion Hill
EC4 ... 116 D6 251 D6
White Lion St
N1 ... 94 C5 234 B3
White Lo 7 Ealing W5 ... 87 C2
Golders Green NW11 ... 47 B1
South Norwood SE19 .. 182 D3
Whitelock Ho 21 E9 ... 74 D2
White Lodge Cl
Hampstead Garden Suburb
N2 ... 48 B3
Isleworth TW7 ... 131 A3
Sutton SM2 ... 218 A1
White Lodge Ct TW16 .. 172 C2
Whitely Ct TW13 ... 151 B1
White Lyon Ct EC2 ... 242 A4
Whiteness Ho 18 SW9 .. 138 C4
White Oak Dr BR3 ... 186 A1
White Oak Gdns DA15 .. 167 D4
Whiteoak Ho SE19 ... 183 A3
Whiteoaks La UB6 ... 86 B5
White Orchards
Barnet N20 ... 13 B3
Stanmore HA7 ... 25 A5
White Post La E9 ... 75 C2
White Post St SE14,
SE15 ... 140 C5
White Rd E15 ... 76 C1
Whites Ave IG2 ... 57 C3
Whites Dr BR2 ... 208 D2
White's Grounds
SE1 ... 117 C4 253 B2
White's Grounds Est
SE1 ... 253 B2
White's Mdw BR1 ... 210 C5
Whitespar DA14 ... 189 D6
White's Row E1 . 95 D2 243 C3
White's Sq SW4 ... 137 D1
White St UB1 ... 106 D4
Whitestile Rd TW8 ... 109 D1
Whitestone La NW3 ... 70 A5
Whitestone Wlk NW3 ... 70 A5
Whitethorn Ave UB7 ... 104 B6
Whitethorn Gdns
Croydon CR0 ... 222 B6
Enfield EN2 ... 17 B6
Whitethorn Pl UB7 ... 104 B5
Whitethorn St E3 ... 97 C2
Whiteways NW4 ... 46 D5
Whitewebbs Way BR5 .. 189 D2
Whitfield Ct
3 Dulwich SE21 ... 183 C6
Redbridge IG1 ... 56 B2
SW4 ... 270 A1
West Barnes SW20 ... 178 D1
Whitfield Gdns W1 ... 239 B4
Whitfield Ho NW8 ... 237 A5
Whitfield Pl W1 ... 239 B5
Whitfield Rd DA7 ... 147 B5
Upton E6 ... 77 C1
Whitfield St W1 . 93 C2 239 B4
Whitford Gdns CR4 ... 202 D6
Whitgift Ave CR2 ... 221 A3
Whitgift Ct CR2 ... 221 A3
Whitgift Ctr CR0 ... 221 A6
Whitgift Ho
Battersea SW11 ... 267 A2
Croydon CR2 ... 221 A3
Lambeth SE11 ... 260 C4
Whitgift Sch CR2 ... 221 A3
Whitgift St
Croydon CR0 ... 221 A5
SE11 ... 116 B2 260 C4
Whiting Ave IG11 ... 78 D1
Whitings Hill Prim Sch
EN5 ... 12 C6
Whitings Rd EN5 ... 12 C6
Whitings The IG2 ... 57 C4
Whitings Way E6 ... 100 C2
Whitington Ave EC3 ... 243 A1
Whitland Rd SM5 ... 202 B1
Whitley Cl TW19 ... 148 A5
Whitley Ho SW1 ... 269 B6
Whitley Rd N17 ... 33 C1
Whitlock Dr SW19 ... 157 A3
Whitman Ho 20 E2 ... 96 C4
Whitman Rd E3 ... 97 A3
Whitmead Cl CR2 ... 221 C2
Whitmore Cl N11 ... 31 B5
Whitmore Gdns NW10 .. 90 C5
Whitmore High Sch HA1,
HA2 ... 42 A1
Whitmore Ho
Friern Barnet N11 ... 30 D6
20 Hoxton E1 ... 95 C6
Whitmore Prim Sch
N1 ... 95 B6 235 D5
Whitmore Rd
Beckenham BR3 ... 207 B6
Harrow HA1 ... 42 A2
Hoxton N1 ... 95 C6
Whitnell Ct 7 SW15 ... 156 D6
Whitnell Way SW15 ... 156 D6
Whitney Ave IG4 ... 55 D5
Whitney Ho 6 SE22 ... 139 C2
Whitney Rd E10 ... 53 D2
Whitney Wlk DA14 ... 191 A4
Whitstable Cl
Beckenham BR3 ... 185 B2
Ruislip HA4 ... 61 C6
Whitstable Ho 11 W10 ... 90 D1
Whitstable Pl 9 CR0 ... 221 A4
Whitsters Ho SE1 ... 253 C2
Whitstone La BR3 ... 207 D4
Whittaker 3 NW9 ... 27 D3
Whittaker Ave TW10,
TW9 ... 153 D6
Whittaker Ct SW4 ... 270 B1
Whittaker Pl 28 TW10 .. 153 D6
Whittaker Rd
Cheam SM3 ... 217 B5
Forest Gate E6 ... 77 D1
Whittaker St SW1 ... 258 A3
Whittaker Way 19 SE1 .. 118 A2
Whittam Ho SE27 ... 183 A5
Whitta Rd E12 ... 77 D4
Whittell Gdns SE26 ... 162 C1
Whitten Lo N12 ... 30 C6
Whittingham 6 N17 ... 34 B3
Whittingham Com Prim Sch E17 ... 35 A2
Whittingham Ct W4 ... 133 C5
Whittingstall Mans
SW6 ... 264 D1
Whittingstall Rd
SW6 ... 135 B4 264 D1
Whittington Ave UB4 ... 83 D2
Whittington Ct
Fortis Green N2 ... 48 D4
Penge SE20 ... 184 B1
Whittington Hospl The
N19 ... 71 C6
Whittington Mews N12 .. 30 A6
Whittington Rd N22 ... 32 A3
Whittington Way HA5 ... 41 A4
Whittle 4 NW9 ... 27 D3
Whittlebury Cl SM5 ... 218 D1
Whittlebury Ho N4 ... 51 A2
Whittle Cl Southall UB1 .. 85 D1
Walthamstow E17 ... 53 A2
Whittle Rd
Heston TW5 ... 128 C5
Southall UB2 ... 107 D4
Whittlesea Cl HA3 ... 24 A3
Whittlesea Path HA3 ... 24 A2
Whittlesea Rd HA3 ... 24 A2
Whittlesey St
SE1 ... 116 C5 251 B3
WHITTON ... 152 A4
Whitton NW3 ... 70 D1
Whitton Ave W UB5,
UB6 ... 64 B3
Whitton Cl UB6 ... 65 B2
Whitton Dene TW3,
TW7 ... 152 B6
Whitton Dr UB6 ... 65 A2
Whitton Manor Rd
TW7 ... 152 A5
Whitton Rd
Hounslow TW3 ... 151 D6
Twickenham TW1 ... 153 A4
Whitton Road Rdbt
TW1 ... 152 D5
Whitton Sch TW2 ... 151 D2
Whitton Sta TW2 ... 152 A4
Whitton Waye TW2,
TW3 ... 151 C5
Whitton Wlk E3 ... 97 C4
Whitwell Ho 11 E5 ... 74 B6
Whitwell Rd E13 ... 99 A4
Whitworth Cres 1 EN3 ... 7 C6
Whitworth Ho SE1 ... 262 B5
Whitworth Rd SE18 ... 144 C5
South Norwood SE25 ... 205 D5
Whitworth St SE10 ... 120 C1
Whorlton Rd SE15 ... 140 B2
Whychcote Point NW2 .. 46 C2
Whymark Ave N22 ... 50 D6
Whytecroft TW5 ... 128 D5
Whyteville Ho E7 ... 77 B2
Whyteville Rd E7 ... 77 B2
Whytlaw Ho 10 E3 ... 97 B2
Wickersley Rd SW11 .. 137 A3
Wickers Oake SE19 ... 183 D6
Wicker St 24 E1 ... 96 B1
Wicket Rd UB6 ... 87 A4
Wickets The TW15 ... 170 A6
Wicket The CR0 ... 223 C3
Wickfield Ho 32 SE16 .. 118 A4
Wickford Ho 5 E1 ... 96 C3
Wickford St E1 ... 96 C3
Wickford Way E17 ... 52 D5
Wickham Ave
Cheam KT4, SM3 ... 216 C3
Croydon CR0 ... 207 A1
Wickham Chase BR4 .. 208 C2
Wickham Cl Enfield EN3 ... 6 C2
New Malden KT3 ... 199 D4
Stepney E1 ... 96 C2
Wickham Common Prim Sch BR4 ... 225 A4
Wickham Court Rd
BR4 ... 224 A6
Wickham Court Sch
BR4 ... 224 B4
Wickham Cres BR4 ... 224 A6
Wickham Ct DA16 ... 145 C3
Wickham Gdns SE4 ... 141 B2
Wickham Ho SW15 ... 156 D5
Wickham La SE2 ... 146 A6
Wickham Mews SE4 ... 141 B3
Wickham Rd
Beckenham BR3 ... 207 D6
Brockley SE4 ... 141 B2
Chingford E4 ... 36 A3
Croydon CR0 ... 207 B1
Harrow HA3 ... 24 B1
Wickham St
Bexley DA16 ... 145 C3
Vauxhall SE11 .. 116 B1 260 C2
Welling DA16 ... 146 A4
Wickham Way BR3 ... 208 A4
Wick Ho 1 KT1 ... 175 D2
Wick La Hackney E3 ... 75 B1
Stratford Marsh E3 ... 97 C6
Wickliffe Ave N3 ... 29 A1
Wickliffe Gdns HA9 ... 66 D6
Wicklow Ct SE26 ... 184 C5
Wicklow Ho N16 ... 51 D1
Wicklow St WC1 . 94 B4 233 C2
Wick Rd Hackney E9 ... 74 D2
Hackney E9 ... 75 A2
Teddington TW11 ... 175 C3
Wicks Cl SE12 ... 187 D6
Wickstead Ho TW8 ... 110 B1
Wicksteed Ho SE1 ... 262 B5
Wickway Ct 7 SE15 ... 139 D6
Wickwood St SE5 ... 138 D3
Widdenham Rd N7 ... 72 B4
Widdicombe Ave HA2 ... 63 A6
Widdin St E15 ... 76 C1
Widecombe Ct N2 ... 48 B4
Widecombe Gdns IG4 ... 56 A5
Widecombe Ho 32
SE5 ... 139 A3
Widecombe Rd SE9 ... 166 A1
Widecombe Way N2 ... 48 B5
Widegate St E1 ... 243 B3
Widenham Cl HA5 ... 40 C4
Wide Way CR4 ... 203 D6
Widewing Cl TW11 ... 175 B3
Widford 8 NW1 ... 71 B2
Widford Ho N1 ... 234 C3
Widgeon Cl E16 ... 99 B1
Widgeon Path SE28 ... 123 B3
Widley Rd W9 ... 91 C3
Widmer Ct TW5 ... 129 A3
WIDMORE ... 188 A1
Widmore Lodge Rd
BR1 ... 187 D1
Widmore Rd BR1 ... 187 C1
Hillingdon UB8 ... 82 D3
Widnes Ho 6 N7 ... 72 C3
Wieland Rd HA6 ... 22 A3
Wigan Ho E5 ... 52 B1
Wigeon Way UB4 ... 84 D1
Wiggins La TW10 ... 153 C2
Wiggins Mead NW9 ... 27 D3
Wigginton Ave HA9 ... 66 D2
Wigham Ho IG11 ... 79 A1
Wightman Rd N4, N8 ... 50 C4
Wighton Mews TW7 ... 130 C3
Wigley Rd TW13 ... 150 D3
Wigmore Ct 4 W13 ... 109 A5
Wigmore Hall* W1 ... 238 C2
Wigmore Pl W1 . 93 B1 238 C2
Wigmore Rd SM5 ... 202 C1
Wigmore St W1 . 93 A1 238 B2
Wigmore Wlk SM5 ... 218 B6
Wigram Ct SW11 ... 267 A2
Wigram Ho 7 E14 ... 119 D6
Wigram Rd E11 ... 55 C3
Wigram Sq E17 ... 54 A6
Wigston Cl N18 ... 33 C5
Wigston Rd E13 ... 99 B3
Wigton Gdns HA7 ... 26 A2
Wigton Pl SE11 ... 261 B1
Wigton Rd E17 ... 35 B2
Wilberforce Ct
Edgware HA8 ... 26 B6
2 SE28 ... 124 C5
Wilberforce Ho 4
SW11 ... 136 B2
Wilberforce Mews 9
SW4 ... 137 D1
Wilberforce Prim Sch
W10 ... 91 A4
Wilberforce Rd
Finsbury Pk N4 ... 72 D6
Hendon NW9 ... 46 A3
Highbury N4, N5 ... 73 A5
Wilberforce Way
SW19 ... 178 D4
Wilbraham Ho SW8 ... 270 A3
Wilbraham Pl SW1 ... 258 A4
Wilbury Prim Sch N18 .. 33 B5
Wilbury Way N18 ... 33 B5
Wilby Mews
W11 ... 113 B5 244 D4
Wilcox Cl SW8 ... 270 B4
Wilcox Gdns TW17 ... 192 B6
Wilcox Ho 5 E3 ... 97 B2
Wilcox Pl SW1 ... 259 B5
Wilcox Rd Sutton SM1 .. 217 D4
SW8 ... 138 A5 270 A4
Teddington TW11 ... 174 B6
Wildcroft Gdns HA8 ... 25 D4
Wildcroft Manor
SW15 ... 156 C4
Wildcroft Rd SW15 ... 156 C4
Wild Ct WC2 ... 94 B1 240 C2
Wilde Cl E8 ... 96 A6
Wilde Pl Edmonton N13 ... 32 D4
Wandsworth SW18 ... 158 B4
Wilder Cl HA4 ... 40 B1
Wilde Rd DA8 ... 147 D5
Wilderness Mews
SW4 ... 137 B1
Wilderness Rd BR7 ... 188 D3
Wilderness The
East Molesey KT8 ... 196 A4
Hampton TW12 ... 173 D6
Wilderton Rd N16 ... 51 C2
Wildes Cotts SM3 ... 217 A2
Wildfell Rd SE6 ... 163 D4
Wild Goose Dr SE14 ... 140 C4
Wild Hatch NW11 ... 47 C3
Wilding Ho 17 E9 ... 74 D2
Wild Marsh Ct EN3 ... 7 A6
Wild's Rents
SE1 ... 117 C3 263 A6
Wild St WC2 ... 94 B1 240 C1
Wildwood Cl SE12 ... 164 D4
Wildwood Gr NW3 ... 48 A1
Wildwood Rd NW11 ... 48 A2
Wildwood Rise NW11 ... 48 A1
Wildwood Terr NW3 ... 48 A1
Wilford Cl EN2 ... 5 B2
Wilford Ho 3 SE18 ... 122 D1
Wilford Rd CR0 ... 205 A2
Wilfred Fienburgh Ho
N7 ... 71 D4
Wilfred Owen Cl
SW19 ... 180 A4
Wilfred St
SW1 ... 115 C3 259 A6
Wilfrid Gdns W3 ... 89 A2
Wilkes Rd 3 TW8 ... 132 A6
Wilkes St E1 ... 95 D2 243 D4
Wilkie Ho SW1 ... 259 D2
Wilkins Cl Hayes UB3 ... 105 D1
Mitcham CR4 ... 180 C2
Wilkins Ho SW1 ... 269 A6
Wilkinson Cl UB10 ... 83 A6
Wilkinson Ct SW17 ... 180 B6
Wilkinson Gdns CR7 ... 183 C2
Wilkinson Ho
Isleworth TW7 ... 130 D2
N1 ... 235 D3
Twickenham TW2 ... 152 B2
Wilkinson Rd E16 ... 99 C1
Wilkinson St
SW8 ... 138 B5 270 C3
Wilkinson Way W4 ... 111 B4
Wilkin St NW5 ... 71 B2
Wilks Gdns CR0 ... 207 A1
Wilks Pl N1 ... 95 C5
Willan Rd N17 ... 33 C1
Willan Wall E16 ... 120 D6
Willard St SW8 ... 137 B2
Willbury Ho 4 N7 ... 71 D3
Willcocks Cl KT9 ... 214 A5
Willcott Rd W3 ... 110 D5
Will Crooks Gdns SE9 .. 143 D1
Willenfield Rd NW10 ... 89 A5
Willenhall Ave EN5 ... 14 A5
Willenhall Ct EN5 ... 14 A5
Willenhall Dr UB3 ... 105 C6
Willenhall Rd SE18 ... 122 D1
Willersley Ave
Blackfen DA15 ... 167 D4
Orpington BR6 ... 227 B5
Willersley Cl DA15 ... 167 D3
WILLESDEN ... 67 D1
Willesden Community Hospl The NW10 ... 68 A1
WILLESDEN GREEN ... 90 B6
Willesden Green Sta
NW2 ... 68 C2
Willesden Junction Sta
NW10 ... 89 D4
Willesden La NW2,
NW6 ... 68 D2
Willes Rd NW5 ... 71 B2
Willett Cl BR5 ... 211 C3
3 Northolt UB5 ... 84 C4
Willett Ho
7 Newham E13 ... 99 A5
Willett Ho *continued*
Stockwell SW9 ... 138 A2
Willett Pl CR7 ... 204 C4
Willett Rd CR7 ... 204 C4
Willett Way BR5 ... 211 C3
William Allen Ho HA8 ... 26 B3
William Ash Cl RM9 ... 80 B2
William Atkinson Ho
N17 ... 33 C3
William Banfield Ho 10
SW6 ... 135 B3
William Barefoot Dr
SE9 ... 166 C1
William Bellamy Jun & Inf Schs RM10 ... 81 C6
William Blake Ho 2
SE15 ... 140 A3
William Bonney Est 10
SW4 ... 137 D1
William Booth Meml Training Coll SE5 ... 139 B3
William Booth Rd
SE20 ... 184 A2
William Brown Ct
SE27 ... 160 D2
William Byrd Sch UB3 .. 127 A6
William Carey Way
HA1 ... 42 C3
William Caslon Ho 28
E2 ... 96 B5
William Channing Ho 6
E2 ... 96 B4
William C Harvey Sch
N17 ... 33 B1
William Cl
26 Finchley N2 ... 30 B1
Lewisham SE13 ... 142 A2
Southall UB2 ... 108 A4
William Covell Cl EN2 ... 4 B5
William Ct
4 Belvedere DA17 ... 125 C2
4 Ealing W5 ... 87 C2
Ilford IG6 ... 57 B5
William Davies Prim Sch
E7 ... 77 D2
William Davis Prim Sch
E2 ... 96 A3
William Dr HA7 ... 25 B5
William Dromey Ct
NW6 ... 69 B1
William Dunbar Ho
NW6 ... 91 B5
William Dyce Mews 1
SW16 ... 181 D6
William Ellis Sch NW5 .. 71 A5
William Ellis Way 16
SE16 ... 118 A3
William Evans Ho 9
SE8 ... 118 D2
William Ford CE Jun Sch
RM10 ... 81 C1
William Gdns SW15 ... 156 B6
William Guy Gdns 47
E3 ... 97 D4
William Harvey Ho 1
SW19 ... 157 A3
William Ho N13 ... 32 D4
William Hogarth Prim Sch
The W4 ... 111 C1
William Hunt Mans
SW13 ... 134 C6
William IV St
WC2 ... 116 A6 250 A5
William Margrie Cl 1
SE15 ... 140 A3
William Marsden Ho 2
SE27 ... 182 D6
William Mews
SW1 ... 114 D4 247 D1
William Morley Cl E6 ... 99 D6
William Morris Acad
W6 ... 112 D1
William Morris Cl E17 ... 53 B6
William Morris Gallery*
E17 ... 53 C6
William Morris Ho
W6 ... 134 D6
William Morris Prim Sch
CR4 ... 203 D6
William Morris Sch
E17 ... 35 A2
William Morris Way
SW6 ... 136 A3
William Patten Prim Sch
N16 ... 73 D6
William Perkin Ct UB6 .. 64 C2
William Pl 37 E3 ... 97 B5
William Rainbird Ho 9
N17 ... 33 D3
William Rathbone Ho 3
E2 ... 96 B4
William Rd
Regent's Pk
NW1 ... 93 C4 232 A1
Sutton SM1 ... 218 A3
Wimbledon SW19 ... 179 A3
William Rushbrooke Ho 4
SE16 ... 118 A2
Williams Ave E17 ... 35 B2
William Saville Ho 2
NW6 ... 91 B5
William's Bldgs 1 E2 ... 96 C3
Williams Cl
SW6 ... 135 A5 264 B4
Williams Coll EC1 ... 241 B3
Williams Dr TW3 ... 129 C1

Williams Gr
Kingston u T KT6 197 C3
Wood Green N22 32 C2
Williams Ho 10 Bow E3 97 C4
9 Hackney E9 96 B6
14 Streatham SW2 160 C3
7 Tottenham N17 33 D3
Willesden NW2 68 C5
Williams La
Morden SM4 202 A4
Mortlake SW14 133 A3
William Smith Ho 10
DA17 125 C3
Williamson Cl SE10 120 D1
Williamson Ct SE17 262 A1
Williamson Rd N4 50 D3
Williamson St N7 72 A4
Williamson Way NW7 29 A4
William Sq 15 SE16 119 A6
Williams Rd UB2 107 A2
William's Rd W13 109 A5
William St Barking IG11 79 A1
Carshalton SM5 218 D5
SW1 114 D4 247 D1
Tottenham N17 33 D3
Walthamstow E10 53 D3
Williams Terr CR0 220 C2
William Torbitt Prim Sch
IG2 57 D4
William Tyndale Prim Sch
N1 72 D1
William Wilberforce Ho 1
SE27 182 D6
William Winter Ct 23
SW2 160 C4
William Wood Ho 3
SE26 162 C1
Willifield Way NW11 47 C4
Willingale Cl IG8 37 C4
Willingdon Rd N22 32 D1
Willingham Cl 4 NW5 71 C3
Willingham Terr NW5 71 C3
Willingham Way KT1 176 C1
Willington Ct E5 75 A5
Willington Prep Sch
SW19 179 B5
Willington Rd SW9 138 A2
Willis Ave SM2, SM5 218 C2
Willis Ct CR7 204 C3
Willis Ho 2 Ilford E12 78 C5
8 Poplar E14 119 D6
Willis Rd E15 98 D5
Thornton Heath CR0 205 A2
Willis St E14 97 D1
Willis Yd N14 15 D4
Willlows The CR0 223 A6
Will Miles Ct 6 SW19 180 A3
Willmore End SW19 179 D1
Willoughby Ave CR0 220 B4
Willoughby Gr N17 34 B3
Willoughby Ho EC2 242 C3
34 Wapping E1 118 B5
Willoughby La N17 34 B3
Willoughby Mews N17 34 B3
Willoughby Park Rd
N17 34 B3
Willoughby Rd
Hampstead NW3 70 B4
Hornsey N8 50 C5
Kingston u T KT2 176 B2
Twickenham TW1 153 D6
Willoughby St WC1 240 A3
Willoughbys The
SW14 133 C1
Willoughby Way SE7 121 B2
Willow Ave
Barnes SW13 133 D3
DA15 168 A5
Yiewsley UB7 104 B6
Willowbank SW6 135 A2
Willow Bank TW10 153 B1
Willowbank Rd SE15 139 D6
Willowbay Cl EN5 12 D5
Willow Bridge Rd N1 73 A2
Willow Brook Prim Sch
E10 53 C1
Willowbrook Rd
Southall UB2 107 C3
Stanwell TW19 148 A2
Willow Bsns Pk SE26 162 C1
Willow Cl BR2 210 B4
Brentford TW8 131 C6
Buckhurst Hill IG9 21 D1
12 Catford SE6 164 D3
Sidcup DA5 169 B5
Willow Cotts
Carshalton CR4 202 D2
Feltham TW13 151 A1
Richmond TW9 132 C6
Willowcourt Ave HA3 43 B4
Willowcroft SE3 142 D1
Willow Ct
Ashford TW16 171 C3
3 Beckenham BR3 185 C2
Brixton SW9 138 C4
Chiswick W4 133 C5
8 Dagenham RM8 58 D2
EC2 243 A6
Edgware HA8 26 A6
6 Finchley N12 29 D6
Harrow HA3 24 D2
Headstone HA2 24 A1
Ilford IG1 79 A3
Islington N7 72 B3
Kingston u T KT3 198 D6
8 London E11 76 C6
Mitcham CR4 202 C5

Willow Ct *continued*
40 Paddington W2 91 C2
3 Streatham SW16 160 B1
Thornton Heath CR7 205 B4
Willow Ctr The CR4 202 D3
Willow Dean HA5 22 D1
Willowdene
Highgate N6 48 D2
1 Peckham SE15 140 B4
5 SE15 140 B5
Willow Dene WD23 8 C4
Willowdene Cl TW2 152 A4
Willowdene Ct N20 14 A4
Willow Dene Sch
SE18 145 C4
Willow Dr EN5 1 A1
Willow End
Northwood HA6 22 A4
Surbiton KT6 198 A1
Totteridge N20 13 C2
Willow Farm La SW15 134 B2
Willowfields Cl SE18 123 C1
Willowfield Sec Sch
E17 52 D6
Willow Gdns
Heston TW5 129 C4
Ruislip HA4 61 D6
Willow Gn
Borehamwood WD6 11 B6
Grahame Pk NW9 27 C2
Willow Gr BR7 188 D4
Newham E13 99 A5
Ruislip HA4 39 D1
Willow Hall NW3 70 B4
Willowhayne Dr KT12 194 B2
Willowhayne Gdns
KT4 216 C4
Willow Ho TW14 150 B6
Willow Ho
17 Finchley N2 30 B1
9 Maitland Pk NW3 70 D2
North Kensington W10 90 D3
Teddington TW11 175 C3
Willow La
Mitcham CR4 202 D3
Woolwich SE18 122 C2
Willow Lo
6 Ashford TW16 171 D3
Fulham SW6 134 D4
New Barnet EN5 14 A6
Putney SW15 134 B2
Willow Lodge 10 SW8 137 B2
Willow Manor SM1 217 B4
Willowmead Cl W5 87 D2
Willowmere
Esher KT10 212 A4
Ladywell SE13 163 D6
Willow Mount CR0 221 C5
Willow Pl SW1 115 C2 259 B4
Willow Rd
Dagenham RM6 59 A3
Ealing W5 110 A4
Enfield EN1 5 C3
Hampstead NW3 70 B4
New Malden KT3 199 A5
Wallington SM6 219 B1
Willows Ave SM4 201 D4
Willows Cl HA5 22 C1
Willows Ct 3 SW19 179 C3
Willows Sch The UB4 84 D3
Willow St
Broadgate
EC2 95 C3 243 A6
Chingford E4 20 B4
Willows Terr NW10 89 D5
Willows The
Beckenham BR3 185 C2
Claygate KT10 212 C2
Loughton IG10 21 D6
Wallend E12 78 C1
Whetstone N20 14 A1
Willowtree Cl UB10 61 A5
Willow Tree Cl
Hayes UB4 84 C3
Northolt UB5 63 A2
14 Old Ford E3 97 B6
Wandsworth SW18 157 D3
Willow Tree Ct DA14 189 D5
5 Wembley HA0 65 D3
Willow Tree La UB4 84 C3
Willow Tree Prim Sch
UB5 63 A2
Willowtree Way SW16 182 C2
Willow Tree Wlk BR1 187 B2
Willow Vale BR7 188 D4
Shepherd's Bush W12 112 A5
Willow View SW19 180 B2
Willow Way Finchley N3 29 D3
Forest Hill SE26 162 C1
9 Shepherd's Bush
W11 112 D6
Sunbury TW16 194 A5
Twickenham TW2 151 D2
Wembley HA0 65 A5
West Ewell KT19 215 B2
Willow Wlk
Bermondsey
SE1 117 D2 263 C4
Cheam SM1, SM3 217 B5
15 Finchley N2 30 B1
Harringay N15 50 D5
Locksbottom BR6 226 D5
Southgate N21 16 B5
Walthamstow E17 53 B4
Willow Wood Cres
SE25 205 C3
Willridge Ct E11 54 B2
Willrose Cres SE2 124 B1
Willsbridge Ct 1
SE15 139 D6

Wills Cres TW3 151 D5
Wills Gr NW7 28 B5
Will Thorne Pav The
E16 100 A1
Wilman Gr E8 74 A1
Wilmar Cl UB4 83 B3
Wilmar Gdns BR4 207 D1
Wilmcote Ho W2 91 D2
Wilment Ct NW2 68 C5
Wilmer Cl KT2 176 B5
Wilmer Cres KT2 176 B5
Wilmer Gdns 22 N1 95 C6
Wilmer Ho 6 E3 97 A5
Wilmer Lea Cl E15 76 B1
Wilmer Pl N16 73 D6
Wilmers Ct 5 NW10 89 B6
Wilmer Way N14 31 D5
Wilmington Ave W4 133 B5
Wilmington Ct SW16 182 A3
Wilmington Gdns IG11 79 C1
Wilmington Sq
WC1 94 C4 234 A1
Wilmington St WC1 234 A1
Wilmot Cl Finchley N2 30 A1
SE15 140 A5
Wilmot Ho 14 SM2 218 A2
Wilmot Pl
Camden Town NW1 71 C1
Ealing W7 108 C5
Wilmot Rd Leyton E10 75 D6
Tottenham N17 51 B6
Wallington SM5 218 D3
Wilmot St E2 96 B3
Wilmount St SE18 122 D2
Wilna Rd SW18 158 A4
Wilnett Ct 4 RM6 58 B2
Wilnett Villas 5 RM6 58 B2
Wilsham St
W11 113 A5 244 A4
Wilshaw Cl NW4 46 A6
Wilshaw Ho 10 SE8 141 C5
Wilshaw St SE14 141 C4
Wilsmere Dr
Harrow HA3 24 C3
Northolt UB5 63 A3
Wilson Ave CR4 180 C2
Wilson Cl Croydon CR2 221 B3
Wembley HA9 44 B2
Wilson Ct 9 SE28 123 A3
Wilson Dr HA9 44 B2
Wilson Gdns HA1 42 A2
Wilson Gr SE16 118 B4
Wilson Ho
39 Clapham SW8 137 D3
2 SE7 143 C6
South Hampstead NW6 70 A1
Wilson Rd
Camberwell SE5 139 C4
Chessington KT9 214 B2
Newham E6 99 D4
Redbridge IG1 56 B2
Wilson's Ave 4 N17 33 D1
Wilson's Pl E14 97 B1
Wilson's Rd W6 112 D1
Wilsons Sch SM6 220 A2
Wilson St
Broadgate
EC2 95 B2 242 D4
Southgate N21 16 C4
Walthamstow E17 54 A4
Wilstone Cl UB4 85 A3
Wiltern Ct NW2 69 A2
Wilthorne Gdns RM10 81 D1
Wilton Ave W4 111 C1
Wilton Cres
Merton SW19 179 B2
SW1 115 A4 248 A1
Wilton Ct
3 Edgware HA8 26 D5
Muswell Hill N10 31 A1
4 Richmond TW10 154 A6
7 Stepney E1 96 B1
7 Woodford IG8 37 A4
Wilton Est E8 74 A2
Wilton Gdns
East Molesey KT8 195 C6
Walton-on-T KT12 194 D1
Wilton Gr
Merton SW19 179 B2
New Malden KT3 199 D3
Wilton Ho
8 Camberwell SE22 139 C2
Chislehurst BR7 189 B2
Ealing W13 109 B6
Wilton Mews
SW1 115 A3 258 B6
Wilton Par TW13 150 B2
Wilton Pl
2 Beckenham BR3 208 A6
4 Harrow HA1 42 D3
SW1 115 A4 248 A1
Wilton Rd
Abbey Wood SE2 124 C2
Cockfosters EN4 2 D1
Hounslow TW4 128 D2
Mitcham SW19 180 C3
Muswell Hill N10 31 A1
Westminster
SW1 115 C2 259 A4
Wilton Row SW1 248 A1
Wilton Sq N1 95 B6 235 C6
Wilton St SW1 115 B3 258 C6
Wilton Terr SW1 258 A6
Wilton Villas N1 235 C5
Wilton Way E8 74 A2
Wiltshire Cl
Edgware NW7 27 D5
SW3 257 C3
Wiltshire Ct
Barking IG11 79 A2

Wiltshire Ct *continued*
2 Finsbury Pk N4 50 B1
Wiltshire Gdns
Stoke Newington N4 51 A3
Twickenham TW2 152 A3
Wiltshire La Pinner HA5 40 A5
Ruislip HA4 39 D6
Wiltshire Rd
Brixton SW9 138 C2
Thornton Heath CR7 204 C6
Wiltshire Row
N1 95 B6 235 D5
Wilverley Cres KT3 199 C3
Wimbart Rd SW2 160 B4
WIMBLEDON 179 B4
Wimbledon Bridge
SW19 179 B4
Wimbledon Central
SW19 179 B4
Wimbledon Chase Prim
Sch SW20 179 A2
Wimbledon Chase Sta
SW20 179 A1
Wimbledon Cl 2
SW20 178 D3
Wimbledon Coll
SW19 178 D3
Wimbledon Common*
SW19 178 B6
Wimbledon Common Prep
Sch SW19 178 D3
Wimbledon High Sch
SW19 179 A4
Wimbledon Hill Rd
SW19 179 B4
Wimbledon Lawn Tennis
Mus* SW19 157 A1
Wimbledon Park Ct
SW19 157 B3
Wimbledon Park
Montessori Sch
SW18 157 C2
Wimbledon Park Prim Sch
SW19 157 D2
Wimbledon Park Rd SW18,
SW19 157 B3
Wimbledon Park Side
SW19 156 D3
Wimbledon Park Sta
SW19 157 C1
Wimbledon Rd SW17 180 A6
Wimbledon Sch of Art
SW19 179 A2
Wimbledon Sch of Art
Annexe SW19 179 C3
Wimbledon Sta SW19 179 B4
Wimbledon Stad
SW17 180 A6
Wimbledon Stadium Bsns
Ctr SW17 157 D1
Wimbledon Windmill
Mus* SW19 156 C1
Wimbolt St E2 96 A4
Wimborne 2 DA14 190 B6
Wimborne Ave
Hayes UB4 84 B1
Southall UB2 107 C2
St Paul's Cray BR5, BR7 211 D5
Wimborne Cl
Buckhurst Hill IG9 21 C2
Lewisham SE12 164 D6
North Cheam KT4 200 C1
Wimborne Ct 1 UB5 63 C2
Wimborne Dr
Pinner HA5 41 A2
Queensbury NW9 44 C6
Wimborne Gdns W13 87 B2
Wimborne Ho
Canning Town E16 120 D6
Croydon CR0 206 C4
Marylebone NW1 237 B5
South Lambeth SW8 270 D3
Upper Tooting SW12 159 C1
Wimborne Rd
Edmonton N9 18 A2
Tottenham N17 33 C1
Wimborne Way BR3 207 A5
Wimbourne Ct
Mitcham SW19 180 B3
N1 235 C4
South Croydon CR2 221 C2
Wimbourne St
N1 95 B5 235 C4
Wimbush Ho 3 N12 29 D5
Wimpole Cl
Bromley BR2 209 C5
1 Kingston u T KT1 176 C1
Wimpole Mews
W1 93 B2 238 C3
Wimpole St W1 93 B1 238 C2
Wimshurst Cl CR0 204 A1
Winans Wlk SW9 138 C3
Winant Ho 19 E14 119 D6
Wincanton Cres UB5 63 C3
Wincanton Ct 2 N11 31 A4
Wincanton Gdns IG6 56 D6
Wincanton Rd SW18 157 B4
Winchcombe Rd SM5 202 C1
Winchcomb Gdns SE9 143 D2
Winchelsea Ave DA7 147 B5
Winchelsea Cl SW15 156 D6
Winchelsea Ho 16
SE16 118 C4
Winchelsea Rd
Becontree NW10 89 B6
Forest Gate E7 77 A4
Tottenham N17 51 C6
Winchelsey Rise CR2 221 D2
Winchendon Rd
Fulham SW6 135 B4 264 D2

Winchendon Rd *continued*
Teddington TW11,
TW12 174 B6
Winchester Ave
Brondesbury NW6 69 A1
Heston TW5 129 B6
Queensbury NW9 44 C6
Winchester Cl
Beckenham BR2 208 D6
Enfield EN1 17 C6
Kingston u T KT2 176 D3
11 Newham E6 100 B1
SE17 261 D3
Winchester Ct
15 Belvedere DA17 125 C1
5 Higham Hill E17 35 A2
Richmond TW9 132 B2
W8 245 C2
Winchester Dr HA5 40 D4
Winchester Ho
5 Barking IG11 80 A1
Bayswater W2 236 A1
Chelsea SW3 266 D5
1 Greenwich SE18 143 D5
24 Tower Hamlets E3 97 B4
Twickenham TW1 153 C4
Winchester Mews
KT4 216 D6
Winchester Pal* SE1 252 C4
Winchester Pk BR2 208 D6
Winchester Pl
6 Dalston E8 73 D3
Highgate N6 49 B1
Winchester Rd
Beckenham BR2 208 D6
Bexley DA7 146 D3
Chingford E4 36 A3
Edmonton N9 18 A3
Harlington UB3 127 C5
Harrow HA3 44 A5
Highgate N6 49 B1
Ilford IG1 79 B5
Northwood HA6 40 A6
South Hampstead NW3 70 B1
St Margarets TW1 153 B5
Twickenham TW13 151 B1
Walton-on-T KT12 194 A1
Winchester Sq SE1 252 C4
Winchester St
Acton W3 111 A4
SW1 115 B1 258 D2
Winchester Wlk SE1 252 C4
Winchet Wlk CR0 206 C3
Winchfield Cl HA3 43 C3
Winchfield Ho SW15 155 D5
Winchfield Rd SE26 185 A5
Winch Ho
Isle of Dogs E14 119 D3
SW10 266 B4
Winchilsea Cres KT8 174 A1
Winchilsea Ho NW8 229 D1
WINCHMORE HILL 16 D4
Winchmore Hill Rd N14,
N21 16 A4
Winchmore Hill Sta
N21 16 D4
Winchmore Sch N21 17 A2
Winchmore Villas N21 16 B4
Winchstone Cl TW17 192 B5
Winckley Cl HA3 44 B4
Wincott St
SE11 116 C2 261 B3
Wincrofts Dr SE9 145 B1
Windall Cl SE20 184 A2
Windborough Rd SM5 219 A1
Windcott Ct HA3 43 C2
Windermere NW1 231 D2
12 Putney SW15 156 D5
Windermere Ave
Golders Green N3 47 C6
Kensal Rise NW6 91 A6
Merton SW19 201 D6
Ruislip HA4 40 D2
Wembley HA9 43 C1
Windermere Cl BR6 226 D5
East Bedfont TW14 149 D3
Stanwell TW19 148 A2
Windermere Ct
Barnes SW13 133 D6
Barnet EN5 1 D1
Carshalton SM5 219 A5
Wembley HA9 43 C2
Windermere Gdns IG4 56 A4
Windermere Gr HA9 43 C1
Windermere Hall HA8 26 B5
Windermere Ho
Isleworth TW1 152 D6
Tower Hamlets E3 97 B3
Windermere Point 3
SE15 140 C5
Windermere Rd
Brentford W5 109 C3
Croydon CR0 205 D1
Kingston u T SW15 177 C5
Mitcham SW16 181 D1
Muswell Hill N10 31 B2
Southall UB1 85 B2
Upper Holloway N19 71 C6
West Wickham BR4 224 C6
Windermere Way UB7 104 B5
Winders Rd SW11 136 C3
Windfield Cl SE26 184 D6
Windham Rd TW9 132 B2
Winding Way RM8 80 C5
Windlass Pl SE8 119 A2
Windlesham Gr SW19 156 D3
Windley Cl SE23 162 C2
Windmill WC1 240 C4
Windmill Alley 7 W4 111 C2
Windmill Ave UB2 108 A4

Windmill Bridge Ho 1
CR0 205 C1
Windmill Bsns Ctr
UB2 108 A5
Windmill Bsns Village
TW16 171 C2
Windmill Cl
Ashford TW16 171 C3
12 Bermondsey SE1 118 A2
Kingston u T KT6 197 C2
4 Lewisham SE13 142 A3
Windmill Ct
Brentford W5 109 C2
Brondesbury NW2 69 A2
Bushey WD23 8 B3
Windmill Dr BR2 225 C4
Clapham SW4 159 B6
Cricklewood NW2 69 A5
Windmill Gdns
Brixton SW2 160 B5
Enfield EN2 4 C2
Windmill Gr CR0 205 A3
Windmill Hill Enfield EN2 5 A2
1 Hampstead NW3 70 A4
Hampstead NW3 70 A5
Ruislip HA4 39 D1
Windmill Ho
4 Millwall E14 119 C2
SE1 251 B3
Windmill La
Barnet Gate EN5 11 D5
Bushey WD23 8 C3
Greenford UB6 86 A2
Isleworth TW7, UB2,
W7 108 C2
Southall UB2 108 A4
Stratford E15 76 B2
Thames Ditton KT7 197 B2
Windmill Lo TW16 171 C2
Windmill Pas 10 W4 111 C2
Windmill Pl UB1 108 A5
Windmill Rd
Brentford TW8, W5 109 C1
Charlton TW16 171 C2
Chiswick W4 111 C2
Edmonton N18 33 B6
Hampton TW12 174 A5
Mitcham CR4 203 C5
Roehampton SW19 156 B1
Thornton Heath CR0 205 A2
Wandsworth SW18 158 B5
Windmill Rd W TW16 171 C1
Windmill Rise KT2 176 D3
Windmill Row SE11 261 A1
Windmill St
Bloomsbury
W1 93 D2 239 C3
Bushey WD23 8 C3
Windmill Terr TW17 193 C2
Windmill Trad Est
CR4 203 C5
Windmill Way HA4 39 D1
Windmill Wlk SE1 251 B2
Windmore Cl HA0 65 A3
Windrose Cl SE16 118 D4
Windrush KT3 199 A5
Windrush Cl
Battersea SW11 136 B1
Chiswick W4 133 A5
Ickenham UB10 60 B4
Windrush Ho NW8 236 D4
Windrush La SE23 162 D1
Windrush Prim Sch
SE28 124 B5
Windrush Rd NW10 89 B6
Windsock Cl 1 SE16 119 B2
Windsor Ave
Cheam SM3 217 A5
East Molesey KT8 195 C6
Edgware HA8 10 D1
Higham Hill E17 35 A1
Hillingdon UB10 60 D1
Merton SW19 180 A2
New Malden KT3 199 A4
Windsor Cl
Brentford TW8 131 B6
Chislehurst BR7 188 D5
Harrow HA2 63 C5
Hendon N3 29 A1
Pinner HA6 22 A1
West Norwood SE27 183 A6
Windsor Cres
Harrow HA2 63 C5
Wembley HA9 66 D5
Windsor Ct
Battersea SW11 136 B3
Bayswater W2 245 C6
Bickley BR1 210 A6
Bushey WD23 8 A4
Chelsea SW3 257 B2
2 Clapham SW4 137 C1
Edgware HA8 26 B3
Friern Barnet N11 30 D5
Fulham SW6 135 A2
Osidge N14 15 C4
20 Rotherhithe SE16 118 D5
17 Sidcup DA14 168 A1
South Norwood SE19 183 C2
Sunbury TW16 172 A3
Temple Fortune NW11 47 A3
Walthamstow E17 53 B6
4 Wandsworth SW18 157 C6
West Hampstead NW3 69 C4
5 West Wickham BR4 207 D1
Windsor Ctr The SE27 183 A6
Windsor Dr EN4 14 D5
Windsor Gdns
Hayes UB3 105 B3
Paddington W9 91 C3
Wallington CR0 220 A5

Windsor Gr SE27 183 A6
Windsor Hall [11] E16 121 B5
Windsor Ho
[4] Acton Green W4 111 A1
Brondesbury NW2 69 A2
[4] Globe Town E2 96 D4
[2] Hendon NW4 28 D1
[7] Northolt UB5 63 C2
Queensbury NW9 44 C5
Regent's Pk NW1 231 D2
Shoreditch N1 235 B4
Stanmore HA7 25 B5
Stoke Newington N4 51 A1
Windsor Lo KT3 199 A4
Windsor Mews
Catford SE6 164 A3
Forest Hill SE23 163 A3
Windsor Park Rd UB3 127 D5
Windsor Pk SW19 180 A2
Windsor Pl SW1 259 B4
Windsor Rd
Ashford TW16 172 A4
Barnet EN5 12 D5
Chingford E4 35 D6
Cranford TW4, TW5 128 C3
DA6 147 A1
Dagenham RM8 81 A5
Ealing W5 110 A6
Forest Gate E7 77 C3
Harrow HA3 24 B2
Hendon N3 29 A1
Ilford IG1 79 A4
Kingston u T KT2 176 A3
Leyton E10 75 D6
Palmers Green N13 16 C1
Richmond TW9 132 B3
Southall UB2 107 B3
South Norwood CR7 182 D1
Teddington TW11 174 B5
Tottenham N17 34 A1
Upper Holloway N7 72 A5
Wanstead E11 77 A6
Willesden NW2 68 B2
Worcester Pk KT4 216 A6
Windsor St N1 94 D6 234 D6
Windsor Terr
N1 95 A4 235 B2
Windsor Way
W14 113 A2 254 A4
Windsor Wharf E9 75 B3
Windsor Wlk
Camberwell SE5 139 B3
Walton-on-T KT12 194 D1
Windspoint Dr SE15 140 B6
Windus Rd N16 51 D1
Windus Wlk N16 51 D1
Windy Ridge BR1 188 A2
Windy Ridge Cl SW19 178 D5
Wine Cl E1 118 C6
Wine Office Ct EC4 241 B2
Winery La KT1 198 B6
Winey Cl KT9 213 C1
Winfield Ho [3] SW11 136 B3
Winford Ct [16] SE15 140 A4
Winford Ho E3 75 B1
Winford Par [6] UB1 85 D1
Winforton St SE10 142 A4
Winfrith Rd SW18 158 A3
Wingate Cres CR0 204 A3
Wingate Ho
[26] Bromley E3 97 D4
[8] Stoke Newington N16 73 B4
Wingate Rd
Hammersmith W6 112 B3
Ilford IG1 78 D3
Sidcup DA14 190 C4
Wingate Trad Est [11]
N17 33 D3
Wingfield Ct
[5] Blackwall E14 120 B6
Sidcup DA15 167 D3
Wingfield Ho
Paddington NW6 91 D5
[16] Spitalfields E2 95 D4
Wingfield Mews SE15 140 A2
Wingfield Prim Sch
SE3 143 B2
Wingfield Rd
Kingston u T KT2 176 C4
Leyton E15 76 C4
Walthamstow E17 53 D4
Wingfield St SE15 140 A2
Wingfield Way HA4 62 B2
Wingford Rd SW2 160 A5
Wingham [3] NW5 71 A2
Wingham Ho [3] SE26 184 B5
Wingmore Rd SE24 139 A2
Wingrad Ho [18] E1 96 C2
Wingrave SE17 262 C3
Wingrave Rd W6 134 C6
Wingreen [15] NW8 91 D6
Wingrove Ho E4 19 D4
Wingrove Rd SE6 164 C2
Wings Cl SM1 217 C4
Winicotte Ho W2 236 D4
Winifred Cl EN5 11 D5
Winifrede Paul Ho [7]
NW5 71 B4
Winifred Pl N12 30 A5
Winifred Rd
Dagenham RM8 59 A1
Hampton TW12 173 C6
Merton SW19 179 C2
Winifred St E16 122 B5
Winifred Terr EN1 17 D4
Winkfield Rd
Newham E13 99 B5
Wood Green N22 32 C2
Winkley Ct
Cranley Gdns N10 49 B5
Winkley Ct *continued*
Harrow HA2 63 C5
Winkley St [6] E2 96 B5
Winkworth Cotts [14] E1 96 C3
Winlaton Rd BR1 186 B6
Winmill Rd RM8 81 B5
Winn Bridge Cl IG8 37 D2
Winn Common Rd
SE18 145 C6
Winnett St W1 249 C6
Winningales Ct IG5 56 A6
Winnings Wlk UB5 63 A2
Winnington Cl N2 48 B3
Winnington Ho
[10] Kensal Town W10 91 A3
[8] SE5 139 A5
Winnington Rd
Enfield EN3 6 C6
Hampstead Garden Suburb
N2 48 B3
Winnipeg Dr [3] BR6 227 D2
Winnipeg Ho UB4 84 B3
Winn Rd SE12 165 B3
Winns Ave E17 53 B6
Winns Mews N15 51 C5
Winns Prim Sch The
E17 35 B1
Winns Terr E17 53 C6
Winsbeach E17 36 B1
Winscombe Cres W5 87 D3
Winscombe Ct W5 87 D3
Winscombe St N19 71 B6
Winscombe Way HA7 25 A5
Winsford Rd SE6 163 B1
Winsford Terr N18 33 B5
Winsham Gr SW11 159 A6
Winsham Ho NW1 232 D2
Winslade Ho [4] E5 74 B6
Winslade Rd SW2 160 A6
Winslade Way SE6 163 D4
Winsland Mews W2 236 C2
Winsland St W2 92 B1 236 C2
Winsley St W1 239 B2
Winslow SE17 263 A1
Winslow Cl
[2] Neasden NW10 67 C5
Pinner HA5 40 B3
Winslow Gr E4 20 C2
Winslow Rd W6 134 C6
Winslow Way TW13 151 A1
Winsmoor Ct EN2 4 D2
Winsor Prim Sch E6 100 C1
Winsor Terr E6 100 C2
Winstanley Rd SW11 136 B2
Winston Ave NW9 45 C2
Winston Cl Harrow HA3 24 D4
Romford RM7 59 D5
Winston Ct [7] BR1 187 B2
Harrow HA3 23 D3
Winston Ho WC1 239 D6
Winston Rd N16 73 B4
Winston Way IG1 79 A5
Winston Wlk [2] W4 111 B2
Winter Ave E6 100 A6
Winterberry Ct [2] N12 29 D6
Winterborne Ave BR6 227 B5
Winterbourne Ho W11 244 A5
Winterbourne Inf Sch
CR7 204 C5
Winterbourne Jun Boys'
Sch CR7 204 C5
Winterbourne Jun Girls'
Sch CR7 204 C5
Winterbourne Rd
Dagenham RM8 80 C6
Forest Hill SE6 163 B3
Thornton Heath CR7 204 C5
Winter Box Wlk TW10 154 B6
Winterbrook Rd SE24 161 A5
Winterburn Cl N11 31 A4
Winterfold Cl SW19 157 A2
Wintergreen Cl [7] E6 100 A2
Winterleys [7] NW6 91 B5
Winter Lo [9] SE16 118 A1
Winter's Ct E4 19 D1
Winterslow Ho [20] SE5 139 A3
Winters Rd KT7 197 B2
Winterstoke Gdns NW7 28 A5
Winterstoke Rd SE6 163 B3
Winterton Ct KT1 175 D2
Winterton Ho [15] E1 96 C1
Winterton Pl SW10 266 B6
Winterwell Rd SW2 160 A6
Winthorpe Rd SW15 135 A1
Winthrop Ho [10] W12 112 B6
Winthrop St E1 96 B3
Winthrop Wlk HA9 66 A5
Winton Ave N11 31 C3
Winton Cl N9 18 D4
Winton Ct [15] KT6 197 D2
Winton Gdns HA8 26 B3
Winton Prim Sch
N1 94 B5 233 C3
Winton Rd BR6 226 D4
Winton Way SW16 182 C5
Wintour Ho HA9 65 D6
Wirrall Ho [15] SE26 162 A1
Wirral Wood Cl BR7 188 C4
Wisbeach Rd CR0 205 B4
Wisbech [5] N4 50 B1
Wisden Ho SW8 270 D5
Wisdom Ct [7] TW7 131 A2
Wisdons Cl RM7, RM9 59 D1
Wise La NW7 28 A4
Wiseman Ct [12] SE19 183 C5
Wiseman Rd E10 75 C6
Wise Rd E15 98 B6
Wiseton Rd SW17 158 D3
Wishart Rd SE3 143 D3
Wishaw Wlk N13 32 A4
Wisley Ho SW1 259 C2
Wisley Rd
Balham SW11 159 A6
St Paul's Cray BR5 190 B3
Wistaria Cl BR6 226 D6
Wisteria Cl
Edgware NW7 27 D4
Ilford IG1 78 D3
Wisteria Ho SE4 141 A2
Wisteria Rd SE13 142 B1
Wistow Ho [14] E2 96 A6
Witanhurst La N6 49 A1
Witan St E2 96 B4
Witchwood Ho [10]
SW9 138 C2
Witcombe Point [14]
SE15 140 A4
Witham Ct Leyton E10 75 D5
Upper Tooting SW17 158 D1
Witham Ho [34] SE5 139 A3
Witham Rd
Dagenham RM10 81 C3
Ealing W13 109 B5
Hounslow TW7 130 B4
Penge SE20 206 C6
Witherby Cl CR0 221 C4
Witherington Rd N5 72 C3
Withers Cl KT9 213 C2
Withers Mead NW9 27 D2
Withers Pl EC1 242 B6
Witherston Way SE9 166 C1
Withington Rd N2 30 C2
Withycombe Rd SW19 156 D4
Withy Ho [4] E1 96 D3
Withy La HA4 39 A4
Withy Mead E4 20 B1
Witley Cres CR0 224 A2
Witley Ct Southall UB2 107 B2
WC1 240 A5
Witley Gdns UB2 107 B2
Witley Ho [2] SW2 160 B4
Witley Ind Est UB2 107 B2
Witley Point [6] SW15 156 B3
Witley Rd N19 71 C6
Witney Cl
Ickenham UB10 60 B4
Pinner HA5 23 B4
Witney Path SE23 162 D1
Wittenham Way E4 20 B1
Witten Ho KT3 199 B1
Wittering Cl KT2 175 D5
Wittering Ho [9] SW11 136 D3
Wittersham Rd BR1 186 D5
Witts Ho KT2 198 B6
Wivenhoe Cl SE15 140 B2
Wivenhoe Ct TW4 129 B1
Wivenhoe Rd IG11 102 B5
Wiverton Rd SE26 184 C5
Wixom Ho SE9 143 C1
Wix Prim Sch SW4 137 B1
Wix Rd RM9 102 D6
Wix's La SW4 137 B1
Woburn W13 87 B2
Woburn Cl Bushey WD23 8 A5
SE28 102 D1
Wimbledon SW19 180 A4
Woburn Ct
[32] Bermondsey SE16 118 B1
Croydon CR0 205 A1
[1] DA6 147 A1
Richmond TW9 132 B2
[4] Woodford E18 37 A1
Woburn Pl WC1 94 A3 240 A5
Woburn Rd
Carshalton SM5 202 C1
Croydon CR0 205 A1
Woburn Sq
WC1 93 D3 239 D5
Woburn Twr [14] UB5 84 D4
Woburn Wlk WC1 232 D1
Wodeham Gdns [1] E1 96 B2
Wodehouse Ave SE15 139 D4
Wodehouse Ct [10] W3 111 A3
Woffington Cl KT1,
KT8 175 C2
Woking Cl SW15 133 D1
Wolcot Ho NW1 232 B3
Woldham Pl BR2 209 C5
Woldham Rd BR2 209 C5
Wolds Dr BR6 226 C4
Wolfe Cl Hayes BR2 209 A3
Yeading UB4 84 B4
Wolfe Cres
Greenwich SE7 121 D1
[34] Rotherhithe SE16 118 D4
Wolfe Ho [19] W12 112 B6
Wolferton Rd E12 78 B4
Wolffe Gdns [2] E15 76 D2
Wolf Fields Prim Sch
UB2 107 B2
Wolfington Rd SE27 182 D6
Wolfram Cl SE13 164 C6
Wolfson Ct
[4] Barnet EN4 14 D3
Golders Green NW11 47 A2
SE1 253 D2
Wolfson Hillel Prim Sch
N14 15 D5
Wolftencroft Cl SW11 136 B2
Wollaston Cl SE1 262 A4
Wollotan Ho N1 234 B4
Wolmer Cl HA8 26 D6
Wolmer Gdns HA8 10 C1
Wolmer Rd HA8 26 D6
Wolseley Ave SW18,
SW19 157 C2
Wolseley Gdns W4 132 D6
Wolseley Rd Acton W4 111 A2
Carshalton CR4 203 A2
Harrow HA3 42 C6
Wolseley Rd *continued*
Hornsey N8 49 D4
Upton E7 77 B1
Wood Green N22 32 B2
Wolseley St
SE1 117 D4 253 D1
Wolsey Ave
Thames Ditton KT7 196 D4
Wallend E6 100 C4
Walthamstow E17 53 B6
Wolsey Cl
Isleworth TW3 130 A1
Kingston u T KT2 176 D2
Southall UB2 108 A3
Wimbledon SW20 178 B3
Worcester Pk KT19,
KT4 216 A4
Wolsey Cres SM4 201 B2
Wolsey Ct Bromley BR1 186 D3
SE9 166 B5
South Hampstead NW6 70 A1
Wolsey Dr
Kingston u T KT2 176 A4
Walton-on-T KT12 194 D1
Wolsey Gr HA8 27 B3
Wolsey Ho
[2] Hampton TW12 173 D4
[3] Kentish Town NW5 71 D2
Wolsey Inf Sch CR0 224 A1
Wolsey Jun Sch CR0 224 A1
Wolsey Mews
Kentish Town NW5 71 C2
Orpington BR6 227 D3
Wolsey Rd
Ashford TW15 170 B6
East Molesey KT8 196 B5
Enfield EN1 6 B3
Hampton TW12 174 A4
Stoke Newington N1 73 B3
Sunbury Comm TW16 171 D4
Wolsey St E1 96 C2
Wolsey Way KT9 214 C3
Wolstenholme HA7 25 B5
Wolstonbury N12 29 C5
Wolvercote Rd SE2 124 D4
Wolverley St E2 96 B4
Wolverton SE17 263 A2
Wolverton Ave KT2 176 C2
Wolverton Gdns
Brook Green W6 112 D2
Ealing W5 110 B6
Wolverton Mans W5 110 B5
Wolverton Rd HA7 25 B3
Wolverton Way N14 15 C6
Wolves La N22 32 C4
Womersley Rd N4, N8 50 B3
Wonford Cl KT2, KT3 177 C2
Wontner Cl [5] N1 73 A1
Wontner Rd SW12,
SW17 158 D2
Wooburn Cl UB8 82 D3
Wooburn Ct N14 15 D3
Woodall Cl
Chessington KT9 213 D2
[15] Poplar E14 119 D6
Woodall Ho TW7 130 D2
Woodall Rd EN3 18 D5
Woodbank Rd BR1 164 D1
Woodbastwick Rd
SE26 185 A5
Woodberry Ave
Edmonton N21 16 D2
Harrow HA2 42 A5
Woodberry Cl
Ashford TW16 172 A4
Mill Hill NW7 28 D3
Woodberry Cres N10 49 B6
Woodberry Down N4 51 A2
Woodberry Down Com
Prim Sch N4 51 A2
Woodberry Gdns N12 30 A4
Woodberry Gr
Finchley N12 30 A4
Stoke Newington N4 51 A2
Woodberry View N6 49 A3
Woodberry Way
Chingford E4 20 A4
Finchley N12 30 A4
Woodbine Cl TW2 152 B2
Woodbine Gr Enfield EN2 5 B5
Penge SE20 184 B3
Woodbine La KT4 216 C5
Woodbine Pl E11 55 A3
Woodbine Rd DA15 167 C3
Woodbines Ave KT1 197 D6
Woodbine Terr E9 74 C2
Woodborough Rd
SW15 134 B1
Woodbourne Ave
SW16 159 D1
Woodbourne Cl SW16 160 A1
Woodbourne Dr KT10 212 D2
Woodbourne Gdns
SM6 219 B1
Woodbridge Cl
[4] Dollis Hill NW2 68 A5
[10] Finsbury Pk N7 72 B6
Woodbridge Ct
Forest Gate E7 77 D3
Stoke Newington N16 73 B5
Woodbridge High Sch
IG8 37 B3
Woodbridge Ho E11 54 D1
Woodbridge Rd IG11 79 D3
Woodbridge St
EC1 94 D3 241 C6
Woodbrook Rd SE2 146 B6
Woodbrook Sch BR3 185 B2
Woodburn Cl NW4 46 D4
Woodbury Cl
Croydon CR0 221 D6
Wanstead E11 55 B5
Woodbury Ct [1] W13 87 B3
Woodbury Gdns
Bromley SE12 187 B6
Eltham SE12 165 B1
Woodbury Ho [4] SE26 162 B1
Woodbury Park Rd
W13 87 B3
Woodbury Rd E17 53 D5
Woodbury St SW17 180 C5
Woodchester Sq W2 91 D2
Woodchurch Cl DA14 167 B1
Woodchurch Dr BR1 187 D3
Woodchurch Ho [15]
SW9 138 C4
Woodchurch Rd NW6 69 D1
Wood Cl
Bethnal Green E2 96 A3
Harrow HA1 42 B2
Kingsbury NW9 45 B2
Woodclyffe Dr BR7 188 C1
Woodcock Ct HA3 44 A2
Woodcock Dell Ave
HA3 43 D2
Woodcock Hill HA3 43 C3
Woodcock Ho [4] E14 97 C2
Woodcocks E16 99 D2
Woodcombe Cres
SE23 162 C3
Woodcote Ave
Mill Hill NW7 28 C4
Thornton Heath CR7 204 D5
Wallington SM6 219 B1
Woodcote Cl Enfield N9 18 C5
Kingston u T KT2 176 B5
Woodcote Ct [14] SM6 219 B2
Woodcote Dr BR6 211 B2
Woodcote Ho [4] SE8 141 B6
Woodcote Mews
Loughton IG10 21 D4
Wallington SM6 219 B2
Woodcote Pl [1] SE27 182 D5
Woodcote Rd
Wallington SM6 219 C1
Wanstead E11 55 A2
Woodcott Ho [1]
SW15 156 A4
Woodcroft SE9 166 B1
South Croydon CR0 221 C5
Southgate N21 16 C3
[17] Stanmore HA7 25 C5
Wembley UB6 65 A2
Woodcroft Ave
Edgware NW7 27 C4
Stanmore HA7 25 A2
Woodcroft Cres UB10 82 D6
Woodcroft Mews SE8 119 A2
Woodcroft Prim Sch
HA8 27 C3
Woodcroft Rd CR7 204 D3
Wood Dene [6] SE15 140 B4
Wood Dr BR7 188 A4
Woodedge Cl E4 20 D3
Woodend
South Norwood SE19 183 A4
Sutton SM1 218 A6
Thames Ditton KT10 212 A6
WOOD END 83 D1
Wood End UB3 83 C1
Wood End Ave HA2 64 A4
Wood End Cl UB5 64 B3
Woodend Gdns EN2 4 A1
Wood End Gdns UB5 64 A3
WOOD END GREEN 83 C2
Wood End Green Rd
UB3 83 C1
Wood End Inf Sch UB5 64 B3
Wood End Jun Sch
UB6 64 B3
Wood End La UB5 63 D3
Wood End Park Com Sch
UB3 105 A6
Woodend Rd E17 36 A1
Wood End Rd HA1, UB5 64 B4
Wood End Way UB5 64 A3
Wooder Gdns E7 77 A4
Wooderson Cl SE25 205 C5
Wooderson Ct [9] BR3 185 C2
Woodfall Ave EN5 13 B6
Woodfall Rd N4 72 C6
Woodfall St SW3 257 C1
Woodfarrs SE5 139 B1
Woodfield SW16 182 B2
Wood Field NW3 70 D3
Woodfield Ave
Colindale NW9 45 C5
Ealing W5 87 C3
Streatham SW16 159 D1
Wallington SM5 219 A1
Wembley HA0 65 C5
Woodfield Cl
[1] Enfield EN1 5 C1
South Norwood SE19 183 A3
Woodfield Cres W5 87 D3
Woodfield Ct SW16 159 D1
Woodfield Dr EN4 15 A3
Woodfield Gdns KT3 199 D4
Woodfield Gr SW16 159 D1
Woodfield Ho
[11] Forest Hill SE23 162 D1
Hinchley Wood KT7 212 D6
New Malden KT3 199 D4
[6] Upper Clapton E5 74 B6
Wood Green N11 31 D4
Woodfield Pl W9 91 B3
Woodfield Rd
Cranford TW4, TW5 128 B3
Ealing W5 87 C3
Woodfield Rd *continued*
Hinchley Wood KT10,
KT7 212 D6
Kensal Town W9 91 B2
Woodfield Rise WD23 8 B4
Woodfield Sch NW9 45 C1
Woodfields Ct SM1 218 A5
Woodfield Way N11 31 D3
WOODFORD 37 D5
Woodford Ave IG2, IG4, IG5,
IG8 56 B5
Woodford Bridge Rd
IG4 56 A5
Woodford Cres HA5 22 B1
Woodford Ct [15] W12 112 D4
Woodford Cty High Sch
IG8 36 D4
Woodforde Ct UB3 105 B1
WOODFORD GREEN 37 B3
Woodford Green Prep Sch
IG8 37 A4
Woodford Green Sch
IG8 36 D5
Woodford Ho [13] SE18 144 D6
[5] Wanstead E18 55 A5
Woodford New Rd
Upper Walthamstow
E17 54 C6
Woodford E18 36 D3
Woodford Pl HA9 44 A1
Woodford Rd
Forest Gate E7 77 B4
Wanstead E18 55 A6
Woodford Sta IG8 37 B4
Woodford Trad Est
IG8 37 D1
WOODFORD WELLS 21 B1
Woodgate Ave KT9 213 D3
Woodgate Cres HA6 22 A4
Woodgate Dr SW16 181 D3
Woodgate Ho [12] KT6 198 A3
Woodger Rd W12 112 C4
Woodget Cl E6 100 A1
Woodglen SM4 202 C4
Woodgrange Ave
Ealing W5 110 C5
Enfield EN1 18 A5
Finchley N12 30 B4
Harrow HA3 43 D4
Woodgrange Cl HA3 43 D4
Woodgrange Ct [1]
BR2 208 D1
Woodgrange Gdns EN1 18 A5
Woodgrange Ho W5 110 B5
Woodgrange Inf Sch
E7 77 B4
Woodgrange Mans
HA3 43 C4
Woodgrange Park Sta
E12 77 D3
Woodgrange Rd E7 77 A3
Woodgrange Terr EN1 18 A5
WOOD GREEN 32 B2
Wood Green Sh City
N22 32 C1
Wood Green Sta N22 32 C1
Woodhall NW1 232 A1
Woodhall Ave
Dulwich SE21 161 D1
Pinner HA5 23 A2
Woodhall Dr
Dulwich SE21 161 D1
Pinner HA5 23 A2
Woodhall Gate HA5 22 D3
Woodhall Ho SW18 158 B5
Woodhall La WD19 23 A6
Woodhall Prim Sch
WD19 23 A6
Woodhall Rd HA5 22 D4
Woodham Ct E11 54 D5
Woodham Rd SE6 164 A1
Woodhatch Cl [16] E6 100 A2
Woodhaven Gdns IG6 57 A5
Woodhayes BR7 188 D4
Woodhayes Rd SW19,
SW20 178 C4
Woodhead Dr BR6 227 C6
Woodheyes Rd NW10 67 C3
Woodhill SE7, SE18 122 A2
Woodhill Cres HA3 43 D3
Woodhill Prim Sch
SE18 122 A2
Wood Ho
[4] Clapham SW4 137 D3
[6] Paddington NW6 91 B5
Woodhouse Ave UB6 86 D5
Woodhouse Cl
Hayes UB3 105 C3
Wembley UB6 86 D5
Woodhouse Eaves HA6 22 A5
Woodhouse Gr E12 78 A2
Woodhouse Rd
Colney Hatch N12 30 C4
Leyton E11 76 D5
Woodhouse Sixth Form
Coll N12 30 B4
Woodhurst Ave BR5 211 A3
Woodhurst Rd
Acton W3 111 A6
SE2 124 A2
Woodington Cl SE9 166 C5
Woodison St E3 97 A3
Woodknoll Dr BR7 188 B2
Wood La
Dagenham RM10 81 A5
Highgate N6 49 B3
Hounslow TW7 130 D5

Wood La continued
Kingsbury NW9 .....45 B2
Ruislip HA4 .....61 C6
Shepherd's Bush W12..112 C6
Stanmore HA7.......9 B2
Woodford IG8.......36 D5
Woodland App UB6...65 A2
Woodland Cl
Kingsbury NW9 .....45 A3
Uxbridge UB10.....60 D6
West Ewell KT19...215 C2
West Norwood SE19...183 C4
Woodford IG8.......21 B1
Woodland Cres
[18] Rotherhithe SE16...118 D4
SE10.............142 C6
Woodland Ct
Cheam SM1........217 C2
Temple Fortune NW4...47 A4
[13] Wanstead E11.....55 A4
Woodland Gdns
Cranley Gdns N10....49 B4
Isleworth TW7.....130 C2
Woodland Gr SE10...120 C1
Woodland Hill SE19...183 C4
Woodland Hts SE3...142 C6
Woodland Mews
SW16.............160 A1
Woodland Rd
Chingford E4......20 A3
Friern Barnet N11....31 B5
Penge SE19.......183 D4
Thornton Heath CR7...204 C5
Woodland Rise
Cranley Gdns N10....49 B5
Wembley UB6......65 A2
WOODLANDS.......130 C2
Woodlands
Beckenham BR3....185 D3
Clapham SW4......137 B1
Finchley N12......30 A4
Harrow HA2.......41 C5
Temple Fortune NW11...47 A4
Walthamstow E11....54 B2
West Barnes SW20...200 D5
Woodlands Ave
Acton W3.........110 D5
DA15.............167 C3
Dagenham RM6.....59 A2
Finchley N3.......30 A2
Kingston u T KT3...177 B2
Ruislip HA4.......40 D2
Wanstead E11......55 B1
Worcester Pk KT4...216 A6
Woodlands Cl BR1...188 B1
Claygate KT10.....212 D1
Temple Fortune NW11...47 A4
Woodlands Ct
[9] Bromley BR1.....186 D2
Brondesbury Pk NW10...90 D4
Dulwich SE22.....162 B4
Southall UB1......107 C5
Woodlands Dr
Harrow HA7.......24 D4
Sunbury TW16......172 C1
Woodlands Fst & Mid Sch
HA8.............26 B2
Woodlands Gdns E17...54 C3
Woodlands Gr TW7...130 C3
Woodlands Gt SW15...157 B6
Woodlands Jun & Inf Schs
IG1.............79 B3
Woodlands Par TW15...171 A4
Woodlands Park Rd
SE10.............142 C6
Tottenham N15.....51 A4
Woodlands Rd
Barnes SW13......133 D2
Bexleyheath DA7....147 A2
Bickley BR1.......188 B1
Enfield EN2.......5 B4
Harrow HA1.......42 D4
Ilford IG1.........79 A5
Isleworth TW7.....130 C3
Leyton E11........76 C6
Lower Edmonton N9...18 C3
Southall UB1......106 D5
Surbiton KT6......197 D2
Walthamstow E17....54 A6
Woodlands St SE13...164 B4
Woodland St [2] E8...73 D2
Woodlands The
East Barnet N14....15 B3
Harrow HA1.......64 C6
Highbury N5......73 A4
[12] Hornsey N8......50 A2
Isleworth TW7.....130 D3
Lewisham SE13.....164 B4
Mitcham CR4......203 A6
South Norwood SE19...183 A3
Stanmore HA7.....25 B5
Thames Ditton KT10...212 A6
Woodlands Way
SW15.............157 B6
Woodland Terr SE7...122 A2
Woodland Way
Abbey Wood SE2....124 D2
Croydon CR0......207 A1
Edgware NW7......27 D4
Merton SM4.......201 B5
Mitcham CR4......181 A3
Petts Wood BR5....211 A4
Southgate N21......16 C2
Tolworth KT5......214 D6
West Wickham BR4...224 A4
Woodford IG8......21 B1

Woodland Wlk
Chessington KT19...214 C2
[9] Greenwich SE10...120 C1
Hampstead NW3.....70 C3
Wood Lane High Sch
W12.............90 B1
Woodlawn Cl SW15...157 B6
Woodlawn Cres TW2...151 D2
Woodlawn Dr TW13...150 D2
Woodlawn Rd SW6...134 D4
Woodlea Dr BR2....208 C4
Woodlea Lo EN1.....17 C5
Woodlea Rd N16.....73 C5
Woodleigh
[1] Kingston u T KT5...198 B4
[3] Woodford E18.....37 A2
Woodleigh Ave N12...30 C4
Woodleigh Ct N22...32 B2
Woodleigh Gdns
SW16.............160 A1
Woodley Cl SW17...180 D3
Woodley La SM1, SM5...218 C5
Woodlodge [4] SW19...179 B5
Wood Lodge Gdns
BR1.............188 A3
Wood Lodge La BR4...224 A5
Woodman La E4.....20 C6
Woodman Mews TW9...132 D4
Woodman Par [4] E16...122 C5
Woodmans Ct HA7....44 A6
Woodmans Gr NW10...67 D3
Woodmans Mews W12...90 B2
Woodman St E16...122 C5
Woodmansterne Prim Sch
SW16.............181 D2
Woodmansterne Rd
Mitcham SW16.....181 D2
Sutton SM5.......218 C1
Wood Mead N17.....34 A4
Woodmere Ave CR0...206 D2
Woodmere Cl
[11] Clapham SW11...137 A2
Croydon CR0......206 D2
Woodmere Ct N14...15 B4
Woodmere Gdns CR0...206 D2
Woodmere Way BR3...208 B4
Woodnook Rd SW16...181 B5
Woodpecker Cl
Bushey WD23.......8 A3
Enfield N9.........18 B5
Harrow HA3.......24 D2
Woodpecker Ct TW2...151 D4
Woodpecker Ho E17...53 C6
Woodpecker Mews
SE13.............142 B1
Woodpecker Rd
[6] SE14...........141 A6
Woolwich SE28.....124 C6
Wood Point [8] E16...99 A2
Woodquest Ave SE24...161 A6
Wood Rd
Littleton TW17.....192 C5
Willesden NW10.....67 A1
Wood Retreat SE18...145 B5
Wood Ride Barnet EN4...2 B4
Orpington BR5.....211 C5
Woodridge Cl EN2....4 C4
Woodridge Prim Sch
N12.............13 C1
Woodridings Ave HA5...23 B2
Woodridings Cl HA5...23 B3
Woodridings Ct N22...31 D2
Woodriffe Rd E11.....54 B2
Wood Rise HA5.....40 A4
Woodrow SE18.....122 B2
Woodrow Ave UB4...83 D3
Woodrow Cl UB6.....65 B1
Woodrow Ct [3] N17...34 B3
Woodruff Ho [12] SW2...160 C5
Woodrush Cl [4] SE14...141 A5
Woodrush Way RM6...58 D5
Woodseer St E1.....96 A2
Woodsford SE17....262 C1
Woodsford Sq
W14.............113 A4 244 B2
Woodshire Rd RM10...81 D5
Woods Ho SW8.....269 A2
WOODSIDE.......206 A4
Woodside
Buckhurst Hill IG9...21 C2
Hampstead Garden Suburb
NW11.............47 C4
Muswell Hill N10....49 A6
Walton-on-T KT12...194 A1
Wimbledon SW19...179 B5
Woodside Ave
Chislehurst BR7....189 A5
Croydon SE25.....206 B4
Fortis Green N6.....48 B5
North Finchley N12...30 A6
Thames Ditton KT10...196 C2
Wembley HA0......88 A4
Woodside Cl Ruislip HA4...39 B3
Stanmore HA7.....25 B5
Tolworth KT5......199 A4
Wembley HA0......88 A4
Woodside Court Rd
CR0.............206 A2
Woodside Cres DA15...167 C1
Woodside Ct
Ealing W5.........110 A5
Enfield EN2.......4 D4
[10] Finchley N12.....29 D6
Palmers Green N13...16 C1
Wanstead E12......55 C1
Woodside End HA0...88 A6
Woodside Gdns
Chingford E4......35 D4
Tottenham N17.....33 D1

Woodside Gn SE25...206 A3
Woodside Gr N12....14 A1
Woodside Grange Rd
N12.............29 D6
Woodside Ho SW19...179 B4
Woodside Jun & Inf Sch
CR0.............206 A2
Woodside La DA5....168 D5
Whetstone N12.....14 A1
WOODSIDE PARK...29 C6
Woodside Park Ave
E17.............54 B5
Woodside Park Int Sch
N11.............30 D5
Woodside Park Rd N12...30 A6
Woodside Pk SE25...206 B3
Woodside Pl HA0....88 A6
Woodside Rd BR1...210 A4
Coombe KT3......177 C1
Croydon SE25.....206 B3
Kingston u T KT2...176 A3
Newham E13......99 C3
Northwood HA6.....22 A3
Sidcup DA15......167 C1
Sutton SM1.......218 A5
Woodford IG8......37 A6
Wood Green N22....32 C3
Woodside Sch
Belvedere DA17....125 D2
Walthamstow E17....54 A6
Woodside Sta SE25...206 B3
Woodside Way
Croydon CR0......206 C3
Streatham CR4.....181 C2
Wood's Mews
W1.............115 A6 248 A6
Wood's Pl SE1......263 B5
Woodspring Rd SW19...157 A2
Wood's Rd SE15.....140 B4
Wood St Barnet EN5...1 A1
Carshalton CR4....203 A2
Chiswick W4......111 C1
City of London
EC2.............95 A1 242 B2
Custom Ho E16....121 B6
Kingston u T KT1...175 D1
Kingston u T KT2...176 A2
Walthamstow E17....54 B5
Woodstar Ho [5] SE15...140 A5
Woodstead Gr HA8...26 A4
Woods The
Eastbury HA6......22 A5
Uxbridge UB10.....60 D4
Woodstock Ave
Brentford W13.....109 A3
Cheam SM3.......201 B2
Golders Green NW11...47 A2
Isleworth TW7.....153 A6
Southall UB1......85 B4
Woodstock Cl DA5...169 B3
Stanmore HA7.....26 A1
Woodstock Cres N9...18 B5
Woodstock Ct
Kingston u T KT2...176 D1
Lee SE12.........165 A5
Vauxhall SE11.....260 D2
Woodstock Dr UB10...60 B4
Woodstock Gdns
Beckenham BR3....185 D3
Hayes UB4.........83 D2
Ilford IG3.........80 A6
Woodstock Gr W12...112 C4
Woodstock Grange
W5.............110 A5
Woodstock Ho
Hayes UB3........83 B2
[2] Highbury N5.....73 A4
Woodstock Lane N
KT6.............198 C2
Woodstock Lane S KT6, KT9,
KT10.............213 C4
Woodstock Mews W1...238 B3
Woodstock Rd
Bedford Pk W4....111 C3
Bushey WD23.......8 D4
Chingford E17.....36 B1
Finsbury Pk N4.....50 C1
Golders Green NW11...47 B1
South Croydon CR0...221 B5
Upton E7.........77 C1
Wallington SM5, SM6...219 A3
Wembley HA0......66 B1
Woodstock Rise SM3...201 B2
Woodstock St W1...238 C1
Woodstock Studios [17]
W12.............112 D4
Woodstock Terr E14...119 D6
Woodstock The SM3...201 B2
Woodstock Way CR4...181 C1
Woodstone Ave KT17,
KT4.............216 A4
Wood Street Sta E17...54 B5
Woodsyre SE26.....183 D6
Woodthorpe Rd
Ashford TW15.....170 A6
Putney SW15......134 B1
Woodtree Cl NW4....28 C1
Wood Vale
Cranley Gdns N10...49 C4
Dulwich SE23.....162 B4
Woodvale Ave SE25...183 D1
Woodvale Ct BR1...188 B1
South Norwood SE25...205 D5
Woodvale Way NW11...68 D5
Woodvale Wlk SE27...183 A5
Woodview Ave E4....36 A6
Woodview Cl
Finsbury Pk N4.....50 D2
Kingston u T SW15...177 B6

Woodview Cl continued
Orpington BR6.....227 A6
Woodville SE3......143 B4
Woodville Cl SE12...165 A6
Teddington TW11...175 A6
Woodville Ct
[3] Lewisham SE10...142 A4
Southgate N14......15 C6
Woodville Gdns
Ealing W5.........88 A1
Hendon NW11......46 D2
Ilford IG6.........56 D5
Ruislip HA4.......39 A2
Surbiton KT6......197 D2
Woodville Gr [2] DA16...146 A2
Woodville Ho SE1...263 C6
Sutton SM1.......217 D4
Woodville Rd Barnet EN5...1 C1
Ealing W5.........87 D1
Golders Green NW11...47 A2
Leytonstone E11....54 D1
Morden SM4......201 C5
Paddington NW6....91 B5
Richmond TW10....153 C1
South Norwood CR7...205 B6
Stoke Newington N16...73 C3
Walthamstow E17....53 B5
Woodford E18......37 B1
Woodville St SE7...122 A2
Woodville The W5....87 D1
Woodward Ave NW4...46 A4
Woodward Cl KT10...212 D2
Woodwarde Rd SE22...161 C5
Woodward Gdns
Dagenham RM9.....80 C1
Harrow HA7.......24 D3
Woodward Rd RM9...80 C1
Wood Way BR6.....226 C6
Woodway Cres HA1...43 A3
Woodwell St SW18...158 A6
Wood Wharf SE10...142 A6
Woodyard Cl NW5...71 A3
Woodyard La SE21...161 C4
Woodyates Rd SE12...165 B4
Woolacombe Rd SE3...143 C3
Woolacombe Way
UB3.............105 C2
Woolcombes Ct [4]
SE16.............118 D5
Woolden St [2] E4....20 C4
Wooler St
SE17.............117 B1 262 D2
Woolf Cl SE28......124 B5
Woolf Ct [7] W3.....111 A3
Woolf Mews WC1....240 A6
Woollaston Rd N4...50 D3
Woolley Ho SW9....138 D2
Woollon Ho [1] E1....96 C1
Woolmead Ave NW9...46 A2
Woolmer Gdns N18...34 A5
Woolmer Ho [2] E5....74 B6
Woolmer Rd N18....34 A5
Woolmore Prim Sch
E14.............120 A6
Woolmore St E14...120 A6
Woolneigh St SW6...135 D3
Woolpack Ho [1] E9...74 C2
Wool Rd SW20.....178 B4
Woolridge Way E9...74 C1
Woolstaplers Way
SE16.............118 A2
Woolston Cl E17....34 D1
Woolstone Ho [7] E2...96 A6
Woolstone Rd SE23...163 A4
Woolven Ho SE3....142 D6
WOOLWICH.......122 A5
Woolwich Arsenal Sta
SE18.............122 A3
Woolwich Church St SE7,
SE18.............122 A3
Woolwich Comm
SE18.............144 C6
Woolwich Ct EN3....7 C5
Woolwich Dockyard Ind
Est SE18.........122 A3
Woolwich Dockyard Sta
SE18.............122 B2
Woolwich High St
SE18.............122 C3
Woolwich Manorway
E16.............122 D4
Woolwich Manor Way
Beckton E6.......100 C1
North Woolwich E16...122 D5
Woolwich New Rd
SE18.............122 D2
Woolwich Poly Sch for
Boys SE28........124 A5
Woolwich Rd
Belvedere DA17....125 C1
DA7.............147 C2
Erith SE2.........125 B1
Greenwich SE7, SE10...121 C2
Wooster Gdns E14...98 B1
Wooster Mews HA2...42 A6
Wooster Pl SE1....262 D4
Wootton Gr N3.....29 C2
Wootton Ho SE9...167 B5
Wootton St
SE1.............116 C5 251 B3
Worbeck Rd SE20...184 C1
Worcester Ave N17...34 A3
Worcester Cl
Croydon CR0......223 C6
Dollis Hill NW2.....68 B5
Mitcham CR4......181 A1

Worcester Ct
Ashford TW15.....170 D5
Ealing W7.........86 D1
Finchley N12......29 D5
Harrow HA1.......42 C6
[44] Paddington W2...91 C2
[12] Sutton SM2.....217 D2
Walton-on-T KT12...194 C1
Worcester Pk KT4...215 C5
Worcester Dr
Ashford TW15.....170 D5
Bedford Pk W4....111 C4
Worcester Gdns
Northolt UB6......64 B2
Redbridge IG1.....56 A2
Wandsworth SW11...158 D6
Worcester Pk KT4...215 C5
Worcester Ho
Bayswater W2.....236 A1
[3] Islington N1.....73 A1
Lambeth SE11.....261 A5
[9] Putney SW15....156 C4
Worcester Mews [2]
NW6.............69 D2
WORCESTER PARK...215 C4
Worcester Park Rd
KT4.............215 B5
Worcester Park Sta
KT4.............200 A1
Worcester Rd
Belmont SM2.....217 D1
Higham Hill E17....34 D1
Ilford E12........78 B4
[11] Wimbledon SW19...179 B5
Worcesters Ave EN1...6 A5
Worcesters Prim Sch
EN1.............5 D5
Wordsworth N8.....50 C5
Wordsworth Ave
Greenford UB6.....86 B5
Plashet E12.......78 A1
Snaresbrook E18....54 D6
Wordsworth Ct
Harrow HA1.......42 B2
New Barnet EN5....14 A6
Wordsworth Dr KT4,
SM3.............216 C4
Wordsworth Gdns WD6...10 C6
Wordsworth Ho
Maida Vale NW6....91 C4
[15] SE18.........144 C6
Wordsworth Par [1]
N15.............50 D5
Wordsworth Pl [11] NW5...70 D3
Wordsworth Rd
Bermondsey SE1...263 C6
Bexley DA16......145 C4
Hampton TW12, TW13...173 B6
Penge SE20.......184 D3
Stoke Newington N16...73 C4
Wallington SM6....219 D2
Wordsworth Way UB7...104 B2
Wordsworth Wlk NW11...47 C5
Worfield St
SW11.............136 C5 267 B3
Worgan St
Rotherhithe SE16...118 D2
SE11.............116 B1 260 C2
Working Men's Coll The
NW1.............93 C5 232 B4
Worland Rd E15....76 C1
World Bsns Ctr TW6...127 A4
WORLD'S END.....4 C1
Worlds End La EN2...4 B1
World's End Pas SE10...266 B4
World's End Pl SW10...266 B4
World Trade Ctr London
E14.............119 D4
Worley Ct NW2.....68 D5
Worleys Dr BR6....227 B4
Worlidge St W6....112 C1
Worlingham Rd SE22...139 D1
Wormholt Park Prim Sch
W12.............112 A6
Wormholt Rd W12...112 A5
Wormwood St EC2...243 A2
Wornington Rd W10...91 A2
Woronzow Rd
NW8.............92 C6 230 A5
Worple Ave
Isleworth TW7.....153 A6
Wimbledon SW19...178 D3
Worple Cl HA2......41 B1
Worple Ct SW19....179 A4
Worple Prim Sch
TW7.............131 A1
Worple Rd
Isleworth TW7.....131 A1
Wimbledon SW19,
SW20.............178 D2
Worple Road Mews
SW19.............179 B4
Worple St SW14....133 B2
Worple Way
Harrow HA2.......41 B1
Richmond TW10....132 A1
Worship St EC2...95 C3 242 A5
Worslade Rd SW17...180 B6
Worsley Bridge Jun Sch
BR3.............185 C3
Worsley Bridge Rd BR3,
SE6.............185 C5
Worsley Ct N3......29 A4
Worsley Gr E5......74 A4
Worsley Grange BR7...189 A4
Worsley Ho [9] SE23...162 B2
Worsley Rd E11.....76 C4
Worsopp Dr SW4...159 C6
Worth Cl BR6......227 C4

Worthfield Cl KT19...215 B1
Worth Gr SE17.....262 C4
Worthing Cl [5] E15...98 C5
Worthing Rd TW5...129 B6
Worthington Cl CR4...203 B6
Worthington Ho EC1...234 B2
Worthington Rd KT6...198 B1
Wortley Rd
Forest Gate E6.....77 C1
Thornton Heath CR0...204 C2
Worton Ct TW7.....130 C1
Worton Gdns TW7...130 B3
Worton Hall Ind Est
TW7.............130 C1
Worton Rd TW7....130 C2
Worton Way TW3,
TW7.............130 B3
Wotton Ct [14] E14...120 B6
Wotton Rd
Cricklewood NW2...68 C5
[18] SE8...........141 B6
Wouldham Rd E16...98 D1
Wragby Rd E11.....76 C5
Wrampling Pl N9....18 A3
Wrangthorne Wlk
CR0.............220 C4
Wray Ave IG5......56 C6
Wrayburn Ho [28] SE16...118 A4
Wray Cres N4......72 B6
Wray Ct N4........72 B6
Wrayfield Rd SM3...216 D5
Wray Ho [11] SW2...160 A4
Wraysbury Cl TW4...151 A6
Wrays Way UB4....83 C3
Wrekin Rd SE18....145 A5
Wren Ave
Cricklewood NW2...68 C4
Southall UB2......107 B2
Wren Cl E16.......98 C1
Lower Edmonton N9...18 D3
Wren Cres WD23.....8 A3
Wren Ct [1] Barnet EN4...14 D3
Croydon CR0......221 B4
Wren Gdns RM9....80 D3
Wren Ho [29] Bow E3...97 A5
[4] Hampton TW12...173 D4
SW1.............259 C1
Wren Landing E14...119 C5
Wrenn Ho SW13....134 C6
Wren Path SE28....123 B4
Wren Rd
Camberwell SE5....139 B4
Dagenham RM9.....80 D3
Sidcup DA14......168 C1
Wrens Ave TW15....171 A6
Wren's Park Ho E5...74 B6
Wren St WC1.....94 B3 240 D6
Wrentham Ave NW10...90 D5
Wrenthorpe Rd BR1...186 C6
Wren View N6......49 C1
Wrenwood Way HA5...40 B5
Wrestlers Ct EC3...243 A2
Wrexham Rd E3.....97 C5
Wricklemarsh Rd SE3...143 C4
Wrigglesworth St
SE14.............140 D5
Wright Cl SE13....142 B1
Wright Gdns TW17...192 C4
Wright Ho SW15...156 B6
Wrighton Ct SM1...217 B2
Wright Rd TW5....128 C5
Wrights Cl RM10....81 D4
Wright's Gn SW4...137 D1
Wright's La
W8.............113 D3 255 C6
Wrights Pl NW10...67 A2
Wright St SE25.....205 C6
Wright's Rd E3.....97 B5
Wright's Row SM5...219 B4
Wrights Wlk SW14...133 B2
Writtle Ho [38] NW9...27 D1
Wrotham Ho
Beckenham BR3....185 B3
SE1.............262 D6
Wrotham Rd Barnet EN5...1 A3
[18] Camden Town NW1...71 C1
DA16.............146 C4
Ealing W13.......109 C5
Wrottesley Rd SE18...145 A6
Willesden Green NW10...90 A5
Wroughton Rd SW11...158 B5
Wroughton Terr NW4...46 B5
Wroxall Rd RM9.....80 C2
Wroxham Gdns N11...31 B1
Wroxham Rd SE28...124 D6
Wroxton St SE15...140 C3
Wr Twr Cl UB8.....60 A3
Wr Twr Hill CR0...221 B4
Wr Twr Pl N1......234 C2
Wrythe Gn [2] SM5...218 D5
Wrythe Green Rd
SM5.............218 D5
Wrythe La SM1, SM5,
SM4.............218 C6
WRYTHE THE.....218 D6
Wulfstan St W12....89 D1
Wyatt Cl Bushey WD23...8 C4
Feltham TW13.....150 D3
Hayes UB4........84 A2
Rotherhithe SE16...119 B4
Wyatt Ct HA0......66 A1
Wyatt Ho
Blackheath Vale SE3...142 D3
NW8.............236 B5
Wyatt Park Mans [1]
SW2.............160 A2
Wyatt Park Rd SW2...160 B2
Wyatt Rd Forest Gate E7...77 B4

Wyatt Rd *continued*
Highbury N5 73 A5
Wyatt's La E17 54 A6
Wybert St NW1 239 A6
Wyborne Ho NW10 67 A1
Wyborne Prim Sch
SE9 166 D3
Wyborne Way NW10 67 A1
Wyburn Ave EN5 1 B2
Wyche Gr CR2 221 A1
Wycherley Cl SE3 142 D5
Wycherley Cres EN5 13 D5
Wychwood Ave
Edgware HA8 25 D4
South Norwood CR7 205 A6
Wychwood Cl
Ashford TW16 172 A4
Edgware HA8 25 D4
Wychwood End N6 49 C2
Wychwood Gdns IG5 56 C5
Wychwood Ho N4 51 A2
Wychwood Way SE19 183 B4
Wyclif Ct EC1 234 C1
Wycliffe Cl DA16 145 D4
Wycliffe Ho 13 N16 73 C4
Wycliffe Rd
Battersea SW11 137 A3
Wimbledon SW19 179 D4
Wyclif St EC1 234 C1
Wycombe Ct SE3 143 A5
Wycombe Gdns NW11 69 C6
Wycombe Ho NW8 237 A6
Wycombe Pl SW18 158 A5
Wycombe Rd
Redbridge IG2 56 B4
Tottenham N17 34 A2
Wembley HA0 88 C6
Wycombe Sq W8 245 A3
Wydehurst Rd CR0 206 B2
Wydell Cl SM4 200 D3
Wydeville Manor Rd
SE12 187 B6
Wye Cl Ashford TW15 170 D6
BR6 211 D2
Ruislip HA4 39 A3
Wye Ct W13 87 B2
Wyemead Cres E4 20 C2
Wyersdale Ho N4 51 A2
Wye St SW11 136 B3
Wyevale Cl HA5 40 A6
Wyfold Ho 8 SE2 124 D4
Wyfold Rd
SW6 135 A5 264 A3
Wyke Cl TW7 130 D6
Wyke Gdns W7 109 A3
Wykeham Ave RM9 80 C2
Wykeham Cl UB7 126 C6
Wykeham Ct
Chislehurst BR7 189 C4
Hendon NW4 46 C4
Wykeham Gn RM9 80 C2
Wykeham Hill HA9 44 B1
Wykeham Ho SW19 179 C2
Wykeham Prim Sch
NW10 67 C5
Wykeham Rd
Harrow HA3 43 B5
Hendon NW4 46 C4
Wykeham Rise N20 13 A3
Wykehurst Ho SW17 180 B5
Wyke Rd
Hackney Wick E3 75 C1
Merton SW20 178 C1
Wylchin Cl HA5 39 D6
Wyldes Cl NW11 48 A1
Wyldfield Gdns N9 17 D2
Wyld Way HA9 66 D2
Wyleu St SE23 163 A4
Wylie Rd UB2 107 C3
Wyllen Cl E1 96 C3
Wylo Dr EN5 12 A5
Wymering Mans 9 W9 91 C4
Wymering Rd W9 91 C4
Wymondham Ct NW8 229 D6
Wymond St SW15 134 C2
Wynan Rd E14 119 D1
Wynash Gdns SM5 218 C3
Wynaud Ct N22 32 B4
Wynbourne Ct SE20 184 B1
Wyncham Ave DA15 167 C3
Wynchgate Harrow HA3 24 C3
Southgate N14 16 A4
Wyncroft Cl BR1 210 B6
Wyndale Ave NW9 44 C3
Wyndcliff Rd SE7 143 B6
Wyndcroft Cl EN2 4 D2
Wyndham Cl
Belmont SM2 217 C1
Orpington BR6 211 A1
Wyndham Cres
Camden Town N19 71 C5
Hounslow TW4 151 C5
Wyndham Ct
Brentford W7 109 A2
1 Thornton Heath
CR0 204 D3
Wyndham Deedes Ho 30
E2 96 A5
Wyndham Ho SW1 258 A3
Wyndham Lo TW7 130 C4
Wyndham Mews W1 237 C3
Wyndham Pl W1 237 C3
Wyndham Rd
Barnet EN4 14 D3
Brentford W13 109 B3
Forest Gate E6 77 D1
Kingston u T KT2 176 B3
SE5 139 A5
Wyndhams Ct 4 E8 73 D1
Wyndham St
W1 92 D2 237 C4
Wyndham Yd W1 237 C3
Wyndhurst Cl CR2 220 D1
Wyneham Rd SE24 161 B6
Wynell Rd SE23 162 D1
Wynford Pl DA17 147 C6
Wynford Rd N1 94 B5 233 D4
Wynford Way SE9 166 B1
Wynlie Gdns HA5 22 B1
Wynndale Rd E18 37 B2
Wynne Ct 6 TW7 131 A2
Wynne Ho SE14 140 D4
Wynne Rd SW9 138 C3
Wynn's Ave DA15 168 A6
Wynnstay Gdns
W8 113 C3 255 B6
Wynter Ho 20 SW9 138 B3
Wynter St SW11 136 A1
Wynton Gdns SE25 205 D4
Wynton Pl W3 88 D1
Wynyard Ho SE11 260 D2
Wynyard Terr SE11 260 D2
Wynyatt Ho EC1 234 C2
Wynyatt St EC1 94 D4 234 C2
Wyre Gr Edgware HA8 10 D1
Hayes UB3 106 A2
Wyresdale Cres UB6 86 D4
Wyteleaf Cl HA4 39 A3
Wytham Ho NW8 236 D5
Wythburn Ct W1 237 C2
Wythburn Pl W1 237 C2
Wythenshawe Rd RM10 81 C5
Wythens Wlk SE9 166 D5
Wythes Cl BR1 188 B1
Wythes Rd E16 122 A5
Wythfield Rd SE9 166 B5
Wyvenhoe Rd HA2 64 A5
Wyvern Est The KT3 200 A5
Wyvil Prim Sch
SW8 138 A5 270 B4
Wyvil Rd SW8 138 A5 270 A4
Wyvis St E14 97 D2

X

Xavier Ho E17 35 B1

Y

Yabsley St E14 120 A5
Yaldam Ho SE1 263 A3
Yalding Ho 20 E5 74 B3
Yalding Rd SE16 118 A2
Yale Cl TW4 151 B6
Yale Ct NW6 69 D3
Yarborough Rd 1
SW19 180 B2
Yardley Cl E4 19 D6
Yardley Ct SM3 216 D4
Yardley La E4 19 D6
Yardley Prim Sch E4 20 A5
Yardley St WC1 234 A1
Yard The N1 233 B3
Yarlington Ct N11 31 A5
Yarmouth Cres N17 52 B4
Yarmouth Pl W1 248 C3
Yarnfield Sq 15 SE15 140 A4
Yarnton Way DA17,
DA18 125 B3
Yarrow Cres E6 100 A2
Yarrow Ho
12 Cubitt Town E14 120 A3
16 North Kensington
W10 90 C2
Yateley St SE18 121 D3
Yatesbury Ct E5 75 A3
Yates Ct NW2 68 D2
Yates Ho 22 E2 96 A4
Yatton Ho 15 W10 90 C2
YEADING 84 D3
Yeading Ave HA2 41 A1
Yeading Ct UB4 84 C3
Yeading Fork UB4 84 C3
Yeading Gdns UB4 84 B2
Yeading Ho UB4 84 D2
Yeading Jun & Inf Schs
UB4 84 C2
Yeading La Hayes UB4 84 B2
Northolt UB4, UB5 84 C4
Yeadon Ho 14 W10 90 C2
Yeames Cl W13 87 A1
Yearby Ho W10 90 C3
Yeate St N1 73 B1
Yeatman Rd N6 48 D3
Yeats Cl NW10 67 C2
Yeend Cl KT8 195 C5
Yeldham Ho W6 112 D1
Yeldham Rd W6 112 D1
Yellowhammer Ct NW9 27 C1
Yelverton Lo TW1 153 C4
Yelverton Rd SW11 136 B3
Ye Market CR0 221 B3
Yenston Cl SM4 201 C3
Yeoman Cl
Newham E16 122 D6
West Norwood SE27 160 D1
Yeoman Ct
Heston TW5 129 B5
8 Sutton SM1 218 B3
Yeoman Dr TW19 148 A3
Yeoman Rd UB5 63 A1
Yeomans Acre HA4 40 A3
Yeomans Mews TW7 152 B6
Yeoman's Row
SW3 114 C3 257 B5
Yeoman St SE8 119 A2
Yeomans Way EN3 6 C3
Yeoman's Yd E1 253 D6
Yeo St E3 97 D2
Yeovil Cl BR6 227 C6
Yeovil Ho Finsbury Pk N7 72 B6
North Kensington W10 90 C3
Yeovilton Pl KT2 175 C5
Yerbury Prim Sch N19 71 D5
Yerbury Rd N19 71 D5
Yeshivo Horomo
Tadmudical Coll N16 51 B1
Yesodey Hatorah Sch
N16 51 D2
Yester Dr BR7 188 A3
Yester Pk BR7 188 B4
Yester Rd BR7 188 B3
Yet Lev Ct E5 52 A1
Yew Ave UB7 104 A6
Yew Cl IG9 21 D2
Yewdale Cl BR1 186 C4
Yewfield Rd NW10 67 D2
Yew Gr NW2 68 D4
Yew Ho SE14 141 B3
Yews The TW15 170 D6
Yew Tree Ave N2 47 D6
Yewtree Cl Harrow HA2 41 D5
Wood Green N22 31 C2
Yew Tree Cl DA16 146 A4
3 Lewisham SE13 142 A2
New Malden KT4 199 C1
Southgate N21 16 C4
Yew Tree Cotts KT10 212 B6
Yew Tree Ct Elstree WD6 9 D5
8 Stoke Newington N16 73 B6
8 Sutton SM2 218 A1
4 Temple Fortune
NW11 47 B4
Yew Tree Gdns RM6 59 A4
Yew Tree Grange 2
W5 109 C6
Yew Tree Ho
New Malden KT4 199 C1
5 Surbiton KT6 198 A1
Yew Tree Lo 10 SW16 181 C6
Yewtree Rd BR3 207 B6
Yew Tree Rd
East Acton W12 111 D6
Hillingdon UB10 82 B6
Yew Trees TW17 192 B5
Yew Tree Wlk TW4 151 B6
Yew Wlk HA1 42 C1
YIEWSLEY 104 A6
Yiewsley Ct UB7 104 A5
Yoakley Rd N16 73 C6
Yoke Cl N7 72 A2
Yolande Gdns SE9 166 A6
Yonge Pk N4, N7 72 C5
York Ave Ealing W7 108 C5
Hayes UB3 83 A1
Mortlake SW14 155 A6
Sidcup DA15 167 D2
Stanmore HA7 25 B1
Walworth SE17 262 B2
York Bldgs
WC2 116 A6 250 B5
York Bridge
NW1 93 A3 238 A6
York Cl
17 Camberwell SE5 139 A3
Ealing W7 108 C5
Morden SM4 201 D5
Newham E6 100 B1
York Ct Beckenham BR3 186 B2
Kingston u T KT2 175 D4
York Ct *continued*
Palmers Green N13 16 A1
Wallington SM6 219 C3
York Gate NW1 238 B5
Southgate N14 16 A4
York Gr SE15 140 C4
York Hill SE27, SW16 160 D1
York Ho Acton W3 111 A6
Chelsea SW3 257 D2
Chingford E4 35 C6
Edgware HA8 26 B4
Enfield EN2 5 B4
Forest Hill SE26 184 C5
1 Hendon NW4 28 D1
1 Ilford IG1 78 D6
Islington N5 72 C3
Kensington W8 245 C2
11 Kentish Town N7 71 D2
Kew TW9 132 C4
4 Kingston u T KT2 176 B3
Lambeth SE1 116 B3 260 D5
Marylebone W1 237 C4
Pentonville N1 233 C3
Richmond TW10 154 C6
South Norwood SE25 205 C5
10 West Acton W3 88 C1
York House Pl
W8 113 D4 245 C2
Yorkland Ave DA16 145 D1
Yorkley Ho 3 W10 90 C3
York Mans
Battersea SW11 268 B2
2 Hendon NW9 46 A3
Marylebone W1 238 A4
Walworth SE17 262 B2
York Mews
Camden Town NW5 71 B3
Ilford IG1 78 C5
York Par
Brentford TW8 109 D1
Hendon NW9 46 A3
York Pl
Battersea SW11 136 B2
Ilford IG1 78 C6
WC2 250 B5
York Place Mans NW1 237 D4
York Rd
Battersea SW11,
SW18 136 B2
Belmont SM1, SM2 217 C1
Brentford TW8 109 D1
Chingford E4 35 C5
Dagenham W3 89 B1
Ealing W5 109 C3
Edmonton N18 34 B5
Forest Gate E7 77 A2
Friern Barnet N11 31 D4
Hounslow TW3 129 D2
Ilford IG1 78 C6
Kingston u T KT2 176 B3
Leyton E10 76 A5
New Barnet EN5 14 B6
Pinner HA6 22 A1
4 Richmond TW10 154 B6
SE1 116 B4 250 D2
Southgate N21 17 B4
Teddington TW11 174 C6
Thornton Heath CR0 204 C2
Walthamstow E17 52 D4
Wimbledon SW19 180 A4
York Rise BR6 227 C6
Dartmouth Pk NW5 71 B5
York Road Bsns Ctr
SW11 136 B3
York St Chambers W1 237 C4
Yorkshire Cl N16 73 C5
Yorkshire Gdns N18 34 B5
Yorkshire Grey SE9 165 D6
Yorkshire Grey Pl 13
NW3 70 A4
Yorkshire Grey Yd
WC1 240 C3
Yorkshire Rd
Limehouse E14 97 A1
Mitcham CR4 204 A5
York Sq 12 E14 97 A1
York St Carshalton CR4 203 A2
Paddington W1 92 D2 237 D4
Twickenham TW1 153 A3
York Terr EN2 5 A5
York Terr E
NW1 93 A3 238 B5
York Terr W
NW1 93 A3 238 A5
Yorkton St E2 96 A5
York Way
Barnsbury N1, N7,
NW1 72 A1
Chessington KT9 214 A1
Friern Barnet N20 14 D1
N1 233 B5
Twickenham TW13 151 B1
York Way Ct
Islington N1 233 C5
Islington N1 233 B5
Youngmans Cl EN2 5 A4
Young Rd E16 99 C1
Young's Bldgs EC1 242 B6
Youngs Brewery Visitor
Ctr* SW18 157 D6
Youngs Ct SW11 268 B1
Youngs Rd IG2 57 B4
Young St W8 113 D4 245 C1
Yoxall Ho 2 W10 90 C3
Yoxford Ct 6 RM6 58 B4
Yoxley App IG2 57 A3
Yoxley Dr IG2 57 A3
Yukon Rd SW12 159 B4
Yunus Khan Cl E17 53 C4

Z

Zambezie Dr N9 18 C1
Zampa Rd SE16 118 C1
Zander Ct E2 96 A4
Zangwill Ho NW6 91 B5
Zangwill Rd SE18, SE3 143 D4
Zealand Ave UB7 126 A5
Zealand Ho
11 Camberwell SE5 139 A3
4 Woolwich SE7 122 A2
Zealand Rd E3 97 A5
Zenith Lo 7 N3 29 D3
Zennor Rd SW12 159 C3
Zenoria St SE22 139 D1
Zermatt Rd CR7 205 A5
Zetland Ho W8 255 C6
Zetland St E14 98 A2
Zeus Ho N1 235 C1
Zion Ho 6 E1 96 C1
Zion Pl CR7 205 B5
Zion Rd CR7 205 B5
Zircon Ct N11 31 D3
ZK Pk CR0 220 B5
Zoar St SE1 117 A5 252 A4
Zodiac Ct CR0 204 D1
Zodiac Ho 3 E3 97 C3
Zoffany St N19 71 D6

List of numbered locations

This atlas shows thousands more place names than any other London street atlas. In some busy areas it is impossible to fit the name of every place.

Where not all names will fit, some smaller places are shown by a number. If you wish to find out the name associated with a number, use this listing.

The places in this list are also listed normally in the Index.

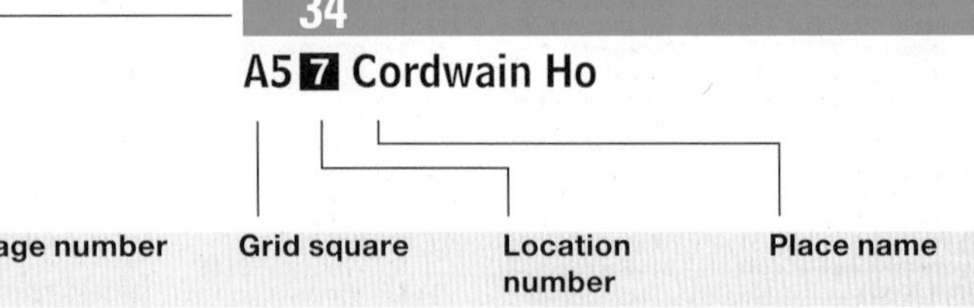

Page number	Grid square	Location number	Place name

1
A1 1 Hertswood Ct
2 Abingdon Lo
3 Sunbury Ct
4 Meriden Ho
5 Norfolk Ct
6 Vanburgh Ct
7 Morrison Ct
8 Kingshill Ct
9 Baronsmere Ct
10 Chartwell Ct
A2 1 Richard Ct
2 Alston Ct
3 Ridgeleigh Ct
4 Bartletts Cotts
5 Leathersellers Cl
6 Holkham Ho
7 Leinster Mews
B1 1 Olivia Ct
2 Tudor Ct
3 Gordon Mans
B2 1 Brake Shear Ho
2 Durham Ct
3 Huntingdon Ct
4 Cambridge Ct
5 Summit Ct
D1 1 Cranleigh Ct
2 Valeside Ct
3 Sherwood
4 Bradbury Ct
5 Chester Ho
6 Graham Ho
7 Highfield Ct
8 Amberley Ho
9 Hadley View
10 Stratton Lo
11 Gainsborough Ct
12 Christopher Ct
13 Bowmar Lo

2
A1 1 Hanover Ho
2 St Giles Ho
3 Henrietta Ho
4 Byron Ct
5 Preston Ct
6 Clivedon Ct
7 Battle House Mews
8 Phoenix Ct
9 Landsdown Cl
10 Comer Ho
11 Basil Ct
12 Russell Ct
13 Alice Ct
C1 1 Braeburn Ct
2 Bramley Ct
3 Cox Ct
4 Golden Ct
5 Pippin Ct
6 Russet Ct
7 High Birch Ct
8 Joystone Ct
9 Mark Lo
10 Edgeworth Ct

4
D3 1 Oakington Ct
2 Elderberry Ct
3 Blueberry Ct
4 Butterfield Ho

5
C1 1 Woodfield Cl
2 Fielders Cl

7
A2 1 Amethyest Ct
2 Bradmore Ct
3 Acer Ct
4 Cornell Ct
5 Durnsford Ct
6 Feldspar Ct
C6 1 Whitworth Cres
2 Polsten Mews
3 Aldis Mews
4 Dundas Mews
5 Colt Mews
6 Warlow Cl
7 Barrass Cl
8 Rigby Pl
9 Gunner Dr
10 Colgate Pl
11 Baddeley Cl
12 Sten Cl
13 Pritchett Cl
14 Rubin Pl
15 Turpin Cl
16 Island Centre Way
17 Hispano Mews
18 Watkin Mews
19 Wallace Ct
20 Needham Ct
21 Dryer Ct
22 Webley Ct
23 Frosbery Ct
24 Jacob Ct
25 Peabody Ct
26 Greener Ct
27 Bren Ct

9
D5 1 Watling Ct
2 Stuart Ct
3 Westview Ct
4 Potters Mews

13
D6 1 Rowan Wlk
2 Ford Ho
3 Glenwood Ho
4 Whitegates
5 Lisa Lo
6 South Lo
7 Hockington Ct
8 Lysander Ct
9 Ashwood Lo
10 Thornbridge Ct
11 Invergarry Ct
12 Eysham Ct
13 Warwick Ct
14 Chaucer Ct
15 Coleridge Ct
16 Springfields
17 Bure Ct
18 Florence Ct
19 Minetta Ct

14
A1 1 Belmont Ct
2 Terrace Ho
3 Croft Mews
4 Bluebell Ct
A2 1 Westview Ct
2 Oakleigh Mews
3 Mountview Ct
4 Mortimer Ct
5 Parklands
A6 1 Chiltern Ct
2 Gills Ct
3 Beaufort Ct
4 St Augustines Ct
5 Somerset Lo
6 Carlyle Lo
7 Stirling Lo
8 St Mirren Ct
9 Wardrew Ct
10 Apex Lo
11 Westbury Ct
B2 1 Davis Ct
2 Deerings Ct
3 Ashcroft Ct
B6 1 Redrose Trad Ctr
2 Lancaster Road Ind Est
C2 1 Mendip Ct
2 Purbeck Ct
3 Brendon Ct
4 Quantock Ct
5 Malvern Ct
6 Chiltern Ct
C5 1 Feline Ct
2 Brookhill Ct
3 Littlegrove Ct
4 Desmond Ho
D1 1 Springfield Ct
2 Victor Ho
3 Malborough Ho
4 Coopers Ct
5 Joiners Ct
D2 1 Bantock Ct
2 Burgess Ct
3 Heaton Ct
4 Bordley Ct
5 Garside Ct
6 Cranston Ct
7 Gleave Ct
D3 1 Wren Ct
2 Homerton Ct
3 Emmanuel Ct
4 Wolfson Ct
5 Robinson Ct
6 Gonville Ct

15
C6 1 Tregenna Cl
2 Catherine Ct
3 Conisbee Ct
4 Ashmead
D3 1 Dennis Par
2 Broadway The
3 Southgate Cir
4 Station Par
5 Bourneside
6 Bourneside Cres

17
C6 1 Wade Ho
2 Newport Lo
3 Halcyon Ho
4 Lerwick Ct
5 Anchor Ct
6 Grassmere Ct
7 Datchworth Ct
8 Trentham Lo
9 Austin Ct
10 Cedar Grange
11 Brookview Ct
12 Chestbrook Ct
13 Paddock Lo
14 Hamlet Ct
15 Haven Lo

18
A1 1 Plevna Ct
2 Lea Ho
3 Brook Ho
4 Valley Ho
5 Chiltern Ho
6 Blenheim Ho
7 Penn Ho
8 Romany Ho
9 Gilpin Ho
10 Anvil Ho
11 Well Ho
12 Passmore Ho
13 Durbin Ho
A2 1 Market Par
2 Beechwood Mews
3 Keats Par
4 Cedars Rd
5 Cross Keys Ct
6 Dorman Pl
7 Concourse The

20
1 Lea Ct
2 Park Ct
3 Conference Cl
4 Berrybank Cl
5 Russell Lo
6 Brunswick Lo
7 Kenilworth Ct
8 Trinity Ct
9 Kingsmead Lo
10 Fairlawns
A3 1 Knight Ct
2 Grant Ct
3 Chantry The
4 Bowyer Ct
5 Pineview Ct
6 Ellen Ct
7 Leeview Ct
8 Chelsea Ct
9 Bramley Ct
10 Garenne Ct
11 Kendal Ct
12 Fairways
13 Avon Ct
B3 1 Maddox Ct
2 Village Arc The
3 Cambridge Rd
4 Crown Bldgs
5 Pentney Rd
6 Scholars Ho
7 Cranworth Cres
C4 1 Connaught Ct
2 Woolden Ho
3 Fairmead Ct
4 Lockhart Lo
5 Cavendish Ct
6 Oakwood Ct
7 Plains The
8 Hadleigh Ct
9 Forest Ho
10 Mathieson Ho

21
B2 1 Stag Hts
2 Shore Point
3 Buckhurst Hill Ho
4 Beech Ave
5 High Road Buckhurst Hill
6 Highclears
C2 1 Westbury Ct
2 Palmerston Ct
3 Ibrox Ct
4 Richard Burton Ct
5 Queens Mews
6 Gunnels Ct & Hastingwood Ct
7 Marlborough Ct
8 Avenue The
9 Tora Ct
10 Somerset Ct
11 Mirravale Ct
C3 1 Rayburne Ct
2 Laurels The
3 Mablin Lo
4 Silvers
5 Makinen Ho
6 Roman Lo
D1 1 Highview Ho
2 Hornbeam Ho
3 Highview Ho
4 Bourne Ho
D2 1 Regency Lo
2 Kings Ct
3 Beech Ct
4 Sycamore Ho
5 Salisbury Gdns
6 Pegasus Ct
7 Buckhurst Ct
8 Mountbatten Ct
9 Atrium
D6 1 Richmond Ct
2 Highview Ct
3 Collins Ct
4 Lower Park Rd
5 Homecherry Ho

22
C1 1 Daniel Ho
2 Hawthorn Ct
3 Northcote
4 Edwin Ware Ct
5 Chalfont Wlk
6 Maple Ct
7 Montesole Ct
8 Viewpoint Ct

23
B3 1 Russettings
2 St Cuthberts Gdns
3 Cherry Croft Gdns
4 Claire Ct
5 Cornwall Ct
6 Falmouth Ho
7 Newlyn Ct
8 Chestnuts The
9 Dunford Ct
10 Stratton Ct
11 Hanover Ct

25
C5 1 Belgrave Gdns
2 Heywood Ct
3 Norfolk Ho
4 Garden Ct
5 Chatsworth Ct
6 Chartridge Ct
7 Hardwick Cl
8 Cheltenham Ct
9 Cargrey Ho
10 Holbein Ho
11 Goodwood Ct
12 Ascot Pl
13 Longchamp Ct
14 Halfacre
15 Burnham Ct
16 Dingle Ct
17 Woodcroft
18 Daneglen Ct
19 Buckingham Par
C6 1 Bickley Ct
2 Kelmscott Ho
3 Elstree Ho
4 Brompton Ct
5 Kenmare Ct
6 Burlington Park Ho
7 Gressenham Ct
8 Amora

26
D5 1 Penshurst Ct
2 Cranbourne Ct
3 Wilton Ct
4 Saxon Ct
5 Abbey Ct
6 Kenlor Ct
7 Daniel Ct
8 Hillcrest Ct
9 Hunters Lo
10 Orion Ct

27
A1 1 Colesworth Ho
2 Crokesley Ho
3 Curtlington Ho
4 Clare Ho
5 Kedyngton Ho
A3 1 Tadbourne Ct
2 Truman Cl
3 Lords Ct
4 Hutton Row
5 Compton Cl
6 Botham Cl
7 Bradman Row
A6 1 Iris Wlk
2 Sycamore Ct
3 Aster Ct
4 Firethorn Cl
5 Berberry Cl
6 Hibiscus Cl
B5 1 Monarchs Ct
2 Kensington Ct
3 Grosvenor Ct
4 Chasewood Ct
C2 1 Rufforth Ct
2 Riccall Ct
3 Lindholme Ct
4 Driffield Ct
5 Jack Ashley Ct
6 Folkingham La
7 Debden Cl
8 Holbeach Ct
9 Shawbury Cl
10 Daniel Ct
11 Leander Ct
12 Nimrod
13 Nisbet
14 Pixton
15 Rapide
16 Ratier
D1 1 Gauntlet
2 Guilfoyle
3 Grebe
4 Gates
5 Galy
6 Folland
7 Firefly
8 Halifax
9 Debussy
10 Crosbie
11 Grant Ct
12 Ham Ct
13 Deal Ct
14 Ember Ct
15 Canterbury Ct
16 Beaumont Ct
17 Cirrus
18 Defiant
19 Dessouter
20 Douglas
21 Cobham
22 Clayton
23 Camm
24 Bradon
25 Boarhound
26 Bodmin
27 Bleriot
28 Blackburn
29 Audax
30 Anson
31 Albatross
32 Arran Ct
33 Mavis Ct
34 Goosander Ct
35 Platt Halls (a)
36 Writtle Ho
37 Platt Halls (b)
38 Platt Halls (c)
D2 1 Slatter
2 Sopwith
3 Saimet
4 Sassoon
5 Roe
6 Orde
7 Osprey
8 Prodger
9 Randall
10 Porte
11 Norris
12 Nardini
13 Noel
14 Nicolson
15 Napier
16 Nighthawk
17 Moorhouse
18 Moineau
19 Mitchell
20 Lysander
21 March
22 Martynside
23 March
24 Kemp
25 Mercury
26 Merlin
27 Hudson
28 Hawker
29 Hawfinch
30 Heracles
31 Hector
32 Concourse The
D3 1 Wellington
2 Wheeler
3 Whittaker
4 Whittle
5 Tedder
6 Cranwell Ct
7 Tait
8 Spooner

28
D1 1 York Ho
2 Windsor Ho
3 Regency Cres
4 Normandy Ho
5 Allerton Ct
6 Beaulieu Ho
7 Dewlands Ct
8 Knightshayes Ho

29
A3 2 Frances & Dick James Ct
3 Farthing Ct
4 Coniston Ct
B1 1 Carlisle Lo
2 Laburnum Lo
3 Eden Ct
4 Moorcroft Ct
5 Clifford Lo
6 Acacia Lo
7 Cumberland Ct
8 Little Dell Lo
9 Cyprus Ct
10 Cyprus Ho
C2 1 Sheringham Ct
2 St Ronan's
3 Crescent Rise
4 Elm Ct
5 Norman Ct
6 Marlow Ct
7 Dancastle Ct
8 Newman Ct
9 Station Mans
10 Alice Ct
D3 1 Hadley Ct
2 Sherbrook Ho
3 Shine Ho
4 Regent Ct
5 Lodge Mead Ct
6 Spencer Ct
7 Zenith Lo
8 Burberry Ct
D5 1 Silverbell Ct
2 Inverey Ho
3 Wimbush Ho
4 Tudor Lo
5 Duncan Ct
6 Phillipson Ho
D6 1 Brookfield Ct
2 Magnolia Ct
3 Dunbar Ct
4 Haughmond
5 Nansen Village
6 Willow Ct
7 Birch Ct
8 Beechcroft Ct
9 Speedwell Ct
10 Woodside Ct
11 Speedwell Ho
12 Rebecca Ho
13 Ashbourne Ct
14 Forest Ct
15 Beecholme
16 Greville Lo
17 St Johnstone Ho
18 Ashbourne Cl
19 Clements Ct
20 Station App
21 Montclair Ct
22 Winterberry Ct
23 Caroline Ct

30
A4 1 Sharon Ct
2 Lydia Ct
3 Beatrice Lo
4 Grange Ct
5 Blissland Ct
A5 1 Archgate Bsns Ctr
2 Robart Ho
3 Danescroft
4 Cornelius Ct
5 Gable Lo
6 Waterville Lo
7 Chand Ho
B1 1 New Trinity Rd
2 Garden Ho
3 Todd Ho
4 Sayers Ho
5 Mowbray Ho
6 Bouchier Ho
7 Cleveland Ho
8 Goodyear Ho
9 Lochleven Ho
10 Berwick Ho
11 Oak Ho
12 Hilton Ho
13 East View Ho
14 Myddleton Ho
15 Willow Wlk
16 Craven Ho
17 Willow Ho
18 Vane Ho
19 Adelphi Ct
20 Annette White Lo
21 Foskett Ho
22 Elmfield Ho
23 Sycamore Ho
24 Netherwood
25 Rew Lo
26 William Cl
B5 1 Murray Ho
2 Damon Ho
3 Wendy Ho
4 Lychgate Ct
5 Clarence Ct
6 Carley Ct
7 Hermiston Ct
8 Cardrew Ct
9 Whitefriars Ct
D5 1 Halliwick Ct
2 Halliwick Court Par
3 Queen's Par
4 St John's Villas
5 Hartland Ct
6 Kennard Mans
7 Bensley Ct
8 Leadbeaters Cl
9 Gibson Ct
10 Burton Ct
11 Knights Ct
12 Constable Ct
13 Alderman Ct

31
A3 1 Campe Ho
2 Betstyle Ho
3 Pymmes Brook Ho
4 Mosswell Ho
5 Cavendish Ho
6 Tudor Ho
7 Kingsfield Ho
8 Peacehaven Ct
9 Hatch Ho
10 Hampden Ct
11 Crown Ct
A4 1 Cheddar Cl
2 Wincanton Ct
3 Whitby Ct
4 Richmond Ct
5 Tadworth Ct
6 Wensley Cl
7 Howeth Ct
8 Kilnsey Ct
9 Harrogate Ct
10 Ripon Ct
B1 1 Cedar Ct
2 Carisbrook
3 St Ivian Ct
4 Barrington Ct
5 Essex Lo
B6 1 Grovefield
2 Lapworth
3 Stewards Holte Wlk
4 Sarnes Ct
5 Stanhope Ho
6 Holmsdale Ho
7 Crosby Ct
8 Leyland Ct
9 Boundary Ct
10 Stateland Ct
C5 1 Barbara Martin Ho
2 Jerome Ct
3 Limes Cl
4 Arnos Grove Ct
5 Cedar Ct
6 Betspath Ho
7 Curtis Ho
8 Mason Ho
9 Danford Ho
10 New Southgate Ind Est
11 Palmer's Ct
12 Swinson Ho
13 Jackson Ho

32
A4 1 Brownlow Lo
2 Brownlow Ct
3 Latham Ct
4 Fairlawns
5 Beaumaris
C1 1 Penwortham Ct
2 Tarleton Ct
3 Holmeswood Ct
4 Kwesi Johnson Ct
5 Sandlings The
6 Suraj Ho
C6 1 Hazelwood Ct
2 Ashbourne Lo
3 Mapledurham Ct

33
D1 1 Kenmare Dr
2 Ashling Ho
3 Honeysett Rd
4 Wilson's Ave
5 Palm Tree Ct
6 Stoneleigh Ct
7 Brook St
D3 1 Charles Ho
2 Moselle Ho
3 Ermine Ho
4 Kathleen Ferrier Ct
5 Concord Ho
6 Rees Ho
7 Williams Ho
8 Nursery Ct
9 William Rainbird Ho
10 Gibson Bsns Ctr
11 Wingate Trad Est
D4 1 Regan Ho
2 Isis Ho
3 Boundary Ct
4 Stellar Ho
5 Cooperage Cl

34
A5 1 Angel Pl
2 Cross St
3 Scott Ho
4 Beck Ho
5 Booker Rd
6 Bridport Ho
7 Cordwain Ho
8 St James's Ct
9 Highmead
A6 1 Walton Ho
2 Alma Ho
3 Brompton Ho
4 Field Ho
5 Bradwell Mews
6 Angel Corner Par
7 Paul Ct
8 Cuthbert Rd
9 Brockenhurst Mews
B3 1 Kenneth Robbins Ho
2 Charles Bradlaugh Ho
3 Woodrow Ct
4 Cheviot
5 Corbridge
6 Whittingham
7 Eastwood Cl
8 Alnwick
9 Bamburgh
10 Bellingham
11 Briaris Cl

35
A1 1 Clayton Ct
2 St Andrew's Ct
3 Aranya Ct
4 Fitzwilliam Ho
A2 1 Romany Gdns
2 Swansland Gdns
3 Garnett Way
4 Claymore Ct
5 Winchester Ct
C5 1 Ainslie Ho
2 Lewis Ho

36
B5 1 Hedgemoor Ct
2 Hewitt Ho
3 Castle Ho
4 Bailey Ct
5 Harcourt Ho
6 Gerboa Ct
7 Wentworth Ct
D1 1 Chatham Rd
2 Washington Rd
3 Cherry Tree Ct
4 Grosvenor Lo
5 Torfell
D2 1 Hillboro Ct
2 Dorchester Ct

37
A1 1 Chiltons The
2 Ullswater Ct
3 Leigh Ct
4 Woburn Ct
5 Alveston Sq
6 Eaton Ct
7 Regency Ct
8 Cowley Ct
9 High Oaks Lo
A2 1 Lindal Ct
2 Hockley Ct
3 Woodleigh
4 Milne Ct
5 Cedar Ct
6 Elizabeth Ct
7 Silvermead
8 Laurel Mead Ct
9 Mitre Ct
10 Pevensey Ct
11 Lyndhurst Ct
12 Manor Court Lo
A3 1 New Jubilee Ct
2 Chartwell Ct
3 Greenwood
4 Clementine Wlk
A4 1 Terrace The
2 Broomhill Ct
3 Clifton Ct
4 Fairstead Lo
5 Hadleigh Lo
6 Broadmead Ct
7 Wilton Ct
8 Fairfield Ct
9 Higham Ct
10 Aston Ct
A6 1 Tree Tops
2 Cranfield Ct
3 Percival Ho
4 Raine Gdns
B1 1 Station Est
2 Station App
3 James Ct
C3 1 Liston Way
2 Elizabeth Ct
3 Coopersale Cl
4 Sunset Ct
5 Lambourne Ct
C4 1 Hope Cl
2 Rex Par
3 Shalford
4 Rodings The
5 Lawrence Ct
6 Cowan Lo

40
C1 1 Salisbury Ho
2 Rodwell Cl
3 Pretoria Ho
4 Ottawa Ho
5 Swallow Ct
6 Wellington Ho
7 Canberra Ho
C6 1 Tulip Ct
2 Hyacinth Ct
3 Rose Ct
4 Iris Ct
D6 1 Ashburton Ct
2 Northend Lodge

42
D3 1 Nightingale Ct
2 St John's Ct
3 Gayton Ct
4 Wilton Pl
5 Murray Ct
6 Cymbeline Ct
7 Knowles Ct
8 Charville Ct
9 Lime Ct
10 Petherton Ct
11 Garth Ct
12 Chalfont Ct
13 Shepherds Ct
D4 1 Crystal Ctr The
2 Blue Point Ct
3 Ryan Ho
4 Rothwell Ct
5 Bruce Ho
6 Middlesex Ct
7 Ingram Ho
8 Arless Ho
9 Leaf Ho
10 Becket Fold
11 Brandan Ho
12 Robert Ho

46
A2 1 Milton Rd
A3 1 Mapesbury Mews
2 York Mans
3 Telford Rd
A5 1 Pilkington Ct
2 Cousins Ct
3 Seton Ct
4 Frensham Ct
5 Chatton Ct
6 Geraldine Ct
7 Swynford Gdns
8 Miller Ct
9 Roffey Ct
10 Peace Ct
11 Rambler Ct
12 Lion Ct
13 Wenlock Gdns
14 Dogrose Ct
15 Harry Ct
16 Tribune Ct
17 Bonville Gdns
18 Pearl Ct
B4 1 Vivian Mans
2 Parade Mans
3 Georgian Ct
4 Florence Mans
5 Park Mans
6 Cheyne Cl
7 Queens Par
8 Central Mans
C5 1 Courtney Ho
2 Golderton
3 Thornbury
4 Ferrydale Lo
5 Studio Mews
6 Brampton La
7 Short St
8 Belle Vue Rd
9 Longford Ct
10 Ashwood Ho
D5 1 Midford Ho
2 Rockfield Ho
3 Lisselton Ho
4 Acrefield Ho

47
B2 1 Berkeley Ct
2 Exchange Mans
3 Beechcroft Ct
4 Nedahall Ct
B3 1 Charlton Lo
2 Clifton Gdns
B4 1 Hallswelle Par
2 Belmont Par
3 Temple Fortune Ho
4 Yew Tree Ct
5 Temple Fortune Par
6 Courtleigh
7 Arcade Ho
8 Queens Ct
9 Temple Fortune Ct
B5 1 Monkville Par
2 Ashbourne Par

48
A6 1 St Mary's Gn
2 Dunstan Ct
3 Paul Byrne Ho
4 Longfield Ct
5 Warwick Ct
6 Branksome Ct
7 Sherwood Hall

49
B6 1 Dorchester Ct
2 Old Chapel Ct
3 Athenaeum Pl
4 Risborough Ct
5 Risborough Ct
C1 1 Calvert Ct
2 Academy The
3 Whitehall Mans
4 Pauntley St
5 Archway Hts
6 Pauntley Ho
D1 1 Louise White Ho
2 Levison Way
3 Sanders Way
4 Birbeck Ho
5 Scholars Ct
D2 1 Eleanor Rathbone Ho
2 Christopher Lo
3 Monkridge
4 Marbleford Ct
5 High London
6 Garton Ho
7 Hilltop Ho
8 Caroline Martyn Ho
9 Arthur Henderson Ho
10 Margaret Mcmillan Ho
11 Enid Stacy Ho
12 Mary McArthur Ho
13 Bruce Glasier Ho
14 John Wheatley Ho
15 Keir Hardie Ho
16 Monroe Ho
17 Iberia Ho
18 Lygoe Ho
19 Lambert Ho
20 Shelbourne Ho
21 Arkansas Ho
22 Lafitte Ho
23 Shreveport Ho
24 Packenham Ho
25 Orpheus Ho
26 Fayetville Ho
27 Bayon Ho
D4 1 Kelland Cl
2 Truro Ct
3 Veryan Ct
4 Coulsdon Ct

50
A1 1 Beeches The
2 Lambton Ct
3 Nugent Ct
4 Lambton Mews
5 Mews The
A2 1 Marie Lloyd Gdns
2 Edith Cavell Cl
3 Marie Stopes Ct
4 Jessie Blythe La
5 Barbara Rudolph Ct
6 Hetty Rees Ct
7 Leyden Mans
8 Brambledown
9 Lochbie
10 Lyngham Ct
11 High Mount
12 Woodlands The
A4 1 Margaret Hill Ho
2 Manray Ct
3 Hermiston Ct
4 Carleton Ho
A5 1 Mackenzie Ho
2 Stowell Ho
3 Campsbourne Ho
4 Palace Gate Mews
B1 1 Lawson Ct
2 Wiltshire Ct
3 Fenstanton
4 Hutton Ct
5 Wisbech
D5 1 Wordsworth Par
2 Spanswick Lo
B6 1 Langham Cl
2 Sidi Ct
3 Ince Terr

51
A2 1 Finmere Ho
2 Keynsham Ho
3 Kilpeck Ho
4 Knaresborough Ho
5 Leighfield Ho
6 Lonsdale Ho
7 Groveley Ho
8 Wensleydale Ho
9 Badminton Ct
B2 1 Selwood Ho
2 Mendip Ho
3 Ennerdale Ho
4 Delamere Ho
5 Westwood Ho
6 Bernwood Ho
7 Allerdale Ho
8 Chattenden Ho
9 Farningham Ho
10 Oakend Ho
C1 1 Godstone Ct
2 Farnham Ct
3 Milford Ct
4 Cranleigh Ct
5 Haslemere Ct
6 Belmont Ct
7 Hockworth Ho
8 Garratt Ho
9 Fairburn Ho
10 Thorndale Ho
11 Oakdene Ho
12 Briardale Ho
C3 1 Oatfield Ho
2 Perry Ct
3 Henrietta Ho
4 Bournes Ho
5 Chisley Rd
6 Twyford Ho
7 Langford Cl
8 Hatchfield Ho
D1 1 Stamford Hill Mans
2 Montefiore Ct
3 Berwyn Ho
4 Clent Ho
5 Chiltern Ho
6 Laindon Ho
7 Pentland Ho
D2 1 Regent Ct
2 Stamford Lo
3 Regent Ct
D3 1 Sherboro Rd
2 Westcott Cl
3 Cadoxton Ave

52 — continued
D4 1 Westerfield Rd
2 Suffield Rd
D5 1 Laseron Ho
2 Greenway Cl
3 Tottenham Gn E
4 Tottenham Gn E South Side
5 Deaconess Ct
6 Elliot Ct
7 Bushmead Cl
8 Beaufort Ho
9 Tynemouth Terr
D6 1 Holcombe Rd
2 Rigby Ho
3 Chaplin Rd
4 Keswick Apartments
5 Ambleside Cl
6 Lauriston Apartments
7 Terrall Apartments
8 Old School Ct
9 Nicholson Ct
10 Reynardson's Ct
11 Protheroe Ho

52
A1 1 Stamford Gr E
2 Stamford Mans
3 Grove Mans
4 Stamford Gr W
B1 1 Hawkwood Mount
2 Holmbury View
3 High Hill Ferry
4 Leaside Ho
5 Courtlands
6 Ivy Ho
7 Shelford Ct

53
A4 1 Hammond Ct
2 St James Apartments
3 Grange The
A5 1 Bristol Park Rd
2 Stoneydown Ho
3 Callonfield
4 Hardyng Ho
C1 1 Wellington Mans
2 Clewer Ct
3 Cochrane Ct
C5 1 Westbury Ho
2 Hatherley Ho
3 Vintry Mews
4 Tylers Ct
5 Merchants Lo
6 Gillards Mews
7 Blacksmiths Ho
8 Central Par
D1 1 Fitzgerald Ct
2 Bechervaise Ct
3 Underwood Ct
D2 1 Staton Ct
2 Howell Ct
3 Atkinson Ct
4 Russell Ct
5 St Catherines Twr
6 St Lukes Ct
7 St Matthews Ct
8 St Mark's Ct
9 St Elizabeth Ct
10 Emanuel Ct
11 St Thomas Ct
12 Beaumont Ho
13 Shelley Ct
14 St Paul's Twr
15 Flack Ct
16 King Ct
17 Osborne Ct
18 Muriel Ct
19 All Saints Twr
20 St Josephs Ct
D5 1 Nash Ho
2 St Columbas Ho
3 Attlee Terr
4 Astins Ho
5 Lindens The
6 Kevan Ct
7 Squire's Almshouses
8 Berry Field Cl
9 Connaught Ct
10 Holmcroft Ho
11 St Mary's Church Ho
D6 1 Hallingbury Ct
2 Mace Ho
3 Gaitskell Ho
4 Hancocke Ho
5 Trinity Ho
6 Fanshaw Ho
7 Hilltop
8 Batten Ho
9 Bradwell Ho
10 Walton Ho
11 Temple Ho
12 Gower Ho
13 Maple Ho
14 Poplars Ho
15 Cedars Ho
16 Kimm Ho
17 O'Grady Ho
18 Latham Ho
19 Powell Ct
20 Crosbie Ho

54
A2 1 Ayerst Ct
2 Dare Ct
3 St Edwards Ct
A4 1 Collard's Almshouses
2 Ellen Miller Ho
3 Tom Smith Ho
A5 1 Northwood Twr
2 Walnut Ct
3 Albert Whicher Ho
4 Pelly Ct
5 Ravenswood Ind Est
6 Holland Ct
7 Emberson Ho
8 St Mark's Ho
9 Alfred Villas
10 Leonard Ct
11 Old Station Yard The
A6 1 St David's Ct
2 Golden Par
3 Chestnuts Ct
4 Matthew Ct
5 Gilbert Ho
6 Manning Ho
7 Southgate Ho
8 Boyden Ho
9 Prospect Ho
10 Newton Ho
D2 1 Buxton Ho
2 Hanbury Dr
3 Forest Lea
4 Watershipdown Ho

55
A3 1 Aldham Hall
2 Parkside Ct
3 Mapperley Ho
4 Weavers Ho
5 Cyna Ct
6 Reed Mans
7 Thornton Ho
8 Hardwick Ct
A4 1 Kingsley Grange
2 Station Par
3 Gwynne Ho
4 Staveley Ct
5 Thurlow Ct
6 Devon Ho
7 Wellington Pas
8 Wanstead Hts
9 Hollies The
10 Little Holt
11 Hunter Ct
12 Mountier Ct
13 Woodland Ct
14 Dudley Ct
15 Struan Ho
16 Westleigh Ct
A5 1 Shernwood Ho
2 Orwell Lo
3 Hermitage Ct
4 Gowan Lea
5 Woodford Ho
6 Eagle Ct
7 Newbury Ct
8 Shelley Ct
9 Hardy Ct
10 Dickens Ct
11 Byron Ct
A6 1 Millbrook
2 Half Acre
3 Elmbrook
4 Grange The
5 Glenavon Lo
6 Glenwood Ct
7 Ferndown
8 Embassy Ct
9 Orestes Ct
10 Walbrook
11 Helmsley
B4 1 Nightingale Ct
2 Chelston Ct
3 Grosvenor Ct
4 Louise Ct
5 St Davids Ct
6 Cedar Ct
7 Shrubbery The
8 Nightingale Mews
B5 1 Great Hall The
2 Clock Ct
3 Langham Ho
B6 1 Victoria Ct
2 Kenwood Gdns
3 Thaxted Ct
4 Albert Rd
5 Albert Ho
6 Falcon Ct
7 Deborah Ct
8 Swift Ho
9 Pulteney Gdns
10 Spring Ct
11 Trinity Gdns

56
B4 1 High View Par
2 Spurway Par
3 Florence Root Ho
4 Rohan Pl
5 Homeheather Ho

57
A3 1 Catherine Ct
2 Lincoln Ct
3 Ivy Terr
4 Newbury Cotts

58
B1 1 Caledonian Cl

2 Talisman Cl
3 Norseman Cl
4 Frank Slater Ho
5 Brook's Mans
6 Brook's Par
B2 1 Mitre Ct
2 Coppins The
3 Stanetta Ct
4 Wilnett Ct
5 Wilnett Villas
B4 1 Sudbury Ct
2 Dunwich Ct
3 Cromer Terr
4 Norfolk Ct
5 Framlingham Ct
6 Yoxford Ct
C4 1 Swaffham Ct
2 Nacton Ct
3 Suffolk Ct
D2 1 Pavement Mews
2 Chadview Ct
3 Granary Ct
4 Bedwell Ct
5 Chapel La
6 Faulkner Cl
7 Maple Ct
8 Willow Ct
9 Cedar Terr

63
C2 1 Wimborne Ct
2 Haydock Green Flats
3 Brighton Dr
4 Blaydon Ct
5 Fakenham Cl
6 Rutland Ho
7 Windsor Ho

65
D3 1 Lowry Lo
2 Morritt Ho
3 Charles Goddard Ho
4 Snow Ct
5 Willow Tree Ct
6 Oak Lo

66
A2 1 Montrose Cres
2 Peggy Quirke Ct
3 Marylebone Ct
4 Waterloo Ct
5 Euston Ct
6 St Pancras Ct
7 Paddington Ct
8 Copland Mews
9 Coronet Par
10 Aylestone Ct
11 Charlotte Ct
A3 1 Wembley Mkt
2 Market Way
3 Lodge Ct
4 Central Sq
5 Manor Ct
6 Rupert Ave
7 Lily Ho
C4 1 Wembley Mkt

67
A5 1 Curie Ho
2 Darwin Ho
3 Priestley Ho
4 Rutherford Ho
5 Fleming Ho
6 Lister Ho
7 Edison Ho
B1 1 Biko Ho
2 Kingthorpe Terr
3 Scott Ho
4 Peary Ho
5 Shackleton Ho
6 Amundsen Ho
7 Brentfield Ho
8 Nansen Ho
9 Stonebridge Ct
10 Newcroft Ho
11 Magellan Ct
12 Leadbetter Ct
13 Jefferies Ho
14 Cowan Ct
15 Prothero Ho
16 Crawford St
17 Clark Ct
18 Diamond St
19 Mary Seacole Villas
C1 1 Beveridge Rd
2 Purcell Mews
3 George Lansbury Ho
4 Charles Hobson Ho
5 Reade Wlk
6 Westbury Ho
7 Bridge Ct
C4 1 Grange Ct
2 Green Ct
C5 1 Hazelwood Ct
2 Winslow Cl

68
A2 1 Regency Mews
2 Tudor Mews
3 Utopia Ho
4 Bell Flats
5 Angel Ct

A5 1 Bourne Ho
2 Carton Ho
3 Bidwell Ho
4 Woodbridge Cl
5 Mackenzie Ho
6 Banting Ho
C2 1 Rutland Park Gdns
2 Rutland Park Mans
3 Queens Par
4 Harcourt Ho
5 Solidarity Ho
6 Electra Ct
7 Cassandra Ct
8 Carlton Ct
D4 1 Oaklands Mews
2 Acer Ct
3 Maple Ct
4 Argyle Mans

69

A1 1 Christ Church Ct
2 Paul Daisley Ct
3 Fountain Ho
4 Kingston Ho
5 Waverley Ct
6 Weston Ho
7 Mapes Ho
8 Athelstan Gdns
9 Leff Ho
B1 1 Alma Birk Ho
2 Brooklands Ct
3 Brooklands Court Apartments
4 Cleveland Mans
5 Buckley Ct
6 Webheath
B5 1 Mortimer Cl
2 Primrose Ct
3 Sunnyside Ho
4 Sunnyside
5 Prospect Pl
C1 1 Linstead St
2 Embassy Ho
3 Acol Ct
4 Kings Wood Ct
5 Douglas Ct
6 King's Gdns
7 Carlton Mans
8 Smyrna Mans
9 New Priory Ct
10 Queensgate Pl
11 Brondesbury Mews
C2 1 Dene Mans
2 Sandwell Cres
3 Sandwell Mans
4 Hampstead West
5 Redcroft
C3 1 Orestes Mews
2 Walter Northcott Ho
3 Polperro Mans
4 Lyncroft Mans
5 Marlborough Mans
6 Alexandra Mans
7 Cumberland Mans
8 Cavendish Mans
9 Ambassador Ct
10 Welbeck Mans
11 Inglewood Mans
12 Dennington Park Mansions
C5 1 Portman Hts
2 Hermitage Ct
3 Moreland Ct
4 Wendover Ct
D2 1 Beswick Mews
2 Worcester Mews
3 Minton Mews
4 Doulton Mews
5 Laurel Ho
6 Sandalwood Ho
7 Iroko Ho
8 Banyan Ho
9 Rosewood Ho
10 Ebony Ho
11 Rosemont Mans
12 Exeter Mews

70

A1 1 Harrold Ho
2 Glover Ho
3 Byron Ct
4 Nalton Ho
A2 1 Petros Gdns
2 Heath Ct
3 Imperial Twrs
4 Fairhurst
5 St John's Ct
6 New College Ct
7 Chalford
8 Rosslyn Mans
9 Sutherland Ho
A4 1 Windmill Hill
2 Highgrove Point
3 Gainsborough Ho
4 Holly Bush Hill
5 Heath Mans
6 Holly Bush Steps
7 Pavilion Ct
8 Holly Berry La
9 New Campden Ct
10 Holly Bush Vale
11 Benham's Pl
12 Prospect Pl
13 Yorkshire Grey Pl
14 Gardnor Mans
15 Ellerdale Cl
16 Monro Ho
17 Prince Arthur Mews
18 Prince Arthur Ct
19 Village Mount
20 Perrin's Ct
21 Wells Ct
22 Bakers Pas
23 Spencer Wlk
24 Bird In Hand Yd
25 Kings Well
26 New Ct
27 Streatley Pl
28 Mansfield Pl
29 Upper Hampstead Wlk
A5 1 Hampstead Sq
2 Stamford Cl
3 Mount Sq The
B1 1 New College Par
2 Northways Par
3 Noel Ho
4 Campden Ho
5 Centre Hts
6 Hickes Ho
7 Swiss Terr
8 Leitch Ho
9 Jevons Ho
10 Langhorne Ct
11 Park Lo
12 Avenue Lo
B2 1 Belsize Park Mews
2 Baynes Mews
3 McCrone Mews
B3 1 Belsize Court Garages
2 Roscommon Ho
3 Akenside Ct
B4 1 White Bear Pl
2 Wells Ho The
3 Boades Mews
4 Flask Cotts
5 Coach House Yd
6 Pilgrim's Pl
7 Rosslyn Mews
C2 1 Banff Ho
2 Glenloch Ct
3 Havercourt
4 Holmefield Ct
5 Gilling Ct
6 Howitt Cl
7 Manor Mans
8 Straffan Lo
9 Romney Ct
10 Lancaster Stables
11 Eton Garages
D1 1 Hancock Nunn Ho
2 Higginson Ho
3 Duncan Ho
4 Mary Wharrie Ho
5 Rockstraw Ho
6 Cleaver Ho
7 Chamberlain St
8 Sharples Hall St
9 Primrose Mews
10 Rothwell St
11 St Georges Mews
D2 1 Alder Ho
2 Hornbeam Ho
3 Whitebeam Ho
4 Aspen Ho
5 Rowan Ho
6 Beech Ho
7 Chestnut Ho
8 Oak Ho
9 Willow Ho
10 Sycamore Ho
11 Maple Ho
12 Hazel Ho
13 Elaine Ct
14 Faircourt
15 Walham Ct
16 Stanbury Ct
17 Priory Mans
18 Wellington Ho
19 Grange The
D3 1 Cayford Ho
2 Du Maurier Ho
3 Isokon Flats
4 Palgrave Ho
5 Garnett Ho
6 Stephenson Ho
7 Park Dwellings
8 Siddons Ho
9 Mall Studios
10 Park Hill Wlk
11 Wordsworth Pl
12 Fraser Regnart Ct
13 St Pancras Almshouses

71

A1 1 Bridge Ho
2 Hardington
3 Mead Cl
4 Rugmere
5 Tottenhall
6 Beauvale
7 Broomfield
A2 1 Silverbirch Wlk
2 Penshurst
3 Wingham
4 Westwell
5 Chislet
6 Burmarsh
7 Shipton Ho
8 Stonegate
9 Leysdown
10 Headcorn
11 Lenham
12 Halstow
13 Fordcombe
14 Cannington
15 Langridge
16 Athlone Ho
17 Pentland Ho
18 Beckington
19 Hawkridge
20 Edington
B1 1 Ferdinand Ho
2 Harmood Ho
3 Hawley Rd
4 Hawley Mews
5 Leybourne St
6 Barling
7 Tiptree
8 Havering
9 Candida Ct
10 Lorraine Ct
11 Donnington Ct
12 Welford Ct
13 Torbay Ct
14 Bradfield Ct
15 Torbay St
16 Water La
17 Leybourne Rd
18 Haven St
19 Stucley Pl
20 Lawrence Ho
B2 1 Ashington
2 Priestley Ho
3 Leonard Day Ho
4 Old Dairy Mews
5 Monmouth Ho
6 Alpha Ct
7 Una Ho
8 Widford
9 Heybridge
10 Roxwell
11 Hamstead Gates
B4 1 Denyer Ho
2 Stephenson Ho
3 Trevithick Ho
4 Brunel Ho
5 Newcomen Ho
6 Faraday Ho
7 Winifrede Paul Ho
8 Wardlow
9 Fletcher Ct
10 Tideswell
11 Grangemill
12 Hambrook Ct
13 Calver
C1 1 Cherry Tree Ct
2 Chichester Ct
3 Durdans Ho
4 Philia Ho
5 Bernard Shaw Ct
6 Foster Ct
7 Bessemer Ct
8 Hogarth Ct
9 Rochester Ct
10 Soane Ct
11 Wallett Ct
12 Inwood Ct
13 Wrotham Rd
14 St Thomas Ct
15 Caulfield Ct
16 Bruges Pl
17 Reachview Cl
18 Lawfords Wharf
C3 1 Eleanor Ho
2 Falkland Pl
3 Kensington Ho
4 Willingham Cl
5 Kenbrook Ho
6 Aborfield
7 Great Field
8 Appleford
9 Forties The
10 Maud Wilkes Cl
11 Dunne Mews
12 Dowdeny Cl
C4 1 Benson Ct
2 Tait Ho
3 Manorfield Cl
4 Greatfield Cl
5 Longley Ho
6 Lampson Ho
7 Davidson Ho
8 Palmer Ho
9 Lambourn Cl
10 Morris Ho
11 Owen Ho
C5 1 Hunter Ho
2 Fisher Ho
3 Lang Ho
4 Temple Ho
5 Palmer Ho
6 Carlisle Ho
7 Durham Ho
8 Suffolk Ho
9 Lincoln Ho
10 Llewellyn Ho
11 Fell Ho
12 Aveling Ho
13 Merryweather Ct
14 Rennards Ct
15 St Christophers Ct
16 Francis Terrace Mews
C6 1 Flowers Mews
2 Archway Cl
3 Sandridge St
4 Bovingdon Cl
5 Cavell Ct
6 Torrence Ho
7 Rowan Wlk
8 Laurel Cl
9 Forest Way
10 Larch Cl
11 Pine Cl
12 Alder Mews
13 Aspen Cl
D1 1 Hillier Ho
2 Gairloch Ho
3 Cobham Mews
4 Bergholt Mews
5 Blakeney Cl
6 Weavers Way
7 Allensbury Pl
D2 1 Rowstock
2 Peckwater Ho
3 Wolsey Ho
4 Pandian Way
5 Busby Mews
6 Caledonian Sq
7 Canal Bvd
8 Northpoint Sq
9 Lock Mews
10 Carters Cl
11 York Ho
12 Hungerford Rd
13 Cliff Road Studios
14 Cliff Ct
15 Camelot Ho
16 Church Studios
17 Camden Terr
D3 1 Blake Ho
2 Quelch Ho
3 Lee Ho
4 Willbury Ho
5 Howell Ho
6 Holmsbury Ho
7 Leith Ho
8 Betchworth Ho
9 Rushmore Ho
10 Dugdale Ho
11 Horsendon Ho
12 Colley Ho
13 Coombe Ho
14 Ivinghoe Ho
15 Buckhurst Ho
16 Saxonbury Ct
17 Charlton Ct
18 Apollo Studios
19 Barn Cl
20 Long Meadow
21 Landleys Field
22 Margaret Bondfield Ho
23 Haywood Lo
D4 1 Fairlie Ct
2 Trecastle Way
3 Dalmeny Avenue Est
4 Hyndman Ho
5 Carpenter Ho
6 Graham Ho
7 Tufnell Mans
D5 1 Melchester Ho
2 Norcombe Ho
3 Weatherbury Ho
4 Wessex Ho
5 Archway Bsns Ctr
6 Harford Mews
7 Opera Ct
8 Rupert Ho
9 All Saints Church
D6 1 Bowerman Ct
2 Gresham Pl
3 Hargrave Mans
4 Church Garth
5 John King Ct
6 Ramsey Ct

72

A3 1 Kimble Ho
2 Saxonbury Ct
3 Poynder Ct
4 Pangbourne Ho
5 Moulsford Ho
A4 1 Arcade The
2 Macready Pl
3 Cardwell Rd
4 Mcmorran Ho
5 Crayford Ho
6 Whitby Ct
7 Prospect Pl
A5 1 Northview
2 Tufnell Park Mans
3 Fulford Mans
4 Tollington Ho
A6 1 Bracey Mews
2 Christie Ct
3 Ringmer Gdns
4 Kingsdown Rd
5 Cottenham Ho
6 St Paul's Ct
7 Rickthorne Rd
8 Stanley Terr
9 Arundel Lo
10 Landseer Ct
B1 1 Kerwick Cl
2 Rydston Cl
3 Skegness Ho
4 Frederica St
5 Ponder St
6 Kings Ct
7 Freeling St
8 Coatbridge Ho
9 Tilloch St
B2 1 Burns Ho
2 Scott Ho
3 Wellington Mews
4 Roman Ct
5 Piccadilly Ct
B3 1 Culverin Ct
2 Garand Ct
3 Mount Carmel
B4 1 Buckmaster Ho
2 Loreburn Ho
3 Cairns Ho
4 Halsbury Ho
5 Chelmsford Ho
6 Cranworth Ho
B6 1 Berkeley Wlk
2 Lazar Wlk
3 Thistlewood Cl
4 Tomlins Wlk
5 Andover Ho
6 Barmouth Ho
7 Chard Ho
8 Methley Ho
9 Rainford Ho
10 Woodbridge Cl
11 Allerton Wlk
12 Falconer Wlk
13 Sonderburg Rd
14 St Mark's Mans
15 Athol Ct
C1 1 Mountfort Terr
2 Avon Ho
3 Buckland Ho
4 Dovey Lo
5 Carfree Cl
6 Mitchell Ho
7 New College Mews
8 Lofting Ho
9 Brooksby Ho
10 Cara Ho
C3 1 Slaney Pl
2 Eastwood Cl
3 Milton Pl
4 Hartnoll Ho
5 St James School Flats
6 Widnes Ho
7 Tranmere Ho
8 Victoria Mans
9 Formby Ct
10 Mersey Ho
11 Birkenhead Ho
12 Drayton Park Mews
C6 1 Brookfield
2 Churnfield
D1 1 Islington Park Mews
2 Evelyn Denington Ct
3 Bassingbourn Ho
4 Cadmore Ho
5 Adstock Ho
6 Garston Ho
7 Flitton Ho
8 Datchworth Ho
9 Battishill St
10 Almeida St
11 Edward's Cotts
12 Hyde's Pl
13 Tyndale Terr
14 Spriggs Ho
15 Barratt Ho
16 Spencer Pl
17 Chadston Ho
18 Whiston Ho
19 Wakelin Ho
20 Tressel Cl
21 Canonbury Ct
22 Halton Ho
23 Shillingford St
24 Highburty Mans
25 Premier Ho
26 Waterloo Gdns
D2 1 Hampton Ct
2 Salisbury Ho
D3 1 De Barowe Mews
2 Fieldview Ct
3 Viewpoint
4 Ashurst Lo
D4 1 Chestnuts The
2 Bowen Ct
3 Peckett Sq
D5 1 Hurlock Ho
2 Blackstock Ho
3 Vivian Comma Cl
4 Monsell Ct

73

A1 1 Astey's Row
2 Lincoln Ho
3 Worcester Ho
4 Melville Pl
5 Wontner Cl
6 Hedingham Cl
7 Laundry La
8 Base Apartments
9 Walkinshaw Ct
10 New Bentham Ct
11 Bentham Ct
12 Haslam Ho
13 Horsfield Ho
14 Riverside Ho
15 Eric Fletcher Ct
16 Annette Cres
17 Ashby Ho
18 Lindsey Mews
19 Cardigan Wlk
20 Red House Sq
A2 1 Crowline Wlk
2 Upper Handa Wlk
3 Handa Wlk
4 Lismore Wlk
5 Bardsey Wlk
6 Walney Wlk
7 Upper Bardsey Wlk
8 Upper Lismore Wlk
9 Sark Ho
10 Guernsey Ho
11 Guernsey Rd
12 Sybil Thorndike Ho
13 Clephane Rd
14 Florence Nightingale Ho
15 Jersey Ho
16 Jethou Ho
17 Islay Wlk
18 Upper Caldy Wlk
19 Caldy Wlk
20 Alderney Ho
21 Gulland Wlk
22 Marquess Rd S
23 Upper Gulland Wlk
24 Church Rd
25 Oransay Rd
A3 1 Pearfield Ho
2 Larchfield Ho
3 Beresford Terr
4 Pondfield Ho
5 Ashfield Ho
6 Elmfield Ho
A4 1 Fountain Mews
2 Woodstock Ho
3 Henson Ct
4 Taverner Sq
B1 1 Downham Ct
2 Trafalgar Point
B2 1 John Kennedy Ct
2 John Kennedy Lo
3 Ball's Pond Pl
4 Haliday Wlk
5 Queen Elizabeth Ct
6 Canonbury Hts
7 Pinnacle The
8 Threadgold Ho
9 Wakeham St
10 Saffron Ct
11 Callaby Terr
12 Tilney Gdns
13 Westcliff Ho
14 Ilford Ho
15 Ongar Ho
16 Greenhills Terr
17 Romford Ho
18 Bute Wlk
19 Upper Ramsey Wlk
20 Rona Wlk
21 Thorndike Rd
B4 1 Ledo Ho
2 Salween Ho
3 Prome Ho
4 Arakan Ho
5 Rangoon Ho
6 Mandalay Ho
7 Karen Ho
8 Wingate Ho
9 Jubet Ho
10 Orde Ho
11 Chindit Ho
12 Mabel Thornton Ho
13 Crawshay Ho
14 Avon Ho
15 Connaught Mans
16 Jonson Ho
17 Herrick Ho
18 Donne Ho
19 Thirlmere Ho
20 Grasmere Ho
B6 1 Chestnut Cl
2 Sycamore Ho
3 Lordship Ho
4 Clissold Ho
5 Beech Ho
6 Laburnum Ho
7 Ormond Ho
8 Yew Tree Ct
9 Oak Ho
C1 1 Dorchester Ct
2 Wareham Ct
3 Dorset Ct
4 Stratton Ct
5 Swanage Ct
6 Blandford Ct
7 Portland Ct
8 Oscar Faber Pl
9 Metropolitan Bsns Ctr
10 Lancaster Cl
11 Palazzo Apartments
C2 1 Kingsland Gn
2 Kingsland Pas
3 Metropolitan Benefit Societies Almshouses
4 Nimrod Pas
5 De Beauvoir Pl
6 Warburton Cl
7 Buckingham Mews
8 Aztec Ct
C3 1 Hewling Ho
2 Matthias Ho
3 Port Royal Pl
4 Cressington Cl
5 King Henry's Yd
6 Bronte Ho
7 Sewell Ho
8 Lydgate Ho
9 Patmore Ho
10 Congreve Ho
11 Elton St
12 Conrad Ho
13 Southwell Ho
14 Neptune Ho
15 Campion Ho
16 Webster Ho
17 Meredith Ho
18 Beckford Ho
19 Ashley Ct
20 Hayling Cl
21 Millard Cl
22 Lydford Cl
23 Salcombe Rd
24 Truman's Rd
25 Templeton Cl
26 John Campbell Rd
27 Gillett Pl
28 Bradbury St
29 Thomas Crowell Ct
C4 1 Londesborough Ho
2 Knebworth Ho
3 Knebworth Rd
4 Bransby Ct
5 Imperial Ave
6 Leonard Pl
7 Shakspeare Mews
8 Binyon Ho
9 Shelley Ho
10 Browning Ho
11 Burns Ho
12 Andrew Marvell Ho
13 Wycliffe Ho
14 Blake Ho
15 Marlowe Ho
16 Fletcher Ho
17 Chaucer Ct
C5 1 Gujarat Ho
2 Marton Rd
3 Painsthorpe Rd
4 Selkirk Ho
5 Defoe Ho
6 Edward Friend Ho
7 Sheridan Ho
8 Barrie Ho
9 Arnold Ho
10 MacAulay Ho
11 Stowe Ho
12 Carlyle Ho
13 Shaftesbury Ho
14 Lillian Cl
15 Swift Ho
16 Dryden Ho
17 Scott Ct
18 Kingsfield Ho
19 Uhura Sq
20 Hartopp Ct
D1 1 Hilborough Rd
2 Shoreditch Ct
3 Evergreen Sq
4 Wyndhams Ct
5 Festival Ct
6 Fortune Ct
7 Rose Ct
8 Ability Plaza
D2 1 Prospect Ho
2 Woodland St
3 Crosby Wlk
4 Kirkland Wlk
5 Bowness Cl
6 Carlisle Wlk
7 Skelton Cl
8 Camerton Cl
9 Buttermere Wlk
10 Houghton Cl
11 Hayton Cl
12 Kingsland Sh Ctr
13 Springfield Ho
14 Parton Lo
15 Sanctuary Mews
D3 1 Miller's Terr
2 Chow Sq
3 Drysdale Flats
4 Gateway Mews
5 Birkbeck Mews
6 Winchester Pl
D4 1 Coronation Ave
2 Morris Blitz Ct
3 Shacklewell Ho
4 Alexandra Ct
D5 1 Lawrence Bldgs
2 Cottage Wlk
3 Batley Pl
D6 1 Garnham St
2 Garnham Cl
3 Sanford La
4 Sanford Wlk
5 Abney Gdns
6 Fleet Wood

74

A1 1 Aldington Ct
2 Bayton Ct
3 Rochford Wlk
A2 3 Burdon Ct
4 Thomson Ct
5 Bruno Ct
A3 1 Kingsdown Ho
2 Glendown Ho
3 Moredown Ho
4 Blakeney Cl
5 Beeston Cl
6 Benabo Ct
7 David Devine Ho

8 Kreedman Wlk
9 Hermitage Row
10 Grafton Ct
11 Lushington Terr
12 Aspen Ct
13 Pykewell Lo
14 Albion Works Studios
A5 1 Ravenscourt
2 Mellington Ct
3 Rendlesham Ho
4 Carroll Ct
A6 1 Cazenove Mans
2 Chedworth Ho
3 Aldergrove Ho
4 Abbotstone Ho
5 Briggeford Cl
6 Inglethorpe Ho
7 Ashdown Ho
8 Epping Ho
9 Cypress Cl
B1 1 Fortescue Ave
2 Pemberton Pl
3 Weston Wlk
4 Bayford St Ind Ctr
5 Bayford St
6 Sidworth St
7 Helmsley St
8 Cyntra Pl
9 Signal Ho
10 All Nations Ho
11 Vanguard Ho
12 Hacon Sq
B2 1 Bohemia Pl
2 Graham Mans
3 Marvin St
4 Boscobel Ho
5 Royal Oak Rd
6 Colonnades The
7 Sylvester Ho
8 Sylvester Path
9 Doctor Spurstowe Almshouses
10 Great Eastern Bldgs
11 Sojourner-Truth Cl
B3 1 Birchington Ho
2 Bicknor Ho
3 Boxley Ho
4 Adisham Ho
5 Cranbrook Ho
6 Marden Ho
7 Broome Ho
8 Crandale Ho
9 Cheriton Ho
10 Ditton Ho
11 Langley Ho
12 Dymchurch Ho
13 Elham Ho
14 Davina Ho
15 Pembury Pl
16 Downs Ct
17 Perrywood Ho
18 Staplehurst Ho
19 Pegwell Ho
20 Yalding Ho
21 Northbourne Ho
22 Monkton Ho
23 Milsted Ho
24 Athlone Cl
25 Clarence Pl
26 Gould Terr
27 Quested Ct
28 Brett Pas
29 Marcon Ct
30 Appleton Ct
B4 1 Ross Ct
2 Downs La
3 Gaviller Pl
4 Robert Owen Lo
5 Apprentice Way
6 Arrowe Ct
7 Gilwell Ct
8 Sutton St
9 St Andrews Mans
10 Kinnoull Mans
11 Rowhill Mans
12 Sladen Pl
13 Mothers Sq The
14 Richborough Ho
15 Sandgate Ho
16 Sheppey Ho
B5 1 De Vere Ct
2 Redcliffe Ct
3 Greville Ct
4 Anthony Kendal Ho
B6 1 Wentwood Ho
2 Woolmer Ho
3 Warwick Ct
4 Winslade Ho
5 Morriss Ho
6 Woodfield Ho
7 Rossendale Ho
8 Ettrick Ho
9 Charnwood Ho
10 Boyne Ho
11 Whitwell Ho
12 Scardale Ho
13 Hendale Ho
14 Brampton Cl
15 Aveley Ct
16 Aldeburgh Ct
17 Dennington Cl
C1 1 Pitcairn Ho
2 Lyme Grove Ho
3 Shakespeare Ho
4 Upcott Ho
5 Loddiges Ho

6 Parkinson Ho
7 Sloane Ho
8 Vanbrugh Ho
9 Cambridge Pas
10 Lyttleton Ho
11 Victoria Park Ct
12 Tullis Ho
13 Fairchild Ho
14 Forsyth Ho
15 Tradescant Ho
16 Mason Ho
17 Capel Ho
18 Cordwainers Ct
19 Bridgeman Ho
20 St Thomas's Pl
21 Barclay Ho
22 Clayton Ho
23 Danby Ho
24 Sherard Ho
25 Catesby Ho
26 Petiver Ct
27 Leander Ct
28 Philip Turner Est
29 Grendon Ho
30 Shore Mews
31 Shore Bsns Ctr
32 Kendal Ho
33 Classic Mans
34 Tudor Ho
35 Park Ho
36 Enterprise Ho
37 Alpine Gr
38 Clarendon Cl
39 Rotheley Ho
40 Bernie Grant Ho
C2 1 Woolpack Ho
2 Elvin Ho
3 Thomas Ho
4 Hockley Ho
5 Retreat Ho
6 Butfield Ho
7 Brooksbank Ho
8 Cresset Ho
9 Brooksbank St
10 Lennox Ho
11 Milborne Ho
12 Collent Ho
13 Middlesex Pl
14 Elsdale Ho
15 Devonshire Hall
16 Brent Ho
C6 1 Haybridge Ho
2 Framlingham Cl
3 Halesworth Cl
4 Harleston Cl
5 Lowestoft Cl
6 Howard Ho
D1 1 Stuart Ho
2 Gascoyne Ho
3 Chelsfield Point
4 Sundridge Ho
5 Banbury Ho
6 Lauriston Ho
D2 1 Musgrove Ho
2 Cheyney Ho
3 Haynes Ho
4 Warner Ho
5 Gilby Ho
6 Gadsden Ho
7 Risley Ho
8 Baycliffe Ho
9 Sheldon Ho
10 Offley Ho
11 Latimer Ho
12 Ribstone Ho
13 Salem Ho
14 Fieldwick Ho
15 Lever Ct
16 Matson Ho
17 Wilding Ho
18 Rennell Ho
19 Dycer Ho
20 Granard Ho
21 Whitelock Ho
22 Harrowgate Ho
23 Cass Ho
24 Lofts on the Park
25 Heathcote Point
26 Ravenscroft Point
27 Vanner Point
28 Hensley Point
29 San Ho
D4 1 Cromford Path
2 Longford Ct
3 Overbury Ho
4 Heanor Ct
5 Wharfedale Ho
6 Ladybower Ct
7 Ilkeston Ct
8 Derby Ct
9 Rushmore Cres
10 Blackwell Cl
11 Belper Ct

75
A2 1 Chigwell Ct
2 Wellday Ho
3 Selman Ho
4 Vaine Ho
5 Trower Ho
B2 1 Mallard Cl
2 Merriam Ave
3 Gainsborough St
D6 1 Hammond Ct
2 Sorensen Ct
3 Hinton Ct

76
B1 1 Service Route No 2
2 Service Route No 3
B4 1 Mulberry Ct
2 Rosewood Ct
3 Gean Ct
4 Blackthorn Ct
5 Cypress Ct
C1 1 Stratford Office Village The
2 Violet Ct
3 Mandrake Way
4 Brimstone Ho
5 Hibiscus Lo
6 Glasier Ct
C3 1 Bordeaux Ho
2 Luxembourg Mews
3 Basle Ho
C5 1 Acacia Bsns Ctr
2 Brook Ct
3 Gainsfield Ct
4 Artesian Wlk
5 Doreen Capstan Ho
6 Apollo Ho
7 Peppermint Pl
8 Denmark St
9 Mills Ct
10 Paramount Ho
11 Robinson Cl
C6 1 Nansen Ct
2 Mallinson Ct
3 Barbara Ward Ct
4 Caradon Ct
5 Noel Baker Ho
6 Corigan Ct
7 Norman Ho
8 Willow Ct
9 Lime Ct
10 Owens Mews
11 Marnie Ct
12 Cotton Cl
D1 1 Flint Cl
2 St Matthews Ct
3 Ammonite Ho
4 Stone Ct
D2 1 Common The
2 Wolffe Gdns
3 College Pt
4 Onyx Mews
5 Candlelight Ct
6 Boltons The

77
A4 1 Bronte Ct
2 Anna Neagle Cl
3 Brownlow Rd
4 Carrington Gdns
5 Vera Lynn Cl
C1 1 Sarwan Ho
2 Bridgepoint Lofts
3 Vineyard Studios

78
C3 1 Stewart Rainbird Ho
2 Abraham Fisher Ho
3 Redo Ho
4 George Comberton Wlk
C4 1 Cardamom Ct
2 Annie Taylor Ho
3 Richard Fell Ho
4 Susan Lawrence Ho
5 Walter Hurford Par
6 John Cornwell VC Ho
C5 1 Charlbury Ho
2 Willis Ho
3 Arthur Walls Ho
4 Blakesley Ho
5 Twelve Acre Ho
6 Beech Ct
7 Golding Ct
D1 1 Aveley Mans
2 Harlow Mans
3 Danbury Mans
4 Mayland Mans
5 Bowers Ho
6 Webber Ho
7 Paulson Ho
8 Collins Ho
9 Jack Cook Ho
D3 1 St Luke's Path
2 Springfield Ct
D5 1 Postway Mews
2 Oakfield Ho
3 Janice Mews
4 Kenneth More Rd
5 Clements Ct
6 Handforth Rd
7 Churchill St
8 Oakfield Lo
9 Langdale Ho
10 Ilford Chambers
D6 1 York Ho
2 Opal Mews
3 Florentine Ho
4 Kingsley Mews
5 Hainault Bridge Par

79
A6 1 Spectrum Twr
2 Thames View
3 City View
4 Centreway
5 Axon Pl
D1 1 Upney Ct
2 Edgefield Ct
3 Manor Ct
4 Lambourne Gdns
5 Westone Mans
6 Loveland Mans
7 Edward Mans
8 Clarke Mans
9 Dawson Gdns
10 Sebastian

80
A1 1 Bristol Ho
2 Canterbury Ho
3 Durham Ho
4 Wells Ho
5 Winchester Ho
6 Rosalind Ct
7 Exeter Ho
8 Wheatley Mans
9 Greenwood Mans
10 Plymouth Ho
11 Graham Mans
12 Portia Ct

81
C5 1 Markham Ho
2 Webb Ho
3 Preston Ho
4 Steadman Ho
5 Hyndman Ho
6 Clynes Ho
7 Henderson Ho
8 Blatchford Ho
9 Rogers Ho
10 Sylvia Pankhurst Ho
11 Mary Macarthur Ho
12 Ellen Wilkinson Ho
D2 1 Picador Ho
2 Centurion Lodge
3 Louis Ct
4 Watsons Lo
5 Carpenters Ct
6 Bell Ho
7 Rounders Ct
8 Oldmead Ho
9 Jervis Ct
10 Bartletts Ho
11 Royal Par
12 Richardson Gdns
13 Forsyth Ct
14 Eldridge Ct
15 Madison Ct
16 Bowery Ct
17 Rivington Ct

82
D3 1 Marlborough Par
2 Blenheim Par
3 Lea Ct
4 Westbourne Par
5 Whiteleys Par
6 Hillingdon Par
7 New Broadway

84
C4 1 Dilston Cl
2 Wells Cl
3 Willett Cl
4 Merlin Cl
5 Glyndebourne Ct
6 Albury Ct
7 Osterley Ct
8 Hatfield Ct
9 Gayhurst Ct
D4 1 Caravelle Gdns
2 Farman Gr
3 Viscount Gr
4 Tomahawk Gdns
5 Martlet Gr
6 Trident Gdns
7 Latham Ct
8 Jupiter Ct
9 Westland Ct
10 Seasprite Ct
11 Convair Wlk
12 Mayfly Gdns
13 Valiant Ct
14 Woburn Twr
15 Brett Cl
16 Friars Cl
D5 1 Medlar Ct
2 Cranberry Cl
3 Lely Ho
4 Girtin Ho
5 Cotman Ho
6 Raeburn Ho
7 Gainsborough Twr
8 Stanfield Ho
9 Millais Ct
10 Hunt Ct
11 Poynter Ct
12 Hogarth Ho
13 Constable Ho
14 Bonnington Ct
15 Romney Ct
16 Landseer Ho

85
B1 1 St Crispins Ct

B3 1 Weaver Ho
2 Caldon Ho
3 Ashby Ho
4 Welford Ho
5 Hertford Ho
6 Wey Ho
7 Middlewich Ho
8 Stourbridge Ho
B4 1 Netherton Ho
2 Keadby Ho
3 Tame Ho
4 Dorset Ct
D1 1 Thurlestone Ct
2 Disley Ct
3 Burgess Ct
4 Bayliss Cl
5 Lytham Ct
6 Winford Par
7 Brunel Pl
8 Rutherford Twr
9 Rountree Ct

86
A1 1 Farnham Ct
2 Gleneagles Twr
3 Birkdale Ct
4 Verulam Ct
5 Hartsbourne Ct
6 Ferndown Ct
7 Deal Ct
8 St David's Ct
9 Portrush Ct
10 Alnmouth Ct
11 Panmure Ct
12 Peterhead Ct
13 Sunningdale Ct
D2 1 Denbigh Ct
2 Devon Ct
3 Dorset Ct
4 Glamorgan Ct
5 Gloucester Ct
6 Hereford Ct
7 Merioneth Ct
8 Oxford Ct
9 Monmouth Ct
10 Paddington Ct
11 Pembroke Ct
12 Chadwick Cl
13 Cotts Cl
D3 1 Berkshire Ct
2 Buckingham Ct
3 Cardigan Ct
4 Carmarthen Ct
5 Cornwall Ct
6 Merlin Ct
7 Osprey Ct
8 Pelham Pl
9 Puffin Ct
10 Fulmar Ct
11 Turnstone Terr
D5 1 Medway Par
2 Brabstone Ho
3 Cotswold Ct

87
B3 1 Woodbury Ct
2 Edward Ct
3 Park Lo
C1 1 Hurley Ct
2 Amherst Gdns
3 Tudor Ct
4 Hilton Ho
C2 1 Hutton Ct
2 Cain Ct
3 Langdale Ct
4 William Ct
5 Castlebar Ct
6 Warren Ct
7 White Lo
8 Queen's Ct
9 King's Ct
10 Cheriton Cl
11 Stanley Ct
12 Juniper Ho
C3 1 Holtoake Ct
2 Pitshanger Ct
3 Holtoake Ho

88
A4 1 Nelson Ho
2 Gordon Ho
3 Frobisher Ho
4 Wellington Ho
5 Fairfax Ho
A5 1 Carlyon Mans
2 Ainslie Ct
3 Millers Ct
4 Priory Ct
5 Tylers Ct
6 Twyford Ct
7 Rose Ct
8 Laurel Ct
9 Sundew Ct
10 Campion Ct
11 Foxglove Ct
C1 1 Buckingham Ho
2 Chester Ct
3 Devon Ct
4 Essex Ho
5 Fife Ct
6 Gloucester Ct
7 Hereford Ho
8 Inverness Ct
9 Warwick Ho
10 York Ho
11 Suffolk Ho
12 Perth Ho
13 Norfolk Ho
14 Thanet Ct
15 Rutland Ho

16 Oxford Ct

89
A1 1 Avon Ct
2 Bromley Lo
3 Walter Ct
4 Lynton Terr
5 Acton Ct
6 Fells Haugh
7 Springfield Ct
8 Tamarind Ct
9 Lynton Ct
10 Aspen Ct
11 Pegasus Ct
12 Friary Park Ct
B1 1 Rosebank Gdns
2 Rosebank
3 Edinburgh Ho
4 Western Ct
5 Kilronan
B6 1 Carlyle Rd
2 Bernard Shaw Ho
3 Longlents Ho
4 Mordaunt Ho
5 Wilmers Ct
6 Stonebridge Ctr
7 Shakespeare Ave
C5 1 Futters Ct
2 Barrett Ct
3 Elms The
4 Fairlight
D5 1 New Crescent Yd
2 Harlesden Plaza
3 St Josephs Ct
4 Jubilee Ct
5 Ellery Cl

90
B1 1 Holborn Ct
2 Clement Danes Ho
3 Vellacott Ho
4 O'Driscoll Ho
5 King Ho
6 Daley Ho
7 Selma Ho
8 Garrett Ho
C1 1 Latimer Ind Est
2 Pankhurst Ho
3 Quadrangle The
4 Nightingale Ho
5 Gordon Ct
6 Ducane Cl
7 Browning Ho
8 Pavilion Terr
9 Ivebury Ct
10 Olympic Ho
C2 1 Galleywood Ho
2 Edgcott Ho
3 Cuffley Ho
4 Addlestone Ho
5 Hockliffe Ho
6 Sarratt Ho
7 Firle Ho
8 Sutton Est The
9 Terling Ho
10 Danes Ho
11 Udimore Ho
12 Vange Ho
13 Binbrook Ho
14 Yeadon Ho
15 Yatton Ho
16 Yarrow Ho
17 Clement Ho
18 Danebury
19 Coronation Ct
20 Calderon Pl
C3 1 Princess Alice Ho
2 Yoxall Ho
3 Yorkley Ho
4 Northaw Ho
5 Oakham Ho
6 Markyate Ho
7 Letchmore Ho
8 Pagham Ho
9 Quendon Ho
10 Redbourn Ho
11 Ketton Ho
12 Hillman Dr
D1 1 Kelfield Ct
2 Downing Ho
3 Crosfield Ct
4 Robinson Ho
5 Scampston Mews
6 Girton Villas
7 Ray Ho
8 Walmer Ho
9 Goodrich Ct
10 Arthur Ct
11 Whitstable Ho
12 Kingsnorth Ho
13 Bridge Cl
14 Prospect Ho
15 St Marks Rd
16 Whitchurch Ho
17 Blechynden Ho
18 Waynflete Sq
19 Bramley Ho
20 Dixon Ho
D4 1 Westfield Ct
2 Tropical Ct
3 Chamberlayne Mans
4 Quadrant The
5 Queens Park Ct
6 Warfield Yd
7 Regent St
8 Cherrytree Ho
9 Artisan Mews
10 Artisan Quarter

91
A1 1 Malton Mews
2 Lancaster Lo
3 Manning Ho
4 Galsworthy Ho
5 Hudson Ho
6 Cambourne Mews
7 Upper Talbot Wlk
8 Kingsdown Cl
9 Lower Clarendon Wlk
10 Talbot Grove Ho
11 Clarendon Wlk
12 Upper Clarendon Wlk
13 Camelford Wlk
14 Upper Camelford Wlk
15 Camelford Ct
A2 1 Murchison Ho
2 MacAulay Ho
3 Chesterton Ho
4 Chiltern Ho
5 Lionel Ho
6 Watts Ho
7 Wheatstone Ho
8 Telford Ho
9 Golborne Mews
10 Millwood St
11 St Columb's Ho
12 Norfolk Mews
13 Lionel Mews
A3 1 Sycamore Wlk
2 Westgate Bsns Ctr
3 Buspace Studios
4 Bosworth Ho
5 Golborne Gdns
6 Appleford Ho
7 Adair Twr
8 Gadsden Ho
9 Southam Ho
10 Norman Butler Ho
11 Thompson Ho
12 Wells Ho
13 Paul Ho
14 Olive Blythe Ho
15 Katherine Ho
16 Breakwell Ct
17 Pepler Ho
18 Edward Kennedy Ho
19 Winnington Ho
A4 1 Selby Sq
2 Severn Ave
3 Stansbury Sq
4 Tolhurst Dr
5 John Fearon Wlk
6 Mundy Ho
7 Macfarren Ho
8 Bantock Ho
9 Banister Ho
10 Batten Ho
11 Croft Ho
12 Courtville Ho
13 Mounsey Ho
14 Bliss Mews
B1 1 Silvester Ho
2 Golden Cross Mews
3 Tavistock Mews
4 Clydesdale Ho
5 Melchester
6 Pinehurst Ct
7 Denbigh Ho
B2 1 Blagrove Rd
2 All Saints Ho
3 Tavistock Ho
4 Leamington Ho
B3 1 Octavia Mews
2 Russell's Wharf
3 Western Ho
4 Kelly Mews
B4 1 Boyce Ho
2 Farnaby Ho
3 Danby Ho
4 Purday Ho
5 Naylor Ho
6 St Judes Ho
7 Leeve Ho
8 Longhurst Ho
9 Harrington Ct
10 Mulberry Ct
11 Kilburn Ho
B5 1 Claremont Ct
2 William Saville Ho
3 Western Ct
4 Bond Ho
5 Crone Ct
6 Wood Ho
7 Winterleys
8 Carlton Ho
9 Fiona Ct
C1 1 Shottsford
2 Tolchurch
3 Casterbridge
4 Sandbourne
5 Anglebury
6 Weatherbury
7 Westbourne Gr Mews
8 Rosehart Mews
9 Viscount Ct
10 Hereford Mans
11 Hereford Mews
C2 1 Ascot Ho
2 Ashgrove Ct

3 Lockbridge Ct
4 Swallow Ct
5 Nightingale Lo
6 Hammond Lo
7 Penfield Lo
8 Harvey Lo
9 Hunter Lo
10 Barnard Lo
11 Falcon Lo
12 Johnson Lo
13 Livingstone Lo
14 Nuffield Lo
15 Finch Lo
16 Polesworth Ho
17 Oversley Ho
18 Derrycombe Ho
19 Buckshead Ho
20 Combe Ho
21 Culham Ho
22 Dainton Ho
23 Devonport Ho
24 Honwell Ho
25 Truro Ho
26 Sunderland Ho
27 Stonehouse Ho
28 Riverford Ho
29 Portishead Ho
30 Mickleton Ho
31 Keyham Ho
32 Moulsford Ho
33 Shrewsbury Mews
34 St Stephen's Mews
35 Westway Lo
36 Langley Ho
37 Brindley Ho
38 Radway Ho
39 Astley Ho
40 Willow Ct
41 Larch Ct
42 Elm Ct
43 Beech Ct
44 Worcester Ct
45 Union Ct
46 Leicester Ct
47 Kennet Ct
48 Oxford Ct
49 Fazerley Ct
C3 1 Westside Ct
2 Byron Mews
3 Sutherland Ct
4 Fleming Cl
5 Hermes Cl
C4 1 Pentland Rd
2 Nelson Cl
3 Pavilion Ct
4 Masefield Ho
5 Austen Ho
6 Fielding Ho
7 Argo Bsns Ctr
8 John Ratcliffe Ho
9 Wymering Mans
C5 1 Wells Ct
2 Cambridge Ct
3 Ely Ct
4 Durham Ct
C6 1 Ryde Ho
2 Glengall Pass
3 Leith Yd
4 Daynor Ho
5 Varley Ho
6 Sandby Ho
7 Colas Mews
8 Bishopsdale Ho
9 Lorton Ho
10 Marshwood Ho
11 Ribblesdale Ho
12 Holmesdale Ho
13 Kilburn Vale Est
14 Kilburn Bridge
D1 1 Vera Ct
2 Alexander Mews
3 Gurney Ho
4 Burdett Mews
5 Greville Lo
6 Hatherley Ct
7 Bridge Field Ho
8 Ralph Ct
9 Peters Ct
9 Pickering Mews
10 Riven Ct
11 Inver Ct
12 Cervantes Ct
13 Bishops Ct
14 Newbury Ho
15 Marlow Ho
16 Lynton Ho
17 Pembroke Ho
18 Pickering Ho
19 Whiteleys Ctr
D3 1 Ellwood Ct
D5 1 Tollgate Ho
2 Regents Plaza
3 Royal Langford Apartments
D6 1 Sylvan Ct
2 Birchington Ct
3 Farndale Ho
4 Abbey Rd Motorist Ctr
5 Greville Mews
6 Goldsmith's Pl
7 Remsted Ho
8 Bradwell Ho
9 Cheshunt Ho
10 Haliwell Ho
11 Broadoak Ho

12 Philip Ho
13 Hillsborough Ct
14 Sandbourne
15 Wingreen
16 Toneborough
17 Silverthorn
18 Kington Ho
19 Marrick Ho

95

C4 1 Pimlico Wlk
2 Aske Ho
3 Hathaway Ho
4 Haberdasher Pl
5 Fairchild Ho
6 Burtt Ho
7 Enfield Cloisters
8 McGregor Ct
9 Royal Oak Ct
10 Hoxton Mkt
11 Bath Pl
12 Chapel Pl
13 Standard Pl
14 Cleeve Workshops
15 Cleeve Ho
16 Printing House Yd
17 Perseverance Works
18 Crooked Billet Yd
19 Drysdale Ho
20 Castlefrank Ho
21 School App
22 Basing House Yd
23 Mail Coach Yd
C5 1 Bracer Ho
2 Scorton Ho
3 Fern Cl
4 Macbeth Ho
5 Oberon Ho
6 Buckland Ct
7 Crondall Ct
8 Osric Path
9 Caliban Twr
10 Celia Ho
11 Juliet Ho
12 Bacchus Wlk
13 Malcolm Ho
14 Homefield St
15 Crondall Pl
16 Blanca Ho
17 Miranda Ho
18 Falstaff Ho
19 Charmian Ho
20 Myrtle Wlk
21 Arden Ho
22 Sebastian Ho
23 Stanway Ct
24 Jerrold St
25 Rosalind Ho
26 Cordelia Ho
27 Monteagle Ct
28 John Parry Ct
29 James Anderson Ct
30 Ben Jonson Ct
31 Sara Lane Ct
32 Walbrook Ct
C6 1 Portelet Ct
2 Trinity Ct
3 Rozel Ct
4 St Helier Ct
5 Corbiere Ho
6 Kenning Ho
7 Higgins Ho
8 Cavell Ho
9 Girling Ho
10 Fulcher Ho
11 Francis Ho
12 Norris Ho
13 Kempton Ho
14 Nesham Ho
15 Crossbow Ho
16 Catherine Ho
17 Strale Ho
18 Horner Hos
19 Stringer Hos
20 Whitmore Ho
21 Nightingale Ho
22 Wilmer Gdns
23 Arrow Ho
24 Archer Ho
25 Meriden Ho
26 Rover Ho
27 Bowyer Ho
28 Tiller Ho
29 Canalside Studios
30 Kleine Wharf
31 Benyon Wharf
32 Quebec Wharf
33 Belvedere Ct
34 Portfleet Pl
D4 1 Gorsuch Pl
2 Strout's Pl
3 Vaughan Est
4 George Loveless Ho
5 Baroness Rd
6 James Brine Ho
7 Arthur Wade Ho
8 Robert Owen Ho
9 Sivill Ho
10 Georgina Gdns
11 Old Market Sq
12 Cuff Point
13 Bakers Rents
14 Leopold Bldgs
15 Dunmore Point
16 Wingfield Ho
17 Gascoigne Pl
18 Mandela Ho

19 Virginia Rd
20 Briggs Ho
21 Packenham Ho
22 Gowan Ho
23 Kirton Gdns
24 Chambord Ho
25 Ducal St
26 Strickland Ho
27 Alliston Ho
28 Gibraltar Wlk
29 Equity Sq
30 Shacklewell St
31 Rochelle St
32 Sonning Ho
33 Culham Ho
34 Hurley Ho
35 Palissy St
36 Taplow Ho
37 Chertsey Ho
38 Sunbury Ho
39 Sunbury Workshops
40 Datchett Ho
41 Hocker St
42 Coll Sharp Ct
43 Marlow Studio Workshops
44 Marlow Ho
45 Shiplake Ho
46 Wargrave Ho
47 Iffley Ho
D5 1 Queensbridge Ct
2 Godwin Ho
3 Kent Ct
4 Brunswick Ho
5 Weymouth Ct
6 Sovereign Mews
7 Dunloe Ct
8 Cremer Bsns Ctr
9 James Hammett Ho
10 Allgood St
11 Horatio St
12 Cadell Ho
13 Horatio Ho
14 Shipton Ho
D6 1 Hilborough Ct
2 Scriven Ct
3 Livermere Ct
4 Angrave Ct
5 Angrave Pas
6 Benfleet Ct
7 Belford Ho
8 Orme Ho
9 Clemson Ho
10 Longman Ho
11 Lowther Ho
12 Lovelace Ho
13 Harlowe Ho
14 Pamela Ho
15 Samuel Ho
16 Acton Ho
17 Loanda Ct
18 Phoenix Cl
19 Richardson Cl
20 Thrasher Ct
21 Mary Secole Cl
22 Canal Path
23 Pear Tree Ct
24 Hebden Ct
25 Charlton Ct
26 Laburnum Ct
27 Mansfield Ct
28 Garden Pl
29 Amber Wharf
30 Haggerston Studios

96

A1 1 Whitechurch Pas
2 Manningtree St
3 Whitechurch La
4 Naylor Bldg W
5 Morrison Bldgs
6 Nayor Bldg E
7 Mulberry St
8 Albany Ct
9 Cornell Bldg
10 Dryden Bldg
11 Weyhill Rd
12 Colefax Bldg
13 Fordham St
14 Myrdle Ct
15 Buckle St
16 Plough St
17 Goodman's Stile
18 Ropewalk Gdns
19 Skyline Plaza Bldg
20 Minet Ho
21 Mitali Pas
22 Basil Ho
23 Bernhard Baron Ho
24 Hogarth Ct
25 Delafield Ho
26 Chandlery Ho
27 Berner Terr
28 Victoria Yd
29 Batson Ho
30 Harkness Ho
31 Drewett Ho
32 Dowler Ho
33 Everard Ho
34 Bicknell Ho
35 Danvers Ho
36 Philchurch Pl
37 Hadfield Ho
38 Kindersley Ho
39 Langmore Ho
40 Halliday Ho

A2 1 Arthur Deakin Ho
2 Albert Cotts
3 Victoria Cotts
4 Boden Ho
5 Vollasky Ho
6 Daplyn St
7 Hobsons Pl
8 Hanbury Ho
9 Huguenot Ct
10 Links Yd
11 Casson Ho
12 Ramar Ho
13 Greatorex Ho
14 Chicksand Ho
15 Spelman Ho
16 Tailworth St
17 Monthope Rd
18 Evelyn Ho
19 Bloomfield Ho
20 Davenant Ho
21 Pauline Ho
22 Tannery Ho
23 Don Gratton Ho
24 Green Dragon Yd
25 Fieldgate Mans
26 Mosque Tower
A3 1 Bentworth Ct
2 Hawksmoor Pl
3 Kerbela St
4 Fuller Cl
5 Kinsham Ho
6 Menotti St
7 Barwell Ho
8 Grimsby St
9 Reflection Ho
10 Fleet Street Hill
11 Bratley St
12 Weaver Ho
13 Cornerstone Ct
14 Stuttle Ho
15 McGlashon Ho
16 John Pritchard Ho
A4 1 Providence Yd
2 Lygon Ho
3 Brabner Ho
4 Delta St
5 Delta Point
6 Tillet Way
7 Mullet Gdns
8 Lampern Sq
9 Kite Pl
10 Elver Gdns
11 Cobden Ho
12 Eversley Ho
13 Lorden Wlk
14 Rapley Ho
15 Dence Ho
16 McKinnon Wood Ho
17 Satchwell Rd
18 Dickinson Ho
19 Hutton Ho
20 Simmons Ho
21 Swinton Ho
22 Yates Ho
23 Johnson Ho
24 Jeremy Bentham Ho
25 Waring Ho
26 St James Ct
27 Ebony Ho
28 Azure Ho
29 Westhope Ho
30 Hague St
A5 1 London Terr
2 Sturdee Ho
3 Maude Ho
4 Haig Ho
5 Jellicoe Ho
6 Ropley St
7 Guinness Trust Bldgs
8 Ion Ct
9 Columbia Rd
10 Moye Cl
11 Morrel Ct
12 Courtauld Ho
13 Drummond Ho
14 Gurney Ho
15 Atkinson Ho
16 Halley Ho
17 Goldsmith's Sq
18 Shahjalal Ho
19 Ken Wilson Ho
20 April Ct
21 Crofts Ho
22 Sebright Ho
23 Beechwood Ho
24 Gillman Ho
25 Cheverell Ho
26 Besford Ho
27 Dinmont Ho
28 Elizabeth Mews
29 Sebright Pas
30 Wyndham Deedes Ho
31 Sheppard Ho
32 Mary James Ho
33 Hadrian Est
34 Blythendale Ho
35 George Vale Ho
36 Lion Mills
37 St Peter's Ave
38 Pritchard Ho
A6 1 Broke Wlk
2 Rochemont Wlk
3 Marlborough Ave
4 Rivington Wlk
5 Magnin Cl
6 Gloucester Sq

7 Woolstone Ho
8 Marsworth Ho
9 Cheddington Ho
10 Linslade Ho
11 Cosgrove Ho
12 Blisworth Ho
13 Eleanor Ct
14 Wistow Ho
15 Muscott Ho
16 Boxmoor Ho
17 Linford Ho
18 Pendley Ho
19 Northchurch Ho
20 Debdale Ho
21 Broadway Market Mews
22 Welshpool Ho
23 Ada Ho
B1 1 Peter Best Ho
2 Mellish Ho
3 Porchester Ho
4 Dickson Ho
5 Silvester Ho
6 Wilton Ct
7 Sarah Ho
8 Bridgen Ho
9 Tylney Ho
10 Greenwich Ct
11 Damien Ct
12 Philson Mans
13 Siege Ho
14 Jacob Mans
15 Proud Ho
16 Sly St
17 Barnett St
18 Kinder St
19 Richard St
20 Hungerford St
21 Colstead Ho
22 Melwood Ho
23 Wicker St
24 Langdale St
25 Chapman Ho
26 Burwell Cl
27 Walford Ho
28 Welstead Ho
29 Norton Ho
30 Turnour Ho
31 Luke Ho
32 Dunch St
33 Sheridan St
34 Brinsley St
B2 1 Wodeham Gdns
2 Castlemaine St
3 Court St
B3 1 Rochester St
2 Weaver Ct
3 Greenheath Bsns Ctr
4 Glass St
5 Herald St
6 Northesk Ho
7 Codrington Ho
8 Heathpool Ct
9 Mocatta Ho
10 Harvey Ho
11 Blackwood Ho
12 Rutherford Ho
13 Bullen Ho
14 Fremantle Ho
15 Pellew Ho
16 Ashington Ho
17 Dinnington Ho
18 Bartholomew Sq
19 Steeple Ct
20 Orion Ho
21 Fellbrigg St
22 Eagle Ho
23 Sovereign Ho
24 Redmill Ho
25 Berry Ho
26 Grindall Ho
27 Collingwood Ho
B4 1 Charles Dickens Ho
2 Adrian Bolt Ho
3 William Rathbone Ho
4 Southwood Smith Ho
5 Rushmead
6 William Channing Ho
7 John Cartwright Ho
8 Charles Darwin Ho
9 Thomas Burt Ho
10 John Fielden Ho
11 Gwilym Maries Ho
12 Joseph Priestley Ho
13 Wear Pl
14 John Nettleford Ho
15 Thornaby Ho
16 Stockton Ho
17 Barnard Ho
18 Gainford Ho
19 Stapleton Ho
20 James Middleton Ho
21 Kedleston Wlk
22 Queen Margaret Flats
23 Hollybush Ho
24 Horwood Ho
25 Norden Ho
26 Newcourt Ho

27 Seabright St
28 Viaduct Pl
29 Sunlight Sq
30 Providence Row Cl
B5 1 Dinmont St
2 Marian St
3 Claredale Ho
4 Keeling Ho
5 Maple St
6 Winkley St
7 Temple Dwellings
8 Argos Ho
9 Helen Ho
10 Lysander Ho
11 Antenor Ho
12 Paris Ho
13 Nestor Ho
14 Hector Ho
15 Ajax Ho
16 Achilles Ho
17 Priam Ho
18 Peabody Est
19 Felix St
20 Cambridge Cres
21 Peterley Bsns Ctr
22 Beckwith Ho
23 Brookfield Ho
24 Parminter Ind Est
25 Ted Roberts Ho
26 Cambridge Ct
27 Millennium Pl
28 William Caslon Ho
29 Hugh Platt Ho
30 West St
31 Mayfield Ho
32 Apollo Ho
33 Tanners Yd
34 Teesdale Yd
B6 1 Welshpool St
2 Broadway Ho
3 Regents Wharf
4 London Wharf
5 Warburton Ho
6 Warburton St
7 Triangle Rd
8 Warburton Rd
9 Williams Ho
10 Booth Cl
11 Albert Cl
12 King Edward Mans
13 Victoria Bldgs
14 Andrews Wharf
C1 1 Woollon Ho
2 Dundalk Ho
3 Anne Goodman Ho
4 Newbold Cotts
5 Kerry Ho
6 Zion Ho
7 Longford Ho
8 Bromehead St
9 Athlone Ho
10 Jubilee Mans
11 Harriott Ho
12 Brayford Sq
13 Clearbrook Way
14 Rochelle Ct
15 Winterton Ho
16 Swift Ho
17 Brinsley Ho
18 Dean Ho
19 Foley Ho
20 Robert Sutton Ho
21 Montpelier Pl
22 Glastonbury Pl
23 Steel's La
24 Masters Lo
25 Stylus Apartments
26 Arta Ho
C2 1 Fulneck
2 Gracehill
3 Ockbrook
4 Fairfield
5 Dunstan Hos
6 Cressy Ct
7 Cressy Hos
8 Callahan Cotts
9 Lindley Ho
10 Mayo Ho
11 Wexford Ho
12 Sandhurst Ho
13 Addis Ho
14 Colverson Ho
15 Beckett Ho
16 Jarman Ho
17 Armsby Ho
18 Wingrad Ho
19 Miranda Cl
20 Drake Ho
21 Ashfield Yd
22 Magri Wlk
23 Jean Pardies Ho
24 St Vincent De Paul Ho
25 Sambrook Ho
26 Louise De Marillac Ho
27 Dagobert Ho
28 Le Moal Ho
29 Odette Duval Ho
30 Charles Auffray Ho
31 Boisseau Ho
32 Clichy Ho
33 Paymal Ho
C3 1 William's Bldgs
2 Donegal Ho
3 Pelican Pas

4 Frederick Charrington Ho
5 Wickford Ho
6 Braintree Ho
7 Doveton Ho
8 Doveton St
9 Cephas Ho
10 Sceptre Ho
11 Bancroft Ho
12 Stothard St
13 Redclyf Ho
14 Winkworth Cotts
15 Amiel St
16 Hadleigh Ho
17 Hadleigh Cl
18 Ryder Ho
19 Mantus Cl
20 Kenton Ho
21 Colebert Ho
22 Ibbott St
23 Rickman Ho
24 Rickman St
25 Stothard Ho
26 Barbanel Ho
27 Stannard Cotts
28 St Peters Ct
29 Rennie Cotts
30 Pemell Cl
31 Pemell Ho
32 Leatherdale St
33 Gouldman Ho
34 Lamplighter Cl
35 Sherren Ho
36 Marlborough Lo
37 Hamilton Lo
38 Montgomery Lo
39 Cleveland Gr
40 Cromwell Lo
41 Bardsey Pl
42 Charrington Ho
43 Hayfield Yd
44 Allport Mews
45 Colin Winter Ho
C4 1 Mulberry Ho
2 Gretton Ho
3 Merceron Ho
4 Montfort Ho
5 Westbrook Ho
6 Sugar Loaf Wlk
7 Museum Ho
8 Burnham Est
9 Globe Terr
10 Moravian St
11 Shepton Hos
12 Mendip Hos
13 Academy Ct
14 Pepys Ho
15 Swinburne Ho
16 Moore Ho
17 Morris Ho
18 Burns Ho
19 Milton Ho
20 Whitman Ho
21 Shelley Ho
22 Keats Ho
23 Dawson Ho
24 Bradbeer Ho
25 Forber Ho
26 Hughes Ho
27 Silvester Ho
28 Rogers Est
29 Pavan Ct
30 Stafford Cripps Ho
31 Sidney Godley (VC) Ho
32 Butler Ho
33 Butler St
34 Thorne Ho
35 Bevin Ho
36 Tuscan Ho
C5 1 Evesham Ho
2 James Campbell Ho
3 Thomas Hollywood Ho
4 James Docherty Ho
5 Ebenezer Mussel Ho
6 Jameson Ct
7 Edinburgh Cl
8 Roger Dowley Ct
9 Sherbrooke Ho
10 Calcraft Ho
11 Burrard Ho
12 Dundas Ho
13 Ponsonby Ho
14 Barnes Ho
15 Paget Ho
16 Maitland Ho
17 Chesil Ct
18 Reynolds Ho
19 Cleland Ho
20 Goodrich Ho
21 Rosebery Ho
22 Sankey Ho
23 Cyprus Pl
24 Royston St
25 Stainsbury St
26 Hunslett St
27 Baildon
28 Brockweir
29 Tytherton
30 Malmesbury
31 Kingswood
32 Colville Ho
C6 1 Halkett Ho
2 Christchurch Sq
3 Helena Pl

4 Swingfield Ho
5 Greenham Ho
6 Dinmore Ho
7 Anstey Ho
8 Weston Ho
9 Carbroke Ho
10 Bluebell Cl
11 Cherry Tree Cl
12 Georgian Ct
13 Park Cl
14 Regency Ct
15 Norris Ho
D1 1 Pattison Ho
2 St Thomas Ho
3 Arbour Ho
4 Bladen Ho
5 Antill Terr
6 Majorie Mews
7 Billing Ho
8 Dowson Ho
9 Lipton Rd
10 Chalkwell Ho
11 Corringham Ho
12 Ogilvie Ho
13 Edward Mann Cl
14 Reservoir Studios
15 Lighterman Mews
D2 1 Roland Mews
2 Beatrice Ho
3 Morecambe Cl
4 Stepney Green Ct
5 Milrood Ho
6 Panama Ho
7 Galway Ho
8 Jacqueline Ho
9 Crown Mews
10 Caspian Ho
11 Darien Ho
12 Riga Ho
13 Flores Ho
14 Taranto Ho
15 Aden Ho
16 Master's St
17 Rosary Ct
D3 1 Raynham Ho
2 Pat Shaw Ho
3 Colmar Ct
4 Withy Ho
5 Stocks Ct
6 Downey Ho
7 Bay Ct
8 Sligo Ho
9 Pegasus Ho
10 Barents Ho
11 Biscay Ho
12 Solway Ho
13 Bantry Ho
14 Aral Ho
15 Pacific Ho
16 Magellan Ho
17 Levant Ho
18 Adriatic Ho
19 Genoa Ho
20 Hawke Ho
21 Palliser Ho
22 Ionian Ho
23 Weddell Ho
24 Carlyle Mews
25 Greencourt Ho
26 Sundra Wlk
D4 1 Stubbs Ho
2 Holman Ho
3 Clynes Ho
4 Windsor Ho
5 Gilbert Ho
6 Chater Ho
7 Ellen Wilkinson Ho
8 George Belt Ho
9 Ayrton Gould Ho
10 O'Brian Ho
11 Sulkin Ho
12 Jenkinson Ho
13 Bullards Pl
14 Sylvia Pankhurst Ho
15 Mary Macarthur Ho
16 Trevelyan Ho
17 Wedgwood Ho
18 Pemberton Ct
19 Leatherdale St
20 Walter Besant Ho
21 Barber Beaumont Ho
22 Brancaster Ho
23 Litcham Ho
D5 1 Kemp Ho
2 Piggott Ho
3 Mark Ho
4 Sidney Ho
5 Pomeroy Ho
6 Puteaux Ho
7 Doric Ho
8 Modling Ho
9 Longman Ho
10 Ames Ho
11 Alzette Ho
12 Offenbach Ho
13 Tate Ho
14 Norton Ho
15 St Gilles Ho
16 Harold Ho
17 Velletri Ho
18 Bridge Wharf
19 Gathorne St
20 Bow Brook The
21 Twig Folly Cl
22 Palmerston Ct
23 Lakeview

24 Peach Walk Mews
25 Caesar Ct
97
A1 1 Hearnshaw St
2 Berry Cotts
3 Causton Cotts
4 Elizabeth Blount Ct
5 Carr St
6 Shaw Cres
7 Darnley Ho
8 Mercer's Cotts
9 Troon Ho
10 Ratcliffe Ho
11 Wakeling St
12 York Sq
13 Anglia Ho
14 Cambria Ho
15 Caledonia Ho
16 Ratcliffe La
17 Bekesbourne St
18 John Scurr Ho
19 Regents Canal Ho
20 Basin App
21 Powlesland Ct
A2 1 Waley St
2 Edith Ramsay Ho
3 Andaman Ho
4 Atlantic Ho
5 Pevensey Ho
6 Solent Ho
7 Lorne Ho
8 Cromarty Ho
9 Dakin Pl
10 Greaves Cotts
11 Donaghue Cotts
12 Ames Cotts
13 Waterview Ho
14 Limehouse Fields Est
A3 1 Formosa Ho
2 Galveston Ho
3 Arabian Ho
4 Greenland Ho
5 Coral Ho
6 Anson Ho
7 Cambay Ho
8 Lindop Ho
9 Moray Ho
10 Azov Ho
11 Sandalwood Cl
12 Broadford Ho
A4 1 Imperial Ho
2 Newport Ho
3 Vassall Ho
4 Maurice Ct
5 Creed Ct
6 Christopher France Ho
7 Beaumont Ct
8 Pembroke Mews
A5 1 Nightingale Mews
2 Bunsen Ho
3 Bunsen St
4 Beatrice Webb Ho
5 Margaret Bondfield Ho
6 Wilmer Ho
7 Sandall Ho
8 Butley Ct
9 Josseline Ct
10 Dalton Ho
11 Brine Ho
12 Ford Cl
13 Viking Cl
14 Stanfield Rd
15 Stoneleigh Mews
16 Ruth Ct
17 School Bell Cloisters
18 Schoolbell Mews
19 Medhurst Cl
20 Olga St
21 Conyer St
22 Diamond Ho
23 Daring Ho
24 Crane Ho
25 Exmoor Ho
26 Grenville Ho
27 Hyperion Ho
28 Sturdy Ho
29 Wren Ho
30 Ardent Ho
31 Senators Lo
32 Hooke Ho
33 Mohawk Ho
34 Ivanhoe Ho
35 Medway Mews
B1 1 Dora Ho
2 Flansham Ho
3 Gatwick Ho
4 Ashpark Ho
5 Newdigate Ho
6 Midhurst Ho
7 Redbourne Ho
8 Southwater Cl
9 Andersens Wharf
10 Whatman Ho
11 Butler Ho
12 Fitzroy Ho
13 Salmon St
14 Mission The
15 Aithan Ho
16 Britley Ho
17 Cheadle Ho
18 Elland Ho
19 Wharf La
20 Docklands Ct
21 Park Heights Ct

22 Grosvenor Ct
23 Lime House Ct
24 Swallow Pl
25 St Anne's Trad Est
B2 1 Wearmouth Ho
2 Elmslie Point
3 Grindley Ho
4 Stileman Ho
5 Wilcox Ho
6 Huddart St
7 Robeson St
8 Couzens Ho
9 Perley Ho
10 Whytlaw Ho
11 Booker Cl
12 Tunley Gn
13 Callingham Cl
14 Bowry Ho
15 Perkins Ho
16 Printon Ho
17 Tasker Ho
B4 1 Trellis Sq
2 Sheffield Sq
3 Howcroft Ho
4 Astra Ho
5 Frye Ct
6 Byas Ho
7 George Lansbury Ho
8 Regal Pl
9 Coborn Mews
10 Tredegar Mews
11 Cavendish Terr
12 Lyn Mews
13 Buttermere Ho
14 Coniston Ho
15 Tracy Ho
16 Hanover Pl
17 St Clair Ho
18 Longthorne Ho
19 Vista Bldgs
20 Verity Ho
21 Icarus Ho
22 Whippingham Ho
23 Hamilton Ho
24 Winchester Ho
B5 1 Roman Square Mkt
2 John Bond Ho
3 McKenna Ho
4 Dennis Ho
5 McAusland Ho
6 McBride Ho
7 Libra Rd
8 Dave Adams Ho
9 Regency Ct
10 Tay Ho
11 Sleat Ho
12 Brodick Ho
13 Ewart Pl
14 Lunan Ho
15 Cruden Ho
16 Anglo Rd
17 Mull Ho
18 Sinclairs Ho
19 Driftway Ho
20 Clayhall Ct
21 Berebinder Ho
22 Partridge Ho
23 Barford Ho
24 Gullane Ho
25 Gosford Ho
26 Dornoch Ho
27 Dunnet Ho
28 Enard Ho
29 Fraserburgh Ho
30 Forth Ho
31 Stavers Ho
32 Rosegate Ho
33 Crowngate Ho
34 Queensgate Ho
35 Towergate Ho
36 Ordell Ct
37 William Pl
B6 1 Hampstead Wlk
2 Waverton Ho
3 Elton Ho
4 Locton Gn
5 Birtwhistle Ho
6 Clare Ho
7 Magpie Ho
8 Hornbeam Sq
9 Rowan Ho
10 Barge La
11 Walnut Ho
12 Birdsfield La
13 Atkins Ho
14 Willow Tree Cl
15 Jasmine Sq
16 Tait Ct
17 Ranwell Ho
18 Ranwell Cl
19 Tufnell Ct
20 Pulteney Cl
21 Vic Johnson Ho
22 Lea Sq
23 Iceni Ct
24 Tamar Cl
25 Roman Rd
26 Valentine Ho
C1 1 Landin Ho
2 Thomas Road Ind Est
3 Vickery's Wharf
4 Abbotts Wharf
5 Limehouse Ct
6 Charlesworth Ho
7 Gurdon Ho
8 Trendell Ho
9 Menteath Ho

10 Minchin Ho
11 Donne Ho
12 Old School Sq
13 Anglesey Ho
14 Gough Wlk
15 Baring Ho
16 Gladstone Ho
17 Hopkins Ho
18 Granville Ho
19 Overstone Ho
20 Pusey Ho
21 Russell Ho
22 Stanley Ho
C2 1 Bredel Ho
2 Linton Ho
3 Matthews Ho
4 Woodcock Ho
5 Limborough Ho
6 Maydwell Ho
7 Underhill Ho
8 Meyrick Ho
9 Ambrose Ho
10 Richardson Ho
11 Carpenter Ho
12 Robinson Ho
13 Bellmaker Ct
14 Lime Tree Ct
15 Bracken Ho
16 Bramble Ho
17 Berberis Ho
18 Bilberry Ho
19 Ladyfern Ho
20 Rosebay Ho
21 Invicta Cl
22 Phoenix Bsns Ctr
23 Metropolitan Cl
24 Busbridge Ho
C3 1 Fairmont Ho
2 Healy Ho
3 Zodiac Ho
4 Buick Ho
5 Consul Ho
6 Bentley Ho
7 Cresta Ho
8 Daimler Ho
9 Riley Ho
10 Jensen Ho
11 Lagonda Ho
12 Ireton St
13 Navenby Wlk
14 Burwell Wlk
15 Leadenham Ct
16 Sleaford Ho
17 Bow Triangle Bsns Ctr
C4 1 Bow Ho
2 Denmark Pl
3 Marsalis Ho
4 Lovette Ho
5 Drapers Almhouses
6 Mallard Point
7 Creswick Wlk
8 Bevin Ho
9 Huggins Ho
10 Williams Ho
11 Harris Ho
12 Marina Ct
13 Electric Ho
14 Matching Ct
15 Wellington Bldgs
16 Grafton Ho
17 Berkeley Ho
18 Columbia Ho
C5 1 Vincent Mews
2 Menai Pl
3 Heathfield Ct
4 Redwood Cl
5 Acorn Ct
6 Primrose Cl
7 Briar Ct
8 Springwood Cl
C6 1 Ironworks
2 Juno Ho
3 Chariot Cl
4 Saturn Ho
5 Hadrian Ct
6 Mercury Ho
7 Forum Cl
8 Venus Ho
9 Vesta Ho
10 Tiber Cl
11 Gemini Ho
12 Crown Close Bsns Ctr
13 Old Ford Trad Ctr
D1 1 Colebrook Ho
2 Essex Ho
3 Salisbury Ho
4 Maidstone Ho
5 Osterley Ho
6 Norwich Ho
7 Clarissa Ho
8 Elgin Ho
9 Shaftesbury Lo
10 Shepherd Ho
11 Jeremiah St
12 Elizabeth Cl
13 Chilcot Cl
14 Fitzgerald Ho
15 Vesey Path
16 Kilmore Ho
17 Cygnet House N
18 Cygnet House S
D2 1 Sumner Ho
2 David Hewitt Ho
3 St Gabriels Cl
4 Limehouse Cut
5 Colmans Wharf

6 Foundary Ho
7 Radford Ho
D3 1 Broxbourne Ho
2 Roxford Ho
3 Biscott Ho
4 Stanborough Ho
5 Hillstone Ct
D4 1 Bradley Ho
2 Prioress Ho
3 Alton Ho
4 Foxley Ho
5 Munden Ho
6 Canterbury Ho
7 Corbin Ho
8 Barton Ho
9 Jolles Ho
10 Rudstone Ho
11 Baxter Ho
12 Baker Ho
13 Insley Ho
14 Hardwicke Ho
15 Glebe Ct
16 Priory St
17 Sadler Ho
18 Ballinger Point
19 Henshall Point
20 Dorrington Point
21 Warren Ho
22 Fairlie Ct
23 Regent Sq
24 Hackworth Point
25 Priestman Point
26 Wingate Ho
27 Nethercott Ho
28 Thelbridge Ho
29 Bowden Ho
30 Kerscott Ho
31 Southcott Ho
32 Birchdown Ho
33 Upcott Ho
34 Langmead Ho
35 Limscott Ho
36 Northleigh Ho
37 Huntshaw Ho
38 Chagford Ho
39 Ashcombe Ho
40 Shillingford Ho
41 Patrick Connolly Gdns
42 Lester Ct
43 Franklin St
44 Taft Way
45 Washington Cl
46 Veronica Ho
47 William Guy Gdns
48 Denbury Ho
49 Holsworthy Ho
50 Padstone Ho
98
A1 1 Glenkerry Ho
2 Carradale Ho
3 Langdon Ho
4 Balfron Twr
5 St Frideswides Mews
6 Tabard Ct
7 Delta Bldg
8 Findhorn St
9 Kilbrennan Ho
10 Thistle Ho
11 Heather Ho
12 Tartan Ho
13 Sharman Ho
14 Trident Ho
15 Wharf View Ct
A2 1 Mills Gr
2 St Michaels Ct
3 Duncan Ct
A4 1 Miller's House Visitor Ctr
B1 1 Lansbury Gdns
2 Theseus Ho
3 Adams Ho
4 Jones Ho
5 Sam March Ho
6 Arapiles Ho
7 Athenia Ho
8 Julius Ho
9 Jervis Bay Ho
10 Helen Mackay Ho
11 Gaze Ho
12 Ritchie Ho
13 Blairgowrie Ct
14 Circle Ho
15 Dunkeld Ho
16 Rosemary Dr
17 Sorrel La
18 East India Dock Road Tunnel
B3 1 Crescent Court Bsns Ctr
2 Ashmead Bsns Ctr
3 Forward Bsns Ctr The
B6 1 Victoria Mills
2 Hallings Wharf Studios
3 Poland Ho
4 Peter Heathfield Ho
5 Burford Rd
C5 1 Abbey Lane Commercial Est
2 Greenway Ct
C6 1 Barnby Sq
2 Barnby St
3 Brassett Point
4 David Lee Point
5 Worthing Cl

6 Bexhill Wlk
7 Old Barrowfield
8 Elmgreen Cl
9 Stafford Morris Ho
10 Nina Mackay Cl
11 Lime Wlk
D1 1 Newton Point
2 Sparke Terr
3 Montesquieu Terr
4 Crawford Point
5 Rathbone Ho
6 George St
7 Emily St
8 Fendt Cl
9 Sabbarton St
10 Briary Ct
11 Shaftesbury Ho
D2 1 Radley Terr
2 Bernard Cassidy St
3 Rathbone Mkt
4 Thomas North Terr
5 Mary St
6 Hughes Terr
7 Swanscombe Point
8 Rawlinson Point
9 Kennedy Cox Ho
10 Cooper St
D6 1 Harris Cotts
2 Moorey Cl
3 Euro Bsns Ctr
4 Ladywell St
5 Caistor Ho
6 Redfern Ho
99
A2 1 Odeon Ct
2 Edward Ct
3 Newhaven La
4 Ravenscroft Cl
5 Douglas Rd
6 Ferrier Point
7 Harvey Point
8 Wood Point
9 Trinity St
10 Pattinson Point
11 Clinch Ct
12 Mint Bsns Pk
A3 1 Webb Gdns
2 Eric Shipman Terr
3 Warmington St
4 Jellicoe Rd
5 Frank St
6 Seaton Cl
7 Tabernacle Ave
8 Upland Rd
9 Clove St
10 Edward St
A4 1 Bob Anker Cl
2 Lea Ct
3 Third Ave
4 Suffolk St
A5 1 Lettsom Wlk
2 Ashburton Terr
3 Grasmere Rd
4 Dimsdale Wlk
5 Rawstone Wlk
6 Scott Ho
7 Willett Ho
8 James Cl
9 Cordwainers Wlk
10 Victoria Point
11 Settle Point
12 Middle Rd
13 Steve Biko Lodge
14 Lady Helen Seymour Ho
A6 1 Royston Ct
B4 1 Barbers Alley
2 Grengate Lodge
3 Augurs La
4 Surrey St
5 Dongola Rd W
6 Bemersyde Point
7 Rowntree Clifford Cl
C2 1 Alliance Rd
2 Salomons Rd
3 Barnes Ct
4 Triangle Ct
5 Moorings The
C5 1 Wellby Ct
2 Northfield Ho
3 Bishop Wilfred Wood Ct
4 Castle Point
5 Moat Dr
C6 1 Tolpuddle Ave
2 Crown Mews
3 Lilac Ct
4 Hamara Ghar
5 Greenleaf Rd
6 Massey Ct
7 Florence Rd
8 Sissulu Ct
9 Austin Ct
D2 1 Partridge Cl
2 Vanbrugh Ct
3 Meadowsweet Cl
4 St Michaels Ct
5 Long Mark Rd
6 Congreve Wlk
D5 1 Foxcombe Cl
2 Rochford Cl
3 Kylemore Cl
4 Stondon Wlk
5 Imperial Mews
6 Dominica Cl

D6 1 Oldegate Ho
2 Gaitskell Ho
3 Cabot Way
100
A1 1 Hadleigh Wlk
2 Hawksmoor Cl
3 Fraser Cl
4 Moncrieff Cl
5 Burlington Cl
6 Dundonald Cl
7 Oakley Cl
8 Ashwell Cl
A2 1 Orchid Cl
2 Bellflower Cl
3 Partridge Sq
4 Larkspur Cl
5 Lobelia Cl
6 Stonechat Sq
7 Wintergreen Cl
8 Garnet Wlk
9 Mavis Wlk
10 Beacons Cl
11 Abbess Cl
12 Elmley Cl
13 Chetwood Wlk
14 Selby Cl
15 Denny Cl
16 Woodhatch Cl
A6 1 Oakwood Cl
2 Harrow Rd
3 Ray Massey Way
4 Madge Gill Way
5 Pilgrims Way
6 St Bartholomews Ct
B1 1 Bowers Wlk
2 Barton Cl
3 Clayton Cl
4 Dixon Cl
5 Gautrey Sq
6 Wakerley Cl
7 Canterbury Cl
8 Goose Sq
9 Coventry Cl
10 Butterfield Sq
11 Winchester Cl
B2 1 Fleetwood Ct
2 Lymington Cl
3 Holyhead Cl
4 Bondfield Rd
5 Tulip Cl
6 Ambrose Cl
7 Sage Cl
8 Lindwood Cl
D1 1 Weymouth Ct
2 Founder Cl
3 Admirals Cl
101
A6 1 Wellington St
2 St Ann's Rd
3 Cooke St
4 Gateway Ho
5 Ardleigh Ho
6 Skipper Ct
7 Hewetts Quay
B5 1 Anderson Ho
2 Rookwood Ho
3 Tasker Ho
4 Crispe Ho
5 Oban Ho
6 Earlsdown Ho
B6 1 Jarvis Cl
2 Mayflower Ho
3 Westbury Ct
4 Millicent Preston Ho
5 Louise Graham Ho
6 Grange Ho
7 Basing Ho
8 Barnes Ho
9 Lexham Ho
10 Ripple Ct
11 Waldegrave Ct
12 Howard Ct
104
A6 1 Milburn Dr
2 Cousins Cl
3 Leacroft Cl
108
C5 1 Marlow Ct
2 Andrewes Ct
3 Vine Cotts
4 Benjamin Cl
5 Broadway Bldgs
6 Clocktower Mews
7 Amberley Ho
8 Diamond Ct
D5 1 Silverdale Cl
2 Burdett Cl
3 Hopefield
4 Maunder Rd
5 Clare Ho
109
A5 1 Glastonbury Ct
2 Evesham Ct
3 Lacock Ct
4 Wigmore Ct
5 Melrose Ct
6 Brownlow Rd
7 Chignell Pl
8 Shirley Ct
9 Trojan Ct

10 Hatfield Rd
11 Pershore Ho
12 Hyde Ho
13 Hugh Clark Ho
14 Rosemoor Ho
15 Leeland Mans
16 Waterford Ct
17 O'Grady Ct
C6 1 Abbey Lo
2 Yew Tree Grange
3 Abinger Ct

110
A1 1 Burford Ho
2 Hope Cl
3 Centaur Ct
4 Phoenix Ct
A6 1 Watermans Mews
2 Hills Mews
3 Grosvenor Ct
4 Elton Lo
5 Hambledon Ct
C1 1 Surrey Cres
2 Forbes Ho
3 Haining Cl
4 Melville Ct
5 London Stile
6 Stile Hall Par
7 Priory Lo
8 Kew Bridge Ct
9 Meadowcroft
10 St James Ct
11 Rivers Ho
C5 1 Grosvenor Par
2 Oakfield Ct
3 Hart Grove Ct
4 Grosvenor Ct
D1 1 Churchdale Ct
2 Cromwell Cl
3 Cambridge Rd S
4 Oxbridge Ct
5 Tomlinson Cl
6 Gunnersbury
Mews
7 Grange The
8 Gunnersbury Cl
9 Bellgrave Lo
D4 1 Cheltenham Pl
2 Beaumaris Twr
3 Arundel Ho
4 Pevensey Ct
5 Jerome Twr
6 Anstey Ct
7 Bennett Ct
8 Gunnersbury Ct
9 Barrington Ct
10 Hope Gdns
11 Park Road E
D5 1 Lantry Ct
2 Rosemount Ct
3 Moreton Twr
4 Acton Central Ind
Est
5 Rufford Twr
6 Narrow St
7 Mount Pl
8 Sidney Miller Ct
9 Mill Hill Terr
10 Cheltenham Pl
11 Mill Hill Gr
12 Benjamin Ho
13 Arlington Ct
14 Lombard Ct
15 Steyne Ho

111
A1 1 Arlington Park
Mans
2 Sandown Ho
3 Goodwood Ho
4 Windsor Ho
5 Lingfield Ho
6 Ascot Ho
7 Watchfield Ct
8 Belgrave Ct
9 Beverley Ct
10 Beaumont Ct
11 Harvard Rd
12 Troubridge Ct
13 Branden Lo
14 Fromow's Cnr
A2 1 Chiswick Green
Studios
2 Bell Ind Est
3 Fairlawn Ct
4 Dukes Gate
5 Dewsbury Ct
6 Chiswick Terr
7 Mortlake Ho
A3 1 Blackmore Twr
2 Bollo Ct
3 Kipling Twr
4 Lawrence Ct
5 Maugham Ct
6 Reade Ct
7 Woolf Ct
8 Shaw Ct
9 Verne Ct
10 Wodehouse Ct
11 Greenock Rd
12 Garden Ct
13 Barons Gate
14 Cleveland Rd
15 Carver Cl
16 Chapter Cl
17 Beauchamp Cl
18 Holmes Ct

19 Copper Mews
A4 1 Belgrave Cl
2 Buckland Wlk
3 Frampton Ct
4 Telfer Ct
5 Harlech Twr
6 Corfe Twr
7 Barwick Ho
8 Charles Hocking
Ho
9 Sunninghill Ct
10 Salisbury St
11 Jameson Pl
12 Castle Cl
A5 1 Rectory Rd
2 Derwentwater
Mans
3 Market Pl
4 Hooper's Mews
5 Cromwell Pl
6 Locarno Rd
7 Edgecote Cl
8 Harleyford Manor
9 Coopers Ct
10 Avingdor Ct
11 Steyne Ho
B1 1 Chatsworth Lo
2 Prospect Pl
3 Townhall Ave
4 Devonhurst Pl
5 Heathfield Ct
6 Horticultural Pl
7 Merlin Ho
8 Garth Rd
9 Autumn Rise
B2 1 Disraeli Cl
2 Winston Wlk
3 Rusthall Mans
4 Bedford Park
Mans
5 Essex Place Sq
6 Holly Rd
7 Homecross Ho
8 Swan Bsns Ctr
9 Jessop Ho
C1 1 Glebe Cl
2 Devonshire Mews
3 Binns Terr
4 Ingress St
5 Swanscombe Rd
6 Brackley Terr
7 Stephen Fox Ho
8 Manor Gdns
9 Coram Ho
10 Flaxman Ho
11 Thorneycroft Ho
12 Thornhill Ho
13 Kent Ho
14 Oldfield Ho
C2 1 Chestnut Ho
2 Bedford Ho
3 Bedford Cnr
4 Sydney Ho
5 Bedford Park Cnr
6 Priory Gdns
7 Windmill Alley
8 Castle Pl
9 Jonathan Ct
10 Windmill Pas
11 Chardin Rd
12 Gable Ho
C3 1 Fleet Ct
2 Ember Ct
3 Emlyn Gdns
4 Clone Ct
5 Brent Ct
6 Abbey Ct
7 Ormsby Lo
8 St Catherine's Ct
9 Lodge The
C4 1 Longford Ct
2 Mole Ct
3 Lea Ct
4 Wandle Ct
5 Beverley Ct
6 Roding Ct
7 Crane Ct
D1 1 Miller's Ct
2 British Grove Pas
3 British Grove S
4 Berestede Rd
5 North Eyot Gdns
D2 1 Flanders Mans
2 Stamford Brook
Mans
3 Linkenholt Mans
4 Prebend Mans
5 Middlesex Ct
D3 1 Stamford Brook
Gdns
2 Hauteville Court
Gdns
3 Ranelagh Gdns

112
A1 1 Chisholm Ct
2 North Verbena
Gdns
3 Western Terr
4 Verbena Gdns
5 Montrose Villas
6 Hammersmith Terr
7 South Black Lion
La
8 St Peter's Wharf
A2 1 Hamlet Ct
2 Derwent Ct
3 Westcroft Ct
4 Black Lion Mews
5 St Peter's Villas

6 Standish Ho
7 Chambon Pl
8 Court Mans
9 Longthorpe Ct
10 Charlotte Ct
11 Westside
12 Park Ct
13 London Ho
A3 1 Elizabeth Finn Ho
2 Ashchurch Ct
3 King's Par
4 Inver Ct
5 Ariel Ct
6 Pocklington Lo
7 Vitae Apartments
A4 1 Becklow Gdns
2 Victoria Ho
3 Lycett Pl
4 Kylemore Ct
5 Alexandra Ct
6 Lytten Ct
7 Becklow Mews
8 Northcroft Ct
9 Bailey Ct
10 Spring Cott
11 Landor Wlk
12 Laurence Mews
13 Hadyn Park Ct
14 Askew Mans
15 Malvern Ct
B1 1 Prince's Mews
2 Aspen Gdns
3 Hampshire Hog La
4 Blades Ct
B2 1 Albion Gdns
2 Flora Gdns
3 Lamington St
4 Felgate Mews
5 Galena Ho
6 Albion Mews
7 Albion Ct
8 King Street Clois-
ters
9 Dimes Pl
10 Clarence Ct
11 Hampshire Hog La
12 Marryat Ct
13 Ravenscourt Ho
B3 1 Ravenscourt Park
Mans
2 Paddenswick Ct
3 Ashbridge Ct
B4 1 Westbush Ct
2 Goldhawk Mews
3 Sycamore Ho
4 Shackleton Ct
5 Drake Ct
6 Scotts Ct
7 Raleigh Ct
8 Melville Court
Flats
9 Southway Cl
B5 1 Arlington Ho
2 Lugard Ho
3 Shabana Ct
4 Sitarey Ct
5 Oaklands Ct
6 Davenport Mews
B6 1 Abercrombie Ho
2 Bathurst Ho
3 Brisbane Ho
4 Bentinck Ho
5 Ellenborough Ho
6 Lawrence Cl
7 Mackenzie Ct
8 Carteret Ho
9 Calvert Ho
10 Winthrop Ho
11 Auckland Ho
12 Blaxland Ho
13 Havelock Cl
14 Hargraves Ho
15 Hudson Ct
16 Phipps Ho
17 Lawson Ho
18 Hastings Ho
19 Wolfe Ho
20 Malabar Ct
21 Commonwealth
Ave
22 Charnock Ho
23 Canning Ho
24 Cornwallis Ho
25 Commonwealth
Ave
26 Champlain Ho
27 Grey Ho
28 Durban Ho
29 Baird Ho
30 Campbell Ho
31 Mitchell Ho
32 Denham Ho
33 Mackay Ho
34 Evans Ho
35 Davis Ho
36 Mandela Cl
C1 1 Bridge Avenue
Mans
2 Bridgeview
3 College Ct
4 Beatrice Ho
5 Amelia Ho
6 Edith Ho
7 Joanna Ho
8 Mary Ho
9 Adela Ho
10 Sophia Ho
11 Henrietta Ho
12 Charlotte Ho
13 Alexandra Ho

14 Bath Pl
15 Elizabeth Ho
16 Margaret Ho
17 Peabody Est
18 Eleanor Ho
19 Isabella Ho
20 Caroline Ho
21 Chancellors Wharf
22 Sussex Pl
C2 1 Phoenix Lodge
Mans
2 Samuel's Cl
3 Broadway Arc
4 Brook Ho
5 Hammersmith
Broadway
6 Broadway Ctr The
7 Cambridge Ct
8 Ashcroft Sq
C4 1 Verulam Ho
2 Grove Mans
3 Frobisher Ct
4 Library Mans
5 Pennard Mans
6 New Shepherd's
Bush Mkt
7 Kerrington Ct
8 Granville Mans
9 Romney Ct
10 Rayner Ct
11 Sulgrave Gdns
12 Bamborough Gdns
13 Hillary Ct
14 Market Studios
15 Lanark Mans
C5 1 Linden Ct
2 Frithville Ct
3 Blomfield Mans
4 Poplar Mews
5 Hopgood St
6 Westwood Ho
7 Stanlake Mews
8 Stanlake Villas
9 Alexandra Mans
D3 1 Grosvenor Resi-
dences
2 Blythe Mews
3 Burnand Ho
4 Bradford Ho
5 Springvale Terr
6 Ceylon Rd
7 Walpole Ct
8 Bronte Ct
9 Boswell Ct
10 Souldern Rd
11 Brook Green Flats
12 Haarlem Rd
13 Stafford Mans
14 Lionel Mans
15 Barradell Ho
D4 1 Vanderbilt Villas
2 Bodington Ct
3 Kingham Cl
4 Clearwater Terr
5 Lorne Gdns
6 Cameret Ct
7 Bush Ct
8 Shepherds Ct
9 Rockley Ct
10 Grampians The
11 Charcroft Ct
12 Addison Park
Mans
13 Sinclair Mans
14 Fountain Ct
15 Woodford Ct
16 Roseford Ct
17 Woodstock Stu-
dios
D5 1 St Katherine's Wlk
2 Dorrit Ho
3 Pickwick Ho
4 Dombey Ho
5 Caranday Villas
6 Mortimer Ho
7 Nickleby Ho
8 Stebbing Ho
9 Boxmoor Ho
10 Poynter Ho
11 Swanscombe Ho
12 Darnley Terr
13 Norland Ho
14 Hume Ho
15 Boundary Ho
16 Norland Rd
17 Helix Ct
D6 1 Frinstead Ho
2 Hurstway Wlk
3 Testerton Wlk
4 Grenfell Wlk
5 Grenfell Twr
6 Barandon Wlk
7 Treadgold Ho
8 St Clements Ct
9 Willow Way
10 Florence Ho
11 Dora Ho
12 Carton Ho
13 Agnes Ho
14 Marley Ho
15 Estella Ho
16 Waynflete Sq
17 Pippin Ho
18 Baseline Business
Studios

118
A1 1 Hope Ct
2 West Point
3 Centre Point

4 East Point
5 Proctor Ho
6 Tovy Ho
7 Avondale Pave-
ment
8 Brettinghurst
9 Colechurch Ho
10 Harman Cl
11 Avondale Ho
12 Lanark Ho
13 George Elliston
Ho
14 Eric Wilkins Ho
15 Six Bridges Ind
Est
16 St James Ind
Mews
17 Winter Lo
18 Fern Wlk
19 Ivy Ct
20 Fallow Ct
21 Culloden Cl
22 Archers Lo
A2 1 Cadbury Way
2 Robert Bell Ho
3 Robert Jones Ho
4 William Rush-
brooke Ho
5 Helen Taylor Ho
6 Peter Hills Ho
7 Charles Macken-
zie Ho
8 Drappers Way
9 Racs Flats
10 Abbey Gdns
11 Mayfair Ho
12 Windmill Cl
13 Maria Cl
14 Townsend Ho
15 Mason Ho
16 Kotree Way
17 Hannah Mary Way
18 Langdon Way
19 Whittaker Way
A3 1 Rudge Ho
2 Spenlow Ho
3 Darnay Ho
4 Carton Ho
5 Giles Ho
6 Bowley Ho
7 Casby Ho
8 Sun Pas
9 Ness St
10 Voyager Bsns Est
11 Dockley Road Ind
Est
12 Spa Ct
13 Discovery Bsns Pk
14 Priter Road Hostel
15 Salisbury Ct
16 William Ellis Way
17 John McKenna
Wlk
18 Toussaint Wlk
19 Gillison Wlk
20 Bromfield Ct
21 Ben Smith Way
22 Major Rd
23 Old Jamaica Bsns
Est
A4 1 Providence
2 Springalls Wharf
3 Flockton St
4 Meridian Ct
5 East La
6 Luna Ho
7 Axis Ct
8 Farthing Alley
9 Peter Butler Ho
10 Brownlow Ho
11 Tapley Ho
12 Copperfield Ho
13 Dombey Ho
14 Fleming Ho
15 Parkers Row
16 Wade Ho
17 Bardell Ho
18 Nickleby Ho
19 John Felton Rd
20 Flockton St
21 Pickwick Ho
22 Oliver Ho
23 Weller Ho
24 Haredale Ho
25 Havisham Ho
26 Tupman Ho
27 Micawber Ho
28 Wrayburn Ho
29 Dartle Ct
30 Waterside Cl
31 Burnaby Ct
32 Wickfield Ho
33 Fountain Ho
34 Fountain Green
Sq
35 St Saviours Ho
36 Providence Sq
A5 1 Trade Winds Ct
2 Spice Ct
3 Leeward Ct
4 Bridgeport Pl
5 Tamarind Yd
6 Cape Yd
7 Nightingale Ho
8 St Anthony's Cl
9 Stockholm Way
10 Miah Terr
11 Seville Ho
12 Douthwaite Sq
13 Codling Cl

14 Hermitage Ct
15 Capital Wharf
16 Cinnabar Wharf
East
17 Cinnabar Wharf
Central
18 Cinnabar Wharf
West
19 Halcyon Wharf
A6 1 Conant Mews
2 Hanson Ho
3 Royal Tower Lo
4 Victoria Ct
5 Swan Pas
6 Royal Mint Ct
7 Peabody Est
8 Florin Ct
9 Flank St
10 Onedin Point
11 Liberty Ho
12 Ensign Ct
13 Sapphire Ct
14 Graces Alley
15 George Leybourne
Ho
16 Fletcher St
17 Hatton Ho
18 Noble Ho
19 Shearsmith Ho
20 Wellclose St
21 Telford's Yd
22 Breezer's Ct
23 Pennington Ct
B1 1 Hockney Ct
2 Toulouse Ct
3 Lowry Ct
4 Barry Ho
5 Lewis Ct
6 Gainsborough Ct
7 Renoir Ct
8 Blake Ct
9 Raphael Ct
10 Rembrandt Ct
11 Constable Ct
12 Da Vinci Ct
13 Gaugin Ct
14 Michelangelo Ct
15 Monet Ct
16 Weald Cl
17 Jasmin Lo
18 Birchmere Lo
19 Weybridge Ct
20 Florence Ho
21 Gleneagles Ct
22 Sunningdale Cl
23 Muirfield St
24 Turnberry Cl
25 St Andrews Cl
26 Kingsdown Cl
27 St Davids Cl
28 Galway Ct
29 Edenbridge Cl
30 Birkdale Cl
31 Tralee Ct
32 Woburn Ct
33 Belfry Cl
34 Troon Cl
35 Holywell Cl
B2 1 Market Pl
2 Trappes Ho
3 Thurland Ho
4 Ramsfort Ho
5 Hambley Ho
6 Holford Ho
7 Pope Ho
8 Southwell Ho
9 Mortain Ho
10 Radcliffe Ho
11 Southwark Park
Est
12 Galleywall Road
Trad Est
13 Trevithick Ho
14 Barlow Ho
15 Donkin Ho
16 Landmann Ho
17 Fitzmaurice Ho
18 Dodd Ho
B3 1 Perryn Rd
2 Chalfont Ho
3 Prestwood Ho
4 Farmer Ho
5 Gataker Ho
6 Gataker St
7 Cornick Ho
8 Glebe Ho
9 Matson Ho
10 Hickling Ho
11 St Andrews Ho
B4 1 Butterfield Cl
2 Janeway Pl
3 Trotwood Ho
4 Maylie Ho
5 Cranbourn Pas
6 Cranbourn Ho
7 Cherry Garden Ho
8 Burton Ho
9 Morriss Ho
10 Dixon's Alley
11 King Edward The
Third Mews
12 Cathay St
13 Mission The
14 Millstream Ho
B5 1 China Ct
2 Wellington Terr
3 Stevedore St
4 Portland Sq
5 Reardon Ho
6 Lowder Ho

7 Meeting House
Alley
8 Farthing Fields
9 Oswell Ho
10 Park Lo
11 Doughty Ct
12 Inglefield Sq
13 Chopin's Ct
14 Welsh Ho
15 Hilliard Ho
16 Clegg St
17 Tasman Ho
18 Ross Ho
19 Wapping Dock St
20 Bridewell Pl
21 New Tower Bldgs
22 Tower Bldgs
23 Chimney Ct
24 Jackman Ho
25 Fenner Ho
26 Franklin Ho
27 Frobisher Ho
28 Flinders Ho
29 Chancellor Ho
30 Beechey Ho
31 Reardon Path
32 Parry Ho
33 Vancover Ho
34 Willoughby Ho
35 Sanctuary The
36 Dundee Ct
37 Pierhead Wharf
38 Scandrett St
39 St Johns Ct
B6 1 Newton Ho
2 Richard Neale Ho
3 Maddocks Ho
4 Cornwall St
5 Brockmer Ho
6 Dellow Ho
7 Bewley Ho
8 Artichoke Hill
9 Queen Anne Terr
10 King Henry Terr
11 King Charles Terr
12 Queen Victoria
Terr
13 Sovereign Ct
14 Princes Court
Bsns Ctr
15 Kingsley Mews
C2 1 Damory Ho
2 Antony Ho
3 Roderick Ho
4 Pedworth Gdns
5 Banner Ct
6 Rotherhithe Bsns
Est
7 Beamish Ho
8 Corbetts Pas
9 Gillam Ho
10 Richard Ho
11 George Walter Ho
12 Westlake
13 Adron Ho
14 McIntosh Ho
C3 1 Blick Ho
2 Neptune Ho
3 Scotia Ct
4 Murdoch Ho
5 Edmonton Ct
6 Niagara Ct
7 Columbia Point
8 Ritchie Ho
9 Wells Ho
10 Helen Peele Cotts
11 Orchard Ho
12 Dock Offices
13 Landale Ho
14 Courthope Ho
15 Hithe Gr
16 China Hall Mews
C4 1 Mayflower St
2 St Mary's Est
3 Rupack St
4 Frank Whymark
Ho
5 Adams Gardens
Est
6 Hatteraick St
7 East India Ct
8 Bombay Ct
9 Stable Ho
10 Grannary The
11 Riverside
12 Cumberland
Wharf
13 Seaford Ho
14 Hythe Ho
15 Sandwich Ho
16 Winchelsea Ho
17 Rye Ho
18 Kenning St
19 Western Pl
20 Ainsty St
21 Pine Ho
22 Beech Ho
23 Larch Ho
24 Turner Ct
25 Seth St
26 Risdon Ho
27 Risdon St
28 Aylton Est
29 Manitoba Ct
30 Calgary Ct
31 Irwell Est
32 St Olav's Sq
33 City Bsns Ctr
C5 1 John Rennie Wlk
2 Malay Ho

3 Wainwright Ho
4 Riverside Mans
5 Shackleton Ho
6 Whitehorn Ho
7 Wavel Ct
8 Prusom's Island
C6 1 Shadwell Pl
2 Gosling Ho
3 Vogler Ho
4 Donovan Ho
5 Knowlden Ho
6 Chamberlain Ho
7 Moore Ho
8 Thornewill Ho
9 Fisher Ho
10 All Saints Ct
11 Coburg Dwellings
12 Lowood Ho
13 Solander Gdns
14 Chancery Bldgs
15 Ring Ho
16 Juniper St
17 Gordon Ho
18 West Block
19 North Block
20 South Block
21 Ikon Ho
D2 1 John Kennedy Ho
2 Brydale Ho
3 Balman Ho
4 Tissington Ct
5 Harbord Ho
6 Westfield Ho
7 Albert Starr Ho
8 John Brent Ho
9 William Evans Ho
10 Raven Ho
11 Egret Ho
12 Fulmar Ho
13 Dunlin Ho
14 Siskin Ho
15 Sheldrake Ho
16 Buchanan Ct
17 Burrage Ct
18 Biddenham Ho
19 Ayston Ho
20 Empingham Ho
21 Deanshanger Ho
22 Codicote Ho
23 Buryfield Ho
D4 1 Schooner Cl
2 Dolphin Cl
3 Clipper Cl
4 Deauville Ct
5 Colette Ct
6 Coniston Ct
7 Virginia Ct
8 Derwent Ct
9 Grantham Ct
10 Serpentine Ct
11 Career Ct
12 Lacine Ct
13 Fairway Ct
14 Harold Ct
15 Spruce Ho
16 Cedar Ho
17 Sycamore Ho
18 Woodland Cres
19 Poplar Ho
20 Adelphi Ct
21 Basque Ct
22 Aberdale Ct
23 Quilting Ct
24 Chargrove Cl
25 Radley Ct
26 Greenacre Sq
27 Maple Leaf Sq
28 Stanhope Cl
29 Hawke Pl
30 Drake Cl
31 Brass Talley Alley
32 Monkton Ho
33 James Ho
34 Wolfe Cres
D5 1 Clarence Mews
2 Raleigh Ct
3 Katherine Cl
4 Woolcombes Ct
5 Tudor Ct
6 Quayside Ct
7 Princes Riverside Rd
8 Surrey Ho
9 Tideway Ct
10 Edinburgh Ct
11 Falkirk Ct
12 Byelands Cl
13 Gwent Ct
14 Lavender Ho
15 Abbotshade Rd
16 Bellamy's Ct
17 Blenheim Ct
18 Sandringham Ct
19 Hampton Ct
20 Windsor Ct
21 Balmoral Ct
22 Westminster Ct
23 Beatson Wlk
D6 1 Barnardo Gdns
2 Roslin Ho
3 Glamis Est
4 Peabody Est
5 East Block
6 Highway Trad Ctr The
7 Highway Bsns Pk The
8 Cranford Cotts
9 Ratcliffe Orch
10 Scotia Bldg

11 Mauretania Bldg
12 Compania Bldg
13 Sirius Bldg
14 Unicorn Bldg
15 Keepier Wharf

119

A2 1 Trafalgar Cl
2 Hornblower Cl
3 Cunard Wlk
4 Caronia Ct
5 Carinthia Ct
6 Freswick Ho
7 Graveley Ho
8 Husbourne Ho
9 Crofters Ct
10 Pomona Ho
11 Hazelwood Ho
12 Cannon Wharf Bsns Ctr
13 Bence Ho
14 Clement Ho
15 Pendennis Ho
16 Lighter Cl
17 Mast Ct
18 Rushcutters Ct
19 Boat Lifter Way
A5 1 Edward Sq
2 Prince Regent Ct
3 Codrington Ct
4 Pennington Ct
5 Cherry Ct
6 Ash Ct
7 Beech Ct
8 Hazel Ct
9 Laurel Ct
A6 1 St Georges Sq
2 Drake Ho
3 Osprey Ho
4 Fleet Ho
5 Gainsborough Ho
6 Victory Pl
7 Challenger Ho
8 Conrad Ho
9 Lock View Ct
10 Shoulder of Mutton Alley
11 Frederick Sq
12 Helena Sq
13 Elizabeth Sq
14 Sophia Sq
15 William Sq
16 Lamb Ct
17 Lockside
18 Adriatic Bldg
19 Ionian Bldg
20 Regents Gate Ho
B1 1 Gransden Ho
2 Daubeney Twr
3 North Ho
4 Rochfort Ho
5 Keppel Ho
6 Camden Ho
7 Sanderson Ho
8 Berkeley Ho
9 Strafford Ho
10 Richman Ho
11 Hurleston Ho
12 Grafton Ho
13 Fulcher Ho
14 Citrus Ho
B2 1 Windsock Cl
2 St George's Mews
3 Linberry Wlk
4 Lanyard Ho
5 Golden Hind Pl
6 James Lind Ho
7 Harmon Ho
8 Pelican Ho
9 Bembridge Ho
10 Terrace The
11 George Beard Rd
12 Colonnade The
13 Pepys Ent Ctr
B6 1 Hamilton Ho
2 Imperial Ho
3 Oriana Ho
4 Queens Ho
5 Brightlingsea Pl
6 Faraday Ho
7 Ropemaker's Fields
8 Oast Ct
9 Mitre The
10 Bate St
11 Joseph Irwin Ho
12 Padstow Ho
13 Bethlehem Ho
14 Saunders Cl
15 Roche Ho
16 Stocks Pl
17 Trinidad Ho
18 Grenada Ho
19 Kings Ho
20 Dunbar Wharf
21 Limekiln Wharf
22 Belgrave Ct
23 Eaton Ct
C1 1 Hudson Ho
2 Shackleton Ct
3 De Gama Pl
4 Mercator Ct
5 Maritime Quay
6 Perry Ct
7 Amundsen Ct
C2 1 Nova Bldg
2 Apollo Bldg
3 Gaverick Mews
4 Windmill Ho
5 Orion Point

6 Galaxy Bldg
7 Venus Ho
8 Olympian Ct
9 Poseidon Ct
10 Mercury Ct
11 Aphrodite Ct
12 Cyclops Mews
13 Neptune Ct
14 Artemis Ct
15 Hera Ct
16 Ares Ct
17 Ringwood Gdns
18 Dartmoor Wlk
19 Rothsay Wlk
20 Ashdown Wlk
21 Radnor Wlk
22 Ironmonger's Pl
23 Britannia Rd
24 Deptford Ferry Rd
25 Magellan Pl
26 Dockers Tanner Rd
C3 1 Bowsprit Point
2 St Hubert's Ho
3 John Tucker Ho
4 Broadway Wlk
5 Nash Ho
6 Fairlead Ho
7 Crosstrees Ho
8 Stanliff Ho
9 Keelson Ho
10 Clara Grant Ho
11 Gilbertson Ho
12 Scoulding Ho
13 Hibbert Ho
14 Cressall Ho
15 Alexander Ho
16 Kedge Ho
C4 1 Anchorage Point
2 Waterman Bldg
3 Jefferson Bldg
4 Pierpoint Bldg
5 Franklin Bldg
6 Vanguard Bldg
7 Edison Bldg
8 Seacon Twr
9 Naxos Bldg
10 Express Wharf
11 Hutching's Wharf
12 Tobago St
13 Bellamy Cl
14 Dowlen Ct
15 Cochrane Ho
16 Beatty Ho
17 Scott Ho
18 Laybourne Ho
19 Ensign Ho
20 Beaufort Ho
21 Spinnaker Ho
22 Bosun Cl
23 Topmast Point
24 Turner Ho
25 Constable Ho
26 Knighthead Point
C6 1 West India Ho
2 Berber Pl
3 Birchfield Ho
4 Elderfield Ho
5 Thornfield Ho
6 Gorsefield Ho
7 Arborfield Ho
8 Colborne Ho
9 East India Bldgs
10 Compass Point
11 Salter St
12 Garland Ct
13 Bogart Ct
14 Fonda Ct
15 Welles Ct
16 Rogers Ct
17 Premier Pl
18 Kelly Ct
19 Flynn Ct
20 Mary Jones Ho
21 Cannon Dr
22 Horizon Bldg
D1 1 Slipway Ho
2 Taffrail Ho
3 Platehouse The
4 Wheelhouse The
5 Chart House The
6 Port House The
7 Beacon Ho
8 Blasker Wlk
9 Maconochies Rd
D2 1 Brassey Ho
2 Triton Ho
3 Warspite Ho
4 Rodney Ho
5 Conway Ho
6 Exmouth Ho
7 Akbar Ho
8 Arethusa Ho
9 Tasman Ct
10 Cutty Sark Ho
D3 1 Turnberry Quay
2 Balmoral Ho
3 Aegon Ho
4 Marina Point
D6 1 Westcott Ho
2 Corry Ho
3 Malam Gdns
4 Blomfield Ho
5 Devitt Ho
6 Leyland Ho
7 Wigram Ho
8 Willis Ho
9 Balsam Ho
10 Finch's Ct
11 Poplar Bath St
12 Lawless St

13 Storey Ho
14 Abbot Ho
15 Woodall Cl
16 Landon Wlk
17 Goodhope Ho
18 Goodfaith Ho
19 Winant Ho
20 Goodspeed Ho
21 Lubbock Ho
22 Goodwill Ho
23 Martindale Ho
24 Holmsdale Ho
25 Norwood Ho
26 Constant Ho

120

A2 1 St John's Ho
2 Betty May Gray Ho
3 Castleton Ho
4 Urmston Ho
5 Salford Ho
6 Capstan Ho
7 Frigate Ho
8 Galleon Ho
A3 1 Cardale St
2 Hickin St
3 John McDonald Ho
4 Thorne Ho
5 Skeggs Ho
6 St Bernard Ho
7 Kimberley Ho
8 Kingdon Ho
9 Killoran Ho
10 Alastor Ho
11 Lingard Ho
12 Yarrow Ho
13 Sandpiper Ct
14 Nightingale Ct
15 Robin Ct
16 Heron Ct
17 Ferndown Lo
18 Crosby Ho
A4 1 Llandovery Ho
2 Rugless Ho
3 Ash Ho
4 Elm Ho
5 Cedar Ho
6 Castalia Sq
7 Aspect Ho
8 Normandy Ho
9 Valiant Ho
10 Tamar Ho
11 Watkins Ho
12 Alice Shepherd Ho
13 Oak Ho
14 Ballin Ct
15 Martin Ct
16 Grebe Ct
17 Kingfisher Ct
18 Walkers Lo
19 Antilles Bay
A5 1 Lumina Bldg
2 Nova Ct W
3 Nova Ct E
4 Aurora Bldg
5 Arran Ho
6 Kintyre Ho
7 Vantage Mews
8 Managers St
9 Horatio Pl
10 Concordia Wharf
A6 1 Discovery Ho
2 Mountague Pl
3 Virginia Ho
4 Collins Ho
5 Lawless Ho
6 Carmichael Ho
7 Commodore Ho
8 Mermaid Ho
9 Bullivant St
10 Anderson Ho
11 Mackrow Wlk
12 Robin Hood Gdns
13 Prestage Way
B2 1 Verwood Lo
2 Fawley Lo
3 Lyndhurst Lo
4 Blyth Cl
5 Farnworth Ho
6 Francis Cl
B6 1 Quixley St
2 Romney Ho
3 Pumping Ho
4 Switch Ho
5 Wingfield Ct
6 Explorers Ct
7 Sexton Ct
8 Keel Ct
9 Bridge Ct
10 Sail Ct
11 Settlers Ct
12 Pilgrims Mews
13 Studley Ct
14 Wotton Ct
15 Cape Henry Ct
16 Bartholomew Ct
17 Adventurers Ct
18 Susan Constant Ct
19 Atlantic Ct
C1 1 Bellot Gdns
2 Thornley Pl
3 King William La
4 Bolton Ho
5 Miles Ho
6 Mell St
7 Sam Manners Ho

8 Hatcliffe Alms-houses
9 Woodland Wlk
10 Earlswood Cl
D1 1 Baldrey Ho
2 Christie Ho
3 Dyson Ho
4 Cliffe Ho
5 Moore Ho
6 Collins Ho
7 Lockyer Ho
8 Halley Ho
9 Kepler Ho
10 Sailacre Ho
11 Union Pk
D3 1 Teal St
2 Maurer Ct
3 Mudlarks Blvd
4 Renaissance Wlk
5 Alamaro Lo

121

A1 1 Layfield Ho
2 Westerdale Rd
3 Mayston Mews
4 Station Mews Terr
A5 1 Capulet Mews
2 Pepys Cres
3 De Quincey Mews
4 Hardy Ave
5 Tom Jenkinson Rd
6 Kennacraig Cl
7 Charles Flemwell Mews
8 Gatcombe Rd
9 Badminton Mews
10 Holyrood Mews
11 Britannia Gate
12 Dalemain Mews
13 Bowes-Lyon Hall
14 Lancaster hall
15 Victoria Hall
A6 1 Clements Ave
2 Martindale Ave
3 Balearic Apts
4 Marmara Apts
5 Baltic Apts
6 Coral Apts
7 Aegean Apts
8 Capital East Apts
B1 1 Phipps Ho
2 Hartwell Ho
3 Nicholas Stacey Ho
4 Frank Burton Cl
B5 1 Beaulieu Ave
2 Charles Whincup Rd
3 Audley Dr
4 Julia Garfield Mews
5 Rayleigh Rd
6 Pirie St
7 Royal Victoria Pl
8 Pankhurst Ave
9 West Mersea Cl
10 Ramsgate Cl
11 Windsor Hall
12 Munning Ho
13 Drake Hall
14 Jane Austen Hall
C1 1 Ransom Rd
2 Linton Cl
3 Cedar Pl
4 Gooding Ho
5 Valiant Ho
6 Chaffey Ho
7 Benn Ho
8 Wellesley Cl
9 Gollogly Terr

122

A2 1 Harden Ct
2 Albion Ct
3 Viking Ho
4 Zealand Ho
5 Glenalvon Way
6 Parish Wharf
7 Elsinore Ho
8 Lolland Ho
9 Denmark Ho
10 Jutland Ho
11 Tivoli Gdns
12 Rance Ho
13 Peel Yates Ho
14 Rosebank Wlk
15 Paradise Pl
16 Woodville St
B2 1 Bowling Green Row
2 Sarah Turnbull Ho
3 Brewhouse Rd
4 Red Barracks Rd
5 Marine Dr
6 Hastings Ho
7 Centurion St
8 Cambridge Ho
9 Churchill Ct
10 Elizabeth Ct
11 Cambridge Barracks Rd
12 Len Clifton Ho
13 Granby Ho
14 Harding Ho
15 Rutland Ho
16 Townshend Ho
17 Rendlebury Ho
18 Milne Ho
19 Mulgrave Rd

20 Murray Ho
21 Chatham Ho
22 Biddulph Ho
23 Carew Ho
24 Eleanor Wlk
C2 1 Preston Ho
2 Lindsay Ho
3 Fraser Ho
4 Pickering Ho
5 Watergate Ho
6 Grinling Ho
7 Glebe Ho
8 Elliston Ho
9 Sir Martin Bowes Ho
10 Jim Bradley Cl
11 Bathway
12 Limavady Ho
13 Slater Cl
14 Vista Bldg The
C5 1 Westland Ho
2 Queensland Ho
3 Pier Par
4 Woodman Par
5 Shaw Ho
6 Glen Ho
7 Brocklebank Ho
D1 1 Branham Ho
2 Ford Ho
3 Wilford Ho
4 Parker Ho
5 Stirling Ho
6 Twiss Ho
7 Hewett Ho
8 De Haviland Dr
9 Schoolhouse Yd
D2 1 Beresford Sq
2 Central Ct
3 Walpole Pl
4 Anglesea Ave
5 Troy Ct
6 Ormsby Point
7 Haven Lo
8 Green Lawns
9 Eardley Point
10 Sandham Point
11 Bingham Point
12 Anglesea Mews
13 Masons Hill
14 Maritime St

123

A1 1 Glenmount Path
2 Claymill Ho
3 St James Hts
4 St Margaret's Path
5 George Akass Ho
A3 1 Wayatt Point
2 Albert Ho
3 Building 50
4 Building 49
5 Building 48
6 Building 47
7 Building 36
8 Blenheim Ho
9 Wilson Ct
B1 1 Bert Reilly Ho
B3 1 Apollo Way
2 Senator Wlk
3 Mallard Path
4 Fortune Wlk
C1 1 Fox Hollow Cl
2 Goldsmid St
C2 1 Gavin Ho
2 Richard Neve Ho
3 Bateson St
4 Lewin Ct

124

B5 1 Rowntree Path
2 MacAulay Way
3 Manning Ct
4 Chadwick Ct
5 Simon Ct
B6 1 Beveridge Ct
2 Hammond Way
3 Leonard Robbins Path
4 Lansbury Ct
5 Raymond Postgate Ct
6 Webb Ct
7 Curtis Way
8 Lytton Strachey Path
9 Keynes Ct
10 Marshall Path
11 Cross Ct
12 Octavia Way
13 Passfield Path
14 Mill Ct
15 Besant Ct
C3 1 Hermitage Cl
2 Chantry Cl
C4 1 Binsey Wlk
2 Tilehurst Point
3 Blewbury Ho
4 Coralline Wlk
5 Evenlode Ho
C5 1 Kingsley Ho
2 Wilberforce Ct
3 Shaftesbury Ct
4 Hazlitt Ct
5 Ricardo Path
6 Nassau Path
7 Malthus Path
8 Bright Ct
9 Cobden Ct
D4 1 Oakenholt Ho

2 Trewsbury Ho
3 Penton Ho
4 Osney Ho
5 St Helens Rd
6 Clewer Ho
7 Maplin Ho
8 Wyfold Ho
9 Hibernia Point
10 Duxford Ho
11 Radley Ho
12 Limestone Wlk
13 Masham Ho
14 Jacob Ho

125

A3 1 Harlequin Ho
2 Dexter Ho
3 Argali Ho
4 Mangold Way
5 Lucerne Ct
6 Holstein Way
7 Abbotswood Cl
8 Plympton Ct
9 Benedict Cl
B1 1 Shakespeare Ho
2 Tennyson Ho
3 Dickens Ho
4 Scott Ho
5 Lansbury Ho
6 Shaw Ho
7 Chestnuts The
C1 1 Stevanne Ct
2 Tolcairn Ct
3 Chalfont Ct
4 Alonso Ho
5 Ariel Ct
6 Miranda Ho
7 Prospero Ho
8 Laurels The
9 Camden Ct
10 Newnham Lo
11 Court Lo
12 Flaxman Ct
13 Hertford Wlk
14 Riverview Ct
15 Winchester Ct
C2 1 Brushwood Lo
2 Bletchington Ct
3 Upper Sheridan Rd
4 William Ct
5 Samson Ct
6 Cowper Rd
7 Venmead Ct
C3 1 Cressingham Ct
2 Telford Ho
3 Kelvin Ho
4 Faraday Ho
5 Jenner Ho
6 Keir Hardie Ho
7 Lennox Ho
8 Mary Macarthur Ho
9 Elizabeth Garrett Anderson Ho
10 William Smith Ho
11 Baden Powell Ho
12 Baird Ho
13 Boyle Ho

129

D1 1 Heathwood Ct
2 Aldermead
3 Northumberland Ct

130

C4 1 Osterley Lo
2 St Andrew's Cl
3 Parkfield
4 Fairways
5 Granwood Ct
6 Grovewood Ct

131

A2 1 Brewery Mews Bsns Ctr
2 Forge Lo
3 Pulteney Cl
4 Tolson Ho
5 Percy Gdns
6 Wynne Ct
7 Wisdom Ct
8 Swann Ct
9 Shrewsbury Wlk
10 King's Terr
11 Van Gogh Cl
12 Holme Ct
C5 1 Canute Ho
2 Spruce Ho
3 Moorings Ho
4 Jessops Wharf
5 Corsell Ho
6 Barnes Qtr
7 Dorey Ho
8 Tanyard Ho
9 Booth Ho
10 Oakbark Ho
11 Bordeston Ct
12 Shire Pl
D5 1 Galba Ct
2 Servius Ct
3 Maurice Ct
4 Leo Ct
5 Otho Ct
6 Nero Ct
7 Romulus Ct

8 Pump Alley
D6 1 Brockshot Cl
2 Westbury Pl
3 Brook La N
4 Braemar Ct
5 Brook Ct
6 Clifden Ho
7 Cedar Ct
8 Cranbrook Ct
9 Somerset Lo
10 Alexandra Rd
11 Berkeley Ho
12 Watermans Ct
13 Ferry Quays Ctyd

132
A1 1 St John's Gr
2 Michel's Row
3 Michelsdale Dr
4 Blue Anchor Alley
5 Clarence St
6 Sun Alley
7 Thames Link Ho
8 Benns Wlk
9 Waterloo Pl
10 Northumbria Ct
A6 1 Ferry Sq
2 Watermans Ct
3 Wilkes Rd
4 Albany Par
5 Charlton Ho
6 Albany Ho
7 Alma Ho
8 Griffin Ct
9 Cressage Ho
10 Tunstall Wlk
11 Trimmer Wlk
12 Running Horse Yd
13 Mission Sq
14 Distillery Wlk
B1 1 Towers The
2 Longs Ct
3 Sovereign Ct
4 Robinson Ct
5 Calvert Ct
6 Bedford Ct
7 Hickey's Alms-shouses
8 Church Estate Almshouses
9 Richmond International Bsns Ctr
10 Abercorn Mews
B4 1 Primrose Ho
2 Lawman Ct
3 Royston Ct
4 Garden Ct
5 Capel Lo
6 Devonshire Ct
7 Celia Ct
8 Rosslyn Ho
9 Branstone Ct
10 Lamerton Lo
11 Kew Lo
12 Dunraven Ho
13 Stoneleigh Lo
14 Tunstall Ct
15 Voltaire
C4 1 Clarendon Ct
2 Quintock Ho
3 Broome Ct
4 Lonsdale Mews
5 Elizabeth Cotts
6 Sandways
7 Victoria Cotts
8 North Ave
9 Grovewood
10 Hamilton Ho
11 Melvin Ct
12 Royal Par
13 Power Ho
14 Station Ave
15 Blake Mews
D1 1 Hershell Ct
2 Deanhill Ct
3 Park Sheen
4 Furness Lo
5 Merricks Ct
D4 1 Terrano Ho
2 Oak Ho
3 Aura Ho
4 Maple Ho
5 Cedar Ho
6 Saffron Ho
7 Lime Ho
8 Lavender Ho
9 Juniper Ho

133
B2 1 Rann Ho
2 Craven Ho
3 John Dee Ho
4 Kindell Ho
5 Montgomery Ho
6 Avondale Ho
7 Addington Ct
8 Dovecote Gdns
9 Firmston Ho
10 Glendower Gdns
11 Chestnut Ave
12 Trehern Rd
13 Rock Ave
D3 1 Melrose Rd
2 Seaforth Lo
3 St John's Gr
4 Sussex Ct
5 Carmichael Ct

6 Hampshire Ct
7 Thorne Pas
8 Brunel Ct
9 Beverley Path

134
D1 1 Olivette St
2 Mascotte Rd
3 Glegg Pl
4 Crown Ct
5 Charlwood Terr
6 Percy Laurie Ho
D6 1 Cobb's Hall
2 Dorset Mans
3 St Clements Mans
4 Bothwell St
5 Hawksmoor St

135
B3 1 Plato Pl
2 Mustow Pl
3 Laurel Bank Gdns
4 Ranelagh Mans
5 Churchfield Mans
6 Bear Croft Ho
7 Elysium Gate
8 Ethel Rankin Ct
9 Arthur Henderson Ho
10 William Banfield Ho
11 Melbray Mews
D3 1 Brightwells
2 Broughton Road App
3 Bulow Ct
4 Langford Rd
5 Elizabeth Barnes Ct
6 Snowbury Rd

136
A2 1 Molasses Ho
2 Molasses Row
3 Cinnamon Row
4 Calico Ct
5 Calico Row
6 Port Ho
7 Square Rigger Row
8 Trade Twr
9 Ivory Ho
10 Spice Ct
11 Sherwood Ct
12 Mendip Ct
13 Chalmers Ho
14 Coral Row
15 Ivory Sq
16 Kingfisher Ho
B1 1 Burke Ho
2 Fox Ho
3 Buxton Ho
4 Pitt Ho
5 Ramsey Ho
6 Beverley Cl
7 Florence Ho
8 Linden Ct
9 Dorcas Ct
10 Johnson Ct
11 Agnes Ct
12 Hilltop Ct
13 Courtyard The
14 Old Laundry The
15 Oberstein Rd
16 Fineran Ct
17 Sangora Rd
18 Harvard Mans
19 Plough Mews
B2 1 Benham Cl
2 Milner Ho
3 McManus Ho
4 Wilberforce Ho
5 Wheeler Ct
6 Sporle Ct
7 Holliday Sq
8 John Parker Sq
9 Carmichael Cl
10 Fenner Sq
11 Clark Lawrence Ct
12 Shaw Ct
13 Sendall Ct
14 Livingstone Rd
15 Farrant Ho
16 Jackson Ho
17 Darien Ho
18 Shepard Ho
19 Ganley Ct
20 Arthur Newton Ho
21 Chesterton Ho
22 John Kirk Ho
23 Mantua St
24 Heaver Rd
B3 1 Archer Ho
2 White Ho
3 Winfield Ho
4 Powrie Ho
5 Morgan Ct
6 Fairchild Ho
7 Musjid Rd
C2 1 Kiloh Ct
2 Lanner Ho
3 Griffon Ho
4 Kestrel Ho
5 Kite Ho
6 Peregrine Ho
7 Hawk Ho
8 Inkster Ho
9 Harrier Ho
10 Eagle Hts

11 Kingfisher Ct
12 Lavender Terr
13 Temple Ho
14 Ridley Ho
15 Eden Ho
16 Hertford Ct
17 Nepaul Rd
C3 1 Meecham Ct
2 McKiernan Ct
3 Banbury St
4 Colestown St
5 Crombie Mews
6 Frere St
D3 1 Stevenson Ho
2 Ambrose Mews
3 Harling Ct
4 Southside Quarter
5 Latchmere St
6 Dovedale Cotts
7 Roydon Cl
8 Castlemaine
9 Wittering Ho
10 Berry Ho
11 Weybridge Point

137
A2 1 Shaftesbury Park Chambers
2 Selborne
3 Rush Hill Mews
4 Marmion Mews
5 Crosland Pl
6 Craven Mews
7 Garfield Mews
8 Audley Cl
9 Basnett Rd
10 Tyneham Cl
11 Woodmere Cl
A3 1 Hopkinson Ho
2 MacDonald Ho
3 Rushlake Ho
4 Bishopstone Ho
5 Dresden Ho
6 Millgrove St
7 Farnhurst Ho
8 Walden Ho
9 Kennard St
10 Langhurst Ho
11 Atkinson Ho
12 Kennard Ho
13 Voltaire Ct
14 Barloch Ho
15 London Stone Bsns Est
B2 1 Turnchapel Mews
2 Redwood Mews
3 Phil Brown Pl
4 Bev Callender Cl
5 Keith Connor Cl
6 Tessa Sanderson Pl
7 Daley Thompson Way
8 Rashleigh Ct
9 Abberley Mews
10 Willow Lodge
11 Beaufoy Rd
B3 1 St Philip Sq
2 Montefiore St
3 Gambetta St
4 Scott Ct
5 Radcliffe Path
6 Moresby Wlk
7 Victorian Hts
C1 1 Polygon The
2 Windsor Ct
3 Trinity Cl
4 Studios The
5 Bourne Ho
C2 1 Clapham Manor Ct
2 Clarke Ho
3 Gables The
4 Sycamore Mews
5 Maritime Ho
6 Rectory Gdns
7 Floris Pl
C3 1 Seymour Ho
2 Lucas Ho
3 Durrington Twr
4 Amesbury Twr
5 Fovant Ct
6 Allington Ct
7 Welford Ct
8 Ilsley Ct
9 Blake Ct
10 Brooklands Ct
D1 1 Kendoa Rd
2 Felmersham Cl
3 Abbeville Mews
4 Saxon Ho
5 Gifford Ho
6 Teignmouth Cl
7 Holwood Pl
8 Oaklands Cl
9 Wilberforce Mews
10 William Bonney Est
D2 1 Chelsham Ho
2 Lynde Ho
3 Greener Ho
4 Towns Ho
5 Hugh Morgan Ho
6 Roy Ridley Ho
7 Lendal Terr
8 Slievemore Cl
9 Cadmus Cl
10 Clapham North Bsns Ctr
D3 1 Haltone Ho

2 Surcot Ho
3 Kingsley Ho
4 Wood Ho
5 Dalemain Ho
6 Falloden Ho
7 Dartington Ho
8 Esher Ho
9 Kneller Ho
10 Lostock Ho
11 Croxteth Ho
12 Donnington Ho
13 Farnley Ho
14 Hardwick Ho
15 Bradfield Ho
16 Brocket Ho
17 Colchester Ho
18 Clive Ho
19 Chessington Ho
20 Rushbrook Ho
21 Stanmore Ho
22 Newton Ho
23 Netherby Ho
24 Oakwell Ho
25 Rydal Ho
26 Rushton Ho
27 Harcourt Ho
28 Metcalfe Ho
29 Lydwell Ho
30 Raleigh Ho
31 Spencer Ho
32 Shipley Ho
33 Naylor Ho
34 Mordaunt Ho
35 Stanley Ho
36 Alderley Ho
37 Effingham Ho
38 Grant Ho
39 Wilson Ho
40 Fraser Ho

138
A1 1 Morris Ho
2 Gye Ho
3 Clowes Ho
4 Thomas Ho
5 Stuart Ho
6 Storace Ho
7 Bedford Ho
8 Ascot Ct
9 Ascot Par
10 Ashmere Ho
11 Ashmere Gr
12 Ventura Ho
13 Vickery Ho
14 Stafford Mans
15 Beresford Ho
A2 1 Callingham Ho
2 Russell Pickering Ho
3 Ormerod Ho
4 Lopez Ho
5 Coachmaker Mews
A3 1 Barling Ct
2 Jeffrey's Ct
3 Brooks Ct
4 Dalmeny Ct
5 Fender Ct
6 Fishlock Ct
7 Bedser Ct
8 Gover Ct
9 Clarence Wlk
10 Barton Ct
11 Allom Ct
12 Garden Ho
13 Otha Ho
14 Hayward Ct
15 Surridge Ct
16 Knox Ct
17 Jephson Ct
18 Holmes Ct
19 McIntyre Ct
20 Richardson Ct
21 Cassell Ho
22 Pakington Ho
23 Bain Ho
24 Enfield Ho
25 Fawcett Ho
26 Sidgwick Ho
27 Jowett Ho
28 Beckett Ho
29 Arden Ho
30 Pinter Ho
31 Barrington Ct
32 Union Mews
B1 1 Freemens Hos
2 Roger's Alms-houses
3 Gresham Alms-houses
4 Exbury Ho
5 Glasbury Ho
6 Dalbury Ho
7 Fosbury Ho
8 Chalbury Ho
9 Neilson-Terry Ct
10 Pavilion Mans
11 Daisy Dormer Ct
12 George Lashwood Ct
13 Marie Lloyd Ct
14 Trinity Homes
15 Lethaby Ho
16 Edmundsbury Ct Est
17 Regis Pl
18 Marlborough Mews
19 Alpha Ho
20 Beta Pl

21 Cedars Ho
B2 1 Turberville Ho
2 Thrayle Ho
3 Percheron Ct
4 Draymans Ct
B3 1 Maurice Ho
2 Thring Ho
3 Paton Ho
4 Huxley Ho
5 Morell Ho
6 Mary Ho
7 Beale Ho
8 Rosa Parks Ho
9 Birrell Ho
10 Waltham Ho
11 Burford Ho
12 Thornicroft Ho
13 Addington Ho
14 Goffton Ho
15 Redmayne Ho
16 Norton Ho
17 Aytoun Ct
18 Colwall Ho
19 Burrow Ho
20 Wynter Ho
21 Crowhurst Ho
22 Lidcote Gdns
23 Cumnor Cl
24 Park View Mews
C1 1 Electric Mans
2 Electric La
3 Connaught Mans
4 Clifton Mans
5 Hereford Ho
6 Chaplin Ho
7 Brixton Oval
8 Lord David Pitt Ho
9 Marcus Garvey Way
10 Montego Cl
11 Bob Marley Way
12 Leeson Rd
C2 1 Buckmaster Cl
2 Albemarle Ho
3 Goodwood Mans
4 Angell Park Gdns
5 Fyfield Rd
6 Howard Ho
7 Harris Ho
8 Broadoak Ct
9 Burgate Ct
10 Witchwood Ho
11 Blacktree Mews
12 Chartham Ct
13 Chilham Ct
14 Northgate Ct
15 Westgate Ct
16 Dover Mans
C3 1 Norval Gn
2 Hilda Terr
3 Burton La
4 Church Gn
5 Lord Holland La
6 Sorrell Cl
7 Burton Rd
8 Holles Ho
9 Leys Ct
10 Warwick Ho
11 Fairfax Ho
12 Wayland Ho
13 Dudley Ho
14 Denchworth Ho
15 Fitzgerald Ho
16 Lambert Ho
17 Chute Ho
18 Bedwell Ho
19 Ferrey Mews
20 Serenaders Rd
21 Boateham Wlk
22 Ireton Ho
23 Marston Ho
24 Morrison Rd
25 Fir Grove Rd
26 Shore Way
C4 1 Hector Ct
2 Jason Ct
3 Creon Ct
4 Hermes Ct
5 Argos Ct
6 Cadmus Ct
7 Appollo Ct
8 Mercury Ct
9 County Ho
10 Seasalter Ho
11 Downbarton Ho
12 Garlinge Ho
13 Moira Ho
14 Alvanley Ho
15 Woodchurch Ho
16 Durlock Ho
17 Hallam Ho
18 Whiteness Ho
19 Bromstone Ho
20 Penelope Ho
21 Melbourne Sq
22 Cloisters The
23 Cliffsend Ho
24 Sacketts Ho
25 Hanway Ho
26 Brickworth Ho
27 Redlynch Ho
28 Stodmarsh Ho
29 Kingsgate Ho
30 Chardin Ho
31 Annesley Ho
32 Knowlton Ho
33 Russell Gr
34 Eamann Casey Ho
C5 1 Swift Ho
2 Listowel Cl

3 Deal Wlk
4 Plover Ho
5 Aigburth Mans
6 Glencoe Mans
7 Glenshaw Mans
8 Cleveland Mans
9 Leda Ct
10 Jupiter Ct
11 Juno Ct
12 Healy Ho
13 Ashton Ho
14 Ramsey Ho
15 Annesley Ho
16 Cowley Rd
C6 1 Sherwin Ho
2 Pegasus Pl
3 Kilner Ho
4 Read Ho
5 Lohmann Ho
6 Hornby Ho
7 Abel Ho
8 Blythe Ho
9 Key Ho
10 Lockwood Ho
11 Alverstone Ho
12 Blades Ho
13 Rothesay Ct
D1 1 Mahatma Gandhi Ind Est
2 Dylan Rd
3 Bessemer Park Ind Est
4 Pablo Neruda Cl
5 Langston Hughes Cl
6 Walt Whitman Cl
7 James Joyce Wlk
8 Alice Walker Cl
9 Louise Bennett Cl
10 Chadacre Ho
11 Burwood Ho
12 Pyrford Ho
13 Wangford Ho
14 Ashford Ho
15 Kenwood Ho
16 Moyne Ho
17 Elveden Ho
18 Carrara Cl
19 Broughton Dr
20 Angela Davis Ind Est
21 Tilia Wlk
22 County Ho
D2 1 Mallams Mews
2 Amberley Ct
3 Harper Ho
4 Leicester Ho
5 Station Ave
6 Wellfit St
7 Loughborough Ct
8 Belinda Rd
9 Higgs Ind Est
D3 1 Langport Ho
2 Iveagh Ho
3 Newark Ho
4 Edgehill Ho
5 Hopton Ho
6 Ashby Ho
7 Nevil Ho
D4 1 Fairbairn Gn
2 Hammerton Ho
3 Foxley Sq
4 Silverburn Ho
5 Butler Ho
6 Dalkeith Ho
7 Turner Cl
8 Bathgate Ho
9 Black Roof Ho
D6 1 Faunce Ho
2 Garbett Ho
3 Harvard Ho
4 Doddington Pl
5 Kean Ho
6 Jephson Ho
7 Cornish Ho
8 Bateman Ho
9 Molesworth Ho
10 Walters Ho
11 Cruden Ho
12 Brawne Ho
13 Prescott Ho
14 Chalmer's Wlk
15 Copley Cl
16 King Charles Ct

139
A3 1 Bergen Ho
2 Oslo Ho
3 Viking Ho
4 Jutland Ho
5 Norvic Ho
6 Odin Ho
7 Baltic Ho
8 Nobel Ho
9 Mercia Ho
10 Kenbury Gdns
11 Zealand Ho
12 Elsinore Ho
13 Norse Ho
14 Denmark Mans
15 Dane Ho
16 Canterbury Cl
17 York Cl
18 Kenbury Mans
19 Parade Mans
20 Winterslow Ho
21 Lilford Ho
22 Bartholomew Ho
23 Guildford Ho
24 Boston Ho

25 Hereford Ho
26 Weyhill Ho
27 Lichfield Ho
28 Lansdown Ho
29 Honiton Ho
30 Pinner Ho
31 Baldock Ho
32 Widecombe Ho
33 Nottingham Ho
34 Witham Ho
35 Barnet Ho
36 Empress Mews
A4 1 Bertha Neubergh Ho
2 Mornington Mews
3 Badsworth Rd
4 Pearson Cl
5 Elm Tree Ct
6 Samuel Lewis Trust Dwellings
7 Milkwell Yd
8 Keswick Ho
9 Mitcham Ho
A5 1 Boundary Ho
2 Day Ho
3 Burgess Ho
4 Carlyle Ho
5 Myers Ho
6 Thompson Ave
7 Palgrave Ho
8 Winnington Ho
9 Brantwood Ho
10 Lowell Ho
11 Jessie Duffett Ho
12 Otterburn Ho
13 Crossmount Ho
14 Venice Ct
15 Bowyer St
16 Livingstone Ho
17 Gothic Ct
18 Coniston Ho
19 Harlynwood
20 Carey Ct
21 Finley Ct
22 Grainger Ct
23 Hayes Ct
24 Moffat Ho
25 Marinel Ho
26 Hodister Cl
27 Arnot Ho
28 Lamb Ho
29 Kipling Ho
30 Keats Ho
31 Kenyon Ho
32 New Church Rd
33 Sir John Kirk Cl
B1 1 Shaftesbury Ct
2 Mayhew Ct
3 Morris Ct
4 Swinburne Ct
5 Perth Ct
6 Tayside Ct
7 Matlock Ct
8 Hunter Ct
9 Turner Ct
B3 1 Selborne Rd
2 Hascombe Terr
B4 1 Joiners Arms Yd
2 Butterfly Wlk
3 Cuthill Wlk
4 Colonades The
5 Artichoke Mews
6 Peabody Bldgs
7 Brighton Ho
8 Park Ho
9 Peabody Ct
10 Lomond Ho
11 Lamb Ho
12 Kimpton Ct
13 Belham Wlk
14 Datchelor Pl
15 Harvey Rd
B5 1 Masterman Ho
2 Milton Ho
3 Pope Ho
4 Chester Ct
5 Marvel Ho
6 Flecker Ho
7 Landor Ho
8 Leslie Prince Ct
9 Evelina Mans
10 Langland Ho
11 Drinkwater Ho
12 Procter Ho
13 Shirley Ho
14 Drayton Ho
15 Bridges Ho
16 Cunningham Ho
17 Hood Ho
18 Herrick Ho
19 Dekker Ho
20 Houseman Way
21 Coleby Path
B6 1 Queens Ho
2 Arnside Ho
3 Horsley St
4 St Peter's Ho
5 St Johns Ho
6 St Marks Ho
7 St Stephens Ho
8 St Matthew's Ho
9 Red Lion Cl
10 Boyson Rd
11 Bradenham
C2 1 Harfield Gdns
2 Karen Ct
3 Seavington Ho
4 Appleshaw Ho
5 Birdsall Ho
6 Whitney Ho

7 Wheatland Ho
8 Wilton Ho
9 Walcot Ho
10 Whaddon Ho
11 Melbreak Ho
12 Ledbury Ho
13 Tidworth Ho
14 Riseholme Ho
15 Ringmer Ho
16 Petworth Ho
17 Stagshaw Ho
18 Ivybridge Ho
19 Inwood Ho
20 Gatcombe Ho
21 Felbridge Ho
22 Cowdray Ho
C3 1 Springfield Ho
2 Craston Ho
3 Walters Ho
4 Edgecombe Ho
5 Fowler Ho
6 Rignold Ho
7 Chatham Ho
C4 1 Barnwell Ho
2 Brunswick Villas
3 St Giles Twr
4 Bentley Ho
5 Dawson Ho
6 Dryden Ho
7 Mayward Ho
8 Longleigh Ho
9 Fairwall Ho
10 Bodeney Ho
11 Sandby Ho
12 Vestry Mews
13 Netley
14 Lakanal
15 Racine
C5 1 Tower Mill Rd
2 Tilson Cl
3 Granville Sq
4 Edgar Wallace Cl
5 Potters Cl
6 Dorton Cl
7 Samuel Jones Ind Est
8 Dibden Ho
9 Marchwood Cl
10 Pilgrims Cloisters
11 Beacon Ho
12 Teather St
13 Stacy Path
14 Rumball Ho
15 Ballow Cl
16 Rill Ho
C6 1 Downend Ct
2 Andoversford Ct
3 Pearse St
4 Watling St
5 Gandolfi St
D1 1 Dulwich Mews
2 St James's Cloisters
D4 1 Colbert
2 Voltaire
3 Finch Mews
4 Charles Coveney Rd
5 Bamber Rd
6 Crane St
7 Curlew Ho
8 Mallard Ho
9 Tern Ho
10 Crane Ho
11 Falcon Ho
12 Bryanston Ho
13 Basing Ct
14 Marcus Ho
15 Sheffield Ho
D5 1 Painswick Ct
2 Sharpness Ct
3 Mattingly Way
4 Hordle Prom N
5 Burcher Gale Gr
6 Calypso Cres
7 Hordle Prom S
8 Cinnamon Cl
9 Savannah Cl
10 Thames Ct
11 Shannon Ct
12 Amstel Ct
13 Danube Ct
14 Tilbury Cl
15 Hordle Prom E
16 Indus Ct
17 Oakcourt
18 Palm Ct
19 Rowan Ct
20 Blackthorn Ct
21 Pear Ct
22 Lidgate Rd
23 Whistler Mews
24 Boathouse Wlk
D6 1 Willsbridge Ct
2 Cam Ct
3 Quedgeley Ct
4 Saul Ct
5 Quenington Ct
6 Westonbirt Ct
7 Wickway Ct

140

A3 1 William Margrie Cl
2 William Blake Ho
3 Quantock Mews
4 Choumert Sq
5 Parkstone Rd
6 Atwell Rd
A4 1 Canal Head Public Sq
2 Angelina Ho
3 Jarvis Ho
4 Richland Ho
5 Honeywood Ho
6 Wakefield Ho
7 Primrose Ho
8 Hardcastle Ho
9 Dunstall Ho
10 Springtide Cl
11 Purdon Ho
12 Flamborough Ho
13 Lambrook Ho
14 Witcombe Point
15 Yarnfield Sq
16 Winford Ct
17 Portbury Cl
18 Robert Keen Cl
A5 1 Thornbill Ho
2 Vervain Ho
3 Woodstar Ho
4 Tamarind Ho
5 Hereford Retreat
6 Haymerle Ho
7 Furley Ho
8 Thomas Milner Ho
9 Applegarth Ho
10 Freda Corbett Cl
11 Rudbeck Ho
12 Henslow Ho
13 Lindley Ho
14 Collinson Ho
15 Sister Mabel's Way
16 Timberland Cl
17 Hastings Cl
18 Sidmouth Ho
19 Bulleigh Ho
20 Stanesgate Ho
21 Breamore Ho
22 Ely Ho
23 Gisburn Ho
A6 1 Bowles Rd
2 Western Wharf
3 Northfield Ho
4 Millbrook Ho
5 Denstone Ho
6 Deerhurst Ho
7 Caversham Ho
8 Battle Ho
9 Cardiff Ho
10 Bridgnorth Ho
11 Exeter Ho
12 Grantham Ho
13 Aylesbury Ho
14 Royston Ho
B2 1 Tilling Ho
2 Goodwin Ho
3 Tyrells Ct
4 Citron Terr
5 Basswood Cl
6 Cheam St
B3 1 Walkynscroft
2 Ryegates
3 Hathorne Cl
4 Pilkington Rd
5 Russell Ct
6 Heaton Ho
7 Magdalene Cl
8 Iris Ct
B4 1 Willowdene
2 Pinedene
3 Oakdene
4 Beechdene
5 Hollydene
6 Wood Dene
7 Staveley Cl
8 Carnicot Ho
9 Martock Ct
10 Cherry Tree Ct
11 Kendrick Ct
B5 1 Tortington Ho
2 Credenhill Ho
3 Bromyard Ho
4 Hoyland Cl
5 Willowdene
6 Ashdene
7 Acorn Par
8 Havelock Ct
9 Springall St
10 Harry Lambourn Ho
11 Grenier Apartments
C3 1 Honiton Gdns
2 Selden Ho
3 Hathway Ho
4 Hathway St
5 Station Ct
C4 1 Trotman Ho
2 Boddington Ho
3 Heydon Ho
4 Boulter Ho
5 Astbury Bsns Pk
C5 1 Ambleside Point
2 Grasmere Point
3 Windermere Point
4 Roman Way
5 Laburnum Cl
6 Juniper Ho
7 Romney Cl
8 Hammersley Ho
9 Hutchinson Ho
10 Hammond Ho
11 Fir Tree Ho
12 Glastonbury Ct
13 Highbridge Ct
14 Filton Ct
15 Chiltern Ct
16 Cheviot Ct
C6 1 Penshurst Ho
2 Reculver Ho
3 Mereworth Ho
4 Camber Ho
5 Chiham Ho
6 Otford Ho
7 Olive Tree Ho
8 Aspen Ho
9 Lewis Silkin Ho
10 Richborough Ho
11 Dover Ho
12 Eynsford Ho
13 Horton Ho
14 Lamberhurst Ho
15 Canterbury Ind Pk
16 Upnall Ho
17 Sissinghurst Ho
18 Rochester Ho
19 Saltwood Ho
20 Leybourne Ho
21 Lullingstone Ho
D1 1 Laxton Path
2 Barlings Ho
3 Bayfield Ho
4 Coston Wlk
5 Coverham Ho
6 Gateley Ho
7 Dereham Ho
8 Greenwood Ho
9 Hilton Ho
10 Goodall Ho
11 Horsley Ho
12 Jordan Ho
D5 1 Richard Anderson Ct
2 Palm Tree Ho
3 Edward Robinson Ho
4 Antony Ho
5 Gerrard Ho
6 Palmer Ho
7 Pankhurst Cl
D6 1 Harrisons Ct
2 Grantley Ho
3 Sunbury Ct
4 Tilbury Ho
5 Graham Ct
6 Connell Ct
7 St Clements Ct
8 Henderson Ct
9 Jemotts Ct
10 Verona Ct
11 Heywood Ho
12 Francis Ct
13 Hind Ho
14 Donne Ho
15 Carew Ct
16 Burbage Ho
17 Newland Ho
18 Dobson Ho
19 Dalton Ho
20 Greene Ct
21 Redrup Ho
22 Tarplett Ho
23 Stunell Ho
24 Gasson Ho
25 Bryce Ho
26 Barnes Ho
27 Barkwith Ho
28 Bannister Ho
29 Apollo Ind Bsns Ctr

141

A4 1 Archer Ho
2 Browning Ho
3 Hardcastle Ho
4 Brooke Ho
5 Wallis Ho
A5 1 Batavia Ho
2 Marlowe Bsns Ctr
3 Batavia Mews
4 Woodrush Cl
5 Alexandra St
6 Primrose Wlk
7 Vansittart St
8 Granville Ct
9 Cottesbrook St
10 Ewen Henderson Ct
11 Fordham Ho
A6 1 Portland Ct
2 Phoenix Ct
3 Rainbow Ct
4 Hawke Twr
5 Chubworthy St
6 Woodpecker Rd
7 Hercules Ct
B5 1 Austin Ho
2 Exeter Way
3 Crossleigh Ct
4 Mornington Pl
5 Maple Ho
B6 1 Chester Ho
2 Lynch Wlk
3 Arlington Ho
4 Woodcote Ho
5 Cornbury Ho
6 Prospect Pl
7 Akintaro Ho
8 Mulberry Ho
9 Laurel Ho
10 Linden Ho
11 Ashford Ho
12 Wardalls Ho
13 Magnolia Ho
14 Howard Ho
15 Larch Cl
16 Ibis Ct
17 Merganser Ct
18 Wotton Rd
19 Kingfisher Sq
20 Sanderling Ct
21 Dolphin Twr
22 Mermaid Twr
23 Scoter Ct
24 Shearwater Ct
25 Brambling Ct
26 Kittiwake Ct
27 Diana Cl
28 Guillemot Ct
29 Marine Twr
30 Teal Ct
31 Lapwing Twr
32 Violet Cl
33 Skua Ct
34 Tristan Ct
35 Rosemary Ct
36 Cormorant Ct
37 Shelduck Ct
38 Eider Ct
39 Pintail Ct
C4 1 Admiralty Cl
2 Harton Lodge
3 Sylva Cotts
4 Pitman Ho
5 Heston Ho
6 Mereton Mans
7 Indiana Bldg
8 St John's Lodge
C5 1 Sandpiper Ct
2 Flamingo Ct
3 Titan Bsns Est
4 Rochdale Way
5 Speedwell St
6 Reginald Pl
7 Fletcher Path
8 Frankham Ho
9 Cremer Ho
10 Wilshaw Ho
11 Castell Ho
12 Holden Ho
13 Browne Ho
14 Resolution Way
15 Lady Florence Ctyd
16 Covell Ct
17 Albion Ho
C6 1 Dryfield Wlk
2 Blake Ho
3 Hawkins Ho
4 Grenville Ho
5 Langford Ho
6 Mandarin Ct
7 Bittern Ct
8 Lamerton St
9 Ravensbourne Mans
10 Armada St
11 Armada Ct
12 Benbow Ho
13 Oxenham Ho
14 Caravel Mews
15 Hughes Ho
16 Stretton Mans
D4 1 Washington Bldg
2 California Bldg
3 Utah Bldg
4 Montana Bldg
5 Oregon Bldg
6 Dakota bldg
7 Idaho Bldg
8 Atlanta Bldg
9 Colorado Bldg
10 Arizona Bldg
11 Nebraska Bldg
12 Alaska Bldg
13 Ohio Bldg
14 Charter Bldgs
15 Flamsteed Ct
16 Friendly Pl
17 Dover Ct
18 Robinscroft Mews
19 Doleman Ho
20 Plymouth Ho
D5 1 Finch Ho
2 Jubilee The
3 Maitland Cl
4 Ashburnham Retreat

142

A2 1 Bankside Ave
2 Elder Wlk
3 Yew Tree Cl
4 Mill Ho
A3 1 Ellison Ho
2 Pitmaston Ho
3 Aster Ho
4 Windmill Cl
5 Hertmitage The
6 Burnett Ho
7 Lacey Ho
8 Darwin Ho
9 Pearmain Ho
A4 1 Penn Almshouses
2 Jervis Ct
3 Woodville Ct
4 Darnall Ho
5 Renbold Ho
6 Lindsell St
7 Plumbridge St
8 Trinity Gr
9 Hollymount Cl
10 Cade Tyler Ho
11 Robertson Ho
A5 1 Temair Ho
2 Royal Hill Ct
3 Prince of Orange La
4 Lambard Ho
5 St Marks Cl
6 Ada Kennedy Ct
7 Arlington Pl
8 Topham Ho
9 Darnell Ho
10 Hawks Mews
11 Royal Pl
12 Swanne Ho
13 Maribor
14 Serica Ct
15 Queen Elizabeth's Coll
A6 1 Crescent Arc
2 Greenwich Mkt
3 Turnpin La
4 Durnford St
5 Sexton's Ho
6 Bardsley Ho
7 Wardell Ho
8 Clavell St
9 Stanton Ho
10 Macey Ho
11 Boreman Ho
12 Clipper Appts
B6 1 Frobisher Ct
2 Hardy Cotts
3 Palliser Ho
4 Bernard Angell Ho
5 Corvette Sq
6 Travers Ho
7 Maze Hill Lodge
8 Park Place Ho
D5 1 Westcombe Ct
2 Kleffens Ct
3 Ferndale Ct
4 Combe Mews
5 Mandeville Cl
7 Pinelands Cl

143

A5 1 Mary Lawrenson Pl
2 Bradbury Ct
3 Dunstable Ct
4 Wentworth Ho
A6 1 Nethercombe Ho
2 Holywell Cl
B6 1 Capella Ho
2 Collington Ho
C6 1 Warren Wlk
2 Wilson Ho
3 Priory Ho
4 Mar Ho
5 Langhorne Ho
6 Games Ho
7 Erskine Ho
8 Ducie Ho
9 Downe Ho
10 Bayeux Ho
11 Elliscombe Mount
12 Harold Gibbons Ct
13 Mascalls Ct
14 Leila Parnell Pl
15 East Mascalls
16 Birch Tree Ho
17 Cherry Tree Ct
18 Elm Tree Ct
19 Cedar Ct
D5 1 Winchester Ho
2 Brentwood Ho
3 Shenfield Ho
4 Chesterford Ho

144

A4 1 Master Gunner's Pl
2 Ross Ho
3 Dickson Ho
4 Horne Ho
5 Pendlebury Ho
6 Roberts Ho
7 Maple Tree Pl
C6 1 Lawson Ho
2 Mabbett Ho
3 Petrie Ho
4 Memess Path
5 Ruegg Ho
6 Nile Path
7 Leslie Smith Sq
8 Spearman St
9 Siedle Ho
10 Watling Ho
11 O'Neill Path
12 Old Clem Sq
13 Jefferson Wlk
14 Milward Wlk
15 Wordsworth Ho
16 Fenwick Cl
D6 1 Acworth Ho
2 Griffiths Ho
3 Squires Ho
4 Cowen Ho
5 Turton Ho
6 Alford Ho
7 Boxshall Ho
8 MacAllister Ho
9 Marvin Ho
10 Kelham Ho
11 Kimber Ho
12 Maxwell Ho
13 Woodford Ho
14 Penfold Ho

146

A2 1 Wellingfield Ct
2 Woodville Gr
3 Midwinter Cl
4 St Leonards Cl

147

A1 1 Woburn Ct
2 Arundel Ct
3 Longleat Ct
4 Upton Villas
5 Whitehaven Ct
6 Shirley Hts
7 Louise Ct
8 Bethany Ct
B6 1 Bevercote Wlk
3 Lullingstone Rd
4 Benjamin Ct
5 Charton Cl
6 Terence Ct
7 Renshaw Cl
8 Grove Rd
C1 1 Friswell Pl
2 Market Pl
3 Geddes Pl
4 Janet Ct
5 Broadway Sh Ctr
6 Mall The
7 Norwich Pl
8 Pincott Rd

148

A5 1 Stranraer Way
2 Deri Dene Cl
3 Lord Knyvetts Ct
4 Tudor Ct
5 Wessex Ct
6 Vanguard Ho
7 Shackleton Ct
8 Fleetwood Ct
9 Clifton Ct
10 Vickers Ct
11 Bristol Ct
12 Sunderland Ct

153

A3 1 Katharine Rd
2 Sandringham Ct
3 Garfield Rd
4 Arragon Rd
5 Flood La
6 John Wesley Ct
7 King Street Par
8 Thames Eyot
A4 1 Perryn Ct
2 Ivybridge Cl
3 Heritage Ho
4 Brook Ho
5 Neville Ho
6 Latham Cl
7 March Rd
8 Berkley Ct
9 Cole Court Lo
10 Cheltenham Ave
11 Railway App
A5 1 Greenways The
2 Cole Park View
B4 1 Melton Ct
2 Amyand Park Gdns
3 Crown Ct
4 Burrell Ho
5 Owen Ho
6 Brentford Ho
7 Leeson Ho
8 Westbourne Ho
9 Orleans Ct
10 Lebanon Ct
B5 1 Grove The
2 Cumberland Cl
3 Westmorland Cl
4 Sussex Cl
5 Norfolk Cl
6 Nicol Cl
7 Old Lodge Pl
8 Kelvin Ct
9 St Margaret's Ct
10 Park Cotts
11 St Margarets Bsns Ctr
12 Amyand Cotts
C1 1 Benson Ho
2 Bowes Lyon Ho
3 Cavendish Ho
4 Bentinck Ho
5 Clarke Ho
6 Secrett Ho
7 Edwards Ho
8 Field Ho
9 Greig Ho
10 Hawkins Ho
11 Newman Ho
12 Leyland Ho
13 Hornby Ho
14 Hatch Ho
C5 1 Howmic Ct
2 Sefton Lo
3 Ravensbourne Ho
4 Arlington Ct
5 Georgina Ct
6 Trevelyan Ho
7 Caradon Ct
8 Green Hedges
9 Old House Gdns
10 Queens Keep
11 Beresford Ct
12 Langham Ct
13 Poplar Ct
D5 1 Richmond Bridge Mans
2 Heatherdene Mans
3 Kenton Ct
4 Lennox Ho
5 Leicester Ct
6 Turner Ho
7 Blanchard Ho
8 Arosa Rd
9 Ashe Ho
10 Bevan Ct
11 Lawley Ho
12 Darling Ho
13 Richmond Mans
14 Beaulieu Cl
15 Roseleigh Cl
16 Mallard Ct
D6 1 Garrick Cl
2 Old Palace Yd
3 Wardrobe The
4 Maids of Honour Row
5 Hunters Ct
6 Queensberry Ho
7 Green The
8 Old Palace Terr
9 Paved Ct
10 Golden Ct
11 Brewers La
12 Square The
13 Lower George St
14 St James's Cotts
15 Church Wlk
16 Church Ct
17 Victoria Pl
18 Castle Yd
19 Lewis Rd
20 Wakefield Rd
21 Church Terr
22 Warrington Rd
23 Ormond Ave
24 Glovers Lo
25 Holbrooke Pl
26 Northumberland Pl
27 Heron Sq
28 Whittaker Pl
29 Water Lane Ho
30 Riverside Ho
31 St Helena Terr

154

A5 1 Lancaster Cotts
2 Lancaster Mews
3 Bromwich Ho
4 Priors Lo
5 Richmond Hill Ct
6 Glenmore Ho
7 Hillbrow
8 Heathshott
9 Friars Stile Pl
10 Spire Ct
11 Ridgeway
12 Matthias Ct
A6 1 Lichfield Terr
2 Union Ct
3 Carrington Lo
4 Wilton Ct
5 Egerton Ct
6 Beverley Lo
7 Bishop Duppa's Almshouses
8 Regency Wlk
9 Clear Water Ho
10 Onslow Avenue Mans
11 Michels Almshouses
12 Albany Pas
13 Salcombe Villas
B5 1 Chester Cl
2 Evesham Ct
3 Queen's Ct
4 Russell Wlk
5 Charlotte Sq
6 Jones Wlk
7 Hilditch Ho
8 Isabella Ct
9 Damer Ho
10 Eliot Ho
11 Fitzherbert Ho
12 Reynolds Pl
13 Chisholm Rd
B6 1 Alberta Ct
2 Beatrice Rd
3 Lorne Rd
4 York Rd
5 Connaught Rd
6 Albany Terr
7 Kingswood Ct
8 Selwyn Ct
9 Broadhurst Cl

156

A3 1 Farnborough Ho
2 Rushmere Ho
3 Horndean Cl
4 Highcross Way
5 Timsbury Wlk
6 Foxcombe Rd
7 Ryefield Path
8 Greatham Wlk
9 Gosport Ho
10 Stoatley Ho
11 Milland Ho
12 Clanfield Ho
13 Fareham Ho
14 Grayswood Point
A4 1 Woodcott Ho
2 Lyndhurst Ho
3 Wheatley Ho
4 Allbrook Ho

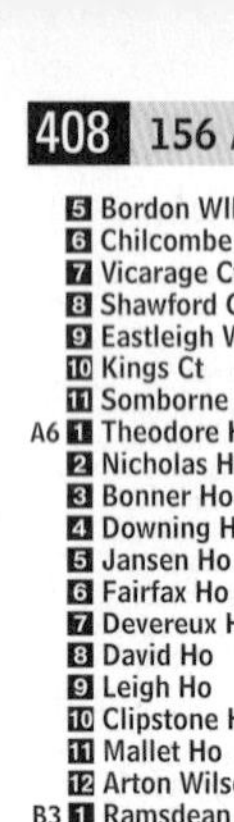

5 Bordon Wlk
6 Chilcombe Ho
7 Vicarage Ct
8 Shawford Ct
9 Eastleigh Wlk
10 Kings Ct
11 Somborne Ho
A6 1 Theodore Ho
2 Nicholas Ho
3 Bonner Ho
4 Downing Ho
5 Jansen Ho
6 Fairfax Ho
7 Devereux Ho
8 David Ho
9 Leigh Ho
10 Clipstone Ho
11 Mallet Ho
12 Arton Wilson Ho
B3 1 Ramsdean Ho
2 Purbrook Ho
3 Portsea Ho
4 Blendworth Point
5 Eashing Point
6 Hindhead Point
7 Hilsea Point
8 Witley Point
9 Buriton Ho
10 Grateley Ho
11 Hascombe Ho
12 Dunhill Point
13 Westmark Point
14 Longmoor Point
15 Cadnam Point
C4 1 Cumberland Ho
2 Devonshire Ho
3 Cornwall Ho
4 Norfolk Ho
5 Leicester Ho
6 Warwick Ho
7 Sutherland Ho
8 Carmarthen Ho
9 Worcester Ho
10 Rutland Ho
11 Paddock Way
C6 1 Inglis Ho
2 Ducie Ho
3 Wharncliffe Ho
4 Stanhope Ho
5 Waldegrave Ho
6 Mildmay Ho
7 Mullens Ho
D3 1 Sandringham Cl
2 Eastwick Ct
3 Oatlands Ct
4 Banning Ho
5 Grantley Ho
6 Caryl Ho
7 Duncombe Ho
8 Chilworth Ct
9 Kent Lo
10 Turner Lo
11 Marlborough
12 Parkland Gdns
13 Lewesdon Cl
14 Pines Ct
15 Ashtead Ct
16 Mynterne Ct
17 Arden
18 Stephen Ct
19 Marsham Ct
20 Doradus Ct
21 Acorns The
22 Heritage Ho
23 Conifer Ct
24 Spencer Ho
25 Chartwell
26 Blenheim
27 Chivelston
28 Greenfield Ho
29 Oakman Ho
30 Radley Lo
31 Simon Lo
32 Admirals Ct
D4 1 Brett Ho
2 Brett House Cl
3 Sylva Ct
4 Ross Ct
5 Potterne Cl
6 Stourhead Cl
7 Fleur Gates
8 Greenwood
D5 1 Balmoral Ct
2 Glenalmond Ho
3 Selwyn Ho
4 Keble Ho
5 Bede Ho
6 Gonville Ho
7 Magdalene Ho
8 Armstrong Ho
9 Newnham Ho
10 Somerville Ho
11 Balliol Ho
12 Windermere
13 Little Combe Cl
14 Classinghall Ho
15 Chalford Ct
16 Garden Royal
17 South Ct
18 Anne Kerr Ho
19 Ewhurst
D6 1 Geneva Ct
2 Laurel Ct
3 Cambalt Ho
4 Langham Ct
5 Lower Pk
6 King's Keep

7 Whitnell Ct
8 Whitehead Ho
9 Halford Ho
10 Humphry Ho
11 Jellicoe Ho

157
A3 1 William Harvey Ho
2 Highview Ct
3 Cameron Ct
4 Galgate Cl
5 Green Ho The
6 King Charles Wlk
7 Florys Ct
8 Augustus Ct
9 Albert Ct
10 Hertford Lo
11 Mortimer Lo
12 Allenswood
13 Ambleside
14 Hansler Ct
15 Roosevelt Ct
A6 1 Claremont
2 Downside
3 Cavendish Cl
4 Ashcombe Ct
5 Carltons The
6 Espirit Ho
7 Millbrooke Ct
8 Coysh Ct
9 Keswick Hts
10 Lincoln Ho
11 Avon Ct
B6 1 Keswick Broadway
2 Burlington Mews
3 Cambria Lo
4 St Stephen's Gdns
5 Atlantic Ho
6 Burton Lo
7 Manfred Ct
8 Meadow Bank
9 Hooper Ho
10 Aspire Bld
C6 1 Pembridge Pl
2 Adelaide Rd
3 London Ct
4 Windsor Ct
5 Westminster Ct
6 Fullers Ho
7 Bridge Pk
8 Lambeth Ct
9 Milton Ct
10 Norfolk Mans
11 Francis Snary Lo
12 Bush Cotts
13 Downbury Mews
14 Newton's Yd
D6 1 Fairfield Ct
2 Blackmore Ho
3 Lancaster Mews
4 Cricketers Mews
5 College Mews
6 Arndale Wlk

158
A2 1 Beemans Row
2 St Andrew's Ct
3 Townsend Mews
4 Sheringham Mews

159
1 Upper Tooting Park Mans
2 Cecil Mans
3 Marius Mans
4 Boulevard The
5 Elmfield Mans
6 Holdernesse Rd
7 Lumiere Ct
A3 1 Heslop Ct
2 St James's Terr
3 Boundaries Mans
4 Station Par
5 Old Dairy Mews
A4 1 Hollies Way
2 Endlesham Ct
A5 1 Rayne Ho
2 St Anthony's Ct
3 Earlsthorpe Mews
4 Nightingale Mans
B3 1 Holbeach Mews
2 Hildreth Street Mews
3 Coalbrook Mans
4 Hub Buildings The
5 Metropolis Apartments
B4 1 Meyer Ho
2 Faraday Ho
3 Hales Ho
4 Frankland Ho
5 Graham Ho
6 Gibbs Ho
7 Dalton Ho
8 Ainslie Wlk
9 Rokeby Ho
10 Caistor Ho
11 Ivanhoe Ho
12 Catherine Baird Ct
13 Marmion Ho
14 Devonshire Ct
15 Blueprint Apartments
C4 1 Limerick Ct
2 Homewoods
3 Jewell Ho
4 Glanville Ho
5 Dan Bryant Ho
6 Olding Ho
7 Quennel Ho

8 Weir Ho
9 West Ho
10 Neville Ct
11 Friday Grove Mews
C5 1 Joseph Powell Cl
2 Cavendish Mans
3 Westlands Terr
4 Cubitt Ho
5 Hawkesworth Ho
6 Normanton Ho
7 Eastman Ho
8 Couchman Ho
9 Poynders Ct
10 Selby Ho
11 Valentine Ho
12 Gorham Ho
13 Deauville Mans
14 Deauville Ct
C6 1 Timothy Cl
2 Shaftesbury Mews
3 Brook Ho
4 Grover Ho
5 Westbrook Ho
6 Hewer Ho
7 Batten Ho
8 Mandeville Ho
9 George Beare Lo
D3 1 Sinclair Ho
2 MacGregor Ho
3 Ingle Ho
4 St Andrews Mews
D4 1 Riley Ho
2 Bennett Ho
3 White Ho
4 Rodgers Ho
5 Dumphreys Ho
6 Homan Ho
7 Prendergast Ho
8 Hutchins Ho
9 Whiteley Ho
10 Tresidder Ho
11 Primrose Ct
12 Angus Ho
13 Currie Ho
D5 1 Parrington Ho
2 Savill Ho
3 Blackwell Ho
4 Bruce Ho
5 Victoria Ct
6 Victoria Ho
7 Belvedere Ct
8 Ingram Lo
9 Viney Ct
10 Bloomsbury Ho
11 Belgravia Ho
12 Barnsbury Ho

160
A1 1 De Montfort Ct
2 Leigham Hall Par
3 Leigham Hall
4 Endsleigh Mans
5 John Kirk Ho
6 Raeburn Ct
7 Wavel Ct
8 Homeleigh Ct
9 Howland Ho
10 Beauclerk Ho
11 Bertrand Ho
12 Drew Ho
13 Dowes Ho
14 Dunton Ho
15 Raynald Ho
16 Sackville Ho
17 Thurlow Ho
A2 1 Wyatt Park Mans
2 Broadlands Mans
3 Stonehill's Mans
4 Streatleigh Par
5 Dorchester Ct
6 Picture Ho
A3 1 Beaumont Ho
2 Christchurch Ho
3 Stapleford Cl
4 Chipstead Ho
5 Coulsdon Ho
6 Conway Ho
7 Telford Avenue Mans
8 Telford Parade Mans
9 Wavertree Ct
10 Hartswood Ho
11 Wray Ho
A4 1 Picton Ho
2 Rigg Ho
3 Watson Ho
4 MacArthur Ho
5 Sandon Ho
6 Thorold Ho
7 Pearce Ho
8 Mudie Ho
9 Miller Ho
10 Lycett Ho
11 Lafone Ho
12 Lucraft Ho
13 Freeman Ho
14 New Park Par
15 Argyll Ho
16 Dumbarton Ct
17 Kintyre Ct
18 Cotton Ho
19 Crossman Hos
20 Cameford Ct
21 Parsons Ho
22 Brindley Ho
23 Arkwright Ho
24 Perry Ho

25 Brunel Ho
26 New Park Ct
27 Tanhurst Ho
28 Hawkshaw Cl
A6 1 King's Mews
2 Clapham Court Terr
3 Clapham Ct
4 Clapham Park Terr
5 Pembroke Ho
6 Stevenson Ho
7 Queenswood Ct
8 Oak Tree Ct
9 Park Lofts
10 Ashby Mews
B1 1 Carisbrooke Ct
2 Pembroke Lo
3 Willow Ct
4 Poplar Ct
5 Mountview
6 Spa View
B3 1 Charlwood Ho
2 Earlswood Ho
3 Balcombe Ho
4 Claremont Cl
5 Holbrook Ho
6 Gwynne Ho
7 Kynaston Ho
8 Tillman Ho
9 Regents Lo
10 Hazelmere Ct
11 Dykes Ct
B4 1 Archbishop's Pl
2 Witley Ho
3 Outwood Ho
4 Dunsfold Ho
5 Deepdene Lo
6 Warnham Ho
7 Albury Lo
8 Tilford Ho
9 Elstead Ho
10 Thursley Ho
11 Brockham Ho
12 Capel Lo
13 Leith Ho
14 Fairview Ho
15 Weymouth Ct
16 Ascalon Ct
17 China Mews
18 Rush Common Mews
B6 1 Beatrice Ho
2 Florence Ho
3 Evelyn Ho
4 Diana Ho
5 Brixton Hill Ct
6 Austin Ho
7 Manor Ct
8 Camsey Ho
9 Romer Ho
10 Gale Ho
11 Byrne Ho
12 Farnfield Ho
13 Marchant Ho
14 Rainsford Ho
15 Springett Ho
16 Mannering Ho
17 Waldron Ho
C3 1 Valens Ho
2 Loveday Ho
3 Strode Ho
4 Ethelworth Ct
5 Harbin Ho
6 Brooks Ho
7 Godolphin Ho
8 Sheppard Ho
9 McCormick Ho
10 Taylor Ho
11 Saunders Ho
12 Talcott Path
13 Derrick Ho
14 Williams Ho
15 Baldwin Ho
16 Churston Cl
17 Neil Wates Cres
18 Burnell Ho
19 Portland Ho
C4 1 Ellacombe Ho
2 Booth Ho
3 Hathersley Ho
4 Brereton Ho
5 Holdsworth Ho
6 Dearmer Ho
7 Cherry Cl
8 Greenleaf Cl
9 Longford Wlk
10 Scarlette Manor Wlk
11 Chandlers Way
12 Upgrove Manor Way
13 Ropers Wlk
14 Tebbs Ho
15 Bell Ho
16 Worthington Ho
17 Courier Ho
18 Mackie Ho
19 Hamers Ho
20 Kelyway Ho
21 Harriet Tubman Cl
22 Estoria Cl
23 Leckhampton Pl
24 Scotia Rd
25 Charles Haller St
26 Worsley Ho
27 Hunter Ct
28 Onslow Lo
29 William Winter Ct
30 Langthorne Lo
C5 1 Eccleston Ho

25 Scarsbrook Ho
2 Purser Ho
3 Rudhall Ho
4 Hardham Ho
5 Heywood Ho
6 Haworth Ho
7 Birch Ho
8 Lansdell Ho
9 Laughton Ho
10 Lomley Ho
11 Woodruff Ho
12 Bascome St
13 Dudley Mews
14 Herbert Mews
15 Blades Lo
16 Dick Shepherd Ct
17 Charman Ho
18 Morden Ho
19 Bishop Ct
20 Blackburn Ct
21 Leigh Ct
22 John Conwey Ho
23 Bristowe Cl
C6 1 Crownstone Ct
2 Brockwell Ct
3 Nevena Ct
4 St George's Residences
5 Hanover Mans
6 Fleet Ho
7 Langbourne Ho
8 Turnmill Ho
9 Walker Mews
10 Cossar Mews
11 Carter Ho
D1 1 Thanet Ho
2 Chapman Ho
3 Beaufoy Ho
4 Easton Ho
5 Roberts Ho
6 Lloyd Ct
7 Kershaw Ho
8 Wakeling Ho
9 Edridge Ho
10 Jeston Ho
11 Lansdowne Wood Cl
12 Rotary Lo

161
B2 1 Welldon Ct
2 Coppedhall
3 Shackleton Ct
4 Bullfinch Ct
5 Gannet Ct
6 Fulmar Ct
7 Heron Ct
8 Petrel Ct
9 Falcon Ct
10 Eagle Ct
11 Dunnock Ct
12 Dunlin Ct
13 Cormorant Ct
14 Oak Lodge
15 Corfe Lodge
C6 1 Velde Way
2 Delft Way
3 Arnhem Way
4 Isel Way
5 Kempis Way
6 Terborch Way
7 Steen Way
8 Deventer Cres
9 Nimegen Way
10 Hilversum Cres
11 St Barnabas Cl

162
A1 1 Tunbridge Ct
2 Harrogate Ct
3 Bath Ct
4 Leamington Ct
5 Porlock Ho
6 Cissbury Ho
7 Eddisbury Ho
8 Dundry Ho
9 Silbury Ho
10 Homildon Ho
11 Highgate Ho
12 Richmond Ho
13 Pendle Ho
14 Tynwald Ho
15 Wirrall Ho
16 Greyfriars
A6 1 Dorothy Charrington Ho
2 Keswick Ho
3 Kendall Ct
4 Halliwell Ct
B1 1 River Ho
2 Fordington Ho
3 Arbury Terr
4 Woodbury Ho
5 Gainsborough Mews
6 Forest Hill Ct
B2 1 Bromleigh Ct
2 Parfew Ct
3 Thetford Ct
4 Attleborough Ct
5 Dunton Ct
6 Frobisher Ct
7 Julian Taylor Path
8 Grizedale Terr
9 Worsley Ho
C1 1 Forest Lo
2 Sydenham Park Mans
3 William Wood Ho
C2 1 Fitzwilliam Hts

2 Taymount Grange
3 McLeod Ho
4 Featherstone Ave
5 Kingswear Ho
6 Salcombe Ho
7 Glynwood Ct
C3 1 Harlech Ct
2 Angela Ct
3 Westwood Ct
4 New Belmont Ho
5 Pearcefield Ave
6 Waldram Pl
7 Horniman Grange
8 South View Ct
9 Heron Ct
10 Katherine Ct
D1 1 Standlake Point
2 Radcot Point
3 Newbridge Point
4 Northmoor
5 Kelmscott
6 Radnor Ct
7 Heathwood Point
8 Ashleigh Point
9 Deepdene Point
10 Rosemount Point
11 Woodfield Ho
12 Clairville Point
13 Trevenna Ho
14 Hyndewood
D2 1 Pikethorne
2 Andrew Ct
3 Valentine Ct
4 Soper Cl

164
C4 1 Beaumont Terr
2 Littlebourne
3 Verdant Ct
D2 1 Kinross Ct
2 Montrose Ct
3 Rattray Ct
4 Rothesay Ct
D3 1 Edinburgh Ct
2 McMillan Ct
3 Rowallan Ct
4 Meridian Ct
5 Braemar Ct
6 Barrow Ct
7 Blair Ct
8 Darlington Ct
9 Hamilton Ct
10 Inverness Ct
11 Oak Cottage Cl
12 Willow Ct
13 Keswick Ct

165
A4 1 Swallow Ct
2 Honeysuckle Ct
3 Venture Ct
4 Cheriton Ct
5 Askham Lo
6 Syon Lo

166
A2 1 Portland Cres
2 Bourdillon Ct
3 Hillary Ct
4 Tenzing Ct
5 John Hunt Ct
6 Everest Ct
A6 1 Horsfeld Gdns
2 Foxhole Rd
C5 1 Roper St
2 Arcade The
3 Elm Terr
4 Imber Ct
5 Ashcroft Ct
6 Fairlands Ct
7 Brecon Ct
8 Newlands Ct
9 Harvard Ct
10 Garden Ct
11 Chiltern Ct
12 Fairway Ct

167
A2 1 Mervyn Stockwood Ho
2 Michael Marshall Ho
3 Keith Sutton Ho

168
A1 1 Ham Shades Cl
2 Aspen Ho
3 Medlar Ho
4 Cornel Ho
5 Stanton Ho
6 Hornbeam Ho
7 Beech Ho
8 Spindle Ho
9 Hunters Lo
10 Edam Ct
11 Monica James Ho
12 Oak Ho
13 Crescent Ct
14 Freeland Ct
15 Montague Ct
16 Windsor Ct
B5 1 Rochester Ct
2 Cobham Cl
3 Shorne Cl
4 Warne Pl

169
C4 1 Close The
2 Parkhurst Gdns
3 Chichester Ct

4 Pound Green Ct

170
B6 1 Station Par
2 Queens La
3 Copthorne Chase
4 Canterbury Ct
5 Church Par
C5 1 St Matthew's Ct
2 Dencliffe
3 Crest Ho
4 Bourne Ho
5 Elms The
6 Roxeth Ct
7 Rowland Hill Almshouses

171
A3 1 Viscount Ct
2 Blackthorne Ct
D3 1 Bishops Ct
2 Ash Lo
3 Lime Lo
4 Oak Lo
5 Elm Ct
6 Willow Lo
7 Sycamore Lo
8 Priscilla Ho
9 Sunbury Cross Ctr
10 Isobel Ho

173
A6 1 Gabriel Cl
2 Metcalfe Wlk
3 Dunmow Cl
4 Burgess Cl
5 Chamberlain Wlk
C2 1 Sherbourne Ct
2 Somerset Ct
3 Jubilee Ho
4 Rushbury Ct
5 Blenheim Ct
6 Hemming Ct
7 Ryedale Ct
8 Norman Ct
C4 1 Begonia Pl
2 Snowdrop Cl
3 Hyacinth Cl
4 Cyclamen Cl
5 Jonquil Gdns
6 Gladioli Cl
7 Daffodil Pl
8 Partridge Rd
D4 1 Acorn Cl
2 Wolsey Ho
3 Lytton Ho
4 Wren Ho
5 Faraday Ho

174
C5 1 Knaggs Ho
2 Keeling
3 Elizabeth Ct
4 Oakhurst Cl
5 Charles Ct
6 Harold Ct
D5 1 Waldegrave Ct
2 Luther Mews
3 Alice Mews
4 Gresham Ho
5 Traherne Lo
6 Fishers Ct
7 Waterhouse Ct
8 Oval Ct
9 Walpole Pl
10 Walpole Cres
11 Bychurch End

175
A5 1 Cherrywood Ho
2 Cambridge Ho
3 Cairngorm Cl
4 Gleneagles Ct
5 Christchurch Ave
6 Hales Ct
7 Plough La
8 Springfield Rd
9 Royal Oak Mews
10 Trinder Mews
C3 1 Belgravia Ho
2 Ash Ho
3 Crieff Ct
4 Maples The
D2 1 Wick Ho
2 Spinnaker Ct
3 Osiers Ct
4 Trent Ho
5 Arun Ho
6 Medway Ho
7 Avon Ho
8 Tyne Ho
9 Clyde Ho
10 Mersey Ct
11 Severn Ct
12 John William Cl
13 Henry Macaulay Ave
14 Seymour Lo
15 Falmouth Ho
16 Earlsfield Ho
D6 1 Byron Ct
2 Coleridge Ct
3 Tennyson Ct
4 Herrick Ct
5 Spenser Ct
6 Marlowe Ct
7 Brooke Ct
8 Gray Ct
9 Shelley Ct
10 Pope Ct

11 Dryden Ct

176
A1 1 Cleave's Almshos
2 Perry Ct
3 Drovers Ct
4 Gough Ho
5 Eden Wlk
6 Alderman Judge Mall
7 Lady Booth Rd
8 Caversham Ho
9 Littlefield Cl
10 Bentall Sh Ctr The
11 Adams Wlk
12 Ceres Ct
A2 1 Regents Ct
2 Walter St
3 Canbury Bsns Pk
4 Sigrist Sq
5 Ashway Ctr
6 Warwick Ho
7 Hedingham Ho
8 Alexander Ho
9 Bramber Ho
10 Carisbrooke Ho
11 Dartmouth Ho
12 Garland Ho
A3 1 Walton Ho
2 Berkeley Cl
3 Canbury Ct
4 King's Penny Ho
B1 1 Vicarage Ho
2 Rayleigh Ct
3 School Pas
4 Chippenham
5 Camm Gdns
B2 1 Onslow Ho
2 Dowler Ct
B3 1 McDonald Ho
2 Elm Ho
3 Dale Ct
4 York Ho
5 Florence Ho
6 Florence Rd
7 Roupell Ho
8 Delft Ho
C1 1 Wimpole Cl
2 Burwell
3 Caldecote
4 Fordham
5 Connington
6 Chesterton Terr
7 Westwick
8 Eureka Rd
9 Fulbourn
10 Comberton
11 Madingley
12 Grantchester
13 Cambridge Grove Rd
14 Oakington
15 Harston
16 Graveley
17 Croxton
18 Brinkley
19 Impington
20 Shelford
21 Duxford
22 Cascadia Ho
C2 1 Farthings The
2 Brae Ct
3 Princeton Mews
4 Station App
C3 1 Queen's Ct
2 St George's Rd
3 Park Road Ho
4 Dagmar Rd
5 Tapping Cl
6 Arthur Rd
7 Borough Rd
8 Belvedere Ct
9 Braywick Ct
10 Dean Ct
11 Rowan Ct
12 Richmond Ct
13 Sunningdale Ct
14 Hawker Ct
15 Cromwell Ct
16 Kings Ct
D2 1 Trevallyn Lo
2 Chichester Ho
3 Beechcroft
4 Cedars The
5 Liddlesdale Ho W
6 Liddlesdale Ho E
7 Deerhurst
8 Brockworth
9 Alderton
D3 1 Bramley Ho
2 Abinger Ho
3 Thursley Ho
4 Ridge Ho
5 Clone The
6 Mount Ct
7 Hillside Ct
8 Hill Ct
9 Royal Ct
10 Lakeside
11 High Ashton
D4 1 Godstone Ho
2 Hambleden Ho
3 Kingswood Ho
4 Leigh Ho
5 Milton Ho
6 Newdigate Ho
7 Farleigh Ho
8 Ockley Ho
9 Effingham Ho
10 Dunsfold Ho

11 Pirbright Ho
12 Clandon Ho
13 Ripley Ho

178
C3 1 Roskeen Ct
2 Chimneys Ct
3 Aston Ct
4 Rosemary Cotts
5 Victoria Lo
D2 1 Beaufort Ho
2 Kinnear Ct
3 Ranmore Ct
4 Lantern Ct
5 Crescent Ho
D3 1 Kings View Ct
2 Wimbledon Cl
3 Beryl Harding Ho
4 Upton Ct
5 Marian Lo
6 Terraces The
7 Lanherne Ho
8 Cumberland Cl
9 Thaxted Pl
10 Rathbone Ho
11 Princess Ct
12 Claremont Lo
13 Downs Ct
14 Ravenscar Lo
15 Haverley
16 Savona Cl
17 Beaumont Ct
18 Gordon Ct
D5 1 Lancaster Pl
2 Haygarth Pl
3 Allington Cl
4 Homefield Pl

179
A3 1 Stretford Ct
2 Brunswick Ct
3 Pavilion Ct
4 Louie Black Ho
5 Warwick Ho
6 Erica Ho
7 Adyar Ct
8 Thornton Lo
9 Ash Ct
10 Broughton Ho
11 Naomi Watts Ho
12 Wellesley Ho
13 Mayfair Ct
A4 1 Walham Rise
2 Grosvenor Ct
3 Sovereign Ho
4 Holly Lo
5 Florence Ct
6 Linden Cotts
7 Sheep Walk Mews
8 Emerson Ct
9 Hill Ct
10 Powell Ho
B4 1 Aspen Lo
2 Gladebury Ct
3 Centre Court Sh Ctr
B5 1 Lawns The
2 Prentice Ct
3 Catherine Ct
4 Woodlodge
5 Pixham Ct
6 Lake Cl
7 Westwood Ct
8 Brambles The
9 Lismore
10 Rose Ct
11 Worcester Rd
12 Leopold Ct
C3 1 Ashbourne Terr
2 Sir Cyril Black Way
3 Willows Ct
4 Harefield Ct
5 Broadway Ho
6 Viscount Point
7 Carrington Ho
8 Cloisters Ho
9 Downing Ho
10 Bickley Ct
11 Palmerston Gr
12 Gladstone Ct
13 Warrington Ct
D2 1 Gilbert Ct
2 Becket Cl
3 Priory Cl
4 Hudson Ct
5 Ryder Ho
6 Eleanor Ho
7 Ramsey Ho
8 Colborne Ct
9 Falcon Ho
10 Spur Ho
D3 1 Hamilton Road Mews
2 Dowman Cl
3 Burleigh Lo
4 Horatio Ho

180
A2 1 Tanner Ho
2 May Ct
3 Marsh Ct
4 Lovell Ho
A3 1 Fiske Ct
2 Mellor Ct
3 Olive Rd
4 Allerton Ho
5 Victory Road Mews
6 Will Miles Ct

7 Vanguard Ho
8 Mychell Ho
9 Merton Pl
10 De Burgh Ho
11 Norfolk Ho
12 Hotham Road Mews
B1 1 Ripley Ct
2 Brooklands Ct
3 Horner La
B2 1 Yarborough Rd
2 Vista Ho
3 Prospect Ho
4 Independence Ho
5 Nonsuch Ho
6 Baron Ho
C2 1 Linford Ct
2 Searle Ct
3 Gunnell Ct
4 Wells Ct
5 Hartley Ct
C3 1 Shere Lo
2 Goodwin Ct
3 Cairn Ho
C4 1 Douglas Ct
2 Lannock Ct
3 Gateway Ho
4 Wellington Ct
C5 1 Robertson Ho
2 Dewar Ho
3 Jean Ho
4 Marion Ct
5 Gravenel Gdns
6 Palladino Ho
D1 1 Elms Cotts
2 Sibthorp Rd
3 Armfield Cotts
4 Sir Arthur Bliss Ct
5 Fountain Ho
6 Gladstone Ho
7 Chart Ho

181
A1 1 Kennedy Cl
2 Pearce Cl
3 Mainwaring Ct
4 Coningsby Ct
5 Laburnum Ct
6 Beaumont Ct
7 Penfold Ct
8 Fitch Ct
10 Lea Cotts
A5 1 Osborne Terr
2 Limetree Wlk
C5 1 Tyers Ho
2 Boothby Ho
3 Adams Ho
4 Burney Ho
5 Boswell Ho
6 Chesterfield Ho
7 Garrick Ho
8 Levett Ho
9 Shelburne Ho
10 Marchmont Ho
11 Ryland Ho
12 Flather Cl
13 Bank Bldgs
14 Carriage Pl
15 Locarno Cl
C6 1 Walmsley Ho
2 Chambers Ho
3 Fordyce Ho
4 Percy Ho
5 Langton Ho
6 Moorfields Ct
7 Hidaburn Ct
8 Salter Ho
9 Tailors Ct
10 Yew Tree Lo
D6 1 William Dyce Mews
2 Doctor Johnson Ho

182
A3 1 Spa Central
A5 1 Oakdene Ct
2 Hopton Par
3 Merton Lo
4 Bouverie Ct
5 Deerhurst
6 Farnan Hall
A6 1 Central Mans
2 Central Par
B3 1 Marqueen Twrs
2 Shirley Ct
3 Sinclair Ho
4 Vantage Ct
5 Pavilion Ct
B6 1 Ashleigh Ho
2 Roseneath Pl
3 Shenley Ho
4 Blytheswood Pl
C5 1 Parkhill Ct
2 Ash Ct
3 Alder Ct
4 Beech Ct
5 Acacia Ct
6 Blackthorn Ct
7 Cypress Ct
8 Hawthorn Ct
9 Hazel Ct
10 Sycamore Ct
11 Maple Ct
12 Laburnum Ct
13 Fern Lo
14 Colyton La
C6 1 James Boswell Cl
2 St Albans Ho
3 Suffolk Cl

4 Rockhampton Cl
5 Delphian Ct
6 Heather Ct
D5 1 Woodcote Pl
2 Joe Hunte Ct
3 Cork Tree Ho
4 Lake Ho
5 Cedars Ho
6 Portobello Ho
7 Cooper Ho
8 Farnsworth Ho
9 Hook Ho
10 Crest The
11 Renshaw Ho
12 Ruscoe Ho
13 Sardeson Ho
D6 1 William Wilberforce Ho
2 William Marsden Ho
3 Samuel Ho
4 Morris Stephany Ho
5 Church Ct

183
A6 1 Moore Ho
2 Chaucer Ho
3 Bushell Ho
4 Bligh Ho
5 Hobbs Rd
6 Hogarth Ho
7 Goodbehere Ho
8 Astley Ho
9 Elder Gdns
10 Elderberry Gr
11 Pavement The
12 Dunkirk St
B6 1 Josef Perrin Ho
2 Jean Humbert Ho
3 Charles Staunton Ho
4 Violette Szabo Ho
5 Lilian Rolfe Ho
6 Odette Ho
7 Robert Gerard Ho
8 St Bernards Ct
9 Champness Cl
10 Pennington Cl
11 Queenswood Ct
C4 1 Northwood Way
2 High Limes
3 Valley Prospect
4 Plane Tree Wlk
5 City Prospect
6 Bankside Way
7 Ridge Way
8 Rochdale
9 Barrington Wlk
10 Gatestone Ct
11 Childs La
12 Carberry Rd
13 Norwood Heights Sh Ctr
C5 1 Oakdene
2 Thorsden Way
3 Oakfield Gdns
4 Georgetown Cl
5 Bridgetown Cl
6 Mountbatten Cl
7 Brabourne Cl
8 Alexandra Wlk
9 Compton Ct
10 Battenburg Wlk
11 Burma Terr
12 Wiseman Ct
C6 1 Linley Ct
2 Mellor Ho
3 Whitfield Ct
4 Michaelson Ho
5 Holberry Ho
6 Hovenden Ho
7 Huntley Ho
8 Telfer Ho
9 Markham Ho
10 Oldham Ho
11 Parnall Ho
12 Pierson Ho
13 Roper Ho
14 Roundell Ho
15 Sawyer Ho
16 Ransford Ho
17 Carmichael Ho
18 Bonne Marche Terr Mews
D3 1 Hetley Gdns
2 Claybourne Mews
3 Highland Lo
4 Mason Ct
5 Kendall Ct
6 High View
D5 1 Glenhurst Ct
2 Marlowe Ct
3 Grenville Ct
4 Raleigh Ct
5 Beechwoods Ct
6 Burntwood View

184
A3 1 Hanover Ct
2 Brunswick Ct
3 New Church Ct
4 Regency Ct
5 Owen Wlk
6 Bargrove Ct
7 Beaver Ct
B2 1 Dorset Ho
2 Collingwood Cl
3 Chartwell Way
4 Essex Twr

4 Appletree Cl
5 Ditton Pl
6 Kelvin Ct
7 Readman Ct
8 Glen Ct
9 Kingsbridge Ho
10 Carlton Ct
11 Benhurst Ct
12 Carole Ho
13 Dover Ho
14 Bettswood Ct
B3 1 Avery Ct
2 Rossal Ct
3 Oakdene Lo
4 Ridgemount Cl
5 Blakewood Ct
6 Trenholme Cl
7 Oakleigh Ct
8 Upchurch Cl
9 Devon Ct
10 Westmoreland Terr
11 Oakfield Road Ind Est
B5 1 Ragwort Ct
2 Firs The
3 Wingham Ho
4 Seath Ho
5 Ripley Ho
6 Lathwood Ho
7 Hurst Ho
8 George Ho
9 Browne Ho
10 Beacon Ho
11 Bailey Ho
12 Agate Ho
C2 1 Challin St
2 Rutland Ho
3 Pine Ct
C3 1 Watermen's Sq
2 St John's Cotts
3 Gladstone Mews
4 Middlesex Ho
5 Bethesda Ct
6 Ospringe Cl
7 Goudhurst Ho
8 Walmer Ho
9 Strood Ho
10 Greatstone Ho
11 John Baird Ho
C4 1 Midhurst
2 Oliver Ct
3 Victoria Ct
4 Wakefield Ct
5 Fountain Ct
6 Newlands Ct
C6 1 Homewalk Ho
2 Grace Path
3 Sycamore Ct
4 Sydenham Station App
5 Greenways
6 Faircroft
D3 1 Groombridge Ho
2 Provincial Terr
3 Smithers Ho
4 West Ho
5 Swallows Ct
6 Hornbeam Ho
7 Blenheim Centre

185
A1 1 Clock House Ct
2 Blandford Ave
3 Old School Ct
4 Lynsted Ct
5 Florence Rd
A6 1 Paxton Ct
2 Kenton Ct
3 Grove Ct
4 Shirley Lo
B2 1 Ashton Ct
2 Coombe Ct
3 Fontaine Ct
4 Richfield Ct
5 Sheridan Way
C1 1 Christ Church Rd
2 Lea Rd
3 Stanmore Terr
C2 1 Erindale Ct
2 Montgomerie Ct
3 Rebecca Ct
4 Sycamore Ct
5 Willow Ct
6 Marlborough Ct
7 Bearsted Terr
8 Berwick Ct
9 Wooderson Ct
10 Beck River Pk
11 Waterside
C3 1 Gardenia Ct
2 Brackendale Ct
3 Daniel Ct
4 Moliner Ct
5 Chartwell Lo
6 Randmore Ct
7 Dover Ho
8 Lucerne Ct
9 Malling Ho
10 Westerham Lo
11 Brasted Lo
12 Milton Ho
13 Bradsole Ho
14 Sandgate Ho
15 Adelaide Ho
16 Nettlestead Ct
17 Warren Ct
18 Alton Ct
19 Rockingham Ct
20 Camellia Ho

21 Sinclair Ct
22 Regents Ct
23 Minshull Pl
24 South Park Ct
D1 1 Parkside
2 Tudors The
3 Oakbrook
4 Tara Ct
5 Redlands The
6 Cambria
7 Hillworth
8 Kelsey Gate
9 Burrells
10 Lincoln Lo
11 Courtlands
12 Fairleas
13 Ashdown Cl
14 Barons
D2 1 Clifton Ct
2 Mayfair Ct
3 Lait Ho
4 Fire Station Mews
D4 1 Warner Ho
2 Clifford Ho
3 Lloyd Ho
4 Thurston Ho
5 Byron Ho
6 Blake Ho
7 Keats Ho

186
A2 1 White House Ct
2 Hunters The
3 Sandringham Ct
4 Glenhurst
5 Copperfields
6 Westgate Ct
A6 1 Dedham Ho
2 Flatford Ho
3 Langthorne Ct
4 Radley Ct
5 Hoover Ho
6 Brunner Ho
7 Waterer Ho
8 Marriott Ho
9 Bourbon Ho
B5 1 Longford Ho
2 Ingrebourne Ho
3 Brent Ho
4 Darent Ho
5 Beverley Ho
6 Wandle Ho
7 Rythe Ho
8 Ember Ho
9 Crane Ho
10 Ravensbourne Ho
C1 1 Warwick Ct
2 Maplehurst
3 Mount Arlington
4 Arundel Ct
D2 1 Weston Gr
2 Gibbs Ho
3 Longfield
4 Hammelton Ct
5 Bracken Hill Cl
6 Townend
7 Treversh Ct
8 Cameron Ho
9 Woodlands Ct
10 Blythwood Pk
11 Bromley Pk
D3 1 Homecoppice Ho
2 Linden Ct
3 Kimberley Gate
4 Inglewood Ct
5 Mavery Ct
6 Glen Ct
7 Marlborough Ct
8 Cawston Ct
9 Blendon Path

187
A1 1 St James Ct
A2 1 Mitchell Way
2 Harrington Ho
3 Newman Ct
4 Uno Apartments
5 Bromley Ho
B2 1 Dainton Cl
2 Rothwell Ct
3 St Timothy's Mews
4 Andringham Lo
5 Kendall Lo
6 Summerfield
7 Winston Ct
8 Vogue Ct
9 Laurels The
C1 1 Westland Ct
2 Eastland Ct
3 Dairsie Ct
4 Northlands
5 Beechfield Cotts
6 Oasis The
7 Cromarty Ct
8 Silverstone Ct

188
A6 1 Beaconsfield Par
2 Cranley Par
3 Kimmeridge Gdns
4 King & Queen Cl
C2 1 Ivybridge Ct
2 Greenbank Lo

190
A6 1 Cyril Lo
2 Hazlemere
3 Milton Ct
4 Marlin Ct
5 Conroy Ct

7 Glenwood Ct
8 Culverton Ct
9 Holmbury Manor
B1 1 Swanscombe Ho
2 Haverstock Ct
3 Arrandene Ho
4 Broomfield Ho
5 Headley Ho
6 Kenley Ho
7 Ladywell Ho
B6 1 Chudleigh
2 Wimborne
3 St John's Par
4 Holly Ct
5 Rectory Bsns Ctr

193
D1 1 Orchard Ct
2 Bridge Ct

197
A2 1 Raleigh Ho
2 Leicester Ho
3 Gresham Ho
D2 1 Napier Ct
2 Darlington Ho
3 Charminster Ct
4 Mulberry Ct
5 Leander Ct
6 Clinton Ho
7 Hollingsworth Ct
8 Gloucester Ct
9 Palmerston Ct
10 Redwood Ct
11 Hursley Ct
12 Westmorland Ct
13 Lawson Ct
14 Alexander Ct
15 Winton Ct
16 Sydenham Ho
17 Caroline Ct
18 Ellswood Ct
19 Masefield Ct

198
A1 1 Ash Tree Cl
2 Shrubbery The
3 Malvern Ct
4 Gate Ho
5 Yew Tree Ho
A3 1 Station App
2 South Bank Lo
3 Bramshott Ct
4 Pandora Ct
5 Wellington Ct
6 Glenbuck Ct
7 Leighton Ho
8 Oakhill Ct
9 Downs View Lo
10 Osborne Ct
11 Surbiton Par
12 Woodgate Ho
13 Godwyn Ho
14 Ashby Ho
A4 1 Effingham Lo
2 Maple Ho
3 Channon Ct
4 Falconhurst
5 Ferndown
6 Viceroy Lo
7 Frensham Ho
8 Kingsley Ho
9 Rannoch Ct
10 Stratton Ct
11 Moray Ho
12 Dulverton Ct
13 Westerham
14 Hill Ct
15 Assheton-Bennett Ho
16 Hatfield Ho
17 Oxford Ct
18 Pennington Lo
19 Austin Ho
20 Wentworth Ct
21 Priory The
22 Sheraton The
23 Christopher Ct
24 Hobart Ho
25 St Mark's Hts
A5 1 Marquis Ct
2 Garrick Ho
A6 1 College Rdbt
2 Edinburgh Ct
3 Weston Ct
4 Grebe Terr
5 Heron Ct
6 Agar Ho
7 St James' Ct
8 Grove Ct
9 Springfield Ct
10 College Wlk
B3 1 Percy Ct
2 Holmwood
3 Middle Green Cl
4 Herbert Ct
B4 1 Woodleigh
2 Highcroft
3 Caernarvon Ct
4 Regency Ct
D1 1 Oakleigh Way
2 Chandler Ct

199
C2 1 Goodland Ho
2 Furzeland Ho
3 Oakcroft Ho

410 199 C2

4 Meadcroft Ho
5 Newhouse
C4 1 Merryweather Ct
2 Roebuck Ct
3 Sable Ct
C5 1 Acacia Ho
2 Kingston Lo
3 Carrington Ct
4 Fairholme Ho
5 Marshall Ho
6 Norton Ho
7 Martin Ho

200
A1 1 Brookside Cres
2 Beverley Gdns
3 Purdey Ct
4 Avenue The
5 Briarwood Ct
6 Station App

202
D6 1 Fair Green Ct
2 Regal Ct
3 Lewes Ct
4 Esher Mews
5 Sibford Ct
6 Deseret Ho
7 Standor Ho
8 Langdale Par
9 Newman Terr

204
A2 1 Barcom Trad Est
2 Croydon Valley Trade Pk
C3 1 Rozelle Ct
2 Dunheved Ct
3 Truscott Ho
C4 1 Brigstock Par
2 Terry Lodge
D3 1 Wyndham Ct
D5 1 Nutfield Pl
2 Braidwood Ho
3 Elliott Ho

205
B1 1 Tavistock Ct
2 Chartwell Cl
3 Speaker's Ct
4 Cumberland Ct
5 Viceroy Ct
6 Oriel Ct
7 Cherry Orchard Gdns
8 Sola Ct
9 Gamma Ct
C1 1 Windmill Bridge Ho
2 Squire Ct
3 Houston Ct
4 Warren Ct
D1 1 Hastings Pl
2 Grant Pl

3 Clive Ho
4 Havelock Ho
5 Bellmore Ct
6 Hereford Ct
7 Chequers Ct
8 Havelock Hall

206
A1 1 Farleycroft
2 Edgecumbe Ct
3 Wesson Ho
4 Sullivan Ct
5 Kenley Ho
6 Christopher Ct
7 Jayson Ct
A6 1 Leybourne Ct
2 Lestock Cl
3 Croftside The
D1 1 Cottongrass Cl
2 Oxlip Cl
3 Eyebright Cl

207
1 North Rd
2 Sussex Rd
3 Riverside Wlk
4 Christie Ho
5 Windsor Ct
6 Sherwood Ct
7 Wheatsheaf Par
D6 1 Linden Ct
2 Park Ct
3 Chilchester Ct
4 Iveagh Ct

208
A6 1 Overbury
2 Wilton Pl
D1 1 Woodgrange Ct
2 Maycroft
3 Farnborough Cres
D4 1 Knowlton Gn
2 Speldhurst Ct
3 Bidborough Cl
4 Penshurst Wlk
D5 1 Wedgewood Ct
2 Birches The
3 Eccleshill
4 Tavistock Rd
5 Montpelier Ct

209
A5 1 Montague Terr
2 Chatsworth Ho
A6 1 Marina Cl
2 Cheveney Wlk
3 Bromley Manor Mans
4 Mall The
5 Westmoreland Pl
B5 1 Reflex Apartments
2 Wheeler Pl
3 Maxim Apartments
4 Exchange Apartments
5 Axiom Apartments
6 Weller Mews

211
B1 1 Gleneagles Gn
2 Tandridge Pl
3 Springfield Wlk
4 Pinehurst Wlk
5 Cromer Pl
6 Oakmont Pl

214
A6 1 St Bernards Ho
2 Wentworth Ct
3 Sunningdale Cl
4 Arklow Mews
5 Edward Pinner Ct

216
1 Lansdowne Copse
2 Lansdowne Ct

217
A2 1 Cheam Court Flats
2 Farnham Ct
3 Tabor Ct
C1 1 Lancaster Ct
2 Redclyffe Terr
3 Kenilworth Terr
4 Lincoln Terr
5 Garden Ct
6 Ashwood Pk
7 Midsummer Apartments
8 Lyndhurst Ct
9 Lorraine Ct
10 Gloucester Ct
11 Banbury Ct
12 Camilla Ct
13 Lorac Ct
14 Kingswood Mans
15 Claremont Ho
16 Holly Ct
17 Castle Ho
18 Balmoral Ct
19 Davington Ct
20 Hereford Ct
C2 1 Norman Ho
2 Hawthorns The
3 Limes The
4 Alexa Ct
5 Kristina Ct
6 Beverley Ct
7 Chestnut Ct
D1 1 Holmeswood
2 Pebworth Lo
3 Addison Ct
4 Kingslee Ct
5 Raeburn Ho
6 Girtin Ho
7 Leith Towers
8 Courtlands
9 Thomas Ho
10 Grayshott Ct
11 Hadrian Ct
12 Sandown Ct
13 Magnolia Ct
14 Dunsfold Ct
15 Camberley Ct
16 Berrylands Ct
17 Brockham Ct

18 Alford Ct
19 Lansdowne Ho
20 Larchvale Ct
D2 1 Portland Ct
2 Durnston Ct
3 Barton Ct
4 Aplin Ct
5 Hannah Ct
6 Honeysuckle Ct
7 Rowans The
8 St Annes Ct
9 Bonnington Ho
10 Pamir Ct
11 Bradbourne Ct
12 Worcester Ct
D3 1 Marian Ct
2 Robin Hood Ct
3 Distin Ct
4 Queensmere
5 Grosvenor Mans
6 Cromer Mans
7 St Nicholas Ct
D5 1 Dorothy Pettingel Ho
2 Margaret Ho

218
A1 1 Beauclere Ho
2 Melford Ct
3 Elmhurst Lo
4 Mansard Manor
5 Tranmere Ct
6 Beechcroft Lo
7 Savin Lo
8 Yew Tree Ct
9 Avondale Ct
10 Devonshire Ho
11 Hidcote Ho
12 Munstead Ct
13 Lodden Lo
14 Steetley Ct
15 Grampian Cl
16 Richard Sharples Ct
A2 1 Grosvenor Ct
2 Forest Dene Ct
3 Cedar Ct
4 Vanborough Ct
5 Shrub Ct
6 Evergreen Ct
7 Grasmere Ct
8 Heathfield Ct
9 Sherbourne Ct
10 Kinsale Grange
11 Linden Ct
12 Jubilee Ct
13 Langley Ct
14 Wilmot Ho
15 Farendon Ho
16 Alexander Ho
A3 1 Goossens Cl
2 Cliffe Wlk
3 Marlins Cl
4 Clowser Cl
5 Montana Gdns
6 Bournemouth Ct
7 Palmerston Ct
A4 1 Lodge The

2 Hazelwood Ho
3 Chesterton Ho
4 Clevedon Ho
5 Staincliffe Ho
6 Denewood Ho
7 Newlyn Ho
8 Manor Ct
9 Glenrose Ho
10 Oak Lo
11 Briar The
12 Fernhead
13 Branch Ho
14 Thicket Ct
15 Adam Ct
16 Arndell Ho
17 Oakwood Ct
B3 1 Hogarth Ho
2 Gillray Ho
3 Cramhurst Ho
4 Ronald Ho
5 Blythewood
6 Hillsde
7 Weldon Ct
8 Yeoman Ct
D5 1 Kynersley Cl
2 Wrythe Gn
3 Bedford Villas
4 Chateau The
5 Nelson Ct
6 Errington Manor
7 Leeds Ct
8 Blair Ct

219
A4 1 Westcroft
2 Westcroft Ho
A5 1 Burnside Ct
2 Millpond Pl
3 Waterside Ct
4 Stable Ct
5 Manor Ct
B2 1 Runnymede Ct
2 Dolphin Ct
3 Kings Ct
4 Cheyne Ct
5 Hendfield Ct
6 Ellerslie Ct
7 Embassy Ct
8 Chandler Ct
9 Hambledon Ct
10 Wallington Ct
11 Jasmine Ct
12 Napier Ct
13 Rosswood Ho
14 Woodcote Ct
15 Surrey Ct
16 Stag Ct
17 Moorlands
B3 1 Cornelion Cotts
2 Walpole Ct
3 Farmstead Ct
4 Derby Ho
5 Salisbury Ho
6 Chatham Ho
B4 1 Loraine Ho
2 Harcourt Lo
3 Coniston Ct
4 Alcester Ct

5 Friars Ct
6 Campbell Ho
7 Brodie Ho
8 Lesley Ct
9 Birch Ct
10 Airborne Ho
C2 1 Rossendon Ct
2 Mulberry Mews
3 Nairn Ct
4 Wallington Sq
5 Rosemount Twrs
6 Connell Ho
7 Ashby Grange
8 Terry Ct
9 Leigham Ct
10 Clyde Works
11 Chandos Bsns Ctr
12 Beech Ho
13 Wendon Ct
D3 1 Torquay Ho
2 Ashburton Ho
D5 1 Goodwood Lo
2 Haydock Lo
3 Kempton Lo

220
A1 1 Phoenix Ctr The
2 Ensign Way
3 Hunter Ct
4 Cirrus Cl
D5 1 Latimer Rd
2 Cromwell Ho
3 Arundel Ct
4 Warrington Ct
5 Grace Ct
6 Stuart Ct
7 Bridge Par

221
A3 1 Trent Ct
2 Sherwood Ct
3 Archers Ct
4 Keepers Ct
5 Lincoln Ct
6 Mount The
7 Fairhaven Ct
8 Brockham Ct
9 Chelwood Ct
10 Marey Ct
11 Landau Ct
A4 1 West Street Pl
2 Maple Ct
3 St Andrew's Rd
4 Albury Ct
5 Chestnut Ct
6 Elgin Ct
7 Beechfield Ct
8 Barham Ct
9 Whitstable Pl
10 Ledbury Pl
A5 1 Fellmongers Yd
2 Halstead Ct
3 Mann Cl
4 Waterworks Yd
5 Chanderia Ct
6 Katherine Ho
A6 1 Otterbourne Rd
2 Charrington Rd

3 Tamworth Pl
4 Priddy's Yd
5 Hospital of the Holy Trinity (Alms-shouses)
B6 1 Wellesley Court Rd
2 Norfolk Ho
3 Station App
4 Suffolk Ho
5 Cherry Orchard Gdns
6 Harrington Ct
D6 1 Cheyne Ct
2 Fourways
3 Princess Ct
4 Tierney Ct
5 Sinclair Ct
6 Guinness Ct
7 Mayfair Ct
8 Bishopscourt
9 Gloucester Lo
10 Beverley Hyrst
11 Melton Ct
12 Cecil Ct
13 Napier Ct

227
A3 1 Westfield
2 Farnborough Ct
3 Fern Hill Pl
4 Churchill Ct
5 Spencer Ct
6 Ladycroft Gdns
7 Crabbs Croft Cl
8 Clifton Cl
D2 1 Brittenden Cl
2 Wardens Field Cl
3 Winnipeg Dr
4 Superior Dr
5 Huron Cl
6 Manitoba Gdns
7 Lynne Cl
8 Flint Cl
9 Bakers Mews
D3 1 Osgood Gdns
2 Amberley Cl
3 Rawlings Cl
4 Beblets Cl
5 Fir Tree Cl
6 Raleigh Mews
7 King Henry Mews
D4 1 Healy Dr
2 Marsden Way
3 Taylor Cl
4 Strickland Way
5 Dryland Ave
6 Adcot Wlk
7 Lichlade Cl

Hospitals

Hospitals with Accident and Emergency departments

✚ **Central Middlesex Hospital** 89 A4
Acton Lane, Park Royal, London NW10 7NS
☎ 020 8965 5733

✚ **Charing Cross Hospital** 112 D1
Fulham Palace Road, London W6 8RF
(A&E entrance off St Dunstan's Road)
☎ 020 8846 1234

✚ **Chase Farm Hospital** 4 C5
The Ridgeway, Enfield, Middlesex EN2 8JL
☎ 020 8375 1010

✚ **Chelsea and Westminster Hospital** 136 A6 266 B5
369 Fulham Road, London SW10 9NH
☎ 020 8746 8080

✚ **Ealing Hospital** 108 B4
Uxbridge Road, Southall, Middlesex UB1 3HW
☎ 020 8967 5613

✚ **Hammersmith Hospital** 90 B1
Du Cane Road, London W12 0HS
☎ 020 8383 1111

✚ **Hillingdon Hospital** 82 B2
Pield Heath Road, Uxbridge, Middlesex UB8 3NN
☎ 01895 238282

✚ **Homerton University Hospital** 74 D3
Homerton Row, E9 6SR
☎ 020 8510 5555

✚ **King George Hospital** 58 A4
Barley Lane, Goodmayes, Ilford, Essex IG3 8YB
☎ 020 8983 8000

✚ **King's College Hospital** 139 B3
Denmark Hill, (A&E in Ruskin Wing) SE5 9RS
☎ 020 3299 9000

✚ **Kingston Hospital** 176 D2
Galsworthy Road, Kingston-upon-Thames, Surrey KT2 7QB
☎ 020 8546 7711

✚ **Lewisham Hospital** 163 D6
High Street, Lewisham, London SE13 6JH
☎ 020 8333 3000

✚ **Mayday University Hospital** 204 D3
Mayday Road, Thornton Heath CR7 7YE
☎ 020 8401 3000

✚ **Moorfields Eye Hospital (eyes only)** 95 B4 235 C1
162 City Rd, London EC1V 2PO
☎ 020 7253 3411

✚ **Newham General Hospital** 99 C3
Glen Road, Plaistow, London E13 8SL
☎ 020 7476 4000

✚ **North Middlesex University Hospital** 33 C5
Sterling Way, Edmonton, London, N18 1QX
☎ 020 8887 2000

✚ **Northwick Park Hospital** 43 A4
Watford Road, Harrow, Middlesex HA1 3UJ
☎ 020 8864 3232

✚ **Princess Royal University Hospital** 226 C5
Farnborough Common, Orpington BR6 8ND
☎ 01689 863000

✚ **Queen Elizabeth Hospital** 144 A5
Stadium Rd, Woolwich SE18 4QH
☎ 020 8836 6000

✚ **Queen Mary's Hospital** 190 A4
Frognal Avenue, Sidcup, Kent DA14 6LT
☎ 020 8302 2678

✚ **Royal Free Hospital** 70 C3
Pond Street, London NW3 2QG
☎ 020 7794 0500

✚ **Royal London Hospital (Whitechapel)** 96 B2
Whitechapel Road, London E1 1BB
☎ 020 7377 7000

✚ **St George's Hospital** 180 B5
Blackshaw Road, London SW17 0QT
☎ 020 8672 1255

✚ **St Helier Hospital** 202 A1
Wrythe Lane, Carshalton, Surrey SM5 1AA
☎ 020 8296 2000

✚ **St Mary's Hospital** 92 B1 236 D2
Praed Street, Paddington W2 1NY
(A&E entrance on South Wharf Rd)
☎ 020 7886 6666

✚ **St Thomas' Hospital** 116 B3 260 C6
Lambeth Palace Road, London SE1 7EH
☎ 020 7188 7188

✚ **University College Hospital** 93 C3 239 B6
235 Euston Road, London NW1 2BU
☎ 0845 155 5000

✚ **West Middlesex University Hospital** 131 A3
Twickenham Road, Isleworth, Middlesex TW7 6AF
☎ 020 8560 2121

✚ **Whipps Cross Hospital** 54 B3
Whipps Cross Road, Leytonstone London E11 1NR
☎ 020 8539 5522

✚ **Whittington Hospital** 71 C6
Highgate Hill, London, N19 5NF
☎ 020 7272 3070

Acton Hospital W3 110 C4
Ashford Hospital TW15 3AA 148 A2
Athlone House (The Middlesex Hospital) N6 48 D1
Atkinson Morley Hospital SW20 178 B3
Barking Hospital IG11 79 D1
Barnes Hospital SW14 133 C2
Beckenham Hospital BR3 185 B1
Bethlem Royal Hospital The BR3 207 C2
Blackheath Hospital SE3 142 C2
Bolingbroke Hospital The SW11 158 C6
Bowden House Hospital (Private) HA1 64 C6
British Home and Hospital for Incurables SW16 182 D5
Bromley Hospital BR2 9AJ 209 B5
Brompton Hospital SW3 114 B1 256 D2
BUPA Bushey Hospital WD2 8 D3
Carshalton, War Memorial Hospital SM5 218 D2
Cassel Hospital TW10 175 D6
Castlewood Day Hospital SE18 144 C4
Central Middlesex Hospital NW10 7NS 89 A4
Central Public Health Laboratory NW9 45 C6
Chadwell Heath Hospital RM6 58 B4
Charing Cross Hospital W6 8RF 112 D1
Charter Nightingale Hospital The NW1 92 C2 237 B4
Chase Farm Hospital EN2 8JL 4 C5
Chelsea Hospital for Women SW3 114 C1 257 A2
Chelsea and Westminster Hospital SW10 9NH 136 A6 266 B5
Chingford Hospital E4 20 A1
Chiswick Maternity Hospital W4 111 D1
Clayponds Hospital and Day Treatment Ctr TW8 110 A2
Clementine Churchill Hospital The HA1 64 D5
Colindale Hospital NW9 45 C6
Connaught Day Hospital E11 54 C3
Coppetts Wood Hospital N10 30 D2
Cromwell Hospital SW5 113 D2 255 C4
Devonshire Hospital W1 93 A2 238 B4
Dulwich Hospital SE22 139 C1
Ealing Hospital UB1 3HW 108 B4
East Ham Memorial Hospital E7 77 D1
Eastman Dental Hospital WC1 94 B4 240 C6
Edgware General Hospital HA8 26 D3
Elizabeth Garrett Anderson and Obstetric Hospital WC1 93 C3 235 B5
Farnborough Hospital BR6 226 C4
Finchley Memorial Hospital N12 30 A3
Fitzroy Nuffield Hospital W1 92 D1 237 C2
Garden Hospital The NW4 46 C6
Goldie Leigh Hospital SE2 146 C6
Goodmayes Hospital IG3 58 A4
Gordon Hospital The SW1 115 D2 259 C3
Great Ormond St Hospital for Children WC1 94 B3 240 C5
Grovelands Priory N14 16 A3
Guy's Hospital SE1 117 B5 252 D2
Hackney Hospital E9 75 A3
Hamlet (Day) Hospital The TW9 132 A2
Hammersmith Hospital W12 90 B1
Harrow Hospital HA2 64 C6
The Heart Hospital W1 93 B2 238 C3
Hillingdon Hospital UB8 82 B2
Homerton University Hospital E9 74 D3

Hornsey Central Hospital N8 49 D4
Hospital for Tropical Diseases WC1 232 C5
Hospital of St John and St Elizabeth NW8 92 B5 229 C3
Inverforth House Hospital NW3 70 A6
Jewish Home and Hospital at Tottenham The N15 51 D5
King George Hospital IG3 58 A4
King's College Hospital SE5 139 B3
Kings Oak Hospital (Private) The EN2 4 C5
Kingsbury Hospital NW9 44 C5
Kingston Hospital KT2 176 D2
Langthorne Hospital E11 76 B5
Lewisham Hospital SE13 163 D6
Lister Hospital SW1 115 B1 258 C1
London Bridge Hospital SE1 117 B5 252 D4
London Chest Hospital E2 96 C5
London Clinic NW1 93 A3 238 B5
London Foot Hospital W1 93 C3 239 A5
London Hospital (Mile End) The E2 96 D4
London Hospital (St Clements) The E3 97 B4
London Independent Hospital The E1 96 D2
Maida Vale Psychiatric Hospital W9 92 A3 236 B6
Manor House Hospital NW11 47 D1
Marlborough Day Hospital NW8 92 A5 229 A4
Maudsley Hospital The SE5 139 B3
Mayday University Hospital CR7 204 D3
Memorial Hospital SE18 144 C3
Mildmay Mission Hospital E2 95 D4
Molesey Hospital KT8 195 C4
Moorfields Eye Hospital EC1 95 B4 235 C1
Morland Road Day Hospital RM10 103 C6
National Hospital for Neurology and Neurosurgery N2 48 C5
National Hospital The WC1 94 A3 240 B5
National Physical Laboratory TW11 174 C4
Nelson Hospital SW20 179 B1
New Cross Hospital SE14 140 C5
New Victoria Hospital KT3 177 C2
Newham General Hospital E13 99 C3
Normansfield Hospital KT8 175 C3
North London Nuffield Hospital EN2 4 C3
North Middlesex University Hospital N18 33 C5
Northwick Park Hospital HA1 43 A4
Northwood Pinner and District Cottage Hospital HA6 22 A2
Norwood Hospital SE19 183 B4
Orpington Hospital BR6 227 D4
Paddington Com Hospital W9 91 C2
Penny Sangam Day Hospital UB2 107 B3
Plaistow Hospital E13 99 C5
Portland Hospital for Women and Children The W1 93 B3 238 D5
Princess Grace Hospital The W1 93 A3 238 A5
Princess Louise Hospital W10 90 C2
Princess Royal University Hospital BR6 226 C5
Priory Hospital The SW15 133 D1
Putney Hospital SW15 134 C2
Queen Charlotte's Hospital W12 90 B1
Queen Elizabeth Hospital for Children The E2 96 A5
Queen Elizabeth Hospital SE18 144 A5
Queen Mary's Hospital DA14 6LT 190 A4
Queen Mary's Hospital NW3 70 A5
Queen Mary's University Hospital SW15 156 A5
Queen's Hospital CR0 205 A3

Roding Hospital IG4 55 D6
Royal Brompton and Nat Heart Hospital The SW3 114 C1 257 A2
Royal Ear Hospital WC1 93 C3 239 B5
Royal Free Hospital NW3 70 C3
Royal Hospital SW15 157 A5
Royal London Homeopathic Hospital The WC1 94 A2 240 B4
Royal London Hospital(Whitechapel) E1 96 B2
Royal Marsden Hospital SW3 114 B1 256 D2
Royal Masonic Hospital W6 112 A2
Royal National Orthopaedic Hospital HA7 9 C2
Royal National Orthopaedic Hospital W1 93 B3 238 D5
Royal Nat TN&E Hospital The W5 87 C2
Royal Nat TN&E Hospital The WC1 94 B4 233 C2
St Andrew's Hospital E3 97 D3
St Ann's General Hospital N4, N15 51 A4
St Anthony's Hospital KT4 200 D1
St Bartholomew's Hospital EC1 94 D2 241 D3
St Charles' Hospital W10 90 D2
St Christopher's Hospice SE26 184 C5
St George's Hospital SW17 180 B5
St Giles Hospital SE5 139 C4
St Helier Hospital SM5 202 A1
St Joseph's Hospice E9, E8 96 B6
St Leonard's Hospital N1 95 C5
St Luke's Hospital W1 93 C3 239 A6
St Luke's Woodside Hospital N10 49 A5
St Mark's Hospital EC1 94 D4 234 D2
St Mark's Hospital HA1 43 A2
St Mary's Cottage Hospital TW12 173 B2
St Mary's Hospital W2 92 B1 236 D2
St Michael's Hospital EN2 5 B4
St Pancras Hospital NW1 93 D6 232 C5
St Thomas's Hospital SE1 116 B3 260 C6
St Vincent's Hospital HA5 39 D6
Samaritan Hospital for Women NW1 237 C4
Shirley Oaks Hospital CR0 206 C2
Sloane Hospital BR3 186 B2
South Western Hospital SW9 138 B2
Southwood Hospital (Geriatric) N6 49 A4
Springfield Hospital SW17 158 C1
Stepney Day Hospital E1 96 C1
Surbiton Hospital KT6 198 A3
Teddington Memorial Hospital TW11 174 C4
Thorpe Coombe Hospital E17 54 A6
Tolworth Hospital KT6 214 C6
Travel Clinic, Hospital for Tropical Diseases WC1 93 C3 239 B5
University College Hospital WC1 93 C3 239 B6
Upton Day Hospital DA6 147 A1
Wanstead Hospital E11 55 B5
Wellington Hospital (North) NW8 92 B5 229 D3
Wellington Hospital (South) NW8 92 B5 229 D3
Wembley Hospital HA0 65 D2
West Middlesex University Hospital TW7 6AF 131 A3
Western Hospital The NW1 92 D2 237 C4
Whipps Cross Hospital E11 1NR 54 B3
Whittington Hospital N19 5NF 71 C6
Willesden Community Hospital The NW10 68 A1
Winifred House Hospital EN5 11 D5

Places of interest

Central

West End

Admiralty Arch SW1 . . . . **249** D4
Apple Market WC2 . . . . **250** B6
Banqueting House SW1 . . . . **250** A3
Big Ben SW1 . . . . **250** B1
British Library NW1 . . . . **93** D4 **232** D2
British Mus WC1 . . . . **94** A2 **240** A3
BT Tower W1 . . . . **93** C2 **239** A4
Buckingham Palace SW1 . **115** C4 **249** A1
Cabinet War Rooms SW1 . **115** D4 **249** D2
Carnaby Street W1 . . . . **93** C1 **239** A1
Cenotaph SW1 . . . . **250** A2
Changing of the Guard
 (site of) SW1 . . . . **249** A1
Chinatown W1 . . . . **115** D6 **249** D6
Clarence House SW1 . . . . . . **115** C5 **249** B3
Cleopatra's Needle WC2 . . **116** B5 **250** C5
Courtauld Galleries WC2 . . . . **250** C6
Covent Garden WC2 . . . . . . **116** A6 **250** B6
Dickens House
 Mus WC1 . . . . **94** B3 **240** D5
Downing Street SW1 . . . . . . **116** A4 **250** A2
Eros W1 . . . . **115** D6 **249** C5
Green Park SW1,W1 . . . . . . **115** B4 **248** D2
Guards Mus SW1 . . . . **115** C4 **249** B1
Holocaust Memorial
 Garden W2 . . . . **114** D4 **247** D2
Horse Guards
 Parade SW1 . . . . **115** D5 **249** D3
Houses of
 Parliament SW1 . . . . **116** A3 **260** B6
Hyde Park W2 . . . . **114** D5 **247** C3
Leicester Square WC2 . . . . **115** D6 **249** D5
London's Transport Mus WC2 . . . **250** B6
Marble Arch W1 . . . . **114** D4 **247** D6
Methodist Central
 Hall SW1 . . . . **115** D4 **249** D1
National Gallery W1 . . . . . **115** D6 **249** D5
National Portrait
 Gallery W1 . . . . **115** D6 **249** D5
Nelson's Monument WC2 . . . . **250** A4
New Scotland Yard SW1 . **115** D3 **259** C6
Parliament Square SW1 . . **116** A4 **250** A1
Pepsi Trocadero W1 . . . . **249** C5
Piccadilly Circus W1 . . . . . **115** D6 **249** C5
Queen Victoria Memorial SW1 . . . **249** A2
Queen's Gallery SW1 . . . . . **115** B4 **248** D1
Rotten Row SW1 . . . . **114** D4 **247** C2
Royal Academy
 of Arts W1 **115** C6 **249** A5
Royal Mews SW1 . . . . **115** B3 **258** D6
Royal United Services
 Mus SW1 . . . . **250** A3
St James's Palace SW1 . . . . **115** C5 **249** B3
St James's Park SW1 . . . . **249** C2
Serpentine Gallery W2 . . **114** B4 **246** D2
Soho W1 . . . . **93** D1 **239** C2
Somerset House WC2 . . . . **116** B6 **250** D6
Speakers' Corner W1 . . . . **114** D6 **247** D6
Tate Britain SW1 . . . . **116** A2 **260** A3
Theatre Mus WC2 . . . . **250** B6
Trafalgar Square WC2 . . . . **115** D5 **249** D4
Tyburn Tree (site of) W2 . . . . **247** C6
Wallace Collection W1 . . . . **238** A2
Wellington Arch SW1 . . . . **248** B2
Wellington Mus
 (Apsley House) SW1 . . . **115** A4 **248** B2
Westminster Abbey SW1 . . **116** A3 **260** A6
Westminster
 Cathedral SW1 . . . . **115** C3 **259** A1

City

Bank of England EC2 . . . . **242** C1
Barbican Arts and
 Conference Centre EC2 . . **95** A2 **242** B4
Central Criminal Court
 (Old Bailey) EC4 . . . . **94** D1 **241** D2
Custom House EC3 . . . . **117** C6 **253** A5

Dr Johnson's House EC4 . . . . **241** B1
Gray's Inn WC1 . . . . **94** B2 **240** D4
Guildhall EC2 . . . . **95** A1 **242** B2
Inner Temple EC4 . . . . **251** A6
John Wesley's House &
 Mus EC1 . . . . **242** D6
Lincoln's Inn WC2 . . . . **94** B1 **240** D2
Lloyd's Building EC3 . . . . . . **95** C1 **243** A1
Mansion House EC4 . . . . **242** C1
Merchant Taylors Hall EC2R **242** D1
Middle Temple EC4 . . . . . . **116** C6 **251** A6
Monument, The EC3 . . . . **252** D6
Mus of London EC2 . . . . **95** A2 **242** A3
Nat West Tower EC2 . . . . **243** A2
National Postal
 Mus EC1 . . . . **95** A1 **242** A2
Petticoat Lane Market EC2 **95** D2 **243** C3
Public Record Office
 Mus EC4,WC2 . . . . **241** A2
Royal Exchange EC3 . . . . **242** D1
St Katharine Dock E1 . . . . **117** D6 **253** D4
St Mary le Bow Church EC2 . . . . . **242** B1
St Paul's Cathedral EC4 . . . **95** A1 **242** A1
Sir John Soane's
 Mus WC2 . . . . **94** B1 **240** C2
Spitalfields Market E1 . . . . . **95** D2 **243** C4
Stock Exchange EC2 . . . . **241** D1
Tower Bridge E1,EC3,SE1 . **117** D5 **253** C4
Tower of London EC3 . . . . **117** D6 **253** C5
Traitors Gate EC3 . . . . **117** D5 **253** C4
Ye Olde Cheshire Cheese EC4 . . . . **241** B2

Northern

Business Design Centre N1 **94** C6 **234** B5
Camden Market NW1 . . . . . **93** B6 **231** D6
London Canal Mus N1 . . . . **94** A5 **233** B4
London Central
 Mosque NW8 . . . . **92** C4 **230** B1
London Zoo NW1 . . . . **93** A5 **231** A4
Lord's Cricket Ground NW8 **92** B4 **229** D2
Madame Tussaud's NW1 . . **93** A3 **238** A5
Open Air Theatre, Regent's
 Park NW1 . . . . **231** A1
Planetarium NW1 . . . . **93** A3 **238** A5
Primrose Hill NW1 . . . . **92** D6 **230** C6
Queen Mary's Gardens NW1 . . . . . **231** A1
Regent's Park NW1 . . . . **93** A4 **231** A3
St George's Cathedral NW1 . . . . . . **231** D2
Sherlock Holmes
 Mus NW1 . . . . **92** D3 **237** D5

Southern

Battersea Park SW11 . . . . . **137** A5 **268** A3
Battersea Power
 Station SW8 . . . . **137** B6 **268** D6
Brompton Oratory SW7 . . **114** C3 **257** A5
Bear Gardens
 Mus SE1 . . . . **117** A5 **252** A4
Bermondsey Market SE1 . . **117** C3 **263** B8
Borough Market SE1 . . . . **252** C3
Design Mus SE1 . . . . **117** D4 **253** D2
Florence Nightingale
 Mus SE1 . . . . **250** D1
Gabriel's Wharf SE1 . . . . **251** A4
George Inn SE1 . . . . **252** C3
Globe Theatre SE1 . . . . **252** A5
Hayward Gallery SE1 . . . . **116** B5 **250** D4
HMS Belfast SE1 . . . . **253** B4
Imperial War
 Mus SE1 . . . . **116** C2 **261** B5
Lambeth Palace SE1 . . . . . **116** B3 **260** C5
London Aquarium SE1 . . . . **250** C1
London Dungeon SE1 . . . **117** B5 **252** D4
London Eye SE1 . . . . **116** B4 **250** C2
London Peace Pagoda SW11 . . . . . **267** D4
Millennium Bridge SE1,EC4 . . . . . **252** A5
Mus of Garden History SE1 . . . . . . **260** C5
National Film Theatre SE1 . . . . **250** D4
National Theatre SE1 . . . . **116** B5 **250** D4
Old County Hall SE1 . . . . **250** C2

Operating Theatre Mus and Herb
 Garret SE1 . . . . **117** B5 **252** D3
Oxo Tower SE1 . . . . **251** B5
Royal Festival Hall SE1 . . **116** B5 **250** D3
Saatchi Gallery SE1 . . . . **250** C2
St George's RC
 Cathedral SE1 . . . . **116** C3 **261** B6
Shakespeare's Globe Theatre
 (site of) SE1 . . . . **252** B4
Southwark Cathedral SE1 **117** B5 **252** C4
Tate Modern SE1 . . . . **116** D6 **251** D4
Vinopolis SE1 . . . . **117** B5 **252** C4

Western

Albert Memorial SW7 . . . . **114** B4 **246** C1
Carlyle's House SW3 . . . . **267** A5
Chelsea Barracks SW1 . . . **115** A1 **258** B1
Chelsea Physic
 Garden SW3 . . . . **115** A1 **267** C6
Commonwealth
 Institute W8 . . . . **113** C3 **255** A6
Geological Mus SW7 . . . . **114** B3 **256** D5
Kensington Gardens W2 . **114** A5 **246** B3
Kensington Palace W8 . . . **113** D5 **245** D3
Leighton House W14 . . . . **254** D6
Lindsey House SW10 . . . . **266** D4
Little Venice W9 . . . . **92** A2 **236** A4
National Army
 Mus SW3 . . . . **136** D6 **267** D6
Natural History
 Mus SW7 . . . . **114** B3 **256** C5
Ranelagh Gardens SW1 . . **115** A1 **258** B1
Royal Albert Hall SW7 . . . **114** B4 **246** C1
Royal Hospital (Army
 Pensioners) SW1 . . . . . . **115** A1 **258** A1
Science Mus SW7 . . . . **114** B3 **256** C5
Victoria and Albert
 Mus SW7 . . . . **114** B3 **256** D5

East

Canary Wharf E14 . . . . **119** D5
Docklands Mus E14 . . . . **119** D6
Epping Forest IG10 . . . . **21** B6
Geffrye Mus E2 . . . . **95** D5
London Docklands Visitor
 Centre E14 . . . . **120** A4
London Gas Mus E16 . . . . **98** B3
Mus of Childhood (V&A) E2 . . . . **96** C4
Museum of the Great Eastern
 Railway E16 . . . . **122** C4
Queen Elizabeth's Hunting
 Lodge Mus E4 . . . . **20** D4
Ragged School Mus E3 . . . . **97** A2
Vestry House (Mus) E17 . . . . **53** D5
Whitechapel Art Gallery E1 . . . . . **95** D1

North

Alexandra Palace N22 . . . . **31** D1
Barnet Mus EN5 . . . . **1** A1
Battle of Britain Mus NW9 . . . . . **27** D1
Bruce Castle Mus N17 . . . . **33** C2
Church Farm House Mus NW4 . . . **46** B6
Coppetts Centre N12 . . . . **30** D3
Forty Hall EN2 . . . . **5** D6
Freud Mus NW3 . . . . **70** A2
Grange Mus of Community History
 NW10 . . . . **67** D4
Hampstead Heath NW3 . . . . **70** B6
Harrow Mus and Heritage Centre
 HA2 . . . . **42** A6
Highgate Cemetery N19 . . . . **71** B6
Kensal Green Cemetery
 (All Souls) NW10 . . . . **90** C4
Kenwood House NW3 . . . . **48** C1
Old Court (Mus and Library) HA0 **65** C3
RAF Mus NW9 . . . . **28** A1

Ruislip Lido HA4,HA5 . . . . **39** B5
Ruislip Lido Railway HA4 . . . . **39** B5
White Cube N1 . . . . **95** C4

South east

Blackheath SE3 . . . . **142** C4
Brockwell Park SE24 . . . . **160** D5
Cutty Sark SE10 . . . . **142** A6
Docklands Heritage Mus SE16 . . . **119** B5
Dulwich Picture Gallery SE21 . . . **161** C4
Eltham Palace SE9 . . . . **166** A4
Flamsteed House SE10 . . . . **142** A5
Gipsy Moth IV SE10 . . . . **142** A6
Greenwich Park SE10 . . . . **142** C5
Horniman Mus and Gardens SE23 **162** B3
Livesey Mus SE15 . . . . **140** B6
Meridian Building SE10 . . . . **142** B5
Millennium Dome SE10 . . . . **120** C5
National Maritime Mus SE10 . . . . **142** B6
Old Royal Observatory
 Greenwich SE10 . . . . **142** B5
Queen's House SE10 . . . . **142** B6
Rotunda Mus SE18 . . . . **122** B1
Scadbury Park Nature
 Reserve BR7 . . . . **189** D4
South Norwood Country
 Park SE25 . . . . **206** C5
Thames Barrier Visitor
 Centre SE18 . . . . **121** D3
Well Hall Pleasance SE9 . . . . **144** A1

South west

Barnes Common SW13 . . . . **134** A2
Clapham Common SW4 . . . . **137** C1
Fulham Palace SW6 . . . . **135** A3
Hampton Court Palace KT8 . . . . . **196** D6
Kingston Mus KT1 . . . . **176** A1
Wandsworth Mus SW15 . . . . **135** A1
Wetland Centre SW13 . . . . **134** B5
Wimbledon Common SW19 . . . . . **178** B6
Wimbledon Lawn Tennis
 Mus SW19 . . . . **157** A1
Wimbledon Windmill Mus SW19 . **156** C1

West

Chiswick House W4 . . . . **133** B6
Eel Pie Island TW1 . . . . **153** A3
Gunnersbury Park Mus W3 . . . . . **110** C3
Ham House TW10 . . . . **153** C2
Kew Bridge Steam Mus TW8 . . . . **110** B1
Kew Gardens
 (Royal Botanic Gardens) TW9 . . **132** A4
Kew Observatory TW9 . . . . **131** C2
Kew Palace TW9 . . . . **132** A5
London Butterfly House TW8 . . . . **131** B4
Marble Hill TW1 . . . . **153** C4
Mus of Richmond TW10 . . . . **153** D6
Musical Mus TW8 . . . . **132** A6
Osterley Park TW7 . . . . **108** B1
Pitshanger Manor Mus and
 Art Gallery W5 . . . . **109** D5
Portobello Road Market W10 . . . . **91** A2
Richmond Park TW10 . . . . **155** A3
Syon House TW8 . . . . **131** C4
Walled Garden TW16 . . . . **194** B6

Screen on
Baker St

MARYLEBONE

PADDINGTON STREET

WEYMOUTH STREET

BAKER STREET

THAYER ST

MARYLEBONE HIGH STREET

NEW CAVENDISH STREET

PORTLAND STREET

GREAT PORTLAND STREET

FITZROVIA

HOWLAND STREET

BERNERS ST

NEW CAVENDISH STREET

MANDEVILLE PL

GEORGE ST

PORTMAN SQUARE

PORTMAN ST

JR ST

PLACE

LANGHAM PLACE

MORTIMER STREET

Wigmore Hall

CAVENDISH CAVENDISH PLACE

REGENT ST

Niketown   Top Shop

HMV

WIGMORE STREET

JAMES ST

STREET

SQUARE

John Lewis   BHS   H&M

OXFORD

Borders

Marks and
Spencer

Marks and
Spencer

ORCHARD ST

Selfridges

House of
Fraser

OXFORD

Oxford
Circus

Laura
Ashley

Palladium

Debenhams

STREET

REGENT STREET

Dickins & Jones

OXFORD

HMV

Liberty

West One
Shopping Centre

DAVIES STREET

Bond
Street

Jaeger

Mothercare

NEW BOND STREET

Fenwick

Sotheby's

Hamleys

CONDUIT STREET

Burberry

Next

KNIGHTSBRIDGE

KNIGHTSBRIDGE

Curzon
Minema

NIGHTSBRIDGE

Knightsbridge

Harvey Nichols

SLOANE STREET

BRUTON ST

MAYFAIR

BERKELEY SQUARE

Asprey and
Garrard

Aquascutum

Austin Reed

BROMPTON ROAD

Cartier

Burlington
Arcade

Waterstones

Harrods

Gucci

Chanel

MAURICE PL

FITZ-

BERKELEY ST

PICCADILLY

Hatchards

Fortnum
and Mason

ST. JAMES'S STREET

Christie's

CHAMP PL

PONT

STREET

SLOANE STREET

CURZON

Curzon
Mayfair

Green
Park

BROMPTON

STREET

PICCADILLY

GREEN PARK

Prada

CLIVEDEN PL

SLOANE

Royal
Court

CONSTITUTION HILL

Peter Jones

SQUARE

KING'S ROAD

WH Smith

Sloane
Square

LOWER SLOANE ST

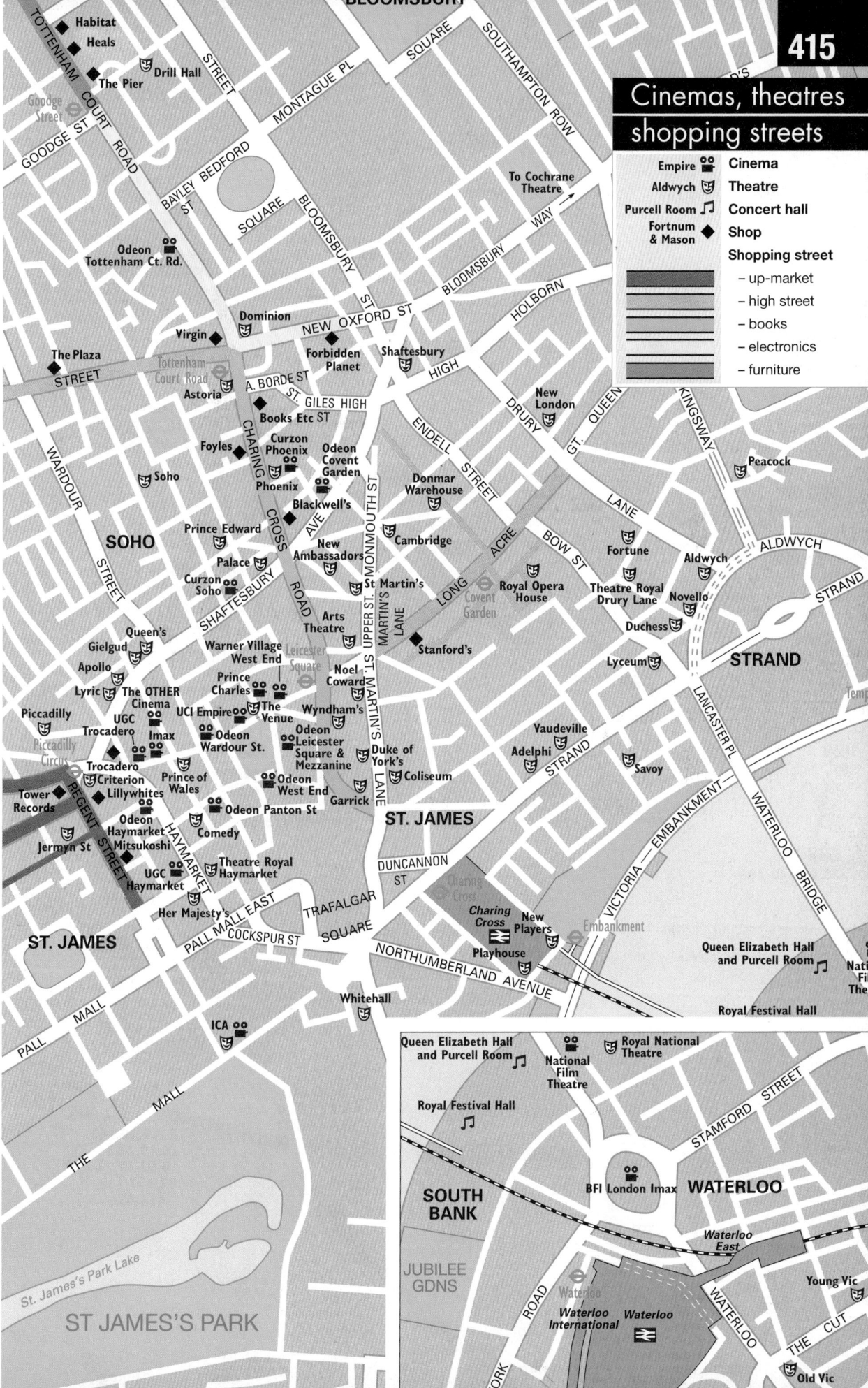

BLOOMSBURY

Habitat
Heals
Drill Hall
The Pier
Goodge
Street
TOTTENHAM COURT ROAD
GOODGE ST
BAYLEY
BEDFORD ST
MONTAGUE PL
BLOOMSBURY SQUARE
SOUTHAMPTON ROW
To Cochrane Theatre
BLOOMSBURY WAY
Odeon Tottenham Ct. Rd.
HOLBORN

Cinemas, theatres shopping streets

Empire — Cinema
Aldwych — Theatre
Purcell Room ♪ — Concert hall
Fortnum & Mason ◆ — Shop
— Shopping street
– up-market
– high street
– books
– electronics
– furniture

The Plaza
STREET
Virgin
Dominion
NEW OXFORD ST
Forbidden Planet
Shaftesbury
HIGH
DRURY
New London
GT. QUEEN
KINGSWAY
Peacock
Tottenham Court Road
Astoria
A. BORDE ST
ST. GILES HIGH ST
Books Etc
Foyles
CHARING
Curzon Phoenix
Odeon Covent Garden
Phoenix
Blackwell's
AVE
Donmar Warehouse
ENDELL STREET
Fortune
LANE
Aldwych
ALDWYCH
Novello
STRAND
WARDOUR
SOHO
Soho
CROSS
Prince Edward
Palace
New Ambassadors
Cambridge
UPPER ST MONMOUTH ST
St Martin's
LONG
ACRE
BOW ST
Royal Opera House
Theatre Royal Drury Lane
Duchess
Curzon Soho
SHAFTESBURY
ROAD
MARTIN'S
LANE
Covent Garden
Lyceum
STRAND
Arts Theatre
Queen's
Gielgud
Apollo
Lyric
The OTHER Cinema
Warner Village West End
Leicester Square
Noel Coward
Stanford's
Piccadilly
UGC Trocadero
Prince Charles
Imax
UCI Empire
The Venue
Wyndham's
Odeon Wardour St.
Odeon Leicester Square & Mezzanine
Duke of York's
Vaudeville
Adelphi
STRAND
Savoy
Piccadilly Circus
Trocadero
Criterion
Lillywhites
Prince of Wales
Odeon West End
Coliseum
Garrick
MARTIN'S LANE
ST. JAMES
LANCASTER PL
Tower Records
Odeon Panton St
REGENT STREET
Odeon Haymarket
Mitsukoshi
Comedy
Jermyn St
HAYMARKET
Theatre Royal Haymarket
UGC Haymarket
Her Majesty's
PALL MALL EAST
TRAFALGAR SQUARE
DUNCANNON ST
Charing Cross
New Players
Embankment
VICTORIA — EMBANKMENT
WATERLOO BRIDGE
Queen Elizabeth Hall and Purcell Room
National Film Thea
ST. JAMES
PALL MALL
COCKSPUR ST
NORTHUMBERLAND AVENUE
Playhouse
Royal Festival Hall
Whitehall
ICA

Inset map (bottom right)

Queen Elizabeth Hall and Purcell Room ♪
National Film Theatre
Royal National Theatre
Royal Festival Hall ♪
STAMFORD STREET
SOUTH BANK
BFI London Imax
WATERLOO
JUBILEE GDNS
Waterloo East
Young Vic
Waterloo Road
Waterloo
Waterloo International
Waterloo
WATERLOO
THE CUT
Old Vic

PALL MALL
THE MALL
St. James's Park Lake
ST JAMES'S PARK
YORK ROAD

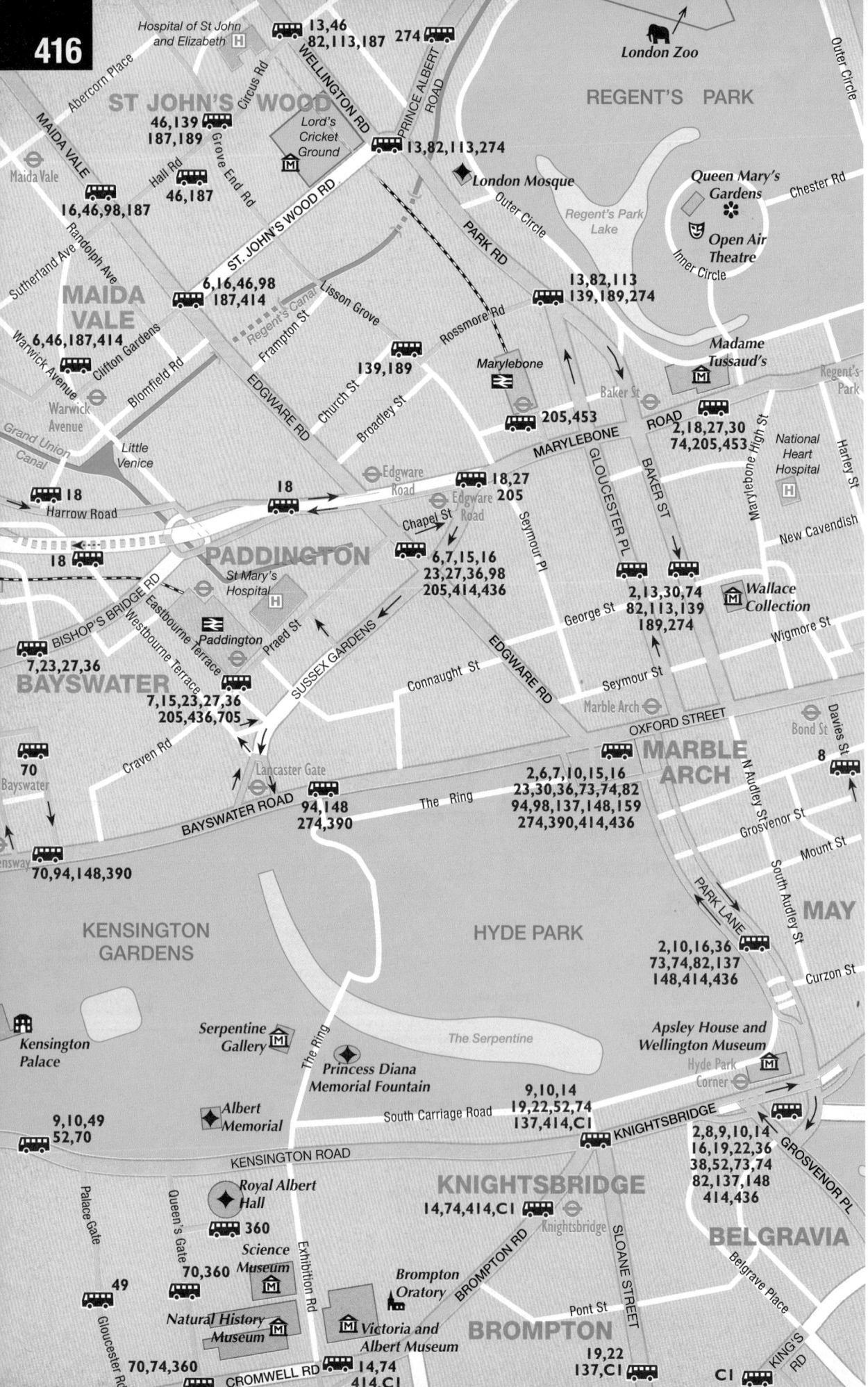

Hospital of St John and Elizabeth
13,46
82,113,187
274
London Zoo
Outer Circle
Abercorn Place
Circus Rd
WELLINGTON RD
PRINCE ALBERT ROAD
ST JOHN'S WOOD
REGENT'S PARK
46,139
187,189
Lord's Cricket Ground
MAIDA VALE
Grove End Rd
13,82,113,274
Maida Vale
Hall Rd
46,187
London Mosque
Queen Mary's Gardens
Chester Rd
16,46,98,187
ST. JOHN'S WOOD RD
Outer Circle
Regent's Park Lake
Open Air Theatre
Randolph Ave
PARK RD
Inner Circle
Sutherland Ave
MAIDA VALE
6,16,46,98
187,414
13,82,113
139,189,274
Regent's Canal
Lisson Grove
Frampton St
Rossmore Rd
6,46,187,414
Clifton Gardens
Madame Tussaud's
Warwick Avenue
Blomfield Rd
139,189
Marylebone
Regent's Park
Warwick Avenue
EDGWARE RD
Church St
Baker St
Grand Union Canal
Little Venice
Broadley St
205,453
ROAD
2,18,27,30
74,205,453
National Heart Hospital
Harley St
MARYLEBONE
Marylebone High St
Edgware Road
18,27
205
GLOUCESTER PL
BAKER ST
18
18
Harrow Road
Edgware Road
Chapel St
Seymour Pl
New Cavendish
18
PADDINGTON
6,7,15,16
23,27,36,98
205,414,436
St Mary's Hospital
BISHOP'S BRIDGE RD
Eastbourne Terrace
2,13,30,74
82,113,139
189,274
Wallace Collection
Westbourne Terrace
Paddington
George St
Praed St
SUSSEX GARDENS
Wigmore St
EDGWARE RD
7,23,27,36
BAYSWATER
Connaught St
Seymour St
7,15,23,27,36
205,436,705
Marble Arch
OXFORD STREET
Bond St
Davies St
Craven Rd
MARBLE ARCH
8
70
Bayswater
Lancaster Gate
2,6,7,10,15,16
23,30,36,73,74,82
94,98,137,148,159
274,390,414,436
BAYSWATER ROAD
94,148
274,390
The Ring
N Audley St
Grosvenor St
Mount St
Queensway
70,94,148,390
PARK LANE
South Audley St
MAY
KENSINGTON GARDENS
HYDE PARK
2,10,16,36
73,74,82,137
148,414,436
Curzon St
Serpentine Gallery
The Serpentine
Apsley House and Wellington Museum
Kensington Palace
The Ring
Princess Diana Memorial Fountain
Hyde Park Corner
9,10,14
19,22,52,74
137,414,C1
Albert Memorial
South Carriage Road
9,10,49
52,70
KNIGHTSBRIDGE
2,8,9,10,14
16,19,22,36
38,52,73,74
82,137,148
414,436
GROSVENOR PL
KENSINGTON ROAD
Royal Albert Hall
KNIGHTSBRIDGE
Palace Gate
Queen's Gate
14,74,414,C1
Knightsbridge
360
BELGRAVIA
Science Museum
Exhibition Rd
BROMPTON RD
SLOANE STREET
Belgrave Place
70,360
Brompton Oratory
49
Natural History Museum
Victoria and Albert Museum
Pont St
BROMPTON
Gloucester Rd
70,74,360
CROMWELL RD
14,74
414,C1
19,22
137,C1
C1
KING'S RD

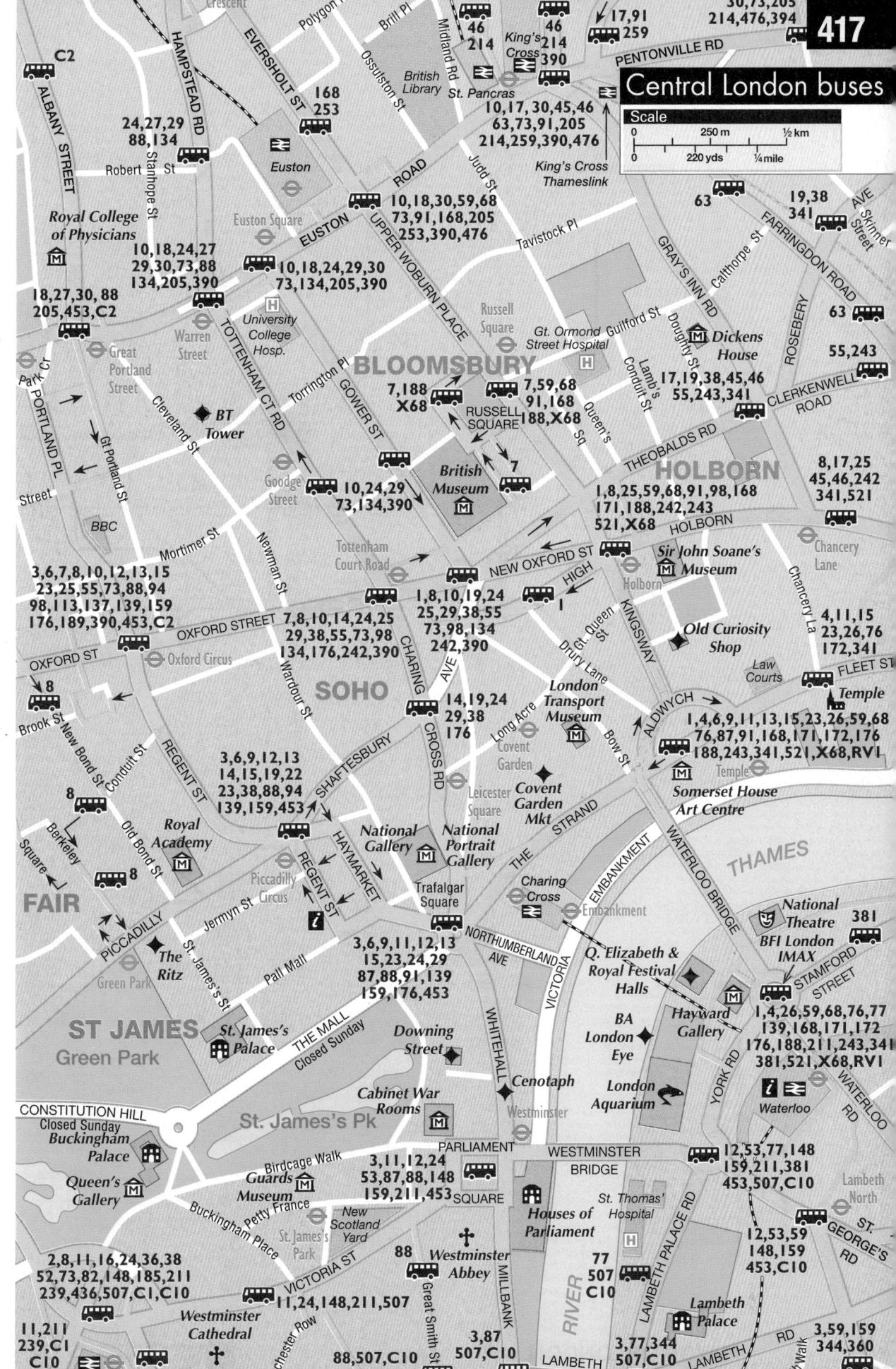

Central London buses

Scale

0 — 250 m — ½ km

0 — 220 yds — ¼ mile

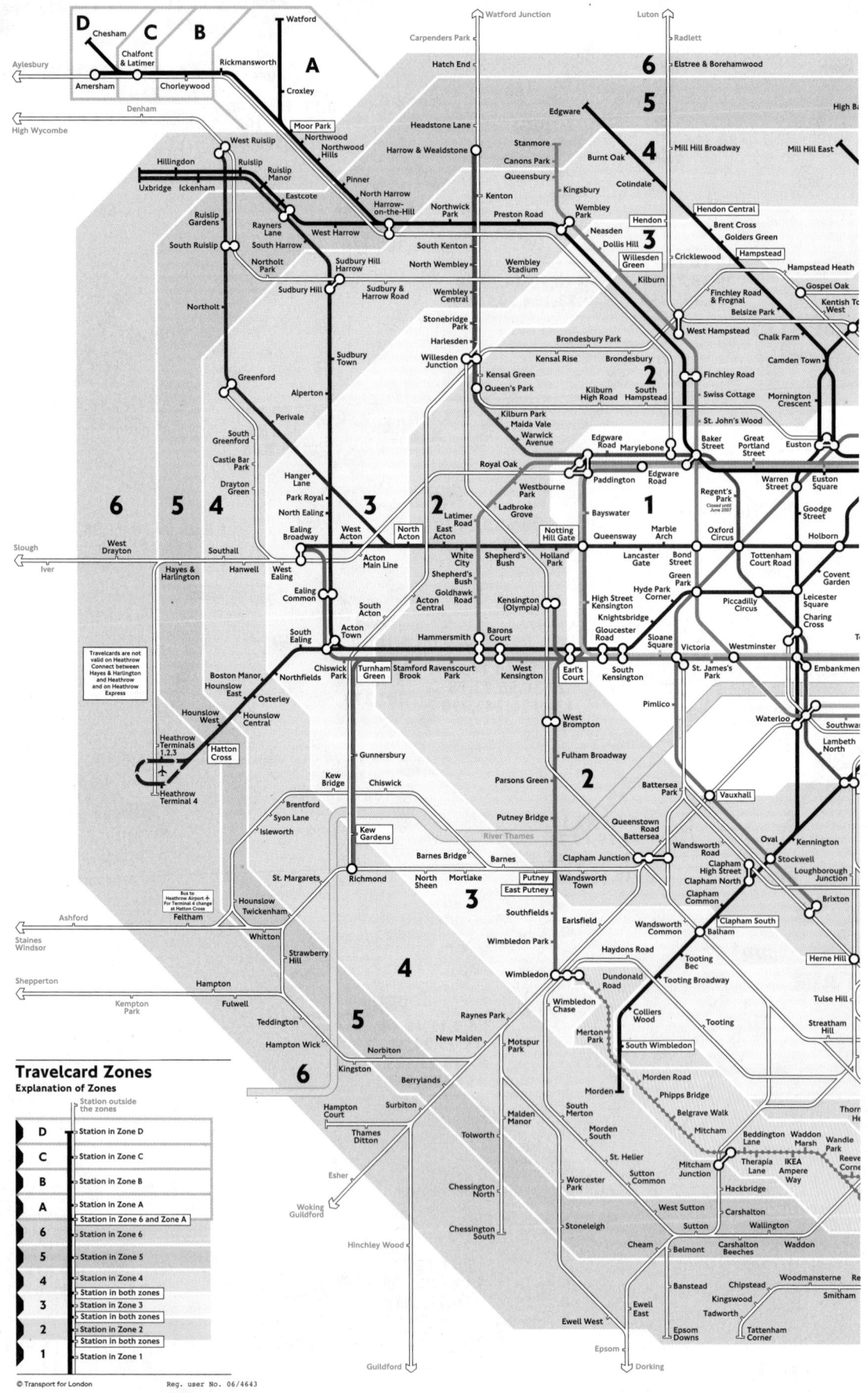

Travelcard Zones

Explanation of Zones

		Station outside the zones
D		Station in Zone D
C		Station in Zone C
B		Station in Zone B
A		Station in Zone A
6		Station in Zone 6 and Zone A
6		Station in Zone 6
5		Station in Zone 5
4		Station in Zone 4
3		Station in Zone 4
3		Station in both zones
3		Station in Zone 3
2		Station in both zones
2		Station in Zone 2
1		Station in both zones
1		Station in Zone 1

© Transport for London   Reg. user No. 06/4643

MAYOR OF LONDON

i 24 hour travel information
020 7222 1234

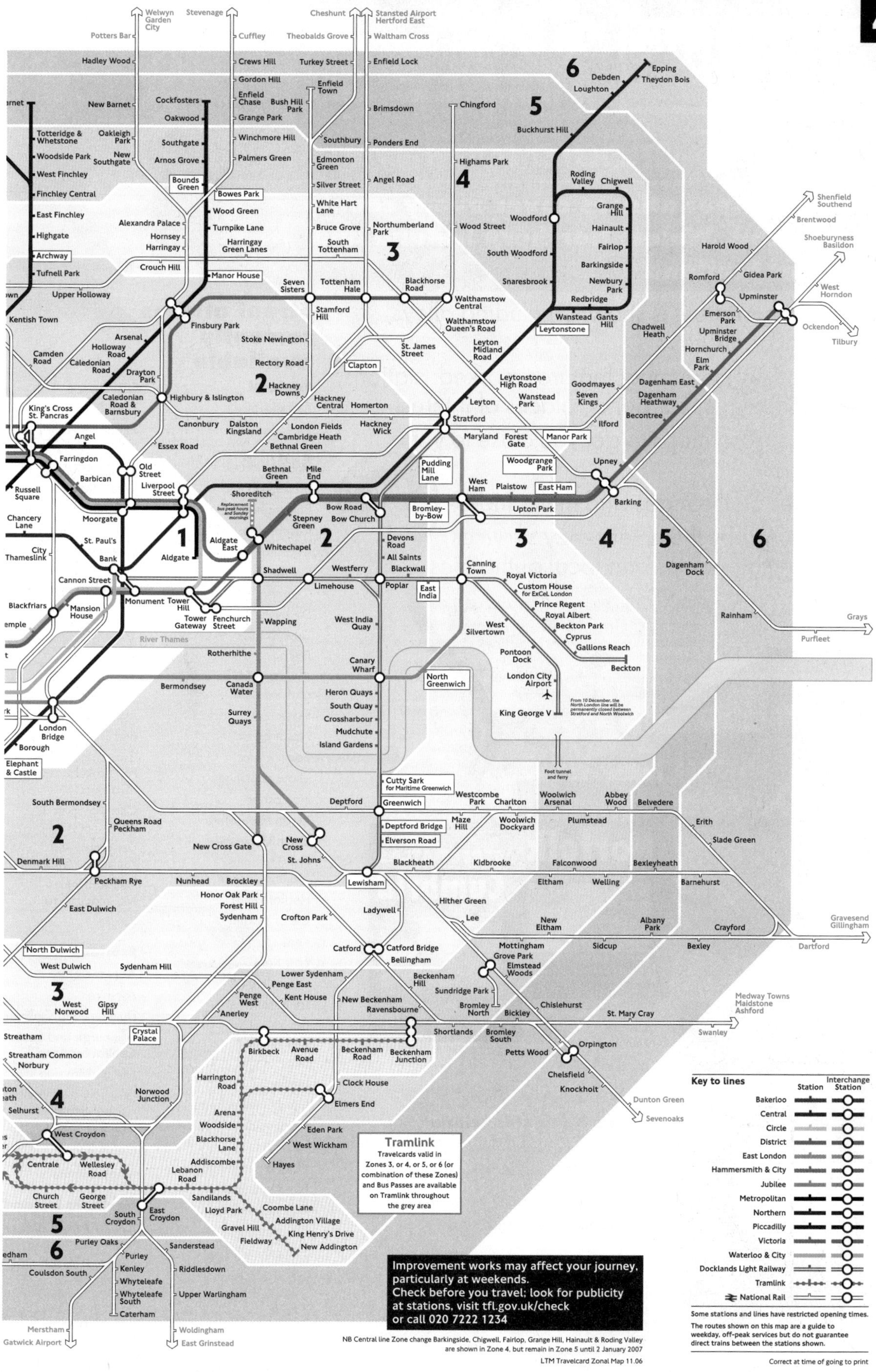

Key to lines

	Station	Interchange Station
Bakerloo		
Central		
Circle		
District		
East London		
Hammersmith & City		
Jubilee		
Metropolitan		
Northern		
Piccadilly		
Victoria		
Waterloo & City		
Docklands Light Railway		
Tramlink		
⩥ National Rail		

Some stations have restricted opening times.

The routes shown on this map are a guide to weekday, off-peak services but do not guarantee direct trains between the stations shown.

Correct at time of going to print

Tramlink
Travelcards valid in Zones 3, or 4, or 5, or 6 (or combination of these Zones) and Bus Passes are available on Tramlink throughout the grey area

Improvement works may affect your journey, particularly at weekends. Check before you travel; look for publicity at stations, visit tfl.gov.uk/check or call 020 7222 1234

NB Central line Zone change Barkingside, Chigwell, Fairlop, Grange Hill, Hainault & Roding Valley are shown in Zone 4, but remain in Zone 5 until 2 January 2007

LTM Travelcard Zonal Map 11.06

From 10 December, the North London line will be permanently closed between Stratford and North Woolwich

River Thames

Website
tfl.gov.uk

Textphone
020 7918 3015

Transport for London

PHILIP'S MAPS

the Gold Standard for drivers

◆ **Philip's street atlases cover every county in England, Wales, Northern Ireland and much of Scotland**

◆ Every named street is shown, including alleys, lanes and walkways

◆ Thousands of additional features marked: stations, public buildings, car parks, places of interest

◆ Route-planning maps to get you close to your destination

◆ Postcodes on the maps and in the index

◆ Widely used by the emergency services, transport companies and local authorities

For national mapping, choose **Philip's Navigator Britain** the most detailed road atlas available of England, Wales and Scotland. Hailed by Auto Express as 'the ultimate road atlas', the atlas shows every road and lane in Britain.

Street atlases currently available

England	
Bedfordshire	East Sussex
Berkshire	West Sussex
Birmingham and West Midlands	Tyne and Wear
	Warwickshire
Bristol and Bath	Birmingham and West Midlands
Buckinghamshire	Wiltshire and Swindon
Cambridgeshire	Worcestershire
Cheshire	East Yorkshire
Cornwall	Northern Lincolnshire
Cumbria	North Yorkshire
Derbyshire	South Yorkshire
Devon	West Yorkshire
Dorset	
County Durham and Teesside	**Wales**
	Anglesey, Conwy and Gwynedd
Essex	Cardiff, Swansea and The Valleys
North Essex	
South Essex	Carmarthenshire, Pembrokeshire and Swansea
Gloucestershire	
Hampshire	Ceredigion and South Gwynedd
North Hampshire	
South Hampshire	Denbighshire, Flintshire, Wrexham
Herefordshire Monmouthshire	
Hertfordshire	Herefordshire Monmouthshire
Isle of Wight	Powys
Kent	
East Kent	**Scotland**
West Kent	Aberdeenshire
Lancashire	Ayrshire
Leicestershire and Rutland	Dumfries and Galloway
	Edinburgh and East Central Scotland
Lincolnshire	
London	Fife and Tayside
Greater Manchester	Glasgow and West Central Scotland
Merseyside	Inverness and Moray
Norfolk	Lanarkshire
Northamptonshire	Scottish Borders
Northumberland	
Nottinghamshire	**Northern Ireland**
Oxfordshire	County Antrim and County Londonderry
Shropshire	
Somerset	County Armagh and County Down
Staffordshire	Belfast
Suffolk	County Tyrone and County Fermanagh
Surrey	

How to order Philip's maps and atlases are available from bookshops, motorway services and petrol stations. You can order direct from the publisher by phoning **0190 828503** or online at **www.philips-maps.co.uk** For bulk orders only, e-mail philips@philips-maps.co.uk